St. James Encyclopedia of Popular Culture

SECOND EDITION

St. James Encyclopedia of Popular Culture

SECOND EDITION

VOLUME 2

CRE–H

Thomas Riggs

EDITOR

ST. JAMES PRESS

A part of Gale, Cengage Learning

GALE
CENGAGE Learning®

Detroit • New York • San Francisco • New Haven, Conn • Waterville, Maine • London

GALE
CENGAGE Learning

St. James Encyclopedia of Popular Culture

Thomas J. Riggs, Editor

Product Manager: Douglas Dentino

Project Editor: Carol A. Schwartz

Editorial: Laura Avery; Dana Barnes; Erin Bealmear; Shawn Corridor; Matthew Derda; Jason Everett; Dana Ferguson; Jennifer Greve; Kristy Harper; Kristin Hart; Alan Hedblad; Andrea Henderson; Monica Hubbard; Jeff Hunter; Victor Ibarra; Reed Kalso; Kristin Key; Debra Kirby; Laurie Malashanko; Kim McGrath; Chelsea Merchan; Kathy Nemeh; Scot Peacock; Jennifer Wisinski

Rights Acquisition and Management: Christine Myaskovsky

Composition: Gary Leach

Manufacturing: Wendy Blurton

Imaging: John Watkins

Product Design: Kristine Julien

LIBRARY OF CONGRESS CATALOGING-IN-PUBLICATION DATA

St. James encyclopedia of popular culture / Thomas Riggs, editor ; with an introduction by Jim Cullen. -- 2nd edition.
p. cm. --
Includes bibliographical references and index.
ISBN 978-1-55862-847-2 (set) -- ISBN 978-1-55862-848-9 (vol. 1) -- ISBN 978-1-55862-849-6 (vol. 2) -- ISBN 978-1-55862-850-2 (vol. 3) -- ISBN 978-1-55862-851-9 (vol. 4) -- ISBN 978-1-55862-852-6 (vol. 5) -- ISBN 978-1-55862-853-3 (ebook)
1. United States--Civilization--20th century--Encyclopedias. 2. United States--Civilization--21st century--Encyclopedias. 3. Popular culture--United States--History--20th century--Encyclopedias. 4. Popular culture--United States--History--21st century--Encyclopedias. I. Riggs, Thomas, 1963- II. Title: Saint James encyclopedia of popular culture.

E169.1.J3 2013
973.9--dc23 2012049921

Gale, a part of Cengage Learning
27500 Drake Rd.
Farmington Hills, MI, 48331-3535

ISBN-13: 978-1-55862-847-2 (set) ISBN-10: 1-55862-847-9 (set)
ISBN-13: 978-1-55862-848-9 (vol. 1) ISBN-10: 1-55862-848-7 (vol. 1)
ISBN-13: 978-1-55862-849-6 (vol. 2) ISBN-10: 1-55862-849-5 (vol. 2)
ISBN-13: 978-1-55862-850-2 (vol. 3) ISBN-10: 1-55862-850-9 (vol. 3)
ISBN-13: 978-1-55862-851-9 (vol. 4) ISBN-10: 1-55862-851-7 (vol. 4)
ISBN-13: 978-1-55862-852-6 (vol. 5) ISBN-10: 1-55862-852-5 (vol. 5)

This title is also available as an e-book.
ISBN-13: 978-1-55862-853-3 ISBN-10: 55862-853-3
Contact your Gale, a part of Cengage Learning, sales representative for ordering information.

Printed in China
1 2 3 4 5 6 7 17 16 15 14 13

Contents

List of Entries

C

VOLUME 2

C *continued*

D

G

VOLUME 3

I

J

M

VOLUME 5

S *continued*

T

Creationism

Creationism is a Christian doctrine holding that the universe and all living things in it—human beings in particular—were created by God. There has been a variety of creationist viewpoints, and some of these viewpoints are in conflict with mainstream scientific theories, especially the theory of evolution. Creationism has developed in five waves, with the first originating in the mid-nineteenth century and the last appearing in the first decade of the 2000s. The first wave began after Charles Darwin published *Origin of Species* (1859), which not only defended the pre-existing theory of evolution but also maintained that evolution took place through natural selection. Many fundamentalist Christians reacted with horror. Anti-evolutionists maintained that evolution was contrary to the Bible, that it was atheistic pseudo-science, and that, by proposing that humans descended from lower animals, it denied human's spiritual nature. Evolutionists denounced creationists for allegedly misinterpreting both the Bible and the scientific evidence.

CREATIONISM ENTERS THE TWENTIETH CENTURY

The second wave of creationism began in the 1920s. During this wave, twenty states passed creationist legislation. William Jennings Bryan, a former Nebraska senator, presidential candidate, and U.S. Secretary of State, joined the movement to prevent the teaching of evolution. In response to lobbyists such as Bryan, the state of Tennessee passed a law making it a crime for a public-school teacher or state-college professor to teach the allegedly un-Scriptural doctrine that man evolved from a lower order of animals. However, under the Butler Act (and similar laws in other states) it remained permissible to teach the theory of evolution as applied to species other than humans.

A test case of the Tennessee law was arranged in Dayton, Tennessee, in 1925. A teacher named John Thomas Scopes was charged with violating the law. Bryan was brought in to help the prosecution, and an all-star legal defense team, including famed attorney Clarence Darrow, was enlisted to defend the young teacher. Scopes was convicted after a highly publicized trial, but his conviction was overturned on a technicality by the Tennessee Supreme Court. A play based on the Scopes Monkey Trial, *Inherit the Wind*, was turned into a movie in 1960. Spencer Tracy, Gene Kelly, and Fredric March were among the cast of this popular and anti-creationist rendering of the trial. The movie altered some of the historical details, but this version was probably better known than the actual trial.

Arkansas had also passed a "monkey law" similar to Tennessee's Butler Act. In *Epperson v. Arkansas* (1968), the United States Supreme Court ruled that the Arkansas law was designed to promote religious doctrine and that therefore it was an unconstitutional establishment of religion that violated the First Amendment. The *Epperson* decision had no effect on the Butler law, because that law had been already been repealed in 1967.

The third wave of creationism developed in the post-Epperson period. Since the Scopes trial, the views of some creationists had been getting closer to the secular scientific position. During World War II a group of scientists who were evangelical Christians formed an organization called the American Scientific Affiliation (ASA). Members pledged support for Biblical inerrancy and declared that the Christian scriptures were in harmony with the evidence of nature. Within this framework, however, the ASA began to lean toward the progressive creation viewpoint—the idea that God's creation of life was accomplished over several geological epochs, that the six "days" of creation mentioned in Genesis were epochs rather than literal days, and that much or all of mainstream science's interpretation of the origins of life could be reconciled with the Bible. These progressive creation tendencies were articulated in *Evolution and Christian Thought Today*, published in 1959. Some of the contributors to this volume seemed to be embracing theistic evolution; two of them were scientists who indicated that Christian doctrine could be reconciled with something resembling evolution.

Other creationists moved toward the theory of flood geology, the idea that God had created the world in six 24-hour days, that all species, including humans, had been specially created, and that the fossil record was a result not of evolution over time but of a single catastrophic flood in the days of Noah. George McCready Price, a Canadian-born creationist, had outlined these ideas in a 1923 book titled *The New Geology*. At the time, Price's ideas had not been widely accepted by creationists outside his own Seventh Day Adventist denomination, but in 1961 his ideas received a boost. Theologian John C. Whitcomb Jr. and engineer Henry M. Morris issued *The Genesis Flood*, which, like *The New Geology*, tried to reconcile the geological evidence with a strong creationist viewpoint.

THE MODERN DEBATE

In 1963 the Creation Research Society (CRS) was formed. The founders were creationist scientists (many of them from the fundamentalist Lutheran Church-Missouri Synod), and voting membership was limited to scientists. The CRS was committed to Biblical inerrancy and a creationist interpretation of the Bible, an interpretation that in practice coincided with the doctrine of flood geology.

The CRS and others began lobbying for the inclusion of creationist ideas in school curricula. This was a delicate task because of the *Epperson* decision, which prohibited the introduction of religious doctrines into the curricula of public schools. Creationists campaigned all over the country, trying to get creationism (now often dubbed creation science) into textbooks on an equal basis with evolution. Some states allowed the use of creationist texts such as Henry M. Morris's *Scientific Creationism.* The Texas Board of Education required that textbooks used by the state must emphasize that evolution was merely a theory and that other explanations of the origins of life existed. On the other hand, California—which together with Texas exerted a great influence over educational publishers due to its mass purchasing of textbooks—rejected attempts to include creationism in school texts.

During the fourth wave of creationism, laws were passed in Arkansas and Louisiana requiring that creation science be discussed whenever evolution was taught. However, the U.S. Supreme Court struck down the Louisiana law in 1987 on the grounds that creation science was a religious doctrine that could not constitutionally be taught in public schools.

In Tennessee, home of the Scopes trial, the legislature passed a law in 1973 that required that various ideas of life's origin—such as creationism—be included in textbooks. A federal circuit court struck down this law. A 1996 bill in the Tennessee legislature authorizing school authorities to fire any teacher who taught evolution as fact rather than theory was also unsuccessful. But in Tennessee and other states the campaign for teaching creationism continued.

The fifth wave of creationism began at the turn of the twenty-first century with a renewed interest and debate on human origins. Professor of biochemistry Michael J. Behe sparked a great deal of controversy in 1996 with the publication of his text, *Darwin's Black Box: The Biochemical Challenge to Evolution.* Situating his discussion in the context of biological systems, Behe argued for intelligent design based on his notion that evolution could not have produced the "irreducibly complex" systems of organic life. The book was championed by creationists as proof of their position.

Attempts at legislation renewed in 2004 with the passage of a creationist law in Dover, Pennsylvania, that required public school teachers to read a specific disclaimer about evolution and direct them toward an alternative text that promoted the theory of intelligent design. The wave came to an abrupt end when a federal district judge overturned the law on the grounds that it violated the separation of church and state guaranteed in the First Amendment. Creationists began gearing up for another round, and scientists responded with the Clergy Letter Project, which involved the cooperation of 940 scientists from all fifty states and thirty other countries and 13,000 members of the American clergy. The statement issued in the Clergy Letter Project accepts evolution as "fundamental scientific truth that has stood up to rigorous scrutiny" and asserts that to ignore it is "to deliberately embrace scientific ignorance" and pass false knowledge on to future generations.

Increased efforts in support of creationism began to pay off by the first decade of the 2000s. As awareness and acceptance developed, the creationist worldview grew closer to the status quo. The 2007 opening of the Creation Museum in Petersburg, Kentucky, provided further evidence of the shift in public perception of creationism from a fundamentalist belief to a theory based on empirical proof. In 2012 a so-called "monkey bill" was passed allowing Tennessee public school teachers to present creationist or intelligent design theories alongside evolution. Whereas creationism and intelligent design gained ever more traction in American culture, ongoing legislation in several states demonstrated that this controversy was far from being resolved.

Eric Longley

SEE ALSO: *Darrow, Clarence; Religious Right; Scopes Monkey Trial.*

BIBLIOGRAPHY

Beckwith, Francis J. *Law, Darwinism, and Public Education: The Establishment Clause and the Challenge of Intelligent Design.* Lanham, MD: Rowman and Littlefield, 2003.

Behe, Michael J., Ph.D. *Darwin's Black Box: The Biochemical Challenge to Evolution.* New York: Touchstone, 1996.

Darwin, Charles. *The Origin of Species by Means of Natural Selection.* New York: Modern Library, [1936].

De Camp, L. Sprague. *The Great Monkey Trial.* Garden City, NY: Doubleday, 1968.

Harrold, Francis B., and Raymond A. Eve, eds. *Cult Archaeology & Creationism.* Iowa City: University of Iowa Press, 1995.

Irons, Peter. *The Courage of Their Convictions.* New York: Free Press, 1988.

Johnston, Robert C. "70 Years after Scopes, Evolution Hot Topic Again." *Education Week*, March 13, 1996.

Johnston, Robert C. "Tenn. Senate to Get New Chance to Vote on Evolution Measure." *Education Week*, March 27, 1996.

Larson, Edward J. *The Creation-Evolution Debate: History and Perspectives.* Athens: University of Georgia Press, 2007.

Lawrence, Jerome, and Robert E. Lee. *Inherit the Wind.* New York: Random House, 1955.

Mitchell, Colin. *The Case for Creationism.* Grantham, UK: Autumn House, 1994.

Numbers, Ronald L. *The Creationists.* New York: Knopf, 1992.

Sommerfeld, Meg. "Lawmakers Put Theory of Evolution on Trial." *Education Week*, June 5, 1996.

Webb, George E. *The Evolution Controversy in America.* Lexington: University Press of Kentucky, 1994.

Witham, Larry. *When Darwin Meets the Bible: Creationists and Evolutionists in America.* New York: Oxford University Press, 2002.

Zimmerman, Michael, and David Loye. "Science and Religion: A New Alliance to Combat the New Wave of Creationism." *World Futures: The Journal of General Evolution* 67, no. 1 (January 2011).

Credit Cards

The small molded piece of polyvinyl chloride known as the credit card has transformed not only the U.S. but also the world economy and promises to be at the heart of the future economic system of the world. Social scientists have long recognized that the things people buy profoundly affect the way they live.

Microwave ovens, refrigerators, air conditioners, televisions, computers, the birth control pill, and antibiotics have all affected peoples' lives in profound ways. The credit card has changed peoples' lives as well, for it allows unprecedented access to a world of goods. The emergence of credit cards as a dominant mode of economic transaction has changed the way people live, the way they do things, the way they think, their sense of well-being, and their values. When credit cards first entered the lives of the U.S. public, ordinary people could only dream of an affluent lifestyle. Paying with plastic changed all that.

Credit cards were born from the embarrassment of Francis X. McNamara in 1950. Treating clients to dinner in a New York City restaurant, he reached for his wallet only to find he had not brought money. Though his wife drove into town with the money, McNamara went home vowing never to experience such disgrace again. To guarantee it, he created the Diners Club Card, a simple plastic card that served in place of cash at any establishment that agreed to accept it. It was a revolutionary concept.

Of course, credit had long been extended to U.S. consumers. Merchants offered credit to neighborhood customers long before McNamara's embarrassing moment. In the 1920s oil companies promoted courtesy cards to induce travelers to buy gas at their stations across the country; department stores extended revolving credit to their prime customers. McNamara's innovation, however, created a multipurpose (shopping, travel, and entertainment) and multilocation card that was issued by a third party independent of the merchant. He took to the road and signed up merchants across the country to save others from his fate.

Credit Card Purchase. *Since their introduction in the 1950s, credit cards have been a shopping staple for items large and small for many consumers.* SCHWEINEPRIESTER/SHUTTERSTOCK.COM.

GROWTH AND TECHNOLOGY

McNamara's success led to a host of imitators. Alfred Bloomingdale of Bloomingdale's department store fame introduced Dine and Sign in California. Duncan Hines created the Signet Club. *Gourmet* and *Esquire* magazines began credit card programs for their readers. But all McNamara's early imitators failed. Bankers, however, saw an opportunity.

Savvy as they are about giving out money for profit, bankers were more successful in offering their own versions of national cards. Success came to Bank of America and Master Charge, which came to dominate the credit card business in the 1960s. In the late 1970s Bank Americard became VISA, and Master Charge became MasterCard. In 1958 American Express introduced its first card. Its success the first year was so great—more than 500,000 people signed up—that American Express turned to computer giant IBM for help. Advanced technology was the only way for companies to manage the vast numbers of merchants and consumers who were linking themselves via their credit cards and in the process creating a mountain of debt. Technology made managing the credit card business profitable.

To make their system work, credit card companies needed to get as many merchants to accept their cards and as many consumers to use them as they possibly could. They were aided by the sustained economic growth of the post–World War II era, which saw the United States realize the potential for becoming a true consumption-based society. Credit card companies competed with each other to get their cards into the hands of consumers. With direct-mail solicitations, televisions advertisements, and the ubiquitous placement of credit applications, these companies reached out to every segment of the consumer market.

Affluent U.S. citizens were flooded with credit card offers at low interest rates, but poorer members of the public were also offered credit, albeit with high interest rates, low credit lines, and annual fees. Since the 1980s banks and credit card companies have marketed their cards more aggressively to college students, stating that using the cards was the best way to establish a good credit score. As the cards filled the wallets and purses of more and more consumers, the credit card became the essential tool of the consumer society. At the same time, the competition for the consumer heated up at the retail end. First to differentiate themselves from and then to keep up with competitors, more and more retailers, businesses, and services began accepting credit cards.

ECONOMIC ASPECTS

As of 2010 there were more than 609 million credit cards issued in the United States. Moreover, more than five billion offers of credit cards were being made annually. VISA administered about 50 percent of the credit cards in circulation. MasterCard had 33 percent, the Discover Card 9 percent, and American Express 8 percent.

The amount of money channeled through credit cards is staggering. By the late twentieth century about $820 billion were charged annually—approximately $11,000 per family—and credit cards accounted for $444 billion of debt. About 17 percent of disposable income was spent making installment payments on credit card balances; the average cardholder owed approximately $150 per month. Eight billion transactions per year involve credit cards. Simply put, credit cards have a profound effect on the economy. To put the force of credit cards into some perspective, in 1998 the Federal Reserve put $20 billion of new money into the economy, while U.S. banks unleashed the equivalent of $20 to $30 billion of new money into the same economy via new credit cards and increased spending limits.

Given the strong tie between credit card spending and the economy, the fact that consumers have freely used credit cards to fuel their lifestyles has been good for the country, for the stock market, and for retirement plans. But spending is more than simply an economic issue. It reflects deeper and broader social and psychological processes. These processes may underlie the true meaning of credit cards in U.S. culture.

SOCIAL PRESTIGE

Spending money to reflect or announce success is certainly not a new phenomenon. Anthropologists have long reflected upon tribal uses of possessions as symbols of prestige. In the past the winners were the elites of the social groups from which they came. But credit cards have leveled the playing field, affording the common people entry into the game of conspicuous consumption. Indeed, the use of credit cards allows people with limited incomes to convince others that they are in the group of winners. Credit cards have thus broken the link that once existed between the possession of goods and success.

Money does buy wonderful things, and many people derive satisfaction from knowing that they can buy many things. Credit cards allow consumption to happen more easily, more frequently, and more quickly. The satisfaction achieved through consumption is not illusory. Goods can be authentic sources of meaning for consumers. Indeed, goods are democratic. The Mercedes the rich person drives is the same Mercedes that the middle-class person drives. Acquiring possessions brings enjoyment, symbolizes achievement, and creates identity.

Because credit cards make all these personal accomplishments possible, they have become a symbolic representation of that achievement. Having a gold card is prestigious and means you have achieved more in life than those with a regular card. (A platinum card is, of course, even better.) Credit cards are more than modes of transaction—they are designer labels of life and thus impart to their user a sense of status and power. People know what these symbols mean and desire them.

The ways that people pay for their goods differ in important social, economic, and psychological ways. Unlike cash, credit cards promote feelings of membership and belonging. Having and using a credit card is a rite of passage, creating the illusion that the credit card holder has made it as an adult and is a success. Unique designs, newsletters, rewards for use, and special deals for holders make owners of cards feel that they are part of a unique group. Prestige cards such as the American Express Gold Card attempt to impress others with how much the user seems to be worth. Finally, credit cards are promoted as being essential for self-actualization. You have made it, card promoters announce, you deserve it, and you should not leave home without it; luckily, it is everywhere you want to be, according to VISA's advertising slogan. Self-actualized individuals with credit cards have the ability to express their individuality as fully as possible.

PROBLEMS AND ABUSES

There are, however, costly, dangerous, and frightening problems associated with credit card use and abuse. For instance, credit cards act to elevate the price of goods. Merchants who accept credit cards must pay anywhere from 0.3 to 3 percent of the value of the transaction to the credit card company or bank. Such costs are not absorbed by merchants but are passed on to all other consumers (who may not own or use credit cards) in the price of products and services. Credit cards also create trails of information in credit reports that reveal much about the lives of users, from the doctors they visit to their choice of underwear. Such reports reveal information that the credit card user might not want made available, and confusion between users can result in embarrassing and costly mistakes.

In addition, credit card fraud creates billions of dollars in costs that are paid for in high fees and interest rates and, eventually, in the price of goods. VISA estimated that these costs amount to between $43 and $100 per thousand dollars charged. Credit card companies charged off more than $75 billion in unpaid bills in 2010, with the rate projected to increase in the future. Finally, consumers pay in direct and indirect ways for the personal bankruptcies to which credit card abuse contributes. Although the number is difficult to determine, analysts estimated that more than nine million consumers sought debt counseling each year with over 1.5 million households filing for bankruptcy, much of it due to credit card debt. The result of these problems is the same: consumers pay more for goods.

One of the untold stories in the history of credit cards is the manner in which the poorer credit card holders subsidize the richer. Payments on credit card balances (with interest rates that normally range from 8 to 21 percent) subsidize those who use the credit card as a convenience and pay no interest by paying their charges within the grace period. The 50 to 60 percent of consumers who pay their balances within the grace period have free use of this money, but they could not do so unless others were paying the credit card companies for their use of the money. The people who pay the highest interest rates are, of course, the people with the lowest incomes.

ENCOURAGE SPENDING

In an obvious way, the convenience of using credit cards increases the probability that consumers will spend more than they might have otherwise. But using credit cards is also a bit like the arms race: the more the neighbors spend, the more consumers spend to stay even. Such competitive spending, while a source of sport for the wealthy, can be potentially devastating to those on more limited incomes.

Interestingly, credit card spending may facilitate spending in a more insidious manner. Research has shown that the facilitation effect of credit cards is both a conscious/rational and unconscious process. At the rational end, credit cards allow easy access to money that may only exist in the future. People spend with credit cards as a convenience and as a means to purchase something that they do not have the money for now but will in the near future. As an unconscious determinant of spending, however, credit cards can irrationally and unconsciously urge consumers to spend more and to do so more frequently.

Credit card spending has become an essential contributor—some would argue a causal determinant—of a good economy. Spending encourages the manufacture of more goods and the commitment of capital and creates tax revenues. By facilitating spending, credit cards are thus good for the economy. Credit cards are tools of economic expansion, even if they do bring associated costs.

ECONOMIC DOWNTURN

In the first years of the twenty-first century as the economy floundered, the use of credit cards declined drastically. This was partly in response to what was widely considered abuses by credit card companies that varied from rapid rate increases to exorbitant over-the-limit fees. Unable to pay such huge bills, scores of U.S. citizens were forced to declare bankruptcy. Congress addressed such issues with the passage of the Credit CARD Act of 2009 and consideration of the Government Charge Card Abuse Prevention Act of 2011/2012. Many consumers opted to use debit cards, which deducted amounts spent immediately from a bank account or from a prepaid plastic card. Both kinds of debit cards functioned like credit cards but without huge usage fees or the temptation to overspend.

Credit card companies responded to this downturn in use by offering rewards and rebates, and by early 2012 usage of credit cards was again outpacing usage of debit cards. The increasing use of technology in the late twentieth and early twenty-first centuries also made it much easier for criminals to steal another person's identity, allowing them to obtain credit cards and run up huge bills while the person whose name appeared on the card remained completely unaware that their credit rating was being demolished.

In a little more than sixty years, credit cards have gone from being a mere convenience to being crucial facilitators of economic transactions. Some would have them do even more. Credit card backers promote a vision of a cashless economy in which a single credit card consolidates all a person's financial and personal information needs. And every day consumers vote for the evolution to a cashless electronic economic and information system by using their credit cards. People in the United States are willing prisoners of and purveyors of credit cards, spending with credit cards because of what they get them; what they symbolize; and what they allow them to achieve, experience, and feel. In many ways credit cards are the fulfillment of the ultimate dream of this country's founders—they offer life, liberty, and the pursuit of happiness. As of 2010, there were 176.8 million cardholders in the United States, accounting for $2 trillion in purchasing goods and services. Credit card debt steadily increased in the twenty-first century, with the average cardholder holding $5,000 worth of debt.

Richard A. Feinberg
Cindy Evans

SEE ALSO: *Consumerism; Department Stores; The Great Recession; IBM (International Business Machines); Online Shopping; The Pill.*

BIBLIOGRAPHY

Buchan, James. *Frozen Desire: The Meaning of Money.* New York: Farrar Straus Giroux, 1997.

Choosing and Using Credit Cards. Washington, DC: FTC, Bureau of Consumer Protection, 2005.

Evans, David S., and Richard Schmalensee. *Paying with Plastic: The Digital Revolution in Buying and Borrowing.* Cambridge, MA: MIT Press, 1999.

Galanoy, Terry. *Charge It!: Inside the Credit Card Conspiracy.* New York: Putnam, 1981.

Hendrickson, Robert A. *The Cashless Society.* New York: Dodd Mead, 1972.

Klein, Lloyd. *It's in the Cards: Consumer Credit and the American Experience.* Westport, CT: Praeger, 1997.

Mandell, Lewis. *Credit Card Use in the United States.* Ann Arbor: University of Michigan, 1972.

Manning, Robert D. *Credit Card Nation: The Consequences of America's Addiction to Credit.* New York: Basic Books, 2000.

Ritzer, George. *Expressing America: A Critique of the Global Credit Card Society.* Thousand Oaks, CA: Pine Forge, 1995.

Simmons, Matty. *The Credit Card Catastrophe: The 20th Century Phenomenon That Changed the World.* New York: Barricade Books, 1995.

Creedence Clearwater Revival

By the late 1960s, when Creedence Clearwater Revival (CCR) released its first album, rock and roll was transforming into rock—the more "advanced" and "sophisticated" cousin of the teenage riot whipped up by Elvis Presley and Little Richard. While the band's contemporaries (The Moody Blues, Pink Floyd, King Crimson, etc.) were expanding the sonic and lyrical boundaries of rock and roll, CCR bucked the trend by returning to the music's roots. On its first album and six subsequent releases, this San Francisco Bay Area–group led by John Fogerty fused primal rockabilly, swamp-boogie, country, R&B, and great pop songwriting and—in doing so—became one of the biggest-selling rock bands of the late 1960s and early 1970s.

Most of the members of CCR played in what were essentially bar bands around San Francisco and its suburbs. Along with El Cerrito, California, junior high school friends Stu Cook and Doug "Cosmo" Clifford, Tom and John Fogerty formed the Blue Velvets in the late 1950s. The group eventually transformed into the Golliwogs, recording a number of singles for the Berkeley, California–based label Fantasy, and then changed its name to Creedence Clearwater Revival in 1967. If the Blue Velvets and the Golliwogs were dominated by Tom Fogerty, then Creedence Clearwater Revival was John Fogerty's vehicle, with John writing and singing the vast majority of CCR's songs. It was clear that John's influence was what made the group popular, because under Tom's control, the Golliwogs essentially went nowhere. Further, when John let other members gain artistic control on CCR's *Mardi Gras* (1972), that album received poor reviews and became the first CCR album not to go platinum.

Like Bruce Springsteen, John's songs tackle subjects that cut deep into America's core, and like any great artist, he was able to transcend his own experience and write realistic and believable songs (for instance, the man who wrote "Born on the Bayou" in 1969 had never even been to Louisiana's bayous). Despite John's talents as a songwriter, CCR's first hits from its eponymous debut album in 1968 were covers—Dale Hawkins's

"Suzie Q" and Screamin' Jay Hawkins's "I Put a Spell on You." But with the release of "Proud Mary," backed with "Born on the Bayou" from CCR's second album (*Bayou Country*, 1969), the group released a series of original compositions that dominated the U.S. Billboard charts for three years.

Despite its great Top 40 success and its legacy as the preeminent American singles band of the late 1960s, CCR was able to cultivate a countercultural and even anticommercial audience with its protest songs and no-frills rock and roll. "Fortunate Son" (1969), "Run through the Jungle" (1970), "Who'll Stop the Rain" (1976), and CCR's other protest songs remain timeless classics because of John's penchant for evoking nearly universal icons (for North Americans, at least) rather than specific cultural references.

John's dominance proved to be the key to the band's success and the seeds of its dissolution, with Tom leaving the group in 1971 and John handing over the reins to be split equally between Cook and Clifford, who equally contributed to the group's last album, *Mardi Gras*, which flopped. Tom released a few solo albums, and so did John, who refused to perform his CCR songs well until the early 1990s as the result of a bitter legal dispute that left control of the CCR catalog in the hands of Fantasy Records. One of the most bizarre copyright infringement lawsuits took place when Fantasy sued John for writing a song for his 1984 *Centerfield* album that sounded too much like an old CCR song. After spending $300,000 in legal fees and having to testify on the stand with his guitar to demonstrate how he wrote songs, John won the case.

In 1990 Tom died from tuberculosis stemming from the HIV he had contracted from a blood transfusion. Creedence Clearwater Revival was inducted into the Rock and Roll Hall of Fame in 1993 and ranked eighty-two on *Rolling Stone*'s 100 greatest artists of all time. Lingering personal and legal disputes prevented the band from reuniting, and John refused to play with Cook and Clifford during the induction ceremony. When Cook and Clifford formed Creedence Clearwater Revisited in 1995, John filed an injunction against the band to force them to change the name; however, the court ruled in favor of Cook and Clifford, and they continued to tour and release albums.

After the breakup, John established an impressive solo career. Following the success of 1997's *Blue Moon Swamp*, he released *Deja Vu (All over Again)* in 2004. Although the record was not as commercially successful as *Blue Moon*, the political overtones of the title track catapulted John into the touring circuit. He received multiple awards for his solo material and continued to play CCR songs alongside his original compositions. Although the band members have since been awarded royalties, Fantasy Records maintains rights to the material and continues to license songs such as "Who'll Stop the Rain" and "Fortunate Son" to sell such products as cars, paint thinner, and blue jeans. The copyright issues surrounding CCR's catalog proved that even a protest song like "Fortunate Son" could be used to sell consumer goods as well as provide the soundtrack to war-based video games such as *Call of Duty: Black Ops*.

Kembrew McLeod

SEE ALSO: *Advertising; Alternative Country Music; Country Music; Pink Floyd; Pop Music; Rhythm and Blues; Rock and Roll;* Rolling Stone; *Springsteen, Bruce; Top 40; Video Games; Vietnam.*

BIBLIOGRAPHY

Bordowitz, Hank. *Bad Moon Rising: The Unauthorized History of Creedence Clearwater Revival.* New York: Schirmer Books, 1998.

Hallowell, John. *Inside Creedence.* New York, London: Bantam, 1971.

Crichton, Michael *(1942–2008)*

Published in 1969, *The Andromeda Strain* established Michael Crichton as a major best-selling novelist whose popularity was due as much to the timing and significance of his subject matter as to the quality of his writing and the accuracy of his research. As Crichton had correctly judged, America was ready for a tale that treated both the rationalism and the paranoia of Cold War scientists' response to a biological threat. From that first success on, Crichton continued to embrace disagreeable or disturbing topical trends as a basis for exciting, thriller-related fiction. That several have been made into highly successful movies and that he expanded his career into film and television made Crichton a cultural fixture in late twentieth-century America. If this was in doubt, his position was cemented by *ER* (1994–2009), the monumentally successful television series that he had created.

Born on October 23, 1942, in Chicago, Crichton had received an AB degree summa cum laude from Harvard, completed an MD at Harvard Medical School, and begun working as a postdoctoral fellow at the Salk Institute for Biological Studies by the time *The Andromeda Strain* was published in 1969. Most impressively, he had already published six novels (under various pseudonyms), written largely during weekends and vacations, while still at medical school. As an undergraduate, he had intended to major in English, but poor grades convinced him that no amount of creative talent would deter Harvard's faculty from altering its absurdly high expectations. Incipient scientist that he was, Crichton tested this hypothesis by submitting an essay by George Orwell under his own name and received a B minus.

This tale, recounted in Crichton's spiritual autobiography, *Travels* (1988), perhaps explains his own lack of interest in producing anything other than commercial fiction. As a result, his journey through medical school seems, in retrospect, more of a detour than a career path, for, by the end of his schooling, he had decided once and for all to become a writer. During his final rotation Crichton concentrated more on the emotional than the physical condition of his patients, research that formed the basis of his nonfiction work, *Five Patients: The Hospital Explained* (1970).

A NEW CAREER TRAJECTORY

But it was *The Andromeda Strain* that permanently changed the trajectory of his career. His previous novels have all fallen out of print, with the exception of *A Case of Need* (1968), published under the pseudonym Jeffrey Hudson and winner of the 1968 Edgar Award from the Mystery Writers of America. Although the success of *The Andromeda Strain* lifted Crichton's career to new heights, it did not prevent him from completing other less successful works already in progress. In 1970 and 1971, using the name John Lange, he finished three more novels (*Drug of Choice*, *Grave Descend*, and *Binary*), and with his brother Douglas co-wrote *Dealing*, under the apparently prescient name of

Michael Crichton. *Michael Crichton poses with a stack of his best-selling books at a book show in 1994.* TAMMIE ARROYO/GETTY IMAGES.

Michael Douglas. (Michael Douglas the actor would star in the film versions of several of Crichton's novels.) With three of his novels already filmed—*The Andromeda Strain* (1971), *Dealing: Or the Berkeley-to-Boston Forty-Brick Lost-Bag Blues* (1972), and *A Case of Need* (retitled *The Carey Treatment*, 1972)—Crichton, who had directed the made-for-TV film *Pursuit* (1972) made his feature film directing debut in 1973 with *Westworld*. Starring Yul Brynner, the film was supposedly inspired by Crichton's visit to Disneyland's Pirates of the Caribbean ride. At this point he pursued a dual career as moviemaker and writer, having published the second novel to appear under his own name, *The Terminal Man*, in 1972. Dealing with a Frankenstein-type experiment gone haywire, it confirmed its author's storytelling powers, sold in the millions, and was adapted for the cinema in 1974.

Through the rest of the 1970s and into the 1980s, Crichton the author continued to turn out such bestsellers as *The Great Train Robbery* (1975), *Congo* (1980), and *Sphere* (1987), but Crichton the director fared less well. His successes with *Coma* (1978), a terrific nailbiter based on Robin Cook's hospital novel and starring the real Michael Douglas, and *The Great Train Robbery* (1979), were offset by such mediocrities as *Looker* (1981), *Runaway* (1984), and *Physical Evidence* (1989). A major turnaround came when he stopped directing and concentrated on writing fiction once again. The fruits of his labors produced bestsellers *Jurassic Park* (1990), *Rising Sun* (1992), *Disclosure* (1994), *Lost World* (1995), *Airframe* (1995), and *Timeline* (1999). In the meantime, Crichton shifted from director to producer, convincing NBC to launch *ER*, which he had created and had been his dream for twenty years. By the end of the 1990s, he was an established and important presence in Hollywood as well as in publishing, enjoying a professional longevity that only a handful of popular novelists and screenwriters experience.

In the new millennium, Crichton turned his attention to the emerging science of genetic engineering and his own personal concerns over the effects of the increasingly emotional global warming debate on scientific discourse. He delivered a number of speeches arguing that, while convincing evidence of global warming did exist, the severity of its effects was being overemphasized, and humanity's contribution to the phenomenon remained in doubt. Crichton was even called to speak before the U.S. Congress in 2005 as an expert on global warming science and again in 2006 as an expert on the possible uses of genetic research. His novels of this period include *Prey* (2002), *State of Fear* (2004), and *Next* (2006).

Crichton was diagnosed with throat cancer in 2008 and died of the disease on November 4 of that year. Two of his novels, *Pirate Latitudes* (2009) and *Micro* (2011), were published posthumously, the latter being completed by science fiction author Richard Preston.

CREATOR OF THE MODERN TECHNO-THRILLER

Not unlike Tom Clancy, whose success came in the 1980s, Crichton was a masterful storyteller who has been credited with the invention of the modern "techno-thriller." His prose is clear and concise; his plotting strong; his research accurate and, at times, eerily prescient. On the other hand, in common with many fiction writers who depend heavily on premises drawn largely from the science fiction genre, his character development has been attacked as weak. Despite his protests to the contrary, his penchant for using speculative science as the basis for much of his fiction landed him willy-nilly within the gothic and science fiction traditions. In *Michael Crichton: A Critical Companion*, Elizabeth Trembley details the extent to which Crichton's work revisits earlier gothic or science fiction classics, from H. Rider Haggard's *King Solomon's Mines*, for example, to *Jurassic Park*, a modern retelling of H. G. Wells's *The Island of Doctor Moreau*.

Crichton's popularity is perhaps best explained by his intuition for presenting through the medium of fiction our own anxieties in consumable form. Often fiction relieves anxieties by reconfiguring them as fantasy. Crichton sensed that people worry about biological weapons (*The Andromeda Strain*), mind control technology (*The Terminal Man*), human aggression (*Sphere*), genetic engineering (*Jurassic Park*, *Next*), and competitive corporate greed (*Rising Sun*, *Disclosure*, and *Prey*). His gift was the ability to turn these fears into a form that lets the audience deal with them from the safety of the reading and moviegoing experience.

Bennett Lovett-Graff

SEE ALSO: *Best Sellers; Brynner, Yul; Cancer; Clancy, Tom; Cold War;* ER*; Global Warming;* The Great Train Robbery*; Hollywood;* Jurassic Park*; Moore, Demi; Science Fiction Publishing; Television.*

BIBLIOGRAPHY

Crichton, Michael. *Travels*. New York: Knopf, 1988.

Golla, Robert, ed. *Conversations with Michael Crichton*. Jackson: University Press of Mississippi, 2011.

Heller, Zoe. "The Admirable Crichton." *Vanity Fair*, January 1994, 32–49.

Trembley, Elizabeth. *Michael Crichton: A Critical Companion*. Westport, CT: Greenwood, 1996.

Crime Does Not Pay

Crime Does Not Pay was a comic book published from 1942 to 1955 by the Lev Gleason Company. Inspired by the MGM documentary series of the same name, *Crime* featured material based loosely on true criminal cases. The stories indulged in graphic violence, sadism, and brutality of a sort that was previously unheard of in children's entertainment. Bullet-ridden corpses, burning bodies, and horrific gangland tortures were among the more predictable themes found in these comic books.

An unusual comic book when it first appeared amid the superheroes of the World War II era, *Crime* found a huge audience after the war. Arguably the first "adult" comic book, *Crime* also became one of the most popular titles ever, selling in excess of one million copies monthly. When *Crime*'s formula became widely imitated throughout the industry, it attracted the wrath of critics who charged that crime comic books caused juvenile delinquency.

Bradford Wright

SEE ALSO: *Comic Books; Comics; Comics Code Authority; DC Comics; EC Comics; Marvel Comics; Underground Comics; World War II.*

BIBLIOGRAPHY

Benton, Mike. *Crime Comics*. Dallas, TX: Taylor Publishing, 1993.

Goulart, Ron. *Over Fifty Years of American Comic Books*. Lincolnwood, IL: Mallard Press, 1991.

Jones, Gerard. *Men of Tomorrow: Geeks, Gangsters, and the Birth of the Comic Book*. New York: Basic Books, 2004.

Crinolines

In 1859 French writer Charles Baudelaire wrote that "the principal mark of civilization . . . for a woman, is invariably the crinoline." The crinoline, or horsehair ("crin") hoop, allowed women of the 1850s and 1860s to emulate the fashionable wife of Napoleon III, Empress Eugénie, in ballooning skirts supported by these Crystal Palaces of lingerie. From Parisiennes to Scarlett O'Hara, women moved rhythmically and monumentally during "crinolineomania" (1856–1868), assuming some power if only by taking up vast space. A culture of boulevards and spectatorship prized the volume of crinolines.

In the 1950s crinolineomania recurred: prompted by Christian Dior's New Look, any poodle skirt or prom dress could be inflated by nylon crinolines, as if to become the female version of mammoth 1950s cars with their flashy fins. A culture of big cars valued the crinoline as well.

Richard Martin

SEE ALSO: *Retro Fashion.*

BIBLIOGRAPHY

Cunningham, Patricia A. *Reforming Women's Fashion, 1850–1920: Politics, Health and Art*. Kent, OH: Kent State University Press, 2003.

Neuberger Museum. *Crinolineomania: Modern Women in Art, 1856–68*. Exhibition Catalogue. Purchase, NY: Neuberger Museum, 1991.

Waugh, Norah. *Corsets and Crinolines*. New York: Routledge/Theatre Arts Books, 1998.

The *Crisis*

Founded in 1910 as the monthly magazine of the National Association for the Advancement of Colored People (NAACP), the *Crisis* has played an important role in the formation and development of African American public opinion since its inception. As the official voice of the leading civil rights organization in the United States, the *Crisis* gained entry into a variety of African American and progressive white homes, from the working class and rural poor to the black middle class. Through the mid-1930s the *Crisis* was dominated by the character, personality, and opinions of its first editor and NAACP board member, W. E. B. Du Bois. Because of his broad stature within black communities, Du Bois and the NAACP were synonymous for many African Americans. One of his editorials or essays could literally sway the opinions of thousands of black Americans.

MIGRATIONS AND WAR

The 1910s were a time of dynamic change within black communities as the Great Migration began to speed demographic shifts from the rural South to the industrialized North and African American institutions grew and expanded. As black newspapers and periodicals gained prominence within these rapidly developing communities, the New York–based magazine the *Crisis* emerged as one of the most eloquent defenders of black civil rights and racial justice in the United States. During this era the magazine led battles for a federal antilynching law, equality at the ballot box, and an end to legal segregation. As World War I approached, the *Crisis* ran vigorous denunciations of racial violence in its columns.

Following a bloody riot in East St. Louis, Illinois, in 1917, Du Bois editorialized with melancholy, "No land that loves to lynch 'niggers' can lead the hosts of the Almighty." In the same year, after black servicemen rampaged through the streets of Houston, Texas, killing seventeen whites and resulting in the execution of thirteen African Americans, the *Crisis* bitterly lamented, "Here at last, white folks died. Innocent, adventitious strangers, perhaps, as innocent as the thousands of Negroes done to death in the last two centuries. Our hands tremble to rise and exult, our lips strive to cry. And yet our hands are not raised in exultation; and yet our lips are silent, as we face another great human wrong."

After the initial success of black troops stationed in France during the summer of 1918, Du Bois penned the controversial editorial "Close Ranks." He wrote, "Let us, while this war lasts, forget our special grievances and close our ranks shoulder to shoulder with our own white fellow citizens and the allied nations that are fighting for democracy. We make no ordinary sacrifice, but we make it gladly and willingly with our eyes lifted to the hills." Appealing to the ideals of patriotism, citizenship, and sacrifice connected to military service, *Crisis* editors argued that by fighting a war "to make the world safe for democracy," African Americans would be in a better position to expect a new era of opportunity and equality after the war's end.

As the war drew to a close and black soldiers returned home, the *Crisis* continued its determined efforts to secure a larger share of democracy for African Americans. In "Returning Soldier," the magazine captured the fighting spirit of the moment: "*We return. / We return from fighting. / We return fighting.* / Make way for democracy! We saved it in France, and by the Great Jehovah, we will save it in the United States of America, or know the reason why."

NEW CHALLENGES

The next two decades, though, did not bear out the optimism of *Crisis* editors. During the 1920s, as racial conservatism set in nationwide and the hopes of returning black soldiers dimmed, the *Crisis* shifted its focus to the development of the cultural politics of the New Negro movement in Harlem. With the addition of celebrated author Jessie Fauset to the editorial board, the *Crisis* printed essays from Harlem Renaissance architect Alain Locke, as well as early works of fiction and poetry by Fauset, Langston Hughes, and Zora Neale Hurston.

The 1930s proved contentious years for the *Crisis* as it went to battle with the Communist Party over the fate of nine African American youths accused of raping two white women in the Scottsboro (Alabama) case. In addition, the Great Depression put the magazine in financial peril. As Du Bois struggled to find solutions to the dire circumstances facing most black Americans, he published a series of essays advocating the creation of "urban black self-determination" through the creation of race-based economic cooperatives. This stance irked many NAACP leaders, who saw the remarks as a repudiation of the organization's integrationist goals. The clash precipitated a split within the group that in 1934 resulted in the resignation of Du Bois from both the magazine and the NAACP board.

What the *Crisis* lost in the departure of Du Bois, it regained with the rapidly increasing membership of the NAACP during World War II and the rising tide of civil rights protest throughout the nation. Although the magazine no longer had the stature, intellectual respect, or skillful writing associated with Du Bois, it remained an important public African American voice. In particular, as the legal attack on segregation engineered by Thurgood Marshall and the Legal Defense Arm of the NAACP crescendoed in 1954 with the *Brown v. Board of Education of Topeka* decision, the *Crisis* ran a special issue dedicated solely to the NAACP victory, featuring the full text of the decision, historical overviews, and analysis. One editorial gloated, "The 'separate but equal' fiction as legal doctrine now joins the horsecar, the bustle, and the five-cent cigar." While the *Crisis* trumpeted the victory, it also kept a pragmatic eye on the unfinished business of racial justice in the United States, stating, "We are at that point in our fight against segregation where unintelligent optimism and childish faith in a court decision can blind us to the fact that legal abolition of segregation is not the final solution for the social cancer of racism."

Over the next decade, as the NAACP struggled to find its place in the post-*Brown* movement, the *Crisis* maintained its support of nonviolent civil rights activity, although it no longer set the agenda. Marshall, in an article on the student sit-in wave sweeping the South in 1960, compared Mississippi and Alabama to South Africa and argued, "Young people, in the true tradition of our democratic principles, are fighting the matter for all of us and they are doing it in the most effective way. Protest—the right to protest—is basic to a democratic form of government." Of the 1963 Jobs and Freedom march on Washington, D.C., the *Crisis* beamed, "Never had such a cross section of the American people been united in such a vast outpouring of humanity." Similarly, in 1964, with the passage of the historic Civil Rights Act, the *Crisis* editorialized, "[the Act] is both an end and a beginning: an end to the Federal Government's hands-off policy; a beginning of an era of Federally-protected rights for all citizens."

LOSS OF POWER

As the movement spun off after 1965 toward Black Power; increasing radicalization; and, in some cases, violence, the NAACP and the *Crisis* began to lose their prominent position in shaping African American attitudes and opinions. Against these new politics, the *Crisis* appeared more and more conservative. Continuing to oppose violent self-defense and separatism, the *Crisis* also came out against radical economic redistribution as well as the Black Studies movement of the late 1960s and early 1970s.

Over the next two decades the *Crisis* evolved into a more mainstream popular magazine, upgrading its pages to a glossy stock and including more advertisements, society articles, and human interest stories. Unable to recapture the clear programmatic focus that had driven its contents during the previous fifty years, articles tended to be more retrospective and self-congratulatory than progressive. In the mid-1990s the *Crisis* took a brief hiatus but reappeared soon after in a revised form, focusing primarily on national politics, cultural issues, and African American history.

In 2001 Victoria L. Valentine, a former White House press agent, took over as editor of the *Crisis*. At the time she worked out of her home because she had no office. Undaunted, she set about revamping and redesigning the magazine with the help of two other full-time employees and a group of freelancers. Publishing only six times a year, the magazine devoted special issues to topics such as the status of black children, the health of African Americans, crime, housing, science and technology, and black/Latino relations. Valentine resigned in 2007, and the *Crisis* was forced to cut back to quarterly publication out of financial necessity. She was replaced by writer Jabari Asim later that year. Regardless of the changes that have occurred in its more than 100-year history, the *Crisis* continues to focus attention on issues that affect the life of African Americans in the United States.

Patrick D. Jones

SEE ALSO: *Civil Rights Movement; Du Bois, W. E. B.; Fauset, Jessie Redmon; The Great Depression; Hughes, Langston; Hurston, Zora Neale; Locke, Alain; Lynching; World War I; World War II.*

BIBLIOGRAPHY

Du Bois, W. E. B. *The Writings of W. E. B. Du Bois.* New York: Crowell, 1975.

Ellis, Mark. "'Closing Ranks' and 'Seeking Honors': W. E. B. Du Bois in WWI." *Journal of American History* 79, no. 1 (1992).

Hughes, Langston. *Fight for Freedom: The Story of the NAACP.* New York: Berkley Publishing, 1962.

Johnson, Brian. *Du Bois on Reform: Periodical-Based Leadership for African Americans.* Lanham, MD: AltaMira, 2005.

Lewis, David Levering. *W. E. B. Du Bois: Biography of a Race, 1868–1919.* New York: Holt, 1994.

Musser, Judith, ed. *"Girl, Colored" and Other Stories: A Complete Short Fiction Anthology of African American Women Writers in the "Crisis" Magazine, 1910–2010.* Jefferson, NC: McFarland, 2011.

Valentine, Victoria L. "Goodbye and Good Luck." *Crisis* 114, no. 1 (2007).

Walden, Daniel, ed. *W. E. B. Du Bois: The "Crisis" Writings.* Greenwich, CT: Fawcett Publishing, 1972.

Wilson, Sondra Kathryn, ed. *The "Crisis" Reader: Stories, Poetry, and Essays from the N.A.A.C.P.'s "Crisis" Magazine.* New York: Modern Library, 1999.

Croce, Jim *(1943–1973)*

Singer and songwriter Jim Croce is remembered for beautiful guitar ballads ("Time in a Bottle") and upbeat character-driven narratives ("Bad, Bad Leroy Brown") that deftly combine folk, blues, and pop influences. Croce's brief but brilliant musical career was tragically cut short by his death in a plane accident in 1973.

Born to James Alford and Flora Croce in Philadelphia, Pennsylvania, Croce's interest in music got off to a slow start. He learned to play "Lady of Spain" on the accordion at the age of five but did not seriously pursue music until his college years. He attended Villanova College in the early 1960s, where he formed various bands and played at parties. Croce was encouraged to focus on his music when one of his bands went on an embassy tour of the Middle East and Africa through a foreign exchange program. He earned a degree in psychology from Villanova in 1965.

Croce's music career was interrupted by the odd jobs he took to make a living. He worked in construction, welded, and joined the army. He spun records as a university disc jockey on a folk and blues show in Philadelphia and wrote ads for a local R&B station. After marrying Ingrid Jacobsen in 1966, the two spent the summer teaching at a children's camp in Pine Grove, Pennsylvania. He taught guitar, and she taught ceramics and leather crafts. The following autumn he served as a teacher for problem students at a high school in Philadelphia.

Finally becoming truly serious about a career in music, Croce moved to New York in 1967. He and Ingrid played together in folk clubs and coffee houses. By 1969 the pair signed to Capital Records and released an album called *Approaching Day.* The album's lack of success led the couple to leave New York and return to Pennsylvania. Jim sold off his guitars, took a job in construction, and later found work as a truck driver. Ingrid learned how to can foods and bake bread to help stretch the budget. On September 28, 1971, they had a son, Adrian James (A. J.) Croce.

Croce never lost his love of music, and he eventually played and sang on some commercials for a studio in New York. His break came when he sent a demo tape to Tommy West, a Villanova college pal who had found success in New York as a record producer. West and his friend Terry Cashman helped Croce land a contract with ABC records. Croce also had a fortuitous meeting with guitarist Maury Muehleisen while working as a studio freelancer. Croce had played backup guitar on Muehleisen's record, *Gingerbread* (1970). The album flopped, but Croce remembered the young guitarist and called him in to collaborate. The two worked closely in the studio, trading rhythm and lead parts. The first album, *You Don't Mess Around with Jim* (1972), was a huge success, giving Croce two Top 10 hits with the title track and "Operator (That's Not the Way It Feels)." Before long Croce was a top-billing concert performer, known as much for his friendly and charming personality as for his songs.

His second album, *Life and Times* (1973), had a hit with the July 1973 chart topper "Bad, Bad Leroy Brown." This first blush of success soon turned bittersweet. Leaving a concert venue at Northwestern State University in Natchitoches, Louisiana, on September 20, 1973, Croce's plane snagged the top of a pecan tree just past the runway. Croce, Muehleisen, and four others were killed in the accident. Croce was buried in Haym Salomon Memorial Park in Frazer, Pennsylvania. His third album, *I've Got a Name* (1973), was released posthumously, and the hits kept coming. The next chart hit was the title track, and "Time in a Bottle" was the number one hit of the year in 1973. The following year "I'll Have to Say I Love You in a Song" and "Workin' at the Car Wash Blues" appeared on the charts. The ongoing string of hits only highlighted the tragic loss of a performer who was just coming into his own.

In 1985 Jim's widow, Ingrid, opened Croce's Restaurant and Jazz Bar in San Diego's Gaslamp Quarter in his memory. The restaurant features musical acts nightly and is decorated with Croce memorabilia. Ingrid also wrote a book of recipes and memories called *Thyme in a Bottle* (1996). Their son, A. J., started his own musical career in the 1990s. He released his eponymous first album in 1993, followed by *That's Me in the Bar* (1995) and *Fit to Serve* (1997). He said of his father, "I think the most powerful lesson I learned from him was the fact there is no reason to write a song unless there is a good story there. He was a great storyteller and, for me, if there is any way that we are similar, it's that we both tell stories."

Emily Pettigrew

SEE ALSO: *Folk Music; Pop Music; Rock and Roll.*

BIBLIOGRAPHY

Croce, Ingrid. *Thyme in a Bottle: Memories and Recipes.* San Francisco: CollinsPublishersSanFrancisco, 1996.

Croce, Jim. *Jim Croce: Greatest Hits.* Milwaukee, WI: Hal Leonard, 2001.

Crockett, Jim. "Talking Guitar." *Guitar Player*, April 1973, 18.

Dougherty, S. "Don't Mess around with A. J." *People*, August 17, 1992, 105–106.

"Epitaph for Jim." *Time*, February 11, 1974, 56.

"Jim Croce." Accessed February 1999. Available from http://www.hotshotdigital.com/WellAlwaysRemember.3/JimCroce-Bio.html

"Jim Croce: The Tribute Page." Accessed February 1999. Available from http://www.jimcrocefans.com

Makarushka, Mary. "At Last, He Got a Name." *Entertainment Weekly*, September 15, 1995, 124.

Nelton, S. "A Legend in Her Own Right." *Nation's Business*, December 1992, 14.

Talevski, Nick. *Knocking on Heaven's Door: Rock Obituaries.* London: Omnibus Press, 2006

Crocs

The squishy, multicolored footwear known as Crocs got their start in 2002, when Scott Seamans encountered a strange clog intended for spa use. It was light and waterproof and made of a resin that got softer from body heat when worn. The little bumps on the clog fought fatigue and helped circulation, and the resin was more resistant to bacteria than either plastic or rubber. Seamans added a strap and recruited friends Lyndon Hanson and George Boekecker to start manufacturing the shoe.

The result was a strange, moderately priced product that sold like crazy and immediately polarized American popular culture. On one hand, Crocs have supporters ranging from the American Podiatric Medical Association, which praised them for their comfort, to fans among celebrities and trend setters. Mario Batali wore his orange Crocs on the cooking show *Iron Chef*, and pop singer Britney Spears bought a pair in every color available (which in 2007 was twenty-seven). Workers who have to stand a lot, such as nurses and cooks, like them, and the fact that they can be hosed off at the end of a shift is highly attractive in many professions. Crocs were so popular that sales broke $1 billion in 2011.

On the other hand, Crocs do not just look unique, they look strange. Some people downright despise them. Journalist Vincenzo Ravina, for example, started the website ihatecrocs.com to express his hatred for the shoes. The site features many pictures and videos of people destroying Crocs in innovative ways and sells T-shirts expressing Croc hatred. The most popular line from this Croc-hating site is, "They are to your eyes what secondhand smoke is to your lungs."

Other critics of Crocs point to the soft clog as a sign of a larger negative trend in American society, which is for people to embrace personal comfort in fashion over style or what is appropriate. This trend has gone so far, the critics observe, that people wear clothes—like Crocs, worn with pajamas—for comfort even if this means looking inappropriately casual in public.

The success of Crocs has spawned many imitators. Cheaper (if less comfortable) knockoff Crocs are widely available, and Crocs Inc. has defended its creation via numerous lawsuits against companies infringing on their patents. The company occupies a curious position in the market. Its clog may have spawned a new footwear category through emphasizing comfort over style, but it is as subject to shifts in the fashion market as anyone else. As a result, the company that made its money by being comfortable rather than cool is continually reinventing itself, producing Crocs for golfing, Crocs with heels, and even Crocs clothing.

Greg Beatty

SEE ALSO: *Casual Friday; Celebrity Chefs; Spears, Britney; T-Shirts.*

BIBLIOGRAPHY

Alsever, Jennifer. "What a Croc!" *Fast Company*, June 2006, 74–78.

"Crocs, Inc. Expects to Surpass $1 Billion in Revenue in 2011." *Business Wire*, January 10, 2012.

Markels, Alex. "Croc and Roll: The Maker of the Popular Funky Footwear Is on the Hunt for Its Next Big Hit." *U.S. News & World Report*, September 16, 2007.

Cronkite, Walter *(1916–2009)*

Walter Cronkite's nineteen-year tenure as anchorman of the *CBS Evening News* was an uncanny match of man and era. Two generations of Americans came to rely upon his presence in the Columbia Broadcasting System (CBS) television anchor chair in times of war and crisis, scandal and celebration. His was a forthright, solemn presence in a time when each new dawn brought with it the prospect of nuclear annihilation or a second American civil war. Yet the master journalist was also a master performer—Cronkite was able and quite willing to display a flash of emotion or anger on the air when it suited him. This combination of stoic professionalism and emotional instinct earned the broadcaster two enduring titles: the man known familiarly as Uncle Walter was also widely considered "the most trusted man in America." When Cronkite closed the *Evening News* each night with his famous sign-off "And that's the way it is," few doubted he was telling them the truth.

Cronkite's broadcasting career had a unique prologue. As a young World War II correspondent, he did what few others dared: he turned down a job offer from Edward R. Murrow. The CBS European chief was already a legend; the radio correspondents known as Murrow's Boys were the darlings of the American press, even as they defined the traditions and standards of broadcast journalism. Cronkite, however, preferred covering the war for the United Press. It was an early display of his preference for the wire-service style and attitude; the preference marked Cronkite's reporting for the rest of his career. When he accepted a second offer from CBS several years later, the budding broadcaster found himself assigned—perhaps relegated—to airtime in the new medium that seemed little more than a journalistic backwater: television.

LAUNCH OF A TELEVISION CAREER

Cronkite anchored the local news at CBS's Washington, D.C., affiliate starting soon after the Korean War began in 1950, his

Walter Cronkite. *Walter Cronkite anchors the evening news from the CBS studios in 1963.* © BETTMANN/CORBIS.

broadcast a combination of journalism and experimental theater. There were no rules for television news, and Cronkite had come in on the ground floor. He had little competition; few of the old guard showed much interest in the new medium. Cronkite was pressed into service to anchor the 1952 political conventions and election for CBS television, and his presence was soon taken for granted in the network anchor chair. He continued to anchor much of CBS's special events coverage, including the 1956 and 1960 political conventions, and established himself firmly as the network's face in the medium which was, by now, quite obviously the wave of the future.

In 1962 Cronkite succeeded Douglas Edwards as anchor of the *CBS Evening News*, then a fifteen-minute nightly roundup that found itself regularly beaten in the ratings by the runaway success of NBC's anchor team of Chet Huntley and David Brinkley. Ratings aside, however, television news was finally coming of age; CBS news was expanding staff and adding bureaus and airtime. TV news veered away from the staged, hackneyed style of its most obvious model, the movie newsreels. Instead it became a straightforward, serious purveyor of hard news, thanks in no small part to the efforts and sensibilities of Cronkite and his colleagues. His *Evening News* expanded to thirty minutes in September 1963, premiering with an exclusive interview of President John F. Kennedy. It was the assassination of Kennedy two months later that caused Cronkite to briefly lose his self-control on the air, reflecting the feelings of the millions of Americans for whom the assassination became a life-defining moment.

Yet Cronkite, like Douglas Edwards before him, regularly spoke to an audience much smaller than that of Huntley and Brinkley. It is true that Cronkite's shirtsleeves pronouncement of the Kennedy assassination—"From Dallas, Texas, the flash, apparently official . . . President Kennedy . . . died . . . at 1:00 pm . . . "—is usually excerpted on retrospective programs and documentaries. But the simple fact is that NBC was the clear audience choice during the early and middle 1960s.

Cronkite's ratings plummeted during the 1964 Republican convention. He was replaced in the anchor chair for the Democratic convention by Robert Trout and Roger Mudd, two fine, veteran broadcasters whose selection nonetheless was a thinly veiled effort to capture some of the Huntley-Brinkley magic. It did not work; viewer protests quickly led to Cronkite's reinstatement.

CRONKITE'S CAREER REIGNITES WITH THE SPACE PROGRAM

Meanwhile Cronkite threw himself into coverage of the American space program. He displayed obvious passion and an infectious, even boyish enthusiasm. His cries of "Go, baby, go!" became familiar accompaniment to the roar of rockets lifting off from Cape Canaveral. Cronkite anchored CBS's coverage of every blast-off and splashdown. Arguably the single most famous quote of his career came as astronauts Neil Armstrong and Buzz Aldrin touched down on the moon on the afternoon of July 20, 1969. "The Eagle has landed," Armstrong radioed, and Cronkite added his benediction: "Gosh! Oh, boy!" He later recalled it as the only time he ever came up speechless on the air. That afternoon Cronkite's audience was greater than that of NBC and ABC combined. Huntley-Brinkley fever had cooled. Walter Cronkite had now gained the public's trust, and his stature in American living rooms resounded throughout the television industry.

This was the age in which local television news departments strove to emulate the networks, and the success of Cronkite's dead-earnest *Evening News* led many local TV newscasts to adopt the Cronkite style. Likewise, there is no official count of how many anchormen or anchorwomen around the world, subconsciously or not, adopted that distinctive Cronkite cadence. Politicians and partisans on all sides complained bitterly that Cronkite and CBS were biased against them; this was perhaps the ultimate tribute to the anchorman's perceived influence on American life in the late 1960s.

While his popularity was rising, however, Cronkite had grown decidedly unenthusiastic about the Vietnam War. A trip to Vietnam in the midst of the Tet offensive led to arguably the most courageous broadcast of the anchorman's career. Cronkite returned home, deeply troubled, and soon used the last few moments of a CBS documentary to call for an end to the war through negotiated peace. It was a shocking departure from objectivity, easily the most brazen editorial stand on television since Edward R. Murrow criticized Senator Joseph McCarthy nearly a decade and a half earlier. At the White House, President Lyndon Johnson is said to have remarked, "If I've lost Cronkite, I've lost middle America." Whether the anecdote is apocryphal is irrelevant; that it is widely accepted as fact is the real testament to Cronkite's influence as the 1960s drew to a close. During the turmoil of the 1968 Democratic convention, Cronkite stood out as the voice of reason and sanity. Even so, his anger was apparent when his colleague Dan Rather was punched in the stomach during one of the many confrontations that broke out.

Cronkite rode the *Evening News* to ratings victory after ratings victory through the 1970s; the whole of CBS news was now at a pinnacle of popularity and influence. Cronkite cut short his summer vacation to preside over the August 8, 1974, resignation of President Nixon. Two years later he anchored an all-day-and-all-night television party for the American bicentennial on July 4, 1976. And after a group of U.S. citizens was taken hostage in Iran in 1979, he stubbornly closed every nightly newscast by counting the number of days they had been held captive. Cronkite's nightly reminders were instrumental in making it clear that Carter was unable to free the hostages. When the hostages were released on January 20, 1981, to coincide with the swearing-in of President Ronald Reagan, Cronkite held forth over his last great news spectacular, calling the event "one of the great dramatic days in our history."

EASED OUT AND SHUT OUT

By then Cronkite was on his way out, giving up the anchor chair to Dan Rather, narrowly forestalling Rather's defection to ABC. Cynics have long speculated that Cronkite was, in fact, pushed aside to make way for Rather, but everyone involved—including Cronkite—clung to the story that the veteran anchorman was genuinely tired of the grind and had repeatedly asked to be replaced. His final *Evening News* came on March 6, 1981. His final utterance of "And that's the way it is" was preceded by a brief goodbye speech in which he asserted, "Old anchormen don't go away, they keep coming back for more."

Cronkite had not intended to retire completely upon stepping down from the anchor chair, but to his astonishment, he found the new CBS news management would not let him back on the air. An exclusive report of Cronkite's from strife-torn Poland was given short shrift; later, his already limited participation in the network's 1982 election-night coverage was reportedly reduced even further when anchorman Rather simply refused to cede the air to him. The new brass feared reminding either viewers or a jittery, ratings-challenged Rather of Cronkite's towering presence; Rather himself was apparently enjoying a little revenge. Uncle Walter had for years been known behind the scenes as a notorious air hog, filling airtime with his own face and voice, even as waiting correspondents cooled their heels. Now, suddenly, he was getting a taste of his own medicine.

It only got worse for Cronkite. CBS's board members completely ignored the elder statesman's heated protests of mid-1980s news budget cuts, and his staid, substance-over-style approach appeared to be falling by the CBS wayside. His legacy was fading before his very eyes. That he never pulled up stakes and left the network (unlike a disgruntled David Brinkley, who had recently bolted from NBC) is a testament either to true professional loyalty or else to an iron-clad contract.

RECOVERY BEFORE THE END

In the 1990s, however, Cronkite made a broadcasting comeback. He produced and narrated a series of cable documentaries, including a multi-part retrospective of his own career, and his 1996 autobiography was a major bestseller. In late 1998 Cronkite accepted CNN's offer to co-anchor the network's coverage of astronaut John Glenn's return to space. On that October day, Cronkite reprised one of his great career triumphs, providing enthusiastic, knowledgeable coverage of a manned spaceflight. It was thrilling for both audience and anchor; yet it was also clear that Cronkite's day had come and gone. He was a bit deaf, and he thoroughly lacked the aura of hype that had become a primary qualification for modern news anchors. His presence that day was, however, a glorious reminder of what Cronkite had been to the nation for so long: the very manifestation of serious, hard news in the most powerful communications medium of the twentieth century.

Walter Cronkite died in 2009 at the age of 92. During his long career, he had won Emmy awards, a Peabody Award, and a Presidential Medal of Freedom (1981). The latter was awarded by President Jimmy Carter because of the role that Cronkite had played in bringing Egyptian president Anwar Sadat and Israeli prime minister Menachem Begin to the negotiating table. Cronkite served as the voice of Benjamin Franklin in *Liberty Kids* on PBS. He made sixty documentaries and was a longtime host of the Kennedy Center Honors. Arizona State University honored Cronkite by naming its school of journalism after him. In July 2006 *American Masters* aired a segment celebrating his career. Even though he had never been close to Dan Rather, Cronkite did support Katie Couric, who succeeded Rather in 2006. It was Cronkite's voice that regularly introduced the *CBS Evening News with Katie Couric*. Until the day he died, Cronkite remained the most trusted man in America.

Chris Chandler

SEE ALSO: *Apollo Missions; Brinkley, David; CNN; Huntley, Chet; Kennedy Assassination; McCarthyism; Murrow, Edward R.; Rather, Dan; Television Anchors; Vietnam.*

BIBLIOGRAPHY

Boyer, Peter. *Who Killed CBS?* New York: Random House, 1988.

Cronkite, Walter. *A Reporter's Life.* New York: Alfred A. Knopf, 1996.

Joyce, Ed. *Prime Times, Bad Times.* New York: Doubleday, 1988.

Kutscher, Austin Ken. *Watching Walter Cronkite: Reflections on Growing Up in the 1950s and 1960s.* New York: Gordian Knot Books, 2009.

Leonard, Bill. *In the Storm of the Eye.* New York: G. P. Putnam's Sons, 1987.

Martin, Douglas. "Walter Cronkite, 92, Dies." *New York Times,* July 17, 2009.

Slater, Robert. *This . . . Is CBS.* Englewood Cliffs, NJ: Prentice Hall, 1988.

Crosby, Bing *(1903–1977)*

Bing Crosby is recognized as one of the most influential entertainers of all time. He emerged as America's most beloved crooner during the 1930s and remained at the forefront of popular culture in the ensuing decades. From 1926 until his death in 1977, he recorded more than 1,600 songs. Crosby also starred in a long string of highly successful movies, including the classic *Going My Way* (1944). After amassing a fortune, he eventually became a major Hollywood presence behind the scenes.

Born Harry Lillis Crosby into a large family in Tacoma, Washington, Crosby grew up to study law at Gonzaga University in Spokane, Washington. However, he soon became more interested in playing drums and singing with a local band. It was during this period that he adopted his professional name, reportedly borrowing the "Bing" from his favorite comic strip, *The Bingville Bugle*. Crosby signed a deal with CBS Radio in the early 1930s, and he was an instant hit. His live performances from New York were broadcast by the national radio network for twenty consecutive weeks in 1932.

Crosby's low-key and spontaneous delivery was widely imitated for decades. At the time of his death, he was considered the world's top-selling singer. Hundreds of millions of Crosby's records have been sold worldwide, and some of his recordings remained in print for decades after his death. He garnered twenty-two gold records (signifying 500,000 sales) and was awarded platinum discs (signifying sales of one million) for his two biggest-selling singles, "White Christmas" (1960) and "Silent Night" (1970).

HOLLYWOOD BECKONS

Crosby's radio success prompted Paramount Pictures to sign him to a film contract. He starred in more than fifty full-length motion pictures, beginning with *The Big Broadcast of 1932* (1932) and ending with the television movie *Dr. Cook's Garden* (1971). Interestingly, his large ears were pinned back during his early films, until partway through *She Loves Me Not* (1934).

His movie career reached its zenith during his association with Bob Hope. Crosby and Hope first met in the summer of 1932 in New York. In December of that year, they performed together at New York's Capitol Theater, doing an old vaudeville routine that included two farmers meeting on the street. They did not work together again until the late 1930s, when Crosby invited Hope to appear with him at the opening of the Del Mar race track north of San Diego. The boys reprised some old vaudeville routines that delighted the celebrity audience. One of the attendees was the production chief of Paramount Pictures, who began searching for a movie vehicle for Crosby and Hope and ended up finding an old script originally intended for George Burns and Grace Allen and then Jack Oakie and Fred MacMurray. The tentative title was *The Road to Mandalay*, but the destination was eventually changed to Singapore. Wanting a love interest in the movie, the producers signed the exotically beautiful Dorothy Lamour. Although *The Road to Singapore* was not considered as funny as the subsequent *Road* pictures, the chemistry among the three actors shined through, and the film was a hit.

At least twenty-three of Crosby's movies were among the top ten box-office hits during the year of their release. Furthermore, Crosby was among the top ten box-office stars in at least fifteen years (1934, 1937, 1940, 1943–1954), and he was the top box-office draw in America for five consecutive years (1944–1948). Critical recognition of his acting talent came with *Going My Way*: his performance as an easygoing priest resulted in the Oscar for Best Actor. His work in *The Country Girl* (1954)—in which Crosby plays a down-on-his-luck alcoholic opposite Grace Kelly—also received excellent reviews.

A MIXED LEGACY

Crosby married singer Dixie Lee in 1930, and the couple had four sons—Gary, Dennis and Phillip (twins), and Lindsay—all of whom unsuccessfully attempted careers as actors. Widowed in 1952, Crosby married movie star Kathryn Grant (thirty years his junior) in 1957. She bore him two more sons—Harry and Nathaniel—and a girl, Mary, who grew up to be a TV and film actress best known for her role as the person who shot J. R. Ewing in the television series *Dallas*.

During his four decades as an entertainer, Crosby accumulated a fortune from radio, records, films, and TV. He invested wisely in an array of business ventures, including real estate, banking, oil and gas wells, broadcasting, and the Coca-Cola Company. At one point he was estimated to be worth between $200 million and $400 million. From the 1940s to the 1960s, Crosby owned 15 percent of the Pittsburgh Pirates baseball team, though golf was his favorite sport. In fact, he died while playing at a golf course outside Madrid—after completing a tour of England that had included a sold-out engagement at the London Palladium.

After his death Crosby's Hollywood persona—established largely by his role as the warmhearted priest in *Going My Way*—underwent much reassessment. Donald Shepherd and Robert F. Slatzer wrote an unflattering biography on Crosby, *Bing Crosby—The Hollow Man* (1981), in which he was portrayed as an egotistical and heartless manipulator. In *Going My Own Way* (1983), Crosby's eldest son, Gary, tells of his experiences as a physically and mentally abused child. When Bing's youngest son by Dixie Lee, Lindsay, committed suicide in 1989 after finding himself unable to provide for his family, it was revealed that Crosby had stipulated in his will that a trust fund he had established for his sons could not be accessed by them before they reached age sixty-five.

Bianca Freire-Medeiros

SEE ALSO: *Coca-Cola;* Dallas; *Hope, Bob; Lamour, Dorothy; Movie Stars; Radio.*

BIBLIOGRAPHY

Crosby, Bing, and Pete Martin. *Call Me Lucky*. New York: Da Capo Press, 1993.

Grudens, Richard. *Bing Crosby: Crooner of the Century*. Stony Brook, NY: Celebrity Profiles Publishing, 2003.

MacFarlane, Malcolm. *Bing Crosby: A Diary of a Lifetime*. Leeds, England: International Crosby Circle, 1997.

Mielke, Randall G. *Road to Box Office: The Seven Film Comedies of Bing Crosby, Bob Hope, and Dorothy Lamour, 1940–1962*. Jefferson, NC: McFarland, 1997.

Osterholm, J. Roger. *Bing Crosby: A Bio-Bibliography*. Westport, CT: Greenwood Press, 1994.

Prigozy, Ruth, and Walter Raubicheck. *Going My Way: Bing Crosby and American Culture*. Rochester, NY: University of Rochester Press, 2007.

Reynolds, Fred. *Road to Hollywood (The Bing Crosby Film Book)*. Gateshead, England: John Joyce & Son, 1986.

Shepherd, Donald, and Robert F. Slatzer. *Bing Crosby: The Hollow Man*. London: W. H. Allen, 1981.

Crosby, Stills, and Nash

David Crosby, Stephen Stills, and Graham Nash came together in the late 1960s as idiosyncratic individual talents in flight from famous groups. Their 1969 debut album arguably initiated the dominance of singer-songwriters in popular music until the mid-1970s. After appearing at the Woodstock festival, augmented by Neil Young, they achieved a wider public role as the artistic apotheosis of the hippie ideals of "music, peace, and love." As the 1970s progressed, however, CSN(&Y) became infamous for an inability to show enough peace and love to one another to continue playing and recording music together.

CSN . . . AND THEN COMES Y

Crosby had been an integral member of folk-rock pioneers the Byrds until he left the group acrimoniously in 1967. He had first encountered Stills when the latter's band, Buffalo Springfield, supported the Byrds in concert in early 1966. In May 1968, just after the demise of Buffalo Springfield, Crosby and Stills met disillusioned Hollies frontman Nash. As suggested by the unassuming name, Crosby, Stills, and Nash was conceived as a loose collective in order to foster creative freedom and forestall the internal strife that each individual had experienced in his previous band. Yet with the release of *Crosby, Stills & Nash* in 1969, CSN was hailed as a "supergroup"—and not just because of their prestigious genealogy. Lyrics that meshed with the ideals of the counterculture were immersed in acoustic guitars and immaculate vocal harmonies. Crosby and Stills's "Wooden Ships" envisioned a new Eden in the aftermath of nuclear apocalypse, while Nash's "Marrakesh Express" less grandly located utopia on the Moroccan hippie trail.

Stills's Buffalo Springfield colleague and rival Young was recruited in June 1969 in order to bolster their imminent live shows. Ominously, there were squabbles over whether Young should get equal billing. With only one recently released record to their name, and in only their second-ever concert performance, CSN&Y wowed the Woodstock festival in July 1969. There was a certain amount of manipulation involved in the rapid mythologization of the group as the epitome of the

Crosby, Stills, and Nash. *Stephen Stills, left, David Crosby, and Graham Nash perform in concert in 1978.* RICHARD MCCAFFREY/MICHAEL OCHS ARCHIVE/GETTY IMAGES.

"Woodstock nation." Their manager, David Geffen, who also represented many of the other acts that appeared, threatened to withdraw his cooperation from the film of the festival unless CSN&Y's cover of Joni Mitchell's "Woodstock" was used over the opening credits. Atlantic, the group's record label, disproportionately featured the band on two very successful soundtrack album sets. In contrast, CSN&Y's appearance at the Rolling Stones' disastrous free festival at Altamont in December 1969 was, as Johnny Rogan has observed, "effectively written out of rock history" by journalists sympathetic to the CSN&Y-Woodstock cause.

There were unprecedented prerelease orders worth more than $2 million for *Déjà Vu*, released in March 1970. Though it was somewhat more abrasive sounding than the debut album, due to the arrival of Young and his electric guitar, *Déjà Vu* was suffused with hippie vibes. These were amusingly conveyed on Crosby's "Almost Cut My Hair," but Nash's "Teach Your Children" sounded self-righteous. In May 1970 CSN&Y rush released the single "Ohio," Young's stinging indictment of President Richard Nixon's culpability in the killing of four student protesters by the National Guard at Kent State University. After completing a highly successful tour in 1970 (documented on the double album *Four-Way Street*), CSN&Y were lauded by the media as the latest American answer to the Beatles, a dubious honor first bestowed on the Byrds in 1965, but which CSN&Y seemed capable of justifying.

"AN AGGREGATE OF FRIENDS"

Instead, the foursome diverged into various solo ventures. While this was informed by their insistence that, in Crosby's words, "We're not a group, just an aggregate of friends," individual rivalries and the tantalizing example of Young's flourishing solo career were also determining factors. The flurry of excellent solo albums in the early 1970s, invariably featuring the "friends" as guests, only increased interest in the enigma of the "aggregate." When CSN&Y finally regrouped in 1974, popular demand was met by a mammoth worldwide tour of sport stadiums that redefined the presentation, scale, and economics of the rock-and-roll spectacle. But CSN&Y failed to complete an album after this tour, and they never again attained such artistic or cultural significance. After further attempts at a recording reunion failed, Crosby, Stills, and Nash eventually reconvened without Young for *CSN* (1977). The album was another huge seller and spawned their first Top 10 single, Nash's "Just a Song before I Go." Nevertheless, each member was past his peak in songwriting terms, and their musical style and political views were being vociferously challenged by punk rock and its maxim, "Never trust a hippie."

Crosby was becoming ever more mired in cocaine and heroin addiction. A farcical series of drug-related arrests culminated in his incarceration in 1986. In that year's "Hippie Dream," Young transformed Crosby's personal fate into a fable of the descent of countercultural idealism into rock-and-roll hedonism ("the wooden ships / were just a hippie dream / capsized in excess"). Crosby's physical recovery resulted in a much-publicized CSN&Y album—the first in eighteen years—*American Dream* (1988). The artistic irrelevance of Crosby, Stills, and Nash, however, was highlighted not only by comparisons between the new CSN&Y record and *Déjà Vu* but also by *Freedom* (1989), the opening salvo of Neil Young's renaissance as a solo artist.

In the 1990s, while Young was being lauded as the "Godfather of Grunge," Crosby, Stills, and Nash operated, as Rogan has noted, "largely on the level of nostalgia." This was typified by their appearance at Woodstock II in August 1994. Young refused to appear with CSN and instead designed a range of hats depicting a vulture perched on a guitar, a parody of the famous Woodstock logo featuring a dove of peace. It was Young's pithy comment on the commodification of a (counter)cultural memory with which his erstwhile colleagues were, even twenty-five years later, inextricably associated.

After twenty-six years apart, Crosby, Stills, and Nash finally reunited with Young at the turn of the twenty-first century for a concert tour. David Fricke of *Rolling Stone* described their combined voices as "bruised gold." He wrote that the four, now in their fifties, rendered "Old Man" with a "reflection on passing youth and lost opportunity, with electrifying honesty." Crosby, Stills, and Nash have begun touring together again, and with Young they released *Greatest Hits* in 2005 and rereleased *Déjà Vu* in 2008. Each has also continued to pursue solo careers. Crosby released the box set *Voyages* in 2006, featuring highlights from his decades-long career. Sills put out *Man Alive!* in 2006, and the following year, a collection of unreleased acoustic demos that had been lost for decades was released as *Just Roll Tape*. Nash followed his 2002 release of *Songs for Survivors* with the box set *Reflections* in 2009.

Martyn Bone

SEE ALSO: *Altamont; Atlantic Records; Buffalo Springfield; The Byrds; Electric Guitar; Hippies; Kent State Massacre; Rock and Roll; The Rolling Stones; Stadium Concerts; Woodstock; Young, Neil.*

BIBLIOGRAPHY

Crosby, David. *Long Time Gone*. London: Heinemann, 1989.

Crosby, David, and David Bender. *Stand and Be Counted: Making Music History: The Dramatic Story of the Artists and Events That Changed America.* San Francisco: HarperSanFranciso, 2000.

Fricke, David. "David Crosby, Stephen Sills, Graham Nash, and Neil Young." *Rolling Stone*, April 13, 2000, 83–84.

Rogan, Johnny. *Crosby, Stills, Nash and Young: The Visual Documentary*. London: Omnibus Press, 1996.

Rogan, Johnny. *Neil Young: The Definitive Story of His Musical Career*. London: Proteus, 1982.

Zimmer, Dave. *Crosby, Stills, and Nash: The Authorized Biography.* New York: St. Martin's, 1984.

Cross-Dressing

SEE: *Drag.*

Crossword Puzzles

Once a peripheral form of entertainment, crossword puzzles have become a popular national institution. They appear in almost every newspaper and have become a focus of many people's daily and weekend rituals. They are also published in stand-alone books and magazines and appear in many foreign languages—including Chinese. Crosswords have inspired other gridded word games, such as acrostic, cryptic, and diagramless puzzles.

The average crossword puzzle involves a total of thirty words. Crosswords are generally divided into American and British (cryptic) styles, which differ in the structure of the grid, the types of words included, and the styles of the clues. The British style is popular throughout Europe and India.

Arthur Wynne constructed the first crossword, which appeared in 1913 in the *New York World.* His word puzzle consisted of an empty grid dotted with black squares. Solvers entered letters of intersecting words into this diagram; when correctly filled in, the answers to the "across" and "down" numbered definitions would complete, and hence solve, the puzzle. The layout and concept of the crossword has not changed since its inception.

Although crossword puzzles appeared in newspapers after Wynne's debut, the *New York Times* legitimized and popularized the pastime. The *Times*'s first Sunday puzzle appeared in the *New York Times Magazine* in 1942, and daily puzzles began in 1950. Being able to do the *Times* puzzle in ink rather than pencil is seen as the mark of a true crossword puzzle devotee.

Wendy Woloson

SEE ALSO: *Leisure Time; The* New York Times.

BIBLIOGRAPHY

Maleska, Eugene T. *Across and Down: The Crossword Puzzle World.* New York: Simon and Schuster, 1984.

Shepard, Richard F. "Bambi Is a Stag and Tubas Don't Go Pah-Pah." *New York Times Magazine.* February 18, 1992, 31–39.

Crouching Tiger, Hidden Dragon

Winner of both a Golden Globe and an Academy Award as best foreign-language film of 2000, the visually dazzling Chinese martial arts movie *Crouching Tiger, Hidden Dragon* surprised audiences with its compelling plot and engaging characterizations. The film's success not only launched Hollywood careers for director Ang Lee and actress Michelle Yeoh but also expanded American interest in Asian culture.

A key theme of *Crouching Tiger, Hidden Dragon* is announced in the title: surprises are concealed everywhere, and nothing is as it seems. Throughout the film, situations turn out to be more complicated than they appear—and the characters all harbor secrets as well. Fearless swordsman Li Mu Bai hides his love for the beautiful female warrior Yu Shu Lien, and Jade Fox is not really a governess but a notorious assassin. Her pupil Jen is not just a pampered young aristocrat, but Jade's secret protégé. In fact, Jen's skills have surpassed those of her teacher, and Jade seeks revenge after discovering that Jen has withheld her knowledge of certain teachings. Set in the early nineteenth century, in locations that range from China's lush mountains and grand palaces to its forbidding Gobi Desert, the film tells a story of secret passions, difficult choices, and ultimate destinies.

Crouching Tiger, Hidden Dragon is an example of *wuxia*, a type of Chinese fiction that features heroic protagonists who are skilled in martial arts and act in accordance with a code of chivalry. In *wuxia*, fighting often goes beyond expert swordsmanship and advanced techniques of physical combat to include seemingly supernatural feats of dexterity by warriors who know how to become very light and to intensify their own internal energy for many purposes. These capabilities are displayed in some of *Crouching Tiger, Hidden Dragon*'s most amazing scenes, where combatants scale sheer walls, skim over water, and fight in the treetops. The style of combat shown in the film is called Wudang ("inner fighting"), which is different from the Shaolin ("outer fighting") style frequently seen in martial arts movies. Fight choreographer Yuen Wo Ping brought to the film some of the same styles and techniques he had used in the popular 1999 film *The Matrix*.

Beyond its impressive special effects, *Crouching Tiger, Hidden Dragon* features an award-winning score, a wealth of authentic cultural detail, and a timeless, tragic love story. The screenplay (adapted from the Crane-Iron series by twentieth-century *wuxia* author Wang Dulu) received numerous award nominations, as did the cinematography, art direction, costumes, and choreography. Filmed in Mandarin, *Crouching Tiger, Hidden Dragon* played in the United States with English subtitles and set a new box-office record for a foreign-language film. The lavish production—a joint effort by Hong Kong, Taiwanese, and U.S. firms—was intended especially for European and North American audiences but was also successful in Asian markets, grossing a worldwide total of more than $200 million in its debut year.

Cynthia Giles

SEE ALSO: *Academy Awards; Hollywood; Martial Arts.*

BIBLIOGRAPHY

Berry, Chris. *Chinese Films in Focus: 25 New Takes*. London: British Film Institute, 2003.

Lee, Ang, and Huiling Wang. *"Crouching Tiger, Hidden Dragon": Portrait of the Ang Lee Film*. New York: Newmarket Press, 2000.

Slampyak, Diana E. "Chivalric Virtues in Female Form: *Crouching Tiger, Hidden Dragon*'s Wudan Warrior Princess as Medieval Hero." *The Medieval Hero on Screen: Representations from Beowulf to Buffy*, ed. Martha W. Driver and Sid Ray. Jefferson, NC: McFarland, 2004.

Crow, Sheryl *(1962–)*

Famous for her genre-blending and often politically charged lyrics, singer-songwriter Sheryl Crow gained national prominence with her 1993 debut album *Tuesday Night Music Club*. Refusing to mold herself after other female performers who dominated the market, Crow created a niche as a strong female role model. Her musical talent has garnered a large fan base, and her public struggle with breast cancer, her failed high-profile romance with cyclist Lance Armstrong, and her openness about her experiences as an adoptive parent have endeared her even further to her fans.

Crow is known for her advocacy of a simple and empowered life. This approach can be traced to her small-town midwestern roots. Born in Kennett, Missouri, on February 11, 1962, to musically inclined parents, Crow pursued her interest in music as a piano and voice student at the University of Missouri at Columbia, graduating in 1984. Her first major break came soon after she moved to Los Angeles in 1986, when she was signed as a backup singer on Michael Jackson's *Bad* (1987) tour, a job that led to work with other well-known musicians, including singer-songwriters Don Henley and Rod Stewart. Eventually, Crow was signed by A & M Records. But after critics panned tracks from what was to be her debut album, the project was abandoned in 1992. In 1993 her work with a group of musicians known as the Tuesday Night Music Club blossomed into an immensely popular album of the same name.

Crow followed up her successful debut with a string of award-winning albums, including *Sheryl Crow* (1996), *The Globe Sessions* (1998), *C'mon, C'mon* (2002), and *Wildflower* (2005). Critics responded to the intelligence behind the lyrics, her generally upbeat messages, and her unique sound. She also established herself as someone unafraid to speak her mind. She stood her ground when Wal-Mart refused to sell her eponymous album because one of its songs implicated the retailer in gun violence involving children.

As an outspoken artist, Crow is not without critics. She has been accused of hypocrisy for lambasting young female pop stars for exploiting their sexuality while at times doing the same thing. Others have noted that her assertion that fame had negatively impacted her creativity is contradicted by her reliance on famous friends to make *C'mon, C'mon*, which featured rock singer-songwriters Liz Phair and Lenny Kravitz.

In 2006 Crow's life shifted course. She went public with her breast cancer diagnosis, and soon after, her engagement to Armstrong crumbled. After successful cancer treatment, she made major changes in her life, adopting her son, Wyatt, in 2007 and taking her political activism to a new level. She famously confronted Karl Rove, then senior adviser to president George W. Bush at the White House Correspondents Dinner in 2007, criticizing the administration's failure to respond to global warming.

Her critique of Bush-era politics would form a central part of her 2008 album *Detours*. Songs on the album take aim at the war in Iraq and the government's failure to adequately respond to Hurricane Katrina. Other tracks offer insight into Crow's personal struggles and triumphs, detailing her cancer treatment, broken engagement, and love for her son. Her fans welcomed the turn in her music, relating to her as a mother and as a survivor of medical and personal traumas. Her political activism even led to an invitation to perform at the 2008 Democratic National Convention.

The singer-songwriter's resurging popularity drove sales of her 2010 album *100 Miles from Memphis*, which is more upbeat in tone than *Detours*. The same year, she adopted a second son, Levi. The changes in her life, which enhanced fans' perception of her as an approachable family woman, have contributed to her success outside of the music industry. In 2011 she coauthored the cookbook *If It Makes You Healthy*, a play on her popular 1996 song "If It Makes You Happy."

In the early 2010s, Crow is respected as one of the foremost female figures in the American music industry, having won nine Grammy Awards over the course of her career. Her facility in multiple genres (as of early 2012 she was said to be working on a country-influenced album) has allowed her to endure in the music industry into the 2010s. It is, perhaps, her personal side, however, that has most endeared her to her fans, proving her a committed activist who is willing to lend her voice to causes ranging from environmental protection to education and medical research.

Greta Gard

SEE ALSO: *Armstrong, Lance; Global Warming; Jackson, Michael; Wal-Mart.*

BIBLIOGRAPHY

Evans, Jerome. "From Sheryl Crow to Homer Simpson: Literature and Composition through Pop Culture." *English Journal* 93, no. 3 (2004): 32.

Scaggs, Austin. "Sheryl Crow's Southern Comfort." *Rolling Stone*, February 21, 2008, 40–44.

"Sheryl Crow." *Contemporary Musicians*, vol. 64. *Gale Biography in Context*. Detroit, MI: Gale, 2008.

Cruise, Tom *(1962–)*

Tom Cruise was perhaps the most charismatic actor of the 1980s and 1990s. He is a media magnet, garnering as much (if not more) interest for his family life, religious beliefs, and behavior as for his acting and producing. Although initially dismissed as little more than a pretty face with a million-dollar smile when he made his screen debut as a member of Hollywood's "Brat Pack" generation in the early 1980s, Cruise made an immediate impact in Hollywood with performances in *Taps* (1981), *The Outsiders* (1983), and *Risky Business* (1983). At one point between 1987 and 1989, four of his films combined to post more than $1 billion in box-office receipts. He became known for playing cocky, swaggering characters in such films as *Top Gun* (1986), *The Color of Money* (1986), *Cocktail* (1988), and *Days of Thunder* (1990). He has also won critical acclaim, earning Academy Award nominations for Best Actor in 1990 for *Born on the Fourth of July*, in which he portrayed disabled Vietnam vet Ron Kovic; in 1997 for a high-energy performance in *Jerry Maguire*; and in 2000 for his supporting role in *Magnolia*.

Cruise made the jump to producer in 1996 with the blockbuster *Mission: Impossible*, a big-screen remake of the popular 1960s television series. The movie spawned sequels in 2000, 2006, and 2011. In 1999 he took on his most challenging leading role to date in Stanley Kubrick's sexual thriller *Eyes Wide Shut*, teaming with his then-wife, Nicole Kidman. He received a Golden Globe nomination for his performance in *The Last Samurai* (2003), which he coproduced with Paula Wagner. Cruise and Wagner had previously teamed up to produce a number of films, including *Without Limits* (1998), *Vanilla Sky* (2001), and *Minority Report* (2002), and in 2006 they partnered with MGM Studios to revive the defunct United Artists production company and film studio. United Artists went on to produce several moderately successful films, including *Lions for Lambs* (2007) and *Valkyrie* (2008), before Wagner departed in 2008 and Cruise was bought out in 2011.

A longtime believer in Scientology, a religion founded by science fiction writer L. Ron Hubbard in the 1950s, Cruise made a number of comments in the early 2000s that threw the religion into the spotlight. He discussed his disbelief in psychiatry and psychiatric medicine, based on Scientology principles, drawing widespread disapproval from the media and society at large. In 2005 he had an emotional argument on *Today* with Matt Lauer concerning actress Brooke Shields's use of antidepressants to counter the effects of postpartum depression, calling psychiatry a "pseudo science" and attacking Lauer as "glib." Just one month before his interview with Lauer aired, Cruise had made headlines for his manic appearance on *The Oprah Winfrey Show*, in which he breathlessly professed his love for actress Katie Holmes by parading through the set and even jumping on a couch. Holmes and Cruise (dubbed "TomKat" by the tabloids) had a daughter, Suri, in early 2006 and were married later that year in a Scientology-based ceremony. The public was both fascinated and appalled by Cruise's behavior and his lawsuit-happy protection of his new family, and his professional life suffered as a result. In 2006 Paramount Pictures declined to renew a longstanding contract with Cruise, citing public backlash over his comments and actions. In 2012, Katie Holmes sued Cruise for divorce and gained full custody of their daughter.

Cruise sought to counter his slipping popularity by authorizing a revealing biography, *Tom Cruise: All the World's a Stage*, but with limited success, as he continued to be the subject of jokes. Nevertheless, he remains a worldwide celebrity, and his films continue to generate interest, as evidenced by the success of *Mission Impossible: Ghost Protocol* (2011), which earned more than $570 million in box-office sales alone.

Sandra Garcia-Myers

SEE ALSO: *Academy Awards; Brat Pack; Celebrity; Celebrity Couples; Depression; Hollywood; Hubbard, L. Ron; Kubrick, Stanley; Media Feeding Frenzies; MGM (Metro-Goldwyn-Mayer);* Mission: Impossible*; Movie Stars; Tabloids; Television;* Today*; Winfrey, Oprah.*

BIBLIOGRAPHY

Broeske, Pat H. "Cruis-ing in the Media Stratosphere." *Los Angeles Times Calendar*, May 25, 1986, 19–20.

Clarkson, Wensley. *Tom Cruise: Unauthorized*. Norwalk, CT: Hastings House, 1997.

Corliss, Richard. "Tom Terrific." *Time*, December 25, 1989, 74–79.

Greene, Ray. "Man with a Mission." *Boxoffice*, April 1996, 12–16.

Johnstone, Iain. *Tom Cruise: All the World's a Stage*. London: Hodder & Stoughton, 2006.

Morton, Andrew. *Tom Cruise: An Unauthorized Biography*. New York: St. Martin's Press, 2008.

Crumb, Robert *(1943–)*

Robert Crumb is one of the most famous and well respected of all underground comic artists and the first to be accepted into the mainstream of popular American culture. His comics are notable for explicit, detailed, and unflattering self-confessions, in which strange sexual fantasies abound. When not writing about himself, he targets the American consumer-culture establishment as well as antiestablishment hippies and dropouts. Crumb's art veers from gritty, grubby realism to extremes of expressionism and psychedelia. As both an artist and a writer, Crumb is a true original. He is relentlessly unrestrained and impulsive, and his work reflects few influences other than the funny animal comics of Carl Barks and Walt Kelley and the twisted, deformed monster people of *MAD* magazine artist Basil Wolverton.

The Philadelphia-born Crumb lived in many different places as a child, including Iowa and California. Seeking refuge from an alienated childhood and adolescence, he began drawing comics with his brothers, Charles and Max. As a young adult he lived in Cleveland, Ohio; Chicago; New York; and San Francisco. He worked for a greeting card company until he was able to produce comic books full time, and his first comic strips

Robert Crumb. *Robert Crumb attends the opening of an exhibition of his work at a museum in Germany in 2004.* TORSTEN SILZ/AFP/GETTY IMAGES.

appeared in underground newspapers, such as New York's *East Village Other*. In 1967 he published the first issues of his *Zap* comic book. Crumb introduced many of his most popular characters in *Zap*, as well as the unforgettable "Keep on Truckin'" logo, making a tremendous impact on the underground comics scene. In 1972 particularly dazzling examples of his bizarre and imaginative art appeared in *XYZ Comics*.

Among Crumb's most notable characters are Mr. Natural, a sort of sham guru who lives like a hedonist and prefers to tease, and occasionally exploit, his devotees rather than enlighten them, and his occasional disciple, Flakey Foont, emblematic of the suburban nebbish fraught with doubts and hang-ups. Others include Angelfood McSpade, a simple African girl exploited by greedy and lecherous white Americans; Mister Snoid, a diminutive sex fiend; and Whiteman, a big-city businessman, proudly patriotic and moralistic yet inwardly repressed and obsessed with sex.

Crumb's most famous character is Fritz the Cat, who first appeared in *R. Crumb's Comics and Stories* (1969). Fritz, a disillusioned college student looking for freedom, knowledge, and counterculture kicks, became popular enough to star in the 1972 animated movie *Fritz the Cat*, directed by Ralph Bakshi. It was the first animated movie ever to require an X rating. While the movie proved a huge success with young people, Crumb hated the film and retaliated in his next comic book by killing Fritz with an ice pick through the forehead.

Although much of Crumb's best-loved work was produced in the late 1960s and early 1970s, he reached a peak of widespread fame in the mid-1990s with the release of filmmaker Terry Zwigoff's mesmerizing documentary, *Crumb* (1994), which intersperses shots of Crumb's works between frank interviews with the artist and his family and comments by media and culture critics. *Crumb* won the Grand Jury Prize: Documentary at the Sundance Film Festival and was widely praised by critics. The film is honest in acknowledging the controversial aspects of Crumb's work, with critics pointing out the racist caricatures; the perverse lust; and, above all, the overt misogyny that runs through much of Crumb's oeuvre. Some of those images have depicted scantily clad buxom women with bird heads, animal heads, or no heads at all.

By the late 1990s Crumb's comic-book work had been published in a host of publications, including *Yellow Dog*, *Home Grown Funnies*, *Mr. Natural*, *Uneeda Comix*, *Big Ass*, *Weirdo*, and *Hup*. He also became well known for his bright, intense album cover for *Cheap Thrills*, released by Janis Joplin's Big Brother and the Holding Company in 1968.

Despite the controversy over content, a multitude of high-quality Crumb compilations and reprints, including coffee-table books, sketchbooks, and complete comics and stories from the 1960s, have been published. His continuing output included the illustration of short stories by Franz Kafka and a book on early blues music. Profiles of Crumb have appeared in *News-*

week, People, the *New Yorker*, and the *Paris Review* and on BBC-TV, while his art has been featured at the Whitney Museum of American Art and Museum of Modern Art in New York, as well as in numerous gallery shows in the United States, Europe, and Japan. His comic characters appear on mugs, T-shirts, patches, and stickers.

In 2009 Crumb surprised longtime fans by publishing *The Book of Genesis*, a faithful and tastefully illustrated transcription of the first book of the Old Testament. A former Catholic, Crumb said he thinks that the story is already strange enough without him trying to make it psychedelic or subversive.

David Elroy Goldweber

SEE ALSO: *Animated Films; Comic Books; Comics; Joplin, Janis;* MAD Magazine*; The* New Yorker*;* Newsweek*;* People*; Psychedelia; Sundance Film Festival; Underground Comics;* Zap Comix.

BIBLIOGRAPHY

Beauchamp, Monte. *The Life and Times of R. Crumb: Comments from Contemporaries.* New York: St. Martin's, 1998.

Crumb, Robert. *Crumb-ology: The Works of R. Crumb, 1981–1994.* Sudbury, MA: Water Row Press, 1995.

Crumb, Robert. *The Complete Crumb*, 17 vols. Seattle, WA: Fantagraphics, 1987–2005.

Crumb, Robert. *The Sweeter Side of R. Crumb.* London: MQ Publications, 2006.

Estren, Mark James. *A History of Underground Comics.* Berkeley: Ronin, 1974.

Fiene, Donald M. *R. Crumb Checklist of Work and Criticism: With a Biographical Supplement and a Full Set of Indexes.* Cambridge, MA: Boatner Norton Press, 1981.

Holm, D. K., ed. *R. Crumb: Conversations.* Jackson: University Press of Mississippi, 2004.

Crystal, Billy *(1948–)*

Billy Crystal went from stand-up comedy to playing Jodie Dallas, American TV's first major gay character, on the sitcom *Soap* (1977–1981). As a cast member on *Saturday Night Live* (1984–1985), he was known for the catchphrases "you look mahvelous" and "I hate it when that happens." After he moved from the small screen to films, Crystal's endearing sensitivity and gentle wit brought him success in movies such as *Throw Momma from the Train* (1987), *When Harry Met Sally* (1989), and *City Slickers* (1991). He made his directorial debut with *Mr. Saturday Night* (1992), the life story of Buddy Young Jr., a fictional Catskills comedian Crystal created on *Saturday Night Live.*

In the late 1990s Crystal continued working in films, costarring with Robert De Niro in *Analyze This* (1999) and its sequel, *Analyze That* (2002). Voicing animated characters in the Pixar film *Monsters, Inc.* (2001) and the English version of *Howl's Moving Castle* has endeared Crystal to a new generation of viewers. His good-natured ribbing and reliability have made him an ideal emcee; as of 2012 Crystal hosted the Grammy Awards three times and the Academy Award ceremony nine times. In 2005 his one-man play, *700 Sundays* won him a Tony Award. The play, based on Crystal's childhood on Long Island, New York, was later adapted as a book, published in 2005 by Warner Books.

Christian L. Pyle

SEE ALSO: *Academy Awards; Animated Films; De Niro, Robert; Grammy Awards;* Saturday Night Live*; Sitcom; Television; Tony Awards.*

BIBLIOGRAPHY

Crystal, Billy, and Dick Schaap. *Absolutely Mahvelous.* New York, G. P. Putnam's Sons, 1986.

Crystal, Billy. *700 Sundays.* New York: Warner Books, 2005.

CSI

CSI: Crime Scene Investigation (2000–), commonly referred to as simply *CSI*, is an American crime drama television series produced by Jerry Bruckheimer and created by Ann Donahue and Anthony E. Zuiker. Since its October 6, 2000, premiere on CBS, the show has become one of the most popular dramatic series in the world, with an estimated global audience of nearly seventy-four million viewers in 2009. The success of the show, which is set in Las Vegas, Nevada, has led CBS to add two spin-off shows, *CSI: Miami* (2002–2012) and *CSI: New York* (2004–).

CSI: Crime Scene Investigation is a variant within the police procedural genre. A team of crime lab specialists with the Las Vegas Police Department solves gruesome murders by collecting and analyzing physical evidence from crime scenes, including fingerprints, DNA samples, blood, and any other artifact that might not have been on the scene before the crime was committed. Unlike traditional police procedurals, which depict the process of identifying perpetrators through interviews with suspects and witnesses, the sleuths in *CSI* are more concerned with determining how a crime was accomplished. The show originally starred Marg Helgenberger and William Petersen (who left in the show's ninth season) as lead investigators. Other featured actors include Jorja Fox, Gary Dourdan, George Eads, Paul Guilfoyle, Eric Szmanda, Robert David Hall, Louise Lombard, Wallace Langham, Lauren Lee Smith, Laurence Fishburne, Liz Vassey, David Berman, Ted Danson, and Elisabeth Harnois.

CSI is a fictionalized version—with a healthy mixture of graphic violence and lurid sex thrown into the mix—of *The New Detectives* (1996–2005), a Discovery Channel program in which real forensic detectives use DNA and other evidence to solve long-standing unsolved crimes. Bruckheimer took Zuiker's pilot script to NBC, Fox, and ABC executives; all decided to pass. However, the head of CBS's drama development department thought the script had possibilities, and Petersen expressed interest in starring in the pilot. CBS executives were pleased with the pilot and added the show to their 2000 program schedule. *CSI* originally aired on Friday evenings after *The Fugitive* (2000–2001). It took off immediately.

The cause of *CSI*'s popularity is no mystery: Americans enjoy watching experts at work, watching crimes being solved, and watching shows that explain insider jargon and offer tidbits of expertise. The show is also popular for its slick look and special effects, as well as for its exemplary ensemble cast. *CSI* has received numerous awards, including Emmy Awards for

Special Visual Effects (2010), Cinematography (2006 and 2010), Sound (2003 and 2007), and Makeup (2002), as well as a Screen Actors Guild Award for Outstanding Ensemble in a Drama Series (2004).

The sex and violence depicted on *CSI* have earned the program a ringing condemnation by the Parents Television Council. Many law enforcement agencies have also found the show's depiction of investigations simplistic and unrealistic, particularly those that involve CSI personnel chasing down suspects and making arrests, tasks that are the province of regular police detectives and uniformed officers. The popularity of the series and its unique approach to crime solving have engendered a phenomenon called the "CSI effect," in which crime victims and jury members who are familiar with the show have unrealistic expectations about what forensic science is capable of proving.

CSI has become a cultural phenomenon and has expanded into a multimedia franchise. In addition to two spin-off series, the show has inspired a video game, a comic book, a published book about the crimes that inspired memorable episodes (*True Stories of "CSI,"* 2008), and a traveling interactive science museum exhibit, "*CSI*: The Experience." In 2011*CSI* remained the most watched drama series in the world and a linchpin for the CBS network. In 2012 CBS announced that it was canceling the *CSI: Miami* series after ten seasons; however, the network renewed both *CSI* and *CSI: New York*. American audiences' unabated appetite for the educational and the macabre continues to propel the enduring popularity of this television show.

Gerald Carpenter

SEE ALSO: *Bruckheimer, Jerry; Comic Books; Emmy Awards; Las Vegas; Television; Video Games.*

BIBLIOGRAPHY

Byers, Michelle, and Val Marie Johnson, eds. *The "CSI" Effect: Television, Crime and Governance.* Lanham, MD: Rowman & Littlefield, 2009.

Cavendar, Gray, and Deutsch, Sarah K. "*CSI* and Moral Authority: The Police and Science." *Crime, Media, Culture* 3, no. 1 (2007): 67–81.

Nichols-Pethick, Jonathan. *TV Cops: The Contemporary American Police Drama.* New York: Routledge, 2012.

Ramsland, Katherine. *True Stories of "CSI."* New York: Berkley Trade, 2008.

Cukor, George *(1899–1983)*

An American film director whose career spanned more than fifty years, George Cukor was particularly adept at female-centered melodrama (*Little Women* [1933] and *The Women* [1939]), romantic comedy (*The Philadelphia Story* [1940] and *Adam's Rib* [1949]), and musicals (*A Star Is Born* [1954] and *My Fair Lady* [1964], for which he received a Best Director Oscar). Cukor was often derided as a competent technician, although revelations about his homosexuality led to reappraisals of his work by, in particular, queer academics. They focused on his predilection for more feminine genres and gender-bending narratives, as seen in *Sylvia Scarlett* (1935), for example. Critics now perceive Cukor (like fellow director Dorothy Arzner) as an auteur, one whose sexual identity influenced the final form taken by the Hollywood material he handled.

Glyn Davis

SEE ALSO: My Fair Lady*;* The Philadelphia Story.

BIBLIOGRAPHY

Levy, Emanuel. *George Cukor: Master of Elegance: Hollywood's Legendary Director and His Stars.* New York: Morrow, 1994.

McGilligan, Patrick. *George Cukor: A Double Life.* London: Faber and Faber, 1991.

Cullen, Countee *(1903–1946)*

Among the most conservative of the Harlem Renaissance poets, Harvard-educated Countee Cullen exploded onto the New York literary scene with the publication of *Color* (1925) and solidified his reputation with *Copper Sun* (1927) and *The Black Christ and Other Poems* (1929). His verse defied the expectations of white audiences. Where earlier black poets like Paul Laurence Dunbar (1872–1906) had written in dialect, Cullen's tributes to black life echoed the classical forms of John Keats (1795–1821) and Percy Bysshe Shelley (1792–1822). The young poet was the leading light of the African American literary community during the 1920s. Although his reputation waned after 1930 as he was increasingly attacked for ignoring the rhythms and idioms of black culture, Cullen's ability to present black themes in traditional European forms made him one of the seminal figures in modern African American poetry.

Jacob M. Appel

SEE ALSO: *Harlem Renaissance; The Twenties.*

BIBLIOGRAPHY

Baker, Houston A. *Afro-American Poetics: Revisions of Harlem and the Black Aesthetic.* Madison: University of Wisconsin Press, 1988.

Ferguson, Blanche E. *Countee Cullen and the Negro Renaissance.* New York: Dodd, Mead, 1966.

Harris, Trudier, ed. *Afro-American Writers from the Harlem Renaissance to 1940.* Detroit, MI: Gale Research, 1987.

Turner, Darwin T. *In a Minor Chord: Three Afro-American Writers and Their Search for Identity.* Carbondale: Southern Illinois University Press, 1971.

Cult Films

Cult films are motion pictures that are favored by groups of audience members who find special meanings in the films of a particular director or star or for those that deal with a particular theme. In practical terms, however, cult status can be conferred on almost any film. In fact, such an occurrence is particularly sought after by filmmakers to maintain interest in the movie once its initial theatrical run has been completed. Thus, cult films might be more accurately defined as those special films that, for one reason or another, "connect" with a hard-core group of fans who never tire of viewing them or discussing them.

Cult films by their very nature deal with extremes, eschewing middle-of-the-road story lines and character stereotypes commonly seen in Hollywood studio products. These normally small movies present unusual—if not totally outrageous—protagonists involved in bizarre story lines that resolve themselves in totally unpredictable ways. According to Daniel López's *Films by Genre*, cult films can be divided into two basic categories: clique movies and subculture films.

CLIQUE FILMS

Generally speaking, "clique" films are either foreign, experimental, or films representative of a neglected genre that have become favored by special interest groups such as film societies, cinephiles, and certain academics. Proponents of a specific film may believe that it has either been overlooked or misinterpreted by filmgoers at large. They also "rediscover" the works of "B" movie directors such as Douglas Sirk or Sam Fuller and, through retrospective screenings and articles in film journals, attempt to make the case for their status as auteurs whose body of works yield a special message heard only by them. In many cases, the cult status awarded these directors has led to a revaluation of their contributions to film by historians and scholars and to the distribution of new prints of their works.

SUBCULTURE FILMS

The second type of cult film and, perhaps, the first one that comes to mind for the average person is the "subculture cult film." These are small films for which every aspect of production, from story themes to casting, exists in a cauldron of controversy, experimentation, and contention. They are often cheaply made and usually do not last long at the box office. Yet to their fans these films contain special messages sent by the filmmakers and stars. Through word-of-mouth contacts and the Internet, cultists recruit new fans for the film, thus serving to keep it alive. What is particularly fascinating, however, is the fact that all over the world, a certain segment of filmgoers will react to these same films in the same way. This is the true measure of a film's cult potential.

The fanatical appeal of these subculture favorites has also altered the traditional patterns of moviegoing and the unique role of the audience. In traditional viewing, the audiences are essentially passive, reacting to on-screen cues about when to laugh or cry and whom to root for. The subculture film audience, however, takes on an auteurial role on a performance-by-performance basis. This is due to the fact that the viewers have seen the film so many times that they know all of the lines and the characters by heart. Thus, they may attend the screening in the attire of their favorite characters and, once that character appears on the screen, begin to shout out new dialogue that they have constructed in their minds. This *new* script, more often than not, alludes to the actor's physical characteristics or foreshadows future dialogue or warnings about plot twists. In many cases audience members will yell out stage directions to the actor, telling him that he should come back and turn out a light or close a door.

Perhaps the most notable example of this auteuristic phenomenon is the undisputed "queen" of cult films, the British production *The Rocky Horror Picture Show* (1975), which concerns the plight of two newlyweds, Brad (Barry Bostwick) and his would-be bride Janet (Susan Sarandon), who become trapped in a spooky house on a rainy night in Ohio. They are met by a group of supposedly fun-loving aliens from the planet Transylvania who are being entertained by one Dr. Frank-N-Furter (Tim Curry), who struts around in sexy female underwear and fishnet stockings while belting out gender-bending tunes such as "I'm just a sweet transvestite from Transsexual, Transylvania." He is in the process of creating a Frankenstein-type monster, Rocky Horror (Peter Hinwood), to be employed strictly for sexual purposes. During the course of the evening, however, he manages to seduce both of the newlyweds and also causes a suddenly liberated Janet to pursue a fling with Rocky Horror.

The film proved to be a box-office disaster when it was released in 1975, but it developed an underground word-of-mouth reputation, causing its American producer, Lou Adler, to convince Twentieth Century Fox to search for alternative ways to publicize it. The film was re-released at the Waverly Theater in Greenwich Village, New York, and soon after at theaters throughout the country for midnight performances. Its first audiences consisted primarily of those groups represented in the film—transvestites, gays, science fiction fans, punk rockers, and college psychology majors (who presumably attended to study the rest of the audience).

For avid viewers of *The Rocky Horror Picture Show*, attendance at a midnight screening began to take on the form of a ritual. In addition to wearing costumes, members of the audience would talk to the screen, create new dialogue, dance in the aisles, and shower their fellow viewers with rice during the wedding scene and water during the rainy ones. Experienced fans, of course, attended with umbrellas, but "virgins" (those new to the film) generally went home bathed in rice and water. In the years since its first screenings, the film become a staple at midnight screenings around the country and achieved its status as the most significant cult film of all time.

Rocky Horror is often paired with *Hedwig and the Angry Inch* (2001), another film in a similar vein, for late-night double features. Directed by John Cameron Mitchell, this film depicts the journey of a transsexual glam rock singer in pursuit of her rock-star former boyfriend and frequently diverges into memorable musical numbers. Both *Rocky Horror* and *Hedwig* began as low-budget stage musicals, and they continue to enjoy revivals ranging from local theater offerings to large-scale Broadway productions.

Performers in subculture films have acquired cult followings as well. Many hard-core fans, in fact, view their favorite performers as only revealing their real personalities in their "special" film. In attempting to interpret the actor's performance in this context, the fans will also bring into play all of the performer's previous characterizations in the belief that they have some bearing on this particular role. To such fans the actor's whole career has built toward this performance, as was the case with Jeff Bridges, whose performance in the 1998 Coen brothers' film *The Big Lebowski* has many fans convinced that he truly is the pot-smoking, jelly-sandal-wearing, Zen-quoting "Dude" that he plays in the film. Although this perception has had little effect on Bridges's career or on that of other major stars in similar defining roles, it has enhanced the careers of such "B" movie icons as transvestite diva Divine and horror film actor Bruce Campbell (*The Evil Dead*), making them the darlings of the midnight theatrical circuit and major draws at fan conventions. Even deceased performers have been claimed by cult film devotees. The screen biography of Joan Crawford, *Mommie Dearest* (1981), elevated—or lowered—her from stardom to cult status, and Bela Lugosi attracted posthumous fame with fans who revisited his old horror films with an eye to the campy elements of his performances.

MAJOR CULT GENRES: HORROR

Although it is difficult to predict which films are destined to achieve special status with subcultures, a great many fall into the horror and science fiction genres. The horror films that appeal to this audience share most of the characteristics of cult films in general. They are only rarely major studio productions, but they frequently "rip off" such larger-budgeted mainstream productions as *The Exorcist* (1973), *The Omen* (1976), or the various manifestations of Bram Stoker's *Dracula*. Cult horror films inhabit the margins of the cinema in pursuit of off-beat themes, controversial subject matter, and shocking scenes of mayhem. They are either so startlingly original as to be too "far out" for most viewers or such blatant derivations of existing films that they are passed over by general audiences and critics alike.

The plots of most horror films involve a demonic disruption in the normal order of things that must be righted by each film's protagonist before the status quo can be restored. This fundamentally safe view of the world allows the audience to write its own text with any number of subjective meanings regardless of what happens in the story as a whole. As most horror film directors do not intend to send out a specific message with their work, their conservative stance leaves plenty of room for rereadings of the text to allow issues incorporating a questioning of authority, a rejection of government and the military-industrial complex, sexism, and a host of environmental concerns that inevitably arise when horror films deal with the impact of humans upon nature.

Perhaps the first cult horror film to raise such issues was Tod Browning's *Freaks* (1932), which was banned for thirty years following its initial release. The film essentially conveys the simple message that beauty is more than skin deep. When the protagonist, a circus trapeze star, attempts to toy with the affections of a sideshow midget, she is set upon by the sideshow "freaks," who transform her physical beauty into a misshapen form to reflect the ugliness within her. Although Browning was clearly attempting an entertaining horror film that stretched the boundaries of the genre, there is no overt evidence that he intended the many metaphysical meanings regarding the relationship of good and evil and body and soul that audiences have brought to the film in the sixty years since its initial release.

Another film, 1956's *Invasion of the Body Snatchers*, has been celebrated by scholars as a tract against the McCarthyism of the 1950s, though it is probably more rightly read as a statement against conformity and repression of individual thought that transcends its period. Similarly, George Romero's legendary *Night of the Living Dead* (1968) was not only the goriest movie of its time but also worked on basic human fears. Like its inspiration, Alfred Hitchcock's *The Birds* (1963), it deals with a group of people confined to a certain geographic area while nature runs amok because humans have transgressed against the natural law. The film is particularly effective because it deals with gradations of insanity, beginning with stark fear and escalating to show that humankind is totally powerless to deal with the things it fears most. Audiences sat riveted to their seats, convinced that there was no way out except death. The film began as the second feature on movie double bills and, through strong word of mouth and gradual acceptance from critics, took on a second life in college retrospectives and museum screenings (where it was declared a masterpiece) before ending up on the midnight movie circuit.

Another reason for the cult appeal of low-budget horror films is the fact that they often push the limits of what is traditionally thought to be acceptable. For example, the legendary *Blood Feast* (1976) became the first film to go beyond merely showing blood to actually showing human entrails, a development that was later picked up by Hollywood for much larger special-effects-laden films. Another low-budget film, *Evil Dead II* (1987), directed by Sam Raimi, surpassed its bloody predecessor by presenting extreme violence at such a fast pace that the human eye could barely register the images flashing by, creating an almost comical frenzy of cartoonish gore. Several other films have managed to achieve cult status by exploiting the comedy inherent in such over-the-top depictions of violence, including Peter Jackson's *Dead Alive* (1992) and Edgar Wright's zombie film *Shaun of the Dead* (2004).

A final appeal of low-budget horror films is the fact that a number of major actors and directors—including Jack Nicholson, Tom Hanks, Francis Ford Coppola, and Roger Corman—got their start in them. Corman once referred to these pictures as a film school where he learned everything he would ever need to become successful in motion pictures. But it worked the other way as well. Many stars on the downslope of their careers appeared in "B" horror films to keep their fading careers alive, hoping that they might accidentally appear in a breakthrough film. Former box-office stars—including Boris Karloff (*The Terror*, 1963), Bela Lugosi (*Plan 9 from Outer Space*, 1959), Yvonne DeCarlo (*Satan's Cheerleaders*, 1977), and Richard Basehart (*Mansion of the Doomed*, 1976)—who had been forgotten by Hollywood received a new type of stardom in these "B" films and often spent the last years of their careers appearing at comic-book and horror film conventions for adoring fans.

MAJOR CULT GENRES: SCIENCE FICTION

Science fiction films also push the cinematic envelope by their very identification with their genre. They are futuristic, technologically driven films that employ astonishing special effects to create a world that does not yet exist but might in the future. Sci-fi movies can be horror films as well. It took technology to create the Frankenstein monster, and it took technology to encounter and destroy the creature in *Alien* (1979). But, like horror films, these movies also question the impact of humans and their technology on the world. They make political statements through their futuristic story lines, saying, in effect, that twenty or more years in the future, this will be humankind's fate if people do not stop doing certain things.

Science fiction films that achieve cult status do so because, even within this already fantastic genre, they are so innovative and experimental that they take on a life of their own. With the exceptions of the *Star Wars*, *Star Trek*, and *Planet of the Apes* series and a number of individual efforts such as *2001: A Space Odyssey* (1968), the films that attract the long-term adulation of fans are generally not large studio products. They are normally small films, such as the Japanese Godzilla pictures, minor films from the 1950s with their dual themes of McCarthyism and nuclear monsters, and low-budget favorites from the 1970s and 1980s. One recent exception to this rule is director Richard Kelly's breakthrough cult film *Donnie Darko* (2001), which incorporates science fiction elements such as time travel into a dark psychological portrait of a troubled adolescent chaffing against the monotony of suburban life.

Again, as in horror, science fiction pictures seem to fall into three categories of fan fascination. These include films such as *Brain Eaters* (1958), *Lifeforce* (1985), and *The Incredible Two-Headed Transplant* (1971) that feature major stars such as Leonard Nimoy; Patrick Stewart; Bruce Dern; or, in the case of *Donnie Darko*, Jake Gyllenhaal, on the way up. Conversely a number of major stars ranging from Richard Burton and Henry Fonda appeared in some otherwise forgettable science fiction films during the twilight of their careers, making their performances memorable to aficionados of embarrassing moments on film. Still other stars, however, are able to turn almost any film into a sci-fi cult film. The list is headed by Zsa Zsa Gabor, Vincent Price, Lugosi, and John Agar.

In the final analysis, cult films say more about the people who love them than about themselves. To maintain a passion for a film that would compel one to drive to the very worst parts of town dressed in outlandish costumes to take part in a communal viewing experience sets the viewer apart as a special person. He or she is one of a select few who has the ability to interpret a powerful message from a work of art that has somehow escaped the population at large. In pursuing the films they love, cultists are making a statement that they are not afraid to set themselves apart and to take on the role of tastemakers for the moviegoers of the future. In many cases the films they celebrate influence filmmakers to employ new subjects, performers, or technology in more mainstream films. In other instances their special films will never be discovered by the mainstream world. But that is part of the appeal: to be different, to be "out there," is to be like the cult films themselves.

Steve Hanson

SEE ALSO: Alien*; "B" Movies; Batman;* Blade Runner*; Blockbusters; Broadway; Capra, Frank; Celebrity; Circus; Coen, Joel and Ethan; Comic Books; Corman, Roger; Crawford, Joan; Divine; Drive-In Theater; Environmentalism;* The Exorcist*; Fonda, Henry; Ford, John; Frankenstein;* Freaks*; Gay Men; Godzilla; Greenwich Village; Hanks, Tom; Hitchcock, Alfred; Hollywood; Horror Movies; The Internet;* It's a Wonderful Life*; Karloff, Boris; Leisure Time; Lucas, George; Lugosi, Bela; McCarthyism; Movie Stars; The Musical; Nicholson, Jack;* Night of the Living Dead*;* Planet of the Apes*; Price, Vincent;* The Rocky Horror Picture Show*; Sarandon, Susan; Science Fiction Publishing;* The Searchers*; Sirk, Douglas; Spinal Tap;* Star Trek*;* Star Wars*; Teenagers; Television;* 2001: A Space Odyssey*; Waters, John; The Western;* The Wizard of Oz.

BIBLIOGRAPHY

Batchelor, Bob, ed. *Cult Pop Culture: How the Fringe Became Mainstream.* Santa Barbara, CA: Praeger, 2012.

Davies, Steven Paul. *A-Z of Cult Films and Film-Makers.* London: Batsford, 2001.

Everman, Welch. *Cult Horror Films: From "Attack of the 50-Foot Woman" to "Zombies of Mora Tau."* Secaucus, NJ: Carol Publishing Group, 1993.

Everman, Welch. *Cult Science Fiction Films.* New York: Carol Publishing Group, 1995.

Hentzi, Gary. "Little Cinema of Horrors." *Film Quarterly,* Spring 1993, 22–27.

Jancovich, Mark; Antonio Lázaro Reboll; Julian Stringer, et al, eds. *Defining Cult Movies: The Cultural Politics of Oppositional Taste.* New York: Manchester University Press, 2003.

Lopez, Daniel. *Films by Genre.* Jefferson, NC: McFarland, 1993.

Margulies, Edward, and Stephen Rebello. *Bad Movies We Love.* New York: Plume, 1993.

Mathijs, Ernest, and Xavier Mendik, eds. *The Cult Film Reader.* New York: Open University Press/McGraw-Hill Education, 2008.

Peary, Danny. *Cult Movie Stars.* New York: Simon & Schuster, 1991.

Peary, Danny. *Cult Movies: The Classics, the Sleepers, the Weird, and the Wonderful.* New York: Gramercy Books, 1998.

Schwartz, Carol, with Jim Olenski, eds. *VideoHound's Cult Flicks and Trash Pics,* 2nd ed. Detroit: Visible Ink Press, 2001.

Weldon, Michael J. *The Psychotronic Video Guide to Film.* New York: St. Martin's Griffin, 1996.

Cults

The 1978 Jonestown massacre, where 913 of the Reverend Jim Jones's followers were forced to commit suicide, marked the high point in the condemnation of cults in the United States. Spread across newspaper front pages and national magazines from coast to coast, the slaughter gave focus to an alarm that had grown throughout the decade.

Sometimes referred to as "new religious movements" (NRMs), cults and splinter groups from established religions have found a fertile cultural terrain. That the modern-day American public finds cults alarming is yet another example of the paradoxical culture. The debate over the tax status of what are generally defined as alternative religions continued into the twenty-first century, as did the issue of defining them as religions or cults.

Cults as they are understood in the popular imagination have some additional characteristics and can include any religious organization that spends an inordinate amount of time raising money; any religion that relies on a virulent us-vs.-them dogmatism, thereby alienating its members further from mainstream society; and any religion where the temporal leader holds such authoritarian sway as to be regarded as a deity capable of treating cult members as financial, sexual, or missionary chattel to be exploited to the limits of their endurance. In this expanded definition, a Pentecostal such as Aimee Semple McPherson, a Los Angeles preacher and not technically a cult leader, fits adequately into the definition, as does Jones, Charles Manson, or Sun Myung Moon.

EARLY RELIGIOUS CULTS

Originally, much of the colonized area that would become the United States was a land of pilgrims and religious proselytizers, and the Plymouth colonists were not the last to view the New World as a holy land. And, as in all times and all religions, religious charlatans were a constant. By the close of the nineteenth century, people in the United States had founded some peculiar interpretations of Christianity. The Mormons, Seventh-Day Adventists, Christian Scientists, and Jehovah's Witnesses all had their origins in the nineteenth century, and by dint of accretion they had developed from dubious, persecuted faiths into mainstream institutions.

The history of Mormonism shows much that is pertinent to understanding modern-day cults; elements of this tale are reminiscent of the histories of Scientology, the Unification Church, and the Peoples Temple, among others. A charismatic leader, claiming divine inspiration and not above resorting to trickery, amasses a following that is often viewed with derision by the general populace. The faith aggressively recruits new members and later attempts to gloss over its dubious origins, building enormous and impressive edifices and going out of its way to convey an image of solidity, eventually securing a sense of respectability.

From time to time, waves of religious fervor have swept across the United States—the Shakers and Pentecostals early in the nineteenth century, for instance, or the Spiritualist and Theosophy movements at century's end. In western New York state, where the Church of Jesus Christ of Latter-day Saints (and its offshoot, the Community of Christ) originated, so many evangelical movements caught fire in the 1820s that it was nicknamed the Burned-over District. The church's founder, Joseph Smith, claimed to have received revelation directly from an angel who left Smith with several golden tablets on which were inscribed the story of Hebraic settlers to the New World. Notes author and journalist Tom Wolfe in his essay in *Mauve Gloves and Madmen, Clutter and Vine*, Smith and his band of youthful comrades were "regarded as wilder, crazier, more obscene, more of a threat than the entire lot of hippie communes of the 1960s put together." Smith's contemporaries called him "a notorious liar" and "utterly destitute of conscience" and cited his 1826 arrest for fortune-telling as evidence of his dishonesty.

Jonestown Massacre. *Bodies of the followers of the Rev. Jim Jones and his People's Temple cult lie amid tubs of cyanide-laced punch after the group's mass suicide in Guyana in 1978.* **DAVID HUME KENNERLY/GETTY IMAGES.**

By the time Smith fled New York in 1839, however, he was accompanied by 10,000 loyal converts who followed him to Nauvoo, Illinois, with an additional 5,000 converts from England swelling their numbers. After Smith began a systematic power grab, using the Mormon voting bloc in gaining several elected positions, he was lynched by the locals, and the Mormons continued westward to Utah, where the only threat was the Native Americans. It was not until 2004 that the state of Illinois officially apologized for its treatment of Smith and the Mormons.

An earnest desire to bring people into the fold has often devolved into hucksterism in the hands of some religious leaders. Throughout the twentieth century, Elmer Gantry-esque religious leaders, from the lowly revivalist preacher to the television ministries of a Jimmy Swaggart or Oral Roberts, have shown as much concern with fleecing their followers as with saving their souls. When Mary Baker Eddy, the founder of the Church of Christ, Scientist, died in 1910, she left a fortune of $3 million. Author George Orwell once mused that the best way to make a lot of money was to start a religion, and L. Ron Hubbard, founder of Scientology, showed Orwell's maxim to be true.

SCIENTOLOGY

A pulp fiction writer by trade, Hubbard originally published his new science of Dianetics, a treatise on the workings of the mind, in the April 1950 issue of *Astounding Science Fiction*. Dianetics was a technique for self-actualization and understanding, and Hubbard couched his theories in scientific rhetoric and obscure phraseology to appeal to a well-educated, affluent constituency. Published in book form, *Dianetics* became an overnight success, and Hubbard quickly set up a research institute and began attracting adherents.

Dianetics, as practiced by Hubbard, straddled the gap between the self-actualization movements typical of later religious cults and religion (though Scientology's mythos was not set down until shortly before Hubbard's death). In Dianetics an auditor ran potential followers through a list of questions, and their emotional response was measured with an e-meter, a simple galvanic register held in both hands. This meter supposedly revealed the negative experiences imprinted in a person's unconscious in an almost pictorial form called an engram, and Dianetics promised to sever the unconscious connection to negative experiences and allow the follower to attain an exalted state similar to enlightenment. Hubbard's idea appeared scientific, and, like psychotherapy, it proved to be an inherently expensive, time-consuming process to adherents.

From the beginning Hubbard ran into all manner of legal troubles. He squabbled with the Internal Revenue Service (IRS) over the church's tax-exempt status and the Food and Drug Administration (FDA) over the use of the e-meter. Scientology met stiff government opposition in every country in which it operated. An Australian Board of Inquiry, convened in 1965, called Scientology "evil, its techniques evil, its practice a serious threat to the community, medically, morally, and socially. . . . Scientology is a delusional belief system, based on fictions and fallacies and propagated by falsehoods and deception"; it was banned from Australia until 1983. The British government banned foreign Scientologists in 1968, and Hubbard was convicted on fraud charges in absentia by a Paris court in 1978. The church lost its tax-exempt status in France and Denmark in the mid-1980s and had to seriously curtail its operations in Germany.

More than most cults, Scientology's travails appeared to be symptomatic of its founder's mental instability. As an institution, Scientology was marked by an extreme fractiousness and a pronounced penchant for litigation. Ruling in a 1984 lawsuit brought by the church, a Los Angeles judge stated, "The organization clearly is schizophrenic and paranoid, and this bizarre combination seems to be a reflection if its founder."

The issue of whether or not Scientology should be recognized as a legitimate religion rose to prominence in a number of countries early in the twenty-first century. Celebrity Scientologists such as actors Tom Cruise and John Travolta were quick to defend their church. Nevertheless, a revolt occurred within the church over the billion-dollar fortune amassed by church leaders. Another scandal erupted in 2009 when Paul Haggis, the Hollywood screenwriter who penned scripts for the award-winning *Million Dollar Baby* and *Crash* (both 2004), left the church and accused Scientologists of being involved in human trafficking and enslavement. He insisted that the Church of Scientology was a cult and should be recognized as such. A subsequent Federal Bureau of Investigation (FBI) inquiry uncovered claims of coercion and harassment, but Haggis's assertion remained unproven.

"MOONIES"

In many ways Scientology anticipated the tactics of the wave of cult groups that rose to prominence the United States in the 1960s and 1970s. A look at two of the most infamous—the Unification Church and the Hare Krishnas—must suffice to explain this religious revival, what Wolfe terms the "Third Wave."

Better known by the pejorative term *Moonies*, the Unification Church, a radical offshoot of Presbyterianism, founded its first American church in California in 1959. Its founder, the Reverend Moon, converted from his native Confucianism as a child after claiming to receive a messianic revelation while in his teens. He was subsequently expelled from his church, but by the late 1950s he had established a large congregation and had gathered the finances necessary to begin missionary work abroad. Like many cults, the church's teachings were culturally conservative and spiritually radical. Initially, it appealed to those confused by the rapid changes in social mores then prevalent, offering a simple theology and rigid moral teachings. One of its more unorthodox beliefs is the idea that all races will eventually become one. Adherents are assigned marriage partners (typically from a different race), and mass weddings are sometimes held in large outdoor stadiums, drawing attention from community members and the press.

The Unification Church was aggressive in its proselytizing. Critics decried its recruitment methods as being callous, manipulative, and deceitful; the charge of brainwashing was frequently leveled against the church. Adherents preyed on college students, targeting the most vulnerable among them—the lonely, the disenfranchised, and the confused. The unsuspecting recruit was typically invited over to a group house for dinner. Upon arrival the recruit was showered with attention (called "love-bombing" in church parlance) and told only in the most general terms the nature of the church. The potential member was then invited to visit a church-owned ranch or farm for the weekend and was continually supervised from early morning until late at night.

Once absorbed, the new member was destined to take a place in the church's vast fund-raising machine—selling trinkets, candy, flowers, or other cheap goods—and witnessing on behalf of the church. Often groups of adherents traveled across the country, sleeping in their vehicles and renting a motel room once a week to maintain personal hygiene—in short, living lives of privation while funneling profits to the church. Moonie proselytizers were known for their stridency and their evasions, typically failing to identify their church affiliation should they be asked. On an institutional level the church resorted to this same type of subterfuge, setting up dozens of front groups and buying newspapers and magazines—usually with a right-wing bias. (Moon was an avowed anticommunist, a result of his spending time in a North Korean prisoner of war camp.)

The Unification Church also developed an elaborate lobbying engine; it was among the few groups that actually supported President Richard Nixon, organizing pro-Nixon demonstrations up until the last days of his administration. Allusive, shadowy connections to Korean intelligence agencies were also alleged. The church, with its curious theology coupled with a rabid right-wing agenda, was and is a curious institution. Like Hubbard, many Christian evangelists, and other cult leaders, Moon taught his followers to be selfless while he himself enjoyed a life of luxury. But the depth and scope of his political influence is profound, and among cults his has achieved an unprecedented level of political power.

HARE KRISHNAS

Like the Unification Church, the International Society for Krishna Consciousness (ISKCON), better known as the Hare Krishna movement, has drawn widespread criticism. Unlike the Unification Church, the Hare Krishnas evince little concern for political exigencies, but their appearance—clean-shaven heads and pink saris—make the Hare Krishnas a visible target for anticult sentiments, and for many years the stridency of their beliefs exacerbated matters.

A devout Hindu devotee of Krishna, A. C. Bhaktivedanta Swami Prabhupada was charged by his guru with bringing Hinduism from India to the United States. He arrived in New York City in 1965, and his teachings became popular with members of the emerging hippie populace, who adopted the movement's distinctive uniform, forswearing sex and drugs for nonchemical bliss. Hare Krishnas lived in communes, practicing a life of extreme asceticism and forsaking ties with family and friends. Complete immersion in the group was de rigueur.

The movement spread rapidly, becoming infamous for its incessant street proselytizing, in which lines of devotees played percussion instruments while chanting for hours. Even ex-Beatle George Harrison, who became a Hare Krishna in the late 1960s, produced a number of singles in support of the group, most notably "My Sweet Lord" (1970). The sect's frequenting of airports and train stations, importuning travelers with flowers or

Prabhupada's translation of the classic Indian text, the Bhagavad-Gita, also drew public scorn. Like the Moonies, the Hare Krishna's fund-raising efforts helped turn public opinion against the cult.

DEPROGRAMMING

In the 1970s, as more and more young people in the United States joined such groups as the Unification Church, the Hare Krishnas, or the Jesus People (an eclectic group of hippies who turned to primitive charismatic Christianity while retaining their dissolute fashions and lifestyle), parental concern intensified. An unsubstantiated but widely disseminated statistic held that a quarter of all cult recruits were Jewish, provoking alarm among Jewish congregations. To combat the threat, self-proclaimed cult experts offered to abduct and deprogram cult members for a fee, and, in the best of American traditions, deprogramming itself became a lucrative trade full of self-aggrandizing pseudo-psychologists.

Nonetheless, the deprogrammers did have some valid points. Many cults used sleep deprivation, low-protein diets, and constant supervision to mold members into firmly committed zealots. By stressing an us-vs.-them view of society, cults worked on their young charges' feelings of alienation from society, creating virtual slaves who would happily sign over their worldly possessions, or, as was the case with a group called the Children of God, literally give their bodies to Christ as prostitutes.

For those who had lost a child to a cult, the necessity of deprogramming was readily apparent. But in time, the logic of the many cult watchdog groups grew a bit slim. If anything, the proliferation of anticult groups spoke to the unsettling aftershocks of the 1960s counterculture as much as to any threat presented by new religions. Were all religious groups outside the provenance of an established church to be equally condemned? Were all religious beliefs that were not intrinsically exoteric to be rejected out of hand? By stressing conformity, many watchdog groups diluted their moral authority.

Ironically, whereas cult watchdog groups focused public outrage on the large, readily identifiable cults—Scientology, ISKCON, the International Churches of Christ, the Unification Church—it was usually the smaller, homegrown varieties that proved the most unstable. Religions are concerned with self-perpetuation. When a charismatic leader dies, stable religious groups often grow more stable and moderate and perpetuate themselves (as has the now respectable Community of Christ). But smaller cults, if they do not dissolve and scatter, have often exploded in self-destruction. The Peoples Temple, the Branch Davidians (actually a sect of Presbyterianism), and the Manson Family were such groups. In 1997 Heaven's Gate, a cult with pronounced science fiction beliefs based in California, committed mass suicide in accordance with the passing of the Hale-Bopp comet.

PUBLIC REACTION

The Jonestown massacre in the Guyanese jungle in 1978 marks the period when cult awareness was at its height, although incidents like the Heaven's Gate mass suicide have kept cults in the headlines. Such is the degree of public suspicion of cults that, when necessary, government agencies could tap into this distrust and steer blame away from their own wrongdoing. This was the case when the Bureau of Alcohol, Tobacco, and Firearms (ATF) and the FBI burned the Branch Davidian compound in Waco, Texas, in 1993 after followers of cult leader David Koresh refused to surrender themselves to authorities on charges ranging from the stockpiling of illegal weapons to physical and sexual abuse. At the time of the massacre, media reportage was uniform in its condemnation of Koresh and vociferous in its approval of the FBI; it was only with the release of *Waco: The Rules of Engagement*, a 1997 documentary on the FBI's mishandling of the situation, that a dissenting note was finally heard.

The United States is not unique in its war between the positive, socializing aspects of religion and the esoteric, ecstatic spiritualism running counterpoint beside it. "As Max Weber and Joachim Wach have illustrated in detail," notes Wolfe, "every major modern religion, as well as countless long-gone minor ones, has originated not with a theology or a set of values or a social goal or even a vague hope of a life hereafter. They have all originated, instead, with a small circle of people who have shared some overwhelming ecstasy or seizure, a 'vision,' a 'trance,' an hallucination; in short, an actual neurological event."

This often-overlooked aspect of the cult experience explains the suspicion with which mainstream religions view the plethora of cults that rolled over the United States since its founding, as well as the aversion cult members show to society at large once they have bonded with their fellows in spiritual ecstasy. It is precisely these feelings of uniqueness, of privileged insight, that fraudulent cult leaders work on in their efforts to mold cult members into spiritual slaves. The problem is this: not all cults are the creation of charlatans, but the opprobrium of society toward cults is by now so ingrained, that on the matter of cults there is no longer any question of reconciling the historical precedent with the contemporary manifestation.

Nevertheless, a portion of the American public is and will continue to be endlessly susceptible to simple, all-encompassing explanations, and what most cults share is a rigid dogmatism that brooks no argument, a hermetically sealed belief system, eternally vulnerable to exposure from the world at large. The rage of a Jones or Manson springs from not only their personal manias but also from their impotence in controlling the world to suit their teachings. When cults turn ugly and self-destructive, it is often in reaction to this paradox. Like a house of cards in a light wind, cults are fragile structures—it does not take much to set them tumbling down. Still, given humankind's pressing spiritual needs, and despite society's abhorrence, it seems likely that cult groups will continue to emerge in new and occasionally frightening ways.

Michael Baers

SEE ALSO: Astounding Science Fiction*;* Crash*; Cruise, Tom; Hare Krishna; Hubbard, L. Ron; Jonestown; Koresh, David, and the Branch Davidians; Manson, Charles; McPherson, Aimee Semple; Moonies/Reverend Sun Myung Moon; New Age Spirituality; Swaggart, Jimmy; Travolta, John; Wolfe, Tom.*

BIBLIOGRAPHY

Barrett, David V. *Sects, "Cults," and Alternative Religions: A World Survey and Sourcebook*. London: Blandford, 1996.

Christie-Murray, David. *A History of Heresy*. Oxford: Oxford University Press, 1976.

Collins, John J. *The Cult Experience: An Overview of Cults, Their Traditions, and Why People Join Them*. Springfield, IL: Thomas, 1991.

Davis, Derek H., and Barry Hankins. *New Religious Movements and Religious Liberty in America.* Waco, TX: Baylor University Press, Dawson Institute of Church-State Studies, 2002.

Jenkins, Philip. *Stoning the Prophets: Cults and Cult Scares in Modern America.* New York: Oxford University Press, 2000.

Lane, Brian. *Killer Cults: Murderous Messiahs and Their Fanatical Followers.* London: Headline, 1996.

Robbins, Thomas. *Cults, Converts & Charisma.* London: Sage Publications, 1988.

Rochford, E. Burke. *Hare Krishna Transformed.* New York: New York University Press, 2007.

Stein, Stephen J. *Communities of Dissent: A History of Alternative Religions in America.* New York: Oxford University Press, 2003.

Stoner, Carroll, and Jo Anne Parke. *All God's Children.* Radnor, PA: Chilton, 1977.

Wolfe, Tom. "The Me Decade and the Third Great Awakening." In *Mauve Gloves and Madmen, Clutter and Vine.* New York: Farrar, Straus & Giroux, 1976.

Yanoff, Morris. *Where Is Joey?: Lost among the Hare Krishnas.* Athens, OH: University Press, 1981.

Zellner, William W., and Marc Petrowsky, eds. *Sects, Cults, and Spiritual Communities: A Sociological Analysis.* Westport, CT: Praeger, 1998.

Cunningham, Merce *(1919–2009)*

Dancer and choreographer Merce Cunningham influenced twentieth-century art with his postmodern dance and collaborations with important figures of the American art scene, such as composer John Cage and artists Robert Rauschenberg and Andy Warhol. Cunningham founded Merce Cunningham Dance Company (MCDC) in 1953 to challenge traditional ideas of dance and the expectations of audiences.

His philosophy declared all elements of a performance—music, dancing bodies, sets, and costumes—to be of equal importance, and he dispensed with conventional plots. His pioneering video work questioned the use of the stage. He and his collaborators also incorporated chance into the elaborate systems of their performances to create abstract and haunting dances. A recipient of numerous awards and honorary degrees, including doctorates from Wesleyan and Bard colleges, Cunningham was always searching for ways to innovate. In 2008 he collaborated with the OpenEnded Group to release *Loops*, an abstract rendering of his dance movements.

He continued to dance with MCDC into the 1990s, choreographing his final work, *Nearly Ninety*, in April 2009. He died shortly after, on July 26, 2009. The same year the Cunningham Dance Foundation, a charitable organization that Cunningham founded in 1964, announced a final world tour of the dancer's work and the subsequent close of MCDC, which occurred in 2012.

Petra Kuppers

SEE ALSO: *Modern Dance; Videos; Warhol, Andy.*

BIBLIOGRAPHY

Kostelanetz, Richard, ed. *Merce Cunningham: Dancing in Space and Time.* New York: Da Capo Press, 1998.

Vaughan, David, and Melissa Harris, eds. *Merce Cunningham: Fifty Years.* New York: Aperture, 1997.

Curious George

Since 1941, when Curious George was first introduced in an eponymous children's book, children and adults have embraced the mischievous monkey. A cultural icon and hero of seven children's books, Curious George was cocreated by husband-and-wife team H. A. and Margret Rey. The character retains his appeal through his timeless, childlike qualities and penchant for doing what readers may be too afraid to try. As children's author Madeleine L'Engle writes in the introduction to *The Complete Adventures of Curious George* (1994), "George, like most true heroes, is a creature of action; he acts, rather than being acted upon."

CREATORS

Often referred to as the father of Curious George, Hans Augusto Rey (1898–1977) began drawing at the age of two. He had a passion for animals evident in his initial drawings and in the menagerie of animals he kept as pets. In his native Hamburg, Germany, H. A. often visited the Hagenbeck Zoo, where he perfected his animal sketches. A love of languages helped him to master four different tongues and fostered his lifelong fascination with linguistics.

As a soldier in World War I, he passed the time studying the constellations. His interest in astronomy would lead him to write two books on the subject, one for a young audience and the other for more advanced readers. Before leaving Germany in 1923 for Rio de Janeiro, H. A. met Margret (1906–1996) through mutual friends. While he sold bathtubs in Brazil for a relative's firm, she studied art in Germany at the Bauhaus in Dessau, at the Academy of Art in Dusseldorf, and at art school in Berlin. She then worked as a newspaper reporter and a copywriter for an advertising agency.

In 1935 Margret left Germany for Rio, where she and H. A. became collaborators in business and in life. According to Margret, they formed "a sort of two-person advertising agency, doing a little of everything" to make ends meet. After their marriage in 1936, the Reys traveled to Paris, planning to spend only a few weeks; instead their visit lasted four years.

While in Paris, H. A. drew funny illustrations of a giraffe for a magazine, catching the attention of French publishing house Gallimard. The publisher approached him about writing a children's story using the drawings, and the result was *Cecily G. and the Nine Monkeys* (1939). The book, which featured a monkey named George, led to other children's books for the same publisher.

EARLY PUBLICATIONS

If not for the start of World War II, the Reys might have remained in Paris. But, in a turn of events that has become as legendary as their fictional creation, the Reys escaped Paris on bicycles one rainy morning in June 1940. Strapped to their bike racks were their manuscripts, which included a draft of their

Curious George. *Creators Margret and H. A. Rey introduced Curious George and the Man with the Yellow Hat to readers in 1941.* SPENCER PLATT/GETTY IMAGES.

first book, *Curious George*. Abandoning their bikes at the French-Spanish border, the Reys hopped a train to Lisbon, Portugal. By October of that same year, they arrived in New York, intent on selling their stories.

Shortly after arriving, the Reys sold *Curious George* to publisher Houghton Mifflin, which released the book in 1941. For the next twenty years, the couple lived and worked in New York, turning out six more books about the curious monkey and his trusted companion, the man with the yellow hat. According to Margret, they initially did not want to write another book about Curious George, and nearly six years passed before they published *Curious George Takes a Job* in 1947.

Despite the books' apparent simplicity, each was a time-consuming process. "Sometimes, it became more like mathematics than writing a book," Margret once told an interviewer. Inspiration came from many places: friends, newspaper stories, even chance conversations with strangers. Generally, H. A. presided over the illustrations and Margret wrote the stories, but most often the books were a complex merger of the couple's various talents.

APPEAL

Since Curious George's first book appeared in 1941, children have enjoyed how the pictures tell the story, liberating nonreaders from relying on their literate older brothers, sisters, or parents. H. A.'s illustrations deftly capture George's mischievousness. In his first book, the little monkey takes an unexpected swim in the ocean on a voyage from Africa to the United States. The illustration of George coughing up seawater and live fish delightfully conveys the results of his curiosity.

Children can relate to George's curiosity and the trouble it frequently inspires. When the Reys wrote, "George promised to be good, but little monkeys sometimes forget," they could have been referring to any little girl or boy. The man with the yellow hat adds a soothing quality to the stories, as George's adventures are thrilling but also can be scary. The man often helps George out of scrapes, and George shows readers that it is okay to be afraid and to cry. George's quick mind demonstrates the benefits of becoming self-reliant.

In the 1960s, after writing nearly all of the seven *Curious George* books, the Reys moved from New York to Massachusetts. After a long illness, H. A. died in 1977. In the 1980s, Margret and collaborator Alan J. Shelleck worked together on a second series of Curious George stories. Through various licensing agreements carefully selected by Margret and secured through a series of legal battles in the 1990s, the instantly recognizable image of the curious little monkey began appearing on greeting cards, children's toys, clothing, and even CD-ROMs.

FILMS AND ANIMATED SERIES

In all the *Curious George* stories have sold more than twenty million copies and continue to have solid sales each year. Sales received a boost in 1994 when the film *Forrest Gump* (1994) featured a scene with Forrest's mother (played by actress Sally Field) reading a *Curious George* book to her son (played as an adult by actor Tom Hanks). Curious George also has appeared in animated television films and series. In the 1980s several animated television movies featured George embarking on new adventures. The movies were later turned into books under the New Adventure series moniker.

In 2006 PBS began airing a new animated program targeted at preschoolers, *Curious George*. The show depicts George's animated misadventures interspersed with live-action scenes of children learning math and science concepts. New plots and real children performing experiments based on George's exploits have attracted young viewers. The series was nominated for a Daytime Emmy Award for Outstanding Children's Animated Program in 2011.

A full-length animated feature film, starring comic actor Will Ferrell as the man in the yellow hat (named Ted), also debuted in 2006. Critics generally approved of the movie, which added modern elements and a lighthearted love plot for Ted, and the film performed well at the box office, spurring a DVD sequel, *Curious George 2: Follow That Monkey!* (2010). The movie's soundtrack, *Sing-a-Longs and Lullabies for the Film "Curious George"* by Hawaiian crooner Jack Johnson, reached the number one position on the Billboard 200 album chart.

Poet W. H. Auden once wrote that a good children's book should also interest a clever adult. The Curious George series has consistently gained new fans, young and old, through classic stories and new media. The little monkey's continued popularity is testament to the universality and timelessness of his charm. His stories have been translated into many languages, further demonstrating his wide appeal.

Alison Macor

SEE ALSO: *Animated Films; Emmy Awards; Ferrell, Will; Field, Sally;* Forrest Gump*; Hanks, Tom; L'Engle, Madeleine; Public Television (PBS); Toys; World War I; World War II; Zoos.*

BIBLIOGRAPHY

Rey, Margret, and H. A. Rey. *The Complete Adventures of Curious George*. Boston: Houghton Mifflin, 1994.

Smee, Sebastian. "'Curious George Saves the Day' Shines with the Life." *Boston Globe*, January 6, 2012.

Williams, Karen. "She Wrote from the Heart and Touched the Child in All of Us." *Christian Science Monitor*, May 23, 1996, B3.

Currier and Ives

The decorative and hugely popular colored lithographs mass produced by Currier and Ives in the nineteenth century and familiar to subsequent generations through Christmas cards and calendars illustrate sporting scenes and sailing ships, noteworthy triumphs and disasters, Native American uprisings and comic vignettes, rustic beauty and domestic bliss. In general they evoke an idealized and sentimental view of life in nineteenth-century America. Typically, a well-known artist's work would be reproduced as a black-and-white lithograph, hand colored by a team of women, and distributed by the thousands at costs ranging from a few cents to a few dollars, depending on size.

The firm was founded in New York City in 1834 by Nathaniel Currier, employed James Merritt Ives in 1852, and became Currier and Ives in 1857. The two were succeeded by their sons, who managed the company until its closing in 1907, by which time more than 7,000 different prints had been produced.

Craig Bunch

SEE ALSO: *Christmas; Pop Art.*

BIBLIOGRAPHY

Baragwanath, Albert K. *Currier and Ives*. New York: Abbeville Press, 1980.

LeBeau, Bryan F. *Currier and Ives: America Imagined.* Washington, DC: Smithsonian Institution Press, 2001.

Reilly, Bernard, and Gale Research Company. *Currier and Ives: A Catalogue Raisonné*. Detroit, MI: Gale Research, 1984.

Cyrus, Miley / Hannah Montana *(1992–)*

As the breakout star of the popular Disney Channel show *Hannah Montana*, Miley Cyrus established herself as a teen icon and role model in 2006. The show served as the launching pad for her career as a pop music performer and television and film actress.

Destiny Hope Cyrus was born in Franklin, Tennessee, on November 23, 1992, to performer Billy Ray Cyrus and Leticia "Tish" Finley. An established country music singer, her father first gained public notoriety and commercial success with the hit "Achy Breaky Heart," in 1992. Cyrus parlayed his brief musical success into an acting career as well, starring in basic cable television series and made-for-television movies. The Cyrus family decided on the name Destiny Hope for their child because they felt she was special and would be a light in the world for others. Constant smiling as a baby, however, led the couple to nickname her Smiley. Eventually, Smiley was shortened to Miley, as she became known to her fans.

Cyrus's first acting work appeared on her father's show, *Doc*, which aired from 2001 to 2004. Citing her father's work as an influence, Cyrus began pursuing acting professionally and auditioning for various roles after this first appearance in front of the camera. Initially trying for the role of Lilly in Disney's *Hannah Montana* show, producers were impressed by her singing ability and eventually cast Cyrus in the lead role. Debuting in 2006, the show became an instant hit. The plot revolves around the life of pop star Hannah Montana, an alias for Miley Stewart, who is an international pop music sensation. Hannah, the alter ego, commands the stage and handles life with aplomb and ease. Miley, however, encounters the typical problems teenagers endure growing up with much less confidence and success.

HANNAH MONTANA AND MUSIC CAREER

The role of Miley's best friend, Lilly, was given to Emily Osment, sister of noted child actor Haley Joel Osment. Mitchel Musso played the role of Oliver, Lilly's boyfriend, and Miley's brother was portrayed by Jason Earles. Rounding out the main cast, Billy Ray Cyrus played the role of Miley's father in the series, and their strong connection and chemistry was apparent during the show's production. The series lasted for ninety-nine episodes, with the final one airing in January 2011.

Hannah Montana was a commercial success for the Disney Channel and continued the company's history of family- and kid-friendly comedies that imparted important messages about family, self-confidence, and friendship. A critical success, the show was nominated for and won several awards for outstanding programming for children.

Hannah Montana. *Miley Cyrus performs as Hannah Montana during her Best of Both Worlds tour in 2007.* KEVIN MAZUR/ WIREIMAGE/GETTY IMAGE.

Cyrus's first two albums, *Meet Miley Cyrus* (2007) and *Breakout* (2008), hit number one on the charts and achieved platinum status. A mix of country and pop, both were popular with preteen and teen audiences. The various *Hannah Montana* soundtracks were also significant commercial successes. Concert tours featuring both personas, Hannah Montana and Miley Cyrus, were popular during the run of the television series. During these shows Cyrus spent half the show singing as Hannah Montana and the other half performing as herself. After the series wrapped, she performed exclusively as herself.

CONTROVERSY

Cyrus became increasingly more scrutinized as she attempted to appeal to a wider audience and evolve from a teen pop star to an adult performer. In 2008 she posed for *Vanity Fair* magazine, but the published photos were viewed as provocative by parents and Cyrus's core audience of children and teens. In the shots, taken by famed celebrity photographer Annie Leibovitz, Cyrus appears to be nude, wrapped only in a sheet with her bare back exposed to the camera. Although Leibovitz was surprised at the reaction, Cyrus issued an apology for the shoot.

Repeatedly, Cyrus's comments and actions, including smoking from a bong and giving a rude hand gesture to photographers, were shared with a wider media audience through camera phones and Internet news and gossip sites. She was the target of lesbian rumors and was accused of being racist toward Asians after a picture of her making slant eyes surfaced on the Internet. Other pictures of her posing in her underwear were also widely circulated. These incidents contributed to damaging public opinion toward Cyrus. She received much criticism for various sexualized performances, such as pole dancing during a performance for the Teen Choice Awards in 2009.

FILM CAREER

Cyrus's first major role in film came with the Disney animated feature *Bolt* in 2008, when she voiced the lead, Penny. She received a Golden Globe nomination for her performance of one of the movie's songs, "I Thought I Lost You." She also starred in the Disney *Hannah Montana & Miley Cyrus: Best of Both Worlds Concert* 3-D concert film, released in 2008. A scripted adaptation of the series was released in 2009 as *Hannah Montana: The Movie*. Both films were successful commercially at the box office and continued to build the Cyrus brand, while the soundtracks for the movies topped the charts.

In 2010 Cyrus made her dramatic debut in the film *The Last Song*. Based on a novel by Nicholas Sparks, the film was a vehicle for Cyrus to demonstrate her acting and singing abilities. Critics did not receive the film well, however, and were especially critical of Cyrus's performance. The movie was a moderate financial success for the studio, with Cyrus starring alongside Oscar-nominee Greg Kinnear, as well as the young actor Liam Hemsworth. Hemsworth and Cyrus were linked romantically during filming and became popular targets for paparazzi after its release.

The success of Cyrus's career can be attributed in large part to the marketing and advertising power of the Walt Disney Company. The *Hannah Montana* show was a highly rated cable television program, and children had easy access to repeat episodes as well as through DVD releases. Because of the show's popularity and Cyrus's audience appeal, Cyrus became a household name with massive appeal among the preteen and teen groups. Like so many other child stars, however, she encountered a rocky transition to adult performer.

Jay Parrent

SEE ALSO: *Bubblegum Rock; Pop Music; Sitcom; Teen Idols.*

BIBLIOGRAPHY

Handy, Bruce. "Miley Knows Best." *Vanity Fair*, June 2008.

Summers, Kimberly Dillon. *Miley Cyrus: A Biography*. Santa Barbara, CA: Greenwood, 2009.

D

The Da Vinci Code

The Da Vinci Code (2003) is a mystery-detective novel by Dan Brown that follows Harvard symbologist Robert Langdon as he investigates a murder committed at the Louvre in Paris. Brown presents a complex conspiracy narrative that places the Roman Catholic Church behind a fictional centuries-long cover-up. Among the church's secrets: Jesus and Mary Magdalene were married and had a child, and the Holy Grail is not the cup used at the last supper but rather a symbol of Magdalene herself and Christ's bloodline.

The Da Vinci Code opens with the killing of Jacques Saunière, the curator of the Louvre, and unfolds over the next twenty-four hours, presented in chapters that alternate between fast-paced adventure and historical explanation. As Saunière dies, he scrawls an encoded message in his own blood. The Paris police call on Langdon to decipher the message. Working with Saunière's granddaughter, police cryptographer Sophie Neveu, Langdon solves a series of riddles and puzzles, slowly discovering that the murder is the latest act in an ongoing power struggle between the Priory of Sion (an amalgamation of real and fictitious secretive Catholic societies) and Opus Dei (an equally clandestine, but real, society employed by the church to guard the secret of Jesus's marriage).

Langdon and Neveu conclude that Saunière's killer was looking for a clue to the location of the Holy Grail. As they work together to solve the murder, they uncover a complex history of deception, political pressure, and assassinations that have served to maintain the mythic, hermetic history of Christ's sanctity and the legitimacy of the Bible. In spite of its open and controversial challenges to Catholic doctrine, the novel ends with the secrets intact, as Langdon and Neveu successfully foil a plot that would have toppled the Vatican and upended a large portion of the Western historical narrative.

By postulating a revised Christian history in which Mary Magdalene plays a key role, Brown engages the late-twentieth-century celebration of the feminine divine, which recasts Christianity's early relationships with goddess worship. *The Da Vinci Code* also reimagines mysticism, revisiting pagan practices that access the sacred through sexually expressive rituals. Finally, Brown suggests that Leonardo da Vinci's paintings can be read as coded clues to the secret history of Western civilization. According to Brown's narrative, these coded messages run through all canonical and popular works of art—a gesture that revives the ideas of subliminal messaging that gained traction in the 1970s.

Brown has defended the validity of every historical statement in his novel. Critics and scholars, however, have demonstrated that the historical "truths" Brown espouses have either been debunked or are gross fabrications that exaggerate the importance of pseudo-histories and rumors that gain traction only through their relationships to arcane organizations such as the Knights Templar and the fraternal order of Freemasons. Because Brown's narrative asserts that the Catholic Church actively engages in the suppression of these truths, every attempt to expose its historical inaccuracies or to challenge its alternative Christian history can be viewed as part of the "conspiracy" and thereby propelled the novel's success. The book has been translated into dozens of languages and has sold tens of millions of copies worldwide, and it spawned a 2006 film adaptation starring Tom Hanks as Langdon.

A few progressive scholars and clergyman who believe that doubt is essential to the existence of faith have embraced the novel, using it as a tool to engage students and parishioners in discussions about doubt and faith. For these exercises, readers do not have to concede the book's claims, but asking "What if?" provides a constructive way to articulate their doubts.

As with many novels, a great disparity existed between public and critical reception of *The Da Vinci Code*. Although it was an immense commercial success, critics such as Stephen Fry lamented its thin characters, forced dialogue, cumbersome expository lumps, and nasty stereotypes (an evil albino, for example). The *New Yorker* lambasted Brown for the historical exaggerations and conflations in the novel. Some critics, however, have been more favorable, focusing on Brown's capacity for suspense and the adeptness with which he handles compression of time. Whatever the reception, *The Da Vinci Code* effectively exploits Western culture's fascination with conspiracy theories and alternative histories.

Greg Beatty

SEE ALSO: *Best Sellers; Conspiracy Theories; Hanks, Tom; Howard, Ron; The Pope; Religious Right.*

BIBLIOGRAPHY

Bethune, Brian. "Cracking *The Da Vinci Code*." *Maclean's*, December 12, 2004, 51.

Ehrman, Bart D. *Truth and Fiction in "The Da Vinci Code": A Historian Reveals What We Really Know about Jesus, Mary Magdalene, and Constantine*. Oxford, UK, and New York: Oxford University Press, 2004.

Lane, Anthony. "Heaven Can Wait." *The New Yorker*, May 29, 2006.

McDermott, Jim. "Krispy Kremes and *The Da Vinci Code*." *America*, September 19, 2005.

O'Neill, Tim. "History versus *The Da Vinci Code*." Accessed on June 8, 2012. Available from http://www.historyversustheda-vincicode.com

Thornbury, Gregory Alan. "The Da Vinci Code Distraction." *American Spectator*, July/August 2006.

Dahmer, Jeffrey *(1960–1994)*

Jeffrey Dahmer was a serial killer who was convicted in 1992 of murdering fifteen young men. He was sentenced to fifteen consecutive life terms in prison. The trial and the gruesome details of Dahmer's crimes, including accounts of cannibalism, fascinated the public and generated books, trading cards, movies, and other products. But behind the monstrous ghoul of popular imagination there lurked a desperately lonely young man whose killings appeared to be the result of years of progressive mental illness.

When Dahmer's mother, Joyce, was pregnant with him, she endured a particularly difficult pregnancy, suffering extended bouts of nausea and nervousness and strange fits of rigidity. Doctors prescribed morphine and phenobarbital, among other medications. At one point Joyce was taking twenty-six pills a day. Despite this, Dahmer was born without complications and appeared to be a happy, normal child. When Dahmer was four years old, however, he had a hernia operation, and his behavior changed profoundly afterward. He became remote, fearful, and distant. He would sit for hours in front of the television without moving. Even his body language changed. His movements grew stiff and labored, like those of an old man.

By the time he began grade school, Dahmer had become so shy and reclusive that a teacher felt compelled to bring his behavior to his parents' attention. Nothing was done, and young Dahmer grew increasingly remote, submerged in a realm of unpleasant fantasies and, in increasing degrees, alcohol. In early adolescence, he often occupied himself by collecting roadkills, stripping the flesh and assembling the bones in the nearby woods. He once mounted a dog's head on a stick as a bizarre totem. In his late teens, Dahmer's obsessions began to overwhelm him. He was so fearful of other people that he could only relate to them as inert objects. In 1978 he committed his first murder, picking up a hitchhiker and taking him back to his parents' house where he killed the boy with a piece of gym equipment.

Unaware of Dahmer's blossoming psychosis, his father, Lionel, continued to counsel the apathetic boy to the best of his ability, insisting on his enrollment at Ohio State University. By the end of the first quarter, Dahmer's grades were so poor that he returned home. Lionel drove to the university to pick up his son's possessions, where he was further dismayed to learn that Dahmer had done little other than drink. In frustration, he insisted that Dahmer join the military. Dahmer seemed to blossom under the rigid discipline of military life, but the improvement was short-lived. While stationed in Germany, his behavior quickly deteriorated, and he received an early discharge for drunkenness.

Now at his wits' end, Lionel sent his son to live with his aging grandmother in a suburb outside Milwaukee, Wisconsin. There, Dahmer's behavior became increasingly bizarre. Once, his grandmother found a fully clothed male mannequin in his closet; another time, she found a gun under his bed. At times the house would have unpleasant odors. As he had in the past, Dahmer lamely explained away his activities, although now no one believed him. Finally he moved out of his grandmother's house.

On Dahmer's first day at his new apartment, he was arrested for drugging and molesting a thirteen-year-old Laotian boy. Dahmer served ten months in a Milwaukee work-release program, during which his father lobbied aggressively, and unsuccessfully, for additional treatment for his alcoholism. In March 1990 Dahmer was released on probation.

HORRIFIC CRIMES REVEALED

After his release, Dahmer killed several men. He would hang out in bars and on street corners, trolling for a likely victim from among the hustlers who worked his neighborhood. To conceal his activities, he bought a freezer, installed an elaborate security system, and separated his bedroom from the rest of the apartment with a heavy metal door. Once secure within his apartment, Dahmer would drug, then strangle his victims; molest the corpses; and finally eat or preserve parts of his victims, disposing of the remains with quicklime in an enormous plastic bucket. He was finally apprehended when a victim escaped and then returned accompanied by police officers, who discovered photographs of dead and dismembered men strewn about Dahmer's bedroom.

Hoping to avoid prison, Dahmer pled not guilty by reason of insanity. He said he wanted to find out why he did the things he did. The public was riveted by the trial and fascinated by the details of his crimes. The jury, unmoved by his plea of insanity, found him guilty in 1992 of murdering fifteen men. Dahmer was sentenced to fifteen consecutive life terms in prison.

In prison, Dahmer found Jesus as well as the death he had long desired. Another inmate bludgeoned him to death in 1994. Dahmer's assailant, himself a convicted killer of questionable mental health, claimed he had acted under God's direction. A figure at once pathetic and monstrous, Dahmer was generally reviled, although there was still something in his deflated appearance that generated sympathy. He received an enormous number of letters after his incarceration that were more often sympathetic than threatening.

In 1996 a judge decided that all of Dahmer's belongings should be sold by his estate and that the money collected would be given to the families of Dahmer's victims. The estate's lawyers originally planned an auction, but many people were horrified by the idea. Included in the hundreds of belongings were items Dahmer had used to torture and kill his victims. A Milwaukee civic group launched a fund-raising campaign and reached a deal with the estate to buy all the belongings for $407,000. The group then destroyed everything.

Dahmer continued to remain an object of public fascination for years after his death. The 2002 movie *Dahmer*, starring Jeremy Renner, explores the origins of Dahmer's psychotic behavior. Another film, *Raising Jeffrey Dahmer*, was released in 2006. It considers his crimes through the intense emotional grief of his parents.

In 2009 Arthur Jay Harris published the book *Jeffrey Dahmer's Dirty Secret*, in which he suggests that Dahmer killed six-year-old Adam Walsh in 1981. Dahmer lived near Walsh at the time of the boy's disappearance, and he was questioned by police. Harris argues that investigators failed to consider numerous inconsistencies surrounding Dahmer's potential involvement in the crime. Although police in Hollywood, Florida, closed Walsh's case in 2008, concluding that Walsh was killed by an indigent man named Ottis Toole, Harris's book raises troubling questions that left many wondering if the Walsh case had in fact been solved.

Michael J. Baers

SEE ALSO: *Serial Killers.*

BIBLIOGRAPHY

Baumann, Ed. *Step into My Parlour.* Chicago: Bonus Books, 1991.

Dahmer, Lionel. *A Father's Story.* New York: Morrow, 1994.

Dvorchak, Robert, and Lisa Holewa. *Milwaukee Massacre: Jeffrey Dahmer and the Milwaukee Murders.* New York: Dell, 1991.

Holewa, Lisa. "Recurring Nightmare: Did Dahmer Kill Adam Walsh?" AolNews. Accessed on March 3, 2012. Available from http://www.aolnews.com/2010/03/30/recurring-nightmare-did-dahmer-kill-adam-walsh/

Masters, Brian. *Killing for Company: The Case of Dennis Nilsen.* New York: Stein and Day, 1985.

Ressler, Robert K., and Tom Shachtman. *I Have Lived in the Monster.* New York: St. Martin's, 1997.

Schwartz, Anne E. *The Man Who Could Not Kill Enough: The Secret Murders of Milwaukee's Jeffrey Dahmer.* New York: Carol Publishing, 1992.

Smith, Jane. "New Book Links Jeffrey Dahmer to Adam Walsh Murder." *Washington Examiner,* October 4, 2009.

Tithecott, Richard. *Of Men and Monsters: Jeffrey Dahmer and the Construction of the Serial Killer.* Madison: University of Wisconsin Press, 1997.

The Daily Show

SEE: *Stewart, Jon.*

Dallas

The 1980 episode that answered the question "Who Shot J. R.?," *Dallas* became the most-watched program in the history of television to that time. *Dallas* was the first prime-time soap opera, and its serial stories about the exploits of a Texas oil family provided fodder for water-cooler gossip as well as for real bookie-joint wagering. The program enjoyed a thirteen-year run, making superstars of virtual unknowns such as Victoria Principal, Patrick Duffy, and others. Larry Hagman, who played J. R. Ewing, had already developed a loyal following from his days playing Major Anthony Nelson opposite Barbara Eden's genie on *I Dream of Jeannie* (1965 to 1970). *Dallas* foundered in the early 1990s and is remembered more than any other program as the epitome of the unabashedly capitalistic Reagan era.

Premiering April 2, 1978, on CBS, the series revolved around the relationships and tribulations of patriarch Jock Ewing and wife "Miss Ellie" (played by Jim Davis and Barbara Bel Geddes, respectively) and their three sons: J. R. (Hagman), a deceitful, conniving businessman, who with his father ran the family oil company; Bobby (Patrick Duffy), a freewheeling playboy in the early days of the series; and Gary (first David Ackroyd, then Ted Shackelford), a weak-willed alcoholic who long ago had fled the family's Southfork Ranch. J. R.'s wife was boozy Sue Ellen (Linda Gray). Bobby, in the first episode of the series, eloped with Pamela (Victoria Principal), the sexy daughter of family archenemy Digger Barnes. Their marriage set the stage for years of conflict, especially with Pamela's brother Cliff (Ken Kercheval).

In early episodes, the series was structured as a traditional weekly drama; each episode presented a stand-alone story, with Pamela ostensibly the focal point of the narrative. It quickly became clear, however, that wily J. R. was the real favorite of both the writers of the series and its audience. By 1979 the series threaded continuing stories through several stand-alone episodes. Alcoholic Sue Ellen turned up pregnant: was the baby J. R.'s or Cliff's? J. R.'s turncoat secretary Julie (Tina Louise) was murdered: would J. R. succeed in framing Cliff for the killing?

Dallas. Dallas *followed the trials of the wealthy Ewing family, played by, clockwise from left, Larry Hagman, Linda Gray, Jim Davis, Patrick Duffy, Victoria Principal, Charlene Tilton, and Barbara Bel Geddes.* LORIMAR/THE KOBAL COLLECTION.

"WHO SHOT J. R.?"

Dallas grew in popularity through the final episode of the 1979–1980 season, when J. R. was shot by an unknown assailant. There was no shortage of suspects: he had spent the season acquiring, then unloading, what proved to be worthless Asian oil leases, swindling everyone from the family banker to his own mother in the process; he had driven Bobby and Pam off Southfork; and he had shipped wife Sue Ellen off to a sanitarium, even as he bedded her younger sister Kristin (Mary Crosby).

During the summer of 1980, *Dallas* fever exploded. "Who Shot J. R.?" was a sensation, the subject of everything from fan speculation to Las Vegas betting. T-shirts bearing the question "Who Shot J. R.?" were seen all around the country. As the press scrambled in vain to uncover details of the fall scripts, elaborate security precautions were put into effect at the studio. Producers took no chances, and each actor was brought in to film scenes of his or her character shooting J. R.

A lingering actors' strike—and Larry Hagman's demand for a raise—threatened to delay the solution to the mystery, but the public finally learned the answer on November 21, 1980. Sue Ellen's sister Kristin, J. R.'s former mistress, had pulled the trigger, infuriated by J. R.'s attempts to run her out of town. Sue Ellen herself solved the mystery, realizing that her sister was plotting to frame her for the crime. When Kristin revealed that she was pregnant with J. R.'s baby, J. R. shipped his assailant off to California, where she could have her illegitimate child in secret. The episode set a ratings record: an unprecedented 53.3 Nielsen mark, meaning more than one-half of U.S. television households were tuned in. (That record was broken a few years later, in 1983, by the final episode of M*A*S*H.)

Dallas had become the most popular series on American television in 1980.

In early 1981 actor Jim Davis passed away, and his character, Jock, was eventually written out of the series. Jock's will set up a power struggle at Ewing Oil that unfolded over most of the 1982–1983 season, arguably the creative peak of the series. Barbara Bel Geddes (Miss Ellie) departed for health reasons in 1984, and she was replaced by Donna Reed. Reed was reportedly livid to discover barely a year later that she was being fired to make way for Bel Geddes's return. Reed sued the producers of the series for breach of contract. Bel Geddes returned to the role, and Reed won a million-dollar settlement.

Meanwhile, J. R. and Sue Ellen divorced, remarried, then divorced again. Bobby and Pam had also divorced , and the characters were moving toward reconciliation when actor Patrick Duffy announced that he was leaving the show. In the final episode of the 1984–1985 season, Bobby was killed—murdered by his deranged former sister-in-law, even as he had just professed his undying love for Pam.

Even as the series spun its larger-than-life stories, it managed to capture the real-life flavor of a turbulent decade: the 1982–1983 recession figured prominently in the story; later, the mid-decade mania of big-business mergers and takeovers was reflected on-screen. The fictional Ewing Oil was now worth $2 billion, but the *Dallas* franchise itself was priceless to CBS and its affiliates.

NEW DIRECTIONS

The series had begotten one spin-off (brother Gary and wife Val set up housekeeping in *Knots Landing* in 1979) and a host of imitators, from *Falcon Crest* to *Flamingo Road* to *Dynasty*. *Dynasty* in particular caught the public's fancy. Whereas *Dallas*'s stories had at least some grounding in real life, *Dynasty* was simply glamorous, over-the-top high camp. By the end of the 1984–1985 season, *Dynasty* ran neck-and-neck with *Dallas* for the number-one position in the ratings.

A behind-the-scenes shakeup followed, and *Dallas* suddenly began looking more like *Dynasty*, with soapier plots and more elaborate costumes. By 1986 a *Cosby*-led sitcom resurgence pushed all the evening soaps down the ratings chart, and the production staff was overhauled again. Much of the old guard returned, and Larry Hagman began assuming some creative control over the series. Hagman himself reportedly engineered one of the biggest television coups of 1986 when he personally convinced Patrick Duffy to return to the series. In the final 1985–1986 episode, Pamela awoke from a night's sleep, only to find the long-dead Bobby lathering up in her shower. The audience was left to wonder all summer: Who was that? How did he get there? The cliffhanger was nearly as big a sensation as "Who Shot J. R." had been six years earlier, and the producers hyped it expertly—going so far as to film fake footage, then allowing it to find its way into the tabloids.

"Bobby in the Shower" was an inspired stunt; the resolution was a disaster. In the opening moments of the fall season, it was revealed that Bobby had never died. Instead, Pamela had simply dreamt the entire 1985–1986 season. An entire year's worth of narrative and character development was simply wiped out. Fans howled in protest, and the move was a critical and creative debacle. The episode also turned out to be the last great moment of the prime-time soap craze. *Dynasty*'s ratings had collapsed, and *Dallas*'s ratings, though still strong, were losing ground. Victoria Principal departed the series in 1987, and several supporting characters were written out about the same time. By this time everyone from Priscilla Presley to a young Brad Pitt had passed through Southfork, but the antics of the characters were becoming sillier. A stranger claimed to be the presumed-dead Jock, but he was revealed as an impostor. J. R's dirty dealings finally cost him Ewing Oil, so he went into business for himself. In 1988 J. R. was held captive by some good ol' boys in Arkansas, and he later married their young sister. His 1990 stay in a mental institution (J. R. had infiltrated it to meet a business contact, only to find himself committed by his disgruntled illegitimate son) was a low point in the series.

Yet even in its later years, the series made waves. Location filming in Europe and the Soviet Union in 1989 drew considerable press. Later that year, CBS switchboards lit up when Linda Gray's final appearance as Sue Ellen was interrupted for news bulletins (the network repented by showing the scenes without the interruption several weeks later). An experimental return to single-story episodes in 1988 drew little attention. An attempt at using several-episode story arcs in 1990 featured a guest appearance by Susan Lucci and a reunion with Hagman's *I Dream of Jeannie* costar Barbara Eden. The venerable series ended its run in May 1991 with a takeoff of *It's a Wonderful Life*. J. R. was visited not by an angel, however, but by a messenger of Satan (Joel Grey), who together with favorite characters from *Dallas*'s past presented a series of vignettes demonstrating what life would have been had J. R. never been born. In the final scene of the series, the mysterious visitor goaded J. R. into an apparent suicide attempt.

A pair of mid-1990s reunion movies (J. R. of course had not killed himself, but merely shot a mirror!) failed utterly to capture the spirit of the series in its best day. In 2012, however, with the tagline "They're back, and no, you're not dreaming," TNT revived the series, reuniting Hagman, Duffy, and Gray, but emphasizing the next generation of Ewings, who continue the battle over Southfork.

Dallas continues to hold a special place in popular culture in the early twenty-first century. When asked why audiences loved J. R. Ewing so much, Hagman replies that he assumed that women wanted to reform him and men wanted to be him. *Dallas* is still shown in reruns around the world and is a mainstay of ABC's Soapnet. DVDs of the various seasons sell well. In a 2008 article for *Macleans*, Jaime Weinman pondered why the character of J. R. Ewing is still significant to contemporary popular culture. He determined that it was because J. R. was created as a character "who never stops being interesting."

Chris Chandler

SEE ALSO: The Cosby Show*;* Dynasty*;* I Dream of Jeannie*;* It's a Wonderful Life*;* Knots Landing*;* M*A*S*H*; Soap Operas; Suicide; Television; T-Shirts.*

BIBLIOGRAPHY

Adams, Leon. *Larry Hagman: A Biography*. New York: St. Martin's, 1987.

Brooks, Tim, and Earle Marsh. *The Complete Directory to Prime Time Network and Cable TV Shows*. New York: Ballantine Books, 1995.

Weinman, Jaime. "Why We Still Care Who Shot J. R." *Macleans*, December 8, 2008,49–50.

The Dallas Cowboys

The Dallas Cowboys of the National Football League (NFL) have been characterized as "America's Team," thanks to their winning ways and once squeaky-clean image. Their immense popularity, which has endured through three owners and eight head coaches, is due largely to the historic success of the franchise, for the team has won five Super Bowls (1972, 1978, 1993, 1994, and 1998). The list of coaches includes Tom Landry, Jimmy Johnson, Barry Switzer, Chan Gailey, Dave Campo, Bill Parcells, Wade Phillips, and Jason Garrett. The first three led the Cowboys to Super Bowl wins, with Landry establishing himself as one of the greatest coaches in the history of the NFL.

Star players also cemented the Cowboys' legacy. A brief list of some of the Cowboys players reads like a Who's Who of the football world: Bob Lilly, Mel Renfro, Roger Staubach, Randy White, Tony Dorsett, Michael Irvin, Emmitt Smith, and Troy Aikman are just a few of the names associated with the success of the franchise. The Cowboys are also well known for the prominence of their cheerleading squad, named simply the Dallas Cowboy Cheerleaders. Emerging in the mid-1970s as beguiling halftime entertainment, the cheerleading squad has thousands of fans of its own, as evidenced by the sales of calendars and the demand for them as performers at promotional events.

THE 1960s

Dallas was awarded a National Football League expansion franchise in 1960. The team got off to a slow start: the Cowboys lost their inaugural game 35–28 to the Pittsburgh Steelers on September 24, 1960, and didn't notch their first win until 1961, with a 27–24 victory over the Steelers in Dallas. In 1966 the Cowboys made it to their first Eastern Conference Championship game and won, but they lost the NFL Championship to the Green Bay Packers 34–27.

Throughout the 1960s the Cowboys were prime contenders for the NFL's top honor. In 1967 they fell to the Green Bay Packers 21–17 in the championship game. That game, generally regarded as one of the greatest in the history of professional football, has become known as the Ice Bowl because it was played in Green Bay in temperatures dropping as low as negative 13 degrees. All-Pro quarterback Don Meredith retired in 1969, going on to further fame announcing *Monday Night Football* with Howard Cosell and Frank Gifford. As an announcer, Meredith was best known for singing the phrase, "Turn out the lights. The party's over," once the outcome of a game was no longer in doubt.

THE 1970s

In 1970 the Cowboys once again won the Eastern Division Championship (their fifth consecutive first-place finish) but lost to the Baltimore Colts in their first Super Bowl appearance, 16–13. In 1971 the team moved from the Cotton Bowl in Dallas to Texas Stadium in suburban Irving, a facility known for the large hole in its roof, which preserved the atmosphere of an outdoor stadium while providing fans with protection from the rain. That year the Cowboys marched through the playoffs and won their first NFL Championship by beating the Miami Dolphins 24–3 in Super Bowl VI in New Orleans. Dallas quarterback (and league Most Valuable Player) Roger Staubach passed for two touchdowns and was named Super Bowl MVP.

The Cowboys missed the playoffs for the first time in eight years when they stumbled to an 8–6 record in 1974. In 1975 the team returned to the playoffs as a wild card. In the opening round, they shocked the Minnesota Vikings on a last-second 50-yard touchdown completion from Staubach to Drew Pearson. One of the most famous plays in NFL history, the pass became known as the Hail Mary. Despite contending for the championship for the next several years, the Cowboys would not win the title again until 1977, when Dallas defeated the Denver Broncos 27–10. Defensive linemen Harvey Martin and Randy White were named co-MVPs.

THE 1980s

On March 31, 1980, legendary quarterback Staubach retired. Behind new quarterback Danny White, the Cowboys made the playoffs as a wild card team and beat the Los Angeles Rams 34–13 and the Atlanta Falcons 30–27 to advance to the NFC Championship, where they lost 20–7 to the Philadelphia Eagles.

In May 1984 Clint Murchison sold the Cowboys to H. R. "Bum" Bright. The Cowboys went on to notch just nine wins for the season, with seven losses, and missed the playoffs for the first time in ten years. In 1986 the team's streak of twenty consecutive winning seasons was broken when they finished 7–9.

Jerry Jones purchased the Cowboys from Bright in 1989 and shocked the city of Dallas, the state of Texas, and Cowboy fans everywhere when he unceremoniously replaced Landry, the Cowboys' only coach for twenty-nine seasons, with University of Miami head coach Jimmy Johnson.

THE 1990s

In 1991, for the first time since 1985, Dallas was back in the playoffs as a wild card. They defeated the Chicago Bears 17–13 in the opening round of the playoffs but then lost 38–6 to the Detroit Lions. The Cowboys claimed the Eastern Division Championship in 1992. They advanced to the NFC Championship, where they beat the San Francisco 49ers 30–20 and then defeated the Buffalo Bills 52–17 in Super Bowl XXVII in Pasadena. The Cowboys repeated as Super Bowl champions the following year, when they again defeated Buffalo, this time by the score of 30–13.

Due to difficulties with owner Jones, Johnson resigned as the Cowboys coach, and Barry Switzer became the third head coach in team history on March 30, 1994. Later that year the Cowboys went on to capture the Eastern Division Championship. However, they fell to San Francisco in the NFC Championship, 38–28.

In 1995 the Cowboys were again Eastern Division Champions. After they beat Green Bay 38–27 to advance to Super Bowl XXX, they knocked off Pittsburgh 27–17. But the Cowboys did not continue to enjoy success under Switzer, and he was replaced by Chan Gailey after the 1997 season. In Gailey's first season as the Cowboys' head coach, Dallas won the NFC Eastern Division but lost in the first round of the playoffs to the Arizona Cardinals, 20–7. In 1999 the Cowboys finished the regular season 8–8, and once again lost in the first round of the playoffs, this time to the Minnesota Vikings, 27–10.

THE TWENTY-FIRST CENTURY

Gailey was replaced as head coach by Dave Campo in 2000, and after the team posted three straight losing seasons, Campo was replaced in 2003 by former New York Giants Super Bowl–winning coach Bill Parcells. In Parcells's first season the Cowboys rebounded, posting a 10–6 record, but they lost in the first round of the playoffs 29–10 to the Carolina Panthers. After missing the playoffs in 2005 with a 9–7 record, the Cowboys again finished 9–7 the next year, but this time made the playoffs, losing 21–20 in the first round against Seattle. Parcells retired at the end of the 2006 season, and Wade Phillips took over as head coach in 2007, leading the Cowboys to thirteen wins in the regular season. However, they faltered in the playoffs, losing 21–17 to the New York Giants in the divisional playoff game.

In 2009 the Cowboys moved from Texas Stadium into Cowboys Stadium in Arlington. Cowboys Stadium, built at a price tag of $1.2 billion and the largest indoor venue in the NFL, is renowned for its retractable roof and end-zone doors (the world's largest) and the massive television screen that hangs above the field, spanning 60 feet. During their inaugural season in the new stadium, the Cowboys finished 11–5 and returned to the playoffs, beating Philadelphia 34–14 before falling to Minnesota 34–3. After a losing start in 2010, Phillips was replaced by Jason Garrett as the Cowboys' head coach.

CROWDING THE HALL

The list of Cowboys enshrined in the NFL Hall of Fame is long. Bob Lilly was first, becoming a Hall of Famer on August 2, 1980. Landry was inducted into the Hall on August 4, 1990, with Tony Dorsett and Randy White following on July 30, 1994, and Mel Renfro in 1996. Former quarterback Troy Aikman was welcomed into the NFL Hall of Fame in 2006, and in rapid succession, Michael Irvin became a Hall of Famer in 2007, Bob Hayes in 2009, Emmitt Smith in 2010, and Deion Sanders in 2011.

Few teams in the NFL have enjoyed the historic record of success and popularity associated with the Dallas Cowboys. They remain one of the preeminent franchises in football history.

Kerry Owens

SEE ALSO: *Cheerleading; The Chicago Bears; Cosell, Howard; Ditka, Mike; Gifford, Frank; The Green Bay Packers; Landry, Tom;* Monday Night Football*; National Football League (NFL); The Pittsburgh Steelers; Professional Football; Sports Heroes; Staubach, Roger; Super Bowl.*

BIBLIOGRAPHY

Donovan, Jim; Ken Sins; and Frank Coffey. *The Dallas Cowboys Encyclopedia: The Ultimate Guide to America's Team*, rev ed. Secaucus, NJ: Carol Publishing Group, 1999.

Golenbock, Peter. *Cowboys Have Always Been My Heroes: The Definitive Oral History of America's Team*. New York: Warner Books, 1997.

Johnson, Jimmy, and Ed Hinton. *Turning the Thing Around: Pulling America's Team out of the Dumps*. New York: Hyperion Press, 1993.

Landry, Tom, and Greg Lewis. *Tom Landry: An Autobiography*. Grand Rapids, MI: Zondervan Publishing House, 1990.

Roselius, J. Chris. *Dallas Cowboys*. Edina, MN: ABDO Publishing, 2011.

St. John, Bob. *Tex! The Man Who Built the Dallas Cowboys*. Englewood Cliffs, NJ: Prentice Hall, 1988.

Stowers, Carlton. *Dallas Cowboys: The First Twenty-Five Years*. Dallas, TX: Taylor Publishing, 1984.

Sugar, Bert Randolph. *I Hate the Dallas Cowboys: And Who Elected Them America's Team Anyway?* New York: St. Martin's Griffin, 1997.

Wolfe, Jane. *The Murchisons: The Rise and Fall of a Texas Dynasty*. New York: St. Martin's Press, 1989.

Damon, Matt *(1970–)*

One of America's most bankable film actors, Matt Damon received a star on the Hollywood Walk of Fame in 2007. His top-notch box-office presence was propelled by his hugely successfully turn as an amnesiac former CIA agent in the action-adventure *Bourne* trilogy (2002–2007), which grossed close to $1 billion worldwide. In a *Commonweal* review of the third installment of the trilogy, *The Bourne Ultimatum*, Rand Richard Cooper wrote of Damon, "For someone blessed with all-American good looks and a brash, winning grin, he can be surprisingly inward, repressed, or weird—or, as in the Jason Bourne trilogy, haunted and violent." Damon has more than fifty films to his credit. In 2011 alone he appeared in five roles: Bill the Krill in the animated *Happy Feet Two*, ambitious congressman David Norris in the fantasy romantic thriller *The Adjustment Bureau*, one of the ensemble cast of the medical disaster thriller *Contagion*, the widower Benjamin Mee of the family comedy *We Bought a Zoo*, and prep school teacher Mr. Aaron in the drama *Margaret*.

His first major success came with the film *Good Will Hunting* (1997), which he cowrote and starred in with actor Ben Affleck, a friend from childhood and former classmate at the Rindge and Latin School in Cambridge, Massachusetts. The pair won an Academy Award for their screenplay, and Damon was nominated for both an Academy Award and a Golden Globe Award for Best Actor for his portrayal of title character Will Hunting, a disaffected twenty-year-old mathematical genius torn between his working-class roots in South Boston and pressures to apply his considerable talents. With the help of best friend Chuckie (Affleck's character) and his therapist (played by actor-comedian Robin Williams), Hunting confronts his past as an abused foster child. *Variety* reviewer Emanuel Levy wrote of Damon, "Perfectly cast, he makes the aching, step-by-step transformation of Will realistic and credible."

Five years before this breakout success, Damon dropped out of Harvard twelve credits short of graduating to take a sizeable role in the Western *Geronimo* (1993), featuring renown actors Gene Hackman and Robert Duvall; however, the film unexpectedly flopped. By this time Affleck had joined Damon in Los Angeles, and the two shared an apartment, struggling to find work. Damon finally landed what critics consider his first memorable role, the heroin-addicted Gulf War veteran in the critically acclaimed *Courage under Fire* (1996), directed by Edward Zwick. Then, with the help of director Rob Reiner and screenwriter William Goldman, Damon and Affleck sold the script of *Good Will Hunting* to production company Miramax.

Matt Damon and Ben Affleck. *Matt Damon, left, and Ben Affleck celebrate their Oscar wins for Best Original Screenplay for* Good Will Hunting *in 1998.* EVAN AGOSTINI/IMAGEDIRECT/GETTY IMAGES.

Since *Good Will Hunting*, Damon has starred in a string of premiere roles with some of Hollywood's most esteemed directors, such as Francis Ford Coppola (*The Rainmaker*, 1997), Steven Spielberg (*Saving Private Ryan*, 1998), Martin Scorsese (*The Departed*, 2006), Robert De Niro (*The Good Shepherd*, 2006), and Joel and Ethan Coen (*True Grit*, 2010). He has received Golden Globe Award nominations for several roles: the titular serial killer and impersonator in *The Talented Mr. Ripley* (1999), the comically unstable whistle-blower in *The Informant!* (2009), and the South African rugby team captain in the Clint Eastwood–directed *Invictus* (2009)—a performance for which Damon was also nominated for an Academy Award for Best Supporting Actor.

Eastwood also cast Damon in the supernatural drama *Hereafter* (2010), in which he plays a medium cursed by the ability to communicate with the dead. Eastwood told Donna Freydkin in *USA Today*, "You get the feeling [in the movie] that he's a common man with an uncommon affliction." Damon has seemed to resist capitalizing on his looks. When he was named *People*'s Sexiest Man Alive in 2007, he responded by writing to the magazine, suggesting it choose quarterback Tom Brady instead: "He's like a taller, better-looking version of me anyway."

Like actor friends Brad Pitt and George Clooney, with whom Damon starred in the blockbuster *Ocean's 11* (2001) and its two sequels, Damon lends his star power to a variety of humanitarian causes. He was named to *Time*'s 2011 list of the 100 most influential people in the world for his work as a founder of Water.org, a nonprofit organization that provides access to safe water and sanitation in many regions in Africa, South America, and Central America. He also has been a spokesperson for the hunger relief agency Feeding America and for the ONE Campaign, which is aimed at fighting AIDS in poverty-stricken countries. He and his mother, a professor of early childhood education, have protested educational reforms they judge damaging to the teaching profession. A liberal who has publicly aired his frustrations with Barack Obama's presidential administration, Damon is considered so charismatic and likeable that filmmaker Michael Moore suggested the actor run for president in 2012.

Janet Mullane

SEE ALSO: *Academy Awards; Bourne Series; Brady, Tom; Celebrity; Clooney, George; Coen, Joel and Ethan; De Niro, Robert; Duvall, Robert; Eastwood, Clint; Hackman, Gene; Hollywood; Moore, Michael; Obama, Barack; Pitt, Brad; Scorsese, Martin; Spielberg, Steven;* Time*;* USA Today*;* Variety*; Williams, Robin.*

BIBLIOGRAPHY

Cooper, Richards Rand. "Identity Crisis: *The Bourne Ultimatum*." *Commonweal* 134, no. 15 (2007): 24.

Freydkin, Donna. "'Hereafter' Star Matt Damon Focuses on the Here and Now." *USA Today*, October 21, 2010, 1D.

Hauser, Brooke. "How Matt Damon Tamed the Celebrity

Beast." *Parade*, December 11, 2011, 8–11, 15.

Levy, Emanuel. Review of *Good Will Hunting*. *Variety*, November 30, 1997.

Schickel, Richard. "*The Adjustment Bureau*: Fate Accompli." *Truthdig*, March 4, 2011.

Dana, Bill *(1924–)*

In the heyday of the network era of broadcasting, writer, actor, and producer Bill Dana created a nationally recognized comic character who endured in the American consciousness for more than a decade. When that character first uttered his signature phrase "My name . . . José Jiménez" on *The Steve Allen Show* in 1959, he became one of the clearest representatives of a familiar American type. Portraying a Mexican immigrant on the bottom half of the social ladder, Dana's Jiménez worked at various times as an elevator operator and a bellboy.

By early twenty-first century standards, that portrayal, which included Jiménez's broken English and naïveté, appears to many as condescending at best. However, Jiménez was a singularly noble character, possessing goodness, wisdom, and sincerity—traits comparatively unusual in the history of American TV characters. Although he exhibited stereotypical racial characteristics common to the period, at the same time Jiménez displayed more positive tendencies. He was confused and clueless but also resourceful and crafty; he had a stereotypically huge family back home, but he supported them faithfully through the sweat of his own brow; he worked as a salaried servant of the wealthier residents of the hotel, but he often proved kinder and smarter than his social superiors.

Born William Szathmary in Quincy, Massachusetts, on October 5, 1924, Dana entered the television industry in 1950 as a page at NBC in New York City. Through the 1950s he performed in nightclubs and played bit parts on television shows. He got his big break when he was hired as a writer on *The Steve Allen Show* in 1956. He moved up to head writer, earning an Emmy nomination for his work, and became a performer on the show in 1959.

Like many film and television actors, the public identity of Dana became inseparable from the celebrated persona he portrayed. What was unusual about Dana/Jiménez, however, was that he was able to escape the show on which he first appeared and move fluidly, and often simultaneously, to an assortment of other venues. After Dana introduced Jiménez on *The Steve Allen Show*, the character resurfaced regularly over the next five years on *The Spike Jones Show*, *The Danny Thomas Show*, and *The New Steve Allen Show*, and he became the principal character of *The Bill Dana Show* (NBC, 1963–1965). Through the 1960s Dana also made guest appearances as Jiménez on a wide variety of contemporary TV series and featured the character in several comedy record albums. Dana (as Jiménez) even showed up briefly in the 1983 feature film *The Right Stuff.*

By 1970 the ethnic humor and dialect comedy upon which Jiménez depended was growing increasingly less fashionable. The fact that Dana was not himself Hispanic intensified developing claims that the character was a racist representation. As American television moved into the more politically conscious "relevance" era of the 1970s with shows such as *All in the Family*, *M*A*S*H*, and *The Mary Tyler Moore Show*, Jiménez became a vestige of a bygone time and all but disappeared.

Although his other achievements were eclipsed by the popularity of Jiménez, Dana also wrote and produced for the several shows in which the character was featured, and, as a character actor of some note, he played guest roles on a number of series, including *Get Smart*, *The Man from U.N.C.L.E.*, and *Batman*. Dana's presence on American TV waned after the retirement of the Jiménez character, though he did continue to play occasional parts in TV series into the 1970s. One of the brightest spots in his career came in 1972 when he wrote the classic episode of *All in the Family* in which Sammy Davis Jr. visits the Bunker household.

In the 1980s, when Jiménez had become a distant memory, Dana moved into a new period of activity. Having appeared in *Get Smart*, he cowrote and acted in *The Nude Bomb* (1980), a feature film based upon the TV comedy. He was in the principal cast of two network comedy series, *No Soap, Radio* (1982) and *Zorro and Son* (1983), but neither lasted longer than a few months. In 1988 and 1989 he wrote for and appeared on a series of specials featuring the Smothers Brothers, who had appeared regularly on *Steve Allen* in 1961. During this decade, Dana was also reunited with many other of his costars from *The Steve Allen Show*, including Allen, Jayne Meadows, Louis Nye, and Tom Poston, all of whom played recurring guest roles with Dana on the hit medical drama *St. Elsewhere*. He also had a recurring role on *The Golden Girls* from 1988 to 1992.

Robert Thompson

SEE ALSO: All in the Family*; Allen, Steve; Batman;* Get Smart*;* The Golden Girls*;* The Man from U.N.C.L.E.*; Sitcom;* St. Elsewhere*; Sullivan, Ed; Television; Thomas, Danny.*

Dance Dance Revolution

Dance Dance Revolution (DDR) is a video game that combines computer technology and body movement. It offers a blend of frenetic dancing, the intense beat of techno music, and an "onstage" performance experience that had a great appeal for teens who played it in video arcades—often at all-night, after-hours events—throughout the United States in the late twentieth century. Home versions of DDR introduced a strenuous physical component to personal video games and countered the image of gaming as a totally sedentary activity, ushering in a new genre of "exertainment." A totally new concept when it was introduced in the late 1990s, DDR was popular with girls and with people who had never been drawn to the world of video games, and it paved the way for a new wave of extremely popular interactive musical games.

Konami, a game-making company in Japan, created DDR and released it in Japan in 1998. It quickly became one of the most popular arcade games in the country, with everyone from teenagers to businesspeople trying their skill. The game consists of a video screen and a dance pad that is designed in 6-inch squares and marked with arrows and colors. As the music pounds, the video screen directs the player where to move his or her feet on the dance pad, resulting in ever-faster dance movements. Crowds frequently gathered to watch and cheer players, and the machine itself calls out encouragement ("You're cool!") to reward successful moves.

In 1999 Konami released DDR in the United States, where its popularity skyrocketed in arcades, movie theaters, and amusement parks around the country. DDR introduced a community aspect to gaming that had not been seen before. In addition to playing the game itself, players participated in Internet message boards, fan websites, and clubs and tournaments devoted to the game.

In 2001 PlayStation launched a popular home version of the game, and new versions, such as DDR Max and DDR UltraMix, have remained best sellers. The home versions further expanded DDR's fan base to those who would not play in public. Later versions also included features that allowed players to plan exercise programs and track calories burned. Based on DDR's popularity, other manufacturers created similar games, such as Samba de Amigo, based on Latin dance music, and Dance on Broadway, which featured show tunes. Even the wildly popular Guitar Hero video game evolved from the DDR innovation.

DDR also appears in music videos, such as "Picture Perfect" by singer Angela Via, and in dozens of videos on the website YouTube. Christian R&B group Out of Eden even took a machine on tour with them in 2004. The movie *The FP* (2011), written and directed by Brandon and Jason Trost, features a futuristic society in which gangs compete in a deadly dance game called Beat-Beat Revolution.

Tina Gianoulis

SEE ALSO: *Computer Games; The Internet; Toys; Video Games; YouTube.*

BIBLIOGRAPHY

Bulik, Beth Snyder. "Dance Dance Revolution: Arcade Craze Swings into the Living Room." *Advertising Age*, June 28, 2004, 3.

Molina, Al. "A 'Fitness' Revolution? Certain Video Games Can Help One Be Physically Fit Instead of Physically Out of It." *American Fitness*, March–April 2004, 26.

Schiesel, Seth. "P.E. Classes Turn to Video Game That Works Legs." *New York Times*, April 30, 2007.

Wolf, Jaime. "The Video-Game Workout." *New York Times Magazine*, December 9, 2001.

Dance Halls

Dancing has been regarded as a social institution in the United States for more than a century. Famous dance venues such as the Cotton Club and Savoy Ballroom in New York City, the Avalon Ballroom on Catalina Island, Ali Baba in Oakland, and the Old Roosevelt Hotel in New Orleans attest to the tremendous influence that dancing has had on American culture. These venues are only a few of the popular meeting spots where people interact socially and can be seen publicly dancing to the popular music of the day. Local community dance halls thrive in recreation centers, churches, and high school gyms as well as commercial night clubs. The primary requirement in any dance hall is to provide ample music and the space for people to dance. Food and beverages are often served as light refreshments, and seating arrangements allow people to meet, to comment, and to view others who are out on the dance floor. An important concept of the dance hall is "to see and be seen," and rites of passage into society, including proms, pageants, and ceremonies such as weddings and musical debuts have centered around dance events and have always been a common function of dance halls.

EARLY DANCE HALLS

The forum of entertainment generally known as the dance hall evolved over the course of several centuries, taking on a distinctive function and purpose in each succeeding generation. The notion of halls as social meeting places may have originated in northern Europe during the Middle Ages, when one large, central room with an elevated ceiling was used for dining, reveling, convening, and even sleeping by large groups of tenants and visitors of no particular relation. The British connotation of the word *hall* more often refers to a large common room used as a meeting place for particular events. By contrast, the American sense of the word conveys a central space or passageway usually into which the front door opens. Both meanings are similar in the sense that the hall is a room common to all people who enter a particular building.

As feudal houses grew in stature and as European nobility became more pronounced, "great halls" were designed as distinct chambers for meeting and gathering. These great halls were featured in many palaces and country manors of the fourteenth through eighteenth centuries and used as places of social gathering for important events, coronations, festivals, and celebrations. Court dancing evolved in these great halls throughout Europe,

Times Square Dance Hall. *A sign beckons dancers to the New Gardens dance hall in New York's Times Square in 1944.* WEEGEE-(ARTHUR FELLIG)/INTERNATIONAL CENTER OF PHOTOGRAPHY/GETTY IMAGES.

developing intricate codes of conduct and rituals that persisted through the beginning of the twentieth century. Grand balls were an important social component of the seventeenth through nineteenth centuries, and dancing was regarded as a prime element of display, courtship, and social manners. Dance balls of the Victorian era usually lasted entire evenings. Hosts served multicourse suppers, and attendees literally danced "until they dropped," finding back rooms and quiet corners to sleep when they could dance no longer. It is notable that dance events in Europe and North America serve as celebrations of social occasions. In the Asia, dancing is generally reserved strictly for religious ceremonies, with elaborate costumes and traditions that have remained intact for centuries.

MODERN DANCE HALLS

The modern dance hall has a more obscure origin. Dance halls in the United States seem to have grown out of refugee immigration from eastern and southern Europe during the mid-1900s. Folk dancing, most particularly the polka, has enjoyed a rich tradition among working-class immigrants, who found dancing to be an essential element of recreation after long hours in labor-intensive jobs. Dance halls naturally grew up around this need to socialize. Many dance hall regulars attribute the Polish immigration of the 1940s and 1950s with the establishment of the American dance hall. The Nazi and Soviet occupations of Poland, leading up to the outbreak of World War II, forced thousands of working-class and minority Poles and Slavs to come to the United States. Once they arrived, Polish immigrants succeeded in venerating traditional customs including social folk dancing. Primary among these was the polka. Polka parties, international polka associations, and dance competitions continued to thrive in the late twentieth century in the United States, whereas in eastern Europe the dance form had virtually died out, most likely because of the influence of foreign political regimes.

During World War I and World War II, USO (United Service Organization) buildings were filled with local girls who demonstrated their patriotism by turning out to dance with soldiers, many of whom were on their way to the front from which they never returned. Scores of romances began in these wartime dance halls.

In the United States during the 1980s and 1990s there was a resurgence in vintage dancing, most notably swing parties from the era of the 1930s and 1940s and nineteenth-century Victorian dance balls. Vintage dance balls tended to emphasize social entertainment through historic recreation. These recreations could be very elaborate, with authentic period attire or costume recreations, selected beverages, and foods of the era. The teaching and calling of traditional dance forms were key elements of vintage dance events, and attendees were often educated professionals or middle-class descendants of European immigrants. Music was most often supplied by live musicians, although recorded music was sometimes featured in regular clubs.

Dance halls in the 1990s often had full calendars featuring a wide variety of dance events. Many dance halls were rented out for rehearsals, parties, social occasions and receptions, or were otherwise used for public recreational evenings that featured both unknown and popular bands. Attendees tended to favor one form or series of forms over others based on cultural bias, perceived social stature, or personal tastes. Fans of noted bands anticipated scheduled appearances and often prepared for occasions months in advance. Most often, attendees gathered at dance halls to celebrate a particular event such as a wedding reception, or as a regular social activity with their friends.

The dance hall's modern cousin, the night club or discotheque (disco), has distinctly urban origins. Discos began in Paris with the advent of the long-playing phonograph album in the late 1950s and early 1960s. Night clubs tend to feature more modern forms of popular music, and many new dances have been invented in reaction to new music. Whether the music is being played live or in recordings, the important feature of all dance halls, night clubs, and discos is the emphasis on dancing and socializing.

In rural areas, dance halls have generally been known for their live bands, and it is not unusual for attendees to drive 50 to 100 miles to be present. Dance halls in rural areas tend to feature food and beverages more prominently, whereas the urban night club or disco emphasizes dance floor decorations, settings, and acoustics.

The state of Texas considers itself the capital of the modern dance hall. In the twenty-first century, Texans of all ages still come together, often in traditional western gear, to enjoy dancing, refreshments, and companionship. The music, often by unknown bands, is functional rather than attention-getting.

Throughout the United States, dance halls, night clubs, and discos continue to play a major role in the sexual mating rites of single adults. One 2009 study by Hendrie and colleagues revealed that 80 percent of individuals entered such events without partners but 50 percent left with a partner at the end of the evening. Researchers also discovered that even at a time when women's roles have changed drastically, males are still more likely to initiate an encounter. In addition, one-fifth of the females were observed wearing tight clothing and dancing in a manner that some people might construe as provocative.

Ethan Hay

SEE ALSO: *The Cotton Club; Disco; Phonograph; Savoy Ballroom; Social Dancing; Swing Dancing; World War I; World War II.*

BIBLIOGRAPHY

Croce, Arlene. *Going to the Dance.* New York: Knopf, 1982.

Folkins, Gail Louise. *Texas Dance Halls: A Two-Step Circuit.* Lubbock: Texas University Press, 2007.

Hendrie, Colin A.; Helena D. Mannion; and Georgina K. Godfrey. "Evidence to Suggest That Nightclubs Function As Human Sexual Display Grounds." *Behavior* 146, no. 10 (2009): 1331–1348.

Jensen, Kimberley. *Mobilizing Minerva: American Women in the First World War.* Urbana: University of Illinois Press, 2005.

Jonas, Gerald. *Dancing: The Pleasure, Power, and Art of Movement.* New York: Harry N. Abrams, 1992.

Keller, Kate Van Winkle, and Genevieve Shimer. *The Playford Ball.* Remington, NJ: A Cappella Books, 1990.

McDonagh, Don. *Dance Fever.* New York: Random House, 1979.

Sallie, Randolph G. *Putting On Perfect Proms, Programs and Pageants.* New York: F. Watts, 1991.

Dancing with the Stars

Dancing had always been an essential ingredient of variety and music shows from television's earliest days, but few expected a reality competition built solely on dance would be so commercially successful. *Dancing with the Stars* has been one of reality television's juggernauts since it began airing in the summer of 2005 on ABC. The series has consistently ranked in the top five on the Nielsen ratings for the year, building a loyal and diverse audience throughout seven years and fourteen seasons.

A SUCCESSFUL BLUEPRINT

Adapted from the British series *Strictly Come Dancing*, which debuted on the BBC in May 2004, the *Dancing with the Stars* format has since been licensed to more than thirty-five countries. In each version celebrities are paired with professional ballroom dancers, who compete against one another each week to remain on the show. A panel of established judges critiques the dancers, and at-home viewers vote for their favorite pair via telephone or text. This interactive audience element has been a hallmark of talent shows since *Major Bowes Amateur Hour* broadcast on radio, but *Dancing with the Stars* and *American Idol* have revitalized such participation for the twenty-first century.

The affable Tom Bergeron has hosted the U.S. version of *Dancing* since the beginning; in 2010 he was joined in his hosting duties by former contestant Brooke Burke. The stable of judges has also remained consistent, featuring former *In Living Color* backup dancer and Fly Girl Carrie Ann Inaba, Italian choreographer Bruno Tonioli, and former British professional ballroom dancer Len Goodman. Both Tonioli and Goodman also serve as judges on the British series. In the first season just six celebrities competed. Over the years that number has varied between ten and a maximum of sixteen in the fall of 2009; on average twelve celebrities compete over ten weeks.

The first *Dancing* contestants provided a formula that the show has sought to replicate each successive season. Those initial selections have evolved into types of celebrity that viewers have come to expect. Among those types are a sports hero (first, boxer Evander Holyfield), a model (Rachel Hunter), a soap star (Kelly Monaco of *General Hospital*), a "B"-list actor (John O'Hurley of *Seinfeld*), a singer and former pop idol (Joey McIntyre of New Kids on the Block), and a reality television personality (Trista Rehn of *The Bachelor*). Over the years the list of celebrity categories has expanded to also include politicians, astronauts, journalists, and business executives. New casts are highly anticipated and announced with great fanfare on ABC's *Good Morning America*.

MADE FOR TV

Like the variety shows of the fifties, *Dancing with the Stars* embraces live television, creating added pressure for performers. The series has maintained high production values throughout its run, with elaborate costumes, a live orchestra, and an energetic studio audience—all of which add to the appeal of a live broadcast. Before each live dance viewers are shown rehearsal footage that typically depicts the celebrities stumbling through practice, often at odds with the choreographer. Dances range from the seductive tango to the elegant waltz and the jaunty two-step. Each dance requires a different skill and attitude, presenting contestants with constant hurdles. One of the pleasures of the show is following the journey of a celebrity as he or she learns a different dance each week. Many surprises have occurred during the live airings, most notably the collapse of Marie Osmond from exhaustion in season five.

As Gia Kourlas of the *New York Times* noted, *Dancing* combines two shows in one: "the reality is the performance, while the actual melodrama of dance is captured during the rehearsals." Both elements depend on the persuasiveness and personality of the choreographer. Sultry Cheryl Burke and the suave Tony Dovolani have appeared in each season of the show, and more than thirty other choreographers have participated over the fourteen-season run. As the series has continued the professional dancers have also developed their own cults. Much has been written about the sexiness of the Ukrainian-born Maksim Chmerkovskiy, as well as the youthful vitality of Derek Hough.

WINNING DANCERS

Although the first athlete, Evander Holyfield, finished a distant fifth out of six competitors, athletes have won the famed "Mirrorball" trophy six times. Hannah Karp wrote in the *Wall Street Journal* that the series has been "completely manhandled by athletes." Second season contestant and NFL receiver Jerry Rice displayed the physical grace and competitive composure that has marked sporting contestants. The following season Dallas Cowboy running back Emmitt Smith was an upset victor over actor Mario Lopez. Since then five athletes from different sports have placed first: Olympic speed skater Apolo Anton Ohno (season four), race car driver Helio Castroneves (season five), figure skater Kristi Yamaguchi (season six), gymnast Shawn Johnson (season eight), and NFL receiver Hines Ward (season twelve). Dancer Cheryl Burke, who was paired with Emmitt Smith, stated that athletes are better suited to the work ethic that dancing demands: "they're used to being coached, and they respond to criticism better than, say, actors."

Entertainers, especially those with dancing backgrounds, have also won the competition frequently. Although many fans have debated how much dancing experience a celebrity should have to be allowed to compete, song-and-dance show people have excelled in competition. Winners include Drew Lachey of the group 98 Degrees (season two), Donny Osmond (season nine), Nicole Scherzinger of the Pussycat Dolls (season ten), and actress Jennifer Grey (season eleven). In fact, only two winners have not been from the musical or sports worlds: model Brooke Burke (season seven) and soldier/actor J. R. Martinez (season thirteen).

Controversy has abounded during the run of *Dancing with the Stars*, but never more than in the first season. Many questions arose concerning the actual winner of that season. Actress Kelly Monaco was favored as the best dancer with her partner Alec Mazo over the popular runner-up John O'Hurley, who was paired with professional Charlotte Jorgensen. In recognition of the protest, ABC created a special "Dance Off" rematch between Monaco and O'Hurley; O'Hurley won in a close vote. Over the years some questions have been raised about the voting process overall, in particular about how judges' scores are balanced with the votes of the fans.

Dancing with the Stars has emerged as a signature show for ABC. The success of the series has allowed the network to dominate two time periods: the competition show on Mondays and the results program on Tuesdays. Its success spawned programs such as Fox's *So You Think You Can Dance* (2005–), MTV's *America's Best Dance Crew* (2008–), Oxygen Network's

Dance Your Ass Off (2009–2010), and the Sundance Channel's *Push Girls* (2012–). *Dancing with the Stars* and reality show phenomenon *American Idol*, along with their many progeny, have proven that song and dance still thrive on television.

Ron Simon

SEE ALSO: American Idol*; "B" Movies;* The Bachelor*; Celebrity; The Dallas Cowboys; Game Shows;* General Hospital*; Gymnastics; Hollywood; Holyfield, Evander; Live Television; National Football League (NFL); The New Kids on the Block; Olympics; Pop Music; Radio; Reality Television; Rice, Jerry;* Seinfeld*; Soap Operas; Sports Heroes; Supermodels; Teen Idols; Television.*

BIBLIOGRAPHY

Bergeron, Tom. *I'm Hosting as Fast as I Can!: Zen and the Art of Staying Sane in Hollywood.* New York: HarperOne, 2010.

Karp, Hannah. "Athletes Dance Better than You." *Wall Street Journal*, March 31, 2010.

Kourlas, Gia. "Cheek to Cheek (and Tongue-In-Cheek)." *New York Times*, April 19, 2010.

Dandridge, Dorothy *(1922–1965)*

Born in Cleveland, Ohio, on November 9, 1922, entertainer Dorothy Dandridge was smart, immensely talented, and alluringly beautiful. In her three-decade career in Hollywood she endured the bittersweet distinction of being the first sexy African American woman film artist of the postwar period. Dandridge attempted to forge a career in Hollywood when the majority of roles for black women were as servants or for those who could sing in brief nonspeaking cameo roles.

Dandridge was the first black woman to grace the cover of *Life* magazine and to appear on stage at the posh Waldorf-Astoria. Her film credits include *Bright Road* (1953); *Carmen Jones* (1954), opposite Harry Belafonte, and for which she received an Oscar nomination for best actress, the first African American to receive a nomination for a starring role; *Tamango* (1958); *Island in the Sun* (1957) with James Mason and Belafonte, the first major interracial film from Hollywood; *The Decks Ran Red* (1958); *Porgy and Bess* (1959), opposite Sidney Poitier; and *Malaga* (1960) with Trevor Howard.

In life Dandridge was a star, and in death she became a legend. Decades after her mysterious demise on September 8, 1965, she continues to evoke the interest of film scholars and fans, resulting in various biographies; website tributes; and a film about her life, *Introducing Dorothy Dandridge* (1999), starring Halle Berry.

Pamala S. Deane

SEE ALSO: *Belafonte, Harry; Hollywood; Poitier, Sidney.*

BIBLIOGRAPHY

Bogle, Donald. *Blacks in American Films and Television: An Encyclopedia.* New York: Garland, 1988.

Bogle, Donald. *Dorothy Dandridge: A Biography*, New York: Amistad, 1997.

Dandridge, Dorothy, and Earl Conrad. *Everything and Nothing: The Dorothy Dandridge Tragedy.* New York: Abelard-Schuman, 1970.

Mills, Earl. *Dorothy Dandridge: An Intimate Biography.* Los Angeles, CA: Holloway House, 1991.

Daniels, Charlie *(1936–)*

Charlie Daniels came to prominence during the early 1970s, at a time when country music was caught up in Vietnam patriotism and anti-hippie sentiment. Rock was the music of the counterculture, whose views of the South were formed through newsreels of civil rights battles and movies like *Easy Rider* (1969). A white southern band had to choose one or the other, and many followed the lead of bands such as the Allman Brothers to create the sound known as Southern Rock. The Charlie Daniels Band began as Southern Rockers with an anti-redneck anthem, "Uneasy Rider" (1973), a song about a longhaired guy going into a bar full of good ol' boys. One of the few musicians to fit into both rock and country genres, Daniels manipulated his image and music brilliantly in an attempt to capture his place in twentieth-century popular culture.

Most of the Southern Rockers separated themselves totally from country music—and they remained separate. Even in the 1980s and 1990s, when rock had become a staple of the new country sound, groups like the Allman Brothers, Little Feat, and the Marshall Tucker Band never showed up at country concerts or on the country charts. Daniels was an exception. Right from the start he managed to keep a presence in both worlds, working as a studio fiddle player on Nashville sessions. When pop came to Nashville, Daniels was there, playing hot fiddle parts on Bob Dylan's album *Nashville Skyline.* Even "Uneasy Rider" made the lower rungs of the country charts (it was in the Top 10 on the pop charts).

Southern Rock faded as a chart phenomenon with the end of the 1970s; it did, however, retain a core audience. Daniels then made his move toward country. In 1980 country music was in the grip of the *Urban Cowboy* phenomenon, and there was a lot of country overlap on the pop charts. Daniels was no Urban Cowboy, but he was an artist with the capacity to play to both audiences, and he made the most of it with his biggest hit—"The Devil Went Down to Georgia," which hit number one on the country charts and was number three as a pop hit. It won him a Grammy for Best Country Music Performance by a Duo or Group and earned the Country Music Association Award for Single of the Year. The single was Daniels's high-water mark as his career was middling through the 1980s. He continued to have a mystique of sorts, remaining signed to the same label (Epic), releasing one record after another without cracking the Top 10—mostly, in fact, languishing near the bottom of the charts.

Then, in 1989, Daniels had another career breakthrough. His hit album *A Simple Man* aggressively advocated the lynching of bad guys and hopped onto the anticommunist bandwagon (a little late) by suggesting that it would not be such a bad idea to assassinate Gorbachev. And, as a final rejection of his youthful fling with the counterculture, he recorded a new version of "Uneasy Rider" in which the hero is himself—one of the good ol' boys from whom the original uneasy rider had his narrow escape. This time, he accidentally wanders into a gay bar. Daniels had made himself over completely, from protest-era rebel to Reagan-era conservative. In 2008 he was invited to be a member of the Grand Ole Opry in Nashville. His latest album, *Land That I Love*, was released in 2010.

Tad Richards

SEE ALSO: *The Allman Brothers Band; Communism; Country Music; Dylan, Bob;* Easy Rider*; Grammy Awards;* Grand Ole Opry*; Pop Music; Rock and Roll.*

BIBLIOGRAPHY

Daniels, Charlie. *Ain't No Rag: Freedom, Family, and the Flag.* Washington, DC: Regnery Publishing, 2003.

Wolff, Kurt, and Duane, Orla. *Country Music: The Rough Guide.* London: Rough Guides, 2000.

Daredevil, the Man without Fear

Daredevil, the Man without Fear is a superhero comic book published by Marvel Comics since 1964. Blinded by a childhood accident involving radioactivity that has also mysteriously enhanced his remaining senses to superhuman levels, defense attorney Matt Murdock trains himself to physical perfection and crusades for justice as the costumed Daredevil.

Daredevil remained a consistently popular but decidedly second-tier Marvel superhero until the late 1970s, when writer/artist Frank Miller assumed the creative direction of the series. By emphasizing the disturbing obsessive and fascistic qualities of the superhero as a modern vigilante, Miller transformed *Daredevil* into one of the most graphic, sophisticated, and best-written comic books of its time. His work on the series became a standard for a new generation of comic-book creators and fans who came to expect more violence and thematic maturity from their superheroes.

A live-action feature film starring Ben Affleck as Murdock/Daredevil was released in 2003, during a period of fascination with superheroes in Hollywood. *Daredevil* received lukewarm reviews from critics but managed to capture the top box-office position for the first two weeks after its release. The film also spawned a hugely successful video game available on Gameboy Advance and a spin-off film, *Elektra*, which follows the adventures of Murdock's girlfriend-turned-crime-fighter, Elektra Natchios. In the 2010s, rumors emerged that another Daredevil film was in the works at Twentieth Century Fox, albeit with an all-new cast.

Bradford Wright

SEE ALSO: *Comic Books; Computer Games; Gameboy; Marvel Comics; Video Games.*

BIBLIOGRAPHY

Daniels, Les. *Marvel: Five Fabulous Decades of the World's Greatest Comics.* New York: Harry N. Abrams, 1991.

Lee, Stan. *Origins of Marvel Comics.* New York: Simon & Schuster, 1974.

Weiner, Robert G. *Marvel Graphic Novels and Related Publications: An Annotated Guide to Comics, Prose Novels, Children's Books, Articles, Criticism and Reference Works, 1965–2005.* Jefferson, NC: McFarland, 2008.

The Dark Knight

The Dark Knight, released in 2008, is the sequel to 2005's *Batman Begins*. Both films were directed by Christopher Nolan and star actor Christian Bale as Bruce Wayne/Batman. However, *The Dark Knight* is no mere retread of what came before. Instead the film is a rare example of a sequel that critics and audiences generally regard as superior to the original, even with the high praise the first film received.

The sequel continues much of what had occurred in the previous film, with the supporting cast of characters largely intact. Actor Gary Oldman is police lieutenant (and later commissioner) James Gordon; Michael Caine is Wayne's butler, Alfred Pennyworth; and Morgan Freeman is Batman's technical assistant, Lucius Fox. Wayne's love interest, Rachel Dawes, also reappears, but actress Maggie Gyllenhaal replaces Katie Holmes in the role. Perhaps most compelling is the addition of new characters Harvey Dent (Aaron Eckhart) and the Joker (Heath Ledger).

The film received particular attention as one of Ledger's last roles and the first of his movies released after his premature death. The performance's notoriety notwithstanding, however,

Heath Ledger as the Joker. *Heath Ledger played the Joker as menacing and demented in* The Dark Knight. WARNER BROS/DC COMICS/THE KOBAL COLLECTION.

Ledger's embodiment of the Joker is the outstanding performance of the film. Far from the madcap portraits previously created by actors Cesar Romero and Jack Nicholson, Ledger's Joker is incredibly grim and without a traditional criminal motivation. He disregards the greed and petty vengeance pursued by other characters, instead embracing chaos as his only goal. Nolan largely attributed the creation of the character to Ledger himself, who worked to create a villain consistent with the somber tone established in *Batman Begins*.

As *The Dark Knight* begins, new district attorney Dent and Batman appear to have largely reduced crime in Gotham City. These successes lead organized crime leaders to turn to the Joker, a mysterious new figure in Gotham's criminal underground, who promises to eliminate Batman for a price. One of the Joker's preferred tactics is forcing people into situations in which they must make hopeless choices. For example, Batman must choose to rescue either Rachel or Dent, and the result is Rachel's death and the severe disfiguration of Dent.

Half of his face gruesomely deformed, Harvey adopts a new moniker, Two-Face, and begins a campaign of terror against those he sees as responsible for Rachel's death. Consistent with the theme of choice, Two-Face effectively waives his free will, relying on the toss of a coin to determine whether or not an individual lives or dies. The character arc of Two-Face is the most dynamic of the film, as the other characters remain generally consistent throughout the narrative. Dent undergoes a complete, tragic reversal of fortune, resulting in a turnabout of his ethical ideals. Initially presented as a kind of white knight, he is absorbed into the darkness of the city, raising the question of how one stays moral when faced with an utterly bleak and corrupted world.

The Dark Knight's answer to the question of maintaining one's morality in the face of adversity is ultimately ambiguous. Two-Face's villainy is not excused, but Batman and Commissioner Gordon attempt to cover it up. Batman insists on taking the blame for Dent's crimes in order to preserve the district attorney's image as a hero who works through the law. Thus, Batman becomes the outlaw, working for justice from the shadows.

The film proved a tremendous success on all fronts, enjoying a box-office gross of more than $1 billion, making it the highest-grossing motion picture of 2008. Additionally, many critics praised *The Dark Knight* as perhaps the finest film version of a comic-book character, suggesting that it both transcended the genre and opened it up for sophisticated storytelling. Among the film's many award nominations were eight Academy Award nods, and it was named Movie of the Year by the American Film Institute. Ledger's performance received nominations for dozens of awards, most of which the actor won, including the Academy Award for Best Supporting Actor, the first time the honor had been posthumously awarded since actor Peter Finch in 1977.

With 2012's *The Dark Knight Rises* director Christopher Nolan reportedly completed his contribution to the Batman legend.

Marc Oxoby

SEE ALSO: *Academy Awards; Batman; Blockbusters; Comic Books; Nicholson, Jack; Romero, Cesar.*

BIBLIOGRAPHY

Byrne, Craig. *"The Dark Knight": Featuring Production Art and Full Shooting Script.* New York: Universe, 2008.

Durand, Kevin K., and Leigh K. Mary. *Riddle Me This, Batman!: Essays of the Universe of the Dark Knight.* Jefferson, NC: McFarland, 2011.

Halbfinger, David M. "Batman's Burden: A Director Confronts Darkness and Death." *New York Times Magazine*, March 9, 2008, AR1, AR6.

Dark Shadows

In the world of continuing daytime drama, aka "the soaps," *Dark Shadows* remains an anomaly. Unlike any other day or evening television show, the program's increasing popularity over the course of its five-year run from 1966 to 1971 led to the creation of two feature films (*House of Dark Shadows* and *Night of Dark Shadows*); a hit record album of themes from the show; and a series of thirty novels, comic books, and other paraphernalia—a development unheard of in the world of daytime television. *Dark Shadows* had unexpectedly evolved from another afternoon soap into a cultural phenomenon and franchise. Indeed, the show was in a genre all by itself during this period of twentieth-century television history.

Like other soaps, *Dark Shadows* dealt with forbidden love and exotic medical conditions. Unlike any other, however, its conflicts tended to extend beyond the everyday material most

***Barnabas Collins of* Dark Shadows.** Dark Shadows *saw its ratings buoyed by the introduction of Jonathan Frid as vampire Barnabas Collins.* DAN CURTIS PROD/THE KOBAL COLLECTION.

soaps cover into more "otherworldly" phenomena. Nestled in the fog-enshrouded coastal town of Collinsport, Maine, the Collins family was repeatedly plagued by family curses that involved ghosts, vampires, werewolves, and "phoenixes"—mothers who come back from the dead to claim and then kill their children. In fact, there were as many curses as there were locked rooms and secret passageways in the seemingly endless family estate known as Collinwood. Characters had to travel back and forth in time, as well as into "parallel dimensions," in order to unravel and solve the mysteries that would prevent future suffering.

Amazingly, despite its cancellation some forty years ago and the fact that during its time on the air it was constantly threatened with cancellation by the management of ABC, *Dark Shadows* is fondly remembered by many baby boomers as "the show you ran home after school to watch" in those pre-DVR days. It is the subject of dozens of fan websites and chat rooms, an online college course, and even a site where fans have endeavored to continue writing episodes speculating what might have transpired after the last episode was broadcast in 1971. There are even yearly conventions held by the International Dark Shadows Society celebrating the show and featuring former cast members who are asked to share their memories.

The concept for *Dark Shadows* originated in the mind of Emmy-winning sports producer Dan Curtis, who wanted to branch out into drama. His dream of a mysterious young woman journeying to an old dark house—which would hold the keys to her past and future—became the starting point, establishing the gothic tone that combined elements of *Jane Eyre* with *The Turn of the Screw*—the latter of which would figure repeatedly in the show's plotlines.

The young woman was known as Victoria Winters (played by Alexandra Moltke). She accepted a post as a governess of ten-year-old David Collins (David Henesy), heir to the family fortune, and companion to Collinwood's stern and secretive mistress, Elizabeth Collins (Joan Bennett). Believing herself to be an orphan (she is in fact the illegitimate daughter of Elizabeth), Victoria senses that the keys to her past and future lie with the Collins family.

While plot complications in the first few months of the show concerned mysterious threats on Victoria's life, there was little in the turgid conflicts between the Collins family and a vengeful local businessman to attract viewers, and ratings declined rapidly. This is when Curtis decided to jazz things up by introducing the first of the series' many ghosts. While exploring an obscure part of the rambling Collins estate, young David encounters the ghost of a young woman, Josette DuPres. As ratings began to rise, Josette becomes integral in helping to protect David from Curtis's next supernatural phenomenon—the arrival of Laura Collins (Diana Millay), David's deceased mother who has risen from the dead as a phoenix to claim him.

ENTER BARNABAS

While this influx of the supernatural buoyed up the flailing ratings, it was the introduction of Jonathan Frid as vampire Barnabas Collins—originally intended to be yet another short-term monster to be dealt with and destroyed—that established the tone for the show and caused its popularity to steadily rise. Cleverly, Barnabas was not depicted as a mere monster but as a man tortured by his conscience. He had once been in love with Josette DuPres and, upon encountering local waitress Maggie Evans (Kathryn Leigh Scott), he attempts to hypnotize her into becoming Josette, hoping to then drink her blood and transform her into his eternal vampire bride. His efforts, however, are thwarted by the intervention of yet another benevolent ghost.

The increasing popularity of the tortured Barnabas and his sufferings in love led the writers to attempt yet another first—during a séance, Victoria is instantaneously transported to 1795, and there, along with the audience, witnesses the events surrounding the original Barnabas/Josette love story. This extended flashback—with the cast of actors playing the ancestors of their present characters—ran for months to high ratings as young, uncursed Barnabas goes to the Caribbean island of Martinique on business and there meets and prepares to marry the young Josette, the daughter of a plantation owner. Simultaneously, he initiates an affair with her maid, Angélique Bouchard (Lara Parker), who is herself in love with Barnabas and attempts to use witchcraft to possess him. When he spurns her, Angélique places an irreversible curse on him, and suddenly a vampire bat appears and bites him. Though he manages to kill Angélique before he can transform Josette into his vampire bride, the spirit of Angélique appears to her and shows her the hideousness of her future. In response, the traumatized girl runs from Barnabas and throws herself off the edge of Widow's Hill, to be dashed on the rocks below. The fateful love triangle of Barnabas, Josette, and Angélique was repeated in various forms throughout the life of the show.

Always searching for a novel twist, the writers then toyed with the concept of a "parallel universe." Barnabas discovers a room on the estate in which he witnesses events transpiring in the present, but the characters are all in different roles—the result of different choices they made earlier. This is essentially a parallel dimension, and he enters it, hoping to learn that there he is not a vampire. Scott later suggested that this innovation proved to be so complex that it hastened the demise of the show, for both the writers and audience were having trouble keeping track of the various characters in "real" time versus the variations they played in alternate dimensions. But as Victoria suggests in her opening voice-over, essentially the past and present were "one" at Collinwood.

ON THE BIG SCREEN

Over the course of its approximately 1,200 episodes, *Dark Shadows*' ratings ebbed and peaked, drawing an extremely diverse audience. By May of 1969 the show was at its peak of popularity as ABC's number one daytime drama, which boasted a daily viewership of some twenty million. It was this status that led producer/creator Curtis to envision a *Dark Shadows* feature film—yet another first for a daytime drama. Despite the show's success, however, most studios laughed off the idea until Metro-Goldwyn-Mayer (MGM) green-lighted it, and *House of Dark Shadows* became the first of the show's movie adaptations. For this big-screen incarnation, Curtis decided to go back to the central and most popular plotline involving Barnabas's awakening/arrival at Collinwood, his meeting Maggie Evans, and his subsequent effort to remake her into his lost love Josette. Curtis did attempt to change the tone of the film version of the story—instead of being the vampire with a conscience, Barnabas would be what Curtis originally envisioned him to be: a monster that would motivate the greater gore ratio Curtis intended for the film audiences.

Released in 1970, *House of Dark Shadows* was such a success that some claim it helped to save a failing MGM, and Curtis was commissioned by the studio to create another film. *Night of Dark Shadows* was a smaller-scale effort. Adapting one of the parallel-dimension plotlines, Quentin Collins (David Selby) inherits the Collins estate and brings his young wife (played by Kate Jackson, later of *Charlie's Angels* and *Scarecrow and Mrs. King*) there to live. He then begins painting the image of Angélique, whose ghost appears to seduce and take possession of him. Less successful than its predecessor, but still a moneymaker, there were plans to make a third film, but *Dark Shadows* was canceled, and Curtis decided to move on to other projects.

Some twenty years later, in 1991, Curtis joined forces with NBC to re-create *Dark Shadows* as a prime-time soap opera. In this incarnation, he attempted to initiate things with the arrival of Barnabas (played by *Chariots of Fire* star Ben Cross) and the subsequent recounting of his history via the 1795 flashback. Veteran screen star (and fan of the original show) Jean Simmons took over the role of Elizabeth, and British scream queen Barbara Steele was cast as Dr. Julia Hoffman. This casting also included Lysette Anthony as Angélique and Adrian Paul (future star of *Highlander: The Series*) as Barnabas's younger brother Jeremiah Collins. Despite much anticipation by fans, the show debuted as a midseason replacement just as the First Gulf War began. It was both preempted and shifted around in its time slot due to low ratings until the producers finally chose to cancel it after twelve episodes.

In 2012 *Dark Shadows* returned to the big screen once again, this time as a film directed by Tim Burton and starring Johnny Depp as Barnabas and Michelle Pfeiffer as Elizabeth.

Rick Moody

SEE ALSO: *Baby Boomers; Camp;* Charlie's Angels*; Goth; Gulf Wars; Horror Movies; Soap Operas; Vampires.*

BIBLIOGRAPHY

Scott, Kathryn Leigh. *My Scrapbook Memories of "Dark Shadows."* Los Angeles: Pomegranate Press, 1986.

Scott, Kathryn Leigh. *The "Dark Shadows" Companion: 25th Anniversary Collection.* Los Angeles: Pomegranate Press, 1990.

Scott, Kathryn Leigh, and Kate Jackson. *The "Dark Shadows" Movie Book.* Los Angeles: Pomegranate Press, 1998.

Scott, Kathryn Leigh, and Jim Pierson. *The "Dark Shadows" Almanac.* Los Angeles: Pomegranate Press, 1995.

Darrow, Clarence *(1857–1938)*

Sometimes reviled for his defense of unpopular people and causes, Clarence Darrow was the most widely known attorney in the United States at the time of his death in 1938. He plied his trade in the Midwest, eventually becoming chief attorney for the Chicago and North Western Railways. By 1900 he had left this lucrative position to defend socialist leader Eugene Debs, who had organized striking American Railway Union workers.

Involved in several other labor-related cases and an advocate of integration, he also worked as a defense attorney, saving murderers Nathan Leopold and Richard Loeb from the electric chair in 1924. His 1925 courtroom battle against bible-thumping politician William Jennings Bryant in the Scopes Monkey Trial—called such because of its focus on the teaching of Charles Darwin's theory of evolution in schools—was immortalized in the play and film *Inherit the Wind.* Darrow wrote several books, including *Crime: Its Cause and Treatment* (1922).

Pamela L. Shelton

SEE ALSO: *Capital Punishment; Debs, Eugene V.; Leopold and Loeb; Scopes Monkey Trial.*

BIBLIOGRAPHY

Kersten, Andrew E. *Clarence Darrow: American Iconoclast.* New York: Hill and Wang, 2011.

Kurland, Gerald. *Clarence Darrow: "Attorney for the Damned."* Charlottesville, VA: SamHar Press, 1972.

Stone, Irving. *Clarence Darrow for the Defense.* Garden City, NY: Doubleday, 1941.

Tierney, Kevin. *Darrow: A Biography.* New York: Crowell, 1979.

Weinberg, Arthur, and Lila Weinberg. *Clarence Darrow, a Sentimental Rebel.* New York: Putnam, 1980.

Dateline

Dateline is a one-hour news magazine television show that premiered on NBC in March 1992. With anchors Jane Pauley and Stone Phillips, *Dateline* aired on Tuesday nights, typically featuring three current-event news stories per episode. Initially ratings were low, but by 1994 *Dateline* had gained enough momentum that NBC aired a second edition of the show on Wednesday with anchors Tom Brokaw and Katie Couric.

In November 1992 *Dateline* became a newsmaker itself when a story about General Motors (GM) trucks was revealed to have been embellished. Titled "Waiting to Explode," the report claimed that gas tanks in GM pickup trucks could explode during vehicle crashes. However, the video accompanying the report showed trucks that had been rigged with remote-controlled explosives in order to dramatize the danger. When the deception came to light, GM filed a trade libel lawsuit against NBC that was settled out of court. Several top NBC executives were dismissed, and Pauley read a lengthy on-air apology to viewers for the show's misrepresentation. The program came under fire in subsequent years for other exaggerated accusations and the use of hidden cameras.

Regardless, *Dateline* remained on the air, and by 1999 it was on five nights a week in the same time slot, a first for any TV news magazine. With *Dateline*'s Nielsen ratings consistently hitting the top ten, rival news magazine shows followed suit by producing midweek spin-off editions. However, alternate editions of *60 Minutes* and *20/20* were short-lived. Five nights proved to be too much for *Dateline* as well, and by the end of 2000, the show was airing only three nights per week.

In the late 1990s and early 2000s *Dateline* began to concentrate more exclusively on human-interest stories, with segments about consumer advocacy, true-crime tales, and individuals' struggles dominating each episode. With this change in focus, the format of the show varied over the years. Some episodes still followed the news magazine format of several short segments, while others focused on a single story for an entire episode. Some interviews extended over multiple shows. In 1999, as part of an effort to attract viewers, *Dateline* pioneered the use of public opinion polls during the show. The anchors asked questions about audience perception regarding the subject matter of the current episode, such as the guilt or innocence of a suspected criminal. The results would then be given at the end of the episode.

With the advent of reality shows in the early 2000s, news magazine programs as well as many traditional television shows lost considerable numbers of viewers. *Dateline* was no exception. As its ratings fell steadily during the first decade of the 2000s, producers scaled the show back even further, airing it only one night a week. The flagship Tuesday night edition ended in 2003. As of 2012, *Dateline* regularly broadcast on Friday night with occasional specials on other evenings. During this time period, several personnel shifts also occurred. Pauley stepped down in 2003, leaving Phillips to anchor alone until Ann Curry joined him as coanchor in 2005. Curry was the solo anchor from 2007 to 2011, when Lester Holt assumed the position.

In 2004 *Dateline* debuted a spin-off series to compete with reality television juggernauts such as *Survivor*. Hosted by Chris Hansen, *To Catch a Predator* is an award winning, yet highly controversial show that capitalizes on parental fears of sexual predators trolling the Internet for teenage victims. Producers of the show impersonate young people on the Internet and make contact with adults under the pretense of meeting for a sexual encounter. The adults then arrive at a prearranged location to find Hansen, who then questions them about why they are there. Law enforcement officers, waiting out of sight, then move in and arrest the predator. Eventually the show's popularity made it increasingly difficult to lure sexual predators, and in 2008 NBC canceled the show.

Although critics have decried *Dateline*'s sensationalism, strong ratings even in the twenty-first century have proven that such coverage is what television audiences want, and in 2012 the show celebrated its twentieth anniversary. During its two-decade run, *Dateline* has been nominated for dozens of awards, including Peabody, Emmy, ALMA (American Latino Media Arts), ASCAP (American Society of Composers, Authors and Publishers), and GLAAD (Gay & Lesbian Alliance Against Defamation) awards. To keep pace with the growing number of reality and true-crime networks, *Dateline* began repackaging the show for syndication on stations such as the Investigation Discovery network, TLC, and Cloo. Despite drops in ratings, changing trends, and an unpredictable world, *Dateline* remains a staple of American evening news entertainment.

Jill Gregg Clever

SEE ALSO: *Brokaw, Tom; Emmy Awards; General Motors; The Internet;* 60 Minutes*;* Survivor*; Television;* 20/20.

BIBLIOGRAPHY

Bartone, Richard C. "Dateline NBC." In *Encyclopedia of Television*, ed. Horace Newcomb. New York: Fitzroy Dearborn, 2004.

Greppi, Michelle. "Decade-Old 'Dateline' Counts Its Blessings." *Electronic Media*, April 22, 2002.

Davis, Bette *(1908–1989)*

Born Ruth Elizabeth Davis in 1908, Bette Davis was one of the biggest stars of the Hollywood Studio era. During her illustrious career, which spanned six decades, she appeared in more than 100 films and made numerous television appearances. Her talents were recognized with nine Academy Award nominations and two awards (1936 and 1939); three Emmy nominations and one award (1979); and a Life Achievement Award from the American Film Institute (1977). In films such as *Marked Woman* (1937), *Jezebel* (1938), and *All about Eve* (1950), she played women who were intelligent, independent, and defiant—often challenging the social order. It is perhaps for these reasons that Davis became an icon of urban gay culture, for more often than not, her characters refused to succumb to the strict restraints placed on them by society.

Frances Gateward

SEE ALSO: *Academy Awards;* All about Eve*; Crawford, Joan; Hollywood; Movie Stars.*

BIBLIOGRAPHY

Davis, Bette. *The Lonely Life: An Autobiography*. New York: Lancer Books, 1962.

Higham, Charles. *Bette: The Life of Bette Davis*. New York: Macmillan, 1981.

Leaming, Barbara. *Bette Davis: A Biography*. New York: Simon & Schuster, 1992.

Ringgold, Gene, and Lawrence J. Quirk *The Complete Films of Bette Davis*. New York: Carol Publishing Group, 1990.

Davis, Miles *(1926–1991)*

Trumpet player Miles Davis became famous among both jazz buffs and people who know very little about the art form. He did so through a combination of intelligence, charisma, awareness of his own abilities, and a feel for the music scene rarely equaled in jazz. Some critics note that he did so with less natural technical ability than most jazz stars.

EARLY STAGES

In spite of attempts to portray himself otherwise, Davis was not a street kid. Rather, he came from comfortable, upper-middle-class surroundings. His father was a dentist in East St. Louis, Illinois, and his mother was a trained pianist who taught school. Davis grew up listening to classical and popular music.

In common with many teens of his day, Davis played in the school band and worked in a jazz combo around town. He learned quickly from older musicians, and many took a liking to a young man they all described as "shy" and "withdrawn." Shy and withdrawn as he may have been, young Davis found the audacity to ask noted vocalist Billy Eckstine to sit in with his band. By all accounts, Davis was "awful," but the musician saw something special beneath the shy exterior and limited technical ability.

In 1944 Davis went to New York to study at the Juilliard School of Music. In a typical move, he tracked down saxophonist Charlie "Bird" Parker and moved in with him. Bird sponsored Davis's career and used him on recordings and with his working band from time to time. Certainly, this work aided Davis in getting jobs with Benny Carter's band and then taking trumpeter Fats Navarro's chair in the Eckstine band. In 1947 Davis was back staying with Bird.

Although he still was not the most proficient trumpet player on the scene, Davis was attracting his own following and learning with each experience. It was, however, becoming obvious that his future fame would not be based on playing in the complex, flashy Dizzy Gillespie style so many other young trumpeters were trying to imitate and develop.

ELEMENTS OF STYLE

In 1949 Davis provided a clear indication of his future distinctive style and pattern. He emerged as the leader of a group of bandleader Claude Thornhill's musicians, and from that collaboration sprang *Birth of the Cool* and the style of jazz named after it. That Davis, still in his early twenties, would assume leadership of the group that boasted Lee Konitz, Gerry Mulligan, Gil Evans, and others was in itself remarkable, but that he had successfully switched styles and assumed leadership of the style that he did so much to shape was a pattern he repeated throughout his life.

Unfortunately, however, Davis's heroin addiction became the predominant force in his life, and for the next few years he did little artistically. Stories about his wrecked life circulated in the jazz world, which Davis confronted in his 1990 autobiography. But the challenge of younger up-and-coming stars such as Clifford Brown stirred up Davis's pride and led to his kicking his habit.

Miles Davis. *Miles Davis performs live in 1986. He is credited with introducing a broad range of music fans to jazz.* EBET ROBERTS/REDFERNS.

By 1954 Miles was back and heading toward the most artistically successful years of his life. The Davis style fully matured; that style of the 1950s and early 1960s was marked by use of the Harmon mute, half valves, soft and fully rounded tones, reliance on the middle register, snatches of exquisite melodic composition, and general absence of rapid-fire runs. Davis attributed his sound to Freddie Webster, a St. Louis trumpet master, and his use of space to Ahmad Jamal, a pianist of great genius.

SIGNATURE RECORDINGS

In the mid-1950s Davis pioneered the funk movement with songs such as "Walkin'." He kept his own rather cool approach, accentuated by unparalleled use of the Harmon mute while typically surrounding himself with "hotter" (more technically flashy) players such as Jackie McClean or Sonny Rollins. In 1955 the style came together with his "classic" quintet at the Newport Jazz Festival, where the quintet's enormous success led to a lucrative contract with Columbia Records, reputedly making Davis the highest-paid jazz artist in history. The Miles Davis Quintet, consisting of John Coltrane on tenor sax, Paul Chambers on bass, Philly Joe Jones on Drums, and Red Garland on piano, was a band of all-stars and the stuff of which jazz legends are made. With the addition of Cannonball Adderly on alto sax, the sextet was able to use combinations and colorations that shaped the course of modern jazz. The ultimate personification of cool, the albums *Bye, Bye, Blackbird* (1956) and *Milestones* (1958) pointed the way to Davis's next experiments.

Davis's 1958 Paris recording of the music for the film *The Elevator to the Gallows* was a high point in his career. His use of unexpected note placement leading to suspended rhythms and simple harmonic structures led logically into the use of modes or scalar improvisation. (In modal improvisation the improviser uses one or two modes, or scales, as the basis for improvisation rather than changing chords each measure or even more frequently.) John Coltrane had taken that style to its logical conclusion, developing the work of Gillespie at a frantic pace. Davis had never been comfortable with playing at frantic speeds.

Kind of Blue, which featured Bill Evans on a number of cuts, fueled the modal explosion in jazz. Considered one of the finest jazz albums ever made, it was a commercial success, and Davis continued to use compositions from the album over a long period of his career. He did not, however, exclusively feature modal tunes in his repertoire. In fact, it should be noted that Davis never totally dropped one style as he moved on to another one, and the challenge of Free Jazz was about to launch him into another phase of his career, a series of records with his friend Gil Evans featuring a big band. The first album, which some consider the best, was *Sketches of Spain* (1960), featuring "Concierto." Davis did not abandon his small-group career, although he did frequently perform with a big band and recorded more albums in that format, including *Porgy and Bess*, featuring his marvelous rendition of "Summertime."

FREE JAZZ AND ROCK

By 1964 Davis was ready to change again. His albums were not selling as they once had. They were receiving excellent reviews, but they were not reaching the pop audience. Davis still refused to try the Free Jazz route of Don Cherry and Ornette Coleman or even of his former colleague, Coltrane. Davis was more inclined to reach out to the audience his friend Sly Stone had cultivated—the huge rock audience, including young blacks.

It was at this point that Davis, already possessing something of a reputation as a "bad dude," truly developed his image of a nasty street tough. He had always turned his back on audiences and refused to announce compositions or performers, but now he exaggerated that image and turned to fusion. Beginning in 1967 with *Nefertiti* and following in 1968 with *Filles de Kilimanjaro*, Davis began incorporating rock elements into his work. He used Chick Corea on electric piano and replaced his veterans with other younger men, including Tony Williams on drums, Ron Carter on bass, and Wayne Shorter on tenor sax.

The success of these records, although somewhat short of his expectations, forced Davis to explore the genre further. That led to his use of fusion guitarist John McLaughlin on *In a Silent Way* in 1969 and the all-out fusion album, *Bitches Brew*, the same year. *Bitches Brew*, which introduced rock listeners to jazz, marked a point of no return for Davis. The 1970s were a period that led to great popular success for his group. Davis changed his clothing and performing styles. He affected the attire of the pop music star, appeared at Fillmore East and West, attracted young audiences, attached an electric amp mike to his horn, and strode the stage restlessly.

LAST DAYS

For a period of years, Davis stopped performing, and rumors once again surfaced regarding his condition. In the early 1980s he made a successful comeback with a funk-oriented group. This was a different sort of funk from "Walkin'" and his other 1950s successes, however. He was still able to recruit fine talent from among young musicians, as his use of saxophonist Kenny Garrett attests. As the 1980s came to an end, however, Davis's loyal jazz followers saw only a few sparks of the Miles Davis whom they revered. Nevertheless, there were still enough of these sparks to fuel the hope that Davis might just once more play in his old style.

Finally, at the Montreux Festival of 1991, Quincy Jones convinced Davis to relive the work he had done with Gil Evans. Davis had some fears about performing his old hits, but as he rehearsed, those fears subsided, and the documentary based on that performance, as well as the video and CD made of it, demonstrate that he gained in confidence as he performed. While not quite the Davis of the 1950s and 1960s, he was "close enough for jazz." These performances as well as the soundtrack of *Dingo* have gone far to fuel the jazz fans' lament for what might have been. They display a Davis filled with intelligence, wit, and emotion who responds to the love of his audience and who is for once seemingly at ease with his own inner demons.

The rest of the Montreux performance featured Davis with members from his various groups over the years. The range of the groups offered proof of his versatility and his self-knowledge of his strengths and weaknesses. After the festival, Davis performed in a group with his old friend Jackie McClean. Rumors persist of tapes they made in Europe that have not yet surfaced commercially.

In September 1991, Davis died of pneumonia, leaving a rich legacy of music and enough fuel for controversy to satisfy jazz fans for many years. The extent of his legacy is felt in almost every genre of music. Artists as disparate as Herbie Hancock, Radiohead, and Busta Rhymes have mentioned Davis as an influence, and numerous hip-hop artists, including Aceyalone and Heavy D, have sampled his music. His ability to continually reinvent his compositions signaled an early prototype for a pop star.

Although he was largely revered for his innovative and pioneering musical compositions, Davis was also inspired by other musicians. He covered numerous artists throughout his career, including Dizzy Gillespie's "A Night in Tunisia," Michael Jackson's "Human Nature," and Cyndi Lauper's "Time after Time." Since his death, Davis has received Grammy Awards for *Doo-Bop* (1992) and *Miles & Quincy Live at Montreux* (1993) and was inducted into the Rock and Roll Hall of Fame in 2006. The fiftieth anniversary of *Kind of Blue* sparked the U.S. House of Representatives to pass a measure commemorating the album as well as preserving and advancing jazz music. In 2010 the fortieth anniversary of *Bitches Brew* was celebrated through the release of two separate multidisc editions: *Legacy Edition* and *40th Anniversary Collector's Edition*.

Frank A. Salamone

SEE ALSO: *Coltrane, John; Eckstine, Billy; Funk; Gillespie, Dizzy; Hancock, Herbie; Jackson, Michael; Jazz; Lauper, Cyndi; Newport Jazz and Folk Festivals; Parker, Charlie; Pop Music; Radiohead; Sly and the Family Stone.*

BIBLIOGRAPHY

Carner, Gary, ed. *The Miles Davis Companion: Four Decades of Commentary*. New York: Schimer Books, 1996.

Carr, Ian. *Miles Davis: The Definitive Biography*. Cambridge, MA: Da Capo Press, 2006.

Chamber, Jack. *Milestones: The Music and Times of Miles Davis*. New York: Da Capo Press, 1998.

Cole, Bill. *Miles Davis: The Early Years*. New York: Da Capo Press, 1994.

Davis, Miles, and Quincey Troupe. *Miles: The Autobiography*. New York: Touchstone Books, 1990.

Kirchner, Bill, ed. *A Miles Davis Reader: Smithsonian Readers in American Music*. Washington, DC: Smithsonian Institution Press, 1997.

Nisenson, Eric. *Around about Midnight: A Portrait of Miles Davis*. New York: Da Capo Press, 1996.

Davy Crockett

Davy Crockett, Walt Disney's mid-1950s television adaptation of the Crockett legend, transformed the coonskin-capped frontiersman into a national role model whose appeal has endured for both historians and popular culture aficionados. The Crockett fad in the 1950s spurred the first real mass-marketing campaign in American history, changing the way both films and television shows were promoted. Many baby boomers can still recite the lyrics to "The Ballad of Davy Crockett" and have passed down their treasured Crockett-related items, such as lunchboxes, to their children.

THE REAL DAVY CROCKETT

Crockett was born on August 17, 1786, near Limestone, Tennessee. He went from a local folk hero to a national sensation when the Whig party made him a political symbol in the early nineteenth century. He served as commander of a battalion in the Creek Indian War from 1813 to 1814, was a member of the Tennessee state legislature from 1821 to 1824, and was a member of the United States Congress from 1827 to 1831 and again from 1833 to 1835. Crockett was renowned for the following motto: "Be always sure you are right, then go ahead."

The myths surrounding Crockett began as the Whig party created his election image through deliberate fabrication so that it could capitalize on his favorable political leanings. His penchant for tall tales also helped to make him a folk legend who was rumored to be capable of killing bears with his bare hands and performing similar feats of strength. Even his trusty rifle, "Betsy," achieved fame and name recognition. Crockett was one of the several hundred men who died defending the Alamo from Mexican attack in March 1836 as Texas fought for independence from Mexico with the aid of the United States. After his heroic, patriotic death at the Alamo, his legend was sealed. His tombstone reads, "Davy Crockett, Pioneer, Patriot, Soldier, Trapper, Explorer, State Legislator, Congressman, Martyred at The Alamo. 1786–1836." His larger-than-life persona soon found its way into folklore, journalism, dime novels, plays, television, movies, and music. Historian Margaret J. King has called him "as fine a figure of popular culture as can be imagined."

DISNEY'S DAVY CROCKETT

Disney understood the ability of popular culture to manipulate historical images and the power of the entertainer to educate. Thus, Disney took the Crockett legend and reshaped it to suit its audience of the 1950s. A three-part television series was planned—"Davy Crockett, Indian Fighter" (aired December 15, 1954); "Davy Crockett Goes to Congress" (January 26, 1955); and "Davy Crockett at the Alamo" (February 23, 1955)—to represent the Frontierland section of the Disneyland theme park. Airing on ABC and starring little-known Fess Parker as Crockett, the series greatly elevated the status of both the network and the actor. The American frontier spirit that formerly had been embodied by Daniel Boone was now transferred to Crockett. Walt Disney himself was surprised by the enormity of the Crockett craze—King quotes him as saying, "It became one of the biggest overnight hits in television history and there we were with just three films and a dead hero." Disney quickly released the series as a feature film, *Davy Crockett: King of the Wild Frontier* (1955), in order to cash in on the sudden popularity of Crockett. The fourth and fifth installments of Disney's TV series spawned another feature film, *Davy Crockett and the River Pirates* (1956).

MARKETING THE LEGEND

Disney's interpretation of the Crockett legend arrived soon after leisure activities had started to center on the television. The series demonstrated TV's ability to capture and influence wide audiences. Television programmers and advertisers discovered sizable new markets in the young baby boomer audience, which became infatuated with all things Crockett. The promotional tie-in has been a mainstay ever since the first young boy placed a coonskin cap on his head and pretended he was Crockett. Practically overnight, raccoon skin prices skyrocketed. Disney was unable to copyright the Crockett name since it was in the public domain, and hundreds of related products saturated the market, including guitars, underwear, clothes, toothbrushes, moccasins, bedspreads, lunchboxes, toys, books, and comics. Many companies simply pasted Crockett labels over existing Western-themed merchandise so as not to miss out on the phenomenon. Sixteen versions of the catchy "The Ballad of Davy Crockett" were recorded. Though the song was written merely as filler for the series, it went on to sell more than four million copies.

The legendary Davy Crockett sprang from a long tradition of national heroes as embodiments of the national character, most in the mold of the great white male. Disney's Crockett is a 1950s-era ideal, a dignified common man known for his congeniality, courage, and civic-mindedness. He demonstrates that God's laws exist in nature. Men such as Crockett, after all, led the American people on their divinely appointed mission into the wilderness and set the cultural standard for the settlements that would follow. However, detractors of Disney's Crockett felt that some of his less-refined qualities should not be passed on to children, which led to a debate over whether he was suitable as a national hero. King terms such controversy as an example of the volatile melding of mass media, national history, and the popular consciousness. Davy Crockett—both Disney's and the earlier versions—represents how Americans perceive their history, and how those perceptions change with the times.

Marcella Bush Treviño

SEE ALSO: *Baby Boomers; Consumerism; Disney (Walt Disney Company); Leisure Time; Television.*

BIBLIOGRAPHY

Cummings, Joe, and Michael A. Lofaro, eds. *Crockett at Two Hundred: New Perspectives on the Man and the Myth.* Knoxville: University of Tennessee Press, 1989.

Hauck, Richard Boyd. *Davy Crockett: A Handbook.* Lincoln: University of Nebraska Press, 1982.

King, Margaret J. "The Recycled Hero: Walt Disney's Davy Crockett." In *Davy Crockett: The Man, the Legend, the Legacy, 1786–1986*, ed. Michael A. Lofaro. Knoxville, University of Tennessee Press, 1985.

Lofaro, Michael A., ed. *Davy Crockett: The Man, the Legend, the Legacy, 1786–1986.* Knoxville: University of Tennessee Press, 1985.

Dawson's Creek

Dawson's Creek was a television drama for teenagers that aired on the WB network from 1998 to 2003. It premiered to mixed reviews but gradually worked its way into pop culture history as one of the most beloved teen shows of all time. Set in the fictional town of Capeside, Massachusetts, this coming-of-age drama follows the struggles of childhood friends Dawson Leery, Joey Potter, and Pacey Witter (played respectively by James Van Der Beek, Katie Holmes, and Joshua Jackson) and their extended group of friends. They were joined in the second season by Andie and Jack McPhee (Meredith Monroe and Kerr Smith). Often considered a soap opera, *Dawson's Creek* focuses on teen love, parental divorce, single parenthood, and the trials and tribulations of becoming an adult. While critics often found the characters unbelievable and emotional, teenagers (girls in particular), identified with the characters and the often melodramatic situations that revolve around their ever-changing romantic relationships.

Screenwriter Kevin Williamson, who achieved success with the *Scream* movie franchise, created *Dawson's Creek*, and many saw it as his homage to predecessors such as *Beverly Hills, 90210* (1990–2000) and to the "brat pack" movies of the 1980s such as *Sixteen Candles* (1984) and *The Breakfast Club* (1985). The adept use of popular culture references in *Dawson's Creek* gave viewers an instant relationship with the characters, turning their fictional world into a mirror for real-life teen experiences and apprehensions. And, as the characters matured, so did their concerns, which grew to include literature, health trends, and political and social issues.

Dawson's Creek drew criticism from conservative media watchdogs, such as the Parents Television Council, for its liberal treatment of sexuality, as evidenced in the story arc in which teenage Pacey has a steamy affair with his thirty-something high school teacher. But for the most part, the show accurately reflected on the changes happening in family life and belief structures of the era. One of the best examples is Jack's acknowledgement that he is gay. The series deals not only with the reaction of Jack's family and friends but also on how his orientation impacts his life. Ultimately, Jack finds happiness, self-worth, and fulfillment raising Jen's daughter, while his partner, Pacey's uptight law enforcement brother Doug, finds himself constantly in denial and fear of discovery.

Dawson's Creek gave television teens a sophisticated voice and fans a new way to interact with each other by introducing a website and message board, on which viewers could discuss episodes and related issues. The impact of *Dawson's Creek* on subsequent teenage television dramas is evident in the more open dialogues that teenage characters in shows such as *The O.C.* (2003–2007) and *Gossip Girl* (2007–) have with each other and the more sophisticated situations that they find themselves in. Viewers also now regularly interact with each other on websites dedicated to their favorite programs.

Linda Martindale

SEE ALSO: Beverly Hills, 90210*; Brat Pack;* The Breakfast Club*; The Internet;* Scream*; Soap Operas; Television.*

BIBLIOGRAPHY

Bindig, Lori. *"Dawson's Creek": A Critical Understanding.* Lanham, MD: Lexington, 2007.

Crosdale, Darren. *"Dawson's Creek": The Official Companion.* London: Ebury, 1999.

Tibbs, Katheë, and Biff L. Peterson. *They Don't Wanna Wait: The Stars of "Dawson's Creek."* Toronto: ECW Press, 1999.

Day, Doris *(1924–)*

Vocalist and screen actress Doris Day, a freckle-faced buttercup blond with a sunny smile who radiated wholesome good cheer, embodied the healthy girl-next-door zeitgeist of 1950s Hollywood. The decade marked the fall of the Hollywood musical, and Day, with her pleasing personality and distinctive voice, huskily emotive yet pure and on note, helped prolong the genre's demise. Thanks largely to her infectious presence, a series of mostly anodyne musical films attracted bobby-soxers and their parents alike during the otherwise somber era of the Cold War and McCarthyism.

Behind the smile, however, Day's life was marked by much unhappiness endured, remarkably, away from the glare of publicity. She was born Doris von Kappelhoff in Cincinnati, Ohio, on April 3, 1924, the daughter of German parents who divorced when she was eight. She pursued a dancing career from an early age, but her ambitions were cut short by a serious automobile accident in her midteens, and she turned to singing as an alternative. She had two disastrous early marriages, the first, at age seventeen, to musician Al Jorden, by whom she had a son. She divorced him because of his violent nature and later married George Weidler in a liaison that lasted eight months. By age twenty-four, she had worked her way up from appearing on local radio stations to becoming a popular big band singer with Bob Crosby and Les Brown and had begun making records.

HOLLYWOOD

In 1948 Warner Brothers needed an emergency replacement for a pregnant Betty Hutton in *Romance on the High Seas.* Day was suggested; won the part; and, true to the cliché, became a star overnight. The movie yielded a huge recording hit in "It's Magic," establishing a pattern that held for most of her films and secured her place as a best-selling recording artist in tandem with her screen career. The songs as sung by Day threaded themselves into a tapestry of cultural consciousness that remained familiar across generations. Notable among her many hits are the wistfully romantic and Oscar-winning "Secret Love" from *Calamity Jane* (1953) and the insidious "Que Sera Sera" from Alfred Hitchcock's *The Man Who Knew Too Much* (1956), which sold more than a million records at the time and earned her a Gold Disc.

No matter what the role or the plot of a movie, Day retained an essentially "virginal" persona about which it was once fashionable to make jokes. She confounded derision, however, with sheer energy and professionalism, revealing a range that allowed her to broaden her scope and prolong her career in nonmusicals—an achievement that eluded her few rivals.

Early on, her string of Warner musicals, which paired her with Jack Carson, then Gordon MacRae or Gene Nelson, were interrupted by a couple of straight roles (opposite Kirk Douglas's Bix Beiderbecke in *Young Man with a Horn* and murdered by the Klan in *Storm Warning,* both 1950), but it was for Metro-Goldwyn-Meyer, in the biopic *Love Me or Leave Me* (1955), that Day won her colors as an actress of some accomplishment and grit. As Ruth Etting, the famed nightclub singer of the 1920s who suffered at the hands of her handicapped hoodlum husband (played by James Cagney), she was able to meet the acting challenge while given ample opportunity to display her vocal expertise. She had, however, no further opportunity to develop the dramatic promise she displayed in this film.

The most effervescent and enduring of Day's musicals, the screen version of the Broadway hit *The Pajama Game* (1957), marked the end of her Warner Brothers tenure, after which she studio-hopped for three undistinguished comedies: *Tunnel of Love* (MGM, 1958, with Richard Widmark), *Teacher's Pet* (Paramount, 1958, with Clark Gable), and *It Happened to Jane* (Columbia, 1959, with Jack Lemmon). A star of lesser universal appeal might have sunk with these leaden enterprises, but her popularity emerged unscathed—indeed, in 1958 the Hollywood Foreign Press Association voted her the world's favorite actress, the first of several similar accolades that included a Golden Globe in 1962.

THE SIXTIES

In 1959 any threat to Day's star status was removed by a series of monumentally profitable comedies in which mildly risqué innuendo stood in for sex, and the generally farcical plots were made to work through the light touch and attractive personalities of Day and her coterie of leading men. The first of these, *Pillow Talk* (1959), teamed her with Rock Hudson, grossed a massive $7.5 million, and won her an Oscar nomination for her masquerade as a buttoned-up interior designer. The Day-Hudson formula was repeated twice more with *Lover Come Back* (1962) and *Send Me No Flowers* (1964). In between, in *That Touch of Mink* (1962) she costarred with Cary Grant, while *The Thrill of It All* and *Move over Darling* (both 1963) added James Garner to her long list of leading men. The last years of the 1960s saw a decline in both the number and quality of her films, and she made her last, *With Six You Get Eggroll*, in 1968, exactly twenty years after the release of her first film.

Her third husband, Martin Melcher, who administered her financial affairs and forced the pace of her career in defiance of her wishes, produced most of Day's comedies. After his death in 1968, nervous exhaustion, coupled with the discovery that he had divested her of her earnings of some $20 million, leaving her penniless, led to a breakdown. She recovered and starred for five years in her own television show, *The Doris Day Show*, to which Melcher had committed her without her knowledge, and in 1974 she was awarded damages (reputed to be $22 million) against her former lawyer who had been a party to Melcher's embezzlement of her fortune.

ANIMAL RIGHTS ACTIVISM

Other than making a series of margarine commercials and hosting a television cable show *Doris Day and Friends* (1985–1986), Day retired from the entertainment profession in 1975 to devote herself to the cause of animal rights. She married Barry Comden in 1976, but they divorced four years later. From her ranch estate in Carmel, California, she founded the Doris Day Animal League and worked tirelessly to lobby for legislative protection against all forms of cruelty. In 2006 she merged her organization with the Humane Society of America.

By the 2010s, Day's recordings continued to sell and her films were often shown on television. In 2011, after a gap of twenty years, she released the album *My Heart*, a compilation of previously unreleased recordings. She has received numerous awards and tributes, including the Presidential Medal of Freedom in 2004 and a Grammy Award for Lifetime Achievement in 2008. To some, Day was a hopeless eccentric, to many a saint, but she continued to enjoy a high profile and the loyalty of her many fans—her celluloid image of goodness lent veracity by her actions.

Robyn Karney

SEE ALSO: *Beiderbecke, Bix; Big Bands; Brown, Les; Divorce; Gable, Clark; Garner, James; Grant, Cary; Hitchcock, Alfred; Hollywood; Hudson, Rock; Movie Stars; The Musical;* Your Hit Parade.

BIBLIOGRAPHY

Bret, David. *Doris Day: Reluctant Star*. London: JR Books, 2008.

Braun, Eric. *Doris Day*. London: Weidenfield & Nicolson, 1992.

Day, Doris, and A. E. Hotchner. *Doris Day: Her Own Story*. New York: Morrow, 1975.

Hirschhorn, Clive. *The Hollywood Musical*. New York: Crown, 1981.

Kaufman, David. *Doris Day: The Untold Story of the Girl Next Door*. New York: Virgin Books USA, 2008.

McGee, Garry. *Doris Day: Sentimental Journey*. Jefferson, NC: McFarland, 2005.

Shipman, David. *The Great Movie Stars: The International Years*. New York: St. Martin's Press, 1972.

The Day the Earth Stood Still

The Day the Earth Stood Still (1951), a fixture of cinema revivals, outdoor summer festivals, and nostalgic cable channels, was at the forefront of the science fiction film explosion of the 1950s. A number of its basic elements, from its moralizing to its music, from its fear of apocalypse to its menacing robot, are aspects of the genre that remain in the early twenty-first century. Although the film did not bring all these elements to science fiction for the first time, the film's strong and sophisticated visual and aural style was to have a lasting impact on how the scenario of alien visitation has subsequently been presented. *The Day the Earth Stood Still* outlined creatively, some might even say factually, the images of alien visitation that fascinated increasing numbers of people in the second half of the twentieth century. Its ongoing influence was made evident by the release of a high-budget remake in 2008.

Between 1950 and 1957, 133 science fiction movies were released. *The Day the Earth Stood Still* was one of the earliest, most influential, and most successful. Its story was relatively simple: the alien Klaatu (with his robot, Gort) arrives on Earth and attempts to warn people, in the face of increasing fear and misunderstanding, that their escalating conflicts, now evolved to potentially nuclear, endanger the rest of the universe. The film was unusual as a science fiction film in this period in that it was produced by a major production company (Twentieth Century Fox) on a large budget, and this is reflected in the pool of talent the film was able to call upon, in terms of scripting, casting, direction, special effects, and music. The commentator Bruce Rux has even claimed, in *Hollywood vs. the Aliens*, that the film's resonance in the depiction of alien visitation reflected testimony and information withheld by the government from the public concerning sightings and contact with "real" UFOs at the time.

Director Robert Wise had worked as an editor for famed actor/director Orson Welles and directed a number of Val Lewton horror films. In *The Day the Earth Stood Still*, Wise was restrained in the use of special effects (although Klaatu's flying saucer cost more than $100,000, a huge expense at the time), maintaining their effectiveness by contrasting them with scenes showing a xenophobic and paranoid Washington in a light one might usually associate with film noir. Edmund North's script, based on the story "Farewell to the Master" by the famous science fiction magazine editor Harry Bates, emphasizes distinct religious parallels while balancing the allegory with Klaatu's direct experience of individual humans' hopes and fears.

The film's mood of anxiety is underlined by the score of Bernard Herrmann, who would later do the music for a clutch of Alfred Hitchcock's films and Martin Scorsese's *Taxi Driver*. Herrmann's use of the precursor of electronic instruments, the

The Day the Earth Stood Still. The Day the Earth Stood Still *was one of the most successful and influential science-fiction films to be released in the 1950s.* **20TH CENTURY FOX/THE KOBAL COLLECTION.**

theremin, as well as the more usual piano, percussion, and brass helped create a disturbing and anxious background. It is not until toward the end of the film that the art direction and special effects take over. More than the spaceship, however, the film's biggest selling point was the 8-foot Gort. Though clumsy and simplistic by today's standards, his huge stature and featureless face give a real sense of presence and menace. The talismanic phrase that had to be memorized and repeated to Gort to prevent him from destroying the world, "Klaatu barada nikto," was on the lips of many a schoolchild of the period.

POPULAR DESPITE DRAWBACKS

In many ways, *The Day the Earth Stood Still* is far from being the most representative or the most original science fiction film of this period. There were many more thematically interesting films that appeared risible because they lacked the budget of Wise's movie. The film's liberal credentials seem rather compromised by its lack of belief in the ordinary individual to avoid panic and suspicion in the face of anything different, while there is something rather paternalistic in the idea that, because Earth cannot be trusted to guard its own weapons of mass destruction, it must be put in the charge of a larger, wiser, scientifically more advanced intergalactic power. This faith in the rationality of science to overcome all the fears and anxieties of the period was far from a unanimously held view.

Despite these drawbacks, *The Day the Earth Stood Still* is a successful film in popular terms for other reasons. Its influence is obvious: Its opening scenes of the flying saucer coming in over the symbols of American democracy in Washington, D.C., resonate all the way down to similar scenes in later films such as *Independence Day* (1996). The alien craft and the tense scenes when figures descend from the craft to face a watching crowd create an archetypal image repeated again and again in science fiction films, most potently in *Close Encounters of the Third Kind* (1977). And finally, Gort is the prototype for the robot in the American science fiction movie, a figure both menacing and protective, a precursor to every humanoid machine from Robbie the Robot to the Terminator, one of the most original and beguiling figures the science fiction genre has offered the moviegoer.

In 2008 Twentieth Century Fox released a remake of the 1951 film, starring Keanu Reeves as Klaatu. While the movie retained many of the elements of the original, it also incorporated contemporary concerns, shifting the threat to humanity from nuclear warfare (a major concern in the post–World War II era) to environmental destruction (inspired by current events such as Hurricane Katrina). As such, the spaceship is no longer portrayed as a machine but as a giant biological sphere that shuts down Earth's electrical capabilities. Reviews of the film were largely negative, but it managed to gross more than $230 million, indicating that *The Day the Earth Stood Still* still resonates with moviegoers worldwide.

Kyle Smith

SEE ALSO: Close Encounters of the Third Kind; *Environmentalism; Hitchcock, Alfred; Hollywood; Hurricane Katrina;* Independence Day; *Scorsese, Martin; Welles, Orson.*

BIBLIOGRAPHY

Biskind, Peter. *Seeing Is Believing: How Hollywood Taught Us to Stop Worrying and Love the Fifties.* London: Pluto, 1983.

Hardy, P. *The Encyclopedia of Science Fiction Movies.* London: Octopus, 1986.

Jancovich, Mark. *Rational Fears: American Horror in the 1950s.* New York: Manchester University Press, 1996.

Pringle, David, ed. *The Ultimate Encyclopedia of Science Fiction.* London: Carlton, 1997.

Redmond, Sean. *Liquid Metal: The Science Fiction Film Reader.* London: Wallflower, 2003.

Rux, Bruce. *Hollywood vs. the Aliens: The Motion Picture Industry's Participation in UFO Disinformation.* Berkeley, CA: Frog, 1997.

Shapiro, Jerome F. *Atomic Bomb Cinema: The Apocalyptic Imagination on Film.* New York: Routledge, 2002.

Days of Our Lives

Developed by Ted Corday, Irna Phillips, and Alan Chase, the daytime drama *Days of Our Lives* premiered on NBC in 1965. With Phillips's *As the World Turns* (created for Procter & Gamble) serving as a model, *Days* proceeded to put increasingly outrageous twists on established formulae for its first three decades. By the mid-1990s its flights into the postmodern and macabre became examples for a struggling genre but failed to avert a ratings downturn. In the first decade of the twenty-first century, however, ratings rebounded, rendering the program secure once again.

EARLY SEASONS

"Like sands through the hourglass, so are the days of our lives," proclaims the show's opening narration, voiced by former film actor MacDonald Carey over the appropriate image. Carey portrayed patriarch Tom Horton, all-purpose physician in the show's midwestern hamlet of Salem, from the program's inception until the passing of both actor and character in 1994. Accompanied by dutiful wife Alice (Frances Reid), the elder Hortons are two of a handful of veterans who evolved over the years as virtual figureheads on a conspicuously youth-oriented program.

After Corday's passing in 1966, and under the stewardship of his widow, Betty, and head writer Bill Bell, *Days* began, in the words of author Gerard Waggett in *The Soap Opera Encyclopedia*, "playing around with the incest taboo." Young Marie Horton (Maree Cheatham) first married and divorced the father of her ex-fiancé and then fell for a man later discovered to be her prodigal brother. Marie was off to a nunnery, and the "incest scare" was to pop up on other soaps, including *The Young and the Restless*, Bell's future creation for CBS.

The incest theme carried the show into the early 1970s with the triangle of Mickey Horton (John Clarke); wife, Laura Spencer (Susan Flannery); and her true desire, Mickey's brother Bill (Edward Mallory)—a story that inspired imitation on *Guiding Light*. Bill's rape of Laura, whom he would later wed, muddied the issue of whether "no" always means "no." Cowriter Pat Falken Smith later penned the similarly controversial "rape seduction" of *General Hospital*'s Laura by her eventual husband, Luke. *Days* soon featured another familial entanglement, in which saloon singer Doug Williams (Bill Hayes) romanced young Julie Olson (Susan Seaforth), only to marry and father a child by her mother before being, predictably, widowed, at which point he returned to Julie's side.

Bell's departure in 1973 provided Smith with interrupted stints as head writer, as the show's flirtations with lesbian and interracial couplings were short-circuited due to network fears of a viewer backlash. The introduction of popular heroine Dr. Marlena Evans (Deidre Hall) late in the decade was a highlight, but the "Salem Strangler" serial killer story line spelled the end for many cast members by the early 1980s. Marlena's romance with cop Roman Brady (Wayne Northrop) created a new "supercouple" and established the Bradys as a working-class family playing off the bourgeois Hortons.

WOOING YOUNGER VIEWERS

General Hospital's Luke and Laura, along with their fantasy story lines—which were attractive to younger viewers in the early 1980s—were emulated, and then some, by *Days*. Marlena and Roman were followed by Bo and Hope (Peter Reckell and Kristian Alfonso), Kimberly and Shane (Patsy Pease and Charles Shaughnessy), and Kayla and Steve (Mary Beth Evans and Stephen Nichols), who anchored Salem's supercouple era and whose tragic heroines are profiled in Martha Nochimson's book *No End to Her*. Their Gothic adventures involved nefarious supervillains such as Victor Kiriakis (John Aniston) and, later, Stefano DiMera (Joseph Mascolo), whose multiple resurrections defied any remaining logic. Kayla and Steve's saga revived the program's sibling triangle and rape redemption scenarios. Identities also became tangled, with Roman returning as the enigmatic John Black (portrayed by another actor, Drake Hogestyn), brainwashed to temporarily forget his "true" identity. When Wayne Northrop was available to reclaim the role, however, Black's identity became a mystery once again.

In the 1990s Ken Corday was at the producer's helm, and with innovative new head writer James Reilly, *Days* crossed a horizon into pure fantasy to woo the next generation. Vivian Alamain (Louise Sorel) had one rival buried prematurely and purloined another's embryo. Marlena, possessed by demons, morphed into animals and levitated. Later she was exorcised by John Black, now found to have been a priest, and imprisoned in a cage by Stefano. Super triangles supplanted supercouples, as insecure and typically female third parties schemed to keep lovers apart. The most notorious of these was teen Sami Brady (Alison Sweeney), whose obsession with Austin Reed (Patrick Muldoon, later Austin Peck) produced machinations plaguing his romance with Sami's sister, Carrie (Christie Clark), and led Internet fans to nickname her "Scami." While many longtime fans lamented the program's new tone, younger viewers adored it. By 1996 the program had risen to second in ratings and first in all-important demographics.

To the chagrin of their fans, other soaps soon found themselves subject to various degrees of "daysification." But overall viewership of the genre had diminished, and when *Days*' ratings dipped in the late 1990s, its creators seemed not to consider that postmodern escapism might work to lure very young fans but not to hold them. In the late 1990s NBC hired Reilly to develop a new soap and threatened its other soaps with cancellation if they did not get up to pace.

Its stories were risky, but *Days of Our Lives* had succeeded in narrowing the genre's purview and with it, perhaps, its pool of potential viewers. Although Reilly returned to *Days* in 2003 and remained until his death in 2008, Jeff Zucker, president of NBC Universal, warned in 2007 that *Days* was in danger of cancellation. However, having then inserted stories chronicling the longstanding feuds of Salem families and eventually introducing the series' first gay male character, the program managed a ratings resurgence. In 2011 it was NBC's last remaining daytime soap.

Christine Scodari

SEE ALSO: As the World Turns; General Hospital; *Radio Drama; Soap Operas; Television;* The Young and the Restless.

BIBLIOGRAPHY

Nochimson, Martha. *No End to Her: Soap Opera and the Female Subject.* Berkeley: University of California Press, 1992.

Russell, Maureen. Days of Our Lives: *A Complete History of the Long-Running Soap Opera.* Jefferson, NC: McFarland, 1995.

Scodari, Christine. "'No Politics Here': Age and Gender in Soap Opera 'Cyberfandom.'" *Women's Studies in Communication* Fall (1998): 168–187.

Waggett, Gerard J. *The Soap Opera Encyclopedia.* New York: HarperPaperbacks, 1997.

Zenka, Lorraine. Days of Our Lives: *The Complete Family Album.* New York: Regan Books, 1996.

Daytime Talk Shows

The daytime television talk show is a uniquely modern phenomenon but one with roots stretching back to the beginning of broadcasting. Daytime talk programs are popular with audiences for their democratic, unpredictable nature; with producers for their low cost; and with stations for their high ratings. They have been called everything from the voice of the common people to a harbinger of the end of civilization. Successful hosts become stars in their own right, while guests play out the national drama in a steady stream of confession, confrontation, and self-promotion.

TYPES OF TALK SHOWS

Daytime talk shows can be classified into two basic formats. Celebrity-oriented talk shows have much in common with their nighttime counterparts. The host performs an opening monologue or number, and a series of celebrity guests promote their latest films, TV shows, books, or other products. The host's personality dominates the interaction. These shows have their roots in both talk programs and comedy-variety series. The basic formula was designed by NBC's Sylvester "Pat" Weaver, creator of both *Today* (1952–) and *The Tonight Show* (1957–). Musical guests and comic monologues are frequently featured along with discussion. Merv Griffin, Mike Douglas, Dinah Shore, and Rosie O'Donnell have all hosted this type of show.

The more common and successful category of talk shows is the issue-oriented talker. Hosts lead the discussion, but the guests' tales of personal tragedy, triumph, and nonconformity are at the center. Phil Donahue was the first, beginning in 1979, to achieve national prominence with this style of talk show. Oprah Winfrey was transformed from local Chicago television personality to national media magnate largely on the strength of her talk program. In the 1990s these shows grew to depend more and more on confession and confrontation. The trend reached its apparent apotheosis with *The Jerry Springer Show*

The Jerry Springer Show. *Jerry Springer tapes an episode of his often outrageous self-titled daytime talk show in 1998.* GETTY IMAGES.

(1991–), on which conflicts between guests frequently turned physical, with fistfights erupting on stage.

Since the tremendous success in the 1980s of *Donahue* (1970–1996), hosted by Donahue (most daytime talk programs are named for the host or hosts), and *The Oprah Winfrey Show* (1996–2011), the form has proliferated. Other popular and influential hosts in the late twentieth and early twenty-first centuries included Maury Povich, Jenny Jones, Sally Jessy Raphael, former U.S. Marine Montel Williams, journalist Geraldo Rivera, actress Ricki Lake, and Jerry Springer, who had previously been mayor of Cincinnati. On the celebrity-variety side, actress-comedienne O'Donnell and the duo of Regis Philbin and Kathie Lee Gifford—and later Philbin and Kelly Ripa—consistently drew large audiences.

Philbin left his show in 2011, and a comprehensive search began for a new male host who demonstrated considerable affinity with Ripa. O'Donnell gave up her highly successful show in 2002 but returned to the air in 2011 with a revamped talk show for the Oprah Winfrey Network. O'Donnell's show ran for a year before being cancelled due to low ratings and the host's frequent clashes with network staff. In 1997 television veteran Barbara Walters introduced *The View*, featuring a multigenerational cadre of women who combined the elements of the issue and variety shows. With the exception of Walters, who appears intermittently, and comedian Joy Behar, the show has had a revolving group of hosts that have included a brief stint by O'Donnell and a longer one by Academy Award–winning actress Whoopi Goldberg, who replaced her.

The list of those who tried and failed at the daytime talk format include a wide assortment of rising, falling, and never-really-were stars. Among those who flopped with issue-oriented talk shows are former *Beverly Hills, 90210* (1990–2000) actress Gabrielle Carteris, actor Danny Bonaduce of *The Partridge Family* (1970–1974), ex-*Cosby Show* (1984–1992) kid Tempestt Bledsoe, actor Mark Wahlberg, actress Rolanda Watts, British journalist Gordon Elliott, Oprah's pal Gayle King, news anchor Charles Perez, pop group Wilson Phillips's Carnie Wilson, retired Pittsburgh Steelers quarterback Terry Bradshaw, the team of gay actor Jim J. Bullock and former televangelist Tammy Faye Baker Messner, and ex-spouses George Hamilton and Alana Stewart. Others have tried the celebrity-variety approach of Douglas and Griffin. Singer-actress Vicki Lawrence and Marsha Warfield of *Night Court* (1984–1992) both failed to find a sufficient audience to ensure their success.

SHOW FORMAT

Issue talk shows such as *Sally Jesse Raphael* (1985–2002) and *The Jerry Springer Show* rely on ordinary people who are, in some way, extraordinary (or at least deviant). Though celebrities do occasionally appear, the great majority of guests are drawn from the general population. They are not celebrities as traditionally defined. The talk show provides a flash of fleeting notoriety, but they have no connection with established media, political, or social elites. The guests become briefly famous for the contradictory qualities of ordinariness and difference.

Show employees called bookers work the telephones and read the great volume of viewer mail in search of the next hot topic or the next great guest. Those chosen tend to either lead nontraditional lifestyles—such as gays, lesbians, bisexuals, prostitutes, transvestites, and people with highly unorthodox political or religious views—or have something to confess to a close confederate, usually adultery or some other sexual transgression. If the two can be combined, such as confessing a lesbian affair—which *The Jerry Springer Show* has featured—then so much the better. The common people gain a voice but only if they use it to confess their sins.

SHOCK VALUE AND REPERCUSSIONS

Like all talk shows, daytime talkers rely on the element of unpredictability. There is a sense that virtually anything can happen. Few shows are broadcast live; rather, they are taped in a studio with a cast of nonprofessional, unrehearsed audience members. The emotional reaction of the audience to the guest's revelations becomes an integral part of the show. The trend in the late 1990s was deliberately to promote the unexpected. The shows traded heavily on the reactions of individuals who had just been informed, on national television, that a friend/lover/relative had been keeping a secret from them. Their shock, outrage, and devastation became mass entertainment. The host became the ringmaster (a term Springer freely applied to himself) in an electronic circus of pain and humiliation.

Sometimes the shock has implications well beyond the episode's taping. In March 1996 *The Jenny Jones Show* (1991–2003) invited Jonathan Schmitz to appear on a program about secret admirers, where someone would confess to having a crush on him. Though he was told that his admirer could be either male or female, the single, heterosexual Schmitz assumed that he would be meeting a woman. During the taping Scott Amedure, a gay male acquaintance, confessed that he was Schmitz's admirer. Schmitz felt humiliated and betrayed by the show and was later enraged by the incident. He subsequently went to Amedure's home with a gun and shot him to death. Schmitz was convicted of murder but was granted a new trial in 1998. In a 1999 civil suit, *The Jenny Jones Show* was found negligent in Amedure's death, and the victim's family was awarded $25 million. The ruling forced many talk shows to consider how far they might go with future on-air confrontations.

DEVELOPMENT OF TALK SHOWS

Since the early days of radio, talk has been an essential element in broadcast media. The world's first commercial radio broadcast, by KDKA Pittsburgh on November 2, 1920, featured an announcer giving the results of the presidential election. Early visions of the future of radio and TV pictured the new media as instruments of democracy that could foster participation in public debate. Broadcasters were, and still are, licensed to operate in "the public interest, convenience and necessity," in the words of the Communications Act of 1934. Opposing views on controversial contemporary issues could be aired, giving listeners the opportunity to weigh the evidence and make informed choices. Radio talk shows went out over the airwaves as early as 1929, though debate-oriented programs took nearly another decade to come to prominence. Commercial network television broadcasts were under way by the fall of 1946, and talk, like many other radio genres, found a place on the new medium.

Television talk shows of all types owe much to the amateur variety series of the 1940s and 1950s. Popular CBS radio personality Arthur Godfrey hosted *Arthur Godfrey's Talent Scouts* on TV in prime time from 1948 to 1958. *The Original Amateur Hour*, hosted by Ted Mack, ran from 1948 to 1970 (at various times appearing on ABC, CBS, NBC, and Dumont). These amateur showcases were genuinely democratic: they offered an opportunity for ordinary people to participate in the new public forums. Talent alone gave these guests a brief taste of the kind of recognition usually reserved for celebrities. Audiences saw themselves in these hopeful amateurs looking for their big break. Winners were a source of inspiration; losers provided a laugh.

Godfrey added another element to this mix: unconventionality. He was unashamedly emotional and unafraid to push the envelope of acceptable (for the era) host behavior. Breaking the rules became part of his persona, and that persona made him a star. The most infamous event to occur on the show took place on October 19, 1953, when Godfrey fired his popular singer Julius LaRosa live on the air. Talk show hosts from Jack Paar to David Letterman to Springer turned Godfrey's provocative lessons to productive use.

One of the earliest daytime talkers was *Art Linkletter's House Party* (1952–1970). Many of the elements of the successful, modern talk show were in place: Linkletter was a genial host who interacted with a live audience. Members of the audience participated in the program by confessing their minor transgressions and foibles. Linkletter responded with calm platitudes, copies of his book (*The Confessions of a Happy Man*), and pitches for Geritol and Sominex.

Whatever the trouble, Linkletter could soothe his audience members' guilt with reassurances that they were, after all, perfectly normal and that "people are funny" (an early title for the series.) Sin (albeit venial) was his subject, but salvation was his game. Each show concluded with his Kids Say the Darnedest Things segment, wherein Linkletter milked laughs from children's responses to questions about grown-up subjects. This bit proved both endearing and enduring; in 1998 it was revived in prime time by CBS as a vehicle for another genial comedian, Bill Cosby.

Linkletter gave the modern talk show confession, but Joe Pyne gave it anger. *The Joe Pyne Show*, syndicated from 1965 to 1967, offered viewers a host as controversial as his guests. Twenty years before belligerent nighttime host Morton Downey Jr., Pyne smoked on the set and berated his guests and audience. The show was produced at KTTV in Los Angeles. At the height of the Watts riots of 1965, Pyne featured a militant black leader; both men revealed, on the air, that they were armed with pistols. Other guests included the leader of the American Nazi Party and Lee Harvey Oswald's mother. Pyne, like Downey, lasted only a short time but made a major impact.

MODERNIZING DAYTIME TALK

In the 1960s and 1970s, the celebrity-variety talk show flourished. This was the era of Douglas, Griffin, and Shore. Douglas was a former big-band vocalist who occasionally sang on his show. *The Mike Douglas Show* ran in syndication from 1961 to 1982. His variation on the daytime talk formula was to have a different celebrity cohost from Monday to Friday each week. For one memorable week in the early 1970s, he was joined by rock superstars John Lennon and Yoko Ono. His guests ran the gamut from child actor Mason Reese to pioneering heavy metal rock band KISS.

In 1980 Douglas's production company replaced him with singer-actor John Davidson in an unsuccessful attempt to appeal to a more youthful audience. Douglas stayed on the air for two more years, then faded from public view. His impact on daytime talk shows was underappreciated by many until 1996, when *The Rosie O'Donnell Show* premiered to immediate acclaim and ratings success. A winner of multiple Emmy Awards, O'Donnell frequently cited both Douglas and Griffin as major inspirations.

The modern issue-oriented daytime talk show began with *Donahue*. From the beginning, Donahue knew he was doing something different, neither purely journalism nor purely entertainment. It was not news, but it was always new. The issues were real, the guests were real, but the whole package was ultimately as constructed a piece of entertainment as any of its predecessors. By making a television spectacle out of giving voice to the voiceless, Donahue found an audience, thus meeting commercial broadcasting's ultimate imperative: bringing viewers to the set. Though the market has since become saturated with the confessional show, Donahue's concept was as radical as it was engaging. For the first time the marginalized and the invisible were given a forum, and the mainstream American public was fascinated.

SUCCESS STORIES

A true heir to Donahue's throne did not appear until 1986, with the premiere of *The Oprah Winfrey Show*. Winfrey was a Chicago TV personality who burst onto the national scene with her Academy Award–nominated performance in Steven Spielberg's *The Color Purple* (1985). She took Donahue's participatory approach and added her own sensibility. Winfrey, an African American and sexual abuse survivor, worked her way out of poverty onto the national stage. When her guests poured out their stories, she understood their pain. Unlike many who followed, Winfrey tried to uplift viewers rather than offer them a wallow in the gutter.

Winfrey sought to avoid the confrontations so popular on later series. After one guest surprised his wife on the air with the news that he was still involved with his mistress and had, in fact, impregnated her, Winfrey vowed such an episode would never occur again. In 1998, in response to the popularity of *The Jerry Springer Show*, she introduced a segment called Change Your Life Television, featuring life-affirming advice from noted self-help authors. *The Oprah Winfrey Show* received numerous accolades, including Peabody Awards and Daytime Emmys. Winfrey also started Oprah's Book Club to encourage viewers to read contemporary works she believed important. She was considered by some to be the most powerful woman in show business, as strong an influence on popular culture as any male Hollywood mogul. In 2011 she left her long-running show to create the Oprah Winfrey Network (OWN).

The next big daytime talk success was *Geraldo* (1987–1998). Host Geraldo Rivera made his reputation as an investigative journalist on ABC's newsmagazine series *20/20* (1978–). After leaving that show, his first venture as the star of his own show was a syndicated special in 1986. The premise was that Rivera and a camera crew would enter Chicago mobster Al Capone's long-lost locked vault. The program was aired live. All through the show Rivera speculated on the fantastic discoveries they would make once the vault was open. When it finally was opened, they found nothing.

What Rivera did find, however, was an audience for the daytime talk series that premiered soon after. He also found controversy, most notably when, during a 1988 episode featuring neo-Nazis, a fight broke out and one skinhead youth hit Rivera with a chair, breaking his nose. In 1996 Rivera ended *Geraldo* and signed with cable network CNBC for a nighttime news-talk hour. Though often accused of sensationalism, even he had become disgusted with the state of talk TV, especially the growing popularity of *The Jerry Springer Show*.

TRASH TELEVISION

The era of so-called trash television began with Springer in 1991. His was the most popular daytime talk show of the late 1990s, often beating *The Oprah Winfrey Show* in the ratings. Springer's program began its life as another undistinguished member of a growing pack. Viewership picked up when the subject matter became more controversial and the discussion more volatile. Confrontation over personal, often sexual, matters was Springer's most popular angle. Guests frequently faced lovers, friends, and family members with disapproval over their choice of lifestyle or romantic partner.

Taking the drama a step beyond other daytime talk shows, these arguments on the show frequently come to physical blows. The fights have become a characteristic, almost expected, part of the program, and Springer is often accused of choreographing them. The content of the series led some stations to banish it from daytime to early morning or late-night hours when children are less likely to be watching. Springer's production company has sold several volumes of *Too Hot for TV* videos, featuring nudity, profanity, and violence edited from the broadcasts.

Critics have declaimed Springer's show as a further symptom of the moral decline of the United States, especially American television. Some bemoaned the *Springerization* of the nation. Springer defends his show as reflecting the lives of his guests and giving his audience what they want to see. The series' consistently receives high ratings, at least partially supporting his claim. Springer saw less success when the show became the first daytime talk program to inspire a feature film version, *Ringmaster* (1998), which failed at the box office.

TWENTY-FIRST CENTURY

By the end of the 1990s, daytime talk shows were more popular than ever. New contenders such as former sitcom star Roseanne, comedian Howie Mandel, and singing siblings Donny and Marie Osmond joined the veteran hosts in the battle for a share of the large talk audience, with a new talk show premiering every season. Although most of these talkers were short-lived, the talk show format continued into the twenty-first century. Springer's show, for example, remains on the air, even though his popularity has declined drastically.

Besides Winfrey and O'Donnell, the only other single host who proved to have discovered the right formula for modern daytime talk shows is comedian Ellen DeGeneres, who debuted in 2003. In 2011 CBS introduced *The Talk* in a format similar to that of *The View*. Host Sharon Osbourne was joined by various women, including actresses Leah Remini and Sara Gilbert and former model Aisha Tylor. Personnel changes, however, took place before the show's sophomore season. When Winfrey left her show in 2011, the media began suggesting that it might be a prime time for another genre to dominate daytime television.

Many people say that they turn on the television for company, and talk shows bring a wide variety of acquaintances into American living rooms, kitchens, and bedrooms. Their revelations, whether it is an unguarded moment with a celebrity or a painful confession from an unknown, give audiences a taste of intimacy from a safe distance. In a world that many U.S. citizens perceive as more and more dangerous, this infiltration is the ultimate paradox of television, the safe invitation of strangers into the house. Whether talk shows inspire sympathy or judgment, they have become a permanent part of the television landscape.

David L. Hixson

SEE ALSO: *Academy Awards;* Beverly Hills, 90210*; Bradshaw, Terry; Capone, Al; Cosby, Bill;* The Cosby Show*; DeGeneres,*

Ellen; Donahue, Phil; Douglas, Mike; Emmy Awards; Godfrey, Arthur; Goldberg, Whoopi; Griffin, Merv; Hollywood; KISS; Lake, Ricki; Lennon, John; Letterman, David; Linkletter, Art; O'Donnell, Rosie; Paar, Jack; The Partridge Family; *Radio; Rivera, Geraldo; Shore, Dinah; Spielberg, Steven; Springer, Jerry; Syndication; Talk Radio; Television;* The Tonight Show; 20/20; The View; *Walters, Barbara; Winfrey, Oprah.*

BIBLIOGRAPHY

Burns, Gary, and Robert J. Thompson. *Television Studies: Textual Analysis.* New York: Praeger, 1989.

Carbaugh, Donal A. *Talking American: Cultural Discourses on "Donahue."* Norwood, NJ: Ablex, 1988.

Fiske, John. *Television Culture.* New York: Metheun, 1987.

Gross, Larry; John Stuart Katz; and Jay Ruby, eds. *Image Ethics in the Digital Age.* Minneapolis: University of Minnesota Press, 2003.

Manga, Julie Engel. *Talking Trash: The Cultural Politics of Daytime Television Talk Shows.* New York: New York University Press, 2003.

Mincer, Deanne, and Richard Mincer. *The Talkshow Book: An Engaging Primer on How to Talk Your Way to Success.* New York: Facts On File, 1982.

Munson, Wayne. *All Talk: The Talk Show in Media Culture.* Philadelphia: Temple University Press, 1993.

Newcomb, Horace, ed. *Television: The Critical View, Fourth Edition.* New York: Oxford University Press, 1987.

Postman, Neil. *Amusing Ourselves to Death: Public Discourse in the Age of Show Business.* New York: Viking Press, 1985.

Slide, Anthony, ed. *Selected Radio and Television Criticism.* Metuchen, NJ: Scarecrow Press, 1987.

Timberg, Bernard M. *Television Talk: A History of the TV Talk Show.* Austin: University of Texas Press, 2002.

Daytona 500

The Daytona 500 is commonly referred to as "the Great American Race." With a well-earned reputation for exciting finishes, horrendous crashes, Florida-in-February weather, and bumper-to-bumper and door-handle-to-door-handle racing, the annual NASCAR race thrills fans and challenges the drivers and mechanics. Thanks to television and professional marketing, the Daytona 500 is the premier stock-car race of the year, bringing the thrills and violence of racing into the homes of millions. Stock-car legends are born on the Daytona International Speedway's 2.5-mile, tri-oval, high-banked track with the long back-straight. Two hundred laps, 600 left turns, three or four stops for gasoline, all lead to one winner. The prize is the Harley J. Earl Daytona 500 trophy and, as of 2012, a minimum $1.4 million. (Earl, 1893–1969, was responsible for the design of the modern American car while at General Motors in the 1930s, 1940s, and 1950s when the "stock car" was born.)

DAYTONA INTERNATIONAL SPEEDWAY

The first official race of the NASCAR season, the Daytona 500 is the final, paramount event of Daytona Speedweeks, which features no less than fifteen days of racing, starting with the world-famous Rolex 24 and two qualifying races. Sponsors of the top cars are afforded what is basically a three-and-a-half-hour commercial as their names and logos loop repeatedly around the track. Although the Indianapolis 500 has a larger viewing audience, in-car cameras at the Daytona 500 allow viewers to watch the driver, the cars in front, and the cars behind from the safety of the roll cage. Cameras mounted on the outside of the cars allow viewers to see the hoods buckling in the wind, virtually ride out a spin at 200 miles per hour, and read bumper stickers on the car behind.

The track was built by Bill France, founder of the National Association for Stock Car Auto Racing (NASCAR) to provide his fledgling franchise a permanent venue off the beach of Daytona and bring it into a legitimate race facility. The first Daytona 500 was run in 1959 and won by Lee Petty. Since that time, the number of fans as well as the speeds of the cars have increased. The cost of racing has gone up, and NASCAR and the Daytona track owners have continued to enlarge their entertainment empire. The corporation that owns Daytona also owns Darlington (South Carolina), Talladega (Alabama), and Watkins Glen (New York) race tracks.

The track design and the high speeds require an appreciation, if not a dread, on the part of the mechanics and drivers of the modern high-speed professional racing leagues that use the track. The turns—wide U-shaped continuous corners—are banked at an imposing 31 degrees, too steep to walk up let alone drive on, and because there are no short chutes between them, they are called "one-two" and "three-four." At 18 degrees, the tri-oval turn is relatively flat, but it is connected by short, flat straights from the exit of turn four to the entrance of turn one. Flipped up on their sides by the banking, the drivers look "up" to see ahead in the turns and have to deal with a down-force caused by the car wanting to sink down into the pavement. Drivers actually steer fairly straight to accomplish a 120-degree change in direction (1,000-foot radius for 3,000 feet of turn). Drivers must do all that and keep their 3,400-pound cars out of the way of surrounding vehicles—at speeds up to 200 miles per hour.

The road abruptly flattens after 3,000 feet of turns one-two. The equally long straight that is the signature of Daytona now requires the driver to draft within a yard of the car in front, race three wide, keep his or her foot to the floor, and relax—for a moment—until the car upends again in turns three-four. The driver and car are subject to gravitational forces that push down and out in the high banks, immediately followed by a tremendous downward slam at the start of the back-straight. In the tri-oval portion of the track, the g-forces are more outward than down. The car's suspension has to keep the wheels evenly on the surface, and the aerodynamics have to keep the car in a line with itself.

THE ACTION

Daytona is the track where "Awesome Bill from Dawsonville" Elliott achieved fame and fortune, and Lee Petty began the Petty dynasty. It is the race Dale Earnhardt took twenty years to win after winning NASCAR races everywhere else. It is the race Mario Andretti won once in 1967, but, like the Indianapolis 500 (1969), never repeated. Two lasting images from the race are Cale Yarborough (1968, 1977, 1983, and 1984 winner) and Donnie Allison duking it out in the back-stretch grass in 1979, and Richard Petty and David Pearson colliding with each other after coming out of turns three-four on the last lap—Petty spinning off the track with a dead motor and Pearson sliding along the track, killing his engine too. As Petty, farther downtrack than Pearson, frantically tried to restart, Pearson ground the starter with his Mercury in gear to creep across the finish line and win the 1976 race.

During the early years of the 2000s the iconic race has seen its share of triumph and tragedy. The new millennium began on a somber note when fan favorite Earnhardt died from injuries suffered in a crash during the last lap of the 2001 race. His son, Dale Earnhardt Jr., won the race three years later—on the sixth anniversary of his father's only win. The 2007 race saw some racing crews disciplined for using illegal methods to try to increase speed. In the race itself, a multicar wreck near the end of the running allowed Kevin Harvick and Mark Martin to sprint to the finish, with Harvick winning by only 0.02 seconds.

The 2010 race was something of an embarrassment, with a pothole opening up in the aging asphalt during the actual race, causing a delay for road repairs. The track was repaved for 2011. The next year was marred by a series of bizarre events that caused headline writers to quip, "I've seen fire, I've seen rain." First, rain forced the race to be postponed a day for the first time in its history. Then an accident caused a massive fireball and a long delay while crews spent two hours using laundry detergent to clean jet fuel off the track. When the race finally resumed, Matt Kenseth won his second Daytona.

The race remains popular and important; the 2006 Daytona 500 attracted the sixth-largest average live global TV audience of any sporting event that year, with twenty million viewers. The rain-delayed 2012 race had an even more impressive viewership of more than 36.5 million.

Charles F. Moore

SEE ALSO: *Advertising; Andretti, Mario; Automobile; Foyt, A. J.; Indianapolis 500; Petty, Richard; Sports Heroes; Stock-Car Racing; Television.*

BIBLIOGRAPHY

Hinton, Ed. *Daytona: From the Birth of Speed to the Death of the Man in Black.* New York: Grand Central Publishing, 2002.

Menzer, Joe. *The Great American Gamble: How the 1979 Daytona 500 Gave Birth to a NASCAR Nation.* Hoboken, NJ: Wiley Publishing, 2009.

Stewart, Mark. *The Daytona 500 (The Watts History of Sports).* New York: Franklin Watts, 2002.

Zeller, Bob. *Daytona 500: An Official History.* Phoenix, AZ: David Bull Publishing, 2002.

DC Comics

As the leading publisher during the first three decades of the comic-book industry, DC Comics was largely responsible for creating the look and content of mainstream American comic books. Simply put, DC is arguably the most important and influential comic-book publisher in history. Home to some of the genre's most popular characters—including Superman, Batman, and Wonder Woman—DC made innovations in the field that were quickly and widely imitated by its competitors. However, few of those wannabes achieved the consistent quality and class of DC's comic books in their heyday.

HUMBLE BEGINNINGS

In 1935 a forty-five-year-old former U.S. Army major and pulp magazine writer named Malcolm Wheeler-Nicholson started up a small operation called National Allied Publishing. From a tiny office in New York City, Wheeler-Nicholson (who friends and colleagues called "the Major") launched *New Fun* and *New Comics*. Although modeled after the new comics magazines, such as *Famous Funnies*, Wheeler-Nicholson's titles were the first to feature original material instead of reprinted newspaper funnies. The Major, remembered by his associates as both an eccentric and something of a charlatan, started his publishing venture with insufficient capital and little business acumen. He met with resistance from distributors still reluctant to handle the new comic books, fell hopelessly into debt, and sold his struggling company to the owners of his distributor, the Independent News Company. The new owners, Harry Donenfeld and Jack Liebowitz, eventually built the Major's tiny operation into a multimillion-dollar company.

In 1937 Donenfeld and Liebowitz put out a third comic-book title, *Detective Comics*. Featuring a collection of original comic strips based on detective-adventure themes that were mostly associated with "B" movies and pulp magazines, *Detective Comics* adapted those genres into a comics format, setting a precedent for all adventure comic books to come. With their own distribution company as a starting point, Donenfeld and Liebowitz developed important contacts with other national distributors to give their comic books the best circulation network in the business. Their publishing arm was officially called National Periodical Publications, but it became better known by the trademark—DC—printed on its comic books and taken from the initials of its flagship title.

SUPERMAN SAVES THE DAY

What truly put DC on top, however, was the acquisition of Superman. In 1938 Jerry Siegel and Joe Shuster reluctantly sold the rights to their costumed superhero to DC for $130. When Superman debuted in the first issue of DC's *Action Comics*, the impact on the market was immediate. Sales of the title jumped to a half-million per issue by year's end, and DC had the industry's first original comic-book star. In 1939 Bob Kane and Bill Finger created Batman for DC as a follow-up to Superman, and this strange new superhero quickly became nearly as popular as his predecessor. DC's competitors took note of the winning formula and promptly flooded the market with costumed imitators. However, DC served notice that it would protect its creative property and its domination of the market by suing the Fox Syndicate for copyright infringement over Wonderman, a flagrant imitation of Superman. It later did the same to Fawcett Publications over Captain Marvel in a lawsuit of dubious merit that dragged on for more than a decade.

DC made it a policy to elevate the standards of its material over that of the increasing competition. In 1941 the company publicized the names of its editorial advisory board, which was made up of prominent educators and child-study experts, and it assured parents that all of DC's comic books were screened for appropriate moral content. The strategy spared the publisher from much of the public criticism being directed at comic books in general, but it also deprived DC's publications of the edgy qualities that had made the early Superman and Batman stories so compelling. DC stayed with this conservative editorial policy for the next several decades.

WAR AND MORALITY

The World War II years were a boom time for DC and for comic-book publishers in general. DC added to its stable of stars such popular characters as Wonder Woman, the Green Lantern, the Flash, and the Justice Society of America. More so than any other publisher, DC worked to educate readers on the issues at stake in the war. Rather than simply bombard young people with malicious stereotypes of the enemy, as most of the competition did (although there was plenty of that to be found in DC's comics as well), the publisher stressed the principles of national unity across ethnic, class, and racial lines, and repeatedly stated a simplified forecast of the postwar vision proclaimed by the Franklin D. Roosevelt administration. DC was also consistent enough to continue its celebration of a liberal postwar order well into the postwar era itself, although it generally did so in dry educational features rather than within the context of its leading adventure stories.

During the 1940s and 1950s, DC strengthened and consolidated its leading position in the industry. The publisher remained aloof when its competitors turned increasingly toward violent crime and horror subjects, and although it made tentative nods to these genres with a few mystery and cops-and-robber titles, DC was rarely a target of the criticism directed at the comic-book industry in the late 1940s and early 1950s. The 1954 publication of Dr. Fredric Wertham's text *Seduction of the Innocent* launched a scathing condemnation of the entire comic-book industry. The text decried comics as a contributor to juvenile delinquency and served to propel anti-comic sentiment. When the industry adopted the Comics Code in 1954, DC's own comic books were already so innocuous as to be scarcely affected. While Wertham attacked several CD heroes specifically, his conceits were too far-flung to cause any real negative impact on the brand. Indeed, spokespeople for DC took the lead in extolling the virtues of the Code-approved comics. With its less scrupulous competitors fatally tarnished by the controversy over crime and horror, DC was able to dominate the market as never before, even though the market itself shrank in the post-Code era. By 1962 DC accounted for more than 30 percent of all comic books sold.

STRENGTHENING ITS HOLD

The company published comics in a variety of genres, including sci-fi, humor, romance, Western, war, and mystery. It even published adaptations of popular television sitcoms and movie star-oriented stories featuring the likes of Jerry Lewis and Bob Hope. However, DC's market strength continued to rest upon the popularity of its superheroes, especially Superman and Batman. Whereas the rise of television hurt comic-book sales throughout the industry, DC enjoyed the cross-promotional benefits of the popular *Adventures of Superman* TV series (1952–1958). Beginning in 1956, DC revised and revamped a number of its 1940s-era superheroes, and the new-look Flash, Green Lantern, Hawkman, and Justice League of America made up the vanguard of what historians have termed the "Silver Age" of superhero comics (as opposed to the "Golden Age" of the 1930s and 1940s).

DC's comic books were grounded firmly in the culture of consensus and conformity. In accordance with the Comics Code and DC's longstanding editorial policies, the superheroes championed high-minded and progressive American values. There was nothing ambiguous about the character, cause, or inevitable triumph of these heroes, and DC took pains to avoid the implication that it glorified vigilantes and, thus, was a harmful role model for children. All of the superheroes held respected positions in society. When they were not in costume, most of them were members of either the police force or the scientific community: Hawkman was a policeman from another planet; the Green Lantern served in an intergalactic police force; the Atom was a respected scientist; the Flash was a police scientist; and Batman and his sidekick, Robin, were deputized members of the Gotham City police force. Superman, of course, was a citizen of the world.

These characters all underscored the importance of the individual's obligation to the community, and did so to an extent that, in fact, minimized the virtues of individualism. All the DC heroes spoke and behaved the same way. Always in control of their emotions and their environment, they exhibited no failings common to the human condition. Residing in clean green suburbs, modern cities with shining glass skyscrapers, and futuristic unblemished worlds, the superheroes exuded American affluence and confidence.

A CULTURAL SHIFT

The pristine comic books promoted by DC were, however, highly vulnerable to the challenge posed by the new "flawed" superheroes of Marvel Comics. Throughout the 1960s, figures such as Spider-Man, the Incredible Hulk, and the Fantastic Four garnered Marvel an anti-establishment image that was consciously in synch with trends in contemporary youth culture. DC's star performers, on the other hand, epitomized the "Establishment," coming off as costumed Boy Scout troop leaders by comparison. By the late 1960s, DC recognized its dilemma and clumsily introduced some obvious ambiguity and angst into its superhero stories, but the move came too late to reverse the company's fall from the top. By the mid-1970s, Marvel had surpassed DC as the industry's leading publisher.

Despite faltering sales, DC's characters remained the most popular and the most lucrative comic-book properties. In 1968 DC was purchased by the powerful Warner Brothers conglomerate, which would later produce a series of blockbuster movies featuring Superman and Batman. Throughout the 1970s, DC enjoyed far greater success with licensing its characters for TV series and toy products than it did with selling actual comics. Jeanette Kahn became the new DC publisher in 1976 and was charged with the task of revitalizing the comic books. In the early 1980s Kahn helped to institute new financial and creative incentives at the company, a move that attracted some of the top writers and artists in the field to DC and set a precedent for further industry-wide benefits for creators.

DC'S NEW LOOK

Starting in the late 1980s, DC found success in the direct-sales market to comic-book stores with a number of titles labeled "For Mature Readers Only," and it also took the lead in the growing market for sophisticated and pricey graphic novels. Established superheroes such as Batman and Green Arrow gained new life as violent vigilante characters and were soon joined by a new generation of surreal postmodern superheroes, such as the Sandman and Animal Man. Such innovative and ambitious titles helped DC to reclaim much of the creative cutting edge from Marvel. Although DC's sales lagged behind Marvel's throughout the 1990s, the company retained a loyal following among discerning fans as well as longtime collectors, who appreciated the company's historical significance as the prime founder of the American comic-book industry.

In 2009 Warner Brothers created DC Entertainment to handle the licensing of projects such as films, DVDs, and television rights connected with DC Comics. Two years later Warner Brothers resumed responsibility for all global licensing. That same year, DC Comics made a bold move that both shocked and delighted generations of fans. "The New 52," as it was dubbed, reintroduced the most popular DC characters, beginning with the first episodes of each comic. *Justice League #1*, featuring Batman and the Green Lantern, was introduced in August 2011. Shortly thereafter, DC issued #1 episodes for *Action Comics* (a prequel to Superman), *Animal Man*, *Batgirl*, *Batwing*, *Detective Comics*, *Green Arrow*, *Hawk and Dove*, *Justice League International*, *Men of War*, *O.M.A.C.*, *Static Shock*, *Star Watch*, and *Swamp Thing*. All reissues were sold at comic-book and general bookstores, and digital copies were also available.

Bradford W. Wright

SEE ALSO: *Batman; Comic Books; Comics; Comics Code Authority; Graphic Novels; Green Lantern; Pulp Magazines; Superman; Wonder Woman.*

BIBLIOGRAPHY

Daniels, Les. *DC Comics: Sixty Years of the World's Favorite Comic Book Heroes*. Boston: Little, Brown & Co., 1995.

Daniels, Les. *The Golden Age of DC Comics: 365 Days*. New York: Harry N. Abrams, 2004.

The Greatest 1950s Stories Ever Told. New York: DC Comics, 1991.

The Greatest Golden Age Stories Ever Told. New York: DC Comics, 1990.

Jacobs, Will, and Gerard Jones. *The Comic Book Heroes*. Rocklin, CA: Prima Publishing, 1996.

Jimenez, Phil, et al. *The DC Comics Encyclopedia: The Definitive Guide to the Characters of the DC Universe*. New York: DK Publishing, 2004.

Kovacs, George, and C. W. Marshall, eds. *Classics and Comics*. New York: Oxford University Press, 2011.

Levitz, Paul. *75 Years of DC Comics: The Art of Modern Mythmaking*. New York: Taschen, 2010.

O'Neil, Dennis, ed. *Secret Origins of the Super DC Heroes*. New York: Warner Books, 1976.

Wertham, Fredric, M.D. *Seduction of the Innocent*. Toronto: Clarke, Irwin, 1954.

De La Hoya, Oscar *(1973–)*

Nicknamed "The Golden Boy" following his Olympic boxing achievement during the 1992 Summer Games, Oscar De La Hoya had promised his dying mother that he would win the gold medal for her and did just that. He then turned pro and cashed in on his amateur fistic glory. The only fighter campaigning below heavyweight to command eight-figure purses since Sugar Ray Leonard, De La Hoya's appeal crossed over from mostly male boxing fans to women attracted by his charm and good looks. Guided by savvy promoter Bob Arum, De La Hoya became one of richest and best-known athletes of the United States even before taking on any of the world's top young fighters.

In addition to exploiting the markets as Leonard did before him, De La Hoya has a huge Latin American fan base as a result of his Mexican American heritage. His willingness to engage opponents in exciting fights makes him a television favorite as well. In the early twenty-first century, De La Hoya was still considered a golden boy, able to draw large audiences even when many arenas were only half filled. In a much-anticipated fight against Floyd Mayweather in 2007, De La Hoya lost his title in a split decision. However, he still raked in a guaranteed purse of $12 million.

Max Kellerman

SEE ALSO: *Boxing; Leonard, Sugar Ray; Olympics.*

BIBLIOGRAPHY

Kawakami, Tim. *Golden Boy: The Fame, Money, and Mystery of Oscar De La Hoya*. Kansas City, MO: Andrews McMeel, 1999.

Mannix, Chris. "Oscar De La Hoya." *Sports Illustrated*, March 12, 2007, 11.

De Niro, Robert *(1943–)*

For approximately a decade, from the mid-1970s to the mid-1980s, screen actor Robert De Niro came to embody the ethos of urban America—most particularly New York City, where he was born, raised, and educated. In a series of performances that demonstrated a profound and introspective intelligence and great power, De Niro became a poster child for method acting—also known as the Stanislavsky System—which stressed realism in developing character roles. One of the most ardent supporters of method acting was Lee Strasberg, who taught the Stanislavsky System to generations of American actors, including De Niro. Known throughout the last quarter of the twentieth century for his gritty, realistic performances, in the twenty-first century he is best known by young Americans for the role of ex-CIA agent and father-in-law-to-be-feared Jack Byrnes in the comedy *Meet the Parents* (2000) and two sequels, *Meet the Fockers* (2004) and *Little Fockers* (2010).

The son of an artist-poet father and an artist mother, De Niro decided in his teens to become an actor and began studying at several institutions, including the Stella Adler Studio and with Strasberg at the Actors Studio in New York City. He worked in obscurity off-Broadway and in touring theater companies before director Brian De Palma discovered him and used him in his first three little-seen films—*The Wedding Party* (1963, released 1969), *Greetings* (1968), and *Hi Mom!* (1970). In these, the young De Niro revealed an affinity with the anarchic, and, indeed, De Palma perhaps came closest to longtime De Niro collaborator Martin Scorsese in being, at that time, a natural director for the actor. They worked together again almost twenty years later when De Niro, honed in cold villainy, enhanced *The Untouchables* (1987) as a mesmerizing Al Capone.

CRIMINALS, MISFITS, AND VILLAINS

In his gallery of characters, which include violent or otherwise troubled men and social misfits, it is in his portrayal of Travis

Bickle in Scorsese's *Taxi Driver* (1976) that his image is likely to remain forever enshrined. As the disturbed, nervy, undereducated Vietnam vet who, through the skewed vision of his isolation and ignorance, sets out on a bloody crusade to cleanse society's ills, De Niro displayed an armory of personal gifts unmatched by any actor of his generation. The film itself was a seminal development in late-twentieth-century cinema, and it is not too fanciful to suggest that, without its influence, certain films in which De Niro excelled for other directors, notably Michael Cimino's *The Deer Hunter* (1978), might not have existed—at least not in as uncompromising a form. It is impossible to catalog or categorize De Niro's work without examining his significant actor-director relationship with Scorsese, for, while the actor's substantial skills and the concentrated intensity of his persona were very much his own, much of his success can be attributed to that symbiotic collaboration. Scorsese explored, interpreted, and recorded the underbelly of Manhattan as no director before him had been able to do.

It was *Mean Streets* (1973), Scorsese's picture of small-time gangster life in New York's Little Italy, that focused major attention on De Niro, even though his role as Johnny Boy, a brash, none-too-bright and volatile hustler, was secondary to Harvey Keitel's role. At the time of *Mean Streets*, De Niro had already appeared in Roger Corman's *Bloody Mama* (1970) and the unfunny Mafia comedy *The Gang That Couldn't Shoot Straight* (1971). His supporting role in *Bloody Mama* brought him his first meaningful attention, and after several more roles in minor movies, he soon became stamped as American cinema's most authoritative and interesting purveyor of criminals, large and small. His first real mainstream appearance came in 1973 as the baseball player in *Bang the Drum Slowly* (1973), which earned him the New York Critics' Circle Best Actor Award. The following year, he won an Academy Award for Best Supporting Actor in *The Godfather: Part II.*

***Robert De Niro in* Goodfellas.** *Robert De Niro starred as a New York mobster in* Goodfellas *in 1990.* WARNER BROS/THE KOBAL COLLECTION.

His rising reputation and compelling presence survived his somewhat uncomfortable inclusion in Bernardo Bertolucci's Italian political epic *1900* and his blank, if elegant, performance in Elia Kazan's disastrous *The Last Tycoon* (both 1976). His Oscar-nominated Travis Bickle, followed by his Jimmy Doyle in Scorsese's *New York, New York* (1977), fortunately superseded both. The director's dark take on a musical genre of the 1940s was badly cut before its release and suffered accordingly. Underrated at the time and a commercial failure, it nonetheless brought plaudits for De Niro, essaying a saxophonist whose humor and vitality masks arrogance, egotism, and an inability to sustain his love affair with, and marriage to, a singer played by Liza Minnelli.

Next came *The Deer Hunter*, giving the actor a role unlike anything he had done before, albeit as essentially another loner. A somber treatment of male relationships, war, and heroism in which a bearded De Niro, voice and accent adjusted to the character, was as tough and tensile as the steel he forged in a small, bleak Pennsylvania town. His Michael is the authoritative leader of his pack of hunting and drinking buddies, a fearless survivor—yet locked into a profound and unexpressed interior self, permitted only one immensely effective outbreak of overt emotion when confronted by the death wish of his buddy (Christopher Walken), which his own heroics are finally powerless to conquer. De Niro earned a second Oscar nomination for Best Actor for his role in the film.

TRIUMPH AND CHALLENGES

De Niro began the 1980s with a triumphant achievement, shared with Scorsese. *Raging Bull* (1980), filmed in black-and-white, dealt with the rise, fall, and domestic crises of middleweight boxing champ Jake LaMotta, an Italian American who copes with his personal insecurities via braggadocio and bullying. It was known that De Niro went to great lengths in preparing his roles, keeping faith with the letter and spirit of the method in his search for authenticity. In preparing to play LaMotta, he trained in the ring, entered some amateur contests, and famously put on 60 pounds for the later-life sequences. It was a bravura performance in one of the best fight films ever made. The actor was lavished with praise and awards, including the Best Actor Oscar. Nine years later the film was voted the best of the decade.

Inexplicably, although widely acknowledged and admired as a great *actor*, De Niro, for all his achievements, did not prove to be a great *movie star*—a label that refers to marquee value and box-office clout. Producers looked to the Stallones and the Schwarzeneggers for big financial returns, which might account for some of De Niro's erratic choices during the 1980s. He was brilliant on familiar ground, aging thirty years as a gangster in Sergio Leone's epic *Once upon a Time in America* in 1984, the same year he starred in *The King of Comedy* for Scorsese. This superb collector's piece for the cognoscenti failed disastrously at the box office, despite De Niro's memorable portrayal of would-be comedian Rupert Pupkin, a pathetically disturbed misfit whose obsessional desire for public glory through television leads him to kidnap TV star Jerry Lewis and demand an appearance on his show as ransom. The film is cynical, its title ironic: tragedy lies at its heart. It lost a fortune, and director and star went their separate ways for seven years.

Until then, and for much of the 1990s, De Niro's career had no discernible pattern. Desirous of expanding his repertoire on the one hand and seeming bored with the ease of his own facility on the other, he appeared in numerous middle-of-the-road entertainments that had little need of him, nor he of them. After *The King of Comedy*, he went into *Falling in Love* (1984) with Meryl Streep, about an abortive affair between two married commuters, largely perceived as a contemporary American reworking of *Brief Encounter* (1945). The result was a disappointment and a box-office failure. *Variety* accurately noted that "the effect of this talented pair acting in such a lightweight vehicle is akin to having Horowitz and Rubinstein improvise a duet on the theme of Chopsticks."

Other attempts to break the mold between 1985 and 1999 included a turn as a Jesuit priest in *The Mission* (1986), worthy but desperately dull; a good-natured bounty hunter in *Midnight Run* (1988), entertaining but unimportant; an illiterate cook in *Stanley and Iris* (1989), a film version of the novel *Union Street* that verged on the embarrassingly sentimental; *Guilty by Suspicion* (1991) an earnest but uncompelling attempt to revisit the McCarthy era in which De Niro played a film director investigated by the House Un-American Activities Committee—and the list goes on.

On the credit side, among the plethora of undistinguished or otherwise unworthy vehicles and performances delivered on automatic pilot, De Niro met a major challenge in Penny Marshall's *Awakenings* (1990), earning an Academy Award nomination for his moving portrayal of a patient awakened from a twenty-year sleep by the drug L-dopa. He did all that could have been expected of him in the political satire *Wag the Dog* (1997), and he gave an accomplished character performance in Quentin Tarantino's *Jackie Brown* (1997). Almost unrecognizable as a shambling wreck of an ex-con, he seemed initially disconcertingly blank, but this proved deceptive as, in one of the film's best moments, he revealed a chilling hole where a man's heart would normally reside.

It was, however, three more films with Scorsese that made public noise. Their long separation was broken by *GoodFellas* (1990), a brilliant and violent evocation of the Mafia hierarchy, but while De Niro shared in the accolades and acquitted himself with the expertise that was to be expected, he was in a sense retreading familiar ground. The same was true of the overlong and less successful *Casino* (1995). In between, he scored his biggest success as Max Cady, the vengeful psychopath in Scorsese's remake of *Cape Fear* (1991). Threateningly tattooed, the actor broke the bounds of any conventional villainy to come up with a character so evilly repellent as to almost, but not quite, flirt with parody. The film, and his uncompromising, Oscar-nominated performance, lifted his star profile once more, only for it to dissipate in the run of largely unmemorable films.

THE OTHER SIDE OF THE CAMERA

An intensely private man, De Niro has eschewed publicity over the years and has been notoriously uncooperative with journalists. His unconventional private life has been noted but caused barely a ripple of gossip. He was married from 1976 to 1988 to Diahnne Abbott, with whom he has a son; he fathered twins by a surrogate mother for his former girlfriend Toukie Smith; and he married Grace Hightower in 1997. They divorced two years later. De Niro seemed to grow restless during these years of often-passionless performances, seeking somehow to reinvent himself and broaden the horizons of his ambition. In 1988 he bought an eight-story building in downtown Manhattan and set up his Tribeca Film Center. Aside from postproduction facilities and offices, it housed De Niro's Tribeca Grill, the sought-after and exclusive haunt of New York's media glitterati. He is also part owner of the restaurants Nobu and Layla.

It was from there that De Niro launched himself as a player on the other side of the camera, producing some dozen films between 1992 and 1999. One of these, *A Bronx Tale* (1993), marked his directing debut. Choosing a familiar milieu, he cast himself this time as the good guy, a bus driver attempting to keep his young son free of the seemingly glamorous influence of the local Mafia as embodied by Chazz Palminteri—a role that he once would have played himself.

After attempting to regain the acting high ground as a tough loner in John Frankenheimer's ambiguous thriller *Ronin* (1998)—material inadequate to the purpose—De Niro began displaying a new willingness to talk about himself. What emerged was a restated ambition to turn his energy to directing because, as he told the respected British broadsheet the *Guardian* in a long interview in the fall of 1998, "Directing makes one think a lot more and I have to involve myself—make my own decisions, my own mistakes. It's more consuming. The actor is the one who has to grovel in the mud and jump through hoops." His words had the ring of a man who had exhausted his own possibilities and was searching for a new commitment, but whatever the outcome, De Niro's achievements had long assured his place in twentieth-century American cultural history.

In the twenty-first century, De Niro continues to bring his own inimitable twist to a variety of roles. He began by appearing as Billy Sunday in *Men of Honor* (2000). Also that year, *Meet the Parents* broke the record for the highest October opening in history. Over the course of the next few years, he appeared in such family fare as *The Adventures of Rocky and Bullwinkle* (2000), *Shark Tale* (2004), *Arthur and the Invisibles* (2006), and *Stardust* (2007). His other projects ranged from the adult comedy *Analyze That* (2002) to the chilling *Hide and Seek* (2005) to the crime drama *Righteous Kill* (2008). Whatever the role, De Niro continues to become that character, which is a testament to his early training in method acting.

Robyn Karney

SEE ALSO: *Academy Awards; Animated Films; Broadway; Capone, Al;* The Deer Hunter*;* The Godfather*;* GoodFellas*; Hollywood; Keitel, Harvey; Leone, Sergio; Lewis, Jerry;* Mean Streets*; Minnelli, Liza; Movie Stars;* Raging Bull*; Scorsese, Martin; Streep, Meryl; Tarantino, Quentin;* Taxi Driver.

BIBLIOGRAPHY

Agan, Patrick. *Robert Di Niro: The Man, The Myth, and the Movies.* London: Hale, 1989.

Dougan, Andy. *Untouchable—A Biography of Robert De Niro.* New York: Thunder's Mouth Press, 1997.

Friedman, Lawrence S. *The Cinema of Martin Scorsese.* New York: Continuum, 1997.

Le Fanu, Mark. "Robert De Niro." In *The Movie Stars Story*, ed. Robyn Karney. New York: Crescent Books, 1986.

Le Fanu, Mark. "Robert De Niro." In *Who's Who in Hollywood*, ed. Robyn Karney. New York: Continuum, 1994.

Rompalske, Dorothy. "Finding the Real Robert Di Niro." *Biography* 5, no. 2 (2001).

Thomson, David. *A Biographical Dictionary of Film*. New York: Alfred A. Knopf, 1994.

The Dead Kennedys

Singer Jello Biafra's politically confrontational lyrics lived up to the provocative billing of his group's name: the Dead Kennedys. Biafra's equal-opportunity outrage reproached a wide collection of targets: callow corporations, the Reagan administration, the Moral Majority, then-California governor Jerry Brown, feeble liberals, punk rockers with fascist leanings, and MTV. When asked if playing a concert on the anniversary of John F. Kennedy's assassination wasn't distasteful, guitarist East Bay Ray responded that the assassination wasn't in particularly good taste either. Generally acknowledged as pioneers in the American hardcore scene, which was centered in Washington, DC, and Los Angeles in the early 1980s, the Dead Kennedys' faster variant of punk never fully matched the fury in Biafra's lyrics. By the mid-1980s, in the midst of a political backlash against rock music, Biafra, the group, and its record label became the targets of a misguided obscenity trial. The Dead Kennedys' case was a forewarning of future prosecutions against musicians and record retailers.

The Dead Kennedys' 1980 debut, *Fresh Fruit for Rotting Vegetables*, was released on the group's own label, Alternative Tentacles, and featured the political sarcasm that became the group's strength. The album's opening track, "Kill the Poor," is a Swiftian proposal about the neutron bomb. "California Uber Alles" imagines Jerry Brown's "Zen Fascist" state: "Your kids will meditate in school . . . You will jog for the master race . . . Mellow out or you will pay." The following year the Dead Kennedys released *In God We Trust, Inc.*, which attacked corporate religion's self-righteousness in the age of televangelism. *Plastic Surgery Disasters* (1982) ridiculed personal identifications such as the preppy, the car enthusiast, and the RV tourist. *Frankenchrist*, the group's first release after a three-year break, was an uneven mixture of scathing commentary and didacticism.

However one felt about his vitriol, Biafra's political carpings often included some sort of constructive solution. For Biafra merely pointing out the shortcomings in American society was not an answer: "Real freedom scares you / 'Cos it means responsibility," he sang in 1985's "Stars and Stripes of Corruption." Even Michael Guarino, the Los Angeles deputy city attorney who unsuccessfully prosecuted the band, was forced to acknowledge the band's social commitment, commenting in the *Washington Post* that, "midway through the trial we realized that the lyrics . . . were in many ways socially responsible, very anti-drug and pro-individual." Biafra's fourth-place run for mayor of San Francisco in 1979 showed that 6,600 people had been equally discontented with the establishment and that Biafra's level of political involvement ran deeper than mere complaint. Although his campaign was farcical at times—Biafra's platform suggested that all downtown businessmen wear clown suits—there were serious proposals from the candidate whose slogan was, "There's always room for Jello." For example Biafra's platform called for neighborhood elections of police officers long before the 1991 Rodney King beating compelled urban leaders to demand that local police departments hold themselves more accountable.

Ultimately the Dead Kennedys' attacks on the status quo did not provoke authorities so much as the H. R. Giger "Landscape #20" poster in *Frankenchrist* did. Commonly referred to as "Penis Landscape," the poster's artwork depicted an endless series of alternating rows of copulating penises and anuses. Biafra decided that the poster merited inclusion for its depiction of everyone getting screwed by everyone else. A Los Angeles parent filed a complaint in 1986, and police raided Biafra's San Francisco apartment, Alternative Tentacles' headquarters, and the label's distributor. Police confiscated copies of *Frankenchrist* and the Giger poster, charging the Dead Kennedys with "distribution of harmful matter to minors."

The year 1985 marked the beginning of a national backlash against rock music that had lasting effects. The Parents Music Resource Center (PMRC), a political action group cofounded by Tipper Gore, held congressional hearings on rock music lyrics. The hearings focused on rap and heavy metal music, but the ensuing publicity questioned rock lyrics in monolithic terms. In 1985 the PMRC succeeded in pressuring the Recording Industry Association of America to voluntarily include warning stickers ("Parental Advisory: Explicit Lyrics") on albums. A series of First Amendment disputes was soon under way as rock and rap artists faced obscenity charges, and retailers who sold stickered albums to minors faced fines and imprisonment.

Biafra soundly contended that the group's political views and the limited resources of their independent record company made them an expedient target. The band found support from other underground musicians who performed benefit concerts to augment the band's defense fund. Pretrial wrangling pushed the trial's length to a year and a half, and with that, the Dead Kennedys were effectively finished. In 1987 the case was dismissed due to a hung jury that leaned toward acquittal. His band finished, Biafra became a spoken-word performer, recording *No More Cocoons* (1987), a collection of political satire in the tradition of Lenny Bruce. Biafra recounted the trial on the album *High Priest of Harmful Matter—Tales from the Trial* (1989).

The history of censorship in rock and roll reverts back to Elvis Presley's first television appearance, when cameras cut off his performance at the waist. New to this history are politically organized forces of censorship. Large superstores such as Wal-mart have compelled artists to change lyrics or artwork by threatening not to sell albums that have warning labels. These gains by the anti-rock forces made the Dead Kennedys' legal victory a crucial one; the case was an invaluable blueprint for rap groups with incendiary or sexually explicit lyrics, such as 2 Live Crew, who faced prosecution in 1990.

Former band members spent years wrangling among themselves over royalties. Finally in 2001 those issues were settled long enough for Manifesto Records to agree to release some of the Dead Kennedys' back catalog, combining *Plastic Surgery Disasters* and *In God We Trust* on one CD. The company also released a remastered version of *Bedtime for Democracy* and a greatest hits album, *Give Me Convenience or Give Me Death.*

That same year, the band reunited without Biafra. The Dead Kennedys appeared in three performances in 2010.

Daryl Umberger

SEE ALSO: *Automobile; The Bomb; Bruce, Lenny; Compact Discs; Heavy Metal; Kennedy Assassination; King, Rodney; Moral Majority; MTV; Pornography; Preppy; Presley, Elvis; Punk; Rap; Reagan, Ronald; RV; Televangelism; Television; 2 Live Crew; The* Washington Post.

BIBLIOGRAPHY

Kester, Marian. *Dead Kennedys: The Unauthorized Version.* San Francisco: Last Gasp of San Francisco, 1983.

Sartwell, Crispin. *Political Aesthetics.* Ithaca, NY: Cornell University Press, 2010.

Segal, David. "Jello Biafra: The Surreal Deal. The Life and Times of an Artist Provocateur; Or, How a Dead Kennedy Got $2.2 Million in Debt." *Washington Post,* May 4, 1997, G01.

Deadwood

Despite the enthusiasm of fans and critics, HBO's original series *Deadwood* ended after just thirty-six episodes. From its debut in 2004 to its cancellation in 2006, however, the acclaimed drama received twenty-eight Emmy nominations, winning eight. *Deadwood* has been widely praised not only for its distinctive visual style and edgy, complex view of frontier America but also for characters and stories that capture the audience.

Deadwood begins in 1876, set in the recently established mining camp for which it is named, and ends about two years later, when Deadwood is on its way to joining the organized Dakota Territory. During this time the camp becomes a town, and an assortment of characters cope with a variety of challenges. Unlike traditional Westerns, *Deadwood* often blurs the line between "good guys" and "bad guys," and its characters struggle with complicated personal relationships as well as the more typical conflicts over land, money, and power.

Although *Deadwood* has a large cast of characters, the series centers on ruthless saloon owner Al Swearengen (Ian McShane) and principled sheriff Seth Bullock (Timothy Olyphant). The two begin as enemies, with sharply different visions for the future of Deadwood, but they become reluctant allies and even develop a grudging respect for each other. Both oppose the big-money interests that descend on Deadwood in pursuit of profit. There are also two central female characters—troubled socialite Alma Garret (Molly Parker) and the compassionate "working girl" Trixie (Paula Malcomson). They, too, are apparent opposites, but Trixie helps Alma overcome her addiction to the narcotic laudanum, and both women must fight for survival in the lawless environment of Deadwood.

Deadwood received a great deal of notoriety for its extensive use of profanity, and although the series is notable for its realism in matters of set, costume, social custom, and historical context, the curse words are taken from the present not the past. Series creators wanted to emphasize the lack of "civilized" manners in frontier Deadwood, but they found that nineteenth-century profanity just did not have much impact for a twenty-first-century audience. Instead they peppered the dialogue with a generous supply of swear words that modern viewers will definitely recognize.

David Milch, who created *Deadwood,* was also one of the minds behind pioneering television drama *NYPD Blue,* in collaboration with noted producer Steven Bochco. That series ran on ABC from 1993 to 2005, introducing television audiences to a level of gritty intensity, realistic violence, and personal-professional conflict that was new at the time but soon became familiar. Although *NYPD Blue* was set in a contemporary urban environment, its exploration of lawless territories and moral quandaries established a path for *Deadwood.*

Deadwood was dropped by HBO in 2006, but the series had strong DVD sales, and when the "Complete Series" set was released in 2008, it contained a feature revealing what had been planned for season four. The short-lived drama introduced unforgettable characters and explored themes that continue to spark critical debate as well as fan loyalty.

Cynthia Giles

SEE ALSO: *Bochco, Steven; Emmy Awards;* NYPD Blue*; Television; The Western.*

BIBLIOGRAPHY

Lavery, David. *Reading "Deadwood": A Western to Swear By.* London: I. B. Tauris, 2006.

Milch, David, and David Samuels. *"Deadwood": Stories of the Black Hills.* New York: Bloomsbury, 2006.

Vest, Jason P. *"The Wire," "Deadwood," "Homicide," and "NYPD Blue": Violence Is Power.* Santa Barbara, CA: Praeger, 2011.

Dean, James *(1931–1955)*

Perhaps no film actor is as emblematic of his own era as is James Dean of his. Certainly, no screen-idol image has been as widely disseminated—his brooding, enigmatic, and beautiful face has sold everything from blue jeans to personal computers, and decades after his death, his poster-size image was still gracing the bedroom walls of millions of teenage girls and beaming down on the customers in coffee bars throughout America and Europe.

Whether or not he intended to take it to its logical and tragic conclusion, Dean's credo was to live fast, die young, and leave a good-looking corpse. Thus, his legendary legacy is composed of only three major motion pictures (though he had small roles in others), a handful of seldom-seen television dramas, and an admired Broadway stage performance seen only by a relative handful of people. But Dean, like Marlon Brando, whom he idolized, was able to blend his life and his art so seamlessly that each seemed an extension of the other. And he harbored a long-festering psychic wound, a vulnerability that begged for redemption. It was the omnipresent wounded child in Dean's persona that made him so appealing and gave his acting such visceral impact.

TROUBLED CHILDHOOD

Born in Marion, Indiana, Dean spent his early childhood in Los Angeles, where his father worked as a dental technician for the Veterans Administration. His mother, Mildred, overly protective

James Dean in **Giant.** *James Dean performs in the 1956 Warner Bros. epic* Giant, *for which he posthumously received his second Academy Award nomination.* AP IMAGES.

of her son and with a preternatural concern for his health, died of cancer when he was nine, and he was sent to live with his father's sister in Fairmount, Indiana. There, he developed the hallmark traits of an orphan: depression, an inexplicable feeling of loneliness, and antisocial behavior.

But Dean's childhood was bucolic as well as tormented. His aunt and uncle doted on him and nurtured his natural talents. Good at sports, particularly basketball (despite his short stature), and theater, the bespectacled teenager nevertheless acquired a reputation for rebelliousness that made him persona non grata with the parents of his classmates—particularly those of female students who, even then, were fascinated by this mysterious, faintly melancholy youth. Dean was also attractive to older men, and it was a local preacher in Fairmount who first sensed the boy's emotional vulnerability, grew fond of him, and showered him with favors and attention. This quality in the young Dean was a dubious asset that he would exploit to his advantage frequently over the course of his brief career.

Dean never entertained the idea of any career but acting. Upon graduating, he rejoined his father in Los Angeles and attended Santa Monica City College and UCLA before dropping out to pursue acting full time. According to his fellow drama students at the latter institution, he showed little talent. After quitting UCLA, he lived hand to mouth, picking up bit parts on television and film. His acting may have been lackluster, but he had a pronounced gift for evoking sympathy, and it was during a lean stretch that he acquired his first patron. Dean had taken a job parking cars at a lot across from CBS, and it was there that he met the director Rogers Brackett, who took a paternal, as well as a sexual, interest in the young man. Eventually Dean moved in with Brackett and was introduced to a sophisticated homosexual milieu. When Brackett was transferred to Chicago in 1951, he supplied Dean with the necessary money and connections to take a stab at New York.

EARLY FORAYS INTO SHOW BUSINESS

There was nothing predestined about Dean's eventual success. He went about just as any other young actor, struggling to eat, relying on the kindness of others, and changing addresses like he changed his clothes. At first he was timid; legend has it that he spent his first week either in his hotel room or at the movies, but just as he had a flair for cultivating older men, he had an impeccable ear for self-promotion and slanting his stories for maximum advantage. Fortunately, his relationship with Brackett gave him entrée to an elegant theater crowd that gathered at the Algonquin and, helped by Brackett's influential contacts, Dean found television work and an agent. In the summer of 1952, he auditioned for, and was accepted into, the prestigious Actors Studio. Once again, the Dean mystique has distorted the facts to fit the legend: he never appeared in a studio production, and his fellow members remembered him only as a vague presence, uncommunicative and sullen.

From a purely practical point of view, Dean's casual morals gave him one advantage over his struggling contemporaries. He was not averse to peddling his sexual favors to further his career, and his first real break came from his seduction of Lemuel Ayers, a successful businessman who invested money in the theater and helped secure the aspiring actor a role in a forthcoming Broadway play called *See the Jaguar*. The play folded after four performances, but 1954 brought him *The Immoralist*, adapted from André Gide's novel, in which he played the North African street Arab whose sexual charisma torments a male married writer struggling with homosexual tendencies. Dean's own sexual charisma was potent, and his performance attracted notice, praise, and Hollywood. By the end of the following year, 1955, he had starred in *East of Eden* for Elia Kazan—mentor to Montgomery Clift and Brando—and, under Nicholas Ray's direction, became the idolized voice of a generation as the "rebel without a cause."

Many writers have attributed Dean's winning combination of vulnerability and bravado to his mother's early death; certainly, he seemed aware of this psychic wound without being able to rectify it. "Must I always be miserable?" he wrote to a girlfriend. "I try so hard to make people reject me. Why?" Following his Broadway success, he abandoned his gay friends, as if in revenge for all the kindness they had proffered, and when he was cast in *East of Eden,* he broke away from his loyal patron, Brackett, then fallen on hard times. When a mutual friend upbraided him for his callousness, his response was, "I thought it was the john who paid, not the whore." But to others, Dean seemed unaffected by success. He was chimerical yet remarkably astute in judging how far (and with whom) he could take his misbehavior. This trait fostered his Jekyll-and-Hyde image—sweet and sensitive on the one hand, callous, sadistic, and rude on the other.

AN UNCONVENTIONAL STAR

The actor's arrival in Hollywood presented a problem for studio publicists unsure how to market this unknown, uncooperative commodity. They chose to focus on inflating Dean's sparse Broadway credentials, presenting him as the New York theater actor making good in Hollywood. In New York, Dean had been notorious for skulking sullenly in a corner at parties and throwing tantrums. Although he could be perfectly delightful given sufficient motivation, he was not motivated to appease the publicists. What were taken for Dean's Actors Studio affectations—his ill-kempt appearance, slouching, and mumbling—was actually his deliberate attempt to deflate Hollywood bombast and pretension. The reigning queens of Hollywood gossip, Louella Parsons and Hedda Hopper, both took umbrage at Dean's behavior.

His disdain for Hollywood was so overt that, before *East of Eden* was even complete, he had managed to set much of the entertainment press squarely against him. The film, however, made a huge impact, won Dean an Academy Award nomination, and launched him into the stratospheric stardom that was confirmed later the same year with the success of *Rebel without a Cause.* In both films, the young actor played complex adolescents, alienated from the values of the adult world around them—tormented, haunted by an extraordinarily mature recognition of pain that comes from being misunderstood and needing to be loved. The animal quality he brought to conveying anguish and frustration struck a chord in the collective psyche of 1950s American youth, and his almost immediate iconic status softened the scorn of journalists. His on-screen charisma brought forgiveness for his off-screen contemptuousness, and his uncouth mannerisms were suddenly accorded the indulgence shown a naughty and precocious child.

Stardom only exacerbated Dean's schizoid nature, which, paradoxically, he knew to be central to his appeal. When a young Dennis Hopper quizzed him about his persona, he replied, "In this hand I'm holding Marlon Brando saying, 'Fuck you!' and in the other hand saying, 'Please forgive me,' is Montgomery Clift. 'Please forgive me.' 'Fuck you!' 'Please forgive me.' 'Fuck you!' And somewhere in between is James Dean." But while playing the enfant terrible for the press, he reacted to his overnight fame with naive wonder, standing in front of the theater unnoticed in his glasses and watching the long queues forming for *East of Eden* with delight. That was Dean's sweet side. He exorcised his demons through speed, buying first a horse, then a Triumph motorcycle, an MG, and a Porsche in short order. He delighted in scaring his friends with his reckless driving. Stories of Dean playing daredevil on his motorcycle (which he allegedly called his "murdercycle") are legion. Racing became his passion, and he managed to place in several events. His antics so alarmed the studios that a "no-ride" clause was written into his contract for fear that he would be killed or disfigured in the middle of shooting.

With the shooting of *Rebel* completed, he made his third film, costarring with Rock Hudson and Elizabeth Taylor in *Giant* (1956). As Jett Rink, the graceless farm laborer who strikes oil and becomes a millionaire, Dean was able to play to type for the first half of the film but was seriously too young to meet the challenge of the second half, in which Rink has become a dissipated, middle-aged tycoon. Nonetheless, he collected a second Oscar nomination—but was no longer alive to hear the announcement. On September 30, 1955, almost immediately after the completion of filming, Dean and a mechanic embarked for a race in Salinas in the actor's new Porsche Spyder. Fate, in the form of a Ford, struck the tiny car head-on, breaking Dean's neck. He was dead at twenty-four years old.

Part of Dean's enduring allure rests in the fact that he was dead before his two biggest films were complete. His legacy as an artist and a man is continually debated. Was he gay or straight? Self-destructive or merely reckless? Perhaps he didn't know himself, but doom hung about him like a shroud, and it came as no surprise to many of his colleagues when they learned of his fatal accident. Kazan, upon hearing the news, sighed, "That figures." After his death, his friend Leonard Rosenman commented, "[Jimmy's main] attraction to the public . . . was his almost pathological vulnerability to hurt and rejection. Enormous defenses on his part to cover it up—hence the leather-garbed motorcycle rider, the tough kid having to reassure himself at every turn of the way by subjecting himself to superhuman tests of survival, the last of which he failed."

Whether Dean had a death wish or simply met with an unfortunate accident will continue to be batted around for eternity; there are as many who will attest to his self-destructiveness as to his hope for the future. So, was it mere bravado or a sense of fatalism that made him remark to his friend and future biographer John Gilmore: "You remember the movie Bogie made—*Knock on Any Door*—and the line, 'Live fast, die young, have a good-looking corpse?' Shit, man, I'm going to be so good-looking they're going to have to cement me in the coffin."

Michael Baers

SEE ALSO: *Academy Awards; Brando, Marlon; Broadway; Cancer; Celebrity; Clift, Montgomery; The Fifties; Gay Men;* Giant*; Gossip Columns; Hollywood; Hopper, Dennis;* Rebel without a Cause*; Sex Symbol; Teen Idols.*

BIBLIOGRAPHY

Alexander, Paul. *Boulevard of Broken Dreams: The Life, Times, and Legend of James Dean.* New York: Plume, 1994.

Dalton, David. *James Dean, the Mutant King: A Biography.* Chicago: A Cappella, 2001.

Gilmore, John. *Live Fast—Die Young: Remembering the Short Life of James Dean.* New York: Thunder's Mouth Press, 1997.

Holley, Val. *James Dean, The Biography.* New York: Saint Martin's Press, 1995.

Howlett, John. *James Dean: A Biography*. London: Plexus, 1975.

McCann, Graham. *Rebel Males: Clift, Brando, and Dean*. New Brunswick, N.J.: Rutgers University Press, 1993.

Perry, George. *James Dean*. Bath, UK: Palazzo, 2011.

Riese, Randall. *The Unabridged James Dean: His Life and Legacy from A to Z*. Chicago: Contemporary, 1991.

Death of a Salesman

Arthur Miller's 1949 masterpiece *Death of a Salesman* has been lauded as one of the greatest plays in all of twentieth-century American drama. The play probes the filial and social realms of American life, exploring and exploding the concept of the American dream. From its debut in New York in 1949 to its many international stagings since, *Death of a Salesman* has spoken to the concerns of middle-class workers and their struggle to live in a capitalist society. The play and its initial production set the tone for American drama for the rest of the century through sociopolitical themes, poetic realism, and focus on the common man.

PLOT

The play tells the story of aging salesman Willy Loman; his wife, Linda; and their sons, Biff and Happy. Willy has reached a critical point in his career: he cannot work as a traveling salesman and is disappointed in Biff's unwillingness to fulfill his father's dreams. When Willy finally summons the courage to ask his employer to transfer him to New York, he is fired. Linda informs Biff that Willy has secretly attempted suicide, and a series of flashbacks reveals that Biff found his father with a mistress, causing Biff to have a breakdown.

The family's story is interwoven with two other subplots—involving Willy's neighbors, Charley and Bernard, and the appearance of Willy's dead brother, Ben. Charley becomes Willy's creditor, and Bernard represents the successful son Willy never had. Conversely, Ben is the pioneering capitalist Willy could never be. Because Willy has a life insurance policy, he decides he is worth more dead than alive. He commits suicide, and Linda is left at his grave uttering the famous lines, "And there'll be nobody home. . . . We're free and clear. . . . We're free."

Miller uses realism for scenes in the present and expressionistic flashbacks for scenes from the past. The flashbacks include visits from Ben and scenes from Willy's affair. Miller's juxtaposition of time and place give the play a dimension of ambiguity: Miller never acknowledges from whose point of view the story is told and whether the episodes are factual or recreations based on Willy's imagination. He also wrote musical directions for flute, cello, and other instruments to punctuate the action of the play.

MILLER'S INSPIRATION

The play's subtitle is "Certain Private Conversations in Two Acts and a Requiem." Miller's first concept was vastly different from his final work. "The first image that occurred to me which was to result in *Death of a Salesman* was of an enormous face the height of the proscenium arch which would appear and then open up, and we would see the inside of a man's head. In fact, *The Inside of His Head* was the first title." Miller instead gives the audience a cross section of the Loman household by creating a realistic setting while maintaining the expressionistic elements of the play.

Many critics have attempted to connect the name Loman to Willy's position in society, though Miller refuted this theory in his 1987 autobiography *Timebends: A Life*. He explained that the origin of the surname was a character called Lohmann in director Fritz Lang's film *The Testament of Dr. Mabuse* (1933). "In later years I found it discouraging to observe the confidence with which some commentators on *Death of a Salesman* smirked at the heavy-handed symbolism of 'Low-man,'" Miller wrote. "What the name really meant to me was a terror-stricken man calling into the void for help that will never come."

Death of a Salesman draws inspiration from two sources: Miller's philosophy of tragedy as expressed in his essay "Tragedy and the Common Man" (1949) and the rags-to-riches stories of nineteenth-century author Horatio Alger Jr. Miller refutes Alger's theory, expressed in such stories as *Ragged Dick* (1867), that through hard work and determination, even the poorest Americans could eventually work their way to the upper class. Willy is the antithesis of this ideal: the more he works toward security, the further he is driven away from it.

In "Tragedy and the Common Man," Miller attempts to define Willy as an Aristotelian tragic figure. "The common man is as apt a subject for tragedy in its highest sense as kings were," he writes. He compares Willy's fall with that of Oedipus or Orestes, claiming that tragedy is "the consequence of a man's total compulsion to evaluate himself justly." Literary critic Harold Bloom, in his book *Willy Loman* (1991), disagrees: "All that Loman actually shares with Lear or Oedipus is agony; there is no other likeness whatsoever. Miller has little understanding of Classical or Shakespearean tragedy."

PRODUCTION AND CRITICAL RECEPTION

The play has a critical place in the history of American drama, bridging the gap between the early melodramatic works of playwright Eugene O'Neill and the Theatre of the Absurd of the 1960s. The original Broadway production of *Death of a Salesman* was directed by filmmaker Elia Kazan and designed by set designer Jo Mielziner. The duo was the same team that made playwright Tennessee Williams's *A Streetcar Named Desire* a Broadway success. Williams's and Miller's works came to define serious Broadway theater of the 1950s and 1960s. However, Miller's refusal to submit to the communist investigations of the House Committee on Un-American Activities and the onslaught of avant-garde theater squelched his dramatic voice.

Several productions of *Death of a Salesman* have received great acclaim, including the 1951 film starring actor Fredric March and the 1975 Broadway production directed by, and starring, actor George C. Scott. Director Michael Rudman's 1984 theater production with actors Dustin Hoffman, John Malkovich, and Kate Reid garnered much praise and was later filmed for television. Other notable productions include the 1983 production at the Beijing People's Art Theatre (directed by Miller himself), the 1997 Diana LeBlanc production at Canada's Stratford Festival, and the 1999 fiftieth anniversary Broadway production of the play by director Robert Falls, starring actors Brian Dennehy, Elizabeth Franz, and Kevin Anderson.

In 2012 a new production by director Mike Nichols premiered on Broadway, starring actors Philip Seymour Hoffman as Willy, Linda Emond as Linda, and Andrew Garfield as Biff. Miller's play continues to ring true to audiences more than half a century since its writing. Critic Ben Brantley of the *New York Times* wrote of Nichols's production, "You admire every detail of construction and leave . . . feeling that you have learned something of worth, dutifully noting the parallels between Miller's portrait of failed American dreams and our own disenchanted times."

Michael Najjar

SEE ALSO: *Broadway; Communism; Consumerism; Hoffman, Dustin; Lang, Fritz; Miller, Arthur; Scott, George C.;* A Streetcar Named Desire*; Suicide; Williams, Tennessee.*

BIBLIOGRAPHY

Bloom, Harold, ed. *Willy Loman.* New York: Chelsea House Publishers, 1991.

Brantley, Ben. "American Dreamer, Ambushed by the Territory." *New York Times,* March 15, 2012.

Kazan, Elia. *Kazan on Directing.* New York: Vintage Books, 2009.

Klaus, Carl H.; Miriam Gilbert; and Bradford S. Field Jr. *Stages of Drama: Classical to Contemporary Masterpieces of the Theater,* 2nd ed. New York: St. Martin's Press, 1991.

Martine, James J. *Critical Essays on Arthur Miller.* Boston: G. K. Hall, 1979.

Miller, Arthur. *Timebends: A Life.* New York: Grove Press, 1987.

Roudanè, Matthew C. "*Death of a Salesman* and the Poetics of Arthur Miller." In *The Cambridge Companion to Arthur Miller,* ed. Christopher Bigsby. Cambridge, UK: Cambridge University Press, 1997.

Debs, Eugene V. *(1855–1926)*

Eugene Victor Debs, labor leader and five-time Socialist candidate for president, was born in Terre Haute, Indiana, on November 5, 1855. Debs started working on the railroads at age fourteen and founded the American Railway Union in 1893. The following year the union was destroyed, and Debs served six months in jail after a failed strike against the Pullman Palace Car Company in Chicago. Subsequently, he joined the Socialist Party of America and was its presidential candidate in 1900, 1904, 1908, and 1912 (when he received about 6 percent of the vote).

In 1918 Debs opposed the United States' entry into World War I and was sentenced to ten years in prison for sedition. From his prison cell in Atlanta, Georgia, in 1920, he ran for president again, gaining about 3.5 percent of the vote. A year later President Warren G. Harding commuted his sentence, and Debs lived in relative obscurity until his death on October 20, 1926. He is remembered as the most viable Socialist Party candidate for the nation's highest office and as a champion of workers' rights.

John F. Lyons

SEE ALSO: *Labor Unions; Political Bosses.*

BIBLIOGRAPHY

Debs, Eugene Victor. *Walls and Bars.* Whitefish, MT: Kessinger Publishing, 2005.

Ginger, Ray. *The Bending Cross: A Biography of Eugene Victor Debs.* New Brunswick, Canada: Rutgers University Press, 1949.

Salvatore, Nick. *Eugene V. Debs: Citizen and Socialist.* Urbana: University of Illinois, 1982.

Debutantes

A debutante is a young woman, usually seventeen or eighteen years old, who is formally introduced to affluent society at a ball or "coming out" party. The original purpose of the "debut" was to announce that young women of prominent social standing were available for courtship by eligible young men. This social ritual was necessitated by the traditional upper-class practice of sending girls away to boarding school, where they were prohibited from dating, attending parties of mixed company, or socializing with adults. A coming out party thus introduced the debutante to her social peers and potential suitors. The custom had been long established among the aristocracy and the upper classes in England, where debutantes were, until the mid-twentieth century, presented at court. In the United States the debutante ball derived from the formal etiquette of the nineteenth century, but the ritual changed as society changed in the generations that followed.

According to the 1880 etiquette reference, *The Manners That Win,* a debutante should have graduated school, sing or play an instrument gracefully, dance with elegance, and know the rules governing polite society. Having mastered these essential skills, she was presumed ready for courtship, leading, of course, to marriage, which was at the time the single vocational avenue open to the well-to-do woman. A second purpose was to display the wealth and prestige of the debutante's family. Until the early twentieth century, debutante balls were held at the family's residential estate or at a fashionable hotel.

By the 1920s, the rules of the debut had relaxed. In her 1922 book *Etiquette in Society, in Business, in Politics and at Home,* author Emily Post describes several ways in which a young woman might be introduced to society. These include a formal ball, an afternoon tea with dancing, a small dance, or a small tea without music. In addition, Post lists a fifth and more modest way for a family to announce that a daughter has reached the age of majority: mother and daughter might simply distribute joint engraved calling cards. For the most part, private debuts were replaced by public cotillions or assemblies that invite prominent young women to make their debuts collectively. These long-established debutante balls include the Passavant Cotillion in Chicago, the Boston Cotillion, the Junior Assemblies in New York, and the Harvest Ball at the Piedmont Driving Club in Atlanta, Georgia.

After World War II, the debutante ball spread to almost every city in the United States and enjoyed a heyday during the conservative years of President Dwight D. Eisenhower's administration. Yet a decade later, antiestablishment sentiment led many young women of even the most affluent status to abandon the event, dismissing it as anachronistic snobbery. In addition, sexual liberation and the feminist movement challenged the very basis of the century-old convention, as women began to seek both sexual and professional fulfillment outside of marriage. In the 1980s the debutante ball witnessed a popular resurgence, and by the end of the twentieth century, charitable

New York Debutantes, 1947. New York debutantes take part in a special dance at a cotillion in 1947. ©BETTMANN/CORBIS.

organizations frequently sponsored cotillions, extending invitations exclusively to philanthropically active women. Only one feature of the debut has not changed over the years: the debutante is required to wear a white or pastel gown. Loud colors and black have always been considered inappropriate.

In the early twenty-first century, college-age women continue to float onto the dance floor in virginal white dresses on the arms of proud fathers. The tradition of debutante balls remains particularly prevalent in the American South, but debutante balls are also held in Texas, California, and New York. Some of these balls are charity events in which parents contribute to a charity and guests purchase tickets to the event with the charity receiving the proceeds. In other cases the debutantes are involved in charity work and community service themselves, and they see such events as a way to raise funds for their favorite causes.

Michele S. Shauf

BIBLIOGRAPHY

The Manners That Win. Minneapolis, MN: Buckeye Publishing, 1880.

Marling, Karal Ann. *Debutante: Rites and Regalia of American Debdom.* Lawrence: University Press of Kansas, 2004.

Post, Emily. *Etiquette in Society, in Business, in Politics and at Home.* New York: Funk & Wagnalls, 1922.

Post, Peggy. *Emily Post's Etiquette.* New York: Harper-Collins, 1997.

Roosevelt, Eleanor. *Eleanor Roosevelt's Book of Common Sense Etiquette.* New York: Macmillan, 1962.

Schlesinger, Arthur M. *Learning How to Behave.* New York: Macmillan, 1947.

Tuckerman, Nancy, and Nancy Dunnan. *The Amy Vanderbilt Complete Book of Etiquette.* New York: Doubleday, 1985.

The Deer Hunter

Before director Michael Cimino's 1978 film *The Deer Hunter*, the only cinematic treatment of the Vietnam War most Americans had seen was John Wayne's *The Green Berets* a decade earlier. By 1978, however, American audiences were finally ready to deal with the war on-screen. *The Deer Hunter* was popular with audiences and critics alike and was nominated for nine Academy Awards, winning five, including Best Picture, Best Director, and Best Supporting Actor (Christopher Walken). *The Deer Hunter* broke new ground in the cinematic treatment of Vietnam, opening the door for films such as *Apocalypse Now* (1979), *Platoon* (1986), and *Full Metal Jacket* (1987). All of these "Vietnam" films share the same shattering emotional impact on audiences, but none is as moving as *The Deer Hunter*.

The Deer Hunter not only deals with Vietnam but also foregrounds the contrast between the soldier's comparatively gentle life at home and the brutal trauma of war. The film opens in the Clairton, Pennsylvania, steel mill where Michael (Robert De Niro), Nick (Walken), and Steve (John Savage) are working their last shift before shipping out to Vietnam. The quotidian details of their working-class lives revolve around work, hunting, drinking, and playing pool. Steve, like so many soldiers before him, is getting married before he leaves for the war. Cinematographer Vilmos Zsigmond beautifully photographs the Russian Orthodox wedding ceremony, but portents of the war intrude upon the revelry. A Green Beret mysteriously appears at the wedding like Coleridge's Ancient Mariner, foreshadowing the death and destruction that await in Vietnam.

The brutal rituals of war replace the rituals back in Pennsylvania; however, Cimino and cowriter Deric Washburn use Russian roulette in a North Vietnamese prison camp as their metaphor for combat. The deadly game is an ironic, terrifying counterpoint to the trio's hunting and pool playing stateside, and the prison camp scenes are a chilling condensation of the Vietnam war itself—bamboo, rain, and death. The spectrum of the Vietnam veteran's experience is exhibited in the three characters at the end of the film: Nick dies, Steve returns home in a wheelchair, and Michael returns emotionally crippled.

Besides the emotional impact of the story and the photography, the film benefits from its excellent ensemble cast. In addition to Oscar winner Walken, Oscar nominee De Niro (Best Actor), and Savage, the film stars Meryl Streep (nominee for Best Supporting Actress), George Dzundza, and John Cazale (Cazale died of cancer right after filming was completed). Stanley Myers's powerful, melancholy musical score, mostly consisting of a solitary, plaintive guitar, adds to the film's heartbreaking effect.

In a 1990 article in *Journal of American Folklore*, literary critic Leslie Fiedler notes that *The Deer Hunter* is "the reenactment of a fable, a legend as old as America itself: a post-Vietnam version of the myth classically formulated in James Fenimore Cooper's *The Deerslayer* and *Last of the Mohicans*." The myth that is played out in the movie is an ancient one: the transition from innocence to experience. War films, according to John Newsinger in his article in *You Tarzan: Masculinity, Movies and Men*, "are tales of masculinity. They are stories of boys becoming men, of comradeship and loyalty, of bravery and endurance, of pain and suffering, and the horror and the excitement of battle. Violence—the ability both to inflict it and to take it—is portrayed as an essential part of what being a man involves." No film before *The Deer Hunter*, and few since, has so brutally captured war as an initiation rite.

Tim Arnold

SEE ALSO: *Academy Awards;* Apocalypse Now*; De Niro, Robert;* Platoon*; Streep, Meryl; Vietnam; War Movies; Wayne, John.*

BIBLIOGRAPHY

Dittmar, Linda, and Gene Michaud, eds. *From Hanoi to Hollywood: The Vietnam War in American Film.* New Brunswick, NJ: Rutgers University Press, 1990.

Eberwein, Robert T. "Ceremonies of Survival: The Structure of *The Deer Hunter*." *Journal of Popular Film and Television* 7 (1979): 352–364.

Fiedler, Leslie. "Mythicizing the Unspeakable." *Journal of American Folklore* 103 (1990): 390–399.

Hellman, John. *American Myth and the Legacy of Vietnam.* New York: Columbia University Press, 1986.

Newsinger, John. "'Do You Walk the Walk?': Aspects of Masculinity in Some Vietnam War Films." In *You Tarzan: Masculinity, Movies and Men*, eds. Pat Kirkham and Janet Thurmim. New York: St. Martin's Press, 1993.

DeGeneres, Ellen *(1958–)*

Ellen DeGeneres attracted massive media attention when she came out as a lesbian on her sitcom *Ellen* in 1997. Known as "the puppy episode," the program stirred controversy and drew criticism from conservative sectors. DeGeneres and her partner, actress Anne Heche, came out at the same time, with DeGeneres appearing on the covers of national magazines. The caption accompanying her photograph on the cover of *Time* read, "Yep, I'm Gay." Her place in history as TV's first gay lead character secured, she went on to become a prominent and outspoken advocate for lesbian, gay, bisexual, and transgender (LGBT) rights and the host of the Emmy Award–winning television talk show*The Ellen DeGeneres Show* (2003–).

FUNNY FOR A REASON

Born in New Orleans, Louisiana, in 1958, DeGeneres had a sometimes difficult upbringing that inspired her to use humor as a coping device. After her parents' divorce when she was thirteen, she and her mother, Betty, moved to Texas. It was a difficult period, and DeGeneres tapped into comedy to buoy her mother's spirits. "My mother was going through some really hard times and I could see when she was really getting down, and I would start to make fun of her dancing," DeGeneres is quoted as saying in the book *Ellen DeGeneres: A Biography* (2009). "Then she'd start to laugh and I'd make fun of her laughing. And she'd laugh so hard she'd start to cry, and then I'd make fun of that. So I would totally bring her from where I'd seen her start going into depression to all the way out of it."

After graduating from high school in 1976, DeGeneres moved back to New Orleans, where she worked a series of dead-end jobs: house painter, secretary, oyster shucker, sales clerk, waitress, bartender, and vacuum salesperson. At the encouragement of friends, she tried out her comedy on an amateur-hour audience in 1981. Her act went over well, and only a year later she entered and won Showtime's "Funniest Person in America" contest. The title was her springboard to stardom.

One of her better-known stand-up routines, "A Phone Call to God," came from a dark moment of personal despair, when her close friend and roommate was killed in a car accident while out on a date. The girl was only twenty-three, which seemed strikingly unfair to DeGeneres. She wanted to question God about a lot of things that seemed unnecessary, and again she turned to humor. DeGeneres sat down one night and considered what it would be like if she could call God on the phone and ask him about some of the things that troubled her. As if it was meant to be, the monologue poured from her pen to paper, focusing on topics such as fleas and what their purpose might be. DeGeneres performed "A Phone Call to God" on *The Tonight Show Starring Johnny Carson* show six years later, in 1986. Everything clicked that night, and Carson signaled her over to sit on the couch after her performance. She was the only female comedian he ever called to come over and talk to him on a first appearance on *The Tonight Show* (1962–).

DeGeneres continued on the comedy circuit and started acting; one memorable performance was with dancing fruit in Very Fine juice commercials. She eventually landed small roles in several short-lived television series: *Duet* (1987–1989), *Open House* (1989–1990), and *Laurie Hill* (1992). Her feature film debut was in *Coneheads* in 1993.

EARLY SUCCESS AND DISAPPOINTMENT

By 1994 she was starring in a series called *These Friends of Mine* (1994–1998) on ABC. The first season was aided by a prime slot following Tim Allen's *Home Improvement* (1991–1999). The network had such confidence in her that it announced that she would be the ABC spokesperson on radio ads and on-air promos, allowing her to introduce the debut of every show in the fall lineup. She also cohosted the 1994 Emmy Awards.

Despite ABC's fervent backing of DeGeneres, *These Friends of Mine* had a number of problems, not the least of which were less than favorable comparisons to *Seinfeld* (1990–1998) and a number of personnel changes on both sides of the camera. The show's name was changed to *Ellen* for its second season, its concept was revamped, and DeGeneres was given more creative input.

By the third season, however, *Ellen* had failed to find an audience. DeGeneres and her producers decided to announce the character's homosexuality to give the show a new edge, as well as to tell the truth. As DeGeneres told *Time*: "I never wanted to be the lesbian actress. I never wanted to be the spokesperson for the gay community. Ever. I did it for my own truth." After months of hinting around on the show, Ellen came out in an hour-long episode featuring guest stars Laura Dern, Melissa Etheridge, k.d. lang, Demi Moore, Billy Bob Thornton, and Oprah Winfrey. The result was a clamor among conservatives and the religious right; evangelist Jerry Falwell called DeGeneres a "degenerate."

The show won an Emmy for Outstanding Writing for a Comedy Series and a Peabody Award for the coming-out episode. *Entertainment Weekly* named DeGeneres its "Entertainer of the Year" in 1997, and the next year, the Gay and Lesbian Alliance against Defamation (GLAAD) awarded DeGeneres the Stephen F. Kolzak Award for being an openly gay celebrity who had battled homophobia. The show was even praised by Vice President Al Gore for forcing Americans "to look at sexual orientation in a more open light."

The following season, the show continued to focus mainly on gay issues despite declining ratings, and ABC decided not to renew it. Critics noted that the show had become one-dimensional, with Ellen's homosexuality overshadowing all other topics. All the while, however, DeGeneres had been branching out, writing a book, *My Point . . . and I Do Have One* (1995), and releasing an album of stand-up material, *Taste This* (1996). She also had her first leading role in a film, a romantic comedy with actor Bill Pullman titled *Mr. Wrong* (1996). Meanwhile, her TV series was picked up in syndication by the Lifetime channel in 1998.

DeGeneres starred in several films in the late 1990s, including *Goodbye Lover* (1998), *Edtv* (1999), and *The Love Letter* (1999) before returning to television in 2001 with the CBS sitcom *The Ellen Show*. While her character, Ellen Richmond, was also a lesbian who faced obstacles and dilemmas with a quirky humor reminiscent of her counterpart on *Ellen*, *The Ellen Show* failed to capture viewers' attention and was cancelled after just twelve episodes.

FINDING A NICHE

In November 2001 DeGeneres returned as host of the Emmy Awards with a performance that was lauded for its sensitive yet resolute treatment of the 9/11 tragedy. She followed this with perhaps her most successful movie role as the voice of Dory, a lovable, bumbling blue tang fish, in *Finding Nemo* (2003). Although Dory was technically a supporting role, moviegoers and critics alike fell in love with the character, and DeGeneres garnered a number of awards and accolades.

Having gradually reestablished herself, DeGeneres settled into another television niche, this time as the host of an offbeat talk show, *The Ellen DeGeneres Show*, starting in 2003. Lighthearted in tone, the show (often abbreviated as simply *Ellen*) features celebrity and musical acts, comedic bits, and frequent interludes showcasing the dancing abilities of DeGeneres and her guests, most notably presidential hopeful Barack Obama in 2007. *Ellen* has earned numerous Daytime Emmy Awards and is consistently among the highest-rated shows in daytime television.

DeGeneres continues to enjoy a great deal of public attention. She hosted the Emmy Awards again in 2005 and the Oscars in 2007, served as a judge on the popular singing competition *American Idol* for the 2009–2010 season, and wrote books—*The Funny Thing Is . . .* (2003) and *Seriously . . . I'm Kidding* (2011)—that were *New York Times* best sellers. In 2008 she once again made headlines by marrying her girlfriend of four years, actress Portia de Rossi.

Included on *Time* magazine's "100 Most Influential People" and *Forbes*'s "100 Most Powerful Women" lists, DeGeneres has made an undeniable mark on American television as a LGBT pioneer and a champion for bullied and abused people and animals, as well as a tireless supporter of breast cancer awareness efforts. Her influence as both a comedian and a humanitarian has become so widespread that she was named special envoy for global AIDS awareness by Secretary of State Hillary Clinton in 2011.

Emily Pettigrew

SEE ALSO: *Carson, Johnny; Coming Out; Daytime Talk Shows; Emmy Awards; Gay and Lesbian Marriage; Gay Liberation Movement; Lesbianism; Outing; Sitcom; Stand-Up Comedy; Syndication; Television;* The Tonight Show.

BIBLIOGRAPHY

Carter, Bill. "At Lunch with Ellen DeGeneres." *New York Times*, April 13, 1994, C1.

DeGeneres, Betty. *Love, Ellen: A Mother/Daughter Journey*. New York: Rob Weisbach, 1999.

DeGeneres, Ellen. *My Point . . . and I Do Have One*. New York: Bantam, 1995.

Handy, Bruce. "He Called Me Ellen Degenerate?" *Time*, April 14, 1997.

Handy, Bruce. "Roll over, Ward Cleaver." *Time*, April 14, 1997.

Hooper, J. "The Dirty Mind of Ellen DeGeneres." *Esquire*, May 1994, 29.

Ianucci, Lisa. *Ellen DeGeneres: A Biography*. Westport, CT: Greenwood, 2009.

Kronke, David. "True Tales of TV Trauma: 3 Comics Chase Roseanne-dom." *Los Angeles Times*, September 4, 1994.

Tracy, Kathleen, and Jeff Rovin. *Ellen DeGeneres up Close: The Unauthorized Biography of the Hot New Star of ABC's "Ellen."* New York: Pocket Books, 1994.

Tracy, Kathleen. *Ellen: The Real Story of Ellen DeGeneres.* Secaucus, NJ: Carol Publishing Group, 1999.

del Río, Dolores *(1904–1983)*

Acclaimed as the female Rudolph Valentino, Dolores del Río starred in more than fifty full-length motion pictures, including *Flying Down to Rio* (1933), *Journey into Fear* (1943), *Las Abandonadas* (1944), *Doña Perfecta* (1951), and *El Niño y la Niebla* (1953). With her first husband, millionaire Jaime Martínez del Río, she traveled around the world, learned several languages, and settled in Mexico City before moving to Hollywood to pursue careers in the movie industry—she as an actress and he as a screenwriter.

del Río had an intense love life, marrying three times and having affairs with actor Gilbert Roland and actor/director Orson Welles, among others. In 1942, when her career started to decline, she returned to Mexico City. del Río dropped her femme fatale image, and through Gabriel Figueroa's camera and Emilio Fernández's direction she helped create the so-called golden age of Mexican cinema, winning the Ariel (the Mexican equivalent of the Academy Award) three times, in 1946, 1952, and 1954. In her later years she was highly praised for her work with orphans.

Bianca Freire-Medeiros

SEE ALSO: *Valentino, Rudolph; Welles, Orson.*

BIBLIOGRAPHY

Gonsior, Marian C. "Dolores del Rio." In *Latinas! Women of Achievement*, ed. Diane Telgen and Jim Kamp. Detroit, MI: Visible Ink Press, 1996.

Hershfield, Joanne. *The Invention of Dolores del Rio.* Minneapolis: University of Minnesota Press, 2000.

Ramon, David. *Dolores del Rio.* Mexico: Clio, 1997.

Reyes, Aurelio de los. *Dolores del Rio.* Mexico City, Mexico: GrupoCondumex, 1996.

DeMille, Cecil B. *(1881–1959)*

Director Cecil B. DeMille epitomized the film epic and Hollywood's "Golden Age." From the 1910s through the 1950s, he was able to anticipate public taste and gauge America's changing moods. He is best known for his spectacularly ambitious historical and biblical epics, including *The Ten Commandments* (1923 and 1956), *The King of Kings* (1927), *The Sign of the Cross* (1932), *Cleopatra* (1934), *The Crusades* (1935), *Unconquered* (1947), and *The Greatest Show on Earth* (1952), but he also made domestic comedies such as *The Affairs of Anatol* (1921). Originating the over-the-top reputation of Hollywood filmmakers, DeMille is famous for his huge crowd scenes, yet his films also clearly demonstrate his mastery as a storyteller. He avoided camera trickery and developed plots in a traditional manner that film audiences appreciated. In narrative skill and action, DeMille had few competitors.

Cecil Blount DeMille was born in Ashfield, Massachusetts, on August 12, 1881. His father was of Dutch descent and an Episcopalian lay preacher, Columbia professor, and playwright. His mother, Beatrice Samuel, also occasionally wrote plays and ran a girls' school. DeMille attended the Pennsylvania Military Academy from 1896 to 1898 and the American Academy of Dramatic Arts in New York from 1898 to 1900. He made his Broadway acting debut in 1900 and struggled to make a living as an actor for the next decade.

Abandoning his acting career in 1913, DeMille went into partnership with vaudeville musician Jesse L. Lasky and glove salesman Samuel Goldfish (later changed to Goldwyn) to form the motion-picture production company that would eventually become Paramount Studios. It was then that DeMille directed his first film, *The Squaw Man* (1914), shot on location in the Los Angeles area, bringing him to the Southern California locale he would help develop into the enclave of Hollywood. The film's success and popularity established DeMille in the nascent motion-picture industry; he was understood to be the creative force at Paramount, not only directing many films but also overseeing the scripts and shooting of Paramount's entire output.

DeMille capitalized on the same themes throughout his lengthy career. He often used a failing upper-class marriage; an

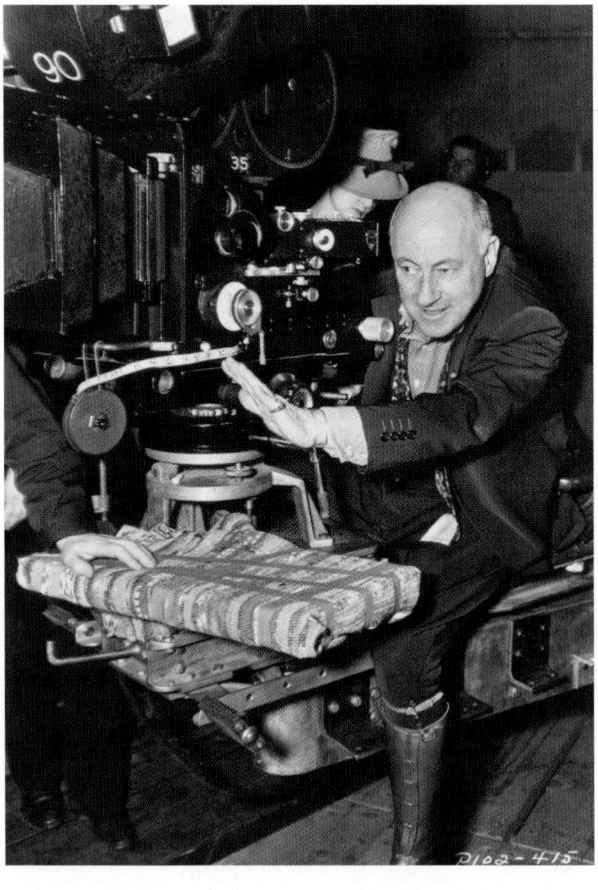

Cecil B. DeMille. *Cecil B. DeMille is known for his work behind the camera on some of the most ambitious epics from Hollywood's "Golden Age," including* The Ten Commandments *and* Cleopatra. © BETTMANN/CORBIS.

exoticized Far East; and obsessive, hypnotic sexual control between men and women. At the same time, he emphasized Christian virtues alongside heathenism and debauchery. He repeatedly mixed Victorian morality with sex and violence. DeMille's popularity can largely be attributed to his dexterity with these seemingly contradictory positions and their appeal to audiences.

Instead of focusing on big-name stars, DeMille tended to develop his own roster of players. With the money he saved, he centered his energies on higher production values and luxurious settings. The players he developed include soprano Geraldine Ferrar in *Carmen* (1915), *Joan the Woman* (1916), *The Woman God Forgot* (1917), and *The Devil Stone* (1917) and Gloria Swanson in *Male and Female* (1919), *Why Change Your Wife?* (1920), *Something to Think About* (1920), and *The Affairs of Anatol.*

DeMille produced and directed seventy films and participated in many more. He cofounded the Screen Directors Guild in 1931, and from 1936 to 1945 he was a producer for Lux Radio Theater of the Air, a position that consisted of adapting famous films and plays to be read by noted actors and actresses. He was awarded the Outstanding Service Award from the War Agencies of the U.S. government, and he also received a Special Oscar for lifetime achievement in 1949. His long list of awards continues with the Irving Thalberg Award from the Academy of Motion Pictures in 1952 and the Milestone Award by the Screen Producers' Guild in 1956.

Liza Black

SEE ALSO: Cleopatra*; Hollywood; Silent Movies;* The Ten Commandments*; Thalberg, Irving G.; Vaudeville.*

BIBLIOGRAPHY

Birchard, Robert S. *Cecil B. DeMille's Hollywood.* Lexington: University Press of Kentucky, 2004.

DeMille, Cecil B. *The Autobiography of Cecil B. DeMille.* Englewood Cliffs, NJ: Prentice-Hall, 1959.

Higashi, Sumiko. *Cecil B. DeMille: A Guide to References and Resources.* Boston: G. K. Hall, 1985.

Higashi, Sumiko. *Cecil B. DeMille and American Culture: The Silent Era.* Berkeley: University of California Press, 1994.

Higham, Charles. *Cecil B. DeMille.* New York: Charles Scribner's Sons, 1973.

Democratic Convention of 1968

SEE: *The Chicago Seven.*

Dempsey, Jack *(1895–1983)*

Boxer Jack Dempsey helped to usher in the "Golden Age of Sports" in the 1920s. Like Babe Ruth in baseball, Red Grange in football, Bill Tilden in tennis, and Bobby Jones in golf, Dempsey was the face of his sport. "In the ring, he was a tiger without mercy who shuffled forward in a bobbing crouch, humming a barely audible tune and punching to the rhythm of the song," wrote Red Smith in the *Washington Post*, adding, "he was 187 pounds of unbridled violence."

Dempsey was also a box-office magnet, attracting the first gates of $1 million and $2 million. He won the world heavyweight boxing title on July 4, 1919, with a third-round knockout of Jesse Willard—who wound up with a broken jaw, two broken ribs, and four teeth missing—and held it until September 23, 1926, when he lost to Gene "The Fighting Marine" Tunney by decision. Of a total of eighty recorded bouts, Dempsey won sixty, lost six, and had eight draws and six no decisions. He knocked out fifty opponents, twenty-five in the first round; his fastest KO came in just fourteen seconds.

William Harrison Dempsey was born in Manassa, Colorado, on June 24, 1895, one of thirteen children in a Mormon family. When Dempsey was fifteen, his brother Bernie (a prizefighter with a glass jaw) started training him. A year later Dempsey got his first serious mining job, earning $3 a day. When he wasn't mining, he was fighting. Nicknamed "Kid Blackie," he had dozens of amateur fights. He would hop freight trains and ride the rails from town to town, announcing his arrival in the nearest gym and boasting that he would take on anyone.

A NEW PERSONA

"Kid Blackie" became "Jack" Dempsey on November 19, 1915, when he beat George Copelin by technical knockout in the seventh round. Dempsey was actually substituting for his brother Bernie, who had been fighting under the name of Jack Dempsey in honor of the great Irish middleweight Jack "Nonpareil" Dempsey. The newly named Jack Dempsey flooded New York sports editors with clippings of his knockouts, though no one noticed him except journalist Damon Runyon, who nicknamed him the "Manassa Mauler."

Late in 1917 Dempsey caught the attention of canny fight manager Jack "Doc" Kearns. Under Kearns, the ballyhoo began: Dempsey fought his way through the top contenders, and within eighteen months he took the heavyweight title from Willard. Dempsey's glory was short-lived, however, for the day after he won the championship, writer Grantland Rice called him a "slacker" in his *New York Tribune* column, referring to his alleged draft evasion. Though a jury found him not guilty of the charge in 1920, it took Dempsey six years to overcome the stigma associated with the label.

Dempsey soon found himself in a peculiarly modern position: he became a sports hero—or antihero—whose image took on extraordinary significance in the climate of publicity and marketing that was coming to dominate big-time sports. Because of his rogue style of fighting and his alleged draft evasion, his title fight against the decorated French combat pilot George Carpentier on July 2, 1921, was hyped as a titanic clash between "good" and "evil." Not only was it the first fight to be broadcast on radio and gross more than $1 million, but it also drew 90,000 people, the largest crowd ever for a sporting event.

Amid a chorus of "Slacker!" jeers, Dempsey dispatched Carpentier in round three and somehow won over the crowd. Dempsey defended his crown several more times, most notably against Luis Angel "The Bull of the Pampas" Firpo. Dempsey sent Firpo to the canvas seven times before Firpo knocked the champ clear out of the ring to close the first round. Dempsey made it back into the ring and ended the fight fifty-seven seconds into the second round with a knockout.

THE TUNNEY FIGHTS

In 1926 Dempsey lost his title by decision to Tunney. The rematch on September 22, 1927, was among the most celebrated fights in boxing history. Chicago's Soldier Field was swollen with the 104,943 fans, resulting in boxing's first $2 million gate. Referee Dave Barry made the terms of the fight clear: "In the event of a knockdown, the man scoring the knockdown will go to the farthest neutral corner. Is that clear, Jack?" Both men nodded.

Tunney outboxed Dempsey in the first six rounds, but in the seventh round, Dempsey unloaded his lethal left hook and sent Tunney to the canvas. Barry shouted, "Get to a neutral corner!" but Dempsey stood still. At the count of three, Dempsey started moving; at five, he was in the neutral corner. In one of the most controversial decisions in boxing history, Barry restarted the count. Tunney got up at "nine," which actually was "fourteen" because of the restart, or four seconds beyond being ruled knocked out. Tunney stayed out of Dempsey's reach for the rest of the round, floored Dempsey briefly in the eighth, and won a ten-round decision.

The bout, immortalized as "the Battle of the Long Count," is described in an HBO documentary as "purely and simply the greatest fistic box-office attraction of all time." Although Dempsey lost, the fight allowed him to reinvent himself, according to Steven Farhood, editor-in-chief of *The Ring* magazine: "He was viewed as a villain, not a hero, but after losing to Tunney, he was a hero and he remained such until his death."

Dempsey retired after the second Tunney bout, although he still boxed exhibitions. A large amount of the $3 million he earned over his career was lost in the Wall Street Crash of 1929, but Dempsey was a shrewd businessman who had invested well in real estate. In 1936 he opened Jack Dempsey's Restaurant in New York City. During World War II he served as a physical education instructor in the coast guard, thus wiping his alleged "slacker" slate clean. Dempsey—whom Farhood calls "the first universally accepted American sports superstar"—died in New York City on May 31, 1983, at the age of eighty-seven.

Rob van Kranenburg

SEE ALSO: *Boxing; Rice, Grantland; Runyon, Damon; Sports Heroes; World War I; World War II.*

BIBLIOGRAPHY

Dempsey, Jack, and Barbara Piattelli Dempsey. *Dempsey.* New York: Harper & Row, 1977.

Evensen, Bruce J. *When Dempsey Fought Tunney: Heroes, Hokum, and Storytelling in the Jazz Age.* Knoxville: University of Tennessee Press, 1996.

Roberts, Randy. *Jack Dempsey: The Manassa Mauler.* Baton Rouge: Louisiana State University Press, 1979.

Smith, Toby. *Kid Blackie: Jack Dempsey's Colorado Days.* Ouray, CO: Wayfinder Press, 1987.

Denishawn

In 1915 dancers Ruth St. Denis and Ted Shawn founded a pioneering company and training school in Los Angeles that became known as Denishawn. The training they provided for their students—who also served as company members—was highly disciplined and extremely diverse in its cultural and stylistic range. Denishawn toured worldwide and was the first dance company to tour extensively in America, bringing the concept of serious dance and an appreciation of unknown cultures to American audiences.

Denishawn students Martha Graham, Doris Humphrey, and Charles Weidman went on to become legendary dancer-choreographers. Musical director Louis Horst led the way in the composition of music for dance, while Pauline Lawrence became a legendary accompanist, costume designer, and dance administrator. These students instructed and inspired succeeding generations, and in this way the "family tree" of Denishawn influenced virtually every American dancer and choreographer in the twentieth century.

Brian Granger

SEE ALSO: *Graham, Martha; Modern Dance; Shawn, Ted; St. Denis, Ruth.*

BIBLIOGRAPHY

Harbin, Billy J.; Kim Marra; and Robert A. Schanke. *The Gay and Lesbian Theatrical Legacy: A Biographical Dictionary of Major Figures in American Stage History in the Pre-Stonewall Era.* Ann Arbor: University of Michigan, 2005.

Sherman, Jane. *The Drama of Denishawn Dance.* Middletown, CT: Wesleyan University Press, 1979.

Sherman, Jane. *Denishawn: The Enduring Influence.* Boston, MA: Twayne Publishers, 1983.

Denver, John *(1943–1997)*

Singer, songwriter, and activist John Denver was a large part of 1970s music. At a time when the simplicity of rock and roll was fading to be replaced with the cynicism of punk rock, Denver carved out his own niche and became the voice of the recently disenfranchised folksinger idealist who believed in love and hope and fresh air. With his flyaway blond hair and signature granny glasses, Denver had a cross-generational appeal, presenting a nonthreatening, earnest message of gentle social protest.

John Denver was born Henry John Deutschendorf Jr. on December 31, 1943, in Roswell, New Mexico. His entire life was shaped by trying to measure up to his father, who was a flight instructor for the air force. In his autobiography, *Take Me Home, Country Roads*, Denver describes his life as the eldest son in a family shaped by a stern father, who could never show his love for his children. It was Denver's mother's family who imbued Denver with a love of music. His maternal grandmother gave him his first guitar when he was a young boy.

Because Denver's father was in the military, the family moved often, making it hard for Denver to make friends and fit in with kids his own age. Constantly being the new kid was agony for the introverted youngster, and he grew up always feeling as if he should be somewhere else but never knowing where that "right" place was. When the family was living in Montgomery, Alabama, Denver finally discovered that music was a way to make friends. When he sang and played his guitar, others paid attention to him.

Denver attended high school in Fort Worth, Texas. He still had a tough time making friends, and when he was a junior, he took his father's car and ran away to California to visit family friends and pursue a musical career. His father flew to California to retrieve him, and he finished high school.

After high school, Denver enrolled in Texas Tech and studied architecture, but he dropped out in his third year to pursue a music career. He managed to get a job at Ledbetter's, a nightclub that was a mecca for folksingers, as an opening act for the Backporch Majority. Denver found himself in the ideal spot for an aspiring young singer, because he was living and working with more established artists who taught the idealistic young entertainer how to survive in his new world.

Denver's big break came when he met Milt Okun, who represented the folk group Peter, Paul, and Mary. Okun was looking for a replacement singer for another group, the Chad Mitchell Trio, and Denver perfectly fit the requirements. Although the group disbanded not long after Denver joined, his experience with them taught him much about the world of professional musicians.

In 1967, while in a Washington airport on a layover, Denver wrote "Oh, Babe, I Hate to Go," the title of which was later changed to "Leaving on a Jet Plane." Both the Mitchell Trio and Spanky and Our Gang recorded the song, but it was Peter, Paul, and Mary who turned it into a number-one hit in 1969. After being turned down by sixteen record companies, Okun negotiated a recording contract for Denver with RCA Records.

MARRIAGE AND PROFESSIONAL SUCCESS

In 1966 Denver met Annie Martell while touring, and they were married in June 1967. In 1970 the couple moved to Aspen, Colorado. They could not afford to build a house on the land they bought, so they rented and saved. Unable to have children, the couple adopted Zachery and Anna Kate. The marriage later ended in a bitter divorce. A subsequent marriage produced a daughter, Jessica Bell, but it also ended unhappily.

Denver admits in his autobiography that he had less trouble talking to large groups of people than to those he loved. This ability that caused him so much damage in his personal life gave him an uncanny ability to connect with an audience, and it set his music apart. His purpose was always greater than simple entertainment. He clothed his messages in everyday scenes to which everyone could relate, whether it was the airport of "Leaving on a Jet Plane," or the forests of "Annie's Song," or the country roads of "Take Me Home, Country Roads." People related to Denver as if he were a friend who shared their personal history. His messages behind the simple pleasures of life were always to protect the world that provides so much beauty and to enjoy life to the fullest every day because life is a gift.

Denver's success would have been impressive at any time, but it was particularly impressive in the changing environment of the 1970s music scene. He had thirteen top hits with the American Society of Composers, Authors, and Publishers (ASCAP), nine platinum albums, one platinum single ("Take Me Home, Country Roads"), thirteen gold albums, and six gold singles. He also had gold records in Canada, Australia, and Germany. In 1975 he was named the Country Music Association's (CMA) Entertainer of the Year and "Take Me Home, Country Roads" won Best Song of the Year. He won a People's Choice Award and the Carl Sandburg's People's Poet Award. He was also named the Poet Laureate of Colorado. He made twenty-one television specials, and he starred in the movies *Oh, God* and *Walking Thunder*. Denver had come a long way from the young boy who could not make any friends.

ACTIVISM AND A TRAGIC DEATH

In the early 1970s Denver also became an activist for the causes he loved, including campaigning against nuclear arms and nuclear energy. In 1976, when he was the country's biggest recording star, Denver established the Windstar Foundation on 1,000 acres in Snowmass, Colorado, to fight world hunger. He was deeply hurt when he was not among the many artists invited to sing in the noted song "We Are the World," which was dedicated to that same cause. Denver was also the moving force behind Plant-It 2000 (later renamed Plant-It 2020), a group that promoted the planting of as many trees as possible by the year 2000. Denver made his first trip to Africa when he was appointed to President Jimmy Carter's Commission on World Hunger. Upon his first visit to Alaska, Denver was captivated by its beauty and worked hard for its preservation. He became the first American musician to perform in the Soviet Union and mainland China and even collaborated with Russian musicians on a project. He often said that he considered himself a "global citizen," because he believed so strongly in an interconnected world.

After the 1970s, Denver's career declined in the United States, but he continued to be a strong presence in the international music scene. With his Wildlife Concert in 1995, he began to reclaim his domestic audience. It was plain to see that he had matured. The glasses were gone, as was the innocence. His hair was shorter and neater. His face was lined and often sad. Yet, his voice was stronger, more sure and arresting. He was still John Denver, and he still knew how to connect with an audience. Denver followed the success of the Wildlife Concert with the hit album, *Best of John Denver* in 1997. Tragically, his comeback was cut short on October 12, 1997, when he crashed his experimental aircraft into Monterey Bay in Monterey, California.

Elizabeth Purdy

SEE ALSO: *Country Music; Folk Music; Peter, Paul, and Mary; Sandburg, Carl.*

BIBLIOGRAPHY

Denver, John, and Arthur Tobier. *Take Me Home: An Autobiography*. New York: Harmony Books, 1994.

Flippo, Chet. "Artist, Activist Denver Lost to Crash." *Billboard*, October 25, 1997, 1.

"John Denver—Poet for the Planet." *Earth Island Journal*, Winter 1997–98, 43.

Kemp, Mark. "Country-Pop Star Dies in Plane Crash." *Rolling Stone*, November 27, 1997, 24.

Department Stores

With the creation of the first department stores at the end of the nineteenth century came the inception of that most American of diversions: shopping. Though people had always purchased necessities, it was the development of the emporium that turned the perusal of a wide variety of goods—the necessary and the frivolous, the affordable and the completely out of reach—into a leisure pastime. Between the late 1800s and the 1970s department stores continued to grow and evolve into a quintessential modern marketplace that was both elite and accessible. Huge department stores, named for the families who founded them, dominated urban centers, and store and city became identified with each other. Filene's of Boston, Macy's and Bloomingdale's of New York, Marshall Field of Chicago, and Rich's of Atlanta are only a few of the stores recognized nationwide as belonging to their cities. The era of the department store is rapidly fading, and those stores are being replaced by consumer choices that are more consistent with modern economics, just as the department stores themselves once replaced their predecessors.

A NEW WAY TO SHOP

As the nineteenth century drew to a close, citizens began to enjoy the benefits of a new cash economy. Improved postal service and a new nationwide rail network allowed for an unprecedented flow of goods. Previously, consumers had been dependent on traveling peddlers, who carried such stock as sewing needles, thread, and fabrics from town to town in bulky packs on their backs or in horse-drawn carts. The peddlers who grew more prosperous eventually began to settle in small storefronts. As economic times improved with the modernizations of the late 1800s, savvy shopkeepers began to expand, offering not only a wider variety of goods but also an air of refinement and personal service that had previously been available only to the very rich.

Macy's Department Store in New York. *Macy's department store dominates 34th Street in New York City in the 1930s.* FPG/GETTY IMAGES.

An example of this was Marble Dry Goods, opened by A. T. Stewart in Manhattan in 1846. Stewart set up posh parlors for his female customers. These included attentive sales clerks and the first Parisian-style full-length mirrors in the United States. Thus, department stores drew all classes of customers by making them feel as if they were part of society's elite while shopping there.

Owners of the new department stores were able to undercut the prices of their competitors in the specialty shops by going directly to the manufacturers to purchase goods, bypassing the wholesalers' markup. Some even manufactured their own products. Where once stores had been slow, sedate places where goods had to be requested from behind the counter, the lively new department store displayed products prominently within reach and encouraged browsing. To keep customers from leaving, stores expanded to sell anything they could possibly need. Smaller stores responded with outraged protests that the larger stores were employing unfair practices and running them out of business, but they had little success in slowing the growth of the giant emporiums.

As the cities grew, so did the stores, becoming multifloor edifices that were the primary generators of retail traffic in newly burgeoning downtown areas. Women, who were enjoying some new rights due to the wave of feminism in the late 1800s and early 1900s, began to have more control over the shopping dollar. By 1915 women did 90 percent of consumer spending in the United States, and the department stores catered to women and began to hire them to work as sales clerks. Stores competed with each other to have the most refined atmosphere, the cheapest bargain basement, the most fashionable tea room, the fastest delivery, and above all the most attentive service.

In 1911 Sears and Roebuck offered credit to its customers for large mail order purchases, and by the 1920s the practice had spread to most of the large department stores. Customers carried an imprinted metal "charge plate" particular to each store. Because they were the only form of credit available at the time, department store charge accounts inspired loyalty and increased their store's customer base.

ALL IN ONE PLACE

In 1946 writer Julian Clare described Canada's famous department store, Eaton's, in *Maclean's* magazine: "You can have a meal or send a telegram; get your shoes half-soled or buy a canoe. You can have your other suit dry cleaned and plan for a wedding right down to such details as a woman at the church to fix the bride's train. You can look up addresses in any Canadian city. You can buy stamps or have your picture taken."

Department stores also developed distinctive departments, with features designed to attract trade. Filene's in Boston made the bargain basement famous, with drastically reduced prices on premium goods piled on tables, where economically minded customers fought, sometimes physically, over the merchandise and even undressed on the floor to try on contested items. Department store toy departments competed to offer elaborate displays to entertain children, who were often sent there to wait for parents busy shopping. Marshall Field's toy department introduced the famous Kukla, Fran, and Ollie puppet act to the

Chicago public before the act found its way onto television screens, while Bullocks in Los Angeles had a long wooden slide from the toy department to the hair salon on the floor below, where children might find their mothers. Department store window displays were also highly competitive, fabulous artistic tableaux that drew "window shoppers" just to admire them.

Department stores even had an effect on the nation's calendar. Ohio department store magnate Fred Lazarus convinced President Franklin Roosevelt to fix Thanksgiving on the fourth Thursday of November rather than the last Thursday, which had been traditional. The extra week of Christmas shopping afforded by the switch benefited the department stores and, Lazarus assured the president, the nation. John Wanamaker of the famous Philadelphia store created Mother's Day, turning a little-known Catholic religious holiday into another national day of spending. Christmas itself became strongly identified with the stores as thousands of department store Santas were photographed holding future customers on their laps.

OUT WITH THE OLD

In the 1950s middle-class families began to abandon the cities for the suburbs. More and more, only less affluent people were left in the urban centers, and as a result the great flagship downtown department stores began to lose money. Suburban shopping malls proliferated, and most department stores opened branches there. For more than twenty years it was considered necessary to have a large department store as an "anchor" for a mall, and customers continued to patronize the department stores as their main retail sources.

Beginning in 1973, however, the oil crisis, inflation, and other economic problems began to cause a slowing of growth in the department stores. The arrival of bank credit cards such as Visa and MasterCard put an end to customer dependence on department store credit. Discount stores—large stores that offered a wide inventory like that of the department stores but without the grand style and attentive service—often had lower prices. In an economy more and more focused on lower prices and fewer amenities, department stores waned and discount stores grew.

Gradually, many of the once-famous department stores went out of business. Gimbels', B. Altman's, and Ohrbach's in New York; Garfinckel's in Washington, D.C.; Frederick and Nelson's in Seattle, Washington; and Hutzler's in Baltimore, Maryland, are just a few of the venerable emporiums that closed their doors or limited their operations. They were replaced, first by discount stores, specialty chains, mail-order businesses, and cable television shopping channels such as QVC and later by the ever-expanding sphere of online retailers.

Huge discount chains such as Wal-Mart inspire the same protests that the department stores drew from their competition at the early part of the twentieth century: they are too big and too cheap, and they run the competition out of business, including the department stores. Chains of specialty shops fill the malls, having national name recognition and offering customers the same illusion of being part of the elite that the department stores once did. Mail-order houses flood potential customers with catalogs and advertisements—more than fourteen billion pieces a year—and QVC reached $5 billion in sales within five years of its inception, a goal department stores took decades to achieve. In the first decade of the 2000s online shopping accounted for a growing percentage of world market share and more than $140 billion in U.S. sales alone.

Besides bringing together an enormous inventory under one roof and customers from a wide range of classes to shop together, department stores helped define the city centers where they were placed. The failure of the department stores and the rise of the suburban shopping mall and superstore likewise defined the trends of late twentieth century society away from the city and into the suburb. Though acknowledgment of class difference is far less overt than it was at the dawn of the age of department stores, actual class segregation is much greater. As the cities were increasingly relegated to the poor, except for those who commuted there to work during the day, public transportation (except for commuter rush hours) and other public services also decreased in the city centers through the 1980s. Big stores that invited everyone to shop together were replaced by rundown markets selling necessities to the poor at inflated prices and specialty shops that catered to middle-class workers on their lunch hour. There are few poor people in the suburbs, where car ownership is a must and house ownership a given. There, too, shopping was more segregated, with the working and lower middle class shopping at discount houses and the upper middle class and wealthy frequenting smaller, service-oriented specialty stores. This trend continued as more well-to-do Americans returned to urban areas in the twenty-first century, bringing with them the process of gentrification.

In many ways the department store is a uniquely nineteenth-century artifact. Many characteristics and amenities of the original stores were put in place because shopping itself was still a novel and luxurious activity. In the twenty-first century low prices and convenience are the primary motives guiding shoppers. As a result department store brands have had to adapt to consumers' changing demands. Among the roughly dozen department stores with a consistent economic presence in the twenty-first century are Macy's, Saks Fifth Avenue, Nordstrom, and Dillard's. Nearly all of these companies have franchised their brand name for smaller satellite stores in malls across the United States and maintained their own catalogs, but most importantly these companies have increased their online presence through efficient and comprehensive retail websites. The physical appearance of the remaining department stores has been altered drastically over their 150-year lifespan. By staying attuned to consumers' priorities and desired shopping experiences, these companies have stayed competitive in a rapidly changing market.

Tina Gianoulis

SEE ALSO: *Amazon.com; Christmas; Consumerism; Credit Cards; eBay; Home Shopping Network/QVC; The Internet; Kmart;* Kukla, Fran, and Ollie*; Leisure Time; Macy's; Mall of America; Malls; Mother's Day; Online Shopping; Saks Fifth Avenue; Sears Roebuck Catalog; Thanksgiving; Wal-Mart.*

BIBLIOGRAPHY

Benson, Susan Porter. *Counter Cultures: Saleswomen, Managers, and Customers in American Department Stores, 1890–1940.* Urbana: University of Illinois Press, 1986.

Cohen, Daniel. "Grand Emporiums Peddle Their Wares in a New Market." *Smithsonian,* March 1993, 22.

Harris, Leon A. *Merchant Princes: An Intimate History of Jewish Families Who Built Great Department Stores.* New York: Kodansha International, 1994.

Leach, William. *Land of Desire: Merchants, Power, and the New American Culture.* New York: Vintage Books, 1994.

Schwartz, Joe. "Will Baby Boomers Dump Department Stores?" *American Demographics*, December 1990, 42.

Soucek, Gayle. *Marshall Field's: The Store That Helped Build Chicago*. Charleston, SC: History Press, 2010.

Whitaker, Jan. *Service and Style: How the American Department Store Fashioned the Middle Class*. New York: St. Martin's Press, 2006.

Whitaker, Jan. *The World of Department Stores*. New York: Vendome Press, 2011.

Depp, Johnny *(1963–)*

Johnny Depp is one of America's most gifted and charismatic actors. Known as an idiosyncratic and uncompromising performer, he achieved prominence by refusing to conform to expectations, often choosing roles in offbeat and independent films that showcased his ability to inhabit a wide range of characters rather than his matinee-idol looks. Worshipped as show-business royalty, Depp was honored in 1999 with a star on Hollywood's Walk of Fame and consistently appears on lists of the world's "most beautiful" people. But Depp stands in a class all of his own as an icon of bohemian chic, the epitome of cool.

Depp rose to superstardom as the swaggering, staggering, swashbuckling Captain Jack Sparrow of *Pirates of the Caribbean: The Curse of the Black Pearl* (2003) by characteristically refusing to play the role in the manner studio executives envisioned it, an artistic decision that earned him his first Academy Award nomination and made Depp such a huge box-office draw that Disney starred him in three sequels to the film. According to Depp, he modeled Jack Sparrow after Rolling Stones guitarist Keith Richards. Depp told Patti Smith in a 2011 *Vanity Fair* interview that his campy version of the character frightened Disney executives who saw the dailies: "They couldn't stand him . . . and me getting phone calls direct from, you know, upper-echelon Disney-ites, going, 'What's wrong with him? Is he, you know, like some kind of weird simpleton? Is he drunk? By the way, is he gay?'"

Depp had earlier encountered a similarly alarmed reaction from producer Stephen J. Cannell, who cast Depp in his breakout role as Detective Tom Hanson on the fledgling Fox television network's high school drama *21 Jump Street*. Depp balked at playing the role squeaky clean, instead adding a dark and rebellious quality to Hanson that immediately won over young viewers. Depp's role on *21 Jump Street* turned him into a teen idol overnight. He detested all the publicity and feared he would be forever labeled a teenage heartthrob. He was therefore relieved when Cannell let him out of his contract after four seasons. In the meantime, hoping to reverse his pretty-boy image, Depp had jumped at the chance to appear as the titular juvenile delinquent in director John Waters's send-up of 1950s teen movies, *Cry-Baby* (1990). Ever since, Depp has continued to make risky choices, most of which have paid off critically, if not always commercially.

Born in 1963 in Owensboro, Kentucky, Depp was raised in Miramar, Florida, where he dropped out of high school at the age of sixteen hoping to become a rock star. He enjoyed some success as lead guitarist of a series of garage bands, including one called the Kids that opened for such big-name acts as the B-52s and Iggy Pop. But when the Kids moved to Los Angeles, the band faltered amid the stiffer competition there. By 1985 Depp's marriage to Lori Anne Allison, the sister of his bass player, had also dissolved. Through Allison, Depp had become acquainted with actor Nicolas Cage, who encouraged him to audition for a part in what was to be Depp's first movie, Wes Craven's *A Nightmare on Elm Street* (1984). Depp was cast in a small but memorable role in the horror hit as a doomed teen swallowed by his bed.

UNUSUAL ROLES

Cast as a Vietnamese interpreter in Oliver Stone's blockbuster *Platoon* (1986), Depp was highly disappointed that most of his scenes were left on the cutting-room floor. Following *Cry-Baby*, he took another role as a quirky outsider, playing a rubber-suited freak with deadly blades for hands in *Edward Scissorhands* (1990), thereby initiating a collaboration with director Tim Burton that would result in several more pictures: *Ed Wood* (1994), *Sleepy Hollow* (1999), *Charlie and the Chocolate Factory* (2005), *Corpse Bride* (2005), *Sweeney Todd* (2007), and *Alice in Wonderland* (2010). Depp received his third Academy Award nomination for his singing part in the musical *Sweeney Todd*, having received his second nomination for his portrayal of Scottish author J. M. Barrie in *Finding Neverland* (2004).

Burton's films have required Depp to wear elaborate, sometimes macabre, makeup and costumes. Such is the case with his portrayal of Barnabas Collins, the vampire in Burton's remake of the 1960s television series *Dark Shadows* (2012). But Depp has also proven himself in mainstream dramatic roles, none of which, however, he has interpreted in conventional leading-man fashion. These include the bank robber John Dillinger in *Public Enemies* (2009); cocaine kingpin George Jung in *Blow* (2001); and the titular undercover FBI agent in *Donnie Brasco* (1997), which is widely considered Depp's finest performance to date.

Depp counts among his mentors actor Marlon Brando, with whom he is frequently compared, and gonzo journalist Hunter S. Thompson. The first association resulted in the Depp-Brando vehicles *Don Juan de Marco* (1995), a romantic comedy, and *The Brave* (1997), which exploited Depp's Cherokee heritage by putting him in the role of a Native American man who sells himself to a snuff film director. The second association resulted in Depp's portrayal of the famously hard-drinking and hard-drugging Thompson in *Fear and Loathing in Las Vegas* (1998) and *The Rum Diary* (2011).

Always shy and modest, Depp was coaxed out of his shell by the spectacular success of the *Pirates* franchise, the fourth-highest-grossing film series of all time, according to figures calculated at the end of 2011. As part of the expansive merchandising for the franchise, he agreed to voice Sparrow in a video game adaptation. Though Depp prefers to keep the focus on his work in television and print interviews, the media is fascinated by his personal life, including past romances with actress Winona Ryder and model Kate Moss. Depp has had a long-term relationship with French singer and actress Vanessa Paradis—the mother of his two children—and the family divides its time between homes in Los Angeles and Plan-de-la-Tour, France, as well as its own private island in the Bahamas.

Janet Mullane

SEE ALSO: *Academy Awards; Blockbusters; Brando, Marlon; Celebrity;* Dark Shadows; *Dillinger, John; Disney (Walt Disney*

Company); Hollywood; Moss, Kate; Pirates of the Caribbean*;* Platoon*; Pop, Iggy; The Rolling Stones; Ryder, Winona; Stone, Oliver; Teen Idols; Thompson, Hunter S.; Waters, John; Wood, Ed.*

BIBLIOGRAPHY

De Baecque, Antoine. "The Actor as Iconoclast: An Interview with Johnny Depp." *Cineaste*, Spring 2012, 30.

Goodall, Nigel. *The Secret World of Johnny Depp: The Intimate Biography of Hollywood's Best-Loved Rebel.* London: Blake, 2006.

Smith, Patti. "The Crowded Mind of Johnny Depp." *Vanity Fair*, January 2011, 48.

Depression

One of the most common modern emotional complaints, depression is sometimes referred to as "the common cold of psychiatric illness." In its everyday usage, the word *depression* describes a feeling of sadness and hopelessness that may or may not have an external cause and usually lasts for weeks or months. Sometimes the word is used casually ("That movie made me depressed") and sometimes it is far more serious ("After I was fired, I was depressed for six months"). Though depression has been recognized as an ailment for hundreds of years, the number of people experiencing its symptoms has been steadily rising since the beginning of the twentieth century. Association with health conditions such as diabetes, coronary disease, stroke, and cancer has increased focus on the illness. Celebrities who have suffered from postpartum depression (PPD) have helped to focus national attention on the condition, which may accompany declining hormone levels and other changes that follow childbirth. Brooke Shields, for example, entered into a high-profile feud with Tom Cruise when he criticized her use of antidepressant medicine to treat PPD, bringing the issue of PPD into the public spotlight and initiating widespread debate over the efficacy of psychotropic drugs.

DEFINITION AND CAUSES

The cause of depression is a controversial topic. Current psychiatric thinking treats depression as an organic disease caused by chemical imbalance in the brain. However, many social analysts argue that the roots of depression can be found in psychosocial stress. They blame the increasing incidence of depression on an industrial and technological society that is isolating and alienating and on the breakdown of community support systems and extended families. Though some depression seems to descend with no explanation, it more often is triggered by trauma, stress, or a major loss, such as of a relationship, job, or home. Many famous artists, writers, composers, and historical figures have reportedly suffered from depressive disorders, and images and descriptions of depression abound in literature and art.

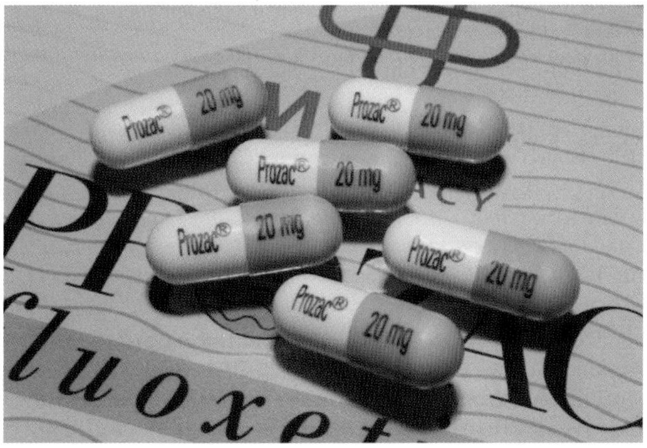

Prozac. *Prozac is one of many medications prescribed by doctors to treat depression.* MEDIPICS/ALAMY.

In its clinical usage, *depression* refers to several distinct but related mental conditions that psychiatrists and psychologists classify as mood disorders. Although the stresses of modern life may leave many individuals with feelings of sadness and hopelessness, psychiatrists and psychologists make careful distinctions between episodes of feeling blue and clinical depression. According to the *Diagnostic and Statistical Manual of Mental Disorders* (*DSM-IV*), an episode of depression is not a disorder in itself but a building block that clinicians use in making a diagnosis. For example, psychiatrists might diagnose a person suffering from a depressive episode with substance-induced depression, a general medical condition, major depression, chronic mild depression (dysthymia), or bipolar disorder (formerly called manic depression). Major depression is diagnosed if a client experiences at least five of the following symptoms for at least two weeks: feeling sad, diminished interest and pleasure in sex and other formerly enjoyable activities, significant changes in appetite and weight, sleep disturbances, agitation or lethargy, fatigue, feelings of worthlessness and guilt, difficulty concentrating, and thoughts of death and/or suicide.

Bipolar disorder has received the most publicity of any type of depression. The theatrical juxtaposition of flamboyant mania and incapacitating depression has captured the public imagination and has been the inspiration for colorful characters in print and film, from fictional detective Sherlock Holmes to *Breakfast at Tiffany's* protagonist Holly Golightly. Clinicians diagnose a bipolar disorder when an individual experiences a manic episode, whether or not there is a history of depression. The *DSM-IV* defines a manic episode as "a distinct period of abnormally and persistently elevated, expansive or irritable mood that lasts at least 1 week" and is characterized by inflated self-esteem or grandiosity, decreased need for sleep, excessive speech, racing thoughts, distractibility, increased goal-directed activity and/or agitation, and excessive pleasure-seeking and risk-taking behaviors (the perfect personality for a dramatic hero). Bipolar disorders are categorized according to the type and severity of manic episodes and the pattern of alteration between mania and depression.

PREVALENCE AND GROUPS AFFECTED

Although people of all ages and backgrounds are diagnosed with major depression, age and culture can affect the way they experience and express their symptoms. Children who suffer from depression often display physical complaints, irritability, and social withdrawal rather than sadness, a depressed mood, or tearfulness. Although they may not complain of problems concentrating, such difficulties may be inferred from their school performance. Depressed children may not lose weight but may fail to make expected weight gains. They also are more likely to exhibit mental and physical agitation than to show lethargy.

Members of different ethnic groups may describe their depressions differently. Complaints of nerves or headaches are common in Latino and Mediterranean cultures. Individuals in many cultures outside North America or Western Europe manifest depression with physical rather than emotional symptoms. Complaints of weakness, tiredness, or imbalance are prevalent among East Asians, whereas Middle Easterners often express problems of the heart. However, certain commonalities prevail: a fundamental change in mood and lack of enjoyment of life.

Studies have shown that depression is often more prevalent in wealthier countries than in middle- or low-income countries. Some explain this trend by saying depression is a disease of the rich. Others state that wealthy countries have large income gaps, giving rise to higher rates of depression. Women from all cultures are much more likely than men to experience depression. *DSM-IV* reports that women have a 10 to 25 percent lifetime risk for major depression, whereas men's lifetime risk is 5 to 12 percent. Some theorists argue that this difference may represent a biological propensity for depressive disorders. Others argue that depression is a result of gender differences in help-seeking behaviors or clinicians' biases in diagnosis.

Feminists have long linked women's depression to social causes. Poverty, violence against women, and lifelong discrimination, they contend, offer ample triggers for depression; moreover, women are socialized to internalize the pain of difficult situations. Whereas men are taught to outwardly express their anger and are more likely to be diagnosed with antisocial personality disorder, women are far more likely to entertain feelings of guilt and thoughts of suicide.

HISTORICAL VIEWS

For centuries, doctors have tried to treat those who suffer from depression. Aaron Beck, author of *Depression: Causes and Treatment*, credits Hippocrates in the fourth century BCE with the first clinical description of melancholia. Beck also notes that Aretaeus and Plutarch—both physicians in the second century CE—described conditions that would today be called bipolar disorders.

Beginning in antiquity, melancholia was attributed to the influence of the planet Saturn. Until the end of the seventeenth century, depression was believed to be caused by an accumulation of black bile, resulting in an imbalance in the four fluid components of the body. Thus, doctors used purgatives and bloodletting to treat depression.

Despite changes in the nomenclature and the attribution of causes for melancholia, contemporary psychiatric criteria for major depression and bipolar disorder are strikingly consistent with the ancient accounts of the condition. In the nineteenth century, such clinicians as Philippe Pinel, Jean-Martin Charcot, and Sigmund Freud described melancholia similarly. In his essay "Mourning and Melancholia," written in the 1920s, Freud distinguishes melancholia from mourning—the suffering engendered by the loss of a loved one. In melancholia, Freud argues, the sufferer perceives a loss of part of the self—a narcissistic injury that results in heightened self-criticism, self-reproach, and guilt; withdrawal from the world; and an inability to find comfort or pleasure.

Freud's psychoanalytic interpretation of melancholia reflected a shift from away from biological explanations. In the early twentieth century, clinicians ascribed primarily psychological causes—such as unresolved mourning, inadequate parenting, or other losses—to the development of depression. To seek out and resolve these causes, they prescribed psychotherapy. In the 1960s and 1970s radical therapy movements, along with feminism and other social movements, began to question many psychiatrists and psychologists' personal interpretation of depression. These activists began to look to society as the cause of and cure for depression, dismissing therapy as a misguided way of teaching patients to cope with unacceptable societal situations.

In the twenty-first century, clinicians incorporate the biological and psychological in their understanding of depressive disorders. Most consider psychological causes to be significant in triggering the onset of depressive episodes. Nevertheless, research has indicated that genetics play a significant role in propensity toward clinical depression. Whatever the cause, the consequences can be deadly: Up to 15 percent of individuals with severe depression commit suicide, and many more are at risk for substance abuse and other self-destructive behavior.

TREATMENT

Although many clinicians treat depression with talk therapy, scientists have continued to search for a medical cure. In the 1930s Italian psychiatrists Ugo Cerletti and Lucio Bini began to experiment with electricity to treat their patients. Electroconvulsive shock therapy (ECT) became a standard treatment for schizophrenia and depression. However, it lost favor in the 1960s when many doctors and antipsychiatry activists lobbied against its use, finding it as barbaric and dangerous as leeches.

Shock therapy became known as a painful and frightening experience, which medical staff sometimes used as a punishment for recalcitrant patients. Public feeling against it was aroused in response to books such as writer Ken Kesey's *One Flew over the Cuckoo's Nest* in 1963, actress Frances Farmer's 1972 autobiography *Will There Really Be a Morning?*, and author Janet Frame's *An Angel at My Table* in 1984. Perhaps as a testimony to the inherent drama of depression and its treatment by ECT, each of these books was made into a film: *One Flew over the Cuckoo's Nest* (1975), *Frances* (1982), and *An Angel at My Table* (1990). The 2001 film *A Beautiful Mind* focused on the famous mathematician John Nash, who was also treated with ECT for schizophrenia.

ECT made a comeback in the 1990s, when proponents claimed that improved techniques made it a safe, effective therapy for the severely depressed. However, the side effects remained, such as loss of memory and other brain functions. In 1999 Italy, the birthplace of ECT, severely restricted its use.

Many medications have been developed in the fight against depression. The tricyclics—imipramine, desipramine, amitriptyline, nortriptyline, and doxepin—have been found to be effective in controlling classic, melancholic depression. However, tricyclics also are known for triggering side effects associated with the flight-or-fight response, such as rapid heart rate, sweating, dry mouth, constipation, and urinary retention.

Another class of antidepressant medication, monoamine oxidase inhibitors (MAOIs), has been shown to be more effective in alleviating nonclassical symptoms of depression. MAOIs—phenelzine, isocarboxazid, nialamide, and tranylcypromine—are more specific than tricyclics in their action. However, they are also more problematic due to their potentially fatal interactions with other drugs, such as alcohol, tricyclics, and anesthetics, and foods containing tyramine.

The most dramatic and widely publicized development in depression drugs has been the debut of selective serotonin reuptake inhibitors (SSRIs). SSRIs increase brain levels of serotonin, a neurotransmitter linked to mood. These medications, such as Prozac, Paxil, and Zoloft, are highly effective for many people in alleviating the symptoms of major depression. In addition, they have been surprisingly successful in lifting chronic depression. SSRIs are touted as having far fewer adverse effects than other drugs used to treat depression, which has contributed to their enormous popularity. However, they have serious side effects, which include reduced sexual drive or difficulty in having orgasms, panic attacks, aggressive behavior, and potentially dangerous allergic reactions.

MEDICATION AND THE MEDIA

Prozac, probably one of the most widely advertised medicinal brand names in history, has had considerable exposure on television talk shows and in other popular media. By 1997, just ten years after it was placed on the market, twenty-four million people were taking Prozac in almost 100 countries. Although most often prescribed for depression, Prozac is also used in a variety of other cases, from aiding in weight loss to controlling adolescent hyperactivity.

In general, psychiatrists do not prescribe antidepressant medications to treat bipolar disorder because of the likelihood of triggering a manic episode. Extreme bipolar disorders are treated with a mood stabilizer, such as lithium. Lithium is a mineral found naturally in the body in trace amounts. In larger amounts it can be toxic, so dosages must be closely monitored to prevent patients from developing lithium toxicity. Lithium has received publicity as a dramatic "cure" for bipolar disorder, notably in television and film star Patty Duke's autobiography, *Call Me Anna* (1987), in which Duke recounts her struggles with violent mood swings.

Other, more extreme drugs continue to be prescribed to fight depression. Antipsychotics, also called neuroleptics or even neurotoxins, may be used to alleviate psychotic symptoms during a major depressive episode. Neuroleptics, such as Thorazine, Mellaril, and Haldol, can have harsh adverse effects, from Parkinson's disease to general immobility. Viewed as extreme measures, these medications are sometimes referred to as a "pharmacological lobotomy." Stereotypical mental patients shown in movies, with glazed eyes and shuffling gait, are based on the effects of drugs such as Thorazine, which are often used to subdue active patients.

By the late 2000s antidepressants represented a global industry of around $27 billion a year. For some, the development of safer and more widely available antidepressant medication has been an important breakthrough. However, three out of ten depression sufferers do not respond to a given antidepressant; many of those who do only partially respond or find that the benefits wear out. Some therapists and activists worry about the implications of a chemical solution to depression, claiming that antidepressants are overprescribed.

Manufacturers' enthusiastic advertisements often downplay the drugs' worrisome adverse effects. Yet research has shown antidepressants are successful in helping victims of rape, war, and other traumatic stress. In a study at Atlanta's Emory University, four out of five rape victims became less depressed after a twelve-week program of the SSRI Zoloft. Although some greet this as a positive development, others are chilled at the prospect of giving victims pills to combat their natural reactions to a social ill. Most responsible psychologists continue to see the solution to depression as a combination of drug therapy and talk therapy, which is used to explore a client's emotional reactions.

A number of studies have supported the tendency of children and young people to react differently than adults when taking antidepressant medications. Children and adolescents may have thoughts of death and suicide when taking the drugs. In 2005 the federal government issued a mandate requiring all drug manufacturers to attach a black-box warning to such drugs. In 2007 the FDA recommended the warning be extended to include anyone under age twenty-four, recommending that anyone under that age who takes antidepressants be closely monitored for worsening depression, suicidal thoughts, or marked changes in behavior.

NOTED INDIVIDUALS AND WORKS

Many famous artists and historical figures have reportedly suffered from depression or bipolar disorder. Aristotle wrote that many great thinkers of antiquity were afflicted by melancholia, including Plato and Socrates. Cultural historians have included in their lists of melancholic figures painters Michelangelo and Vincent Van Gogh; early women's rights advocate Mary Wollstonecraft; composers Hector Berlioz and Robert Schumann; novelist Virginia Woolf; and poets Dante Alighieri, Charles Baudelaire, Samuel Coleridge, John Donne, Sylvia Plath, and Anne Sexton.

Depression has also been described in literary texts. In his seminal essay "Mourning and Melancholia," Freud refers to playwright William Shakespeare's Hamlet as the archetype of the melancholic sufferer. Freud also called playwright Molière's *The Misanthrope* (1666) "atrabilious," a term denoting the black bile that medieval medicine considered the cause of melancholia. Descriptions of characters suffering from depression can also be found in novelist Gustave Flaubert's *Madame Bovary* (1856) and novelist Franz Kafka's *The Metamorphosis* (1915).

The poetry of Edna St. Vincent Millay presents a depressed cynicism, perhaps the result of personal loss and the wider cultural losses posed by disillusion and war. Plath's *The Bell Jar* (1963) is one of the most finely crafted modern portraits of the depressed heroine, "the perfect setup of a true neurotic . . . wanting two mutually exclusive things at one and the same time." Perhaps in response to increasing discussion of depression in the 1990s, a new genre appeared: the memoir of depression. In *Darkness Visible* (1990) by William Styron, *Prozac Nation: Young and Depressed in America* (1994) by Elizabeth Wurtzel, and *An Unquiet Mind* by Kay R. Jamison (1995), the authors explore their bleak mood, its causes, its effects on daily life, and sometimes a personal remedy.

Whether defined as a biological tendency activated by personal experience or as a personal experience activated by sociopolitical realities, depression has long been a significant part of human experience. Coping with the complexities and contradictions of life has always been a formidable prospect, and as society becomes more complex, the job of living becomes even more staggering. In words that still ring true, Woolf, who ended her own recurrent depressions with suicide at age fifty-nine, described the feeling: "Why is life so tragic; so like a little strip of pavement over an abyss. I look down; I feel giddy; I wonder how I am ever to walk to the end."

Tina Gianoulis
Ava Rose

SEE ALSO: Breakfast at Tiffany's*; Celebrity; Feminism; Freud, Sigmund; Kesey, Ken;* One Flew over the Cuckoo's Nest*; Plath, Sylvia; Prozac; Suicide.*

BIBLIOGRAPHY

Badal, Daniel W. *Treating Chronic Depression: Psychotherapy and Medication*. Northvale, NJ: Jason Aronson, 2003.

Beck, Aaron T. *Depression: Causes and Treatment*, 2nd ed. Philadelphia: University of Pennsylvania Press, 2009.

Diagnostic and Statistical Manual of Mental Disorders: DSM-IV. Washington, DC: American Psychological Association, 1994.

Freud, Sigmund. "Mourning and Melancholia." In *Collected Papers, Vol. 4*. London: Hogarth Press, 1950.

Hermsen, Lisa M. *Manic Minds: Mania's Mad History and Its Neuro-Future*. New Brunswick, NJ: Rutgers University Press, 2011.

Ingram, Allan; Stuart Sim; Clark Lawlor; et al. *Melancholy Experience in Literature of the Long Eighteenth Century: Before Depression, 1660–1800*. New York: Palgrave Macmillan, 2011.

Jackson, Stanley. *Melancholia and Depression: From Hippocratic Times to Modern Times*. New Haven, NY: Yale University Press, 1986.

Miletich, John J. *Depression: A Multimedia Sourcebook*. Westport, CT: Greenwood Press, 1995.

Oddenino, Kathy. *Depression: Our Normal Transitional Emotions*. Annapolis, MD: Joy Publications, 1995.

Schwartz, Arthur. *Depression: Theories and Treatments: Psychological, Biological, and Social Perspectives*. New York: Columbia University Press, 1993.

Derleth, August *(1909–1971)*

A better description of August Derleth's massive output could not be found than in Alison M. Wilson's *August Derleth: A Bibliography*:

> August Derleth . . . one of the most versatile and prolific American authors of the twentieth century, is certainly one of its most neglected. In a career that spanned over forty years, he produced a steady stream of novels, short stories, poems, and essays about his native Wisconsin; mystery and horror tales; and biographies, histories, and children's books, while simultaneously writing articles and reviewing books for countless magazines and newspapers, and running his own publishing house.

Despite the flood that streamed from his pen, none of Derleth's critically acclaimed regional novels ever sold more than 5,000 copies, whereas his fantasy, children's, and mystery fiction fared only marginally better. Since his death in 1971, he is best remembered for his Solar Pons stories, modeled closely on Arthur Conan Doyle's Sherlock Holmes tales, and for his founding with Donald Wandrei in 1939 of Arkham House, a publishing concern that specialized in macabre fiction. Arkham House was notable for publishing the work of neglected pulp fiction horror and fantasy writers of the 1930s such as H. P. Lovecraft, as well as European weird fiction writers such as Arthur Machen and Lord Dunsany.

Bennett Lovett-Graff

SEE ALSO: *Lovecraft, H. P.; Science Fiction Publishing;* Weird Tales.

BIBLIOGRAPHY

Arkham House. *August Derleth: Thirty Years of Writing, 1926–1956*. Sauk City, WI: Arkham House, 1957.

Derleth, August William. *Arkham House: The First Twenty Years: 1939–1959*. Sauk City, WI: Arkham House, 1959.

Derleth, August William. *Thirty Years of Arkham House, 1939–1969*. Sauk City, WI: Arkham House, 1970.

Roberts, James P. *Famous Wisconsin Authors*. Oregon, WI: Badger Books, 2002.

Wilson, Alison M. *August Derleth: A Bibliography*. Metuchen, NJ: Scarecrow Press, 1983.

Desert Storm

SEE: *Gulf Wars.*

Desperate Housewives

Desperate Housewives was a comedy/drama television show that aired on ABC for eight seasons, from 2004 to 2012. Created by writer and producer Marc Cherry and starring Teri Hatcher, Felicity Huffman, Marcia Cross, and Eva Longoria, it follows the lives and misadventures of four female friends who live on the same street. The show, its cast and crew, and its guest stars received numerous award nominations, including Emmy Awards, Golden Globes, ALMA (American Latino Media Arts) Awards, GLAAD (Gay & Lesbian Alliance against Defamation) Media Awards, Screen Actors Guild Awards, and People's Choice Awards. The show's awards include the 2005 People's Choice Award for Favorite New Drama; the 2005 and 2006 Golden Globe Award for Best Television Series, Musical or Comedy; the 2009 GLAAD Media Award for Outstanding Comedy Series; and the 2011 ALMA Award for Outstanding Television Series.

The housewives of *Desperate Housewives* are Susan Mayer (Hatcher), Lynette Scavo (Huffman), Bree Van de Kamp (Cross), and Gabrielle Solis (Longoria). They live on the fictional Wisteria Lane in the fictional town of Fairview. Susan, a single working mother, tries to make a good life for her daughter. Lynette, a former corporate executive, is raising her four children. Bree, the perfect housewife, has problems with her two children and her husband. Gabrielle, a former high-fashion model, is a bored housewife who is having an affair with her young gardener. Throughout its run, the show is narrated by the original Wis-teria Lane housewife, Mary Alice Young (Brenda Strong), who commits suicide in the pilot episode.

By the start of season five, a number of changes have occurred in the ladies lives. Susan has a new husband, Mike Delfino (James Denton), and they are struggling financially while raising their son. Lynette tackles cancer, a pregnancy, and marriage problems with her husband (Doug Savant), while trying to build a new career. Bree has turned her avocation into her vocation and become a successful cookbook writer and entrepreneur. Gabrielle is now faithful to her husband (Ricardo Antonio Chavira) and has become the mother of two daughters.

Although *Desperate Housewives* was primarily focused on the lives of the four friends, other story lines infused the show with mystery and suspense. Wisteria Land resident Edie Britt (Nicollette Sheridan) blackmails herself into the group of four friends before getting killed in a car accident. Betty Applewhite (Alfre Woodard) moves onto the lane with her family, hiding her mentally disabled son in her basement. Seemingly perfect Katherine Mayfair (Dana Delany), a former Wisteria Lane resident, returns with her husband and daughter. Angie Bolen (Drea de Matteo) unintentionally brings violence to the neighborhood, while Lynette inadvertently offers a home to a young man who is revealed to be the notorious Fairview Strangler. Paul Young (Mark Moses), Mary Alice's husband, seeks revenge for the slights he experienced after his wife's suicide. The resident gay couple, Lee McDermott (Kevin Rahm) and Bob Hunter (Tuc Watkins), suffer relationship problems and yearn for a child of their own.

Desperate Housewives tackled difficult topics, such as alcoholism, cancer, organ transplants, gay marriage, and spousal abuse. Accordingly, the show was not without controversy. During the first season, Kellogg's, Tyson Foods, and Lowe's Foods canceled their advertising, claiming that plots regarding blackmail, adultery, and murder do not fit their projected family image. The series also came under fire from women's groups and the American Family Association due to the use of dark humor and concern regarding the portrayal of women as catty and shallow.

Whereas *Desperate Housewives* is a fictional account of suburban women's lives, many critics have cited it as an influence on reality shows such as *The Real Housewives of Orange County*, which debuted on the Bravo cable network in 2006 and highlights the day-to day lives of high-profile housewives in Orange County, a wealthy community in Southern California. The show was so successful that it spawned additional shows in Beverly Hills, California; Atlanta, Georgia; Washington, D.C.; Miami, Florida; New York City; and New Jersey.

Producers of *Desperate Housewives* capitalized on the show's enduring popularity by releasing a range of *Desperate Housewives* merchandise, including dolls; video games; and even a perfume, aptly named *Forbidden Fruit* after the show's title sequence, which depicts each of the four main characters as a kind of Eve figure, holding an apple plucked from the tree of knowledge of good and evil.

Linda Martindale

SEE ALSO: *Emmy Awards;* The Real Housewives of . . . ; *Suburbia; Television.*

BIBLIOGRAPHY

Dalton, David. *Desperate Housewives: Behind Closed Doors*. New York: Hyperion, 2005.

Hill, Lisa. "Gender and Genre: Situating Desperate Housewives." *Journal of Popular Film and Television* 38, no. 4 (2010): 162–169.

McCabe, Janet, and Kim Akass, eds. *Reading "Desperate Housewives": Beyond the White Picket Fence*. London: I.B. Tauris, 2006.

Detective Fiction

Mysteries and their solutions have always been used in fiction, but detective fiction as a recognizable genre first appeared in the mid-nineteenth century. Despite detective fiction becoming one of the most popular of literary genres of the twentieth century, disputes over the point at which a story containing detection becomes a detective fiction story have continued. In its most obvious incarnation detective fiction is to be found under the heading "Crime" in the local bookstore; it includes tales of great detectives, such as Sherlock Holmes and C. Auguste Dupin, of police investigators, of private eyes, and of little old ladies with a forensic sixth sense. But detective fiction can also be found disguised in respectable jackets, in the "Classic Literature" section under the names Dickens and Voltaire. Within detective fiction itself, there are many varieties of detectives and methods of detection; in its short history, the genre has shown itself to be a useful barometer of cultural conditions.

EARLY DETECTIVE FICTION

Defining detective fiction, then, is fraught with problems. Even its history is in dispute, with critics claiming elements of detective fiction in ancient Greek tragedies and in Geoffrey Chaucer. Part of the problem is that although the category "Crime Fiction" includes all fiction involving crime, and, very often, detective work as well, "Detective Fiction" must be restricted only to those works that include, and depend upon, detection. Such a restrictive definition leads inevitably to arguments about what exactly constitutes "detective work" and whether works that include some element of detection, but are not dependent on it, should be included. Howard Haycraft is quite clear on this in his book *Murder for Pleasure* (1941), when he says, "The crime in a detective story is only the means to an end which is—detection."

Perhaps the first work in English to have its entire plot based around the solution to a crime is a play, sometimes attributed to William Shakespeare, called *Arden of Faversham*. The work, first published in 1592, is based on the true story of the murder of a wealthy and much disliked landowner, Thomas Arden, which took place in 1551. Arden's body is discovered on his land, not far from his house. The fact that the body is outside points to his having been murdered by neighboring farmers and laborers, jealous about Arden's acquisition of nearby land. What the detective figure, Franklin, sets out to prove is that Arden was murdered in his house, by his adulterous wife, Alice, and her lover. He manages to achieve this by revealing a clue, a piece of rush matting lodged in the corpse's shoe, which could only have found its way there when the body was dragged across the floor of the house.

Although the plot of *Arden of Faversham* revolves around the murder of Arden and the detection of its perpetrators, Julian Symons suggests in *Bloody Murder: From the Detective Story to the Crime Novel* that the purpose of the play itself lies elsewhere, in characterization, and, among other things, the moral issues surrounding the allocation of land following the dissolution of the monasteries. Because the element of crime and detection is merely a vehicle for other concerns, the place of *Arden of Faversham* in the canon of detective fiction remains marginal. But this is a debatable point. As Symons says, the exact position of the line that separates detective from other fiction is a matter of opinion. Nevertheless, early detective stories such as this play, and others by writers such as Voltaire, certainly prefigure the techniques of detectives like Sherlock Holmes and Philo Vance.

MODERN POPULAR DETECTIVE FICTION

What critical consensus there is on this topic suggests that the earliest writer of modern popular detective fiction is Edgar Allan Poe. In three short stories, or tales—"The Murders in the Rue Morgue" (1841), "The Mystery of Marie Rogêt" (1843), and "The Purloined Letter" (1845)—Poe established many of the conventions that became central to what is known as classic detective fiction. Perhaps reacting to the eighteenth-century idea that the universe is a mechanical system and as such can be explained by reason, Poe devised a deductive method, which, as he shows in the stories, can produce seemingly miraculous insights and explanations. This deductive method, sometimes known as ratiocination, goes some way in defining the character of the first "great detective," C. Auguste Dupin, whose ability to solve mysteries borders on the supernatural but is, as he insists to the narrator sidekick, entirely rational in its origins. The third important convention Poe established is that of the locked room, in which the solution to the mystery lies in the detective's working out how the criminal could have left the room unnoticed and leaving it locked from the inside.

Other writers, such as Wilkie Collins and Emile Gaboriau, began writing detective stories after Poe in the mid-nineteenth century, but rather than making their detectives aristocratic amateurs like Dupin, Inspectors Cuff and Lecoq are professionals, standing out in their brilliance from the majority of policemen. Gaboriau's creation, Lecoq, is credited with being the first fictional detective to make a plaster cast of footprints in his search for a criminal. Perhaps the most famous of the "great detectives," however, is Sir Arthur Conan Doyle's creation Sherlock Holmes, whose method of detection, bohemian lifestyle, and faithful friend and narrator, Watson, all suggest his ancestry in Poe's creation, Dupin, but also look forward to the future of the genre. Although Doyle wrote four short novels involving Holmes, he is best remembered for the short stories, published as casebooks, in which Holmes's troubled superiority is described by Watson with a sense of awe that the reader comes to share. Outwitting criminals, and showing the police to be plodding and bureaucratic, what the great detective offers to readers is a sense both that the world is understandable and that they themselves are unique, important individuals. If all people are alike, Holmes could not deduce the intimate details of a person's life from their appearance alone, and yet his remarkable powers also offer reassurance that, where state agents of law and order fail, a balancing force against evil will always emerge.

While Holmes is a master of the deductive method, he also anticipates detectives such as Sam Spade and Philip Marlowe by his willingness to become physically involved in solving the crime. Where Dupin's solutions come through contemplation and rationality alone, Holmes is both an intellectual and a man of action, and Doyle's stories are stories of adventure as well as detection. Holmes is a master of disguise, changing his appearance and shape, and sometimes engaging physically with his criminal adversaries, famously with Moriarty at the Reichenbach Falls.

The Poe-Gaboriau-Doyle school of detective fiction remained the dominant form of the genre until the late 1920s in America, and almost until World War II in England, although the influence of the short story gradually gave way to the novel during that time. Many variations on the great detective appeared, from G. K. Chesterton's priest-detective, Father Brown, solving crime by intuition as much as deduction, through Dorothy L. Sayers's return to the amateur aristocrat in Lord Peter Wimsey and Agatha Christie's unlikely detective Miss Marple, and her eccentric version of the type, Hercule Poirot. In Christie's work in particular, the locked room device that appeared in Poe occurs both in the form of the room in which the crime is committed and at the level of the general setting of the story—a country house, an isolated English village, a long-distance train, or a Nile riverboat, for example. This variation of the detective story became so dominant in England that classic detective fiction is often known as the English or Country House type.

Detective fiction of the classic type was very popular on both sides of the Atlantic, however, and the period from about 1900 to 1940 has become known as the Golden Age of the form. In America writers such as R. Austin Freeman, with his detective Dr. Thorndike, brought a new emphasis on forensic science in the early part of the twentieth century. Both Freeman and Willard Huntingdon Wright (also known as S. S. Van Dine), who created the detective Philo Vance, wrote in the 1920s that detective fiction was interesting for its puzzles rather than its action. Van Dine in particular was attacked by critics for the dullness of his stories and the unrealistic way in which Vance could unravel a case from the most trivial of clues. Nevertheless, huge numbers of classic detective stories were published throughout the 1920s and 1930s, including, in the United States, work by such well-known figures as Ellery Queen (the pseudonym for cousins Frederic Dannay and Manfred B. Lee), John Dickson Carr (Carter Dickson), and Erle Stanley Gardner, whose series detective, Perry Mason, has remained popular in print and on-screen since he first appeared in 1933. Elsewhere the classic detective story developed in the work of writers such as Georges Simenon, Margery Allingham, and Ngaio Marsh.

Whereas all of these writers have their own particular styles and obsessions—Carr is particularly taken by the locked room device, for example—they all conform to the basic principles of the classic form. Whatever the details of particular cases, the mysteries in works by these writers are solved by the collection and decoding of clues by an unusually clever detective (amateur or professional) in a setting that is more or less closed to influences from outside.

HARD-BOILED DETECTIVE FICTION

Just as the classic form of the detective story emerged in response to late eighteenth- and early nineteenth-century beliefs in the universe as rationally explicable, so hard-boiled detective fiction appeared in the United States in the 1920s perhaps in response to doubts about that view. Significantly, just as the influence of the short story was declining in the classic form, early hard-boiled detective fiction appeared in the form of short stories or novellas in pulp magazines such as *Dime Detective* and *Black Mask*. These magazines were sold at newspaper stalls and station bookstores, and the stories they published took a radical turn away from the sedate tone of classic detective fiction.

Hard-boiled detective stories, as they became known for their clipped, unembroidered language, focus not on the detective's intellectual skill at interpreting clues but on his—and, mostly since the 1980s (aside from Miss Marple), her—experiences. This type of detective fiction encourages the reader to identify with the detective rather than look upon him or her as a protective authority; it champions the ability of ordinary people to resist and combat the influences of crime and corruption on their lives. As part of their rejection of the puzzle as a center for their narratives, hard-boiled detective stories are also concerned with the excitement generated by action, violence, and sex. So graphic did their description of these things seem in the 1920s that some stories were considered to border on the pornographic.

The effect of this on detective fiction as a genre, however, was profound for other reasons. Hard-boiled detective stories described crimes taking place in settings that readers could recognize. No longer was murder presented as a remote interruption to genteel village life, but, as Raymond Chandler points out in his essay "The Simple Art of Murder," something that happened to real people, for real reasons. Crime was no longer the subject of an interesting and challenging puzzle but something with real human consequences, not only for the victim but for the detective as well as society at large. This new subject matter had limited impact within the restricted space of the short story but came to the fore in the hard-boiled detective novels that gained popularity from the late 1920s onward.

Carroll John Daly is usually credited with the invention of the hard-boiled detective, in his series character Race Williams, who first appeared in *Black Mask* in 1922. But Dashiell Hammett, another *Black Mask* writer, did the most to translate the hard-boiled detective to the novel form, publishing his first, *Red Harvest*, in 1929. The longer format, and the hard-boiled form's emphasis on the detective's actions, meant that Hammett's detectives, who include the famous Sam Spade, could confront, more directly than classic detectives, complex moral decisions and emotional difficulties. Chandler, who in the 1930s also began his career writing for *Black Mask*, took this further, creating in his series detective, Philip Marlowe, a sophisticated literary persona and moving the focus still further away from plot and puzzle and on to the detective's inner life. Chandler is also well known for his realistic descriptions of Southern California and his view of American business and politics as underpinned by corruption and immorality.

Other writers picked up where Hammett and Chandler left off; some began using their work to explore particular issues, such as race or gender. Ross MacDonald, whose Lew Archer novels are generally considered to follow on from Chandler in the 1950s and 1960s, addresses environmental concerns. Mickey Spillane, who began publishing in the late 1940s and continued until his death in 2006, took the subgenre further by having his detective, Mike Hammer, not only confront moral dilemmas but also take the law into his own hands. Sara Paretsky, who published her first novel, *Indemnity Only*, in 1982, reinvents the masculine hard-boiled private eye in V. I. Warshawski, a female detective whose place in a masculine environment enables her to explore feminist issues, whereas Walter Mosley uses a black detective to explore problems of race. While hard-boiled detective fiction shifts the focus from the solution of the problem to the search for that solution, and in doing so is able to address other topics, it remains centered on the idea of the detective restoring order in one way or another. Hard-boiled detectives do, in most cases, solve mysteries, even if their methods are more pragmatic than methodical.

POLICE PROCEDURALS

In the 1920s hard-boiled detective fiction was considered a more realistic approach to crime and detection than the clue-puzzles of the classic form. Since the early 1970s, however, the idea that a single detective of any kind is capable of solving crimes has seemed more wishful than realistic. In the three decades that followed, the police procedural became the dominant form of detective fiction, overturning the classic depiction of the police as incompetent and the hard-boiled view of them as self-interested and distanced from the concerns of real people. Police procedurals adapt readily for TV and film and come in many forms, adopting elements of the classic and hard-boiled forms in the police setting. They range from the tough "precinct" novels of Ed McBain to the understated insight of Colin Dexter's Inspector Morse series or P. D. James's Dalgliesh stories. The type of detection ranges from the violent, chaotic, and personal approach of the detectives in James Ellroy's L.A. series to the forensic pathology of Kay Scarpetta in Patricia Cornwell's work. What all of these variations have in common, however, is that the detectives are backed up by state organization and power; they are clever, unusual, inspiring characters, but they cannot operate as detectives alone in the way that Holmes and Marlowe can.

This suspicion that detectives are not the reassuring figures they once seemed is explored in a variation of the classic form known as antidetective fiction. In the 1940s Jorge Luis Borges produced clue-puzzle detective stories whose puzzles are impossible to fathom, even by the detective involved. At the time, the hard-boiled novels of Hammett and Chandler were also challenging the idea that the detective could know or fathom everything, but Borges's work undermines even the very idea of finding truth through deductive reasoning. In one well-known story, "Death and the Compass" (1942), Borges's detective unwittingly deduces the time and place of his own murder. In the 1980s Paul Auster's *New York Trilogy* (1988) explored contemporary theories about language and identity to produce detective stories with no solution, no crime, and no detective. Antidetective fiction provides an interesting view of detection and a comment on the futility of trying to understand the universe, but it is of limited scope and popular appeal.

In the twenty-first century, police procedurals remained popular, though the detectives themselves, and their wider examination of their local cultures, have in many cases, become the real subject of the novels. Ian Rankin's Scottish detective, Inspector Rebus, for example, often finds himself up against local criminals who operate against a background of wider political apathy and petty corruption. Rebus struggles with his place in a police force organized according to the latest management theory, while others, such as Harry Hole, the creation of Norwegian writer Jo Nesbo, battle private demons and establishment forces determined to cover up inconvenient truths. In the United States, Michael Connelly's detective Hieronymus "Harry" Bosch is a similarly confrontational figure.

Despite the dominance of fictional police detectives in Europe and the United States, the best-known detective fiction author of the first decade of the twenty-first century was Stieg Larsson, a Swedish writer whose unconventional detectives, Mikael Blomkvist and Lisbet Salander, are, respectively, an investigative journalist and a damaged, abused young woman, who is identified by a dragon tattoo across her shoulder. Salander's many attributes, besides her survival instinct, include high-level computer hacking and a propensity for cold-blooded revenge. The three novels of the so-called Millennium trilogy explore corruption, violence, and malignant secrecy at the heart of Swedish society, a society more widely known for its peaceful, open-minded liberalism. Larsson's posthumously published best-selling novels, the first of which is called *The Girl with the Dragon Tattoo*, are part of a self-examining turn in Swedish detective fiction that is also represented by Henning Mankell and his disillusioned police detective Kurt Wallander. Larsson's novels, however, have a more explicitly political edge.

In the 1990s detective fiction began to be appreciated in literary terms; it appeared as a matter of course on college literature syllabi; was reviewed in literary journals; and individual writers, such as Conan Doyle and Chandler, were published in "literary" editions. Much of that academic attention might seem to go against the popular, commercial origins of the form, but it also reflects the burgeoning popularity of detective fiction. In the hands of writers such as Mankell and Rankin (in Europe) or Ellroy and George Pelecanos (in the United States), detective fiction has shown itself capable of considerable sophistication as a literary form. Whatever its appeal, detective fiction seems to reflect society's attitudes to problems of particular times. That was as true in the 1840s for Poe, exploiting his culture's fascination with rationality and science; for the police procedural and its concerns with corruption and power in the late twentieth century; and current concerns about corporate power, terrorism, violence, and justice in the first decades of the twenty-first century.

Chris Routledge

SEE ALSO: *Best Sellers;* Black Mask*; Carr, John Dickson; Chandler, Raymond; Christie, Agatha; Doyle, Arthur Conan;* The Girl with the Dragon Tattoo*; Hammett, Dashiell; Hard-Boiled Detective Fiction; Hillerman, Tony; Himes, Chester; Kantor, MacKinlay; Leonard, Elmore; MacDonald, John D.; McBain, Ed; Mosley, Walter; Paretsky, Sara; Perry Mason; Pulp Magazines; Queen, Ellery; Spillane, Mickey; Stout, Rex;* True Detective*; Van Dine, S. S.; World War II.*

BIBLIOGRAPHY

Chandler, Raymond. "The Simple Art of Murder." *Atlantic Monthly*, December 1944.

Haycraft, Howard. *Murder for Pleasure: The Life and Times of the Detective Story*. New York: Appleton-Century, 1941.

Horsley, Lee. *Twentieth-Century Crime Fiction*. Oxford, UK: Oxford University Press, 2005.

Klein, Kathleen Gregory. *The Woman Detective: Gender and Genre*. Urbana: University of Illinois Press, 1988.

Knight, Stephen. *Form and Ideology in Crime Fiction*. London: Macmillan, 1980.

Knight, Stephen. *Crime Fiction 1800–2000: Detection, Death, Diversity*. New York: Palgrave Macmillan, 2004.

Messent, Peter, ed. *Criminal Proceedings: The Contemporary American Crime Novel*. Chicago: Pluto Press, 1997.

Symons, Julian. *Bloody Murder: From the Detective Story to the Crime Novel*. London: Faber and Faber, 1972.

Winks, Robin W., ed. *Detective Fiction: A Collection of Critical Essays*. Woodstock, VT: Foul Play Press, 1988.

The Detroit Tigers

Baseball—with its cheap bleacher seats, Sunday doubleheaders, and working-class heroes—has a blue-collar tradition. It is, therefore, no surprise that one of the most famous, durable, and successful baseball teams is from a quintessential blue-collar city: Detroit, Michigan. The Detroit Tigers date back to 1894 and were one of the charter members of the American League in 1901. While never as successful as the New York Yankees, the Tigers have a rich history. Like the city's dominant economic entity, General Motors, the Tigers have been a conservative force, resisting change. When free agency arrived in the 1970s, the Tigers reacted to the new high salaries, according to baseball writer Bill James, "like a schoolmarm on a date with a sailor." However, those days may have ended in the new millennium when the Tigers began signing high-profile free agents from others teams, notably slugger Prince Fielder to a contract worth more than $200 million.

ESTABLISHING A TRADITION

While the Tigers have not always had the best teams, they have often had the brightest stars. Ty Cobb was baseball's first

Detroit Tigers Win 1968 World Series. *Tigers teammates mob pitcher Mickey Lolich after his game-seven victory over the St. Louis Cardinals in the 1968 World Series. Lolich also won the second and fifth games in the series to earn MVP honors.* FOCUS ON SPORT/ GETTY IMAGES.

superstar: he *was* Tigers baseball from 1905 to 1928, the team's top player and, in his later years, its manager. Though he was a hero at home, he played the role of villain on road trips when his intensity led to many violent confrontations, some with fans. Cobb was suspended in 1912 for punching a fan, but the team backed him and went on strike, forcing management to put together a roster of sandlot players for a game against the Philadelphia Athletics.

The year 1912 was also significant because the Tigers moved into Navin Field on the corner of Michigan and Trumbull. Named after team owner Frank Navin, the ballpark would remain in use for the rest of the century. Although it had Cobb, as well as stars such as Sam Crawford, the team went from 1910 through 1933 without capturing an American League pennant. In the 1930s three more superstars—Charlie Gehringer, Hank Greenberg, and Mickey Cochrane—played for the Tigers. The decade was also notable for giving birth to an ignominious tradition: when spectators hurled garbage onto the field during the 1934 World Series, they initiated a practice of hooliganism among Tigers fans that persisted for years afterward.

After the team won the World Series in 1935, Walter Briggs, an auto parts manufacturer, became the new owner. His family also owned the team's playing field, which was renamed Briggs Stadium. Although they enjoyed another World Series win in 1945, the Tigers—like the rest of the teams in the American League—were overshadowed by the dominance of the Yankees from 1949 to 1964. The only real highlight for the Tigers during this period was outfielder Al Kaline, who joined the team in 1953 and put together a career that resulted in his induction into the National Baseball Hall of Fame in 1980. The Briggs family sold the team in 1956 to a group of eleven radio and television executives led by John Fetzer, a transaction that foreshadowed the marriage of media and sports in the ensuing decades.

TURBULENT TIMES

A mark against the Tigers was their slowness to integrate black players. Despite a steady increase in the city of Detroit's black population, the team rarely had more than a handful of African American players throughout the 1960s. The contradictions of racial politics in Detroit exploded with riots in 1967 that changed the history of the city. The violence resulted in unprecedented white flight that left parts of the city, including the neighborhoods around Tiger Stadium, devastated. Though ravaged and divided, the city came together as the Tigers won the 1968 World Series. The factual basis for the team's role in uniting Detroit communities remains debatable, but sports historian Patrick Harrigan noted that "the myth of unity is important, illustrating the importance many Detroiters give to baseball as a bonding element."

The key to the 1968 team was Denny McLain, an immature kid with a great arm who won thirty-one games that year but whose career later self-destructed. McLain was baseball's equivalent of football's Joe Namath—brash, cocky, quotable, and unconventional. After 1968 the Tigers remained competitive and, managed by Billy Martin—another brash, cocky, and quotable figure—won the American League Eastern Division on the last day of the 1972 season. Over the next decade, however, the Tigers endured many setbacks. Racial tensions and economic conditions in the city worsened, attendance at games declined, and the Tigers lost 100 games in the 1975 season. Yet in 1976 another shining star emerged from the mire: Mark "The Bird" Fidrych. Nicknamed after the *Sesame Street* character Big Bird because of his lanky build and curly blond mane, Fidrych was a right-handed pitcher with the eccentric on-field habit of talking to the baseball. He quickly made the cover of *Sports Illustrated*, and his games, both at home and on the road, were sellouts. Yet, like McLain before him, Fidrych's immaturity (he injured his knee horsing around in the outfield) led to his rapid decline.

The devastation of the economy in Detroit in the late 1970s led to the dispersal of Tigers fans to other parts of the country, but the team's enduring popularity was validated when Tom Selleck's character on *Magnum, P.I.* (1980–1988) donned the familiar Tigers cap with the Old English "D" on it. As with many sports franchises, however, the Tigers' logo was adopted as a gang symbol, in this case for the Gangster Disciples.

A GLIMMER OF HOPE

In 1979 the Tigers hired manager Sparky Anderson, and the team's outlook began to brighten. With a stable of great young players, the Tigers exploded in 1984, starting 35–5 en route to the World Series title. This was the first year under owner Tom Monaghan, a lifelong Tigers fan who made his fortune with the Domino's Pizza franchise. The 1984 World Series was known as the "fast food series"—the Kroc family of McDonald's fame owned the opposing San Diego Padres. The 1984 season was marked by two significant spectator developments. Fans at Tiger Stadium popularized "the wave," a coordinated mass cheer in which sections of people jump from their seats in succession with their hands in the air. Less happily for the game, Tigers fans also popularized the ritual of turning victory celebrations into all-night melees. In the wake of the World Series win, there were near-riots in Detroit.

Monaghan ran into financial problems and sold the team to his business rival, Mike Ilitch, owner of the Little Caesar's pizza chain, in 1992. The franchise was damaged not only by the stumbling Michigan economy but also by, according to Harrigan, "a series of public relations disasters, including the botched dismissal of popular announcer Ernie Harwell that alienated its most loyal followers." At the same time, Harrigan added, the city was harming rather than helping as "a bellicose mayor alienated the suburbanites and outsiders. A few highly publicized incidents in the downtown area magnified fear of coming to the Stadium. . . . The club became separate from the city, and the wider community divorced itself from the city." Though in the early 1990s the Tigers had slugger Cecil Fielder, their first black superstar in more than twenty years, interest in the team primarily concerned its future. By the late 1990s, following years of bitter debate, lawsuits, and public hearings, construction of a new stadium started in downtown Detroit. Although the 1994 baseball strike and a series of poor teams had devastated attendance, the opening of Comerica Park in 2000 signified that better days were ahead.

INTO THE FUTURE

Whereas attendance increased following the opening of Comerica Park, the number of wins by the Tigers did not. In 2003 the Tigers lost 119 games, only one defeat shy of the record established by the 1962 New York Mets. However, just as the auto industry made a brief comeback in the middle of the first decade of the 2000s, so did the Tigers. With new manager Jim Leyland in the dugout and strong-armed Justin Verlander on the mound, the 2006 squad upset the Yankees and Oakland A's in the playoffs to reach the World Series, where it lost in five games to the St. Louis Cardinals. In 2011 Verlander again led the Tigers to the postseason; this time, they were stopped by the Texas Rangers in the American League Championship Series.

Hopes for the next decade are pinned on Cecil Fielder's son Prince, who signed a $214 million contract in early 2012. It is among the most lucrative deals in baseball history. Though Detroit faces severe challenges due to high unemployment and an alarming crime rate, people in the area still cheer on the Tigers, just as they have been doing for more than a century.

Patrick Jones

SEE ALSO: *Baseball; Cobb, Ty; Fidrych, Mark "The Bird"; Greenberg, Hank; Race Riots; Sports Heroes.*

BIBLIOGRAPHY

Anderson, William M. *The Detroit Tigers: A Pictorial Celebration of the Great Players and Moments in Tigers' History.* Detroit, MI: Wayne State University Press, 2008.

Cantor, George. *The Good, the Bad, and the Ugly Detroit Tigers.* Chicago: Triumph Books, 2008.

Falls, Joe. *The Detroit Tigers: An Illustrated History.* New York: Walker and Company, 1989.

Harrigan, Patrick. *The Detroit Tigers: Club and Community, 1945–1995.* Toronto: University of Toronto Press, 1997.

James, Bill. *This Time Let's Not Eat the Bones.* New York: Villard Books, 1989.

Parrish, Lance, and Phil Pepe. *Few and Chosen: Defining Detroit Tigers Greatness across the Eras.* Chicago: Triumph Books, 2010.

Devers, Gail *(1966–)*

Labeled "the world's fastest woman" after she won the 100-meter dash and a gold medal in the Summer Olympics at Barcelona in 1992, Gail Devers has become an exemplar of excellence, grace, and courage and has served as an inspiration to other athletes, especially women, throughout the world. In 1988 she set an American record in the 100-meter hurdles (12:61). What happened to Devers between 1988 and 1992, however, created a story "that exemplifies the triumph of the human spirit over physical adversity," noted Walter Leavy in *Ebony*, for Devers was sidelined with Graves disease, a debilitating thyroid disorder. After nearly having to undergo amputation of both feet in March 1991, she not only recovered to run triumphantly in 1992 but went on to win her second gold in the 100 meter at the Atlanta Olympics in 1996, becoming only the second woman to win back-to-back gold medals in the event.

Devers continued to compete in the early years of the twenty-first century, placing fourth in the 2006 Millrose Games shortly after giving birth to a daughter. The following year, at the age of forty, she took first place in the 60-meter hurdles with the best time recorded for any competitor that year (.786 seconds).

John R. Deitrick

SEE ALSO: *Olympics; Sports Heroes.*

BIBLIOGRAPHY

Gutman, Bill. *Gail Devers.* Austin, TX: Raintree Steck-Vaughn, 1996.

Leavy, Walter. "The Many Splendored Faces of Today's Black Woman." *Ebony*, March 1997, 90.

Woolum, Janet. *Outstanding Women Athletes: Who They Are and How They Influenced Sport in America.* Phoenix, AZ: Oryx Press, 1998.

Devo

Proving that America's most engaging and original artists do not have to come from culture industry hubs such as New York and Los Angeles, Ohio's Devo crawled out of the Midwest industrial city of Akron to become one of the most well-known conceptual-art-rock outfits of the late twentieth century. Formed in 1972 by two sets of offbeat art-student brothers and their drummer friend, Devo began making soundtracks for short films such as *In the Beginning Was the End: The Truth about De-evolution.* Over the course of the 1970s the group went from being an obscure Midwest oddity to, for a brief moment, one of new wave's most popular exports. While the group did adopt a more accessible sound at its commercial peak, it never toned down its weirdness factor, something that may have alienated mainstream audiences once it ran out of ultra-catchy songs.

Devo was formed by brothers Jerry and Bob Casale (bass and guitar, respectively) and Mark, Jim, and Bob Mothersbaugh (vocals, drums, and lead guitar, respectively—Alan Myers replaced Jim Mothersbaugh early in Devo's career). The name Devo is derived from the group's guiding conceptual principle, "de-evolution." As a concept, de-evolution is based on the notion that, rather than evolving, human beings are actually *devolving*—and the proof is manifest in the myriad social problems of the late twentieth century that, from Devo's point of view, are the result of a conformist American ideology that renders its population mindless clones. De-evolution was derived from a crackpot text the brothers found titled *The Beginning Was the End: Knowledge Can Be Eaten*, which maintained that humans are the evolutionary result of a race of mutant brain-eating apes.

Part joke, part art project, part serious social commentary, Devo went on to make the short film *In the Beginning Was the End: The Truth about De-evolution*, which won a prize at the Ann Arbor Film Festival in 1976, garnering the band significant—though small-scale—attention. This helped push the group to move to Los Angeles, where Devo gained even more attention as a bizarre live act that, in turn, led to a hit British single on the Stiff label and, soon after, an American contract with Warner Brothers Records. Between the band's formation and its Brian Eno–produced debut album in 1978, the band recorded a number of tracks in a basement studio on a four-track recorder; many of these songs were documented on Rykodisc's two-volume *Hardcore Devo* series. These unearthed songs showcase a band that, with the exception of the arty weirdos the Residents, created music without precedent. During an era dominated by prog-rock bands, disco acts, and straightforward pop/rock, Devo was crafting brief, intense bursts of proto-punk noise that fused electronic instruments, rock-and-roll fervor, and ironic detachment.

The Eno-produced *Q: Are We Not Men? A: We Are Devo!* announced to the world the de-evolution philosophy and sold respectably, though not spectacularly. Sonically speaking, the group's second album, *Duty Now for the Future*, matched Devo's conceptual weirdness to the point that it was its most challenging album. The breakthrough came with the ironically titled *Freedom of Choice*, in which the group adopted a more New Wave synth-pop sound that did not reduce the musical punch but made Devo more accessible to a wider audience. The success of "Whip It," the group's sole Top 40 hit, was in part due to the edgy video, making Devo one of the few American groups to embrace music videos during the early stages of MTV.

Devo's popularity and artistic quality steadily dropped off with the release of *New Traditionalists*, *Oh, No! It's Devo*, and *Shout*, all of which replace the playful quirkiness of earlier albums with a more heavy-handed rendering of the de-evolution philosophy (which may have been a reaction to the band's brief popularity). During the mid-1980s when Devo was largely inactive, Mark Mothersbaugh made a name for himself composing music for Pee-Wee Herman's Saturday morning live action vehicle *Pee-wee's Playhouse*, which led to numerous other scoring jobs.

In 1988 Devo returned with *Total Devo* on the indie label Enigma, which did not restore anyone's faith in the band's relevance. An even less worthwhile effort followed, the live *Now It Can Be Told*. Still, Devo produced a few decent songs, such as "PostPost-Modern Man" from the 1990 album *Smooth Noodle Maps*. In 1996 Devo released a CD-ROM and soundtrack album, *Adventures of the Smart Patrol*, and played a few dates at the Lollapalooza alternative music festival.

Devo continued producing new projects, "Whip It" was used in a Swiffer commercial, and the band teamed with Disney in 2006 in a project dubbed Devo 2.0, in which kids rerecorded Devo songs (changing the lyrics on some to make them more family friendly). Mark and Bob Mothersbaugh worked together on the score for the television show *Rugrats*, and Mark worked on Wes Anderson films such as *Bottle Rocket*, *Rushmore*, and *The Royal Tenenbaums*. Casale directed videos for the Foo Fighters, the Cars, and Soundgarden. He created a side project, Jihad Jerry & the Evil Doers, and released two albums, *Army Girls Gone Wild* (2005) and *Mine Is Not a Holy War* (2006).

Throughout the early 2000s Devo toured and released new recordings. The act's genre-defying and wacky portrayals continue to surprise people, even if none of the band's recent work has become as popular as its 1980s song and odd music videos.

Kembrew McLeod

SEE ALSO: *Album-Oriented Rock; Alternative Rock; The Cars; Disco; Disney (Walt Disney Company); MTV; New Wave Music;* Pee-wee's Playhouse*; Punk; Rock and Roll; Top 40.*

BIBLIOGRAPHY

Bourgoin, Suzanne M. *Contemporary Musicians: Profiles of the People in Music*, vol. 13. Detroit, MI: Gale, 1995.

Heylin, Clinton. *From the Velvets to the Voidoids: A Pre-Punk History for a Post-Punk World.* New York: Penguin, 1993.

Dexter

Dexter is a television drama series that debuted on October 1, 2006, on the Showtime cable network. The series features Dexter Morgan, a blood-spatter analyst for the Miami Metro Police Department who lives a double life as a serial killer targeting violent criminals. Although Dexter lacks most recognizable human emotions, he mimics them well as he juggles the demands of his job, his personal life, and his after-hours murders of other killers. By having a serial killer who elicits audience identification and sympathy as a central character, the series has achieved remarkable success as a drama, morality play, and dark comedy.

Dexter is based on author Jeff Lindsay's *Dexter* novels. The first season of *Dexter* is adapted from the first *Dexter* novel, *Darkly Dreaming Dexter* (2004). The season introduces the characters central to Dexter's life, including his adopted sister, Debra Morgan, a vice squad officer in Miami Metro who later transfers to the Homicide Department; his girlfriend, Rita Bennett, a divorcée raising two young children; Angel Batista, a detective in the Homicide Division; Lieutenant Maria LaGuerta, in command of the Homicide Division; Vince Masuka, the lead forensics investigator; James Doakes, a sergeant in the Homicide Division who also sees through Dexter's masquerade and loathes him; and Harry Morgan, Dexter's deceased adoptive father, who appears to him in flashbacks and apparent visions. During Dexter's adolescence, his father instilled in him the Code of Harry, a series of rules designed to camouflage Dexter from detection and to compel him to target only proven killers for murder.

The main antagonist in the first season is the so-called Ice Truck Killer, a serial killer who murders prostitutes, leaving their bodies to be found with clues that only Dexter recognizes as having connections to himself. The Ice Truck Killer is revealed at the season's end to be Dexter's long-lost biological brother. Dexter kills his brother for his crimes but not without regret.

The following seasons take Dexter in a different direction than Lindsay's novels. Dexter narrowly escapes detection and arrest, finds and loses a new best friend, becomes a father, becomes a widow and single father, and wrestles with the mysteries of faith. The episodes pit Dexter in a cat-and-mouse game with a guest villain or villains, all of whom invariably end up in his "kill room."

Dexter consistently generates strong ratings. In 2008 the third-season finale drew 1.5 million viewers, then a record for Showtime. Critical and entertainment industry acclaim for *Dexter* has paralleled the strong ratings. The show has been nominated for Emmy Awards, including Outstanding Drama Series and Best Actor for Michael C. Hall, who plays Dexter, and Screen Actors Guild Awards.

When *Dexter* debuted in the United Kingdom in 2007, the television station FX launched a viral ad campaign that allowed fans to customize a video clip and name a friend as Dexter's next "victim," sparking controversy. When the CBS television network, owner of Showtime, announced in 2008 it would run edited episodes of *Dexter* late on Sunday nights, the Parents Television Council denounced CBS for contributing to a "culture of violence."

The show's success rests on a number of factors. Dexter's vigilantism is in keeping with the long American tradition of seeking justice when institutions of law and justice are lacking. The Miami Metro Police Department depicted in the show is largely dysfunctional, cumbersome, and even corrupt. This opens a void in public safety that Dexter steps in to fill. That Dexter targets other killers goes a long way in allowing the audience to exonerating him of blame. Even his occasional regrettable mistake in target selection is not held against him, given his covert public service.

Perhaps more important to Dexter's appeal, however, is his psychological vulnerability. As a survivor of a hideous childhood trauma, Dexter is himself a victim. His flawed adoptive father perhaps further damaged him by assuming Dexter was destined to be a killer. Finally, because he lacks the range of normal human emotions, Dexter continually finds himself seeking to understand the mystery of other people's motivations and feelings, a quest for shared humanity to which audiences can relate.

Philip L. Simpson

SEE ALSO: *Cable TV; Emmy Awards; Serial Killers; Television.*

BIBLIOGRAPHY

DePaulo, Bella, ed. *The Psychology of Dexter.* Dallas, TX: Smart Pop, 2010.

Greene, Richard; George A. Reisch; and Rachel Robison-Greene, eds. *Dexter and Philosophy: Mind over Spatter.* Chicago: Open Court, 2011.

Howard, Douglas L., ed. *Dexter: Investigating Cutting Edge Television.* New York: I.B. Tauris Publishers, 2010.

Diamond, Neil *(1941–)*

Singer and songwriter Neil Leslie Diamond has produced a collection of hits that range from schmaltzy to openly patriotic. Whether performed by Diamond himself or another artist, many of his songs are well known to the American public. Beginning his career while still a student at New York University, Diamond worked as a Tin Pan Alley writer before starting his solo career. The songs that he wrote or cowrote, such as "Solitary Man" (1966) and "Headed to the Future" (1986), reflect the era in which they were written and performed, whereas songs such as "Heartlight" (1982) reflect a nation's consciousness. Known for his pop hits, Diamond also tried his hand at country music and traditional Christmas songs. In the early 1970s he ventured into film, recording the soundtrack for *Jonathan Livingston Seagull* (1973), which earned him a Grammy Award. For *The Jazz Singer* (1980), Diamond not only wrote and performed the soundtrack but also starred in the movie.

Diamond's songs have been performed by such diverse groups as the Monkees and UB40. In 2011 he was inducted into the Rock and Roll Hall of Fame and received the Kennedy Center Honors.

Linda Ann Martindale

SEE ALSO: *Country Music; Grammy Awards;* The Jazz Singer*; The Monkees; Pop Music; Rock and Roll.*

BIBLIOGRAPHY

Grossman, Alan. *Diamond: A Biography.* Chicago: Contemporary Books, 1987.

Harvey, Diana Karanikas, and Jackson Harvey. *Neil Diamond.* New York: Metro Books, 1996.

Miller, Jim, ed. *The Rolling Stone Illustrated History of Rock and Roll.* New York: Rolling Stone Press, 1980.

Neil Diamond: The Official Neil Diamond Website. Accessed September 23, 2011. Available from www.neildiamond.com/home

Wiseman, Rich. *Neil Diamond: Solitary Star.* New York: Dodd, Mead, 1987.

Diana, Princess of Wales *(1961–1997)*

The most charismatic and publicly adored member of the British royal family for decades, Diana, Princess of Wales, imposed her own distinctly modern style and attitudes on Great Britain's traditionalist monarchy during her brief marriage to Prince Charles. Later, after the Royal couple divorced, Diana's alienation from the monarchy led much of the public, both in the United Kingdom and abroad, to view the royal family with

Princess Diana. *Diana personalized and modernized the image of Britain's royal family with public persona that blended her roles as princess, wife, mother, goodwill ambassador for England, and international humanitarian.* JAYNE FINCHER/PRINCESS DIANA ARCHIVE/GETTY IMAGES.

disapproval, fueling support for Republicanism and, after her death, forcing the royal family to moderate its aloof image.

As a glamorous and sympathetic icon of an image-driven and media-fueled culture, Diana's celebrity status and considerable influence traveled across continents. Her fame, matched by only a handful of women during the twentieth century—notably Jacqueline Kennedy Onassis and Princess Grace of Monaco (Grace Kelly)—made her a significant popular figure in the United States, where her visits were welcomed with the fervor once reserved for the most famous stars of the Golden Age of Hollywood. During her lifetime Diana was among the most photographed women in the world, and from the time of her marriage until her premature and stunning death in 1997, she forged a public persona that blended her various roles as princess, wife, mother, goodwill ambassador for England, and international humanitarian.

Diana's combination of beauty and glamour; her accessible, sympathetic, and vulnerable personality; and an ability to convey genuine concern for the affairs of ordinary people and the world's poor and downtrodden set her apart decisively from the distant formality of the British monarchy. She became an object of near worship, and her lasting fame was ensured. Ironically, the intense media attention and public adulation that came to define her life were widely blamed for the circumstances of her death. Her untimely demise, however, served only to amplify the public's romantic perception of her as a modern goddess cruelly destroyed by a faithless husband, unsympathetic in-laws, and prying paparazzi. The life and death of the Princess of Wales, is, indeed, a monument to sad contradictions and ironies.

STORYBOOK ROMANCE

Lady Diana Spencer was born into aristocratic privilege, the daughter of Viscount Althorp, on July 1, 1961, at the remote and spacious family estate near Sandringham in Norfolk. Her parents divorced when she was still a child, leaving Diana and her siblings in the care of her father and his second wife. She was a shy child, unhappy about the absence of her mother, and early on developed a passion for children, which led her to become a nursery school teacher in London. At eighteen she became reacquainted with Prince Charles, thirteen years her senior and heir to the British throne, whom she had known slightly in childhood. Their courtship became public, and she had the first taste of the media circus that was to dog her every move for the rest of her life.

On July 29, 1981, three weeks after her twentieth birthday, Diana married her prince—the first English woman in 300 years to become the wife of a future English king—in a wedding aptly described by the Archbishop of Canterbury as "the stuff of which fairy tales are made." The ceremony took place before an overflowing congregation of some 2,500 in London's St. Paul's Cathedral and drew a record-breaking global radio and television audience of nearly one billion. A worldwide media event, the wedding affirmed Diana's value as an internationally marketable personality whose image soon not only appeared in magazines, newspapers, and television programs across the globe but also adorned an unending stream of merchandise ranging from postage stamps to coffee mugs.

Diana's married life revolved around her official Court duties and, increasingly, her own public causes. Twenty days after her twenty-first birthday, the princess gave birth to the next heir apparent, Prince William, and two years later to Prince Henry (known as Harry). She insisted on taking her young sons on "normal" outings to cinemas and theme parks and on informal holidays abroad, and she bestowed lavish affection on them in public. Her conduct represented a sharp break from the stiff conventions of royalty and contributed to her position as the media's darling as well as to the discomfiture of her less demonstrative mother-in-law. On the one hand, Diana seemed determined to protect her sons from the harsh glare of public scrutiny; on the other, she kept the people abreast of the family's life by granting interviews and making numerous public appearances. She fed the media's hunger even while expressing despair at its persistence.

ROYAL AFFAIRS

By the mid-1980s, rumors of a rift between Charles and Diana were growing, accompanied by whispers of infidelity and reports that the princess was far from well or happy. By the end of the decade, it was public knowledge that Diana was suffering from bulimia, a fact that she courageously admitted in public in hopes of helping other sufferers; that Charles had resumed his long-standing love affair with Camilla Parker-Bowles early in his marriage; and that Diana had sought solace in an affair with an army officer named James Hewitt, who cooperated in a scandalous tell-all book about their relationship.

For a time, Diana was cruelly treated by the media and criticized by the public, who simultaneously relished and disapproved of a spate of further revelations. When, however, Charles consented to an in-depth television interview with his biographer Jonathan Dimbleby, and confessed to the Parker-Bowles affair, Diana retaliated with her own interview that effectively put the knife into the royal family and reestablished her position in the public affection. To the evident distress of the queen, the couple announced a separation in 1992, the year in which Britain and America were agog at the publication of Andrew Morton's book, *Diana, Her True Story*. The royal divorce followed four years later.

Her marital woes and personal troubles only served to raise Diana's public profile even higher, and she took advantage of the media's relentless coverage of her every move by redirecting their attention from her private life to her charity work. Though no longer "Her Royal Highness," she continued to upstage her beleaguered husband and his family in the public eye. She ruffled the feathers of politicians with her international campaign for the banning of land mines, she visited lepers, and she indicated her sympathy and support for AIDS sufferers.

A TRAGIC LEGACY

But even as Diana worked to focus the world's attention on her pet causes, people remained most keenly interested in her post-divorce love life. The public's seemingly insatiable appetite for detail was both whetted and offended by Diana's sudden whirlwind romance with Egyptian playboy Dodi Al-Fayed, which hit the headlines in 1997. Her new lover was the son of Mohammed Al-Fayed—the owner of Harrod's department store and the Ritz Hotel in Paris, from where the couple left on their last fateful car journey—and had long been a figure of ugly controversy in Britain. When the Mercedes in which Diana and Al-Fayed were traveling crashed at high speed in a Paris tunnel on the night of August 30, 1997, immediate blame was laid at the door of the press photographers who were giving chase to the car and gave rise to protracted legal hearings in Paris in a futile attempt to charge somebody with the couple's senseless deaths.

The news of Princess Diana's death sent shock waves around the world and plunged millions into a near-hysterical frenzy of grief. The profound sense of loss that was experienced, particularly in Britain, elevated Diana's mythic-martyr status to unprecedented levels. In the aftermath of her death, her brother, Earl Spencer, remembered his sister as "the very essence of compassion, of duty, of style, and of beauty." Indeed, when in the eyes of the public, the queen failed to show the requisite level of emotion at the news of Diana's death, she endured outraged criticism for "not responding to the pain of Britons." To quell the anger, she spoke publicly about Diana's death on television and agreed to lower the Union Jack atop Buckingham palace to half-mast—an honor that had up until that time been reserved solely for reigning monarchs.

As further evidence of Diana's impact on staid British institutions, although a divorcée, she was given a state funeral on September 5, 1997. Her coffin was borne, in a simple but ceremonial procession, from her home at Kensington Palace to Westminster Abbey, where the service was conducted in the presence of television cameras. The cameras then followed the cortege to her final resting place at Althorp, and two-and-a-half billion television viewers in 210 countries worldwide watched the hours of filmed coverage. In Britain, in memory of the princess, sporting events were postponed, bells chimed every minute, and a moment of silence was observed before the takeoff of each British airline flight.

In death, Diana hardly eluded the international cult of celebrity and the whispers of scandal that had haunted her during her life. Thriving on the controversy over who was to blame for her death, the international media sold more magazines and newspapers worldwide than they had at any time during her life. In an attempt to quell persistent tabloid rumors that the British Secret Intelligence Service and the royal family had conspired to cause the fatal crash, the British Metropolitan Police and the royal coroner launched separate inquests in 2004 and 2007 that, predictably, found no evidence of foul play but did little to quiet rampant conspiracy theories at their conclusion in 2008. Even the Diana, Princess of Wales Memorial Fund, established to endow a suitable memorial in 1997, was riven by indecision and controversy throughout the 1990s and early 2000s, while her name and likeness were continually exploited by the souvenir market and opportunistic artists and authors who churned out scores of biographies, memoirs, portraits, songs, documentaries, and biopics well into the twenty-first century. The most notorious of these figures may have been Diana's former butler, Paul Burrell, who was accused of stealing more than 300 items from Buckingham Palace that once belonged to the princess. Burrell was exonerated by the Queen herself and went on to write a revealing autobiography about his years in service of Diana, titled *A Royal Duty*.

While Diana's status as an exemplary mother and world-class humanitarian became cemented in the popular imagination, she left behind a darker legacy, that of a public figure who became a master at manipulating the media and the celebrity culture that had both exploited and promoted her. As the object of the world's infatuation, Diana was, in the words of her brother, "the most hunted person of the modern age." British prime minister Tony Blair, however, addressing the nation on the Sunday morning following the accident, dubbed her "The People's Princess." So she was, and so she is remembered.

Lauren Supance

SEE ALSO: *AIDS; Divorce; Kelly, Grace; Media Feeding Frenzies; Onassis, Jacqueline Lee Bouvier Kennedy; Tabloid Television; Tabloids.*

BIBLIOGRAPHY

Battiscombe, Georgina. *The Spencers of Althorp*. London: Constable, 1984.

Brown, Tina. *The Diana Chronicles*. New York: Doubleday, 2007.

Burrell, Paul. *A Royal Duty*. New York: G. P. Putnam's Sons, 2003.

Campbell, Lady Colin. *Diana in Private: The Princess Nobody Knows*. New York: St. Martin's Press, 1992.

Davies, Nicholas. *Diana: A Princess and Her Troubled Marriage*. Secaucus, NJ: Carol Publishing Group, 1992.

Holden, Anthony. *The Tarnished Crown: Princess Diana and the House of Windsor*. New York: Random House, 1993.

Martin, Ralph G. *Charles and Diana*. New York: Putnam, 1985.

Morton, Andrew. *Diana: Her True Story*. New York: Simon & Schuster, 1992.

DiCaprio, Leonardo *(1974–)*

After his critically acclaimed performances in the movies *This Boy's Life* (1993) and *What's Eating Gilbert Grape* (1993), actor Leonardo DiCaprio quickly gained a reputation for playing tormented young men in such films as *The Basketball Diaries* (1995), *Total Eclipse* (1995), and *William Shakespeare's Romeo and Juliet* (1996). His boyish good looks and sensitive, troubled persona made him a favorite of young women. Starring in the romantic tragedy *Titanic* (1997), which grossed more money than any film ever had before, broadened his popularity even further.

DiCaprio was born on November 11, 1974, in Los Angeles. He began acting when he was young, first appearing on the children's television show *Romper Room* (1953–1994). He made commercials as a teen before being added as a recurring character on the sitcom *Growing Pains* in 1991. From that point his career quickly took off and he moved to films.

Following the success of *Titanic*, DiCaprio starred in a number of relatively small-budget films throughout the late 1990s and early 2000s, including *The Man in the Iron Mask* (1998) and *The Beach* (2000). He reentered the spotlight with featured roles in the Steven Spielberg caper comedy *Catch Me If You Can* (2002) as well as in Martin Scorsese's *Gangs of New York* (2002), *The Aviator* (2004), and *The Departed* (2006). He continued to collaborate with high-profile directors throughout the first decade of the 2000s, performing in the Ridley Scott thriller *Body of Lies* (2008) and the Sam Mendes dramatic adaptation *Revolutionary Road* (2008). In 2010 DiCaprio appeared in his fourth Scorsese film, the thriller *Shutter Island*, and also starred in the visually appealing Christopher Nolan blockbuster *Inception*. Often praised for his ability with difficult accents and in assuming the identity of historical figures, DiCaprio was tapped to play the notorious FBI director J. Edgar Hoover in the 2011 biopic *J. Edgar*.

In just two decades DiCaprio grew from a relatively unknown, baby-faced upstart into an internationally recognized leading man. He was nominated for multiple Academy Awards, Golden Globes (he won in 2004), and Screen Actors Guild Awards. He was also recognized for his efforts to promote environmental awareness and an eco-friendly lifestyle. His production company, Appian Way, produced a number of films and documentaries, including *Gardener of Eden* (2007), *The 11th Hour* (2007), *Orphan* (2009), and *Red Riding Hood* (2011).

Christian L. Pyle

SEE ALSO: *Academy Awards; Scorsese, Martin; Scott, Ridley; Sitcom; Spielberg, Steven; Television; The* Titanic.

BIBLIOGRAPHY

Bego, Mark. *Leonardo DiCaprio: Romantic Hero.* Kansas City, MO: Andrews & McMeel, 1998.

Catalano, Grace. *Leonardo DiCaprio: Modern-Day Romeo.* New York: Bantam Books, 1997.

Catalano, Grace. *Leonardo: A Scrapbook in Words and Pictures.* New York: Dell, 1998.

Furgang, Kathy, and Adam Furgang. *Leonardo DiCaprio: Environmental Champion.* New York: Rosen, 2009.

Krulik, Nancy. *Leonardo DiCaprio: A Biography.* New York: Archway/Pocket Books, 1998.

Looseleaf, Victoria. *Leonardo: Up Close and Personal.* New York: Ballantine, 1998.

Dick, Philip K. *(1928–1982)*

Author of forty-four novels and approximately 121 short stories, Philip K. Dick started his career as a science fiction writer in 1952. He was awarded the Hugo Award, a presentation made by sci-fi fans, for his novel *The Man in the High Castle* in 1962, but he had to wait until the late 1970s to receive critical acclaim rivaling his popular reputation. His novels are uneven in quality, most containing powerful social satire. Dick has been immensely influential in contemporary science fiction writing, identifying many of the prominent concerns of cyberpunk, particularly consumerism, the cyborg, issues surrounding memory, surveillance, and mediated or artificial reality. *Blade Runner* (1982), the film version of his novel *Do Androids Dream of Electric Sheep?* (1968), has become a central reference point for critical discussions of both science fiction and modern technologically driven society.

Dick's career began in the 1950s after he had been expelled from the University of California at Berkley for his aversion to the required ROTC training and began to produce fiction for magazines and Ace Books. Writing against a backdrop of McCarthyism, the first novels Dick produced present satirical dystopias, exaggerating aspects of contemporary social experience. *Solar Lottery* (1955) presents an economic dystopia; *The World Jones Made* (1956) concerns the power of the police; *Vulcan's Hammer* (1956), the rise of a computer technocracy; and *The Man Who Japed* (1956) examines the totalitarianism inherent in democracy. These novels also established his interest in themes of political power and messianic figures.

It is, however, the consideration of different levels of reality and the world of appearances imposed upon ordinary characters that marks out Dick's work as radically creative and culturally astute. *The Eye in the Sky* (1957), *The Cosmic Puppets* (1957), and *Time out of Joint* (1959), which all have structural inconsistencies in the worlds they portray, each deal with shifting realities and characters who defy illusion. These convoluted plots circle the issue of defining the real from the ersatz, which is a predominant theme throughout Dick's work.

The Man in the High Castle, which earned Dick his Hugo Award, also debates the same theme. It is an alternate history, where the Allies have lost World War II. The novel stands out

Books by Philip K. Dick. *A collection of some of the twenty-six science-fiction novels written by Phillip K. Dick line a bookshelf.* MICK SINCLAIR/ALAMY.

from his earlier work because it is less allegorical; its length allows Dick the space for deeper characterization and to dwell on ambiguity and irony. From this point Dick writes about existence within depleted environments and derelict worlds, particularly the harshness visualized in the Martian colonies. In *The Three Stigmata of Palmer Eldritch* (1965), Dick concentrates on the use of drugs that allow Martian colonists to escape the severity of their lives. His fiction often explores the social use of drugs, including their economic and psychological effects. This interest culminates in *A Scanner Darkly* (1977), where drugs promote such powerful illusions that they preempt reality.

Flow My Tears the Policeman Said (1974) was nominated for both the Nebula (writers) and the Hugo (fan) Awards, and it won the John W. Campbell Award, which is presented by academic writers for the best science fiction novel of the year. The book marked a stage in which Dick was ready to cast aside the more traditional conventions of science fiction—for example, time travel, space colonies, technology, aliens, and telepathy—in order to focus on the more philosophical concerns of mainstream writing. He wrote a series of nongeneric novels during the 1950s, but only one, *Confessions of a Crap Artist* (1975), was published in his lifetime. His last novels, *VALIS* (1981), *The Divine Invasion* (1981), and *The Transmigration of Timothy Archer* (1982) combine autobiography and realism with the metaphysical search for God.

Dick will likely be most remembered for *Do Android's Dream of Electric Sheep?* which best exemplifies his preoccupation with the nature of humanity, realized in the dystopia of a society that has wiped out animal life and supplanted it with androids. It is a novel of deep existential insight that expands its hard-boiled genre for the popular market. Dick died of a stroke just before the completion of *Blade Runner*. In acknowledgment of his achievements and influence, the Philip K. Dick Award was established in 1982 to recognize the best science fiction novel of the year published originally in paperback.

Although Dick's work is popularly known through highly profitable film adaptations such as *Blade Runner*, *Minority Report*, and *Total Recall* (the ten films based on his works have grossed more than a billion dollars), he spent most of his life in poverty. His reach has spanned across disciplines and genres, immeasurably influencing postmodern writers and thinkers. He was the first science fiction writer canonized in the Library of America in 2007, and in 2010 the first American Philip K. Dick Festival was held in Colorado.

Nickianne Moody

SEE ALSO: *Best Sellers;* Blade Runner*; Consumerism; McCarthyism; Science Fiction Publishing.*

BIBLIOGRAPHY

Dick, Anne. *The Search for Philip K. Dick, 1928–1982: A Memoir and Biography of the Science Fiction Writer*. San Francisco: Tachyon Press, 2010.

Dick, Philip K. *Selected Letters, 1938–1982*, 6 vols. Grass Valley, CA: Underwood Books, 1991–2010.

Gillespie, Bruce, ed. *Philip K. Dick: Electric Shepherd.* Melbourne: Norstrilia Press, 1975.

Jackson, Pamela, and Jonathan Lethem, eds. *The Exegesis of Philip K. Dick*. New York: Houghton Mifflin Harcourt, 2011.

Mason, Darryl. *The Biography of Philip K. Dick*. London: Gollancz, 2006.

Olander, J. D., and M. H. Greenberg, eds. *Philip K. Dick*. New York: Taplinger, 1983.

Robinson, K. S. *The Novels of Philip K. Dick*. Ann Arbor, MI: UMI Research Press, 1984.

Rossi, Umberto. *The Twisted Worlds of Philip K. Dick: A Reading of Twenty Ontologically Uncertain Novels*. Jefferson, NC: McFarland, 2011.

Sutin, Lawrence. *Divine Invasions: A Life of Philip K. Dick*. London: Gollancz, 2006.

Vest, Jason P. *The Postmodern Humanism of Philip K. Dick*. Lanham, MD: Scarecrow Press, 2009.

Wittkower, D. E., ed. *Philip K. Dick and Philosophy: Do Androids Have Kindred Spirits?* Chicago: Open Court, 2011.

Dick and Jane Readers

From 1930 through about 1970, more than 85 million American schoolchildren learned to read using the *Dick and Jane* readers that were part of a series published by the Scott Foresman Company. The books took their name from the series' lead characters, who, with a dog named Spot and a kitten named Puff, inhabited a nostalgic, innocent American landscape of white picket fences and neighborliness. So deeply have the *Dick and Jane* stories been etched into the minds of the baby boomer generation and their immediate predecessors that repetitive phrases like "See Spot run! Run, Spot, run!" are today remembered by millions as the very first sentences they could read on their own. It has been estimated that four-fifths of the nation's schools used *Dick and Jane* readers, ranking the books with the venerable *McGuffey Readers* of the nineteenth century as a tool of universal literacy.

SERIES DEVELOPMENT

With an emphasis on methodology over content, the *Dick and Jane* series was conceived in part as a rebellion against didactic traditions that relied heavily on moralistic and patriotic texts drawn from the Bible, Shakespeare, and American historical legends. The *Dick and Jane* readers emphasized non-phonic sight reading and repetitive, limited vocabulary, a formula that had become a parody of itself by the time the approach was jettisoned in the tumultuous 1960s and replaced by phonics and books with more diverse characters and situations. The fact that method trumped content in the choice of story lines for the *Dick and Jane* readers provoked frequent criticism, such as this acerbic remark from educational critic Arther S. Trace Jr.: "Students could learn a great deal indeed from early American readers, but the only possible answer to what children can learn from the *Dick and Jane*–type reader is, 'Nothing of any consequence.'"

The *Dick and Jane* program was developed by three people—Dr. William S. Gray, an authority on pedagogy; Zerna Sharp; and Harry B. Johnston. Working with teachers and school psychologists, the team developed the Scott Foresman series, using the limited vocabulary technique advocated by Gray. Thus, the first grade *Dick and Jane* reader had only about 300 words, the third grade reader had about 1,000, and the sixth grade reader had about 4,000. Writers for the series had to adhere to strict guidelines about using limited words, and they were required to introduce only a few of them on each page, then repeat them frequently on subsequent pages. The formulaic nature of the books, along with their lack of poetry and imagination, led to criticism that they were uninteresting and unnatural.

Dick and Jane made their first appearance in 1930, in a pre-primer of the *Elson-Gray* basic reader series, with stories in large type under vividly colored heavy-line illustrations set in boxes according to 1920s graphics conventions. It was not until 1941, when Eleanor Campbell began illustrating the series, that the Dick and Jane characters, appearing in pastels, took on the rounder, "cuter" form known to most baby boomers, inviting comparisons with Norman Rockwell for their evocation of idyllic small-town life and situations. Within a short time, books were added to the series, including *More Dick and Jane Stories* (1934) and *Dick and Jane* (1936). In 1937 a pre-primer, *Before We Read*, was introduced. The concept caught on, and by the end of the 1930s half of America's schoolchildren were learning to read with Dick and Jane.

MODIFICATIONS AND CRITICISM

The *Dick and Jane* series was completely revised in 1940, introducing Campbell's illustrations and three paper-bound preprimers—*We Look and See, We Work and Play*, and *We Come and Go*—which prepared students for the 160-page primer *Fun with Dick and Jane*. In this edition "Baby" became known as "Sally," Spot became a long-haired spaniel, and the kitten previously known as "Little Mew" was renamed "Puff." In 1950 another revision introduced *The New Basic Readers*, with updated story lines and illustrations to reflect a more suburban postwar lifestyle.

In 1941 a special edition of the *Dick and Jane* readers was developed for Roman Catholic schools, the nation's largest private school system. Called the *Cathedral* series, this version featured Catholic situations and children with more "Catholic" names—John, Jean, and Judy.

The universe of the *Dick and Jane* readers was one of optimism and innocence, inviting criticism that the situations were unreal and stereotypical. As Sara Goodman Zimet writes in *What Children Read in School*: "Dick and Jane's world is a friendly one, populated by good, smiling people who are ready and eager to help children whenever necessary . . . There are no evil impulses to be controlled. Instead, free rein and encouragement is given for seeking more and more fun and play." Trace complained that the *Dick and Jane* readers ironically painted authority figures in an unfavorable light, noting that "Father behaves like a candidate for the all-American clown. He acts, in fact, like an utter ass, and Mother is almost as good a representative of the female of the species . . . These stories do, of course, help adjust students to life if their fathers and mothers are fools . . . The *Dick and Jane* readers for the early grades are comic books in hard covers."

City life is generally ignored in the *Dick and Jane* readers, leading other critics to implicate the books as partially responsible for low reading scores in inner-city schools. The series was not adapted for racial diversity until shortly before its demise: in 1965 African American characters were introduced in the form of Dick and Jane's neighbors, Mike, Pam, and Penny.

MODERN VALIDATION

The *Dick and Jane* readers fell into general disfavor in the late 1960s, partly due to changes in reading pedagogy that advanced more realistic and relevant story lines, and partly because of complaints of the books' racial and sex-role stereotyping. Still, the books have retained a sentimental hold over the millions of Americans who learned their first words within their covers, and the *Dick and Jane* readers have become both collectors' items and cultural icons.

In the late 1990s some educators began revisiting the concept of controlled vocabulary as used in the *Dick and Jane* series. Marlow Ediger, for instance, identified five major advantages to the philosophy: high word recognition, new vocabulary development, advancement of speaking vocabulary, supplementation by library books, and homogeneous reading groups. Because *Dick and Jane* books—many of which have been reissued for a contemporary generation of early readers—are success- and achievement-oriented, they give children a sense of accomplishment that some people feel is lacking in modern educational techniques. Harry Roman maintains that contemporary scientists are finding that the *Dick and Jane* readers were on the right track after all because they let children learn on their own.

Edward Moran

SEE ALSO: *Baby Boomers; Golden Books; Rockwell, Norman.*

BIBLIOGRAPHY

Ediger, Marlow. *The Controlled Vocabulary: A Reexamination.* Washington, DC: ERIC Clearinghouse, 1999.

Henderson, Harold. *Let's Kill Dick & Jane: How the Open Court Publishing Company Fought the Culture of American Education.* South Bend, IN: St. Augustine Press, 2006.

Kismaric, Carole, and Marvin Heiferman. *Growing Up with Dick and Jane.* San Francisco: Collins, 1996.

Roman, Harry T. "*Dick and Jane* and Technology Education." *Technology Teacher* 62, no. 1 (September 2002).

Trace, Arther S., Jr. *Reading without "Dick and Jane."* Chicago: Henry Regnery, 1965.

Zimet, Sara Goodman, ed. *What Children Read in School: Critical Analysis of Primary Reading Textbooks.* New York: Grune & Stratton, 1972.

Dick Tracy

Dick Tracy has been called America's most famous detective, but his fame does not stop at the border. With his chiseled countenance and tough-guy morality, Tracy has become recognizable throughout the world. When Chester "Chet" Gould created the character—the first *Dick Tracy* comic strip ran on October 4, 1931—he could not have foreseen the influence of his tough but honest police detective. In fact, the influence extends well beyond the comics, into film, radio, and television.

The timing of the comic strip's release was perfect. The Great Depression paved the way for a character who upheld traditional values even as he fell hard into the sordid underworld—he was just a regular guy fighting to make the world a better place. Moreover, Prohibition, though nearing its demise, had established heretofore unknown levels of underground criminal activity. The strip also suggested better times with its presentation of new inventions; tools to continue the war against crime; and, more importantly, inspiring signs of progress to come. *Dick Tracy* was created as a reflection of his time, and Gould's genius is reflected in the fact that the comic strip has survived for so long.

Gould always regarded himself as a cartoonist, and he had done quite a number of odd illustration jobs before showing a strip called *Plainclothes Tracy* to Captain Joseph Medill Patterson, cofounder and director of the *New York Daily News*. Patterson was himself something of a powerhouse in the world of comics. He was the editorial force behind the development of such strips as *Little Orphan Annie*, *Moon Mullins*, and *Gasoline Alley*. Patterson saw promise in *Plainclothes Tracy* and set up a meeting with Gould. It was Patterson who was responsible for the name change. The name "Dick" was slang for a detective and complemented "Tracy," Gould's play on the word "tracing." Patterson also suggested a basic outline for the first story, in which the father of Tess Trueheart, Tracy's sweetheart, is robbed and murdered and, consequently, Tracy goes into the crime-fighting business. Dick Tracy made his premiere in the Detroit *Sunday Mirror* and about a week later, on October 12, 1931, began as a daily.

COMIC STRIP

Dick Tracy quickly became not only Gould's claim to fame but also Patterson's greatest success in the field. For readers, *Dick Tracy* was something completely different. Moral tales in the comics, nearly half of which at the time were serial strips like *Dick Tracy*, were not uncommon. But *Dick Tracy* presented a rough kind of morality. Tracy was always good, the villains were always evil, and the confrontations were always flamboyant. The level of violence was new to the comics, and Gould was not above bringing his villains to the cruelest of all possible ends. Audiences were also fascinated by the details of police procedure. Fisticuffs and gunfire were there, but Gould always remembered that Dick Tracy was first and foremost a detective.

The strip also gained notoriety for its take on technology and its pageant of some of the most bizarre villains to appear anywhere. Of the inventions, the most famous was the two-way wrist radio, which later became a television and, finally, a computer. Gould believed that technology was the key to the future. Because of this, he was always experimenting with new fictional inventions that ranged from items that would eventually find equivalents in the real world—such as the Voice-O-Graph voice print recorder—to absurd "inventions" that were destined to remain purely fictional. His placement of an antennaed race of humanoids and giant snails on the moon is, however, regarded by many as the low point of the strip. At any rate, Gould lent the strip a gruesome edge with the villains, whose corrupted morals were reflected by their physical deformities. The names of the criminals are evocative in and of themselves: the Blank, Flyface, the Mole, Pruneface, and B-B Eyes.

When Chester Gould retired from *Dick Tracy* in December 1977, its artistic responsibilities were taken over by Gould's longtime assistant, Rick Fletcher, while the writing became the responsibility of Max Allan Collins. Collins was a young mystery novelist who went on to script comic books, including *Batman*, along with his own detective creation, Ms. Tree. Fletcher was eventually replaced by Pulitzer Prize–winning editorial cartoonist Dick Locher in 1983, and Collins was later replaced by Mike Killian. Locher took over the writing chores upon Killian's death in 2005 and continued producing art until 2009 (he was replaced by Jim Brozman) and retired from writing in 2011. His replacements were writer Joe Staton and artist Mike Curtis.

OTHER FORMATS

Although Gould himself did not give it much consideration, Dick Tracy refused to be simply confined to the comics page. He appeared on radio and television, in books and movies—serial and feature—and in animated cartoons. He has been personified by the likes of Ralph Byrd; Morgan Conway; Ray MacDonnell; and, in a 1990 motion picture, Warren Beatty. In addition, Dick Tracy has been the basis for a great multitude of licensed products, from toys to clothing, and, of course, watches.

Clearly, the influence of *Dick Tracy* can be seen across a spectrum of media. Although the serial strip has lost much of its foothold in American newspaper comics, comic books owe much to *Dick Tracy*. Though perhaps not the greatest draftsman to work in comics, Gould was, without a doubt, original. His use of shadows opened doors for comics to explore darker visuals. Gould's work can even be seen as a precursor of sorts to the techniques of film noir, and the police procedure of Dick Tracy became a staple of detective stories in virtually all narrative media.

Dick Tracy also served as the model for yet another icon of American culture. Bob Kane credited Dick Tracy as the inspiration for his own creation, the Batman, and Gould's menagerie of grotesque villains found reflection in the likes of the Joker and Two-Face, a virtual duplicate of Gould's Haf-and-Haf. It could be argued that *Dick Tracy* invented the look that came to be associated with both an era and a type of character: the term "hard-boiled detective" immediately conjures up an image of the trench coat and fedora pioneered by the famed Dick Tracy.

Marc Oxoby

SEE ALSO: *Batman; Beatty, Warren; Comic Books; Comics; Detective Fiction; Film Noir; The Great Depression; Hard-Boiled Detective Fiction; Little Orphan Annie; Madonna; Mafia/Organized Crime; Radio; Television.*

BIBLIOGRAPHY

Crouch, Bill, Jr. *Dick Tracy: America's Most Famous Detective.* New York: Citadel, 1987.

Roberts, Garyn G. *Dick Tracy and American Culture: Morality and Mythology, Text and Context.* Jefferson, NC: McFarland, 1993.

Dickinson, Angie *(1931–)*

An attractive and talented film actress of the 1960s and 1970s, Angie Dickinson was also the star of the popular television show *Police Woman* (1974–1978). Fans' most indelible image of Dickinson came courtesy of the 1980 Brian De Palma film *Dressed to Kill.* By then an elegant and sophisticated presence, she starred as a woman who is brutally and shockingly slashed to death in an elevator. Competing with the shower scene in *Psycho* (1960) as one of the most uncomfortably enduring celluloid murders of modern times, Dickinson's bloody demise guaranteed her immortality.

Earlier in her career, Dickinson (born Angeline Brown in North Dakota), exuded a unique blend of upfront acting, all-

American charm, sympathetic femininity, and good-natured sex appeal. She was perfect as both foil and comfort to the men in her several male-oriented films, beginning with *Rio Bravo* (1959). Although she played many sympathetic characters, a tougher quality was exploited in *The Killers* (1964) and *Point Blank* (1967). She was married for a time to musician Burt Bacharach.

Dickinson continued to act in the twenty-first century, playing small parts in movies such as *Pay It Forward* (2000) and *Oceans 11* (2001) and occasionally guest starring in television shows, including *Judging Amy* (1999–2005).

Robyn Karney

SEE ALSO: *Celebrity Couples; Hollywood; Movie Stars;* Psycho*; Television.*

BIBLIOGRAPHY

"Angie Dickinson." In *Who's Who in Hollywood*, ed. Robyn Karney. New York: Continuum, 1993.

"Angie Dickinson." IMDb. Accessed January 2012. Available from http://www.imdb.com/name/nm0001141/

Diddley, Bo *(1928–2008)*

Best known for the "shave-and-a-haircut, two bits" beat that bears his name, Bo Diddley, vocalist, guitarist, songwriter, and inventor, helped build the rhythmic foundations of rock and roll with a string of hits during the mid-1950s. Diddley came out of the Chicago blues scene but also brought the African American traditions of children's game songs, tall-tale telling, and ritualized rounds of bragging and insults into popular music (the latter perhaps making him a precursor of today's rappers). His chunky riffs and use of distortion and tremolo effects on his signature square guitar were unique at the time and later became popular with many rock guitarists, most notably Jimi Hendrix.

The history of Diddley's beat has been traced to the African Yoruba and Kongo cultures, and from there to Cuba, where the clave (KLAH-vay) rhythm was the basis for the conga, rumba, mambo, and other Afro-Cuban musical styles. Early New Orleans jazz composer Jelly Roll Morton employed it in his tune "Black Bottom Stomp" in the early twentieth century, and it was a common rhythm played by children in rural Mississippi on so-called diddley bows—homemade single-stringed instruments of probable African origin. The rhythm is also commonly referred to as "hambone," a method of slapping and stomping often used by black shoeshine boys.

Diddley was born Ellas Otha Bates in McComb, Mississippi, in 1929 but was mostly raised by his cousin Gussie McDaniel. When McDaniel moved to Chicago with Ellas and her own children, she became his legal guardian and changed his name to Ellas McDaniel. As Chicago was then the hotbed of the blues, it was there that he was undoubtedly exposed to the Afro-Cuban musical traditions and influences. "Truthfully, I don't know where it came from exactly. I just started playing it one day," Diddley said in George R. White's biography *Bo Diddley: Living Legend*. "I figured there must be another way of playing, and so I worked on this rhythm of mine. I'd say it was 'mixed-up' rhythm: blues, and Latin American, and some hillbilly, a little spiritual, a little African and a little West Indian calypso. . . . I like gumbo, you dig? Hot sauces, too. That's where my music come from: all the mixture."

Young Ellas was entranced one day shortly after moving to Chicago by a man playing a violin. He signed up for classical lessons from Professor O. W. Frederick at the Ebenezer Baptist Church, where he studied for at least twelve years. After hearing blues legend John Lee Hooker on the radio, however, he decided to play guitar instead. Diddley's sister, Lucille, bought him his first guitar when he was twelve. According to Diddley, "The violin was the railroad track, or lifeline, to me playing a guitar. . . . I used the bow licks with the guitar pick, and that's the reason for the weird sounds [he got on his guitar]. That was my way of imitating the bow on the violin strings, and that was the closest I could get to it."

Diddley attended Foster Vocational High School, where he learned to build violins and guitars, but quit school to work manual labor jobs and play on street corners. He formed a small group and played in neighborhood taverns, ultimately recording a demo that got the attention of Chess Records. Diddley, along with maracas player Jerome Green, joined Otis Spann on piano, Lester Davenport on harmonica, and Frank Kirkland on drums to record "Bo Diddley" and (on the flip side) "I'm a Man" in 1955.

Chess was prepared to issue the single under McDaniel's real name, but harmonica player Billy Boy Arnold suggested the name Bo Diddley, possibly a take-off on the primitive stringed instrument mentioned above or slang for a short, bow-legged guy, but no one seems to be sure. At any rate, the name and the single caught on, reaching number two on *Billboard*'s rhythm-and-blues singles chart. He charted many more singles on Checker, a Chess subsidiary, and recorded twenty-seven albums for Chess/Checker through 1974.

Countless artists have had hits using Diddley's rhythm, including Buddy Holly ("Not Fade Away") and Johnny Otis ("Willie and the Hand Jive"). Many more, including the Rolling Stones and Eric Clapton, have had hits covering his tunes. The Who, the Yardbirds, Ronnie Hawkins, and the Doors all employed Diddley's beat at one time or another. Unfortunately for Diddley, American copyright law does not cover a beat or rhythm—only lyrics or a melody—and he therefore never received royalties from these songs.

Diddley released a few albums in the 1980s and 1990s with his own company, BoKay Productions, and other small labels, but he found it difficult to fit in with the new style of popular music. He returned to form with the release of *A Man amongst Men* on Atlantic Records in 1996. Featuring guest musicians Jimmie Vaughan, Ron Wood, Richie Sambora, Billy Boy Arnold, Johnnie Johnson, and Johnny "Guitar" Watson, the album was nominated for a Grammy Award for Best Traditional Blues Album.

On June 2, 2008, Diddley died of heart failure at his home in Archer, Florida. Later that summer, the University of Florida posthumously awarded him a doctor of fine arts degree for his influence on American popular music.

Jon Klinkowitz

SEE ALSO: *Atlantic Records; Blues; Clapton, Eric; The Doors; Electric Guitar; Grammy Awards; Hendrix, Jimi; Holly, Buddy; Hooker, John Lee; New Orleans Rhythm and Blues; Pop Music; Rhythm and Blues; Rock and Roll; The Rolling Stones; The Who; The Yardbirds.*

***Bo Diddley.** Bo Diddley's trademark beat, guitar sounds, and singing style went on to influence rock and rap music.* MICHAEL OCHS ARCHIVES/GETTY IMAGES.

BIBLIOGRAPHY

DeCurtis, Anthony. "Living Legends." *Rolling Stone*, September 21, 1989, 89–99.

Kiersh, Edward. *Where Are You Now, Bo Diddley? The Stars Who Made Us Rock and Where They Are Now*. Garden City, NY: Doubleday, 1986.

Lydon, Michael. *Boogie Lightning*. New York: Dial, 1974.

Ratliff, Ben. "Bo Diddley—Who Gave Rock His Beat—Dies at 79." *New York Times*, June 3, 2008.

White, George R. *Bo Diddley: Living Legend*. Chessington, UK: Castle Communications, 1995.

Didion, Joan *(1934–)*

Joan Didion has proven herself one of the most acute observers of and commentators on American life in the latter half of the twentieth century and into the twenty-first century. Her widely anthologized essays have been required reading for generations of college students. Combining old-fashioned investigative reporting and New Journalistic subjectivity, she has brought her trademark style and deeply skeptical intelligence to bear on a variety of cultural phenomena, from her own marriage and the rock group the Doors to the terror in El Salvador, Cuban exiles in Miami, and the Central Park jogger case.

Her highly cinematic novels are stylistically and tonally of a piece with her nonfiction and have become increasingly journalistic and more political over the years. Focusing on women who are affluent but adrift, Didion's decidedly pessimistic novels expose not just her characters' self-delusions but the political and psychological shortcomings of an American Dream gone sour. As such, her novels, along with her essays, give laconic voice to the disillusionment and pessimism that is the other face of the radicalism of the 1960s.

Didion's most recent work has all been nonfiction: starting with *Political Fictions* (2002), *Fixed Ideas: America since 9.11* (2003), and *Where I Was From* (2004) before, brilliantly but painfully, taking a more personal turn. In *The Year of Magical Thinking* (2005), Didion deals with the sudden loss of her husband, the writer John Gregory Dunne, who died in 2003. The work received the National Book Award in 2005, and Didion adapted it for the stage in 2007. The death of her husband was followed by another tragic loss, that of her daughter, Quintana Roo, in 2005. In *Blue Nights* (2011), Didion writes of her struggle to cope with life after the tragedy. More than examples of the memoirs and therapeutic-grieving accounts that have become popular, the two books turn personal loss into self-examination that, like her books about her native California and her writing, evoke larger social concerns.

Robert A. Morace

SEE ALSO: *The Doors; Hippies.*

BIBLIOGRAPHY

Berman, Jeffrey. *Companionship in Grief: Love and Loss in the Memoirs of C. S. Lewis, John Bayley, Donald Hall, Joan Didion, and Calvin Trillin*. Amherst: University of Massachusetts Press, 2010.

Felton, Sharon, ed. *The Critical Response to Joan Didion*. Westport, CT: Greenwood, 1994.

Winchell, Mark Roydon. *Joan Didion*. Boston: Twayne, 1989.

Didrikson, Babe *(1911–1956)*

Babe Didrikson was a sports hero in the grandest American tradition: larger than life, with supersized faults to match her virtues. Carrying a chip on her shoulder from her rough-and-tumble upbringing, she approached life with swagger and wisecracks. Didrikson brought controversy and excitement to the refined world of women's golf, and she challenged assumptions everywhere she went. In addition to breaking world records regularly, she broke barriers for women. Her statistics are an inspiration to female athletes, but her personality—angry, cocky, competitive, and irrepressible—is what truly forged her place in sports history.

"Before I was even into my teens I knew exactly what I wanted to be when I grew up," Didrikson wrote in her 1955 autobiography, *This Life I've Led*. "My goal was to be the greatest athlete who ever lived." Didrikson achieved that goal. The

Mildred "Babe" Didrikson. *Mildred "Babe" Didrikson Zaharias achieved outstanding success in basketball, professional golf, and track and field, including winning three medals in the 1932 Summer Olympics.* HARRY WARNECKE/NY DAILY NEWS ARCHIVE VIA GETTY IMAGES.

Associated Press named her Female Athlete of the Year six times between 1932 and 1954, and in 1950 it christened her Female Athlete of the Half Century. She was an All-American basketball player, an Olympic gold medal winner in track and field, a record-breaking golf champion, and a proficient dabbler in other sports such as swimming and billiards. Didrikson's achievements transcend the footnote status usually given to women in sports.

Mildred Didrikson was born in the southern Texas town of Beaumont. The sixth of seven children in a working-class family, she learned early the value of toughness and self-reliance. Roaming the streets of Beaumont, she taught herself to run by racing streetcars and to jump hurdles by leaping over hedges. It was the boys in her hometown who gave her the nickname "Babe," because she hit so many home runs in their sandlot games.

Didrikson dropped out of high school and was playing semiprofessional basketball when she was made an All-American in 1932. That year she participated in an Amateur Athletic Union track-and-field championship as a one-woman team. She entered eight events and won six to capture the overall title. A team of twenty-two women came in second, eight points behind Didrikson. That day, the smart-alecky kid from southern Texas set world records in the high jump, the 80-meter hurdles, the javelin, and the baseball throw. Competing in the Olympics in Los Angeles a few weeks later, she won gold medals in the javelin and the 80-meter hurdles and a silver in the high jump. Didrikson would have won the gold in the high jump, but her best jump was disqualified because her head went over the bar before her feet.

Starting in 1935, Didrikson took the golf world by storm. Over the course of her career, she won fifty-five professional and amateur tournaments and set a record with seventeen victories in a row. Staid golfing audiences were put off by her irreverent, wisecracking style, but they could not argue with her talent. Didrikson's drives were regularly 50 to 100 yards longer than those of her opponents, and it was not uncommon for her to come in well under the men's par. The upper-class golf establishment tried to exclude Didrikson because she played professionally and women's golf was made up primarily of amateur events, but she combated this with her typical aggressiveness. In 1949 she helped found the Ladies Professional Golfers Association, giving women's golf its own venue and putting it on more of an equal footing with the men's game.

Didrikson always remained the cocky, streetwise, tough kid from Texas. Her style was both confrontational and comic—sometimes she would charm her audiences with silly trick golf shots, sometimes she would shock them with her directness. Many of her opponents hated her, perhaps because she was an egotistical and graceless winner. The press nicknamed her "muscle moll," and college physical education departments warned women against emulating her. Didrikson, however, was unfazed. She continued to start her golf matches with a grin and the quip, "Well, I'm just gonna have to loosen my girdle and let 'er fly!" She also continued to play almost every sport available, including exhibitions in baseball, football, and pool. She even sang and played harmonica on the vaudeville stage. When asked if there was anything she didn't play, Didrikson answered dryly, "Yeah, dolls."

Didrikson married professional wrestler George Zaharias in 1938. They had met when they were partnered in a golf tournament, the Los Angeles Open. In 1953 Didrikson underwent surgery for colon cancer, and doctors told her that her athletic career was over. With her typical lack of concern for the opinions of naysayers, she continued in athletics and won five golf tournaments in 1954 despite playing with pain, fatigue, and a colostomy bag. Two years later, she died. The epitaph on her tombstone in Galveston, Texas, reads: "Babe Didrikson Zaharias—1911–1956—World's Greatest Woman Athlete."

Tina Gianoulis

SEE ALSO: *Basketball; Golf; Olympics; Sports Heroes.*

BIBLIOGRAPHY

Cayleff, Susan E. *Babe: The Life and Legend of Babe Didrikson Zaharias.* Urbana: University of Illinois Press, 1995.

Knudson, R. Rozanne. *Babe Didrikson: Athlete of the Century.* New York: Viking Kestrel, 1985.

Lynn, Elizabeth A. *Babe Didrikson Zaharias.* New York: Chelsea House, 1989.

Sutcliffe, Jane, and Jeni Reeves. *Babe Didrikson Zaharias: All-Around Athlete.* Minneapolis, MN: Carolrhoda Books, 2000.

Dieting

While Americans have long been trying to meet standards of beauty imposed on them by the media, the diet craze has grown and expanded its influence over the past several decades. In the early 2010s, television talk shows regularly feature diet gurus and people offering weight-loss testimonials, and glossy publications such as *Cosmopolitan* and *Men's Health* typically contain advice on how to eat right to maintain one's figure. Despite the fact there is little evidence that diets promoted by the experts featured in these sources actually work in long term—and, in fact, with quite a bit of evidence to the contrary—a multibillion-dollar industry has grown up around the modern obsession with thinness. Men also participate in the craze, but most data indicate that women comprise the majority of consumers in the diet industry.

BEFORE THIN WAS IN

Although for contemporary Americans, thinness has been presented as an ideal of health and beauty, the lean look is a relatively new concept that was not held in such high regard 100 years ago, when having a certain amount of body fat was widely viewed as signaling health, success, and sensuality. To this day many modern cultures do not place the same value on thinness as Americans and Europeans do. Some, such as those in Polynesia and east and central Africa, value heavy women to the extent of fattening up daughters to make them more marriageable.

Evolutionary science suggests that human bodies developed in response to a struggle to survive with an uncertain food supply. One could logically surmise that in prehistoric eras the ability to store fat was a valued genetic trait that contributed to human survival. As long ago as 30,000 to 10,000 BCE, statues such as the so-called *Venus of Willendorf* show an ideal of feminine beauty that includes large thighs, broad buttocks, and pendulous breasts. The biblical book of Proverbs says, "He that putteth his trust in the Lord shall be made fat." Even in medieval Europe, when religious art showed lank, acetic Marys and Eves, secular art pictured round, fleshy women, brimming with laughter and sexuality. It seems reasonable to conclude from such artifacts that a dimpled buttock or thigh was a symbol of sex appeal.

There is also evidence to suggest that thinness, on the other hand, was viewed as a sign of weakness, disease, and poverty. Eighteenth-century diet specialist Jean-Anthelme Brillat-Savarin called thinness "a terrible misfortune" for a woman. "Every thin woman wishes to put on weight," he said, "This is an ambition that has been confided to us a thousand times." He obliged them by prescribing fattening diets. By the end of the nineteenth century, women had begun to slim their waists through the use of tightly laced corsets, but ample cleavage and voluminous hips were still very much the style, helped along by contrivances called farthingales, panniers, and bustles. These were wire frames worn under clothes to add desirable inches (or feet) to hips and buttocks. Indeed, most changes deemed necessary in the body were effected by additions to the costume.

STANDARDS BEGIN TO CHANGE

As the 1900s began, the country was in an era of tremendous growth and change. Rapid industrial growth in the United States was creating more jobs and making more products available to more people. A feminist age was beginning as women entered the workforce in unprecedented numbers. Along with these changes came a new look in women's fashions. The corsets and cumbersome contraptions were gone. By the 1920s women were supposed to be slim, straight, and boyish. Hair was bobbed, breasts and hips were bound, and women began to try to lose weight. Along with such extreme treatments as electrotherapy, tapeworm pills, and hot baths to melt off the fat, miracle diets promised to fatten the scrawny as well as slim the stout.

The Roaring Twenties' dieting craze, which never penetrated much beyond the upper classes, waned during the late 1930s and early 1940s, as the poverty of the Depression years deepened. But by the 1950s, the preference for thinness was becoming more common. The number of magazine articles about weight and diet increased dramatically. Weight-loss products and diet foods began to appear on grocery shelves. Pharmaceuticals firm Mead and Johnson created an all-liquid diet food called Metrecal that boosted their earnings more than 300 percent from 1958 to 1960. Just as quickly, however, profits dropped again, as unsuccessful dieters moved on to try other products. Amphetamines, a fairly new drug about which little was known, were prescribed as a weight-loss aid.

THE DIET CRAZE GROWS

The latter half of the twentieth century saw the continued increase of the thinness obsession. By the 1990s the diet fad had become so prevalent that young children were known to monitor their weight compulsively. Studies have been done that show a high percentage of girls as young as eight years old have begun to diet. It is likely that the popular media are at least in part culpable for this phenomenon. Fashion models routinely appear acutely undernourished, and some of them are known to have their pictures airbrushed to appear even more gaunt. Eating disorders such as anorexia (the rejection of food to achieve ever-increasing thinness) and bulimia (binge eating followed by forced vomiting or laxative-induced diarrhea), which once were rare, became more common. Surgical procedures such as stomach stapling and liposuction were also in greater demand, despite reliable evidence indicating that such procedures can have dangerous side effects.

By the turn of the twenty-first century, the diet business had grown from a few companies to a multibillion-dollar industry. With ads seemingly promising that users can "lose ten pounds for only ten dollars," or even knock off the pounds while still eating "whatever you want, whenever you want," these diet companies have made a tremendous profit by selling a series of unrealistic solutions to many gullible consumers.

The success of products such as Metrecal in the 1950s led to a boom in diet products and organizations. Whereas some products, such as SlimFast and Lean Cuisine, specialize in diet food, others have entered the market by offering light or low-fat versions of their products. Soft drink companies were among the first to profit from offering alternatives to their high-sugar products. Diet sodas are guzzled in considerable quantities by Americans of all sizes, even though their artificial sweeteners—first saccharin, then cyclamates, and most recently aspartame—have in some cases been found to have damaging effects on the body. While many of these products have been marketed to women, the beer industry, which serves more male than female consumers, has also launched several successful "lite" beer campaigns. Among the most popular of these was the Miller Lite commercials from the 1970s and early 1980s, which typically featured two famous sports icons arguing about why they preferred the beverage. One would say because the beer "tastes great" while the other would argue that it was "less filling." Another popular commercial, for Michelob Lite, featured two groups of men in an athletic competition and ran with the tag line "Michelob Lite for the Winner."

Drugs have always been an important adjunct to dieting, from amphetamines prescribed to suppress the appetite during the last half of the twentieth century to pills purporting to contain tapeworms (bought by weight-loss hopefuls in the early 1990s). During the mid-1990s a new drug called Fen Phen (fenfluramine and phentermine) seemed to be the long-sought miracle drug for weight loss. Doctors prescribed the drug for more than six million people, until it was found to cause serious heart damage in users. By 1999 the first of many class-action suits had been brought against the makers of the drug, which had to pay millions in damages to those who had been harmed.

Another form of diet business is the dieter's organization or "club." Affluent dieters often pay high prices to attend spas and "fat farms" to help them lose weight. For middle- and working-class dieters, there are more affordable alternatives. Organizations such as Weight Watchers and Jenny Craig offer counseling and group support for a price, plus a line of food products that is required or strongly suggested to go with the program. The twelve-step approach of Alcoholics Anonymous is emulated by groups such as Take off Pounds Sensibly (TOPS) and Overeaters Anonymous, which tend to view being overweight as a result of being addicted to food.

CELEBRITIES SPEAK UP

Over the years, many weight-loss "gurus" have risen to media prominence, producing books or videos to promote their personal recommendation for weight loss. As early as 1956, Roy de Groot published his low-protein "Revolutionary Rockefeller Diet" in *Look* magazine, leading the way for Robert Atkins's *Dr. Atkins' Diet Revolution* in 1972, Herman Tarnower's "Scarsdale" diet in 1979, Jane Fonda's books and videos in the 1980s and 1990s, and David Zinczenko's *Eat This, Not That* series in the opening decades of the 2000s. Trading on medical credentials or celebrity, these self-proclaimed diet experts often become corporations in themselves, profiting handsomely from sales and public appearances.

In the early years of the twenty-first century, reality television got into the diet business with a number of voyeuristic weight-loss programs. *The Biggest Loser*, where a group of obese people compete in exercise and diet challenges to lose the most weight, debuted in 2004 on NBC. By its thirteenth season in 2012, the show had spawned more than a dozen spin-offs around the world, in addition to copycats, such as ABC's *Extreme Makeover: Weight Loss Edition*. These shows claimed to focus on increasing public awareness and health, but many health care professionals worried that the public competitions are exploitative and dangerous for contestants.

NEGATIVE EFFECTS OF DIETING

Yet, in spite of ever-frantic attempts at dieting, increasing numbers of Americans are still overweight. In fact, diets have never been successful at making fat people thin. Only about 10 percent of dieters lose anything close to their goals, and only about half of those keep the weight off for an extended period of time. The body is an efficient processing machine for food, and its response to the starvation message sent by dieting is to become even more efficient, thereby needing less food to maintain the same weight. The World Health Organization's definition of starvation is 1,200 calories per day, the same intake as an average weight-loss diet. Even when caloric reduction causes the body to use stored resources, there is no guarantee that unwanted fat will be used. The body might as easily draw from muscle tissue, even from the brain or heart, with life-threatening results.

Some researchers claim that the rising instances of obesity are caused by the incessant dieting practiced by most Americans. Each bit of weight loss causes the body to respond as it would to recurring famine, by storing food, and fat, more efficiently. Even aside from overtly dangerous diets, such as liquid protein diets or extreme 400- to 500-calorie-per-day diets, any sort of weight-loss diet can have seriously negative effects. Depression, irritability, and fatigue are frequent side effects, along with amenorrhea (cessation of monthly periods) for women, muscle damage, and stress on liver, kidneys, and the cardiovascular system.

Though dieting has become entrenched in American culture, some voices are being raised in protest. The "fat-positive movement" (also called the size-acceptance or size-diversity movement) is growing, energized by people who are no longer willing to devote their lives to fitting an impossible ideal. Publications such as Marilyn Wann's *Fat!So? Because You Don't Have to Apologize for Your Size!* offer alternative approaches to living a healthy life in a fat body. Even the fashion industry has begun to embrace more realistic body types, frequently employing "plus-sized" models such as Whitney Thompson, 2008 winner of the reality competition show *America's Next Top Model*, and Emme Aronson, host of the E! Network's *Fashion Emergency*. An anti-diet movement has arisen, drawing attention to the dangers of dieting, with an annual International No-Diet Day. Concerned by the rising numbers of young girls afflicted with anorexia and bulimia (more than eleven million in the 1990s), some parents and educators are calling for more focus on raising the self-esteem of adolescents. Such advocates will likely always be in competition with the large segments of the media that send a different message about the ideal human form.

Tina Gianoulis

SEE ALSO: *Advertising;* The Biggest Loser*; Bodybuilding; Feminism; The Great Depression; Low-Carb Diets; Reality Television.*

BIBLIOGRAPHY

Atrens, Dale. *Don't Diet.* New York: William Morrow, 1988.

Bennett, William, and Joel Gurin. *The Dieter's Dilemma: Eating Less and Weighing More.* New York: Basic Books, 1982.

Chernin, Kim. *The Obsession: Reflections on the Tyranny of Slenderness.* New York: Harper and Row, 1981.

Farrell, Amy. *Fat Shame: Stigma and the Fat Body in American Culture.* New York: New York University Press, 2011.

Foxcroft, Louise. *Calories and Corsets: A History of Dieting over 2,000 Years.* London: Profile Books, 2012.

Schuyler, Nina. "Marilyn Wann Is Fat. Got a Problem with That?" Stanford Magazine. Accessed April 2012. Available from http://www.stanfordalumni.org/news/magazine/2003/julaug/features/wann.html

Seid, Roberta Pollack. *Never Too Thin: Why Women Are at War with Their Bodies.* New York: Prentice Hall, 1989.

Dietrich, Marlene *(1901–1992)*

Marlene Dietrich worked hard to become a mythological Hollywood figure. The German-born Dietrich emerged as a screen idol in the 1930s, was an entertainer of Allied troops during World War II, and ended her career as an age-defying concert

Marlene Dietrich. *Marlene Dietrich's Hollywood films capitalized on her glamour and exotic looks, making her one of the highest-paid actresses of her era.* PARAMOUNT PICTURES/GETTY IMAGES.

singer in the 1950s, 1960s, and 1970s. Her many decades of stardom were predicated on her ability to remain sexually ambivalent and mysterious, and she influenced modern pop icons such as Madonna.

Born in Berlin, Maria Magdalene "Marlene" Dietrich was the daughter of a policeman who died when she was young. During World War I her stepfather, a colonel, died of battle wounds. Although Dietrich played the violin and the piano, she was not accepted to music school. Thus, following the war, she forsook her middle-class background and embarked on a more dangerous and decadent path: the stage. She gained entry into the Max Rheinhardt School, a renowned theater institution with good connections. Dietrich was on the stage by 1922. With tireless energy, she worked her way through small roles and, as many stage actors did at the time, appeared in silent films.

THE MOVE TO HOLLYWOOD

By 1927 Dietrich's sensuous appearance had won over Berlin audiences. Two years later a successful Hollywood director, Josef von Sternberg, came to Berlin to look for someone to star in the film *The Blue Angel* (1930). He found Dietrich, and one of Hollywood's legendary collaborations began. Dietrich was already well aware of her ability to exude an ambiguous sexuality. Her risqué cabaret performances with well-known lesbian Maro Lion in their duet "It's in the Air" had been deliciously scandalous. Under the guidance of her Svengali, von Sternberg, this ambivalence became the core of Dietrich's persona. Together, they fashioned the myth of Dietrich—one of sex, sadomasochism, cool poise, and darkness. It traveled surprisingly well from the permissive Weimar culture of Berlin to the stricter environment of Hollywood.

In *The Blue Angel*, Dietrich plays Lola Lola, the ruin of a professor who falls desperately in love with her and, in return, is treated cruelly and dismissively. In the film Dietrich establishes her gender-bending image by donning tails and a top hat. She also liberally reveals what would become another part of the Dietrich myth: her long, sensual legs. Trousers added to the myth. Dietrich wore slacks outside the studio and, as a result, was called by some "the best dressed man in Hollywood."

At a time when morality clauses allowed studios to void the contracts of stars who behaved questionably, Dietrich's open bisexual affairs were indulged. Her foreign ancestry and dangerous sexuality were recognized as her main box-office appeal. Films such as *Morocco* (1930) and *Blonde Venus* (1932) cemented her image as the cool, poised femme fatale in feathers and fur.

After her relationship with von Sternberg ended, Dietrich continued to be an infamous and successful star, though she was occasionally labeled "box-office poison." Her desire to broaden her appeal led to starring roles in productions by Ernst Lubitsch—*Desire* (1936) and *Angel* (1937)—that enabled her to display humor as well as sexuality. Other ventures into different genres included a Western parody, *Destry Rides Again*, directed by George Marshall and released in 1939.

THE WAR YEARS AND BEYOND

During World War II Dietrich added a new dimension to her identity. Her foreign origin and accent, as well as the decadent sexual persona that was fueled by her continental European ancestry, had been part of her draw, but now her vehemently anti-Nazi stance and her belief in the American way of life led her to assist in the war effort. She worked for the United States Entertainment Organization, appeared at fund-raising events, and entertained the troops on the front lines in Europe. Her most famous song, "Lili Marleen," stems from this period. The head of the German Nazi Ministry of Culture had earlier asked her to return to her homeland to be a great Nazi star, even after some of her films had been banned in Germany. As an answer, Dietrich became a U.S. citizen in 1937. In 1945 she returned to Germany to bury her mother and, according to her daughter Maria Riva, to bury her connection to the country she once knew and loved.

After the war Dietrich's film roles were sporadic. Movies such as *Rancho Notorious* (1952) and *A Touch of Evil* (1958) are tongue-in-cheek takes on her carefully constructed persona. Dietrich's main focus was now the stage: she recaptured her original calling from the years in Weimar and embarked on a successful career as an international cabaret star. Although her singing voice was criticized, she had a full-blown cabaret delivery.

Her repertoire consisted of sexy songs, often originally written for male singers, allowing her to exhibit her worldly charm and eroticism. Numbers recorded by Dietrich include "One for My Baby," "One More for the Road," and "Makin' Whoopee." However, the image of Dietrich as a femme fatale shifted somewhat when she began performing a strand of antiwar songs, such as *"Sag mir wo die Blumen sind"* ("Where Have All the Flowers Gone") and other tunes by Pete Seeger and Bob Dylan. During a concert in Israel, she broke a taboo against the German language by singing against the war in her mother tongue. She also went back to Germany for what would be a successful performance, even though she was still called a traitor by some.

Dietrich ended her stage career in 1975 when she broke a leg on stage. With many of her old friends dead, including her husband from her Weimar years, she led a somewhat reclusive life in her adopted home of Paris until her death in 1992.

AN INDELIBLE IMAGE

For decades Dietrich had been a focal point of the famous—her rumored lovers included Ernest Hemingway, Greta Garbo, and Jean Gabin. At the end of her career, however, she became camera-shy. She claimed this was not due to vanity but rather her need to protect her image as an icon of glamour, ambivalent sexuality, erotic sophistication, and mystery. Her skill was well rewarded. Later generations of artists have plundered and recycled the rich image of Dietrich. Her most well-known "interpreter" has been Madonna—another star of sexual ambivalence and mystery.

In her book *ABC*, Dietrich writes: "Dietrich—In the German language the name for a key that opens all locks. Not a magic key. A very real object, necessitating great skill in the making."

Petra Kuppers

SEE ALSO: *Garbo, Greta; Hemingway, Ernest; Madonna; Sex Symbol; von Sternberg, Josef; World War II.*

BIBLIOGRAPHY

Bach, Steven. *Marlene Dietrich—Life and Legend*. New York: William Morrow, 1992.

Riva, Maria. *Marlene Dietrich*. New York: Alfred A. Knopf, 1992.

Spoto, Donald. *Blue Angel: The Life of Marlene Dietrich.* New York: Doubleday, 1992.

Diff'rent Strokes

For eight seasons and 189 episodes, Americans tuned in to *Diff'rent Strokes,* a sitcom chronicling the family life of a wealthy white industrialist who adopts two African American children. The tepid comedy's lengthy television run made many cultural observers wonder if its creators had made a deal with the devil. Certainly the show's trinity of child stars seems to have spent the ensuing years in show business purgatory.

Developed by Norman Lear, the brains behind *All in the Family, Diff'rent Strokes* began as a well-meaning, if patronizing, look at America's racial and economic divides. Conrad Bain, a veteran of Lear's *Maude,* was cast as Philip Drummond, the white Daddy Warbucks to black ragamuffins Arnold and Willis Jackson, played by Gary Coleman and Todd Bridges. Stringy Dana Plato rounded out the main cast as Drummond's natural daughter, Kimberly. A succession of brassy housekeepers, vanguarded by Charlotte Rae, commented mordantly on the goings-on.

Conceived as an ensemble, *Diff'rent Strokes* quickly became a star vehicle for the adorable Coleman, a natural comedic talent relegated to Lilliputian stature by a congenital kidney condition. "What'chu talkin' about, Willis?," Coleman's Arnold would bellow repeatedly at his older, worldlier sibling. Eventually this interrogative came to be something of a catchphrase, flung promiscuously by Coleman at any of the show's characters and accompanied by a mugging double take. As the years went by, however, Coleman's stunted growth began to take on an eerie, sideshow quality. Only at the very end of the eight-year run was his character allowed to grow up, date girls, and behave like something other than a mischievous eight-year-old. Coleman was seventeen at the time.

Medical oddities aside, *Diff'rent Strokes* was little more than light entertainment for the home-on-Saturday-night crowd. It did, however, occasionally tackle meaningful subject matter. In one memorable episode, Arnold converted to Judaism after attending a friend's bar mitzvah. Pleased with his complimentary "yamaha," the diminutive adoptee was dissuaded from his change of faith only after Drummond engineered a visit from Milton Berle as a wisecracking rabbi. Terrified by the prospect of Hebrew School and Jewish dietary obligations, the impressionable tyke opted to forego his opportunity to celebrate "harmonica."

Not all series installments, however, addressed weighty issues with such rampant insensitivity. Rotund *WKRP in Cincinnati* fixture Gordon Jump played a child molester in one topical episode, while First Lady Nancy Reagan herself dropped by for a memorable 1983 show about drug abuse. The jaded Coleman was nonplussed by the visit from the power-suited astrology enthusiast, who stiffly hugged a group of child actors for the cameras and accepted a pair of *Diff'rent Strokes* T-shirts from Conrad Bain before departing in a four-car motorcade. "It was just another show," Coleman shrugged after Reagan's visit. "We didn't talk about much. She came in, did her job, and left."

When the program's three young stars made their exits following *Diff'rent Strokes*'s 1986 cancellation by ABC, they had no way of knowing that a living tabloid hell awaited them. Dana Plato posed nude for *Playboy* in 1989 to pay off her mounting personal debt and then robbed a Las Vegas video store at gunpoint in 1991 after being turned down for a job cleaning toilets. Her career reached a nadir in 1998 with an appearance in a porno film entitled *Different Strokes: The Story of Jack and Jill . . . and Jill.* (Plato died of an accidental drug overdose in 1999.) Todd Bridges was arrested for cocaine possession and later for shooting an accused drug dealer in a crack house. (He was subsequently acquitted of the latter crime.) He later blamed his problems on a cocaine habit. In 2010 Bridges wrote an autobiography called *Killing Willis,* which details his attempts to overcome his addictions and forge his own identity.

Even Gary Coleman, the little pixie with the atrophied kidney, could not escape controversy. In 1989 he sued his real-life adoptive parents and his former business manager, claiming they had stolen more than $1 million from him. Tabloid rumors began to circulate reporting that Coleman had legally changed his name to Andy Shane and asked a female housemate if he could suck her toes. In 1998 the tubby actor, now working as a mall security guard, was himself sued by a Los Angeles bus driver who alleged that he had assaulted her after she asked him for an autograph. In 2008 the 40-year-old Coleman married a 22-year-old woman named Shannon Price. It was his first marriage. In 2010 Coleman, who had suffered numerous health problems over the years, died of a brain hemorrhage.

"The world don't move to the beat of just one drum," went the theme to *Diff'rent Strokes,* the television show. "What might be right for you, may not be right for some." The program's troubled stars seem to have been following a rhythm all their own in their personal lives as well.

Robert E. Schnakenberg

SEE ALSO: All in the Family*; Berle, Milton; Child Stars; Lear, Norman;* Maude*;* Playboy*; Sitcom; Tabloids; Television;* WKRP in Cincinnati.

BIBLIOGRAPHY

Armstrong, Lois. "For Gary Coleman, Acting with the First Lady Is No Big Deal." *People Weekly,* March 28, 1983.

Bridges, Todd, and Sarah Tomlinson *Killing Willis: From "Diff'rent Strokes" to the Mean Streets to the Life I Always Wanted.* New York: Touchstone, 2010.

Sporkin, Elizabeth. "Diff'rent Strokes, Fallen Stars." *People Weekly,* March 25, 1991.

Dilbert

Dilbert's subject matter "strikes a nerve," as *Newsweek*'s cover story shouted in August 1996, because it "portrays the bedrock truth of the American workplace, at least in the white-collar caverns where clerks, engineers, marketers, and salespeople dwell." This comic strip presents aspects of the corporate culture that veterans of the cubicle easily identify with: company monitoring of employee e-mail, management double talk, carpal tunnel syndrome, endless and pointless meetings, inane team-building exercises, and lower-back pains resulting from excessive hours in front of the computer screen. Since his initial appearance in the early 1990s as the creation of MBA-trained and former Pacific Bell software engineer Scott Adams, Dilbert, a nerdy engineer and the strip's main character, has become a sort of corporate everyman.

THE CHARACTERS

The strip centers on an anonymous company where Dilbert is employed in an unnamed department. With coworkers, he struggles to meet deadlines, withstand management trends, and endure other indignities. Each of the strip's main characters is described in Adams's 1997 retrospective, *Seven Years of Highly Defective People*, and was inspired and shaped by bits and pieces of his own experience at Pacific Bell. Much of the subject matter is supplemented by "war stories" taken directly from reader e-mail and visitors to the "Dilbert Zone," Adams's website. Each character, therefore, embodies some facet of corporate reality, which is probably why readers familiar with the environment identify with the strip's material so readily.

The more significant of Dilbert's coworkers are Wally, a fellow engineer and "thoroughly cynical employee who has no sense of company loyalty and feels no need to mask his poor performance or his total lack of respect," and Alice, a no-nonsense go-getter known for her "pink suit, her fluffy hair, her coffee obsession, her technical proficiency, and her take-no-crap attitude." Other characters include the "generic guy" Ted, whose manic work habits go unnoticed by the company bigwigs; Tina, the technical writer who resents the engineers for their failure to appreciate her talents; and Asok, who is competent but not taken seriously because he is only an intern.

This motley cast struggles to withstand the whimsical machinations and inane directives of Dilbert's dog, the annoying know-it-all Dogbert; his cat, the head of the Evil Human Resources, Catbert; the troglodytes of the Accounting Department; the Teflon-coated PR types in marketing who have no clue about what engineers do; and the "Pointy-Haired Boss," whose coif reflects his ultimately demonic stature as a figure of management inanity and cluelessness. Together, these characters represent the worst face of corporate culture and are frequently seen drafting dehumanizing policies, issuing obscure directives, arbitrarily demonstrating their authority, and generally making life miserable for the employees who nonetheless "see through" their motives.

MANAGEMENT TAKES NOTICE

Dilbert's world isn't too different from that of his audience of real-life counterparts who identify with his struggle to maintain his sanity. In the mid-1990s, *Dilbert* became a hot topic for discussion among management strategists and human resources officers, and a voice of late-capitalist corporate worker cynicism. Management consultant Tom Brown notes in *HR focus* that Adams's strip "take[s] virtually every HR issue of the past 20 years and catapults it to the top of many management agendas via trenchant cartoons and scathing essays in books. . . . *Dilbert* is about human rights, human purpose, and human potential. It's what the human resources profession is about, or ought to be, as well." Indeed, Adams's comic lampoons of corporate America achieved status as mandatory reading for those in the management and human resources professions.

Along with his stature as an embodiment of worker frustration, Dilbert has become a prosperous commodity as a merchandising icon. In the late 1990s the nerdy engineer's visage could be found on everything from ties to mouse pads to coffee mugs, and his website was both the bane and a boon to corporations, some of which advertised on it while others blocked employee access to it. An article in the *Economist* in April 1997 observed, "There are Dilbert dolls, Dilbert calendars and ties, a $20m contract for another five Dilbert books, plus plans for Dilbert-based television programmes and computer software. There is even talk of a Dilbertland theme park, complete with boss-shooting galleries. Mr. Adams's only real worry is over-exposure—and, as he happily points out, 'you can't get to over-exposure without going through filthy rich first.'" The prediction of a television show came true in 1999 when the pilot for *Dilbert* was aired on UPN. The TV series ran for two seasons before being canceled. In 2001 Adams collaborated with a design firm to come up with a better office cubicle. He also gave readers a peek into the workings of his mind in 2004 with *It's Not Funny If I Have to Explain It*, a collection of some of his favorite strips with handwritten commentary about each.

FINDING FAULT IN *DILBERT*

Given its success, the strip has inevitably prompted criticism from those who see it as yet another management tool. In his 1997 critique *The Trouble with Dilbert: How Corporate Culture Gets the Last Laugh*, author Norman Solomon contends that with *Dilbert*, "corporate America is not selling us the rope to hang it with; corporate America is selling us the illusions to exculpate it with. To mistake pop-culture naughtiness for opposition to the corporate system is an exercise in projection—and delusion." Others have also found it easy to point to the strip's popularity and overexposure as signs that it represents not a paean to disenfranchised workers but just another capitalist success story.

Within its series of strategies for avoiding work while still looking busy, *Dilbert*'s ultimate message is that the greater the technological and organizational sophistication in the workplace, the more opportunities exist to create the false image of actual productivity, as well as the documentation to validate it as production. Whether regarded as a subversive attack on the corporation or merely as a "steam valve" to give release to the corporate worker's frustrations, *Dilbert* continues to provide an important voice in the dialogue between the corporation and those at the lower levels who make it run.

Warren Tormey

SEE ALSO: *Comics.*

BIBLIOGRAPHY

Adams, Scott. *The Dilbert Principle: A Cubicle's-Eye View of Bosses, Meetings, Management Fads, and Other Workplace Afflictions.* New York: HarperBusiness, 1996.

Adams, Scott. *Seven Years of Highly Defective People: Scott Adams' Guided Tour of the Evolution of Dilbert.* Kansas City, MO: Andrews McMeel, 1997.

Adams, Scott. *It's Not Funny If I Have to Explain It: A Dilbert Treasury.*. Kansas City, MO: Andrews McMeel, 2004.

Adams, Scott. *Dilbert 2.0: 20 Years of Dilbert.* Kansas City, MO: Andrews McMeel, 2008.

"The Anti-Management Guru: Scott Adams Has Made a Business of Bashing Business. Why Does the Hand He Bites Love to Feed Him?" *Economist*, April 3, 1997, 64.

Brown, Tom. "What Does Dilbert Mean to HR?" *HR focus*, February 1997, 12–13.

Levy, Steven. "Working in Dilbert's World." *Newsweek*, August 11, 1996, 52–57.

Solomon, Norman. *The Trouble with Dilbert: How Corporate Culture Gets the Last Laugh*. Monroe, ME: Common Courage Press, 1997.

Dillard, Annie *(1945–)*

One of the best-known writers of the twentieth century and winner of the 1975 Pulitzer Prize for general nonfiction, Annie Dillard has developed a following unique among writers. Her readers embrace her mixture of literary, philosophical, theological, and scientific themes regardless of the genre in which they appear, from the essays of *Pilgrim at Tinker Creek* (1974), *Holy the Firm* (1977), and *Teaching a Stone to Talk* (1982), to the poetry of *Tickets for a Prayer Wheel* (1974) and *Mornings Like This* (1995), and from the autobiographical prose of *Encounters with Chinese Writers* (1984), *An American Childhood* (1987), and *The Writing Life* (1989) to the literary criticism of *Living by Fiction* (1982) and the fiction of *The Living* (1992). In part, Dillard achieved her popularity because of her ongoing interest in spiritual experience, interdisciplinary knowledge, and aesthetic creation, all topics that mirror the concerns of a growing segment of the reading public.

EARLY YEARS AND CAREER

Born Meta Ann Doak in Pittsburgh, Pennsylvania, on April 30, 1945, Dillard was the oldest of Frank and Pam Doak's three daughters. She spent her youth reading books, studying the natural world, and "getting religion"—experiences she recounts in detail in *An American Childhood*. After graduating from the Ellis School in Pittsburgh, she attended Hollins College in Roanoke, Virginia, where she received a BA (1967) and an MA (1968) in English literature. While there, she met her first husband—her writing teacher, Richard Dillard—whom she married in 1965 and whose name she retained after the marriage ended.

Her first book, the slim volume of poetry titled *Tickets for a Prayer Wheel* (1974), was well received, but its publication was overshadowed by *Pilgrim at Tinker Creek*, released only a few months later. Described by Dillard, quoting Thoreau, as "a meteorological journal of the mind," the book recounts the year (1972) she spent walking, reading, and journal keeping while living on Tinker Creek in the Blue Ridge Mountains of Virginia. After advance chapters were published in *Harper's* and the *Atlantic Monthly*, the book was widely and enthusiastically reviewed, launching its twenty-nine-year-old author into instant literary celebrity.

UNCOMFORTABLE SUCCESS

Disturbed by the attention she was receiving, especially after winning the Pulitzer Prize, Dillard accepted a position as scholar in residence at Western Washington University in 1975 and moved to an isolated island in Puget Sound. There she wrote *Holy the Firm*, a short but powerful prose narrative about the relationship between beauty and violence, a topic she had previously begun to explore in *Pilgrim*. Inspired by a plane crash in which a neighbor's child was badly burned, the book relates Dillard's process of coming to terms with the seeming contradiction between the existence of human suffering and the idea of a loving and all-powerful God.

In 1979 Dillard accepted a new post as visiting professor of creative writing at Wesleyan University in Middletown, Connecticut, where she subsequently remained as writer in residence. Having divorced her first husband in 1975, Dillard married anthropologist Gary Clevidence in 1980. In 1982 she published two books, *Teaching a Stone to Talk: Expeditions and Encounters* and *Living by Fiction*. The first, a collection of essays, received excellent reviews; the second, a work of literary criticism, garnered more muted praise. She followed these two works in 1984 with *Encounters with Chinese Writers*, an account based in part on her visit to China in 1982 as a member of a cultural delegation.

In 1988, having published *An American Childhood*, Dillard divorced Clevidence and married Robert D. Richardson Jr., whom she had met after reading his biography, *Henry Thoreau: A Life of the Mind* (1986). At this time she also worked on *The Writing Life*, a description of the writing process and the creative energies it entails.

Dillard published her first novel, *The Living*, in 1992. Expanding a short story of the same name that she had written for *Harper's* in 1978, the story spans forty-two years, from 1855 to 1897, and explores the frontier history of Whatcom, a town on Bellingham Bay in Washington state. Although the tale is related by an omniscient narrator, *The Living* nonetheless reflects Dillard's continuing concerns throughout her books with the arbitrariness of death, the insignificance of individuals in an indifferent universe, and the necessity of faith despite the knowledge of these uncomfortable truths.

The popularity of Dillard's writing during the late 1980s and 1990s can be judged by the frequency with which her work was reprinted during these decades. As well as excerpts included in multiauthor collections, the four-volume *Annie Dillard Library* appeared in 1989, followed by *Three by Annie Dillard* (1990), and *The Annie Dillard Reader* (1994). During these years she also served as the coeditor of two volumes of prose—*The Best American Essays* (1988), with Robert Atwan, and *Modern American Memoirs* (1995), with Cort Conley—and crafted *Mornings Like This: Found Poems*, a collection of excerpts from other writers' prose, which she reformatted into verse.

Though a minor work, *Mornings Like This* could be said to encapsulate all of the qualities that have made Dillard's work consistently popular among readers: clever and playful, it displays her wide learning and eclectic tastes, her interest in the intersection of nature and science with history and art, and her desire to create beauty and unity out of the lost and neglected fragments of human experience.

Most recently, Dillard has published *For the Time Being* (1999), a collection of narrative nonfiction similar to *Holy the Firm*, and *The Maytrees* (2007), her second novel, which was named one of the Top Ten Books of the Year by the *New York Times Book Review*.

Daniel J. Philippon

SEE ALSO: Atlantic Monthly*; Best Sellers;* Harper's.

BIBLIOGRAPHY

Dillard, Annie. *Pilgrim at Tinker Creek*. New York: Harper's Magazine Press, 1974.

Dillard, Annie. *An American Childhood*. New York: Harper and Row, 1987.

Dillard, Annie. *The Annie Dillard Reader.* New York: HarperCollins, 1994.

Johnson, Sandra Humble. *The Space Between: Literary Epiphany in the Work of Annie Dillard.* Kent, OH: Kent State University Press, 1992.

Parrish, Nancy C. *Lee Smith, Annie Dillard, and the Hollins Group: A Genesis of Writers.* Baton Rouge: Louisiana State University Press, 1998.

Smith, Linda L. *Annie Dillard.* Boston: Twayne, 1991.

Thompson, Roger, and J. Scott Bryson. *Twentieth-Century American Nature Writers: Prose.* Detroit, MI: Gale, 2003.

Diller, Phyllis *(1917– 2012)*

Comedienne Phyllis Diller occupies a unique position in the annals of American stand-up comedy as the first woman to make her name in that previously all-male preserve. Remarkably, her show business career began in 1955 when she was thirty-seven years old. Diller progressed from being the only touring female comedienne in the United States to one of the world's most successful and best-loved comics, and she is the acknowledged forerunner to the many female comics who have followed her.

Phyllis Ada Driver was born in Lima, Ohio. She studied classical piano at the Sherwood Conservatory of Music and received a music education degree from Buffton College, but she shelved her music career to marry Sherwood Diller and start a family. Almost fifteen years and five children later, in California, desperation—rather than dormant ambition—drove her to reconsider a stage career.

Phyllis Diller. *Phyllis Diller is most noted for her stage persona of a wild-haired, eccentrically dressed housewife who makes self-deprecating jokes.* TIME & LIFE PICTURES/GETTY IMAGES.

As a housewife and mother, Diller's life began to fall apart in 1953. Her husband had lost his job, bills were past due, and it began to look as if the family would lose their house. Diller found a job writing for a local radio station; two years later she quit that job to pursue a career as a stand-up comic. She auditioned at San Francisco's Purple Onion, and, though female comedians were extremely rare, she was engaged for a two-week stint. Her instant popularity with audiences turned the two weeks into an eighty-seven-week run. In 1959 she appeared before the nation on *The Jack Paar Tonight Show* (1957–1962), and in 1960 she performed at Carnegie Hall, not at the piano but on it—vamping and slithering and singing satirical songs interspersed with rapid-fire comic patter.

Calling her comedy "tragedy revisited," Diller based her act on her experiences as a housewife. Dressed in outrageous costumes, with wildly disheveled bleached-blond hair and a raucous, maniacal laugh, she lampooned housework; her neighbors; a fictitious husband she called "Fang"; and, most of all, herself. She has always written her own material, and the jokes come fast and furious, sometimes as many as twelve punch lines a minute. She takes pride in the fact that her jokes are "clean," though she has been criticized by feminists for her self-deprecating put-downs of her own looks and abilities. Though "Fang" is a creation of her act and, she claims, not based on either of her two husbands, the family of her first husband once brought an unsuccessful lawsuit against her for denigrating him in her routine.

Diller continued to perform her comedy act in arenas as diverse as Las Vegas supper clubs and Madison Square Garden. She did, however, return to her classical music roots from 1971 to 1982, when she played as a soloist with more than 100 different symphony orchestras around the country, using the "virtuoso" name Illya Dillya. She has also performed in stage shows and many films. Her one dramatic role was a surprising tour de force as the wife of Zero in the film version of Elmer Rice's expressionistic play *The Adding Machine* (1969); a high point of her stage career was on Broadway in 1970 where, for several months, she played Dolly Levi in *Hello Dolly!*. Diller played a number of roles in various television productions, including a long-term stint on the soap opera *The Bold and the Beautiful* (1987–) between 1999 and 2004 and a much-loved 2007 cameo on *Boston Legal* (2004–2008). She has a recurrent gig as the voice of Thelma Griffin on the animated series *Family Guy* (1999–).

Though it was the comedic projection of herself as a frumpy grotesque that won Diller her fame and fortune, her cultivated image masked an intense insecurity about her looks. Determined to change the things she did not like about her face and body, she became notorious for her relationship with cosmetic surgery. Blatantly outspoken, she has always admitted to having herself "fixed," saying, "I used to be young and ugly. Now I'm old and gorgeous." Her very public admission of her many procedures—facelifts, nose job, tummy tuck, cheek implants, and straightened teeth among them—have caused plastic surgeons to hail her as a boon to their business. She has written humor books and made many best-selling comedy albums. A gourmet chef, she turned entrepreneur to market her own chili and has sold her own lines of cosmetics and jewelry. There is, however, another side to Diller. Like many celebrities, she has used her fame and wealth to support humanitarian causes and has been honored accordingly.

Diller had suffered health problems since the late 1990s, and in 2002 she retired from stand-up comedy. In 2005 she published a memoir titled *Like a Lampshade in a Whorehouse.* She was still making occasional television appearances, including a 2011 appearance on CNN's *Anderson Cooper 360*, up until she died peacefully at her home at age 95 on August 20, 2012.

Tina Gianoulis

SEE ALSO: *Broadway; Carnegie Hall; Celebrity; CNN;* Family Guy*; Feminism;* Hello, Dolly!*; Plastic Surgery; Radio; Soap Operas; Stand-Up Comedy; Television;* The Tonight Show.

BIBLIOGRAPHY

Borns, Betsy. "Phyllis Diller." *Interview*, September, 1986, 25.

Diller, Phyllis, and Richard Buskin. *Like a Lampshade in a Whorehouse: My Life in Comedy.* New York: JP Tarcher/Penguin, 2005.

Smith, Ronald L. "Diller's Choice." *Writer's Digest*, November 1982, 20.

Dillinger, John *(1902?–1934)*

During the Great Depression, many Americans, nearly helpless against forces they did not understand, made heroes of outlaws who took what they wanted at gunpoint and stole from institutions that they felt were oppressing them. Of all these lurid desperadoes, John Dillinger more than any other came to evoke this gangster era, stirring mass emotion to a degree rarely seen in this country. That admiration was drawn partly from Dillinger's keen enjoyment of his status as a celebrity. In truth, he was not the leader of a crime syndicate but was merely a brutal thief and a cold-blooded murderer. From September 1933 until July 1934, he and his violent gang terrorized the Midwest, killing ten men and wounding seven others, robbing banks and police arsenals, and staging three memorable jail breaks in which they killed a sheriff and wounded two guards. Dillinger was so determined to remain free that he resorted to plastic surgery on his nose, cheeks, and chin to disguise his appearance. He also tried to burn away his fingerprints with acid. He became something of a folk hero because he successfully thwarted his pursuers, but it was only for a time.

BEGINNINGS

John Herbert Dillinger was born on either June 28, 1902, or June 22, 1903, in the middle-class Oak Hill section of Indianapolis. His father, a hardworking grocer, raised him in an atmosphere of disciplinary extremes, harsh and repressive on some occasions but generous and permissive on others. Dillinger's mother died when he was three, and he resented his stepmother when his father remarried six years later. He loved to read of the Old West, and his hero was the outlaw Jesse James. In adolescence, Dillinger was frequently in trouble. Finally, he quit school and obtained a job in a machine shop in Indianapolis. Although intelligent and a good worker, he soon became bored, often staying out all night. His father, worried that the temptations of the city were corrupting his teenage son, sold his property in Indianapolis and moved his family to a farm near Mooresville, Indiana. However, Dillinger responded no better to rural life than he had to that in the city, and he soon began to run wild again.

After being arrested for auto theft, Dillinger was given the opportunity to enlist in the navy, where he soon got into more trouble, deserting his ship when it docked in Boston. Returning to Mooresville, he married sixteen-year-old Beryl Hovius in 1924 and moved to Indianapolis. Finding no work in the city, Dillinger joined the town pool shark, Ed Singleton, in his quest for easy money. They tried to rob a Mooresville grocer but were quickly apprehended. Singleton pled not guilty, stood trial, and was sentenced to two years. Dillinger, following his father's advice, confessed, was convicted of assault and battery with intent to rob and conspiracy to commit a felony, and received joint sentences of two to fourteen years and ten to twenty years in the Indiana State Prison. Stunned by the harsh sentence, Dillinger became a tortured, bitter man in prison, where he learned the tricks of the trade that stood him in good stead when he was back on the streets.

CRIME SPREES

Dillinger's notoriety grew when he made a successful prison break. On May 10, 1933, he was paroled from prison after serving eight and a half years of his sentence. He almost immediately robbed a bank in Bluffton, Ohio. Dayton police arrested him on September 22, and he was lodged in the county jail in Lima, Ohio, to await trial. While frisking him, the Lima police found a document outlining a plan for a prison break, but Dillinger denied knowledge of any plan. Four days later, using the same plans, eight of his friends shot two guards and escaped from the Indiana State Prison, using shotguns and rifles that had been smuggled into their cells.

On October 12, three of the escaped prisoners and a parolee from the same prison, Harry Pierpont, Russell Clark, Charles Makley, and Harry Copeland, showed up at the Lima jail where Dillinger was incarcerated. They told the sheriff that they had come to return Dillinger to the Indiana State Prison for violation of his parole. When the sheriff asked to see their credentials, one of the men pulled a gun, shot the sheriff, and beat him into unconsciousness. Then, taking the keys to the jail, the bandits freed Dillinger; locked the sheriff's wife and a deputy in a cell; and, leaving the sheriff to die on the floor, made their getaway.

Dillinger and his gang pulled several bank robberies and also plundered police arsenals at Auburn and Peru, Indiana, stealing several machine guns, rifles, and revolvers; a quantity of ammunition; and several bulletproof vests. On December 14, John Hamilton, a Dillinger gang member, shot and killed a police detective in Chicago. A month later the Dillinger gang killed a police officer during the robbery of the First National Bank of East Chicago, Indiana. Then they made their way to Florida and, subsequently, to Tucson, Arizona. There, on January 23, 1934, a fire broke out in the hotel where Clark and Makley were hiding under assumed names. Firemen recognized the men from their photographs, and local police arrested them along with Dillinger and Pierpont. Police also seized three Thompson submachine guns, two Winchester rifles mounted as machine guns, five bulletproof vests, and more than $25,000 in cash, part of it from the East Chicago robbery.

Dillinger was sequestered at the county jail in Crown Point, Indiana, to await trial for the murder of the East Chicago police officer. Authorities boasted that the jail was "escape proof," but on March 3, 1934, he cowed the guards with what he claimed later was a wooden gun he had whittled. He forced them to open the door to his cell, then grabbed two machine guns, locked up the guards and a trustee, and fled in the sheriff's car, hightailing it to nearby Illinois. The stunt captured headlines around the world and earned Dillinger top priority on FBI director J. Edgar Hoover's hit list.

By stealing the sheriff's car and driving it across a state line, Dillinger had violated the National Motor Vehicle Theft Act, which made it a federal offense to transport a stolen motor vehicle across a state line. A federal complaint was sworn, charging Dillinger with the theft and with interstate transportation of the sheriff's car, which actively involved the FBI in the nationwide search for Dillinger. Meanwhile, Pierpont, Makley, and Clark were returned to Ohio and convicted of the murder of the Lima sheriff. Pierpont and Makley were sentenced to death and Clark to life imprisonment. But in an escape attempt, Makley was killed and Pierpont was wounded. A month later, Pierpont had recovered sufficiently to be executed.

ENDINGS

Hoover protégé Melvin Purvis was put in charge of capturing Dillinger, and in late April "Nervous" Purvis received a tip that the bandit was holed up at Little Bohemia, a lakeside resort in Wisconsin. Purvis and his team blundered onto the resort grounds and blazed away indiscriminately at what proved to be innocent customers leaving a restaurant. While an agent was reporting on the debacle, the operator broke in to tell him there was trouble at another cottage about 2 miles away. FBI Special Agent W. Carter Baum, another FBI agent, and a constable arrived to find a parked car, which the constable recognized as belonging to a local resident. They pulled up and identified themselves. Inside the other car, "Baby Face" Nelson, a member of Dillinger's gang, was holding three local residents at gunpoint. He turned, leveled a revolver at the lawmen's car, and ordered them to step out. But without waiting for them to comply, Nelson opened fire. Baum was killed, and the constable and the other agent were severely wounded. Nelson jumped into the Ford they had been using and fled.

For the second time in three weeks, Dillinger had made the feds look like fools. Hoover appointed a trusted Washington inspector, Sam Cowley, to take thirty handpicked men and form a special Dillinger squad in Chicago, though Purvis remained Agent in Charge. He was rated Public Enemy Number One and was featured on wanted posters all over the United States. Eliminating him had become a public relations imperative, despite the lack of proof that he personally had ever killed anyone.

Late in the afternoon of Saturday, July 21, 1934, the madam of a brothel in Gary, Indiana, contacted one of the police officers with information. This woman called herself Anna Sage but was actually Ana Cumpanas, who had entered the United States from her native Romania in 1914. Because of the nature of her profession, she was considered an undesirable alien by the Immigration and Naturalization Service, and deportation proceedings were underway. Sage was willing to sell the FBI information about Dillinger for a cash reward, plus the FBI's help in preventing her deportation. As Public Enemy Number One, there was a $10,000 price on Dillinger's head.

At a meeting with Sage, Cowley and Purvis were cautious. They promised her the reward if her information led to Dillinger's capture, but they cautioned her that all they could do was call her cooperation to the attention of the Department of Labor, which at that time handled deportation matters. Satisfied, Sage told the agents that a girlfriend of hers, Polly Hamilton, had visited her establishment with Dillinger. Sage said she had recognized him from a newspaper photograph. She told the agents that she, Hamilton, and Dillinger probably would be going to the movies the following evening at either the Biograph Theater or the Marbro Theater. She said that she would notify them when the theater was chosen. She also said that she would wear a red dress so she would be easy to identify.

On Sunday, July 22, Sage called to confirm the plans, but she still did not know which theater they would attend. Therefore, agents and policemen were sent to both theaters. At 8:30 p.m., Sage, Dillinger, and Hamilton strolled into the Biograph Theater to see Clark Gable in *Manhattan Melodrama* (1934). Purvis phoned Cowley, who shifted the other men from the Marbro to the Biograph. Cowley also phoned Hoover for instructions, who cautioned them to wait outside rather than risk a shooting match inside the crowded theater. Each man was instructed not to unnecessarily endanger himself and was told that if Dillinger offered any resistance, it would be each man for himself.

At 10:30 p.m., Dillinger, with his two female companions on either side, walked out of the theater and turned to his left. As they walked past the doorway in which Purvis was standing, Purvis lit a cigar as a signal for the other men to close in. Dillinger quickly realized what was happening and acted by instinct. He grabbed a pistol from his right trouser pocket as he ran toward the alley. Five shots were fired from the guns of three FBI agents. Three of the shots hit Dillinger, and he fell face down on the pavement. At 10:50 p.m. on July 22, 1934, Dillinger was pronounced dead in a little room in the Alexian Brothers Hospital.

AFTERMATH

The agents who fired at Dillinger were Charles B. Winstead, Clarence O. Hurt, and Herman E. Hollis. Each man was commended by Hoover for fearlessness and courageous action. None of them ever said who actually killed Dillinger. The events of that sultry July night in Chicago marked the beginning of the end of the gangster era. Eventually, twenty-seven persons were convicted in federal courts on charges of harboring, aiding, and abetting Dillinger and his cronies during their reign of terror. Nelson was fatally wounded on November 27, 1934, in a gun battle with FBI agents in which Special Agents Cowley and Hollis also were killed.

Dillinger was buried in Crown Point Cemetery in Indianapolis. In his 1970 book *The Dillinger Dossier*, Jay Robert Nash, citing flaws in the autopsy evidence and detailed testimony, even offers the thesis that Dillinger did not die in Chicago at all, positing that the victim was really an underworld fall guy sent to take Dillinger's place.

In 1945 former bootleggers turned filmmakers the King Brothers, Frank and Maurice, produced a low-budget, largely nonfactual biography of Dillinger called *Dillinger*, which starred Lawrence Tierney and was scripted by famous front Philip Yordan. It surprised the film industry by turning a tidy profit. A third of the film consisted of stock footage lifted from other classic gangster films, from Howard Hawks's *Scarface* to Fritz Lang's *You Only Live Once*. The film's nonstop action set a pattern for future gangster epics from the 1960s onward but was unique for its time.

Writer-director John Milius made his film debut with another biography of Dillinger called simply *Dillinger* (1973) and starring Warren Oates, though it too owes little to the actual facts of Dillinger's life. His noted demise also inspired Lewis Teague's film *The Lady in Red* (1979; also known as *Guns, Sin and Bathtub Gin*), scripted by John Sayles with Robert Conrad playing the famed bank robber. Other treatments of Dillinger on film include *Young Dillinger* (1965), *Dillinger and Capone* (1995), *Public Enemies* (2009), and the documentary *Appointment with Death: The Last Days of John Dillinger* (1971).

Dillinger's legacy continues to be enshrined in song and story; Hoover even put a plaster cast of the gangster's face on display at FBI headquarters. Dillinger had been inflated from a simple bank robber into a legend and remains one to this day.

Dennis Fischer

SEE ALSO: *FBI (Federal Bureau of Investigation); The Great Depression; Hoover, J. Edgar; Mafia/Organized Crime.*

BIBLIOGRAPHY

Block, Lawrence, ed. *Gangsters, Swindlers, Killers, & Thieves: The Lives and Crimes of Fifty American Villains.* New York: Oxford University Press, 2004.

Cromie, Robert, and Pinkston, Joseph. *Dillinger: A Short and Violent Life.* New York: McGraw-Hill, 1962.

Girardin, G. Russell, and Helmer, William J. *Dillinger: The Untold Story.* Bloomington: Indiana University Press, 1994.

Gorn, Elliott. *Dillinger's Wild Ride: The Year that Made America's Public Enemy Number One.* New York: Oxford University Press, 2009.

Matera, Dary. *John Dillinger: The Life and Death of America's First Celebrity Criminal.* New York: Carroll and Graf Publishers, 2004.

Nash, Jay Robert. *The Dillinger Dossier.* Highland Park, IL: December Press, 1983.

Nash, Jay Robert, and Ron Offen. *Dillinger: Dead or Alive?* Chicago: Henry Regnery, 1970.

Peterson, Linda. "John Dillinger. " *Biography*, February 2002.

Summers, Anthony. *Official and Confidential: The Secret Life of J. Edgar Hoover.* New York: G. P. Putnam's Sons, 1993.

Toland, John. *The Dillinger Days.* New York: Random House, 1963.

DiMaggio, Joe *(1914–1999)*

Joe DiMaggio is one of the few athletes who truly transcended their sport. His Hall of Fame career, during which he led the New York Yankees to nine World Series in thirteen years, bridged two great eras of baseball—the last years of Babe Ruth and the post-integration days of Jackie Robinson. He will always be known as "Joltin' Joe," whose record-breaking fifty-six-game hitting streak in 1941 captivated the country. DiMaggio's fame only grew after retirement, with his brief but highly publicized marriage to movie star Marilyn Monroe and his frequent public appearances. The cool, classy ballplayer was immortalized in music and literature as an enduring symbol of decency and order during a confusing era. In the words of the *New York Times* on the day of his retirement, DiMaggio had "something that no baseball averages can measure."

THE MOST POPULAR PLAYER IN BASEBALL

He was born Giuseppe Paolo DiMaggio in San Francisco in 1914, one of nine children; his parents were part of a wave of Sicilian immigrants to immigrate to the United States at the turn of the twentieth century. DiMaggio's parents expected him to go into the family fishing business, but the shy, unsociable boy's only true interest was baseball. The story of DiMaggio's discovery has become baseball legend; a member of the San Francisco Seals organization spotted the thin seventeen-year-old peaking through a hole in the outfield fence, hoping to find his brother Vince, a Seals player. The Seals offered the talented sandlot player an opportunity to play, and he stayed for four years, becoming a hero in the Italian community in San Francisco. The year 1933 proved to be a harbinger of things to come; DiMaggio chalked up a minor-league record with a sixty-one-game hitting streak.

At the end of the 1935 season, the New York Yankees signed DiMaggio, hoping he would lead the team into the post-Ruth era. Despite the pressures of following Ruth, DiMaggio had a fabulous rookie season in 1936, hitting .323 with twenty-nine home runs, 125 RBI, and a league-leading fifteen triples. Writers across the country marveled at his exceptional clutch

Joe DiMaggio. *Joe DiMaggio, who played his entire thirteen-year career for the New York Yankees, is perhaps best known for his record fifty-six-game hitting streak in 1941.* **PHOTO FILE/GETTY IMAGES.**

hitting, skilled base running, and graceful defensive play. The shy, conservative DiMaggio, a sharp contrast from the wild, gregarious Ruth, became an instant celebrity. He led the Yankees to four straight World Series titles from 1936 to 1939 and constantly appeared among the leaders in batting, home runs, and RBI.

DiMaggio became one of the most popular players in baseball, although he angered fans in 1938 by sitting out the beginning of the season due to a contract dispute, a theme repeated throughout his career. Despite his new celebrity status, he continued to live a very normal life, returning to San Francisco to live with his family during the winter. At the end of the 1939 season, DiMaggio married Dorothy Arnold, and two years later, they had a son, Joe Jr.

All of the fanfare could not prepare DiMaggio for the 1941 season, in which he racked up an astonishing fifty-six-game hitting streak, recording a hit in every game from May 15 to July 16. Never before had an individual sports record received so much public attention; radio stations across the country regularly interrupted broadcasts to give updates on "the streak." It seemed to come at a perfect time for a nation on the brink of war. Songwriter Alan Courtney wrote "Joe, Joe DiMaggio! we want you on our side!" as if his hitting streak could protect America from the turmoil overseas. DiMaggio himself joined the air force at the end of the 1942 season, while in the prime of his baseball career. Like many ballplayers, he saw no combat, spending the majority of his service time entertaining the troops in exhibition games. But the distance from his family was frustrating, and in 1944 his wife filed for divorce.

When DiMaggio returned to baseball in 1946, his finest years were clearly in the past. He did, however, add to his fame by continually playing through injury. In 1949 he made a remarkable comeback from a leg injury and "took his place in that select circle of athletes, like Babe Ruth and Jack Dempsey, who are not only admired but also beloved," according to *Life* magazine. He continued to show flashes of his former brilliance, even as he lost consistency and fought with Yankee manager Casey Stengel. DiMaggio retired at the end of the 1951 season, having amassed a .325 lifetime average and 361 home runs in thirteen seasons. That same year, he was immortalized in the Ernest Hemingway classic *The Old Man and the Sea*, the tale of a tired, aging fisherman, stuck at seas for days, who turned to "the Great DiMaggio" for solace.

LIFE AFTER BASEBALL

Unlike many former players, DiMaggio had little trouble adjusting to life after baseball. He spent his first year of retirement working as a broadcaster for the Yankees, and he went on to work in public relations with a variety of companies and charitable foundations. DiMaggio reentered the public consciousness in 1952 when he met a young Marilyn Monroe. The relationship between these two very different celebrities—the quiet, conservative former ballplayer and the beautiful but troubled movie star—was instant front page news. They married on January 14, 1954, but constantly fought over DiMaggio's traditional views of marriage and views of the Hollywood life and divorced just nine months later. DiMaggio remained a close, dependable friend to Monroe, right until her death in 1962. He made all the funeral arrangements, excluding the Hollywood crowd in the hope it would restore some dignity to her tragically short life.

In 1967 a new generation of Americans was introduced to DiMaggio in Paul Simon and Art Garfunkel's "Mrs. Robinson," a song from the film *The Graduate*. Simon and Garfunkel asked "Where have you gone, Joe DiMaggio?" lamenting lost innocence and looking for a hero to guide them through troubled times. More than twenty-five years after the magical summer of 1941, Joltin' Joe became a symbol of fundamental good to a confused generation. His image continued to grow through the 1970s and 1980s through his charitable work and public appearances. DiMaggio's cultural importance received another nod when memorabilia of the Dimaggio-Monroe marriage was featured in the plot of Michael Chabon's best-selling novel *Wonder Boys* (1995), which was made into a movie in 2000.

DiMaggio died on March 8, 1999, after a bout with cancer. In August 2011 the U.S. Postal Service announced it would issue a commemorative stamp in his honor.

Simon Donner

SEE ALSO: *Baseball; Celebrity; Celebrity Couples;* The Graduate; *Hemingway, Ernest; Monroe, Marilyn; The New York Yankees; Ruth, Babe; Simon and Garfunkel; Sports Heroes; Stengel, Casey.*

BIBLIOGRAPHY

Allen, Maury. *Where Have You Gone Joe DiMaggio?: The Story of America's Last Hero.* New York: E. P. Dutton, 1975.

Cramer, Richard Ben. *Joe Dimaggio: The Hero's Life.* New York: Simon & Schuster, 2001.

Engelberg, Morris and Marv Schneider. *Dimaggio: Setting the Record Straight.* St. Paul, MN: Motorbooks International, 2003.

Moore, Jack B. *Joe DiMaggio: A Bio-bibliography.* Westport, CT: Greeenwood Press, 1986.

Schoor, Gene. *Joe DiMaggio: A Biography.* Garden City, NY: Doubleday, 1980.

Seidel, Michael. *Streak: Joe DiMaggio and the Summer of '41.* New York: McGraw-Hill, 1988.

Whittingham, Richard, ed. *The DiMaggio Albums: Selections from Public and Private Collections Celebrating the Baseball Career of Joe DiMaggio.* New York: G. P. Putnam and Sons, 1989.

Dime Novels

A popular form of literary entertainment in the late nineteenth and early twentieth centuries, dime novels were works of sensational fiction published in paper-covered booklets, issued at regular intervals, and priced between five and ten cents. Profitable mainstays of the American publishing industry for many years, dime novels gradually waned as pulp magazine consumption increased, and by 1915 motion pictures had replaced dime novels as inexpensive forms of entertainment. Since that time, dime novels have become significant resources for examining the development of American popular culture in that they exemplify early printing methods, serve as rudimentary forms of genre fiction, and reflect aspects of the social history of the United States.

Published in four basic formats between 1860 and 1915, dime novels usually possessed pictorial covers with black-and-white or colored illustrations, ranged in size from 4-by-6 inches to 8-by-12 inches, and varied in length from 32 to 250 pages.

Initially produced for an adult market, early versions detailed life on the American frontier. Later publications, however, featured detective mysteries, adventure stories, and science fiction tales and were primarily read by juveniles.

The idea of producing cheap paper-covered novels in a continuous series was conceived by Irwin P. Beadle. In 1860 Beadle, along with his older brother, Erastus, and Robert Adams, established the publishing firm Beadle & Adams in New York City and launched *Malaeska, the Indian Wife of the White Hunter* by Mrs. Ann S. Stephens as the first entry in a series titled Beadle's Dime Novels. Achieving success with the publication of this story and others, Beadle & Adams were for a time the principal publishers of dime novels until competitors George P. Munro, his brother Norman L. Munro, Frank Tousey, and Street & Smith began to publish dime novels as well.

Dime novel authors had strict guidelines to follow—stories had to be exciting, entertaining, and moral. Each of the major publishers employed regulars who wrote for a particular series. In some instances, authors published stories for several firms. Prolific contributors to Beadle's Dime Novels (1860–1874) included Stephens, Mrs. Metta Victor, Edward S. Ellis, Edward L. Wheeler, Philip S. Warne, and Ned Buntline. George P. Munro's Old Sleuth Library (1885–1905) highlighted the detective adventures of Old Sleuth, a pseudonym for Harlan Page Halsey, and other authors.

Munro's brother, Norman, published works by W. I. James in the Old Cap Collier Library (1883–1899), another dime novel detective series. Tousey's small group of authors wrote under so many pseudonyms that the number of contributors to the Wide Awake Library (1878–1898) appeared greater than it actually was. Street & Smith, as the last major publishing firm to produce dime novels, featured authors Horatio Alger Jr., Ned Buntline, Gilbert Patten, and Colonel Prentiss Ingraham, among others, in several series between 1883 and 1899. When dime novel production ceased, most of the once-prolific authors faded into obscurity.

Often, characters appearing in dime novel series were better known than their authors were. Buntline's famous Western hero, Buffalo Bill, based on U.S. scout and performer William Frederick Cody, appeared in numerous publications by Beadle & Adams, Street & Smith, and Tousey. Amateur detective Nick Carter proved to be so popular after his first appearance in *The Old Detective's Pupil* (1886) that Street & Smith featured his adventures in three different series between 1891 and 1915: The Nick Carter Library, The New Nick Carter Weekly, and Nick Carter Stories. Similarly, the exploits of Deadwood Dick, Kit Carson Jr., Jesse James, Old Sleuth, Young Wild West, Frank Reade Jr., Tiger Dick, and Frank Merriwell appeared in more than one dime novel.

Covering a wide variety of subjects, dime novels promoted traditional American values of patriotism, rugged individualism, and moral behavior. Many of the early dime novel stories focused on historical events such as the Revolutionary War, the War of 1812, and conflicts with Native Americans. Others were set in gold mining camps or towns within the expanding western frontier and featured gunfighters, villains, and damsels in distress. Reflecting the urbanization of cities, the Industrial Revolution, and increased transportation modes, subsequent dime novel subjects included circuses, railroad workers, firefighters, sports, science fiction, fantasy, sea or polar explorations, and mysteries with detectives from every walk of life. Moving beyond the borders of America, a few detail adventures in distant places.

Few original dime novels exist outside of libraries and personal collections. Moreover, owing largely to their sheer numbers and past popular appeal, dime novels are seldom considered by literary scholars to be good examples of American literature. Their value as historical artifacts, however, is considerable.

Marlena E. Bremseth

SEE ALSO: *Cody, Buffalo Bill, and His Wild West Show; Pulp Magazines; Science Fiction Publishing; Street and Smith.*

BIBLIOGRAPHY

Cox, Randolph J. *The Dime Novel Companion: A Source Book.* Westport, CT: Greenwood Press, 2000.

Denning, Michael. *Mechanic Accents: Dime Novels and Working Class Culture in America.* London: Verso, 1987.

Johannsen, Albert. *The House of Beadle & Adams and Its Dime and Nickel Novels: The Story of a Vanished Literature*, vol. 1. Norman: University of Oklahoma Press, 1950.

Sullivan, Larry E., and Lydia C. Schurman. *Pioneers, Passionate Ladies, and Private Eyes: Dime Novels, Series Books, and Paperbacks.* New York: Haworth Press, 1996.

Dime Stores/Woolworth's

Dime stores, or five-and-dimes, maintained a central place in American life from before 1900 until after World War II. Woolworth (also known as Woolworth's) was the original and dominant dime-store chain. In the first half of the twentieth century, the main street of virtually every town and city in the United States featured a Woolworth; it was the first place many people went to look for basic merchandise of all sorts. Woolworth offered its customers a wide assortment of very affordable household items, and the working class appreciated finding basic things at basic prices. The dime store's lunch counter was a common meeting place, its toys made it a favorite destination of children, and its endless locations meant it served as the neighborhood store for many. Although part of Woolworth's appeal was in its ubiquitous presence, stores were also encouraged to remain local institutions. They varied widely from region to region and from city to town. Each filled a particular role and developed its own character.

In 1919, when F. W. Woolworth died, his chain of five-and-dimes consisted of 1,081 stores in the United States and Canada. At that time, department stores were all regional; Woolworth's was one of a very few nationwide retail chains. Department stores were also notably more lavish and expensive than dime stores. Millions of working people depended on Woolworth's and other five-and-dimes for many basic needs. As the nation's largest food-service retailer by the 1940s, Woolworth maintained nearly 1,000 inexpensive lunch counters across the United States before the first McDonald's restaurant opened.

BEGINNINGS

Before Woolworth, shopping usually meant bartering. Merchandise was kept behind counters or on inaccessible shelves, and customers had to ask clerks to show them an item. Fixed pricing had begun appearing in a few places in the 1870s, notably in Michigan, but was sporadic and unorganized. Other merchants had set up five-cent counters inside their stores from time to time for limited runs, but no one had worked hard to make the approach consistently profitable, and certainly no one had devoted an entire variety store to the same fixed price. Frank Woolworth was not a natural salesman or bargainer, but he had a strong Yankee work ethic and recognized and exploited a good idea. He assiduously sharpened his bargaining skills until he became known for them. They helped him negotiate endless deals with wholesalers, which allowed Woolworth to make a profit on items priced less than ten cents.

Woolworth opened his first "five cent store" in Utica, New York, on February 22, 1879, using a $300 loan from his former employer. That first store failed, but a second attempt the next year in Lancaster, Pennsylvania, succeeded and spawned twenty-one over the next ten years. His fourth store, opened in Scranton, Pennsylvania, on November 6, 1880, was the first "five & ten cent store." Woolworth never stopped opening or buying new stores: he ran twelve in 1890, fifty-four in 1900, 238 in 1910, and 319 by the December 1911 merger that created F. W. Woolworth & Co.

Combined with 254 previously franchised stores, Woolworth became the first retail company to operate stores in all forty-eight states. As he planned for the merger that created F. W. Woolworth & Co., Woolworth also oversaw the construction of the Woolworth Building in Manhattan. It was the tallest building in the world at the time of its completion in 1913, because Woolworth insisted that it surpass the Metropolitan Life Building—a company that had refused him a policy when he was laying the foundation for his retail empire.

Woolworth said that he aimed "to open a store in every civilized town throughout the world." He expanded into England in 1909, then Germany, Canada, South Africa, and elsewhere. Woolworth's critics complained that Woolworth was creating a monopoly, and Congressman John J. Cochran championed legislation that would have taxed Woolworth into collapse. Many people were dismayed by "the chain store menace" of Woolworth's in the 1930s, just as many people in the twenty-first century recoil when Wal-Mart builds a store in their communities.

In 1935 Representative Cochran led a congressional investigation into the "super-lobby" of chain store interests. Woolworth's and grocery-store chain A&P were the primary targets. Fortunately for the chains, a 1939 bill that would have broken them up died in committee. Woolworth did indeed try to drive out or buy out much of its competition. The company knew that many of the towns and districts where it opened could not support more than one dime store.

SUCCESS, CONTROVERSY, AND DECLINE

Woolworth remained literally a dime store for more than fifty years, until 1933, when the top price was raised to twenty-four cents. In 1935 the limited price policy ended as the company expanded into higher-priced merchandise such as furniture and appliances. Despite fixed, low prices, Woolworth paid better wages than most of its competitors. The company introduced paid vacations, Christmas bonuses, and minimum wages for all positions long before there was a federal minimum wage. These things were far from standard early in the twentieth century. Nevertheless, Woolworth did not escape labor trouble, including serious Detroit and New York City strikes in 1937. Woolworth was a major employer of women, although by the 1950s many were protesting their lack of promotion in the company.

Woolworth's lunch counters will be long remembered as the site of civil rights sit-ins in 1960. The first one began at the Woolworth in Greensboro, North Carolina, on February 1, 1960. Soon protesters throughout the South were occupying Woolworth's and other lunch counters and calling for a nationwide boycott against the company, which announced it would "abide by local custom." Woolworth's earnings dropped 8.9 percent in March 1960. Sit-ins and demonstrations continued in Greensboro and elsewhere until July 25; all of Woolworth's lunch counters officially desegregated on July 26.

Woolworth perfectly filled a key place in American culture in the first half of the twentieth century, but as the culture changed after World War II, its importance waned. As other chains emulated Woolworth's low-cost approach, it became little more than another department store. The 2,850 Woolworth stores of the early 1960s sold enormous quantities of merchandise but held onto a very thin profit margin.

In the postwar era, Woolworth seemed stale and staid; its workforce aged with its clientele as it failed to change with the times. A succession of company-trained presidents found it impossible to halt the gradual decline. The last 400 Woolworths in North America were closed in 1997 and 1998, although the company survives in the United States as Footlocker Inc. In Great Britain Woolworth remained a major variety store until its bankruptcy in 2009. Woolworths Limited, the largest retail corporation in Australia and New Zealand, has never been associated with the original Woolworth company.

The legacy of the dime store thrives in the myriad discount department stores throughout the world; in the many "dollar stores" now occupying the neighborhood malls that have taken the place of downtown shopping districts; and in the merchandise purchasing, display, and pricing policies that have become standards of modern commerce.

Paul Gaffney

SEE ALSO: *Civil Rights Movement; Consumerism; Department Stores; McDonald's; Wal-Mart; World War II.*

BIBLIOGRAPHY

Brough, James. *The Woolworths.* New York: McGraw-Hill, 1982.

Pitrone, Jean Maddern. *F. W. Woolworth and the American Five and Dime: A Social History.* Jefferson, NC: McFarland, 2003.

Raucher, Alan R. "Dime Store Chains: The Making of Organization Men, 1880–1940." *Business History Review* 65, no. 1 (1991).

Winkler, John K. *Five and Ten: The Fabulous Life of F. W. Woolworth.* New York: Robert McBride, 1940.

Wolff, Miles. *Lunch at the 5 & 10.* Chicago: Ivan R. Dee, 1990.

Diners

Restaurants commonly referred to as "diners" have held a special place in American popular culture since the 1930s. Once sleek, futuristic icons of postwar optimism, in the early 2000s these establishments have become objects of nostalgia. As the precur-

Hollywood Diner, Baltimore, Maryland. *The Hollywood Diner in Baltimore, Maryland, has a stainless steel exterior that gives it a nostalgic look.* SUSAN WATTS/NY DAILY NEWS ARCHIVE VIA GETTY IMAGES.

sor to fast-food restaurants, diners were one of the unique building types spawned by the burgeoning automobile society. Their very appearance—with streamlined, movement-implying shapes and bright neon lights—captured the spirit of the new mobile culture.

The diner evolved from horse-drawn night lunch wagons of the late nineteenth century, which served walk-up customers in downtown areas after restaurants had closed for the evening. The next generation of wagons featured indoor seating; by the turn of the twentieth century, many lunch wagons had become stationary. The early diners' forte was the quick, inexpensive meal—atmosphere was not important. The clientele consisted of night workers and late revelers, and sandwiches, hamburgers, pies, hot dogs, and breakfast fare were standard items. By the 1890s Thomas H. Buckley was mass-producing lunch wagons and had placed them in at least 275 cities across the United States. Early diners were also converted from railroad or trolley cars.

The diner that has become the object of popular affection dates to the 1930s and 1940s. The machine-influenced, Art Deco or Streamline Moderne design style, which emphasized smooth curves, simplicity, and shiny surfaces, was inherent in much product design of the time, but in the diner it was integrated into a total environment. Diners from this golden age were long and low in shape, with streamlined effects and clean surfaces, evoking a feeling of both futurism and movement. Formica, stainless steel, and Naugahyde were the most popular interior materials. Diners contained booths, but the highlight of the interior was a long, shiny counter. Meals were simple and inexpensive. The imagery of speed and progress fit perfectly with the rapidly developing mobile society, in which the automobile was reshaping the landscape and creating opportunities for new building.

In the 1950s, as more families began to eat outside the home and the diner became more "respectable," diners expanded in size and menu. The 1960s marked a turning point for the diner, as the fast-food restaurant industry proliferated. Fast food represented standardization, as opposed to the uniqueness of diners. The McDonald's menu was a known quantity, whereas every diner had a specialty and a different atmosphere.

In response, many diners tried to emphasize their individuality by expanding their menus and adopting more conservative imagery. Apart from their smaller size and the word *diner* in their names, many of these establishments became difficult to distinguish from standard restaurants. Booth and table service came to predominate over the traditional counter. Colonial and Mediterranean architectural styles often replaced the Art Deco model familiar from past decades.

Beginning in the 1970s diners began to make a comeback as nostalgic reminders of a more innocent time. They also became legitimate subjects of study by architectural and popular culture scholars. In 1978 the Cooper-Hewitt branch of the Smithsonian held an exhibit on architectural packaging, which looked at four popular American building types: fast-food restaurants, diners, gasoline stations, and museum-village restorations. An article by Richard Oliver and Nancy Ferguson, the curators of the exhibit, appeared in *Architectural Record* in February 1978 and also appeared as a reprint catalog. Barry Levinson's 1982 movie *Diner* also helped introduce the phenomenon to a new audience.

In the early twenty-first century, diners were still being manufactured and patronized. Many older models have been restored, and diners continue to be the subject of books and museum exhibitions. The Henry Ford Museum in Dearborn, Michigan, now includes a 1946 diner as part of its collection of twentieth-century cultural artifacts in an exhibition titled "Driving America." Diners have thus been recognized as unique cultural inventions that, like the gas station and fast-food restaurant, are byproducts of the automobile revolution of the twentieth century.

Dale Allen Gyure

SEE ALSO: *Automobile; Coffee; Fast Food; The Fifties; Gas Stations; Hamburger; Hot Dogs; Leisure Time; McDonald's.*

BIBLIOGRAPHY

Baeder, John. *Diners*, 2nd ed. New York: Harry N. Abrams, 1995.

Gutman, Richard J. S. *American Diner Then and Now.* New York: HarperCollins, 1993.

Gutman, Richard J. S.; Elliott Kaufman; and David Slovic. *American Diner.* New York: Harper and Row, 1979.

Hurley, Andrew. *Diners, Bowling Alleys and Trailer Parks: Chasing the American Dream in the Postwar Consumer Culture.* New York: Basic Books, 2002.

Dionne Quintuplets

Yvonne, Annette, Cécile, Émilie, and Marie Dionne (1934–) are the first monozygotic—all from a single fertilized egg—quintuplets known to have survived to adulthood. They were nearly sextuplets, but the sixth fetus miscarried in the third month of pregnancy. Born May 28, 1934, to Oliva and Elzire Dionne, French Canadian peasants, in their seven-room farmhouse near Callander, Ontario, the premature babies weighed a total of 13 pounds, 6 ounces. They owe their survival to the quick and intelligent care of the local general practitioner, Dr. Allan Roy Dafoe, who collected virtually every incubator in the province and kept the tiny girls alive through his excellent scientific care.

Nevertheless, the significance of the Dionne quintuplets rests not in their place in medical history but as examples of exploitation and publicity. Their birth and survival created a worldwide sensation, and their father collected a fortune by serving as their "manager," selling the right to photograph them, to have them appear in motion pictures, and to secure their "endorsement" of various products. They were made wards of the Canadian government in 1935, and for their first ten years were raised in a special nursery built for them out of public funds. After a protracted lawsuit, their parents recovered custody in 1944.

The birth of multiple children in the United States never garnered as much interest as that of the Dionne quintuplets. However, the subsequent birth of the Thompson sextuplets and the McCaughey septuplets in 1997 brought to light racial tensions in the United States. Unlike the worldwide attention given to the Dionne family, the birth of the first African American sextuplets on May 8, 1997, came with little fanfare. Living in a three-bedroom apartment, the Thompson family struggled to make ends meet with the money Linden Thompson made from his two jobs. Only after the much-publicized birth of the white McCaughey septuplets seven months later did corporations extend the same free products and aid to the Thompson sextuplets. Although they represent a small fraction of the riches given to the Dionne family, the lifetime of free diapers, college scholarships, and use of a minivan relieved some of the stresses on the newly enlarged families.

Gerald Carpenter

SEE ALSO: *The Duggar Family;* Jon & Kate Plus 8*; Octomom.*

BIBLIOGRAPHY

Barker, Lillian. *The Dionne Legend: Quintuplets in Captivity.* Garden City, NY: Doubleday, 1951.

Berton, Pierre. *The Dionne Years: A Thirties Melodrama.* Toronto: McClelland and Stewart, 1977.

Blatz, W. E. *Collected Studies on the Dionne Quintuplets.* Toronto: University of Toronto Press, 1937.

Braudy, Leo. *The Frenzy of Renown: Fame and Its History.* New York: Oxford University Press, 1986.

Nihmey, John, and Stuart Foxman. *Time of Their Lives: The Dionne Tragedy, a True-Life Fairy Tale.* Ottawa, Canada: NIVA, 1986.

The Dirty Dozen

Directed by Robert Aldrich, *The Dirty Dozen* tells the story of Major Reisman (Lee Marvin) and the twelve hardened convicts he selects to join him on a suicide mission behind German lines in 1944. *The Dirty Dozen* remains an interesting and popular film because it is meticulously crafted and deftly edited and it features several future stars at the beginning of their careers (including Donald Sutherland, Charles Bronson, and Telly Savalas). Although it was released in 1967 at the height of the anti–Vietnam War movement, *The Dirty Dozen* was nevertheless a success, becoming one of the biggest box-office hits in the history of MGM (Metro-Goldwyn-Mayer). War protesters readily accepted the film's depiction of officers as indiscriminate killers, while more militaristic moviegoers approved of the film's brutal combat scenes.

Robert C. Sickels

SEE ALSO: *Bronson, Charles; Brown, Jim; MGM (Metro-Goldwyn-Mayer); War Movies; World War II.*

BIBLIOGRAPHY

Aldrich, Robert; Edwin T. Arnold; and Eugene L. Miller. *Robert Aldrich: Interviews.* Jackson: University Press of Mississippi, 2004.

Basinger, Jeanine. *The World War II Combat Film: Anatomy of a Genre.* New York: Columbia University Press, 1986.

Manuell, Roger. *Films and the Second World War.* South Brunswick, NJ: A. S. Barnes, 1974.

Disaster Movies

In disaster movies, natural disasters, accidents, and terrorist actions provide the setting for daring escapes and incredible heroism. Disaster films rely heavily on special effects to recreate on-screen the violent consequences of earthquakes, plane crashes, and meteorite storms; the category also includes monster disaster movies in which an enraged oversized creature destroys buildings and other large objects. It is an important plot device of disaster movies that heroic acts are performed by unlikely heroes—by people with psychological wounds, with limited experience of the things they are asked to do, and in situations in which the odds against success seem impossibly high.

Because these films are about averting and surviving disaster, it may be significant that disaster movies began to be produced in large numbers in the years after the horrors of World War II. If the modern era has seen great advances in technology, disaster movies reflect a fear that technology alone will not save humankind. Although their plots are often unrealistic and the acting and special effects unconvincing, disaster movies offer the message that, through self-belief and the right moral choices, people have the ability to save themselves.

EARLY HISTORY

Disasters featured in disaster movies can be divided into three main types: natural disasters, disasters caused by the failure of or accidental damage to a technological innovation, and disasters caused by terrorism or by the recklessness of an individual or agency. The most successful disaster movies are usually the simplest, but popular disaster films can contain elements of any or all of these scenarios. The actual type of disaster involved is only one of many reasons for a particular film's popularity. Among other things, audiences want to know how the characters will escape with their lives; they watch for the special effects and for sentimental reasons—popular disaster movies almost always include a love affair developing alongside the disaster plot.

When the type of disaster is significant, it is often because it reflects current or local concerns. In the 1990s, for example, perhaps cashing in on premillennium fears, a rash of films such as *Independence Day* (1996) and *Deep Impact* (1998) appeared, with plot lines based around threats to life on Earth posed by attacks from extraterrestrials or from asteroids. Similarly, in the 1980s films such as *Testament* (1983) and *The Day After* (1983) appeared in response to the threat posed by the nuclear arms race. Because most disaster movies are made in Hollywood and Japan, it is probably no coincidence that a large number of them feature earthquakes, tidal waves, and volcanic eruptions.

The history of disaster movies is a relatively short one. Although disasters have featured in movies since the beginning of the twentieth century, films in which the disaster is the reason for making and watching the film did not become common until the 1950s, when alien invasion and monster movies were popular. Until then, disasters of various kinds had appeared in adventure films and films about war, but true disaster movies were rare. One precursor to modern monster disaster movies such as *Jurassic Park* (1993) is Merian Cooper and Ernest Schoedsack's *King Kong* (1933), but the film is really an exotic adventure thriller with only a small element of disaster movie action. Such extravagant special effects as were needed to make the famous scene on the Empire State Building are remarkable for their time, but it was not until the 1950s that such effects could be achieved with regularity.

In the 1950s advances were made in film technology that allowed filmmakers to better use special effects techniques pioneered in the 1930s. Many of the resulting films were a combination of science fiction and horror, but disaster was often at their heart, as titles such as *When Worlds Collide* (1951) and *War of the Worlds* (1953) suggest. Under the perceived threat of nuclear destruction, filmmakers and audiences became concerned with global rather than local conflicts, and many of the monster-based disaster movies of the 1950s involve a world under attack by mutant creatures. New film techniques such as 3-D, made possible by improvements in color film, made monster movies still more thrilling as giant creatures appeared to step off the screen and into the audience. Perhaps because of Japan's own experience of nuclear destruction, the Japanese film industry has been prolific in the field of atomic monsters, its most famous being Inoshiro Honda's *Godzilla, King of the Monsters* (1956).

1960s AND 1970s

In the 1960s science fiction disaster movies and nuclear accident films remained popular in Japan, where Honda's *Godzilla* and other monster series continued until late in the decade. Although extra footage of well-known American actors was added to Honda's films for American distribution, disaster movies in the United States generally did less well during this period. American disaster movies in the 1950s had mostly upheld Hollywood's conservative values, and in the 1960s the genre perhaps seemed less suitable for exploring the new moral climate than, for example, the Westerns of Sam Peckinpah or the thoughtful science fiction of Stanley Kubrick's *2001: A Space Odyssey* (1968). It was not until 1970, with the release of *Airport*, that disaster movies became popular again.

The golden age of American disaster movies was the 1970s. As Hollywood embraced once again the idea of making popular, big budget features, the disaster movie became an important format for demonstrating spectacular special effects and for drawing in audiences to watch destruction on a large scale. Exactly what appeals to audiences in watching planes crash, ships sink, trains collide, and tall buildings burn will probably never be known for sure, but films such as *The Poseidon Adventure* (1972), *The Towering Inferno* (1974), and the *Airport* series gave Hollywood some of its most lucrative successes.

Unlike the futuristic films of the 1950s, disaster movies in the 1970s often dealt with familiar events and situations, ones that already caused anxiety for many people. For example, the number of miles Americans traveled by air doubled between 1965 and 1970, and air travel is one of the most common themes for disaster movies of the 1970s. Similarly, at a time when many new high-rise buildings were being planned and built, Paul Newman and Steve McQueen braved flames and smoke to rescue people from a party on the top floor of "the tallest building in the world" in John Guillermin's *The Towering Inferno*.

RISE OF CGI

While the special effects in *The Towering Inferno* are impressive for their time, as with many disaster movies, the biggest challenge its makers faced was to prevent the record-breaking skyscraper—the "Tower of Glass"—from looking like a model. In the 1990s the situation was helped by improvements in digital technology—in particular the ability to mix live action with computer-generated imagery (CGI). CGI has become widely used in the production of many kinds of films, but it is used most spectacularly in disaster movies, which have become much more realistic in terms of sound and vision.

The turning point in the relationship between conventional filmmaking and CGI was James Cameron's deep-sea disaster movie *The Abyss* (1989). The plot of Cameron's film peripherally involves a research team working on the edge of a deep ocean trench, whose seabed living quarters seem certain to be dragged down into the abyss. The discovery of friendly aliens living at the bottom of the trench allows the opportunity for some impressive effects, such as a suspended column of seawater known as a "pseudopod," which explores the corridors of the deep-sea craft. Cameron also used CGI and improved digital sound technology to excellent effect in his 1997 disaster film *Titanic*, creating convincing footage of the great ship's final hours. Director Steven Spielberg used similar techniques to bring dinosaurs back to life in *Jurassic Park* (1993) and the more overtly disaster-based *The Lost World: Jurassic Park* (1997).

MODERN DISASTER MOVIES

Since the turn of the twenty-first century, disaster movies have benefited from advances in CGI and the development of more convincing 3-D effects, especially in movie theaters. Staples of disaster movies, such as alien invasion, disaster at sea, in the sky, in space, and on the roads, have remained immensely popular. Dramatic developments in special effects and increasing concerns about environmental catastrophe, have led to many disaster movies about apocalyptic weather, including *The Day after Tomorrow* (2004), in which New York is first struck by a tsunami and then plunged into an ice age. Reflecting real fears of global pandemics, perhaps spread by terrorists or perhaps simply by an increasingly urbanized and mobile population, disaster movies about medical disasters, including mystery viruses, and the undead have become popular. Examples include *28 Weeks Later* (2007), *I Am Legend* (2007), *Quarantine* (2008), *Carriers* (2009), and *Contagion* (2011). One new source of material for this kind of disaster movie in the new millennium has been the computer gaming industry. For example, several spin-off movies have been made based on the survival horror game *Resident Evil.*

Disaster movies have a tendency to take themselves too seriously, and though improvements in special effects have made comical visual effects more rare, disaster movie plots have improved very little. Emotions are still crudely acted and contrived situations—such as the appearance of a dinosaur in San Diego in *The Lost World*—still challenge audiences to believe. Because of these weaknesses and in response to the popularity of disaster movies in the 1970s, parodies of disaster movies have also proved popular. In particular, the *Airport* series of films, the last of which appeared in 1979, was parodied in 1980 by *Airplane!*, a film advertised with the tagline "What's slower than a speeding bullet, and able to hit tall buildings in a single bound?" The film spoofs the typical disaster movie plot when a pilot who is afraid of flying becomes the only person capable of flying the plane, while the score by Elmer Bernstein parodies the melodramatic music that accompanies all popular disaster movies.

While disaster movies have tended to be made as fictional entertainment, other categories of disaster movie have taken a more serious approach. There are films based on the Exxon *Valdez* oil spill and the Mount St. Helens volcanic eruptions. The films*United 93* (2006) and *World Trade Center* (2006) portray the terrorist attacks of September 11, 2001. Other movies, such as the many Titanic disaster films, add a fictional or semifictional dramatic element to the real-life story. *The Perfect Storm* (2000) features a natural disaster, while *2012* (2009) dramatically explores the Mayan calendar's prediction of the cataclysmic end of the world. Still others, such as the British-made semidocumentary *Threads* (1984), mix documentary reporting with dramatization to make a serious point, in this case about the threat of nuclear war and its long-term effects.

Whatever the reason for their appeal, disaster movies continue to be produced in large numbers and with great commercial success. Hard-core disaster movie fans will argue that they watch for the scenes of destruction and to revel in the special effects, but the importance of even a basic human story unfolding alongside the disaster suggests that the popularity of disaster movies has as much to do with sentiment as with spectacle.

Chris Routledge

SEE ALSO: Airplane!*; Godzilla; Hollywood; Horror Movies;* Independence Day*;* Jurassic Park*;* King Kong*; Kubrick, Stanley; McQueen, Steve; Newman, Paul; 9/11; Spielberg, Steven; The* Titanic*;* 2001: A Space Odyssey*;* War of the Worlds*; World Trade Center; World War II.*

BIBLIOGRAPHY

Annan, David. *Catastrophe: The End of the Cinema?* New York: Bounty Books, 1975.

Broderick, Mick. *Nuclear Movies: A Critical Analysis and Filmography of International Feature Length Films Dealing with Experimentation, Aliens, Terrorism, Holocaust and Other Disaster Scenarios, 1914–1989.* Jefferson, NC: McFarland, 1991.

Cook, David A. *A History of Narrative Film.* New York: Norton, 1996.

Keyser, Lester Joseph. *Hollywood in the Seventies.* San Diego, CA: A. S. Barnes, 1981.

Law, John William. *Disaster on Film.* San Francisco: Aplomb Publishing, 2010.

Disc Jockeys

Since the early days of radio broadcasting, the disc jockey, or DJ, has been an essential part of the medium—not just playing records but serving as an intermediary between the audience and the stars of popular music. Disc jockeys enjoyed their greatest influence in the 1950s and 1960s, when they made rock and roll an important force in American youth culture.

THE RISE OF DISC JOCKEYS

In the early days of radio in the United States in the 1920s and 1930s, the person introducing records and making station announcements was usually a technician who worked the broadcast equipment. It was the policy of large radio networks to avoid recorded sound as much as possible and rely on live programming, so there was little call for disc jockeys. However, in the 1940s, as studio musicians were called up to join the armed forces, radio networks were forced to drop their opposition to canned music. Thus began the rise of the radio announcer who played recordings on the air, the so-called disc jockey.

The most popular early disc jockey was Martin Block, whose "Make Believe Ballroom" invited listeners to a pretend concert and entertained them with humor and records. His program went national in 1935. The monopoly of the three national radio networks—NBC, CBS, and ABC—was broken up in the 1950s, and this allowed many small, independent stations to go on the air. Lacking the programming resources of the networks, the independent stations relied on recorded music. The person spinning the records also made commercial announcements and read the news. At this time, an estimated 75 percent of all programming on American radio came from records, providing many job opportunities for young people with ambitions in the music industry. Many important entertainers, record producers, and entrepreneurs of the 1950s received their starts playing records on local radio stations, including Bill Haley, Norman Petty, and Sam Phillips.

African Americans in southern cities and urban areas in the Northeast were important new markets for independent radio stations. Many of these urban stations altered their programming to suit predominately African American audiences. The ownership of these stations remained in the hands of whites, but gradually, black disc jockeys populated the scene. It was this group that began to play rhythm-and-blues (R&B) records and create a new kind of radio personality who would inaugurate the era of rock and roll.

Most radio announcers maintained a dignified demeanor and spoke in proper English, but some African American disc jockeys broke all the rules of on-air behavior and invented outrageous alter egos for themselves. Their antics were rapidly copied by their white counterparts, who also stole the most commercial songs from their playlists and introduced them to white teenage audiences.

THE PERIOD OF POWERFUL DJS

It is significant that the term *rock and roll* was coined by a white disc jockey from Cleveland, Ohio—Alan Freed—who played R&B records and created an entertaining on-air personality for himself. Attuned to telephone requests and the sales of records in local stores, Freed responded quickly to the growing appeal of R&B and turned his show into a showcase for the music. In 1952 he started to call it rock and roll. Such was the success of his *Moondog's Rock and Roll Party* that he moved to New York in 1954 and a much larger audience. The program climbed to the top of the ratings as rock music became increasingly popular. Freed was America's most influential disc jockey, a conduit through which the "race" music of the 1940s became the rock-and-roll music of the 1950s.

The disc jockey of the late 1950s and early 1960s was an extremely important figure in the business of popular music. Radio play was the main way to promote a record, and many stations allowed the disc jockey to choose what songs would be broadcast. The mythology of rock and roll is full of stories of unknown performers becoming stars overnight because of a radio personality who "broke" their record to the listening audience. However, disc jockeys did a lot more than play records—they managed bands, promoted tours and public appearances, and acted as master of ceremonies at rock shows. At concerts in the 1950s and early 1960s, the disc jockey serving as the promoter or master of ceremonies would typically share equal billing with the band. Several disc jockeys, such as Freed and Murray "the K" Kaufman, became stars in their own right. Kaufman, working for WINS in New York, played an important part in introducing American youth to the Beatles during their first tour of the United States in 1964.

SCANDAL HITS THE AIRWAVES

The great power enjoyed by disc jockeys in the marketing of recordings encouraged corruption. The practice of "payola" (from the words *pay* and *Victrola*), in which a disc jockey was bribed with money or a share of the publishing rights of a song in return for airplay, was widespread. Smaller record companies commonly paid disc jockeys and jukebox operators to use their recordings. This practice came under scrutiny of the U.S. House of Representatives at the end of the 1950s, and the ensuing scandal ended the careers of several influential disc jockeys, including that of Freed.

The payola scandal was only one of the factors that reduced the power of disc jockeys in the 1960s. The move to the Top 40 format—in which playlists were based on the *Billboard* charts—narrowed the choices of which records to play. Additionally, the gradual consolidation of the radio industry, with one company controlling several stations, often took record-playing decisions out of the hands of the on-air staff.

CHANGING ROLES

The great technological watershed of the late 1960s and 1970s was the migration from AM to FM broadcast bands, which brought a significant improvement in sound quality and encouraged stations to use high-fidelity, long-playing records rather than the forty-five rpm singles that had been the staple of commercial radio for two decades. The typical disc jockey on an album-oriented FM station was quiet and unobtrusive compared to the radio personalities of the 1950s and 1960s. More than histrionics, knowledge of the music was now the key attribute for a disc jockey. As the role of the disc jockey changed, women found it easier to break into the profession.

Although disc jockeys were still instrumental in exposing listeners to new music, their power steadily declined in the 1970s and 1980s. Commercial radio came to rely less on the individual in front of the microphone and more on the programming director and market analyst to choose what records to play. The flamboyant radio personality survived only on the morning format; the rest of the day belonged to anonymous interchangeable voices. Disc jockeys did, however, find opportunities as independent businesspeople who played parties and clubs. Rap and hip-hop came out of the activities of New York–area disc jockeys, who kept the records playing while masters of ceremonies, or "toasters," spoke over and in between the music. The advent of music television in the 1980s raised expectations that the presenter would again wield some influence, but the video jockey, or VJ, proved to be disposable too.

The radio industry's pattern of consolidation continued in the 1990s, further marginalizing disc jockeys. This situation intensified in the early twenty-first century, when hundreds of DJ jobs at local stations were eliminated so that the conglomerates could broadcast the same programming throughout the country. Critics fear that these cost-cutting measures signal the end of disc jockeys as America has known them.

Andre Millard

SEE ALSO: *Freed, Alan "Moondog"; Haley, Bill; Hip-Hop; Kasem, Casey; MTV; Radio; Rap; Rock and Roll; Top 40; Wolfman Jack.*

BIBLIOGRAPHY

Brewster, Bill, and Frank Broughton. *Last Night a DJ Saved My Life: The History of the Disc Jockey.* New York: Grove Press, 2000.

Chapple, Steve, and Reebee Garofalo. *Rock 'n' Roll Is Here to Pay.* Chicago: Nelson-Hall, 1977.

Gillett, Charlie. *The Sound of the City: The Rise of Rock and Roll.* New York: Pantheon, 1984.

Passman, Arnold. *The Deejays.* New York: Macmillan, 1971.

Sterling, Christopher H., and John M. Kittross. *Stay Tuned: A Concise History of American Broadcasting.* Belmont, CA: Wadsworth, 1990.

Williams, Gilbert Anthony. *The Legendary Pioneers of Black Radio.* Westport, CT: Praeger, 1998.

Disco

Derived from the French word *discotheque*, "disco" refers not only to a musical style but also to a unique brand of dance club decor, a sexy-synthetic manner of dress, a style of dance, and an attitude toward sexual promiscuity and night life. All of these elements came together during the 1970s in one of the glitziest and most celebrated fads in the history of American popular culture.

Between 1975 and 1979 the established sensibilities of rock and pop—which emphasized sincerity, emotion, and rebellion—gave way to the enchantment of dance floor rhythms. Disco colonized the popular imagination as an alluring dreamscape of pleasure and sexual utopia, and the boundary between commercial fabrication and real experience became blurred. Disco ushered in a post-1960s concept of hedonistic weekends and exciting after-hours activity that was open to anyone with a reasonable income, a basic sense of rhythm, and a good body. However, for all its fashionable accouterments, the disco craze was driven by the music. Characterized by a hypnotically repetitive beat that was overlaid with teasing and sexy vocals, disco music captivated and mesmerized its adherents.

THE TOTAL DISCO EXPERIENCE

Though psychedelic dance bars had experimented with combinations of dance, music, and lighting since the 1960s, it was during the 1970s that the technological, musical, and fashion elements were refined and popularized. In the early 1970s discos began expanding their equipment to include a wider array of musical and visual props. The "mirror ball," which fragmented a white spotlight into a million rotating dots, became the symbol of the new disco, along with synchronized lights that were matched to the bass track of a record. Later came the "pin spot" light, which pierced a cloud of smoke from a dry ice-generated smoke machine to cast an illuminated shaft across a darkened room.

Throughout the 1970s dance clubs sprang up across the country, ranging from fashionable and exclusive big-city venues such as New York's Studio 54 to more modest establishments in hotels or revamped bars. The larger venues included advanced lighting and music systems controlled by a disc jockey, or DJ, who lorded over the collective euphoria from an elevated booth and cajoled the crowd to "get down and boogie." Disco fashions highlighted tight-fitting clothes, high heels, platforms, and the funky "gentleman's" three-piece suits and displayed an unabashed preference for polyester.

Pop music had always been danceable and flamboyant, but disco offered something different. Not only was disco music *for* dancing, but it was also music *about* dancing. The disco beat was the anthem of the dancers, and the disco floor was a wonderland of sexual promise where anything might happen. Unlike the "be-ins," pot parties, and other escapades favored by hippies in the 1960s, disco promised an experience of the exotic that could be easily slotted into a well-ordered work week. Film titles such as *Thank God It's Friday* and *Saturday Night Fever* reflected the compartmentalized nature of this package-tour utopia.

Though disco's dreamland of sexual fulfillment is often remembered as the longing of the heterosexual male libido, the real origins of the genre's sexual imagery can be traced to the gay club scenes in New York and San Francisco, where the camp atmosphere of sexual reverie was born. Disco audiences were largely oblivious to this fact. In hindsight, it is astonishing that middle-class, heterosexual listeners did not notice the homoerotic suggestions that permeate the songs of such widely accepted groups as the Village People ("Macho Man," "In the Navy," and "YMCA"). Disco became sanitized and commercialized as it matured; at its peak, it targeted an age group that was too young to be admitted to real dance clubs and had no clue as to what separated gay from straight dance culture.

DOMINATING THE AIRWAVES

Disco's real ground zero was not the concert hall or even the dance floor—it was the AM radio dial. Mainstream radio started playing disco music in the mid-1970s, and by December 1978, 200 disco-only formats aired across the country. Six months later, the number had increased by another fifty. In 1974 and 1975, respectively, George McCrae's "Rock Your Baby" and Van McCoy's "The Hustle" introduced the sounds of disco to AM radio, though it was a few years before artists such as Kool & the Gang, Gloria Gaynor, Donna Summer, the Bee Gees, KC and the Sunshine Band, Sister Sledge, Diana Ross, and the Village People rode the wave of disco mania. By the time disco dominated the airwaves in 1979, even rockers such as Rod Stewart and the Rolling Stones had hopped onto the bandwagon.

No group is more emblematic of the disco period than the Bee Gees, who began the 1970s as a British-Australian pop act with moderate sales and made a sensational breakthrough on the soundtrack of *Saturday Night Fever* (1977). The film focuses on a working-class youth (John Travolta, in the role that turned him into a star) who escapes the mundane reality of life by becoming a demigod on the local disco scene. The album was released as a double LP and became the industry's biggest-selling soundtrack ever, producing ten hits from its seventeen tracks, including "How Deep Is Your Love," "Stayin' Alive," and "Night Fever." An image of Travolta from the movie—in which he is wearing a white polyester suit, his pelvis thrust forward and his finger raised skyward against a background of disco lights—came to define disco's garish eroticism. The Bee Gees, whose thumping and squealing ballads of sexual enterprise saturated the film, also became symbols of disco for the remainder of the decade. Ironically, both Travolta and the Bee Gees fell victim to the fickleness of fads and fashion, becoming objects of ridicule for many years after disco faded.

DISCO'S DECLINE AND LEGACY

By the end of 1979 disco's celebration of the fanciful and the fake was beginning to wear thin. After a stream of "one-hit wonders," disco seemed to be more the product of producers and promoters than of the artists themselves. One of the problems was that disco music seemed to lack talented musicians: electronically manipulated sounds replaced the bass, drums, and guitar that typified rock, and disco stars came to rely increasingly on prerecorded tracks and off-stage musical support in their live performances. The Village People, for example, kept backup singers entirely out of view of the audience. Moreover, disco succumbed to a variety of commercial marketing devices. A record called *Hooked on Classics*, whose cover features a Mozart-like character mimicking Travolta's famous pose from *Saturday Night Fever*, mixes well-known classical music pieces to a disco beat. Novelty songs such as "Disco Duck" climbed the AM charts, and the theme from the film *2001: A Space Odyssey* was even rerecorded to a disco beat.

The demise of disco came swiftly. Its commercialism, ersatz sexuality, and reliance on radio rather than albums to reach the average music consumer seemed to violate everything rock stood for, and it provoked a powerful backlash from fans of "real" rock. The hostility came to a head in 1979 when a "Disco Demolition Derby" was organized by DJ Steve Dahl before a baseball game at Chicago's Comiskey Park. Anti-disco fans burned more than 100,000 albums, hoisted "disco sucks" banners, and rioted, forcing the cancellation of the game. The precise nature of this spontaneous outburst remains unclear: Dahl's event, which has since been compared to fascist book burnings, may have been homophobic, sexist, or racist, or perhaps it expressed a widespread disappointment with the increasing commercialism of a supposedly rebellious musical form. It was most likely a combination of all these factors. Regardless, not since John Lennon's fateful remark about the Beatles being more famous than Christ had there been such a sweeping consumer revolt against the music industry.

The backlash against disco's commercialism, cheap sentiment, and *faux* sexuality fueled the emergence of other more "authentic" expressions of youth culture, such as punk and heavy metal. By 1981 the disco boom was bust, though the genre's legacy has lived on. Music critics cite disco as one of the influences on early hip-hop and rap music, as well as some indie rock performers.

Sam Binkley

SEE ALSO: *The Bee Gees; Disc Jockeys; Heavy Metal; Hip-Hop; Indie Music; Leisure Suit; Polyester; Pop Music; Punk; Radio; Rock and Roll;* Saturday Night Fever*; Studio 54; Summer, Donna; Travolta, John.*

BIBLIOGRAPHY

Echols, Alice. *Hot Stuff: Disco and the Remaking of American Culture*. New York: W. W. Norton, 2010.

Haden-Guest, Anthony. *The Last Party: Studio 54, Disco, and the Culture of the Night*. New York: William Morrow, 1997.

Disney (Walt Disney Company)

When it was founded in 1923, Walt Disney Productions consisted of a tiny studio in Hollywood housing a small group of creative artists headed by a young visionary who had recently arrived from the Midwest to produce cartoons for the movies. Beyond that, there was little more than a paper menagerie of barnyard animals and a mouse nicknamed Mickey, who emerged at night to seek crumbs left behind by the artists. Five years later that mouse had made the jump to the silver screen when he starred in *Plane Crazy* (1928), helped along with the assistance of artist Ub Iwerks, who supplied the artwork, and Walt Disney, who came up with the trademark squeaky voice. The company was on its way.

At the beginning of the twenty-first century, the Walt Disney Company was considered by many to be one of the most influential companies in the world, surpassing even its founder's vision as it established footholds not only in motion pictures but also in such diverse industries as television, electronic media, book publishing, hotels, transportation, tourism, amusement parks, real estate, and communications. In an industry where vertical integration had become increasingly important, Disney and its chief rival, Time Warner, had their corporate interests well diversified, more so than any other entertainment entities. Yet, the mouse continued to lead the way.

WALT DISNEY MOVES TO HOLLYWOOD

Perhaps the most recognizable logo in the history of the world, Mickey Mouse has left his footprints on almost every country and culture in the world. The road to success, however, was not entirely without its share of ups and downs. Disney was born in Chicago in 1901, the son of a ne'er-do-well father who drifted from one job to another. He learned to work hard early in life and had little escape from the everyday drudgery except for the drawings he created. This early experience instilled two traits in Disney that would follow him for all his life: one was that he learned the value of hard work and became a compulsive workaholic; the other was a firm belief that the public thirsted for escapism and happy endings.

In 1919 Disney went to work for the Kansas City Film Ad Company, where he put his drawing talents to use working on short animated commercials for local merchants. He also met Iwerks, another young artist. Together the two learned the fundamentals of animation and decided to strike out on their own, producing a series of ads and comic shorts called Newman's Laugh-O-Grams for the local Newman's Theater. In 1922 Disney took the Newman's concept further by creating pure entertainment-oriented theatrical cartoons satirizing popular fairy tales. Unfortunately, he spent more money than he earned on the production and technical aspects of each film. The result was that, artistically, the films were quite polished for their time, with full background detail and a broad spectrum of wash tones that served to establish the basic Disney style. Financially, however, the company was forced to go out of business because its production costs were simply too high.

In 1923 Disney moved to Hollywood with his brother Roy and formed the Disney Brothers studio to produce short subjects that combined both live action and animation. These first short films were based on *Alice in Wonderland* and featured a live Alice character juxtaposed with cartoon backgrounds and animated characters. This method was a reversal of rival animator Max Fleischer's *Out of the Inkwell* series, which featured a cartoon clown having adventures against a live background. The Disney series, which was dubbed *Alice in Cartoonland*, was picked up by a Los Angeles distributor named M. J. Winkler.

After the formation of the company, both Disney brothers realized that animation was not a one- or two-person job. Ad-

Walt Disney at Disneyland. *Walt Disney poses in front of the Fantasyland castle at the grand opening of Disneyland in 1955.* ALLAN GRANT/TIME & LIFE PICTURES/GETTY IMAGES.

ditionally, they knew that they needed to hire the best talent, so they brought in a small staff, including Iwerks and an up-and-coming animator named Hugh Harmon. Some of the titles in the Alice series include *Alice's Wild West Show* (1924), *Alice's Egg Plant* (1925), and *Alice Chops the Suey* (1925). These shorts were innovative in that they integrated the real and animated action, showing a live girl jumping out of an animated inkwell, blowing animated smoke rings, or being splattered with cartoon eggs. Yet, at the speed that the small studio was required to produce them (approximately one every two weeks), the staff could not experiment with too many ideas, and the novelty began to wear off.

LOSING OSWALD, INVENTING MICKEY

Disney quickly introduced a new character and series featuring Oswald the Lucky Rabbit. These cartoons reflected a higher quality of animation and experimented with a variety of visual effects, particularly the manipulation of light and shadow, not seen in the Alice series. In addition, the use of an animated central character as opposed to a live figure made a certain reality-defying flexibility possible. In one adventure Oswald attempts to kiss a medieval maiden's hand and arm and keeps pulling more and more arm out of her sleeve until he has a seemingly endless expanse of arm to kiss. In another cartoon his car expands and contracts to fit a variety of continuously changing road conditions.

Like the cartoons themselves, the planning sessions for them were equally flexible. Instead of formal scripts, the stories were conceived at what amounted to corporate bull sessions consisting of Disney and four other animators. Ideas were tossed into the ring until a basic plot evolved. Disney would then divide the elements into four sequences, with each animator responsible for his own area of the cartoon's action. Each animator could then freely improvise within his own area subject to Disney's approval.

The Oswald series was so fresh and innovative that it made Disney's company a modest success. Yet, when he approached his current distributor, Charles Mintz—who had taken over the Winkler Company—for larger production budgets, Mintz refused and took both Oswald and all the key animators who participated in the project away from Disney. Only Iwerks remained. The experience made the Disney brothers determined to own all their own films and copyrights in the future.

In 1928 Disney and Iwerks fashioned another animal character to replace Oswald—Mortimer Mouse, whose name was quickly changed to Mickey. Mickey Mouse, who first appeared in the silent cartoons *Plane Crazy* and *Gallopin' Gaucho*, was not an immediate success. Although the animation and story ideas were good, the character itself looked like Oswald with shorter ears and a longer nose. There was nothing intrinsically interesting about the character to separate it from the multitudes of other animals cavorting on the screen.

It took the introduction of synchronized motion picture sound in 1926 to make Mickey Mouse a superstar. Whereas the first live-action sound films such as *The Jazz Singer* (1927) put the sound in somewhat gratuitously, counting on the technology to thrill the audience, Disney created an integrated film in which sound and images worked together. When *Steamboat Willie* was released at the end of the year, audiences were captivated by the idea that a character plainly drawn with pen and ink could actually sing and dance in rhythm. The secret was that Disney began with song and music first and then drew the characters and backgrounds to reflect the sounds.

Disney built on the success of *Steamboat Willie* by working with his musical director, Carl Stallings, to create animated cartoons based on specific musical pieces. The first of these was *Skeleton Dance* (1929), a noncharacter cartoon that demonstrated animation's ability to evoke mood and atmosphere. Suddenly, cartoons were no longer the poor relative of live-action feature films but works of art in themselves. In the years that followed, Disney created the *Silly Symphonies* series of music-based animation and introduced new characters, including Pluto (1930), Minnie Mouse (1933), and Donald Duck (1934). In 1932 he switched to the new medium of Technicolor for *Flowers and Trees* and won the Academy Award for best short subject. After that the young company maintained an exclusive agreement with Technicolor for all their animated productions.

EXPANDING BEYOND SHORT CARTOONS

Cartoon shorts, however, could only evolve so far. Disney became determined to create a feature-length animated film. Although conventional Hollywood wisdom dictated that an animated cartoon could not hold audience interest beyond seven minutes, Disney envisioned a fairly simple structure as a viable formula to capture attention. This structure would allow one sequence to flow into another and would have musical numbers that would evolve from and add to character development.

In *Snow White and the Seven Dwarfs* (1937), Disney created seven distinctly individual personalities in addition to his main characters, a feat that never before had been accomplished in animation. To gain such distinction, Disney crafted the characters, particularly Snow White, with such a degree of detail that they could convey human emotions in a believable manner. Audiences reacted to *Snow White* as if the characters were real, showing a variety of emotions ranging from horror at the sight of the queen's transformation into a witch to happiness as Snow White frolics with the dwarfs and charms the woodland animals.

After *Snow White* came a steady flow of features, each one expanding the techniques of animation. By the beginning of the 1940s, the company geared up to produce a constant stream of animated features and literally become a factory employing hundreds of artists and technical personnel even though the studio had not gained major status as a full production/distribution entity on par with Warner Brothers or Columbia. *Pinocchio* and *Fantasia* appeared in 1940, blazing a trail for other notable productions such as *Dumbo* (1941), *Bambi* (1942), *Cinderella* (1950), *Sleeping Beauty* (1959), and *101 Dalmatians* (1961). Interspersed with these animated features were documentary and live action productions, including *The Living Desert* (1953), *20,000 Leagues under the Sea* (1954), and *Mary Poppins* (1964). During the early 1950s, Disney founded his own distribution company, Buena Vista, to release these films, thus freeing him from his reliance on RKO and other larger companies to determine the venues for his products.

But Disney did not confine himself to one medium. In 1954 he made the jump to the newly developed television airwaves with a weekly series called *Disneyland*, which would be followed by an afternoon children's series titled *The Mickey Mouse Club*. In 1955 he fulfilled his personal vision by creating an escapist world in Anaheim, California, in which reality dare not intrude. The Disneyland theme park featured a nostalgic Main Street USA and four thematically constructed lands: Adventureland, Fantasyland, Frontierland, and Tomorrowland. Each of these lands reflected motifs first delineated in Disney films or television programs. It was the first time that viewers could actually enter the world of their favorite Disney films and interact with fictional characters. The company also created spin-off products from the films and theme parks, including lines of toys, clothing, and records. By the end of the 1950s, Disney was the undisputed king of family entertainment in the United States.

DISNEY AFTER WALT'S DEATH

After its founder's death in 1966, the company coasted along for a number of years, turning out acceptable products and fulfilling several of Disney's unrealized dreams. These included an updated East Coast version of Disneyland—Walt Disney World in Orlando, Florida—in 1971 and the futuristic Epcot Center several years later. Under the management of Disney's successor, E. Cardon Walker, the company was faced by a defection of a number of its leading animators led by Don Bluth, who felt that the company's standards had deteriorated after Disney's death. After venturing out on their own, however, they quickly discovered that while they could duplicate the legendary Disney animation, they could not capture the elusive Disney touch that transformed drawings into real characters capable of expressing human emotions within innovative story lines.

Walker's successor, Ron Miller, was faced with declining film revenues, and he created a new division called Touchstone in 1984 to turn out more adult products than the Disney image would allow. This prompted Roy Disney, still a major shareholder in the company, to resign from the board of directors, initiating a management struggle for control of the company that by the mid-1980s was producing only four films a year and was reliant on the theme parks for the bulk of its revenue (87 percent in 1983 alone).

Miller resigned under pressure in September 1984 just as Touchstone's first release, *Splash*, boosted the film division's earnings to record highs and became the highest-grossing film in Disney history while also making a star of Tom Hanks. Miller's successor, Michael Eisner, lured from Paramount Pictures, appeared cut from the Disney mold. He followed up on the success of *Splash* with two more nontraditional features, *Down and Out in Beverly Hills* (1986) and *Three Men and a Baby* (1987). These would be followed by the worldwide mega-hit *Pretty Woman* (1990), a story of a romance between a prostitute and a millionaire that took the old Cinderella story in a modern direction.

With chairman Jeffrey Katzenberg, Eisner brought about a renaissance of the animated feature at a time when conventional wisdom had declared it moribund. Beginning with the critically acclaimed *The Black Cauldron* in 1985, Eisner started a new golden age of animation that surpassed the box-office successes of the 1930s and 1940s. Yet, the formula was much the same: realistic characters that tugged at the viewers' emotions, superb animation, and memorable music. Films such as *The Little Mermaid* (1989), *Beauty and the Beast* (1991), *Aladdin* (1992), *The Lion King* (1994), *Pocahontas* (1995), *Mulan* (1998), *Lilo & Stitch* (2002), *Bolt* (2008), and *Tangled* (2010) generated grosses in the hundreds of millions, prompting many of Hollywood's major studios to jump into animation in order to compete. *Beauty and the Beast* became the first animated feature to be nominated for an Academy Award.

EXPANDING THE DISNEY EMPIRE

By the mid-1990s, production at Disney had risen from the four films per year of a decade earlier to more than twenty per annum. Eisner's strategy of producing tightly budgeted films pairing low-cost name talent such as Richard Dreyfuss and Bette Midler, who were in temporary career lulls, with widely appealing stories paid major dividends. Films such as the aforementioned *Pretty Woman*, *Stakeout* (1987), *Honey, I Shrunk the Kids* (1989), and *Sister Act* (1992) achieved grosses that greatly exceeded their small (by Hollywood standards) production budgets. The success of these features prompted the studio to open a third production entity, Hollywood Pictures, in 1990.

Disney had at last acquired major studio status by the 1990s. Its distribution company, Buena Vista, was regularly in the top one or two in film grosses, and it was out-producing all the studios in Hollywood in sheer number of films. With its ownership of a cable TV channel and a successful video distribution empire, as well as with the ability to distribute its product worldwide via satellite, Disney became one of the earliest studios to realize the financial value of a large library. In 1996 the company purchased the ABC television network for $19 billion, giving it a national outlet for its product as well as an all-encompassing venue for plugging its upcoming films. Although the network never regained the top spot it held in the 1970s, it nonetheless presented some of the more innovative new shows on television and was a leader in sports and news programming.

Eisner also took major steps to revitalize the theme park side of the company by creating EuroDisney outside of Paris in 1992 and a wild animal theme park in Florida in 1997. On the West Coast he started a project to expand the original Disneyland in Anaheim. Hong Kong Disneyland opened in 2005, becoming the company's second theme park in Asia; Tokyo Disneyland had opened in the 1980s. The ancillary markets for Disney products were expanded as well. The company refurbished El Capitan Theater in Hollywood as a showcase for its new releases and added promotional stage acts as well as a place to buy the company's products in the lobby. To expand its vacation offerings, Disney opened the Disney Cruise Line in 1998.

In New York Disney refurbished a Broadway theater and began to turn its film hits, including *Beauty and the Beast* and *The Lion King*, into musical plays with new numbers and scenes added to make them successful on the stage. Similarly, several of the animated productions were turned into ice extravaganzas that toured the country, blending the traditional stories and songs with fancy skating numbers arranged specifically for the frozen medium.

The ultimate spin-off of a motion picture concept occurred in the early 1990s when Eisner bought an Anaheim National Hockey League (NHL) franchise and named it after the moderately successful live action feature *The Mighty Ducks*. The company also purchased the Anaheim Angels baseball team and the highly popular cable TV station Entertainment and Sports Network (ESPN). Disney sold the Angels in 2003 and the Ducks in 2005 but retained ownership of ESPN. In a much more profitable cross-pollination of its various enterprises, Disney turned one of its most popular theme-park rides into the blockbuster movie *Pirates of the Caribbean*, starring Johnny Depp. As of 2012, the movie had spawned three sequels.

By the twenty-first century the Walt Disney Company had grown from the small Hollywood studio of 1923 to a recreational empire. With holdings so expansive, the nostalgic Disney vision was applied beyond mere entertainment. The company's theme-oriented steamship line (floating Disneylands); Disney Stores; innovative theme parks; and music, video, and television endeavors allowed the company unprecedented power to shape the perceptions of consumers, offering people the chance to see, experience, and purchase Disney-styled versions of Americana.

Steve Hanson

SEE ALSO: *Academy Awards; Amusement Parks; Animated Films;* Davy Crockett*; Depp, Johnny; ESPN;* Fantasia*; Hanks, Tom; Hockey; Hollywood;* The Jazz Singer*;* The Lion King*;* Mary Poppins*;* The Mickey Mouse Club*; Midler, Bette; National Hockey League (NHL);* Pirates of the Caribbean*;* Snow White and the Seven Dwarfs*;* Steamboat Willie*; Television;* The Three Caballeros*; Toys; Winnie-the-Pooh.*

BIBLIOGRAPHY

Bailey, Adrian. *Walt Disney's World of Fantasy*. New York: Everest House, 1982.

Coleman, Todd. "Mouse Trap." *Hollywood Reporter*, November 25, 1996, 29+.

Gabler, Neal. *Walt Disney: The Triumph of the American Imagination*. New York: Knopf, 2006.

Hanson, Steve. "The Mouse That Roared." *Stills*, October 1984, 24–27.

Koepp, Stephen, "Do You Believe in Magic? Starring in Its Own Cinderella Story, Disney Transforms Itself." *Time*, April 25, 1988, 66–75.

Maltin, Leonard. *Of Mice and Magic: A History of American Animated Cartoons*. New York: New American Library, 1980.

Schickel, Richard. *The Disney Version*. New York: Simon, 1968.

Smith, Dave. *Disney A to Z: The Official Encyclopedia*. New York: Hyperion, 1996.

Solomon, Charles. *The Disney That Never Was: The Stories and Art from Five Decades of Unproduced Animation*. New York: Hyperion, 1995.

Taylor, John. *Storming the Magic Kingdom: Wall Street, the Raiders and the Battle for Disney*. New York: Knopf, 1987.

Veness, Susan. *The Hidden Magic of Walt Disney World: Over 600 Secrets of the Magic Kingdom, Epcot, Disney's Hollywood Studios, and Animal Kingdom*. Avon, MA: Adams Media, 2009.

West, John G., Jr. *The Disney Live-Action Productions*. Milton, WA: Hawthorne & Peabody, 1994.

Disney Channel

SEE: *Cyrus, Miley / Hannah Montana; High School Musical; The Jonas Brothers.*

Ditka, Mike *(1939–)*

Football player turned football coach "Iron" Mike Ditka is described in his Pro Football Hall of Fame enshrinee data as a "fast, rugged, outstanding blocker [and a] great competitor." In 1960 he was a consensus All-American at the University of Pittsburgh and became the Chicago Bears' number one draft pick the following year. From 1961 through 1972 Ditka was a hard-nosed tight end for the Bears, Philadelphia Eagles, and Dallas Cowboys. He was the National Football League (NFL) Rookie of the Year in 1961, starred on the Bears' 1963 NFL title squad, and scored the final touchdown for the Cowboys in Super Bowl VI. During his career he caught 427 passes for 5,812 yards and 43 touchdowns. He made all-NFL four times, played in five straight Pro Bowls, was named to the NFL 75th Anniversary Team, and in 1988 became the first tight end to enter the Pro Football Hall of Fame. Two years earlier he was enshrined in the College Football Hall of Fame, and in 1999 Ditka was ranked number ninety on a *Sporting News* list of the 100 Greatest Football Players.

Despite his eminence as a player, Ditka is best known today as an NFL head coach. He worked as an assistant under Tom Landry in Dallas from 1973 through 1981 and was hired to lead the Bears in 1982. While he has willingly parodied his in-your-face, bullying, drill-instructor coaching style on television shows and particularly in TV commercials, he is all business when it comes to winning football games. During eleven seasons coaching the Bears, he led the team to six NFC Central crowns, three trips to the NFC Championship game, and a 46–10 whipping of the New England Patriots in Super Bowl XX. Additionally, he won NFL Coach of the Year honors in 1985 and 1988. After retiring from the Bears in 1992 and working as an NBC sports broadcaster, he was lured back onto the field in 1997 as coach of the New Orleans Saints, where he remained for three years.

Since leaving coaching permanently, Ditka has offered game analysis and commentary on various CBS and ESPN football programs and frequently appears on radio shows in Seattle and Chicago. He is also a high-profile advocate for increasing awareness of the financial and medical needs of indigent ex-NFL players. He sits on the board of directors of the Gridiron Greats Assistance Fund, which offers financial support and social services to these players.

Rob Edelman

SEE ALSO: *The Chicago Bears; College Football; The Dallas Cowboys; Landry, Tom; National Football League (NFL); Professional Football; Radio; The* Sporting News*; Sports Heroes; Super Bowl; Television.*

BIBLIOGRAPHY

Ditka, Mike, and Jim Stamborski. *Don't Get Me Wrong: Mike Ditka's Insights, Outbursts, Kudos and Comebacks.* Chicago: Chicago Review Press, 1988.

Ditka, Mike, and Don Pierson. *Ditka: An Autobiography.* Chicago: Bonus Books, 1986.

Ditka, Mike, and Rick Telander. *Mike Ditka: Reflections on the 1985 Bears and Wisdom from Da Coach.* New York: Sports Publishing, 2007.

Keteyian, Armen. *Ditka: Monster of the Midway.* New York: Pocket Books, 1992.

Divine *(1945–1988)*

The obese transvestite character actor Divine personified self-consciously campy underground films and ushered in a new threshold of bad taste in cinema. Starring mainly in the films of offbeat director John Waters, Divine cultivated an outrageous drag-queen image, with gaudy makeup, a blond mane the texture of cotton candy, and tight dresses on his 300-plus-pound frame. He played female characters in the majority of his films and dressed in women's garb during his short-lived career as a singer. Though Divine was poised to break into mainstream film and television at the end of his life, most of his appearances were in films with shocking subject matter. He will likely remain famous for his role as the "Filthiest Person Alive" in the 1972 Waters's

***Divine in* Pink Flamingos.** *Divine was the star of John Waters's* Pink Flamingos *in 1972.* DREAMLAND PRODUCTIONS/THE KOBAL COLLECTION.

film *Pink Flamingos*, especially due to the notorious scene at the end in which he consumes freshly excreted poodle dung.

Divine was born Harris Glenn Milstead on October 19, 1945, and raised in an upper-middle-class home in a suburb of Baltimore, Maryland, the city that provided the backdrop for the bulk of his films. As a teen, Divine was active in school plays and began associating with Waters, who lived nearby. They were both outcasts, and Divine noted in Waters's book *Shock Value* that he required a daily police escort to and from school to avoid constant beatings by other students.

After high school Divine graduated from beauty school and became known as an excellent stylist. His parents even bought him his own salon, but he became bored with it. He later opened a fashion boutique in Provincetown, Massachusetts. Meanwhile, he also began acting in Waters's independent movies. His first role was in *Roman Candles* (1966), a home movie of Waters's friends stealing and then modeling dresses. It was at this time that Waters recognized the actor's potential and renamed his friend "Divine."

After that unceremonious induction into film, Divine starred in *Eat Your Makeup* (1968), in which he played the part of Jacqueline Kennedy in the movie's central scene, which reenacted President John F. Kennedy's assassination. Subsequently, Waters made another film of questionable taste that is rarely noted in official sources, *The Diane Linkletter Story*, named after Art Linkletter's daughter, who committed suicide allegedly after taking large amounts of hallucinogenic drugs.

In 1969 Waters and his troupe, known as the Dreamlanders, made *Mondo Trasho*, which established Divine's bizarre look. In *Not Simply Divine*, Bernard Jay quotes Divine as saying that his new image was based on Waters's concept of a blend of "the wicked stepmother in *Cinderella*, the evil queen of *Snow White*, and the bad witch in *The Wizard of Oz*," combined with a touch of Jayne Mansfield. Continuing down a slippery slope of poor taste, *Mondo Trasho* was followed by *Multiple Maniacs* in 1970, which professed that Divine was the actual killer in what were later dubbed the Manson Family murders. It also featured Divine being raped by a fifteen-foot-tall lobster.

After *Multiple Maniacs*, Divine and Waters garnered a good deal of attention from underground publications. Their next collaboration, though, dwarfed their previous efforts. *Pink Flamingos* was the tale of a battle for the title of "Filthiest Person Alive" and featured a couple who kidnaps women, impregnates them, and sells the babies to lesbians on the black market to raise money for their elementary school heroin ring. They want to take the distinction away from Divine, an incestuous, trailer-dwelling matriarch who firmly maintains her disgusting reputation with the dog excrement scene. *Pink Flamingos* generated a flurry of attention and became one of the premier cult films of all time.

Divine had acted in stage plays in San Francisco in the early 1970s, and after *Pink Flamingos* began appearing in off-Broadway productions such as *Women Behind Bars* (1976) and *The Neon Woman* (1978). He also launched a disco singing career. In fact, he often attended the legendary Studio 54 disco in full drag and mingled with other icons of the day. Divine made a number of other films with Waters throughout the years, including *Female Trouble* (1974), *Polyester* (1981), and *Lust in the Dust* (1985), as well as a few on his own.

Although Divine made his mark as the garish caricature of himself that people usually saw, he grew weary of dressing in drag and yearned to be accepted as a talented character actor. Finally, in 1988 he was noticed for his dual role in Waters's *Hairspray* as both proud stage mother Edna Turnblad and bigoted television executive Arvin Hodgepile. After that, he was slated to appear on the popular television program *Married . . . with Children* and was eager to line up other work as well. Just as he seemed on the verge of making an entrance into the mainstream, however, Divine died of a heart attack in a hotel room in Los Angeles on March 7, 1988.

Geri Speace

SEE ALSO: *"B" Movies; Cult Films; Drag; Linkletter, Art; Waters, John.*

BIBLIOGRAPHY

Clark, John. "Ready for the Return of 'Flamingos'?" *Los Angeles Times*, April 10, 1997.

Jay, Bernard. *Not Simply Divine: Beneath the Make-Up, above the Heels, and behind the Scenes with a Cult Superstar.* New York: Simon & Schuster, 1993.

Waters, John. Hairspray; Female Trouble; *and* Multiple Maniacs: *Three More Screenplays.* New York: Thunder's Mouth Press, 2005.

Waters, John. *Shock Value: A Tasteful Book about Bad Taste.* New York: Thunder's Mouth Press, 2005.

Divorce

Marriage, generally considered the legally sanctioned and structured pairing of heterosexual couples, has long been an established practice all over the world. Divorce, the dissolution of this pairing, is as old as marriage itself and has become particularly prevalent in modern times. Following World War II, divorce rates began to climb, partly in response to quickie wartime marriages and partly due to the changing roles of women in society. In the 1970s California passed its innovative no-fault divorce law and instituted major reforms of family laws; other states soon followed suit. With slight variations, the divorce rate remained high from the mid-1970s until the mid-1990s. In 1996, however, divorces occurred less frequently, and this trend has continued in the twenty-first century. Many couples put off divorces because of the economic downturn late in the first decade of the 2000s.

Nevertheless, divorce has become among society's most common rituals since the 1960s. Roughly 41 percent of first marriages end in divorce, and that number rises to 60 percent with second marriages and 73 percent with third marriages. The prevalence of divorce has altered not only the dynamic of marriage but the definition of family as well. It has also wreaked economic havoc.

THE HISTORY OF DIVORCE

Early cultures often permitted divorce with relative ease. Roman law allowed couples to divorce simply by mutual consent, whereas Jewish Talmudic law granted the dissolution of a marriage on a variety of grounds, including adultery and desertion.

Greek, Germanic, and Frankish laws recognized a couple's right to divorce, as did the laws of Islam and the Orthodox Church. The Roman Catholic Church became one of the first institutions to outlaw divorce, claiming marriage as a sacrament of the church. Dissolution of marriage could only be granted by the church under special circumstances, such as an annulment if one's spouse was a close relative or a "judicial separation" in which the husband and wife were permitted to live apart without remarrying. The attitude of the Catholic Church toward divorce had repercussions that carried into future centuries and influenced lands as far-flung as Ireland, Latin America, and parts of the South in the United States.

The Protestant Reformation brought new perspectives on marriage. Whereas Catholics had viewed marriage as a sacred sacrament, taken on for life, Protestants saw it as a contract that was changeable if it no longer met the needs of the two parties. Likewise, whereas Catholics had primarily defined the purpose of marriage as procreation, Protestants included in it such functions as companionship, support, and sexual pleasure, inspiring radical Protestants such as poet John Milton to argue that divorce should be allowed for simple incompatibility.

In the United States, starting in colonial times, divorce has been widely permitted but traditionally frowned upon socially. By the time of the Civil War, divorces were granted in most parts of the country on grounds of cruelty, abandonment, drunkenness, nonsupport, or verbal threats or insults. As legal divorces became easier to obtain, they began to increase steadily. By the early 1900s, more divorces were granted in the United States than in any other European or North American country—six times as many as in France, which had the second-highest rate. The number of divorces in the United States rose from 7,380 in 1860 to 83,045 by 1910.

DIVORCE AFTER WORLD WAR II

In the 1950s the divorce rate in the United States was 1,070 per 100,000 for males and 1,373 per 100,000 for females. Women had entered the workplace in unprecedented numbers during the war, but there was a major effort to force them back into the home in the 1950s. Betty Friedan, the mother of the women's rights movement, later identified the guilt saddled on American women during the 1950s and 1960s as "the problem that had no name." By the 1960s early baby boomers were leaving home, and for the first time in history, large numbers of females were graduating from college with career aspirations and the skills to achieve them. The divorce rate shot up as these women no longer felt forced to remain in unhappy marriages. The number of divorces also increased among their parents, who were freed from the responsibility of raising children.

Despite its prevalence, divorce was still stigmatized in some segments of American society and was pathologized by experts who defined these suddenly single people as neurotics who needed counseling. This perception finally began to change in the 1970s when feminism and the sexual revolution combined to give divorce a more positive image that reflected the right of women to be liberated and independent. The divorce rate peaked in 1981 and then began to dip as the threat of AIDS encouraged monogamy. In addition, married baby boomers of the 1980s began to find financial reasons to stay together: two incomes were needed to support the lifestyles to which they had grown accustomed. These factors, coupled with political conservatism and a backlash against feminism in the 1980s, caused more couples to seek counseling to save their marriages.

The lull did not last, however. As the twenty-first century approached, generation Xers, many the children of divorce themselves, attempted to determine the boundaries of commitment. Divorce became so commonplace that many couples used mediators instead of lawyers in order to end their marriages amicably. A number of states began mandating the use of mediators when couples could not reach agreements on child custody or financial distributions. However, the use of mediation cannot always guarantee an amicable divorce. There were even rare cases of children divorcing their parents and vice versa.

Some experts have suggested that cohabitation and open marriages may help reduce the number of divorces that occur in the United States. Between 1960 and 2000 the number of cohabitating couples increased tenfold. By the twenty-first century, the majority of couples were cohabitating before marriage. According to the U.S. Census Bureau, between 2005 and 2007 more than twelve million unmarried couples were living together. In open marriages, both partners agree that a marriage will be nonmonogamous. Such couples do not consider it cheating when they have affairs. Experts have pointed out, however, that many so-called open marriages involve outside liaisons for only one partner. High-profile open marriages that end in divorce, such as those of Newt and Marianne Gingrich and Demi Moore and Ashton Kutcher, have given weight to the argument that they do not always preclude divorce.

THE EVOLUTION OF THE MODERN DIVORCE

Until the last half of the nineteenth century, wives were considered little more than the property of their husbands, and the treatment of women in the divorce process reflected that attitude. Though many women were unhappy in the marital roles assigned them, they often had more to lose financially from divorce than men. Less valued in the marketplace than males to begin with, women lost further ground by removing themselves from the workforce to be homemakers. When a woman divorced, the standard of living for her and her children fell an average of 73 percent, often placing them below the poverty line. Men, in contrast, were free to put more energy into their existing jobs when they were released from familial obligations. After divorce, a man's average standard of living rose 42 percent. The devaluing of a woman's role in the home also contributed to an unfair distribution of assets after divorce. Except in "community property" states, where any property acquired by either partner during the marriage was divided equally, a woman often received little or none of the family resources, which may have been in the husband's name. However, reforms to divorce and family law have dealt with these inequities in a number of ways.

Beginning with the so-called "tender years" legislation of the nineteenth century, custody of young children traditionally was awarded to the mother in divorce settlements. However, in what some feminists consider a backlash against the women's movement, most states have passed legislation requiring that fathers be considered as equal to mothers as potential custodial parents. In practice, though, small children generally remain with the mother. Alimony is generally not awarded in the twenty-first century except in lengthy marriages where one spouse remained at home, in cases where one spouse supported another's education/training, or in instances of a disabled or elderly spouse. No-fault divorce, a concept developed in the 1970s, has further eroded the system of spousal support by removing the factor of blame and responsibility for the end of a marriage. Although these changes have been widely applauded, they often have resulted in worsening economic conditions for women following divorce.

Some couples are now opting for a collaborative divorce, which generally involves lawyers for the two parties agreeing beforehand to consider what is best for entire families rather than engaging in an adversarial process inside a courtroom. Another product of the rising divorce rate has been the prenuptial agreement. Here, couples plan for the possibility of a divorce before they are even married and agree upon a future division of property. Originated by the lawyers of wealthy people who felt they had lost unfair amounts in divorces, the "prenup" is now as much a part of an upper-class wedding as the cake.

SOCIETY AND THE MEDIA

Social attitudes toward men and women have tended to be quite different when it comes to divorce, especially prior to the 1970s. Divorced men have often been viewed as roguish or even slightly dangerous, not undesirable qualities in a male. Moreover, the addition of another available man to the social pool is generally viewed in a positive light. Divorced women, on the other hand, have been traditionally perceived as promiscuous; the addition of an unattached woman to the pool is usually viewed as a threat to other females.

Images of divorce in the media have contributed to these perceptions. Entertainers have always lived by their own rules, and even in decades when divorce was stigmatized in ordinary society, the public avidly followed the marital adventures of celebrities. Even in the repressive 1950s, actors such as Elizabeth Taylor and Mickey Rooney seemed to be constantly marrying and then divorcing. Fascinated fans reacted with outrage when divorcee Taylor broke up the "idyllic" marriage of Eddie Fisher and Debbie Reynolds. In the mid-1970s many Americans formed strong opinions about the so-called "palimony" suit following the breakup of unmarried lovers Lee Marvin and Michelle Triola; Triola insisted that she was entitled to spousal support after their six-year relationship ended.

Films have tended to both reflect and mold social attitudes. In the 1934 movie *The Gay Divorcee*, Fred Astaire and Ginger Rogers dance their way through lighthearted marital misunderstandings. In *The Parent Trap* in 1961, antidivorce attitudes win out when twin daughters (played by Hayley Mills) of a divorced couple manage to reunite their parents, whose breakup was clearly ill advised. The backlash in the 1980s is inaugurated deftly by *Kramer vs. Kramer* (1979), the Oscar winner for Best Picture in which Dustin Hoffman and Meryl Streep play divorcing parents. Both characters are motivated by their own selfishness, but in the end, it is the husband who is redeemed by learning the joys of family, and he is rewarded with custody of the couple's son.

By the 1990s divorce was so commonplace that it had lost much of its social stigma and much of its value as scandal. Fans still followed the love lives of the stars, but it took an exceptionally short marriage or brutal breakup to arouse much public interest. Celebrity-watchers felt vindicated when superstar actress Julia Roberts walked away from her unlikely spouse, musician Lyle Lovett, after only a few months, and they cheered for entertainer Carol Channing when she left her forty-one-year marriage at age seventy-seven, citing lack of sex as one of the reasons. Film portrayals tended to show divorce as a positive solution to a bad situation. The 1989 film *The War of the Roses* is a black comedy about the violent breakup of marriage in which neither partner is presented positively, whereas *The First Wives Club* (1996) is a sort of revenge comedy in which mistreated and abandoned wives take action against their boorish ex-husbands.

FAMILY CHANGES

In past centuries, when the family was an economic unit, marriage was a pragmatic agreement. Members had unique functions and derived stability and protection from their place in the unit, which most often was an extended family made up of elders, adults, and children. Marriage was an essential part of a family's survival. As American society evolved, the nuclear family replaced the extended family as the major social unit, and its function increasingly became that of emotional support and physical caretaking rather than working together. As partners entered marriage, they had higher expectations of happiness and satisfaction. Some sociologists cite these heightened expectations as the reason for rising rates of divorce, whereas others contend that since marriage and family are no longer a necessity of physical survival, it is natural that couples tend to drift apart.

As divorce becomes more prevalent, the image of the family continues to change. Though political and religious conservatives have tried to restore a more traditional concept of the nuclear family, they have not been able to stop these changes. Many of these observers bemoan the ill effects of divorce on children, but most modern studies show that children do not benefit from growing up in a traditional nuclear family where the parents are unhappy together. The definition of family is broadening to include unmarried heterosexuals and gays living together, single-parent families, stepfamilies, foster and adoptive families, childless couples, non-monogamous relationships, and multiple-adult households. Family is not only biological but also chosen—a complex network of economic support and affection that is no longer easily categorized.

THE NEW NORMAL

By the 1990s Madison Avenue had even started to understand and speak to these changes, as companies such as Hallmark Greeting Cards and John Hancock Insurance developed advertising campaigns directed at families of divorce and other nontraditional units. A 1998 Rite-Aid ad shows two girls helping their mother get ready for her first post-divorce date, while a 1991 MCI Communications ad depicts a workaholic father sadly explaining how his personal toll-free number helps him keep in touch with his son, who now lives with his mother far away. These images show how the reality of divorce has been incorporated into American culture and, indeed, into culture worldwide.

Divorce remains a fixture in the twenty-first century, but statistics released by the U.S. Census Bureau indicate that among higher-educated two-earner families, the institution of marriage has become more stable. Overall in 2009, 52 percent of males and 58 percent of females had been married only once. Twelve percent of Americans had been married twice, and 3 percent had been married more than three times. Most divorces occurred in the thirty-five to forty-four age group (31.0 percent), followed by forty-five to fifty-four (27.5 percent) and twenty-five to thirty-four (23.6 percent). Almost 80 percent of couples that divorced had no children under the age of eighteen living in the household. The numbers, it seems, do not lie: despite fluctuations, divorce is here to stay.

Tina Gianoulis

SEE ALSO: *AIDS; Baby Boomers; Celebrity Couples; Feminism; Generation X; Kutcher, Ashton; Moore, Demi; Sex Scandals; Sexual Revolution; Taylor, Elizabeth.*

BIBLIOGRAPHY

Basch, Norma. *Framing American Divorce: From the Revolutionary Generation to the Victorians.* Berkeley: University of California Press, 1999.

Celello, Kristin. *Making Marriage Work: A History of Marriage and Divorce in the Twentieth-Century United States.* Chapel Hill: University of North Carolina Press, 2009.

Chused, Richard H. *Private Acts in Public Places: A Social History of Divorce in the Formative Era of American Family Law.* Philadelphia: University of Pennsylvania Press, 1994.

Davis, Rebecca L. *More Perfect Unions: The American Search for Marital Bliss.* Boston: Harvard University Press, 2010.

DiFonzo, J. Herbie. *Beneath the Fault Line: The Popular and Legal Culture of Divorce in Twentieth-Century America.* Charlottesville: University Press of Virginia, 1997.

Ganong, Lawrence H., and Marilyn Coleman. *Changing Families, Changing Responsibilities: Family Obligations following Divorce and Remarriage.* Mahwah, NJ: Lawrence Erlbaum Associates, 1999.

May, Elaine Tyler. *Great Expectations: Marriage and Divorce in Post-Victorian America.* Chicago: University of Chicago Press, 1980.

Metz, Tamara. *Untying the Knot: Marriage, the State, and the Case for Their Divorce.* Princeton, NJ: Princeton University Press, 2010.

"Number, Timing, and Duration of Marriages, and Divorces: 2009." United States Census Bureau. Accessed February 2012. Available from http://www.census.gov/prod/2011pubs/p70-125.pdf

Phillips, Roderick. *Putting Asunder: A History of Divorce in Western Society.* Cambridge, UK: Cambridge University Press, 1988.

Riley, Glenda. *Divorce: An American Tradition.* New York: Oxford University Press, 1991.

Talbot, Margaret. "Love, American Style: What the Alarmists about Divorce Don't Get about Idealism in America." *New Republic*, April 14, 1997, 30.

Dixieland

Dixieland jazz is a style that blends New Orleans, Louisiana, jazz with the classic variety—also called "Chicago jazz"—of the 1920s. The music is generally thought of as a collective improvisation during the choruses, with individual solos that include riffing by the horns and a two- to four-bar call-and-response tag game between the drummer and the full group at the closing of the song. Although almost any song can be played in the dixieland style, the music is most often associated with certain tunes, including "That's a Plenty" and "Tin Roof Blues." Most dixieland bands are composed of a trumpet or cornet, a harmonizing trombone, a clarinet, and a piano, string bass, or tuba. Occasionally a guitar or banjo is also included.

DEFINING THE STYLE

"Dixieland" is a blanket term for the earliest blending of New Orleans and Chicago jazz between 1917 and 1923, and the style has enjoyed many revivals throughout the years. Despite the wide use of the term, some confine the definition of dixieland jazz to New Orleans music played by white New Orleans performers or in their style. Others limit the definition to the earliest white players in Chicago. Some of the most important albums of the dixieland style include Louis Armstrong's *Hot Fives and Hot Sevens, Vol. 3* (1927), Eddie Condon's *Dixieland All-Stars* (1939), Kid Ory's Creole Jazz Band's *Legendary Kid* (1956), and Pete Fountain's *Standing Room Only* (1965).

Despite the controversy surrounding how the term should be used, many musicians have been associated with dixieland music. The white Chicago musicians usually included as dixieland musicians are Jimmy McPartland, Bud Freeman, and Frank Teschemacher. These musicians first heard the white New Orleans bands of the 1920s associated with Nick LaRocca in the Original Dixieland Jass (later Jazz) Band, which began recording in 1917, and with Paul Mares in the New Orleans Rhythm Kings (originally the Friar's Society Orchestra), which recorded between 1922 and 1923. This "white" style had a great influence on the development of jazz and was not too far removed from the style of the great black pioneers. White New Orleans bands and their dixieland followers drew less on ragtime and ethnic African sources than did the black pioneers; they drew quite heavily on European sources. One of the most inspirational musicians of the dixieland sound of the 1920s was Armstrong, who noted opera as a strong influence on his style.

SPREADING BEYOND NEW ORLEANS

The popularization of jazz beyond the New Orleans area and the development of dixieland can be traced to the U.S. Navy's 1917 closure of the Storyville base near New Orleans' red light district, which put many musicians out of work. Seeking work, musicians relocated to Chicago. Joe "King" Oliver was the hottest cornetist in New Orleans in 1917; by 1918 he had moved to Chicago. Jelly Roll Morton, jazz's first noted composer and an innovative pianist, had moved to Chicago at the turn of the twentieth century. Many of New Orleans' best musicians followed and played for a time in Chicago. Others went elsewhere: from 1919 to 1924 Kid Ory worked in Los Angeles, whereas Sidney Bechet, the fine clarinetist and soprano saxophonist, played in London. As the musicians moved, the music they played changed, and dixieland became a discernable style.

The carefree style of dixieland music soon lost favor to swing, especially after the stock market crashed in 1929, but it did not disappear. From 1945 through 1960 dixieland actually became one of the more popular forms of jazz. The revival of dixieland in the 1940s can be traced to Lu Watters's Yerba Buena Jazz Band out of San Francisco. Much of the music was based on King Oliver's Creole Jazz Band, but Watters developed his own style, sometimes called San Francisco Jazz. Eddie Condon was also influential in the revival of dixieland; he featured a dixieland band on his weekly half-hour radio broadcast, *Town Hall Concerts*, from 1944 to 1945 and led a band at his Chicago nightclub for a few decades. And though there were many styles of jazz at the time, Armstrong disbanded his big band in 1947 and led his All-Stars as a Dixieland-style sextet for the rest of his career. Despite the overwhelming popularity of rock and roll after the 1950s, Armstrong proved dixieland's lasting appeal in 1964 with the popularity of his "Hello Dolly!"

THE BEAT GOES ON

The success of the dixieland style in the mid-1940s ignited the release of a flurry of hasty and uninspired imitations of the music. By the 1950s dixieland was often associated with embarrassingly garish groups that played amateurishly and donned straw hats and wore vintage clothing. Nevertheless, serious and competent musicians still played dixieland music. In 1974 the first Sacramento Dixieland Jubilee was held, the success of which inspired similar events. By the end of the twentieth century, jazz festivals featuring dixieland along with other styles could be found throughout the year, and many record labels—such as Stomp Off, GHB, and Jazzology—continued to release dixieland music. Many of the greatest players and innovators of dixieland are dead, but younger musicians such as Wynton Marsalis and Jim Cullum continue to incorporate the style into their music.

People across America still associate dixieland music with New Orleans, a link that played a part in efforts to help the city recover from the devastation caused by Hurricane Katrina in 2005. As part of the Bush-Clinton Katrina Fund, a New Orleans band named the Dukes of Dixieland went on a multistate tour aboard a steam-powered riverboat to help raise money for their hometown.

Frank A. Salamone

SEE ALSO: *Armstrong, Louis; Chicago Jazz;* Hello, Dolly!*; Hurricane Katrina; Jazz; Original Dixieland Jass (Jazz) Band.*

BIBLIOGRAPHY

Charters, Samuel Barclay. *A Trumpet around the Corner: The Story of New Orleans Jazz.* Jackson: University Press of Mississippi, 2008.

Condon, Eddie, and Thomas Sugrue. *We Called It Music.* New York: Henry Holt, 1947.

Deffaa, Chip. *Voices of the Jazz Age: Profiles of Eight Vintage Jazzmen.* Urbana: University of Illinois Press, 1990.

Gottleib, Bill. "Dixieland Nowhere, Says Dave Tough." *Down Beat,* September 23, 1946.

Griffiths, David. *Hot Jazz: From Harlem to Storyville.* Lanham, MD: Scarecrow Press, 1998.

Hadlock, Richard. *Jazz Masters of the Twenties.* New York: Da Capo Press, 1988.

Hennessey, Thomas J. *From Jazz to Swing: Afro-American Jazz Musicians and Their Music, 1890–1935.* Detroit, MI: Wayne State University Press, 1994.

Schuller, Gunther. *Early Jazz: Its Roots and Musical Development.* New York: Oxford University Press, 1986.

Wilber, Bob, and Derek Webster. *Music Was Not Enough.* New York: Oxford University Press, 1987.

DIY/Home Improvement

The term "do-it-yourself" (DIY) applies in its broadest sense to a range of tasks, usually domestic projects of repair or improvement, completed by individuals who are amateurs in the field. Instead of hiring professional contractors, many homeowners enjoy the challenge of learning new skills, adapting individual styles, and incorporating materials and techniques from local sources to beautify and improve their homes. The high degree of personal satisfaction, not to mention the lower cost of labor, provides substantial incentives to many do-it-yourselfers. Many view the work they do on their homes as a hobby, and do-it-yourselfers can now learn and master home improvement methods and techniques from an enormous variety of books, television shows, and multimedia computer programs.

Though people relied on manual skills before industrialization, personal skills and expertise gave way to organized labor and specialized craftsmanship in the early nineteenth century when the infusion of power-driven machinery created a revolution in manufacture. Items that had previously been hand-crafted and individually created could be produced by machine automation. The novelty of mass production generated a craze in the purchase of prefabricated goods. By the 1950s in America, mass production had spread to home building, as evidenced by the first neighborhood tract homes.

People have turned to hand-crafting in times of hardship such as the Great Depression and World War II, when there were shortages of building materials and sundry items. Shortages fostered the development of independent home improvement solutions ranging from construction using found materials to the brewing of homemade beer. Propaganda during wartime also encouraged individual thrift and problem solving as important contributions to the war effort. In addition, following the Allied victory, many people returned home with new skills gained through military service and focused on rebuilding their homes and families. DIY home-building kits were available in America as early as the late 1940s.

During the prosperity of the 1950s, home improvement was enjoyed as a family hobby and social activity among neighbors. By the 1960s young homeowners had begun home-crafting and personalized home improvement less as a hobby and more as a statement of individuality. While rebelling against what was generally called "the establishment," young people saw opportunities in home industry that provided an avenue of freedom from commercial and industrial ventures. Homemade

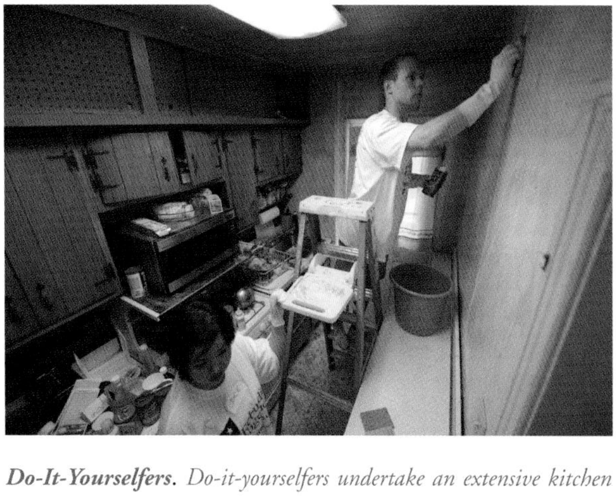

Do-It-Yourselfers. *Do-it-yourselfers undertake an extensive kitchen renovation project.* MANDEL NGAN/AFP/GETTY IMAGES.

items from clothing to bread to wall hangings and interior decorations enjoyed popularity throughout the 1960s and 1970s.

Interest in homemade items waned in the 1980s as Americans returned to more conservative politics, but the spirit of being able to "do it yourself" continued not only among first-time home-buyers, who were principally interested in saving money (not to mention putting a personal "stamp" on their new homes), but also among the wealthy who continued the trend in home improvement as a personal hobby. Many chose to develop home improvement projects themselves not because politics or economics dictated that they do so, but out of the personal satisfaction derived from individual achievement. A weekend painting project, for example, provided the opportunity to enhance one's self-esteem as well as to reduce stress. People who do it themselves tend to see themselves as competent, capable, and goal-oriented.

In this light many women increased their involvement in home improvement activities throughout the 1990s, taking on plumbing, minor carpentry, and mechanical repair jobs that were previously considered to be men's jobs. Through these projects women have been able to express their self-confidence and ability in ways that had previously been discouraged. Since the late 1990s, DIY projects have been supported by a growing network of home improvement stores. With vast inventories and knowledgeable salespeople providing instruction, stores like the Home Depot, HomeBase, and Lowe's help people finish their own projects.

Nationwide, the popularity of home improvement projects slumped during the Great Recession—a prolonged economic downturn that began in late 2007, triggered by a housing bubble that caused home prices to fall. Because people often rely on home equity loans to fund home improvement projects, the drop in housing values dried up that source of financing. As a result, homeowners made fewer changes to their residences. In an effort to bolster the sagging economy, beginning in 2009 the U.S. government offered tax credits to people who installed equipment and features that would improve the energy efficiency of their homes. Also, because the housing market was slow to recover from the recession, some homeowners began to embrace DIY remodeling as a way to get the home of their dreams without "trading up" by simply buying a new house.

Ethan Hay

SEE ALSO: *Catalog Houses; Consumerism; The Great Depression; The Great Recession; Suburbia; World War II.*

BIBLIOGRAPHY

Consumer's Guide, eds. *Do-It-Yourself and Save Money!* New York: Harper & Row, 1980.

Creative Publishing, eds. *Black & Decker: The Complete Photo Guide to Home Repair.* Minneapolis, MN: Creative Publishing International, 2008.

Family Handyman Magazine, eds. *The Family Handyman Home Improvement Book.* New York: Scribner, 1973.

Gladstone, Bernard. *The Simon and Schuster Complete Guide to Home Repair and Maintenance.* New York: Simon and Schuster, 1984.

Holmes, Mike. *Make It Right: Expert Advice on Home Renovations.* New York: Time Home Entertainment, 2006.

Price, Bernard. *Do-It-Yourself Projects from Attic to Basement.* New York: Rodale Press/Popular Science Books, 1986.

Reader's Digest, eds. *New Fix-It-Yourself Manual.* Pleasantville, NY: Reader's Digest Association, 1996.

Roberts, Jason, ed. *The Learn 2 Guide: How to Do Almost Anything.* New York: Villard, 1999.

Schultz, Morton. *Fix It Yourself for Less.* Yonkers, NY: Consumer Reports Books, 1992.

Tompkins, Susie. *I Can Fix That: A Guide for Women Who Want to Do It Themselves.* Toronto/New York: Harlequin Books, 1996.

Vivian, John, ed. *Living on Less.* Arden, NC: Mother Earth News, 1997.

Do the Right Thing

As many film scholars have noted, the Hollywood film industry's portrayal of race has been problematic, reflecting the racial divisions of the wider culture. While whites have been considered as representing the "norm," people of color have been rendered invisible, stereotyped, and maligned in every decade and in every genre. A major shift occurred in the 1980s, when an unprecedented number of studio-backed films written and directed by African American filmmakers were released. This movement was led by Spike Lee, whose art house success *She's Gotta Have It* opened doors previously closed to black filmmakers. Able to control the images presented in his films, Lee and the African American directors who followed brought to the screen issues and concerns often ignored by Hollywood. One such film, *Do the Right Thing,* written and directed by Lee and released in 1989, is a postmodern masterpiece and a controversial film about issues of race, gender, class, and politics.

The film is set in the predominantly African American Bedford Stuyvesant neighborhood of Brooklyn, New York. It covers twenty-four hours of the hottest day of the year, which is communicated well by the award-winning cinematography of Ernest Dickerson, with its use of highly saturated reds and oranges. Featuring an ensemble cast—Ossie Davis, Ruby Dee, Giancarlo Esposito, Rosie Perez, Danny Aiello, John Turturro, Bill Nunn, Robin Harris, Roger Guenveur Smith, and Lee himself—the film presents a tense atmosphere of varied characters with differing political outlooks.

Full of numerous confrontations, the main conflict concerns the decor of the local hangout, Sal's Pizzeria, owned by an Italian American. Buggin Out, who wants the pizzeria's "wall of fame" to display pictures of African Americans rather than Italian Americans, tries to organize the community in a boycott of the business. Incensed, Buggin Out enters the pizzeria with Radio Raheem, who carries with him a portable stereo blaring the anthem "Fight the Power" by hip-hop artists Public Enemy. When the young men refuse to lower the stereo's volume, Sal smashes it with a baseball bat. Radio Raheem retaliates by physically attacking Sal. The police arrive and in the midst of the struggle, Radio Raheem is killed by a policeman's stranglehold. A riot ensues, and Sal's Pizzeria is burned to the ground.

As noted above, the film created a controversy in both critical and popular circles: What is the right thing? Does the film advocate violence? Some panned the film because it did not make use of well-rounded, complex characters; did not support productive collective action; and presented less than positive images of women. Yet the film elicited a dialogue about one of the most ingrained aspects of American culture—racism—and is generally considered a masterpiece. It presents racism as a complex and multifaceted issue, while at the same time questioning the ideologies personified by the numerous characters.

Frances Gateward

SEE ALSO: *Lee, Spike; Public Enemy; Race Music; Race Riots.*

BIBLIOGRAPHY

Jones, K. Maurice. *Spike Lee and the African American Filmmakers: A Choice of Colors.* Brookfield, CT: Millbrook Press, 1996.

Lee, Spike; Lisa Jones; and David Lee. *"Do the Right Thing": The New Spike Lee Joint.* New York: Simon & Schuster, 1989.

Reid, Mark, ed. *Spike Lee's "Do the Right Thing."* New York: Cambridge University Press, 1997.

Dobie Gillis

The Many Loves of Dobie Gillis is a classic sitcom of the late 1950s. If on the surface the show seems unassuming and standard early sitcom fare, just below is a show that breaks new ground in television. Two significant aspects set it apart from other shows of that era and make it watchable and influential into the new millennium. First is the show's focus on teenagers. Second is the addition of a new type of character in the form of Maynard G. Krebs, the outsider.

Dobie Gillis is a teenager in small-town America; the plot revolves around Dobie's life and thoughts. In the course of the show Dobie graduates from high school, briefly joins the army, and returns to the same town to attend college. The show was adapted from Max Shulman's short stories of the 1930s and was updated for teenagers of the 1950s. It premiered in September of 1959 and ran until 1963. The main characters were Dobie (Dwayne Hickman), the forever-girl-chasing and money-short lead; his best friend and sidekick Maynard (Bob Denver), the cool jazz beatnik; Dobie's hardworking father Herbert T. Gillis (Frank Faylen); and Zelda Gilroy (Sheila James), who was determined to marry Dobie one day.

Before Dobie there had been teenagers on television shows but always in secondary roles and usually within the confines of a very structured family, such as *The Adventures of Ozzie and Harriet* and *Father Knows Best.* Although there were occasional episodes dealing with teenage issues, they were usually reserved for comic relief or family homilies. *Dobie Gillis* offered an entirely different way of viewing the subject. Although most of the stories deal with the basic trials and tribulations of teenage life—getting a date, getting money, and getting out of work—they are taken seriously; each show starts and ends with Dobie speaking to us from a pose near a replica of the Rodin sculpture known as "The Thinker." In this way, he tells the viewers that the problems of money, girls, and work are important to the youth.

Dobie's world includes several recurring characters who provide the basic themes for the show. His father runs the Gillis Grocery Store and cannot understand his son (he continually tries to instill in him the need for hard work), while his mother (Florida Friebus) attempts to mediate between father and son. In the beginning of the series Tuesday Weld plays Thalia Meninger, Dobie's dream girl, whom he hesitates to pursue because he does not have enough money. As one might expect, there are several rivals who do—Milton Armitage (Warren Beatty), followed by Chatsworth Osborne Jr. (Stephen Franken). It is their presence that generates many of the show's conflicts.

As the series unfolds a more striking character also takes form, that of Maynard. Maynard is the classical beatnik: he has the goatee, ripped sweatshirt, love of jazz, and the "like" vocabulary. He seems out of place in this little town, and that is the point. Maynard (played by Denver, later of *Gilligan's Island*) is Dobie's "good buddy," and he is loyal to him to the end. While Dobie dreams of money so that he can get the girls, Maynard has no need for either. His mannerisms and clothes make him stand out from everyone, and his simple ways and shuddering at the thought of work seem to hold him apart from the suburban dream. Maynard sets a standard for every other outsider with a message in shows to come.

Despite the concentration on themes of money and dating, or perhaps because of it, the show occasionally slides into uncharted areas. Dobie tends to think and speak about life in terms of big questions, or more accurately, he tends to make whatever he is thinking about seem big. Dobie, like many teenagers, is in search of many things, including an understanding of himself and the world in which he lives.

The impact of this show extends far beyond the 1950s. Shows that centered on teens and tried to attract the baby-boomer market would be a staple from the 1960s on. The outsider beatnik character could easily metamorphose into the hippie of the 1960s or even to "The Fonz" of *Happy Days.* Dobie resurfaced in two sequels: a thirty-minute pilot for a revival of the show in 1977 named *Whatever Happened to Dobie Gillis?* and a reunion movie in 1988 called *Bring Me the Head of Dobie Gillis.*

Frank E. Clark

SEE ALSO: The Adventures of Ozzie and Harriet*; The Beat Generation; Beatty, Warren;* Father Knows Best*;* Gilligan's Island*;* Happy Days*; Shulman, Max; Sitcom; Teenagers; Television.*

BIBLIOGRAPHY

Denver, Bob. *Gilligan, Maynard & Me.* New York: Carol Publishing, 1993.

Hickman, Dwayne, and Joan Roberts Hickman. *Forever Dobie: The Many Lives of Dwayne Hickman.* Secaucus, NJ: Carol Publishing, 1994.

Kieley, Genny Zak. *Green Stamps to Hot Pants: Growing up in the 50s and 60s.* Minneapolis, MN: Nodin Press, 2008.

Marschall, Rick. *The Golden Age of Television.* New York: Exeter Books, 1987.

McNeil, Alex. *Total Television: A Comprehensive Guide to Programming from 1948 to the Present.* New York: Penguin Books, 1991.

Putterman, Barry. *On Television and Comedy: Essays on Style, Theme, Performer, and Writer.* Jefferson, NC: McFarland, 1995.

Doby, Larry *(1923–2003)*

African American baseball player Larry Doby was an improbable civil rights pioneer. Unlike the fiery Jackie Robinson, the first African American to play in the major leagues, Doby was a low-key figure.

Doby grew up in integrated Patterson, New Jersey; attended predominantly white Long Island University; and lived a life far more sheltered from racial prejudice than most African Americans did. Yet it was Doby, even more so than Robinson, who helped transform baseball into the national pastime for people of all races. On July 5, 1947, approximately eleven weeks after Robinson's debut with the National League's Brooklyn Dodgers, Doby became the first black in the American League and the first player to jump straight from the Negro Leagues to the majors. He later helped integrate pro baseball in Japan and became the second black manager in the major leagues and one of its first black executives. However, he made his greatest impact as a player. His debut in the majors demonstrated to the American public that Robinson's entrance into white baseball had not been an anomaly and that the sport's color barrier was permanently shattered.

When integration-minded Cleveland Indians owner Bill Veeck sought to sign a black player in 1947, the Newark Eagles' Doby was the obvious choice. The twenty-two-year-old Doby, a former high school football and basketball star, was leading the Negro National League with a batting average of .458 and thirteen home runs. He was the top black prospect who was not under contract with the Dodgers (after Robinson came to the majors, the Dodgers acquired several other talented African Americans for their minor-league affiliates). Unlike Dodgers general manager Branch Rickey, Veeck was determined to integrate his organization from the top down. On July 5 he purchased Doby's contract from the Eagles for $10,000. Three hours later he sent the surprised young athlete onto the field as a pinch hitter against the Chicago White Sox. This courageous decision, coming without warning, drew 20,000 letters of protest from irate fans.

Larry Doby. *Larry Doby of the Cleveland Indians was the first African American to play for an American League team.* KIDWILER COLLECTION/DIAMOND IMAGES/GETTY IMAGES.

Doby's sudden entrance into the majors relieved much of the pressure that had been on Robinson. Both men faced extraordinary adversity that first season in 1947, including open hostility from teammates and opposition players, and they formed a close relationship that endured through their lifetimes. Upon Doby's signing with the Indians, Robinson stated, "I no longer have the feeling that if I don't make good it will kill the chances of other Negro players." Doby's debut opened the way for three more blacks to enter the majors within a month, making it clear that widespread integration in baseball was inevitable. His presence on the Indians also contributed to the civil rights movement in general. For example, the exclusive Hotel Statler, a whites-only establishment in Washington, D.C., permitted Doby to room with his teammates.

After a rough first season in which he was limited to 32 at-bats and batted only .156, Doby found his stride and emerged as one of the game's marquee figures. In 1948 he batted an impressive .301 with 14 home runs and 66 runs batted in. He led the Indians to a victory over the Boston Braves in the World Series, becoming the first African American to play on a championship team. Doby led the American league in home runs in 1952 (32) and 1954 (32). When he retired in 1959 after 13 seasons with the Indians, White Sox, and Detroit Tigers, he had a formidable career batting average of .283 and 253 home runs. In 1998 he was inducted into the National Baseball Hall of Fame.

After retiring from the major leagues, Doby continued to be a pioneer among black athletes. In 1962 he was one of the first blacks to play professional baseball in Japan. Later, he returned to the United States and served in front-office roles with the Montreal Expos, Indians, and White Sox. He became the second African American ever to manage a big-league club (following Frank Robinson) when he took over the White Sox in 1978. Doby later returned to the role of an executive, as a special assistant to Dr. Gene Budig, president of the America League. Throughout the 1960s and 1970s—when blacks were welcome on the field but not in the front office—Doby continued to push for expanded opportunities for African Americans.

After Robinson's death in 1972, Doby stood out as a living symbol of the early civil rights movement. Until his death in 2003 at age 79, he was one of baseball's chief attractions at special events and old-timers' games.

Jacob M. Appel

SEE ALSO: *Baseball; Civil Rights Movement; Negro Leagues; Robinson, Jackie.*

BIBLIOGRAPHY

Briley, Ron. *The Politics of Baseball: Essays on the Pastime and Power at Home and Abroad.* Jefferson, NC: McFarland & Co., 2010.

Boundreau, Lou, with Ed Fitzgerald. *Player-Manager*. Boston: Little, Brown, 1952.

Frommer, Harvey. *Rickey and Robinson: The Men Who Broke Baseball's Color Barrier*. New York: Macmillan, 1982.

Moore, Joseph Thomas. *Pride Against Prejudice: The Biography of Larry Doby*. New York: Greenwood Press, 1988.

Tygiel, Jules. *Baseball's Great Experiment*. New York: Oxford, 1997.

Veeck, Bill, and Edward Linn. *Veeck—As in Wreck: The Autobiography of Bill Veeck*. New York: G. P. Putnam's Sons, 1962

Young, Andrew "Doc." *Great Negro Baseball Stars and How They Made the Major Leagues*. New York: A. S. Barnes, 1953.

Doc Martens

More than just functional footwear, Doc Martens shoes and boots have been a staple for decades in style-conscious subcultures and eventually emerged as a fashion phenomenon. Once synonymous with angry British youth, Doc Martens, like their sturdy leather uppers, have mellowed with age. Bavarian physician Klaus Maerten designed the clunky, cushiony, thick-soled boot out of old tires in 1945 after a skiing accident necessitated more comfortable footgear. Bunion-plagued customers became converts until the 1960s, when fascist skinheads appropriated the boots.

Rock stars soon followed the trend, and after punk rockers in the 1970s began painting their own designs on the boots, the company came out with wildly colored and patterned models. The brand was a must-have for the young and hip throughout the 1980s, from hip-hop to grunge fans. By the late 1990s women accounted for 70 percent of the fast-growing market, picking up pairs at upscale department stores. In the 2000s, sales dipped somewhat, causing the company to close its British factories and relocate production to Asia. However, the company has remained solvent and celebrated its fiftieth anniversary in 2010.

Geri Speace

SEE ALSO: *Grunge; Hip-Hop; Punk; Retro Fashion; Rock and Roll.*

BIBLIOGRAPHY

Morais, Richard C. "What's Up, Doc?" *Forbes*, January 16, 1995, 42.

Van den Bergh, Joeri, and Mattias Behrer. *How Cool Brands Stay Hot: Branding to Generation Y*. Philadelphia: Kogan Page, 2011.

Doc Savage

During the sixteen-year run of *Doc Savage Magazine* (1933–1949), Clark Savage Jr. (better known as Doc) was one of the most exciting and popular pulp magazine characters. The appeal of Doc Savage is succinctly stated in the promotional blurb that appears on the back of the Bantam Books paperback editions that reprint his pulp adventures: "To his fans he is the greatest adventure hero of all time, whose fantastic exploits are unequaled for hair-raising thrills, breathtaking escapes, and bloodcurdling excitement." Doc is a transitional hero who unites the intellect of Sherlock Holmes and the physical prowess of Tarzan with the best gadgets imagined by the then-new genre of science fiction. In bringing together all of these elements, Doc Savage served as a model for the superheroes that followed.

IN THE BEGINNING . . .

Doc Savage was the creation of Street & Smith business manager Henry Ralston and editor John Nanovic, who hoped to duplicate the success of the company's first single-character pulp magazine, *The Shadow*. While Ralston and Nanovic created the concept, the characters, and even many of the colorful details, it was a young writer named Lester Dent who brought Doc Savage to life. The house byline used was Kenneth Robeson; there were six different authors who contributed Doc Savage stories under that byline. Dent, however, wrote the vast majority of the Doc tales and edited, or at least approved, the work of the writers who ghosted for him. It was also Dent who established the distinctive style of the Doc Savage adventures.

Overall, Doc Savage appeared in 181 fantastic pulp magazine adventures. In October 1964 Bantam Books began paperback reprints of all the pulp Doc stories, plus one previously unpublished manuscript by Dent (*The Red Spider*). Bantam later started publishing original Doc Savage material. *Escape from Loki* was written by longtime Doc aficionado Philip Jose Farmer, and Doc Savage fan and scholar Will Murray authored seven books based on Dent story fragments and outlines. Other Doc Savage offerings have included a radio show in the 1930s, a movie in the 1970s, and comic books from at least six different publishers, but the true adventures of this hero are the 182 stories written for the pulps.

THE DOC SAVAGE STORY

Doc Savage is a hero of mythical proportions. Clark Savage Jr. is born one stormy night aboard a tiny schooner anchored off Andros Island in the infamous Bermuda Triangle. Doc dwells far above ordinary humans on the eighty-sixth floor of the Empire State Building. Both his strength and intellect are Herculean. As a young child he begins his strenuous, lifelong training. Even after Doc reaches adulthood and begins traveling the globe to right wrongs and help the oppressed, he adheres faithfully to a two-hour routine of intensive exercises for his muscles, senses, and mind. Though he excels in virtually every endeavor, Doc displays his most prodigious talent in the practice of medicine. By the time he is thirty, he is the world's most brilliant surgeon. In fact, he "rehabilitates" criminals using an intricate type of brain surgery only he has the skill to perform.

When Doc first appears in 1933, he is 6 feet tall and weighs 200 pounds. In later tales, however, Doc is usually described as standing around 6 feet, 8 inches and weighing 270 pounds. His build has such symmetry and proportion that he does not look big unless he is standing next to someone. Beneath his sun-bronzed skin, his muscles are "like cables" or "bundles of piano wire." When he flexes those great muscles, he often rips his shirt and coat. Gently swirling flakes of gold in his eyes are Doc's most riveting characteristic. Thanks to the dynamic covers painted by James Bama for the Bantam reprints, a virtual costume is established for Doc. On most paperback covers, he wears boots, aviator pants, and a very precisely ripped shirt.

The first Doc Savage story, *The Man of Bronze*, establishes that the men who compose Doc's amazing crew are "the five greatest brains ever assembled in one group." They include Long Tom, the wizard of electricity who looks frail but is a wildcat in a fight; Renny, a grim-faced giant of a man who likes to smash his huge fists through solid panel doors and is the greatest engineering expert of his time; the tall, gaunt, bespectacled Johnny, who, with his bulging forehead and big words, is one of the world's foremost experts on geology and archaeology; Ham, who is a dapper clothes horse and possibly the greatest lawyer Harvard has ever produced; and the most remarkable of Doc's companions, Monk, a short, barrel-chested man whose knuckles nearly drag along the ground. Monk looks like a red-haired ape pretending to be a man, but he is one of the world's top chemists, though he would much rather work with his fists than with test tubes. The frontispiece of the Bantam paperbacks gives this characterization of the men who join Doc Savage in his work: "Together with their leader, they would go anywhere, fight anyone, dare everything—seeking excitement and perilous adventure."

THE SUPERHERO PATRIARCH

Although Doc Savage is a relatively minor fictional character, he has influenced some major popular culture icons. Superman is the most obvious "descendant" of Doc—in fact, in the stories themselves and in the advertisements for the magazine, Doc is often referred to as a "superman." In addition to sharing the first name Clark, both heroes have a Fortress of Solitude somewhere in the Arctic. Both also have female cousins who look like them, have their powers, and want to horn in on their adventures. Doc is known as the Man of Bronze, while Superman is recognized as the Man of Steel.

Doc's connection to Batman is less obvious but more fundamental. Both heroes are "self-made supermen" who, beginning in childhood, devote themselves to intense training. They also have considerable scientific know-how, as evidenced by Doc's utility vest and Batman's very similar utility belt. It is even possible that the Batmobile is patterned after Doc's bulletproof and gadget-filled sedan.

Randy Duncan

SEE ALSO: *Batman; Kenneth Robeson; Paperbacks; Pulp Magazines; Science Fiction Publishing; The Shadow; Street and Smith; Superman; Tarzan.*

BIBLIOGRAPHY

Cannaday, Marilyn. *Bigger than Life: The Creator of Doc Savage.* Bowling Green, OH: Bowling Green State University Popular Press, 1990.

Farmer, Philip Jose. *Doc Savage: His Apocalyptic Life.* New York: Playboy Paperbacks, 1973.

Murray, Will. *Secrets of Doc Savage.* Greenwood, MA: Odyssey Publications, 1981.

Robeson, Kenneth, and Will Murray. *The Man of Bronze, and, the Land of Terror: Classic Debut Adventures of Doc Savage.* Encinitas, CA: Sanctum Productions for Nostalgia Ventures, 2008.

Doctor Who

Doctor Who is the world's longest continually produced science fiction serial. It aired on the British BBC network from 1963 until 1989, was revived briefly as a television movie in 1996, and returned to the BBC as a series in 2005. In the United States, *Doctor Who* first began broadcasts on independent channels in the 1970s and was broadcast on some local PBS affiliates into the late 1990s. In the early 2000s, it was shown on the BBC America cable channel. It has, like *Star Trek*, engendered movies, radio dramas, lucrative novel series, nonfiction, comic books, and an extensive home video market.

Doctor Who revolves around the adventures of the mysterious time-traveling title character, simply known throughout as the Doctor. The Doctor, as first seen in the 1963 pilot episode, broadcast in the midst of the BBC's coverage of the Kennedy Assassination, is outwardly human. William Hartnell, the actor to first portray the Doctor (1963–1966), presented audiences with a cranky old man who had a gross lack of basic human kindness. Initially, the Doctor is accompanied on his travels through time and space by his granddaughter and her human schoolteachers. In the serial's second episode, he seems to encourage his companion to kill an incapacitated caveman. Later, his selfish, obsessive desire to learn places him and his companions in danger when they meet the alien Daleks. The character begins to soften his edges as he is exposed to the ideals and attitudes of his human companions. His scientific curiosity and towering ego remain, but his ego has become tempered with an increasing respect for his companions and the races that he encounters.

When Hartnell became too ill to continue the role, the producers came up with the ingenious idea of having the character "regenerate" into a new body with a new personality. Since 1966 the Doctor has been played by ten more actors: Patrick Troughton (1966–1969), Jon Pertwee (1970–1974), Tom Baker (1974–1981), Peter Davison (1982–1984), Colin Baker (1984–1986), Sylvester McCoy (1987–1989), Paul McGann (1996), Christopher Eccleston (2005), David Tennant (2005–2010), and Matt Smith (beginning in 2010). Richard Hurndall also played the role of the first Doctor in place of the late William Hartnell in the 1983 anniversary serial "The Five Doctors." This change in the lead actor (and usually in the rest of the cast and the production teams) allowed the show to adapt to and change with the times.

Hartnell's serials began originally as a children's program, but by the mid-1970s Tom Baker's serials were also targeted toward the science fiction aficionado. Low ratings and lack of support from the BBC (it went on an eighteen-month hiatus in the middle of Colin Baker's tenure) soon saw the serial descending into self-parody. Toward the end it began to recover some of its ground, but in 1989 it was taken off the air, though it was never officially canceled. The 1996 television movie was coproduced by the BBC and the Fox network in the United States at a sum of $5 million (an unusual amount for such a production), but it did not achieve great ratings. The serial continued in original novels published first by Virgin Books and later by BBC Books. In 2005, after resolving some issues related to ownership of the property, the BBC revived the series in a contemporary setting.

Two theatrical movies were made in the 1960s based on the scripts of two of the television serials, *Dr. Who and the Daleks* (1965) and *Daleks—Invasion Earth, 2150 A.D.* (1966), starring Peter Cushing as the Doctor. In the television serial, it was the popularity of the Daleks, created by writer Terry Nation and a BBC special effects wizard, that propelled the Doctor to instant stardom in the United Kingdom. It was not until the first Tom Baker serials began broadcasting in the United States, however, that the show earned anything more than a cult audience there. The Doctor has since earned cameos in episodes of *The Simpsons*, and cancellation of the serial usually results in a PBS station being inundated with masses of fan mail.

As is the case with *Star Trek*, the fans of *Doctor Who* run major conventions every year attended by thousands of fans sporting scarves and cricket jackets. Instantly recognizable at these conventions is the Doctor's unique TARDIS (time and relative dimension in space). On the outside it resembles a battered London police call box. Inside, however, TARDIS is, in reality, a large ship, its cavernous interior seemingly endless. The Doctor and his fans also have a strong presence on the Internet, where hints about new television seasons compete for attention with spoilers of the novel plots.

Icons of the show include the pepperpot-shaped Daleks and the silver-enshrouded Cybermen. Also earning a place in history was the show's electronic theme music, which evolved over the years but still retained an eerie hint of the otherworldly. On the whole, the show was a hodgepodge of what is good and bad about long-running serial television: devoted audiences, a long history, and very bad continuity. The video market ensures that older episodes of the show can still be seen by the new audiences captured by the current version of the series, thus bringing everyone up to date with the ongoing adventures of the Doctor.

John J. Doherty

SEE ALSO: *Kennedy Assassination; Public Television (PBS); Science Fiction Publishing;* Star Trek*;* Star Trek: The Next Generation.

BIBLIOGRAPHY

Corry, Neil, et al. *Doctor Who: The Visual Dictionary*. New York: DK Publishing, 2010.

Howe, David J., and Stephen James Walker. *Doctor Who: The Television Companion*. London: BBC Books, 1998.

Russell, Gary. *Doctor Who Encyclopedia (New Edition)*. London: Random House UK, 2011.

Tulloch, John, and Manuel Alvarado. *Doctor Who: The Unfolding Text*. New York: St. Martin's, 1983.

Doctor Zhivago

The only novel by famed Russian poet Boris Pasternak, *Doctor Zhivago* received the Nobel Prize in Literature in 1958. The story traces the experiences of a Moscow doctor, Yuri Zhivago, during the Russian Revolution of 1917 and throughout the ensuing civil war, which took place between 1918 and 1921.

Pasternak initially submitted his work to leading Soviet literary journal *Novy Mir*. However, editors there considered Zhivago's independence, religious convictions, and conflict with the Soviet regime too controversial for publication, despite the fact that the Soviet Union was experiencing greater openness following the death of dictator Joseph Stalin in 1953. Pasternak had the manuscript smuggled out of the Soviet Union in late 1956, and it was first published in Italy in November 1957. In the two years that followed, the book was translated into more than twenty languages and became an international best seller. A 1965 film adaptation of the book, directed by David Lean, received five Academy Award nominations.

Jason George

SEE ALSO: *Academy Awards; Best Sellers.*

BIBLIOGRAPHY

Clowes, Edith W. *Doctor Zhivago: A Critical Companion*. Evanston, IL: Northwestern University Press, 1995.

Fleishman, Lazar. *Boris Pasternak: The Poet and His Politics*. Cambridge, MA: Harvard University Press, 1990.

Hingley, Ronald. *Pasternak: A Biography*. New York: Alfred A. Knopf, 1983.

Pasternak, Boris. *Doctor Zhivago*. New York: Pantheon Books, 1991.

Doctorow, E. L. *(1931–)*

As Matthew Henry noted in the fall 1997 issue of *Critique*, "E. L. Doctorow has made a career out of historical fiction, and he is renowned for both examining and rewriting the American past . . . because for Doctorow there is no fact or fiction, only narrative." In his attempt to examine the cultural myths of America and their impact on society, Doctorow has created some of the most noted works of postmodern historical fiction through his unique ability to weave documented historical facts and figures with invented ones. As Henry observed, this brand of historical fiction has allowed Doctorow to present different histories—not only those accepted by consensus. His approach to history and his style of writing mark him as a significant contributor to the postmodern literary movement.

Edgar Lawrence Doctorow was born in 1931 in New York City, the setting of many of his novels. He began his writing career within a decade graduation from Kenyon College in 1952. Doctorow's first three books were experiments with different fiction genres. The first novel, *Welcome to Hard Times* (1960), was a Western and focused on the common theme of man's relationship to evil. *Big as Life* (1966), Doctorow's second novel, was a science fiction work about two giants materializing in New York City. Yet it was not until Doctorow experimented with the historical form in his third novel, *The Book of Daniel* (1971), that he achieved commercial and critical success. Here, in his account of Julius and Ethel Rosenberg and their children, Doctorow first experimented with what was later called postmodern historical fiction—historical facts blended with contemporary fiction styles and elements.

POSTMODERN HISTORICAL FICTION

Doctorow approaches this writing style as a reconstitution of history. Unlike the many historical fiction writers before him, he does not attempt to present history as fact. Doctorow preferss not to write from research, but rather uses memory and inspiration. As he did with the Rosenbergs in *The Book of Daniel*, Doctorow's style is the interweaving of historical facts and figures with fictional ones. This was best done in his fourth novel, *Ragtime* (1975). This work intertwines the lives of many famous historical figures, including Harry Houdini, Henry Ford, and Emma Goldman, with three fictional families—an upper-class white family, a poor immigrant family, and a black ragtime

E. L. Doctorow. E. L. Doctorow's work has been published in over thirty languages and includes such award-winning novels as The Book of Daniel, Ragtime, *and* Billy Bathgate. EVAN AGOSTINI/ GETTY IMAGES.

musician's family. By mixing history with fiction, he confuses—and to a degree, falsifies—history as he investigates the myths and realities of the American dream in *Ragtime*; this theme was further explored in his next novel, *Loon Lake* (1980).

Doctorow's approach to history and his writing style are what make his novels postmodern. Just as Toni Morrison did in her novel *Jazz* (1992), Doctorow uses the combination of the repetition and improvisation in music to create a relentless narrative prose style in *Ragtime*, a style he continued in his following novels. At first read, Doctorow's writings may seem like out-of-control prose due largely to his professed dislike for the look of punctuation on the printed page. In her article in *Guardian*, critic Sarah Crown views him as the "master of the run-on sentence," seeing his finely crafted prose at work on multiple levels of meaning and interpretation. In a *New Republic* article, Andrew Delbanco agrees, calling the author more associative than sequential. In Doctorow's biography, Michelle Tokarczyk labels his style "accessible experimentation." Doctorow also experiments with point of view and voice, so there are many instances in his novels where it is difficult to ascertain who is saying what to whom, where the narrative does not instantly reveal itself. This postmodern language play adds to the historical reconstructions, sometimes labeled allegorical romances, of American life as it occurs in Doctorow's novels.

SOCIAL COMMENTARY

In addition to writing novels, in the 1990s Doctorow used his position in American society to take on many social issues. Citing what he called a "gangsterdom of the spirit," he wrote that American life was suffering from a loss of cohesion and morality. Some of his social projects of the 1990s included saving Walden Woods in Massachusetts, developing a cable television channel dedicated to books, peacefully settling the American conflict with Iraq, and analyzing the presidencies of Ronald Reagan and Bill Clinton.

Since the turn of the century, Doctorow has let his novels do much of the talking. Although he has denied writing works of social commentary, critic Steven Kurutz argued in the *New York Times* that novels such as *City of God* (2000) and *Homer & Langley* (2009) are ripe with cautionary tales of excessive consumption and unchecked materialism.

Through Doctorow's works, readers get fanciful explanations of the past that resonate with the author's take on the present and his vision of the future. In this way, Doctorow's works provide a unique account of history, making him one of the most influential writers of his time.

Randall McClure

SEE ALSO: *Best Sellers; Morrison, Toni;* The Nation*; Postmodernism; Rosenberg, Julius and Ethel; Saratoga Springs.*

BIBLIOGRAPHY

Crown, Sarah. "E. L. Doctorow: 'I Don't Have a Style, but the Books Do.'" *Guardian*, January 23, 2010.

Delbanco, Andrew. "Necropolis News—'The Waterworks' by E. L. Doctorow." *New Republic*, July 18, 1994, 44.

Doctorow, E. L. *Welcome to Hard Times*. New York: Simon & Schuster, 1960.

Doctorow, E. L. *Big as Life*. New York: Simon and Schuster, 1966.

Doctorow, E. L. *The Book of Daniel*. New York: Random House, 1971.

Doctorow, E. L. *Ragtime*. New York: Random House, 1975.

Doctorow, E. L. *Loon Lake*. New York: Random House, 1980.

Doctorow, E. L. "A Gangsterdom of the Spirit." *Nation*, October 2, 1989, 348–354.

Doctorow, E. L. *City of God*. New York: Random House, 2000.

Doctorow, E. L. *Homer & Langley*. New York: Random House, 2009.

Fowler, Douglas. *Understanding E. L. Doctorow*. Columbia: University of South Carolina Press, 1992.

Henry, Matthew A. "Problematized Narratives: History as Fiction in E. L. Doctorow's *Billy Bathgate*." *Critique*, Fall 1997, 32–40.

Kurutz, Steven. "At Home with E. L. Doctorow: Writing about the Stuff of Legend." *New York Times*, September 3, 2009.

Morris, Christopher D. *Conversations with E. L. Doctorow*. Jackson: University of Mississippi Press, 1999.

Siegel, Ben. *Critical Essays on E. L. Doctorow*. New York: G. K. Hall, 2000.

Tokarczyk, Michelle M., and E. L. Doctorow. *E. L. Doctorow: An Annotated Bibliography.* New York: Garland Publishing, 1988.

Docudrama

Docudrama is a film genre that plays out primarily, though not exclusively, on television. *Brian's Song* (1971)—the story of the tragic death of football player Brian Piccolo—was the first notable example in the United States, and it proved that the made-for-television, reality-based "telefilm" could be both a critical and commercial success. However, the docudrama has been controversial in North America and Britain because of its mixture of truth and fiction, drama and documentary—a case of blurred boundaries that some viewers and critics find cavalier and unsettling. The genre has gone by many names, including drama-documentary, dramatized documentary, dramadoc, faction, infotainment, reconstruction, historical drama, biographical drama, historical romance, thesis drama, problem play, and based-on-fact.

DIFFICULT TO DEFINE

For many of those who do not like it, the television docudrama is a tacky replacement for the more distinguished Hollywood social-issue picture. However, docudramas have been extremely popular with audiences (and, in turn, advertisers), and they are less expensive to produce than theatrical feature films. Because the majority of docudramas are based on a well-known recent event and the audience already knows at least part of the story, they require much less promotion. The turnaround time in producing these docudramas has become incredibly brief. An infamous example of this is *Ambush in Waco: In the Line of Duty* (1993), a docudrama about the violent clash between the government and a religious cult in Waco, Texas, that was filmed while events were still unfolding.

Initially, the docudrama was generally considered to be a hybrid form, caught somewhere between documentary and drama and often doing justice to neither. Film and television critics have tried with mixed success to define its conventions. Andrew Goodwin and Paul Kerr, authors of *Drama-Documentary*, say the genre defies definition because of "the break up of consensual views of social reality" in a postmodern world. Critics maintain that the mixture of fact and fiction leads to the creation of a "hyper-reality" in which audiences can no longer distinguish between truth and fiction—the docudrama becomes its own reality. Steven Spielberg's *Schindler's List* (1993) is often cited as a prime example because the only information many people have about the Holocaust comes from this film, which is known for its fictionalizing of "the truth."

THE "TRAUMA DRAMA"

Arts critic Derek Paget has argued that the docudrama has been around long enough to be considered a genre in itself with well-established conventions. He traces the history of the form in the United States from early documentary-like television anthology programs such as *Armstrong Circle Theatre* (1950–1963) and *Kraft Television Theatre* (1947–1958) through made-for-TV movies such as *Brian's Song* and *Roots* (1977) to, finally, a more controversial type of "trauma drama," which has been largely influenced by tabloid television with stories based upon well-known scandals. Falling into this category are docudramas about Amy Fischer's attempted murder of her lover's wife, *Amy Fisher: My Story* (1992) and *The Amy Fisher Story* (1993), and about the O. J. Simpson murder trial, *The O.J. Simpson Story* and *The Trial of O.J. Simpson* (both 1995).

Critical quibbling aside, the docudrama is one of the most popular and lucrative genres in North America, perhaps because it blurs the boundaries between reality and fiction and, in the process, draws attention to the media's manipulation of "fact." Consider the controversy over docudramas such as Oliver Stone's *JFK* (1991) or *Nixon* (1995). The docudrama has become a culturally important form that sparks debate over the nature of truth, reality, and the tabloidization of everyday life.

Jeannette Sloniowski

SEE ALSO: JFK*;* Kraft Television Theatre*; Made-for-Television Movies;* Roots*;* Schindler's List*; Simpson, O. J.; Spielberg, Steven; Stone, Oliver; Television.*

BIBLIOGRAPHY

Breitbart, Eric. "From the Panorama to the Docudrama: Notes on the Visualization of History." *Radical History Review* 25 (1981): 115–125.

Brode, Douglas. "Video Verite: Defining the Docudrama." *Television Quarterly* 20, no. 4 (1984): 7–26.

Carveth, Rod. "Amy Fisher and the Ethics of 'Headline' Docudramas." *Journal of Popular Film and Television* 21, no. 3 (1993): 121–127.

Corner, John. *The Art of Record: A Critical Introduction to Documentary.* Manchester, UK: Manchester University Press, 1996.

Edgerton, Gary. "High Concept Small Screen: Reperceiving the Industrial and Stylistic Origins of the American Made-for-TV Movie." *Journal of Popular Film and Television* 19, no. 3 (1991): 114–127.

Gomery, Douglas. "Brian's Song: Television, Hollywood, and the Evolution of the Movie Made for Television." In *American History, American Television: Interpreting the Video Past*, ed. John E. O'Connor. New York: Frederick Ungar, 1983.

Goodwin, Andrew; Paul Kerr; and Ian Macdonald, eds. *Drama-Documentary.* London: British Film Institute, 1983.

Hartley, John. *Tele-ology: Studies in Television.* New York: Routledge, 1992.

Hoffer, Thomas W., and Richard Alan Nelson. "The Evolution of Docudrama on American Television Networks: A Content Analysis, 1966–1978." *Southern Speech Communication Journal* 45 (1980): 149–163.

Izod, John, and Richard Kilbourne, eds. *From Grierson to the Docu-Soap: Breaking the Boundaries.* Luton, Bedfordshire, UK: University of Luton Press, 2000.

Kerr, Paul. "F for Fake? Friction over Faction." In *Understanding Television*, ed. Andrew Goodwin and Gary Whannel. London: Routledge, 1990.

Lipkin, Steven N. "Real Emotional Logic: Persuasive Strategies in Docudrama." *Cinema Journal* 38, no. 4 (1999): 68–85.

Margulies, Lee. "Academy of Television Arts & Sciences Docu-Drama Symposium." *Emmy: The Magazine of the American Academy of Arts & Sciences*, Summer 1979, D1–D40.

Paget, Derek. *No Other Way to Tell It: Dramadoc/Documentary Drama on Television.* Manchester, UK: Manchester University Press, 1998.

Petley, Julian. "Fact Plus Fiction Equals Friction." *Media, Culture and Society* 18, no. 1 (1996): 11–25.

Rapping, Elayne. *The Movie of the Week: Private Stories, Public Events.* Minneapolis: University of Minnesota Press, 1992.

Rosenthal, Allen, ed. *Why Docudrama? Fact-Fiction on Film and TV.* Carbondale: Southern Illinois University Press, 1999.

Stewart, Michael, and Richard Butt, "We Had It Coming: Hypothetical Docudrama as Contested Form and Multiple Fantasy." *Critical Studies in Television* 6, no. 1 (2011): 72–88.

Domino, Fats *(1928–)*

The music of Fats Domino embodies the spirit of early rock and roll. His work reveals the links between rock and roll, rhythm and blues, and the black southern singers of the early twentieth century. His music was recorded by most of the rock artists of the 1950s, who recognized his significant contribution to establishing the rock-and-roll sound, and he is acknowledged as a pioneer in crossing the racial barriers of the music industry. With more than sixty-five million record sales, Domino was second only to Elvis Presley in popularity during the 1950s, and he is credited with bringing mass attention to the New Orleans, Louisiana, sound, inspiring many other southern black singers to record for white audiences.

Domino's New Orleans style of piano playing is a combination of traditional jazz, Latin rhythms, blues, Cajun, and boogie-woogie that reflects that city's rich heritage of cultural amalgamation. From the mid-1940s through the early 1950s, he was an established rhythm-and-blues recording artist who had successfully toured the nation, but his pounding playing style made him well suited to crossover into the emerging rock format. Domino's greatest popularity arrived in 1955 with the release of "Ain't That a Shame," which became an early rock hit, and although his career began to fade somewhat in the 1960s, he continued to record into the 1990s.

The man considered the most famous New Orleans–born musician since Louis Armstrong was born Antoine Domino, one of a large family, on February 26, 1928. He developed an early interest in music, began playing the piano at age nine, and was performing publicly at local honky-tonks a year later. He quit school at fourteen and took a job at a bedspring factory so that his nights would be free to play the area bars and clubs. A large young man, he acquired the nickname "Fats" from bandleader Bill Diamond. The entertainer was spotted in 1949 by trumpeter Dave Bartholomew and then Lew Chudd of Imperial Records, who soon signed him to a recording contract. His first hit song, "The Fat Man," sold more than a million copies. Domino formed an especially close professional relationship with Bartholomew, and the pair cowrote, arranged, and produced most of the singer's material for the next two decades. Among his hits of this period are "Goin' Home," "Goin' to the River," and "Every Night about This Time."

Domino's rollicking piano playing allowed him to cross onto the pop charts in the mid-1950s, the time when young white audiences were discovering rock and roll. However, white artists were also covering his initial pop records—Teresa Brewer recorded "Bo Weevil," and Pat Boone's mild version of "Ain't That a Shame" sold even more copies than Domino's own—but he broke into the pop Top 10 himself with the release of "I'm in Love Again." Domino became a national sensation and was one of the first black recording stars to prove that he could appeal to white listeners. He proceeded to enjoy a string of major hits from 1955 to 1960, of which the most instantly recognizable are "Blueberry Hill," "Blue Monday," "I'm Walkin'," "My Blue Heaven," "Whole Lotta Loving," and "Walking to New Orleans."

The second half of Domino's career lacked the continuous commercial success of the first. Although he continued to tour and occasionally produced some notable recordings, more magnetic (and frenetic) performers such as Little Richard, Chuck Berry, and Jerry Lee Lewis eclipsed his gentle, laid-back stage persona. In the late 1960s he released a New Orleans–style version of the Beatles' "Lady Madonna" that gained some attention.

In 1993 he returned to the recording studio for the first time in nearly twenty-five years to produce his *Christmas Is a Special Day* set. The results received much critical acclaim. In his later years Domino was much honored for his achievements: in 1986 he was in the inaugural group of artists inducted into the Rock and Roll Hall of Fame, and in 1998 President Bill Clinton awarded him the National Medal of Arts. By the late 1990s, though entering his seventies, Domino was still performing while enjoying life in his palatial New Orleans home.

As Hurricane Katrina approached New Orleans in 2005, Domino refused to evacuate. Rumors swirled that the entertainer had perished in the massive storm, but they proved untrue. (He had been rescued by boat from his home in in the city's devastated Lower Ninth Ward but had lost most of his belongings, including his National Medal of Arts; he later received a replacement from President George W. Bush.) In 2006 Domino released an album titled "Alive and Kickin'," which benefited local indigent musicians. Illness prevented him from returning to the stage until 2007.

Charles Coletta

SEE ALSO: *The Beatles; Berry, Chuck; Boone, Pat; Hurricane Katrina; Lewis, Jerry Lee; Little Richard; New Orleans Rhythm and Blues; Presley, Elvis; Rhythm and Blues; Rock and Roll.*

BIBLIOGRAPHY

Aquila, Richard. *That Old Time Rock & Roll: A Chronicle of an Era, 1954–1963.* New York: Schirmer Books, 1989.

Coleman, Rick. *Blue Monday: Fats Domino and the Lost Dawn of Rock 'n' Roll.* Cambridge, MA: Da Capo Press, 2006.

Gulla, Bob. *Icons of R&B and Soul: An Encyclopedia of the Artists Who Revolutionized Rhythm.* Westport, CT: Greenwood Press, 2008.

Donahue, Phil *(1935–)*

Talk show host Phil Donahue is credited with pioneering the daytime television talk show format. His programs introduced viewers to sensitive and intelligent discussions of topics and issues that had never before been seen on the small screen. From the debut of *The Phil Donahue Show* in 1967, Donahue challenged, informed, and entertained daytime audiences and helped establish the talk show as one of television's most prolific and profitable formats.

Beginning in the 1970s, his promotion of feminism and the frequent airing of women's health issues on his program identified him as the embodiment of the "sensitive man." As daytime TV shows became raunchier in the 1990s, Donahue came to be viewed as the patriarch of the genre. Although he did present programs with outrageous content—senior citizen strippers, for example—he continued to offer sober conversations about politics and social concerns and a mix of celebrity interviews. Donahue's decision to treat the female television viewer as an intelligent, active, and aware participant in society challenged those programmers wedded to the conviction that women would only watch soap operas and cooking demonstrations.

Phil Donahue. *Phil Donahue's self-titled show, the first television program to use a talk-show format, had a nearly thirty-year run.* RON GALELLA, LTD./WIREIMAGE.

EARLY INNOVATOR

For a man who later symbolized the modern era's willingness to talk openly about the most personal issues, Donahue's beginnings were very traditional. He was born Phillip John Donahue, the son of a furniture salesman in Cleveland, Ohio, on December 21, 1935. He was an altar boy and, after graduating high school, studied theology at the University of Notre Dame. After completing his degree, he found work as a radio announcer in Cleveland and, later, Dayton. (One of his first professional positions involved delivering the 5 a.m. hog report.) His first talk show was a Dayton radio program titled *Conversation Piece*, which aired from 1963 to 1967. He later accepted a position with Dayton's WLWD television station to host a local call-in talk show, but, unable to attract top guests, he and his producers focused each episode on relevant issues of the day.

The Phil Donahue Show premiered in November 1967 with an appearance by celebrated atheist Madalyn Murray O'Hair, who was considered by some the most hated woman in America. That first week also included film of a woman giving birth and a discussion on the appropriateness of anatomically correct male dolls. Donahue's likable personality and his ease in addressing often-uncomfortable issues tempered the daring subject matter. A further innovation was his solicitation of questions and comments from the studio audience, previously regarded as little more than background for hosts and their guests. Donahue's charm, coupled with his bold choice of topics, attracted national attention when he moved his show, renamed simply *Donahue*, to Chicago in 1974. The program was soon syndicated nationwide and boasted millions of viewers, of whom 85 percent were women.

In a career that spanned more than 6,000 hours of programming, there was no subject that Donahue was unwilling to confront and present to mainstream America. Some complained that his choices were often inappropriate or too outlandish. Talk show host Merv Griffin expressed the opinion of many when he complained that Donahue and his imitators were most interested in controversy and titillation. Griffin stated, "What they have to resort to in subject matter is sometimes a pain in the neck. You know, the sex lives of Lithuanian doctors and dentists is not all that interesting." Donahue did, indeed, parade bizarre guests at times and was not above risking offense to capture high ratings. He interviewed nudists, drag queens, neo-Nazis, and strippers of all sorts. The episode that caused the most controversy and hysteria was titled "Transvestite Fashion Show" and featured Donahue wearing a dress.

However, complaints that daytime talk shows peddled only salacious material ignored Donahue's many episodes that focused on serious issues such as race relations, class differences, and feminist causes. In 1982 he presented the first national program devoted to the AIDS crisis, and a high point of his series was a 1988 discussion of the disease in children, led by the HIV-positive boy Ryan White. Over the years the series also welcomed politicians and advocates from across the political spectrum to express their views. In the late 1980s Donahue initiated a series of "space bridge" shows with Russian TV host Vladimir Pozner, designed to promote understanding between the people of the United States and the Soviet Union. The host's own stand on abortion rights, the Equal Rights Amendment, and other feminist causes identified him as one of TV's outstanding liberal voices.

DONAHUE VS. OPRAH

Donahue's success continued into the 1980s and 1990s. In 1980 the divorced father of five married actress Marlo Thomas, best known for TV's *That Girl.* The couple had met several years earlier when Thomas was a guest on Donahue's program. The series relocated to New York in 1985, but the following year saw the first real challenge to Donahue's ratings dominance with the arrival of Oprah Winfrey. The pair battled for the position of TV's top daytime talk show host for a decade until Donahue announced his retirement in 1996. The final episode of his show was a national event.

Donahue returned to television in 2002 to host a show on MSNBC. Although it was the highest-rated talk show on the new network, the series was canceled in 2003. Donahue and others complained the series was removed from the airwaves when NBC executives feared that the host's liberal political leanings would be criticized during the Iraq War. In 2007 he served as the executive producer of *Body of War,* a documentary that told the story of a severely disabled Iraq War veteran. He briefly returned to daytime television for a November 2010 guest appearance on *The Oprah Winfrey Show.* He reminisced with Winfrey and other daytime hosts Sally Jessy Raphael, Geraldo Rivera, Montel Williams, and Ricki Lake about the genre he had created.

After Donahue's departure, daytime talk shows sank into a mire of freak shows, fights, and shocking behavior. The intelligence, curiosity, and humane probing that characterized Donahue's approach were sadly absent in an era filled with hosts such as Rivera, Jenny Jones, and Jerry Springer. Where Donahue had sought to inform and entertain, others set out to demean, provoke, and shock—an unworthy tribute to Donahue's ability to present often controversial subjects to the mass American audience, which had once appeared to mark the nation's growing willingness to confront previously taboo topics.

Charles Coletta

SEE ALSO: *Daytime Talk Shows; Feminism; Griffin, Merv; Lake, Ricki; Rivera, Geraldo; Springer, Jerry; Thomas, Marlo; Winfrey, Oprah.*

BIBLIOGRAPHY

Andersen, Christopher. *The New Book of People: Photographs, Capsule Biographies, and Vital Statistics of Over 500 Celebrities.* New York: Putnam, 1986.

Donahue, Phil. *Donahue: My Own Story.* New York: Simon & Schuster, 1979.

Winship, Michael. *Television.* New York: Random House, 1988.

Donovan *(1946–)*

The rise and fall of British singer Donovan's career and popularity paralleled that of the 1960s counterculture. In the dreamy world of the late sixties, the exotic performer embodied the image of the earthy flower child. Appearing simultaneously wide eyed and cynical, a little silly but nobody's fool, and as an intensely commercial hippie, he seemed to embrace antithetical categories in popular culture. From 1965 to 1970 he lived so close to the cutting edge of each new trend that it almost seemed as if he had initiated them. Then, with shocking rapidity, he became irrelevant, discarded—like the counterculture—by critics and audiences alike as passé and uncool. Despite being so identified with a specific time and worldview, however, his best songs never lost either their catchiness or their ability to charm.

EARLY FAME

Donovan Leitch was born in an old section of Glasgow, Scotland, and his family moved to the outskirts of London in 1955. He learned the rudiments of music at folk enclaves in St. Albans, north of London, and in the coastal artists' colony of St. Ives in Cornwall. At age eighteen he began recording demo records that were heard by talent scouts from the British rock television show *Ready Steady Go!,* and by 1965 he was appearing regularly on the program. Initially, Donovan's music was entirely acoustic, and—while noting his English accent and more romantic attitude—critics labeled him "Britain's answer to Bob Dylan." Thousands of youngsters learned to play the guitar using the chords of his first hit, "Catch the Wind." Follow-up singles included the folksy "Colours"; Buffy St. Marie's "Universal Soldier" (a standard of the antiwar movement); and the jazzy drug tour of "Sunny Goodge Street," which featured one of the first explicit references to hashish in rock music. Donovan made his American debut at the Newport Folk Festival in 1965, the same year the crowd booed Dylan for performing with electric accompaniment.

By 1966 the twenty-year-old Donovan had shed his anti-bomb rhetoric and completely reinvented himself as a psychedelic troubadour of "flower power," the epitome of 1960s mysticism. With the help of Mickie Most, his new producer at Epic Records (with whom he worked until 1969), he retained the folklike refrains of his songs but added quirky pop instrumentation (sitars, flutes, cellos, and harps). His work during this period often exhibited brilliant musical inventiveness and a fine ear for lyrical phrasing, although he occasionally crossed the line into pomposity and pretension. His biggest hit, "Sunshine Superman," reached number one in the United States and number two in the United Kingdom in July 1966; it remains one of the most engaging and innovative singles of the 1960s. The album of the same name also includes such drug favorites as "The Trip," as well as the ominous "Season of the Witch."

Later that year Donovan released "Mellow Yellow" (with the phrase "quite rightly" supposedly whispered by Paul McCartney in the background), a number two hit on the Billboard charts. Baby boomers everywhere debated whether the lyrics advocated smoking banana peels; Donovan later claimed that the song was about an electric dildo. His subtle drug references endeared him to the hippie movement, although some complained that his songs were mawkish, the lyrics overloaded with images of trees, sunny days, and laughing children.

PHENOM OF THE 1960s

Donovan seemed omnipresent in the late 1960s, hanging out with the Byrds, the Rolling Stones, and Dylan. Peter, Paul, and Mary parodied him in "I Dig Rock 'n' Roll Music." The hits kept coming, including the druggie "Epistle to Dippy" and "Young Girl Blues," with its perfectly captured sense of rock ennui set off by shocking (for the times) sexual imagery. Donovan was a "must" to headline at the 1967 Monterey Pop Festival, but his visa was revoked because of a drug charge. He traveled to India at the same time as the Beatles to study with the Maharishi Mahesh Yogi. Shortly thereafter, he publicly renounced drug use, requested that his followers substitute meditation for getting stoned, and appeared onstage wearing flowing robes and love beads.

Nowhere was Donovan's versatility better displayed than in the hit singles he penned in rapid succession in 1968. His acoustic skill was featured in the sweet hymn to childhood "Jennifer Juniper." "Wear Your Love Like Heaven" layered soft harmonies consisting of little more than the names of exotic colors; the song later gained wide circulation as the ubiquitous advertising jingle for Love cosmetics. At the other end of the pop music spectrum, Top 10 hit "Hurdy Gurdy Man," with its drug and fairy-tale imagery, featured Jimmy Page's wailing guitars as a backdrop for Donovan's distinctive, tremulous intonation. Three-quarters of the future Led Zeppelin band played on the single, and the group later used the same contrast between acoustic and electric sound to great effect.

Donovan's work continually displayed an original bent and a desire to move beyond traditional popular forms while retaining commercial appeal. "There Is a Mountain," a hypnotic calypso-based song with lyrics inspired by Japanese haiku, reached number eleven on the charts in 1967. "Rikki-Tikki-Tavi" (1970) also borrowed successfully from West Indian traditions. The unique, albeit bizarre story-song "Atlantis" (1969) was the last of Donovan's efforts to make the Billboard Top 10. That year he also experimented with jazz-based sound, most noticeably in "Goo Goo Barabajagal (Love is Hot)," a searing collaboration with the Jeff Beck Group that marked the end of his string of popular hits.

NEW INCARNATIONS

Ironically, just as the singer-songwriter movement reached a peak in the early 1970s, Donovan fell from commercial grace. After his audience failed to appreciate 1970's *Open Road*, the release of a poorly reviewed double album of children's songs (*HMS Donovan*, 1971) triggered a critical backlash. His sparsely attended 1971 American tour drove him into the movie business; he wrote scores for—among other films—Franco Zeffirelli's *Brother Sun, Sister Moon* (1972). Subsequent albums met with mixed critical acclaim and declining sales. Among these was *7-Tease* (1974), a conceptual album about a young hippie and his search for inner peace, which also toured as a stage revue with some collaboration from David Bowie. By 1980 Donovan was no longer a concert attraction and lacked any major record company affiliation. He recorded only sporadically in the next decade.

After several inactive years, the singer enjoyed a minor renaissance in the 1990s. The spacey British dance band Happy Mondays brought him back into favor by praising his work and touring with him. In 1991 they paid an irreverent tribute to him on *Pills 'n' Thrills and Bellyaches*; the hit album precipitated a flood of Donovan reissues. There was considerable interest in *Sutras*, his 1996 "comeback" effort, but ultimately the purely acoustic work, filled with cosmically sincere and occasionally cloying material, found no audience. Throughout the 1990s and into the twenty-first century, he continued to make new music and tour small clubs, as he had done at the beginning of his career.

Donovan's music took a commercial turn as his old hits were recycled in various movie soundtracks and advertisements. In 2007 alone four songs were featured in commercials for such "un-hippie"-like companies as Coca Cola, Target, General Electric, Delta Airlines, and Cheerios. "Hurdy Gurdy Man" was used in the movies *Sleepers* (1996), *Bobby* (2006), *Man of the Year* (2006), and *Zodiac* (2007), while the gentle "Atlantis" played as the backdrop for a violent scene in *GoodFellas* (1990).

Despite being a consistently imaginative lyricist who pioneered and popularized novel musical forms, Donovan will forever be associated with naive psychedelia. His career may have fit the typical rock star paradigm, but the best of his work remains uniquely original. With his induction into the Rock and Roll Hall of Fame in 2012, his place in music history was secured. The museum's website pays this tribute to him: "The first British folk troubadour who truly captured the imaginations of early Beatles-era fans on both sides of the Atlantic, Donovan Leitch made the transition from a scruffy blue-jeaned busker into a brocaded hippie traveler on Trans Love Airways."

Jon Sterngass

SEE ALSO: *Advertising; Baby Boomers; The Beatles; Bowie, David; The Byrds; Coca-Cola; Dylan, Bob; Electric Guitar; Folk Music;* GoodFellas*; Hippies; Jazz; Led Zeppelin; Marijuana; McCartney, Paul; Newport Jazz and Folk Festivals; Peter, Paul, and Mary; Pop Music; Psychedelia; Rock and Roll; The Rolling Stones; Sexual Revolution.*

BIBLIOGRAPHY

Donovan. *Troubadour: The Definitive Collection, 1964–1976.* Epic/Legacy E2K 46986, 1992, compact disc.

Friedenberg, Edgar. "Current Patterns of a Generational Conflict." *Journal of Social Issues* 25 (1969): 21–38.

Lee, Linda. "Hurdy Gurdy Man." *New York Times*, October 12, 2008, 4(L).

Leitch, Donovan. *Dry Songs and Scribbles.* Garden City: NY: Doubleday, 1971.

Leitch, Donovan. *The Autobiography of Donovan: The Hurdy Gurdy Man.* New York: St. Martin's Press, 2005.

Sunshine Superman: The Journey of Donovan. DVD. Hanover, Germany: SPV, 2008.

The Doobie Brothers

The Doobie Brothers, or the Doobies, formed in California in 1970 and became one of the definitive rock bands of the ensuing decade. Many of their songs, including hits such as "Listen to the Music" (1972), "Long Train Running" (1973), "China Grove" (1973), and "Takin' It to the Streets" (1976), have an upbeat, easygoing sound influenced by R&B and soul. Their two songs that went to number one on the charts, "Black Water" (1975) and "What a Fool Believes" (1979), have become soft-rock classics.

Not quite as original or as influential as the Eagles, the Allman Brothers Band, or Steely Dan, the Doobie Brothers must nevertheless be counted among the best American light-rock and country-rock groups of the 1970s. The Doobies continue to tour and record even though the peak of their popularity has passed. In 2010 they released *World Gone Crazy*, their first album in a decade. The album captures enough of the band's classic sound to be pleasing to die-hard fans.

Dave Goldweber

SEE ALSO: *The Allman Brothers Band; Rock and Roll.*

BIBLIOGRAPHY

Bego, Mark. *The Doobie Brothers.* New York: Fawcett, 1980.

Buckley, Jonathan. *The Rough Guide to Rock.* London: Rough Guides, 2003.

Christgau, Robert. *Rock Albums of the '70s.* New York: Da Capo Press, 1981.

Edwards, John W. *Rock 'n' Roll, 1970–1979.* Jefferson, NC: McFarland, 1993.

Doonesbury

On October 26, 1970, Garry Trudeau's comic strip *Doonesbury* debuted in twenty-eight newspapers around the United States, revolutionizing the language and cultural significance of cartoon art forever with its depth of focus, breadth of satirical targets, and richness of character development. From its roots as a *Yale Daily News* strip satirizing college life, *Doonesbury* expanded the horizons of its content and its popularity until, more than forty years after its first national appearance, it was a feature in nearly 1,400 newspapers across the country.

A HUGE CAST OF CHARACTERS

Following on ground broken by Walt Kelly's *Pogo*, Trudeau challenged the definition of the comic page as escape and silliness by bringing sharp satire, social commentary, and adult issues into his strip. His heroes, and their quirky responses to the ups and downs of life in the late twentieth century, have stood the test of time, chronicling the changing priorities and dilemmas of the baby boom generation from college into middle age. His style of cartooning, with panels of complex artwork and extensive bubble-free dialogue, has been much imitated.

In the 1970s the initial *Doonesbury* focus was on the inhabitants of an anonymous eastern college campus and its nearby Walden commune. Conservative, gung-ho football star B. D. (a tribute to a real Yale athlete, Brian Dowling) and his loopy, girl-crazy roommate Mike Doonesbury formed the initial core of the strip. Soon they were joined by "Megaphone Mark" Slackmeyer, a campus radical; Calvin, a revolutionary Black Panther; and Zonker, a stoned, irreverent hippie. B. D.'s cheerleader girlfriend, Boopsie, and her intellectual roommate, Nicole, have perpetual disagreements about women's liberation, while the clueless college president constantly tries to sidestep controversy. As time passes, Mike learns about economics, racism, and class when he tutors a savvy inner-city black kid, while B. D. takes his raging drive to win from the football field to Vietnam, where he is captured by Phred, a charming Viet Cong terrorist who teaches him something about the history of Vietnam and the absurdities of war. Those still left at school move to a communal house on idyllic Walden Puddle, where they are joined by still more refugees of the turbulent 1970s. One such is Joanie Caucus, an older housewife who has left her stifling life and her husband behind to return to college, and she becomes the spokesperson for women's liberation while she tries to get into law school.

Across the decades, these core characters, and many others, tracked the trends and current events of their time and place in history, graduating from college; surviving the yuppie years; and experiencing marriage, divorce, and parenthood. Through many thousands of ingeniously created panels, Doonesbury has offered complex insights into personal relationships together with incisive social commentary. Joanie Caucus, remarried to *Washington Post* columnist Rick Redfern, bemoans the difficulty of nonsexist child rearing as her young son, holding the doll she gave him for Christmas as if it were the rifle she would never buy him, aims it straight at her. Radio talk-show host Mark Slackmeyer, still the leftist radical, comes out as gay late in the 1980s, but his boyfriend is a dyed-in-the-wool conservative who gets along with Mark's right-wing father better than Mark ever did. In the 1990s and early 2000s, B. D. served in both Gulf Wars, eventually losing a leg in Iraq. Trudeau chronicled B. D.'s recovery in the book *The Long Road Home* (2005), which contains a forward by former Trudeau critic John McCain. The quandaries of everyday modern life ring true, as does Trudeau's ironic, "wish-I'd-said-that" dialogue.

POLITICS AND PRESIDENTS

Interspersed with the "personal" stories of the characters are direct visitations from public figures. A favorite *Doonesbury* scenario is a four-panel strip with the White House in each panel, unchanged except for dialogue. In these, presidents from Nixon to Clinton are effectively skewered by the words Trudeau puts in their mouths. In later years, with a technique possibly inspired by the icons of modern computer jargon, presidents and others have been represented only by meaningful icons—a floating feather for Vice President Dan Quayle, for example, or a buttery waffle for President Bill Clinton, proving perhaps that a symbol may be worth a thousand caricatures. Trudeau further satirized the political process by having his character Duke run for president in 2000 and by going so far as to create a website and campaign videos.

One of the most powerful symbols Trudeau created is that of Mr. Butts, the talking spokes-cigarette for the tobacco lobby. Mr. Butts originally appeared in a troubled Mike Doonesbury's nightmares when Mike, by then an advertising agent, is asked to design a campaign to improve tobacco's image. The cynical Mr. Butts reappeared frequently thereafter to lampoon the tobacco lobby, becoming a powerful image in the antismoking campaign. Indeed, *Doonesbury* has frequently been a catalyst for change as well as presaging events. Senator Bob Dole once called the strip the "best source for what's going on in Washington."

In 1971, well before the conservative Reagan years, a forward-looking B. D. called Ronald Reagan his "hero." In 1984, almost ten years before Congressman Newt Gingrich became speaker of the house and decades before his 2012 presidential bid, another character worried that he would "wake up someday in a country run by Newt Gingrich." When repressive laws in the wealthy town of Palm Beach, Florida, allowed people of color to be stopped regularly by police and required domestic servants to register with local authorities, Trudeau focused the bright light of *Doonesbury*'s satire on the town's policies, and the laws were repealed.

Because of its mission to attack difficult issues and mock public figures, *Doonesbury* has always roused controversy. Many newspapers place the strip on their editorial page, considering it inappropriate for the comics, while others regularly pull individual strips when the content is judged too extreme. In the 1990s, when *Doonesbury* came out with a series of strips in support of the legalization of marijuana for medical use, the attorney general of California railed against the strip and tried unsuccessfully to have it pulled from papers in the state. It is this hard-hitting political satire that earned Trudeau the Pulitzer Prize for Editorial Cartooning in 1975, the first time that honor had ever been conferred on a comic strip.

DOONESBURY'S PLACE IN AMERICAN CULTURE

Trudeau, born into a family of physicians in New York City in 1948, came honestly by his gift for trouble-causing satire—his great-great-grandfather was driven out of New York because of the caricatured sculptures he made of his colleagues. Known for his avoidance of the press, Trudeau, an avid student and researcher of the U.S. political scene, also writes editorials and draws editorial cartoons for the *New York Times*. He has written film scripts and the book for a Broadway musical of *Doonesbury* in 1983, though many critics did not think the cartoon translated well to the stage. He has also created *Doonesbury* television specials and a musical revue called *Rap Master Ronnie*, spoofing the Reagan years. For decades he refused to compromise the principles of his creation by allowing merchandising, but he finally succumbed in 1998, when he permitted *Doonesbury* products to be sold, with all proceeds going to the campaign for literacy.

In 1988, when Vice President George Bush said of Trudeau, "He speaks for a bunch of Brie-tasting, Chardonnay-sipping elitists," he was simply referring to the most negative baby boomer stereotype of the 1980s, the pampered yuppie. But Trudeau's strip speaks for more than the elite, clearly addressing a far wider audience than liberal Americans of a certain generation. *Doonesbury* fills a need in the American press for progressive readers who appreciate the demystification of complex issues through no-nonsense, direct language and humor. Though by the late 1990s many other comics had appeared who attempted to fill this need (even one especially for conservative readers), *Doonesbury* paved the way for these and for a comics page that explores adult issues through humor. The characters who inhabit the panels of *Doonesbury* are old friends to its readers, and one of Trudeau's great talents is his ability to make these characters—with the possible exception of faceless politicos—lovable to his readers. They keep reading to enjoy a cynical and satirical take on current events. And they keep reading to see how life is turning out for the old gang.

Tina Gianoulis

SEE ALSO: *Advertising; Broadway; Cigarettes; Comics; Gulf Wars; Hippies; Marijuana; The* New York Times*; Quayle, Dan; Reagan, Ronald; Teenagers; Vietnam; Yuppies.*

BIBLIOGRAPHY

Satin, Allan D. *A "Doonesbury" Index: 1970–1983*. Metuchen, NJ: Scarecrow Press, 1985.

Soper, Kerry D. *Garry Trudeau: "Doonesbury" and the Aesthetics of Satire (Great Comic Artists)*. Jackson: University Press of Mississippi, 2008.

Trudeau, G. B. *Flashbacks: Twenty-Five Years of "Doonesbury."* Kansas City, MO: Andrews and McMeel, 1995.

Trudeau, G. B. *The Long Road Home*. Kansas City, MO: Andrews and McMeel, 2005.

Walker, Brian. *"Doonesbury" and the Art of G. B. Trudeau*. New Haven, CT: Yale University Press, 2010.

The Doors

With their mix of music, poetry, theater, and daring, the Doors emerged as America's most darkly innovative and eerily mesmerizing rock group of the 1960s. The college-educated, Los Angeles–based group stood apart from the folk-rock movement of Southern California and the hippy bands of San Francisco. In exploring death, doom, fear, and sex, the Doors' music reflected the hedonistic side of the era. Writing for the *Saturday Evening Post* in 1967, Joan Didion called them "the Norman Mailers of the Top 40, missionaries of apocalyptic sex." The group's flamboyant lead singer, Jim Morrison, put it another way, saying, "Think of us as erotic politicians." Morrison was a seminal rock figure whose dark good looks and overt sexuality catapulted him to the status of sex symbol.

Morrison's provocative stage presence—combined with the group's mournfully textured, blues-rooted music—suggested the musical theater of Kurt Weill and Bertolt Brecht and the edginess of the avant-garde troupe The Living Theater. However, the complicated and troubled Morrison could not overcome his personal demons, which he sated with drugs and alcohol. By late 1968 his frequently "stoned" demeanor became off-putting, his onstage rants pretentious. His behavior during a concert in Miami, Florida, in March 1969, and his resulting arrest on charges including indecent exposure, represented not only his downfall but also the Doors' looming disintegration. Nevertheless, though the group's rise and fall was fast and furious, encompassing just four years, its anarchist influence is undeniable.

THE BAND'S BEGINNINGS

The saga of the Doors began in the summer of 1965 on the beach at Venice, California, where singer-musician Ray Manzarek ran into his former UCLA classmate, Morrison. After listening to Morrison sing the haunting lyrics to a song he had written called "Moonlight Drive," Manzarek proposed they start a band and "make a million dollars." Manzarek then approached two other musicians who were studying with him at a Maharishi

The Doors. *The Doors were one of the most interesting rock acts of the 1960s, due mostly to singer Jim Morrison's wild lyrics and unpredictable stage persona.* MICHAEL OCHS ARCHIVES/GETTY IMAGES.

meditation center. Thus, with Manzarek on organ, Robby Krieger on guitar, John Densmore on drums, and Morrison singing, the group was in place. It was Morrison who came up with the band's moniker, derived from a William Blake passage that had inspired the title of Aldous Huxley's book about his mescaline experiences, *The Doors of Perception*. As paraphrased by Morrison: "There are things that are known and things that are unknown, in between [are] the doors."

Working their way through the Los Angeles club scene, the Doors initially performed blues and rock-and-roll standards in addition to material written by Morrison. They were playing the London Fog on the Sunset Strip, making $5 apiece on weeknights and $10 apiece weekends, when they were spotted by a female talent booker who was especially struck by the star quality of Morrison. Hired to work the Strip's popular Whisky a Go Go, the Doors became the club's unofficial house band, billed behind groups such as the Turtles, Them, and Love. During their sets, the Doors were an anomaly; the four members appeared disparate, as if each was on his own plane, but their sound had a synchronicity. There also was no denying the allure of the group's pretty-boy singer.

In his earliest performances, Morrison was so introverted that he performed with his back to the audience. Some nights his baritone was barely audible. However, his confidence grew with the group's reputation, and his stage presence became unique. He had languid body movements, tended to throttle the microphone, and often emoted with closed eyes as if in a spectral trance. Moreover, he was unpredictable. Sometimes he dropped to the floor to sob out his lyrics; other times he danced with abandon, like he was possessed. One night at the Whisky in late 1966, he delivered an improvised rendition of his oedipal song "The End." The eleven-and-a-half-minute epic climaxed with a young man's screaming threat to kill his father and rape his mother (Morrison used a word other than *rape*), bringing the entire club, including the go-go girls in hanging cages, to a stunned silence. That very night the Doors were fired. Ultimately, however, they would have left on their own accord, for they already had a contract with Elektra Records.

POETRY AND ROLE PLAYING

Released in January 1967, the band's debut album, *The Doors*, includes "Light My Fire," which, at six minutes and fifty seconds, was considered too long for Top 40 airplay. As the group toured nationally, a shorter version began climbing the AM charts; meanwhile, the full-length rendition became a favorite of FM. Eschewing the matching costumes that were then in vogue among pop and rock bands, the Doors also had no official leader. However, in interviews and on the stage, it was invariably Morrison who took the spotlight. Shrewdly, the photogenic singer-songwriter exploited his rapport with the camera, as well as his appeal to journalists, who found him sensual, mystical, and eminently quotable. After all, the erudite rock star was also a poet who read and quoted nineteenth-century French poets Arthur Rimbaud and Charles Baudelaire and German philosopher Friedrich Nietzsche. Moreover, when not waxing metaphysical or apocalyptic, Morrison could be surprisingly playful. When asked how he had prepared for stardom, he quipped, "I stopped getting haircuts."

In his Elektra Records publicity biography, he claimed to have no family; in fact, he was the son of a navy rear admiral and from a family of career militarists. As a performer, Morrison assumed various alter egos. For a while, he called himself the "King of Orgasmic Rock," and as the "Lizard King," he donned tight-fitting snakeskin pants. He also claimed to be possessed by the spirit of a dead Native American, the result of a childhood trip across the desert. He and his family had once passed an overturned truck, which had resulted in fatalities, and Morrison claimed that the spirit of one of the dead Native Americans somehow entered him. He accessorized that persona by donning a concho belt and leather pants and dancing in a ritualistic style.

OUT OF CONTROL

The role Morrison played best was that of the rebel. When the Doors appeared on *The Ed Sullivan Show* in September 1967, Morrison defied the famed host's request that a particular line be deleted from "Light My Fire" due to perceived drug connotations. Three months later the singer made headlines when he was arrested on stage in New Haven, Connecticut, on charges including breach of the peace and indecent and immoral exhibition. In August 1968 he was again arrested, this time for disorderly conduct on a flight to Phoenix, Arizona.

Increasingly, Doors concerts became known for their dangerous atmosphere, as an incorrigible and no-longer-slender Morrison staggered across the stage, taunting the audience, inciting it to riot, screaming, "Wake up!" He also clutched at his crotch and tugged threateningly at his pants. The Doors were in a slump when they embarked on a tour in March 1969, and following the arrest of a bloated and bearded Morrison in Miami, the rest of the tour was canceled. The group's symbiosis was on the wane when it recorded its blues-oriented collection *L.A. Woman*. Afterward, a burned-out Morrison headed for Paris to concentrate on his poetry.

Morrison was just twenty-seven when he died in Paris on July 3, 1971, reportedly of a heart attack suffered while in the bathtub. Because of his penchant for substance abuse, and the curious handling of his death and burial by several close friends, questions persist over how he actually perished. Morrison's body was found by his common-law wife, who died in 1974 of a heroin overdose, and there have long been theories that drugs were a factor. Whatever the cause, his death was yet another reminder of the perils of the dark side of rock and roll. It was the third untimely passing of a rock star in less than a year following those of guitarist Jimi Hendrix and singer Janis Joplin, both of whom died of overdoses.

THE LEGEND OF JIM MORRISON

Following Morrison's death, the surviving Doors recorded two additional albums. Manzarek also sought to reinvent the group with Iggy Pop as lead singer, but it was clear that the magic had died with Morrison. It was Morrison's mystique that led to the discovery of the Doors by subsequent generations and his enshrinement as a modern-day Dionysus, the Greek god of revelry and wine who was dismembered and later resurrected. The 1980 Morrison biography *No One Here Gets Out Alive*, by rock journalist Jerry Hopkins and Doors associate Danny Sugerman, spurred one revival of the band's popularity and sent other writers in search of similarly debauched rock subjects.

The 1980 album *Greatest Hits*, which featured ten Doors classics and made it into *Billboard's* Top 10, proved that defunct groups could sell as well as active groups. Other attempts were made to capitalize on the enduring interest in Morrison and the Doors. In 2000 the surviving members of the band released a tribute album called *Stoned Immaculate: The Music of the Doors*.

It includes contemporary artists doing covers of Doors hits, as well as new music dubbed over old recordings of Morrison reading his poetry. In 2007, in honor of the fortieth anniversary of the band's debut album, a compilation called *The Very Best of the Doors* was released.

Rolling Stone acknowledged the continuing power of Morrison with its cover story on him in September 1981 that proclaimed, "He's hot, he's sexy and he's dead." Hollywood heralded Morrison in 1990 when a decade-long quest to make a feature film about him was realized with *The Doors*, directed by Oliver Stone and starring Val Kilmer.

In death, Morrison has been depicted as a poet trapped in the image of rock star. He is, after all, buried in Père Lachaise Cemetery in Paris, the famous final resting place of such notable artists as Edith Piaf, Oscar Wilde, Honoré de Balzac, and Frédéric Chopin. Moreover, the poetry he self-published in 1970 was republished in the late 1980s and during the 1990s. His writings have also been the subject of scholarly studies, including one in which he is compared to his idol, the French symbolist Rimbaud.

Although the spotlight remains on Morrison more than anyone else in the Doors, his musical legacy came from his collaborative work with Manzarek, Krieger, and Densmore. Many Doors hits—including "Light My Fire," "Hello, I Love You," "Touch Me," "Love Her Madly," "People Are Strange," and "Riders on the Storm"—have remained accessible. These songs attest to the power of provocative music and to the enduring interest in sex, drugs, and rock and roll.

Pat H. Broeske

SEE ALSO: *Blues; Hendrix, Jimi; Hippies; Joplin, Janis; Rock and Roll; Stone, Oliver; Sullivan, Ed; Whisky a Go Go.*

BIBLIOGRAPHY

Breslin, Rosemary. "Jim Morrison, 1981: Renew My Subscription to the Resurrection." *Rolling Stone*, September 17, 1981, 31–34.

Broeske, Pat H. "Jim Morrison: Back to the Sixties, Darkly." *Los Angeles Times*, January 7, 1990, 6–7, 19–24.

Didion, Joan. "Waiting for Morrison." *Saturday Evening Post*, March 9, 1968, 16.

Doors, and Ben Fong-Torres. *The Doors*. New York: Hyperion, 2006.

Hopkins, Jerry, and Daniel Sugerman. *No One Here Gets Out Alive*. New York: Warner, 1980.

Marcus, Greil. *The Doors: A Lifetime of Listening to Five Mean Years*. New York: PublicAffairs, 2011.

Rocco, John M., ed. *The Doors Companion: Four Decades of Commentary*. New York: Schirmer, 1997.

Sugerman, Danny. *The Doors: The Illustrated History*. New York: William Morrow, 1983.

Doo-wop Music

"Doo-wop" is a form of close-harmony singing that is rooted in rhythm and blues. The style became popular during the 1950s, originating among African American vocal groups in urban centers. As one of the most common rhythm phrases used by 1950s-era groups, "doo-wop" came to be the name of the musical style. In the doo-wop style, phonetic or nonsensical words are used as rhythmic parts in harmonic arrangements. Usually this is done by three or four vocalists, over whom a soloist sings a melody. The melody is expressed through understandable words and is often accented by the nonsensical phrasing of the vocal accompaniment.

By the end of the 1960s, doo-wop groups were losing popularity. Yet rock-and-roll musicians would often use doo-wop for their background vocal arrangements, and in this way, the style continued to develop beyond the 1950s and to exert its influence on popular music.

Brian Granger

SEE ALSO: *Pop Music; Rock and Roll.*

BIBLIOGRAPHY

Gribin, Dr. Anthony J., and Dr. Matthew M. Schiff. *Doo-wop: The Forgotten Third of Rock 'n' Roll*. Iola, WI: Krause Publications, 1992.

Morrow, Cousin Bruce, and Rich Maloof. *Doo Wop: The Music, the Times, the Era*. New York: Sterling Publishing, 2007.

Pruter, Robert. *Doowop: The Chicago Scene*. Urbana: University of Illinois Press, 1996.

Dora the Explorer

For more than a decade, posters, lunchboxes, backpacks, T-shirts, and television screens around the world have sported the ever-smiling face of bright, confident seven-year-old Dora the Explorer. The cartoon Latina's eponymous animated television series, which incorporates Latin American themes and Spanish language terms, is primarily aimed at an English-speaking preschool audience. Although it follows in the well-trod footsteps of educational children's shows such as *Sesame Street* (1969–) and *Blue's Clues* (1996–2006), *Dora the Explorer* has become a media sensation. Its bilingual (English and Spanish) script and its brown-skinned, brown-eyed Latina protagonist stand out against a field of Anglophone cartoon animals and culturally generic human hosts.

After debuting on August 14, 2000, on the Nickelodeon network, the show attracted millions of young Latino and non-Latino fans, garnering the highest cable TV ratings among preschoolers. Soon it ascended to the status of most watched TV show (broadcast or cable) among viewers two to five years old. The backpack-donning adventurer even graced the November 11, 2002, cover of *Newsweek* magazine. In 2005 she became the first Latina character balloon in the Macy's Thanksgiving Day Parade. By 2012 the show had garnered several coveted Peabody Awards and a global audience of more than twenty-five million. The show has captivated audiences in dozens of countries, despite altering its format from bilingual to monolingual in many overseas translations.

In the United States and beyond, Dora has been held up as a model for young Latinas as a protagonist who instills curiosity, a desire to learn, and a spirit of geographic exploration in young children of different, and often mixed, cultural backgrounds. The show's characters often voice Spanish words and phrases without translation, and in some plotlines, the terms acquire magical power. Cocreator Valerie Walsh states, "For many of our preschool viewers, Dora is their first encounter with a foreign language. As such, the show might teach them a little Spanish and make them curious and interested in learning more." Dora is also meant to help Spanish-speaking preschoolers "take pride in being bilingual," Walsh states, and to stand out as an "alternative to Barbie and the blond, princess myth often hammered into young girls." To further strengthen her appeal as a role model across ethnic groups, Dora is designed to be generally Latin American rather than specifically Mexican American.

Each episode is presented in a simple, easy-to-follow story line suitable for young viewers. The show also has a pseudo-interactive, play-along format. Dora often turns to the viewer to ask for help, such as in finding a lost item ("Do you see it? Where?"). She pauses for a few seconds to allow viewers to voice answers. Then an arrow or a cursor appears and clicks on the item in question as Dora voices positive reinforcement ("Yeah, there he is! *Sí. Allí está!* Come on! *Vamonos!*").

As a strategy for discouraging passive TV viewing, Dora and her friends encourage movement and interaction, such as pointing, clapping, jumping, and dancing. Sing-alongs, stand-in-place marches, and simple children's dances are incorporated into each episode, along with the "We Did It" dance and song at each episode's end. The characters also attempt to elicit viewers' help with rhyming, practicing polite manners, and direction following while teaching basic Spanish and math skills. The show's creators purport to give viewers problem-solving skills and confidence through modeling behaviors such as courage, empathy, and resourcefulness.

Dora's animated friends are brightly colored, peppy characters. Boots, a five-year-old English-speaking monkey, follows Dora like a little brother. Diego Marquez is Dora's bilingual eight-year-old cousin, and Swiper is a sneaky fox who is foiled by calls of "Swiper, no swiping!" Tico, a four-year-old Spanish-speaking squirrel, can operate any vehicle; Benny, a little blue bull, hiccups loudly; and Isa, a smart six-year-old iguana, is a vegetarian. Dora is almost always seen with her anthropomorphized exploring equipment—Backpack and Map—who have friendly, wide smiles and blinking eyes.

In 2005 *Go, Diego, Go!* was spun off to feature Dora's cousin. Diego is aided by Alicia, his eleven-year-old sister who is a computer whiz, and Baby Jaguar, Diego's inexpert but fiercely roaring friend. Diego and his viewers learn about Latin American culture, including animal mythology, while using scientific observations and high-tech equipment to rescue animals. His love for animals is equaled by what the show's creators call his "adventurous, fearless spirit"—qualities that he shares with his more famous female cousin.

Stephen P. Davis

SEE ALSO: *Barbie; Cable TV;* Newsweek*;* Sesame Street*; Television; Thanksgiving.*

BIBLIOGRAPHY

"*Go Diego Go!*" Nick Jr. Accessed May 2012. Available from http://www.nickjr.com/go-diego-go

"Meet the Creators of *Dora the Explorer.*" Nick Jr. Accessed May 2012. Available from http://www.nickjr.com/dora-the-explorer/about-dora-the-explorer/meet-doras-creators_ap.html

Dorsey, Jimmy *(1904–1957)*

Jimmy Dorsey was a leading jazz performer who played alto saxophone, clarinet, and trumpet and influenced musicians such as Charlie Parker and Lester Young. During the 1920s he toured with the Paul Whiteman and Red Nichols bands. In 1934 he and his brother Tommy founded the Dorsey Brothers Orchestra, which featured Glenn Miller on trombone and Ray McKinley on drums. After Tommy left to form his own orchestra in 1935, Jimmy led the band to national stardom in the 1940s behind the popular singing duo of Helen O'Connell and Bob Eberly. The song "Green Eyes" was the band's most requested number. In 1953 the brothers reunited.

Benjamin Griffith

SEE ALSO: *Big Bands; Dorsey, Tommy; Jazz; Miller, Glenn; Parker, Charlie; Whiteman, Paul.*

BIBLIOGRAPHY

Atkins, Ronald, ed. *All That Jazz: The Illustrated Story of Jazz Music.* New York: Smithmark, 1996.

Balliett, Whitney. *American Musicians.* New York: Oxford Press, 1986.

Dicaire, David. *Jazz Musicians of the Early Years, to 1945.* Jefferson, NC: McFarland, 2003.

Simon, George T. *The Big Bands.* New York: Macmillan, 1974.

Dorsey, Tommy *(1905–1956)*

A trombone player known for his warm, silken tone on ballads as well as upbeat improvisations, Tommy Dorsey, "the Sentimental Gentleman of Swing," led one of the most versatile orchestras of the big band era. With its premier jazz stars, the band could swing with the best, and none equaled its style on ballads, as sung by Frank Sinatra and Jo Stafford.

By age twenty-five, Dorsey had become a successful radio and recording star, and in 1933 he and his brother Jimmy formed the Dorsey Brothers Orchestra. Soon Tommy left to start his own group. His band's best-selling record was the swinging *Boogie-Woogie,* which sold more than four million copies, but the most requested number was the poignant "I'll Never Smile Again." The brothers reunited in 1953.

Benjamin Griffith

SEE ALSO: *Big Bands; Dorsey, Jimmy; Jazz; Sinatra, Frank.*

BIBLIOGRAPHY

Atkins, Ronald, ed. *All That Jazz: The Illustrated Story of Jazz Music.* New York: Smithmark, 1996.

Balliett, Whitney. *American Musicians: Fifty-Six Portraits in Jazz.* New York: Oxford University Press, 1986.

Dicaire, David. *Jazz Musicians of the Early Years, to 1945.* Jefferson, NC: McFarland, 2003.

Simon, George T. *The Big Bands.* New York: Macmillan, 1974.

Double Indemnity

Double Indemnity (1936) is one of the classic, tough-talking murder stories of the late 1930s. Written by controversial

Double Indemnity. *Barbara Stanwyck, Fred MacMurray, and Edward G. Robinson star in the film noir classic* Double Indemnity. **APIC/GETTY IMAGES.**

mystery novelist James M. Cain (1892–1977), *Double Indemnity* is based upon a true story about a weak-willed insurance agent, Walter Huff, who falls for sultry, murderous blond Phyllis Nirdlinger. Nirdlinger's inconvenient husband has to be eliminated so that his wife and her lover can collect on his life insurance, a policy that doubles in value if the holder dies by accident.

As is the case with Cain's *The Postman Always Rings Twice* (1934), upon which *Double Indemnity* is modeled, *l'amour fou*, or sexually charged obsessive love, is at the heart of this psychologically realistic novel. Cain, Raymond Chandler, and Dashiell Hammett have been called, perhaps unjustly in Cain's case, members of the hard-boiled school of detective novelists. Critic Edmund Wilson once referred to them as "the poets of the tabloid murder" because of their interest in the low-life aspects of American culture and the often-sordid stories of murder, eroticism, and adultery that fascinated them.

Cain has been compared to Chandler (who wrote the screenplay for the film version of *Double Indemnity*), but Cain's writing is deeply pessimistic and far less romantic than Chandler's. His characters are terribly flawed yet very human in their failings, and the eroticism of many of Cain's novels made them controversial in their day. His interests and lean writing style also made him stand apart from much of the popular writing of his time. Cain's gritty, downbeat stories such as *The Postman Always Rings Twice*, *Mildred Pierce*, and *Double Indemnity* had a pictorial quality that made them attractive for adaptation to the movies. All, however, underwent considerable sanitation before the more censorship-plagued Hollywood studios could make them into films.

In the case of *Double Indemnity*, the novel ends with Huff and Phyllis on a freighter going nowhere in particular. They are unable to return to the United States because of their murderous pasts and are contemplating suicide by jumping off the boat into shark-infested waters. As Phyllis says, "There's nothing ahead of us, is there Walter." And Walter replies, "No, nothing." This existential gloom did not survive in the film version, where Walter, after narrating his sordid tale of adultery and betrayal, lies dying from a gunshot wound inflicted by, perhaps, Phyllis, who he has murdered a few hours before.

Director Billy Wilder turned the novel into a convention-setting film noir in 1944, starring Fred MacMurray, Barbara Stanwyck, and Edward G. Robinson. Told in the first person in a confessional flashback by the dying insurance agent, Wilder's more cynical but less gloomy version helped establish flashback as a convention in film noir. The unusual casting of MacMurray, who was noted for his roles in comedy, helped the audience identify with the amoral but ruthless Huff, who in the film is called Walter Neff.

In the movie version the first-person narration helps draw the audience into a morally complex position. As the events unfold through Neff's eyes, viewers viscerally experience the amoral world in which he and Phyllis operate. To put the spectator on edge, Wilder sets the rigid and righteous Barton Keyes (Robinson), an insurance investigator and Neff's boss and friend, up against the Neff character, giving the audience a choice between identifying with a slippery, ruthless, and greasily charming insurance salesman or his cold and obsessive nemesis. As is the case with an Alfred Hitchcock film, the audience becomes ethically involved with the criminals, hoping that they will elude the ever-present, relentless Keyes. With its raw, more naturalist flavor and serious, unsentimental prose, the novel makes identification with the characters more difficult. Thus in the film, when Neff sets out to kill Phyllis, the audience is uncomfortably aware that they have identified with a hero who is a callous and brutal loner.

Jeannette Sloniowski

SEE ALSO: *Chandler, Raymond; Hammett, Dashiell; Hard-Boiled Detective Fiction; MacMurray, Fred;* Mildred Pierce*;* The Postman Always Rings Twice*; Robinson, Edward G.; Stanwyck, Barbara; Wilder, Billy.*

BIBLIOGRAPHY

Cain, James M. *Double Indemnity.* New York: Vintage Books, 1978.

Evans, Peter William. "Double Indemnity (or Bringing up Baby)." In *The Book of Film Noir*, ed. Ian Cameron. New York: Continuum, 1993, 165–173.

Irwin, John T. *Unless the Threat of Death Is behind Them: Hard-boiled Fiction and Film Noir.* Baltimore, MD: Johns Hopkins University Press, 2006.

Johnston, Claire. "*Double Indemnity.*" In *Women in Film Noir*, ed. E. Ann Kaplan, 100–111. London: British Film Institute, 1980.

Palmer, R. Barton. *Hollywood's Dark Cinema.* New York: Twayne Publishers, 1994.

Schickel, Richard. *Double Indemnity.* London: British Film Institute, 1992.

Silver, Alain, and Elizabeth Ward, eds. *Film Noir: An Encyclopedic Reference to the American Style.* Woodstock, NY: Overlook Press, 1992.

Wilder, Billy; Raymond Chandler; and Jeffrey Meyers. *Double Indemnity.* Berkeley: University of California Press, 2000.

Douglas, Lloyd C. *(1877–1951)*

With the publication of *The Robe* in 1942, Lloyd C. Douglas became the most influential religious novelist in the world. Following in the tradition of Lew Wallace's *Ben Hur* (1880), Douglas's novels satisfied a reading public's demands for rollicking adventure and historical romance combined with piety. *The Robe* purports to tell what happened to the Roman soldier who acquired Jesus's garment at the Crucifixion. After many adventures, this soldier meets St. Peter and accepts Christianity, later to die a happy martyr's death.

Douglas, who retired from the Congregational ministry to write, never pretended his novels were refined works of literature. He graciously suffered the attacks of reviewers, who found him loquacious and sentimental. Yet he proved incapable of writing a book that did not become a best seller; the public loved his vintage narratives of decent characters who worked through problems to happy resolutions.

In 1953 Henry Koster directed a major Hollywood film adaptation of *The Robe*, which is still highly regarded. Douglas's continuing though diluted influence may be seen in books by Fulton Oursler, Taylor Caldwell, and Frank G. Slaughter.

Allene Phy-Olsen

SEE ALSO: Ben-Hur*; Best Sellers.*

BIBLIOGRAPHY

Douglas, Lloyd C. *Time to Remember.* Boston: Houghton Mifflin, 1951.

Hackett, Alice P. *60 Years of Best Sellers, 1895–1955.* New York: R. R. Bowker, 1956.

Schneider, Louis, and Sanford M. Dornbusch. *Popular Religion: Inspirational Books in America.* Chicago: University of Chicago Press, 1958.

Douglas, Melvyn *(1901–1981)*

Although he acted in motion pictures from the early 1930s to the late 1970s, Melvyn Douglas was never especially fond of most of the more than seventy movies in which he starred. He much preferred the theater and returned to the stage whenever he got the chance. A versatile actor, he excelled in both dramatic and comedic roles. He appeared in horror films, mysteries, and melodramas but is best remembered for playing opposite Greta Garbo in the comedy *Ninotchka* (1939). Later in his screen career, when he had ceased playing dapper leading man roles and was showing up in character parts, Douglas earned two supporting actor Oscars. A dedicated liberal, he was active in politics; his wife, Helen Gahagan Douglas, ran against Richard Nixon for the U.S. Senate but was defeated.

Born Melvyn Edouard Hesselberg in Macon, Georgia, Douglas grew up in the Midwest. He served in the army during World War I but never went overseas. "The closest I personally came to death during World War I was in the kitchen, not at the battlefield, narrowly avoiding a meat cleaver thrown at me by a furious cook," he remembers in *See You at the Movies.* After the war he joined his family—his father was a modestly successful concert pianist—in Chicago. Douglas had not yet picked a career and had "no idea what to do with [his] life." By the early 1920s he had decided on the theater and was touring the Midwest. After several years of touring with an assortment of companies, Douglas reached Broadway in 1928 in *A Free Soul.* He played the gangster, a role that made Clark Gable a star when he appeared later in the movie version.

Douglas's work in the 1930 Broadway comedy *Tonight or Never* changed his life in two important ways. During the play he met Helen Gahagan, his costar, and fell in love with her. When the play was filmed, Douglas repeated his role in Hollywood. He went on to make several films in the early 1930s, including *The Vampire Bat* (1933), *The Old Dark House* (1932), and *As You Desire Me* (1932), in which he first starred opposite Garbo. Unimpressed with the movie business, the actor left Hollywood for a time to return to the New York stage. "I had gotten disgusted with being photographed at close range," he later explained, "with a microphone down my throat."

Douglas was lured back to Hollywood in the late 1930s and began working in a wide variety of films. He played reformed rogues such as the Lone Wolf and Arsene Lupin and a range of sleuths in mystery movies such as *Fast Company* (1938), *Tell No Tales* (1939), and *There's That Woman Again* (1939). He also starred in a string of successful screwball comedies. He worked opposite Irene Dunne in *Theodora Goes Wild* (1936), with Marlene Dietrich in *Angel* (1937), and with Myrna Loy in *Third Finger, Left Hand* (1940). In 1939 he made Garbo laugh in Ernst Lubitsch's *Ninotchka.*

Douglas said that he didn't become politically active until "just before Roosevelt's reelection in 1936." His wife was a singer as well as an actress, and he had accompanied her on a tour that took her to Germany. Once they saw Adolph Hitler's campaign against the Jews firsthand, Helen cancelled her tour and the couple returned home. Douglas joined the Hollywood Anti-Nazi League, worked for the rights of migrant workers, and campaigned for the Democratic candidate for governor. In June 1938 he organized the Motion Picture Democratic Committee, the earliest group of movie people to campaign for a specific political party.

Never a communist, Douglas found himself attacked by the local members of the party when he called Russia as big a totalitarian threat as Germany and Italy. For his criticisms of Nazi Germany he was labeled a "premature anti-Fascist." When Helen ran against fledgling politician Richard Nixon for the U.S. Senate in 1950, some of Nixon's campaigners introduced a strong note of anti-Semitism. In speaking of his opponent, Nixon would often refer to her as "Mrs. Hesselberg." One of Nixon's more extreme supporters, the racist Gerald L. K. Smith, told his followers that they must "*not* send to the Senate the wife of a Jew."

During World War II Douglas enlisted in the army and was eventually stationed in the China-Burma-India war area. He returned to the movies after the war—notably in *Mr. Blandings Builds His Dream House* (1948) with Cary Grant and Loy. After 1951 he concentrated on the stage again, winning a Tony for his performance in Gore Vidal's political drama *The Best Man.* Older, and letting his age show, Douglas returned to motion pictures once again in the early 1960s. He made more than a dozen films in his last years, including *Hud* (1963), for which he won his first Oscar, and *Being There* (1979), for which he won his second.

Ron Goulart

SEE ALSO: *Academy Awards; Dietrich, Marlene; Dunne, Irene; Garbo, Greta; Grant, Cary; Hollywood; Loy, Myrna; Lubitsch, Ernst; Tony Awards; Vidal, Gore.*

BIBLIOGRAPHY

Ciment, James, and Thaddeus Russell. *The Home Front Encyclopedia: United States, Britain, and Canada in World Wars I and II.* Santa Barbara, CA: ABC-CLIO, 2007.

Douglas, Melvyn, and Tom Arthur. *See You at the Movies.* Lanham, MD: University Press of America, 1986.

Mitchell, Greg. *Tricky Dick and the Pink Lady.* New York: Random House, 1998.

Douglas, Mike *(1925–2006)*

Daytime television talk show host Mike Douglas personified mainstream popular entertainment during the twenty-one-year run of *The Mike Douglas Show* from 1961 to 1982. The show, which initially originated from Cleveland, Ohio, and later moved to Philadelphia, was a ninety-minute syndicated program that dominated the ratings during the important weekday afternoon/early evening time slots. Douglas served as an affable midwestern everyman who welcomed guests from show business, politics, and current events. *The Mike Douglas Show* offered viewers a mixture of thoughtful conversation and wholesome entertainment. Douglas once described his personality and appeal to a mass audience by stating, "I'd have to say I'm a square and I'm happy that I am." His charming "Mr. Nice Guy" image made him the quintessential TV host and encouraged such personalities as Marlon Brando, John Lennon, Barbra Streisand, Rose Kennedy, and Princess Grace of Monaco to choose his program for their rare talk show appearances.

Born Michael Dowd on August 11, 1925, in Chicago, Mike Douglas served in the navy during World War II and, upon leaving the service in 1945, joined Kay Kyser's big band as a featured male singer. For five years Douglas, whose professional name was bestowed upon him by Kyser during a performance, sang on the radio and television versions of *Kay*

Mike Douglas. *Mike Douglas came to fame as a big band–era singer and entertainer before hosting his own self-titled variety show.* HULTON ARCHIVE/GETTY IMAGES.

Kyser's Kollege of Musical Knowledge. Among his most popular songs with Kyser and his own spin-off group, Michael Douglas & the Campus Kids, were "Ole Buttermilk Sky" (1946) and "The Old Lamplighter" (1947). Upon Kyser's retirement in 1950, Douglas began a solo singing career. His most noteworthy performance of this period occurred when he provided the singing voice for Prince Charming in Walt Disney's animated fairytale classic *Cinderella* (1950).

Douglas moved into television in the early 1950s and appeared on numerous programs originating from Chicago. In 1961 he arrived in Cleveland to launch his own talk show. Westinghouse, which syndicated the Douglas show, owned KYW-TV in Cleveland and believed it would be most cost effective to originate the program from those facilities. Later, an FCC ruling on a legal technicality forced Westinghouse and NBC to swap their stations in Cleveland and Philadelphia. In 1972 Douglas and his successful program relocated to Philadelphia's Independence Mall. Each episode of *The Mike Douglas Show* began with Douglas singing an opening number (most often "On a Wonderful Day Like Today") and then commenting on his personal life with his wife, Genevieve, and their three daughters. He then welcomed various guests and participated in comedy-variety segments.

One of the most noteworthy elements of the *Douglas Show* was the inclusion of a celebrity guest cohost each week. Performers such as Rosemary Clooney, Jim Nabors, Fred Astaire, Gene Kelly, and Gloria Swanson would join Douglas in this role for five days. Perhaps his most unconventional cohosts were Lennon and Yoko Ono, who appeared for a week in February 1972. The couple introduced Douglas and his Middle American audience to such counterculture figures as Jerry Rubin, Black Panther Bobby Seale, and several segments of performance art. Highlights of the unusual week included Lennon playing with his rock idol Chuck Berry and Douglas joining the couple in an unrehearsed segment in which they phoned strangers to say they loved them. In 1978 Douglas welcomed a two-year-old Tiger Woods to the program, where the golf prodigy demonstrated his putting skills to Bob Hope and Jimmy Stewart.

Douglas symbolized family entertainment during the turbulent 1960s and 1970s. He was extremely popular and prominent on the American scene. Beyond his own afternoon program, he often substituted for Johnny Carson on *The Tonight Show.* Douglas produced a hit record, "The Men in My Little Girl's Life," a song about fatherhood that reached number three on Billboard's adult contemporary chart in 1966. He was seen on the big screen when he made a cameo appearance as a southern governor in the Burt Reynolds film *Gator* (1976).

After *The Mike Douglas Show* ceased production in 1982, the host moved to the fledgling CNN cable network to briefly host an interview show. Douglas remained out of the spotlight until 1996, when he made a special guest appearance during the premiere week of *The Rosie O'Donnell Show.* O'Donnell credited Douglas as the inspiration for the positive, entertainment-based, family-friendly show she hoped to create. Her great success proved the daytime talk show format pioneered by Douglas still resonated with many Americans.

Mike Douglas died in 2006 on his eighty-first birthday in Palm Beach Gardens, Florida. In 2007 PBS broadcast a documentary film, *Mike Douglas: Moments and Memories.*

Charles Coletta

SEE ALSO: *Astaire, Fred, and Ginger Rogers; Berry, Chuck; Black Panthers; Brando, Marlon; Carson, Johnny; Clooney, Rosemary; CNN; Daytime Talk Shows; Hope, Bob; Kelly, Gene; Kelly, Grace; Lennon, John; O'Donnell, Rosie; Reynolds, Burt; Stewart, Jimmy; Streisand, Barbra; Television;* The Tonight Show; *Woods, Tiger.*

BIBLIOGRAPHY

Douglas, Mike. *Mike Douglas: My Story.* New York: Putnam, 1978.

Douglas, Mike; Thomas Kelly; and Michael Heaton *I'll Be Right Back: Memories of TV's Greatest Talk Show.* New York: Simon & Schuster, 1999.

White, Mel. *Mike Douglas: When the Going Gets Tough.* Waco, TX: Word Books, 1982.

Downey, Robert, Jr. *(1965–)*

Robert Downey Jr. has orchestrated one of the most spectacular comebacks in recent Hollywood history. Nominated for an Academy Award at the age of twenty-seven for his role in the 1992 biopic *Chaplin* (1992), Downey spent the last half of the decade in and out of jail and court-ordered rehabilitation on charges related to his cocaine, heroin, and alcohol addictions. "Even by movie industry standards," Jon Wilde of the *Guardian* wrote in 2003, "his appetite for illegal substances was mammoth, unquenchable, riotously insatiable." Downey finally got lasting sobriety after spending a year at a live-in treatment facility (2001–2002). His prodigious talent, soldered by a twelve-step program and wise career moves, has since regained center stage in rave movie reviews. The jewel in this "karmic turnaround," to quote *Entertainment Weekly*'s Benjamin Svetkey, has been his starring turn in Marvel Comics' hugely successful *Iron Man* franchise.

Downey was born in New York City in 1965 to parents in the film industry. His father, Robert Downey Sr., directed underground films in which his mother, Elsie Ford Downey, frequently appeared. Downey had minor roles in these films as a young boy and, with his father, began smoking pot and abusing alcohol before he was in his teens. (In retrospect, Downey has interpreted his father's indulgence as a seriously misguided attempt to make an emotional connection with him.) After his parents' divorce Downey moved to California with his mother. In 1982 he dropped out of Santa Monica High School and returned to New York intent on pursuing a career as an actor.

Within a few years Downey started getting noticed with a series of coming-of-age films, including two from 1985, *Tuff Turf* and *Weird Science*, and 1987's *The Pick-up Artist*, in which he assumed his first lead role, playing opposite Molly Ringwald. He had earlier tapped his comedic side with a short-lived stint as a *Saturday Night Live* cast member (1985–1986) and with the role of prankster Derek Lutz in *Back to School* (1986).

DRUG ADDICTION

Downey's first substantial critical attention came with *Less than Zero* (1987), the film based on Bret Easton Ellis's drug-fueled novel about jaded, affluent California teenagers. He was widely praised for his performance as Julian Wells, a crack-addicted rich boy who turns to a life of male prostitution after his parents cut him off. Downey was himself struggling with multiple drug dependencies at the time he made the film. While his performance benefited—*Chicago Sun-Times* film critic Roger Ebert described his acting as "so real, so subtle and so observant that it's scary"—Downey later explained to the *Guardian*'s Wilde that the part marked the start of his serious dissipation. "Until that movie," Downey revealed, "I took my drugs after work and on the weekends. . . . That changed on *Less than Zero*. I was playing this junkie-faggot guy and, for me, the role was like the ghost of Christmas future. The character was an exaggeration of myself. Then things changed and, in some ways, I became an exaggeration of the character."

Still, Downey managed to function professionally and was rewarded for his work in *Less than Zero* with roles in higher-profile films that led to his breakout success in *Chaplin*. He continued to impress, even in movies that were generally panned—most notably *Natural Born Killers* (1994)—until his very public unraveling, which began in 1996 with his arrest in Los Angeles on drugs and weapons charges. One month later police found him unconscious on a neighbor's lawn, and he was ordered into treatment. More violations under bizarre circumstances followed, with corresponding jail time, including a 2001 arrest in Culver City, California, that got him fired from his recurring role on *Ally McBeal* and shut down Mel Gibson's stage production of *Hamlet*.

It was Gibson who paved the way for Downey's comeback by putting up his own money to insure him on the set of the semi-independent 2003 film *The Singing Detective*, in which Downey stars as a hospitalized detective novelist suffering from hallucinations. Downey followed *The Singing Detective* by playing opposite Halle Berry in the more mainstream *Gothika* (2003), a psychological thriller produced by Susan Levin, who would become Downey's second wife in 2005. *Kiss Kiss Bang Bang* (2005), a murder mystery with Val Kilmer, was a commercial flop, but critics were enthralled by Downey's penetrating performance as Harry, a petty thief pretending to be an actor. Anthony Lane of the *New Yorker* called the movie a "slithery treat," praising Downey as compellingly watchable. The Edward R. Murrow story *Good Night, and Good Luck* (2005) with George Clooney also helped advance Downey back up the ladder to "A"-list stature.

IRON MAN

Director Jon Favreau, who was searching for someone to play Iron Man, was so impressed by Downey's work in *Kiss Kiss Bang Bang* that he insisted on casting him as Tony Stark, the playboy weapons-manufacturing magnate who transforms into the crime-fighting superhero. Downey's hipster spin on the character was roundly applauded in the press and sent fans flocking to theaters. Along with the enormous commercial success of *Iron Man* (2008) and *Iron Man 2* (2010), Downey received a second Academy Award nomination for his work in Ben Stiller's *Tropic Thunder* (2008) and was named that same year to *Time* magazine's list of the 100 most influential people in the world. Adding to this, Downey starred with Jude Law in 2009 in another sequel-spawning blockbuster, the Guy Ritchie–directed *Sherlock Holmes*. *Sherlock Holmes: A Game of Shadows* was released in 2011.

Downey is far from smug about his return to Hollywood's graces. He credits wife Susan with helping to keep him focused and is vocal in interviews about how he finally managed to stop his downward spiral of addiction and self-destructive behavior. He and his wife became the parents of their first child, Exton Elias, on February 7, 2012. Downey is also the father of a son, Indio, from his previous marriage to actress Deborah Falconer.

Janet Mullane

SEE ALSO: *Academy Awards;* Ally McBeal*; Brat Pack; Celebrity; Chaplin, Charlie; Clooney, George; Comic Books; Gibson, Mel; Hollywood; Murrow, Edward R.;* Natural Born Killers*;* Saturday Night Live*; Siskel and Ebert; Stiller, Ben;* Time.

BIBLIOGRAPHY

Ansen, David. "Putting the Irony in *Iron Man*." *Newsweek*, April 30, 2008.

Ebert, Roger. Review of *Less than Zero*. *Chicago Sun-Times*, November 6, 1987.

Lane, Anthony. "Troublemakers." *New Yorker*, October 31, 2005: 94.

Svetkey, Benjamin. "Robert Downey Jr.: EW's 2008 Entertainer of the Year." *Entertainment Weekly*, November 14, 2008.

Wilde, Jon. "More than Skin Deep." *Guardian* November 8, 2003.

Downs, Hugh *(1921–)*

Throughout his more than sixty years in broadcasting, Hugh Downs was the embodiment of reassurance and congeniality. Learning his craft as a radio announcer in the late 1930s and 1940s, Downs became the master host of television. After serving as announcer on *Caesar's Hour* and *The Tonight Show*, he simultaneously hosted an early morning series, *Today*, and a daily game show, *Concentration*. Always curious about health and science, Downs oversaw the first successful series on aging, *Over Easy*, for PBS. When the magazine series *20/20* was floundering, ABC lured the affable Downs out of semiretirement to anchor the show in 1978. He reported on many of his special interests, including sailing, psychology, and astronomy, for *20/20*, helping to make it the network's signature prime-time newsmagazine for more than two decades.

After his retirement from *20/20* in 1999, Downs continued to write inspirational books and host infomercials. Because of his decency and trustworthiness, he was one of the most familiar and reassuring figures in the history of television, clocking more hours on the air than any other network personality, according to *The Guinness Book of World Records* (a record that was later broken by Regis Philbin in 2004).

Ron Simon

SEE ALSO: *Public Television (PBS); Radio; Television; Television Anchors;* Today*;* The Tonight Show*;* 20/20.

BIBLIOGRAPHY

Downs, Hugh. *My America: What My Country Means to Me, by 150 Americans from All Walks of Life*. New York: Scribner, 2007.

Downs, Hugh. *On Camera: My 10,000 Hours on Television*. New York: Putnam, 1986.

Doyle, Arthur Conan *(1859–1930)*

So great is the influence of Sherlock Holmes that only the truest of the great detective's fans know that his creator, Arthur Conan Doyle, thought far less of Holmes than he did of his other creative efforts. Doyle was not a stock-in-trade mystery writer, a genre that was still finding its legs. He certainly had not "invented" the genre of detective fiction, a privilege that belonged to Edgar Allan Poe and his own creation, master detective Auguste Dupin. Although Doyle claimed that Holmes was modeled on his medical school teacher, Dr. Joseph Bell, the writings of Poe, as well as Émile Gaboriau, Charles Dickens, Eugene Vidocq, and Wilkie Collins, were what provided Doyle with the basic elements for building his mythic detective.

DOYLE'S EARLY WRITINGS

Arthur Conan Doyle was born on May 22, 1859, in Edinburgh, Scotland, the eldest son of Charles Altamont Doyle and his wife, Mary Foley. Doyle's father, a builder and designer in the Edinburgh Public Works Office, was from a staunchly Catholic family. In 1868 Doyle was enrolled in Hodder Preparatory, a Jesuit school in Lancashire. Two years later he attended the Jesuit college Stonyhurst School, also in Lancashire. Upon graduating, he traveled to Austria, where he spent a year studying German in Feldkirch School, before entering Edinburgh University in 1876 to study medicine. Doyle's year in Austria proved a major turning point, as a crisis of faith led him to abandon his Catholic upbringing, despite his Jesuit education, for a studied agnosticism. This change in religious perspective, based on his own faith in scientific reasoning, prepared Doyle for the rigors of medical school.

Sir Arthur Conan Doyle. *Although most noted for his* Sherlock Holmes *series, Sir Arthur Conan Doyle was a prolific writer whose works include science-fiction stories, plays, romances, poetry, nonfiction, and historical novels.* E. O. HOPPE/MANSELL/TIME LIFE PICTURES/GETTY IMAGES.

Interestingly, it was Doyle's avowed agnosticism and unwavering commitment to honest dealing that led to his becoming a writer. After he informed his father's well-to-do family of his religious disillusionment, all social and financial help was withdrawn. Barely able to support himself, in his third year of medical school he turned to writing fiction for extra cash, using as material his own adventures serving as a ship's doctor on a whaling vessel to the Arctic and later on an African freighter. Between the few stories he published, which paid just enough to keep him and his family afloat, Doyle racked up a good number of rejections before achieving steady work as a writer.

In 1882 Doyle established a private practice in Southsea, Portsmouth. Three years later he married Louisa Hawkins, whose own small family income offered him greater freedom to write more. His first novel, *The Firm of Girdlestone*, written in 1886, was soundly rejected by the British publishing industry and did not see publication until 1890. His next work was his first Sherlock Holmes story, the novella *A Study in Scarlet*, which, after several initial rejections, was published in the 1887 issue of *Beeton's Christmas Annual.* Despite Doyle's faith in the quality and originality of the story's hero, *A Study in Scarlet* gained little notice among readers. His next novel, however (*Micah Clarke*), caused a great stir. It was published in 1889—following the usual round of rejections by British publishers—by Andrew Lang, chief editor at Longmans Publishing Company. *Micah Clarke*, a story about the dangers of fanaticism, was Doyle's first work of historical fiction and was an immediate success, propelling the author into literary stardom in England.

TAKEN OVER BY SHERLOCK HOLMES

Meanwhile, despite the poor showing Holmes had made in his creator's home country, Doyle's detective fared quite well in the United States, and a request for another story about the master detective was made to Doyle while he was deep in his next historical novel, *The White Company* (1891). As soon as Doyle had completed *The White Company*, which was to be his personal favorite, he dashed off *The Sign of Four* (1890), which was, once again, well received in America. Fortunately for Doyle, Holmes's stock was beginning to rise in England by leaps and bounds. In July 1891 he wrote his first of six Holmes tales for the *Strand* magazine, making him England's most popular serialized fiction writer. Doyle continued to write Holmes stories over the next two years until he decided to have Holmes killed by his archnemesis, Dr. Moriarty, in December 1893, with the story "The Final Problem."

Doyle's decision was a momentous one. Holmes's death was met with howls of outrage and large-scale subscription cancellations of the magazine. The pressure on the author to continue the series was enormous, but he was adamant about letting Holmes rest in peace. The production of a Holmes story for serial publication had proved to be an enormous strain on Doyle's creative powers, draining precious energy that he thought better spent on his now-little-known historical novels, such as *Rodney Stone* (1896) and *Uncle Bernac* (1897). Ironically, the character that Doyle once tried to kill off has lived on long past his author's death. In fact, Holmes has gained new popularity in the twenty-first century with a new set of Holmes movies, starring Robert Downey Jr. as the detective and Jude Law as Watson, launched in 2009. The following year, the BBC created a television series starring Benedict Cumberbatch that features Holmes in a modern setting.

In the early 1900s he added to his output two works of historical nonfiction, *The Great Boer War* (1900) and *The War in South Africa* (1902), which sought not only to document the Boer War but also to defend England's role in it. In 1901 Doyle published *The Hound of the Baskervilles*, in which Holmes was reintroduced to solve one of his older cases. By 1903 he had accepted an American offer of $5,000 per story for a series of new tales about the great detective, regardless of how many Doyle wrote or how often. He continued to write stories about Holmes and his companion Watson over the next twenty years, although they tended to appear in short bursts, when they appeared at all.

DOYLE'S SPIRITUALISM

After Holmes's resurrection, Doyle sought an outlet in other genres for his early passion for historical fiction, such as the scientific romance, resulting in the writing of *The Lost World* (1912), *The Poison Belt* (1913), and *The Land of Mist* (1926). Concurrent with these he began a spate of spiritualist works that included *The New Revelation* (1918), *The Vital Message* (1919), *The Wanderings of a Spiritualist* (1921), *The Coming of the Fairies* (1922), and the two-volume *History of Spiritualism* (1926).

Many consider Doyle's turn to spiritualism at the end of his life one of the strangest events to occur in the life of a man whose greatest creation was a detective who drew his conclusions from a hard and cold reality that disavowed all things supernatural. Few recognize the important nuances in Doyle's thoughts about spiritualism, as well as the nuances within the spiritualist movement itself, which sought to treat spirits as a scientific reality, a view that Doyle favored. He was, after all, an agnostic not an atheist, and there is little doubt that, his medical training and belief in scientific method notwithstanding, he remained unable to reconcile the loss of his childhood Catholic faith with his belief in a greater good that directed human conduct and morals. Indeed, Holmes's own work as a detective of "setting the world to rights" suggests a moral imperative that is explained more by Doyle's faith—in goodness, in mankind, and perhaps even in God—than his reason.

Bennett Lovett-Graff

SEE ALSO: *Best Sellers; Detective Fiction; Downey, Robert, Jr.; Movie Stars; Television.*

BIBLIOGRAPHY

Carr, John Dickson. *The Life of Sir Arthur Conan Doyle*. New York: Harper, 1949.

Clausen, Christopher. "Sherlock Holmes, Order, and the Late-Victorian Mind." *Georgia Review* 38, no. 1 (1984): 104–123.

Green, R. L., ed. *A Bibliography of A. Conan Doyle*. London: Oxford University Press, 1983.

Lycett, Andrew. *The Man Who Created Sherlock Holmes: The Life and Times of Sir Arthur Conan Doyle*. New York: First Free Press, 2007.

Nordon, Pierre. *Conan Doyle: A Biography*, tr. Frances Partridge. London: John Murray, 1966.

Stashower, Daniel. *Teller of Tales: The Life of Arthur Conan Doyle*. New York: Henry Holt, 1999.

Dr. J

SEE: *Erving, Julius "Dr. J".*

Dr. Jekyll and Mr. Hyde

The phrase *Dr. Jekyll and Mr. Hyde* is a popular metaphor to express the dual nature of human beings, who are capable of great goodness and almost unbelievable evil. It is derived from the respectable Victorian doctor with a demonic alter ego who first appeared in the eponymous novella (1886) by Scottish writer Robert Louis Stevenson. The story of a scientist who finds a formula to isolate his evil side but fails to control it has also been told in the movies. The first film, *Dr. Jekyll and Mr. Hyde*, was released in 1908. It is a sixteen-minute, black-and-white, silent movie, directed by Otis Turner and starring Hobart Bosworth. A 1931 version, also titled *Dr. Jekyll and Mr. Hyde*, garnered two Academy Award nominations and one win for Fredric March for Best Actor. In 1996 TriStar Pictures released *Mary Reilly*, starring John Malkovich as the doctor and Julia Roberts as his housemaid, and in 2008 the story was told in a television movie with Dougray Scott in the title role.

The presence of Jekyll and Hyde can be detected in many other films, novels, and comics over the last 100-plus years. Stories dealing with scientists involved in fatal accidents, tormented serial killers, and even secret superheroes are ultimately indebted to Stevenson's Gothic masterpiece.

Sara Martin

SEE ALSO: *Comic Books; Comics; Horror Movies; Made-for-Television Movies; Roberts, Julia; Television.*

BIBLIOGRAPHY

Campbell, James. "The Beast Within." *Guardian*, December 12, 2008.

Frayling, Christopher. *Nightmare: The Birth of Horror*. London: BBC Books, 1996.

Geduld, Harry M. *The Definitive Dr. Jekyll and Mr. Hyde Companion*. New York: Garland, 1983.

King, Charles. "Dr. Jekyll and Mr. Hyde: A Filmography." *Journal of Popular Film and Television* 25, no. 1. (1997).

Rose, Brian A. *Jekyll and Hyde Adapted: Dramatizations of Cultural Anxiety*. Westport, CT: Greenwood Press, 1996.

Skal, David J. *The Monster Show: A Cultural History of Horror*. London: Plexus, 1993.

Veeder, William, and Gordon Hirsch, eds. *Dr. Jekyll and Mr. Hyde after One Hundred Years*. Chicago: University of Chicago Press, 1988.

Dr. Kildare

In 1938 Metro-Goldwyn-Mayer (MGM) acquired the rights to author Max Brand's creation, *Dr. Kildare*, and began a series of popular films about a young intern in a metropolitan hospital and his struggle to learn his profession and earn the respect of a crusty senior doctor in his specialty, internal medicine. In 1961 the same characters, with different actors, made a nationwide success of the television adaptation of *Dr. Kildare,* becoming the forerunner of the many medical dramas, such as *St. Elsewhere, ER,* and *Grey's Anatomy,* that have lit up the small screen since the 1980s.

In the cinema version, Lew Ayres stars in the title role and Lionel Barrymore plays Dr. Gillespie, a sharp-tongued old curmudgeon with a heart of gold, which he tries to conceal. The first in the series, *Young Dr. Kildare* (1938), presents a cast of regular characters that includes Nat Pendleton as the ambulance driver. Laraine Day appears as nurse Mary Lamont in the next film, *Calling Dr. Kildare*; she stayed in the troupe for five pictures. MGM released three Kildare pictures in 1940 alone, including *Dr. Kildare Goes Home, Dr. Kildare's Crisis,* and *Dr. Kildare's Strange Case. Dr. Kildare's Wedding Day,* Day's last in the series, was among the most popular and is notable as one of Red Skelton's early on-screen appearances. Ayres, who had chosen to be a conscientious objector and refuse certain military duties in 1941, left the cast. Van Johnson and Keye Luke vied to become Dr. Gillespie's assistant in two films, *Dr. Gillespie's Criminal Case* and *Dr. Gillespie's New Assistant.*

Finding the right stars to play Kildare and Gillespie on television was a challenge. The first pilot shot for the series had Ayres return to his role as a more mature Kildare, but executive producer Norman Felton said, "The result was a clinical sort of film, too much like a documentary." The producer decided on a second pilot and quickly signed Raymond Massey, a Canadian actor famous for his portrayal of Abraham Lincoln, as Dr. Gillespie. More than thirty-five actors read for the Kildare part, and William Shatner was the leading contender for the role until he accepted the captain's chair in the new science fiction series *Star Trek.* One of the remaining actors was a nervous newcomer named Richard Chamberlain, who had done a few minor television roles and was then collecting "$38 a week at the unemployment office. Despite his lack of experience, the producer thought he had just the right physical appearance and decided to let him take the lead in the pilot.

The show was an overnight success, and Chamberlain found himself the object of mobs of squealing women wherever he went. His boyish, blond good looks attracted 4,500 fan letters a week. The character of Dr. Kildare, however, a medical crusader and straight-arrow idealist, did not entirely appeal to Chamberlain. He told an interviewer in the *Saturday Evening Post* that Kildare is "nobler than humans prefer other humans to be. If I were to mold Kildare, I would make him more subject to faults and weaknesses—like the rest of us. I might even have him pinch a nurse or two." It was an attitude Dr. Gillespie would not have endorsed.

Despite the development of the show into a worldwide hit, the series ended in 1966 after a five-year run. Toward the end, the ratings declined somewhat as the show strayed from the key relationship between Kildare and Gillespie and focused more on the medical problems of its guest-star patients. During the final season, some of the episodes were serialized in a thirty-minute format rather than the hour-long version that had been so effective. Following the show's demise, Chamberlain went on to become the "king of the miniseries" in the 1970s and 1980s, starring in such blockbusters as *Shogun, The Thornbirds,* and *Centennial.*

In 1972 MGM tried to revive the series in a new format called *Young Dr. Kildare,* starring Mark Jenkins as Kildare and Gary Merrill as Gillespie, but the series had a brief run, followed by a short afterlife in syndication. Many have commented on the coincidence that two of the most successful medical shows ever to air on television arrived in the year 1961, with *Ben Casey* premiering four days after *Dr. Kildare.*

Benjamin Griffith

SEE ALSO: *Brand, Max;* ER*;* Grey's Anatomy*; MGM (Metro-Goldwyn-Mayer);* St. Elsewhere.

BIBLIOGRAPHY

Berkowitz, Edward D. *Mass Appeal: The Formative Age of the Movies, Radio, and TV.* New York: Cambridge University Press, 2010.

Brooks, Tim, and Earle Marsh. *The Complete Directory of Prime Time Network TV Shows: 1946–Present.* New York: Ballantine, 1979

Sackett, Susan. *Prime-Time Hits: Television's Most Popular Network Programs, 1950 to the Present.* New York: Billboard Books, 1993.

Dr. Seuss *(1904–1991)*

As an author, an illustrator, an editor, and a publisher, Dr. Seuss revolutionized materials directed at young readers by introducing humorous, rhymed, and colorful books using limited vocabularies and simple, appealing illustrations. Uniquely innovative in the annals of twentieth-century children's books, Seuss openly acknowledged that helping to kill off the predictable "Dick and Jane" primers of the 1950s was one of his proudest accomplishments. His stories, which contained subtle moral messages that could be read on different levels, included casts of bizarre creatures that often acted with what their author termed "logical insanity." For example, if an animal had two heads, he must also have two toothbrushes.

A SLOW START

Twice-married but childless, Seuss had not started out to be a children's book innovator. He was born Theodor Seuss Geisel in Springfield, Massachusetts, the son of a German immigrant who ran a brewery until the arrival of Prohibition. He later commented that his father was on track to become company president until circumstances forced him to switch his careers and become commissioner of parks. This helped instill an early cynicism in the future Dr. Seuss, while his frequent trips to the zoo thereafter helped to stimulate his fertile imagination.

His mother, Henrietta Seuss Geisel, unwittingly lent him her maiden name, which he first used when writing a humorous scientific piece. While studying for a bachelor's degree in English from Dartmouth College, Seuss contributed to the school humor magazine, *Jack O'Lantern,* then studied literature for a year at Oxford. Returning to the United States in 1927, he sold cartoons to the *Saturday Evening Post, Judge,* and *Vanity Fair.* He always considered himself to be an artist first and an author second. This belief is confirmed by the fact that many of his books were initially composed of his sketches, to which he afterward added dialogue. When he later wrote books that he did not illustrate himself, Seuss used the pseudonym Theo LeSieg ("Geisel" spelled backward.)

Seuss composed advertising illustrations for Standard Oil of New Jersey for fifteen years after a company executive saw his cartoon of a knight trying to kill dragons with the insecticide Flit. This led to one of the 1930s most famous ad slogans, "Quick, Henry, the *Flit*." In 1932 Seuss wrote an ABC book for children but could not find a publisher. In 1936, while crossing the Atlantic by ship, he composed *And to Think That I Saw It on Mulberry Street* in rhyme inspired by the rhythm of the vessel's engines. About a boy whose imagination transformed a horse and wagon into various beasts, the book became his first published monograph, bought by Vanguard Press after nearly thirty other publishing houses had turned it down.

Vanguard also published his next book, *The 500 Hats of Bartholomew Cubbins*, in 1938. Seuss then moved on to Random House, where he remained for the rest of his life, founding its Beginner Books division in 1958. The year 1939 witnessed both *The King's Stilts* and Seuss's only novel, *The Seven Lady Godivas*, a commercial failure and one of only two books he wrote for adults. From 1940 to 1942 he worked as a political cartoonist for the anti-isolationist *PM* newspaper, revealing both his political concerns and his preference for drawing. The perennial favorite *Horton Hatches the Egg* appeared in 1940. Critics variously regard this first Horton book as a parable about the virtue of intervening in crises, about protecting unborn life, about perseverance and integrity, or as just an amusing story.

Theodore Geisel/Dr. Seuss. *Theodore Seuss Geisel was an American writer, poet, and cartoonist most widely known for his children's books written under the pen name Dr. Seuss.* JOHN BRYSON/TIME LIFE PICTURES/GETTY IMAGES.

A PERFECTIONIST FINDS SUCCESS

During a stint in the army, Seuss worked with Warner Brothers cartoonist Chuck Jones (who later brought *How the Grinch Stole Christmas* to television) on training films. He also collaborated on documentaries in the Army Signal Corps with film director Frank Capra, from whom he learned the importance of plot development. One could also argue that Seuss's penchant for depicting the triumph of physically weak protagonists and the essential goodness of most people reflect a Capraesque sensibility. Seuss garnered three Academy Awards in his lifetime: for two documentaries, *Hitler Lives* (1946) and *Design for Death* (1947, about the Japanese), and for his cartoon *Gerald McBoing-Boing* (1951).

His postwar book production continued with *McElligot's Pool* (1947), *Thidwick the Big-Hearted Moose* (1948), *Bartholomew and the Oobleck* (1949), *If I Ran the Zoo* (1950), *Scrambled Eggs Super!* (1953), *Horton Hears a Who* (1954), *On Beyond Zebra* (1955), *If I Ran the Circus* (1956), and *How the Grinch Stole Christmas* (1957). But the debut of *The Cat in the Hat* in 1957 was the event that established Seuss's reputation. Produced as a supplementary first-grade reader with a controlled vocabulary of 223 words, it was the tale of a mischief-maker who teaches children to misbehave while their mother is away. Its success allowed Seuss to establish Beginner Books.

According to E. J. Kahn Jr., writing in December 17, 1960, issue of the *New Yorker*, Seuss was a perfectionist. He often labored more than a year on a book and threw away 99 percent of his material before he was satisfied, afterward haunting the production department to ensure that it got his material right. He later observed that his favorite book was *The Lorax* (1971), which came almost effortlessly to him, allegedly taking only forty-five minutes to compose. This environmentally conscious allegory about trees so loved that they are all cut down and become extinct was also the only one of his books that anyone ever tried to ban. That effort occurred in 1989 in the Northern California logging town of Laytonville. Other direct-message books such as *Yertle the Turtle and Other Stories* (1958), about a deceitful leader, and *The Sneetches and Other Stories* (1961), about a hateful competition between two kinds of creatures, have received uniformly welcome responses.

CHARACTERS AND THEMES

The characters in the Dr. Seuss books often encounter fearful situations, but wit and good luck see them through. Even the baddies are not irredeemably evil. The Grinch, for example, who starts out with a heart two sizes too small, ends up with one three sizes bigger than before. Seuss's trademarks are nonsense, humor, mischief, galloping rhymes, and tongue twisters. Some of his words are his own inventions; others, such as *burp*, had never before been used in children's books.

His illustrations—gangling cartoon-style figures, generally depicted in simple primary colors—are of ordinary characters with which children readily identify. All of his people look very much alike, which perhaps is part of the message. The lead characters are also invariably male, if they can be identified by gender at all. The novelist Alison Lurie asserted in the December 20, 1990, *New York Review of Books* that there was an inherent sexism in his characters' roles. One book with a female protagonist, however, *Daisy-Head Mayzie* (1995), was published posthumously. Seuss's focus on the issues of aging, tolerance, laziness, individuality, and persistence were usually subtly intertwined in his stories.

In a career that spanned six decades, Dr. Seuss published forty-eight books, including his second for adults, this time the successful *You're Only Old Once: A Book for Obsolete Children* (1986). Altogether, his body of work has sold 100 million copies in eighteen languages. According to *Publishers' Weekly* in 2001, of the top ten best-selling children's books of all time, Seuss wrote two: *The Cat in The Hat* and *Green Eggs and Ham* (1960, written in response to a challenge from Random House publisher Bennett Cerf to write a book using fifty words or less). Many others of his works were not far behind in popularity.

The last of Seuss's books to be published in his lifetime, *Oh, the Places You'll Go!* (1990), addresses the highs and lows of human experience—facing fear, loneliness, and confusion—and, fittingly, appealed to both adults and children. With its presence on the *New York Times* adult best-seller list for two years (1990–1992), its author could say: "I no longer write for children, I write for people!" Older readers could appreciate the satire, younger readers the charm. In the end, Seuss's hegemony over the picture-book market was challenged by lushly illustrated and more pragmatic books with more direct messages, but his books have retained their popularity.

The enduring appeal of Seuss's themes and messages has led to an entire market surrounding the licensing of Seuss characters. Many successful television specials and feature-length films have been made, based on several of his most revered texts. Cartoon versions of stories such as *Horton Hatches the Egg* (1942), *The Lorax* (1972), and perennial Christmas favorite *How the Grinch Stole Christmas* (1966) frequently appear on television into the twenty-first century. In 2000 Seuss's stories arrived on Broadway in the musical adaptation of several books titled *Seussical*. And as of 1999 children can even walk in a Seuss-ified world at the Islands of Adventure theme park in Orlando, Florida.

In 2000 *How the Grinch Stole Christmas* was made into a live-action feature film starring Jim Carrey, who later also provided the voice for a new animated version of *Horton Hears a Who* (2008). Comedian Mike Myers portrayed the eponymous Cat in the 2003 live-action film *The Cat in the Hat*, and *The Lorax* was released as an animated film in 2012. The latter film was met with some controversy regarding its use of promotional advertising tie-ins, such as partnerships with car company Mazda and tech giant Apple, that seemed at odds with its message of reducing consumption. The film also brought Seuss's family some unpleasant attention when a Lorax sculpture crafted by his step-daughter was stolen from in front of his widow's home shortly after the film's release.

At the age of eighty-seven, in 1991, Theodor Seuss Geisel died of complications due to cancer, but his work stands out among the most recognized and beloved of children's books. The fantastically imaginative world of Seuss's stories continues to captivate new generations of readers, and the variety of adaptations and licensing of his works ensures that audiences will continue to be familiar with the world of Dr. Seuss for years to come.

Frederick J. Augustyn Jr.

SEE ALSO: *Academy Awards; Amusement Parks; Animated Films; Apple Computer; Best Sellers; Broadway;* Dick and Jane *Readers; Judge; The* New Yorker*; Prohibition; The* Saturday Evening Post*;* Vanity Fair.

BIBLIOGRAPHY

Fensch, Thomas, ed. *Of Sneetches and Whos and the Good Dr. Seuss: Essays on the Writings and Life of Theodor Geisel.* Jefferson, NC: McFarland, 1997.

Kahn, E. J., Jr. "Children's Friend." *New Yorker*, December 17, 1960.

Lurie, Alison. "The Cabinet of Dr. Seuss." *New York Review of Books*, December 20, 1990.

Martin, Patricia Stone. *Dr. Seuss: We Love You*. Vero Beach, FL: Rourke, 1987.

Morgan, Judith, and Neil Morgan. *Dr. Seuss & Mr. Geisel*. New York: Random House, 1995.

Pease, Donald E. *Theodore Seuss Geisel.* New York: Oxford University Press, 2010.

Wheeler, Jill C. *Dr. Seuss*. Edina, MN, Abdo, 1992.

Dr. Strangelove or: How I Learned to Stop Worrying and Love the Bomb

Produced and directed by Stanley Kubrick, this dark satire on Cold War relations paints a searing portrait of a world accidentally plunged into nuclear warfare. Intermingling sex, love, and war in unexpected ways (for example, its characters' names often suggest "strange loves" of various types), *Dr. Strangelove* (1964) is a rich, provocative film that stands up well to repeat viewings.

Dr. Strangelove tells the story of an insane air force general, Jack D. Ripper, who orders a bomber wing to drop a nuclear bomb on the Soviet Union. Ripper, who favors rainwater as a drink mixer, believes the Soviets are poisoning "our precious bodily fluids," an allusion to an actual Cold War belief that the fluoridation of America's water supply was a communist plot. As the bomber unit headed by Major T. J. "King" Kong relentlessly approaches its primary target—a missile complex called Laputa, a reference to a place in Jonathan Swift's satiric 1726 novel *Gulliver's Travels*—Soviet Ambassador de Sadesky confronts the president of the United States in the latter's war room and tells him that a nuclear strike will detonate a doomsday device and annihilate all living things on the surface of the planet.

The wheelchair-using Dr. Strangelove, a presidential adviser on international political affairs and weapons development, explains the ramifications of the doomsday device while attempting to keep his bionic arm under control; during tense moments, the prosthesis has a tendency to choke its owner or to give Nazi salutes. While making plans with others in the war room for living underground in the post-Armageddon world, Strangelove unexpectedly rises out of his wheelchair and takes a few steps. "Mein Führer, I can walk!" he exclaims to the president, but his excitement is short-lived; Major Kong's bomber wing completes its grim mission at that moment, and a series of thermonuclear bomb blasts accompanied by the strains of the schmaltzy Vera Lynn tune "We'll Meet Again" concludes the film.

Kubrick began developing *Dr. Strangelove* in 1961 after reading *Red Alert* (also known as *Two Hours to Doom*), a 1958 Cold War novel written by former Royal Air Force officer Peter George. Kubrick purchased the novel's screen rights and began working with George on the script with the hope of maintaining the book's solemn tone. His plans changed, though, as the screenplay took shape. As Kubrick told *New York Times* reporter Eugene Archer, "I was fascinated by the book—*Red Alert*, a serious suspense novel about what happens when one of the great powers pushes the wrong button. The film keeps the same suspense frame. But the more I worked on it, the more I was intrigued by the comic aspects—the facade of conventional reality being pierced." Shortly before filming started in early 1963, Kubrick brought in Terry Southern, a writer known for his sardonic humor, to play up the script's sense of absurdity.

Kubrick assembled an eclectic group of actors for his film, including Sterling Hayden as General Ripper, Slim Pickens as Major Kong, Keenan Wynn as Colonel "Bat" Guano, George C. Scott as General Buck Turgidson, Peter Bull as Ambassador de Sadesky, and James Earl Jones as Lieutenant Lothar Zogg. Heading the cast was Peter Sellers, a highly versatile actor at the peak of his powers. Sellers played three roles: British Colonel Lionel Mandrake, U.S. president Merkin Muffley, and German presidential adviser Dr. Strangelove—Kubrick wanted him to play a fourth character, Major Kong, but eventually assigned the role to Slim Pickens after Sellers begged off.

Kubrick, who shot the movie in Great Britain mainly to accommodate Sellers, allowed the actor to improvise much of the Strangelove character, including the dramatic rise from the wheelchair. Sellers greatly appreciated the artistic license. "I especially enjoyed doing the mad scientist in *Dr. Strangelove* because Stanley Kubrick likes free improvisation that can be so stimulating," he told *New York Times* writer Howard Thompson. "Given a free hand, you can build, construct into the characterization. It's all any actor could ask for." Sellers's improvisation, in turn, helped Kubrick develop a strong finish for the film (he had originally filmed a monumental pie fight in the war room but abandoned it, believing its slapstick tone would conflict with the rest of film).

Though its power has diminished somewhat during the post–Cold War era, *Dr. Strangelove*—with its nightmarish visions of a world gone mad—remains an important milestone in screen satire.

Martin F. Norden

SEE ALSO: *The Bomb; Cold War;* Fail-Safe*; Kubrick, Stanley; Scott, George C.; Sellers, Peter; Southern, Terry; War Movies.*

BIBLIOGRAPHY

Archer, Eugene. "How to Learn to Love World Destruction." *New York Times*, January 26, 1964, B-13.

Falsetto, Mario. *Stanley Kubrick: A Narrative and Stylistic Analysis*. Westport, CT: Greenwood Press, 1994.

Kagan, Norman. *The Cinema of Stanley Kubrick*. New York: Holt Rinehart and Winston, 1972.

Nelson, Thomas A. *Kubrick: Inside a Film Artist's Maze*. Bloomington: Indiana University Press, 1982.

Rasmussen, Randy Loren. *Stanley Kubrick: Seven Films Analyzed*. Jefferson, NC: McFarland, 2001.

Thompson, Howard. "Pause for Reflection with Peter Sellers." *New York Times*, October 25, 1964, B-7.

Dracula

Cursed to an endless life, Count Dracula is eternally resurrected in film and fiction, as well as in the vampire myth. Bela Lugosi's Dracula has become an indelible figure haunting the popular imagination since the release of the film *Dracula* in 1931. The definitive vampire, Lugosi's well-groomed Count has spawned a diverse group of vampires, including Sesame Street's Count, Grandpa Munster, Blacula, Duckula, and Count Chockula. One of the few vampires people know by name, Dracula has sold innumerable books, plays, movies, costumes, toys, consumer products, and even tours of Romania.

INITIAL ADAPTATIONS

Tod Browning's 1931 film *Dracula* is probably the most famous version of Bram Stoker's 1897 novel. Often criticized for its over-resemblance to the drawing-room melodrama from which it was derived, the film has nevertheless had a tremendous and lasting impact on both film and popular culture. The film follows the journey of Renfield, a British businessman, who visits Count Dracula in Transylvania in order to sell the Count some London property. Slowly, Renfield realizes that he is a prisoner and that the Count is a vampire. Once in London, the Count must battle Professor Van Helsing, a doctor who specializes in ferreting out and eradicating the undead. Van Helsing and Count Dracula fight over the soul of the innocent Mina, and finally Van Helsing kills the Count by plunging a wooden stake through the vampire's heart.

Dracula was so successful that, almost single-handedly, it rescued Universal Studios from folding, giving the studio its first profit in two years. More importantly, it established talking horror movies as a popular and profitable genre. Lugosi's quintessential Dracula set the stage for the filmic and fictional vampires that followed. Certainly, Lugosi's sartorial elegance has become a trademark of Count Dracula—as George Hamilton complains in *Love at First Bite* (1979), "How would you like to spend 700 years dressed like a head waiter?" From the 1950s forward, Lugosi's image graced a staggering number of incongruous consumer goods, including swizzle sticks, jewelry, card games, decals, transfers, tattoos, cleaning products, Halloween costumes, albums, pencil sharpeners, greeting cards, plastic and wax figurines, clothing, puzzles, wind-up toys, candy, comic books, and bath products. By the 1960s Dracula had become such a marketable image that he could be co-opted to sell just about anything.

POP VAMPIRISM

The late 1950s and 1960s saw a resurgence of interest in monster culture, centered on television showings of classic horror movies by hosts including Vampira and Ghoulardi; the proliferation of magazines such as *Famous Monsters of Filmland*; and the development of popular television series such as *The Munsters* and *The Addams Family*, which parodied the American nuclear family.

Dracula. *Bela Lugosi as Dracula prepares to bite the neck of Maila Nurmi as Vampira in 1956.* HULTON ARCHIVE/GETTY IMAGES.

Lugosi's disdainful Count (barely even interested in his female victims) was re-created by Christopher Lee in seven films, beginning with *Horror of Dracula* (1958); by Jack Palance in a primetime version of *Dracula* (1974); and by Louis Jourdan in a BBC miniseries, *Count Dracula* (1977).

While the kitsch market bearing Dracula's image continues to spread seemingly unabated, like vampirism itself, a new vampire emerged who bears a resemblance to Lugosi's elegant, aristocratic Dracula and yet who is markedly sympathetic as well as erotic. Beginning with Anne Rice's *Interview with the Vampire*, published in 1976, novels and movies told from the vampire's point of view have become increasingly popular, as have vampire stories and films created by and for women—such as the films *Lust for a Vampire* (1971) and *The Hunger* (1983), and the novels *The Vampire Tapestry* (1983) and *A Taste of Blood Wine* (1992). Francis Ford Coppola's *Bram Stoker's Dracula* (1992) sought to be a more authentic film adaptation of the novel. Although the screenplay took some creative liberties, the movie was successful at the box office and went on to receive a variety of awards, bespeaking the resilient popularity of the Dracula character.

In the first decade 2000s Stephenie Meyer's *Twilight* series of novels for teenage girls became runaway best sellers (the film versions were equally popular), and HBO's drama *True Blood* became an instant sensation. Dracula has appeared in every form of media, from movies and television to novels and comics. The ubiquity of his presence and his various manifestations speak larger about cultural attitudes than about the fascination with the original monster.

SOCIOLOGICAL RELEVANCE

The repeated adaptation of a text can serve as a guide to changes in popular understandings of psychological and social issues. Vampirism has been read as a metaphor for gender and racial "otherness"; the simultaneous desire and fear of female sexuality, male sexuality, and/or homosexuality; contagion of all sorts; and the relationship between the "new" worlds of Western Europe and North America and the "old" world of Eastern Europe.

Dracula itself has been variously interpreted as a parable of the oppression and resistance of marginalized groups, the power and alienation resulting from technological reproduction, the repression of sexuality and desire, the effects of industrial capitalism on the working class, and the complex interdependencies of colonialism. Of course, on one level, *Dracula*'s popularity lies in its face value: the fear of (and possible desire for belief in) the notion that the dead are not really dead. Like much horror and monster culture, *Dracula* deals in the (linked) questions of sex and death. And as in most horror films, *Dracula* tells the story of a contest between good and evil, between the normal and the abnormal or pathological.

Dracula also follows generic conventions by installing normalcy at the end of its story, reinstating and reaffirming the good and the true after an anxious yet enjoyable period of peril. Yet *Dracula* plays with the boundary between good and evil, between the normal and the pathological, in a way that goes a long way in explaining the story's popularity. The story blurs and transgresses the distinctions between living and dead, East and West, male and female, heterosexual and homosexual, aristocratic and professional, healthy and diseased, and British and foreign before finally reinstating those terms as pairs of fixed opposites with the (apparent) death of the Count. It is Dracula's ability to appear normal, after all, to pass in the nighttime streets of London, which makes him both so dangerous and fascinating. He does not look like a monster—in fact, he looks like an upscale version of his victims. It is, in the end, Dracula's very adaptability, his ability to confuse epistemological and social categories, that ensures his everlasting capacity to both frighten and entertain.

Austin Booth

SEE ALSO: *The Addams Family; Horror Movies; Lugosi, Bela; Television;* Twilight*; Vampires.*

BIBLIOGRAPHY

Beresford, Matthew. *From Demons to Dracula: The Creation of the Modern Vampire Myth*. London: Reaktion, 2008.

Clements, Susannah. *The Vampire Defanged: How the Embodiment of Evil Became a Romantic Hero*. Grand Rapids, MI: Brazos Press, 2011.

Glut, Donald F. *The Dracula Book*. Metuchen, NJ: Scarecrow Press, 1975.

Gordon, Joan, and Veronica Hollinger, eds. *Blood Read: The Vampire as Metaphor in Contemporary Culture*. Philadelphia: University of Pennsylvania Press, 1997.

Skal, David J. *Hollywood Gothic: The Tangled Web of Dracula from Novel to Stage to Screen*. New York: Norton, 1990.

Stoker, Bram. *The New Annotated Dracula*, ed. Leslie S. Klinger. New York: Norton, 2008.

The Draft

From America's founding through the twentieth century, the draft, also known as conscription, has been a familiar way to ensure the country's safety in terms of the numbers of soldiers it can mobilize to fight in wars. In the twentieth century, the draft was used—in one way or another—during many of the major wars, from World War I to Vietnam. Naturally, then, draft dodging has also played a part in American war history. From the famous to the infamous, numerous Americans have used whatever means they could to change their lot in the military during times of war or to avoid participation in war altogether.

HISTORY OF THE DRAFT

The draft existed before American independence. In the colonies, young and middle-age (white) men were declared by law to constitute the militia of the colony, and such men were subject to compulsory militia training. After the adoption of the federal Constitution, Congress left militia matters largely to the judgment of the states.

In response to the Civil War, a federal draft law was passed in 1863 (and modified in 1864). The Civil War draft was not particularly effective: the draft law brought 46,000 draftees and 118,000 substitutes into the Union Army, which was less than 10 percent of the federal army's total strength.

Congress passed a draft law in May 1917 that lasted throughout America's participation in World War I. A majority of American troops who went to France during this war were draftees. The draft was administered by a decentralized civilian agency, the Selective Service System, whose power was largely exercised by local draft boards. In 1940 Congress again passed a draft law. Except for a draft-free period in 1947 and the first half of 1948, this law was renewed at four-year intervals until 1971, when it was renewed for two years. The draft then expired in 1973, when Congress failed to renew it. A Selective Service System, similar to that of World War I, supervised the draft.

During both world wars, the government eventually chose to rely solely on the draft for its military needs. In 1953 (the last year of the Korean War), more than half of enlisted men were draftees. After Korea, the military increasingly came to rely on volunteers (some of them motivated by the desire to avoid the draft), and the proportion of draftees in the armed forces was further reduced. There was an upsurge in the use of draftees during the Vietnam period, but the majority of enlisted men remained volunteers.

At the beginning of the Iraq War (2003–2011), some people called for a reinstatement of the draft. Because of the difficulty of keeping sufficient numbers serving in an all-volunteer army, soldiers during the wars in Iraq and Afghanistan (which began in 2001) often had to serve repeated tours of duty rather than the single tour that was common during the Vietnam War. Using conscription might have changed that, but a draft law remained too unpopular to pass.

DODGING THE DRAFT

Draft dodging means deliberately modifying one's behavior—legally or illegally—for the purpose of avoiding the draft. It is different from draft resistance, which involves the open defiance of the draft law. Over the years, men discovered various techniques for draft dodging. One popular method was to volunteer for military service before the draft caught up with them. To enter military service voluntarily had certain advantages over the draft. A volunteer had some control over which branch of the service to enter, whereas draftees tended to end up in the army rather than the navy or air force. A volunteer could choose a branch of the armed services, or a specialty, where there was less of a danger of doing infantry combat duty. For those who volunteered for the National Guard, one's tour of duty would be done in the United States. A Vietnam-era study of those who had volunteered for the armed forces found that 40 percent of the respondents indicated that the draft led them to enlist. According to a 1964 Defense Department survey, the number of Vietnam-era draft dodgers who enlisted in the National Guard and reserves was even higher.

Another method of dodging the draft was simply ignoring the law. According to one estimate, more than 160,000 men on the side of the Union failed to appear when summoned by their draft boards during the Civil War. During the World War I draft, between 2.4 and 3.6 million men failed to register for the draft as required. The federal government held "slacker raids" during World War I, in which federal authorities (civil and military), with help from vigilantes, would stop and detain draft-age men and find out if they were properly registered. In other periods, the draft laws were enforced by more conventional law enforcement techniques.

Married men were more likely to get deferments, a fact that did not escape the notice of draft dodgers. The draft law of 1940 seems to have prompted some marriages: in 1939 there was a total of 1,404,000 marriages in the United States, and in 1940 there were more than five million marriages in the eighteen- to twenty-nine-year-old group alone. The Selective Service, aware that some men were using marriage and fatherhood to avoid their military responsibilities, tightened the regulations in response. By the Vietnam era, marriage and having children were not particularly effective ways of dodging the draft.

Fleeing abroad was another method of avoiding the draft. Mexico was a destination for some draft dodgers during World War I, while Canada was a destination during the Civil War and Vietnam War. Sweden was also a popular destination for some Vietnam-era draft dodgers.

Under the old militia laws in the various states, a man who had enough money could avoid militia duty by paying someone to go in his place. This method of hiring substitutes was included in the federal draft law in the Civil War. Until June 1864, those who could not afford substitutes could avoid the draft by paying a commutation fee of $300. Many local and state governments gave financial assistance so that draftees could hire substitutes.

After World War II attending a postsecondary school could also be a method of draft dodging. If a college student proved he had a good academic record to the Selective Service, he could stave off the draft at least until graduation (in 1967, Congress made deferments available to all undergraduates regardless of their academic standing).

Draft dodgers (and draft resisters) have sometimes benefitted from presidential amnesties, including Franklin Roosevelt's limited amnesty for World War I offenders in 1933, Harry Truman's limited amnesty for World War II offenders in 1947, and Jimmy Carter's complete amnesty for nonviolent Vietnam-era offenders in 1977.

Eminent draft dodgers include President Grover Cleveland, who hired a substitute so as to avoid the Civil War draft; President Bill Clinton, who made use of student exemptions and the ROTC program to avoid the Vietnam War; and Vice President Dan Quayle, who joined the Indiana National Guard.

Eric Longley

SEE ALSO: *Gulf Wars; Quayle, Dan; Vietnam; War in Afghanistan; World War I; World War II.*

BIBLIOGRAPHY

Chambers, John Whiteclay II. *To Raise an Army: The Draft Comes to Modern America.* New York: Free Press, 1987.

Curry, G. David. *Sunshine Patriots: Punishment and the Vietnam Offender.* Notre Dame, IN: University of Notre Dame Press, 1985.

Flynn, George Q. *The Draft, 1940–1973.* Lawrence: University Press of Kansas, 1993.

Gold, Philip. *The Coming Draft: The Crisis in Our Military and Why Selective Service Is Wrong for America.* New York: Presidio Press, 2006.

Haig-Brown, Alan. *Hell No, We Won't Go: Vietnam Draft Resisters in Canada.* Vancouver: Raincoast Books, 1996.

Polner, Murray, ed. *When Can I Come Home? A Debate on Amnesty for Exiles, Antiwar Prisoners, and Others.* Garden City, NY: Anchor Books, 1972.

Drag

"Drag" was originally a theatrical term used to describe the women's clothing a man wore onstage. It came into use in the 1870s at the same time that cross-dressing, or dressing as the opposite sex, became popular in vaudeville variety shows. Men would dress in "drag" and women would "wear breeches," each one poking fun at the foibles and anxieties of the opposite sex. By the 1940s drag had come to describe professional female impersonators and had begun to take on meanings associated with male homosexuality. By mid-century gay men who wore women's clothes off-stage started to be characterized as men in "drag."

DRAG QUEENS (AND KINGS)

Since the 1950s the term "drag" has come to describe a form of cross-dressing for both men and women that intends to expose itself as false. In other words, men and women in drag broadcast the fact that they are *dressed up* as one sex or the other. Unlike some cross-dressers, they are not interested in wearing costumes that disguise who they "really" are underneath. Instead they make costumes that are clearly costumes, putting on clothes that are stereotypically men's or women's, such as floor-length evening gowns, high heels, bow ties, or three-piece suits. Men and women in drag work to exaggerate masculine and feminine gestures, facial expressions, tones of voice, and scenarios in order to simultaneously enhance their performance and underline the fact that they are performing. Drag is most commonly associated with "drag queens," or male performers who dress up as women. But it can also describe women dressed as men, or even women dressed as women or men dressed as men as long as their outfits are designed to produce the sense that the gender they are performing is self-consciously acted out.

Gay male nightclubs often host "drag shows" as part of their nightly or weekly ritual, especially in urban areas with large gay populations such as San Francisco or New York. These variety shows usually feature a lineup of drag queens who "lip-synch" to popular songs by female artists, moving their lips and performing along with previously recorded music. These numbers are often outrageously dramatic, extremely sentimental, or bitingly satirical. Each one is treated as an opportunity to experiment with the meanings of gender onstage. Sometimes performers make fun of mainstream gender relations; at other times they take the insights of the songs they sing very seriously. Drag shows are usually emceed by a drag performer, who often presents a comedy routine on topics ranging from gay sex to contemporary politics. Some clubs only hire professional performers, and others are strictly amateur.

There are many fewer drag kings than drag queens, and they are far less visible. However some lesbian clubs do sponsor drag shows that provide a forum for drag king performances.

These shows often feature women dressed up in female drag as well as male drag. In other words women dress in "campy" or exaggerated female clothes that draw attention to the ways that they must perform their femininity as they interact with other women who are dressed as men and who are drawing attention to their self-conscious decision to dress as their chosen gender rather than their biological sex.

Ultimately, drag exposes the ways that everyone "performs" their gender, even when they are "wearing" the socially appropriate role. Rather than being a natural extension of biological sex, sex-role behavior is learned, performed, and always unreal. If gender can be successfully understood through sex-role behavior that is outrageous and clearly fake, then logically it follows that those traits and characteristics that people uncritically associate with one sex or the other are being put on or taken off by everyone.

DRAG IN MAINSTREAM CULTURE

Drag has become more mainstream in the new millennium, both within the gay community specifically and in American culture more generally. RuPaul was a crossover sensation in the early 1990s and was, according to *People* magazine "the first drag queen ever to land on the pop charts." Her album *Supermodel of the World* brought her into the limelight in 1993, and her perfectly accessorized seven-foot frame has kept her in the public eye. Like other drag performers, RuPaul often openly reflects on the meaning of drag. "Drag queens," she once explained, "are like the shamans of our society, reminding people of what's funny and what's a stereotype." In 2009 RuPaul hosted a TV reality show called *Drag Race*, which was a competition to name the best cross-dresser in the United States.

A number of movies have also caught the national eye. The popularity of the 1994 Australian film *The Adventures of Priscilla, Queen of the Desert* in the United States as well as the success of *To Wong Foo, Thanks for Everything, Julie Newmar* (1995) attest to the American cultural interest in drag and particularly drag queens in the 1990s. Both films feature a group of drag queens traveling across their respective countries and ultimately finding themselves stranded in backward small towns. *To Wong Foo*, especially, captures the bland moral most commonly associated with drag queens in popular culture. By first experiencing discrimination and then "educating" the provincial residents with whom they come into contact, the three drag queens represent American cultural fantasies about victimized people. Confronting and overcoming their oppression by drawing on the drag queen "spirit," the queens of *To Wong Foo* tell Americans what they already think they know: that a good attitude on the part of oppressed people is the best way to overcome injustice.

Although mainstream movies make these simple connections, drag queens and kings themselves discuss the disruptive potential of drag. Rather than reinforcing Americans' comfort with oppression and their resolve not to take responsibility for victimization, drag underlines American cultural anxieties about difference and forces men and women to think critically about how cultural ideas structure their identities and their sense of possibility.

Karen Miller

SEE ALSO: *Divine; The Fifties; Gay Men;* People; *Pop Music; Reality Television; RuPaul; Television; Vaudeville.*

BIBLIOGRAPHY

Brown, Susan, and Steven Reinberg. *Persona*. New York: Rizzoli, 1997.

Bullough, Vern L., and Bonnie Bullough. *Cross Dressing, Sex, and Gender*. Philadelphia: University of Pennsylvania Press, 1993.

Chermayeff, Catherine; Jonathan David; and Nan Richardson. *Drag Diaries*. San Francisco: Chronicle Books, 1995.

Ekins, Richard, and Dave King, eds. *Blending Genders: Social Aspects of Cross-Dressing and Sex-Changing*. New York: Routledge, 1996.

Ferris, Lesley, ed. *Crossing the Stage: Controversies on Cross-Dressing*. New York: Routledge, 1993.

Garber, Marjorie B. *Vested Interests: Cross-Dressing & Cultural Anxiety*. New York: Routledge, 1992.

Pettiway, Leon E. *Honey, Honey, Miss Thang: Being Black, Gay, and on the Streets*. Philadelphia: Temple University Press, 1996.

Rupp, Leila J., and Verta A. Taylor. *Drag Queens at the 801 Cabaret*. Chicago: University of Chicago Press, 2003.

Drag Racing

Drag racing, an acceleration contest that takes place from a standing start and covers a measured distance, is probably as old as the automobile itself. However, it wasn't until June 19, 1950, that it got its start as a legal and commercially organized sport. On that day C. J. Hart and two partners hosted the Santa Ana Drags at an airstrip near Santa Ana, California. A year before that a drag race was held in Goleta, California, on a closed-off section of road with approval of the police, but it was only a one-time event. The surge of returning veterans at the end of World War II—many of whom could afford an automobile and had a sense of adventure as well as a desire to test the performance of their machines—gave rise to street racing or "hot rodding." It was street racing, illegal and dangerous, which led to the need for safely organized events. In the early 2010s drag meets take place all across the United States, with some contests attracting upward of 50,000 spectators.

Although drag racing has become more professional and commercialized over time, many hobbyists still have the opportunity to participate. There are various race classes, each held to certain rules regarding the weight of the vehicle, engine size and modification, and body configuration. In any major drag-race event there are dozens of class winners. Drag meets in the United States are sanctioned by the National Hot Rod Association (NHRA), the American Hot Rod Association (AHRA), or the International Hot Rod Association (IHRA). These associations establish and enforce contest and safety rules. The NHRA, founded in 1951 by Wally Parks, remains the most influential drag-racing entity; the first NHRA national championship meet was held in Great Bend, Kansas, in 1955.

The measured course for most races is a quarter mile, though some competitions are limited to one-eighth of a mile. The track is a straight strip made of asphalt or concrete. Race events usually begin with each class conducting trials; the sixteen drivers with the lowest times are allowed starting positions in the official competition. After the sixteen compete, eight winners advance to the semifinals until the two remaining victors drag for the championship. The format and rituals of the race are generally the same for all race classes.

In the "burnout box" behind the starting line, drivers will spin their rear tires to generate heat for better traction. Then, on signal by the electronic starting pole (called the Christmas tree), they will advance to the staging area and then to the starting line. The race begins when three amber lights, mounted in a vertical row for each driving lane, flash in quick secession from top to bottom, followed by the green light. Should a racer start too soon, a red light at the very bottom of the Christmas tree will turn on, meaning automatic disqualification for the driver at fault. Most races, which last from five to ten seconds, are won and lost at the starting line for either "red lighting" or for not "attacking the green," respectively.

RACER CATEGORIES

The main professional categories of racers are pro stock, top fuel, and funny cars. The pro stockers are production cars in which the engine is made by the same manufacturer as the body, with the wheel base remaining unaltered. Many performance modifications are otherwise allowed, including rebuilt engines, hood scoops, and header exhaust systems. Whereas pro stockers must run only on gasoline, top fuel dragsters burn nitro, an explosive mixture of nitromethane and alcohol commonly known as rocket fuel. The V-shaped racers—known as dragsters, rails, stilettos, or slingshots—are 25 feet long, 3 feet wide, and 3 feet high, and can clock speeds in excess of 300 miles per hour. Funny cars, sometimes called floppers, also run on nitro, but they have a body made of one piece of lightweight fiberglass or carbon fiber, not metal, that is mounted over the top of the driver and hooked to the chassis, or frame, of the vehicle. Both top fuelers and funny cars must use parachutes to aid in braking at the end of the race.

Three legendary top-fuel competitors are Don "Big Daddy" Garlits of Tampa, Florida; Don "The Snake" Prudhomme of Southern California; and Shirley Muldowney of Mount Clemens, Michigan. In 1964 Garlits was the first to break the barrier of 200 miles per hour. Later Prudhomme would clock a speed of 300 miles per hour. During the 1980s Muldowney won the top-fueler championship three times. Both Prudhomme and Muldowney got their start racing funny cars. Muldowney's life story was dramatized in the Hollywood movie *Heart Like a Wheel* (1983), starring Bonnie Bedalia. In 1984 Garlits opened his Museum of Drag Racing and International Drag Racing Hall of Fame in Ocala, Florida.

DRAG RACING IN POP CULTURE

The culture of drag racing has been represented in various media, from a plethora of specialized magazines—including *Hot Rod Magazine*—and novels such as Henry Gregor Felsen's *Street*

Dragsters Smoke Tires. *Dragsters can cover the quarter mile track in about 4.5 seconds at speeds exceeding 330 mph.* RUSTY JARRETT/ GETTY IMAGES.

Rod (1953) to recording group Tommy Dugan and the Hot Rodders. In the early 1960s Charlie Ryan recorded several songs on car racing, including the popular "Hot Rod Lincoln." During the 1960s and 1970s, the California rock band the Beach Boys further glamorized hot rodding with the hits "Little Deuce Coup," "409," "Shut Down," and "Fun, Fun, Fun." Mattel, one of the first toy manufacturers to recognize the appeal of drag racing to young people, introduced Hot Wheels, a line of miniature die-cast cars, which included replicas of funny cars raced by Don "The Snake" Prudhomme and Tom "Mongoose" McEwen. In 1992 the NHRA established the Junior Drag Racing League, where drivers between the ages of eight and seventeen could race half-sized copies of top fuelers, funny cars, and pro stockers.

Roger Chapman

SEE ALSO: *Automobile; The Beach Boys; Extreme Sports; Hollywood; Hot Rods; Leisure Time; Muscle Cars; Stock-Car Racing; Toys; World War II.*

BIBLIOGRAPHY

Madigan, Tom. *Fuel and Guts: The Birth of Top Fuel Drag Racing.* St. Paul, MN: Motorbooks, 2007.

Miller, Timothy. *Drag Racing: The World's Fastest Sport.* Richmond Hill, Ontario: Firefly Books, 2009.

National Hot Rod Association. *Fast Lane: The History of NHRA Drag Racing.* New York: Regan Books, 2001.

Post, Robert C. *High Performance: The Culture and Technology of Drag Racing, 1950–1990.* Baltimore, MD: Johns Hopkins University Press, 2001.

Wallace, Dave. *Petersen's History of Drag Racing.* Los Angeles: Petersen Publishing, 1981.

Dragnet

Created by actor Jack Webb, the original *Dragnet* ran on the radio from 1949 to 1957 and on television from 1951 to 1959. The series broke new ground from the outset, offering radio listeners rare authenticity of experience as they accompanied the police in following a case from beginning to final sentencing. Each episode unfolded at a measured pace as detectives Friday and his partner followed clues, interviewed both friendly and hostile witnesses, and checked with various branches of law enforcement for information. Documentary realism was a key element of the show's appeal, with Jack Webb's own deadpan delivery and opening gambit, "This is the city. Los Angeles, California," making the mundane routine seem hip and cool.

THE RADIO SERIES

The idea for *Dragnet* came to Webb after he had played a police lab technician in Anthony Mann's film *He Walked by Night* (1948). Webb shared a belief with the film's technical adviser, Sergeant Marty Wynn of the Los Angeles Police Department (LAPD), that pure investigative procedure was dramatic enough without introducing the traditional melodrama of the fictional hard-boiled private eye. In early 1949 Webb secured the cooperation of the LAPD and its chief, William H. Parker. As long as Webb did not compromise confidentiality or portray the police in "unflattering entanglements," Parker granted him access to all actual case files. Thus armed, early in 1949 Webb approached the National Broadcasting Company (NBC) with his radio pilot for *Dragnet.*

Webb's style was to underplay the role of the policeman. He told *Time* magazine that "underplaying is still acting. We try to make it as real as a guy pouring a cup of coffee." In addition, the series was realistic. When Webb and his partner walked up the steps to police headquarters, for example, listeners heard each step they took. To further the sense of realism, Webb had everything recorded at a distance so that ambient sounds could be heard.

DRAGNET ON TELEVISION

With his tremendous success on radio, Webb took *Dragnet* to television in 1951.Within two years of its debut, it had become TV's number-one rated program. On television *Dragnet* was extraordinarily conservative. Webb put the hard-boiled edge of nonconformist heroes like Sam Spade and Philip Marlowe into the mouth of a downtown cop: "My name's Friday. I carry a badge." The Friday character had no tolerance or sympathy for anyone outside the system. Los Angeles lawbreakers had to be punished, and Friday's investigations were carried out with a terse, no-nonsense approach. "Just the facts, ma'am," he often said to witnesses who digressed from the point. He had no interest in witnesses as personalities, nor did he have any interests in life outside police work. His whole duty was to "serve and protect." By contrast, his partner Frank Smith, played by former child star Ben Alexander, was much more human and often fretted over his health or his wife, Fay. Friday's diligence, however, fit well within a period of conformity during the Cold War of the 1950s. At a time when Americans feared the spread of Communism and atomic weapons, Friday was a figure of dependability and stability. During *Dragnet*'s run Webb's image was so pervasive that, despite a rise in the national crime rate, the public came to believe that crime had diminished and that city streets were safer than ever before.

The conservative tenor adopted by Webb could be seen in several episodes that suggested a hysterical and paranoid vision. In "The Big Producer," for example, "dirty" joke books and nude photographs had made their way into a high school, but Friday and Smith could not bring themselves to label the materials pornography. Instead, a series of omissions in the dialogue between the two convey their fear over this "filth." In "The Big Seventeen" the two cracked down on drugs, "H" standing for heroin, in the schools, although they were too late to save a seventeen-year-old boy from overdosing. The ending of the episode, as with several others, was downbeat, and in a 1950s context it worked. When *Dragnet* was revived in a later period, 1967–1970, the hysterical mood was far too judgmental for audiences. Similarly, a second revival of the series aired in 2003–2004 but failed to find its niche amid the numerous crime shows on television at the time.

EFFECTS OF *DRAGNET*

Through its use of abbreviations and codes, *Dragnet* generated a unique syntax in American English. MO (modus operandi), DMV (Department of Motor Vehicles), and APB (All Points Bulletin) became parts of everyday speech, along with 211 (robbery), 459 (burglary), and 311 (lewd conduct). Walter Schumann's four-note musical theme, "Dum-de-dum-dum," was a motif that evoked justice and retribution but also a sense of agitation. The motif was taken up in popular culture as a signal of trouble. In "Better Living through TV," an episode of *The Honeymooners*, for example, the character Norton hummed Schumann's *Dragnet* motif as Alice caught wind of another of Ralph's harebrained schemes. And in the 1980s a series of ads for Tums antacid modified Schumann's theme to "Tum-te-tum-tum."

The series was immensely popular. Parodies of it abounded in the 1950s. *Mad Magazine* attacked its conformity and its shilling for Chesterfield cigarettes. Radio comedians such as Stan Freberg and Bob Elliott and Ray Goulding—of the *Bob and Ray Show*—had fun with its narrative excesses. In the classic Chuck Jones cartoon *Rocket Squad* (1956), featuring Daffy Duck and Porky Pig in the Friday and Smith roles, the two intrepid heroes become villains. Moreover, the look of *Dragnet*, with its reliance on shots and reverse shots and with eye line matches to suggest judgment—a witness said something; Friday shook his head and looked at Smith offscreen; Smith shook his head and looked in return at the offscreen Friday—became an industry standard in shooting such scenes with effective economy of style.

There is no doubt that the success in the early 1950s of *Dragnet* and of its chief rival in the ratings, the comedy series *I Love Lucy*, helped shape the direction of television cop shows and sitcoms for years to come. The series also contributed to the positive portrayal of law enforcement that prevailed until such later events as the shocking images of Rodney King's beating in the early 1990s helped shake Americans' faith in the police. When Jack Webb, who had always been a loyal defender of the police, died of a heart attack on December 23, 1982, the LAPD flew its flags at half-staff.

Grant Tracey

SEE ALSO: *Bob and Ray; Cold War;* The Honeymooners*;* I Love Lucy*; King, Rodney; Webb, Jack.*

BIBLIOGRAPHY

Dunning, John. *On the Air: An Encyclopedia of Old-Time Radio.* New York: Oxford University Press, 1998.

Hayde, Michael J. *My Name's Friday: The Unauthorized but True Story of "Dragnet" and the Films of Jack Webb.* Nashville, TN: Cumberland House Publishing, 2001.

"Jack, Be Nimble!" *Time*, March 15, 1954, 47–50.

Marc, David. *Demographic Vistas: Television in American Culture.* Philadelphia: University of Pennsylvania Press, 1996.

Stark, Steven D. "Dragnet and the Policeman as Hero." In *Glued to the Set: The 60 Television Shows and Events That Made Us Who We Are Today.* New York: Free Press, 1997, 31–36.

Dragon Lady

In movies and comic strips, the Dragon Lady epitomizes the legend of the seductive, exotic, and deadly Asian woman. Although there is no evidence that an actual Dragon Lady ever existed, the character was treated as real by actress Anna May Wong in the 1931 Fu Manchu thriller *Daughter of the Dragon*. The Dragon Lady persona gained additional popularity in Milton Caniff's 1930s-era comic strip *Terry and the Pirates*. In this comic, the Dragon Lady "captivates men with her beauty then tramples them like insects when they cross her." During World War II the Dragon Lady persona became associated with an English-speaking radio announcer for Radio Tokyo, whose voice was broadcast to American soldiers. The American media dubbed her Tokyo Rose and portrayed her as an Asian Mata Hari. Rose turned out to be a naive Japanese American girl named Iva Ikuko Toguri.

Midori Takagi

SEE ALSO: *Caniff, Milton; Comics; Fu Manchu;* Terry and the Pirates*; Tokyo Rose; Wong, Anna May; World War II.*

BIBLIOGRAPHY

Cao, Lan, and Himilce Novas. *Everything You Need to Know about Asian American History.* New York: Plume, 1996.

Hodges, Graham Russell. *Anna May Wong: From Laundryman's Daughter to Hollywood Legend.* New York: Palgrave Macmillan, 2004.

Kutler, Stanley I. "Forging a Legend: The Treason of 'Tokyo Rose.'" *Wisconsin Law Review* 6 (1980): 1341–1382.

Dream Team

America's so-called Dream Team—the greatest collection of basketball talent ever assembled—rolled to a gold medal in the 1992 Olympics in Barcelona, Spain. Composed of eleven National Basketball Association (NBA) players and one collegian, the Dream Team came to be because of a 1989 agreement with the International Amateur Basketball Federation that allowed professionals to participate in the Olympics. While the U.S. team was the greatest beneficiary of the rule change, its international organization, USA Basketball, had voted against the inclusion of NBA players. As Olympic television commentator David Wallechinsky noted, concerns were expressed that financial support for women's and junior basketball programs would diminish and that one-sided games would markedly reduce the TV audience.

BUILDING THE DREAM TEAM

The American team averaged 117.3 points per game and held its opponents to 73.2 en route to a sweep of eight consecutive wins in Barcelona. The margins of victory probably would have been even greater if several U.S. players had not been held back due to injury concerns. The Dream Team featured ten players who would eventually be inducted into the Naismith Memorial Basketball Hall of Fame, including Michael Jordan, Larry Bird, Magic Johnson, Charles Barkley, Karl Malone, Patrick Ewing, David Robinson, Scottie Pippen, Clyde Drexler, and John Stockton. NBA star Christopher Mullin and Duke University's Christian Laettner also played on the team. Meanwhile, Chuck Daly of the Detroit Pistons was the head coach, while Lenny Wilkens of the Atlanta Hawks, P. J. Carlesimo of the Portland Trail Blazers, and Mike Krzyzewski of Duke served as his assistants.

The United States had come up short in the 1972 and 1988 Olympics, as well as in a subsequent series of international events. Jordan, who had recently led the Chicago Bulls to their second consecutive NBA championship, asserted prior to the Barcelona Olympics, "We've got to regain our sense of pride, our dignity. Some way—even if it's just basketball. We can at

1992 Dream Team Wins Olympic Gold. *The 1992 United States men's Olympic basketball team, nicknamed the "Dream Team," defeated its opponents by an average of almost 44 points en route to winning the gold medal.* RICHARD MACKSON/SPORTS ILLUSTRATED/GETTY IMAGE.

least show the world that *we can take control of something*." National pride aside, it was the possibility of a financial windfall that undoubtedly led the NBA to support sending its greatest players to Barcelona. Commissioner David Stern envisioned the possibility of a transoceanic league, and the NBA had already started to create an international presence by adding Lithuania's Sarunas Marciulionis, Croatia's Drazen Petrovic, Germany's Detlef Schrempf, and Yugoslavia's Vlade Divac to its team rosters.

GIANTS AMONG MEN

Off the court, the Dream Team players were treated like rock stars. On the court, opponents were often thoroughly intimidated before the first jump ball—they seemed thrilled just to be playing against the Dream Team. As the U.S. team was crushing Argentina 128–87 in an Olympic qualifier in Portland, Oregon, called the Tournament of the Americas, a dunk by Jordan resulted in wild cheering from Argentina's bench. Argentina center Hernan Montenegro declared, "I played with great happiness against the monsters." Argentina guard Marcelo Milanesio added, "When we met at the center of the court, I was very excited that it was Magic Johnson shaking my hand." After his team was shellacked 136–57 by the United States in the Tournament of the Americas, Cuba coach Miguel Gomez philosophized, "One finger cannot cover the sun." American observers also waxed poetic about the Dream Team, including Princeton coach Pete Carril, who said, "This is not a great team. This is the greatest team ever."

Despite playing under international rules—two 20-minute halves as opposed to four 12-minute quarters in the NBA, a shorter three-point line, and zone defenses—the Americans scored more than 100 points in each of their games during the Barcelona Olympics. The two closest games involved Croatia, which had Petrovic and future NBA player Toni Kukoc, but those margins of victory were both better than thirty points. The only real controversy surrounding the Dream Team's run came in its 116–48 rout of Angola in the opener, when Barkley elbowed an opponent. Afterward Jordan remarked, "Charles is Charles. He's not crazy. He just likes to push his behavior to the edge." Angola coach Victorino Cunha dismissed the issue, saying, "We know Charles Barkley. No problem. He does this ten times a year in the NBA."

ETCHED IN HISTORY

Following the Dream Team's 117–85 win over Croatia in the gold medal game, Mullin mused that "everybody [was] willing to throw egos, individual statistics, and all that other stuff out the window to prepare to be the best team ever. Nope, it won't happen again." When asked by reporters, "When will there be another Olympic team like this one?" Johnson responded, "Well, you guys won't be around, and neither will we." While Barkley led the team in scoring with an 18.0-point average, Jordan contributed 14.9 points per game and provided a tournament-high thirty-seven steals. According to *Sports Illustrated*'s Jack McCallum:

> On the most star-studded team in history, Jordan was, simply, the star stud. When Magic was on the floor running the fast break. Jordan was his finisher. When Jordan was called upon to run the offense, he did so with control and a few dazzling no-look passes. When Daly gave the ball to Scottie Pippen, Jordan acted as a

> decoy. When the U.S. needed a defensive stopper, as it did in the semifinal against Lithuania, Jordan got the call—and made life miserable for Marciulionis. And when the team need a scoring jolt, as it did against both Lithuania and Croatia, Jordan went out early and kick-started the offense.

Indeed, the Dream Team was, as Daly described it, "a majestic team." Following the 1992 Olympics, the term *Dream Team* entered the American lexicon. For example, the NBA's Miami Heat was called a "Dream Team" after stars LeBron James and Chris Bosh were signed before the 2010–2011 season to join Dwyane Wade. For many basketball fans, however, there will always be only one Dream Team: the star-studded squad that captivated the world during the 1992 Olympics.

Robert C. Cottrell

SEE ALSO: *Barkley, Charles; Basketball; Bird, Larry; Johnson, Earvin "Magic"; Jordan, Michael; National Basketball Association (NBA); National Collegiate Athletic Association (NCAA); Olympics; Pippen, Scottie; Sports Heroes;* Sports Illustrated.

BIBLIOGRAPHY

Bradley, Michael. "It's in the Bag for Now: The Future of American Basketball in Olympic Competition." *Sport* 83 (1992): 56, 58, 60, 62.

Daly, Chuck, and Alex Sachare. *America's Dream Team: The Quest for Olympic Gold.* Atlanta, GA: Turner Publications, 1992.

Deford, Frank. "Team of Dreams." *Newsweek,* July 6, 1992, 26–28.

McCallum, Jack. "Barcelona Dreamin'." *Sports Illustrated,* August 3, 1992, 22.

McCallum, Jack. *The Dream Team: The Inside Story of the 1992 U.S. Olympic Basketball Team.* Boston: Little, Brown, 1992.

Stauth, Cameron. *The Golden Boys: The Unauthorized Inside Look at the U.S. Olympic Basketball Team.* New York: Pocket Books, 1992.

Williams, Pat, and Peggy Rose Matthews. *Daly Wisdom: Life Lessons from Dream Team Coach and Hall-of-Famer Chuck Daly.* Charleston, SC: Advantage, 2010.

Witteman, Paul A. "Basketball Are They Kidding?" *Time,* July 27, 1992, 60–61.

Dreiser, Theodore *(1871–1945)*

A journalist turned novelist, Theodore Dreiser was at the forefront of the battle for social realism and sexual candor in the early twentieth-century novel, treating popular sentimental and realist subjects with a refreshing lack of moralizing. Dreiser produced a number of dense, uneven, and controversial novels about the attempts of men and women to adapt themselves to the new urban, secular order of industrial capitalism. His most popular novel, *An American Tragedy* (1925), is one of the first serious psychological studies of an American murderer.

Dreiser escaped a very poor and deeply religious upbringing through a successful career in journalism in the 1890s, publishing his first novel, *Sister Carrie,* in 1900. Although the book had been recommended by rising author Frank Norris, publisher Doubleday's management was unhappy with what it considered the immorality of the story and published it without publicity. With no advertising and reviews critical of both its moral tone and its scrappy prose, the book achieved initial sales of only nine hundred. This fiasco and Dreiser's failing marriage caused a nervous breakdown, and he returned to journalism, not publishing another novel for a decade. His second novel, *Jennie Gerhardt* (1911), began an increasingly fruitful period, though his sexual frankness and social criticism continued to hamper his success. Over the next fourteen years Dreiser published several novels, including *The Financier* (1912), *The Titan* (1914), *The Genius* (1915), and most successfully, *An American Tragedy.* This last draws from a number of real-life murder cases to tell the fictional story of Clyde Griffiths—his youth, the murder of his pregnant girlfriend, and the court case that followed. The novel was adapted for both stage and screen. Two notable screen versions include that directed by Josef von Sternberg in 1931 and the George Stevens version, *A Place in the Sun* (1951), starring Elizabeth Taylor and Montgomery Clift. After this surge of novels, Dreiser's output dropped as he became involved with various left-wing causes.

Dreiser's career grew out of the newspaper and magazine revolution of the 1880s and 1890s Thus, whereas his novels reflect many of the themes of the sentimental tradition (marked by the love of the rags-to-riches story), they are inflected by issues highlighted in the best journalism of his day (crime, disease, prostitution, vagrancy, and the violence and double-dealing behind huge wealth). Dreiser's subject matter also appears journalistic in its use of personal experience (*Sister Carrie* was based on one of his sisters) and real-life stories (*The Financier* is the first of a trilogy of novels based on Chicago financier Charles T. Yerkes, and *An American Tragedy* was largely based on the murder trial of Chester Gillette). Dreiser's novels, though criticized for their circumlocution, inversion, uncertain vocabulary, and overburdened syntax, are noteworthy for their singular level of excited detail and documented fact. This reliance on facts and details reflects a contemporary scientific methodology pursued eagerly by Dreiser who read widely on the subjects of biology, psychology, and sociology. Although Honoré de Balzac, Émile Zola, Leo Tolstoy, and Thomas Hardy were all important literary models for him, literary allusions are much less prevalent in his work than scientific ones; his interest in every minute detail of biological and sociological influences on his characters pushes the literary into the background.

Dreiser's main achievement is the characterization of his central figures. His interest in what drives Carrie Meeber or Clyde Griffiths makes the figures around them appear little more than phenomena affecting them, while these major characters themselves become little more than the drives and desires brought on by economic, genetic, and psychological circumstances. These desires were not necessarily beautiful, imaginative, or morally right, and it was this, combined with Dreiser's unflinching candor, that made his books so controversial. Dreiser simply ignored genteel aspirations and probity, logically and objectively drawing characters whose aspirations were powerful enough to lead a poor girl to become a kept woman, or a boy to kill a pregnant lover. Such desires destroy everything in their paths and do not bring happiness—certainly not the familial stability and financial security of the middle classes.

Dreiser was not the first novelist of his generation to write of the squalor, poverty, and violence of the city; both Stephen

Crane and Frank Norris had done that before him. He was, however,unique in his personal experience of poverty. This is undoubtedly a major reason he was able to capture in such detail the desire to escape poverty and to possess wealth in a society that was in a period of transformation. The tide of migration from country to city; the impersonal nature of the urban setting of factories, tenements, and department stores; the contrast of poverty and wealth; and the new culture of conspicuous consumption were all at the center of Dreiser's work. Where many of the new journalistic, realist writers around him attempted to represent the nature and effects of want, Dreiser investigated wanting, one of the central mechanisms of the twentieth century. His attempts to delineate desire are what made him interesting and influential to many writers, from F. Scott Fitzgerald to Saul Bellow. Dreiser's illustration of a less intellectualized, aspirational amorality deep within the American way of life makes him the most radical as well as the most realistic writer of his generation.

Kyle Smith

SEE ALSO: *Norris, Frank;* A Place in the Sun*; von Sternberg, Josef.*

BIBLIOGRAPHY

Gogol, Miriam, ed. *Theodore Dreiser: Beyond Naturalism.* New York: New York University Press, 1995.

Moers, Ellen. *Two Dreisers.* New York: Viking, 1969.

Pizer, Donald. *The Novels of Theodore Dreiser: A Critical Study.* Minneapolis: University of Minnesota Press, 1976.

Pizer, Donald. *Theodore Dreiser: Interviews.* Urbana: University of Illinois Press, 2004.

Salzman, Jack, ed. *Theodore Dreiser: The Critical Reception.* New York: David Lewis, 1972.

The Drifters

When Clyde McPhatter formed the Drifters in 1953, a new musical voice emerged. Combining doo-wop with gospel stylings, rhythm and blues changed. Songs such as "Money Honey" (1953) and "White Christmas" (1954), the latter second only to Bing Crosby's version, increased their popularity. McPhatter left the group in 1954, after which a series of other lead singers fronted the group until the arrival of Ben E. King in 1959. King changed the Drifters' image and sound. The baion, a Brazilian rhythm, and the addition of strings made such songs as "There Goes My Baby" (1959) a success. From 1953 to 1966 the group provided the music for a southeastern coastal dance known as the shag and proved a driving force for Atlantic Records, from which many rising musicians gained inspiration. The Drifters were inducted into the Rock and Roll Hall of Fame in 1988.

Linda Ann Martindale

SEE ALSO: *Atlantic Records; Doo-wop Music; Gospel Music; Rhythm and Blues; Rock and Roll.*

BIBLIOGRAPHY

Barnard, Stephen. *Rock: An Illustrated History.* New York: Schirmer Books, 1986.

Hirshey, Gerri. *Nowhere to Run: The Story of Soul Music.* New York: Da Capo Press, 1994.

Warner, Jay. *American Singing Groups: A History from 1940s to Today.* Milwaukee, WI: Hal Leonard Corporation, 2006.

Drive-In Theater

As early as 1928, Richard Hollingshead Jr., owner of an auto products business, was experimenting with screening films outdoors. In the driveway of his New Jersey home, he mounted a Kodak projector atop his car and played the image on a nearby screen. In time, Hollingshead refined and expanded his idea, registering his patent for a drive-in theater in 1933. In doing so, he not only re-created an American pastime, but he also contributed to American popular culture for some time to come.

Drive-in theaters, also known as ozoners, open-air operators, fresh-air exhibitors, outdoorers, ramp houses, under-the-stars emporiums, rampitoriums, and auto havens, were just that—places where people drove their cars to watch movies on a huge outdoor screen. This was a seemingly preposterous idea—people would drive to a gate, pay an admission fee, park their car on a ramp to face the movie screen, and watch the movie from the car, along with hundreds of other people. But the drive-in caught on because it tapped into America's love for both automobiles and movies; going to the drive-in became a wildly popular pastime from its inauguration in the 1930s through the 1950s.

THE GOLDEN AGE OF DRIVE-INS

The first drive-in opened on June 6, 1933, just outside Camden, New Jersey. The feature film was *Wife Beware*, a 1932 release starring Adolphe Menjou. This movie was indicative of those commonly shown at drive-ins: the films were always second rate ("B" movies like *The Blob* [1958] or *Beach Blanket Bingo* [1965]) or second run. However, people did not object. Throughout the drive-in's history, its films were always incidental to the other forms of attractions it offered its patrons.

Around 1935, Richard Hollingshead sold most of his interest in the drive-in, believing that the poor sound and visuals, the great expense of construction, the limited choice of films, and other factors (like reliance on good weather) were enough to keep investors and customers alike from embracing this new form of entertainment. But people did not mind that viewing movies outdoors was not qualitatively as "good" as their experiences watching movies at indoor theaters. Just a few years after the first New Jersey drive-in opened, there were others in Boston and Cape Cod, Massachusetts; Cleveland, Ohio; Detroit, Michigan; Galveston, Texas; Los Angeles; and Miami, Florida. By 1942 there were ninety-five drive-ins in more than twenty-seven states; Ohio had the most (eleven), and the average lot held 400 cars.

Drive-ins peaked in 1958, numbering more than 4,000. They proved to be popular attractions for many reasons. After World War II industries turned back to the manufacture of domestic products and America enjoyed a burgeoning car culture. In addition, the postwar baby boom meant that there

Drive-In Movie. *Night falls on a drive-in movie theater in Baltimore, Maryland, in 2005.* J. R. EYERMAN//TIME LIFE PICTURES/GETTY IMAGES.

were more families with more children who needed cheap forms of entertainment. Packing the family into a car and taking them to the drive-in was one way to avoid paying a babysitter, and it was also a way that a family could enjoy a collective activity "outdoors." Indeed, in the 1940s and 1950s, many owners capitalized on this idea of the drive-in being a place of family entertainment and offered features to attract more customers. Drive-ins had playgrounds; baby bottle warmers; fireworks; and concession stands that sold hamburgers, sodas, popcorn, candy, hot dogs, and other refreshments.

Although owners emphasized family activities, by the 1940s and 1950s, teenagers had taken over rows at the drive-in to engage in more private endeavors. Drive-ins became known for their "passion pits"—places where kids went to have sex, because they could not go to their parents' houses but did have access to automobiles. Therefore, families parked their cars in the front rows, dating teens sat in the middle rows, and teens having sex occupied the dark back rows. Sneaking into drive-ins was another popular teenage activity, with kids hiding in the trunk until the car was parked well away from the entrance booth in order to avoid paying the entrance fee. Teenagers from the 1960s on also used drive-ins as places to drink alcohol and smoke marijuana.

In the late 1940s drive-ins became more popular than indoor theaters. One improvement that led to this was the development of a viable in-car speaker through which to hear a movie's sound. Before the implementation of individualized speakers, drive-in owners used directional sound: three central speakers that projected the movie's soundtrack over the entire drive-in. The sound not only was distorted but also was nearly impossible for the cars in the back rows to hear. In addition, it was so loud that owners received complaints from neighbors, many of whom were unhappy about a drive-in's presence to begin with. The first in-car speakers were put into production by RCA in 1946. In the 1950s people began experimenting with transmitting movie sound over radio waves; this was not feasible until 1982, when 20 to 30 percent of drive-ins asked viewers to tune in their radios. By 1985, 70 percent of drive-ins were using this sound transmission technique.

COMPETITION LEADS TO DECLINE

The drive-in business started to stagnate in the 1960s and began its decline in the 1970s. Land prices were increasing, and drive-ins took up a lot of space that could be made more profitable with other ventures. By this time the original drive-ins were also in need of capital improvements, in which many owners chose not to invest. In addition, theaters continued to get only "B" movies or second- or third-run pictures, and the industry charged higher rental fees and required longer runs, making it extremely difficult to compete with the indoor multiplex cinemas.

The drive-ins lost most of their key audiences in the 1980s—by 1983 there were only 2,935 screens. Families could stay home and watch movies on cable television or on their video cassette recorders. The later developments of DVD players and DVRs provided even more entertainment options. When teenagers found other places to have sex and fool around, the drive-in was no longer a necessary locale for this activity. Due to gasoline shortages, many people opted for compact cars, which were not comfortable to sit in during double or triple movie features. By the 1990s there were few drive-ins left; those that remained were reminders of an American era that revered cars and freedom, with a little low-budget entertainment thrown in. Even so, in the first decade of the 2000s, about 400 remained in operation, and new ones were still being opened. Some groups of enthusiasts began to organize what were called "guerrilla drive-ins" by taking over empty lots and showing movies in an effort to bring back the nostalgic form of entertainment. As of the early 2010s, it was unclear whether such efforts would succeed in keeping the drive-in alive.

Wendy Woloson

SEE ALSO: *Automobile; "B" Movies; Baby Boomers;* The Blob; *Marijuana; Teenagers.*

BIBLIOGRAPHY

Jonas, Susan, and Marilyn Nissenson. *Going, Going, Gone: Vanishing Americana.* San Francisco: Chronicle Books, 1994.

Sanders, Don, and Susan Sanders. *The American Drive-in Movie Theater.* Osceola, WI: Motorbooks International, 1997.

Segrave, Kerry. *Drive-in Theaters: A History from Their Inception in 1933.* Jefferson, NC: McFarland, 1992.

Drudge, Matt *(1966–)*

Online journalist Matt Drudge offers news on politics and entertainment on his website, *The Drudge Report.* Launched before most Americans had even visited the Internet, *The Drudge Report* republished news stories available elsewhere, bypassing mainstream news outlets with insider reports that soon brought Drudge notoriety. His name became a household word in early 1998, when he broke the story of President Bill Clinton's involvement with White House intern Monica Lewinsky, and Drudge—an underachiever in high school—became a multimillionaire. Yet his conservative politics and his defiant attitude toward mainstream news outlets have made him many powerful enemies.

Matthew Nathan Drudge was born on October 27, 1966, in Takoma Park, Maryland, the only child of Jewish liberal Democrats. His father, Robert Drudge, was a social worker who then went on to operate the website refdesk.com, and his mother worked as a staffer for Senator Ted Kennedy. Despite his parents' divorce when he was six (he went to live with his mother), Drudge has described his as an idyllic childhood.

His first job in the world of journalism was as a paperboy for the *Washington Star,* and he fondly remembered reading the editorial page to feed an avid interest in current events. But his paper route closed along with the *Star* itself in August 1981. By then Drudge had become a gangly teenager with a bad case of acne and little interest in his studies. He graduated near the bottom of his class at Northwood High School in Silver Spring, Maryland, and did not even attempt to go to college.

The mid-1980s saw Drudge in a series of dead-end work situations, including the night shift at a 7-Eleven, a job selling *Time-Life* books over the telephone, and a stint as a sales assistant at a grocery store in New York City. (He worked for *Time-Life* alongside another future journalist of sorts, Craig Seymour, who later came to fame writing about celebrities and his experience as a stripper in the gay clubs of Washington, D.C.) Drudge moved to Los Angeles in 1989 and got a job in the gift shop at the CBS studios in Hollywood. This position gave him exposure to a wealth of TV insider gossip, and that, along with the Packard Bell computer his father bought him in 1994, set him on the path to what became his life's work.

The Drudge Report began in 1995 with an e-mail newsletter and postings to Usenet, which at the time was still a major part of the online world. His work so impressed another future conservative superstar, Andrew Breitbart, that the latter e-mailed him and asked for a job. Breitbart, who continued to work with Drudge even after launching his own highly successful sites, has referred to himself as "Matt Drudge's bitch."

Drudge moved his focus to the World Wide Web, where he soon came to prominence with stories such as his report (thanks to a tip from a stagehand) that Jerry Seinfeld had begun demanding $1 million an episode for his highly successful NBC sitcom. Greater notoriety followed in 1996, when Drudge was

Matt Drudge. *Matt Drudge is the force behind the* Drudge Report, *which began as an e-mail newsletter in the mid-1990s.* © LARRY DOWNING/SYGMA/CORBIS.

one of the first journalists to break the story that Bob Dole, Republican candidate for the presidency, had chosen Jack Kemp as his running mate.

The true turning point in Drudge's career, however, came on January 17, 1998, when he broke what came to be known as the Monica Lewinsky scandal. As Drudge reported, *Newsweek* was sitting on a story about the president's sexual involvement with the young White House intern but had refused to run it.

In the years since, Drudge (who describes himself as a conservative with populist leanings) has often infuriated detractors on the Left. During the 2004 presidential campaign, he reported on allegations by Swift Boat Veterans for Truth that Democratic candidate John Kerry had misrepresented aspects of his service in Vietnam. Four years later, *The Drudge Report* published a photo—supposedly provided by Hillary Clinton's campaign staff—of Barack Obama in Somali tribal dress. More than once, Drudge has gotten a story wrong. For example, in October 2008, he reported allegations by Ashley Todd, a volunteer for the John McCain presidential campaign, that she had been physically assaulted by a black male Obama supporter. Todd's claims turned out to be a hoax.

Drudge hosted a show on Fox News Channel in 1998 and 1999, and in the early 2000s had a radio program syndicated by Premiere Radio Networks. In 2000, with Julia Phillips, he published *Drudge Manifesto*, a quirky presentation of his views that became a best seller.

Drudge has been ridiculed—for example, by the creators of the parody website *The Drudge Retort*—and attacked. Keith Olbermann has called him "an idiot with a modem," and Michael Isikoff, author of the Lewinsky story *Newsweek* suppressed, described him as "a menace to honest, responsible journalism." In 1997 White House staffer Sidney Blumenthal launched an ultimately unsuccessful lawsuit against Drudge for a story alleging that Blumenthal was involved in spousal abuse. (Drudge had immediately retracted the story, which he said was based on bad information.) In March 2010 the sergeant-at-arms of the Democratic-controlled U.S. Senate issued a warning to staffers not to visit *The Drudge Report* because of alleged viruses on the site.

Despite attempts to discredit him, Drudge has benefited enormously from his site, which makes its money primarily through advertising sales. As of 2012 he owns two luxury properties in Miami and reportedly earns more than $1 million a year. He has never been married.

Judson Knight

SEE ALSO: *Fox News Channel; The Internet; Lewinsky, Monica;* Newsweek*; Talk Radio.*

BIBLIOGRAPHY

Drudge, Matt, and Julia Phillips. *Drudge Manifesto*. New York: New American Library, 2000.

The Drudge Report. Accessed February 2012. Available from http://www.drudgereport.com/

Gale Biography in Context. Detroit, MI: Gale, 1999.

Kinsley, Michael. "In Defense of Matt Drudge." *Time*, February 2, 1998.

Porter, Ethan. "Drudge Has Lost His Touch." *Columbia Journalism Review* 48, no. 3 (2009).

Weiss, Philip. "Watching Matt Drudge." *New York* 40, no. 31–32 (2007).

Du Bois, W. E. B. *(1868–1963)*

William Edward Burghardt "W. E. B." Du Bois was one of twentieth-century America's foremost black leaders and intellectuals. During his long life, the multitalented Du Bois worked as a sociologist, a historian, a poet, a short-story writer, a novelist, an autobiographer, and an editor—and was a champion of racial justice in each of these roles. Though his ideological outlook changed many times—through phases of Darwinism, elitism, socialism, Pan-Africanism, self-segregation, and communism—Du Bois consistently reiterated his view that the major issue of the twentieth century was "the problem of the color-line." As historian Eric Sundquist notes in *The Oxford W. E. B. Du Bois Reader*, Du Bois was born in Great Barrington, Massachusetts, in 1868, the same year the Fourteenth Amendment to the Constitution was adopted, and he spent his life attempting to make the principles, promises, and protections of this landmark political article a reality for black Americans.

A RACIAL AWAKENING

Despite the complex mixture of a racial background he summarized as "a flood of Negro blood, a strain of French, a bit of Dutch, but thank God! no 'Anglo-Saxon,'" the young Du Bois soon learned that his black ancestry assumed the greatest significance in the minds of his white schoolmates, with his darker skin placing a "vast veil" between their social worlds. An exceptional student, Du Bois enrolled in Fisk University on a scholarship in 1885. This black college, located in Nashville, Tennessee, gave him the experience of extreme southern racism and a new racial identity fostered by exposure to the region's strong sense of African American culture and community. Moved by the religious faith and "sorrow songs" he came across during his stay in Tennessee, Du Bois later used these distinctive cultural expressions to recover, highlight, and discuss the meaning of the black historical experience in *The Souls of Black Folk (1903)*—which, in turn, inspired an increased popular interest in black vernacular art forms.

After graduating from Fisk in 1888, Du Bois took a second undergraduate degree at Harvard in 1890. In 1895 he became the first African American to gain a doctoral degree from Harvard, and with the publication of his thesis in 1896, *The Suppression of the African Slave Trade to the United States, 1638–1870*, Du Bois launched successful academic and publishing careers.

After accepting an invitation from the University of Pennsylvania to conduct a study examining the condition of the black population in Philadelphia, Du Bois published *The Philadelphia Negro: A Social Study* (1899). This seminal critical survey cemented his academic reputation and was cited as an influential model by sociologist Gunnar Myrdal some forty-five years later. Between 1897 and 1910, Du Bois taught history and economics at Atlanta University. This was one of his most productive periods as a writer, and he began to advance a political program that insisted on higher education as the foundation for black racial progress. His emphasis on higher education—together with his political activity in the Niagara Movement and then as one of the founders of the National Association for the Advancement of Colored People (NAACP)—placed Du Bois in opposition to the more vocationally oriented Booker T. Washington.

ASSUMING A LEADERSHIP ROLE

Editing and directing the publication of a multivolume study of African Americans under segregation known as the Atlanta University Studies series, as well as the journal the *Horizon* from 1907 to 1910, Du Bois was gaining prominence as the self-appointed spokesperson for what he called the black community's "Talented Tenth"—"developing the Best of this race that they may guide the Mass away from the contamination and death of the Worst, in their own and other races." Du Bois enhanced his leadership position as editor of the *Crisis* from 1910 to 1934, the official organ of the NAACP that grew to have more than 100,000 subscribers by the end of World War I. In this magazine, Du Bois highlighted the indignities and atrocities of racism in the United States, including regular reports and investigations into lynchings, yet his appeal remained, for the most part, limited to the privileged, literate black middle class of the North and its white supporters.

As a scholar, a propagandist, and an organizer of the Pan-Africanist movement, Du Bois sought to unite and make sense of the apparent disparate experiences of diaspora blacks. Unlike Marcus Garvey, one of his African American political rivals of the 1920s, Du Bois did not advocate a return to Africa as the route to black American liberation. For him, Africa was more a source of common identity for blacks, and in the continent's battle against European colonial domination, he found parallels with African Americans struggling for civil rights.

INTELLECTUAL EXILE

Following his departure from the NAACP and the *Crisis* in the mid-1930s, Du Bois no longer commanded a popular audience. In this period, however, he produced some of his most significant work, returning to Atlanta University as a professor of sociology and writing *Black Reconstruction in America* (1935) and the autobiographical *Dusk of Dawn* (1940) while also founding *Phylon: The Atlanta University Review of Race and Culture* (1940). Although he briefly returned to the NAACP during World War II, his politics of self-segregation and a Marxist interpretation of history soon put him at odds again with the organization's leadership, and he was dismissed at the age of seventy-nine in 1948. Du Bois's life ended in intellectual exile from the United States. He joined the Communist Party in 1961 and moved to Ghana, where he died in 1963, the day before Martin Luther King Jr. led the long-planned Civil Rights March on Washington, D.C.

The Souls of Black Folk is perhaps Du Bois's most valuable literary legacy. Its recovery of the neglected black voices from the days of slavery, potent idea of "double-consciousness," and critique of modernity have influenced generations of black novelists (including Jean Toomer, Richard Wright, Ralph Ellison, and Alice Walker), historians, and scholars of culture and civilization.

Stephen C. Kenny

SEE ALSO: *Civil Rights Movement;* The Crisis; *Garvey, Marcus; King, Martin Luther, Jr.; Protest Groups; Walker, Alice; Wright, Richard.*

BIBLIOGRAPHY

Du Bois, W. E. B. *The Autobiography of W. E. B. Du Bois.* New York: International Publishers, 1968.

Du Bois, W. E. B. *The Souls of Black Folk.* New York: Bantam, 1989.

Gilroy, Paul. *The Black Atlantic: Modernity and Double-Consciousness.* Cambridge, MA: Harvard University Press, 1993.

Marable, Manning. *W. E. B. Du Bois: Black Radical Democrat.* Boston: Twayne, 1986.

Randolph, Ryan P. *W. E. B. Du Bois: The Fight for Civil Rights.* New York: PowerPlus Books, 2005.

Sundquist, Eric J., ed. *The Oxford W. E. B. Du Bois Reader.* New York: Oxford University Press, 1996.

Duck Soup

Though it failed at the box office upon its release, the Marx Brothers' 1933 feature *Duck Soup* is widely regarded as the comedy team's masterwork. By turns madcap, scathingly satirical, and genially surreal, the film chronicles the war fever that engulfs the mythical nation of Freedonia when Groucho becomes its dictator. Harpo and Chico play bumbling spies, with Zeppo relegated to the romantic subplot. Some critics found an antiwar subtext in the proceedings, but the brothers always denied any political agenda. Classic scenes abound, including the famous "mirror routine" and a rousing musical finale. Woody Allen paid homage to *Duck Soup*'s enduring comedic power by including scenes from it in the climax of his own classic *Hannah and Her Sisters* in 1986.

Robert E. Schnakenberg

SEE ALSO: *Allen, Woody; Marx, Groucho; The Marx Brothers.*

BIBLIOGRAPHY

Adamson, Joe. *Groucho, Harpo, Chico, and Sometimes Zeppo: A History of the Marx Brothers and a Satire on the Rest of the World.* New York: Simon & Schuster, 1973.

Seaton, George, et al. *The Marx Brothers:* Monkey Business, Duck Soup, *and* A Day at the Races. London: Faber & Faber, 1993.

The Duggar Family

The Duggar family are the stars of the TLC reality program *19 Kids and Counting.* Conservative Christians whose lifestyle reflects their fundamentalist beliefs, Jim Bob and Michelle Duggar quit using birth control while still a young married couple, and their family soon began growing at the rate of one child approximately every year and a half. They and their children, all of whose names begin with *J,* appeared on a number of Discovery Health and TLC programs from 2004 on. In 2008 they got their own show, *17 Kids and Counting.* Twice renamed to reflect the growth of the burgeoning clan, the program began its ninth season in the fall of 2012.

James Robert Duggar was born in Springdale, Arkansas, on July 18, 1965, the son of entrepreneur Jimmy Lee and homemaker Mary Duggar. Jimmy Lee passed away in 2009, and his funeral was the subject of a poignant episode from the show's second season. Mary makes regular appearances on the show, as do Jim Bob's older sister and only sibling, Deanna, and her daughter Amy. Michelle Annette Ruark was born on September

13, 1966, in Ohio, the youngest of five sisters and one brother. Her mother, Ethel, died in 1991, but her father, Garrett Floyde Ruark, appeared on one episode of the TV series before his death in 2010.

The couple met after Michelle converted to Christianity and received a follow-up visit from two church members, one of whom was Jim Bob. They were married on July 21, 1984. Initially Michelle used birth control pills, then stopped when they were ready to start a family. After the birth of Joshua in February 1988, she went back on the pill but got pregnant again and suffered a miscarriage. The couple then decided to quit birth control entirely because, as they later explained, they wanted God to determine how many children they would have. The result is a family that includes two sets of fraternal twins, for a total of ten boys and nine girls. In raising them, the Duggars apply a buddy system whereby each of the older children is assigned responsibility for one of the younger ones.

Jim Bob, who served in the Arkansas state legislature from 1999 to 2003, is a real estate agent who derives his primary income from property rentals. The family lives free of debt, a fact Jim Bob credits to the influence of the Institute in Basic Life Principles (IBLP), an extremely conservative Christian fundamentalist group. The Duggars also apply the teachings of the IBLP in the raising of their family. The children dress modestly, and teenagers are not allowed to date; rather, they practice chaperoned courtship, and physical contact with the opposite sex is forbidden prior to marriage. Such was the case with Josh, whose courtship of Anna Keller figured heavily in the first season.

Josh and Anna married in September 2008 and as of February 2012 have two children, both of whose names begin with *M*. In November 2011, Michelle announced that she was pregnant with another child, but miscarried the following month. The unborn girl was named Jubilee Shalom.

Judson Knight

SEE ALSO: *Celebrity; Fundamentalism; The Pill; Reality Television; Television.*

BIBLIOGRAPHY

Duggar, Michelle, and Jim Bob Duggar. *The Duggars: 20 and Counting! Raising One of America's Largest Families: How They Do It.* New York: Howard Books, 2008.

Duggar, Michelle, and Jim Bob Duggar. *A Love That Multiplies: An Up-Close View of How They Make It Work.* New York: Howard Books, 2011.

The Duggar Family. Accessed 16 May 2012. Available from http://www.duggarfamily.com

"Jim Bob Duggar." *Gale Biography in Context.* Detroit, MI: Gale, 2011.

"Michelle Duggar." *Gale Biography in Context.* Detroit, MI: Gale, 2011.

"19 Kids & Counting." TLC. Accessed 16 May 2012. Available from http://tlc.howstuffworks.com/tv/19-kids-and-counting

Dukes of Hazzard

The Dukes of Hazzard television show, airing on CBS from 1979 to 1985, blended down-home charm, handsome men, beautiful women, rip-roaring car chases, and the simple message of good triumphing over evil; this successful combination made the program a ratings success and a long-standing campy cult favorite. The Dukes were country cousins Bo, Luke, and Daisy Duke, who lived in backwoods Hazzard County on their Uncle Jesse's farm. The formula story line usually involved the Dukes versus the town's gluttonous bigwig, Boss Hogg, and his lackey, Sheriff Rosco P. Coltrane. Episodes were liberally punctuated with raucous car chases in the Dukes' orange 1969 Dodge Charger, the "General Lee," and Daisy's trademark short shorts inspired a 1993 hit rap song, "Dazzey Duks," which led to the term's use as a synonym for such apparel. The cast reunited for a television movie on CBS in 1997.

In 2005 Warner Brothers produced a feature film adaptation of the television show, starring Johnny Knoxville (of MTV's *Jackass* fame) as Luke and singer Jessica Simpson as Daisy. Geared toward a young-adult audience, *The Dukes of Hazzard* is a raunchier, highly sexualized interpretation of the original series that drew the ire of conservative groups; critics; and even an original cast member, who called the film "a sleazy insult" to the family-oriented TV show. Despite being almost universally panned by reviewers, the film debuted at number one in box-office sales. A prequel, *The Dukes of Hazzard: The Beginning* was released directly to video in 2007.

Geri Speace

SEE ALSO: *Celebrity; Hollywood; Made-for-Television Movies; MTV; Simpson, Jessica; Television.*

BIBLIOGRAPHY

Baldwin, Kristen. "Bringing up Daisy: Bach Puts up Her *Dukes*." *Entertainment Weekly*, April 25, 1997, 54.

Bark, Ed. "*Seinfeld, Dukes*, Yada, Yada, Yada." *Dallas Morning News*, April 24, 1997, sec. 1.

Bates, Billie Rae. *Them Dukes! Them Dukes!: A Guide to TV's "The Dukes of Hazzard."* North Charleston, SC: Booksurge, 2006.

Graham, Jefferson. "The *Dukes* Ride High Again in Nashville Network Reruns." *USA Today*, August 14, 1996.

Hofstede, David. *"The Dukes of Hazzard": The Unofficial Companion.* Los Angeles: Renaissance Books, 1998.

Werts, Diane. "Hazzard-ous Material." *Newsday*, April 20, 1997.

Duncan, Isadora *(1877–1927)*

Isadora Duncan, the great American icon of dance, rose to prominence early in the twentieth century and met a tragic death at age fifty. She was ahead of her time in her artistic ideals, modes of physical expression, and controversial private life. Though greatly admired by many, she also became an object of scorn and derision, mocked for her uninhibited approach to her work and pilloried for her scandalous love affairs and "bohemian" associations and lifestyle. Ironically, Duncan's art has always been more highly valued abroad than in her native land, but her cultural influence in America was nevertheless considerable. The development of the modern dance form as exemplified by Martha Graham and her contemporaries and successors owed much to Duncan's unshakable belief in the power of female self-expression.

INTO THE ARTS

Angela Isadora Duncan was born in San Francisco, the daughter of poor but liberal, art-loving parents who gave relatively free rein to their children. Duncan and her siblings became involved with movement and dance early on and taught the waltz and the mazurka to their friends. Meanwhile, Duncan attended sessions in gymnastics, a vigorous and increasingly fashionable form of exercise that was free of the constraints of corsets or heavy clothing. This contrast with the rigidly formal balletic style that she and her family saw on the stages of local theaters was marked, and it appealed to her. Duncan was still in her teens when she and her sister Elisabeth were listed in a San Francisco directory as teachers of dance, an occupation in which their brothers soon joined them. The Duncans loved to perform, and soon she was part of a small family variety show touring California.

It did not take Duncan long to combine her love of expressive movement with the relative freedom offered to the female body by gymnastics. François Delsarte's movement vocabulary, which sought exact expressions of emotions and inner states through physical actions, was much in fashion during the 1880s, and Duncan's later dances showed this influence in her use of a trained body, able to single out and intensify a whole-body expression. Another influence from her early years could be traced to the 1893 World's Columbian Exposition in Chicago. There, the Art Nouveau displays made a strong impression on her imagination, and her dances later reflected the organic lines and swirls that characterized Art Nouveau design.

A NEW STYLE OF DANCE

After two years with a touring company and many excursions into acting, singing, and dancing, Duncan became bored with a theatrical environment that did not allow for the expression of her individuality. She began to develop her own style and work on a dance repertoire, and in 1899 she gave a solo performance in New York in which she danced to poetry. Her bare arms and legs caused some ladies to leave the auditorium, but those people who remained were entranced by the classical purity of her art. Duncan had found her way out of the "low art" of club and theater dance to a new high form of dancing, whose form was influenced by Greek statues, classical music, and poetry and whose physical disciplines were rooted in calisthenics. Her favorite poet, Walt Whitman, inspired her to use her body as the instrument of a new poetry.

Later in 1899, declaring the dedication of her life to art and beauty, Duncan embarked on a world journey, taking her style of dance to the sophisticated centers of London, Paris, Berlin, and Moscow. She caused a sensation wherever she went and became an inspiration to poets, musicians, and painters, taking a succession of lovers from among their ranks. One of her most famous liaisons was with the famed English stage designer of the time, Gordon Craig, and she married Russian poet Esenin (Yesenin).

In performance, Duncan was a euphoric dancer of sensual dreams. A freethinking woman and an artistic visionary, she focused on the concerns of her time and translated them into movement, deserting the relatively static displays of the period for generous, sensitive dances in which she brought the accompanying music to three-dimensional life. To music that ranged from Schubert to Wagner to Chopin, she filled the stage, her voluptuous body dressed in a Greek-style tunic or veils and expressing her feelings and emotions through movement. The influence of this style, while considerable, was concealed within the images of free, gracious, sensuous, and powerful dancing that mesmerized her audience through its simplicity—the Duncan approach could not be studied through preserved step patterns, finished dances, or her writings.

Parallel with her position as an exponent of a new form of dance, Duncan became an early symbol of personal women's liberation and of general political freedom. Duncan's writings attacked the constraints imposed on women, and she exercised no limitations in the conduct of her permissive sexual life. She even danced while pregnant. Although Duncan advocated the equality of both men and women in a new morality, she did not perceive her own work as erotic—her freedom was the freedom of the naked Greeks. Her audiences appreciated her in different ways, some for her purity of expression, others undoubtedly with prurient interest as they waited (successfully) for her breasts to fall out of her loose costume. It was not only gender politics that excited her—she saw communism as a way forward and offered her services to the Russian republic.

A TRAGIC ENDING

After a wandering life filled with ideas, achievements, personal tragedies such as the death of her children, many men, and few places to call home, Duncan died in a horrible yet appropriately flamboyant way. Her trademark flowing silk scarf became entangled in the wheels of a Bugatti sports car, causing her spine to be fatally broken.

The schools Duncan founded did not do very well, and few of her adopted daughters took on the mantle of teaching the next generation. Ballet masters dismissed her dances of free expression for their lack of technique—these people viewed Duncan as a mere amateur. Her writings were revived in the back-to-nature days of the 1970s, though they had little sustained influence on the further development of modern dance. Nevertheless, her powerful, free, and beautiful image has stayed with dancers all over the world. Duncan is cemented as one of the great feminine myths of the twentieth century. In fact, she was played by Vanessa Redgrave in Karel Reisz's 1968 film, *The Loves of Isadora* (a.k.a. *Isadora*).

Petra Kuppers

SEE ALSO: *Graham, Martha; Modern Dance.*

BIBLIOGRAPHY

Daly, Ann. *Done into Dance. Isadora Duncan in America.* Bloomington: Indiana University Press, 1995.

Duncan, Isadora. *The Art of Dance*, ed. Sheldon Cheney. New York: Theatre Arts Books, 1977.

Isadora, Rachel. *Isadora Dances.* New York: Viking, 1998.

Dungeons and Dragons

Dungeons and Dragons, a fantasy role-playing game created by Gary Gygax and Dave Arneson, was first published in 1974 by their company, Tactical Studies Rules (TSR). Affectionately known by its players as D&D, it is a game of imagination, strategy, and tactics. Available in more than twelve languages and sold in fifty countries, D&D has been played by millions of people around the world. Its success led to the creation of a billion-dollar, role-playing game industry in the United States.

To play D&D one player assumes the role of Dungeon Master (DM). This person sets up the adventure, narrates the action, controls the monsters and the enemies, and serves as a type of referee, ensuring that all players adhere to the rules. The other players create characters for themselves based on a variety of traits; strength, intelligence, and endurance are three key qualities. The level of each trait that a character possesses is determined by a roll of dice before the game starts. Players then select a role for their character, such as thief, assassin, fighter, or cleric, and they choose the character's race, such as human, elf, or dwarf. The players then embark on adventures as their characters, interacting with each other in the setting created by the DM. They may find themselves fighting battles, stealing treasure, or outwitting monsters. The game can be played with varying degrees of complexity, depending on the experience of the players and the DM.

D&D was extremely successful. TSR sold all 1,000 games it first produced within a year of the game's debut. D&D also turned out to be very controversial. One game can take hours, days, or sometimes even weeks to finish. Tales arose of promising college students flunking out of school because they spent all their time playing D&D. Other criticisms were even harsher. Many people accused it of instilling violence in the minds of the players; others said it produced suicidal tendencies, especially when a player overidentified with a character who was killed during a game. Organizations and religious groups accused the game of being Satanic because it sometimes dealt with demons and conjuring devils. Objections to D&D eventually spawned a group known as BADD (Bothered about Dungeons and Dragons), founded by a woman who claimed that her child killed himself because of the game.

The game endured more bad publicity when the television movie *Mazes and Monsters* (1982), starring Tom Hanks, came out. The movie is about D&D players who take their role-playing too seriously and start acting out their campaigns in the tunnels and sewers of their college. Proponents of the game fought back, arguing that a game alone could not be the main cause of any psychological problems certain players were exhibiting. Advocates emphasized that the game helped stimulate imagination and problem-solving skills. Others claimed it helped people vent violent feelings through imaginary play instead of acting such feelings out. Despite the positive support of the game, many parents were still concerned and did not want their children playing it. Although TSR generated its own positive publicity for the game, it did tone down some of its user manuals and game-based fiction, especially the parts that dealt with demons and conjuring.

To capitalize on the popularity of D&D and to assist players in playing the game, D&D's publisher, which became TSR Hobbies, Inc., in 1975, also published books and magazines about the game. The books *Monster Manual* (1977), published in later years as *Monstrous Manual*; *The Player's Handbook* (1978); and *Dungeon Master Guide* (1979) became known as the "core rule books," even though they are not required in order to play the game. The *Dragon* magazine, which debuted in 1976, and *Dungeon Adventures* magazine, first published in 1986, were still producing new issues as of early 2012. To keep players interested and challenged, Wizards of the Coast, which acquired TSR Hobbies in 1997, also released new versions and editions of the game over the years. The second edition was published in 1989, the third appeared in 2000, and a fourth version was released in 2008. Subsequent editions of the core rule books have also been published.

D&D has appeared on television and in movie theaters with limited success. In 1983 it appeared on Saturday mornings as an animated series for kids, called *Dungeons and Dragons*. It lasted for twenty-seven episodes over three seasons, and reruns continued to air until 1990. A much-anticipated movie called *Dungeons & Dragons*, starring Jeremy Irons, was released in 2000, but fans and critics alike were disappointed in its quality. Despite the poor reception to the movie, a sequel, *Dungeons & Dragons: Wrath of the Dragon God* appeared in 2005, which aired on television, but it did not do well either.

While D&D was not well received on-screen, another form of D&D entertainment has been extremely successful—competitive game playing. Every year die-hard D&D players participate in the Dungeons and Dragons tournament at Gen Con, the largest annual adventure, fantasy, and sci-fi gaming convention for consumers. Players compete as teams in rounds of play, and prizes are D&D products. The convention, which premiered in 1976 and is hosted by TSR Hobbies, is a four-day event that enjoyed record-breaking attendance in 2011 with more than 119,000 attendees. Gen Con, which has an agreement with Indianapolis, Indiana, to hold its conventions there through 2020, is evidence of the continuing success of the role-playing game industry, an industry spawned by the creation of Dungeons and Dragons.

P. Andrew Miller

SEE ALSO: *Board Games; Hanks, Tom; Leisure Time; Saturday Morning Cartoons; Television.*

BIBLIOGRAPHY

Advanced Dungeons and Dragons Players Handbook, 2nd ed. Lake Geneva, WI: TSR, 1989.

Martin, Daniel, and Gary Alan Fine. "Satanic Cults, Satanic Play: Is 'Dungeons and Dragons' a Breeding Ground for the Devil?" In *The Satanism Scare*, eds. James T. Richardson, Joel Best, and David G. Bromley. New York: Aldine De Gruyter, 1991.

Dunkin' Donuts

Associated with the blue-collar coffee break, Dunkin' Donuts catered to Americans' desire for a strong cup of coffee and a sweet treat long before Starbucks coffee shops first started selling fancy pastries and gourmet coffee. Started in 1950, Dunkin' Donuts was ranked by *Entrepreneur* and *Franchise Times* magazines as one of the top franchises of 1998, when it was operating more than 3,700 stores in twenty-one countries worldwide. In addition to coffee and doughnuts, the retail chain, with its ubiquitous pink-and-orange signs, sells muffins, bagels, and other bakery products.

Founder William Rosenberg developed the chain after World War II from a string of canteen trucks into the world's largest chain of coffee and doughnut shops in the 1990s. In 1988 he turned the business over to his son Robert, who had managed doughnut shops during summer breaks from Harvard

Business School. In 1989 Allied Domecq PLC, a British-based food and beverage conglomerate, acquired Dunkin' Donuts. Allied Domecq sold the chain, together with Baskin-Robbins, to a private equity group in 2006, and in 2011 Dunkin' Brands—which became the parent company of Dunkin' Donuts and Baskin-Robbins—was formed by raising capital in an initial public offering of stock. In 2010 Dunkin' Donuts had 9,760 locations in thirty-one countries and earned $6 billion in annual sales.

Courtney Bennett

SEE ALSO: *Bagels; Coffee; Diners; Ice Cream Cone; Starbucks.*

BIBLIOGRAPHY

Allen, Robin Lee. "It's Time to Leave the Donuts: Dunkin's Rosenberg Retires." *Nation's Restaurant News*, June 29, 1998.

Rosenberg, William, and Jessica Keener. *Time to Make the Donuts: The Founder of Dunkin' Donuts Shares an American Journey*. New York: Lebhar-Friedman Books, 2001.

Dunne, Irene *(1898–1990)*

Dubbed "The First Lady of Hollywood" for her charm, sweetness, resourcefulness, and dignity, Irene Dunne gave movie audiences a romantic escape from the harsh realities of the Great Depression. Before entering films in 1930, the Kentucky-born Dunne carved out a successful career on Broadway. She famously starred as Magnolia Hawks in *Show Boat* and reprised the role in the film version of the musical in 1936.

Dunne was in the first rank of sympathetic screen heroines throughout the 1930s. She suffered gracefully through several sentimental and sometimes tragic love stories, including *Back Street* (1932), *Magnificent Obsession* (1935), and *Love Affair* (1939). In addition, she displayed an exceptional aptitude for comedy in such films as *Theodora Goes Wild* (1936) and *The Awful Truth* (1937). Dunne received her fifth Oscar nomination for *I Remember Mama* (1948), which marked her last big success. After retiring from movies in the early 1950s, she devoted herself to civic, philanthropic, and political causes. Beyond her accomplishments in film and on the stage, she was a prolific radio and television performer. In 1985 she was given a lifetime achievement award by the Kennedy Center Honors for her work in the performing arts.

Robyn Karney

SEE ALSO: *Broadway; The Great Depression; Hollywood; The Musical; Radio;* Show Boat; *Television.*

BIBLIOGRAPHY

Gehring, Wes D. *Irene Dunne: First Lady of Hollywood*. Lanham, MD: Scarecrow Press, 2003.

Schultz, Margie. *Irene Dunne: A Bio-Bibliography*. New York: Greenwood Press, 1991.

Thomson, David. *A Biographical Dictionary of Film*. New York: Alfred A. Knopf, 1994.

Durán, Roberto *(1951–)*

Roberto "Manos de Piedra" (Stone Hands) Durán is one of the few boxers in history to win world boxing titles in four different weight divisions—lightweight, welterweight, junior middleweight, and middleweight. Born in a poverty-stricken barrio of Panama on June 16, 1951, Durán only received a third-grade education, after which he became a "street kid," making his living selling newspapers, shining shoes, committing petty theft, and doing whatever else he could to earn some money for his mother and eight siblings. Clearly one of the most talented boxers to enter the ring, Durán is also well known for his contributions to the poor and his loyalty to family and friends.

Durán eventually followed an older brother into boxing and turned professional at the age of sixteen. A wealthy ex-athlete, Carlos Eleta, befriended Durán and arranged for his training with one of the best tacticians in American boxing, Ray Arcel, who taught Durán to become ambidextrous in the ring. Arcel also hired Freddie Brown, a trainer for world-champion boxers including Rocky Marciano, to work with Durán.

All of the attention paid off in 1972, when Durán won his first title as a lightweight against Ken Buchanan. Durán defended his title eleven times and won seventy of his first seventy-one fights. He reigned as a national hero in Panama, where he fed the poor, gave to numerous charitable causes, and was more than generous to his family. He made sure, in addition, to employ residents from his old barrio on his estate and in his various enterprises.

In 1975 the most famous (or infamous) promoter in the fight game—Don King—took on Durán. Durán's appetite for food forced him to move up in the weight divisions, as did the larger prizes that were offered through the assistance of King. One of the highlights of Durán's career was his victory over one of the greatest boxers of all time, Sugar Ray Leonard, in 1980 for the WBC (World Boxing Council) welterweight championship.

After this pinnacle of success, Durán gorged himself and could not control his weight before his rematch with Leonard; he trained in a rubber corset and took diuretics before the weigh-in, but he soon stuffed himself with steaks and, by the time of the match, was too bloated and exhausted from the desperate training to put up a credible fight. He walked out of the ring in the eighth round, exclaiming a now infamous phrase: "No más . . . no peleo más" (No more . . . I don't want to fight anymore). Durán explained to the press that he had stomach cramps, but his reputation was sullied in the world sports press and among late-night television hosts, who satirized his surrender mercilessly. Durán, nevertheless, had earned $3 million for the fight, but he also lost Brown and Arcel from his team. In Panama, he was shunned, and all of his acts of charity and goodwill were quickly forgotten.

In 1983 Durán made a comeback by winning the junior middleweight title from Davey Moore at Madison Square Garden, but soon after he lost a round of bouts. He came back once again to win the WBC middleweight title in 1989, after twenty-two years in the ring. Durán continued to fight into his forties. He was involved in car crash in 2001, suffering a collapsed lung and other injuries that caused him to retire from the sport. In 2006 he was inducted into the World Boxing Hall of Fame.

Nicolás Kanellos

SEE ALSO: *Boxing; Leonard, Sugar Ray; Marciano, Rocky; Sports Heroes.*

BIBLIOGRAPHY

Giudice, Christian. *Hands of Stone: The Life and Legend of Roberto Duran.* Wrea Green, UK: Milo Books, 2009.

Tardiff, Joseph C., and L. Mpho Mabunda, eds. *Dictionary of Hispanic Biography.* Detroit, MI: Gale, 1996.

Durbin, Deanna *(1921–)*

Deanna Durbin's overnight rise to fame as an adolescent movie star began with *Three Smart Girls* (1936) and *One Hundred Men and a Girl* (1937). Her box-office success was widely credited with saving Universal Studios from bankruptcy. Fans and critics alike were taken by her mature soprano voice and her wholesome yet feisty characters. Born Edna Mae Durbin in Winnipeg, Canada, she was dubbed "America's Kid Sister" and in 1939 was awarded a miniature Oscar. Although Durbin was praised for her successful transition to adult roles in the 1940s, her popularity declined. In 1948 she permanently traded her thirteen-year, twenty-one-film career for a private life in France with her third husband, French filmmaker Charles David, and their family.

Kelly Schrum

SEE ALSO: *Academy Awards; Child Stars; Movie Stars.*

BIBLIOGRAPHY

Nash, Ilana. *American Sweethearts: Teenage Girls in Twentieth-Century Popular Culture* Bloomington: Indiana University Press, 2006.

Scheiner, Georganne. "The Deanna Durbin Devotees: Fan Clubs and Spectatorship." In *Generations of Youth: Youth Cultures and History in Twentieth-Century America*, ed. Joe Austin and Michael Nevin Willard. New York: New York University Press, 1998.

Shipman, David. "Nostalgia: Deanna Durbin." *Film and Filming*, December 1983, 24–27.

Durocher, Leo *(1905–1991)*

Throughout his colorful and often contentious baseball career, Leo Durocher often found himself at the center of the game's most exciting events. His major-league career spanned nearly fifty years and saw him serve as player, manager, coach, and television commentator. But it was his tenure as a manager in New York City from 1941 to 1955 that made him a national sports celebrity and placed him at the heart of so many significant baseball events. In *The Era, 1947–1957*, baseball writer Roger Kahn fondly remembers that era "when the Yankees, Giants, and Dodgers ruled the world." On the field, Durocher managed both the Brooklyn Dodgers and the New York Giants; was directly involved in the controversy surrounding the game's first black player, Jackie Robinson; and was a participant in what many sportswriters consider the greatest game in baseball history—the last game of the 1951 playoff series between the Giants and the Dodgers.

Born in the industrial slums of West Springfield, Massachusetts, the young Durocher worked in factories and hustled pool to make money. He was suspended from high school for slapping a teacher and never returned. He began playing baseball on a railroad company team and made it to the major leagues in 1925. His playing career was mediocre at best, and his hitting was weak, but his flashy and acrobatic fielding was enough to make him an All-Star in 1936, 1938, and 1940.

LIFE IN THE MAJORS

Durocher played for two of the most celebrated teams of the early twentieth century: In 1928 he spent his first full season in the major leagues with the legendary New York Yankees, led by Babe Ruth, and in 1934 he captained the St. Louis Cardinals, a team better known as the "Gas House Gang." Those boisterous Cardinals were a hell-raising group that played hard on and off the field. Durocher and the Cardinals won the 1934 World Series.

In 1939 Durocher became player-manager for the Brooklyn Dodgers. He helped the Dodgers to a National League pennant in 1941 and, in what was perhaps his finest moment in baseball, quashed a 1947 rebellion by some Dodgers players protesting the presence of Jackie Robinson on the team. During spring

Chicago Cubs Manager Leo Durocher. *Chicago Cubs manager Leo Durocher walks back to the dugout after arguing with an umpire in 1970.* FOCUS ON SPORT/GETTY IMAGES.

training, Durocher discovered that several players were circulating a petition vowing not to play on the same team as Robinson. Durocher called the team together and told them that Robinson was a great player and would help them to victory. He declared:

> He's only the first, boys, only the first! There are many more colored ballplayers coming right behind him and they're hungry, boys. They're scratching and diving. Unless you wake up, these colored ballplayers are gonna run you right out of the park. I don't want to see your petition, I don't want to hear anything else. This meeting is over.

But he never had the opportunity to manage Robinson. A controversial figure, Durocher was suspended by the baseball commissioner for the entire 1947 season on the vague charge of "moral turpitude." He had been under suspicion for being too friendly with New York gamblers and other shady characters, such as mobster Bugsy Siegel, and he had married movie actress Laraine Day in Mexico before her California divorce was final. Already a twice-divorced Catholic, Durocher had made enemies of powerful Roman Catholic Church officials and politicians in Brooklyn. Thus, public pressure, and the threat of Catholic youth organizations being kept away from the ballpark, forced his year-long sabbatical.

When he returned in 1948, the Dodgers faltered and he was fired early in the season. To the amazement of New York fans, however, he was immediately hired as manager of the Dodgers' cross-town rival, the New York Giants. And he led the Giants when they faced off against his former team in the legendary playoff game on August, 12, 1951. The Giants, who had trailed the first-place Dodgers by thirteen games, tied their rivals by season's end and forced a three-game playoff. In game three, with the Dodgers leading 4–1 in the final inning, Bobby Thomson hit a dramatic home run to win the pennant for the Durocher-led Giants. Durocher took the team to one more World Series, winning the 1954 contest, but after these successes, the Giants finished a weak third in 1955 and he was fired at the end of the season.

LEAVING NEW YORK

After working as a television commentator and coaching for several years with the Los Angeles Dodgers, Durocher returned to manage the Chicago Cubs in 1966. The Cubs had been one of the worst teams in baseball for nearly three decades, but Durocher helped turn them into winners—almost. In 1969 his Cubs held a nine-and-a-half-game lead in early August, but they collapsed in the last two months of the season and lost the National League pennant to the New York Mets. Durocher was criticized for not resting his players during the humid days of summer. He left the Cubs in 1972 and managed one more season with the Houston Astros before retiring.

Durocher remains among the all-time leaders in games managed (3,740) and games won (2,010). In addition, he is the only baseball player cited in Bartlett's Quotations. His quote "Nice guys finish last" is also the title of his autobiography, which he wrote after leaving baseball. Durocher first uttered the words in 1947, describing his opinion of then Giants manager Mel Ott, whose team had been underachieving during the season. "Leo the Lip," as the irascible Durocher was called, maintained that Ott and most of the Giants players were nice guys, but they would never be winners because nice guys finish last.

David E. Woodard

SEE ALSO: *Baseball; The Brooklyn Dodgers; The Chicago Cubs; The New York Mets; Robinson, Jackie; Siegel, Bugsy; Sports Heroes; Thomson, Bobby; World Series.*

BIBLIOGRAPHY

Durocher, Leo, and Ed Linn. *Nice Guys Finish Last.* Chicago: University of Chicago Press, 2009.

Hynd, Noel. *The Giants of Polo Grounds: The Glorious Times of Baseball's New York Giants.* New York: Doubleday, 1988.

Kahn, Roger. *The Era, 1947–1957: When the Yankees, the Giants, and the Dodgers Ruled the World.* New York: Ticknor & Fields, 1993.

Neft, David, and Richard Cohen, eds. *The Sports Encyclopedia: Baseball,* 16th ed. New York: St. Martin's Griffin, 1996.

Shatzkin, Mike, ed. *The Ballplayers: Baseball's Ultimate Biographical Reference.* New York: Arbor House, William Morrow, 1990.

Thorn, John; Pete Palmer; and David Reuther, eds. *Total Baseball,* 2nd ed. New York: Warner Books, 1991.

Duvall, Robert *(1931–)*

Veteran American actor Robert Duvall has been an integral part of a large portion of Hollywood cinema throughout his lengthy career, thanks to his ability to metamorphose fully into each character he plays. He is also a skilled director, producer, screenwriter, singer, and songwriter. His film debut came in *To Kill a Mockingbird* (1962), in which he played the troubled recluse Boo Radley. In the 1970s he played attorney Tom Hagen in *The Godfather* (1972) and *The Godfather, Part II* (1974). One of his most memorable roles is as Colonel Kilgore in the 1979 Francis Ford Coppola film *Apocalypse Now,* in which he uttered the classic line, "I love the smell of napalm in the morning."

Duvall won an Academy Award for Best Actor for his turn as a country singer in 1983's *Tender Mercies,* for which he wrote and performed some of the songs. One of his favorite roles was Texas Ranger Gus McCrae in the television miniseries *Lonesome Dove* (1989), for which he received an Emmy nomination. He was also nominated for playing the lead in the HBO movie *Stalin* (1992). In 1997 Duvall won critical plaudits for *The Apostle,* a pet project that was a long time coming. He wrote, directed, starred in, and funded the picture about a flawed southern minister. In 2005 President George W. Bush awarded Duvall a National Medal of Arts.

Geri Speace

SEE ALSO: *Academy Awards;* Apocalypse Now*; Cable TV; Country Music; Emmy Awards;* The Godfather*; Hollywood; Made-for-Television Movies; Movie Stars;* To Kill a Mockingbird.

BIBLIOGRAPHY

Duvall, Robert. "The *Apostle* Speaks." *Newsweek,* April 13, 1998, 60.

Moritz, Charles, ed. *Current Biography Yearbook 1977*. New York: H.W. Wilson, 1977.

DVRs

First introduced in 1999, the digital video recorder, or DVR, revolutionized television viewing. More flexible than its predecessor, the tape-driven videocassette recorder (VCR), DVRs offered a new range of options, including the ability to pause and then resume viewing of programs while they aired, without missing any part of the shows; to record programs without commercials; and to have a menu of prerecorded programs available. The new technology resulted in changes in viewing habits which, in turn, resulted in advertisers changing their marketing strategies in order to reach the viewing audience.

A DVR is essentially a hard drive connected to a television and operated via a remote control and an on-screen menu. It is also typically connected to the Internet so that it can obtain program listings, allowing the user to select television shows to record for the upcoming two weeks. The DVR records a program when it is broadcast and then lists it in a menu. Users can then watch the recorded programs at any time. Because of the convenience of DVRs, fewer viewers watch shows on the day and time they actually air on television, a phenomenon known as time shifting.

Before DVRs, people used VCRs to record televisions shows. While the purpose of the DVR and VCR is the same, there are important differences. Unlike VCRs, most DVRs automatically record the program currently being watched on the television set, even if the viewer has not specifically chosen to record the show. This allows viewers to pause any show for up to half an hour. Viewers can also "rewind" the show. Most DVRs offer search features, ways for users to rate shows and receive viewing suggestions, and other more personalized features than VCRs.

One of the more popular features of the DVR is the ability to skip commercials in recorded shows. Whereas a VCR user could fast forward through the commercials of a recorded show (an option also available to DVR users), many DVRs can also be programmed to jump forward in a recording for the length of a typical commercial, making it easier to avoid seeing commercials at all.

By 2011 almost half of U.S. households owned DVRs. As DVR use increased, the ability to avoid commercials made advertisers nervous. This contributed to the rapid increase in product placement in both television and film throughout the early 2000s. Many car companies began sponsoring television shows. In the popular forensic detective show *Bones*, for example, the characters drive to crime scenes discussing the features of their new cars, essentially making every episode a minicommercial for their sponsor, Toyota. In addition, the use of TV "bugs," small logos or ads in the bottom quarter of the viewing screen, has increased.

Advertisers also had to develop new strategies to address time shifting. Because more and more viewers were watching shows whenever it suited their schedule rather than when shows actually aired on television, time-sensitive advertising was affected. This phenomenon caused advertisers to use other ways to reach DVR users, including placing ads in the DVR menus themselves or enabling pop ups when a user fast forwards through a recorded commercial.

Kim Keeline

SEE ALSO: *Television; TiVo; Videos.*

BIBLIOGRAPHY

McMillan, Graeme. "Only One-Third of TV-Watching in the U.S. Is Realtime." *Time*, January 11, 2012.

Miller, Paul. "Commercial Skipping to Cost $8 Billion in TV Ads This Year?" Engadget.com. Accessed May 23, 2012. Available from http://www.engadget.com/2006/05/05/commercial-skipping-to-cost-8-billion-in-tv-ads-this-year/

Rock, Margaret. "Live TV Viewing Declines as Mobile Video Takes Off." Mobiledia.com. Accessed May 23, 2012. Available from http://www.mobiledia.com/news/124050.html

Schaeffler, Jimmy. *Digital Video Recorders: DVRs Changing TV and Advertising Forever*. Burlington, MA: Focal Press, 2009.

Strickland, Jonathan, and James Bickers. "How DVR Works." Howstuffworks.com. Accessed May 23, 2012. Available from http://electronics.howstuffworks.com/dvr.htm

Trombino, Stacy. "Watching the TiVo Effect." *Bloomsberg Business Week*, March 2, 2006.

Dyer, Wayne *(1940–)*

Charismatic and camera-friendly, Wayne Dyer became well known after the publication of his first best-selling book, *Your Erroneous Zones*, in 1976. Since then, he has been a proponent of such typical New Age concepts as "living in the moment" and making "choices that bring us to a higher awareness," as he told a reporter for the *St. Petersburg Times* in 1994. In addition to books, Dyer has used audio recordings and the broadcast media to his advantage, securing his position as a cultural icon and leading light in the areas of motivation and self-awareness.

Dyer was born in Detroit, Michigan, and began his professional career in that city in 1965 as a high school guidance counselor. In 1971, after earning a doctorate of education, he was appointed a professor of counselor education at St. John's University in Jamaica, New York, and began contributing articles to professional journals and coauthoring books on counseling with his colleague, John Vriend. These endeavors established his credentials in academia, and at the same time, he ran a lucrative private clinical psychology practice. His lectures at St. John's taught exercises in motivational speaking, complete with an upbeat, positive message that was well received. Students began bringing their friends to Dyer's lectures, and he amassed a small following.

News of these lectures intrigued a literary agent, who approached Dyer about the possibility of writing a book based on their content. The result was *Your Erroneous Zones*, sales of which were initially abysmal. Undaunted, the author bought up all the copies and, quitting both his teaching position and his practice, set out on the road with the books to make publishing and self-marketing history. Dyer covered all of the contiguous United States, making personal appearances at bookstores and giving radio and television interviews. By the end of his journey,

Dr. Wayne Dyer. *Dr. Wayne Dyer gained celebrity with a string of successful books, audiotapes, and lecture tours touting his self-help philosophies.* ANGELA WEISS/GETTY IMAGES.

he had been a guest on nationally televised talk shows and had been interviewed by the likes of Phil Donahue, Johnny Carson, and Merv Griffin.

Dyer's status as a celebrity allowed him to publish more books on the same theme and to generate audiences for his informal lecture tours. These tours cemented his following, becoming the basis for the many acclaimed, high-selling audio sets that he recorded. His message offered something for everyone, since it was not specific to a religion or a particular portion of society. This was in contrast to self-help gurus such as Dale Carnegie and Stephen Covey, whose philosophies were somewhat hemmed in by their affiliations and concerns with the business and corporate worlds. Dyer even resisted the New Age tag, warning his audience in one of his audios that the New Age phenomenon and its proponents were often superficial and could be dangerously misleading.

Dyer's theme became more convoluted and esoteric as his career continued, accruing a certain degree of mysticism to accompany his pop psychology. In *Real Magic* (1993), for example, he discusses the potential for spiritual experience, whereas *Your Sacred Self* (1995) further expounds on the benefits of attaining a higher consciousness. Having remarried, he and his wife were raising a family of eight children throughout the 1980s, and his books largely recounted experiences and anecdotes culled from his domestic life. In 1998 he published *Wisdom of the Ages*, a collection of essays reflecting on the essence of certain literary quotations.

Dyer has often said that his own life is his best example. In fact, much of his appeal can be attributed to his life experiences, which he has used consistently as entry points into his discussions and writings. Many of his preteen years were spent in an orphanage, and although he grew up to be successful, he was also profoundly unhappy until he decided to take responsibility for his life in the mid-1970s. Because his ideas have been based on the psychological mechanisms that have worked so well for him, he has gained added credibility among the consumers of self-development media.

Nevertheless, Dyer has had his share of critics. In a 1983 article in *Life* magazine, Campbell Geeslin suggested that Dyer's message is "a gospel in praise of the superficial" and that "Dyer is selling simplistic solutions to life's inevitable difficulties." Dyer, who was his own best advertisement in the late 1970s, turned out to be his own saboteur in the 1990s and beyond. While remaining a hugely successful author, publishing a book per year since 2001, his increasingly mystical approach to his subject matter has made him less desirable as a guest on the talk-show circuit. Dyer is still visible—he has waged a highly publicized battle against leukemia—but his voice and message no longer saturate the airwaves.

Dan Coffey

SEE ALSO: *Best Sellers; Carnegie, Dale; Carson, Johnny; Covey, Stephen; Daytime Talk Shows; Donahue, Phil; Griffin, Merv; Me Decade; New Age Spirituality; Popular Psychology;* The Tonight Show.

BIBLIOGRAPHY

Alim, Fahizah. "Breaking Free." *Sacramento Bee*, May 16, 1993.

Dyer, Wayne W. *Your Erroneous Zones*. New York: HarperPerennial, 1991.

Dyer, Wayne W. *Real Magic*. New York: HarperCollins, 1993.

Dyer, Wayne W. *Your Sacred Self*. New York: HarperCollins, 1995.

Fidelman, Charlie. "Self-Help Guru Touts Power of Imagination in Our Lives." *Montreal Gazette*, September 22, 2011, C4.

Geeslin, Campbell. "Dr. Wayne Dyer; Pulling Those Same Old Strings with a New Book." *Life*, April, 1983, 19–22.

Reynolds, Cynthia Furlong. "You Can Choose to Become a New Person." *St. Petersburg Times*, October 26, 1994.

Dykes to Watch Out For

In the mid-1980s, lesbian cartoonist Alison Bechdel began to create the family of lesbians who comprise her popular comic strip, *Dykes to Watch Out For*. By the time Bechdel put it on hiatus in 2008, the strip—the first continuing lesbian cartoon—had been syndicated in more than fifty lesbian, gay, and alternative periodicals and had been published in over ten separate collections. *Dykes to Watch Out For* was, and remains, an institution.

The strip is a little like a soap opera, with a developing story line, and a lot like a peek behind the scenes of any lesbian community. The cast of characters is a group of lesbian friends in a nameless midsized city in the United States. Just as in any real group of friends, pairings change and priorities evolve, influenced by events both internal and external. Much of the action takes place at Madwimmin Books, a feminist bookstore owned by Jezanna, a no-nonsense lesbian entrepreneur. Among the staff at Madwimmin are Mo, a lovable curmudgeon filled with leftist angst, and Lois, a butch rake with a girl in every port. Their friends include Toni and Clarice, an accountant and a lawyer with a baby boy—however uncomfortably, they are upwardly mobile and nuclear-family-bound. Lois lives in a group house with Ginger, an academic, and Sparrow is a pagan spiritualist who works at a battered-women's shelter.

These women, and the friends who ebb and flow around them, form a diverse community. Through them, Bechdel pokes gentle fun at the foibles of lesbians, be they politically earnest, promiscuous, or pretentious. She also allows them to change as they experience the events of the real world, mirroring real changes that occur both among lesbians and in the larger community. Just as traditional media reflects the effects of phenomena on the larger culture, *Dykes to Watch Out For* reflects lesbian culture. Presidential elections, the O. J. Simpson trial, Prozac, sadomasochism, transsexuality—all appear in the panels of the comic strip, analyzed and digested by Bechdel's family of lesbians.

Bechdel calls her strip "half op-ed column and half endless, serialized Victorian novel." While her primary alter ego is clearly Mo, the anguished leftist, Bechdel does not take herself or her characters too seriously. She occasionally has her characters break the "fourth wall" and address her readers directly or interact with each other as if they are quite different characters performing in the strip. One of the strip's calendars shows a large panel of the "green room" where characters display heretofore unseen personality traits as they wait for their "entrance" onto the strip. In another strip, characters of color, a Jewish character, and a disabled character bewail their token status in the story line.

It is a tribute to Bechdel's skill as an artist and a writer that she can bring her characters enough life to argue with her from the page. Her drawings are clean yet complex, filled with subtle references and in-jokes for her audience, and the dialogue is lively and incisive. In fact, Bechdel's work and the success of *Dykes to Watch Out For* drew the attention of the mainstream press when Universal Press Syndicate approached her with an offer that could have placed her in the daily "funny papers." Though its interest was exciting to Bechdel, it only took a moment's thought to realize that whittling down her work to fit the narrow niche of the mainstream would have changed her work beyond recognition. The title would have to go, "dykes" being far too controversial, and out of six main characters only two would have been allowed to be lesbians. Unwilling to give up her vision of a strip that reflected the realities of lesbian life, Bechdel refused the offer and remained in the alternative press, where her uncensored style was welcome.

In 2006 Bechdel published a graphic memoir of her upbringing and family life, titled *Fun Home: A Family Tragicomic*, that was hailed as a masterpiece and named the best book of the year by *Time* magazine. The mainstream exposure that such accolades afforded her led Bechdel to issue *The Essential Dykes to Watch Out For*, a kind of best-of compendium for hardcore fans and newcomers alike, in 2008. Citing the decline of newspaper sales, Bechdel then announced that she was placing *Dykes to Watch Out For* on indefinite hiatus and completed another graphic memoir, *Are You My Mother?: A Comic Drama*, in 2012.

Bechdel's works—be they books, strips, collections, or calendars—have always been eagerly awaited by her fans, and the uncertain future of *Dykes to Watch Out For* has done little to diminish their enthusiasm.

Tina Gianoulis

SEE ALSO: *Alternative Press; Comics; Gay and Lesbian Press; Graphic Novels; Lesbianism.*

BIBLIOGRAPHY

Bechdel, Alison. *The Indelible Alison Bechdel: Confessions, Comix, and Miscellaneous "Dykes to Watch Out For."* Ithaca, NY: Firebrand Books, 1998.

Bechdel, Alison. *Fun Home: A Family Tragicomic.* Boston: Houghton Mifflin, 2006.

Beirne, Rebecca. "'Dykes to Watch Out For' and the Lesbian Landscape." In *Lesbians in Television and Text after the Millennium.* New York: Palgrave MacMillan, 2008.

Rhoads, Heather. "Cartoonist to Watch Out For." *Progressive,* April 1992, 13.

Dylan, Bob *(1941–)*

Bob Dylan was the most influential musician to emerge out of the social unrest of the early 1960s, dramatically expanding the aesthetic and political boundaries of popular song. Recognized almost immediately as the voice of his generation, Dylan began his brilliant career by performing blues, folk ballads, and his own topical compositions, many of which addressed issues of racial injustice and protested against the threat of nuclear war. By 1965 he had transformed himself into a rock star, the first of many metamorphoses he would undergo over the following five decades. Mercurial, iconoclastic, and enigmatic, Dylan variously presented himself as a poet, gospel singer, bluesman, country musician, and minstrel, recording more than forty albums that would make him one of the most popular and influential recording artists of the twentieth century. Above all else, Dylan changed songwriting. In 1988 musician Bruce Springsteen noted, "Bob freed your mind the way [legendary entertainer Elvis Presley] freed your body. . . . To this day, wherever great rock music is being made, there is the shadow of Bob Dylan."

"Dylan has invented himself. He's made himself up from scratch," writes author Sam Shepard in his book, *Rolling Thunder Logbook*. The point, Shepard suggests, "isn't to figure [Dylan] out but to take him in." Dylan began his extraordinary odyssey as Robert Zimmerman, the son of Jewish merchants from Hibbing, Minnesota, where he enjoyed a comfortable middle-class life. Although he was bar mitzvahed, Dylan listened to prophets who were unfamiliar to his parents. Musicians Little Richard, Elvis Presley, and Hank Williams Sr. inspired the young guitar player, while actors James Dean and Marlon Brando shaped the attitude he carried to the University of Minnesota in 1959.

Dylan's days as a student were few. Having received an assortment of Huddie "Leadbelly" Leadbetter's recordings as high school graduation gifts, he was more interested in music than his studies and promptly matriculated to Dinkytown, a hip section of Minneapolis renowned for its folk scene. It was here that he obtained a copy of folk singer and songwriter Woody

Guthrie's autobiography, *Bound for Glory* (1943), a book that inspired him to learn the Dust Bowl balladeer's compositions and to perform them in local coffeehouses. By 1960 nineteen-year-old Dylan had changed his name and adopted Guthrie's nomadic ways, embarking on a cross-country trip that ended in New York City in early 1961.

Dylan then immersed himself in the bohemian culture of Greenwich Village, where leftists old and new were participating in the folk-music revival. Folk singers Pete Seeger, Ramblin' Jack Elliott, Ralph Rinzler, and scores of other young people enamored with folk music attended jam sessions in Washington Square Park and gathered regularly to pay homage to Guthrie, the movement's patron saint. Hospitalized with Huntington's disease, Guthrie made weekend visits to the East Orange, New Jersey, home of Bob and Sidsell Gleason, where Dylan temporarily resided. The two men established a warm relationship. Disease had nearly destroyed Guthrie's creative and communicative abilities, but he managed to express his enthusiasm for his admirer. When Dylan debuted at Gerde's Folk City in April 1961, he donned one of his mentor's old suits for the occasion.

Bob Dylan. *Bob Dylan has explored a variety of musical styles over the course of his lengthy career, including folk and rock as well as gospel, blues, and country.* MICHAEL OCHS ARCHIVES/GETTY IMAGES.

AN AUTHENTIC TRADITIONAL ARTIST

A self-described "Woody Guthrie juke box," Dylan recalls that he was "completely taken over by his spirit," a claim to which his self-titled album of 1962 attests. Released soon after he signed a recording contract with Columbia Records, this collection of folk standards and two original songs established Dylan's credentials as an authentic traditional artist and as a nasal-voiced, road-weary traveler who had hoboed for most of his young life. The album includes the poignant "Song to Woody," a ballad written to the tune of Guthrie's "1913 Massacre" that musically, stylistically, and lyrically declared Dylan's intent to carry his hero's mantle. Cover versions of songs by bluesmen Blind Lemon Jefferson and Bukka White placed Dylan firmly in the folk tradition, as did a 1961 press interview, during which he claimed to have played with Jefferson and the Texas songster Mance Lipscomb.

Bored with the predictability and sheltered nature of his middle-class life, Dylan fabricated a past full of hard traveling and hard living. If, like his fellow baby boomers, his life was smothered by relative affluence and haunted by the specter of nuclear war, his ersatz travels were filled with adventure and possibility. But if Dylan responded to his generation's ennui and malaise, he also began to absorb and shape its politics. "Whether he liked it or not, Dylan *sang for us*," writes Todd Gitlin, the former president of Students for a Democratic Society, in his book, *The Sixties: Years of Hope, Days of Rage*. "We followed his career as if he were singing our song; we got in the habit of asking where he was taking us next."

In 1963 Dylan's album *The Freewheelin' Bob Dylan* was released. Born out of his emerging political consciousness, it features the song "Masters of War," perhaps the most stinging indictment of the U.S. government ever released by the commercial recording industry. It condemns those who produce weapons of mass destruction and warns them that even the most benevolent God would not absolve their transgressions. The politics of *Freewheelin'* did not stop there. The song "Oxford Town" mocks segregation at the University of Mississippi; "A Hard Rain's a-Gonna Fall" imagines a stark and terrifying post-nuclear landscape; and "Blowin' in the Wind," which became a hit for the group Peter, Paul, and Mary, is a simple, though poetic, call for racial harmony. After becoming the star of the 1963 Newport Folk Festival, Dylan actively supported a number of political causes, performing at a voter registration rally in Mississippi and at the March on Washington that summer. Meanwhile, the song "The Times They Are a-Changin'" from his third album of the same name (1964) furnished the anthem for a generation dedicated to transforming the social order.

Dylan's fourth album, *Another Side of Bob Dylan*, also released in 1964 suggests, however, that the artist was moving in new directions. Bitter love songs, such as "It Ain't Me Babe" replaced the moralism of *Freewheelin'* and *The Times*, while "Chimes of Freedom" cloaked its social concerns beneath a virtuosic lyricism. Both the album and Dylan's promotion of it at the 1964 Newport Festival were poorly received by members of the folk press, many of whom opined that their hero's preoccupation with aesthetics forsook his political commitment. Their accusations were not unfounded. Unwilling to be shackled with the duties of generational spokesman, Dylan publicly renounced his involvement with the New Left and, after shedding his denim shirt for black leather and sunglasses, repackaged himself as a poet and rock star.

A ROCK STAR

By the end of 1965, perhaps the most important year in Dylan's career, the transformation was complete. Following the release of the album *Bringing It All Back Home* that March, Dylan embarked on a tour of England, where he was met by transfixed crowds, screaming girls, and adoring musicians. The documentary film, *Don't Look Back* (1967), directed by D. A. Pennebaker, chronicles the tour. It shows an increasingly arrogant artist who sounds more like an existentialist than a proponent of civil rights. In his interactions with the press, an irreverent Dylan attacked those who tried to categorize and explain his art. In fact, his material at the time seemed to question the ability of language to convey a sense of reality. Rather than writing topical songs, he assailed the social order by intimating that it was unreal and absurd, a mere construction of language. The song "Mr. Tambourine Man" from *Bringing It All Back Home* suggests that drugs may have been helping Dylan alter his own private reality.

Those who followed Dylan's career closely were not surprised when he turned his back on the folk revival at Newport in 1965. The end of his romantic relationship with folk singer Joan Baez, his work on a collection of poems titled *Tarantula* (eventually published in 1971), his arcane lyrics, and his interest in the musical arrangements of the Beatles, whom he had met on his British tour, all pointed to his intention to leave the movement. So his followers were shocked when Dylan appeared with an electric guitar. Among the stalwarts who suggested that rock-and-roll musicians had sold out to commercial interests, Seeger was rumored to have been so outraged that he tried to cut the power supply. The audience nearly booed Dylan from the stage.

Although shaken, Dylan remained resolute about his artistic decision. After meeting the group the Hawks in the summer of 1965, he took his electric show on a tour of England, during which he continued to incur the wrath of folk purists. This reaction, as well as the stunning music that Dylan and the Hawks produced, is documented on the album *Live 1966* (released in 1998). Recorded at Manchester's Free Trade Hall, this concert includes a riveting acoustic set that ultimately yields to a full-blown rock show, in which Dylan's voice and the masterful playing of his musicians soar above the audience's cries of betrayal.

Exhausted from the tour, Dylan returned to the United States. Then, starting in the summer of 1967, he and the Hawks, now called the Band, spent several months writing and recording songs, most of which were released eight years later on the critically acclaimed album *The Basement Tapes* (1975). The search for personal redemption (reflected in the song, "I Shall Be Released"), a sense of disillusionment and abandonment ("Tears of Rage"), and a persistent existential angst ("Too Much of Nothing"), remained prominent themes, but if the Dylan of 1966 was trying to inter the musical past, the Dylan of *The Basement Tapes* exhumed it. Traditional musicians Dock Boggs, Clarence Ashley, and Jefferson have a palpable presence on these recordings.

In 1968 Dylan released *John Wesley Harding* (1968), a largely acoustic collection of parables and allegories, one of which, "All Along the Watchtower," became a standard in guitarist and singer Jimi Hendrix's repertoire. The next year Dylan traveled south to record *Nashville Skyline* (1969), a collection of country-tinged love songs that includes a duet with musician Johnny Cash.

THE 1970s

The albums that Dylan produced in the 1970s showed sporadic signs of the genius that characterized his earlier work. The soundtrack to *Pat Garrett and Billy the Kid* (1973), a movie in which Dylan plays a bit part, is notable for the inclusion of "Knockin' on Heaven's Door," a song later performed by guitarist Eric Clapton and the hard rock band Guns N' Roses. *Before the Flood* (1974), a live album recorded with the Band, suggests that Dylan was perhaps undergoing a creative renaissance, an assessment that *Blood on the Tracks* (1975) confirms. Here again are songs of love, but crisp acoustic guitar, wailing harmonica, and a voice filled with doubt and disappointment convey the pain, anguish, and longing of "Tangled up in Blue" and "Shelter from the Storm" with remarkable weight and precision.

The album *Desire* (1976) indicates that Dylan's interest in politics was renewed. "Hurricane," the lengthy centerpiece, is the angriest song Dylan had recorded since "Masters of War." Co-written with Jacques Levy, this fierce narrative impugns the American justice system because of the murder trial of former professional boxer Rubin "Hurricane" Carter. Contending that Carter's trial was conducted unfairly, Dylan publicized the jailed athlete's case by marshaling the forces of his Rolling Thunder Revue, a mélange of some seventy artists, including Baez, Shepard, Elliot, and poet Allen Ginsberg, that toured the United States under Dylan's direction. Dylan, who performed most of the shows with his face covered in white pancake makeup, designated appearances at Madison Square Garden and the Astrodome as benefits for Carter. Although the revue's efforts may have played a part in convincing a New Jersey court to throw out Carter's first conviction, a second jury found the boxer guilty in 1976. In 1985, however, a judge threw out Carter's conviction, and he was released.

Dylan teamed with Shepard to write the script for the movie *Renaldo and Clara* with the Rolling Thunder Review as the backdrop for the story. Released in a four-hour version in 1978, critics savaged it, and it was later released featuring mostly concert footage. Then on Thanksgiving Day in 1976, Dylan and the Band gave their last concert, called the Last Waltz. Director Martin Scorsese filmed the farewell concert, and the documentary *The Last Waltz* was released in 1978. It has been hailed as the greatest rock concert film ever.

Dylan had spent much of the early 1970s exploring his Jewish roots, and then suddenly he became a born-again Christian. Fans and critics had little tolerance for the musician's choice, particularly when he proselytized at concerts and refused to play his better-known songs. The dogmatic lyrics may have made audiences uneasy, but the music on *Slow Train Coming* (1979) was triumphant and exhilarating. Backed by powerful gospel arrangements, Dylan sings with a passion that convinces the congregation that he had finally found his direction. "Gotta Serve Somebody," the single from *Slow Train Coming*, earned Dylan his first Grammy Award.

THE 1980s AND 1990s

Dylan was busy in the early 1980s, releasing *Saved* (1980), *Shot of Love* (1981), and *Infidels* (1983). Receiving warm praise from critics, *Infidels* features "Jokerman," "License to Kill," and "I and I"—some of the most innovative songs of his career. In 1985 he released *Empire Burlesque* and *Biograph*, a retrospective of his career that included much previously unreleased material and initiated the "boxed-set" format to the recording industry.

With his popularity again peaking, he participated in efforts to alleviate famine in Ethiopia, joining the chorus for the song "We Are the World," recorded for the charity USA for Africa in 1985.

In the mid-1980s Dylan launched separate but noteworthy tours with Tom Petty and the Heartbreakers and the Grateful Dead. Perhaps his most interesting work from this period came as a member of the Traveling Wilburys, a group composed of Petty, George Harrison, Roy Orbison, and Jeff Lynne. Released in 1988, the first of the Wilburys two albums includes the foot-tapping singles "Handle Me with Care" and "End of the Line." Dylan capped the 1980s with the critically acclaimed *Oh Mercy* (1989), which includes the socially conscious "Political World" as well as "What Was It You Wanted," a song that recalls the bitterness of such earlier compositions as "Don't Think Twice, It's All Right."

In the 1990s Dylan received accolades and experienced continued success. In 1991 the Recording Academy, an organization that supports the music industry and honors achievements in music, presented him with a Lifetime Achievement Award. In October 1992 a panoply of artists, including Harrison, Cash, Petty, Lou Reed, and Neil Young, assembled at Madison Square Garden to celebrate the thirtieth anniversary of Dylan's first album. When the honoree opened his own set with "Song for Woody," his career had come full circle. To be sure, his next two albums returned to his roots: *Good as I Been to You* (1992) and *World Gone Wrong* (1993) are both collections of traditional folk songs. Because these releases contained no new material, critics opined that Dylan's creative powers were again on the wane. Their diagnosis was premature.

In 1997 Dylan was one of the recipients of the Kennedy Center Honors, which ranks among the most prestigious tributes paid to American artists. Soon after he experienced a life-threatening illness and responded with the Grammy Award–winning *Time out of Mind* (1997). Here the aging Dylan tries to come to terms with the emptiness of love and the limits of his own humanity. At this time he also released a set of official bootleg compilations that featured some of his best material. *The Bootleg Series, Volumes 1–3: Rare and Unreleased, 1961–1991* appeared in 1997. Volume 4, a recording of a 1966 concert in Royal Albert Hall, followed in 1998.

THE TWENTY-FIRST CENTURY

As Dylan entered his fifth decade in the public eye, his creative energies remained strong. His song "Things Have Changed" for the 2000 film *Wonder Boys* won both a Golden Globe Award and an Academy Award, while his 2001 album *Love and Theft* was nominated for several Grammy Awards. Both *Newsweek* and *Entertainment Weekly* magazines named it one of the best albums of the decade. His next release, *Modern Times* (2006), earned two Grammy Awards, was named Album of the Year by *Rolling Stone* magazine, and entered the music charts at number one. Dylan's 2009 album, *Together through Life* also entered the charts at number one, making Dylan, who was sixty-seven years old at the time, the oldest artist to achieve that feat. From 2006 through 2009 Dylan also hosted *Theme Time Radio Hour*, a one-hour program on satellite featuring a wide range of musical genres including rap, country, and blues. The playlist for each episode was built around a theme such as "danger," "the big city," or "dreams, " to name just a few. On October 13, 2009, he released *Christmas in the Heart*, which included covers of popular Christmas carols. Proceeds from the album were donated to charity.

Nearly fifty years after his first record, Dylan continued to provide audiences with a "means to adventure" as he lived life on the road with his Never Ending Tour, performing more than 2,300 shows all around the world from 1988 to 2011. He also focused on other pursuits in the twenty-first century. Movies continued to be a passion as he cowrote and starred in *Masked and Anonymous* (2003). Most critics hated it, whereas some proclaimed it a work of art. In 2004 he published *Chronicles*, his memoirs. The book reached number two on the *New York Times* best-seller list and received a National Book Award nomination.

Dylan, a folk singer, a rock star, a religious convert, an author, an artist, a filmmaker, and a road warrior, is the true renaissance man of popular culture. Perhaps it was Bill Clinton, the first president to come of age under Dylan's influence, who summed up his impact best when presenting him with the Kennedy Center Honors in 1997. Clinton stated, "With searing lyrics and unpredictable beats, he captured the mood of a generation. Everything he saw—the pain, the promise, the yearning, the injustice—turned to song. He probably had more impact on people of my generation than any other creative artist."

Bryan Garman

SEE ALSO: *Academy Awards; Baez, Joan; The Beatles; Brando, Marlon; Cash, Johnny; Clapton, Eric; Dean, James;* Entertainment Weekly*; Folk Music; Ginsberg, Allen; Grammy Awards; The Grateful Dead; Guthrie, Woody; Hendrix, Jimi; Leadbelly; Little Richard; March on Washington; The* New York Times*;* Newsweek*; Orbison, Roy; Peter, Paul, and Mary; Presley, Elvis; Reed, Lou; Rock and Roll;* Rolling Stone*; Scorsese, Martin; Seeger, Pete; Shepard, Sam; Springsteen, Bruce; Williams, Hank, Sr.; Young, Neil.*

BIBLIOGRAPHY

Cott, Jonathan, ed. *Bob Dylan: The Essential Interviews*. New York: Wenner Books, 2006.

Dettmer, Kevin J. H. *The Cambridge Companion to Bob Dylan*. Cambridge, UK: Cambridge University Press, 2009.

Cantwell, Robert. *When We Were Good: The Folk Revival.* Cambridge, MA: Harvard University Press, 1996.

Gitlin, Todd. *The Sixties: Years of Hope, Days of Rage*. New York: Bantam, 1987.

Dylan, Bob. *Chronicles, Volume One*. New York: Simon & Schuster, 2004.

Epstein, Daniel Mark. *The Ballad of Bob Dylan*. New York: Harper, 2011.

Gray, Michael. *The Bob Dylan Encyclopedia*. New York: Continuum, 2006.

Hajdu, David. "Forever Young? In Some Ways, Yes." *New York Times*, May 23, 2011.

Heylin, Clinton. *Bob Dylan: Behind the Shades: A Biography.* New York: Summit Books, 1991.

Marcus, Greil. *Invisible Republic: Bob Dylan's Basement Tapes.* New York: Holt, 1997.

Shelton, Robert. *No Direction Home: The Life and Music of Bob Dylan*. New York: Beech Tree Books, 1986.

Shepard, Sam. *Rolling Thunder Logbook*. New York: Limelight Editions, 1987.

Thomson, Elizabeth, and David Gutman, eds. *The Dylan Companion.* New York: Delta, 1990.

Wilentz, Sean. *Bob Dylan in America.* New York: Doubleday, 2010.

Dynasty

Produced by Aaron Spelling for the ABC television network, *Dynasty* was introduced to American television as a three-hour movie and lasted nine seasons in the form of a weekly one-hour drama serial, from 1981 to 1989. Perfect for the decade, which, despite the conservatism and family values of the Reagan years, was characterized by increasing mass consumption, materialism, and the "me generation," *Dynasty* celebrates glamour, wealth, and capitalism.

Inspired by the monumentally popular CBS program *Dallas*, *Dynasty*, along with *Dallas* and *Falcon Crest* (also on CBS), helped to define a new genre—the prime-time soap opera—while reaching unprecedented heights of melodramatic, over-the-top, escapist absurdity. Like their daytime counterparts such as *General Hospital*, the prime-time soaps present serialized narratives, with each episode ending on a cliffhanger, or story line left unresolved at the highest point of tension, to be taken up in the next installment. The technique ensures a captive audience, and *Dynasty* came to be one of the most popular shows of the decade, dominating television screens not only in the United States but also in more than seventy other countries.

The show centers on the lives of the dynastic Carrington family, headed by patriarch Blake Carrington (John Forsythe), a Denver oil tycoon. To the traditional story formula of the daytime soaps is added a potent brew of adultery, murder, and deceit, as well as complicated plotlines dominated by corporate greed, rivalries, takeovers, and mergers consonant with the patina of outrageous wealth that is evident everywhere. Women are integral to *Dynasty*, no more so than the character of Alexis, whose name became a byword for female power and high-octane glamour. Ruthless, vengeful, and cunning, she is played by Joan Collins, and the role made her a major star and a household name around the world.

Much of *Dynasty*'s action involves the rivalry between Alexis, as Blake's ex-wife, and Krystle (Linda Evans), his current spouse, as they battle for dominance, both figuratively and literally, in numerous cat fights. One of the most interesting aspects of their characters is their presentation as glamorous and sexy, albeit that they are over forty—a rare departure for American television, which, like the movies, has tended to regard such attributes as belonging to the younger generation (of whom *Dynasty* has its fair share of both sexes). Audiences found the character of Alexis so deliciously conniving that she became the center of the weekly spectacle.

Because of their highly stylized representations of domesticity and personal problems, often characterized by excess, soap operas have been much denigrated by the high-minded. However, *Dynasty* was enjoyed by huge numbers of educated and intellectual viewers and, as many scholars have pointed out, it is the soap opera that brought to American television those inflammatory issues so often ignored by more seriously intentioned programs. Toward the end of its run, it featured the first significant African American character in a prime-time soap, Dominique Deveraux, played by Diahann Carroll. Though the program does not directly confront issues of racism, Deveraux's presence raised the subject of interracial relationships, while in Steven Carrington (played by Al Corley and, later, Jack Coleman), it introduced one of popular television's first regular homosexual characters.

Frances Gateward

SEE ALSO: *Consumerism;* Dallas; *Gay Men; Reagan, Ronald; Soap Operas; Spelling, Aaron; Television.*

BIBLIOGRAPHY

Shapiro, Esther. *Dynasty: The Authorized Biography of the Carringtons.* Garden City, NY: Doubleday, 1984.

Geraghty, Christine. *Women and Soap Opera: A Study of Prime Time Soaps.* Cambridge, UK: Polity, 1991.

Gripsrud, Jostein. *The Dynasty Years: Hollywood Television and Critical Media Studies.* New York: Routledge, 1995.

E

Eames, Charles and Ray

The husband-and-wife team of Charles (1907–1978) and Ray (1916–1988) Eames created a multitude of artistic works in various fields from the 1940s to the 1970s. Charles Eames was trained as an architect; Ray (Kaiser) was an artist. After their marriage in 1941 they formed an unparalleled design team. Together the Eameses designed stage and film sets, furniture, exhibitions, interiors, houses, multimedia presentations, short films, graphic designs, industrial products, and books. Their greatest impact may have come from their work in two particular areas—architecture and furniture. The Eames's two Case Study Houses (1945–1950), designed in collaboration with architect Eero Saarinen, incorporated prefabricated elements into a simple rectangular box; the houses became internationally famous as premier examples of domestic modernism. The Eames's furniture work evolved out of a series of experiments with molded plywood done for the navy during World War II. Eames Chairs were widely praised in the 1940s and 1950s for their curving plywood forms, light weight, simplicity, and inexpensive price; they were also widely imitated.

Dale Allen Gyure

SEE ALSO: *Industrial Design; Modernism; World War II.*

BIBLIOGRAPHY

Albrecht, Donald, ed. *The Work of Charles and Ray Eames: A Legacy of Invention*. New York: Harry N. Abrams, 1997.

Demetrius, Eames. *An Eames Primer*. New York: Universe, 2002.

Kirkham, Pat. *Charles and Ray Eames: Designers of the Twentieth Century*. Cambridge, MA: MIT Press, 1998.

Neuhart, John; Marilyn Neuhart; and Ray Eames. *Eames Design: The Office of Charles and Ray Eames 1941–1978*. New York: Harry N. Abrams, 1989.

Earth Day

Inspired by antiwar "teach-ins" and the activist culture of the late 1960s, U.S. Senator Gaylord Nelson of Wisconsin organized the first Earth Day on April 22, 1970, to raise awareness of environmental issues and elevate the state of the environment into mainstream political discourse. Rachel Carson's book, *Silent Spring* (1962), which examines the increasing levels of smog in the nation's cities and focuses attention on environmental disasters such as the Santa Barbara oil spill (1969) and the fire on Cleveland's Cuyahoga River due to oil and chemical pollution (1969), had given rise to local groups of concerned citizens and activists. Enlightening photographs of Earth taken by astronauts underscored the fact that humans inhabit a finite system, small in comparison with the vastness of the solar system; this in turn changed the way people visualized the planet.

On that first Earth Day an estimated twenty million people participated in peaceful demonstrations, lectures, and celebrations all across the country—10,000 grade schools and high schools, 2,000 colleges, and 1,000 communities were involved. Extensive media coverage of the events succeeded in alerting people to the deteriorating condition of the environment and increased the influence of environmental groups on government and industry. For many, Earth Day 1970 radically altered the image of nature and how society should treat it, marking the beginning of the modern environmental movement.

The dramatic rise in citizen awareness after Earth Day made pollution a major news story. Programs on pollution appeared on television, newspapers hired environmental reporters, advertisements stressed the ecological qualities of products, and books and magazines addressed the protection of nature. Within months of the original Earth Day, the Environmental Protection Agency was created. The Clean Air Act, the Clean Water Act, and several other important environmental laws were passed in the early 1970s. Politicians spoke out on ecological issues in their campaigns and speeches. Companies that violated pollution laws were taken to court, and membership in many environmental groups doubled and tripled. The construction of nuclear power plants in the United States halted in the late 1970s. Many experienced activists, trained in the antiwar, civil rights, and women's movements, used civil disobedience to combat polluters. Subsequent Earth Days continued to put pressure on government and industry to act responsibly with regard to the environment.

Along with some environmental organizations, Earth Day lost steam during the pro-environmental Carter administration, as people perceived that ecological problems were being addressed. Some conservation efforts also prompted an angry backlash by conservative groups. During the 1980s the Reagan and Bush administrations systematically dismantled many environmental laws. When Reagan named James Watt to the position of Secretary of the Interior, however, environmental organizations were rejuvenated, and their membership rolls increased. In 1989 the editors of *Time* magazine abandoned their tradition of featuring a man or woman of the year in favor of featuring "The Endangered Planet."

Earth Day. Environmental advocates celebrate Earth Day in 2011. JAY DIRECTO/AFP/GETTY IMAGES.

In reaction to such environmental concerns as global warming and the depletion of the ozone layer and such eco-disasters as Bhopal, Chernobyl, and the Exxon Valdez oil spill, organizers of Earth Day intensified their efforts on the twentieth anniversary in 1990. That year Earth Day turned global, uniting more people concerned about a single cause than any other event in the history of the world—more than 140 nations participated. The *New York Times* reported that 200 million people took part in the largest grassroots demonstration in history. More than one million people gathered in Central Park to hear speakers and entertainers.

Earth Day 2000 focused on global warming and the push for clean energy, making use of the Internet to organize activists globally. Earth Day 2010, the fortieth anniversary, brought 225,000 people to the National Mall, where forty million "environmental service actions" were pledged toward the 2012 goal of "A Billion Acts of Green." The 2010 Earth Day celebration also launched a million tree planting initiative with the help of film director James Cameron.

The environmental movement was one of the most successful and enduring reform movements of the twentieth century. Due to the movement's continued prominence in the early twenty-first century, a majority of Americans now believe that the poor quality of the environment is one of our most serious national problems. Millions of families take for granted the policy of reduce, reuse, and recycle. Although Earth Day is not responsible for all of the environmental accomplishments that have taken place since 1970, it has succeeded in transforming a fairly specialized interest into a pervasive, popular one and has made ecological consciousness part of the American value system.

Ken Kempcke

SEE ALSO: *Advertising; Central Park; Civil Disobedience; Civil Rights Movement; Eco-Terrorism; Environmentalism; Global Warming; The Internet; NASA; Reagan, Ronald; Recycling; Student Demonstrations; Television;* Time.

BIBLIOGRAPHY

Cahn, Robert, and Patricia Cahn. "Did Earth Day Change the World?" *Environment*, September 1990, 16–42.

Devall, Bill. "Twenty-Five Years since Earth Day." *Humboldt Journal of Social Relations* 21, no.1 (1995): 15–34.

Dunlap, Riley, and Angela Mertig, eds. "The Evolution of the U.S. Environmental Movement from 1970 to 1990: An Overview." In *Society and Natural Resources*. New York: Taylor & Francis, 1992.

Earth Day Network. Accessed January 10, 2012. Available from http://www.earthday.org

Gilbert, Bill. "Earth Day Plus 20, and Counting." *Smithsonian*, April 1990, 46–52.

Hayes, Denis. "Earth Day 1990: Threshold of the Green Decade." *World Policy Journal* 7, no. 2 (1990): 289–304.

Nelson, Gaylord; Susan Campbell; and Paul R. Wozniak. *Beyond Earth Day: Fulfilling the Promise*. Madison: University of Wisconsin Press, 2002.

Earth Shoes

The Earth Shoe was brought to America in 1970, and the advertising campaign for it promised that wearing the shoe would bring its owner closer to nature. With a negative heel that sits lower than the front, the Earth Shoe claimed to offer the wearer a more natural posture, closer to aboriginal human locomotion.

The shoe was a startling multimillion-dollar success for two reasons. First, the back-to-nature promise of the Earth Shoe resonated with members of the burgeoning environmental movement. Second, the boxy appearance of the shoe was viewed as an antifashion statement; as such, it was a social statement favoring simplicity over image, substance over style. In time the square, broad shape of the Earth Shoe was emulated in a wide range of other shoes, and for a few years its look became a hallmark style of the 1970s.

Dylan Clark

SEE ALSO: *Environmentalism.*

BIBLIOGRAPHY

Lofaro, Lina. "The Fate of the Earth Shoe." *Time*, May 1, 1995, 32.

Mansour, David. *From Abba to Zoom: A Pop Culture Encyclopedia of the Late 20th Century*. Kansas City, MO: Andrews McMeel Publishing, 2005.

Trasko, Mary. *Heavenly Soles: Extraordinary Twentieth Century Shoes*. New York: Abbeyville Press, 1989.

Eastman Kodak Company

SEE: *Kodak.*

Eastwood, Clint *(1930–)*

In the course of a career that has spanned more than half a century, Clint Eastwood rose from obscure bit-part movie actor to box-office star in the United States, became a producer for his own highly successful company, and established himself as a film director of some accomplishment. He has often been compared to Gary Cooper—both men have been frequently and accurately identified as long, lean, and laconic—but Eastwood's dark good looks and granite-like persona, often self-mocking under a cloak of grim impassivity, is different from the earlier icon, whose career ended as Eastwood's began.

Eastwood's own iconic associations are, most famously, the silent, detached, cheroot-chewing Man with No Name—poncho-clad, unkempt, and unshaven as he goes about his bloody business—and Harry Callahan, dark avenger of the San Francisco police force, clean-cut and neatly suited as he undertakes even bloodier business. His true significance in the history of Hollywood filmmaking, however, is shown in the fact that, as both actor and director, he breathed new life into a dying U.S. art form: the Western. Finally, with *Unforgiven* (1992), Eastwood subverted the myth of this historic canon, inverting his own practiced characterization to transmit a moral message for a modern age. His now reluctant avenging gunslinger had grown weary of violence—a capitulation that, perhaps, paved the way for Frank Horrigan protecting the U.S. president (*In the Line of Fire*, 1993) or, further expanding his range, Robert Kincaid surrendering to a woman's love (*The Bridges of Madison County*, 1995).

Born in San Francisco on May 31, 1930, Clinton Eastwood Jr. passed an itinerant, Depression-hit childhood with schooling to match. After high school he earned his keep variously logging wood, stoking furnaces, and pumping gas before joining the army for four years, where he coached athletics and swimming. Subsequently, he briefly attended Los Angeles City College and married his first wife, Maggie Johnson (the mother of his actress daughter, Alison).

In the mid-1950s, on the strength of his looks and physique, Eastwood was signed to a $75-a-week contract—dropped after eighteen months—by Universal Studios, one of a standard, low-paid intake of good-looking men whose screen potential studios neglected to nurture. For four years he passed unnoticed in a string of parts, ranging from tiny to small, in ten or so largely forgotten films. These parts began with *Revenge of the Creature* (1955) and ended with *Lafayette Escadrille* (1958), while taking in along the way the Rock Hudson vehicle *Never Say Goodbye* (1956) and his first (and some say worst) excursion into cowboy territory, *Ambush at Cimarron Pass* (1958).

THE MAN WITH NO NAME

During this time Eastwood supplemented his income with odd jobs until he was cast in a new TV Western series. *Rawhide* ran for eight seasons—from 1959 to 1966—and Rowdy Yates, played by Eastwood, became a familiar figure to followers of the series. More importantly, he was noticed by the Italian director Sergio Leone, offered a part in Italy, and found himself launched as the Man with No Name in *A Fistful of Dollars* (*Per un pugno di dollari*, 1964).

The film emerged from a genre newly popular in Italy during the 1960s that imitated U.S. cowboy films in a peculiarly bloody way and came to be known as spaghetti Westerns. *A Fistful of Dollars*, given a face-lift by the presence of a U.S. actor-hero and Leone's particular facility with celluloid violence, was astonishingly successful. Two sequels—*For a Few Dollars More* (*Per qualche dollaro in più*) and *The Good, the Bad, and the Ugly* (*Il Buono, il brutto, il cattivo*)—both starring Eastwood, followed in 1965 and 1966, bringing Leone a fortune and an invitation to Hollywood and catapulting Eastwood to international stardom.

The first two films of the Leone trilogy were released in the United States in 1967; the third followed a year later. Eastwood returned to the United States, set up his Malpaso production company, and, in a lucrative deal with United Artists, relaunched himself on home soil with *Hang 'em High* (1968), an unashamed attempt to emulate the noisy gore of his Italian vehicles. In this movie the newly minted star, saved from a lynching and appointed as a deputy sheriff, grimly sets out to take revenge on nine men. The film was slick, violent, and not particularly good, but, coinciding as it did with the popularity of the spaghetti Westerns, it established Eastwood with the moviegoing public. Indeed, by this time he began to set up the first seeds of the avenging angel—or devil—that would come to mark his more serious and ambitious midperiod Westerns.

When the box-office Top 10 list was issued in 1968, the cowboy star was in at number five, having begun his association with director Don Siegel in *Coogan's Bluff* (1968). This urban Western let Eastwood loose in Manhattan as an Arizona sheriff whose methods clash with those of Lee J. Cobb's city detective. It was an explosive crime melodrama with Eastwood seen, for the first time, in modern clothes and minus his hat. Attempts to broaden his range in 1969 took him to World War II in *Where Eagles Dare* and back to the gold rush days in the musical *Paint Your Wagon*. The first was a soldiering potboiler, the second a visually attractive failure, but neither dented his popular image.

He retained his number five position and, by 1970, after the crude war film *Kelly's Heroes* and *Two Mules for Sister Sara*, in which he reverted to cowboy hat and five o'clock shadow to play a taciturn mercenary protecting a supposed nun (Shirley MacLaine), he rose to number two.

BRANCHING OUT

A key time in Eastwood's career came in 1971. Displaying the business acumen and Midas touch that would in time make many millions of dollars for Malpaso, he rejoined director Siegel for *Dirty Harry*, bringing to the disillusioned character Harry Callahan the same implacable qualities that had been displayed in his cowboy roles. The film is uncompromisingly brutal and raised questions in certain quarters as to its morality, perceived by some as favoring the vigilante methods of the ultraconservative Right. A closer look confirms that it is, rather, a protest against messy loopholes in law enforcement. The moral message aside, however, the film was monumentally successful, catering to audiences' taste for psychopathic serial killers and tough antiheroes, and was followed by four increasingly formulaic and cynical sequels over the next sixteen years.

More importantly for the long term, 1971 brought Eastwood's directorial debut with the film *Play Misty for Me*. As he would continue to do in all but a couple of his self-directed films, he cast himself in the lead, here as a radio disc jockey who becomes the obsessive object of a murderously psychotic fan's infatuation. The film demonstrated that he had learned much from Siegel—it was taut, tense, entertaining, and beautifully photographed in Carmel and Monterey, California.

From 1971 to 2011 Eastwood acted in thirty-seven feature films, directed thirty-three, and produced more than thirty. While bent, successfully, on proving he was not just the gruff, taciturn hero of the *Dirty Harry* franchise, he veered between the ambitious, the worthwhile, and the purely commercial. In the last category, his judgment sometimes faltered, as evidenced by the poorly received *The Eiger Sanction* (1975). Although his screen presence only grew more charismatic with age, he made a number of films that were essentially retreads of familiar ground—*The Gauntlet* (1977), *City Heat* (1984), *The Rookie* (1990), and *A Perfect World* (1993)—in all of which he played cops of one sort or another.

At the same time Eastwood experimented, not always successfully, with material that, in the context of his recognized oeuvre, was distinctly off the wall. In the film *Every Which Way but Loose* (1978), for example, he crosses the country accompanied by an orangutan won in a bet. There was, however, a wistful sweetness about the small-scale *Honkytonk Man* (1982), in which he directed himself as an aging alcoholic country singer and allowed himself to play guitar and sing to touching effect.

During the 1980s Eastwood the actor retained his superstar status, undamaged by the tabloid headline-making scandal of his affair with actress Sondra Locke, for whom he left his wife of twenty-six years. Indeed, he seemed to rise above gossip and escape mockery, despite court cases—Locke sued him, he sued the *National Enquirer*—and other personal difficulties. Included in the latter was a liaison with actress Frances Fisher, which produced a child, only for him to leave and marry Dina Ruiz in 1996, becoming a father for the seventh time.

For Eastwood the director, meanwhile, his best work was yet to come, and he was held in increasing esteem by his peers, who acknowledged his unshowy professionalism. As early as 1980 the Museum of Modern Art in New York held a retrospective of his films; in 1985 he was given a retrospective at the elite Cinémathèque Française in Paris and made a Chevalier des Arts et Lettres by the French government. From 1986 to 1988 he served as the elected mayor of his beloved Carmel. Also during the decade he made *Pale Rider* (1985), which, with *High Plains Drifter* (1972) and *The Outlaw Josey Wales* (1976), form a trio of classic Westerns. The three are spare in execution against an epic landscape, and in all of them the actor plays the mysterious loner pitting himself against dark forces and giving no quarter.

Long a jazz aficionado (he plays jazz piano in *In the Line of Fire*), in 1988 Eastwood directed *Bird*, a biopic of Charlie Parker (played by Forest Whitaker). Somewhat restrained and overlong—a recurring weakness of his more ambitious films—it was nevertheless lovingly crafted and raised his status as a serious director. He had his failures, too, however. The public did not respond to *White Hunter, Black Heart* (1990), an interesting fiction about the making of the 1951 movie classic *The African Queen*, and he was unable to find the key to capturing on film John Berendt's enthralling Savannah, Georgia, odyssey, *Midnight in the Garden of Good and Evil* (1997).

PEAK OF SUCCESS

As the end of twentieth century neared, Eastwood had, however, earned universal respect and admiration for his achievements. The holder of four Academy Awards (including best picture and director for *Unforgiven*) and a figure of gravitas and impeccably groomed dignity, he had become the elder statesman of the industry's creative arm, a position that was, as David Thomson puts it in *A Biographical Dictionary of Film*, "rendered fitting by his majesty."

In the first decade of the 2000s Eastwood entered one of the most successful stages of his career. In a nod to his longevity and changing career ambitions, he directed and acted alongside senior stars Tommy Lee Jones, Donald Sutherland, and James Garner in *Space Cowboys* (2000). The movie tells the story of four aging test pilots who are called upon to save the earth from a failing satellite. He also directed and played a similar role in *Blood Work* (2002), a crime thriller about a retired Federal Bureau of Investigation (FBI) agent who returns to complete a long unsolved case. While *Space Cowboys* and *Bloodwork* received mixed reviews, Eastwood's next several projects would propel him into the upper echelons of Hollywood lore.

Eastwood remained behind the camera and earned Best Director and Best Picture Oscar nominations for the brooding crime drama *Mystic River* (which he also scored) in 2003. The following year he directed and starred in *Million Dollar Baby* (2004), a film that many consider his masterpiece. In it Eastwood plays Frankie Dunn, a tormented boxing trainer who pins his hopes on a young female fighter (played by Hillary Swank). The film garnered Eastwood Best Director and Best Picture Oscars and also earned Academy Awards for Swank and Morgan Freeman, on its way to becoming a massive box-office hit.

Eastwood then directed two films depicting the World War II battle of Iwo Jima, *Flags of Our Fathers* (2006) and *Letters from Iwo Jima* (2006), before directing Angelina Jolie and providing the score for the mystery film *Changeling* (2008). He once again tapped into his tough guy past to direct and star in *Gran Torino* (2008), in which he plays a Korean War veteran who attempts to rid his neighborhood of gangs. Next, he devoted himself to producing and directing three well-received films: *Invictus* (2009), *Hereafter* (2010), and the biopic *J. Edgar* (2011), which he also scored.

While for some Eastwood will forever remain the cigar-chomping cowboy or the hand-cannon-wielding cop, his work of the last several decades firmly established him as one of the most prolific, versatile, and highly regarded figures in Hollywood history. He won the Screen Actors Guild's Life Achievement Award in 2003, received the Lifetime Achievement Award from the Directors Guild of America in 2006, and was awarded the National Medal of Arts and the National Humanities Medal by President Barack Obama in 2010.

Robyn Karney

SEE ALSO: *Academy Awards;* The African Queen*;* The Bridges of Madison County*; Cooper, Gary; FBI (Federal Bureau of Investigation);* A Fistful of Dollars*; Garner, James;* The Good, the Bad, and the Ugly*; The Great Depression; Hollywood; Hoover, J. Edgar; Hudson, Rock; Jazz; Leone, Sergio; Obama, Barack; Parker, Charlie;* Shane*; Spaghetti Westerns; Television;* Unforgiven*; The Western; World War II.*

BIBLIOGRAPHY

Cornell, Drucilla. *Clint Eastwood and Issues of American Masculinity.* New York: Fordham University Press, 2009.

Eliot, Marc. *American Rebel: The Life of Clint Eastwood.* New York: Three Rivers Press, 2009.

Foote, John H. *Clint Eastwood: Evolution of a Filmmaker.* Westport, CT: Praeger, 2009.

Locke, Sondra. *The Good, the Bad and the Very Ugly: A Hollywood Journey.* New York: Morrow, 1997.

Schickel, Richard. *Clint Eastwood: A Biography.* New York: Knopf, 1996.

Thompson, Douglas. *Clint Eastwood, Sexual Cowboy.* London: Smith Gryphon, 1992.

Thomson, David. *A Biographical Dictionary of Film.* New York: Knopf, 1994.

Zmijewsky, Boris, and Lee Pfeiffer. *The Films of Clint Eastwood.* New York: Citadel Press, 1993.

Easy Rider

In the film *Easy Rider*, writers and costars Peter Fonda and Dennis Hopper capture in a popular medium many of the ideals of the youth-oriented "counterculture" circa 1969. *Easy Rider* presents both the hedonism of drug use and the serious-minded idealism of the hippie movement. The film also uses a coterie of cutting-edge rock groups to articulate its indictment of conformist American culture. Ironically, however, *Easy Rider*'s continuing cultural resonance and cinematic influence owes much to its evocation of more traditional myths of American identity.

Hopper first gained notice for his precocious performance in an earlier film about youthful rebellion, *Rebel without a Cause* (1955), which starred James Dean. After appearing again with Dean in *Giant* (1956), Hopper became a proto-hippie dropout from the Hollywood system, smoking pot and eating peyote instead of making mainstream movies. In 1967 Hopper acted

***Fonda and Hopper in* Easy Rider.** *Peter Fonda, left, and Dennis Hopper ride their machines through the desert in a scene from the counterculture classic* Easy Rider. SILVER SCREEN COLLECTION/ HULTON ARCHIVE/GETTY IMAGES.

with his friend Peter Fonda, scion of Hollywood icon Henry, in *The Trip*. Director Roger Corman refused to spend time or money on pivotal scenes concerning LSD "trips," so Hopper and Fonda shot the scenes themselves at their own expense, garnering valuable experience and ideas for their future masterpiece.

The Trip was cowritten by Jack Nicholson, who in the same period scripted another avant-garde psychedelic film, *Head* (featuring the previously straitlaced band the Monkees). Nicholson also starred in *Hells' Angels on Wheels*, an excruciating attempt to combine two types of cultural rebels—bikers and drug-taking hipsters—in one film. Fonda and Hopper worked on two more motorcycle movies—the high-grossing *Wild Angels* and *The Glory Stompers*, respectively—before reuniting as cowriters (with Terry Southern, author of the 1958 novel *Candy*) and costars (with Nicholson) for what Hopper called "another bike film. But a *different* one."

A NEW KIND OF FILM

Easy Rider was "different" because, unlike *Hells' Angels on Wheels*, it successfully infused the "bike film" genre with the psychedelic surrealism of *The Trip* to produce a movie that could viably claim to reflect the ethos of contemporary youth culture. The film begins with two bikers, Wyatt/Captain America (Fonda) and Billy (Hopper), receiving payment for their role as middlemen in a cocaine deal before setting off for Mardi Gras in New Orleans, Louisiana. Thereafter, the deliberately loose narrative focuses on the bikers' heroic desire to win freedom from the moral strictures of American society, which Wyatt and Billy periodically encounter in assorted, prejudiced provincials. When Billy complains that "all we represent to them, man, is somebody who needs a haircut," alcoholic ACLU lawyer George Hanson (Nicholson), who joins the bikers' odyssey in Texas, explains, "What you represent to them is freedom. . . . It's real hard to be free when you're bought and sold in the marketplace. . . . They're not free. . . . They're gonna get real busy killin' and maimin' to prove to you that they are."

Easy Rider's clarion call to "freedom" was also expressed by the titles of soundtrack songs such as "Born to Be Wild" (Steppenwolf) and "Wasn't Born to Follow" (the Byrds). This utilization of rock and roll, the most popular mode of expression for youth culture in the late 1960s, was inspired. The *Village Voice*'s Robert Christgau enthused, "*Easy Rider* is a double rarity . . . not only does it use rock successfully, it also treats the youth drop-out thing successfully. You can't have one without the other."

However, like its literary, beat generation antecedent, Jack Kerouac's *On the Road* (1957), *Easy Rider* taps into more traditional American notions of liberty and individualism. It is no accident that the heroes' names echo Wyatt Earp and Billy the Kid. Billy and Wyatt move from the urbanized, un-Wild West to the Deep South, reclaiming rural America (lovingly filmed by director of photography Laszlo Kovacs) as a frontier. Early in *Easy Rider*, Wyatt and Billy stop at a ranch, where an elaborate comparison is constructed between the rancher's horses and the bikers' machines. *Easy Rider* evinces some unease as to whether being perpetually on the road, astride a product of modern technology, is the most satisfactory form of "freedom." Wyatt lauds the rancher: "It's not every man who can live off the land. You do your own thing in your own time." Here, the free man is no less than Thomas Jefferson's ideal, the yeoman farmer.

The hippie commune that Wyatt and Billy later visit is a countercultural reconstruction of this agrarian ideal: disillusioned young urbanites ("All cities are alike," says one) going back to the garden, even if this Eden is the desert landscape of the Southwest. As writer Frederick Tuten observed in 1969, "the commune scene is at the center of the film's nostalgic values." *Easy Rider*'s "nostalgia for a still beautiful America" (Tuten) and for a pre-urban, precapitalist American hero is apparent in the doom-laden climax of the movie. Whereas Billy rejoices, "We're rich. . . . You go for the big money and you're free," his brooding compadre insists, "We blew it." For Wyatt, the tainted cash gained from the cocaine deal has not facilitated liberty. Finally, even Wyatt and Billy have been "bought and sold in the marketplace," just like the stereotypical Southern rednecks who murder the outlaws in the movie's final scene.

THE AFTERMATH

In addition to catapulting Nicholson from art-house obscurity to Hollywood stardom, *Easy Rider* was extremely influential in establishing the road movie as the modern paradigm of the frontier freedom fable. *Vanishing Point* (1971) replaces *Easy Rider*'s pot fumes with amphetamine-fueled paranoia appropriate to the decline of the hippie dream, whereas *Badlands* (1973) and *Natural Born Killers* (1994) both combine *Easy Rider*'s legacy with that of another neo-Western counterculture allegory, *Bonnie and Clyde* (1967). *Thelma and Louise* (1991) partially revises the insidious sexism of *Easy Rider* and the genre in general, but in attempting to reveal what director Ridley Scott called "the vanishing face of America," this "feminist road movie" retains the convention of the heroes' gloriously tragic demise.

Martyn Bone

SEE ALSO: *The Beat Generation; Hippies; Hopper, Dennis; LSD; Nicholson, Jack;* On the Road*; Rock and Roll; Southern, Terry.*

BIBLIOGRAPHY

Colley, Iain. *Easy Rider*. Harlow, England: Longman, 2000.

Dalton, Stephen. "Endless Highway." *Uncut*, September 1998, 30–35.

Hardin, Nancy, and Marilyn Schlossberg. *Easy Rider: Original Screenplay by Peter Fonda, Dennis Hopper, and Terry Southern Plus Stills, Interviews, and Articles*. New York: Signet, 1969.

Hill, Lee. *Easy Rider*. London: BFI Publishing, 1996.

eBay

Born at a moment of enormous growth in the new medium of communication called the Internet, the web-based auction site eBay introduced an intensely personal and practical use for the new technology. One of the earliest Internet shopping sites, eBay provided a space for buyers and sellers of an unimaginably wide variety of items to find each other. In the process the site resulted in the creation of a new kind of virtual community based on person-to-person commerce and may have helped initiate a fundamental change in society's habits of consumption.

Though eBay's vast online presence makes it seem to exist virtually everywhere, its headquarters are located in San Jose, California. The company was founded during the mid-1990s by software designer Pierre Omidyar. Born in 1967 in France to Iranian parents, Omidyar was six when his family moved to the United States. In 1988 he graduated from Tufts University with a degree in computer science and worked developing software for an Apple subsidiary.

In 1991, together with a group of friends, Omidyar launched his own company, Ink Development Corporation, with an online shopping arm called eShop Inc. He became interested in the potential of Internet commerce, particularly the unexplored area of direct trade between individuals. The result of his work on the concept was AuctionWeb, which he introduced as a website in 1995. AuctionWeb's first sale was a broken laser pointer, sold to a person who collected broken laser pointers. Perhaps there is no better symbol for what eBay would become—a place where buyers could find what they wanted no matter how unusual. AuctionWeb was an instant success, and Omidyar was soon working on it full time. By 1997, when he changed its name to eBay, the site had hosted two million sales.

The Internet saw an explosion of activity during the late 1990s, and eBay was on the crest of the wave, growing from 340,000 registered users at the beginning of 1998 to more than one million by the end of the year. In 1998 the company went public. At a time when the stock market was sluggish, eBay's initial public offering was wildly successful, with stocks rising from $18 a share to $54 the first day. By the end of the year the company was worth more than $7 billion.

ENABLING BUYING AND SELLING

eBay makes it easy for sellers to arrange an auction. All contact is directly between buyer and seller, with the site simply facilitating the connection. Both buyers and sellers are required to register with name, contact information, and credit card number or other payment information. Sellers pay a small insertion fee for each item listed and a commission on each item sold. Sellers set a minimum price and establish the length of time for the auction. Buyers register their bids, and the highest bid at the time the auction ends buys the item, which the sellers ships. Bidders who swoop in to raise a bid and snatch an item just before an auction closes are dubbed *snipers* by eBay regulars.

Merchandise is divided into a number of categories—such as Antiques, Entertainment Memorabilia, or Pet Supplies—to make it easy for buyers to browse. Because eBay has almost everything for sale, the site appeals to a huge diversity of shoppers, from collectors seeking a particular esoteric item to the budget-conscious looking for a bargain on a necessary purchase. The auction format adds an element of competition to the transaction that many buyers find fun, stimulating, and even addictive. Feedback forums and a rating system help protect both buyers and sellers from dishonest or unreliable users.

eBay has continued to refine and expand its operation, weathering bad economic times and slumps in Internet commerce. In 2002 the company bought the payment service PayPal to help make the payment process more secure. The same year the original auction rules were relaxed to allow sellers to offer items for sale at a fixed price. In 2005 eBay added categories for surplus office and industrial equipment, so that businesses began to shop there as well as individuals. In 2012 the governor of New York listed 450 vehicles, retired from the state fleet, for sale on eBay.

eBay has also introduced a number of related person-to-person sites, including StubHub, where shoppers can buy and sell tickets to events; eBay Classifieds, where users can access items and services near where they live; and eBay Celebrity, where stars auction memorabilia or tickets to events to raise money for charities. In 2011 the company purchased Hunch, a personal advice service that uses software to gather information and make shopping recommendations. Another service is Trading Assistants, featuring experienced eBay sellers who charge a fee to handle sales for those who do not wish to sell their own items. In 2011, just before Christmas, the first eBay pop-up (temporary) store opened in London, allowing customers to browse before ordering items to be delivered.

By the middle of the first decade of the 2000s, eBay's popularity seemed to plateau. The novelty of auctions appeared to have worn off, and eBay's plethora of offerings overwhelmed buyers and buried vendors' goods. In response to changes made in 2008, including increased sellers' fees and the elimination of negative reviews, users boycotted the service. As a result, the number of items for sale diminished and stock shares briefly slumped. However, the introduction of new user-friendly features such as member blogs and discussion boards helped to create a sense of community that attracted users back to the site. A new "Buy It Now" button that sidestepped the auction process also contributed to solidifying eBay's prominence among person-to-person sales sites.

Throughout its tenure, eBay has undergone continual modifications; those who frequent the site have evolved as well. Buyers and sellers have become more savvy about pricing and product promotion, and in the 2010s the majority of merchants were no longer individuals unloading their used wares but rather professionals selling new goods.

CULTURAL ICON

As eBay's popularity endures, it has become a recognized cultural presence. In 2003 singing satirist Weird Al Yankovic documented the public fascination with the auction site in his song, "eBay," which includes the lyrics (to the tune of the Backstreet Boys' "I Want It That Way"): "A used pink bathrobe, a rare mint snow globe, a Smurf TV tray, I bought on eBay." CNBC explored the phenomenon in the 2005 documentary *The eBay Effect: Inside a Worldwide Obsession*. Trends in eBay sales based on gender, geography, and race have been fodder for market research and academic studies. Dozens of books have been published about various aspects of eBay, from the basic, *eBay for Dummies* (Marsha Collier, 2012); to the specialized, *How to Start a Bonsai Tree Nursery and Sell on eBay* (Bruce Bullock, 2011); to the metaphorical, *I Sold My Soul on eBay: Viewing Faith through an Atheist's Eyes* (Hemant Mehta, 2007).

Some social analysts theorize that the eBay model of online commerce has done more than just introduce a convenient and entertaining way to shop—it has altered consumerism around the globe. Internet entrepreneur Daniel Nissanoff predicts that an economy is developing where more and more people will buy and sell used merchandise rather than saving money to buy new items. Internet commerce websites such as eBay that facilitate the transfer of goods between individuals are vital to this new concept of temporary ownership. In addition, the eBay lifestyle has given rise to an increasing number of eBay entrepreneurs who have turned individual online sales into a full-time business.

Person-to-person Internet commerce continues to grow, and by the 2010s eBay had competition from a number of other successful sites, such as Amazon, Craigslist, eBid, and QuiBids.

However, eBay continues to thrive and remains almost synonymous with online sales for most Internet users.

Tina Gianoulis

SEE ALSO: *The Internet; Online Shopping.*

BIBLIOGRAPHY

Cohen, Adam. *The Perfect Store: Inside eBay.* New York: Little, Brown, 2002.

Collier, Marsha. *eBay for Dummies,* 7th ed. Hoboken, NJ: Wiley & Sons, 2012.

Gibson, Owen. "E-Commerce: eBay Changes Aim for Fewer Critics and More Sellers." *Guardian.* Accessed May 2012. Available from http://www.guardian.co.uk/business/2008/aug/20/ebay.efinance

Hasker, Kevin, and Robin Sickles. "eBay in the Economic Literature: Analysis of an Auction Marketplace." *Review of Industrial Organization* 37, no. 1 (2010): 3–42.

Levy, Steven, and Brad Stone. "Risky Bidness: You Can Get Anything You Want on the Auction Site EBay. But Proceed with Caution." *Newsweek,* December 21, 1998.

Nissanoff, Daniel. *FutureShop: How the New Auction Culture Will Revolutionize the Way We Buy, Sell, and Get the Things We Really Want.* New York: Penguin Books, 2006.

Spencer, Christopher Matthew. *The eBay Entrepreneur.* Chicago: Kaplan, 2006.

Surowiecki, James. "Going, Going, Gone: Who Killed the Internet Auction?" *Wired,* May 17, 2011.

Ebbets Field

From 1913 to 1957 Ebbets Field was home to Major League Baseball's Brooklyn Dodgers. The venue was considered by many to be the heart and soul of Brooklyn, New York, but that does not tell the whole story. Perhaps more so than with any other franchise in sports history, the players, the fans, and their stadium were intertwined. Ebbets Field symbolized the unique and independent character of Brooklyn, a borough that was different from the others in New York. The ballpark provided a setting where everyone in the ethnically and racially diverse community was equal. The electricity of the Dodgers and their home field helped to maintain interracial unity. At Ebbets Field, the Dodgers and their fans pulled together for a common cause: the establishment of a baseball tradition in Brooklyn that would best reflect the people and the culture of the borough.

Charles Ebbets, owner of the Dodgers from 1898 to 1925, moved the team to a new venue after the old ballpark, Washington Park, proved to be too small. Named after the team's owner, Ebbets Field opened on April 9, 1913, with a seating capacity of 25,000. Later, the capacity was expanded to more than 30,000. Renovations over the years transformed the ballpark from a pitcher's to a hitter's stadium. Although Ebbets Field was smaller than many other major-league stadiums, it was acceptable to the citizens of Brooklyn because it was comfortable. When fans went to the stadium, they saw not only a game but also many different types of interesting characters rooting for the Dodgers. The "Dodger Symphony," for example, was made up of five hardcore fans who danced and played music in the stands and on top of the dugout. Before each game, fans lined up along the railing to shake the hands of and get autographs from the players. The players and fans had a bond that was unique in the major leagues. Dodgers fans loved their team because the players symbolized the working-class ethos of Brooklyn.

Ebbets Field was the setting for several milestones that affected both major-league baseball and American popular culture. The first-ever televised Major League Baseball game was played at Ebbets Field on August 26, 1939, when Brooklyn met the Cincinnati Reds in the first game of a Saturday afternoon doubleheader. Televised by NBC, the contest paved the way for the array of sports broadcasts that exists in the early 2010s. Another event that occurred at Ebbets Field was even more significant: on April 15, 1947, Jackie Robinson became the first African American to play in a major-league game. Dodgers president and general manager Branch Rickey was the man behind this historic move, and soon the rest of baseball would be integrated. Given that it was already known for ethnic and racial diversity among the fans, Ebbets Field was a fitting place for the major-league color barrier to be broken.

Although winning was certainly important to Dodgers fans, they supported their team through thick and thin. Luckily for those fans, the team had many winning years, highlighted by nine National League pennants and a World Series title (1955). The people of Brooklyn did much celebrating after that championship, including giving their beloved players a victory parade. The joy was short-lived, however. After the 1957 season, the Dodgers left Brooklyn and Ebbets Field for Los Angeles. Attendance was not the issue—the Dodgers had always drawn well. There simply was greater profit potential on the West Coast. The Dodgers took with them the heart of Brooklyn—life in the borough has never been quite the same. Ebbets Field had served as the ideal for what an American ballpark should be: a place that truly united the community. Sadly, it was demolished in 1960.

David Treviño

SEE ALSO: *Baseball; The Brooklyn Dodgers; Robinson, Jackie.*

BIBLIOGRAPHY

Golenbock, Peter. *Bums, an Oral History of the Brooklyn Dodgers.* New York: Putnam, 1984.

Kahn, Roger. *The Boys of Summer.* New York: Harper & Row, 1972.

McCauley, Joseph. *Ebbets Field: Brooklyn's Baseball Shrine.* Bloomington, IN: Author House, 2004.

McNeil, William. *The Dodgers Encyclopedia.* Champaign, IL: Sports Publishing, 1997.

Prince, Carl. *Brooklyn's Dodgers: The Bums, the Borough, and the Best of Baseball, 1947–1957.* New York: Oxford University Press, 1996.

Ebert, Roger

SEE: *Siskel and Ebert.*

Ebony

Bucking the trend against print, *Ebony* was the predominant African American magazine in the early twenty-first century. With a total paid circulation of more than one million readers—down from around two million at the turn of the century—*Ebony* and its sister publication, *Jet*, evolved from strident civil rights to lifestyle, celebrity, and general interest publications. *Ebony* still reports on racism and the economic disparities between blacks and whites, but it also documents the accomplishments and achievements and the rich cultural heritage of African Americans. Published by Linda Johnson Rice, daughter of founder John Harold Johnson, *Ebony* promotes itself as a platform for African Americans to express themselves and their individual and collective identities and experiences.

The first African American magazines and newspapers appeared before the Civil War. Some were linked to abolitionism, but others reported on literature and political issues. New titles began appearing after the war and emancipation. Some of the more successful included *Southern Workman*, *African Methodist Episcopal Church Review*, and *Voice of the Negro*. By the early twentieth century the NAACP's *Crisis* briefly attracted more than 100,000 readers, but it and others could not boast of sustained mass circulations. They were read and supported by relatively small numbers of the better educated, upper-class black people.

JOHN HAROLD JOHNSON

Johnson was born into poverty in rural Arkansas in 1918. His father was killed in a sawmill accident when he was eight years old. The curriculum for black students in his segregated school district stopped at the eighth grade, so Johnson and his family became part of the early twentieth-century black diaspora to the North and moved to Chicago in 1933, in part to view the world's fair. Johnson became an honor student at DuSable High School in Chicago. At a convocation he delivered a speech heard by Harry H. Pace, president of the Supreme Liberty Life Insurance Company, a business that sold to blacks who would not have been otherwise able to get life insurance.

Pace had encouraged a number of talented young blacks, including singer and actor Paul Robeson, and gave Johnson a part-time job at his insurance company. Among Johnson's duties was to collect news and information about African Americans and prepare a weekly digest for Pace, loosely based on the format of the popular *Reader's Digest*. Johnson reasoned that such a black digest could be marketed and sought a $500 bank loan in late 1942. The only collateral that he could offer was some new furniture that he had helped his mother buy. According to Johnson's 1989 autobiography, *Succeeding against the Odds*, his mother considered helping him but first needed to pray on the matter. Unable to wait, Johnson offered to pray with her, and shortly thereafter *Negro Digest* was born. The magazine reached $50,000 in sales within a year and survived until 1951.

Meanwhile, with the end of World War II in 1945, Johnson predicted that returning black veterans would need a new magazine to help them cope with the racism back home. "We believed in 1945 that Black Americans needed positive images to fulfill their potential," he wrote. "We believed then—and we believe now—that you have to change images before you can change acts and institutions." Johnson also recognized that the great magazines of words such as *Time*, *Reader's Digest*, and his own *Negro Digest* had reached their peak and were giving way to what he called the "blitzkrieg of the photograph." *Life*, a weekly magazine founded in 1936, and *Look*, which first appeared in 1937, featured full-page pictures by the leading photographers of the day and developed massive circulations. Johnson believed that the photographic magazines of the 1940s "opened new windows in the mind and brought us face to face with the multicolored possibilities of man and woman."

THE BIRTH OF *EBONY*

Ebony first appeared on November 1, 1945, and featured a front cover photograph of seven boys—six white and one black—from a New York City settlement house. Johnson was eager to imitate the success of *Life*, which devoted a significant portion of each weekly issue to the activities of rich and famous people, and he emphasized the glamorous aspects of African American life. He also concentrated on black accomplishments in the worlds of entertainment and business.

Johnson's elitist perspective was criticized for failing to represent the aspirations of middle- and lower-class blacks, who could only buy the magazine for escapism. Black press historian Walter C. Daniel observes in *Black Journals of the United States* that the early *Ebony* advanced a two-society portrait of U.S. life, one black and another white. "*Ebony* extracted a journalism model and economic clout from one and used these to propel the accomplishments and aspirations of the other without the encumbrances of philanthropy that had obligated almost every previous black institution," Daniel writes. Still, the early *Life* and *Look* had much the same rose-colored perspective and did not begin to practice more serious photojournalism until the 1950s and 1960s.

Johnson barely broke even in the first few years of his second magazine. He wanted to publish full-page four-color ads such as those that appeared in *Life*, but most black companies could not afford the cost. Johnson wrote to the chief executives of large white corporations trying to convince them to consider his as well as white publications for their advertising. He struck pay dirt with Eugene F. McDonald of Chicago-based Zenith Corporation. MacDonald was a former arctic explorer and personal friend of Matthew Henson, a black man who was one of the first to step on the North Pole. A long-term contract with Zenith opened doors to other white corporations such as Chrysler, General Motors, and Sears Roebuck and ensured *Ebony*'s profitability. The magazine meant prestige to its advertisers even as it was criticized for an excess of alcoholic beverage ads and the use of lighter-hued black models.

Ebony provided reliable news on the battle against segregation and the rise of the civil rights movement during the 1950s and 1960s. Staff writer Clotye Murdock Larrson supplied monthly coverage of the Emmett Till trial in 1955. Johnson's pictorial editorials praised student activism and condemned so-called Uncle Tom faculty and administrators in traditional African American colleges and universities. The magazine presented news and analysis on the rise of nationalism among former African colonies. Johnson traveled with Vice President Richard Nixon to Africa and Russia in 1957 and 1959, respectively. Martin Luther King Jr. published an article on a visit to India in *Ebony* and contributed a regular question-and-answer column titled "Advice for Living By." In addition, Johnson endorsed political candidates in *Ebony*, beginning with Harry Truman in 1948, and met with every subsequent president

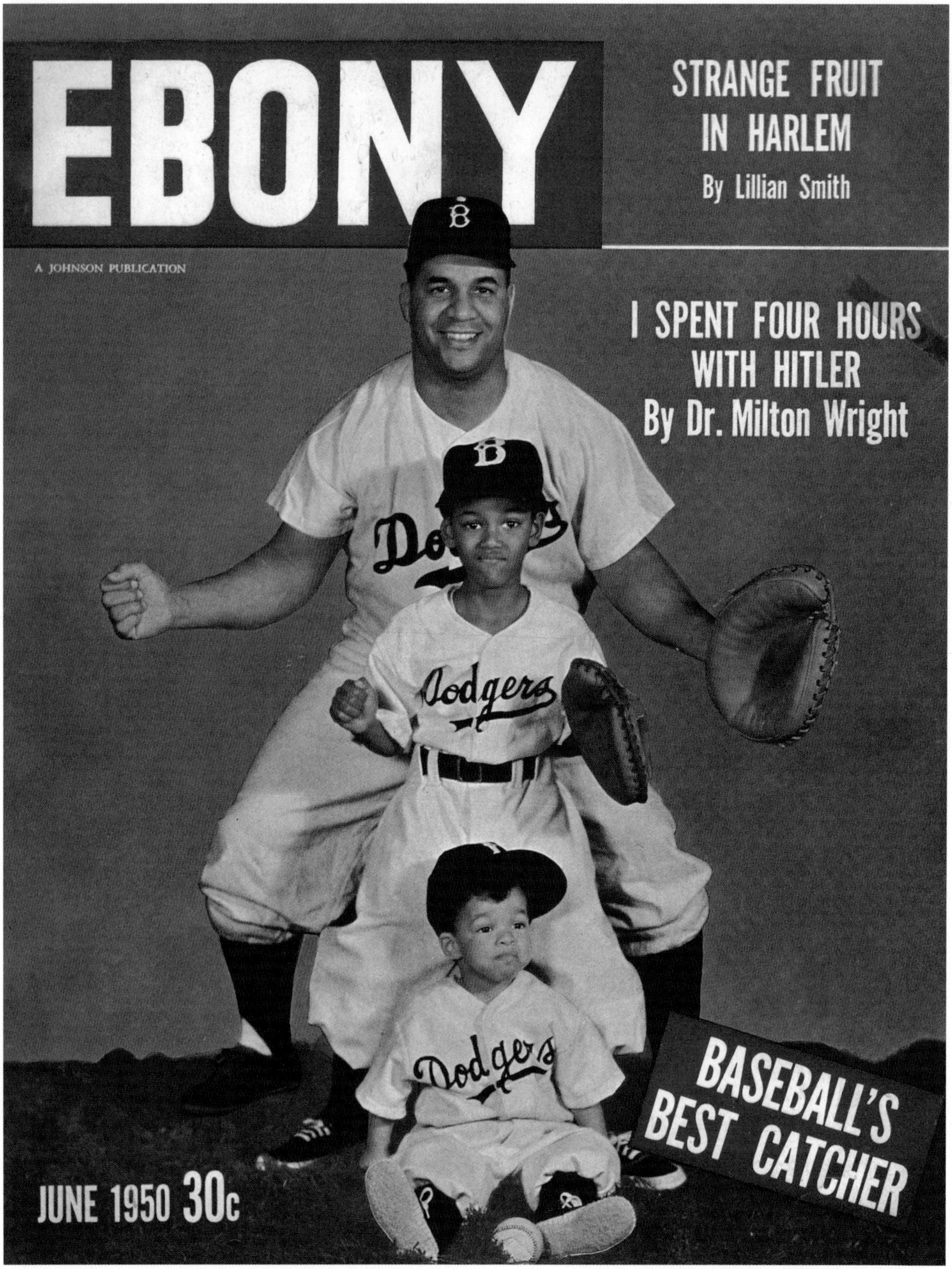

Ebony *Magazine*. *Brooklyn Dodgers catcher Roy Campanella and his sons appear on the cover of an issue of* Ebony *magazine from 1950.* TRANSCENDENTAL GRAPHICS/GETTY IMAGES.

up to George W. Bush, including fellow Arkansas native Bill Clinton.

Johnson was the first black person to construct a major building on Chicago's South Michigan Avenue, in 1971, and he housed *Ebony* in the structure with the magazine's name (and *Jet*) painted prominently outside of the top floor. He was unable to purchase the land for the building because of his race and had to hire a white lawyer to buy it in trust. In addition to *Ebony* and other publishing and broadcast ventures, Johnson and his wife, Eunice, started the *Ebony* Fashion Fair in 1958, a traveling fashion show that has raised millions of dollars for charities and scholarships. Johnson was added to *Forbes* magazine's list of the 400 richest people in the United States in 1982.

THE MAGAZINE'S REFOCUS

Johnson reduced the physical size and redirected the focus of *Ebony* during the 1970s with the demise of *Life* and *Look*. The magazine's 1975 bicentennial issue presented "200 Years of Black Trials and Triumphs." On its thirty-fifth anniversary in 1980, *Ebony* claimed a total readership of more than six million readers, the most ever. The magazine celebrated its fiftieth anniversary in 1995 with Johnson's daughter as president and chief operating officer. The issue featured "50 Who Have Changed America," a list of prominent blacks that included Rosa Parks, Michael Jordan, Colin L. Powell, and Oprah Winfrey.

In the twenty-first century the magazine concentrated more on celebrities, with actors Denzel Washington, Halle Berry, and Jamie Foxx appearing on its 2005 sixtieth anniversary issue cover. It reported the campaign of Illinois U.S. Senator Barack Obama beginning in 2007 and featured Obama with the caption "Mr. President" on the cover of its January 2009 issue, said to be the best-selling issue in the magazine's history. To provide its revamped content, *Ebony* drew staff members from several mainstream publications. Editor Amy DuBois Barnett, former deputy editor for *Harper's Bazaar*, was named editor-in-chief in 2010, and she introduced the magazine's first ever cover-to-cover redesign in 2011.

Howard University named its communication school after Johnson in 2003, the same year he was selected as the greatest minority entrepreneur in U.S. history by Baylor University. He died in 2005. The Johnson building was sold to Columbia College in 2012, and *Ebony* editorial offices were relocated a few blocks north in Chicago's century-old Cliff Dwellers Club building. Johnson was recognized with his own U.S. Postal Service stamp in 2012. "We try to seek out good things," Johnson once said of *Ebony*, "even when everything seems bad."

Richard Junger

SEE ALSO: *Civil Rights Movement;* The Crisis*; General Motors;* Jet*; Jordan, Michael; King, Martin Luther, Jr.;* Life*; Obama, Barack; Parks, Rosa;* Reader's Digest*; Robeson, Paul; Sears Roebuck Catalog; Washington, Denzel; Winfrey, Oprah; World War II; World's Fairs.*

BIBLIOGRAPHY

Daniel, Walter C. *Black Journals of the United States*. Westport, CT: Greenwood Press, 1982.

"The *Ebony* Story." *Ebony*, November 1995, 80–87.

Hughes, Langston. "Publishing History of Ebony." *Ebony*, November 1965.

Johnson, John H., and Lerone Bennett Jr. *Succeeding against the Odds*. New York: Warner Books, 1989.

"John H. Johnson." In *International Directory of Business Biographies*, ed. Neil Schlager. Vol. 4. Detroit, MI: St. James Press, 2005.

Pride, Armistead S., and Clint C. Wilson II. *A History of the Black Press*. Washington, DC: Howard University Press, 1997.

Roeder, David. "Johnson Publishing to Move." *Chicago Sun-Times*, January 6, 2012.

EC Comics

EC Comics was arguably the most innovative and controversial company in the history of mainstream comic-book publishing. Although EC thrived for only a half decade in the early 1950s, it accounted for a body of comic-book work that shook up the industry and has continued to influence popular culture artists since. EC's publications featured some of the cleverest writing and most accomplished artwork ever to appear in comic books, and they attracted a fanatically enthusiastic following. They also provoked harsh criticism, however, from those who charged that the comic books degraded the morals of the nation's youth. Whatever might be said of EC's comic books, they certainly left few readers disinterested.

NEW TREND COMIC BOOKS

EC began in 1946 as a company called Educational Comics. Its founder, Max C. Gaines, was one of the original entrepreneurs responsible for the development of comic-book magazines. In 1947 his son William M. Gaines inherited the company and soon thereafter embarked upon a new editorial direction for the line. Keeping the imprint as *EC*, the younger Gaines changed the full name of the company in 1950 to Entertaining Comics and launched a series of new titles promoted as EC's New Trend comic books. These titles eventually included three horror comics, called *Tales from the Crypt*, *The Vault of Horror*, and *The Haunt of Fear*; the crime titles *Crime SuspenStories* and *Shock SuspenStories*; the science fiction series *Weird Fantasy* and *Weird Science*; the war comics *Two-Fisted Tales* and *Frontline Combat*; and a humor comic called *MAD*.

The New Trend titles were different from anything that had come before them. All featured quality artwork—some of the most innovative and accomplished ever seen in the medium—and writing that, though often crude, was still far more sophisticated than the norm for comic books. Gaines and his chief collaborator, Al Feldstein, wrote most of the stories for the horror, crime, and science fiction titles, and they obviously enjoyed their work. As Feldstein later explained, "We always wrote to our level." They aimed the stories at adolescents and young adults, although their audience doubtless included many children as well. The stories commonly incorporated such adult themes as murder, revenge, lust, psychosis, political intrigue, and scathing satire.

An alternative, irreverent, and even confrontational perspective on American Cold War culture informed the stories in EC comics, which criticized, satirized, and subverted prevailing values, conventions, and institutions. At a time when the mass-entertainment industry in general remained captive to conservative financial and political concerns, such social criticism was seldom to be found in popular media offerings, and EC comic books rank collectively as perhaps the most subversive work produced for profit by an entertainment enterprise during the McCarthy era.

A VARIETY OF GENRES

The war comics, published concurrently with the Korean War, qualified as the first truly antiwar comic books ever produced. Harvey Kurtzman wrote and drew many of these comics, bringing to them both his penchant for historical accuracy and his gift for irony. In Kurtzman's hands, historical stories, ranging from Julius Caesar to the Battle of Little Big Horn to the atomic bombing of Hiroshima, became parables on the dangers inherent in military authority and the utter futility and horror of war—weighty material for comic books.

In their science fiction and crime titles, Gaines and Feldstein often attacked such social ills as racism and bigotry, and they even dared to point the finger at McCarthyism. *Shock SuspenStories* in particular was a vehicle for realistic and damning portrayals of the violence and injustice inflicted upon African Americans, Jews, and Latinos. No other comic book even began to approach this kind of social commentary, and few contemporary movies or television series did so either.

Under the editorial direction of Kurtzman, *MAD* became the first and best satirical comic book ever published. Besides mocking many of the conventions, institutions, and icons held dear by the American mainstream, *MAD* also took aim at its own competition, with devastating parodies of such inviting targets as Superman, Batman, and Archie. This irreverence branded EC as a maverick within the comic-book industry, a distinction that Gaines welcomed.

EC became best known, however, for its horror comic books. Titles such as *Tales from the Crypt* offered readers some of the most grotesque and grisly images available in mass culture. To say that violence and murder were commonplace in these comics hardly begins to do justice to stories wherein people were chopped to pieces, ground into pulp, deep-fried, and even eaten. One infamous story, called "Foul Play," ended with a baseball team murdering a rival player, disemboweling his corpse, and playing a baseball game with his body parts. There was usually a tongue-in-cheek quality about these atrocities, as evidenced by the ghoulish narrators who introduced and concluded each tale with gallows humor and bad puns. Husbands murdered wives, wives murdered husbands, parents abused their children, and children rose up to murder their parents.

Stories like these sold more than a half million copies per issue and found a revealingly large audience within a society dominated elsewhere by images of affluence and vapid suburban conformity. They also made EC the most controversial publisher in the business and the one most vulnerable to the charges of the critics of the industry. It was, therefore, perhaps unsurprising that EC was unable to survive the crisis that engulfed the comic-book industry from 1954 to 1955, spurred on by the publication of psychiatrist Fredric Wertham's 1954 text *Seduction of the Innocent.*

CONTROVERSY AND LEGACY

In 1954 Gaines testified before the U.S. Senate subcommittee that was investigating the alleged influence of crime and horror comic books on juvenile delinquency. At one point he found himself in an absurd (and often recounted) debate with Senator Estes Kefauver over the artistic merits of an EC horror comic with an image of a severed head on the cover. At the same time, public opinion was increasingly anti-comic, and particularly anti-EC, due to the ringing condemnation put forth in Wertham's text. His assertion that reading about gruesome acts would promote such behavior in adolescents was especially damaging for EC because of its uniquely shocking content. When Gaines's competitors formed the Comics Magazine Association of America and adopted the self-censoring Comics Code, he initially refused to join the organization. He subsequently relented, but nervous distributors nevertheless refused to handle the EC publications, code-approved or not. In 1955 Gaines canceled the entire EC line except for *MAD*, which continued to enjoy a long run of success, first in a black-and-white magazine format and then, beginning in 2001, in a color format. The magazine became a quarterly publication in 2009 and switched to a bimonthly schedule in 2010.

Long after its demise as a comic-book publisher, the influence of EC remained evident. Successive generations of comic-book creators drew inspiration from the imaginative ideas of EC writers and artists. Hard rock acts such as Alice Cooper and Rob Zombie incorporated the grotesque world view of EC into their own musical tributes to American junk culture, whereas horror novelist Stephen King has cited EC as a profound early influence on his imagination; he paid tribute to their horror titles in his 1982 movie *Creepshow.* Many of EC's crime and horror stories have been adapted into the successful live-action anthology series *Tales from the Crypt* on the HBO and Fox networks, and the original comic books themselves continue to be reprinted and sold in comic-book stores into the twenty-first century. As an exemplar of mass entertainment of the most inspired, gutsy, and irreverent sort, EC's place in comic-book immortality is assured.

Bradford W. Wright

SEE ALSO: *Cable TV; Cold War; Comic Books; Comics Code Authority; Cooper, Alice; King, Stephen;* MAD Magazine; *McCarthyism;* Tales from the Crypt; *Television.*

BIBLIOGRAPHY

Barker, Martin. *A Haunt of Fears: The Strange History of the British Horror Comics Campaign.* London: Pluto Press, 1984.

Benton, Mike. *Horror Comics: The Illustrated History.* Dallas, TX: Taylor Publishing, 1991.

The Complete EC Library. West Plains, MO: Russ Cochran, 1979–1987.

Jacobs, Frank. *The Mad World of William M. Gaines.* Secaucus, NJ: Lyle Stuart, 1972.

Sadowski, Greg, and John Benson. *Four Color Fear: Forgotten Horror Comics of the 1950s.* Seattle, WA: Fantagraphics, 2010.

Trombetta, Jim, and R. L. Stine. *The Horror! The Horror!: Comic Books the Government Didn't Want You to Read!* New York: Abrams ComicArts, 2010.

Wertham, Fredric, M.D. *Seduction of the Innocent.* Toronto: Clarke, Irwin, 1954.

Eckstine, Billy *(1914–1993)*

Although he was best known after 1948 as a singer of popular ballads, Billy Eckstine was also a fine jazz artist. From 1939 to 1943 Eckstine sang jazz with Earl Hines's band, achieving success with recordings such as "Jelly, Jelly." The Pittsburgh-born Eckstine also led a jazz orchestra of his own in the mid-1940s that was many years ahead of its time. During this transitional bebop era, Eckstine assembled such cutting-edge jazz stars as trumpeters Dizzy Gillespie and Miles Davis, saxophonists Charlie Parker and Dexter Gordon, and drummer Art Blakey. Unfortunately, Eckstine's band was so poorly recorded that no evidence remains of its extraordinary music. Among his many other accomplishments, Eckstine helped launch the career of Sarah Vaughan, one of history's most innovative of jazz singers.

Benjamin Griffith

SEE ALSO: *Davis, Miles; Gillespie, Dizzy; Jazz; Parker, Charlie; Vaughan, Sarah.*

BIBLIOGRAPHY

Balliett, Whitney. *American Musicians: Fifty-Six Portraits in Jazz.* New York: Oxford Press, 1986.

Simon, George T. *The Big Bands.* New York: Macmillan, 1974.

Studwell, William E., and Mark Baldin. *The Big Band Reader: Songs Favored by Swing Era Orchestras and Other Popular Ensembles.* New York: Haworth Press, 2000.

Eco-Terrorism

In 2002 the Federal Bureau of Investigation defined *eco-terrorism* as "the use or threatened use of violence of a criminal nature against innocent victims or property by an environmentally oriented, subnational group for environmental-political reasons, or aimed at an audience beyond the target, often of a symbolic nature."

Despite this effort to solidify the meaning of the term, eco-terrorism remains highly contested. Ron Arnold, a leader of the antienvironmental "Wise Use" movement, has argued for a broad definition of eco-terrorism that includes almost every crime committed on behalf of the environment, even acts of civil disobedience. Many environmentalists, however, have disagreed with this usage, preferring to distinguish between *eco-sabotage* (an assault on inanimate objects) and eco-terrorism (an assault on living things). The environmentalist David Brower has argued that the real terrorists are those who pollute and despoil the earth, not those who seek to protect it.

ENVIRONMENTALISM AS SELF-DEFENSE

This distinction between violence toward property and violence toward living things reflects the influence of *deep ecology*, a philosophy upon which much radical environmental action has been based. In 1973 Norwegian Arne Naess distinguished between what he called *shallow ecology* (or human-centered environmentalism) and *deep ecology* (or earth-centered environmentalism). A central component of deep ecology, according to Naess, is the idea of *self-realization*, in which the *self* is understood to include not just an individual consciousness but all of human and nonhuman nature. Some environmentalists, therefore, argue that eco-sabotage cannot be labeled terrorism, because from this perspective it is actually an act of "self"-defense.

The roots of eco-sabotage or eco-terrorism can be traced back to the early nineteenth century, when bands of English craftsmen known as Luddites destroyed the textile machinery that was rendering their skills increasingly unnecessary. Generally masked and operating at night, the Luddites claimed to be led by Ned Ludd, an apparently mythical figure whom many modern eco-saboteurs have taken as their namesake. Henry David Thoreau, though by no means an eco-terrorist, has also been cited as a forerunner of the radical environmental movement. In *A Week on the Concord and Merrimack Rivers* (1849), Thoreau mourned the inability of shad to bypass the Billerica Dam in the Concord River. "I for one am with thee," Thoreau wrote of the fish, "and who knows what may avail a crow-bar against that Billerica Dam?"

INFLUENTIAL ECO-TERRORISM GROUPS

Modern eco-terrorism came into being after the first Earth Day, held in 1970, when a handful of environmentalists in the United States began using force to achieve their political goals. In Arizona, the "Arizona Phantom" tore up railroad tracks and disabled equipment in an attempt to stop construction of a coal mine in the desert highlands. A group of college-age men calling themselves the "Eco-Raiders" burned billboards, disabled bulldozers, and vandalized development projects in and around Tucson, causing more than half a million dollars of damage. In Illinois, a man going by the name of "The Fox" plugged drainage pipes, capped factory smokestacks, and dumped industrial waste from a U.S. Steel plant into the office of the company's chief executive. In Michigan the "Billboard Bandits" cut down roadside signs with chainsaws, and in Minnesota a group of farmers calling themselves the "Bolt Weevils" disabled fourteen electrical towers that were part of a high-voltage power line being built across the prairie.

These early eco-radicals may have been inspired by the 1971 founding of the environmental group Greenpeace, which encouraged nonviolent, direct action against high-profile targets. They may also have been influenced by the publication of several books, including *The Anarchist Cookbook* (1971), by William Powell; *Ecotage!* (1972), edited by Sam Love and David Obst; and *The Monkey Wrench Gang* (1975), by Edward Abbey, a novel about four "ecoteurs" who roam the southwestern United States blowing up bridges and vandalizing bulldozers in the name of environmental protection.

The Monkey Wrench Gang not only gave the activity of eco-sabotage its popular moniker ("monkeywrenching"), it also inspired the founding of Earth First!—the environmental group most closely associated with eco-terrorism in the popular imagination. Founded in 1979 by Dave Foreman and other disenchanted activists, Earth First! took as its motto the phrase "No Compromise in Defense of Mother Earth," and its journal served as a clearinghouse for monkeywrenching tactics, though the group never officially advocated the practice. In 1985, however, Foreman edited the first of several editions of *Ecodefense: A Field Guide to Monkeywrenching*, which contained instructions on how to spike trees, close roads, and burn machinery. By 1990 monkeywrenching was estimated to be costing business and industry from $20 to $25 million a year, and it had spawned federal legislation against tree-spiking and caught the attention of the FBI, Scotland Yard, and other intelligence organizations.

Since the terrorist attacks of September 11, 2001, federal prosecutors have increasingly labeled crimes committed in the name of the environment as eco-terrorism, and defendants have received stiffer sentences as a result. As part of "Operation Backfire," for example, the FBI targeted members of the Animal Liberation Front (ALF) and the Earth Liberation Front (ELF), the latter of which began as a splinter group of Earth First! One such target was Chelsea Dawn Gerlach, who in 2007 was sentenced to nine years in prison for engaging in arson and other destructive activities throughout the West, including the 1998 burning of a Vail, Colorado, ski resort, which caused some $12 million in damage. Other activists received equally lengthy sentences under a "terrorism enhancement," enacted in 1995, which allowed judges to increase prison time if an offense "involved, or was intended to promote, a federal crime of terrorism," as defined by Congress.

Whether or not such enhanced sentences will deter acts of eco-terrorism in the future, their appearance in such films as Terry Gilliam's *Twelve Monkeys* (1995), such novels as Tom Clancy's *Rainbow Six* (1998) and Michael Crichton's *State of Fear* (2004), and such computer games as Eidos Interactive's *Final Fantasy VII* suggests that this highly contested term has quite clearly hit a popular cultural nerve.

Daniel J. Philippon

SEE ALSO: *Clancy, Tom; Crichton, Michael; Environmentalism.*

BIBLIOGRAPHY

Abbey, Edward. *The Monkey Wrench Gang*. New York: Avon, 1975.

Arnold, Ron. *Ecoterror: The Violent Agenda to Save Nature: The World of the Unabomber*. Bellevue, WA: Free Enterprise Press, 1997.

Foreman, Dave, ed. *Ecodefense: A Field Guide to Monkeywrenching*, 2nd ed. Tucson, AZ: Ned Ludd Books, 1987.

Lee, Martha F. *Earth First! Environmental Apocalypse*. New York: Syracuse University Press, 1995.

Manes, Christopher. *Green Rage: Radical Environmentalism and the Unmaking of Civilization*. Boston: Little, Brown, 1990.

Potter, Will. *Green Is the New Red: An Insider's Account of a Social Movement under Siege*. San Francisco: City Lights Books, 2011.

Eddy, Duane *(1938–)*

Known as a master of the "twang" electric guitar sound, Duane Eddy was a leading rock-and-roll instrumentalist in the late 1950s and early 1960s, with fifteen Top 40 hits between 1958 and 1963. The songs Eddy recorded were excessively similar, and only two ever reached the major success of the Top 10: "Rebel Rouser" in 1958 and "Forty Miles of Bad Road" in 1959.

Born in upstate New York, Eddy later moved to Arizona. He was an early experimenter with natural sources of echo and reverberation, which resulted in the "twangy" sound that quickly became his trademark. Eddy recorded on the Jamie label through 1961 and moved to the more prestigious RCA Victor label for his last few records in 1962 and 1963.

Eddy, who was inducted into the Rock and Roll Hall of Fame in 1994, continued to perform and write music into the 2000s. In 2011 *Road Trip*, a new album featuring eleven songs, was released. It was his first album release in more than two decades. His popularity and good looks led to a few supporting roles in motion pictures, including *Because They're Young*, for which he also performed the main theme song. In 2004 Gibson introduced a custom line of Duane Eddy signature guitars.

David Lonergan

SEE ALSO: *Rock and Roll; Top 40.*

BIBLIOGRAPHY

Ingram, Adrian. *A Concise History of the Electric Guitar*. Pacific, MO: Mel Bay Publications, 2001.

Stambler, Irwin. *The Encyclopedia of Pop, Rock and Soul*, rev. ed. New York: St. Martin's Press, 1989.

Eddy, Mary Baker *(1821–1910)*

Mary Baker Eddy is regarded among the most influential women in U.S. history. In 1992 the Women's National Book Association recognized her book *Science and Health* as one of the seventy-five books by women "whose words have changed the

Mary Baker Eddy. *Mary Baker Eddy founded the Christian Science Publishing Society in 1898.* HULTON ARCHIVE/GETTY IMAGES.

world." In 1995 she was elected into the National Women's Hall of Fame as the only American woman to have founded a religion that is recognized worldwide.

Eddy was born the sixth child of a Puritan family outside of Concord, New Hampshire, on July 16, 1821. As a child she was extremely frail and suffered from persistent illnesses. In 1843 she married her first husband, George Washington Glover, who died of yellow fever six months after their marriage, leaving her penniless and pregnant. After years of trying to raise her son George on her own, she lost track of him when the family he was living with moved to the West. (She later wrote that as an adult, George realized that his mother had not died and began looking for her. They met again when he was thirty-four years old and the father of two.) In 1853 she wed her second husband, Daniel Patterson, a Baptist dentist. Because her health was persistently in decline, Eddy began to investigate many "mind over matter" theories that were popular at the time. She even went so far as to consult a psychic healer in 1862.

EPIPHANY

Eddy's struggle with illness lasted until her epiphany experience on February 4, 1866. Bedridden after having sustained critical spine injuries from a fall on an icy sidewalk, she came across a story in the Bible about a palsied, bedridden man who is forgiven by Christ and made to walk. She then formed her theory that the power to heal sin is the same power that heals the body. Indeed, she believed and got out of bed. Patterson left her that year, and seven years later, Eddy divorced him. After her transforming spiritual realization, she preached her discovery of Christian Science. She had found the answer to her quest for health, and she wrote her first book on the subject, *Science and Health with a Key to the Scriptures* (1875). In 1877 Eddy married her third and last husband, Asa Gilbert Eddy.

Christian Science is based on her beliefs that anything associated with the physical world is an illusion (including pain) and that mind, life, and spirit are all that exist and are all part of God. Healing for her meant recognizing the error of believing in the flesh. Eddy's philosophy, however, cannot be considered a mind over matter one because, in Christian Science, the concept of matter does not exist.

Eddy's writings and beliefs quickly helped her become the leader of thousands of people in the Christian Science movement. By the year 1900, only thirty-four years after her revelation and twenty-five years after the publication of her first book, more than 900 churches were actively participating in the Christian Science movement. Eddy had obtained a nearly god-like status within her churches by the time of her death in 1910.

A WORLDWIDE PRESENCE

The Christian Science Church, from its "Mother Church" headquarters in Boston, has been a major media influence. *Science and Health*, reissued in 1994, immediately became an annual best seller among religious books. Eddy wrote twenty other books and pamphlets, including works of theology and a book of her poetry and letters. In 1883 she published the first issue of the *Christian Science Journal*. In 1890 she established the *Christian Science Quarterly* and later the *Christian Science Sentinel* (1898). She had a strong influence as editor of these periodicals. Finally, in 1908 she requested that a daily newspaper be started called the *Christian Science Monitor*. Both the *Christian Science Journal* and the *Christian Science Monitor* are still in print and continue to be well respected.

In 1991 the *Christian Science Monitor* launched The Monitor Channel, a cable network that collapsed in 1992. At the same time, the church started a radio network and a public affairs magazine that both failed to catch on with the public. Although Christian Science has remained politically powerful, estimated membership totals have shown a drop, from 270,000 members before World War II to 170,000 in the 1990s. Branch churches have declined from 3,000 in thirty-seven countries to fewer than 2,400 in the 1990s.

A major criticism of Christian Science is that its members are often unwilling to seek medical help for themselves or their critically ill children. In the last half of the twentieth century, Christian Scientists have succeeded in most states in establishing the right to deny their children medical treatment. Part of the decline in church population is due to an increasing trust of traditional medicine.

The followers of Christian Science revere Eddy, and her ideas, although spawned and proliferated in her time, have outlived her. In *Science and Health*, she pushed for the equality of the sexes, female suffrage, and the right of women to hold and dispose of property. She also advocated both the motherhood and the fatherhood of God. Many feminists continue to praise Eddy for her insistence that women, despite teachings to the contrary, were equal to men both in intelligence and in being worthy of receiving divine revelations directly from God.

In 2002 the Mary Baker Eddy Library for the Betterment of Humanity was opened in Boston in the renovated facility that houses the Christian Science Publishing House. In addition to providing access to Eddy's papers and historical church records, the library offers a nostalgic look at what life in America was like in the 1930s via a walk-through stained-glass Mapparium built in 1935.

Adam Wathen

SEE ALSO: *Feminism.*

BIBLIOGRAPHY

Beasley, Norman. *Mary Baker Eddy*. New York: Duell, Sloan, and Pearce, 1963.

Milmine, Georgine, and Willa Cather. *Mary Baker G. Eddy and the History of Christian Science*. New York: S. S. McClure, 1906–1908.

Dakin, Edwin Franden. *Mrs. Eddy: The Biography of a Virginal Mind*. New York: Charles Scribner's Sons, 1929

D'Humy, Fernand Emile. *Mary Baker Eddy in a New Light*. New York: Library Publishers, 1952.

Gottschalk, Stephen. *Rolling away the Stone: Mary Baker Eddy's Challenge to Materialism*. Bloomington: Indiana University Press, 2006.

Orcutt, William Dana. *Mary Baker Eddy and Her Books*. Boston: Christian Science Publishing Society, 1991.

Peel, Robert. *Mary Baker Eddy*. New York: Holt, Rinehart, and Winston, 1974.

Schoepflin, Rennie B. *Christian Science on Trial: Religious Healing in America*. Baltimore, MD: Johns Hopkins, 2002.

Silberger, Julius. *Mary Baker Eddy: An Interpretive Biography of the Founder of Christian Science*. Boston: Little, Brown, 1980.

Thomas, Robert David. *"With Bleeding Footsteps": Mary Baker Eddy's Path to Religious Leadership.* New York: Knopf, 1994.

Wilbur, Sibyl. *The Life of Mary Baker Eddy.* New York: Concord, 1908.

Zweig, Stefan. *Mental Healers: Franz Anton Mesmer, Mary Baker Eddy, Sigmund Freud.* New York: Viking Press, 1932.

Eddy, Nelson *(1901–1967)*

With his good looks, military uniform, and baritone voice, Nelson Eddy was the epitome of the Hollywood musical hero in the 1930s and 1940s. He and Jeanette MacDonald became known as "America's Singing Sweethearts" because of their eight MGM film collaborations.

Born in Providence, Rhode Island, on June 29, 1901, Eddy grew up in a musical household. He sang major roles at New York's Metropolitan Opera before becoming known as a radio singer and eventually a film star. Although he performed with such esteemed leading ladies as Eleanor Powell and Rise Stevens, he was most strongly associated with MacDonald. The films the so-called "Beauty and the Baritone" made together include *Naughty Marietta* (1935), *Rose Marie* (1936), *Maytime* (1937), *The Girl of the Golden West* (1938), *The New Moon* (1940), *Bitter Sweet* (1940), and *I Married an Angel* (1942). Among Eddy's other movies are *The Chocolate Soldier* (1941) and *Phantom of the Opera* (1943). In addition to his film appearances, Eddy made numerous recordings and sang frequently in concert and on the nightclub circuit. He died in Miami, Florida, on March 6, 1967.

William A. Everett

SEE ALSO: *MacDonald, Jeanette; MGM (Metro-Goldwyn-Mayer);* The Phantom of the Opera.

BIBLIOGRAPHY

Castanza, Philip. *The Complete Films of Jeanette MacDonald and Nelson Eddy.* Secaucus, NJ: Carol Publishing Group, 1990.

Hamann, G. D. *Nelson Eddy in the 30s.* Hollywood, CA: Filming Today Press, 1996.

Kiner, Larry F. *Nelson Eddy: A Bio-Discography.* Metuchen, NJ: Scarecrow Press, 1992.

Knowles, Eleanor; J. Peter Bergman; John Robert Cocchi; et al. *Films of Jeanette MacDonald and Nelson Eddy.* South Brunswick, NJ: A. S. Barnes, 1975.

Rich, Sharon. *Sweethearts: The Timeless Love Affair—On-Screen and Off—Between Jeanette MacDonald and Nelson Eddy.* New York: Bell Harbour Press, 2001.

The Edge of Night

The Edge of Night, one of the top-ten longest-running soap operas in daytime television history, debuted April 2, 1956, on CBS, along with *As the World Turns.* The two shows were the first soaps to air for a full half hour on a major television network, and the enthusiastic audience response marked a new trend in the orientation of popular television. *The Edge of Night*'s original time slot, 4:30 p.m., inspired the show's title, but the title reflected the content, which was at times graphically violent. While some television critics, including the redoubtable *TV Guide,* have argued that *The Edge of Night* was technically a serialized melodrama rather than a soap opera, over its almost three-decade run the show turned to themes most commonly associated with soap opera drama: sex, romance, and family turmoil.

Set in Monticello, a turbulent midwestern town, *The Edge of Night* revolved around the criminal investigations of Mike Karr and his sometimes unorthodox detective work and courtroom tactics. After the first couple of seasons, Karr married his devoted assistant, Sara Lane, though the writers had her run over by a bus on an episode first airing on February 17, 1961. Lane was the first major soap character to be killed off, and the high realism of the accident—the show was broadcast live until 1975—sent the audience into shock. Thousands of letters and phone calls deluged the network and prompted a televised announcement by Teal Ames and John Larkin (the actors who played Sara and Mike), explaining that Ames was fine in real life and had left the show to pursue other opportunities.

Over the years Mike Karr was played by three different actors: John Larkin, 1956–1961; Laurence Hugo, 1961–1972; and Forrest Compton, 1972–1984. Exemplifying a paradox that television audiences have simply come to accept, the three replacements were neither announced nor explained, which did nothing to disturb the sense of realism so central to *The Edge of Night*'s success. By the 1970s, however, the show's writers perhaps did push the limits of believability in the popular Adam-Nicole love story. Nicole (Maeve McGuire; later Jayne Bentzen and Lisa Sloan) had been killed off in a drowning during the explosion of a yacht, only to rejoin the show two years later when it was discovered that in fact she had survived the drowning, joined a gang in France, and suffered a long bout of amnesia before returning to Monticello.

After the show's sponsor, Procter & Gamble, requested a time change in the 1970s, *The Edge of Night* experienced a ratings slump from which it never recovered. The show moved to ABC on December 1, 1975, the first daytime serial to change networks, but was canceled on December 28, 1984. A few years later it enjoyed a short-lived cult revival in syndication on the USA cable network. Among the sophisticated luminaries who had early on enjoyed some of its 7,420 episodes were Cole Porter, P. G. Wodehouse, Tallulah Bankhead, and Eleanor Roosevelt.

Michele S. Shauf

SEE ALSO: As the World Turns*; Porter, Cole; Soap Operas; Television;* TV Guide*; Wodehouse, P. G..*

BIBLIOGRAPHY

Erickson, Hal. *Encyclopedia of Television Law Shows: Factual and Fictional Series about Judges, Lawyers and the Courtroom, 1948–2008.* Jefferson, NC: McFarland, 2009.

Hyatt, Wesley. *The Encyclopedia of Daytime Television.* New York: Billboard Books, 1997.

McNeil, Alex. *Total Television: The Comprehensive Guide to Programming from 1948 to the Present.* New York: Penguin Books, 1996.

Edison, Thomas Alva *(1847–1931)*

Thomas Alva Edison—inventor of the phonograph in 1877, the incandescent lightbulb in 1879, and electrical power distribution to the public in 1880—is considered one of America's greatest creative minds. He is the only American to have patented an invention every year for sixty-five consecutive years, beginning in 1869 with his electrical vote recorder. In all, Edison held 1,093 patents, including those for a stock ticker, a component of mimeograph systems, and a telephone transmitter that led to commercial telephone and radio broadcasting. Using a mobile studio and a photographic device he designed, Edison also created the first apparatus for projecting motion pictures. This invention, along with George Eastman's refinement of film, provided the foundation for the motion picture industry.

It is appropriate that the creator of so many products, a man whose impact on America proved to be revolutionary, should have provided a symbol of originality and intelligence: the shining lightbulb, used in illustrations to represent a bright idea.

Sharon Brown

SEE ALSO: *Phonograph; Radio.*

BIBLIOGRAPHY

Baldwin, Neil. *Edison Inventing the Century.* New York: Hyperion, 1995.

Israel, Paul. *Edison: A Life of Invention.* New York, John Wiley & Sons, 1998.

Jonnes, Jill. *Empires of Light: Edison, Tesla, Westinghouse, and the Race to Electrify the World.* New York: Random House, 2003.

Josephson, Matthew. *Edison: A Biography.* New York: John Wiley & Sons, 1992.

Stross, Randall E. *The Wizard of Menlo Park: How Thomas Alva Edison Invented the Modern World.* New York: Crown, 2007.

The Edsel

Announced with great fanfare in 1957 after almost a decade of planning, the Ford Motor Company's Edsel model car became one of the great flops in automotive history. The car was forecasted to sell more than 200,000 units in its first year but sold less than 85,000 during its three-year run.

Despite massive advertising—including preempting *The Ed Sullivan Show* with *The Edsel Show* featuring Bing Crosby and Frank Sinatra—the Edsel was the wrong car at the wrong time. The auto industry, after years of massive sales, hit a post-Sputnik slump, and the new car, with its strange oval grille, was doomed. Named after Henry Ford's son Edsel, the name is now synonymous with failure. As such, Edsel is often used as a punch line and visual gag. The car can be seen in films such as *Pee Wee's Big Adventure* and *Airplane II*, where the engine from a 1959 Edsel is used to jumpstart a space shuttle.

Patrick Jones

SEE ALSO: *Advertising; Automobile; Crosby, Bing; The Fifties; Ford, Henry; Ford Motor Company; Sinatra, Frank.*

BIBLIOGRAPHY

Baughman, James L. "The Frustrated Persuader: Fairfax M. Cone and the Edsel Advertising Campaign, 1957–1959." In *The Other Fifties: Interrogating Midcentury American Icons,* ed. Joel Foreman. Urbana: University of Illinois Press, 1997.

Bonsall, Thomas E. *Disaster in Dearborn: The Story of the Edsel.* Stanford, CA: Stanford General Books, 2002.

Brooks, John. *The Fate of the Edsel and Other Business Adventures.* New York: Harper & Row, 1963.

Deutsch, Jan G. *Selling the People's Cadillac: The Edsel and Corporate Responsibility.* New Haven, CT: Yale University Press, 1976.

Warnock, C. Gayle. *The Rest of the Edsel Affair.* Paradise Valley, AZ: Pro West, 2007.

Edwards, James *(1918–1970)*

With his thoughtful, intelligent manner and splendid good looks, African American actor James Edwards came to epitomize the "new Negro" in post–World War II Hollywood. Edwards performed in theater, on radio and television, and in feature films. He also made spoken-word recordings, operated his own acting school, directed and produced plays, and worked as a singer. Most significantly, Edwards was a groundbreaker whose work helped to forge positive change during a volatile period in the social history of postwar America.

Edwards began his acting career in theater. He was born in Muncie, Indiana, and attended Indiana and Northwestern universities, earning a bachelor of science degree in 1938 for dramatics. As a lieutenant in the army during World War II, he was wounded in battle; surgeons had to rebuild his face, and he endured a long, painful convalescent period. Recovered, he pursued an acting career and appeared in the controversial 1945 stage production of *How Deep Are the Roots* (in which he portrayed the love interest of a very white Barbara Bel Geddes).

POSTWAR HOLLYWOOD SUCCESS

After honing his craft on the stage, Edwards enjoyed a moderately successful career in the film industry. After two small speaking roles in the 1949 films *Manhandled* and *The Set-Up*, he burst into prominence with his portrayal of a tortured soldier in Stanley Kramer's *Home of the Brave* (1949). Edwards was cast as Peter Moss, a World War II army private who becomes paralyzed after an attack—not from the Japanese enemy but from the racial prejudice he endured. As the first film to deal honestly with racism during a time when the subject was considered taboo, *Home of the Brave* made box-office history, breaking attendance records, drawing huge audiences, and earning thoughtful praise from many sectors of society. Moreover, Edwards, an everyday guy from Indiana, as he liked to call himself, became a Hollywood movie star. He was proclaimed the "Bronze Valentino" by black newspapers across the country.

For many reasons, Edwards was never again to achieve such success in another film. Still, he would continue to find work and appeared alongside such film luminaries as Robert Ryan, Frank Sinatra, Raymond Massey, Ethel Waters, Humphrey Bogart, Rock Hudson, Eartha Kitt, Gregory Peck, and Sammy Davis Jr. Some of Edwards's films include issues of race as a main or secondary story line. In *Night of the Quarter Moon* (1959), his brilliant portrayal of a lawyer who defends a woman in a case of miscegenation won him kudos, even though the film was little more than a "B"-grade exploitation vehicle. In *Bright Victory* (1951), Edwards portrays a blinded black soldier whose sightless friend rejects him when he learns he is black. In his role as Corporal Thompson in Sam Fuller's Korean War cult classic *The Steel Helmet* (1951), a communist officer chides Edwards for risking his life for a country that requires him to sit in the back of bus. Edwards appeared in a number of war and combat films, including *Battle Hymn* (1957), *Men in War* (1957), *Blood and Steel* (1959), and the star-studded *Pork Chop Hill* (1959).

More significantly, Edwards appeared as "Joe Everyman" in films such as *The Phenix City Story* (1955); Stanley Kubrick's *The Killing* (1956); *The Manchurian Candidate* (1962); and *The Sandpiper* (1965), in which a tormented Elizabeth Taylor confides in him as she would her best friend. Indeed, these uncommon appearances were applauded by the African American community, which appreciated the inclusion of black characters in Hollywood pictures—not as stereotypes or victims of racial prejudice but as everyday people.

However, Edwards was no Hollywood Negro poster boy. He was a forthright critic of racism and discrimination. He spoke disparagingly against the controversial *Amos 'n' Andy* television show. As Congress sought to root out the supposed influence of communism in Hollywood, he refused to cooperate with federal investigators who wanted him to testify against Paul Robeson. In regard to his cocky persona, he was quoted in the December 1953 issue of *Our World* magazine as saying, "If arrogance means that I try at all times to maintain a pride and dignity that would exemplify favorably my person and my people—I say, yes, I am arrogant and shall remain so." The FBI maintained a file on this handsome, intelligent, outspoken actor who dated white women, hobnobbed with big-name movie stars, and got into fights when he couldn't control his liquor.

SHIFT TO TELEVISION

During the volatile period of school integration, bus boycotts, racial violence, and hateful rhetoric, Edwards joined a small cadre of black performers who earned dramatic roles on prime-time television. For his efforts Edwards earned the praise of an African American community still reeling from the *Amos 'n' Andy* debacle and encouraged to see the new medium's inclusion of black characters in "dignified" settings. Some of Edwards's performances were uncommonly good, such as his 1963 role in the program *The Fugitive*. Appearing with Ruby Dee, he plays as a boxer so consumed with his need to earn the respect usually denied a black man that he puts his health in danger.

Along with an appearance on *The Ed Sullivan Show* and roles in a number of early television's dramatic anthologies, Edwards's other television appearances include *The Outcasts*; *The Virginian*; *Cowboy in Africa*; *Burke's Law*; *Dr. Kildare*; *Death Valley Days*; *The Nurses*; *East Side, West Side*; and *Alfred Hitchcock Presents*.

In 1970 Edwards appeared as a personal aide to George C. Scott's General George Patton in the Academy Award–winning film *Patton*. He died before the picture was released of an apparent heart attack, leaving behind devastated Indiana family members to whom he had remained close throughout his career. Edwards was a multitalented artist, a pioneer of the entertainment industry, and excellent actor who cared about his craft.

Pamala S. Deane

SEE ALSO: The Amos 'n' Andy Show; *Bogart, Humphrey; Civil Rights Movement;* Dr. Kildare; The Fugitive; *Hollywood; Hudson, Rock; Kubrick, Stanley;* The Manchurian Candidate; *McCarthyism; Movie Stars;* Patton; *Peck, Gregory; Robeson, Paul; Sinatra, Frank; Taylor, Elizabeth; Television; Valentino, Rudolph; War Movies; World War II.*

BIBLIOGRAPHY

Bogle, Donald. *Bright Boulevards, Bold Dreams: The Story of Black Hollywood.* New York: One World Ballantine Books, 2005.

Deane, Pamala-Suzette. *James Edwards: African American Movie Icon.*. Jefferson, NC: McFarland, 2010.

Edwards, James. "Hollywood. So What!" *Our World*, December 1953.

Nesteby, James R. *Black Images in American Films, 1896–1954: The Interplay between Civil Rights and Film Culture.* Washington, DC: University Press of America, 1982.

Edwards, Ralph *(1913–2005)*

Television producer Ralph Edwards is best known for creating the game show *Truth or Consequences*. Born on June 13, 1913, Edwards began his career in the entertainment industry as a radio announcer while attending the University of California, Berkeley. After graduating, he moved to New York and became a nationally syndicated radio personality. In 1940 Edwards produced, wrote, and emceed the radio version of *Truth or Consequences*, which aired for thirty-eight consecutive years on radio and television. He introduced the "live on film" technique by having *Truth or Consequences* filmed before a live studio audience when it debuted on television in 1950; the show was hosted for eighteen years by Bob Barker, who went on to become television's most durable game show host with *The Price Is Right*.

Edwards produced dozens of television game shows, including *This Is Your Life*, *Knockout*, *Place the Face*, and *It Could Be You*. In 1981 he teamed up with producer Stu Billett to create a show that introduced a new form of the reality genre to television; they called their show *The People's Court*. Edwards died of heart failure on November 16, 2005, in Los Angeles.

Lara Bickell

SEE ALSO: *Game Shows;* The Price Is Right; *Radio; Reality Television;* This Is Your Life.

BIBLIOGRAPHY

Fabe, Maxene. *TV Game Shows*. New York: Doubleday, 1979.

Graham, Jefferson. *Come on Down!!!: The TV Game Show Book.* New York: Abbeville Press, 1988.

Schwartz, David; Steve Ryan; Fred Wostbrock; et al. *The Encyclopedia of Television Game Shows.* New York: New York Zoetrope, 1987.

The Eight

SEE: *Ashcan School.*

8 Mile

SEE: *Eminem.*

Eight-Track Tape

During the 1960s the eight-track tape player was an ambitious attempt to employ magnetic prerecorded tape in a convenient format for use in home and automobile stereos. The eight-track was significant evidence that Americans now demanded music while they traveled and that the automobile had become a place to experience entertainment. By the early 1980s, however, the eight-track became a symbol of obsolescence in audio technology and an artifact of 1960s and 1970s nostalgia.

Several manufacturers developed tape cartridges in the 1960s as a format for recorded sound. The Lear Company, a manufacturer of executive jet airplanes, produced a continuous-loop cartridge with four sets of paired stereo tracks—thus, the name eight-track. In 1965 representatives from Lear approached Ford Motor Company with a plan to introduce this format into automobiles. People wanted to select their own music to listen to while traveling, and the eight-track tape was convenient for the driver because it could be inserted into the player with one hand.

Ford equipped millions of automobiles with eight-track players, and millions more were manufactured for use in home audio systems. Although the eight-track format became a major format for prerecorded popular music in the 1960s and 1970s, it was not an entirely satisfactory product for the user. A user could not record on it and could not access selections easily. By the end of the 1970s, the eight-track tape had been overtaken by the compact cassette and dropped by audio manufacturers and record companies.

Andre Millard

SEE ALSO: *Automobile; Cassette Tape; Ford Motor Company; Long-Playing Record; Radio.*

BIBLIOGRAPHY

Kusisto, Oscar P. "Magnetic Tape Recording: Reels, Cassettes, or Cartridges?" *Journal of the Audio Engineering Society* 25 (1977): 828–835.

Millard, Andre J. *America on Record: A History of Recorded Sound.* Cambridge, NY: Cambridge University Press, 1995.

Morton, David L., Jr. *Sound Recording: The Life Story of Technology.* Baltimore, MD: The Johns Hopkins University Press, 2006.

Einstein, Albert *(1879–1955)*

In the 1910s Albert Einstein proposed a series of theories that led to new ways of thinking about space, time, and gravitation. For the first time the scientific world raced far beyond the theories of the seventeenth-century English scientist Sir Isaac Newton, who began his study of gravity by observing an apple fall from a tree. Einstein's famous energy-mass equation, which asserts that a particle of matter can be transformed into an astounding quantity of energy, led to the construction of atomic and hydrogen bombs with unimaginable capacities for destruction. In his own time he was widely recognized as one of the most innovative geniuses in human history. Today, in the realm of popular culture, his name is synonymous with genius, and many a young prodigy has been called an "Einstein."

Einstein was born in Ulm, Germany, on March 14, 1879, and grew up in Munich, where he was educated in public schools that he found to be boring, as well as highly regimented and intimidating. He showed such little ability as a student that his mother recommended that he study music, and he became an accomplished violinist, playing throughout his life for relaxation, not for public performance. Under the influence of two uncles, as a boy Einstein began to develop a curiosity about science and mathematics, and at age twelve he announced that he would concentrate his mind on solving the riddle of the *huge world.*

At age fifteen—with poor grades in languages, history, and geography—Einstein left his German school without a diploma and moved with his family to Milan. He resumed his education at the famous Federal Polytechnic Academy in Zurich, where he completed four years of physics and mathematics. After graduating in the spring of 1900, Einstein began a two-month tenure

Albert Einstein. *Einstein's famous energy–mass equation led to the development of the nuclear bomb.* ERNST HAAS/ERNST HAAS/GETTY IMAGES.

as a mathematics teacher before being employed as an examiner in the Swiss patent office in Bern. He continued his research and writing and in 1905 published a thesis titled *A New Determination of Molecular Dimensions* that won him a PhD from the University of Zurich. Four more important papers were published that year in the prestigious German journal *Annalen der Physik*, forever changing human's view of the universe.

THEORY OF RELATIVITY

Now accepted by his colleagues as one of Europe's leading physicists and much sought after as a consultant, Einstein left the patent office and returned to teaching in universities in Switzerland and Germany. In 1914 he moved to Berlin, where he worked at the Prussian Academy of Sciences, doing his research on the general theory of relativity and lecturing occasionally at the University of Berlin. He published his findings in 1916 in an article titled (in translation) "The Foundation of the General Theory of Relativity." He postulated that gravitation was not a force, as Newton had thought, but a curved field in a space-time continuum. This could be proved, he wrote, by measuring the deflection of starlight during a period of total eclipse. In 1919 British scientists photographed a solar eclipse from Principe Island in the Gulf of Guinea, and their calculations verified Einstein's predictions. Einstein was amazed at the worldwide acclamation he received, but he resented the constant interruptions his new fame brought. In 1921 he was awarded the Nobel Prize for Physics.

During the 1920s Einstein worked toward finding a mathematical relationship between electromagnetism and gravitation, thus relating the universal properties of matter and energy into a single equation or formula. This quest for a unified field theory, which occupied the rest of his life, proved futile. The rapidly developing quantum theory showed that the movement of a single particle could not be predicted because of the uncertainty in measuring both its speed and its position at the same time. The first version of the unified field theory was published in 1929, but the tentative, preliminary nature of the work was apparent to the scientific community.

In the 1930s Einstein spent as much time championing the cause of peace as he did discussing science. He established the Einstein War Resisters International Fund to bring massive public pressure on the World Disarmament Conference, scheduled to meet in Geneva in 1932. After the failure of the conference, which he termed "farcical," Einstein visited Geneva to focus world attention on the failure and on the necessity of reducing the world's firepower.

FLEEING NAZI GERMANY

When Adolf Hitler became chancellor of Germany in 1933, Einstein warned the world that Nazi Germany was preparing for war. He then renounced his German citizenship and moved to America. He accepted a full-time position at the newly formed Institute for Advanced Study at Princeton, New Jersey. Nazi storm troopers ransacked his summer home near Berlin in reprisal.

Einstein's life at Princeton remained the same for the next twenty years. He lived in a simple frame house, walking daily a mile or so to the Institute, where he worked on his unified field theory and talked with colleagues. In a 1994 movie titled *I.Q.*, Walter Matthau played the role of Einstein enjoying his intellectual life at Princeton. He rarely traveled, preferring to relax with his violin and sail on a local lake. He took no part in the work at Los Alamos, New Mexico, where the nuclear fission bombs were being made. When he died in his sleep on April 18, 1955, his wife found an incomplete statement, written to honor Israeli Independence Day, on his desk. It included this statement: "What I seek to accomplish is simply to serve with my feeble capacity truth and justice at the risk of pleasing no one."

Benjamin Griffith

SEE ALSO: *The Bomb; Cold War; World War II.*

BIBLIOGRAPHY

Brian, Denis. *Einstein: A Life.* New York: J. Wiley, 1996.

Calaprice, Alice. *The Einstein Almanac.* Baltimore, MD: Johns Hopkins University Press, 2005.

Holton, Gerald James. *Einstein, History, and Other Passions: The Rebellion against Science at the End of the Twentieth Century.* New York: Springer-Verlag, 1995.

Pais, Abraham. *"Subtle Is the Lord . . . : The Science and Life of Albert Einstein.* New York: Oxford University Press, 1982.

Rowe, David E., and Robert J. Schulmann, eds. *Einstein on Politics: His Private Thoughts and Public Stands on Nationalism, Zionism, War, Peace, and the Bomb.* Princeton, NJ: Princeton University Press, 2007.

Eisner, Will *(1917–2005)*

With a career as a writer and an artist that spanned virtually the entire history of the medium, Will Eisner was one of the most innovative and influential creators of comic books and graphic novels. From his earliest work on the newspaper supplement *The Spirit,* Eisner strove to understand and develop his chosen art form. His career was driven by a canny business sense and by his belief that sequential art (as he preferred to call comic books and graphic novels) is a valid medium of artistic expression that deserves wider acceptance and respect.

As a teenager, Eisner's artistic talent simply represented a way out of the grim reality of Bronx, New York, tenement life during the Great Depression. After a brief stint studying at the Art Students League and working in a magazine advertising department, Eisner began writing and drawing comics for *Wow, What a Magazine!* in 1936. Samuel "Jerry" Iger was editing *Wow*, and when the magazine folded after four issues, Eisner and Iger formed their own studio to package comic-book material for Fiction House, Fox Comics, and other publishers. At first, the prolific Eisner produced most of the work under different pen names. As the Eisner-Iger Shop flourished, however, the young Eisner began supervising a staff of artists that included Bob Kane and Jack Kirby.

COMIC-BOOK SUPPLEMENT

In 1939 Eisner was approached by a features syndicate about producing a comic-book supplement for newspapers. He jumped at the chance to reach a more mature audience through newspaper distribution. Because the syndicate had approached him—it was not likely to find anyone else capable of producing a complete comic book every week—Eisner was able to retain ownership and creative control of the feature. He sold his interest in the Eisner-Iger Shop to Iger and took four of the staff artists with him to form Will Eisner Productions.

The newspaper supplement that debuted in 1940 was simply called *The Comic Book Section*, but it became better known by the title of the lead feature, *The Spirit*. The syndicate saw the supplement as a way to benefit from the growing national market for comic books that was sparked by the appearance of *Superman* in 1938 and *The Batman* in 1939, and it envisioned the Spirit as a superhero very much in the mold of these two characters. Eisner was more interested in telling good stories, and his only concessions to the superhero concept were a simple domino mask and a pair of gloves.

When Eisner was drafted in 1942, his assistants, primarily Lou Fine, took over for the duration of World War II. Fine was true to the style Eisner had set for the book, and it was a subtle change compared to what happened when Eisner returned from the army. Many early stories from *The Spirit* were whimsical and fantasy-oriented, but when Eisner returned from the war, his stories had greater realism and concern for the human condition—in his work, that usually meant the condition of humans crowded together by big city life. As Catherine Yronwode puts it in *The Art of Will Eisner*, "New York, or more properly, Brooklyn and the Bronx, was, in Eisner's metaphoric world, transformed into a stage upon which the most wide-sweeping and the most intimate dramas of human life were enacted."

Eisner stopped producing *The Spirit* in 1952 and devoted his time to his new venture, American Visuals Corporation, which was a successful producer of educational and corporate comics for the next twenty-five years. One of his chief clients was the U.S. Army, for which he produced *P*S, the Preventive Maintenance Monthly* for more than twenty years.

SEQUENTIAL ART TRAILBLAZER

In 1974 Eisner began teaching comics courses at the School of Visual Arts in New York. He reworked his lecture material and published two books, *Comics and Sequential Art* (1985) and *Graphic Storytelling* (1995), that have helped advance both artistic and critical understanding of the comics medium.

Eisner had used art as a means of escape from the tenements of New York, but eventually he used his art to explore the personal and universal meanings of life in the big city. In 1976, inspired by the decidedly nonadolescent material that he discovered in the underground comics of the late 1960s and early 1970s, he began creating a major comic-book work that he hoped would find an adult audience. His 192-page work *A Contract with God* (1978) was groundbreaking in that it deviated from the usual adventure material to present more realistic and intimate human dramas. At sixty, Eisner began blazing a new trail in the medium and followed *Contract* with more than two dozen original and deeply felt graphic novels, including *A Life Force* (1983), *To the Heart of the Storm* (1991), and *The Name of the Game* (2001). He had finished his final work, *The Plot*, in 2005 and was starting on a new project when he died of complications following open heart surgery.

Eisner remains one of the most widely respected masters of the comics art form. In 1988 the major artistic awards of the American comic-book industry, the Eisners, were established in his honor. The National Cartoonists Society gave him the Milton Caniff Lifetime Achievement Award in 1995, and in 2002 he was given a lifetime achievement award from the National Federation of Jewish Culture, only the second such award given in the history of the organization.

Eisner's experimentation with layout and composition in *The Spirit* stories clearly established the comic book as a medium distinct from its comic strip origins. His championing of new forms and mature content in the graphic novel helped establish comics as an art form. Much of the visual language of the form was invented, or at least perfected, by Eisner. In the afterword to Eisner's *New York the Big City*, acclaimed comic-book writer Alan Moore provides an eloquent statement of Eisner's importance to the medium: "He is the single person most responsible for giving comics their brains."

Randy Duncan

SEE ALSO: *Batman; Comic Books; Graphic Novels; The Great Depression; Kirby, Jack; Superman; Underground Comics; World War II.*

BIBLIOGRAPHY

Andelman, Bob. *Will Eisner: A Spirited Life*. Milwaukie, OR: M Press, 2005.

Couch, N. C. Christopher, and Stephen Weiner. *The Will Eisner Companion: The Pioneering Spirit of the Father of the Graphic Novel*. New York: DC Comics, 2004.

Eisner, Will; Jack Kirby; Lloyd Greif; et al. *Will Eisner: Portrait of a Sequential Artist*. DVD. Montilla Pictures, 2010.

Inge, M. Thomas, ed. *Will Eisner: Conversations*. Jackson: University Press of Mississippi, 2011.

Schumacher, Michael. *Will Eisner: A Dreamer's Life in Comics*. New York: Bloomsbury, 2010.

Yronwode, Catherine, and Denis Kitchen. *The Art of Will Eisner*. Princeton, WI: Kitchen Sink Press, 1982.

El Teatro Campesino

The annexation of Mexico's northern territories by the United States in 1848 marked the beginning of the Mexican American theater arts tradition. Mexican American (California Chicano, Texas Tejano, and New Mexico Hispano inclusive) theater evolved as an amalgamation of Mexican street theater arts such as the *carpa* (traveling tent theater) and the zarzuela (Spanish comedic opera) with a European, Bertolt Brechtian brand of sociopolitical drama. Until the 1960s civil rights movements, however, Mexican American theatrical arts had not received mainstream recognition.

In 1965 two Chicano activists—the young, fiery new actor-director, Luis Valdez, and the powerful farmworkers' organizer Cesar Chavez—teamed up during California's "Great Delano Strike" and founded El Teatro Campesino Cultural (The Workers' Cultural Center). Drawing on his firsthand experience as an actor-director working in San Francisco's Mime Troupe and his broad knowledge of Mexican drama, history, and myth, Valdez trained striking farmworkers to perform and write politically savvy bilingual performances. He writes in his 1971 book, *Actos: El Teatro Campesino*, of the group's mission: "Chicano theater must be revolutionary in technique as well as in content. It must be popular, subject to no other critics except the pueblo itself; but it must also educate the pueblo toward an appreciation of social change, on and off the stage."

El Teatro Campesino's performances became well known among those involved in the "Brown Power Movement" of the

1960s. For example, one of its first productions, *Las dos caras del patroncito* (*The Two-Faced Boss*), fully embodied El Teatro Campesino's ideal of developing a socially aware dramatic art form combining Aztec and European traditions. The loosely improvised, bilingually acted piece—composed of ten- to fifteen-minute *actos*, or skits—not only candidly addresses a farmworker's plight at the hands of a money-grubbing boss, but it does so with a tinge of humor. The influence of satirically playful Italian commedia dell'arte allows the piece to both incite action and offer the audience the possibility of laughing at "The Boss," who dons a yellow pig-face mask and hides behind a rent-a-goon bodyguard.

In the late 1960s and early 1970s, El Teatro Campesino performed a series of plays that used the *mito*, or culturally anchored act, to explore the plight of the Chicano dwelling increasingly in inner-city barrios. For example, in *Los vendidos* (*The Sell-Outs*), the audience not only meets a Chicana Republican named Miss Jiménez; a *pachuco*, or Chicano gang member; and a revolutionary but also gets a big taste of Aztec mythology and Mexican culture.

El Teatro Campesino won a special Obie Award in 1968. In 1971 Valdez and a professionalized El Teatro Campesino troupe moved to San Juan Bautista, California, where a range of performances continued to infuse the mythical dimension of Chicano identity. Figures such as *Huitzilopochtli* (Aztec sun and war god), Quetzalcoatl, and the Virgin de Guadalupe would appear symbolically to explore the everyday struggles of survival, from border-crossing tragedies to romances to family breakups.

El Teatro Campesino's professionalization and broadened scope quickly led to recognition by mainstream critics. In the mid-1970s the famed British artistic director and drama critic Peter Brooks traveled to San Juan Bautista to work with the group. The result: *The Conference of the Birds*, whose nationwide success opened doors outside the Americas. El Teatro Campesino's follow-up production, *La carpa de los rasquachis* (*The Tent of the Underdogs*), toured eight European countries. And in 1979 its *Zoot Suit*—a music-infused drama that retells the story of the 1942 Zoot Suit riots in Los Angeles of 1942 from a Chicano, Aztec-mythic point of view—was the first Chicano play to open on New York's Broadway. While *Zoot Suit* only had a short run, flopping at the box office, it received glowing critical reviews from drama critics.

After many years as a professional theater-arts organization, El Teatro Campesino is recognized as a major contributor to dramatic arts. While the troupe continues with performances in the Old Mission at San Juan Bautista—at Christmas they regularly perform their Chicano-reenvisioned miracle plays such as the *La virgen del Tepeyac* (The virgin of Tepeyac) and *La pastorela* (The pastoral)—the members continue to experiment with new forms and techniques.

El Teatro Campesino has moved into television, and Valdez has directed several films. Finally, it is largely due to the troupe's struggle to clear a space in the dramatic arts terrain that opportunity has opened up for many contemporary Chicano playwrights—Cherríe Moraga, Ricardo Bracho, and Octavio Solis, to name a few—to express a more complicated (queer sexuality and gender-inclusive) vision of what it means to be Latino and Latina in the United States.

Frederick Luis Aldama

SEE ALSO: *Broadway; Chavez, Cesar; Valdez, Luis; Zoot Suit.*

BIBLIOGRAPHY

Aldama, Frederick Luis. *Spilling the Beans in Chicanolandia: Conversations with Writers and Artists.* Austin: University of Texas Press, 2006.

Krasner, David. *A Companion to Twentieth-Century American Drama. Blackwell Companions to Literature and Culture.* Oxford, England: John Wiley & Sons, 2007.

Tatum, Charles. *Chicano Literature.* Boston: Twayne Publishers, 1982.

Valdez, Luis. *Actos: El Teatro Campesino.* San Juan Bautista, CA: Cucaracha Publications, 1971.

El Vez *(1960–)*

Unlike most Elvis Presley impersonators, Robert Lopez has created his own successful and unique character from the legacy of the legendary performer. Looking back on his uneventful life growing up in Chula Vista, California, Lopez recalls that his uncles would wear "continental slacks and slight pompadours in that Elvis style." Considering this, perhaps it is not surprising that the shy boy from Chula Vista would one day transform himself into the nationally acclaimed jumpsuit-wearing, sombrero-sporting, pencil-line-mustachioed Chicano musician/performance artist El Vez.

In 1988, while showcasing an Elvis-inspired kitsch/folk art exhibition at La Luz de Jesús Gallery on Melrose in Los Angeles, a twenty-nine-year-old Lopez embraced his true calling: to combine his talents as a musician (he used to play for the Southern California punk band the Zeroes) with his taste for Mexican kitsch and reinvent himself as El Vez. Just in time for Weep Week (the annual celebration of Presley's birthday), Lopez traveled to Memphis, Tennessee, where he secured a spot for himself at Graceland's hot spot for Elvis impersonators, Bob's Bad Vapors. Lopez's over-the-top costume, super-gelled hair coif, "Mexican Elvis" identifying sign, and corrido music (Mexican ballads) cut and mixed into Elvis tunes were a huge success. With the help of newspaper wire services, Lopez became an overnight, nationally recognized celebrity.

Certain of his destiny, El Vez—along with his Memphis Mariachis and the hip-gyrating Lovely Elvettes (Gladysita, Lisa María, Prescillita, and Qué Linda Thompson)—began touring all over the United States and Europe. He has received critical recognition from the *New York Times* and *Rolling Stone* and has appeared on such television shows as *The Tonight Show* and *Oprah* and the cable network CNN. El Vez has released numerous CDs, with titles such as *El Vez Is Alive, Not Hispanic, G.I. Ay, Ay Blues*, and *A Merry Mex-Mus* (in which reindeer named Poncho and Pedro join Santa's team).

El Vez is not merely a novelty act. Along with Mexican mariachi tunes, he has used a range of popular music sounds from the likes of Elvis, David Bowie, T. Rex, Queen, and the Beatles to address issues such as California's anti-immigration act and former California governor Pete Wilson's racism. For example, the lyrics in his song "Chicanisma" (set against the music of Elvis's "Little Sister") are critical of the male-dominated Chicano community's oppression of women, whereas his revision of "Mystery Train" (called "Misery Train") tells the story of Pancho Villa and Los Zapatistas destroying *los capitalistas.* "Viva Las Vegas" is a crash course in preconquistador Mexican civilization, mixing musical styles and speeches to discuss the plight of the Mexican immigrant worker. On his album *Graciasland*—a rockabilly/country version of Paul Simon's *Graceland*—El Vez identifies the southwestern United States as the spiritual homeland Aztlán for Chicanos. As the *New York Times* reported in December 1995, "He may look and dress like a young Elvis Presley (though Elvis never had El Vez's pencil-thin mustache), but El Vez is his own creation."

Frederick Luis Aldama

SEE ALSO: *Pop Music; Presley, Elvis.*

BIBLIOGRAPHY

Homan, Shane. *Access All Eras: Tribute Bands and Global Pop Culture.* Maidenhead, England: Open University Press, 2006.

Muñoz, José, and Celeste Fraser Delgado. *Everynight Life: Dance, Music, and Culture.* Durham, NC: Duke University Press, 1997.

Electric Appliances

By the turn of the twentieth century, it was common knowledge that the American home did not function efficiently. In an attempt to improve this, homemaking became more scientific. Home economists and other observers began to analyze the processes of managing the home and determine how these tasks could be carried out more effectively. This sensibility provided the crucial opportunity for technological innovation to find its way into the American home.

Household technology, especially in the form of new electric appliances, radically altered the American home in the twentieth century. These innovations, of course, relied on the inventions of Thomas Alva Edison and others who perfected the generation and transferal of electric energy for home use in the early 1900s. Although many American households remained without electricity through World War II, the American ideal of the electrified home had been firmly established.

REFRIGERATION

To say that any single electric appliance transformed American life more than another is difficult, but a good case can be made for the electric refrigerator. As it took form in the 1920s, the refrigerator revolutionized food storage capabilities in a dramatic fashion. Improving on the "icebox," which was limited by the melting of a block of hand-delivered ice, electricity enabled the use of pumps that relied on centrifugal pressure to push cooling fluids throughout an insulated box. Enhanced for safety and efficiency, the refrigerator soon became a household mainstay. It allowed homemakers to stock perishable items, ending the necessity of frequent trips to the market. Moreover, the addition of the "deep freeze" (freezer) in the 1940s allowed for the creation of the frozen-food market. In 1941, 52 percent of American families owned refrigerators; ten years later, this number had risen to 80 percent, and by 1980 refrigeration was almost universal.

THE NEW AMERICAN HOME

Shifts in home technology after World War II were heavily based on labor-saving devices. Increased electrification, spurred by President Franklin D. Roosevelt's New Deal policies of the 1930s, provided the power source, and a new model of the American housewife, promoted when soldiers returned to civilian jobs, offered a suitable rationale. Whereas domestic servants had aided many homemakers previously, the contemporary American housewife relied predominantly on the assistance of electric appliances. During these years the growing middle class elevated the ideal standard of living to include the trappings of affluence, among them kitchen appliances, washing machines, and televisions. The reformed cultural values defined the modern middle-class home as self-sufficient; in addition, it was expected to ease the pressures of everyday life through the application of technology.

The idealization of the new American home was crystallized in what is known as "the kitchen debate." In this astonishing 1959 Cold War conversation, Vice President Richard Nixon and Soviet Premier Nikita Khrushchev discussed ideology and domestic technology through the medium of a "model American home" constructed in Moscow. Nixon drew attention to the washing machines as work-saving devices. Khrushchev countered Nixon's boasts with pride in the productivity of Soviet female laborers. Summing up the capitalist ideal, Nixon responded, "What we want is to make easier the life of our housewives."

No apparatus embodies the desire to ease domestic pressures more than the microwave. Perfected in 1946 but reaching widespread acceptance only in the 1980s, these ovens heat water and chemical molecules in food with short-wave radio energy similar to that used in radar and television. In addition to cooking foods rapidly without heating the environment, microwaves make defrosting frozen foods easier, again altering American patterns of life. For many people the ubiquitous microwave is the most indispensable item in the kitchen.

ENTER THE COMPUTER

An entirely new class of home electric appliances involving computer components began to emerge in the 1990s. Computers and other electronic and information technologies did not stop at revolutionizing the workplace; they have come to be considered essential to American home life. Internally, most home appliances now use computer controls to improve reliability and service, and the computer itself has also become part of the domestic landscape. The Internet, at first available only when funneled through routers to personal computers, now controls entertainment in many households, supplying electronic games, music, movies, and television programming to television sets and handheld devices. In addition, some Americans have integrated their smartphones (mobile phones with computer-enabled features) into home management, allowing them to use the Internet to adjust thermostats and turn off lights from anywhere.

In the twenty-first century, the plethora of electronic appliances and devices has also contributed to a new awareness of the implications of "e-Waste." The staggering pace of technological innovation has aggravated the problem of planned obsolescence (in which products are engineered not to last) as Americans toss out the old in order to acquire the new. This tendency, combined with dropping prices, has significantly increased the volume of outdated gadgets in landfills. In some instances electronic appliances containing valuable—and often toxic—materials are shipped to developing societies to be dismantled and scrapped.

Although some portions of the devices can be recycled in this process, the rest is disposed of improperly.

Electric appliances have completely changed the workings of the American household since 1945. They continue to be a source of innovation and gadgetry as engineers work to enhance, create efficiency in, and solve the problems of home life.

Brian Black

SEE ALSO: *Cold War; Computer Games; Edison, Thomas Alva; The Internet; New Deal; Smartphones; Television; Video Games; Videos; World War II.*

BIBLIOGRAPHY

Cowan, Ruth Schwartz. *More Work for Mother: The Ironies of Household Technology from the Open Hearth to the Microwave.* New York: Basic Books, 1983.

Grossman, Elizabeth. *High-Tech Trash: Digital Devices, Hidden Toxics, and Human Health.* Washington, DC: Island Press, Shearwater Books, 2006.

Matranga, Victoria Kasuba, and Karen Kohn. *America at Home: A Celebration of Twentieth-Century Housewares.* Rosemont, IL: National Housewares Manufacturers Association, 1997.

Postman, Neil. *Technopoly: The Surrender of Culture to Technology.* New York, Vintage, 1993.

Russell, Loris S. *Handy Things to Have around the House.* Toronto: McGraw-Hill Ryerson, 1979.

Slade, Giles. *Made to Break: Technology and Obsolescence in America.* Cambridge, MA: Harvard University Press, 2006.

Electric Guitar

The electric guitar has dominated the production of popular music since its invention in the 1930s. Although primarily identified with both the sound and the image of rock and roll, the electric guitar has made its mark on all genres of popular music, from country to world beat. Combined with an amplifier and armed with a large inventory of special effects, the electric guitar is an extremely versatile instrument that can produce an infinite variety of sounds. Its ease of playing and low cost have made it an important consumer good of the twentieth and twenty-first centuries. It has given the baby boom generation the means to make their own music and emulate the great guitar heroes of their times.

GOING ELECTRIC

Musicians began to consider electric amplification of the acoustic guitar during the 1930s when guitar players sat in the rhythm sections of the big bands and struggled to be heard. The Western Electric system of amplification was readily available and was soon employed to power the signal coming from the first primitive guitar pickups. The first electric guitars were hollow-bodied acoustic models with pickups attached, but in the 1940s guitars were made with solid bodies to better suit electric amplification. Leo Fender was the first to mass produce solid bodied electric guitars, and his Telecaster (1950) and Stratocaster (1954) models remained in production into the twenty-first century. Fender established the basic layout of the electronics, and the shape of his Stratocaster has been the most copied by other manufacturers of electric guitars.

Fender Stratocaster. *Jeff Beck plays a Fender Stratocaster at a concert in 2003.* CLAYTON CALL/REDFERNS/GETTY IMAGES.

The increased volume of the electric guitar was soon heard in popular music. Les Paul used a model of his own design to make successful records in both country and pop music in the 1940s and 1950s, but it took rock and roll to showcase the power of the instrument and the great number of new sounds it could make. The electric guitar figured large in the two well springs of this new popular music: rhythm and blues from the black urban centers and rockabilly from the country. Blues musicians such as Muddy Waters electrified a traditional music and brought it into the urban context, using the harder sounds of the electric guitar to make the blues more urgent and menacing. Country players had been the first to adopt the electric guitar, perhaps because their audiences were used to the metallic sounds of the steel guitar, which was extremely popular in the 1940s and 1950s. The high, ringing tones of the Fender guitar became the trademark of a new type of country music that was both more traditional than the popular records made in Nashville and more modern in its stark metallic tone. The Bakersfield sound of players such as Merle Haggard and Buck Owens was created not far from the Fender factory in California and soon spread across the country.

The first rock guitarists—players like Scotty Moore, Chuck Berry, and Buddy Holly—were inspired by both sides of the racial divide in popular music, and the successful hybrid they produced came to be called rock and roll. Holly was the most influential exponent of the rock guitar, not only because of his playing, which used basic chords in an energetic and exciting way, but also because he popularized the all guitar lineup of the rock-and-roll band: lead, bass (and later rhythm) guitars playing through the same amplification system in front of the drums. Holly's music was widely disseminated on records, and the simplicity of his playing made it easy to copy; thousands of teenagers learned how to play rock guitar by listening to his recordings, and many of them went on to form their own bands.

THE SOUNDS

Leo Fender had designed his solid bodied guitars with ease of manufacture in mind and quickly moved into mass production. The unprecedented appeal of rock and roll created an enormous demand for electric guitars, and by the 1960s the production of instruments had become a highly profitable and crowded industry. Most of the manufacturers of acoustic guitars, such as Gibson and Gretsch, had moved into electric models, and a host of new companies entered the field, including Mosrite and Peavey. There were also many new manufacturers of amplifiers and the effects boxes, which added reverberation and echo to the sound of the guitar.

But rock-and-roll music never relied on the sound of the electric guitar alone—the amplifier created the sound, and the signal it received could be altered by the electronic circuits of the effect boxes. Thus the clear, high "Fender sound" heard on surf guitarist Dick Dale's records is not just the sound of his Fender Stratocaster but also of the Fender Showman or Bassman amplifier and the 6G15 Reverb unit plugged in between guitar and amplifier. Musicians began to experiment with this technological system in their continual attempts to find new sounds. Pete Townshend of the Who was the great innovator in using all parts of the system to generate new sounds; his rapid turning on and off of the power switch on his guitar made a memorable ending to several of the Who's songs.

THE PLAYERS

The person playing an electric guitar became a universally recognized image of rock and roll and the instrument itself became a symbol of empowerment for a generation of teenagers who yearned for the abilities and successes of their guitar-playing heroes. The myths of rock and roll leaned heavily on the rags to riches tradition in the United States, whereby ambitious immigrants could, with "luck and pluck," rise to the top of their profession and achieve the affluence and security of the American dream. The stories of the stars of rock and roll followed this tradition and placed totemic importance on the tool of the trade: the electric guitar. Berry's "Johnny Be Goode," one of the great anthems of rock and roll, tells the story of a young boy who leaves home, with only a guitar on his back, to seek out fame and fortune. This story resonated in thousands of other songs, most of which cast the hero as a guitar player.

The mass adulation of a few leading guitar players in the 1960s was a measure of the size of audience for the music and the market for the instruments. It also marked a return to an older tradition in the popular culture of the guitar, when the solitary bluesman was the center of attention. Several English musicians, including Jeff Beck and Eric Clapton, had spearheaded a blues revival in the early 1960s. This invigorated both blues and pop music and also created a new wave of guitar heroes who reflected some of the characteristics of the blues musicians who inspired them: outlaws and outcasts who traveled from place to place living on their wits and enjoying the rewards of their virtuosity on the guitar. The bluesman was a special person, either gifted or damned by the gods, whose freedom and powers (especially over women) were highly valued in the popular culture of the 1960s. Jimi Hendrix was the greatest of all the guitar heroes; his unequalled virtuosity on the instrument was only matched by the excesses of his lifestyle, which were also embodied in his songs.

The steady advance of the technology of electric guitars was centered on two main goals: increasing the volume and finding more electronic effects. In the 1960s amplifiers were made larger and more efficient, and the separate amplifier unit and speaker boxes replaced the old amplifiers, which had electronics and speakers in the same box. The banks of Marshall 4X12 speaker units became the backdrop for the typical rock-and-roll performance. More complicated devices were used to manipulate electronic feedback and create new sounds. Guitar players could surround themselves with effects boxes, such as "fuzz" and "wah wah," that were operated by foot switches. The sound of psychedelic music of the 1960s was essentially the sound of controlled feedback from the electric guitar.

EVOLUTION OF THE SOUND

The increasing popularity of other methods of manipulating electronic sounds in the 1970s, such as the Moog synthesizer and electric organ, threatened to end the dominance of the electric guitar in popular music. But there were several sub genres of rock and roll that were still completely dominated by its sound: heavy metal, which made a cult of loudness and made futuristic guitars the center of theatrical stage shows, and punk, which returned to the basic guitar sound of early rock and roll. Punk musicians made a virtue out of amateurism in their rejection of the commercialization of pop music and the elevation of guitar virtuosos. They encouraged everybody to pick up a guitar and advised the aspiring musician that only a few chords needed to be mastered before forming a band. On the other hand, advocates of heavy metal wanted to be transported to an imaginary world of outlandish stage shows, outrageous costumes, and unusual guitar shapes. Both groups of musicians used exactly the same equipment but to different ends.

Although each decade after the 1960s produced an "alternative" music to rock and roll, the electric guitar's ubiquitous presence in popular music was not challenged. Disco (1970s) and rap (1980s) still relied on the supple rhythm lines of the electric bass, whereas the guitar-based rock band continued to dominate both professional and amateur music into the twenty-first century.

While the electric guitar has remained a staple in popular music, it has undergone a few minor transformations. In the middle of the first decade of the 2000s Gibson developed and released the first digital guitar, which produced a crisper sound and allowed for musicians to avoid the noise associated with analog cables. Amps and effects devices also converted to digital, enabling the guitarist to combine multiple effects and to preset their effects. Oddly enough, many of the digital upgrades attempted to mimic the older analog sounds. In spite of the stardom of vocalists such as Justin Timberlake and Christina Aguilera, guitarists were still the backbone of rock and roll. Performers such as Jack White, John Mayer, and Johnny Greenwood emerged as some of the best performers of the early 2000s. White merged garage rock with the blues into a frenzied outburst; Mayer relied on technical, sound-playing skills; and Greenwood performed some of the most experimental popular music with Radiohead. Their creative impulses and technical skills helped them sell millions of records and illustrated the electric guitar's foundational presence in modern music.

Female guitarists gained more notoriety as well. Although lists such as *Rolling Stone*'s "Top 100 Guitarists of All Time" tended to be dominated by their male counterparts, female guitarists such as Marnie Stern, Joan Jett, Sleater-Kinney's Carrie Brownstein, and Poison Ivy of the Cramps helped to change the image of the guitar as a particularly masculine instrument. Bolstered by the Riot Grrrl bands of the 1990s, female lead guitarists became more commonplace and inspired younger generations of women to play the guitar.

Andre Millard

SEE ALSO: *Berry, Chuck; Blues; Clapton, Eric; Country Music; Hendrix, Jimi; Holly, Buddy; Paul, Les; Pop Music; Rock and Roll; Timberlake, Justin; Waters, Muddy; The Who.*

BIBLIOGRAPHY

Gill, Chris. *Guitar Legends*. London: Studio Editions, 1995.

Gruhn, George, and Walter Carter. *Electric Guitars and Basses: A Photographic History*. San Francisco: Miller Freeman, 1994.

Millard, Andreé, ed. *The Electric Guitar: A History of an American Icon*. Baltimore, MD: Johns Hopkins University Press, 2004.

Shaughnessy, Mary Alice. *Les Paul: An American Original*. New York: Morrow, 1993.

"100 Greatest Guitarists of All Time." *Rolling Stone*, November 11, 2011.

Smith, Richard R. *Fender: The Sound Heard around the World*. Fullerton, CA: Garfish, 1995.

Trynka, Paul, ed. *The Electric Guitar: An Illustrated History*. San Francisco: Chronicle Books, 1993.

Wheeler, Tom. *American Guitars: An Illustrated History*. New York: Harper, 1992.

Electric Trains

Even as transportation improvements accelerate through the twenty-first century, the railroad still symbolizes the ability of mechanized invention to conquer distance. Thus, electric trains continue to be popular among hobbyists. From children's playthings, they have evolved into accurately scaled and finely detailed models. Several gauges provide size options for modeling railroads, from the tiny N-scale and the highly popular HO at 1/87 scale up to O-gauge and Standard gauge.

In Europe in 1901, Märklin manufactured the first model trains run by small electric motors. Nine years later the Ives Corporation of Bridgeport, Connecticut, introduced electric trains to the United States. The Ives Corporation remained the leading manufacturer of electric trains until World War I. As the hobby caught on, others entered the mix, including Marx, Varney, Mantua, American Flyer, and Lionel. Collecting and operating model trains is a pastime now enjoyed by people around the world.

Robert Kuhlken

SEE ALSO: *Consumerism; Leisure Time; Lionel Trains; Toys.*

BIBLIOGRAPHY

Bagdade, Susan, and Al Bagdade. *Collector's Guide to American Toy Trains*. Radnor, PA: Wallace-Homestead Book Company, 1990.

Carlson, Pierce. *Toy Trains: A History*. New York: Harper & Row, 1986.

Souter, Gerry, and Janet Souter. *The American Toy Train*. Osceola, WI: Motorbooks International, 1999.

Williams, Guy. *The World of Model Trains*. New York: G. P. Putnam's Sons, 1970.

Elizondo, Hector *(1936–)*

Hector Elizondo, who delighted audiences and gained fame with his polished performance as the hotel manager in *Pretty Woman* (1990), is a versatile actor and an accomplished singer and guitarist. *Pretty Woman* was one of several films he made for Garry Marshall, who considers Elizondo his good-luck charm.

Elizondo, of Hispanic ancestry, was born in New York and trained at the Actors Studio. He has played a wide range of supporting roles, using different accents and dialects and capturing the essence of a character, whether in drama or comedy, by an expert flick of expression. His multitude of television appearances include Sandy Stern in *Burden of Proof* (1992) and the put-upon hospital chief Dr. Philip Watters, authoritative, weary, and not always wise, in *Chicago Hope* (1994–2000). He came to television and film with an impeccable Broadway provenance, beginning his career in *Mister Roberts* (1961) with distinguished director Edwin Sherin.

In 2008 Elizondo replaced the late Stanley Kamel on USA Network's *Monk*, playing compulsive Adrian Monk's wise and patient psychiatrist. He played Carlos Torres on ABC's *Grey's Anatomy* from 2007 to 2011 and has appeared in movies including *The Celestine Prophecy* (2006), *Love in the Time of Cholera* (2007), and *New Year's Eve* (2011).

Robyn Karney

SEE ALSO: Grey's Anatomy; *Marshall, Garry; Television.*

BIBLIOGRAPHY

Charity, Tom. "Hector Elizondo." *The Hollywood Who's Who*, ed. Robyn Karney. New York: Continuum, 1993.

Eichenbaum, Rose. *The Actor Within: Intimate Conversations with Great Actors.* Middletown, CT: Wesleyan University Press, 2011.

Elkins, Aaron *(1935–)*

Aaron Elkins is the creator of the Gideon Oliver and the Chris Norgren mystery series. His forté lies in combining intriguing characters and plots with exotic settings, as far-flung as England, Germany, Mexico, Alaska, Egypt, Tahiti, and the Pacific Northwest.

The Gideon Oliver series features a forensic anthropologist who is frequently compelled to investigate modern murders instead of ancient bones. *Fellowship of Fear* (1982) initiated the series, followed by *The Dark Place* (1983), an unusually poetic mood piece, and *Murder in the Queen's Armes* (1985). *Old Bones* (1987) received the 1988 Edgar Award for Best Mystery Novel. Subsequent Gideon Oliver novels include *Curses!* (1989), *Icy Clutches* (1990), *Make No Bones* (1991), *Dead Men's Hearts* (1994), *Twenty Blue Devils* (1997), *Skeleton Dance* (2000), *Good Blood* (2004), *Where There's a Will* (2005), *Unnatural Selection* (2006), *Little Tiny Teeth* (2007), *Uneasy Relations* (2008), and *Skull Duggery* (2009). The hero of the Chris Norgren novels is a museum curator. This series includes *A Deceptive Clarity* (1987), *A Glancing Light* (1991), and *Old Scores* (1993).

Additionally, Elkins has cowritten golf mysteries with his wife, Charlotte Elkins: *A Wicked Slice* (1989), *Rotten Lies* (1995), *Nasty Breaks* (1997), *Where Have All the Birdies Gone?* (2004), and *On the Fringe* (2005). His other novels include *The Worst Thing* (2011), a thriller about a man who designs hostage-negotiation programs.

Michael R. Collings

SEE ALSO: *Best Sellers; Detective Fiction.*

Ellen

SEE: *DeGeneres, Ellen.*

Ellington, Duke *(1899–1974)*

Heralded by many as the greatest composer in jazz history, pianist and bandleader Duke Ellington composed and arranged most of the music played by his famous orchestra. His 1932 recording of "It Don't Mean a Thing (If It Ain't Got That Swing)" is often credited with introducing the term *swing*, which foreshadows the Swing Era, when jazz music and jitterbug dancing swept the nation in the late 1930s and early 1940s.

Edward Kennedy Ellington was born into a modestly prosperous family in Washington, DC. Encouraged by his parents, he began studying piano at age seven. His graceful demeanor earned him the aristocratic nickname Duke. Continuing to study piano formally, as well as learning from the city's ragtime pianists, Ellington formed his own band at age nineteen and soon was earning enough playing for parties and dances to marry Edna Thompson. The band's drummer was his friend Sonny Greer, who would anchor Ellington's rhythm section for the next thirty-three years.

After moving to New York City in 1923, Ellington began assembling jazz musicians whose unique sounds enhanced his own arrangements. With his new ensemble, he launched Duke Ellington and the Washingtonians. The band first worked for the legendary singer Ada Smith (better known later in European clubs as Bricktop). In 1924 Ellington wrote his first score for a revue, *Chocolate Kiddies*, which ran for two years in Germany but was never produced on Broadway.

The band's big break came in 1927, when it began a five-year engagement at Harlem's Cotton Club, the site of frequent national radio broadcasts. Soon the group was widely known for Ellington's signature style of improvisational and ensemble jazz. His earliest arrangements included what he at first called the "jungle style," which achieved unusual effects and rhythms

Duke Ellington. *Ellington's music stretched into various genres, including blues, gospel, film scores, pop, and classical.* MICHAEL OCHS ARCHIVES/GETTY IMAGES.

through the use of plunger mutes on the trumpets and trombones. Major sidemen who joined the Duke Ellington Band in the Cotton Club era included Barney Bigard on clarinet, Johnny Hodges on alto and soprano sax, and Cootie Williams on the trumpet. The ensemble's first great recorded hit was 1930's "Mood Indigo," which featured the band's inimitable tonal colors, made possible by the special sounds and styles of each individual musician. In 1933 a tour of Europe brought the band worldwide fame.

With little change in personnel over the beginning years, the orchestra was able to play with unheard-of ensemble precision. Such melodic recordings as "Solitude," "Sophisticated Lady," and "In a Sentimental Mood" won Ellington and his band a wide audience. But it was the uniquely orchestrated ensemble jazz in such pieces as "Daybreak Express," "Harlem Speaks," and "Rockin' in Rhythm" that impressed fellow jazzmen such as Billy Strayhorn, who joined the band as assistant arranger in 1939. Strayhorn's composition "Take the A Train" became the orchestra's theme song.

In 1943 the band began a series of annual concerts in Carnegie Hall that would continue until 1950. The first concert included Ellington's earliest attempt at a nearly hour-long jazz composition, *Black, Brown, and Beige*, which he envisioned as a "musical history of the Negro." It was his most ambitious work to date, one which musicologist and composer Gunther Schuller, in his article included in the book *Jazz*, believes has "not been surpassed" in "scope and stature." In subsequent Carnegie Hall concerts Ellington played such lengthy compositions as *Deep South Suite*, *Blutopia*, and *New World A-Comin'*. *Harlem*, another suite, was the centerpiece of an Ellington concert at the Metropolitan Opera House in 1951.

Although the Ellington ensemble continued to be ranked as one of the top two or three jazz orchestras during the 1950s, their difficult repertoire, coupled with frequent personnel changes, led to spotty performances that were often disappointing to their fans. After giving a smash-hit performance at the Newport Jazz Festival in 1956, however, followed by a 1957 television special on Ellington titled *A Drum Is a Woman*, the band's fortunes were revived, and Ellington began a period of prolific composing. He and Strayhorn wrote a suite based on Shakespearean characters, *Such Sweet Thunder*, performed at New York's Town Hall in 1957. In 1958 his first European tour in eight years proved a stunning success—one that he repeated the following year. Also in 1959 Ellington wrote his first score for a film, director Alfred Hitchcock's *Anatomy of a Murder*, which was recorded by Ellington's band.

Up until his death of lung cancer in May 1974, Ellington continued to write important music, much of it devoted to other cultures and to religious themes. For more than a half century, he had led one of America's most popular and successful bands. As George T. Simon writes in his book *The Big Bands*, "No other bandleader ever did this nearly so long so well as Duke Ellington. No other bandleader created as much and contributed as much to American music." A chorus of jazz critics agrees that Ellington may be the greatest single talent in the history of jazz.

Benjamin Griffith

SEE ALSO: *Big Bands; Carnegie Hall; The Cotton Club; Jazz; Swing Dancing; Zoot Suit.*

BIBLIOGRAPHY

Balliett, Whitney. *American Musicians: Fifty-Six Portraits in Jazz.* New York: Oxford University Press, 1986.

Howland, John Louis. *"Ellington Uptown": Duke Ellington, James P. Johnson, and the Birth of Concert Jazz.* Ann Arbor: University of Michigan Press, 2009.

Schuller, Gunther. "The Ellington Style: Its Origins and Early Development." In *Jazz*, ed. Nat Hentoff and Albert J. McCarthy. New York: Da Capo Press, 1974.

Simon, George T. *The Big Bands*, 4th ed. New York: Schirmer Books, 1981.

Ellis, Bret Easton *(1964–)*

Though he was born and raised in Los Angeles, writer Bret Easton Ellis belongs with novelists Jay McInerney and Tama Janowitz in New York's literary "brat pack"—writers who achieved early success with their portraits of lonely types isolated in sparkling 1980s New York. Ellis has published the novels *Less than Zero* (1985), *The Rules of Attraction* (1987), *American Psycho* (1991), *Glamorama* (1998), *Lunar Park* (2005), and *Imperial Bedrooms* (2010) and the short story collection *The Informers* (1994).

Ellis's first novel, *Less than Zero*, which was published when the author was twenty-one, narrates the sorry lives of a group of twenty-somethings living in Los Angeles. These characters epitomize *Generation X*, a term first used by fellow novelist Douglas Coupland. The lives of the main character, Clay, and his well-to-do friends revolve around the use of sex and drugs in an effort to find the essence of a world that eludes them. Similar empty people populate the short stories of *The Informers*. Outstanding among them is the satirical "The End of the Summer," in which the Californians of *Less than Zero* appear as happy vampires.

Ellis's popularity ebbed in 1987 when both the film adaptation of *Less than Zero* and his novel about a triangular relationship, *The Rules of Attraction*, failed. But in 1991 he became a social phenomenon thanks to the publication of *American Psycho*, a first-person narration of the exploits of serial killer and Manhattan yuppie Pat Bateman.

AMERICAN PSYCHO

The extreme graphic violence and nihilism of *American Psycho* were controversial even before its publication: following complaints by people working on the manuscript, Simon & Schuster withdrew the book from publication, losing a $300,000 advance. The book was finally published as a Vintage paperback, becoming a best-selling novel in the United States and abroad. Its publication was greeted with a barrage of criticism, especially from feminists, and lukewarm reviews that missed much of the book's originality to focus only on its nastier passages. Ellis himself confessed in an interview with Leslie White in 1994 that the controversy felt "like a joke, a huge postmodernist irony—the book was so badly misread."

David Skal complains in *The Monster Show* that "although the whole incident [involving Ellis's novel] was endlessly discussed in terms of taste, misogyny, and political correctness, a subtext of class snobbery predominated." Skal argues that what really irritated feminists and moral guardians alike is the fact that Bateman is a member of the upper class and that Ellis's book is "literature"—unlike books by popular authors such as Stephen King. This explanation may have some merit, yet *American Psycho*'s status as a literary text is still ambiguous. The book has sold remarkably well in many countries, creating a cult reflected in the many websites devoted to its discussion, but critics and academics show an equivocal attitude toward it. Arguably, the book is commendable if only because it questions in depth what constitutes *literature*, along with the meaning of homophobia, racism, misogyny, and classism.

American Psycho is essentially a radical indictment of the American culture of the Ronald Reagan era, a very bleak portrait of a time and place filled with people obsessed with money. Bateman's insanity is close to the existentialism of characters such as the anonymous protagonist of Albert Camus's novel *The Outsider* (1946). In his lucidity Bateman is also a brother to the infamous Hannibal Lecter of the novel and film *Silence of the Lambs* (1991) and of Mickey Knox in Oliver Stone's *Natural Born Killers* (1994).

Bateman's diary narrates his frivolous life and the yuppie crowd that surrounds him. He engages in a series of increasingly grisly murders of homosexuals, women, and male business colleagues, which he describes with stark, functional prose. Bateman's descriptions of characters and places abound with information about designer objects seemingly taken straight from catalogs. Violent passages that were published in isolation missed much of the irony of the book: characters mistake each other all the time because they all wear the same expensive clothes; Bateman's appraisals of pop idols such as Whitney Houston make them appear trivial and boring; and restaurant scenes are enriched by funny dialogue with plenty of non sequiturs showing the abysmal depth of the yuppies' ignorance.

POPULAR RECEPTION

Many of the scenes in *American Psycho*—the book and the 2000 movie adaptation—have offended the sensibilities of readers and viewers. But Ellis offers them some hope in that Bateman is addicted to Valium and Halcion, suggesting that the bloodbaths might be just a product of his imagination, which is why nobody suspects him. In the midst of such adamant criticism, it is also interesting that few reviewers noted Ellis's fierce attack against yuppiedom. *American Psycho* shows no mercy at all with a society that allows people like Bateman a room at the top.

Any reading of *American Psycho* is complicated by Ellis's risky choice of Bateman as both his mouthpiece and his target. The deep morality of the book is purposely blurred in a literary game of mirrors, but readers should not make the mistake of identifying character and author. Ellis challenges the reader to face Bateman's cruelty for the sake of reaping the reward of the character's final observation: "Surface, surface, surface was all that anyone found meaning in. . . . This was civilization as I saw it, colossal and jagged."

Ellis has continued to attract and repel readers with a style that is difficult to define. Criticized by some critics for his recycled characters and gratuitous pop-culture references, his books *Glamorama*, *Lunar Park*, and *Imperial Bedrooms* nonetheless offer critiques of contemporary cultural fixations with celebrity. *Glamorama* follows Victor Ward, a self-involved and disconnected model who becomes embroiled in international terrorism. *Lunar Park* does not venture far from Ellis's literary preoccupations. The novel is a semiautobiographical work in which Ellis, wrestling with his celebrity, moves to the suburbs, where he and his family are haunted by his father's ghost. *Imperial Bedrooms*, a quasi-sequel to *Less than Zero*, elicited negative reactions from critics for its focus on Hollywood decadence and for its difficult prose style; however, other critics found it to be a trenchant narrative whose detached protagonist reflects society's uncritical acceptance of the status quo.

Sara Martin

SEE ALSO: *Best Sellers; Generation X; Houston, Whitney; The Internet; King, Stephen;* Natural Born Killers*; Reagan, Ronald; Serial Killers;* The Silence of the Lambs*; Stone, Oliver; Yuppies.*

BIBLIOGRAPHY

Baelo-Allué, Sonia. *Bret Easton Ellis's Controversial Fiction: Writing between High and Low*. New York: Continuum International Publishing Group, 2011.

Clarke, Jamie. "Interview with Bret Easton Ellis." *Mississippi Review* 27, no. 3 (1999): 61–102.

Ellis, Bret Easton, and Camille Silvy. "Interview with Mark Lawson." *Front Row*, BBC Radio 4, July 14, 2010.

Forrest, Emma. "On the Psycho Path." *Sunday Times*, October 23, 1994, sec. 10, 18.

Grant, Barry Keith. "Rich and Strange: The Yuppie Horror Film." *Journal of Film and Video* 28, no. 1/2 (1996): 4–16.

Mandel, Naomi. *Bret Easton Ellis: "American Psycho," "Glamorama," "Lunar Park."* New York: Continuum Publishing, 2011.

Punter, David. "Contemporary Gothic Transformations." In *Literature of Terror*, vol. 2. London: Longman, 1980.

Skal, David J. *The Monster Show*. London: Plexus, 1994.

Twitchell, James B. *Carnival Culture: The Trashing of Taste in America*. New York: Columbia University Press, 1992.

White, Leslie. "Bleak as He Is Painted (An Interview with Bret Easton Ellis)." *Sunday Times*, October 23, 1994, 20–21.

Ellis, Perry *(1940–1986)*

Virginia-born Perry Ellis took his talents from fashion merchandising to fashion design in 1975. In 1978 he founded Perry Ellis Sportswear, a name that immediately recognized his fashion niche. Strong color, luxury fabrics, and a rich-suburban nonchalance were chief characteristics. Women prized his cashmere and silk hand-knitted sweaters and throws. He offered a young outlook on old-money styles. He also designed menswear and home fashions.

A ruggedly handsome man and a famously affable figure in American fashion, he fell gravely ill in the mid-1980s. He denied that the cause was AIDS, then a scourge of New York design talent. Ironically, despite his denials, Ellis's struggle with disease and his early death was a point of conscience and conversion for the fashion industry, which began to aggressively raise funds for AIDS research. In 2002 Ellis was honored with a commemorative bronze plaque on the Fashion Walk of Fame on New York's Fashion Avenue (Seventh Avenue). Since his death Ellis continues as a popular licensing name.

Richard Martin

SEE ALSO: *AIDS; Lauren, Ralph.*

BIBLIOGRAPHY

Moor, Jonathan. *Perry Ellis*. New York: St. Martin's Press, 1988.

Ellison, Harlan *(1934–)*

Author Harlan Ellison has been called one of the great living American short-story writers. He has also been called a lot worse by the many enemies with whom he has sparred in print, online, and in countless combative science fiction convention appearances. Ellison, whose major works include the short stories "I Have No Mouth and I Must Scream" (1967), which was made into a video game in 1995, and "Jeffty Is Five" (1977), began writing professionally at age fifteen, when his first published story appeared in the *Cleveland News*. Since then he has been a prolific, at times logorrheic, presence on the American literary scene, penning essays, reviews, and teleplays in addition to his speculative fiction. He has written scripts for television series including *The Outer Limits* (1963–1965), *The Twilight Zone* (1985–1989), *Star Trek* (1966–1969), and *Babylon 5* (1994–1998).

A self-proclaimed humanist, Ellison writes dark fantasies that challenge the technological optimism prevalent in the science fiction genre. His idiosyncratic style has put off many mainstream science fiction readers, but few living writers have been nominated for as many different honors as this complex, controversial figure. The Science Fiction and Fantasy Writers of America honored Ellison with the Bradbury Award in 2000 for his radio show *2000X* and with the Nebula Award for Best Short Story for "How Interesting: A Tiny Man" in 2011. Filmmaker Erik Nelson documented Ellison's life over a period of twenty-five years in the 2008 release *Harlan Ellison: Dreams with Sharp Teeth*.

Robert E. Schnakenberg

SEE ALSO: The Outer Limits*; Science Fiction Publishing;* Star Trek*; Television;* The Twilight Zone*; Video Games.*

BIBLIOGRAPHY

Ellison, Harlan. *The Essential Ellison*. Beverly Hills, CA: Morpheus International, 1991.

Sabelle, Robert. *Who Shaped Science Fiction*. Commack, NY: Kroshka Books, 2011.

Slusser, George Edgar. *Harlan Ellison: Unrepentant Harlequin*. San Bernardino, CA: Borgo Press, 1977.

Weil, Ellen, and Gary K. Wolfe. *Harlan Ellison: The Edge of Forever*. Columbus: Ohio State University Press, 2002.

Ellison, Ralph

SEE: *Invisible Man.*

Elway, John *(1960–)*

During his sixteen-year career in the National Football League (NFL), quarterback John Elway earned a reputation as a fearless competitor, leading the Denver Broncos to five Super Bowls. When the Broncos lost the first three, Elway seemed destined never to earn a championship ring. However, in 1998 and 1999, the final two seasons of his career, his team beat the Green Bay Packers and Atlanta Falcons, respectively, to win the Super Bowl. Those championships assured Elway of his place in NFL history, and he was enshrined in the Pro Football Hall of Fame in 2004.

Although Elway often chose to run with the ball and sacrifice his body for an extra yard or two, he became more of a finesse quarterback as he matured. He set several records during his NFL career, including most come-from-behind victories (47), and as of 2012 is fourth on the all-time list for passing yards (51,475). He held the record for most wins by an NFL quarterback (148) until 2007 when he was passed by Brett Favre (who eventually racked up 186). In addition to being the league's most valuable player for the 1987 season, Elway was named to nine Pro Bowls.

Elway retired from the NFL in 1999 and was inducted in the Pro Football Hall of Fame in 2004. From 2003 through 2008, he was a co-owner and chief executive of the Colorado Crush, an arena football league team. Financial difficulties caused the indoor league to cancel its 2009 season, and the Crush did not resume playing in 2010. In 2011 Elway became the executive vice president of Football Operations for the Denver Broncos. Elway caused a stir in Denver in the spring of 2012 when he signed former Indianapolis Colts star quarterback Peyton Manning to a long-term deal. Manning's arrival made it possible for Elway to trade Tim Tebow to the New York Jets. A charismatic figure with a woefully inaccurate passing arm, Tebow had led the Broncos to an improbable playoff spot the previous season and stunned the football world with a victory in the first playoff match against the Pittsburgh Steelers, the defending AFC champions. Tebow is a devout Christian and was immensely popular in Denver.

Jason McEntee

SEE ALSO: *National Football League (NFL); Professional Football; Sports Heroes; Super Bowl.*

BIBLIOGRAPHY

Latimer, Clay. *John Elway: Armed and Dangerous*. Lenexa, KS: Addax Publishing Group, 1998.

Saccomano, Jim. *Denver Broncos: The Complete Illustrated History*. Minneapolis, MN: MBI Publishing, 2009.

E-mail

The most important new medium of mass communication of the late twentieth century was not in any way connected with television, moving pictures, or the recording industry; it initially emerged, instead, as a project of the U.S. Defense Department. In the 1960s the department's Advanced Research Projects Agency (ARPA), in coordination with several research institutions, came up with a system called ARPANET, a network of distantly located computers connected to each other by independent, dedicated telephone lines. Researchers experimented by sending simple text messages to one another over the network. Soon the trickle of research-oriented messages and data became a tidal wave of information exchange of all kinds. The new medium of "electronic mail" eventually changed the way people interacted with friends, coworkers, and families. It also brought everyday reality much closer to Marshall McLuhan's pipedream of a genuine worldwide community rooted in technology.

RUDIMENTARY PRECURSORS

The practice of sending electronic messages from one person to another actually predated computer networking. A few years before ARPANET, users of time-sharing-style computer consoles developed a simple system of sending memos to a central mailbox located on a mainframe computer used by a variety of users at different times. Each user had a file to which messages were directed; those messages could be retrieved any time the user was logged in to the computer. The practice was important to the future development of electronic messaging but had little or no utilitarian value at the time. The ARPANET engineers later picked up on the idea, and after successfully sending small messages and memos from one computer to another, they then began sending messages over the nationwide span of ARPANET itself. To paraphrase one beneficiary of ARPA's research, it was a small step for a few computer geeks, a giant leap for the global village.

The system was not only useful for the researchers but also proved to be a pleasant pastime—so pleasant, in fact, that ARPA director Stephen Lukasik worried that it could jeopardize the entire enterprise. In their history of the Internet, *Where Wizards Stay up Late*, Katie Hafner and Matthew Lyon quote Lukasik, who told the researchers that if "you're going to do something that looks like it's forty thousand miles away from defense, please leave our name off of it." It was clear early on that e-mail was useful for much more than just the military and technological research for which ARPA was founded in 1958.

By the mid-1970s engineers discovered that messages could be sent through ARPANET by those without official authorization to use it. The message-sending capability of this network was obviously universal and, through the demonstrated use of satellite technology, global. Anyone could tap into the network to send messages of any sort to anyone else in the world who had access to the network. The message of this medium was limitless interactivity, not mere broadcasting. ARPANET eventually gave way to a new, more enveloping network known as the Internet. The use of e-mail quickly mushroomed.

The possibilities of the Internet were soon tested. In the early 1970s individuals wrote antiwar messages and mass mailed them; one electronically advocated the impeachment of President Richard Nixon. Other mass mailings became routinized around a variety of subject headings that were of interest only to certain groups: this later became that part of the Internet known as Usenet. On Usenet, e-mail messages were sent to a central server and mass posted to a kind of electronic message board where anyone could read and even reply to the message. Other forms of mass e-mailings included discussion lists; users subscribed privately to a list and would receive messages directly via e-mail rather than via a public message board.

E-mail also entertained in more traditional ways. Many used the Internet's e-mail capabilities early on to play fantasy role-playing games such as Dungeons and Dragons. More serious uses of e-mail soon came to the attention of the U.S. Postal Service, leading President Jimmy Carter—who used a primitive e-mail system during his 1976 campaign—to propose ways of integrating the new technology into a postal system that originally delivered messages on the backs of ponies.

THE INTERNET BOOM

During the 1980s and 1990s the computer culture began to flourish among a worldwide community of users. Hundreds of thousands of people now understood what it meant to be "flamed" (told off in a vicious manner). Multitudes decoded the meanings of emoticons, which are text symbols used to convey facial expressions. For example, the emoticon ;-) means a wink and a smile and indicates that the sender was just kidding. As the medium matured, private companies such as CompuServe and America Online built private networks for individuals to dial in to send and receive electronic messages. The phrase "you've got mail"—notifying users of America Online's e-mail service that a new message had arrived—entered into common usage, even becoming the title of a hit romantic comedy starring Tom Hanks and Meg Ryan in 1998.

New electronic communities were soon burdened with such "real-world" issues as free speech, crime, and sexism. Many women complained of electronic abuse by the predominantly male online community. Predators sent electronic messages to children in attempts to commit crimes against them. Some of the private networks regulated speech in "public" forms of electronic communication, and this met with scorn from the online community. Others used e-mail as an advertising medium, mass mailing ads to hundreds of thousands of Internet users. This practice, known as "spam," was held in almost universal disrepute but became almost unavoidable.

Seeking to provide increased protection to e-mail users from scam artists and spammers, the U.S. Congress passed the Controlling the Assault of Non-Solicited Pornography and Marketing (CAN-SPAM) Act of 2003, officially placing e-mail communications under the authority of the Federal Trade Commission. Though the bill outlined several stipulations for e-mail marketing and was used to successfully prosecute repeat offenders, experts estimated that in the early twenty-first century, anywhere from half to 90 percent of all e-mail was spam.

E-mail became ubiquitous by the late 1990s, and the lines blurred between public, corporate, and private networks. Many large corporations standardized their e-mail systems on Internet protocols, allowing employees to send e-mail beyond the confines of the office. E-mail allowed some workers to telecommute rather than physically move from home to a separate workplace each day. In 1997 Microsoft's Outlook software merged scheduling and task management functions with the standard e-mail experience, indicating the centrality of e-mail in the business world, while the launch of the free, World Wide Web–based Hotmail service extended the convenience of e-mail for personal use. Internet service providers soon joined the fray, offering e-mail addresses to subscribers, and Internet-based companies such as Yahoo and Google followed suit with their own free e-mail services in the early 2000s.

With e-mail established as the primary form of written communication by the middle of the first decade of the 2000s, problems arose. Managing e-mail began to take up larger periods of workers' time, and employers worried about the toll of high-volume e-mail use on their servers. Security concerns increased as sensitive information—personal and business related—was transmitted via vulnerable accounts. Resourceful Internet users could easily trespass through the largely unsecured private e-mail accounts of others. A famous example of such e-mail hacking occurred during the 2008 presidential campaign when a twenty-two-year-old college student accessed vice presidential candidate Sarah Palin's personal Yahoo account by correctly guessing her password. He posted his findings, including some information from Palin's stint as governor of Alaska, on an online message board.

During the first decade of the twenty-first century, the rise of instant-messaging services, text messaging on cell phones, and social networking sites such as MySpace, Facebook, and Twitter allowed users to share media and information in new ways, but e-mail remained a prominent component of electronic communication, particularly in the workplace. The continuing need for efficient e-mail management techniques inspired books, instructional videos, and seminars.

Robin Markowitz

SEE ALSO: *Dungeons and Dragons; Google; Hanks, Tom; The Internet; McLuhan, Marshall; Microsoft; Palin, Sarah; Pornography; Ryan, Meg; Texting.*

BIBLIOGRAPHY

Abbate, Janet. *Inventing the Internet.* Cambridge, MA: MIT Press, 1999.

Baty, S. Paige. *E-mail Trouble: Love & Addiction @ the Matrix.* Austin: University of Texas Press, 1999.

Brook, James, and Iain Boal, eds. *Resisting the Virtual Life: The Culture and Politics of Information.* San Francisco: City Lights Books, 1995.

Grey, Victor. *Web without a Weaver: How the Internet Is Shaping Our Future.* Concord, CA: Open Heart Press, 1997.

Hafner, Katie, and Matthew Lyon. *Where Wizards Stay up Late: The Origins of the Internet.* New York: Simon & Schuster, 1996.

Johnson, Paul. *Email Survival Guide.* Brighton, UK: Book Guild, 2007.

Mann, Merlin. *Inbox Zero: Cutting through the Crap to Do the Work That Matters* New York: HarperCollins, 2012.

Shipley, David, and Will Schwalbe. *Send: Why People Email So Badly and How to Do It Better.* New York: Alfred A. Knopf, 2008.

Wolinsky, Art. *The History of the Internet and the World Wide Web.* Springfield, NJ: Enslow Publishers, 1999.

Eminem *(1972–)*

A rap artist, record producer, and songwriter, Marshall Bruce Mathers III—known professionally as Eminem, or sometimes Slim Shady—has been one of the most iconic musical performers of the early twenty-first century. Although some observers laud his rags-to-riches story, others see his life and success as metaphors for the moral and cultural decline of postindustrial America.

A TOUGH CHILDHOOD

Eminem's childhood has inspired many of his lyrics. He was born on October 17, 1972, in St. Joseph, Missouri. His father left him as an infant with his mother, Deborah R. Nelson Mathers. Deborah changed jobs frequently, and her son spent his childhood moving between apartments, public housing projects, and relatives. A 1982 lawsuit filed by her claimed that he suffered a concussion, headaches, and temporary loss of vision and hearing as a result of bullying in school. As Eminem sings in his 1999 song "Brain Damage," "Beat up in the bathroom, beat up in the hallways." A Michigan judge dismissed a defamation lawsuit filed by the alleged bully in 2003 on the grounds that the lyrics to that song are a literary exaggeration of repeated bullying as a child.

In his 2000 song "Kill You," Eminem blames the departure of his father on his mother. "She used to tell me my daddy was an evil man," he writes, "but then I got a little bit older, and I realized she was the crazy one." In his music, he also accuses his mother of emotionally and physically abusing him while she was addicted to prescription drugs. She sued her son twice for defamation, for some $11 million. Both cases were settled for $25,000.

Eminem attended Lincoln High School in Warren, Michigan, failing ninth grade three times and dropping out of school at age seventeen (he has since earned a GED). While in high school, Eminem discovered a passion for language and storytelling and gifts for wit and pathos. He began performing his own rap lyrics at age fourteen, using the initials M&M, a nickname that was later changed to Eminem for trademark reasons. He recorded a single in 1995 and an album, *Infinite*, the following year. Both efforts failed to attract attention, but they provided material for the 2002 semiautobiographical *8 Mile*, a film about the Detroit, Michigan, rap scene in which Eminem performs and won an Oscar for the song "Lose Yourself."

FAME AND FORTUNE

His breakout album was 1999's *The Slim Shady LP*, produced by rap artist Dr. Dre. The lyrics make extensive references to drug abuse, sex acts, violence, and mental illness, and the album went triple platinum. Within months, he went from a minimum-wage restaurant worker to an international star. His next album, *The Marshall Mathers LP* (2000), sold more than six million copies and won the Grammy for Album of the Year, though it was criticized in some corners for its homophobic lyrics. Eminem responded by performing with Elton John at the 2001 Grammys. In 2002 he released *The Eminem Show*, which won another Grammy and became the best-selling album of the year. He was the first white artist to appear on the cover of the rap magazine the *Source*, which contributed to critics accusing him of trying to "act black."

Eminem was also criticized for misogynist lyrics that have, among other horrors, called women "whores" who need to be choked "'til the vocal cords don't work" or murdered with chain saws. He and his high school girlfriend, Kimberly Scott, had a child in 1995 and married in 1999. In 2001 Eminem pleaded guilty to a reduced charge of illegal gun possession for an incident in which he witnessed a nightclub bouncer kissing Scott. They divorced, remarried, and divorced again in 2006. Following their first divorce, Scott charged him with defamation for accusing her of adultery in the 2000 song "'97 Bonnie & Clyde." He later claimed to have "trust issues" with women.

Eminem released *The Eminem Show* in 2002, which won another Grammy, followed by *Encore* in 2004. He also became involved in other financial ventures. Following an addiction to a prescription sleeping medication in 2005, he entered rehabilitation and stopped performing for several years. After declaring himself clean of drugs and alcohol, he released *Relapse* in 2009, another Grammy winner, and *Recovery* in 2011.

PRAISE AND CRITICISM

Eminem has been recognized repeatedly for the power of his lyrics. The emotional "Stan," from the *The Marshall Mathers LP*, was called "a cultural milestone" by the music website *Pitchfork* in 2005. He was named artist of the decade by *Billboard* in 2009 and anointed the "King of Hip-Hop" by *Rolling Stone* in 2011. Eminem has sold nearly 100 million albums worldwide, and he reached a new audience when Chrysler cast him and his song "Lose Yourself" in a commercial that first aired during Super Bowl XLV in 2011.

On the other hand, Eminem was ranked fifty-eighth in Bernard Goldberg's book *100 People Who Are Screwing up America* (2005), and *New York Times* columnist Bob Herbert called his music "poisonous, the equivalent of developing one's self-image by looking into a toilet." Eminem is probably best described, in his own words, as "a lyricist without a clue."

Richard Junger

SEE ALSO: *Academy Awards; Advertising; Grammy Awards; Rap; Super Bowl; Top 40.*

BIBLIOGRAPHY

Abrams, Dennis. *Eminem*. New York: Chelsea House Publishers, 2007.

Bozza, Anthony. "Eminem Blows Up." *Rolling Stone*, April 29, 1999, 42–46.

Bozza, Anthony. *Whatever You Say I Am: The Life and Times of Eminem*. New York: Three Rivers Press, 2004.

Eells, Josh. "Eminem on the Road Back from Hell." *Rolling Stone*, November 25, 2010, 48–54.

Eminem, and Sacha Jenkins. *The Way I Am*. New York: Penguin Books, 2008.

Goldberg, Bernard. *100 People Who Are Screwing up America*. New York: HarperCollins, 2005.

Hasted, Nick. *The Dark Story of Eminem*. London: Omnibus Press, 2003.

Nelson, Debbie. *My Son Marshall, My Son Eminem: Setting the Record Straight on My Life as Eminem's Mother*. Beverly Hills, CA: Phoenix House, 2008.

Emmy Awards

The movies have their Oscars. Broadway has its Tonys. Off-Broadway has its Obies. And television has its Emmys. Ever since January 1949, when the Academy of Television Arts & Sciences first presented them at the Hollywood Athletic Club, the Emmy Awards have remained the most highly visible and coveted honor earned for achievement in television. The trophy's name was derived from *Immy*, a word routinely employed to signify the image orthicon camera tube, which was in use during the early years of television. The statuette—a gold-plated winged lady hoisting a globe—was designed by television engineer Louis McManus, using his wife as a model. McManus himself was honored during that first ceremony with a special award "for his original design of the Emmy."

Over the years the Emmy Awards have expanded and evolved. In 1949 six trophies were handed out; in the 2010s scores of Emmys are won each year for both national and local programs. Walter O'Keefe, a long-forgotten radio quiz show emcee and celebrity interviewer, was the initial master of ceremonies for the awards. In the decades since, the ceremony has been hosted by a gallery of star names, including Lucille Ball, Desi Arnaz, Phil Silvers, Danny Thomas, Johnny Carson, Bill Cosby, Art Linkletter, and Ed Sullivan; more recent masters of ceremony include Ellen DeGeneres, Conan O'Brien, Ryan Seacrest, Neil Patrick Harris, Jimmy Fallon, and Jane Lynch. The very first Emmy recipient was Shirley Dinsdale and her puppet, Judy Splinters, who won for Most Outstanding Television Personality. Since then, many acting legends have won Emmys, including Helen Hayes, John Gielgud, Julie Harris, Laurence Olivier, Dustin Hoffman, Bette Davis, Anthony Hopkins, Hume Cronyn, Jessica Tandy, Ingrid Bergman, Judith Anderson, Jack Lemmon, William Holden, Maggie Smith, Helen Mirren, Al Pacino, and Meryl Streep.

THE EARLY YEARS

The Emmy categories, particularly during the early years, were frequently and somewhat arbitrarily renamed. Actor William Frawley, for example, was nominated for five successive years for his role as Fred Mertz on *I Love Lucy*. His first nomination in 1954 was as Best Series Supporting Actor; the following four

Emmy Awards. *Kyle Chandler gives his acceptance speech after winning an Emmy Award in 2011. The Emmys recognize outstanding achievement in television.* KEVIN WINTER/GETTY IMAGES.

awards were redesignated annually as Best Supporting Actor in a Regular Series, Best Actor in a Supporting Role, Best Supporting Performance by an Actor, and Best Continuing Supporting Performance by an Actor in a Dramatic or Comedy Series.

The procedure for securing nominations and naming winners also changed, and the number and variety of categories expanded. As the awards evolved, the most popular and high-profile prizes—as with the Oscars—remained those for best performers and best programs, but established Emmy Award categories have come to include directing, writing, casting, and hairstyling. Technological expertise is also acknowledged with awards for technical direction, electronic camerawork, film editing, and videotape editing.

CRITICS AND CONTROVERSY

The Emmys have been fraught with controversy and internal conflict, characterized by in-fighting between the New York and Hollywood chapters of the Academy of Television Arts & Sciences and disputes between other Academy factions, followed by lawsuits, rule changes, and separations of power and responsibility. Some of the most publicized Emmy squabbles have involved boycotts. Upon learning that their awards would not be handed out during the televised broadcast, TV directors and writers banded together and threatened to boycott the 1974–1975 show. In the previous decade, the news branches of CBS and ABC snubbed the 1963–1964 Emmys. At the time, CBS News President Fred Friendly alleged that voting practices were "unrealistic, unprofessional and unfair," and CBS News again refused to participate in 1964–1965 and 1965–1966. The 1979–1980 affair was also boycotted—on that occasion by performers wishing to coerce the TV networks to resolve a strike by the Screen Actors Guild and the American Federation of Television and Radio Artists.

Other brouhahas have centered on the actions of individual performers. In 2006–2007 Kathy Griffin earned the Outstanding Reality Program Emmy for *Kathy Griffin: My Life on the D List*. She stirred up a storm with her acceptance speech when she comically knocked performers who "come up here and thank Jesus for this award." Then in 2010–2011 Alec Baldwin was set to appear in a previously taped skit in which he joked about the phone-hacking scandal that had enveloped News Corp., the parent company of Fox, the network broadcasting the show. Fox ordered that the bit be cut, and Baldwin insisted that the show's producers eliminate the skit completely.

Critics also take issue with the fact that certain actors have amassed more trophies than can fit on their mantels for playing the same character year after year, whereas other equally fine performers have remained un- or under-rewarded. Beginning in 1984–1985 Angela Lansbury earned twelve consecutive Emmy nominations for playing Jessica Fletcher on *Murder, She Wrote*. Between 1982–1983 and 2004–2005 she was nominated on six additional occasions for other television appearances. Not once did Lansbury collect a statuette, and her failure to do so has become an industry joke. Similarly in 1977–1978, Susan Lucci earned the first of eighteen nominations for her performance as Erica Kane on the soap opera *All My Children* but remained statueless until 1998–1999; she was nominated twice more, in 2000–2001 and 2001–2002, but did not win.

And in an incident that echoed the censure of the nomination process four decades earlier, Ellen Burstyn was nominated in 2005–2006 as Outstanding Supporting Actress in a Miniseries or Movie for playing a character billed as "Former Tarnower Steady" in *Mrs. Harris*—despite the fact that the role was essentially a cameo. In the film, Burstyn appears on-screen for all of fourteen seconds. Her dialogue consists of thirty-eight words. Critics alleged that many of the 13,000 Academy members who selected the nominees did not view the shows and performances but merely checked off the most familiar names, one of which was Burstyn.

Nonetheless, echoing the annual hype that surrounds the Oscars, critics and viewers continue to speculate as to the nominees and winners, gathering before their television sets for the star-studded prime-time ceremony. And the winners—from Lucille Ball, Sid Caesar, Danny Thomas, Loretta Young, and Phil Silvers in the 1950s through Tina Fey, James Gandolfini, Kelsey Grammer, Edie Falco, and Julianna Margulies more than a half century later—set aside any behind-the-scenes tension and beam proudly for the cameras as they gratefully accept their gold-plated statues.

Rob Edelman

SEE ALSO: *Academy Awards;* All My Children*; Arnaz, Desi; Baldwin, Alec; Ball, Lucille; Bergman, Ingrid; Broadway; Caesar, Sid; Carson, Johnny; Celebrity; Cosby, Bill; Davis, Bette; Daytime Talk Shows; DeGeneres, Ellen; Fey, Tina; Frawley, William; Grammy Awards; Griffin, Kathy; Hairstyles; Hoffman, Dustin; Holden, William; Hollywood;* I Love Lucy*; Linkletter, Art; Made-for-Television Movies;* Murder, She Wrote*; O'Brien, Conan; Olivier, Laurence; Pacino, Al; Sitcom; Soap Operas; Streep, Meryl; Sullivan, Ed; Television; Thomas, Danny; Tony Awards; Young, Loretta.*

BIBLIOGRAPHY

Gelman, Morrie, and Gene Accas. *The Best in Television: 50 Years of Emmy*. Los Angeles: General Publishing, 1998.

Hyatt, Wesley. *Emmy Award Winning Nighttime Television Shows, 1948–2004*.Jefferson, NC: McFarland, 2006.

O'Neil, Thomas. *The Emmys: Star Wars, Showdowns and the Supreme Test of TV's Best*. New York: Penguin Books, 1992.

Emo

The musical style emo (short for *emotional* or *emotive*) has become somewhat of a dirty word among music aficionados, who largely regard the term as shorthand for a group of whiney, eyeliner-wearing rock bands that captured the airwaves in the first decade of the twenty-first century and spawned legions of fans distinguishable by their lopsided haircuts and goth-meets-skater fashion choices. But emo has its roots in some of the most influential and revered bands of the 1980s and 1990s, many of which managed to transform the raw energy and militant disposition of punk rock into a more intricate and introspective form of music.

Most music historians agree that emo music originated in Washington, D.C., in the so-called Revolution Summer of 1985, as politically minded hardcore punk bands such as Bad Brains and Minor Threat gave way to more melodic "emotional hardcore," "post-hardcore," or "emocore" bands such as Rites of Spring, whose lead singer, Guy Picciotto, combined the gravelly screams and yelps of the traditional punk front man with poetic, brooding lyrics about lost love and personal torment. Former

Minor Threat singer Ian MacKaye recognized the potential inherent in this new direction and soon formed his own melodic punk band, Embrace, and released records by similar-sounding groups on his record label, Dischord Records.

By the early 1990s, emo music had infiltrated the punk underground on the West Coast. In Seattle, Washington, a band called Sunny Day Real Estate honed a slower, more deliberate brand of emo built around plucked guitars and lead singer Jeremy Enigk's plaintive vocal melodies. Their debut album, *Diary* (1994), was a critical and financial success and helped to move emo music into the mainstream spotlight. In San Diego, California, Jawbreaker developed a fuzzy, upbeat sound that would later make its way into the commercial pop-punk of the late 1990s. As emo bands gained airplay on college radio stations and the occasional MTV feature, the genre produced several stylistic offshoots, including "screamo"—a more frenetic version of emo punctuated by syncopated guitar riffs and screamed vocal melodies, developed by such bands as Heroin, Saetia, the Swing Kids, Hot Cross, Orchid, and Drive Like Jehu—and a gentler, more literate sound that incorporated piano and acoustic guitar, among other instruments, as performed by such groups as the Promise Ring, Mineral, Weezer, Cursive, and Jimmy Eat World.

The mainstream crossover of emo music in the late 1990s and beginning of the twenty-first century introduced legions of high school and college-aged listeners to a musical subset that spoke directly to the inner turmoil caused by puberty, young love, and the emotional stress of leaving home for good. Fans soon began to emulate the fashion choices of their favorite bands: tight-fitting T-shirts, cuffed jeans, tattoo "sleeves," and thick-rimmed glasses replaced the unkempt look popularized by grunge music. By the first few years into the twenty-first century, record executives began to take notice of the growing trend, and emo/screamo bands including Saves the Day, Dashboard Confessional, Glassjaw, Coheed and Cambria, the Blood Brothers, Thrice, and Taking Back Sunday all made their way to major labels or elevated once-obscure labels such as Vagrant, Jade Tree, and Saddle Creek Records to powerful new heights.

The popularity of emo music peaked sometime around 2005. As the genre reached global audiences, it also became increasingly commercialized, and the third wave of emo bands sounded more and more like a campy parody of their influences. Such groups as My Chemical Romance, the Used, Panic! at the Disco, and Fall Out Boy were touted as the new face of emo, but in truth they bore little resemblance to the emo core bands that were often cited as their forebears. Emo fashion at the time also began to evolve away from the clean-cut, nerd-inspired look of the early twenty-first century toward a darker style more akin to the all-black clothing of goth groups, including Bauhaus and the Cure. Clothing marketed directly to the emo crowd became widely available in malls, and soon tattered black clothes, leather wristbands, studded belts, wallet chains, and uneven black haircuts highlighted with streaks of white or hot pink rose to prominence. My Chemical Romance took the commercialization of emo culture to its inevitable extreme with the release of a series of action figures in the early 2010s.

As a result of its rapid co-option by mainstream culture, emo music has largely fallen out of favor with musical tastemakers, and even those bands and labels that once proudly associated themselves with the genre now shy away from it. Criticism over the style's lack of female voices and borderline misogynistic lyrics, as well as accusations that its turn toward all things dark and depressive have contributed to a rash of teen suicides, has further pushed emo music out of the limelight. But for every band that has held some responsibility for the demise of the genre, there are countless others that helped make it one of the most influential rock music styles of the late twentieth century.

Jacob Schmitt

SEE ALSO: *Goth; Grunge; Punk; Rock and Roll; Suicide.*

BIBLIOGRAPHY

Azerrad, Michael. *Our Band Could Be Your Life: Scenes from the American Indie Underground 1981–1991.* Boston: Little, Brown, 2001.

Greenwald, Andy. *Nothing Feels Good: Punk Rock, Teenagers, and Emo.* New York: St. Martin's Griffin, 2003.

Grubbs, Eric. *Post: A Look at the Influence of Post-Hardcore 1985–2007.* New York: iUniverse, 2008.

Simon, Leslie, and Trevor Kelley. *Everybody Hurts: An Essential Guide to Emo Culture.* New York: HarperEntertainment, 2007.

Empire State Building

Constructed in 1930 and 1931, the Empire State Building, located in New York City, was the tallest skyscraper in the world for forty years, until the appearance of New York's World Trade Center in 1973. After the September 11, 2001, attacks on the World Trade Center, the Empire State Building once again stood as the tallest building in the city. Despite being overtaken in terms of its height by other international structures, both in the United States and abroad, the Empire State Building has remained one of the most internationally famous architectural icons in the United States. It is both a shining example of the aesthetic and functional possibilities of the skyscraper form and a potent symbol of the Manhattan metropolis it inhabits. The Empire State Building has played a prominent role in several Hollywood movies and has been the subject of countless essays and artworks, while an infinite number of products have been marketed, capitalizing on its familiar image.

CONCEPTION AND CONSTRUCTION

The building demonstrated the extent to which corporate capitalism came to represent the United States to the rest of the world. It was the fruit of a speculative real estate venture by the Empire State Company, an organization whose major investors were John J. Raskob of General Motors and businessmen Coleman and Pierre du Pont. The former New York governor and presidential candidate Alfred E. Smith served as the company's president and figurehead. The project began with the purchase of land, formerly owned by the Astor family, on Fifth Avenue between 33rd and 34th streets in midtown Manhattan. From the start there was no anchor tenant or large company to occupy and associate with the building, unlike the nearby Chrysler Building or the famous downtown Woolworth Building. The Empire State venture was announced in 1929 and coincided with the beginning of the Great Depression, but the developers gambled on an economic turnaround and proceeded with their plans.

On May 1, 1931, at a ceremony attended by President Herbert Hoover and New York Governor Franklin Delano

Roosevelt, the Empire State Building was officially opened. Construction had taken only eight months—a remarkable rate of progress, during which the building's steel skeleton was erected in a mere twenty-three weeks. (During one period in 1930, workers put up fourteen floors in ten days.) For promotional purposes the developers had specifically set out to build the tallest building in the world. They achieved their goal. Reaching a height of 1,250 feet, the Empire State Building was almost 200 feet taller than its rival, the glitteringly flamboyant Chrysler Building; but compared to the latter, the Empire State, designed by the architectural firm of Shreve, Lamb and Harmon, was relatively sedate in appearance.

The building's form was determined by its height and the setbacks required by the 1916 New York Zoning Laws. There was no elaborate decoration on the limestone exterior to attract the eye; instead, the building relied on its graceful form, enlivened by the conscientious use of setbacks, to provide an aesthetic effect. At the top, on the 102nd floor, was an open-air observation deck beneath a huge mooring mast intended by the developers to serve as an enticement for zeppelin landings (although no zeppelin ever docked there).

Empire State Building. *New York City's Empire State Building was the first building to have more than 100 floors.* MLADEN ANTONOV/AFP/GETTY IMAGES.

IMPACT

The first years, however, were lean. The Empire State Building was only half full when it opened and, with only a 23 percent occupancy rate during the 1930s, was often dubbed the Empty State Building. At times it seemed that only the income from the popular 86th and 102nd floor observation decks was keeping the premises alive. Nonetheless, almost immediately after opening, the Empire State Building became a cultural icon. In its first year of operation, more than one million sightseers visited the observation decks, and Hollywood soon spotted its movie potential. The building's association with the film industry famously began with *King Kong* in 1933 and surfaced as an integral plot strand many times since, including in *An Affair to Remember* (1957) and *Sleepless in Seattle* (1993). The building is a ubiquitous icon of the city's tourist trade, and millions of replicas of varying sizes have been sold to visitors and native New Yorkers alike.

There is no obvious explanation as to why the Empire State Building has continued to attract successive generations of visitors and admirers. People remain fascinated by the sheer (and ever increasing) size of skyscrapers, but impressive edifices such as Chicago's Willis Tower or New York's former World Trade Center have failed to capture the public affection in the same manner. The Empire State has not been the world's tallest building in decades; neither is it universally considered to be the most beautiful or the most interesting of the world's skyscrapers. Nevertheless, its special place in the hearts of Americans has not been superseded.

During the Great Depression, the building was a stalwart symbol of optimism. As Smith said at the dedication ceremony, the Empire State Building is "the greatest monument to ingenuity, to skill, to brain power, to muscle power." And, he might have added, to triumph in the face of adversity. After World War II it was the emblem of the triumphant emergence of the United States as the world's preeminent economic and cultural power; from the 1950s onward the building's elegant beauty put to shame the forest of impersonal glass boxes that came to alter the face of Manhattan. With its many historic and romantic resonances, the Empire State Building represents much more than just a pioneering triumph of scale.

Dale Allen Gyure

SEE ALSO: *Chrysler Building; General Motors; The Great Depression; Hollywood;* King Kong*; Sears Tower; Skyscrapers; World Trade Center.*

BIBLIOGRAPHY

Douglas, George H. *Skyscrapers: A Social History of the Very Tall Building in America.* Jefferson, NC: McFarland, 1996.

Goldman, Jonathan. *The Empire State Building Book.* New York: St. Martin's Press, 1980.

James, Theodore, Jr. *The Empire State Building.* New York: Harper, 1975.

Pacelle, Mitchell. *Empire: A Tale of Obsession, Betrayal, and the Battle for an American Icon.* New York: Wiley, 2001.

Tauranc, John. *The Empire State Building: The Making of a*

Landmark. New York: St. Martin's Griffin, 1997.
Willis, Carol, ed. *Building the Empire State*. New York: Norton, 1998.

Energy Drinks

As modern life became increasingly hurried, complex, and stressful, people of all ages began to seek ways to overcome exhaustion and boost flagging energy levels. Soft drink manufacturers rushed to fill this need with a number of performance-enhancing energy drinks, which started to gain widespread popularity in the late 1900s. From the introduction of Red Bull to the United States in 1997, energy drink sales quickly grew into a multibillion-dollar industry with more than 100 brands from which to choose. Though energy drinks are advertised to help with everything from athletic performance to concentration, some industry analysts claim that they contain few helpful ingredients and may have damaging health effects.

The forerunners of modern energy drinks were tonic drinks that became popular among Asian workers during the 1980s. Dietrich Mateschitz, an Austrian businessman, discovered the energy-boosting tonic drinks while traveling in Thailand and recognized their potential for sales in Europe and North America. He partnered with Chaleo Yoovidhya, a Thai pharmaceutical maker who had formulated his own brand of tonic drink called Krating Daeng, or Red Bull, and the two began to market the drink, first in Austria, then around the world.

The success of Red Bull led to an explosion of new energy drink brands. Most contained similar ingredients: sugar or artificial sweeteners, the stimulant caffeine, the amino acid taurine, B vitamins, and various other nutritional supplements. Marketed primarily to trendy young consumers, the new drinks had outlaw names, such as Zombie, Monster, Rock Star, No Fear, and Adrenaline Rush. Associated with athletes, such as snowboarder Shaun White who endorsed Red Bull, and rock musicians, such as rapper Nelly who introduced his own drink called Pimp Juice, the first energy drinks appealed largely to young men, who appreciated their rebellious macho image. Later, manufacturers reached out to female consumers with drinks purporting to be more natural, such as Ocean Spray's Cran Energy and Volvic Revive.

Along with their defiant image, young users of energy drinks were drawn to the caffeine rush the drinks gave them and often combined them with alcohol for a more intense mood-altering experience. Some products, such as Four Loko, introduced in 2005, combined caffeine and other typical energy drink ingredients with alcohol and rapidly gained popularity on college campuses. Caffeine masked the effects of the alcohol in the drink, however, and users frequently overdosed, leading to Four Loko's implication in dozens of hospitalizations and even some deaths. Several states banned the drink, leading to a federal Food and Drug Administration ban on combining alcohol and caffeine in 2010.

Even without alcohol, parents and consumer groups continued to express concern over the effects of frequent use of energy drinks. Though marketed as sports drinks, experts questioned the usefulness of energy drinks for athletes. Unlike true sports drinks, such as Gatorade and 10K, which, though often sugary, do replenish electrolytes lost through perspiration, energy drinks provide only a brief artificial caffeine boost, which often leaves the body even more depleted afterward. In addition, critics pointed to other dangers connected to overuse of caffeine, such as addiction, high blood pressure, heart damage, and increased risk of blood clots. Some researchers suspected the common ingredient taurine of being a dangerous stimulant as well, and high energy drink consumption has also been tied to weight gain and damage to tooth enamel. These health concerns led a number of nations, including France, Germany, Denmark, Norway, and Uruguay, to ban some energy drinks. Others, such as Canada, have required the addition of labels to warn consumers of possible health hazards.

Tina Gianoulis

SEE ALSO: *Snowboarding; White, Shaun.*

BIBLIOGRAPHY

Duchan, Erin C., and Neil D. Patel. "Energy Drinks." *Food Engineering & Ingredients*, October 2010, 30.

Gidus, Tara. "Energy Drinks: Do They Really Deliver Energy?" *Golf Fitness Magazine*, November–December 2008, 42.

Kelly, Alice Lesch. "Behind the Buzz; Energy Drinks with Caffeine and Sugar Pack a Punch, But at What Cost?" *Los Angeles Times*, August 23, 2004, F1.

O'Rourke, Kevin. "An Energized Category: Energy Drinks Are Blazin', and Here's What's Happening." *Beverage Aisle*, February 15, 2004, 20.

Reid, T. R. "Caffeine: What's the Buzz?" National Geographic. Accessed June 4, 2012. Available from http://science.nationalgeographic.com/science/health-and-human-body/human-body/caffeine-buzz/#page=5

Enron Scandal

In October 2001, 20,000 workers lost their jobs and over a million investors lost their nest eggs when the energy trading company Enron declared bankruptcy after years of using false accounting measures to cover up billions of dollars in debt. Its shocking collapse led to criminal investigations and convictions of several Enron executives, as well as a wave of new regulations to protect investors from similar manipulations. Enron became the prime example of late-1990s corporate corruption and greed.

Before its fall, Enron represented a new development in the commodification of energy. Taking the concepts that were at the root of John D. Rockefeller's Standard Oil Trust a century earlier, Enron and others created the field of energy trading, which was now possible with electronic stock trading. In mastering this process, Enron contributed mightily to a demonization of energy and oil companies in American popular culture. A symbol of "Big Oil" (though better called "Big Energy" in this case), the Enron scandal showed American consumers how vulnerable their energy addictions made them—whether to foreign exporters of oil or large domestic companies most concerned with their own profits. Energy became a touchstone for a consumer base that felt under siege.

A POWERHOUSE

After being founded in Houston, Texas, in 1985, Enron became the nation's seventh-biggest company in revenue by emphasizing the transmission and distribution of electricity and gas throughout the United States and the development, construction, and operation of power plants and pipelines worldwide. Following the trend toward energy deregulation, particularly in states such as California, Enron became the essential middleman between energy producers and consumers. As a result, Enron was named "America's Most Innovative Company" by *Fortune* magazine for five consecutive years, from 1996 to 2000. Viewed as a great technological and business innovator, Enron, under the direction of its chairman, Kenneth Lay, was credited with creating the energy markets that it grew to dominate the investment world.

For most of the twentieth century, utility companies had generated, transmitted, and sold electricity as state-regulated monopolies. They also built and maintained the "electrical grid"—the network of transmission wires that carries electricity to homes and businesses. With deregulation, companies needed to make sure that their supplies of power on the grid would remain consistent. Energy trading—buying and selling resources without necessarily owning power plants or supplies of raw material—was Enron's route to success and, ultimately, failure.

With its transactions taking place entirely on paper, Enron's business was highly susceptible to illegal manipulation. For instance, the company has been accused of manipulating energy prices to create shortages in California in the summer of 1999. These practices, however, earned Enron great sums of money, which made the company even more enticing to investors.

Traders at Enron took advantage of the poorly conceived energy market system created by the California Deregulation Plan of the late 1990s. This law allowed traders to manipulate the supply of energy to increase prices—and Enron profits. Actions such as shutting down plants to increase demand contributed to California's energy crisis of 2000 and 2001, in which rolling blackouts occurred. Enron traders gave these schemes code names such as Fat Boy and Death Star. Publicly released audiotapes of internal conversations also revealed that the traders joked about stealing from California and overcharging for power.

THE BOTTOM FALLS OUT

In a six-week downward spiral during 2000, Enron disclosed a stunning $638 million third-quarter loss, the Securities and Exchange Commission opened an investigation into the partnerships, and the company's main rival backed out of an $8.4 billion merger deal. After a series of scandals involving irregular accounting procedures bordering on fraud involving Enron and its accounting firm, Arthur Andersen, Enron filed for protection from creditors on December 2, 2001, in the biggest corporate bankruptcy in U.S. history.

The company's stock, worth more than $80 per share only a year earlier, tumbled to less than $1 per share. Enron's collapse left investors burned and its 20,000 employees out of work and with lost retirement savings. In addition, Enron barred its employees from selling Enron shares from their retirement accounts as the stock price plunged, saying the accounts were being switched to a new plan administrator. Former Enron chief financial officer Andy Fastow was indicted on November 1, 2002, by a federal grand jury in Houston on seventy-eight counts, including fraud, money laundering, and conspiracy. He was ordered to serve a ten-year prison sentence and forfeit $23.8 million. Lay was similarly convicted of securities and wire fraud but died of heart disease in 2006 before he could be sentenced.

The swift fall of this corporate giant caught investors by surprise. Maybe the best symbol of how quickly corporate entities can come and go is the baseball stadium opened in Houston in 2000, which was named Enron Field. After the Enron collapsed the following year, the Houston Astros baseball team removed company's name from the stadium. The team cited the need to do so in order to avoid the negative publicity associated with the former model of corporate success. Additionally, Enron's headquarters stood empty for years before Houstonians converted it into diversified office spaces.

During the ensuing financial difficulties of the early twenty-first century, banks, mortgage companies, and financial advisers, among others, were found to have exploited the trust of investors in order to gain enormous personal profit. Enron was one in a continuing litany of businesses willing to rely on questionable ethics in order to maximize profits. Observers called Enron's leaders "the smartest guys in the room," which was just the latest term—following "masters of the universe" for the junk-bond traders of the 1980s—to describe the willingness of certain executives to bilk the system for their own good.

THE LESSON

In the end, the questionable actions of Enron's energy traders did not directly cause its downfall; in fact, they earned hundreds of millions of dollars for the company. However, their practice of speculating on energy prices was symptomatic of the company's freewheeling culture, which was more pointedly demonstrated by aggressive and fraudulent accounting practices that involved risky long-term contracts. It was those practices that made Enron vulnerable to collapse. Even though Enron became a symbol of society's angst about corporate ethics, its business of trading on energy prices was a product of a new era in resource management. This approach has outlived the company that perfected it.

Possibly the most farsighted accomplishment of Enron was to perceive energy as an increasingly valuable commodity. In much the same fashion, over a century earlier, Rockefeller identified profit to be made in the increasingly popular and available resource of petroleum. The plan for his Standard Oil Trust had little to do with owning oil wells. Instead, Standard came to dominate the commodity of crude by controlling the infrastructure necessary to use it: refining and transportation. Similarly, Enron operated in an era when electricity—made in any fashion, really—became so integral that its supply could be used as leverage for prices and, thereby, profits.

Enron introduced its state-of-the-art trading floor on national television. Energy companies such as Centaurus have learned from Enron's example. Since its founding in 2002, Centaurus has amassed $1.5 billion in assets but has done so with a low profile. Energy trading is springing to life again, though without the flamboyance Enron displayed.

Volatile energy markets and record-high commodity prices are prompting renewed interest from investors. That has pushed banks and a growing number of hedge funds to hire more energy traders to maximize their ability to profit from the unpredictable sector. Whether Americans agree with such ethics, many appreciate the growth energy trading provides in their investment portfolios; and they continue to recognize energy as an essential part of society.

Brian Black

SEE ALSO: *Media Feeding Frenzies.*

BIBLIOGRAPHY

McLean, Bethany. *The Smartest Guys in the Room.* New York: Portfolio, 2004.

Munson, Richard. *From Edison to Enron: The Business of Power and What It Means for the Future of Electricity.* New York: Praeger, 2008.

Swartz, Mimi. *Power Failure.* New York: Crown, 2004.

Entertainment Tonight

Five days a week, *Entertainment Tonight,* commonly called *ET,* televises reports on the entertainment industry, celebrating the deeds and misdeeds of celebrities. An entertainment newsmagazine, *Entertainment Tonight* is the longest running of all such programs and the number one syndicated entertainment news show. Its success has helped to blur the differences in network television programming between news and entertainment, creating a hybrid nicknamed "infotainment."

ET was first broadcast on September 14, 1981, with Tom Hallick and Marjorie Wallace cohosting the show's first season. They sat at what appeared to be a local television news set and introduced what looked like local reporters to air their stories, a practice that continues. They were soon replaced by Mary Hart, who anchored until 2011, when she was replaced by Nancy O'Dell. During her tenure Hart was joined by several cohosts, including John Tesh (1986–1996) and Mark Steines (2004–). In its earliest years *ET*'s coverage was limited primarily to famous actors and musicians, but eventually the show began doing investigative reporting into entertainment industry practices, fashioning itself as an industry watchdog.

By the mid-1990s *ET* had expanded its coverage to include political and other noteworthy topics. As such, its typically optimistic entertainment news was tempered by more sober topics such as political scandals. The reporting was inflected with sensationalism, and *ET* openly courted controversy through paid interviews with infamous figures such as Amy Fisher, a teenager who shot her older boyfriend's wife, and Mary Kay Letourneau, a teacher who had an affair with her student. In some cases *ET* even scooped regular news shows with their exclusive paid for access, a practice called checkbook journalism.

True crime also became fodder for the show, as it reported on national—and often salacious—stories such as JonBenet Ramsey, a young girl and beauty pageant contestant who was murdered, and Susan Smith, a mother found guilty of killing her two young sons. One result of this genre blending was that the designation of celebrity was expanded to include people working outside the entertainment industry, including criminals and their victims. Such coverage further blurred the line the line between entertainment and news.

Although *Entertainment Tonight* is derided by some critics as a "fluff" news program, it is enormously influential on other entertainment and gossip newsmagazines and on the global culture of celebrity. The *ET* format spawned a variety of imitators including *Insider* and *Showbiz Today.* In the twenty-first century many countries also broadcast either the U.S. version or their own versions of the show. Not only a pioneer of infotainment television, *Entertainment Tonight* has also been influential for its style and syndication process. Its sets are jazzy and change frequently to maintain a fresh feel, as does its theme music. Moreover, instead of airing the program at a predetermined time, as is the case with most syndicated programs, local stations can tape the broadcast and air the program any time that day. The show has also come under criticism over the years for its use of the paparazzi, a practice subsequently imitated by shows such as *TMZ on TV.*

After thirty years on air, *Entertainment Tonight* remains popular with audiences. While tabloid newspapers and magazines, as well as Internet gossip blogs, vied for the public's attention, the rapacious desire for celebrity news and Hollywood-insider perspective continued to propel television shows such as *ET,* securing its place in U.S. culture. By keeping up-to-date in looks, calling on famous special correspondents to help report, and offering exclusive insights into the hottest topics, *ET* remains a forerunner of infotainment and celebrity news and gossip.

Jill Gregg Clever

SEE ALSO: *Blogging; Celebrity; The Internet; Media Feeding Frenzies; Syndication; Tabloid Television; Television.*

BIBLIOGRAPHY

Bartone, Richard C. "Entertainment Tonight." In *Encyclopedia of Television,* ed. Horace Newcomb. New York: Fitzroy Dearborn, 2004.

Stark, Steven D. "*Entertainment Tonight* and the Expansion of the Tabloid, Celebrity Culture." In *Glued to the Set: The 60 Television Shows and Events That Made Us Who We Are Today.* New York: Free Press, 1997.

Entertainment Weekly

After two years of planning, the magazine *Entertainment Weekly* (*EW*), the brainchild of noted journalist Jeff Jarvis, was first published on February 16, 1990. Jarvis saw the magazine as a way to guide the U.S. public through a maze of entertainment venues that included premium and cable channels as well as traditional network offerings, the Internet, compact discs, and videocassettes. Instead of focusing on the personal lives of celebrities, *Entertainment Weekly* reports on what celebrities are doing professionally. Each issue provides reviews and rankings of movies, television shows, music, books, and theater. Regular features include reader feedback; highlights from the website; the Must List, which discusses the week's Top 10 list of movies, books, television shows, and electronic applications (apps); a television schedule of selected programming; and feature stories. In September 2010 more than 100,000 individuals downloaded *EW*'s Must List app to their smartphones, iPods, or iPads.

When Time Inc. announced the upcoming publication of *Entertainment Weekly* in July 1989, Jarvis promised that the magazine would be "brash and browsable." From the onset the mission statement for the magazine was "We help you have fun." Guest reviewers were regularly invited to add their ratings of popular media to those of *EW* staff. In the Critical Mass section, ten reviewers from newspapers such as the *Boston Globe* and the *Los Angeles Times* join *Entertainment Weekly* staffers and readers in rating current movies from A to F to create an average.

The Chart section reports box-office earnings so that readers have a point of comparison to critical reviews. A second charting system relates the number of viewers and rankings for television shows.

In 1998 *Entertainment Weekly* was one of the first media giants to recognize that it could generate additional revenue through its existing website by adding an exclusive section for subscribers only. The website offered free access to its blogs, extensive photo galleries, a Games and Gadgets section, and full-length episodes of current television shows. In 2011 *EW* won a Media Vanguard Award for building what *Advertising Age* labels "one of the most sophisticated and well-rounded social-media strategies" instituted among any form of media. In response to the explosion of social networking, *Entertainment Weekly* established a presence on Twitter, where it had 1.7 million followers. On Facebook, where *EW*'s Friends list reached 30,000 in 2012, *EW* set up a Fans Only site that offered exclusive content and contests. In the blogging genre the magazine partners with Tumblr and GetGlue.

Entertainment Weekly's circulation grew to 1,798,643 by 2010. Sixty-one percent of its readers were female as compared to 39 percent who were male. The median age of readers of the print version was 36.9. Some 60 percent had attended college. The demographics of regular visitors to the website were similar. Registered members were 57 percent female and 43 percent male, with a median age of thirty-five. Many social commentators view the massive increase in *Entertainment Weekly*'s circulation—and the popularity of other periodicals and television shows similar to it—as evidence of a growing trend in American culture to worship celebrities and to value personality more than character. Others disagree, claiming that the United States has a long tradition of celebrating popular culture and that publications like *Entertainment Weekly* are harmless diversions and do not contribute to the breakdown of society.

Elizabeth Rholetter Purdy

SEE ALSO: *Celebrity; Facebook;* The Girl with the Dragon Tattoo; *Hollywood; The Internet; iPad; iPod / iTunes;* People; *Public Television (PBS); Smartphones; Social Media; Television; Twitter.*

BIBLIOGRAPHY

Cain, Susan. *Quiet: The Power of Introverts in a World That Can't Stop Talking.* New York: Crown, 2012.

Entertainment Weekly. Accessed May 2, 2012. Available from http://www.ew.com

"News That You Can Choose: Time, Inc., Announces Plans to Start *Entertainment Weekly.*" *Time,* July 24, 1989, 49.

Snyder, Beth. "*Entertainment Weekly* Rolls Out New Model." *Advertising Age,* May 11, 1998, 46–50.

"2011 Media Vanguard Awards." *Advertising Age,* November 14, 2011, 10–16.

Environmentalism

More than three-quarters of Americans refer to themselves as *environmentalists.* In the twenty-first century, this term can mean a variety of things. Environmentalism has grown to encompass a diverse group of activities and ideas and has become so influential that it has a countermovement.

JEFFERSONIAN IDEALS

American environmental concern traces back to Jeffersonian ideas of a unique American connection to land and the romantic ethos of the nineteenth century. Open land, sometimes viewed as "wilderness," defined the New World for many European settlers. Thomas Jefferson argued that this open land could be transferred into an American strength if development were directed toward an agrarian republic. Much of the nation would pursue land use similar to the landscape of Jefferson's ideal, and some urban Americans remained intrigued by his idea of a unique American connection to the natural environment. This can be seen in the adoption of European forms such as parks and gardens and in the intellectual tradition of romanticism and transcendentalism. By the end of the 1800s, wealthy urbanites pursued "wild" adventures in sites such as the Adirondacks; initiated organizations to conserve animal species or limit pollution; and, finally, set aside areas of nature from development. While the first national parks, Yellowstone and Yosemite, proved to be watershed events in environmental history, they were not initially set aside to protect wilderness areas.

Much nineteenth-century environmentalism occurred without a strict organization or philosophy, and the first national parks are a primary example of this. Some scholars have chosen to view nineteenth-century environmentalism as a product of Gilded Age decadence and not an emerging new consciousness toward natural resource use. For instance, Yellowstone, established as the first national park in 1872, developed closely with railroad interests in the hope that it would attract tourists to the American West. Its oddities, such as geysers and waterfalls, proved more important to observers than its unspoiled wilderness. They also made its utility for settlement questionable, which allowed its sponsors to dub the area "worthless for development." Such a designation made lawmakers more willing to sponsor setting it aside for altruistic reasons.

CONSERVATIONISM VS. PRESERVATIONISM

The progressive period energized many Americans to identify social ills and use the government to correct them. The impulse to stop wasting resources and the desire to halt pollution, physical and spiritual, of American communities rapidly became an expression for Americans' unique connection to the land. The leadership of President Theodore Roosevelt and his chief of forestry Gifford Pinchot in the early 1900s galvanized the upper-class interest with national policies. These policies deviated in two directions: preservation and conservation. Roosevelt greatly admired the national parks as places where "bits of the old wilderness scenery and the old wilderness life are to be kept unspoiled for the benefit of our children's children." With his spiritual support, preservationists linked the prevention of natural areas from development to the spirit of "Americanness," including Jeffersonian ideals and romanticism. Finally, though, preservationists argued that a society that could exhibit such restraint as to cordon off entire sections of itself had ascended to the level of great civilizations in world history. Whereas Roosevelt is thought to have had preservationist convictions, his main adviser on land management, Pinchot, argued otherwise for the good of the nation.

Conservationists, including Pinchot, sought to qualify the preservationist impulse with a dose of utilitarian reality. The mark of an ascendant society, they argued, was the awareness of limits and the use of the government to manage resources in danger. Forest resources were Pinchot's primary concern. The first practicing American forester, Pinchot urged Americans to manage forests differently than had Europe. Under his advice, President Roosevelt moved the few national forests created in 1891 out of the jurisdiction of the Department of Agriculture and into an independent Forest Service. During his administration, Roosevelt added 150 million acres of national forests. Under Pinchot's direction, the U.S. Forest Service became one of the most publicly recognized government agencies of the Roosevelt era. A mailing list of more than 100,000, frequent public appearances, and penning articles for popular magazines combined with Pinchot's personal connections to help make forests a national cause célebrè. This public standing, created through forest conservation, further inflamed the approaching altercation that would define the early environmental movement.

Although the difference between preservation and conservation may not have been clear to Americans at the beginning of the twentieth century, popular culture and the writings of muckraking journalists clearly reflected a time of changing sensibilities. After the San Francisco fire in 1906, the nation confronted its feelings in order to define national policy. San Francisco, in search of a dependable supply of water, requested that the Hetch Hetchy Valley, located within the boundaries of Yosemite National Park, be flooded in order to create a reservoir to protect against future fires. Preservationists, rallied by popular magazine articles by naturalist John Muir, boisterously refused to compromise the authenticity of a national park's natural environment. Reviving romantic notions and even transcendental philosophies, Muir used this pulpit to spread his message: "Thousands of tired, nerve-shaken, over-civilized people are beginning to find out that going to the mountains is going home; that wildness is a necessity; and that mountain parks and reservations are useful not only as fountains of timber and irrigating rivers, but as fountains of life." He called those wishing to develop the site "temple destroyers." In reaction, Pinchot defined the conservationist mantra by claiming that such a reservoir represented the "greatest good for the greatest number" of people and, therefore, should be the nation's priority. The dam and reservoir were approved in 1913, but the battle had fueled the emergence of the modern environmental movement.

INCORPORATING SCIENTIFIC STUDIES

Environmentalism continued to emerge as a part of twentieth-century culture throughout the period leading up to World War II. The New Deal brought the connection of scientific understanding to the popular appeal of not abusing natural resources. As New Deal agencies strove to win public approval for their back-to-work programs, popular periodicals were deluged with science-based articles discussing land-use practices being carried out by New Deal agencies. This development incorporated the emergence of ecology, also taking place in the 1930s, with federal policies to manage watersheds, maintain forests, teach agriculture, and hold fast the flying soils of the Southern Plains. Press coverage of the "dust bowl" of the 1930s, for instance, presented a natural disaster caused by drought and bad luck. Through government-made documentary films such as *The Plow that Broke the Plains*, the New Deal infused a bit of ecological background to explain desertification and agricultural practices that can be used to combat it. In the midst of a natural disaster, the American public learned a great deal about its role within the natural environment.

This lesson became more pronounced as Americans increased their lifestyle standards and their expectations for safety. Historians point to a clear correlation between the growth of the middle class in the 1950s and the popularity of environmentalism. Samuel P. Hays wrote that this era "displayed demands from the grass-roots, demands that are well charted by the innumerable citizen organizations" that grew out of such public interest. Within growing suburbanization, middle-class Americans expected health and home safety. While there was as yet little regulative authority available, grassroots environmentalists demanded their government to intercede and ensure community safety. The groundswell of interest mobilized with the counterculture movements of the 1960s, and activists seized a national stage to link scientific data with environmental concern.

PASSING LEGISLATURE

The initial interest of the public in the 1940s and 1950s was garnered through an event similar to Hetch Hetchy. The Bureau of Reclamation, an agency developed by applying Pinchot's idea of conservation to waterways of the American West, set out to construct the Echo Park Dam along the Utah-Colorado border and within a little-used national monument named Dinosaur, most of whose fossils and bones had been stolen. As Congress neared a vote on the issue in 1950, seventy-eight national and 236 state conservation organizations expressed their belief that national parks and monuments were sacred areas.

David Brower, executive director of the Sierra Club, and Howard Zahniser of the Wilderness Society used the opportunity to create a model for environmental lobbyists to follow. Direct-mail pamphlets asked: "What Is Your Stake in Dinosaur?" and "Will You DAM the Scenic Wildlands of Our National Park System?" Additionally, a color movie and a book of lush photos, each depicting the Echo Park Valley's natural splendor, were widely viewed by the public. Such images and sentiments forced Americans to react. With mail to Congress late in 1954 running at eighty-to-one against the dam, the bill's vote was suspended and the project eventually abandoned. The issues had been packaged by environmentalists to connect concerns with romantic images of the American past. The American public reacted as never before.

Zahniser identified this moment as the best to press for the environmental movement's greatest goal: a national system of wilderness lands. Based on the idealistic notion of pristine wilderness, such a system had been called for beginning with Aldo Leopold in the 1910s. With increased recreation in parks and public lands, Zahniser argued, it had become even more crucial that some of the land be set aside completely. His bill, introduced to Congress in 1956, precluded land development and offered recreational opportunities only for a few rather than for the great mass of travelers. Such an idealistic goal required great salesmanship, and Zahniser was perfect for the job.

As the political climate shifted in the early 1960s, lawmakers became more interested in wilderness. Finally, in 1964, President Lyndon Johnson signed the Wilderness Act into law. The United States had taken one of the most idealistic plunges in the history of environmentalism: nearly 10 million acres were immediately set aside as "an area where the earth and its community of life are untrammeled by man, where man himself is a visitor who does not remain." Additional lands were preserved in similar fashion by the end of the decade.

THE EPA

While the concept of wilderness forced the general American public to begin to understand ecosystems and the webs of reliance operating within natural systems, the application of scientific understanding to environmentalism occurred most often in other realms. Pollution was the most frequent complaint, but its nuisance derived more from physical discomfort than a scientific correlation with human health. Rachel Carson, a government biologist turned nature writer, presented the American public with its lesson in science in 1962 with the publication of *Silent Spring*. The best seller told the story of pollution (particularly that caused by the popular pesticide DDT) and its effect on ecological webs of life. The study linked water runoff to declining fish health and then to depletion of the bald eagle population. Readers were left to infer the effects of such chemicals on humans.

Flexing their increased environmental awareness, the American public scurried to support Carson's parade through television talk shows. The Kennedy administration appointed a commission to study her findings and a year later banned DDT from use in the United States. Carson became identified with "mother nature" and a maternal impulse to manage the natural environment through federal regulation.

Over the next decade, a deluge of environmental legislation was passed in response to the public's demand for action. The public outcry was so severe that even a conservative such as Richard Nixon could be deemed "the environmental president" as he signed the National Environmental Protection Act in 1969, creating the Environmental Protection Agency (EPA). The public anointed the EPA its environmental regulator to enforce legislation monitoring air and water purity, limiting noise and other kinds of pollution, and monitoring species in order to discern which required federal protection. The public soon realized just how great the stakes were. During the 1970s, oil spills, river fires, nuclear accidents, and petroleum shortages made it appear as if nature were in open rebellion. Americans, already possessing a growing environmental sensibility, rapidly learned that humans—just as Carson had instructed—needed to live within limits. A watershed shift in human consciousness occurred as "green" philosophies infiltrated companies that wanted to create products that appealed to the public's environmental priority. Recycling, daylight saving time, carpooling, and environmental impact statements became part of everyday life after the 1970s.

GLOBAL IMPACT

The culture expressing this environmental priority has taken many forms since the 1970s. Earth Day 1970 introduced a tradition that has evolved into an annual reminder of humans' tenuous existence. As many as twenty million Americans participated in the first celebration. Some celebrants protested polluting companies, others planted trees, and still others cleaned up trash. Particularly for school-age children, a single day has evolved into continuous awareness. Ideas such as highway trash cleanup and recycling have become part of everyday American society. Many parents find children acting as environmental regulators within a household. Mixing science with action, environmentalism proved to be excellent fodder for American educators.

More importantly, though, the philosophy of fairness and living within limits merged with cultural forms to become mainstays in entertainment for young people, including feature films such as *FernGully: The Last Rainforest* (1992) and *The Lion King* (1994), environmental music, and even clothing styles. The audience of children and youths quickly became an outlet for ideals for which many adults longed but from which society limited their access. Many American parents expressed their own convictions by supporting the environmental idealism of youth culture.

Earth Day 1990 continued such traditions but also marked an important change in environmentalism's scope. Worldwide, 141 nations and 200 million humans marked some kind of celebration on Earth Day 1990. While a global perspective seemed inherent in the web of life put forward by Carson and others, it took global issues such as the Chernobyl nuclear accident in 1986 and shared problems such as greenhouse gasses and global warming to bind the world into a common perspective, fueled to action by the European and American environmental consciousness.

The United Nations presented a tool for facilitating such efforts. With its first meeting on the environment in 1972, the global organization created its Environmental Programme, which sponsored the historic Rio Conference on the Environment in 1992 and a meeting on global warming in New York in 1997. In response to such activities, the U.S. federal government declared the environment a genuine diplomatic risk in global affairs by creating the position of state department undersecretary for the environment in 1996. What began as an intellectual philosophy had so impacted the human worldview that it now influenced global relations.

ENVIRONMENTAL ORGANIZATIONS

By the late 1990s polls revealed that nearly 70 percent of Americans referred to themselves as "environmentalists." But of those who called themselves environmentalists, most did not hold deep philosophical commitments. More often, they expressed themselves in reaction to mass mailings put out by any of the hundreds of environmental special interest groups. Starting from associations of conservation hunters, including the Audubon Society (founded in 1905), organizations such as the Sierra Club, Wilderness Society, and National Wildlife Federation have evolved with the environmental movement. Additionally, the global emphasis spawned Greenpeace, the world's largest environmental organization. Financial support from membership dues broadens the cultural impact of environmental philosophies and allows many Americans to define themselves as supporters while possessing little of the movement's primary convictions.

As policymakers reacted to grassroots demand for environmental reform in the 1970s and 1980s, many late-twentieth-century Americans sought ways to integrate their newfound environmental ethics into their everyday lives. More than at any other time in American history, the living patterns of everyday American life in the 1980s included a thought or awareness of humans' impact on the world around them. Once this environmental awareness made it into basic patterns of American mass culture, it often held little identifiable connection to its roots in the ecological principles. However, many Americans clearly had added "impact on the environment" to their list of considerations when they made choices about which product to buy, where to eat, and what to do in their free time. This cultural foundation would serve as a critical tool as humans began to wrestle with large-scale environmental problems such as climate change.

GREEN CULTURE

When these choices reflected a bit of environmental conscience or reflection, they could be grouped with a cultural pattern termed *green culture*. Often this change was marked by alterations to tradition and practices already ingrained in American life, including residential patterns, leisure culture, and film preferences. Many scientists and active environmentalists decried such energies as depthless efforts to exploit environmental greenness without understanding the real issues. They described green culture as a consumer America's example of "green washing" seen in corporate America.

By the twenty-first century, though, environmentalists did not need to fight among themselves; instead, they needed to fight an onslaught of criticism. In particular, efforts to publicize the issue of climate change were reconfigured as an environmental assault on economic development. As environmental concerns moved into popular culture, criticism of them did as well.

The twentieth century witnessed the development of a consciousness that transcended the preservation of special places and the regulation of damaging pollutants. From romantic beginnings, Americans have been moved to ask serious questions about their very basic idea of progress. For many, increased environmental awareness has moved them to alter their actions and priorities. In the twenty-first century, the passionate ideals of environmentalism have evolved into ideas such as sustainability, and proponents work against genuine threats to human survival such as climate change.

Brian Black

SEE ALSO: *Animated Films; Earth Day; Eco-Terrorism; Global Warming; Greenpeace;* The Lion King*; National Parks; Recycling; Yellowstone National Park.*

BIBLIOGRAPHY

Fox, Stephen. *The American Conservation Movement: John Muir and His Legacy*. Madison: University of Wisconsin Press, 1986.

Nash, Roderick. *Wilderness and the American Mind*, 3rd ed. New Haven, CT: Yale University Press, 1982.

Opie, John. *Nature's Nation*. Fort Worth, TX: Harcourt Brace, 1998.

Sale, Kirkpatrick. *The Green Revolution: The American Environmental Movement, 1962–1992*. New York: Hill and Wang, 1993.

Steinberg, Ted. *Down to Earth: Nature's Role in American History*. New York: Oxford University Press, 2009.

Worster, Donald. *Nature's Economy: A History of Ecological Ideas*, 2nd ed. New York: Cambridge University Press, 2008.

Equal Rights Amendment

While the history of slavery is well known in the United States, the fact that married women were legally subservient until the nineteenth century is less well known. The doctrine of *coverture*, practiced throughout the United States, meant that married women were covered by their husbands and had no separate legal existence. In practice this resulted in the inheritance of women being assigned to their husbands, the guardianship of minor children being decided by the father, and earnings of wives and minor children being claimed by the father. Furthermore, women lacked protection from abusive husbands. Many states allowed husbands to beat their wives to correct them as long as the means of punishment was no thicker than his thumb. This is where the concept of the rule of thumb derived.

ERA INTRODUCED

The Seneca Falls Convention in 1848 paved the way for the rights of women, but it was not until 1920 that women won

Equal Rights Amendment Supporters. *Supporters of the Equal Rights Amendment wave signs at the 1980 Democratic National Convention.* BILL PIERCE/TIME LIFE PICTURES/GETTY IMAGES.

the right to vote, with the Nineteenth Amendment. Once the vote was assured, women's groups launched a campaign to provide for equal rights amendments at both state and national levels.

The push for equal rights was led by the National Women's Party (NWP), which in 1923 convinced Congress to hold the first congressional hearings on the Equal Rights Amendment (ERA). The amendment stated that "men and women shall have equal rights throughout the United States and every place subject to its jurisdiction." The National Association for Women's Suffrage of America (NAWSA), headed by Carrie Chapman Catt, also worked for the passage of the Equal Rights Amendment. Alice Paul, a veteran of the English campaign for women's rights, joined Catt in her struggle and accepted the presidency of the NWP. Paul introduced the first version of the Equal Rights Amendment to Congress, arguing that the purpose of the amendment was to allow women to be all that they could be. Opponents of the ERA could be found both in and out of the women's movement. From within, Florence Kelly led the fight against it, believing that it would take away existing protections for which women had fought.

In 1940 the Republican Party endorsed the Equal Rights Amendment, and the Democrats followed in 1944. In 1946 an attempt to steer the amendment through the Senate failed. By 1950 the intent of the amendment had been weakened by a rider that exempted all laws designed to protect women. Then in 1953 the amendment was sent to congressional committees, where it remained for the next two decades.

When the "second wave" of the women's movement was launched in 1963 with the publication of Betty Friedan's *The Feminine Mystique*, new attention was focused on the Equal Rights Amendment. In 1923 support for the ERA had been considered radical, but in the 1970s support came from mainstream America as well as from more liberal elements. Advocates included the League of Women Voters, the Business and Professional Women, the Young Women's Christian Association (YWCA), the American Association of University Women (AAUW), Common Cause, and United Auto Workers (UAW).

ERA REINTRODUCED

Representative Martha Griffiths reintroduced the Equal Rights Amendment in 1970, with a slight rephrasing: "Equality of rights under the law shall not be denied or abridged by the United States or by any state on account of sex." In 1972 the new version of the Equal Rights Amendment passed both houses of Congress with large majorities. The stiffest battle was still ahead, however, as supporters of the amendment set out to garner the necessary approval of three-fourths of the fifty states. This was not to be. Thirty-five states ratified, but the sophisticated organization of the opposition prevented passage in the three additional states needed for ratification.

Opponents to the Equal Rights Amendment pointed out that the Fourteenth and Fifth Amendments to the U.S. Constitution contained guarantees of equality and that existing laws, such as the Civil Rights Act of 1964 and the Equal Pay Act, already provided practical protections of rights. They painted horrifying portraits of women in combat, coed restrooms, and working mothers who neglected their families. To no avail, supporters countered with arguments that laws were more transitory than amendments and that women had an equal responsibility to protect their countries. They pointed out that women already worked outside the home and that traditional families were still the norm.

Most amendments are given seven years from the date of congressional approval to win ratification by the necessary thirty-eight states. The Equal Rights Amendment was given an unprecedented three-year extension. But in 1982 the extension expired, and the Equal Rights Amendment was not made a part of the U.S. Constitution.

Supporters of the amendment continue to offer it up for approval at both the national and state levels, but the urgency for its passage has dissipated. As a whole, women no longer feel as threatened by the lack of an ERA, because they have enjoyed the successes of a society more open to women's rights and have reaped the benefits of Title VII of the Civil Rights Act of 1964, which bans discrimination based on sex. In a landmark case in 1972, the Supreme Court held in *Reed v. Reed* that legal classifications could not arbitrarily be based on sex. Subsequent cases have upheld women's right to serve on juries, to practice law and medicine, to work in bars, to be protected from pregnancy discrimination, and to take control of their reproductive lives.

Ruth Bader Ginsburg, appointed to the U.S. Supreme Court by President Bill Clinton in 1993, successfully argued as a practicing lawyer that the Equal Protection Clause of the Fourteenth Amendment should protect individuals from sexual discrimination. Even though the Equal Rights Amendment was never added to the U.S. Constitution, protection for those rights has now become part of the fabric of American law and society. While women continue to be discriminated against in practice, they are legally protected from intentional discrimination. It could be argued that the defeat of the ERA paved the way for the success of the goals of the amendment.

Elizabeth Purdy

SEE ALSO: *Civil Rights Movement; Feminism.*

BIBLIOGRAPHY

Becker, Susan D. *The Origins of the Equal Rights Amendment: American Feminism between the Wars.* Westport, CT: Greenwood Press, 1981.

Evans, Sarah M. *Born for Liberty: A History of Women in America.* New York: The Free Press, 1989.

Keller, Kristin Thoennes. *Carrie Chapman Catt: A Voice for Women.* Minneapolis, MT: Compass Point Books, 2006.

Stetson, Dorothy McBride. *Women's Rights in the USA: Policy Debates and Gender Roles.* New York: Garland Publishing, 1997.

ER

The Emmy Award–winning television drama *ER* premiered in the fall of 1994 and concluded on April 2, 2009. Over the course of its run, it was nominated for 124 Emmy Awards, winning twenty-two. It became the most richly compensated show in television history in 1998 when NBC agreed to pay the program's production company, Warner Brothers, $13 million per episode for three seasons. Best-selling author and film producer Michael Crichton—the author of *Jurassic Park* (1990) and *Disclosure* (1994)—created the hour-long drama, which centers on a staff of young medical professionals who work in the emergency room of an inner-city hospital in Chicago.

A collection of talented actors, writers, and producers garnered *ER* an average of thirty million viewers per episode. The show's blockbuster ratings and critical acclaim accelerated the trend in the 1990s toward cross-pollination between the television and film industries. Many members of the cast branched into film work while honoring contracts with the show. Crichton shared duties as executive producer with legendary Hollywood producer and director Steven Spielberg and veteran television producers John Wells, Lydia Woodward, and Carol Flint.

The NBC–Warner Brothers financial agreement concerning *ER* signaled a shift in television economics. In the decade leading up to the deal, increased competition brought about by cable and satellite technology found traditional networks straining to maintain their dwindling audiences. Suddenly, exceptionally popular programs such as *ER* enjoyed increased bargaining power. As a result, a two-tiered system took shape in which one show or a handful of shows would carry a network—not necessarily by generating direct profits (although advertisers did pay $500,000 per thirty-second spot during *ER* broadcasts) but by luring viewers to the network. This generated interest among advertisers to invest in less popular shows.

Frenzied pacing and frankness in depicting emergency medical procedures characterizes *ER*'s narrative. The show's immediate popularity also afforded its directors considerable room for artistic experimentation. In attempting to reproduce an edgy documentary style, for instance, "Ambush," the opening episode of the fourth season, was broadcast live and shot on video rather than on traditional film stock. The daring episode received mixed reviews, as some critics called it a publicity stunt. Ultimately, producers shifted the focus of the drama away from its hyperactive emergency scenes and toward the soap-opera-like personal lives of the characters.

Websites centering on the show's doctors and nurses proliferated. Viewers enjoyed the medical heroics performed by the characters but also sympathized with the tragic humanity of their flaws and their weekly attempts to hold together their neglected personal lives. The most popular of these characters include Dr. Mark Greene (Anthony Edwards), a senior attending physician whose career cost him his marriage; Dr. Doug Ross (George Clooney, whose 1999 departure from the show was one of the most-watched episodes), a handsome, philandering pediatrician; Dr. Peter Benton (Eriq La Salle), an intense and egotistical surgeon; Dr. John Carter (Noah Wyle), a well-intentioned but naive son of one of Chicago's wealthiest families; Carol Hathaway (Julianna Margulies), a compassionate, earthy nurse who struggles to determine her own self-worth; Jeanie Boulet (Gloria Reuben), an HIV-positive physician's assistant; Dr. Kerry Weaver (Laura Innes), an abrasive attending physician and administrator; and Dr. Elizabeth Corday (Alex Kingston), a winsome and intelligent visiting surgeon from England who is perplexed by the seriousness of her American colleagues.

Adrienne Russell

SEE ALSO: *Clooney, George; Crichton, Michael; Networks; Spielberg, Steven; Television.*

BIBLIOGRAPHY

Collins, Scott. "*ER* Calls Its Time of Death." *Los Angeles Times*. Accessed December 2011. Available from www.latimes.com/entertainment/news/la-et-er28-2009mar28,0,1083134.story

Newitz, Annalee. "ER, Professionals, and the Work-Family Disaster." *American Studies* 39, no. 2 (1998): 93–103.

Pourroy, Janine. *Behind the Scenes at "ER."* New York: Ballatine Books, 1995.

Erdrich, Louise *(1954–)*

Of mixed Chippewa and German American ancestry, writer Louise Erdrich addresses the concerns of modern Native Americans in a way that appeals equally, if somewhat differently, to Native American and mainstream readers alike. "Indianness" matters in her work, but Erdrich is far more interested in affirming important aspects of the Native American experience—in particular, attitudes toward sexuality and nature, women's power, and communal ethics and aesthetics—than in accusing European American culture (and readers) of past wrongs.

Erdrich's Faulknerian preoccupation with place has led her to create a sprawling, loosely connected multinovel saga that deals mainly, though not exclusively, with Native American life in the latter half of the twentieth century. Her fiction (she also writes poetry and essays) weaves together realism and fantasy, sensuality and lyricism, the short story and novel, oral and written traditions, and comic sensibilities and tragic awareness. The commercial and critical success of her National Book Award–winning first novel, *Love Medicine* (1984), and her physical attractiveness, which led *People* magazine to include her on its "Most Beautiful" list in 1990, have helped to make her one of the most recognizable and influential Native American writers of her generation. Although Erdrich continues to write fiction, poetry and children's literature, interest in her work has decreased slightly in recent years as the popularity of Native American literature in general has waned.

Robert A. Morace

SEE ALSO: *Faulkner, William;* People.

BIBLIOGRAPHY

Beidler, Peter G. *A Reader's Guide to the Novels of Louise Erdrich*. Columbia: University of Missouri Press, 2006.

Chavkin, Allan Richard, and Nancy Feyl Chavkin, eds. *Conversations with Louise Erdrich and Michael Dorris*. Jackson: University Press of Mississippi, 1994.

Chavkin, Allan Richard, ed. *The Chippewa Landscape of Louise Erdrich*. Tuscaloosa: University of Alabama Press, 1999.

Wong, Hertha Dawn. *Louise Erdrich's Love Medicine: A Casebook*. New York: Oxford University Press, 2000.

E-Readers

E-readers are specialized, portable, handheld touch-screen devices that are similar to tablet computers but meant primarily for reading digitized books and periodicals. Any device capable of displaying text on a screen may function as an e-book reader, but specialized e-book reader designs offer optimized portability, readability (especially in sunlight), and battery life. Thanks to their portability, selection, and ease of use, within just a few years of appearing on the consumer market e-readers could be seen in the hands of citizens and celebrities, everywhere from the classroom to the coffee shop to the beach.

The slow development of e-readers was closely linked to the limited availability of texts. Project Gutenberg, an online, open-source library, offered the first e-text when it digitized the Declaration of Independence in 1971. Other texts surfaced in the mid-1980s on CD-ROM, and full-text reference books began appearing on the Internet in the mid-1990s; however, most of the texts were of little interest, consisting mainly of how-to books and instruction manuals.

The first e-texts had to be entered by hand, but as scanning and optical-character-recognition technology were developed, the process of digitizing books became easier. Through efforts such as Project Gutenberg, a wide variety of texts was made available to the public. At first, people read the books from their computers. However, consumer demand for convenience and portability led to the development of e-readers.

The SoftBook reader, the first known specialized e-reader, appeared in 1998. Modeled after a traditional book, the device featured a leather cover and a large touch screen but offered limited access to subscription content via a standard telephone jack. Although the device was largely unsuccessful and despite the fact that several manufacturers offered alternatives in the early 2000s, their high cost, bulky design, and limited selection of titles made early e-readers largely unpopular.

By late in the first decade of the 2000s e-readers had advanced significantly, often incorporating multimedia players, Web browsers, and Wi-Fi connectivity. And with the debut of the Sony Reader in 2006, the Amazon Kindle in 2007, and Barnes & Noble's Nook in 2009, e-readers gained widespread popularity. The new compact, lightweight designs, coupled with larger storage capacities and a greater selection of titles, offered consumers unprecedented convenience. These newer models offered up to two weeks of reading time on a single charge and many measured approximately 8 inches by 5 inches—about the size of a book—and weighed only 8 ounces. Some allowed users to "turn" pages, bookmark and highlight passages, make the text larger or smaller, and change the font as desired, while others could convert text to voice, simulating the experience of an audiobook.

By 2009 there were more than two million digitized books freely available on the Internet, with many other copyrighted books available for a fee. Because of the lower production costs and decreased time required to bring a new book to market, publishers issued more of their titles, including best sellers, as digitized editions. Ease and expediency of electronic publishing also allowed writers to forego traditional publication houses in favor of self-publishing. Greater selection directly translated to higher device sales, and by the end of 2010 approximately six million e-readers had sold in the United States; worldwide, sales had reached thirteen million.

By 2011 the textbook industry, mass-market publishers, and newspapers were increasingly interested in e-publishing as a means of expanding their readership. As with MP3 players in the music industry, e-readers and e-books presented challenges in publishing. Although print books still maintained a market share of 80 percent, purchases of e-books doubled between 2010 and 2011. By May 2011 Amazon announced it had sold more Kindle e-Book editions than print editions, and e-book versions frequently appeared in the top ten on national best-seller lists. In addition, electronic publishing soon faced copyright concerns and diminished revenues at the hands of piracy.

Despite their many advantages, early e-readers did suffer a few drawbacks. Some could not display color or did not display page numbers, and e-books with large pictures or graphs were more difficult to view and read. In addition to the myriad e-book formats, advances in technology led to the development of new file types and to new proprietary formats, creating occasional compatibility issues. Each manufacturer adapted its device to specific file formats, but as of 2012 there was no standardized format. Proprietary formats, such as Amazon's .azw, require the user to purchase either a new version of the e-book or a new e-reader, and other e-readers are limited by digital-rights-management software, preventing interoperability between e-readers.

Additionally, the shelf life of a print book can easily exceed that of an e-reader. The batteries in e-readers have a limited lifespan, and e-books and e-readers can malfunction, resulting in significant data loss. While manufacturers of e-readers are quick to point to deforestation as an environmental concern surrounding print publications, e-readers depend on the extraction of toxic metals such as lithium, mercury, cadmium, and lead, and the plastic shells and components contain a variety of toxic substances that are difficult to recycle.

As e-readers improve new features appear, and some of the early drawbacks have diminished. Advanced technology has allowed e-readers to become more like tablets, enabling them to incorporate social media, games, music, and movies into their functionality. Improvements to the touch screen, including durability and flexibility, have increasingly enticed more consumers to purchase the device. Even colleges and high schools have begun to use e-readers for class assignments.

Byron Anderson

SEE ALSO: *Amazon.com; Best Sellers; The Internet; iPad; MP3.*

BIBLIOGRAPHY

"Amazon Kindle e-Book Downloads Outsell Paperbacks." *BBC News*. Accessed June 2012. Available from http://www.bbc.co.uk/news/business-12305015

Fowler, Geoffrey, and Marie C. Baca. "The ABCs of E-Reading." *Wall Street Journal*, August 24, 2010.

Gielen, Nina. *Handheld E-Book Readers and Scholarship: Report and Reader Survey*. American Council of Learned Societies. Accessed June 2012. Available from http://www.humanities-ebook.org/heb-whitepaper-3.html

Stern, Joanna. "Among E-Readers, Competition Heats Up." *New York Times*, June 9, 2010.

Erector Sets

Sets of metal girders, nuts, bolts, gears, and electric motors that could be used to build numerous structures and vehicles, Erector Sets were a popular construction toy for decades and spawned other lines of construction sets, including Legos.

In 1909 A. C. Gilbert founded the Mysto Magic Company, which sold magic trick equipment. Inspired by the girders he saw being installed along the New Haven railroad, Gilbert introduced the Erector Set in 1913. He was influenced by similar toy construction sets already on the market, including the English Meccano, which was made up of strips of metal, bolts, and nuts that could be put together to build various small models. Gilbert's Erector Set, however, could use gears and electric motors, a feature that made Erector a leader among construction toys.

The success of the Erector Set was due to its versatility and response to new technological developments. Gilbert originally created pieces and designs for his sets that could be put together to create square girders that allowed for the construction of impressive buildings and bridges in imitation of the engineering feats of the burgeoning skyscraper architecture. In the 1920s, Erector Sets could build models of trucks, Ferris wheels, and zeppelins. In the 1940s, Gilbert introduced the Parachute Jump model, based on an amusement park ride that had been built for the 1939 New York World's Fair. Gilbert and his company produced his toys until his death in 1961. In 1965 Gabriel Industries purchased the A. C. Gilbert Company, but by the end of the twentieth century, Meccano S.A., which had purchased the Erector trademark around 1990, produced Meccano sets labeled with the Erector name. The nostalgia surrounding the original Erector Sets made them collectors' items.

Wendy Woloson

SEE ALSO: *Legos; Skyscrapers; Toys.*

BIBLIOGRAPHY

Hertz, Louis H. *The Handbook of Old American Toys.* Wethersfield, CT: Mark Haber & Co., 1947.

Hertz, Louis H. *The Toy Collector.* New York: Funk & Wagnalls, 1969.

McClintock, Inez, and Marshall McClintock. *Toys in America.* Washington, DC: Public Affairs Press, 1961.

Ertegun, Ahmet *(1923–2006)*

Ahmet Ertegun is remembered as the foremost music entrepreneur of the rock-and-roll age. He and partner Herb Abramson founded Atlantic Records in 1947 on a loan of $10,000. Under Ertegun's guidance, Atlantic Records was a key force in making rhythm and blues (R&B) and rock and roll part of the American mainstream, ultimately becoming one of the top labels in the world.

However, Ertegun's impact extends well beyond Atlantic Records. His astute guidance helped shape the careers of dozens of music executives, including David Geffen. He is also a founding member of the Rock and Roll Hall of Fame and served as its chairman. Ertegun was inducted into the hall in 1987, and the main exhibition area of the Rock and Roll Hall of Fame and Museum in Cleveland, Ohio, bears his name. Interestingly, he was instrumental in bringing soccer to the United States—he was president of the highly successful New York Cosmos team during the 1970s. Ertegun also won many prestigious humanitarian awards for his tireless efforts on a number of civil rights and civil liberties fronts.

THE BIRTH OF A RECORD LABEL

Ertegun's unique ear for talent and his penetrating insight into the music industry were developed early. A child of a Turkish ambassador, he and his older brother Nesuhi spent many of their formative years in Washington, D.C., where they became ravenous jazz and blues fans. Their record collection as teenagers reportedly numbered in the thousands, and long before they were of legal age, the brothers had seen many of the great jazzmen of the era, including Louis Armstrong and Duke Ellington.

While studying philosophy at St. John's College, Ertegun became increasingly frustrated in his search for the recordings of many of the jazz and blues performers he had seen live. Thus, he started Atlantic Records in 1947 in order to record many of these unrecognized talents. Atlantic, however, was never intended to be an archival label—he envisioned it as a vehicle for mainstreaming blues and jazz. To realize this goal, Ertegun concentrated on finding and recording musicians who did not easily fit into the dominant black music styles of the day.

Ertegun's reputation in the industry was built upon his great "ears" for talent. His intimacy with the black musical idiom and his willingness to scour clubs and juke joints in any neighborhood and any region of the country set him apart from other talent scouts of the day. His success in the field of A&R still stands as the measuring stick for others. Among the more influential artists Ertegun brought to Atlantic during the early years were Ray Charles, Big Joe Turner, Ruth Brown, the Drifters, the Clovers, and the Coasters. Jazz masters John Coltrane and Professor Longhair also recorded for Atlantic during this era. Once artists were contracted with Atlantic, Ertegun continued to work closely with them in the studio. On occasion, he even wrote songs for them. Under the pseudonym Nugetre (Ertegun spelled backward), he penned several hits, including "Don't Play That Song (You Lied)," "Chains of Love," "Sweet Sixteen," and "Mess Around."

THE ATLANTIC SOUND

More important, though, was Ertegun's ability to coax from a variety of musicians a sound that found widespread appeal among white audiences. The Atlantic sound evolved into a "danceable" compromise that borrowed from both country blues and big-band jazz. It laid critical groundwork for the development of R&B and ultimately rock and roll. By successfully bringing R&B to the mainstream, Atlantic established itself as one of the first and most successful of the emergent "independent" record labels. Along with Chess Records and Sun Records, Atlantic eroded the corporate oligopoly of the recording industry (for example, Columbia, RCA, and Decca).

THE BEAT GOES ON

In the early 1960s, when many independent labels faltered, Atlantic's successes mounted. Ertegun's musical instincts kept Atlantic from buying too heavily into the faddish teenybopper rock of that period. Instead, the label concentrated on popularizing the emergent soul sound. During this era, Atlantic signed soul legends Otis Redding; Wilson Pickett; Sam and Dave; and, perhaps most importantly, Aretha Franklin.

In the later 1960s Ertegun's insight into the nature of the British Invasion prompted him to lead scouting missions to England, where Atlantic tapped into London's blues revivalism. The label's discoveries during this era include megastars Cream and Led Zeppelin. Ertegun was also instrumental in bringing art rock to American shores, signing or helping to sign Genesis, Yes, and King Crimson. From the West Coast scene, the label signed artists such as Buffalo Springfield; Crosby, Stills and Nash; and Neil Young.

Although he sold the label in 1967 to Warner-Seven Arts, Ertegun stayed on as chairman of the Atlantic group and guided it to greater glories in the 1970s. Atlantic's climb toward preeminence among rock labels was largely a product of Ertegun's personality and professional reputation. By the early 1970s he had come to be regarded as one of the most knowledgeable, charismatic, and trustworthy industry executives. His abiding love of the music itself, his street savvy, and his legendary hedonism won him respect and admiration from musicians everywhere. In addition, his long-term friendship with Mick Jagger helped Atlantic steal the Rolling Stones from Decca, a deal that sealed Atlantic's standing as the preeminent rock label of the era.

By the end of the twentieth century, Ertegun was still CEO of Atlantic, as well as a vital personality on the New York nightclub circuit, and the label he had founded five decades earlier was the top market-share holder. In 2006 Ertegun died in New York of a head injury.

Steve Graves

SEE ALSO: *A&R Men/Women; Atlantic Records; Blues; British Invasion; Charles, Ray; Coltrane, John; Crosby, Stills, and Nash; Franklin, Aretha; Jazz; Led Zeppelin; Redding, Otis; Rhythm and Blues; Rock and Roll; The Rolling Stones; Soccer; Soul Music; Young, Neil.*

BIBLIOGRAPHY

Ertegun, Ahmet. *What'd I Say: The Atlantic History of Music.* New York: Welcome Rain, 1998.

Gillett, Charlie. *Making Tracks: Atlantic Records and the Growth of a Multi-Billion-Dollar Industry.* New York: E. P. Dutton, 1974.

Greenfield, Robert. *The Last Sultan: The Life and Times of Ahmet Ertegun.* New York: Simon & Schuster, 2011.

McCourt, Tom. *A Man of Wealth and Taste: Ahmet Ertegun.* New York: Taylor & Francis, 2007.

The House That Ahmet Built. DVD. Burbank, CA: Rhino Entertainment, 2007.

Wade, Dorothy, and Justine Picardie. *Music Man: Ahmet Ertegun, Atlantic Records, and the Triumph of Rock 'n' Roll.* New York: W. W. Norton, 1990.

Erving, Julius "Dr. J" *(1950–)*

Julius Erving led a revolution in the style and substance of basketball, beginning in 1971 when he joined the Virginia Squires of the American Basketball Association (ABA) following his junior year at the University of Massachusetts. It was while playing college basketball that he earned his famous nickname, "Dr. J." Erving is one of only six players in National Collegiate Athletic Association history to average more than twenty points and twenty rebounds per game. During his professional career, which spanned two leagues and sixteen years, Erving redefined the role of a forward in basketball. He had an artistic playing style the likes of which basketball fans had never seen. In addition to becoming an ambassador for basketball, Erving helped the pro game realize its financial potential.

During his five years in the ABA with the Squires (1971–1973) and New York Nets (1973–1976), Erving was voted the league's Most Valuable Player (MVP) three times (1974, 1975, and 1976) and led the Nets to the ABA championship twice (1974 and 1976). He was credited by many for singlehandedly keeping the financially strapped ABA afloat. Because the league had no national television exposure, most of its teams struggled at the box office. However, arenas throughout the ABA consistently sold out games involving the Nets and the flamboyant Erving. In his ABA career, Erving averaged 28.7 points and 12.1 rebounds per game, led the league in scoring three times (1973, 1974, and 1976), and was named to the All-Star first team four times (1973, 1974, 1975, and 1976).

Following the 1975–1976 season, four ABA teams merged with the larger and more financially stable National Basketball Association (NBA). The merger, which had always been the goal of the ABA's founders, was due in large part to the popular and charismatic play of Erving and a handful of other star ABA

Julius "Dr. J" Erving. *Julius "Dr. J" Erving won three championships, four Most Valuable Player Awards, and three scoring titles while playing with the ABA's Virginia Squires and New York Nets and the NBA's Philadelphia 76ers.* FOCUS ON SPORT/GETTY IMAGES.

stars. Erving joined the Philadelphia 76ers, with whom he spent his entire eleven-year NBA career. He was named to the NBA All-Star first team five times (1978, 1980, 1981, 1982, and 1983) and was voted the league's MVP in 1981. In 1983 Erving and Moses Malone led the 76ers to the NBA title. It was Erving's only championship in the league, though he appeared in the NBA Finals three other times (1977, 1980, and 1982). All told in the NBA, Erving averaged 22.0 points and 6.7 rebounds per game. He left his mark on the combined NBA-ABA record book, ranking third in career scoring and field goals made, fifth in field goals attempted, and first in steals. At the time of his retirement in 1987, Erving was one of only three players to have scored more than 30,000 points (30,026) as a professional.

There was, however, much more to Erving than statistics. He is primarily remembered as a player who helped establish the individual artistry that has permeated professional basketball since the 1980s. While still in the ABA in 1976, Erving put his creative genius on full display when he became the first player to win a leaguewide slam-dunk contest. In addition to his physical gifts, Erving's magnetism and sense of dignity made him one of the most beloved players in basketball history. The equally talented and charismatic Michael Jordan has said that he would have never developed his high-flying basketball style if he had not grown up watching Erving.

Since retiring as a player, Erving has continued to be a worldwide ambassador for the game, both through his personal business dealings and his work as a television commentator on NBA broadcasts. In 1993 Erving was inducted into the Basketball Hall of Fame in Springfield, Massachusetts.

G. Allen Finchum

SEE ALSO: *Basketball; Jordan, Michael; National Basketball Association (NBA); National Collegiate Athletic Association (NCAA).*

BIBLIOGRAPHY

Dickey, Glenn. *The History of Professional Basketball Since 1896.* Briarcliff Manor, NY: Stein and Day, 1982.

Hareas, John. *Basketball.* New York: DK, 2005.

Sachare, Alex. *The Naismith Memorial Basketball Hall of Fame's 100 Greatest Basketball Players of All Time.* New York: Pocket Books, 1997.

Escher, M. C. *(1898–1972)*

With his fantastically precise yet hallucinatory and illusional imagery, graphic artist M. C. Escher became a favorite of students and those who indulged in chemically altered states. Escher was best known for his tessellation, or repeating geometric patterns, and he also liked to draw scenes that incorporated several different spatial perspectives. Over time his work became some of the most recognizable in the art world. In the early 2010s, decks of playing cards and T-shirts decorated with his distinctive black-and-white patterns are often found in museum gift stores next to the Van Gogh items—somewhat ironic considering that, during his lifetime, Escher was dismissed by the traditional arts establishment as "too cerebral." Escher died in 1972, not long after the heady counterculture of the 1960s had elevated his art to iconic status.

EARLY INTEREST IN ARCHITECTURE

Born Maurits Cornelis Escher in the Dutch city of Leeuwarden in 1898, as a youth he studied architecture but later switched to graphic art. From 1922 to 1935 Escher lived in southern Italy, where he sketched traditional landscapes and architectural sites, from which he made woodcuts or lithographs. Some of this work, however, foreshadowed his later creativity; the pattern he painstakingly reproduced in *St. Peter's, Rome* (1935), for example, served as a precursor to his penchant for infinitely repeated abstractions, while his fascination with the hallucinatory is presaged in the 1935 woodcut *Dream*, in which an enormous insect visits the body of a recumbent bishop.

In the mid-1930s the artist spent time in Spain, and his visits to Granada's Alhambra and the famed La Mezquita (mosque) of Cordoba gave him fresh inspiration. Both of these impressive architectural legacies from Spain's Moorish past housed a treasure of decorative art in abstract patterns, as Islamic art avoided any representational imagery. At this point Escher began to think more about spatial relationships and the depiction of the infinite. His work soon took another direction when he began to fill space entirely with a repeating image.

In other works he would create a fantastical scene that had no counterpart in reality. The 1938 woodcut *Day and Night* depicts checkerboard farm fields that morph into birds; the black birds are flying to the left into daylight, while the white flock heads toward darkness. Escher also somehow managed to mirror the opposite but concurrent hours into the landscape below them. Another famous work from this era, the 1942 lithograph *Verbum*, represents his fascination with the "closed cycle" in its images of reptiles that become fish that then become birds. Amphibians always remained a particular favorite for the artist; in the 1943 lithograph *Reptiles*, his subjects crawl off a piece of paper in a circular trajectory, during which they become three-dimensional; one exhales a little smoke before it returns to two dimensions.

A CULT AUDIENCE

These and other creations, wrote Robert Hughes in *Time*, "are scientific demonstrations of how to visualize the impossible." Yet far from being a capricious fantasist, Escher was deeply interested in the hard sciences. The artist regularly corresponded with mathematicians and had little contact or respect for other artists, especially those working in modernism. "I consider sixty percent of the artists nuts and fakes," he once said of those whose work hung in Amsterdam's famed Stedelijk Museum.

Escher handled much of the business of art himself, selling his images directly to college professors who had requested them for use in mathematical textbooks. He also sold inexpensive prints of his works in college bookstores, which helped give him a certain cachet among the brainy. One of the most enthusiastic of American collectors during his lifetime was the engineer grandson of Theodore Roosevelt, Cornelius Van Schaak Roosevelt, but for the most part, Escher was largely ignored by the art world. In the 1960s among the very few periodicals that ran articles on him were *Life*, *Scientific American*, and *Rolling Stone*.

A 1968 retrospective of Escher's work in The Hague gave his popularity something of an international boost, and the Escher Foundation was established in 1968 to market and promote his prints. Rock album covers began using his imagery, which further popularized it, and items with his signature double helixes or reptilian nightmares began appearing in the hippie mail-order bible *The Whole Earth Catalog*. In 1971 the staid art-book publisher Abrams issued a well-received tome, *The World of M. C. Escher*.

Shortly after Escher's death in 1972, the National Gallery in Washington, D.C., hosted an exhibition of his graphics. "Once the focus of a small, rather cultish, mostly non-art-world audience . . . Escher has in recent years become the focus of a *vast* rather cultish, mostly non-art-world audience," wrote Peter Schjeldahl in the *New York Times* that same year. The art critic, noting that Escher's fan base seemed confined to "scientists and stoned kids," observed dryly that the "psychedelic young" had seized upon Escher imagery in part because of his "terrific virtuosity" and "gamut of fanciful imagery," not to mention accessibility. "Renditions of easily grasped intellectual and sentimental conceits, laced with the bizarre, they yield their essences, it might be said, with alacrity," Schjeldahl declared. "They play intricate tricks in a direct, even blatant way, thus teasing the viewer and flattering him at once."

Carol Brennan

SEE ALSO: *Psychedelia;* The Whole Earth Catalog.

BIBLIOGRAPHY

Escher, M. C., and J. L. Locher *The World of M. C. Escher*. New York: Abrams, 1971.

Escher, M. C., et al. *M. C. Escher: His Life and Complete Graphic Work*. New York: Abradale Press/Abrams, 1992.

Davis, Douglas. "Teasing the Brain." *Newsweek*, July 31, 1972, 59–60.

Gardner, Martin. "Mathematical Games: Extraordinary Non-Periodic Tiling That Enriches the Theory Tiles." *Scientific American*, January 1977, 110–121.

Hughes, Robert. "n-Dimensional Reality." *Time*, April 17, 1972, 64.

Schattschneider, Doris, and M. C. Escher. *M. C. Escher: Visions of Symmetry*. New York: H. N. Abrams, 2004.

Schjeldahl, Peter. "The Games M. C. Escher Plays." *New York Times*, July 23, 1972.

ESPN

From humble beginnings, the Entertainment and Sports Programming Network (ESPN) has become a media empire. The sports network started in 1979, when cable television was available to less than 10 percent of the population. Since then, its irreverent style, brilliant advertising, and shrewd programming and business decisions have catapulted it into about 100 million homes in the United States and to more than 200 countries around the world.

EXPECTED TO FAIL

When ESPN debuted its 24/7 sports format, most industry experts concluded the network had little chance of survival. With a limited budget and no connections to major sports programming, ESPN was forced to run such oddities as Australian Rules football, college lacrosse, and other rarely watched athletic endeavors. Most of its resources were poured into *SportsCenter*, the flagship news show for the network. In addition, network executives turned events such as college basketball games and the National Football League (NFL) draft into must-see television theater.

As ESPN grew in popularity, more and more sports fans began to subscribe to cable simply to gain access to the network's

ESPN at the Home Run Derby. *ESPN baseball commentators, from left, Bobby Valentine, Joe Morgan, and Chris Berman broadcasting during the 2010 Home Run Derby.* MICHAEL ZAGARIS/ GETTY IMAGES.

excellent news coverage. ESPN deftly used this leverage: By 1983 it had become the first basic cable network to demand an operating fee from cable franchisers. As cable television continued to expand throughout the United States, ESPN became an integral part of basic cable packages.

CREATING A BRAND

In 1987 the network made two brilliant moves. The first was acquiring the rights to televise NFL games on Sunday nights, which catapulted ESPN into the realm of big-time sports coverage. The addition of the NFL dramatically increased the network's visibility and drew millions of new viewers to its other shows. (In 2006 *Monday Night Football* moved to ESPN, while *Sunday Night Football* migrated to NBC.) The second move was the hiring of John Walsh, who would transform *SportsCenter* into the must-see sports show on television. Walsh brought his background as managing editor of the weekly news magazine *U.S. News & World Report* to *SportsCenter*, transforming it into a broadcast about sports rather than a sports broadcast.

Under Walsh, the network covered sports like major nightly news shows covered news. ESPN added investigative coverage with *Outside the Lines*, a show whose mission was to examine such controversial issues as racism and gambling in sports. In addition, an interview program, *Up Close*, was created to showcase the greatest names in sports on a daily basis. Walsh built an organization that covered sports at a level of detail never before seen on television.

Walsh endeavored to give ESPN its own personality, one that was humorous, intelligent, and absolutely in love with all types of sports. He hired anchors for *SportsCenter* who could convey this personality, including Dan Patrick and Keith Olbermann, who would become the star anchors on ESPN, throwing out catchphrases, humor, and information at a rapid-fire pace. Olbermann and Patrick's 11 p.m. edition of *SportsCenter* soon became known as the "Big Show" among sports fans, and audience devotion to the two anchors reached almost obsessive levels.

UNPRECEDENTED GROWTH

By the late 1980s ESPN had become *the* network for serious sports fans and players alike. Professional athletes made it clear that being on the *SportsCenter* highlight reel was important to them, and fans held up signs at games that were addressed to the *SportsCenter* anchors and featured the catchphrase of the week. The power of *SportsCenter* was such that the anchors could literally create a trend overnight. During one broadcast, Olbermann and Craig Killborn shouted the word "Salsa!" every time they showed someone scoring a basket in college basketball. The very next night, college basketball fans throughout the country were seen holding up "Salsa!" signs whenever the home team made a basket. ESPN had clearly become a cultural phenomenon.

In the 1990s ESPN exerted even more of an influence. ESPN Radio debuted in 1992, and ESPN2, a second all-sports TV network, began broadcasting in 1993. Additionally in 1993, the network introduced its own annual award, the ESPY, for outstanding sports achievements, and invited fans to take part in the voting. The network's expansion continued as ESPN Sportszone became a presence on the Internet in 1995, the all-news network ESPNews began in 1996, and *ESPN: The Magazine* emerged as a major competitor to the industry giant *Sports Illustrated* in 1998. In addition, ESPN opened ESPN Zone restaurants and began selling licensed sportswear and other products. The first decade of the 2000s brought a series of specialized cable channels: ESPN HD in 2003, ESPNU (focused on college sports) in 2005, and ESPN 3-D in 2010. As of 2012 both ESPN and ESPN2 were reaching some ninety-nine million households in the United States. The demand for ESPN programming is so high that the network now commands the highest operating fees and advertising rates on cable. Through saturation and careful marketing, ESPN has become virtually synonymous with sports in the United States.

CHANGING THE CULTURE OF SPORTS

Before ESPN, most sports coverage was limited to eight minutes on local news channels. Although the major broadcast networks would occasionally run half-hour sports shows on the weekends, these were little more than compilations of highlights. ESPN provided the serious sports fan with a wide variety of news and sports coverage that was unmatched on the airwaves. Fans tuned in to *SportsCenter* to see a full hour of highlights and analysis focused exclusively on sports. Such comprehensiveness had never before been available on TV.

Although ESPN's sheer amount of coverage sets the network apart, volume is no substitute for quality. If *SportsCenter* had simply been another bland collection of highlights, ESPN would not have made such a large impact. Clearly, the secret to the network's success is its ability to cater to the serious sports fan. *SportsCenter* runs several times per day, from 5 a.m. to midnight, with each show covering the latest news from the sporting world. In addition, the personnel have a true love for the sports they cover, and this is made apparent to the viewer. Anchors constantly rattle off detailed histories, statistics, and biographies, demonstrating their levels of knowledge. Although ESPN viewers are predominantly male, the network's coverage of women's sports—including basketball, soccer, and gymnastics—has drawn legions of females into its ranks.

Finally, the anchors are not afraid to inject humor into their coverage. However, rather than resorting to the slapstick "blooper" reels so commonly seen on local television, ESPN anchors take a more cerebral and nuanced approach. They even make fun of themselves, which has created a bond with their audience. The inside jokes and catchphrases created by the anchors have become the common language of the serious sports fan.

NO SIGN OF SLOWING

Timing has also been critical to ESPN's ascent. The 1980s were a decade when sports franchises around the country experienced increases in popularity. Some of the greatest sports figures of all time emerged in the 1980s, including Michael Jordan, Wayne Gretzky, Joe Montana, and Barry Bonds. Fans were flocking to sporting events in larger numbers than ever before, and ESPN was a clear beneficiary of it. However, ESPN also served as a catalyst in this growth. Its regular coverage of college basketball, professional hockey, auto racing, and professional soccer was at least partially responsible for the rise in popularity of those sports.

ESPN remains the dominant force in sports media. Other cable networks have attempted to duplicate its success, but none of them have achieved anything close to its ratings. As the sports industry continues to grow, ESPN will grow with it.

Geoff Peterson

SEE ALSO: *Baseball; Basketball; Bonds, Barry; Cable TV; College Football; Gretzky, Wayne; Jordan, Michael;* Monday Night Football*; Montana, Joe; National Basketball Association (NBA); National Collegiate Athletic Association (NCAA); National Football League (NFL); Networks; Professional Football; Soccer;* Sports Illustrated*; X Games.*

BIBLIOGRAPHY

Carvell, T. "Prime Time Player." *Fortune*, March 2, 1998, 135–144.

"ESPN International at 15." *Variety*, January 19, 1998.

Freeman, Michael. *ESPN: The Uncensored History*. Dallas, Texas: Taylor Trade Publishing, 2000.

Mandalese, J. "Cable TV." *Advertising Age*, April 13, 1998, 6–18.

Miller, James Andrew, and Tom Shales. *Those Guys Have All the Fun: Inside the World of ESPN*. New York: Back Bay Books, 2011.

Esquire

From its Depression-era origins as a men's fashion magazine with high literary aspirations, through a brief period when it threatened to devolve into a semi-girlie pulp magazine, *Esquire* had emerged by the 1960s as one of America's brashest and most sophisticated monthlies, with hard-hitting articles by the nation's leading writers and journalists on the hot-button cultural and political issues of the decade. At the same time, the periodical served as a Baedeker of sorts to a new generation of leisure-driven, style-conscious, sexually sophisticated men who were abandoning the austerity of the 1930s, the wartime privations of the 1940s, and the conformity of the 1950s for the more carefree, swinging lifestyle of the 1960s.

APPEALING TO A NEW MARKET

Esquire magazine was founded in Chicago in 1933 by Arnold Gingrich and David Smart, who conceived of the publication as a magazine for the "new leisure," one that would be distributed largely through men's clothing stores, a plan that was quickly reversed when newsstands quickly and unexpectedly sold out their limited allotment of 5,000 of the 105,000 initial press run. From the beginning the magazine was known for its literary excellence—publishing such authors as Erskine Caldwell, John Dos Passos, F. Scott Fitzgerald, Dashiell Hammett, and Ernest Hemingway. Exhibiting its lack of bigotry, *Esquire* also featured cartoons by E. Simms Campbell, the only black artist whose work appeared regularly in a mainstream national magazine, and fiction by Langston Hughes, best known for his poetry and as a founder of the Harlem Renaissance.

Perhaps most notable, though, was the magazine's virtual reinvention of American masculinity. In place of the hardworking man of character who plodded through the pages of most American magazines, *Esquire* promoted men who were interested in leisure, were avid consumers, and had a keen interest in sex. Such representations of manhood were soon to become commonplace in American culture, but they first appeared regularly in *Esquire*.

Despite a cover price of fifty cents, double that of most magazines, circulation soared to 675,000 within a decade, emboldening its entrepreneurial founders to launch several other lifestyle magazines, including *Coronet*, *Verve*, and *Ken*. Another circulation-boosting factor was a series of controversial incidents in the early 1940s over the issue of censorship. *Esquire* first became the target of a boycott led by Roman Catholic leaders when *Ken* published articles the church found unpalatable. In another well-publicized case, *Esquire*'s practice during World War II of printing double-page pinups as a morale booster for its military readership prompted the U.S. Post Office to deny the publication its second-class mailing privileges, a decision that was eventually reversed by the Supreme Court.

Gingrich withdrew from the publishing partnership soon after World War II, and Smart appointed Frederic A. Birmingham to assume the editorship. Under Birmingham's direction, the publication veered away from its original stylish and literary format in favor of more Western and detective stories, as in other popular pulp magazines of the time. "The design was garish, confused," writes Carol Polsgrove in her 1995 book *It Wasn't Pretty Folks, but Didn't We Have Fun: "Esquire" in the Sixties*. She notes that "circulation stayed high—around 800,000 in the early 1950s—but blue-chip advertisers, wary of Esquire's naughty wartime reputation, stayed away."

POSTWAR REINVENTION

In 1950 *Esquire* moved from Chicago to New York, with Gingrich returning as publisher just a few months before Smart's death. Gingrich took on the task of trying to restore polish to the magazine, which over the next few years was forced to weather challenges from television and other upscale periodicals, such as Hugh Hefner's *Playboy*. With his first priority the reestablishment of *Esquire*'s literary reputation, Gingrich asked authors such as Paul Gallico, Aldous Huxley, and George Jean Nathan to come onboard as regular contributors. By this time, L. Rust Hills had been hired as literary editor, taking on responsibility for organizing the magazine's annual literary symposia on college campuses.

In 1956 Harold Hayes, who had worked for *Picture Week* and *Pageant* magazines, was hired by Gingrich, who writes in his memoir, *Nothing but People*, "I took him in like the morning paper, knowing that in a Southern liberal who was also a Marine reserve officer I had an extremely rare bird." Gingrich began to withdraw in favor of a younger generation of editors. Ralph Ginzburg and Clay Felker became editors in 1957, and the young Robert Benton took over as art editor, solidifying a team that, despite an acrimonious working style and the sudden firing of Ginzburg soon afterward, succeeded in remolding the magazine to appeal to younger demographics, turning *Esquire* into the power magazine it became over the course of the following decade.

By 1960 *Esquire* was already earning a reputation for publishing serious, even philosophical, articles that appealed to a more educated audience, such as the correspondence between Elia Kazan and Archibald MacLeish during the production of MacLeish's drama *J.B.* The new editorial policy prompted Polsgrove to declare that the *Esquire* editors were trying to:

> make thought entertaining. In an age where a whole generation of young men had gone to college on the GI Bill, why not put out a magazine for an audience that cared about rock and roll and the spiritual position of modern man, an audience that had heard of French playwrights and existentialists, an educated audience weary of television and eager to taste the

delights of the mind, the cultivations of spirit and sense—and have fun doing it, too?

Hayes vowed to publish a magazine that would help America, particularly its men, resolve "a period of self-doubt and anxiety of great magnitude." His prescription was an *Esquire* with "humor, irreverence, fashion, fine writing, controversy, topicality and surprise." Diane Arbus was commissioned to do a photo spread of offbeat New York scenes and characters for a special July 1960 issue on the city that included articles by James Baldwin, Gay Talese, and John Cheever. Among the many notable writers and journalists who contributed to Hayes's mission over the next several years were Saul Bellow, Richard Rovere, Gloria Steinem, Malcolm Muggeridge, Dwight Macdonald, John Updike, Gore Vidal, and Norman Mailer. The latter had been assigned to cover the 1960 Democratic National Convention, which nominated a youthful John F. Kennedy for president. Mailer vehemently resigned from the project when *Esquire*'s editors changed the word *supermarket* to *supermart* in his title. However, Mailer was persuaded to return to the fold. Beginning in 1962 he signed up to write a monthly column, which quickly attracted critical attention for its audacity and imagination; Mailer later wrote a report on the 1964 Republican National Convention that nominated Barry Goldwater for president.

It was also in 1962 that *Esquire* began bestowing its annual Dubious Achievements Awards, a semihumorous feature concocted largely by a new member of the editorial staff, David Newman. By this time, Hayes had assumed the role of editor-in-chief and brought in John Berendt as editor. It was also during the early 1960s that *Esquire* gained a widespread reputation for publishing both serious and satirical articles on fashion, making the magazine the de facto arbiter of sartorial style for sophisticated and would-be sophisticated American men.

By the fall of 1963, when a fledgling writer named Tom Wolfe began to publish his onomatopoetic "new journalism" pieces in *Esquire*, the magazine's circulation had risen to 900,000 and was regarded as one of America's most influential publications. It devoted many pages over the next few years to the controversial social issues cleaving the American body politic, such as the militant Black Power movement and the Vietnam War. Michael Herr went to Southeast Asia as a war correspondent for the magazine, and Tom Hedley contributed in-depth reports about unrest on American college campuses. Another young writer, Garry Wills, began his career under contract for *Esquire*, covering strife in the nation's black ghettos and the assassination of Martin Luther King Jr. in 1968.

Publication of contentious articles by the feuding William F. Buckley Jr. and Vidal in the summer of 1969 led to libel suits that were eventually settled in Buckley's favor. The following year, the magazine published John Sack's interviews with Lieutenant. William L. Calley about atrocities allegedly committed by American soldiers in My Lai, Vietnam. About that time, Gordon Lish, the new fiction editor, helped establish the career of writer Raymond Carver by publishing his short stories in *Esquire*, often over the objections of Hayes.

DECLINE AND REBOUND

During most of the 1960s the provocative and offbeat covers by George Lois were credited with helping stimulate newsstand impulse sales, and by 1972 the magazine's circulation had peaked at 1.25 million. Newsstand sales soon began to decline, however, perhaps in part because the issues that had fueled *Esquire* during the turbulent 1960s were running out of steam. Many of the prominent writers who had brought the periodical to the pinnacle of literary and journalistic prominence, such as Wolfe, Talese, and Vidal, could no longer be relied upon as regular contributors, and Mailer had again become estranged. In 1974, with the retirement of Gingrich, Hayes became editor and assistant publisher and Don Erickson was appointed executive editor. Hayes left *Esquire* in April 1973 due to "irreconcilable differences" with management. Soon afterward, Lois ended his connection with the publication.

Over the next three years, the magazine suffered sharp declines in readership and advertising lineage. In 1977 *Esquire* was sold to Associated Newspapers, a British concern that had a partnership agreement with Clay Felker. In 1979 the magazine was sold to Sweden's Bonnier Newspaper Group and a firm owned by Phillip Moffitt and Christopher Whittle, with Moffitt becoming editor. In 1987 *Esquire* was purchased by the Hearst Corporation, which continues as its publisher. By the end of the twentieth century, editor-in-chief David Granger contended that "*Esquire* is special because it's a magazine for men. Not a fashion magazine for men, not a health magazine for men, not a money magazine for men. It is not any of these things; it is all of them. It is, and has been for nearly seventy-five years, a magazine about the interests, the curiosity, the passions, of men."

Proving that *Esquire*'s collective sense of humor survived into the twenty-first century, in 2011 the staff launched the Logo Project, in which top artists and designers were asked to put their talents for innovation into use by designing a new logo for the magazine. The fruits of those labors were made available on *Esquire*'s website. Tom Geismar of Charmayeff and Geismar, for instance, used Esky, the magazine's mascot since 1934, allowing his changing colors and expressions to represent the new logo without the title of the magazine ever appearing. Graphic designer Aaron Rayburn opted to include the title in his design, carving it out of 300-year-old black walnut and supplementing it with three blocks and a life-sized carving of an issue of *Esquire*. Rayburn's sculpture is now on display at the magazine's headquarters in New York. Even the Angry Birds team got in on the action, having the animated letters of the title chase floating Esky heads.

Esquire demonstrates that it is not irrelevant to the twenty-first century in other ways also, providing both iPad and digital copies for modern readers and offering advice on everything from making pancakes from scratch to installing solar panels.

Edward Moran

SEE ALSO: *Baldwin, James; Buckley, William F., Jr.; Caldwell, Erskine; Fitzgerald, F. Scott; Hammett, Dashiell; Hemingway, Ernest; Hughes, Langston; Mailer, Norman; Mass Market Magazine Revolution; My Lai Massacre;* Playboy; *Pulp Magazines; Steinem, Gloria; Updike, John; Varga Girl; Vidal, Gore; Wolfe, Tom.*

BIBLIOGRAPHY

Breazeale, Kenon. "In Spite of Women: *Esquire* Magazine and the Construction of the Male Consumer." *Signs* 20, no. 1 (1994): 1–22.

Cieply, Stefan K. "The Uncommon Man: *Esquire* and the Problem of the North American Male Consumer, 1957–63." *Gender & History* 22, no. 1 (2010): 151–168.

Gingrich, Arnold. *Nothing but People: The Early Days of*

"Esquire": A Personal History, 1928–1958. New York: Crown, 1971.

Heller, Steven. "*Esquire* and Its Art Directors: A Survivor's Tale." In *Graphic Design History*, ed. Steven Heller and Georgette Balance. New York: Allworth Press, 2001.

Kimball, Penn T. "The Non Editing of *Esquire*." *Columbia Journalism Review* 3 (1964): 32–34.

Lish, Gordon, ed. *The Secret Life of Our Times: New Fiction from "Esquire."* New York: Doubleday, 1973.

Merrill, Hugh. *Esky: The Early Years at "Esquire."* New Brunswick, NJ: Rutgers University Press, 1995.

Mikin, Mark. "The Logo Project." *Esquire*, February 2011, 74.

Pendergast, Tom. "'Horatio Alger Doesn't Work Here Any More': Masculinity and American Magazines, 1919–1940." *American Studies* 38, no. 1 (1997), 55–80.

Polsgrove, Carol. *It Wasn't Pretty Folks, but Didn't We Have Fun? "Esquire" in the Sixties.* New York: W. W. Norton, 1995.

Tebbel, John William. *The American Magazine: A Compact History.* New York: Hawthorn Books, 1969.

est

Werner Erhard established est (Erhard Seminar Training) in 1971 in San Francisco. Latin for "it is," est epitomized the "me decade," a time when people began to focus on self-improvement and the articulation of identity. One of the more successful motivational therapy groups to spring from the "human-potential movement," est used strict training within a group format to build self-awareness and offer individual fulfillment, while training people to get "It." Est was a type of program called large group awareness training, in which dozens of people are given intense instruction aimed at helping them discover what is hindering them from achieving their full potential. Est later evolved into the Landmark Forum, the flagship program offered by Landmark Education, a company that provides seminars and training courses. Formed in 1991, Landmark Education offers its programs in 125 cities around the world, and more than 175,000 people attend those programs every year.

Like many people, Jack Rosenberg was interested in human development and potential. Confused about his own identity, Rosenberg, a used car salesman, walked away from his family and his life in 1960, in search of answers. Changing his name to Werner Erhard (taken from Werner Heisenberg, a German physicist, and Ludwig Erhard, a German economist and politician), he went to California to dabble in various human potential disciplines and Eastern religions. He became very interested in L. Ron Hubbard, the founder of the Scientology religion, and the Church of Scientology, which catalyzed the birth of his own teachings, causing some controversy with the church as to their origins. Erhard insisted the two were different: "Ron Hubbard seems to have no difficulty in codifying the truth and in urging people to believe in it. . . . In presenting my own ideas . . . I hold them as pointers to the truth, not as the truth itself." Scientologists have accused Erhard of stealing his main ideas from Hubbard, while Erhard has claimed the church was behind attempts to discredit him, even hiring hit men to kill him.

An avid reader, Erhard has said he used a mixture of ideas culled from existential philosophy, motivational psychology, Zen Buddhism, American philosopher Alan Watts, and Austrian neurologist Sigmund Freud, among others, to build est. His own proverbial "enlightenment" occurred while driving across the Golden Gate bridge in San Francisco, where he says he was "transformed" into a state he described as "knowing everything and knowing nothing." The result was est.

The militant sessions of est (trainees were not allowed to speak to each other or take bathroom breaks) were rigorous and took place over two consecutive weekends. Participants were egged on by confrontational trainers, who told them flatly "your life doesn't work" and to "wipe that stupid smile off your face, you a-hole." But the goal was "to get rid of old baggage" and to learn a "more profound sense of responsibility, a sense of potency," said Erhard in a 1988 interview. "My theory is that a person's vitality will generally equal their commitments, and if you'd like to have more vitality, make bigger commitments." Besides personal fulfillment, another benefit touted by the seminars was strengthening relationships.

Part of the controversy surrounding est (besides whether or not it should be classified as a cult) was its offering of quick-fix solutions in a psychologically manipulative setting and its overly aggressive approach, which often continued after participants finished their sessions. Est employees would persistently call former participants, haranguing them to sign up for "follow-up" seminars and encouraging them to become recruiters for the program. Despite these tactics, many people who went through the program maintained their loyalty.

Critics often satirized the organization, its lingo, and its zealous followers as self-obsessed cultists, who sported glazed, exuberant demeanors that made people uncomfortable. Characteristic of other similar movements, est attracted its share of celebrities who became public advocates of the program, such as actress Valerie Harper, singer John Denver, and artist Yoko Ono, which helped to publicize the organization and its beliefs. Est and its buzzwords started to become popular culture when advertisers capitalized on its popularity; for example, one ad campaign for MasterCard used "master the possibilities," one of Erhard's famous aphorisms.

Erhard saw himself as a strict but passionate coach for people receptive to exploring life's possibilities through self-awareness and "transformation." Est "transformed" Erhard's life, making him a rich guru who reigned over his self-help empire. In 1991 he sold the rights to est to Landmark Education.

Sharon Yablon

SEE ALSO: *Cults; Denver, John; Freud, Sigmund; Hubbard, L. Ron; Me Decade; Popular Psychology.*

BIBLIOGRAPHY

Ayella, Marybeth F. *Insane Therapy: Portrait of a Psychotherapy Cult.* Philadelphia: Temple University Press, 1998.

Carroll, Robert Todd. "est and Werner Erhard." The Skeptic's Dictionary. Accessed November 29, 2011. Available from http://skepdic.com/est.html

Renton, Jane. *Coaching and Mentoring: What They Are and How to Make the Most of Them.* London: Profile, 2009.

Streissguth, Thomas. *Charismatic Cult Leaders.* Minneapolis, MN: Oliver Press, 1995.

Termayer, Charlotte Fal. "The Best of est?" *Time*, March 16, 1996, 52–53.

Yalom, Irvin D. *The Theory and Practice of Group Psychotherapy*. New York: Basic Books, 1995.

E.T. The Extra-Terrestrial

Released in 1982, Steven Spielberg's *E.T. The Extra-Terrestrial* touched the emotions and the collective imagination of moviegoers of all ages, breaking all previous box-office records to become the most profitable film of its time until it was ousted by Spielberg's own *Jurassic Park* eleven years later. Exciting, moving, thought-provoking, and funny, as well as inventive and skillful, the film has an importance that transcends that of box-office success or entertainment value.

Made and released early in the Reagan years, *E.T.* exemplified a shift in America's cultural values after the 1960s and 1970s, during which the Vietnam War, the Watergate scandals, and the Iran hostage crisis had convulsed the nation. The emergence, too, of the new youth culture that had accompanied these turbulent decades had manifested itself in a new cinema that began with *Easy Rider* in 1969. With the onset of the 1980s, Americans were seeking reconciliation and a reassertion of family values. The perceived message of the times, albeit clothed in political conservatism, was one of hope, love, and nostalgia for a gentler past, which was faithfully reflected in the majority of Hollywood movies.

Thus it was that Spielberg's film proved timely to its age, reflecting the spirit and values that were being so eagerly sought by a troubled nation and thereby appealed to adults and children alike. The expertise and imagination with which it was made, however, gave it lasting properties well beyond the 1980s and has made it a favorite film of audiences throughout the world. Indeed, it might be seen as serving the same purpose and exerting the same degree of magic as the perennially beloved *Wizard of Oz* (1939), although it is a product of the technological age in both its vision and its realization.

Considered at the time to be Spielberg's masterpiece, and undoubtedly his most personal film, this story set in middle-class suburbia grew out of the director's own lonely childhood in Scottsdale, Arizona, as the son of a father who left the family home. Spielberg has said, "I use my childhood in all my pictures, and all the time. I go back there to find ideas and stories. My childhood was the most fruitful part of my entire life. All those horrible, traumatic years I spent as a kid became what I do for a living today, or what I draw from creatively today."

AN IDEA IS BORN

E.T. was the culmination of several ideas that had germinated, been explored, and even filmed over a number of years. One of Spielberg's major contributions to late-twentieth-century culture is the concept of the benign alien. Virtually all previous science fiction films grew out of fears of invasion, war, and the threat of nuclear annihilation that loomed large during the Cold War years. It was posited that aliens with the technology to reach Earth would also have the technology to unleash incredible destruction, and these fears were reflected in stories of invasion, aggression, colonization, and extermination. In Spielberg's mind, however, "comics and TV always portrayed aliens as malevolent [but] I never believed that. If they had the technology to get here, they could only be benign."

Spielberg's first creative expression of this concept resulted in one of the most profoundly searching and brilliantly executed films of the century, *Close Encounters of the Third Kind* (1977), at the end of which an alien creature steps off the ship—allowing Spielberg the opportunity to create and show an alien, even though the scene lasted only a half minute or so. Then, in 1979, after dreaming up an idea he called "Night Skies," a tale about eleven aliens terrorizing a farm family, he put the project into development at Columbia and turned it over to writer/director John Sayles to flesh out the script. Sayles made a number of changes that included the introduction of an alien who befriends an autistic child, and he ended his script with the kindly alien being stranded on Earth. This last scene became the first scene of *E.T.*, though Sayles never pursued screen credit, considering his script "more of a jumping-off point than something that was raided for material."

In 1980, while filming *Raiders of the Lost Ark* on location in Tunisia, Spielberg was turning over the idea of following *Raiders* with a simpler, more personal project. Looking for someone as a sounding board for his idea of an interplanetary love story, he turned to Harrison Ford's girlfriend, screenwriter Melissa Mathison, who had accompanied Ford to Tunisia. Mathison subsequently said the story was already half created in Spielberg's mind, but she spent weeks pitching ideas back and forth with him for both the story and for the creature's visual image. Among other things, they decided that the creature's neck should elongate like a turtle's, so that the audience would instantly know that they were not watching an actor in costume, while Spielberg knew that he wanted the creature's communication to rest in emotion rather than intellect.

Back in the United States, while Spielberg edited *Raiders*, Mathison began writing the screenplay in earnest. An earlier version depicted E.T. as an interplanetary botanist stranded on Earth, at first more empathetic with plants than animals and discussing with artichokes and tomatoes whether he should make contact with the humans. He finally does so by rolling an orange toward the boy Elliott's feet. In the hours spent by Spielberg and Mathison discussing changes, the orange became a baseball.

Spielberg went to Columbia, which had already spent $1 million in development of "Night Skies," and offered it *E.T.* instead, but the studio, perceiving the idea as a children's picture with only limited commercial potential, said no. Universal was interested, but Columbia, because of its investment in "Night Skies," retained the rights to the property and refused to coproduce with Universal. Columbia finally relinquished the rights in exchange for 5 percent of the net profits and earned a fortune. (Spielberg, meanwhile, also convinced MGM (Metro-Goldwyn-Mayer) to produce "Night Skies," which, after extensive rewrites to distance its subject matter from *E.T.*, became director Tobe Hooper's 1982 film *Poltergeist*.)

THE STORY DEVELOPS

The story line of *E.T.* is simple enough: One night, in the woods behind a hillside development of split-level homes, a spacecraft lands, disgorging a group of strange little creatures who shuffle off into the night until the appearance of humans—menacing from their point of view—forces them to reenter their craft and take off, with one of their number left behind. The terrified creature hides out in a backyard and is found by Elliott (Henry Thomas), the youngest boy of the family and a child at once sensitive, bold, and canny. They form a close friendship, communicating largely through instinctive understanding (E.T.

has telepathic powers), which ends when Elliott becomes sadly aware that the creature wants to go home.

Within this plot, Spielberg unfolds an empathetic tale of love and sympathy, pitted against fear and suspicion. The characterizations, including those of Elliott's mother (Dee Wallace), his siblings (Drew Barrymore and Robert MacNaughton), and an initially menacing authority figure played by Peter Coyote, are richly three-dimensional. But the high ground is shared between Thomas's enchanting, fatherless Elliott and the bizarre little alien, an Oscar-winning triumph of imagination, created and made by artist Carlo Rambaldi in accordance with Spielberg's humane vision.

More than one creature was built: a mechanically controlled version for scenes requiring large body movements, one with electronic controls for subtler articulation, and another to contain an actor (one of three used for the purpose) for the few scenes in which E.T. has to lurch across the floor. Commentators have drawn parallels between E.T. and Jesus Christ, pointing to, among other aspects, the creature's arrival, healing touch, persecution by civil authorities, and ascension into the heavens. Spielberg gave E.T. an appearance "only a mother could love," then wisely made him as afraid of earthlings as they are of him, disarming Americans conditioned by years of Cold War sci-fi films to fear extra-terrestrials. Interestingly, unlike the main character in *Close Encounters*, Elliott does not heed E.T.'s request, "Come," but chooses to stay behind with his family, perhaps reflecting Spielberg's own maturity and sense of responsibility. At the end, to lessen the pain of E.T.'s departure, Coyote's character, Keys, is subtly transformed from the antagonist to a possible new father, linked in two shots with Elliott's mother as they watch the spaceship fly off.

A LASTING MESSAGE

The logistics, statistics, and tales both apocryphal and accurate surrounding the genesis and the making of *E.T.* have been frequently recounted in books and articles, but its importance lies in the finished product and the response it evoked, and continues to evoke, in all who see it. There is not a dry eye in the house at the film's climax, but the message is one of hope, within which is a serious subtext (shared by *Close Encounters*) that aims to diffuse the viewer's nameless and parochial fears of "otherness." The film embodies its director's excursion into the wishes, dreams, and fantasies of his own past; but, significantly, that excursion brought audiences a return to innocence, love, and faith within a realistic contemporary social context.

With rare exceptions, the film, which was originally unveiled at the Cannes Film Festival, collected only superlatives from reviewers; it grossed millions for Spielberg personally as well as for Universal studios. When the Academy Awards came around, *E.T.* lost out to *Gandhi*, but by the end of the twentieth century it had become established as an acknowledged classic of the cinema.

In 2002 *E.T.* was rereleased in celebration of its twentieth anniversary, and plans for a thirtieth-anniversary edition for 2012 were in place. The film, as well as its then-young stars, struck a chord with audiences. Both Thomas and Barrymore continued with acting, but they will always be remembered as the kids from *E.T.*

Bob Sullivan

SEE ALSO: *Academy Awards;* Close Encounters of the Third Kind*; Cold War;* Easy Rider*; Ford, Harrison;* Jurassic Park*; Kotzwinkle, William; MGM (Metro-Goldwyn-Mayer);* Raiders of the Lost Ark*; Spielberg, Steven; UFOs (Unidentified Flying Objects); Vietnam; Watergate;* The Wizard of Oz.

BIBLIOGRAPHY

Baxter, John. *Steven Spielberg*. London: HarperCollins, 1996.

Ferber, Elizabeth. *Steven Spielberg*. Philadelphia: Chelsea House Publishers, 2000.

McBride, Joseph. *Steven Spielberg: A Biography*. New York: Simon & Schuster, 1997.

Taylor, Philip M. *Steven Spielberg*. London: Batsford, 1992.

Yule, Andrew. *Steven Spielberg: Father of the Man*. London: Little, Brown, 1996.

Etiquette Columns

Etiquette columns have appeared in American newspapers and magazines since the mid-nineteenth century. Targeted primarily at women, the columns sought to guide readers through the tangled thickets of social convention and polite behavior. They began in part as a response to the cultural anxieties of a newly emerging middle class and also derived from the related American mythologies of moral perfection and self-improvement. And despite contemporary society's avowed indifference to propriety, these concerns clearly persist, as evidenced by the enthusiastic readership of Judith Martin's etiquette column "Miss Manners."

Godey's Lady's Book was among the first periodicals to dispense etiquette advice to American women. In the years before the Civil War literacy rates in the United States reached 66 percent, and *Godey's* enjoyed a circulation of 150,000. *Godey's* editor, Mrs. Sarah Josepha Hale, avoided references to the day's political unpleasantness and frequently turned to contributor Mrs. James Parton, known to readers as Fanny Fern, for her sharp and amusing column "Rules for Ladies."

Following the Civil War there was widespread concern about the moral decay presumed to be an inevitable result of bad manners, and etiquette columns began to appear further afield. *Appleton's Journal*, the *Atlantic*, the *Galaxy*, and the *Round Table* all tendered advice on appropriate behavior, though social education continued to be the special purview of women's magazines. Readers who had questions on both fine and general points of etiquette began sending their inquiries directly to the magazines. Among the first to address these questions in a regular column was *Ladies' Home Journal*, whose editor Edward Bok created Side-Talks with Girls, written by "Ruth Ashmore" (actually Isabel A. Mallon), but it was not until 1896 that newspapers began to include subjects of special interest to female readers. That year "Dorothy Dix" (Mrs. Elizabeth M. Gilmer) started her etiquette column in the *New Orleans Picayune*, and soon etiquette columns appeared in newspapers throughout the country.

The nineteenth century's true expert on etiquette, however, was undoubtedly Mary Elizabeth Wilson Sherwood. Sherwood first offered etiquette advice in a series of features for *Harper's Bazaar*, which at the time was primarily known for presenting European fashions to American women. Readers immediately accepted her advice as authoritative. Sherwood greatly embellished her writing with florid details so that readers could visualize the fork or finger bowl she was describing, but it was not only this attention to detail that made her such a popular columnist. Unlike her predecessor, Henry Tomes, Sherwood was convinced that American women were not crude by nature. She believed they desperately wanted wise advice on manners and deportment, arguing that existing articles and books were either inaccessible or fraught with error. Sherwood thus set out to do more than codify the rules of good behavior: In *Manners and Social Usages* (1884), she sought to whet the nation's appetite for gracious living.

MODERNIZING ETIQUETTE

The rules of etiquette changed dramatically over the course of the twentieth century, but during the first decade of the 1900s, Americans were seemingly obsessed with the subject. More than seventy books and at least twice as many magazine articles on etiquette appeared between 1900 and 1910. Of these books, Marion Harland's *Everyday Etiquette* (1905) had the widest appeal. Miss Harland (the nom de plume of Mrs. Edward Payson Terhune, wife of a prominent clergyman) also wrote for many magazines. Another popular etiquette columnist at the time was Gabrielle Rozière, whose articles in the *Delineator* centered on the "E. T. Quette" family. Columns in *Current Literature*, *Munsey's*, the *Independent*, and *Century Magazine* all decried the decline of manners, especially the manners of women.

The best known of the early twentieth-century etiquette columnists were Florence Howe Hall; her sister Maud Howe; and their mother, Julia Ward Howe, better remembered for her "Battle Hymn of the Republic." Like their fellow writers, the Howes avoided the term *society*, which had, by the turn of the century, become equated with showy extravagance and vulgarity. The members of society likewise avoided "etiquette"—reasoning that those who required such advice did not really belong in society. But none of the hundreds of etiquette books and thousands of advice columns had the cultural impact of Emily Post's *Etiquette: The Blue Book of Social Usage* (1922). Almost immediately, Post became synonymous with etiquette. No one, it seemed, was embarrassed to have Emily Post on their shelves, and her book shot to the top of the nonfiction best-seller list.

As Post saw it, etiquette was nothing less than "the science of living," and her systematic approach to the subject promised firm guidance to everyone afloat in a sea of social uncertainty. Yet perhaps most important was the way Post dramatized etiquette. She introduced characters such as the Oldnames, Mr. Richan Vulgar, and Mrs. Cravin Praise to personify elegance, rudeness, or gaucherie so readers understood that these were not abstractions but very real qualities (or shortcomings) embodied in real people. If earlier writers had used this technique, no one had deployed so extensive a cast. Post's *Etiquette* thus enjoyed popularity for two reasons: it was an authoritative manual of taste and decorum, and it allowed average readers to glimpse through a keyhole the world of footmen and debutante balls that they were unlikely to experience directly. Post's success might also be traced to the burgeoning advertising industry. Her book was heavily advertised and easily played into an advertising strategy as common then as now: exploiting the insecurities of the socially inexperienced.

Like Sherwood before her, Post was a socialite, and, until she came to write her own book, she had always considered etiquette advice to be an act of sabotage, an easy way for parvenus and social climbers to worm their way into society. She steadfastly maintained this view until she was approached by Frank Crowninshield, the editor of *Vanity Fair*, and Richard Duffy of Funk and Wagnalls to write an etiquette book. She refused until they sent her a copy of a new etiquette manual to review, which she found condescending and useless. Only then did she agree that a new book was badly needed.

THE POST DYNASTY

With her impeccable background, Post was an obvious choice for the job. Born in 1872 to wealthy architect Bruce Price and his wife, Josephine Lee Price, Emily Price made her debut into society in 1892 and shortly thereafter married Edwin Post, an affluent financier. The couple eventually divorced amid alleged indiscretions committed by Edwin. After her divorce, Post, who had been drawn to intellectual and artistic pursuits since childhood, turned to writing and enjoyed success as a novelist and feature writer before turning to etiquette. After the enormous popularity of *Etiquette*, she published many revisions of the book and in 1932 began a syndicated etiquette column that eventually appeared in some 200 newspapers.

In its first twenty years *Etiquette* sold 666,000 copies, and after its fiftieth anniversary, the book had been through twelve editions and ninety-nine printings and had sold twelve million copies. For a time it was used as a textbook in poise and good manners for high school classes throughout the country, and by the late 1990s Post's great-granddaughter-in-law Peggy was writing the latest editions of the book. Emily Post, the name now a registered trademark, remains the authoritative voice on all matters of good taste and polite behavior.

In 1946 Post and her son Ned established the Emily Post Institute (EPI), which has evolved over the years into an etiquette dynasty. With five generations of Posts involved in the effort, EPI conducts seminars and training sessions throughout the United States. Collectively the Post family has written twenty-five books, and they publish regular columns in *Good Housekeeping*, the *New York Times*, *USA Weekend*, the *Boston Globe*, and on the *Brides* magazine website. Because of her exposure through the "Ask Peggy" column that appears monthly in *Good Housekeeping*, Peggy Post, like her great-grandmother-in-law before her, has become a household name, but the questions she answers are more likely to be about e-mail etiquette than about setting the table for fine dining. In 2011 she coauthored the eighteenth edition of *Emily Post's Etiquette*. Peggy has also published a number of books dealing with parenting and wedding planning.

Michele S. Shauf

SEE ALSO: *Advice Columns;* Atlantic Monthly*;* *Divorce;* Good Housekeeping*;* Harper's*;* *The* New York Times*;* Vanity Fair.

BIBLIOGRAPHY

Aresty, Esther B. *The Best Behavior.* New York: Simon & Schuster, 1970.

Cable, Mary. *American Manners and Morals.* New York: American Heritage Publishing, 1969.

Carson, Gerald. *The Polite Americans.* Westport, CT: Greenwood Press, 1966.

Claridge, Laura P. *Emily Post: Daughter of the Gilded Age, Mistress of American Manners.* New York: Random House, 2008.

Emily Post Institute. "About Us." Accessed February 2012. Available at http://www.emilypost.com/about-us

Lynes, Russell. *The Domesticated Americans.* New York: Harper & Row, 1963.

Post, Peggy, and Emily Post. *Emily Post's Etiquette.* New York: Harper-Collins, 1997.

Schlesinger, Arthur M. *Learning How to Behave.* New York: Macmillan, 1947.

Evangelism

From frontier camp meetings of the early 1800s to the urban revivals of the late 1800s and early 1900s to late twentieth-century Christian radio and television networks, evangelism has been a prominent feature of American religious culture. The process of evangelism focuses primarily on encouraging others to accept a particular sect of Christianity, usually through a personal conversion experience, but in the United States, evangelism has also been closely related to revivalism, the process of encouraging existing believers to renew their commitment to particular forms of Christian practice and belief. Though most commonly associated with Protestantism, other groups such as Mormons, Jehovah's Witnesses, and so-called "Jews for Jesus" practice forms of evangelism, actively seeking to bring new members into their fold.

Billy Graham, 1958. *Evangelist Billy Graham delivers a sermon at Madison Square Garden in 1958.* GJON MILI//TIME LIFE PICTURES/GETTY IMAGES.

Evangelism emerged as an important feature of American religious culture for several reasons. The American policy of religious voluntarism, which rendered religious affiliation a matter of personal choice rather than civic obligation, precluded even large denominations from taking their membership for granted. Evangelical efforts to acquire new members and to retain existing ones became an important church function, particularly within the Protestant churches and among interdenominational movements such as fundamentalism and Pentecostalism. In addition, secular influences have had pronounced affects on American society as it has gone through the processes of modernization and urbanization. The weakening role of religion in many aspects of American life has in turn motivated religious leaders and institutions to increase their involvement in evangelistic endeavors. Finally the evangelical Protestant denominations, which defined the nation's religious establishment during most of the nineteenth and early twentieth centuries, placed a strong doctrinal emphasis on evangelism and the conversion experience.

SPREADING THE MESSAGE

In promoting evangelism, different groups and individuals have developed diverse approaches to spreading their message. The most conspicuous form of evangelism early in the nineteenth century was the camp meeting, where believers would gather for several days of sermons, prayer, and religious testimony. Although the camp meetings were primarily a phenomenon of the frontier, many of their features persisted in the efforts of the itinerant evangelists who staged so-called tent meeting revivals in small towns and rural communities throughout the nineteenth century and well into the twentieth.

As the United States became increasingly urbanized during this period, however, so did evangelistic activity. By the early 1900s the most prominent evangelists worked primarily in urban settings. The urban revivals they staged retained the focus on charismatic leadership and personal conversion, including the climactic "altar call" during which participants declared their faith, but the urban revivals reached audiences numbering in the millions and produced converts by the thousands. The urban evangelists also incorporated a greater degree of showmanship, perhaps best exemplified by the garrulous, dramatic style of Billy Sunday during the 1910s.

TELEVANGELISM

Changing social conditions led to a decline in professional evangelism after World War I, particularly in urban settings. After World War II, however, a new generation of evangelists appeared on the American religious scene. These new crusaders became highly influential during the religious resurgence of the 1950s, although more so within the conservative wing of American Protestantism than among the mainstream churchgoers targeted by earlier revivalists. The leading figure in this new evangelical movement was Billy Graham, a conservative Baptist minister who spread his message through a wide variety of mass media, including radio, television, the cinema, and mass market publications. Graham's early use of television to promote evangelistic activities proved to be particularly important. By the 1970s television had become a primary medium of mass evangelism in the United States—a position that was strengthened in the following decade as cable television enabled various Christian broadcasting networks to reach audiences dispersed throughout the country.

As televangelism expanded, it also became increasingly associated with conservative perspectives in both religion and politics, and it generated considerable controversy during the 1970s and 1980s after a number of its major proponents lent their support to conservative political causes. Dubbed the "Religious Right," this strand of conservative politics, which was influenced by (but wary of fully embracing) the dominionism movement—the belief that secular government should be replaced by a strict Christian theocracy—made its mark on the presidential election of Ronald Reagan. Though not overtly religious, Reagan and his administration came to stand for the emerging synthesis of conservative politics and evangelical cultural values.

Emboldened by the role evangelicals played in electing Ronald Reagan, televangelist Pat Robertson, founder of the Christian Broadcasting Network (CBN), entered himself as a Republican candidate in the 1988 presidential election. Though he failed to earn the Republican nomination, he went on to create a highly influential political organization called the Christian Coalition (later renamed the Christian Coalition of America, or CCA). The Christian Coalition worked closely with conservative (mostly Republican) politicians, linking their campaigns to the fight against such hot-button issues as abortion and gay marriage.

This technique was particularly successful between 2000 and 2004, when the CCA distributed millions of voter guides in support of George W. Bush and mobilized evangelical voters by placing several antigay and antiabortion laws on the ballot in key states. The CCA has since fallen into decline under accusations of racial discrimination and mounting debt, but its influence on the political climate of the twenty-first century is undeniable, as the debate over abortion and gay marriage remains a central feature of political campaigns on all levels of government in America.

THE INTERNET AND SOCIAL MEDIA

The advent of the Internet as a major mode of communication in the late 1990s provided evangelicals with a new method of spreading the conservative Christian message. The Internet Evangelism Coalition, founded in 1999, encourages religious groups and individuals alike to flood message boards, comment sections, social media sites, and e-mail in-boxes with the Christian message and invitations to "search for Jesus." It has even instated an Internet Evangelism Day, which is held on the last Sunday of April each year. Internet evangelicals also advocate for a number of conservative political and cultural causes on the Web, using private Web sites and mass e-mail campaigns to attract and influence conservative voters and to speak out against issues such as Internet pornography.

The shift in focus of mass evangelism during the twentieth century from a broad connection to the Protestant mainstream to a narrower association primarily with religious conservatives has had significant implications for its relationship to American culture. The leading television, radio, and Internet evangelists especially have become less exclusively concerned with the individual conversion experience and increasingly concerned with general trends within American popular culture. In this sense evangelism, though still centered on an interpretation of Biblical imperatives, has evolved from a primarily religious phenomenon to one that has had significant impacts on politics and public policy in the United States.

Roger W. Stump

SEE ALSO: *Abortion;* Bush v. Gore *(2000); Cable TV; E-mail; Gay and Lesbian Marriage; Graham, Billy; The Internet; McPherson, Aimee Semple; Pornography; Radio; Reagan, Ronald; Religious Right; Robertson, Pat; Social Media; Sunday, Billy; Televangelism; Television; World War I; World War II.*

BIBLIOGRAPHY

Ahlstrom, Sydney. *A Religious History of the American People.* New Haven, CT: Yale University Press, 1972.

Bruns, Roger. *Preacher: Billy Sunday and Big-Time American Evangelism.* New York: W. W. Norton, 1992.

Evensen, Bruce J. *God's Man for the Gilded Age: D.L. Moody and the Rise of Modern Mass Evangelism.* New York: Oxford University Press, 2003.

Hankins, Barry. *American Evangelicals: A Contemporary History of a Mainstream Religious Movement.* Lanham, MD: Rowman & Littlefield, 2008.

Hardman, Keith. *Seasons of Refreshing: Evangelism and Revivals in America.* Grand Rapids, MI: Baker Books, 1994.

Lambert, Frank. *Religion in American Politics: A Short History.* Princeton, NJ: Princeton University Press, 2010.

Schultze, Quentin J., and Robert Woods, eds. *Understanding Evangelical Media: The Changing Face of Christian Communication.* Downers Grove, IL: IVP Academic, 2008.

Smith, Christian. *Christian America?: What Evangelicals Really Want.* Berkeley: University of California Press, 2000.

The Everly Brothers

One of the greatest singing brother duos of all time, the Everly Brothers' close harmonies became one of the most identifiable sounds of the early rock-and-roll era of the late 1950s and early 1960s. Hits such as "Bye Bye Love," "Wake up Little Susie," and "Love Hurts" are long ingrained in the memories of Americans who grew up listening to the Everly Brothers. They went on to influence such groups as the Beatles and Simon and Garfunkel (who covered "Wake up Little Susie" on their *Bridge over Troubled Water* album). After their pop stardom declined, they followed the same path as Jerry Lee Lewis and other early rock and rollers, becoming country music artists. Although they temporarily went solo, they reunited in 1983 and have been touring together ever since.

Phil (born January 19, 1939) and Don (born February 1, 1937) were raised in a musical family, singing with their guitarist father Ike and other family members on radio broadcasts in the early 1950s. Raised in Brownie, Kentucky, the brothers were heavily influenced by such country legends as the Louvin Brothers (and the Louvin's inspiration, the Delmore Brothers), as well as a number of other singing brother duo acts. After a very brief and unsuccessful stint at Columbia Records, the two hit their commercial stride when they joined Cadence records, which released the number two Billboard hit and rock-and-roll classic, "Bye Bye Love." The brothers had a number of hits for Cadence, including "Wake up Little Susie," "Bird Dog," "('Til) I Kissed You," "All I Have to Do is Dream," and "When Will I Be Loved."

In 1960 the two joined Warner Brothers Records, hitting their commercial peak with songs such as "Cathy's Clown" and helping to establish Warner Brothers as a major player in the music business in the process. Unfortunately, Don soon succumbed to the pressure, turning to drinking and drugs (in much the same way that Ira Louvin did); he nearly died of an intentional overdose in 1962. This was among a number of career setbacks the Everly Brothers experienced after signing with Warner Brothers, including being drafted into the marines. However, after only six months in the military, they began a European tour, where they found the British Invasion led by the Beatles was in full swing and the era of early rock and roll was on the wane.

After their last Top 10 hit, the aptly titled 1962 song "That's Old Fashioned," the brothers' career floundered as they released a series of albums that were nothing less than careless contract fillers. In 1968 the Everly Brothers revived themselves, artistically at least, with *Roots*, a country-rock album that—along with the Byrd's *Sweetheart of the Rodeo*—became a major influence on the country-rock movement that inspired such groups as Poco and the Flying Burrito Brothers, as well as pioneering artists such as Gram Parsons. Sibling rivalry and record-industry-induced pressure led to the duo's dramatic demise at a 1973 concert in which Phil smashed his guitar and stormed offstage. Afterward the brothers pursued solo careers. Don remained in Nashville with his Dead Cowboys band, and Phil devoted himself to songwriting. However, after a decade of poorly received solo albums, the two resumed singing together in 1983, primarily performing on the oldies circuit.

The Everly Brothers were inducted into the Rock and Roll Music Hall of Fame in 1986 and into the Country Music Hall of Fame in 2001. That same year they were among a group of songwriters inducted into the Nashville Songwriters Hall of Fame.

Kembrew McLeod

SEE ALSO: *The Beatles; The Byrds; Country Music; The Draft; The Fifties; Lewis, Jerry Lee; Pop Music; Radio; Rock and Roll; Simon and Garfunkel; Top 40.*

BIBLIOGRAPHY

"The Everly Brothers Biography." Country Music Hall of Fame. Accessed February 2012. Available from http://countrymusichalloffame.org/full-list-of-inductees/view/-everly-brothers

Karpp, Phyllis. *Ike's Boys: The Story of the Everly Brothers*. Ann Arbor, MI: Popular Culture, 1988.

Spies, Jerry. *Phil & Don, Home Again*. Shenandoah, IA: World Publishing, 1986.

Everson, Cory *(1959–)*

The best known of all Ms. Olympia winners, bodybuilder Corinna (Cory) Kneuer Everson grew up in Deerfield, Illinois, where she was an outstanding athlete throughout high school and college. She attended the University of Wisconsin, where she won the Big Ten Championship in the pentathlon for four consecutive years. While attending the university, Cory met Jeff Everson, a competitive weightlifter and bodybuilder who worked there as a strength coach. Following her marriage to Everson and her graduation from college, she began to train seriously as a bodybuilder. Blessed with outstanding genetics for bodybuilding, she made rapid progress, especially after the couple moved to Los Angeles. She won the Ms. Olympia competition in 1984, the first time she entered, and won every year until 1989, when she retired.

Everson soon became part of the fitness show phenomenon on cable television with her *Bodyshaping* program. She has served as the fitness expert on *Cory Everson's Gotta Sweat* (ESPN) and as host of Fox Sports and FIT-TV's *Body Waves*. She has also had roles in such films as *Double Impact* (1991), *Natural Born Killers* (1994), and *Tarzan, the Epic Adventures* (1996). In the late 1990s she authored several fitness and health books, including *Cory Everson's Lifebalance* (1998). In 2007 Everson became the first woman to win a Lifetime Achievement Award at the Arnold Classic. Now in her fifties, she runs a chain of health and wellness clinics.

Jan Todd

SEE ALSO: *Bodybuilding; Cable TV; ESPN; Television.*

BIBLIOGRAPHY

Hurd, Lyle. "A Fitness Adventure." *Total Health*, July/August 2000.

"Biography." *JamzProducts*. Accessed February 2012. Available from http://www.jamzproducts.com/Articles.asp?ID=250

Evert, Chris *(1954–)*

One of the greatest female tennis players of all time, Chris Evert ruled the sport for more than ten years (1973–1985) and established herself as a cultural icon in America and around the world. Born December 21, 1954, in Fort Lauderdale, Florida, Christine Marie Evert started playing tennis at the age of six. With her father (teaching professional Jimmy Evert) as coach, Evert showed promise early on, rising to number two in the United States in the twelve-and-under age group. By the time she was fifteen, she had established herself as the country's top amateur player by defeating such stars as Billie Jean King; Virginia Wade; and the world's number one player at the time, Margaret Smith Court. At sixteen, Evert made it all the way to the semifinals of the U.S. Open. In 1972 she was a winner at both the Virginia Slims Championship and the United States Clay Court Championship. In December of that same year, on her eighteenth birthday, Evert turned professional.

TENNIS PHENOM

In 1974, still only nineteen years old, Evert won singles titles at Wimbledon, the French Open, and the Italian Open; lost in the finals at the Australian Open; and was a semifinalist at the U.S. Open. Already a popular player, the poise and intense concentration exhibited by Evert that year made her a favorite of sportswriters and spectators alike. Her engagement to budding American tennis hero Jimmy Connors (who was then twenty-one) in late 1973 also contributed to Evert's rising fame. Dubbed the "King and Queen of tennis" by columnists, the couple called off the engagement in 1975. Four years later, Evert wed British Davis Cup player John Lloyd; the union lasted until 1987.

Evert won her first U.S. Open singles title in 1975, defeating Yvonne Goolagong in the finals at Forest Hills. She retained that crown for the next three years and finished her career as a six-time U.S. Open champion. However, her best surface was clay, and the French Open was where she had the most success. Evert made it to the finals at Roland Garros nine times, losing only twice; her seven French Open singles titles remain a record. Evert's career highlights also include two Australian Open titles (1982 and 1984) and three Wimbledon titles (1974, 1976, and 1981). This last is all the more impressive considering her reluctance to come up to net, a practice that according to conventional wisdom is essential on Wimbledon's grass surface. Nor did her preference for staying at the baseline prevent Evert from winning three Grand Slam doubles titles. All told, she won at least one Grand Slam title per year for thirteen straight years (1974–1986), a statistic that testifies to her legendary consistency.

Evert's combination of charm and intensity helped attract large audiences and significant prize money to women's tennis. Nicknamed the "Ice Maiden" and the "Ball Machine" by her peers, she was extremely disciplined and almost never lost her composure on court. In this respect, she stood in stark contrast to other American tennis stars of the time, in particular to Connors and John McEnroe. At risk of turning fans off because winning came almost *too* easily for her, the ongoing rivalry with Martina Navratilova took on increasing importance. After sixteen years and dozens of hard-fought battles, Evert's career record against Navratilova ended at thirty-seven wins and forty-three losses. It should be noted, however, that the majority of these matches were not played on clay.

RETIREMENT AND LEGACY

One year after a disappointing early exit in the 1988 Olympics, Evert retired from competitive tennis ranked number four in the world—her lowest ranking since turning pro seventeen years earlier. Among her immense list of on-court accomplishments, the following stand out: for 133 consecutive weeks (starting in 1975) she held the number one ranking in singles; she won 125 consecutive matches on clay—no one has won more matches consecutively on *any* surface; she took home a total of 157 singles titles, second only to Navratilova; and her career winning percentage of .900 (1,309 victories against a mere 146 losses) ranks first in the history of the game. In 1995 Evert earned a rare unanimous selection to the International Tennis Hall of Fame.

It would be nearly impossible to overestimate Evert's popularity during her playing career. In 1985 the Women's Sports Foundation voted her the Greatest Woman Athlete of the Last 25 Years. In November 1989 she became the first female athlete to host television's *Saturday Night Live*. In 1991 a poll conducted by American Sports Data found her to be the most widely known athlete in the nation. What accounted for her high degree of fame? One of the first players to rely on a two-handed backhand, Evert's unprecedented success with this stroke encouraged a generation of novices to copy her. Her grace and professionalism on and off the court led to her unofficial canonization as a role model for young people of both sexes.

Further, her high-profile romances with male sports stars (in 1988 she married ex-Olympic skier Andy Mill, with whom she had three children) kept her in the gossip columns as well as the sports pages. The couple divorced in 2006 after eighteen years of marriage. Two years later Evert married professional golfer Greg Norman; they divorced after fifteen months.

Evert's seventeen-year-long reign at or near the top of women's tennis is what ultimately ensures her celebrity status. Although not blessed with prodigious athletic ability, her honed-to-perfection strokes, along with a fierce will to win and an uncanny ability to exploit opponents' weaknesses, gave her an air of dominance that eventually became a source of national pride. After her retirement, Evert worked as a color commentator for network-television broadcasts of major tennis tournaments. In her more recent work with ESPN, she is frequently praised for her honest critiques. She is also host of the annual Chris Evert Celebrity Tennis Classic in Boca Raton, Florida, a charity event that raises money to help drug-exposed, abused, and neglected children. She and her brother John run Evert Academy, a training school for aspiring tennis champions.

Steven Schneider

SEE ALSO: *Connors, Jimmy; ESPN; King, Billie Jean; McEnroe, John; Navratilova, Martina; Olympics; Sports Heroes; Tennis.*

BIBLIOGRAPHY

Collins, Bud, and Zander Hollander, eds. *Bud Collins' Modern Encyclopedia of Tennis*. Detroit, MI: Gale Research, 1994.

Evert, Chris, and Neil Amdur. *Chrissie: My Own Story*. New York: Simon & Schuster, 1982.

Lloyd, Chris Evert; John Lloyd, and Carol Thatcher. *Lloyd on Lloyd*. New York: Beaufort Books, 1986.

Wertheim, L. Jon. "Chris Evert." *Sports Illustrated*, December 12, 2011.

Woolum, Janet. *Outstanding Women Athletes: Who They Are and How They Influenced Sports in America*. Phoenix, AZ: Oryx Press, 1998.

Everybody Loves Raymond

Everybody Loves Raymond was an award-winning situation comedy created and produced by Phil Rosenthal. The show starred comedian Ray Romano, whose family-centered material served as the basis for the plots. The program ran on CBS from September 13, 1996, to May 16, 2005. After a slow start, it became a major hit for the network and ranked in the top ten for its last five seasons, winning an Emmy Award for Outstanding Comedy Series in 2003 and 2005. So successful was the show that advertisers paid as much as $1.3 million for a thirty-second spot in the series finale. The show was syndicated in more than 140 countries and continues to be seen in reruns.

Unlike other popular sitcoms that focused on interactions within a nuclear family, *Everybody Loves Raymond* centered on the extended Italian American family of Ray Barone (Romano), a sportswriter for *Newsday* living in Long Island, New York. Raymond and his wife, Debra (Patricia Heaton), are the parents of three children, a daughter and twin sons, but the children were strictly minor characters. In another break with sitcoms of earlier periods, Raymond is not a wise, involved father. When he does interact with his children, he is usually inept. He does not fare much better as a husband. There is something of the eternal adolescent in his character. He and Debra bicker endlessly about their sex life, about the choices Raymond makes, and about his family. He uses humor to avoid confronting the consequences of his irresponsibility.

Much of the humor involves Raymond's parents, interfering Marie (Doris Roberts) and curmudgeonly Frank (Peter

Boyle), who live across the street. Older brother Robert (Brad Garrett), a cop, lives with his parents in the early years of the series, unable even as an adult to overcome his jealousy of Raymond, their mother's favorite son. Clashes between Debra and Marie, who criticizes Debra at every turn, are standard, and Raymond is caught in the middle, trying to appease his wife but unable to stand up to his mother.

Romano, Heaton, Garrett, and Roberts all received Emmy Awards for their performances, a total of ten among them, with Roberts taking home television's highest honor four times. Although *Everybody Loves Raymond* never attracted the kind of media attention enjoyed by the sitcoms *Seinfeld* or *Friends*, the character-driven comedy about a dysfunctional but loving family drew a wide audience and had a loyal fan base. Romano was the highest-paid actor on television the last two seasons, earning $2.7 million per episode in the final season.

Romano attributes the success of the show to its realism. It seemed natural to him to draw upon his experiences with his own family in writing material for his stand-up act, and he built his comedic reputation upon humor that allowed his audience to see themselves and their families in the material, albeit in exaggerated form. It was this humor that persuaded David Letterman to see sitcom potential in Romano's act and sign him to a deal with his production company. Producer Rosenthal and Romano, both New Yorkers of about the same age, found more commonality in their family experiences. Eventually, the entire writing staff of *Raymond* was contributing family stories to serve as grist for the episodes.

Heaton concurs, acknowledging the show's lack of hipness and insisting that hipness was never the goal in a series that portrayed in its bickering spouses and imperfect family something much closer to the lives of its viewers than found in other, more sophisticated shows. When the filming of the 210th episode ended, Romano walked away with 12.5 percent of the show's syndication profits, approximately $130,000 a year. Heaton, Boyle, Roberts, and Garrett all shared a considerably smaller but still impressive portion of the profits.

Wylene Rholetter

SEE ALSO: *Emmy Awards;* Friends*; Letterman, David;* Seinfeld*; Sitcom; Television.*

BIBLIOGRAPHY

Freydkin, Donna. "Does Everybody Love Raymond?" *USA Today*, December 8, 2002.

Keveney, Bill. "'Raymond': Sweet Run, and Now, Sweet Dreams." *USA Today*, May 15, 2005.

Lipton, Mike, and Tom Cunneff. "Everybody Leaves Raymond." *People*, May 23, 2005, 125–128.

The Exorcist

The first major blockbuster in the history of horror cinema, William Friedkin's *The Exorcist* (1973) has exerted a powerful influence on the subsequent development of the genre and on public reception of it. Never before had a horror film been the subject of so much prerelease hype, so much gossip about post-production strife, so much speculation as to why people of all ages would stand in line for hours to watch something reputed

The Exorcist. *Max Von Sydow casts a foreboding silhouette in a scene from* The Exorcist*, the first horror film to receive an Academy Award nomination for Best Picture.* WARNER BROTHERS/GETTY IMAGES.

to induce fits of vomiting, fainting, even temporary psychosis. The cultural impact of *The Exorcist* can hardly be overestimated: it challenged existing regulations specifying what was acceptable to show on the big screen; stole U.S. newspaper headlines away from the ongoing Watergate scandal (at least for a little while); led to a detectable increase in the number of "real-life" possessions reported; and, in the words of gross-out film expert William Paul, "established this push-pull aspect of disgust as mass entertainment for a large audience."

In 1949 reports came out in the press about a thirteen-year-old Maryland boy whose body was said to have been taken over by demonic forces. After seeing household objects fly around his room, the boy's distraught parents called in a Jesuit priest, who conducted a thirty-five-day-long exorcism with the help of numerous assistants. While the priests recited their holy incantations, the boy spit, cackled, urinated, writhed in his bed, and manifested bloody scratch marks on his body that spelled out words such as "Hell," "Christ," and the far more mysterious "Go to St. Louis." Fortunately for everyone involved, the alleged demon departed shortly after Easter. Novelist William Peter Blatty, inspired by this tale, made the possessee a girl (supposedly to protect the boy's anonymity, though his readiness to disclose information in later media interviews suggests this was unnecessary), sensationalized many of the details, added heavy doses of philosophical-theological speculation on the nature of evil, and came out with *The Exorcist* in 1971. An instant sensation, Blatty's novel would remain on the *Publishers Weekly* best-seller list for almost an entire year.

Even before the book's publication, Blatty signed a deal with Warner Brothers for the rights to make a film version of the novel. Warner agreed to Blatty's choice of director, Friedkin, on the strength of his not-yet-released action movie, *The French Connection*, for which he won an Academy Award in 1971. After numerous and painstaking rewrites of the original script, Blatty finally came up with a screenplay of *The Exorcist* that managed to meet Friedkin's exacting demands for more mystery, more drama, and above all more direct confrontation between (good) priest and (evil) demon than were in the novel. For his own part—and with Warner's considerable financial backing—Friedkin employed a range of sophisticated cinematic techniques, along with state-of-the-art special-effects technology, to give the film's supernatural occurrences and gory physical details a degree of realism never before achieved.

The plot of *The Exorcist* is deceptively simple and has its roots in storytelling conventions well established in American cinema. After a lengthy prologue that is nearly incomprehensible to anyone who has not read the book, the first half of the film methodically develops the essential character relationships and establishes the crisis situation. Regan MacNeil (Linda Blair) is the adorable, almost-pubescent daughter of divorcee and well-known film star Chris MacNeil (Ellen Burstyn). After Regan prophesies the death of her mother's acquaintance and urinates (standing up, no less) in front of a roomful of shocked dinner guests, Chris starts to wonder what has "gotten into" her daughter. More odd behavior, and a wildly shaking bed, lands Regan in the hospital, where she is subjected to a battery of extremely invasive procedures best described as "medical pornography." A brain lesion is suspected, but the tests turn up nothing.

When Regan, supposedly under hypnosis, responds to the smug questions of a hospital psychologist by grabbing his scrotum and rendering him immobile, it is recommended that Chris seek the church's help. She does, pleading with doubt-ridden Jesuit priest Damien Karras (Jason Miller, Pulitzer Prize–winning playwright of *That Championship Season*, 1972) to perform an exorcism. The second half of the film culminates in an intense one-to-one fight to the finish between Karras and Regan's demonic possessor, after the more experienced exorcist on the scene, Father Merrin (Bergmanian actor Max von Sydow) dies in the struggle. Karras finally saves Regan by accepting the demon into his own body, only to throw himself (or at least allow himself to be thrown) out of a window to his death.

Although the Catholic Church originally supported Friedkin's efforts in the hopes that he would present Catholicism in a positive light, they ended up retracting that support after viewing the infamous scene in which Regan-demon violently masturbates with a crucifix in front of her powerless mother. For many audience members, the highly sexualized profanities spewing out of twelve-year-old Regan's mouth (the voice of the demon, Mercedes McCambridge, had to sue for credit) were as offensive as the green bile she vomited on Karras's face. In an era of student protest, experimental drug use, and general questioning of authority, *The Exorcist* allowed viewers to take pleasure in the terrible punishments inflicted on the rebellious ("possessed") Regan. But by making Regan-demon so fascinating to watch, so filled with nasty surprises, *The Exorcist* also allowed viewers to take pleasure in that rebelliousness.

The Exorcist did not merely give rise to a slew of imitations and variants on the possession theme; it made the child with special powers a dominant motif in modern horror cinema. Two mediocre sequels—*The Exorcist II: The Heretic* (1977) and *The Exorcist III* (1990)—followed, the second one written and directed by Blatty; neither involved Friedkin at all. Richard Donner's highly polished *The Omen* (1976) added an apocalyptic edge to the demonic infiltration theme. Linda Blair, who attained cult-figure status with her role as Regan, reprised it in a Leslie Nielsen spoof titled *Repossessed* (1990).

Two attempts were made at a prequel, 2004's *Exorcist: The Beginning* (directed by Renny Harlin) and 2005's *Dominion: Prequel to the Exorcist* (directed by Paul Schrader)—both starring Stellan Skarsgård as the young Father Merrin.

Steven Schneider

SEE ALSO: The French Connection*; Horror Movies; Watergate.*

BIBLIOGRAPHY

Blatty, William Peter. *William Peter Blatty on "The Exorcist" from Novel to Film.* New York: Bantam, 1974.

Bowles, Stephen. "*The Exorcist* and *Jaws*." *Literature/Film Quarterly* 4, no. 3 (1976): 196–214.

Kermode, Mark. *The Exorcist.* London: BFI, 1997.

Newman, Howard. *"The Exorcist": The Strange Story behind the Film.* New York: Pinnacle, 1974.

Paul, William. "Possession, Regression, Rebellion." In *Laughing, Screaming: Modern Hollywood Horror and Comedy*, 287–318. New York: Columbia University Press, 1994.

Travers, Peter, and Stephanie Reiff. *The Story behind "The Exorcist."* New York: Crown, 1974.

Twelftree, Graham H. *In the Name of Jesus: Exorcism among Early Christians.* Grand Rapids, MI.: Baker Academic, 2007.

Extreme Sports

No universally accepted definition of *extreme sports* yet exists, and that is not likely to change soon. The term came into common usage in the late twentieth century to encompass various strenuous, sometimes competitive, activities that present the participants with a much higher-than-usual risk of physical stress, injury, or death.

In the middle of the fifteenth century the word *sport* implied a "pleasant pastime, entertainment or amusement." A century later it connoted an "amorous dalliance or intercourse." After another hundred years, it also came to mean a "pastime afforded by the endeavor to take or kill wild animals, game, or fish." In the later nineteenth century *sport* meant—in the United States, especially—"participation in games or exercises, especially those of an athletic character or pursued in the open air."

Extreme is Latin in origin and denotes, among other things, "being in or attaining the greatest or highest degree; very intense." In the last decade of the twentieth century and the beginning of the twenty-first, this particular sense of extreme became current among American youth as a term of approval—in the same sense that earlier generations had used the word *cool*, but with the added prestige of being unrestrained, out of control, or even anarchic. Hoping to attract a young demographic, the media began attaching the word to various activities that otherwise would have sounded mundane or even dull: *extreme shopping* or *extreme lunch*. The first uses were mostly tongue-in-cheek, almost satirical, but as is often the case with satire in the mass media, the wacky fringe being mocked moved steadily to the center and became the norm. "Moderate," long considered a virtue, now became a sign of weakness and cowardice; *extreme* was the watchword of the new culture heroes.

In his 1926 novel *The Sun Also Rises*, Ernest Hemingway describes his characters at the annual bullfighting festival in Pamplona, Spain. Hemingway may have been the first to identify an extreme sport, when he writes of how young men at the festival, to prove their virility, run along with the chosen bulls of each festival as they gallop through the streets of Pamplona from their pens into the bullring. The male characters in *The Sun Also Rises* join in the run, which has inspired readers of the novel to make the pilgrimage to Spain to run with the bulls, risking their lives—the danger is real and constant—to establish their courage. Requiring little or no training and no equipment, running with the bulls qualifies as a primitive ancestor of twenty-first century extreme sports.

A list of contemporary extreme sports includes air sports such as base jumping, bungee jumping, gliding, hang gliding, high wire, ski jumping, skydiving, skysurfing, and sky flying; land sports such as indoor climbing, adventure racing, aggressive inline skating, BMX, caving, motocross, extreme skiing, freestyle skiing, land and ice yachting, mountain biking, mountain boarding, outdoor climbing, sand boarding, skateboarding, snowboarding, snowmobiling, speed biking, speed skiing, scootering, and street luge; and water sports such as barefoot water skiing, cliff diving, free diving, jet skiing, open-water swimming, powerboat racing, round-the-world yacht racing, scuba diving, snorkeling, speed sailing, surfing, wakeboarding, whitewater kayaking, windsurfing, and kite surfing. Since 1995 the cable channel ESPN has sponsored an annual extreme sports competition called the X Games that has produced some of the more thrilling athletic feats in recent memory and influenced the International Olympic Committee to add such extreme-sports-inspired events as half-pipe snowboarding and ski cross to the Winter Olympics and BMX racing to the Summer Olympics.

The level of risk in these activities varies widely. Some seem scarcely to qualify as risky at all; others border on life threatening. The unifying principle among them is that they allow the participants to push themselves to their physical limits and stimulate the flow of adrenaline.

Gerald Carpenter

SEE ALSO: *ESPN; Generation X; Hemingway, Ernest; Jet Skis; Mountain Biking; Olympics; Rock Climbing; Skateboarding; Snowboarding; X Games.*

BIBLIOGRAPHY

Bane, Michael. *Over the Edge: A Regular Guy's Odyssey in Extreme Sports.* New York: Macmillan, 1996.

Browne, David. *Amped: How Big Air, Big Dollars and a New Generation Took Sports to the Extreme.* New York: Bloomsbury, 2004.

Gutman, Bill, and Shawn Frederick. *Being Extreme: Thrills and Danger in the World of High-Risk Sports.* New York: Citadel Press, 2003.

Rinehart, Robert E., and Synthia Sydnor. *To the Extreme: Alternative Sports, Inside and Out.* Albany: State University of New York Press, 2003.

Tomlinson, Joe *Extreme Sports: In Search of the Ultimate Thrill.* Buffalo, NY: Firefly Books, 2004.

F

Fabares, Shelley *(1944–)*

In 1958, when Shelley Fabares was cast as Mary Stone in television's *The Donna Reed Show* at the age of fourteen, she was already an acting veteran. Born in Santa Monica, California, this niece of actress Nanette Fabray had been working in movies and on television since childhood, but it was as Mary Stone that she established her image as the ideal teenager: pretty, perky, smart, and sweet. After four years of the show's five-year run, its producer (and the husband of Donna Reed), Tony Owen, persuaded Fabares to record "Johnny Angel," and she lip-synched the tune on an episode in January 1962. By March the single had climbed to number one on the Billboard Hot 100 chart.

Fabares grew up on *The Donna Reed Show* and, as Mary, went away to college. In real life she moved to the big screen, donning a bikini to costar with Fabian in *Ride the Wild Surf* (1964) and playing the female lead to Elvis Presley in *Girl Happy* (1965), *Spinout* (1966), and *Clambake* (1967)—the only actress to star with the legendary entertainer three times—but her film career never fulfilled the promise of her teenage years. Fabares appeared in a number of TV roles through the 1980s and 1990s, most notably as one of the central characters on the popular ABC comedy *Coach*. When the show ended in 1997, she took on voice-over work, playing the role of Ma Kent in a number of Superman productions, including *Superman: The Animated Series* (1998).

Jennifer Davis McDaid

SEE ALSO: *Fabian; Pop Music; Presley, Elvis; Reed, Donna; Superman; Teen Idols; Television.*

BIBLIOGRAPHY

Bartel, Pauline. *Reel Elvis! The Ultimate Trivia Guide to the King's Movies.* Dallas, TX: Taylor Publishing, 1994.

Fultz, Jay. *In Search of Donna Reed.* Iowa City: University of Iowa Press, 1998.

Geri, Brian. Liner notes for *The Best of Shelley Fabares.* Los Angeles: Rhino Records, 1994.

Lisanti, Tom. *Fantasy Femmes of Sixties Cinema: Interviews with 20 Actresses from Biker, Beach and Elvis Movies.* Jefferson, NC: McFarland, 2001.

"Teens Are Looking at . . . [Shelley Fabares]." *Seventeen,* November 1962, 52.

Fabian *(1943–)*

Perhaps the quintessential teen idol of the 1950s, Fabian was only fourteen when he was plucked from obscurity and thrust into the idol-making machinery by Philadelphia record producer-promoter Bob Marcucci. Though he had failed his high school chorus classes, the darkly handsome Fabian Forte hit the national charts with the off-key single "I'm a Man." The hits "Turn Me Loose" and "Tiger" followed. Critics savaged him; *Time* labeled him a "tuneless tiger." But to teenage girls lamenting Elvis Presley's tenure in the U.S. Army, Fabian filled a void. Aware that he was being marketed like "a thing," Fabian left music in the early 1960s to pursue a Hollywood career. But after he had proved to be an affable costar in popular movies such as *High Time* (1960) and *North to Alaska* (1960), his career stalled.

Fabian's career was revived in the 1980s by "golden oldies" tours, which continued into the twenty-first century. Married three times, he and his third wife, Andrea Patrick, have been actively engaged in charity work for the American Diabetes Association, the American Heart Association, and supporting veterans.

Pat H. Broeske

SEE ALSO: *Hollywood; Pop Music; Rock and Roll; Teen Idols.*

BIBLIOGRAPHY

Farley, Ellen. "The Story of Frank and Fabe and Bob." *Los Angeles Times,* November 23, 1980, 30–31.

"Tuneless Tiger." *Time,* July 27, 1959, 33.

Fabio *(1961–)*

The boom in romance novels in the mid-1980s propelled Italian-born cover model Fabio, who appeared on hundreds of book covers, to the heights of superstardom. With his broad, bare chest and long (dyed) blond hair, Fabio became an international sex symbol. Although his subsequent film and television career was limited to cameos playing himself, he parlayed his fame into a job as a spokesperson for I Can't Believe It's Not Butter in the 1990s and made it onto MTV with a spot in Jill Sobule's music video for "I Kissed a Girl." As his career as a model faded, Fabio returned to romance novels, this time as an author. He also appeared on television shows such as *Arli$$* (1996–2002) and *The Suite Life on Deck* (2008–) and served as a spokesperson for

Best Buy's Geek Squad. In 2006 Nationwide Insurance hired him to appear as a 120-year-old-man as part of their "Life Is Short" commercials during Super Bowl XL. That commercial became the most downloaded video from the 2006 game.

Deborah Broderson

SEE ALSO: *Advertising; Bodybuilding; MTV; Romance Novels; Sex Symbol; Super Bowl; Television; Videos.*

BIBLIOGRAPHY

Fabio. "The Trouble with American Women." *Penthouse*, September 1994, 130–136.

"Nationwide Ad Finds Fabio's Flowing Locks Flattened." *USA Today*, February 2, 2006.

Paul, Peter. *Fabio*. Livonia, MI: Stabur, 1993.

Romantic Conventions. Bowling Green, OH: Bowling Green State University Popular Press, 1999.

Facebook

With 845 million active users (and growing) worldwide, Facebook is by far the most popular social networking site on the Internet, and it is among the most visited websites in the world. Founded by Harvard University students Mark Zuckerberg, Chris Hughes, Andrew McCollum, Dustin Moskovitz, and Eduardo Saverin on February 4, 2004, Facebook was originally intended to serve as a version of bound student directories known as "face books" and was open to only to Harvard students. Since it became publicly available in 2004, however, Facebook use has grown exponentially. By the end of 2004 it had more than a million registered users; by the end of 2006 that total reached twelve million; in 2008 it jumped to 145 million; and in 2010 there were more than 600 million active Facebook users. It is impossible to quantify the impact that Facebook has had on life in the twenty-first century. The service has shaped developments in nearly every aspect of culture including art, entertainment, business, politics, and even language (the word *friend* is now in the Oxford English Dictionary as a verb as well as a noun).

Facebook allows anyone over the age of thirteen to create a profile that includes photos and personal information such as age, education, relationship and employment status, and interests. Users cultivate their Facebook identities by posting text, photos, or links to online content such as articles, music, or videos on a personal page known as the user's "wall." Users can then "friend" each other. Facebook friends have access to each other's walls and receive notifications when changes are made to each other's status or wall. Users can create or join an unlimited number of groups that cater to people who share specific backgrounds, interests, or views; attend the same school or work for the same company; or just want to show support for a project or idea. The site also features instant-messaging and video-calling services, and Facebook-specific applications allow users to play games against each other. The average user spends more than seven hours per month on the site, a number twice as high as Facebook's closest competitor.

EARLY YEARS

The earliest iteration of Facebook took shape in 2003 when Zuckerberg, a computer programmer (he built a computer network called ZuckNet for his family at the age of eleven) and self-professed hacker, accessed the Harvard student directory and posted photos of students on a website he called Facemash, which encouraged users to vote on the most attractive students. When Facemash was shut down due to privacy concerns and the strain that its high user rates put on the school's servers, Zuckerberg began developing a social network site for Harvard students similar to what was offered by sites such as Friendster and MySpace. Thefacebook.com launched in early 2004 and was an immediate success with Harvard students. One month later Zuckerberg and his business partners decided to expand the service to other Ivy League campuses. In May 2004, Facebook caught the attention of entrepreneur Sean Parker (the developer behind the notorious music-sharing service Napster), who served as president of the company until 2005.

In the summer of 2004 Zuckerberg and company moved to Palo Alto, California, a haven for start-up technology companies, and promptly received a $500,000 investment from venture capitalist Peter Thiel. In May 2005 Accel Partners invested $12.7 million in Facebook, citing its "tremendous underlying, organic growth." Parker advised Zuckerberg to drop the "the" from his website's name, and in the fall of 2005 Facebook.com expanded to high school campuses and added its popular photo-uploading function. In 2006 Facebook developed an application that allowed users to access the site from their mobile phones. Zuckerberg then hired his former teacher, Andrew "Boz" Bosworth, who developed the site's news-feed feature, which updates users on their friends' activities—an addition that initially drew criticism from users concerned about privacy but has since become a central feature of the service. In September 2006 Facebook opened registration to anyone age thirteen or older, and in November it introduced the "share" feature, allowing users to share content from partnering sites with the click of a button.

Early on, Facebook embraced hacker culture, which promotes openness through the sharing of the type of software code that is typically guarded with great intensity by tech companies. The site sponsored regular "hackathons," in which hackers would attempt to develop the most interesting or useful piece of software in a single, frantic overnight coding session. Some features that emerged from hackathons include Facebook's chat service and an algorithm that automatically suggests new friends to a user based on the user's existing circle of friends. The Facebook Platform, launched in May 2007, encourages third-party developers to create applications that enhance the user experience and integrate the site with other popular services, such as the Spotify music service.

MAINSTREAM CROSSOVER

Impressed by Facebook's precipitous growth, Microsoft bought a 1.6 percent share of the company in October 2007 for a reported $240 million. The following month Facebook launched Facebook Ads, which allows advertisers to target specific users based on their online activities. In 2008 the website expanded its service into Europe by launching Spanish, French, and German versions of the site and opening international headquarters in Dublin. The company also debuted a completely revamped user interface in 2008 that gave users increased control over what appeared in their news feeds and allowed them to customize the look of their pages by organizing features into adaptable tabs.

In February 2009 Facebook introduced one of its most used features, the "like" button, which allows users to quickly signal their approval of content posted on the site. That same year the company announced that it was officially making more money through strategic advertising than it was paying out in salaries and development costs. To accommodate the site's 360 million active users, Facebook also began building a massive data center in Prineville, Oregon. In March 2009 Facebook once again redesigned its user interface, incorporating an automatically updating news feed.

Facebook continued to expand its reach into external websites in 2010. That year, Internet marketing researcher comScore reported that half of the top 100 websites in the world had integrated Facebook Connect, which allows users to log on to external sites using their Facebook identity. Facebook also launched a new feature, Facebook Places, that lets users "check in" to Facebook from places they visit, and the user profile page was redesigned to give it a more streamlined look. In September 2011 Facebook changed user profile pages further by incorporating what it called the "timeline," giving users the ability to create a narrative of their lives by highlighting the most important content on their profiles in chronological order.

A WORLDWIDE PHENOMENON

In less than a decade Facebook grew from a dorm room project into one of the most powerful (and valuable) technology companies in the world. Zuckerberg was named *Time*'s 2010 Person of the Year, and renowned filmmaker David Fincher released an Oscar-winning film, *The Social Network* (2010), tracing the rise of Facebook. In a sign of its reputation for innovation and creativity, the company was invited to perform hackathons with organizations ranging from the Ford Motor Company to the U.S Congress in 2011. Facebook acquired the popular photo-sharing application Instagram for $1 billion in April 2012 and made waves among investors when it announced plans to go public by offering shares of the company on the NASDAQ stock market in May 2012. The company's anticipated $100 billion value would rank it among the largest publicly owned companies in the world.

Such success, however, has not come without controversy. Just weeks after the site launched in 2004, two Harvard students, twin brothers Cameron and Tyler Winklevoss, claimed that Zuckerberg had stolen the idea for a Harvard-only social network from a project they had invited him to work on called HarvardConnection (later called ConnectU). They filed a lawsuit against Facebook in 2004 claiming that Zuckerberg had stolen large portions of the code for ConnectU. The two parties later settled out of court. Another of Zuckerberg's Harvard classmates, Aaron Greenspan, has made similar claims, and Internet company Yahoo! has filed copyright infringement suits against Facebook.

Beyond assertions of intellectual property theft, Zuckerberg and Facebook have been subject to a wide range of cultural criticism: some claim that the site promotes isolation and loneliness among users; others contend that it is a kind of Big Brother–like data-mining program aimed at tracking users' every move. It has been argued that Facebook use decreases attention span and destabilizes users' sense of self. Cases of so-called Facebook bullying, in which (typically young) users are harassed by other users, have been reported, with some of the victims driven to suicide. Perhaps the most common complaint is that the site simply wastes users' time, making them feel as if they are socially active when in fact they are simply pressing buttons on their home computers or mobile phones.

Facebook has had an undeniably profound impact on the way its users view themselves, their friends, and the world around them. It has changed the way they communicate, gather, learn, shop, and vote, and with current studies projecting that the site will reach one billion active users by the end of 2012, it is fair to say that Facebook is well on its way to achieving its stated goal of making the world a "more open and connected" place.

Jake Schmitt

SEE ALSO: *Advertising; Ford Motor Company; The Internet; Microsoft; Napster; Online Dating; Online Gaming; Online Shopping; Social Media;* Time.

BIBLIOGRAPHY

Baloun, Karel M. *Inside Facebook: Life, Work and Visions of Greatness.* Victoria, BC: Trafford, 2007.

Cooke, Tanya. *Help! I'm a Facebookaholic: Inside the Crazy World of Social Networking.* London: John Blake, 2011.

Kirkpatrick, David. *The Facebook Effect: The Inside Story of the Company That Is Connecting the World.* New York: Simon & Schuster, 2010.

Mezrich, Ben. *The Accidental Billionaires: The Founding of Facebook, a Tale of Sex, Money, Genius and Betrayal.* New York: Doubleday, 2009.

Rice, Jesse. *The Church of Facebook: How the Hyperconnected Are Redefining Community.* Colorado Springs, CO: David C. Cook, 2009.

Wittkower, D. E. *Facebook and Philosophy: What's on Your Mind?* Chicago: Open Court, 2010.

Facelifts

SEE: *Botox; Plastic Surgery.*

Factor, Max *(1877–1938)*

Best known for the cosmetic line that bears his name, Max Factor also pioneered screen makeup for motion pictures. When films were in their infancy, stage makeup was generally used on film actors, but it did not photograph well. Factor created a makeup more suitable for film lighting. He also popularized the use of human hair in wigs. He won a special Oscar in 1928 for his panchromatic makeup and made what would become his most famous product, Pancake Makeup, when the advent of Technicolor film required another new type of makeup. His line of skin-toned foundations disguised facial imperfections and was soon marketed for home use to mainstream Americans. Still creating "firsts" in makeup technology, Max Factor has remained one of the most popular brands of stage and street makeup into the new millennium.

Jill A. Gregg

SEE ALSO: *Hollywood; Mary Kay Cosmetics.*

BIBLIOGRAPHY

Basten, Fred E. *Max Factor: The Man Who Changed the Faces of the World.* New York: Arcade Publishers, 2008.

Basten, Fred E.; Robert Salvatore; and Paul A. Kaufman. *Max Factor's Hollywood: Glamour, Movies, Makeup*. Los Angeles: General Publishing Group, 1995.

Fadiman, Clifton *(1904–1999)*

Clifton Fadiman was a man of letters whose effectiveness as a broadcast personality helped him spread the gospel of the rewards of book reading to a wide public. A book reviewer for the *New Yorker* and other distinguished periodicals, Fadiman found fame in the late 1930s and most of the 1940s as the host of the radio quiz program *Information, Please!* Taking advantage of his radio popularity, he appeared in magazines as an essayist and critic and between hardcovers as an anthology editor and introduction writer. Through his introductions and prefaces to the world's great books, he became one of the first and most distinguished of that unique breed of twentieth-century scribes: the "popularizer." The advent of television kept Fadiman in the public eye, and he continued to be an unpretentious but fervent advocate for the joys of reading and the pleasures of the civilized life.

Clifton (Paul) Fadiman ("Kip" to his friends) was born May 15, 1904, in Brooklyn, New York. Before he had graduated Phi Beta Kappa from Columbia University in 1925, he had already managed a bookstore; devised the standard translation of Friedrich Nietzsche's *Ecce Homo*; and begun selling articles to national periodicals, including book reviews for the *Nation*. In 1927 Fadiman began a fruitful association with publisher Simon & Schuster when he was hired as a reader and an assistant editor. Within two years he had been promoted to general editor, a position he held until the mid-1930s. While still with Simon & Schuster, Fadiman wrote book reviews for *Harper's Bazaar* and *Stage*; in 1933 he began a ten-year stint as the *New Yorker*'s book editor.

Urbane yet unpretentious, Fadiman claimed that, "I look for clarity above all in what I read." These qualities—plus his penchant for the "atrocious" pun—made him the perfect person to peddle erudition to the masses when, in 1938, he was hired to moderate a distinguished but good-humored panel—Franklin P. Adams, John Kieran, and Oscar Levant—on the NBC radio program *Information, Please!* Aided considerably by Levant's iconoclastic wit, the show, in which listeners competed for sets of the *Encyclopaedia Britannica* by submitting questions with which they hoped to "stump the experts," became both a critical and popular success, running for the next ten years.

During this period Fadiman expanded his activities to include writing introductions for such classics as *War and Peace* and *Moby-Dick*. He left the *New Yorker* to join the editorial board of the Book-of-the-Month Club, but he continued to promote the classics through the writing and editing of various introductions and anthologies and the creation of *The Lifetime Reading Plan*. *Information, Please!* faded in the late 1940s, and the 1950s found Fadiman writing a series of essays in *Holiday* magazine under the title "Party of One." He also had no trouble making the transition from radio to television, where he contributed his witty presence to quiz shows such as *What's in a Word?* and *The Name's the Same*, although probably closer to his heart was the radio show he cohosted concurrently on NBC with Columbia professor Jacques Barzun, *Conversation*.

In his writings, Fadiman came across as learned but genial and far from snobbish. His inclusion of science fiction stories in his anthologies, *Fantasia Mathematica* and *Mathematical Magpie*, probably helped create the atmosphere in which that once-despised genre began acquiring literary respectability. To the general public, Fadiman so personified the world of great books that when one man was asked to name his favorite work of literature, he responded: "Clifton Fadiman's introduction to *War and Peace*."

Preston Neal Jones

SEE ALSO: *Book-of-the-Month Club; The* New Yorker*; Radio.*

BIBLIOGRAPHY

Fadiman, Clifton. *Reading I've Liked*. New York: Simon & Schuster, 1941.

Fadiman, Clifton. *Party of One: The Selected Writings of Clifton Fadiman*. Cleveland, OH: World Publishing, 1955.

Fadiman, Clifton. *Enter, Conversing*. Cleveland, OH: World Publishing, 1962.

Fadiman, Clifton, and John S. Major. *The New Lifetime Reading Plan*. New York: HarperCollins, 1997.

Sterling, Christopher H.; Michael C. Keith; and Museum of Broadcast Communications. *Encyclopedia of Radio*. New York: Fitzroy Dearborn, 2004.

Fail-Safe

Director Sidney Lumet's taut nuclear thriller *Fail-Safe* (1964) is based on the 1962 Eugene Burdick and Harvey Wheeler novel of the same title. *Fail-Safe* depicts the changing face of war in the nuclear age, specifically the possible consequences of the military's ever-increasing reliance on computers. This is where *Fail-Safe* differs from its famous film cousin, *Dr. Strangelove or: How I Learned to Stop Worrying and Love the Bomb*, in which a lone military madman plots an atomic attack against the Soviet Union. In *Fail-Safe*, the nuclear apocalypse is at hand because a malfunctioning machine—not a malfunctioning person—directs a squadron of U.S. long-range bombers to drop their nuclear payloads on Moscow. Through sharp dialogue, the concepts of limited war in the nuclear age, the ability to analyze potential nuclear strikes in mere moments, and the survival of a nation's culture after the bomb are effectively challenged.

In April 2000 director Stephen Frears staged a teleplay of the Burdick and Wheeler novel titled *Fail Safe*, which aired live on CBS. Shot entirely in black and white on two Warner Brothers' soundstages, *Fail Safe* is introduced by legendary news anchor Walter Cronkite and stars such prominent actors as George Clooney, Richard Dreyfuss, Harvey Keitel, and Noah Wyle. *Fail Safe* was the first live teleplay to appear on CBS in nearly forty years. It received mixed reviews from critics, many of whom found the live broadcast to be an unnecessary hindrance to an otherwise well-crafted remake.

Lori C. Walters

SEE ALSO: *The Bomb; Cold War;* Dr. Strangelove or: How I Learned to Stop Worrying and Love the Bomb*; Fonda, Henry; Live Television; Television.*

BIBLIOGRAPHY

Burdick, Eugene, and John Harvey Wheeler. *Fail-Safe*. New York: McGraw-Hill, 1962.

The "New York Times" Television Reviews 2000. Chicago: Fitzroy Dearborn, 2001.

Fairbanks, Douglas Jr. *(1909–2000)*

Although swashbuckling actor Douglas Fairbanks Sr. did not want him to go into the business, Douglas Fairbanks Jr. wound up becoming Hollywood's first second-generation movie star. When Fairbanks Jr. was barely a teenager, the studios sought to cash in on the famous family name by casting him in swashbuckling films. Ultimately, however, he managed to carve his own niche as a debonair actor in supporting and leading roles. Movie audiences enjoyed his work, even though he was often overshadowed by similar actors of his era. When his acting career began to fade, he gracefully shifted his primary focus to producing and writing.

AN INAUSPICIOUS BEGINNING

Born to one of the world's first movie stars, Fairbanks Sr., and his first wife, Beth, Fairbanks Jr. was not initially interested in acting. Eventually, however, he was drawn to it because he hoped it would make him closer to his distant father. Paramount Pictures executive Jesse Lasky, eager to attract the loyal fans of Fairbanks Sr., cast Fairbanks Jr. in *Stephen Steps Out* (1923) when he was only thirteen. The film was a failure, but Fairbanks Jr. continued to try to make a name for himself. He was able to secure a contract with Paramount, although his career did not go anywhere.

At seventeen he costarred in the silent version of *Stella Dallas* (1925), receiving critical acclaim but no notable follow-up jobs. Fairbanks continued to be cast in small parts, but he was forced into work as a title writer to make ends meet. Although he also did some stage work in Los Angeles, his career remained stagnant until he met and married a young starlet, Joan Crawford. The couple became the darlings of the Hollywood gossip columns and fan magazines.

BREAKING THROUGH

The attention he received because of his marriage led to some good parts, usually as villains. Metro-Goldwyn-Mayer (MGM) capitalized on fan interest in the couple by pairing Fairbanks and Crawford in the motion picture *Our Modern Maidens* (1929). However, it wasn't until Fairbanks played strong supporting parts in *Dawn Patrol* (1930) and the hit gangster film *Little Caesar* (1931) that his talent was finally noticed. Although his marriage was ending by this time, his career was progressing.

Warner Brothers gave Fairbanks a contract that allowed the actor more control over his career, but most of the roles that followed were forgettable. He appeared with Katharine Hepburn in *Morning Glory* (1933), a film that produced an Academy Award for her but did little for his career. In 1937 he played a memorable villain in *The Prisoner of Zenda*. He then costarred with Cary Grant in the 1939 hit *Gunga Din*, arguably Fairbanks's most famous performance. That same year he married his second wife, Mary Hartford. World War II was looming, and Fairbanks put his acting career on hold to join the U.S. Navy. He rose to the rank of lieutenant commander and was among the most decorated of the Hollywood stars who served in the armed forces.

A CAREER SHIFT

Fairbanks was knighted by the British Empire following the war. By the late 1940s, however, his career as an actor was in sharp decline. Although Fairbanks appeared in the successful *Sinbad the Sailor* (1947), he had fallen out of the public eye during his time in the service, and his career had suffered. After appearing in *Mister Drake's Duck* in 1951, he virtually retired from the screen, going twenty years before acting in another feature film.

Fairbanks began producing films, mostly for television, and occasionally acted in stage productions. In 1981, when he starred in the supernatural film *Ghost Story* with Fred Astaire, Fairbanks enjoyed somewhat of a career resurgence. He also appeared with some regularity on popular television programs of the 1970s and early 1980s. Interest in his life and career was further revived by two well-received autobiographies, *The Salad Days* (1988) and *A Hell of a War* (1993). His wife, Mary, died in 1988, and he married Vera Shelton in 1991.

Although he may be best remembered as the son of his famous father, Fairbanks proved to be a worthy carrier of the family name. As an actor, a producer, and a writer, he epitomized the elegance and manners of a bygone era in film history.

Jill A. Gregg

SEE ALSO: *Astaire, Fred, and Ginger Rogers; Crawford, Joan; Fairbanks, Douglas, Sr.; Gossip Columns; Hepburn, Katharine; World War II.*

BIBLIOGRAPHY

Connell, Brian. *Knight Errant: A Biography of Douglas Fairbanks, Jr.* New York: Doubleday, 1955.

Fairbanks, Douglas, Jr. *The Salad Days*. New York: Doubleday, 1988.

Fairbanks, Douglas, Jr. *A Hell of a War*. New York: St. Martin's, 1993.

Wise, James E., Jr., and Anne Collier Rehill. *Stars in Blue: Movie Actors in America's Sea Services*. Annapolis, MD: Naval Institute Press, 2007.

Fairbanks, Douglas Sr. *(1883–1939)*

The person who would become famous for his tireless energy, all-American attitude, and action-packed silent movies was born Douglas Ulman in Denver, Colorado, in 1883. In a 1926 article in *Ladies' Home Journal*, poet Vachel Lindsay described Douglas Fairbanks Sr.'s on-screen persona as architecture in motion and sculpture in motion. In the 1910s and 1920s Fairbanks's acrobatic and extroverted performance style seemed to mirror the flickering images and seemingly endless possibilities of the emerging form of film. Known for his insistence on maintaining control over his movies, Fairbanks founded a studio, United Artists, with Mary Pickford, Charlie Chaplin, and D. W. Griffith.

THE ROAD TO FAME AND FORTUNE

After leaving his mother and stepfather behind in Colorado, Fairbanks tried his hand on the New York stage and soon made it to Broadway. In 1907, however, he married Anna Beth Sully and attempted to transform himself into her father's protégé, first working as an executive in the family's soap company and then as a broker on Wall Street. The couple had a son, actor Douglas Fairbanks Jr., in 1909. Following several years of trying to conform to his wife's wishes for him, Fairbanks returned to Broadway, achieving a successful comeback in *He Comes Up Smiling* (1913).

Despite his prejudice against the nascent film industry, Fairbanks signed a contract with Triangle-Fine Arts in 1915 and made his debut in *The Lamb*, playing a wealthy, idle, relatively effeminate fellow who is disenchanted with life on Wall Street but decides to build himself up for the woman he loves. Fairbanks would develop this theme throughout the 1910s, both with director Allan Dwan in films such as *The Half Breed* (1916) and *Manhattan Madness* (1916) and with director John Emerson and screenwriter Anita Loos in *His Picture in the Papers* (1916) and *The Americano* (1916).

His screen stories reinforced the philosophies he espoused in fan magazines and advice manuals (such as *Laugh and Live* in 1917 and *Making Life Worthwhile* in 1918), which followed Theodore Roosevelt's emphasis on clean living and rugged individualism. Fairbanks became a role model for young boys everywhere, evangelically touting, "To be successful you must be happy . . . to be happy you must be enthusiastic; to be enthusiastic you must keep mind and body active." His intense love of activity was probably easier to read about in articles or watch on-screen than to confront personally. Foreign dignitaries and other guests were obligated to accompany the star to his private gymnasium on the studio lot and endure "basic training" that left many of them crawling to the steam room.

Douglas Fairbanks Sr. and Jr. *Douglas Fairbanks Sr., right, poses with his son and fellow actor Douglas Fairbanks Jr. in the 1930s.* MPI/GETTY IMAGES.

TAKING CONTROL

In 1917 Fairbanks signed on as his own producer with Artcraft films, a subsidiary of Famous Players-Lasky. There, he continued his tradition of acrobatic stunts and masculine transformation in films such as *Wild and Woolly* (1917), *Reaching for the Moon* (1917), and *A Modern Musketeer* (1918). He gained full control of his career when he cofounded United Artists in 1919. Fairbanks went on to star in *The Mollycoddle* (1920) and *The Nut* (1921), among other films, while making the transition to the swashbuckler genre, for which he became famous. These costume dramas, such as *The Mark of Zorro* (1920), *The Three Musketeers* (1921), and *The Thief of Bagdad* (1924), offered him a formula by which he could continue his traditions of physically demanding stunts and chases but tailor them to his maturing persona.

Fairbanks was lauded for being an auteur, one of Hollywood's first actors to exercise control over the development and production of his films. He participated in the scripting of many of his early films under the pseudonym Elton Thomas. By the mid-1920s Fairbanks was demonstrating a keen understanding of the importance of publicity. He went so far as to finance a New York City screening of *The Thief of Bagdad*, for which he reportedly had the female ushers dress in harem costumes, serve Arabian coffee in the lobby, and spray perfume inside the auditorium.

Fairbanks married "America's Sweetheart," Pickford, in 1920, and they reigned over Hollywood from their palatial Pickfair estate for more than a decade. His interest in overseas travel and international celebrity associations meant that the couple made a number of renowned world tours throughout the 1920s. Later, Pickford preferred to remain in California, and her husband embarked on these trips with his comrades and often stayed in Europe for months, or even years, at a time.

A SCANDALOUS LIAISON

After the silent-film era passed, Fairbanks was relatively successful in talkies. He and Pickford made their sound debuts together in *The Taming of the Shrew* in 1929. As for his work behind the scenes, he was named president of the Academy of Motion Pictures, Arts, and Sciences in 1927. However, because of his international interests, he was viewed as something of an expatriate by 1930. Fairbanks fell out of public favor to a greater extent in 1933, when he was named correspondent with British noblewoman Lady Sylvia Ashley in a divorce suit filed by Lord Ashley. An ex-chorus girl, Lady Ashley had been married three times by the time she was romantically linked to Fairbanks. The crumbling marriage between Fairbanks and Pickford played out turbulently in America's press, with tabloid newspapers intercepting their private telegrams and publishing them as headlines. Pickford and Fairbanks divorced in 1936, after which he promptly married Lady Ashley. Though many of Fairbanks's friends said he was content in his third marriage, it also was reported that the star spent many afternoons sitting by the pool at Pickfair repeatedly mumbling his apologies to Pickford.

Once middle age required him to curtail his physically demanding on-screen antics, Fairbanks starred in two travelogue-inspired films, *Around the World with Douglas Fairbanks* (1931) and *Mr. Robinson Crusoe* (1932). His final film, *The Private Life of Don Juan* (1934), was directed by Alexander Korda and parodies the romantic image of Don Juan as he comes to terms with his age and receding popularity. The release of this commentary on the fleeting nature of fame coincided with Fairbanks's own downward spiral.

Fairbanks died of a heart attack in 1939 at the age of fifty-six. The consensus at the time was that Fairbanks had pushed his body so hard for so many years that his muscles literally turned in on him and caused his organs to degenerate.

Christina Lane

SEE ALSO: *Broadway; Celebrity Couples; Chaplin, Charlie; Divorce; Fairbanks, Douglas, Jr.; Griffith, D. W.; Movie Stars; Pickford, Mary; Silent Movies; United Artists.*

BIBLIOGRAPHY

Carey, Gary. *Doug and Mary: A Biography of Douglas Fairbanks and Mary Pickford.* New York: E. P. Dutton, 1977.

Cooke, Alistair. *Douglas Fairbanks: The Making of a Screen Character.* New York: Museum of Modern Art, 1940.

Dimare, Philip C. *Movies in American History: An Encyclopedia.* Santa Barbara, CA: ABC-CLIO, 2011.

Fairbanks, Douglas, Jr. *The Salad Days.* New York: Doubleday, 1988.

Hancock, Ralph, and Letitia Fairbanks. *Douglas Fairbanks: The Fourth Musketeer.* London: Peter Davies, 1953.

Herndon, Booten. *Mary Pickford and Douglas Fairbanks: The Most Popular Couple the World Has Ever Known.* New York: W. W. Norton, 1977.

Lindsay, Vachel. "The Great Douglas Fairbanks." *Ladies' Home Journal,* August 1926, 12, 114.

Schickel, Richard. *His Picture in the Papers: A Speculation on Celebrity in America Based on the Life of Douglas Fairbanks, Sr.* New York: Charterhouse, 1974.

Tibbets, John C., and James M. Welsh. *His Majesty the American: The Cinema of Douglas Fairbanks, Sr.*. New York: A. S. Barnes, 1977.

Fake Memoirs

Fakes and forgeries have a long literary history—but few have received more notoriety than *A Million Little Pieces* (2003), an addiction "memoir" by James Frey (1969–). The book became a runaway best seller thanks to the recommendation of talk-show host Oprah Winfrey (1954–), who later confronted Frey on the air after the book was revealed to be mostly fictitious. The "Holocaust romance" *Angel at the Fence* also drew raves from Winfrey for writer Herman Rosenblat (1929–). The film rights sold for millions before *Angel at the Fence* was revealed as a fake and its planned 2009 publication was cancelled.

In an age of heightened media scrutiny, it is increasingly difficult to maintain a hoax for long. Yet the potential payoff for sensational "true" stories is enough for writers to keep trying. These books are aggressively promoted by publishers, leading to huge sales and lucrative deals for future books. Even after their deceptions are discovered, some authors continue to profit—from their notoriety. Frey, for example, went on to write several best-selling novels.

Fake memoirs often tell moving stories that capitalize on problems such as addiction, abuse, and war by taking common situations to an extreme. These stories make amazing events seem believable because they "really" happened, and they often depict triumph over unimaginable adversity. By dramatizing serious social issues, fake memoirs also allow readers to believe they are learning about realities that are very different from their own or to feel that their problems are simpler by comparison.

In many cases, fake memoirs are based on a kernel of truth. Frey, for example, was actually an addict and did have some of the realizations recorded in his book, but he exaggerated his experiences so much that "memoir" became a novel. Rosenblat was a Holocaust survivor, but his actual experience was not very unusual, so he added an amazing (and completely impossible) love story.

In another type of fake memoir, the narrator is entirely invented. Timothy Patrick Barrus (1950–) wrote *The Blood Runs Like a River through My Dreams* (2000) and two other books under the pen name Nasdijj, claiming to be a contemporary Native American who overcame a tragically difficult life. The books drew critical praise, but in reality, Barrus had no connection with Native American culture, and the entire story of Nasdijj's life seems to have been invented.

A third kind of fake memoir takes advantage of a famous name. The best-known example is *The Autobiography of Howard Hughes* (1972), a complete fabrication penned by Clifford Irving (1930–). An even more dramatic hoax was carried out by Michael Pelligrino (1966–), who sold a fake memoir of mob life (*The Honored Society*, 2001) by pretending to be a grandson of Mafia boss Carlo Gambino (1902–1976); Pelligrino even used the pen name "Michael Gambino" to perpetuate the hoax.

Even if they are not literally true, fake memoirs very often reflect the realities of human nature. And as long as readers want to read exciting memoirs, and publishers are eager to sell books, it seems likely that fakes will continue to be published.

Cynthia Giles

SEE ALSO: *Best Sellers; Oprah's Book Club; Winfrey, Oprah; World War II.*

BIBLIOGRAPHY

Rothe, Anne. *Popular Trauma Culture: Selling the Pain of Others in the Mass Media.* New Brunswick, NJ: Rutgers University Press, 2011.

Ruthven, Kenneth K. *Faking Literature.* Cambridge, UK: Cambridge University Press, 2001.

Fallout Shelters

Part of American culture since 1949, fallout shelters were developed due to fear of nuclear attack. Their subsequent waxing and waning popularity was directly related to U.S.–Soviet relations. A fallout shelter, sometimes known as a bomb shelter, is a structure designed to enable those inside it to survive a nuclear blast and its likely aftermath: fire, radiation, and societal disruption.

Although some large shelters were built by the U.S. government during the Cold War, most were smaller, designed to protect individual families. A prototypical fallout shelter was located in a family's backyard and was made of concrete and steel. Shelters were often sunk in the earth for added protection, although those who could not afford such a construction project sometimes set aside a corner of their basement or dug a makeshift shelter under the crawlspace of a house. A shelter would usually be stocked with canned food, bottled water, medical supplies, a radio, a Geiger counter, and a chemical toilet, among other necessities.

THE TRUMAN ADMINISTRATION

The initial interest in fallout shelters within the United States can be traced to 1949, the year that President Harry Truman informed the nation that the Soviets had exploded an atomic bomb. This ended the American monopoly on nuclear weapons and introduced the world to the possibility of nuclear war between the two superpowers. Aside from the attack on Pearl Harbor, the United States had never, in all its wars, suffered such an attack from the air, but the nuclear age—with its long-range bombers and intercontinental ballistic missiles—made that threat very real.

Truman responded to the heightened public anxiety by creating the Federal Civil Defense Administration in 1951. Although scientists disagreed as to the effectiveness of shelters in the event of a nuclear war, Truman and his advisers knew public belief that shelters worked would be a boon to morale in an otherwise nervous age. In fact, Truman was walking a tightrope in dealing with American public opinion about the Soviet menace. On the one hand, he was convinced that massive defense spending was essential if the United States was to stop communist expansion throughout Europe. But postwar America was tired of high taxes and huge military budgets and would only support these if the danger to the nation's security was both obvious and grave. On the other hand, Truman did not want fear of nuclear war to lead the public to outbreaks of panic, pacifism, or "better red than dead" fatalism. Thus, fallout shelters were portrayed as realistic protection if worst should come to worst.

THE EISENHOWER ADMINISTRATION

After President Truman left office in 1953, Americans' interest in shelters blew hot or cold in keeping with the temperature changes of the Cold War. There was relatively little interest in shelters during much of the Eisenhower administration until 1957—the year that saw both the launch of the first orbiting satellite (the Soviet *Sputnik*) and the release of the Gaither Report in the United States. The latter was the work of a blue-ribbon panel selected by Eisenhower to assess the relative nuclear capability and civil defense preparedness of the United States and the Soviet Union. The report concluded that the Soviets would soon surpass America in all categories of nuclear weaponry and that civil defense preparations in the USSR were already far ahead of American efforts. The supposedly secret document, which was leaked to the press a week after being presented to President Eisenhower, led to an upsurge in public concern about fallout shelters, even though Eisenhower himself believed that true national security lay in U.S. superiority in offensive nuclear weapons.

THE KENNEDY ADMINISTRATION AND BEYOND

The heyday of the fallout shelter occurred during the administration of John F. Kennedy, which saw a rise in international tension. Kennedy advocated for shelters as part of the American response. During the Berlin crisis of 1961, precipitated by Soviet Premier Nikita Khrushchev's aggressive moves toward West Berlin, Kennedy gave a nationally televised speech explaining the gravity of the situation. He also endorsed the construction of fallout shelters, saying, "In the event of an attack, the lives of those families which are not hit in a nuclear blast and fire can still be saved if they can be warned to take shelter and if that shelter is available." The world came closer to nuclear war than ever before during the Cuban missile crisis of 1962, providing further inducement to build shelters.

The popular culture of the late 1950s and early 1960s also contributed to public concern about nuclear war and thus increased interest in fallout shelters. The best-selling novel *Fail-Safe* (1962), which was also made into a popular film, features a technical glitch that results in the nuclear destruction of both Moscow and New York. Other novels portrayed the aftermath of a nuclear exchange. Some, such as Pat Frank's *Alas, Babylon* (1959), were guardedly optimistic. Others, such as Nevil Shute's *On the Beach* (1957) and Walter Miller's *A Canticle for Leibowitz* (1959), presented bleak and pessimistic visions.

Civil defense programs, sponsored by both federal and state governments, were designed to increase both Americans' optimism and their chances for survival in the event of nuclear attack. In addition to encouraging the building of shelters, the Federal Office of Civil and Defense Mobilization advised communities to conduct air-raid drills. The importance of such drills was emphasized by government-produced instructional films that were shown on television and in schools. Some of these films manifest a degree of naive optimism about nuclear war that today seems absurd, such as a short animated film in which a character named "Bert the Turtle" (a talking amphibian in a civil defense helmet) tells children that a nuclear blast can be survived by those who learn to "Duck and Cover" (crouch down and cover one's face and head).

Although concern about "The Bomb" was gradually replaced in American consciousness by the Vietnam War, interest in fallout shelters was revived in the 1980s. Consistent with its vigorously anticommunist foreign policy, the Reagan administration devoted considerable rhetoric and resources to civil defense. This effort included the development of evacuation plans for people living near probable nuclear targets as well as a new shelter program designed to protect the rest of the population. However, the program languished during Reagan's second term as U.S. relations with the Soviet Union dramatically improved.

In the 1990s and beyond, the limited interest in fallout shelters (as evidenced by the dozen or so websites devoted to them) was apparently restricted to hard-core "survivalists," who wished to be prepared for anything, even the end of the world.

Justin Gustainis

SEE ALSO: *The Bomb; Cold War; Communism;* Fail-Safe*; Reagan, Ronald;* Sputnik*; Vietnam.*

BIBLIOGRAPHY

Johnson, Stephen P. *Silent Steel: The Mysterious Death of the Nuclear Attack Sub USS* Scorpion. Hoboken, NJ: John Wiley, 2006.

Scheer, Robert. *With Enough Shovels: Reagan, Bush and Nuclear War.* New York: Random House, 1982.

Weart, Spencer R. *Nuclear Fear: A History of Images.* Cambridge, MA: Harvard University Press, 1988.

Winkler, Allan M. *Life under a Cloud: American Anxiety about the Atom.* New York: Oxford University Press, 1993.

Fame

SEE: *Celebrity.*

Family Circle

Family Circle is one of the most widely circulated magazines in the United States. Like its sister magazines—*Ladies' Home Journal, Good Housekeeping, Better Homes and Gardens,* and *Woman's Day*—*Family Circle* has not only disseminated and popularized expert knowledge about children, but it has also been a major contributor to the nation's parent-education curriculum and an exporter of American culture. It has been a medium through which information and ideas about children, adolescents, parenting, and the family have been transmitted to parents—especially, though not exclusively, to mothers. Since its beginning, *Family Circle* has offered parents advice about children's development and behavior. Its first issue (September 1932) included both Dr. Julius D. Smith's "Judging the Health of Your Baby" and Dr. Arnold Gesell's assessment of what parents could expect from a child at six months.

SUPERMARKET CIRCULATION

After World War II, the economy was booming, and *Family Circle* served as a guide and manual for families at the lower end of the economic scale who were trying to make comfortable homes for themselves and their children. Its readers proved to be good users of price-off coupons. Through most of its history, the magazine has been distributed in a way that has made it accessible to a wide segment of the population. When *Family Circle* first appeared, it was not available by subscription but rather was confined to chain grocery stores—it was nearly impossible to miss at the checkout counter.

In large measure *Family Circle*, like *Woman's Day*, has been overlooked by scholars and has not received the attention it deserves, perhaps because the publication was available for so many years only in grocery stores. Yet the circulations of both magazines have been greater than those of virtually all other similar offerings. While each has been described as belonging to the "seven sisters"—*Ladies' Home Journal, McCall's, Good Housekeeping, Better Homes and Gardens* (at times not included in this grouping), and *Cosmopolitan*—it may be more appropriate to view them as stepsisters. Both *Family Circle* and *Woman's Day* may justly be described as store-distributed magazines, but neither is insignificant. There is no doubt that the practice of distributing magazines at the supermarket checkout stand has been successful. In the 1930s and 1940s, that spot was the exclusive domain of *Family Circle* and *Woman's Day*. Other magazines were added in the 1950s, including *TV Guide* and *Reader's Digest*. By the early 1950s, according to *Business Week*, *Family Circle* and *Woman's* Day were "hard on the heels of the big women's service magazines." Subsequently, other magazines saw the desirability of being placed near checkout stands.

MAKING ITS MARK

Family Circle's appearance in September 1932 was, as Roland E. Wolseley reports in *The Changing Magazine*, the beginning of "the big boom in store-distributed magazines." Of the many founded since the 1930s—perhaps as many as 100—*Family Circle*, like *Woman's Day*, has survived and prospered. In *Magazines in the Twentieth Century*, Theodore Peterson notes that "when the old *Life* was undergoing one of its periodic readjustments, its managing editor, Harry Evans, joined with Charles Merrill, a financier with an interest in grocery chains, to start a magazine that would be distributed free but that would carry advertising." At the time, Merrill was a member of Merrill, Lynch, Pierce, Fenner, & Smith, which controlled Safeway

Family Circle *Magazine*. Family Circle, *which began publication in 1932 with a focus on homemaking and child rearing, remains as one of the most widely circulated magazines.* DANIEL ACKER/ BLOOMBERG VIA GETTY IMAGES.

stores. Evans reasoned that since radio programs were broadcast to listeners without charge, it should be possible to secure advertisers for a magazine for which the reader did not pay. His hope that *Family Circle* would reach a circulation of three million was quickly realized. By the end of 1933, its circulation was nearly a million (964,690); it was slightly over a million (1,068,106) a few weeks later, on February 9, 1934.

Family Circle's initial circulation of 350,000 was distributed through Piggly Wiggly, Sanitary, and Reeves grocery stores in Richmond, Virginia; Baltimore, Maryland; and New York City. The first issue of the twenty-four-page gravure-printed tabloid weekly contained recipes and items on beauty, fashion, food, humor, movies, and radio and was mostly written by Evans. It survived the years of the Great Depression and was clearly prospering by the 1940s. *Family Circle* lost its giveaway status on September 3, 1946; became a monthly; and sold for five cents. It then assumed its present format and began its use of color.

In the postwar era, *Family Circle* grew with the baby boom. When the Kroger stores joined the other chains in selling it in 1949, its distribution was national. By 1952 the magazine was available in 8,500 grocery stores and was able to guarantee its advertisers a circulation of 3.5 million. In 1958, when it took over *Everywoman's*, it announced a circulation rate base of five million and was then able to claim that *Everywoman's Family Circle* was available in nearly 12,000 chain stores (almost all of which were self-service establishments) in more than 1,800 counties, where 93 percent of all retail sales in the United States occurred. By the end of the 1950s, the publication's circulation was 5.1 million; by the end of the 1970s, it had reached more than eight million. *Family Circle* continued only to grow, and at the end of the 1980s, its audience was more than twenty-one million. It then claimed it was the "world's largest women's magazine."

THE POSTWAR YEARS

Family Circle began to assume its present form when the United States was in the midst of its new consumer culture, rearing the children who would express themselves as young adults in the late 1960s and early 1970s. It was a time when the American household was, as historian William E. Leuchtenburg observes in *A Troubled Feast: American Society Since 1945*, adopting "a style of consumption that was more sophisticated, more worldly [and] more diversified" than ever before. As Landon Y. Jones records in *Great Expectations: America and the Baby Boom Generation*, the United States became a "vast maternity ward" during this era. By the end of the 1950s, forty million new babies had arrived, and the number of children between ages five and thirteen was increasing by a million per year. *Family Circle* provided parents with information on how to feed, bathe, educate, and entertain these children and how to raise them without spoiling them.

The ways in which Americans lived changed significantly between the end of World War II and the beginning of the 1960s. Those who gave birth to the baby boomers were mostly born in the 1920s and experienced the Great Depression and World War II. These baby boomers had no such experiences of hardship, and many were brought up in what seemed destined to become an increasingly affluent society. A new culture was being made. Parents who were reared in urban neighborhoods or small towns were now living in the suburbs, and *Family Circle* served as an inexpensive and handy directory and manual for families that were adjusting to and embracing a new and more affluent way of life. According to *Business Week*, magazines such as *Family Circle* told "the housewife how to cook economically, how to bring up her children, how to clothe them and herself, how to take care of her house. To the budget-minded, this makes good sense." It was a "good formula today for new housewives, many of them young, who want[ed] help at their new job."

THE CELEBRITY TOUCH

Family Circle used celebrities as either authors or on its covers to increase its appeal and to satisfy the interests of readers. Covers of early issues featured Bing Crosby, Joan Crawford, Douglas Fairbanks Jr., Eleanor Roosevelt, and Amelia Earhart. During the presidency of Franklin D. Roosevelt, Eleanor Roosevelt contributed articles to *Family Circle*, as well as to *Woman's Day*. In the April 1955 issue, Quentin Reynolds wrote about the problems of adolescence in an article called "Help over the Teen-Age Hurdle." The next month, Art Linkletter addressed humor in "Why People Are Funny," and in September of that year, Herman Hickman tackled football in "Football Is a Ladies' Game." When *Everywoman's* told its readers in 1958 that the next issue would be *Everywoman's Family Circle*, it also promised that in the first issue of the merged magazines Ivy Baker Priest, treasurer of the United States, would switch to her role as a "successful mother" and ask, "Are we neglecting our children enough?"

The use of celebrities has endured, and on many occasions it has amounted to free advertising for *Family Circle*. The *New York Times* reported in February 1976 that Susan Ford, daughter of President Gerald Ford, was in Palm Beach, Florida, "working as a model . . . for *Family Circle* magazine." It also reported in 1981 that Nancy Reagan told *Family Circle* that she "had just gotten out of the tub" and Ronald Reagan was in the shower when "President Jimmy Carter went on national television to concede the election."

CONTENT AND CULTURE

Charges that *Family Circle*'s content has traditionally been about economical cooking and styling hair—that it is, in short, a magazine about women's issues—do not ring true. In *Magazines in the United States* (1956), James Playsted Wood writes that *Family Circle* was "a full magazine, carrying romantic fiction with housewife appeal, feature articles on such subjects of family interest as sports, law, divorce, teen-age problems, gardening, and travel." Its largest department was "All around the House," which included material on food and its preparation, household equipment, decoration, home building, and home furnishings. Another department, "Your Children and You," included articles on child care, parent-child relationships, and organizing successful parties for children. A typical issue contained sections by contributors called "The Personal Touch," notices of new movies under "The Reel Dope," beauty and health departments, and a buying guide that told where and how the products mentioned in the magazine could be acquired. As was announced in the premiere issue, *Family Circle* was designed to have something for all members of the family. While a large portion of its editorial content has been devoted to food, needlework, and other activities identified with women, it has not ignored fathers and men's pursuits.

Family Circle also has included material directed to children and teenagers. For example, when the first monthly issue appeared in September 1946, it included "Teen Scene" by Betsy Bourne, a feature addressed not to parents but to teenagers themselves. It was similar to the feature *Woman's Day* introduced in 1939, Susan Bennett Holmes's "School Bus." Bourne, however, addressed only a portion of the nation's teenagers—there was no mention or acknowledgment of race. This may be partially explained by the period during which she worked, one that ended with the *Brown v. Board of Education* decision in 1954. Furthermore, she tacitly accepted that the families of the teenagers she wrote about were all basically alike. There certainly was no significant acknowledgment of the great variety of familial forms and styles that prevailed throughout the nation. The topic that received most attention—social skills—told teenagers, especially girls, how to manipulate and manage their parents and peers and how to get their own way. Girls were given instructions on how to catch boys and what to give and not to give boys.

Teenage girls who followed Bourne's advice were being prepared to be good middle-class wives who could understand their husbands; be considerate; and know how to dress and groom themselves, give parties, and participate in volunteer work. However, while they were being told how to manage, manipulate, and get their own way, they were not being instructed on how to become independent or to pursue their own careers. Boys, meanwhile, were given instructions on how to please girls, lessons that would someday translate to their marriages.

INTERNATIONAL APPEAL

Family Circle has always served as a successful exporter of American culture. In 1965 its Canadian circulation was 350,000. A British edition appeared late in 1964, and by early 1966 it was the most successful monthly for housewives in Britain. Its initial circulation was 700,000 and was distributed through 9,000 markets, but those numbers increased to 850,000 and 13,000 stores by the beginning of 1966. On March 24, 1966, 5,000 self-service stores in Germany began distributing a German edition, *Ich und meine familie*, with a circulation of 500,000 guaranteed through 1967. Most of its editorial content was provided by the Germans, but a significant portion of the material on health and infant care came directly from *Family Circle*. An Australian edition appeared in May 1973. *Family Circle* and Vanchen Associated of Hong Kong entered into a licensing agreement in 1984 to make it available in Hong Kong and Taiwan. The first issue was written in Chinese, but the recipe headings were in English.

By 2006 *Family Circle* was seventy-four years old, and young women had begun associating it with their grandmothers' era. The average age of readers had reached fifty-one. When Meredith Corporation bought the magazine from G + J USA Publishing that same year, the publisher refreshed its look and narrowed its target audience to mothers of teens and tweens. Under the guidance of editor-in-chief Linda Fears, advertising rose by 6.5 percent as retailers such as Hewlett-Packard, Home Depot, and Sears came into the fold. Color-coded tabs were added to page margins to make it easier to find specific material, and the lengths of stories were shortened. Fears also added sections that taught readers how to cook or purchase large-ticket items. By 2012 circulation had risen to 3.8 million, a sign that this venerable magazine had managed to maintain its relevance in the twenty-first century.

Erwin V. Johanningmeier

SEE ALSO: *Advertising; Baby Boomers;* Better Homes and Gardens*; Bok, Edward; Consumerism;* Cosmopolitan*;* Good Housekeeping*;* McCall's Magazine*; Teenagers;* Woman's Day.

BIBLIOGRAPHY

"Food-Store Magazines Hit the Big Time." *Business Week*, February 9, 1952.

Jones, Landon Y. *Great Expectations: America and the Baby Boom Generation.* New York: Ballantine Books, 1981.

Leuchtenburg, William E. *A Troubled Feast: American Society since 1945.* Boston, Little, Brown, 1979.

Moses, Lucia. "A Family Affair." *Media Week*, November 13, 2006.

Peterson, Theodore. *Magazines in the Twentieth Century.* Urbana: University of Illinois Press, 1964.

Sumner, David E. *The Magazine Century: America's Magazines since 1900.* New York: Peter Lang, 2010.

Taft, William H. *American Magazines for the 1980s.* New York: Hasting House Publishers, 1982.

Wolseley, Roland E. *The Changing Magazine.* New York: Hasting House Publishers, 1973.

Wood, James Playsted. *Magazines in the United States.* New York: Ronald Press, 1956.

The Family Circus

Bil Keane's daily single-frame comic strip began chronicling the mild misadventures of a white, middle-class suburban family on February 19, 1960, and is currently distributed to more than 1,500 newspapers, making it the most popular panel in the world. Comics historian Ron Goulart has called *The Family Circus* "one of the gentlest and most heartwarming panels in comics history." The strip's wryly humorous perspective has made Keane's creation among the clearest, most significant examples of the deep-seated American belief in the nuclear family as the moral center of domestic life. If a circus can accurately be described as a form of entertainment that displays human beings in control of both wild beasts and their own fears, then the ring surrounding each panel of Keane's strip is apt indeed, for *The Family Circus* takes everything that might be threatening or frightening about children or parenting and tames it with the whip crack of a grin and the safety net of a smile.

Keane reported that the idea for a comic strip poking fun at the foibles of family life occurred to him as early as 1952 while he was still involved in producing *Channel Chuckles*, a daily comic that encouraged readers to laugh at the new medium of television as well as at their own compulsive interest in it. When *The Family Circus* debuted in 1960 (as *The Family Circle*), the Keane family's ink-drawn counterparts consisted of a Daddy in horn-rimmed glasses, a pert and neatly dressed Mommy, and three children—seven-year-old Billy, five-year-old ponytailed Dolly, and three-year-old Jeffy. Another baby arrived two years later, and PJ has since been permanently fixed at a toddling eighteen months. Barfy the Dog and Kittycat are the family pets, and all are occasionally visited by a stereotypical crew of in-laws, neighbors, and school chums—with the principal focus remaining exclusively on the central family of parents and children.

The perpetual preadolescence of the brood enabled Keane to ignore the more disturbing issues of parenting that arise with puberty, and a typical *Family Circus* panel has always been a simple illustration of a child's malapropism, mild misunderstanding of the adult world, or parental eye-rolling. Any variation from this formula has usually been confined to the more experimental (and larger) format offered by the Sunday panel, and here Keane made regular, innovative use of an overhead perspective tracing one child's path through the neighborhood and of a version of the strip "as drawn by" little Billy—usually as a Father's Day "present" to the hardworking Bil.

Keane helped define the unique tenor of his strip by noting that "there's a general tendency among people who want to be funny to exaggerate. I do just the opposite. I tone down every idea I get." While the resulting moderation can easily lull a reader into taking the strip for granted, the comic industry and the American public have always been generous in their persistent recognition of Keane's consistently popular, understated art. The National Cartoonists Society (NCS) awarded Keane its highest honor, the Reuben, as Outstanding Cartoonist of the Year (1982). Keane also hosted the Reuben Award Show for NCS for many years; in 2000 the group turned the tables on him with a good-natured roasting. *The Family Circus* characters themselves have appeared in three television specials; more than forty book collections; and countless calendars, figurines, advertisements, greeting cards, and Christmas ornaments.

While an occasional reference to contemporary matters has helped to keep the panel meaningful to its wide audience (for instance, a caption of Dolly advising Jeffy that "conscience is e-mail your head gets from Heaven"), the strip has continued to focus on the timeless center "ring" of the family—the mild pleasures, sighing frustrations, and deep love that makes the "circus" a place we want to visit whenever it comes to town or is delivered to our doorstep.

Bil Keane died on November 8, 2011, at the age of eighty-nine. Since 1981 he had been sketching out the strip before giving it to his youngest son, Jeff, to finish and prepare for publication. Jeff announced that he would take over *The Family Circus* so that it could continue to entertain its legions of fans.

Kevin Lause

SEE ALSO: *Advertising; Christmas; Circus; Comic Books; Comics; E-mail; Father's Day; Greeting Cards; Pets; Suburbia; Television.*

BIBLIOGRAPHY

Goulart, Ron, ed. *The Encyclopedia of American Comics from 1897 to the Present.* New York: Facts On File, 1990.

Goulart, Ron. *The Funnies: 100 Years of American Comic Strips.* Holbrook, MA: Adams Media, 1995.

Herei, Dennis. "Bil Keane, Creator of *The Family Circus* Dies at 89." *New York Times*, November 9, 2011.

Horn, Maurice, ed. *100 Years of American Newspaper Comics.* New York: Random House, 1996.

Family Guy

Often dismissed as a *Simpsons* and *South Park* retread when it first aired in early 1999, Seth MacFarlane's *Family Guy* has become a popular and critically acclaimed animated television show. The program is centered on the Griffins, a typical sitcom-style family complete with an oafish, beer-guzzling father (Peter), his doting and outspoken wife (Lois), their dimwitted son (Chris), outcast daughter (Meg), devious toddler bent on world domination (Stewie), and a dog (Brian) that also happens to be a quasi-intellectual novelist. It features a simple, unadorned animation style and emphasizes jokes over stories, often using abrupt cutaways and flashbacks for the sake of gags unrelated to the plot. *Family Guy* often builds its humor around obscure pop culture references and the characters' awareness that they exist in a fictional animated world, earning it frequent designations as a postmodern animated series.

MacFarlane worked as a writer and an animator for Hanna-Barbera in the early 1990s, during which time he developed story ideas for a blissfully ignorant character named Larry and his talking dog, Steve, who had been the subject of his art school thesis, an animated short called *The Life of Larry.* In 1996 the Cartoon Network aired a nine-minute cartoon by MacFarlane titled *Larry & Steve,* which caught the attention of talent scouts at Fox, who offered MacFarlane the opportunity to produce a fifteen-minute pilot episode based on *Larry & Steve.* He drew the pilot in his kitchen in six months. Fox ordered thirteen episodes, and a remake of the pilot was aired on January 31, 1999, immediately after Super Bowl XXXIII.

Some viewers decried *Family Guy*'s decidedly politically incorrect humor (the toy factory that Peter works for produces an action figure called "G.I. Jew") and unwholesome family image (Peter is falling-down drunk in the first five minutes of the episode and is subsequently fired from his job for being too hung over to work), but the show was praised for its rapid-fire humor and fragmented story lines in comparison to the more meticulous humor and plots found in shows such as *The Simpsons* or *King of the Hill.*

Fox struggled to find a permanent time slot for *Family Guy*, moving it from Sunday nights to Thursday nights and finally to Tuesday nights during the second season. Despite winning Emmy Awards in 2000 and 2002, the show was unable to secure a regular audience and was briefly canceled by Fox before the network decided to bring it back for what was to be a third and final season. In 2003 Cartoon Network bought the rights to air reruns of all three seasons during its late-night programming block, Adult Swim, and it was there that *Family Guy* finally found its core audience, garnering an average of 1.9 million viewers each night. The DVD collections of seasons one and two sold more than two million copies, and soon Fox offered MacFarlane a contract for thirty-five new episodes, the first of which premiered on May 1, 2005.

The show has followed a similar arrangement ever since, with new episodes airing on Fox and (often uncensored) reruns airing on Adult Swim several weeks later. As it began its tenth season in 2011, *Family Guy* had been nominated for thirteen Emmy Awards—including one for Outstanding Comedy Series, the first such nomination for an animated series since *The Flintstones*—and had won five. Its success has spawned video games, live appearances by cast members, a series of books and action figures, and a spin-off titled *The Cleveland Show*, which follows the life of the Griffins' former neighbor Cleveland Brown. In 2011 MacFarlane announced plans for a *Family Guy* feature film.

Jake Schmitt

SEE ALSO: *Animated Films; Cable TV; Emmy Awards; Hanna-Barbera; Political Correctness;* The Simpsons; *Sitcom;* South Park; *Super Bowl; Television.*

BIBLIOGRAPHY

Booker, M. Keith. *Drawn to Television: Prime-Time Animation from "The Flintstones" to "Family Guy."* Westport, CT: Praeger, 2006.

Callaghan, Steve, and Seth MacFarlane. *"Family Guy": The Official Episode Guide, Seasons 1–3.* New York: HarperCollins, 2005.

Wisnewski, Jeremy. *"Family Guy" and Philosophy: A Cure for the Petarded.* Malden, MA: Blackwell, 2007.

Family Matters

Family Matters debuted in 1989 and aired on prime-time television for a total of nine years. Created by William Bickley and Michael Warren, the sitcom featured a multigenerational, working-class black family living under the same roof. Originally a spin-off from *Perfect Strangers* (1986–1993), in which actress JoMarie Payton-France played an elevator operator, the series placed her character of Harriette Winslow in her own home with her husband, a Chicago police officer (Reginald VelJohnson), and three children (Kellie Shanygne Williams, Darius McCrary, and Jaimee Foxworth). Other family members were Carl's mother, Estelle (played by Rosetta LeNoire), and an adult sister (Telma Hopkins).

Jaleel White as Steve Urkel. *Jaleel White played the nerdy Steve Urkel in the 1990s sitcom* Family Matters. **FOTOS INTERNATIONAL/ARCHIVE PHOTOS/GETTY IMAGES.**

Much as Henry Winkler's character Fonzie unexpectedly stole the *Happy Days* thunder from his costars in the 1970s, *Family Matters* also witnessed the breakout performance of an actor named Jaleel White during its first season. Written into the script as the world's worst blind date—arranged for Laura by her father—twelve-year-old Urkel was a neighborhood goofball who fell instantly in love with the Winslows' daughter.

For his audition, White borrowed a pair of oversized work glasses from his dentist father, hiked his pants up inches off the floor, and proceeded to wheeze and snort his way into a character who would soon become television's most famous nerd. Urkel was an instant hit. In fact, White's performance was so stellar that producers quickly snatched him up as a regular cast member. Bickley claimed that he knew Urkel would be big after overhearing some teenagers imitating him in a shopping mall. As one reviewer put it, kids took to the character like quarters to arcade games. Before long there were Urkel T-shirts, jigsaw puzzles, and even a talking doll that recited favorite Urkel phrases such as "No sweat, my pet."

In the midst of an otherwise unremarkable series, it was Urkel who drew both the bulk of criticism and praise for the program. Denounced as cartoonish by many, he was, in some ways, a stereotypical buffoon. It could also be argued, however, that Urkel challenged racial stereotypes. Depicted as the son of a neurosurgeon, he was a studious bookworm with geniuslike abilities in math and science—traits that made him a rare representation of black youth for prime-time television. Even more insulting to many critics, however, was the show's clichéd portrayal of the Winslow family's matriarch. Whereas her husband was often bumbling and unsure, Harriette was the sassy decision maker—the domineering "powerhouse of reality" in the home.

Nestled between *Full House* (1987–1995) and *Perfect Strangers* on ABC's Friday night lineup, *Family Matters* was a black-cast series that found mainstream success among white American audiences. Although it never won critical praise or Emmy Awards, viewers were warmed by the show, which was a consistent favorite in its time slot. Unlike some of the more politicized black series of its era, such as *The Cosby Show* (1984–1993) and *A Different World* (1987–1993) , *Family Matters* did not emerge from a black sensibility. In fact, the white producing team of Bickley and Warren (who later created *On Our Own*, another black comedy for ABC, which ran from 1994 to 1995) made a conscious effort to fashion a universal family, unmarked by racial difference. As VelJohnson notes, *Family Matters* was never nominated for any National Association for the Advancement of Colored People (NAACP) Image Awards. He goes on to state that despite its all-black cast, the show was perhaps seen as being "too white . . . to be considered a black show."

Even after its retirement from prime time, *Family Matters* continued to be a hit on cable. After a brief and unsuccessful run on the white-dominated CBS, the series migrated to the Turner Broadcasting System (TBS) cable network, where it ranked high in its appeal for children.

Kristal Brent Zook

SEE ALSO: The Cosby Show; Happy Days; *Sitcom; Television.*

BIBLIOGRAPHY

Curry, Jack, and Walter T. Middlebrook. "*Family Matters.*" *USA Today*, September 13, 1989, 4D.

McNeil, Alex. *Total Television.* New York: Viking/Penguin, 1996.

Moore, Barbara; Marvin R. Bensman; and Jim Van Dyke. *Prime-Time Television: A Concise History.* Westport, CT: Praeger, 2006.

Spigel, Lynn. *Make Room for TV: Television and the Family Ideal in Postwar America.* Chicago: University of Chicago Press, 1992.

Family Reunions

A family reunion is a special event that a family organizes so that all members of the family can meet in the same place and spend some time together. Families usually have reunions because their members, such as grandparents, parents, brothers, sisters, aunts, uncles, and cousins, live far apart and do not get to see each other very often. Sometimes families organize reunions to celebrate a special occasion, such as a family member's birthday or a wedding anniversary.

In the United States families have been holding reunions since the 1880s. In the 1960s they became a popular pastime. Throughout the 1970s, 1980s, and 1990s, family reunions grew in both popularity and scale as the baby boomer generation aged.

During the 1980s the development of the Internet made it easier for people to research their family history and find lost relatives. Many Americans who traced their heritage often became the primary organizers of family reunions. They wanted to meet their lost relatives, share their family history findings, and gather new information through personal contact. The Internet also made it easier to organize reunions.

Family reunions are held in many different places and for different lengths of time. Where and how long they are held depend on the family. Some families are very large, so their reunions may take place over several days in a hotel, where family members can participate in different activities either on-site or in the surrounding area. Smaller families may make a mealtime a special occasion, either eating out at a restaurant or organizing a meal at a family member's home. Regardless of the place and type of reunion, many family members find that the most enjoyable part of a reunion is sitting around talking. Recalling memories of youth and passing those memories on to the next generation are important goals of many family reunions. Many adults want their children to get to know their cousins or other extended family members, particularly those who influenced their own lives.

By the 1990s reunions involved much careful planning and organization. Near the end of a reunion, families would often plan the next one and perhaps set a date and a place. Some families have a member who serves as family historian. This person is usually responsible for recording the events of the reunion, as well as keeping the family history and genealogy up-to-date. Some large families even organize fund-raising events to help pay for the costs of the reunion.

To commemorate the occasion, some families create souvenirs for their reunion. T-shirts printed with the family name and the date and place of the reunion are common, while other popular items are caps, bumper stickers, tote bags, complete genealogies, and family recipe books. Family members also take many photographs and videos to preserve the memory of the reunion.

By the early twenty-first century, family reunions had become big business. More and more families were holding their reunions onboard cruise ships or at large hotels that cater to families. Hotels and inns often provided chefs to cook family recipes, photographers to take pictures and make videos, and activities planners to organize events for family members. Some places even offered on-site genealogy experts. For those families needing a little help with planning a reunion, there are even companies that will teach them how to organize one. The YMCA of the Rockies in Colorado offers classes on how to plan ideal reunions at its Family Reunion University.

Angela O'Neal

SEE ALSO: *The Internet.*

BIBLIOGRAPHY

Ayoub, Millicent R. "The Family Reunion." *Ethnology* 5, no 4. (1966): 415–433.

Mergenhagen, Paula. "The Reunion Market." *American Demographics*, April 1966, 30–34.

Swenson, Greta E. *Festivals of Sharing: Family Reunions in America.* New York: AMS Press, 1989.

Weingarten, Tara. "An Affair to Remember." *Newsweek* 144, no. 25 (2004).

Family Ties

U.S. President Ronald Reagan (served from 1981 to 1989) once named NBC's *Family Ties* his favorite show, despite the fact that the sitcom was originally intended as a parody of Reagan-style values.

The premise of the Emmy Award–winning series, which ran from 1982 to 1989, is the generation gap between the Keaton parents and their children. Elyse (Meredith Baxter) and Steven (Michael Gross) came of age in the 1960s (their hippie leanings are evident from the opening sequence of the show), while their children are products of the materialistic 1980s. The eldest child, Alex (Michael J. Fox, who became a star because of the series), wears suits, reads the *Wall Street Journal*, and worships former president Richard Nixon and conservative political pundit William F. Buckley. Middle child Mallory (Justine Bateman) is rather dim and obsessed with shopping. The youngest, Jennifer (Tina Yothers), is a precocious sitcom kid. As viewers became more interested in the kids, the generation-gap theme was dropped.

The main characters all continued working in television—to varying degrees—after *Family Ties* ended. Fox, who was diagnosed with Parkinson disease in 1991, has become involved in research for the disease.

Karen Lurie

SEE ALSO: *Buckley, William F., Jr.; Emmy Awards; Reagan, Ronald; Sitcom; Television; The* Wall Street Journal.

BIBLIOGRAPHY

Brooks, Tim, and Earle Marsh. *The Complete Directory to Prime Time Network and Cable TV Shows 1946–Present*, 6th ed. New York: Ballantine Books, 1995.

McNeil, Alex. *Total Television: The Comprehensive Guide to Programming from 1948 to the Present*. New York: Penguin Books, 1996.

Fan Magazines

Although many fields of entertainment, including sports, auto racing, radio, and music, have spawned special-interest magazines that provide inside information for devotees, it is to the motion picture industry that the United States owes the long-established concept of the fan magazine. Conceived to promote, popularize, and trade off the fledgling art of film in early Hollywood, fan magazines date to 1911, when *Motion Picture Story* and *Photoplay* first appeared. These magazines provided readers with the illusion of intimacy with the stars and fed their fantasies about the opulent lifestyles and sometimes scandal-ridden private lives of famous actors and actresses. At the same time they purported to reveal the mechanics of the star-making process, allowing the average reader—an outsider looking in—to claim knowledge of and to form judgments about a player's screen image, talent, and off-screen personality and character, as well as to form opinions about the best career moves for their favorite stars.

EARLY SCREEN MAGAZINES

Fan magazines initially relied on a formula that packaged a portrait gallery of movie stars with illustrated stories of popular motion pictures, as well as specialized features such as reader inquiries. Each issue included short fictional pieces. As early as 1912, however, the magazines began to print interviews with stars, articles on various phases of film production, and even motion picture scenarios. The magazines were targeted primarily to female readers who, in the belief of most film industry executives, formed the large majority of the filmgoing public. By the same token most of the contributors were also women. They included such notable writers as Adela Rogers St. Johns, Hazel Simpson Naylor, Ruth Hall, and Adele Whitely Fletcher, all of whom wrote for various publications under a variety of pen names. Other contributors came from the ranks of press representatives for both actors and film studios.

A magazine occasionally published an article purportedly written by a star or printed an interview in which an actor or actress solicited readers' opinions on such matters as career moves. Although these pieces were normally the result of collaboration between the editorial staff and the subject's press agent, there was an accompanying photograph or a set of handwritten responses to questions, supposedly supplied by the star, in order to lend authenticity to the enterprise. These editorial ploys gave the impression that the magazines were essentially uncritical mouthpieces, fawning over an industry that fed them tidbits so as to heighten public interest in films.

While this was not without some truth, fan magazines were, for the most part, published independently of the studios, although this did not always guarantee objectivity. The publications depended on the studios to organize interviews with actors and to supply publicity releases and information about stars and films. Nonetheless, the magazines could be critical at times, particularly after they began publishing film reviews in 1915. It was not uncommon to see both *Photoplay* and *Motion Picture Story* giving a "thumbs down" to pictures they did not think readers would enjoy, although the sort of harsh criticism or exposé that became a feature of the tabloids in the late twentieth century was generally avoided. Articles that dealt with the private lives of screen personalities tended to overlook sordid matters and, instead, placed the emphasis on family values, domestic pursuits, and the aesthetics of home life in Hollywood. From the 1930s onward, it was commonplace to see major photographic features showing stars hard at work gardening, cooking, washing the car, or playing with the baby.

This type of journalism contrasted with the coverage of Hollywood by the national press. Tabloid newspapers thrived by titillating their readers with detailed reporting on the numerous scandals that erupted in Hollywood. One notorious example of this was the murder trial of Roscoe "Fatty" Arbuckle during the 1920s. The magazine *Screenland*, published from 1921 to 1927, took Hollywood's side against the sensationalism of the Arbuckle case by publishing an article in defense of the comedian, who was later found not guilty. Other fan publications, notably *Photoplay*, took a neutral stance toward Hollywood scandals. Such incidents as the murder of the director William Desmond Taylor—with Mabel Normand briefly suspected as the murderer—Rudolph Valentino's divorce, and Wallace Reid's drug-related death were largely neglected by the fan magazines or treated in general terms within an article that presented a star and his family bravely overcoming adversity. (Early scandals did, however, help prompt the implementation of a production code in the 1930s.) That this approach worked as well as it did demonstrates the devotion of film fans to the romanticized image of their screen idols. Most readers were well aware of current scandals, and when a fan magazine alluded to a star's "brave fight" or "lingering illness," they were knowledgeable enough to translate the terms into "drug addiction" or to know that "young foolishness" or "hot-headed wildness" meant sexual indiscretions of one kind or another.

Most film historians view the fan magazines of the silent era as having more scholarly validity than those after the advent of sound. Such publications as *Filmplay Journal*, *Motion Picture Classic*, *Motion Picture*, and *Movie Weekly* gave readers well-written film reviews and factual, biographical information that could not be found anywhere else. They have come to provide modern scholars with fascinating sociological insights into the phenomenon of film in the first two decades of the history of American motion pictures.

CHANGES WITH THE COMING OF SOUND

After the advent of sound, fan magazines became less serious and more concerned with sensationalism and sex. During the 1930s the magazines played a major role in creating the lasting impression of Hollywood as a center of glamour. To a country mired in the economic consequences of the Great Depression, fan magazines presented an image of the American dream as something the average person could attain. They treated as gospel such myths as Lana Turner having been discovered by a producer while she was eating a sundae at Schwab's Drug Store or Hollywood talent scouts combing the country for "unknowns" to be turned into stars. Mythmakers were preaching the messages of the so-called Dream Factory to a nation only too willing to believe them. In the make-believe world that formed the

Photoplay ***Magazine.*** *Joan Crawford appears on the cover of the fan magazine* Photoplay *in August 1931.* TRANSCENDENTAL GRAPHICS/ GETTY IMAGES RM/.

setting of the majority of popular movies of the period, crime was punished, courage was rewarded, and lovers lived happily ever after.

Fan magazines presented movie actresses as icons of perfect beauty. At one end of the scale they were pictures of fresh prettiness (Fay Wray, Deanna Durbin); at the other, stylish and glamorous sophisticates (Greta Garbo, Marlene Dietrich, Myrna Loy). Their handsome male counterparts were either debonair (Cary Grant, Errol Flynn) or the epitome of masculine strength (Gary Cooper, Clark Gable). Everything about the stars was larger than life—their homes, their lifestyles, their passions, even their sins. In short, they had everything except the ability to visit with their fans. Hence, such magazines as *Modern Screen, Movie Action Magazine, Movie Classic, Movie Mirror, Silver Screen,* and *Motion Picture Classic* came into being to reveal the inside scoop on their lives. Articles such as "Jean Harlow—From Extra to Star," "Shirley Temple's Letter to Santa," "Motherhood: What It Means to Helen Twelvetrees," and "The Bennetts Answer Hollywood Gossip" allowed readers to forget their drab lives, at least for a moment, during the Great Depression and to live vicariously through the pages of the magazines.

On the other hand, the magazines let the public know that these glamorous stars did not have perfect lives; indeed, the stars envied the simple pleasure enjoyed by their fans. Temple, the magazines reported, wished that she could visit a department store Santa. Durbin longed to eat fudge like an ordinary teenager but could not lest she put on weight, and Loy wanted the freedom to walk into a department store without being recognized. The conspiracy between editors and publicists that created communication between the stars and their fans was a significant factor in keeping movie theaters filled with customers.

During the 1940s and 1950s the pattern continued. The leading magazines during this period were *Photoplay, Modern Screen, Silver Screen, Movie Fan, Movie Stars Parade, Screen Album, Screen Stars,* and *Movie Story.* With the arrival of affluence after World War II, however, the public grew less impressed with the wealth of the stars and more appreciative of pinup poses of both sexes and of stories that revealed the less savory antics of stars such as Elizabeth Taylor, Flynn, and Frank Sinatra. It was the beginning of the end of fan magazines as they had been known and loved for almost half a century. With the onset of the 1960s, they came increasingly to resemble tabloids, trumpeting banner headlines such as "Liz Will Adopt a Negro Baby" (*Movie Mirror,* April 1967) and containing little real news. It was in the 1960s, too, that a number of specialty magazines began to appear. *Screen Legends* and *Film and TV Careers* devoted each issue to only one or two personalities and included filmographies and interviews. *Famous Monsters of Filmland* dealt only with horror films and monsters, and *Serial Quarterly* concentrated on "cliff-hangers" and Saturday matinee serials.

NEW MAGAZINES AND THE INTERNET

As the traditional fan magazines declined, eventually disappeared, and left the market to specialist publications and to scandal-mongering tabloids, a new style of movie magazine was created in the 1980s, one that has continued to fill the void. By the 1990s film fans were buying magazines such as *Entertainment Weekly, Movieline,* and *Premiere,* publications that offered a combination of interviews, filmographies, and production pieces, with serious analyses of film trends and fashion. They largely avoided sensationalism, but they were not above criticism of people and their work. The magazines became the new reading material for the fans of an industry that had become almost unrecognizable after the end of the traditional studio-based Hollywood. In turn, these magazines came to be challenged by websites such as Film in Focus (launched in 2007 by Faber and Faber and *Filmmaker* magazine) and Alt Film Guide (which provided information on independent films).

The Internet also provided opportunities for fans to communicate with one another and to construct their own versions of fan magazines. This gave credence to those who claimed that the contemporary model of fandom was much more interactive, if not democratic, than the old system of studio-constructed narratives and images. Furthermore, the Internet offered a mechanism by which celebrity could be claimed by anyone who captured the media's attention for a moment or garnered hits on a website, Facebook page, or Twitter account. Meanwhile, the great gossip magazines, highly prized by collectors, have taken their place in Hollywood legend along with the stars who populated their pages.

Steve Hanson

SEE ALSO: *Arbuckle, Fatty; Celebrity;* Entertainment Weekly*; Gossip Columns; Movie Stars;* People*;* Photoplay*; Tabloids; Teen Idols; Turner, Lana.*

BIBLIOGRAPHY

Hellekson, Karen, and Kristina Busse, eds. *Fan Fiction and Fan Communities in the Age of the Internet: New Essays.* Jefferson, NC: McFarland, 2006.

Levin, Martin, ed. *Hollywood and the Great Fan Magazines,* rev. ed. New York: Wings Books, 1991.

Older, Jon. "Children of the Night." *Magazines of the Movies* 4 (1993): 14–16.

Slide, Anthony, ed. *They Also Wrote for the Fan Magazines: Film Articles by Literary Giants from E. E. Cummings to Eleanor Roosevelt, 1920–1939.* Jefferson, NC: McFarland, 1992.

Slide, Anthony. *Inside the Hollywood Fan Magazine: A History of Star Makers, Fabricators, and Gossip Mongers.* Jackson: University Press of Mississippi, 2010.

Studlar, Gaylyn. "The Perils of Pleasure? Fan Magazine Discourse as Women's Commodified Culture in the 1920s." *Wide Angle,* January 1991, 6–33.

Tohill, Cathal. "Sleaze Town, USA." *Magazines of the Movies* 4 (1992): 91–93.

Fantasia

Walt Disney's *Fantasia* (1940) was a seminal film in the development of animated features and a cultural cornerstone in leading children to classical music. The work has entranced multiple generations of viewers in America and Europe. Named one of the American Film Institute's Top 100 Movies of All Time in 1998, *Fantasia* served as the inspiration for subsequent animated classics including Bruno Bozzetto's 1976 *Allegro Non Troppo* and Osamu Tezuka's 1994 *Legend of the Forest.* Although influential, *Fantasia* remains unique, one of the most masterful combinations of sound and images ever committed to celluloid.

Fantasia was Walt Disney's third full-length animated feature. The film was from its inception one of the most significant experiments by the Hollywood film industry since the introduction of sound in *The Jazz Singer* in 1927. The finished film, with scenes introduced by composer and music critic Deems Taylor and with the Philadelphia Orchestra under Leopold Stokowski providing the music, grew out of a chance meeting between Stokowski and Disney. The conductor had expressed an interest in working with Disney, and Disney, the master of animation, was looking to restore Mickey Mouse to his former level of popularity. They felt that a visual realization of composer Paul Dukas's symphonic poem "The Sorcerer's Apprentice" (1897) might do the trick.

Stokowski and Disney were both world-class showmen and in love with technological gimmickry. Stokowski was one of the earliest experimenters in stereophonic sound and suggested that the film's sound re-create that of a concert hall. This was done by recording the orchestra on three separate channels (right, left, and surround). Unfortunately recording the sound to the conductor's satisfaction cost more than a short subject could possibly recoup. Disney then committed to making what he initially called a "concert feature," a collection of shorts that would make up a concert. Stokowski wondered why Disney planned to stop at short subjects; why not a full-length film with several other musical works to suggest "the mood, the coloring, the design, the speed, the character of motion of what is seen on the screen." In short, a fantasia—a free development on a given theme.

MUSIC

Disney decided to open the film with Stokowski's own orchestral transcription of Johann Sebastian Bach's "Toccata and Fugue in D Minor," complemented by visual detailing suggestive of falling asleep at the orchestra. As Disney recalled, "All I can see is violin tips and bow tips—like when you're half asleep at a concert," not, apparently, an uncommon occurrence for the easily bored studio executive. In preparing for *Fantasia* Disney subscribed to a box at the Hollywood Bowl, where, he told a colleague, he invariably fell asleep, lulled by the music and the warmth of the polo coat he liked to wear. After the film opened Disney told a reporter from the *New York World Telegram*, "I never liked this stuff. Honest, I just couldn't listen to it. But I can listen to it now. It seems to mean a little more to me. Maybe it can give other people the same thing."

The final film, a glorious marriage of sound and image, is not without flaws. Oskar Fischinger, an avant-garde painter who had worked with director Fritz Lang on the special effects for *Die Frau im mond* (*Woman in the Moon*) in Germany in 1929, helped design *Fantasia*'s opening sequence. However, the literal-minded Disney, who denied Fischinger credit and had his designs altered, considered his vision too abstract.

There were musical compromises too. Bach, best experienced with the original instrumentation, was given a bombastic transcription for full orchestra, and Igor Stravinsky's "Rite of Spring" was seriously distorted under Stokowsky's baton. Disney reportedly offered Stravinsky $5,000 for his work, pointing out that because it was copyrighted in Russia but not in the United States, he could simply pirate the music if he wanted to. Ludwig van Beethoven's "Pastoral Symphony" was truncated, a problem exacerbated later when a pickaninny centaur was excised from the film on subsequent reissues as being in poor taste. The female centaurs in that sequence were originally bare-breasted, but the censors insisted that discreet garlands be hung around their necks.

IMAGERY

Other aspects of the film have remained a continual source of delight. The design for the excerpts from Peter Ilyich Tchaikovsky's "Nutcracker Suite," an enchanted forest peopled by mushroom Chinamen and Cossacks as dancing flowers, is a visual and aural feast; "The Sorcerer's Apprentice" starring, as intended, Mickey Mouse, is wonderfully inventive and amusing; "The Dance of the Hours" (from Amilcare Ponchielli's opera *La Gioconda*) is a memorably comic sequence, with balletic ostriches and dancing hippopotami lampooning cultural pretensions.

Modest Mussorgsky's "A Night on Bald Mountain," remains the high spot of the film, with its gargoyles, demons, and other frightening creatures of the night in a visual battle between the forces of good and evil. The spirits of the night rise from the local graveyard and travel to Bald Mountain for a celebration of Evil, a ritualistic bow to Chernobog, the Black God. The flames transform into dancers, then animals, and then lizards at the whim of the great Black God, who revels in the passionate exhibition. However, as morning approaches and church bells are rung, the Black God recoils in horror and is driven back until he is vanquished. The music segues into Franz Schubert's "Ave Maria," scored for solo voice by the composer but here given a choral treatment (with new lyrics by Rachel Field) that blasts the preceding crescendo of magnificent malevolence out of existence.

Bela Lugosi was hired to perform the part of Chernobog, a figure of ultimate evil. He was photographed miming the actions of the character—the legendary horror star's expressions on the character's face are unmistakable—and his image was then altered and incorporated by Vladimir Tytla, one of Disney's greatest master animators. Disney had been rotoscoping (tracing) live-action figures as guides to animation as far back as *Snow White and the Seven Dwarfs* (1937), and for *Fantasia* members of the Ballet Russe, notably Roman Jasinsky, Tatiana Riabouchinska, and Irina Baranova, modeled for the elephants, hippos, and ostriches (respectively) in the "Dance of the Hours" sequence.

The finale is an anticlimactic version of Schubert's "Ave Maria," which was innovatively filmed as one long continuous take, requiring several days to shoot. The first time the sequence was filmed someone had placed the wrong lens on the camera, thus exposing the background on each side of the artwork. A second attempt was made mere days before the film's opening and was briefly disrupted by an earthquake on the third day of filming, fortunately with no ill effect. Disney had wanted to shoot the film in widescreen and offer it on a reserved-seat basis before giving it a general release; however, his bankers objected and the only innovation Disney was able to offer was "Fantasound," an early stereo process that was available in only a few theaters.

LEGACY

By the time *Fantasia* opened, Disney had spent a fortune building his dream studio, but World War II shut down his foreign markets and a significant portion of his revenues. The banks closed off his line of credit in 1940, and he was forced to offer stock to the public for the first time. *Fantasia* fared badly on its initial release, trimmed to eighty-eight minutes, pleasing neither the audience (who wanted and expected more films like *Snow White*) nor the critics (who decried the misuse of classical music). However, Disney and *Fantasia* both survived, with the latter achieving classic status and more than recouping its costs (about $2.25 million). Until the film became available on video, it remained one of the classic Disney perennials, screened as a staple of children's vacation time.

Fantasia stands acknowledged as one of cinema's undisputed works of art visually, musically, and technically, and its influence was far-reaching. One of Disney's goals for the *Fantasia* project was to periodically rerelease it with varying musical selections, and a number of classical standards were considered for insertion into future releases. However, only Sergei Prokofiev's "Peter and the Wolf" reached the animation stage in Disney's lifetime, featured in the 1946 animated film *Make Mine Music*, narrated by Sterling Holloway. Claude Debussy's "Clair de Lune" formed the basis for Bobby Worth and Ray Gilbert's "Blue Bayou" in the same film. In 2010 actor Nicolas Cage, who had long been an admirer of *Fantasia*, brought *The Sorcerer's Apprentice* to theaters as a real-life family adventure. Cage played the master magician who had been a student of Merlin's.

In 1987 Lillian Disney, Walt Disney's widow, donated $50 million to the city of Los Angeles to fulfill her husband's desire to bring classical music to a wider audience. The bequest stipulated that groundbreaking for what was envisioned as a "concert hall for the masses" must take place by 1992. In order to meet that deadline, a symbolic groundbreaking took place, but the project remained on the drawing board. With major fund-raising efforts and additional donations by the Disney family, the concert hall was finally finished at a cost of $274 million under the guidance of architect Frank Gehry. Designed as an acoustical masterpiece, the exterior is made up of stainless-steel curves. On October 23, 2003, Esa-Pekka Salonen led the Los Angeles Philharmonic at the first concert at Walt Disney Concert Hall. Classical music and other genres including jazz, pop, holiday, and world music are regularly scheduled there.

Dennis Fischer

SEE ALSO: *Animated Films; Ballet; Cage, Nicolas; Disney (Walt Disney Company); Lugosi, Bela;* The Mickey Mouse Club*; Stokowski, Leopold.*

BIBLIOGRAPHY

Alan, Robin. *Walt Disney and Europe: European Influences on the Animated Feature Films of Walt Disney*. Bloomington: Indiana University Press, 1999.

Beck, Jay, and Tony Grajeda. *Lowering the Boom: Critical Studies in Film Sound*. Urbana: University of Illinois Press, 2008.

Culhane, John. *Walt Disney's "Fantasia."* New York: Abradale Press, 1983.

Haithman, Diane. "Disney's *Fantasia*." *Opera News* 68, no. 1 (2003).

Heath, Robert. *"Fantasia": The Making of a Masterpiece*. Burbank: CA: Walt Disney, 1990. Videocassette (VHS).

Maltin, Leonard. *The Disney Films*. New York: Popular Library, 1978.

Peary, Danny. *Cult Movies*. New York: Dell, 1981.

Schickel, Richard. *The Disney Version*. New York: Avon Books, 1968.

Taylor, Deems. *Walt Disney's "Fantasia."* New York: Simon & Schuster, 1940.

The Fantastic Four

The Fantastic Four is a comic book published by Marvel Comics since 1961. Created by Stan Lee and Jack Kirby, the Fantastic Four are a family of superheroes—Mr. Fantastic, Invisible Girl (later renamed the Invisible Woman), Human Torch, and the Thing. The series departed significantly from previous superhero comic books by casting characters as distinct individuals plagued by human failings such as self-doubt, jealousy, and even occasional antipathy toward the society they have sworn to protect. With his monstrous orange rock-skinned appearance, the Thing especially was prone to alienation and periods of self-loathing, and he quickly emerged as the favorite among fans of the comic.

The Fantastic Four was the first of the Marvel comic books to predict the anticonformist themes soon to become prevalent in the youth culture of the 1960s and subsequent decades. Along with *The Incredible Hulk* and *The Amazing Spider-Man*, *The Fantastic Four* formed the core of Marvel's 1960s comic-book publishing boom. It remained one of the company's most popular titles in the 1990s and first decade of the 2000s.

There have been numerous attempts to expand *The Fantastic Four*'s audience through adaptations in various types of media. Four animated television series were produced between 1967 and 2006, and video games featuring the Fantastic Four were released in 1997, 2005, and 2007, the latter two to accompany the feature films *Fantastic Four* (2005) and *Fantastic Four: Rise of the Silver Surfer* (2007). Both films debuted at number one in box-office sales but received mostly poor reviews from critics.

Bradford Wright

SEE ALSO: *Comic Books; The Incredible Hulk; Kirby, Jack; Lee, Stan; Marvel Comics; Spider-Man.*

BIBLIOGRAPHY

Daniels, Les. *Marvel: Five Fabulous Decades of the World's Greatest Comics*. New York: Harry N. Abrams, 1991.

DeFalco, Tom. *Fantastic Four: The Ultimate Guide*. New York: DK, 2005.

Lee, Stan. *Origins of Marvel Comics*. New York: Simon & Schuster, 1974.

Starbuck, Alex; Fred Van Lente; John Romita; et al. *Origins of Marvel Comics*. New York: Marvel Worldwide, 2011.

Fantasy Island

Producer Aaron Spelling once said that of all the characters he created, *Fantasy Island*'s Mr. Roarke was the one he most identified with because he made dreams come true. Airing after *The Love Boat* on Saturday nights on ABC from 1978 to 1984, *Fantasy Island* offered viewers a chance to imagine romantic escapes and gave "B"-list celebrities such as Bill Bixby, Joseph Campanella, Adrienne Barbeau, Karen Valentine, and Victoria Principal another opportunity to appear on the small screen. Unlike the comedic *Love Boat*, however, *Fantasy Island* was a romantic drama, complete with suspense and ironic twists. Each episode carried an implicit warning: be careful what you wish for.

The premise of *Fantasy Island* is simple: each of the three weekly visitors to the tropical island pays $10,000 to make a lifelong dream come true. Awaiting the visitors is their host, Mr.

***Mr. Roarke and Tattoo from* Fantasy Island.** *Ricardo Montalbán, left, and Hervé Villechaize star as the mysterious Mr. Roarke and his sidekick Tattoo on* Fantasy Island. **SILVER SCREEN COLLECTION/GETTY IMAGES.**

Roarke (Ricardo Montalbán), a suave, mysterious man in a white suit, and his similarly white-suited midget (Villechaize's preferred term) attaché, Tattoo (Hervé Villechaize). Mr. Roarke manages the visitors' fantasies, directing his retinue to smile as the seaplane lands to Tattoo's now-infamous call of "The Plane! The Plane!" From show to show the visitors' fantasies vary: one visitor is an ugly duckling who longs to be a sex symbol, another is a frustrated salesperson looking for the business coup of a lifetime, and yet another is a henpecked family man looking for a little respect. The visitors have one thing in common: they all imagine a life more glamorous or exciting than the one they left behind.

Mr. Roarke provides the magic that makes fantasies come true, but he also proves a wise adviser to guests who realize that their fantasies often lead them where they do not want to go. When a pregnant woman certain to die during childbirth asks to see the life of her unborn child, for example, she is horrified at the way the child's life turns out. As the fantasies go awry—and they always go awry—Mr. Roarke is there to help his guests realize that some fantasies are best left fantasies.

As the seasons passed the show delved more into the supernatural. Mr. Roarke was suddenly able to bring about events from the future and the past; cast spells and mix up magic potions; and even do battle with the devil, played in a recurring role by a sinister Roddy McDowall. Was Roarke God? An angel? Or just a figure who let viewers indulge their taste for tropical fantasy while reassuring them that they were better off in the lives they had?

Fantasy Island was very much a product of its times. It attempted to indulge the popular appetite for wealth and glamour that brought shows such as *Dallas* and *Dynasty* success. At the same time the show addressed the age-old fears of those who worried that greed could only bring trouble. ABC brought back a revamped and "edgier" *Fantasy Island* in the fall of 1998, featuring Malcolm McDowell as Mr. Roarke (wearing a black suit this time), along with a few disgruntled assistants. Although the show had the same basic premise, it was far more interested in exploring the horror of a fantasy realized than its predecessor. The revival was short-lived, leaving the air after just one season.

Karen Lurie

SEE ALSO: Dallas*;* Dynasty*;* The Love Boat*; Montalbán, Ricardo; Spelling, Aaron; Television.*

BIBLIOGRAPHY

Brooks, Tim, and Earle Marsh. *The Complete Directory to Prime Time Network and Cable TV Shows 1946–Present*, 6th ed. New York: Ballantine Books, 1995.

McNeil, Alex. *Total Television: The Comprehensive Guide to Programming from 1948 to the Present.* New York: Penguin, 1996.

Spelling, Aaron, and Jefferson Graham. *Aaron Spelling: A Prime-Time Life.* New York: St. Martin's Press, 1996.

Fantasy Sports

First emerging during the late 1950s and early 1960s as a hobby for a few obsessive fans, fantasy sports expanded exponentially until, by the end of the first decade of the twenty-first century, tens of millions of players were avidly and meticulously "managing" fantasy teams in almost every professional sport. Becoming involved in fantasy sports brought an immediacy and personal involvement to sports fans, which in turn gave a boost to professional athletics and resulted in the creation of a multimillion-dollar parallel fantasy sports industry.

Players of fantasy sports create teams by choosing, or "drafting," real-life players and then competing with other teams by comparing their players' scores and statistics in real games. These comparisons are made using various tally systems that award points for touchdowns, runs, points, or the like (depending on the sport), as well as other achievements. In baseball, for example, points might be awarded based on batting average or earned run average; in basketball they might be given for number of points, rebounds, and assists; and in football for passing, receiving, touchdowns, or yards gained. Fantasy team members are also vulnerable to their real-life counterparts' injuries, slumps, and setbacks, and team managers can trade, bench, or recall players in order to keep team statistics high. Members of fantasy sports leagues generally begin by paying an upfront fee, and winning teams often receive a prize. Entry fees and prizes vary widely from league to league.

Some say fantasy sports got their start during the 1950s when Wilfred "Bill" Winkenbach, a limited-partnership owner of the Oakland Raiders football team, devised a simple fantasy golf game. The idea was popular among sports fans who loved studying player strengths, weaknesses, and statistics. In 1962, Winkenbach and a group of sports journalists and Raiders administrators adjusted the rules for the more complex variables of football and launched the Greater Oakland Professional Pigskin Prognosticators League (GOPPPL). The GOPPPL began as a friendly competition among colleagues but soon spread throughout the San Francisco bay area.

On the East Coast in the early 1980s freelance writer and editor Dan Okrent turned a friendly baseball rivalry into a fantasy game, devising a fantasy league as a way to judge who would be the best general manager. They called it Rotisserie Baseball, after the New York restaurant La Rotisserie Francaise, where the group liked to meet. The idea of a fantasy sports "franchise" quickly gained popularity. By 1984 there were fifty-five authorized Rotisserie Leagues, and the idea spread to sports fans across the country. Enthralled with the idea of "owning" their own baseball teams, some Rotisserie players actually went to Florida to scout players at spring training.

"Running" early fantasy sports teams was time consuming and painstaking, as it required poring over pages of statistics to choose and manage a roster of players as well as to check the box scores and track scores and results. The development of personal computers gave a boost to fantasy sports enthusiasts, simplifying the work of keeping tabs on constantly changing statistics. In 1988 Center Field Software became one of the first companies to introduce software specifically designed for fantasy sport fans. That program, the rotisserie-style Grand Slam! was soon followed by numerous others.

The first decade of the 2000s saw an explosion in the popularity of fantasy sports. Though fantasy leagues still exist in the form in which they originated—small groups of friends and coworkers who gather for fun and friendly competition—the rise of the Internet and dozens of fantasy sport websites have expanded fantasy sports and made it almost as important a part of popular culture as real sports. In the late 1990s Yahoo! and CBS launched major fantasy websites, which were soon followed by ESPN.com and NFL.com. Sports network ESPN legitimized fantasy competition in 2007 by naming writer Matthew Berry their director of fantasy sports.

The popularity of fantasy sports continues to rise, with players from all classes and careers in countries all over the world. Though predominantly a male obsession, more and more women have become involved. In 2005 experts estimated that 95 percent of fantasy players were men, but by 2011 the estimated percentage of female players had grown to 25. In 2009 the FX network launched the comedy series *The League*, about members of a fantasy football league. The BBC comedy *Fantasy Football League* aired from 1994 through 1996, with revivals in 1998 and 2004. In 2011 an Indian reality show, *Bigg Toss*, challenged two households of contestants to pick fantasy cricket teams.

Tina Gianoulis

SEE ALSO: *Baseball; Basketball; Cable TV; ESPN; Golf; The Internet; National Basketball Association (NBA); National Football League (NFL); The Oakland Raiders; Professional Football; Reality Television; Sports Heroes; Television.*

BIBLIOGRAPHY

Cavanaugh, Maureen, and Hank Crook. "Fantasy Sports Growing from Hobby to Multi-Million Dollar Industry." KPBS .com, August 12, 2009. Accessed May 2012. Available from http://www.kpbs.org/news/2009/aug/12/fantasy-sports-growing-hobby-multi-million-dollar-/

Cobb, Nathan. "Rotiss: The Greatest Game for Baseball Fans since Baseball." *Smithsonian*, June 1990, 100.

Crupi, Anthony. "Billion Dollar Draft: Some 27 Million Americans Play Fantasy Football—And Media Companies Are Cashing In on Their Obsession." *Adweek*, November 7, 2011, 18.

Hendricks, Sam. *Fantasy Football Guidebook: Your Comprehensive Guide to Playing Fantasy Football.* Austin, TX: Extra Point Press, 2010.

Mass, A. J. *How Fantasy Sports Explains the World: What Pujols and Peyton Can Teach Us about Wookiees and Wall Street.* New York: Skyhorse Publishing, 2011.

The Far Side

Debuting in 1980, *The Far Side*, a single-panel comic strip written and drawn by Gary Larson, was different from anything previously seen on a comics page. Its offbeat and obscure humor drew epithets such as "tasteless," "sick," or "demented," but the cartoon became immensely popular during its fifteen-year tenure, appearing in more than 1,900 daily and Sunday newspapers and being translated into seventeen languages. More than twenty *Far Side* collections and anthologies reached the best-seller lists and were available in bookstores long after Larson stopped producing the cartoon in 1995. *The Far Side* made its way to greeting cards, T-shirts, and calendars—including the especially popular desk calendars of 365 daily *Far Side* cartoons, which are produced and sold each holiday season.

Unlike other comics, *The Far Side* did not feature the same characters in each installment, although it did repeat types of characters. Farm animals, especially cows, chickens, and ducks, made frequent appearances. Among other animals featured were snakes and squids. Larson's love of biology showed itself in numerous insect jokes. (An entomologist even named a species of chewing lice after Larson for his contributions to biology. The insect was named *Strigiphilus garylarsoni*. Larson considered it a great honor.) The people who appeared in *The Far Side* usually were similar in appearance: most of the children had big heads and glasses; the women had big hair and glasses; the men had long noses and often wore glasses. In fact, most of Larson's characters fit the stereotypical image of the nerd. Neanderthal men and aliens appeared as well.

The jokes found in *The Far Side* ranged from puns to the silly to the intellectual to the morbid. A cartoon about a sticky widget (a strange device covered in honey) could be followed by a joke referencing archaeologists Mary and Louis Leakey and their discovery of the skeleton of a prehistoric being nicknamed Lucy. (That particular cartoon showed the Leakeys uncovering a cave painting of Lucy from the *Peanuts* cartoon strip.)

On the morbid side, Larson often had animals or people meet their end in untimely and ironic ways. One panel showed a mother bear using the skulls of two young hunters to entertain her cubs. She had her hand inside each skull and mimicked the boys' last words about entering the cave. In fact, the panels that drew the most complaints usually depicted some cruelty done to an animal, usually by another animal. For example, one cartoon with the caption "Tethercat" showed a cat tied to a pole by its neck while two dogs batted it around. And as often as he got complaints, Larson got letters asking for him to explain the joke.

During his career Larson also created an animated television special titled *Gary Larson's Tales from the Far Side* (1994). Among his many accolades, he won the Reuben Award for best cartoonist in 1991 and 1994. *The Far Side* was awarded the Max & Moritz Prize for best international comic strip/panel in 1993 and best syndicated panel in 1985 and 1987.

After Larson's retirement from the comics page, other single-panel comics that took up his style included *Off the Mark* and *Speed Bump*. Larson went on to other projects, including publishing the book *There's a Hair in My Dirt: A Worm's Story* in 1998. He also occasionally accepted new commissions, such as the prestigious November 17, 2003, *New Yorker* cover.

P. Andrew Miller

SEE ALSO: *Comics; The* New Yorker*;* Peanuts.

BIBLIOGRAPHY

Larson, Gary. *The Far Side*. Kansas City, KS: Andrews and McMeel, 1982.

Larson, Gary. *The PreHistory of* The Far Side: *A 10th Anniversary Exhibit*. Kansas City, KS: Andrews and McMeel, 1989.

Fargo

In order to gain a piece of his father-in-law's fortune, a financially desperate husband (William H. Macy) hires two hit men (Steve Buscemi and Peter Stormare) to fake the kidnapping of his wife in Joel and Ethan Coen's 1996 noir-comedy film *Fargo*. Frances McDormand won a 1996 Best Actress Oscar for her portrayal of the pregnant police chief who cracks the botched-kidnapping, multiple-homicide case. More than murders, people-pulverizing wood chippers, and snowstorms, *Fargo* brought allegedly genuine midwestern mannerisms and dialect to urban America and an Academy Award for Best Original Screenplay to the native-Minnesotan Coen brothers.

Daryna M. McKeand

SEE ALSO: *Academy Awards; Coen, Joel and Ethan; Film Noir; Hollywood.*

BIBLIOGRAPHY

Bennun, David. "Coen for Gold." *Melody Maker*, June 1, 1996, 24.

Russell, Carolyn R. *The Films of Joel and Ethan Coen*. Jefferson, NC: McFarland, 2001.

Farley, Chris *(1964–1997)*

A Wisconsin-born comedian who honed his improvisational skills in nearby Chicago, Chris Farley gained fame as one of the NBC *Saturday Night Live* (*SNL*) Bad Boys of the 1990s with comedians such as David Spade and Adam Sandler. Farley appeared in two successful films with Spade and was cast to voice the lead character in the animated *Shrek*, but before that project commenced he died of a drug overdose in Chicago in 1997. Due to his appearance, image, and cause of death, Farley continues to be compared to John Belushi, an earlier *SNL* cast member who also died of a drug overdose at the age of thirty-three.

Christopher Crosby Farley was born to a large Irish Catholic family in Madison, Wisconsin, in 1964. It was said that he gained his father's attention as a child by impersonating Belushi's character John Blutarsky from the 1978 *Animal House*. Farley graduated from Catholic Edgewood High School and Marquette University, the latter with a degree in communications and theater in 1986, and he performed improvisational comedy in Madison and Chicago, joining the Second City improv group in 1989. A training ground for numerous other *SNL* cast members, including Belushi, Farley was personally scouted by *SNL* producer Lorne Michaels.

Farley made more than 100 appearances on the nationally televised program beginning in 1990, showcasing his intense personal energy through numerous dumber-than-life personas. His Matt Foley character was an in-the-face motivational speaker who reminded his audience that he "lived in a van, down by the river." Todd O'Connor was a sausage eating, beer-guzzling Chicago sports fan on the faux sports program "Bill Swerski's Superfans" who worshipped "da Bears" and "da Bulls" in an exaggerated Chicago dialect. Another character was Bennett Brauer, a commentator on the simulated news program "Weekend Update" who complained of personal hygiene problems. Farley also parodied himself in the mock television talk program "The Chris Farley Show" and performed a memorable Chippendales male-dancer routine with actor and dancer Patrick Swayze.

Farley was released from his *SNL* contract in 1995 as part of an effort to revamp the program and as a result of his growing addictions. He had made minor appearances in several *SNL*-inspired films, including *Wayne's World* (1992), *Coneheads* (1993), and *Billy Madison* (1995), but his first and most successful major film role was as underdog Tommy Callahan in *Tommy Boy* in 1995. A Marquette University graduate, as was Farley, the character Callahan went through several life-changing experiences in the process of saving a Sandusky, Ohio, automotive-parts manufacturing firm from closing. *Black Sheep*, released the following year, tried but failed to repeat the same loser-turned-winner formula. Set in Washington State, it featured Farley as the reckless brother of a defrauded gubernatorial candidate. *Chicago Tribune* film critic Gene Siskel wrote that it was one of only two movies he had ever walked out of in twenty-six years of reviewing.

However, both movies grossed more than $30 million each, and Farley was cast as the lead character in the early 1997 *Beverly Hills Ninja*. The film, the story of a blond-haired, light-skinned ninja hired to protect a Beverly Hills socialite, was almost universally panned by critics but grossed another $30 million, evidence of Farley's comedic talents and dedicated fan base. By this time the emotionally vulnerable Farley was coming under increasing scrutiny for his obesity and chronic alcohol and drug abuse. Production on *Almost Heroes*, a story of two frontiersmen competing with the Lewis and Clark expedition, was halted several times so that Farley could attend rehabilitation. Released after Farley's death, the film grossed only $6 million and was labeled "a dreadful motion picture" by at least one critic.

Meanwhile, Farley made a final *SNL* guest appearance on October 25, 1997, although producers, concerned he was too intoxicated, almost canceled the live show. On December 18,

1997, his body was found by a brother in his apartment in Chicago's John Hancock Center. His death was attributed to a four-day binge of alcohol, morphine, and cocaine, along with advanced atherosclerosis. He was buried in Madison. More than 500 people attended his funeral, although Spade did not, saying he did not want to "be in a room where Farley was in a box." Farley was awarded a star on the Hollywood Walk of Fame in 2005, and his *SNL* skits continued to be cited as some of the funniest ever. His brother Tom established the Chris Farley Foundation in 1998 to communicate the dangers of substance abuse to young people.

Richard Junger

SEE ALSO: *Belushi, John;* Saturday Night Live*; Second City;* Shrek*; Siskel and Ebert; Television;* Wayne's World.

BIBLIOGRAPHY

Chris Farley Foundation. Accessed May 2012. Available from http://www.chrisfarleyfoundation.org/

"Curators Favorites." Wisconsin Historical Society. Accessed May 2012. Available from http://www.wisconsinhistory.org/museum/artifacts/archives/003176.asp/

Farley, Tom, Jr., and Tanner Colby. *The Chris Farley Show: A Biography in Three Acts.* New York: Viking Press, 2008.

Mohr, Jay. *Gasping for Airtime: Two Years in the Trenches of "Saturday Night Live."* New York: Hyperion, 2004.

Shales, Tom, and James Andrew Miller. *Live from New York: An Uncensored History of "Saturday Night Live."* New York: Little, Brown, 2002.

Farm Aid

Farm Aid is a nonprofit organization that supports family farms in the United States. It was founded in 1985 by musicians Willie Nelson, Neil Young, and John Mellencamp. The idea for Farm Aid evolved from a comment made by musician Bob Dylan at the 1985 Live Aid concert, a benefit held to raise money to help starving people in Africa. Dylan said, "Wouldn't it be great if we did something like this for our own farmers right here in America?"

At the time, American farmers were struggling. Poor markets and high operating costs were driving an estimated 500 family farmers out of business every week. In response to Dylan's comment, Nelson, Young, and Mellencamp quickly organized a benefit concert for American farmers, and six weeks after the Live Aid concert, the first Farm Aid concert was held in Champaign, Illinois, attracting 80,000 people and raising more than $9 million. A second concert, Farm Aid II, was held the next year in Austin, Texas, and Farm Aid III was held in Lincoln, Nebraska, in 1987. A wide variety of artists turned out to perform at the Farm Aid concerts, including Dylan, Lyle Lovett, Steppenwolf, Hootie & the Blowfish, Wilco, Loretta Lynn, the Beach Boys, Steve Earle, Elton John, Stevie Ray Vaughan, Johnny Cash, the Grateful Dead, Ringo Starr, Martina McBride, and Phish.

Over the years, Farm Aid evolved into a two-part organization: one part produces annual fund-raising concerts, and the other part administers support programs for family farmers and lobbies for political change. In 1987 Farm Aid began to influence U.S. farm policy when Nelson, Mellencamp, and a group of family farmers testified before Congress about the state of family farming in the United States. Congress later passed the Agricultural Credit Act of 1987. This act mandates that the Farmer's Home Administration cannot foreclose on a family farm unless the administration would make more money through foreclosure than it would by investing in the farm to make it profitable. Farm Aid saw this as a significant step forward.

John Mellencamp at Farm Aid. *John Mellencamp performs at the 2011 Farm Aid Concert in Kansas City, Kansas.* EBET ROBERTS/REDFERNS/GETTY IMAGES.

In 1989 Nelson took Farm Aid on the road with sixteen of his own shows, asserting that "the fight to save family farms isn't just about farmers. It's about making sure that there is a safe and healthy food supply for all of us. It's about jobs, from Main Street to Wall Street. It's about a better America."

In the 1990s Farm Aid concerts were held in Indianapolis, Indiana (1990); Dallas, Texas (1992, 1997); Ames, Iowa (1993); New Orleans, Louisiana (1994); Louisville, Kentucky (1995); Columbia, South Carolina (1996); and Tinley Park, Illinois (1998). In 1991 Farm Aid focused on dairy farmers, who had experienced a sharp drop in prices, and teamed with ice-cream maker Ben & Jerry's. In 1993 Farm Aid raised money to aid farmers affected by the Mississippi River floods that destroyed or damaged millions of acres of crops. In 1994 Nelson, on behalf of Farm Aid, successfully urged President Bill Clinton to pardon Nebraska farmer Ernest Krikava, who had been imprisoned for illegally selling hogs during a bankruptcy proceeding to feed his desperate and starving family.

By 2012 Farm Aid had raised nearly $40 million with its benefit concerts. The organization continued to provide direct aid to farmers through small grants, an online Farmers Resource Network, and a national hotline. Through interaction with governments, farmers, and the American people, Farm Aid has been a positive influence on all aspects of growing and marketing food in the United States. Its efforts have resulted in a rise in the number of farmers' markets, an increase in the number of community-supported agricultural groups, and a rise in the number of farm-to-table restaurants. Most importantly it has increased public awareness of sustainable farming in the United States.

S. Renee Dechert

SEE ALSO: *The Beach Boys; Cash, Johnny; Dylan, Bob; Farmers' Markets; The Grateful Dead; Mellencamp, John; Nelson, Willie; Steppenwolf; Vaughan, Stevie Ray; Young, Neil.*

BIBLIOGRAPHY

Duffy, Thom. "Deeply Rooted." *Billboard*, November 19, 2011.

Hoekstra, Dave; Holly George-Warren; Willie Nelson; et al. *Farm Aid: A Song for America.* Emmaus, PA: Rodale, 2005.

Farmers' Markets

A long-standing human tradition, farmers' markets offer a place to purchase produce and other food from the people who grew it. Perhaps surprisingly, such markets continue to grow and prosper in a twenty-first-century America chock full of grocery stores and restaurants. To support this system, today's farmers' markets have turned an economic paradigm on its head.

A farmers' market consists of individual vendors—mostly farmers—who set up booths, tables, or stands outdoors or indoors to sell produce, meat products, fruits, and sometimes prepared foods and beverages. In the past, centralized markets were primarily created to provide producers with the opportunity to sell their products. Although this is still accomplished, most of today's markets are driven by consumers who are specifically looking for locally grown and organic products.

The marketplace, of course, grows from an ancient tradition: public markets are known to have existed 6,000 years ago in Mesopotamia, where they played a critical part in the development of local economies. In Europe centuries later, markets became a mechanism for protecting consumers from high prices. Typically, these markets were scheduled to coincide with community events, including local fairs or festivals. When European powers such as France and Spain extended their empires through colonization, the markets moved throughout the globe. With European influence, American markets gathered on empty lots along major thoroughfares. Often, these roads became formalized and were referred to as "Market Streets."

The market tradition bound together many American communities. Even more important in such a rural nation, the markets tied towns and cities to outlying farmlands. This was important economically and sociologically. Boston, Massachusetts, is credited for having the first American market, which was established in 1634. In 1643 the General Court of Connecticut required Hartford to hold its market on Wednesdays. In Philadelphia, Pennsylvania, the entire city plan was organized around a market along High Street, which was later renamed Market Street. And the oldest ongoing market in the United States was established in the 1730s in Lancaster, Pennsylvania. Carrying the tradition west of the Mississippi River, the Soulard Farmers Market in St. Louis, Missouri, was established in 1779.

Changes to the tradition of farmers' markets came with alterations to American agriculture. When large corporate interests streamlined agriculture through the use of chemicals and machines during the twentieth century, farmers' markets nearly died. There seemed to be little use for small-scale products because consumers placed scarce value on them. However, the evolution of modern environmentalism into green consumerism after 1970 brought a new reason for farmers' markets to exist.

Americans' interest in chemical-free, organic—or at least local—products brought new life to this ancient institution. Additionally, many communities began to appreciate the worth of such markets in a decentralized consumer world. Beginning in the 1980s many states emphasized investment in farmers' markets and local agriculture through initiatives designed to promote the growing and marketing of local produce. An increased awareness of the importance of diet and nutrition also led to an increased interest in farmers' markets in the 1980s and 1990s.

Today green consumerism joins with dietary consciousness in an exciting new trend. Starting with communes and other small-scale, anti–big agriculture efforts in the late 1960s, organic foods have become part of a popular movement that includes the slow food movement and efforts to buy locally produced agriculture. Even First Lady Michelle Obama has focused attention on such ideas: She installed an organic garden at the White House in 2009. She encouraged Freshfarm Markets, a group that runs a number of farmers' markets in the Washington, D.C., area, to set up near the White House, and then arrived at the market to shop for food. She also initiated a call for the regulations for school lunches across the nation to begin to incorporate organic and local products.

Farmers' markets have become mainstream thanks to green consumerism. In 1994 there were only 1,755 farmers' markets in the United States. That number surged to 5,274 in 2009. The growth is mainly due to an increased interest in more heathful foods, a desire to protect local cultivars, and an increased understanding of the importance of small, sustainable farming. This ancient tradition continues to find ways to bind people together, country and city.

Brian Black

SEE ALSO: *Communes; Consumerism; Environmentalism; Flea Markets; Foodies; Organic Food.*

BIBLIOGRAPHY

Petrini, Carlo. *Slow Food Nation.* New York: Rizzoli Ex Libris, 2007.

Pollan, Michael. *The Omnivore's Dilemma.* New York: Penguin, 2006.

Robinson, Jennifer Meta, and J. A. Hartenfeld. *The Farmers' Market Book.* Bloomington, IN: Quarry Books, 2007.

Rodale, Maria. *Organic Manifesto.* Emmaus, PA: Rodale Press, 2011.

Schlosser, Eric. *Fast Food Nation: The Dark Side of the All-American Meal.* Boston: Houghton Mifflin, 2001.

Farmville

SEE: *Online Gaming.*

Fast Food

Even more than hot dogs and apple pie, the hamburgers and french fries found at ubiquitous fast-food restaurants represent America's quintessential food and, in many ways, the country's quintessential culture. Because it is both affordable and convenient, fast food has become a regular part of family life. The undisputed king of the fast-food world, McDonald's, sells seventy-five burgers every second of the day to forty-seven million customers throughout the world. As the economy worsened in the first decade of the 2000s, fast-food chains were the only restaurants in the United States that continued to show increased sales. In response to criticism, some of these establishments have begun offering more healthful options such as salads, fruits, and oatmeal and have agreed to use less saturated food in their cooking. However, customers continue to exhibit preferences for less healthful items such as burgers, chicken nuggets, and fries.

MOBILITY AND CHANGING LIFESTYLES

The rise of the fast-food restaurant would not have been possible without concomitant changes in U.S. culture. In the 1920s, thanks in large part to developments in technology and industry, the American lifestyle began to change. Formerly distinctive regional and ethnic cultures merged, blurring differences in ethnic and cultural identities. Many people moved away from farms and into cities in search of lucrative and exciting careers. In addition, the widespread use of the telephone and other modern conveniences and the increasing acceptance of mass media meant that there was a larger degree of cultural interaction.

The development of an affordable automobile and the simultaneous governmental support of new road systems physically reinforced this cultural melding, enabling people—especially car owners—to go to places they had never been before. This sparked a boom in the tourist industry: travelers who once went by rail, boat, or horse were moving faster by car, and they began to value speed and convenience as part of their trips. These travelers needed affordable and reliable places to stay—and to eat.

While local diners and eateries offered good, wholesome, home-cooked meals, they were often located far away from main thoroughfares, making them inconvenient for the interstate traveler. Travelers, however, were not the only ones eating on the run; private dining, once a formal ritual among family members and close friends, was becoming a thing of the past, and eating in public was becoming much more acceptable for everyone. The increased pace of life, especially in urban areas, meant that people no longer ate as a group around the table but favored sandwiches and other foods that could be eaten quickly and on the go. Food carts had been familiar in urban areas since the late 1800s, eventually evolving into more permanent short-order joints and diners. Cafeterias such as Horn and Hardart in Philadelphia featured Automat systems in the early 1900s that allowed people to extract pies, sandwiches, and entrées from vending machines for a penny or nickel. Food quickly became a means of fueling human beings in the same way that gasoline fueled automobiles.

The need for fast, reliable, affordable, and convenient food, along with an increasing acceptance among Americans of a more homogenous culture, led to the rise of the fast-food industry and, in particular, to the hamburgers and fries that it served. Purveyors of fast food sprang up in urban areas and along the nation's highways. During the 1920s the hamburger experienced a complete change of identity that attested to Americans' collective willingness to accept the new culture of food service. At the beginning of the decade, the humble meat patty, served between layers of a bun and often garnished with onions, ketchup, and mustard, was considered a lowly, working-class food—most hamburger stands were located close to factories and in working-class neighborhoods. By the end of the decade, the hamburger had come into its own, gaining widespread popularity and being considered a staple food, as evidenced by the overwhelming success of the "hamburger stand." The cartoon *Popeye*, which was popular at the time, even features a character, Wimpy, who gorges himself on hamburgers.

WHITE CASTLE

The most successful of these hamburger stands quickly multiplied, taking advantage of the growing popularity of "fast" food and applying industrial principles of standardization to its development. White Castle, founded in Wichita, Kansas, in 1921 by Billy Ingram and Walt Anderson, is considered the first fast-food restaurant in America. Anderson was originally a fry cook and perfected one version of the hamburger—square with small holes for better cooking, topped with fried onions and placed on a bun of soft white bread. Ingram recognized the potential of this relatively simple food, devised a limited menu around it, and standardized its production so that the uniform White Castle hamburger could be found in many different cities. While White Castle was never the largest of the fast-food chains, it was the first and most influential, beginning the franchise system and inspiring many imitators, including White Tower, White Clock, Royal Castle, and White Palace.

The methods and success of White Castle outlets had many implications for business and culture. They sold their five-cent burgers "by the sack," and encouraged carry-out for those customers on the go. They also developed standard floor plans and architectural designs that could be easily duplicated wherever a new White Castle was erected. They standardized the operations of the cooks so that even human workers behaved like machine mechanisms. All of these processes were implemented in order to make a uniform product and to divest the hamburger of its formerly negative reputation as a working-class foodstuff made of dubious ingredients. In order to implement these ideas, White Castle even adopted a system of vertical integration: the company produced the white porcelain and steel panels used for its buildings, owned the bakeries that made its buns, and even started a company to make the disposable paper hats and aprons worn by its employees.

White Castle hamburgers were so tasty, affordable, and increasingly ubiquitous that there was a marked increase in beef production in addition to the mass consumption of hamburgers. As historian David Hogan remarks in *Selling 'Em by the Sack: White Castle and the Creation of American Food*, "White Castle advanced food production and distribution to the volume demanded by the expanding population, and it gave an American democracy an accessible, egalitarian, and standardized style of eating. It also supplied America with a distinctive ethnic symbol: people the world over now readily identify fast-food hamburgers as the food of Americans." By the end of the decade, White Castle had brought its burgers and cultural ethos to Omaha, Nebraska; Kansas City, Kansas; St. Louis, Missouri; Minneapolis, Minnesota; Indianapolis, Indiana; Louisville, Kentucky; Cincinnati, Ohio; and Chicago. The chain also expanded to the East Coast in 1929, inspiring successful imitators wherever it went and making *White Castle* almost a generic name for hamburgers by the end of the 1920s.

RISE OF AN INDUSTRY

The hamburger fulfilled economic as well as cultural needs. During the Great Depression, affordable food such as that found at the local hamburger stand was a godsend, especially to those who were unemployed; White Castle's hamburgers, for example, cost just five cents each until 1946, when the price doubled due to beef shortages imposed during World War II. By the end of 1930, the company had sold more than twenty-one million hamburgers; at the end of 1937, this number had increased to more than forty million.

The rise of White Castle led to another development in the fast-food front: the drive-in restaurant. Even though the first drive-in restaurant, Royce Hailey's Pig Stand in Dallas, Texas, was opened in 1921, it was not until nearly three decades later that the drive-in restaurant enjoyed a degree of success. Drive-ins, another fast-food institution, celebrated the cultural importance of the automobile, allowing the car itself to be a dining room of sorts, from which people could order their food and eat it in the open air. These drive-ins, at which the servers were known as car hops, became familiar hangouts for American teenagers.

Various businesspeople, impressed by the enduring success of hamburger stands, especially White Castle, capitalized on these cultural shifts by developing sophisticated franchise operations to run new fast-food companies. The franchise was a distinct business strategy that standardized not only the specific product sold but also the very institution that sold it. This form of organization exploited economies of scale and therefore was highly successful; as one entrepreneur remarked, there was "more money to be made selling hamburger stands than in selling hamburgers."

Franchises were not unique to the 1950s; they had been around since the early decades of the twentieth century, patronized by a public increasingly used to and insistent upon the supposed reliability and trustworthiness of branded goods. White Castle was one of the first successful franchises, but it was quickly followed by A&W Root Beer in 1924 and Howard Johnson's, which began operations in 1935. But it took the ideals of postwar culture to wholly support the fast-food franchises and make many of them into companies worth billions of dollars. The idea of the franchise operation itself was attractive, melding otherwise conflicting postwar desires: after the war, the business economy was a reiteration of American power, and the fact that this economy was made up of small businesses simultaneously expressed traditional American values.

McDONALD'S

McDonald's, the most successful fast-food franchise, was started in 1955 by Ray A. Kroc (1902–1984), a Chicago milk shake machine salesman. While Kroc did not invent the hamburger, the concept of the hamburger stand, or even the franchise system, he combined these elements in such an astute way as to make both his name and his company synonymous with fast food. When Kroc sold some of his milk shake equipment to Richard and Maurice McDonald of San Bernardino, California, for their popular hamburger stand, he was so impressed with their operation that he joined them in partnership in 1955. The first McDonald's outlet opened in Des Plaines, Illinois, that same year.

By 1960 Kroc had opened 228 "golden arches" drive-ins, selling fifteen-cent hamburgers, ten-cent french fries, and twenty-cent milk shakes; in 1961 Kroc bought out the McDonald brothers, name and all. The original McDonald's architecture was red-and-white tile with a golden arch abutting each end of the building. Patrons and critics found it to be too gaudy, so McDonald's moved to a more modest brown brick design with a shingled mansard roof in the mid-1960s but kept the golden arches, now attached to form an "M," as the company's widely recognized logo.

Kroc's success lay in his approach not specifically to cooking individual food items but in conceiving of his franchise operation in its entirety. His outlets were food factories—everything was systematized to ensure uniformity, even the smiles on the clerks' faces. Kroc did not promise the best burger in the world, but he did promise identical burgers throughout the world; indeed, the public came to accept this dictum, preferring predictability over quality. Every McDonald's had the same menu and the same general layout (with minor variations to acknowledge regional differences). The workers, all dressed alike, used the same techniques and equipment to prepare the food in the same way. In addition, Kroc established the chain as "family" restaurants that were clean, well-lit, and free from pay phones and pinball machines that might encourage loitering.

McDonald's periodically introduced new products in response to perceived consumer demand and competition from other chains. The Filet-O-Fish entered the menu in 1962 in an attempt to attract Catholic customers on Fridays. The "Chevy of Hamburgers," the Big Mac, appeared in 1967 to directly compete with Burger King's Whopper. In 1971 McDonald's introduced the Egg McMuffin and developed an entire breakfast line from it. Chicken McNuggets were added in 1983.

GOLDEN AGE

The 1960s through the 1990s was the golden age of fast food and saw the explosion of various fast-food chains and the subsequent creation of "the strip" in almost every town—the piece of road or highway flanked by franchise after franchise—which became a trademark feature of the suburban landscape. Fast-food restaurants along the strip sold not only hamburgers but also hot dogs, fish, pizza, ice cream, chicken, and roast beef sandwiches. Their brightly colored neon signs advertised such businesses as A&W, Arby's, Big Boy, Blimpie, Burger Chef, Burger King, Carrol's, Church's Chicken, Dairy Queen, Domino's Pizza, Hardee's, House of Pizza, Howard Johnson's, Jack in the Box, Kentucky Fried Chicken (KFC), Long John Silver's, Pizza Hut, Ralley's, Red Barn, Roy Roger's, Royal Castle, Sandy's, Shakey's Pizza, Taco Bell, Taco Time, Taco Tito's, Tastee Freez, Wendy's, White Castle, and White Tower.

McDonald's experienced its stiffest competition in the 1960s from Burger Chef, which was eventually sold to General Foods and absorbed by Hardee's in the early 1980s. Burger King was a more enduring rival for McDonald's than other chains had been. It began in 1954 as a "walk-up" called InstaBurger King and offered no interior seating. Dave Edgerton and Jim McLamore, its Miami founders, shortened the name to Burger King in 1957. While the business featured hamburgers, similar to McDonald's and White Castle, it set itself apart by offering the "flame-broiled" Whopper—a much larger hamburger (4 ounces compared to the 1.6-ounce McDonald's hamburger)—and instituted an advertising campaign that promised people could "Have It Your Way," by letting customers choose their own toppings.

Kentucky Fried Chicken (KFC), also a viable competitor to McDonald's, took a different approach by offering stereotypical southern food—buckets of fried chicken, coleslaw, mashed potatoes, and biscuits and gravy. Founded by "Colonel" Harland Sanders (1890–1980) in 1954, the franchise that made chicken "Finger Lickin' Good" consisted of more than 300 outlets by 1963 and was enjoying revenues of more than $500,000; by 1966 KFC had a gross income of $15 million.

GROWING COMPETITION

Other fast-food franchises also bear mentioning. Arby's first appeared in 1964 in Boardman, Ohio, and was the brainchild of Forrest and Leroy Raffel, who tried to attract a more discriminating clientele by offering roast beef sandwiches, using an Old West decor, and featuring more expensive menu items. Dairy Queen, started in 1944 by partners Harry Axene and John McCullough of Davenport, Iowa, sold hot dogs and ice cream and had 2,500 outlets by 1948. Domino's, with delivery-only pizza service, was founded by Tom Monaghan, who opened his first shop in 1960 and turned to franchising in 1967. By the end of 1986, Domino's had sold more than 189 million pizzas, accruing sales of $2 billion. The sale of pizza has become heavily associated with sporting events. On Super Bowl Sunday, 350 slices of pizza are sold every second in the United States.

Hardee's, largely an imitation of Burger King, began in Greenville, North Carolina, in 1960, and its outlets numbered more than 900 by 1975. Howard Johnson's, named for its founder and known for its bright orange rooftops and homemade ice cream, started out as a set of franchised roadside restaurants in 1935. By 1967 "HoJo's" boasted more than 800 restaurants but was a victim of the "burger wars" in the late 1970s and 1980s, eventually going out of business.

Taco Bell originated in 1962 in Downey, California. Even though Taco Bell was the idea of Glen Bell, a telephone repairman, it was John Martin who understood how to merchandise the company, beginning in 1983, and he was responsible for much of its success. Among other things, Martin omitted all ethnic symbols to counteract the negative associations people made with Mexican restaurants and changed the logo from a sleeping Mexican with a sombrero to a pastel-colored bell. Wendy's, specializing in bigger, better, and more expensive hamburgers, introduced the first drive-through windows at its restaurants, which were so popular that Burger King and McDonald's followed suit. Founded in 1972 by R. Dave Thomas in Columbus, Ohio, Wendy's had nine outlets and sales of $1.8 million by the end of that same year.

McDonald's, Burger King, Taco Bell, Wendy's, and KFC have remained the most successful fast-food chains, edging out most of their competitors during the burger wars, a time when large companies bought up fast-food franchises and either made them more successful or put them out of business. Other factors also led to many franchise downfalls. Beginning in the 1970s, these operations were faced with increasing criticism about everything from employees' working conditions and the nutritional value of the food they served to the impact the "fast food" mentality was having on the public at large.

CRITICISM

Franchise success was almost wholly based on the principles of standardization and a machine ethic. This included the laborers working inside fast-food restaurants who were treated as parts of a machine meant to run as efficiently as possible. Training was based on the idea that basic skills substituted for high turnover rates—the guarantee that the food could still be made the same even from unskilled hands. The short-order cook of the early diners, who was considered an artisan of sorts, was replaced by teenagers working for minimum wage and no benefits.

Nutritionists targeted the composition of the meals themselves, identifying them as laden with too much fat, cholesterol, and sugar and not enough vegetables. They worried that people eating a steady diet of fast food would go without basic nutrients and also become too accustomed to unhealthy meals. Hogan underscores this point, noting, "Americans consumed 50 percent more chicken and beef in 1976 than they had in 1960, mainly because the fast-food chains usually served only those two meats."

Critics coined the pejorative phrase "fast-food culture" as a metaphor for the quick-service industries and excessive standardization of culture and consumption. This homogenization, they believed, not only affected American culture, erasing once-vibrant ethnic and regional traditions, but also influenced the entire world—a cultural imperialism enacted on an international level. Books such as Eric Schlosser's *Fast Food Nation* (2001) and documentaries like Morgan Spurlock's *Super Size Me* (2004) sought to challenge the emergent fast-food culture by portraying its adverse effects on personal and community health, as well as its consequences on the environment and local and international economies.

The major franchises combated these critiques with varying degrees of success. They hired older workers in an attempt to seem beneficent, giving job opportunities to those past retirement age while never addressing the real issue of wages. To counter the protests of nutritionists, they introduced salad bars and "lean" burgers, which were largely ignored by customers. They tried to soften their images in a number of ways, chiefly by marketing themselves as family restaurants.

They also targeted children, creating loyal future consumers. Most chains had mascots. McDonald's has Ronald McDonald, a clown who debuted in 1963. (Ronald was so successful that a study conducted in the early 1970s found that 96 percent of American children recognized him—he came in second only to Santa Claus.) Ronald's friends who live in McDonaldland with him include Grimace, the Hamburglar, Mayor McCheese, Captain Crook, and the Professor. McDonald's also built brightly colored playgrounds at its restaurants beginning in the 1970s. Burger King's mascot is the Magic Burger King. KFC has continued to use the colorful Colonel himself as a spokesman long after he had sold the rights to his company and many years after his death.

Most fast-food franchises also introduced specially packaged children's meals that contain prizes; many serve as popular sites for children's birthday parties. In the 2010s, a new movement to stop fast-food companies from marketing to children gained momentum. The city of San Francisco went so far as to enact a Healthy Food Incentive Ordinance, which banned fast-food chains from including toys in children's meals, in 2010. McDonald's, however, found a way around the law by charging just 10 cents to add a toy to their Happy Meals. Nevertheless, many fast-food chains have adopted a number of healthful, kid-friendly options on their menus in recent years, such as bite-sized fruit or veggie slices.

In addition, these franchises have openly founded or contributed to charitable organizations. McDonald's established Ronald McDonald Houses, which provide lodging to parents whose critically ill or injured children are getting treatment in nearby hospitals. Both Burger King and Wendy's support programs for needy children, and Colonel Sanders was an outspoken supporter of the March of Dimes.

FAST-FOOD CULTURE

By the final decades of the twentieth century, Americans had fully embraced their fast-food culture. In 1994 alone, fast-food restaurants in the United States sold more than five billion hamburgers, making fast food a favorite meal and an important commodity. In 1996, 7 percent of the population ate at the 11,400 McDonald's franchises each day; males from their mid-teens to their early thirties comprised 75 percent of this business.

Fast food is a cultural phenomenon that reaches beyond America's borders. By 1996 McDonald's owned more than 7,000 restaurants in other countries, including 1,482 in Japan; 430 in France; 63 in China; 2 each in Bulgaria and Andorra; and 1 in Croatia. These outlets have acknowledged some cultural differences—in Germany they sell beer, in France they sell wine, and in Saudi Arabia they have separate sections for men and women and close four times a day for prayers. But for the most part the fare is the same, homogenizing culture on an international level. The overwhelming success of the fast-food culture invasion, and of McDonald's in particular, was fully realized when that chain opened its first store in India in 1996 and sold no hamburgers at all.

The greatest concern surrounding the ubiquitous nature of fast-food restaurants is that the most popular foods are unhealthful. This has led to what some are calling "globesity" because fast food has now circled the globe. Particular attention is being paid to childhood obesity. The Centers for Disease Control and Prevention reports that obesity among children six to eleven rose from 7 percent in 1980 to almost 20 percent in 2008. During that same period, obesity among young people in the twelve-to-nineteen age bracket rose from 5 percent to 18 percent. By 2008 more than one-third of American children and adolescents were overweight. Very few children get enough fruit, vegetable, and dairy products in their diets.

In spite of the fact that most fast-food chains offer more healthful options, the most popular choices are hamburgers, chicken nuggets, and fries. For instance, McDonald's Big Mac packs 540 calories, 10 grams of saturated fat, 43 grams of carbohydrates, and 1,040 milligrams of sodium. Adding an order of regular fries increases the meal by 570 calories, 6 grams of saturated fat, 70 grams of carbohydrates, and 330 milligrams of sodium. Despite repeated warnings by the federal government and various watchdog groups, fast-food restaurants keep introducing choices that are even more unhealthful. Stroke, heart attacks, diabetes, high blood pressure, and other such conditions are on the rise in the United States, and those upswings have occurred in conjunction with the rise in the consumption of fast food.

Wendy Woloson

SEE ALSO: *Automobile; Burger King; Diners; French Fries; The Great Depression; Hamburger; Hot Dogs; Ice Cream Cone; Kentucky Fried Chicken; McDonald's; Pizza; Pop-Up Restaurants; Super Bowl;* Super Size Me*; White Castle; World War II.*

BIBLIOGRAPHY

Boas, Max, and Steve Chain. *Big Mac: The Unauthorized Story of McDonald's.* New York: E. P. Dutton, 1976.

Costley, Kevin C., and Timothy Legett. *Childhood Obesity: A Heavy Problem.* Washington, DC: ERIC Clearinghouse, 2010.

Dicke, Thomas S. *Franchising in America: The Development of a Business Method, 1840–1980.* Chapel Hill: University of North Carolina Press, 1992.

Fishwick, Marshall, ed. *Ronald Revisited: The World of Ronald McDonald.* Bowling Green, OH: Bowling Green University Popular Press, 1983.

Hogan, David. *Selling 'Em by the Sack: White Castle and the Creation of American Food.* New York: New York University Press, 1997.

Jackson, Kenneth T. *Crabgrass Frontier: The Suburbanization of the United States.* New York: Oxford University Press, 1985.

Kline, Stephen. *Globesity, Food Marketing and Family Lifestyles.* New York: Palgrave Macmillan, 2011.

Kroc, Ray. *Grinding It Out: The Making of McDonald's.* Chicago: Contemporary Books, 1977.

Love, John. *McDonald's: Behind the Arches.* New York: Bantam Books, 1995.

Luxenberg, Stan. *Roadside Empires.* New York: Viking, 1985.

McLamore, James W. *The Burger King: Jim McLamore and the Building of an Empire.* New York: McGraw-Hill, 1998.

Millstone, Erik, and Tim Lang. *The Atlas of Food: Who Eats What, Where, and Why.* Berkeley: University of California Press, 2008.

Monaghan, Tom, and Robert Anderson. *Pizza Tiger.* New York: Random House, 1986.

Pearce, John. *The Colonel: The Captivating Biography of the Dynamic Founder of a Fast-Food Empire.* Garden City, NY: Doubleday, 1982.

Schlosser, Eric. *Fast Food Nation: The Dark Side of the All-American Meal.* Boston: Houghton Mifflin, 2001.

Fatal Attraction

Released by Paramount Pictures and directed by Adrian Lyne, *Fatal Attraction* was one of the biggest box-office hits of 1987. The film was more than just a commercial success, however; it was also a cultural phenomenon, inspiring heated discussions across the nation.

Fatal Attraction tells the story of an extramarital affair between Dan Gallager (played by Michael Douglas), a married attorney and father of one, and Alex Forrest (Glenn Close), a single, successful professional. After a brief and seemingly casual two-night fling, Dan is stalked and terrorized by Alex. The film sparked a new genre—that of the female psychopath—which included offerings such as *The Hand That Rocks the Cradle* (1992), *Single White Female* (1992), and *Basic Instinct* (1992). Though dangerous cinematic women predate *Fatal Attraction,* the murderous female characters in earlier films are more violent, sexualized, and devious.

Many critics view *Fatal Attraction* as characteristic of the backlash against the feminist movement in the 1980s and 1990s. The character of Alex—with her gender-neutral name, financial independence, and ability to express and act on her desires—makes female power seem destructive and deadly. She is a far cry from the traditional Hollywood depictions of women as passive sexual objects.

Frances Gateward

SEE ALSO: *Feminism; Sexual Revolution.*

BIBLIOGRAPHY

Hirschberg, Jeffrey. *Reflections of the Shadow: Creating Memorable Heroes and Villains for Film and TV.* Studio City, CA: Michael Wiese Productions, 2009.

Holmlund, Chris. "Reading Character with a Vengeance: The *Fatal Attraction* Phenomenon." *Velvet Light Trap,* Spring (1991): 25–36.

Father Divine *(1880?–1965)*

Despite certain ambiguities of character, the self-appointed Father Divine was undoubtedly both charismatic and clever and prospered in one of the few leadership roles open to black males in early twentieth-century America. Father Divine's theology blended various Christian traditions with a belief in positive thinking in ways that foreshadowed a number of contemporary New Age spiritual trends. His career demonstrated how a promise of religious salvation, political progress, and the philanthropic provision of basic social services can attract a large following in times of racial and economic turmoil. From obscure and humble origins, Father Divine fashioned himself into a cult leader of godlike pretensions and created a controversial church whose beliefs fascinated America throughout the 1930s and 1940s.

There are a number of competing versions of the history of Father Divine's early life. Sources conflict as to his birthdate—variously noted as between 1874 and 1882—but the most plausible account is that Divine was born George Baker to ex-slave parents in a Maryland African American ghetto in about 1880. By the early years of the twentieth century, he was traveling with a wandering evangelist who styled himself Father Jehovia, while the young Baker called himself the Messenger. After some years of preaching together they parted, and Baker began to refer to himself as Major Jealous Devine and to proclaim himself as God. With a small band of followers in tow, he moved to New York, where he changed his name yet again to Father Divine.

By 1919 he had obtained a base for his new Peace Mission Movement in Sayville, Long Island, where his preaching initially attracted a mainly black audience. The years following World War I had seen a massive migration of southern African Americans to northern industrial cities, and Father Divine's message of self-respect and racial equality drew an increasingly large following. The Peace Mission mandated celibacy and modesty and shunned improvidence and debt, but it was its provision of employment, cheap lodgings, and inexpensive food to its adherents during the Great Depression that brought thousands of worshippers, white as well as black, flocking to Sayville.

The influx aroused the ire of local residents whose complaints resulted in Father Divine's arrest. He was charged with disturbing the peace, convicted in 1932, and sentenced to a year in jail. The court proceedings brought him widespread notoriety when, two days after sentencing him, the judge suffered a fatal heart attack. From his prison cell, the self-styled "God" proclaimed "I hated to do it"—a remark that, trumpeted by the media, confirmed their leader's claims to divine being among his followers.

Moving the mission's headquarters to Harlem, New York, Father Divine continued to attract national attention on two fronts: by his lavish lifestyle and rumors of his sexual adventures and by the progressive social ideas his believers practiced. The mission's services were scrupulously integrated racially, and the movement led the way in pressing for antilynching laws and for public facilities to be open to all races. In a time of economic disaster, it rejected relief and welfare and bought hotels, which it termed "heavens," where its members could live modest, mutually supportive lives free of alcohol, tobacco, and reliance on credit.

In 1946 Father Divine was again in the headlines when he married one of his young followers, a white Canadian woman named Edna Rose Ritchings, also known as Sweet Angel. By the 1950s, however, he was in deteriorating health. His public profile dwindled alongside the importance of his movement as other, less outrageous African American leaders rose to prominence. Father Divine died in 1965 at his Philadelphia estate. As of 2012, his wife, known as Mother Divine, was still presiding over the remains of the Peace Mission Movement.

Gerry Bowler

SEE ALSO: *Cults; The Great Depression; New Age Spirituality; World War I.*

BIBLIOGRAPHY

Burnham, Kenneth E. *God Comes to America: Father Divine and the Peace Mission Movement.* Boston: Lambeth Press, 1979.

Hall, Timothy L. *American Religious Leaders.* New York: Facts On File, 2003.

Watts, Jill. *God, Harlem, U.S.A.: The Father Divine Story.* Los Angeles: University of California Press, 1992.

Weisbrot, Father. *Father Divine and the Struggle for Racial Equality.* Urbana: University of Illinois Press, 1983.

Father Knows Best

Father Knows Best, which began life as a radio series in 1949, evolved into a CBS television sitcom in 1954. An archetypal representation of 1950s ideals of family life, it came to be regarded as an important influence on American family values. Actor Robert Young (the only member of the original radio cast who continued his role on television) starred as Jim Anderson, an agent for the General Insurance Company. Anderson lives with his wife, Margaret, and their three children at 607 South Maple Lane in Springfield, a wholesome midwestern suburban community. Jane Wyatt costarred as Margaret Anderson, and their offspring—seventeen-year-old Betty (called "Princess" by her father); fourteen-year-old Jim Jr. (or "Bud"); and Kathy, the baby of the family at age nine and fondly known as "Kitten" to her dad—were played by Elinor Donahue, Billy Gray, and Lauren Chapin, respectively. The stories revolve around the various exploits of the Anderson family, whose problems are neatly solved in each thirty-minute episode by listening to father (and, by extension, mother) and doing the right thing.

Although the show was critically acclaimed, its initial season on television in the Sunday 10 p.m. slot was considered a ratings failure, and CBS canceled it in the spring of 1955. Despite the low ratings the cancellation brought protests from viewers, who demanded not only the return of the show but also an earlier time slot to allow youngsters to watch it. This audience reaction brought a response from NBC, which picked up the show and aired it earlier and was rewarded with a hit. Young decided to leave in 1960, but such was the show's popularity that CBS (in a highly unusual move for network television) aired reruns in prime time for two more years.

The most remarkable episode of *Father Knows Best,* however, was never seen on television. In a move that pointed toward the national importance it had assumed because of its healthy depiction of family life, the U.S. Treasury Department commissioned a special episode in 1959 to be distributed to schools and civic organizations throughout the country. Titled "24 Hours in Tyrantland," the story disseminated a masterful piece of Cold War propaganda through the plot device of Jim Anderson being asked to head Springfield's U.S. Savings Bond drive. Delighted at being charged with this worthwhile task, Jim decides to enlist the help of his family in the campaign. Predict-

Father Knows Best. *The cast of* Father Knows Best *included, clockwise from lower left, Billy Gray, Elinor Donahue, Robert Young, Jane Wyatt, and Lauren Chapin.* SCREEN GEMS/GETTY IMAGES.

ably, Margaret is entirely supportive, but the kids, caught up in other concerns, are less than enthusiastic. Upset by their unwillingness to help, Jim strikes a bargain: he gives them each the cost of a U.S. savings bond but decrees their home a communist state for twenty-four hours. If, he tells them, they can stand to live in "Tyrantland" for twenty-four hours, they can keep the money to use however they choose. If they don't make it, they have to use the money to buy a bond and help him in the drive.

Throughout the day, "tyrant" Jim works them to the bone and taxes them into poverty, while they repeatedly assert the unfairness of the situation. Jim reacts to their complaints as would a man who has no concept of fairness. The children make it through the twenty-four hours, but just when time is up and Betty is about to go out on her Saturday evening date, Jim turns back the clock an hour. The tyrant is all powerful; he can even reverse time. This is too much for Betty, who breaks down and sees the error of her ways. She is now proud to help sell bonds, and her siblings follow suit.

Like many a sitcom of its period, *Father Knows Best* came to acquire the camp appeal of the quaintly outmoded, particularly in its treatment of gender issues. Women know their place in the Anderson family (and seemingly in 1950s America), and in the rare instances when they momentarily lose sight of that place, some revelatory incident gently nudges them into submission, because "father knows best."

Joyce Linehan

SEE ALSO: *Camp; Cold War; Radio; Sitcom; Young, Robert.*

Father's Day

The origin of Father's Day represents a grassroots phenomenon that characterizes American reverence for the family. Although deeply rooted in North American social culture, the popularity—and, some might say, commercial exploitation—of Father's Day has crossed national boundaries to become popular in other countries such as Canada and the United Kingdom. Americans and Canadians set aside the third Sunday in June as the day children show their appreciation and gratitude for their fathers, but the earliest Father's Day celebration on record appears to have been held on July 5, 1908, in a church in Fairmont, West Virginia.

Father's Day was first celebrated in towns and cities scattered across America. The citizens of Vancouver, Washington, claim to have been the first to officially hold a townwide Father's Day ceremony, beginning in 1912. In 1915 the president of the Uptown Lions Club in Chicago was hailed as the "originator" of Father's Day when he suggested that the Lions hold a Father's Day celebration on the third Sunday in June.

Perhaps the most famous promoter of this holiday, though, was Sonora Smart Dodd of Spokane, Washington. Her inspiration for a Father's Day celebration came while she was listening to a Mother's Day sermon in 1909. Dodd wished to show appreciation to her own father because he had raised six children after their mother died in 1898. Dodd's father's birthday was June 5, so she petitioned the Spokane Ministerial Association to set aside that day in June 1910 as a special day to honor fathers. The association honored her request but changed the date of the celebration to June 19. On that day, Spokane became the first city to honor fathers in this way, beating Vancouver's official claim by two years.

The governor of Washington took note of the celebration and declared that the entire state should observe the day as Father's Day. Newspapers around the country carried stories about Spokane's celebration of Father's Day, and the celebration soon received national recognition. In 1916 President Woodrow Wilson joined in a celebration of Father's Day by pressing a button in Washington, D.C., that caused a flag to unroll in Spokane. In 1924 President Calvin Coolidge recommended that the third Sunday in June be set aside as Father's Day in all states.

In the years that followed, there were several attempts to pass a resolution in Congress declaring Father's Day an official holiday. In 1957 Senator Margaret Chase Smith attempted to pass such a resolution, arguing that it was the "most grievous insult imaginable" that Father's Day had not been recognized as an official holiday, despite the fact that Mother's Day had been celebrated as a holiday nationwide since 1914. Finally, in 1972, President Richard Nixon signed a proclamation designating the third Sunday in June as Father's Day.

This holiday is marked by many interesting traditions. Roses are worn to honor fathers: red for living fathers and white for those who have died. Many families celebrate the day by preparing the father's favorite meal, while children often buy special gifts for their fathers. The necktie is a perennial favorite, though power tools have become a popular choice in smaller towns, especially in the northern states. In larger cities, where a growing number of employers allow casual dress at work, sports shirts have become popular gifts. Thus, the customs of Father's Day can be seen to have evolved to reflect social change.

Thousands of different Father's Day cards are available each year—albeit less than the variety offered for Mother's Day and Valentine's Day—and Father's Day cards hold the distinction of having the highest percentage of humor. Approximately 100 million of these cards are sold annually, compared to sales of around 150 million Mother's Day cards; both are far outstripped by the almost 900 million Valentine's Day cards given each year.

Numerous churches continue the century-long tradition of recognizing fathers. Sermons often honor fathers and deliver encouragement to strengthen family relationships. Indeed, for all the commercial and private family aspects of Father's Day, churches in America have remained the backbone of organized Father's Day celebrations, continuing to pay tribute to the work and dedication of fathers in a society that continues to see many changes and upheavals in family life.

James H. Lloyd

SEE ALSO: *Greeting Cards; Mother's Day; Valentine's Day.*

BIBLIOGRAPHY

Christianson, Stephen G., and Jane M. Hatch. *American Book of Days*, 4th ed. New York: Wilson, 2000.

Klebanow, Barbara, and Sara Fischer. *American Holidays: Exploring Traditions, Customs, and Backgrounds.* Brattleboro, VT: Pro Lingua Associates, 1986.

Myers, Robert J., and the Editors of Hallmark Cards. *Celebrations: The Complete Book of American Holidays.* New York: Doubleday, 1972.

Santino, Jack. *All Around the Year: Holidays and Celebrations in American Life*. Urbana: University of Illinois Press, 1995.

Faulkner, William *(1897–1962)*

William Faulkner is regarded not only as one of the greatest American novelists but also among the world's greatest modernist writers. Born September 25, 1897, in New Albany, Mississippi, Faulkner spent most of his life in Oxford, Mississippi, the small town that provided inspiration for his novels. He began his writing career as a poet, and although he soon turned to prose, he retained a poetic, flowery style.

His first novel, *Soldiers' Pay* (1926), reflects postwar disillusion. *Mosquitoes* (1927), a book of ideas similar in style to the works of Aldous Huxley, concerns a group of artists and intellectuals. Not until *Flags in the Dust* did Faulkner find inspiration in his southern heritage. He invented the town of Jefferson, Mississippi, modeled after his own Oxford, and peopled it with dozens of characters based on his family and townspeople, most of whom reappear in later novels. In the southern setting Faulkner found the great themes that would occupy him for the remainder of his career: family curses, the burden of guilt that slavery had left upon whites, the romance of the southern aristocracy and its ghostly influence upon modern social codes, the transmission of a defeated culture through the telling of stories and gossip, and the intrusion of the automobile upon the settled ways of the rural South. In these themes one finds the clashes of old and new, past and present, fiction and reality, and absolutism and relativity that Faulkner developed in later novels. *Flags* was a long, complex, and fragmented manuscript that editors refused to publish without abridging it drastically; it first appeared as *Sartoris* in 1929, and a partially restored edition was published posthumously as *Flags in the Dust* in 1973.

THE SOUND AND THE FURY

Upset by the changes and convinced that he would never make money from novels, Faulkner began writing for himself rather than for the public. *The Sound and the Fury* (1929) was a book he thought no one would ever understand. It is indeed one of the most difficult novels ever published, but it is also one of the greatest. Abandoning the rambling, omniscient style of *Sartoris*, Faulkner used several modernist techniques, such as multiple narrators and jumbled chronology—both of which had been used so successfully by Joseph Conrad—and a stream-of-consciousness narrative that meticulously reports the thoughts of characters without the filter of dialogue or paraphrase. Thus, the simple story of Caddy, a rebellious girl who loses her virginity, becomes complex: each of the first three sections of the novel is told by one of her three brothers, whose thoughts reveal what Caddy's loss of virginity means to them. The final section is told by an omniscient narrator but focuses on the family's servant, an aged black woman who knows that Caddy's loss of virginity does not *mean* anything at all.

It is ironic, but highly significant, that Caddy does not tell her own story. This decentralization of the main character implies that there is no objective reality, that all exists in the eyes of the perceiver, and that meaning does not inhere in facts and deeds but is assigned to them by the perceiver—hence Faulker's borrowing of the title from a Shakespearean monologue, wherein Macbeth intones that life is fleeting and meaningless, "a tale told by an idiot, full of sound and fury, signifying nothing." In such a subjective context, concepts like virginity, honor, and sin are not God-given constants; they are social constructs created within a patriarchal society. These modernist ideas reverberated throughout the century. However, *The Sound and the Fury* is no mere novel of ideas. It is a gripping, passionate tale of human love and suffering. Faulkner's genius lies in the artistic union of the universal and the particular: the treatment of cosmic themes through vivid, sympathetic portraits of believable characters.

After *The Sound and the Fury*, Faulkner continued to experiment with narrative techniques and explore universal themes through the microcosm of the South. *As I Lay Dying* (1930), *Light in August* (1932), *Absalom, Absalom!* (1936), and *Go Down, Moses* (1942) are all considered masterpieces of modernist fiction. Less experimental but also great are *Sanctuary* (1931), *The Unvanquished* (1938), and *The Hamlet* (1940).

Unfortunately, only *Sanctuary*, a stark potboiler about gangsters and prostitutes, sold well, and Faulkner was forced to write for Hollywood in order to make money. His screen credits included *To Have and Have Not* (1944) and *The Big Sleep* (1946). The drunken screenwriter in the Coen brothers' film *Barton Fink* (1991) seems to be based on Faulkner during his Hollywood years; he struggled throughout his life with alcoholism.

ANTHOLOGY AND LATER CAREER

In 1946, when all his novels were out of print, *The Portable Faulkner* was published. This anthology gradually exposed him to a wider audience, and Faulkner was awarded the 1949 Nobel Prize in Literature, followed by the Pulitzer Prize in 1955. Faulkner's career in the 1950s was devoted to filling in the history of the mythic town of Jefferson and Yoknapatawpha County. This work is marked by continuing experimentation, including a hyperbolic rhetoric that makes some of these novels almost unbearable. When Faulkner died on July 6, 1962, he bequeathed scholarships for African American students and grants for the advancement of American literature.

Because of his radical experiments; his recondite diction; and his long, convoluted sentences that sometimes last several pages, Faulkner is notoriously difficult and has never attained widespread readership. Nevertheless, his books sell by the thousands each semester in college bookstores, and students find their efforts rewarded by a powerful intellectual experience. He had a great influence on the French "New Novelists" of the 1950s and Latin American authors of the "Boom" period of the 1960s. As one of the great modernists, Faulkner has influenced almost every writer today, whether they have read him or not. Often noted for his cinematic qualities, many of Faulkner's techniques are now used routinely in TV programs and movies (notably *The Godfather: Part II*, 1974). Whether we realize it or not, we are more sophisticated viewers and readers because of Faulkner.

Another, more amusing legacy is the annual Faux Faulkner contest, sponsored by the Jack Daniels Distillery, which awards a prize to the writer of the funniest parody of Faulkner's distinctive style.

Douglas Cooke

SEE ALSO: *Coen, Joel and Ethan;* The Godfather*; Hollywood; Modernism.*

BIBLIOGRAPHY

Blotner, Joseph. *Faulkner: A Biography*. New York: Vintage, 1991.

Cowley, Malcolm. *The Faulkner-Cowley File: Letters and Memories, 1944–1962*. New York: Viking, 1966.

Faulkner, John. *My Brother Bill: An Affectionate Reminiscence*. New York: Trident, 1963.

Kawin, Bruce F. *Faulkner and Film*. New York: Frederick Ungar, 1977.

Millgate, Michael. *William Faulkner*. New York: Grove, 1961.

Volpe, Edmond L. *A Reader's Guide to William Faulkner*. New York: Noonday, 1964.

Fauset, Jessie Redmon *(1882–1961)*

Writer Jessie Redmon Fauset represented the emergence of an authentic African American voice in American literature. She corresponded with W. E. B. Du Bois while attending language courses at Cornell University. Impressed by her writing, Du Bois invited Fauset to join the staff of *Crisis*, the magazine of the National Association for the Advancement of Colored People (NAACP). As literary editor from 1919 to 1926, Fauset encouraged black writers and served as a mentor to such artists as Langston Hughes, who said she was one of the "midwives" of the Harlem Renaissance.

Fauset wrote four novels: *There Is Confusion* (1924), *Plum Bun* (1929), *The Chinaberry Tree* (1931), and *Comedy, American Style* (1933). Racial identity was a major theme of her work. Her writing stressed her belief that middle-class African Americans could overcome prejudice but not self-loathing. Through her characters, Fauset revealed the complex literary and artistic lives of Harlem Renaissance figures, including herself. Hoping to mitigate racism, she wanted to enlighten white Americans about the realities of African Americans' experiences. Fauset also developed the *Brownies' Book*, a monthly publication for black children in 1920 and 1921. Her novels were reprinted during the 1960s civil rights movement.

Elizabeth D. Schafer

SEE ALSO: *Civil Rights Movement;* The Crisis*; Du Bois, W. E. B.; Harlem Renaissance; Hughes, Langston.*

BIBLIOGRAPHY

Allen, Carol. *Black Women Intellectuals: Strategies of Nation, Family, and Neighborhood in the Works of Pauline Hopkins, Jessie Fauset, and Marita Bonner*. New York: Garland Publishing, 1998.

McLendon, Jacquelyn Y. *The Politics of Color in the Fiction of Jessie Fauset and Nella Larsen*. Charlottesville: University Press of Virginia, 1995.

Myree-Mainor, Joy R. "Jessie Redmond Fauset," in *Encyclopedia of African American Women Writers*, Volume 1, ed. Yolanda Williams Page. Westport, CT: Greenwood Press, 2007.

Sylvander, Carolyn Wedin. *Jessie Redmon Fauset, Black American Writer*. Troy, NY: Whitston Publishing Company, 1981.

Fawcett, Farrah *(1947–2009)*

Perhaps best known for her role in the television series *Charlie's Angels*, which ran on ABC from 1976 to 1981, Farrah Fawcett became one of the biggest influences on style in the United States during the late 1970s. With a plot that revolved around a trio of female private investigators—Fawcett and costars Kate Jackson and Jaclyn Smith—the campy TV show relied heavily on the physical attributes of its leading actresses. As the standout on the series during its first season, the blond, attractive Fawcett set the trend for millions of women, who copied her trademark feathered hair and bought hair care products marketed under her name.

But it was not only women who liked Fawcett. One of the most popular posters of the decade, featuring Fawcett's toothy smile; flipped-back, bushy mane; and slim, athletic physique shown off in a wet swimsuit, became a staple on untold numbers of boys' bedroom walls during the era. After becoming a superstar on the top-rated show during the 1976–1977 season, Fawcett left to pursue more serious acting roles but met with little success. She never reclaimed the status that she once held, although she continued to appear regularly on television and in films into the first decade of the 2000s and retained a cult following by those enamored with 1970s nostalgia.

EARLY CAREER

Mary Farrah Leni Fawcett was born on February 2, 1947, in Corpus Christi, Texas. She attended Catholic school until the

Farrah Fawcett. *Although her looks made her an iconic sex symbol of the 1970s, Fawcett was a formidable actress, earning two Emmy nominations and six Golden Globe nominations during her career.* HULTON ARCHIVE/GETTY IMAGES.

sixth grade, after which she went to public school. She then enrolled at the University of Texas in Austin, where she planned to study microbiology but later changed her major to art. In college she began modeling for newspaper advertisements and art classes. When she was voted one of the ten most beautiful women on campus, a publicist contacted her and suggested that she pursue a career in entertainment. At the end of her junior year, Fawcett went to Hollywood, landed an agent, and met actor Lee Majors, who helped jump-start her acting career. They married in 1973 but divorced in 1982.

During the 1960s Fawcett guest starred on a number of popular television shows, while maintaining a lucrative career on the side as a model. She appeared in top magazines and in television commercials promoting products such as Noxzema shaving cream, Ultra-Brite toothpaste, and Wella Balsam shampoo. In 1969 she saw her screen debut in the French film *Love Is a Funny Thing*, and in the early 1970s she began to find work in television movies. Her big break came in 1976, when she was cast as one of three attractive female private eyes in *Charlie's Angels*. Playing the athletic Jill Munroe, Fawcett's character was known for her sense of humor and card skills. Jackson was cast as the intelligent Sabrina Duncan, and Smith provided street smarts as Kelly Garrett.

CHARLIE'S ANGELS POPULARITY

Charlie's Angels became the top-rated show of the 1976–1977 season, thanks to its appeal to both men and women. Men enjoyed watching the women clad in scanty costumes as they went undercover as prostitutes or go-go dancers, and they relished the melodramatic situations that found the trio tied up by ne'er-do-wells. Women, however, also enjoyed the program, finding a feminist slant amid the eroticism because the program broke ground as a prime-time action-adventure program that featured the women in a variety of daring situations. Women viewers appreciated the Angels' courage, quick thinking, and resourcefulness—they were quick draws and could hold their own in a fight—in addition to their stylish sensuality.

Fawcett quickly emerged as the most popular of the three stars. Her wholesome likeness spawned a cottage industry of merchandise, including one of the defining pieces of 1970s popular culture: the famous Fawcett poster. An estimated six million of these pictures were eventually sold, and her image also landed on items such as T-shirts and lunch boxes. In addition, salons nationwide turned out scores of women with the curled-back, mussed-up coiffure. With her career at its peak, Fawcett left *Charlie's Angels* after the first season to pursue more serious drama.

MADE-FOR-TV ROLES

Fawcett initially found it hard to break away from her *Charlie's Angels* image, and at first her foray into serious acting met with little luck. Finally, in 1981 she landed a role in the comedy *The Cannonball Run*, starring Burt Reynolds, and also that year starred in the made-for-television movie *Murder in Texas*. She subsequently found her niche in made-for-TV movies, particularly those based on true stories, and was highly acclaimed for her role in the 1984 television movie *The Burning Bed*, an emotional tale of domestic abuse. Her acting in *Extremities* (1986), a dramatic film about a woman who is attacked by a rapist in her own house, was also highly praised.

Fawcett made news again in 1995 after posing for nude pictures in *Playboy* magazine. Two years later the media focused positive attention on her acting again for her role in *The Apostle* (1997), and she received an Emmy nomination in 2003 for her performance in the television drama *The Guardian*. She starred in the reality television series *Chasing Farrah* in 2005, but the show received poor reviews and was promptly cancelled.

Fawcett began a long-term relationship with actor Ryan O'Neal in the early 1980s and had a son, Redmond O'Neal, with him. The couple broke up in 1997 but remained close throughout their lives. Fawcett later began dating producer James Orr, who was convicted of assaulting her in 1998 in a highly publicized scandal that was played up in the tabloids. In 2006 Fawcett was diagnosed with anal cancer, and she captured her battle with the disease in an Emmy-nominated documentary titled *Farrah's Story*. Though the cancer went into remission on several occasions, Fawcett ultimately succumbed to it. She died on June 25, 2009.

Though Fawcett was never one of Hollywood's leading actresses and enjoyed only a sporadic television career, she made a lasting imprint on the style of the 1970s during her heyday. She is remembered fondly by nostalgia buffs and long-standing fans.

Geri Speace

SEE ALSO: *Camp;* Charlie's Angels*; Feminism; Hairstyles; Made-for-Television Movies;* Playboy*; Reynolds, Burt; Sex Symbol; Supermodels; Television.*

BIBLIOGRAPHY

Mortiz, Charles, ed. *Current Biography Yearbook*. New York: Wilson, 1978.

Stewart, Alana. *My Journey with Farrah: A Story of Life, Love, and Friendship*. New York: Morrow, 2009.

Fawlty Towers

Fawlty Towers was a British television comedy starring John Cleese as hotel proprietor Basil Fawlty. Cleese, one of the original members of *Monty Python's Flying Circus*, returned to television as the writer and star of *Fawlty Towers*. Although only twelve episodes were produced (six in 1975 and six in 1979), it remains one of the most widely syndicated comedy series in television history. The show continues in syndication on public television stations throughout the United States to this day.

Much as *All in the Family* broke ground by portraying a flawed family, *Fawlty Towers* took the premise to its comedic extreme. Fawlty and his wife constantly argued, insulted each other's intelligence, and generally made each other miserable. Their pointed barbs and insults marked a new high (or low) in television dialogue. *Fawlty Towers* proved critically, if not commercially, successful. The series garnered two British Academy of Film and Television Arts awards for Best Comedy Series, and Cleese received an award from the Royal Television Society for his writing and acting.

In 2009, in recognition of the thirtieth anniversary of the series, a special remastered DVD edition of the show was released as *Fawlty Towers: The Complete Collection Remastered*. By 2012 syndication of the show had slowed, but episodes were readily available via video-streaming services such as Netflix.

Geoff Peterson

SEE ALSO: All in the Family; Monty Python's Flying Circus; *Netflix; Public Television (PBS); Sitcom; Syndication; Television.*

BIBLIOGRAPHY

Berman, Garry. *Best of the Britcoms: From "Fawlty Towers" to "The Office."* Lanham, MD: Taylor Trade Publishing, 2011.

Cleese, John, and Connie Booth. *The Complete "Fawlty Towers."* London: Methuen, 1988.

Margolis, Jonathan. *Cleese Encounters.* New York: St. Martin's, 1992.

McCann, Graham. *"Fawlty Towers": The Story of the Sitcom.* London: Hodder & Stoughton, 2007.

FBI (Federal Bureau of Investigation)

The Federal Bureau of Investigation (FBI) is housed under the U.S. Department of Justice with field offices throughout the country. Its agents are responsible for investigating federal crimes that occur within the United States. FBI cases are as diverse as white-collar crime, serial killing, terrorism, and espionage. The forerunner of the FBI was established in 1908 when Attorney General Charles Bonaparte and President Theodore Roosevelt hired thirty-four investigators and designated them as a special agent force, ordering the Department of Justice to refer their cases to these agents for investigation. The pair's desire to create a bureau of agents to strengthen the federal government's crime-fighting capabilities grew out of the need for reform during the Progressive Era of the late-nineteenth and early twentieth centuries.

The Department of Justice named this force the Bureau of Investigation in 1909; renamed it the United States Bureau of Investigation in 1932; and finally, in 1935, the Federal Bureau of Investigation. The American public calls the agency by its initials or identifies it simply as "the bureau." Since the terrorist attacks on the United States on September 11, 2001, the role of the FBI has been increasingly involved with intelligence and with the war on terror. As part of the reforms that were put in place after that event, the FBI now cooperates closely with other government agencies and with state and local officials.

GOOD VERSUS EVIL

The FBI gained power and popular notoriety during the gangster era of the 1920s and 1930s. This era was characterized by a general sense of lawlessness accompanying ratification of the Eighteenth Amendment (Prohibition), which forbade the manufacture, sale, transport, export, and import of alcohol, as well as by the despair and fear precipitated by the 1929 stock market crash and the Great Depression. Organized crime took root more strongly than ever because of its involvement in the production and distribution of illegal alcohol. Americans felt that they were witnessing illegal activity with increasing frequency and that criminals were lurking on every corner. The famous kidnapping and murder of Charles Lindbergh's infant son and the crimes of the legendary gangster Al Capone had captured American imaginations, and the public demanded revenge. There was widespread fear that the exploding crime wave was undermining the country's moral base. These developments led to a desire for a strong national crime-fighting presence. The people increasingly looked to the FBI to bring order to their chaotic world.

J. Edgar Hoover. *FBI director J. Edgar Hoover reviews a map in his office locating the bureau's offices and operations across the United States in 1942.* AP IMAGES.

FBI agents have enjoyed a leading role in American popular culture almost since the bureau's inception—the dashing secret agent who saves America from communism; the mysterious man in black; the image of a "G-man." Radio shows, movies, novels, magazines, and television shows have all featured FBI agents and their adventures. The FBI's popularity demonstrates the American public's fascination with crime and punishment as moral conflict between good and evil. As scholar Richard Gid Powers notes in *G-Men: Hoover's FBI in American Popular Culture*, "a formula adapts the universal myth to the national experience so that national history might be understood as an instance of the eternal struggle between good and evil." The FBI and its agents became potent forces in this eternal struggle as it played out in American popular culture.

People also sought escape from the troubling times through popular entertainment. Popular culture anointed the FBI as the nation's solution to the problem of the mythical public enemy. Gangsters and their FBI pursuers quickly found their way into movies, detective fiction, magazines, and radio shows. Popular culture helped the FBI agent become a beacon of hope that American values would survive the crime wave and the economic despair of the nation.

THE HOOVER ERA

No figure has been more closely associated with the popular image of the FBI as the major force in defending the nation against crime than J. Edgar Hoover, the bureau's most controversial leader. Attorney General Harlan Fiske Stone selected Hoover to head the FBI in 1924. Hoover quickly gave the bureau a more professional image and solidified its strength by firing unqualified agents and establishing formal training for all agents at the newly created National Academy in Quantico, Virginia. He also oversaw the creation of the FBI's Technical Laboratory and the establishment of a nationally centralized fingerprint database to aid in tracking criminals. Hoover was not only a great leader, but he was also a great publicity agent who carefully presided over the growing public popularity of both himself and his organization. In his day, Hoover was a dominant presence that the government, his agents, and the public both feared and admired.

Though Hoover and his G-men set the early standard for the quintessential FBI agent, Hoover's image dipped after his death in 1972 and a subsequent public reevaluation of his methods. He became widely associated with the negative image of government as "Big Brother," spying on the average citizen and maintaining secret files, and he gained much notoriety due to his widely rumored penchant for cross-dressing. Hoover's legacy also became entwined with the increasingly negative popular images of American government that began in the late 1950s and 1960s.

THE BUREAU'S TAINTED IMAGE

In the middle decades of the twentieth century, there was a growing public distrust of government and its official representatives for a number of reasons. The FBI was not immune to this image problem. Some of the government's most notorious actions involved the witch hunts for suspected communists that dominated the World War I, World War II, and Cold War periods. The bureau assisted Attorney General A. Mitchell Palmer during World War I in the quest to expose American communists and communist sympathizers. Hoover, an assistant to Palmer at this time, was a key figure in the endeavor and was responsible for compiling the list of alleged subversives. The FBI then gained its own power to investigate subversives during World War II. When Senator Joseph McCarthy and the House Un-American Activities Committee went too far in the minds of most Americans, all government officials involved in the hunt for communists were caught in the scandal.

The FBI's role in detecting subversion, sabotage, and espionage had at first enhanced its image as protector of the American way of life but ultimately led to a more negative image of the FBI as Big Brother. During the 1960s the FBI's image suffered again. Many Americans found the bureau's overall treatment of minorities and people the bureau and/or Richard Nixon labeled as subversives to be questionable at best. Many citizens felt that the FBI unjustly persecuted antiestablishment groups such as anti–Vietnam War demonstrators, radical students, and minority activists. The FBI was also involved in such controversial 1960s civil rights investigations as the Mississippi murders of three civil rights workers later immortalized in the movie *Mississippi Burning* (1988). The FBI conducted these investigations under the auspices of a secret FBI program known as COINTELPRO (counterintelligence program), which ran between 1956 and 1971 with the purpose of identifying and infiltrating domestic groups considered to be threats to national security. The culmination of the growing popular cynicism toward government and authority, however, is widely regarded as the 1970s Watergate scandal that brought down the presidency of Nixon; it is not without irony that the Watergate scandal was blown open by a source in the FBI.

The FBI also garnered a negative image by figuring prominently in a number of conspiracy theories that captured the American imagination. Perhaps the most famous of these theories have revolved around the 1963 assassination of President John F. Kennedy. Much controversy surrounded the official Warren Commission's report of the events responsible for Kennedy's death and the naming of Lee Harvey Oswald as the sole killer. Oliver Stone offered one of the most famous treatments of these conspiracy theories in his movie *JFK* (1991).

Conspiracy theories have also circulated widely on the question of whether UFOs exist and whether the government was responsible for covering up any such knowledge. Many rumors centered on the alleged crash of one such UFO at Roswell, New Mexico. The popularity of the television show *The X-Files* (1993–2002) proved that the popularity of these theories of alien contact continued to thrive into the late twentieth century. The show portrayed two FBI agents assigned to investigate unexplained X-File cases of possible paranormal and extraterrestrial activity as well as government conspiracies to conceal the truth.

REESTABLISHING THE "TOUGH GUY" IMAGE

The latter decades of the twentieth century witnessed a revival of the get-tough-on-crime stance that first made the FBI popular in the 1920s and 1930s. The largely positive response from the American public to this stance was due to an alarming growth of terrorist incidents, the illegal drug trade, and white-collar crime. Infamous serial killers such as Ted Bundy and Jeffrey Dahmer also instilled fear into the American public. But crime-fighting techniques were developed to combat these threats. The FBI behavioral sciences unit pioneered the technique of profiling violent and serial offenders, and DNA technology greatly aided the fight against crime. The television show *America's Most*

Wanted as well as the bureau's Ten Most Wanted lists involved the public in the FBI's manhunts.

Despite the events that reestablished the "tough guy" image of the FBI, other incidents challenged the public's views of the bureau's policies. The 1992 death of a U.S. marshal led to a standoff at Ruby Ridge, Idaho, between the FBI and fugitive Randall Weaver, during which Weaver's wife was accidentally killed by a sniper's bullet. The Branch Davidians, led by David Koresh, isolated themselves in their compound near Waco, Texas, leading to another FBI siege in 1993. This siege ended amid much controversy when some cult members deliberately set fire to their compound rather than surrender. The negative publicity garnered by these events led to governmental inquiries into the FBI's conduct. They also quickly became made-for-television movies. While the FBI's role has always centered on the struggle between the forces of good and evil, the FBI's changing image shows that it is often difficult to distinguish between these seemingly diametrically opposite forces.

NEW CHALLENGES

The FBI took on a more prominent role in counterterrorism following the 1993 bombing of the World Trade Center and the 1995 Oklahoma City bombing. In both cases, technological advancements and traditional on-the-ground measures improved the agency's public image. The FBI informant network led to the conviction of Ramzi Ahmed Yousef and his conspirators for the Trade Center bombing. In the Oklahoma City case, agents investigated identification numbers from remnants of the vehicle used in the attack and linked the Ryder rental truck to Timothy McVeigh. In 1996, the agency concluded the most expensive investigation in its history by tracking down and capturing Ted Kaczynski, known as the Unabomber, who committed a series of mail bombings between 1978 and 1995. Although Kaczynski's brother David assisted in the investigation, he was initially reluctant to involve the FBI due to its track record at Waco and Ruby Ridge. The agency's reputation was again clouded in 1996, when a suspect's name was leaked to the media during the investigation of the bombing of Centennial Olympic Park in Atlanta, Georgia.

The FBI was one of the intelligence agencies that underwent public scrutiny in the wake of the terrorist attacks of September 11, 2001. Analysts called for the dissolution of the clear division of power between the FBI and the Central Intelligence Agency (CIA), demanding that a single director of National Intelligence be created at the cabinet level. President George W. Bush responded by creating the U.S. Department of Homeland Security and instituting a major reorganization of government agencies. In its 2004 report, the 9/11 Commission concluded that the FBI failed to pursue numerous leads that might have prevented the attacks. The commission offered numerous recommendations to improve the FBI's organizational structure. Since the report, members of the commission, watchdog groups, and politicians have questioned the FBI's willingness to commit to the changes.

Also in 2001, the FBI faced a security breach that threw into doubt its ability to maintain the public trust. Robert Hanssen, a high-ranking agent, was caught selling secret information to the Russian government. After his arrest, it was revealed that Hanssen had been selling documents since 1979 and had received close to $1.5 million from the Russians. The reports of Hanssen's activities and the manner in which he was caught brought to life the mythic image of the FBI that most American's held. The media reports read like a cloak-and-dagger tale, complete with moles, secret drop sites, and familial betrayal.

The FBI has been a constant source of fascination for the media. Aside from *The FBI*, a pro-FBI television show that aired from 1965 to 1974 and was sanctioned by the bureau, since 1935's G-Men and Hoover's propaganda the popular image of the FBI has been altered by televisions shows, including *The X-Files*, *Bones* (2005–), and *The Sopranos* (1999–2007), and movies such as *The Silence of the Lambs* (1991), *The Siege* (1998), *Breach* (2007), and *Public Enemies* (2009). Not surprisingly, the 2011 film *J. Edgar* proved financially successful in spite of its mixed reviews. Popular culture has consistently depicted the bureau performing clandestine investigations or unearthing spectacular secrets.

Marcella Bush Treviño

SEE ALSO: *Bundy, Ted; Capone, Al; Civil Rights Movement; Cold War; Communism; Conspiracy Theories; Cults; Dahmer, Jeffrey; Detective Fiction; Dillinger, John; The Great Depression; Hoover, J. Edgar;* JFK*; Koresh, David, and the Branch Davidians; Made-for-Television Movies; Mafia/Organized Crime; McCarthyism; 9/11; Olympics; Prohibition; Radio; Roswell Incident; Serial Killers;* The Silence of the Lambs*;* The Sopranos*; Stone, Oliver; Television; UFOs (Unidentified Flying Objects); Vietnam; Watergate; World Trade Center; World War I; World War II;* The X-Files.

BIBLIOGRAPHY

Breuer, William B. *J. Edgar Hoover and His G-Men*. Westport, CT: Praeger, 1995.

Cook, Fred J. *The FBI Nobody Knows*. New York: Macmillan, 1964.

Jeffreys-Jones, Rhodri. "The FBI's Continuing Challenge." *Chronicle of Higher Education* 51, no. 20 (2005).

Jeffreys-Jones, Rhodri. *The FBI: A History*. New Haven, CT: Yale University Press, 2007.

North, Mark. *Act of Treason: The Role of J. Edgar Hoover in the Assassination of President Kennedy*. New York: Carroll and Graf, 1991.

Peykar, Edward V., ed. *The FBI: Past, Present, and Future*. Hauppauge, NY: Nova Publications, 2005.

Potter, Claire Bond. *War on Crime: Bandits, G-Men, and the Politics of Mass Culture*. New Brunswick, NJ: Rutgers University Press, 1998.

Powers, Richard Gid. *G-Men: Hoover's FBI in American Popular Culture*. Carbondale: Southern Illinois University Press, 1983.

Sullivan, William C., and Bill Brown. *The Bureau: My Thirty Years in Hoover's FBI*. New York: Norton, 1979.

Turner, William W. *Hoover's FBI: The Men and the Myth*. New York: Dell, 1971.

Zegart, Amy B. *Spying Blind: The CIA, the FBI, and the Origins of 9/11*. Princeton, NJ: Princeton University Press, 2007.

Feliciano, José *(1945–)*

José Feliciano is one of the most passionate balladeers and guitar virtuosos on the popular music scene. Because of his bilingual abilities, Feliciano has achieved popularity throughout the Americas, where his English- and Spanish-language albums have often topped the charts. His 1968 *Feliciano!* is considered a classic, as is his number one hit single "Light My Fire."

Born the second of twelve children on September 10, 1945, in Puerto Rico, Feliciano was raised on the Lower East Side of New York City. He was born blind from congenital glaucoma but nevertheless was a musical prodigy who by age six was playing instruments. Today he is known to perform credibly not only on his favorite, the guitar, but also on the bass, banjo, organ, mandolin, harmonica, piano, harpsichord, and several Afro-Caribbean percussion instruments. Because of his exposure to both Latin and American pop musical traditions, Feliciano developed an eclectic taste and style and has been able to master folk, flamenco, salsa, rock guitar, and vocals.

His folk-rock performances got him onto stages at the beginning of his career during his teens, in Greenwich Village cafés. At age seventeen Feliciano dropped out of high school to become a professional musician, with his first road show booked at the Retort Coffee House in Detroit in 1963. He soon signed a recording contract with RCA Victor and became a frequent performer at coffee houses and night clubs around the country and in San Juan, Puerto Rico, resort hotels.

Feliciano's first album, *The Voice and Guitar of José Feliciano*, appeared and went unnoticed in 1964, and both he and RCA experimented for the next few years in finding an appropriate niche for the eclectic singer and musician. In those years the greatest success came with Feliciano's Spanish-language recordings and his Latin American tours; in 1966, for instance, his concert in Buenos Aires drew an audience of 100,000. Finally in 1968, his album *Feliciano!*, which included "Light My Fire" (a 1967 Doors hit song), achieved mainstream success. "Light My Fire" became the third most popular single that year, and *Feliciano!* reached number two on the album charts. To top this, Feliciano won Grammy Awards for Best New Artist of 1968 and Best Contemporary Male Pop Vocal Performance for "Light My Fire."

After 1968 Feliciano continued as a standard and recognized artist in both American and Latin pop music, but he never again achieved the popularity or success in the United States that he had that stellar year. One tune, however, did make Feliciano a seasonal staple—his bilingual classic "Feliz Navidad (I Wanna Wish You a Merry Christmas)." He has, however, remained enormously popular internationally, especially in Latin America and Europe. In the mid-1970s Feliciano left RCA and began recording with a number of other houses. At times, his relationships with the studios have been rocky because the performer insists on his unique style and on doing things "his way."

Feliciano has earned forty international gold and platinum records and won Grammys for Best Latin Pop Performance in 1983, 1986, 1989, and 1990. In 1991, at the First Annual Latin Music Expo, he was presented with a lifetime achievement award. In 1998 he released the album *Señor Bolero* and completed a European tour. In 2006 the Hispanic Heritage Foundation awarded a lifetime achievement award to Feliciano at the Kennedy Center in Washington, D.C., and in 2007 he released the album *The Soundtrax of My Life*. Feliciano's "way" pioneered a place for intercultural musicians and opened up a new space for Hispanics in American pop culture.

Nicolás Kanellos

SEE ALSO: *The Doors; Folk Music; Grammy Awards; Greenwich Village; Pop Music; Rock and Roll.*

BIBLIOGRAPHY

Otfinoski, Steven. *Latinos in the Arts*. New York: Facts On File, 2007.

Rees, Dafydd, and Luke Crampton. *Rock Movers and Shakers*. Santa Barbara, CA: ABC-CLIO, 1991.

Rubiner, Julia M., ed. *Contemporary Musicians*. Detroit, MI: Gale Research, 1994.

Tardiff, Joseph T., and L. Mpho Mabunda, eds. *Dictionary of Hispanic Biography*.New York: Gale Research, 1996.

Felix the Cat

The creation of Otto Messmer (1892–1983) and Pat Sullivan (1887–1933), Felix the Cat first appeared as an animated cartoon character (under another name) in 1919 in *Feline Follies*. Felix had a lively personality and an expressive manner, and he solved problems in a creative fashion. For this latter facet of Felix's personality, his creators took full advantage of the animation medium and metamorphosed body parts into useful tools. The first major funny animal character to star in a series of animated cartoons, Felix appeared in some 150 shorts in the 1920s before the introduction of new sound technology saw his popularity wane. In the meantime, however, King Features had commenced a Felix the Cat comic strip in 1923, and his trademark likeness had been licensed to many products.

Not only was Felix the first star of animation, but he was also the product of a particular business arrangement that would become commonplace in animation studios. Messmer and Sullivan were the creative force behind the character. Messmer, a talented artist, took creative control of the movies, and Sullivan, a lesser artist but a driven entrepreneur, arranged distribution and licensing. Sullivan retained all rights for the character, and for many years his was the only name publicly associated with Felix. Messmer remained an employee.

Messmer, the son of German immigrants, was born just across the river from New York in Union City. Before joining Sullivan he worked variously as a scene painter, a cartoonist, and an animator for Henry "Hy" Mayer. Sullivan, of Irish heritage, was born in a tough working-class neighborhood of Sydney, Australia. In 1907, after some limited success as a cartoonist, during which time he shortened his name from O'Sullivan, he departed Australia for London. By 1909 he was in New York, where, about two years later, he found work as an assistant to William F. Marriner on his comic strip *Sambo and His Funny Noises*. Felix would later demonstrate some of Sambo's trickster qualities.

When Messmer and Sullivan joined forces in 1916, the worldly Sullivan had established his own animation studio, releasing animated shorts based on the Sambo strip but renaming the title character Sammie Johnsin to avoid litigation. Sullivan's studio, however, was put on hold in 1917, when he was convicted of rape and sentenced to two years in Sing Sing. Messmer went back to work for Mayer before being drafted. The two met up again in 1919 on Messmer's return from World War I and Sullivan's release from jail. They collaborated on the aforementioned *Feline Follies*, which helped reestablish the Sullivan studio.

The 1920s were Felix's decade. Sullivan shopped his character around to various film distributors. Historian John Canemaker has estimated that some thirty Felix shorts were released through Famous Players–Lasky from 1919 to 1921. In 1922, finding himself without a distributor but with the ownership of an established character, Sullivan struck a deal with distributor Margaret J. Winkler, and from 1922 to early 1925 her company distributed approximately fifty Felix animations. In these years Bill Nolan influenced Messmer to soften Felix's features, and a rounder Felix became the cartoon norm.

In 1925 Sullivan broke his ties with Winkler and signed a new distribution contract with Educational Films. Winkler turned to a young Walt Disney, who had already turned out a Felix clone named Julius in a series distributed by Winkler. Disney's new character, Oswald the Lucky Rabbit, had many similarities to Felix. In 1928 Disney lost control of Oswald to Winkler and had to create a new character: Mickey Mouse.

Meanwhile, Felix had been licensed extensively to doll, toy, and pencil manufacturers, as well as cigarette companies. Also the subject of popular songs, the character generated income for Sullivan from sheet music sales. The comic strip, which, according to Canemaker, was not widely popular, nonetheless appeared from coast to coast in the papers of William Randolph Hearst. Felix was also extremely popular in the United Kingdom and Sullivan's native Australia. In 1928 Felix was at the height of his fame. So ubiquitous was his fame and appearance that NBC used a Felix doll to test television cameras and transmission. In the strong visual presence of Felix lay the seeds of his downfall.

Disney's debut of Mickey Mouse in the sound film *Steamboat Willie* introduced a new dimension to animated shorts. Felix embodied the perfect characteristics for silent animation. To meet the challenges of sound he had to change, and the change undermined his character. Moreover, whereas Disney carefully planned his animation to fit music and sound effects, the Sullivan studio, when it eventually introduced sound, did so as a postanimation process. Inevitably the Disney product was superior.

By 1930 Felix had faded from the screen. Sullivan died in early 1933 from the effects of alcoholism. His heirs and lawyer briefly revived Felix in film in 1936, but the lackluster efforts were short lived. Felix lived on in weekly and daily comic strips, which ran to 1943 and to 1967, respectively. He also appeared monthly in a Dell comic book. In 1959 Joe Oriolo revived Felix in a series of cartoons for television. Oriolo resurrected Felix again in another television series in 1982. Retrospectives of early Felix shorts were held at the Whitney Museum of American Art and at the Museum of Modern Art in 1976. In the late 1980s Felix cropped up in a number of licensed merchandise ventures.

Felix is an icon of twentieth-century American popular culture. That he was created by an Irish Australian and a German American and was popular worldwide reminds us of the transnational character of popular culture.

Ian Gordon

SEE ALSO: *Animated Films; Comics; Disney (Walt Disney Company); Hearst, William Randolph;* Steamboat Willie*; Television; Toys; The Twenties; World War I.*

BIBLIOGRAPHY

Canemaker, John. *Felix: The Twisted Tale of the World's Most Famous Cat.* New York: Pantheon, 1991.

Lenburg, Jeff. *Who's Who in Animated Cartoons: An International Guide to Film and Television's Award-Winning Legendary Animators.* New York: Applause Theatre and Cinema Books, 2006.

Fellini, Federico *(1920–1993)*

Italian film director Federico Fellini helped bring the cinema to a mature state of expressive quality, introducing an eye-opening kaleidoscope of psychological symbolism and sometimes bawdy imagery to popular audiences and art-house denizens alike. His films are noted not only for their autobiographical elements but also for their integration of a surreal, fantasy world with real life.

Fellini began his career as a journalist and an editor. His first foray into the film world was as a screenwriter for famed filmmaker Roberto Rossellini. Fellini's work was critically praised, and in the 1950s he directed a number of masterpieces that expanded upon the natural, visually stark style of Italian neorealism pioneered by Rossellini. Most notable of these films are *La Strada* (1954) and *Nights of Cabiria* (1957), both of which boasted emotionally rich performances by Fellini's wife, Giulietta Massina. It was during the 1960s, however, that Fellini reached the height of his international stature with films such as *La Dolce Vita* (1960), *8 1/2;* (1963), and *Juliet of the Spirits* (1965), wherein he evinced a circuslike, highly personal vision of the world that could be achieved only through the cinema. Fellini continued directing films until his death in 1993, consistently creating worlds so distinctively characteristic that the word Felliniesque found its way into the popular vocabulary.

Shaun Frentner

SEE ALSO: *Cult Films; Fosse, Bob.*

BIBLIOGRAPHY

Baxter, John. *Fellini.* London: Fourth Estate, 1993.

Bondanella, Peter E. *The Cinema of Federico Fellini.* Princeton, NJ: Princeton University Press, 1992.

Cooke, Mervyn. *A History of Film Music.* New York: Cambridge University Press, 2008.

Fellini, Federico, and Costanzo Costantini. *Fellini on Fellini.* London: Faber and Faber, 1995.

Feminism

Feminism, the ideology that supports uplifting the status and improving the rights of women, has been one of the most influential political forces of the nineteenth, twentieth, and twenty-first centuries. It is based on a rejection of patriarchy, which dictates that males are innately superior to females, and promotes legal, political, and social equality. Since its inception, feminism has been both hailed as a profoundly liberating force and condemned as a philosophy of victimhood that has been responsible for the breakdown of the nuclear family and the degradation of society in general. There is no doubt, however, that the work of activists and reformers has been responsible for enormous improvements in the position of women in the United

Feminist Activists Protest IMF. *Feminist activists demonstrate in front of the International Monetary Fund (IMF) headquarters in May 2011 demanding the removal of managing director Dominique Strauss-Kahn from his post with the organization after he was arrested on rape charges.* STR/AFP/GETTY IMAGES.

States over the past 200 years. Equally indisputable, a glance at the power structures of most of the world's governments and businesses shows that male dominance is still very much a reality. Nevertheless, feminism has changed the American social order—from the seemingly superficial, such as media portrayals of women, to the deepest underlying assumptions of science and religion.

EARLY HISTORY

Throughout Europe and the United States, the eighteenth and nineteenth centuries were a time of sweeping ideological changes. A new humanism was developing, with a focus on the "rights of man." The principles of both the American and French revolutions of the late 1700s and the publication of *The Communist Manifesto* in 1848 were examples of this new atmosphere of brotherhood and justice. However, as white males were discovering and outlining their inalienable rights, white women were still largely trapped within a patriarchal system, kept there by economic necessity and rigid social convention. Basically considered the property of husbands or fathers, women were not permitted to vote, own property, operate businesses, attend college, or make legal decisions concerning their children or themselves.

Even in the eighteenth century, politically aware women had already begun to work to change these conditions. In the United States, figures such as Abigail Adams and Mercy Otis Warren spoke out for women. In a letter dated March 31, 1776, that is considered one of the first written expressions of American feminism, Abigail Adams wrote to her husband, John Adams, who was attending the Second Continental Congress in Philadelphia, "I desire you would remember the ladies and be more generous and favorable to them than your ancestors." In Europe, Mary Wollstonecraft published the landmark *Vindication of the Rights of Women* in 1792 in response to an emerging focus on the rights of man as articulated by classical liberal thinkers such as Thomas Paine and Jean-Jacques Rousseau.

MAKING PROGRESS

By the early 1800s many progressive men and women began to join the abolitionist movement to work for the end of slavery. One liberation ideology led naturally to another, and a number of abolitionist women drew parallels between the slavery they fought and the plight of white women. "The investigation of the rights of the slave has led me to a better understanding of my own," wrote antislavery activist Angelina Grimké in 1836. This growing understanding of the condition of women led to the first Women's Rights Convention in Seneca Falls, New York, in 1848. Organized by abolitionists Elizabeth Cady Stanton and Lucretia Mott, the convention drew dozens of women and a number of supportive men as well. Together, convention participants drew up the "Declaration of Sentiments," outlining both the rights of women and a set of demands, such as equality in law, education, and wages and the right to vote. Much of the focus of the early women's rights movement was on passage of Married Women's Property Acts because suffrage was seen as too radical by many early feminists.

In the 1860s the fight for women's rights led to a split in the abolition movement. Some antislavery activists felt that women should step back and focus on the fight against slavery, even if that meant prioritizing the rights of black men, whereas others argued that changes in the status of slaves and changes in the status of women must go hand in hand. Foreshadowing a recurrent issue in the struggle for women's rights, the role of men in the women's movement also became a source of controversy. With the ratification of the Fifteenth Amendment in 1868 and the removal of barriers to suffrage only for black males, the women's rights movement split. The National Woman Suffrage Association, led by Stanton and Susan Brownell Anthony, was an all-women organization that opposed the Fifteenth Amendment. The American Woman Suffrage Association, led by Lucy Stone and Julia Ward Howe, supported legalization of black male suffrage and included men in its membership.

By the 1890s, however, both factions reunited to push for the still-elusive women's suffrage. Women's clubs began to form to foster discussions about politics, culture, and education. In 1896 the National Association of Colored Women formed, uniting the separate black women's clubs. Women's temperance societies also became an important element in the activism of the period. Often mocked as prim and puritanical, the temperance societies were in reality an attempt to protect women and children from the abuse and poverty that were often a result of male drunkenness. Toward the end of the suffrage battle, the word *feminism* first came into use. The feminists of this period had a more comprehensive agenda than those suffragists who believed that the right to vote should be given the highest priority.

THE MOVEMENT WANES

Gradually, some states, particularly those in the West, began to grant women the right to vote in local or state elections. Wyoming, for instance, had granted women territorial suffrage in 1869; state officials refused to take away the right as a stipulation of statehood when Wyoming was admitted to the United States in 1890. In 1917 Jeannette Rankin of Montana, a pacifist, became the first woman elected to the U.S. Congress, and in 1920 women finally won the vote. Within three years of the ratification of the Nineteenth Amendment to the Constitution, the National Woman's Party proposed an Equal Rights Amendment, which was defeated.

Once suffrage was won, many women felt that the battle was over. Activism declined, resulting in what came to be known as a "feminist wasteland." However, some individuals continued on, laboring to gain a measure of control over the lives, bodies, and property of all females. Gradually, they chipped away at the laws that put women in the power of men, and women won many of the rights that Stanton and Anthony had demanded at the Seneca Falls convention. Because childbirth and the work of raising children affect women's lives so deeply, birth control and abortion have always been central issues in the feminist movement. The American Birth Control League, organized by Margaret Sanger in 1921, was one of the earliest attempts to make family planning available to U.S. women.

The 1920s brought newfound independence for women, and young females shed many restrictions of earlier periods. Fashion designers such as Coco Chanel discarded the painful, restrictive corsets women had once laced around themselves. The new fashions emphasized freedom and even androgyny, as women cut off their long, time-intensive tresses and sported the free and easy bobs that symbolized the era. During the Great Depression of the 1930s, the feminist movement subsided into quiescence. Though women were given unprecedented opportunities to work in male-dominated industries during World War II, they were unceremoniously sent back home when the war ended.

REBIRTH

The 1950s were a paradoxical decade, conventional and conformist on the exterior yet seething underneath with repressed rebellion. In the white upper and middle classes, more women than ever were attending college, where they developed an intellectual camaraderie with each other and learned to take themselves seriously before being isolated and often ignored while raising families in suburban homes. In the working class, women were frequently stuck in repetitive dead-end jobs, which generally paid around fifty cents for every dollar earned by the men working next to them. Many women began to awake to the knowledge that living the American dream and doing as they were told had not brought them happiness.

The dilemma of the middle-class woman was articulated powerfully in a pivotal book published in 1963. *The Feminine Mystique* by Betty Friedan marked the official beginning of the second wave of U.S. feminism. Describing the stultifying life of white, educated, middle-class women in American suburbs, Friedan captured the deep longing within girls and women for "something more" than their prescribed roles as cheerleaders and helpmates for men and caretakers for children. It was a message females around the country had been waiting to hear, and they began to discuss the innovative concept of women's liberation.

Just as nineteenth-century feminism had been a part of a larger social liberation movement, the second wave of feminism was fired by the same energy that fueled the civil rights movement, the antiwar movement, and the gay and lesbian liberation movement. In the same way that the female abolitionists had been inspired by the fight against slavery to stand up for their own rights, women in the civil rights and other movements began to feel empowered to challenge their own second-class citizenship, not only in the larger world but even among their male colleagues within the movement.

Following the passage of Title VII of the Civil Rights Act of 1964, prohibiting discrimination based on sex, race, religion, or national origin, government agencies began to document cases of sex discrimination. Even women themselves were appalled to see the evidence of so much blatant discrimination. They began to gather in "consciousness-raising" groups to discuss their own experiences. The isolation of women was breaking down—the competition and mistrust that had been fostered among females by a patriarchal society began to be replaced by communication and alliance. Though the National Organization for Women (NOW) was formed by Friedan and others in 1966, it was the solidarity created by the consciousness-raising groups that was the heart of the new movement. Threatened males of every political stripe ridiculed the personal and revelatory nature of the groups, but feminists responded by saying "the personal is political." The phrase became the very basis of women's liberation, meaning that each individual life has political meaning and each personal action requires responsibility.

SWEEPING CHANGES

By the early 1970s NOW had more than 400 chapters around the country, all of which worked to change the laws that oppressed women and to raise women's consciousness about their own potential. In 1972 Title IX of the Education Amendments prohibited sex discrimination in all education programs receiving federal funds, an act that promised to revolutionize women's education. In 1973 the landmark *Roe v. Wade* decision in the Supreme Court made legal abortions available to women throughout the United States, ending decades of dangerous and traumatic illegal abortions and unwanted childbirths. Based on the right to privacy, the *Roe v. Wade* decision grew out of the notion that abortion access should be dependent on the development of the fetus. Thus, unrestricted abortion was available only in the first three months of pregnancy.

The ideas and energy of women's liberation spread around the country, touching females from the universities to the suburbs, from the PTA to the factory floor. Feminists began to create a "woman's culture" in which females could gather to discuss and disseminate the new ideas. Women's bookstores, coffeehouses, journals, publishing houses, and community centers were energized by the burgeoning spirit of sisterhood. Women's studies courses were introduced at colleges and universities to focus on women's history and perspectives. Feminist health-care workers created women's clinics to prioritize female health issues. Women, who had been encouraged to view their bodies as inferior and even slightly disgusting, attended classes where they learned to appreciate and understand their physical shapes. Feminist psychotherapists developed feminist therapy, which included an analysis of women's oppression. Rape crisis centers opened to publicize and combat violence against women. From family to language to religion, no nook or cranny of modern society or history escaped the critique of feminists who sought to reinterpret a male-defined world from a woman's perspective.

THE MEDIA REACTION

The media responded to the new movement at first with ridicule but then with more serious analysis. In 1971 the premiere issue of *Ms.*, the first national feminist magazine, appeared on newsstands. Even on television, that most conservative organ of the status quo, independent women began to spring up on sitcoms and dramas of the 1970s. Mary Richards, the solid and sensible heroine of *The Mary Tyler Moore Show* (1970–1977), is a single career woman who has real friendships with females, not just double dates or competitions over boyfriends. Mary Tyler Moore had fought to have her character be divorced rather than recovering from a failed relationship, but it was decided that America was not yet ready for such a bold stroke.

Maude Findlay—outspoken, bitchy, and unashamedly middle-aged—appeared first on *All in the Family* (1968–1979) and then was given her own spin-off, *Maude* (1972–1978), as audiences responded enthusiastically to the non-stereotypical portrait of a wife and mother. In 1972 episodes, a personal view of abortion is presented when Maude is forced to grapple with an unexpected pregnancy. Though it did not debut until 1981, *Cagney and Lacey* was also part of the wave of feminist television. The innovative police drama pairs tough-talking, hard-drinking single woman Chris Cagney with down-to-earth, happily married mother Mary Beth Lacey. *Cagney and Lacey* brought an element of compassion to the police genre that drew audiences for eight years.

SELECTIVE EQUALITY

Though the feminist ideal of sisterhood was exhilarating, it also appeared to be based on the notion that all women were white, straight, and from the middle class. Lesbians had been among the first activists of women's liberation, but straight women immediately sought to disassociate them from the movement. Calling the issue the "lavender menace," many heterosexual feminists were uncomfortable with the idea of lesbianism and feared that inclusion of gay women would discredit the cause. Lesbians fought for their place within the movement, but many were hurt by being shunned and remained mistrustful. Some even withdrew from feminism, calling themselves lesbian separatists, and began focusing on homosexual issues only.

African American and working-class women also had to fight for their places in the women's liberation movement of the 1970s. The intellectual ideology of the movement had been developed chiefly by white academics and middle-class suburban housewives, but working-class and black women had the largest stake in the feminist cause. Issues of pay and advancement at work, abortion and birth control, and abuse at home were often matters of survival for black and working-class women. Though these women were active in the movement, white feminists often had to be compelled to confront their own racism and classism, and many did not rise to the occasion.

The 1980s saw a sharp backlash against the advances of the 1970s. While most people professed to believe in "equal pay for equal work," many were threatened by the deeper societal changes suggested by feminist thought. Using the age-old weapons of ridicule and threat, antifeminist writers and pundits announced that women had achieved equality and no longer needed to be liberated. (This cheery mythology has continued.) In the 1980s feminism's critics described a world in which women had unprecedented equality in the workplace but were frustrated, unhappy, and unfulfilled in their personal lives. Conservative religious leaders assured women that their place in the home was divinely ordained. Popular feminist novels of the 1970s, such as Erica Jong's *Fear of Flying* (1973) and Marilyn French's *The Women's Room* (1977), were replaced the following decade by grim tales of the price of independence, such as Gail Parent's *A Sign of the Eighties* (1987) and Freda Bright's *Singular Women*. In film, *Kramer vs. Kramer* (1979), which won the Oscar for Best Picture, features a narrative that punishes a confused mother who leaves her child with his father so that she can explore her own identity.

THE THIRD WAVE

Despite the backlash and the divisions within the feminist movement, many women united to fight the antifemale policies of the Ronald Reagan and George H. W. Bush administrations, which slashed social programs and used views on abortion as litmus tests for positions on the federal courts. In 1991 the Anita Hill–Clarence Thomas hearings before the U.S. Senate Judiciary Committee rejuvenated the women's movement, propelling it into what became known as the third wave. This new phase was more inclusive, embracing women of all races, classes, and sexual persuasions.

Many third wavers rejected the label of *feminist* at the same time they accepted the equality that had been fought for so vigorously by earlier activists. Since the 1970s, in polls where women are asked if they are feminists, only 25 to 30 percent reply in the affirmative. However, in polls such as one taken in 2005 by CBS News, in which the definition of a feminist is expanded to include someone who believes in social, political, and economic equality, affirmative responses rise to 65 percent. It seems the antifeminist media has at least partially succeeded in turning the word *feminist* into a pejorative; thus, the term *postfeminism* has come to be widely accepted.

UNFINISHED BUSINESS

In the twenty-first century, many of the old issues remain: women are still paid less than men for identical or comparable work; career advancement is slower for women, and the glass ceiling prevents their advancement beyond a certain point; sexual harassment, domestic violence, and rape continue at alarming rates; and child care remains prohibitively expensive and is often stigmatized as the choice of selfish mothers. Even battles that seemingly had been already won, such as those concerning abortion rights and welfare rights for single mothers, are having to be fought again as conservatives attempt to restore the old order.

Even though feminism has not totally succeeded in achieving economic and political equality, there is no denying that the position of women in American society has dramatically improved. Feminism has challenged patriarchal interpretations of history and science, and it has likewise embraced the issues of children's rights, the politics of the family, and internationalism. Like the abolitionists/suffragists of the nineteenth century, feminists of the early twenty-first century continue to advocate for the helpless and the disenfranchised.

Tina Gianoulis

SEE ALSO: *Abortion; Androgyny; Anita Hill–Clarence Thomas Senate Hearings; Bra;* Cagney and Lacey*; Chanel, Coco; Consciousness Raising Groups; Equal Rights Amendment; Hite, Shere; Lesbianism;* The Mary Tyler Moore Show*;* Maude*;* Ms.*; National Organization for Women (NOW); Pants for Women;* Playgirl*;* Roe v. Wade*; Sexual Harassment; Sexual Revolution; Steinem, Gloria.*

BIBLIOGRAPHY

Baumgardner, Jennifer, and Amy Richards. *Manifesta: Young Women, Feminism, and the Future.* New York: Farrar, Straus & Giroux, 2000.

Berg, Barbara J. *The Women's Movement and Young Women Today: A Hot Issue.* Berkeley Heights, NJ: Enslow Publishers, 1999.

Berkeley, Kathleen C. *The Women's Liberation Movement in America.* Westport, CT: Greenwood Press, 1999.

Collins, Patricia Hill. *Black Feminist Thought: Knowledge, Consciousness, and the Politics of Empowerment.* New York: Routledge, 1999.

Crowley, Karlyn. *Feminism's New Age: Gender, Appropriation, and the Afterlife of Existentialism.* Albany: State University of New York, 2011.

Faludi, Susan. *Backlash: The Undeclared War against American Women.* New York: Doubleday, 1991.

Marilley, Suzanne M. *Woman Suffrage and the Origins of Liberal Feminism in the United States, 1820–1920.* Cambridge, MA: Harvard University Press, 1996.

Purdy, Elizabeth Rholetter, ed. *Celebrating Women in American History. Volume V: Modern Feminist Movement and Contemporary Issues, 1961 to the Present.* New York: Facts On File, 2011.

Ridgeway, Cecilia L. *Framed by Gender: How Gender Equality Persists in the Modern World.* New York: Oxford University Press, 2011.

Scott, Joan Wallach. *The Fantasy of Feminist History.* Durham, NC: Duke University Press, 2011.

Yeo, Eileen Janes, ed. *Mary Wollstonecraft, and 200 Years of Feminism.* New York: Rivers Oram Press, 1997.

Fenway Park

Together with Chicago's Wrigley Field, Boston's Fenway Park is one of the last two remaining archetypal American baseball facilities from the early twentieth century. Called "a lyric little bandbox" by author John Updike, the park's idiosyncratic design is as legendary among baseball aficionados as was the futility endured by its home team, the Boston Red Sox, for most of the twentieth century.

FENWAY'S EARLY YEARS

The ballpark derived its name from the Fenway Realty Company, the business that owned the plot of marshland on which the ballpark was constructed. The Osborn Engineering Company of Cleveland designed the concrete and steel structure, which was modeled in part on Philadelphia's Shibe Park. The famous wall in left field, popularly known as the Green Monster, was not part of the original ballpark. Fenway's asymmetrical configuration was largely a function of location, nestled as it was just across the Massachusetts Turnpike from bustling Kenmore Square.

Fenway Park opened on April 20, 1912. The sinking of the *Titanic* was still front-page news in the *Boston Globe* that morning as the Red Sox prepared to play the New York Highlanders before a crowd of 27,000. Boston Mayor John F. "Honey Fitz" Fitzgerald threw out the ceremonial first pitch, and the hometown club went on to win 7–6 on an extra-inning single by Tris Speaker. The Highlanders, later rechristened the Yankees, would remain integrally intertwined with the ballpark's history over the ensuing decades.

At first, the new park seemed to be a good-luck charm for the Red Sox. The team won the American League pennant in 1912, and Fenway played host to its first World Series that year. An error by Fred Snodgrass of the New York Giants in the tenth inning of the deciding game gave the series to the Sox, four games to three. The Red Sox subsequently won the World Series in 1915, 1916, and 1918, but the auspicious beginning to the Fenway Era would be followed by one of the longest championship droughts in the history of baseball.

TWENTIETH CENTURY

Fenway Park took a major step forward in its evolution in 1934, when the original wall in left field was leveled and a 37-foot-high metal fence was installed. Initially covered with advertising signs, the wall was painted green in 1947, and it became known as the Green Monster. The Green Monster is today one of the most distinctive features of any American ballpark. Officially listed as 315 feet from home plate (though some aerial photographs have indicated that 300 feet is more likely), the Green Monster continues to bedevil American League left fielders while providing an all-too-tempting target for right-handed power hitters looking to pull a ball out of the park.

One such power hitter was New York Yankee Bucky Dent, a diminutive shortstop who clouted one of the signature home runs in Fenway Park's history on October 2, 1978. The towering pop fly off Red Sox pitcher Mike Torrez landed on the screen above the Green Monster and helped the Yankees capture the American League East Division championship in a one-game playoff. Dent's blast was just one in a long line of tragic moments for the Red Sox's long-suffering fans, who watched their beloved team fail time and time again in their long quest to capture the franchise's first World Series title after 1918.

The Red Sox returned to the World Series in 1946 and again in 1967 but were turned away in seven games on both occasions. In the 1975 World Series the Red Sox played the Cincinnati Reds. That series saw Fenway host one of the most dramatic games in baseball history, the sixth game of the series, in which Boston catcher Carlton Fisk clouted a twelfth-inning, game-winning home run just inside the left-field foul pole. True to form, however, the Red Sox proceeded to lose the seventh, decisive game in heartbreaking fashion.

At the end of the twentieth century, Fenway Park remained one of Major League Baseball's oldest and most revered ballparks. In addition to the Green Monster, its distinctive features included one of the last remaining hand-operated scoreboards in the majors. In typically eccentric Fenway fashion, the initials of the club's longtime former owner, Thomas A. Yawkey, and his wife, Jean R. Yawkey, were inscribed vertically in Morse code on the face of the scoreboard.

Despite its aesthetic and historic value, the park was facing an uncertain future. Its seating capacity (about 35,000) was woefully small by modern ballpark standards, and there were few provisions for such revenue-generating gewgaws as luxury boxes and interactive entertainment centers. The club was said to be actively seeking a new home for the new millennium, and Red Sox fans could only hope that a new facility would retain the charming architectural features and rich sense of place that marked the original.

TWENTY-FIRST CENTURY

In 2002, after much deliberation, the Boston Red Sox were sold to John Henry, Tom Werner, and Larry Lucchino. The new owners undertook plans to renovate Fenway Park. They worked with Janet Marie Smith, an architect with experience in maintaining the old-fashioned feel in new ballparks. In the following year, 269 Green Monster seats replaced the old netting above the wall. Painted in what had become "Fenway green," the seats were selling for $165 a game by the time all of the renovations were finished in 2011.

A concession and seating area with about 300 picnic tables shaped like home plate was added in the right-field corner high above the field in 2004. Before the 2011 season, the seating behind home plate was renovated and three high-definition video boards were installed. Other changes included extended concourse areas and expanded food offerings. The total cost of the renovations was $285 million. The revamped Fenway managed to retain the feeling of the old ballpark, and the Green Monster was still there.

Robert E. Schnakenberg

SEE ALSO: *Baseball; Boston Red Sox; Fisk, Carlton; The New York Yankees; Updike, John; World Series; Wrigley Field.*

BIBLIOGRAPHY

Boer, Michael Ian. *Faithful to Fenway: Believing in Boston, Baseball, and America's Most Beloved Ballpark.* New York: New York University Press, 2008.

Foulds, Alan E. *Boston's Ballparks and Arenas.* Hanover, NH: University Press of New England, 2005.

Gershman, Michael. *Diamonds: The Evolution of the Ballpark.* Boston, Houghton Mifflin, 1995.

Higgins, George V. *The Progress of the Seasons: A Partisan's View of Forty Years of Baseball at Fenway Park.* New York: Henry Holt, 1989.

Huntington, Tom. "There Is No Finer Place in the World to Watch Baseball." *Smithsonian,* October 1994.

Lowry, Philip J. *Green Cathedrals: The Ultimate Celebrations of All 273 Major League and Negro League Ballparks Past and Present.* Reading, MA: Addison-Wesley, 1992.

Reiter, Ben. "The New New Fenway." *Sports Illustrated,* November 24, 2011, 54–86.

Ferrante and Teicher

Piano stylings of pop music themes, sometimes called lounge music or mood music, were in vogue during the post–World War II years, and Arthur Ferrante (1921–2009) and Louis Teicher (1924–2008) were the duo-piano team that capitalized most prolifically on this genre during the 1960s. Imitating the sound of the Romantic-era piano concerto, and at times including novelty effects such as "prepared" pianos, Ferrante and Teicher, who were known alternately as the "Movie Theme Team" or the "Grand Twins of the Twin Grands," recorded lush arrangements of film themes, Broadway tunes, and other melodies backed by full orchestra and chorus.

Both pianists pursued their early training at the Juilliard School in New York but gradually dropped their classical repertoire in favor of pop and light comedy performance elements. After signing with United Artists in 1960, they had their first American chart hits with the million-plus-seller theme from *The Apartment* and Ernest Gold's main theme from *Exodus;* in 1969 their arrangement of "Midnight Cowboy" was a Billboard Top 10 single. By the time they retired in 1989 to set up the Avant-Garde record label, Ferrante and Teicher had recorded more than 150 albums and sold eighty-eight million records, of which twenty-two went gold or platinum. They had also performed more than 5,000 concerts. Their music continues to be released on albums that include *Great 1970s Motion Picture Themes* (2001) and *All-Time Greatest Hits Live on Stage* (2005).

Ivan Raykoff

SEE ALSO: *Broadway;* Midnight Cowboy*; Pop Music.*

BIBLIOGRAPHY

Ferrante, Arthur, and Louis Teicher. "Two Pianos? It'll Never Sell!" *Music Journal,* September 1965, 42–43.

Noland, Claire. "Arthur Ferrante Dies at 88; Half of the Popular Piano Duo Ferrante and Teicher." *Los Angeles Times,* September 21, 2009.

Ferrell, Will *(1967–)*

Among the most recognizable cast members in the history of the television series *Saturday Night Live,* Will Ferrell built a successful comedic film career working frequently with director and cowriter Adam McKay. Ferrell's generation of comedians, which included Jack Black and Ben Stiller, was often called the "Frat Pack" because of their skillfully rendered low-brow humor that lampoons the eternally adolescent American male who refuses to grow up.

John William Ferrell was born on July 16, 1967, in Irvine, California, to parents Betty Kay, a teacher, and Roy Lee Ferrell Jr., a musician who played with the popular 1960s and 1970s duo the Righteous Brothers. Ferrell's parents divorced when he was eight years old, and he initially had little interest in show business, witnessing the effects that the unstable nature of the work had on his father. He did, however, have a knack for entertaining, as exemplified through his reading of school announcements in high school and his postcollegiate work with the Groundlings, a Los Angeles–based improvisation comedy troupe that helped launch the careers of Jon Lovitz, Phil Hartman, and Lisa Kudrow.

After graduating from the University of Southern California in 1990 with a degree in sports journalism, Ferrell worked a series of odd jobs, including parking attendant and bank teller, before earning a spot on *Saturday Night Live* (*SNL*) in 1995. He remained with the show for seven seasons, building his reputation on celebrity impersonations of U.S. president George W. Bush, sports announcer Harry Caray, *Jeopardy!* game show host Alex Trebek, and singers Robert Goulet and Neil Diamond, as well as on original characters such as Craig Buchanan, the Spartan cheerleader, and nightclubbing lothario Steve Butabi. It was at *SNL* that Ferrell first teamed with McKay, with whom he would later collaborate on a number of his most successful ventures.

COMEDY ACTOR

In 1997 Ferrell made his film debut as Mustafa in *Austin Powers: International Man of Mystery*, a movie written by and starring fellow *SNL* cast member Mike Myers. Ferrell made minor appearances in other *SNL* spin-off movies, such as *Superstar* (1999) and *The Ladies Man* (2000), before leaving the show for good in 2002. His breakthrough on the big screen came in 2003 when he starred in director Todd Phillips's *Old School* as Frank "the Tank" Ricard, a thirtysomething former frat boy who cannot outgrow his drunken college ways. In one of the film's most memorable scenes, Frank's life unravels when his new wife discovers him streaking downtown as she is returning home from a night out with her friends. Kicked out of his home, Frank and fellow midlife failures Mitch (Luke Wilson) and Bernard (Vince Vaughn) start a college-style fraternity for anyone in town who wants to join. A series of hilarious misadventures follow, and the film suggests that Frank has finally begun to grow when he assumes a leadership position in the fraternity. In *Elf*, a Christmas movie from the same year, Ferrell plays Buddy, a human who has mistakenly been raised as one of Santa's helpers in the North Pole. Unskilled as a toymaker, Buddy returns to New York as an adult donning his elf apparel to look for his biological parents. Together *Old School* and *Elf* grossed more than $300 million at the box office.

EXPANDING CAREER

Following the success of these two films, Ferrell cowrote—with McKay—and played the comic lead in *Anchorman: The Legend of Ron Burgundy* (2004) and *Talladega Nights: The Ballad of Ricky Bobby* (2006). In both movies he plays essentially the same character to perfection: an oversized, incompetent boor who is somehow at or near the top of his profession. The protagonists are lovably vain; astoundingly oblivious to their circumstances (Ricky Bobby, for example, thinks he is paralyzed when he is not); and, at the last possible moment, kindhearted and generous. *Blades of Glory* (2007), which casts Ferrell as the street-fighting figure skater Chazz Michael Michaels, follows a similar formula under the direction of Josh Gordon and Will Speck.

Throughout his career Ferrell tested his range and took chances on parts other than the stock characters he played in his comedies. He tried his hand at drama opposite Maggie Gyllenhaal in director Marc Forster's *Stranger than Fiction* (2006), in which he plays Harold Crick, an Internal Revenue Service agent plagued by an omniscient voice warning him of his imminent death. Ferrell made his Broadway debut in 2009 with a comedic production, *You're Welcome America: A Final Night with George W. Bush*, which earned critical acclaim and was nominated for a Tony Award for Best Special Theatrical Event. At the end of the play, Ferrell's Bush asks in a pitch-perfect Texas drawl, "Can you go to sleep at night, knowing the decisions you've made?" Staying in character, he replies, "I can, because I can sleep anywhere. I'm a really good sleeper."

PRODUCTION COMPANY

In 2006 Ferrell and McKay founded Gary Sanchez Productions, which has produced and distributed a number of Ferrell comic vehicles, such as *Step Brothers* (2008) and *The Other Guys* (2010). The company also promoted the work of aspiring comic actors with the release of *The Foot Fist Way* (2006) and *The Virginity Hit* (2010), starring relative unknowns Danny R. McBride and Matt Bennett, respectively. In 2007 Ferrell and McKay founded the Funny or Die video website, which airs sketches and short films by some of the most popular modern comics, including Zach Galifianakis, Jack Black, John C. Reilly, Amy Poehler, and Aubrey Plaza.

As of 2012, Ferrell continued to serve as an actor and a producer on films, TV shows, and web-based shorts, with numerous movies in postproduction. For all his success on the big screen, however, many of his best-remembered laughs date back to his days on *SNL*, including his portrayal of game show host Trebek picking a fight with actor Sean Connery and his rendition of Goulet, a singer of Broadway musicals, covering songs by the Notorious B.I.G.

Ron Horton

SEE ALSO: *Black, Jack; Broadway; Caray, Harry; Diamond, Neil; Hollywood;* Jeopardy!*;* Saturday Night Live*; Stiller, Ben; Television; Television Anchors; Tony Awards.*

BIBLIOGRAPHY

Epstein, Dwayne. *Will Ferrell: People in the News*. San Diego: Lucent Books, 2005. Print.

Funny or Die. Accessed May 30, 2012. Available from http://www.funnyordie.com

Hedegaard, Erik. "The Beautiful Empty Mind of Will Ferrell." *Rolling Stone*, March 6, 2012, 44–47.

Mitchell, Susan K. *Will Ferrell: Today's Superstars*. New York: Gareth Stevens Publishing, 2009.

Raab, Scott. "Will Ferrell." *Esquire*, December 2003.

"Will Ferrell News." *New York Times*, February 9, 2009.

Winters, Kelly. "Will Ferrell." In *Newsmakers*. Farmington Hills, MI: Gale, 2004.

Fetchit, Stepin *(1902–1985)*

Comic actor Stepin Fetchit was arguably the first African American movie star in the United States. Appearing in more than fifty films in the early twentieth century, he usually played slow-talking, dim-witted, shuffling slaves and servants. While praised for opening doors for other black actors, Fetchit was also criticized for perpetuating America's perception at the time that blacks were servile, lazy, feckless, and stupid.

Fetchit was born Lincoln Theodore Monroe Andrew Perry in Key West, Florida, on May 30, 1902. He left home at age fourteen to perform in traveling medicine shows and in vaudeville. By the mid-1920s he was in Hollywood, using the stage name Stepin Fetchit and getting small roles in films. His first major role was as Gummy in *Hearts of Dixie* (1929), the first all-black musical. Fetchit stole the show, but none of the several subsequent musicals in which he was cast gave him a similar opportunity to shine with such prominence.

Fetchit worked steadily throughout the 1930s, rapidly becoming one of the best-known, best-loved, and most instantly recognizable black actors. He was, however, often confined to cameos and small-featured roles, because he was black, a common occurrence for black actors at the time. His films include *Marie Galante* (1934), starring Spencer Tracy; *Stand up and Cheer* (1934) and *Dimples* (1936) with popular child actress Shirley Temple; and *David Harum* (1934), *Judge Priest* (1934), *The Country Chairman* (1935), and *Steamboat 'round the Bend* (1935) with popular actor Will Rogers.

Actor Stepin Fetchit circa 1930. *Stepin Fetchit was the first African American actor in history to receive a screen credit, even as most of his movie roles perpetuated a negative black stereotype.* AMERICAN STOCK/GETTY IMAGES.

Usually typecast as a servant wearing a grin and hand-me-down clothes too large and loose for his tall, lanky frame, Fetchit quickly developed a servile image that eventually alienated him from black audiences and offended civil rights advocates. The National Association for the Advancement of Colored People (NAACP) declared that Fetchit's flunky roles reinforced white people's racist image of blacks, while the black press repeatedly criticized his perpetration of unwelcome stereotypes. By the mid-1940s these protests against his racist caricatures had curtailed his career. Moreover, his income from his movie career had allowed him to adopt such an extravagant lifestyle—at one time he owned six houses and twelve cars and employed sixteen Chinese servants—that he was forced to declare bankruptcy in 1947, the year he starred in *Miracle in Harlem.*

In the early 1950s Fetchit disappeared from the screen. The 1970s brought something of a renaissance to the then almost forgotten actor. He returned to the Hollywood screen with roles in *Amazing Grace* (1974) and *Won Ton Ton the Dog Who Saved Hollywood* (1976); in 1976, his earlier perceived slights on African Americans forgiven, the NAACP awarded him a special image award, and in 1978 he was inducted into the Black Filmmakers Hall of Fame.

In November 1985 Fetchit died in Woodland Hills, California, from complications from pneumonia and congestive heart failure. Over time film scholars have come to recognize Fetchit's comic talent and his flawless timing. African American writer, actor, and director Robert Townsend paid him lasting tribute with his brilliant impersonation of Fetchit in his independent film, *Hollywood Shuffle* (1987), and, thanks to television reruns of his movies, Fetchit lives on for future generations.

Peter C. Holloran

SEE ALSO: *Hollywood; Medicine Shows; Rogers, Will; Temple, Shirley; Tracy, Spencer; Vaudeville.*

BIBLIOGRAPHY

Bogle, Donald. *Toms, Coons, Mulattos, Mammies, and Bucks: An Interpretive History of Blacks in American Films.* New York: Continuum, 1989.

Cripps, Thomas. *Slow Fade to Black: The Negro in American Film, 1900–1942.* New York: Oxford University Press, 1977.

Gates, Henry Louis, Jr., and Evelyn Brooks Higginbotham, eds. *Harlem Renaissance Lives.* New York: Oxford University Press, 2009.

Leab, Daniel J. *From Sambo to Superspade: The Black Experience in Motion Pictures.* Boston: Houghton Mifflin, 1975.

Patterson, Lindsay, ed. *Black Films and Film-Makers: A Comprehensive Anthology from Stereotype to Superhero.* New York: Dodd, Mead, 1975.

Watkins, Mel. *Stepin Fetchit: The Life and Times of Lincoln Perry.* New York: Pantheon Books, 2005.

Fey, Tina *(1970–)*

The first female lead writer for the television sketch comedy show *Saturday Night Live* (*SNL*, 1975–), Tina Fey joined the popular series in 1997 after a successful stint with Second City, a comedy club based in Chicago. After appearing as an extra in a 1998 *SNL* skit, she became a regular on the show's famous mock news sketch "Weekend Update," which she coanchored with comedian Jimmy Fallon from 2000 to 2006. She left the show to pursue a career in film acting and to create and star in *30 Rock* (2006–), a sitcom based in part on her *SNL* tenure. She has become known on-screen and off as the cerebral and unexpectedly beautiful woman next door. She has won several Golden Globe, Emmy, Screen Actors Guild, and Writers Guild awards and received the 2010 Mark Twain Prize for American Humor.

Born on May 18, 1970, in Upper Darby, Pennsylvania, to Zenobia, an employee at a brokerage firm, and Donald, a grant writer, Elizabeth Stamatina Fey got the idea to become a comedienne in middle school, when she would stay up late watching *SNL* and Canadian sketch-comedy show *SCTV* (1976–1984). Her hero was Catherine O'Hara, a writer and an actor on *SCTV* who also starred as the mother in the *Home Alone* film franchise (1990–1992). Fey remembers herself as a flat-footed, short-permed, bushy-browed schoolgirl who failed in romance. She filled her time writing and participating in school-related activities and eventually earned a bachelor's degree in drama from the University of Virginia in 1992.

Tina Fey. *Tina Fey stars as comedy writer Liz Lemon in the NBC sitcom* 30 Rock. MARY ELLEN MATTHEWS/NBC/NBCU PHOTO BANK VIA GETTY IMAGES.

She moved to Chicago and took improv classes at the renowned Second City Training Center, working a dull desk job at a suburban YMCA. Soon she joined Second City's professional comedy troupe, and in 1997 Lorne Michaels, the producer of *SNL*, hired Fey as a writer at the request of head writer Adam McKay. In 1999, after McKay left the show, Michaels gave the post to Fey, making her the show's first female head writer. The following season she began coanchoring "Weekend Update," and by 2006 many ranked her alongside popular alumni Chevy Chase and Dennis Miller as one of the best anchors in the show's history. Others were not as impressed by her comedy chops, blaming her for the show's preponderance of awkwardly paced skits and flat jokes in the late 1990s and early in the first decade of the 2000s.

Nevertheless, Fey earned acclaim for her work outside of the show as well, first by writing and acting in the antibullying comedy *Mean Girls* (2004), which starred actress Lindsay Lohan. Fey also headlined in the films *Baby Mama* (2008), with *SNL* costar Amy Poehler; *The Invention of Lying* (2009), with comic actors Ricky Gervais and Christopher Guest; and *Date Night* (2010), with comedian Steve Carell. She also has voiced characters for animated films such as *Ponyo* (2008) and *Megamind* (2010).

In the fall of 2008, during the U.S. presidential campaign, Fey returned to *SNL* as a guest to do a series of impersonations of Republican vice presidential candidate Sarah Palin. In the most famous of these skits, Fey appears as Palin alongside Poehler, who plays former first lady Hillary Clinton. The biggest laugh came when Poehler's Clinton said, "I believe that diplomacy should be the cornerstone of any foreign policy," and Fey's Palin responded, "I can see Russia from my house." The video of the performance went viral almost immediately, receiving more hits than any other *SNL* skit in history. Even Palin was amused by Fey's impersonation, and the candidate appeared on an episode in October 2008 to show she could take a joke.

However, Fey's greatest success has been *30 Rock*, an NBC network sitcom in which she plays Liz Lemon, a neurotic head writer for a comedy variety series called *The Girlie Show*. Much of the show's humor derives from Fey's repartee with costar Alec Baldwin, who plays Jack Donaghy, a condescending studio executive who develops a "work spouse" relationship with Lemon, complete with repeated backhanded compliments and patronizing comments about her love life and other personal matters. Curtis Sittenfeld wrote in the *New York Times* in 2011 that Lemon "straddles a fine line between role model and pathetic stereotype of single womanhood."

Fey's work ethic and wit have driven her career, though her good looks have not hurt her. Despite claiming to have been homely in her young adulthood, she regularly lands on "most beautiful celebrities" lists. Aware that she is a role model for young female performers, she began hosting the public radio show *The Hidden World of Girls* in 2011, and her best-selling autobiographical book *Bossypants* (2011) has received acclaim as both humorous and fiercely feminist.

Stephen P. Davis

SEE ALSO: *Animated Films; Baldwin, Alec; Carell, Steve; Chase, Chevy; Emmy Awards; Gervais, Ricky; Guest, Christopher; Lohan, Lindsay; Palin, Sarah; Radio;* Saturday Night Live*; Second City; Sitcom; Television;* 30 Rock.

BIBLIOGRAPHY

Fey, Tina. *Bossypants.* New York: Reagan Arthur Books, 2011.

Sittenfeld, Curtis. "Tina Fey and Me." *New York Times*, April 8, 2011.

Fibber McGee and Molly

Out of Fibber McGee's famous closet came a twenty-four-year radio run whose success and innovation were matched by few broadcasters in the 1930s and 1940s. The series *Fibber McGee and Molly* helped forge the genre later called "situation comedy." It also paved the way for the concept of the "spin-off," as two popular supporting characters from *Fibber McGee and Molly* won their own series in the 1940s. Through it all, Jim and Marian Jordan played Fibber and Molly, and their program set both ratings records and a patriotic example during the war years. The Jordans were perhaps more deserving of the title "beloved" than any other performers during network radio's glory days.

The Jordans' early broadcasting careers were inauspicious at best. They were already battle-worn vaudevillians when, on a bet, they performed on a Chicago radio station in 1924. Their obvious talent soon earned them their own music and patter series. By the early 1930s the Jordans had hosted or appeared on numerous local music and banter programs, and their work gradually evolved into a series that would finally win them a spot on a national NBC hookup.

For *SmackOut*, the Jordans teamed with Don Quinn, the gifted writer with whom they would collaborate for more than fifteen years. In this new series, the couple played multiple roles, among them the proprietors of a Depression-era grocery always "smack out" of everything. An existing 1931 recording reveals that Marian perfected her Teeny character, the precocious adolescent she continued to portray when *SmackOut* gave way to *Fibber McGee and Molly* in 1935.

GOING NATIONAL

After years of work, *Fibber McGee and Molly* was an undeniably big break for the Jordans and Quinn. From Chicago on April 16, 1935, *Fibber McGee and Molly* was broadcast nationwide over the NBC network to middling reviews. The premiere was an uneasy mix of swing music and comedy segments in which Molly was an unadulterated battle-ax who spoke in a thick Irish brogue and Fibber was a tale-spinning loudmouth who more closely resembled his *SmackOut* character Uncle Luke than the character the nation would come to know as Fibber McGee. Yet the series became a moderate success, earning enough time to develop its style and characters. Within a year, Quinn and the Jordans had shaped the characters into the warmer, funnier personas they would inhabit for the rest of the series' run.

The cornball scripts for *Fibber McGee and Molly* revolve around the thinnest of plots. Fibber is a big-talking but inept spinner of yarns; Molly is his long-suffering but big-hearted companion. The couple has no obvious source of income; most of their Tuesday night adventures take place in the McGee home at 79 Wistful Vista, with a company of popular supporting characters parading through the house for brief appearances. Even announcer Harlow Wilcox was made into a character, his job being to work in a clever plug for sponsor Johnson's Wax. Many of the supporting characters were played by Bill Thompson, a genuine vocal acrobat who brought life to, among others, Wally Wimple, a perpetually henpecked husband whose every syllable bespeaks his suffering, and the Old Timer, a talkative curmudgeon whose catchphrase "That ain't the way I hear'd it!" became national slang by 1940.

CRISIS AND TRIUMPH

In the late 1930s the series weathered a crisis that threatened its very existence. Health issues forced Marian off the show for eighteen months starting in November 1937. Fans and historians have spent the ensuing decades debating the true nature of her absence. Press accounts from the time say only that Marian was sent to a "sanitarium" for a "rest," while fans have long whispered that she suffered a nervous breakdown. In 1998 radio historian John Dunning, citing an impeccable but anonymous source, revealed that Marian was actually battling alcoholism during her absence. The show limped along without her under the title *Fibber McGee and Company*. Marian—and Molly—returned on April 18, 1939, drawing both press attention and a huge ovation from the studio audience.

Then, seemingly out of the blue, the series' popularity simply exploded. Paired with Bob Hope's new NBC series on Tuesday nights, *Fibber McGee and Molly* shot to the very top of the ratings chart—part of a spate of new radio hits in the late 1930s that featured stars such as Hope, Red Skelton, and Edgar Bergen. One of the Jordans' supporting characters proved to be so popular that he received his own show, becoming broadcasting's first "spin-off." The program was titled *The Great Gildersleeve* (1941), in which Harold Peary reprised his role of bombastic but lovable Throckmorton P. Gildersleeve, who had delighted audiences for several years as Fibber's ever-feuding next-door neighbor.

THE WAR YEARS

Fibber's famous closet was opened for the first time on March 5, 1940, a sound-effects extravaganza in which years of piled-up junk came pouring out, much to the delight of the audience. It became one of the best-known gags in broadcast history. *Fibber McGee and Molly* was among the first series to go for all-out flag waving during World War II. On December 9, 1941, two days after the Japanese bombed Pearl Harbor, Marian uttered what may have been the first broadcast joke of World War II. (Gale Gordon, as Mayor LaTrivia, tells Molly he's shopping for a globe. "You want a globe with Japan on it?" Molly asks. "Then you better get one quick!") The series almost always featured patriotic themes during the war years. For example, during an episode from April 1943, Fibber buys and then gets sick from black market meat. The McGees even take in a war-plant worker, Alice, at one point.

By February 1943 *Fibber McGee* was drawing record ratings—quite a feat considering a significant percentage of the population was off fighting the war. The series suffered a major hit during this period when actor Bill Thompson joined the service, but the slack was taken up in large part by the appearance of the McGees' feisty African American maid Beulah, a giggly, vivacious bundle of energy whose catchphrases "Somebody bawl fo' Beulah?" and "Looovedatman!" became immensely popular. The character's popularity only increased when the audience learned that she was actually portrayed by a white man, Marlin Hurt, who became so famous in the role that he, too, was given his own series. *Beulah* premiered in 1945, and upon Hurt's sudden death the next year, it became the first radio comedy to feature a black actress (Hattie McDaniel) in a starring role, perhaps making up somewhat for the unapologetic caricature that had first given the series life.

THE DECLINE OF RADIO

The late 1940s proved to be troublesome for *Fibber McGee and Molly*. Hope never recaptured the overwhelming success of his war-years tours of service camps, and the entire NBC Tuesday schedule suffered as his popularity declined. By 1950 the previously obscure CBS sitcom *Life with Luigi* was besting Hope's ratings. However, the biggest threat was television: the new medium's first real sensation—Milton Berle's *Texaco Star Theater*—was slotted on Tuesday night, directly opposite Hope's and the Jordans' shows. *Fibber McGee and Molly* performed impressively against long odds, but NBC radio's Tuesday-night glory days were clearly over.

Nevertheless, *Fibber McGee and Molly* had long since crossed the line from popular entertainment to American institution. The Jordans stayed with NBC when many of the network's top comedians bolted to CBS in the 1948–1949 talent raids, though writer Quinn departed in 1950. Longtime sponsor Johnson's Wax dropped the series in 1950, and later sponsors included Reynolds Aluminum (which used its commercial time to introduce a revolutionary new product called Reynolds Wrap) and Pet Milk. In 1953, with network radio dying, the Jordans gave up their weekly series and started a nightly fifteen-minute version of *Fibber McGee and Molly*. In 1958 and 1959 the McGees were featured in short segments on NBC's innovative *Monitor* series.

Marian died in 1961; Jim lived another quarter century. During their careers, they set a decent, honest example for their audience and also invented and honed many of the formats and techniques broadcast writers and comedians utilize to this day. The phrase "Fibber's closet" may be a distant memory, but the legacy of *Fibber McGee and Molly* is alive and well.

Chris Chandler

SEE ALSO: *Berle, Milton;* Beulah*; The Great Depression; Hope, Bob; McDaniel, Hattie; Radio; Sitcom; World War II.*

BIBLIOGRAPHY

Dunning, John. *On the Air: The Encyclopedia of Old-Time Radio*. New York: Oxford University Press, 1998.

Price, Tom. *Fibber McGee's Closet: The Ultimate Log of Performances by Fibber McGee and Molly, 1917–1987*. Monterey, CA: T. A. Price, 1987.

Smith, Mickey C. *How Fibber McGee and Molly Won World War II*. Albany, GA: BearManor Media, 2010.

Stumpf, Charles, and Tom Price. *Heavenly Days!: The Story of Fibber McGee and Molly*. Waynesville, NC: World of Yesterday, 1987.

Fiddler on the Roof

One of the most important musicals of the 1960s, *Fiddler on the Roof* in many ways represents the end of the classic mid-twentieth-century American musical theater. The tale of Tevye, a Jewish peasant in turn-of-the-century Russia, and his difficulties with maintaining tradition in the midst of change, has had universal appeal ever since its premiere in 1964. The score includes the hit songs "Tradition," "To Life," "If I Were a Rich Man," and "Sunrise, Sunset."

In the early 1960s composer Jerry Bock, lyricist Sheldon Harnick, and librettist Joseph Stein decided that they wanted to write a musical together. After looking at numerous potential plot sources, they chose Sholom Aleichem's short story "Tevye and His Daughters." The trio persuaded Harold Prince to produce the show, who in turn advised them to engage Jerome Robbins as director-choreographer. With Prince and Robbins—two of Broadway's most significant creative personalities—involved with the production, its success was virtually guaranteed.

Fiddler on the Roof takes place in the Jewish village of Anatevka, Russia, in 1905. Its plot revolves around Tevye (a dairy farmer); his wife, Golde; and their five daughters. Tevye reveals his creed in his opening monologue:

> A fiddler on the roof. Sounds crazy, no? But in our little village of Anatevka, you might say every one of us is a fiddler on the roof, trying to scratch out a pleasant, simple tune without breaking his neck. It isn't easy. You may ask, why do we stay here if it's so dangerous? We stay because Anatevka is our home. And how do we keep our balance? That I can tell you in a word—tradition!

Tevye's world is challenged by impending change. Tzeitel, his eldest daughter, marries a poor tailor after Tevye had promised her to a wealthy widowed butcher. Hodel, his second daughter, marries a revolutionary and follows him to Siberia. Chava, his third daughter, marries a Christian. At the end of the musical, the czar's Cossacks destroy Anatevka as Tevye and his family leave for an unknown future in America. The show's title image—a fiddler on the roof who tries to maintain his balance while playing—suggests the desire for constancy in the face of mutability. The image itself was inspired by Marc Chagall's painting *The Green Violinist*.

Fiddler on the Roof opened on Broadway on September 22, 1964, at the Imperial Theater, where it played for 3,242 performances—the longest run in the history of the American musical theater to that time. Zero Mostel created the role of Tevye. Other original cast members included Maria Karnilova, Beatrice Arthur, Joanna Merlin, Julia Migenes, Bert Convy, and Tanya Everett. The musical garnered numerous Tony Awards, including for best musical, score, book, actor (Mostel), featured actress (Karnilova), choreographer (Robbins), and costumes (Patricia Zipprodt). Topol starred in the London production, which ran for more than 2,000 performances, as well as in the 1971 film version.

The success of the show was due largely to its superb musical score. The opening number, "Tradition," is a joyous celebration of life, as is the wedding number "To Life." The waltzes "Matchmaker" and "Sunrise, Sunset" capture the nostalgia of bygone traditions and the passing of time. Tevye's splendidly dramatic monologue, "If I Were a Rich Man," is one of the great soliloquies of the musical theater. Tevye and Golde's comic duet "Do You Love Me?" is a frank expression of the love that can develop between two people over a lifetime. This expression of matrimony based on traditional matchmaking is contrasted with the more modern concept of marriage based on love and choice in "Now I Have Everything" and "Miracle of Miracles."

The music of *Fiddler on the Roof* does not generally fit into the standard mold of Broadway show tunes; traditional folk idioms fill the score and infuse it with a particular yet accessible ethnic character that distinguishes it from other shows of its era. As such, it opened the door for more variations on the traditional American musical theater genre through the end of the century.

Fiddler on the Roof is embedded within its Jewishness without being parochial. The show's emphasis on family and religious interactions against a backdrop of a disintegrating social order gives it a universality that transcends time, place, and ethnicity. Its popularity through professional, amateur, and school productions remains as strong as ever decades after its premiere.

William A. Everett

SEE ALSO: *Arthur, Bea; The Musical; Prince, Hal; Tony Awards.*

BIBLIOGRAPHY

Robbins, Jerome, and Jerry Bock. *Harold Prince Presents Zero Mostel in* Fiddler on the Roof: *Director's Book.* New York: J. Robbins, 1970.

Shandler, Jeffrey. *Jews, God and Videotape: Religion and Media in America.* New York: New York University Press, 2009.

Slobin, Mark. "Some Intersections of Jews, Music, and Theater." In *From Hester Street to Hollywood: The Jewish-American Stage and Screen,* ed. Sarah Blacher. Bloomington: Indiana University Press, 1983.

Suskin, Steven. *Opening Night on Broadway: A Critical Quotebook of the Golden Era of the Musical Theatre,* Oklahoma! *(1943) to* Fiddler on the Roof *(1964).* New York: Schirmer Books, 1990.

Swain, Joseph P. *The Broadway Musical: A Critical and Musical Survey.* New York: Oxford University Press, 1990.

Fidrych, Mark "The Bird" *(1954–2009)*

The American League's Rookie of the Year for 1976, pitcher Mark Fidrych briefly captured the imagination of baseball fans with his bizarre on-the-field antics. Dubbed the "The Bird" for his lanky, ostrich-like frame resembling *Sesame Street*'s Big Bird, Fidrych was a 6-foot, 3-inch right-hander. He won nineteen games for the Detroit Tigers that season, compiling twenty-four complete games and a 2.34 earned run average.

It was the *way* he pitched more than his pitching results that filled ballparks that summer. Fidrych was far more animated than any pitcher before him: he talked to the baseball and shook hands with his infielders when good plays were made. After one stellar season, however, Fidrych blew out his arm and never regained his rookie form. He retreated to the minors for a while and attempted several abortive comebacks before he retired in 1983.

After retiring from the game, Fidrych held a variety of jobs, including running a farm in his hometown of Northborough, Massachusetts. In 2009 he appeared in the low-budget film *Dear Mr. Fidrych,* directed by Mike Cramer. The film concerns a man who as a twelve-year-old boy was greatly inspired by Fidrych's success and as a middle-aged adult travels together with his son to find Fidrych and new optimism in life. Fidrych died on his farm about two months before the release of the film.

Robert E. Schnakenberg

SEE ALSO: *Baseball; The Detroit Tigers;* Sesame Street.

BIBLIOGRAPHY

Amos, Ken. "Still the Bird." *Los Angeles Times,* November 3, 1996.

Nugent, Karen. "A Natural." *Worchester Telegram and Gazette,* June 15, 2010.

Pepe, Phil. *Talkin' Baseball: An Oral History of Baseball in the 1970s.* New York: Ballantine Books, 1998.

Ziegel, Vic. "Former Tigers Goofball Fidrych Remains a Different Sort of Bird." *St. Louis Post-Dispatch,* July 23, 1993.

Field, Sally *(1946–)*

From perky, surf-loving Gidget in 1965 to gray-haired, frumpy Mrs. Gump in 1994, the Academy Award–winning actress Sally Field has exhibited a wide range of talent and an enduring likability in a profession that too often ignores women over the age of forty. If her roles have a common theme, it is that women are intelligent, strong, and capable of heroic deeds.

Born in Pasadena, California, on November 6, 1946, Field was brought up by her actress mother and her stepfather, Jock Mahoney. At eighteen, while most young women were deciding whether to go to college or to get married, Field won the starring role in the television show *Gidget* (1965–1966), a role originally played by Sandra Dee in the hit movie of the same name. Gidget epitomized the typical teenager of the early 1960s, and Field was ideal for the part, establishing herself as a television star who gave young women a positive role model: enthusiastic and slightly goofy but always inherently obedient and moralistic.

The role of Gidget was followed by the even more endearing role of Sister Bertrille in *The Flying Nun* (1967–1970). Ironically Field was pregnant with her son Peter while flying through the air around the convent. She had married her high school sweetheart, Steven Craig, in 1968. Field gave birth to a second son, Eli, but the couple divorced in 1975. Field's next series was *The Girl with Something Extra* (1973–1974), which told the story of a young newlywed who had extrasensory perception (ESP).

BREAKING OUT

The breakout performance of Field's early career came with the role of Sybil in 1976. Playing a young woman with multiple-

Sally Field. *In addition to her two Academy Awards for Best Actress, Sally Field has won three Emmy Awards, two Golden Globes, a Screen Actors Guild Award, and the Best Female Performance Prize at the Cannes Film Festival for* Norma Rae *(1979).* JAMES DEVANEY/WIREIMAGE/GETTY IMAGES.

personality disorder, Field sealed her place in American television history and won an Emmy for her efforts. Sybil was as different from Gidget as it was possible to be. Bound up in her mental illness, Sybil took no pains with her appearance and had very few people skills—traits that were the essence of Gidget. While she met the challenges of this difficult role with apparent ease, Field paid a price for playing against type. She was no longer perceived as an attractive leading lady.

In 1977 she took on a different type of challenge with the role of young, attractive, fun-loving Carrie, who accepts a ride from a trucker, played by Burt Reynolds, while fleeing her wedding in *Smokey and the Bandit* (1977). Field would appear with Reynolds in a sequel to the film in 1980, and offscreen the duo became romantically involved. However, while Field was entering her prime as an actress, Reynolds entered a period of decline, and the romance ended after several years.

In 1980 Field won her first of two Academy Awards for Best Actress for her role in *Norma Rae*, the story of an Alabama textile worker who fights for unionization. When Field, as Norma Rae, stood up, holding her placard for union rights, and faced down irate mill owners, no one thought of Gidget. It was a moment that cemented the maturity of Field as an actress and illustrated the gains made by women in American film. Unlike earlier female stars, who had become known mostly for romantic and maternal roles, women of the 1970s and beyond were allowed to become heroes by standing up for what they thought was right.

Field's second Academy Award for Best Actress came with *Places in the Heart* (1984). Playing Edna Spalding, a Depression-era widow and mother of two who fights to save her farm with only the help of a black man and a blind man, Field demonstrated that heroes could be more traditional than Norma Rae and still be memorable. She said in a 1984 interview that Edna was her favorite role because she identified with her fierce love for her children and her strong will to survive. Accepting the honor as proof that she had surpassed the roles of Gidget and Sister Bertrille, Field effused, "You like me—You really like me!" That same year Field married the producer Alan Greisman and gave birth to a third son, Sam. The couple divorced in 1993.

TAKING CHANCES

Throughout her career Field has demonstrated versatility as an actress. In *Absence of Malice* (1981) with Paul Newman, she plays a reporter determined to get her story even at the cost of destroying innocent people. In *Murphy's Romance* (1985), Field is the much-younger love interest of the veteran actor James Garner. Even though the movie is a romantic comedy, Field managed to strike a blow for women's rights with the role of a single mother trying to raise her son by boarding horses. In 1989 she led an all-star cast in *Steel Magnolias*, a fact-based story of six southern women who hang out at a beauty shop, loving and supporting one another and remaining strong even when death claims one of their group.

Continuing to take chances, Field plays the stable wife of a forever-youthful Robin Williams in *Mrs. Doubtfire* (1993), the voice of Sassy the cat in the two *Homeward Bound* (1993, 1996) movies, and a justice-seeking mother of an abducted daughter in *Not without My Daughter* (1991) and of a slain daughter in *Eye for an Eye* (1996). She again became involved in an Academy Award–winning movie in 1994 when she accepted the role of Mrs. Gump in *Forrest Gump*. Ironically Field played the mother of Tom Hanks, who had played opposite her six years before in *Punchline*.

In 1998 Field continued to hold her own in the world of entertainment. She directed and starred in a segment of Hanks's phenomenal *From the Earth to the Moon* (1998). The turn of the twenty-first century saw her starring in the television movie *David Copperfield*, and in 2003 she returned to the big screen in the Reese Witherspoon vehicle *Legally Blonde 2: Red, White & Blonde*.

Although Field had become a critically acclaimed film actress, by the twenty-first century she recognized that there were few starring film roles for even gracefully aging actresses. She returned to television, appearing as the fragile and self-destructive Maggie Wyczenski in twelve episodes of the medical drama *ER* (1994–2009). She also briefly starred in the legal drama *The Court* in 2002, but she found her true niche in 2006 playing the matriarch Nora Walker in *Brothers and Sisters*, garnering her third Emmy Award in 2007 and winning a Screen Actors Guild Award in 2009.

Field remains active in improving the image of women in the entertainment industry and in a number of charitable works. After being diagnosed with osteoporosis in 2005, she became an advocate for educating women about health issues.

Elizabeth Rholetter Purdy

SEE ALSO: *Academy Awards; Emmy Awards;* ER*;* The Flying Nun*;* Forrest Gump*; Garner, James; Hanks, Tom; Made-for-Television Movies; Newman, Paul; Reynolds, Burt; Television; Williams, Robin; Witherspoon, Reese.*

BIBLIOGRAPHY

Bandler, Michael J. "Sally Field: Sweetness and Might." *Ladies' Home Journal*, February 1, 1991, 73–76.

Craig, Peter. *The Martini Shot.* New York: William Morrow, 1998.

Hallett, Lisa. "Field Day." *Emmy*, January 1, 1995, 18.

Roberts, Russell. *Sally Field.* Hockessin, DE: Mitchell Lane Publishers, 2004.

Sachs, Aviva. "Spunky Sally Field." *McCall's*, November 1989, 10.

Field and Stream

Field and Stream magazine, America's fishing and hunting bible, was born in a Minnesota duck blind in 1895. With contemporaries such as *Sports Afield* and *Outdoor Life*, it challenged the nineteenth-century stereotype that hunting and fishing were the domain of fur trappers and frontiersmen or amusements for the idle rich. Coupled with technological innovations that made shooting and fishing more accurate and easier, the new magazines demonstrated that hunting and fishing were recreational activities that could be enjoyed by all, especially the growing middle class. With a circulation of still more than a million in the early twenty-first century, *Field and Stream* continues to crusade for conservation measures, provides a library of wildlife video, and commissions wildlife images by well-known artists and photographers without forgetting its basic purpose—to provide the stuff of dreams for generations of hunters and fishermen.

INCREASED INTEREST IN SPORTS

The Civil War marked a new interest among Americans in sporting activities, most notably horse racing, boxing, track and field, and the relatively new sport of baseball, but also in hunting, fishing, and other outdoor activities. The *Sporting News* debuted in St. Louis, Missouri, in 1886, and its quick success encouraged newspaper publishers such as Joseph Pulitzer to add sporting news sections to their daily newspapers. Sports were considered entertainment and a form of escapism from what the late nineteenth century considered a frantic lifestyle, but they also taught an important lesson, especially to the young. Like life, sports had rules, and one needed to learn and obey them to succeed and win. The alternative—disobedience—meant failure, disgrace, and perhaps even death in a society obsessed with social Darwinism.

Magazine publishers were not far behind their newspaper counterparts in filling the new void for sports information. *Sports Afield* was founded in 1887, followed by *Outdoor Life*, which began as a Denver-based bicycling magazine in the early 1890s. John P. Burkhard and Henry W. Wack were talking in their duck blind in September 1895 about the wholesale slaughter of wildlife by so-called sportsmen. The conservation movement was in full swing, inaugurated by the establishment of Yellowstone National Park in 1872 and fanned by advocates such as John Muir and Gifford Pinchot. Burkhard and Wack disapproved of thrill shooting and set out to preach the new gospel of conservation to middle-class hunters and fishermen in their publication *North Western Field and Stream: A Journal of the Rifle, Gun, Rod and Camera*, which was published in their hometown of St. Paul, Minnesota.

Theodore Roosevelt was the first of many notable conservationists to appear in the publication. Writing in 1899, the president-to-be noted of the grizzly bear, "He has been hunted for sport, and hunted for his pelt, and hunted for the bounty, and hunted as a dangerous enemy to stock, until, save in the very wildest districts, he has learned to be more wary than a deer." Another article on childhood hunting observed a few years later, "All little boys crave the out-of-doors—when they don't get enough of it." The magazine was moved to New York in the first years of the twentieth century and its title modified, but it continued to struggle financially. Reportedly Henry Ford offered Burkhard and Wack $1,200 worth of stock in his new motor car company in 1905 in exchange for twenty full-page advertisements, but the pair turned him down because they were desperate for cash. Eltinge Warner, a printing salesman and circulation manager, took over the business side of the magazine in 1906 and purchased the publication upon Burkhard's death in 1907.

Circulation climbed, and *Field and Stream* prospered as conservation measures advocated by the magazine increased animal and fish populations. Warner became involved in the motion picture industry and published other magazines using profits from *Field and Stream*, but his first magazine kept to its original course. "When trout are rising, hope is strong in the angler's heart, even though he may not have determined in what position or upon what insects the fish are feeding," a *Field and Stream* article on fly-fishing maintained in 1912. An article on a shark attack in 1933 portended "terrible things . . . there in the murky water and the misty moonshine." The magazine also featured the self-deprecating humor of Gene Hill and the off-the-wall antics of Ed Zern. It absorbed its chief rival, *Forest and Stream*, in 1930.

CIRCULATION UPS AND DOWNS

A boon in men's magazines during and after World War II expanded the circulation of *Field and Stream*. By 1963 *Sports Afield*, *Outdoor Life*, and *Field and Stream* had a combined circulation of 3.7 million. In 1951 Warner sold *Field and Stream* to the book publishing house of Holt, Rinehart, and Winston, which was subsequently absorbed and reorganized into the CBS magazine division in 1971. The title peaked in size at about 200 hundred pages per issue during the 1970s, due to its payment method for writers. "We don't pay by the word anymore," managing editor Margaret Nichols said in 1995. "Long ago, when we paid a nickel a word, some people let their stories drag on and on. Fish would jump, then jump again and again and again."

Circulation plateaued at two million before the turn of the twenty-first century, but competition from televised sporting programs and, more recently, digital sources forced a downward trend in readership. The magazine was sold to Times Mirror Magazines, the publisher of *Outdoor Life*, in 1987 and in turn to Time Inc. in 2001. The Bonnier Group purchased it along with seventeen other titles in 2007, but the license for use of the *Field and Stream* name was sold to another private investment group. While styling itself as the world's leading outdoor magazine, *Field and Stream* entered the digital age with Web, smartphone, and tablet editions providing advice, reviews, and adventure stories along with videos and blogs. Still "there are certain things a magazine does better than anything else," editor Anthony Licata said in 2007, "[not] only to teach and instruct, but also [to] inspire sportsmen with great photography and long-form journalism."

Richard Junger

SEE ALSO: *Leisure Time; Smartphones; The* Sporting News.

BIBLIOGRAPHY

Egan, D'Arcy. "Hunting, Fishing Bible Turns 100: Field & Stream Takes Readers Back to the Adventures They Grew Up On." *Cleveland Plain Dealer*, July 14, 1995, 9D.

Merritt, J. I., and Margaret G. Nichols. *The Best of "Field & Stream": 100 Years of Great Writing from America's Premier Sporting Magazine.* Guilford, CT: Lyons, 2002.

Mott, Frank L. "The Argosy." *A History of American Magazines*, vol. 4, 417–423. Cambridge, MA: Harvard University Press, 1957.

Nickens, T. Edward, and Philip Bourjaily. *"Field and Stream": The Total Outdoorsman Manual.* San Francisco: Weldon Owen, 2011.

Peterson, Theodore. *Magazines in the Twentieth Century.* Urbana: University of Illinois Press, 1964.

Field of Dreams

Released in 1989, *Field of Dreams* is a movie about faith, forgiveness, and redemption. Directed by Phil Alden Robinson and starring Kevin Costner, James Earl Jones, and Ray Liotta, the film was a huge success, garnering three Academy Award nominations and making more than $64 million at the box office. After leaving movie theaters, *Field of Dreams* earned another $40 million in video rentals and sales.

Field of Dreams is based on W. P. Kinsella's book *Shoeless Joe* and is a fantasy-drama featuring Ray Kinsella (Costner), an Iowa corn farmer, and his family. They lead a normal, if boring, existence until Kinsella hears a ghostly voice in his cornfield whispering, "If you build it, he will come." At first Kinsella assumes he is hallucinating, but the voice returns. After seeing a vision of a baseball diamond in the middle of his cornfield, Kinsella plows a portion of his corn and builds a baseball field, complete with bleachers. Pretty soon the ghost of "Shoeless" Joe Jackson (Liotta), who was a baseball player with the Chicago White Sox in the early twentieth century, walks out of the corn in uniform. He is soon joined by his teammates, and they play baseball on the field.

Kinsella, meanwhile, continues to hear messages from the voice in the cornfield. The voice eventually leads him to Boston and Terence Mann (Jones), an author who was an activist in the 1960s. Kinsella convinces Mann to return to Iowa with him, and on their way, they are told by the voice to find an old country doctor, Moonlight Graham (Burt Lancaster), who played one game in the major leagues but never got to bat. Although the doctor is long dead, he appears as a young man to Kinsella. After Kinsella, Mann, and the teenage Graham return to Iowa, Kinsella meets the ghost of his father as a young minor-league baseball player. For the first time, he understands his father and the deeper meaning behind his father's obsession with baseball and Jackson. Not long after this, bankers come to foreclose on Kinsella's farm. As he begins to realize the situation he is in, a long line of cars leading to the farm begins to form—people willing to pay to watch "Shoeless" Joe and his fellow ghosts play baseball on Kinsella's field.

Field of Dreams touched a particular chord with baby boomers. Kinsella himself represents the average boomer male who has forgotten how important baseball was to him as a child. Mann is clearly symbolic of all of the activists in the 1960s who sold out their principles to make money. The bankers represent the faceless corporations that own baseball teams, focusing entirely on profits rather than a love of the game. The connection between boomer children and baseball is perhaps best explained by Mann, who looks out onto the field of ghost players and proclaims, "The one constant through all the years, Ray, has been baseball. America has rolled by like an army of steamrollers. It's been erased like a blackboard, rebuilt, and erased again. But baseball has marked the time. This field, this game, is a part of our past, Ray. It reminds us of all that was once good, and what could be good again."

Field of Dreams started a resurgence of baseball nostalgia, with dozens of books and movies recounting the "good old days" when children collected baseball cards for trading. The location where the movie was filmed, a 193-acre farm owned by Don and Becky Lansing in Dyersville, Iowa, became a tourist attraction, drawing about 65,000 visitors a year. The baseball diamond, built for the film, is also there. In late 2011 the Lansings sold their farm, which they had named Field of Dreams Movie Site, to an investment group that planned to change the site's name to All-Star Ballpark Heaven and add a youth training facility for baseball and softball and a dozen ball fields.

Geoff Peterson

SEE ALSO: *Academy Awards; Baby Boomers; Baseball; Baseball Cards; Black Sox Scandal; Costner, Kevin; Jackson, "Shoeless" Joe; Lancaster, Burt.*

BIBLIOGRAPHY

Kinsella, W. P. *Shoeless Joe.* Boston: Houghton Mifflin, 1982.

Will, George F. *Men at Work: The Craft of Baseball.* New York: Macmillan, 1990.

Wood, Stephen C., and David J. Pincus. *Reel Baseball.* Jefferson, NC: McFarland, 2003.

Fields, W. C. *(1880–1946)*

One of film comedy's best-loved performers, W. C. Fields has inspired countless impersonators but few imitators. In more than forty films over three decades, the bulbous-nosed actor perfected a unique comic persona marked by a love of whiskey, a hatred of small children and animals, and a love of underhanded chicanery. Among the memorable quotes attributed to Fields are "Anyone who hates dogs and kids can't be all bad" and "A thing worth having is a thing worth cheating for." His famous epitaph, "All things considered, I'd rather be in Philadelphia," paid mocking tribute to his birth city.

Born William Claude Dukenfield, Fields left home at age eleven to escape his abusive father. By thirteen he was a skilled pool player and juggler and was soon entertaining customers at amusement parks. By the age of twenty-one, he was one of the leading lights of vaudeville. He played the Palace in London and starred at the Folies-Bergère in Paris. Fields appeared in each of the Ziegfeld Follies from 1915 through 1921. His stage act, which featured both comedy and juggling, was immortalized in 1915 in his first silent film, *Pool Shark*. He devoted himself to films throughout the 1920s, though his comic persona did not find full flower until the advent of sound in the next decade.

Fields's best silent feature, *It's the Old Army Game* (1926), was later remade as his breakthrough talkie, *It's a Gift* (1934). That film, which cast Fields as a grocery clerk who moves his family west to manage a chain of orange groves, established for all time the incomparable W. C. Fields persona. His nose reddened by excessive drink, speaking sarcastic asides in a comic snarl, forever bedeviled by animals and children, Fields was the cantankerous bastard inside of every moviegoer, the personification of the male id unleashed. This emerging comic identity was also on view in a series of classic shorts he made for Mack Sennett. Most notable among these are *The Dentist* (1932), and *The Barber Shop* and *The Pharmacist* (both 1933).

Fields proved himself more than a mere clown, however. He also found a niche playing character roles in adaptations of the classics. He portrayed Humpty Dumpty in the all-star 1933 film version of *Alice in Wonderland*, then replaced Charles Laughton as Micawber in the 1935 adaptation of *David Copperfield.* Fields was also given serious consideration for the title role in 1939's *The Wizard of Oz*, though that part eventually went to Frank Morgan.

As the 1930s drew to a close, he began work on one last stretch of classic films. He teamed up with ventriloquist Edgar Bergen and his dummy Charlie McCarthy for the 1939 circus farce *You Can't Cheat an Honest Man. My Little Chickadee* (1940) paired Fields with Mae West, an inspired bit of casting that produced some of their best work. *The Bank Dick* (1940), which Fields wrote using an alias, was perhaps his finest starring vehicle. His last full-length starring feature was 1941's *Never Give a Sucker an Even Break*, an anarchic comedy with a plot outline that Fields reportedly sketched on a cocktail napkin.

Battling poor health, Fields continued acting in bit parts well into the 1940s. His infirmities eventually caught up with him, and he died of pneumonia on Christmas Day in 1946. In the decades after his death, Fields's filmic oeuvre generated a vibrant cult following. His works became a staple of late-night art house film festivals, and he was particularly beloved on college campuses. In 1976 Rod Steiger gamely impersonated the comic legend for a well-received biopic *W. C. Fields and Me.*

Robert E. Schnakenberg

SEE ALSO: *Bergen, Edgar; Charlie McCarthy; Sennett, Mack; Silent Movies; Vaudeville; West, Mae;* The Wizard of Oz; The Ziegfeld Follies.

BIBLIOGRAPHY

Curtis, James. *W. C. Fields: A Biography.* New York: A. A. Knopf, 2003.

Deschner, Donald. *The Complete Films of W. C. Fields.* Secaucus, NJ: Citadel Press, 1989.

Louvish, Samuel. *Man on the Flying Trapeze: The Life and Times of W. C. Fields.* New York: W. W. Norton, 1997.

Fierstein, Harvey *(1954–)*

The gravel-voiced Harvey Fierstein was one of the first openly homosexual American actor/playwrights who lent his name and support to gay rights and AIDS (acquired immunodeficiency syndrome) activism during the 1980s and 1990s. His breakthrough work was the autobiographical 1982 play *Torch Song Trilogy*, dealing with a young man's coming out and his relationship with his mother. For the work, Fierstein won Tony Awards for Best Playwright and Best Actor.

Fierstein became familiar to moviegoers for his role as a supporting actor in such blockbuster hits as *Mrs. Doubtfire* (1993) and *Independence Day* (1996), and he narrated the 1984 Oscar-winning documentary *The Times of Harvey Milk*, about an assassinated gay politician. He later played Edna Turnblad in the Broadway production of *Hairspray* (2003) and won another Tony for Best Book of a Musical for *La Cage aux folles* (2011), in which he appeared in more than 400 performances. Fierstein won the Drama League Award for Distinguished Production of a Musical for *A Catered Affair* in 2007 before signing on to adapt *Newsies* as a musical for Disney.

Andrew Milner

SEE ALSO: *Academy Awards; AIDS; Broadway; Gay Men;* Independence Day*; Milk, Harvey; Outing; Tony Awards.*

BIBLIOGRAPHY

Fierstein, Harvey. *Torch Song Trilogy.* London: Methuen, 1984.

"Harvey Fierstein." *Current Biography Yearbook*, vol. 45. New York: H.W. Wilson, 1984.

Sternlicht, Sanford. *A Reader's Guide to Modern American Drama.* Syracuse, NY: Syracuse University Press, 2002.

The Fifties

The 1950s were a time of rapid change and lockstep conformity, of new forms emerging out of old, and technical innovations proceeding at a breakneck pace. For all the talk of traditional American values, the country was shedding its past as a snake sheds its skin. By the decade's end, so much had changed—internationalism replacing isolationism; rampant consumerism replacing thrift; the extended family network, once the social glue binding the country, superseded by the suburban nuclear family—that the country was scarcely recognizable. Yet the 1950s continues to be perceived by many as the ultra-American decade.

Nostalgic for a time when America was without question the most powerful nation on earth and, like the biblical land of

Teens in the 1950s. *A teenage couple shares an ice cream drink at a soda shop in 1958.* BOB BARRETT/FPG/HULTON ARCHIVE/GETTY IMAGES.

milk and honey, overflowing with bounty, America has projected its anxieties back to this supposedly golden age. This perception does not bear scrutiny. At the time it seemed as if overnight a familiar way of life had been replaced by shopping malls and prefabricated suburbs, the atom bomb and television sets—especially television sets.

TELEVISION

It is almost impossible to calculate the effect television had in the first decade of its usage. Television intruded into every aspect of American life, leaving almost nothing untouched. Book sales declined; radio listenership slumped precipitously; the film industry, already in shambles, was dealt a staggering blow. By 1951 movie theaters had begun to close throughout the country—134 in Southern California alone—and even cities with only one television station were reporting drops in film attendance of between 20 and 40 percent. So fascinated was the public with this new medium, according to a 1951 study, that when a popular program was on, toilets would flush throughout the city as if on cue, in concert with commercial breaks or the conclusion of a program.

Television altered the country's mores and conventions, its collective vision of the nation and the world, and the very nature of electoral politics. Television brought America the wars abroad and conflict at home—the Arkansas National Guard blocking court-ordered school desegregation in Little Rock, Arkansas; the French catastrophe at Dien Bien Phu—and the confluence of these forces, racial tension and American internationalism, would foster the more radical changes of the 1960s.

Nowhere was the effect of television so pervasive as in advertising; so great was the effect of television advertising on consumer habits, it was almost Pavlovian. "Television was turning out to be a magic machine for selling products," writes David Halberstam, author of an exhaustive survey of the decade, "and the awareness of that was still dawning on Madison Avenue in the late 1950s." Six months after Revlon began sponsoring the popular game show *The $64,000 Question*, for instance, the company's revenues had risen 54 percent. The next year sales had risen to $85.7 million (a $33 million increase)—a figure close to Revlon's total profits prior to television. Obviously, there were winners and losers in this equation. The companies that could afford national advertising gained market share, and smaller companies lost it. In short, television furthered the subsumption of market capitalism under the hegemony of national and multinational corporations, a profound blow to the free market that television so zealously trumpeted.

Television advertising was also used to great effect in politics. The campaign commercial became an integral part of American electioneering, as did television coverage, replacing the whistle-stop tour as a tool of effective voter outreach. Television could make or break a candidate: it was Richard Nixon's famous televised "Checkers" speech that saved his 1952 vice-presidential candidacy and television again that proved his undoing against John F. Kennedy in 1960. In their debate, Nixon, exhausted by his arduous campaign schedule and with sweat washing away his makeup, appeared so haggard and pale that acquaintances called afterward to inquire after his health. Kennedy, on the other hand, having spent the previous week relaxing poolside in

Southern California, literally radiated vitality; the choice was apparently between a derelict used-car salesman and a bronzed demigod.

ENEMIES AT HOME AND ABROAD

There was a schizoid quality to life in the 1950s, a manic oscillation between paranoia and omnipotence. The disjunct was fueled by the long shadow of the Depression and, among certain parties, a blind, unreasoned hatred of communism. "You and I were trained for a conflict that never came," writes D. J. Waldie in his memoir of life in Lakewood, California, the second mass-produced suburb built in America (Levittown, New York, was first). "At my grade school, the Sisters of St. Joseph made me hate Communists, then intolerance, and finally everything that could break the charmed pattern of our lives. I am not sure the Sisters of St. Joseph expected this from their daily lessons on the Red threat." One might attribute this hypervigilance to a form of collective post-traumatic stress disorder, a reaction to defeating the Nazis and Japanese, as if prosperity—linked as it was to war production—was contingent on possessing a worthy enemy to defeat.

In fact, this was precisely the case. The U.S. economy had become beholden to perpetual war production. As it was, America had already experienced a series of recessions since the end of World War II. The more leftist historians of the age would argue that the bellicose nature of our foreign policy—in Korea, our material support of France's struggle in Indochina, our numerous covert actions in places like Guatemala and Iran—and our strident anticommunism was in fact a method of keeping the war machine chugging away full blast. It was the Monroe Doctrine expanded to include the entire world.

In addition, our numerous foreign interventions coincided with vested interests, and it was often at the behest of large corporations that foreign policy was molded. One seldom-mentioned proof of this thesis was the new zeal with which Americans were taxed—they were spending more, but they were also, many for the first time, paying an income tax, much of which went to supporting our foreign excursions. By the end of the decade, even President Dwight Eisenhower could not ignore the changes the Cold War had wrought, and his farewell address carried a dire warning.

Above all else, red-baiting made for effective campaign politics. Nixon, perhaps America's most opportunistic politician, first saw the value of red-baiting, using the Alger Hiss hearings before the House Un-American Activities Committee as a bully pulpit, pushing anticommunist legislation through subcommittee when the matter seemed all but dead. Nixon then seized the moral high ground in his 1950 senatorial race, mercilessly baiting his liberal opponent, Helen Gallagher Douglas, at every opportunity.

Senator Joseph McCarthy became the most notorious red-baiter of all, stepping into the role of what Halberstam calls an "accidental demagogue" when he casually mentioned a fictitious list of State Department communists at a Lincoln Day celebration in Wheeling, West Virginia. McCarthy's campaign to ferret out communism lasted four long years, fueled as much by a lust for headlines as by ideological conviction. It ended with his ill-conceived attack on the U.S. Army, leading to his censure by the Senate and political disgrace. The red scare was, as Maryland Senator Millard Tydings said of McCarthy, "a hoax and a fraud . . . an attempt to inflame the American people with a wave of hysteria and fear on an unbelievable scale." As such, it was a smashing success. Nixon was victorious in his senatorial campaign against Douglas in 1950. Tydings, whose comments exposed him to the full brunt of Far Right wrath, was not: he lost his seat in 1956.

MORE OF EVERYTHING

If America was exporting saber rattling abroad, at home the good life was being rationalized as never before. Technology and the mania for speedy service had crept into almost every facet of commerce, from restaurants (McDonald's) to motels (Holiday Inn) to shopping (E. J. Korvett and the many discount department stores Korvett inspired) to farming itself. Family farms disappeared at a staggering rate, replaced by large agribusiness conglomerates, whose indiscriminate use of pesticides and feed additives, along with promotion of the beef industry, changed forever the American diet. Whatever product or service could be performed could be performed better and more efficiently as part of a chain, or so it was thought. Ray Kroc, the original franchiser of McDonald's, demonstrated this with stunning success. It was part of a democratization of goods and services. What had formally been the province of the upper-middle class—leisure, cars, houses—was now available to the working man, albeit in a watered-down form. Nowhere was this dual relationship of technology and egalitarianism in commerce more apparent than in the housing industry.

THE SUBURBS

Housing had suffered from the paucity of building supplies during World War II. In 1948 there had been a mere 11,400 new house starts, and with the return of America's soldiers, the housing shortage became a housing crisis. Bill Levitt, himself a veteran of the Seabees, began thinking about applying assembly-line techniques to housing before the war, and he had bought a plot of farmland on Long Island, New York, with his brother for that very purpose. He wanted to bring housing to the working class and emancipate them from the inner city. Following the war, Levitt, with the aid of federally insured mortgages, began building a community of 17,311 minimalist Cape Cod houses, a scale of production heretofore unknown. Everything was prefabricated and transported to the building site, where specialized crews moved from one lot to the next in assembly-line fashion performing their single task. Construction was finished within a matter of months.

"This is Levittown! All yours for $58. You're a lucky fellow, Mr. Veteran," proclaimed an ad in the *New York Times*. "Uncle Sam and the world's largest builder have made it possible for you to live in a charming house in a delightful community without having to pay for them with your eye teeth." Veterans stormed Levitt's sales office; in one day alone 1,400 contracts were drawn up. The new owners were pioneers in what became a mass exodus from city to suburb as all across the nation similar projects were initiated. Levitt himself built several other Levittowns along the East Coast. It was a revolutionary change in living for the nuclear family. In 1955 Levitt-type suburbs accounted for 75 percent of the new housing starts. Within thirty years some sixty million people had moved to the prefabricated suburbs Levitt had helped to create, while eighteen of the twenty-five largest cities had declined in population, a massive migration that would have dramatic consequences in the ensuing years.

The ranks of the suburbanized middle class were swelling, but what was the price of this newfound affluence? The suburbs were clean and safe, but living in them could be enervating, especially to college-educated women who had forsaken careers for domesticity and child rearing. Nor were men spared the malaise. It was ironic, an irony not lost on many returning veterans, that having risked their lives in war, they had returned to another kind of death, that of the colorless organization man.

In 1950 sociologist David Reisman published *The Lonely Crowd*, his psychological exploration of middle-class anomie. Shortly thereafter, Sloan Wilson wrote *The Man in the Gray Flannel Suit*, his 1955 novel portraying the emptiness of the suburbs. "Have we become a nation of yes-men?" these books asked. Was solace to be found in blind materialism? Many sensed the danger but could not resist the allure. Writes Richard Schickel in his biography of Marlon Brando:

> *The Lonely Crowd* was anatomized in 1950, and the fear of drifting into its clutches was lively in us. *White Collar* [C. Wright Mills's truculent attack on conformist culture] was on our brick and board bookshelves, and we saw how the eponymous object seemed to be choking the life out of earlier generations . . . though of course, even as we read about these cautionary figures, many of us were talking to corporate recruiters about entry-level emulation of them."

REBELLION

While the nation fell further under the sway of homogeneity, it was no surprise that a kind of exaggerated rebel would become a popular cultural icon, an omnipresent figure in literature (the Beats), in rock and roll, and the movies. Stars such as James Dean, Brando, and Montgomery Clift assayed a new type of masculinity—sensitive, brooding, and rebellious—while Elvis Presley, and to a greater degree, Jerry Lee Lewis, comported themselves with a haughty menace. These sneering film and music stars were America's surrogate rebels, acting out in ways most people could ill afford to chance. America's contempt for what it had become was caught in the sneer, an expression that, when employed by Brando or Dean or Presley, contemptuously leveled the organization man and the carrot-on-a-stick world of nine to five.

Rock and roll was this rebellious spirit's most potent manifestation. The culmination of years of cross-cultural evolution, teenagers in the early 1950s began enthusiastically seeking out "race" music, one of a variety of blues and rhythm and blues, an enthusiasm all the more attractive for the disapprobation with which parents reacted to it. Rock and roll was unabashedly sexual, exuberant, and raucous. To parents everywhere it represented a threat, an insidious menace crawling up from the cellars of the lower classes.

In 1951 a Cleveland record store owner reported this new craze to DJ Alan Freed, then playing classical music on a late-night show, and prevailed upon him to change his show to the nascent rock and roll, making Freed one of the first DJs in the country to program biracially. Previously, Memphis DJ Dewey Phillips had devised a radio show, *Red, Hot and Blue*, that had become the rage among Memphis's hip youth. The city was thoroughly segregated, but on Phillips's show one could hear Ike Turner, Fats Domino, and B. B. King alongside Bill Haley, Hank Williams, and Johnny Cash; in short, the two styles from which rock and roll derived played side by side.

Presley, who listened religiously to Phillips's show, exemplified this hybrid, blending country and western, blues, and evangelical mania, presented with a sneer ripped straight off the face of Dean, whom the young Elvis worshipped. Linking the surliness of Dean with the frenzy of the gospel revivalist was an inspired combination. "This cat came out in a coat and pink shirt and socks and he had this sneer on his face and he stood behind the mike for five minutes, I'll bet, before he made a move," said country singer Bob Luman in recalling an early Elvis show. "Then he hit his guitar a lick and he broke two strings. . . . So there he was, these two strings dangling, and he hadn't done anything yet, and these high school girls were screaming and fainting and running up to the stage, and then he started to move his hips real slow like he had a thing for his guitar." This was the threat that parents worried over—why religious groups burned rock-and-roll records, why the music was ineluctably attractive to the kids, and why the nature of music and musical celebrity would never be the same.

THE BEATS

The change in rock and roll over the course of the decade, from unbridled passion to commercial product, was an early lesson in co-optation. Yet for the Beat writers, defiance to American values, such as they were, was a central tenet of their thinking, and they were regularly castigated for it. Writing in the November 1959 issue of *Life*, Paul O'Neill called the Beat writers "undisciplined and slovenly amateurs who have deluded themselves into believing their lugubrious absurdities are art simply because they have rejected the form, styles, and attitudes of previous generations."

The Beats rejected American consumerism and the plastic world of mortgages and car payments, living instead on the periphery. "In their discontent with American values," writes Ted Morgan, William S. Burroughs's biographer, "with cold-war suspicion, with loving the bomb, with a society shaped by corporate power and moral smugness, they had come up with something more vital. . . . In their rejection of the boring, the conventional, and the academic, in their adoption of a venturesome lifestyle, they gave everyone the green light to plumb their own experience." Although the Beats were derided in the 1950s, endlessly examined for moral failings, labeled as naysayers, and saddled with the diminutive "Beatnik" (after Sputnik), America could not be rid of them. Within a few short years, their progeny—the baby boomers who read them in high school—were omnipresent.

1950s NOSTALGIA

The most common representation of the 1950s is a sort of glossy coffee table *histoire*, heavy on photographic images and short on historical fact. It is these images of tail fins and spotless kitchens and poodle skirts that endure, as if the other America, the America of violent racist attacks, of Little Rock and Montgomery, Alabama—the incipient racism and paranoia of the most powerful country on earth—never existed. According to Halberstam:

> One reason that Americans as a people became nostalgic about the 1950s more than twenty-five years later was not so much that life was better in the 1950s (though in some ways it was), but because at the time it had been portrayed so idyllically on television. It was the television images of the era that remained so

remarkably sharp in people's memories, often fresher than memories of real life. Television reflected a world of warm-hearted, sensitive, tolerant Americans, a world devoid of anger and meanness of spirit and, of course, failure.

Those aficionados of the decade who dress in vintage clothing, drive 1950s-era cars, and listen to the music have made of the 1950s a virtual cult of style. Their strivings to elude the present constitutes a nostalgic retreat, a harkening back to a golden age through the mute power of artifacts. This beneficent image, the make-believe world represented by movies and television shows such as *Grease* (1978), *Happy Days* (1974–1984), *Sha Na Na* (1977), and *Laverne and Shirley* (1976–1983), constitutes an evasion, a return to a time of clear-cut values, which is all the more insidious for being fictional. As a decade, the 1950s represents a sort of idealized America, but this image has more to do with the 1970s television show *Happy Days* than with any objective reality.

It is perhaps to be expected, then, that compared to the abundance of memoirs, histories, and analyses published about the 1960s, there is such a paucity of historical material on the 1950s. Ironic, and unsettling, because the America we have inherited, and with which some take umbrage, was shaped in great part by the 1950s. Much of the landscape we take for granted—fast-food franchises and foreign policy, corporate hegemony and interstate highways—was brought into being during that era, as was the generation that went to college, protested the war, took acid, and wrote their memoirs. They prefer to remember the 1950s as a bad dream.

Michael Baers

SEE ALSO: American Graffiti; *Army-McCarthy Hearings; Blues; The Bomb; Brando, Marlon; Burroughs, William S.; Cash, Johnny; Clift, Montgomery; Dean, James; Domino, Fats; Freed, Alan "Moondog"; Ginsberg, Allen; Haley, Bill;* Happy Days; *Holiday Inns; King, B. B.;* Laverne and Shirley; *Levittown; Lewis, Jerry; Live Television; McCarthyism; McDonald's;* The Organization Man; *Presley, Elvis; Red Scare; Rhythm and Blues; Rock and Roll;* The $64,000 Question; Sputnik; *Suburbia; Television; Turner, Ike and Tina; Williams, Hank, Sr..*

BIBLIOGRAPHY

Arnold, Eve. *The Fifties: Photographs of America.* New York: Pantheon, 1985.

Carter, Paul A. *Another Part of the Fifties.* New York: Columbia University Press, 1983.

Escott, Colin, and Martin Hawkins. *Sun Records: The Brief History of the Legendary Recording Label.* New York: Omnibus Press, 1980.

Ginsberg, Allen. *Journals Mid-Fifties, 1954–1958*, ed. Gordon Ball. New York: HarperCollins, 1995.

Gruen, John. *The Party's over Now: Reminiscences of the Fifties: New York's Artists, Writers, Musicians, and Their Friends.* New York: Viking Press, 1972.

Friedan, Betty. *The Feminine Mystique.* New York: W. W. Norton, 1963.

Halberstam, David. *The Fifties.* New York: Villard Books, 1993.

Harvey, Brett. *The Fifties: A Women's Oral History.* New York: HarperCollins, 1977.

Jezer, Marty. *The Dark Ages: Life in the United States 1945–1960.* Boston: South End Press, 1982.

Kaplan, Fred M. *1959: The Year Everything Changed.* Hoboken, NJ: Wiley, 2009.

Mills, C. Wright. *White Collar: The American Middle Classes.* New York: Oxford University Press, 1951.

Morgan, Ted. *Literary Outlaw: The Life and Times of William S. Burroughs.* New York: Henry Holt, 1988.

Riesman, David. *The Lonely Crowd: A Study of the Changing American Character.* New Haven, CT: Yale University Press, 1950.

Schickel, Richard. *Brando: A Life in Our Times.* New York: Atheneum, 1991.

Waldie, D. J. *Holy Land: A Suburban Memoir.* New York: W. W. Norton, 1996.

Whyte, William H. *The Organization Man.* New York: Simon & Schuster, 1956.

Wilson, Edmund. *The Fifties: From Notebooks and Diaries of the Period.* New York: Farrar, Straus & Giroux, 1986.

Wilson, Sloan. *The Man in the Gray Flannel Suit.* New York: Simon & Schuster, 1955.

50 Cent *(1975–)*

Curtis James Jackson III—better known as 50 Cent—was born July 6, 1975, in Jamaica Queens, New York. His mother, Sabrina, dealt drugs and was killed in 1983 when Jackson was only eight years old. He moved in with his grandparents and began splitting his time between boxing at a local gym and dealing crack on the streets. His boxing career was cut short after he was arrested twice in 1994 on drug and weapons charges. Jackson escaped a lengthy prison sentence by attending juvenile boot camp, where he was given the name "50 Cent" after a famous Brooklyn robber from the 1980s.

50 Cent began rapping in his early twenties under the tutelage of Run-DMC's Jam Master Jay, who taught him the technical aspects of the craft and produced an unreleased album of his early work. 50 Cent's first underground single, "How to Rob" (1999), drew instant attention by poking fun at other rappers and actors by name, including Sean "P. Diddy" Combs, Will Smith, and Master P. The song garnered negative reactions from Jay-Z, DMX, and other rappers who each responded in their own songs. The Fugees' Wyclef Jean jested, "I stay so hungry that if 50 Cent came to rob me, he'd be part of my charity," while Jay-Z got more graphic with, "I'm about a dollar, what the F— is 50 Cent?" On May 24, 2000, 50 Cent was shot nine times by an unknown assailant. He spent nearly two weeks in the hospital, and it took him five months to recover. He claims the shooting was a holdover from his drug-dealing days and not part of a rap feud.

50 Cent worked his way up the rap ladder by making underground mix tapes using other artists' beats with his lyrics dubbed over them. After listening to one of these mix tapes in 2002, Eminem introduced 50 Cent to Dr. Dre, signed him to a $1 million contract with Interscope Records, and put one of his tracks on the *8 Mile* (2002) movie soundtrack. 50 Cent's first album, *Get Rich or Die Tryin'* (2003) debuted at number one on the Billboard chart. The album's breakout hit, "In Da Club," won Best Rap Video, and 50 Cent won Best New Artist at the

2003 MTV Music Awards. That same year he started his own label, G-Unit Records.

50 Cent's second album, *Massacre* (2005), spent a record six weeks at number one, and his third album, *Curtis* (2007), debuted at number two, battling with Kanye West's *Graduation*, which was released on the same day. *Before I Self Destruct* (2009) debuted at number five and was not well received by critics. 50 Cent won a Grammy in 2010 for his work with Dr. Dre and Eminem on the song "Crack a Bottle."

Apart from his music career, 50 Cent is an entrepreneur with the G-Unit brand on a record label, a clothing line, a book publisher, a film company, and a shoe endorsed by Reebok. The artist has two namesake video games—50 Cent: Bulletproof and 50 Cent: Blood on the Sand. In 2011 he began endorsing Street King energy drinks, whose mission to end global hunger provides one meal to a starving child per shot purchased.

50 Cent has appeared as himself in multiple television shows, including *Entourage* (2004–2011); *The Simpsons* (1989–); and his own MTV reality show, *The Money and the Power* (2008–2009). His 2005 film debut, *Get Rich or Die Tryin'* was semiautobiographical, documenting his early years dealing drugs and rapping. He has since acted in nearly a dozen films, supporting some of the biggest stars in Hollywood, including *Home of the Brave* (2006) with Samuel Jackson, *Righteous Kill* (2008) with Robert De Niro and Al Pacino, and *Streets of Blood* (2009) with Sharon Stone.

50 Cent is also the writer or coauthor of nearly a dozen books, including *From Pieces to Weight: Once upon a Time in Southside Queens* (2006), *The 50th Law* (2009), and *Playground* (2011). *Rolling Stone*'s Nathan Brackett explained the artist's commercial appeal: "It helps that 50 Cent is the most likable rapper ever to need a bulletproof vest. . . . 50 has charisma . . . is cool and easy to be around—you get the sense that if he weren't so busy getting shot, stabbed and selling millions of albums, he would be an enormously successful fraternity president or restaurateur."

Ron Horton

SEE ALSO: *Boxing; Cocaine/Crack; Combs, Sean "P. Diddy"; De Niro, Robert; Eminem; Gangsta Rap; Grammy Awards; Hollywood; Jay-Z; MTV; Pacino, Al; Rap; Reality Television; Run-DMC; Smith, Will; West, Kanye.*

BIBLIOGRAPHY

50 Cent, and Chris Ex. *From Pieces to Weight: Once upon a Time in Southside Queens.* New York: Pocket Books, 2006.

50 Cent, and Noah Callahan-Bever. *50 X 50.* London: Simon & Schuster, 2007.

Fight Club

Fight Club is a 1999 motion picture directed by David Fincher and starring Edward Norton, Brad Pitt, and Helena Bonham Carter. Based on Chuck Palahniuk's 1996 novel of the same name, it involves themes of masculinity, identity, alienation, anticonsumerism, and nihilism. Despite a poor initial showing at the box office, *Fight Club* ultimately became a cult classic.

In the context of the film, the unnamed narrator (Norton) is an accident investigator for an automobile company whose demanding travel schedule combined with the emptiness of his life contribute to a severe case of insomnia. However, instead of prescribing pills, his doctor insists that he visit a disease support group and observe "genuine" suffering. Ironically, once he makes the transition from observer to faux victim, involvement in such groups does provide a cure, until he finds himself stymied by another disaffected "poser"—Marla Singer (Carter).

On a business trip, the narrator meets and finds himself inexplicably drawn to the vibrant and enigmatic Tyler Durden (Pitt), who seems to possess all of the lust for life that the narrator has lost. When he returns home to find that his apartment has been destroyed in a freak explosion, he calls Tyler and the two meet at a bar. There Tyler asks a strange favor: he wants Norton's character to hit him as hard as possible. A fistfight ensues, and by the time the two men walk back to Tyler's ramshackle, abandoned mansion, a friendship has begun. Soon the two begin living together and regularly fighting outside the bar, which attracts other men. Thus, "fight club" is born.

From the beginning it is clear that Tyler has the upper hand. He cements his role as leader of the fight club at its first meeting, where he makes the now-famous announcement: "The first rule of Fight Club is: you do not talk about Fight Club." And though the narrator claims to have no interest in Marla, he is chagrined when Tyler meets her and they begin an intensely sexual relationship.

Under Tyler's leadership, the Fight Club grows and evolves into an international brotherhood of anarchists and saboteurs known as "Project Mayhem," which initiates a series of clandestine attacks on official institutions. When Tyler suddenly disappears and the narrator finds Project Mayhem to be out of control, he embarks on a desperate search to find Tyler, only to discover that everyone he encounters—including Marla—believes *he* is Tyler—and his world begins to unravel.

Made on a budget of $63 million, *Fight Club* grossed just $37 million by the end of its domestic theatrical run—however, it brought in more than $100 million worldwide and more than half that much in video and DVD sales and rentals. *Fight Club* ultimately generated enormous profits, as well as and controversy, as numerous "fight clubs" were rumored to have formed worldwide. It has since become a pop culture phenomenon that has inspired dozens of scholarly pieces analyzing a film that is at once nihilistic and homoerotic, intensely violent and bitingly satirical.

Judson Knight

SEE ALSO: *Cult Films; Film Noir; Pitt, Brad; Videos.*

BIBLIOGRAPHY

Fight Club. DVD. Directed by David Fincher. Burbank, CA: Twentieth Century Fox Film, 1999.

Gronstad, Asbjorn. "One-Dimensional Men: *Fight Club* and the Poetics of the Body." *Film Criticism* 28, no. 1 (2003): 1.

Palahniuk, Chuck. *Fight Club.* New York: Norton, 1996.

Rothe-Kushel, Jethro. "*Fight Club*: A Ritual Cure for the Spiritual Ailment of American Masculinity. *Film Journal.* Accessed May 28, 2012. Available from http://www.thefilmjournal.com/issue8/fightclub.html

Schuchardt, Read Mercer, ed. *You Do Not Talk about Fight Club: I Am Jack's Completely Unauthorized Essay Collection.* Dallas, TX: BenBella Books, 2008.

File Sharing

File sharing is the exchange of information in digital files between individuals whose computers are connected to the Internet. The formats of the files vary, ranging from documents and photos to music and videos, and the sharing is either legal or prohibited by copyright laws. Around the turn of the twenty-first century, the sharing of media files increased dramatically, in part as a result of increased Internet access and in part due to peer-to-peer file-sharing services, and the music and film industry took legal action to stop it. However, even illegal file sharing is deemed by many of those raised in the computer age to be a vital part of the freedom of the Internet, and they continue to find ways to do it.

When personal computers became available during the 1970s, many of the first users developed a subculture based on their fascination with the new technology. One of the first objectives of these "computer geeks," as they came to be called, was to communicate with each other and share information. The rise of the Internet provided the technology to do so, and Bulletin Board Systems (BBS) were the venue. BBS were networks managed by systems operators dubbed SYSOPS, or administrators who oversaw network users in a shared online community. They allowed people far apart from each other geographically to connect via computer modems in order to exchange messages, download and upload software, play games, and receive technical support. Some BBS were commercial ventures that charged subscription fees, while others were operated by hobbyists for free.

As computer use expanded, file sharing remained an important part of the culture. In 1979 Tom Truscott and Jim Ellis, students at Duke University, had the idea of connecting individual computers to share information, creating Usenet, or User Network. Unlike BBS, Usenet systems had no centralized SYSOP. Instead, they were peer-to-peer (P2P) systems that allowed users to form "newsgroups" to communicate and share files on a wide range of topics. Usenet groups are still an effective Internet tool in the twenty-first century.

Though Internet communication through bulletin boards and newsgroups became more widespread, complex file sharing remained largely an underground activity, the province of computer professionals or amateur hackers. These users continued to search for better sharing methods. In 1999, Shawn Fanning, a student at Northeastern University in Boston, designed a simple program for P2P sharing of music files. With two friends, he launched Napster, a centralized service that allowed users to exchange music files for free.

Friends had been sharing music with each other for decades, through unauthorized copies of cassette tapes and compact discs, but Napster expanded the practice to millions of users, and the music industry began to take notice. As Napster was followed by other similar P2P file-sharing services, such as Gnutella and LimeWire, the Recording Industry Association of America (RIAA) began filing lawsuits for copyright infringement against the service and its users. By 2001 Napster had been shut down and reorganized as a legal music subscription service. Purchased by Best Buy in 2008, Napster later merged with on-demand streaming music service Rhapsody in 2011. Despite such renovations, Napster never enjoyed the same level of success as it did as a free service.

Other P2P services, such as KaZaA and Grokster, tried to avoid being held responsible for users' file sharing by decentralizing their services, but many were forced to shut down. The increased sharing of video files caused the Motion Picture Association of America to join the RIAA in bringing thousands of suits against P2P services and their users. Most users were offered settlements, but one, a Minnesota mother of four named Jammie Thomas-Rasset, fought the charges in 2005, hoping to point out the unfairness of such suits. She lost her case and, after a number of lengthy court actions, was fined $1.92 million for violating copyright laws by downloading twenty-four songs. A judge reduced her fine to $54,000, but the RIAA appealed in 2011.

In spite of such legal actions, the freedom to share information through the Internet remains important to the new generation of computer users, many of whom resist the notion of the ownership of ideas through copyright laws. Services such as Dropbox, MediaFire, and Rapidshare still exist, treading the fine line between the permissible and the illegal. When the P2P service eDonkey was abandoned by its operator, the MetaMachine Corporation, because of music industry litigation in 2005, it was taken over by users and continued as a decentralized system. Online users' resolve to share with one another in new ways demonstrates the belief held by many that the Internet should be a community of free information exchange. In 2012 a group of Swedish file-sharing advocates founded the Church of Kopimism, whose major tenet is the right to share computer files.

Tina Gianoulis

SEE ALSO: *MP3; Napster.*

BIBLIOGRAPHY

Allen, Danny. "A Guide to Better File Sharing." *Australian PC World*, May 2003, 144.

Fisk, Nathan W. *Understanding Online Piracy: The Truth about Illegal File Sharing*. Santa Barbara, CA: Praeger/ABC-CLIO, 2009.

Sisario, Ben. "Supreme Court Passes on File-Sharing Case, but Still No End Is in Sight." *New York Times*. Accessed May 21, 2012. Available from http://mediadecoder.blogs.nytimes.com/2012/05/21/supreme-court-passes-on-file-sharing-case-but-still-no-end-is-in-sight/

Strang, Martin. *Usage of Peer-to-Peer Networks for Music File-Sharing: "Piracy or Revolution?"* Munich: Grin Verlag, 2008.

Wang, Wallace. *Steal This File Sharing Book: What They Won't Tell You about File Sharing*. San Francisco: No Starch Press, 2004.

Film Noir

The genre known as film noir emerged from economic, political, and moral crises in European and American cultures in the years leading up to World War II. Its American origins are in the "tough-guy" and "hard-boiled" novels that became popular in the 1920s and 1930s and that, as Hollywood became more liberal in the 1940s and 1950s, could more easily be adapted for the movies than before. Such novels were also popular in Europe, particularly in France, where they were known as *romans noirs* and were published under imprints with titles such as *La Série noire*. When the embargo on American films that existed in

France under German occupation was lifted in 1944, many of the films that first arrived were based on hard-boiled novels, and it seems natural for French critics to have begun categorizing these films as film noir.

The European influence on film noir is not restricted to its name, however. Many of the cinematic techniques, and the overall pessimistic outlook of these movies, can be found in French poetic realist films made in the 1930s and, more especially, the work of German Expressionist filmmakers, many of whom immigrated to the United States to escape the Nazis and went on to work in Hollywood. German directors such as Fritz Lang and Robert Siodmak and cinematographers such as Hungarian-born John Alton used contrasting light and shade, odd camera angles, and scenes dominated by shadow to reproduce on-screen the bleak vision of writers such as Dashiell Hammett and Cornell Woolrich.

Movies in the film noir style can be recognized by their visual dependence on the effect of chiaroscuro, the contrast between light and shade. Characters and objects in film noir are often backlit so that they cast long shadows and their features are obscured, or the principals are brightly lit from the front so that the background is dark. Faces are pictured half obscured by darkness or crosshatched by the shadows of prison bars, window frames, or banister rods; the corners of rooms are dark and the interiors of cars provide a gloomy, claustrophobic setting.

DEFINING THE GENRE

Although many of its visual codes are familiar, the overall concept of film noir is notoriously difficult to pin down; their plots usually center on crime, but films included in the corpus cannot easily be identified as belonging to one particular genre. For example, Howard Hawks's *The Big Sleep* (1946), an adaptation of Raymond Chandler's novel of the same name, is a detective thriller, while Charles Laughton's *The Night of the Hunter* (1955) concerns an ex-con's search for the proceeds of a robbery committed by his former cellmate. Billy Wilder's *Sunset Boulevard* (1950) depicts a vain and aging star of silent movies obsessed with loyalty, her lost beauty, and star status; it ends with her murder of the young man who rejects her, and it is narrated, famously, by the victim, face down in the swimming pool. What these films do have in common, however, is a fascination with psychological instability, sexual obsession, and alienation. Unlike the "Hollywood Gothic" of films such as *Dracula* (1931) or *The Bride of Frankenstein* (1935), what appears as monstrous in film noir derives not from the half-human horrors of the vampire or Frankenstein's monster but from the all-too-human characteristics of jealousy, greed, lust, and ruthless self-interest.

Such themes are by no means exclusive to film noir, of course, and film categories must be defined as much by their technical and visual features as by thematic and formal tendencies. If film noir is difficult to define in terms of the plots of the films it includes, the problem is hardly eased by critics' reliance on terms such as *style, mood,* and *sensibility* when discussing films of noir pedigree. Rather than seeing film noir as a genre, many critics instead view it as a movement, a set of films and filmmakers expressing a common approach to life using similar literary sources, narrative structures, and visual codes.

The difficulties of describing film noir as a genre combine the problem of the sheer variety of different types of stories such

***Humphrey Bogart in* The Maltese Falcon.** *Humphrey Bogart stars in 1941 film noir classic* The Maltese Falcon. WARNER BROTHERS/COURTESY OF GETTY IMAGES.

films encompass and the question of what it is exactly that distinguishes them from other films. Many films, for example, use chiaroscuro but can be described only as noir-ish, whereas others, such as *Gilda* (1946), are accepted as film noir but betray their otherwise pessimistic tone with a happy ending of sorts.

A further complication is that while genres seem not to be trapped in a particular time or place, film noir is very closely linked with the Hollywood of the 1940s. A significant proportion of films in the film noir mode that have been made since then refer back, in some way, to the immediate postwar period, and many of the reasons for film noir's appearance at that time and place have to do with the particular culture of Hollywood. Financial restrictions on filmmakers during the war have already been mentioned, but other factors, such as the perception of German expressionist style as "quality" and the need among the smaller studios for new and distinctive film products, are also important. The opportunities film noir gave for directors and cinematographers to show off their talents, combined with the gradual relaxation of the Hays Code, which controlled the "moral content" of movies, made Hollywood cinema receptive to the content, mood, and style of film noir in the 1940s.

Because most noir films were "B" movies or at least made much of their money in the so-called grind houses—small theaters playing a rolling program and catering to people on the move from one town to another—budgets for sets, costume, and film stock were limited. This was particularly the case with films made during and just after the war, when money for new sets was restricted to $5,000 per film. The shadowy look of what has become known as film noir could be used to conceal props and sets that were lacking in detail or perhaps missing altogether. While much of this could be achieved by lighting effects alone, cinematographers such as Alton or Gregg Toland, who worked on Orson Welles's famous early noir film, *Citizen Kane* (1941), enhanced and spread out the darkness in their pictures by underexposing slow film. Faster film stock, which had only recently become available, was, in any case, much more expensive.

EXPOSING THE DARKNESS OF HUMANITY

Besides economic considerations, the visual style of film noir owes much to the ideas and techniques of émigré directors such as Lang, Siodmak, and Wilder. Lang's German film *M* (1931), for example, uses shadowy streets, empty and darkened office buildings, and unlit attics to depict the inner turmoil of the child murderer, played by Peter Lorre. If the chaos of the murderer's mind is represented by the cluttered attics in which he hides, so the dank, half-lit cellar in which he is lynched by a mob of "decent" people suggests that humanity at large is troubled by a dark inner life. This view of the human psyche as dark and troubled, brought by directors such as Lang and Siodmak from Nazi Germany, appears too in the "tough" stories written in America during the 1920s and 1930s. Combining such a view of humanity with the American themes of urban alienation, organized crime, and fear of failure, such stories became ideal vehicles for the émigrés and their followers, and it is from this combination that the mood and sensibility of film noir developed.

Siodmak's 1946 film of Ernest Hemingway's short story "The Killers" (1927) is a good example of the interplay between the look of film noir and its exploration of the ambiguities of the human psyche. *The Killers* concerns a man known as "The Swede" (Burt Lancaster) who waits in his small, dark room for his killers to arrive, accepting his fate because "I did something wrong once." Hemingway's story takes us only to the moments before the killers arrive, whereas the film uncovers what it was he did wrong through a narrative constructed mainly from flashbacks. The images of The Swede's last moments include shots of him, in a darkened room, lying half-dressed on the bed, deep in thought. The impenetrable shadows around him suggest the impenetrability of his thoughts. His enigmatic and ambiguous answer to the man who warns him of his approaching death suggests the possibility of regret for a criminal past but turns out to refer to his obsession with a woman. Through flashbacks, and the insurance investigator's haphazard reconstruction of events, it emerges that what The Swede has "done wrong" has nothing to do with the fact of his criminal past but with the psychological reasons for it.

This emphasis on The Swede's psychological state is representative of film noir's fascination with psychoanalysis. Frank Krutnik suggests in *In a Lonely Street* (1991) that Freudian psychoanalysis became popular in America during the late 1930s and 1940s and coincided with the adaptation of hard-boiled crime stories such as "The Killers" by Hollywood. Krutnik argues that the shift in crime thrillers toward highlighting the psychological reasons for and consequences of crime can be attributed to this popularization of psychoanalysis. This is evident, he thinks, in the complex narrative structures of many film noirs, including *The Killers*. In these films "the process of storytelling becomes submerged"; it becomes unclear who is telling the story, whose version is true, and what their motives are for telling it in a particular way.

Citizen Kane, for example, addresses directly the process of telling and retelling stories, being the story of the rise and fall of a newspaper magnate. In *Citizen Kane*, as in film noir in general, the margins between fantasy, psychosis, and reality become blurred; the film emerges as the story of Kane's psychological flaws, centering on an incident from his childhood. All of these signs of unstable psychological states are enhanced by film noir's adoption of techniques from expressionist cinema: exaggerated darkness and light/shade contrast; strange camera angles; and plain, unrealistic sets.

While the political conditions of Europe in the 1930s affected the American film industry through the arrival of talented filmmakers, film noir is also a product of the political instability of the period during and after World War II. Critics point to a crisis in American national identity, the problems of war veterans readjusting to civilian life, and the new threats of the atom bomb and the Cold War as possible cultural reasons for the flourishing of film noir in the period 1941 to 1958. Certainly the aftermath of war meant that large numbers of young men, to some extent institutionalized by life in the forces and often physically or psychologically damaged, now had to look after themselves and find work in a competitive labor market that included many more women than before. They returned from war anxious that their contribution be acknowledged yet questioning what they had fought for, given the new threat that was emerging in Eastern Europe and the Far East. On a more personal level, many returned to wives and families who were no longer dependent on them for financial or emotional support, whose lives had continued without them for several years, and who were unable to understand the ordeal they had suffered. All of this contributed to a sense of instability and hostility in the culture at large that is a central feature of film noir.

Like many films of the time, *The Blue Dahlia* (1946) makes direct reference to the concerns and problems associated with returning war veterans. The story revolves around the return of Johnny Morrison (Alan Ladd) from service in the navy and his discovery of his wife's infidelity. Helen Morrison (Doris Dowling) represents the new moral possibilities for women in the years following the war, abandoning the traditional roles of wife and mother and declaring her freedom to go where she wants and do what she wants. She goads Johnny into using violence against her and so unwittingly makes him a suspect for her murder. The exchanges between her and Johnny represent a challenge to old-fashioned versions of masculinity based on physical strength and power over women and the family. While Johnny's violence is presented in the film as unacceptable and excessive, the idea that he is in some way struggling to come to terms with a changed world presents itself as a way of understanding his actions.

The male characters in this film, like The Swede in *The Killers* and men in film noir in general, command our sympathy because they have all in some way been deprived of their defining masculine roles by forces beyond their control. As is also common in film noir, Johnny finds emotional support in his relationships with other men. Krutnik suggests that the problems Johnny experiences in his conventional family are offset by the stability of the "all-male navy family" that consists of his friends George and Buzz.

PORTRAYAL OF WOMEN

Women in film noir tend to fall into two main categories: those who support the hero as good wives or pliant molls and those who use their sexuality in an explicit way to manipulate men and get what they want. Women in this second group, a key feature of film noir, are known as "femmes fatales," dangerous women who encourage the hero's obsessive sexual interest to the point where he will risk his job, his freedom, or even his life for her. The insecurity of the hero's identity, outlined above in the case of The Swede in *The Killers*, leads him to "over-invest" in a version of her sexuality that he himself has invented; the femme fatale is awarded power over the hero by the (weakened) hero himself. Her inevitable death can be seen as punishment for her "unfair" exploitation of her advantage.

The many examples of cheating wives such as Helen Morrison, and more obvious femmes fatales whose overt sexuality plays a part in the hero's misery, is often given as evidence of film noir's inherent misogyny, of a conservative core in what otherwise appears to be a subversive alternative to classical Hollywood cinema. But the femme fatale is usually drawn in at least as much psychological detail as her male counterpart, and the emergence of that unexpected complexity often takes the place of the quest or mystery plot at the center of the hero's attentions. She rejects classical Hollywood cinema's version of passive womanhood and, by whatever means she has at her disposal, actively seeks independence and freedom from men. She is remembered by audiences not for her death but for her strength in life, her sexual power and the deadly challenge she represents to the male's attempt to solve the mystery or reach the end of his quest. If film noir is concerned with exploring ambiguities of perspective (through voice-overs and flashbacks), the limits of subjective vision (through the use of shadow and unnatural camera angles), and the instability of the human psyche, then the femme fatale represents a further interference with clarity of vision. Like the heroes of film noir, the femme fatale is an ambiguous figure, at once the victim of society's restrictions and the defiant answer to them. Her strength, sexual independence, and freedom pose a direct challenge to the masculine gaze of the hero and the male majority of film noir's original audience.

The origins of film noir in the political turmoil of prewar Europe and postwar America and Hollywood would seem to limit its scope to the historical period from which it springs. Although film noir was at its most popular during the late 1940s and 1950s, the production of noir and "neo-noir" films has persisted beyond that era. Some of these, like *Farewell, My Lovely* (1975), have been remakes of films made in the 1940s; others, such as *Chinatown* (1974), re-create the look of 1930s Los Angeles. *Taxi Driver* (1976) and *Seven* (1995) bring noir sensibilities to their contemporary settings, while *Blade Runner* (1982) adds a futuristic, science fiction setting that compounds the ambiguities, instabilities, and uncertainties of more conventional film noir. If film noir viewed 1940s America through the bleak sentiments of prewar Europe, it remains a "dark mirror" in which we look to find out who we are and what we might become.

Chris Routledge

SEE ALSO: *"B" Movies;* The Big Sleep*;* Blade Runner*; Chandler, Raymond;* Chinatown*;* Citizen Kane*; Dracula; The Fifties; Hammett, Dashiell; Hard-Boiled Detective Fiction; Hawks, Howard; Hemingway, Ernest; Hollywood; Ladd, Alan; Lancaster, Burt; Lang, Fritz;* Laura*; Lorre, Peter;* Mildred Pierce*;* The Postman Always Rings Twice*;* Sunset Boulevard*;* Taxi Driver*;* The Third Man*; The Twenties; Welles, Orson; Wilder, Billy; World War II.*

BIBLIOGRAPHY

Christopher, Nicholas. *Somewhere in the Night: Film Noir and the American City*. New York: Free Press, 1997.

Copjec, Joan, ed. *Shades of Noir: A Reader*. London: Verso, 1993.

Crowther, Bruce. *Film Noir: Reflections in a Dark Mirror*. London: Columbus Books, 1988.

Fay, Jennifer, and Justus Nieland. *Film Noir: Hard-Boiled Modernity and the Cultures of Globalization*. London: Routledge, 2009.

Hannsberry, Karen Burroughs. *Femme Noir: Bad Girls of Film*. Jefferson, NC: McFarland, 1998.

Kaplan, E. A., ed. *Women in Film Noir*. London: British Film Institute, 1980.

Krutnik, Frank. *In a Lonely Street: Film Noir, Genre, Masculinity*. London: Routledge, 1991.

Naremore, James. *More than Night: Film Noir in Its Contexts*. Berkeley: University of California Press, 1998.

Stephens, Michael L. *Film Noir: A Comprehensive, Illustrated Reference to Movies, Terms, and Persons*. Jefferson, NC: McFarland, 1995.

Tuska, Jon. *Dark Cinema*. Westport, CT: Greenwood Press, 1984.

Finding Nemo

In 2003 *Finding Nemo* set box-office records, won the Academy Award for Best Animated Feature, and became one of the best-selling DVDs of all time. Funny, heartwarming, and visually amazing, this family film is all about fish, but it tells a very human story. *Finding Nemo* also introduced audiences to the fascinating world of the Great Barrier Reef off the coast of Australia, and despite some inaccuracies, the film has drawn praise for calling attention to the earth's fragile ocean ecology.

The story revolves around problems faced by a family of clownfish living on the Barrier Reef. After young Nemo's mother is eaten by a barracuda, his father, Marlin (voiced by Albert Brooks), becomes overprotective, and Nemo tries to prove his independence but ends up being caught by a diver. Marlin sets out in search of his son, accompanied by Dory, a helpful but forgetful regal tang (voiced by Ellen DeGeneres). Nemo ends up in a dentist office aquarium but eventually uses his wits to escape, while Marlin, after many adventures, learns to take risks.

Finding Nemo's computer-generated animation delighted audiences, but the creators at Pixar Studios had to overcome many challenges in order to achieve the final effect. For one, most of the characterization had to be done through facial expressions, because fish have little in the way of body language. At the same time, however, animators had to avoid making the sea creatures look too human or too "cartoonish." They also had to create a very detailed and highly realistic underwater world. In preparation for the project, animators watched hours of underwater photography, and some learned scuba diving in order to explore the underwater world firsthand.

Writer and director Andrew Stanton drew on his experiences as a parent to construct the basic story of Marlin and Nemo. Then, after deciding to make his characters fish, he saw the opportunity to include an environmental message. *Finding Nemo* suggests some of the ways that technology and climate change have affected the oceans, and the film also shows how human activities—even when they are well intended—can adversely affect animals. These topics are explored further in the *Finding Nemo* DVD package, which includes a short film titled *Exploring the Reef with Jean Michel Cousteau*, along with features that provide information on fish species and their habitats.

The popularity of *Finding Nemo* had a few unfortunate consequences—for example, some young viewers tried to release their freshwater fish into the ocean or sent them down the drain thinking they would "escape" like Nemo. Overall, however, the film has become an enduring example of artful, educational entertainment. In 2008 the American Film Institute named *Finding Nemo* to its list of the ten greatest animated films, noting that "*Nemo* swam its way into America's heart by combining a razor sharp script . . . and a stunning animated world that entrances with each shift in the light."

Cynthia Giles

SEE ALSO: *Academy Awards; Animated Films; CGI; DeGeneres, Ellen; Environmentalism; Global Warming.*

BIBLIOGRAPHY

Bruckner, Lynne Dickson. "*Bambi* and *Finding Nemo*: A Sense of Wonder in the Wonderful World of Disney?" In *Framing the World: Explorations in Ecocriticism and Film*, ed. Paula Willoquet-Maricondi. Charlottesville: University of Virginia Press, 2010.

Vaz, Mark C. *The Art of Finding Nemo.* San Francisco: Chronicle Books, 2003.

Firearms

The right to carry a gun, whether for purposes of self-protection or hunting animals, is an emotional issue embedded deep in the cultural consciousness of the United States. By the twenty-first century, after nearly a century of destruction wrought by the use of guns by organized crime, political assassins, and dangerous psychopaths, many Americans were growing disturbed by their gun heritage, but they remained a minority when it came to efforts to enact antigun legislation.

The American love of firearms probably originated in a combination of frontier actuality and propaganda coup. When English colonists and Native American cultures collided, the usual result was gunfire from the colonists, who won the Pequot and King Philip's wars and secured their toeholds in North America. When revolutionaries created an icon of independence, it was the Minute Man, usually portrayed with plow in the background and long rifle in hand. That heroic figure of the liberty-loving citizen-soldier hovers over every discussion of gun control and the Second Amendment to the U.S. Constitution, whose complete text reads, "A well-regulated Militia, being necessary to the security of a free State, the right of the people to keep and bear Arms, shall not be infringed." Those organizations, such as the National Rifle Association (NRA), and individuals who favor individual gun ownership stress the last two phrases of the Second Amendment. Those who support gun control or elimination argue that the complete amendment provides for police organization, not for an individual right. However, in *District of Columbia v. Heller*, 554 U.S. 570 (2008), the Supreme Court held that the Second Amendment to the U.S. Constitution protects an individual's right to possess a firearm for lawful purposes, such as self-defense within the home.

RIFLES

In the twentieth century, certain specific weapons achieved iconic status for Americans. In popular military imagination, there are only two American rifles. The first is the M1, or Garand semiautomatic rifle, which General George S. Patton memorialized in his famous assertion, "In my opinion, the M1 rifle is the greatest battle implement ever devised." The M1 is the final development of infantry doctrine that stresses target selection, accuracy, and measured fire. (The original design specifications excluded full automatic firing.) For perhaps twenty-five years after World War II the M1 was a symbol of American might, rooted in GI grit and bravery, and reluctantly deployed in order to save the world. Some of the best movie images of M1s in skilled acting hands can be seen in William Wellman's *Battleground* (1949) and Samuel Fuller's *Fixed Bayonets* (1951).

The second legendary American military weapon is the M16 rifle. Imaginatively speaking, the M16, which can be toggled for either semiautomatic or full automatic firing, figures in the moral ambiguities of the late Cold War and post–Cold War periods. Late twentieth-century infantry doctrine took as fundamental the statistical fact that, under fire, the majority of riflemen in World War II did not fire their weapons, and those who did tended to fire high. The M16, with its automatic-fire

Handguns for Sale. *Handguns hang on a display wall for sale at a gun shop in Dallas, Texas, in 2008.* RICK GERSHON/GETTY IMAGES.

option and light recoil, lets a soldier "cover" a target area without particular target selection. Probability, more than aim, determines the results.

One of the most enduring and disturbing images of the M16 resides in a television interview during the 1968 Tet Offensive in Vietnam. The reporter questions a rifleman who repeatedly jumps into firing position, shoots a burst of automatic fire, and drops down to relative safety. He first tells the reporter the hardest thing is "not knowing where they are." After another burst he says, "The whole thing stinks, really."

When such confusion, which must be common to the experience of all soldiers in the field, is replayed uncensored on television, the iconography shifts from democratic dogface to enduring but victimized grunt, doing the will of (at best) deluded leaders. The M16 shares in this imaginative legacy of the Vietnam War, whereas M16s in the hands of young, drug-busting Colombian soldiers or crowd-controlling Israeli soldiers are more likely to provoke sympathy for peasants and protesters than concerns for enlisted men.

The counterpart to the M16 is the Soviet AK47, which expresses the same combat doctrine. With its characteristic banana clip and crude wooden stock and fore piece, the AK47 has a somewhat sharper emblematic presence than the high-industrial M16, perhaps because it is associated with the uprising of the oppressed. It was the weapon of the victorious North Vietnamese Army and figures in the artful, controlled imagery from that side of the war. In contemporary Mexico the contrast between M16 and AK47 is stark. The army is equipped with M16s. When one of the army's most militant opponents, Subcommander Marcos of the Zapatista National Liberation Army, appears for photo opportunities, he does so "in full military garb with an AK-47 automatic rifle strapped across his chest," according to the *New York Times*.

The M16 carries its ambiguous military significance into equivocal imaginations of civilian life. While there are relatively few images of the M1 deployed on American streets, the M16 figures prominently in urban American drug movies. Police SWAT (special weapons and tactics) teams carry the weapons in various configurations, ever more technically advanced. In such nihilistic gangster movies as Michael Mann's *Heat* (1995), Val Kilmer's split devotion to family and to casually murderous excitement has him emptying uncounted magazines of .223 ammunition at expendable policemen, his weapon always toggled to full automatic. The camera delights in shattered windshields, while the exquisite audio track records the counterpoint of firing with the clinking sound of spent cartridges hitting the streets and sidewalks.

HANDGUNS

Moving from long guns to hand guns, the American pistol that probably holds pride of place in civilian imagination is the ".45 automatic," Colt's model 1911 semiautomatic military sidearm, whose high-caliber, relatively low-velocity cartridge was meant to knock a man down, wherever it struck him. It had a name-recognition advantage, since the other Colt .45, a six-shooter, is the favorite gun of such Western movies as *High Noon* (1952). A presentation-grade version of the 1911 semiautomatic Colt .45 appears in the movie *Titanic* (1997) and again in *Indiana Jones and the Kingdom of the Crystal Skull* (2008). The counter-image to the .45 automatic is the German Luger, officer issue in the German army. The pistol's narrow barrel and curved trigger guard give it a sinuous, European quality, in contrast to the bluff (and heavy) American .45. In cinematic imagination, seductively evil men use Lugers in such movies as Clint Eastwood's *Midnight in the Garden of Good and Evil* (1997) and Joe Johnston's *Captain America: The First Avenger* (2011), in which the villain Red Skull wields a modified Luger that fires laser beams.

The more visually and audibly stimulating weapon associated with mid-twentieth-century urban mayhem is the tommy gun, whose movie and comic-strip "rat-a-tat-tat!" lights up the seemingly countless gangster-versus-cops movies. A tommy gun is the .45 caliber fully automatic Thompson submachine gun. The *sub* simply means that it is smaller in size and magazine capacity than a military machine gun. There is a famous photograph of smiling John Dillinger, with a drum-magazine tommy gun in one hand, a small Colt automatic pistol in the other. The most eroticized, cinematic realization of the tommy gun's power is in the slow-motion shooting of Warren Beatty and Faye Dunaway at the end of Arthur Penn's *Bonnie and Clyde* (1967).

Other handguns permeated late-twentieth and early twenty-first-century popular culture. The James Bond novels and movies briefly popularized the Walther PPK, and Eastwood's *Dirty Harry* series gave us "Go ahead, make my day," but few know the make of the gun down which he speaks (it is a Smith & Wesson .44 Magnum). As urban gang activity—and police attention to such activity—rose in the 1990s and early in the first decade of the 2000s, handgun manufacturer Glock became a cultural icon. Police departments often distribute the Glock 9-millimeter (mm) semiautomatic pistol as a standard-issue firearm, and the company's .40 caliber semiautomatic pistol has become a staple (together with the 9-mm) of both gangs and protective homeowners. There are Uzis (Israeli micro submachine guns) and the MAC-10, but none of these weapons has the imaginative staying power of the M1, M16, AK47, Colt .45, Luger, and tommy gun, many of which are central features of so-called shooter video games like the popular Call of Duty and Battlefield series.

GUN CONTROL

In the twenty-first century the role of guns in society has once again returned to the forefront of political debate. The 2004 expiration of a federal ban on so-called assault weapons (semiautomatic or fully automatic firearms with high-capacity magazines such as the AK-47, AR-15, Tec-9, or Uzi) and two high-profile Supreme Court rulings (*District of Columbia v. Heller* in 2008 and *McDonald v. Chicago* in 2010) that struck down bans against handguns in Washington, D.C., and Chicago and asserted that the Second Amendment was not just applicable to federal laws but also to state and local laws have made gun control one of the most prominent and contentious political issues in America.

In 2008 presidential hopeful Barack Obama made statements that suggested that he supported gun-control legislation, making certain to emphasize the need of keeping firearms out of the hands of violent criminals, not from average citizens. This was met with resistance from conservatives and pro-gun groups such as the NRA, who feared that it was empty rhetoric. Republican vice presidential candidate Sarah Palin was frequently filmed and photographed firing semiautomatic weapons and was even presented with a personalized .50 caliber semiautomatic rifle (illegal under the assault weapons ban) by the NRA in 2009. After Obama took office in 2009, gun sales increased by nearly 50 percent amid fears that he would enact strict gun-control laws. However, Obama has yet to succeed in getting any sweeping gun-control laws passed, and in 2010 he signed into law a bill that permits carrying loaded firearms in national parks.

During the highly contentious congressional elections of 2010, conservative voters (particularly those associated with the nascent Tea Party movement) protested gun-control laws by brandishing assault weapons at political events and rallies. One conservative politician, Sharron Angle, sparked outrage from gun-control advocates when she proposed using "Second Amendment remedies" as a method of returning Congress to Republican control, a phrase now held as an example of the extreme rhetoric surrounding the firearms debate.

Events such as the 2011 shooting of U.S. Representative Gabrielle Giffords at a political rally in Arizona and the 2012 killing of unarmed teenager Trayvon Martin by armed civilian George Zimmerman, a Florida neighborhood watch member, continue to fuel national discourse over how to reconcile the rights ensured by the Second Amendment with the dangers that firearms introduce into society. With studies showing Americans evenly divided over the question of whether it is more important to protect gun ownership rights or to install strict gun-control laws, the issue is bound to occupy a major portion of the American political conversation, just as firearm use is sure to be romanticized in popular films and video games, for decades to come.

Jonathan Middlebrook

SEE ALSO: Annie Get Your Gun*; Beatty, Warren;* Bonnie and Clyde*; Cold War;* The Deer Hunter*; Eastwood, Clint;* High Noon*; James Bond Films; Obama, Barack; Rambo; The Tea Party; Video Games; Vietnam; World War II.*

BIBLIOGRAPHY

Barnes, Robert. "Justices Reject D.C. Ban on Handgun Ownership." *Washington Post*, June 27, 2008.

Bellesiles, Michael A. *Arming America: The Origins of a National Gun Culture.* New York: Alfred A. Knopf, 2000.

Cramer, Clayton E. *Armed America: The Remarkable Story of How and Why Guns Became as American as Apple Pie.* Nashville, TN: Nelson Current, 2006.

Crosby, Alfred W. *Throwing Fire: Projectile Technology through History.* New York: Cambridge University Press, 2002.

D'Este, Carlo. *Patton: A Genius for War.* New York: HarperCollins, 1995.

Homsher, Deborah. *Women & Guns: Politics and the Culture of Firearms in America.* Armonk, NY: M. E. Sharpe, 2001.

Karnow, Stanley. *Vietnam: A History*, rev. ed. New York: Penguin Books, 1997.

Lepore, Jill. *The Name of War.* New York: Alfred A. Knopf, 1998.

Lewis, Paul. *The Grand Incendiary: A Biography of Samuel Adams.* New York: Dial Press, 1973.

Newton, Michael. *Armed and Dangerous: A Writer's Guide to Weapons.* Cincinnati, OH: Writer's Digest Books, 1990.

Pauly, Roger. *Firearms: The Life Story of a Technology.* Westport, CT: Greenwood Press, 2004.

Reporting World War II, 2 vols. New York: Literary Classics of the United States, 1995.

Toland, John. *The Dillinger Days.* New York: Random House, 1963.

Wellford, Charles F.; John Pepper; and Carol Petrie; eds. *Firearms and Violence: A Critical Review.* Washington, DC: National Academies Press, 2005.

Firesign Theatre

With their education, artfulness, attention to detail, and full use of the newly emerging multitrack recording technologies, the four members of the Firesign Theatre—Peter Bergman (1939–2012), David Ossman (1936–), Phil Proctor (1940–), and Phil Austin (1941–)—were the Beatles of recorded comedy. Writing and performing their own material, they created multilayered surrealist satires out of the very stuff of popular culture, including television shows, the Golden Age of Radio, old movies, commercials, literature, and music.

At a time when the Who was pioneering the rock concept album, Firesign was pioneering the comedy concept album. Their humor reflected the times. Though Firesign was sometimes criticized for its occasional drug references, such criticism may have been misplaced because it would be difficult to represent Southern California in the 1960s and 1970s without mentioning drugs. The group's comedy, however, was much more than an amalgam of cultural references. One forty-minute album might be as tightly structured as a one-act play, achieving real poignancy, conveying new ways of looking at things, and making new connections. The first cut on Firesign's debut album, for example, presents the novel perspective provided by a brief aural history of the United States from the view of Native Americans. The group's comedy albums can be listened to repeatedly and still be enjoyed, each new listening revealing subtle asides, missed connections, and hidden messages.

THE GROUP'S BEGINNINGS

Bergman and Proctor first met while studying playwriting at Yale University, but Bergman went on to work on a British radio show with Goon Show alumnus Spike Milligan. In England, Bergman saw the Beatles for the first time, and he vowed someday to become part of a four-man comedy team. The foursome came together in 1966 as part of "Radio Free Oz," a freeform late-night FM radio show on KPFK in Los Angeles that was hosted by Bergman.

Although the radio show included such guests as Andy Warhol and Buffalo Springfield, it was because of the comedy group and its improvisations that the show developed a cult following. No one was aware of the size of this audience until the group promoted a *love-in* (a term coined by Bergman) in Elysian Park in Los Angeles, and 40,000 people showed up. Seeing the commercial potential of this audience, CBS record producer Gary Usher signed the group to a record contract.

The group found that when each of the members was contributing and each had ultimate veto power (if any one of them did not like a line, it was out), a tangible entity emerged that was much more than the sum of its parts: the Fifth Crazee Guy. As a result, the Firesign Theatre's publishing company was given the name *4 or 5 Crazee Guys Publishing*. According to Austin, "It's like, suddenly there is this fifth guy that actually does the writing." And who is the Fifth Crazee Guy? He is Clem riding the bus; he is George Leroy Tirebiter; he is Mr. and Mrs. John Smith from Anytown, USA; he is the audience's laughter; he is an everyman (and everywoman) reflecting society's culture and society's collective unconscious.

THE FIRST FOUR ALBUMS

The first four albums that the group created for CBS remain the core of its work and include its best material. The albums document the group's evolution—the transition from shorter pieces to album-length fantasies and the emergence of the Fifth Crazee Guy. Firesign Theatre's first album, *Waiting for the Electrician or Someone Like Him* (1968), contains several short pieces on side one, including the Native Americans' view of American history and some drug humor. All of side two is taken up by a comic nightmare journey through Turkish security, complete with the now-classic game show send-up called "Beat the Reaper."

The first album sold poorly, but the group's sophomore effort, *How Can You Be in Two Places at Once When You're Not Anywhere at All* (1969), benefited from the emergence of FM radio as a significant force and the willingness of FM disc jockeys to play long cuts. The title piece is a sonic delight that puts the listener behind the wheel of a motor home with climate control that changes the climate as never before in a motor vehicle. Side two contains the piece that is most likely to convert the uninitiated: "Nick Danger, Third Eye," a pun-filled satire of noir radio dramas involving a Peter Lorre soundalike and bizarre time-travel convolutions.

The third and fourth albums, considered to be the group's best, each contains one long cut (interrupted only by the pre-CD need to turn the album over). *Don't Crush That Dwarf, Hand Me the Pliers* (1970), the first of their albums recorded on sixteen tracks, mingles the recollections of film producer George Leroy Tirebiter with footage from one of his teen comedies, "High School Madness," to produce a moving nostalgia piece loaded with laughs.

However, nothing could prepare fans for the total sonic immersion of *I Think We're All Bozos on This Bus* (1971), a sensurround trip to and through the Future Fair—a cross between Disneyland and a World's Fair—complete with clones, computers, and holograms. In this extravaganza, Clem, the established hero, eventually has a showdown with the computer that controls everything. Repeated listenings reveal hidden subtleties. For example, the listener may suddenly realize that, although passengers are warned to pump their shoes before walking across the water, Clem gave up shoes years ago. Further listenings might then reveal that when Clem talks about how he is going to just "sink in" to a bus seat and the public address system says to get "in sync," the words *sink* and *sync* are, in fact, in sync.

LATER WORK

In the 1990s Firesign produced the Grammy-nominated album *Give Me Immortality or Give Me Death* (1998). The setting is the last hour of the last day of 1999 at Radio Now, a station so cutting-edge that it changes formats every commercial break. Individual members of the group continued to lend their vocal talents to a variety of projects, including *The Tick* TV series (1994) and *A Bug's Life* (1998).

Firesign experienced a resurgence in the early twenty-first century. In 2001 the group was not only supporting public television fund-raising efforts by regularly appearing in *Firesign Theatre Weirdly Cool* but also was airing a live radio show on digital satellite. That same year the group received a Grammy nomination for *Bride of Firesign*. Sony Legacy rereleased the group's first four albums in 2006 and Shout! Factory released the Nick Danger story in a four-CD box set in 2008.

Bob Sullivan

SEE ALSO: *The Beatles; Buffalo Springfield; Concept Album; Grammy Awards; Lorre, Peter; Public Television (PBS); Radio; Warhol, Andy; The Who; World's Fairs.*

BIBLIOGRAPHY

"Firesign Reignites Counterculture Flame." *USA Today*, February 19, 2002.

Firesign Theatre. Accessed February 26, 2012. Available from http://www.firesigntheatre.com

Smith, Ronald L. *Comedy on Record: The Complete Critical Discography*. New York: Garland Publishing, 1988.

Fireworks

SEE: *Fourth of July Celebrations.*

Fischer, Bobby *(1943–2008)*

In 1972 American Robert "Bobby" James Fischer became the world's chess champion after defeating Soviet Boris Spassky. This match, set against the backdrop of Cold War rivalries, marked the pinnacle of Fischer's often turbulent career. In 1975 he was stripped of his title after refusing to defend it. Despite his eccentricities, Fischer's demands initiated improvements in playing conditions and the financial rewards of professional chess. In the United States and Europe, Fischer's dramatic rise to international prominence revitalized popular interest in chess.

In 1992 Fischer, still claiming to be the legitimate world champion, ended his self-imposed exile to play a return match against Spassky. Played in war-torn Yugoslavia in violation of U.S. and United Nations (UN) sanctions, this match again made Fischer the center of popular controversy. He defeated Spassky with 10 wins, 5 losses, and 15 draws and received $3.65 million as the winner's share of the prize fund. Although he was later indicted for his violation of U.S. sanctions, he spent the remainder of the 1990s traveling freely between Eastern Europe, the Philippines, and Japan. Following a series of increasingly vitriolic and irrational verbal attacks on the United States, Fischer was detained in Japan in July 2004. After months of legal procrastination, Japan extradited him to Iceland, which had granted him citizenship following his arrest. On January 17, 2008, Fischer succumbed to degenerative renal failure.

Christopher D. O'Shea

SEE ALSO: *Board Games; Cold War; Leisure Time; Toys.*

BIBLIOGRAPHY

Brady, Frank. *Profile of a Prodigy: The Life and Games of Bobby Fischer*. New York: David McKay, 1965.

Brady, Frank. *Endgame: Bobby Fischer's Remarkable Rise and Fall—from America's Brightest Prodigy to the Edge of Madness*. New York: Crown Publishers, 2011.

Edmonds, David, and John Eidinow. *Bobby Fischer Goes to War: How a Lone American Star Defeated the Soviet Chess Machine*. New York: HarperCollins, 2005.

Roberts, Richard; Bobby Fischer; and Boris Vasilyevich Spassky. *Fischer/Spassky: "The New York Times" Report on the Chess Match of the Century*. New York: Quadrangle Books, 1972.

Steiner, George. *Fields of Force: Fischer and Spassky at Reykjavik*. New York: Viking Press, 1974.

Fisher, Eddie *(1928–2010)*

Eddie Fisher was the most popular male vocalist in America for a brief time in the 1950s, but for a longer period, the affable crooner was the center of a highly publicized series of romantic entanglements involving some of the most famous celebrities of his generation.

SEEKING STARDOM

One of seven children of a Jewish grocer in South Philadelphia, Edward Fisher had a Depression-era childhood of poverty and frequent moves. He sought a singing career from an early age and became a regular performer on Philadelphia radio by the age of fifteen. Two years later, the seventeen-year-old Fisher obtained a tryout with the Buddy Morrow band in New York, but he was only employed for a few weeks.

Calling himself Sonny Edwards, Fisher haunted the city's nightclubs for months, searching for work. In an audition at the Copacabana, Fisher impressed the owner with his voice, but his immature looks and manner detracted from his talent. Fortunately, the nightclub owner put him in touch with publicist and celebrity manager Milton Blackstone, who in turn found the youthful entertainer a summer job at Grossinger's resort hotel in the Catskills. There Fisher set about learning as much as possible, not only by honing his own skills but also by studying the behavior of the famous acts that performed at Grossinger's.

In the fall of 1946 Fisher returned to the Copacabana, where he was given a small job, and the ambitious young singer spent the next three years trying in vain to become a star. Frustrated with his slow progress, in 1949 he put himself fully under the control of Blackstone and made one last effort at establishing himself as a singing sensation. Now twenty-one, he was more mature and his stage presence had greatly improved, so Blackstone decided to manufacture a groundswell of popularity for Fisher and persuaded the famous comedian Eddie Cantor to "discover" Fisher during a performance at Grossinger's.

Blackstone paid for "fans" to sit throughout the hall and cheer wildly during Fisher's act. Cantor set up the audience to love Fisher, and Fisher performed very well. Several reporters, who had been alerted by Blackstone of a breaking show-business story, covered the "discovery" for major newspapers. A star was born in one hour of conniving, where four years of talented and honest effort had achieved nothing.

FISHER'S CAREER TAKES OFF

Cantor then took Fisher under his wing, giving him a place on his current national tour and television show, and even wrangling invitations for the young singer on other major television programs. Finally, Cantor and Blackstone arranged for Fisher to sign with RCA Victor, one of the biggest recording companies. Throughout the rest of 1949 and all of 1950, Fisher's career grew at a rapid pace. He had several hit records, performed frequently on television and on tour, and was given *Billboard* magazine's award as Most Promising Male Vocalist of 1950.

Fisher was drafted into the army early in 1951, during the Korean War. But Blackstone used his influence to ensure that Fisher would spend his two years in the military crooning with the U.S. Army Band. In fact—given that his recording dates, television appearances, and tours continued without a hitch—

Fisher's career probably benefited from his military service. Not until he made a personal request to President Harry Truman was he allowed to visit Korea and entertain fighting troops.

Returning to civilian life in early 1953, Fisher found that his handlers had set up a television program for him to host, a twice-weekly show on NBC. Sponsored by the Coca-Cola corporation, the show was called *Coke Time*, as Fisher's popularity with teenagers made soft drinks a logical sponsor. The show lasted four years on radio as well as on television; when it ended, NBC found another show (albeit a less successful one) for him until 1959.

Television was just part of Fisher's hectic performance schedule, which included tours and frequent live shows in New York. After excessive singing began to harm his voice, he was taken to celebrity physician Dr. Max Jacobson and given an injection of special vitamins, or so he was told. He felt better immediately, and he turned to Dr. Jacobson more and more often in the years to come. The shots were a mixture of substances, but it turned out that they were mostly amphetamines, or "speed"; Jacobson would eventually lose his license to practice medicine, but not before Fisher had become a confirmed drug addict.

Fisher's youth, fame, and wealth carried him through the next several years, and his records continued to sell well. Drug use made Fisher easier for his handlers, who booked him into almost continuous performances, to manage. His income and popularity soared. In 1954 he won the *Cash Box* magazine Top Male Vocalist Award.

ROMANTIC ENTANGLEMENTS

In the same year, Fisher began seeing a young but already established movie star named Debbie Reynolds. His base of operations in New York and hers in Los Angeles limited their interaction, but they became close. The media quickly promoted Fisher and Reynolds as America's sweethearts, but when marriage began to appear imminent, Fisher's fans (mostly young and female) turned on him. Record sales declined, and Fisher's managers attempted to block the marriage. Finally, in late 1955, Fisher and Reynolds were married at Grossinger's resort.

Throughout 1956 Fisher experienced a career decline. Coca-Cola canceled his program, his records were not selling well, and rock and roll was erupting into the popular music scene. Almost from the outset, Fisher's marriage was in trouble too. The media once again made much of this celebrity couple, chronicling the supposed ups and downs of the marriage, casting Fisher as the thoughtless villain and Reynolds, whose film career as a sweet young thing was at its height, as the put-upon wife. There was a lot of truth in what the reporters wrote. Fisher was a dope addict, an irresponsible husband and father, and a compulsive gambler. He still made a huge income, but he was spending virtually all of it. The couple's daughter, Carrie, would go on to become famous as Princess Leia in *Star Wars* and as a best-selling author. They also had a son, Todd, named after Fisher's close friend Mike Todd, who was married to actress Elizabeth Taylor.

After Todd was killed in a plane crash in 1958, Fisher embarked on an affair with Taylor and his marriage disintegrated completely. The media responded predictably to this notorious romantic triangle, casting Taylor as the evil "other woman." Fisher and Reynolds were divorced in 1959, and he quickly married Taylor. His career had slipped so badly by that point that he was never able to make an effective comeback.

Fisher had hoped to parlay his singing success into a movie career, and in 1956 he had starred with then-wife Reynolds in *Bundle of Joy*. It was no more successful than his performance opposite Taylor in *Butterfield 8* in 1960; she won the Academy Award for Best Actress, but Fisher was never again invited to act in a major film. In 1963, on the film set of the epic *Cleopatra*, Taylor switched allegiances once more, this time to costar Richard Burton. Fisher was the media's innocent, sympathetic character this time amid an orgy of gossip.

A LONG FIGHT AGAINST ADDICTION

The next several decades followed a sad pattern for Fisher—one high-profile romance after another—and he proved unable to restart his singing career. His third marriage, in 1967 to actress Connie Stevens, lasted only two years but produced two daughters—now actresses in their own right: Tricia Leigh Fisher and Joely Fisher. He followed that union with a ten-month marriage to Terry Richard, a twenty-one-year-old beauty queen (Fisher was forty-seven at the time). He declared bankruptcy in the early 1970s, and an attempt at a music comeback in 1983 failed. In 1981, while still battling drug addiction, Fisher published his first autobiography, *Eddie: My Life, My Loves*—a memoir he would reportedly later hardly remember writing—highlighting his romantic entanglements with numerous celebrities (beyond his wives), as well as discussing his forty years of drug abuse and his gambling addiction.

Even a former celebrity can earn a lot of money in America, but Fisher could never get ahead. His drug habit and erratic behavior kept him from building a strong second career from the wreckage of the first. He was the last of the old-style crooners and the least capable of recovering from changes in American popular music. It was not until the 1990s that Fisher would finally conquer his cocaine habit with a trip to the Betty Ford Clinic. He credited fifth wife, Betty Lin, with helping him maintain a drug-free life. He published a second autobiography in 1999 titled *Been There, Done That*, which contained even more salacious details than the previous version and was not received well by his ex-wives and daughters. Fisher died September 22, 2010, at the age of eighty-two, due to complications from hip surgery.

David Lonergan

SEE ALSO: *Academy Awards; Celebrity; Celebrity Couples;* Cleopatra*; Coca-Cola; Divorce; Hollywood; Media Feeding Frenzies; Movie Stars; Pop Music; Radio;* Star Wars*; Taylor, Elizabeth; Television.*

BIBLIOGRAPHY

Fisher, Eddie. *Eddie: My Life, My Loves*. New York: Harper & Row, 1981.

Fisher, Eddie, and David Fisher. *Been There, Done That*. New York: St. Martin's Press, 1999.

Greene, Myrna. *The Eddie Fisher Story*. Middlebury, VT: Paul S. Eriksson, 1978.

Fisher-Price Toys

One of the most famous American toymakers, Fisher-Price has been part of children's play for almost a century. While Fisher-

Price is still creating low-cost and durable playthings for infants and preschoolers, older Fisher-Price toys have become prized collectibles, coveted by the same owners—now adult toy aficonados—who once clutched them in cribs and playpens. From Granny Doodle and Snoopy Sniffer in the 1930s; through the decades with Tick Tock Clock, Pull-a-Tune Xylophone, and Little People; to computer software for toddlers in the 1990s and digital applications in the first decade of the 2000s, the Fisher-Price name has long been in the forefront of imaginative and educational play for children.

The company was founded in 1930 in East Aurora, New York, by Herman G. Fisher, Irving Price, and Helen M. Schelle, who began with $5,000 and the idea of creating an innovative line of toys for very young children. The company had only fifteen employees, but one of those was Margaret Evans Price, the wife of Irving Price and, more importantly, a writer and an illustrator of children's books. Although they managed to build their factory and began producing toys during the difficult Depression years, few consumers had money to spend on "luxuries." During World War II, the factory was refitted to produce goods needed for the war effort.

By the 1950s, however, toy production was up and running again, coinciding with the arrival of the baby boomer generation. During this more prosperous period, more disposable income was available for leisure-time products such as toys. With the demand for toys skyrocketing, Fisher-Price was forced to build another plant. For the first time, the company began to make its own parts for toys, producing them with plastic, an exciting and popular new material.

By the 1960s Fisher-Price was producing twice as many toys as during the three previous decades combined. Discretionary income of American families continued to vary, but by the 1960s the idea had been firmly established that "store-bought" toys were necessities for children. Further, television commercials for toys began to be directly aimed at children; thus, children became the best lobbyists for toy companies. A play laboratory was opened in New York, and every year since some 2,000 children have tested Fisher-Price toys before they reach the market. In 1969 Quaker Foods bought the toy company, and the 1970s saw the opening of new Fisher-Price plants in New York, Mexico, Belgium, and England.

Much of Fisher-Price's success was due to its focus on and understanding of toys for infants and preschool children. The darkest days for the company came in the 1980s when it attempted to branch out into toys for older children. This new line included makeup kits and battery-powered sports cars and even a toy video camera that used audiotapes that could be played back through a television. The new products failed miserably. This failure, coupled with large order cancelations caused by Fisher-Price's inability to meet delivery deadlines, gave competing toy manufacturers Mattel and Hasbro a significant advantage. In 1991 Fisher-Price went back to its specialty: producing simple toys beloved by infants and toddlers. The company streamlined its operation and regained its status among toymakers. In 1993 competing toy giant Mattel acquired Fisher-Price and expanded the Fisher-Price niche in the United States and abroad.

As toys have grown more and more sophisticated, Fisher-Price has kept up, producing educational computer games for two and three year olds. Yet the familiar Fisher-Price standbys remain its most popular items. Such items include the Bubble Mower, which emits a stream of soap bubbles as it "mows" the floor; the Corn Popper, a clear plastic dome in which colored balls jump energetically as it is pushed; and SnapLock Beads, which teach dexterity. Perhaps the most popular of all Fisher-Price toys are Little People, small wooden figures that are essentially colorful heads on wooden pegs that fit into various vehicles and toy houses. Created decades ago, the older Little People are valued by adult toy collectors, while the newer ones, little changed except for racial diversity and wider plastic bodies, are equally in demand in the playroom. These toys are durable in every sense, as their appeal is diminished neither by time nor by the vigorous chewing of a two-year-old. Little People toys are packaged with videos starring such favorites as Michael, Sara Lynn, Sonya Lee, Eddie, and Maggie.

In the twenty-first century, Fisher-Price extended its line to include cribs, car seats, high chairs, baby monitors, and lamps. The company remained modern by entering the digital age, maintaining an interactive website (www.fisher-price.com) that is geared to appeal to children, parents, and grandparents. An application for the social media giant Facebook allows parents to create a digital time line of memories so that families and friends can watch children grow. In 2005 Fisher-Price branched out into "experimental marketing," forming partnerships with national zoos, Lowe's Hotels, and Royal Caribbean cruise lines to reach preschool children at play.

Regardless of the sophistication of Fisher-Price's marketing strategies, the company continues to adhere to the guidelines laid down by Irving Fisher when he served as the company's first CEO: all toys sold by Fisher-Price must have intrinsic play value, exhibit ingenuity, be durable, provide good value, and promote active play.

Tina Gianoulis

SEE ALSO: *Baby Boomers; Facebook; Leisure Time; Toys.*

BIBLIOGRAPHY

Bulik, Beth Snyder. "Fisher-Price Plays, Laughs, and Grows into Global Brand." *Advertising Age*, March 29, 2010, 14.

Fox, Bruce R., and John J. Murray. *Fisher-Price: A Historical, Rarity, and Value Guide, 1931–Present.* Iola, WI: Krause Publications, 2002.

Fisk, Carlton *(1947–)*

Despite the fact that he set the all-time major-league career marks for most games played as a catcher and most home runs by a catcher, Carlton Fisk will always be remembered for his dramatic, extra-innings game-winning home run in game six of the 1975 World Series. With the score tied in the bottom of the twelfth inning and his Boston Red Sox trailing the Cincinnati Reds three games to two, he hit a long line drive down the left-field line. As the ball started curving foul, Fisk hopped down the first base line and waved his arms toward fair territory, *willing* the ball to stay in play. After the ball bounced off of the foul pole for the series-tying home run, he jumped in the air, arms outstretched in celebration.

Although the Sox would lose the series the next day, Fisk's spontaneous and joyous reaction captured the public's imagination, as it seemed to exemplify the purity and innocence of baseball during a time of contentiousness and increasing labor strife in the game. Fisk was traded to the Chicago White Sox in 1980 after nine years with the Red Sox and retired in 1993.

Gregory Bond

SEE ALSO: *Baseball; Bench, Johnny; Boston Red Sox; World Series.*

BIBLIOGRAPHY

Gammons, Peter. *Beyond the Sixth Game*. Boston: Houghton Mifflin, 1985.

McKelvey, G. Richard. *Fisk's Homer, Willie's Catch and the Shot Heard Round the World: Classic Moments from Postseason Baseball, 1940–1996*. Jefferson, NC: McFarland, 1998.

Remy, Jerry, and Corey Sandler. *Red Sox Heroes: The RemDawg's All-Time Favorite Red Sox, Great Moments, and Top Teams*. Guilford, CT: Lyons Press, 2010.

Thorn, John; Pete Palmer; Michael Gershman; et al. *Total Baseball*. New York: Viking Penguin, 1997.

A Fistful of Dollars

The film *A Fistful of Dollars*, released in 1964, was the first of the spaghetti Westerns to gain a large audience in the United States. Directed by Sergio Leone, it starred Clint Eastwood, who was then best known to American audiences as a supporting actor on the television Western *Rawhide*. Eastwood's television character, the fresh-faced Rowdy Yates, was far removed from his first starring film role as the unshaven, cigarillo-smoking, deadly bounty hunter known only as "The Man with No Name."

The plot was blatantly lifted from Akira Kurosawa's Japanese classic *Yojimbo*. In both films, a mercenary shows up in a town that is being terrorized by two rival gangs. The stranger cleverly plays each gang off against the other, then ruthlessly wipes out those who are left standing. This story line was revived yet again for the 1996 Bruce Willis film *Last Man Standing*.

The worldwide success of the *A Fistful of Dollars* led to Eastwood's reprising his role in two Leone-directed sequels: *For a Few Dollars More* (1965) and *The Good, the Bad, and the Ugly* (1966).

Justin Gustainis

SEE ALSO: *Eastwood, Clint;* The Good, the Bad, and the Ugly; *Leone, Sergio; Spaghetti Westerns; The Western.*

BIBLIOGRAPHY

Stempel, Tom. *American Audiences on Movies and Moviegoing*. Lexington: University Press of Kentucky, 2001.

Weisser, Thomas. *Spaghetti Westerns: The Good, the Bad, and the Violent*. Jefferson, NC: McFarland, 1992.

Fitzgerald, Ella *(1917–1996)*

The flawless voice and delivery of singer Ella Fitzgerald is woven tightly into the tapestry of American popular music. Her place in the canon of jazz artists was ensured early in her career, while she reached a wider audience throughout the world with her renditions of those enduring songs that have come to be known as standards. Her name is almost synonymous with the compositions of Irving Berlin, George Gershwin, Rodgers and Hart, and Cole Porter, as well as the music of Duke Ellington. Her interpretation of their music is forever enshrined in her famous "songbook" series of albums, in which she uniquely included the verses to the songs. Billed as "The First Lady of Song," she commanded sellout attendance at concerts at home and abroad, touring extensively from the mid-1940s onward, but her unique integrity to the music and the high standards she set never wavered in the face of her immense popularity.

EARLY YEARS

Born in Newport News, Virginia, and raised in Yonkers, New York, Fitzgerald was discovered at the age of sixteen while singing in a talent contest at the Apollo Theater in Harlem. She joined the Chick Webb band in 1935 and became the idol of Harlem's Savoy Ballroom. She was featured on most of Webb's recordings, and Decca was committed to pushing her recording career, which began with "Love and Kisses" in 1935. She had her first hit with the humorous and perkily tuneful ditty "A-Tisket, A-Tasket" in 1938, which propelled her to the top of the charts. In the course of her subsequent recording career, she made more than 250 albums and won thirteen Grammy Awards.

Ella Fitzgerald in the 1940s. *Over the course of her fifty-nine-year recording career, Ella Fitzgerald won thirteen Grammy Awards and was presented with the National Medal of Arts and the Presidential Medal of Freedom.* WILLIAM GOTTLIEB/REDFERNS/GETTY IMAGES.

Fitzgerald inherited Webb's band after his death in 1939 and muddled along until Norman Granz, later her manager (and instigator of her "songbook" albums), began to feature her in his Jazz at the Philharmonic Concerts. Mingling with great jazz musicians at a time when jazz drew enormous audiences and dominated the popular music scene gave her the exposure and education that allowed her to move to the front rank of vocalists.

ADMIRED BY HER PEERS

Fitzgerald was blessed with a crystal clear voice and perfect pitch. Indeed, the Memorex Corporation capitalized on her ability to break glass in their famous commercials that asked whether it was Fitzgerald or Memorex tape. Her tone was generally bright and cheerful, and some critics caviled that her sense of fun got in the way of her overall art, depriving her of emotional depth. In fact, her technique enabled her to do anything she desired with a song, and she loved what has come to be termed the Great American Songbook (that is, songs by Berlin, Porter, et al.). Her clarity of diction was the admiration of her peers, including her male counterpart of perfection, Frank Sinatra, and her live performances were suffused with warmth and a quality of youthful vulnerability that she never lost.

Fitzgerald is often bracketed with Billie Holiday, her contemporary, as among the greatest of jazz vocalists, but although she could, and did, swing and scat with the best of them, her repertoire was not jazz dominated. Holiday is generally defined as the more emotional and sensual of the two, implying her greater depth and sophistication, whereas Fitzgerald is considered to have greater simplicity and directness. Her dexterity was considered equal to that of the best horn players, and Bing Crosby was not alone in saying she had "the best ear of any singer ever" and called her "the greatest."

Speaking of Fitzgerald's skill, Ellington noted that "her artistry brings to mind the words of the maestro, Mr. Toscanini, who said concerning singers, 'Either you're a good musician or you're not.' In terms of musicianship, Ella Fitzgerald was beyond category." Mel Torme marveled that "anyone who attempts to sing extemporaneously—that is, scat—will tell you that the hardest aspect is to stay in tune. You are wandering all over the scales, the notes coming out of your mouth a millisecond after you think of them. . . . Her notes float out in perfect pitch, effortlessly and, most important of all, swinging."

RECORDINGS

Her live recordings demonstrate the musical affection she and her audience shared. On *Ella in Berlin*, for example, she forgets the words to her version of "Mack the Knife," but she keeps going, making it up as she playfully teases herself. The audience loved it. This moment would probably have been cut out of a studio recording. Fitzgerald enjoyed touring and continued to do so for most of her life until ill health prohibited it. She generally appeared with a trio but was also frequently found at festivals where she would join groups of varying sizes. Fortunately, many of these live performances, in which she was in great form, were recorded.

Fitzgerald loved Louis Armstrong, and the three albums and many radio checks she made with him can be placed with her best work. The respect and affection these artists had for each other shines through their recordings, and their *Porgy and Bess* album remains essential to any jazz collection.

A favorite guest artist on television programs—Dinah Shore and Crosby featured her often—Fitzgerald was in particularly good form on the *Swing into Spring* programs of 1958 and 1959 and in a program produced by Norman Granz on PBS in November 1979, which featured Count Basie and his Orchestra, Roy Eldridge, Zoot Sims, Joe Pass, and many other leading jazz artists. She also made a number of cameo appearances in movies and was featured more substantially in *Pete Kelly's Blues* (1955) and *St. Louis Blues* (1958).

Fitzgerald came of age in a period that respected elegance and artistry. She continued to hone her craft throughout her long career, and her fans instinctively appreciated her note-perfect musicianship and precise technique that was so admired by the cognoscenti. Her long career saw her singing in numerous and varied settings and winning fans across several generations. She rose from simple origins to become a goodwill ambassador for the United States.

In 1947 Fitzgerald married bass player Ray Brown and the couple adopted a son, Ray Brown Jr., before divorcing in 1953. She suffered some eye trouble in the 1970s but continued to perform happily at concerts and festivals until the late 1980s, when she grew debilitated as a consequence of the diabetes from which she had suffered for a number of years. She continued to perform, even after both her legs were amputated below the knee in 1987, until she retired a few years before her death in 1996 the age of seventy-nine.

Frank A. Salamone

SEE ALSO: *Apollo Theater; Armstrong, Louis; Basie, Count; Berlin, Irving; Big Bands; Crosby, Bing; Ellington, Duke; Holiday, Billie; Porter, Cole; Rodgers and Hart; Savoy Ballroom; Shore, Dinah; Sinatra, Frank; Webb, Chick.*

BIBLIOGRAPHY

Colin, Sid. *Ella: The Life and Times of Ella Fitzgerald.* London: Elm Tree Books, 1986.

Fidelman, Geoffrey Mark. *First Lady of Song: Ella Fitzgerald for the Record.* Secaucus, NJ: Carol Publishing Group, 1994.

Gourse, Leslie, ed. *The Ella Fitzgerald Companion: Seven Decades of Commentary.* New York: Schirmer Books, 1998.

McDonough, John. "Ella: A Voice We'll Never Forget." *DownBeat*, September 1996.

Nicholson, Stuart. *Ella Fitzgerald: A Biography of the First Lady of Jazz.* New York: Da Capo Press, 1995.

Otfinoski, Steven. *African Americans in the Performing Arts.* New York, Facts On File, 2003.

Fitzgerald, F. Scott *(1896–1940)*

Perhaps because so much of his writing is autobiographical, F. Scott Fitzgerald is as famous for his personal life as he is for his writing. In his career as a writer, he proved to be gifted in a number of forms—he excelled as a novelist, a short-story writer, and an essayist. Because his personal and professional histories paralleled the times in which he lived and wrote, Fitzgerald will be forever identified with the Jazz Age of the 1920s and the ensuing Great Depression of the 1930s.

F. Scott Fitzgerald was born on September 24, 1896, the namesake and distant cousin of Francis Scott Key, the author of the U.S. national anthem. Fitzgerald's father, Edward, who viewed himself as an old southerner, was from Maryland, and his mother, Mary (Mollie) McQuillan, was the daughter of an Irish immigrant who was a successful grocery wholesaler in St. Paul, Minnesota. After Fitzgerald's father failed as a businessman in St. Paul, he relocated the family to upstate New York, where he worked as a salesman for Procter and Gamble. In 1908 his father was let go by the company, and he moved the family back to St. Paul. After two years at the Newman School, a Catholic prep school in New Jersey, Fitzgerald enrolled at Princeton University in the fall of 1913.

COLLEGE AND THE MILITARY

It was during his years at Princeton that Fitzgerald first applied himself to the pursuit of a literary life. He wrote for the Princeton Triangle Club's musicals and also contributed pieces to the *Princeton Tiger* and the *Nassau Literary Magazine*. In addition, he cultivated life-long relationships with fellow students who also went on to achieve literary success, including Edmund Wilson and John Peale Bishop. Unfortunately, Fitzgerald's dedication to the literary life resulted in his neglecting his studies. In 1917, after being placed on academic probation and realizing that he was unlikely to graduate, he dropped out of Princeton and joined the army, earning a commission as a second lieutenant in the infantry.

Like so many others who were slated to see action in Europe during World War I, Fitzgerald was certain his days were numbered. Accordingly, he quickly turned out a novel titled *The Romantic Egoist*, which was an autobiographical work chronicling the Princeton years of "Armory Blaine." Although the novel was rejected by Charles Scribner's Sons, it was praised for its originality, and Fitzgerald was invited to resubmit it after revisions. In the summer of 1918 he was assigned to Camp Sheridan, outside Montgomery, Alabama. While there he met Zelda Sayre, a debutante and the youngest daughter of an Alabama Supreme Court judge. Thus began one the most famous and tragic romances in American history.

Fitzgerald pursued Zelda with vigor but was not particularly well liked by her family, who thought he was an ill-suited match for their daughter. He had high hopes that Scribner's would accept his revised novel, which would, he hoped, make him worthy of Zelda's hand. Scribner's rejected it, which ultimately resulted in Zelda breaking off their engagement. Shortly before Fitzgerald was to go overseas, the war ended and he was discharged. In 1919 he left for New York intending to make his fortune in order to persuade Zelda to marry him.

SUCCESS IN THE JAZZ AGE

Amazingly, Fitzgerald succeeded. After a brief stint in New York, he returned to St. Paul to dedicate himself to rewriting his novel yet again. The finished product, *This Side of Paradise*, was published on March 26, 1920. The novel was an immediate smash hit, making Fitzgerald suddenly famous as the voice of his generation. A week later he married Zelda in New York, and the couple began their life together as young celebrities. In order to support their lavish lifestyle, Fitzgerald wrote short stories for mass-circulation magazines, which he did for the remainder of his life.

Most of his stories were published in the *Saturday Evening Post*, which resulted in his becoming known as a "*Post* writer." Because he wrote many of them for money, Fitzgerald often felt that his short stories were not artistic achievements on par with his novels. However, literary history has proven his low estimation of his short stories wrong. Fitzgerald published some 160 magazine stories in his lifetime, an extraordinarily high number by any count. Although many of these works are second rate, his finest pieces nevertheless rank at the forefront of American short stories. Among his best are "Bernice Bobs Her Hair," "May Day," "The Diamond as Big as the Ritz," "Winter Dreams," "The Rich Boy," "Babylon Revisited," and "Crazy Sunday."

After spending a summer in Connecticut, the Fitzgeralds moved to New York City, where Fitzgerald wrote his second novel, *The Beautiful and the Damned* (1922), which tells the story of the dissipation of Anthony and Gloria Patch. Much of the book's events were inspired by the Fitzgeralds' drunken lifestyle, particularly during their time in Connecticut. The novel was not particularly well received, nor did it make much money. The Fitzgeralds, especially Scott, were quickly gaining a well-deserved reputation as hard drinkers. Although he claimed never to have worked while under the effects of "stimulant"—and judging by the quality of his work it may be true—Fitzgerald's reputation as a carouser did damage his literary standing.

After their first trip to Europe, the couple returned to St. Paul, where in October 1921 Zelda gave birth to their only child, a daughter named Frances Scott (Scottie) Fitzgerald. In the meantime, Fitzgerald wrote *The Vegetable*, a play he was sure would result in financial riches. The family moved to Great Neck, Long Island, in order to be closer to Broadway. Unfortunately, the play bombed at its tryout in November 1923. Fitzgerald was bitterly disappointed. The distractions of New York City proved too much for him. He was not making progress on his third novel, and he and Zelda were increasingly fighting, often after heavy drinking. The Fitzgeralds retreated to Europe in an attempt to find peace.

In April 1925 Fitzgerald published *The Great Gatsby*, the book that was to become his literary legacy. Through the recollections of Nick Carraway, *The Great Gatsby* recounts the history of Jay Gatsby (born James Gatz) and his love for Daisy Buchanan. As Matthew Bruccoli writes in his introduction to *A Life in Letters*, "Fitzgerald's clear, lyrical, colorful, witty style evoked the emotions associated with time and place. . . . The chief theme of Fitzgerald's work is aspiration—the idealism he regarded as defining American character. Another major theme was mutability or loss. As a social historian Fitzgerald became identified with 'The Jazz Age.'"

Gatsby is the essential Jazz Age document—the work most commonly considered an accurate reflection of the ultimately irresponsible optimism of the boom years of the Roaring Twenties. Jay Gatsby starts off with a traditional American work ethic, but in his pursuit of the American Dream, his ethic eventually gives way to the pursuit of money. The inevitable failure of his dreams, which are all along founded on a fallacy, anticipate the demise of the postwar prosperity of the 1920s. That prosperity officially came to a close with the stock market crash of October 29, 1929.

Fitzgerald knew that *Gatsby* was good, but the reviews were lukewarm and sales were extremely disappointing. In fact, at the time of Fitzgerald's death the book had sold fewer than 23,000 copies. In the end, though, he was proved correct. In the years following his death, *The Great Gatsby*, along with the rest of his work, underwent a remarkable renaissance. Beginning in the 1950s, Fitzgerald's literary reputation skyrocketed. Book after book was reissued and numerable new collections of his stories were released to keep up with demand. In the 1990s *The Great Gatsby* remained by far the most frequently assigned book in American high schools and colleges.

THE DEPRESSION YEARS

After being labeled the voice of his generation and experiencing fame and notoriety as someone whose life was representative of the Jazz Age, Fitzgerald, like the country around him, fell on extremely hard times. In addition, in 1930 Zelda experienced her first mental breakdown. Her mental problems lasted the remainder of her life, which she spent in and out of sanitariums. Zelda's medical condition was of great concern to Fitzgerald, who by all accounts never stopped loving her. Unfortunately, his drinking increased concurrently with his need for more money. Scottie was in private school, and Zelda's medical expenses were immense.

Following the publication of *Gatsby* in 1925, Fitzgerald began writing short stories almost exclusively in order to counteract cash-flow problems. In the early 1930s his fee, which had peaked at $4,000 per story for his *Post* stories, began to plummet. Fitzgerald's *Post* stories no longer had an audience; the country, deep in economic depression, no longer wanted to read about the Jazz Age. In truth, his stories were not often optimistic, nor did they always end happily. Fitzgerald's reputation as a Jazz Age figure, however, could not be separated from his fiction. Thus, his star fell rapidly.

His final completed novel was *Tender Is the Night*, a tale about the fall of Dick Diver that is loosely based on Fitzgerald's experiences with Zelda's various breakdowns. The 1934 publication was a critical and financial failure. Although not as well crafted as *Gatsby*, *Tender* has since earned its proper place as an American masterpiece. For the remainder of his life, Fitzgerald scrambled to make a living, writing essays and stories for magazines and spending time in Hollywood as a contract writer. Toward the end of his life, he appeared to have finally put things in order. He was sober; in a stable relationship with Hollywood movie columnist Sheilah Graham; and in the midst of writing *The Last Tycoon*, which even in incomplete form has the characteristics of his finest work. Just as the United States appeared to be coming out of the Great Depression, so too did Fitzgerald seem to be on the brink of making a return to his former glory. However, on December 21, 1940, Fitzgerald died of a heart attack in Graham's apartment. He was forty-four years old.

LEGACY AND ADAPTATION OF WORK

Despite his meteoric posthumous rise to the forefront of American letters, the myth of Fitzgerald as an irresponsible writer has endured. In fact, he was a meticulous craftsman—a dedicated reviser who went through countless drafts of everything he ever wrote. However, the image of Fitzgerald as a raucous prodigy whose Jazz Age excesses became larger than life continues.

One cannot easily forget the tragic figure of the 1930s whose fall from grace somehow seemed to be the inevitable price he had to pay for his earlier actions. Either way, Fitzgerald's art ultimately supersedes his life. The events of his life continue to fascinate as legend, but the grace and beauty of his uniquely American works forever serve as a testament to the truth of Fitzgerald's opinion of himself: "I am not a great man, but sometimes I think the impersonal and objective quality of my talent and the sacrifices of it, in pieces, to preserve its essential value has some sort of epic grandeur."

Both Fitzgerald's talent and "epic grandeur" are due to be brought to life for twenty-first-century movie audiences by director Baz Luhrman—best known for his lavish musical production of *Moulin Rouge* (2001)—in a 3-D adaptation of *The Great Gatsby*. The film stars Leonardo DiCaprio as Jay Gatsby, Carey Mulligan as Daisy Buchanan, and Tobey Maguire as Nick Carraway. Even before its release, the film made an influence on fashion; in early 2012 some fashion shows featured models wearing Ralph Lauren and Gucci versions of drop waists and beaded chiffon dresses. Luhrman studied Fitzgerald for several years to develop a feeling for his time and to present the author's masterpiece faithfully. However, many purists have criticized the use of 3-D technology in the movie, seeing it as a detraction from the amazing talent that Fitzgerald demonstrated in *The Great Gatsby*.

Robert C. Sickels

SEE ALSO: *Broadway; DiCaprio, Leonardo; The Great Depression; Gucci; Hollywood; Jazz; Lauren, Ralph; The* Saturday Evening Post*; Stock Market Crashes; The Twenties.*

BIBLIOGRAPHY

Berman, Ronald. *The Great Gatsby and Modern Times.* Urbana: University of Illinois Press, 1994.

Bloom, Harold, ed. *F. Scott Fitzgerald.* New York: Chelsea House, 1985.

Bruccoli, Matthew J. *Some Sort of Epic Grandeur: The Life of F. Scott Fitzgerald.* Columbia: University of South Carolina Press, 1981.

Bruccoli, Matthew J., ed. *F. Scott Fitzgerald: A Life in Letters.* New York: Simon & Schuster, 1995.

Bruccoli, Matthew J., and Judith S. Baughman, eds. *Conversations with F. Scott Fitzgerald.* Jackson: University of Mississippi Press, 2004.

Canterbery, E. Ray, and Thomas D. Birch. *F. Scott Fitzgerald: Under the Influence.* St. Paul, MN: Paragon House, 2006.

Donaldson, Scott. *Fool for Love: F. Scott Fitzgerald.* New York: St. Martin's Press, 1983.

Donaldson, Scott, ed. *Critical Essays on F. Scott Fitzgerald's "The Great Gatsby."* Boston: G. K. Hall, 1984.

Donaldson, Scott. *Fitzgerald and Hemingway: Works and Days.* New York: Columbia University Press, 2009.

Kuehl, John. *F. Scott Fitzgerald: A Study of the Short Fiction.* Boston: Twayne, 1991.

Kundu, Gautam. *Fitzgerald and the Influence of Film: The Language of Cinema in the Novels.* Jefferson, NC: McFarland, 2007.

Mellow, James R. *Invented Lives: F. Scott and Zelda Fitzgerald.* Boston: Houghton Mifflin, 1984.

Seiters, Dan. *Image Patterns in the Novels of F. Scott Fitzgerald.* Ann Arbor, MI: UMI Research Press, 1986.

Tate, Mary Jo. *F. Scott Fitzgerald A to Z: The Essential Reference to His Life and Work.* New York: Facts On File, 1998.

Flack, Roberta *(1939–)*

One of the most popular female singers of the early 1970s, Roberta Flack was critically praised for her impressively beautiful and classically controlled voice, as well as her performance style: powerful yet intimate in its delivery. Flack was a musical prodigy on the piano. In 1969, after years of study and working as a music teacher, she began using her voice to record professionally. Her biggest success came in 1971 with the song "The First Time Ever I Saw Your Face." By the following year, it was the number one song in the United States, popularized in part through its inclusion in the soundtrack of Clint Eastwood's *Play Misty for Me*.

Over the next two decades Flack's successes were sporadic, but interest in her music surged again in the late 1990s, inspired by the Fugees' popular hip-hop remake of her 1973 song "Killing Me Softly." In 1999 Flack was honored with a star on the Hollywood Walk of Fame.

In the early twenty-first century, Flack continued to record and tour all over the world. She released *Holiday* in 2003 and *Friends: Roberta Flack Sings Mariko Taka* three years later. In 2012 she saluted the Beatles with the release of *Let It Be Roberta: Roberta Flack Sings the Beatles*. She also continued to support the Roberta Flack School of Music at Hyde Leadership Charter School (New York City), where underprivileged young people study music for free.

Brian Granger

SEE ALSO: *The Beatles; Eastwood, Clint; Pop Music.*

BIBLIOGRAPHY

Altman, Linda Jacobs. *Roberta Flack: The Sound of Velvet Melting*. St. Paul, MN: EMC, 1975.

Weisbard, Eric. *Listen Again: A Momentary History of Pop Music*. Durham, NC: Duke University Press, 2007.

Whitburn, Joel. *The Billboard Book of Top 40 Hits*. New York: Billboard Publication, 1996.

Flag Burning

Although the burning of the American flag does not occur very often, when it does, the act leads to strong emotions from both supporters and detractors. The issue first reached the mainstream when flags were burned in the 1960s at protests against the Vietnam War, leading to the passage by Congress of the federal Flag Protection Act in 1968. Over the next twenty years, flag burning became an emotional issue, as well as an increasingly complicated legal question about the extent to which the First Amendment protects freedom of speech. The issue first reached the Supreme Court in 1989 in *Texas v. Johnson*, in which Texas resident Gregory Johnson was convicted of flag desecration. The court ruled that a person has the right to burn the flag as an act of political protest. Justice William Brennan, writing for the court, said, "To say that the Government has an interest in encouraging proper treatment of the flag, however, is not to say that it may criminally punish a person for burning a flag as a means of political protest."

Many groups have led the charge to add a flag desecration amendment to the Constitution. The proposed amendment, which has passed the House of Representatives in numerous congressional terms, had not, by the end of 2011, achieved the sixty-seven votes needed in the Senate to be sent to the states for ratification. Those who do not endorse the amendment believe that the right to protest, which is protected under the First Amendment, should not be limited. As Robert Justin Goldstein notes in *Burning the Flag*, "forbidding flag burning as a means of peaceful political protest will surely diminish the flag's symbolic ability to represent political freedom." The issue is sure to spark heated debate for some time to come.

D. Byron Painter

SEE ALSO: *Protest Groups; Student Demonstrations.*

BIBLIOGRAPHY

Corn-Revere, Robert. *Implementing a Flag-Desecration Amendment to the U.S. Constitution: An End to the Controversy—or a New Beginning?* Nashville, TN: First Amendment Center, 2005.

Goldstein, Robert Justin. *Burning the Flag: The Great 1989–90 American Flag Desecration Controversy*. Kent, OH: Kent State University Press, 1996.

Lockhart, William B.; Yale Kamisar; Jesse H. Choper; et al. *Constitutional Rights and Liberties: Cases, Comments, Questions*. St. Paul, MN: West Publishing, 1991.

Flag Clothing

In the United States, flag clothing is highly subjective; it can be either seditious or patriotic, depending upon context. The activist Abbie Hoffman was arrested in the disestablishment year 1968 for wearing a flag shirt; beginning in 1990 the designer Ralph Lauren had the flag knitted into or applied to sweaters and sportswear almost as a brand logo, and by 1995 the designer Tommy Hilfiger was producing flag clothing as well. The actress Sherilynn Fenn appeared on the July 7, 1990, cover of *New York* magazine wearing only the Lauren hand-knitted "Betsy" throw. In 1998 Lauren gave the Smithsonian Institution $13 million to restore the Star-Spangled Banner (the flag that flew over Fort McHenry during the War of 1812), a less than equal return on the money Lauren had made on the flag.

The Desecration Amendment, often referred to as the "Flag Burning Amendment," would amend the U.S. Constitution by allowing Congress to prohibit the expression of political views if such views took the form of "desecrating" the flag. Instances of desecration include using the flag for clothing or napkins. Between 1995 and 2005 six efforts were made to pass the amendment in Congress. In 2006 the amendment failed to pass in the U.S. Senate by only one vote. Critics continue to ponder whether flag clothing amounts to desecration or exaltation or whether it is equivalent to flag burning or flag waving.

Richard Martin

SEE ALSO: *Flag Burning; Lauren, Ralph; Smithsonian Institution.*

BIBLIOGRAPHY

Bodenhamer, David J. *Our Rights*. New York: Oxford University Press, 2007.

First Amendment Center at Vanderbilt University. Accessed January 2012. Available from http://www.firstamendmentcenter.org

Hulse, Carl, and John Holusha. "Amendment on Flag Burning Fails by One Vote." *New York Times*, June 27, 2006.

Flagpole Sitting

One of the more outlandish fads associated with the Roaring Twenties, flagpole sitting—like marathon dancing and bunion derbies—was an endurance feat performed for fame and money during a decade of change and restlessness. Alvin "Shipwreck" Kelly traveled across America, setting up and sitting on flagpoles through extremes of weather for increasingly longer periods of time. Seated atop a flagpole, he took only liquids for nourishment (hoisted to him by rope and pail), voiding his waste through a tube attached to the pole. In 1929 he perched on a flagpole in Baltimore for twenty-three days and seven hours, while thousands stood and gaped, a feat that has become a metaphor for an American obsession with endurance feats and records, crazy thrills, and outlandish exploits.

John R. Deitrick

SEE ALSO: *College Fads; Dance Halls; Houdini, Harry; Jones, Bobby; Leisure Time; Lindbergh, Charles; Ruth, Babe; The Twenties.*

BIBLIOGRAPHY

Allen, Frederick Lewis. *Only Yesterday*. New York: HarperCollins, 1957.

Flappers

In the 1920s a new and popular model of modern womanhood dominated the American cultural scene. Although not all American women of the early twentieth century would emulate the flapper model, it quickly came to represent the youthful exuberance of the post–World War I period. According to F. Scott Fitzgerald—the author whose novels set a tone for the 1920s—the ideal flapper (and by extension, the ideal modern woman) was "lovely, expensive, and about nineteen." Originally merely a symbol of young and daring female chic, the flapper came to embody the radically modern spirit of the 1920s. Not merely a fashion trend, "flapperhood" corresponded to an entire new set of American values.

The term *flapper* originated in England, where it was used simply to describe girls of an awkward age. American writers like Fitzgerald transformed the term into an iconic phrase that glorified the fun-loving youthful spirit of the postwar decade. The flapper ideal, along with the look, first became popular with chic young moderns, then with a larger body of American women. The flapper was remarkably identifiable. Clara Bow, with her bobbed hair, short skirts, and penchant for lipstick, was the starlet who had "it." Other celebrity women, from the

Flappers. *Flappers dance in a Charleston contest in 1926.* HULTON ARCHIVE/GETTY IMAGES.

film star Louise Brooks to the author Dorothy Parker, cultivated and popularized the devil-may-care attitude and fashion of the flapper. America's young women rushed to emulate the flapper aesthetic. They flattened their chests with tight bands of cloth in order to look as young and boyish as possible. They shortened the skirts on their increasingly plain frocks, and they bought more cosmetics than American women ever had before.

But flapperhood was more than mere fashion. To an older generation of Americans, the flapper symbolized a "revolution in manners and morals." Flappers did not just look daring, they were daring. In the 1920s growing numbers of young American women began to smoke, drink, and talk slang. And they danced—not in the old style, but in the new mode inspired by jazz music. The popularity of jazz and dancing hinted at new attitudes toward sexuality. The image of the "giddy flapper, rouged and clipped, careening in a drunken stupor to the lewd strains of a jazz quartet" gave license to new ideas about female sexuality. As Fitzgerald claimed, "None of the Victorian mothers . . . had any idea how casually their daughters were accustomed to being kissed." Flappers presented themselves as sexual creatures, radically different from the stable maternal women who epitomized the ideal of the previous generation.

And yet the popularity of the flapper did not, as one might suppose, signal the triumph of feminism in the early twentieth century. For all her sexual sophistication and her rejection of her mother's Victorian values, the flapper did not pose any real threat to the gender status quo. With her athleticism and her adventurous spirit, she may have presented a positive image for modern women, but she remained a soft creature who demurred to men. Indeed, it was precisely the flapper's "combination of daring spirit and youthful innocence that made her attractive to men." She was a highly sexualized creature, but that sexuality retained an innocent, youthful, romantic quality. Ultimately, flappers married and became the mothers of the 1930s.

The new prototype of single womanhood had positive ramifications, giving women license to work and play alongside men, but the model had its limits. Like the fashion for short skirts and short hair, the transformative cultural promise of the flapper moment receded. In the long years of the Great Depression, the desire to emulate reckless rich girls faded along with the working girl's ability to afford even the cheapest imitation of flapper chic. Remnants of the flapper lifestyle, however, remained popular—a youthful taste for music and dancing, smoking and swearing, and sex and sexiness. And the market for goods that had emerged to meet the consuming passions of flapper women gained in strength and power. Even after the flapper disappeared from the American scene, the feminine ideal that she had popularized lingered, along with a culture of consumption designed to help women pursue that impossibly impermanent idea. The ideal modern woman of America's imagination, although no longer officially a "flapper," was to remain infuriatingly "lovely . . . and about nineteen."

Jackie Hatton

SEE ALSO: *Bow, Clara; Brooks, Louise; Cigarettes; Consumerism; Fitzgerald, F. Scott; The Great Depression; Hairstyles; Jazz; Lipstick; Parker, Dorothy; Sex Symbol; Slang; The Twenties; World War I.*

BIBLIOGRAPHY

Allen, Frederick Lewis. *Only Yesterday: An Informal History of the 1920s.* New York: Harper Brothers, 1931.

Coben, Stanley. *Rebellion against Victorianism: The Impetus for Cultural Change in 1920s America.* New York: Oxford University Press, 1991.

Fass, Paula S. *The Damned and the Beautiful: American Youth in the 1920s.* New York: Oxford University Press, 1977.

Marchand, Roland. *Advertising the American Dream: Making Way for Modernity, 1920–1940.* Berkeley: University of California Press, 1985.

Melosh, Barbara. *Gender and American History since 1890.* London: Routledge, 1993.

Robinson, Thomas A., and Lanette R. Ruff. *Out of the Mouths of Babes: Girl Evangelists in the Flapper Era.* New York: Oxford University Press, 2011.

Flash Gordon

The most successful of the *Buck Rogers* imitators, *Flash Gordon* began as a Sunday comic strip in early 1934. It was drawn by Alex Raymond, written by erstwhile pulp magazine editor Don Moore, and syndicated by King Features. The strip commences with handsome, blond Flash and lovely Dale Arden, destined to be his love interest for the life of the strip, taking off in a rocket ship with brilliant, bearded Dr. Zarkov. Due to a miscalculation they end up on the planet Mongo, a considerable stretch of which is ruled over by a ruthless dictator known as Ming the Merciless. A combination of all the terrible qualities of Fu Manchu, Adolf Hitler, and the villain of a Victorian melodrama, Ming becomes Flash's prime antagonist.

Flash and his friends undergo a series of picaresque adventures that take them, often while aiding local guerrilla activities, to dense jungles thick with monsters, to strange arboreal kingdoms, to realms beneath the sea, and to whatever other stock science fiction locales Moore could borrow from the pulps. While the writing, which appears in captions below the drawings, is stodgy and noticeably purple, Raymond quickly developed into a first-rate illustrator. Within a year the feature was one of the best looking and most impressive in the Sunday funnies.

Flash Gordon soon began being reprinted in comic books and Big Little Books and within two years was also in the movies. Universal Studios produced three extremely popular serials based on the strip. Loosely adapted from some of Moore's newspaper continuities, they star Buster Crabbe, his hair dyed blond, as Flash. Jean Rogers is Dale in the initial two; Frank Shannon portrays Zarkov in all three; and Charles Middleton, a veteran cinema villain, brings just the right degree of camp to the part of Ming.

The first of the film serials, titled simply *Flash Gordon*, was released in 1936. *Flash Gordon's Trip to Mars* came along in 1938, followed by the more flamboyantly titled *Flash Gordon Conquers the Universe* in 1940. Filled with rocket ships, ray guns, mad-doctor apparatus, and young women in skimpy costumes, the Flash Gordon serials are not noted for their state-of-the-art special effects. Yet they do possess a sort of tacky charm and the performances make up in exuberance for what they lack in dramatic depth.

Such was the popularity of the strip that King decided to add a daily in the spring of 1940. Raymond chose to devote all of his time to the Sunday strip, while his longtime assistant Austin Briggs, an established magazine illustrator in his own right, drew the weekday version. Never a particular success, the weekday strip was dropped in 1944. About that time Raymond entered the marines, and Briggs took over the Sunday *Flash Gordon*. Determined to abandon comics eventually and devote himself full time to illustration, Briggs never signed the page. He quit in 1948 and went on to become one of the highest-paid magazine and advertising artists in the country, as well as a founder of the Famous Artists School.

Mac Raboy, a comic-book artist who had drawn such superheroes as Captain Marvel Jr. and the Green Lama, followed Briggs on the Sunday page, doing a flamboyant and formidable job. In the early 1950s the daily version was revived with Dan Barry, another alumnus of comic books, as the artist. Various science fiction writers, including Harry Harrison, wrote the scripts. Barry added the Sunday page to his chores after Raboy's death in 1967; he eventually turned over the drawing to Bob Fujitani. In the late 1990s *Flash Gordon* was once again only a Sunday comic strip, appearing in a handful of newspapers and written and drawn by Jim Keefe.

Ron Goulart

SEE ALSO: *Big Little Books; Camp; Captain Marvel; Comic Books; Comics; Fu Manchu.*

BIBLIOGRAPHY

Barry, Dan, and Harvey Kurtzman. *Flash Gordon*. Princeton, NJ: Kitchen Sink Press, 1988.

Kinnard, Roy; Tony Crnkovich; and R. J. Vitone. *The Flash Gordon Serials, 1936–1940: A Heavily Illustrated Guide*. Jefferson, NC: McFarland, 2008.

Marschall, Richard. *America's Great Comic Strip Artists*. New York: Abbeville Press, 1989.

Raymond, Alex. *Flash Gordon*. Franklin Square, NY: Nostalgia Press, 1967.

Flashdance Style

The 1983 film *Flashdance* was an instant phenomenon in the United States. It not only created a new fashion style quickly embraced by females of all ages, but it also introduced the world to actress Jennifer Beals and the wholesome but sexy character she played. Her character welded by day and danced by night. The look consisted of worn-in sweatshirts ripped at the neckline that slipped off the shoulder casually, revealing some but hinting at more. Combining comfort with sexuality, the style also embraced athleticism for women by making workout wear sexy.

In the early 1980s punk music and its fashions were starting to fade, and break dancing was the new fad—and with it, a new style was born: sportswear worn as everyday wear. Moving away from lace and other classic feminine clothing, the Flashdance look celebrated a new kind of woman, independent and down-to-earth, athletic and sexy.

Sharon Yablon

SEE ALSO: *Punk; Retro Fashion; Social Dancing; Sweatshirt.*

BIBLIOGRAPHY

Bailey, William G., and Frank W. Hoffman. *Arts and Entertainment Fads*. New York: Haworth, 1990.

Fresh, Mr. *Breakdancing*. New York: Avon, 1984.

Morrison, Sasha Charnin. *Secrets of Stylists: An Insider's Guide to Styling the Stars*. San Francisco: Chronicle Books, 2011.

Sewall, Gilbert T., ed. *The Eighties: A Reader*. Reading, MA: Addison-Wesley, 1997.

Traube, Elizabeth G. *Dreaming Identities: Class, Gender, and Generation in 1980s Hollywood Movies*. Boulder, CO: Westview, 1992.

Flatt, Lester *(1914–1979)*

Born in Sparta, Tennessee, musician Lester Flatt was known for his friendly, down-home vocal style; solid rhythm guitar; and songwriting ability, all of which were instrumental in both creating and popularizing bluegrass music. Flatt joined Bill Monroe's Blue Grass Boys in 1945, where his warm lead vocals were an integral part of the original bluegrass sound, as was "the Lester Flatt G-run," a guitar figure used to punctuate song verses. Together with Earl Scruggs, he departed the group in 1948 to form the Foggy Mountain Boys, and throughout the 1950s and early 1960s the ensemble was one of the most visible and successful bluegrass acts. Creative differences led to a breakup in 1969, and Flatt formed a new band, the Nashville Grass, to pursue the earlier act's more traditional sound. With both former Foggy Mountain Boys and new musicians backing him up, Flatt remained a popular elder statesman of bluegrass until his death.

Jon Weisberger

SEE ALSO: *Bluegrass; The Foggy Mountain Boys; Monroe, Bill; Scruggs, Earl.*

BIBLIOGRAPHY

Cantwell, Robert. *Bluegrass Breakdown: The Making of the Old Southern Sound*. Urbana: Univerity of Illinois Press, 1984.

Kochman, Marilyn, ed. *The Big Book of Bluegrass*. New York: William Morrow, 1984.

Rosenberg, Neil V. *Bluegrass: A History*. Urbana: University of Illinois Press, 1985.

Willis, Barry R. *America's Music, Bluegrass*. Franktown, CO: Pine Valley Music, 1992.

Flava Flav *(1959–)*

William Jonathan Drayton Jr.—known almost exclusively by his stage name, Flava Flav—is a hip-hop artist and reality television star. He rose to prominence in the late 1980s as the flamboyant hype man of groundbreaking hip-hop group Public Enemy. Founded in 1982, the group transformed hip-hop with militant lyrics, proving rap music was a significant cultural phenomenon, not just a passing fad. With the help of a production crew known as the Bomb Squad, Public Enemy introduced hip-hop audiences to violent noise and hard-edged sounds by using aggressive beats, turntable scratches, and sirens. The group succeeded in large part because of the unique rapport between serious front man Chuck D (born Carlton Ridenhour) and his comic foil, Flava Flav.

In hip-hop a hype man is responsible for generating audience enthusiasm—and Flav performed the role like no other, pumping up crowds with his jerky dances, chants, and catchy slang phrases, such as "Yeah boyeeee!" He livened up the atmosphere with his outrageous dress, including oversized sunglasses and hats and his now-legendary Viking horned headdress and 15-inch clock necklace. He is also credited with starting the trend of wearing a grill—teeth made of gold, silver, and/or diamonds.

Flav was born in 1959 in Long Island, New York. A musical prodigy and classically trained pianist, he is said to have mastered fifteen different instruments. Petty theft and burglary arrests interrupted his high school years, and he dropped out of high school. On the campus of Long Island's Adelphi University, he met Chuck D, who was hosting a college radio show. The two began rapping together, and with the addition of DJ Terminator X and choreographer Professor Griff, the group Public Enemy was formed.

They signed with Def Jam Records, and by the late 1980s they were already superstars. Their hit single "Fight the Power" brought them even greater acclaim as the theme music for director Spike Lee's controversial film *Do the Right Thing* (1989). However, their fortunes changed in the mid-1990s amid member rivalries, record label disputes, and Flav's worsening addiction to drugs, mainly crack cocaine. For much of the next decade, he spent time in and out of jail and treatment centers. A move from New York to Los Angeles in 2003 helped him to finally kick his habit.

After his recovery he reclaimed his high-profile status in hype-man fashion, reinventing himself as one of the hottest and most flamboyant stars of reality television. In 2004 he joined the cast of the VH1 network's *The Surreal Life* (2003–), which features a group of has-been celebrities living in close quarters. Flav, sporting outrageous costumes, jewelry, and his trademark clock and grill, fell in love with one of his housemates on the show, Danish model and actress Brigitte Nielsen. The romance continued with their globe-trotting misadventures as featured in the 2005 spin-off series *Strange Love*, at the end of which Nielsen decided to return to her Italian fiancé. The breakup spawned another series, *Flavor of Love* (2006–2008), which brought women into Flav's mansion to compete for his affections. The show became the model for several celebrity dating shows that later appeared on VH1.

The success of his comeback was confirmed in 2007 when he was the subject of a Comedy Central network roast featuring such big-name performers as rapper Snoop Dogg and comedian Jimmy Kimmel. Flav's other credits include regular roles on MYNetworkTV's *Under One Roof* (2008) and on BET's *Nite Tales* (2009). He continues to record and tour with Public Enemy, which had a comeback with the soundtrack for Lee's 1998 film *He Got Game*. The group celebrated its thirtieth anniversary in 2012. Although their fan base has dwindled since their early years, their performances continue to electrify audiences thanks to Chuck D's booming voice and politically charged lyrics and Flav's showstopping antics and teasing vocals.

Janet Mullane

SEE ALSO: *Cable TV; Chuck D; Cocaine/Crack;* Do the Right Thing; *Hip-Hop; Lee, Spike; Public Enemy; Rap; Reality Television; Television.*

BIBLIOGRAPHY

Ciccariello, George. "Public Enemy." In *Icons of Hip Hop: An Encyclopedia of the Movement, Music, and Culture, Vol. 1*, ed. Mickey Hess. Westport, CT: Greenwood, 2007.

Davis, Johnny. "Hip-Hop, You Don't Stop." *Guardian* (London), June 18, 2006.

Flavor Flav. *Flavor Flav: The Icon: The Memoir.* Las Vegas, NV: Farrah Gray, 2011.

Myrie, Russell. *Don't Rhyme for the Sake of Riddlin': The Authorized Story of Public Enemy.* Edinburgh, UK: Canongate, 2008.

Flea Markets

Markets where hundreds and sometimes thousands of people gather to buy and sell goods, flea markets are literally a material accumulation of American culture in a concentrated area. At a single flea market one can see—and buy—just about anything imaginable, such as lamps, cookbooks, shoes, tools, clocks, toys, uniforms, salt-and-pepper shakers, cookie jars, ratchet sets, tarpaulins, radios, paintings, porcelain sinks, drinking glasses, bookends, duct tape, and candy dishes. The variety of goods constitutes the very nature of the flea market. New but discounted merchandise is common and runs the gamut from pet supplies, housewares, and tube socks to boxes of laundry detergent, canned goods, and toothpaste. Used items are generally household castoffs, including baby clothes, furniture, stereo equipment, carpeting, and automobile tires. Flea markets contain objects of both the past and the present, revealing obsolete technologies (e.g., eight-track players and Atari video games) and out-of-date clothing (e.g., bell-bottom pants, wide ties, and polyester shirts). Some people even sell antiques—not higher-end goods like Tiffany lamps and fine china, but more affordable collectibles like vintage pottery and prints. Flea markets may offer fresh produce from local farms, plants, and sometimes pets. Flea market operators often put restrictions on the types of things that are sold and usually prohibit the sale of firearms and other deadly weapons, stolen property, illicit drugs, pornography, and liquor. While most also officially prohibit "gray market" (counterfeit) items, these goods are usually in evidence at every flea market, with vendors selling imitation designer sunglasses, T-shirts, watches, and jewelry. Many medium-sized towns hold their own weekly or monthly flea markets.

Also known as swap meets, trade days, and peddlers' fairs, the flea market derives from the Greek *agoras* and other open-air markets of ancient times. It is believed that the term *flea market* comes from the French *Marché aux Puces*, the name of an outdoor bazaar known for the fleas that infested the upholstery of used furniture sold there. A popular pastime for people who frequent them regularly, flea markets allow people of all classes to enjoy a degree of economic power and autonomy—being able to buy or sell what they want at a price they more or less determine—outside of the highly regulated, inflexible, and taxable sphere of retail commerce.

Ubiquitous across the country for more than a century, one of the first American flea markets was the Monday Trade Days in Canton, Texas, which began in 1873 as a place where people

Flea Market in New Orleans. *Bargain hunters shop at a flea market in the French Quarter of New Orleans, Louisiana, in 2006.* DANIEL ACKER/BLOOMBERG VIA GETTY IMAGES.

would go to buy horses; later they brought their own goods to sell or trade. Other towns quickly adopted this pattern of trade, but the modern flea market was supposedly the brainchild of Russell Carrell, an East Coast antique show organizer. Working as an auctioneer in Connecticut, Carrell thought to run an antique show like an outdoor auction, only forgoing the tent, which because of fire hazards was too expensive to insure. Carrell's 1956 Salisbury open-air antiques market, he claimed, was the first modern incarnation of the flea market, although the true flea market does not consist of professional antique dealers but rather of people looking to make some extra money on the side.

The different characteristics of flea markets reflect the diversity of the goods they offer and the people who attend them. Some take place completely outside, others are indoors, while still others have both inside and outside areas for selling goods. They usually take place at drive-ins, parking lots, race tracks, or fairgrounds. Paying a flat fee to the flea market's organizer (about $10 to $20 per day in the 1990s), vendors come equipped with tables, racks, and shelves on which to display their merchandise or merely a sheet or blanket to cover the ground. Flea markets usually take place on the weekends, although not always; some convene on Fridays or on particular weekdays. Northern markets sometimes shut down during the winter while southern ones do the same in the hot summer months.

While flea markets have been touted as a good way to save money during the economic recession that began in 2007, many sellers say that even their industry has been adversely affected by the poor economy. According to a number of dealers interviewed in 2008 at a Massachusetts flea market, while the number of customers is increasing, those customers are not willing to pay very high prices. As one dealer put it, "They want it for less than you pay for it."

For all of their differences, flea markets and the people who frequent them have some things in common. Flea markets are characterized by the unpredictability in goods offered and the prices asked. Most certainly, every buyer is looking for a bargain—some hope to find valuable antiques and collectibles hidden among the castoffs, while others look for utilitarian goods that are cheaper than in the retail marketplace. To this end, haggling is commonplace at flea markets, with buyer and seller both working to agree on a fair price, but using their own strategies. The seller "talks up" his or her merchandise to make it as appealing as possible, while the buyer points out defects or claims to have only a certain amount of money left to spend. Other tactics include, conversely, coming early to get first pick of the goods or staying late, hoping that sellers will be more willing to unload items cheaply rather than taking them home.

Wendy Woloson

SEE ALSO: *Baseball Cards; Farmers' Markets; Retro Fashion.*

BIBLIOGRAPHY

Freund, Thatcher. *Objects of Desire: The Lives of Antiques and Those Who Pursue Them.* New York: Penguin, 1995.

LaFarge, Albert. *U.S. Flea Market Directory.* New York: Avon Books, 1996.

Stanton, Maureen. *Killer Stuff and Tons of Money: Seeking History and Hidden Gems in Flea-Market America.* New York: Penguin Press, 2011.

Fleetwood Mac

Founded in 1967 as a British blues band, Fleetwood Mac exploded as an American rock-and-roll phenomenon in 1975, after a pair of young Californian songwriters joined the group. The bewitching Stevie Nicks and guitar genius Lindsey Buckingham rounded out the band of songwriter-keyboardist Christine McVie, bassist John McVie, and drummer Mick Fleetwood. Their first album together, the eponymous *Fleetwood Mac* (1975), hit number one with three hit singles, but its merits were far overshadowed by the follow-up album, *Rumours* (1977). Songs of love, anger, heartbreak, and hope launched the band into superstardom, but the drama between the grooves mirrored that raging between the members of the band: Christine and John McVie divorced after seven years of marriage, Nicks and Buckingham ended their longtime romance, and Fleetwood split with his wife, Jenny Boyd.

Audiences sang along and sympathized, sending *Rumours* to the top of the charts and making it the best-selling album of all time to date; it also won the Grammy Award for album of the year. Fleetwood Mac continued to tour and make music together for the next ten years, while four of the five members also began solo careers. Of these, Nicks—with her husky voice, boots and shawls, and mystical lyrics—garnered the greatest success. Throughout the 1980s she toured in support of her albums, which included *Bella Donna*, and *The Wild Heart*, magnifying her identity as a popular culture icon. (New York City holds a "Night of 1,000 Stevies" each year, when thousands of men and women pay tribute to the woman and her style by emulating her dress and gestures.) Buckingham self-produced two albums, *Law and Order* and *Go Insane*, during this period as well, and Christine McVie made a self-titled album.

Continuing tensions and creative dissention caused Buckingham to leave after the *Tango in the Night* (1987) album, and Nicks and Christine McVie followed not long after. As he had in the past, Fleetwood again scouted out new talent to keep the band going: Bekka Bramlett, Billy Burnette, and Rick Vito toured and recorded with the band's founders, but the *Rumours* lineup rejoined to perform "Don't Stop" at President Bill Clinton's inauguration gala in 1993 and continued to flirt with group projects, culminating in a CD, tour, and video called *The Dance* in 1998. Although Christine McVie left the band in 1998, Fleetwood Mac continued to record, producing the popular album *Say You Will* (2003), followed by a successful world tour. The "Unleashed" tour of 2009, though not associated with an album, was also successful internationally. Fleetwood Mac, which remains one of the most influential and beloved American rock bands, was inaugurated into the Rock and Roll Hall of Fame in 1998.

Celia White

SEE ALSO: *Blues; Pop Music; Rock and Roll.*

BIBLIOGRAPHY

Brackett, Donald. *Fleetwood Mac: 40 Years of Creative Chaos.* Westport, CT: Praeger, 2007.

Carr, Roy, and Steve Clarke. *Fleetwood Mac: Rumours n' Fax.* New York: Harmony Books, 1978.

Fleetwood, Mick, and Stephen Davis. *Fleetwood: My Life and Adventures in Fleetwood Mac.* New York: Morrow, 1990.

Furman, Leah. *Rumours Exposed: The Unauthorized Biography of Fleetwood Mac.* New York: Citadel Press, 2000.

Graham, Samuel. *Fleetwood Mac: The Authorized History.* New York: Warner Books, 1978.

Fleming, Ian *(1908–1964)*

Writer Ian Fleming created one of the major male icons of the second half of the twentieth century, the spy James Bond. As Alan Barnes suggests in *Kiss Kiss Bang! Bang!: The Unofficial James Bond Film Companion*, Bond is "the only fictional character of the 20th century to have acquired the aura of myth." The series of novels featuring the character not only concocted a new heroic figure, but their immense success and popularity (Fleming had sold thirty million books by the time of his death) kick-started indigenous spy writing in America. Bond on film was also hugely successful, adding to the luster of the spy and increasing the popularity of British music and cinema in 1960s America.

Fleming was the son of a major and member of the British Parliament and younger brother of author Peter Fleming. His English background was privileged and reflected the expected route of one of his class (Eton, Sandhurst, a job in the "City") rather than the adventurous spirit of his most famous creation. It was Fleming's periods as a journalist in Moscow at the beginning and end of the 1930s, along with his work in World War II as a high-ranking officer in naval intelligence, that provided much of the background for the novels. Fleming was in his forties when he began his writing career with *Casino Royale* in 1953, followed by ten more Bond novels (the best of which were written in the 1950s) and two collections of short stories. Fleming also wrote a column under the pseudonym Atticus for the London *Sunday Times* in the 1950s and contributed to other magazines.

The plots of the Bond stories reflect the heritage of the previous half century of British popular spy and thriller writing. Fleming laid out "the right ingredients" for these works in *Dr. No* (1958): "physical exertion, mystery and a ruthless enemy . . . a good companion" and a certainty that the "cause was just." The Bond character was based on a number of soldiers and agents Fleming knew during the war, but the author, as quoted in Andrew Lycett's biography, wanted the character to be "unobtrusive": "Exotic things would happen to and around him, but he would be a neutral figure—an anonymous blunt instrument wielded by a government department."

Bond's enemies and their conspiracies took their power from an almost mythical badness, and the battles were more parables of good and evil than political thrillers. Yet Fleming covered these parables with a veneer of reality, which, in its intensity, was perhaps his biggest influence on the genre. His prose closely depicts many of the most attractive and expensive places in the world, from beautiful islands to expensive restaurants. He also describes in detail the possessions of the rich and successful, whether they be the most reliable guns or smoothest cigarettes, the finest car or best mixed cocktail. Comparable to this closely described visible consumption was the depiction of women, built to *Playboy* specifications, whom Bond seduced, bedded, and discarded with astonishing ease. There was something of the *Playboy* philosophy to Fleming's novels, of men as adventurous and potent while still at ease with consumer society.

Fleming's work did much to change attitudes toward the figure of the spy in American culture. Bond was praised by John F. Kennedy and recommended by Allen Dulles, head of the Central Intelligence Agency (CIA). The character made the spy acceptable, shifted the perception from 1950s associations with the Rosenbergs and muddied the moral problems the spy had always held in the American psyche. Bond was a very English figure, of class and with imperial concerns, but he was also an international, professional figure fighting evil. As America moved to the forefront of world politics, its own intelligence service could be drawn in such a light—an international, professional movement against evil.

The Bond novels reflect a moment in time after World War II, beyond rationing in Britain and beyond the darkest days of the Cold War in America when tourism, visible consumption, and sexual freedom came to the fore. It was at this point in the early 1960s that they made it onto the screen. Cubby Broccoli, producer of the majority of the Bond movies, pinpoints the strengths Fleming's work offered in his biography *When the Snow Melts*: "a virile and resourceful hero, exotic locations, the ingenious apparatus of espionage and sex on a fairly sophisticated level." It was these elements that would sell the films as the racism and misogyny (in their most extreme forms) and much of Fleming's British imperial nostalgia were sloughed off. Bond, as a character, was fleshed out by Sean Connery into a less one-dimensional personality with a more attractive and humorous rebelliousness.

Dr. No, the initial film, came out in 1962, quickly followed by *From Russia with Love* (1963) and *Goldfinger* (1964). These films showed the British industry turning away from the "kitchen sink" dramas of the previous few years to more slick and upbeat movies that were enormous commercial successes in America, where interest in British pop music and culture was growing. *Dr. No* had been made cheaply, but a great deal of American money was pumped into its sequels—money well spent, as the series became successful on an increasingly global scale.

Kyle Smith

SEE ALSO: *Best Sellers; Cold War; James Bond Films;* Playboy; *Watergate.*

BIBLIOGRAPHY

Barnes, Alan, and Marcus Hearn. *Kiss Kiss Bang! Bang!: The Unofficial James Bond Film Companion.* London: Batsford, 1997.

Broccoli, Albert R. (Cubby), and Donald Zec. *When the Snow Melts: The Autobiography of Cubby Broccoli.* London: Boxtree/Macmillan, 1998.

Lycett, Andrew. *Ian Fleming.* London: Weidenfield & Nicholson, 1995.

Slifkin, Irv. *VideoHound's Groovy Movies: Far-Out Films of the Psychedelic Era.* Detroit, MI: Visible Ink, 2004.

Fleming, Peggy *(1948–)*

Peggy Fleming remains one of the best-known and most widely respected American figure skaters in history. After an outstanding amateur career capped by her winning the 1968 Olympic Ladies' Figure Skating gold medal at Grenoble, France, she

Peggy Fleming at 1968 Olympics. *Peggy Fleming practices her routine at an outdoor rink at the 1968 Winter Olympics in Grenoble, France. Her gold medal was the only one that was won by the U.S. women's figure skating Olympic team at those games.* **STAFF/AFP/GETTY IMAGES.**

embarked on a career as a professional skater, signing first with the Ice Follies and then pioneering as a solo act on television specials when the professional skating field was largely limited to ice shows. Corporate endorsements were minute compared to the enormous financial rewards available to most competitors today, but Fleming broke new ground here too, becoming the spokesperson for at least thirty sponsors during her career. In 1981 she became an anchor on ABC Television's figure-skating coverage, usually paired with Dick Button, two-time men's Olympic champion and skating entrepreneur. Known for her poise, elegance, and professionalism, Fleming has maintained a presence in the world of figure skating since the 1960s and has been an inspiration for generations of skaters.

Peggy Gale Fleming was born July 27, 1948, in San Jose, California, the second of four daughters. The Fleming family was often short on cash, and one summer the entire family had to camp out in Oregon while her father worked. Fleming began skating at the age of nine and won her first competition at ten. Her mother, Doris, described by Button as forceful and domineering, was considered the quintessential skating mother. She pushed her daughter to excel, making all her costumes, driving her to practices, grilling her coaches, and generally managing her career. Her father, Al, a newspaper pressman, strongly believed that a working-class girl like Peggy could succeed in a sport of the well-to-do. Fleming's family moved constantly to support her career. Many skaters might not have done well with such an unsettled lifestyle, but Fleming seemed to thrive on it.

PROPELLED INTO THE SPOTLIGHT

In 1961 an unprecedented tragedy in the sports world pushed Fleming to the forefront of skating: a plane carrying the entire U.S. Figure Skating Team crashed near Brussels, killing all aboard, including Fleming's coach. Fleming was soon noticed as an up-and-coming competitor, and in 1964 she had a stunning victory at the U.S. National Figure Skating Championships. At the age of fifteen, she was suddenly propelled into the international spotlight when she headed the American team at the Olympics in Innsbruck, Austria. Fleming placed sixth, performing with a high fever but gaining invaluable experience on the world stage.

After the Olympics, Doris sought a top-notch coach for her daughter and selected Carlo Fassi, whom she believed would help Fleming with "school figures"—the grueling and precise art of tracing figures in the ice. At that time this kind of technical skating made up a major part of a skater's marks in competitions. Fassi and Fleming proved to be a perfect match in every respect—a coach of rare ability and artistic refinement, he brought out the best in her. Fleming continued to improve and won every title in her progress toward the 1968 Olympics in Grenoble. In a major upset, she became world champion in 1966 and retained her national and world titles in 1967.

Grenoble was the pinnacle of her amateur career—in a chartreuse costume that Doris had sewed, Fleming won the gold medal (the only one for the United States in those Winter Games). Known for a balletic style that incorporated superior jumps with graceful moves, such as her trademark layback spin (the pose made famous by a well-known Olympic photo), Fleming achieved a new level of excellence that has been approached by few skaters, such as Dorothy Hamill, Kristi Yamaguchi, and Michelle Kwan.

Fleming attained tremendous popularity and was almost immediately signed to make television skating specials, which drew critical approval and high ratings—her Sun Valley special won two Emmy Awards. *Peggy Fleming in the Soviet Union* (1974), a cooperative venture between the United States and the Soviet Union, made history as a television first. Fleming's professional success was important far beyond skating; she was arguably the first female sports superstar in history. In 1994 *Sports Illustrated* named her one of "40 for the Ages": "40 individuals who have most significantly altered or elevated the world of sports in the last 40 years."

PERSONAL HIGHS AND LOWS

Fleming's private life has been quietly successful as well. She met Dr. Greg Jenkins, her future husband, when both were pupils of Fassi. They married in 1970, and she gave birth to two sons, Andy (born 1977) and Todd (born 1988). She managed to remain active as a skater without significant interruption to her family life. Although her relationship with her mother was often strained by Doris's need to control her daughter's life, she speaks with great affection of both her parents, now deceased. Her father died at forty-one of a heart attack shortly after driving across country to see his daughter perform after capturing a world title.

Fleming made news on the eve of the Michelle Kwan–Tara Lipinski battle for the Olympic gold medal in 1998. Diagnosed with breast cancer, she withdrew from her commentator duties for ABC and had successful surgery and chemotherapy. Immediately she began to speak out on breast cancer awareness; her self-detection and candor about her experience have motivated a noticeable increase in women seeking medical attention. In addition, she has worked for numerous charities (March of Dimes, Osteoporosis Foundation, Kidney Foundation) throughout her career.

Mary Hess

SEE ALSO: *Hamill, Dorothy; Ice Shows; Kwan, Michelle; Olympics; Skating; Sports Heroes;* Sports Illustrated.

BIBLIOGRAPHY

Brennan, Christie. *Inside Edge: A Revealing Journey into the Secret World of Figure Skating.* New York: Anchor Books, 1997.

Guthrie, Patricia. "Fleming Speaks Out on Breast Cancer." *Atlanta Journal and Constitution*, October 8, 1998.

Hiestand, Michael. "Cancer Surgery Can't Ruin Fleming's Upbeat Outlook." *USA Today*, February 18, 1998.

Hines, James R. *Historical Dictionary of Figure Skating.* Lanham, MD: Scarecrow Press, 2011.

Lessa, Christina, ed. *Women Who Win: Stories of Triumph in Sport and Life.* New York: Universe Publishing, 1998.

U.S. Figure Skating Association. *The Official Book of Figure Skating.* New York: Simon & Schuster, 1998.

Vecsey, George. "New Role in Sports for Peggy Fleming." *New York Times*, September 6, 1981.

The Flintstones

Every prime-time animated television series traces its lineage back to *The Flintstones*, the first show to disprove the notion that cartoons are suited only for children. From 1960 to 1966, the comical adventures of the stone-age Flintstone family unfolded weekly on ABC. Essentially a prehistoric version of *The Honeymooners*, the program revolved around Fred Flintstone, an irascible blowhard (voiced by Alan Reed), his pliant pal Barney Rubble (voiced by Mel Blanc), and their long-suffering spouses, Wilma and Betty. Cartoon veterans William Hanna and Joseph Barbera produced the cheaply animated half hour.

A live-action movie version, starring John Goodman as Fred and Rosie O'Donnell as Betty, was produced in 1994, but was not as popular with audiences as the original cartoon, and a follow-up film, *The Flintstones in Viva Rock Vegas*, was released in 2000. *The Flintstones* was syndicated on Cartoon Network from 1992 until 2004 and began to be broadcast again in January 2012. As well as serving as a model for the next generations of family-based animated television shows such as *The Simpsons* and *Family Guy*, in the early twenty-first century *The Flintstones* remained one of the most popular and beloved cartoons of all time.

Robert E. Schnakenberg

SEE ALSO: *Blanc, Mel;* Family Guy*; Hanna-Barbera;* The Honeymooners*; O'Donnell, Rosie; Saturday Morning Cartoons;* The Simpsons*; Sitcom.*

BIBLIOGRAPHY

Adams, T. R. *"The Flintstones": A Modern Stone Age Phenomenon*. Atlanta: Turner Publishing, 1994.

Lenburg, Jeff. *William Hanna and Joseph Barbera: The Sultans of Saturday Morning*. New York: Chelsea House, 2011.

Flip-Flops

Cheap, lightweight, and often brightly colored, flip-flops are a vktype of sandal with a sole of polyurethane rubber, a band over the front of the foot, and a thong between the big toe and the adjacent toe. Because flip-flops have no heel strap, they make a slapping sound against the foot when the wearer is walking. The unique sandals are commonly used around swimming pools, at sports facilities, and on beaches because they are simple to put on and take off and are easily rinsed. In developed countries flip-flops are so cheap that they are usually considered disposable, but in less affluent regions they are frequently repaired, modified, or constructed from alternative materials such as car tires, wood, rope, or leather.

There is some dispute over the origin of flip-flops. They first appeared in the United States after World War II, when designers copied traditional sandal designs from the Asian Pacific region. Some claim that English businessman John Cowie was the first to manufacture the Japanese-style sandals from plastic and rubber, which he produced in Hong Kong in the late 1940s. However, New Zealander Morris Yock first patented the modern flip-flop design, using plastic and rubber, in 1957. The open-toed shoes became known in New Zealand as *jandals*, a combination of *Japanese* and *sandals*.

Jandals quickly became a central feature of New Zealand's surf and beach culture. Soon they spread to other parts of the world where water sports were popular. In Australia the sandals became known as thongs, and in the burgeoning California surfing culture of the 1950s, they became known as flip-flops. The ubiquity of flip-flops has linked them to leisure and relaxation. For this reason they are generally considered unacceptable in formal situations. In 2005 the Northwestern University lacrosse team was widely criticized for wearing the minimalist sandal during a meeting with President George W. Bush.

The low cost and customizability of flip-flops make them popular options for sports team branding and other promotional uses. However, long-term wear of flip-flops can put stress on parts of the foot, ankle, hip, and lower back. For this reason elite athletes are often forbidden from wearing them. Moreover, because of the lack of foot support flip-flops afford, children may be susceptible to injuries or even permanent damage from prolonged wearing. Some sportswear manufacturers have attempted to improve the footwear by creating contoured soles to increase comfort. Nevertheless, no matter where they are made or worn, the basic design remains the same.

Chris Routledge

SEE ALSO: *College Fads; Swimming Pools; World War II.*

BIBLIOGRAPHY

"New Claims Rock Jandal Orthodoxy." *Stuff*, January 1, 2009. Accessed May 2012. Available from http://www.stuff.co.nz/oddstuff/146213

Ward, Julie. "Next Big Step in Team Spirit: Flip Flops." *USA Today*, September 13, 2005. Accessed May 2012. Available from http://www.usatoday.com/sports/2005-09-13-flip-flops_x.htm

Flipper

The bottlenose dolphin star of two 1960s feature films, a television series from 1964 to 1967, and a 1996 film revival, Flipper educated Americans about the intelligence, loyalty, and compassion toward humans that characterizes the several dolphin species. Flipper rescued people from perilous situations, fought sharks, and warned individuals about impending dangers. Through Flipper, viewers were entertained by an unusual animal friend with a built-in smile and were made aware of a dolphin's ability to communicate with and respond to people.

Flipper was born of the vision of movie and television underwater stuntman Ricou Browning. While watching *Lassie* on television with his children, Browning was inspired to invent an underwater counterpart to the courageous collie and wrote a story about a boy and a dolphin named Flipper. He offered the property to Ivan Tors, the producer of the successful television series *Sea Hunt* (1958–1961). Tors was fascinated by the idea and agreed to produce a feature film.

Browning acquired a dolphin named Mitzi and began training her for the stunts in the film, which included having a boy ride on her back. The training for this stunt required Browning to get into the water with the dolphin, a technique that was highly unusual for the time—trainers who worked with dolphins generally remained outside the water. Browning discovered, however, that being in the water with Mitzi seemed to accelerate her learning process.

Flipper. *Television's Flipper was played at first by a female dolphin named Suzy, then by another female named Kathy, and occasionally by other females named Patty, Scotty, and Squirt.* NBC TELEVISION/ COURTESY OF GETTY IMAGES.

The stunt that required Mitzi to carry a boy on her back was one that gave her the most difficulty. Browning finally overcame the problem by employing a variation of the retrieving behavior with the assistance of his son, Ricky. He picked up Ricky, commanded Mitzi to fetch, and then threw the boy into the water near the dock where the training session was being conducted. After several attempts, Mitzi grabbed Ricky, he took hold of her fins, and she pulled him back to Browning. The trainer was thrilled that his dolphin had been able to master this routine, which had been considered to be an impossible feat.

Mitzi starred, with Luke Halpin as the boy, in the feature film *Flipper* (1963) and in the sequel, *Flipper's New Adventures* (1964), both filmed in the Bahamas. The commercial success of the movies led to the television series, *Flipper* (1964–1967), which aired on NBC, starring Brian Kelly as Porter Ricks, a ranger in Coral Key Park, Florida; Halpin as his elder son, Sandy; and Tommy Norden as his younger son, Bud. The episodes related the adventures of the boys and their aquatic pet, who rescued them from many dangerous situations.

A dolphin named Suzy was selected as the lead dolphin for the television series, and she quickly learned the thirty-five to forty behaviors necessary for any script circumstance. However, some behaviors she seemed to exercise on her own. For example, before diving with Suzy, Halpin gulped air from the surface then plunged beneath the water, holding onto the dolphin as she swam toward the bottom. The actor noticed that whenever he needed more air, Suzy returned to the surface. Since she repeated this behavior regularly, Halpin concluded that Suzy's keen hearing and sonar ability probably allowed her to monitor his heart and respiration rates and thus know when the boy needed air. Offscreen, Suzy demonstrated a newly learned trick to producer Tors. While visiting the set, Tors walked down to the dock and greeted Suzy, who returned the courtesy by squirting water on his shoes.

Flipper enthralled, entertained, and enlightened millions. For three consecutive years from 1965 to 1967 Flipper was honored with three PATSY Awards (Performing Animal Top Stars of the Year), the animal equivalent of the Academy Awards, given by the American Humane Association. The Flipper idea was revived in the 1990s—as part of a general revival of television shows from the 1960s—with the movie *Flipper* (1996) and the television series of the same name (1995). The Flipper legacy lives on in increased interest, awareness, and concern for dolphins.

Pauline Bartel

SEE ALSO: *Lassie; Television.*

BIBLIOGRAPHY

Annino, Jan Godown. *Florida's Famous Animals.* Guildford, CT: Globe Pequot Press, 2008.

Brooks, Tim, and Earle Marsh. *The Complete Directory to Prime Time Network and Cable TV Shows 1946–Present,* 6th ed. New York: Ballantine Books, 1995.

Edelson, Edward. *Great Animals of the Movies.* Garden City, NJ: Doubleday, 1980.

Paietta, Ann C., and Jean L. Kauppila. *Animals on Screen and Radio: An Annotated Sourcebook.* Metuchen, NJ: Scarecrow Press, 1994.

Rothel, David. *Great Show Business Animals.* San Diego, CA: A. S. Barnes, 1980.

Terrace, Vincent. *Encyclopedia of Television Series, Pilots, and Specials 1937–1973.* New York: Zoetrope, 1986.

The Flying Nun

Julie Andrews, Whoopi Goldberg, and Mary Tyler Moore all portrayed nuns on the big screen, but the most famous TV nun was played by Sally Field, much to her chagrin. The sitcom *The Flying Nun* soared on ABC from 1967 to 1970, bringing viewers a concept that still seems ridiculous years later.

Sister Bertrille (Field) is a bubbly, young, ninety-pound novice at the ancient Convent San Tanco, which sits on a hilltop in Puerto Rico. Whenever a stiff wind catches the starched cornette worn by her order, Bertrille is lifted into the air, becoming the "flying nun." The convent's conservative Mother Superior, the Reverend Mother Placido (Madeleine Sherwood), isn't too impressed, but Sister Bertrille does get along well with wise and humorous Sister Jacqueline (Marge Redmond) and Sister Sixto (Shelley Morrison), a Puerto Rican nun who has trouble with English. And because even a show about nuns needs to have a little sex appeal, Bertrille is admired from a distance by Carlos Ramirez (Alejandro Rey), who is a wealthy and handsome playboy, the owner of a discotheque in town, and a patron of the convent.

Bertrille's avian ability gets her into some hot water, sometimes literally: she is occasionally dunked into the ocean.

Once she is almost shot down because she is mistaken for an enemy aircraft; another time a pelican falls in love with her. The character takes it all in sunny stride, but Field was anything but sunny about this role, as she explained to *Playboy* in 1986:

> In *Gidget*, I had things to play, scenes with fathers and people; here I had nothing. Just complete silliness—someone got into the convent who shouldn't have and we'd have to hide him. . . . There were no life problems going on, nothing I could relate to. It made no sense to me. I started refusing press interviews and getting a bad reputation. But I couldn't go and hype the show, saying, 'I'm having such a good time' when I wanted to say, 'Let me out of here!' *Flying Nun* was a one-joke show, and I don't know why it was successful.

Field took the role because she was a teenager and believed she'd never work again after *Gidget* made her, or at least her character, the butt of jokes. Comics such as Bob Hope had a field day with *The Flying Nun*, making cracks about the series and turning all of the standard nun jokes into flying-nun jokes. Besides being hurt by the jibes and feeling the ennui of an actor with no challenges, Field had another problem during her holy tenure: she was pregnant with her first child. During filming, she had to carry books in front of herself to hide her growing midsection.

The role did, however, produce one positive result for Field: castmate Sherwood took her to the Actors Studio, where she honed her craft with the likes of Ellen Burstyn, Jack Nicholson, Sally Kellerman, Bruce Dern, and Lee Strasberg. "It changed my life," she said in *Playboy*. "I found a place where I could go and create." However, before Field left the world of light, gimmicky sitcom fare to begin her career as an Academy Award–winning actress, she completed her wacky TV trilogy with *The Girl with Something Extra* (1973–1974), in which her character has ESP.

Not everyone hated *The Flying Nun* as much as Field; after all, it did last three years. In a 1996 article in *Psychology Today*, Will Miller writes, "This show is actually a provocative lesson about personal power. . . . This show says, if you'll stop resisting the environment, if you'll only attune yourself to nature, to the direction and flow of the world's winds, you too can fly!" *The Flying Nun* was also commended by religious orders for "humanizing nuns and their work." The series was based on the book *The Fifteenth Pelican* (1965) by Tere Ríos.

Karen Lurie

SEE ALSO: *Field, Sally; Nicholson, Jack; Sitcom; Television.*

BIBLIOGRAPHY

Brooks, Tim, and Earle Marsh. *The Complete Directory to Prime Time Network and Cable TV Shows, 1946–Present*, 6th ed. New York: Ballantine Books, 1995.

McNeil, Alex. *Total Television*. New York: Penguin, 1996.

Miller, Will. "Mental TV." *Psychology Today*, November–December 1996, 56.

Nelson, Craig. *Bad TV*. New York: Dell, 1995.

"Playboy Interview: Sally Field." *Playboy*, March 1986.

Flynn, Errol *(1909–1959)*

Errol Flynn's place in popular culture was assured equally by fame and notoriety. A heroic swashbuckler on-screen, seducing audiences with his fresh charm, devil-may-care personality, athleticism, and dazzling good looks, he scandalized the public and his peers with his private exploits. A boon to gossip columnists he undoubtedly was, but while they charted his barroom brawls and questionable boudoir escapades (which gave the English language the expression "In like Flynn"), he steadily disintegrated, dying of drink, drugs, and despair at the age of fifty.

From an early age, Flynn's nature—adventurous, reckless, unstable—was evident. Born into a comfortable and well-educated family in Hobart, Tasmania, Australia, he was expelled more than once from the good schools to which he was sent and became a shipping clerk at the age of seventeen. He had an affinity with boats and sailing and, still in his midteens, went wandering in search of gold. At twenty-one he bought a boat in which he made a seven-month journey to New Guinea, where he worked on a tobacco plantation and became a correspondent for an Australian newspaper. Back in Sydney, his looks brought an offer to play Fletcher Christian in a semidocumentary film (*In the Wake of the Bounty*, 1933), and there he caught the acting bug. Flynn went to England, joined a provincial repertory company, and played the lead in a "B" picture, which led to a contract with Warner Brothers.

Flynn arrived in Hollywood in 1935, married actress Lili Damita, and made brief appearances in a couple of low-budget

Errol Flynn. *Errol Flynn was known as much for his dashing on-screen persona as he was for his scandalous personal life.* GEORGE HURRELL/JOHN KOBAL FOUNDATION/GETTY IMAGES.

movies. Before the year was out, he played *Captain Blood*, surgeon-turned-pirate during the reign of James II, and became a star. This first foray into swashbuckling adventure demonstrated his grace and agility in wielding a sword, notably in a brilliant duel with Basil Rathbone's villain, and the public responded favorably to the combination of Flynn and then-relative newcomer Olivia de Havilland. Backed by a stirring score from composer Erich Korngold, Warner Brothers' experienced craftsman Michael Curtiz directed with panache.

The studio was quick to grasp that they had found a winning formula and the natural heir to Douglas Fairbanks Sr. De Havilland costarred with Flynn in another eight films, and, more significantly, Curtiz directed him in a further ten, beginning with *The Charge of the Light Brigade* (1936) and ending with *Dive Bomber* (1941). These included the actor's first Western, *Dodge City*, and the same year—1939—*The Private Lives of Elizabeth and Essex*, in which Flynn, bravado substituting for skill and experience, played second fiddle to Bette Davis's awesome Virgin Queen. He was never a great actor and his range was limited, but when the beguiling personality matched well with the vehicle, it did not seem to matter. Such was the case with the most memorable of the Curtiz collaborations, *The Adventures of Robin Hood* (1938). Indeed, the film endures as a classic in its own right, distinguished by outstanding Technicolor and Academy Award–winning design, a host of marvelous supporting performances, and what David Thomson aptly calls Flynn's "galvanizing energy" and "cheerful gaiety." It is as Robin Hood—handsome, dashing, brave, and humorous—that Flynn is, and should be, best remembered.

Many commentators consider that the actor owed much of his success to the good fortune of being assigned first to Curtiz, then to the more serious-minded Raoul Walsh. They made seven films together, beginning with *They Died with Their Boots On* (1941), in which the star was a sympathetic General Custer, and including what is arguably his best performance, as prizefighter *Gentleman Jim* (1942). *Objective Burma* (1945), however, gave much offense to the British for creating the impression that the Americans single-handedly conquered the Japanese in Burma, and Flynn, although winningly portraying the heroic leader of a crucial and life-endangering mission, already looked weary and older than his years.

In truth, his notoriety had been rising in direct proportion to his stardom. He was tried, and eventually acquitted, for the rape of two teenage girls in 1942, the year he was divorced from Damita (by whom he had a son). In 1943 he married Nora Eddington (they divorced in 1949, and he married Patrice Wymore in 1950); meanwhile, his heavy drinking and smoking was on the increase, and he began experimenting with drugs.

From the late 1940s Flynn's life and career reflected a downward slide. Weary of swashbuckling and looking for new directions in his work, he left Hollywood for Europe in 1952, played in several films probably best forgotten, and bankrupted himself in a failed attempt to finance a production of *William Tell*. He sailed around aimlessly in his yacht, returning to Hollywood in 1956, a ravaged shadow of his former self, to face the final irony of his self-destruction: praise for his performance as a drunken wastrel in *The Sun Also Rises* (1957). He played two more drunks the following year—in *Too Much, Too Soon* (as John Barrymore) and in John Huston's *The Roots of Heaven*—and ended his career, shortly before his death, with the nadir of his achievements, a semi-documentary about Fidel Castro called *Cuban Rebel Girls*, which he wrote, coproduced, and narrated.

In the 2004 Oscar-winning film *The Aviator* (directed by Martin Scorsese), which depicts Hollywood life in the 1930s and 1940s through the eyes of film magnate Howard Hughes, Flynn was played by British actor Jude Law.

Robyn Karney

SEE ALSO: *Barrymore, John; Celebrity; Davis, Bette; Hughes, Howard; Huston, John; Movie Stars;* Mutiny on the Bounty; *Scorsese, Martin; Sex Scandals.*

BIBLIOGRAPHY

Flynn, Errol. *My Wicked, Wicked Ways*. New York: G. P. Putnam's Sons, 1959.

Godfrey, Lionel. *The Life and Crimes of Errol Flynn*. New York: St. Martin's, 1977.

McNulty, Thomas. *Errol Flynn: The Life and Career*. Jefferson, NC: McFarland, 2004.

Thomas, Tony; Rudy Behlmer; and Clifford McCarty. *The Films of Errol Flynn*. New York: Citadel, 1969.

Thomson, David. *The New Biographical Dictionary of Film*. New York: Knopf, 2002.

Flynt, Larry

SEE: *Hustler*.

The Foggy Mountain Boys

Created in 1948 by Lester Flatt and Earl Scruggs, the Foggy Mountain Boys were one of bluegrass music's most popular acts, introducing millions of listeners to the style through their association with well-known movies and television shows in the 1950s and 1960s. Though the act's full name was Flatt and Scruggs and the Foggy Mountain Boys, they were widely referred to as Flatt and Scruggs, as the two coleaders were the sole permanent members of the band during its almost twenty-year existence.

GRAND OLE OPRY

The Foggy Mountain Boys' first recordings were made shortly after Flatt and Scruggs left Bill Monroe's Blue Grass Boys in 1948. In the space of little more than a year, they created twenty-eight of the most influential and enduring songs in the style, virtually all of which have become standards. With John Ray "Curly" Seckler singing tenor harmony to Flatt's genial lead vocals and Scruggs providing the lower, baritone harmony part, the band sought to distinguish itself from Monroe's by downplaying the role of his instrument, the mandolin, and instead featuring Scruggs's dazzling banjo picking and the work of a succession of fiddlers, including Benny Sims, "Chubby" Wise, "Howdy" Forrester, and Benny Martin. Whereas Monroe's sacred ("gospel") songs were performed with spare backing featuring the mandolin, Flatt and Scruggs opted to retain the full band's sound, with the substitution of Scruggs's bluesy, finger-picked lead guitar for his banjo. Working for a succession of radio stations in places such as Danville, Virginia; Bristol, Tennessee; Atlanta, Georgia; and Versailles, Kentucky, they quickly built a devoted following that made them an attractive acquisition for Columbia, on whose label they joined in 1950 and remained for the duration of the band's career.

While the Foggy Mountain Boys scored their first charting record in 1952, "'Tis Sweet to Be Remembered," their real breakthrough came when Martha White Mills signed on as their sponsor, a relationship that was to continue for as long as the band existed. The deal gave Flatt and Scruggs an early morning show on Nashville's WSM, the radio home of the Grand Ole Opry. The program began in the spring of 1953 and led to regular weekly appearances on a Martha White–sponsored portion of the Opry, as well as a series of television shows that aired in cities around the south. Together with a busy touring schedule and regular recording sessions and releases, these appearances kept the Foggy Mountain Boys before an increasingly devoted audience, while the security of their Martha White sponsorship allowed them to retain a relatively stable lineup—Paul Warren on fiddle, Burkett "Uncle Josh" Graves on dobro (resonator guitar), Seckler and English "Jake" Tullock on string bass—at a time when other bluegrass acts were suffering the economic effects of the rock-and-roll boom of the late 1950s.

SURVIVING ROCK AND ROLL

Indeed, Flatt and Scruggs defied conventional wisdom by achieving their greatest success during a period when many country and bluegrass acts were suffering hard times. On the one hand, their increasingly sophisticated recorded sound—often augmented by drums, additional guitars, and other instruments—found favor on the country charts (they placed numerous singles in the Top 40 between 1959 and 1962). On the other hand, Scruggs's brilliance on the banjo brought the act attention from the growing numbers of urban folk revival enthusiasts, which was carefully tended to by his wife, Louise. The greatest boost to their popularity, however, was their recording of the theme song for television's *Beverly Hillbillies*, which spent three weeks at the top of the country charts and exposed millions of viewers to their music; Scruggs and Flatt even made several guest appearances on the show. When they appeared at Carnegie Hall in New York the same week in December 1962 that "The Ballad of Jed Clampett" reached number one, it was apparent that the Foggy Mountain Boys had reached hitherto unattained heights of popularity for a bluegrass act.

From then on, the band led what amounted to a double life, aiming single records at country radio and LPs at the folk audience and making appearances at both folk and country venues, including at the prestigious and increasingly well-attended Newport Folk Festivals in the mid-1960s. Though the strategy worked well from a commercial point of view, many of their fans were dismayed by the resultant changes to their music, which drew increasingly from the folk realm—both older, traditional numbers as well as songs written by newer, urban folk artists such as Bob Dylan. The Foggy Mountain Boys' sound moved increasingly in the direction of folk-rock, with an ever-growing number of studio musicians playing a prominent role in their recordings; the change was further sharpened as Scruggs, encouraged by his teenage sons, began to develop a greater interest in contemporary popular styles, while Flatt yearned for a return to the more countrified, strictly bluegrass sound of the 1950s and early 1960s editions of the band.

TRADITION VS. EXPERIMENTATION

By 1969, despite even greater popularity resulting from the prominent use of their "Foggy Mountain Breakdown" as background music in the movie *Bonnie and Clyde*, both Flatt and Scruggs were unwilling to maintain their association, and the Foggy Mountain Boys disbanded shortly after Scruggs's appearance with his sons at an anti–Vietnam War demonstration in Washington, D.C. Both of the leaders established their own groups: Flatt formed the Nashville Grass, with a more traditional sound, and Scruggs created the Earl Scruggs Revue with his sons and other young musicians interested in a bluegrass-rock hybrid. The Foggy Mountain Boys passed into history. The band's reputation, tarnished by the end, rebounded as their earlier recordings were reissued, and their influence has proven to be both immense and enduring; most of the recordings from the band's first fifteen years of existence have become staples of the bluegrass repertoire, and virtually no bluegrass festival takes place without the performance of a healthy number of the Foggy Mountain Boys' classic songs.

Flatt and Scruggs were inducted into the Country Music Hall of Fame in 1985. Flatt had passed away in 1979, and Scruggs later said that it was his own need to experiment that had caused their breakup but that there were no hard feelings. The Coen brothers' 2000 film *O Brother, Where Art Thou?* made reference to the Foggy Mountain Boys when the jailbird characters, led by actor George Clooney, formed a band called the Soggy Bottom Boys that, though comical, helped to make the film's soundtrack an unexpected success. In 2005 Flatt and Scruggs's 1949 signature song, "Foggy Mountain Breakdown," became part of the Library of Congress National Recording Registry. Scruggs passed away in 2012 at the age of eighty-eight.

Jon Weisberger

SEE ALSO: The Beverly Hillbillies; *Bluegrass; Clooney, George; Coen, Joel and Ethan; Country Music; Dylan, Bob; Flatt, Lester; Monroe, Bill; Newport Jazz and Folk Festivals; Scruggs, Earl; Vietnam.*

BIBLIOGRAPHY

Cantwell, Robert. *Bluegrass Breakdown: The Making of the Old Southern Sound.* Urbana: University of Illinois Press, 1984.

Kochman, Marilyn, ed. *The Big Book of Bluegrass.* New York: William Morrow, 1984.

Rosenberg, Neil V. *Bluegrass: A History.* Urbana: University of Illinois Press, 1985.

Willis, Barry R. *America's Music, Bluegrass.* Franktown, CO: Pine Valley Music, 1992.

Folk Music

Before the twentieth century, a dichotomy prevailed between cultivated music (by educated, formally trained musicians and composers) and folk music (by everyone else). Cultivated music was created by and for the upper classes and was taught and transmitted within a written tradition, whereas folk music was created by and for the lower classes and was transmitted orally. Since folk songs were remembered rather than written down, they changed over time—sometimes gradually over centuries, sometimes all at once at the hands of a particularly innovative interpreter. The changes might have been accidental, resulting

Peter, Paul, and Mary. *The folk trio Peter, Paul, and Mary became popular during the folk-music revival of the 1960s.* OWEN FRANKEN/ARCHIVE PHOTOS/GETTY IMAGES.

from a lapse of memory, or a deliberate improvement. This communal re-creation is one of the defining characteristics of folk music.

Whereas the names of great classical composers were transmitted in the written tradition along with their compositions, traditional folk songs are anonymous. Cultivated music had to please the wealthy patron who paid the composer, but a folk song had to appeal to the entire community in order to survive over generations. Thus, cultivated music was aristocratic and folk music was communal. Each reflected its audience's values: cultivated music was often quite complex and required specialized musicians who were hired to perform it; folk songs remained simple so that anyone could memorize, sing, or play them.

An innovation that compromised the oral nature of folk music was the broadside. Broadsides were lyrics printed on large sheets of paper and sold at the marketplace. There was often an instruction to sing the lyrics to the tune of a well-established song. This introduced a degree of literacy to folk music, and many "broadside ballads" exhibit literary qualities. However, the major change that permanently affected folk music was the advent of mass media. Records, movies, radio, and television all gave rise to popular music that was accessible to everyone from coast to coast. Individuals were able to become rich, or at least make a living, by performing music that appealed to millions of people. This has caused difficulty for musicologists in defining folk music. Popularity itself does not disqualify a song as folk music, but some musicologists claim that it ceases to be folk when it conforms to mainstream styles and tastes.

There are very few communities today that are unaffected by mainstream culture. One may be immersed in his or her own regional or ethnic tradition, but hardly anyone is completely sheltered from mass media. Consequently, individual traditions have shed their particularities and conformed to mainstream tastes. Folk has given way to folk rock and folk pop. The same can be said of blues, bluegrass, and country. These were originally types of folk music that have been popularized into mainstream genres.

AMERICAN FOLK

American folk music is among the richest and most variegated in the world, owing to the many ethnic groups that make up the American people. The major strains of American folk music are Irish, Scottish, English, and African. Other European traditions, notably Spanish, have also exerted some influence. Native Americans have a rich musical heritage, but it was never integrated with the European or African traditions. Some instruments of American folk music are the guitar, string bass, mandolin, autoharp, dulcimer, fiddle, and banjo.

The most intriguing genre of American folk is the ballad, a song that tells a story. The earliest American ballads came from the British Isles and thrived for centuries in Appalachian areas. Ballads are often rooted in mythic or epic traditions. "Polly Vaughan" (Peter, Paul, and Mary) can be traced to Celtic mythology. (In this discussion, examples of ballads will be followed by popular performers who have recorded the song. More traditional versions of many of these ballads may be explored in Francis James Child's *English and Scottish Popular Ballads.*) "Polly Vaughan" tells the story of a hunter who accidentally kills his wife, having mistaken her for a swan. The story has a supernatural element: in some versions, Polly is resurrected as a swan; in others, her ghost visits the courtroom where her husband is tried. "John Riley" (Joan Baez, the Byrds) tells of a man who, returning from a expedition, disguises himself from his wife to find out if she has been faithful. John Riley has obvious parallels with the Greek Odysseus. Many ballads derive from the biblical tradition, as in "Samson and Delilah," also called "If I Had My Way" (Grateful Dead; Peter, Paul, and Mary).

THE POWER OF THE BALLAD

Although there are some comic ballads, most are tragic and have a tone of inevitability that exerts a strange power over the listener. Many depict the hero's ruin and seek to deter the listeners from a similar fate by delivering a moral at the end. "The House of the Rising Sun" (Bob Dylan, Baez, Odetta, the

Animals) is about a woman lured into prostitution who warns the listener "not to do what I have done." The fidelity of women is a common theme, as in "John Riley" and "Gallows Tree," also called "Hangman" (Peter, Paul, and Mary; Odetta), which tells of a man at the gallows who has been abandoned by father, mother, and brother but whose true love finally comes to pay his fee. (A very different version of this song is recorded by Led Zeppelin as "Gallows Pole.") The infidelity of men is an equally common motif, as in "Come All Ye Fair and Tender Ladies," also known as "Tiny Sparrow" (Peter, Paul, and Mary).

Ballads may be inspired by local events, such as battles, uprisings, disasters, train wrecks, and shipwrecks (including the *Titanic*). A shipwreck is the subject of "Sir Patrick Spens," one of the oldest and most famous of all British ballads, often included in literature anthologies for its deft, concise poetry and symbolism. Train songs are extremely common. The advent of the train captured the folk imagination because of its great economic and cultural impact upon rural America. "John Henry" (Odetta) is about a railroad laborer who tries to outperform the steam drill using his bare hands to drill the railroad tracks. "Casey Jones" tells of an engineer who dies in a train wreck. (The Grateful Dead's "Casey Jones," from the album *Workingman's Dead* [1970], is their own composition and is only marginally related to the original.) The Badman Ballad was also popular. Often petty criminals and bandits attained legendary status and became tragic or ironic antiheroes in ballads such as "Jesse James" or "Pretty Boy Floyd."

THE PROTEST SONG

A major genre of American folk music is the protest song. Wars have always been a topic of protest songs—"Cruel War" (Peter, Paul, and Mary), for example, goes back to the American Revolution. However, in the twentieth century, it was the "union singers," declaiming the atrocious labor conditions of the Industrial Age, who made protest songs notorious. One of the first union singers was Swedish immigrant Joe Hill. He was a member of the Industrial Workers of the World and contributed to its book, *Songs to Fan the Flames of Discontent*. He was executed in 1915, accused of murdering a businessman. (Baez commemorated him in the song "I Dreamed I Saw Joe Hill.")

However, the hardships of the Great Depression are what truly led to the flowering of protest songs. Notable among these are the Dust Bowl ballads of Woody Guthrie, who added his own lyrics to folk and country songs to convey what he saw and suffered in his travels across America during the Depression. He modified the Badman Ballad to write songs about good people down on their luck—thus, one of his major contributions was the emphasis on new lyrics. Guthrie traveled with folksingers such as Ramblin' Jack Elliott, Cisco Houston, and Huddie "Leadbelly" Ledbetter.

In 1941 Guthrie joined the Almanac Singers, who played topical songs that informed people of current events that might not be covered honestly in the media. They formed a commune in Greenwich Village in New York City and charged thirty-five cents for daylong performances, which demanded audience participation. (Such group participation in folk music is called a hootenanny.) The purpose of these folksingers was to promote group solidarity and rally listeners into supporting workers' rights by joining unions. Though Guthrie and his companions would be hailed as "authentic" folksingers by a later generation, many folk musicologists of the time objected to this popularization of folk music for the sake of political causes. Guthrie himself denied that he was a folksinger. He hated the beautifully sad songs of the "silk-stocking balladeers" of an ancient British tradition that held no hope of social mobility for the lower classes.

Another important folksinger of this period was Pete Seeger, a musicologist and Harvard dropout who, like Guthrie, was bent upon traveling and recording his experiences in song. He traveled to other countries, learned their traditions, and included them in his repertoire. Seeger also joined the Almanac Singers, though he was more famous for his next band, the Weavers. Seeger, Guthrie, and others were affiliated with communism, as were many left-wing activists of the time. In 1953 the Weavers disbanded, effectively silenced by the House Committee on Un-American Activities. In 1954 Guthrie entered the hospital, debilitated by Huntington's disease. He ceased to write songs, though he did not die until 1967. Without these major players, folk music subsided in the mid-1950s, forgotten by the mainstream amid the excitement of a thrilling new sound called rock and roll.

A NEW ERA OF FOLK

In the late 1950s folk music became chic among certain middle-class college students who disdained rock and roll as an inane, fleeting fad. Eventually, folk scenes arose in Berkeley, California, and Cambridge, Massachusetts, and Albert Grossman opened the Gate of Horn folk club in Chicago. Grossman was also responsible for producing the Newport Folk Festival, which became an annual event. The first festival, in 1959, introduced Baez.

However, the most exciting folk scene was in Greenwich Village, in coffeehouses such as the Bitter End and the Gaslight Cafe. (This scene was later satirized in Dylan's "Talking New York" and commemorated more abstrusely in Simon and Garfunkel's "Bleecker Street.") Grossman visited Greenwich Village and, moved by the devotion of college students buying expensive coffee while watching grubby folksingers, decided the time was right to cash in on folk. He converted three clean-cut California boys into the Kingston Trio in 1957. They recorded "Tom Dooley" (1958), a traditional ballad about a man sentenced to death, which sold more than three million copies. Soon a proliferation of polished, clean-cut folkies imitated the Kingston Trio: the Folkswingers; the Limeliters; the Ramblers Three; the Brothers Four; the Chad Mitchell Trio; the New Christy Minstrels; and Peter, Paul, and Mary.

A remarkable new talent distinguishing himself from the crowd was Dylan, who wrote his own material in addition to covering traditional songs. He was audacious, perhaps even pretentious: his "Song for Woody" compared his own travels to the hardships Guthrie endured during the Depression. However, Dylan soon proved to be a poet of true worth. When his songs were covered by Peter, Paul, and Mary in the mid-1960s, they became hits, and Dylan finally received his deserved recognition. Soon other folk popularizers and then mainstream acts were covering his material.

A more significant outgrowth of Dylan's success was the emergence of folksingers who, rather than simply covering his songs, were inspired by his example to write and perform their own music. Tom Paxton, Tim Hardin, Phil Ochs, Judy Collins, and Gordon Lightfoot were all indebted to the standard of originality, creativity, and intelligence established by Dylan. Peter, Paul, and Mary's reputation hovered between that of popularizers and the earnest folkies until Dylan's nostalgic poem commemorating their performances at the Gaslight was published on their album *Blowin' in the Wind* and boosted their credibility. In February 1964 Peter, Paul, and Mary were at the height of their popularity, with all three of their albums in the Top 10, when the Beatles invaded America and awoke the sleeping giant of rock and roll.

THE ROCK-AND-ROLL INFLUENCE

It was inevitable that folk and rock would merge. Rock was always an eclectic genre, born of blues and country music. After the Beatles began to dominate the charts, other bands sought something new to hook fickle teen tastes. In September 1964 the Animals attacked "House of the Rising Sun" with electric guitars and organ. The song was a hit and suggested to the folkies that they, too, could cash in on the hybrid.

In 1965 folk rock exploded. Dylan shocked the folkies in January of that year by "going electric" on the single "Subterranean Homesick Blues." They hoped the new style was a put-on, a satire of the rock craze, but these hopes were shattered in March by the equally electric album *Bringing It All Back Home.* At the Newport Folk Festival in July, Dylan and his electric guitar were booed offstage after three songs, even though Muddy Waters had played an electric guitar at the 1964 festival.

Meanwhile, the Byrds had released *Mr. Tambourine Man* (1965), featuring Dylan songs and other folk tunes revitalized by the band's electric twelve-string guitars and vocal harmonies. The Byrds followed this up with another fine album in December of that year, *Turn! Turn! Turn!* The Byrds were essentially folk musicians who shrewdly recognized rock as the new direction in popular music. Simon and Garfunkel were also urban folkies transformed into folk rockers. Their first album, *Wednesday Morning, 3 A.M.*, was, like Dylan's first album, a mixture of traditional folk songs and authentic-sounding original compositions. In spite of its great musical and lyrical qualities, the album did not sell well. However, when the duo's producer added electric guitars and drums to one of the songs, "The Sounds of Silence," and rereleased it as a single, it reached the top of the charts. Fortunately, Paul Simon was able to live up to the expectations stirred by the folk-rock version. He had been uncomfortable with the "authenticity" demands of the folkniks and proved to be an original and intelligent songwriter, free of Dylan's evasiveness and posturing. Simon created much of folk rock's finest music throughout the rest of the 1960s.

Meanwhile, the Beatles also had come under the influence of Dylan. Inspired by his mellow introspection and elusive symbolism, John Lennon responded with "You've Got to Hide Your Love Away," and Paul McCartney offered the folksy, wordy "I've Just Seen a Face" (*Help!*, August 1965). By December 1965 the Beatles were rising to the challenge established by the upstart Byrds, and they exhibited a more pronounced folk influence on *Rubber Soul.* It never occurred to the Beatles to explore their own British tradition of folk music. This task was taken up by the Scottish troubadour Donovan Leitch, who combined the ballad tradition of the British Isles with Dylanesque lyrics and was quickly hailed as the "Scottish Dylan."

THE DILUTION OF FOLK

By 1966 folk rock was seemingly everywhere. Worthy folk rockers included the Lovin' Spoonful, the Mamas and the Papas, Buffalo Springfield, and the Turtles. However, the "folk" label was often abused as a marketing device applied to anyone slightly eclectic, from Janis Joplin to the Youngbloods. Even Sonny and Cher were classified as folk rock. On the other hand, the Grateful Dead are rarely mentioned as part of the genre, yet they produced great folk rock on *Workingman's Dead, American Beauty* (1970), and *Reckoning* (1981) by mingling blues, country, jug-band, bluegrass, and Appalachian styles. The Dead's lyricist, Robert Hunter, was a poet whose literary qualities rivaled those of Simon and Dylan. His terse, ironic tales of the struggles and adventures of simple people were closer to genuine folk songs than many others ever came.

Much of what passed for folk rock was the appropriation of several features with varying relevance to traditional folk. First, anyone holding an acoustic guitar was called a genuine folkie, and the electric twelve-string guitar was also labeled folk, based on the Byrds' precedent. Then there were the vocal harmonies associated with Peter, Paul, and Mary (though these were just as often borrowed from the Beatles or the Everly Brothers). Finally, "sensitive" lyrics, whether political or personal, were a sure sign of folkdom. Dylan's songwriting was the widest and most enduring influence, though not always for the best: his style of protest—detached, ironic, and accusing—was eventually imitated in every area of popular music, reaching a crescendo of sanctimony in the art rock of the 1970s. *Another Side of Bob Dylan*, his cryptic autobiographies, also exerted an unfortunate influence, as less skilled writers began to bare their souls with diminishing subtlety and sophistication.

The 1960s-era spirit of togetherness, embraced by everyone from Peter, Paul, and Mary to Crosby, Stills, and Nash, was abandoned in the 1970s as these and so many other groups splintered into solo artists. Retreating from the political chaos of the late 1960s, the singer/songwriters resorted to whiny introspection and self-infatuation. Some of them, such as John Prine and Jim Croce, maintained a sense of humor and irony that made them worthy folksingers. Others, such as Joni Mitchell and Leonard Cohen, relied on their literary prowess to grace their gloom with a little dignity.

Folk rockers of the British Isles tended to avoid the singer/songwriter malady. In the late 1960s and 1970s, Fairport Convention, the Incredible String Band, Jethro Tull, Led Zeppelin, and Irish guitar maestro Rory Gallagher successfully blended folk influences into their eclecticism. These were usually musical influences, without the ideological baggage associated with folk music. The folk spirit of protest, homespun integrity, and anticorporate independence was eventually seized by a new and very different breed of "simple folks"—the punk rockers.

FOLK TANGENTS

In the early twenty-first century, a subgenre known as "freak folk" arose in the United States. Associated with artists such as Joanna Newson, Animal Collective, and Devendra Banhart, freak folk blends traditional folk elements such as the ballad and the use of mainly acoustic instruments with forms taken from experimental music and psychedelic pop. Freak folk often deploys found sounds, unusual musical themes, unique vocal styles, and complex instrumentation.

Douglas Cooke

SEE ALSO: *Baez, Joan; The Beatles; Bluegrass; Blues; Buffalo Springfield; The Byrds; Country Music; Croce, Jim; Crosby, Stills, and Nash; Donovan; Dylan, Bob; Folkways Records;*

The Grateful Dead; Greenwich Village; Griffith, Nanci; Guthrie, Woody; The Kingston Trio; Led Zeppelin; The Mamas and the Papas; Newport Jazz and Folk Festivals; Peter, Paul, and Mary; Protest Groups; Punk; Rock and Roll; Seeger, Pete; Simon, Paul; Simon and Garfunkel; The Weavers.

BIBLIOGRAPHY

Anthology of American Folk Music. Folkways Records, 1952.

Cantwell, Robert. *When We Were Good: The Folk Revival*. Cambridge, MA: Harvard University Press, 1996.

Child, Francis James. *English and Scottish Popular Ballads*. New York: Dover Publications, 1965.

Folk Song and Minstrelsy. Vanguard, 1962, 4 record albums.

Laing, Dave; Karl Dallas; Robin Denselow; et al. *The Electric Muse: The Story of Folk to Rock*. London: Methuen Paperbacks, 1975.

Nettl, Bruno. *Folk Music in the United States*. Detroit, MI: Wayne State University Press, 1976.

Pollock, Bruce. *When the Music Mattered: Rock in the 1960s*. New York: Holt, Rinehart and Winston, 1984.

Vassal, Jacques. *Electric Children: Roots and Branches of Modern Folkrock*, trans. Paul Barnett. New York: Taplinger, 1976.

Folkways Records

Founded by Moses "Moe" Asch in 1948, Folkways Records evolved into perhaps the most important independent record label in the history of American popular culture. Determined to document the authentic musical traditions of the world, Asch assembled an eclectic catalog of more than 2,200 titles that featured such artists as Huddie "Leadbelly" Ledbetter, Woody Guthrie, Pete Seeger, Coleman Hawkins, Mary Lou Williams, and John Cage. In addition to assembling an impressive collection of children's and world artists, Folkways played a prominent role in shaping the canon of American folk music; exerted tremendous influence on left-wing culture; and, in part, inspired the folk revival of the 1960s.

ASCH RECORDS

Born in 1905 in Warsaw, Poland, Moses Asch immigrated in 1914 (when he was nine years old) with his family to New York City, where his father, the renowned Yiddish novelist Sholem Asch, sought to forge relationships with other Jewish intellectuals. In 1923 Sholem sent his son to Germany to study electronics, and when Moe returned to New York in 1926, he opened a radio repair shop and pursued a career as a sound engineer. Eager to gain his father's approval, he then sought a more literary occupation. During his sojourn in Germany, he had read John Lomax's *Cowboy Songs* (1910), which sparked his interest in American folklore and convinced him that folk music constituted the literature of the "common" people. In 1939 he established Asch Records to document their voices, recording traditional Yiddish folk songs and cantorials. Asch's repertoire expanded in 1941 when he released a collection of children's songs performed by Leadbelly, the former Lomax protégé who became central to the label's success.

The release of Leadbelly's material in addition to *The Cavalcade of the American Negro* (1940) underscored Asch's commitment to preserving the cultural heritage of African Americans. Such actions on matters of race were indicative of his general leftist sympathies. Reared in a family of socialists, he enthusiastically embraced the Popular Front, a loose affiliation of left-wing and liberal artists and intellectuals who, at the suggestion of the Communist Party International, committed themselves to the defeat of European fascism and the promotion of racial and economic equality. The alliance essentially fell apart in August 1939 when the Soviet Union signed the nonaggression pact with Nazi Germany, who then proceeded to invade Poland. In 1945 he opened his studio, now under the banner of Disc Records, an integral element of the leftist American Folk Song Movement. Seeger and his Almanac Singers (Cisco Houston, Brownie McGhee, Sonny Terry, and Woody Guthrie) gathered to record both traditional tunes and politically inflected songs. Folkways was particularly supportive of Guthrie's career and, between 1944 and 1945, Asch recorded nearly 140 Guthrie selections and meticulously archived the musician's voluminous notebooks, letters, and drawings.

FOLKWAYS RECORDS

Disc Records was dissolved by bankruptcy, but when Asch and his assistant, Marian Distler, launched Folkways in 1948, he refused to make efforts to sign commercially successful artists. Marquee performers, he worried, would compromise the label's integrity among academics as well as his attempts to chronicle the lives of "real" folk. As a result, he continued to record music that appealed to small but well-defined audiences: white leftists, jazz aficionados, librarians, and teachers. In its fledgling years, Folkways rereleased Guthrie's *Dust Bowl Ballads* (which RCA originally recorded in 1940); expanded its jazz catalog; and, under the direction of ethnomusicologist Harold Courlander, promoted the Ethnic Series.

In 1952 Asch hired Harry Smith to assemble the *Anthology of American Folk Music*, a compendium that introduced a new generation, notably Bob Dylan and Bruce Springsteen, to the genre. This seminal album became a cultural touchstone for the many white students who, inspired by the success of the Weavers and the Kingston Trio, sought to celebrate folk musicians and their traditions. Under Asch's auspices, Mike Seeger, Pete's half-brother, reclaimed and recorded southern traditions, while Ralph Rinzler documented such virtuosos as Clarence Ashley and Arthel "Doc" Watson. A burgeoning interest in folk music opened a new market to Asch, impelling him to rerelease older materials and to issue new recordings by such legends as Sam "Lightnin'" Hopkins and Big Joe Williams.

This renaissance gained momentum when, in the early 1960s, Dylan and Joan Baez began to write and perform topical songs that both reflected and shaped the politics of the Ban the Bomb and civil rights movements. Interested in the New Left's use of the folk idiom, Folkways created the Broadside label to document songs written for the radical underground publication of the same name. Replete with Dylan compositions, the *Broadside Ballads* featured a host of folksingers, including Seeger, Phil Ochs, and Dylan himself, performing under the pseudonym Blind Boy Grunt. Folkways captured other sounds of the decade by employing Guy and Candie Carawan to record the music and speeches of the civil rights movement.

A sizable catalog, a vault of vintage recordings, and a handful of new projects sustained Folkways through the 1970s, but as the 1980s approached, Asch focused on finding a way to preserve his life's work. Moe Asch died in 1986. Before his death he donated his entire collection, which includes African

American music, gospel music, mountain ballads, sea chanteys, Native American ritual songs, Caribbean dance music, and avant-garde poetry, as well as folk music, to the Smithsonian Institution with the stipulation that every single record, regardless of its popularity, remain in print and commercially available.

With the Smithsonian in charge of the collection, the company was reorganized under the rubric Smithsonian-Folkways. To fund the venture, the Smithsonian enlisted a coterie of popular musicians to cover material for an album titled *A Vision Shared: A Tribute to Woody Guthrie and Leadbelly* (1988). The artists who participated in this effort attest to the enduring legacy that Folkways and its most recognizable legends passed to American popular music. Dylan, Springsteen, Willie Nelson, Little Richard, John Mellencamp, and Emmylou Harris were among those who identified Leadbelly and Guthrie as their cultural forebears. The Smithsonian regularly issues unreleased materials from the Folkways archives. From 1988 to 2000, Anthony Seeger, a member of the celebrated Seeger clan, served as curator and director of the Smithsonian Folkways label, and is now curator and director emeritus.

Bryan Garman

SEE ALSO: *Blues; Civil Rights Movement; Dylan, Bob; Folk Music; Guthrie, Woody; Hawkins, Coleman; Hopkins, Sam "Lightnin'"; The Kingston Trio; Leadbelly; Little Richard; Mellencamp, John; Nelson, Willie; Ochs, Phil; Seeger, Pete; Smithsonian Institution; Springsteen, Bruce; The Weavers.*

BIBLIOGRAPHY

Burdick, Alan. "Now Hear This." *Harper's*, July 2001.

Goldsmith, Peter. *Making People's Music: Moe Asch and Folkways Records*. Washington, DC: Smithsonian Press, 1998.

Hale, Grace Elizabeth. *A Nation of Outsiders: How the White Middle Class Fell in Love with Rebellion in Postwar America*. New York: Oxford University Press, 2011.

Slobin, Mark. *Folk Music: A Very Short Introduction*. New York: Oxford University Press, 2011.

Follett, Ken *(1949–)*

Writer Ken Follett began his career as a fiction writer while working for the *London Evening News*. He produced a series of mysteries and thrillers under various pseudonyms until he felt he had learned enough and written well enough to author under his own name. His early works were, in Follett's words, "intentionally very racy, with lots of sex."

Each of his best works grew out of news stories and historical events. Cinematic in conception, they follow a hunter-hunted pattern that leads to exciting chase scenes and games of wit and brinkmanship. Some of his most successful works have dealt with World War II, perhaps because he requires a wide backdrop and world-shaking events to justify the tumultuous passions he instills in his characters. At its best, Follett's prose is lean and driven. His forte lies in setting up a chain of events in chronological sequences. Follett's ideal is a compromise between the serious and the popular, the "plot, story, excitement, sensation and the world outside the mind" that he believes serious writers often ignore merged with the graceful, powerful prose and more complex "character development" that mass-market writers fail to take time for.

Follett burst upon the American fiction scene in 1978 with his mystery spy story *Eye of the Needle*. A taut thriller, it portrayed a central female character rising to heroism and a humanized villain together with a convincing image of World War II lifestyles, sensibilities, and attitudes. Characterized by fast-paced action and an economic, readable style, the book was greeted with enthusiasm by the public and reviewers alike. It became an American Literary Guild selection, garnering sales of more than ten million copies. This was to be the start of Follett's continued success in America. With *Eye of the Needle*, he gained the coveted Edgar Award from the Mystery Writers of America, a prize honoring the father of the American detective story, Edgar Allan Poe. The novel was later adapted for the screen by Stanley Mann, starring Donald Sutherland and Kate Nelligan. With its release in 1981, the film secured Follett's reputation as a top-notch writer in the spy genre.

He followed his first success with four more best-selling thrillers: *Triple* (1979), *The Key to Rebecca* (1980), *The Man from St. Petersburg* (1982), and *Lie Down with Lions* (1986). American television movies of both *The Key to Rebecca* in 1985, starring Cliff Robertson and David Soul, and *Lie Down with Lions* in 1994, starring Timothy Dalton, enhanced his popular reputation. A miniseries of *On Wings of Eagles* (1986), a true story of an Iranian rescue mission, cemented his standing and following.

Pillars of the Earth, which has since achieved a worldwide cult status, was published in 1989. It was a radical departure from Follett's spy stories. The novel about building a cathedral in the Middle Ages was on the *New York Times* best-seller list for eighteen weeks. *World without End* (2007), the sequel to *Pillars of the Earth*, which follows the descendants of the previous novel in the time of the Black Death, was an international best seller. *Pillars of the Earth* was followed by *Night over Water*, *A Dangerous Fortune*, and *A Place Called Freedom*, which again were not in the spy genre but had elements of suspense and intrigue. In 1996 Follett's thriller *The Third Twin*, a suspense novel about a young woman scientist who stumbles over a genetic engineering experiment, was ranked number two in the world, beaten only by John Grisham's *The Partner*. Miniseries rights for the book were sold to CBS for $1.4 million, and its broadcast in 1997 was a further indication of Follett's rank in American popular culture. *The Hammer of Eden* (1998) is a contemporary suspense story with the fast pace and intriguing characters established in his earlier efforts.

In 2010 Follett published *Fall of Giants*, the first book in a projected three-volume project titled The Century Trilogy, which will tell the history of the twentieth century through the eyes of five interconnected families. *Winter of the World*, the second book in the trilogy, appeared in 2012 and traces the lives of the five families spanning from the rise of the Third Reich through the Cold War.

Born in Cardiff, Wales, on June 5, 1949, Follett was encouraged to read from a very early age. He openly acknowledging his debt to the access to free books he had from the local library, often saying in lectures that it is axiomatic that a writer is also a reader. He attended University College, London, where he received a BA in philosophy in 1970. While at the university, he married his first wife, Mary Elson, and had a son and a daughter. His second wife, Barbara Follett, became the member of parliament for Stevenage in Hertfordshire. Follett has interests in music, playing bass guitar in a band called Damn Right I Got the Blues; the theater, especially William Shakespeare; and his work as president of Dyslexia Action.

Jim Sinclair
Joan Gajadhar

SEE ALSO: *Best Sellers; Clancy, Tom; Detective Fiction; Grisham, John; Made-for-Television Movies.*

BIBLIOGRAPHY

Atkins, John. *The British Spy Novel: Studies in Treachery.* London: Calder, 1984.

"Ken Follett." Accessed April 2012. Available from http://www.ken-follett.com

McCormick, Donald. *Who's Who in Spy Fiction.* London: Elm Tree/Hamilton, 1977.

Fonda, Henry *(1905–1982)*

Although cast in a mold similar to that of his contemporaries Gary Cooper and Jimmy Stewart, Henry Fonda was one of the most distinctive American screen actors. Tall, dark, good-looking, and quietly spoken, he exuded decency, sincerity, and understated authority and spent much of his forty-six-year career being offered up as a repository of honesty, a quiet American hero and a man of the people. He will forever be remembered as the incarnation of the president in *Young Mr. Lincoln* (1939) and as John Steinbeck's Tom Joad in *The Grapes of Wrath* (1940)—both for John Ford, with whom he did much of his finest work—and also as the subtly persuasive jury member in *12 Angry Men* (1957).

Henry Fonda. *In his nearly fifty-year movie career, Henry Fonda created a legacy of decent, heroic, distinctly American characters.* THE KOBAL COLLECTION.

Fonda's roles ranged wide, and his successes were numerous. He was an engagingly absentminded dupe, turning the tables on Barbara Stanwyck in Preston Sturges's sparkling comedy *The Lady Eve* (1941); the voice of conscience in William Wellman's *The Ox-Bow Incident* (1943); and a memorable Wyatt Earp for Ford in *My Darling Clementine* (1946). He created the role of *Mister Roberts* on Broadway and on-screen and played presidential candidates in two of the best political films of the 1960s, *Advise and Consent* (1962) and *The Best Man* (1964).

Fonda was born on May 16, 1905, in Grand Island, Nebraska. After high school, he enrolled at the University of Minnesota, intending to get a degree in journalism, but he dropped out and became an office boy. Asked to play a role in an amateur production with the Omaha Community Playhouse, he found his calling; went on to work in summer stock; and joined the University Players, a new group of students who aspired to the theater. The guiding light was future director Joshua Logan, and the young company included Jimmy Stewart and Margaret Sullavan. From there, with his friend Stewart, he made his way to New York and the Broadway stage in the early 1930s. Fonda married Sullavan, the first of his five wives, in 1931 (the marriage would end just two years later). In 1934, after having enjoyed a Broadway success in *The Farmer Takes a Wife*, he signed a contract with film producer Walter Wanger.

EARLY FILM CAREER

Victor Fleming's film version of *The Farmer Takes a Wife* (1935) marked Fonda's screen debut. He repeated his lead role, cast opposite Janet Gaynor, and progressed steadily to popularity and stardom through the rest of the decade. He played a backwoods pioneer in the first outdoor Technicolor adventure movie, *The Trail of the Lonesome Pine* (1936), the film that established his idealistic resolute persona (cartoonist Al Capp later claimed that he had based L'il Abner on Fonda), and in 1937 he was invited to star in the first British Technicolor picture *The Wings of the Morning*. In 1939 he played Frank James in the first Technicolor Western, *Jesse James*.

His best work of this early period, however, was in Fritz Lang's social conscience drama *You Only Live Once* (1937). Set against the background of the Depression, Fonda played a fundamentally decent young man driven to crime because of circumstances and on the run with his wife (Sylvia Sidney). Other career highlights of the 1930s were William Wyler's Civil War melodrama *Jezebel* (1938), in which he costarred as the exasperated but intractable beau of a willful Bette Davis, and the start of his collaboration with Ford. *Young Mr. Lincoln*, in which Fonda limned a dreamy, political calm while maintaining a commitment to justice and decency, found him perfectly cast. His frontier pioneer in *Drums along the Mohawk* (1939) followed and confirmed (after his portrayal of Frank James) that Fonda, who detested guns and didn't care much for horses, was nonetheless a sympathetic candidate for the Western genre.

He played Frank James again in *The Return of Frank James* (1940), a memorable but sadly underrated Western from Lang, but it was indubitably Ford who engraved Fonda's image on the

Western. In Ford's hands, Fonda was a kind of Sir Galahad of the Prairie: polite, laconic, slow to anger, but a man of his word who meant what he said. They made only one more Western together (*Fort Apache*, 1948), but Fonda's mature postwar demeanor served Anthony Mann's *The Tin Star* (1957) and Edward Dmytryk's uneven *Warlock* (1959). Meanwhile, there was Tom Joad.

THE GRAPES OF WRATH

Although a major star by 1940, Fonda, dissatisfied with his material, wanted out of his contract with Twentieth Century Fox and Wanger. He desperately wanted to play Joad, however, and reluctantly signed a seven-year deal with Fox in order to get it. Ford directed *The Grapes of Wrath* from his own screenplay adaptation of the novel. It was a powerful depiction of the plight of the Dust Bowl migrants, in which Fonda's Joad, a decent man just out of jail after killing in self-defense, is dismayed to find his family farm a ruin. Undaunted by adversity, he helps his family make it to California against the odds, only to find the poor are oppressed there too. Following the death of Casey (John Carradine), an inspirational figure, Joad, in a classic speech lifted directly from Steinbeck's novel, vows to fight injustice wherever it may be. Fonda was nominated for an Oscar for his performance but lost, ironically, to his close friend Stewart, who won for his comedic performance in *The Philadelphia Story* (1940).

In 1936 Fonda had married socialite Frances Brokaw. The marriage lasted until 1950 when, following a mental breakdown, she committed suicide. Brokaw was the mother of future actors Jane and Peter Fonda. In the early 1940s Fonda was able to escape from a couple years of his contractual obligations to Fox thanks to being called to active service during World War II. His postwar return was *My Darling Clementine*, and after a handful of feature films, ending with *Fort Apache*, he deserted Hollywood for the Broadway stage and was off the screen for eight years. During this time, his notable successes included *The Caine Mutiny, Court Martial* and *Mister Roberts*, the play that brought him back to the screen when Ford insisted he re-create his stage role for the Warner Brothers 1955 film version (Warner Brothers had wanted William Holden or Marlon Brando to star). Sadly, the filming was marked by dissension between star and director, as well as Ford's increasing illness, and the picture was completed by Mervyn Le Roy.

In 1956 the actor starred as Pierre, opposite Audrey Hepburn's Natasha, in King Vidor's lumbering, multimillion-dollar version of *War and Peace*. Fonda insisted on wearing spectacles to give the character a suitably distracted, intellectual air but, unfortunately for the film, as *Time* magazine noted, Fonda gave "the impression of being the only man in the huge cast who had read the book." Also in 1956 Fonda's third wife divorced him, citing his affair with Afdera Franchetti, who became his fourth wife in 1957. That year, he starred in one of his biggest successes of the decade, Alfred Hitchcock's *The Wrong Man*, playing the victim of a case of mistaken identity, fighting to save himself from a wrongful charge of murder. The 1960s began with a fourth divorce and brought marriage (in 1965) to his fifth and last wife, Shirlee Mae Adams. During this decade, too, his public profile became somewhat eclipsed by those of his children, notably his daughter, Jane, who was a prominent political activist as well as an increasingly successful actress. Both children were publicly outspoken in their criticism of their famous father, and his image as the nicest guy in town was somewhat tarnished.

On the professional front, Fonda remained active. He made a number of television specials, including *Clarence Darrow*, and produced and starred in *The Deputy* from 1959 to 1961. He alternated between the live theater and films, but the Hollywood glory days were over and the good roles were few and far between. There were exceptions, notably in three overtly political films to which the gravitas of his demeanor was perfectly suited and in which he was uniformly excellent. He was the candidate running for the office of secretary of state while dogged by a dark secret in Otto Preminger's *Advise and Consent* (1962); an Adlai Stevenson–like presidential nominee with high ideals in Franklin Schaffner's adaptation of Gore Vidal's Broadway play *The Best Man* (1964); and a heroic president staving off a nuclear holocaust by extreme means in Sidney Lumet's *Fail-Safe* (1964). He made cameo appearances in such major, all-star productions as *The Longest Day* and *How the West Was Won* (both 1962) and *Battle of the Bulge* and *In Harm's Way* (both 1965). In a late reprise of his Western career, but in a reversal of his "good guy" image, he starred as a ruthless gunman in Sergio Leone's epic *Once upon a Time in the West* (1968).

LATER CAREER HIGHLIGHTS

During the 1970s, with ill health gradually creeping up on him, Fonda's illustrious career gradually wound down, though never quite out. In 1974 he was a presenter at the Tony Awards, was honored by the American Civil Liberties Union, and narrated a history film series for colleges and universities. That year he also opened on Broadway in the one-man show *Clarence Darrow*, but the show closed after twenty-nine performances when Fonda collapsed in his dressing room from total exhaustion. He was rushed to the hospital and had a pacemaker implanted. He revived the play at the Huntington Hartford Theater in Los Angeles, where it was taped and presented on NBC later in 1974. In 1977 he made a splash as a crusty old Supreme Court judge in Robert E. Lee and Jerome Lawrence's *First Monday in October*, which played in Los Angeles, on Broadway, and in Chicago.

In between work Fonda found time to paint (his watercolors hang in several galleries), do needlework, and experiment with haute cuisine. He was honored by the American Film Institute with a Lifetime Achievement Award in 1978 and by the Kennedy Center for the Performing Arts, and he was given an honorary Oscar at the 1981 Academy Awards ceremony "in recognition of his brilliant accomplishments."

Fonda stepped into the Hollywood spotlight once more to costar with Katharine Hepburn in *On Golden Pond* (1981). The film went some way to healing the rift with his daughter, Jane, who played his daughter in the film, and at age seventy-six, he became the oldest recipient of the Best Actor Oscar—the first of his long and distinguished career—for his performance as a retired professor grown curmudgeonly with age and the fear of approaching death. He was, alas, too ill to attend the Oscar ceremony in March 1982, and Jane, herself a nominee that year, collected the statuette on her father's behalf. Henry Fonda, one of the best loved actors of Hollywood's Golden Age and of the Broadway theater, died in August of that year.

Dennis Fischer

SEE ALSO: *Boston Strangler; Brando, Marlon; Cooper, Gary; Darrow, Clarence; Davis, Bette;* Fail-Safe*; Fonda, Jane; Ford, John;* The Grapes of Wrath*; The Great Depression; Hepburn,*

Audrey; Hepburn, Katharine; Hitchcock, Alfred; Holden, William; Hollywood; How the West Was Won*; Lang, Fritz;* My Darling Clementine*; Perot, Ross; Preminger, Otto; Stanwyck, Barbara; Steinbeck, John; Stewart, Jimmy; Sturges, Preston; Suicide; Vidal, Gore; The Western.*

BIBLIOGRAPHY

Fonda, Henry, and Howard Teichmann. *Fonda: My Life.* New York: New American Library, 1981.

Goldstein, Norm, and Associated Press. *Henry Fonda.* New York: Holt, Rinehart and Winston, 1982.

Parish, James Robert; Don E. Stanke; and Michael R. Pitts. *The All-Americans.* New Rochelle, NY: Arlington House, 1977.

Sweeney, Kevin. *Henry Fonda: A Biobibliography.* New York: Greenwood Press, 1992.

Thomas, Tony, and Henry Fonda. *The Complete Films of Henry Fonda.* Secaucus, NJ: Citadel Press, 1983.

Fonda, Jane *(1937–)*

A popular culture icon alternately revered and reviled by American audiences, Jane Fonda is an actress whose career often has been overshadowed by her very public personal life. The quintessentially mod 1960s cinematic sex symbol in *Barbarella* (1968), Fonda soon became one of America's most controversial figures following her highly publicized trip to Vietnam during which she spoke out against the war. Despite public disapproval, Fonda nonetheless became one of Hollywood's most popular actresses, nominated for seven Academy Awards and winning two. Offscreen, she has been known as a dedicated political activist, a hugely successful workout guru, and wife to three prominent men—French film director Roger Vadim, progressive politician Tom Hayden, and media mogul Ted Turner.

EARLY LIFE

A member of Hollywood's aristocracy, Jane was born in New York City to the legendary actor Henry Fonda and his socialite wife, Frances Seymour Brokaw. She spent her early years at the Fonda home in the mountains above Santa Monica, California, where as a tomboy she and her younger brother, Peter, spent an idyllic childhood climbing trees and riding horses. After World War II, her father returned to Broadway to star in *Mister Roberts* (1948), and the family moved to Connecticut, where the Fondas hoped to raise their children away from the Hollywood limelight. However, the marriage quickly disintegrated after Henry fell in love with Susan Blanchard, the twenty-one-year-old stepdaughter of composer Oscar Hammerstein. Shortly thereafter, Frances, who had long suffered from depression, had a series of nervous breakdowns and was committed to a sanatorium, where she committed suicide by slashing her throat. Feeling that his twelve-year-old daughter and ten-year-old son were too young to know the truth, Henry told them their mother had died of a heart attack. Both Jane and Peter later learned the truth through the press.

As a teenager, Fonda showed little interest in following in her father's footsteps. Educated at the elite girls' school Emma Willard and later at Vassar, she earned a reputation as a free spirit and rebel whose chief interests were boys and art. Yet when the opportunity came to costar with her father and Dorothy McGuire at the theater where the two stars had made their debuts, Fonda accepted and, in 1954, made her own acting debut in the Omaha Playhouse production of *The Country Girl.* She continued to envision a career as a painter, studying at L'École des Beaux Arts in Paris and the Art Students League in New York.

ACTING CAREER

After meeting famed acting teacher Lee Strasberg in 1958, Fonda became interested in acting but was afraid of being compared to her famous father. It wasn't until Strasberg told the twenty-one-year-old Fonda she had talent that she decided to become an actress. She joined the Actors Studio in 1958 and two years later made her film debut opposite Anthony Perkins in *Tall Story.* Fonda soon found regular work on Broadway and in Hollywood, where her beauty and talent won her a growing public following. During the 1960s she starred in such popular films as *Walk on the Wild Side* (1962), *Cat Ballou* (1965), and Neil Simon's *Barefoot in the Park* (1967) with Robert Redford.

In 1965 Fonda married French director Roger Vadim, and it was her controversial nudity in his futuristic film *Barbarella* that catapulted her to international stardom. Her next two films, *They Shoot Horses, Don't They?* (1969) and *Klute* (1971), revealed her growing reputation as one of Hollywood's top actresses, earning her two Academy Award nominations; she took home the Oscar for Best Actress for *Klute.* Fonda's reputation as an actress continued to grow throughout the 1970s, and in the latter part of the decade, she appeared in such film classics as *Julia* (1977); *Comes a Horseman* (1978); *Coming Home* (1978), for which she won her second Oscar; *The China Syndrome* (1979); and *Nine to Five* (1980).

In 1972 Fonda traveled to North Vietnam. Shocked by the devastation, she agreed to make ten propaganda broadcasts to U.S. servicemen. This earned her the pejorative nickname "Hanoi Jane," and her speeches, calling U.S. soldiers war criminals and urging them to disobey orders, were carried around the world, along with pictures of her on a North Vietnamese gun used to shoot down American planes. Fonda's fame skyrocketed as she became both the darling of the antiwar movement and the sworn enemy of the Establishment, the U.S. military, and countless Vietnam veterans. For the rest of her life, she would be associated with her trip to Vietnam, greeted with praise or literally shunned and spit upon.

In 1981 Fonda finally was given the opportunity to act opposite her father on film. *On Golden Pond,* starring Henry, Jane, and the inimitable Katharine Hepburn, would be Henry's last film and would earn the ailing actor an Academy Award. Jane continued to make movies throughout the 1980s, appearing in *Agnes of God* (1985), *The Morning After* (1986), and *Old Gringo* (1989), but much of her time was taken up with a new role, as she once again became an iconic figure in a new movement—the fitness revolution. She produced "The Jane Fonda's Workout" series of fitness videos, which became national best sellers even as the money they earned benefited the liberal political causes she espoused.

LATER LIFE

Following her divorce from Vadim in 1973, Fonda married radical politician Tom Hayden later that year and became increasingly politically active. The Haydens supported countless liberal causes, becoming one of Hollywood's most outspoken political couples. In 1988, sixteen years after her trip to Vietnam, during an interview with Barbara Walters on television's *20/20,* Fonda publicly apologized for her bad judgment in going to Vietnam and particularly rued the effects her trip had had on Vietnam veterans. She would later meet with Vietnam veterans in a semisuccessful effort to heal old wounds.

In 1989 Fonda and Hayden divorced. After a difficult period of adjustment, she married Ted Turner in 1991 and retired from acting for nearly fifteen years, preferring to devote her time to marriage and the social causes she continued to support. She returned to acting after their 2001 divorce, starring in *Monster-in-Law* (2005) and *Georgia Rule* (2007). In 2001 Fonda publically announced that she had converted to Christianity, though she remains opposed to dogmatic interpretations of scripture, bigotry, and intolerance. She protested against the Iraq War and, in 2005, helped to cofound the Women's Media Center, which works to increase the number of female voices in the media. Fonda has also published several books, including a memoir in 2005, *My Life So Far*, and 2011's *Prime Time*, which contains anecdotes and advice for living well in later life. As Jennet Conant wrote in an April 1997 *Vanity Fair* article, Fonda has become "the star turned supporting player, the activist turned philanthropist." After a lifetime in the public eye, the more private Jane Fonda nonetheless remains one of America's most intriguing popular culture icons.

Victoria Price

SEE ALSO: *Academy Awards; Aerobics; Celebrity; Celebrity Couples;* The China Syndrome*; Dieting; Fonda, Henry; Hepburn, Katharine; Hollywood;* Julia*; Protest Groups; Redford, Robert; Simon, Neil; Turner, Ted; Vietnam.*

BIBLIOGRAPHY

Als, Hilton. "Queen Jane, Approximately." *New Yorker*, May 9, 2011, 54–63.

Andersen, Christopher P. *Citizen Jane: The Turbulent Life of Jane Fonda.* New York: Henry Holt, 1990.

Bosworth, Patricia. *Jane Fonda: The Private Life of a Public Woman.* New York: Houghton Mifflin Harcourt, 2011.

Conant, Jennet. "Married . . . with Buffalo." *Vanity Fair*, April 1997, 210–230.

Fonda, Jane. *My Life So Far.* New York: Random House, 2005.

Fonda, Jane. *Prime Time.* New York: Random House, 2011.

Freedland, Michael. *Jane Fonda: A Biography.* New York: St. Martin's Press, 1988.

Fonteyn, Margot *(1919–1991)*

Prima ballerina of the British Royal Ballet for more than forty years, Margot Fonteyn was one of greatest dramatic dancers of the twentieth century. She was the first ballerina trained in a British school and company to achieve international stature. Artistic partnerships were integral to her career; her forty-year collaboration with Frederick Ashton was the longest between a ballerina and choreographer in dance history. As she prepared to retire at age forty-three in 1962, her career was revitalized by her partnership with Rudolf Nureyev, who, at age twenty-four, had just defected from the Soviet Union. "It was an artistic love affair conducted in public," said dance critic Clement Crisp. Fonteyn's career was unusually long for a ballet dancer—she continued to perform all the way up to her mid-sixties.

Jeffrey Escoffier

SEE ALSO: *Ballet; Nureyev, Rudolf.*

BIBLIOGRAPHY

Daneman, Meredith. *Margot Fonteyn: A Life.* New York: Penguin Books USA, 2005.

Franchi, Cristina, and Royal Opera House. *Margot Fonteyn: Prima Ballerina Assoluta of the Royal Ballet.* London: Oberon Books, 2004.

Tony Palmer's Film about Margot Fonteyn. DVD. West Long Branch, NJ: Kultur Video, 2006.

Foodies

The origin of the term *foodie* is most commonly believed to have been coined around 1982 by British writers Paul Levy and Ann Barr, although Levy admits that U.S. restaurant critic Gael Greene may have begun using the term independently around the same time. *Foodie* describes with modern informality a concept once defined by words such as *epicure* and *gourmet*; that is, a person with a passion for eating, cooking, and learning esoterica about food and cuisine. The number of people defining themselves as foodies dramatically increased at the end of the twentieth century and the beginning of the first decade of the twenty-first. These modern connoisseurs have been aided in their quest for a deeper appreciation of gastronomy by a host of television cooking shows and by an online network of websites and bloggers devoted to exploring foodie culture. In addition to studying cooking techniques and sampling exotic fare, foodies concern themselves with the origins of their ingredients, and many have become activists in a movement for using fresh local products and sustainable agriculture.

The foodie explosion has its roots as far back as author and chef Julia Child's revolutionary cooking show *The French Chef*, which ran on National Educational Television from 1963 to 1973 and sparked an interest in gourmet cooking at home. The 1980s saw another fad of cosmopolitan food preparation and fine dining (and the publication of Barr and Levy's book *The Official Foodie Handbook* [1985]). Another 1980s event that would have a significant influence on future foodies was the 1985 Farm Aid concert, organized by musicians Willie Nelson, Neil Young, and John Mellencamp. Farm Aid was a fund-raising event that drew attention to the economic plight of small farmers in the United States who had been hard hit by dropping commodities prices and land takeovers by giant agribusiness corporations.

In addition, an outbreak of so-called mad cow disease in the United Kingdom during the 1980s and a deadly incidence of *E. coli* contamination in fast-food hamburgers in the United States in 1993 generated concern about the safety of big-business farming methods. A progressive movement to buy locally and support small farmers became intertwined with a burgeoning fascination with diverse cuisine, and modern foodie culture was born.

In 1993 the Providence Journal Company launched the first cooking-centered cable channel, the Television Food Network. Combining the classic cooking shows of Julia Child, French chef Jacques Pépin, and American culinary expert James

Beard with exercise shows and other programming, the Food Network took a few years to get its footing, but by the turn of the twenty-first century it was firmly established, and by 2012 it had more than 100 million viewers. Programming has expanded to include not only celebrity chef programs but also a number of reality competition shows, during which professional and amateur foodies vie in cooking challenges. In 2010, the Food Network introduced a spin-off network, the Cooking Channel, to provide even more cooking programming.

The rise of the Internet provided another arena for foodies of all types to find each other. In addition to an abundance of cuisine-related websites, in the late 1990s devoted foodies began creating hundreds of blogs on which they could share recipes, philosophies, and their general love of all things epicurean. One of the earliest of these blogs was Jim Leff and Bob Okumura's *Chowhound*, which discussed the New York food scene, and one of the most famous was *The Julie/Julia Project*, in which regular working girl Julie Powell blogged about cooking her way through Child's famous *Mastering the Art of French Cooking*. Powell's blog attracted the attention of the *New York Times* and went on to become a book, *Julie and Julia*, and later a 2009 film of the same title, directed by Nora Ephron and starring Amy Adams and Meryl Streep (in a Golden Globe–winning performance) as the respective titular characters. It was a case of a foodie inspiring a foodie to write a book to inspire other foodies.

The foodie movement for sustainable agriculture has led to a rapid growth of local farmers' markets, such as Chicago's Green City Market, which began in 1998 with a handful of farmers setting up booths in an alley. By the second decade of the 2000s, Green City had grown to a year-round enterprise with 200 farmers selling produce to more than 200,000 visitors. Similar markets have arisen in other cities across the United States, with many having markets in different neighborhoods almost every day of the week. One of the best-known spokespersons for the so-called locavore movement to support local producers is author Michael Pollan, whose books *The Omnivore's Dilemma* (2006) and *In Defense of Food* (2008) explore both the politics and the pure sensual joy of food.

Tina Gianoulis

SEE ALSO: *Blogging; Cable TV; Celebrity Chefs; Child, Julia; Farm Aid; Farmers' Markets; Fast Food; Gourmet Grocery Stores; The Internet; Mellencamp, John; Nelson, Willie; The* New York Times*; Organic Food; Public Television (PBS); Ray, Rachael;* Top Chef*; Young, Neil.*

BIBLIOGRAPHY

Barr, Ann, and Paul Levy. *The Official Foodie Handbook*. Westminster, MD: Arbor House, 1985.

Johnston, Josée, and Shyon Baumann. *Foodies: Democracy and Distinction in the Gourmet Foodscape*. New York: Routledge, 2009.

Pollan, Michael. *The Omnivore's Dilemma: A Natural History of Four Meals*. New York: Penguin, 2006.

Suthivarakom, Ganda. "A Brief History of Food Blogs." *Saveur*, May 9, 2011.

Football

SEE: *College Football; National Football League (NFL); Professional Football.*

Ford, Glenn *(1916–2006)*

One of the most pleasing, consistent, thoughtful, and prolific of screen actors, Glenn Ford (born Gwyllyn Samuel Newton Ford in Quebec City, Canada) was a regular feature of the Hollywood landscape—particularly the sagebrush, given the large number of Westerns in which he starred. Initially a leading man of the second rank, he enjoyed full stardom from the mid-1940s until the late 1950s.

Ford owed his elevation to *Gilda* (1946), Charles Vidor's classic film noir in which Ford tangles angrily and enigmatically with Rita Hayworth in a seedy South American nightclub. He subsequently demonstrated his worth and versatility in a wide range of material. He subsumed his natural likability to play hard men (as in *3:10 to Yuma*, 1957) and revealed comedic talent (in *Teahouse of the August Moon*, 1956; and *The Courtship of Eddie's Father*, with Ron Howard, 1963). Important Western roles included those in *Fastest Gun Alive* (1956) and *Cimarron* (1960). Yet his most memorable performances were as the revenge-obsessed detective in Fritz Lang's *The Big Heat* (1953) and as the new teacher tangling with delinquents in an urban high school in *Blackboard Jungle* (1955). His star waned in the 1960s, owing to poor material, but he proved his durability on television and made a noteworthy appearance in *Superman* (1978). Ford died at his home in Beverly Hills, California, on August 30, 2006.

Robyn Karney

SEE ALSO: The Blackboard Jungle*; Film Noir; Hayworth, Rita; Howard, Ron; Lang, Fritz; Superman; The Western.*

BIBLIOGRAPHY

Ford, Peter. *Glenn Ford: A Life*. Madison: University of Wisconsin Press, 2011.

Shipman, David. *The Great Movie Stars*. Boston: Little, Brown, 1995.

Ford, Harrison *(1942–)*

Starring in two of the most successful film trilogies of all time, the *Star Wars* and *Indiana Jones* adventures, actor Harrison Ford became the action hero for a new generation of blockbusters in the 1970s and 1980s. Throughout the 1990s he further consolidated his film star appeal and was voted "The Greatest Movie Star of All Time" by *Empire* magazine in September 1997.

FROM CARPENTER TO MOVIE STAR

Ford's most notable roles prior to *Star Wars* were appearances in George Lucas's *American Graffiti* (1973) and Francis Ford Coppola's *The Conversation* (1974), establishing him as a competent character actor and, more importantly, making him known to the so-called "movie brat" directors who came to dominate commercial cinema in the 1970s and 1980s. Ford was working as a carpenter to the stars when Lucas called him in to take part in auditions for a new science fiction project. Breaking all box-office records and establishing the trend for special-effects blockbusters, *Star Wars* (1977) was a much bigger film than any of its actors; but Ford's Han Solo clearly had the edge as an attractive rogue—a cowboy in the first film, a romantic hero in

The Empire Strikes Back (1980), and a freedom fighter in *Return of the Jedi* (1983).

Apart from a lighthearted cowboy role in *The Frisco Kid* (1979), for a while it seemed that Ford was going to be typecast in war movies—he was the Vietnam veteran in *Heroes* (1977); the action man in *Force 10 from Navarone* (1978); the romantic hero in *Hanover Street* (1979); and, as the sum of his associations, Captain Lucas in Coppola's *Apocalypse Now* (1979). But it was with the release of Steven Spielberg's *Raiders of the Lost Ark* in 1981 that Ford was able to take center screen in an altogether different, but still highly familiar, set of adventures. As an archaeologist in the 1930s, the Indiana Jones character combined all of the essential action fantasies of the Lucas-Spielberg team; as typified by the first film, for example, this adventurer could take part in a mythic quest against the Nazis—fantasy and war movie heroics lovingly packaged in Saturday morning serial form.

The first two sequels, *Indiana Jones and the Temple of Doom* (1984) and *Indiana Jones and the Last Crusade* (1989), clearly established Ford as the family action hero of the decade, an actor who combined elements of Humphrey Bogart, Gary Cooper, and Cary Grant, partly in his looks and his acting style, partly in the types of pastiche films he chose, and all in contrast to the solely muscle-bound poundings of Sylvester Stallone and Arnold Schwarzenegger.

Ford's performances in Ridley Scott's *Blade Runner* (1982) and Peter Weir's *Witness* (1985) may, in fact, remain his most interesting in this respect. Not overtly commercial films, they nevertheless established Ford as an actor with understated authority, earning comparisons to 1940s film noir with the former and to *High Noon* (1952) with the latter, serving to enhance rather than detract from his contemporary "everyman" appeal. Although possibly Ford's least favorite film, *Blade Runner* nevertheless gained cult and now classic status, and for *Witness* he gained his only Academy Award nomination. Ford perhaps demonstrated his greatest acting range as a stubborn inventor in Weir's *The Mosquito Coast* (1986). His next two films were Mike Nichols's romantic comedy *Working Girl* (1988) and Roman Polanski's Hitchcockian thriller *Frantic* (1988).

RELUCTANT STAR

Ford's attractiveness lies in the fact that he's something of a reluctant star who can nevertheless bring authority and appeal to the most generic of films. Part of his ongoing success has been due to the deliberation and discrimination with which he has chosen his films, taking care to alternate action with light comedy and drama and to work with the most professional directors available. After two of his most mediocre films, Alan J. Pakula's solid courtroom drama *Presumed Innocent* (1990) and Nichols's sentimental *Regarding Henry* (1991), Ford had the sense to move on to action thrillers, starring as Jack Ryan in the high-tech Tom Clancy adaptations *Patriot Games* (1992) and *Clear and Present Danger* (1994) and as the innocent doctor on the run in *The Fugitive* (1993).

Two of Ford's most ill-received films appeared in 1995 and 1997; in the remake of 1954's *Sabrina* he played the Bogart role, and in *The Devil's Own* he courted controversy as a New York police office harboring an Irish Republican Army (IRA) assassin. Though Ford often has noted that he chooses films with "strong" stories, some of his films have had controversial political agendas. Both *Patriot Games* and *The Devil's Own* offer a simplistic vision of the IRA situation in Ireland. *Clear and Present Danger* is quite radical in its attack on sub-Republican government, and *Air Force One* (1997) offers a more populist political agenda. Directed by Wolfgang Petersen, *Air Force One* is an undeniably professional action film, but with Ford playing a U.S. president who gets to fight back at terrorists, it was too contemporary, perhaps, to avoid "political" readings. From these films with deliberate political currents, Ford moved on to Ivan Reitman's lightweight "castaway" comedy *Six Days Seven Nights* (1998), playing the sort of cantankerous figure Cary Grant played in his later years—another classic comparison for an actor who also happens to be one of the most important stars of the contemporary era.

FORD'S SUCCESS CONTINUES

Ford's first two thrillers of the next decade, *What Lies Beneath* (2000) and *K-19: The Widowmaker* (2002), earned respectable reviews and fared better than his 2003 crime comedy, *Hollywood Homicide*, and 2006 thriller, *Firewall*. In 2008 he returned as one of his favorite characters in *Indiana Jones and the Kingdom of the Crystal Skull*. He played dramatic leads in *Crossing Over* (2009) and *Extraordinary Measures* (2010); starred in a romantic comedy, *Morning Glory* (2010); and saved humanity from a new frontier threat in a graphic-novel-inspired sci-fi–Western hybrid, *Cowboys & Aliens* (2011). Most of these films performed better at the box office than they did in critical reviews, "but they were adventures," he told *USA Today* in 2008 about some of the earlier works.

Ford has starred in several of the highest-grossing films in history. He attributes his extraordinary success at the box office to his midwestern work ethic (he grew up in Park Ridge, Illinois, a Chicago suburb). Nor does he mind no longer being the star: age has made him a character actor, and he says he is happy in that role. In late 2011 a fifth installment of the *Indiana Jones* series was announced, with Ford again reprising his role as Indy, much to his fans' delight.

Ford received the American Film Institute's Life Achievement Award in 2000, the Golden Globe Cecil B. DeMille Award in 2002, and several People's Choice Awards for favorite actor. He is married to actress Calista Flockhart and is a noted environmental activist, happiest on his 800-acre ranch in Jackson, Wyoming, or in the air, where he flies private airplanes and helicopters. In 2000 and 2001 Ford piloted his helicopter to join searches for missing, stranded hikers. The headlines about the rescues annoyed him because he felt the other members of the search parties were unfairly ignored. It is indeed a paradox that Ford is a movie star, because his down-to-earth refusal to take his movie star status too seriously makes him so likeable. His characters are most successful when they are like him—playful, witty, cantankerous, heroic, and renegade.

Stephen Keane

SEE ALSO: *Academy Awards;* American Graffiti*;* Apocalypse Now*;* Blade Runner*; Blockbusters; Bogart, Humphrey; Celebrity; Celebrity Couples; Clancy, Tom; Cooper, Gary; Environmentalism; Film Noir;* The Fugitive*; Grant, Cary;* High Noon*; Hollywood; Lucas, George; Movie Stars; Nichols, Mike, and Elaine May;* Raiders of the Lost Ark*; Schwarzenegger, Arnold; Scott, Ridley; Spielberg, Steven; Stallone, Sylvester;* Star Wars*; War Movies; The Western.*

BIBLIOGRAPHY

Clinch, Minty. *Harrison Ford: A Biography.* London: New English Library, 1987.

Duke, Brad. *Harrison Ford: The Films.* Jefferson, NC: McFarland, 2008.

Jenkins, Garry. *Harrison Ford: Imperfect Hero.* London: Simon & Schuster, 1997.

Ford, Henry *(1863–1947)*

As the founder of Ford Motor Company, Henry Ford epitomized the can-do optimism of the industrial age. His homespun, folksy persona charmed Americans and defined an alternate image of the wealthy industrialist. His Model T automobile, which rolled out of his Michigan headquarters in 1908, was the first car to capture the national imagination and the first to sell in mass quantities. Upon doubling his workers' wages in 1914, Ford became an overnight celebrity.

Though he earned his fame as a wealthy industrialist, Ford grew up on a modest family farm. Born July 30, 1863, in Dearborn, Michigan, he spent his early years doing chores and tinkering with watches and steam engines. At age sixteen he left home to take a job in Detroit for a manufacturer of railroad boxcars. For the next twenty years he worked at a succession of technical jobs, eventually landing the position of chief engineer at a power company. All the while, he tinkered in his off hours with homemade steam and, ultimately, gasoline-powered engines and vehicles.

In 1899, at age thirty-eight, Ford quit the power company and, with some partners, founded his first automobile manufacturing enterprise. While this attempt failed, as did a second, his third try, Ford Motor Company, founded in 1903, grew into one of the largest, wealthiest companies of the century. The introduction of the Model T in 1908 revolutionized the young industry. Ford quite intentionally set out to, in his words, "build a motor car for the great multitude." Ford continually reduced the retail price, bragging, "Every time I reduce the charge for our car by $1, I get a thousand new buyers." Each price decrease was heralded by national press coverage. The first car aimed at the middle class, the Model T was an immediate best seller—so much so that building enough cars to meet public demand became a significant challenge.

Ford worked with his team to develop a number of refinements to the production process, culminating in 1913 with the assembly line, a system in which each worker had one small task to repeatedly perform and remained in place while an automated belt rolled the cars past. These improvements cut production time by 90 percent. Ford's competitors were forced to adopt the same methods, and the assembly line became a standard of manufacturing operations.

Previously, craftspeople had worked on a job from beginning to end, but the division of labor necessary to boost efficiency on an assembly line required the breaking of the production process into a series of repetitive, boring tasks that required only moderate skill. The implementation of the assembly line increased worker turnover and absenteeism. By 1914 Ford Motor Company was spending $3 million a year training new workers to replace those who had quit. In response, Ford raised the daily wage of his laborers from $2.35 to $5. While the success of the Model T gained Ford some renown as a successful inventor and industrialist, the "$5 day," as it became known, heralded his arrival as a national celebrity. All the newspapers of the day reported it, many editorializing for or against the practice.

Once he became a household name, Ford was asked to opine on all manner of popular issues and eagerly did so with a commonsensical folk wisdom that endeared him to many. Ford's populist pronouncements, such as "the right price is the lowest price an article can be steadily sold for and the right wage is the highest wage the purchaser can steadily pay," set him in stark contrast to the monopolistic robber barons of the previous era, such as Andrew Carnegie, John D. Rockefeller, and Cornelius Vanderbilt. The left-wing magazine the *Nation* marveled that this "simple mechanic" didn't need "combination or manipulation or oppression or extortion" to dominate his market but instead "distanced his competitors by no other art than that of turning out his product by more perfect or more economical methods than they have been able to devise or execute."

Ford basked in the favorable attention lavished on him, but he was unprepared for the increased scrutiny he received in the public eye. In 1915 the national press ridiculed him when, in an effort to avoid war with Germany, he chartered an ocean liner to take himself and his "delegates" to Europe to mediate and negotiate for peace. In 1918 he was chastened by the personal attacks he and his family endured as a result of his narrowly unsuccessful run for U.S. Senate. In 1919 Ford sued the *Chicago Tribune* when it labeled him "ignorant." In the ensuing trial and surrounding media circus, the *Tribune*'s lawyer proceeded to humiliate Ford by exposing his utter lack of historical knowledge.

Ford nonetheless became a folk hero to the public in the 1910s and 1920s. He was a man of little formal education who, through his own wits, became one of the richest men in the country yet continued to espouse populist values, paying his workers well and lowering the price of his cars nearly every year. A 1923 *Collier's* poll showed him far ahead of Warren G. Harding, Herbert Hoover, and everyone else in a theoretical presidential race. In part because of Ford's influence, it has become routine to accept populist political and social wisdom from wealthy titans of industry, such as Lee Iacocca and Ross Perot.

Ford, the farmer, tinkerer, inventor, industrialist, and populist social critic, died in 1947. The automobile had long since become an American icon, as had the man himself.

Steven Kotok

SEE ALSO: *Automobile; Conspiracy Theories; The Edsel; Ford Motor Company; Iacocca, Lee; Model T; Perot, Ross.*

BIBLIOGRAPHY

Collier, Peter, and Chris Horowitz. *The Fords: An American Epic.* New York: Summit Books, 1987.

Lewis, David L. *The Public Image of Henry Ford.* Detroit, MI: Wayne State University Press, 1976.

Nevins, Allan. *Ford: The Times, the Man, the Company.* New York: Scribner, 1954.

Sward, Keith. *The Legend of Henry Ford.* New York: Russell & Russell, 1968.

York, M. J. *Henry Ford: Manufacturing Mogul.* Minneapolis, MN: ABDO, 2011.

Ford, John *(1894–1973)*

Director John Ford's influence on American culture extends far beyond his prolific, wide-ranging, and often impressive output of movies in a fifty-year career that began in the silent era with *The Tornado* (1917). Despite the variety of subjects he tackled for the screen, he remains best known as the architect of the Western, the genre in which he cut his teeth during the silent era. His romantic vision of the Old West has crept into the perception of American history, blending idealized fiction into the harsher truths for generations of people in the United States and beyond.

Ford is one of the most decorated directors in Hollywood history. His four Academy Awards for Best Director illustrate his range while curiously ignoring his Westerns. He won his first Oscar for a return to the political roots of Ireland with *The Informer* (1935), a tale of a simpleminded Irishman (Victor McLaglen) who betrays an Irish Republican Army (IRA) leader. It was lavished with critical praise for its stylization and grim atmosphere. Ford returned to Ireland again for his Oscar-winning *The Quiet Man* (1952), a Technicolor comedy. His other Best Director Oscars were for *The Grapes of Wrath* (1940), from John Steinbeck's novel about a family that treks to California to escape the Dust Bowl of the 1930s, and *How Green Was My Valley* (1941), a nostalgic tearjerker set in a Welsh mining community.

Ford's other acclaimed films include *The Whole Town's Talking* (1935), a comedic melodrama with Edward G. Robinson; the Shirley Temple vehicle *Wee Willie Winkie* (1937), set in colonial India; *Young Mr. Lincoln* (1939); *What Price Glory* (1952); *Mogambo* (1953); and his last feature, *Seven Women* (1966), set in an isolated Chinese mission in the 1930s. This canon shows the depth and range of his interests and film-making skills.

John Ford. *During his career of more than fifty years, John Ford won a record four Academy Awards for Best Director.* **HULTON ARCHIVE/GETTY IMAGES.**

HIS FIRST FILMS

Ford was born Sean O'Feeney in Portland, Maine, on February 1, 1894, one of the many children of his first-generation Irish immigrant parents. Of his siblings, he was closest to his brother Francis, who was twelve years his senior. The restless Francis ran away from home at an early age to seek his fortune, changed his last name to Ford, and forged a modestly successful acting career in the theater before moving into the film business with Thomas Edison and Biograph. By 1913 he was in Hollywood writing, directing, and acting in silent action serials at Universal Studios; in 1914, his younger brother joined him.

Known initially as Jack Ford (he changed his first name to John in 1923), he learned the rudiments of filming as an apprentice to Francis, eventually being allowed a hand in acting, writing, and camera work. In 1917, just as Francis Ford's star was fading, Universal's founder and chief, Carl Laemmle, entrusted the younger Ford with directing *The Tornado*, a two-reel short. The film was a success, and what would become a prolific directing career was launched.

In Ford's four and a half years at Universal, he made his reputation as a director of Westerns and forged a significant creative relationship with actor Harry Carey, whom he later frequently cited as having been the most important influence on his work besides his brother Francis. When the fledgling director met Carey, sixteen years his senior, the actor had already worked in almost 200 films. He would appear in the majority of Ford's films for Universal. Ford's stock rose considerably during his time at Universal, as his films generally came in on time and under budget and turned a profit.

REDEFINING THE WESTERN

In 1920 Ford jumped to Fox, for which he made fifty films. The move was perfectly timed: within a few years after his arrival, Fox rose from a second-tier studio to an industry leader. Although Ford, always stubborn, had run-ins with management from time to time, he enjoyed freedom that few of his counterparts could claim. By 1939 his stock had risen to new heights. Ford had taken a break from his first love, the Western, since 1927, partially because the genre was not taken seriously by critics. However, he now was determined to use his reputation and influence to bring prestige to the Western.

Ford achieved this goal with *Stagecoach* (1939), a watershed film that marked the first of his famous collaborations with John Wayne. It was also the first of nine films that Ford set in Monument Valley, a rocky, wide-open region of the Colorado Plateau that is located on the Arizona-Utah border. Thanks mostly to Ford, contemporary audiences think of Monument Valley as the quintessential setting for a cowboy movie. As Jane Tompkins argues in *West of Everything: The Inner Life of Westerns*, "not just any space will do [for a Western film]. Big sky country is a psychological and spiritual place known by definite physical markers. It is the American West, and not just any part of that but the West of the desert, of mountains and prairies, the West of Arizona, Utah, Nevada, New Mexico, Texas, Colorado, Montana, Wyoming, the Dakotas, and some parts of California." Ford's repeated use of the valley turned it into an archetypal landscape. Never identified by name in any of the Ford films in which it is featured, Monument Valley represents locations as diverse as Tombstone, Arizona *(My Darling Clementine*, 1946), and the Texas plains (*Rio Grande*, 1950, and *The Searchers*, 1956).

In many ways, *Stagecoach* is a "B" Western: it is rife with stereotypes and follows the structure of what would later be known as the "road movie." However, Ford was fully aware of these stereotypes, the use of which, as Richard Slotkin observes in *Gunfighter Nation*, "allowed him to take advantage of genre-based understandings—clichés of plot, setting, characterization, and motivation—to compose an exceptional work marked by moral complexity, formal elegance, narrative and verbal economy, and evocative imagery." The characters were given rich life by a superb cast led by Wayne, Claire Trevor, and Thomas Mitchell, who won an Oscar for Best Supporting Actor. The film also earned an Oscar for its music score and garnered five additional nominations, including for Best Picture and Best Director. *Stagecoach* was exquisitely photographed. In a 1939 review for the *New York Times*, critic Frank Nugent called it "a motion picture that sings the song of camera."

After the immense critical and commercial success of *Stagecoach*, Ford had the freedom to make just about any Western he wanted. In 1941, however, his Hollywood career was put on hold while he served as a lieutenant commander in the navy during World War II. Appointed chief of the Field Photographic Branch of the Office of Strategic Services, he made two Academy Award–winning documentary propaganda films, *The Battle of Midway* (1942) and *December 7* (1943).

After the war, Ford returned home and focused primarily on the Western, beginning with *My Darling Clementine*, starring Henry Fonda. This film marked the beginning of a nearly ten-year period of filmmaking by Ford that frequently reflected mainstream America's postwar optimism. As Mark Siegel notes in *American Culture and the Classic Western Movie*:

> *Clementine* seems to reflect an America looking back on the recent world war. One image Americans held of their participation in World War II was that . . . America needed not just to revenge itself but to make the world a safe and decent place in which to live. . . . The hopefulness of this movie, which shows Tombstone as an increasingly civilized social center, seems typical of American optimism immediately after World War II.

Ford's optimism continued throughout the late 1940s and early 1950s, as evidenced by such films as his marvelous "Cavalry Trilogy," starring Wayne—*Fort Apache* (1948), *She Wore a Yellow Ribbon* (1949), and *Rio Grande*—and *Wagon Master* (1950).

FADING OPTIMISM

According to Peter Stowell in a 1986 biography of Ford, most of the director's Westerns present America as a "strong, vibrant, frontier culture that must retain its strength through a wilderness frontier hero, while it demonstrates its progress through a series of civilizing factors." Thanks to Ford's influence, most classic Hollywood Westerns share these traits. However, toward the end of his career, his optimism turned to cynicism, and he began lamenting the progress he had once celebrated.

In his later films, most notably *The Searchers*—a bitter revenge Western starring Wayne and considered by many to be the director's masterpiece—*The Man Who Shot Liberty Valance* (1962), and *Cheyenne Autumn* (1964), he began to question the myths that he had played such a central role in creating. As Jon Tuska observes in *The Filming of the West*, "memories, instead of being cherished, became bitter; progress became a hollow drum that beat mechanically." While Ford's earlier films established the tone and morality that typify the classic Hollywood Western, these late works, particularly *The Man Who Shot Liberty Valance*, paved the way for the moody revisionism that has since characterized much of the genre.

Ford died of cancer on August 31, 1973. Shortly before his death, he received the first American Film Institute Lifetime Achievement Award. Since his passing, Ford's reputation as a filmmaker has continued to grow, and he is widely considered to be the most influential director in Hollywood history. His gifts and his influence have been acknowledged over the decades by the finest of his peers. Orson Welles spoke for many when, in answering a question about which American directors most appealed to him, he said, "The old masters . . . by which I mean John Ford, John Ford, and John Ford."

Robert C. Sickels

SEE ALSO: *Edison, Thomas Alva; Fonda, Henry;* The Grapes of Wrath*;* How the West Was Won*;* The Man Who Shot Liberty Valance*;* My Darling Clementine*;* The Searchers*;* She Wore a Yellow Ribbon*; Silent Movies;* Stagecoach*; Wayne, John; The Western.*

BIBLIOGRAPHY

Bogdanovich, Peter. *John Ford*. Berkeley: University of California Press, 1967.

Darby, William. *John Ford's Westerns: A Thematic Analysis with Filmography*. Jefferson, NC: McFarland, 1996.

Davis, Ronald L. *John Ford: Hollywood's Old Master*. Norman: University of Oklahoma Press, 1995.

Gallagher, Tag. *John Ford: The Man and His Films*. Berkeley: University of California Press, 1986.

McBride, Joseph, and Michael Wilmington. *John Ford*. New York: Da Capo Press, 1975.

McBride, Joseph *Searching for John Ford*. Jackson: University Press of Mississippi, 2011.

Siegel, Mark. *American Culture and the Classic Western Movie*. Tokyo: Eihosha, 1984.

Slotkin, Richard. *Gunfighter Nation*. New York: Atheneum.

Stowell, Peter. *John Ford*. Boston: Twayne, 1986.

Tompkins, Jane. *West of Everything: The Inner Life of Westerns*. New York: Oxford University Press, 1992.

Tuska, Jon. *The Filming of the West*. New York: Doubleday, 1976.

Yawn, Mike, and Bob Beatty. "John Ford's Vision of the Closing West: From Optimism to Cynicism." *Film & History* 26, nos. 1–4 (1996): 6–19.

Ford, Tennessee Ernie *(1919–1991)*

With his smooth bass voice and warm country charm, Ernest Jennings "Tennessee Ernie" Ford became one of the first country music stars to cross musical boundaries to reach a truly national audience during the 1950s. Working as a disc jockey and radio performer in California after World War II, Ford came to the attention of Capitol Records, which signed him in 1949. A string of hits followed, most of them in the "country boogie" style he helped pioneer that married boogie-woogie rhythms with country music themes and instrumentation. Some of his most famous songs include "The Shot Gun Boogie," "Anticipation Blues," and "I'm Hog-Tied Over You." Tennessee Ernie Ford became a national figure when his recording of "Sixteen Tons" became both a country and pop hit in 1955. He starred in his own television programs between 1956 and 1961 and later recorded a number of highly successful gospel albums.

Timothy Berg

SEE ALSO: *Country Music; Gospel Music.*

BIBLIOGRAPHY

Ford, Jeffrey Buckner. *River of No Return: Tennessee Ernie Ford and the Woman He Loved.* Nashville, TN: Cumberland House Publishing, 2008.

Ford, Tennessee Ernie. *Sixteen Tons of Boogie: The Best of Tennessee Ernie Ford.* Rhino Records R2 70975, 1990, compact disc.

Malone, Bill C. *Country Music U.S.A.: A Fifty-Year History.* Austin: University of Texas Press, 1968.

Stambler, Irwin, and Grelun Landon. *Country Music: The Encyclopedia.* New York: St. Martin's Press, 1997.

Ford, Whitey *(1928–)*

Edward Charles "Whitey" Ford was the dominating left-handed pitcher for the New York Yankees from 1950 to 1967, a seventeen-year period that coincided with the team's greatest success. Manager Casey Stengel nicknamed Ford "Slick"—and with good reason: Ford, born and raised in New York, was a city slicker who often relied on guile—and perhaps a scuffed ball on the mound—and liked to take a drink now and then. "The Chairman of the Board," as he was also known, chalked up a career record of 236–106, the highest winning percentage for any twentieth-century pitcher, and came to hold a nearly unsurpassable World Series record for wins, strikeouts, and consecutive scoreless innings.

Whitey Ford, Mickey Mantle, and Billy Martin constituted a New York trio in the 1950s that shared a public passion for baseball, drinking, and women. They did much to establish the image of the baseball player as an overgrown boy: silly, crude, and outrageous but basically harmless. Ford was inducted into the Baseball Hall of Fame in 1974, at which point the Yankees retired his number (16).

Jon Sterngass

SEE ALSO: *Baseball; Mantle, Mickey; The New York Yankees; Sports Heroes; Stengel, Casey; World Series.*

BIBLIOGRAPHY

Ford, Whitey, and Phil Pepe. *Slick: My Life in and around Baseball.* New York: William Morrow, 1987.

Vincent, Fay. *We Would Have Played for Nothing: Baseball Stars of the 1950s and 1960s Talk about the Game They Loved.* New York: Simon & Schuster, 2008.

Ford Motor Company

Founded in 1903 by Henry Ford with money from twelve other investors, Ford Motor Company grew from a modest factory in Detroit, Michigan, into a multinational corporation that boasted more than $180 billion in annual global sales by 2011. During Ford Motor Company's early years, it was virtually indistinguishable from its founder, who was widely recognized as a genius in the early part of the twentieth century. The success of the company has been attributed to a system of mass production that combined new manufacturing technology, such as the assembly line, with the principles of "scientific management," a process developed by American mechanical engineer Frederick Taylor that streamlined workflow to maximize worker efficiency and thereby increase production and profits. Ford's methods were so successful that his management style came to be known as "Fordism" and was widely imitated by other entrepreneurs.

Made famous by his signature vehicle, the Model T, which was produced between 1908 and 1927, the Ford Motor Company controlled the car market of the 1920s and, in the process, helped to make the automobile an essential component of American culture. After Ford's resignation in 1945 and a series of problems throughout the 1950s, the remarkable success of the Mustang in the 1960s reestablished the prominence of Ford Motor Company. Since then, the company has remained one of the most successful automobile manufacturers in the world, eventually producing more than five million cars and trucks per year and continually receiving high ranks in customer satisfaction surveys.

THE MODEL T

The rapid growth of Ford Motor Company during the first twenty years of the twentieth century was due to the astounding sales record of the Model T, or "Tin Lizzie," as it came to be known. Because the cost of early automobiles was prohibitive for most Americans, cars were essentially luxury items. Thus, few manufacturers saw the potential for mass appeal of the motorized vehicle. Introduced in 1908 with a debut price of only $850, significantly less expensive than those of its competitors, the Model T was within the budget of many consumers. Because Ford's ingenious labor-saving techniques were not yet available—the assembly line, for instance, would later quadruple productive capacities and reduce labor expenses—Ford kept costs for the Model T low by producing only one type of car (other companies tried to build several different models simultaneously) but assembling it with interchangeable body styles. Due to its functional simplicity, the car was often ridiculed for its aesthetic shortcomings, and Ford himself joked that consumers could purchase the Model T "in any color they want so long as it's black."

Despite its competitive price, the Model T did not sell particularly well until Ford developed an aggressive marketing scheme that broadened the appeal of the Model T and eventually made it the best-selling car in history. Ford had originally won financial backing for Ford Motor Company by racing cars, and he turned to racing once again in an effort to sell his new product. This competition, however, was a much publicized transcontinental race. Though the winning Ford car was later disqualified for irregularities, the Model T gained enormous notoriety for its victory, which Ford turned into massive sales.

By 1911 the popularity of the Model T began to present fresh challenges to Ford Motor Company and its management

Ford Motor Company's 300 Millionth Vehicle. *Ford Chairman and CEO Bill Ford addresses workers and the media to mark the production of the company's 300 millionth vehicle, a Mustang GT convertible, in 2003.* BILL PUGLIANO/GETTY IMAGES.

team. The young company had already moved its base of operations to Highland Park, Michigan, after reaching productive capacity at its Detroit shop and was rapidly approaching its limit once again. The appetite of consumers was far from sated, but labor shortages and productivity ceilings were arresting further plans for expansion. Over the next five years or so, Ford began to streamline the assembly process, enabling his workers to produce one car every ninety-three minutes.

To a large extent, the evolution of America's car culture can be traced to Ford and the Model T. It was the first car marketed to a large consumer audience, and this alone redefined the role of the automobile industry in the United States. In their famous sociological study *Middletown* (1929), Robert and Helen Lynd conclude that by 1925 the automobile was already an accepted and indispensable part of American life. It is no exaggeration to suggest that the Model T permanently changed the geography of the United States: the popularity of the car made the huge suburban building booms of the 1920s possible, as millions of miles of paved roads were built in response to the demands of new motorists.

EARLY WORKING CONDITIONS

In its early years, the philosophy of Fordism rested on two simple strategies: the invention of the assembly line and the increase of wages. Before the introduction of line work at Ford, the bodies of cars remained stationary while teams of workers moved from station to station. By simply putting the unfinished body on rails and attaching it to a drive train, Ford could move the car from point to point while groups of laborers remained at their assigned posts. This new method allowed for greater specialization of tasks among the workers and permitted management to monitor the efficiency of laborers. Though Ford did not invent the assembly line, he has been credited with its development and refinement.

One of the earliest and most persistent critiques of the assembly line came from craftspeople who complained that the division of labor reduced the level of skill required for employment. The assembly line created a distinct division of labor, and the standardization of tasks it required led to a more general deskilling of workers. In order to induce workers to accept this new industrial regime, Ford decided to raise wages. Although this contradicted the logic of supply and demand (with the assembly line, fewer workers could produce more), Ford reasoned that workers would accept more mundane work only in return for better compensation. With the introduction of the eight-hour, $5 day (more than doubling the average daily pay) in 1914, Ford singlehandedly revolutionized wage structures. Thousands of job seekers flooded employment offices across the Detroit area looking for positions at Ford, and Ford himself later said that the $5 day was the best idea he had ever had.

Ironically, the concept of higher wages also permitted the company to discriminate in the workplace. Employees of Eastern European and Middle Eastern descent were given the most dangerous and physically taxing jobs, while African Americans were not hired until World War I and women were a rarity before World War II. Meant to bring stability to the organization, the $5 day was introduced as part of a larger profit-sharing scheme: workers were eligible only after six months at the company and had to pass a battery of tests in order to qualify.

To this end, Ford Motor Company recruited an army of social workers, whose ranks included physicians, nurses, and sociologists, to inspect the habits and living arrangements of its employees. To his credit, Ford seemed genuinely concerned with the safety of his employees and built a hospital where they could receive treatment at any time of day. However, his paternalistic attitude toward his employees had more questionable results in other areas. The company produced a series of instructional manuals during the 1910s and 1920s that encouraged its employees to practice thrifty lifestyles and conform to "American" ways of living. Employees who were unmarried or did not live in "sanitary" homes were consistently denied a share of profits. To assist its many immigrant employees, Ford established an official program of "Americanization" that included English-language training, courses on household thrift, and moral instruction. Not surprisingly, employees of British descent often qualified for profit sharing with little scrutiny; most other immigrants had to pass the course of Americanization before they could hope to realize the $5 wage.

THE 1930s AND BEYOND

The glory years of Ford ended during the 1930s, and the next three decades were a very tumultuous time for the company. In keeping with his philosophy, Ford actually raised wages after the stock market crash of 1929 in an effort to stimulate demand. Unwilling to find other supporters in industry, he was compelled to reverse his policy shortly thereafter. Labor unrest and unionization during the 1930s forced Ford to reassess his authoritarian discipline and recognize the power of organized labor. He stepped down as president of the company in 1945, and though profits had been maintained during the war, his arcane organizational structure was limiting profitability. The ensuing power struggle eventually led to the company's public stock offering.

The Edsel, the company's intermediate model of the late 1950s, named after Ford's son, was the most spectacular failure in the history of American automobile production, symbolizing the mood within the company and its public reputation. Although Ford kept its position as an industrial giant (it has consistently been the third-largest American manufacturer during the postwar era), General Motors established itself as a much larger and more profitable rival.

On the road, Ford maintained its visibility during the 1950s with the Thunderbird. Its eight-cylinder engine was one of the most powerful in its time, but its size necessitated a fairly large body. Because it was priced in the range of other luxury cars (the Chevrolet Corvette was the only true sports car made in the United States), the Thunderbird faced stiff competition from sleek foreign models, though it always achieved high sales figures. New technology in the early 1960s allowed for more streamlined vehicles, and Ford responded by releasing the Mustang in 1963 (under the direction of a young Lee Iacocca). Smaller and more affordable than the Thunderbird, the Mustang became all things to all people: at once a sports coupe and a touring sedan, it offered a unique combination of practicality and flair. Featured in the 1964 Bond film *Goldfinger*, its remarkable success helped to create the category of the sports sedan, reinvigorating Ford's lagging profits.

Although the 1970s and early 1980s were a difficult time for Ford and the other American auto manufacturers—the oil crisis of 1973 and competition from Japanese firms sapped profits, while the well-publicized safety problems of the Pinto did little to enhance the company's image—Ford reemerged during the 1980s with the Escort, a functional economy car designed for the growing legions of suburban Americans. The Escort was the best-selling car in the world for a number of years, and it helped catapult Ford into a period of renewed profitability. With the Escort, Ford returned to its roots, using the principles of functionality and reliability to once again capture a mass consumer audience.

FORD IN THE TWENTY-FIRST CENTURY

As with many car manufacturers, Ford was hit hard by the economic downturn of the early twenty-first century. Even before the recession that began in 2007, the company saw substantial profit losses. By 2005 corporate bond-rating agencies had downgraded the bonds of both Ford and General Motors to junk status. In late 2008 Ford, General Motors, and Chrysler attended congressional hearings in Washington, D.C., at which the companies sought financial aid. While this request was ultimately denied, GM and Chrysler received aid through the Troubled Asset Relief Program. Ford refused the aid, saying it had sufficient funds to make a comeback.

Although Ford posted a profit in 2009 for the first time in four years, its economic recovery was largely due to a reduction in production and job cuts. The company developed long-term plans that included dropping less profitable models such as the sport utility vehicle (SUV), increasing production of hybrid models, and creating more fuel-efficient and environmentally friendly technologies. In 2011 Ford saw its sales rise 17 percent by the end of the year, and in 2012 the company had its rating raised from junk to investment-grade status. Following in Henry Ford's original vision, the firm continued to find innovative ways to engage its employees and customers. In 2012 it launched a partnership with the Detroit Tech Shop to develop a program that encouraged employees to design features for its automobiles. Ford also partnered with Microsoft to create mobile technologies that would facilitate the charging of its electric cars. Throughout its history, Ford has maybe not invented the wheel, but it has continually remained relevant by improving upon it.

Peter Kalliney

SEE ALSO: *Automobile; Consumerism; The Edsel; Ford, Henry; General Motors; Hybrid Cars; Iacocca, Lee; Model T; Muscle Cars; Sport Utility Vehicles (SUVs).*

BIBLIOGRAPHY

Ford, Henry. *My Life and Work: An Autobiography of Henry Ford.* Sioux Falls, SD: NuVision Publications, 2007.

Flink, James J. *The Automobile Age.* Cambridge, MA: MIT Press, 1988.

Miller, Ray. *Mustang Does It: An Illustrated History.* Oceanside, CA: Evergreen Press, 1978.

Nevins, Allan. *Ford: The Times, the Man, the Company.* New York: Scribner, 1954.

Nevins, Allan. *Ford: Expansion and Challenge, 1915–1933.* New York: Scribner, 1957.

Nevins, Allan. *Ford: Decline and Rebirth, 1933–1962.* New York: Scribner, 1963.

Raushenbush, Carl. *Fordism, Ford, and the Community.* New York: League for Industrial Democracy, 1937.

Stern, Philip Van Doren. *Tin Lizzie: The Story of the Fabulous Model T Ford.* New York: Simon & Schuster, 1955.

Foreman, George *(1949–)*

Boxer George Foreman is best known not as the fierce young heavyweight fighter of his youth but as the oldest man ever to claim the heavyweight championship. He has had a boxing career in two distinct eras, the first spanning the glory years of heavyweight boxing in the late 1960s and the 1970s and the second defined by his astonishing comeback in the 1990s. The forty-plus-year-old Foreman's return earned him the status of an American icon, and as he boxed and boasted about his ability to eat, he became a symbol of determination for a generation many considered over the hill.

In 1968 Foreman won an Olympic gold medal in Mexico City. After turning professional he beat Joe Frazier to capture the world heavyweight championship. In one of the most publicized fights in history, Foreman lost his championship to Muhammad Ali in 1974. By 1977 Foreman had retired from boxing and become a preacher. But he returned to the ring a decade later, an object of ridicule because of his weight and age. In 1994—at the age of forty-five—he recaptured the heavyweight crown.

Foreman was born on January 10, 1949, and was reared in an impoverished area known as the Fifth Ward of Houston, Texas, by his mother. Foreman dropped out of school in junior high and earned a reputation as a fighter. He joined the Job Corps, where he was shipped first to the Fort Vanney Training Center outside Grants Pass, Oregon, then to the Parks Job Corps Center outside Pleasanton, California. After years of being a bully, he finally released his energy in a beneficial way and began to box. He graduated from the Job Corps and worked at the Pleasanton Center while continuing to train as a fighter. As an amateur, Foreman went on to win the gold medal in the tumultuous 1968 Olympics. During the games John Carlos and Tommie Smith, two American sprinters, had been expelled from the Olympic Village for flashing the Black Power salute during their medal ceremony. Foreman waved a small American flag after winning his gold medal match.

George Foreman. *George Foreman was the oldest heavyweight champion in boxing history, winning the title in 1994 at age forty-five.* BOB THOMAS/GETTY IMAGES.

After the Olympics Foreman turned professional, and in his first fight on June 23, 1969, in Madison Square Garden, he knocked out Don Waldheim. Foreman advanced through the heavyweight ranks, and on January 22, 1973, in Kingston, Jamaica, he knocked out Frazier in the second round to win the heavyweight championship.

After compiling a record of 40–0, Foreman lost his first professional fight and the heavyweight crown to Ali on October 30, 1974, in Kinshasa, Zaire (now the Democratic Republic of the Congo), in a match dubbed the "Rumble in the Jungle." His second loss came to Jimmy Young in March 1977 in San Juan, Puerto Rico. Afterward, Foreman experienced a religious conversion, retired from boxing, and became a street preacher and ordained minister. He eventually moved into radio evangelism in Los Angeles and Houston and established his own church in the latter city. He also founded the George Foreman Youth and Community Center.

In an effort to raise money for his youth center—at the age of thirty-seven and ten years removed from professional boxing—Foreman decided to return to the ring. His comeback began in March 1987 in Sacramento, California, against Steve Zouski. The first loss after Foreman's return came on April 19, 1991, in Atlantic City, New Jersey, when he lost a twelve-round decision in a heavyweight championship bout with Evander Holyfield. On November 5, 1994, however, at the age of forty-five, Foreman recaptured the heavyweight championship with a tenth-round knockout of Michael Moorer.

Foreman's return to boxing prominence was accompanied by a rush of media attention, and he proved himself as adept a media celebrity as he was a boxer. With his bald pate, broad smile, and massive physique, he made good copy as he boasted about the numbers of hamburgers he loved to eat. Quipped Foreman to a reporter, "Today the biggest decisions I make aren't related to the heavyweight title. They are whether I visit McDonalds, Burger King, Wendy's, or Jack-in-the-Box." It might have all seemed a joke had he not backed up his words with a powerful punch. In 1999, with a career record of 76–5, Foreman's fans wondered if he could win his next championship while in his fifties. The boxer went on to defend his second heavyweight championship twice before retiring. He maintained his ministry and became known for marketing his George Foreman Grill, which has sold more than 100 million units.

Kerry Owens

SEE ALSO: *Ali, Muhammad; Boxing; Burger King; Frazier, Joe; Holyfield, Evander; McDonald's; 1968 Mexico City Summer Olympic Games; Olympics.*

BIBLIOGRAPHY

Foreman, George, and Joel Engel. *By George*. New York: Villard Books, 1995.

Foreman, George, and Ken Abraham. *God in My Corner*. Nashville: Nelson, 2007.

George Foreman Official Website. Accessed January 2012. Available from http://www.georgeforeman.com

Mailer, Norman. *The Fight*. Boston: Little, Brown, 1975.

Forrest Gump

The film *Forrest Gump* (1994) represents the ultimate American dream. It is a history lesson that takes the viewer from Alabama—where Forrest Gump, an idiot savant and improbable modern hero, is born—across America and beyond, and back to Alabama.

Forrest Gump masterfully weaves together fact and fiction. Governor George Wallace stands in a schoolhouse door as he vows, "Segregation now, segregation tomorrow, and segregation forever"; Paul "Bear" Bryant, the legendary University of Alabama football coach, sees how fast Forrest can run and makes him a Crimson Tide gridiron star. After serving in Vietnam, Forrest comes home to Alabama and earns a fortune in the shrimping business. He had promised his "best good friend" Bubba that they would go into shrimping business together when they returned from the war. Bubba, however, is killed in action, so Forrest goes it alone and gives half of the money he makes to his fallen friend's family.

Based upon the 1986 novel *Forrest Gump* by Winston Groom, the story was transformed into a screenplay by Eric Roth. The movie was a huge hit both commercially and critically, grossing more than $677 million and winning the Oscar for Best Picture. *Forrest Gump*'s message connected with audiences: no matter how grim things may seem, it is possible, as Forrest says, "to put the past behind you and move on." He shows that a gimpy kid in leg braces can become a football hero; win a Congressional Medal of Honor for bravery in Vietnam; become a table tennis champion; crisscross America from sea to shining sea; and marry his childhood sweetheart, who bears him a son to carry on the father's good name.

Despite its notion that life is "like a box of chocolates," *Forrest Gump* is no exercise in candy-coated sentimentality. The viewer witnesses the assassinations of John F. Kennedy and Robert Kennedy, as well as the attempted assassination of Wallace; the struggles over civil rights; and the brutality of the war in Vietnam. Lieutenant Dan (Gary Sinise), who loses both legs in Vietnam, depicts the postwar horror many veterans faced. Jenny (Robin Wright), born in poverty and molested by her father, becomes a stripper and a drug addict after being caught up in the counterculture of love-ins and psychedelics, flower power, and antiwar demonstrations. Though Jenny becomes pregnant with Forrest's child and eventually marries him, she lives a short, unhappy life that serves as questionable testimony to the overriding power of love. Forrest tells her, "I'm not a smart man, but I know what love is." Such words, however, are not enough to save her or his friend Bubba or to prevent Lieutenant Dan from losing his legs.

At the beginning of *Forrest Gump*, a feather floating in the wind lands at Forrest's feet; he picks it up and places it in his worn copy of *Curious George*, the book his mother used to read to him. At the end of the film, he passes the book and the feather on to his son. The lesson is that every person, extraordinary or ordinary, is blown around by the winds of chance, but that it is still possible to prevail.

In addition to the Oscar for Best Picture, *Forrest Gump* earned five other Academy Awards, including Best Actor for Tom Hanks, Best Director for Robert Zemeckis, Best Film Editing, Best Adapted Screenplay, and Best Visual Effects. The masterful visual effects enable Forrest to shake the hand of President Kennedy, Lyndon B. Johnson to place a Congressional Medal around Forrest's neck, and Forrest to meet Richard Nixon and Ronald Reagan, not to mention John Lennon, Dick Cavett, Bob Hope, Captain Kangaroo, and Chairman Mao. Elvis Presley even learns to swivel his hips by watching a young, handicapped Forrest dance.

Although some critics dismiss *Forrest Gump*, the movie affirms the values that Americans hold dear. For example, Forrest's mother (played by Sally Field) exemplifies the ideals associated with motherhood. Forrest repeatedly says, "My Mama always said," his words acting as a refrain. Even though Forrest has an IQ of seventy-five, his mother tells him, "Don't ever let anybody tell you they're better than you." Life, after all, is a box of chocolates, even if "you never know what you're gonna get." *Forrest Gump*'s enduring appeal comes down to this: it gives people hope.

Sue Walker

SEE ALSO: *Academy Awards; Field, Sally; Hanks, Tom; Kennedy Assassination; Vietnam.*

BIBLIOGRAPHY

Groom, Winston. *Forrest Gump*. Garden City, NY: Doubleday, 1986.

Forsyth, Frederick *(1938–)*

Frederick Forsyth shot to fame in America in 1971 as a top thriller writer with the publication of *The Day of the Jackal*, which dealt with the attempt by a hired killer, the Jackal, to murder French president Charles de Gaulle. In the novel, Forsyth precisely describes how things worked, ranging from the construction of a special rifle to the last detail of the "procedure" the Jackal used to acquire his new passport—a style that was to be the hallmark of his books, a meticulous attention to realistic detail. In researching the book, Forsyth consulted a professional assassin, a passport forger, and an underground armorer. In later best sellers he improvised car bombs (*The Odessa File*, 1972), gunrunning (*The Dogs of War*, 1974), the innards of oil tankers (*The Devil's Alternative*, 1979), and the assembly of miniature nuclear bombs (*The Fourth Protocol*, 1984). These novels were followed by a series of books addressing current events, including the first Persian Gulf War (*The Fist of God*, 1994), civil unrest in post-Soviet Russia (*Icon*, 1996), the war in Afghanistan (*The Afghan*, 2006), and the international drug trade (*The Cobra*, 2010). Forsyth's popular appeal has been fueled by the blockbuster films made of his books. He has twice won the Edgar Allan Poe Award from the Mystery Writers of America.

Forsyth's books have been criticized for containing recipes for forged passports and explosive bullets. Some actual crimes seem to have been copycats of crimes described in his books, as in the following examples:

> After Yigal Amir was arrested for the assassination of Yitzhak Rabin in 1995, Israeli police searching his apartment found a copy of *The Day of the Jackal* among his Orthodox Jewish literature.

John Stonehouse, former British labor minister, faked his death in Florida and began a new life in Australia with a new partner.

When geophysicist Karen Reid was shot dead in May 1994, mercury bullets were found near the scene.

Forsyth's research methods when he was writing *The Dogs of War* came under scrutiny in 1978, when a London *Times* story argued that the author had actually commissioned the coup d'état in Equatorial Guinea—an event described in his book. While the truth of this story is difficult to determine, files released from the UK National Archives in 2005 demonstrate that such a coup was in fact planned, and Forsyth has since claimed that he was involved.

Forsyth's interests lay in the relationship of an individual to the organization. In his suspense thrillers, a man of action, a consummate professional, is pitted against an establishment, a bureaucracy, or an organization. The hero, a maverick who succeeds by cutting through standard procedure, often has difficulty fitting into society. Forsyth suggests that it is the lone professionals, whether opposed to the organization or part of it, who truly create history, but a history that is only barely represented on the front pages of newspapers. His technique suggests a hidden pattern governing a great event, a pattern not always obvious even to the participants, much less to newspaper readers or devotees of CNN. It is a style similar to a docudrama, which was popular in the United States in the 1960s with such books as Truman Capote's *In Cold Blood* (1966) and Norman Mailer's experiments with fact and the novel form.

Forsyth was born in Ashford, Kent, in 1938 and educated at Tonbridge School, where he studied French and German. He ended his formal education at the age of seventeen. His background as pilot, journalist, world traveler, and speaker of several languages has served him well in his writing career, where he employs a terse journalistic style using real people, places, and events. From 1958 to 1961 he was a reporter for the *Eastern Daily Press*, first in Norwich and later in King's Lynn, Norfolk. In 1961 he was a Reuters correspondent traveling between Paris, London, and East Berlin, serving as bureau chief in the East German capital because of his knowledge of languages. Next he acted as a BBC radio reporter in London between 1965 and 1967. After that he served a brief stint as an assistant diplomatic correspondent for BBC television, in 1967 and 1968, when he was recalled after his pro-Biafran coverage offended Sir David Hunt, British high commissioner in Lagos.

Forsyth enjoys fishing in the streams on his leafy country estate in Hertfordshire, where he lives with his second wife, Sandy, and two sons, Frederick and Shane. A serious angler who also enjoys the calm of fishing in the Caribbean, Mauritius, and the Andaman Sea, he has commented that the plots of some of his best sellers gel in his mind during hours of staring into space. He also says that the weirdest and loneliest job in the world is that of being a writer. An actor has a cast, a pilot a crew, and a doctor a patient, but a writer has only himself. His own life is reflected in the characters depicted in his thrillers and his anthology of short stories, *No Comebacks* (1982). The effect he achieves is less that of fiction than a projection into real lives.

Joan Gajadhar
Jim Sinclair

SEE ALSO: *Best Sellers; Capote, Truman; Detective Fiction; Docudrama; Gulf Wars; Mailer, Norman; War in Afghanistan; War on Drugs.*

BIBLIOGRAPHY

Atkins, John Alfred. *The British Spy Novel: Styles in Treachery.* London: Calder, 1984.

McCormick, Donald. *Who's Who in Spy Fiction.* New York: Taplinger, 1977.

Merry, Bruce. *Anatomy of the Spy Thriller.* Dublin: Gill & Macmillan, 1977.

Panek, LeRoy L. *The Special Branch: The British Spy Novel, 1890–1980.* Bowling Green, OH: Bowling Green University Popular Press, 1981.

Pate, Janet. *The Book of Spies and Secret Agents.* London: Gallery Press, 1978.

Stade, George, and Karen Karbiener. *Encyclopedia of British Writers, 1800 to the Present, Volume 1.* New York: Facts On File, 2009.

Fortune

Despite an inauspicious launch in February 1930, just four months after the Wall Street crash, *Fortune* magazine became established as the premier business publication in the United States. Symbolic of the success and status of *Fortune*, its annual listing of the top performing companies—the Fortune 500 (established in 1955)—rapidly became, and remains, the highest accolade of American business. Determined to avoid the banality of the trade journal, *Fortune* aimed instead to become "the literature of enterprise." To this end, the magazine publishes high-quality copy, written by established intellectual figures such as Dwight MacDonald, in a high-quality, glossy format. *Fortune* humanizes the world of commerce by combining its stories and values with those of the broader social and political world, and it presents the face of business through the inventive use of photojournalism. Both approaches profoundly influenced Time Inc.'s next publication, the more populist *Life* magazine, which in turn impacted a whole generation of journalists and publishers.

In 2009, during the economic slowdown that came to be known as the Great Recession, *Fortune* experienced a drop in advertising revenues as ad pages fell almost 35 percent. In response, Time Inc. announced that it was cutting costs by changing *Fortune*'s publication schedule from biweekly to triweekly, or eighteen issues a year. As of 2010 the magazine had an average paid circulation of more than 850,000.

Emma Lambert

SEE ALSO: *The Great Depression; The Great Recession;* Let Us Now Praise Famous Men*;* Life.

BIBLIOGRAPHY

Augspurger, Michael. *An Economy of Abundant Beauty: "Fortune" Magazine and Depression America.* Ithaca, NY: Cornell University Press, 2004.

Tebbel, John, and Mary Ellen Zuckerman. *The Magazine in America, 1741–1990.* New York: Oxford University Press, 1991.

Fortune Tellers

SEE: *Psychics.*

42nd Street

The first of a series of Depression-era musicals released by Warner Brothers Pictures, *42nd Street* is notable for its role in reviving and redefining a cinematic genre that had begun to fade by 1933. Following the industry-wide adaptation of sound films in 1929, Hollywood promptly released a plethora of musicals to excited audiences. Unfortunately, the majority of these products were hastily conceived and often hindered by the still unresolved technical mysteries of "talking" pictures. Such artistic shortcomings conspired with a saturation of the marketplace, and the public's enthusiasm for such fare rapidly faded.

The successful release of *42nd Street* in March 1933 reversed this trend and convinced the major studios to reexamine the commercial possibilities for screen musicals. By the end of the year, Warner had released two follow-up films: *Gold Diggers of 1933* and *Footlight Parade.* Other studios embraced this trend, most notably RKO Radio, which began production of a series of pictures starring Fred Astaire and Ginger Rogers. In general, musicals would remain a significant component of Hollywood's product well into the World War II era.

THE SHOW

The plot of *42nd Street* revolves around the efforts of a Broadway director (Warner Baxter) struggling to revive his failing reputation with the creation of a lavish extravaganza. The majority of the film details the rigors and hardships of backstage life with a clear eye for the steamier side of show business. On the eve of the show's debut, the leading lady breaks her leg, leaving the director no recourse but to take a chance on a neophyte yet determined chorus girl (Ruby Keeler). Following Baxter's now-legendary warning—"You're going out a youngster, but you've got to come back a star!"—Keeler takes the stage and delights the audience. Although this should provide Baxter's triumph, the film ends on a somber note. As the director stands outside of the theater to assess the comments of the exiting crowd, the loudest sentiments are complaints about the position of Baxter's name on the marquee. To the audience, it was the dancer, not the director, who deserved the credit for the show's success.

While the backstage setting of *42nd Street* would be used in dozens of subsequent musical films, the basic story was not an innovation at the time. Earlier productions, most notably MGM's *Broadway Melody* (1929), had focused on a similar theme without such lasting impact. What set *42nd Street* apart from its predecessors was a unique collaboration of actors, songwriters, and directors. The film benefited from a strong cast; Baxter and Keeler shared the screen with Bebe Daniels, Ginger Rogers, Dick Powell, Allen Jenkins, Una Merkel, and Guy Kibbee. The team of Al Dubin and Harry Warren composed the music. Although the picture was directed by the dependable craftsman Lloyd Bacon, the musical numbers, which were the main focus of the film, were staged and created by Busby Berkeley.

This assemblage of talent formed a reliable unit that continued to produce highly successful musicals throughout most of the 1930s. Although actors came and went over time, Powell and Keeler were often the focus of these films. Joan Blondell soon joined the stock company as a frequent costar, while Jenkins and Kibbee routinely provided support. Dubin and Warren were prolific songwriters and seldom failed to include at least one tune per film that would become a popular standard. For *42nd Street,* the duo provided "Shuffle off to Buffalo." In subsequent movies, they debuted soon-to-be-familiar titles such as "We're in the Money," "I Only Have Eyes for You," "Don't Give up the Ship," and "The Lullaby of Broadway."

Although Bacon continued to direct musicals such as *Footlight Parade, Wonder Bar* (1934), and *In Caliente* (1935), he was a versatile filmmaker, and the studio often used his talents on other projects. At various times, Mervyn LeRoy, Ray Enright, and Frank Borzage directed musicals for Warner.

THE RISE OF BUSBY BERKELEY

The dominant figure in the creation of the Warner musicals was Berkeley. Rising to prominence as dance director for Broadway showman Florenz Ziegfeld, Berkeley came to Hollywood in 1930 to work for Samuel Goldwyn. In 1933 Warner signed Berkeley to a lucrative seven-year exclusive contract, with *42nd Street* as his initial assignment. Berkeley's work is best described as kaleidoscopic. Employing a system of overhead and moving cameras, he organized his dancers into a dizzying array of geometric patterns. Such activity could occur on stages as diverse as an indoor waterfall or a gigantic typewriter. The dancers might possess props as innocuous as parasols or as surreal as neon-trimmed violins. Berkeley's imagination seemed endless, and with each film the musical numbers became increasingly outlandish.

The fantasy world of Berkeley's dance numbers provided the perfect counterpart to the back stage grittiness of *42nd Street.* As a tremendously popular film released in the depths of the Great Depression, the movie remains a valuable key to the needs and tastes of the American public at a specific time in history. The story focuses on the hopes of the downtrodden, and through luck and determination, a hero emerges. At the same time, the swirling elegance of the elaborate musical numbers provided a healthy dose of escapism from the worries of the day.

However, the topical nature of the film should not be exaggerated. Some fifty years later, the story would be revived as a major Broadway play, written and directed by Mark Bramble in 2001. *42nd Street* opened on May 2 and ran for 1,524 performances at the Foxwoods Theater. It was nominated for eight Tony Awards, winning Best Revival of a Musical and Best Featured Actress in a Musical. Its success translated into a tour of the United Kingdom in 2007 and a tour through China and South Korea between 2007 and 2008.

J. Allen Barksdale

SEE ALSO: *Astaire, Fred, and Ginger Rogers; Berkeley, Busby; Broadway; Goldwyn, Samuel; The Great Depression; MGM (Metro-Goldwyn-Mayer); The Musical; Powell, Dick; Tony Awards; World War II.*

BIBLIOGRAPHY

Barrios, Richard. *A Song in the Dark: The Birth of the Musical Film.* New York: Oxford University Press, 1995.

Rubin, Martin. *Showstoppers: Busby Berkeley and the Tradition of the Spectacle.* New York: Columbia University Press, 1993.

Sennett, Ted. *Hollywood Musicals.* New York: H. N. Abrams, 1981.

Spivak, Jeffrey. *Buzz: The Life and Art of Busby Berkeley.* Lexington: University of Kentucky Press, 2010.

Fosse, Bob *(1927–1987)*

In the late twentieth century, director-choreographer Bob Fosse forever changed the way audiences around the world viewed dance on the stage and on film. Visionary, intense, and unbelievably driven, Fosse was an artist whose work was always provocative, entertaining, and quite unlike anything ever before seen. His dances were sexual, physically demanding of even the most highly trained dancers, full of joyous humor as well as bleak cynicism—works that addressed the full range of human emotions. Through his films he revolutionized the presentation of dance on screen and paved the way for a whole generation of film and video directors, showing dance through the camera lens as no one had done before, foreshadowing the rise of the MTV-era of music video dance.

EARLY LIFE AND CAREER

Robert Louis Fosse was born in Chicago, Illinois, on June 23, 1927. Bob was the youngest of six children and quickly learned to win attention from his family through his dancing. It was not long before he was recognized as a child prodigy. His parents sent him to formal lessons, where he immersed himself in tap dancing. A small boy who suffered from nagging health problems, he nevertheless was so dedicated that by the time he reached high school, he was already dancing professionally in area nightclubs as part of their sleazy vaudeville and burlesque shows. The sexually free atmosphere of these clubs and the strippers with whom Fosse was in constant contact made a strong impression on him. Fascinated with vaudeville's dark humor and teasing sexual tones, he would later develop these themes in his adult work. After finishing high school, Fosse enlisted in the navy in 1945. Shortly after he arrived at boot camp, V-J day was declared, and World War II officially came to an end. Fosse completed his two-year duty and moved to New York City.

For the next seven years, Fosse went through two rocky marriages with dancers Mary Ann Niles and Joan McCracken, all the while performing in variety shows on stage and on television. He had a few minor Broadway chorus parts, but his big break came with his brief appearance in the 1953 MGM movie musical *Kiss Me Kate.* Fosse caught the immediate attention of two of Broadway's acknowledged masters: George Abbott and Jerome Robbins.

CHOREOGRAPHER AND DIRECTOR

Fosse's first fully choreographed show was *The Pajama Game* (1954). Directed by Abbott, the show made Fosse an overnight success and showcased his trademark choreographic style: sexually suggestive forward hip-thrusts; the vaudeville humor of hunched shoulders and turned-in feet; the mimelike articulation of hands. He often dressed his dancers in black and put them in white gloves and derbies, recalling the image of Charlie Chaplin. He incorporated all the tricks of vaudeville that he had learned—pratfalls, slights-of-hand, double takes. Fosse received the first of his many Tony Awards for Best Choreography for *The Pajama Game.*

His next musical, *Damn Yankees,* brought more awards and established his life-long creative collaboration with Gwen Verdon, who had the starring role. With her inspiration, Fosse created a stream of classic dances. By 1960 Fosse was a nationally

Bob Fosse. *Bob Fosse won an unprecedented eight Tony Awards for his choreography, as well as one for direction. He was nominated for an Academy Award four times, winning Best Director for* Cabaret. EVENING STANDARD/GETTY IMAGES.

known and respected choreographer, and he married Verdon (by then a beloved Broadway star). Yet Fosse struggled with many of his producers and directors, who wished him to tone down or remove the controversial parts of his dances. Tired of subverting his artistic vision for the sake of "being proper," Fosse realized that he needed to be the director as well as the choreographer in order to have control over his dances.

From the late 1960s to the late 1970s, Fosse created a number of groundbreaking stage musicals and films. These works reflected the desire for sexual freedom that was being expressed across America and were huge successes as a result. His 1966 stage production of *Sweet Charity* was based on an earlier movie by Italian director Federico Fellini about a prostitute's search for love. After the success of the stage version, Universal Studios commissioned Fosse to produce a new film version. Before Fosse, dance was always filmed either in a front-facing or overhead view. In his 1969 film version of *Sweet Charity* and in later works, Fosse introduced unique perspective shots and jump cuts. These film and editing techniques would become standard practice for music video directors decades later.

His 1972 film *Cabaret* was based on Christopher Isherwood's stories of pre-Weimar Germany. Articles on the film appeared in all the major magazines. Photos appeared on the covers of *Time* and *Newsweek*. The film was Fosse's biggest public success and won eight Academy Awards. Fosse's *Pippin* (1972) became the highest-earning Broadway show in history as well as the first Broadway show to advertise on national television. *Pippin* was awarded five Tony Awards for the 1972–1973 season, one of them given to Fosse for best direction and choreography. Fosse staged and choreographed a variety show special for NBC starring Liza Minnelli, *Liza with a Z*, which brought Fosse an Emmy Award and made him the first person to ever win top honors in three entertainment mediums—stage, film, and television.

LATER WORKS

Two stage musicals followed: *Chicago* (1975) and *Dancin'* (1978). During rehearsals for *Chicago*, Fosse suffered a heart attack. He survived and used much of that traumatic experience in 1979 in his semiautobiographical dance film *All That Jazz* (1979). Two other films, *Lenny* (1974) and *Star 80* (1983), were not the popular successes that his other shows had been. *Big Deal*, Fosse's last musical, was also poorly received. During a rehearsal for a revival of *Sweet Charity* in 1987, Fosse suffered a massive heart attack and died on the way to the hospital.

Fosse's contribution to American entertainment continued after his death via show revivals and dance classes. His most prominent contribution was through the body of his work recorded on film and video, which continued to influence other artists for decades. For example, in 2009 the pop star Beyoncé Knowles was inspired by seeing an old recording of Gwen Verdon dancing Fosse's choreography and used it to inspire her own music video for "Single Ladies." In 2007 Bob Fosse was inducted into the National Museum of Dance in Saratoga Springs, New York.

Brian Granger

SEE ALSO: *Academy Awards; Broadway; Burlesque; Chaplin, Charlie; Emmy Awards; Fellini, Federico; Knowles, Beyoncé; Minnelli, Liza; MTV; The Musical;* Newsweek*; Tap Dancing; Television;* Time*; Tony Awards; Vaudeville; World War II.*

BIBLIOGRAPHY

Beddow, Margery. *Bob Fosse's Broadway*. Portsmouth, NH: Heinemann, 1996.

Gottfried, Martin. *All His Jazz: The Life and Death of Bob Fosse*. Cambridge, MA: Da Capo Press, 2003.

Grubb, Kevin Boyd. *Razzle Dazzle: The Life and Work of Bob Fosse*. New York: St. Martin's Press, 1989.

Foster, Jodie *(1962–)*

Actress Jodie Foster earned a reputation as a precocious, complicated preteen in Martin Scorsese's *Taxi Driver* (1976) and went on to prove herself as a no-nonsense actress, producer, and director in the 1990s. When, in 1981, the tabloid spotlight unexpectedly hit her following John Hinckley Jr.'s attempt to assassinate President Ronald Reagan, she displayed a grace and reserve to the media that reinforced her status as an intelligent woman. Having won two Academy Awards for Best Actress, Foster has established herself as one of Hollywood's most powerful women and one of the few female stars able to guarantee exceptional box-office receipts in the increasingly important global market.

CHILD ACTRESS

In 1962 Alicia Christian Foster was born the youngest of four siblings in Los Angeles. She was tightly bonded to her mother, Evelyn "Brandy" Foster, in part because her father had abandoned the family before she was born and because her mother actively promoted her acting talents from an early age. Foster made a popular Coppertone commercial when she was three years old and garnered a minor television role on *Mayberry RFD*, a program in which her brother Buddy was also a star.

Her film debut came with Disney's *Napoleon and Samantha* (1972), and she later played a number of children's roles onscreen. It was her infamous performance as Iris, a child prostitute who soberly and unaffectedly carries her pain and powerlessness through a New York City world of moral corruption, opposite Robert De Niro in *Taxi Driver*, that won her a National Society of Film Critics Award. This part also affirmed the fact that, in addition to the capricious, nimble-witted characters she took on at Disney, she was incredibly well suited for more adult material. After *Taxi Driver*, she starred in *Freaky Friday* (1977), a family film in which her character finds herself in the skin of her mother (Barbara Harris) for a day, as she humorously confronts the realities of being an adult housewife.

While actively pursuing her career as a performer, Foster graduated and was valedictorian at the Lycée Français in Los Angeles and earned a magna cum laude degree in literature at Yale University. It was while she was at Yale that she was stalked by Hinckley, whose obsession with *Taxi Driver* motivated him to shoot President Reagan in 1981. Though Foster was trying to carry on the life of a "normal college student," she immediately held a press conference on campus in hopes of containing the publicity and wrote an article titled "Why Me?" for *Esquire* magazine, which explained her experiences as one of Hinckley's targets.

THE ADULT ACTRESS-DIRECTOR-PRODUCER

Once out of college, in an attempt to recharge her acting career, Foster lobbied for the role of a working-class rape victim in *The Accused* (1988). She won a difficult competition among a number of up-and-coming female stars, even dropping weight for the part upon request from studio executives, and scored her first Academy Award. She battled yet again for another role—that of FBI agent Clarice Starling in the thriller *The Silence of the Lambs* (1991)—convincing director Jonathan Demme that she had a better psychological understanding of the "rising heroine" character than the other top-notch stars he preferred. This performance garnered her a second Best Actress Oscar.

Foster moved into the role of director in a range of Hollywood feature films, including *Little Man Tate* (1991); *Home for the Holidays* (1995); and *The Beaver* (2011), in which she also starred, alongside Mel Gibson. *Little Man Tate* tells the story of a young child prodigy and his complicated relationship with his struggling, little-educated, waitress-mother, played by Foster. At the release of the film, Foster admitted that her interest in it partially stemmed from her own experiences as a child living in a world beyond her years. With *Home for the Holidays*, which was produced through Foster's company, Egg Pictures, the director follows an insecure single mother (Holly Hunter) as she journeys home to her eccentric family for Thanksgiving.

While increasing her power as a producer-director, Foster continued to turn in remarkable performances in films such as *Nell* (1994), in which she plays a rugged wild child brought painfully into contemporary society (and for which she was nominated for a Best Actress Oscar); and *Contact* (1997), an adaptation of Carl Sagan's science fiction story about a woman who explores the possibility of life in outer space.

Foster developed a reputation as an antiestablishment pragmatist who remained within the Hollywood system in order to transform its representations of women and bring unconventional character pieces to the screen. She is also known as a down-to-earth, democratic star who, throughout her twenties, lived in the less-than-glamorous "valley" of Los Angeles and reportedly refused to rely on a personal assistant for mundane tasks, such as picking up dry cleaning or going to the post office. Foster fiercely protects her private life, having earned the respect and protection of Hollywood trade reporters and mainstream journalists. She became mother to a boy, Charles Foster, in the summer of 1998, provoking a relatively minor outcry when she refused to name the baby's father.

In films such as *Silence of the Lambs* and *Contact*, Foster drew on the androgyny and maturity of her childhood characters and solidified a reputation as an actress who rebelled against traditional feminine stereotypes and sought out complex acting opportunities that had been relatively unexplored by female stars. She became notorious for taking disenfranchised, scrappy characters and moving them closer to heroic self-empowerment. Her roles diversified as she sought out a range of prominent directors to work with, in films such as Spike Lee's thriller *Inside Man* (2006), Neil Jordan's *The Brave One* (2007), and Roman Polanski's *Carnage* (2011).

In a 1993 discussion of Hollywood, Foster explained:

> 95 percent of the people will always try to maintain the status quo. It's the other 5 percent that move the art form further. . . . What's different about [women] is that we identify with the underdog, so we spend a lot of time thinking about who's left out. When you sit around a table like this with a bunch of guys, they spend a lot of time thinking about who's on top.

Foster's career leaves little doubt that she stands within "the other 5 percent" and that, despite her immense Hollywood power, she has spent considerable efforts "thinking about who's left out."

Christina Lane

SEE ALSO: *Academy Awards; De Niro, Robert; Disney (Walt Disney Company); FBI (Federal Bureau of Investigation); Gibson, Mel; Hollywood; Lee, Spike; Reagan, Ronald; Sagan, Carl; Scorsese, Martin;* The Silence of the Lambs*;* Taxi Driver.

BIBLIOGRAPHY

Chunovic, Louis. *Jodie: A Biography*. Chicago: Contemporary Books, 1995.

DeAngelis, Therese. *Jodie Foster*. Philadelphia: Chelsea House Publishing, 2000.

Foster, Buddy. *Foster Child*. New York: Penguin Group, 1997.

Kennedy, Philippa. *Jodie Foster: A Life on Screen*. New York: Carol Publishing Group, 1996.

Lane, Christina. "The Liminal Iconography of Jodie Foster." *Journal of Popular Film and Television*, Winter 1995, 149–153.

Rich, B. Ruby. "Never a Victim: Jodie Foster, A New Kind of Female Hero." *Sight & Sound*, December 1991, 50–61.

Smolen, Diane. *The Films of Jodie Foster*. Seacaucus, NJ: Carol Publishing Group, 1996.

Fourth of July Celebrations

As the day designated to commemorate the signing of the Declaration of Independence and the anniversary of America's birth, the Fourth of July has been celebrated since the Revolutionary War era. For a couple of decades after the war, however, it was only sporadically celebrated, and the day did not become a regular observance in many parts of the country until after the turn of the nineteenth century.

Although the Continental Congress formally passed the resolution for independence on July 2, 1776, it was not until July 4 that Congress voted to approve the Declaration of Independence, which stated the reasons for the break with England. In fact, on July 3 John Adams wrote his wife, noting that the previous day would be "the most memorable epocha in the history of America," according to historian Daniel Boorstin. Adams then outlined the contours of the "great anniversary festival," which he thought should include "solemn acts of devotion to God Al-mighty . . . with pomp and parade, with shows, games, sports, guns, bells, bonfires, and illuminations from one end of this continent to the other."

FROM PARTISAN TO COMMUNITY CELEBRATIONS

While it is still a mystery to some historians why July 4 was the designated date to commemorate independence and the signing of the Declaration, it marked the annual official celebration during the Revolutionary War period. Afterward, official festivities became irregular and eventually evolved into incredibly partisan

Fourth of July Celebration. A fireworks display lights up the night sky over the Hudson River as part of a Fourth of July celebration in 2009. BOBBY BANK/WIREIMAGE/GETTY IMAGES.

events, which persisted for more than three decades. These often included separate observances held by the different political parties. As a day of political dissension, the celebrations at times erupted into violence. In particular, Independence Day was used by both the Federalist and Republican parties to hold what amounted to political rallies, with separate orations, dinners, and processions.

It was not until 1826, after another war with Britain and the commemoration of the fiftieth anniversary of the new nation, that newspapers across the country called for an end to partisanship. They encouraged plans for orations, military processions, private gatherings, public dinners, and picnics to celebrate American independence. As this day became popular as a community event, its rituals affirmed community ties as well as national identity and became linked to other community events such as groundbreakings, building dedications, and rededications of historic sites.

Communitywide celebrations continued in popularity from the early nineteenth century until the Civil War and included parades, ceremonies, sporting events, and fireworks. During the Civil War, Independence Day celebrations were no longer held in many parts of the country, especially in the South.

CELEBRATORY STYLES

In the postwar era, the urban celebrations on the East Coast were often sites for clashes between the upper and middle classes and the working class (especially immigrants) over the style of celebration and the use of public space. A genteel, or respectable, celebration was favored by the middle and upper classes, with an emphasis on picnics, private gatherings, games such as croquet and lawn tennis, and retreats into the countryside. The working class, however, typically favored rowdy and carnivalesque festivities such as unruly parades, drunkenness, rough games, and noisy discharges of firecrackers and fireworks.

Significantly, celebratory styles were debated back in the Revolutionary era in hopes of standardizing festivities throughout the Colonies. Members of the Continental Congress weighed the advantages of the rowdy or carnival style of celebration—with its ability to stimulate crowds and allow the venting of tensions—in contrast to the solemn style—with its ability to unify a diverse populace. Eventually, in the interests of national unity, the solemn style was favored and became associated with the notion of civil religion. In newspaper accounts of Independence Day thereafter, celebrations in this style were typically emphasized, while coverage of regional Fourth of July observances and their local variations in the carnival style were often neglected.

Although incompatible with urban order, the rowdy style of celebration regained popularity with immigrants in many urban areas in the early nineteenth century. Rooted in the European carnival customs of the working class, these celebrations included masking, charivaris (noisy demonstrations to humiliate someone publicly), and callithumpian parades (parades of urban maskers whose "rough music" mocked "real music").

Over time, tamed versions of these working-class practices were adopted and modified to accommodate urban order and to avert class conflicts that had previously erupted over the clash of styles.

In the early twentieth century, the Safe and Sane Fourth of July Program promoted standardized Fourth of July commemorations across the country that emphasized the solemn style. Aimed at the socialization and Americanization of immigrants, the program developed as part of the progressive reform movement that emerged in the late nineteenth century. A major goal of the Safe and Sane program was to legitimate the respectable style as preferred American behavior by promoting safety and noise abatement with a ban on all firecrackers. A standardized format for Independence Day celebrations stressed a formal program devoted to promoting the values of social order, solemn patriotism, and moderation. In addition, the program emphasized speeches and orations related to the Declaration of Independence. Progressive reformers also encouraged parades featuring patriotic pageantry with selected folk traditions to model the respectable version of America's history.

TOWN RITUALS

In many small towns and remote areas, the Fourth of July has typically been a communitywide celebration in which distinctive rituals and traditions have reflected the interests of the residents. In Lititz, Pennsylvania, for example, in a tradition dating back to 1843, community members prepare for the day during the winter by producing thousands of tallow candles in old-fashioned molds. In 2011 this town marked its 200th celebration, 194 of which were continuous. Festivities there typically begin with a baby parade highlighting children dressed in patriotic costumes riding on floats decorated in red, white, and blue. A queen of candles is chosen from the senior high school class to preside over the evening ceremony, in which boys of the town light many of the candles in the park and float them on the water. In 2007 more than 7,000 candles were used to illuminate the park.

The town of Bridgeport, California, celebrated its 149th Independence Day in 2011 with events that included an arts and crafts festival, a turkey shoot, and a rodeo. For years, Biwabik, Minnesota, a town of less than 1,000, has seen its population grow to more than ten times its size during the Fourth of July. Its traditional celebration includes patriotic and callithumpian parades, fireworks, and games such as egg-tossing contests and three-legged races. In some of the western states, including Colorado and Texas, Fourth of July observances have often revolved around rodeos featuring events such as roping and riding contests. In 1959, when Alaska became the forty-ninth state and in 1960 when Hawaii was added as the fiftieth state, commemorations of these occasions were held across the country on the Fourth of July.

Although Independence Day has been celebrated since the Revolutionary War era, it was not made a federal holiday until 1870, and it was not made a federal paid holiday until 1941. Its status as a holiday from work sometimes takes precedence over the emphasis on commemorating America's birthday, and in some parts of the country celebrations are no longer held. In addition, a pattern of waxing and waning of interest in holding Independence Day programs is evident in many urban areas. The years in which its popularity has peaked were during periods of patriotic fervor such as the centennial in 1876, the years after both World War I and World War II, the country's 175th anniversary in 1951, and the bicentennial in 1976. The turn of the twenty-first century evoked a resurgence in the popularity of Fourth of July celebrations across the country, especially in the years following the September 11, 2001, terrorist attacks on New York City and Washington, D.C.

Mary Lou Nemanic

SEE ALSO: *9/11; Parades; Thanksgiving; Valentine's Day; World War I; World War II.*

BIBLIOGRAPHY

Bodnar, John E. *Remaking America: Public Memory, Commemoration and Patriotism in the Twentieth Century.* Princeton, NJ: Princeton University Press, 1992.

Boorstin, Daniel J. *The Americans: The National Experience.* New York: Random House, 1965.

Cohen, Hennig, and Tristram Potter Coffin, eds. *The Folklore of American Holidays.* Detroit, MI: Gale Research Company, 1987.

Davis, Susan G. *Parades and Power: Street Theatre in Nineteenth-Century Philadelphia.* Philadelphia: Temple University Press, 1986.

Glassberg, Philip. *American Historical Pageantry: The Uses of Tradition in the Early Twentieth Century.* Chapel Hill: University of North Carolina Press, 1990.

Litwicki, Ellen M. *America's Public Holidays: 1865–1920.* Washington, DC: Smithsonian Institution Press, 2000.

Matthew, Dennis. *Red, White and Blue Letter Days: An American Calendar.* Ithaca, NY: Cornell University Press, 2002.

Nemanic, Mary Lou. *One Day for Democracy: Independence Day and the Americanization of Iron Range Immigrants.* Athens: Ohio University Press, 2007.

Fox News Channel

A part of the international media empire of Rupert Murdoch, the Fox News Channel (FNC) was the most popular cable and satellite news channel in the United States in the early twenty-first century. Among all viewers, Fox had the top thirteen cable news programs on cable in 2011, and among the prized twenty-five- to fifty-four-year-old demographic, it had the top nine programs. The channel has generated controversy since its founding in 1996 for intense partisanship. Given Murdoch's longstanding conservatism, critics allege that FNC promotes his political agenda and that its news product is biased. Others, including employees, contend that its reporting and political commentary functions operate independently and deny institutional bias in its news. Regardless, FNC has been a powerful media voice in the nation's stormy political debates of the early twenty-first century.

A HISTORY OF MEDIA BIAS

Partisanship, the advocacy of a political party or cause, in the news media is almost as old as newspapers themselves. Early Americans read an intensely partisan press as the two parties of the day battled for dominance. With more efficient mass printing methods in the nineteenth century, newspapers tried to increase their circulation through more neutral, less partisan reporting, but editorial pages and selected newspapers continued to adhere to fervent party lines well into the twentieth century. It was the introduction of broadcast news, especially television, coupled with a decline in circulation that forced newspapers to tone down their partisanship. By the latter years of the twentieth century, most American cities and towns had only one paper, making rabid partisanship unprofitable. Radio and television news were prevented from explicit partisanship by Federal Communications Commission regulations from 1949 until 1987.

Sky News, Murdoch's first twenty-four-hour television news channel, was established in the United Kingdom in 1989 and criticized for a conservative bias even though UK broadcasting regulations require content neutrality. In the United States, Murdoch had purchased Twentieth Century Fox Filmed Entertainment in 1985 and used the name to establish his Fox broadcast television network in 1986. Ten years later, Murdoch announced his intention to launch a twenty-four-hour U.S. cable news channel. He hired Roger Ailes, a CNBC executive and Republican political consultant, as its chief executive and architect. Ailes had gained fame for coaching Ronald Reagan in the 1984 presidential debates and was involved in the production of the Willie Horton "Revolving Door" ad used by George H. W. Bush in his successful 1988 presidential campaign. Ailes observed in 1989 that candidates get more news coverage for making mistakes or attacking opponents than for discussing their own positions, and critics have observed that such a philosophy helped build FNC's viewership.

Ailes took eighty-nine NBC employees with him to form the new channel, and FNC debuted to a potential cable viewership of seventeen million on October 7, 1996. It emphasized breaking news, then a novelty in a medium that relied on prewritten, pre-edited content; graphical presentations for viewers who could not hear the broadcast; and visual summarizations of speaking points. FNC initially paid cable systems to carry it, in contrast to normal distribution practices. Early in its existence FNC became involved in an acrimonious court battle with Time Warner, parent company of CNN, over the inclusion of FNC on its cable systems. At one point, Time Warner's Ted Turner compared Murdoch to Adolf Hitler, while Murdoch's *New York Post* questioned Turner's mental capacities.

PERSONALITIES OF FNC

FNC has always depended on a stable of popular anchors and commentators to maintain its ratings. Bill O'Reilly, a former network and syndicated TV reporter, debuted in October 1996. His *The O'Reilly Report*, renamed *The O'Reilly Factor* in 1998, was one of the most popular cable news programs during the first decade of the 2000s for its energetic tone and willingness to discuss controversial political issues. O'Reilly has been cited as one of the most influential talk show hosts in the nation, and he has been accused of distorting facts and using propaganda techniques in his program. Sean Hannity, a conservative radio and television talk show host noted for his polemic views, debuted with FNC in a panel program with Alan Colmes, a self-described moderate who provided a more liberal perspective. Their program ran until 2008. Shepard Smith, a regional broadcast journalist, joined the network in 1996 as well. His *The Fox Report with Shepard Smith* was the top-rated newscast in cable news, and Smith has ranked as high as second in most-trusted ratings among cable and network anchors.

Brit Hume, a former ABC correspondent, worked as the network's managing editor from 1996 until 2008. He also hosted *Special Report*, which featured political conversation among a group of commentators Hume called "The Fox All-Stars." Hume generated attention for his sign-off, which went in part, "more news is on the way—fair, balanced, and unafraid," and which became one of FNC's taglines. Chris Wallace, a former network reporter and son of *60 Minutes* correspondent Mike Wallace, joined FNC in 2003, commenting that "Fox News wouldn't exist if it weren't for [media bias] in the mainstream media." In a well-publicized interview of Comedy Central's Jon Stewart in 2011, Wallace admitted to FNC's conservative bias.

FNC'S GROWING AUDIENCE

Beyond commentary, FNC built an audience through spirited coverage of major domestic and international events. Its success was tied in part to a growing viewer preference for cable rather than network news early in the first decade of the 2000s, based on the constant availability of the twenty-four-hour news networks. Coverage of President Bill Clinton and the Whitewater scandal, Clinton's impeachment trial, and the contested 2000 presidential election gave the network a wider viewer base. It surpassed CNN in total viewership in 2002 and saw another increase the following year after the start of the Iraq War, its viewership climbing temporarily by 300 percent. Viewers demonstrated their loyalty during the 2004 election campaign when some seven million watched President George W. Bush's acceptance speech at the Republican National Convention on FNC, compared to 1.4 million on NBC. The 2006 Lebanon War helped regain viewers lost in 2005, and FNC continued to hold its popularity through further international crises. It was the most viewed cable channel the week of the 2008 presidential election, and it reached that level again during the 2010 Massachusetts special elections.

CRITICISMS OF FNC

FNC's news programming has come under criticism for its conservative bias. Former employees allege that editors encouraged them to manipulate stories so that Democrats appeared as villains or the butt of jokes and Republicans as the objects of unfair liberal media attacks or as heroic figures. The network has been accused of using pejorative labels or misleading descriptions to color stories. Critics have also argued that FNC's conservative commentators cast a shadow over its news content, suggesting that reporters such as Washington correspondent Jim Angle, whose stories were said to be indistinguishable from other networks', are overlooked. Research studies have suggested that FNC is perceived by more viewers as being the most conservative and ideological cable news channel and more sympathetic to Republicans and Republican administrations even though more than 10 percent of viewers considered it liberal.

Critics have also pointed to the network's predominant political content and use of on-set experts within news segments, blurring viewer perception between anchors and sources in lieu of prewritten and edited stories. The Australian-born Murdoch has maintained that the majority of American media have a hidden liberal bias, and Ailes has said that FNC was created to correct that liberalism and report stories missed by other journalists, making it appear conservative.

Other studies have suggested a higher level of misinformation among loyal FNC viewers on issues such as global warming, health care, the Iraq War, and the 2010 election compared to viewers of rivals CNN and MSNBC. Controversy remains among scholars over whether the misinformation was related to FNC's coverage of such issues or whether misinformed people gravitate toward FNC. The network has also been accused of increased racism in its news coverage following President Barack Obama's election in 2008. It came under fire in particular when commentator Glenn Beck compared America under Obama to the 2010 film *Rise of the Planet of the Apes.*

FNC continued to prosper in the second decade of the twenty-first century as American political dialogue became more virulent. It added a high-definition simulcast in 2008, and an international version was available in more than forty countries. Journalist William Raspberry called America's increasing political incivility "Foxidation," and FNC's assertive attitude, graphics, and O'Reilly's "no spin zone" were said to have inspired the fictional *Onion News Network* FactZone parody on cable channel IFC. CNN's Aaron Brown labeled the era one "when people only want to hear that which they agree with." If true, such a phenomenon has not hurt FNC. "Fox News is after all a private channel and our presenters are quite open about where they stand on particular stories," FNC's London bureau chief Scott Norvell once explained. "People watch us because they know what they're getting."

Richard Junger

SEE ALSO: *Beck, Glenn;* Bush v. Gore *(2000); Cable TV; CNN; O'Reilly, Bill;* 60 Minutes*; Television; Turner, Ted.*

BIBLIOGRAPHY

Auletta, Ken. *Backstory: Inside the Business of News.* New York: Penguin, 2003.

DellaVigna, Stefano, and Ethan Kaplan. "The Fox News Effect: Media Bias and Voting." *Quarterly Journal of Economics,* August 2007, 122.

Jaramillo, Deborah. *Ugly War, Pretty Package: How CNN and Fox News Made the Invasion of Iraq High Concept.* Bloomington: Indiana University Press, 2009.

Mooney, Chris. *The Republican War on Science.* New York: Basic Books, 2005.

Sheppard, Si. *The Partisan Press: A History of Media Bias in the United States.* Jefferson, NC: McFarland, 2008.

St. Clair, Duane. "GOP Media Consultant Roger Ailes says Democrats Are out to Get Him." *Columbus Dispatch,* October 26, 1989, 3C.

Weprin, Alex. "The Top Cable News Programs of 2011." *TVNewser,* December 28, 2011.

Foxx, Jamie *(1967–)*

Jamie Foxx first gained national fame during the 1990s on the Fox sketch comedy show *In Living Color* (1990–1994), inhabiting such outlandish characters as T-Dog Jenkins and Wanda, the ugliest woman in the world. Few of those who laughed at Foxx's antics then realized the depth of his versatility not only as an actor but also as a skilled musician and singer. Throughout his career Foxx has met each success by reaching for another challenge, becoming the star of his own television show, an Academy Award–winning actor, and a recording artist with two platinum records.

Foxx was born Eric Marlon Bishop in Terrell, Texas, in 1967. Though he was abandoned by both parents when he was a baby, he was raised in a loving home by his mother's adoptive parents, Mark and Estelle Talley. It was Estelle who suggested music as a positive channel for her grandson's youthful energy, and Foxx devoted himself to the piano, becoming choir leader and music director for their church. After finishing high school he got a scholarship to the U.S. International University in San Diego, California, where he studied classical music.

While in San Diego, Foxx went onstage at a comedy club open mic on a dare and discovered he was good at making people laugh. He made the rounds of comedy clubs, trying to get as much stage time as he could. Because men greatly outnumbered women on the club circuit, Foxx reasoned that he would have a greater chance of being called up if emcees thought he was a woman. "Jamie Foxx" was one of a number of androgynous aliases he used, and he eventually chose it for his stage name.

Foxx is a dead-on impressionist and a quick-witted comic who learned to read his audience and respond to their mood. In 1991 he won the Bay Area Black Comedy Competition, which led to acting roles in the Barry Levinson comedy *Toys* (1992) and in the Fox series *Roc* (1991–1994). In the early 1990s Foxx got his greatest exposure on Keenen and Damon Wayans's sketch comedy series *In Living Color.* In 1993 he got his own comedy special on HBO, *Straight from the Foxxhole.*

Foxx continued to showcase his comic skill in episodes of a number of television shows, prompting the WB network to offer him his own sitcom in 1996. *The Jamie Foxx Show* (1996–2001) drew record-setting audiences. The show remained on the air for five seasons, depicting the adventures of Jamie King, a show business hopeful who works in his aunt and uncle's Los Angeles hotel while trying to find his big break. The comedy ended on a high note, with Jamie marrying longtime love interest Fancy, the hotel desk clerk, on the 100th episode.

Foxx continued to seek work in films, starring in Jeff Pollack's comedy *Booty Call* (1997). His first dramatic role came when famed director Oliver Stone tapped him to play a troubled quarterback in *Any Given Sunday* (1999). His skillful handling of that sensitive role led Michael Mann to seek him out to play opposite Will Smith in *Ali* (2001). Similarly, his standout performance as Bundini Brown in *Ali* convinced director Taylor Hackford that Foxx could handle the lead role in *Ray* (2004), a biopic of the legendary musical genius Ray Charles.

The film version of the life and career of the acclaimed father of soul music was fifteen years in the making. Critics and audiences were stunned by Foxx's impeccable performance, theatrically and musically. Foxx and Charles were both black artists from poor southern roots trying to deal with the complexities of success, and in playing Charles, Foxx seemed not so much to portray as to inhabit him; Charles himself approved the performance. Foxx won the Academy Award for Best Actor for his work in *Ray,* becoming the third African American man to have earned that honor. He was also the second male actor in history to be nominated for both Best Actor and Best Supporting Actor (for Mann's *Collateral*) in the same year.

His performance in *Ray* changed Foxx's career dramatically. Not only did he gain recognition as a serious actor, leading to more dramatic roles in such films as *Jarhead* (Sam Mendes, 2005), but his musical work in the film offered him the opportunity to develop himself as a singer and musician. Foxx had released his first album of original songs, *Peep This* (1995) without much fanfare, but *Ray* showcased him as a musician to a wider audience, and his second album, *Unpredictable* (2005), sold more than a million copies. Foxx also reached number one on the Billboard Hot 100 with the single "Gold Digger" (2005), a duet with popular hip-hop artist Kanye West. In 2010 Foxx released *Best Night of My Life*, which, like *Unpredictable*, showcased a number of his musical friends—including Ludacris and Justin Timberlake—and received positive critical reviews.

Tina Gianoulis

SEE ALSO: *Academy Awards; Charles, Ray; Hip-Hop;* In Living Color*; Smith, Will; Stand-Up Comedy; Stone, Oliver; Television; Timberlake, Justin; Top 40; The Wayans Family; West, Kanye.*

BIBLIOGRAPHY

Collier, Aldore. "Jamie Foxx: Year of the Foxx." *Jet*, December 5, 2005, 56.

Cruz, Clarissa. "Oscar on My Mind: How Jamie Foxx Transformed for 'Ray.'" *Entertainment Weekly*, October 29, 2004.

Hirschberg, Lynn. "All the Right Moves." *New York Times Magazine*, March 12, 2006.

True, Cynthia. "Foxx, Whole." *Texas Monthly*, November 1998, 88.

Young, Josh. "Jamie Foxx's Oscar Hunt." *Variety*, October 4, 2004, S46.

Foxx, Redd *(1922–1991)*

Born John Elroy Sanford in St. Louis, Missouri, in 1922, Redd Foxx was one of America's most beloved comedic figures in the 1970s. Called "Redd" because of his complexion, he took the last name of baseball star Stan Fox—adding his distinctive double "x"—and left home at the age of sixteen to join a New York street band. In the 1940s and 1950s Foxx worked as a stand-up comedian and became known for his many "party records": recordings of his bawdy stand-up act. The most famous of these was 1955's *Laff of the Party*. More than fifteen million copies of his records were reportedly sold, although Foxx claimed to have never received any of the royalties.

Foxx is best remembered for his role as junk dealer Fred G. Sanford, the cantankerous but lovable elderly widower on NBC's hit comedy *Sanford & Son* (1972–1977). The show was the second smash hit (after *All in the Family*, 1968–1979) for Norman Lear and Bud Yorkin, whose topical 1970s comedies addressed issues such as bigotry, race, gender, and sexuality to a degree that had never been seen on American television. (Sanford was a kind of black counterpart to Archie Bunker, *All in the Family*'s grouchy star character.)

Sanford & Son was based on the hit British comedy *Steptoe & Son* (1962–1974), which revolved around a cockney junk dealer. The American version was set in the Watts section of Los Angeles, where Fred and his son Lamont (played by Demond Wilson) are partners in the junk business. Fred ekes out a living but constantly hatches all kinds of get-rich-quick schemes. Lamont is seeking a more reasonable path to a better life, and many of the sitcom's conflicts arise from Lamont's struggle to leave the junk business while Fred tries to make him stay. Their arguments frequently end with Fred feigning a heart attack, clutching his chest, and calling to his dead wife, "I'm coming to join you Elizabeth!" With this conflict between family and ambition at the center, the Sanfords interact with other engaging characters, many of them played by older black actors who worked with Foxx in his early stand-up days. The results are hilarious.

Redd Foxx. *Redd Foxx was a popular stand-up comedian for several decades before he took the role of cantankerous junk dealer Fred Sanford in* Sanford and Son *in 1972.* MICHAEL OCHS ARCHIVES/GETTY IMAGES.

Foxx left *Sanford and Son* at the end of the 1976–1977 season amid reported contract disputes with the producers and an argument with NBC over an appropriate dressing room. He signed with ABC for the *Redd Foxx Comedy Hour* (1977–1978), in which he showcased some of his old show-business friends and explained his take on American history in a regular spot called "The History of the Black in America." Unfortunately, the show was a ratings bomb and ended after a few months.

After a few years working in Las Vegas clubs and making guest appearances on other variety shows, Foxx returned to television in 1980 on *Sanford*, NBC's revival of the earlier hit series. A new cast of characters and poor writing doomed the show, which lasted only a few months. In 1986 *The Redd Foxx Show* presented its star in an entirely new guise as a kindly newsstand operator with a white foster daughter. The show was retooled after a couple of episodes when network research showed that Americans liked Foxx better as a grumpy character. The writers took out the daughter and put in a nagging ex-wife, but the series lasted only one season.

In the late 1980s Foxx filed for bankruptcy after three divorces, an extravagant lifestyle, and the seizure of most of his assets by the Internal Revenue Service (IRS). In a reversal of fortune, his appearance in Eddie Murphy's film *Harlem Nights* (1989) received good reviews and led to a role in the Murphy-produced series *The Royal Family* (1991). On October 11, 1991, Foxx collapsed on the set during rehearsals, at first provoking laughter from cast and crew who thought he was doing his "Elizabeth, I'm coming to join you!" routine from *Sanford and Son*. However, he had suffered a fatal heart attack, dying in harness as he no doubt would have wished.

Joyce Linehan

SEE ALSO: All in the Family*; Lear, Norman; Murphy, Eddie;* Sanford and Son*; Sitcom; Stand-Up Comedy; Television.*

BIBLIOGRAPHY

Travis, Dempsey J. *The Life and Times of Redd Foxx*. Chicago: Urban Research Press, 1999.

Foyt, A. J. *(1935–)*

A. J. Foyt is one of the premier names in motor sports, having enjoyed an auto racing career that spanned four decades, beginning in the 1950s. No other driver achieved such a unique combination of longevity, dominance, and versatility in motor sports, on which he left a permanent mark wherever he raced. Known as "Supertex" to his many fans, Foyt gained a reputation for a uniquely tough and aggressive style that brought a new excitement to the sport, and he is probably the most popular driver ever to have run at "The Greatest Spectacle in Racing," the Indianapolis 500.

Anthony Joseph Foyt Jr. was born on January 16, 1935, in Houston, Texas, where he became familiar with racing cars from an early age. His father owned the Burt and Foyt Garage that specialized in the vehicles, and Foyt had already decided to make a career of racing when he was no more than five years old. By his late teens he was driving midget racers on the midwestern circuit.

In the years that followed, Foyt firmly established himself in various aspects of the sport: midgets, sprints, stock cars, sports cars, and IndyCars. He emerged from quarter-mile dirt ovals to become arguably the most dominant driver in the history of the Indianapolis 500. At Indianapolis, Foyt qualified for a record thirty-five consecutive races and was the first driver to win Indianapolis four times, a feat later matched only by Al Unser and Rick Mears. As of 2011, Foyt still held the record for the most United States Auto Club (USAC) wins, with sixty-seven victories, and remained the only driver in the history of the sport to win seven national USAC titles.

Foyt was also highly successful in other areas of car racing. He won the 24 Hours at Le Mans in 1967, captured the 24 Hours at Daytona in 1983 and 1985, and was victorious at the 12 Hours of Sebring in 1985. Perhaps one of the most amazing aspects of his career is that such a successful IndyCar driver was also able to achieve victories in major stock car events. After recording forty-one wins in USAC stock car racing, he joined the famous Wood Brothers team and became a significant force on the NASCAR circuit, winning seven NASCAR Winston Cup races, including the 1972 Daytona 500. His astonishing record was enhanced even further when he captured the world closed-course speed record for an Oldsmobile in 1987, recording a 257-miles-per-hour lap in a Quad-4-powered Aerotech.

In 1993, at the age of fifty-eight, Foyt announced his retirement from race-car driving. However he retained his connection with the sport through business interests in A.J. Foyt Enterprises and A.J. Foyt Racing Ltd. He was also the proprietor of A. J. Foyt Honda in Houston; owned several cattle and horse ranches in Texas; and was appointed to the boards of both Riverway Bank and Service Corporation International, the nation's largest funeral service business. After retirement Foyt continued living in Houston with his wife, Lucy. Of Hoyt's four children, three followed in their father's footsteps: Jerry had a brief racing career, Larry was a NASCAR driver, and A. J. Foyt IV was an IndyCar and NASCAR driver.

James H. Lloyd

SEE ALSO: *Automobile; Daytona 500; Indianapolis 500; Sports Heroes; Stock-Car Racing; Unser, Al.*

BIBLIOGRAPHY

"A. J. Foyt." Motorsports Hall of Fame. Accessed December 2011. Available from http://www.mshf.com/hof/foyt_aj.htm

"Anthony Joseph Foyt Jr." A. J. Foyt Racing. Accessed December 2011. Available from http://www.foytracing.com/aj/

Engle, Lyle Kenyon. *The Incredible A. J. Foyt*. New York: Arco, 1977.

Foyt, A. J. "A. J. Foyt: Champion for Life." Greenwich, CT: Cabin Fever Entertainment, 1992. Videocassette.

Foyt, A. J. *My Checkered Past: An Autobiography*. New York: HarperCollins, 2006.

Foyt, A. J., and William Neely. *A. J.* New York: Times Books, 1983.

Libby, Bill. *Foyt*. New York: Hawthorn Books, 1974.

Wilker, Josh. *A. J. Foyt*. Race Car Legends series. New York: Chelsea House, 1996.

Francis, Arlene *(1907–2001)*

During her long career as one of television's most versatile hostesses, Arlene Francis was the quintessence of wit and style. Beginning her career as an actress on the stage and screen, Francis hosted a precursor to *The Dating Game*, called *Blind Date*, for three years in the early 1950s while also emceeing the talent shows *By Popular Demand* and, later, *Talent Patrol*. At the same time she radiated sophistication and good cheer as a regular panelist on *What's My Line?*, the popular game show with which she was associated for twenty-five years. In 1954 NBC president Sylvester "Pat" Weaver chose Francis as host and editor-in-chief for a new concept in daytime television, *Home*, a serious talk show for women. The three-year run of *Home* established Francis's credentials as a pioneer in the talk format.

She returned to public affairs television in the early 1980s when she hosted a New York program, *The Prime of Your Life*, a noteworthy series for senior citizens. She was also the host of a popular New York radio show for twenty-four years. When Francis died in 2001, the *New York Times* obituary recognized her "upbeat charm and humor," qualities she displayed in several media.

Ron Simon

SEE ALSO: *Daytime Talk Shows; Game Shows; Radio; Talk Radio; Television;* What's My Line?

BIBLIOGRAPHY

Francis, Arlene, and Florence Rome. *Arlene Francis: A Memoir.* New York: Simon & Schuster, 1978.

Timberg, Bernard, and Bob Erler. *Television Talk: A History of the TV Talk Show.* Austin: University of Texas Press, 2002.

Francis, Connie *(1938–)*

In the late 1950s and early 1960s, singer Connie Francis reigned as America's top-selling female vocalist and the female counterpart to teen idols such as Frankie Avalon and Fabian. Cute—as opposed to glamorous—the diminutive brunette with the perky demeanor typified the girl next door. Teenage girls wanted to be her best friend; teenage boys dreamed of dating her. The media called her "America's sweetheart."

Connie Francis. *Her image as "America's sweetheart" helped to make Connie Francis the best-selling female artist in the late 1950s and early 1960s.* SILVER SCREEN COLLECTION/ARCHIVE PHOTOS/ GETTY IMAGES.

Born Concetta Rosa Maria Franconero in Newark, New Jersey, Francis was three years old when her Italian roofing-contractor father presented her with an accordion. Soon she was performing at family events, churches, and hospitals. She was eleven when her father took her to Manhattan to meet the producer of the television show *Startime,* which featured child performers; she appeared on the program for the next four years. The young musician was later showcased on TV variety shows, including Arthur Godfrey's *Talent Scouts.* It was Godfrey who suggested that she change her name. He also recommended that she put away her accordion to concentrate on singing.

Francis began her recording career cutting demo records for various music publishing companies. Then came a 1955 recording contract with MGM (Metro-Goldwyn-Mayer) and ten failed singles. At her father's suggestion, she performed an up-tempo version of the 1923 standard "Who's Sorry Now?" for what she anticipated would be her final recording session for the label. To her surprise the record found favor with Dick Clark, congenial host of the popular *American Bandstand.* Touting the new "girl singer," Clark played her single on a 1958 New Year's Day telecast. The recording quickly sold a million copies to become Francis's first gold record. Francis, who became a frequent guest on *Bandstand,* later admitted that were it not for Clark and his support, she would have given up on her music career.

Instead, she became a perennial on the charts. In addition to outselling all other female artists from 1958 to 1964, she was the first female singer to produce consecutive number one hits with the 1960 songs "Everybody's Somebody's Fool" and "My Heart Has a Mind of Its Own." Francis became household name, and her likeness appeared on paper dolls, diaries, and other merchandise aimed at teenage girls. Roles in a quartet of MGM films followed. First and most memorable was *Where the Boys Are* (1960), a story of college girls looking for love during spring break in Fort Lauderdale, Florida. Though the film is best known today for its heartfelt title song, performed by Francis, its plot and setting were mimicked myriad times in succeeding decades, especially during the 1980s, when youth-oriented movies were the rage.

As her fame grew, Francis began recording songs that appealed to adults; she also recorded albums in numerous foreign languages. As a result, the mature singer was able to establish herself as a strong nightclub draw. In the late 1960s, during the cultural revolution that saw American audiences clamoring for performers with British accents, Francis took her act overseas.

There were personal trials, however, including failed marriages and disagreements with her domineering father-manager. Then came an emotionally shattering rape and beating, which she suffered hours after performing at Long Island's Westbury Music Fair in late 1974. The headline-making experience left Francis psychologically unable to perform. Three years later she suffered another setback when cosmetic surgery on her nose affected her voice. In 1978 she returned to her career, appearing on a television concert show hosted by longtime friend Clark; unbeknownst to audiences, though, the still-fragile Francis had to lip-sync to a prerecorded medley of her hits. She went through yet another crisis in 1981 with the gangland-style murder of her younger brother, but she faced a live audience later that year; in fact, she bravely played the same venue where she had performed the night of her rape and beating, explaining, "I had to put my fears to sleep."

Sadly, various fears continued to resurface. The recipient of sixteen gold records suffered nervous breakdowns and involuntary confinements in mental facilities. She was diagnosed with bipolar disorder. In interviews and in her 1984 autobiography, she attributed some of her woes to her relationship with her overprotective father: "Thanks to my father, I [grew up] the typical horribly repressed Italian girl. I was this nice little girl that no man was supposed to touch. . . . Probably the biggest regret of my life is that I allowed him to exercise all that control. It was a form of emotional abuse."

During the 1990s Francis made intermittent comebacks, and in 2007 she played to an enthusiastic audience at San Francisco's Castro Theater. In performance, the woman who led the way for today's female superstars, including Madonna, Janet Jackson, and Céline Dion, continues to project the engaging demeanor of the girl next door, though a sadder and wiser girl.

Pat H. Broeske

SEE ALSO: American Bandstand; *Avalon, Frankie; Clark, Dick; Fabian; Godfrey, Arthur; Jackson, Janet; Madonna; MGM (Metro-Goldwyn-Mayer); Teen Idols; Television.*

BIBLIOGRAPHY

Bronson, Fred. *The Billboard Book of Number One Hits.* New York: Billboard Publications, 1988.

Francis, Connie. *Who's Sorry Now?* New York: St. Martin's Press, 1984.

Hunt, Dennis. "Connie Francis Gets It All out of Her System." *Los Angeles Times*, November 23, 1984, 22.

Levinson, Bill. "Where the Boys Aren't." *American Weekly*, January 1, 1961, 7.

Parish, James Robert, and Michael R. Pitts. *Hollywood Songsters.* New York: Routledge, 2003.

Francis the Talking Mule

Francis was the smart, sassy talking mule who led a bumbling but sincere human sidekick into and out of trouble in seven films for Universal Pictures from 1949 to 1956. For all but the last film the sidekick was played by singer and dancer Donald O'Connor, and the voice of Francis was supplied by character actor Chill Wills. The special effect of talking was achieved by feeding a strong thread from the bridle to the mule's mouth. A gentle off-camera tug on the thread caused the animal to try to dislodge the annoyance by moving its lips.

The film series was considered silly by the critics, but moviegoers enjoyed the antics of a mule who not only talked but who was more intelligent than his owner. As the first noncartoon-talking movie animal, Francis paved the way for television's talking horse, *Mister Ed.*

Pauline Bartel

SEE ALSO: Mister Ed.

BIBLIOGRAPHY

Edelson, Edward. *Great Animals of the Movies.* Garden City, NY: Doubleday, 1980.

Kimball, Cheryl. *The Complete Horse: An Entertaining History of Horses.* St. Paul, MN: Voyageur Press, 2006.

Rothel, David. *Great Show Business Animals.* San Diego, CA: A. S. Barnes, 1980.

Frankel, Bethenny *(1970–)*

Bethenny Frankel may have come in second on *The Apprentice: Martha Stewart* in 2005, but she has since proven that her business sense is unsurpassed. The natural foods chef, entrepreneur, author, and star of several reality shows climbed from struggling obscurity to fame, wealth, and power within a few years, using reality television as her springboard. Exhibiting an ability—rare in reality programming—to avoid pretention and pettiness, Frankel won viewers' hearts with her unforced candor and dry humor, exposing her private life and building her brand at the same time. By 2012 Frankel had constructed an extensive empire around that brand and achieved her ambition of appearing on the cover of the respected business journal *Forbes.*

Frankel's painful childhood, frequently exposed during her reality career and countless interviews, was perhaps one of the factors that motivated her determination to succeed. Born in 1970 in New York City, Frankel was the daughter of Bernadette and Bobby Frankel. Her father was a respected trainer of thoroughbred racehorses who left the family when Frankel was only four. Even after her mother's remarriage to horse trainer John Parisella, Frankel's family life remained unstable, with frequent relocations and issues of alcoholism and eating disorders. Frankel herself, growing up in the racetrack environment, was introduced to alcohol and gambling at a young age and developed issues around food and dieting.

In the early 1990s Frankel went to Los Angeles to pursue an acting career. Though she did get roles in a few films, such as Barry Roskin Blake's 1994 film *Hollywood Hills 90028*, she supported herself chiefly by working as nanny and assistant to such celebrities as Paris Hilton and Jerry and Linda Bruckheimer. Already full of business ideas, she soon launched a party planning business called In Any Event and began importing popular pashmina scarves to sell to her friends under the name Princess Pashmina.

After moving back to New York at the turn of the twenty-first century, Frankel entered culinary school, graduating in 2001, and began to market natural, low-calorie cookies under the brand BethennyBakes. As an up-and-coming chef, she auditioned for *The Apprentice*, Donald Trump's NBC reality show. She was not accepted the first time but made the cut two years later on the spin-off *The Apprentice: Martha Stewart*, where she finished in second place.

Bravo network executives had noted Frankel's drive and engaging screen presence on *The Apprentice*, and in 2008 they approached her to join the cast of the upcoming *Real Housewives of New York City*, one of several reality shows inspired by the success of ABC's nighttime soap *Desperate Housewives.* Frankel was hesitant at first, fearing the exposure might damage her growing career, but she finally agreed and soon became the show's breakout star. Alongside sister "housewives" LuAnn de Lesseps, Alex McCord, Ramona Singer, and real-life friend Jill Zarin, Frankel demonstrated an acerbic wit and blunt openness that engaged audiences immediately. The only one of the group that was not married, Frankel had few acting ambitions and avoided much of the drama associated with reality programming. Instead she showcased her career, and such products as her new line of Skinnygirl margaritas made regular appearances.

Frankel appeared in three seasons of *Real Housewives* while at the same time building her Skinnygirl brand; writing books such as *Naturally Thin: Unleash Your Skinnygirl and Free Yourself from a Lifetime of Dieting* and *The Skinnygirl Dish: Easy Recipes for Your Naturally Thin Life* (with Eve Adamson) in 2010; and *Skinnydipping*, a novel, in 2012. She also released DVDs, such as *Body by Bethenny* (2010) and launched a number of Skinnygirl products, from cocktails to nutritional supplements to undergarments. Though she sold her cocktail line to Beam Global Spirits & Wine in 2011, she shrewdly kept the rights to the Skinnygirl name for all other products. In addition, she made lucrative endorsement and promotion deals with such companies as Pepperidge Farm, Procter & Gamble, and British Airways.

While appearing on *Real Housewives* in 2009, Frankel began dating sales representative and real estate agent Jason Hoppy. When she became pregnant and the two got engaged the following year, Bravo gave Frankel her own reality show, *Bethenny Getting Married?* With typical bravado, Frankel opened every aspect of her life to the cameras, from the difficulties of urinating in a wedding dress to the delivery of her baby Bryn Casey Hoppy. Frankel's show soon surpassed *Real Housewives*, with 2.7 million viewers tuning in to the wedding episode and 2.4 million watching as baby Bryn was born. Once the wedding was over, the young family's life continued to be televised on the popular *Bethenny Ever After*. Finally succumbing to the drama so central to reality programming, Frankel left *Real Housewives* after the third season amid public disputes with several cast members.

Tina Gianoulis

SEE ALSO: The Apprentice; *Bruckheimer, Jerry;* Desperate Housewives; *Divorce; Foodies; Gambling; Hilton, Paris; Hollywood;* The Real Housewives of . . . ; *Reality Television; Soap Operas; Stewart, Martha; Television.*

BIBLIOGRAPHY

Casserly, Meghan. "Can Bethenny Crack a Billion?" *Forbes*, June 6, 2011.

McNeil, Liz. "Bethenny Frankel: Love Saved My Life." *People Weekly*, July 19, 2010.

Rosman, Katherine. "As Seen on TV: Brand Bethenny." *Wall Street Journal*, November 24, 2010.

Frankenstein

On the shores of Switzerland's Lake Geneva in the summer of 1816, nineteen-year-old Mary Wollstonecraft Godwin (1797–1851); her future husband, Percy Bysshe Shelley; and their charismatic friend Lord Byron engaged in a ghost-story contest. After seeing a vision of what she called "the hideous phantasm of a man," the woman who would be known as Mary Shelley began writing *Frankenstein; or, The Modern Prometheus*, the gothic novel that would bring her lasting fame. Even before Shelley's name was widely known, theatrical versions of her novel—the tale of Victor Frankenstein and his monster—frightened and appalled audiences all over Europe.

The popularity of stage adaptations in the nineteenth century foreshadowed the emergence of the Frankenstein monster as an icon of film, television, and other forms of popular culture in the twentieth century, including everything from comic books to Halloween costumes. Indeed, the creature's deformity and pathos have earned it such an indelible position in the popular imagination that the name "Frankenstein" has come to denote not the scientist who bears the name or even the novel that gave it life but rather the image of a scarred and lumbering monster in angry revolt against its creator and society. On one level, the creature exists simply as a horror-movie staple, like Dracula or the Wolf Man. But it is the monster's value as a powerful symbol of our fears regarding the dangers of science, technology, and industrialization, as well as the perils of man's hubristic attempts to control nature, that has given Shelley's "hideous progeny" such an enduring and ubiquitous afterlife.

FILM VERSIONS

No other medium exploited, influenced, and perpetuated the Frankenstein myth like film. One of the first movies ever made, Thomas A. Edison's sixteen-minute silent film *Frankenstein* (1910), began the transformation of Shelley's literary creation into its numerous cinematic offspring. But it was the 1931 Universal Studios release of director James Whale's *Frankenstein* that exerted the greatest impact on Frankenstein mythmaking. In his career-making performance as the monster, Boris Karloff reduced Shelley's articulate, intelligent, and agile creature to a silent brute that was nevertheless endearing in its childlike innocence. Karloff's monster—furnished with a protruding and stitched forehead, eyes devoid of intelligence, and electrodes in his neck—all but replaced Shelley's original creation in the popular imagination. As well as cementing Karloff's creature as a cinematic icon, the film gave rise to enduring "Frankenstein movie" conventions such as the elaborate creation scene; the mad doctor's laboratory; his demented hunchback assistant, Fritz; his infamous ecstatic cry at the moment of creation ("It's alive!"); and the angry torch-carrying rabble who pushed the monster to its fiery death. For two decades, Universal profited immensely from the Frankenstein series with the much-praised *Bride of Frankenstein* (1935) and several lesser but popular sequels, such as *Frankenstein Meets the Wolf Man* (1943). The film series also yielded several spin-off characters, including Elsa Lanchester's Bride of Frankenstein, whose teased-up hair with white "lightning streaks" made her a comparable, though lesser known, pop icon.

REFLECTIONS OF SOCIOPOLITICAL CLIMATES

Embodying the postwar optimism and prosperity of the late 1940s, the Frankenstein monster shifted into the comic genre when Universal released *Abbott and Costello Meet Frankenstein* in 1948. This "horror-comedy" approach to the Frankenstein myth, complete with slapstick gags, marked a departure from Whale's more serious pictures of the 1930s. But the title's explicit focus on the Frankenstein monster—and the film's positive reception with audiences and critics—evinced the creature's ongoing mass-market appeal and presaged the onslaught of low-budget films such as *I Was a Teenage Frankenstein* (1957) in the following decades.

After Abbott and Costello's satire of "classic" monster movies proved that the more serious Frankenstein formula had grown tired, Frankenstein films suffered a hiatus until the British studio Hammer Films released *The Curse of Frankenstein* in 1957. The movie marked the beginning of a more serious and gory approach to big-screen versions of the Frankenstein story. Peter Cushing, who played Baron Frankenstein in numerous films for the Hammer series, captured the psychological struggle of the "mad" scientist so memorably that his character soon overshadowed the monster in much the same way that Karloff's creature had usurped the fame of his creator in the Whale films.

This focus on the psychology of the mad scientist, however, was short-lived. Capitalizing on the prevailing countercultural climate and the renewed popularity of classic horror characters in the 1960s and 1970s, the Frankenstein monster made a comeback as a popular symbol of nonconformity. Exemplary of this new trend, interpretations of Frankenstein in the 1970s subverted and even perverted more traditional representations. In 1973 cult artist Andy Warhol produced *Flesh for Frankenstein* (or *Andy Warhol's Frankenstein*), an ultra-gory retelling in which Baron Frankenstein and his "zombies" display overtly homoerotic, sensual, and necrophiliac behavior. The following year, Mel Brooks's *Young Frankenstein* cleverly parodied the Frankenstein myth and answered the long-unspoken question about the monster's sexual girth. The cult film *The Rocky Horror Picture Show* (1975) even featured a transvestite named Frank-n-Furter and his creation, Rocky Horror.

TELEVISION VERSIONS

The Frankenstein monster also infiltrated America's rising TV culture in two very similar shows about eccentric nuclear families. Both *The Munsters* (CBS, 1964–1966) and *The Addams Family* (ABC, 1964–1966) featured a Frankenstein-like character that was essentially a nostalgic reproduction of Karloff's famous creature. In telling the weekly stories of these suburban families who were, besides their monster-movie appearance, normal in every respect, these shows satirized the quaint, white, middle-class family sitcoms of an earlier decade and capitalized on the comic implications of a "domesticated" Frankenstein monster. (In *The Addams Family*, for instance, the creature named Lurch served as the terse family butler.) The popularity of such series in TV reruns and feature films suggested that the Frankenstein monster, and its attending creature culture, had become a cuddly household commodity now endlessly recycled for comic effect and commercial gain.

RETURNING TO THE SOURCE

It was not until the 1990s that any significant attempt was made to reestablish a more serious approach to this material. Kenneth Branagh's 1994 film *Mary Shelley's Frankenstein* returned to Shelley's original novel and captured much of its gothic terror but also added popular movie formulas such as the creation of the monster's bride. *Frankenstein* continues to be portrayed and adapted in television, film, stage, and print forms, including a television miniseries in 2004 and a London Royal National Theatre play in 2011.

Despite the endless dilutions, distortions, and recyclings, the force of the Frankenstein myth remains undiminished as contemporary society continues to incorporate technological advances—in fields such as genetic engineering—into everyday life while growing increasingly apprehensive about their potential dangers. Each version of Frankenstein's monster acts not only as a potent reminder of the dark side of man's creative idealism—the dangers of trying to play God—but also as a powerful representation of the collective fears and desires of the particular era in which it was conceived. The Frankenstein legend continues to endure as a deformed mirror held up to human nature, *re*-formed from parts of the dead past—with our imagination providing the electrical spark.

Kristine Ha

SEE ALSO: *Abbott and Costello; The Addams Family; Brooks, Mel; Dracula; Hollywood; Horror Movies; Karloff, Boris;* The Rocky Horror Picture Show*; Science Fiction Publishing; Silent Movies; Sitcom; Television; Warhol, Andy.*

BIBLIOGRAPHY

Bloom, Harold, ed. *Mary Shelley's Frankenstein.* New York: Chelsea House Publications, 2006.

Glut, Donald. *The Frankenstein Legend: A Tribute to Mary Shelley and Boris Karloff.* Metuchen, NJ: Scarecrow Press, 1973.

Glut, Donald. *The Frankenstein Catalog.* Jefferson, NC: McFarland, 1984.

Haining, Peter, ed. *The Frankenstein File.* London: New English Library, 1977.

Levine, George, ed. *The Endurance of Frankenstein: Essays on Mary Shelley's Novel.* Berkeley: University of California Press, 1979.

Mellor, Anne Kostelanetz. *Mary Shelley, Her Life, Her Fiction, Her Monsters.* New York: Methuen, 1988.

Seymour, Miranda. *Mary Shelley.* New York: Grove Press, 2002.

Shelley, Mary W. *Frankenstein: or, the Modern Prometheus.* New York: Penguin Books, 1992.

Franklin, Aretha *(1942–)*

As the career of singer, songwriter, and pianist Aretha Franklin makes evident, the black church, its ministers, its members, and its music have had a profound influence on popular music. A fruit of the black Baptist church, Franklin is one of the most important female artists to translate gospel music, with all its intensity, into so-called soul music. Her talent was nurtured by a who's who of gospel music, from Clara Ward, James Cleveland, and Mahalia Jackson to her own father, the Reverend C. L. Franklin, who was a gospel singer in his own right. For nearly fifty years, Franklin has reigned as the Queen of Soul, winning more Grammy Awards than any other female vocalist (at least one a year from 1967 through 1974 and then in 1981, 1985, and 1987). From 1960 to 1992, eighty-nine of her songs were in the pop or R&B Top 40, with nearly twenty of them reaching number one on the rhythm-and-blues (R&B) chart.

Franklin was the first African American woman to appear on the cover of *Time* magazine (in June 1968), and in 1987 she became the first woman to be inducted into the Rock and Roll Hall of Fame. By the mid-1980s, Franklin had racked up a total of twenty-four gold records; she has had forty-three singles in the Top 40. The state of Michigan has designated her voice as a natural resource.

REARED BY GOSPEL

One of three sisters, Aretha Franklin was born in Memphis, Tennessee, on March 25, 1942. During her childhood, her family moved to Buffalo, New York, and then to Detroit, Michigan,

Aretha Franklin. *The "Queen of Soul" performs at New York's Madison Square Garden in 1971.* WALTER IOOSS JR./GETTY IMAGES.

where she grew up. Her father, the celebrated Reverend C. L. Franklin, ministered to the 4,500-member New Bethel Baptist Church. He was one of the first ministers to have a nationally broadcast radio program, and at one time he earned up to $4,000 per sermon. His eldest daughter taught herself to play the piano at the age of eight.

Her father's national stature and influence drew such well-known gospel singers as Cleveland, Jackson, and Ward to their home for improvisational praise sessions. Two of the Clara Ward Singers helped rear a young Franklin after her mother's separation from the family. Franklin absorbed the rich musical experience in her father's church and by the age of twelve began touring with him, singing solos.

Her recording career began in the early 1950s when she and her sisters, Carolyn and Erma, made a 78 rpm record, singing behind their father on the Gotham label. In 1956 Franklin recorded the hymn "Where We'll Never Grow Old," in a style profoundly influenced by her mentor, Ward. Following the path of one of her idols, Sam Cooke, who had made a successful transition from gospel to pop, at the age of eighteen Franklin left Detroit for New York, where Major Holley, a bass player for jazz pianist Teddy Wilson, helped look after her while she made the rounds in an attempt to be discovered. John Hammond, the legendary impresario who had encouraged Columbia Records to sign Jackson, among other talents, heard Franklin and encouraged the company to sign her. While with Columbia, Franklin released a number of recordings: "Today I Sing the Blues" and "Won't Be Long" were moderately successful R&B hits.

STARDOM ARRIVES

After her contract with Columbia expired, Franklin signed with Atlantic Records in 1966. With the savvy producing skills of Jerry Wexler, Franklin recorded "I Never Loved a Man (The Way I Love You)" with the Muscle Shoals, Alabama; rhythm section, her own piano accompaniment; and the backup vocals of her sisters. The single and the album of the same title achieved gold status, and Aretha had arrived. A string of gold records followed, including "Respect," her first single to top both the R&B and pop charts. The album also included such popular hits as "Dr. Feelgood," "Baby, I Love You," "Chain of Fools," and "Since You've Been Gone." Her next hit songs, "Think" and "I Say a Little Prayer," went gold, along with her *Lady Soul* album in 1968.

In 1969 "See Saw" and the album *Aretha Now* similarly attained gold status. "Don't Play That Song" in 1970 and her 1971 version of Simon and Garfunkel's "Bridge over Troubled Water" also were hits. In 1972 she won two Grammys for the albums *Young, Gifted, and Black* and *Amazing Grace*. In 1973 Franklin scored again with "Master of Eyes" and in 1974 with "Ain't Nothin' Like the Real Thing."

The mid- to late 1970s saw a dry spell in Franklin's creative hit making. Disco had begun to gain favor, adversely impacting the sale and popularity of soul and R&B. In 1980 she signed with Arista Records, and by 1982 she had made a successful comeback with the album *Jump to It*. In 1985 the *Who's Zooming Who* album, with the hit "Freeway of Love," went gold. But in 1987 Franklin returned to her roots with the album *One Lord, One Faith, One Baptism*, her first gospel collection in fifteen years. A duet with George Michael titled "I Knew You Were Waiting" became her second number one pop hit.

Franklin was awarded a Lifetime Achievement Award at the 1994 Grammy Awards, and for much of the 1990s she made only sporadic recordings. She released a gold single, "A Rose Is Still a Rose" in 1998, produced by Lauryn Hill of the Fugees, followed by an album of the same name. Franklin recorded her final album for Arista with *So Damn Happy* in 2003 and shortly thereafter formed her own label, Aretha Records. Franklin's first releases on her own label were a duet compilation in 2007 and her first-ever holiday album in 2008. At the fiftieth Grammy Awards in 2008, she received her eighteenth Grammy for "Never

Gonna Break My Faith," a collaboration with Mary J. Blige. In 2011, as a celebration of her fifty years in the music industry, she released *A Woman Falling out of Love.*

SHOWCASING THE VOICE

Franklin's relentless productivity, diverse repertoire, and sheer volume of recordings make a simplified overview of her style difficult. To be sure, if one were to distill her style, it would boil down to her rhythmic gospel piano style and arrangements that accompany her voice with all its ecstatic tension. Beginning with her recordings for Atlantic, Franklin essentially defined soul music as vital, genuine, sexual, and visceral, reflecting the struggles and triumphs of the human spirit. "It is her fierce, gritty conviction. . . . She flexes her rich, cutting voice like a whip; she lashes her listeners—in her words—'to the bone,' for deepness," *Time* magazine observed in June 1968. All in all, it has been Franklin's faith and "hard knocks" that enabled her to embrace a song, dramatizing it and making it her own.

The early Columbia sessions were a fallow period in terms of her individual stylistic development, persistently marred by the company's attempt to pigeonhole her style into jazz and pop arrangements rather than allowing her freedom of expression. But at Atlantic, the arrangements of Franklin's music were based on her piano accompaniment to her voice. Upon her arrival at the studio to record, arrangers such as Arif Mardin would base everything around her piano and voice renditions, adding the backup vocals of sisters Carolyn and Erma. Atlantic allowed Franklin to exercise a great deal of artistic control, encouraging her creativity and a selection of songs that meant something to her. The first album, *I Never Loved a Man (The Way I Love You)*, paid homage to her musical idols Cooke (in "A Change Is Gonna Come" and "Good Times") and Ray Charles—who had previously merged gospel with pop, beginning with the recording of "I've Got a Woman"—which is represented in a moving and undeniably convincing "Drown in My Own Tears."

KEEPING THE PERSONAL PRIVATE

Franklin's personal life has been a turbulent one. During her childhood she faced one traumatic experience after another. At the age of six, her mother abandoned the family, leaving Franklin's father to provide the nurturing and support of the children. From a young age, she toured on the gospel highway, where the attendant pitfalls that she encountered on the road were not always in her best interest. She was the mother of two boys by the time she reached seventeen. Her marriage to her manager, Ted White, who had been known to rough her up from time to time, ended in divorce. Her second marriage, to actor Glynn Turman, also ended in divorce.

In 1979 her father was shot by a robber in his home and remained in a coma for several years, never recovering. Franklin had to drop out of a tour in 2011 due to her undergoing major, and unannounced, surgery. She announced plans for her third marriage, to Willie Wilkerson, her companion of twenty-seven years, in 2012 but called it off a few weeks later. This was followed by news of her goddaughter Whitney Houston's untimely death on February 11, 2012. Through it all, Franklin has ardently guarded her privacy and remained the Queen of Soul.

Franklin has been active for several social causes and an activist for black pride and civil rights. Her father was a friend of Martin Luther King Jr.; Franklin sang at King's funeral. She recorded "Young, Gifted and Black" as an affirmation of positive black consciousness and pride. Her unabashed celebration of sexual liberation with the lyrics "sock it to me" in "Respect" and "taking care of business is really this man's game" in "Dr. Feelgood" was liberating to many women. Franklin sang for the Democratic National Convention in 1968, for the inauguration of President Jimmy Carter in 1977, again for the inauguration of President Bill Clinton in 1993, and again for the inauguration of President Barack Obama in 2009.

Franklin's career has been honored not only by the music industry but also as an important cultural contribution. She was awarded the Presidential Medal of Freedom by President George W. Bush in 2005, and Yale University awarded her an honorary doctorate in music in 2010. Three television specials (*Aretha* in 1986; *Aretha Franklin: The Queen of Soul* in 1988; and *Duets* in 1993) have featured Franklin's life and music, and she also appeared in cameos in both *The Blues Brothers* (1980) and *Blues Brothers 2000* (1998).

Franklin has shared her songs of love, hurt, respect, and pride but not much of her personal life. In 1999 the Queen of Soul finally released a long-awaited autobiography, in collaboration with David Ritz, biographer of fellow musical greats B. B. King, Marvin Gaye, Etta James, and Ray Charles. Those expecting a deeper glimpse into her private life, however, would ultimately be disappointed, for while she shares many musical anecdotes about her peers (and rivals), as well as delving deep into her own career, the personal revelations are minimal. Whether singing gospel or pop, music is a balm and an alter ego for Franklin. "It does get me out of myself," she has said. "I guess you could say I do a lot of traveling with my voice."

Willie Collins

SEE ALSO: *Atlantic Records; Blues; The Blues Brothers; Charles, Ray; Civil Rights Movement; Gaye, Marvin; Gospel Music; Grammy Awards; Jackson, Mahalia; King, B. B.; King, Martin Luther, Jr.; Motown; Pop Music; Rhythm and Blues; Simon and Garfunkel; Soul Music.*

BIBLIOGRAPHY

Bego, Mark. *Aretha Franklin, the Queen of Soul.* New York: St. Martin's Press, 1989.

Franklin, Aretha, and David Ritz. *Aretha: From These Roots.* New York: Villard, 1999.

"Lady Soul Singing It Like It Is." *Time*, June 28, 1968.

McNeil, W. K. *Encyclopedia of American Gospel Music.* New York: Routledge, 2005.

Franklin, Bonnie *(1944–)*

An actress and a dancer best known for her portrayal of Ann Romano—TV's first "Ms."—on Norman Lear's sitcom *One Day at a Time* (1975–1984), Bonnie Franklin was born January 6, 1944, in Santa Monica, California. She started tap dancing when she was nine years old, appearing with Donald O'Connor on the *Colgate Comedy Hour* (1950–1955). Franklin acted in the original *Munsters* (1964–1966) and *Man from U.N.C.L.E.* (1964–1968) but became a household name from 1975 to 1984 on Lear's sitcom.

She dabbled in directing (*The Munsters Today* [1987–1991]), TV movies (*Portrait of a Rebel: The Remarkable Mrs.*

Sanger [1980]), and exercise videos (*I Hate to Exercise—I Love to Tap*). She also did some regional theater during the 1990s. In 2011 she reunited with her *One Day at a Time* costar Valerie Bertinelli for one episode of the TV series *Hot in Cleveland* (2010–). That same year Franklin appeared in the musical *My History of Marriage* at the New York Musical Theatre Festival.

Karen Lurie

SEE ALSO: *Lear, Norman; Made-for-Television Movies; The Musical;* One Day at a Time*; Sitcom; Tap Dancing; Television.*

BIBLIOGRAPHY

Buck, Jerry. "It 'Gives Me a Second Career': Bonnie Franklin Directing *Munsters Today.*" *Los Angeles Times*, July 19, 1989.

Oppenheimer, Peer J. "Bonnie Franklin Knows Where She's Going" *Tuscaloosa News*, May 1, 1977.

Frasier

Frasier, a popular situation comedy starring Kelsey Grammer as pompous, insecure psychiatrist Dr. Frasier Crane, premiered on NBC in September 1993. The character had appeared originally in the long-running and much-loved comedy show *Cheers*, with which *Frasier* shared the same creative team. *Frasier* relocated the doctor from his original *Cheers* setting in a Boston tavern to Seattle, Washington, where he became the host of a call-in radio show on fictional local station KACL. *Frasier* immediately won accolades for its sophisticated humor and literate dialogue and secured a consistent position in the top fifteen network shows. In 1998 the show became the first to win five consecutive Emmy Awards for Outstanding Comedy Series, ensuring its place in television history.

Grammer's character was moved to Seattle in order to give the show enough distance with which to create a sense of identity separate from *Cheers*, yet the choice of Seattle also meant that the show reflected (and contributed to) the heightened profile of the Pacific Northwest city in the 1990s and a range of popular accounts that hailed Seattle as a desirable and sophisticated place to live. For example, in place of the Cheers tavern, one of the main settings of *Frasier* is the upscale Café Nervosa, where Frasier and his snobbish brother, fellow psychiatrist Niles (David Hyde Pierce) sip their cappuccinos and lattes. Much of the show's best comedy is found in the conversations between the two brothers, with sharp retorts flying as each tries to undermine and outdo the other in everything, from successful careers to suit fabrics.

The brothers are of one mind, however, when dealing with their father, retired ex-cop Martin Crane (John Mahoney). Gruff and blue collar, Martin was forced to move into Frasier's expensive, tony apartment after being injured in the line of duty. With his dog Eddie (recipient of much fan mail) and his fondness for beer, hot dogs, and *Monday Night Football*, Martin constantly frustrates Frasier's attempts to create a tasteful, chic ambience for the apartment. Martin's English live-in home-care provider, Daphne Moon (Jane Leeves), also serves as the object of Niles's frustrated affection, adding another hilarious dimension to the complex domestic dynamics.

Critics have noted the way that the best episodes feel like little twenty-two-minute plays because of the combination of high-quality writing and ensemble acting. The episodes often take place within one confined, high-pressure setting, such as Frasier's apartment or the radio station, where the doctor battles against a constant stream of irritating callers with his slightly jaded producer, Roz (Peri Gilpin).

Offscreen, Grammer had some well-publicized battles with substance abuse; he checked himself into the Betty Ford Clinic in the fall of 1996. On-screen, the show continued to move smoothly from strength to strength, and in November 1997 celebrated its 1,000th episode by uprooting from its studio in Hollywood to shoot on location in Seattle. Eschewing its usual stage-bound format, the episode takes in the sights of the city and stars the real mayor of Seattle, Norm Rice, who declares it "Frasier Crane Day" in Seattle.

The show's reward for continued critical and ratings success was taking over *Seinfeld*'s coveted NBC prime-time slot in the fall 1998 schedule. This slot had been filled previously by some of the most successful and critically acclaimed series in American television history, including *The Cosby Show*, *Hill Street Blues*, and *L.A Law*. What made *Frasier*'s rise to the number one comedy slot all the more unusual was that it bucked the trend in situation comedy in the 1990s. Instead of building itself around a celebrity personality (often a stand-up comedian), as in the case of *Seinfeld*, *Roseanne*, and *Ellen*, *Frasier* relied upon the continuing appeal of a well-drawn fictional character.

For five consecutive years, from 1994 to 1998, *Frasier* won the Emmy for Outstanding Comedy Series. In 2002 *TV Guide* ranked it number thirty-four on its list of the fifty greatest TV shows of all time. The show's run concluded at the end of its eleventh season in 2004, a season that resulted in six additional Emmy Awards, leaving the show with a final total of thirty-seven, the most ever Emmy wins by one series. A forty-four-disc DVD set of the complete series was released in 2007.

James Lyons

SEE ALSO: Cheers*;* The Cosby Show*; DeGeneres, Ellen; Emmy Awards;* Hill Street Blues*;* L.A. Law*;* Monday Night Football*;* Roseanne*;* Seinfeld*; Sitcom; Television;* TV Guide.

BIBLIOGRAPHY

Bailey, David, and Warren Martyn. *Goodnight Seattle: The Unauthorized Guide to the World of Frasier*. London: Virgin, 1998.

Graham, Jefferson. *Frasier*. London: Simon & Schuster, 1996.

The Frat Pack

SEE: *Black, Jack; Carell, Steve; Ferrell, Will; Stiller, Ben.*

Frawley, William *(1887–1966)*

William "Bill" Frawley made his mark in the 1930s as one of American cinema's first character actors. Appearing in more than 150 films, from *The Adventures of Huckleberry Finn* (1939) to *Miracle on 34th Street* (1947), the strong-faced Iowan often depicted surly, middle-aged men who hid their compassion behind masks of crustiness. He later adapted his trademark persona to the small screen, where he appeared in two of television's most memorable supporting roles: Fred Mertz on *I Love Lucy* (1951–1957) and "Bub" O'Casey on *My Three Sons* (1960–1964).

Lucille Ball and Desi Arnaz picked Frawley to play Fred Mertz after their first choice, Gale Gordon, was unavailable. CBS executives warned Ball and Arnaz against the choice: Frawley had a reputation for heavy drinking. Yet the veteran actor rose to the occasion and successfully performed as the perfect stick-in-the-mud husband and penny-pinching landlord. Frawley even managed to tolerate Vivian Vance, who played his on-screen wife, Ethel Mertz, although the two strongly disliked each other. "She's one of the finest girls to come out of Kansas," he once said, "but I often wish she'd go back there."

After *I Love Lucy*, Frawley played Michael Francis "Bub" O'Casey, Fred MacMurray's gruff father-in-law and housekeeper, on the sitcom *My Three Sons*. William Demarest replaced him when Frawley retired in 1964. Fittingly, Frawley's last television appearance was a cameo on a 1965 episode of Ball's *The Lucy Show* titled "Lucy and the Countess Have a Horse Guest." On that episode, Lucy Carmichael (Ball) jokes about how familiar Frawley seems to her. As Fred Mertz, a character almost synonymous with the old neighborhood landlord, Frawley is familiar to all those who love classic comedy.

Jacob M. Appel

SEE ALSO: *Arnaz, Desi; Ball, Lucille;* I Love Lucy*;* My Three Sons*; Sitcom; Television; Vance, Vivian.*

BIBLIOGRAPHY

Andrews, Bart. *Lucy & Ricky & Fred & Ethel: The Story of "I Love Lucy."* New York: Dutton, 1976.

Crisp, Tom. *The Book of Bill: Choice Words Memorable Men.* Kansas City, MO: Andrews McMeel, 2009.

McClay, Michael, and Deanna Gaffner-McClay. *I Love Lucy: The Complete Picture History of the Most Popular TV Show Ever.* New York: Warner Books, 1995.

Wyman, Ric B. *For the Love of Lucy: The Complete Guide for Collectors and Fans.* New York: Abbeville Press, 1995.

Frazier, Joe *(1944–2011)*

Joe Frazier was a quintessential pressure fighter. He came forward at all costs, throwing his vaunted left hook at opponents until he broke their spirits or bodies or—as was often the case—both. A great heavyweight champion by any standard of measurement, Frazier left his mark in his three-fight series against Muhammad Ali. In 1967 Ali had been stripped of his heavyweight crown and his license to box for refusing induction into the U.S. Army during the Vietnam War. In Ali's absence an elimination tournament was held to determine his successor to the heavyweight throne. Frazier won the tournament, tearing through the division's contenders and establishing himself as the best active heavyweight in the world.

When Ali's license to box was reinstated, a superfight was made between Frazier, the undefeated reigning champion, and Ali, the undefeated former champ. The fight, which promised to be a thrilling encounter pitting Ali's speed and athleticism against Frazier's strength and determination, was billed as the "Fight of the Century." On March 8, 1971, at New York City's Madison Square Garden, Ali and Frazier split what was then a record-setting purse of $5 million and staged a fight that may have even exceeded its hype.

The fight was of such import that singer, actor, and pop culture icon Frank Sinatra was enlisted as a photographer for *Life* magazine. The bout's significance owed not merely to the high quality of the match itself but also to the social and political symbolism attached to its participants. Whereas Ali's refusal of induction into the armed forces and his outspoken stances on various political and religious issues made him a representative, in the eyes of many, of oppressed people all over the world, Frazier unwittingly came to represent the establishment and the status quo of the white American power structure. Smokin' Joe, as he was nicknamed for his relentless style, resented the perception of himself as the "white hope." Frazier was proud of his racial identity and noted on several occasions that, ironically, he was darker complected than Ali. Nevertheless, Ali vilified Frazier as representing white America, and in turn an enraged Frazier handed Ali his first professional loss, a fifteen-round unanimous decision defeat. Frazier even knocked Ali down in the last round for good measure.

The two boxers fought a rematch three years later, this time with no title on the line (as Frazier had lost his title in a humiliating knockout at the hands of the murderous-hitting George Foreman). This time Ali took revenge with a twelve-round unanimous decision victory. The third and final meeting rivaled their first encounter as the most famous heavyweight title fight in history. Dubbed by Ali "The Thrilla in Manilla," this 1975 classic was a contest of wills unlike anything witnessed in the division's illustrious history.

Joe Frazier. *Joe Frazier remains in the ring after his victory over Jerry Quarry in New York's Madison Square Garden in 1974.* **HERB SCHARFMAN/SPORTS IMAGERY/GETTY IMAGES.**

Ali was champion by this time, having knocked out Foreman, who so easily beat Frazier. Figuring that Frazier would be old and ineffective this time around (though Ali himself was the elder of the two by two years), Ali took him lightly and did not expect a tough fight. To add insult to injury, Ali took to calling him "The Gorilla." Frazier's pride was hurt once again by his antagonist, and he presented Ali with the toughest test of his career—fourteen grueling rounds, ending only when Frazier's chief corner man, the venerable Eddie Futch, refused to let Joe—whose eyes were swollen nearly shut—come out for the last round. Cast unwillingly in a role he despised, Frazier nevertheless etched his name into the American consciousness. If Ali was the greatest heavyweight champion who ever lived (and even if he was not), then Frazier was his greatest rival. Their names go down in history together.

Although the two fighters never became friends, Ali issued a public apology in 2001 for having called Frazier names in the heat of the moment. Many years later, in March 2011, Frazier said that he forgave Ali and would "love to see him." The former adversaries never did have a reunion. In November of that year, Frazier died of liver cancer.

Max Kellerman

SEE ALSO: *Ali, Muhammad; Boxing; Cancer; Foreman, George;* Life*; Sinatra, Frank; Sports Heroes; Vietnam.*

BIBLIOGRAPHY

Arkush, Michael. *The Fight of the Century: Ali vs. Frazier March 8, 1971.* Hoboken, NJ: John Wiley & Sons, 2008.

Frazier, Joe. *Smokin' Joe: The Autobiography of a Heavyweight Champion of the World.* New York: Macmillan, 1996.

Kram, Mark. *Ghosts of Manila: The Fateful Blood Feud between Muhammad Ali and Joe Frazier.* New York: HarperCollins, 2002.

Pepe, Phil. *Come out Smokin': Joe Frazier—The Champ Nobody Knew.* New York: Coward, McCann & Geoghegan, 1972.

Frazier, Walt "Clyde" *(1945–)*

Walt "Clyde" Frazier was the epitome of "cool" in his basketball era. The flamboyant player created a style that fans worshipped and other players emulated. Frazier began his career as an all-American at Southern Illinois University, where he led his team to the 1967 National Invitational Tournament (NIT) Championship. Coincidentally, the games took place in New York's Madison Square Garden, where he would continue his career as a professional.

Frazier became an All-Star guard for the New York Knicks from 1967 to 1977 and was the undisputed floor leader of the Knick teams that won National Basketball Association (NBA) titles in 1970 and 1973. In addition to his smooth and explosive offensive talents, he was one of the league's premier defensive players and was always assigned to control the opposing teams' primary outside offensive threat. Frazier is fondly remembered for his resplendent wardrobe and the calm, dignified demeanor that earned him the nickname "Clyde." He was inducted into the Naismith Memorial Basketball Hall of Fame in 1987.

G. Allen Finchum

SEE ALSO: *Basketball; National Basketball Association (NBA); National Collegiate Athletic Association (NCAA); The New York Knickerbockers.*

BIBLIOGRAPHY

Dickey, Glenn. *The History of Professional Basketball.* Briarcliff Manor, NY: Stein and Day, 1982.

Frazier, Walt, and Dan Markowitz. *The Game within the Game.* New York: Hyperion, 2007.

Sachare, Alex. *100 Greatest Basketball Players of All Time.* New York: Byron Preiss Visual Publications, 1997.

Freak Shows

By the mid-twentieth century the display for profit and entertainment of people known in the United States as "freaks" had for the most part become an anachronism. Parading disabled people before a staring public for amusement has, along with public executions, become socially unacceptable.

As our lingering collective memory of P. T. Barnum suggests, however, from about 1830 to 1940 in the United States and Europe, people with congenital disabilities or other physical traits that could be turned into curiosities were displayed on stages, in dime museums, in circuses, and at fairs as a part of a growing culture of popular performance that was driven by the increased commercialism, leisure, and urbanization of modernity. Whereas the term *freak* now connotes a negative departure from the norm, in the nineteenth century *freak* meant a whimsical fancy. This shift in meaning suggests the long history of exhibiting people whose bodies are presented as extraordinary and the enduring interest that they inspire in the popular imagination.

HISTORICAL ATTITUDES

Extraordinary bodies have been an obsession of humankind since antiquity. The nineteenth-century "freak" was known as a "monster" in ancient times and considered to be a prodigy. The birth of such an individual, as with natural events such as comets and earthquakes, was thought to portend grave or disastrous events. Stone Age cave drawings record monstrous births, and prehistoric grave sites evince elaborate ritual sacrifices of such bodies.

As the narrative of the natural world shifted from one of divine determination to secular explanations, early science viewed exceptional bodies not only as indices to the order of things or proof of God's abundance but also as sources upon which to hone medical expertise. Early scientists and philosophers kept cabinets of curiosities full of items such as shark teeth, shrunken heads, and bottled fetuses that they regarded with a mixture of awe and curiosity. At the same time, these extraordinary bodies were commercialized at public fairs, such as London's famous Bartholomew Fair, and on streets by monster mongers who charged for viewings and sold pamphlets called monster ballads, which offered morals drawn from the wondrous bodies.

Well into the seventeenth century, congenitally disabled newborns, called monstrous births, continued to be interpreted as exegeses of the divine and natural orders by figures as respected as Cotton Mather and John Winthrop. Disabled people and dwarfs were often celebrities and kept at court as "fools" or in the role of pets. For example, a powdered and wigged Matthew Buchinger, who was virtually armless and legless, dazzled eighteenth-century Europe with his conjuring, musical performances, calligraphic skills, and marksmanship with the pistol. These monsters filled their viewers with awe and curiosity; they were seen as "marvels" and "wonders," not as what the twenty-first-century observer would interpret as abnormal or inappropriate to stare at.

DIME MUSEUMS AND CIRCUS SIDESHOWS

In the 1840s P. T. Barnum opened his American Museum in New York, thereby institutionalizing the once itinerant practice of showing monsters in halls and on streets. The museum aspired to middle-class status with temperance tracts, appeals to education, entrepreneurship, and other gestures toward bourgeois respectability. An entertainment industry in freaks and other curiosities flourished in dime museums and later as circus sideshows throughout Victorian America. The secularizing, mobile, rapidly changing social order dominated increasingly by market economics, individualism, and a developing mass culture generated this boom in staring at curiosities. It was part of a larger culture of display manifest in museums, circuses, grand expositions, photographs, parades, theater, department-store displays, and what Thorstein Veblen called "conspicuous consumption."

These shows gathered an astonishing array of wonders, from Wild Men of Borneo to Fat Ladies, Living Skeletons, Fiji Princes, Albinos, Bearded Women, Siamese Twins, Tattooed Circassians, Armless and Legless Wonders, Chinese Giants, Cannibals, Midget Triplets, Hermaphrodites, Spotted Boys, and much more. Augmenting these marvels were ancillary performers such as ventriloquists, performing geese, mesmerists, beauty contestants, contortionists, sharpshooters, trained goats, frog eaters, sword-swallowers, and tumbling monkeys. From Queen Victoria and Henry James to families and the humblest immigrants, people gathered together in this most democratizing institution to gaze raptly at freaks on display.

Freaks were the highest-paid performers in the industry. Many, such as Tom Thumb, were celebrities who made their handlers rich. Freaks were more than simply disabled people; they were figures created by the shows' sensationalized and exaggerated conventions of display. Elaborate costuming, exotic sets, bizarre pamphlets, the hyperbolic rant of the pitchmen, photographs for audiences to collect, and scientific testimonials all surrounded these bodies to produce freaks and marvels from people who had unusual bodies that could be appropriated for the shows.

Scientists and doctors participated in the show culture into the nineteenth century by examining the performers for scientific study and by verifying the freaks' authenticity, lending prestige to the exhibitions. Alongside its involvement with the entertainment industry, however, science had institutionalized its preoccupation with monsters by 1832 with the development of teratology, the scientific study of monsters. Teratology endeavored to harness the ancient power of prodigies by creating pigs with cleft palates and elaborate taxonomies of physical deviation. As science and medicine began to separate from the shows and become more elite, such developments as statistics, the idea of the average man, the pathologizing of disabilities, and the eventual belief that extraordinary bodies should be standardized for the good of both the individual and society helped turn the wondrous freak into a medical problem.

CONTEMPORARY REEMERGENCE

A complex, interrelated combination of historical and social factors diminished the immense popularity and proliferation of the freak show by the mid-twentieth century. The medicalization of disability, the rise of the bourgeoisie, the sentimentalizing of disabled people as pathetic rather than wondrous, and the sinking of freak shows to lowbrow culture, among other developments, nearly eliminated the form of the freak show that Barnum so masterfully exploited. Its allure lingered nevertheless in such transmuted forms as talk shows, bodybuilding, wrestling matches, science fiction narratives such as *Star Trek*, and even performers such as Michael Jackson.

In spite of the increasingly widespread sense that freak shows were not politically correct, the 1990s saw a renewed interest in such entertainment. This renewal took the dual form of traveling sideshows—such as the Jim Rose Circus in the United States—and reality television—such as the *BodyShock* series on British television, which featured such anomalies as a Half-Ton Man.

Scholars saw this revival as not only a reemergence of the freak show but also a redefinition of it, as the performers participated in and benefited from a cultural reevaluation of what "normal" is and how one should respond to those who are different. One point of contention is that advocates for the disabled believe that people with congenital abnormalities should not be labeled "freaks" or put on public exhibition. Some performers, however, view their differences as the source of their very ability to make a living. Perhaps, in the end, one of the reasons freak shows endure and have value for society is that they force us to consider such questions.

Rosemarie Garland Thomson

SEE ALSO: *Beauty Queens; Bodybuilding; Circus; Daytime Talk Shows;* Freaks*; Jackson, Michael; Reality Television; Ringling Bros., Barnum & Bailey Circus;* Star Trek*; Traveling Carnivals.*

BIBLIOGRAPHY

Adams, Rachel. *Sideshow U.S.A.: Freaks and the American Cultural Imagination.* Chicago: University of Chicago Press, 2001.

Altick, Richard D. *The Shows of London.* Cambridge, MA: Belknap Press, 1978.

Bogdan, Robert. *Freak Show: Presenting Human Oddities for Amusement and Profit.* Chicago: University of Chicago Press, 1988.

Daston, Lorraine, and Katharine Park. *Wonders and the Order of Nature: 1150–1750.* New York: Zone Books, 1998.

Dennett, Andrea Stulman. *Weird and Wonderful: The Dime Museum in America.* New York: New York University Press, 1997.

Fiedler, Leslie. *Freaks: Myths and Images of the Secret Self.* New York: Simon & Schuster, 1978.

Hartzman, Marc. *American Sideshow: An Encyclopedia of History's Most Wondrous and Curiously Strange Performances.* New York: Jeremy P. Tarcher, 2005.

Jay, Ricky. *Learned Pigs and Fireproof Women.* New York: Villard Books, 1986.

Mannix, Daniel P. *Freaks: We Who Are Not as Others.* San Francisco: Re/Search Publications, 1990.

Mitchell, Michael, and Charles Eisenmann. *Monsters of the Gilded Age: The Photographs of Charles Eisenmann*. Toronto, Canada: Gage Publishing, 1979.

Paré, Ambroise. *On Monsters and Marvels*. Chicago: University of Chicago Press, 1982.

Thomson, Rosemarie Garland, ed. *Freakery: Cultural Spectacles of the Extraordinary Body*. New York: New York University Press, 1996.

Thomson, Rosemarie Garland. *Extraordinary Bodies: Figuring Physical Disability in American Culture and Literature*. New York: Columbia University Press, 1997.

Freaks

Perhaps the most unsettling horror film to follow in the wake of director Tod Browning's enormously financial success of *Frankenstein* in 1931, *Freaks* (1932) tells the story of seemingly childlike carnival "freaks" who wreak unspeakable revenge on two able-bodied swindlers. Adapted from the Tod Robbins short story "Spurs" and directed by Tod Browning, this untidy little film shocked audiences with its use of actual disabled performers: little people, an armless woman, a "living torso" (a man whose body ended slightly below his ribcage), and many others. Receiving mostly negative reviews and faring poorly at the box office, *Freaks* ran afoul of censorship boards across the United States and was banned in the United Kingdom for three decades. After playing the exploitation-film circuit for years, it received acclaim at the 1962 Venice Film Festival and enjoyed some popularity among counterculture "freaks" during the late 1960s and early 1970s. The Library of Congress honored *Freaks* by adding it to the National Film Registry in 1994.

Martin F. Norden

SEE ALSO: *Cult Films; Frankenstein; Freak Shows; Horror Movies; Traveling Carnivals.*

BIBLIOGRAPHY

Bombaci, Nancy. *Freaks in Late Modernist American Culture: Nathaniel West, Djuna Barnes, Tod Browning, and Carson McCullers*. New York: Peter Lang, 2006.

Hertzogenrath, Bernd, ed. *The Films of Tod Browning*. London: Black Dog Publishing, 2006.

Norden, Martin F. *The Cinema of Isolation: A History of Physical Disability in the Movies*. New Brunswick, NJ: Rutgers University Press, 1994.

Skal, David J., and Elias Savada. *Dark Carnival: The Secret World of Tod Browning*. New York: Anchor Books, 1995.

Frederick's of Hollywood

Frederick's of Hollywood is an innovative lingerie company established by Frederick N. Mellinger on New York's Fifth Avenue in 1946. A year later he moved his business to the West Coast. Originally a mail-order house—the company still sends out about fifteen million catalogs per year—by 2010 it included more than 125 retail outlets and an online presence. For many years, corporate headquarters were located at 6608 Hollywood Boulevard and were housed in an Art Deco building, which was informally known as the Purple Palace for its garish lavender facade.

During World War II Mellinger was stationed in Europe, where he noticed the French preference for black undergarments at a time when Americans preferred white. Mellinger formulated a theory of female pulchritude centered on proportional perfection. When he returned to the United States, he studied

Frederick's of Hollywood. *Models pose in Christmas-themed lingerie by Frederick's of Hollywood in 1997.* MIKE NELSON/AFP/GETTY IMAGES.

anatomy in order to be better prepared to contend with such phenomena as sagging breasts, midriff bulges, lackluster posteriors, and something that he referred to as "piano legs," to name a few. Jane and Michael Stern, in *The Encyclopedia of Bad Taste*, offer the following quote, which addresses the issue of Mellinger's motivation: "I knew there had to be ways to reproportion women and give every lovable one of them EQUAL OPPORTUNITY in the eyes of men." A popular Mellinger slogan—"Came in looking like a Chevy and left looking like a Cadillac"—epitomizes the Frederick's of Hollywood philosophy.

Frederick's-style perfection can be achieved with the assistance of a number of innovative products. For poorly contoured buttocks, there is the Living End padded girdle. For the woman who requires flexibility in regard to bust size, there is the Light 'N' Lovely Air-Lite Inflatable Bra, whose cups can be expanded to the desired degree with the aid of straws. Or, for those who prefer a brassiere that more nearly approximates tactile perfection, there are Liquid Lift bras, which feature pads containing a water-and-gel mixture. A salient nipple effect can be achieved with the aid of prosthetic nipple pad bra inserts.

The Mellinger concept of femininity, the one that Frederick's of Hollywood projected throughout much of its history, extolled the symmetrical, the curvaceous, the buxom, and the docile: the image of the sex kitten and the harem girl, adumbrations of which were even evident in some of the company's product names—Sheik's Choice pajamas, for instance. Males made many of the purchases or told the women in their lives what to buy. The image of Mellinger as "Mr. Frederick" appeared throughout the catalog, proffering tips on such subjects as male preferences and drooping breasts. The male orientation of the firm was unmistakable.

In an era when many American women are financially independent of their male partners and rapid progress has been made toward sexual equality, it is not surprising that Frederick's of Hollywood, with the death of Mellinger in 1990, tried to alter its image. *New York Times* contributor Jennifer Steinhauer related Frederick's CEO Terry Patterson's plans for the company: "Over all . . . Frederick's of Hollywood stores would attempt to whisper seductively to the modern female consumer, instead of simply leering salaciously at her boyfriend. 'I'm dressed, I'm corporate, I'm successful, I can play with the big boys. . . . And you don't know I'm a Frederick's woman.' That is where I see the company now."

Despite that attempt to shift directions, changing tastes have remained problematic for the lingerie company, and in 2000 it filed for bankruptcy, from which it emerged in 2003. In 2006 Frederick's of Hollywood merged with a New York manufacturer of sleepwear called Movie Star Inc. to become a publicly traded company. The firm sold its Movie Star division in 2010.

William F. O'Connor

SEE ALSO: *Advertising; Bra; Online Shopping; Victoria's Secret; World War II.*

BIBLIOGRAPHY

Farrell-Beck, Jane, and Colleen Gau. *Uplift: The Bra in America*. Philadelphia: University of Pennsylvania Press, 2002.

Steinhauer, Jennifer. "What Becomes a Legend?" *New York Times*, February 13, 1998, D-1.

Stern, Jane, and Michael Stern. *The Encyclopedia of Bad Taste*. New York: HarperCollins, 1990.

Free Speech Movement

The free speech movement (FSM) started as a dispute over twenty-six feet of sidewalk and escalated into a pitched battle for control of the University of California at Berkeley. In the process, an entire school—students and faculty alike—was polarized into two camps fundamentally at odds with each other, both ideologically and in terms of rhetoric. The free speech movement represented the adoption of civil rights protest techniques—pickets, sit-ins, and other nonviolent methods—in a hitherto untested arena, the university. As it turned out, it was the opening salvo in a long, drawn-out battle, a tumult that would ultimately affect one out of every ten college and university campuses nationwide (a conservative figure), rending the country in two along ideological and generational lines.

The early 1960s were a time of cultural and political upheaval in the United States. Cold War tensions remained between the United States and Russia, as well as with China and Cuba. Conflict in Vietnam had escalated to full-scale war by 1964. And while the civil rights movement was finally reaping results from years of peaceful protest through anti-discriminatory legislation, the movement continued to meet with violent opposition. It was a confusing time, and for young people many traditional American values seemed moot. Counterculture youth movements began to form in the mid-1960s, many of which were based on a rejection of what were perceived to be oppressive regulations. Liberation was a theme among these groups; free love, free press, and free speech were all championed by young dissenters. Nowhere were these youthful rebellions more evident than on college campuses.

In 1958 UC Berkeley students formed SLATE, a group that advocated for students' ability to support nonschool issues on campus. The group did not endorse a single political position but rather supported democracy and human rights more holistically. Some of the issues SLATE endorsed created controversy and provoked changes to university policy. During the summer of 1964, the administration of UC Berkeley changed its rules on political activism on campus, eliminating a narrow strip of sidewalk at the intersection of Telegraph Avenue and Bancroft Way that had been a main point of egress to the campus and a traditional location for political activity. To the student activists, the administration's ruling was an attack not only on their individual rights but also on the civil rights movement itself. Concerned student activists met with administrators and were able to win back their right to set up tables, but the administration refused to budge on matters of fund-raising or political advocacy.

This set the stage for a series of escalating protests, as students tested the power of their as-yet-untried political muscle. Fund-raising and advocacy activities resumed at the Bancroft/Telegraph intersection under the auspices of the United Front, an ad-hoc organizing committee, and after more than a week had passed without incident, new tables were set up at Sather Gate, a hundred yards inside the campus. On September 30, five students were cited for staffing them. More than 500 students signed a letter of complicity, crowded Sproul Hall—which they occupied until early morning—and demanded that the administration discipline all of them. Eight students were suspended indefinitely, and the following day Jack Weinberg, a recent graduate and a leader of the campus Congress of Racial Equality (CORE), was arrested as he staffed a table. Hundreds of students surrounded the police car containing Weinberg, and for the next thirty-two hours the crowd maintained a vigil, with speakers holding forth from atop the car's hood.

The more intransigent the administration appeared, the more radicalized the movement became. "Beginning with concern about rights to a small strip of territory," wrote Max Heirich, a sociologist who studied the movement as it was happening, "the students had shifted their focus to freedom of expression and advocacy on the campus as a whole. After the arrest of October 1, they began to talk about the proper purpose of the university." The weeks wore on without resolution, and more students were swept up in the conflict, forced to choose a side amid the growing rancor. Chancellor Edward Strong remained firmly opposed to any concessions, convinced that student opinion was volatile and would peter out of its own accord. There were indeed indications that the protest was losing steam: after the UC Board of Regents ruled against the FSM in a November 20 meeting, a rally and sit-in the following Monday ended in disarray, with the student leadership disheartened and student support flagging. Over the Thanksgiving break, however, disciplinary letters were sent to four FSM leaders, rekindling the fickle flames of student unrest and inflaming the FSM leadership by this show of bad faith. The FSM reacted by submitting an ultimatum to the administration—if the charges were not dropped, a sit-in would begin on Wednesday, December 2, followed by a general strike.

OCCUPYING SPROUL HALL

The administration did not deign to respond, and students set about occupying Sproul Hall. Far from housing an angry mob, the occupied premises had a festive air as the students passed the time square dancing, and conducting teach-ins and religious services. Joan Baez led a folk sing-along; Laurel and Hardy films were shown. On Governor Pat Brown's orders, police officers began clearing Sproul Hall early Thursday morning. By daybreak the exhausted police officers were growing rough with the students—who went limp in classic civil rights fashion—and those en route to their morning classes were treated to the sight of fellow students being manhandled by the California Highway Patrol, as well as to cries of police brutality echoing through Sproul Hall. The next day pickets appeared.

In the end the administration capitulated. Perhaps it was the threat of a prolonged strike, perhaps the pressure of faculty members, who voted at an Academic Senate to support the students' demands. However the tenor of the conflict can be summed up in a single event: at an assembly on the Monday following the successful strike, the entire student body watched as Mario Savio, one of the most charismatic of the movement's leaders, strode to the lectern, only to be tackled by Berkeley police officers and quickly hustled offstage. Savio had been forbidden to address the students, and his decision to take the platform appeared to be calculated for maximum impact. The incident had the desired effect, cementing student support for the FSM. In the weeks following the strike, Chancellor Strong was relieved of his duties by the regents, and a chancellor who was sympathetic to FSM goals was appointed. In the elections held the week following the strike, FSM candidates swept into the Senate of the Associated Students of UC office. In the space of a semester, the climate of UC Berkeley changed irrevocably from comfortable complacency to overt radicalism. The campus would remain at war for the next five years.

FALLOUT OF THE MOVEMENT

The triumph of the free speech movement against Berkeley's administration encouraged a wave of protests over alleged administrative abuses nationwide. The following year, additional schools experienced outbreaks of student unrest, and student revolt developed into a worldwide phenomenon, culminating in the massive protests, strikes, and general unrest of 1968. Berkeley itself became the site of bitter, protracted battles that eventually led to fatalities. Heirich wrote of the protests that followed, "With increasing momentum each side seemed to create its own 'self-fulfilling prophecies' of what opponents would do," adding to the rampant paranoia.

Nowhere, then, was the revolt as typical as at Berkeley, where the privileged sons and daughters of the middle class had risen up with such force and determination. Theirs was a political conversion unique in world history—a revolution fomented by abundance. "We were the first generation in the history of the world that had never gone hungry," wrote David Lance Goines, one of the eight students suspended on October 2, 1964. "Our parents trembled at the memory of the Great Depression, but it meant nothing to us. We didn't have much notion of not getting what we wanted, when we wanted it." True to Goines's appraisal, Berkeley students got what they wanted.

The urge to record and memorialize these eventful days in the nation's history gained momentum in the 1990s with a $3.5 million gift from Stephen M. Silberstein to preserve and make accessible records of the free speech movement. This resulted in an endowment to the Bancroft Library, which now curates the free speech movement digital library at UC Berkeley, an oral history project, and a series of lectures (the Mario Savio Lecture Fund), as well as a Free Speech Café dedicated to the exchange of political ideas and free speech. In this way the project that started in the 1960s continues and thrives just as free speech finds its place on the Internet and across social media sites around the world. In the 2010s, a strikingly similar set of political and cultural battles were being waged in the United States as those that gave rise to the FSM. Wars in Iraq and Afghanistan, demonstrations for and against abortion, and a new gay and lesbian equal rights campaign were all contemporary issues that made the free speech cause feel as relevant and important in the new century as it had in the 1960s.

Michael Baers

SEE ALSO: *Baez, Joan; Civil Disobedience; Civil Rights Movement; The Great Depression; The Internet; Laurel and Hardy; McCarthyism; Shock Radio; Social Media; Student Demonstrations.*

BIBLIOGRAPHY

Cohen, Robert. *The Free Speech Movement: Reflections on Berkeley in the 1960s.* Berkeley: University of California Press, 2002.

Cohen, Robert. *Freedom's Orator: Mario Savio and the Radical Legacy of the 1960s.* New York: Oxford University Press, 2009.

Draper, Hal. *Berkeley: The New Student Revolt.* New York: Grove Press, 1965.

Foner, Eric. *The Story of American Freedom.* New York: W. W. Norton, 1999.

Goines, David Lance. *The Free Speech Movement: Coming of Age in the 1960s.* Berkeley, CA: Ten Speed Press, 1993.

Heirich, Max. *The Beginning: Berkeley, 1964.* New York: Columbia University Press, 1970.

Kitchell, Mark. *Berkeley in the Sixties.* Los Angeles: Pacific Art, 1992. Documentary.

Rorabaugh, W. J. *Berkeley at War: The 1960s.* New York: Oxford University Press, 1989.

Steffens, Bradley. *The Free Speech Movement.* Farmington Hills, MI: Cengage Gale, 2004.

Warshaw, Steven. *The Trouble in Berkeley.* Berkeley, CA: Diablo Press, 1965.

Freed, Alan "Moondog" *(1921–1965)*

One of the most popular and influential pioneering radio disc jockeys, Alan "Moondog" Freed helped make Cleveland, Ohio, an early hotbed of rock-and-roll music through the programs that he hosted on radio station WJW there in the 1950s. Moving to WINS Radio in New York, he soon became a nationally known celebrity as one of the first important supporters of the new youth-oriented music that was sweeping the country during that decade. His theory that white teenagers would listen to and purchase rhythm-and-blues (R&B) records by black artists proved insightful.

For more than a decade, Freed constantly promoted the emergent music format via stage shows, national radio, television, and in a series of movies. Although he did not coin the phrase "rock and roll," he is credited with popularizing the term, which had originally been a euphemism for sexual intercourse on "race" records beginning in the 1920s. Freed's talent for promotion soon became his downfall as he and other disc jockeys across the nation were implicated in the payola scandals in 1959. In *Big Beat Heat,* author John Jackson underscores Freed's contribution to contemporary American music by stating he "proved how essential the disc jockey was to the growth of rock & roll."

EARLY YEARS

Aldon James Freed was born on December 21, 1921, and raised in rural Salem, Ohio. He had a strong interest in music from childhood. While attending Ohio State University he became fascinated with the activity at WOSU Radio, the university station. He did not become involved with the station during his stay at the university but instead enrolled in a broadcasting school in Youngstown, Ohio.

Throughout the 1940s he toiled at a variety of small local radio stations in Pennsylvania and Ohio, where he did numerous jobs such as sweeping floors, announcing news and sports, and playing music. The young announcer's fortunes changed dramatically when he took a position with Cleveland's WJW (850 AM) as host of an R&B program in 1951. He adopted the name "Moondog" from a raucous recording featuring a howling dog titled "Moondog Symphony."

Freed's on-air antics soon made him a popular personality with Cleveland's young black community. Six months after the debut of his late-night radio broadcast, he and the owner of the area's largest record store entered a partnership to promote a dance called the "Moondog Coronation Ball." On March 21, 1952, more than 10,000 mostly black teens packed the Cleveland Arena to see R&B performers Paul Williams, Varetta Dillard, and the Dominoes. The arena became so overcrowded with the unexpectedly large mass of people that city officials were forced to stop the show for safety reasons. The Moondog Coronation Ball is considered a significant moment in the development of rock and roll. Bill Randle, one of the nation's most respected DJs in the 1950s, characterizes Freed's 1952 event as the first show that proved to the music industry that rock and roll could be big business.

By 1954 Freed's relentless promotion of himself and the R&B style cemented his position as the music's chief spokesperson. Increasingly, young white record buyers began to cross the racial barrier that had separated mainstream pop songs from R&B. Freed was further able to enlarge his growing white audience when he moved his program to the powerful WINS radio station in New York. The disc jockey became a national figure through his syndicated radio program, many television appearances, and his role in the film *Rock around the Clock* (1956). Playing himself, Freed portrayed a disc jockey encouraging adults to accept the new rock-and-roll music as sung by Bill Haley and the Comets. The film's great success in the United States and across Europe significantly boosted the exposure of rock music to new audiences.

PAYOLA SCANDAL

As the influence of rock and roll spread worldwide, Freed became embroiled in a scandal that would tarnish the remainder of his career. The House Subcommittee on Legislative Oversight, which in 1959 had concluded its investigation of corruption on television quiz shows, began to probe charges that songs heard and heavily promoted on the radio were selected for airplay due to commercial bribery. These secret payments in return for record promotion were known as "payola," a portmanteau word combining "payoff" and "victrola."

After years of legal wrangling and a steadily diminishing career, Freed eventually pleaded guilty on December 10, 1962, in the New York Criminal Court to accepting payments and gifts from Superior Record Sales and the Cosant Distributing Corporation "without the knowledge and consent" of his employers. He was sentenced to a six-month suspended jail term and fined $500. He later noted that payola practices had not been ended despite all the government's efforts. Freed never regained his earlier prominence and died on January 20, 1965, after a long illness.

Freed has secured a place in American music history as the first important rock-and-roll disc jockey. His ability to tap into and promote the emerging black musical styles of the 1950s to a white mainstream audience is seen as a vital step in rock's increasing dominance over American culture. Freed's contribution to the music he sold so successfully was honored in 1986 by the Rock and Roll Hall of Fame, which selected him as one of the first inductees in the special "nonperformer and early influences" category. In 1995 the city of Cleveland hosted the Rock and Roll Hall of Fame and Museum's dedication not far from the site of Freed's Moondog Coronation Ball and the radio station where he popularized the phrase "rock and roll."

Charles Coletta

SEE ALSO: *Disc Jockeys; The Fifties; Haley, Bill; Radio; Rhythm and Blues; Rock and Roll; Top 40.*

BIBLIOGRAPHY

Jackson, John. *Big Beat Heat: Alan Freed and the Early Years of Rock & Roll.* New York: Schirmer Books, 1991.

Scheurer, Timothy E. *American Popular Music, Vol. 2: The Age of Rock.* Bowling Green, OH: Bowling Green University Popular Press, 1989.

Sklar, Robert. *Rocking America.* New York: St. Martin's Press, 1984.

Freedom Rides

Throughout the long struggle for civil and political rights, African Americans used a number of protest methods. These methods included the Freedom Rides that captured the country's attention and imagination in the early 1960s and that successfully influenced the cultural consciousness of the nation with regard to matters of racial prejudice. The goal of the Freedom Rides was simply to end segregation in interstate travel. Although the United States ruled the segregation of interstate facilities unconstitutional, the edict went largely ignored in the Jim Crow South.

In 1949 the Congress of Racial Equality (CORE) and the Fellowship of Reconciliation (FOR) launched a Freedom Ride throughout the upper South to highlight the discrimination African Americans faced when traveling below the Mason-Dixon Line. However, the efforts of these interracial, nonviolent, and pacifist organizations were unsuccessful, largely because they were unable to attract press attention. Nonetheless, the foundation was laid for a tactic that came to achieve amazing results in the early 1960s.

As the federal government began to illustrate a sincere concern for the rights of African Americans in the aftermath of the 1954 *Brown v. Board of Education* decision, CORE once again launched the idea of Freedom Rides to the same purpose as before. For CORE leader James Farmer the concept was simple: (1) have an interracial group take a bus across the South; (2) demand service at all terminals; and (3) if arrested, refuse bail and fill up the jails. The entire program was designed to attract media attention to the brutal conditions that black people faced in the southern states.

CORE's initial Freedom Riders left Washington, D.C., in May 1961 and headed for the South. All was well until they approached Anniston, Alabama, on Mother's Day, when they were greeted by mobs of whites who beat them severely. They encountered further trouble in Birmingham, Alabama, where the local Ku Klux Klan (which had been granted fifteen minutes of immunity by the local police force) unleashed their frustrations upon the riders. The protest was postponed when the riders could not find a driver to continue the trip. Ironically, however, the brutality was instrumental in awakening the consciousness of Americans to the appalling plight of the Freedom Riders because the national media gave extensive coverage to the incident and disseminated the images of the badly beaten protesters.

After a cooling-off period, the Freedom Ride continued from Birmingham to Montgomery, Alabama. Upon arriving in Montgomery the courageous protesters were hit with pipes, baseball bats, billy clubs, and other such objects, and once again the national media was there to give the incident widespread coverage. In the aftermath of the Alabama beatings, young Student Nonviolent Coordinating Committee (SNCC) activists wanted to continue the rides, in spite of the reluctance of CORE and the Southern Christian Leadership Conference (SCLC). They did. In late May SCLC initiated a ride from Montgomery to Jackson, Mississippi, hoping to encounter brutality that would then be broadcast to the world. Contrary to their expectations, however, on their arrival they were peacefully arrested. This response by the Jackson Police Department established a pattern for future Freedom Rides.

In the summer of 1961 the traditional civil rights organizations created the Freedom Rides Coordinating Committee, which sponsored Freedom Rides throughout the country. As a result of the continued protest, the Interstate Commerce Commission (ICC) banned racial segregation and discrimination in interstate travel. Although many civil rights leaders took credit for the legislation, the victory belonged to CORE, which had initiated the protest, and to the young activists in SNCC who were persistent in their quest for civil rights. The ruling by the ICC dealt a massive blow to Jim Crow.

Leonard N. Moore

SEE ALSO: *Civil Rights Movement; King, Martin Luther, Jr.*

BIBLIOGRAPHY

Arsenault, Raymond. *Freedom Riders: 1961 and the Struggle for Racial Justice.* New York: Oxford University Press, 2011.

Carson, Clayborne. *In Struggle: SNCC and the Black Awakening of the 1960s.* Cambridge, MA: Harvard University Press, 1981.

Fairclough, Adam. *To Redeem the Soul of America: The Southern Christian Leadership Conference and Martin Luther King, Jr.* Athens: University of Georgia Press, 1987.

Farmer, James. *Lay Bare the Heart: An Autobiography of the Civil Rights Movement.* New York: Arbor House, 1985.

The French Connection

The French Connection, the 1971 Best Picture Oscar winner, remains one of the best existential cop films ever made, contains arguably the best chase sequence ever committed to film, and turned Gene Hackman into a major star. The film is based on a real-life French connection heroin bust made by New York Police Department narcotics division detectives Eddie "Popeye" Egan and Sonny "Cloudy" Grosso. Off-duty detectives Egan and Grosso noticed Pasquale Fuca talking with some known drug dealers in the Copacabana nightclub. Several months later, Fuca and five others were arrested for drug trafficking.

Producer Philip D'Antoni owned the rights to Robin Moore's book about the case, and when William Friedkin agreed to direct the film, a succession of writers was hired. Ernest Tidyman finally wrote a screenplay good enough to get the project green-lighted by Twentieth Century Fox. Friedkin, who began his career making documentaries on topics ranging from law enforcement to pro football for a Chicago television station and later for ABC, brought a documentarian's sensibilities to the

***Gene Hackman in* The French Connection.** *Gene Hackman stars as Popeye Doyle in the 1971 film* The French Connection, *for which he won the Academy Award for Best Actor.* **20TH CENTURY FOX/HULTON ARCHIVE/COURTESY OF GETTY IMAGE.**

project. When he decided to direct the film, he strapped on a .38 pistol and spent nearly a year riding around with Egan and Grosso, visiting drug houses and shaking down bars.

Once production began, Friedkin had immediate problems directing his actors. We first see Jimmy "Popeye" Doyle (Hackman) dressed as Santa Claus. He and his partner, Buddy "Cloudy" Russo (Roy Scheider), are sprinting after and catching a fleeing suspect. Friedkin decided to stage the interrogation scene as it usually happens in real life, with the suspect sitting in the squad car and being grilled by the two detectives. Dissatisfied with the dialogue as written, Friedkin wrote some dialogue based on actual interrogations he had seen Egan and Grosso conduct, dialogue that he later referred to as Pinteresque. But thirty-two takes later, Friedkin still didn't have anything on film that satisfied him. According to Friedkin, he realized later that night what was wrong with the scene: "This is not Harold Pinter. This is a street show. I've got to let them improvise that scene." The scene was reshot in an open courtyard—one take, two cameras—and Friedkin used the best moments captured on film. Many other scenes were likewise improvised, with Hackman and Scheider taking their cues from Egan and Russo: Egan really did dress up as Santa and really did ask suspects if they "picked their feet in Poughkeepsie."

The film itself is brilliantly photographed and edited, making superb use of visual storytelling. Friedkin has pointed out that, of the film's twelve reels, six contain no dialogue at all, yet the silence isn't conspicuous because the acting is so good that viewers can almost hear what the characters are thinking. An excellent example of this is the cat-and-mouse game Popeye plays with Frog One (Fernando Rey) on the New York City subways, an incident that actually happened the way it was shown on film.

Another example of a scene that is light on dialogue is a car chase that D'Antoni and Friedkin agreed to include in the film even though it never happened in real life and wasn't in the book or screenplay. The sequence starts when Frog Two (Marcel Bozzuffi) tries to shoot Popeye from a rooftop. Popeye runs after him, Frog Two hops on an elevated train, and Popeye commandeers a car to chase him. The ten-minute virtually wordless sequence has pedestrians and other cars in almost every shot, so Friedkin knew he couldn't undercrank the camera to simulate speed. The desired fast pace was ultimately obtained by having someone drive through New York streets at speeds approaching ninety miles per hour. What was to have been a near-miss accidentally became the chase sequence's first collision. Most of this sequence, like 70 percent of the film itself, was shot with handheld cameras, adding to the documentary feel.

Although Hackman wanted to humanize his character, Friedkin kept insisting, "No, this man is a pig. He's as rotten as the criminals he's chasing." This characterization also adds to the realism and is perhaps the most divisive aspect of the film. Popeye is portrayed as brutal, racist, foulmouthed, lecherous, and continuously violating suspects' rights—unlike the way cops are usually portrayed on film. Many saw the film as being right-wing because it humanized cops trampling on civil liberties, and many saw it as being left-wing because it showed cops as they really are, so Friedkin thought he'd achieved the correct balance. What he was striving for was a kind of hyperkinetic activity for its own sake, to little or no avail. Friedkin has said that the police really work hard, killing themselves and sometimes other people, "yet basically they're involved in a line of work that is frustrated, ineffectual." He believes narcotics enforcement is an impossible job, with too many ways to get drugs into the country and too many people wanting them. Friedkin and his actors capture this frustration while telling a gripping tale that proves a police procedure can be fast-paced and riveting if the storytelling and performances are so good that viewers really care what happens to the characters.

Bob Sullivan

SEE ALSO: *Academy Awards; Hackman, Gene; War on Drugs.*

BIBLIOGRAPHY

Clagett, Thomas D. *William Friedkin: Films of Aberration, Obsession and Reality.* Jefferson, NC: McFarland, 1990.

Moore, Robin. *The French Connection.* Boston: Little, Brown, 1969.

Segaloff, Nat. *Hurricane Billy: The Stormy Life and Films of William Friedkin.* New York: William Morrow, 1990.

French Fries

America's love affair with french fries started in 1789 when Thomas Jefferson, fancier of French cuisine and especially of *pommes frites,* introduced the delicacies to his fellow citizens when he returned home after serving as American ambassador to France. Two centuries later, french fries, those thin strips of potato cut lengthwise that have been deep-fried until crisp, are internationally associated with hamburgers and fast-food meals.

The popular success of french fries benefited from advances in food processing and the growth of the fast-food trade. They became a fetish of the McDonald's Corporation: "The french fry would become almost sacrosanct for me, its preparation a ritual to be followed religiously," writes Ray Kroc in his book *Grinding It Out: The Making of McDonald's* (1977). Famous for their high quality, McDonald's french fries are essential to the chain's success, with millions of pounds prepared every day.

On the eve of the twenty-first century, french fries changed national identity as fast-food ventures in Japan and Southeast Asia promoted them as American fries. The food was also involved in political controversy. During the debate over whether or not Allied forces should enter Iraq in 2003, the French government advised negotiation rather than force. As a result, supporters of military action in the United States who were disappointed with France's viewpoint renamed french fries as freedom fries in private and public eating venues. Republican Representative Robert (Bob) Ney of Ohio changed all references to french fries and french toast in the House cafeteria to freedom fries and freedom toast; in 2006 the names were changed back.

Catherine C. Galley
Briavel Holcomb

SEE ALSO: *Fast Food; Gulf Wars; McDonald's;* Super Size Me.

BIBLIOGRAPHY

Bellantoni, Christina. "Hill Fries Free to Be French Again." *Washington Times*, August 2, 2006, A1.

Kroc, Ray. *Grinding It Out: The Making of McDonald's.* Chicago: Contemporary Books, 1977.

Meltzer, Milton. *The Amazing Potato: A Story in Which the Incas, Conquistadors, Marie Antoinette, Thomas Jefferson, Wars, Famines, Immigrants and French Fries All Play a Part.* New York: HarperCollins, 1992.

Salaman, Redcliffe N. *The History and Social Influence of the Potato.* Cambridge, UK: Cambridge University Press, 1985.

Schlosser, Eric. *Fast Food Nation: The Dark Side of the All-American Meal.* Boston: Houghton Mifflin, 2001.

The Fresh Prince

SEE: *Smith, Will.*

Freud, Sigmund *(1856–1939)*

Sigmund Freud is widely known as the founding father of psychoanalysis and is probably the most famous and influential theorist and practitioner in the field of psychology to date. His works are studied not only by mental health professionals but

Sigmund Freud. *Sigmund Freud's theories on personality and human development are considered among the most influential in modern psychology.* IMAGNO/GETTY IMAGES.

also by students of philosophy, humanities, art, literature, and culture. Freud's most widely known contributions are probably his theories about the motivating force of the libido; his descriptions of the effect of childhood experiences on the adult psyche; and his theories of dreams, the mind, and the unconscious. His writings have been translated into most modern languages and are collected in twenty-four volumes in *The Standard Edition of the Complete Works of Sigmund Freud*, but people who have never read a word Freud wrote or even an essay about him are likely familiar with the Freudian implications of dreams. Many of his concepts have been popularized by their usage in novels, movies, and self-help movements, and Freud himself is a widely recognized icon in European and North American societies.

Freud's theories have always aroused controversy. Many of his contemporaries greeted his ideas with overt hostility and ridicule. Some of this was because of widely prevalent anti-Semitism and some was because of the Victorian sexual standards of his day, which found his graphic discussion of sexuality distasteful. Since the women's liberation movement of the 1970s, feminists have questioned Freud's understanding of women and blamed his male-identified theories for much of the damage done to women by mental health institutions. Other psychiatrists and psychologists began to challenge what they call the "hero worship" of Freud. Writers such as Richard Webster and Frederick Crews accuse the father of psychotherapy of fraud, saying he stole many of his ideas and often forced patients to conform to his theories.

EARLY INFLUENCES

Freud was born on May 6, 1856, in the small town of Freiberg in the Austro-Hungarian Empire. The son of a moderately successful Jewish wool merchant, he was raised in Vienna. Though an innovative thinker, Freud was most definitely a product of his time. The mid-nineteenth century was at a crossroads between the romantic movement and a new orientation toward the scientific. Freud was deeply interested in romantic subjects such as philosophy and the humanities, and he felt it necessary to balance this passion with the study of science. His work came from that blending of the intensely humanistic notion of the value of the individual experience and the new growth of medical science, along with influences from Germanic Naturphilosophie (natural philosophy) and the Jewish philosophers of his own heritage. Though his contributions were in part scientific, the way his theories have shaped the public imagination for decades may have more to do with their mythical power.

Freud studied medicine at the University of Vienna and later worked at the Salpêtrière hospital in Paris, where Jean-Martin Charcot was director. Charcot's influence on Freud was significant: the famous French professor of neurology was the leading expert on hysteria, the study and treatment of which eventually led Freud to develop the theory and method of psychoanalysis. Hysteria was an ailment presumed to afflict a large number of women at the time. While its symptoms—such as paralysis, seizures, anorexia, and aphasia—had previously been viewed as resulting from a literal irritation of the uterus (the word *hysteria* derives from the Latin for "uterus"), Charcot viewed hysteria as a neurological disorder that was caused by trauma and could be treated through hypnosis. Charcot's idea that a person's experiences, thoughts, or emotions might cause physiological symptoms had a profound influence on Freud's subsequent work.

HYSTERIA

In *Studies on Hysteria* (1895), Freud and his colleague, Josef Breuer, proposed the radical thesis that hysteria was in fact caused by sexual traumas—specifically, childhood sexual abuse and quite often incest—that the patients were reenacting through their bodily symptoms. Freud's radical insight about the origins of hysteria led to his revolutionary theory of the unconscious mind, which he conceived as a literal place in the brain to which intolerable memories, thoughts, feelings, desires, and conflicts were relegated. Freud's and Breuer's treatment of women diagnosed with hysteria also led to the development of the so-called talking cure, the cornerstone of the psychoanalytic method. The talking cure began with Breuer's treatment of "Anna O." (Bertha Pappenheim), a hysteric patient who was resistant to hypnotic suggestion but who found that talking about her memories and experiences had the cathartic effect of "talking away her symptoms."

In 1896 Freud renounced his original theory that hysteria was caused by the patient's real traumatic experiences of childhood sexual abuse and instead began explaining patients' symptoms in terms of their own incestuous desires and fantasies. This evolved into Freud's well-known theories of infantile sexuality—which include the oral, anal, and phallic drives—and the postulation of a universal Oedipus complex, named for the Greek tragic hero who killed his father and married his mother. According to this theory, childhood development involves a progression from oral desires (for the mother's breast) through anal drives (the desire for mastery and control of one's bodily products) and culminates in overtly genital sexuality, which for Freud is always phallic.

OEDIPUS COMPLEX

For boys, the Oedipus stage of development as Freud describes it involves incestuous desires toward the mother and feelings of rivalry toward—and fear of retaliation from—the father. This retaliation is also understood in terms of male genital sexuality as the threat of castration. According to Freud's theory, the psychological conflicts of desire, guilt, and castration anxiety must be resolved in favor of the boy's gender identification with his father and sublimation of his incestuous desires toward his mother. Freud postulates that the lack of such resolution is the root of much adult male psychopathology.

In the female version of the Oedipus complex, Freud believed the young girl must first shift away from her primary (originally oral) desire for her mother toward a more mature oedipal desire for her father. The girl's normal development involves a recognition that because she lacks a penis, she cannot fulfill her sexual desire for her mother nor identify with her father but must accept her role as the passive recipient of men's desire. Further, in discovering that she lacks a penis, the girl must contend with the realization that she is "already castrated," mutilated, and inferior. Freud described the inability of some female patients to accept their lack of a penis, to renounce their "phallic" (clitoral) desire, and to accept and embrace the passive feminine role as "penis envy," which he considered a common female psychopathology.

CRITICAL DEBATE

Freud's theories of female sexual development have engendered decades of debate both within psychoanalysis and beyond. For example, feminists have pointed out that Freud's conceptualization of both normal and pathological female development require the female's renunciation of some part of herself—either her agency as an active, desiring subject or her feminine gender identity. Freud has been sharply criticized for his equation of sexual activity with masculinity; for his arguments that women are biologically, intellectually, and morally inferior to men; and for his insistence that, in female development, "Anatomy is destiny." From Freud's contemporaries Karen Horney and Joan Riviere to modern feminists such as Nancy Chodorow and Jean Baker Miller, Freud's theories of female psychology have undergone intense scrutiny and revision.

The shift in Freud's focus from real sexual traumas to infantile sexuality and incestuous desires has itself been the subject of controversy. Freud's followers believe that his shift from reality to fantasies reflected a more mature and sophisticated understanding of the mind and of personality formation and allowed for the recognition of infantile sexuality and the psychological importance of fantasies, guilt, and repression. Many contemporary scholars, however, have argued that Freud's original belief in the reality and psychological significance of child sexual abuse was scientifically valid, while his later reversal was personally, professionally, and culturally motivated. According to his critics, Freud's reversal denied the role that actual incestuous abuse had played in the emotional problems of his patients and contributed to a cultural refusal to acknowledge the realities of widely prevalent sexual abuse and other traumas experienced predominately by women and children in a patriarchal society.

Despite Freud's theoretical shift from exploring real traumas to emphasizing unconscious desires and conflicts, Freud continued to develop and employ the talking cure that he and Breuer had used in treating hysterics. This cathartic method evolved into the technique of free association and interpretation that characterizes psychoanalytic practice and has had a profound influence on nearly all other forms of psychotherapy. While subsequent practitioners have differed from Freud in their use of techniques—such as free association, hypnosis, the analytic couch, and interpretation—the essential practice of encouraging patients to talk about their experiences and express their deepest thoughts, feelings, wishes, and fears has remained a central part of psychotherapy since Freud.

ID, EGO, AND SUPEREGO

While Freud's psychoanalytic method had a profound influence on psychotherapeutic practice, it is his theories of the mind—and particularly his conceptualization of the unconscious—that have arguably been his most important and influential contributions to contemporary thought. Freud conceived of the mind in spatial terms, viewing the unconscious as the area to which socially unacceptable desires and fantasies are relegated, as well as the area from which jokes, slips of the tongue, dream imagery, and much of creative ideas flow. Freud elaborated a schematic of the mind that corresponded with his view of personality development. The id consisted of the primary drives and impulses, such as oral and sexual desire and the aggressive instincts. The superego was the internalization of familial and social rules, particularly the prohibitions against primitive desires and instincts. And the ego was essentially the socialized self, capable of defenses, sublimation, rational thought, and creativity. While these theories have been elaborated and debated within psychoanalytic circles, the rudimentary concepts are familiar to most people in European and North American cultures and have been largely, if crudely, incorporated into contemporary thinking about the mind and the personality.

THEORIES AND ART

In addition to Freud's profound influence on ideas of the mind, the significance of early life events, and the dynamics of personality development, contemporary culture owes many of its assumptions about the symbolism of dreams, jokes, and cultural products to Freud's writings. Freud considered his seminal and perhaps most famous text, *The Interpretation of Dreams* (1899), to be the key to his work and pronounced dreams "the royal road to the knowledge of the unconscious." His understanding of dreams, jokes, and slips of the tongue as laden with unconscious meanings has permeated contemporary thinking. Terms such as repression, projection, ego, and superego have become part of everyday parlance; it is common for inadvertent—yet potentially significant—errors in speech to be referred to as Freudian slips (such as the postcard from the erring husband to his unsuspecting wife that reads, "wish you were her"). Freud himself applied many of his theories to the study of art and literary texts—including the works of Italian artists Leonardo da Vinci and Michelangelo; German author Johann Wolfgang von Goethe; and, of course, English dramatist William Shakespeare—and many scholars since Freud have used psychoanalytic ideas about desire, fantasy, language, and the unconscious in their interpretations of an artist's work.

The notion of repression of memory has particularly grasped the modern imagination. From American writer Henry James's *Turn of the Screw* (1898), which was written in Freud's time, to such modern classics as *The Manchurian Candidate* (published 1959; filmed 1962) and Alfred Hitchcock's film *Psycho* (1960), audiences have been fascinated with the potential depths of the mind and the horrors that can be stored there, just out of reach. Even Homer Simpson, paterfamilias of the wacky animated television family portrayed on the series *The Simpsons* (1989–), understands the uses of repression, when he tells his daughter: "The important thing is for your mother to repress what happened, push it deep down inside her, so she'll never annoy us again."

POPULARIZATION OF PSYCHOTHERAPY

One of Freud's most significant impacts on modern culture has been the popularization of psychotherapy. While once reserved for the rich and introspective, psychotherapy is now widely available to a broad spectrum of people. As the stigma of seeing a headshrinker has lessened, therapy has become an increasingly popular way of dealing with life's troubles. In the United States alone, millions of people talk out their problems with psychiatrists, psychologists, and psychiatric social workers. Untold numbers of others see marriage counselors and other, often self-styled, therapists. All these counselors are direct descendants of Freud's talking therapy.

The idea that people's adult actions are influenced by their childhood experiences has become a widely held social belief. While this has led to a certain democratization of mental and emotional problems and has inspired social reform movements, some social critics believe it also has led to a failure to take personal responsibility for one's actions, since everything can be traced back to parental abuse or rejection. From the notorious Menendez brothers, who insisted that constant childhood abuse led them to murder their parents, to Kitty Dukakis, wife of

1988 presidential candidate Michael Dukakis, who wrote an autobiography attributing her adult alcohol and drug abuse to her mother's rejection, the idea that parental failings cause our adult pain has taken root in society. Freud's belief that our lives are determined by how we come to terms with our sexuality shows up at the center of serious social analysis as well as cocktail party chat and in cultural representations from Broadway theater (*Equus* and *Who's Afraid of Virginia Woolf?*) to soap operas.

FREUD'S INFLUENCE

Much is known about Freud's life because of his prolific correspondences with friends, colleagues, students, and patients—many of whom were famous figures in their own right—and because of his self-analysis. At the same time, much about Freud has been obscured—both by his own silences and contradictions and by the deliberate obfuscations of those who have wished to discredit or protect him. Freud himself was sharply aware of his place in history and zealously guarded his image, hoping to control the picture of him that would be written down in history. Some critics accuse Freud of failing to acknowledge the contributions of his mentors, while others even charge him with outright theft of his ideas of the unconscious and his talking therapy from such influential teachers as Breuer and Wilhelm Fliess. Many of Freud's detractors also point to his practice of bullying patients into agreeing with his preconceived theories. They quote Freud himself, who advised his students:

> The work [of therapy] keeps coming to a stop and they keep maintaining that this time nothing has occurred to them. We must not believe what they say, we must always assume, and tell them too, that they have kept something back. . . . We must insist on this, we must repeat the pressure and represent ourselves as infallible, till at last we are really told something.

Critics contend that this image of the infallible psychiatrist has been the most damaging influence of psychotherapy. Still others call psychotherapy itself a fraud, especially Freud's model of psychoanalysis, saying that there is no real evidence that it works.

Freud's persona itself shows up regularly in the popular media, whether it is the actual character of Freud assisting fellow cocaine addict Sherlock Holmes with cases (as in *The Seven Percent Solution*, 1976) or merely his voice speaking through controversial television heroine Murphy Brown when she intones the famous Freud quote, "Sometimes a cigar is just a cigar." Freud has been the prototype for many popular culture representations of psychologists, psychiatrists, and psychoanalysts. His face and habits—such as his cocaine use and his cigar smoking—are widely recognized icons even decades after his death in 1939.

Many have argued that Freud was the most influential thinker of the twentieth century. Others have insisted that his theories reflect a decidedly nineteenth-century emphasis on biological determinism, sexuality, and bourgeois patriarchal values. For better or worse, Freud has had a profound impact not only on psychological theory and practice but also on culture and the way society understands it.

Tina Gianoulis
Ava Rose

SEE ALSO: *Depression; Hitchcock, Alfred;* Murphy Brown*; Popular Psychology;* Psycho*;* The Simpsons.

BIBLIOGRAPHY

Brennan, Teresa. *The Interpretation of the Flesh: Freud and Femininity.* London: Routledge, 1992.

Chodorow, Nancy. *Femininities, Masculinities, Sexualities: Freud and Beyond.* Lexington: University of Kentucky Press, 1994.

Freud, Sigmund. *Standard Edition of the Complete Psychological Works of Sigmund Freud*, ed. James Strachey. London: Hogarth Press, 1953–1974.

Gay, Peter. *Freud: A Life for Our Time.* New York: Norton, 1988.

Masson, Jeffrey Moussaieff. *The Assault on Truth: Freud's Suppression of the Seduction Theory.* New York: Harper Perennial, 1984.

Roazen, Paul, ed. *Sigmund Freud.* New York: Da Capo Press, 1985.

Slavet, Eliza. *Racial Fever: Freud and the Jewish Question.* New York: Fordham University Press, 2009.

Slipp, Samuel. *The Freudian Mystique: Freud, Women, and Feminism.* New York: New York University Press, 1993.

Thurschwell, Pamela. *Sigmund Freud.* New York: Routledge, 2009.

Webster, Richard. *Why Freud Was Wrong: Sin, Science, and Psychoanalysis.* New York: BasicBooks, 1995.

Friday, Nancy *(1933–)*

There is a cliché in American culture that men are principally interested in sex, whereas women are mostly looking for love. Nancy Friday is one of the relatively small number of modern writers who has gathered and published evidence that women's fantasies are often as sexually explicit as men's are. Her books devoted to relating women's sexual fantasies work effectively on several levels: as psychology, as sociology, and as pornography. In addition, Friday has produced several other important books on subjects of interest to modern women, including jealousy, beauty, and the mother-daughter relationship.

Friday grew up in Charleston, South Carolina, the child of a single mother. She moved to New York City in the 1960s, where she was simultaneously introduced to the sexual revolution and the women's movement, both of which would influence her life—and writing—profoundly. She worked at *Cosmopolitan* magazine and the *Examiner* before deciding to devote her energies to writing books.

Friday's first book, *My Secret Garden: Women's Sexual Fantasies*, appeared in 1973. It attracted considerable attention, partly because of its sexually explicit language and subject matter, but mostly because these "nasty" words and scenarios were coming from the minds of women. In 1973 the idea that so-called respectable, normal women had such steamy, even "kinky" thoughts was considered something of a revelation. The book was a best seller, as was its 1975 sequel, *Forbidden Flowers.*

Her third book was something of a departure. *My Mother/My Self,* which appeared in 1977, was an exploration of the mother/adult daughter relationship, including the ways that mothers' implicit messages can influence their daughters long after childhood. The book was a huge success, and interest in the subject was suddenly on the public agenda, spawning workshops, TV programs, and books by a host of authors.

In her next work, Friday returned to familiar territory, but with a twist. *Men in Love* (1980) was a collection of male sexual fantasies. Friday's choice of title was a reflection of her conclusions after reading the anonymously submitted fantasy material. Contrary to widely held belief, she asserted, men's fantasies about women were not mostly violent, hateful, or exploitative; instead, they were passionate, inventive, and, yes, even loving.

Friday waded into another subject of intense interest to many women with her 1985 book *Jealousy*. An immense volume (running more than 500 pages), the book combines a discussion of the psychological literature on the subject with interview material and Friday's own brutally honest account of how jealousy has played a major role in her own life. She admits that her principal reasons for approaching the project were personal, and much of the book is a description of her own personal struggles with the "green-eyed monster."

With *Women on Top* (1991), Friday returned to the milieu of women's sexual fantasies, but the book's subtitle—*How Real Life Has Changed Women's Sexual Fantasies*—reveals her reasons for visiting the territory again. Friday wanted to find out whether the landscape of women's private sexual longings had changed over the fifteen or so years since she had last visited the topic. Her conclusion: women have ceased to dream of passivity and submission. They now are excited by thoughts of sexual power, aggression, and dominance. The fantasies submitted for consideration this time, she found, were much more likely to portray the woman as taking charge of her partner, her relationship, and her own sexual satisfaction.

The year 1996 saw the publication of *The Power of Beauty*, possibly Friday's most ambitious work yet. As with her earlier books on mother/daughter relationships and jealousy, Friday combines survey research, psychological insights, and her own personal history into a meditation on the ways that physical attractiveness (or the lack thereof) influences, for good or ill, many aspects of modern life—from whom you will marry to where you will work to the degree of success you will enjoy in your job.

In 2009 Friday published *Beyond My Control: Forbidden Fantasies in an Uncensored Age*, a return to her earlier explorations of women's (and this time, men's as well) most taboo-shattering sexual fantasies. She concludes that such fantasies do not indicate something missing in one's sex life as much as the need to explore to fulfill oneself.

Justin Gustainis

SEE ALSO: *Best Sellers; Feminism; Popular Psychology; Pornography; Sexual Revolution.*

BIBLIOGRAPHY

Friday, Nancy. *Men in Love: Men's Sexual Fantasies: The Triumph of Love over Rage*. New York: Delacorte Press, 1980.

Friday, Nancy. *Jealousy*. New York: William Morrow, 1985.

Friday, Nancy. *Women on Top: How Real Life Has Changed Women's Sexual Fantasies*. New York: Simon & Schuster, 1991.

Friday, Nancy. *Beyond My Control: Forbidden Fantasies in an Uncensored World*. Naperville, IL: Sourcebooks, 2009.

Winks, Cathy, and Anne Semans. *The Good Vibrations Guide to Sex: The Most Complete Sex Manual Ever Written*. San Francisco: Cleis Press, 2002.

Friday the 13th

Made on a budget of less than $600,000, with mostly unknown actors, corny dialogue, and a hastily prepared script (completed in less than two weeks), the original installment of *Friday the 13th* in 1980 nevertheless went on to gross more than $70 million at box offices around the world and launched a cottage industry of sequels, spoofs, spin-offs, and outright rip-offs. No modern horror film monster, save perhaps Freddy Krueger, has managed to capture American culture's collective imagination as much as Jason Voorhees, the speechless, seemingly immortal psychopath with a hatred for promiscuous adolescents.

Along with John Carpenter's *Halloween* (1978), *Friday the 13th* is credited with initiating the notorious "stalker cycle" of horror films—an immensely popular and heavily criticized subgenre that would continue to draw huge audiences through the mid-1980s. Whereas *Halloween* is best known for the cinematic conventions it helped to establish, *Friday the 13th* has managed to transcend the world of film. The series has come to serve as a point of departure in public debates over the consequences of exposing youths to representations of graphic violence in the name of entertainment.

THE LAUNCH OF A FRANCHISE

Sean Cunningham, producer, director, and cowriter of the original *Friday the 13th*, had gained a measure of infamy in film circles for producing Wes Craven's ultraviolent underground hit *Last House on the Left* in 1972. (Craven, who would go on to direct *A Nightmare on Elm Street* in 1984 and *Scream* in 1996, returned the favor by doing some uncredited editing on the first *Friday*.) But this infamy turned out to be a benefit, as Paramount, United Artists, and Warner Brothers—all eager to repeat the commercial success of the independently produced *Halloween*—entered into a bidding war for Cunningham's low-budget vehicle about a psychopath determined to kill off all the counselors at Camp Crystal Lake (otherwise known as "Camp Blood"). Paramount won the war and launched *Friday the 13th* with a $4 million advertising campaign. The studio's confidence was quickly rewarded, as the film grossed $31 million in its first six weeks alone, surpassing such major productions as Stanley Kubrick's *The Shining* and James Bridges's *Urban Cowboy*. On the strength of Tom Savini's makeup and special effects wizardry, the progressively gory murders taking place in *Friday the 13th* ensured that whatever the movie lacked in narrative sophistication, it more than made up for in violent spectacle.

Although it was not the very first stalker film, *Friday the 13th* is widely regarded as the prototype of the subgenre. In sharp contrast to *Halloween*, fans, critics, and theorists alike have emphasized the movie's essential reliance on formula and convention, denying it any claim to cinematic originality. Andrew Tudor, in his influential history of the horror film, *Monsters and Mad Scientists*, writes that "in practice, however, *Friday the 13th* is no more than a crude template for the creation of formula *Halloween* clones." It is true that the subjective ("point-of-view") camera work; the cat-and-mouse-style killing of vapid, horny teenagers; and the prolonged final battle pitting psychopath against virginal, sensible, ultimately victorious "good girl" all come straight out of *Halloween.*

But it is also important to note the ways in which *Friday the 13th* breaks with stalker convention and establishes precedents of its own. Contrary to popular belief, the killer in Part One is not Jason, but Mrs. Voorhees, who blames her son's 1958 drowning death on the camp counselors who neglected their responsibilities. Twenty years later, she seems not to care that the counselors have changed, nor does she seem to care about the gender of her victims. All this creates difficulties for those who would argue that modern horror film monsters represent nothing more than the sadistic wish fulfillments of misogynistic male viewers. Furthermore, the surface normality of Mrs. Voorhees—she looks and talks just like a conservative, middle-class mom when she's not slitting people's throats—anticipates the all-too-realistic serial killers populating such films as *The Stepfather* (1987), *White of the Eye* (1987), and *Henry: Portrait of a Serial Killer* (1990).

SEQUELS AND SPIN-OFFS

With the disfigured Jason taking over his mother's murderous attacks in *Friday the 13th Part 2* (1981), and especially after his decision to don a goalie mask in *Friday the 13th Part 3: 3-D* (1982), the series' transformation was complete. Under the direction of Steve Miner, these films saw the replacement of a human psychopath whose actions are at least somewhat explicable in quasi-Freudian terms with a supernatural agent of evil whose sole intent seems to be the violent eradication of America's adolescents. In *Terror and Everyday Life,* Jonathan Crane asserts that "Jason, as well-known as any prominent American personality, ranks among the foremost of all popular signs embodying meaning's demise." It is not only the apparent randomness with which Jason chooses his victims that leads Crane to this conclusion. It is also Jason's single-minded devotion to murder, his virtual indestructibility, and above all his inevitable return from the dead that serve as prime sources of pleasure for the mostly teenage audiences who, well into the first decade of the 2000s, came out in droves to see the further adventures of their "hero."

In 2003 filmmakers even pitted Jason against another horror film icon, Freddy Krueger of the *Nightmare on Elm Street* franchise, in *Freddy vs. Jason.* Then, in 2009 director Marcus Nispel, fresh off of a reboot of the *Texas Chainsaw Massacre* horror franchise, attempted to revitalize *Friday the 13th* with a similar remake. The resulting film, *Friday the 13th* (2009), combined elements from the first three films, featured a more agile Jason, and attempted to provide some explanation for his bloodlust. The film received mixed reviews but was a box-office success, spawning persistent rumors of a sequel.

In addition to its record number of sequels (ten) and its reboot, *Friday the 13th* has been the inspiration for parodies such as *Saturday the 14th* (1981), generic rip-offs such as *Campsite Massacre* (1983), a Canadian television show (1987–1990), a series of young adult novels, a heavy-metal song by Terrorvision, and a successful run of pornographic movies that began with *Friday the 13th: A Nude Beginning* (1987). In the late 1990s blockbuster "neo-stalkers" such as *Scream* and *I Know What You Did Last Summer* (1997) scored points with audiences by explicitly foregrounding a number of *Friday*'s plot devices. All of this supports the view that *Friday the 13th,* despite being nominated as worst picture at the 1981 Razzie Awards, inaugurated the most successful franchise in modern horror cinema.

Steven Schneider

SEE ALSO: *Blockbusters;* Halloween*; Heavy Metal; Hollywood; Horror Movies; Kubrick, Stanley; Pornography;* Scream*; Slasher Movies; Teenagers; United Artists.*

BIBLIOGRAPHY

Bracke, Peter M. *Crystal Lake Memories: The Complete History of "Friday the 13th."* Los Angeles: Sparkplug Press, 2005.

Crane, Jonathan Lake. *Terror and Everyday Life: Singular Moments in the History of the Horror Film.* Thousand Oaks, CA: Sage Publications, 1994.

Dika, Vera. *Games of Terror: "Halloween," "Friday the 13th," and the Films of the Stalker Cycle.* East Rutherford, NJ: Fairleigh Dickinson University Press, 1990.

Grove, David. *Making "Friday the 13th": The Legend of Camp Blood.* Godalming, UK: FAB Press, 2005.

Tudor, Andrew. *Monsters and Mad Scientists: A Cultural History of the Horror Movie.* Oxford, UK: Basil Blackwell, 1989.

Friedman, Kinky *(1944–)*

Founder and leader of the Texas Jewboys, an iconoclastic country-and-western band of the 1970s, Richard "Kinky" Friedman has since become better known as a comic novelist. Born in Chicago (not—as often claimed—in Palestine, Texas) on Halloween, Friedman is the son of a psychology professor and a speech therapist. The family moved to Texas during his childhood, buying a ranch near Medina to create the Echo Hill Ranch summer camp for boys and girls. Interested in both music and chess from an early age, seven-year-old Friedman was chosen as one of fifty local chess players to challenge Polish-born U.S. grandmaster Samuel Reshevsky to simultaneous matches in Houston. Reshevsky won all fifty matches. Friedman was by far the youngest competitor.

While he was an honors psychology student at the University of Texas at Austin, Friedman played in a moderately successful rock-and-roll band, King Arthur and the Carrots. The band had a local hit with "Schwinn 24," a parody of Beach Boys–type drag racing songs, this one about a boy and his bicycle. After receiving a BA in 1966, Friedman traveled to the Southwest Pacific as an agricultural extension agent for the Peace Corps. In his own opinion, his greatest achievement in the Peace Corps was to introduce the Frisbee to Borneo. Upon his return to America, he pursued a career in country music.

In the early 1970s Friedman formed his own band, the Texas Jewboys. The name is a multilayered pun on Bob Wills and His Texas Playboys, a famed Depression-era country band. Many musicians performed with Friedman during the band's tenure. A central factor in their material, almost all of which was at least cowritten by Friedman, is the tension in his background as a Jewish intellectual raised in rural Texas. His songs explore diverse topics, including feminism, race relations, the stresses of a musician's life, and nostalgia for the past, but anti-Semitism and clashes with rednecks are frequent concerns. Among his most famous songs are "They Ain't Makin' Jews Like Jesus Anymore" and "Ride 'Em Jewboy." The latter song, a beautiful ballad with eerie lyrics in which the Holocaust is compared to a cattle drive, is considered to be his most affecting song.

Some of Friedman's songs are strictly played for laughs, and a few are more traditional country tunes; most have some kind of social message embedded in them. His audiences have frequently taken his singing persona as a representation of his authentic feelings and social agenda; the National Organization for Women gave him its Male Chauvinist Pig of the Year award in 1974 for "Get Your Biscuits in the Oven and Your Buns in the Bed," a satirical song about a redneck and his women's-libber girlfriend. The band was heckled for this and other songs, and some of their bookings were canceled, but this notoriety led to greater success.

In 1973 Friedman obtained a recording contract with Vanguard, releasing *Sold American* later that year. Another album followed in 1974, and in 1976 Friedman achieved his musical high-water mark with an album on the Epic label, *Lasso from El Paso*. (The song was originally titled "Asshole from El Paso," a parody of Merle Haggard's "Okie from Muskogee," but Epic required a title change before it would issue the record.) On *Lasso* Friedman featured such famed guest artists as Eric Clapton and Bob Dylan—he had met Dylan and gone on the counterculture icon's Rolling Thunder Revue tour the year before. Other important songs on Friedman's early albums include "Sold American," "Wild Man from Borneo," and "Homo Erectus." Later in his musical career, he released a greatest hits compilation titled *Old Testaments and New Revelations* (1992) and *From One Good American to Another* (1995).

Friedman spent several years living in a Greenwich Village loft in New York City after the band broke up in the mid-1970s. While there, he was a frequent performer at the Lone Star Cafe, a Texas-themed hangout in Manhattan. His act and a bit of his lifestyle are described in *Thin Ice: A Season in Hell with the New York Rangers* (1982), by his close friend Larry Sloman, and *No Laughing Matter* (1986), by Joseph Heller and Speed Vogel.

In the early 1980s Friedman returned to the Echo Hill Ranch, eager to make a radical change in his life after seeing several friends die of drug-related causes. Back in Texas he began writing comic mystery novels set in New York, with a fictionalized version of himself as the sleuth. He published one nearly every year from 1986 on, with such memorable titles as *A Case of Lone Star* (1987), *Elvis, Jesus, and Coca-Cola* (1993), and *God Bless John Wayne* (1995). The fame resulting from his second career helped create a renewed demand for his recorded music, and in 2011 he launched his "Springtime for Kinky" Tour.

Friedman has nonartistic interests as well: he was one of two independent candidates for governor of Texas in 2006, placing fourth in the final polling; he also runs the Utopia Animal Rescue Ranch, which saves abandoned dogs from euthanasia.

David Lonergan

SEE ALSO: *The Beach Boys; Clapton, Eric; Country Music; Dylan, Bob; Feminism; Frisbee; Greenwich Village; Haggard, Merle; National Organization for Women (NOW); Rock and Roll; Wills, Bob, and His Texas Playboys.*

BIBLIOGRAPHY

"Friedman, Kinky." *Contemporary Authors*, vol. 147. Detroit, MI: Gale Research, 1995.

"Kinky Friedman." *The Illustrated Encyclopedia of Country Music*. London: Salamander Books, 1977.

Sloman, Larry. *On the Road with Bob Dylan: Rolling with the Thunder*. New York: Bantam Books, 1978.

Stambler, Irwin, and Grelun Landon. *The Encyclopedia of Folk, Country and Western Music*, 2nd ed. New York: St. Martin's Press, 1983.

Friends

Six attractive, barely employed but financially comfortable Manhattanites in their twenties constituted the eponymous core of *Friends*, the TV sitcom created by Marta Kauffman and David Crane. *Friends* burst onto NBC for the first time during the 1994–1995 season and rocketed to instant "must-see" popularity. Single young viewers, bored with sitcoms about family life, latched enthusiastically onto this group of pals in cute clothes and trendy haircuts, who spent much of their time sitting around in a coffee bar conversing and exchanging banter and who treated each other like family. *Friends* was an ensemble show that appeared to have been directly modeled after the Fox sitcom *Living Single*, which began its run a year earlier and featured an almost identical premise except that the cast was African American.

In the series, the group of friends is divided equally between the sexes. The women are Monica Geller (Courteney Cox), a chef and a neat freak; her old high school friend and roommate, Rachel Green (Jennifer Aniston); and flighty Phoebe Buffay (Lisa Kudrow). Phoebe is Monica's college friend and a massage therapist and guitarist who plays at the coffee bar/hangout Central Perk (her signature song is "Smelly Cat"). Rachel began the series by leaving her dentist fiancé at the altar and giving up her father's financial support to make it on her own. Monica's slightly older brother, Ross (David Schwimmer), is a well-meaning paleontologist whose wife divorced him upon realizing that she was a lesbian; Ross's college pal Chandler Bing (Matthew Perry) lives across the hall from Monica and is the wise guy of the group, while his roommate, Joey Tribbiani (Matt LeBlanc), is a none-too-bright aspiring actor who completes the sextet.

The show's theme song, the Rembrandts' Beatles-esque "I'll Be There for You," is insidiously infectious, a suitable metaphor for the show itself. Each week, this clique of attractive idlers discussed life in general and relationships in particular, with the on-again, off-again romance between Ross and Rachel a recurrent theme and an almost constant cliffhanger. Ross was wild about Rachel, so much so that even when he was at the altar about to marry Emily (Helen Baxendale) in 1998, Ross said, "I, Ross, take thee, Rachel."

The best-known cast member when the show started was Cox, who had made a few movies and was on *Family Ties* (1982–1989) for a season as Michael J. Fox's girlfriend. She no doubt felt immediately at home with Perry's Chandler, whose comic timing and delivery is heavily reminiscent of Fox. And Kudrow's Phoebe appears to have borrowed most of her mannerisms from Teri Garr, who was brought on to play Phoebe's long-lost mother in a few 1997 episodes.

Cox, Aniston, Perry, LeBlanc, Kudrow, and Schwimmer became household names as a result of *Friends*. Not only were they a beguiling and talented assembly, but the show had the weight of an incomparable publicity machine behind it, and these six people, together and separately, appeared on the cover of almost every entertainment magazine in the United States.

The Stars of **Friends**. *The cast of* Friends *included, from left, Matt LeBlanc, Jennifer Aniston, David Schwimmer, Courteney Cox, Matthew Perry, and Lisa Kudrow.* GERALD WEINMAN/NBC/NBCU PHOTO BANK/GETTY IMAGES.

All have tried to cultivate movie careers, with Aniston having had the most success with big-screen ventures.

All the episode titles of *Friends* start with "The One with . . . " as in, "The One with the Embryos" and "The One with George Stephanopoulos." The only exception to this pattern was the show's final episode, titled appropriately "The Last One," which aired in May 2004. Many critics might well name the whole series "The One with the Hairdos." No television show has influenced hairstyles as much as *Friends*, with variations on "the Rachel" still in evidence years after the show premiered. The enormous popularity of the series spawned dozens of imitator shows in the 1990s, all of which featured attractive, witty young men and women hanging out together, but *Friends* outlasted them all. This can mostly be credited to the high standard of funny, imaginative, and well-constructed scripts, which helped garner critical acclaim and ratings success for the series, which received more than sixty Emmy nominations and six Emmy Awards during its ten-year run.

Notwithstanding its popularity and success, the series did have its share of vehement detractors. Certainly, not much happened on the show, and the charm of its stars, along with the witty one-liners, was what carried it. For those who failed to find the *Friends* charming, there was not much reason to tune in (but the same could be said of *Seinfeld* [1990–1998]). Critics maintained that the show bore no resemblance to reality, from the trouble these gorgeous people had finding love interests (so much so that they often turned to each other), to the one-dimensional nature of the characters, to the fact that no one ever seemed to be working and, those who did, did not seem to do it much. The fans answered that there were plenty of workplace comedies out there but that this show was about hanging out with your friends. And that was just what the characters did—hang out with their friends.

Karen Lurie

SEE ALSO: *Emmy Awards;* Family Ties; Seinfeld; *Sitcom; Television.*

BIBLIOGRAPHY

Brooks, Tim, and Earle Marsh. *The Complete Directory to Prime Time Network and Cable TV Shows 1946–Present*, 6th ed. New York: Ballantine Books, 1995.

McNeil, Alex. *Total Television*. New York: Penguin, 1996.

Wild, David. *"Friends" 'Til the End: The Official Celebration of All Ten Years*. New York: Time Home Entertainment, 2004.

Fringe

SEE: *Abrams, J. J.*

Frisbee

The Frisbee, a plastic flying disc, has been a required component of any American child's toy collection for most of the latter half of the twentieth century. It is widely believed that Ivy League students began flinging and catching pie and cookie tins in the 1920s and 1930s, naming the practice "Frisbee-ing" after a local pie company. Wham-O Toy Company, producers of the Hula Hoop, bought the original Frisbee (called the Pluto Platter) from its inventor, Walter Frederick Morrison, in 1957 and almost immediately began mass production of the toy. Wham-O has sold more than 200 million Frisbees since then.

An affordable and portable toy with no set rules, the Frisbee enjoyed a boom in sales and public familiarity in the antiestablishment atmosphere of the late 1960s. This new generation of Frisbee fans invented Frisbee Golf, Guts, and Ultimate Frisbee, but it was Freestyle Frisbee—with its behind-the-back and between-the-legs catches; trick throws; and leaping, Frisbee-catching dogs—that did the most for visibility of the growing sport. By the end of the twentieth century, dozens of colleges featured interscholastic Ultimate Frisbee teams, and Frisbee Golf courses peppered suburbs across the continent. It is still a mark of pride among American youth to be able to fling a Frisbee straight and far.

Colby Vargas

SEE ALSO: *College Fads; Hula Hoop; Ivy League; Leisure Time; Toys.*

BIBLIOGRAPHY

Johnson, Stancil E. D. *Frisbee: A Practitioner's Manual and Definitive Treatise.* New York: Workman Publishing, 1975.

McLellan, Dennis. "Walter Frederick Morrison Dies at 90: Father of the Frisbee." *Los Angeles Times*, February 13, 2010.

Morrison, Walter F., and Phil Kennedy. *Flat Flip Flies Straight!: True Origins of the Frisbee.* Wethersfield, CT: Wormhole Publishers, 2006.

Frizzell, Lefty *(1928–1975)*

One of country music's greatest vocal stylists, Lefty Frizzell's syllable-stretching, note-bending style has influenced singers such as Merle Haggard, George Jones, Willie Nelson, George Strait, and Randy Travis. Frizzell's meteoric rise to fame may be unparalleled in country music. Both sides of his first single ("If You've Got the Money I've Got the Time" and "I Love You a Thousand Ways") for Columbia Records in 1950 hit number one on the country charts, and at one point in 1951, he had four singles in the Top 10. Largely because of his alcoholism and brushes with the law, Frizzell's career suffered ups and downs. From 1953 to 1958, though he continued to tour and record, he had no hits. In 1959 he staged a comeback with "Long Black Veil," followed a couple of years later by the number one hit "Saginaw Michigan." Frizzell continued to work until his death from a stroke in 1975.

Joyce Linehan

SEE ALSO: *Country Music; Haggard, Merle; Jones, George; Nelson, Willie; Strait, George.*

BIBLIOGRAPHY

Cooper, Daniel. *Lefty Frizzell: The Honky-Tonk Life of Country Music's Greatest Singer.* Boston: Little, Brown, 1995.

Green, Douglas B. *Classic Country Singers.* Salt Lake City, UT: Gibbs Smith, 2008.

From Here to Eternity

First as a novel and then as a film, *From Here to Eternity* enjoyed enormous critical and popular success in the early 1950s. The novel, the first published work of James Jones, is a long and powerful fictional treatment of the U.S. Army, climaxing with the December 7, 1941, Japanese attack on U.S. military installations at Pearl Harbor. The bulk of Jones's novel relentlessly exposes the exploitation of enlisted men by a cynical officer class. Its naturalistic descriptions of an inhumanly brutal stockade constitute some of the most harrowing passages in American fiction. Still the novel is to a large degree a kind of elegy for the sustaining camaraderie among enlisted men as well as for the sanctuary that the army offered the economically destitute during the Great Depression. It is, then, a unique variation on proletarian fiction, with officers equated to corrupt capitalists and enlisted men to oppressed workers.

THE BOOK

Jones's book was awarded the National Book Award for 1952, received overwhelmingly favorable reviews, and became a sensational best seller (in no small part because of an elaborate publicity campaign by its publisher, Scribner's). The novel's two central characters, Robert E. Lee Prewitt, a boxer and bugler of unusual talent and unyielding principles, and Sergeant Milton Anthony Warden, also a man of integrity but a master manipulator and covert enemy of the officer class as well, are exceptionally well realized.

Largely because of its unrelenting exposé of the corrupt officer class in the old peacetime army and the frankness of its treatment of sexuality, *From Here to Eternity* benefited, in its popular success, from the public's appetite for sensationalism. These two motifs are carefully intertwined in Jones's text. For instance, Warden sets out to seduce Karen Holmes, the allegedly promiscuous wife of his corrupt commanding officer, merely as a political statement, but quickly finds himself falling in love with her. Prewitt, after being forced to desert the army following a horrendous experience in the stockade during which he experiences physical torture and sees another soldier die at the hands of Sergeant "Fatso" Judson, seeks refuge with his prostitute girlfriend, Alma Schmidt, who has taken the professional name of Lorene. The novel contains a comically graphic scene in the brothel where Alma works and in which Prewitt finds relief from the endless harassment that he is receiving at the direct orders of Lieutenant "Dynamite" Holmes. In the scene, Prewitt is accompanied by the only friend that he has in C Company, Private Angelo Maggio, an enormously likable but recklessly defiant young man from Brooklyn.

THE MOVIE

Despite (or because of) the novel's sensational elements, producer Harry Cohn of Columbia Pictures eagerly purchased the film rights to it and hired Jones, who had by then become something of a celebrity (partly because of extensive coverage in *Life* magazine) to write the screenplay. Cohn also acquired the services of Fred Zinnemann, the acclaimed director of *High Noon* (1952) and other successful films. Jones's original screenplay was rejected in favor of a subsequent effort by film writer Daniel Taradash. Because of the novel's emphasis upon memorable characters, Cohn and Zinnemann realized that casting would be a crucial element in the success of their final work. In this, they were to be extremely fortunate.

For the crucial role of Prewitt, Cohn initially pushed for actor Aldo Ray but ultimately yielded to Zinnemann's insistence upon casting Montgomery Clift, whose ability to project a threatened sensitivity had been established in films such as

***Burt Lancaster and Deborah Kerr in* From Here to Eternity.** *Burt Lancaster and Deborah Kerr share a passionate kiss in the iconic beach scene from the 1953 film* From Here to Eternity. COLUMBIA PICTURES/ARCHIVE PHOTOS/GETTY IMAGES.

George Stevens's *A Place in the Sun* (1951). Burt Lancaster and relative film newcomer Ernest Borgnine were easy choices to portray Sergeant Milt Warden and "Fatso" Judson, but the casting of the two female roles surprised many Hollywood observers. Initially, Joan Crawford was chosen to play Holmes, but she withdrew from the project before filming began and was replaced by Deborah Kerr, unquestionably a fine actress but one best known for portraying genteel and sometimes aloof characters. The choice of Donna Reed for the role of Alma was unexpected for comparable reasons. Reed was known for such "wholesome" performances as the wife of Jimmy Stewart in Frank Capra's *It's a Wonderful Life* (1946). Even though the script overtly made her a dance-hall hostess instead of a prostitute, the character's original identity as conceived by Jones in his novel was more than implied.

The process of choosing the actor to play Angelo Maggio became the stuff of Hollywood and pop legend. Then at the nadir of his singing career, Frank Sinatra, who had read Jones's novel and identified with Maggio, campaigned tirelessly for the part and was somewhat reluctantly given it. His campaign would later be fictionalized by Mario Puzo in his novel *The Godfather* (1969).

Taradash's screenplay downplayed Jones's depiction of military corruption. For instance, the corrupt Captain "Dynamite" Holmes is exposed and disgraced in the film, whereas Jones's novel last shows him rising higher in the military command, and the stockade sadism is largely kept offscreen. Still, the finished film, released in 1953, captures much of the novel's emotional power primarily because of Zinnemann's directing and the exceptional performances of his cast. Critics Pauline Kael and Michael Gebert, in *I Lost It at the Movies* and *The Encyclopedia of Movie Awards*, respectively, correctly observe that Clift's inspired interpretation of Prewitt is the real heart of the film and is so intense as to be almost unbearable at times. Lancaster and Kerr are exceptional in playing off each other. A scene in which, dressed in bathing suits, they kiss while lying on a beach with the waves splashing over them is probably the movie's best-known single image (ironically the scene does not exist in the novel). Sinatra, Reed, and Borgnine are perfect in their secondary roles.

SUCCESS

Not surprisingly, the film gathered a number of major awards. Out of thirteen Academy Award nominations, it won eight, including Best Picture, Best Director for Zinnemann, Best Screenplay for Taradash, and Best Supporting Actor (Sinatra) and Actress (Reed). Clift, Lancaster, and Kerr were also nominated. The movie also received the Best Picture award from the New York Film Critics Circle, and Zinnemann was named the year's Best Director by that organization and by the Directors Guild of America. In 1953 much of the film's power originated in its being filmed in black and white in a Technicolor-dominated age. This deliberately anachronistic approach achieved the realistic effect that Zinnemann wanted.

Both as a novel and a film, *From Here to Eternity* occupies an important place in American culture. In the conformist and sexually repressive 1950s, its advocacy of oppressed enlisted men and its frank depiction of their sexual hunger seemed daring and even revolutionary. Some of the images from the film (Lancaster and Kerr on the beach, Clift playing "Taps" for the dead Sinatra) are indelibly engraved on the consciousness of a generation of moviegoers, and Jones's novel remains perhaps the best fictional treatment of the U.S. Army. Despite its considerable length, it was, in fact, conceived by Jones as the first volume in an "army trilogy," the last two volumes of which appeared as *The Thin Red Line* (1962) and *Whistle* (published posthumously in 1978).

James R. Giles

SEE ALSO: *Academy Awards; Capra, Frank; Clift, Montgomery; Crawford, Joan; The Fifties;* The Godfather; *The Great Depression;* High Noon; *Hollywood;* It's a Wonderful Life; *Lancaster, Burt;* Life; *Reed, Donna; Sinatra, Frank; Stewart, Jimmy; War Movies; World War II.*

BIBLIOGRAPHY

Carter, Steven R. *James Jones: An American Literary Orientalist Master.* Urbana: University of Illinois Press, 1998.

Garrett, George P. *James Jones.* Orlando, FL: Harcourt Brace Jovanovich, 1984.

Gebert, Michael. *The Encyclopedia of Movie Awards.* New York: St. Martin's, 1996.

Giles, James. *James Jones.* Boston: Twayne, 1981.

Giles, James, and J. Michael Lennon. *The James Jones Reader.* Secaucus, NJ: Carol Publishing, 1991.

Harkness, John. *The Academy Awards Handbook.* New York: Windsor, 1994.

Hendrick, George, ed. *To Reach Eternity: The Letters of James Jones.* New York: Random House, 1989.

Kael, Pauline. *I Lost It at the Movies.* Boston: Little, Brown, 1965.

LaGuardia, Robert. *Monty: A Biography of Montgomery Clift.* New York: Arbor House, 1977.

McShane, Frank. *Into Eternity: The Life of James Jones.* Boston: Houghton Mifflin, 1985.

Whipple, A. B. C. "James Jones and His Angel." *Life*, May 7, 1951, 143ff.

Frost, Robert *(1874–1963)*

The image of Robert Frost nurtured by most Americans is of a white-haired, rustic saint writing poems about the mellow glories of nature and the pastoral idylls of New England rural life. When not shining in this bucolic light, he glows with a patriotic aura as America's poet laureate. Frost read his work at the inauguration of John F. Kennedy, presaging through his presence the imminent wonders promised by the young president's election. But this idealistic image of Frost was more the product of marketing by the poet himself than a true reflection of any innate homespun charm. Frost was, indeed, a great poet, but he was also a bitter, egotistical writer who resented the late recognition of his genius. To understand how he came to be both a great poet and a bitter man requires foraging in the woods of his life.

EARLY DAYS

Robert Frost was born in San Francisco on March 26, 1874, the son of William Prescott Frost and Isabelle Moodie. Frost's father was a journalist whose drinking habits led to an early death by tuberculosis in 1885 at age thirty-four. After his death Frost's mother moved the family to Massachusetts, where Frost graduated in 1892 as one of two valedictorians from Lawrence High School. His covaledictorian was his future wife, Elinor Miriam White. After high school Frost enrolled at Dartmouth College, while Elinor attended St. Lawrence. Frost left Dartmouth early, unable to contain his bouts of jealousy over Elinor's refusal to leave her studies and marry him.

After Elinor graduated in 1895, she took a teaching position at the school Frost's mother had started and shortly afterward married Frost. At the time he worked as a teacher and reporter, publishing what little poetry could get past the stodgily Victorian editors who ruled the world of American letters. The Frosts started having children shortly after their marriage, increasing the pressure on Frost to make good on his own evolving opinion of himself as a poet worth serious consideration. Financial strains were eased when Frost's grandfather let the entire family reside at Derry Farm in New Hampshire. (The farm was shortly afterward bequeathed, with a small annuity, to the still growing family.)

By 1907 he had six children and still no steady form of income beyond the annuity. On August 23, 1912, Frost—fed up with the obtuseness of the American poetry establishment—left America for England. In England he discovered an entirely new and altogether exciting world of letters. There were the modernist giants—Ezra Pound, T. S. Eliot, Ford Maddox Ford, William Butler Yeats—fashioning with great, broad strokes a new poetic reality.

Frost published his first book of poetry, *A Boy's Will*, in April 1913; it was favorably reviewed in Pound's *Poetry* within a month. Many of the poems featured in *A Boy's Will* had been written during Frost's years at Derry Farm, as were the poems in his next two works, *North of Boston* (1914) and *Mountain Interval* (1916). *North of Boston* offers some of Frost's best work, including "After Apple-Picking" and "The Wood-Pile," whereas *Mountain Interval* features "The Road Not Taken" and "An Old Man's Winter Night."

CRITICAL PRAISE AND THE PULITZER PRIZE

After the publication of *North of Boston*, Frost returned to the United States to resounding critical praise. He was named Phi Beta Kappa Poet by Tufts University and a few years later at Harvard as well. His election to the National Institute of Arts and Letters and appointment as a professor at Amherst College assured the recognition he had always craved and the income he and his family had done without for so long. In 1922 he received his first of four Pulitzer Prizes for poetry with his collection *New Hampshire*, which includes "Fire and Ice"; "Two Witches"; and his most famous work, "Stopping by Woods on a Snowy Evening."

Five years later *West-Running Brook* appeared, again to high praise. Like *New Hampshire*, this volume features individual poems with a decidedly political cast. In 1930 Frost received his second Pulitzer Prize for *Collected Poems of Robert Frost*, and in 1936 a third was awarded for the much more openly political *A Further Range*. Despite the obvious compliment implied in winning a third Pulitzer, *A Further Range* drew fire from major literary critics such as Newton Arvin and R. P. Blackmur for Frost's conservative overtones, which ran contrary to the general political feeling during the Great Depression.

In 1942 Frost received his fourth and last Pulitzer Prize for *A Witness Tree*, which includes "Beech"; "The Most of It";

"November"; and the poem he would read at Kennedy's inauguration twenty years later, "The Gift Outright." Afterward Frost was never quite the same as a poet, despite the occasional powerful lyric. *Steeple Bush* (1947), *A Masque of Mercy* (1947), *A Masque of Reason* (1948), and *In the Clearing* (1962) were themselves vitiated by a writer whose creative genius had run its course. The final twenty years of his life seemed to consist of putting out collections of his earlier poetry and racking up all of the remaining accolades except the one he desired most: the Nobel Prize in Literature.

Frost's genius emanated in large part from his conscious decision during the modernist era not to follow the lead of his fellow poets and experiment with *vers libre*. His poems were thematically and metrically unified by his belief in the idea—shared by other American modernists such as Wallace Stevens—that the chaos of reality is given order by the extension of the perceiver's will. A cross between the stoic naturalism of Jack London and Frank Norris and the Americanized Nietzcheanism of William James and John Dewey, Frost's poetry illustrates the ways in which the decaying effects of nature are held at bay by the forms into which we mold our understanding of our environment. As a result, Frost integrates the formal rigidities of blank verse and sonnet with a distinctly regional coloration that depends heavily on the use of common speech, standard word order, and metaphors grounded in natural events.

Although, like other contemporaries, Frost saw in free verse an opportunity to retreat from the high diction of earlier poetical traditions; the chaotic freedom of its metrical format could not accommodate a personal philosophy that saw the economy and rhythm of poetry as an instrument for taming the uncertainties of lived reality. Thus, in a poem like "Nothing Gold Can Stay," it is the simple rhyme scheme that staves off the decay of nature. Another example, "Once by the Pacific," attempts to contain the dark irony of the inherent destructiveness of nature in a highly structured metrical format. Even "Stopping by Woods on a Snowy Evening" manages to restrain the suicidal intensity of the narrator's tone, rhythmically counterbalancing his response to the woods "lovely, dark and deep" with the "promises" left "to keep." Frost's dark vision may belie the idyllic sweetness that has grown up around the image of him, but in many ways they represent far more closely the anxieties he attempted to capture of the American spirit seeking to understand the limits of freedom and the wisest use of it.

Bennett Lovett-Graff

SEE ALSO: *Capote, Truman; The Great Depression; London, Jack; Norris, Frank.*

BIBLIOGRAPHY

Fagan, Deirdre. *Critical Companion to Robert Frost: A Literary Reference to His Life and Work.* New York: Facts On File, 2007.

Frost, Robert. *Selected Letters of Robert Frost*, ed. Lawrance Thompson. New York: Holt, Rinehart and Winston, 1964.

Greiner, Donald J. *Robert Frost: The Poet and His Critics.* Chicago: American Library Association, 1974.

Lentricchia, Frank. *Robert Frost: Modern Poetics and the Landscapes of Self.* Durham, NC: Duke University Press, 1975.

Pritchard, William H. *Frost: A Literary Life Reconsidered.* New York: Oxford University Press, 1984.

Thompson, Lawrance. *Robert Frost: The Early Years, 1874–1915.* New York: Holt, Rinehart and Winston, 1966.

Thompson, Lawrance, and Robert Frost. *Robert Frost: The Years of Triumph, 1915–1938.* New York: Holt, Rinehart and Winston, 1970.

Thompson, Lawrance, and R. H. Winnick. *Robert Frost: The Later Years, 1938–1963.* New York: Holt, Rinehart and Winston, 1976.

Frosty the Snowman

Frosty the Snowman has entertained American children during the winter holidays since his creation in 1950. Frosty originated in the song, "Frosty the Snowman," written by Steve Nelson and Jack Rollins and recorded by Gene Autry. The song then inspired the 1951 Golden Book adapted by Annie North Bedford and illustrated by Corine Malverne and a series of comic books published by Dell Comics, also in 1951. The song and book tell of a snowman that comes alive and takes the children who created it on sledding and ice-skating adventures. But Frosty melts when he and the children go to the village to see the shop windows. For half a century, the song has been included on Christmas albums by popular performers, including such diverse artists as Bing Crosby, Ella Fitzgerald, Nat King Cole, the Beach Boys, the Jackson Five, Leon Redbone, and Michael Bublé.

The image and story of Frosty remained popular for later generations with the animated film *Frosty the Snowman*, which was narrated by Jimmy Durante and featured the voice of Jackie Vernon as Frosty (1969). Other animated films followed: *Frosty's Winter Wonderland* (1976), *Rudolph and Frosty's Christmas in July* (1979), *Frosty Returns* (2005), and *The Legend of Frosty the Snowman* (2005). The concept was also used in *Jack Frost* (1998), a motion picture starring Michael Keaton as a deceased father who comes back to life in the snowman built by his children. In addition there are Frosty the Snowman action figures, jigsaw puzzles, plush dolls, screensavers, and a Facebook page titled "Frosty the Snowman :D" for fans.

Sharon Brown

SEE ALSO: *Animated Films; The Beach Boys; Christmas; Cole, Nat King; Crosby, Bing; Fitzgerald, Ella; Golden Books.*

BIBLIOGRAPHY

Bedford, Annie North, and Corinne Malverne. *Frosty the Snowman.* New York: Golden Press, 1951.

Collins, Ace. *Stories behind the Greatest Hits of Christmas.* Grand Rapids, MI: Zondervan, 2010.

Frozen Entrées

Frozen entrées, appetizing or otherwise, have revolutionized the social culture of America and much of the rest of the world. Although the science of quick-freezing had its beginnings in the early twentieth century, by the 1950s the development of the process and the successful marketing of frozen food products came both to reflect and advance wider changes in working, family, and social habits. Despite the criticism that has always been attached to frozen cuisine by those with more discerning palates, convenience has triumphed over considerations of taste in sufficient quantity to support a massive frozen food industry. For contemporary America, these "instant meals" are an accepted constituent of domestic life.

ICY BEGINNINGS

People who live in harsh winter conditions with access to ice and snow have always slow-frozen foods as a means of preserving them. Slow-freezing, however, causes irreparable harm to the cellular structure of organic material, making it barely edible when thawed. Clarence Birds Eye, inspired by his work as a naturalist in Montana and then as a fur trader in Labrador, Canada, from 1910 to 1917, was the first to accomplish quick-freezing.

When Birdseye noticed that fish caught at temperatures of 50 degrees below zero froze almost immediately and, upon being thawed, were still fresh and tasty, he was inspired to develop his own quick-freezing techniques. He first employed these techniques in 1924, freezing fish, fruits, and vegetables. He had two methods: to chill foods by means of a very cold calcium chlorate solution or through the vaporization of ammonia. The other important component of successful quick-freezing, Birdseye discovered, was to encase the food in protective packaging before freezing it, thus protecting it from the deleterious effects of direct contact with the gases used for freezing.

In 1929 the Postum Company (founded by C. W. Post) bought Birdseye's frozen haddock factory and became General Foods. The first line of Birds Eye frozen foods, which included peas, spinach, raspberries, cherries, meats, and fish, appeared in 1930 but struggled to catch on in the marketplace for several reasons. The public was inclined to view the frozen foods with suspicion, considering that they were inferior in quality and fit only for institutional use or even that they had been accidentally exposed to cold and then resold as "frozen." In addition, during the 1930s fewer than half of Americans had iceboxes or electric refrigerators, and fewer still had mechanical freezers in which to store frozen food. The first dual-compartment, dual-temperature refrigerator came on the market in 1939, promising greater success for frozen foods, but World War II forced appliance manufacturers to turn their production efforts toward war materials instead.

The end of the war brought a boom in retail manufacturing and sales, as well as a new American ethos that began to value convenience over quality. General Foods had offered a few frozen dinners, such as Irish stew, in the 1930s, but the postwar culture saw a great expansion in frozen dinner lines. In 1945 Maxson Food Systems introduced Strato-Plates, individual frozen meals on trays for military and civilian airplane passengers. In 1951 Swanson came up with pot pies and followed them with mass-marketed TV dinners in 1954.

A turkey dinner with cornbread dressing, gravy, peas, and sweet potatoes constituted Swanson's first offering, which sold for about $1. Roast beef, fried chicken, Salisbury steak, and ham with raisin sauce quickly followed as additional entrée choices. Other companies eventually joined in the trend, among them Stouffer's, Banquet, and On-Core. According to *Consumer Reports*, "by 1959 frozen dinners had become the best-selling of all frozen food items, outstripping the ever-popular meat pot pie." Americans bought seventy million dinners in 1955 and 214 million in 1960. Since that time, the popularity of frozen foods has only increased: contemporary Americans eat an average of six frozen meals per month.

EVOLUTION OF FROZEN ENTRÉES

The first frozen dinners came in compartmentalized aluminum trays, which held meat, vegetables, a starch (usually mashed potatoes), and dessert. The entire meal was baked in an oven, a process that generally took between forty-five minutes and two hours. These dinners represented a revolution in food preservation technology and, more significantly, a change in American eating patterns. The frozen dinner meant that American family members no longer had to eat the same thing at the same time and that the American housewife did not have to cook every meal. Children and husbands could prepare frozen dinners, and they could be eaten in front of the television on "TV trays" rather than at the dining room table. Further, people were no longer tied to the seasons or regions for their choice of food—quick-freezing meant that they could have any meat, fruit, or vegetable at any time.

Swanson launched the Hungry Man's Dinner in 1972, appealing to those who wanted larger quantities of meat and potatoes. During the 1970s the company also changed its product name from TV dinner—which had become a generic term in the American vocabulary—to frozen dinner. The 1980s saw an influx of new products. Dinners were broken up into individual components, with "frozen entrées" overtaking dinners in popularity.

In 1986 the four-section aluminum tray was superseded by plastic serving dishes, which could be placed in the microwave oven for quicker heating. These dishes contained more specialized meals to suit various palates and dietary needs, and by 1990 more than 650 new entrées were on the market, compared with just over fifty dinners that same year. Companies introduced ethnic cuisine, pizzas, gourmet meals, side dishes, cakes, and pies. Lean Cuisine, Budget Gourmet, Le Menu, Weight Watchers, and Healthy Choice were among the main market competitors producing these ranges. As American tastes shifted in the 1990s and the first decade of the 2000s, ethnic offerings became increasingly popular.

For all the apparent variety that frozen entrées offer, people generally agree that the food is mediocre at best. In many brands, meats contain fillers and constitute only a small percentage of the total food in the dinner, while vegetables taste bland. Manufacturers often try to compensate for the loss of taste by adding large amounts of salt, which makes frozen entrées an unhealthy choice for many people. Another health concern is that many frozen foods are made with hydrogenated vegetable oil, which increases the stability of the foods and improves their ability to be stored for long periods; however, hydrogenated fats have been linked to many medical problems. To answer such concerns, some companies have specialized in frozen entrées that have lower sodium and fat content. Others, such as Kashi Frozen Entrées and Amy's Kitchen, offer all-natural, organic, or vegetarian foods.

Where once the evening dinner was a requisite social activity that reinforced familial bonds, it also involved a time-consuming process of preparation. With the development of domestic technologies—particularly freezers and microwaves—frozen entrées have permanently changed the way Americans eat. Though critics are quick to say that today's families are content to eat their individual meals alone, sacrificing taste and conviviality for standardization and convenience, the frozen food industry has continued to improve its freezing methods. Consumers can look for the best-quality products by checking the packaging for the label IQF, which means that the product was individually quick frozen, a process that better preserves texture and flavor and does not allow large lumps of ice to form.

Wendy Woloson

SEE ALSO: *Advertising; Electric Appliances; Fast Food; Foodies; TV Dinners; World War II.*

BIBLIOGRAPHY

"Better than TV Dinners?" *Consumer Reports*, March 1984, 126–127, 170.

Evans, Judith Anne. *Frozen Food Science and Technology.* Oxford, UK: Blackwell, 2008.

I'll Buy That! 50 Small Wonders and Big Deals That Revolutionized the Lives of Consumers. Mount Vernon, NY: Consumers Union, 1986.

Stern, Jane, and Michael Stern. *The Encyclopedia of Bad Taste.* New York: HarperCollins, 1990.

Volti, Rudi. "How We Got Frozen Food." *Invention and Technology*, Spring 1994, 47–56.

Fu Manchu

First introduced to reading audiences in 1913 by British author Sax Rohmer (pseudonym of Arthur Sarsfield Wade, 1883–1959), the character of Fu Manchu quickly grew in the public's imagination as the quintessential sinister Chinese villain. Fu Manchu was featured in numerous short stories and novels, using blackmail, kidnapping, and murder in his efforts to achieve world domination. The popularity of Fu Manchu increased when the character with the long face, goatee, and wispy mustache hit the silver screen (1920s), radio airwaves (1920s to 1930s), comic books (1930s), and television (1950s). Since his creation, Fu Manchu has become a damaging stereotype for Asians, suggesting that they are inscrutable and evil. Fu Manchu has also become the name for a style of beard (a goatee with a thin mustache).

Midori Takagi

SEE ALSO: *Comic Books; Dragon Lady; Radio; Television.*

BIBLIOGRAPHY

Lee, Jonathan H. X., and Kathleen M. Nadeau. *Encyclopedia of Asian American Folklore and Folklife.* Santa Barbara, CA: ABC-CLIO, 2011.

Van Ash, Cay; Elizabeth Sax Romer; and Robert E. Briney. *Master of Villainy: A Biography of Sax Rohmer.* Bowling Green: OH: Bowling Green University Popular Press, 1972.

The Fugitive

A man wrongly convicted of the murder of his wife escapes the train taking him to death row. He wanders America in search of the real killer, a one-armed man, and is pursued by the lieutenant who investigated the murder and lost the prisoner. This was the story of the ABC television drama *The Fugitive.* The saga of Dr. Richard Kimble and Lieutenant Gerard, a mix of *Les Misérables* (1862) and a real-life case, produced not only the highest-rated television series broadcast of the 1960s but also a hit movie and a sequel in the 1990s.

The series first aired September 17, 1963. Roy Huggins, who had created *Maverick* (1957–1962) and would cocreate *The Rockford Files* (1974–1980), devised *The Fugitive* based heavily on the Victor Hugo novel *Les Misérables*, with Lieutenant Gerard modeled on Inspector Javert, the indefatigable pursuer. But *The Fugitive* was also inspired by the real-life case of Dr. Sam Shepard, who was sentenced to prison for killing his wife, after a sensational trial. He always maintained someone else had killed her, and in fact he was later acquitted after winning a new trial. The appeal, based on the circuslike atmosphere of the original trial, went to the U.S. Supreme Court and launched the career of F. Lee Bailey. Shepard died a few years after his release, tarnished by the case. His son is still trying to clear his father's name.

Huggins devised the basic plot, explained in the opening narration of each episode. Dr. Richard Kimble, convicted of killing his wife, is riding to prison on a train, shackled to Lieutenant Gerard. Kimble maintains his innocence and insists that a one-armed man killed his wife. The train crashes, Kimble is thrown clear, and he escapes. Dyeing his hair and changing

The Fugitive. *David Janssen starred as Dr. Richard Kimble, a man on the run after being wrongly convicted of his wife's murder, in* The Fugitive. **GETTY IMAGES.**

his name, he travels America, working a series of odd jobs, intruding on crises featuring guest stars, and always eluding Lieutenant Gerard.

David Janssen, with his world-weary manner and voice, played Kimble; Barry Morse showed up several times a season as Gerard. Bill Raisch played the one-armed man. The series trademark was actor William Conrad's dramatic voiceover in the title sequence, explaining the backstory and announcing "The Fugitive—A QM Production" (*QM* stood for producer Quinn Martin.) The series won an Emmy for Outstanding Dramatic Series of 1965 (its only nomination), and Janssen was nominated several times for Best Actor (1963–1964, 1964–1965, and 1966–1967).

In 1967 ABC canceled the series, and the producers decided to go out with a flourish, wrapping up the story in a two-part episode airing at the very end of *The Fugitive*'s last season. The final episode, airing August 29, 1967, has Kimble corner the one-armed man and Gerard arrive in time to hear the man confess. Conrad reads the closing words, "August 29. The day the running stopped." It was the most viewed episode of a regular series until that time, and its 72 percent share of the viewing audience stood as a landmark until the "Who Shot JR?" resolution episode of *Dallas*. Ironically, the show's famous ending was said to have worked against it. While ABC ran daytime repeats of the series the following year (April 1967 to March 1968), the series was never a big hit in syndication.

In the 1990s, with the burgeoning market for revivals of old TV series, *The Fugitive* seemed to be a natural, despite the death of Janssen in 1980. However, it was as a movie that *The Fugitive* was reincarnated, making it to the screen in August 1993. Dr. Richard Kimble becomes a top-notch surgeon in Chicago, whose wife is murdered by a one-armed man as part of a plot to cover up a medical company's corruption. Again, Kimble escapes in a spectacular train crash. However, he's hunted by a federal officer this time, U.S. Marshal Sam Gerard, who has no connection with the case. Famously, when Kimble insists "I didn't kill my wife," Gerard responds, "I don't care."

The movie focuses on Kimble's efforts to track the one-armed man while Gerard and his oddball team try to track Kimble. Gerard investigates the crime in an effort to find Kimble, but he uncovers more and more evidence that Kimble didn't commit the crime until, like the original Gerard, he is on Kimble's side when he confronts the villain. The presence of Harrison Ford as Kimble, plus the taut script, made the movie a hit, but it was Tommy Lee Jones as Gerard who stole the show, and the Oscar and Golden Globe for Best Supporting Actor. The film's other Oscar nominations were for Best Picture, Sound Effects Editing, Film Editing, Original Score, and Sound. After much wrangling over whether Ford would be back for the inevitable sequel, it was Jones and his ragtag team who made it into the 1998 sequel, *U.S. Marshals*, in which they sought another fugitive.

The 2000 season brought yet another renewal of the series, this time on CBS. This version of *The Fugitive* went back to its TV roots: Gerard (Mykelti Williamson) is with Kimble (Tim Daly) when he escapes and is part of the original case. Taking a cue from the first film's conspiracy plot, there are others trying to stop Kimble from finding the one-armed man, and his ex-father-in-law is also out to get him. The first season ended in a cliff-hanger in which Gerard is shot, but the show was not renewed for a second season. While receiving much publicity and tipped to be a hit, it was instead the series paired with *The Fugitive* on Friday nights, *CSI: Crime Scene Investigation*, that became the sensation. The new *Fugitive* aired from October 6, 2000, through June 1, 2001.

Michele Lellouche

SEE ALSO: CSI*;* Dallas*; Emmy Awards; Ford, Harrison; Garner, James;* Les Misérables*; Shepard, Sam; Television.*

BIBLIOGRAPHY

Brooks, Tim, and Earle Marsh. *The Complete Guide to Prime Time Network and Cable TV Shows*, 8th ed. New York: Random House, 2003.

Robertson, Ed. *The Fugitive Recaptured: The 30th Anniversary Companion to a Television Classic.* Beverly Hills, CA: Pomegranate Press, 1993.

Fuller, Buckminster *(1895–1983)*

Best known as the inventor of the geodesic dome, engineer, architect, inventor, and philosopher Buckminster Fuller epitomized old-fashioned American know-how and was an apostle of the democratizing possibilities of technology. Convinced his inventions and designs might prove the salvation of the human race, for more than fifty years the diminutive autodidact talked a blue streak, tirelessly lecturing to audiences around the world, all the while churning out a seemingly endless procession of designs and elaborations on earlier designs. Circumnavigating the globe twice in the year of his death, Fuller went to his grave convinced of the efficacy of these beliefs—that one day, his inventions would revolutionize human life.

Born to an illustrious New England family, Richard Buckminster Fuller (nicknamed "Bucky" in his youth, an appellation he never outgrew) was an awkward child with poor eyesight and mismatched legs requiring the insertion of a lift in one shoe. His physical defects were countered by a precocious intelligence and startling discernment, abetted, in fact, by his poor eyesight, which taught him not to trust only by physical appearances. A late bloomer, Fuller was twice sent down from Harvard, and at nineteen his family apprenticed him to a Canadian cotton mill.

In 1922 Fuller was out of work when his four-year-old daughter, Alexandra, died during the postwar influenza epidemic. He later credited this event with sparking his interest in housing; he became obsessed with the part drafty houses played in spreading the contagion. As a salesman for his father-in-law's company, selling a new building technique, he rose to president before his father-in-law sold his shares and Fuller was let go. Contemplating suicide on the shores of Lake Michigan, a "private vision" spoke to Fuller, saying, "You do not have the right to eliminate yourself. You do not belong to you. You belong to the universe." Like Saul's vision on the road to Damascus, this experience galvanized Fuller into action.

MASS-PRODUCED HOUSING IDEA

He moved his small family (a second daughter was born in 1927) to a Chicago tenement and began a year of intense introspection. Fuller devoured books at a fantastic rate and emerged from his year of unceasing cerebration the author of an impenetrable essay alternately titled "4-D" or "Timelock" and the designer of a mass-produced house, also called "4-D." The former was privately published and sent out to 200 notables, many of whom professed incomprehension. The latter, whose patent application had been turned down, was presented as a gift to the American Institute of Architects, which imperiously rejected it, saying it could not endorse "pea in a pod" designs.

Fuller was nothing if not resolute. He spent the 1930s refining his Dymaxion house design—interrupted by three years devoted to a revolutionary but flawed vehicle called, fittingly enough, the Dymaxion car. He frequently wrote about technology for *Fortune* magazine and published his own journal, *Shelter*. During World War II Fuller served under Henry J. Kaiser on the Board of Economic Warfare and used his position to promote the Dymaxion house.

In 1944 Fuller submitted a proposal to Kaiser in which he craftily combined the exigencies of economic conversion with the anticipated housing shortage brought on by the legions of returning veterans. His solution was to refit aircraft manufacturing facilities to mass-produce his house, using the same lightweight duralumin used to manufacture planes. Kaiser thought enough of the idea to finance its development. The 1946 Wichita house, produced at Beech Aircraft's Wichita facility, was the first successful application of Fuller's precepts, anticipating the mass-produced suburbs of the 1950s. Some 60,000 houses were ordered, but Fuller insisted on further refinements; the banks funding the development, uneasy at the delay, withdrew funding, and eventually Fuller Houses, Inc., was dissolved.

ON THE LECTURE CIRCUIT

This failure drove Fuller into the world of academia. The job of lecturer was perfectly suited to the loquacious Fuller and gave him the opportunity to refine his ideas without the fickle backing of industry. He moved from university to university, and while in residence at the now-famous experimental Black Mountain College, Fuller built his first geodesic dome. It was made from vinyl louvers and collapsed within seconds of erection. But in 1949 Fuller received a patent for the geodesic dome and founded Geodesics, Inc. He received royalties for each dome built, so for the first time in his life, Fuller was free from economic woes. He could devote more time to what he called "thinking out loud." Traveling incessantly, circling the globe so often he was given to wearing three watches at a time, he would talk to audiences for four or five hours at a stretch.

By the 1960s Fuller had become a counterculture legend, the messiah of modern technology. Film exists of the diminutive Fuller, with his thick glasses, close-shorn white hair, and conservative three-piece suits, lecturing to auditoriums full of ecstatic hippies. His commission for the 1967 Montreal Expo, and perhaps his crowning achievement, was a magnificent 76-meter-wide dome encased in transparent plastic tiles; it was photographed endlessly and graced magazine covers worldwide. One visitor wrote: "Inside the dome the walls start going away from you . . . suddenly you realize the walls are not really there. . . . And it was not done according to the aesthetics of architecture as it had been practiced up to then. It was done simply in terms of doing the most with the least."

For the rest of his life, Fuller refined and expanded upon the implications of this idea. Martin Pawley writes in his biography, "Fuller had converted the Bauhaus epigram 'Less is more' into its Dymaxion derivative 'More for less.'" The domes themselves were the first link in this thought chain; "tensegrity," a building application using continuous tension and discontinuous compression, was a further refinement. Tensegrity made building structures of enormous size and tensile strength—for instance, a 3-kilometer dome that could enclose a part of Manhattan—a possibility. Fuller published elaborate schemata for these and other ideas verging upon science fiction. He envisioned enormous housing developments, self-sufficient islands set offshore, or kilometer-high pyramids, one of which he imagined as replacing a blighted Harlem. Fuller had developed a logarithm of human need, and he followed its varied implications to their logical conclusions. In 1983 he collapsed and died at his wife's bedside; she died thirty-six hours later.

From his "silent year" in Chicago onward, Fuller worked ceaselessly for the betterment of humanity, seeing in his creations the means to realize a more equitable society. But outside of certain limited applications (the geodesic dome house enjoyed a brief vogue with hippies, although industrial applications have proved more enduring), Fuller's inventions failed to revolutionize modern culture. The philosophical underpinnings of his inventions (altruism, ephemeralization, mass housing) remained unpopular ideas—if intermittently expedient. But Fuller saw his creations as part of the evolutionary process, envisioning that his revolutionary designs would inevitably supplant conventional architecture. One day history may prove him correct.

Michael Baers

SEE ALSO: *Fallout Shelters; Gated Communities; Hippies; Manufactured Homes; Suburbia.*

BIBLIOGRAPHY

Fuller, R. Buckminster, and Robert Marks. *The Dymaxion World of Buckminster Fuller*. Garden City, NY: Anchor Press, 1973.

Kenner, Hugh. *Bucky: A Guided Tour of Buckminster Fuller*. New York: Morrow, 1973.

Meller, James, ed. *The Buckminster Fuller Reader*. London: Jonathan Cape, 1970.

Pawley, Martin. *Buckminster Fuller*. New York: Taplinger, 1990.

Ward, James, ed. *The Artifacts of R. Buckminster Fuller*, vols. 1–4. New York: Garland Publishing, 1985.

Zung, Thomas T. K. *Buckminster Fuller: Anthology for a New Millennium*. New York: St. Martin's Press, 2001.

Fundamentalism

The growth of fundamentalism in the twentieth century as an active ideological stance became a source of controversy within the United States. As the twentieth century began, the effects of modernism and secularism on American culture produced a growing sense of alarm among conservative Protestants, who believed that these innovations threatened to undermine the traditional values and moral authority of evangelical Christianity. They responded by reasserting their unyielding commitment to certain fundamental beliefs, such as the divine authorship and literal truth of the Bible, and by working to ensure the survival of those beliefs in American institutions and public life.

By the 1920s, this movement came to be known as fundamentalism, and, since that time, its views have permeated swathes of the social and cultural fabric of America. The fundamentalists' stand against innovations in theology and their strict adherence to biblical doctrine have repeatedly placed them in conflict with mainstream trends in American popular culture—not only in religion but also in the realms of education, politics, entertainment, and the arts. In resisting such trends, fundamentalists have also engaged in various forms of activism, from public demonstration to political organization, and in the process have made their influence felt throughout American society. Although the driving force behind the fundamentalist movement in the United States is rooted in conservative Protestantism, several other religions—including Catholicism, Judaism, and Islam—have produced significant fundamentalist offshoots.

A LIBERAL/CONSERVATIVE SPLIT

The fundamentalist movement originated within the evangelical Protestant churches, particularly among Baptists and Presbyterians. An emphasis on revivalism and the conversion experience had contributed to the rapid growth of evangelical churches during the 1800s, and by the end of the nineteenth century they defined the mainstream of religious life in the United States. As they grew, however, these groups found it increasingly difficult to maintain a denominational consensus on certain theological issues. One major source of controversy was the doctrine of biblical inerrancy, which asserted that the Bible is an infallible source of historical, legal, spiritual, and moral fact. Liberal adherents of the evangelical churches gradually abandoned this doctrine, arguing that the Bible must be theologically, but not necessarily scientifically, true. In their view, for example, the biblical account of creation could not be taken literally because it conflicted with the findings of modern science. Conservatives, on the other hand, rejected modernist revisions of the meaning of scripture, holding to the idea that the Bible contains factual truth and believing that to say otherwise undermined the certainties of their faith.

Another important controversy developed around the doctrine of *dispensational premillennialism*, which became widely accepted among conservative Protestants in the late 1800s and early 1900s upon the release of the Scofield Reference Bible, an annotated version of the Bible edited by American Bible scholar Cyrus I. Scofield. According to this doctrine, human history comprises a series of distinct eras, or dispensations. During each dispensation, humanity is subjected to a divine test, which it ultimately fails, resulting in a catastrophic event such as the banishment from Eden, the Flood of Genesis, or the Crucifixion of Christ. Dispensational millennialism asserts that the end of the next-to-last dispensation is approaching and will be followed by the final dispensation, the "Millennial Age," during which Christ will rule on earth for 1,000 years. Although this doctrine was not universally accepted by conservatives, it became a major theme in the thinking of key fundamentalist leaders during the late nineteenth and early twentieth centuries, clearly setting them apart from moderate and liberal Protestants. Nevertheless, American religious leaders warned of the impending "end times" throughout the 1900s, and many identified the turn of the twentieth century, with all of its attendant "Y2K" hysteria, as a prime era for the return of Christ.

As these theological controversies developed, liberals and conservatives within the evangelical Protestant denominations found themselves increasingly at odds with one another. Both sides tried to ensure that their point of view would define their denomination's policies and statements of faith; as a result, bitter disputes developed within several of the larger Protestant groups. Some of the evangelical denominations actually experienced little conflict, because one side or the other dominated their membership so thoroughly. The widespread acceptance of modernist theology by Congregationalists, for example, precluded extensive debate within that group, as did, conversely, the widespread rejection of modernism by the Southern Baptists. But within other groups, such as the Northern Baptists, Northern Presbyterians, and Disciples of Christ, the diversity of beliefs led to serious conflict. In each of these denominations, however, fundamentalists in the end lacked the numbers needed to ensure that their views would prevail. Realizing that the spread of modernism had made it impossible for them to take control of these groups, the fundamentalist faction within each split off from its parent body to start a new denomination.

SPREADING THE WORD

The fundamentalists' failure to control most of the large evangelical denominations did not deter them from promoting their views. They established a variety of programs and organizations that focused on advancing the fundamentalist cause outside of the existing structure of Protestant denominations. An early example of these nondenominational efforts was the publication of a series of booklets titled *The Fundamentals*, which described and justified various conservative theological positions. Distributed to religious leaders, students, and pastors throughout the English-speaking world, these booklets helped spread the fundamentalist message and provided the source of the fundamentalist movement's name. Fundamentalists also established dozens of nondenominational Bible institutes and colleges (Graham Bible College, Moody Bible Institute, God's Bible School and College) during the early twentieth century, in part to provide clergy for the many independent fundamentalist churches organized during this period. As the century progressed, fundamentalists became very active in religious broadcasting and Internet outreach, which enabled them to disseminate their beliefs to much larger audiences than they could reach within the confines of their own congregations.

THE SCOPES MONKEY TRIAL

While developing its own institutional structure, the fundamentalist movement adopted an increasingly oppositional stance with respect to contemporary culture and began to develop strategies to reform American society. The first major issue raised by the fundamentalists in this context was the teaching of scientific concepts that contradicted traditional interpretations of the Bible. They focused in particular on the teaching of evolution in public schools and universities, which they sought to ban either by legislation or through the regulations of local school districts. Anti-evolution laws were subsequently enacted in a number of states, primarily in the South, where the influence of fundamentalism was greatest.

The controversy surrounding these laws became widely publicized during a celebrated case in Tennessee, the so-called Scopes monkey trial, in which biology teacher John Scopes was tried in 1925 for violating the state ban on teaching Charles Darwin's theory of evolution. Although this event provided a forum for one of the most eloquent supporters of the fundamentalist position, William Jennings Bryan, it also subjected fundamentalists to widespread criticism and ridicule in the national and international press, perhaps most notably by columnist H. L. Mencken. As a result, the movement lost much of its credibility and became increasingly alienated from the mainstream of American popular culture.

TELEVANGELISM

Following their early defeats within the mainstream denominations and in the public debate over the teaching of evolution, fundamentalists entered a period of withdrawal and consolidation. Rather than attempting to reform society at large, they concentrated on building a separate structure of religious institutions consisting of Bible colleges and institutes, nondenominational fundamentalist churches, independent missionary organizations, revival meetings, and the like. They also became increasingly involved in religious broadcasting, first in radio and then television.

Televangelism provided an especially effective outlet for the fundamentalists' efforts to expand their base of support. By enabling them to operate outside traditional institutional structures, it gave them a means of addressing new, untapped audiences as well as their existing followers. The broadcast media also suited the preaching style of many of the leading fundamentalist evangelists, who relied heavily on their personal charisma. Through such efforts, fundamentalism remained an active if unobtrusive force within American culture during the 1950s and 1960s.

THE "RELIGIOUS RIGHT"

A conservative turn in American politics during the 1970s gave fundamentalists a new opportunity to bring their agenda before the public. In response to a number of social concerns, most notably the U.S. Supreme Court's lifting of federal and state laws against abortion in *Roe v. Wade* (1973), fundamentalist movements such as the Moral Majority and the Christian Coalition became extensively involved in political action during the 1970s and 1980s and formed the core of the new "Religious Right." Although the Religious Right supported a range of conservative positions on policy issues, the fundamentalists' primary goal was again to reform American society by addressing issues of faith and morality. They were especially concerned with trends that appeared either to undermine traditional religious belief or to limit the traditional role of religion in American life. They again confronted the issue of teaching evolution in public schools, now cast as a conflict between Darwinian theory and creationism, a defense of the biblical account of creation presented in scientific terms; in a number of locales, primarily in the South and West, they succeeded in influencing curricular policies, although not to the point of banning evolution from science classes.

Fundamentalists' concern with the public role of religion not only involved them most directly in the effort to restore prayer to the public schools but also engaged them in the debates over a variety of social issues and public policy that they believed should be guided by religious principles. These issues included gay rights, pornography, immorality in the entertainment industry, and equal rights for women. They continued to face strong opposition from moderates and liberals on these issues, but, nonetheless, their efforts to organize politically substantially enhanced their influence on American culture, particularly during the Reagan administration of the 1980s and the George W. Bush administration of the first decade of the 2000s, when fundamentalist candidates such as Pat Robertson and Rick Santorum entered the active political arena.

During the 1990s and the first decade of the 2000s, fundamentalists maintained their commitment to political action, although developments at the national level, such as Robertson's failed bid for the Republican presidential nomination in 1988, led many to focus on local or grassroots efforts. Control of local school boards became one of the most common objectives of fundamentalists in their attempts to influence public policy. Around the turn of the twenty-first century, conservative school board members once again organized nationwide challenges to the teaching of evolution in public schools, insisting on controversial disclaimers describing evolution as an unproven theory and instituting "intelligent design" counter-curriculums in a number of school districts. Such actions were met with resistance from the academic and secular communities and challenged in federal court cases, including *Kitzmiller v. Dover Area School District* (2004), which struck down the teaching of intelligent design in Dover, Pennsylvania, science classes, with the finding that it represented "a religious view, a mere re-labeling of creationism, and not a scientific theory."

CRITICIZING MAINSTREAM CULTURE

Fundamentalists also adopted a more direct approach to expressing their opposition to cultural trends through boycotts and protests of entertainment production companies and their advertisers, retail stores, and secular events. One extreme group representing the Westboro Baptist Church of Topeka, Kansas, even engaged in several highly controversial demonstrations at funerals and military ceremonies decrying the increasing acceptance of homosexuality on all levels of society.

Although its prominence in national politics has declined, fundamentalism continues to offer a substantive critique of mainstream American culture. It has also provided a model for understanding the resurgence of militant religious traditionalism in other regions of the world, within religious cultures as different as Islam, Judaism, and Hinduism. For some observers, the rise of militant Islamic fundamentalist groups such as the Taliban, al-Qaeda, and the Muslim Brotherhood and its policy of "jihad," or religious war to defend Islam from external threats (particularly the influence of North American and Western European countries), contains echoes of Christian fundamentalism's fervent renunciation of modern cultural developments. In this sense, the term *fundamentalism* applies not only to a conservative wing of evangelical Protestantism in the United States but also to a variety of analogous social trends, sometimes accompanied by the violence of "Holy war," that have developed around the globe and that have intensified in the years since the attacks of September 11, 2001, on the World Trade Center and the Pentagon.

Roger W. Stump

SEE ALSO: *Darrow, Clarence; Feminism; Gay Liberation Movement; Mencken, H. L.; Moral Majority; 9/11; Pornography; Religious Right; Robertson, Pat; Scopes Monkey Trial; Sunday, Billy; Televangelism.*

BIBLIOGRAPHY

Ammerman, Nancy T. *Bible Believers: Fundamentalists in the Modern World.* New Brunswick, NJ: Rutgers University Press, 1987.

Armstrong, Karen. *The Battle for God: A History of Fundamentalism.* New York: Ballantine Books, 2001.

Brasher, Brenda E. *Godly Women: Fundamentalism and Female Power.* New Brunswick, NJ: Rutgers University Press, 1998.

Carpenter, Joel A. *Revive Us Again: The Reawakening of American Fundamentalism.* New York: Oxford University Press, 1997.

Davidson, Lawrence. *Islamic Fundamentalism.* Westport, CT: Greenwood Press, 2003.

Harris, Harriet. *Fundamentalism and Evangelicals.* New York: Oxford University Press, 2008.

Herriot, Peter. *Religious Fundamentalism: Global, Local and Personal.* New York: Routledge, 2009.

Lawrence, Bruce B. *Defenders of God: The Fundamentalist Revolt against the Modern Age.* San Francisco: Harper & Row, 1989.

Marsden, George M. *Fundamentalism and American Culture: The Shaping of Twentieth Century Evangelicalism, 1870–1925.* New York: Oxford University Press, 1980.

Marty, Martin E., and R. Scott Appleby, eds. *Fundamentalisms Comprehended.* Chicago: University of Chicago Press, 1995.

Milton-Edwards, Beverly. *Islamic Fundamentalism since 1945.* New York: Routledge, 2005.

Sandeen, Ernest R. *The Roots of Fundamentalism: British and American Millenarianism, 1800–1930.* Chicago: University of Chicago Press, 1970.

Funicello, Annette *(1942–)*

During the height of her fame at Walt Disney Pictures, *Mickey Mouse Club* star Annette Funicello received more mail than the studio's two most popular "leading men": Mickey Mouse and Zorro. To young people she was, quite simply, the quintessential dream girl. Males liked her because, over the course of the series' run from 1955 to 1959, she blossomed into a buxom beauty before their eyes. Females liked her for her sweetness and sincerity and for her winning smile. She was so beloved that she became known, and was often billed, by her first name alone.

Born in Utica, New York, Funicello was twelve years old when Walt Disney saw her dancing the lead in *Swan Lake* at a school recital. She had dreamed of becoming a ballerina. Instead, Funicello donned mouse ears to become an original member of Disney's pioneering children's show. Emerging as the series' most popular performer, Funicello was increasingly showcased, even starring in her own *Mickey Mouse Club* serial, "Annette." Disney also licensed Funicello merchandise, including paper dolls, lunch boxes, and jewelry. And in the tradition of "girl detectives" Nancy Drew and Trixie Belden, a fictional Funicello starred in a series of books in which she helped solve mysteries.

Meanwhile, fan magazines recounted the seemingly fairy-tale existence of the real-life teen idol. Readers learned of her romance with another teen idol, Paul Anka, which was the inspiration for his hit tune "Puppy Love." Fans likewise were treated to details about her customized Ford Thunderbird, with its forty coats of purple paint, purple tuck-and-roll upholstery, and purple carpeting. Along with cruising the streets of Burbank, California, home to the Disney studio, Funicello cruised the airwaves. It was her popularity, more than vocal talents, that led to strong record sales for songs including "Tall Paul," "First Name Initial," "How Will I Know My Love?" and "Pineapple Princess." Among the albums she turned out on the Disneyland/Vista label were *Hawaiiannette*, *Italiannette*, and *Danceannette*.

When the *Mickey Mouse Club* ended its run, Funicello was the only Mouseketeer to remain under contract to Disney. She appeared in a string of movies for the studio, including *The Shaggy Dog* (1959) and *Babes in Toyland* (1961), and then segued to American International Pictures for *Beach Party*. That 1963 sand-and-surf youth flick found her cast opposite Frankie Avalon, whom she had dated in the 1950s. In *Beach Party*, the raven-haired Funicello managed to be both voluptuous and wholesome. Honoring the request of her mentor, Walt Disney, she would not wear a navel-baring bikini. Nor would her screen character succumb to her boyfriend's romantic advances. As an unapologetic Funicello once related, "My big line was always, 'Not without a ring you don't' . . . [and] I believed what I was saying wholeheartedly."

In large part because of the Avalon-Funicello chemistry, *Beach Party* spawned a series of sequels, including *How to Stuff a Wild Bikini* (1965) and *Pajama Party* (1964). Funicello also ventured into the fast track with a pair of innocuous car-racing movies opposite Avalon and Fabian, respectively. And she put in a cameo appearance in the 1968 cult picture *Head*, starring the Monkees.

Annette Funicello. *Annette Funicello grew from Mouseketeer in the 1950s to a teen idol in the 1960s, starring in a string of hit beach-party movies.* RB/REDFERNS/GETTY IMAGES.

During the 1970s and for much of the 1980s, the twice-married mother of three made only intermittent appearances on TV, including as a pitchwoman for products such as Skippy peanut butter. She did not return to the screen until 1987's *Back to the Beach*, in which she and Avalon poked fun at their anachronistic images. Their reunion prompted a wave of nostalgic publicity. In fact, such was Funicello's status that her watershed moments have become media milestones. When she was married for the first time, the famed *Peanuts* comic strip depicted Snoopy the dog lamenting, "I can't stand it! This is terrible! How depressing—Annette Funicello has grown up!" A more sobering milestone was Funicello's 1992 disclosure that she suffered from multiple sclerosis (MS). An entire generation suddenly felt much older, as well as sadder.

Despite her illness, Funicello went on to launch several new business ventures, including a line of collectible teddy bears. She also authored an optimistic, scandal-free autobiography, which became a highly rated TV movie. With hopes of finding an eventual cure for MS and other neurological disorders, she set up the Annette Funicello Research Fund for Neurological Diseases.

Pat H. Broeske

SEE ALSO: *Anka, Paul; Avalon, Frankie; Disney (Walt Disney Company); Fabian; Fan Magazines;* The Mickey Mouse Club*; The Monkees; Nancy Drew;* Peanuts*; Teen Idols; Trixie Belden; Zorro.*

BIBLIOGRAPHY

Anderson, Nancy. "What Is an Annette? Who Is She? How Did She Get That Way?" *Photoplay*, September 1959, 57–58, 71–72.

Broeske, Pat H. "Annette, Frankie on Nostalgia Wave in Beach Film Update." *Los Angeles Times*, August 3, 1987.

Funicello, Annette, and Patricia Romanowski. *A Dream Is a Wish Your Heart Makes: My Story*. New York: Hyperion, 1994.

Hollis, Tim, and Greg Ehrbar. *Mouse Tracks: The Story of Walt Disney Records*. Jackson: University Press of Mississippi, 2006.

Santoli, Lorraine. *The Official Mickey Mouse Club Book*. New York: Hyperion, 1995.

Funk

A rhythmically driven, bass-heavy form of black music, funk provided the bridge between 1960s soul music and late-1970s disco. Emerging in America at the same time as the civil rights movement, funk became implicitly associated with black pride because of its unapologetic celebration of traits that were often negatively associated with black people. The key attributes that separated funk from other forms of popular music were expressiveness; unbridled sexual energy; and a raw, gritty attitude. After its 1970s commercial heyday, funk continued to influence a variety of genres, most notably hip-hop—with the massive back catalog of funk records providing a large reservoir of different sounds.

As a musical form, funk is said to have originated with James Brown. As a bandleader, he developed the use of the guitar, horns, and keyboards as purely rhythmic instruments intended to support the bass and drum rhythm section. Brown's 1965 single "Papa's Got a Brand New Bag" is often recognized as one of the first funk recordings. This single provided the syncopated blueprint for many of his later recordings, including "Cold Sweat," "Funky Drummer," and the quintessential black pride song "Say It Loud, I'm Black and I'm Proud." The rhythmic experimentalism of these songs was imitated and expanded upon by the likes of Sly and the Family Stone, Parliament-Funkadelic, and Curtis Mayfield.

As a genre, funk's lineage can be traced relatively easily, but the origins of the term *funk* are more uncertain. It is likely that—just like jazz and rock and roll—funk was used as a euphemism for sexual activity in many African American communities throughout much of the twentieth century. Funk was used to connote something dirty and sexual, and by the late 1960s it became associated with the most earthy, gritty, and raw danceable forms of black music.

Though it is possible to overemphasize Brown's importance in the development of funk, it is hard to overlook the fact that many of the players pulled into Brown's orbit and schooled by him eventually became key players in the genre. Most notably Fred Wesley, Pee Wee Ellis, Maceo Parker, and Bootsy Collins went on to play in Parliament-Funkadelic, Fred Wesley's Horny Horns, Bootsy Collins's Rubber Band, and a slew of lesser-known but no less significant outfits.

Funk was rife with fusion. Jazz musicians immediately gravitated toward funk, with Miles Davis, Herbie Hancock, Lonnie Smith, and Donald Byrd pioneering jazz-fusion. Jimmy Castor and Rufus Thomas used funk to score a number of weird, danceable novelty hits, while acts such as War, Graham Central Station, and Mandrill fused rock with funk by adding a heavier beat and more distorted guitars.

Artists such as Collins, particularly during his tenure in the George Clinton–masterminded operation Parliament-Funkadelic, pushed the envelope of what was acceptable in black and popular music. Others such as Sly and the Family Stone blurred the lines between rock, soul, and funk music on dense, high-concept albums like *There's a Riot Goin' On*. Silky-smooth soul stars soon incorporated funk into their music, with musicians such as Curtis Mayfield, Stevie Wonder, Al Green, and Marvin Gaye making some of the best music of their careers using strains of funk. Although the genre was dominated by men, which was typical of any genre of the time, Millie Jackson, Betty Davis, and Jean Knight proved that women could add a female-centered perspective to the music and still be just as tough and assertive as their male counterparts.

By the late 1970s the experimental left-of-center nature of funk had been largely smoothed over by the standardized pulsating beat of disco. During the 1980s, when slickness ruled the R&B and pop airwaves, the raw crudeness that characterized funk made it a dirty word again—commercially speaking, at least. By this time many of the most essential funk recordings had gone out of print, and interest in the genre had waned. But the emergence of hip-hop, with its widespread use of 1960s and 1970s funk samples, rejuvenated interest in classic funk recordings by the late 1980s. Referring to a hip-hop song by Eric B. & Rakim that sampled Brown, hip-hop group Stetsasonic rapped in their 1988 song, "Talkin' All That Jazz": "Tell the Truth / James Brown was old / Til Eric B. came out with 'I Got Soul' / Rap brings back old R&B / If we would not / People could have forgot."

As the result of hip-hop artists sampling old funk records and the extensive reissues of funk albums on compact disc, Collins, Clinton, Parker, Brown, and others maintained modestly successful careers throughout the 1990s, touring and releasing records. In the twenty-first century, hybrid styles have emerged, including "punk funk," performed by such bands as Out Hud and Mongolian MonkFish. Women became increasingly influential as well, incorporating urban pop and R&B in their music, as illustrated by Beyoncé Knowles's 2003 hit "Crazy in Love" and Jennifer Lopez's 2005 "Get Right."

Kembrew McLeod

SEE ALSO: *Brown, James; Civil Rights Movement; Clinton, George; Collins, Albert; The Commodores; Davis, Miles; Disco; Gaye, Marvin; Green, Al; Hancock, Herbie; Hip-Hop; Jazz; Knowles, Beyoncé; Mayfield, Curtis; Pop Music; Rhythm and Blues; Rock and Roll; Sly and the Family Stone; Soul Music; Wonder, Stevie.*

BIBLIOGRAPHY

Bolden, Tony. *The Funk Era and Beyond.* New York: Palgrave Macmillan, 2008.

George, Nelson. *The Death of Rhythm and Blues.* New York: Pantheon, 1988.

Vincent, Rickey. *Funk: The Music, the People and the Rhythm of the One.* New York: St. Martin's Griffin, 1996.

Fusco, Coco *(1960–)*

Born Juliana Emilia Fusco Miyares in New York City, Coco Fusco is a Cuban American performance artist, writer, teacher, and cultural critic. Fusco earned a BA in semiotics and literature and society from Brown University in 1982, an MA from Stanford University's modern thought and literature program in 1985, and a doctorate in visual culture from Middlesex University in England in 2007. She has been a full-time faculty member at Parson's The New School for Design. Fusco first worked as a curator and writer and then turned primarily to developing sociopolitically infused performance art that would, as she writes in her book *English Is Broken Here* (1995), "make sense out of the clashes between cultures" that shape Latin identities in the United States. Some of her work has addressed issues of war and gender.

One of her more controversial early works, a pair of *tableaux vivants* titled "Two Undiscovered Aborigines Visit . . . ," was first performed in 1992 to critique the quincentennial celebration of Christopher Columbus's discovery of America. Fusco and collaborator Guillermo Gómez-Pena posed as "exotic" Caribbean islanders in a museum cage for three days, performing what anthropologists call "traditional tasks." As a symbolic act expressing 500 years of resistance to colonial oppression, the piece, as Fusco states in *English Is Broken Here*, performs a "reverse ethnography," blurring the distinctions between art object and body, reality and fantasy, history and dramatic enactment. "Two Undiscovered Aborigines Visit . . . " was invited to several international exhibitions, including the 1993 Whitney Biennial, the 1992 Sydney Biennale, and the 1992 Edge Festival in London and Madrid.

Fusco has brought her performance art on tour to Europe, Australia, the United States, New Zealand, South Africa, Canada, and Latin America. She is also actively committed to identifying—through her journalism, teaching, and curatorial work—films and other art media that have been censored in the United States and abroad. Fusco has published extensively. Her books include *The Bodies That Were Not Ours and Other Writings* (2001); *Only Skin Deep: Changing Visions of the American Self* (2003), which she coedited; and *A Field Guide for Female Interrogators* (2008). Fusco's performance art and other critical inquiries into Latin culture have complicated the erstwhile notion of an "authentic" Latin identity. Her interrogation of identity as formed by senses of nation, race, sexuality, gender, and class has helped to dramatically alter the way ethnicity is understood.

Frederick Luis Aldama

SEE ALSO: *Performance Art.*

BIBLIOGRAPHY

Cotter, Holland. "Caught on Video: Fantasy Interrogation, Real Tension." *New York Times*, May 30, 2006, E3.

Fusco, Coco. *English Is Broken Here: Notes on Cultural Fusion in the Americas.* New York: New Press, 1995.

Fusco, Coco, ed. *Corpus Delecti: Performance Art of the Americas.* London: Routledge, 1999.

Fusco, Coco. *The Bodies That Were Not Ours and Other Writings.* London: Routledge, 2001.

Fusco, Coco, and Brian Wallis, eds. *Only Skin Deep: Changing Visions of the American Self.* New York: Harry Abrams, 2003.

Fusco, Coco. *A Field Guide for Female Interrogators.* New York: Seven Stories Press, 2008.

G

Gable, Clark *(1901–1960)*

An icon of Hollywood's Golden Age, Clark Gable was dubbed "The King," and so he remained, a symbol of commanding virility through dozens of films, three generations of leading ladies, and the eventual decline—but never the end—of his popularity. His own golden age occurred during the 1930s, and his image—tough, confident, and handsome—reached its peak and has spoken to all generations since through the character of Rhett Butler, famously and frankly not giving a damn about loving and leaving the ravishing Scarlett O'Hara (Vivien Leigh) in *Gone with the Wind* (1939).

THE YOUNG GABLE

The word *macho*, not yet in use in the 1930s, might have been coined for Clark Gable. The rough-hewn independence of his screen persona mirrored his own background. Born William Clark Gable in Ohio, the son of an itinerant oil-driller, he left school at sixteen to labor in an Akron factory. It was there that he first saw a play, decided he was destined for a life in the theater, and got himself some bit parts with a stock company before his father took him away to drill oil until he was twenty-one. Penniless, he worked at lumberjacking and other odd jobs until he joined a touring theater company run by Josephine Dillon, a veteran actress seventeen years his senior.

The young Gable was then a gangly youth with jug ears and bad teeth, which Dillon paid to have fixed. She also coached him in acting and, in 1924, became his first wife. (They divorced in 1930.) The couple settled in Hollywood, where Gable picked up a few engagements as a movie extra before going on the road again, eventually making it to Broadway and thereafter to the lead in the Los Angeles production of *The Last Mile*. MGM (Metro-Goldwyn-Mayer) and Warner Brothers both rejected him after screen tests, but he played a villain in a William Boyd Western, *The Painted Desert* (1931), and MGM came back with a contract.

THE MGM YEARS

In 1931 Gable began his twenty-three-year tenure at MGM with a bit part as a laundry man in *The Easiest Way*, and by the end of the year he was a star. Not yet sporting his trademark mustache, the actor had a threatening mien well suited to playing brutes and roughnecks, which he did in several supporting roles before starring as Norma Shearer's gangster lover, slapping her around in *A Free Soul*; costarring in two films—*Laughing Sinners* and *Possessed*—with Joan Crawford, a pairing that made for a potent sexual charge on-screen (and off); and portraying a nobler character as Greta Garbo's ill-used swain in *Susan Lenox (Her Fall and Rise)*. Also that year, he married wealthy socialite Ria Langham, seventeen years his senior.

Swiftly established as the archetypal "man's man"—tough, rugged, and confident, whose good looks and earthy sex appeal also fed the fantasies of legions of women—Gable's rating rose even higher in 1932 with the studio's incendiary combination of the actor with Jean Harlow, their newest female star, in *Red Dust*. They made three more films together before Harlow's untimely death during the filming of their last, *Saratoga* (1937). However, despite Gable's popularity, MGM's choice of vehicles for their premier male star often appeared decidedly odd. Throughout his career, much of the material foisted upon him was run-of-the-mill, and it seemed as though, rather than capitalizing on his charisma to create films of real quality, the

Clark Gable. *With his rugged good looks and confident swagger, Clark Gable was MGM's premier male star in the 1930s.* RUSSELL BALL/JOHN KOBAL FOUNDATION/GETTY IMAGES.

bosses exploited his drawing power to sell the mediocre. Efforts in 1932 to lift him out of the rut of his typecasting were even odder: reunited with Norma Shearer in the film version of Eugene O'Neill's *Strange Interlude* and quaintly, even bizarrely miscast as a clergyman restoring a fallen woman (Marion Davies) to grace in *Polly of the Circus*. But nothing seemed bad enough to tarnish his image or diminish his popularity.

FRANKLY, MY DEAR

Gable, though, was increasingly unhappy and made his dissatisfaction known. In what studio head Louis B. Mayer viewed as disciplinary action to contain his moneymaking asset's recalcitrance, Mayer lent a reluctant Gable to Columbia, which was then a Poverty Row studio, for a comedy to be directed by Frank Capra. The film was *It Happened One Night* (1934) featuring Claudette Colbert as a runaway heiress who finds herself mixed up with a down-on-his-luck journalist looking for a scoop. The film was a masterpiece of screwball comedy, and Capra took full advantage of Gable's range. With the famous mustache now well in place, he delivered a thoroughly delightful characterization embodying his down-to-earth practicality, good-natured cockiness, recklessness, charm, humor, and tenderness. It was neither the first nor last newspaperman he played, but this one brought Gable his only Academy Award and the first of his two most enduring successes.

Back at MGM, Gable turned in an Oscar-nominated performance in *Mutiny on the Bounty* (1935), was perfectly cast in *San Francisco* (1936), survived a disaster as the Irish politician *Parnell* (1937), and was everybody's ideal *Test Pilot* (1938). But 1939 was the year in which Gable ensured his immortality as a Hollywood icon. *Gone with the Wind* swept the board at the Oscars, except for Gable as Rhett Butler, who, though nominated, lost out to Britain's Robert Donat.

Gable, separated from his second wife since 1935, had become involved with Carole Lombard, his costar in *No Man of Her Own* (1932). She proved the great love of his life, and, in the midst of filming *Gone with the Wind*, Gable married her in a partnership that was swiftly recognized as a fairy-tale romance. Three years later the beautiful and gifted Lombard was killed in a plane crash. A devastated Gable dealt with the shock by joining the U.S. Air Force, where he rose to the rank of major, and was off the screen until 1945.

RETURN TO HOLLYWOOD

His return to MGM in *Adventure*, publicized with the phrase "Gable's Back and [Greer] Garson's Got Him," was not successful and marked the start of the slow decline of the star's postwar career. Prematurely aged and drinking heavily, he attempted unsuccessfully to find happiness in a brief fourth marriage to Lady Sylvia Ashley, something of a Lombard lookalike, while his film output steadily decreased, despite teamings with stars such as Lana Turner and Hedy Lamarr. His public still held him in affection, however, and there were a few last successes, notably *The Hucksters* (1947), with Deborah Kerr, and *Mogambo* (1953), a remake of *Red Dust* with Ava Gardner subbing for Harlow, in which Gable was as charismatic as ever.

Gable's MGM contract expired in 1954, and his last years were spent as a freelancer in films of little distinction except for a few interesting Westerns (*The Tall Men*, 1955) in the "veteran cowboy" tradition to which he had proved himself well suited. In 1955 he married his fifth wife, Kay Spreckels, another Lombard type, who was pregnant in 1960 when Gable joined Marilyn Monroe and Montgomery Clift on location in the Nevada desert for John Huston's *The Misfits*. Written by Arthur Miller, the bleak and powerful portrait of lost men roping wild stallions to sell was deeply ironic in that the protagonists were as doomed off-screen as their characters were in the film. The production was fraught with difficulties, and Gable, who insisted on doing his own stunts, was exhausted by the physical demands this made on him. His weighty performance, considered by some to be his best ever, was his last. He suffered a fatal heart attack at age fifty-nine, shortly after *The Misfits* finished shooting. Hollywood mourned the passing of its only king.

Robyn Karney

SEE ALSO: *Academy Awards; Broadway; Capra, Frank; Celebrity Couples; Clift, Montgomery; Colbert, Claudette; Crawford, Joan; Garbo, Greta; Gardner, Ava;* Gone with the Wind*; Harlow, Jean; Hollywood; Huston, John;* It Happened One Night*; Lamarr, Hedy; Lombard, Carole; Mayer, Louis B.; MGM (Metro-Goldwyn-Mayer); Miller, Arthur; Monroe, Marilyn; Movie Stars;* Mutiny on the Bounty*; O'Neill, Eugene; Sex Symbol; Turner, Lana; Young, Loretta.*

BIBLIOGRAPHY

Samuels, Charles. *The King, a Biography of Clark Gable*. New York: Coward-McCann, 1962.

Shipman, David. *The Great Movie Stars: The Golden Years*. London; Sydney: Angus & Robertson, 1982.

Spicer, Chrystopher J. *Clark Gable: Biography, Filmography, Bibliography*. Jefferson, NC: McFarland, 2002.

Thomson, David. *A Biographical Dictionary of Film*. New York: Alfred A. Knopf, 1994.

Tornabene, Lyn. *Long Live the King*. London: W. H. Allen, 1977.

Gambling

From television programs such as *Wheel of Fortune* and state lotteries to online casinos and televised poker tournaments, the gambling spirit is everywhere in American life and culture. Gambling has spread from tawdry, out-of-the-way locations such as Las Vegas, Nevada, to major U.S. cities. Online gambling has evolved from simple computer games of chance to an estimated $35 billion industry still considered illegal by the U.S. Department of Justice. Variously blamed on deindustrialization, a decline in the American work ethic, and a lapse in moral values, gambling's something-for-nothing mentality has become an important element of the American consciousness. Long considered a refined diversion for the wealthy or a last chance for the down-on-their-luck, only technology and style separate twenty-first-century gambling from its primeval counterparts.

ROOTS

Gambling, the betting or staking of something of value, is as old as humankind itself. Betting on horses began as soon as the animals were domesticated, and gambling's ties to sports date back as far as 1450 BCE, when Egyptians competed against each other in jumping, wrestling, and ball game competitions, centuries before the first Greek Olympics. As many as 250,000 spectators watched, and gambled on, chariot races in Rome's Circus Maximus. Gospel writers Matthew and Mark report that Roman guards gambled for Jesus's garments following his Crucifixion, "casting lots upon them, what every man should take." Towns challenged towns in medieval archery matches, and gambling was an ever-present accompaniment as sports competitions became organized in Europe during the Renaissance and early modern periods.

In the New World, special days were set aside by the Northwest Coast Indians for *mook-te-lo*, or wagering on games. The Iroquois played a betting game called *hubbub* with dice made from peach stones. Participants hit themselves on the chest and thighs, crying "Hub Hub Hub!" so loudly that they could be heard a quarter of a mile away, according to a contemporary report. The first deck of cards to be manufactured in the Western Hemisphere was made by Christopher Columbus's crew in 1492. According to the story, the sailors threw their European cards overboard because they believed gambling was bringing them ill fortune during their long voyage. Once ashore in the New World, they regretted their impulsive behavior and made substitute decks from the large leaves of the copas tree. Lotteries, begun in England in 1566, were approved for the new Jamestowne settlement in Virginia by King James I in 1612. Proceeds were used to sustain the struggling colony until the king withdrew his permission in 1621.

The Puritans first objected to popular recreations like gambling during the seventeenth century because they violated sabbatarian principles. In the Puritans' distinctive mixture of capitalism and Calvinism, gambling was a double sin: a violation of the Lord's day of rest and an ungodly diversion from work the other six days of the week. Puritans had little success convincing Europeans to stop betting, but they established strict statutes against gambling and other worldly distractions in their early American settlements beginning in 1638. The Puritans' holy opposition to gambling faded in the New England colonies during the eighteenth century, and they never had as much influence on mid-Atlantic and southern colonists, but the Puritan association of gaming and wagering with alcoholism, idleness, and ungodliness became a recurrent theme in numerous antigambling crusades during the nineteenth and twentieth centuries.

Lotteries were a common recourse for eighteenth-century American colonists in search of funds for wars, schools, charities, or other purposes. George Washington himself bought and sold lottery tickets, and Benjamin Franklin spoke in favor of a lottery to finance the purchase of a cannon battery for Philadelphia in 1748. Once-Puritan Massachusetts authorized a lottery in 1758 to fund an expedition against Canada during the French and Indian Wars.

Gambling was still considered a vice, however, and during the first days of the American Revolution, various colonial committees of safety opposed it. General George Washington, a frequent gambler at cards, forbade gambling among his soldiers when it distracted them from their military duties, even during the grueling winter at Valley Forge. However, the Continental Congress sponsored a national lottery in 1777. They promoted it as a contribution "to the great and glorious American cause," only to be disappointed by the proceeds: it seems the loosely knit colonists failed to gamble as freely as their more sophisticated English counterparts.

GAMBLING IN EARLY AMERICA

Gambling was a primary diversion throughout the rough-and-tumble new American country. Thoroughbred horse racing, cockfights, card games, and billiards, as well as fighting over the outcome of such contests, were favorite pastimes of eighteenth-century frontier inhabitants. Gambling, alcoholism, prostitution, and related social vices continued to be associated with the frontier as it spread westward throughout the nineteenth century. The Louisiana Purchase of 1803 opened the western Ohio River and the Mississippi River, and as commerce developed on the waterways, so did gambling. New Orleans, Louisiana, evolved as America's first gambling city, as flatboat men, farmers, and plantation owners played a French card game of *poque*. With a few modifications, draw poker became the quintessential American card game. Gambling was outlawed in the rest of the huge Louisiana territory in 1811 in the wake of a popular antigambling tract written by Mason Locke Weems (better known for authorship of the myth about Washington chopping down the cherry tree), but gambling remained a critical component of New Orleans's economy and politics for another century.

The first American gambling casino was opened in New Orleans around 1822. Owner John Davis provided gourmet food, liquor, roulette wheels, faro tables, poker, and other games; made certain that prostitutes were never far away; and kept his clubhouse open twenty-four hours a day. Dozens of imitators soon made gaming, drink, and women of easy virtue the primary attractions of New Orleans. The city's status as an international port and its thriving gambling industry created a new profession, the card sharper. Professional gamblers and cheats gathered in a waterfront area known as the Swamp, an area even the police were afraid to frequent, and any gambler lucky enough to win stood a good chance of losing his earnings to thieves outside of the gambling rooms and saloons. The slot machine, invented by Charles Fey in San Francisco in 1894, first became popular with New Orleans gamblers. Reform movements struggled to limit gambling and prostitution to a red-light district, until military restrictions put the halls and brothels out of business during World War I.

The nineteenth-century relationship between gambling and western expansion was epitomized by the early West's favorite son, President Andrew Jackson. Although not the first president to gamble openly, Jackson bet with such intensity that he created an image that came to stereotype all Westerners. He bet on cards, lotteries, and cockfights, but he preferred horse racing, a sport suited to his western Tennessee roots. Jackson hated losing, and his advice to a nephew summarized not only his personality but also the mood of the entire nation during his presidential term: "You must risk to win."

New frontier settlements risked everything for success, and those that prospered almost always embraced gambling. Chicago was founded in 1837, the same year it ostensibly outlawed gambling, but gaming "hells" continued to flourish, along with drunkenness and prostitution. By 1849 there were as many gambling establishments in Chicago per capita as in New York City, and more than 1,000 women were said to be employed as prostitutes in 1856.

Gambling thrived in the South as well. Horse racing was the most popular sport for betting, and formal racing sessions were organized by the upper class in Williamsburg, Fredericksburg, and Alexandria, Virginia, and Annapolis, Maryland, well before the Revolutionary War. Slaves rode southern racehorses until replaced by white riders after the Civil War, inspiring the black-jockey lawn ornaments that persisted well into the twentieth century. The development of the telegraph, especially with a modification permitting the transmission of more than one message at a time, allowed gambling from a distance and made betting on the races a major business in the South. (The first sports pages in U.S. newspapers were reports on horse racing.)

As interest in professional baseball increased after the Civil War, the sport began attracting gamblers. The Chicago "Black Sox" scandal of 1919, which saw the best team in baseball lose a World Series on purpose, was predated by the 1877 Louisville Greys, who threw enough games to slide from a comfortable first-place lead in the National League to being a late season also-ran.

Steamboats and riverfront gambling houses along the lower Mississippi attracted swarms of professional gamblers. A host of companies specialized in manufacturing and selling card-cheating devices. One riverboat gambler named George Devol was so proud of his ability to slip a stacked deck into a game that he once used four of them in one poker hand, dealing four aces to each of his four opponents. Devol bragged of his exploits in his 1887 memoir, *Forty Years a Gambler on the Mississippi*. Children looked upon such professional gamblers as heroic figures. "To me as a boy, the gambler was an object of awed admiration," sportswriter Hugh Fullerton recalled of his southern boyhood in the 1870s. But anxious townsfolk viewed the presence of such men as a vestige of an unruly frontier past. Five cardsharps were lynched by vigilantes in Vicksburg, Mississippi, in 1835, less for religious reasons than to preserve civic respectability, and other river cities applied similar, if less stringent, preventives. Still, the riverboat gambler came to symbolize freedom in dime novels and other popular literature, even though most died poor.

California established a reputation for professional gambling as well. In the wake of the 1848 gold rush, European traveler Friedrich Wilhelm Christian Gerstacker observed that "gambling houses are now to California what slave-holding is to the United States." Professional gamblers became so wealthy and influential that they managed to become controlling political forces in the state for short periods.

In San Francisco gamblers played all day and all night at games that were refined into a high-volume industry. Rather than cheating and deceit, the city's gambling saloons relied on percentages and odds for their profits, foreshadowing the Las Vegas casinos a century later. Miners did not seem to mind. San Francisco gambling mirrored the entire gold-rush mentality that "the fun would be worth a fortune almost," as one contemporary wrote. Professional gamblers were an implicit, if not sanctioned, part of the casino scene, until journalist and businessman James King launched such a vigorous crusade against them that he was murdered in 1856. In response, his alleged killer and a professional dealer named Charles Cora were lynched by vigilantes. Nonetheless, gaming continued in San Francisco, on a less ostentatious scale, into the 1910s.

TWENTIETH-CENTURY GAMBLING

Gambling continued to flourish throughout the frontier West during the remainder of the nineteenth century. Virginia City, Comstock, and Deadwood became as well known for faro and gunfights over card games as they did for mineral wealth. Even cattle towns such as Dodge City, Kansas, had forty saloons and gambling houses to cater to the cowboys, buffalo hunters, and railroad workers who visited it in 1875. But prohibition was in the wind. Scandals involving lottery ticket sales, including a massive fraud in the Louisiana lottery in 1894; the rise of baseball and other spectator sports; and a revival of moral concerns about idleness, drunkenness, and debauchery led to laws against lotteries and gambling in most states by 1910. "Puritanism [was] the inflexible doctrine of Los Angeles," one historian noted. By 1908, 289 of the nation's 314 Thoroughbred horse race tracks had been closed.

Horse racing was the first gambling industry to be reborn. Colonel Matt J. Winn, president of Churchill Downs, dusted off old pari-mutuel machines stored in the back of the track's storehouse, banished illegal bookmakers, and made sure that the state of Kentucky got a share of every bet made at his track. Pari-mutuel horse wagering was legalized in other states, especially during the cash-strapped Depression years. State racing boards or commissions supervised the tracks, reducing cutthroat competition and providing an aura of respectability for a public concerned about the connection between gambling and crime.

Professional gamblers remained, epitomized by George E. Smith, better known as "Pittsburgh Phil," who made horse betting into a science. Bookmakers prospered off track as well, aided by advances in communication such as radio. Numbers games were introduced to Harlem, New York, by West Indian immigrants in the 1920s and spread to other cities. Manufactured games such as pull tabs and punch boards appeared in rural areas, as did illegal slot machines and other electronic devices. Nearly one out of three Americans admitted gambling on church-sponsored bingo games and lotteries in a 1938 Gallup poll.

Most casinos and "gambling hells" were shut down during the early 1900s, even in such obscure locations as French Lick, Indiana, and Canton, Ohio. True to the worst fears of the Puritans, gangsters combined liquor and gambling in New York; Cleveland, Ohio; Chicago; and other cities during the 1920s. Florida temporarily legalized slot machines during the depths of the Depression at about the same time that El Monte and Gardena, California, licensed poker. But it was a dusty little Nevada town located on the Old Spanish Trail that reintroduced casinos and gambling to twentieth-century America.

THE RISE OF LAS VEGAS

What would become Las Vegas was established as a Mormon mission before the Civil War. Its future was assured when the San Pedro, Los Angeles & Salt Lake Railroad laid track to it in 1904, and three other railroads, including the Union Pacific, followed suit. The railroads were initially the town's primary employer. Although gambling was banned in Nevada in 1909, Las Vegas continued to grow, reaching a population of 5,165 in 1930. It remained a railroad town until divorce and gambling laws were relaxed, and in that year the federal government began the construction of Hoover Dam. The first major hotel, the 100-room Apache, opened in 1932 to augment an active red-light district patronized by dam workers. Still, Las Vegas continued to be outpaced by its primary competitor, Reno, and boasted only six casinos and sixteen saloons in 1939.

Post–World War II improvements in automobiles and highways, especially to and from Los Angeles, forever changed Las Vegas. Downtown's Fremont Street became "Glitter Gulch" and the vacant Las Vegas Boulevard was renamed the "Strip." Three casinos opened in 1946, including mobster Benjamin "Bugsy" Siegel's Flamingo Hotel. Motion pictures such as the 1952 *Las Vegas Story*, starring Jane Russell and Victor Mature, and the 1960 *Ocean's Eleven*, which featured the "Rat Pack"—Peter Lawford, Sammy Davis Jr., Frank Sinatra, Dean Martin, and Joey Bishop—promoted the growing sophistication of Las Vegas. The movies helped establish gambling as adult entertainment in a decade noted for its juvenile attractions. They also helped erase gambling's disreputable, low-class image. Las Vegas's gambling industry survived and even thrived under scrutiny from investigators led by Senator Estes Kefauver (Democrat from Tennessee). His Special Committee on Organized Crime in Interstate Commerce leaned heavily on gambling during the early 1950s, but only a few of the committee's proposals were enacted.

The Golden Nugget was the first Las Vegas property created specifically as a hotel-casino, but every hotel provided gambling. Eventually all would feature big-name entertainment, led by pianist Liberace, who headlined the new Riviera in 1955. The city's reputation as the "last frontier" not only served as a recurring casino and hotel theme but also intensified the gambling experience. Just as thrill seekers had swarmed San Francisco's casinos a century earlier, gamblers escaped their ordinary lives in the fantasy world of Las Vegas, surrounded by flashing lights and jingling coins, visual and auditory noise that heightened the thrills of gambling.

Sports betting became popular, influenced in part by the banning of Pete Rose from baseball in 1989. Beginning with construction of the Mirage that same year, more than a dozen mega-resorts were built in Las Vegas before 2010. While some were aimed at families, most were opulent playgrounds designed and marketed for adults, leading to the city's "What happens here, stays here" 2003 advertising slogan. Motion pictures such as *Showgirls* (1995); *Rat Race* (2001); the remade *Ocean's Eleven* (2001), along with *Ocean's Twelve* (2004) and *Ocean's Thirteen* (2007); and *The Hangover* (2009), as well as the television series *CSI: Crime Scene Investigation* (2000–), all glamorized Las Vegas as one of the world's top gambling cities. They also helped make it the second-most-recognized brand in the United States, after Google, even as the city suffered through the 2008 Great Recession and the home mortgage crisis.

NEWER DEVELOPMENTS

Beginning with New Hampshire in 1964, lotteries spread to more than forty states and jurisdictions, usually claiming to devote a percentage of the profits to state education or other activities. Critics pointed to a practice in some states of reducing public education funding by roughly the same amount as lottery contributions, effectively negating them. Others suggested that state lotteries contributed to gambling addictions or promoted an ethos of luck rather than work among the young. Multistate lotteries offered payouts of as much as $390 million in the early twenty-first century.

The first legal casino in the United States outside of Nevada opened on the Boardwalk of Atlantic City, New Jersey, in 1978. Gaming on Indian Reservations, the so-called return of the buffalo, was relegalized by Congress in 1988. Tribes across the country constructed casinos and hotel-casinos almost as glitzy as those in Las Vegas and used the profits to bolster their dying cultures and communities. Around 400 Native American gaming establishments operated in the United States in the early twenty-first century, representing some 220 federally recognized tribes. Meanwhile the numbers of river and lake boats, off-track and bingo parlors, and dog- and horse-racing tracks vying for what economists call discretionary funds declined due to competition from more opulent casinos and natural complications such as Hurricane Katrina.

The first online gambling casino appeared in 1994 and was followed by sports-betting, poker, and other individual game sites, many based in foreign countries. In comparison to nonvirtual gaming, regulations on Internet gambling were difficult to enforce. As online gaming spread, the U.S. Justice Department held that a 1961 federal law banned online bets that crossed state or national borders, and a 2006 law made it illegal for American businesses to accept payments from online betting sites. However, the Justice Department softened its position in 2012, allowing states to sell lottery tickets online. Proponents argued that online poker and other sites could generate $2 billion or more in new tax revenues for cash-strapped governments and provide protection for players at risk of unscrupulous operators.

Altogether, gambling generated more revenues in the early twenty-first century than theme parks, video games, movie tickets, and music recordings combined. What had once been a sin was remerchandised into an economic and social virtue. However, the qualities of desperation and greed that guarantee success to gambling enterprises also impel those who become their victims. "Gambling is the child of avarice, the brother of iniquity, and the father of mischief," wrote George Washington, and, whether the gambling is for fun or charity, that argument seems to remain the same.

Richard Junger

SEE ALSO: *Atlantic City; Black Sox Scandal; CSI; Dime Novels; Great Recession; Las Vegas; Liberace; Lottery; Rose, Pete; Siegel, Bugsy; Twelve-Step Programs.*

BIBLIOGRAPHY

Brenner, Reuven, and Gabrielle A. Brenner. *Gambling and Speculation: A Theory, a History, and a Future of Some Human Decisions.* Cambridge, UK: Cambridge University Press, 1990.

Burnham, John C. *Bad Habits: Drinking, Smoking, Taking Drugs, Gambling, Sexual Misbehavior, and Swearing in American History.* New York: New York University Press, 1993.

Christiansen, Eugene Martin. "Gambling and the American Economy." *Annals of the American Academy of Political and Social Science* 556, no. 1 (1998): 36–52.

Cooper, Michael. "As States Weigh Online Gambling, Profit May Be Small." *New York Times*, January 17, 2012.

Fabian, Ann. *Card Sharps, Dreambooks, & Bucket Shops: Gambling in 19th-Century America.* Ithaca, NY: Cornell University Press, 1990.

Haley, James. *Gambling: Examining Pop Culture.* San Diego, CA: Greenhaven Press, 2004.

Lane, Ambrose I., Sr. *Return of the Buffalo: The Story behind America's Indian Gaming Explosion.* Westport, CT: Bergin and Garvey, 1995.

McGowan, Richard. *The Gambling Debate.* Westport, CT: Greenwood Press, 2008.

Weyler, Karen A. "'A Speculating Spirit': Trade, Speculation, and Gambling in Early American Fiction." *Early American Literature* 31, no. 3 (1996): 207–242.

Game Shows

It is not surprising that the game show has been one of the most enduring mass media formats. Combining entertainment and competition, celebrities and ordinary people, populism and the promise of instant success, game shows have tapped into elemental parts of the collective American psyche. America's most acute "quiz mania" occurred during the decades from the 1930s until the mid-1950s as a new incarnation of the American dream in which ordinary people, through luck and pluck, could rise from rags to riches overnight.

EARLY QUIZ SHOWS ON THE RADIO

One of the first quiz programs appeared fairly early in radio's history. To increase its readership, *Time* magazine aired current events quizzes over the radio with *The Pop Question Game*, which lasted from 1923 to 1926. Other early radio contests of the 1920s included *The Brunswick Hour Musical Memory Contest*, *Do You Know*, and *Ask Me Another*. The Depression years also encouraged Americans' interest in game shows and quiz contests. Because listening to the radio was still free in an era of tight budgets and unemployment, people flocked to their sets for diversion. Local movie theaters picked up on the game craze by offering bingo games and bank nights to lure people in with the promise of affordable entertainment and the possibility of winning prize money.

People were attracted to quizzes for these practical purposes, but the shows also tapped into more elemental needs and desires, such as the pursuit of fame. During the Depression people experienced both economic and social hardships. They often felt like they were "lost in the crowd," their individual needs abandoned by governmental and financial institutions. In 1932 workers at the Houston radio station KTRH tried to counteract this malaise by taking a microphone outside and asking passersby their opinions on the Franklin Roosevelt–Herbert Hoover election and other more random questions. First called *Sidewalk Interviews* and later renamed *Vox Pop*, the show, which offered prize money to its participants, lasted until 1948 and spawned similar interview shows all across the country.

Professor Quiz, originating in the mid-1930s in Washington, D.C., was the first genuine money quiz. The show not only awarded money to individual contestants but also sent money to people who submitted questions used on the air, immediately increasing participation from the on-air contestants to, potentially, the entire listening audience. In this way even the early radio quiz shows spurred national interest and involvement, making them games of mass culture and mass appeal. *Professor Quiz*, for example, was so successful that within two years it had inspired more than 200 variations, including a very popular version called *Dr. I.Q.* Other shows emphasized mental acuity by asking difficult questions. Of these, *The Answer Man*,

The Price Is Right. *Host Bob Barker watches a contestant spin the wheel on the popular television game show* The Price Is Right. CLIFF LIPSON/CBS PHOTO ARCHIVE/GETTY IMAGES.

running for almost twenty years, was one of the most popular. It combined information and entertainment, becoming a frequent bet settler and voice of authority.

The format of another show, *Information Please*, was designed to stump a panel of experts rather than the common man. Indeed, appearing as the weekly guest on the panel was a source of prestige and often attracted entertainers and politicians to sit with the regular panelists. Created by Dan Golenpaul and launched in 1938, *Information Please* was so popular that in 1939 it had boosted sponsor Canada Dry's sales by 20 percent. In addition, in one of the first quiz show promotional tie-ins, there were items of spin-off merchandise, including *Information Please* home games and the still-active *Information Please Almanac and Yearbook*. This game and others like it (including a version for younger participants called *Quiz Kids*) gave the public new role models beyond sports and film stars, adding credibility and worth to intellectuals and academicians. Quiz language even entered the vernacular: the phrase "the $64 question," meaning a particularly tough question, came from *Take It or Leave It*, a popular gambling-based game show.

Like other media programming, quiz shows reflected the interests of the times. The big band influence of the late 1930s led to the creation of Kay Kyser's *Kollege of Musical Knowledge*, which ran for several seasons; *Melody Puzzle*; *Beat the Band*; and *So You Think You Know Music*, among others. During World War II "quiz programs and audience-participation shows stressed themes of patriotism and sacrifice, while boosting morale and offering a measure of 'escapist' cheer," notes historian Thomas DeLong in *Quiz Craze: America's Infatuation with Game Shows*. These shows often featured members of the armed forces, asked questions about the war itself, encouraged men to enlist, raised money for war bonds, and frequently awarded war stamps and bonds as prizes.

QUIZ SHOWS ON TELEVISION

After the war, quiz shows once again returned to emphasizing individual pursuits and pleasures, clearly expressing America's postwar preoccupations. Consumption and the possession of goods were seen as a solution to many personal problems and served as psychological and material relief after wartime rationing. Beginning in 1946 manufacturers shifted their production away from military products and back to domestic goods, but these items were still in short supply. Many game shows whetted the consumer appetite by taking place on location in department and grocery stores—traditional sites of merchandise display and mass consumption. Their titles included *Bride and Groom*, *Second Honeymoon*, *Missus Goes a-Shopping*, and *Give and Take*. In 1948 the four major radio networks alone gave away about $83,000 a week in merchandise spread over fifty-four programs, totaling more than $4.2 million by year's end. *Go for the House* offered the grand prize of a fully furnished house; *Break the Bank* presented the chance at a $5,000 jackpot; and *Stop the Music*, hosted by Bert Parks, featured, in addition to a wealth of prizes, a jackpot that accrued weekly. This show and others like it, in which the studio called a random person who was listening to the show at home, even sparked an increased purchase of telephones so that people could feel as if they had an equal chance of participating.

Encouraging women's return to the domestic sphere after their wartime factory work, many shows blatantly pandered specifically to perceived female desires. *Ladies Be Seated*, hosted by Johnny Olson, involved women performing pranks for merchandise. Perhaps the most unfortunate example of this genre was *Queen for a Day* (1945–1964), which was more an audience-participation show than a quiz show. On this program women told various tales of woe, from dead or out-of-work husbands to sick relatives and impending house foreclosures. The "winner"—the woman deemed by the judges to be in the worst straits—received prizes meant to fulfill her special wishes. *Queen for a Day* did not showcase the intellect of the common man but instead spotlighted and exploited the financial and emotional burdens of the common woman, an early form of mass media therapy and confessional that presaged the daytime television talk shows of the 1980s and 1990s.

Another show, *Strike It Rich*, similarly exploited people's misfortunes but also required them to answer questions to receive cash and prizes. Various sponsors telephoned the "Heart Line," offering donations to these needy people while at the same time receiving on-air promotions. *New York Times* critic Jack Gould said at the time that the show "callously exploits human anxiety to sell the products of a soap manufacturer and does it with a saccharine solicitude that hits the jackpot in bad taste."

Successful radio emcees of the 1940s included John Reed King, Parks, Bud Collyer, Jack Barry, Olson, Bill Slater, and Bill Cullen, and many of them were equally successful when the quiz shows went to televised broadcasts. The first televised quiz shows appeared in 1941: *Uncle Jim's Question Bee* (hosted by Slater) and *Truth or Consequences* (hosted by Ralph Edwards). Indeed, many of these former radio shows easily translated to television and were often broadcast simultaneously in both mediums. New shows were also developed to take advantage of the visual aspects of television and its burgeoning stable of talent. *Telequizzicals* and *Pantomime Quiz* were both based on charades, and the latter featured guest appearances by actors such as Roddy McDowall, Lucille Ball, Steve Allen, and Danny Thomas. In 1949 *Pantomime Quiz* won television's first Emmy Award as its most popular show.

Tremendous popularity often brings a backlash, however, and in the late 1940s game shows experienced a wave of negative publicity. People began to feel that the shows emphasized money at the expense of talent and intellect. The 1950 film *The Jackpot*, starring Jimmy Stewart, depicts the problems a man faces after winning prize money, which, far from bringing instant happiness, almost ruins his life. In effect a morality tale, the film points out many of the reservations people had about instantly winning, rather than earning, money and merchandise. Additionally, the Federal Communications Commission (FCC) in 1948, in an attempt to improve the quality of programming in general, tried to outlaw most quiz shows as a form of a broadcast lottery, which was then illegal. After many legal maneuverings, the courts ruled in 1953 that banning quiz shows from the airwaves would constitute censorship and thus allowed them to continue.

The standard game shows of the late 1940s and early 1950s nevertheless sank in popularity and were replaced with comedy shows. The game shows that did appear on the air were, not surprisingly, influenced by this new trend and included such offerings as *Tag the Gag*, *Stop Me if You've Heard This One*, *Draw Me a Laugh*, *Draw to Win*, *Quixie Doodles*, Groucho Marx's *You Bet Your Life*, and *Beat the Clock*. The last, the most popular of the comedy quiz shows, was born of the prolific game show production team of Mark Goodson and Bill Todman. *Beat the Clock*, combining circus influences and sight gags, required people to successfully perform very difficult stunts in a limited time. Future playwright Neil Simon helped write the show's stunts, while future actor and screen idol James Dean auditioned them in front of test audiences.

The early 1950s also saw the winning combination of Hollywood talent and intellectual prowess in popular panel games, which featured celebrities and were hosted by academicians. The number of veterans who had recently completed their studies with the help of the GI Bill meant that there were more educated people who found entertainment both as contestants and as audience members for quiz shows. The stars who appeared on these panels also benefited from this arrangement—the work paid well, afforded good publicity for an entertainer, showcased comedic talent, and often helped revitalize the careers of older comedians and actors.

What's My Line? which began in 1950, was one of the longest-running shows on television, becoming a Sunday night fixture on CBS for more than seventeen years. In this program, panels, by asking yes or no questions, were enlisted to guess the unusual occupation of the night's guest. Over the years panelists included such well-known entertainers as Steve Allen, Fred Allen, Arlene Francis, Errol Flynn, Ronald Reagan, Ernie Kovacs, and Jane Powell. Special guests included actor Fredric March, Mike Todd and his new wife Elizabeth Taylor, Frank Lloyd Wright, Gerald Ford, Jimmy Carter, Milton Berle, and Art Carney. *What's My Line?* inspired a slew of more and less successful imitations, including *The Name's the Same*, *I've Got a Secret* (with Bess Myerson, Henry Morgan, Betsy Palmer, and Bill Cullen), and *To Tell the Truth* (with Kitty Carlisle, Peggy Cass, Tom Poston, and Orson Bean). The panel shows amassed devoted followers who tuned in every week to witness the banter of their old friends; these followers were so loyal that they guaranteed the success of the shows even in the face of the quiz show scandals of the mid- and late 1950s.

BIG MONEY AND BIGGER SCANDALS

The $64,000 Question (1955–1958) was the first big-money television quiz show and was inspired by *Take It or Leave It*'s "$64 question." Incorporating a televisual aesthetic that would reappear in such shows as *The Price Is Right* and *Wheel of Fortune*, *The $64,000 Question* was described by *Newsweek*, at the time of its first airing, as "vaguely sleazy . . . compounded of beaverboard and sequins, liberally decorated with the name of the sponsor." The show was also referred to as the "Mount Everest" of quizzes because, to reach the peak prize, contestants had to return in subsequent weeks to risk their winnings to date for double the amount, beginning at $8,000. *The $64,000 Question*, along with *The $64,000 Challenge* and *Twenty-One*, created ongoing televisual dramas that pitted contestants against each other and provided suspense for the viewing audience. In addition, these shows created overnight folk heroes in their winners, who were equal parts intellectual and common man. Many were offered university lectureships, commercial endorsements, and guest appearances on television shows.

Although audiences believed that the player-against-player drama was naturally inspired by the tension of the games themselves, in actuality many of the contestants were coached by show producers. *Twenty-One* was the first show to blatantly use coaching as a method to create more on-air drama and to force larger stakes in order to draw a larger viewership. Out of greed and actual financial need, Herbert Stempel, a homely Jewish ex-soldier working his way through the City College of New York, knowingly participated in the fraud perpetuated by producer Daniel Enright. Enright coached Stempel, who had a photographic memory, about the correct answers to questions to be posed on air. When Enright realized that Stempel was not a popular contestant, he recruited Ivy League graduate Charles Van Doren, who was tall and aristocratically handsome—and wanted the prize money to be financially independent of his family. Although Van Doren was at first reluctant to cheat, the producers convinced him that his repeated appearances on *Twenty-One* would be a good influence on national attitudes about teachers, education, and intellectual life. Relenting, he lasted for fifteen telecasts, accumulating $143,000 (the largest amount won on a quiz show up to that time). He also received marriage proposals and was offered a regular spot on the *Today* show.

Stempel, angered at having to "take a dive," began to expose the quiz show rigging to journalists, who in 1957 discovered more jilted contestants and began formal investigations into the fraud at this and many other shows, including *Tic Tac Dough* and *Dotto*. Van Doren, after numerous protestations to the contrary, finally testified before a grand jury in 1959, admitting his collusion in the rigging of *Twenty-One*. He resigned his position at Columbia and the day after that was fired from *Today*. Eventually he took a position as a columnist for *Leisure* magazine and found regular employment as an editor at the *Encyclopaedia Britannica*. Ironically, Van Doren was seen by many as a sympathetic figure, and the media compared him to Chicago White Sox player "Shoeless" Joe Jackson, who fixed the 1919 baseball World Series, in what came to be known as the Black Sox Scandal.

The scandals not only ended the impressive reign of the quiz shows but also forced larger cultural discussions about the nature of American morality and the role of television "entertainment." To the media's chagrin, the general public lacked outrage, believing the issue to be irrelevant. Some in the television industry, in fact, claimed that the print media exaggerated the scandal in order to penalize a rival medium; yet these same people took steps to minimize the scandal's fallout, canceling all dubious shows and temporarily banning canned laughter and applause. CBS even went so far as to cancel Edward R. Murrow's six-year-old and respected *Person to Person* interview show because it was "rehearsed."

The Price Is Right, which first aired in 1956, weathered the scandal days to become one of the most popular game shows in America. Originally hosted by Cullen, it encouraged the American consumer ethos by not only awarding prizes but also rewarding people who were good shoppers—people who could come closer than their rivals to guessing the retail prices of goods (anything from a box of detergent to a yacht), without going over, would then win those goods. After a seven-year hiatus, *The Price Is Right* returned to the air in 1972 hosted by the avuncular Bob Barker. It featured a glitzy studio and beautiful models who caressed the items "offered up for bid" and were as objectified as the goods themselves. Chosen Middle-American audience members were exhorted by the announcer to "Come on down!" to be the next contestant, echoing the populist strains of the early quiz shows.

REIMAGINING THE GENRE

The quiz shows of the 1960s, in order to distance themselves from the scandals, renamed themselves "game" shows and stayed away from big money prizes. *Jeopardy!*, created by former game show host Merv Griffin in 1964, reversed the normal question-and-answer format by providing an answer and requiring contestants to supply the question. It was wildly popular, especially among college students who regularly skipped class to watch it. Its original host, Art Fleming, was replaced by Alex Trebek in 1984. The 1970s saw a decrease in the number of and enthusiasm for game shows. As DeLong writes, "It seemed clear that prize money had become less of a riveting attraction to viewers and contestants alike. For the thousands who lined up at a game show studio with the hope of being selected as a contestant, it was less the promise of dollars and merchandise. The lure was television itself."

Producer and game show host Chuck Barris, who referred to his shows as "popcorn for the mind," capitalized on this new attitude with the double entendre–filled *The Dating Game*, *The Newlywed Game*, and *The Gong Show*. *Let's Make a Deal* with Monty Hall also lured Americans looking for televised attention—the most outlandishly costumed people were chosen out of the audience by Hall to be the day's contestants. These shows reflected the increasing desire among the populace for fame rather than fortune. The longing to appear on television in front of millions of viewers seemed to take precedence over anything else—even prize money.

Notable shows of the 1970s and 1980s included *The $100,000 Pyramid* with Dick Clark and new versions of old shows, including *Super Password*, *The $1,000,000 Chance of a Lifetime*, *The $128,000 Question*, and *Tic Tac Dough* (with game show veteran Wink Martindale). *Family Feud* with Richard Dawson added a twist that seemed particularly suited to the conformist backlash of the late 1970s. Rather than coming up with the *right* answer to a question, *Feud*'s teams of families had to guess which answer most people would give.

Among the most outstanding shows beginning in the 1970s was the wholesome *Wheel of Fortune*, combining the children's game of Hangman with a Las Vegas–like spinning wheel to determine prize money. Originally hosted by Chuck Woolery (who later went on to host *Love Connection* and *Scrabble*), *Wheel* gained its greatest popularity in prime time when it was hosted by Pat Sajak and featured the fashionably bedecked former beauty-pageant contestant Vanna White as the letter turner. Still a favorite in the early twenty-first century, this show is often televised in conjunction with *Jeopardy!* during early prime-time hours, and the two together are a study in contrasts: *Wheel* relies partly on luck, celebrates the simple accomplishments of the common man, and encourages a camaraderie wherein contestants clap in support for one another. *Jeopardy!*, in contrast, maintains a more reserved atmosphere. It is strictly an answer-and-question game that hearkens back to the intellectual challenges of *Twenty-One* and *Information Please*, requiring smart players to answer difficult questions before their opponents do.

Game shows had a difficult time competing with the drama found in the daytime talk shows of the 1980s and 1990s. No longer did producers have to pay or reward people to come on television and tell their stories—people do it for free just for the temporary chance at fame and the spotlight. *The Price Is Right* remained daytime television's game show mainstay, accompanied mostly by soap operas and talk shows. Prime-time hours during these decades witnessed the entrenchment of *Wheel of Fortune* and *Jeopardy!* and the resurgence of *Hollywood Squares*, a celebrity-based show, modeled on tic-tac-toe. In addition, in the late 1990s, shows such as *Jeopardy!* and *Wheel of Fortune* developed interactive computer games that allow people to play at home. The Gameshow Network, which televised both classic and new game shows, debuted in 1998, at once reviving the game show format and relegating it to a single marginalized cable network.

In 1999, however, a little-known British quiz show offering exorbitant cash prizes took America by storm. *Who Wants to Be a Millionaire* took several elements from traditional trivia shows and made them more interactive, allowing participants to "phone a friend" and "ask the audience" for input on the increasingly challenging general knowledge questions. Though rare, the possibility of contestants earning the million-dollar grand prize and the show's melodramatic music and lighting reinvigorated viewers. *Who Wants to Be a Millionaire* remained on prime-time television for several years. Other shows, such as the team-oriented *Weakest Link* and the negotiation-based *Deal or No Deal*, attempted, with limited success, to re-create the high-stakes drama of *Who Wants to Be a Millionaire* in the first decade or so of the twenty-first century.

Also during the early twenty-first century, the increasing popularity of reality television led producers to couple the genre's emphasis on the twists and turns in the lives of everyday people with the challenges and potential for elimination inherent in the game show. The first of these reality TV–game show hybrids to gain widespread popularity in America was *Survivor*, in which contestants are sent to a remote location and asked to participate in a series of challenges, working together in "tribes" or alone as individuals. The participants then vote someone off of the show until only one, the "Sole Survivor," remains. The competition proved incredibly popular in America and remained in production well into the 2010s.

While traditional game shows such as *Jeopardy!* and *Wheel of Fortune* remain fixtures of the television landscape, the twenty-first century has seen major shifts in the format of the game show genre. Gone are the days of endless streams of anonymous contestants competing for cash and consumer products. Now a proliferation of competition shows—for example, *American Idol*, *The Bachelor* or *The Bachelorette*, *The Apprentice*, *Last Comic Standing*, *Top Chef*, and *The Biggest Loser*—allow viewers to follow the experiences of a set of participants over an entire season, with the winning participants getting a chance at fame and fortune seldom matched in the history of the game show.

Wendy Woloson

SEE ALSO: *Allen, Steve;* American Idol*;* The Apprentice*;* The Bachelor*; Ball, Lucille; Berle, Milton; Big Bands;* The Biggest Loser*; Black Sox Scandal; Cable TV; Clark, Dick; Daytime Talk Shows; Dean, James; Edwards, Ralph; Emmy Awards; Flynn, Errol; Francis, Arlene; Gambling; Goodson, Mark; The Great Depression; Griffin, Merv; Hollywood;* Hollywood Squares*; Jackson, "Shoeless" Joe;* Jeopardy!*; Kovacs, Ernie; Lottery; Marx, Groucho; Murrow, Edward R.;* The Newlywed Game*;* Newsweek*;* The Price Is Right*;* Queen for a Day*; Quiz Show Scandals; Radio; Reagan, Ronald; Reality Television; Simon, Neil;* The $64,000 Question*; Stewart, Jimmy;* Survivor*; Taylor, Elizabeth; Television; Thomas, Danny;* Time*;* To Tell the Truth*;* Top Chef*;* What's My Line?*;* Wheel of Fortune*;* Who Wants to Be a Millionaire*; World War II.*

BIBLIOGRAPHY

Anderson, Kent. *Television Fraud: The History and Implications of the Quiz Show Scandals.* Westport, CT: Greenwood Press, 1978.

DeLong, Thomas A. *Quiz Craze: America's Infatuation with Game Shows.* New York: Praeger, 1991.

Hoerschelmann, Olaf. *Rules of the Game: Quiz Shows and American Culture.* Albany: State University of New York, 2006.

Holbrook, Morris. *Daytime Television Game Shows and the Celebration of Merchandise: The Price Is Right.* Bowling Green, OH: Bowling Green State University Popular Press, 1993.

Holmes, Su. *The Quiz Show.* Edinburgh: Edinburgh University Press, 2008.

Stone, Joseph, and Tim Yohn. *Prime Time and Misdemeanors: Investigating the 1950s TV Quiz Scandal—a D.A.'s Account.* New Brunswick, NJ: Rutgers University Press, 1992.

Gameboy

When Nintendo introduced the Gameboy in Japan on April 21, 1989, the company revolutionized the video gaming industry by offering a portable system that was generally affordable, fun to play, and easy to use. The Gameboy was introduced in the United States in August of that same year. Part of the popularity of the device came from the inclusion of *Tetris*, an addictive game in which players tried to fit blocks of different sizes together to clear rows before the screen filled and the game ended. Eventually, 650 games were available for the Gameboy.

Nintendo had introduced its first handheld system, the Game and Watch, in 1980 with considerably less success. The most popular games for it included *Donkey Kong, Mario Brothers*, and *Balloon Fight*. The original version sold for about $100 but was subsequently reduced to about half that amount. After the Game and Watch was introduced, Nintendo redesigned the product several times, adding color, accessories, and increased function and capabilities to keep the product competitive with other handheld devices. By July 2001 Nintendo had sold 11.5 million Gameboys. That number rose to 150 million by 2012. Gameboy became the most popular video gaming system of all time, and it stood as a ubiquitous symbol of U.S. culture. In 2009 the Gameboy was added to the National Toy Hall of Fame in New York.

The developers of the Game Boy were Gunpei Yokoi, the creator of the popular arcade game *Donkey Kong*, and Nintendo Research and Development. The 1989 version offered a Z80 processor, a green LCD screen, and a gray hard-shell body. Over the course of the next decade, the device underwent a series of modifications. In 1994 Naki Electronics introduced the Mini-Arcade that allowed Gameboy users to dock their game and turn it into a tabletop game. The arcade included a miniaturized version of the joystick used with standard gaming consoles. By 1995 consumers had a choice of body colors. The following year Nintendo introduced the Gameboy Pocket that could run on two AAA batteries for ten hours and replaced the green screen with a black-and-white version. Sales of Gameboy systems rose significantly after the 1996 launch of the Japanese animated sensation *Pokémon*, which required the use of multiple Gameboys to complete the different versions of the game. In 1998 Gameboy Color doubled the processing speed and offered three times the memory of earlier versions.

The first major redesign of the Gameboy occurred in 2001 with the Gameboy Advance, which reflected technological breakthroughs as well as intensifying competition from makers of other handheld gaming systems. The Advance had a 32-bit ARM processor and was backward compatible so that earlier games could be played on the new model. The Advance went on sale on June 13, 2001, two days later than originally announced. Retail stores that had bundled the Advance with two games and a battery pack for a cost of approximately $200 sold out quickly. As a stand-alone product, the Advance could be purchased for about $70. Ironically, many customers arriving to purchase the Nintendo Gameboy Advance also bought rival Sony's PlayStation 2, pushing those sales up by 8 percent.

In 2003, Nintendo introduced the Gameboy Advance SP (Special) at a cost of about $100. The foldable system was front-lighted and offered extended battery life. By October 2004 eight million Gameboy Advance SP systems had been sold. The introduction of the Gameboy Advance Action Pack offered players a single bag that held the Advance, eight game cartridges, and accessories such as a charger and extra batteries. In 2005 Nintendo introduced the Gameboy Micro. Unable to compete with Nintendo's own DS system, which had been introduced in 2004, the Micro was discontinued in 2005.

By 2004, Nintendo's Gameboy Advance and the Gameboy Advance SP were offering full media platforms. Kid-friendly games such as *SpongeBob SquarePants, Jimmy Neutron*, and *Fairly Odd Parents* were also available. Within a few months Nintendo had partnered with 4Kids Entertainment to offer Saturday morning cartoon shows that could be streamed through the Advance and Advance SP in both the United States and Europe. Although Nintendo had sold more than 81.5 million Gameboy Advance units worldwide by the end of the first decade of the 2000s, Nintendo DS had significantly outpaced sales of Gameboy units. In 2008 the Gameboy Advanced and Gameboy Advanced SP were discontinued, and it was announced that no new games would be released. While some newer Nintendo DS games can be played on the Gameboy systems, by the 2010s all of the Gameboy devices were largely a thing of the past. They have come to be regarded fondly among gamers as a cultural marker of the 1990s and as the original handheld gaming system.

Elizabeth Rholetter Purdy

SEE ALSO: *Pokémon; Toys; Video Games.*

BIBLIOGRAPHY

"Another Step in Gameboy's Evolution." *Courier Mail* (Brisbane, Australia), April 8, 2009, 67.

Daily, Geoff. "Gameboy Advance: Not Just Playing with Content." *EContent*, May 2004.

Marriot, James. "The Gameboy: The True Soundtrack of the 90s." *Oxford Student*, April 26, 2012.

Provenzo, Eugene F., Jr. *Video Kids: Making Sense of Nintendo.* Boston: Harvard University Press, 1991.

Robertson, Andy. "Kid Discovers Gameboy Micro, Convinces Classmates It's the Next 3DS." *Wired*, April 28, 2012.

Tarr, Greg. "Newest GameBoy Gets Snapped Up by Consumers." *This Week in Consumer Electronics*, June 25, 2001.

Gammons, Peter *(1945–)*

In the 1980s and 1990s baseball writer and television analyst Peter Gammons became virtually synonymous with America's pastime. He first made a name for himself in the 1970s at the *Boston Globe*, for which he covered the Boston Red Sox and baseball in general. From 1989 to 2009 Gammon served as a studio analyst and regular reporter for the cable television network ESPN, offering a popular segment called "Diamond Notes" during the *SportsCenter* program. In 2009 he agreed to provide commentary for the MLB Network and NESN, the television home of the Red Sox.

Gammons grew up a Red Sox fan in Groton, Massachusetts. He attended the University of North Carolina in the late 1960s, and after graduating in 1969 he began his stint with the *Boston Globe*. In 1976 Gammons left the *Globe* to work for the prestigious national weekly magazine *Sports Illustrated* until 1978, during which time he covered college basketball, the National Hockey League, and Major League Baseball. He returned to the magazine as a senior writer from 1986 to 1990, this time concentrating solely on baseball. In 1990 he went back to the *Globe* and stayed there until 2000.

In addition to covering the day-to-day aspects of baseball, Gammons offers penetrating insights on the past and future of the game. He has been highly critical of skyrocketing player salaries and the emphasis of baseball owners on television revenues, as evidenced by his book with Jack Sands, *Coming Apart at the Seams: How Baseball Owners, Players, and Television Executives Have Led Our National Pastime to the Brink of Disaster* (1993). Gammons has written several other books, such as *Beyond the Sixth Game* (1985), which deals with the issue of free agency in baseball. Additionally, he helped former Red Sox pitcher Roger Clemens write his autobiography, *Rocket Man: The Roger Clemens Story* (1987).

Gammons was voted the National Sportswriter of the Year in 1989, 1990, and 1993 by the National Sportscasters and Sportswriters Association. He is a recipient of an honorary Poynter Fellowship from Yale University, and in 2004 he was given the J. G. Taylor Spink Award for outstanding baseball writing.

In a July 1998 chat session on the *ESPN SportsZone* website, Gammons offered the following advice for aspiring sportswriters: "Take as many English, political science and history classes as you can. Then try to write for as many publications that will take your copy. Doesn't matter if it's a small-town, weekly newspaper or collector's news or *Sports Illustrated*. The more you write, the better you get."

Jason George

SEE ALSO: *Baseball; Boston Red Sox; ESPN;* Sports Illustrated.

BIBLIOGRAPHY

Coleman, Ken, and Dan Valenti. *The Impossible Dream Remembered: The 1967 Red Sox*. Lexington, MA: Stephen Greene Press, 1987.

Gammons, Peter. *Beyond the Sixth Game*. Boston: Houghton Mifflin, 1985.

Sands, Jack, and Peter Gammons. *Coming Apart at the Seams: How Baseball Owners, Players, and Television Executives Have Led Our National Pastime to the Brink of Disaster*. New York: Macmillan, 1993.

Shaugnessy, Dan. *At Fenway: Dispatches from Red Sox Nation*. New York: Crown Publishers, 1996.

Gangs

Youthful street gangs have become a seemingly ineradicable fixture of American urban life. There are countless stories of well-armed teenagers locked in heated battle—often to the death—with their rivals, growing rich off drug dealing and increasing the population of already overcrowded state prisons. By the end of the twentieth century, as hysteria over the existence of these gangs increased, a sort of historical amnesia appeared to take hold of the news media and the general public. It is easy to forget that the existence of gangs has been a consistent social phenomenon since the nineteenth century, causing sociologists to debate the origins and motivation of the street gang. Common sense, however, dictates that any group, such as deprived inner-city youth, excluded from the general prosperity, will compensate for deprivation by staking a claim to their neighborhood, to the square blocks of ghetto they can control with relative impunity, and will profit from their position by any means at hand.

ORIGINS: NEW YORK CITY

Prior to the Civil War, gangs of young Irish toughs were common in New York City. (In the field of gang studies, New York virtually monopolized the attention of sociologists, criminologists, psychologists, and others until the mid-twentieth century.) These youths had, by all accounts, provoked and fanned the draft riots that consumed New York in 1863, leaving more than 100 dead. Martin Scorsese's 2002 film *Gangs of New York*

L.A. Gangs. *A tattooed gang member poses with a pistol held against his forehead in East Los Angeles, California, an area known for turf wars among rival gangs.* CHRIS RAINIER/GETTY IMAGES.

captures something of the milieu of this period, focusing on the Five Points section of New York City and the extraordinary violence that prevailed between gangs.

Many East Coast gangs had colorful names, such as the Pug Uglies (who took their name from their battered pug hats), the Dead Rabbits, and the Swamp Angels. The different gang contingents wore distinctive costumes, making them easily recognizable to each other and unnerving the rest of the people in their neighborhood. They engaged in street crime and extortion, murder and mayhem for hire, their services itemized in a price list that gang members often carried with them. Such a list carried by one Piker Ryan priced ear removal at $15; murder itself commanded a mere $100.

As an additional source of revenue, certain gangs leased their services to Tammany Hall politicians, intimidating voters and controlling elections. With the support of the corrupt Tammany Hall politicians and payoffs to local police, the street gangs could indulge in all manner of petty larceny and were much feared in the neighborhoods they controlled. In reading accounts of their activities, the parallel with gang activities in the South Central area of Los Angeles in the late twentieth century is striking, but with two major differences: the early gangs were white and they did not carry automatic firearms.

IMMIGRATION AND GANG DIVERSIFICATION AND GROWTH

By the turn of the twentieth century, politicians were forced to buckle under public pressure and withdraw their patronage from the gangs; in the process, gangs lost police protection for their illicit activities. By then the hegemony of Irish gangs throughout the East Coast was being challenged by successive waves of immigrants from Europe, and Italian and Jewish street gangs mushroomed, impinging on Irish territory and profits. In a perverse example of market demand, the price for strong-arm services fell to a new low. Many gangs began diversifying their activities, adding union busting (or striker protection) to their racketeering in extortion and protection. It was a volatile situation. "By the latter part of 1913," wrote historian Herbert Asbury, "it is likely that there were more gangs in New York than in any other period in the history of the metropolis; their number and the ramification of their alliances were so bewildering that of hundreds there now [1927] exists no more than a trace."

Less than ten years later, gangs were spoken of in the past tense—an overly optimistic assessment, as many gang members, cognizant of street crime's limitations, had simply gone professional, attaching themselves to one or another of the Irish, Jewish, or Italian mobs. In the 1920s Prohibition provided ample and lucrative opportunities in the bootlegging trade, and with newfound wealth came a patina of respectability. The now fully fledged criminals abandoned their unconventional outfits for ostentatious, business wear, bought fancy cars, and acquired a certain prestige in their communities; money brought them the temporary illusion that they had transcended their marginal social position.

However, this balance of power was disrupted by new arrivals. In New York waves of Puerto Rican and black immigrants arrived throughout the 1930s, 1940s, and 1950s. They came to seek an escape from rural impoverishment but found, instead, its urban corollary. Following a by-then familiar pattern, neighborhood youths organized under distinctive names, using the local candy store or soda shop as a base from which to enforce their territorial prerogative. They established alliances and bitter rivalries, often but not exclusively along race or ethnicity lines, and made war in the time-honored fashion. Now street fighting was called "rumbling," and it was fought with knives, chains, and homemade zip guns, but seldom with actual firearms. Of course, in this more civilized age, mayhem no longer had the same fiduciary incentive, and street gang crime was petty rather than serious. In short, the newer generations seemed more driven by the emotional need to form bonds and establish a distinctive identity.

GANGS IN/AS MASS CULTURE

The public, however, reacted to the mid-twentieth-century gangs as if they were some fascinating new phenomenon. Their very existence may have been seen as an affront by the police, but sociologists studied them intently, and a regular cottage industry was composed of professors writing about "alienation and the juvenile delinquent." Hollywood capitalized on the Sturm und Drang of disturbed youth, romanticizing their fashions, their primitive chivalry, and their violence. To all appearances, it was as if the term *juvenile delinquent,* having been thus coined, made the problem more comprehensible, but it was never clearly understood.

Perhaps Hollywood came closest to doing the topic justice. Broadway's hit musical (and later film) *West Side Story* gives a romantic gloss to the subject of gang warfare by very virtue of the music, dance, and love story at its center. On the other end of the spectrum, *Blackboard Jungle* (1955) catches the tenor of urban alienation, while *Rebel without a Cause,* released the same year, captures the flavor of suburban teendom and the ways in which it apes the anomie of the ghettoes. A consequence of these films was to inspire teenagers everywhere to adopt the "delinquent" style of dress—black leather jacket, greased hair, tight jeans—and to unleash a wave of mindless and destructive middle-class hooliganism.

By the 1950s and 1960s many gangs had assumed a radical agenda, as much a sign of the changing times as the radicalization of the poor. The Beatniks were a group who operated on the fringes of mainstream society. Although not a gang in the typical sense, they were an underground conformist youth movement that later morphed into the student movement of the 1960s. In an inversion of this trend, the Black Panther Party adopted a stylized version of gang wear, sporting uniform black leather suit jackets and berets. The Panthers, who could not technically be considered a gang, as well as bona fide gangs, initiated community self-protection (and self-help) programs while joining the throngs in search of War on Poverty grants and lobbying the federal government for funding. In his long essay, *Mau-Mauing the Flak-Catchers,* Tom Wolfe notes the methods of intimidation—not so different from the tactics adopted when extorting money from neighborhood businesses—used by gang members to cash in on the federal largesse. With the collapse of the War on Poverty, economic and territorial imperatives reasserted themselves, and gangs returned to the petty crimes and drug dealing that had long supported them.

Another group, the Hells Angels Motorcycle Club, started in 1948 and in the twenty-first century continues to inspire moral panic and threaten the status quo. Its members typically ride Harley-Davidson motorcycles, and the U.S. Department of Justice considers the club an organized crime syndicate. The group gained prominence during the 1960s counterculture movement in San Francisco. Its members have included Beat poet Allen Ginsberg, Jerry Garcia and the Grateful Dead, and American psychologist Timothy Leary, who was known for advocating the use of psychedelic drugs.

"GANGSTAS": DRUGS AND GUNS

Out of the wreckage of the 1960s, new gangs emerged and, with them, a new hysteria. Left to their own devices, gangs in public housing projects, such as the infamous Cabrini Green in Chicago, turned to drug dealing, especially after the introduction in the early 1980s of crack cocaine—a cheap, smokable, and virulent form of the drug. Projects and ghetto neighborhoods such as South Central Los Angeles became no-go areas, patrolled by the new breed of gangster, or "gang bangers" as they called themselves—well-armed, tightly organized cadres inured to violence and ready to give their lives for their colors. Especially in Los Angeles, the new breed of gangs—the Crips, the Bloods, the Mexican Mafia—introduced a paramilitary discipline to their activities, enforcing the age-old territorial imperative with an impressive array of weaponry. These gangs became one of Los Angeles' most talked-about exports, with Crips and Bloods appearing as far afield as small towns in the Midwest.

The "rumble" was a thing of the past. Now gangs engaged in a sort of automotive warfare, the drive-by shooting, that bore as much resemblance to the rumble as a duel to an air raid. And once again Hollywood turned the social unrest to its advantage, churning out a string of dystopic (*The Warriors*, 1979) or topical (*Colors*, 1988; *New Jack City*, 1991) gang films, whereas gangsta rap, a subgenre of rap that celebrates the gang-banging lifestyle in graphic terms, made billions for record companies. Young white suburbanites did not fail to appreciate the nuances of "the life," and gangster slang and fashion overran white America, much to the distress of suburban parents. As in the 1950s, a cognitive dissonance developed between the fictitious depiction of gangs in music and film, enormously popular among white suburban teenagers, and the gangs themselves, who were vilified in the press and subjected to increasingly restrictive police measures. But no one would argue that cost in human life merited the celebration, especially after several high-profile rappers died (most prominently, Tupac Shakur, the son of a Black Panther, who had already survived one murder attempt) as the result of bicoastal gang feuding. Was it art imitating life or life imitating art?

It would appear that few social problems have remained as intractable as the street gang. But are street gangs a genuine danger or simply a bugbear, conveniently trotted out to justify the growth of police departments? This is of some import because, historically, gangs are depicted in the language of crisis. It becomes difficult to separate the phenomenon itself from the overlay of media coverage that concurrently obscures and defines the street gang. But for the atomized middle-class public toward whom most media is slanted, gangs remain a disturbing phenomenon. That the media hysteria itself might not have an agenda is seldom discussed.

In the twenty-first century, the public's reaction to gang influence has become more restrictive. Many schools forbid certain types of clothing that could be considered "gang related" such as baggy clothing, bandannas, and jackets with insignias on them. These preventative measures are in large part due to the violence that has become more alarming. Since the early 2000s the citizens of New York City have experienced a rash of random assaults and murders resulting from "wilding," a practice in which young gangs hunt in packs for their human prey. However, many sociologists point out that gang activity is often the result of socioeconomic factors such as lack of education and job opportunities. Also, people forget that gangs have been a part of America's history since the nineteenth century and are not a sign of impending societal doom.

Michael Baers

SEE ALSO: *Automobile; Black Panthers;* The Blackboard Jungle*; Cocaine/Crack; The Draft; Firearms; Gangsta Rap; Hairstyles; Hells Angels; Hollywood; Labor Unions; Leather Jacket; Mafia/ Organized Crime; Political Bosses; Prohibition; Rap;* Rebel without a Cause*; Scorsese, Martin; Shakur, Tupac; Soda Fountains; Suburbia; Teenagers; War on Drugs;* West Side Story*; Wolfe, Tom.*

BIBLIOGRAPHY

Hagedorn, John. *A World of Gangs: Armed Youth and Gangsta Culture*. Minneapolis: University of Minnesota Press, 2008.

Haskins, James. *Street Gangs: Yesterday and Today*. New York: Hastings House, 1974.

Kontos, Louis, and David Brotherton. *Encyclopedia of Gangs*. Westport, CT: Greenwood Press, 2008.

Kontos, Louis; David Brotherton; and Luis Barrios. *Gangs and Society: Alternative Perspectives*. New York: Columbia University Press, 2003.

National Gang Center. Accessed January 10, 2011. Available from http://www.nationalgangcenter.gov

Salisbury, Harrison E. *The Shook-Up Generation*. New York: Harper & Row, 1958.

Shakur, Sanyika (aka Kody Scott). *Monster: The Autobiography of an L.A. Gang Member*. New York: Penguin Press, 1994.

Soliz, Adela. *Gangs*. Detroit, MI: Greenhaven Press, 2009.

Whyte, William Foote. *Street Corner Society*. Chicago: University of Chicago Press, 1943.

Wolfe, Tom. *Radical Chic and Mau-Mauing the Flak-Catchers*. New York: Farrar, Straus & Giroux, 1970.

Gangsta Rap

Gangsta rap is the most controversial style of the rap music genre. It has achieved global prominence through its vivid sexist and homophobic lyrics, as well as its violent depiction of urban ghetto life in America. Gangsta rap has also helped bring attention to other styles of rap music.

BICOASTAL ORIGINS

Although gangsta rap originated on the East Coast in the late 1970s, it has widely become associated with California, particularly Los Angeles, due to the multimillion album sales of West Coast rappers such as Ice Cube, Ice T, Dr. Dre, and Snoop Dogg. Los Angeles might proclaim itself as the home of gangsta rap, but gangsta lyrics and style were part of the hip-hop scene from its origins in the South Bronx, New York in the mid-1970s. The inspiration behind the specific style known as gangsta rap in the late 1980s came from Philadelphia's Schoolly D's *Smoke Some Kill* (1988) and the Bronx's Boogie Down Production's *Criminal Minded* (1987). In particular, the latter's track "9mm Goes Bang" has been seen as a pioneering force in gangsta rap's development.

However, it was West Coast–based Ice T's *Rhyme Pays* (1987), which ranged from humorous boasts and tales of crime and violence to outright misogyny, together with N.W.A.'s (Niggaz with Attitude) underground album *Straight Outta Compton* (1988) that established gangsta rap firmly within the American music scene. Its keynote track "F*** Tha Police" was considered so shocking that radio stations and MTV refused to play it. Nonetheless, the album went platinum. N.W.A. and gangsta rap's popularity was compounded with the release of their second album *EFIL4ZAGGIN* in 1991, which debuted at number two on the *Billboard* chart with neither a single nor a video and became the first rap album to reach number one. Snoop Dogg then became the first rapper to go straight to number one with his album *Doggystyle* (1993).

GLORIFYING GHETTO LIFE

Gangsta rap is distinctive for its rich, descriptive storytelling laid over heavy funk samples from Parliament-Funkadelic, Sly Stone, James Brown, Rick James, Average White Band, Ohio Players, and George Clinton. Its roots can be traced to early depictions of the hustler lifestyle and low-budget blaxploitation movies of the 1970s, which portrayed blacks as criminals, pimps, pushers, prostitutes, and gangsters. And since many of rap's early pioneers were gang members, gangsta rap came from the life experiences of the rappers. Gangsta rappers have become high-profile figures, many of them featured in Hollywood films such as *Boyz 'n' the Hood* (1991), *New Jack City* (1991), and *Menace II Society* (1993), which have brought views of ghetto life to the masses.

That the lyrics of much gangsta rap are centered on crime fuels much of the controversy surrounding the musical style. Rappers Too Short, Above the Law, Mr. Scarface, and Big Daddy Kane, for example, all celebrated pimping. Although it has been criticized for glorifying the negativity of the streets, gangsta rap's defenders claim that the rappers are simply reporting what really goes on in their neighborhoods; that drugs, prostitution, violence, and sexual promiscuity are all features of their daily existence. As N.W.A. proclaim, "It's not about a salary, it's all about reality." Nonetheless, this has led to suggestions that rap reinforces negative stereotypes of the black community and lionizes antisocial behavior.

Many of gangsta rap's high-profile rappers have acquired public notoriety. Some, including Snoop Dogg, have been implicated in gangland murders, while others, such as Tupac Shakur (1971–1996) and the Notorious B.I.G. (1972–1997), have been killed. Unfolding in the wake of the "East Coast/West Coast" scene wars, gangsta rap spread from the strongholds of New York and Los Angeles into New Orleans, Louisiana; Chicago; and Memphis, Tennessee. Rappers like Eminem, DMX, 50 Cent, Jay-Z, Master P, and Three 6 Mafia carried the torch into the mainstream. Master P and Jay-Z retained an almost pop-hardcore sound, sampling soul, rhythm-and-blues, and pop artists over steadier, slower beats. Relying on the notoriety of shock and controversy, rappers like Eminem and 50 Cent pushed the content of their songs into more graphic depictions of violence.

A MOVE TOWARD THE MAINSTREAM

In an ironic twist, many of gangsta raps' founding fathers moved into roles that were a far cry from their street origins. Ice-T became a household name through his role in *Law & Order: Special Victims Unit*; and, as well as starring in films, Ice Cube produced TV shows and movies such as *Friday* (and its sequels) and the TBS comedy *Are We There Yet?* based on the movie of the same name. Rappers who went mainstream through commercials or TV were accused by their fans of selling out, but many of the legends of gangsta rap claimed they were using their social positions to develop positive alternatives to the gangsta icon.

Gangsta rap has become popular with those who have no direct experience with the lifestyle it depicts. The sexually explicit lyrics combined with graphic portrayals of gang killings have appealed to many middle-class white male youths. Indeed, some critics have suggested that a directly proportional relationship has developed between gangsta rap's explicitness and the sale of its records. Critics note that the violence and gangsterism have been exaggerated as a highly effective marketing ploy by the white-owned record companies. This has been helped by the addition of "parental advisory" stickers to many of their albums.

For the middle-class white male youths, gangsta rap possibly fulfills the same role blaxploitation films used to, attracting listeners for whom the "ghetto" is a location of adventure, violence, and erotic fantasy—an alternative to the conformity and banality of suburbia. This voyeurism helps explain gangsta rap's large following outside its communities of origin.

Nathan Abrams

SEE ALSO: *Blaxploitation Films; Eminem; Gangs; Ice-T; Jay-Z; Public Enemy; Rap; Run-DMC; Shakur, Tupac; Snoop Dogg.*

BIBLIOGRAPHY

Fernando, S. H., Jr. *The New Beats: Exploring the Music Culture and Attitudes of Hip-Hop.* Edinburgh: Payback Press, 1995.

Kelley, Robin D. G. "Kickin' Reality, Kickin' Ballistics: 'Gangsta Rap' and Postindustrial Los Angeles." In *Race Rebels: Culture, Politics and the Black Working Class.* New York: Free Press, 1994.

Oliver, Richard, and Tim Leffel. *Hip-Hop Inc.: Success Strategies of the Rap Moguls.* New York: Thunder's Mouth Press, 2006.

Toop, David. *Rap Attack 2: African Rap to Global Hip Hop.* London: Serpent's Tail, 1991.

The Gap

The Gap casual apparel stores have become a ubiquitous fixture in malls and urban shopping districts around the world. The Gap's high-quality, classic designs have remained wardrobe staples for youthful customers, older shoppers, and their children, bridging the generation gap that originally gave rise to its name. Founded in San Francisco in 1969 by Donald and Doris Fisher as a place for youngsters to buy jeans in a variety of sizes, the Gap has earned a place in popular culture, with mentions and appearances in films and television shows, including the hit movie *Reality Bites* (1994) and a satire on *Saturday Night Live* (1975–). Detractors criticize the store's style as generic, but steadily increasing sales have made it a multibillion-dollar company. Gap Inc., parent company of the Gap, also manages the Piperlime, Banana Republic, Old Navy, and Athleta brands.

In 2012 the company reported that its five brands combined had more than 3,100 stores and 134,000 employees worldwide.

Geri Speace

SEE ALSO: *Advertising; Jeans; Malls; Old Navy; Online Shopping;* Saturday Night Live.

BIBLIOGRAPHY

Caminiti, Susan. "Competition: Will Old Navy Fill the Gap?" *Fortune*, March 18, 1996, 59.

Nevaer, Louis. *Into—and Out of—the GAP: A Cautionary Account of an American Retailer*. Westport, CT: Praeger, 2001.

Rudnitsky, Howard. "Widening the Gap." *Forbes*, September 13, 1982, 205.

Garbo, Greta *(1905–1990)*

Swedish actress Greta Garbo accomplished in less than two decades what advocates for women's rights had sought for centuries: she showed the American public that feminine sexuality was compatible with intelligence. During the 1920s, when liberated flappers still attracted scorn from mainstream society, Garbo's depiction of independent yet feminine beauties helped convince millions of American women that sexual initiative was not a man's prerogative. According to biographer Karen Swenson, Garbo's popularity with both sexes allowed her to successfully challenge traditional gender roles. At the same time, Hollywood's highest-paid female star eschewed media attention. Her indifference to public opinion gave her an air of mystery, and by the age of thirty-six, she had retired to an almost hermetic seclusion. Film critic David Thomson saliently observed that "in making the journey away from fame into privacy she established herself forever as a magical figure, a true goddess, remote and austere, but intimate and touching."

Greta Garbo. *Despite her popularity and acclaim as an actress in the 1920s and 1930s, Greta Garbo preferred to distance herself from the Hollywood social scene.* GENERAL PHOTOGRAPHIC AGENCY/GETTY IMAGES.

Hollywood's Viking beauty began life as Greta Lovisa Gustafsson on September 18, 1905. She grew up in an impoverished Stockholm household and went to work as a lather girl in a barber shop at age fourteen. By seventeen the aspiring actress had garnered admission to Sweden's exclusive Royal Dramatic Theater Academy. She soon impressed Scandinavia's foremost director, Mauritz Stiller (1883–1928), with her perfect instincts and dignified beauty. He gave her the stage name Garbo and cast her as Elizabeth Dohna in the silent screen masterpiece *The Saga of Gosta Berling*. A leading role in G. W. Pabst's *Joyless Street* (1925) soon followed. The part, that of a struggling Viennese woman on the verge of prostitution, permitted Garbo to explore sexuality on screen for the first time. The film itself shattered box-office records and became an enduring masterpiece of realistic cinema. Garbo's great break occurred when Louis B. Mayer (1885–1957) of Metro-Goldwyn-Mayer recruited Stiller for his Hollywood studios. The established director insisted that his relatively obscure nineteen-year-old starlet accompany him to the United States. Stiller was soon exported back to Stockholm, while Garbo became a box-office sensation.

The silent movies that Garbo filmed between 1925 and 1929 earned her critical claim as Hollywood's most talented female actress. Starring with leading man John Gilbert (1899–1936) in *Flesh and the Devil* (1926) and *Love* (1927), she awed audiences and shocked censors with her forthright sexuality. Garbo displayed her wide acting range playing a Spanish opera singer in *Torrent* (1926), a Russian spy in *The Mysterious Lady* (1928), an English aristocrat in *A Women of Affairs* (1928), and a Southern belle in *Wild Orchids* (1929). The star's appearance influenced an entire generation, as millions of female fans copied her tastes in clothing and hair styles. Crazes for artificial eye lashes and cloche hats swept the nation. Meanwhile Garbo, whom playwright and politician Clare Boothe Luce (1903–1987) described as "a deer in the body of a woman, living resentfully in the Hollywood zoo," distanced herself from both the public and the Los Angeles social scene.

Garbo may have been one of the leading box-office draws of the silent era, but few critics expected her to make the transition to talkies. The advent of sound ended the careers of most silent stars, and the Swede's deep voice and heavy accent were expected to turn off audiences. Instead, the twenty-five-year-old actress gave her most compelling performance in an adaptation of the play *Anna Christie* (1930) by Eugene O'Neill (1888–1953). Garbo played a waterfront streetwalker searching for her barge-captain father. Her opening words, at that time the longest sound sequence ever heard on film, are cinematic legend: "Gimme a whiskey, ginger ale on the side. And don't be stingy, baby!" Other hits followed. *Mata Hari* (1932), *Queen Christina* (1933), *Anna Karenina* (1935), and *Camille* (1936) confirmed her reputation as the leading lady of the early sound era. Garbo's greatest role, that of the suicidal Russian dancer Grusinskaya in *Grand Hotel* (1932), ranks among the best female leads ever seen on the big screen. It is here that she declares her haunting wish: "I want to be alone." After surprising success as the comic lead in *Ninotchka* (1939), Garbo filmed the lackluster *Two-Faced Woman* (1941) and then retired from the public eye.

During the last five decades of Garbo's life, "The Swedish Sphinx" established herself as cinema's leading enigma. She traveled extensively but turned down all requests for public appearances. Instead, she entertained such close friends as Winston Churchill (1874–1965) and dancer Martha Graham (1894–1991) in her posh New York City apartment. As one of the grande dames of American cinema, her intimates included William S. Paley (1901–1990), Anthony Eden (1897–1977), Jean Cocteau (1889–1963), Irwin Shaw (1913–1984), Dag Hammarskjöld (1905–1961), Cole Porter (1891–1964), and Jacqueline Kennedy (1929–1994). She also devoted herself to amassing an internationally renowned art collection, which boasted masterpieces by Pierre-August Renoir (1841–1919) and Pierre Bonnard (1867–1947). Garbo received an honorary Academy Award in 1955 for "unforgettable screen performances." She died in New York City on April 15, 1990.

Garbo entered the American consciousness during the mid-1920s at a historical moment when gender roles were in flux. The young actress came to represent a palatable form of female liberation and brought the icon of the independent woman home to Middle America. Garbo's influence endured long after she became film's most celebrated recluse. Throughout her life, she remained private, elusive, and conspicuously unmarried. "There is no one who would have me. . . . I can't cook," she once joked—displaying the combination of independence and feminine intelligence that made her famous.

Jacob M. Appel

SEE ALSO: *Douglas, Melvyn; MGM (Metro-Goldwyn-Mayer); Sex Symbol; Silent Movies; The Twenties.*

BIBLIOGRAPHY

Affron, Charles. *Divine Garbo.* Paris: Ramsay, 1985.

Bainbridge, John. *Garbo.* New York: Holt, Rinehart and Winston, 1971.

Brion, Patrick. *Garbo.* Paris: Chêne, 1985.

Broman, Sven. *Garbo on Garbo.* London: Bloomsbury, 1991.

Carr, Larry. *Four Fabulous Faces: The Evolution and Metamorphosis of Garbo, Swanson, Crawford and Dietrich.* New Rochelle, NY: Arlington House, 1970.

Durgnat, Raymond, and John Kobal. *Greta Garbo.* New York: E. P. Dutton, 1965.

Gronowicz, Antoni. *Garbo.* New York: Simon & Schuster, 1990.

Paris, Barry. *Garbo: A Biography.* New York: Knopf, 1994.

Sands, Frederick. *The Divine Garbo.* New York: Grosset and Dunlap, 1979.

Sjölander, Ture. *Garbo.* New York: Harper & Row, 1971.

Swenson, Karen. *Greta Garbo: A Life Apart.* New York: Scribner, 1997.

Vickers, Hugo. *Loving Garbo: The Story of Greta Garbo, Cecil Beaton and Mercedes de Acosta.* London: Cape, 1994.

Vieira, Mark A. *Greta Garbo: A Cinematic Legacy.* New York: Harry N. Abrams, 2005.

Gardner, Ava *(1922–1990)*

Film actress Ava Gardner was the last, and least typical, of the screen's Love Goddesses, superseding Rita Hayworth and outliving Marilyn Monroe. As the hard-bitten press agent (Edmond O'Brien) in *The Barefoot Contessa* (1954) says of the Madrid slum gypsy (Gardner) elevated to screen stardom, "Whatever it is, whether you're born with it, or catch it from a public drinking cup, she's got it; and the people with the money in their hands put her there." Joseph L. Mankiewicz's film was dubbed "a trash masterpiece" by critic Pauline Kael, but trash or not, it perhaps gave the fullest expression to the magic sensuality of its titular star. Tall and lissome, Gardner was frequently likened to a panther, and her sinuous grace inspired publicists for *The Barefoot Contessa* to trumpet her as "The World's Most Beautiful Animal." Dark-haired, smokily glamorous, and husky-voiced, she had sex appeal that was subtly come-hither, and with her "natural" quality she was a beauty both dazzling and refreshingly uncontrived.

To quote from *The Barefoot Contessa* again, "Life, every now and then, behaves as though it had seen too many bad movies." Spoken by Humphrey Bogart, the words might well have reflected the less happy aspects of Gardner's life, although by all accounts she was a warm, generous, witty, and life-loving free spirit. She was as famed for her torrid love affairs and her heavily publicized marriages, however, as for her legendary looks. Indeed, fame first came her way not for her work but for her first marriage, to an unlikely husband, the pint-sized Mickey Rooney, in 1942. It lasted seventeen months. Her second marriage, to bandleader Artie Shaw in 1945, was even shorter. Most famously her third and last husband was Frank Sinatra. They married in 1951, separated in 1954, and divorced in 1957, but it was a grand passion and a tempestuous liaison that resonated for years to come in their lives and in the pages of an eager tabloid press.

HUMBLE BEGINNINGS

Popular myth has it that Ava Gardner (her real name) suffered an unhappy childhood as a daughter of dirt-poor tenant farmers in North Carolina. In reality, life was a struggle for her Depression-hit family, but nobody went hungry. In 1940, at the age of eighteen, Gardner visited her married sister in New York, where she intended to become a secretary. Her photographer brother-in-law took pictures of her and sent them to somebody at MGM (Metro-Goldwyn-Mayer), resulting in a screen test and a seven-year contract with the studio that boasted "more stars than there are in the heaven." It took six years before Gardner was one of them.

She was put through the usual rigors of studio training in how to walk, how to talk, how to pose for publicity pictures (of which, in her case, there would be thousands), but MGM initially failed to realize her potential. She was given small roles in a variety of films and was lent to other studios. It was only after Gardner, on loan to Universal, played the sultry temptress opposite Burt Lancaster in *The Killers* (1946) that stardom beckoned. The path to the top was uneven, as she played leads alternating with supporting roles. She played her first starring role, appropriately as a goddess, in *One Touch of Venus* (1948). Although the movie was none too successful, the public was entranced by her. Whether playing secondary parts or leads in less than distinguished films, she retained top star status until her career ended, her beauty matured but intact.

BEYOND HER LOOKS

Gardner's high public profile, arising from her private life (after parting from Sinatra she lived for a time among the jet set in Madrid, romancing with playboys and matadors), tended to obscure her professional accomplishments. In *The Great Movie Stars, the International Years*, cinema historian David Shipman writes, "Ava Gardner has seldom been accused of acting," and many considered that she held the world in thrall with her ravishing looks but had little talent. Time proved this a common misperception. Although her range was limited, her intelligence was unmistakable, and she revealed a touching vulnerability that enhanced characters as diverse as her critically well-received Julie in *Show Boat* (1951), her gutsy Hemingway woman in *The Snows of Kilimanjaro* (1952), the half-caste Anglo-Indian of George Cukor's *Bhowani Junction* (1956), and the small but significant role of the patriotic discarded mistress of a deranged general (Lancaster) in *Seven Days in May* (1964).

Gardner was never more beautiful than as Pandora in the mythical, mystical hokum that was *Pandora and the Flying Dutchman* (1951), in which she ensnared and redeemed the eternally wandering sea captain, played by James Mason. She was nominated for an Academy Award for her performance as a tough-talking, witty, good-time girl opposite Clark Gable in *Mogambo* (1953), a remake of his outing with Jean Harlow in *Red Dust* (1932). To Gardner's detractors, the biggest surprise was her performance in John Huston's screen version of *The Night of the Iguana* (1964). No longer youthful, but still oozing sexual charisma, she did creditable justice to Tennessee Williams's play, at the center of things as the heavy-drinking hotel keeper lusting after Richard Burton's defrocked priest.

Gardner retired from the screen in 1982, and in 1985, late in her career, she made her television debut in *Knots Landing*. She played three more television roles, notably as the scheming Agrippina in the miniseries *A.D.*, before settling into a reclusive life in London, where she died of pneumonia at the age of sixty-seven. Her autobiography, compiled by Alan Burgess and Kenneth Turan from interview tapes, was published posthumously.

Robyn Karney

SEE ALSO: *Academy Awards; Bogart, Humphrey; Cukor, George; Gable, Clark; The Great Depression; Harlow, Jean; Hayworth, Rita; Hemingway, Ernest; Huston, John;* Knots Landing*; Lancaster, Burt; MGM (Metro-Goldwyn-Mayer); Monroe, Marilyn; Movie Stars; Shaw, Artie; Sinatra, Frank; Williams, Tennessee.*

BIBLIOGRAPHY

Daniell, John. *Ava Gardner*. New York: St. Martin's Press, 1982.

Gardner, Ava. *Ava: My Story*. New York: Bantam Books, 1990.

Server, Lee. *Ava Gardner: Love Is Nothing*. New York: St. Martin's Press, 2006.

Shipman, David. *The Great Movie Stars, the International Years*. London: Angus & Robertson, 1980.

Garfield, John *(1913–1952)*

The original movie rebel, John Garfield rose to fame with his post-Depression portrayals of cynical men who reflected the era's social unrest. As depicted by the ruggedly handsome Garfield, characters no longer were readily identifiable as either good or evil—the rebel characterization that became the calling card of iconoclastic actors such as Marlon Brando, Montgomery Clift, James Dean, Steve McQueen, and Al Pacino. Garfield also endures as a lasting sex symbol, particularly in his teaming with Lana Turner in the 1946 adaptation of James M. Cain's steamy *The Postman Always Rings Twice* and, a year later, opposite Joan Crawford in *Humoresque*.

Garfield was born Julius Garfinkle on New York's Lower East Side. His father was a coat presser and cantor; his mother died when he was seven. He spent much of his childhood on the streets, where he ran with Bronx gangs. As a teenager his life took a turn for the better when he came under the tutelage of noted educator Angelo Patri, who encouraged him to study drama. "Julie" (as Garfield was called throughout his life by friends and family) earned a drama scholarship at the Heckscher Foundation Drama Workshop. Here he met Clifford Odets, a playwright who would help pave Garfinkle's way into the innovative Group Theater.

It was in the February 1935 Group Theater performance of Odets's play *Awake and Sing* that Garfield first caught the attention of reviewers. Yet, he might have remained a stage performer if not for his disappointment over the casting of Odets's *Golden Boy*. Though the central role had been written with Garfield in mind, it instead went to the director's brother-in-law. After taking a lesser role, Garfield was primed for a career change when he was approached by Warner Brothers, then known for its movies for and about the working class. The studio signed him to a contract.

FILM CAREER

Garfield's vast talents and rebellious persona were apparent with his first film, *Four Daughters* (1938), for which he earned a Best Supporting Actor Oscar nomination. As Mickey Borden—an orchestrator who comes into the life of a sunny blond and her musical family—he sardonically surmises, "The fates are against me. They tossed a coin—heads, I'm poor, tails I'm rich. So what did they do? They tossed a coin with two heads." That sense of fatalism would become a Garfield motif. Indeed, he enjoyed his only traditionally heroic role in the 1945 film *Pride of the Marines*, which follows the return home and rehabilitation of real-life marine Al Schmid. Blinded during a bloody night attack on Guadalcanal, Schmid nonetheless machine-guns some 200 Japanese soldiers.

While he was an actor who identified with characters living on the edge, Garfield also tackled roles because of his admiration for particular artists and themes. He starred in *The Sea Wolf* (1941) because he revered the writings of Jack London. He took a supporting role in the seminal movie *Gentleman's Agreement* (1947) because it examined anti-Semitism. Said Garfield, "That was a part I didn't act. I felt it with all my heart."

Frequently, the men he played were on the run—from themselves as well as from the law. In *They Made Me a Criminal* (1939) Garfield plays a prizefighter who heads west following his involvement with a murder. In *Dust Be My Destiny* (1939) he is an escapee from a prison work farm. In *The Breaking Point* (1950) he plays the role of a boat captain who smuggles illegal aliens. In his final film, the 1951 *He Ran All the Way*, his character goes into hiding following his involvement in a payroll robbery in which a policeman is killed.

Within the Garfield oeuvre, redemption came at a significant price. *Body and Soul* (1947), about an unscrupulous prizefighter, climaxes when Garfield's character refuses to throw a fight. "What are you gonna do? Kill me? Everybody dies," he says, in a defiant but downbeat climax. Renowned for its realistic boxing sequences, the movie earned Garfield a Best Actor Oscar nomination. In the similarly dark *Force of Evil* (1948), Garfield is a crooked lawyer involved in a numbers syndicate. Both movies were produced by Garfield's own company, and they continue to enjoy cult status in part because of the involvement of filmmaker Abraham Polonsky, who was later blacklisted.

BLACKLISTING

Because of his own outspoken, liberal views, Garfield also came under the scrutiny of the House Un-American Activities Committee during its investigation of the communist infiltration of Hollywood. During his 1951 testimony, Garfield surprised friends and associates by contradicting his well-known viewpoints. In the aftermath of his testimony, he ceased receiving major film offers. The actor was estranged from his family when he succumbed to a heart attack at age thirty-nine. Those closest to him claimed that the stress of the investigation contributed to his death.

Because Garfield died in the bed of a female friend, there have long been rumors regarding details of his death. In the 1993 movie *Indecent Proposal*, in which multimillionaire Robert Redford has a contract drawn up regarding a pending sexual liaison with Demi Moore, the lawyer adds a "John Garfield clause," explaining, "That's if you die in the act." But the lore about Garfield's shadowy affairs pales alongside his fiercely memorable screen images. With his tousled hair, ubiquitous cigarette, and embittered world-weariness, he became a reminder that life is a survival course.

It could also be said that the original movie rebel helped to make possible a far more legendary career: Garfield originally was sought for the role of Stanley Kowalski in the Broadway play *A Streetcar Named Desire*. He turned it down, believing that the character of Blanche du Bois overshadowed Kowalski. The role went to a twenty-four-year-old unknown named Marlon Brando. In essence, one rebel passed the torch to another.

Pat H. Broeske

SEE ALSO: *Blacklisting; Brando, Marlon;* The Postman Always Rings Twice*; Sex Symbol;* A Streetcar Named Desire*; Turner, Lana.*

BIBLIOGRAPHY

Beaver, James N., Jr. *John Garfield: His Life and Films*. South Brunswick, NJ: A. S. Barnes, 1978.

McGrath, Patrick J. *John Garfield: The Illustrated Career in Films and on Stage*. Jefferson: NC: McFarland, 1993.

Morella, Joe, and Edward Z. Epstein. *Rebels: The Rebel Hero in Films*. New York: Citadel Press, 1971.

Swindell, Larry. *Body and Soul: The Story of John Garfield*. New York: William Morrow, 1975.

Garland, Judy *(1922–1969)*

For generations of film audiences, Judy Garland was a symbol of hope and tragedy, a gay icon, and most of all a star. A triple threat, she acted, danced, and sang her way through more than two dozen feature films for the Metro-Goldwyn-Mayer (MGM) studio from 1938 to 1950. Many of her films are considered classics of the Hollywood musical genre. She possessed a powerful singing voice full of pain and vulnerability, recording nearly 100 singles and more than two dozen albums. She remarked, "I have a voice that hurts people where they think they want to be hurt."

CHILDHOOD

Garland was born Frances Ethel Gumm on June 10, 1922, in Grand Rapids, Minnesota, to former vaudevillians Frank and Ethel. From the time she was a toddler, Garland, nicknamed "Baby," performed with her sisters in a stage act called the Gumm Sisters. As a two-year-old, she performed "Jingle Bells" on stage at New Grand Theater (her father's cinema) and brought down the house.

At twelve she changed her name to Judy after the title of a contemporary Hoagy Carmichael song. Comedian George Jessel is credited with giving her and her sisters the moniker Garland at the 1934 World's Fair in Chicago. In late 1935 she performed in several radio broadcasts, singing "Broadway Melody" and what would later become one of her signature songs, "Zing! Went the Strings of My Heart." A few days later, her father died of spinal meningitis. Her reaction was a day-long crying binge.

***Judy Garland in* The Wizard of Oz.** *Judy Garland starred in 1939's* The Wizard of Oz *as Dorothy, which would become the defining role of her career.* MGM STUDIOS/MGM STUDIOS/GETTY IMAGES.

CAREER WITH MGM

Months before her father's death, Garland, only thirteen, signed a contract with MGM. At first, MGM (led by producer Louis B. Mayer) was unsure how to use her. Her voice sounded so adult that executives feared audiences would not believe it could come from a child. Finally, in the fall of 1936, the studio loaned her to rival Twentieth Century Fox for a role in *Pigskin Parade* (1936), a college football romp.

In early 1937 she won hearts at MGM's birthday party for famous actor Clark Gable by singing "Dear Mr. Gable / You Made Me Love You." The same year, Garland's first MGM film, *Broadway Melody of 1938*, became a big hit. She also starred in the studio's Andy Hardy series, playing girl-next-door Betsy Booth alongside actor Mickey Rooney, famous for his line "Let's put on a show!"

But the film that elevated the little girl with the grown-up voice to superstardom was *The Wizard of Oz* (1939), for which she sang the immortal "Somewhere over the Rainbow" and received a special juvenile Academy Award. (Shirley Temple was briefly considered for the role, but Garland was always MGM's first choice for Dorothy.) It was the defining role of her life. For many fans, she would always be the plucky girl from Kansas who yearned for a place where "the dreams that you dare to dream really do come true."

"Somewhere over the Rainbow" became an anthem of hope in England during World War II. Later, Garland would sing the last eight bars of it over the phone to President John F. Kennedy whenever he needed cheering up. In her stage concerts, she used the song as a finale, as it had profound personal significance for her and often brought tears to the audience's eyes.

Garland made millions of dollars for MGM in the 1940s. She filmed two features per year, including *Strike Up the Band* (1940) and *Meet Me in St. Louis* (1944). The latter made almost as much money as *Gone with the Wind* (1939) and contained the later standard "Trolley Song." It also added a new carol to the holiday pantheon, "Have Yourself a Merry Little Christmas." Her other titles included *For Me and My Gal* (1942) with actor/dancer Gene Kelly, *The Harvey Girls* (1946), and *Easter Parade* (1948) with Broadway legend Fred Astaire.

FIRING AND COMEBACK

Plagued by ill health and addictions, Garland's private life was never stable. From her teen years, at MGM's insistence, she used pills to control her weight and to help her sleep; at times, her use of drugs got out of control. Soon after her nineteenth birthday, she wedded musician David Rose, although the marriage ended three years later. In 1945 she married director Vincente Minnelli, and they had a daughter, Liza. However, the couple separated in 1949.

On the MGM sets, she had a reputation for unreliability. She was often late for or absent from rehearsals and caused no end of consternation with her diva-like behavior. Finally, MGM fired her in 1950. Soon after she published a somewhat disingenuous open letter to her fans in the magazine *Modern Screen*, saying she had suffered from depression and a "mild inferiority complex" and needed a vacation. She thanked her fans for their stalwart support, saying, "I am still Judy Garland, a plain American girl from Grand Rapids, Minnesota, who's had a lot of good breaks, a few tough breaks, and who loves you with all her heart for your kindness in understanding that I am nothing more, nothing less."

In 1951 she and her third husband, Sid Luft, staged her first big comeback, a concert appearance at the Palace Theater on Broadway. The record-breaking show ran for nineteen weeks. In addition selling out concerts, she nabbed the role of Esther Blodgett/Vicki Lester in Warner Brothers' remake of *A Star Is Born* (1954), which put her back on the map with the songs "The Man That Got Away" and "Born in a Trunk."

In the early 1960s she had a television variety program on CBS. Placed opposite the popular Western series *Bonanza* (1959–1973), however, *The Judy Garland Show* (1963–1964) was short-lived. Nevertheless, she continued to stage comebacks, once remarking she had so many that every time she came back from the bathroom it was regarded as a comeback.

One of her greatest successes was her 1961 Carnegie Hall appearance, the recording of which received an unprecedented five Grammy Awards, including Album of the Year. At this concert and those at the Palace and the London Palladium, the audience's hysterical screaming and crying were comparable to the reaction rock stars received. Despite a real possibility that the star, dubbed "The World's Greatest Entertainer," would collapse or fall onstage, audiences were rooting for her. They loved her voice, her talent, and her persona. Legend has it that once, when she called for requests, an audience member yelled, "Just stand there!"

FANS

Garland's mystique related in part to her combustible personality. Her relationship with her mother was poor, and at one point they were involved in a lawsuit over money. She had five husbands altogether (the last two were Mark Herron and Mickey Deans) and several affairs. Detractors called her temperamental and "a compulsive weeper"; fans loved her even so.

Her fan base was a cross-section of the American population, but she appealed in particular to gay men. Today her status as gay icon is unquestionable and possibly unmatched. She had a gay following from early in her career. The association may have started with her role as the girl who wants to go over the rainbow in *The Wizard of Oz*. The rainbow from the film is mirrored in the gay pride rainbow symbol, and the phrase "friend of Dorothy" was accepted in the 1970s as code for being gay.

Garland's simultaneous mix of vulnerability and emotional intensity was another aspect that made her popular in the gay community. Her sincerity in her stage act made her a character beloved by drag queens. Her appeal in the community was so ubiquitous that in the film *The Boys in the Band* (1970), one character wonders, "What's more boring than a queen doing a Judy Garland imitation?"

Garland's frequent suicide attempts in the last twenty years of her life became part of her legend. With each new attempt reported in the tabloids, gay fans wore Band-Aids on their wrists in solidarity. On June 22, 1969, when her husband found her collapsed in the bathroom, dead of a drug overdose, no one was very surprised. Vincent Canby wrote in the *New York Times*, "The greatest shock about her death was that there was no shock." She was forty-seven years old and millions of dollars in debt.

Some argue that her New York City funeral contributed to the power of the pivotal Stonewall Rebellion. With emotions running high in the aftermath of the funeral, gay and lesbian patrons at the Stonewall Inn in Greenwich Village fought gay-bashing police and sparked a series of riots in New York that heralded the beginning of the gay liberation movement. True or not, director Nigel Finch's 1995 film *Stonewall* played up the effect of Garland's death on the events of that day.

Garland had three children—Liza Minnelli, Lorna Luft, and Joey Luft. Like her mother, Liza became a triple threat—an actress, a singer, and a dancer. She had roles in *Cabaret* (1972) and *Arthur* (1981) and a cameo in *The Muppets Take Manhattan* (1984). She was part of Andy Warhol's Club 54 entourage, and her reputation was similar to her mother's in many ways.

Lorna had a show-business career and made concert appearances. She also had a role in *Grease 2* (1982) and wrote a tell-all book about her mother, *Me and My Shadows: A Family Memoir* (1998). The book was made into an Emmy Award–winning television film, *Life with Judy Garland: Me and My Shadows* (2001), starring Judy Davis.

In 2006 musician Rufus Wainwright performed Garland's entire 1961 program at Carnegie Hall, garnering a Grammy nomination for the subsequent recording. The abundance of tributes to Garland has ensured the continued value of her memorabilia. Manufactured and sold during her early movie career and after her death, her memorabilia includes limited-edition dolls, paper doll sets, coloring books, and of course *Oz*-related products. A pair of her ruby slippers from the film is on permanent display at the Smithsonian Institution. Perhaps singer Frank Sinatra best summed up public feeling about her when he said, "the rest of us will be forgotten—never Judy."

Jessy Randall

SEE ALSO: *Academy Awards; Andy Hardy; Astaire, Fred, and Ginger Rogers;* Bonanza*; Broadway; Carmichael, Hoagy; Carnegie Hall; Celebrity; College Football; Depression; Drag; Emmy Awards; Fan Magazines; Gable, Clark; Gay Liberation Movement; Gay Men;* Gone with the Wind*; Grammy Awards; Jessel, George; Kelly, Gene; Lesbianism; Made-for-Television Movies; Mayer, Louis B.;* Meet Me in St. Louis*; Minnelli, Liza; Minnelli, Vincente; The Musical; Radio; Sinatra, Frank; Stonewall Rebellion; Suicide; Tabloids; Television; Temple, Shirley; Vaudeville;* The Wizard of Oz*; World War II.*

BIBLIOGRAPHY

Clarke, Gerald. *Get Happy: The Life of Judy Garland.* New York: Random House, 2000.

Fricke, John. *Judy Garland: World's Greatest Entertainer.* New York: Holt, 1992.

Goldman, William. *The Season: A Candid Look at Broadway.* New York: Harcourt, Brace, and World, 1969.

Kaiser, Charles. *The Gay Metropolis: 1940–1996.* San Diego, CA: Harcourt Brace and Company, 1997.

Shipman, David. *Judy Garland: The Secret Life of an American Legend.* New York: Hyperion, 1993.

Vare, Ethlie Ann, ed. *Rainbow: A Star-Studded Tribute to Judy Garland.* New York: Boulevard Books, 1998.

Garner, James *(1928–)*

Playing wandering gambler Bret Maverick in the television western *Maverick* (1957–1960), James Garner established the persona of the cynical, witty antihero. He would carry this persona with him in the majority of his later roles, both on television and in movies.

James Scott Bumgarner was born on April 7, 1928, in Norman, Oklahoma. He served in the army during the Korean War and upon his return to the United States decided to pursue a career in acting. After appearing in some commercials, he made his film debut in *Toward the Unknown* (1956). The next year he became well known to major audiences with the television series *Maverick*. He left the show after only three years, however, following a dispute with the studio. Some of the movies he starred in during the 1960s included *The Great Escape* (1963), *The Americanization of Emily* (1964), and *Support Your Local Sheriff!* (1969).

Garner enjoyed television success again in *The Rockford Files* (1974–1980) as crusty private eye Jim Rockford, a role that earned him an Emmy Award in 1976. In films such as *H.E.A.L.T.H* (1979) and *Victor/Victoria* (1982), and the TV film *Barbarians at the Gate* (1993), he proved that his trademark persona had an enduring popularity. Later in his career he took on supporting roles, playing Jim Egan in the television sitcom *8 Simple Rules* (2002–2005) following the death of John Ritter and providing the voice for Chevrolet truck advertisements. The Screen Actors Guild nominated Garner as the Best Supporting Male Actor for his performance in the film *The Notebook* (2004) and presented him with a Lifetime Achievement Award in 2005. His memoir, *The Garner Files* (2011), was warmly received by critics, who praised his candidness and self-deprecating humor.

Christian L. Pyle

SEE ALSO: *Advertising; Emmy Awards; Sitcom; Television; The Western.*

BIBLIOGRAPHY

Garner, James, and Jon Winokur. *The Garner Files: A Memoir.* New York: Simon & Schuster, 2011.

Strait, Raymond. *James Garner: A Biography.* New York: St. Martin's Press, 1985.

Garvey, Marcus *(1887–1940)*

As an activist who promoted black pride, Marcus Garvey founded one of the largest mass movements of black Americans. Garvey's Universal Negro Improvement Association (UNIA) offered new hope for working-class blacks in the 1920s. At the same time, Harlem Renaissance artists encouraged racial pride, but within that movement opportunities came to only a limited number of creative African American individuals. Garvey's clarion call for black nationalism resonated primarily among lower- and working-class blacks and inspired numerous black mass-appeal leaders and movements. The appeal of Garvey himself faded by the late 1920s, but he remained a complex and controversial figure for his views on black nationalism and cultural militancy, which energized many black Americans in the post–World War I era.

Although he would become a pioneering black nationalist in the United States, Garvey grew up in rather inauspicious surroundings in Jamaica. He was born on Saint Ann's Bay, Jamaica, on August 17, 1887. As a young man, Garvey moved to Kingston, where he worked as a printer and an editor. After traveling extensively in the West Indies and Central America and living briefly in England, Garvey became convinced that black people suffered a sort of universal cultural and economic exploitation wherever they lived outside of Africa. He worked to resolve this by preaching cultural unification of blacks worldwide, stressing the idea of going back to Africa.

In 1914 Garvey organized UNIA in Jamaica as the organizational arm of his black nationalist "Back to Africa" Movement. Soon his oratorical skills drew many supporters. By the time Garvey moved to the United States in 1916, UNIA had become a budding international movement for downtrodden blacks seeking help in improving their lives as a collective voice. It was the desperate post–World War I black population of inner-city New York that provided Garvey with the most recruits and support.

By the early 1920s Garvey had made Harlem the home base for UNIA. During numerous rallies, parades, and similar demonstrations, he preached a message of racial pride and cultural unity to millions of blacks throughout the United States and the world. Garvey's then-radical message appealed especially to black Americans who, as a result of the "Great Migration" of the early twentieth century (which had moved millions of blacks from the rural South to the urban North), could easily spread Garvey's message through their new urban-based culture. Garvey's fervent nationalism became epitomized in his cry, "Up, Up You Mighty Race! You Can Accomplish What You Will!" By the mid-1920s UNIA claimed almost two and a half million members and sympathizers, although in retrospect that number seems inflated.

Yet by the late 1920s, the mass cultural appeal of Garvey and UNIA quickly decreased. In 1923 Garvey received a five-year prison sentence for mail fraud, even though the evidence indicated that his subordinates may have committed the crimes without Garvey's knowledge. In 1927 President Calvin Coolidge commuted Garvey's sentence and ordered him deported to Jamaica. Without the dynamic Garvey as its leader, the UNIA quickly disintegrated into a moribund movement. As the Great Depression swept America in the 1930s, Garvey's once forceful movement slipped into anonymity. He sought to resurrect the movement in London in 1935 but gained little success and died a largely forgotten man in London in 1940.

Though Garvey faded from popularity after his incarceration in 1925, his teachings and ideas became a lasting legacy. His emphasis on racial pride, understanding the African heritage, and black unity shaped the thinking of Malcolm X (whose father was a Garveyite) and the program of the black Muslims in the 1930s. Garvey's memory also inspired the Black Power movement of the 1960s. Moreover, his stress on self-reliance is still an important theme among many African American community leaders. Garvey remains an undisputed icon of black pride.

Irvin D. Solomon

SEE ALSO: *Civil Rights Movement; The Great Depression; Harlem Renaissance; Malcolm X.*

BIBLIOGRAPHY

Cronon, Edmund David. *Black Moses: The Story of Marcus Garvey and the Universal Negro Improvement Association.* Madison: University of Wisconsin Press, 1969.

Garvey, Amy Jacques, ed. *Philosophy and Opinions of Marcus Garvey, or, Africa for the Africans.* London: Cass, 1967.

Hill, Robert A., ed. *The Marcus Garvey and Universal Negro Improvement Association Papers,* 7 vols. Berkeley: University of California Press, 1983–1990.

Huddle, Mark Andrew. *Marcus Garvey: Black Nationalism and the New Negro Renaissance.* Chicago: Ivan R. Dee, 2009.

Jamaica Library Service. *Garvey Centenary, 1887–1987: A Select Bibliography.* Kingston: Jamaica Library Service, 1987.

Martin, Tony. *Race First: The Ideological and Organizational Struggles of Marcus Garvey and the Universal Negro Improvement Association.* Westport, CT: Greenwood Press, 1976.

Stein, Judith. *The World of Marcus Garvey: Race and Class in Modern Society.* Baton Rouge: Louisiana State University Press, 1986.

Garvey, Steve *(1948–)*

Baseball great Steve Garvey was among the most popular and successful players in Major League Baseball during the 1970s and 1980s. He was named the National League's Most Valuable Player in 1974 and went on to play in four World Series as first baseman with the Dodgers. He was voted to the All-Star team eight times as a Dodger and was named the All-Star Game's Most Valuable Player twice, in 1974 and 1978. Garvey, with 1,207, holds the record for consecutive games played for a National League player.

He and his wife, Cyndy Garvey, became known as the "Ken and Barbie" of baseball because of their good looks and apparent perfect lifestyle. Marital infidelity plagued both of the Garveys, however, and the couple eventually split up and engaged in an ugly divorce and custody battle. Garvey completed his playing career with the San Diego Padres, where he retired in 1988. Post-baseball, he worked for his beloved Dodgers until his public criticism of ownership led to his dismissal in 2011. Garvey was a member of a group who unsuccessfully attempted to buy the Dodgers in 2012.

Jay Parrent

SEE ALSO: *Baseball; Divorce; Sports Heroes.*

BIBLIOGRAPHY

Garvey, Cynthia, and Andy Meisler. *The Secret Life of Cyndy Garvey.* New York: Doubleday, 1989.

Garvey, Steve, and Skip Rozin. *Garvey.* New York: Times Books, 1986.

McNeil, William F. *The Dodgers Encyclopedia.* Champaign, IL: Sports Publishing, 2003.

Gas Stations

Gas stations are embedded in our urban and rural landscape, pervasive symbols of the automobile's domination of twentieth-century society. Like fast-food restaurants, motels, and shopping malls, their very existence was engendered by the automobile. They demonstrate the extent of corporate control over our lives, and, on a more philosophical note, they represent what the

Gas Station, 1945. *A roadside gas station lights up the Utah night in 1945.* HULTON ARCHIVE/ GETTY IMAGES.

book *The Gas Station in America* (1994) refers to as "a potential point of pause" in our unceasingly mobile culture.

EARLY FILLING STATIONS

Gas stations have changed over the course of their existence, from strictly functional to multipurpose. Their evolution allows us to glimpse the development of a consumer society in the United States that is fueled by the power of advertising and increasing corporatization. Early motorists purchased their gasoline by the bucket from a dry goods or hardware store. The first filling stations were simple sheds or shacks with a gas pump. By the 1910s, however, they began to take on a unique identity in the landscape. Oil companies created standardized buildings for the distribution of their product. The Texas Company (Texaco), for example, constructed its first station in 1911. Since the motorist was in no position to judge the quality of gasoline and therefore distinguish one brand from another, the oil companies then had to instill brand loyalty in their customers. The distribution of gasoline was therefore linked from the beginning to marketing and advertising systems.

Corporate logos and slogans were created to help the public identify with the company producing the gasoline. "Visible" gasoline pumps, with a clear glass cylinder at the top, allowed the motorist to see the product as it was pumped into the car, which led to the practice of dyeing gasoline such colors as red, blue, or purple. Companies also began to diversify the range of products and services available to the public. Maintenance and repair services turned filling stations into all-around car-care stations.

The standardization of the 1910s gave way to eclecticism in the 1920s. Oil companies' drive to make their product identifiable led to the creation of exotic, eye-catching buildings designed to look like Greek temples, Chinese pagodas, and Swiss chalets. By the end of the 1920s, a nationwide gasoline distribution system was in place in the United States that has not changed since. At the same time, a highway construction boom allowed motorists to expand their range of travel. Gas stations were built along the new roads to provide necessary and convenient services. These more out-of-the-way stations were dedicated as much to the customer as the car—they offered amenities for the new long-distance traveler unnecessary in urban locales, such as clean rest rooms, free maps, soft drinks, and snacks.

As traffic increased and the automobile culture expanded, gas stations attracted other businesses, such as motels and diners, to the same location. The desire to make patrons feel comfortable also prompted these early stations to clothe their employees in military-style uniforms, which added an air of legitimacy to a still relatively novel enterprise. Slogans such as Texaco's "You can trust your car to the man who wears the star" also encouraged consumer comfort.

THE MODERN GAS STATION

In the 1930s and 1940s the eclectically styled gas stations of the previous decade diminished as a new, "modern" design aesthetic—reflecting public fascination with images of the future—swept through the industry. Stations emphasized clean surfaces and streamlined curves as Art Deco or Moderne-style structures became popular symbols of the new machine age. Oil companies hired famous designers to update and promote their image. In 1934 Norman Bel Geddes provided a new look for the Socony-Vacuum Oil Company (which became Mobil) that proved too avant-garde and was never used. That year, Texaco hired Walter Dorwin Teague for the same purpose. His streamlined box design was an instant success and was implemented in more than 10,000 stations across the country. Teague created a universally adaptable form and an immediately recognizable symbol for Texaco products. Other companies attempted to duplicate this achievement but were not as successful.

By the 1950s a functional aesthetic began to prevail in the design of gas stations across the country. Historic and modern elements were rejected in favor of a design that emphasized utility. Logos became more important as symbols of corporate identity. The impact of television as an advertising medium lessened the need for the gas station to serve as a three-dimensional billboard. For example, the Pure Oil Company sponsored a television quiz show in 1950 in which the company's slogan "Be Sure with Pure" was constantly repeated. The Texaco Star Theater, with Milton Berle, was the most successful of these ventures—it became the most popular television program in the country in the 1950s.

The nature of the gas station changed again in the 1960s with the emergence of self-service stations and convenience stores. Self-service actually originated in the 1930s, but in the interim most states had passed legislation requiring that only station personnel attend the pumps. The link between gas station and grocery store was even older: in the 1910s many general stores in rural areas also had a gas pump. Truck stops and "highway hubs"—small consumer areas at highway interchanges—developed during this time period.

In the late twentieth century, repair and maintenance services moved increasingly within the purview of specialty shops and automobile dealerships, and gasoline pumps were added to convenience stores as a secondary service. The traditional filling station has become almost extinct, but as long as American society remains dependent on the gasoline-powered automobile, the filling station, in whatever form it may take, will remain a part of our landscape.

Dale Allen Gyure

SEE ALSO: *Advertising; Automobile; Berle, Milton; Consumerism; Diners; Fast Food; Highway System; Industrial Design; Malls; Sunday Driving; Television.*

BIBLIOGRAPHY

Jakle, John A., and Keith A. Schulle. *The Gas Station in America.* Baltimore, MD: Johns Hopkins University Press, 1994.

Jennings, Jan, ed. *Roadside America: The Automobile in Design and Culture.* Ames: Iowa State University Press, 1990.

Russell, Tim. *Fill 'er Up! The Great American Gas Station.* St. Paul, MN: Voyageur Press, 2007.

Vieyra, Daniel I. *"Fill 'er Up": An Architectural History of America's Gas Stations.* New York: Collier Macmillan Publishers, 1979.

Witzel, Michael Karl. *The American Gas Station: History and Folklore of the Gas Station in American Car Culture.* Osceola, WI: Motorbooks International Publishers & Wholesalers, 1992.

Gated Communities

Gated communities are residential areas, ranging in size from individual streets and neighborhoods to entire cities, enclosed by walls and gates that are intended to prevent unauthorized entry by nonresidents. In many gated communities further protection against the outside world is provided by private security guards and electronic security systems. Most such communities operate as common interest developments (CIDs), in which residents collectively own the common spaces or shared amenities and a private homeowner association oversees community affairs. The population of these fortified enclaves tends to be overwhelmingly middle- or upper-class, white, and middle-aged or older. The primary reason these groups settle in such places, according to surveys, is to escape the crime, traffic, and noise of the cities and ungated suburbs. To many observers, the rising number of gated communities constitutes, in the words of Robert Reich, the Clinton administration's labor secretary, "the succession of the successful" away from the civic life of the broader society.

Although gated communities in one form or another have existed in America since the colonial era, up until the late 1960s they were popular only with the ultra-rich and privacy-conscious celebrities. In the 1970s developers began building a few master-planned walled subdivisions aimed primarily at senior citizens and retirees. By the 1980s and 1990s gated communities designed for ordinary middle-class families were proliferating at a rapid rate, particularly throughout the Sun Belt states. Researchers agree that middle-class fears about rising crime and concerns about the deterioration of municipal services are the most important factors in explaining the boom in gated developments. In *Fortress America,* Edward Blakely and Mary Gail Snyder estimate that by 1997 the United States had approximately 20,000 gated communities with some three million units of housing and 8.4 million residents.

Some 1990s gated developments attempted to incorporate all the traditional features of city living behind their walls. An excellent example of this trend is Green Valley, Nevada (a sprawling walled suburb outside Las Vegas), which is divided by house size and cost into prefabricated "villages," each with its own meeting hall, recreational center, school, and park, as well as, in the more exclusive tracts, an entrance with a manned guardhouse. By 2011 the population of Green Valley had reached 40,225. At the same time, more and more preexisting neighborhoods and suburbs are walling themselves off from surrounding cities by barricading public streets and installing gates and security systems.

In the majority of gated developments that are organized as CIDs, homeowner associations function as a kind of private government. People who buy property in such developments are forced to join the association, pay dues, and agree to abide by its rules. Homeowner associations deliver traditional public services, such as trash collection, policing, snow removal, road maintenance, and street lighting. They also make regulations governing all aspects of life in the community, including rules limiting the hours and frequency of visitors, setting the minimum age of residents, banning the display of flags, prohibiting certain kinds of pets, and specifying the paint color that owners can use on their houses. Fairbanks Ranch, an affluent gated community in Southern California, is patrolled by private security officers who enforce a speed limit set by the homeowner association. These officers have the authority to fine repeat speeders $500, and violators can be banned from the community's streets for a month. A few gated communities have succeeded in incorporating themselves as full-fledged municipalities with elected city government usually deferring to the rule-making authority of the homeowner association.

CONTEMPORARY TRENDS

As the proportion of the population living in them has risen, gated communities have gradually become a political force to be reckoned with. In California, private homeowner associations have lobbied state legislatures for the right to deduct homeowner dues from state income taxes. In 1990 New Jersey private homeowner associations pushed legislation through the state legislature that entitles members to rebates on property taxes paid to support city services.

Yet even as gated communities were beginning to enjoy the fruits of their newfound power, there were signs in the late 1990s of a growing backlash against what planner Norman Krumholz has called the "balkanization" of America's cities. Four communities in suburban Dallas—Addison, Plano, Richardson, and Southlake—decided to prohibit barriers on public roads and even placed moratoriums on the construction of private gated developments. In 1995 both San Diego, California, and Portland, Oregon, began studying policies designed to limit the spread of gates within their boundaries. Proposals to erect walls around existing communities and close public streets have been successfully fought in courts and city councils in Los Angeles; Chicago; Atlanta, Georgia; Sacramento, California; and elsewhere.

Ultimately, however, whether the number and population of America's fortified enclaves continues to expand will be determined less by political battles than by the desires and decisions of millions of home buyers in the years to come. As long as fear of crime and the desire for peace and quiet outweigh the lure of public life in the minds of those who can afford to choose where they live, gated communities will continue their inexorable spread across the nation's landscape.

By the early twenty-first century, the rate of gated communities was continuing to rise. In the West, South, and Southeast, more than 40 percent of all new residential developments were being built as gated communities. The trend has led to a burgeoning body of literature on the issue of why Americans, along with residents of many other countries, are hiding behind walls. Critics point out that there is little sense of community spirit within these gated communities. Others insist that the rise of gated communities results in a tendency to ignore the greater social problems that create the need for them in the first place. The chief reason continues to be security. People have become increasingly afraid of being victimized by street gangs, crazed drug addicts, and other criminals. Cities beef up their police forces and spend millions on installing cameras in public places, and individuals buy guns. In the United States the rate of gun owners rose from 76 per 100 in 1994 to 90 per 100 by 2007. Forty states passed laws that permit the carrying of concealed weapons. Those who can afford it escape by living in gated communities, where they feel a modicum of safety from the larger world that terrifies them.

Steve Macek

SEE ALSO: *Gangs; Suburbia; War on Drugs.*

BIBLIOGRAPHY

Bagaeen, Samer, and Ola Uduku. *Gated Communities: Social Sustainability in Contemporary and Historical Gated Developments*. Washington, DC: Earthscan, 2010.

Blakely, Edward, and Mary Gail Snyder. *Fortress America: Gated Communities in the United States*. Washington, DC: Brookings Institution Press, 1997.

Judd, Dennis. "The Rise of the New Walled Cities." *Spatial Practices: Critical Explorations in Social/Spatial Theory*, ed. Helen Liggett and David Perry, 144–166. Thousand Oaks, CA: Sage, 1995.

Low, Setha. *Behind the Gates: Life, Security, and the Pursuit of Happiness in Fortress America*. New York: Routledge, 2003.

May, Elaine Tyler. "Anger and Security." *Chronicle of Higher Education* 56, no. 40 (2010).

McKenzie, Evan. *Privatopia: Homeowner Associations and the Rise of Residential Private Government*. New Haven, CT: Yale University Press, 1994.

Stark, Andrew. "America, the Gated?" *Wilson Quarterly*, Winter 1998, 58–79.

Gay and Lesbian Marriage

The issue of same-sex marriage is a complex one, involving not only the affirmation of love and commitment between two people but also access to rights granted to married opposite-sex couples. These rights range from financial, such as sharing social security benefits, to medical, such as the right to make decisions for a disabled partner. Although some legislatures have attempted to avoid the question of same-sex marriage by introducing domestic partnerships and other forms of civil unions, many gays and lesbians have continued to demand marriage equality. The increasing legal acceptance of same-sex marriage has marked one of the major cultural and social changes of the twenty-first century in the United States.

In 1970, as the gay right movement was gaining strength, the Los Angeles County clerk requested the California legislature tighten the state's marriage laws because so many same-sex couples were applying for marriage licenses. In the late 1980s homosexual marriage was again hotly contested in the courts, in state and national legislatures, by the public at large, in the mass media, and within the gay and lesbian community. By 2012 eight states had laws permitting same-sex marriage, with the number changing almost monthly, as new states introduced legislation allowing the marriages and right-wing groups continued to challenge each new law.

EARLY LEGALIZATION EFFORTS

In 1971 Richard John Baker and James Michael McConnell brought the first case of same-sex marriage to court in Minnesota. Along with arguing their constitutional rights, the plaintiffs cited recent antimiscegenation laws in support of their plea, all of which the court rejected. The first lesbian marriage case, *Jones v. Hallahan*, was brought in Kentucky in 1973. The case was lost on the grounds of falling outside the dictionary definition of *marriage*—as would happen many more times over the next decades.

Although a number of other court cases were lost in the 1970s, there were a few small victories, such as a county clerk granting a marriage license to a gay couple in Boulder, Colorado, encouraging other gay and lesbian couples to apply for—and receive—marriage licenses. However, the state's attorney general

Same-Sex Marriage. *A gay couple exchanges marriage vows at San Francisco City Hall in 2004.* DEBORAH COLEMAN/GETTY IMAGES.

later revoked all of the licenses. In 1975 the Arizona legislature passed an emergency bill defining marriage as only between a man and a woman, setting a precedent for other state legislatures.

The rise of radical lesbian feminism, coupled with concerns about AIDS, dominated political discourse within the lesbian and gay communities from the late 1970s to the mid-1980s. Early feminist theory argued against the institution of marriage in general, and many lesbians questioned the importance of lesbian and gay marriage rights. Moreover, the graver issue of the AIDS epidemic so dominated the gay community that issues such as marriage rights became secondary.

Ironically, the lesbian feminist movement and AIDS activism provoked the reemergence of the issue of same-sex marriage by encouraging gay individuals to come out. Also, by politicizing homosexuality, raising public consciousness about lesbian and gay issues, and fighting the image of gays—particularly men—as promiscuous people incapable of long-term relationships, the lesbian and gay rights movement helped reassert the marriage issue. In addition, the feminist movement's push toward passing the Equal Rights Amendment influenced a prominent same-sex marriage case in Hawaii, *Baehr v. Lewin*, in the 1990s.

LEGISLATION AND RESISTANCE

In 1986 the American Civil Liberties Union declared it would seek to eliminate legal barriers preventing lesbians and gays from marrying. In 1989 the San Francisco Bar Association called for legalizing gay and lesbian marriage. The same year, two gay Chicago journalists filed complaints with the Illinois Department of Human Rights accusing the state of sex discrimination for refusing to allow gay marriages. The issue began to gain momentum in the general public, and in 1989 a *Time* magazine poll reported 69 percent of Americans disapproved of same-sex marriage, 23 percent approved, and 8 percent were unsure. Three years later, a 1992 *Newsweek* survey found 58 percent against, 35 percent for, and 7 percent unsure.

The most well-known court case to advance the cause of same-sex marriage was *Baehr v. Lewin*, heard in Hawaii in 1991. Three same-sex couples sued the state for refusing to issue them marriage licenses, claiming that the refusal violated Hawaii's equal rights amendment barring discrimination on the basis of sex. In May 1993, for the first time in U.S. legal history, the Hawaii Supreme Court ruled in favor of lesbian and gay marriage.

Antigay groups and political leaders feared that lesbians and gays would flock to Hawaii to marry. Gay marriage opponents worked to change the constitutional mandate that provided interstate recognition of marriage (whereby each state must recognize and honor a marriage license granted in any other state). However, the largest blow to the gay and lesbian community came with the passage of the U.S. Defense of Marriage Act (DOMA) in 1996, which defined marriage for federal purposes as a legal union between one man and one woman. DOMA also permitted states to ignore out-of-state gay and lesbian marriages despite constitutional laws that ruled otherwise. Activists immediately began working to challenge DOMA, and in 2011 President Barack Obama announced that his administration would no longer defend the antigay law.

By the late 1990s more than thirty states enacted some type of anti-same-sex-marriage legislation, explicitly limiting marriage to one man and one woman. These 1990s laws differed from those passed in the 1970s because they addressed marriages within the state as well as interstate recognition of marriages. In November 1998 Hawaii voters passed a ballot saying there should be a constitutional amendment defining marriage as between one man and one woman.

LEGALIZATION IN SEVERAL STATES

The first decade of the 2000s was a time of heated debate and tremendous change on the issue of same-sex marriage, resulting in a confused flurry of legislation, challenges, and court decisions. In 2000 Vermont became the first state to give same-sex unions all the rights of heterosexual marriages. In 2004 Massachusetts, in the wake of a state supreme court decision, began allowing same-sex couples to marry. Connecticut followed in 2008.

In California a long effort by gay rights supporters to legalize same-sex unions seemed to end in success when the state supreme court ruled favorably in June 2008. More than 10,000 lesbian and gay couples were married before Proposition 8, a state initiative prohibiting same-sex marriage, was voted into law a few months later. Court challenges that Proposition 8 was discriminatory, and therefore illegal, were upheld in 2012, giving hope to activists that gay marriage would soon be legal in California once again. In Maine a similar scenario occurred, with the legislature approving same-sex unions in 2009 only to have a popular vote rescind the law.

In the years between 2009 and 2012, a number of states passed laws giving same-sex couples the right to marry, including Iowa in 2009; New Hampshire and Washington, D.C., in 2010; New York in 2011; and Maryland and Washington in 2012. Each of these laws faced challenges from conservatives and religious groups. Even within LGBT communities, debate continued over the importance of marriage in the struggle for human rights. Although many fought for marriage rights, believing such rights were an important part of societal acceptance, other individuals saw marriage as a distraction from broader human rights issues and a capitulation to the conservative desire to conform. In 2012 President Obama became the first U.S. president to publicly declare support for gay marriage.

Celebrities also have taken part in the gay marriage debate. Some have hastened to legalize their own unions, such as comedian Ellen DeGeneres and her partner, actress Portia de Rossi, who married in 2008 during California's window of legality. Others have publicly declared their support. Some, such as celebrity couple Brad Pitt and Angelina Jolie, even stated that they would not marry until their gay and lesbian friends had the same right. Talk-show host Conan O'Brien used the issue to gain a few ratings points by marrying one of his gay staffers and his partner on his New York–based show in 2011.

Hollywood, notoriously homophobic as an institution, has done little to highlight the issue. Comedies such as *I Now Pronounce You Chuck & Larry* (2007), in which a straight couple pretends to be gay in order to get the benefits of a civil union, have done little to contribute to the national conversation about same-sex marriage. However, a number of thoughtful documentaries on the subject, such as *The Gay Marriage Thing* (2005), directed by Stephanie Higgins, and *Mission to Matrimony* (2006), directed by Noah Pohl and Jerri Sher.

tova gd stabin

SEE ALSO: *Equal Rights Amendment; Gay Men; Lesbianism.*

BIBLIOGRAPHY

Feldblum, Chai R. "A Progressive Moral Case for Same-Sex Marriage." *Temple Political & Civil Rights Law Review* 7, no. 2 (1998): 485.

"Fever: Why Gay Marriage Is Scaring America to Death." *Advocate*, July 23, 1996, 22.

Goldstein, Richard. "The Great Gay Marriage Debate." *Village Voice*, January 9, 1996, 24.

Kopels, Sandra. "Wedded to the Status Quo: Same-Sex Marriage after *Baehr v. Lewin*." *Journal of Gay & Lesbian Social Services* 8, no. 3 (1998): 69.

Marcus, Eric. *Together Forever: Gay and Lesbian Marriage*. New York: Doubleday, 1998.

Martinac, Paula. *The Lesbian and Gay Book of Love and Marriage: Creating the Stories of Our Lives*. New York: Broadway Books, 1998.

Patten, James M. "The Defense of Marriage Act: How Congress Said 'No' to Full Faith and Credit, and the Constitution." *Santa Clara Law Review* 38, no. 3 (1998): 939.

Rich, Frank. "Whitewashing Gay History." *New York Magazine*, March 5, 2012.

Stiers, Gretchen A. *From This Day Forward: Commitment, Marriage, and Family in Lesbian and Gay Relationships*. New York: St. Martin's Press, 1999.

Wolfson, Evan. *Why Marriage Matters: America, Equality, and Gay People's Right to Marry*. New York: Simon & Schuster, 2004.

Gay and Lesbian Press

For more than sixty years, gay and lesbian presses in America have published papers and magazines that have given a distinctive voice to the homosexual community. Their editorial approaches and journalistic styles—unabashed, irreverent, and confrontational—reflect a commitment to bolstering the strength of the readerships they serve and to documenting and opposing the homophobic attitudes of society. The dissemination of ideas through the words of the gay and lesbian presses has been a building block in the development of gay culture. The publications act as powerful resources in the promotion of homosexual rights on national and international scales and as coalescing agents in bringing together gay and lesbian activists and closeted individuals, both from rural areas and urban ghettos. Mirroring the diversity of the gay and lesbian community, the presses are varied. While many publishers in the early twenty-first century still concentrate mostly on gay or lesbian issues, others have broadened their coverage to a wider community that includes bisexual, transgender, and intersex peoples.

The core of the press group is a small collection of specialist presses, along with a widespread offering of more general local and national newspapers and magazines. Historically, the distribution of gay and lesbian books was primarily through privately owned gay and lesbian bookstores, located in urban gay neighborhoods. There was initially strong opposition by regular booksellers to stocking gay and lesbian titles, but this had changed by the 1990s, when booksellers, along with other commercial enterprises, recognized gay and lesbian readers as a vast untapped resource. By the first decade of the 2000s more and more "straight" publishers had entered the gay market.

PUBLISHING ROOTS

During the first half of the twentieth century, most of the materials published that provided a positive viewpoint on homosexuality were issued through private presses. These publications were often of poor quality, frequently printed by hand, typed, or copied on mimeograph machines. The print runs were discreetly small, though there were notable exceptions in the literary field, where homosexual concerns were explored under the guise of metaphorical language and symbolism.

The precursor to the modern-day gay and lesbian presses can be observed in two late-nineteenth-century German periodicals, *Der Eigene* and *Jahrbuch für Sexuelle Zwischenstufen.* The sexologist Magnus Hirschfeld was the editor of *Jahrbuch für Sexuelle Zwischenstufen* from 1899 to 1923. Published in Berlin, the journal contained an academic perspective on homosexuality and featured full-length articles, bibliographies of new books, and articles by Eugen Wilhelm. *Der Eigene*, headed by Adolf Brand, was devoted to the field of arts and later developed into a publication reflecting a German homosexual movement called *Gemeinschaft der Eigenen*. The publication was of high quality, with many black-and-white, sepia, and color illustrations. *Der Eigene* was published from 1898 to 1930, when the rise of the National Socialist movement in Germany, which culminated with the upswing of Nazi persecution of homosexuals in the mid-1930s, brought the flourishing gay presses to an abrupt halt.

During the 1920s small and secretive gay presses started to emerge in the United States. The first was Henry Gerber's short-lived *Friendship and Freedom* (1924), which was founded in Chicago and published by the Society for Human Rights. Produced on a mimeograph machine and with a circulation of about 100, two issues were published. When police learned of the activities of the Society for Human Rights, they seized the remaining copies of *Friendship and Freedom* and arrested the membership of the group, including Gerber, who was dismissed from his postal job as a result of his activities. During the 1930s he also worked on another publication, *Chanticleer*, which devoted about 50 percent of its content to homosexual issues and the rest to atheistic advocacy. In addition, Gerber published a single-sheet mimeographed newsletter for Contacts pen-pal club from 1930 to 1939. The newsletter contained a few short news articles and was distributed among thirty to seventy members of the club.

None of these publications garnered a large readership due to the limited press runs, geographic constraints, and the restrictive attitudes of society. Indeed, the threat of police or government intervention under one pretext or another forced such publications to the margins of journalism.

THE MODERN PRESS

Following World War II, there was a revival of the homophile movement in the United States, and new gay and lesbian journals began to emerge. The earliest surviving publication, *Vice Versa*, dates to 1947 and was edited initially by Lisa Ben in Los Angeles. Ben was the editor's pseudonym, an anagram for *lesbian* used to conceal her actual identity. Small press runs of *Vice Versa* were printed from 1947 to 1948. The periodical was typed on a dozen carbon copies, a technique that was not uncommon in publishing during this time, and distributed by hand at several Los Angeles lesbian bars. *Vice Versa* helped to lay the groundwork for the creation of a gay and lesbian press in the United States.

Early in 1953 Martin Block, Dale Jennings, and Bill Lambert planned what would become the first openly sold gay and lesbian magazine in the nation. The title, *ONE Magazine*, was derived from a Thomas Carlyle quote, "A common bond of brotherhood makes all men one." Block edited the first issues of *ONE* in 1953 and Jennings took over in the final part of the year. It was a 6-by-7-inch pamphlet that sold for twenty cents and had a circulation of about 500 copies. Distribution was limited primarily to gay and lesbian bars and organized homophile meetings. Most of the issues focused on news, homosexual persecution, and police harassment, but the journal went further than some of its predecessors by including fiction, poetry, and theoretical and political articles. The mission of *ONE* was to remove homophobic attitudes from within the homosexual community, as well as from society at large, while simultaneously creating and nurturing the community and its culture. From *ONE Magazine* sprang the membership newsletter *ONE Confidential* and the first scholarly treatment of homosexual issues, *ONE Institute Quarterly of Homophile Studies*.

UNITING THE COMMUNITY

Jim Kepner joined the staff of *ONE Magazine* in 1954. A victim of police harassment in a bar raid, Kepner wrote pieces that promoted the need for self-respect, education, community building, and identity among gays. Whereas the writings of Kepner and others at *ONE* took a militant stance, the *Mattachine Review*, established by Harold Call in 1955, subscribed to an assimilationist and conformist viewpoint. A squeaky-clean image was advocated by the *Mattachine Review*—and by the *Ladder*, a Daughters of Bilitis publication—as the tool for gays and lesbians to gain entry into a society known to repress homosexuals. Though these early gay presses worked collegially, *ONE* was frequently chastised by *Mattachine*, and some members of the Daughters of Bilitis for its aggressive and confrontational attitudes. The women of the Daughters of Bilitis, *Mattachine*, and *ONE* denied that there were separate women's issues during this period and maintained a strong sense of commitment to a united community. Many women were included as authors in *One Magazine*, highlighted by an all-women's issue in February 1954. Moreover, topical coverage of women was a key facet of *ONE Magazine*.

By the end of the 1950s, monthly homosexual magazines were being discreetly mailed in plain brown wrappers to avoid interception by postal authorities. The contents mainly were news articles, editorials, literature, and illustrations that were subtly suggestive rather than graphic. Personal ads did not appear due to legal and societal constraints.

THE 1960s AND 1970s

The turbulence of the 1960s saw both a changing attitude toward homosexuality and the development of an underground press, which acted as fertile ground for new gay publishers. These unprecedented materials had a harder edge. Obscene language appeared frequently in the articles, and personal ads became fixtures, in which intimate desires and fetishes were expressed. The Gay Liberation Movement had found its voice by the end of the decade in publications such as the *Advocate*, the *Body Politic*, *Come Out!*, *Gay Community News*, *Gay Sunshine*, and *Gay Times*.

During the 1970s gay and lesbian presses continued to grow and flourish. Many magazines, newspapers, and newsletters began to appear that had their own unique identities, specializing in topics such as religion, politics, or professional interests. Local and regional publications also burgeoned, and as the number of gay and lesbian periodicals increased, so did the "in your face" frankness of the content. New homosexual organizations were created, many of which distributed their own publications. Some of these periodicals had short lives, but others are still being produced.

Glossy illustrated magazines featuring male nudity, erotic illustrations, short stories, and personal and classified advertisements rich in graphic details became common in the gay male press during this period. Magazines such as *Blueboy*, *In Touch*, and *Mandate* were more readily accessible, available either on newsstands or by subscription. Their articles and editorials quickly reached a nationwide audience, facilitating norms in taste and attitude within the gay community.

Beyond the major urban centers, many smaller cities began producing local gay newspapers. Often distributed at gay bars, some became known as "bar rags." Many of these newspapers joined forces in 1981 as part of the Gay and Lesbian Press Association. New scholarly journals, such as the *Gai Saber*, *Gay Books Bulletin/Cabirion*, and *Journal of Homosexuality*, provided an academic basis for in-depth gay and lesbian research and university studies.

THE BURGEONING LESBIAN PRESS

The women's liberation movement of the late 1960s and early 1970s was a powerful catalyst for lesbian political activity, and many lesbian publications first appeared under the feminist banner. Signs of a developing lesbian press could be observed from Marie Kuda's Lesbian Writers Conferences, which were held annually from 1974 until 1978. The Women in Print conferences, held in Omaha, Nebraska, during the mid-1970s, provided further space for lesbian publishers to make important contacts. The establishment of lesbian-friendly presses made it possible for fiction and nonfiction to be published in book form, as well as in a number of widely circulated literary journals, such as *Sinister Wisdom* and *Calyx*. Political publications such as *Lesbian Tide* and *Dyke: A Quarterly* explored issues of lesbian feminism and separatism, while others such as *Lesbian Connection* helped lesbians across the country reach out to each other.

Support for lesbian writing was due in large part to a nationwide network of women's bookstores, which made lesbian books more accessible than ever. These bookstores have continued to play a significant role in the sale of lesbian materials, though many fell prey to the emergence of giant chains. Overall, however, lesbian writers still struggle against invisibility. Though many small lesbian presses, such as Bywater and Alyson (which publishes LGBT fiction and nonfiction), survived into the twenty-first century, many mainstream publishers still fail to recognize lesbian writers, as pointed out by the *Washington Blade* in 2011.

THE 1990s AND EARLY 2000s

During the late 1990s and early 2000s, many young people felt less affinity with the gay and lesbian community as such and began to consider themselves queer, an identity that also includes transgenderism and bisexuality. Publishers began to reflect this change; many houses, such as Cleis and Firebrand, that had once limited their coverage to gay and lesbian issues began to reach out to queer writers. Computer technology made the publication of handmade zines easier, and hundreds of local publications, such *Push* in Seattle, Washington, sprang up across the country. The Queer Zine Archive Project maintains an online record of many of these publications.

The rise of the Internet has changed the face of all types publishing, including that of the gay and lesbian community. Anyone who wants to create a website or publish an online zine can do so, and the results include offerings such as *Echelon: The Source for GLBT Business Professionals* and *Flash*, aimed at what the publishers refer to as the "Deaf Queer Community." Book publishing has also become more accessible, as vanity sites allow authors to self-publish. One such outfit, a British transgender publisher called Way Out, offers a range of editorial services to aspiring queer authors.

Through the power of the written word, gay and lesbian presses have created a common language and a shared frame of reference for their readerships. Bonding together through periodicals and books banishes the specter of isolation and replaces it with a sense of gay identity. The presses have also created an informative window through which the outside world can look at the many aspects of gay life.

Michael A. Lutes

SEE ALSO: *Alternative Press; Feminism; Gay Liberation Movement; Gay Men; Lesbianism.*

BIBLIOGRAPHY

Enszer, Julie R. "Publishers Ignoring Lesbian Writers." *Washington Blade*. Accessed April 2012. Available from http://www.washingtonblade.com/2011/06/23/publishers-ignoring-lesbian-writers/

Harris, Paul, ed. *The Queer Press Guide 2000*. New York: Painted Leaf Press, 1999.

Kepner, Jim. *Rough News, Daring Views: 1950s Pioneer Gay Press Journalism*. New York: Haworth Press, 1998.

Malinowsky, H. Robert. *International Directory of Gay and Lesbian Periodicals*. Phoenix, AZ: Oryx Press, 1987.

Miller, Alan. *Our Own Voices: A Directory of Lesbian and Gay Periodicals, 1890–1990: Including the Holdings of the Canadian Gay Archives*. Toronto: Archives, 1991.

"Publishers Ignoring Lesbian Writers." Queer Zine Archive Project. Accessed April 2012. Available from http://www.qzap.org/v6/index.php

Streitmatter, Rodger. *Unspeakable: The Rise of the Gay and Lesbian Press in America*. Boston: Faber & Faber, 1995.

Thompson, Mark. *Long Road to Freedom: The Advocate History of the Gay and Lesbian Movement*. New York: St. Martin's Press, 1994.

Gay Liberation Movement

The tidal wave of social change that began with the black civil rights movement of the early 1960s carried many other social movements on its crest. These included the anti–Vietnam War protests, women's liberation, and the gay and lesbian liberation movement, and all of these movements owed tremendous debts to each other. Many gay men and lesbians worked in the civil rights, antiwar, and feminist movements, and their labor to fight oppression in these movements sparked dissatisfaction with the hidden oppression in their own lives. Many people, even those working politically in other movements, saw sexual orientation as a personal issue, removed from politics. Even progressive activists, who were sympathetic and respectful of many differences among people, often ridiculed gays as savagely as their conservative counterparts. The rise of feminism, in particular, began to change this perception, with its emphasis on the political meaning in each person's experience. Gays began to view their sexuality as a political issue rather than a shameful personal secret.

THE STONEWALL REBELLION

Though there had been work historically to improve the status of homosexuals, the beginning of the gay liberation movement is often officially marked on the night of June 28, 1969, at the Stonewall Inn, a gay bar in New York's Greenwich Village. In the pre-gay liberation 1950s and 1960s, even in known gay neighborhoods like the Village, gay bars were shadowed places. Gay people kept their sexuality hidden, and much about homosexuality was illegal, from cross-dressing to same-sex dancing. Gay bars were one of the few places gays could meet in public, and these bars were often run by members of organized crime, who were happy to profit from the illegitimate status of homosexuality.

Police frequently raided gay bars, where proprietors sometimes had warning systems so that men and women could switch partners quickly when the police entered a bar. Gay bar raids were also often an opportunity for police to brutalize gays, with little fear that their victims would report them and chance being publicly labeled "queer." Those who looked most obviously gay—the drag queens in dresses and high heels and the lesbians in men's clothes—were singled out for the harshest treatment. That June night at the Stonewall Inn, the patrons of the bar did not respond in the passive way gays had usually responded to attacks by the police. Tired of being helpless victims, the gays fought back, rioting in the streets of "their" neighborhood, shouting the new rallying cry, "Gay Power!" The riots lasted for three days and received unprecedented media coverage.

Popular mythology says that the riots occurred on the day that singer Judy Garland died from a drug overdose. Many gays, especially gay men, identified strongly with Garland's ravaged vulnerability and passionate singing style, and the story goes that when the police arrived to harass a gay community grieving over the loss of an idol, something snapped, and anger and pride welled up to take the place of shame. In fact, Garland's death took place almost a week before the riots, on June 22. But there is a truth that underlies all mythology, and the truth is that the Stonewall riots were a watershed that marked a change in gays' and lesbians' perceptions of themselves. The status of homosexuals did not change overnight, but neither could things ever go back to the way they had been before the riots. Almost as if they had been waiting for a catalyzing event, gay liberation organizations began to spring up across the United States and around the world.

HOMOSEXUALITY IN EARLIER TIMES

Though they may not have identified themselves as such, there had always been gay men and lesbians, and they had been more or less visible and more or less oppressed, depending on their time in history and their cultural context. In previous centuries, for example, upper-class women had lived together in lesbian relationships called "Boston marriages," which were socially

Gay Liberation Front. *A member of the Gay Liberation Front displays a poster and banner from the group in 1971.* EVENING STANDARD/GETTY IMAGES.

tolerated. It was not uncommon for women in pioneer country to pass as men to attain some of the freedom of movement and financial independence denied to them as women, and frequently these women married and lived with their "wives." Many Native American cultures made a place for both women and men who did not identify with their traditional gender role or who had same-sex lovers.

In the early part of the twentieth century, African American drag "debutante" balls were major social events that drew elite society, straight and gay alike. These balls were satirical reproductions of the traditional balls where young women were presented to society, and it is from them that the term *coming out* derived, for gays and lesbians publicly announcing their gayness. The more repressive connotation, that of gays coming out of a dark closet, did not arrive until the 1950s, with the less socially lighthearted atmosphere of that decade.

In Europe, World War II brought Nazi aggression and the attempted genocide of European gays. However, the upheaval of war brought a degree of awareness and opportunity to gays in the United States, whether in the military or on the home front. Military service had always provided a same-sex environment, and the necessities of war did not permit an antigay campaign that would reduce U.S. forces. The defense industry attracted thousands of people to urban centers, where gays who had formerly been isolated in small towns around the country could find each other. Once the war was over, society took on the job of repressing gays as well as straight women who had found unusual freedom during wartime. Heterosexual women were sent home to be housewives, and gays and lesbians were the subject of a concerted "witch hunt" by the Truman administration. Hundreds of gays working for the government lost their jobs.

THE FIRST GAY LIBERATION ORGANIZATIONS

Gay and lesbian organizing itself did not originate with the 1970s gay liberation movement, as many people believe. As early as 1924 Henry Gerber was jailed and fired from his job for founding the gay and lesbian Society for Human Rights in Chicago. In Los Angeles in 1950, foreshadowing the connection of gay liberation and leftist politics, a group five men, three of them Communist Party members, founded the Mattachine Society. The group's goal was "to promote a sense of solidarity and group identity among homosexuals." Mattachine was one of a number of early "homophile" associations that included the lesbian group Daughters of Bilitis, founded in San Francisco in 1955. These groups promoted acceptance of homosexuals; their members wrote, spoke, and even picketed in defense of that cause. Their other function was to provide a safe place for lesbians and gays to meet, apart from the bars. Certainly the idea of social safety for gays was radical enough, but by the 1970s, influenced by the civil rights movement and feminists, gays demanded more.

Following the Stonewall Riots, new gay liberation organizations began forming. Some, like New York's Gay Liberation Front and Radical Fairies, had chapters across the country. Others were smaller, local organizations, created by activists in many urban areas and progressive small towns nationwide. The Furies in Washington, D.C.; the Lesbian Alliance in St. Louis, Missouri; and the Atlanta (Georgia) Lesbian Feminist Alliance (ALFA) were only a few of hundreds of groups that formed. Gays and lesbians began by reclaiming the names that had been used against them. The word *gay* itself, once a general term for sexual looseness, had been used by gay men in the 1920s and 1930s as a code word to identify each other. Once the term had been reclaimed by homosexuals to describe themselves, radicals began to look for ways to disempower the antigay epithets that had been hurled at them. They began to reclaim words such as *dyke* and *faggot* for use among themselves, thus denying the words their negative power, much as African Americans had reclaimed racist slurs for an exclusive usage that reinforced black solidarity.

DECRIMINALIZING HOMOSEXUALITY

With few exceptions, homosexuality had previously been treated in American society as either a crime or a disease. Homosexuals who did not regularly end up in jail often ended up in mental hospitals subjected to various brutal "cures," such as aversion therapy and electroshock therapy. Since any deviation from their prescribed societal role often landed women in mental hospitals, many lesbians suffered this form of oppression. After the Stonewall Rebellion, gay activists began to work not only for social acceptance but also for legal rights. They demanded the right to live and work, free from discrimination, and they demanded that homosexuality be removed from the American Psychiatric Association's (APA) list of mental diseases. In 1973, thanks to the work of lesbian and gay activists, the APA removed homosexuality from the list.

Gays also began to work on decriminalizing homosexuality, which was illegal in many states. In 1962 Illinois became the first state to repeal its antigay laws, and activists kept up the pressure until, by 1998, only nineteen states still had antigay laws on the books. In 2003 the U.S. Supreme Court overturned a Texas antisodomy law, thus making all such remaining state laws unconstitutional. Not content with mere legality, gay rights activists continued to work for gay rights protections with varying degrees of success. One example: in 1974 the city council in the liberal university town of Boulder, Colorado, voted in a gay rights law. Outraged, the conservative citizenry not only repealed the law but also voted to recall every member of city council who voted for it. However, by the early 2000s seventeen states included sexual orientation in their antidiscrimination laws, and six included transgender persons.

SPLITS IN THE MOVEMENT

With the new movement and the increasing number of new organizations inevitably came differences and conflict. Older gays who had come out without the support of a very public movement resented the often dismissive attitudes of the young "liberated" gays. Younger gays challenged the political conservatism and "butch" and "femme" gender roles that had often been practiced by their predecessors. Some gays, many of them white men, were fairly comfortable with their place in society and felt that changing society's attitudes about homosexuality was all that was needed. Others saw many things about American society that needed to be changed and viewed gay liberation as inevitably connected to other progressive liberation movements. This argument over whether gay rights was a "single issue" fight or part of a larger leftist liberation struggle was to become perhaps the second-biggest split in the movement.

Possibly the biggest split was between men and women. Some lesbians, coming to the movement through feminism, questioned their commonalities with gay men, preferring to ally themselves with heterosexual women instead. Insisting that *gay* was a word that defined gay men, many chose to distinguish themselves by using the words *lesbian* or *dyke*, and others began to use alternate spellings such as *womin* or *womyn* to remove the word *man* from *woman*. The feminist movement began resisting accusations of lesbianism in its ranks, fearful that identification of lesbians with feminism would undermine the legitimacy of women's liberation. However, many of the feminist leaders were lesbians, and, in the increasing atmosphere of gay openness, they demanded recognition.

More divisions followed: lesbian feminists threatened not only the heterosexual male establishment but also heterosexual feminists and nonfeminist lesbians. Lesbian feminists themselves split, dividing those who still identified with heterosexual women's issues from the separatists, who tried to have as little as possible to do with men or straight women. While these splits created discord and discomfort, they also created an energy that propagated dozens of groups, conferences, newspapers, bookstores, and small presses throughout the country. The new atmosphere of gay liberation was creating a frenzy of dialogue on subjects that had once been shrouded in silence.

SUBGROUPS IN THE MOVEMENT

As was the case with feminism, the gay liberation movement was usually presented by the press as a white and middle-class movement. However, gay activists came from all classes, races, and ethnic backgrounds. Many of these activists attempted in their agendas to focus on the racism, classism, and sexism within the movement, though their attempts were not always successful. Some gays of color and Jewish gays formed their own groups, seeking solidarity and support. Events such as the 1976 West Coast Conference on Faggots and Class Struggle in Wolf Creek, Oregon, and the Dynamics of Color lesbian conference in San Francisco in 1989 are examples of the many efforts made to address difficult intramovement conflicts.

Perhaps the most controversial aspect of the gay and lesbian liberation movement was its connection to the counterculture. Movement gays were no longer content to ask for acceptance by society; they demanded that society change to reflect the evolving definitions of gender and gender roles. Radical gays challenged the ideas of nuclear family, of monogamy, and of capitalism. Although not all gays agreed, the movement brought up topics of discussion, and those discussions would forever change the way American culture saw itself.

Most lesbians were intent on creating and developing "women's culture," which included new forms of spirituality, literature, and music, all stemming from and connected to lesbian feminist politics. Lesbian music became a growing art form, and women's recording artists gained popularity on both coasts and in the Midwest. In 1975 hundreds of women attended Michigan Womyn's Music Festival. The festival, organized by lesbians, combined concerts and political workshops and was the largest of many regional women's cultural events.

THE SCOURGE OF AIDS

The notion of free sex espoused by the counterculture hippies opened up acceptance of differing sexual lifestyles among the young, as well as legitimizing styles of dress and appearance formerly considered outlandish. Gay men in particular reveled in the new sexual openness. Their celebratory exuberance resulted in the rocketing popularity of the disco phenomenon. As gay identity became more proud and less shameful, the image of the gay bar as a dark hideaway also changed. Gay disco bars, which had flashing lights and loud music with a driving sexual beat, became the social centers for gay men and, to a lesser extent, lesbians. The trendy, exciting bars also attracted straight people, and this moved gay culture into the mainstream in a way that demonstrations could not accomplish. The disco scene was also heavily associated with casual sex and recreational drug use, which in part was responsible for its end.

By 1981 medical authorities were beginning to identify a new virus they called gay-related immunodeficiency (GRID). Soon they changed the name of the disease to acquired immunodeficiency syndrome (AIDS) and reevaluated its connection to the gay community. Though AIDS is not a "gay" disease, it is sexually transmitted, and the promiscuous lifestyle and drug use common within many gay male communities made them an ideal place for the virus to spread. It did spread, and, as thousands of gay men died, AIDS became a focus for the work of gay rights activists.

By the late 1970s, the revolutionary fervor that had characterized early gay liberation politics had succumbed to the same backlash that had quieted much of the 1960s activism. Fundamentalist Christians were particularly threatened by any legitimization of gay lifestyles, and the antigay agenda became a platform issue for conservative Republicans. Right-wing Christian activist Anita Bryant launched her antigay Save Our Children campaign in 1977, and many gay-rights advances were threatened. Though leftist gay activists continued to fight the challenges of the right wing, the excitement of the nationwide movement had been dampened.

In 1987 the AIDS Coalition to Unleash Power (ACT-UP) formed to fight for destigmatization of the AIDS virus, money for AIDS research, and other AIDS-related issues. The arrival of ACT-UP, with its 1960s-like aggressive street tactics, politicized the gay male community and many supportive lesbians around the issue of AIDS and led the way to other "second generation" activist organizations such as the Lesbian Avengers, which originated in New York and expanded to chapters across the country. The first gay and lesbian rights march in Washington, D.C., in 1979, attracted 100,000 marchers. By 1993, when the third march on the capital was held, almost a million people attended.

NEW DIRECTIONS FOR THE MOVEMENT

Of all the contributions that gay activism has made to society, one of the most unexpected is that it has given young gays a very public older generation. As in every other grouping, an older generation supplies mentors and role models—and something to rebel against. Like other children of the baby boom generation, the 1970s gay activists have been nonplussed to find their own "children" espousing quite different politics and beliefs than the ones that drove them. Where post-Stonewall gays rejected gender roles, 1990s gay youth rediscovered and embraced "butch" and "femme." And whereas feminism provided the foundation for many 1970s lesbians to discover and acknowledge their own identities, some lesbians in the 1990s called themselves "postfeminist" and rejected what they saw as the unnecessary polarity feminism espouses.

Furthermore, the gay liberation movement expanded to include bisexuals and transgender people. By the second decade of the 2000s it was considered most correct to speak of the lesbian, gay, bisexual, and transgender (LGBT) community, and young radicals simply referred to themselves as "queer," once again reclaiming an epithet often used by bigots. Meetings of queer activists began to open with participants stating which pronoun they preferred: masculine, feminine, or a variety of neutral indicators such as "hir" or "zie."

The rise in the number of female-to-male transgender young people has been a challenging reality for some of the older lesbian generation to face. Many of those who came of age in an era of embracing womanhood and extolling sisterhood have found it painful to see turn-of-the-twenty-first-century gays deconstructing gender and choosing to identify as men, often using hormones and surgery to complete their transition. Venerable feminist institutions, such as the Michigan Womyn's Music Festival, were challenged by both female-to-male and male-to-female transgenders to expand their definition of women.

SAME-SEX MARRIAGE

In a move that would have been unthinkable in the 1960s, many twenty-first-century LGBT activists began to demand marriage equality, or the right to contract same-sex marriages. Activist groups such as Human Rights Campaign identify more than 1,000 benefits couples receive through marriage, including tax benefits, the right for surviving spouses to receive pensions, the right to make medical decisions for an incapacitated spouse, access to health care coverage, and protected parental rights. Some long-term same-sex couples began to ask why they could not commit to each other legally and receive the same benefits that heterosexual couples do.

In 2004 Massachusetts became the first U.S. state to legalize same-sex marriage. Connecticut and California followed suit in 2008, although California's law was repealed six months later after a strong opposition campaign led to the passage of Proposition 8, a law banning same-sex marriages. A federal court overturned Proposition 8 in 2012, but the decision was expected to be appealed. By early 2012, seven states and the District of Columbia had legalized same-sex marriage. Many other states had passed laws recognizing either civil unions or domestic partnerships, which, although not legal marriages, do afford some legal protections to same-sex couples. (Domestic partnerships can also be entered into by heterosexual couples who wish to make a commitment but not marry.) As the repeal of the California law demonstrates, the passage of same-sex marriage laws has provoked a strong backlash among religious and political conservatives. Groups such as the National Organization for Marriage campaigned to legally define marriage as taking place only between a man and a woman.

During the 2010s the battle over same-sex marriage in the United States continued to rage, becoming one of the hottest topics in political races. Amid much controversy, President Barack Obama expressed his support for gay marriage in 2012 as the issue loomed as a hot-button topic in the electoral campaigns. The subject was also debated within the LGBT movement, as many radical gays rejected what they saw as a move toward the mainstream. Many viewed the focus on the right to marry as a polarizing distraction from the larger issue of equal rights for LGBT people.

STRENGTHENING THE FIGHT AGAINST DISCRIMINATION

More than forty years after Stonewall, prejudice against gays and lesbians continues to take ugly forms. One disturbing challenge faced by the LGBT community has been the rise in bullying of young people because of their real or perceived sexual orientation. Much of this bullying occurred in schools, but social media also played a part, as online harassment of teens perceived as "different" skyrocketed.

Beginning in the early 2000s, the nation was shocked by headline after headline about students who had killed themselves because of harassment over their sexuality. One of the most highly publicized cases involved Tyler Clementi, a Rutgers student whose roommate videotaped him having sex with another man and streamed that video over the Internet. Distraught at being "outed" in such a brutal fashion, Clementi jumped off a bridge. However, his was not an isolated case. For example, in February 2012, *Rolling Stone* published an exposée about a Minnesota school district with a rash of teen suicides that some experts linked to an extremely antigay climate in the town.

Gays and their allies have worked to combat antigay harassment and its painful results. The Safe Schools Coalition, founded in 1988 to support LGBT youth in the Seattle area, soon spread throughout the state and beyond, until by the early 2000s there were member groups across the country. The Gay-Straight Alliance Network (GSAN), founded in 1998, is a peer group that challenges hateful behavior by creating clubs where heterosexual and homosexual students can get to know each other in a safe environment and thus build on their common humanity. GSAN also works to educate school communities about sexual orientation and the damaging effects of homophobia and harassment. January 25, 2012, was the first annual National Gay-Straight Alliances (GSA) Day. The "It Gets Better Project" stemmed from a 2010 YouTube video created by Seattle, Washington, journalist and activist Dan Savage and his partner, Terry Miller, to encourage youths facing homophobia and bullying. The project resulted in the creation of more than 40,000 personal videos offering support to gay youth. Famous personalities who contributed videos to the project include President Obama and Matthew Morrison of the teen hit TV series *Glee*. The Stonewall riots are commemorated each year around the end of June on Gay Pride Day, and in cities all over the world gays gather for parades, marches, celebration, and political action.

The early twenty-first century has brought renewed energy to right-wing attacks on gay rights as well as "gay bashing" and other violent attacks on gays. Disagreements among gays regarding gender, race, class, and politics continue. Gay and lesbian identity is still stigmatized, and "coming out of the closet" is often an act of personal courage and risk that many feel unable to perform. However, gays are no longer invisible figures of the shadows. Gay characters appear on many prime-time network television shows and on the covers of national magazines, not only as political figures or as curiosities but as celebrities and role models. LGBT youth, while still at risk in many ways, no longer have to rely on whispered epithets to learn what the words *gay* and *lesbian* mean. The decades of secrecy, shame, and oppression that culminated in three days of rioting in Greenwich Village ended that summer, and a new era began. That era is still unfolding.

Tina Gianoulis

SEE ALSO: *Civil Rights Movement; Equal Rights Amendment; Feminism; Gay Men; Lesbianism; Stonewall Rebellion.*

BIBLIOGRAPHY

Cruikshank, Margaret. *The Gay and Lesbian Liberation Movement.* New York: Routledge, 1992.

D'Emilio, John. *Sexual Politics, Sexual Communities: The Making of a Homosexual Minority in the United States, 1940–1970.* Chicago: University of Chicago Press, 1983.

Grahn, Judy. *Another Mother Tongue: Gay Words, Gay Worlds.* Boston: Beacon Press, 1990.

Johnston, Jill. *Lesbian Nation: The Feminist Solution.* New York: Simon & Schuster, 1973.

Kissack, Terence. "Freaking Fag Revolutionaries: New York's Gay Liberation Front, 1961–1971." *Radical History Review* 62 (1995): 114.

Rimmerman, Craig A. *The Lesbian and Gay Movements: Assimilation or Liberation?* Boulder, CO: Westview Press, 2008.

Sullivan, Andrew. *Same-Sex Marriage: Pro and Con*, rev. ed. New York: Vintage Books, 2004.

Vaid, Urvashi. *Virtual Equality: The Mainstreaming of Gay and Lesbian Liberation.* New York: Anchor Books, 1995.

Wilchins, Riki Anne. *Queer Theory, Gender Theory: An Instant Primer.* New York: Alyson Books, 2004.

Gay Men

Homosexual behavior has been documented in most cultures throughout history. Although ancient civilizations appear to have been more accepting of same sex relationships, the people known to have homosexual desire have been persecuted in Western civilizations since the twelfth century. Perceived as immoral and marginalized in historical records, gay men were forced to develop clandestine social networks that employed a variety of codes in order to maneuver within the larger heterosexual society. First battling biblically structured morals and laws and then a surge of psychological theories in the nineteenth century that defined homosexuality as abnormal behavior, gay men slowly overcame widespread prejudices held by the dominant culture. In the United States the modern gay male community began to form in the early 1900s. The word *gay*, once widely used in the nineteenth century to describe any sort of sexual behavior that challenged particular social and moral codes, gained new meaning when homosexual men in the 1920s and 1930s began using it as a code word to identify each other and later became an umbrella term to describe the LGBT (lesbian, gay, bisexual, transgender) community. Despite the fact that their communities were hidden from the larger society, , gay men have exerted a tremendous influence on American culture through the arts, fashion, literature, entertainment, and politics.

FOUNDATIONS OF THE COMMUNITY

In the late nineteenth century, literature and the arts provided gay men with their most accessible avenue of expression within society. Writers like Walt Whitman celebrated both platonic and homosexual love within the passages of *Leaves of Grass*. Although his poems were originally labeled as obscene and criticized for their sexual content, he served as an inspiration for gay writers and artists and remains one of the most influential American poets. Gay men, however, were largely associated with urban settings and high culture. Gay men living in rural areas received very little social support and were even more closeted than their urban counterparts. Around the 1920s, urban gays began to search for ways to meet and socialize. Prohibition provided gay men with a variety of meeting places, such as speakeasiesand private parties. However, straight society tolerated, and even considered fashionable, certain gay events, such as the African American drag debutante balls of the early twentieth century. These major social gatherings drew members of elite society, straight or gay.

Throughout the 1920s gay men continued to live dual lives. They suffered through Hollywood stereotypes; however, the same stereotypes provided them with a public presence and a passing level of tolerance by the mainstream society. In the more populated urban areas, like New York and Chicago, clubs catering to gay men operated openly and freely. By the 1930s the United States became more conservative, and gay men, fearing legal and social repercussions, once again concealed their identities. A variety of "sodomy" laws were amended to explicitly prohibit same sex relationships, and the Hays Code effectively targeted depictions of sexuality in Hollywood. The 1940s were a galvanizing time for gay communities. In the United States they faced various levels of prejudice and oppression not only from sodomy laws but also from the medical establishment who attempted to treat and cure homosexuality through measures that included shock therapy, lobotomies, and castration. Similarly, the armed forces adopted polices that stipulated that men and women could be discharged for being gay or lesbian. World War II, however, caused major population shifts as young people left rural areas to join the army or find defense industry jobs in cities. Having made connections with other homosexual men in urban areas, gays were reluctant to return to the isolation of small-town life. Many remained in cities and developed communities, opening clubs and bars to facilitate social interaction.

Americans' desire to return to the status quo after World War II led to oppression of, and even witch hunts for, gays in the late 1940s and 1950s, including federal monitoring of the gay community. But repression soon led to release. The African American civil rights movement of the 1960s, and later the antiwar movement and women's liberation, inspired gays to seek their rights. In 1969 decades of repression exploded in the Stonewall Rebellion., In response to a police raid on the Stonewall Inn, New York City's Greenwich Village was consumed by three days of protests. The protests opened up an opportunity for gay men to publicly affirm their identities and to form groups that would demonstrate for equal civil liberties. Within a short time, openly gay publications were established, and gay rights organizations sprouted across the United States. One year later marches commemorating Stonewall took place in New York, Chicago, and San Francisco. Following Illinois in 1961 and Connecticut in 1969, a majority of states rescinded their sodomy laws during the 1970s and 1980s, with the remaining thirteen states forced to decriminalize homosexuality by the 2003 Supreme Court decision in *Lawrence v. Texas*, which invalidated the Texas sodomy law.

By the 1970s gays were enjoying a visibility and freedom previously unknown. The gay liberation movement challenged oppression of homosexuals and offered gay men a new pride in their sexuality. The image of the gay bar as a dark hideaway changed as gays fought against stigma. Gay disco bars, bolstered by the expansion of disco culture and style into popular culture, became social centers, attracting straight people and dramatically moving gay culture into the mainstream.

HIV/AIDS

By 1981 medical authorities were beginning to identify a new viral disease called gay-related immunodeficiency, which they soon renamed acquired immunodeficiency syndrome (AIDS) upon reevaluating its connection to the gay community. Researchers discovered that anyone could contract human immunodeficiency virus (HIV), the virus responsible for AIDS, regardless of sexual orientation. HIV is transmitted through bodily fluids such as blood and semen, putting individuals who use intravenous drugs and have unprotected sex, in particular anal intercourse, at a higher risk of contracting the virus.

Gay men encountered a harsh environment once again. As HIV spread, thousands of gay men developed AIDS and died. The disease soon became a focus for the work of gay rights activists. Galvanized by the deaths of their friends and lovers, gay men began to organize to fight for destigmatization of HIV-positive status and money for AIDS research, among other causes. In addition to the painful deaths, gay men were ridiculed in the public arena. Some members of the Religious Right insisted that HIV/AIDS was God's way of punishing immoral behavior and targeted homosexuals as something to be feared. Gay men were further stigmatized in the reports on AIDS since little was known about how it was caused or passed on between people. Gay men were made into poster children for high-risk behavior, insinuating that being gay also meant being indiscriminately promiscuous. As the number of deaths continued to rise, including both homosexuals and heterosexuals, and images of those suffering through the disease became more prevalent in the media, the cultural backlash against gay men slowly subsided. The gay community responded with outreach programs and support networks, educating gay men on safe sex and the necessity of testing.

During the early twenty-first century, professionals in the medical community focused on the role of drugs and alcohol in the practice of unsafe or anonymous sex among gay men.

SOCIAL AND CULTURAL INFLUENCE

As society became more accepting of gay men, the term *gay* came to connote more than simply sexual orientation but encompassed a variety of cultural expressions, including dress, occupations, and neighborhoods. Americans have traditionally accepted, even expected, gay men to gravitate toward certain occupations. Many assume male hairdressers and interior decorators to be gay, and fields such as music, art, and theater are perceived to be more accepting of gay men. Notably, the cultural acceptance of gay men relies upon an image in which they are portrayed as affluent and educated. The popular TV show *Queer Eye for the Straight Guy* exploited the stereotype that gay men possessed a better sense of fashion and style. Creative icons such as writers Walt Whitman and James Baldwin, musician Cole Porter, and playwright Noel Coward made unparalleled cultural contributions and paved the way for other artists.

Gay men also have been influential in areas where they had to keep their sexual preference secret. Civil rights leader Bayard Rustin and FBI director J. Edgar Hoover represent two ends of this spectrum: activists who thought Rustin's gay identity would harm the struggle for black rights forced him to downplay his public identification with the civil rights movement. Hoover hid his longtime relationship with Clyde Tolson, his second in command, while using the secrets of other closeted public figures as leverage to manipulate public policy.

Perhaps because gay men can identify with female stars' public vulnerability, Americans have associated gay male culture with the glorification of the diva. Singers Barbra Streisand and Bette Midler owe their propulsion into stardom, in part, to gay male audiences. Iconic actresses Judy Garland, as the vulnerable waif, and Joan Crawford, as the tough bitch, earned popularity among gay men during the late twentieth century. Recognized for her outlandish outfits, pop music, and outspoken politics, Lady Gaga ascended to be one of the biggest gay icons in the first decade of the twenty-first century.

Increased visibility of gay men led to another cultural phenomenon: the fag hag relationship, or friendship between gay men and straight women. Traditionally, these friendships allow straight women to seek nonthreatening relationships with men who may offer more emotional depth than the typical heterosexual men. Similarly, gay men may find it comforting to receive emotional support from someone who is not a sexual partner. Such relationships between straight women and gay men have been depicted in films such as *Breakfast at Tiffany's* (1961), *Cabaret* (1972), and *My Best Friend's Wedding* (1997), even though the men may not always be overtly gay. Even on television, which was slow to adopt images of homosexuality, shows like *Love, Sidney* (1981–1983) and *Will & Grace* (1998–2006) found success by pairing gay men with straight women. Broader acceptance of gay relationships allowed for the media to depict openly gay relationships in movies such as *Brokeback Mountain* (2005) and television shows like *Six Feet Under* (2001–2005).

CONTINUED STRUGGLE

Gay men have been severely punished for their sexual preference through ridicule, threats, and physical abuse. Perhaps because of misogyny in U.S. society, tomboyish behavior in girls may be tolerated and even rewarded, whereas feminine behavior in boys may be condemned. Gay bashing, or launching vicious physical attacks on those suspected of being gay, remains common in the twenty-first century. Many states continue to allow the "gay panic" defense for such assaults on the basis that flirtation or propositions from gays is so repugnant that a violent response could be excusable.

In situations where a same-sex environment is enforced, such as prisons and all-male boarding schools, Americans have recognized, if not accepted, that some men and boys engage in sex with other men. The idea that environments in which women are unavailable compel straight men to engage in homosexual behavior alludes to the dominant view of male sexuality as a driving force that must be satisfied irrespective of affection and romance. Many have presumed that the creation of gay clubs and bathhouses, as well as the claiming of public parks areas for gay cruising, is a result of gay men's supposed freedom from constraints on their male sexuality—despite the fact that many gays are celibate or monogamous, entering into long-term relationships, sometimes to marry and to raise children.

Some social analysts have argued that in spite of Americans' persistent homophobia, society has a male homosexual perspective that stems from its sexism and patriarchy. Like ancient Greece, where love between men was viewed as the highest form of spiritual and physical connection, American society endows male friendships with a loyalty and honor deemed impossible in heterosexual relationships. Many male-bonding rituals in the United States are physical and exclude women. Ironically, the openness and acceptance of women exhibited by many gay men threaten the good old boy mentality that still permeates American society. Thus, gay liberation has been linked to a wider liberation of the social order.

Tina Gianoulis

SEE ALSO: *AIDS; Baldwin, James; Bathhouses;* Breakfast at Tiffany's; *Bromance; Civil Rights Movement; The Closet; Coming Out; Crawford, Joan; Disco; Drag; FBI (Federal Bureau of Investigation); Garland, Judy; Gay and Lesbian Marriage; Gay and Lesbian Press; Gay Liberation Movement; Greenwich Village; Hoover, J. Edgar; Metrosexual; Midler, Bette; Porter, Cole; Religious Right; Safe Sex; Sexual Revolution; Singles Bars; Stonewall Rebellion; Streisand, Barbra; Vietnam;* Will & Grace; *World War II.*

BIBLIOGRAPHY

Gottlieb, Andrew R. *Out of the Twilight: Fathers of Gay Men Speak.* New York: Haworth Press, 2000.

Halperin, David M. *What Do Gay Men Want? An Essay on Sex, Risk, and Subjectivity.* Ann Arbor: University of Michigan Press, 2007.

Hardy, Robin, and David Groff. *The Crisis of Desire: AIDS and the Fate of Gay Brotherhood.* Boston: Houghton Mifflin, 1999.

Harris, Daniel. *The Rise and Fall of Gay Culture.* New York: Hyperion, 1997.

Nardi, Peter M. *Gay Men's Friendships: Invincible Communities.* Chicago: University of Chicago Press, 1999.

O'Byrne, Patrick, and Dave Holmes. "Desire, Drug Use and Unsafe Sex: A Qualitative Examination of Gay Men Who Attend Gay Circuit Parties." *Culture, Health and Sexuality* 13, no. 1 (2011): 1–13.

Gaye, Marvin *(1939–1984)*

During his tenure at Motown records, vocalist and songwriter Marvin Gaye expanded the boundaries of what soul music could address and how it could sound. His early Motown hits "How Sweet It Is (To Be Loved by You)," "Ain't That Peculiar," and "Ain't Nothing Like the Real Thing" (with Tammi Terrell) helped define the 1960s Motown sound. His 1968 "I Heard It through the Grapevine" became Motown's biggest-selling record up to that point. On genre-defying albums such as 1971's *What's Going On*, Gaye opened soul music to allow for overt political protest. On 1978's *Here, My Dear* he reduced his subject matter to a level of pain and honesty that had rarely been touched in any form of popular music. During his lifetime Gaye battled many demons—the most significant of which was an ongoing, troubled relationship with his father. That relationship ended tragically on April 1, 1984, when Gaye's father gunned down his son in the home Marvin had bought for his mother after a heated argument.

Born Marvin Pentz Gay Jr. (he later added the "e" to his surname) to a devoutly religious family that belonged to the House of God (a conservative Christian sect that drew from Pentecostalism and Orthodox Judaism), Marvin had a troubled childhood growing up in Washington, D.C. Beaten almost daily by his father, an ordained minister at the local House of God church, Marvin felt stigmatized and out of place among his peers because of his shy nature and the gossip-attracting, flamboyant personality of his father. Gaye grew up amid perpetual confrontations with his father and, by most accounts, was an unhappy child, except when he was singing.

Starting at a very early age Gaye buried himself deep in music, learning to play drums and piano in church. He later became a soloist in his father's church choir. Upon graduating from high school, Gaye enlisted in the air force to escape his family life, but after his discharge he returned to Washington, D.C, and sang around town in a number of doo-wop groups. During a tour stop as a backing vocalist with the Moonglows in Detroit, Michigan, Gaye caught the attention of Motown founder Berry Gordy Jr., who hired him as a session musician and eventually signed him as a Motown artist in 1961. Gaye got to know, and fell in love with, Gordy's sister, Anna (who was seventeen years Gaye's senior). They were married in late 1961.

MOTOWN SUCCESS

After a few minor hit singles and a poor-selling album in the style of his hero, Nat King Cole, Gaye scored his first Top 10

Marvin Gaye. *Marvin Gaye's music ranged from sweet ballads and dance tunes to statements of social conscience and sensuality.* JIM BRITT/MICHAEL OCHS ARCHIVE/GETTY IMAGES.

hit with the up-tempo "Pride and Joy." But Motown's pigeonholing of Gaye as an upbeat party-song singer ran in opposition to his desire to sing sweet romantic ballads and resulted in Gaye's long-running conflicts over artistic direction and control of his career. In addition to churning out up-tempo numbers, Gaye became known as a duet singer, his most beautiful and gut-wrenching songs sung with Terrell. This pairing generated such classics as "Ain't No Mountain High Enough," "Your Precious Love," and "You're All I Need to Get By." Their musical affair sadly ended when she collapsed in his arms onstage, eventually dying of a brain tumor in 1970. By all accounts, Gaye never emotionally recovered from the loss of Terrell, a woman with whom he had a deep emotional connection, though not a romantic relationship.

By the end of the 1960s, America was in the middle of a social upheaval generated by, among other things, the civil rights movement and the Vietnam War. Gaye wanted to find a way to musically address his social concerns but found Motown's assembly-line hit-making method increasingly constraining. He fought against Motown for the release of *What's Going On* (1971), his personal testament against the horrors of the Vietnam War, environmental destruction, and the indignities of ghetto life. Opening with the strains of his tenor voice singing "Mother mother / there's too many of us dying," *What's Going On* was a landmark album. Released to universal critical praise in magazines from *Rolling Stone* to *Time* (which devoted a long, two-column review to the album), the album freed soul music from the limiting subject matter of simple love songs. It also featured more complex and jazzy arrangements that used strings, as well as songs that seamlessly segued into each other. The album became the best-selling album of Gaye's career, a demonstration that an artist's muse and commerce could successfully coexist.

RAW EMOTION

In 1972 Gaye followed up *What's Going On* with the soundtrack to the blaxploitation film *Trouble Man*, and in 1973 he released the deeply erotic *Let's Get It On*. It, too, was a massive hit. Now at the high point of his career, he sank to one of the lowest points in his life. Severely depressed, he increasingly took large amounts of cocaine while his marriage to Anna dissolved. During the course of his marriage, Gaye's weakness for women made him unfaithful, but the last straw for Anna occurred when he had a second child with Janis Hunter (whom he later married).

In a bizarre divorce settlement, Gaye agreed to pay the entirety of royalties for his next album to Anna. Briefly contemplating making a toss-off album, he instead delved deep into their relationship and created what is among the most unusual albums in popular music history, *Here, My Dear*, a concept double album that documented the rise and fall of their marriage, his unfaithfulness, his cocaine habit, his obsession with prostitutes, and other very personal subjects. Songs on the album include "When Did You Stop Loving Me, When Did I Stop Loving You?" and "You Can Leave, but It's Going to Cost You." Even the album's cover art visually represented their crumbling marriage. Confronting an audience that was clearly unprepared for such a display of raw emotion and dirty laundry, the album flopped.

Gaye sank deeper into a drug-induced depression and financial collapse. He moved to Europe, where he pulled himself out of his hole and recorded 1982's *Midnight Love*, an album that contained his last big hit and winner of two Grammy Awards, "Sexual Healing." Gaye was shot and killed by his father in 1984; he was posthumously inducted into the Rock and Roll Hall of Fame in 1987.

Kembrew McLeod

SEE ALSO: *Blaxploitation Films; Civil Rights Movement; Cole, Nat King; Doo-wop Music; Funk; Gordy, Berry; Motown; Rhythm and Blues; Soul Music; Vietnam.*

BIBLIOGRAPHY

Davis, Sharon. *Marvin Gaye*. New York: Proteus, 1984.

Gaye, Frankie, and Fred E. Basten. *Marvin Gaye, My Brother*. San Francisco: Backbeat Books, 2003.

Ritz, David. *Divided Soul: The Life of Marvin Gaye*. New York: McGraw-Hill, 1985.

Ward, Brian. *Just My Soul Responding: Rhythm and Blues, Black Consciousness and Race Relations*. Berkeley: University of California Press, 1998.

Gehrig, Lou *(1903–1941)*

Baseball great Lou Gehrig (the "Iron Horse") was, along with teammate Babe Ruth, a powerhouse player on the New York Yankees during the 1920s and 1930s until his career was cut short by the degenerative disease that bears his name.

Born Henry Louis Gehrig in 1903, he was the son of German immigrants who were living in New York City. Gehrig's high school accomplishments earned him an opportunity to play sports at Columbia University, but he was coaxed into signing a professional contract with Hartford of the Eastern League under the surname Lewis. Gehrig hid his identity but not his talent, and the ruse was soon discovered. Columbia University promptly declared him ineligible for the 1921–1922 school year, but in his second year of college, he played exceptionally in both football and baseball.

Paul Krichell of the New York Yankees discovered Gehrig in 1923 and offered him a $1,500 signing bonus, which Gehrig accepted despite his parents' objections. He played most of the year in the minors before making his Yankee debut in September. Likewise, Gehrig spent most of the 1924 season playing in the minors, but in June 1925, he began a consecutive game streak that did not end until 1939.

Gehrig made an immediate impact on the Yankees, and his ability to hit propelled him to national stardom by the late 1920s. He hit behind Babe Ruth on baseball's most powerful lineup, which the press nicknamed "Murderers' Row," and succeeded in outhitting Ruth by the early 1930s. Gehrig compiled a streak of thirteen consecutive years with more than 100 runs and runs batted in, and a twelve-year streak of hitting over .300. He led the American League in home runs three times and in runs four times and ranks third on the all-time list for runs batted in (RBIs) and slugging percentage. The durable first baseman was selected as the American League's Most Valuable Player twice, won the Triple Crown (leading the league in home runs, RBIs, and batting average) in 1934, and won six world championships as a Yankee.

Statistics alone did not endear Gehrig to the nation. Representing the tireless worker during the Great Depression, the Iron Horse established a record for the number of consecutive games played: 2,130 games in succession from 1925 to 1939. Gehrig's consecutive game streak continued despite back spasms, a broken toe, a broken thumb, and seventeen different hand fractures. This record stood for more than half a century until it was surpassed in 1995 by Cal Ripken Jr. of the Baltimore Orioles.

Gehrig's statistics began to slip in 1938, and he lacked his usual strength and mobility. When Gehrig's teammates congratulated him on a routine ground ball in 1939, he knew it was time to take himself out of the game, and he never again played for the Yankees. His ailing health led him to the Mayo Clinic, where doctors diagnosed him with a rare and fatal degenerative disease, amyotrophic lateral sclerosis (ALS). Since his diagnosis, ALS has been commonly called Lou Gehrig's disease.

On July 4, 1939, the Yankees honored the newly retired Gehrig in front of nearly 62,000 fans. He received awards, retired his number, and then gave one of the most famous speeches in baseball history. Gehrig thanked the many people who touched his life, telling the crowd, "Yet today I consider myself the luckiest man on the face of the earth." The powerful speech electrified the nation and epitomized his humble nature.

Gehrig spent the remaining two years of his life working for the New York City Parole Commission and spending time with family and friends. The Baseball Hall of Fame exempted him from the five-year waiting period, and he was honored by induction in Cooperstown in 1939. The unconditional love between Gehrig and his wife, Eleanor, received national attention, and shortly after his death, Hollywood made *The Pride of the Yankees*, a movie about his life and marriage that starred Gary Cooper as Gehrig. The movie was a box-office success and was nominated for an Oscar for Best Picture.

Nathan R. Meyer

SEE ALSO: *Baseball; The New York Yankees; Ruth, Babe.*

BIBLIOGRAPHY

Gallico, Paul. *Lou Gehrig, Pride of the Yankees*. New York: Grosset and Dunlap, 1942.

Gehrig, Eleanor. *My Luke and I*. New York: Crowell, 1976.

Kashatus, William C. *Lou Gehrig: A Biography*. Westport, CT: Greenwood Press, 2004.

Robinson, Ray. *Iron Horse: Lou Gehrig in His Time*. New York: W. W. Norton, 1990.

Geisel, Theodor

SEE: *Dr. Seuss.*

The General

Johnnie Gray (Buster Keaton) has two loves: his locomotive—the General—and Annabelle Lee (Marion Mack). As the American Civil War begins, both the General and Annabelle are captured by Union spies and taken north across enemy lines. Johnnie follows and rescues both his loves.

Although it was a flop when it was first released in the United States in 1927, *The General* is the best known and most critically acclaimed of Keaton's films; it has a more cohesive plot than many of his other works and a larger background with an elaborate battle sequence. Johnnie is consistent with other Keaton characters: he meets every adversity with a solemn lack of facial expression and an unbeatable determination.

Christian L. Pyle

SEE ALSO: *Keaton, Buster; Silent Movies; War Movies.*

BIBLIOGRAPHY

Meade, Marion. *Buster Keaton: Cut to the Chase*. New York: HarperCollins, 1995.

Moews, Daniel. *Keaton: The Silent Features Close Up*. Berkeley: University of California Press, 1977.

Rubinstein, E. *Filmguide to* The General. Bloomington: Indiana University Press, 1973.

General Hospital

Created by writers Frank and Doris Hursley, *General Hospital* was one of two hospital-based daytime dramas to premiere on April 1, 1963 (the other was *The Doctors*). Though predating the height of the feminist movement by several years, the series nonetheless appealed to a female audience that enjoyed broadening its attention beyond the home by shifting the conventions of the soap opera from the kitchen to the workplace and from a focus on family dynamics to one on relationships between coworkers. The show's developers created the hospital staff as a large surrogate family and wrote story lines that were in a constant state of flux between the personal and professional challenges presented to the main characters.

THE EARLY YEARS

During its first few years, the drama centered on the friendship of Dr. Steve Hardy and nurse Jessie Brewer and on their complicated love lives. The self-sacrificing Brewer had suffered for years in a marriage to an unfaithful husband who was much younger than her; although she went on to have a number of relationships and several marriages, she always seemed to return to her original spouse and to further abuse until his death finally freed her. Dr. Hardy faced his own problems due to an on-again, off-again relationship with an ex-stewardess named Audrey March. In one story line Audrey becomes pregnant by artificial insemination during a separation from Steve, goes to Vietnam, returns, marries someone else, becomes pregnant again as a result of marital rape, leaves that husband, and reconciles with the always understanding Steve, who adopts her child.

General Hospital seemed to lose its focus during the late 1970s despite the efforts of the Hursleys and later writers, including their daughter Bridget, to stick to themes that had brought the show success in the past. When ratings hit rock bottom in 1977 and ABC was considering canceling the program, a last-ditch effort at resuscitation brought in writer Douglas Marland, who had created a number of highly successful, youthful story lines on *The Doctors*, and producer Gloria Monty, who had directed *The Secret Storm* (1954–1974). Monty infused the show with prime-time production values by introducing new scenery, crosscutting, and new lighting and by demanding that the actors speed up the pace of the show. Marland created a new story line centered on fourteen-year-old Laura Vining (Genie Francis), a previously peripheral character, and her relationship with Scotty Baldwin (Kin Shriner). The story was further complicated by the introduction of a new rival for Laura, the scheming Bobbie Spencer. When Laura killed a taunting older lover in a rage and allowed her self-sacrificing mother to take the blame, the show's ratings really took off, bringing in a younger audience who became particularly hooked on the unfolding tragedy of the mother and daughter.

Marland continued to develop the stories into the 1980s, and Monty continued to shorten scenes, emphasize action over dialogue, and synthesize emerging trends into the show's plots. The efforts of the two practitioners revived *General Hospital*, and it became one of ABC's top serial dramas.

GROWING POPULARITY AND CONTROVERSIAL PLOTS

The show reached its peak popularity in the early 1980s following the departure of Marland and the hiring of his replacement, Pat Falken Smith. Smith created what many consider the most controversial story in soap opera history: Laura marries Scotty only to become fascinated with an older, more sophisticated man—antihero Luke Spencer (Anthony Geary)—who rapes her in his deserted disco. The show couldn't afford to slow its pace by having a trial or ordering the incarceration of Luke, so the incident was passed off as a seduction, though Laura subsequently spent a year in therapy trying to recover from the emotional damage done by the attack. Nonetheless, whether it was rape or seduction, the chemistry between the two characters incited fan interest to a fever pitch, and—despite critical outcries denouncing the producers for condoning rape—the show began to increase its focus on Luke and Laura. As this happened, mainstay characters Steve and Jessie were demoted to supporting status with but a few lines of dialogue each week.

Luke and Laura's wedding on November 16 and 17, 1981, became the most-watched event in the history of daytime TV, even attracting a guest appearance by Elizabeth Taylor, a fan of the show. Monty then steered the show in a more fanciful direction by having Luke and Laura confront the efforts of a mad scientist who, in an attempt at global domination, decides to freeze the world. Although the story line disappointed *General Hospital* purists, the theme attracted a new teenage audience, and ratings soared. Within a couple of years, however, both actress Francis and writer Smith departed the show to further develop their careers. Monty assumed the role of head writer. Although plots were both hit-and-miss among fans, the ratings continued to increase.

By early 1985, after a succession of writers had tried to move the show in different directions with limited success, Smith returned many of the original characters to prominent roles while continuing to focus on action-adventure themes. When Smith was succeeded by Claire Labine in the 1990s, the emphasis shifted to social issues such as AIDS, organ transplants, and other emerging medical/ethical concerns, and *General Hospital* came full cycle, returning—at least in part—to its original premise of drama in the lives of hospital personnel. Critics and viewers alike approved of the show's return to its original themes, and *General Hospital* garnered numerous Emmy Awards for Outstanding Drama, winning five out of six times between 1995 and 2000.

Throughout the first decade of the 2000s and into the second, writer Robert Guza infused *General Hospital* with a new source of intrigue to replace the dwindling saga of Luke and Laura: the rise of organized crime in Port Charles, led primarily by Michael "Sonny" Corinthos. The show also absorbed several characters and their attendant story lines from the defunct soap opera *One Life to Live*, which was canceled in early 2012. Although a similar demise has been predicted for *General Hospital* since the show's ratings hit an all-time low in 2009, fan support for the series remains strong and has made it the longest-running American soap opera currently in production.

Sandra Garcia-Myers

SEE ALSO: *AIDS; Disco; Emmy Awards; Feminism; Soap Operas; Taylor, Elizabeth; Teenagers; Television; Vietnam.*

BIBLIOGRAPHY

Allen, Robert C. *Speaking of Soap Operas*. Chapel Hill: University of North Carolina Press, 1985.

Ford, Sam; Abigail de Kosnik; and C. Lee Harrington, eds. *The Survival of Soap Opera: Transformations for a New Media Era*. Jackson: University Press of Mississippi, 2011.

Groves, Seli. *The Ultimate Soap Opera Guide*. Detroit, MI: Visible Ink Press, 1995.

LaGuardia, Robert. *Soap World*. New York: Arbor House, 1983.

Lee, Anna, and Cooper B. Roisman. *Anna Lee: Memoir of a Career on "General Hospital" and in Film*. Jefferson, NC: McFarland, 2007.

Mumford, Laura Stempel. *Love and Ideology in the Afternoon: Soap Opera, Women, and Television Genre*. Bloomington: Indiana University Press, 1995.

Schemering, Christopher. *The Soap Opera Encyclopedia*. New York: Ballantine Books, 1985.

Warner, Gary. *General Hospital: The Complete Scrapbook*. Los Angeles: General Publishing Group, 1995.

General Motors

The impact of auto manufacturer General Motors (GM) on U.S. culture, the economy, and politics is staggering, as is the sheer size of the corporation. For years GM was the largest corporation on the earth, its value greater than most nations. It was the first company to gross more than $1 billion a year. After GM had a bad year in 1957, a reporter suggested that "when GM sneezed the US economy caught a cold," so interdependent were the U.S. gross national product and the fortunes of GM.

Controlling more than half the market and creating more cars than its domestic rivals combined, GM made and sold cars everywhere in the world. Although regulation, foreign competition, and oil shocks have rocked GM the past few decades, for most of its history it has towered over not just the auto industry but all industry. From the farmer-friendly, half-ton pickups of the late 1930s; to the luxurious Cadillac Coupe de Ville or the space-age looking Buick LeSabre of the 1950s; to the Pontiac GTO for the youth longing for muscle cars in the late 1950s; to the uniquely American 1957 Chevy; to sports cars such as the Pontiac TransAm of the 1970s; to the rapper's car of choice, the

General Motors. Several GM models are displayed on the factory floor at the company's Detroit-Hamtramck Assembly Plant in 2011. FABRIZIO COSTANTINI/BLOOMBERG VIA GETTY IMAGES.

Cadillac Escalade of the first decade of the 2000s, GM has produced not just cars but symbols of U.S. culture.

COMPANY BEGINNINGS

Whereas Henry Ford staked his claim on manufacturing genius, the father of General Motors, William "Billy" Durant, was an expert dealmaker who merged companies and formed GM as a large holding company. GM started with Olds and Buick in 1908, then added Cadillac a year later. Durant expanded too quickly, however, and was forced out by bankers. Undeterred, he hired Louis Chevrolet to design a new car, and in 1915 Durant merged the two companies and regained control. He continued to buy auto companies and suppliers until he was forced out once again in 1920. Pierre S. du Pont replaced him, but then du Pont's place was soon taken by Alfred Sloan.

If Ford created modern manufacturing techniques to conquer the massive scale of making automobiles, then Sloan created management techniques to master the managing of a large-scale firm. Sloan's management ideas on hierarchical line authority became the model for all large corporations for years. He also became the first GM president to engage in collective bargaining when the United Auto Workers staged a series of successful sit-down strikes in GM plants in Flint, Michigan, in 1937.

His greatest triumph, however, was his creation of a styling and color department under the direction of designer Harley Earl in 1927. From this concentration on styling, thus on marketing, GM cemented in the U.S. psyche the fact that, according to David Halberstam in *The Fifties*, "the car was not merely transportation, but a reflection of status, a concept to which most Americans responded enthusiastically as they strove to move up into the middle class, and then the upper middle class." With the annual model changes—which were often only cosmetically different from the previous year—new car buyers were hooked. It was Sloan and Durant's vision of a car for every market niche: new car buyers could start cheap with a Chevy and then, as they earned more, work their way up to an Olds, and everyone would dream of owning a Cadillac.

TWENTIETH-CENTURY ADVANCES

The war years of the 1940s made GM rich, but its wealth became unprecedented in the 1950s with a combination of pent-up demand, the need for a car for suburban living, and the coming of the interstate highway system. With Earl's love of the jet engine look, GM cars came to resemble planes, loaded with chrome and fins. Advances in engineering could have made cars more fuel efficient; instead, the company opted to make cars more powerful and loaded with expensive options such as air-conditioning. GM promoted its cars with road shows called Motoramas, which annually drew more than one million spectators. The Motoramas ended in 1961 as GM concentrated its advertising dollars on television. With famous ads such as "See the U.S.A. in your Chevrolet," the company created a national car culture, made even more attractive with the coming of color television.

Yet, the events of the 1960s also brought about the first chinks in GM's armor. The poorly designed Corvair inspired consumer advocate Ralph Nader to write a book about auto safety called *Unsafe at Any Speed*. While the book was troubling to GM, more embarrassing was the company's clumsy attempt to investigate and intimidate Nader. This led to the spectacle of GM issuing Nader a public apology. The safety issues led to more government regulation of the auto industry, which escalated with emissions and other standards enacted in the 1960s and 1970s. Like all large institutions, GM found itself under attack in the 1960s, but nothing compared to the shocks it would face in the next decades.

BRUISED, BUSTED, AND BAILED OUT

Starting in the 1970s, GM started to falter because foreign competition was producing more popular and higher-quality cars. The company began to shrink, closing factories and cutting its workforce in North America. The devastating effect of GM's layoffs was best chronicled in Michael Moore's bitterly funny 1989 film *Roger & Me*. The heads of GM who were once treated like gods began to look like fools. GM had tried to reinvent itself with the Saturn project in 1984, which was an attempt to develop not just a new car but a new method of manufacturing and selling automobiles based on the Japanese model. The Saturn project never took off, however, and after a brief comeback because of sport utility vehicle (SUV) sales, GM limped into the twenty-first century.

Starting in 2001 GM resembled a corporate *Titanic*. It kept shedding companies and subsidiaries, but the floodwaters continued to rise. Despite more layoffs, the burden of high labor costs because of health care, expensive pension obligations, and shrinking market share left the company on the edge. Then came the financial meltdown in 2008–2009, which pushed GM—as well as rival Chrysler—over the cliff.

In 2008, nearing the end of the George W. Bush presidency, a bridge loan was given to GM. When the company went looking for more money from Barack Obama's administration, the new president demanded very tough terms, including the ousting of CEO Richard Wagoner. Despite opposition from many in Congress, the Obama administration engineered a bailout of GM that saved the company. On June 1, 2009, the chrome colossus filed for chapter 11 bankruptcy. In the reorganization, the U.S. government took a large equity stake in the company, several brands (such as Pontiac and Saturn) closed, and hundreds of dealerships were to be shuttered. Resources were poured into hybrid vehicles and the Volt electric car.

The company that Durant put together in 1908 in many ways resembled the GM of 2012: leaner and facing more competition. As long as GM survives, the company's products will fuel pop culture as they have done for more than 100 years. In 2011, just two years after GM emerged from bankruptcy, the company reported a record profit of $7.6 billion. In addition to government programs such as Cash for Clunkers and problems with some of its main Japanese competitors, the profit demonstrated the impact of the changes made during bankruptcy when it closed plants, won changes in labor contracts, and shed weaker brands and dealerships.

GM IN POPULAR CULTURE

In reflecting upon the 100-year anniversary of GM, *Detroit News* writer Susan Whitall noted in 2008, "For a century, General Motors Corp. has cast a huge shadow over American popular culture, its cars inspiring songs, movies, cartoons and TV shows. . . . The image of GM's cars in popular culture would alternate between the dangerous glamour of fast cars and wild youth and the more wholesome virtues—the idea that a Chevy or Buick would deliver you to freedom and escape out on the open road of an expansive, optimistic America." Robert Thompson, professor of public communications at Syracuse University, has argued that "General Motors made cars about a dream, a myth, a lifestyle. . . . They really did usher in the automobile culture because they put the culture into it. The '57 Chevy became so emblematic of the rock and roll era."

Later, in the 1970s and 1980s, singer Bruce Springsteen's car fascination led to plenty of GM references, in particular to Chevy in "Racing in the Streets" and to Cadillacs in songs such as "Cadillac Ranch" and "Pink Cadillac," the latter also a hit for Detroit, Michigan–raised soul singer Aretha Franklin. Prince's "Little Red Corvette" in 1983 ushered in the celebration of a GM product in urban music. Brands such as Hummers and the Cadillac Escalade became standard props in hip-hop videos as rappers boasted about their rides, including in "Two Dope Boyz in a Cadillac" by Outkast and "Do You Wanna Roll?" by Snoop Dogg. Low riders, in particular models such as the Chevy Impala from the 1960s—affiliated with both hip-hop and Chicano culture—were also celebrated in song.

Cars, in particular car chases, were popular features in early silent films. While the '57 Chevy was celebrated in the bootlegger flick *Thunder Road* (1958), it was not until the 1970s that young directors began to celebrate car culture and GM brands. Films including *American Graffiti*, *Two-Lane Blacktop*, *The Gumball Rally*, *Eat My Dust*, and *Smokey and the Bandit* idolized GM sports cars such as the Pontiac Firebird and Chevy Camaro. The Camaro would star in the sci-fi blockbuster *Transformers* (2007). Sports cars also took front and center in 1970s and 1980s TV shows such as *The Rockford Files* and *Knight Rider*. Another GM sports car, the Corvette, was featured in the early 1960s TV show (and tribute to road culture) *Route 66*.

While GM may fall behind other companies such as Japanese automaker Nissan in producing cars, it is doubtful that it will ever be replaced as a popular culture icon. As Mark LaNeve, who headed GM's North American marketing, has commented, the company's influence on popular culture is "part of the automobile being woven into the fabric of American culture." He adds, "You know, there aren't too many songs about your first Toyota. That's a big advantage for us."

Patrick Jones

SEE ALSO: *Automobile; Cadillac; The Corvette; Labor Unions; Moore, Michael; Muscle Cars.*

BIBLIOGRAPHY

Cray, Ed. *Chrome Colossus: General Motors and Its Times.* New York: McGraw-Hill, 1980.

Halberstam, David. *The Fifties.* New York: Villard Books, 1993.

Holstein, William J. *Why GM Matters: Inside the Race to Transform an American Icon.* New York: Walker Books, 2009.

Ingrassia, Paul. *Crash Course: The American Automobile Industry's Road to Bankruptcy and Bailout . . . and Beyond.* New York: Random House, 2011.

Keller, Maryann A. *Rude Awakening: The Rise, Fall, and Struggle for Recovery of General Motors.* New York: Morrow, 1989.

Kushma, David. "America's 100-Year Love Affair with the Car Often Put to Music: Spotlighted in Songs, Movies and TV, GM Vehicles Have Become Part of Pop Culture." *Advertising Age*, September 15, 2008, C-50.

Whitall, Susan. "Driven by Culture: GM's Cars Take Center Stage in Popular Music, Movies, TV Shows." *Detroit News*, September 8, 2008, B1.

Generation X

Throughout the twentieth century, American historians and social commentators have placed labels on various generations in an effort to capture their characteristic spirit. *Generation X*—roughly defined as the more than seventy-nine million people born between 1961 and 1981—has been characterized by the media as lazy, laconic, and unfocused, but in the eyes of many, the pejorative label represents propaganda rather than reality. For those outside this generation, the *X* stands for some unknown variable, implying young adults searching aimlessly for an identity. Many members of Generation X think otherwise, however, and they fill in the blank with such descriptors as diverse, individualistic, determined, independent, and ambitious.

WHAT'S IN A NAME?

The term *Generation X* worked its way into popular vernacular after the release of Douglas Coupland's 1991 novel, *Generation X: Tales for an Accelerated Culture*, about three twentysomethings who are underemployed, overeducated, and unpredictable. Other nicknames have emerged, such as the more neutral *13ers* (which indicates the thirteenth generation since the Pilgrims landed at Plymouth Rock). However, most of the other markers have negative overtones, such as *slackers*, *latchkey generation*, *MTV generation*, and *baby busters*. Many members of this generation reject these labels because they not only stigmatize and stereotype, but they also reinforce the negative behavior they describe. On the other hand, Karen Ritchie, author of *Marketing to Generation X* (1995), actually prefers the label *Generation X*, for she sees "something anticommercial, antislick, anti-Boomer, and generally defiant about the 'X' label." She also predicts that soon enough, and rightly so, this generation "will name themselves."

MODERNISM VS. POSTMODERNISM

The members of Generation X can be seen as natural products of the intellectual atmosphere in which they have grown up, for they are the first generation to be raised in the age of postmodernism—a widespread cultural development of the last quarter of the twentieth century. Understanding the often rocky transition from modern to postmodern culture is necessary to understanding how many members of Generation X think and operate. Whereas modernism values a single world view rooted in objective science, postmodernism values multiple world views based on subjective experiences and contingencies. Information and knowledge are gathered in a linear fashion by the modernists, but for postmodernists, particularly those of Generation X, information comes from fragmented and nonlinear sources, often in the form of hypertext or visual images.

While the modernists revere the classics of art and literature, postmodernists have a broader frame of reference: they not only revere the classics, but they also grant status and value to the productions of popular culture. Ethics for the modernists can be rigid, even self-righteous, but postmodernists have a more situational ethic that resists the concept of "Universal Truth." Monolithic institutions such as government, education, corporations, and the press, which are seen as authoritative by the modernists, are viewed with caution and distrust by members of Generation X.

Xers have grown up during the cultural transformation from modernism to postmodernism, and the sensibilities of postmodernism are naturally appealing to many members of Generation X because their young adulthood has been constructed by the postmodern society. Paradoxically, they have simultaneously been victimized by a society trying to come to terms with a paradigm shift that many find threatening. Members of Generation X often represent that threat to their elders. As a result, Xers are both the product and the scapegoat of a culture in a state of flux.

True to this variable spirit of postmodernism, Generation X defies homogeneity. Extremely diverse in race, class, religion, ethnicity, and sexual orientation, Xers often feel a collective uniqueness that has emerged from shared experiences and cultural circumstances. The unrest of the late 1960s and early 1970s, followed by the uneasy discomfort of the late 1970s and the self-involved consumption of the 1980s, were the foreground to the 1990s—a decade laden with problems. Social ills such as the rise in teen suicide, widespread homelessness, proliferating toxic waste, violent crime, the AIDS epidemic, and a "downsizing" workforce, coupled with fundamental changes in social structures, such as the family, caused by rising divorce rates and working parents, have been the realities of the world as Generation X came of age. Like most younger generations, many Xers resent their parental generation—the baby boomers—for leaving them to repair or endure a society on the brink of collapse. Considering the problems Xers face, it is perhaps no wonder that a favorite T-shirt slogan is "NO FEAR," and it is also representative of the contradictions of their culture that NO FEAR is the corporate brand name of a line of sports clothes.

POLITICAL CLIMATE

Lack of fear, however, is not enough to manage America's social problems, and many baby boomers voice concern that most members of Generation X evince distaste for politics and public affairs. The trust of all Americans in their government reached increasingly low levels in the 1990s, as members of Generation X came of age politically. Because they view politics as a hostile and corrupt environment, Xers have tended to be disgusted by political machinations, and thus often disengaged.

Political apathy among young people is not a new phenomenon; personal challenges such as education, careers, and relationships often consume their time and energy, leaving little left over for political affairs. Furthermore, political scientists report that, historically, levels of public participation increase with age. However, Xers have never experienced political innocence and have lived within a negative climate of politics their entire lives. This climate caused many to turn their backs on political involvement, in turn causing a potentially devastating problem in terms of Xers' future civic and political responsibility. As the generations grew older, however, they turned their disenfranchised angst into a political spirit that was immensely independent, challenging the partisan bickering in American political campaigns. Highly educated and entrepreneurial, strong convictions were beneath the slacker image. Xers championed feminist causes, pushed for changes in environmental policies, and continued to push for racial and sexual equality. Arguably the first Generation X president, President Barack Obama tapped into the energy of the generation, promising hope and change by raising expectations and giving voice to their collective frustration.

Neil Howe and Bill Strauss provide a more pragmatic perspective in their oft-cited *13th Gen: Abort, Retry, Ignore, Fail?* (1993), in which they lay out a five-point political credo of Xers: (1) "Wear your politics lightly"; (2) "Survival comes first"; (3) "Try to fix only what's fixable"; (4) "Clean up after your own mess"; and (5) "Personal style matters." Howe and Strauss posit that for the thirteenth generation, "national politics will drift toward the personal, no-nonsense, survivalist approach."

Xers are already employing this do-it-yourself attitude by saving early for their retirement. According to Richard Thau, in a 1994 poll of eighteen- to thirty-four-year-olds, 82 percent believed that Social Security, the U.S. government's largest benefit program, would deconstruct before their retirement.

Thau is the executive director of the Third Millennium, a political advocacy group centered in New York with hundreds of members who are dedicated to speaking out on behalf of the interests of the Generation X age group. Likewise, Hans Riemer and Chris Cuomo cofounded 2030, which they describe as a "political action-tank" for Generation X. In Riemer's words, "so much of what is going wrong today requires innovation and new thinking, and we can respond to these requirements at a more rapid pace than other generations could." These informed Xers are responding to the concerns of "massive ignorance" through practical action.

IRONY AND ENTERTAINMENT

Xers' cautious and fiscally conservative sensibility has been a challenge to America's mostly middle-age advertisers and marketers who have recognized Generation X as a viable and large market. However, they are also the best-educated generation in America's history and were raised on commercial hyperbole. While Xers might respect and enjoy advertisements that are crisp, sophisticated, humorous, and informative, they are savvy enough to realize when hype or insincerity is at work. Ritchie recognizes that "no icon and certainly no commercial is safe from their irony, their sarcasm or their remote control. These are the tools with which Generation X keeps the world in perspective."

Gen Xer Thau confirms such use of satire and irony in explaining the wild popularity of the "fictional buffoons" who have largely defined Generation X for the nation: Beavis and Butt-Head, Bill and Ted, Wayne and Garth, Bart Simpson, and the children who live in South Park. Members of Generation X, claims Thau, are clearly educated enough to enjoy "watching these morons because they satirize the image older generations have of us." Shows such as *Friends* (1994–2004), *ER* (1994–2009), *Seinfeld* (1990–1998), *Melrose Place* (1992–1999), *The X-Files* (1993–2002), and *Party of Five* (1994–2000) were popular among Xers because they employ friends as family and serialized story lines: ingredients favored by Generation X viewers. The effect of Generation X on TV programming could clearly be measured by the launching of three broadcast networks—Fox, UPN, and WB—specifically targeted at Generation X.

Perhaps one of the more joyful memories from the early days of Xers is those three-minute jingles that provided Saturday morning lessons in grammar, math, civics, and science: ABC's *Schoolhouse Rock!* (1973–1985). Rob Owen, author of *Gen X TV* (1997), claims that "these little ditties entered the Gen X consciousness and stayed there." He also posits that these musical education segments were the forerunner to what we later came to know as music videos.

"I WANT MY MTV"

Unlike any preceding generation, the visual element is essential to Xers. Since they grew up with television, video games, and computers, it is natural that theirs is the generation that added pictures to rock songs. Owen contends that the introduction of the Music Television channel (MTV) "raised the ante" in the entertainment industry when television producers blended music, visuals, and quick cuts for the sophisticated viewing demands of Generation X. When MTV went on the air in August 1981, targeting the twelve-to-thirty-four age group, members of Generation X responded immediately—so much so that Xers are criticized for having an MTV-attention span, alluding to the quick-cut and fast-paced conventions of music videos. Despite this criticism, the attraction of MTV remains constant, explains Meredith Bagby in *Rational Exuberance*, because MTV quite literally made it their business to keep up with the changes in Generation X.

The musical interests of Xers are as diverse as the members themselves. In the early 1990s many members of Generation X revered grunge rock groups such as Nirvana, with their furious, angst-ridden lyrics and wailing guitar licks. Nirvana railed against the establishment and a decaying society—issues with which Xers could readily identify. Kurt Cobain was their poet, but his suicide in April 1994 brought his anguished alienation to a crashing halt. The bullet that ended Cobain's life created a collective heartache for many members of Generation X.

While Cobain screamed in despair, rappers continue to provide their version of the nightly news concerning the happenings on America's urban streets. Hip-hop and rap music appealed to members of Generation X across all race and ethnic lines, for, like Cobain, rappers speak of the issues of the day while simultaneously affirming black identity. Howe and Strauss describe inner-city Xers as "unmarried teen moms and unconcerned teen fathers; lethal gangsters . . . and innocent hiphoppers who have no illusions about why older white guys cross the streets to avoid them." Rappers such as Tupac Shakur, Queen Latifah, Snoop Dogg, Master P, Puff Daddy, and Dr. Dre are significant voices for many members of Generation X. The success of Black Entertainment Television (BET), a music network launched in 1980 that focuses on urban contemporary sounds, attests to the far-reaching appeal of black music among Generation X. In addition to alternative rock and rap, other genres of Gen X music include ska, techno, industrial, country, reggae, and goth.

ENTREPRENEURIAL SPIRIT

Though many Xers have a deep connection to music, they are not merely tuning in to the various music networks and dancing at all-night raves. Some have a strong entrepreneurial spirit that belies their media reputation for laziness and lack of focus. For example, Jerry Yang and David Filo, both graduate students at Stanford, cofounded Yahoo!, the first online navigational guide to the Web. Google was founded in 1998 by another duo from Stanford, Larry Page and Sergey Brin. Xer Adam Werbach was elected as the youngest president of the Sierra Club, the largest grassroots environmental organization, and later went on to assist the advertising firm Saatchi & Saatchi in their efforts to "green" large corporations. Xer Eric Liu edited a collection of essays about Generation X called *Next* and was a foreign-policy speechwriter for President Bill Clinton.

At age twenty-five, Steve Frank became a journalist for the *Wall Street Journal*. Jonathan Karl was hired as a reporter for CNN to represent his generation. Xer David Mays founded the *Source*, the immensely popular magazine of hip-hop music, culture, and politics, in 1988. Kevin Smith financed his first movie, *Clerks*, on his credit card in 1994 and then went on to make *Chasing Amy* (1997), which earned him the respect of mainstream moviemakers. Beth Kobliner, a contributor to the *New York Times* and the Huffington Post, also wrote the best seller on personal finance for Generation X, *Get a Financial Life: Personal Finances in Your Twenties and Thirties* (2009). She was also appointed by President Obama to serve on the Advisory Council on Financial Capability in 2010. At only twenty-six,

Jeff Shesol is considered an acclaimed historian for his book *Mutual Contempt* about Robert Kennedy and Lyndon Johnson. Although the title of the 1991 movie *Slackers* has been used to label members of Generation X, these accomplishments clearly negate such a reputation.

Indeed, films that might be classified as "The Cinema of Generation X," according to writer Peter Hanson, are complex in their portrayal of Gen X themes. The "spiritual wanderlust" that defines the cinema of Generation X—a body of work that includes *sex, lies and videotape* (1989), *Pulp Fiction* (1994), *Reality Bites* (1994), *The Sixth Sense* (1999), *The Usual Suspects* (1995), *American Beauty* (1999), and *The Matrix* (1999)—is what Hanson describes as perhaps the ultimate expression of Generation X's collective identity. *The Matrix* asks, after all, the essential question: how to overthrow the powers that be?

In the face of dismissive and stereotypical media portrayals, Generation X not only learned how to navigate the increasingly fast-paced world around them but also helped construct its identity. Members of Generation X have learned to cope with guarded optimism and practical confidence, assuming leadership positions left open by their aging boomer counterparts. Although they may be cynical about the conditions of the world in which they came of age, most do embrace an American dream, albeit a different one from that of their predecessors.

Judy L. Isaksen

SEE ALSO: *Advertising; Alternative Country Music; Alternative Rock;* American Beauty*; Baby Boomers;* Beavis and Butt-Head*; Best Sellers; CNN; Ellis, Bret Easton; Environmentalism;* ER*;* Friends*; Goth; Grunge; Hip-Hop; The Internet;* The Matrix*; Modernism; MTV; Nirvana; Postmodernism;* Pulp Fiction*; Queen Latifah; Rap;* The Real World*; Reggae; Saturday Morning Cartoons;* Schoolhouse Rock!*;* Seinfeld*;* sex, lies and videotape*; Shakur, Tupac;* The Simpsons*;* The Sixth Sense*; Snoop Dogg;* South Park*; Television; Video Games; The* Wall Street Journal*;* Wayne's World*;* The X-Files*; Zines.*

BIBLIOGRAPHY

Bagby, Meredith. *Rational Exuberance: The Influence of Generation X on the New American Economy.* New York: Dutton, 1998.

Bennett, Stephen Earl, and Eric W. Rademacher. "The *Age of Indifference* Revisited: Patterns of Political Interest, Media Exposure, and Knowledge among Generation X." In *After the Boom: The Politics of Generation X*, 21–42. Lanham, MD: Rowman & Littlefield, 1997.

Chamberlain, Lisa. *Slackonomics: Generation X in the Age of Creative Destruction.* New York: Harvard Business Review Press, 2009.

Coupland, Douglas. *Generation X: Tales for an Accelerated Culture.* New York: St. Martin's Press, 1991.

Hanson, Peter. *The Cinema of Generation X.* Jefferson, NC: McFarland, 2002.

Howe, Neil, and Bill Strauss. *13th Gen: Abort, Retry, Ignore, Fail?* New York: Vintage Books, 1993.

Owen, Rob. *Gen X TV: The Brady Bunch to Melrose Place.* Syracuse, NY: Syracuse University Press, 1997.

Ritchie, Karen. *Marketing to Generation X.* New York: Lexington Books, 1995.

Stephey, J. J. "Gen-X: The Ignored Generation?" *Time*, April 16, 2008.

Thau, Richard. "So-Called Generation X: How Do You Target a Market That Wants to Be Left Alone?" *Vital Speeches of the Day* 62, no. 21 (1996): 664–667.

Gentlemen Prefer Blondes

Novel, stage play, and popular 1953 film *Gentlemen Prefer Blondes* began as a series of satiric sketches written by Anita Loos and published by *Harper's Bazaar* in 1925. The series featured two pretty and bright but unschooled flappers, Lorelei Lee and Dorothy Shaw, who joyfully infiltrated the bastions of the ruling class. "The strength behind Loos's heroines lies not in their sexuality per se," as writer Regina Barreca has noted, "but on the fact that they remain on the periphery of social and cultural structures." Their profound hunger to be fully accepted into society is at odds with their outsider's recognition of society's entrenched moral hypocrisy. The series struck a chord with readers, and by the third installment *Harper's Bazaar* had tripled its newsstand sales.

Loos developed the premise into a novel, which was translated into thirteen languages and adapted into a stage play the following year. The narrative took the form of a diary written by Lorelei, whose attempts to sound cultured resulted in malapropisms ("A girl like I") and whose childlike observations satirized the surrounding society ("He really does not mind what a girl has been through, as long as she does not enjoy herself at the finish"). The first film version premiered in 1928 to rave reviews. "Those two energetic and resourceful diamond diggers, Lorelei and Dorothy, have come to the Rivoli Theatre in a splendid pictorial translation of Anita Loos's book," wrote Mordaunt Hall for the *New York Times*. He continued, "This film is an infectious treat."

The story was transformed into a Broadway musical that made Carol Channing a star in 1949. It was produced as an elaborate Technicolor film by Twentieth Century Fox in 1953, revived as a musical titled *Lorelei* in 1974, and enacted as a stage play by the National Actors Theatre in 1995. But the most influential vehicle for the story is undoubtedly the 1953 film.

1953 MOVIE

Directed by Howard Hawks, *Gentlemen Prefer Blondes* starred Marilyn Monroe as Lorelei and Jane Russell as Dorothy. The film gained instant success, generating more than $5 million for Fox by the end of the year. Monroe got second billing, earning less than one-tenth of Russell's $200,000 for her work on the film. She was even refused her own dressing room, since she was not considered a star. By the end of the year, however, Monroe had starred in three hit films, appeared on the cover of *Look* magazine, and was voted top female box-office star by American film distributors.

Playboy magazine took advantage of Monroe's sudden celebrity by putting her on the cover of its first issue in December 1953 and printing five-year-old nude photographs of her as its first centerfold. The embodiment of the *Playboy* philosophy—combining desirability with vulnerability and exuding sexuality as something natural and innocent—Monroe was perfect for the role of Lorelei, who, as one critic remarked, sometimes "employs an imploring expression, one which seems to imply that she is totally ignorant of her physical attraction." Monroe's star persona coalesced with the film, and thereafter roles such as Pola in *How to Marry a Millionaire* (1953), the Girl in *The Seven Year Itch* (1955), and Sugar in *Some Like It Hot* (1959) were written with her specifically in mind.

FEMINIST VIEWS

In the early 1970s film critics such as Molly Haskell criticized Monroe for "catering so shamelessly to a false, regressive, childish, and detached idea of sexuality." It might seem surprising, then, that *Gentlemen Prefer Blondes* was revived as a feminist text by film scholars a decade later. Lucie Arbuthnot and Gail Seneca, for example, point out in their essay in *Issues in Feminist Film Criticism* that "given the mammary madness of the fifties, it is striking that Hawks chose to dress Monroe and Russell in high-necked sweaters and dresses." Actually, the costumes—including skin-tight, red-sequined dresses with thigh-high slits—are far from modest. And the high necklines were not Hawks's choice but rather the result of the Motion Picture Association of America's self-censorship.

Feminist scholars made a stronger case for the film's progressive depiction of female friendship: "the absence of competitiveness, envy and pettiness" between Dorothy and Lorelei. By many accounts, this reflects a genuine affinity between Russell and Monroe, belying rumors that Monroe could not get along with other women. The popular press predicted a giant feud between the two stars during filming, a "Battle of the Bulges" as one male columnist inevitably called it. In fact, according to Todd McCarthy in *Howard Hawks: The Grey Fox of Hollywood*, Russell "welcomed Monroe at once and gained her confidence professionally and personally." In Monroe's last interview with *Life* magazine, conducted just two days before her death in August 1962, she recalled that Russell "was quite wonderful to me."

Perhaps most strikingly for contemporary feminists, *Gentlemen Prefer Blondes* can be said to draw a moral parallel between the motivations of women who pursue men for their money and men who pursue women for their beauty. Hollywood, of course, has traditionally vilified the former as gold digging and celebrated the latter as love at first sight. But songs like "Diamonds Are a Girl's Best Friend" suggest that men are fickle and women have but one commodity to exchange under patriarchal capitalism: their youthful beauty. "Men grow cold as girls grow old / And we all lose our charms in the end / But square-cut or pear-shaped / These rocks won't lose their shape / Diamonds are a girl's best friend." Proving that she is not as dumb as her future father-in-law thinks, Lorelei proclaims that "a man being rich is like a girl being pretty. You might not marry a girl just because she's pretty, but my goodness, doesn't it help?"

"The line which separates celebration from satire in American culture is perniciously thin," Maureen Turim writes in her essay in *Wide Angle*, and "no place is that lack of differentiation more evident than in Hawks's *Gentlemen Prefer Blondes*." It is not surprising, then, that Madonna, whose work is characterized by a similar ambiguity, chose to restage Monroe's "Diamonds Are a Girl's Best Friend" performance in her 1985 hit music video for the song "Material Girl."

Jeanne Hall

SEE ALSO: *Broadway; Hawks, Howard; Hollywood; Loos, Anita; Madonna; Monroe, Marilyn; Movie Stars;* Playboy; *Russell, Jane;* The Seven Year Itch; Some Like It Hot.

BIBLIOGRAPHY

Arbuthnot, Lucie, and Gail Seneca. "Pretext and Text in *Gentlemen Prefer Blondes*." In *Issues in Feminist Film Criticism*, ed. Patricia Erens. Bloomington: Indiana University Press, 1990.

Dyer, Richard. *Heavenly Bodies*. New York: St. Martin's Press, 1986.

Haskell, Molly. *From Reverence to Rape: The Treatment of Women in the Movies*. New York: Penguin Books, 1974.

Loos, Anita. *Gentlemen Prefer Blondes*. New York: Penguin Books, 1998.

Loos, Anita; Cari Beauchamp; and Mary Loos. *Anita Loos Rediscovered: Film Treatments and Fiction*. Berkeley: University of California Press, 2003.

McCarthy, Todd. *Howard Hawks: The Grey Fox of Hollywood*. New York: Grove Press, 1997.

Rollyson, Carl E. *Marilyn Monroe: A Life of the Actress*. Ann Arbor, MI: UMI Research Press, 1986.

Turim, Maureen. "Gentlemen Consume Blondes." *Wide Angle* 1, no. 1 (1979): 52–59.

Gere, Richard *(1949–)*

Actor Richard Gere evolved from a brash young leading man whose career was based primarily on his sexy good looks into a devoted Buddhist and champion of oppressed people. A deft musician, composer, and gymnast in high school, Gere attended college on a gymnastics scholarship and then dropped out to pursue a career in music. Acting and composing in summer stock led to a position as an understudy for the lead in the Broadway production of the rock musical *Grease* in 1972 and then the opportunity to play the lead in the London production the following year. This was followed by the rare opportunity (for an American actor) to play a season with the Young Vic Company in such offerings as *The Taming of the Shrew* in 1974.

His film debut in 1974 was in a bit part as a pimp in *Report to the Commissioner*, which was followed by a more high-profile but similar role as a sexually charged street hustler involved with Diane Keaton in 1977's *Looking for Mr. Goodbar*. While his subsequent role as a Depression-era con man in Terence Malick's acclaimed *Days of Heaven* (1978) brought him some serious critical attention, his status as a sex symbol was confirmed by his starring role in the breakthrough hit *American Gigolo* in 1980. Over the next few years his career began to decline. Critics claimed that it was because his film work came second after his burgeoning interest in Buddhism. Having studied the religion, Gere made a visit to the Tibetan refugee camps in Nepal in 1978, and after meeting with the Dalai Lama, declared himself a disciple.

Following his embrace of Buddhism, Gere attempted to break free of his sex-symbol status and try more character-driven work. Returning to the stage in a highly praised performance as a gay concentration camp prisoner in the Broadway play *Bent*, he then accepted an equally challenging role as a desperate young man struggling to get through brutal military officer's training in *An Officer and a Gentleman* (1982), which proved a box-office hit (grossing almost $130 million) and suggested that

Gere possessed untapped skills as an actor. Subsequent misfires, however, such as the remake of *Breathless* (1983), *Beyond the Limit* (1983), *King David* (1985), and Francis Ford Coppola's ill-fated *The Cotton Club* (1984), lowered his credibility until his unexpected breakthrough performance opposite Julia Roberts in 1990's megahit *Pretty Woman* caused producers to take notice.

From there Gere reestablished his leading-man status in respectable films such as 1993's *Sommersby* and thrillers such as *Primal Fear* (1996) and *The Jackal* (1997). But Gere's "heart project" was *Red Corner* (1997), which allowed him to bring his career and private concerns together in the story of an American businessman visiting China who is framed for a murder, wrongly imprisoned, and forced to struggle against China's rigidly oppressive legal system.

After receiving unexpected distinction as *People* magazine's "Sexiest Man Alive" in 1999 (at the age of fifty), Gere had three of his biggest box-office hits during the ensuing decade. Drawing on the song and dance skills of his youth, he was cast as flamboyant lawyer Billy Flynn in the film version of the stage musical *Chicago* in 2002. The film won the Oscar in 2003 for Best Picture, and Gere won a Golden Globe for Best Actor in a Comedy or Musical. Subsequently, *Shall We Dance?*—about a middle-aged man who is revitalized by taking ballroom dance lessons—grossed more than $150 million. Reteaming with occasional costar Diane Lane (*Unfaithful*, *The Cotton Club*), Gere made *Nights in Rodanthe* in 2008. Adapted from a Nicholas Sparks best seller, the film received a critical bashing for its contrived and clichéd romance novel plotting but was nevertheless a financial success.

Richard Gere. *Richard Gere signs his name before placing his hands and feet in cement during a ceremony at Mann's Chinese Theatre in Hollywood, California, in 1999.* VINCE BUCCI/AFP/GETTY IMAGES.

Devout in his religion, Gere maintained that he meditated daily and spent time between projects in India with the exiled Tibetans. His very public twenty-year devotion to the faith led the Dalai Lama to personally request Gere's high-profile assistance in the crusade to end China's tyrannous rule of Tibet—a cause that Gere championed to the extent of making a very public plea at the 1993 Academy Awards, which in turn led to his banishment from future Oscar ceremonies. He was also actively involved in campaigning to raise public awareness of the religious and cultural heritage of Tibet in an effort to push for an American boycott of China. This led to Gere's publishing a book of photographs he took of Tibetans, *Pilgrim*, the proceeds of which were donated to the cause of Tibetan autonomy.

Gere's sense of universal responsibility also extended to his taking up the cause of Central American refugees and oppressed tribal peoples worldwide. His concern for the international AIDS crisis also resulted in his launching an AIDS-awareness program in India, for which he received a Harvard Award in 1995.

Rick Moody

SEE ALSO: *Academy Awards; Broadway; The Cotton Club; Crawford, Cindy;* People; *Roberts, Julia; Sex Symbol.*

BIBLIOGRAPHY

Gere, Richard. *Pilgrim.* Boston: Little, Brown, 1997.

Parker, John. *Richard Gere: The Flesh and the Spirit.* New York: Headline Book Publishing, 1996.

Gernsback, Hugo *(1884–1967)*

An American publisher, editor, and author, Hugo Gernsback is perhaps best known as the founder of the modern science fiction literary genre. It was his publication of *Amazing Stories* (1926) that gave him this distinction and drew Americans into reading stories about an unknown future. Indeed, Gernsback's imagination was not only limited to the abstract—not in the sense that what he wrote about was impossible—but his speculation about future technological advancements had a solid basis in science . . . as any good science fiction does. In this sense he was one of the twentieth century's greatest visionaries.

Gernsback immigrated to the United States from Luxembourg in 1904 and established the Electro Importing Company, the first electrical importing business in America. In 1905 he designed and produced the world's first home radio set and began publishing a mail-order catalog, which he filled with articles discussing new technologies. By 1908 Gernsback's mail-order catalog had grown and evolved into *Modern Electrics*, the first electronics magazine of its kind in the world.

Gernsback began experimenting with science fiction as a way to speculate on the new technologies that exploded on the scene at the start of the twentieth century. He serialized his first such story, "Ralph 124C 41+: A Romance of the Year 2660," in *Modern Electrics* from April 1911 to March 1912. Though clumsy and simplistic by today's standards, "Ralph 124C 41+" was based on solid scientific principles and made a number of remarkable technological predictions: fluorescent lighting, plastics, synthetic fabrics, stainless steel, jukeboxes, hydroponics, tape recorders, loudspeakers, microfilm, television, radio networks, vending machines, nuclear weapons, and solar energy. Gernsback's story proved so popular among his mostly young and technologically curious readers that he began including at least one such story in each issue.

BIRTH OF *AMAZING STORIES*

Gernsback sold *Modern Electrics* in 1912 and started a larger periodical, the *Electrical Experimenter*, in 1913, which he retitled *Science and Invention* in 1920 (later absorbed into *Popular Electronics*). By this time Gernsback was publishing two or more stories in each issue of *Science and Invention* as well as in its companion publication *Radio News*, and he began to suspect there might be a market for an all-fiction science magazine. In August 1923 he found out when he published a special "Scientific Fiction Number" of *Science and Invention*, which contained six new *scientifiction* stories (Gernsback's term for the new genre) and cover art depicting a man in a space suit. It was so successful that on April 5, 1926, the enterprising Gernsback launched the first magazine in the world devoted exclusively to science fiction, *Amazing Stories*.

Aware of the "historical interest" posterity would have in this new genre, Gernsback stressed both literary quality and scientific accuracy in his new magazine. At first he filled its pages with reprints of stories by Jules Verne, Edgar Allan Poe, and H. G. Wells. But Gernsback quickly attracted such visionary writers as E. E. "Doc" Smith, Jack Williamson, Ray Cummings, and John W. Campbell, whose groundbreaking stories would map out science fiction's major themes. Gernsback also hired Austrian-born artist Frank R. Paul to provide illustrations for many of the magazine's covers and interior stories. Paul's bold style, vivid use of color, and imaginative depiction of scientific gadgetry, future cities, and alien worlds gave *Amazing Stories* a distinctive look and was an important factor in the magazine's success. Bolstered by that success Gernsback followed *Amazing Stories* with an expanded edition of the magazine titled *Amazing Stories Annual*, which was so popular Gernsback immediately changed it to the more frequent *Amazing Stories Quarterly*.

Gernsback lost control of *Amazing Stories* in 1929 in a bizarre legal maneuver rumored to have been orchestrated by one of his competitors. Within a month, however, the crusading editor launched four new science fiction magazines: *Science Wonder Stories*, *Air Wonder Stories* (both merged in 1930 as *Wonder Stories)*, *Science Wonder Quarterly*, and *Scientific Detective Monthly*. Gernsback's new magazines were overnight successes, in part because of his solid reputation but also because he took with him Paul and many of the best science fiction writers from *Amazing Stories*. But it is Gernsback's editorial in the first issue of *Science Wonder Stories* that is of particular interest to the history of popular culture. It is there he gave the world the term *science fiction*.

HIGHER CALLING

Scholars have noted that if Gernsback had not launched the first science fiction magazine in 1926, someone else would have seen the market opportunities and published something very similar. As important as timing was in the success of Gernsback's magazine publishing, however, his contribution to the genre goes far beyond having an uncanny business sense. Gernsback had a genuinely altruistic, though perhaps simplistic, belief that technology could bring about a human utopia, and he saw it as his role to instill a love of science and technology in his mainly adolescent readers. His argument that science could not only be extrapolated but also taught through fiction was one he returned to over and over and one that was not lost on his readers.

Throughout his life Gernsback continued to invent electronic devices, patenting nearly eighty before his death in 1967. And though he published more than fifty magazines devoted to such diverse topics as radio, humor, sex, economics, crime detection, and aviation, it was with the publication of *Amazing Stories* that he achieved his lasting fame and exerted his most profound influence on popular culture. Shortly after its publication, magazines and newspapers began to carry science fiction stories geared for a wider audience. Science fiction quickly began appearing in nearly every artistic medium, including books, radio, film, comic books, and television. Moreover, Gernsback's actions inspired two generations of readers and writers and played a major role in establishing science fiction as an independent literary genre. As a tribute to Gernsback's overall contribution to the field, in 1953 the prestigious Science Fiction Achievement Awards were named the Hugo Awards.

Anthony Ubelhor

SEE ALSO: Amazing Stories*; Pulp Magazines; Science Fiction Publishing.*

BIBLIOGRAPHY

Aldiss, Brian W. *Trillion Year Spree*. New York: Avon Books, 1988.

Gernsback, Hugo. *Hugo Gernsback: A Man Well Ahead of His Time*, ed. Larry Steckler. Marana, AZ: Poptronix, 2007.

Moskowitz, Sam. *Explorers of the Infinite: Shapers of Science Fiction*. Westport, CT: Hyperion Press, 1974.

Gertie the Dinosaur

Billed as "The Greatest Animal Act in the World," the animated cartoon *Gertie the Dinosaur* premiered in Chicago in February 1914. "She eats, drinks, and breathes! She laughs and cries! Dances the tango, answers questions and obeys every command! Yet, she lived millions of years before man inhabited this earth and has never been seen since!!" claimed the posters. Though Gertie was not the first cartoon character to come alive on-screen, she might as well have been. As American film critic Leonard Maltin writes in *Of Mice and Magic*, "One might say that Gertie launched an entire industry."

Created by the American comic-strip artist Winsor McCay, Gertie's silent film debut preceded Walt Disney's Mickey Mouse sound film *Steamboat Willie* by fourteen years. Though animated cartoons date to experiments in Thomas A. Edison's film studio as early as 1906, it was McCay's sophisticated drawings, charming story, and ingenuity that first really gave "life" to animated characters. It was Gertie's charming personality that captured the imagination of audiences.

Popular comic strips were made to move early in the history of cinema, but the development of the art and craft of animation was initially inhibited by economic constraints. While audiences and exhibitors expected animated cartoons to be produced with the same frequency as newspaper comic strips, one minute of an animated cartoon required about 1,000 drawings (each film frame was one drawing and passed at the speed of sixteen frames per second). The speed of production precluded much analysis of the art, and early animators had to depend on visual gags and dialogue balloons to get a laugh.

McCay, a well-known newspaper cartoonist, inspired by his son's flip-up books and the pioneering films of J. Stuart Blackton, began experimenting with cartoons and motion pictures in 1907. Four years later, in April 1911, he premiered his first animated cartoon, *Little Nemo*, based on one of his popular comic strip characters. This short film had no story. Instead, the character asked the audience, in a dialogue balloon, to watch him move as he jumped, flipped, ran, and bounced. To create this short film, McCay hand-colored 4,000 frames of 35-millimeter film. He incorporated *Little Nemo* into his vaudeville act, and audiences loved it.

Next, McCay created *The Story of a Mosquito*, which took him about a year to make. This new cartoon advanced the techniques used for *Little Nemo*, this time telling a story of a mosquito's experience with a drunken man. Although McCay's second film, which also premiered as part of his vaudeville act, was well received, audiences and critics had a hard time accepting that drawings could be brought to life on film, and they suspected that the movement was some sort of trick produced with wires and figures.

Gertie the Dinosaur was McCay's answer to those skeptics. He chose a dinosaur as his character because the animal was long extinct and no one could claim that the artist was employing trickery to make her move. To create his memorable character, McCay inked drawings on rice paper and then mounted them on cardboard. He invented a flip machine to check the animation. Most astonishing, perhaps, for current aficionados accustomed to animation cells and computer-generated animation, McCay had to redraw the dinosaur and her background for every frame. He drew more than 10,000 Gerties himself and enlisted an assistant to reproduce the backgrounds, often by tracing.

The idea of a dinosaur as the subject of an animated drawing was far-fetched. McCay's ingenuity, however, lay in the manner in which he presented the one-reel, twelve-minute film in his vaudeville act. As Maltin describes it, McCay performed onstage with the cartoon, playing Gertie's trainer and interacting with the motion picture. Gertie "obeyed" his commands, cried when he reprimanded her, ate the snacks he tossed her, and playfully teased her trainer. At the end of the film, McCay walked onto the screen, becoming part of the animation, and together he and Gertie walked away.

The film and its "leading lady" were wildly popular, and the dinosaur became an instant star. McCay, however, had little desire to remain involved in the industry that his work had spawned. He preferred instead to continue with his newspaper comic strips and vaudeville acts and to work on his films for his own satisfaction. In further developing the art of animation, McCay created, among others, *The Sinking of the* Lusitania (1918) and *The Centaurs* (1921). In these, as in *Gertie*, his graphic precision was far more sophisticated than that of his contemporaries.

Eventually, McCay stopped making films altogether, although early animators, including John Randolph Bray, the inventor of the cell, considered McCay to be the father of their art and their craft. Indeed, McCay himself is reported to have proudly christened himself "the creator of animated cartoons."

Ilene S. Goldman

SEE ALSO: *Animated Films; Comics; Disney (Walt Disney Company); Edison, Thomas Alva; McCay, Winsor; Silent Movies;* Steamboat Willie*; Vaudeville.*

BIBLIOGRAPHY

"A Brief History of Gertie the Dinosaur." Van Eaton Galleries. Accessed November 8, 2011. Available from http://vegalleries.com/gerthistory.html

Maltin, Leonard. *Of Mice and Magic: A History of American Animated Cartoons*, rev. ed. New York: Penguin, 1987.

McCay, Winsor. *Winsor McCay: Early Works.* Miamisburg, OH: Checker, 2003.

Pilling, Jayne, ed. *A Reader in Animation Studies.* London: John Libbey, 1997.

Gervais, Ricky *(1961–)*

British comedian Ricky Gervais is a pioneer of a caustic style that took hold in the early part of the twenty-first century. As cowriter, producer, and star of the groundbreaking British television show *The Office* (2001–2003), he brought a sarcastic, faux-documentary style to the situation comedy. In that landmark series, which was adapted for American television, and his other work, Gervais has used humiliation, social embarrassment, and delusion to drive his biting comedy. Although he has often provoked controversy, Gervais has thrived on both sides of the Atlantic Ocean, a rare accomplishment for a comedian.

Gervais's stinging humor has succeeded in many different arenas of show business. He is a popular stand-up comic and has created and starred in acclaimed series for both radio and television. In addition, he has explored podcasts, animation, and directing (*The Invention of Lying*, 2009). Gervais is also the author of a popular children's book series, *Flanimals*, which debuted in 2004.

Gervais was born on June 25, 1961, in Berkshire England. Unlike the lives of many comedians, his childhood was without much stress or family tension. During his final year at University College London, he formed a pop band that had a few minor hits. One of his early jobs was at the commercial radio station Xfm, where he hired Stephen Merchant, who would become his longtime collaborator. In 1999 Merchant and Gervais contributed comedy sketches to the BBC radio series *The Breezeblock.* Their first television project was a comedy special in which Gervais played Clive Meadows, an obsessed David Bowie fan. During that period, he also created the persona of an angry reporter for the British series *The 11 O'Clock Show*. Meanwhile, Merchant produced a documentary parody of office work, with Gervais playing the boss. This short film led to a pilot for a comedy that eventually became *The Office.*

Audiences were not entirely ready for *The Office* when it premiered on BBC Two. Shot as a mockumentary, the show features Gervais as David Brent, a tactless, insufferable boss who parades before the documentary crew that follows him around work filming as he offends his employees and embarrasses himself. The English edition of the show consisted of only twelve episodes, plus two specials, but as word spread about its innovative brand of humor, it built up a cult following and, eventually, an international audience. By 2012 there were American, French, German, Chilean, and Israeli versions of the show.

The American adaptation, set in Scranton, Pennsylvania, and originally featuring Steve Carell as the boss (Gervais's role), premiered in 2005 and had aired more than 170 episodes by 2012. Gervais attributes the longevity of the show's American version to the fact that many of his influences came from the States, including the mockumentary *This Is Spinal Tap*, the animated show *The Simpsons*, and the comic team of Laurel and Hardy.

After the first season of the British version of *The Office*, Gervais and Merchant returned to radio, where they engaged in sometimes raunchy, inappropriate conversation and made fun of the show's producer, Karl Pilkington, who eventually joined the duo in their broadcasts. In 2005 the trio began a series of podcasts for the website Guardian Unlimited. With its ridiculous and often crass recurring segments, such as "Monkey News" (which reported on purported news about monkeys) and "Knob News" (which did the same for male genitalia), the show became the world's most downloaded podcast, according to Guinness World Records. Over the ensuing years, the partnership of Gervais, Merchant, and Pilkington has created audiobooks and video podcasts. Many editions of the audiobooks were turned into an animated series for HBO beginning in 2010.

Ricky Gervais Hosting the Golden Globe Awards. *Ricky Gervais hosts the 68th Annual Golden Globe Awards show in 2011.* PAUL DRINKWATER/NBC/NBCU PHOTO BANK/GETTY IMAGES.

In addition to the podcasts, Gervais and Merchant launched their second TV comedy series, *Extras* (2005–2007), which was broadcast in England by the BBC and by HBO in the United States. Gervais plays the lead character, Andy Millman, a struggling actor bitterly frustrated by his fortunes. Merchant also appears as an incompetent agent named Darren Lamb. Each episode features a guest celebrity, who is asked to play a "twisted" version of his or her persona. Guest celebrities included Kate Winslet, Samuel L. Jackson, Dame Diana Rigg, and Bowie. For his work on the show, Gervais received the 2007 Emmy Award for Outstanding Lead Actor in a Comedy Series.

Many other projects followed *Extras*. In 2010 Gervais and Merchant created *An Idiot Abroad*, an outlandish travel mockumentary with Pilkington in the lead role. At the start of each episode, Pilkington offers ostensibly serious reportage and social commentary from an exotic locale. However, he is soon interrupted by a call from Gervais or Merchant that diverts him from his assignment. For example, when reporting from the beaches of Rio, Pilkington is told to enroll in samba classes to prepare for Carnival.

In 2010 the duo wrote and directed a feature film, *Cemetery Junction*, about English working-class life in the 1970s. The following year Gervais and Merchant joined with actor Warwick Davis to create the sitcom *Life's Too Short* about the tribulations of a dwarf in show business. Gervais drew criticism as host of the 2011 Golden Globe Awards for relentlessly mocking a wide range of celebrities, including Charlie Sheen and Johnny Depp. Robert Downey Jr., among others, called his performance "mean-spirited." Gervais lashed back at his critics, repeating his familiar refrain: "Just because you're offended, that doesn't make you right."

Ron Simon

SEE ALSO: *Bowie, David; Depp, Johnny; Downey, Robert, Jr.; Laurel and Hardy; Mockumentaries;* The Office*;* The Simpsons*; Sitcom; Spinal Tap; Stand-Up Comedy; Television; Winslet, Kate.*

BIBLIOGRAPHY

Brockes, Emma. "Ricky Gervais: 'Bring on the Haters.'" *Guardian*, November 4, 2011.

Heatley, Michael. *Ricky Gervais: The Story So Far*. London: Michael O'Mara, 2007.

Lyall, Sarah. "Ricky Gervais's Life, after 'The Office.'" *New York Times*, March 21, 2005.

Get Smart

The James Bond craze of the 1960s produced a host of spy heroes eager to cash in on the popularity of 007. Some were slavish imitations, but others reflected a willingness to poke fun at the genre. One of the most successful satires, created by Mel

Brooks and Buck Henry, was the television series *Get Smart*, which ran on NBC from 1965 to 1969 and on CBS from 1969 to 1970.

Don Adams (1993–2005) played Maxwell Smart, Agent 86 of CONTROL, a U.S. counterintelligence agency. Barbara Feldon (1933–) was Smart's partner, Agent 99. The inept spy and his far more capable partner fought against the evil organization KAOS. They usually won, mostly because of Smart's tendency to do the right thing for the wrong reason. The show made two contributions to popular culture in the late 1960s—the phrase "Sorry about that, Chief" and a running gag built around the question "Would you believe," as in, "Would you believe you're surrounded by 100 armed agents?" "No, I wouldn't." "Would you believe four Boy Scouts and an angry nun?"

Several attempts were made to relaunch the series over the years. The 1980 film *The Nude Bomb* starred Adams in a reprisal of the role of Agent 86 and was retitled *The Return of Maxwell Smart* when it aired on television in 1982. All the surviving cast members from the original television series reunited for the made-for-TV movie *Get Smart, Again!* (1989), and in 1995 Fox television aired several episodes of a sitcom starring Andy Dick as the son of Maxwell Smart (again played by Adams). The series, however, was cancelled during its first season because of a lack of viewer interest.

In 2008 Warner Brothers Pictures released a major motion picture adaptation of the original series, starring Steve Carell as Agent 86 and Anne Hathaway as Agent 99. The film received lukewarm reviews from critics but was a hit among fans of the original series as well as a younger generation of viewers, and it won the Teen Choice Award for comedy. Adams, who passed away in 2005, was unable to witness the triumphant return of Agent 86, but his distinctive delivery and impeccable comedic timing provided a solid model for Carell's successful interpretation of the role.

Justin Gustainis

SEE ALSO: *Brooks, Mel; James Bond Films; Made-for-Television Movies; Sitcom; Television.*

BIBLIOGRAPHY

Britton, Wesley Alan. *Spy Television*. Westport, CT: Praeger, 2004.

Green, Joey. *The "Get Smart" Handbook*. New York: Collier Books, 1993.

Meyers, Richard. *TV Detectives*. San Diego, CA: Barnes, 1981.

GI Joe

The GI Joe action figure, a plastic doll twelve inches tall and dressed as a military man, was the first action figure and the first exclusively boy's doll, disguised as a war toy. Extremely popular, it was at the same time controversial because of the fighting in Southeast Asia: Its introduction by Hassenfeld Brothers in 1964 coincided with the U.S. Congress's passing of the Gulf of Tonkin Resolution, which escalated American involvement in the Vietnam War. Invented by Stanley Weston, GI Joe was inspired by Mattel's Barbie, which made its debut in 1959, but GI Joe was different from Barbie in that it had twenty-one movable joints, enabling it to be configured in various combat poses. In the "razor and razor blade" principle of marketing, GI Joe, like

GI Joe. *GI Joe action figures are displayed at the FAO Schwarz toy store in Chicago, Illinois, in 2001.*
TIM BOYLE/GETTY IMAGES.

Barbie, was "accessorized"—that is, designed to need additional paraphernalia. "Items sold separately" was the saying that accompanied every advertisement for the dolls.

JOE CAPTURES WWII NOSTALGIA

Although the GI Joe action figure originated during the Cold War, it was nonetheless made in the image of the World War II fighting man. According to Hassenfeld's promotional campaign, the face of GI Joe constituted a composite of the faces of twenty Medal of Honor recipients from the war. American television and cinema were, at the time, frequently glorifying the soldier of the "Good War" in adventure series (*Combat!*, 1962–1967; *The Lieutenant*, 1963–1964; and *The Rat Patrol*, 1966–1968), docucameo-epics (*The Longest Day*, 1962; *Battle of the Bulge*, 1965; and *In Harm's Way*, 1965), and big-war films (*The Great Escape*, 1963; and *Von Ryan's Express*, 1965). Comic books—such as DC Comics' "Sgt. Rock" and Marvel Comics' "Sgt. Fury"—made the World War II fighter a hero as well. Americans' fascination with World War II may have been linked to the uncertainties felt during the Cold War era.

A year after its introduction, the GI Joe line was augmented by an action nurse, featuring blond rooted hair and painted green eyes, and a black soldier heralded as "Action Negro." Neither sold well, and the nurse was discontinued soon thereafter. However, GI Joe accessories such as the plastic jeep and space capsule were very popular. Later, the Talking Joe offered combat discourse—eight phrases per action figure, produced by the pull of a color-coded string. Not everything that GI Joe said was celebratory (for example, "Medic, get that stretcher up here" and "Prepare wounded for helicopter pickup"), although it was certainly less negative than what a real soldier would have said while slogging in the mire of Vietnam. When war protests grew more bitter, fighting Joe dolls were converted into the Adventure Team to look for buried treasure or to capture wild animals. The logo worn by the Adventure Team uncannily resembled a peace sign. By 1976 the GI Joe action figure had become Super Joe and had been reduced in size to eight inches, both for cheaper production and to enable the selling of more affordable accessories. Two years later, with Kenner dominating the market with its Star Wars action figures, racking up nearly $100 million in sales, GI Joe was discontinued.

A REAL AMERICAN HERO

The GI Joe story does not end there, however. Many children wrote Hasbro (Hassenfeld's later name) asking for the toy soldier's return. In the year of Ronald Reagan's first inauguration, GI Joe was reintroduced as "A Real American Hero." Standing at less than four inches tall, a size based on the Star Wars figures, the new GI Joe was the best-selling toy of the 1982 holiday season. This was quite a feat considering that Mattel at the same time introduced its He-Man and the Masters of the Universe action figures. The following year, Mattel hired a film company to create a TV cartoon series based on the Masters of the Universe, inspiring Hasbro to do the same for Joe. In 1984 Tonka entered the competition with its GoBots, and Hasbro responded with its Transformer line featuring "good" Autobots and "evil" Decepticons.

In the meantime, the second wave of GI Joe dolls continued to fill a niche, dealing with new foes such as "Destro" and "Drednoks." In 1986, GI Joe had $185 million in sales. Two years later Hasbro claimed that two-thirds of American boys between the ages of five and eleven owned GI Joe dolls. What was new was the official narrative offered by the GI Joe animation series (airing intermittently starting in 1983) and the comic book *G.I. Joe: A Real American Hero* (1982–1994), creating a need for clear enemies. Also, there were videos, including *G.I. Joe: The Movie* (1987), *Spy Troops: The Movie* (2003), and *Valor vs. Venom* (2004); the Hollywood films *G.I. Joe: The Rise of Cobra* (2009) and *G.I. Joe: Retaliation* (2012); and video and computer games, beginning with *G.I. Joe: Cobra Strike* (1983).

If by the Reagan years it was necessary for a story line to be more explicit, World War II seemed too remote for development. However, a plot directly focusing on the Cold War was considered risky. The comic book and animation series created fictional events and a line of enemy soldiers known as Cobra, a group of warriors who sought "to conquer the world for their own evil purposes!" The first Gulf War did inspire Hasbro to create a "Duke" figure, a friendly soldier dressed in camouflage fatigues, back at the original twelve inches of height. By alluding to the film actor John Wayne, Duke linked not only World War II (à la *Sands of Iwo Jima*) with the Cold War (as in *The Green Berets*), but also the New World Order (represented by the international coalition that opposed Iraq). The twelve-inch figure remained in production through 2005. In the film *G.I. Joe: The Rise of Cobra*, the story line was the fight against terrorism. In 2004 the GI Joe doll was inducted into the National Toy Hall of Fame in Rochester, New York.

Roger Chapman

SEE ALSO: *Barbie; Cold War; Gulf Wars; Toys; Transformers; Wayne, John; World War II.*

BIBLIOGRAPHY

Chapman, Roger. "From Vietnam to the New World Order: The GI Joe Action Figure as Cold War Artifact." In *The Impact of the Cold War on American Popular Culture*, ed. Elaine McClarnand and Steve Goodson. Carrollton: State University of West Georgia, 1999.

Clark, Eric. *The Real Toy Story: Inside the Ruthless Battles for America's Youngest Consumers*. New York: Free Press, 2007.

Cross, Gary. *Kids' Stuff: Toys and the Changing World of American Childhood*. Cambridge, MA: Harvard University Press, 1997.

Hall, Karen J. "A Soldier's Body: GI Joe, Hasbro's Great American Hero, and the Symptoms of Empire." *Journal of Popular Culture* 38, no. 1 (2004): 34–54.

Miller, G. Wayne. *Toy Wars: The Epic Struggle between G.I. Joe, Barbie and the Companies That Make Them*. New York: Times Books, 1998.

Young, Robert. *Action Figures*. New York: Dillon Press, 1992.

Giant

George Stevens's 1956 film *Giant* reveals the ethics and personalities of the Texas oil industry as it shifted from individually driven concerns to large-scale corporate dominance. Including an important subplot, the film also tackles the Tex-Mex border culture that formed during the twentieth century. Today the immigration and labor situations depicted in *Giant* remain touchstones of regional politics.

Rock Hudson plays Bick Benedict, who presides over the 595,000-acre Benedict Reata Ranch. James Dean plays the film's most memorable character, Jett Rink, the rebellious upstart who labors on the ranch before striking oil on his small plot of land. Drenched in crude, Rink arrives at Reata in a great moment in American film. Rink becomes the symbol of new money—a corrupt, flamboyant oil tycoon—and he and Benedict battle for the affections of Leslie Lynton, played by Elizabeth Taylor.

Whereas the nation focused on the Great Depression and then a world war, a growing number of independent oilmen in Houston and Dallas were acquiring spectacular fortunes that in the postwar years attracted the interest of reporters and writers seeking to expose this new center of money and power. The wealth, success, and boundless possibilities that many writers found in Texas only sickened the novelist and playwright Edna Ferber. During the 1950s her novel, which would become the film *Giant*, was serialized in *Ladies' Home Journal* before publication and quickly became a critical and commercial success in 1952.

In the book the undercurrent of racism was a primary concern of Ferber's. In Stevens's film, he scaled down the Benedicts' view of their Mexican American workers and emphasized Rink's openness. Ultimately, he even inserted a narrative in which Benedict comes around to be open to diversity.

Giant was Dean's last film; he died in a car accident just as the filming was completed.

Brian Black

SEE ALSO: *Dean, James; The Great Depression; Hopper, Dennis; Hudson, Rock; Taylor, Elizabeth.*

BIBLIOGRAPHY

Moss, Marilyn Ann. *Giant: George Stevens, a Life on Film.* Madison: University of Wisconsin Press, 2004.

Gibson, Althea *(1927–2003)*

Althea Gibson is one of the foremost names in American tennis and in African American history. In a prejudiced, segregated society—and in the even more segregated world of tennis—she carved out a place for herself with her aggressive serve-and-volley game. She won eleven Grand Slam tournaments and several international titles in both singles and doubles. However, in the United States of the 1950s and 1960s, there were few financial rewards for a black woman athlete, and Gibson grew discouraged and reclusive. Although her name is known and celebrated by many people, few know of the poverty and obscurity in which she lived until her death in 2003.

EARLY LIFE

Gibson was born in August 1927 on a Silver, South Carolina, cotton farm, the oldest of five children. In 1930 her family moved to Harlem in New York City, where her aunt made a living selling bootleg whiskey. The difficulties of growing up on the streets were tempered by the supportive black community in Harlem. Tall and strong, Gibson played basketball with the boys and shot pool in the corner pool halls, but it was in the game of paddle ball, played in streets blocked to traffic, that she excelled. When blues musician Buddy Walker observed how she easily defeated all comers, he bought her a tennis racquet and arranged for lessons for her at the Cosmopolitan Tennis Club in Harlem.

Gibson once said, "No matter what accomplishments you make, somebody helps you." In her own case, she received encouragement not only from Walker but also from boxer Sugar Ray Robinson and doctors Hubert Eaton and Robert Johnson, all of whom took particular interest in encouraging young black athletes. With their support, she began to play in tournaments through the American Tennis Association, the oldest black sports organization in the United States. Gibson won the girls' singles championship in 1944 and 1945 and then, starting in 1947, captured the title ten years in a row.

BREAKING INTO TENNIS

Though Gibson dropped out of high school, her mentors helped her to return, and in 1949 she received a tennis scholarship to Florida Agricultural and Mechanical University in Tallahassee. In 1950 she broke into the world of white tennis. Former tennis champion Alice Marble pleaded her case to the U.S. Lawn Tennis Association (USLTA), and Gibson was allowed to play in its famous tournaments at Forest Hills, New York. Though she won her first tournament, she lost the second and became discouraged. The pressure of serving as a role model for her race, in addition to persistent money troubles, almost prompted her to quit the game, but in 1955 the USLTA and the U.S. State Department chose Gibson to represent the United States on a goodwill tennis tour of Asia. This sign of acceptance by the white tennis establishment restored much of her confidence and renewed her commitment to the sport.

Gibson was almost thirty years old when she began the most dramatic phase of her career. She became the first African American to earn an international championship when she won the French Women's Singles in 1956. She went on to win the Italian championship in 1957 and Wimbledon and the U.S. Nationals in 1957 and 1958. She was part of the winning doubles team for three years at Wimbledon, as well as in the French Open and the Australian Open. Her powerful game became legendary. "People thought I was ruthless," she wrote later, "which I was. I didn't give a darn who was on the other side of the net. I'd knock you down if you got in my way."

In 1958 Gibson was the top-ranked women's tennis player when she decided to turn professional. Financially, she simply could not afford to continue on a strictly amateur basis. Her professional tennis career never took off the way she had hoped, though she did have a successful run touring with the famous Harlem Globetrotters, playing exhibition tennis matches as an opening act for their novelty basketball games. Otherwise, Gibson did not receive many offers to play for money and had little success in her bids to initiate a film or recording career. In the 1960s she played professional golf, becoming the first African American member of the Ladies Professional Golfers Association, but her career in that sport was undistinguished. After that, she earned a living by working as a tennis coach and for state governmental sports agencies in her home state of New Jersey.

TOUGH TIMES

Gibson was elected to the Tennis Hall of Fame in 1971. In 1997 she was honored as a barrier-breaking African American athlete at the dedication of Arthur Ashe Stadium in New York

City. Gibson did not attend the ceremonies, and few knew it was because she had suffered several strokes and was living in poverty in East Orange, New Jersey, depressed, reclusive, and gravely ill. Some women athletes and coaches were horrified to learn of Gibson's circumstances. Pooling their energies and resources, these women staged a benefit and tribute for Gibson, raising more than $35,000 to help with medical bills and other expenses and to found an Althea Gibson Trust Fund to grant scholarships for women athletes. When she learned of the work that had been done on her behalf and was given a video in which old friends and young newcomers alike spoke of how her life had inspired their own careers, her spirits were lifted immeasurably. On September 28, 2003, Gibson died of circulatory collapse at the age of seventy-six.

Though Gibson contributed greatly to the sport of tennis, she had to fight against prejudice every step of the way, whether it was a hotel that refused to book a luncheon in her honor or the unwritten rule against women earning money from sports. Her career is both an inspiration and a cautionary tale for aspiring young athletes: some games cannot be won simply with skill and determination.

Tina Gianoulis

SEE ALSO: *Golf; The Harlem Globetrotters; Sports Heroes; Tennis; Wimbledon.*

BIBLIOGRAPHY

Biracree, Tom. *Althea Gibson.* New York: Chelsea House, 1989

Davidson, Sue. *Changing the Game: The Stories of Tennis Champions Alice Marble and Althea Gibson.* Seattle, WA: Seal Press, 1997.

Gibson, Althea. *I Always Wanted to Be Somebody.* New York: Harper, 1958.

Gibson, Althea. *So Much to Live For.* New York: Putnam, 1968.

Gray, Frances Clayton, and Yanick Rice Lamb. *Born to Win: The Authorized Biography of Althea Gibson.* Hoboken, NJ: John Wiley & Sons, 2004.

Gibson, Bob *(1935–)*

Bob Gibson's pitching for the St. Louis Cardinals earned him a dominant place in baseball history. The 6-foot, 1-inch right-hander used an overwhelming fastball and a peerless array of breaking pitches to strike fear in the hearts of National League batters throughout the 1960s and early 1970s. Gibson reserved his finest performances for the biggest games, outshining all competitors in the three World Series in which he pitched.

A frail child who suffered from a heart murmur, Gibson was encouraged to pursue sports by his older brother, a YMCA athletic director. He signed with the St. Louis Cardinals in 1957 for $4,000 but did not crack into the team's starting rotation until 1961. His breakthrough season came in 1963 when he went 18–9 and the Cardinals emerged as a contender for the National League pennant.

Gibson earned a reputation as the ultimate big-game pitcher by winning the clinching games of the 1964 and 1967 World Series. In 1964 he held a powerful New York Yankees lineup in check on only two days of rest. In 1967 he beat the Boston Red Sox almost single-handedly, recording three of the Cardinals' four victories. All these wins were just a prelude for what was to come.

In 1968 Gibson enjoyed one of the finest seasons ever registered by a major-league pitcher. He won twenty-two games against only nine losses and recorded thirteen shutouts, highlighted by a stretch of ninety-two innings in which only two runs were scored against him. His 1.12 earned run average set a National League record and was the lowest recorded for a pitcher since 1914. For his efforts Gibson was voted the National League Cy Young Award by the Baseball Writers Association of America.

As impressive as he was in the regular season, Gibson was even more dominant in the World Series. He struck out a record seventeen Detroit Tigers in the opening game of the Fall Classic, prevailing 4–0 over thirty-one-game winner Denny McLain. He won Game Four as well, 10–1, to run his World Series record to 7–1. But when he tried to pitch the deciding seventh game on just two days of rest, even the unhittable Gibson met his match. He carried a shutout into the seventh inning but was beaten by the Tigers' Mickey Lolich, 4–1. It was Gibson's last World Series game.

Bob Gibson. *Nine-time All-Star and two-time World Series champion Bob Gibson won two Cy Young Awards and the 1968 National League Most Valuable Player Award.* FOCUS ON SPORT/ GETTY IMAGES.

Thanks in large measure to Gibson's efforts, 1968 went down in baseball history as the "Year of the Pitcher." To compensate for the perceived imbalance in the game, the next season Major League Baseball lowered the pitcher's mound to give batters a fighting chance against the new breed of power pitchers led by Gibson and the New York Mets' Tom Seaver. Despite these adjustments Gibson continued to dominate National League batters well into the 1970s. He won twenty games in each of the next two seasons and was named to the All-Star team both years.

Gibson was feared around the league as one of the most intense, aggressive competitors in baseball. He believed it was a pitcher's right to knock down a batter with a high, inside fastball if the occasion demanded it. His intimidating demeanor extended to his own teammates. Once when catcher Tim McCarver approached the mound for a conference, Gibson glared at him. "The only thing you know about pitching is you can't hit it," he reportedly told the terrified receiver. McCarver slunk back behind the plate, perhaps with Gibson's words of advice still stuck in his gullet.

Although Gibson and the Cardinals did not return again to the World Series, Gibson continued to reach personal milestones. He registered fifty-six total shutouts and became the second pitcher in major-league history to amass 3,000 strikeouts. When injuries to his arms and legs began to impair his performance, Gibson realized the end of his career was at hand. After Pete LaCock, a light-hitting first baseman best known for being the son of *Hollywood Squares* host Peter Marshall, crushed a grand slam off him in September 1975, Gibson decided to call it quits. He retired as the winningest pitcher in St. Louis Cardinals history.

In recognition of his achievements, Gibson was elected to the Baseball Hall of Fame in 1981. He later worked as a baseball broadcaster a major-league pitching coach, and an adviser to the baseball commissioner.

Robert E. Schnakenberg

SEE ALSO: *Baseball; Boston Red Sox; The Detroit Tigers; The New York Mets; World Series; Young, Cy.*

BIBLIOGRAPHY

Deane, Bill. *Bob Gibson.* New York: Chelsea House, 1994.

Gibson, Bob; Reggie Jackson; and Lonnie Wheeler. *Sixty Feet, Six Inches: A Hall of Fame Pitcher & a Hall of Fame Hitter Talk about How the Game Is Played.* New York: Knopf Doubleday, 2011.

Shatzkin, Mike; Stephen Holtje; and James Charlton. *The Ballplayers: Baseball's Ultimate Biographical Reference.* New York: William Morrow, 1990.

Gibson, Mel *(1956–)*

With his piercing blue eyes, rich speaking voice, and humorous "bad boy" manner, American-born, Australian-reared actor Mel Gibson was one of the world's most popular film stars for nearly twenty years. In 1985 he became *People* magazine's first ever "Sexiest Man Alive," and by the late 1990s his reputation as a producer and director was on the ascendance. However, during the first decade of the twenty-first century, questionable professional choices coupled with personal scandal caused many of Gibson's fans and colleagues to view him as a bigot, an abuser, and an unstable personality. Though he continued to make movies and still has loyal fans, his reputation has been deeply damaged.

ACTION HERO

Gibson first came to international attention in his second picture, the low-budget 1979 Australian film *Mad Max.* As Max Rockatansky, a highway patrolman living in postapocalyptic Australia, the twenty-three-year-old Gibson was a bit wooden, but his screen charisma, good looks, and emotional intensity were a hit with audiences throughout the world. Despite the fact that Gibson's then-strong Australian accent was overdubbed by an American for U.S. release, the film has remained a cult favorite. Gibson has maintained the "Mad Max" persona, portraying characters on the edge, from *Lethal Weapon*'s Martin Riggs, his most financially successful characterization, to Scottish patriot William Wallace in *Braveheart* to the lovable paranoid cabby Jerry Fletcher in *Conspiracy Theory.*

Following *Mad Max*, Gibson appeared in several more Australian films. He won an Australian Film Institute Award for Best Actor for *Tim*, a sentimental love story about a slow-witted man who falls in love with a middle-aged business woman. This was followed in 1981 by an outstanding performance in Peter Weir's antiwar masterpiece *Gallipoli* and an enormously popular cult film *The Road Warrior* (released internationally as *Mad Max 2*).

Although Gibson's early post-Australian films were critically and financially mixed, his reputation grew internationally. Some of his early U.S. films faltered at the box office: *The River, Mrs. Soffel, The Bounty*, and the Australian-made Warner Brothers release *Mad Max beyond Thunderdome* were made within an eighteen-month period in the mid-1980s, but only *Thunderdome* proved financially successful.

The stress of work, success, and long separations from his wife and growing young family proved troublesome for Gibson personally. An arrest for drunk driving in Toronto while filming *Mrs. Soffel* and subsequent bouts of erratic behavior and drinking almost brought his career to an end and earned Gibson the moniker "Mad Mel." To address his problems, he returned to his ranch in Australia and did not make any pictures for almost two years. His next film, the 1987 Richard Donner–directed *Lethal Weapon*, costarring Danny Glover, proved to be his greatest career success to that time and placed him on the level of solid international stardom.

In the early 1990s Gibson moved permanently from Australia to the United States and began to take charge of his career, moving into the area of producing and directing. With partner Bruce Davey, Gibson had formed Icon Productions in 1989. In addition to producing or coproducing many of Gibson's own star vehicles, Icon turned out more than a dozen films in the mid- to late 1990s, including some small films such as *Immortal Beloved* and *87.* Its most financially and critically successful film was Gibson's second directorial effort, *Braveheart* (1995), which grossed more than $200 million worldwide and earned five Oscars, two of which went personally to Gibson, as director and as producer, along with Davey and Hollywood veteran Alan Ladd Jr.

Following on the heels of *Braveheart*'s success, Gibson made the intense action drama *Ransom*, directed by Ron Howard. The film was an immediate hit, earning more than

$130 million in the United States and bringing Gibson his first Golden Globe Award nomination for Best Actor. The period between 1994 and 1998 was a high point in Gibson's career, with three of his films earning more than $100 million domestically, including a fourth installment of the *Lethal Weapon* series. In addition, Gibson cemented his position as a Hollywood mainstay by winning his second People's Choice Award for favorite actor and a firm position near the top of the annual Harris poll of America's favorite actors and the world's list of top box-office stars.

CONTROVERSIES

Throughout the 1990s Gibson's personal life seemed remarkably solid, especially by Hollywood standards. He and Robyn Moore had married in 1980 and they had seven children. A devout Catholic with antiabortion views, Gibson had deeply conservative libertarian values that were often unpopular in the more liberal atmosphere of the movie industry. He tended to dismiss criticism of his blunt judgments as political correctness, but gays, feminists, and other minorities bristled at the comments that became public.

In 2004 Gibson melded his politics and his career when he produced, wrote, and directed the controversial *The Passion of the Christ*. The film's critics, who included many Christians, decried what they viewed as the film's gratuitous violence in depicting the events leading up to the Crucifixion of Jesus. Many felt that the film (and the point of view of its maker) was anti-Jewish. Though some reviewers judged *The Passion* to be powerful filmmaking, Gibson's reputation had received a blow. In 2006 he released another controversial film *Apocalypto*, a bloody epic loosely based on Mayan culture prior to the arrival of the Spanish invaders. Again, many critics, especially Mayans and other experts on Mayan culture, decried the film as racist and historically inaccurate.

In 2006 Gibson's image was more seriously damage when he was stopped by the police for speeding. Not only was his blood alcohol level well above the legal limit, but he was also taped shouting anti-Jewish epithets for several minutes. The event made big news, and the public was further disgusted by accusations of an attempted cover-up on the part of the Los Angeles Sherriff's Department. Gibson quickly issued a full public apology for the incident. Shortly after the arrest, Gibson and Moore separated, divorcing in 2011. Gibson became involved with pianist and songwriter Oksana Grigorieva, and the two had a daughter. In 2010 Gibson was caught on tape again, shouting abuse and racist epithets at Grigorieva. Once again, the news spread quickly, and Gibson's reputation for instability grew. He and Grigorieva subsequently separated.

An interesting contradiction in Gibson's personality is his longtime friendship with actor/director Jodie Foster. Foster has remained supportive through all of Gibson's missteps, and in 2011 she cast him in *The Beaver*, a quirky and poignant comedy about a disturbed man who is given new life when he begins talking through a beaver hand puppet. The role seemed tailor-made for that troubled period in Gibson's life, and he gave a nuanced and vulnerable performance at a time when his career was faltering.

Steve Hanson

SEE ALSO: *Abortion; Blockbusters; Foster, Jodie; Howard, Ron;* The Passion of the Christ*; Political Correctness; Sex Symbol.*

BIBLIOGRAPHY

Cieply, Michael. "When Art Imitates an Actor's Troubled Life." *New York Times*, March 17, 2011.

Clarkson, Wensley. *Mel: The Inside Story*. London: Blake Publishing, 1993.

Grobel, Lawrence. "Mel Gibson." *Playboy*, July 1995, 51–63.

McCarty, John. *The Films of Mel Gibson*. New York: Citadel Press, 2001.

Pendreigh, Brian. *Mel Gibson and His Movies*. London: Bloomsbury Publishing, 1997.

Plate, S. Brent, ed. *Re-Viewing the Passion: Mel Gibson's Film and Its Critics*. New York: Palgrave Macmillan, 2004.

Ragan, David. *Mel Gibson*. New York: Dell Publishing, 1985.

Gibson, William *(1948–)*

American science fiction writer William Gibson is most renowned for coining the term *cyberspace* in *Neuromancer* (1984), the book hailed by many critics and technology buffs as the seminal work in the cyberpunk genre. Gibson is most poignant in simultaneously relishing and demonizing the technologies that increasingly shape human relationships at the beginning of the new millennium. The now-legendary idea of cyberspace, defined in *Neuromancer* and employed throughout his fiction, anticipated the Internet as a virtual playground where information is exchanged and where corporations rise and fall: "A consensual hallucination experienced daily by billions of legitimate operators, in every nation, by children being taught mathematical concepts. . . . A graphic representation of data abstracted from the banks of every computer in the human system. Unthinkable complexity. Lines of light ranged in the nonspace of the mind, clusters and constellations of data. Like city lights, receding." In a November 1994 interview for the Swedish news program *Rapport* (which is appropriately available on the Internet), Gibson calls the Internet "as significant as the birth of cities" and "a new kind of civilization" in its being primarily user-driven and transnational. Nevertheless, he also admits to not using "too glamorous" e-mail or even "browsing the 'Net," despite their correlation to his fiction, because of their great time investment and tendency to mark elitist distinctions of social class. As quoted by many of the Internet sites dedicated to his work, Gibson has said, "I'm not a techie. I don't know how these things work. But I like what they do, and the new human processes that they generate."

Gibson grew up in a small town on the edge of the Appalachian Mountains, dropped out of high school in 1967, and ended up in Toronto, Canada. There he married Deborah Thompson in 1972. The couple has two children. He later earned a BA in 1977 from the University of British Columbia. By the early 1980s, Gibson was making a name for himself with stories such as "Johnny Mnemonic" and "Burning Chrome," many published in *Omni* magazine.

In his debut novel *Neuromancer*, Gibson evokes a near-future world organized by technological-corporate enclaves that circulate power through an elite of specialized information-manipulators. The players are typically "console cowboys" (cyberspace operators) who navigate the hallucinatory data-field which is cyberspace, "razor girls" (freelance cybernetic assassins) who roam the "Sprawl" (the extended and dirty metropolis of discarded and constantly renovated technology), and a myriad of

Japanese and Chinese syndicates who pull the strings. Hailed by the science fiction community at its inception and increasingly studied at the university setting, *Neuromancer* won the prestigious Hugo Award, the Philip K. Dick Memorial Award, and the Nebula Award for Best Novel. It is the first of the Sprawl trilogy, a series that charts how disconnected members of a technological elite inadvertently make possible an AI (artificial intelligence) that covertly seeks to revolutionize human-machine relations. The equally compelling *Count Zero* (1986) and *Mona Lisa Overdrive* (1988) complete the trilogy.

Gibson's real-life fear of technology-born inequality also shows itself in his fiction. Written during a robust 1980s economy, which saw unprecedented economic mergers, the Sprawl trilogy resonates with a new sense of the corporation (*zaibatsu*) as an indomitable Hydra: "the multinationals that shaped the course of human history, had transcended old barriers. Viewed as organisms, they had attained a kind of immortality. You couldn't kill a zaibatsu by assassinating a dozen key executives; there were others waiting to step up the ladder, assume the vacated position, access the vast banks of corporate memory." In the *Rapport* interview though, Gibson reveals more real-world optimism in having "great hopes for the Internet" of individual initiative and "very little hope for commercial versions." Making a prophetic gesture before the National Academy of Sciences in May 1993 with colleague Bruce Sterling, Gibson advocated enhanced online teaching, free software to *all* teachers, and corporate-provided computers to *only* the most economically disadvantaged school districts as an equalizing move for the United States.

Hollywood brought Gibson to the silver screen with *Johnny Mnemonic* (1995), an adaptation of his short story published in the Nebula award-winning *Burning Chrome* (1982), a collection of Gibson's short fiction. The film stars Keanu Reeves as an "information-courier" whose cerebral data capacity is dangerously overloaded with information critical to an antitechnology resistance movement. Despite its often lethargic plot and juvenile characterization, the film is most successful in casting rapper Ice-T and singer Henry Rollins as prominent "Lo Teks," a band of renegade fighters that quietly undermines corporate power. The film therefore continues the idea of an "underground" use of discarded technology, established in his fiction, as the ground for resisting larger institutions.

Gibson also has written *Dream Jumbo* (1989), a text to accompany performance art; *Agrippa: A Book of the Dead* (1992), a poem about his father that was encoded on computer disc and eroded rapidly after being read; and, with novelist Bruce Sterling, *The Difference Engine* (1990), a retroactive science fiction novel set in Victorian England. Gibson's latest prose works, *Virtual Light* (1993), *Idoru* (1996), *All Tomorrow's Parties* (1999), *Pattern Recognition* (2003), and *Spook Country* (2007) continue the provocative vision established in the Sprawl trilogy. Although he spends no time there, the Internet is fertile with talk of Gibson and is itself resonant with the implications of his work.

Anthony Cast

SEE ALSO: *E-mail; Hollywood; Ice-T; The Internet; Science Fiction Publishing.*

BIBLIOGRAPHY

Cavallaro, Dani. *Cyberpunk and Cyberculture: Science Fiction and the Work of William Gibson.* London: Athlone Press, 2000.

Henthorne, Tom. *William Gibson: A Literary Companion.* Jefferson, NC: McFarland, 2011.

Trosky, Susan M., ed. *Contemporary Authors.* Vol. 133. Detroit: Gale Research, 1991.

Gibson Girl

A creation from the pen of illustrator Charles Dana Gibson (1867–1944), the Gibson Girl came to be viewed as an ideal image of youthful femininity in the early 1890s. Statuesque and athletic, she was a contemporary incarnation of the beautiful, desirable, modern woman. In one drawing from around 1900 she is pictured on the golf course in her signature long skirt and blouse. She stands tall and straight, one hand planted firmly on her hip, and lifts her head majestically. Her male partner stands well to the side and stares in rapt admiration. The captivating Gibson Girl appealed to the imagination of a nation that craved an image of femininity that was fresh and uniquely American.

Gibson, the most popular illustrator in the United States at the turn of the twentieth century, began his career in New York during the early years of what has come to be known as the golden age of American illustration—the mid-1880s. By 1890 he was drawing for *Life*, *Scribner's Magazine*, *Century*, *Harper's*

Gibson Girl Drawing. *Charles Dana Gibson's "Gibson Girl" illustrations in the late 1800s and early 1900s came to epitomize the feminine ideal of that era.* AMERICAN STOCK/GETTY IMAGES.

Magazine, and *Harper's Weekly*. He began drawing the Gibson Girl in the early 1890s. She was featured in the first folio edition of his work, which appeared in 1894, and soon became a national sensation. Gibson's wife, the aristocratic Irene Langhorne Gibson, whom he met in 1893 and married in 1895, was widely believed to have been the inspiration behind her husband's creation, but she could not have been his original model. There was, in fact, no single model for the Gibson Girl, and the artist himself claimed that he had used several; moreover, he said that he had never intended to represent any one particular type of woman. Many young society women did actually seek out the illustrator, hoping to enhance their social standing further by posing for him as the famous Gibson Girl.

As Lois Banner observes, the Gibson Girl has often been identified with high society, the American "aristocracy" to which Gibson himself belonged. Nonetheless, she had qualities that also endeared her to the working class. Two working-class women, in particular, were thought to have been her inspiration: Minnie Clark, a professional model with an Irish working-class background, and the unnamed personal maid to the dancer Loie Fuller. The Gibson Girl, however, was rarely pictured as a working girl, and the settings in which she appeared were almost invariably fashionable. We see her at fancy dress balls, at musical and theatrical events, and engaged in then-elite sporting activities. She was essentially a privileged socialite, and her image, despite its modern trappings, incorporated traditional aspects of femininity. Contemporary feminists, such as writer Charlotte Perkins Gilman, saw in her the strength, ability, and freedom of the "new woman," although her fundamental appeal was her feminine beauty. Charles Dana Gibson emphasized her decorative qualities when he designed wallpaper for bachelors' rooms featuring a dense pattern of Gibson Girl faces.

The popularity of the Gibson Girl was reflected in many related phenomena in American popular culture. She was a paragon of beauty and style for millions of American women, who sought to emulate her in dress and hairstyle. Songs and plays were written about her, and her image was reproduced everywhere: on dishes and clothing, tablecloths and pillow covers, ashtrays and umbrella stands. For almost two decades she wielded a powerful influence in American popular culture. In the late 1910s, however, her vogue began to wane as a new image of femininity emerged—one that culminated in the liberated and daring Jazz Age flapper of the 1920s.

Laural Weintraub

SEE ALSO: *Feminism; Flappers; Hairstyles;* Harper's*; The Pin-Up;* Scribner's*; Sex Symbol.*

BIBLIOGRAPHY

Banner, Lois W. *American Beauty*. Chicago: University of Chicago Press, 1983.

Banta, Martha. *Imaging American Women: Idea and Ideals in Cultural History*. New York: Columbia University Press, 1987.

Gibson, Charles Dana. *The Gibson Girl and Her America: The Best Drawings of Charles Dana Gibson*. New York: Dover Publications, 1969.

Patterson, Martha H. *Beyond the Gibson Girl: Reimagining the American New Woman, 1895–1915*. Urbana : University of Illinois Press, 2008.

Van Hook, Bailey. *Angels of Art: Women and Art in American Society, 1876–1914*. University Park: Pennsylvania State University Press, 1996.

Gifford, Frank *(1930–)*

Frank Gifford was a football star for the New York Giants in the 1950s and early 1960s, playing both offense and defense during the final days of the two-way player. Away from the game his movie-idol visage made him a larger-than-life sports hero, often paired with another famous New Yorker of the 1950s, baseball player Mickey Mantle. But it was a book about failure that cemented Gifford's cultural standing, when he was cast as a central figure in Frederick Exley's autobiographical novel, *A Fan's Notes* (1968). After retiring from the Giants in 1964, Gifford married television personality Kathie Lee Johnson and joined the *Monday Night Football* broadcasting team helmed by Howard Cosell. He made headlines again in the late 1990s when a tabloid newspaper paid a former flight attendant to seduce him in a bugged hotel room. When the scandal hit, Gifford was forced to leave *Monday Night Football* and his fairy-tale marriage seemed to be over, but Kathie Lee stood by her man. Gifford's late-life sin did little to change his standing as an all-American icon.

Geoff Edgers

SEE ALSO: *Celebrity Couples; Cosell, Howard; Daytime Talk Shows; Mantle, Mickey;* Monday Night Football*; National Football League (NFL); Professional Football; Sports Heroes; Tabloids.*

BIBLIOGRAPHY

Exley, Frederick. *A Fan's Notes*. New York: Harper & Row, 1968.

Gifford, Frank, and Peter Richmond. *The Glory Game: How the 1958 NFL Championship Changed Football Forever*. New York: Harper, 2008.

Gifford, Frank, and Harry Waters. *The Whole Ten Yards*. New York: Random House, 1993.

Gifford, Kathie Lee, and Jim Jerome. *I Can't Believe I Said That!* New York: Pocket Books, 1992.

Gillespie, Dizzy *(1917–1993)*

Onstage—wearing his black beret, goatee, and horn-rimmed glasses—Dizzy Gillespie was the much-imitated archetype of the jazz hipster. When he raised his trademark bent horn and began to play, with his cheeks puffed out like a giant chipmunk, he created a sound that defined American jazz, and many of his compositions become lasting jazz standards.

Gillespie came of age during a golden time in jazz. In the 1930s and 1940s brilliant musicians such as Gillespie, Charlie Parker, Thelonious Monk, Miles Davis, and Max Roach were playing together in wildly creative jam sessions that would change the face of American music. Though Gillespie's technical expertise and soaring harmonies on the trumpet made him an integral part of this new movement, perhaps his greatest contribution was his ability to thrive as an African American musician and public figure in the inhospitable climate of the

Dizzy Gillespie. *Dizzy Gillespie, considered to be one of the greatest jazz trumpeters of all time, performs in London, England, in 1982.* MICHAEL PUTLAND/GETTY IMAGES.

United States before and during the civil rights era. During a career that lasted six decades, Gillespie displayed an upbeat attitude, personal stability, and charismatic showmanship that were major factors in the popularization of jazz.

Gillespie was born John Birks Gillespie, the youngest of nine children, in the small town of Cheraw, South Carolina. His working-class parents had little energy to devote to their youngest son's education, but Gillespie's father was a part-time bandleader on his weekends off from his bricklaying job. Young John practiced on the band instruments around the house, learning piano and percussion before finally settling on the trumpet as his favorite. When a Works Progress Administration job convinced him he did not want to do manual labor, Gillespie got a scholarship to attend the all-black Laurinburg Technical Institute in North Carolina. There he began to study music theory and the principles of harmony with which he would experiment throughout his career.

DIZZY IN NEW YORK

In 1935 Gillespie quit school to move to Philadelphia, where he honed his skills on the horn in jam sessions and joined his first band. By 1937 he had arrived at the new jazz mecca: Harlem, New York. Gillespie began to prove himself to the great New York bandleaders and soon had a job in Cab Calloway's band, wowing audiences and musicians alike with his creative virtuosity and stage antics. Fellow trumpeter Palmer Davis gave him the name Dizzy because of his childlike exuberance and zaniness on stage. "Man, this is a dizzy cat," Davis said, and the name stuck. Adding to Gillespie's eccentric image was his unique trumpet, the horn of which was bent almost straight up. Created by accident when a drunken reveler stepped on it, Gillespie insisted on keeping his bent horn, claiming he could hear his own sound better.

Though it endeared him to fans, Gillespie's unbridled humor got him in trouble more than once, and he lost his job with Calloway in the mid-1940s when the bandleader tired of being the butt of jokes. It was then that Gillespie joined the famous Harlem jam sessions that produced the wildly radical, urgent beat that came to be known as bebop. Polished and developed by Gillespie and saxophonist Charlie "Bird" Parker, bebop got its name from Gillespie's chanted intro to the songs: "Dee-ba-pa-'n-bebop. . . . " Soon fans were yelling, "Play some of that bebop music." Bebop gave jazz a deeper and more complex dimension, and Parker's and Gillespie's innovations continue to influence the development of jazz. Though jazz is perhaps the most intrinsically American of all music forms, it is a combination of many influences.

Early in his career Gillespie was introduced to Cuban music, with its roots in the rhythms of Africa. Together with Cuban musicians such as Chano Pozo, Gillespie was instrumental in developing the genre of Afro-Cuban jazz, which he worked to popularize up until his death. In 1946 Gillespie started his first successful big band, where he introduced Pozo on the conga drum. This was an historic event because African-style drums had been banned since the days of slavery, and Gillespie's band marked the first time a jazz drummer had used his hands rather than sticks to play his instrument. It was by such subtle yet joyously radical maneuvers that Gillespie managed to challenge the racist system while keeping his good nature and popularity. The 1989 film *A Night in Havana* documents Gillespie's connection to Cuban music and culture.

GOODWILL AMBASSADOR

Unlike many other jazz musicians, Gillespie did not fall victim to substance abuse or a self-destructive lifestyle. He married dancer Lorraine Willis in 1940 and remained happily married to her until his death in 1993. In the 1960s he converted to Baha'i, a religion of Persian origin that focuses on tolerance and love. Gillespie himself was widely loved and respected, even in unexpected places. In 1956 the State Department chose Gillespie as a goodwill ambassador and sent him to the Middle East and Latin America. Principled as ever, the jazz man refused to speak for the government. Instead, he got to know individuals, played free concerts for children and the poor, and brought back rhythms such as the samba and bossa nova to enrich American musical culture.

In 1964 Gillespie surprised the public by running for president. Running on a platform that included abolishing racism and uniting the world's people, Gillespie as always had his tongue in cheek, proposing that the White House be renamed the Blues House and suggesting Miles Davis as CIA chief and Malcolm X as attorney general. One of his campaign songs advised, "Your politics oughta be a groovier thing / So get a good President who's willing to swing."

Until his death from cancer in 1993, Gillespie maintained a vigorous schedule, releasing more than 500 recordings and performing in close to 300 live concerts a year. His contribution to jazz and to American music in general resides not only in his considerable legacy of classic hits such as "A Night in Tunisia," "Groovin' High," and "Salt Peanuts" but also in his down-to-earth ability to make his music accessible and transcendent at the same time. Drummer Max Roach said of him, "Dizzy was the catalyst, the man who inspired us all."

Tina Gianoulis

SEE ALSO: *Calloway, Cab; Davis, Miles; Jazz; Parker, Charlie.*

BIBLIOGRAPHY

Gillespie, Dizzy, and Al Fraser. *To Be or Not . . . to Bop: Memoirs.* Garden City, NY: Doubleday, 1979.

Gourse, Leslie. *Dizzy Gillespie and the Birth of Bebop.* New York: Atheneum, 1994.

McRae, Barry. *Dizzy Gillespie: His Life and Times.* New York: Universe Books, 1988.

Shipton, Alyn. *Groovin' High.* New York: Oxford University Press, 1999.

Yanow, Scott. *Afro-Cuban Jazz.* San Francisco: Miller Freeman, 2000.

Gilligan's Island

Airing only three seasons, from 1964 to 1967, *Gilligan's Island* is one of the best-known shows in television history. The premise of the show is basic: seven castaways are shipwrecked on an uncharted island following a storm and have to survive until they are rescued. The show is remarkable in its popularity and longevity almost in spite of itself. In its first season it received terrible reviews from most television critics. It is still considered by many to be one of the dumbest and most absurd shows on television, but its ninety-eight episodes have been in constant syndication since it went off the air. Three reunion television movies in the late 1970s and early 1980s all received good ratings, and the show was the inspiration for two children's animated series.

Gilligan's Island was created and nurtured by Sherwood Schwartz, who would go on to create that other astounding hit of the 1960s and 1970s, *The Brady Bunch.* The show would not have been made at all except for Schwartz's persistence; in his book, *Inside Gilligan's Island,* he describes the long struggle to get the show made against the desires of the CBS network chief. Winning its time slot in each of its three seasons, it was abruptly cut from the lineup to make room for the network president's favorite show, *Gunsmoke.*

In describing *Gilligan's Island,* Schwartz said that his plan was to create a microcosm of society, and the people in this society would each represent a different segment of society. There was the leader, Skipper (Alan Hale Jr.); the bumbling sidekick, Gilligan (Bob Denver); the wealthy businessman and his socialite wife, Mr. and Mrs. Howell (Jim Backus and Natalie Schafer); the simple country girl, Mary Ann (Dawn Wells); the sophisticated movie star, Ginger (Tina Louise); and the intellectual academic, Professor (Russell Johnson). Indeed, the Skipper tries to lead, the Professor solves most of the problems, the rich couple and the movie star act as if they are on vacation at a resort, and Gilligan and Mary Ann are left to do much of the manual labor.

The episodes rely on slapstick humor. The castaways want to be rescued, and in almost every episode they are presented with a possibility of rescue or escape. Invariably something happens to foil the plan, usually involving an innocent accident caused by Gilligan. Quite often the viewer is required to suspend disbelief and accept the fact that while these people can create elaborate equipment and solve a variety of problems with items available on the island, they are incapable of successfully seizing the many opportunities for rescue. And, while upset at the failings, they seem content with their island home. They accept each other for their characteristics and their weaknesses and persist.

Even though the island is uncharted, many episodes feature the arrival and departure of a new person, who leaves the main characters behind. These guests include Russian cosmonauts, natives from other islands, Hollywood producers, foreign spies, and South American dictators, and they all allow for comment on contemporary issues and events of the day, such as space flight, South American politics, radioactivity, surfing, spies, and pictures of Mars.

One of the highest-rated television movie specials history, *Rescue from Gilligan's Island* finally brought the castaways home in 1978 where each one found unhappiness with his or her former way of life. At the end of the movie, they are contentedly shipwrecked again on the same island. In *The "Castaways" on Gilligan's Island* (1979) the castaways are rescued again, only this time they deliberately return to the island and turn it into a resort. *The Harlem Globetrotters on Gilligan's Island* followed in 1981.

Frank E. Clark

SEE ALSO: The Brady Bunch; Gunsmoke; *Sitcom; Television.*

BIBLIOGRAPHY

Denver, Bob. *Gilligan, Maynard & Me.* New York: Carol Publishing Group, 1993.

Froug, William. *How I Escaped from Gilligan's Island: And Other Misadventures of a Hollywood Writer-Producer.* Madison: University of Wisconsin Press, 2005.

Green, Joey. *The Unofficial "Gilligan's Island" Handbook: A Castaway's Companion to the Longest-Running Shipwreck in Television History.* New York: Warner Books, 1988.

Marc, David, and Robert J. Thompson. *Prime Time, Prime Movers: From "I Love Lucy" to "L.A. Law"—America's Greatest TV Shows and the People Who Created Them.* Boston: Little, Brown, 1992.

McNeil, Alex. *Total Television: A Comprehensive Guide to Programming from 1948 to the Present,* 3rd ed. New York: Penguin Books, 1991.

Schwartz, Sherwood. *Inside "Gilligan's Island": From Creation to Syndication.* Jefferson, NC: McFarland, 1988.

Stoddard, Sylvia. *TV Treasures: A Companion Guide to "Gilligan's Island."* New York: St. Martin's, 1996.

Ginny Dolls

Ginny is an American-made, 8-inch doll that was immensely popular from 1951 through 1959. Produced by Jennie Graves, owner of Vogue Doll Company, Ginny was made of hard, durable plastic. The doll's size and durability made it convenient for a child to bring everywhere. Storybooks relating Ginny's activities, such as a trip around the country, piqued children's imaginations while quantities of meticulously designed outfits and accessories encouraged play related to the doll's adventures.

Ginny was a forerunner of action figure dolls that contribute to children's development by encouraging reality-based play. The reasonably priced Ginny dolls were sold in many places, including drugstores and department stores. After Graves's retirement, her daughter and son-in-law ran the company until Vogue Dolls was sold to the Tonka Corporation in 1972. The company shifted owners several times over the next couple of decades. In 1995 the rights to produce Ginny were sold back to a revitalized Vogue Doll Company. Since that time Ginny has been slowly but steadily regaining popularity both with collectors and a new generation of doll enthusiasts.

Taylor Shaw

SEE ALSO: *American Girl Series; Barbie; Kewpie Dolls; Toys.*

BIBLIOGRAPHY

Izen, Judith, and Carol Stover. *Collector's Encyclopedia of Vogue Dolls: Identification and Values.* Paducah, KY: Collector Books, 2004.

Mandeville, A. Glenn. *Ginny, America's Sweetheart.* Grantsville, MD: Hobby House Press, 1998.

Smith, Patricia R. *Vogue Ginny Dolls: Through the Years with Ginny.* Paducah, KY: Collector Books, 1985.

Ginsberg, Allen *(1926–1997)*

The poet Allen Ginsberg, an iconoclast in both his politically charged writing and unconventional lifestyle, epitomized the antiestablishment Beat movement of the 1950s and 1960s. In the midst of a generation shaped by the aftermath of the Holocaust and the creation of the atomic bomb, mass conformity, the hysteria of McCarthyism, and government censorship of personal liberties and civil rights, Ginsberg became a popular voice of artistic defiance. In American popular and academic culture, his influence as a poet, a musician, an artist, a professor, and an agitator has continued to grow even after his 1997 death. Bearing unofficial titles such as the "father of the Beat Generation," the "prophet of the 1960s," and the "guru of the counterculture movement," Ginsberg remains a cultural icon of one of America's most socially and politically turbulent eras.

AWAKENING TO THE UNIVERSE

Along with other Beats such as Jack Kerouac and William S. Burroughs, Ginsberg embraced Eastern philosophies and African American culture, experimented with various drugs, used the raw materials of life as the basis for his art, and subverted numerous societal and middle-class conventions in order to achieve spiritual, political, and sexual liberation. The opening lines of Ginsberg's *Howl,* the poetic manifesto of Beat attitudes and Ginsberg's most widely known work, exemplifies the gritty nature of his poetry: "I saw the best minds of my generation destroyed by madness, starving hysterical naked, dragging themselves through the negro streets at dawn looking for an angry fix." Because of its graphic sexual references, *Howl,* became the subject of a 1957 obscenity case that resulted in a landmark acquittal of the poem's publisher, Lawrence Ferlinghetti of City Lights Books. The trial's notoriety pushed Ginsberg into the public spotlight and ensured his status as a popular poet, an indelible symbol of Beat defiance, and a lasting representative of the rebellious spirit of the 1960s.

Despite his reputation as a boisterous nonconformist, Ginsberg was shy growing up. He was born in New Jersey on June 3, 1926, to Louis Ginsberg, a moderate socialist and an accomplished lyric poet, and to Naomi Ginsberg, a radical communist during the Depression who suffered from paranoid delusions until her death. Ginsberg discovered the poetry of Walt Whitman in high school, which sparked his interest in becoming a poet. However, upon his father's advice, he entered Columbia University in the mid-1940s with the intent of becoming a labor lawyer. At Columbia he joined a circle of friends that included Kerouac, Burroughs, and Neal Cassady. They exposed him to Manhattan's varied subcultures and fostered his artistic, philosophical, and sexual development; each man would contribute greatly to the Beat movement a decade later.

Ginsberg eventually changed his major to literature, and after receiving a bachelor's degree in 1948, he was hired as a market researcher in New York City. During this time Ginsberg experienced a vision of William Blake and awoke, in his own words, "into a totally deeper real universe." He introduced himself to New Jersey poet William Carlos Williams, whose poem about Paterson, New Jersey, moved Ginsberg greatly; Ginsberg would eventually incorporate Williams's broad narrative style into his own poetry. He quit his job and left New York in 1953, traveling to Cuba and Mexico. Bearing a letter of introduction from Williams, he arrived at San Francisco in 1954 to meet Kenneth Rexroth and the group of poets, writers, artists, filmmakers, and avant-gardists who would later be at the core of the Beat movement. It was here that Ginsberg composed and first read *Howl* as part of the Six Gallery reading in October 1955.

THE BEAT MOVEMENT

Not since Brook Farm (a transcendentalist utopian community established in Massachusetts in 1841) had an American cultural-literary group enjoyed such cohesion as the Beat and counterculture movements. At the center of the community was Ginsberg—who coined the term *flower power* in 1965—promoting free love, LSD, and group living in San Francisco's Haight-Ashbury district, the national epicenter of counterculture. He also stood out as a major figure in Vietnam War protests. Ginsberg was arrested in 1967 in an antiwar demonstration in New York City along with Dr. Benjamin Spock, the famed child psychologist.

In the post–Vietnam War years, Ginsberg's reputation as an agitator grew even more widespread when countries such as Cuba, the Soviet Union, and Poland deported him for speaking against communism and the persecution of homosexuals while he attempted to establish residency. Within the United States, he participated in the antinuclear, environmental, and gay liberation movements in the 1970s and 1980s. During the first term of the Reagan administration, the FBI placed him on a list of people deemed "unsuitable" as government-paid speakers abroad, a list on which black leader Coretta Scott King, feminist Betty Friedan, and consumer advocate Ralph Nader also appeared.

Ginsberg wrote more than forty books of poetry in his lifetime. His uncensored free-verse style produced as much controversy among academics as his profanity did among the government authorities. However, despite the stones of disdain and censorship thrown in his path, *Howl* has become required reading on college campuses throughout the United States, and his *Fall of America* won the National Book Award in 1972. Ginsberg was also a member of the American Institute of Arts and Letters.

Ginsberg's love for poetry inspired him to take an active and highly public role in its promotion. In 1974 he helped found the Jack Kerouac School of Disembodied Poetics at the Naropa Institute, the first accredited Buddhist college in Europe or America, located in Boulder, Colorado. He also taught English at Brooklyn College in New York. During the 1970s and 1980s, Ginsberg recorded spoken words and songs, and sometimes toured with popular musicians such as the Clash and Bob Dylan, who cited Ginsberg as one of the few literary figures he could stand. In the 1990s Ginsberg made more recordings, collaborating with Paul McCartney and Philip Glass, among others.

Ginsberg also had a talent in photography; he depicted his subjects—many of whom were people—with great depth of character, expressing visually what he achieved poetically. In 1996 his photographs were displayed in Beat Culture and the New America: 1960–1965, an exhibition organized by the Whitney Museum of Art, suggesting that Ginsberg's antiestab-

Allen Ginsberg. *Allen Ginsberg participates in a mass poetry reading in London, England, in 1965.* POPPERFOTO/GETTY IMAGES.

lishment life and work had, near the end of his life, become fully embraced by the country's most entrenched cultural institutions. In 2006 his *Collected Poems 1947–1997* was published, the first comprehensive single-volume edition of his work. In 2008 and 2010 collections of his letters were also released.

Nancy Lan-Jy Wang

SEE ALSO: *The Beat Generation; Burroughs, William S.; Haight-Ashbury; LSD; McCarthyism;* On the Road*; Vietnam.*

BIBLIOGRAPHY

Ginsberg, Allen. *Howl and Other Poems.* San Francisco: City Lights Pocket Bookshop, 1956.

Ginsberg, Allen. *Collected Poems 1947–1997.* New York: HarperCollins, 2006.

Holmes, John Clellon. *Nothing More to Declare.* New York: Dutton, 1967.

Kramer, Jane. *Allen Ginsberg on America.* New York: Random House, 1969.

Rasking, Jonah. *American Scream: Allen Ginsberg's "Howl" and the Making of the Beat Generation.* Berkeley: University of California Press, 2004.

Girl Groups

Girl group is a popular descriptive term referring to a genre of all-female singing groups and to the distinctive style of music such a group performs. Sexual desire is essential to the girl-group image and sound. The genre was nonexistent in the sexually restrictive first half of the twentieth century, although some all-female groups (such as the Boswell Sisters and Andrews Sisters) existed. The rise of the genre helped challenge sexual mores in society and helped nurture the growth of a youth-driven culture in the United States. By 1960 the image of the girl group had been spread across the country through radio and television. The genre had its ultimate expression in the Supremes in the 1960s. By the 1990s the image of girl groups such as the Spice Girls had become an established musical and cultural symbol.

THE DREAM-DATE IMAGE

The girl-group image alludes to both youthful innocence and sexual desire (desire usually for the heterosexual men for whom the groups were originally marketed). The members of a girl group, typically forming a trio or quartet, are young, attractive women who are groomed in a noticeable way, such as appearing in matching clothes or wearing designer dresses. Their hair is styled fashionably, and they usually wear makeup. Each young woman in the group represents the heterosexual man's ideal, or dream date. She is pretty, and she is dressed for a lovely dinner, a night of dancing, or a romantic movie. Sex is always a part of the image, although this theme has been used in different degrees through the genre's history. The dream date is reinforced in the image of her sister singers, and together the group appears as a harem of sorts, ready to entertain and please the man lucky enough to choose (or be chosen by) the women.

Musically, the girl group sound is meant to complement this narrow but highly identifiable physical image of youthful, desirable women. To emphasize the notion of youth, all members generally have young-sounding voices: thin, high alto to soprano range, sometimes nasal in tone. The thinness of each woman's voice allows for easy blending and a uniformity of tone. A voice that is low or too full or distinctive is uncommon in the genre, because such a voice is considered too mature to convey qualities of youth or too individualistic to blend invisibly into the sound of the other members' voices. To emphasize the notion of sex, sometimes the voices are decidedly breathy, borrowed from the popular images of the Hollywood sex symbols (such as Marilyn Monroe) of the first half of the twentieth century.

As with much popular music, the songs themselves are short and repetitive, making them memorable. They usually immediately address or convey a situation or an emotion, allowing the remainder of the song to be used as a showcase for the group's romantic or sexual appeal. The lyrics of girl-group songs deal with predicaments of love and sexual relationships, often revolving around precoital stress. Before the sexual revolution many lyrics were controversial, for it was not considered proper for a woman—whose American cultural image had long been synonymous with virginity—to consider or give voice to her own thoughts about sexual intercourse, especially in a public forum.

The barriers to what was lyrically acceptable came down in the 1950s with male musicians such as Chuck Berry, Elvis Presley, and Jerry Lee Lewis. They were solo artists who wrote and performed songs that were entertaining and relevant to teenage experience, particularly the desires for freedom and sexual expression that teenagers were developing from beneath the oppressive morality of the 1940s and early 1950s. By the mid-1950s the themes of love and sexual relationships were being explored by groups of male singers, and the genre of all-male singing groups became popular.

Finally, five classmates at a school in Harlem, New York, decided to form an all-female group similar to the male groups that were so popular. Known as the Bobbettes, they recorded their smash Top 10 hit song "Mr. Lee" in 1957. The song had both the flavor of doo-wop (a style many male singing groups were having success with at that time) and many of the characteristics of what would become the girl-group style: the lyrics were simple and repetitive, and the song emphasized youthful innocence and budding sexual desire. In this case, the song concerned a girl's affection for her favorite teacher. The later recordings of the Bobbettes never achieved the level of success that their first single reached, but another girl group called the Chantels released their first song only a few months after the appearance of "Mr. Lee," and so a trend had begun.

GIRL GROUPS OF THE 1960s

A year later, four other high school girls formed a group of their own. Fans of the Bobbettes and the Chantels, they called themselves the Shirelles and soon became one of the most popular girl groups in the rock-and-roll era. Their biggest hit was "Will You Still Love Me Tomorrow?" The lyrics described a young girl musing on the loss of her virginity and were well ahead of the times. The song raced to the top spot on the record charts, making the Shirelles the first black all-female group to have a number one record. Within a few years, dozens of girl groups formed and recorded records, with varying degrees of success. All followed the girl-group format, using slight variations to distinguish themselves from one another. Some of the most popular groups were the Crystals, the Marvelettes, the

Chiffons, and the Shangri-Las. Two groups—Martha and the Vandellas and the Ronettes—brought their own self-confident, "tough girl" innovation to the girl-group sound.

Before the 1960s audiences knew a singer's physical image from the live performance. Records were popular, but artists were, in the beginning, rarely shown on the covers of rock-and-roll records. As girl groups began to appear more regularly on teen-oriented television shows such as Dick Clark's *American Bandstand* and as their pictures began to show up on record covers, the idea of developing a visual image that supported either a group's tough or softly sweet (but in any case, sexually appealing) sound also became common.

Motown Records knew exactly how to use public visual image to their advantage. With shrewd business savvy, the company turned the Supremes (one of the many groups they managed) into the most successful girl group in popular music history. The Supremes capitalized on the use of a group name that implied divinity, on a public image that strove for larger-than-life beauty and sexual appeal, and through the sheer number of record-breaking achievements (including twelve number one hit records). Their music was true to the girl-group mold—simple, highly repetitive songs about love—and audiences everywhere especially took notice of lead singer Diana Ross's breathy, seductive voice.

A charm school run by Motown Records taught the three young women how to behave, dress, dance, and present themselves as young ladies, and their performances showcased their graceful, thoroughly choreographed routines and their often dazzling designer dresses. Motown owner Berry Gordy assembled a gifted team of writers to supply the Supremes with a long stream of popular songs, and the group appeared frequently on television variety shows and commercials. By the end of the 1960s their image largely epitomized the term *girl group*: three beautiful women, shining in sequined dresses, singing seductively to the listener. So completely did the Supremes embody the concepts of the girl-group ideal that other girl groups suffered in comparison by being perceived as mere imitators.

LATER DEVELOPMENTS

Through the 1970s and 1980s, a number of innovative all-female or female-led groups appeared, including the Pointer Sisters, Heart, the Go-Gos, and the Bangles, but they were very different from the girl-group image of the Supremes. Girl groups were often hired by other musicians to perform as background singers, so even when the genre began to move out of the public's eye, its influence was present in much of the subsequent popular musical work that was done in the United States. By the 1990s the term *girl group* had developed a negative connotation for some, drawing on the worst stereotypes of the style: music thought of as shallow, low on talent or vocal beauty but high on studio polish and gimmickry; highly sexual lyrical content; simplistic lyrical texture; and heavy emphasis on public image and physical sexual appeal rather than on the quality of the musical product or performance. In the 1990s a resurgence in the girl-group style occurred in rhythm-and-blues music. Of these groups, there arose a talented few (such as En Vogue) that embodied the best of what the genre had to offer.

A British group called the Spice Girls brought new life to the genre in the late 1990s. Espousing the motto "Girl Power," the band's members adopted descriptive names to convey their individual personas: Ginger Spice, Sporty Spice, Posh Spice, Scary Spice, and Baby Spice. From 1996 to 2000, their catchy dance songs and playful sexuality made them a worldwide phenomenon. The band broke up in 2000 to pursue individual interests. Following the demise of the Spice Girls, the Pussycat Dolls, with their first album *PCD* (2005), became one of the most successful girl groups in the United States. In recent years girl groups have also proven popular in Asian countries such as Japan and South Korea.

Brian Granger

SEE ALSO: American Bandstand; *The Andrews Sisters; Berry, Chuck; Boy Bands; Clark, Dick; Doo-wop Music; Gordy, Berry; Lewis, Jerry Lee; Martha and the Vandellas; Monroe, Marilyn; Motown; The Pointer Sisters; Presley, Elvis; Rock and Roll; Ross, Diana, and the Supremes; Sex Symbol; The Shirelles; The Spice Girls.*

BIBLIOGRAPHY

Clemente, John. *Girl Groups: Fabulous Females That Rocked the World.* Iola, WI: Krause Publications, 2000.

Gaar, Gillian G. *She's a Rebel: The History of Women in Rock & Roll.* Seattle, WA: Seal Press, 1992.

Grieg, Charlotte. *Will You Still Love Me Tomorrow?: Girl Groups from the 50s On.* London: Virago, 1989.

O'Brien, Lucy. *She Bop: The Definitive History of Women in Rock, Pop and Soul.* New York: Penguin Books, 1995.

Ryan, Thomas. *American Hit Radio: A History of Popular Singles from 1955 to the Present.* Rocklin, CA: Prima Publishing, 1996.

Warner, Jay. *The Billboard Book of American Singing Groups: A History 1940–1990.* New York: Billboard Books, 1992.

Warwick, Jacqueline C. *Girl Groups, Girl Culture: Popular Music and Identity in the 1960s.* London: Routledge, 2007.

Girl Scouts

The Girl Scouts would probably never have come into being if the Boy Scouts had not been exclusively for boys. During the first decade of the twentieth century, several thousand girls wanted to join the new youth group created by General Sir Robert Baden-Powell in England shortly after the Boer War in South Africa, and a parallel organization called the Girl Guides was quickly organized, with Baden-Powell's sister Agnes at its head.

By the time Juliette Gordon Low, a transplant to England from Savannah, Georgia, met the Baden-Powells in 1910, she was a wealthy widow who had survived her increasingly abusive marriage and now had both energy and funds to spare. After a turn at leading a Guides group in Scotland, Low threw herself with gusto into creating an American analogue to the organization. On returning to Savannah in 1912, she formed the first troops in the United States with the eager support of a distant cousin, Nina Anderson Pape, and a naturalist, W. J. Hoxie. Hoxie also collaborated with Low on revising Agnes Baden-Powell's Girl Guides handbook for American consumption, including writing some new chapters on camping and nature lore. The first edition of *How Girls Can Help Their Country* was published in 1913. In 1915 the name of the American organization was changed from Girl Guides to Girl

Girl Scouts Celebrate 100th Anniversary. A group of Girl Scouts attend an event marking the organization's 100th anniversary in Washington, D.C., in February 2012. PAUL MORIGI/GETTY IMAGES FOR GIRL SCOUTS OF AMERICA.

Scouts and its headquarters moved from Savannah to Washington; in 1916 the national office moved to New York, where it remains.

SCOUTING VALUES

Robert Baden-Powell saw scouting for boys as a means to a specific end: "to help them become handy, capable men and able to hold their own with anyone," he wrote, adding that a woman with similar training as a Girl Guide "can be a good and helpful comrade to her brother or husband or son along the path of life" and that the Girl Guides during World War I had "quickly showed the value of their training by undertaking a variety of duties which made them valuable to their country in her time of need." So Girl Scouts, like Boy Scouts, were taught how to survive in the wilderness and the basics of water safety and first aid and were encouraged to learn how to handle firearms. With the motto "Be prepared," members of both organizations still promise "to do my duty to God and my country, to help other people at all times, and to obey the Girl Scout Laws." Both groups award merit badges for the acquisition of particular skills. And both sexes wear uniforms—the Girl Scouts' originally were blue like the Girl Guides' but were soon switched to khaki. Green uniforms, which remain the standard today, were selected in the late 1920s.

The separation of the two branches meant that there was less emphasis on a military agenda for the Girl Scouts and more on developing proficiency in skills rooted in a gendered division of labor. In addition to scout craft (woods lore, trailblazing, mapping, Morse and semaphore flag signaling, and other outdoor skills), the first Girl Scout handbooks contained highly practical instructions in hygiene, cooking, housekeeping, gardening, and child care.

As in England, girls flocked to join the movement in America. Like female suffrage, scouting implicitly challenged the Victorian ethos of women's assignment to a male-protected domestic sphere. By getting girls outdoors and into each other's company, the Girl Scouts offered mastery of real-world skills and gender solidarity. The separate governance of the two organizations also allowed the Girl Scouts to continue to follow a policy of inclusiveness when, in the early 1990s, the Boy Scouts took a stand against membership for religious nonbelievers and homosexuals (losing, as a result, some financial support from corporations and foundations with nondiscrimination policies).

SCOUTING IN PRACTICE

Funding for the Girl Scouts was seeded by Low's personal fortune, but the organization remained throughout the twentieth century the only entity of its size supported primarily by a bake sale: the annual Girl Scout Cookie drive. The shortbread Trefoils and chocolate Thin Mints became as much a part of American popular culinary culture as apple pie. Individual member dues are *not* a major source of revenue: in the 2010s, membership was just $12 a year.

Original Girl Scout Laws mandating kindness to animals and thrift were later broadened into the ecological and social directives to "use resources wisely" and to "make the world a better place." A significant difference is the extension of the old "clean in thought, word, and deed" rule from personal and public health to include instruction on how to deal with sexual harassment and psychological challenges of adolescence such as stress, moodiness, and self-esteem issues. One clause that has not changed is the commitment to "be a sister to every Girl Scout," a fellowship that transcends national barriers. Girl Scouts of the USA is a member of the World Association of Girl Guides and Girl Scouts (WAGGGS), which has ten million members in 145 countries and international meeting centers in the United Kingdom, Switzerland, India, and Mexico.

Girl Scouts range in age from kindergarten-age Daisies (named after Low, whose childhood nickname was Daisy), Brownies (ages six to eight), Junior Girl Scouts (ages eight to eleven), Cadettes (ages eleven to fourteen), and Senior Girl Scouts (ages fourteen to seventeen). A girl may become an Adult Scout at age eighteen. Not all Scouts follow the progression from Daisy all the way up through Senior, as the many other activities of adolescence make competing claims on their time. And some girls abandon scouting because of what they see as excessively religious undercurrents, despite the organization's efforts to be nonsectarian and inclusive. Nevertheless, many American women regard scouting as a happy aspect of their childhood and one they would readily see their own daughters experience as well.

MODERN SCOUTS

At the turn of the twenty-first century, the Girl Scouts faced some controversy regarding their policies on religious and other women's issues. The Girl Scouts of America oath includes the phrase "to serve God," which some have found limiting to personal religious practices. In 1993 the group allowed girls to substitute any phrase that would express their own beliefs. In 2011 the Colorado state branch of the group declared that transgender children who identify as girls were welcome to join the Scouts. Both decisions were met with supporters as well as hecklers; some feel the group sets an inclusive example, whereas others find that such measures violate their own beliefs.

In the face of the changing and modernized experience of contemporary young women, the Girls Scouts program reevaluated its entire brand to better meet girls' needs and to be a more efficient organization. Among the changes undertaken were to improve volunteer and fund-raising methods, as well as to significantly realign the community-based council model. Amid these changes, in preparation for their centennial anniversary Girl Scouts declared 2012 "The Year of the Girl." Plans to celebrate the 100th anniversary include parades, campouts, concerts, and numerous other events across the country. To mark the milestone, the U.S. Treasury plans to produce and sell commemorative silver coins in 2013 at the end of the celebratory year. Part of the proceeds have been slated to pay for renovations to the Low birthplace in Savannah.

Nick Humez

SEE ALSO: *Boy Scouts of America; Camping; Feminism.*

BIBLIOGRAPHY

Bacon, Josephine Daskam, ed. *Scouting for Girls.* New York: Girl Scouts, 1920.

Baden-Powell, Agnes. *The Handbook for Girl Guides, or, How Girls Can Help Build the Empire.* London: Thomas Nelson and Sons, 1912.

Bergerson, Chris, and Girl Scouts of the United States of America. *Junior Girl Scout Handbook.* New York: Girl Scouts of the USA, 1994.

Christiansen, Betty, and Girl Scouts of the USA. *Girl Scouts: A Celebration of 100 Trailblazing Years.* New York: Stewart, Tabori & Chang, 2011.

Ciraco, Candace White; Betty De Araujo; and Kathy Allert. *Outdoor Education in Girl Scouting.* New York: Girl Scouts of the USA, 1984.

Ciraco, Candace White; Betty De Araujo; and Kathy Allert. *Brownie Girl Scout Handbook.* New York: Girl Scouts of the USA, 1986.

Cloninger, Kathy. *Tough Cookies: Leadership Lessons from 100 Years of the Girl Scouts.* Hoboken, NJ: Wiley, 2011.

Cordery, Stacy A. *Juliette Gordon Low: The Remarkable Founder of the Girl Scouts.* New York: Viking Adult, 2012.

Degenhardt, Mary, and Judith Kirsch, eds. *Girl Scout Collector's Guide.* Lombard, IL: Wallace-Homestead, 1987.

Eubanks, Toni, and Girl Scouts of the United States of America. *Cadette Girl Scout Handbook.* New York: Girl Scouts of the USA, 1995.

Girl Scouts of the USA. *The Wide World of Girls Guiding and Girl Scouting.* New York: Girl Scouts of the USA, 1980.

Low, Juliette Gordon; Agnes Smyth Baden-Powell; and Robert Stephenson Smyth Baden-Powell. *How Girls Can Help Their Country.* Savannah, GA: Press of M. S. & D. A. Byck, 1916.

Philmus, H. C. *Brave Girls: The Story of the Girls Scouts and Girl Guides in the Underground.* New York: Girl Scouts National Organization, 1947.

Shultz, Gladys Denny, and Daisy Gordon Lawrence. *Lady from Savannah: The Life of Juliette Low.* New York: Lippincott, 1958.

The Girl with the Dragon Tattoo

Swedish journalist Stieg Larsson's distinctive crime thriller *The Girl with the Dragon Tattoo* is the first novel in a best-selling trilogy known as the Millennium Series. The three books, which were published posthumously after Larsson's sudden death in 2004, feature an unusual heroine: the brilliant, relentless, and emotionally damaged Lisbeth Salander. Although opinions differ on the literary quality of Larsson's novels, critics and readers agree that Salander is one of the most original and compelling female characters in modern fiction. The trilogy gathered an enthusiastic audience in Europe, and American readers became equally enthralled when English translations appeared in 2008 and 2009 (*The Girl Who Played with Fire* and *The Girl Who Kicked the Hornet's Nest*, respectively). As of 2012, the novel has been translated into thirty-five different languages.

Although the original title of *The Girl with the Dragon Tattoo*—which translates as "Men Who Hate Women"—was changed for marketing reasons, it effectively captures the central theme of the novel. Salander, a computer hacker with a photographic memory, teams up with investigative reporter Mikael Blomkvist to investigate the decades-old disappearance of a young woman who vanished from the island retreat of her wealthy, dysfunctional family. As the novel unfolds, Salander and Blomkvist not only uncover a series of heinous murders but also identify the perpetrator (who is killed); find the missing woman (who is still alive); and, in a separate subplot, bring down a corrupt corporate magnate and save Blomkvist's political magazine, *Millennium.* Salander develops feelings for Blomkvist but retreats when she sees him with another woman.

Blomkvist is generally regarded as an alter ego for Larsson, a social activist and outspoken opponent of right-wing radicalism. Throughout the trilogy both Blomkvist and Salander are threatened by various corporate and criminal forces, and in Europe the books are viewed not only as a series of crime thrillers but also as a commentary on contemporary Swedish society. For both European and American audiences, however, the popularity of the Millennium Series is driven primarily by a fascination with the bisexual, anorexic, and socially inept Salander, who is determined to overcome her own victimization. A subplot of *The Girl with the Dragon Tattoo* concerns her successful revenge against a cruelly exploitative guardian. The novels have been seen as a powerful indictment of violence against women, but some have argued that Larsson's critique of misogyny is too simplistic, while others condemn his graphic depictions of rape and torture.

A number of critics have approved *The Girl with the Dragon Tattoo* as an intelligent page-turner, but others have found it confusing, far-fetched, or tiresome—and even enthusiasts have acknowledged its flaws. Nevertheless, the novel clearly strikes a resonant note for many readers. Commentators have observed that Salander's character combines feminist rage with traditionally masculine traits such as a mastery of technology and a willingness to act without hesitation or compunction. She appeals equally to men and women, offering a new kind of protagonist, whose ambiguities reflect the complexity of twenty-first-century culture. The cerebral, idiosyncratic Salander can also be seen as an updated version of literature's most iconic sleuth, Sherlock Holmes.

Blomkvist and Salander's investigative partnership and complicated personal connection continue in the second and third novels, but it appears that fans will never know what was intended for them in the long term. Although a fourth installment was partially written at the time of Larsson's death, and there were notes for a fifth and sixth, he reportedly intended the series to extend over ten volumes. In 2011 a big-budget film adaptation of *The Girl with the Dragon Tattoo* received critical praise and showed strong box-office performance.

Cynthia Giles

SEE ALSO: *Best Sellers; Detective Fiction.*

BIBLIOGRAPHY

Bronson, Eric. *"The Girl with the Dragon Tattoo" and Philosophy: Everything Is Fire.* Hoboken, NJ: John Wiley & Sons, 2012.

O'Neill, Maggie, and Lizzie Seal. *Transgressive Imaginations: Crime, Deviance and Culture.* New York: Palgrave Macmillan, 2012.

Rosenberg, Robin S., and Shannon O'Neill. *The Psychology of "The Girl with the Dragon Tattoo": Understanding Lisbeth Salander and Stieg Larsson's Millennium Trilogy.* Dallas, TX: Smart Pop, 2011.

Girls Gone Wild

One of the first amateur video series featuring college girls as the subject, *Girls Gone Wild* made creator Joe Francis wealthy and became a mainstay of popular culture. Marketed primarily toward young adult males, the series highlights the impromptu actions of college girls and young women in various party scenes. *Girls Gone Wild* has been in some form of continuous production since 1997. Several television programs and movies have satirized the *Girls Gone Wild* brand and the behavior exhibited by women who participate in the filming of the videos. The title of the series has also become synonymous with partying and scandalous behavior, especially by college students.

Using common spring break and vacation spots as sites for the videos, the *Girls Gone Wild* production teams identify nightspots, dance clubs, and other gathering places to ask females if they are willing to participate. This participation usually begins with the girls baring their breasts. It often continues with more graphic sexual activity taking place in hotel rooms or the *Girls Gone Wild* party bus in exchange for *Girls Gone Wild*–branded hats, shorts, T-shirts, or other giveaways. Each vignette typically begins with producers asking the women questions as they appear in various stages of undress. The questions continue as the subjects disrobe or engage in other sexual acts, either alone or with other women. Additional scenes of women baring breasts in exchange for beads or other items are included in some episodes.

The *Girls Gone Wild* infomercial was a mainstay on late-night television and contributed to the success of the franchise, earning millions of dollars for Francis and his production company. The videos were sold through a subscription format that provided a certain number of videos per month or as single episodes. Complaints from consumers regarding the subscription program eventually lead to the Federal Trade Commission taking action against Francis and the parent company, Mantra Films, for sending unwanted videos to subscribers and continuing to charge monthly fees. These cases were eventually settled.

Many feminist critics have condemned the *Girls Gone Wild* brand and videos for objectifying women. They have also pointed out that the women in the videos are often drunk when they consent to participate. Despite the criticism, the popularity of the series remained strong through the early 2000s. Even the growth of new online websites offering free pornographic content to viewers and others that engage in real-time, Web-camera activities with viewers has not stopped its expansion. The publication of a *Girls Gone Wild* magazine and an expanding online presence indicates that the demand for this material is not waning. Some of the volumes have also included celebrity guest hosts such as comedian Doug Stanhope and rapper Snoop Dogg.

In 2008, a video of New York escort Ashley Dupre surfaced in a volume of *Girls Gone Wild.* Dupre was a principal figure in the prostitution scandal that eventually led to the resignation of former New York governor Eliot Spitzer. Dupre claimed her consent was not given in the video and subsequently sued Mantra Films, Francis, and others for $10 million. Dupre dropped the suit when video evidence proved that she had, indeed, given consent.

The legality of *Girls Gone Wild* videos has been challenged in several lawsuits in many different states. Litigants have questioned the legally binding nature of the releases participants sign and the approval given, even though in many cases, permission is given on camera. Questions of indecent exposure, lewd conduct, and legal age of consent have been the subject of several of these challenges. Despite these legal problems, *Girls Gone Wild* continues to attract participants for the videos and holds market share in a competitive adult entertainment environment.

Jay Parrent

SEE ALSO: *Breast Implants; Celebrity; College Fads; Feminism; The Internet; Pornography; Reality Television; Sex Scandals; Sex Symbol; Snoop Dogg; Spring Break; Television; T-Shirts; Videos.*

BIBLIOGRAPHY

Internet Movie Database. *Girls Gone Wild.* Accessed May 2012. Available from http://www.imdb.com/title/tt0338066/

Simkin, Ryan. *FLASH! Bars, Boobs and Busted: 5 Years on the Road with "Girls Gone Wild."* Santa Monica, CA: 4 Park Publishing, 2010

Gish, Dorothy *(1898–1968)*

One of the pioneering actresses of silent film, Dorothy Gish starred in more than twenty films directed by legendary filmmaker D. W. Griffith. Like her older sister and costar, Lillian, Gish played roles that embodied Griffith's vision of ideal womanhood—charming, chaste, and strong-willed. In particular, Gish earned acclaim for her comic portrayal of "The Little Disturber" in Griffith's *Hearts of the World* (1918) and as the blind Louise in *Orphans of the Storm* (1921). Although Gish left film for a successful stage career in the 1930s, she remained forever Griffith's gamine in the eyes of the public.

Samantha Barbas

SEE ALSO: *Gish, Lillian; Griffith, D. W.; Silent Movies.*

BIBLIOGRAPHY

Borden, DeWitt. *More from Hollywood: The Careers of 15 Great American Stars.* South Brunswick, NJ: A. S. Barnes, 1977.

Gish, Lillian. *Dorothy and Lillian Gish.* New York: Scribner, 1973.

Waldman, Harry. *Beyond Hollywood's Grasp: American Filmmakers Abroad 1914–1945.* Metuchen, NJ: Scarecrow Press, 1994.

Gish, Lillian *(1893–1993)*

Frail and tough, innocent and powerful, charming and serious, actress Lillian Gish defied both categorization and convention. Best known for her work with director D. W. Griffith in silent films, in her younger years Gish portrayed pale, waiflike heroines who used emotional strength, hard work, and persistence to protect their chastity—and spirit—from destruction at the hands of lustful men. To many filmgoers, Gish served as a bridge between nineteenth- and twentieth-century values, uniting Griffith's Victorian views on sexual purity with the strong-willed independence of the "modern" girl. Even after Gish left Griffith's studios in 1923, she continued to shy away from overtly sexual roles and for the rest of her career remained an icon of propriety—and a firm believer in the dignity of acting. Gish pioneered many of the acting techniques of silent films and worked tirelessly to elevate the cinema from the status of mere entertainment to serious art.

For an actress who championed the respectability of film, Gish's introduction to the world of drama was less than highbrow. At the age of five, she debuted in a vaudeville melodrama called "In Convict's Stripes," and a few years later Gish, her mother, and her sister Dorothy had joined vaudeville touring companies and were traveling around the country with a child actress named Gladys Mary Smith. In New York in 1912, Lillian and Dorothy went to visit Smith, who had been renamed Mary Pickford and was working at D. W. Griffith's Biograph Studios. Pickford urged Griffith to hire the Gish sisters, and during the next three years Lillian and Dorothy appeared in more than thirty-five short films.

In 1914 Gish starred in her first feature-length film, *Judith of Bethulia*, and in 1915 she played heroine Elsie Stoneman in Griffith's controversial film *The Birth of a Nation.* During the next seven years Gish developed and refined her on-screen persona: In *Hearts of the World* (1918), *Broken Blossoms* (1919), and *Orphans of the Storm* (1921), Gish played downtrodden characters who survive poverty, abandonment, and abuse through tenacity, sacrifice, and luck. In the most famous of these roles, in *Way Down East* (1920), Gish's character, Anna Moore, floats down a river on an ice floe, hand and hair dragging in the frigid water, until she is saved by her lover. Prevented by the silent-film medium from using spoken words, Gish perfected the art of facial expression, and Griffith, the pioneer of the close-up shot, used Gish's wide eyes and cautious smile to create a depth and intensity unparalleled in early films.

In 1923 a dispute with Griffith over her salary drove Gish to Inspiration Pictures, where she appeared in *Romola* (1924) with William Powell. In 1926 she moved to MGM and starred in *La Bohème* (1926), *The Scarlet Letter* (1926), and *The Wind* (1928). Gish's films at MGM, though, were largely box-office failures, and production head Irving Thalberg suggested that the studio invent a scandal for Gish to boost her popularity. Gish refused to go along, however, and left MGM, signing with rival United Artists in 1930. Soon afterward, when *One Romantic Night* (1930) proved a commercial disappointment, Gish asked to be released from her contract, thus concluding her most productive and creative years in film. As actress Louise Brooks lamented, "Stigmatized as a grasping, silly, sexless antique . . . the great Lillian Gish left Hollywood forever, without a head turned to mark her departure." Brooks, however, turned out to be wrong.

Although Gish devoted most of the next five decades to the stage, she returned to Hollywood for a few notable films. In 1947 she received an Academy Award nomination for her role in *Duel in the Sun*, and in 1955 she gave a powerful performance as an old woman protecting a group of children from a maniacal killer in *The Night of the Hunter.* No longer the gamine, Gish increasingly portrayed mature, if not spinsterish, characters. In 1960 she played the mother of Burt Lancaster's character in *The Unforgiven*, and in 1969 she appeared in a television version of *Arsenic and Old Lace*, playing one of the two spinster sisters along with Helen Hayes. In real life Gish did not marry, although she was courted by many suitors. When asked in the 1920s why he was so fascinated with Gish, actor John Gilbert, one of her more ardent followers, replied, "Because she is unattainable."

Lillian Gish. *Silent-film star Lillian Gish began her show business career on the stage at age five.* HULTON ARCHIVE/GETTY IMAGES.

By the 1970s Gish was widely celebrated as "the First Lady of the silent screen," and in 1971 she received an honorary Academy Award for her contribution to motion pictures. "This beautiful woman so frail and pink and so overwhelmingly feminine has endured as a working artist from the birth of the movies to their transfiguration," actor Melvyn Douglas read at the ceremony, "for underneath this wisp of a creature there is hard steel." Gish's iron constitution served her well: In her eighties she continued to act in television, theater, and film, giving her final performance in the movie *The Whales of August* in 1987. She died in 1993, leaving a legacy of hard work, creativity, and versatility. While Hollywood vamps, goddesses, and bombshells came and went, Gish remained a testament to the timelessness of the fine art of acting.

Samantha Barbas

SEE ALSO: The Birth of a Nation*; Brooks, Louise; Douglas, Melvyn; Gish, Dorothy; Griffith, D. W.; Hollywood; Lancaster, Burt; MGM (Metro-Goldwyn-Mayer); Movie Stars; Pickford, Mary; Silent Movies; Thalberg, Irving G.; United Artists; Vaudeville.*

BIBLIOGRAPHY

Affron, Charles. *Star Acting: Gish, Garbo, Davis.* New York: Dutton, 1977.

Gish, Lillian. *Dorothy and Lillian Gish.* New York: Scribner, 1973.

Gish, Lillian, and Ann Pinchot. *The Movies, Mr. Griffith, and Me.* Englewood Cliffs, NJ: Prentice Hall, 1969.

Oderman, Stuart. *Lillian Gish: A Life on Stage and Screen.* Jefferson, NC: McFarland, 2000.

Shipman, David. *The Great Movie Stars: The Golden Years.* New York: Crown, 1970.

The Glass Menagerie

Tennessee Williams's 1944 drama *The Glass Menagerie*, his self-described "memory play," has been considered a classic of the American theater ever since its premiere. The play centers on Tom Wingfield's reminiscences of his youth in the 1930s, when he lived in a St. Louis tenement with his domineering mother, Amanda, and his handicapped sister Laura, a character based on Williams's own sister Rose. Williams called it "the saddest play I have ever written. It is full of pain. It's painful for me to see it."

The play premiered at Chicago's Civic Theatre and then moved to Broadway, where it was awarded the New York Drama Critics' Circle Award for Best American Play. Laurette Taylor's performance as Amanda is considered the finest of her career. The play has gone on to be performed often internationally and has been adapted several times to film, including a highly acclaimed 1987 version directed by Paul Newman and starring Joanne Woodward, John Malkovich, and Karen Allen. A 2009 stage production at Connecticut's Long Wharf Theatre, starring Judith Ivey and directed by Gordon Edelstein, was a great success, and the play transferred to the Roundabout Theatre in New York and the Mark Taper Forum in Los Angeles for extended runs. *The Glass Menagerie*'s longevity is attributed in part to its poetic language and vivid characterizations.

Michael Najjar

SEE ALSO: *Broadway; Newman, Paul; Williams, Tennessee.*

BIBLIOGRAPHY

Bloom, Harold. *Tennessee Williams's "The Glass Menagerie."* New York: Chelsea House Publishers, 2007.

Leverich, Lyle. *Tom: The Unknown Tennessee Williams.* New York: Crown Publishers, 1995.

Martin, Robert A., ed. *Critical Essays on Tennessee Williams.* New York: G. K. Hall, 1997.

Parker, R. B., ed. *The Glass Menagerie: A Collection of Critical Essays.* Englewood Cliffs, NJ: Prentice-Hall, 1983.

Presley, Delma E. *The Glass Menagerie: An American Memory.* Boston: Twayne Publishers, 1990.

Williams, Tennessee. *Memoirs.* Garden City, NY: Doubleday, 1975.

Williams, Tennessee. *The Glass Menagerie: The Deluxe Centennial Edition.* New York: New Directions, 2011.

Gleason, Jackie *(1916–1987)*

As his sobriquet, The Great One, implies, Jackie Gleason was a comedian of superlative talents, but his persona housed enormous contradictions. A literally larger-than-life performer who became a star on the small screen when he failed to achieve

Jackie Gleason. *Among many of Jackie Gleason's memorable characters was irascible bus driver Ralph Kramden of* The Honeymooners. **DARLENE HAMMOND/GETTY IMAGES.**

headline status onstage and in the movies during the 1940s, Gleason became "Mr. Saturday Night" during the next two decades and helped to define the comic possibilities of television. Although he hosted a variety series for more than twenty years, the corpulent comedian is best remembered for a situation comedy that lasted only one season: *The Honeymooners.* A high-living bon viveur, Gleason achieved success by never forgetting the lowly "Ralph Kramden" types who populated his boyhood.

In a medium in which understatement is the cool virtue, broad physicality and verbal bombast were the red-hot core of Gleason's game. Even as the medium became more refined, extravagance was Gleason's badge of distinction. His programs were always lavish spectacles, highlighted by gaudy dance numbers and glamorous starlets. Onstage and off, he presided like a monarch.

But poverty and abandonment defined Gleason's childhood and his later conception of himself. Even in his glitziest productions, there was always a reminder somewhere of the mean streets of his youth. He was born in an impoverished section of Brooklyn, New York, on February 26, 1916. His brother died when he was three, and his father, an insurance clerk, deserted the family when he was eight. Gleason's mother supported her son by working in a subway token booth and living with rented furniture.

Gleason quit school at an early age and worked as a pool hustler, comic high diver, and carnival barker to pay the rent. He found his calling as a master of ceremonies at Brooklyn's Folly Theater and across the Hudson River at Newark's Miami Club. His quick wit with hecklers and his energetic charm landed him steady employment at Club 18, a cabaret in Manhattan. Movie executive Jack Warner caught his act and signed him to a Hollywood contract. Beginning in 1941 he played minor parts in a series of movies, including the musical *Navy Blues* (1941) with his idol, Jack Oakie, and *All through the Night* (1942), a gangster yarn with Humphrey Bogart.

Unrecognized by the movie crowd, he returned to New York in 1944 and began to attract notice on Broadway. His appearance in *Artists and Models* led to a larger role in the musical comedy *Follow the Girls*, for which *Time* lauded him as a "likably loony comic." Gleason stole the show by impersonating a female naval officer, proving to himself that he could "get away with more as a fat man." Offers began to pour in: he replaced Bob Crosby on a Sunday night radio show and emceed at Billy Rose's Diamond Horseshoe. In 1949 he was featured in the Broadway revue *Along Fifth Avenue* with comedienne Nancy Walker. Brooks Atkinson of the *New York Times* recognized Gleason's ability to move onstage as "a priceless accomplishment in a man who wants to be funny."

EARLY TELEVISION WORK

Later in 1949 Gleason returned to Los Angeles to star in a blue-collar situation comedy, *Life of Riley*, a television adaptation of a popular radio series about a bumbling aircraft worker. Producer Irving Brecher was unable to sign the lead of the original radio program, William Bendix, because of movie commitments. Gleason was recruited to play the goodhearted but incompetent Chester A. Riley. Chester's catchphrase, "What a revoltin' development this is!" caught on, but Gleason's edginess and joie de vivre were missing without an audience. Although the series received an Emmy Award for Best Film Made for and Viewed on Television (there wasn't much competition), *Life of Riley* was canceled after twenty-six weeks. Bendix revived the role for television in 1953, and that incarnation ran for five years.

Several months after the cancellation, Gleason landed a television role that was totally suited to his strengths. He was hired as host of the live variety series *Cavalcade of Stars* on the DuMont television network. DuMont was a struggling fourth network with little money for programming, but it proved an excellent training ground for future stars on the established networks. Both previous hosts of *Cavalcade*, Jack Carter and Jerry Lester, were stolen by NBC for big-time variety shows. In the two years that Gleason hosted the low-budget DuMont show, he laid the groundwork for his impending future success.

On *Cavalcade* the comedian developed the variety format along with the repertory of characters that would serve him well for the next twenty years. Unlike other variety hosts such as Milton Berle or Sid Caesar who relied mostly on new sketches each week, Gleason based his comedy on recurring characterizations, many of which were comic extensions of people he grew up with in Brooklyn. There was the ever-complaining Charlie Bratton, known as the Loudmouth; the sweetly meek Fenwick Babbitt, who would sometimes explode; the hapless Bachelor, a silent figure struggling to cope alone; and garrulous Joe the Bartender, caught in an endless monologue about the idiosyncratic patrons of his establishment. Two creations revealed the polar sides of Gleason's sensibility: the innocent savant the Poor Soul, a silent homage to the vulnerable, saintly Little Tramp of Charlie Chaplin, and the ostentatious playboy Reginald Van Gleason III, a baroque vision of wealth and grandeur.

BIRTH OF *THE HONEYMOONERS*

Gleason's most famous character, Ralph Kramden, debuted later than the others but was probably his best understood creation. There were, as he explained, "hundreds of them in my neighborhood." Gleason was so close to the yearning and unquiet desperation of his bus driver character that he gave him the same address as his boyhood residence, 358 Chauncey Street. *The Honeymooners* began modestly enough as a six-minute sketch portraying a long-married working-class couple who stayed together despite life's blows and disappointments. Unlike the foolishness of *Life of Riley*, Gleason wanted this pair to be based on realism; he instructed his writers "to make it the way people really live." Pert Kelton first played Alice, the wife, and gave her a battle-scarred feistiness. To everyone's surprise, the audience identified with the Kramdens' struggles, and *The Honeymooners* sketches became longer and richer in comic incident.

For an early Reggie Van Gleason sketch, the show hired Art Carney, an agile player from *The Morey Amsterdam Show*. Gleason and Carney hit it off immediately and remained partners in one way or another until the end. Carney had a cameo in the first *Honeymooners* sketch as a policeman, but he was so adept at playing sidekicks that the role of Ralph's buddy, the sewer worker Ed Norton, was quickly created for him. This pairing eventually developed an archetypal resonance in Carney, who would be a Sancho Panza to Gleason's Don Quixote.

VARIETY SHOWS

The other networks quickly recognized Gleason's popularity on DuMont. He appeared as a special guest star on CBS's *The Frank Sinatra Show*, and there was talk about making him a regular. He also hosted *The Colgate Comedy Hour* on NBC. In 1952 William Paley, chairman of CBS, lured Gleason and his staff to CBS by quintupling his salary. The bigger budget for *The Jackie Gleason Show*, which premiered on September 20, 1952, allowed for splashier production numbers, including an opening extravaganza with the June Taylor dancers that Busby Berkeley would have been proud to own. Gleason also employed beautiful chorines, known as the Glea Girls, to introduce segments of the show, while he himself became one of the show's grand inventions, sipping his "tea" as if it were laced with alcohol and uttering his trademark phrases "How sweet it is," "You are a dan-dan-dandy crowd," and "And away we go!" Soon the Gleason show owned Saturday nights and was second in the overall ratings behind *I Love Lucy*.

On top for the first time, Gleason pushed himself into other creative arenas. Although he could not read music, he composed the signature melody for his variety show, *Melancholy Serenade*. Deciding that the common man needed background music for his pleasures, he composed more than forty mood albums, beginning with *Music for Lovers Only*, whose collective sales reached 120 million. He scored an "original symphony in ballet" titled *Tawny*, which the *New York Times* called "a poem for eye and ear, a simply superb example of inspired television artistry." In 1954 Gleason also produced a summer music show for the Dorsey brothers, Tommy and Jimmy, which became the regular series *Stage Show*. The comedian took personal credit for giving Elvis Presley his first network exposure on the Dorsey program.

In 1953 Gleason made his dramatic acting debut, portraying a manipulative comic in a *Studio One* production. He starred in several live television dramas, which led to the resurrection of his movie career. He received an Academy Award nomination for his role as Minnesota Fats in *The Hustler* (1961) and critical acclaim for his sleazy boxing manager in *Requiem for a Heavyweight* (1962), but he was less successful as a deaf mute in *Gigot* (1962), a sentimental tale that he also wrote. In 1959 he made a triumphant return to the stage as an irresponsible drunk in *Take Me Along*, a musical adaptation of Eugene O'Neill's *Ah, Wilderness!*

Gleason strayed several times from his successful variety formula. In 1955 Buick offered him one of the largest contracts in television history to produce *The Honeymooners* on film, but Ralph and Alice (played by Audrey Meadows since the move to CBS) did not click with the audience. Eventually, however, these thirty-nine episodes of *The Honeymooners* became a financial bonanza in syndication. In 1961 Gleason inexplicably tackled the quiz show format, and his *You're in the Picture* became one of television's most notorious debacles, lasting only one week. During the early 1960s he launched *The American Scene Magazine*, using his characters to comment on societal change. In 1964, when he relocated his television series to Miami Beach, Florida ("the sun and fun capital of the world"), he reverted to his characteristic brand of splashy entertainment. Although the variety format was losing its luster, Gleason remained in the Nielsen top ten throughout the decade.

After his move to CBS, Gleason insisted on total control of his variety series. He participated in every aspect of production, from casting to set design to merchandising. With bravado, his end credit proclaimed, "Entire Production Supervised by Jackie Gleason." As he once explained, "I have no use for humility. . . . In my work, I stand or fall by my own judgment."

Gleason emerged in an era of live television when comedians dominated the airwaves. Despite changes in American culture and television, he was able to produce and star in his type of variety program until 1970. After that, he revived *The Honeymooners* for holiday specials and starred as a southern sheriff in several *Smokey and the Bandit* movies. When he died on June 24, 1987, the country was rediscovering the "lost" episodes of *The Honeymooners* from the 1950s.

Gleason remains relevant in the twenty-first century. In 2000 a statue of him as Ralph Kramden was erected at the entrance of New York City's Port Authority Bus Terminal. In 2002 a television movie starring Brad Garrett as Gleason delved into the comedian's life. Such current performers as Kevin James have been directly influenced by Gleason's work. Gleason demonstrated that commercial television could be a medium for original comic expression, and his work has spoken to the American everyman. As critic Tom Shales has noted, "Gleason was perhaps as much the auteur as Chaplin was or as Woody Allen is."

Ron Simon

SEE ALSO: *Academy Awards; Amsterdam, Morey; Berkeley, Busby; Berle, Milton; Bogart, Humphrey; Broadway; Caesar, Sid; Chaplin, Charlie; Dorsey, Jimmy; Dorsey, Tommy; Emmy Awards; Hollywood;* The Honeymooners*;* I Love Lucy*;* The Life of Riley*; Meadows, Audrey; O'Neill, Eugene; Paley, William S.; Presley, Elvis; Sinatra, Frank; Syndication; Television.*

BIBLIOGRAPHY

Bacon, James. *How Sweet It Is: The Jackie Gleason Story*. New York: St. Martin's Press, 1985.

Bishop, Jim. *The Golden Ham: A Candid Biography of Jackie Gleason*. New York: Simon & Schuster, 1956.

Crescenti, Peter, and Bob Columbe. *The Official Honeymooners Treasury*. New York: Perigee Books, 1985.

Henry, William. *The Great One: The Life and Legend of Jackie Gleason*. New York: Doubleday, 1992.

McCrohan, Donna. *The Honeymooners' Companion*. New York: Workman, 1978.

Meadows, Audrey, and Joseph A. Daley. *Love, Alice: My Life as a Honeymooner*. New York: Crown Publishers, 1994.

The Museum of Broadcasting. *Jackie Gleason: "The Great One."* New York: Museum of Broadcasting, 1988.

Weatherby, W. J. *Jackie Gleason: An Intimate Portrait of the Great One*. New York: Pharos Books, 1992.

Glee

Cocreated and executive produced by Ryan Murphy, Brad Falchuk, and Ian Brennan, *Glee* (2009–) is a musical "dramedy" series that premiered on the Fox network in May 2009. In just four seasons the show has generated hordes of fans (who affectionately refer to each other as "gleeks"—a combination of *Glee* and *geek*) and a string of awards, including six Emmys, four Golden Globes, and two GLAAD Media Awards for its nuanced and fair treatment of openly gay characters. With episodes punctuated by musical performances of both traditional show tunes and chart-topping hits, *Glee* has been cited as a catalyst for renewed popular interest in musical theater and film.

Glee tells the story of Spanish teacher Will Schuester (played by Matthew Morrison) and his desire to revive the glee

Glee. *The cast of* Glee *performs one of the show's trademark musical numbers. The show is credited for sparking a renewed interest in musical theater and film.* FOX-TV/THE KOBAL COLLECTION/BAER, CARIN.

club at McKinley High. Sue Sylvester (played by Jane Lynch) immediately launches an attack to stop this because she feels it will cut funding to her award-winning cheerleading squad. Marginalized students like goody-goody Rachel Berry (played by Lea Michele), closeted gay Kurt Hummel (Chris Colfer), and African American diva Mercedes Jones (Amber Riley) are thrilled that they can shine musically at a school where slushies in the face are the norm for outsiders. They are joined by paraplegic Artie Abrams (Kevin McHale) and Asian American goth Tina Cohen-Chang (Jenna Ushkowitz).

The group does not entirely coalesce until guidance counselor Emma Pillsbury (Jayma Mays) recruits star quarterback Finn Hudson (Cory Monteith). Detecting a threat, Sue sends three cheerleaders (known as "Cheerios"), Quinn Fabray (Dianna Agron), Santana Lopez (Naya Rivera), and Brittany Pierce (Heather Morris), to infiltrate and sabotage the group. Noah "Puck" Puckerman (Mark Salling) and Mike Chang (Harry Shum Jr.), teammates of Finn, then become members, and the New Directions show choir is born.

During season two a competitive squad, the Warblers, is introduced with Blaine Anderson (Darren Criss) as featured singer. Subsequent seasons of *Glee* developed story lines that addressed such issues as bullying, harassment, teen pregnancy, underage drinking, teen sex (heterosexual and homosexual), adoption, suicide, and other topics that impact the characters' lives and deliver subtle messages to the viewing audiences.

Glee has also been lauded for its innovative practices in promotion and merchandising. Joe Earley, Fox's executive vice president of marketing, sought to transform *American Idol* viewers into "brand ambassadors" for *Glee* by airing the pilot episode directly after the *Idol* season finale, despite the fact that the rest of the season would not air for several months. During the summer of 2009 the pilot could be viewed on the Internet at Hulu and on the Fox website. Preview featurettes aired before summer blockbusters, and promotion was particularly heavy on related Fox shows such as *So You Think You Can Dance*. The network found real merchandising success not with the usual posters and T-shirts but with the musical performances themselves. Paying only for the performance rights of popular songs allowed Fox to release albums of music at incredibly low production costs, and in 2010 alone the show released a mind-boggling eighty different singles that ended up on the Billboard Hot 100, primarily as a result of digital song purchases made on iTunes. Downloads of an episode's songs often become available before the episode airs as a promotional move, and individual songs may be purchased during the week it airs. DVD releases and cast tours to major cities also proved to be financially lucrative and continue to provide marketing for the network and the program.

The show, however, has not been without controversy. Although it has brought teens and adults alike back to the love of musicals and has won Golden Globes, Emmys, and GLAAD awards, it has also garnered negative criticism. The Parents Television Council called *Glee* "reprehensible" for its depiction of teen sexuality. A racy *GQ* spread featuring Michele, Monteith, and Agron was labeled pornography by critics and upset parents of preteens. Detractors have even blamed *Glee* for the rise in slushie bullying in high schools.

Nevertheless, *Glee* continues to exert a major influence on popular culture. In 2011 *Glee* spun off a successful audition show on the Oxygen network, *The Glee Project*, which places the winner of each season as a character on the subsequent season of *Glee*. A similar British show, *Don't Stop Believing*, aired in 2010, seeking to compile a group of singers that could compete with American glee clubs, which have seen a major resurgence during the *Glee* era.

Linda Ann Martindale

SEE ALSO: American Idol*; Cheerleading; Emmy Awards; Gay Men; Goth; Hulu; The Internet; The Musical; Reality Television; Suicide; Teenagers; Television; Top 40; T-Shirts.*

BIBLIOGRAPHY

Adalian, Josef. "*Glee* Pilot Doubles as Marketing Trial." *Television Week*, April 27, 2009.

Rickman, Amy. *Gleeful!: A Totally Unofficial Guide to the Hit TV Series "Glee."* New York: Villard Trade Paperbacks, 2010.

Steinberg, Brian. "How *Glee* Married TV and Music to Create a New Moneymaking Model." *Advertising Age*, February 1, 2010.

Wilson, Leah. *Filled with Glee: The Unauthorized "Glee" Companion.* Dallas, TX: BenBella, 2010.

Glitter Rock

From 1972 to 1974 a wave of primarily British rock acts—dubbed glitter rock—emerged to enjoy massive success with a sound that marked a radical departure from the peace/love/sandals vibe of the recent past. The new movement celebrated the superficial, made androgyny look cool, and marked a complete departure from the more earnest "save the world" sentiments of the hippie era. *Rolling Stone* writer David Fricke described glitter rock as "the tidal splash of pop guitars, raging puberty, and elegant anarchy." Male singers often sported shag haircuts, eyeliner, lipstick, outrageous clothing, and towering platform shoes with abandon. Yet the music that came out of this era—David Bowie and Roxy Music would create some of glitter's greatest sonic legacies—would land an assured place in the annals of rock history, and the genre has been posited as the most innovative event to sweep through the pop music landscape before punk rock.

EVOLUTION OF GLITTER

"Glitter was urban panic music," wrote Jon Savage in *Gadfly*, in describing the marked distinction between glitter rock and hippie rock. "Instead of natural fibers, you had crimplene, glitter, fur; instead of LSD, alcohol and downers; instead of albums, singles were the focus; instead of authenticity, synthetic plasticity ruled; in place of a dour, bearded machismo, you had a blissful, trashy androgyny." The summer of 1972 is usually tagged as the moment of glitter's genesis, and London the place, but the chart-success version of glitter—called "glam" in the United Kingdom—did owe a small debt to an obscure young American band, the New York Dolls. Living in New York City's Greenwich Village and originally playing Otis Redding covers in what was called the Oscar Wilde Room at the Mercer Art Center, the Dolls had long hair, dressed in platform shoes, and wore a great deal of makeup. Part of their inspiration came from the late 1960s Greenwich Village theater scene—particularly the gross doings of the Ridiculous Theater Company—and they became the next hot band to catch when Andy Warhol and his entourage began frequenting the Mercer shows.

A management team thought it better to launch the Dolls first in London, and they flew over and found instant success. Contracted to open for Rod Stewart, they became the first group in music history to tour with a major rock act without ever having produced an album or even a single. Then one of the Dolls, Billy Murcia, died of a quaalude overdose, and the band was eulogized in the music press for a time. They emerged again with a new drummer in December 1972 and signed to the Mercury label, but their career fizzled after just two albums. To add to the band's troubles, American audiences assumed that they were gay at a time when homosexuality was a new and very controversial topic for many. Back in London, however, the vibe was quite different. Glitter/glam rock was huge by the summer of 1972. Its precursor came in the spring of 1971 with a young and attractive singer, Mark Bolan, and his band T. Rex. "Get It On (Bang the Gong)" and subsequent tracks, such as "20th Century Boy" (1973), came to be deemed classics of glitter.

Like most pop culture movements, glitter originated as a reaction against something else. In this case it was the ubiquity of the hippie. By 1972 the long-hair-and-granola look was even being co-opted in advertising images. The Beatles were gone, and bands like Yes, the Moody Blues, Fleetwood Mac, and Led Zeppelin were huge, as was country rock; long dirge-like tunes were in vogue. Glitter celebrated artifice and the soignée, and through it ran strong elements of camp. Furthermore, the spectacle of men wearing makeup was still enough to make people halt on the street and cause periodic uproars in the mainstream press. Homosexuality had only been decriminalized in Britain in the late 1960s, and the gay-rights movement in the United States dated back only to the summer of 1969. The average man or woman of a certain age still found it dreadfully uncomfortable even admitting that gay men and women existed at all, so taboo was the topic prior to these years. Thus glitter rock and its accoutrements—the weird album covers, the high-resolution rock poster, the aping of the look of one's favorite singer—found great resonance with the teen generation.

THE KEY YEAR: 1972

Several crucial albums were released in 1972 that portended a new era in rock. Roxy Music, led by Bryan Ferry and at the time including Brian Eno, has been termed the ideological vanguard of the movement. Their self-titled debut album and the single "Virginia Plan" both arrived in the summer of 1972 to massive success. Rock guitar chords and booming drums melded with Ferry's arch, almost poetic lyrics, and made Roxy perhaps the most enduring of all glitter bands and one that virtually never fell out of critical favor. This Eno period is usually termed their zenith; they disbanded after the release of *Country Life* in 1974, and subsequent reformations never really achieved the initial edge.

David Bowie is also inextricably linked with glitter rock through his Ziggy Stardust persona. His massive success with androgynous outfits and spacey lamé bodysuits was the mainstream rock manifestation of the whole glam movement. The 1972 album *The Rise and Fall of Ziggy Stardust and the Spiders from Mars* is deemed one of the quintessential releases of the genre. Moreover, Bowie would produce a number of significant albums in a short span, also vital to the glam-rock discography: Mott the Hoople's *All the Young Dudes*, Lou Reed's *Transformer*, and Iggy Pop and the Stooges' *Raw Power*, all released in 1972. That same year Bowie told an interviewer in the British music paper *Melody Maker* that he was gay (later amending it to bisexual), which caused a huge stir. He became the first pop star to ever to make such an admission.

Further musical events that summer made glam/glitter a commercially viable movement. Gary Glitter, a forgotten English singer from the 1950s and 1960s, had a huge hit with the kazoo-like guitars and one-word lyrics ("Hey!") in "Rock and Roll (Part II)." A massive success in England that reached the Top 10 in the United States, the single would go down in history as the essential sports-stadium rouser. "Instantly nostalgic, but like nothing else on earth, 'Rock and Roll' cut through everything that was around that English summer, through the T. Rex sparkle and David Bowie sashay, through Slade's patent stomp and Sweet's candied pop," wrote Dave Thompson in *Goldmine*, "and though it didn't quite make #1, it hung around the chart so long there's not another song on earth that recaptures the moment like [this] one."

Several other tracks signify the glitter rock moment, such as the cult favorite "Baby's on Fire," from an Eno solo project. Other British bands quickly climbed onto glam once its money-making potential had been established, but they produced music with far less panache and artistic endurance than Bowie, Roxy, or T. Rex. Slade and Sweet were two such acts and would become the begetters of the 1980s glam metal movement; Queen also grew out of this era and surprised many by successfully riding the glitter rock movement well past its announced demise. Glitter rock also marked a turning point in pop music: prior to 1972, American and British tastes had more or less corresponded. Yet glam failed to catch on in the United States as it did in Britain, and the shock-rock proto-goth Alice Cooper was its only true homegrown commercial success.

GLITTER'S DECLINE AND LEGACY

By 1974 the New York Dolls had disintegrated after more problems with drugs, the Stooges broke up, Bowie released an album of vintage cover tunes, and Elton John—perhaps the most commercial and internationally successful manifestation of glitter rock—was a huge success. The cross-dressing camp of glitter rock was successfully translated into a stage play in London, *The Rocky Horror Picture Show* (1973), which was adapted into a film in the United States that debuted in 1975 and became a cult favorite almost immediately. The last gasp of real glam in the United States came with Sweet's Top 10 hit "Ballroom Blitz" in the summer of 1975.

Already by that summer, punk was in its nascent stages in England and would hit full force the following year. Hallmarked by vulgarity; tattered clothing; and almost unlistenable, anything-but-melodic music, punk was, not surprisingly, a reactionary movement—against the satiny, coiffed look of glitter, with its electric pianos and Wildean sentiments. A little more than a decade later the outlandishness and alternative sexuality of glitter rock were standard pop music clichés, embodied most successfully by Boy George, Prince, and even Madonna.

Velvet Goldmine, a 1998 film by Todd Haynes, borrowed its title from a Bowie song of the era and was heralded as a sign of glitter rock's revival. Set in London in the early 1970s, it follows the rock-and-roll love story of a bisexual rock star in space-age apparel and his far punker American friend, a clear stand-in for Iggy Pop. Numerous luminaries from alternative music stepped in to create and/or record for the *Velvet Goldmine* soundtrack, and Haynes recalled in interviews how profoundly some of the music and imagery from the glitter rock era had affected his adolescent years. "It was a moment when it was cool even for straight people to appear bisexual," the film's editor, Jim Lyons, told Amy Taubin in the *Village Voice*. "There's a clear nostalgia for that period when we believed that we were going to have a better and better society, and that feminism would win, and homosexuality would be completely accepted."

The pop music scene of the first decade of the 2000s became one in which artists developed eclectic styles by pulling from a variety of earlier trends, and glitter rock once again played a role in shaping contemporary music. Lady Gaga, one of the most commercially successful new artists of the twenty-first century, cites the 1970s style as one of her biggest influences. She has incorporated glitter rock elements into her performances—in her harmonies, her use of outrageous costumes, and her championing of gay rights in songs like "Born This Way" (2011). Glitter rock may never make a full comeback, but its legacy lives on.

Carol Brennan

SEE ALSO: *Androgyny; Bowie, David; Boy George; Cooper, Alice; Country Music; Fleetwood Mac; Gay Liberation Movement; Gay Men; Greenwich Village; Hippies; John, Elton; Lady Gaga; Led Zeppelin; Madonna; Pop, Iggy; Pop Music; Prince; Punk; Redding, Otis; Reed, Lou; Rock and Roll;* The Rocky Horror Picture Show*;* Rolling Stone*; Teenagers; Warhol, Andy; Yes.*

BIBLIOGRAPHY

Auslander, Philip. *Performing Glam Rock: Gender and Theatricality in Popular Music.* Ann Arbor: University of Michigan Press, 2006.

Fricke, David. "Weird Scenes from the Velvet Goldmine." *Rolling Stone*, November 26, 1998, 64–67.

Goldman, Albert. "Rock Goes Holl-Ly-Wooood!" In *Sound Bites.* New York: Random House, 1992.

Klawans, Stuart. "All that Glitters." *Nation*, November 30, 1998, 32–34.

Lim, Dennis. "The Music Choice Artifacts and Inspired Counterfeits." *Village Voice*, November 3, 1998, 50.

McCormick, Moira. "International *Velvet* Mines Glam's Riches." *Billboard*, October 3, 1998, 22.

McNeil, Legs, and Gillian McCain. *Please Kill Me: The Uncensored Oral History of Punk.* New York: Penguin, 1997.

Rock, Mick, and David Bowie. *Glam! An Eyewitness Account.* London: Vision on Publishing, 2006.

Savage, Jon. "Divine Decadence: Memories of Glam." *Gadfly*, October 1998.

Stambler, Irwin. "David Johansen." In *The Encyclopedia of Pop, Rock & Soul*, 339–341. New York: St. Martin's, 1989.

Taubin, Amy. "All that Glitters." *Village Voice*, November 18, 1997, 64–66.

Thompson, Dave. "Gary Glitter." *Goldmine*, July 4, 1997, 20–30.

Global Positioning System

SEE: *GPS.*

Global Warming

Environmental issues come in many shapes and sizes. After the late 1960s, lawmakers and activists asserted ethics and controls on many human activities to clean up messes and to improve human health. Increasing scientific understanding allowed humans to clarify the implications of their everyday living patterns. Environmentalists used these new understandings to demand regulation and action. A backlash grew out of the 1980s, when some Americans came to feel that such responsibilities weighed down the federal government and slowed economic development. By the start of the twenty-first century, these dynamics led to consistent confrontation, particularly during the administration of President George W. Bush.

In such a contentious moment for all environmental considerations, the issue of climate change emerged as the most divisive of all. Growing from new technologies that allowed scientists the opportunity to make dramatic new hypotheses, the issue of climate change often seemed to pit pro- and antidevelopment forces against one another. Relative to all other environmental issues, climate change is the largest in terms of its global scale and its varied implications, and it has become a centerpiece of the cultural discourse on environmentalism.

GLOBAL ACTION FOR A GLOBAL ISSUE

The year 1988 came as if on cue. First, the heat waves and droughts of the American summer of 1988 made a great deal of news. The National Climatic Data Center estimated around $40 billion in economic losses and between 5,000 and 10,000 deaths. At the start of that difficult summer, James E. Hansen, director of NASA's Goddard Institute for Space Studies, gave testimony to Congress in which he asserted that it was virtually certain that human activity was responsible for the global-warming trends and that this might bring more storms, floods, and heat waves in the future. Hansen made the now-famous remark that "It's time to stop waffling . . . and say that the greenhouse effect is here and is affecting our climate now." Polls indicated that public awareness of global warming rose considerably over the next year.

The rising scientific interest and political concern about global warming gave rise to the foundation of the Intergovernmental Panel on Climate Change (IPCC) in 1988 by the World Meteorological Organization and the United Nations. The IPCC's task was to organize the work of an international group of scientists to produce periodic reports summarizing the best knowledge on the world's climate in order to help political leaders make policy decisions. Over the next two decades the IPCC's reports brought reliable knowledge about climate change to the world.

CLIMATE CHANGE AND GREEN CULTURE

After 1995 American and global efforts to mitigate climate change have worked at every level of society. These efforts have built on some existing elements of popular culture but also created some new ones. In addition, the role of science and scientific findings has come to represent a crucial new portrayal of trust in our culture. Anxieties over the uncertainty related to climate change have played out in popular culture similarly to the way fears of atomic technology played out.

Though the concept began in scientific circles, the emphasis on the moral implications of climate change was brought to the American people through popular culture. Although many Americans who called themselves environmentalists would not change basic consumptive patterns such as the size of their vehicles, upper-middle-class consumers and particularly their children possessed an awareness of environmental issues that translated into a passive style of concern. Often they would emphasize recycling, animal stewardship, or gardening and celebrate Earth Day. As this ethic, or interest, moved into popular culture in the 1990s, corporations, films, and television programs began to exploit this "green" consciousness, sometimes falsely (greenwashing) and other times authentically. Primarily due to luck of timing, global warming was one of the first large-scale environmental concerns to emerge in cultural soil made ready by green marketing.

In the case of climate change, the first well-known example was a feature film titled *The Day after Tomorrow* (2004). Like many science fiction films that seize on a remote possibility and use the genre to imagine what would happen if it came to pass, the big-budget feature film is loosely based on an unlikely scenario related to climate change: the theory of "abrupt climate change." In the film, global warming has resulted in massive shifts in Earth's basic organization: primarily, the Gulf Stream (part of the Atlantic thermohaline circulation) has shut down. This causes the North Atlantic region to cool while heat builds up in the tropics. The result is a severe storm, the likes of which have never been seen, and a dramatic change in the global climate. As the scenario spins forward, expansive portions of Earth are plunged into a momentary ice age. In the United States, surviving Americans flee to Mexico in order to take shelter south of the equator.

However, somewhat lost in the wake of the terrorist attacks of September 2001 and the seemingly impossible scale of the devastation's connection with climate change, *The Day after Tomorrow* did not register fully with the viewing public. Science fiction writer Michael Crichton contributed to the discourse with the 2004 novel *State of Fear*, which cautions the public against believing all of what scientists tell them. This discourse set the stage for a different type of film: the documentary *An Inconvenient Truth* (2006).

AN INCONVENIENT TRUTH

Produced by Laurie David and directed by Davis Guggenheim, *An Inconvenient Truth* grew from a slideshow presentation about the problem of global warming that was being presented around the country by former senator and vice president Al Gore. Gore and film producer David created *An Inconvenient Truth* to serve as a counterbalance to the misinformation about global warming that they felt was being sent to Americans through popular and political culture. By designing a film that would receive a large release and teaming it with other outlets, including a book authored by Gore, they brought new energy and awareness to the issue.

An Inconvenient Truth took great care not to make the debate only a moral one. Shifting to new energy sources and systems was depicted as a great engine for economic growth and development. Using the film as a mobilizing device, Gore and

David created Web-based modules to give individuals ideas on how to actively combat climate change in their communities. In addition, massive workshops took place to train a corps of inspired Americans to give talks, show the film, and generally fuel community awareness about climate change at the grassroots level. The film's astonishing popularity, reception of an Oscar in documentary filmmaking, and massive sales were topped only by human civilization's greatest stamp of moral correctness: in 2007 the IPCC and Gore, for his work with *An Inconvenient Truth*, were awarded the Nobel Peace Prize. Clearly the issue of global warming had transcended any other environmental issue in global awareness.

CONTRARY VIEWS TAKE SHAPE

Even though there could be little dispute over much of the scientific findings, climate change proved a volatile topic in popular culture. In the U.S. Senate, for instance, many pro-development Republicans refused to allow the United States to become involved in the global discussion on finding a political remedy to climate change. By far the most outspoken opponent of the effort to develop such policy solutions was U.S. Senator James M. Inhofe, a Republican from Oklahoma, particularly when he served as chairman of the Committee on Environment and Public Works. Therefore, as forces gathered in favor of political action aimed at mitigating global warming, an opposite set of forces began to mobilize against such action.

The pro-development stance was also stimulated by organizations such as the Cato Institute, which prioritizes free markets. Publishing its own books on the topic of climate change, the institute produced Patrick J. Michaels's *Meltdown: The Predictable Distortion of Global Warming by Scientists, Politicians, and the Media* (2005) and Michaels and Robert C. Balling Jr.'s *Climate of Extremes: Global Warming Science They Don't Want You to Know* (2009).

By the early twenty-first century, naysayers and deniers were able to categorize the global warming faction as "alarmists" in much the same fashion that nonconformists had been called "red" or "commie" in previous decades. The difference, of course, was that the basic ethic behind the effort to craft policies to help put off climate change was not devious or un-American. History has shown that many of the naysayers were more a product of fearing change and uncertainty than of actual scientific findings.

The front lines of the cultural battle over global warming moved swiftly into politics when President Bush took office in 2001. He was publicly skeptical of the alarm and panic over global warming; privately, he led a profound effort by the executive branch to stifle scientific findings by other branches of the government. In particular, with the support of large energy interests, the Bush administration focused significant effort in tempering and even squelching scientists from NASA who worked with the modeling and satellite imagery related to the government's investigation of climate change.

In 2006 Hansen went public with accusations that the executive branch was prohibiting him from bringing his findings on global warming to the public. Although not all scientists agreed with Hansen's findings, NASA's models provided convincing evidence to many that the situation merited immediate attention. In his criticism, Hansen argued that it was immoral for the federal government not to report the information it had found, which could influence the lives of every human.

GLOBAL WARMING BECOMES MAINSTREAM

In *Hot, Flat, and Crowded* (2009), *New York Times* columnist Thomas Friedman designated 2007–2008 the first year of the "Energy-Climate era" (E.C.E), an era when "we now understand that these fossil fuels are exhaustible, increasingly expensive, and politically, ecologically, and climatically toxic." In the past, he writes, "We wanted everyone to be converted to the American way of life, although we never really thought . . . it would herald a climate and biodiversity disaster." Ironically, change has come quicker to other nations, and the United States finds itself lagging behind—even trying to imitate other nations that have more readily modeled their economies on Friedman's E.C.E.

A 2008 commercial summed up how rapidly the debate on global warming was changing: Created by Gore's Alliance for Climate Protection, the public relations entity he created to manufacture green culture concerning climate change, the ad featured former House Speaker (and unofficial spokesman of the Republican conservatives) Newt Gingrich sitting on a small couch with then-House Speaker (and representative of the Democrats' more liberal thinkers) Nancy Pelosi, with the capitol looming large in the background. They confess that they do not "always see eye-to-eye," but—Gingrich states directly into the camera—"we do agree our country must take action to address climate change." Gingrich and many other former naysayers altered their discourse to accept the concept of climate change—and often also the need for action—but debated what role the federal government should take in such action. The ad functions as a symbol of how broadly known the issue of climate change had become, and, it seemed, how mainstream had become the consensus for action.

The closing decade of the twentieth century and the first of the twenty-first were marked by public divisiveness and discussion on the issue of climate change. Major breakthroughs occurred when leaders such as Gore enabled the general public to relate to and appreciate the magnitude of the issue of global warming. This cultural acceptance set the stage for dramatic political action at the start of the twenty-first century. Thus far, though, economic struggles have joined with political divisiveness to keep Americans from taking any cohesive action on climate change. Meanwhile, initiatives by nations throughout the world have made certain that climate change will be a critical aspect of global politics moving forward.

Brian Black

SEE ALSO: *Academy Awards; Crichton, Michael; Earth Day; Environmentalism;* An Inconvenient Truth*; NASA; Recycling.*

BIBLIOGRAPHY

Black, Brian, and Gary Weisel. *Global Warming.* New York: Greenwood, 2010.

Bowen, Mark. *Censoring Science: Inside the Political Attack on Dr. James Hansen and the Truth of Global Warming.* New York: Plume, 2008.

Friedman, Thomas. *Hot, Flat, and Crowded: Why We Need a Green Revolution—and How It Can Renew America.* New York: Picador, 2009.

Gore, Albert. *An Inconvenient Truth: The Planetary Emergency of Global Warming and What We Can Do about It.* New York: Rodale, 2006.

Gore, Albert. *Our Choice: A Plan to Solve the Climate Crisis.* Emmaus, PA: Rodale, 2009.

Steinberg, Ted. *Down to Earth: Nature's Role in American History.* New York: Oxford University Press, 2008.

Gnagy, Jon *(1907–1981)*

Jon Gnagy was a man who taught himself how to draw and then taught millions of youngsters how to draw on television. With his plaid shirt and Vandyke beard, Gnagy was one of the fixtures of television in the late 1940s and early 1950s, demonstrating simplified techniques of line and shade to children, many of whom were drawing along in front of their television sets at home with the aid of one of Gnagy's Learn to Draw kits that included an instruction booklet, a sketch pad, and other supplies.

The Kansas-born Gnagy taught himself how to draw while recovering from a childhood illness. The skill later helped him earn a living as a sign painter and later as an advertising art director. He first appeared on television in a seven-minute segment called "Learn to Draw" on the NBC variety show *Radio City Matinee* in 1946. Standing in front of an easel, Gnagy explained his drawing techniques and proceeded to draw an oak tree. He said that anyone can learn to draw using basic shapes: a cube, a ball, a cylinder and a cone. He was so popular that NBC gave him his own show, called *You Are an Artist.* In 1949 NBC canceled the show, so Gnagy found a partner to help him produce a similar show called *Draw with Me*, a name that was later changed to *Learn to Draw*. Although criticized for oversimplification and for promoting imitation rather than creativity, Gnagy thought that his methods were appropriate for his medium and his audience. There was no quarrel from the many youngsters who faithfully watched his shows and had their parents buy his drawing kits. While Gnagy stopped filming his show in 1955, it lived on for many years in syndication, and his Learn to Draw sets continued to sell well into the twenty-first century. After leaving television, Gnagy traveled around the United States giving lectures on drawing. He died in 1981 at age seventy-four.

Preston Neal Jones

SEE ALSO: *Baby Boomers; Television.*

BIBLIOGRAPHY

Grossman, Gary H. *Saturday Morning TV.* New York: Dell Publishing, 1981.

Spigel, Lynn. *TV by Design: Modern Art and the Rise of Network Television.* Chicago: University of Chicago Press, 2008.

The Godfather

One of American popular culture's most resilient narratives is that of the Mafia and its antiheroic gangsters, and one of this genre's most popular and poignant products is Francis Ford Coppola's *Godfather* trilogy, based on Mario Puzo's novel *The Godfather.* Released in 1972 to universal acclaim and rewarded with several Academy Awards, including Best Picture, *The Godfather* instantly fixed its place in the American cultural psyche, establishing itself as the de facto gangster film to which all other subsequent exercises in the genre would be compared.

MAFIA AS METAPHOR

Powered by Marlon Brando's timeless delivery of the film's namesake, Godfather Vito Corleone, the film established the futures of Hollywood royalty Al Pacino (Michael Corleone), Robert Duvall (Tom Hagen), and James Caan (Sonny Corleone), all of whom are most recognized for the roles they played in this sprawling and sensitive study of two generations of Mafia membership and power. Pacino would go on to star in the last two films of the trilogy: *The Godfather Part II* (1974) and *The Godfather Part III* (1990). The blinding success of the first two *Godfather* films immediately marked Coppola as a major player in Hollywood, allowing him green lights on almost any project he set his hands on. This led to the legendary conflicts with his producers as well as Brando during the shooting of *Apocalypse Now* (1979) and his ambitious attempt to form his own studio-distributor conglomerate, Zoetrope Studios, in 1980.

In 1972 Coppola adapted Puzo's popular novel for the screen, and although the two worked together on the script, Coppola dramatically shaped the project during the shooting. The second installment was entirely his creation. Cutting out much of the novel's romanticized violence, the director decided to instead focus on the Corleone family dynamics, personalizing the film in accordance with his own experience growing up as the second-generation son of an Italian immigrant. The Mafia, as always, was the perfect vehicle for the consideration of American culture and values, Coppola asserted in an interview:

> I feel that the Mafia is an incredible metaphor for this country. Both America and the Mafia have roots in Europe . . . both the Mafia and America feel they are

***Marlon Brando in* The Godfather.** *Marlon Brando starred as crime family leader Vito Corleone in* The Godfather, *which set the standard for the gangster film genre.* PARAMOUNT/GETTY IMAGES.

benevolent organizations. Both the Mafia and America have their hands stained with blood from what it is necessary to do to protect their power and interests. Both are totally capitalistic phenomena and basically have a profit motive.

Indeed, the strength of the *Godfather* trilogy's appeal lay in the collusion of the two phenomena, one that ran throughout the genre in its most moving expressions, from Paul Muni's bravura performance in *Scarface* (1932) to Martin Scorsese's immediately canonical *GoodFellas* (1990). All installments in the gangster genre engaged the audience's sympathies for the lead character as an independent businessman living out his version of the American dream. In fact, there is a built-in bias toward the Mafia, especially within *The Godfather*, as a conglomerate of well-intentioned businessmen looking out for the best interests of their families, as critic Roger Ebert has explained: "During the movie we see not a single actual civilian victim of organized crime . . . The only police officer with a significant speaking role [Sterling Hayden] is corrupt."

The ideas of law and order are specific to the machinations of the various families of the Mafia, replacing the exterior world with the cloistered, fiercely loyal world of organized crime. In fact, one of the first scenes in *The Godfather* involves Brando castigating an undertaker, who describes himself as a "good American," for going to the police for help. Interestingly enough, the film's violent finale, which juxtaposes the exhaustive murders of each of Michael's opponents (a figurative baptism of Corleone power through death) with the literal baptism of his sister's child, was cheered by audiences as a shining example of American triumph. This moral ambiguity and veiled criticism of the American legal and political system's inefficacy is one that has coursed through popular culture's fascination with organized crime, one that was an interesting accident to Coppola, who had actually structured his movie to be a criticism of the ethnic and religious hypocrisy within the Mafia. Instead audiences were attracted by the poignant scenes of family cohesion in the face of social and economic pressure; in this sense Coppola's film had the endearing, if violent, nature of some of the best work of Frank Capra, including his classic *It's a Wonderful Life* (1946).

EXTENDING THE SERIES

The Godfather Part II applied Coppola's intended criticisms of organized crime and religious hypocrisy even further, culminating in Michael's assassination of his own brother Fredo and the disruption of his marriage for the sake of the family business. There is no noble figure in the second installment, except possibly Vito Corleone, played by Robert De Niro, in flashback sequences that reveal his early years as an immigrant. In the more contemporary scenes, everyone from Michael, his family, the Nevada senator, and the local citizenry is completely corrupt. The ethnic cohesion and protection that coursed through the first installment is totally disrupted, a monumental disappointment augmented by Coppola's insertion of an earlier scene of a cheerful birthday party for Vito at the end of the film.

An ultimately tragic figure, Michael, by the end of *The Godfather Part II*, not only has compromised his Italian heritage, his ethnic identity, and his family but also has positioned himself as the type of win-at-all-costs American immigrant criticized in the first installment—one who, even in the possession of unquestionable power and influence, can no longer trust anyone because he can be trusted by no one. By *The Godfather Part III*, Michael has extended his power as far as the Vatican, which he implores for redemption for the murder of his brother, but he still ends up powerless as his daughter is murdered at his side by the end of the film.

Resistant for years to the idea of establishing his *Godfather* series as a trilogy (Coppola asserted that if he ever did make a third installment, it would have to be a farce), the failure of his Zoetrope Studios (in which a good deal of his personal funds were invested) and the relative failure of his artistic product following *The Godfather* and *The Godfather Part II* (*The Outsiders* in 1983 was his only film following the first two *Godfather* films to meet with any measurable mainstream success), Coppola capitulated to the American infatuation with the Corleone family business and released *The Godfather Part III*, inciting further controversy by casting his own daughter, Sofia, as Andy Garcia's love interest. Sofia Coppola's mediocre delivery further damaged the prodigious but deteriorating reputation of her father, whose legendary status seemed to exist parallel to the lasting impact of the trilogy. But it did not diminish the technical skill, daunting vision, and deeply personal attention that Coppola nevertheless employed in his following films. He also turned that technical skill toward preserving his masterpiece, releasing a boxed set in 2008 that contained restorations of *The Godfather* and *The Godfather Part II* and a remaster of *The Godfather Part III*.

Regardless of his future projects, Coppola ensured himself immortal status in film history on the strength of the *Godfather* trilogy alone. The first two films are listed on the American Film Institute's prestigious "100 Years, 100 Movies" list, with *The Godfather* ranking at number two on the 2007 version of the list. Although criticized sharply, *The Godfather Part III*, predictably, was a moderate success at the box office, garnering $70 million, but it was another star vehicle for Pacino as well as for newcomer Garcia. It also fulfilled American popular culture's desire for closure while fulfilling Coppola's desire for a sharp critique of the inherent destruction and corruption within the relentless pursuit of power and wealth that lies at the heart of the American dream.

Scott Thill

SEE ALSO: *Academy Awards;* Apocalypse Now*; Best Sellers; Brando, Marlon; Capra, Frank; Duvall, Robert;* GoodFellas*;* It's a Wonderful Life*; Lansky, Meyer; Mafia/Organized Crime; Muni, Paul; Pacino, Al; Scorsese, Martin; Siskel and Ebert.*

BIBLIOGRAPHY

Bergan, Ronald. *Francis Ford Coppola—Close Up: The Making of His Movies.* New York: Thunder's Mouth Press, 1998.

Browne, Nick. *Francis Ford Coppola's "The Godfather" Trilogy.* Cambridge Film Handbooks. Cambridge, UK: Cambridge University Press, 1999.

Cowie, Peter. *Coppola: A Biography.* New York: Da Capo Press, 1994.

Lebo, Harlan. *The Godfather Legacy.* New York: Simon & Schuster, 1997.

Lewis, Jon. *Whom God Wishes to Destroy: Francis Coppola and the New Hollywood.* Durham, NC: Duke University Press, 1995.

Phillips, Gene D. *Godfather: The Intimate Francis Ford Coppola.* Lexington: University Press of Kentucky, 2004.

Godfrey, Arthur *(1903–1983)*

The arrival of genial, folksy entertainer Arthur Godfrey on television was the most publicized event of the 1948–1949 season. The reviewers pulled out all the stops in praising the old redhead, and he became the only personality in TV history to have two top-rated programs run simultaneously in prime time for an extended period. *Arthur Godfrey's Talent Scouts* aired on Mondays and *Arthur Godfrey and His Friends* on Wednesdays for just over eight seasons. In 1952–1953 the programs ranked two and three, just behind *I Love Lucy*. Even more remarkably, Godfrey's morning radio show, every Monday through Friday, continued during this time with high ratings, his fan base growing with multiple exposures.

Godfrey was born on August 31, 1903, in New York City. As a teenager, he ran away from home and a few years later joined the navy, where he was trained to be a radio operator. He eventually switched to the coast guard, where he concentrated on entertainment duties. After leaving the military he found employment with a Baltimore, Maryland, radio station. By the time he obtained his own programs, he was known for his pleasant personality and affable manner. TV critic Ben Gross of the *New York Daily News* summed up Godfrey's appeal: "It is his friendliness, his good cheer, his small-boy mischievousness, and his kindly philosophy."

Arthur Godfrey's Talent Scouts brought little known or newly discovered professional talent to perform before a live nationwide audience, with an applause meter deciding the winner. The host's witty banter and interviews with contestants plus high-quality talent delighted the listeners. Some of the winners—including Pat Boone, Carmel Quinn, the Chordettes, and the McGuire Sisters—later became regulars on *Arthur Godfrey and His Friends*. Also appearing on the show were many other soon-to-be-famous performers, including Rosemary Clooney, Tony Bennett, Connie Francis, Steve Lawrence, Leslie Uggams, and Patsy Cline. Two big stars missed by the screening staff, Elvis Presley and Buddy Holly, both flunked the show's auditions.

For his weekly variety hour, Godfrey assembled a personable group of talented regulars, chosen with an eye to audience demographics. Frank Parker and Marion Marlowe sang romantic duets for the mature audience, and Julius LaRosa was the bright young singer with appeal to bobby-soxers. There was also the bashful Hawaiian singer, Haleloke, as well as the Chordettes, a squeaky-clean barbershop quartet from Wisconsin. Other popular regulars were Janette Davis, Bill Lawrence, and the Toppers. Tony Marvin was the mellow-voiced announcer, while Godfrey enhanced the proceedings, sometimes playing his ukulele and singing in a gravelly croon. As he had on radio, Godfrey kidded his sponsors' products, but he refused to endorse any product he did not like personally.

When Godfrey underwent surgery for a hip replacement in May 1953, he received get-well cards from people throughout the country. The press continued to revere him until October of that year, when a dramatic turnaround occurred and he became controversial—suddenly maligned by columnists who had praised him. The controversy was ignited when he fired members of his popular TV show for what seemed to be petty reasons. He dismissed LaRosa on the air, charging that he "had become too big a star." He told the press that LaRosa had lost his humility, a remark that was to come back and plague Godfrey for the rest of his career. LaRosa made immediate well-publicized appearances on *The Ed Sullivan Show*, cut several hit records, and was given a series of his own before his career faded a few years later. In April 1955 Godfrey fired Marlowe and Haleloke.

Part of the public forgave Godfrey. His *Talent Scouts* continued until July 1958 and the *Friends* show until April 28, 1959, but his popularity never matched that of the sensational early 1950s. He survived a bout with lung cancer in 1959, but, except for a brief interval on television's *Candid Camera* (1960–1961), his television career was over. He worked on radio until 1972, when he broadcast a tearful farewell over CBS. Coincidentally, it had been tears that brought him to national attention as he gave a touching description of President Franklin D. Roosevelt's funeral in 1945.

In his later years Godfrey was a major supporter of public broadcasting as well as an advocate for environmental causes, serving as a member of the National Advisory Committee on Oceans and Atmosphere and the Citizens' Advisory Committee on Environmental Quality. He died from emphysema on March 16, 1983, and was cremated in Leesburg, Virginia. In 1988 Godfrey was posthumously inducted into the Radio Hall of Fame.

Benjamin Griffith

SEE ALSO: *Bennett, Tony; Boone, Pat;* Candid Camera*; Cline, Patsy; Clooney, Rosemary; Daytime Talk Shows; Francis, Connie; Holly, Buddy;* I Love Lucy*; Presley, Elvis; Radio; Sullivan, Ed; Television.*

BIBLIOGRAPHY

Brooks, Tim, and Earle Marsh. *The Complete Directory to Prime Time Network and Cable TV Shows: 1946–Present*, 6th ed. New York: Ballantine Books, 1995.

Lackmann, Ron. *Same Time . . . Same Station: An A–Z Guide to Radio from Jack Benny to Howard Stern*. New York: Facts On File, 1996.

Lowenstein, Larry, and Ken Huggins. *Famous People Who Knew Me: Adventures of a PR Man*. Lake Worth, FL: Legacies Books, 2007.

Sackett, Susan. *Prime-Time Hits: Television's Most Popular Network Programs*. New York: Billboard Books, 1993.

Singer, Arthur J. *Arthur Godfrey: The Adventures of an American Broadcaster*. Jefferson, NC: McFarland, 1999.

Godzilla

Godzilla is the lead monster character in a series of successful Japanese science fiction movies. The character's popularity and recognition rivals that of Superman and Mickey Mouse. Godzilla has inspired toys, games, clothes, model kits, comic books, novels, fan magazines, candy, television commercials, and countless imitations. In Japan, where he is known as Gojira, he has dominated popular fantasy for every generation to come of age since the 1950s.

In the United States Godzilla movies are often considered "B" movies, and audiences almost exclusively see edited, badly dubbed versions of the Japanese originals. Fans who investigate the series carefully have discovered that many of the movies, particularly the early ones, are thoughtful, well-crafted efforts by respected members of the Japanese film community. Even though an American remake in 1998 did not fare as well as expected, Godzilla maintains a loyal following in the United States and abroad.

Godzilla. *Godzilla arrives on the scene to battle pollution in* Godzilla vs. the Smog Monster, *1971.* TOHO/GETTY IMAGES.

Godzilla's screen debut was in *Gojira* (1954), made by the Toho Company (later Toho Pictures) of Seijo, Japan. The movie's name, meaning "whale-ape," was allegedly inspired by a burly studio employee. *Gojira* was, at the time, the most expensive movie ever produced in Japan, costing around $900,000. The movie was a huge success, and it spawned a new style of Japanese cinema: the *kaiju eiga*, or giant monster genre.

Toho producer Tomoyuki Tanaka was first inspired to make a monster movie by the successful reissue of *King Kong* (1933) in 1952. By the next year, a new breed of American science fiction creature, the giant monster, was drawing audiences to U.S. theaters and the newly popular drive-ins. Movies such as *The Beast from 20,000 Fathoms* (1953) and *Them!* (1954) played off Cold War anxieties; the monsters' creation and/or release on the world was the result of nuclear energy. The terror of nuclear war took physical form as the atomic mutant. As the only nation ever attacked by atomic weapons, Japan had its own reasons to fear such mutations, and memories of the Hiroshima and Nagasaki bombings during World War II were still fresh in the early 1950s. *Gojira* turned these fears and memories into cinematic terror.

Godzilla is largely the product of four men. Tanaka oversaw the original *Gojira* and remained with the series through the 1990s. Director Ishirō Honda was a friend and colleague of Akira Kurosawa, arguably Japan's greatest director. A visit to Hiroshima in 1946 inspired in Honda a desire to tell the story of atomic devastation on film. He regarded monsters as tragic figures, the result of humans' abuse of technology.

Special effects director Eiji Tsuburaya's work in the Godzilla films pioneered what would come to be called "suitmation," a combination of the words *suit* and *animation*, because actors who played his monsters wore molded latex suits. The process eventually became synonymous with Japanese monster movies, although not everyone could do it as well as Tsuburaya. Composer Akira Ifukube was a respected classical musician and scholar. His score, parts of which reappear in the series, became nearly as recognizable as Godzilla himself. The booming contrabass perfectly symbolizes the monster's rumbling gait.

COMING TO AMERICA

Gojira came to America in 1956 as *Godzilla, King of the Monsters.* "B"-movie producers Richard Kay and Harold Ross purchased the American distribution rights from Toho and, along with producer Joseph E. Levine, adapted the film for U.S. audiences. The dialogue was dubbed in English (as were all successive U.S. theatrical and television releases of Godzilla movies). The producers reconstructed the original sets to shoot new footage with Canadian actor Raymond Burr as American newspaper reporter Steve Martin and edited out all mentions of the atomic bombs dropped on Hiroshima and Nagasaki. *Godzilla, King of the Monsters* opened in New York City in April 1956. Levine promoted the film heavily, and it proved a huge hit, becoming the first Japanese picture to play in mainstream first-run theaters.

In the movie industry success breeds sequels. Toho released a second Gojira film, *Gojira No Gyakushū* (Gojira's counterattack), in 1955 only months after the first and a year before the creature's American debut. With this movie, Toho began its long-standing practice of selling the rights to each of its monster movies individually. Warner Brothers acquired *Gojira No Gyakushū* for the American market. It did not, however, acquire the name Godzilla, even though Toho owned it and could have sold it. Consequently, Warner Brothers released the movie as *Gigantis the Fire Monster* (1959).

The sequel received a somewhat shabbier treatment than its predecessor. Warner Brothers originally intended to construct an entirely new movie using only the special effects sequences from *Gojira No Gyakushū*, but it was never made. Instead the studio had the Japanese original dubbed in English. Voice performers include George Takei, who gained fame as *Star Trek*'s Mr. Sulu, and Keye Luke, best known for playing Number One Son in the Charlie Chan movies. Daws Butler, who gave voice to a number of Hanna Barbera's animated characters, was the narrator.

Warner Brothers also added stock footage of rockets and creature effects and replaced the original score by Masaru Sato. The studio released *Gigantis the Fire Monster* as a double feature with the American movie *Teenagers from Outer Space* (1959), a movie so bad its director was never allowed to make another.

Godzilla disappeared from theaters until 1962, while Toho and Honda branched out to other creature features, such as *Radon* (1956), known as *Rodan* in the United States, and *Daikaijū Baran* (1958), known as *Varan the Unbelievable*. Godzilla's return came about due to the efforts of stop-motion photography artist Willis O'Brien. Toho purchased his concept for a *King Kong* sequel, wherein the giant ape fights a rebuilt Frankenstein monster. Toro took out Frankenstein and added Gojira. Tanaka, Honda, Tsuburaya, and Ifukube all returned to the positions they held on *Gojira*. The film they made, *Kingu Kongu tai Gojira* (1962), departed from the atomic-age terror themes of the first two films, taking a more comedic, family-friendly tone with elements of slapstick and satire. It became the most widely seen Gojira film in Japan.

GODZILLA MEETS MOTHRA

In 1962 Universal International released *King Kong vs. Godzilla*, the U.S. version of *Kingu Kongu tai Gojira*, a movie that loses much in the translation. Sequences are cut, and scenes of English-speaking television reporters are added in an attempt to clarify the truncated action. Ifukube's score is gone, replaced by music from the distributor's previous films. Without the subtleties of the original, the film is little more than an extended build up to a fight between two men in monster costumes. For the first time, American audiences received a taste of what the genre would devolve into in a few short years.

For years after the movie's release, a rumor circulated among fans that there were two different endings to *King Kong vs. Godzilla*. Allegedly, Godzilla is triumphant in the Japanese version but not in the U.S. version. The outcome was changed to please U.S. audiences by having "their" monster win. The story, though, is apocryphal. Kong is, and always was, the winner.

Gojira returned in 1964 in *Mosura tai Gojira*, known in the United States as *Godzilla vs. the Thing*. This time Godzilla's enemy is a benevolent giant moth, the title creature of *Mosura* (1961), which was released as *Mothra* (1962) in the United States. In this movie the creative team of Tanaka, Honda, Tsuburaya, and Ifukube deliver a somewhat different, but extremely enjoyable, spin on the *kaiju eiga* motif. Mothra is called upon to fight Godzilla, even though she has just laid an egg and is about to die. A battle royal ensues. In what is likely the most touching sequence in the entire series, Mothra sacrifices herself fighting Godzilla. Soon after she dies, her egg hatches, and two larval Mothras emerge. They spin a cocoon around Godzilla, who falls into the ocean in defeat.

The movie reprises the more purely fantasy atmosphere of *Mothra*, bringing back the two pretty, 6-inch-tall female fairies who act as heralds to the creature. The fairies are as memorable a part of the film as the monsters: They speak in unison and sing a song to Mothra whenever they wish to call her. The emotional core of *Godzilla vs. the Thing* has long made it a favorite of fans, many of whom regard it as the high point in the series.

Godzilla, Mothra and her fairies, and Rodan return in *San daikaijū: Chikyū Saidai no Kessen* (1964), released in the United States as *Ghidorah, the Three-Headed Monster* (1965). It is an exciting film with much action and excellent suitmation effects. It is most notable as the beginning of Godzilla's "good monster" phase. Godzilla, Mothra, and Rodan team up to rid Earth of the menace of Ghidorah, a golden, fire-breathing dragon from outer space.

In Japan, audiences understood that Ghidorah was a metaphorical representation of China, symbolizing Japanese fears of Maoist expansionism. This symbolism was largely lost on American audiences. Mothra, always a good monster, jumps into the fray immediately, but Godzilla and Rodan fight only each other at first. They eventually experience a change of heart (after a "discussion" in monster growls and roars) and the three Earth creatures drive Ghidorah back into space.

DECREASING QUALITY

For the rest of the 1960s and into the 1970s, the Godzilla films closely followed a formula established by the next movie, *Kaiju Daisenso* (1965). The title translates as "The Giant Monster War" even though the U.S. title is *Monster Zero*, or *Godzilla vs. Monster Zero* when the film was release on home video. In this movie an alien race tries to take over Earth, using a monster. Godzilla stops them. It was the first Godzilla movie to use an American actor, Nick Adams, in the original cast. Honda left the series for a time after this movie, citing his reluctance to humanize Godzilla.

Godzilla releases had become an annual event for Toho, but with increased quantity came decreased quality. Jun Fukuda directed *Ebirah, Horror of the Deep* (1966), better known as *Godzilla vs. the Sea Monster*, and Ifukube was not involved with the movie. Godzilla is missing from the first half of the story, which involves a group of young men who discover an island where the natives are being enslaved by a vaguely defined paramilitary organization based on another island. Godzilla fights their monster and puts things right.

Son of Godzilla (1967) is a children's movie. Godzilla and his little mutant lizard son, Minira (Minya in the U.S. version), battle a giant spider. The baby Godzilla is laughable; he resembles Barney the Dinosaur far more than he does Godzilla. His freakish appearance and strange, crying noises make him Toho's most annoying creation.

Kaijū Sōshingeki (1968), released in the United States as *Destroy All Monsters*, was the last vestige of the exciting and creative original Godzilla series. In an attempt to regain its older fans, Toho pulled out all the stops. Honda returned, and so did most of Toho's stable of monsters. As the movie begins, all of the monsters are exiled to a peaceful life on a remote island. But aliens again attack Earth, taking control of the monsters and unleashing them on major cities. After much destruction, the people on Earth regain control of the creatures and turn them on the aliens—only to have Ghidorah appear out of space, leading to a final decisive showdown. Naturally, the good monsters win. The movie offers more action than the previous two combined.

From *Godzilla's Revenge* in 1969 and through the 1970s, the quality of Godzilla films went steadily downhill. Tsuburaya died and Honda left Toho. Fukuda returned as director. *Godzilla vs. the Smog Monster* (1971) tries, unsuccessfully, to integrate antipollution messages with its juvenile monster story. While the monster Hedora (*hedora* means "pollution") is an interesting amalgamation of aquatic creature and industrial waste, he is not nearly enough to redeem the movie.

GODZILLA'S RETURN

Godzilla on Monster Island (1972), known on home video and cable as *Godzilla vs. Gigan*, sees the lizard destroying an amusement park (complete with a Godzilla attraction) that serves as a base for aliens and their monster. In a creative move perhaps more misguided than the creation of Minira, Godzilla speaks. In *Godzilla vs. Megalon* (1973) he is teamed with Jet Jaguar, a robotic rip-off of the popular television character Ultraman (who was, ironically, the creation of Tsuburaya). The series was now firmly lodged in juvenile territory.

Godzilla vs. Megalon, along with *Godzilla vs. the Sea Monster*, would eventually become fodder for the television show *Mystery Science Theater 3000* (1988–1999), wherein a man and his robot puppets mercilessly mock the worst movies ever made. *Godzilla vs. the Cosmic Monster* (1974) features a robotic "Mechagodzilla." Honda and Ifukube returned for *Terror of Mechagodzilla* (1975), but it was too late. There would be no more Godzilla movies for nine years.

Godzilla was temporarily gone but definitely not forgotten. By this time his name and image had entered the popular consciousness. In the United States the movies played as reruns on local television. In the fall of 1978, NBC offered the television show *The Godzilla Power Hour*, an animated adventure from Hanna-Barbera, as part of its Saturday morning children's lineup. Actor Ted Cassidy provides Godzilla's roars.

Godzilla's true return came with the remake *Gojira* (1984), released in the United States a year later as *Godzilla 1985: The Legend Is Reborn*. Based on an original story by Tanaka, the movie takes Godzilla back to his origins as a city-stomping bad monster. Burr returns (in the American version) as the reporter Martin (but not Steve this time), the only living American who had seen Godzilla during his initial attack. The story ignores the sequels. Heavy promotion in both Japan and the United States helped the movie achieve some financial success, despite a nearly universal critical drubbing. Godzilla's new profile even earned him appearances in television advertisements for Nike shoes and the soft-drink Dr. Pepper.

The King of the Monsters was back. Toho's new sequels, however, never reached American theaters, and only the first sequel, *Gojira tai Biorante* (1989), received an official U.S. home video release (as *Godzilla vs. Biollante*). As the sequels became available on VHS and laserdisc in Japan (and sometimes before), the new Godzilla movies began to be traded with tape-collecting fans in the United States. These unauthorized copies, known as bootlegs, kept Godzilla alive in front of the eyes of a small but very dedicated and resourceful group of American monster-movie lovers.

Toho continued making Godzilla movies through the early 1990s, as its famous monster once again met Ghidorah, Mothra, and Mechagodzilla, as well as Space Godzilla. The new series climaxed with *Gojira tai Desutoroiâ* in 1995. Godzilla is apparently wiped out by a weapon called the "oxygen destroyer," the same device that had dispatched him in the 1954 film. His end came mainly to make way for yet another incarnation: a big-budget, Hollywood treatment of the story.

AN AMERICAN GODZILLA MOVIE

The creation of an American Godzilla movie in the 1990s seemed only logical given the success of director Steven Spielberg's dinosaur epic *Jurassic Park* (1993). Digital technology made realistic monsters possible on the screen. The American movie has Godzilla being discovered in the Pacific and shipped to New York City for study, where he breaks loose and wreaks havoc.

Tri-Star Pictures hired Jan de Bont, fresh from his success on the movie *Speed* (1994), to direct. De Bont believed only a huge epic could sell Godzilla to a 1990s audience. "You can do a Godzilla movie two ways," he declared, either "like the Japanese do it with men in costumes and miniatures," or "the other way is to do it right." Although he stressed the need for a compelling story, he seemed to view the digital special effects as key. Fortunately for him, it was two other filmmakers who would learn firsthand how wrong he was.

De Bont left the project over Tri-Star's refusal to let the budget exceed $100 million. The studio was subsequently acquired by Sony, who could afford to put that and more into a movie. The project fell into the hands of Dean Devlin and Roland Emmerich, creators of the hugely successful alien invasion movie *Independence Day* (1996). Hopes were high among fans and studio executives when the pair announced that their next project would be a Godzilla adaptation. It soon became the most anticipated film of 1998.

Posters, merchandise, and theatrical trailers (which did not show the monster) whetted the public's appetite. Other studios shuffled their summer release schedules; none wanted to open their movies opposite the King of the Monsters. Trouble appeared even before the movie's release. Devlin and Emmerich scrambled to make the announced release date of May 18, 1998. Time to finish the digital effects grew short, and they replaced many full-body shots of the monster with quicker, cheaper ones of the feet or tail. Fans and the press wondered why no still photos of the monster were being released. The budget reached $125 million, with tens of millions more spent on promotion.

Godzilla opened on May 20, 1998, to disparaging reviews and bad word-of-mouth. Many fans were unimpressed by the redesigned Godzilla, who looked and moved like a *Tyrannosaurus rex*. The scaled-down effects were further diminished by much of the action taking place at night, in the rain. The slim plot lifts elements from previous science fiction hits, including *Alien* (1979) and *Jurassic Park*. Large quantities of tie-in merchandise went unsold. Hard-core fans took to referring to the new monster by the acronym GINO (Godzilla in Name Only).

The dank, charmless film earned more than $130 million in the United States. *Godzilla* became the latest example of a relatively new species in Hollywood: the $100-million-plus grossing flop. Most in Hollywood agreed that, at least in the immediate future, a sequel was unlikely.

GODZILLA IN THE TWENTY-FIRST CENTURY

All was by no means lost for Toho's best-known creation. The 1998 American movie was released on VHS, laserdisc, and DVD, earning more than respectable figures on sales and rentals. An animated spin-off, titled *Godzilla: The Series*, aired on American and Japanese television from 1998 to 2000. Fan publications, such as *G-Fan*, and countless websites fed the public's appetite for news and discussion on the character.

Then, in 1999 Toho announced tentative plans for a new Japanese film that would take Godzilla into the new millennium. Titled in English, *Godzilla 2000* (1999) depicts Godzilla's battle with Orga, a mutated sea creature who takes on some of Godzilla's regenerative powers, and it was particularly successful in Japan. It was followed by another popular offering, *Godzilla vs. Megaguirus* (2000), as well as *Godzilla against MechaGodzilla* (2002), *Godzilla: Tokyo S.O.S.* (2003), and *Godzilla: Final Wars* (2004), the latter being a modernized, fast-paced take on the Godzilla franchise that was intended to celebrate the fiftieth anniversary of the original film. In 2009 Godzilla received a star on the Hollywood Walk of Fame.

Without a doubt, Godzilla is alive in the imagination of moviegoers worldwide. The subject of more than fifty films and video games, Godzilla is like Dracula or the Frankenstein monster: He is a part of American popular culture, and he will never die, no matter how many times movie heroes might kill him.

David L. Hixson

SEE ALSO: *Blockbusters; The Bomb; Burr, Raymond; Cold War; Comic Books; Disaster Movies; Fan Magazines; Frankenstein; Hanna-Barbera; Hollywood;* Jurassic Park; King Kong; *Nike; Spielberg, Steven;* Star Trek; Star Wars; *Superman; Video Games; World War II.*

BIBLIOGRAPHY

Aberly, Rachel. *The Making of Godzilla.* New York: HarperPrism, 1998.

Bock, Audie. *Japanese Film Directors.* New York: Kodansha International, 1978.

Bueher, Beverly Bare. *Japanese Films: A Filmography and Commentary, 1921–1989.* Jefferson, NC: McFarland, 1990.

Galbraith, Stuart, IV. *Japanese Science Fiction, Fantasy, and Horror Films: A Critical Analysis of 103 Features Released in the United States, 1950–1992.* Jefferson, NC: McFarland, 1994.

Glut, Donald. *Classic Movie Monsters.* Metuchen, NJ: Scarecrow, 1978.

Greenberger, Robert. *Meet Godzilla.* New York: Rosen Publishing, 2005.

Harmon, Jim. *The Godzilla Book.* San Bernardino, CA: Borgo Press, 1986.

Kalat, David. *A Critical History and Filmography of Toho's Godzilla Series.* Jefferson, NC: McFarland, 1997.

Lees, J. D., and Marc Cerasini. *The Official Godzilla Compendium.* New York: Random House, 1998.

Lent, John A. *The Asian Film Industry.* London: Christopher Helm, 1990.

Lovece, Frank. *Godzilla: The Complete Guide to Moviedom's Mightiest Monster.* New York: Morrow, 1998.

Mellen, Joan. *Voices from the Japanese Cinema.* New York: Liveright, 1975.

Tsutsui, William M. *Godzilla on My Mind: Fifty Years of the King of Monsters.* New York: Palgrave Macmillan, 2004.

Tsutsui, William M., and Michiko Ito, eds. *In Godzilla's Footsteps: Japanese Pop Culture Icons on the Global Stage.* New York: Palgrave Macmillan, 2006.

Tucker, Guy Mariner. *Age of the Gods: A History of the Japanese Fantasy Film.* Brooklyn, NY: Daikaiju Publishing, 1996.

Waldecki, Michael E. *Godzilla Goes to Hollywood.* M. E. Waldecki, 1985.

Gold, Mike *(1893–1967)*

Born to Jewish immigrants on New York's Lower East Side, Itzok Isaac Granich changed his name to Mike Gold to avoid persecution in the Red Scare of 1919. A Harvard dropout, he entered Greenwich Village circles in 1914 and became perhaps the most influential leftist literary critic of the 1920s. After authoring "Towards Proletarian Literature" (1921), a radical manifesto that encouraged writers to promote revolution, Gold assumed editorship of *New Masses* in 1926. In 1930 he published *Jews without Money*, a work of autobiographical fiction inspired by his tenement-house childhood. He spent the Depression decade writing for the communist *Daily Worker*. Brash, irreverent, and dogmatic, he praised the class-conscious radicalism of Woody Guthrie and Langston Hughes and assailed Ernest Hemingway and Thornton Wilder for failing to promote social change.

Gold's politics confined him to France in the late 1940s and 1950s and to relative obscurity in American literary history. His influence on radical writers, however, was recovered in the late 1990s.

Bryan Garman

SEE ALSO: *Communism; The Great Depression; Guthrie, Woody; Hemingway, Ernest; Hughes, Langston;* The Masses; *Red Scare; Wilder, Thornton.*

BIBLIOGRAPHY

Bloom, James D. *Left Letters: The Culture Wars of Mike Gold and Joseph Freeman.* New York: Columbia University Press, 1992.

Folsom, Michael, ed. *Mike Gold: A Literary Anthology.* New York: International Publications, 1972.

Goldberg, Rube *(1883–1970)*

Rube Goldberg was a professional cartoonist for more than sixty years, the creator of over a dozen nationally syndicated comic strips, and the winner of a Pulitzer Prize for political cartooning, yet he is remembered chiefly for one thing—the Rube Goldberg Invention. In various strips over the years, he concocted elaborate, multipart machines to perform the simplest of tasks. These struck readers as extremely apt comments on the overly complicated and often circuitous lives led by just about everybody in modern society. Eventually Goldberg's inventions earned him a listing in most dictionaries and made his name part of the language. Rube Goldberg Machine competitions continue to be held in high schools and colleges around America, and Purdue University has an annual national competition for the best Goldberg variations.

Born Reuben Lucius Goldberg to an affluent San Francisco family, Goldberg attended the University of California at Berkeley, and majored, at his father's urging, in engineering. But he was also in on the founding of the college humor magazine, the *Pelican*, to which he became a contributing cartoonist. By 1904, in spite of his engineering degree, young Goldberg was working on the *San Francisco Chronicle*, and a year later he was drawing sports cartoons for the *San Francisco Bulletin*. Soon he moved to New York City to draw for an assortment of newspapers, starting with the *Evening Mail*, at impressive increases in salary each time he moved to the next publication. He drew such daily strips and panels as *Mike and Ike, They Look Alike*, *Lunatics I Have Met*, *I'm the Guy*, *Cartoon Follies*, *The Candy Kid*, and *Foolish Questions*. This last-named panel, much imitated over the years, offered rude answers to obvious inquiries—"Q. Did your hat fall in the water? A. No, I threw it in there for some frogs to use as a ferry boat. Q. Is this number 99? A. No, mister, it's number 66—we turned the house upside down just for a change."

Goldberg began including inventions in his strips, often attributing them to Professor Lucifer Gorgonzola Butts, a sort of screwball anagram of his own full name. The inventions, which were presented in cartoon diagram form, involved not only sundry mechanical devices—especially pulleys—but ingredients that were not always readily available to more conventional inventors. These included a hungry goat, a dancing Eskimo, a miniature elephant, waltzing mice, a college boy, a penguin, an electric eel, Miss Las Vegas, and a palooka hound, plus numerous bowling balls, pistols, midgets, fish, and umbrellas. The components of each mechanism were labeled with letters of the alphabet so that readers could construct their own intricate machines to perform such simple tasks as opening a can, uncorking a bottle, or slicing bread. The typical description accompanying a Goldberg invention is exemplified by that for a device designed to wash dishes while one is out. It begins, "When spoiled tomcat (A) discovers he is alone he lets out a yell which scares mouse (B) into jumping into basket (C), causing lever end (D) to rise and pull string (E)," and so forth. Goldberg sometimes admitted that an invention might not function perfectly and so he offered alternatives. The dishwashing instructions concluded with, "If the cat and turtle get on to your scheme and refuse to cooperate, simply put the dishes on the front porch and pray for rain."

Goldberg's major Sunday page, *Boob McNutt*, began in 1915 and survived until 1934. The strip was syndicated in the Hearst papers by the McNaught Syndicate. It starred a plump, redheaded, and accident-prone young man, dressed somewhat like a silent movie comedian, who, as his name implied, was naive and none too bright. In *The Funnies: 100 Years of American Comic Strips*, Ron Goulart describes the feature as "an eclectic jumble of satire, burlesque, fantasy and cockeyed technology." From 1922 onward Boob was preoccupied with the courtship of a pretty girl named Pearl, who was the target of many a fiendish scheme constructed by the strip's villains. Mike and Ike—their panel defunct—joined the cast, along with Bertha the Siberian Cheesehound. Goldberg had done a mock adventure strip, *Bobo Baxter*, in the mid-1920s, and in the early 1930s he drew a serious daily, *Doc Wright*, which was ahead of its time, trying soap-opera continuities years before *Mary Worth* made them fashionable; it lasted less than two years.

LalaPalooza came along in 1936, daily and on Sundays, and concerned itself with the humorous adventures of the plump, rich Lala and her layabout brother Vincent. Even though Vincent came up with an invention in the Professor Butts vein now and then, *Lala* was not successful and ended in 1939. Next came Goldberg's last go-round in the funny papers with *Side Show*, a Sunday page that offered a hodgepodge of different features under one roof: *Little Butch*; *Brad and Dad*; and, of course, *Weekly Invention*. By then Goldberg was getting considerable help with the drawing from his longtime assistant Johnny Devlin. He and Devlin also had a hand in putting together *Feature Funnies* in 1937. When the comic book ceased reprinting *LalaPalooza* pages in its lineup, Devlin drew new ones, glamorizing and streamlining Lala considerably.

Goldberg began drawing political cartoons in the early 1940s for the *New York Sun*, and after the paper suspended publication he signed with the *New York Journal American* and King Features Syndicate. He had quite a bit of help from Warren King, who later became the political cartoonist for the *New York Daily News*. One of these collaborations won Goldberg a Pulitzer Prize in 1948. He also put together many cartoon books, wrote a novel, and helped found the National Cartoonist Society (NCS). The highest annual NCS award is called a Reuben in his honor.

Ron Goulart

SEE ALSO: *Comics; Hearst, William Randolph; Leisure Time; Mary Worth.*

BIBLIOGRAPHY

Goulart, Ron, ed. *The Encyclopedia of American Comics*. New York: Facts On File, 1990.

Goulart, Ron. *The Funnies: 100 Years of American Comic Strips*. Holbrook, MA: Adams, 1995.

Kinnaird, Clark, ed. *Rube Goldberg vs. the Machine Age*. New York: Hastings House, 1968.

Wolfe, Maynard Frank, and Rube Goldberg. *Rube Goldberg: Inventions*. New York: Simon & Schuster, 2000.

Goldberg, Whoopi *(1955–)*

Rising to prominence in the mid-1980s, Whoopi Goldberg has become one of the most recognizable faces in the entertainment industry as she moved easily between comedy and drama on both stage and screen. Her outspoken humor reflects her experiences as a former drug addict and welfare mother who moved from the depths of poverty to the heights of celebrity. Goldberg first gained significant critical attention in 1982 with the premiere of *Spook Show*, a one-woman review in which she played several characters. In 1985 she made her film debut in *The Color Purple*. Goldberg was one of the first African American actresses to achieve mainstream success, and her willingness to present her offscreen persona to the public has made her one of the most high-profile African Americans in popular culture.

Whoopi Goldberg. *Whoopi Goldberg poses with the Best Supporting Actress Oscar that she won in 1991 for her performance in* Ghost. RON GALELLA/WIREIMAGE/GETTY IMAGES.

EARLY LIFE AND CAREER

Born Caryn Johnson on November 13, 1955, Goldberg was raised in an area of New York City called Chelsea. She was an imaginative child who was encouraged by her mother to become a performer. Her life took a downward spiral, however, when she dropped out of school in the ninth grade. She began to use drugs, had several abortions, and found herself living on the streets. By age seventeen she had weaned herself off heroin, and she eventually married her drug counselor. The couple had one daughter, but the marriage was short-lived.

As a young single mother, Goldberg survived on welfare and a series of temporary jobs, including working as a bricklayer and as a mortician's makeup artist. Throughout this period she was determined to have a career in theater, and in 1974 she moved to the West Coast to perform with several drama and improvisation groups in the San Diego and San Francisco areas. About this time she began to use the professional name "Whoopi Cushion" so that agents and audiences would remember her. She subsequently changed her last name to "Goldberg" on the suggestion of her mother because it sounded more serious. Biographer James Robert Parish notes that Goldberg's gimmicky name soon gained her great attention: "Audiences were forever surprised that the owner of this odd Jewish-sounding name turned out to be an African American who had a strange hairdo and a very special look."

RISE TO SUCCESS

Goldberg's reputation grew with the premiere of *Spook Show*, which showcased her range of characterizations. Among her most popular personas were "Little Blonde Girl" and "Fontaine," an educated junkie. Goldberg populated each performance with more than a dozen alter egos who engaged audiences with their provocative views on contemporary society. In early 1983 director Mike Nichols saw her show and immediately offered to produce it on Broadway. Nichols's interest in Goldberg gained her much media attention and shifted her career into high gear. Steven Spielberg soon cast her as the abused Celie in the film version of Alice Walker's *The Color Purple* (1985). Goldberg's movie debut won raves, and she was nominated for the 1996 Academy Award for Best Actress. Meanwhile, in 1985 she won a Grammy Award for her comedy album *Whoopi Goldberg*.

After her promising start in film, Goldberg's career began to skid as she appeared in a series of forgettable and overly broad comedies such as *Jumpin' Jack Flash* (1986), *Burglar* (1987), and *Fatal Beauty* (1987). She rebounded in 1990 as Oda Mae Brown, a storefront medium, in the popular film *Ghost*. This performance earned her an Academy Award for Best Supporting Actress and made her the first black woman to win an Oscar since Hattie McDaniel in 1940. Goldberg's subsequent film work offered audiences a strong mix of comedy and drama. In *The Long Walk Home* (1990) she played a southern maid in the 1950s, and in Robert Altman's 1992 *The Player*, she had the role of a no-nonsense detective. Goldberg endeared herself to children as the voice of a hyena in *The Lion King* (1994) and enjoyed much acclaim for her *Sister Act* film comedies in 1992 and 1993, in which she plays a lounge singer who pretends to be a nun to avoid the mob.

In the 1990s Goldberg also performed in television programs. She starred in *Bagdad Café*, a mediocre sitcom, in 1990, and 1992 saw her as host of *The Whoopi Goldberg Show*, a syndicated talk show. She found some small-screen success through a recurring role as an alien on *Star Trek: The Next Generation* (1987–1994) and as the center square in a revival of the game show *Hollywood Squares* (1998–2004).

CONTROVERSIAL FIGURE

Goldberg's on-screen persona has tended to be that of a sassy, self-reliant, and always likable woman. However, she has also been known for being unafraid to court controversy. A number of prominent African Americans criticized her for a 1993 presentation at the Friars Club with then-companion Ted Danson, who appeared in blackface mouthing offensive jokes written by Goldberg. The pair later apologized for the incident. Later that year she angered some Jewish organizations with ethnic jokes in her contribution titled "Jewish American Princess Fried Chicken" for a fund-raising cookbook called *Cooking in Litchfield Hills*. In 2004 Goldberg made a controversial sexual joke about President George W. Bush at a Democratic fund-raiser for presidential candidate John Kerry. Slim-Fast, a weight-loss product for which Goldberg was a celebrity endorser, took offense at her comments and removed the comic from its ad campaign.

CAREER IN THE EARLY 2000s

Goldberg earned one of comedy's highest honors in 2001 when she became the first woman to be awarded the Mark Twain Prize for American Humor. The following year she won both a

Daytime Emmy Award for her role as host in *Beyond Tara: The Extraordinary Life of Hattie McDaniel* and a Tony Award as a producer for the musical *Thoroughly Modern Mille.* In 2002 she hosted the Academy Awards ceremonies for the fourth time. She reunited with Billy Crystal and Robin Williams in 2006 to co-host a Comic Relief telethon for the homeless as they had done in the late 1980s through late 1990s. Goldberg found success beginning in 2007 as a moderator on the popular daytime talk show *The View*, and as a producer, she helped bring a musical version of the *Sister Act* to Broadway. In 2011 the musical received five Tony Award nominations, including for Best Musical.

Charles Coletta

SEE ALSO: *Academy Awards; Altman, Robert; Animated Films; Apollo Theater; Broadway; Celebrity; Crystal, Billy; Daytime Talk Shows; Emmy Awards; Game Shows; Grammy Awards;* Hollywood Squares*;* The Lion King*; McDaniel, Hattie; Spielberg, Steven; Stand-Up Comedy;* Star Trek: The Next Generation*; Television; Tony Awards;* The View*; Walker, Alice; Williams, Robin.*

BIBLIOGRAPHY

Adams, Mary Agnes. *Whoopi Goldberg: From Street to Stardom.* New York: Dillon Press, 1993.

Bogle, Donald. *Blacks in American Films and Television.* New York: Garland Publishing, 1988.

Goldberg, Whoopi. *Is It Just Me?: Or Is It Nuts out There?* New York: Hyperion, 2011.

Parish, James Robert. *Whoopi Goldberg.* Secaucus, NJ: Carol Publishing Group, 1997.

Golden Books

From its humble beginnings in the Midwest, Golden Books developed into the most successful publisher and entertainment company for children in North America, with such classics as *Pat the Bunny* and *The Poky Little Puppy*. By the end of the twentieth century, in addition to storybooks, Golden Books Entertainment products included children's television productions, audio and video recordings, interactive software, educational workbooks, craft products, puzzles, party accessories, gift-wrap products, invitations, and stationery. At the time of Golden Books' fiftieth anniversary in 1992, there were more than 1,000 Golden Books titles.

In 1907 Edward Henry Wadewitz purchased a small printing company for less than $3,000. He and his partner, Roy A. Spencer, operated it in the basement of a building in Racine, Wisconsin. Incorporating small publishers, puzzle makers, playing-card manufacturers, and stationery engravers and adding high-volume printing equipment, the company grew under the name of Western Printing and Lithographing. The leap toward children's publishing began in 1933, when Wadewitz signed a contract with Walt Disney for exclusive book rights to all Disney-licensed characters. In 1939, with Simon & Schuster, Western printed Walt Disney's *Bambi*, the precursor to the Golden Books that would dominate the juvenile book market for the rest of the twentieth century. The series developed, by 1942, into Simon & Schuster's "Little Golden Books" line of hardcover, forty-two page, illustrated story books for children.

Little Golden Books became standard fare in home libraries from that decade on through the 1960s. In part, their appeal went beyond entertainment to include a smattering of educational value: the books' title pages included a note that the stories were "prepared under the supervision of Mary Reed, Ph.D., [who was associated with] Teachers College of Columbia University." But the main attraction came in owning these brightly illustrated, neatly bound, and affordable stories at a time before local public libraries included much in the way of children's literature. For the children who read them and the adults who purchased them, they suggested a value beyond their twenty-five-cent price. The books appeared to be expensive, with a distinct, gold-colored, foil trim along their spines. They contained a decorative space on the inside cover that read "This Little Golden Book belongs to," with a line for the child to personalize. And children loved the famous characters in the stories. With these features, the company created a sense that Golden Books provided a special treasure for each child who owned one.

In association with Whitman Publishing Company, Dell Publishing Company, Simon & Schuster Incorporated, and Walt Disney, Western Printing maintained the lead in children's favorites. Western moved its corporate headquarters to Fifth Avenue offices in New York and changed its name to Golden Books Family Entertainment Incorporated. Golden Books printed many popular titles that continue to be sold, from generation to generation. *Pat the Bunny*, first published in 1940, is noteworthy as one of the first touch-and-feel books for children and has been a continual best seller among children's books. *The Poky Little Puppy* (1942), one of the original twelve Golden Books, tells the story of an adventurous puppy; its sales exceeded fourteen million copies by the end of the twentieth century. Other celebrated publications from the company's early years include books about Lassie, the Lone Ranger, Mickey Mouse, Donald Duck, and other animated Disney characters, and a holiday collection including *Frosty the Snow Man*, *Rudolph the Red-Nosed Reindeer*, and *Baby's First Christmas*. Religious titles include *David and Goliath*, *Noah's Ark*, and *My Little Golden Book about God.*

The company's early domination of the children's book market enabled it to continually secure contracts with well-known children's authors, illustrators, and entertainers. Golden Books produced popular works by Margaret Wise Brown, Richard Scarry, and Mercer Mayer. The books often reflected popular culture by using children's television shows and toys for content. For example, in the 1950s Little Golden Books appeared featuring the following television characters: Howdy Doody, the Lone Ranger, and Captain Kangaroo. The 1960s books included Huckleberry Hound, Yogi Bear, the Flintstones, and Bozo the Clown. Later additions included books about Dora the Explorer, Thomas the Tank Engine, Barbie, Jim Henson's Muppets, and Sesame Street characters. Other popular stories to which Golden Books secured printing rights were Winnie-the-Pooh, Tarzan, and Star Wars. In the 1990s Golden Books bought rights to Shari Lewis productions, including videos and television shows featuring the famous Lamb Chop and Charlie Horse puppets. Even a European favorite, Ludwig Bemelmans's *Madeline*, became property of Golden Books with the production of Golden Books Entertainment videos based on Bemelmans's books.

As an indication of their place in American life, Little Golden Books was the focus of an exhibit at the Smithsonian Institution titled *Little Golden Books and American Culture 1942–*

1992. In 2001 the series was sold to Random House, which reports that, as of 2002, sales of Little Golden Books has surpassed two billion.

Sharon Brown

SEE ALSO: *Big Little Books; Disney (Walt Disney Company); Frosty the Snowman; Lassie; The Lone Ranger;* The Mickey Mouse Club; *Toys.*

BIBLIOGRAPHY

Jones, Dolores Blythe. *Bibliography of the Little Golden Books.* Westport, CT: Greenwood Publishing Group, 1987.

"Little Golden Books." Random House. Accessed November 13, 2011. Available from http://www.randomhouse.com/golden/lgb/

Marcus, Leonard S. *Golden Legacy: How Golden Books Won Children's Hearts, Changed Publishing Forever, and Became an American Icon along the Way.* New York: Golden Books, 2007.

Santi, Steve. *Collecting Little Golden Books: A Collector's Identification and Price Guide.* Iola, WI: Krause Publications, 2003.

Santi, Steve. *Warman's Little Golden Books: Identification and Price Guide.* Iola, WI: Krause Publications, 2006.

Golden Gate Bridge

The Golden Gate Bridge—with its soaring Art Deco design, its ability to sway 27.5 feet in high winds, and its arches posed against the backdrop of the sea—symbolizes San Francisco more than any other monument. The bridge, whose construction was overseen by chief engineer Joseph Strauss, spans a submerged cleft in the coastal mountain range, dubbed the "Golden Gate" by prospectors on their way to California's gold fields in the mid-1800s. When the bridge was completed in 1937, it was the world's longest suspension bridge (1.7 miles) and the highest structure west of New York (745 feet), a record it held until 1964 and the construction of the Verrazano-Narrows Bridge in New York.

The Golden Gate Bridge's daily load of approximately 100,000 vehicles is supported by cables that are 3 feet in diameter. When the thick fog pours in, rendering it invisible from land, the bridge's distinct color, "international orange," keeps seagulls from crashing into it.

Adrienne Russell

SEE ALSO: *Haight-Ashbury.*

BIBLIOGRAPHY

Golden Gate Bridge Official Website. Accessed January 2012. Available from http://goldengatebridge.org

Starr, Kevin. *Golden Gate: The Life and Times of America's Greatest Bridge.* New York: Bloomsbury Press, 2010.

The Golden Girls

The situation comedy *The Golden Girls,* which aired on NBC from 1985 to 1992, was one of television's first successful representations of the lives of older women and an unlikely hit in a television landscape populated by young, sexy performers in shows designed to appeal to a youthful audience. The series focused on four single women living together in Miami as they faced the issues of aging in America. Created by veteran television writer and producer Susan Harris, the show balanced controversial social themes with raucous, often ribald, humor. Starring a cast of seasoned actresses, who were all in their late fifties or early sixties, *The Golden Girls* emphasized that life does not end with menopause and that older women are still vital, energetic, and worthy of the attention of the mass viewing audience. Audience acceptance of the series was immediate. It placed in the top ten its premiere season by winning a following among all age groups. Strong public approval was matched by much critical praise. The series was thrice honored with a Best Comedy Emmy, and all of the leads earned Emmy Awards for their performances.

One of TV's dominant female voices, Harris (who wrote for *All in the Family* and *Maude* and created *Soap*) earned her greatest critical and commercial success with *The Golden Girls,* representing a breakthrough for women on television both in front of and behind the camera. In 1984 actress Selma Diamond appeared in a brief sketch titled "Miami Nice" at an NBC affiliates meeting. The performance was designed to test the audience's reaction to a comedy revolving around an older woman. The positive response to the piece encouraged NBC to purchase a pilot of the premise written by Harris.

Harris assembled a strong cast of actresses to play the group of women facing their "golden years" together. Bea Arthur, the star of *Maude,* played Dorothy, a loud divorcée and substitute teacher. She lived with housemates Blanche (Rue McClanahan), a lusty southern widow, and Rose (Betty White), a naive widow from a tiny town in Minnesota. The trio was joined by Sophia

The Golden Girls. *The cast of* The Golden Girls *included, clockwise from left, Estelle Getty, Bea Arthur, Betty White, and Rue McClanahan.* **THEO WESTENBERGER/NBC/NBCU PHOTO BANK/GETTY IMAGES.**

(Estelle Getty), Dorothy's Sicilian mother who moved in after a nursing-home fire. The pilot episode also featured actor Charles Levin as the women's gay housekeeper, but the character was dropped by the second show. The friendship of the "girls" as they supported each other through various problems became the core of the series.

The series' humor grew from Harris's distinctive writing and her actresses' strong characterizations. Arthur's Dorothy was an extension of her Maude character. Divorced from a husband who betrayed her with a younger woman, no-nonsense Dorothy embodied the sense of reason for the series as she demonstrated that a woman did not need a man to be happy. Throughout the series her more flighty roommates tested her patience. Blanche, as the southern belle struggling to hold onto her former glory, appeared to have stepped out of a Tennessee Williams play. Much of the show's raunchy humor came from her recounting a lifetime of wild sexual exploits. Rose provided a contrast to Blanche in that she was more innocent and conservative. A highlight of many episodes consisted of her telling stories about the loony inhabitants of her hometown of St. Olaf. The series' most popular character was the octogenarian Sophia, played by the much younger Getty. Her sarcasm was said to come from the effects of a stroke that destroyed the "tact" portion of her brain. This allowed the character to speak her mind and make jokes at the others' expense.

Harris gave her characters many opportunities to discuss issues beyond aging. Dorothy faced clinical depression, Rose befriended a lesbian, Blanche was distant with her children, and Sophia briefly remarried. Most of all, they displayed the strength of female bonding. In 1992 the series ended as Dorothy married and moved away. The remaining cast returned to TV the following year with the short-lived sitcom *The Golden Palace*, in which Rose, Blanche, and Sophia ran a small hotel on Miami Beach. *Empty Nest*, a more successful spin-off that featured the housemates' next-door neighbors, aired on NBC from 1988 to 1995. During its final two seasons Getty joined the cast to reprise her signature role of Sophia. This allowed her the rare opportunity to play the same character on three different television series.

LIFE AFTER THE SERIES

In 2010 White returned to sitcoms as a star of TVLand's *Hot in Cleveland*. Like *The Golden Girls*, it featured four women sharing a house. White's character, a wisecracking octogenarian, offered a contemporary spin on Getty's Sophia character. As for the other actresses, Arthur and McClanahan worked steadily for the remainder of their lives. Arthur had several notable television guest appearances late in her career. She played Larry David's mother on *Curb Your Enthusiasm*, voiced a malevolent "Femputer" on the animated *Futurama*, and was nominated for an Emmy as Outstanding Guest Actress in a Comedy Series for her role as a babysitter on *Malcolm in the Middle*. In 2002 she returned to Broadway starring in *Bea Arthur on Broadway: Just between Friends*, a collection of songs and stories from her life and career. She died in 2009.

McClanahan devoted herself to charity work and made occasional media appearances until her death in 2010. Most notably, she had a cameo role in the science fiction film *Starship Troopers*. Getty's later life saw the actress facing numerous health problems, such as Parkinson's disease and Alzheimer's. White, Arthur, and McClanahan last appeared together at the 2008 TVLand Awards to accept an award for their contributions to television history. Getty's failing health prevented her from attending, and she passed away later that year.

The Golden Girls proved both that audiences would accept older female characters on series television and that a woman could helm a series and provide it with a distinctive voice and personality. In *Prime Time, Prime Movers*, television historians David Marc and Robert Thompson view the series as an indicator of future programming as baby boomers age and begin to demand more senior characters on the small screen.

Charles Coletta

SEE ALSO: All in the Family; *Arthur, Bea; Baby Boomers; Emmy Awards;* Maude; *Sitcom; Television; White, Betty.*

BIBLIOGRAPHY

Cotter, Bill. *The Wonderful World of Disney Television.* New York: Hyperion, 1997.

Huryk, Harry R. *The Golden Girls: The Viewing Guide.* Los Angeles: Harry Huryk, 2006.

Marc, David, and Robert Thompson. *Prime Time, Prime Movers.* Boston: Little, Brown, 1992.

White, Betty. *Here We Go Again: My Life in Television.* New York: Scribner, 1995.

Goldwyn, Samuel *(1879–1974)*

One of the most successful early independent film producers, Samuel Goldwyn will be remembered for many of his classic films, for his uncultured style, and for his misuse of the English language—so-called Goldwynisms, such as "a verbal contract isn't worth the paper it's written on." Goldwyn was among a pioneering group of immigrant men who came to America and helped shape the Hollywood studio system.

Goldwyn was born Samuel Gelbfisz in Warsaw, Poland. In 1895 he immigrated to London and then New York State to make his fortune. Once in the United States, "Goldfish," as he was then called, obtained work at Louis Meyers and Son as a glovemaker, and by age eighteen he was one of the top glove salesmen in the world and a sales manager in the Elite Glove Company. When the woman he was trying to court married Jesse Lasky instead, Goldfish was introduced to Lasky's sister, Blanche. They married in 1910 and had a daughter, Ruth.

In 1913 Goldfish became interested in a career in the motion picture industry. His initial idea of owning movie theaters progressed to a desire to be a motion picture producer. Eventually he persuaded his brother-in-law to join him, and together they formed the Jesse Lasky Feature Play Company, with Goldfish managing sales for the company. In 1914 the company had its first release: Cecil B. DeMille's successful *The Squaw Man*, one of the first feature-length films made in Hollywood. In 1915 the Goldfishes divorced, and it was only a matter of time before Goldfish had a falling out with Lasky. The company's partners overthrew him, but when the company merged with Adolph Zukor's Famous Players to form Famous Players-Lasky Corporation, Zukor named Goldfish chairman of the board. By the end of 1916, however, Goldfish had managed to sabotage his position there and was forced to resign.

In November 1916 Goldfish established a partnership with the Selwyn brothers and formed Goldwyn Pictures. The company selected the original Leo the Lion as its company logo, and eventually Goldfish changed his last name to Goldwyn. He broke away from Goldwyn Pictures in 1922 after a contract dispute and was therefore only a stockholder when it merged to form Metro-Goldwyn-Mayer (MGM). He immediately formed a new Goldwyn Pictures Company and produced projects independently through United Artists. His first success as an independent producer, *The Dark Angel*, starred Ronald Colman and was released in 1925, the same year he married Frances Howard. The couple later had a son, Samuel Jr.

Although his output could not match the major studios, Goldwyn produced several successful movies. Colman, the only star he had under contract, starred in several of these: *Bulldog Drummond* (1929), *Stella Dallas* (1925), and *Dodsworth* (1936). In the early 1930s Goldwyn had what was perhaps his greatest failure. He discovered a Swedish actress named Anna Sten and was convinced he had found a star who would be greater than Greta Garbo. Unfortunately, Sten had a problem with the English language and did not show much talent. It took Goldwyn several years and several bad films before he admitted his mistake and released her from her contract.

The year 1939 is considered special for the number of classic films it produced. One of these was the Goldwyn film *Wuthering Heights*, which starred Laurence Olivier and Merle Oberon. That same year James Roosevelt, son of the U.S. president, was selected as president of United Artists. By 1940 Goldwyn and United Artists were calling it quits, and Goldwyn thereafter distributed his work through RKO Studios. He continued producing films that would become classics, such as *The Little Foxes* (1941) and *The Best Years of Our Lives* (1946), generally considered his finest. Its unflinching look at veterans returning home after World War II won nine Academy Awards.

In 1954 Goldwyn paid $1 million plus 10 percent of profits for the film rights to the Broadway musical *Guys and Dolls*—the largest sum paid up to that time. Although that film in 1955 and Goldwyn's final film, *Porgy and Bess*, in 1959 were minor successes, Goldwyn's time had passed, and he knew it. The golden era of Hollywood was over, and many of his contemporaries were dead. Goldwyn would survive until 1974, but his career was finished.

Jill A. Gregg

SEE ALSO: *Mayer, Louis B.; MGM (Metro-Goldwyn-Mayer); Olivier, Laurence; United Artists.*

BIBLIOGRAPHY

Berg, A. Scott. *Goldwyn: A Biography*. New York: Knopf, 1989.

Easton, Carol. *The Search for Sam Goldwyn: A Biography*. New York: Morrow, 1976.

Marx, Arthur. *Goldwyn: A Biography of the Man behind the Myth*. New York: Norton, 1976.

Golf

Golf is the strangest of games. Invented by the Scots perhaps as early as the twelfth or thirteenth century, it is played in an area that can vary in size anywhere from 30 to 200 acres; it can be an individual or a team sport; it is essentially a mental game rather than a physical one; and it pays homage to a concept largely ignored in other sports: aesthetics. Golf also has an established code of honor that is a rarity in most sports. A player who breaks a rule, accidental or not, is expected to penalize himself or herself.

To the eye, golf appears a sedate game devoid of action. To the player, it is a mind-numbing; physically demanding; and, more often than not, demeaning sport—a test of character more than athletic ability. It is game played in the mind, on a field awash with lush grass, stately trees, meandering creeks, and manicured greens, each of which are physically endearing but taken together represent an obstacle course to be negotiated for eighteen arduous holes. The ultimate and all-too-simple goal: to hit the ball as few times as possible.

THE LONG HISTORY OF GOLF

The story of golf is as much a tale about change as it is about great players, miraculous shots, and dramatic victories. Great players have been the constant in a game that has changed dramatically over the last 700 years. From wooden balls (prior to 1440), to feather-stuffed, leather-covered balls known as "featheries" (1440–1848), to gutta-percha balls made from the sap of trees indigenous to Malaysia (1848–1901), to rubber balls made from winding rubber thread around a solid rubber core (1901 to the present), to the solid core balls commonly used today, the game and its equipment has relentlessly evolved. And, of course, as balls changed, so did clubs.

The first clubs had shafts made of wood, probably ash. Wood clubs had long, broad heads, while the irons tended to have large faces, square toes, and nicked sockets. Sometime during the feather-ball period, perhaps in the late 1770s, clubmaking became profitable enough that artisans began taking up the craft. By the 1800s most shafts were made from ash or hickory, while all sorts of woods—beech, pear, apple—were used to fashion the heads of wooden clubs. Depending on the course, the number of holes also varied, usually ranging from five to eighteen. The shape and size of club heads were regularly changed in the early years of the game in order to improve accuracy, to increase distance, or both.

As time passed, the number of clubs also increased: from two or three in the 1600s, to four or five in the 1700s, to five or six in the 1800s, to eight or nine or even ten by the late 1900s. Today, a normal set of clubs numbers fourteen and can be made of materials with space-age sounding names like graphic, tungsten, and titanium. Every year hundreds of companies produce thousands of variations of golf clubs in what appears to be a never-ending technological war, all with the purpose of helping a golfer hit a little white ball toward a very small hole a long distance away.

Not surprisingly, the first golf club and course was established at St. Andrews, Scotland, in 1754, the place many golf historians believe the game was first played. (Some historians argue that the game may have been invented much earlier by the Romans, but there exists little substantial evidence to support this theory.) More than 100 years later, in 1857, St. Andrews hosted the first National Club Championship with eleven clubs participating. Three years later Willie Park became the first British Open champion when he won at Prestwick. The popularity of golf in the British Isles spread throughout the second half of the nineteenth century, and by 1888 the first club in the United States, also called St. Andrews, was open for play.

In 1895 the United States Golf Association (USGA) sponsored its first championship: the Men's Amateur. Before the end of the year, however, two other championships were contested: the Men's Open and the Women's Amateur. Championship golf was embraced by both the British and the Americans and laid the groundwork for golf's vast growth in the twentieth century on both the amateur and the professional levels.

Although the history of the game is difficult to compartmentalize because of its longevity, once golf clubs began to open and championships were initiated, three distinct periods can be discerned—the early period (1896–1916), the golden age (the 1920s, 1930s, and 1940s), and the television era. The beginning of the early period is marked by Harry Vardon's victory in the British Open in 1896 and ends with the formation of the Professional Golfers' Association (PGA) in 1916. The golden age was marked by some of the greatest legends the game has seen. In the 1920s two players dominated the game, Bobby Jones and Walter Hagen. By the 1930s, men like Gene Sarazen, Lawson Little, Sam Snead, Ben Hogan, Ralph Guldahl, Craig Wood, Henry Picard, and Jimmy Demaret pushed the game to even greater popularity.

In the early 1950s, Hogan and Snead held sway, but the popularity of the game reached an all-time high with the coming of Arnold Palmer and the television era. With his trademark attacking style and charismatic personality, Palmer revolutionized the game from a marketing standpoint, and television rushed in to capitalize. Although the game was still considered one played by the well-to-do, Palmer's dynamic style of play and his incredible popularity brought the game to millions of Americans who previously displayed little interest in the game.

PROFESSIONALS AND AMATEURS

Palmer's emergence in the 1950s as the dominant player also laid the groundwork for a recurring theme in golf—head-to-head competition for the top spot. In the 1920s Jones and Hagen battled; in the 1940s it was Hogan and Snead. By the 1960s Palmer and Jack Nicklaus had become the marquee players. In each instance the result was the same—the game grew in popularity. Although Nicklaus has since been named golfer of the twentieth century, he, too, was challenged by players like Tom Watson, Johnny Miller, and later Greg Norman. In the 1990s the newest "personalities" in golf—Tiger Woods and the Ryder Cup (a team competition between the best golfers in Europe and the United States)—were responsible for popularizing the sport to heights never previously attained.

Another popular personality on the PGA tour was American golfer Phil Mickelson. For years he was labeled "the best golfer never to win a major," but in 2004 he broke through by winning the Masters. By 2010 he had also racked up a PGA tournament and two more Masters wins. Mickelson further endeared himself to the public by his strong support for his wife, Amy, during her struggle with breast cancer. Woods continued to rule the golf world through the first decade of the 2000s as he seemed on track to surpass Nicklaus's record number of major victories by winning his fourteenth in 2008. Then in the 2010s Woods abruptly fell from dominance after a series of personal problems came to light in late 2009. Since then, the focus has been on which of the rising young stars, such as Rory McIlroy of Northern Ireland, would capture the public's fancy as the face of golf.

At the professional level, golf appears to be in an upward growth pattern. Besides the PGA pro tour in the United States, professionals play on tours in Asia, Europe, Africa, and Latin America. There is a women's tour (the LPGA); a senior tour; and the Nationwide tour, for players attempting to earn their way into the more lucrative PGA tour. The late 1990s and first decade of the 2000s saw winners coming from new regions, with Fijian Vijay Singh, Argentine Angel Cabrera, and South Korean Y. E. Yang all winning major championships on the PGA tour. The first decade of the twentieth century also saw a couple of older players make improbable runs at major wins. In 2009 fifty-nine-year-old Tom Watson led the British Open for most of the tournament, only to lose in a four-hole playoff. The year before, fifty-three-year-old Greg Norman led the tournament after the third round.

Golf, however, still exists primarily for the amateur player. Perhaps the most dramatic change in recent years (besides the ongoing technological changes in club design and composition) has been demographic. More Americans than ever play—28.6 million in 2008—and more blue-collar workers—about 34 percent of all golfers—have taken up what once was once termed the "Royal and Ancient Sport." In the United States, women now constitute about 20 percent of the golfing population, and more minorities and children are playing the game due to the influence of players such as Woods.

Since 1970 the number of players has increased by more than seventeen million, while the number of golf courses has risen to about 16,000 in 2012. (The number was higher in the peak year of 2006, but a number of courses closed because of the recession that began in late 2007.) While the game has traditionally been considered one played by rich people on private courses, more than 70 percent of the courses in the United States are open to the public, and four out of every five courses being built are public facilities.

However, the exclusion of minorities and women from many private clubs, at least until recently, had for years been golf's "dirty little secret." The original constitution of the PGA of America required that members be Caucasian, and not until black golfer Bill Spiller filed suit against the PGA did that change in the early 1950s. Unfortunately, conservative traditionalism blended with elitism to keep most private country clubs "white only" facilities well into the 1980s. When it was revealed that Shoal Creek Country Club near Birmingham, Alabama, the site of the 1990 PGA championship, had no black members, adverse publicity seemed to accomplish what years of criticism failed to yield—a realization among many private clubs that exclusionary policies were both racist and nonproductive. Within a year of the 1990 PGA, both Shoal Creek and Augusta National, the home of the Masters tournament and generally considered the last bastion of segregated golf, had black members. Other clubs around the country followed suit. With the emergence in the 1990s of Woods, who is part African American, as one of the best players in the world and the biggest drawing card since Palmer, the golfing public is more integrated than ever before.

Lloyd Chiasson Jr.

SEE ALSO: *Didrikson, Babe; López, Nancy; The Masters Golf Tournament; Nicklaus, Jack; Palmer, Arnold; Rodríguez, Chi Chi; Sports Heroes; Treviño, Lee; Vardon, Harry; Watson, Tom; Woods, Tiger.*

BIBLIOGRAPHY

Atha, Antony. *The World of Golf.* London: Reed, 1997.

Barkow, Al. *Gettin' to the Dance Floor: An Oral History of American Golf.* New York: Atheneum, 1986.

Browning, Robert. *History of Golf.* Stamford, CT: Classics of Golf, 1985.

Concannon, Dale. *Golf: The Early Days.* New York: Smithmark, 1995.

Frost, Mark. *The Match: The Day the Game of Golf Changed Forever.* New York: Hyperion, 2007.

Grimsley, Will. *Golf: Its History, People, and Events.* Englewood Cliffs, NJ: Prentice-Hall, 1966.

Jerris, Rand, and United States Golf Association. *Golf's Golden Age: Bobby Jones and the Legendary Players of the 10s, 20s, and 30s.* Washington, DC: National Geographic, 2005.

Gone with the Wind

Gone with the Wind, the epic Civil War–era novel and film, has no equal when it comes to longevity and profitability. The film continues to captivate audiences and generate profits more than seventy years after its release in 1939. Meanwhile, for many readers, Margaret Mitchell's novel, published in 1936, supersedes history in its depiction of the Civil War. Though it has been called racist and inaccurate by historians who find its sugarcoating of the Old South and the Ku Klux Klan appalling, *Gone with the Wind* has created an industry of literary and commercial output that shows no sign of slowing down. It is popular worldwide, particularly in Japan, Germany, and Russia, perhaps indicating that it has a special resonance for nations that have experienced defeat and occupation. In fact, *Gone with the Wind*'s most powerful moment comes when a famished, exhausted, and defiant Scarlett O'Hara vows: "As God is my witness they are not going to lick me. . . . If I have to lie, steal, cheat, or kill . . . I'll never be hungry again!"

A PHENOMENON

Mitchell only reluctantly allowed her *Gone with the Wind* manuscript to be published and was stunned and overwhelmed by its success. The winner of the Pulitzer Prize in 1937, it was a Depression-era sensation. Overall, only the Bible has sold more copies than *Gone with the Wind.* The film adaptation premiered to immediate acclaim, culminating with ten Academy Awards. *Gone with the Wind* reigned as the box-office champion until the 1970s and remains the most popular film of all time (when dollars are adjusted for inflation). Nevertheless, the love story between Scarlett O'Hara and Rhett Butler has suffered the barbs of some critics, who have described the novel as "slick, successful but essentially mediocre fiction . . . ; [*Gone with the Wind*] wobbles badly like an enormous house on shaky underpinnings."

Gone with the Wind is a rich, sentimental, and starkly partisan story of a charming and selfish Southern belle, Scarlett, who recklessly pursues the wrong man, the genteel Ashley Wilkes, throughout the narrative, which spans the Civil War and Reconstruction. She marries three times, enduring war, famine, and personal tragedy. At the story's end—after the death of the saintly Melanie Wilkes, who resolutely stood by Scarlett despite her pursuit of Melanie's husband—Scarlett finally recognizes that Rhett is indeed her true love. By then, however, it is too late—Rhett is weary of her contrivances and is

Gone with the Wind. *Clark Gable as Rhett Butler works his charm on Vivien Leigh's Scarlett O'Hara in the 1939 classic* Gone with the Wind. **HULTON ARCHIVE/GETTY IMAGES.**

about to leave her. As he is walking out the door, Scarlett asks him the heartfelt question, "Oh, where shall I go, what shall I do?" His answer is one of the most famous exit lines in literary history: "Frankly, my dear, I don't give a damn." True to form, Scarlett sniffs a bit but then declares brightly: "I'll get him back. . . . I'll think about that tomorrow. After all, tomorrow is another day!"

WRITING THE BOOK

Much has been made of the connections between the flirtatious and determined Scarlett and her creator. Mitchell (who had first named her character Pansy) was a young reporter who stubbornly went her own way through life: routinely flying in the face of Atlanta, Georgia, society; marrying (and divorcing) the unsuitable and abusive Red Upshaw; and then marrying his best friend, John Marsh. Marsh is best known for his literary midwifery: he brought a typewriter to his restless wife, who at the time was mending from an accident, and suggested she write her novel. From these modest beginnings sprang the phenomenon of *Gone with the Wind*: "I would go to the apartment and frequently she was at that little table where she worked," recalled Harvey Smith, a friend of Mitchell's. "We all joked about it: 'Well, you know she's writing the world's greatest novel.' . . . And, by God, she was."

Mitchell furtively wrote her epic novel in a tiny, cramped apartment in a down-at-the-heels house in midtown Atlanta; she affectionately called the place "The Dump." While she drew on her own life to create her characters, her primary inspiration was her family lore: her mother Maybelle and particularly her grandmother Fitzgerald were her models for Scarlett. Mitchell's Irish Catholic background allowed her to further enhance her tale: Gerald O'Hara, a successful immigrant plantation owner, rebukes his frivolous daughter and stirs within her a spiritual connection to Tara, the family plantation. "Why, land's the only thing in the world worth working for, worth fighting for, worth dying for, because it's the only thing that lasts," he tells her. Indeed, this connection to land is the unifying theme of *Gone with the Wind.*

SEARCHING FOR SCARLETT

Ignoring the standard wisdom that Civil War films were "box-office poison," producer David O. Selznick fought to bring the novel to the screen. In his wheeling and dealing, he lost the majority of the financial rights to the film to Metro-Goldwyn-Mayer in return for the coveted services of the "King of Hollywood," Clark Gable. The film's preproduction is legendary in itself—most notably because of the "Search for Scarlett," a publicity stunt dreamed up by publicist Russell Birdwell in which there was a nationwide search for the right woman to portray Mitchell's heroine. The episode was portrayed amusingly by Garson Kanin in his novel and television film *Moviola: The Scarlett O'Hara War* (1979 and 1980, respectively). The screen tests of actresses both famous and relatively unknown are an indication of how fiercely this battle raged in Hollywood: Paulette Goddard, Bette Davis, and Alabama-born Tallulah Bankhead claimed they alone could portray Scarlett, and even arch-Yankee Katharine Hepburn was discussed.

Although there is considerable dispute about the way Selznick found Vivien Leigh, the exquisite British actress who would win an Oscar for her portrayal of Scarlett, the legend is that his brother Myron, a leading agent, brought her to the set of the "Burning of Atlanta" scene, arguably the most famous sequence of the film. "I want you to meet Scarlett O'Hara," Myron said as the flames consumed old sets and illuminated Leigh's lovely face. In fact, she had been brought to Selznick's attention earlier, but the contrived "introduction" may indeed have persuaded him, as he confided to his wife, Irene, in a letter, calling her "the Scarlett dark horse, she looks damn good."

FILLING OUT THE CAST

Securing the other leads proved to be problematic as well, especially in the case of Leslie Howard, who resisted being cast as Ashley. Howard believed himself to be too old and miscast as the hopelessly idealistic and weak-willed character. Gable, the overwhelming choice of the public for Rhett, was also hesitant about joining the film. He feared he wouldn't be able to handle the part of the blockade-running romantic lead. Said Gable: "It wasn't that I didn't appreciate the compliment the public was paying me. It was simply that Rhett was too big an order. I didn't want any part of him. . . . Rhett was too much for any actor to tackle in his right mind." Olivia de Havilland, under contract by Warner Brothers, effectively wore down the resistance of the studio heads with her persistence to be cast as Melanie. She knew the role would establish her as a serious performer. One of the film's finest performances is Hattie McDaniel's Mammy; her sensitive and slyly subversive portrayal won the Academy Award for Best Supporting Actress, the first Oscar ever by a black actor. Butterfly McQueen, both memorable and controversial as Scarlett's skittish and indolent servant Prissy, similarly transformed what might have been a one-note characterization by a lesser talent.

Further complicating matters, the production had three directors. George Cukor was fired early on, although de Havilland and Leigh secretly sought his advice afterward. His replacement was Victor Fleming, Gable's close friend and a "man's director," but he walked off the picture, and Sam Wood was brought in. Leigh, featured in nearly every scene, worked constantly and permanently damaged her fragile health. Sidney Howard's script trimmed some characters and the plot, yet it remained remarkably faithful to the book. Finally, after eleven months of shooting and more than $4 million spent, *Gone with the Wind* premiered in a much-ballyhooed spectacle in Atlanta that was attended by the stars, Selznick, and Mitchell.

AN ENDURING APPEAL

The cultural impact of the film cannot be overestimated. In southern theaters as late as the 1960s, the technically astonishing and highly effective crane shot of the ragged Confederate flag fluttering over the vast assembly of Atlanta's dead and wounded provoked sobs, applause, and spontaneous emotion, including the occasional "rebel yell." The film's length of 222 minutes (broken up by an intermission) was not a deterrent, as audiences were swept up in the story line. Max Steiner's stirring "Tara's Theme" has become an iconic movie score. Film historian Leonard Maltin calls *Gone with the Wind* "if not the greatest film ever made, certainly one of the greatest examples of storytelling on film." Even in numerous rereleases and after being shown on television many times, *Gone with the Wind* continues to do well. In 1998 a restoration of the film's original negative led to lucrative video and DVD releases, as well as a theatrical rerelease. A spectacularly visual film, *Gone with the Wind* uses Technicolor to its greatest effect; William Cameron Menzies's brilliant cinematography remains a landmark achievement.

Gone with the Wind has unlimited kitsch potential: from Madame Alexander dolls and Scarlett Christmas ornaments to souvenir books (including the *Gone with the Wind Cookbook*, which has plenty of recipes from Mammy and Melanie but none from Scarlett); fan clubs; websites crammed with trivia and news; and professional Scarlett, Melanie, and Rhett look-alikes, the story continues to fascinate. Bed and breakfasts (notably the Inn Scarlett in Georgia) offer fans a *Gone with the Wind* immersion experience, and exact replicas of the famed "Green Curtain" and "Barbecue" dresses are widely available. The movie has been the subject of many parodies—memorably by comedian Carol Burnett, who lampooned Scarlett while wearing the "Green Curtain" dress with the rod intact. "The Dump," handsomely restored by the German company Daimler-Benz, survived two arson attempts and opened in 1997. It is a favorite tourist destination.

The literary merit of Mitchell's book has been favorably reassessed by numerous critics, and with the rise of Southern history and literature as a subject of scholarship, *Gone with the Wind* has become a touchstone, spawning many symposiums and studies, with Scarlett lionized as "modern" and a feminist heroine. In 1988 the Mitchell estate finally authorized a sequel, and *Scarlett*, by romance writer Alexandra Ripley, appeared three years later. Though it was panned by critics, the book was commercially successful. A CBS 1994 miniseries based on the book was similarly popular. In 2007 a second authorized sequel, *Rhett Butler's People* by Donald McCaigretold, was published. The novel is told from Butler's point of view. In 2011, for the seventy-fifth anniversary of the publication of the book, a commemorative edition was released featuring the original cover art.

Mary Hess

SEE ALSO: *Academy Awards; Best Sellers; Blockbusters; Cukor, George; Gable, Clark; McDaniel, Hattie; McQueen, Butterfly; MGM (Metro-Goldwyn-Mayer); Mitchell, Margaret; Romance Novels; Selznick, David O.; War Movies.*

BIBLIOGRAPHY

Behlmer, Rudy, ed. *Memo from David Selznick*. New York: Viking Press, 1972.

Brown, Ellen F., and John Wiley Jr. *Margaret Mitchell's "Gone with the Wind": A Bestseller's Odyssey from Atlanta to Hollywood*. Lanham, MD: Taylor Trade Publishing, 2011.

Dooley, Roger. *From Scarface to Scarlett: American Films in the 1930s*. New York: Harcourt, Brace, Jovanovich, 1979.

Dowling, Claudia Glenn. "The Further Adventures of Scarlett O'Hara." *Life*, May 1988.

Flamini, Roland. *Scarlett, Rhett, and a Cast of Thousands: The Filming of "Gone with the Wind."* New York: Macmillan, 1975.

Hanson, Elizabeth I. *Margaret Mitchell*. Boston: Twayne Publishers, 1991.

Haskell, Molly. *Frankly, My Dear: "Gone with the Wind" Revisited*. New Haven, CT: Yale University Press, 2009.

Haver, Ronald. *David O. Selznick's "Gone with the Wind."* New York: Bonanza Books, 1986.

King, Richard H. *A Southern Renaissance: The Cultural Awakening of the American South, 1930–1955*. New York: Oxford University Press, 1980.

Mitchell, Margaret. *Gone with the Wind*. New York: Macmillan, 1936.

Myrick, Susan, and Richard Harwell, eds. *White Columns in Hollywood: Reports from the "GWTW" Sets*. Macon, GA: Mercer University Press, 1982.

O'Dowd, Niall. "Frankly, Scarlett . . . We Do Give a Damn." *Irish America*, November 1981.

Pratt, William. *Scarlett Fever: The Ultimate Pictorial Treasury of "Gone with the Wind," Featuring the Collection of Herb Bridges*. New York: Macmillan, 1977.

Pyron, Darden Asbury, ed. *Recasting "Gone with the Wind" in American Culture*. Miami: University Presses of Florida, 1983.

Taylor, Helen. *Scarlett's Women: "Gone with the Wind" and Its Female Fans*. New Brunswick, NJ: Rutgers University Press, 1989.

Good Housekeeping

By dint of its very title, *Good Housekeeping* magazine stands as a symbol of a past era in American life. Along with *Redbook*, *Woman's Day*, *Ladies' Home Journal*, and others, *Good Housekeeping* belongs to what is known in industry parlance as the "Seven Sisters" of women's service magazines and achieved its most pervasive success in an era when the bulk of middle-class women stayed at home and focused their energies on cooking, cleaning, and raising their children. *Good Housekeeping* and its cohorts "gradually built up the power of the matriarchy," writes John Tebbel and Mary Ellen Zuckerman in *The Magazine in America, 1741–1990*. "Mom was . . . a figure of responsibility, dignity, and authority in the magazines." *Good Housekeeping*, however, differed from the other women's service magazines in its slightly elitist air; clearly aimed at women running economically stable households, in its heyday the periodical featured articles on such topics as how to choose a children's camp and understanding the capital gains tax.

EARLY FOCUS

Good Housekeeping began in 1885 as a ten-cent biweekly founded in Holyoke, Massachusetts, by Clark W. Bryan, a local journalist. Following on the heels of the success of *Ladies' Home Journal*, from the start *Good Housekeeping* catered to the young, affluent homemaker, a distinction that set it apart from its competitors in the field. It did not shy away, for instance, from feature stories on how to deal with hired household help. The first edition solicited reader contributions for a write-in contest on the topic "How to Eat, Drink and Sleep as a Christian Should." In 1891 the magazine became a monthly, and in 1911 it was acquired by the Hearst publishing empire, and its offices relocated to New York City.

From the start *Good Housekeeping* offered domestic guidance in the form of recipes, etiquette advice, and child care issues; it also contained more fiction and poetry in its pages than other women's magazines. In 1900 the magazine founded its famous Good Housekeeping Institute (GHI), which moved to state-of-the-art facilities in New York in 1912 and came under the guidance of a renowned former chemist from the U.S. Department of Agriculture. The GHI conducted research into food purity, tested products for safety, and in general brought a scientific approach to housekeeping. Its findings often became editorial features in the magazine itself, and starting in 1902 the magazine offered its "Ironclad Contract," the promise that any product advertised in *Good Housekeeping* would perform as promised. The "Seal of Approval" evolved over the next few decades in legal language and scope of guarantee in order to deal with the enforced compromises that result from this problematic mix of editorial focus and advertising revenue.

Circulation hit one million in the 1920s, and the magazine—like much of the old-money, upper-middle class in America—was virtually unaffected by the Great Depression of the 1930s, though its competitors suffered. Much of *Good Housekeeping*'s tone was set in the years between 1913 and 1942 under editor William Frederick Bigelow. (The magazine did not have its first female editor until 1994.) Bigelow introduced renowned writers such as W. Somerset Maugham and Booth Tarkington to the roster of fiction contributors, and the illustrations came from the pens of celebrated American artists such as Charles Dana Gibson. Keeping true to the magazine's focus on the sanctity of motherhood, its cover featured illustrations of children, at least through the 1950s; adult celebrities began appearing in the 1960s, but the December issue almost always still features an elaborate gingerbread house or a tray of Christmas cookies, with recipes inside the magazine.

CONTINUING EVOLUTION

In the golden era of the Seven Sisters—the 1950s and 1960s, when circulation and advertising pages reached an all-time high—*Good Housekeeping* continued to set itself apart from, and above, its competitors in the field. It maintained its policy against liquor or tobacco advertising and shied away from the tragic first-person tales found in other women's magazines, though it did have an advice column written by Dr. Joyce Brothers. An etiquette column from Elizabeth Post, a descendant of the legendary authority Emily Post, gave readers advice about table manners and dealing with nosy neighbors; Elizabeth Post's daughter-in-law Peggy took over the column in the late 1990s.

After reaching a circulation high of 5.5 million in 1966, *Good Housekeeping* lost readership—and advertising revenues—over the subsequent decades, as more American women entered the workforce on a full-time, permanent basis. *Redbook* and other service publications responded to the trend, focusing their features and advice on how to manage both a household and a job outside the home, but *Good Housekeeping* did not. By the early 1990s this orthodoxy had served the magazine well, and it began promoting itself to a new demographic: career women who were giving up work in their thirties to become full-time suburban moms. During this period the magazine launched its "New Traditionalist" ad campaign to attract readers and revenue with this focus.

Beginning in 2006 the magazine underwent another overhaul by updating its look and dividing content among several departments, all of which had "Good" in their names, including "Good Health," "Good Food," and "Good Buzz." In tandem with these changes, the magazine renewed focus on the trustworthiness of the Good Housekeeping Seal and the product tests conducted in its laboratory. As a result, *Good Housekeeping*'s circulation has remained strong, at four million in 2010, and it is still one of the top performers in the Hearst media empire.

Carol Brennan

SEE ALSO: *Bok, Edward; Brothers, Dr. Joyce; Etiquette Columns;* Family Circle*; The Great Depression; Hearst, William Randolph;* Redbook*; Tarkington, Booth;* Woman's Day.

BIBLIOGRAPHY

Endress, Kathleen L., and Therese L. Lueck, ed. "Good Housekeeping." In *Women's Periodicals in the United States: Consumer Magazines.* Westport, CT: Greenwood Press, 1995.

McCracken, Ellen. "*Good Housekeeping* and *McCall's*: Safe Consumerism and Ideological Formation." In *Decoding Women's Magazines: From "Mademoiselle" to "Ms."* New York: St. Martin's Press, 1993.

Mott, Frank Luther. "Good Housekeeping." In *A History of American Magazines*, vol. 5. Cambridge, MA: Harvard University Press, 1968.

Peterson, Theodore Bernard. *Magazines in the Twentieth Century*, 2nd ed. Urbana: University of Illinois Press, 1964.

Tebbel, John William, and Mary Ellen Zuckerman. *The Magazine in America, 1741–1990.* New York: Oxford University Press, 1991.

Walker, Nancy A. *Women's Magazines, 1940–1960: Gender Roles and the Popular Press.* New York: Palgrave Macmillan, 1998.

"The Way We Were! The Way We Are!" Special supplement. *Good Housekeeping*, February 1990.

Wood, James Playsted. *Magazines in the United States*, 3rd ed. New York: Ronald Press, 1971.

The Good, the Bad, and the Ugly

The last and most expensive of director Sergio Leone's "Dollar" trilogy of films grossed a respectable $6.1 million in 1966 and solidified Clint Eastwood's status as a major Western star. Following the success of Leone's *A Fistful of Dollars* (*Per un pugno di dollari*, 1964) and *For a Few Dollars More* (*Per qualche dollaro in più*, 1965), *The Good, the Bad, and the Ugly* (*Il buono, il brutto, il cattivo*, 1966) represents the aesthetic high point of the Italian-produced Western, or Spaghetti Western. The film revitalized the Western hero through Eastwood's portrayal of the calculating "Man with No Name," and its international influence, energized by Leone's vibrant film style and Ennio Morricone's didactic score, permanently altered popular conception of the Western genre and its themes.

DIRECTION BY LEONE

The plot of *The Good, the Bad, and the Ugly* follows the progress of three ruthless gunfighters racing to seize $200,000 in stolen Confederate gold that has been buried. Beginning the film with a series of three murder scenes carefully constructed with his signature style of bravado exposition, Leone employs extreme long shots and close-ups, piercing sound spikes, and dramatic freeze frames to introduce Tuco "the Ugly" (Eli Wallach), Angel Eyes "the Bad" (Lee Van Cleef), and Blondie "the Good" (Clint Eastwood). As the story unfolds, the three characters form and break alliances as they seek the treasure.

The epic design of Leone's scenarios reshaped the image of the Western in film. After early collaborations with innovators such as Michelangelo Antonioni and Robert Aldrich, Leone gave the scenes in his Westerns an obviously distorted, often frenetic perspective. Unlike the stagy studio sets of "B"-grade Hollywood

The Good, the Bad, and the Ugly. *Clint Eastwood, Lee Van Cleef, and Eli Wallach play out the climactic scene from* The Good, the Bad, and the Ugly, *the last of Sergio Leone's "Dollar" trilogy, released in 1966.* UNITED ARTISTS/GETTY IMAGES.

Westerns, Leone's camera expanded adobe farmhouses and barren deserts into exaggerated oceans of space peopled by minuscule though deadly specks of humanity. No Western since John Ford's dramatic Monument Valley films had offered such profoundly dynamic compositions.

Leone's wild spectacles of dueling gunfighters, public hangings, Civil War battles, and prison camps create a darkly comic, self-consciously chaotic view of Western society. At one point, Tuco and Blondie fight off a pack of assassins in the middle of a ghost town under artillery fire. As artillery shells demolish the buildings around them, Tuco and Blondie nonchalantly utilize the rising dust as cover and peep out of newly formed craters to survey their enemies. Leone's freewheeling camerawork reaches its expressive heights during the montage of whip pans and zooms that depict the finale of an absurdly bloody Civil War battle on a bridge and during the tension-building long shots that commence the climactic three-way gunfight in a sprawling deserted cemetery.

SCORE BY MORRICONE

Much of *The Good, the Bad, and the Ugly*'s success depends upon Morricone's infamously parodic score. In a discordant aural accompaniment to the title sequence's crazed animations and incongruous antique fonts, Morricone's campy revision of distinctive Western sounds gives the film a Monty Python–flavored musical edge. For *The Good, the Bad, and the Ugly,* Morricone deconstructs clichés of the Western soundtrack to create a distinctively catchy theme of shriek-propelled, psychedelic yodeling that became as popular as Eastwood's nameless hero. In 1968 the album of the soundtrack reached number four on the American Billboard 200. With all its crazed energy, Morricone's score thematically accentuates key moments of Leone's narrative through its invocation of familiar Western harmonies. In *Once upon a Time: The Films of Sergio Leone,* Robert Cumbow explains:

> The score to *The Good, the Bad, and the Ugly* taps Civil War movie conventions in its use of a lilting sentimental ballad played off a recurring march tune. The ballad, "Story of a Soldier," is derivative of the Confederate standard "Lorena" (a leading motif in Max Steiner's score to *The Searchers* . . . and in David Buttolph's music for *The Horse Soldiers*, for which it is the main theme). Sung phonetically by an Italian chorus, the lyrics of the song are only sporadically intelligible, but they reflect an antiwar tone consistent with both the film's treatment of war and the prevailing mood of ballads appearing during the period.

Cumbow also notes that the innovative use of human voices and unconventional instruments in the soundtracks to all three "Dollar" films is an especially affecting element of "Morricone's offbeat orchestration." In *The Good, the Bad, and the Ugly,* Morricone's campy vocal orchestrations amplify not only the opening credits but also the introductory vignettes and Tuco's frantic, nearly orgasmic search for the buried gold in the cemetery.

THE ROLE OF TUCO

In many ways, the spectacle of Wallach's drunken, disheveled Tuco embodies the heart of Leone's film. Eastwood is undoubtedly the box-office star, but the plot and the camera continually privilege Tuco's furious escapades. Grinning, chuckling, and thieving his way through crowds of bitterly serious supporting characters, his vulgarity, tenacity, and humor make him the most endearing of the three principal characters. Leone gives Tuco the most entertaining scenes as he crashes half-shaven through a barbershop window after plugging three bounty hunters, makes faces at an appalled elderly bystander during his own execution, and surprises a would-be assassin by hiding his pistol under the froth of his bubble bath. Tuco even rules the final moments of Leone's 161-minute film as his cursing of Blondie rises in a shocking echo that initiates the last flourish of Morricone's score. Tuco clearly personifies the aesthetic agenda of Leone's entire "Dollar" trilogy.

In *The Good, the Bad, and the Ugly*, themes of war, murder, and greed fuse into a pseudo-serious, gore-punctuated epic that intercuts Tuco's torture scene with the lilting strains of a band in a Civil War prison camp. Combining the deadly serious with the sickly comic, Leone's entertaining, anarchic Western formula parallels James Whale's horror films from Universal Studios, Stanley Kubrick's satirical science fiction, and Tim Burton's gothic Batman series.

Daniel Yezbick

SEE ALSO: *Eastwood, Clint; Ford, John; Kubrick, Stanley; Leone, Sergio; Spaghetti Westerns; The Western.*

BIBLIOGRAPHY

Cumbow, Robert. *Once upon a Time: The Films of Sergio Leone.* Metuchen, NJ: Scarecrow Press, 1987.

Frayling, Christopher. *Spaghetti Westerns.* Boston: Routledge & Kegan Paul, 1981.

Leinberger, Charles. *Ennio Morricone's "The Good, the Bad and the Ugly": A Film Score Guide.* Lanham, MD: Scarecrow Press, 2004.

Newman, Kim. *Wild West Movies, or, How the West Was Found, Won, Lost, Lied about, Filmed, and Forgotten.* London: Bloomsbury, 1990.

Good Times

The television sitcom *Good Times* was the creation of independent producer Norman Lear, whose controversy-provoking shows helped revolutionize American prime-time television during the 1970s. *Good Times* was developed as a spin-off of another hit Lear sitcom, *Maude* (aired 1972–1978), which starred Bea Arthur and Bill Macy. *Maude* presented the often provocative machinations of a well-appointed, middle-aged, married couple. Veteran actress Esther Rolle played their African American housekeeper, Florida, until 1974, when the character was spun off into her own sitcom, *Good Times*. The program is noteworthy in that, along with *The Jeffersons* and *Sanford and Son* (both developed by Lear), it featured a mostly African American cast, something not seen on the air since the notorious cancellation of *The Amos 'n' Andy Show* in 1953.

Good Times was groundbreaking. While the story lines of early television sitcoms provided little more than cautious counsel on the minor vicissitudes of family life, the 1970s ushered in what came to be known as the era of relevancy in television programming. In *Good Times*, which aired on CBS Television from February 1974 to August 1979, racial discrimination, inflation, unemployment, Black Power, and criticism of the government were frequent and resounding themes. *Good Times* stretched the boundaries of television comedy and provided an unconventional glimpse of the life of a particular African American family. At the same time it depicted images of the changing social fabric of 1970s American society in general.

The Evans family lived in a high-rise tenement apartment in an urban Chicago housing project. They traded jokes and clever repartee about being poor and not having enough money for rent, about the rats and roaches that inhabited the inside of their building and the street crime that caused them to be reluctant to go outside their building. In addition to Florida and James (John Amos), her frequently unemployed but looking-for-work husband, the cast of *Good Times* included their teenage son, J. J., portrayed by comedian Jimmie Walker; their grown daughter, Thelma (Bernadette Stanis); and an adolescent son, Michael, portrayed with gusto by a talented young Ralph Carter. A fortyish woman named Wilona (Ja'net Dubois) made frequent appearances as the Evanses' supportive neighbor. Later in the series, a young Janet Jackson of the musical Jackson family fame joined the cast as Wilona's adopted daughter.

Good Times's popularity and good ratings were rooted in the fact that it offered solace for a TV audience fed up with the Vietnam War, Watergate, high interest rates, and unemployment. Indeed, Americans of all races could identify with the difficulties the Evans family faced, and the show became a champion for the plight of the underclass. Black viewers especially appreciated how the program highlighted the good parenting skills of James and Florida. In spite of their difficult situation, they never shirked on their responsibility to teach their children values and accountability. The Evanses' ability to remain stalwart in the face of difficult odds was the underlying theme of many episodes.

Good Times is also significant for the controversy that haunted the show's production. Disputes developed about the program's changed direction, in particular the increasingly popular J. J. character. J. J.'s comical but at times undignified antics raised the resentment of some viewers. With his toothy grin, ridiculous strut, and bug-eyed semblance, he metamorphosed into a racial stereotype of former times. More and more episodes were centered on his farcical exploits, featuring his trademark exclamation, "Dy-No-Mite!" All but forgotten was the daughter Thelma, James's search for a job, Michael's scholastic interests, and family values. "We felt we had to do something drastic," Rolle stated in the *Los Angeles Times* in 1978: "We had lost the essence of the show." Amos left the program in protest after the third season, and Rolle did likewise after the fourth season. Attempts were made to soften the J. J. character and continue the program without the characters of James and Florida. But even with an employed and more mature-acting J. J. and the return of Rolle for the sixth season, ratings for *Good Times* declined. The series was canceled, but it continues to enjoy success in syndication.

Pamala S. Deane

SEE ALSO: The Amos 'n' Andy Show*; Arthur, Bea; Jackson, Janet;* The Jeffersons*; Lear, Norman;* Maude*; Rolle, Esther;* Sanford and Son*; Sitcom.*

BIBLIOGRAPHY

Barnouw, Erik. *Tube of Plenty.* Oxford: Oxford University Press, 1982.

Brooks, Tim, and Earle Marsh. *The Complete Directory to Prime*

Time Network and Cable TV Shows, 1946–Present, 9th ed. New York: Ballantine Books, 2007.

MacDonald, J. Fred. *Blacks and White TV: African Americans in Television since 1948*, 2nd ed. Chicago: Nelson-Hall Publishers, 1992.

Marc, David, and Robert J. Thompson. *Prime Time, Prime Movers: From "I Love Lucy" to "L.A. Law"—America's Greatest TV Shows and the People Who Created Them.* Boston: Little, Brown, 1992.

Margulies, Lee. "Esther Rolle: Coming Home." *Los Angeles Times*, May 12, 1978.

Taylor, Ella. *Prime Time Families: Television Culture in Postwar America.* Berkeley: University of California Press, 1989.

Goodbye, Columbus

Philip Roth's first book, *Goodbye, Columbus* (1959), is a collection of five stories and one novella that introduces the basic themes that are more fully explored in his later novels and that have in turn been shaped by the critical response to Roth's debut work.

Published at a time when anti-Semitism was still prevalent in the United States and memories of the Holocaust still fresh, *Goodbye, Columbus* led a number of influential Jewish readers to question Roth's depiction of American Jews from the perspective of a writer for whom Jewishness was more cultural than religious and assimilation and individual identity more pressing matters than survival and collective memory. While some charged Roth with disloyalty and self-hatred, others welcomed him into the diverse group of Jewish American writers then beginning to dominate American fiction. The less specifically Jewish implications of Roth's comic genius and irreverence were underscored by the release of the successful film version of the title novella in 1969, two years after Mike Nichols's comedy-drama *The Graduate.*

Robert A. Morace

SEE ALSO: *Nichols, Mike, and Elaine May.*

BIBLIOGRAPHY

Cooper, Alan. *Philip Roth and the Jews.* Albany: State University of New York Press, 1996.

Halio, Jay L. *Philip Roth Revisited.* New York: Twayne, 1992.

Milowitz, Steven. *Philip Roth Considered: The Concentrationary Universe of the American Writer.* In *Studies in Major Literary Authors*, ed. William Cain. New York: Garland Publishing, 2000.

Gooden, Dwight *(1964–)*

During the 1980s pitcher Dwight Gooden enjoyed one of the fastest rises to stardom in baseball history, but his career was derailed by cocaine use. Gooden won the National League Rookie of the Year Award in 1984 for the New York Mets; the following year, at the age of twenty, he became the youngest pitcher ever to win the Cy Young Award. Nicknamed "Doctor K" because of all the strikeouts he posted, Gooden became the toast of New York. In 1987, however, the young pitcher was forced to enter a drug rehabilitation center for his cocaine addiction. Repeated violations of Major League Baseball's drug policy limited Gooden's effectiveness and ultimately resulted in his suspension from baseball for the 1995 season.

Gooden subsequently enjoyed some success with the New York Yankees and Cleveland Indians, highlighted by a no-hitter against the Seattle Mariners on May 14, 1996. He also played for the Houston Astros and Tampa Bay Devil Rays before retiring in 2001. Five years later Gooden served seven months in prison for a drug-related violation of his probation for a drunk-driving conviction. His cocaine use again got him into trouble in 2010, when he pleaded guilty to driving under the influence and received five years' probation.

Scott Tribble

SEE ALSO: *Baseball; Cocaine/Crack; The New York Mets; The New York Yankees.*

BIBLIOGRAPHY

Gooden, Dwight, and Bob Klapisch. *Heat: My Life on and off the Diamond.* New York: William Morrow, 1999.

Shatzkin, Mike, ed. *The Ballplayers: Baseball's Ultimate Biographical Reference.* New York: Arbor House, 1990.

GoodFellas

Chosen by the American Film Institute as one of the "100 Greatest American Films of the Last 100 Years," Martin Scorsese's *GoodFellas* (1990) has done more to demythologize organized crime than any other major contemporary film and has cemented its maker's reputation as, arguably, America's greatest director still living and working at the beginning of the twenty-first century.

SYNOPSIS AND RECEPTION

GoodFellas was based on Nicholas Pileggi's 1985 best seller *Wiseguy: Life in a Mafia Family*, which recounted the true story of Henry Hill. A low-level mobster who rose up through the ranks, Hill was involved in the biggest cash robbery in America's history, was caught dealing cocaine, turned state's evidence, and entered the federal witness protection program. Behind its glossy and absorbing gangster-thriller surface, the film offered an unvarnished account of Mafia brutality that came to set a standard—seldom achieved since—for the moral focus of serious crime films and illuminated public understanding of the culture in which organized crime flourishes.

Set in Scorsese's home ground of New York City, whose underbelly he had so successfully exploited in many of his films—including the early *Mean Streets* (1973) and the masterly *Taxi Driver* (1976)—*GoodFellas* marked the climactic contribution to the director's cycle of underworld subjects and the one to which he successfully brought an epic approach. His by-now practiced craft and brilliantly individual brand of expressionistic realism imbued *GoodFellas* with black comedy; often memorably ironic, sharp social observation; and scenes of deeply shocking but never gratuitous violence. While the film is very long, it absolutely enthralls as it unfolds a tale in which audiences watch the young Hill grow to manhood in the Mafia.

The film was further empowered by a large cast. At the center was Ray Liotta as Hill, surrounded and supported by a bevy of actors that included a menacingly detached Robert De Niro as James Conway, Oscar-winning Joe Pesci as the viciously manic Tommy DeVito, Paul Sorvino as Mafia boss Paul Cicero, and a superb Lorraine Bracco as Hill's middle-class Jewish wife Karen. Together these actors vividly and realistically impersonated the real-life sociopaths they were portraying, articulating a world of men whose daily business embraces every known felony from arson and extortion through dealing in drugs and firearms to cold-blooded killing in the pursuit of money and power. The film was nominated by the Academy of Motion Picture Arts and Sciences for Best Picture, Best Director, Best Supporting Actor (Pesci), and Best Supporting Actress (Bracco), as well as for film editing and best nonoriginal screenplay. Only Pesci walked away a winner, but the film was well received by critics, performed beyond expectations at the box office, and remains a cult classic into the twenty-first century.

BOOK TO FILM

Hill was an insider who remained outside; although he was involved in the mob's scams, thefts, and murders, he was half-Irish and half-Sicilian, and only thoroughbred Sicilians could become "made men" within the Mafia. While the book dealt with the facts of the case, Scorsese puts flesh on the bones by making choices as to what he includes and how he treats it. The book, for example, detailed the 1978 theft of $6 million from Lufthansa cargo at Kennedy Airport, but where a lesser director would show the theft in all its detail, Scorsese shrewdly omits it entirely; his concern is with the lives of the perpetrators and how they are affected in the aftermath of the operation. The haul is so huge that a number of the participants, despite being warned to lie low, start living extravagantly, thus causing De Niro's Jimmy Conway to worry that their behavior will tip off the cops. He deals with their indiscretion by having each of them—some ten in all—killed, fully aware that their elimination will bring the added advantage of increasing his own percentage of the take.

This expert and imaginative ability to transpose and select creates dramatic juxtapositions from the start. Pileggi's book began with Henry describing his childhood living across the street from a cab stand controlled by the Mob. He reveals how he was attracted by the apparent glamour of the mobsters' lives, admiring them for their power and wealth so much that, from the age of twelve, his dream was to become one of them. By contrast, on film *GoodFellas* opens midway through the story, with the adult Henry driving along a deserted road at night, accompanied by Jimmy and Tommy. He hears a strange thumping sound, speculates on its cause (a flat? Did he hit something?), and they pull over to investigate. The three men climb out, circle to the back of the car, and Henry opens the trunk to reveal a beaten and bloody cohort who, to their collective astonishment, is still breathing. Tommy lunges forward with a huge knife and brutally stabs him, after which Jimmy pumps four bullets into him. As the stunned Henry moves to close the trunk, he says in voice-over, "As far back as I can remember, I always wanted to be a gangster."

The story then flashes back to Henry's formative years across from that cab stand, his first youthful errands for the mob, and his meeting Jimmy and Tommy. In a now-classic scene, Tommy is first spotted telling an anecdote that has his fellow mobsters in stitches and Henry saying, "You're funny." Tommy suddenly becomes threateningly confrontational. "I'm funny how, I mean funny like I'm a clown? I amuse you? I make you laugh?" The tension builds until Henry finally realizes that Tommy is putting him on, and everyone laughs. From then on, whenever Tommy starts down the same confrontational road with someone else, audiences are lulled into thinking he's kidding again, so that his eventual explosion into uncompromisingly bloody violence is all the more shocking.

The film moves at a dazzlingly fast but perfectly controlled pace, its imagery enhanced by freeze-frames, jump cuts, continuous takes, voice-overs, and on-screen date-and-place information that emphasizes its biographical origins. Unlike the book, which ends with Henry purporting to be happily ensconced in the witness protection program, the movie ends with a distraught Henry trapped in suburbia. As he picks up the morning paper from the front porch of a row of identical houses, he says in voice-over, "I'm an average nobody. I get to live the rest of my life as a schnook."

GOODFELLAS AND THE MOB

Comparisons with Francis Ford Coppola's *The Godfather* and its sequel proved inevitable—they are both great films, epic in scope, and they both make much of the family's code of honor. But as Pileggi told the *New York Times*, "The honor code is a myth. These guys betray each other constantly. Once Henry's life is threatened, he has no qualms about testifying. He does no soul-searching, because he has no soul." *GoodFellas* is mired in the minutiae of everyday life, set among the lawns and shrubs of suburbia and stripped of all but the most fleeting, vulgar, and spurious glamour. The beatings and killings are always sick and brutal, never macho or alluring. The effect is to expose the sickening reality of the criminal lifestyle, revealing it in all of its violence, dishonor, and empty aspirations.

Americans' fascination with the Mafia archetype has served Hill and *GoodFellas* well over the years. In the wake of the film's release and wide success, Hill found ample opportunity to profit from his cultivated mafioso persona: he opened Italian restaurants in Nebraska and Connecticut, he sold his own recipe of pasta sauce on the Internet, and, until his death on June 12, 2012, he continued to be called upon by media outlets for commentary on the Mob and Mob-related movies. The film itself has often been grouped with similar Mafia-themed films. *Goodfellas*, however, has propelled others to explore the archetype in an increasingly gritty and honest fashion in both film and television. The movie remains popular and well regarded by critics and viewers alike and has made it onto many top ten lists. It is even archived in the Library of Congress's National Film Registry for its cultural significance.

Bob Sullivan

SEE ALSO: *Academy Awards; The Big Apple; De Niro, Robert;* The Godfather*; Mafia/Organized Crime; Scorsese, Martin;* Taxi Driver.

BIBLIOGRAPHY

Brunette, Peter, ed. *Martin Scorsese: Interviews.* Conversations with Filmmakers Series. Jackson: University Press of Mississippi, 1999.

Ebert, Roger. *Scorsese.* Chicago: University of Chicago Press, 2008.

Friedman, Lawrence S. *The Cinema of Martin Scorsese.* New York: Continuum, 1997.

Linfield, Susan. "'Goodfellas' Looks at the Banality of Mob Life." *New York Times*, September 16, 1990.

Pileggi, Nicholas. *Wiseguy: Life in a Mafia Family.* New York: Pocket Books, 1985.

Thompson, David, and Ian Christie, eds. *Scorsese on Scorsese.* London: Faber and Faber, 1989.

Goodman, Benny *(1909–1986)*

Known as the "King of Swing," bandleader Benny Goodman left his mark on the swing era of the late 1930s and early 1940s in several important areas. He adapted both jazz and popular songs into a unique style of big band jazz. His superb technique and distinctive solo style made him the outstanding clarinetist of that era. During a time of racial segregation, he became the first leader to include African Americans in his orchestra. He innovatively returned jazz to its roots by using band members in small combos—from trios to sextets. His career was long-lasting, and when almost seventy, he impressed jazz critic John McDonough with his ability to still fill a concert hall all by himself.

A JAZZ STAR RISES

When Chicago-born Goodman was ten he joined a synagogue boys' band, immediately showing a natural aptitude for the clarinet. Within a year he enrolled in the boys' band at the famous Hull House, a settlement house that offered free instruction in the arts to children of immigrant families. There his teacher was Franz Schoepp, an instructor of woodwinds in the Chicago Symphony. Benny was twelve when he appeared on stage in Chicago doing an impersonation of clarinetist Ted Lewis, even then attracting the attention of bandleader Ben Pollack, who later hired him. At thirteen Goodman was playing phenomenal jazz solos with the famous Austin High Gang, which included such future stars as saxophonist Bud Freeman, drummer Dave Tough, cornetist Jimmy McPartland, and clarinetist Frank Teschemacher. When he first jammed with the band, McPartland said, "This little monkey played about sixteen choruses of 'Rose' and I just sat there with my mouth open."

At thirteen he was a full member of the musicians' union and working several nights a week in clubs and dance halls. In August 1925 the sixteen-year-old prodigy left Chicago wearing adolescent knickers to join Pollack's band in Los Angeles. Pollack led one of the best jazz bands in the United States during the late 1920s and early 1930s, and by 1927 Goodman was gaining the respect of other musicians. In 1928 he left Pollack briefly for the Isham Jones band, but when Pollack got a job that year in New York City, young Goodman rejoined him for the chance to play regularly with such standout jazzmen as Freeman, McPartland, Glenn Miller, and Jack Teagarden. He was undaunted by his fellow stars, and Pollack commented that "Benny Goodman was getting in everybody's hair about this time, because he was getting good and took all the choruses."

In 1929 he began a successful career as a freelancer in New York City, playing in Broadway pit bands and on recordings and radio. Of the 130 recording sessions that Goodman was part of during this period, only about fifteen were genuine jazz sessions. In these, however, he played with such jazz musicians as Bix Beiderbecke, Red Nichols, Joe Venuti, and Fats Waller; blues queen Bessie Smith; and even his early idol, Ted Lewis.

FORMING HIS OWN BAND

By 1933, having determined the kind of music he wanted to play, Goodman began making plans to organize his own band, and in 1934 the Benny Goodman Orchestra was featured on an ongoing NBC radio series called *Let's Dance*. After a few recordings on Columbia, he signed a long-term contract with RCA Victor in 1935 and took his band on the road. Success was gradual at first, but with the extraordinary arrangements of Fletcher Henderson—enhanced by the solos of Goodman; trumpeters Bunny Berrigan, Ziggy Elman, and Harry James; pianists Jess Stacy and Teddy Wilson, and drummer Gene Krupa—the band attained nationwide success in 1936. On January 16, 1938, Goodman, wearing white tie and tails, led his band into Carnegie Hall for the first pure jazz concert ever held there. The vocals of Peggy Lee—including "Why Don't You Do Right?" and "My Old Flame"—helped the orchestra remain a prime attraction until it was disbanded in mid-1944 to allow Goodman to focus on concerts with his combo groups.

He reorganized his big band in 1945 and appeared as its leader off and on until 1950, when he toured Europe with a sextet. After that he fronted the big band on one brief tour in the spring of 1953, involving himself in a number of other projects. He assembled a special band in 1955 to record the soundtrack for the film *The Benny Goodman Story*, starring Steve Allen as Goodman. A wide variety of projects drew his attention: In the winter of 1956–1957 he toured the Far East and in

Benny Goodman. *Bandleader Benny Goodman poses with his clarinet in 1939.* GILLES PETARD/REDFERNS/GETTY IMAGES.

1962 the Soviet Union, both under the auspices of the U.S. State Department; sandwiched between were appearances with the Budapest String Quartet as well as concerts of works he had commissioned from composers Béla Bartók, Paul Hindemith, and Aaron Copland.

In the early 1970s he presented a television show from Carnegie Hall in which he reunited his original quartet and played a memorable version of "I'm a Ding Dong Daddy from Dumas." The same group, with an ailing Krupa, also played the 1973 Newport Jazz Festival in Rhode Island. By the 1980s Goodman's health problems began to increase, but as late as 1986 he continued to play with a big band on occasional radio broadcasts. His biographer, D. Russell Connor, found these performances "brilliant, effortless, faultless, inspiring," adding that the sidemen were "visibly impressed."

The respect of his peers was far more important to Goodman than the long string of victories in jazz polls taken by *Downbeat, Metronome, Playboy*, and *Esquire* magazines. His special niche in history is to have changed the course of jazz during the swing era. He was the King of Swing, who, as James L. Collier wrote in his book *Benny Goodman and the Swing Era*, "opened the door for the bands which rushed through the gap—among them [Count] Basie, [Woody] Herman, [Charlie] Barnet, [Jimmie] Lunceford, [Bunnie] Berigan, [Bing] Crosby, [Chick] Webb, [Artie] Shaw, and eventually [Stan] Kenton, [Boyd] Raeburn and the modernists."

Benjamin Griffith

SEE ALSO: *Addams, Jane; Allen, Steve; Basie, Count; Beiderbecke, Bix; Big Bands; Chicago Jazz; Copland, Aaron; Crosby, Bing; James, Harry; Jazz; Krupa, Gene; Lee, Peggy; Lunceford, Jimmie; Miller, Glenn; Newport Jazz and Folk Festivals; Shaw, Artie; Smith, Bessie; Webb, Chick.*

BIBLIOGRAPHY

Collier, James Lincoln. *Benny Goodman and the Swing Era.* New York: Oxford University Press, 1989.

Connor, D. Russell. *Benny Goodman: Listen to His Legacy.* Lanham, MD: Scarecrow Press, 1988.

Firestone, Ross. *Swing, Swing, Swing: The Life & Times of Benny Goodman.* New York: Norton, 1993.

Schuller, Gunther. *The Swing Era.* New York: Oxford University Press, 1989.

Goodrich, William

SEE: *Arbuckle, Fatty.*

Goodson, Mark *(1915–1992)*

Fondly known as the godfather of television game shows, Mark Goodson produced and created some of television's top-rated and most enduring programs, including *The Price Is Right, The Match Game*, and *Family Feud.*

Born in Sacramento, California, to Russian immigrant parents, Goodson was a shy and introverted child. Despite his reserved character, he pursued a career in the radio industry. In 1937 he landed his first job as a disc jockey at radio station KCBS in San Francisco. Two years later he was hired by the Mutual Broadcasting System as an announcer, newscaster, and station director. In 1941 Goodson moved to New York to work as a radio announcer. It was here that he first became involved with game shows. In 1943 he created his first network show for ABC, *Appointment with Life*, a dramatic series based on the files of a marriage counselor. During this time Goodson also wrote and directed installments of *The Kate Smith Variety Hour.*

In 1946 Goodson teamed up with Bill Todman to form Goodson-Todman Productions. Their first creation was a radio game show titled *Winner Take All*, which aired on CBS. During the next couple of years, the two created several more successful radio shows, thereby creating a strong network presence. Goodson created the duo's first television program, *What's My Line?*, which premiered on CBS on February 1, 1950. The program was an overnight success, airing weekly for seventeen years. Over the next thirty years, Goodson-Todman Productions continued to produce hit game shows and develop their widely used formats.

Complementary opposites, Todman managed the business side, while Goodson was the creative and productive force. Goodson created many of the essential attributes that define game shows; for example, Goodson-Todman Productions was one of the pioneers in set design, using bright colors and flashing lights. Goodson also pioneered the celebrity panel on the game show. In an attempt to boost ratings, he introduced the celebrity panel in the 1950s on *What's My Line?* The program featured a panel of four celebrity guests who guessed the occupations of the contestants. Over the years Goodson perfected the use of the celebrity panels on programs such as *Password* and *The Match Game.* His celebrity panels were and still are imitated by other game show producers.

In 1979 Todman died, and Goodson acquired sole ownership of the company, renaming it Mark Goodson Productions. Goodson continued to focus on producing game shows and expanding his media group. In 1986 he created the Goodson Newspaper Group, which consolidated several daily and weekly newspapers. By 1992 the group was publishing eight daily, six Sunday, and twenty-five weekly newspapers.

Two weeks before his death in December 1992, Goodson was inducted into the Academy of Television Arts and Sciences Hall of Fame. This topped a long list of achievements that included three Emmy Awards, Great Britain's National Television Award, and a star on the Hollywood Walk of Fame. Yet nothing represents Goodson's contribution to television better than the longevity of the shows themselves. There has not been a weekday since 1946, when *Winner Take All* premiered on the radio, that a Goodson program has not been on the air.

Goodson-Todman's thirty-plus game shows include *Winner Take All* (1948–1950); *Beat the Clock* (1950–1962, 1968–1971, and 1979–1980); *What's My Line?* (1950–1967); *The Price Is Right* (1956–1965 and 1972–); *To Tell the Truth* (1956–1977); *Password* (1961–1967, 1971–1975, 1979–1982 [as *Password Plus*], 1984–1989 [as *Super Password*], and 2008–2009 [as *Million Dollar Password*]); *The Match Game* (1962–1969 and 1973–1982); *He Said, She Said* (1969–1970); *Concentration* (1973–1979); *Tattletales* (1974–1978 and 1982–1984); *Mindreaders* (1979); *Blockbusters* (1980–1982 and 1987); *Match Game/Hollywood Squares Hour* (1983–1984); and *Trivia Trap* (1984–1985).

Goodson-Todman also produced a few episodic shows: *The Rebel* (1959–1961), *Jefferson Drum* (1958–1959), *The Richard Boone Show* (1963–1964), *Philip Marlowe* (1959–1960), and *The Don Rickles Show* (1968–1969).

Lara Bickell

SEE ALSO: *Emmy Awards; Game Shows;* Hollywood Squares; The Price Is Right; To Tell the Truth; What's My Line?

BIBLIOGRAPHY

Broughton, Irv, ed. *Producers on Producing: The Making of Film and Television.* Jefferson, NC: McFarland, 2001.

Fabe, Maxene. *TV Game Shows.* New York: Doubleday, 1979.

Graham, Jefferson. *Come on Down!!! The TV Game Show Book.* New York: Abbeville Press, 1988.

Scheuer, Steven H., ed. *Who's Who in Television and Cable.* New York: Facts On File, 1983.

Schwartz, David, et al. *The Encyclopedia of Television Game Shows.* New York: New York Zoetrope, 1987.

Google

Stanford University graduate students Larry Page and Sergey Brin designed a search engine in 1996 called BackRub. In 1997 they renamed their creation Google, a play on the word *googol,* which is a mathematical term for the number represented by the numeral one followed by 100 zeros. The use of the term reflects Page and Brin's mission to organize a seemingly infinite amount of information on the Internet.

In 1998, after receiving $100,000 in funding from Sun cofounder Andy Bechtolsheim, Page and Brin incorporated their company as Google, Inc. They set up Google in a rented garage and hired their first employee. In December 1998 *PC Magazine* reported that Google "has an uncanny knack for returning extremely relevant results" and recognized it as the search engine of choice in its Top 100 Web Sites for 1998. From that point on, Google expanded rapidly, and in 2004 the company moved its more than 800 employees to offices in Mountain View, California.

By 2006 Google had become so influential that *google* was added as a verb to *Merriam-Webster Collegiate Dictionary* and *Oxford English Dictionary.* Both dictionaries note that the word means "to search for information on the Internet using the Google search engine." In 2009 the Global Language Monitor, a media company that tracks cultural trends in language all over the world, named the word *google* as number seven on its "Top Words of the Decade" list. Despite its formal definition in dictionaries, *google* quickly evolved into a generic term used to indicate searching on the Internet regardless of the actual search engine used.

In 2004 Google launched Google Print, making books that are in the public domain available for free online along with free limited content from other books. The product was renamed Google Books the next year. In 2010 the company estimated that it had scanned and uploaded more than fifteen million books and announced it wanted to have all books in the world, estimated by Google to be 130 million, scanned by 2020. In 2005 Google got into the mapping business with Google Maps, which offers maps, directions, and photos, and Google Earth, which is a satellite imagery-based mapping service.

Other products developed by the company include Gmail, a free e-mail service, in 2005; Google Voice, phone service over the Internet, in 2009; and Google+, a social media sharing site, in 2011. Many of the company's products came out of Google Labs, a beta-testing section of the Google website, where users try out features and products, some of which are eventually released and some of which fail. The company is unusual in its encouragement of products in open betas; its willingness to allow features and products to fail publicly; and its launching of some projects, such as Gmail, through invitation only (perceived scarcity increasing product popularity, as an invite from a current user was needed to set up a new account). Between its own products and its purchase of the video site YouTube in 2006, Google has become a true powerhouse on the Internet.

LOGO AND FOOLERY

Google's logo is the name of the company, and each letter of the name is a different color. It has undergone minor changes over the years, including a change of font, but the most significant change has been the repeated manipulation of the logo as it appears on the Google search page into images that commemorate people and events. These variations of the logo have become known as Google Doodles.

The first Google Doodle appeared in 1998 for Burning Man, an annual event in Nevada that celebrates community, art, self-expression, and self-reliance, and was created mostly to notify users that the founders of the company would be away and not available to respond to problems. Google Doodles have celebrated everything from major figures and holidays to popular culture topics, such as Pac-Man (the Google logo was redesigned into a 2010 tribute for the video game's thirtieth birthday with a re-creation of the game that could be played right on the Google search page). The doodles have become increasingly popular and elaborate, including an April 2011 video doodle for actor Charlie Chaplin's birthday and a September 2011 interactive Muppet tribute to Muppet creator Jim Henson. Since each doodle also links to search results about the topic, some websites achieve unexpected gains in Internet traffic due to a Google Doodle.

Starting in 2000, Google began a tradition of pulling April Fool's Day hoaxes. The first one involved inviting website visitors to try the MentalPlex search engine, where they stared at an animated image while mentally envisioning what they wanted; they were then greeted with one of several creative error messages. Since then, Google has released hoaxes for its search engine and other products every year, gaining a good deal of attention on the Internet with its range of jokes.

In 2004 Google went public in an unconventional public offering at $85 per share, raising nearly $2 billion in the largest technology initial public offering (IPO) ever recorded to date. In less than a year the stock soared to more than $300 per share, making Google one of the most successful technology companies ever. In late 2011 shares were trading at more than $600 per share.

Google's unofficial motto until 2009 was "Don't Be Evil." The company's 2004 IPO announcement states, "Don't be evil. We believe strongly that in the long term, we will be better served—as shareholders and in all other ways—by a company that does good things for the world even if we forgo some short term gains." The founders of Google said that "Don't Be Evil" was a core value that guided their company. The company's success can also be attributed to its engineering mind-set and its adoption of Internet values such as speed, openness, experimentation, and risk taking. It is also notoriously picky in its hiring process and pampers its engineers, giving them all the resources they need to succeed. Employees also enjoy free food, free dry cleaning, and on-site doctors and masseuses. Google's corporate culture, the company's philanthropy, and the luxuries of it offices have become as famous as its products.

GROWING INFLUENCE AND POWER

As Google's influence grew, a number of critics argued that the company was acquiring too much power over the lives of the public by invading privacy, shaping preferences, and controlling information about the world. In a June 2008 article for Boston.com, journalist Drake Bennett quotes Kevin Bankston, a lawyer with the advocacy group Electronic Frontier Foundation: "What worries me about Google is that they have access to an incredibly sensitive range of personal data, the depth and breadth of which is unlike anything we've ever seen before." Google's growing power brought out many critics concerned about privacy and the seemingly monopolistic hold Google had on Internet searching.

Google also faced criticism regarding its interactions with China. In 2005 the company launched a version of its website in China, and it quickly became the country's second-most popular search engine. In order to operate in China, however, Google had to agree to allow search results to be censored by the Chinese government, which made some politically sensitive material unavailable. Many Americans thought that Google should not be doing business in a country where the government censors information. And, while the Chinese government had given permission for Google to operate in the country, it made actually operating in China difficult. After struggling with the government for five years, Google finally withdrew from China in 2010.

In the early twenty-first century, Google's search engine was the number-one gateway to the Internet's vast commercial potential. It's been compared to the Gutenberg printing press in discussing its importance to America's modern culture. Greg Lastowka, an associate professor of law at Rutgers University in New Jersey, notes that Google "tells us what words mean, what things look like, where to buy things, and who or what is most important to us. Google's control over 'results' constitutes an awesome ability to set the course of human knowledge," as quoted by Bennett.

By the end of 2010, the company had more than eighty-five offices in forty countries and over 24,000 employees. It sold its products and services in more than fifty countries, regions, and territories, and its revenue for fiscal 2010 was over $29 billion. In May 2011 unique visitors of Google surpassed the one-billion mark for the first time, an 8.4 percent increase from the prior year. As one of the most powerful and influential technology companies, Google and its products have had a tremendous impact on the world.

Kimberlee Diane Keeline

SEE ALSO: *Chaplin, Charlie; E-mail; Henson, Jim; The Internet; The Muppets; Pac-Man; YouTube.*

BIBLIOGRAPHY

Bennett, Drake. "Stopping Google." Boston.com. Accessed December 17, 2011. Available from http://www.boston.com/bostonglobe/ideas/articles/2008/06/22/stopping_google/?page=full

Edwards, Douglas. *I'm Feeling Lucky: The Confessions of Google Employee Number 59.* Boston: Houghton Mifflin Harcourt, 2011.

Girard, Bernard. *The Google Way: How One Company Is Revolutionizing Management as We Know It.* San Francisco: No Starch Press, 2009.

"Google History." Google. Accessed December 14, 2011. Available from http://www.google.com/about/corporate/company/history.html

Levine, Robert. "Google's Spreading Tentacles of Influence." *Bloomsburg Business Week.* Accessed December 17, 2011. Available from http://www.businessweek.com/magazine/googles-spreading-tentacles-of-influence-10272011.html

Levy, Steven. *In the Plex: How Google Thinks, Works, and Shapes Our Lives.* New York: Simon & Schuster, 2011.

Van Veelen, Ijsbrand. *Google Documentary.* Google Videos. Accessed December 14, 2011. Available from http://video.google.ca/videoplay?docid=1508211417393454786&ei=duDCSMqQOojkAH0lqy8BQ&q=google

Vise, David A., and Mark Malseed. *The Google Story.* New York: Delta, 2008.

Gordy, Berry *(1929–)*

Founder of the Motown music empire, Berry Gordy was for many years America's most successful black businessman. Gordy was one of eight children from a middle-class family in Detroit, Michigan; his father, Berry Gordy Sr., was a contractor and entrepreneur. The elder Gordy's gospel of achievement and competition found a respectful audience in his son, but Berry Gordy Jr. set his sights on wealth rather than on merely middle-class success. Gordy dropped out of high school to pursue a career in boxing and fought in fifteen professional bouts, but he quit the ring after concluding that he would never be great. Shortly afterward he was drafted into the armed services and saw combat in the Korean War.

Returning to Detroit in 1953, Gordy started a jazz record store with borrowed money. It failed after a short time, and he next took an assembly-line job at a Ford plant. Gordy's sisters had by then obtained the cigarette concession at one of Detroit's better black nightclubs, and he began spending much of his free time there. He was composing songs in his head during his long, boring shifts at Ford and attempted to persuade the nightclub's talent to use his material. In 1957, with the first of his several marriages falling apart, Gordy quit his Ford job to devote himself to composing full time.

It was singer Jackie Wilson, an old acquaintance from his boxing days, who first recorded Gordy's songs. Wilson was just on the brink of success when Gordy gave him "Lonely Teardrops" and several other of his songs to perform. Gordy quickly discovered, however, that a composer's royalties were very small, especially in the frequently corrupt music business of the day, so he started doing freelance record producing as well, learning valuable lessons but still not making much profit.

FOUNDING MOTOWN

In 1959 Gordy founded his own music production company on a shoestring budget. He named it Motown after Detroit, the Motor City, and brought several of his siblings and their spouses into the business. One brother-in-law was writer/producer/singer Harvey Fuqua of Harvey and the Moonglows; another was Marvin Gaye, who would become one of Motown's biggest stars. Gordy also employed a number of would-be singers and writers in secretarial and production capacities, thus assuring a constant supply of willing talent at very little cost to himself.

Gordy's earlier jobs had prepared him well for Motown. From the outset he was a stickler for high production values and quickly created a recognizable "Motown sound." He also sought to broaden his appeal beyond his core customer base of young black people to a larger audience, especially an older, more affluent white one. In order to mask how many records Motown was releasing, Gordy created and managed a variety of labels, such as Tamla, Soul, Gordy, and Rare Earth.

Early acts produced by Motown included Smokey Robinson and the Miracles, Mary Wells, Marvin Gaye, the Temptations, Martha and the Vandellas, the Spinners, the Marvelettes, and Stevie Wonder. In the years to come, Gordy would sign such performers as the Four Tops, Gladys Knight and the Pips, Junior Walker and the All Stars, the Isley Brothers, the Commodores, and the Jackson Five. In many cases, after a few years in Motown's strange brew of production wizardry and tight-fisted, arbitrary control, the now-established stars left for greener pastures. Some critics argue, however, that few ever sounded as good elsewhere as they had at Motown.

CREATING DIANA ROSS

Gordy retained almost complete ownership of his company, making him a very wealthy man. When his struggling female group, the Supremes, finally began to make a name for themselves, he determined to make the group's lead singer, Diana Ross, into a major star. Ross was a skinny schoolgirl when the Supremes started with Gordy's record label and was plunged, like many other new acts, into Motown's whirlwind of star-making training.

Following the practice of the big Hollywood film studios, Motown's Artist Development Department coached the youngsters on speech, choreography, stage behavior, costumes, and singing. Ross was Motown's greatest success story, rising from poverty in Detroit to international superstardom, just as Gordy had willed it. His strategy was methodical. First, he put Ross's name ahead of the group, then he fired Florence Ballard, Ross's equal and arguably the best singer ever to call herself a Supreme. Next, he separated Ross from the group and built her up as a solo act. Finally, he began to invest some of his millions in motion picture production, but only when Ross was given the lead in each film.

Lady Sings the Blues (1972), a biographical film about singer Billie Holiday with Ross in the lead role, was a smash hit. During production of Gordy's next film, *Mahogany* (1975), which also starred Ross, the producer's suggestions came so often that the director resigned. Gordy himself eventually took directorial credit for the film, which was quite successful. Other films in which Gordy was involved were less so. *The Wiz* (1978) was an abject flop, losing millions despite the presence of Ross and Michael Jackson. Gordy left the movie business shortly thereafter. In 1972, much to the chagrin of Detroit residents and his employees, Gordy relocated Motown to Los Angeles.

Gordy lived through many changes in the American recording industry and left an indelible mark on popular music. A list of the artists who recorded for Motown's many labels over the years would include a disproportionate number of major stars whose songs created a musical dynasty. Motown was sold to media conglomerate MCA in 1988, the same year Gordy was inducted into the Rock and Roll Hall of Fame.

Gordy continued his involvement in the music and entertainment industries into the twenty-first century. He spoke at Michael Jackson's funeral in 2009 and appeared in a number of television documentaries about Motown and musicians, including *Michael Jackson: King of Pop* and *An Even of Stars: Tribute to Lionel Richie*. In 2012 the popular television series *Dancing with the Stars* honored Gordy with a show dedicated to Motown hits. Also in 2012 there was talk of Gordy working on a Broadway musical based on the history of Motown.

David Lonergan

SEE ALSO: *The Commodores; Gaye, Marvin; Jackson, Michael; The Jackson Five; Martha and the Vandellas; Motown; Robinson, Smokey; Ross, Diana, and the Supremes; Soul Music; The Temptations; Walker, Junior, and the All Stars; Wells, Mary; Wonder, Stevie.*

BIBLIOGRAPHY

Benjaminson, Peter. *The Story of Motown*. New York: Grove Press, 1979.

George, Nelson. *Where Did Our Love Go? The Rise and Fall of the Motown Sound*. New York: St. Martin's Press, 1985.

Gordy, Berry. *To Be Loved: The Music, the Magic, the Memories of Motown: An Autobiography*. New York: Warner Books, 1994.

Posner, Gerald. *Motown: Music, Money, Sex, and Power*. New York: Random House, 2002.

Gospel Music

Gospel music is arguably the most important African American musical tradition. Throughout the twentieth century and into the twenty-first, it has managed to instill a vision in African Americans with its message of hope, love, and compassion through the power of Jesus Christ. The genre has also had a profound influence on religious and secular music, enabling it to become a part of the broader American culture.

During the Antebellum period, African Americans used religious and sacred songs as a tool of liberation in order to help them survive the terrible institution of slavery. Once emancipation had been achieved, they relied upon spirituals such as "Nobody Knows the Trouble I See," "Steal Away," "Didn't My Lord Deliver Daniel," "Ezekiel Saw the Wheel," and "In that Great Gettin' up Morning" to help them make the transition from slavery to freedom.

PENTECOSTAL INFLUENCE

Beginning in the early twentieth century, however, African American religious music would enter a new age with the birth of black Pentecostal churches and denominations. With a strong worship emphasis on emotionalism and speaking in tongues,

Gospel Choir. *Members of a gospel choir look to their choirmaster for direction as they perform.* DAVID REDFERN/REDFERNS/GETTY IMAGES.

many traditional hymns were instantly gospelized by increasing the tempo and, at times, by adding percussion accompaniment. Instrumental in this phenomena was Charles Price Jones of Jackson, Mississippi. Founder of the Church of Christ (Holiness) USA and crucial in furthering African American Pentecostalism, he composed more than 1,000 songs for his congregation. Jones's songs—such as "I'm Happy with Jesus Alone" and "Jesus Only"—were unique in that they expressed the feelings and expressions of African Americans after slavery.

Beginning in the 1920s, black religious music was introduced to the quartet movement. Whereas most sacred music was sung by congregations, the Fisk Jubilee Singers of Nashville were responsible for popularizing the groups. Because of their amazing popularity, record companies such as RCA Victor, Paramount, and Columbia cashed in on the demand for this type of music in the urban north by recording and promoting the quartet sound. Radio stations also sought to capitalize on the growing popularity of black religious music. Stations such as WLAC of Nashville, Tennessee, with its 50,000 watts, played the music at night to listeners as far away as Chicago, Philadelphia, and New York.

GOSPEL IS BORN

Seeking to take advantage of the growing popularity of black religious music, Tommy Dorsey of Chicago took African American religious music to a new level by combining blues and jazz rhythms to traditional hymns; he labeled his sound *gospel.* Dorsey, a former jazz and blues pianist, decided to give his talents to the Lord in 1932; that same year he organized a gospel choir at Chicago's Pilgrim Baptist Church. One year later he organized the National Convention of Gospel Choirs and Choruses. Thus, he had begun a career that would eventually lead him to compose more than 500 songs. One of his most famous was "Take My Hand Precious Lord."

In addition to directing and composing, Dorsey opened a gospel music publishing house, and soon thereafter he was labeled the father of gospel music. Although Dorsey was indeed a prolific songwriter, he did not operate in isolation. He worked with artists such as Sallie Martin and the popular Mahalia Jackson. Between 1938 and 1947 Jackson made several recordings, but her most popular—"Move on up a Little Higher"—catapulted her into gospel music fame. On the heels of the popular recording, she secured a weekly CBS radio program, and she also made a number of appearances at the famed Apollo Theater and on the *Ed Sullivan Show.* Since she was one of the first gospel artists to take her work to a secular audience, Jackson quickly became an international star, and many today consider her the world's greatest gospel singer.

GOSPEL EXPANDS

Beginning in the 1950s, other artists—the Dixie Hummingbirds, the Blind Boys of Alabama, and the Sensational Nightingales—filled churches, auditoriums, and jazz festivals with their unique style as they followed Jackson's lead in taking their message to a broader audience. Again, the media sought to take advantage of the popularity of gospel music by establishing such nationally syndicated television programs as *TV Gospel Time.* Although the show had a short existence, it was nonetheless instrumental in bringing gospel music to a nonreligious crowd.

While some artists were bringing gospel to new listeners, others such as James Cleveland were gaining notoriety within traditional gospel circles. Born in 1931 in Chicago, Cleveland served as composer, arranger, and pianist for several gospel groups before starting his own, the James Cleveland Singers, which performed many of his 500 songs. What made Cleveland unique was that he introduced the nation to the gospel choir. At times, his choirs would number several hundred as they entertained audiences with their hand clapping, dancing, and singing while arrayed in fashionable robes. In 1968 Cleveland organized the Gospel Music Workshop of America, and because of his success he received three Grammy Awards; in 1981 he was awarded a star on the Hollywood Walk of Fame.

MAINSTREAM MUSIC

In spite of Cleveland's broad appeal, there was a faction inside the gospel music industry that wanted to take gospel into the mainstream; quite simply, they wanted to imitate the more popular rhythm-and-blues songs. Leading this movement was Edwin Hawkins, who in 1969 recorded "Oh Happy Day." This song quickly rose on the Top 40 chart with its catchy beat and rhythmic sound that lacked references to God or Jesus. A new generation of gospel was born.

Other artists such as Andrae Crouch followed Hawkins's crossover success by writing gospel lyrics for more popular secular songs. Although Hawkins and Crouch were forerunners of this new gospel music, their popularity was still largely confined to the ears of black churchgoers. Beginning in the late 1980s, however, contemporary gospel groups such as Take 6 and the Winans began to take the gospel message to an ever-wider audience. During their heyday both groups could easily fill a concert hall as they played their new style to the sacred and the secular.

By the 1990s gospel music had grown to a billion-dollar industry, thanks in part to such artists as Kirk Franklin, whose debut album, *Why We Sing*, reached number one on the Billboard Gospel Chart. Recent inductees to the Gospel Music Hall of Fame include Al Greene, Amy Grant, Sandi Patty, and the Blind Boys of Alabama. Gospel music continues to be an important thread in the fabric of American popular music.

Leonard N. Moore

SEE ALSO: *Apollo Theater; Brown, James; Contemporary Christian Music; Cooke, Sam; Franklin, Aretha; Grammy Awards; Grant, Amy; Jackson, Mahalia; Jazz; Little Richard; Race Music; Rhythm and Blues; Sullivan, Ed.*

BIBLIOGRAPHY

Allen, Ray. *Singing in the Spirit: African-American Sacred Quartets in New York City.* Philadelphia: University of Pennsylvania Press, 1991.

Boyer, Horace, and Lloyd Yearwood. *How Sweet the Sound: The Golden Age of Gospel.* Washington, DC: Elliott and Clark, 1995.

Darden, Robert. *People Get Ready! A New History of Black Gospel Music.* New York: Continuum, 2005.

Harris, Michael. *The Rise of Gospel Blues: The Music of Thomas Andrew Dorsey in the Urban Church.* New York: Oxford University Press, 1992.

McNeil, W. K., ed. *Encyclopedia of American Gospel Music.* New York: Routledge, 2005.

Reagon, Bernice Johnson, ed. *We'll Understand It Better By and By: Pioneering African-American Gospel Composers.* Washington, DC: Smithsonian Institution Press, 1992.

Zolten, Jerome. *Great God A' Mighty! The Dixie Hummingbirds: Celebrating the Rise of Soul Gospel Music.* New York: Oxford University Press, 2003.

Gossip Columns

Gossip columns have existed since the advent of the printing press, if not before. In his book *Scandal: A Scurrilous History of Gossip* (2002), Roger Wilkes points to a Mesopotamian tablet discussing the mayor's extramarital affair. His discussion points to the symbiotic relationship between popular figures and public gossip, suggesting that the desire to gossip about famous people can be traced through the entire history of written language. Writers and journalists have flirted with the private lives of people from Julius Caesar to George Washington. During the 1880s Louis Keller, a New York patent attorney, published a weekly rag (sleazy newspaper) called *Town Topics* that was devoted exclusively to the goings-on of high society and the nouveau riche. Soon most of the major papers had society columns, but most stayed clear of sleazy gossip. In 1890 media gossip had risen to such a level that Louis Brandeis found it necessary to write an article titled "The Right to Privacy" for the *Harvard Law Journal.* In the article Brandeis laments that "Gossip is no longer the resource of the idle and of the vicious, but has become a trade, which is pursued with industry as well as effrontery. To satisfy a prurient taste the details of sexual relations are spread broadcast in the columns of the daily papers."

As the United States entered the modern era, the media emerged as one of the twentieth century's most powerful forces. In the early 1920s Walter Winchell, an ambitious young New York newspaperman, brought gossip into the mainstream media, breaking long-standing conventions about what was acceptable news. During Winchell's heyday, two-thirds of the adult population of the United States listened to his radio broadcast or read his newspaper column, clamoring to learn more about rich, famous, and powerful people.

The ultimate tool of a democracy, gossip became the great leveler, breaking down distinctions of class, race, and gender in favor of a society where no one is above reproach and everyone is the subject of gossip. Winchell's influence was pervasive, spawning such hugely successful gossipmongers as Hollywood's Hedda Hopper and Louella Parsons, whose fame soon came to exceed even Winchell's. Information that was once considered shocking soon became expected, and over the course of the twentieth century, gossip became an integral component of mainstream journalism. Members of less reputable media were willing to do almost anything to uncover every detail of the lives of individuals they deemed newsworthy.

The emergence of gossip columns and columnists as powerful new journalistic forces and voices during the early twentieth century would not have been possible without celebrities. In the past, famous people were famous because of heroism, genius, talent, wealth, or aristocratic birth. The invention of motion pictures and television and their subsequent development into immensely popular forms of entertainment, however, gave birth to a new kind of fame, known as celebrity. People in movies and on television were often more beautiful, more ambitious, and more talented than the average American, but as a rule, they were generally no better born. Celebrities were thus tantalizing to the American public that saw in them the breakdown of an old social order and new possibilities for themselves. The public clamored to know as much as possible about celebrities, and the media tried to meet the demand. This reciprocal relationship spawned the mass-media frenzy that defined the twentieth century.

Gossip has always existed, but it did not become a big business in the United States until Winchell made gossip a staple of the modern press. Neal Gabler, Winchell's biographer, notes in his book, *Winchell: Gossip, Power, and the Culture of Celebrity* (1994), that the tough-talking Winchell "no more invented gossip than he invented slang." In the 1920s Stephen Clow started the monthly tabloid newspaper *Broadway Brevities and Social Gossip*, on the premise that he could make money by getting people to pay him not to print gossip about them.

According to Gabler, the media in the early 1920s was

> exerting an almost inexorable pressure toward gossip by engendering a fascination with personalities. In the movies, magazines and the tabloids, personalities were sales devices; once the public became aware of these personalities, its curiosity was insatiable. With the interest in place, all that was needed to cross the line to gossip was someone with the audacity and nerve to begin writing frankly about the various private doings of the celebrated—someone who would defy the taboo. That was where Winchell came in.

WALTER WINCHELL

Although respectable papers refused to have anything to do with reporting gossip, for the tabloids the line was a little less blurred. In 1924 a new tabloid emerged called the *Graphic*, a publication dedicated to the masses that was not afraid to splash sex across its front page. On the staff of the *Graphic* was a twenty-seven-year-old former vaudevillian named Walter Winchell, who had spent the past four years establishing his reputation as a Broadway reporter. Winchell loved gossip, and he longed to print it in his column.

Inspired by the *Graphic*'s dictum to print "Nothing but the Truth," Winchell's Monday column, "Mainly about Mainstreeters," stunned the theater and journalism worlds. He printed straight gossip. Sex, extramarital affairs, and illegitimate children all found their way into Winchell's Monday pieces. Nothing was out-of-bounds. And Winchell made it additionally juicy by printing the gossip in bold type, virtually creating a new gossip lingo composed of innuendo, double entendre, and slang.

Gabler writes that the "journalistic Old Guard was enraged by the affront to privacy." Winchell, however, had struck a voyeuristic chord in many Americans, and readers devoured his column. They were eager to read about the celebrities created by the entertainment industry. Urbanization was also a factor in the popularity of Winchell's column. According to Gabler, America was being transformed "from a community into a society," with gossip providing a standard frame of reference and empowering readers to see into the lives of the rich and famous.

During the height of his power, Winchell was untouchable. He struck fear into the hearts of the rich, famous, and vulnerable, even as he delighted a national audience of millions. He became one of the most powerful men in America. He was a friend of J. Edgar Hoover, the director of the Federal Bureau of Investigation (FBI); an adviser to President Franklin Delano Roosevelt; and, later, a staunch supporter of McCarthyism. The puissance of his pen became the scourge of his enemies, for although he could make someone's reputation, he could also break it. Yet, as journalist Alistair Cooke once wrote, Winchell's devastating power "was the promise of American freedom and uninhibited bounce; he was Americanism symbolized in a nose-thumbing at the portentousness of the great." Winchell himself once said, "Democracy is where everybody can kick everybody else's ass. But you can't kick Winchell's."

There were, of course, many others who jumped on the gossip bandwagon. Ed Sullivan, host of the long-running variety television show *The Ed Sullivan Show*, began his career writing a theater column for the *Graphic*. Other major gossip columnists included Dorothy Kilgallen; Sidney Skolsky; and, of course, Louella Parsons and Hedda Hopper, who would later rule Hollywood much as Winchell did New York.

PARSONS AND HOPPER

Parsons was a large, strong-willed woman who carved out a career for herself when she was in her thirties, working as a Chicago reporter on the fledgling movie business. When she moved to New York in 1918, she began campaigning to earn the attention of media mogul William Randolph Hearst by inserting glowing praises and weekly mentions of his paramour, actress Marion Davies, in her weekly column. By the early 1920s Hearst had given Parsons a job, and by the mid-1920s she had moved to Hollywood and become globally syndicated. She quickly became the most powerful woman in Hollywood, demanding and receiving every scoop in the movie business. Like Winchell, she was unafraid to print the truth, sniff out scandal, or tell secrets.

In the mid-1930s Hopper, a former actress, was hired to write a column to compete with Parsons's. Although Hopper and Parsons had once been friends, they soon became archenemies, competing for every scoop. Their rivalry upped the ante immediately, and gossip flew from their dueling pens. For almost thirty years, Hopper and Parsons held Hollywood in their hands, making and ruining careers. When Parsons broke the story of actress Ingrid Bergman's illegitimate child with director Roberto Rossellini, Bergman did not work in Hollywood for almost a decade. Neither Parsons nor Hopper was above being vindictive and destructive, and both could inspire genuine rage among members of the motion picture community, who were helpless to fight them. Actor Joseph Cotten once kicked the chair on which Hopper had been sitting to bits after she announced his extramarital affair in her column. His house was soon filled with flowers and telegrams from others who had been similarly maligned. But like Winchell, Hopper and Parsons went out of their way to help those they liked, and their power could become a boon for someone struggling to make it in the movies.

CONTEMPORARY TRENDS AND CONTROVERSIES

As the Golden Age of Hollywood ended and the studio system crumbled, Hopper and Parsons no longer wielded the clout they had once had when studio moguls were forced to kowtow to them. Winchell, too, began to lose his former hegemony, as his New York connections no longer gave him the edge on gossip in movies and television. But the die was cast. Writers were emboldened by the 1964 ruling in *New York Times v. Sullivan* that established a malice standard that placed all the burden on the plaintiff to prove that the author or publisher knowingly printed an outright falsehood. In 1974 *People* magazine hit the shelves; jettisoning any focus on issues, the magazine devoted itself completely to examining the lives of the people who made the news. *Us Magazine* appeared shortly after in 1977. Founded by the New York Times Company, it was eventually sold to Wenner Media in 1986. Originally *Us* covered Hollywood industry news, but by 2000 it changed from a monthly to a weekly publication, *Us Weekly*, devoting its content to celebrity gossip. Perhaps no one performed the role of the gossip columnist more effectively than Liz Smith. Her popularity translated to both newspapers and television. At the height of her career, her column was syndicated in over seventy newspapers, and she held the highest contract for a columnist in history. Gossip had become an integral part of the media, carried on not only by actual gossip columnists but also by mainstream journalists, eager to spice up the news to make a good read. Gossip spilled onto television as early as 1982 with the highly successful *Entertainment Tonight* (*ET*). Like many of its print counterparts, *ET* focused on reviewing movies and television shows, but it soon progressed into covering more scintillating topics and obtaining exclusive interviews with notorious figures like Tonya Harding and Amy Fisher.

In 1997 Princess Diana, the former wife of Prince Charles of England, died in a car crash while trying to evade paparazzi. The incident raised international concerns about the activities of paparazzi and their efforts to snap a picture of a celebrity. With the evolution of the Internet, gossip found another outlet. After Internet gossipmonger Matt Drudge began to spread rumors of President Bill Clinton's extramarital affairs, they became mainstream news, adding fuel to the ongoing debate about whether or not the media goes too far in reporting the private affairs of public people.

The Internet proved to be fertile ground for gossip writers, establishing websites such as Yahoo!, OMG!, TMZ, Perez Hilton, and Gawker. Top sites like Yahoo!, OMG!, and TMZ boasted more than twenty million unique visitors per month, while Perez Hilton accounted for close to ten million visitors, and Gawker close to five million. TMZ proved to be integral in exposing Mel Gibson's anti-Semitic tirades. In 2009 TMZ released a photo of pop singer Rihanna, who had been assaulted by her boyfriend, sparking a celebrity rights activist group to petition for a law, known as "Rihanna's Law," to prohibit photos involved in legal cases from being leaked to the media.

The debate concerning the ethics of gossip took on new momentum in 2011 when it was revealed that employees of Rupert Murdoch, the owner of the British newspapers the*News of the World* and the *Sun*, had been engaged in bribery, wiretapping, and other unscrupulous practices in their voracious search for news. Celebrity targets included Prince William of England, actor Hugh Grant, and author J. K. Rowling. The scandal spread, resulting in the arrest of a former press chief to the prime minister of England and top-ranking members of the London police. Murdoch was forced to shut down the 168-year-old *News of the World*. By early 2012 employees at the *Sun* were also under investigation, and eight people had been arrested.

Victoria Price

SEE ALSO: *Bergman, Ingrid; Cotten, Joseph; Diana, Princess of Wales; Etiquette Columns; FBI (Federal Bureau of Investigation); Hearst, William Randolph; Hollywood; Hoover, J. Edgar; The Internet; McCarthyism; Media Feeding Frenzies; Sullivan, Ed; Tabloid Television; Tabloids; Vaudeville; The* Wall Street Journal*; Winchell, Walter.*

BIBLIOGRAPHY

Bernstein, Carl. "Murdoch's Watergate." *Newsweek*, July 10, 2011. Accessed March 7, 2012. Available from http://www.thedailybeast.com/newsweek/2011/07/10/murdoch-s-watergate.html

Collins, Amy Fine. "Idol Gossips." *Vanity Fair*, April 1997, 357–375.

Eells, George. *Hedda and Louella: A Dual Biography of Hedda Hopper and Louella Parsons.* New York: Putnam, 1972.

Gabler, Neal. *Winchell: Gossip, Power, and the Culture of Celebrity.* New York: Knopf, 1994.

Inglis, Fred. *A Short History of Celebrity.* Princeton, NJ: Princeton University Press, 2010.

Sennett, Robert S. *Hollywood Hoopla: Creating Stars and Selling Movies in the Golden Age of Hollywood.* New York: Billboard Books, 1998.

Spacks, Patricia Meyer. *Gossip.* New York: Knopf, 1985.

Goth

Although members of the Goth youth subculture may differ in their own definitions, Goth can be characterized by a fascination with all things otherworldly, from vampires to magic and beyond. Partly because of the link to the Goth students who opened fire on classmates at Columbine High School in 1999, public perceptions of Goth often carry connotations of a fondness for violence that have little to do with actual fact. Proponents of Goth embrace certain fashions and lifestyles that affect their interests in art, literature, and film. Within the music world, Goth, like punk, comprises a musical genre as well as an attitude, represented by somber acts such as Bauhaus, Dead Can Dance, Christian Death, and Faith and the Muse.

Often perceived by the general public as little more than "kids who wear black clothes," the Goth scene is a fusion of attitudes stemming from the sublime emotion of Romantic poetry, the macabre images of decadent Victorian poetry, and the contempt for normative bourgeois complacency found in the punk movement. While it is true that Goth has been centered on themes of death and morbidity, what often goes unnoticed is Goth's sense of humor—albeit a decidedly black one. Since the late twentieth century, the Goth subculture has been irrevocably intertwined with new technologies, particularly with the Internet. Through online communities, Goths are able to share interests via bulletin boards, newsgroups, music, fashion, and member websites.

Several books examining the Goth lifestyle have been published in the first years of the twenty-first century. Mick Mercer's *21st Century Goth* (2002) contains a detailed look at recent developments in the Goth scene. It has been called the most comprehensive handling of the Goth scene to date, but it has been criticized for its lack of true scholarship. A more scholarly work is Paul Hodkinson's *Goth: Identity, Style, and Subculture* (2002), which examines Goth through interviews, surveys, and participant observation.

Shaun Frentner

SEE ALSO: *The Internet; Punk; Teenagers;* Twilight*; Vampires.*

BIBLIOGRAPHY

Edmundson, Mark. *Nightmare on Main Street: Angels, Sadomasochism, and the Culture of the Gothic.* Cambridge, MA: Harvard University Press, 1997.

Goodlad, Lauren M. E., and Michael Bibby, eds. *Goth: Undead Subculture.* Durham, NC: Duke University Press, 2007.

Hodkinson, Paul. *Goth: Identity, Style, and Subculture.* New York: Berg, 2002.

Mercer, Mick. *The Hex Files: The Goth Bible.* Woodstock, NY: Overlook Press, 1997.

Mercer, Mick. *21st Century Goth.* Surrey, UK: Reynolds and Hearn, 2002.

Poole, W. Scott. *Monsters in America: Our Historical Obsessions with the Hideous and the Haunting.* Waco, TX: Baylor University Press, 2011.

Gotti, John *(1940–2002)*

Known as the "Teflon Don" because he was acquitted in several criminal trials and as the "Dapper Don" for his penchant for expensive, custom-tailored suits, John Gotti was the most visible organized crime figure of the late twentieth century. A media celebrity in the late 1980s and early 1990s, the boastful Gotti offered a public image of macho ultra-confidence that many admirers associated with the iconic American figure of the rebel. In fact, crowds of his supporters often gathered outside the court during his trials. Within the Mob, Gotti was reportedly a ruthless enforcer who controlled New York's Gambino crime family after the 1985 assassination of Paul Castellano outside a Manhattan restaurant.

Gotti was ultimately betrayed by his closest associate, Salvatore "Sammy the Bull" Gravano, and convicted on federal racketeering and murder charges in 1992. In addition to Gravano's devastating testimony, thousands of hours of taped conversations in which Gotti discussed criminal activities with his top associates secured the government's case against him. He received a life sentence in a maximum security federal penitentiary in Marion, Illinois, where he remained until his death from throat cancer on June 10, 2002.

Laurie DiMauro

SEE ALSO: *Mafia/Organized Crime.*

BIBLIOGRAPHY

Capeci, Jerry, and Gene Mustain. *Gotti: Rise and Fall.* New York: Penguin Group, 1996.

Davis, John H. *Mafia Dynasty: The Rise and Fall of the Gambino Crime Family.* New York: HarperCollins, 1993.

Dorigo, Joe. *Mafia.* Secaucus, NJ: Chartwell Books, 1992.

Nash, Jay Robert. *World Encyclopedia of Organized Crime.* New York: Da Capo Press, 1993.

Gourmet Grocery Stores

Supermarkets were unheard of at the beginning of the twentieth century, and grocery shopping typically involved many trips to local providers—the butcher, the greengrocer, the baker, the general store, and so on. By the mid-twentieth century, however, most urban areas had self-serve stores that brought food items under one roof, and standardized, mass-produced food items were widely available. A variety of friendly, affordable brands such as Pillsbury, Campbell's, and Green Giant became staples of the middle-income kitchen.

At the same time, however, an increasing number of consumers were learning about different styles of cooking, and eventually they began to supplement standard food products with more adventurous purchases. As the twentieth century progressed, a growing number of cooking magazines, television programs, cookbooks, and ethnic restaurants speeded up this process, and the term *gourmet* moved away from connotations such as "expensive," "snobbish," and "indulgent" toward associations such as "high quality," "well made," and "healthful."

A major turning point took place in the early 1960s, when Julia Child's popular television series *The French Chef* encouraged ordinary Americans to develop an interest in "fine cuisine." Around the same time, California entrepreneur Joe Coulombe decided to convert his three struggling convenience stores into outlets for bargain-priced specialty foods, tapping into a rising demand that eventually made the stores (Trader Joe's) a retail phenomenon. On the other side of the country, in New York City, a neighborhood store owned by the Balducci family had combined a top-quality butcher shop, seafood shop, produce market, and bakery under one roof, along with a variety of specialty products. Balducci's became a prototype for the gourmet grocery store, offering convenient one-stop shopping for both premium cooking ingredients and delicious prepared foods.

By the 1980s packaged specialty foods were available in trendy urban areas and upscale suburbs, mostly in gourmet kitchenware stores such as Williams-Sonoma, high-end department stores like Neiman Marcus, and boutique gift shops. There was very little access to premium fresh items, however, and mainstream customers shopped in conventional supermarkets, which typically offered nothing more exotic than olive oil and anchovies in their "gourmet" sections. Consumers were not yet demanding access to more gourmet-type specialty items—but there *was* a growing market for the category of high-quality, nonstandard items described as "natural foods." Several upscale chains emerged to supply the market for healthier shopping options, and these stores soon began stocking a variety of specialty and exotic items as well.

Whole Foods Market, for example, started out in 1980 as a small health-food store in Texas, grew into a festive two-story marketplace, and within two decades was opening its 100th location. The Fresh Market chain began in 1982 as an independent North Carolina grocery designed to create a "European" shopping experience—by 2011 there were 110 Fresh Market stores in twenty-one states. In 2012 Whole Foods had more than 300 stores in the United States and the United Kingdom, and Trader Joe's, which had increased its offerings to court the natural foods shopper, boasted 365 locations across more than thirty states.

As this market trend continued, the national chains paid attention. In 2002 grocery giant Kroger added natural-food departments to 120 of its existing stores and began increasing the space allocation for specialty products in hundreds of other locations. Taking a different approach, regional chain H-E-B developed a gourmet-concept spin-off called Central Market in

1994 and gradually added stores to the line in urban areas of Texas, as well as increasing the selection of specialty foods in its 300-plus H-E-B supermarkets. Like Whole Foods, Fresh Market, and Trader Joe's, Central Market offers a festive shopping atmosphere, with frequent tastings, seasonal celebrations, and even live entertainment. The major chains stock their own product lines along with nationally known gourmet brands, and many locations have an in-store restaurant, a flower shop, and extensive take-out offerings. Retaining their connection to the natural foods category, these gourmet grocery stores also offer a wide selection of organic, vegetarian, vegan, and sustainably farmed products.

Although specialty food sales are affected by economic conditions, this segment of the grocery industry consistently enjoys modest annual gains—and the success of gourmet chains has encouraged other retailers to provide shoppers with a broader selection and a more engaging environment. The study "Gourmet, Specialty and Premium Foods, Beverages and Consumer Trends in the U.S.," published in 2010 by the market research firm Packaged Facts, reports that about 20 percent of consumers actively seek gourmet products—and 30 percent say they are willing to pay more for premium items. Among the specialty items categorized as "gourmet," cheeses, condiments, coffees, and boutique confections consistently dominate sales.

Cynthia Giles

SEE ALSO: *Child, Julia; Consumerism; Foodies; Organic Food; Television; Vegetarianism.*

BIBLIOGRAPHY

Pegler, Martin M. *Gourmet & Specialty Shops.* New York: Visual Reference, 2001.

Watson, James L., and Melissa L. Caldwell. *The Cultural Politics of Food and Eating: A Reader.* Malden, MA: Blackwell, 2005.

Wemischner, Robert, and Karen Karp. *Gourmet to Go: A Guide to Opening and Operating a Specialty Food Store.* New York: John Wiley, 1998.

GPS

Since the 1970s the Global Positioning System (GPS) has been used as a navigation tool by the U.S. government, which reserved the highest-quality signal for itself and provided civilians with a lesser-quality signal. This selective ability (SA) ended at midnight on May 1, 2000, by order of President Bill Clinton, and the system entered the American mainstream. The goal was to make the system more reliable for civil and commercial users. Since that day, its popularity has steadily increased, and by 2008 more than 15.1 million GPS devices were sold in the United States.

GPS is a navigational system consisting of at least twenty-four space satellites maintained by the U.S. government and freely available worldwide to anyone with a GPS receiver. The system allows receivers to calculate users' positions through a one-way satellite transmission of location and time. The satellites are arranged in an orbit around the earth in such a way that, theoretically, there are four satellites within reach of receivers from any point on the globe.

People with a GPS receiver within the sightline of the satellites can have their location pinpointed with great precision. This is often displayed as an overlay on a map. GPS helps air-traffic controllers guide airplanes, allows for more accurate missile targeting in wartime, and enables authorities to track prisoners wearing specially equipped ankle monitors. It is also commonly used by people who simply need directions. Personal GPS devices began as stand-alone navigation systems designed to be mounted in a car and supported by subscription services. More recently, cars and cell phones now come with GPS receivers built in, raising increasing concerns about privacy. Police have located suspects by tracking the GPS chip in their cell phones. In the consumer sector, some smartphone applications can access individual users' GPS data, allowing them to be tracked and even targeted with advertising based on their current location. Despite these concerns, the popularity of GPS has not declined.

GPS has become a crucial part of the global infrastructure not only for pinpointing location but also for time synchronization in communications networks, banking systems, and power grids. However, the GPS signal can be blocked by natural phenomena such as sunspots or by mechanical intervention in the form of GPS jammers—illegal for consumer use but common in warfare. These vulnerabilities are a major concern for those who rely on GPS data.

On May 3, 2000, one day after SA was turned off, Dave Ulmer created another use for the system. A GPS enthusiast, Ulmer decided to test the accuracy of the newly available system. He hid a navigational target in the woods and posted it on a GPS user-group's website. This was the beginning of the immensely popular sport of geocaching. Enthusiasts, known as geocachers, hide small prizes in parks or other public areas and then post clues about the location and its GPS coordinates online. Searchers use their GPS devices to find the prize and register their discovery. This treasure-hunting game depends on the GPS technology's ubiquitous nature. Geocaching has become a popular hobby, with more than five million people participating worldwide in 2012.

Kim Keeline

SEE ALSO: *Air Travel; Automobile; Cell Phones; Consumerism; Hiking; Satellites; Smartphones.*

BIBLIOGRAPHY

Denny, Mark. *The Science of Navigation: From Dead Reckoning to GPS.* Baltimore, MD: Johns Hopkins University Press, 2012.

Kaplan, Elliott. *Understanding GPS: Principles and Applications,* 2nd ed. Boston: Artech House, 2005.

Maltais, Michelle. "Police Tracking of Cellphones Raises Concerns." *Los Angeles Times,* April 4, 2012.

Maltais, Michelle. "California Location Privacy Bill Moves to Full Senate Vote." *Los Angeles Times,* May 1, 2012.

Grable, Betty *(1916–1973)*

The most popular pinup of American servicemen during World War II, actress, dancer, and singer Betty Grable was the symbol of an era. Dressed in a bathing suit and looking over her shoulder at the camera in her famous pinup, she radiated the optimism of an all-American girl and gave the servicemen a vision of what they were fighting for. Not only did her image adorn barracks all over the world, but her likeness was used by the military to teach soldiers how to read grid maps.

The star of Technicolor musicals at Twentieth Century Fox, she reigned supreme, registering as the number one box-office star in 1943 and appearing on the list of top stars from 1942 to

Betty Grable. *Betty Grable, known for her pin-up looks and shapely legs, was a top box-office star of the 1940s.* SILVER SCREEN COLLECTION/GETTY IMAGES.

1951. Her legs were considered so close to perfection that they were insured by Lloyd's of London for $1 million as a publicity stunt.

Born Ruth Elizabeth Grable in St. Louis, Missouri, she was called Betty. Her starstruck mother, Lillian, was determined to make one of her daughters a star. She failed with elder daughter Marjorie, but Betty had both talent and enthusiasm for a show business career. She studied dance, singing, and the saxophone. She appeared in her first movie at the Fox Studios in the chorus of *Happy Days* (1929) in a black-face number. She was signed to a one-year contract after lying about her age, but when the executives discovered she was only thirteen, they dropped her option.

Her mother was not deterred, however, and arranged for her to appear in entertainer Eddie Cantor's movie *Whoopee* (1930). Grable was then signed by mogul Samuel Goldwyn as a Goldwyn Girl with a five-year contract, but her career still did not take off. She appeared in a few other films, then signed to the Frank Fay stage musical *Tattle Tales*, which closed after only a few performances.

During the mid- to late 1930s she appeared in more than a dozen films, but it was her appearance in a 1934 Fred Astaire/ Ginger Rogers film titled *The Gay Divorcee* that first brought her some notice. In the film, Grable does a dance number with comic character actor Edward Everett Horton called "Let's K-knock K-knees." In 1937 she married former child actor Jackie Coogan, who at the time was embroiled in a lawsuit against his parents regarding his earnings, and this put much strain on the marriage. Coogan and Grable appeared together in *Million Dollar Legs* (1939), but they later divorced.

Grable was finally getting noticed, and Darryl F. Zanuck of Twentieth Century Fox signed her to a contract. He did not have any immediate plans for Grable, so he allowed her to appear in a musical called *DuBarry Was a Lady* on Broadway. The show starred Ethel Merman and Bert Lahr, but it was Grable who caused a sensation performing the number "Well Did You Evah" with Charles Waters. In 1940 Grable left the show to replace an ailing Alice Faye in the movie *Down Argentine Way*. The film was a huge sensation, and Grable immediately became a superstar.

To capitalize on her overnight success, Grable appeared in musicals such as *Moon over Miami* and *Springtime in the Rockies*. It was during the latter film that she met bandleader Harry James, whom she married in 1943 and with whom she had two daughters.

Although her famous pinup may have been her greatest contribution to the war effort, Grable joined other stars at war-bond rallies; in entertaining the troops; and for appearances at the Hollywood Canteen, a service members' nightclub. Grable continued to make successful films, although after the late 1940s her popularity began to wane.

In an attempt to make Grable toe the line, Zanuck brought several blond starlets into the studio, including one Marilyn Monroe. Grable appeared with Monroe in *How to Marry a Millionaire* (1953), and rather than being threatened she took the younger woman under her wing. Grable had tired of Twentieth Century Fox, however, and left shortly after. When *Millionaire* was released, it was Grable who received the most critical praise, and she was persuaded to return for the film *How to Be Very, Very Popular* (1955), a flop that was her last film.

Grable continued to make successful appearances on television and in live theater productions such as *Guys and Dolls* and in a touring company of *Hello Dolly*. Whereas her career was still going well, her personal life was not. In October 1965 she divorced James after more than twenty years of marriage.

In 1969 Grable went to London for the production of a new musical, *Belle Starr*, which was written especially for her. It flopped and closed after sixteen performances. In 1972, shortly after appearing on the Academy Awards telecast, Grable was diagnosed with cancer. After extensive treatments she decided to return to work, appearing in *Born Yesterday*. Unfortunately, the cancer had spread, and within a few months she was dead.

Jill A. Gregg

SEE ALSO: *Academy Awards; Astaire, Fred, and Ginger Rogers; Broadway; Goldwyn, Samuel;* Hello, Dolly!*; Hollywood; James, Harry; Lahr, Bert; Monroe, Marilyn; The Pin-Up; Sex Symbol; Zanuck, Darryl F.*

BIBLIOGRAPHY

Hill, Constance Valis. *Tap Dancing America: A Cultural History* New York: Oxford University Press, 2010.

McGee, Tom. *Betty Grable: The Girl with the Million Dollar Legs*. New York: Vestal Press, 1995.

Pastos, Spero. *Pinup, the Tragedy of Betty Grable*. New York: Putnam, 1986.

Warren, Doug. *Betty Grable, the Reluctant Movie Queen*. New York: St. Martin's Press, 1981.

Graceland

Graceland mansion, home to rock-and-roll phenomenon Elvis Presley for the twenty years preceding his death in 1977, became world famous after it was opened to the public in 1982. Before the end of its first decade as a tourist attraction (or pilgrimage destination for some fans), Graceland had hosted more than one million tourists, and by the late 1990s it served as a symbol of both the indefatigable hope and immense costs of the American Dream.

Named after the first owner's aunt Grace, Graceland was built in the 1930s to resemble an antebellum, plantation-style manor home. Elvis paid $100,000-plus for the mansion in 1957. Located on "Elvis Presley Boulevard," a portion of Highway 51 South in Memphis, Tennessee, the majestic-looking Georgian mansion sits amidst an extraordinarily overflowing mass of plasticized suburban sprawl. There are an astounding number of fast-food establishments within a one-mile radius of the estate.

Inside, the front rooms of the house have been designed for the eyes of "company"; in this case, company that would be curious to know how a poor farmhand's son would live in an atmosphere of newly acquired wealth. There is the obligatory glitzy chandelier in the foyer, an elegant dining room, marble and glass-topped tables, fine porcelain statuary, a gilded piano, overdone white carpeting, yards of gilt-edged draperies hanging about the rooms—in fact, just about everything is trimmed in gold—and much else to indicate wealth and status. A television set sits smack in the middle of one of the front rooms.

Visitors are guided down a dark staircase with carpeted walls and a mirrored ceiling to Elvis's pleasure palace in the basement. One room sports a blinding yellow, white, and black color scheme; one wall of the room houses three built-in TV sets, side by side. Elvis got the idea from President Lyndon Johnson, who needed to monitor all of the evening newscasts at the same time, but Elvis wanted to watch all of the Sunday football games at once. The billiards room is entombed in yards of printed, pleated fabric that covers the walls and ceilings and that enforces a sensation of profound claustrophobia even in those not ordinarily afflicted. The felt on the surface of the pool table was torn years before Presley's death, and he never had it fixed; the keepers of Graceland decided to maintain most such flaws to create a sense that the home is frozen in time. This is a well-intended, though inaccurate, depiction of Graceland as it was when Elvis lived there; many of Elvis's latter-day decorating decisions have been swept away. The blood-red carpeting and drapes were changed to a more pleasing blue hue, and a rotating glass statue in the foyer that spurted water was simply discarded as an embarrassment.

There was no way, though, that the keepers could enforce any more than the smallest degree of upper-class nobility upon Graceland. The coup de grace is what everyone at Graceland calls "the jungle room." According to Graceland-approved legend, in the early 1960s Elvis and his father happened upon an intriguing collection of "Polynesian" wooden and fake fur furniture at a Memphis establishment called Donald's Furniture. Vernon Presley remarked that it was the ugliest furniture he had ever seen in his life. Elvis arranged to buy the entire collection. The "throne," as it might be called, features a wooden owl's head at the top and claws dangling from each arm. Fake greenery languishes about the room, and a small waterfall flows behind the throne. The jungle room is at once horrifying and hilarious.

Graceland served as the obsessive focus of a teenage couple on a pilgrimage from Japan in Jim Jarmusch's 1989 film *Mystery Train*. In 2005 Elvis's daughter, Lisa Marie Presley, sold the majority of her father's estate—including global rights to the image and likeness of Elvis—to media mogul Robert F. X. Sillerman. She kept Graceland but turned its management over to Sillerman's company CKX Inc. In 2006 CKX announced it would turn Graceland into an international tourist destination on par with the Disney or Universal theme parks. Graceland was made a National Historic Landmark on March 27, 2006.

Robin Markowitz

SEE ALSO: *Presley, Elvis.*

BIBLIOGRAPHY

Eggleston, William, and Martin Filler. "Elvis Presley's Graceland—An American Shrine." *House and Garden*, March 1984.

Marcus, Greil. *Mystery Train—Images of America in Rock 'n' Roll Music*. New York: E. P. Dutton, 1975.

Marling, Karal Ann. *Graceland: Going Home with Elvis*. Cambridge, MA: Harvard University Press, 1996.

Mills, C. Wright. *The Power Elite*. New York: Oxford University Press, 1956.

Rushing, Wanda. *Memphis and the Paradox of Place: Globalization in the American South*. Chapel Hill: University of North Carolina Press, 2009.

Sims, Judith. "At Last—The First Elvis Presley Movie." *Rolling Stone*, November 9, 1972.

The Graduate

The 1967 film *The Graduate* is at once a sex farce, a generation gap comedy, and a ballad of alienation and rebellion. The film tells the story of Benjamin Braddock (Dustin Hoffman), a recent graduate of an eastern college who returns to his parent's California home with no ambition, no plans, and no self-esteem. He wanders through a maze of suburban clichés and expectations looking for something to care about, feeling like a pawn in society's chess game. Along comes Mrs. Robinson (Anne Bancroft), the wife of Ben's father's business partner. She has just the cure for Ben's stupor: herself.

Content for a while, Ben soon finds his tryst depressing; he is, after all, still aimless. Meanwhile his parents have picked the perfect girl for him: Elaine Robinson (Katharine Ross), Mrs. Robinson's daughter. Mrs. Robinson forces a promise from Ben that he will not date her daughter, but the pair end up going out together nevertheless. The date ends in disaster, with Ben humiliating Elaine at a strip club. Despite this false start, they end up connecting, and Ben finally feels something. Mrs. Robinson tries to end the relationship by telling her daughter about the affair, but Ben has decided that only Elaine can save him.

Ben pursues Elaine to Berkeley, where he learns she's about to be married and barges in on the wedding. Elaine leaves the altar and runs off with Ben; they hop on a passing bus and ride off together. Happy ending? Those who wanted this to be a romantic comedy thought so. But these virtual strangers barely look at each other on the bus. The triumphant smiles fade from their faces, and they don't utter a word as the haunting beginning of the song "Sounds of Silence" rises on the soundtrack: "Hello darkness, my old friend."

This late 1960s movie took a different look at the generation gap than, say, *Easy Rider*. There were no hippies or protests in this film, no talk of the Vietnam War, and no rock music—easy-listening bards Simon and Garfunkel provided the soundtrack. All of that might have kept the film from being dated, but it still managed to tell a tale of distinctly generational woe.

The Graduate, which was directed by Mike Nichols, is filled with delightful moments: the fleeing lovers use a giant cross to lock their families in the church; an alienated Ben is decked out in scuba gear like an astronaut landing on the Planet of the Parents; a corporate wonk at his parents' party tells Ben that he should think about one word, "plastics"; a classic shot views Ben as a small, frightened man seen under the arch of Mrs. Robinson's bent leg; Ben calls his now-regular lover by the appellation "Mrs."; and perpetual landlord Norman Fell asks Ben if he's "one of those outside agitators." He's not; in fact, Ben may not even be a rebel. He seems to enjoy the products of the corporate culture he despises, such as his graduation present, a new Alfa Romeo, and his parents' swimming pool. The real rebel against the status quo, at least at first, is Mrs. Robinson. When had a woman with such sexual authority, confidence, and cool intelligence ever been portrayed on screen? But Mrs. Robinson is transformed into a demon. She forbids Ben to see Elaine, not because she wants him to herself, but because the guy she commits adultery with is no longer good enough to date her daughter.

As an odd representative of purity, Elaine falls into a marriage with someone she's "sort of" engaged to, mostly because it's what her parents want. She seems to represent everything Ben hates, but instead he sees her as safe, clean, and forgiving—nothing like her mother. Young Ben, hating everything his parents stand for but never articulating why, gets to screw them in the person of his father's partner's wife. But ultimately, he ends up with the girl his parents picked for him, and he's still

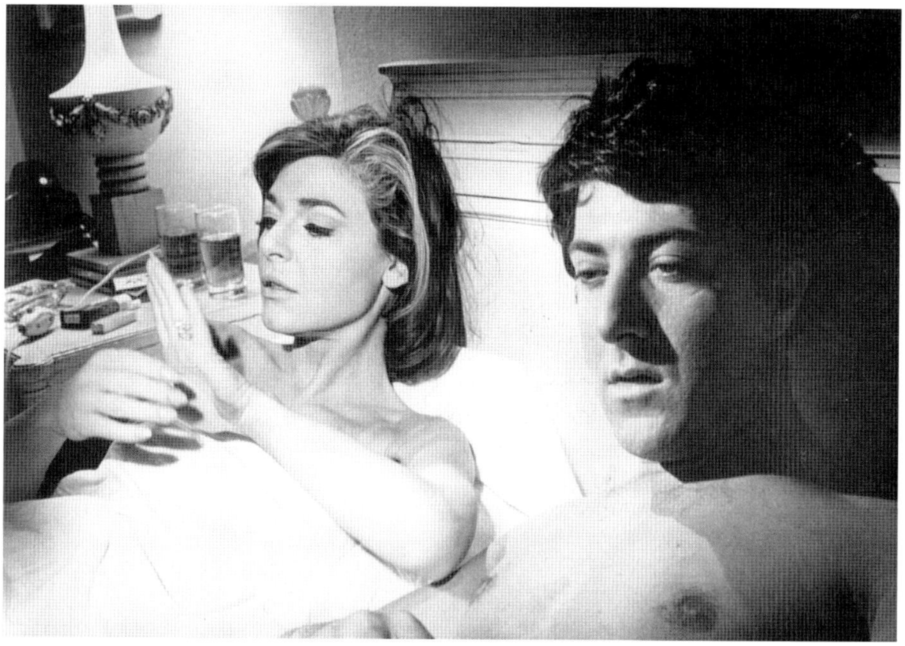

The Graduate. *Anne Bancroft, left, as the seductive Mrs. Robinson beds Dustin Hoffman's aimless college graduate Benjamin Braddock in a scene from* The Graduate. EMBASSY PICTURES/GETTY IMAGES.

aimless. The film seems to deliberately sow confusion, leaving viewers with unanswered questions that become part of the meaning of the film.

Though Hoffman had been in a few movies, Ben is the role that brought him (and director Nichols, who won an Oscar) fame. Hoffman was thirty when he played the twenty-year-old Ben, and Bancroft was only thirty-six. The role of Ben was initially offered to Robert Redford, who turned it down for fear that he wouldn't be able to convey Ben's naïveté. Charles Grodin was then cast in the role, but there was a salary dispute. Bancroft wasn't the first choice for Mrs. Robinson either. The role was offered to Patricia Neal, who was ill, and Doris Day, who was reportedly offended by the character.

Written by Calder Willingham with help from Buck Henry (who has a cameo as the hotel clerk), the film was based on the novel by Charles Webb. Ironically, the Simon and Garfunkel song "Mrs. Robinson," as we know it, was not on the movie's soundtrack, which included only an instrumental version. After the film's successful release, Nichols persuaded Paul Simon to write an actual song with lyrics for use as a marketing tool. It became a huge hit.

Karen Lurie

SEE ALSO: *Day, Doris;* Easy Rider*; Hoffman, Dustin; Nichols, Mike, and Elaine May; Redford, Robert; Simon, Paul; Simon and Garfunkel.*

BIBLIOGRAPHY

Carr, Jay, and National Society of Film Critics. *The A List: The National Society of Film Critics' 100 Essential Films.* Cambridge, MA: Da Capo Press, 2002.

Macklin, F. Anthony. "'Benjamin Will Survive . . . ': Interview with Charles Webb." *Film Heritage* 4, no. 1 (1968): 1–6.

Webb, Charles. *The Graduate.* New York: New American Library, 1963.

Graffiti

People have been scribbling on walls for as long as they have been building them. Graffiti, which comes from the Italian verb *graffiare* (to scratch), covers a wide range of public inscriptions, from the early paintings on the walls of caves at Lascaux, France, to quips hastily inked on contemporary bathroom stalls. In the late twentieth century, a market for graffiti as an art form bloomed, although the majority of graffiti remains unsolicited and anonymous.

Historically, graffiti has been used primarily as a form of personal communication. One of the earliest uses in the United States developed among hobos who rode the rails across the country in the first decades of the twentieth century. The complicated symbolic language of these transients was scratched in chalk on fence posts and in other unobtrusive spots to communicate the receptivity of the townspeople to future travelers.

One of the most famous examples of graffiti in the twentieth century involved the image of James J. Kilroy. Kilroy, a shipyard inspector during World War II, wrote the words "Kilroy was here" in chalk on bulkheads to indicate that he had inspected the riveting. U.S. troops added the scribbled drawing of Kilroy leering over a wall to accompany the inscription "Kilroy was here," and Kilroy became an internationally known phenomenon during the 1940s and 1950s, denoting an American presence. Kilroy turned up in some very odd places; his first appearance is reputed to have been on the side of the battleship *New Yorker*, discovered by U.S. inspectors after the atomic bomb test at the Bikini atoll, but he has also appeared on top of the torch of the Statue of Liberty and under the Arc de Triomphe.

While American soldiers were spreading Kilroy across the globe, another, ultimately more influential, form of graffiti was developing in the United States during the 1940s. The exterior walls of buildings in Hispanic communities in postwar Los Angeles were increasingly decorated with a kind of marking subsequently designated as "old school." Before the advent of spray paint, these black-and-white drawings were realized entirely in marker to communicate the boundaries of neighborhoods controlled by rival gangs.

Although graffiti continued during the 1960s, it was not until the 1970s that it started attracting public attention as a serious social problem. The visibility of graffiti steadily increased as graffiti artists started using spray paint to cover larger areas more colorfully than was previously possible. One of the first graffiti artists to achieve notoriety was a tagger, or name writer, whose signature "Taki 183" began appearing on walls in all five boroughs of New York in 1971. Taki was followed by a hoard of fellow taggers, and by the mid-1970s the primary target of graffiti artists hungry for name recognition had become the trains of the New York City subway system. Throughout the decade, the city of New York fought a battle with enterprising taggers, whose projects grew rapidly from quick signatures to elaborately stylized versions of their street names, dubbed "wild style," that could cover an entire subway car. Even as the transit authorities struggled to remove the colorful paintings, or "throw-ups," New York graffiti was achieving international recognition as part of a nascent hip-hop culture that included rap music and break dancing. Several films immortalize this period, including *Wild Style* (1983) and *Beat Street* (1984).

Eventually, a coating was developed that inhibited the application of spray paint onto the surfaces of trains, and in the 1980s a booming art market developed an interest in graffiti marketed as an art form. Several galleries in Manhattan began specializing in graffiti art, and former graffiti artists such as Keith Haring, known for quick marker drawings in his characteristic outline style, and Jean-Michel Basquiat, a graffiti poet/musician of Haitian/Puerto Rican descent, became instant celebrities, with their works selling for hundreds of thousands of dollars. The public fascination with graffiti faded by the end of the decade, as graffiti became increasingly associated with the activity of urban gangs.

By the twenty-first century, the issue of graffiti had become a hot-button topic for many cities around the world. Despite the criminalizing of such acts, graffiti artists, street gangs, and hate groups continued to use graffiti as a way of expressing themselves. Anti-graffiti groups such as Graffiti Hurts have been established to work with local governments to protect public property from what is viewed as defacement and destruction. In South Africa, white supremacists used graffiti as a way of reminding blacks that apartheid is not far in their past. Thus, the battle continues over whether graffiti is art or vitriol.

Deborah Broderson

SEE ALSO: *Gangs; Haring, Keith; Hip-Hop; Pop Art; Rap; World War II.*

BIBLIOGRAPHY

Ensminger, David. *Visual Vitriol: The Street Art and Subculture of the Punk and Hard Core Generation.* Jackson: University of Mississippi Press, 2012.

Phillips, Susan. *Wallbangin': Graffiti and Gangs in LA.* Chicago: University of Chicago Press, 1999.

Reisner, Robert. *Graffiti: Two Thousand Years of Wall Writing.* New York: Cowles Book, 1971.

Silverman, Jonathan. *The World Is a Text: Writing, Reading, and Thinking about Visual and Popular Culture.* Boston: Prentice Hall, 2012.

Wiese, Markus. *New York: Graffiti 1975–1995.* Moers, Germany: Edition Aragon, 1996.

Wimsatt, William. *Bomb the Suburbs: Graffiti, Freight-Hopping, Race and the Search for Hip-Hop's Moral Center.* Chicago: Subway and Elevated Press, 1994.

Grafton, Sue *(1940–)*

In 2011 the author Sue Grafton's *"V" Is for Vengeance* was published. This novel continued her popular Kinsey Millhone alphabet mystery series. If Grafton continues at her current pace of a novel every two years, she should finish the series with *"Z" Is for . . .* in 2019.

Along with fellow writers Sara Paretsky and Marcia Muller, Grafton has been credited with popularizing the mystery subgenre of the female private eye. Although there have been female detectives almost from the beginning of mystery fiction, in the past they were almost exclusively amateur sleuths rather than detectives for hire. The tough female private eye, written in the tradition of a Mike Hammer or a Philip Marlowe, was unheard of until the late 1970s. Women writers of this type of mystery were also rare. Because of the growing popularity of Grafton, Paretsky, and Muller, however, other authors have begun to introduce many new female detectives. Nevertheless, Grafton's Kinsey Millhone remains among the most popular.

It now seems almost inevitable that Grafton would become a mystery writer. She was born in Louisville, Kentucky, the daughter of teacher Vivian Harnsberger and attorney C. W. Grafton, himself a mystery writer of some note who had several books published in the 1940s and 1950s. Grafton earned a bachelor of arts from the University of Louisville in 1961 with a major in English literature. After graduation she worked in the medical field in various capacities while pursuing her writing. She also married three times and began a family that would eventually include three children.

Grafton's initial forays into novel writing were not in the mystery realm. Her first novel, *Keziah Dane*, was published in 1967. Her second novel, *The Lolly-Madonna War*, published in 1969, was made into the motion picture *Lolly-Madonna XXX* in 1973, with Grafton cowriting the screenplay. This experience led to her early career as a writer for television. During that time she wrote episodes for several television programs, including *Rhoda* (1974–1978) and *Seven Brides for Seven Brothers* (1982–1983). Grafton was also a prolific writer of made-for-television movies, including *Sex and the Single Parent* (1979); *Walking through Fire* (1979), for which she won a Christopher Award; and the critically acclaimed *Nurse* (1980), which starred Michael Learned. With third husband and writing partner Steven Humphrey, she adapted two Agatha Christie novels for TV: *Sparkling Cyanide* (1983) and *A Caribbean Mystery* (1989). The experience of working as a writer of television and movies later made Grafton vow that no Kinsey Millhone novel would ever be used for a motion picture.

Although she was a successful screenwriter, Grafton was determined to leave Hollywood. She planned to try her hand at writing a mystery novel, as her father had forty years before, and she decided her main character would be a female private detective. Grafton based Kinsey Millhone largely on herself. In 1982 she began the alphabet mystery series with *"A" Is for Alibi*, for which she won an Anthony Award. She has continued to win some of the mystery genre's biggest awards, including a Grand Master Award from the Mystery Writers of America in 2009.

Grafton has had an impact on television and its culture with her screenplays and television shows. However, with the popular Kinsey Millhone series, she has continued to stretch not only the boundaries of mystery fiction but also those of acceptable behavior for women, whether fictional or flesh and bone.

Jill Gregg Clever

SEE ALSO: *Best Sellers; Detective Fiction; Hard-Boiled Detective Fiction; Made-for-Television Movies; Paretsky, Sara.*

BIBLIOGRAPHY

Drew, Bernard A. *The 100 Most Popular Contemporary Mystery Authors.* Santa Barbara, CA: Libraries Unlimited, 2011.

Kaufman, Natalie Hevener, and Carol McGinnis Kay. *"G" Is for Grafton: The World of Kinsey Millhone.* New York: Henry Holt, 1997.

Graham, Bill *(1931–1991)*

Bill Graham revolutionized the music industry by providing a forum for the explosion of artistic expression in rock and roll during the 1960s. Though Graham was a teetotaler, he was a prime mover of the psychedelic movement. He used his shrewd business acumen to present music to the world and make it profitable and self-sustaining. In the process, Graham drew attention to this brilliant period of cultural revolution and focused its creative energy into a live-performance ethic that has become the standard.

Born Wolfgang Grajonca on January 8, 1931, in Berlin, Graham was the only son in a large Russian-Jewish family. Graham was sent away to school to escape the Hitler Youth movement, and later, when Germany invaded Poland in 1939, he and his younger sister were transported to France as deportation to labor camps became inevitable. Graham developed few memories of his family, having spent his formative years surrounded by air raids and bomb shelters. As the Nazis pushed into France in 1941, he was separated from his ailing sister when he fled (mostly on foot) with other refugees. Meanwhile, all but two of his sisters were deported to the concentration camp at Auschwitz.

COMING TO AMERICA

Like many Jewish refugees during World War II, Graham was sent to New York City. He languished in a foster home until he was adopted by Alfred and Pearl Ehrenreich in 1941, whereupon he quickly learned English from the Ehrenreichs' son, Roy. Though Graham was not a U.S. citizen and was ridiculed for his heavy German accent, he became an active, integral part of his ethnic community. When World War II ended, he corresponded and was later reunited with his surviving sisters.

In high school and community college, Graham was a hard worker if not a stellar pupil. He held several jobs and enjoyed the positive reinforcement of a good tip for a task well done, especially as a waiter at various resorts in the Catskill Mountains in the late 1940s. Here, he also developed his passion for show business, immersing himself in theater, film, and Latin music while rubbing elbows with high-society vacationers and the stars they came to see. In 1950, however, Graham was drafted at the onset of the Korean War. While in the military, he changed his name to Bill (the American equivalent of Wolfgang) Graham (closest to G-r-a-j in the phonebook) and served until 1953, receiving a Bronze Star for valor and—at last—U.S. citizenship.

FINDING HIS NICHE

Discharged and aimless, he hitchhiked across America and worked with theater troupes in New York City and San Francisco. Eventually, he met his future wife, Bonnie, and found a steady job with the San Francisco Mime Troupe, a politically aware artists' collective. It was when the group was arrested for performing in a public park without a permit that Graham discovered his true organizational calling.

In 1965 Graham arranged a benefit to raise bail money for the Mime Troupe and, seeing a business opportunity, set to work organizing larger and more elaborate community events. A strange synthesis was brewing in San Francisco, as the rising counterculture aimed to change society. Performers did more than entertain—they also educated and informed, though too often without a legitimate venue in which to express themselves. Graham filled this void by opening the Fillmore Auditorium, which quickly became the performance space for important cultural and musical events.

Charging nominal fees, Graham exposed the general public to local groups such as the Grateful Dead and Jefferson Airplane, as well as eclectic opening bands such as Ravi Shankar and Miles Davis, claiming "vegetables before dessert" were important. He also supported performance artists, acid tests, be-ins, love-ins, and any other human social experiment in need of a decent sound system. Light shows backed up the music, and performances were advertised by local artists in psychedelic poster art. The Fillmore thus became the entertainment nexus of San Francisco counterculture.

As the 1960s progressed and more people were "turned on" to the hippie aesthetic, Graham branched out and opened an auditorium in New York City, the Fillmore East. He made a sizable profit from the flower power phenomenon, which caused tension between him and his more obstinate cohorts from the early days. As ticket prices increased, so did the pretensions of many performers, and Graham was often regarded as one of "them," a member of the establishment. Yet he managed to straddle the line between exploiter and exploited, earning the trust of many musicians and artists whom he helped to foster.

A ROCK-AND-ROLL PIONEER

Inevitably, his grassroots business went national and then global. Graham was an integral organizer of the legendary Monterey Pop Festival, and though he only advised the organizers of Woodstock, he made that seminal event possible as well. Due to the widening gulf between audiences and performers in the 1970s, Graham closed his Fillmores and began promoting tours to properly present rock and roll to the world. In the 1980s, as behemoth sports arenas seating thousands of people became the standard for the most popular bands, Graham's production company, Bill Graham Presents, pioneered the rock concert as a social statement while his T-shirt and poster business boomed. He promoted some of the first rock concerts in Eastern Europe and organized historic benefits such as Amnesty International's Conspiracy of Hope tour and the Live Aid concert that brought famine relief to Ethiopia.

On October 25, 1991, while leaving a concert he had promoted, Graham was killed in a helicopter crash. A week later, Bill Graham Presents put on a massive free concert in his honor at the Polo Field in Golden Gate Park in San Francisco, the site of many benefit concerts he had organized. Though no announcement was made in advance regarding who would play, the crowd was estimated at nearly half a million. Many important groups to which Graham had given their first break paid tribute to this capitalist who played no instrument but forever changed the public presentation of bands and the influence they exerted on popular culture. He was inducted into the Rock and Roll Hall of Fame in 1992.

Tony Brewer

SEE ALSO: *Davis, Miles; The Grateful Dead; Hippies; Jefferson Airplane/Starship; Rock and Roll; Stadium Concerts; Woodstock.*

BIBLIOGRAPHY

Glatt, John. *Rage & Roll: Bill Graham and the Selling of Rock.* Secaucus, NJ: Carol Publishing Group, 1993.

Graham, Bill, and Robert Greenfield. *Bill Graham Presents: My Life inside Rock and Out.* New York: Doubleday, 1992.

Graham, Billy *(1918–)*

Billy Graham was arguably the most prominent of America's Protestant evangelists and one of the most successful evangelists in the history of Christianity. By the time he retired in 2005, he had preached to nearly 215 million people (he may hold the record for addressing the most people face-to-face) and to countless other millions through the media of radio and television. He conducted his famous "crusades" in more than 185 countries and territories and is admired even by many who do not share his religious beliefs. For more than five decades, Americans named him to the Gallup Poll's lists of the Ten Most Admired Men in the World, placing his total number of appearances on the list well above those of former President Ronald Reagan and Pope John Paul II, who hold second and third place, respectively. Graham has spoken intimately with many of the most powerful figures of the twentieth century, including twelve American presidents, Winston Churchill, Mikhail Gorbachev, Kim Il Sung, and Pope John Paul II. Former President George H. W. Bush has called him "America's pastor," but Graham's influence is global.

A COUNTRY BOY AND HIS CALLING

When he was born on November 7, 1918, in Charlotte, North Carolina, there was nothing to suggest that William Franklin Graham Jr. would become a world-renowned personality. His parents were country people, devout Christians who reared Billy Frank and his siblings to read the Bible, pray often, and work hard on the family's dairy farm. Graham was sixteen years old when Mordecai Ham, a fire-and-brimstone evangelist, came to Charlotte. Like most adolescent males, Graham was more interested in cars, baseball, and girls than in anything an evangelist had to offer. Even after his confession of faith at a Ham service, visible changes in him were slight. Graham admits in his 1997 autobiography, *Just as I Am*, "Although I had been converted, I did not have much of a concept of my life coming under some kind of divine plan. . . . I had no inkling of what my life work was to be." He was certain, he says, that becoming an undertaker or a preacher could be ruled out.

Nevertheless, by 1938, Graham (who by this time had dropped the "Frank") felt that God had called him to preach. From that moment forward his commitment was unswerving. During his years at the Florida Bible Institute, young Graham preached in small churches, in mission services, and on street corners. Later studies at Wheaton College in Illinois gave him a liberal arts background and reinforced his conservative biblical interpretation. Time would mellow Graham in many respects; his staccato delivery would become more conversational, his Protestantism would become more ecumenical, and his social views would become less judgmental, but he would never swerve from his allegiance to what "the Bible says."

Another significant event of his Wheaton years was his encounter with Ruth Bell, the daughter of medical missionaries, who had spent her first seventeen years in Asia and was planning to return as a missionary to Tibet. Instead, in 1943 she married Graham. He served briefly as a pastor, but he soon resigned his church position to become a charter vice president and the first full-time evangelist of Youth for Christ International (YFC). He traveled the country, conducting YFC meetings in Atlanta, Georgia; Norfolk, Virginia; Indianapolis, Indiana; Princeton, New Jersey; and dozens of other cities.

A MAN FOR HIS TIME

It was a fortuitous moment. Post–World War II America was a nation of seekers. Church membership, sales of religious books, and enrollment at religious institutions were all on the rise. Predictably, so were evangelists. Some were no more than confidence men, and others soon fell prey to life's temptations. Concerned with what he referred to as the Elmer Gantry (an opportunistic, dissolute minister in a 1927 Sinclair Lewis novel of the same name) problem, Graham called together his associates during a 1948 Modesto, California, campaign. In what came to be known as the Modesto Manifesto, team members concurred that the sponsoring committee would be asked to handle funds, with no contributions passing through the hands of the Graham team. They further agreed that each would avoid situations that would place him alone with a woman who was not his wife. These simple but effective measures protected the Graham team from the scandals that toppled many other evangelists.

A year later California was again the setting for a Graham milestone. The young evangelist was invited to be the featured speaker at the annual Christ for Greater Los Angeles revival. The Graham team initiated a plan that would in its general shape become their operating policy for the next five decades: it included preparatory revivals, small-group prayer meetings, area-wide choir recruitment, and counselor training. The campaign required nine months of groundwork coupled with thousands of dollars worth of publicity. Despite these efforts, attendance at the services was not extraordinary. Celebrity conversions resulted in only a flurry of interest.

Then William Randolph Hearst gave the order that became part of Graham legend: "Puff Graham," he instructed his papers. The result was media saturation that no amount of money could have purchased: headlines in Hearst papers, wire service coverage, and exposure in national newsmagazines. By the time Graham left Los Angeles, the revival had run for eight weeks, the aggregate congregation had reached into the hundreds of thousands, and Billy Graham had become a national celebrity.

Graham's team launched a twelve-week crusade in London, followed by a European tour, during which the evangelist preached to record crowds in Stockholm, Amsterdam, and Berlin; clearly, his appeal was not limited to Americans. His greatest triumph was probably the 1957 New York crusade: he preached to almost two and a half million people during services that lasted from mid-May through Labor Day. The crusade was important for more than its numbers. Graham, whose critics had long faulted him for failing to use his status more aggressively for social causes, added black evangelist Howard O. Jones to his team, an act that led to a wave of protests from segregationists. Graham also met privately with the Reverend Dr. Martin Luther King Jr. and invited King to be a platform guest. Graham was unquestionably uncomfortable with confrontation, and the concept of civil disobedience troubled the evangelist, whose patriotic fervor and anticommunist rhetoric had been part of his early appeal. He was convinced of the immorality of racism, however; as early as 1952 he had refused to hold segregated services in Jackson, Mississippi, and, by 1953, in other southern cities. Graham's actions may have made a stronger statement to other moderates than his critics have recognized.

THE MESSAGE AND THE MEDIA

The New York crusade was also important in that it was Graham's first broadcast on network television. He had already shown himself to be astute in promulgating his message through the media. His *Hour of Power* radio broadcasts reached millions, as did his syndicated newspaper column, "My Answer." The Billy Graham Evangelistic Association (BGEA) would later use film, video, and the Internet to reach target audiences. The intimate medium of television, however, which brought his crusades into the living rooms of Americans of all creeds, classes, and colors, was probably the most successful in making him so widely known and admired.

During the fifty years after the New York crusade, Graham preached in hundreds of countries. He organized campaigns in the former Eastern bloc nations; in the People's Republic of China; and, in 1973, in South Korea, where he addressed more than a million people, the largest public religious gathering up to that time. He also served as an unofficial spiritual adviser to President Richard M. Nixon during the Watergate crisis. Graham had literally taken his message to the world.

THE GRAHAM LEGACY

The evangelist's reputation suffered a blow in 2002, and again in 2009, when audio recordings surfaced of two conversations he had had with Nixon in the White House. Made in 1972 and 1973 without his knowledge, the tapes reveal him expressing anti-Semitic views. In 2002 Graham said he did not recall the remarks but apologized for any offense they may have caused, insisting that they did not reflect his views and admitting that he should have disagreed with the president. In a separate apology to the Anti-Defamation League (ADL), Graham said that "racial prejudice, anti-Semitism or hatred of anyone with different beliefs has no place in the human mind and heart." The ADL accepted his apology, describing Graham's words as "full of sadness and repentance."

In 2005 Graham preached his final crusade; during the three days in New York City, the crowds were estimated at more than 230,000. Since his wife's death in 2007, he has been plagued by failing vision, hearing loss, Parkinson's disease, and other health problems. He has become increasingly reclusive, rarely leaving his home in Montreat, North Carolina. Graham's twelfth presidential visit, which occurred in his own home, was from Barack Obama; the two men prayed for one another. Three former presidents—Jimmy Carter, George H. W. Bush, and Bill Clinton—spoke at the dedication of the $27 million, 40,000-square-foot Billy Graham Library in Charlotte. The plan for the library was initiated by Franklin Graham, Graham's eldest son and the president and chief executive of the BGEA.

The apparent heir to the Graham legacy, Franklin is a more abrasive and confrontational figure than his father. He has drawn heavy criticism for his statements about Islam and has linked himself politically with the "Religious Right," a move his father carefully avoided. Franklin is also his father's successor as head of Samaritan's Purse, a relief organization. All the Graham children followed their father into evangelism, however. Virginia (GiGi) Leftwich Graham Tchividjian is an author and a popular speaker at women's conferences. Nelson "Ned" Graham is president of East Gates International, which distributes bibles and other Christian literature in China. Anne Graham Lotz, founder and president of AnGel Ministries, has led women's revivals in more than thirty cities in twelve countries. Named by the *New York Times* as one of the five most influential evangelists of her generation and called by some an "evangelical feminist," she is generally considered to be the one who has inherited the best of her father's oratorical gifts.

None of the Graham children nor any other evangelist is likely to prove the elder Graham's equal in influence. He has been variously described as a one-in-a-century preacher and the last of the mass evangelists. Meanwhile, he celebrated his ninety-third birthday on November 7, 2011, and believes the God he has served for most of his long life still has work for him to do. His thirtieth book, *Nearing Home: Life, Faith, and Finishing Well*, written in the aftermath of his wife's death, was published in 2011. Graham says that old age is "not for wimps" but that it compensates for its challenges with "remembrance, observation and reflection" in the knowledge that the believer's task is still to serve God's purpose.

Wylene Rholetter

SEE ALSO: *Celebrity; Civil Disobedience; Evangelism; Feminism; Hearst, William Randolph; The Internet; King, Martin Luther, Jr.; Lewis, Sinclair; Megachurches; Networks; Obama, Barack; The Pope; Radio; Religious Right; Syndication; Televangelism; Television; Videos; Watergate; Wire Services; World War II.*

BIBLIOGRAPHY

"ADL Accepts the Rev. Graham's Apology." Anti-Defamation League, March 19, 2002. Accessed January 12, 2012. Available from http://www.adl.org

Aikman, David. *Great Souls*. New York: Word, 1998.

Frady, Marshall. *Billy Graham: A Parable of American Righteousness*. Boston: Little, Brown, 1979.

Gibbs, Nancy, and Michael Duffy. *The Preacher and the Presidents: Billy Graham in the White House*. New York: Center Street, 2007.

Graham, Billy. *Just as I Am: The Autobiography of Billy Graham*. New York: HarperCollins, 1997.

Graham, Billy. *Nearing Home: Life, Faith, and Finishing Well*. Nashville, TN: Thomas Nelson, 2011.

Martin, William. *A Prophet with Honor: The Billy Graham Story*. New York: William Morrow, 1991.

Miller, Steven P. *Billy Graham and the Rise of the Republican South*. Philadelphia: University of Pennsylvania Press, 2009.

Wacker, Grant. "Billy Graham's America." *Church History* 78, no. 3 (2009), 489–511.

Graham, Martha *(1894–1991)*

The greatest and most influential choreographer of modern dance, Martha Graham built on the foundations created by American pioneers such as Isadora Duncan, Ruth St. Denis, Ted Shawn, and Doris Humphrey. She created and codified a dance language that stressed the downward pull of gravity and balance—and along with it she identified a series of gestures and movements to express particular emotions in dance. Early in her career she explored American experience in such works as *Steps in the Streets* (1936) about homelessness, *El Pentitente* (1940) about a religious cult in the Southwest, and *Appalachian Spring* (1944) about a Shaker wedding. Later, Graham examined the spiritual and psychological meaning of classical myths, including the story of Oedipus in *Night Journey* (1947) and *Clytemnestra* (1958). She began dancing in 1916 and retired as a dancer in 1970, although she continued to choreograph for her company until her death at age ninety-six.

Jeffrey Escoffier

SEE ALSO: *Duncan, Isadora; Modern Dance; Shawn, Ted; St. Denis, Ruth.*

BIBLIOGRAPHY

De Mille, Agnes. *The Life and Work of Martha Graham*. New York: Random House Vintage Books, 1991.

Horosko, Marian. *Martha Graham: The Evolution of Her Dance Theory and Training*. Gainesville: University Press of Florida, 2002.

Grammy Awards

Commonly called "music's biggest night," the Grammy Awards ceremony is an annual event recognizing outstanding achievements in the field of audio recording. The four biggest honors are Album of the Year, Song of the Year, Record of the Year, and New Artist of the Year, but the live televised performances by various musical acts have become almost as anticipated as the awards presentations.

The Grammys are given by the National Academy of Recording Arts & Sciences (NARAS), which was founded in 1957 by a group of record executives. Their aim was to raise the standard in recorded music while ignoring the new phenomenon of rock and roll, which was thought to be the "devil's music," catering to people's baser instincts. Originally, the award was to be called the Eddie (after Thomas Edison), but the NARAS settled on the Gramophone (after Edison's invention). The award then became known simply as the Grammy. The ceremony was first telecast in 1959 as a series of specials throughout the year, and the first live telecast was in 1971.

Early Grammy winners were mainstream acts such as Ella Fitzgerald and Frank Sinatra. Even as rock and roll grew in popularity in the 1950s and 1960s, it was largely overlooked by the NARAS. A Grammy was not bestowed upon a rock-and-roll recording until 1961, when Chubby Checker won for his song "Let's Twist Again." As the culture wars of the 1960s escalated on college campuses and city streets, the war between "popular" music and rock and roll played out in the Grammy Awards. Even today, the NARAS is often criticized for making safe choices for its winners. Critic Paul Grein of the *Los Angeles Times* once said, "They like their music right down the middle—not too hard too funky too adventurous."

In the late 1960s, this trend was evident when middle-of-the-road performers such as country music's Glen Campbell took home the Grammy hardware. Awards were not being given to the more controversial rock-and-roll acts that were sweeping the nation, such as the Rolling Stones. Cutting-edge performers such as Jimi Hendrix never won the award, and even the Beatles, the most influential rock band of all time, received very little Grammy recognition.

By the 1970s the Grammys had started to grow in prestige, though the NARAS was still often accused of honoring the most popular performers rather than those who had garnered critical praise. As rock and roll became ingrained in mainstream culture, acts such as Fleetwood Mac began winning Grammys. Nevertheless, the televised awards show featured performances mainly by music's biggest acts in order to bolster ratings.

The show grew in scale in the 1980s, and with the advent of MTV and the rise of pop superstars such as Michael Jackson, a generational gap developed. The producers staged elaborate, video-like production numbers in order to draw in the young MTV generation. In 1988, for example, Whitney Houston gave a highly choreographed performance of her hit song "I Wanna Dance with Somebody (Who Loves Me)." The 1990s and the first decade of the 2000s saw the Grammy telecasts drop in the ratings. The live performances continue to grow in grandeur, but the NARAS still has a reputation for rewarding "safe" acts. In 2011 the NARAS restructured its awards, giving out seventy-eight Grammys as opposed to 109 in previous years. Some jazz and blues awards were among the casualties, much to the chagrin of the artists from those genres.

Though often criticized for being behind the times and for awarding commercial rather than critical success, the Grammy Awards have been a microcosm of the music industry and its changing tastes. The Grammys remain the most prestigious music awards ceremony, even as other events, such as the American Music Awards and Billboard Music Awards, attract high-profile acts and large television audiences.

Jill Gregg Clever

SEE ALSO: *The Beatles; Campbell, Glen; Checker, Chubby; Contemporary Christian Music; Country Music; Fitzgerald, Ella; Fleetwood Mac; Funk; Gangsta Rap; Glitter Rock; Gospel Music; Grunge; Hendrix, Jimi; Hip-Hop; Houston, Whitney; Jackson, Michael; Jazz; MTV; New Wave Music; Pop Music; Punk; Rap; Rhythm and Blues; Rock and Roll; The Rolling Stones; Sinatra, Frank; Television; Top 40.*

BIBLIOGRAPHY

Ehrlich, Ken, and Bono. *At the Grammys!: Behind the Scenes at Music's Biggest Night.* New York: Hal Leonard Books, 2007.

O'Neil, Thomas. *The Grammys.* New York: Perigree Books, 1999.

Wild, David. *And the Grammy Goes to . . . : The Official Story of Music's Most Coveted Award.* New York: State Street Press, 2007.

Grand Ole Opry

The longest-running radio show in broadcasting history, the *Grand Ole Opry* has long been the symbolic center of country music. It represents the pinnacle of success for performing artists, for whom the Grand Ole Opry is the country music equivalent of playing Carnegie Hall. The Opry is, however, much more than simply a prestigious performance venue. Since its inception in 1925, it has brought country music to listeners all across the United States, helping to transform the genre from a regional musical form to a national one. For its rural listeners, spread out across vast stretches of open space, the *Opry* became part of the common bond that united rural folk across the country, not only providing musical entertainment but also creating a collective cultural home.

EARLY HISTORY

In the early 1920s radio was still a new means of communication. As its commercial potential grew, certain radio stations began to broadcast programs with special appeal to rural listeners. In 1925 George D. Hay, formerly an announcer at WLS in Chicago, which featured a country music program called *The National Barn Dance*, took a job as station director at the new WSM radio station in Nashville, Tennessee. Hay's first program was the WSM *Barn Dance*, a copy of the WLS show in Chicago that featured just two performers, seventy-seven-year-old fiddle player Uncle Jimmy Thompson and his niece, pianist Eva Thompson Jones. The hour-long show consisted of nothing more than fiddle tunes with piano accompaniment, but the show drew such a favorable response that the format was continued for several weeks. Soon, however, the roster and the repertoire broadened, as other local musicians, including banjo and guitar players, came to perform on the show. Most were amateurs, and none was paid.

The image of *Barn Dance* as a rural program was important, and Hay made sure his performers kept things "down to earth." The show's success continued, and in 1927 Hay changed the

Grand Ole Opry. *Country music fans fill the Grand Ole Opry to watch Alan Jackson perform during a celebration to mark the Opry's 75th anniversary in 2000.* ROBERT ALEXANDER/ARCHIVE PHOTOS/ GETTY IMAGES.

name of the show to the *Grand Ole Opry.* The name *Opry* was an intentional jibe at the world of classical music, often perceived as pretentious, and the *Grand Ole Opry* followed NBC's national *Musical Appreciation Hour,* a show devoted to classical music and opera. Hay announced one evening that although listeners had spent the past hour hearing grand opera, he would now present what he called the "Grand Ole Opry." The name proved popular, and it became the official name of the show that year.

Hay, who called himself the "Solemn Old Judge," opened the show every Saturday night with the words "Let her go, boys." And off they went. Among the early popular favorites were banjo player and singer Uncle Dave Macon; African American harmonica player Deford Bailey (the only African American performer until Charley Pride in the mid-1960s); and Dr. Humphrey Bate, who hosted one of the many string bands featured on the early *Opry.* As the show grew in popularity, the station's power grew as well. By the early 1930s the station's signal could reach more than thirty states and parts of Canada.

IN SEARCH OF STARS

In the 1930s the emphasis of the *Grand Ole Opry* shifted away from its rough rural edge and moved more in the direction of modern country music. The *Opry* had proved that country music had a wide appeal, and the potential of that appeal to turn profits for country musicians and for the corporate sponsors of radio programs like the *Opry* moved the show in a new direction—toward the creation and marketing of country music "stars." In 1928 Harry Stone joined WSM as an announcer and quickly assumed supervisory duties, replacing Hay, who was relegated to announcing duties on the *Grand Ole Opry.* With his brother David Stone and stage manager Vito Pellettieri, Stone furthered the commercial potential of the *Opry.* In 1934 Pellettieri began dividing the show into sponsored segments as a way of increasing revenue. Commercial sponsorship of the *Grand Ole Opry* was still very inexpensive in the mid-1930s; a fifteen-minute segment cost a sponsor only a $100.

Promoting new star talent, however, was where the real money was made. Stone moved the *Opry* away from the amateur string-band sound favored during the 1920s and began promoting new individual stars such as singer Roy Acuff. Stone also managed WSM's Artist Service, which booked *Opry* stars for personal appearances within the territory reached by WSM's radio signal. He used the *Opry* as an avenue to promote individual stars whose personal appearances could make good money, of which the *Opry* got a cut. Performers were paid very little for their appearances on the show, but the exposure was invaluable in providing opportunities for stardom while ensuring that the artists made a living from concert appearances.

This star system, very much akin to the system used to promote Hollywood movie stars at the time, brought talented new acts to the *Opry* in the 1930s and 1940s. Notable among them were the Delmore Brothers, Eddy Arnold, Hank Snow, Pee Wee King, Ernest Tubb, Minnie Pearl, Bill Monroe, and others, all of whom were among the biggest names in country music. The biggest newcomer to the *Opry* in the 1930s was Acuff, who joined it in 1938. Acuff had worked earlier in his life as a musician with a traveling medicine show. He recorded his first songs in 1936 and had an early hit with "The Great Speckled Bird." With his band the Tennessee Crackerjacks (later renamed the Crazy Tennesseans and, later still, the Smoky Mountain Boys), Acuff became the leading performer on the *Grand Ole Opry.* At a time when cowboy music was sweeping country music, Acuff managed to prosper under the *Opry*'s new star system while keeping close ties to his own southern rural roots, which he had in common with his listeners.

Those rural roots were also kept alive by the emerging bluegrass sound of Bill Monroe and his Bluegrass Boys, who were developing a new, hard-driving, string-band sound that combined virtuoso musicianship with close harmony vocals. Among the *Opry*'s biggest female stars in the 1940s and beyond was Minnie Pearl, one of country music's greatest comedians, known for her flowered hats with the price tags attached, her high-pitched "Howdeee!" greeting, and her routines that lovingly chronicled rural life. In the late 1940s one of country music's biggest stars, Hank Williams, became an *Opry* regular, thrilling audiences with his honky-tonk sound until his unreliable appearance schedule led to his dismissal in 1952, followed by his death in 1953.

CONTINUING EVOLUTION

The *Opry* continued to grow during the 1940s and 1950s, playing to a continually expanding audience. In October 1939 the *Opry* went national when a half-hour of the show was featured on NBC's national Saturday night lineup. This was known as the *Prince Albert Show* and was sponsored by Prince Albert Tobacco. The *Opry* was also the subject of a motion picture in 1940, called simply *Grand Ole Opry*, which featured Macon, Acuff, Hay, and others. In 1943 the show moved its location to Nashville's historic Ryman Auditorium in order to accommodate the increased demand among fans to attend the live performances. In 1948 the *Opry* expanded to include a spin-off show on Friday nights on WSM called *Friday Night Frolics*.

During the 1950s the *Opry*'s sound moved further and further from its rural origins. New *Opry* managers Jim Denny and Jack Stapp attempted to modernize the show, and although old-timers like Acuff, Monroe, and Snow still made appearances, often hosting their own segments, the *Opry* continued to use its star system approach, promoting younger stars to add to the roster of older, established stars. The *Opry* in the 1950s remained a crucial stepping-stone for country talent, hosting such emerging stars as George Jones, Johnny Cash, Webb Pierce, Stonewall Jackson, Little Jimmy Dickens, and Porter Wagoner. These trends continued in the 1960s, a decade that saw the emergence of Loretta Lynn, Jim Reeves, Patsy Cline, and Dolly Parton.

By the late 1960s, however, even though the Grand Ole Opry remained a prestigious performance venue for country musicians, it no longer had the same star-making power. This was a reflection of the declining influence of Nashville, brought about by the realization that it was not the nation's sole preserve of country music. In the 1960s California country artists such as Buck Owens and Merle Haggard demonstrated that country music talent could come from anywhere and often with a more authentic sound than the more commercial country-pop Nashville had been offering since the late 1950s.

DECLINING INFLUENCE

Other factors reduced the *Opry*'s influence. The *Opry* refused to acknowledge the growing popularity of rockabilly and rock-and-roll music in the 1950s, both of which had country influences, and as a result the show lost a portion of its younger audience. Early in the 1960s the *Opry* lost two major stars with the deaths of Cline and Reeves. Matters were not made any easier by the fact that the *Opry* paid its performers poorly. Contracts with musicians stipulated a certain number of appearances each year, but the high number of appearances at union scale wages made touring difficult for some of the stars. Consequently, staying close to Nashville in order to fulfill their contractual obligations cut into their income potential from concert performances.

In the 1970s, 1980s, and 1990s, the *Opry* largely redefined itself as a repository for country music's historic traditions. The show moved out of the Ryman Auditorium in 1974 and into more modern and spacious accommodations in the new Opryland amusement park outside Nashville. There, it continued to draw huge crowds each week, an indication that many were hungry for a taste of this country past. By the end of the 1990s, the Opry was still a prestigious venue for both established and up-and-coming stars. The relaxation of contractual obligations, put in place by *Opry* manager Hal Durham during the 1970s and 1980s, allowed such younger stars as Clint Black, Reba McEntire, Vince Gill, Alan Jackson, Alison Krauss, and Garth Brooks, to make occasional appearances on the show without cutting too heavily into their concert schedules.

Despite the rarity of appearances by country stars of this stature, and the fact that the *Opry* has become home more regularly to older or lesser stars who are no longer making hit records, the *Grand Ole Opry* remains one of the greatest country music traditions. In 2004 the Opry organization contracted with Cracker Barrel to be its "presenting sponsor," a position now held by Humana, Inc. Most importantly, the *Grand Ole Opry* has preserved the old-time radio show format that began entertaining country music audiences back in the 1920s.

Timothy Berg

SEE ALSO: *Black, Clint; Bluegrass; Brooks, Garth; Cash, Johnny; Cline, Patsy; Country Music; Haggard, Merle; Jones, George; Lynn, Loretta; Macon, Uncle Dave; McEntire, Reba; Monroe, Bill; Owens, Buck; Parton, Dolly; Pearl, Minnie; Pride, Charley; Rock and Roll; Williams, Hank, Jr..*

BIBLIOGRAPHY

Hagan, Chet. *Grand Ole Opry*. New York: Owl Books, 1989.

Malone, Bill C. *Country Music U.S.A.: A Fifty Year History*. Austin: American Folklore Society, University of Texas Press, 1968.

Stambler, Irwin, and Grelun Landon. *Country Music: The Encyclopedia*. New York: St. Martin's Press, 1997.

Wolfe, Charles K. *A Good-Natured Riot: The Birth of the Grand Ole Opry*. Nashville, TN: Country Music Foundation Press and Vanderbilt University Press, 1999.

Grandmaster Flash *(1958–)*

Hip-hop pioneer Grandmaster Flash (Joseph Saddler) has used his skills as an electronic engineer to perfect the art of punch phasing (a practice that accentuates the music's rhythm and beat) and mixing. He constructed the first twin-deck turntable using a mixer, headphones, and a monitor switch. Flash polished his technique on the "wheels of steel," or turntables, and took the art of "scratching"—manipulating records under a phonographic needle—to a new level. He has been imitated by rap DJs ever since.

His quick mixing and scratching skills can be heard on *The Adventures of Grandmaster Flash and the Wheels of Steel*, the first rap record to use samples—excerpts from other recordings. Flash began to add snippets of rhyme and boasting to his disc jockeying and soon formed the Furious Five, who did the rapping for him. Together they released the seminal track "The Message" (1982), a vivid portrayal of the underside of the American Dream in New York's urban ghettos. Flash's early experimenting with the new hip-hop genre helped to bring it out of abandoned buildings in the South Bronx and into the homes of millions worldwide. In 2007 Grandmaster Flash and the Furious Five were inducted into the Rock and Roll Hall of Fame.

Nathan Abrams

SEE ALSO: *Disc Jockeys; Hip-Hop; Phonograph; Rap.*

BIBLIOGRAPHY

Fernando, S. H., Jr. *The New Beats: Exploring the Music Culture and Attitudes of Hip-Hop*. Edinburgh: Payback Press, 1995.

Flash, Grandmaster, and David Ritz. *The Adventures of Grandmaster Flash: My Life, My Beats*. New York: Crown Archetype, 2008.

Larkin, Colin, ed. *The Guinness Who's Who of Rap, Dance and Techno*. London: Guinness Publishing, 1994.

Toop, David. *Rap Attack 2: African Rap to Global Hip-Hop*. London: Serpent's Tail, 1991.

Grant, Amy *(1960–)*

Bringing a flamboyant and youthful sound to what had generally been considered a stiff and formal genre, Amy Grant changed the face of Christian music. When Grant emerged on the Christian music scene in the 1980s, four categories existed: classical, traditional, gospel, and Jesus rock. Seeing the need for the expression of personal feelings, Grant developed a unique style that made the old form of Jesus rock acceptable to a wider audience. The Christian message reached a mainstream following of teenagers, college students, and twentysomethings through Grant's use of a rock beat. At last, contemporary Christian music had a young, visible performer with a vibrant sound.

Born in Augusta, Georgia, on November 25, 1960, Amy Lee Grant moved to Nashville, Tennessee, as an infant. Religion played an important role in her family life, and her strong convictions were reflected in the songs she wrote as a teenager. These songs were an outlet through which Grant sometimes expressed intensely personal feelings. Grant's career was launched during her teenage years, when record producer Chris Christian played a tape she had made for her parents to the Christian music company Word. Word and the Myrrh label offered her a contract, and she recorded her first album, *Amy Grant*, in Christian's home basement studio. After the release of the album in 1977, a gradual change took place in contemporary Christian music, one that revitalized its image.

Throughout her high school and college years, Grant continued to record and perform, and with each new album, her audience grew. People began to accept her style and unique sound, as well as the fresh messages in her lyrics. Grant also branched out to record works written by others, most notably her first husband, Gary Chapman ("Father's Eyes," 1979), and Michael W. Smith ("Thy Word," 1984), who eventually became a star in his own right. Grant's popularity continued to increase, as did her awards, honors, and media recognition. She has won Grammys and Gospel Music Association Dove Awards, and many of her albums have been designated as Gold and Platinum by the Recording Industry Association of America.

Grant's earlier recordings include deeply religious songs such as "El Shaddai" (1982) and "Thy Word," but her music began to change with the album *Unguarded* in 1985. This album created controversy, especially its song "Find a Way," whose video concerned Christian traditionalists because of the lack of references to God in both the lyrics and imagery. That same year Grant recorded "Next Time I Fall" with Peter Cetera from the pop band Chicago, which raised more questions about the type of music she was choosing to perform.

Despite these concerns in the Christian community, Grant's popularity continued to surge. What's more, she countered the worries of Christian traditionalists with the album *Lead Me On* (1988), which was less pop oriented. In 1991, however, A & M Music, in conjunction with Word, released Grant's first pop collection, *Heart in Motion*, in both the Christian and secular markets. With songs such as "Baby, Baby," which Grant wrote for her infant daughter, the album was a mainstream hit. Her critics, however, found "Baby, Baby" to be too sexual for a Christian singer. While the album is not overtly religious, it still carries messages of hope, love, and family. In 1994 Grant released *House of Love*, which combines secular and Christian music with powerful messages regarding all varieties of love, including God's. With *Behind the Eyes* (1997), Grant returned to her musical roots as a solo performer, using acoustical guitar accompaniment.

Grant's live performances have evolved over the years. At the beginning of her career, she performed as a solo act on a bare stage. By 1981, however, she had added a band and adopted a performing style in which she exhibited dance moves more commonly associated with rock than the Christian genre. Using intense facial expressions and heartfelt pleadings, Grant was not afraid to display her emotions. This exuberance led to a steady increase of young adults at her concerts, which brought more exposure to contemporary Christian music in general. Grant's performance at the Grammys in 1985, which reached a prime-time network audience, gave contemporary Christian music an unprecedented boost. She has served as a pioneer in the genre, opening the door for a wider range of contemporary Christian artists, including the pop stylings of Smith, the hard rock sound of Petra, and the rap of DC Talk.

Grant filed for divorce from Chapman in 1999 and married country singer Vince Gill the following year in Williamson County, Tennessee. Grant and Gill have supported a wide range of humanitarian organizations, such as the Red Cross and Samaritan Ministries. In 2009 they hosted a concert for Challenge America, a charity that works with injured veterans, in Washington, D.C. Returning to her gospel roots as a performer, Grant has continued to tour while recording albums such as *Legacy . . . Hymns and Faith* (2002) and *Somewhere Down the Road* (2010) in celebration of her faith.

Linda Ann Martindale

SEE ALSO: *Celebrity Couples; Contemporary Christian Music; Gospel Music; Grammy Awards.*

BIBLIOGRAPHY

Grant, Amy. *Mosaic: Pieces of My Life So Far*. New York: Doubleday/Flying Dolphin Press, 2007.

Long, Jim, and Michael Long. "Amy Grant: Another New

Beginning." *Campus Life*, July/August 1994, 17–22.
Millard, Bob. *Amy Grant: A Biography*. Garden City, NY: Doubleday, 1986.

Grant, Cary *(1904–1986)*

Cary Grant was the quintessential leading man during Hollywood's golden age. Darkly handsome with that trademark cleft chin, elegantly attired whether in dinner clothes or a soldier's uniform, meeting every challenge with self-deprecating savoir faire, ready with witty banter or an eloquent gesture, and possessing a unique flair for comic timing, Grant was adored by women and admired by men during his box-office reign from the 1930s through the 1960s. Though he occasionally veered from his popular image by attempting more serious roles, Grant's forte was light, romantic comedy. He brought to his films a buoyant charm and an effortless improvisational quality that belied the hard work he put into making it look so easy. He was Fred Astaire minus the music and plus the chiseled good looks.

BECOMING CARY GRANT

The persona the world came to know as "Cary Grant" was the carefully crafted creation of Alexander Archibald Leach, born in Bristol, England, in 1904. As a teenager Leach forsook a bleak existence in Bristol for the uncertainties of a theatrical career, joining Bob Pender's troupe in vaudeville performances throughout England. Pender's troupe eventually played in America, and the young Leach went with it. After deciding to settle in the United States, Leach occasionally found vaudeville work, but just as often, he encountered hard times. At one point he earned his keep as a Coney Island stilt walker. By the late 1920s his perseverance was finally paying off with leading roles on Broadway. His first film appearance, as a sailor in the musical short *Singapore Sue* (1932), led to a contract with Paramount Pictures in Hollywood, California, where he began acting under his new moniker, Cary Grant.

Grant's earliest film roles reveal that he had already developed his "Cary Grant voice," with its unique inflection of Americanized Cockney, which was impossible to place geographically and, therefore, concealed his humble origins. However, the process of becoming Cary Grant was slow—the persona evolved from film to film. "I guess to a certain extent, I did eventually become the characters I was playing," Grant once confessed. "I played at being someone I wanted to be until I became that person. Or he became me."

At first, nothing more was required of Grant than that he be the stalwart leading man, though he soon displayed hints of the charm to come in his badinage with Mae West in *She Done Him Wrong* and *I'm No Angel* (both 1933). Under George Cukor's direction, Grant began to loosen up and find himself, portraying a Cockney con man opposite Katharine Hepburn in *Sylvia Scarlett* (1935). Playing a devil-may-care ghost in 1937's *Topper* seemed to free Grant still further. That same year's *The Awful Truth* featured Grant's first full-out comedy role. Leo McCarey's direction encouraged improvisation, and the interplay between Grant and Irene Dunne delighted audiences. This hit was immediately followed by Howard Hawks's *Bringing Up Baby* (1938), again costarring Hepburn. Though the film was a box-office disappointment, it is now recognized as one of the archetypal classics of screwball comedy.

A HOLLYWOOD MAVERICK

Once he hit his stride, Grant became one of the first big stars to be a "free agent" and shop his wares at different studios, which enabled him to have his pick of the best scripts, directors, and costars. He proved he could shift suavely from the knockabout Kipling adventure of *Gunga Din* (1939) to the sophisticated romance of *The Philadelphia Story* (1940). Alfred Hitchcock was the first director to take advantage of a certain dark undercurrent in Grant by casting him as a murder suspect in *Suspicion* (1941), though the studio insisted the story be rewritten to exonerate Grant's character at the fadeout. Hitchcock and Grant would team memorably thrice more, in *Notorious* (1946), *To Catch a Thief* (1955), and *North by Northwest* (1959).

Highlights of Grant's romantic-comedy filmography include *His Girl Friday* (1940, with Rosalind Russell), *The Bachelor and the Bobby-Soxer* (1947, Shirley Temple and Myrna Loy), and *That Touch of Mink* (1962, Doris Day). Grant's long run as a top box-office draw was sustained partly by his shrewd emphasis on the light romantic fare his public seemed to favor most. There were, however, occasions when Grant attempted to "stretch," as with Ernie Mott, the impoverished Cockney he played in Clifford Odets's *None but the Lonely Heart* (1944).

LIFE BEYOND FILM

In many ways, Ernie Mott was the man Archie Leach might have become had he never left Bristol. An important element of *Lonely Heart* is Ernie's relationship with his mother, played by Ethel Barrymore. Leach's own mother had strangely disappeared

Cary Grant. *With his suave, charming persona and flair for comic timing, Cary Grant was Hollywood's ultimate leading man from the 1930s into the 1960s.* SILVER SCREEN COLLECTION/HULTON ARCHIVE/GETTY IMAGES.

for a time when he was a boy, and as an adult, his relations with women were not as effortless in real life as they were on the screen; he was married five times and divorced four. Grant's search for meaning led him to participate in early clinical experiments with LSD, which he claimed were beneficial. Still handsome in his sixties but growing uncomfortable with playing love scenes with younger actresses, Grant retired from the screen after *Walk, Don't Run* in 1966. Film offers kept coming his way, but he was content to pursue other business interests and, more importantly, spend time with his daughter, Jennifer, the product of his marriage to his fourth wife, actress Dyan Cannon. In 1986, while at a speaking engagement in Davenport, Iowa, with his wife Barbara Harris, Grant suffered a fatal stroke.

As much as he embraced his real-life role as a father, Grant's image in the public mind is the dashing chap in the tuxedo who is never at a loss for the right words to charm Grace Kelly or Audrey Hepburn. Grant's *An Affair to Remember* (1957) remains in the popular consciousness as the epitome of movie romance. Grant has also come to symbolize the power of creating one's own persona, thus giving a world of Archie Leaches hope for the fulfillment of their own dreams. Once, when told that every man would like to be Cary Grant, the actor replied, "So would I."

Preston Neal Jones

SEE ALSO: Bringing Up Baby*; Hawks, Howard; Hepburn, Audrey; Hepburn, Katharine; Hitchcock, Alfred; Kelly, Grace;* North by Northwest*;* The Philadelphia Story*; Screwball Comedies; Sex Symbol.*

BIBLIOGRAPHY

Deschner, Donald. *The Films of Cary Grant.* Secaucus, NJ: Citadel Press, 1973.

Donaldson, Maureen, and William Royce. *An Affair to Remember: My Life with Cary Grant.* New York: G. P. Putnam's Sons, 1989.

Harris, Warren G. *Cary Grant: A Touch of Elegance.* New York: Doubleday, 1987.

McCann, Graham. *Cary Grant: A Class Apart.* New York: Columbia University Press, 1996.

Nelson, Nancy. *Evenings with Cary Grant: Recollections in His Own Words and by Those Who Knew Him Best.* New York: William Morrow, 1991.

Peary, Danny, ed. *Close-Ups: The Movie Star Book.* New York: Simon & Schuster, 1978.

Wansell, Geoffrey. *Haunted Idol: The Story of the Real Cary Grant.* New York: William Morrow, 1983.

The Grapes of Wrath

Written by John Steinbeck and published in 1939, *The Grapes of Wrath* describes the Depression-era journey of the fictional Joad family from the Dust Bowl of Oklahoma to the agricultural fields of California. A film version of the novel, directed by John Ford and starring Henry Fonda, followed in 1940. Together with evocative photographs by Dorothea Lange, the novel and film focused national attention on the plight of migrant farm workers in California and earned Steinbeck the Pulitzer Prize for Fiction in 1940.

The novel recounts the westward journey of the Joads, a three-generation Oklahoma family pushed off their land through a combination of dust storms and foreclosures. Eldest son Tom returns home from the state penitentiary to find the family preparing to head to California in the hopes of obtaining work and eventually a farm of their own. Tom, along with parents, grandparents, an uncle, siblings, and a brother-in-law, is joined in his trek by Jim Casy, an ex-preacher looking to fill the void left by his loss of "the Holy sperit." After leaving Oklahoma, the family discovers that California is not a land of milk and honey where they can become independent farmers. Rather, it is a cold, harsh, uninviting environment in both the towns and the countryside.

Throughout their journey, Tom and Casy learn about the exploitative practices of landowners and the avenues open to farm laborers to challenge the power of the farm owners. Ma Joad learns, over the course of the novel, that her responsibilities extend beyond the limits of the "family" to "the people." She learns the importance of solidarity in regaining and maintaining human dignity, just as Tom learns the value of solidarity in gaining respect in labor. This message is reinforced in the novel's final scene, in which Tom's sister, Rosasharn (Rose-of-Sharon), having just given birth to a stillborn child, gives her maternal breast to a dying man. By the end of the novel, the Joad family has grown to include the family of man.

The Grapes of Wrath is a prime example of the proletarian novel that was popular during the Great Depression, in which ordinary working-class families (especially agricultural workers) became the focus. Steinbeck strongly believed in the power of literature to bring about change in society through education and example. By exposing the corrupt ways of agribusiness and the benefits of government intervention into the agricultural economy, Steinbeck sought to bring about the creation of a farm labor proletariat. The novel ignited an explosion of controversy surrounding the problems of migrant labor. Accusations about the novel's accuracy led to debates such as the 1940 radio broadcast of "America's Town Meeting of the Air," which addressed the issue "What should America do for the Joads?" Criticisms about the representations of California growers and Oklahoma natives resulted in bans on the book in communities across the nation and most publicly in Kern County, California, a heavily agricultural region of the state.

Stylistically, the novel also recalls the documentary movement of the 1930s in its use of interchapters that depart from the narrative of the Joad family and describe phenomena representative of the migrant population as a whole. The interchapters authenticate the narrative by placing the plight of the Joads within the larger context of Dust Bowl migrants, the agricultural economy, and the American proletariat. Steinbeck portrays the "Okie" migrants as uneducated, unsophisticated, earthy, and decent folk whose humanity provides a counterpoint to the inhumanity of industrial/agribusiness exploitation. Much like the photography of Margaret Bourke-White, Lange, and Walker Evans and documentary books such as Bourke-White and Erskine Caldwell's *You Have Seen Their Faces* (1937), Lange and Paul Taylor's *An American Exodus: A Record of Human Erosion* (1939), and Evans and James Agee's *Let Us Now Praise Famous Men* (1941), *The Grapes of Wrath* sought to improve society through the presentation of information in a highly emotionally charged narrative.

Upon publication, Darryl Zanuck of Twentieth Century Fox studios acquired the rights to the novel and set screenwriter

Nunnally Johnson to the task of adapting Steinbeck's prose into a screenplay. Production proceeded under tight security conditions as controversy over the novel mounted. Renowned Western director John Ford gathered together a cast of actors, including Henry Fonda (Tom Joad), Jane Darwell (Ma Joad), and John Carradine (Preacher Casy). The film's look, through the stark cinematography of Greg Toland, recalls the documentary vision of government photographers such as Russell Lee, Arthur Rothstein, and Lange. While more optimistic in tone than the novel, the film presents a bleak look at the conditions of migrant farm workers during the Great Depression. Ford received the Academy Award for Best Director for the 1940 movie adaptation.

Charles J. Shindo

SEE ALSO: *Academy Awards; Caldwell, Erskine; Fonda, Henry; Ford, John; The Great Depression; Steinbeck, John; Zanuck, Darryl F.*

BIBLIOGRAPHY

Benson, Jackson J. "'To Tom Who Lived It': John Steinbeck and the Man from Weedpatch." *Journal of Modern Literature* 5 (1976): 151–224.

French, Warren, ed. *A Companion to* The Grapes of Wrath. New York: Viking Press, 1963.

French, Warren. *Filmguide to* The Grapes of Wrath. Bloomington: Indiana University Press, 1973.

Heavilin, Barbara A. *The Critical Response to John Steinbeck's* The Grapes of Wrath. Westport, CT: Greenwood Press, 2000.

Millichap, Joseph. *Steinbeck and Film.* New York: Frederick Unger, 1983.

Steinbeck, John. *Working Days: The Journals of* The Grapes of Wrath, ed. Robert DeMott. New York: Viking, 1989.

Wyatt, David, ed. *New Essays on* The Grapes of Wrath. New York: Cambridge University Press, 1990.

Graphic Novels

Although words and pictures started out together, adult literature was eventually reduced to words alone, while pictures stayed in the nursery. Graphic novels bring words and pictures back together for an adult audience—but beyond that statement, there is considerable disagreement about just what a graphic novel is or should be. To understand why the matter is complicated, it helps to understand how the term developed.

The background begins in the later nineteenth century, when comic strips started to appear in newspapers. Reduced to essentials, a comic strip is a sequential series of drawings called "cartoons," telling a story through visual content, combined with verbal embellishments such as captions and dialogue bubbles. By the 1930s strips were combined into comic books, which typically focused on the humorous antics of cartoon characters (such as Donald Duck) or the exploits of action heroes (such as Superman). Rapid growth followed in the comics market over the next few decades, not only in number of readers but also in the variety of comic genres, eventually including horror comics, Westerns, science fiction, mysteries, movie tie-ins, and even illustrated classics. Although some of these mass-market comic books were skillfully drawn and well written, most were merely disposable entertainment.

From the early days, however, some comic creators wanted to use the cartoon medium in a more innovative way, combining high-quality art with thoughtful word content, and during the 1960s and 1970s their so-called underground or experimental comics gained a following. To differentiate their work from mass-market cartoon strips and comic books, some artists used the term *comix.* Comix were typically adult oriented, featuring mature topics and sophisticated humor, but most still had a comedic or satiric aspect. As comix artists came out with more serious works, the term did not seem to fit very well, so creators and publishers tried out a variety of other names to describe long-form, adult-audience cartoon art. By the 1980s *graphic novel* had taken hold as the standard label, even though almost everyone agrees that it does not work very well as a description.

With a few exceptions—such as Will Eisner's *A Contract with God* (1978)—most of the books marketed as graphic novels during the early days of the category were really just collections of popular comic-book stories, printed on better paper with a nicer binding. Experimental and alternative uses of the cartoon medium remained underground for practical purposes, until the publication of Art Spiegelman's *Maus* in 1986. Spiegelman, who had long been a force in the comix world, recounted his father's story of captivity and survival during the Holocaust, depicting Nazis as cats and Jews as mice. He also wove into the narrative his own experiences as a child of Holocaust survivors and as an artist trying to convey terrible realities in a completely new way. The result was a work so extraordinary that *Maus* received a special award from the Pulitzer Prize committee and became the first widely read graphic novel.

Two other classic examples from the 1980s—Frank Miller's *Batman: The Dark Knight Returns* (1986) and *Watchmen* (1987), by Alan Moore and Dave Gibbons—significantly raised the quality of series compilations and superhero stories by placing more mature protagonists in dystopian scenarios. These works were not typical, however. Most titles published in the graphic novel category during the 1990s continued to be popular entertainment rather than innovative literature. A particular type of Japanese comic art called *manga* was soon included in the graphic novel category and accounted for a significant percentage of its steadily growing sales.

Plenty of upscale comic books are still marketed as graphic novels, but the twenty-first century has seen increasing creative energy in the field, which has produced a number of groundbreaking works. Reporter Joe Sacco's *Safe Area Goražde* (2000) provides a visual account of the people and events he encountered during the Balkan Wars. Jason Lutes's *Berlin: City of Stones* (2001) begins a sweeping work of historical fiction set in Germany between World War I and World War II. In addition to historical topics, serious graphic novels frequently focus on biography and autobiography, as exemplified in Chester Brown's *Louis Riel* (2003), a fascinating portrait of Canada's most ambiguous hero; *Persepolis* (2003), Marjane Satrapi's poignant memoir of growing up in postrevolutionary Iran; and *Epileptic* (2005), David Beauchard's account of life with an older brother suffering from epilepsy. These are just some of the graphic novels receiving critical acclaim for their innovative portrayals of culture, politics, and personal experience.

In his now-classic graphic book *Understanding Comics: The Invisible Art* (1994), Scott McCloud offers a thoughtful exploration of how comics are composed, read, and understood. As he explains, it is the special nature of visual language—presented by the creative artist and interpreted by the reader—that links the most ordinary comic book with the most extraordinary graphic novel.

Cynthia Giles

SEE ALSO: *Animé; Batman; Comic Books; Comics; Eisner, Will;* Maus; *Superman.*

BIBLIOGRAPHY

Baetens, Jan. *The Graphic Novel.* Louvain, Belgium: Leuven University Press, 2001.

Booker, M. K. *Encyclopedia of Comic Books and Graphic Novels.* Santa Barbara, CA: Greenwood Press, 2010.

Fingeroth, Danny. *The Rough Guide to Graphic Novels.* London: Rough Guides, 2008.

Kannenberg, Gene. *500 Essential Graphic Novels: The Ultimate Guide.* New York: Collins Design, 2008.

McCloud, Scott. *Understanding Comics: The Invisible Art.* New York: HarperPerennial, 1994.

The Grateful Dead

The Grateful Dead, with its notorious founding member Jerry Garcia, was a band that epitomized the psychedelic era of American rock-and-roll music from the 1960s to the 1990s. Even after Garcia's death in 1995, members of the band continued to tour, in part to satisfy the yearnings of the most dedicated group of fans ever to bind themselves to a musical group, the so-called Deadheads.

ORIGINS

Garcia and friends Bob Weir, Ron "Pigpen" McKernan, Bill Kreutzmann, and Phil Lesh formed the band in the San Francisco Bay Area in 1965 after various incarnations as a blues- and bluegrass-influenced jug band (Mother McCree's Uptown Jug Champions) and a blues/rock ensemble (the Warlocks). The various members, especially keyboard players, who were to come and go included Tom Constanten, Donna and Keith Godchaux, Brent Mydland, Bruce Hornsby, and Vince Welnick. Mickey Hart joined the band shortly after its inception, complementing Kreutzmann as a second drummer; left for a while after his father ripped off the band; and later rejoined them. Pigpen died and the band kept on playing, but with the death of Garcia the remaining members finally disbanded. They kept playing in their various individual bands, however, and in a combined band called the Other Ones, which approximated the Grateful Dead and continued the Dead's summer tour tradition.

According to Garcia, he found the name "Grateful Dead" by randomly opening a book and coming upon a dictionary entry describing the legend of those who, returned from the dead, reward a living person who had unwittingly aided them. The folk derivation of the name was fitting, since it summed up the roots of the founding members in the bluegrass, blues, and folk music that was performed in the early 1960s by artists such as Bob Dylan and Joan Baez. The Dead continued to play folk classics like "Peggy-O," "Jack-a-Roe," and "Stagger Lee" until the end. The grounding of the Grateful Dead in the American folk tradition contradicts its image as a corrupt purveyor of hallucinatory drugs, but their roots can also be traced to free-spirited Ken Kesey's Merry Pranksters and Beat figures like Neal Cassady. Garcia acknowledged this very explicitly in a 1991 interview with *Rolling Stone*: "I owe a lot of who I am and what I've been and what I've done to the beatniks from the Fifties

The Grateful Dead. *The Grateful Dead set the standard for psychedelic jam bands and became known for their extensive touring and legions of devoted fans.* WARING ABBOTT/MICHAEL OCHS ARCHIVES/GETTY IMAGES.

and to the poetry and art and music that I've come into contact with. I feel like I'm part of a continuous line of a certain thing in American culture." Like the Beats, the hippies and their house band the Grateful Dead continued the rebellion against the conformist 1950s and the middle-class culture that had by and large given birth to them.

Some of the Grateful Dead's first concerts were known as the Acid Tests of the San Francisco Bay Area, where psychedelic music, visuals, and hippies all came together as harbingers of the raves of the 1990s and the Dead's concerts between the 1970s and the 1990s. They spawned bands like Phish, which re-created the Dead's spontaneity in improvisation, and in its nomadic fans and epic tours that extended across America and sometimes Europe.

DEADHEADS

The Grateful Dead cult started after a call to fans, "Dead Freaks Unite—Who Are You? Where Are You?" was published in the 1971 album *Grateful Dead* (also known as *Skull and Roses*). The Dead fans who answered received concert updates and news that would eventually result in the band's formation of Grateful Dead Ticket Sales, which successfully bypassed music company and corporate control by selling up to half the tickets to concert venues by mail. From 1973 to 1976 the band also had its own recording company, Round Records/Grateful Dead Records. However, this collective thumbing of noses at the recording industry came at a price, costing them the respect of critics who saw the band as an aberration and a throwback.

There was another downside to the burgeoning Grateful Dead industry. In his last few years Garcia occasionally wearily commented on the fact that a whole group of people—not just the traveling circus of Deadheads and unauthorized vendors, but the Grateful Dead ticketing and merchandising industry controlled by the band—were dependent on the Dead. Ironically, as the Dead found more popular success after issuing *In the Dark* (1987), problems abounded with unruly fans who crashed the concert gates and participated in uncontrolled vending, sometimes even of controlled substances.

The Grateful Dead's cult following was almost religious in its intensity. Deadheads showed their loyalty (or perhaps obsession) by reading Dead-themed magazines such as *Relix* and *Golden Road* and the compendium of Dead statistics known as *DeadBase*; tuning into the nationally broadcast Grateful Dead radio hour, aired weekly from the San Francisco Bay Area's KFOG radio station by long-time fan and Dead historian David Gans; buying the recordings that continued to be issued even after Garcia's death from the band's own master soundboard tapes of concerts in the "Dick's Picks" series; and trading the bootleg tapes of Dead concerts recorded by fans almost from the beginning, a practice the band in the end condoned. Deadheads also religiously watched *DeadTV*, a television cable program that first aired in 1988, and visited Grateful Dead–related online groups like Dead-Flames, DeadBase, and Dead.net;. Garcia didn't make the mistake John Lennon did of comparing his band's popularity to that of Jesus Christ, but he did remark on the ritualistic nature of its concerts in *Rock & Roll: An Unruly History*: "For some people, taking LSD and going to a Dead show functions like a rite of passage. . . . Each person deals with the experience individually; it's an adventure that you can have that is personalized. But when people come together, this singular experience is ritualized. I think the Grateful Dead serves a desire for meaningful ritual, but it's *ritual without dogma*."

Also unlike the Beatles, fans were allowed this great road adventure because the band preferred making its money by touring (or perhaps was forced to tour because of the lack of conventional success) rather than by recording studio albums. Garcia explained in an interview published in *Rock Lives*, "Mostly we're always on the road, because we earn our living by playing. So we haven't had much of the luxury where you just go into the studio for no particular reason to screw around." At the time of Garcia's death, the band was in its thirtieth year.

In a 1989 *Rolling Stone* interview, Garcia talked about the last adventure in America that touring with the band allowed. Asked why the fans kept coming back, he answered:

> They get something. It's their version of the Acid Test, so to speak. It's kind of like the war-stories metaphor. Drug stories *are* war stories, and the Grateful Dead stories are their drug stories, or war stories. It's an adventure you can still have in America, just like Neal [Cassady] *On the Road*. You can't hop the freights any more, but you can chase the Grateful Dead around. . . . You can have something that lasts throughout your life as adventures, the times you took chances. I think that's essential in anybody's life, and it's harder and harder to do in America. If I were providing some margin of that possibility, then that's great. That's a nice thing to do.

MEMBERS

Though Garcia was certainly the charismatic spokesman for the band in its later years, early on Pigpen was the draw for the band. The son of a San Francisco Bay Area disc jockey, McKernan was steeped in the blues, playing organ and harmonica and singing in a harsh, anguished voice perfect for the medium. It was Pigpen who largely set the tone of albums like *Workingman's Dead* and *American Beauty*, classic Dead recordings. It wasn't until 1970 with *Live/Dead* and *Workingsman's Dead* that the band's records really began attracting a sizable number of fans outside of the San Francisco Bay Area, and the band toured extensively. Pigpen sang many of the tunes that characterized the Dead at that time, as well as some that they kept playing until the end—covers such as "Good Morning Little School Girl," "Viola Lee Blues," "In the Midnight Hour," "Beat It on down the Line," and "Cold Rain and Snow."

Pigpen's death at twenty-seven in 1973 from liver damage was a serious blow, although before he passed, his absence from gigs due to deteriorating health had begun to lessen his influence on the band. After Pigpen's death, Donna and Keith Godchaux joined the band as vocalist and keyboard player, respectively. As William Ruhlmann points out in *The History of the Grateful Dead*, both events caused the band to diversify its repertoire and approach. Hank Harrison puts it differently in *The Dead*, claiming that the old band also died with Pigpen.

Other neglected de facto "members" of the band included their frequent lyricists, Robert Hunter and John Barlow. Hunter collaborated with Garcia, while Barlow worked with Weir, and, while he was in the band, Mydland. Hunter, himself a musician, was a member of the San Francisco scene from the beginnings of the Grateful Dead. He never played with them but penned several of their trademark songs, including "Terrapin Station," "Touch of Grey," "Jack Straw," "Tennessee Jed," "It Must Have

Been the Roses," "Playing in the Band," and "Truckin'." Most of the time Hunter collaborated with Garcia in composing songs.

In a 1988 interview with Gans, published in *Conversations with the Dead,* Hunter was asked why he didn't collaborate with other members of the band more often. He replied that "Garcia makes it easy. You know, he makes himself available to do it, and when I give him a piece of material he'll either reject it or set it, and he gives me changes, which I *will* set, generally—he doesn't give me anything I don't like. . . . He's a genius, he's got an amazing musical sense, and no one else makes themselves available or particularly easy to work with."

Hunter was probably referring to the Dead's other primary singer, Weir. Barlow, a childhood friend of Weir, explains that although sometimes Weir may abuse him, he is "only that way when he's feeling a bit uptight and overworked. Then he gets very headstrong about certain creative decisions, and I'm not in a position to gainsay him because he's got to get out in front of a whole bunch of people and sing that stuff." Barlow, active online by the late 1990s, started out as a poetry and fiction writer, but Weir persuaded him to try his hand at song lyrics after Weir joined the Dead. Barlow's patience was in evidence when the very first song he wrote, "Mexicali Blues," was transformed into a polka number by Weir, something that Barlow hadn't envisioned. As with those lyrics, Barlow often infuses a western flavor into his songs, which include "Estimated Prophet," "Looks Like Rain," "Cassidy," "Hell in a Bucket," "Heaven Help the Fool," and "Black-Throated Wind." Collaborations with Mydland include "Easy to Love You" and "Just a Little Light," while "Throwing Stones" was a Barlow, Weir, and Mydland effort. Mydland's death in 1990 of a drug overdose ended what had promised to be a fruitful collaboration.

POST-GARCIA

Studio albums present polished versions of the Dead's songs, but the concert experience was the essence of the Dead. Improvisation was their chosen method; they claimed never to perform with a set list (although drummers Hart and Kreutzmann admitted practicing the famous extended drum solo features known as "Space" that were a capstone of a Dead show's second set). This is one reason why, perhaps, the Dead could keep filling large stadiums on their tours, even in the early 1990s when the live concert industry hit a slump. In 1991 they were the top-grossing concert band in the United States. The Dead never had a number one hit—in 1987 the Hunter/Garcia song "Touch of Grey" went only to number nine—but their music was being listened to, and no one knows how many bootleg tapes were trading, and continue to trade, hands.

Every former member of the Grateful Dead, except Kreutzmann, formed a separate band with which they performed, toured, and recorded, including the Mickey Hart Band and Weir's band Ratdog. Lesh, the only classically trained musician in the group, played on occasion with the San Francisco symphony until he underwent a liver transplant in 1998; upon his recovery, Lesh began performing occasional gigs with a roving cast known as "Phil and Friends." Hart, the most eclectic member of the band, went on to compose and perform experimental pieces, even contributing a composition used in the opening ceremony of the 1996 Olympic Games in Atlanta, Georgia. He also composed music for Francis Ford Coppola's film *Apocalypse Now* (1979).

At the end of the twentieth century, members of the Grateful Dead were continuing as an industry unto themselves. The band is the most complete and longest-lasting representation of the San Francisco counterculture, begun in the 1950s with the Beats and flowering in the 1960s with the hippies. The band helped to propagate and preserve the spirit of 1960s America at home and abroad with its recordings and tours. That it was never in need of reviving, and continues to thrive in various guises, attests to a thread of continuity in fast-paced American pop culture.

In 2010 the surviving members of the band resolved to donate the archives of the band—including recordings, press clippings, stage sets from concerts, video, correspondence, business records, and numerous other items—to the University of California at Santa Cruz. The donation provided a stable locus of source material for a growing academic field, including philosophers; musicologists; sociologists; and, surprisingly, business and management scholars, who studied the Dead's music as well as its cultural and economic impacts. The band's willingness to allow for an organic culture and marketplace to form around their music, rather than dictating the cultural participation, prefigured Internet and social media marketing strategies. Their creative business model not only provided for fans to feel that they too possessed an investment in the music but also allowed for the Grateful Dead to retain ownership of its merchandising and publishing rights.

Radio stations across the country have featured the Grateful Dead radio hour, which features live concert recordings from "classic" shows. Sirius radio has an entire channel dedicated only to the band, hosted by Grateful Dead tape archivist David Lemieux, with programming including interviews; "Today in Grateful Dead History"; concert rebroadcasts; and Grateful Dead Tales, a feature to which Deadheads are invited to contribute. The band has an official website as well, Deadnet.

In addition to their solo projects, the remaining members have also composed various reunion ensembles. Weir, Hart, and Lesh toured as the Other Ones in 1998, swapping Kreutzmann for Lesh in 2000, and then again with all four of the members in 2002. The Other Ones changed their name to the Dead and toured during 2003, 2004, and 2009. Lesh and Weir formed Further in 2009, and Kreutzmann and Hart reunited the Rhythm Devils in 2010. A massive set of recordings from the Grateful Dead's 1972 European tour was also released in 2011 to supplement the live recording issued as a two-album set, *Europe '72.*

Josephine A. McQuail

SEE ALSO: *Blues; Ginsberg, Allen; Hippies; Kesey, Ken; LSD; Marijuana; Rock and Roll;* Rolling Stone; *Woodstock.*

BIBLIOGRAPHY

Brandelius, Jerilyn Lee. *The Grateful Dead Family Album.* New York: Warner, 1989.

Editors of *Rolling Stone. Garcia.* Boston: Little, Brown, 1995.

Gans, David. *Conversations with the Dead: The Grateful Dead Interview Book.* New York: Citadel, 1991.

Gans, David, and Peter Simon. *Playing in the Band: An Oral and Visual Portrait of the Grateful Dead.* New York: St. Martin's Press, 1985.

Green, Joshua. "Management Secrets of the Grateful Dead." *Atlantic,* March 2010, 64–67.

Harrison, Hank. *The Dead.* Millbrae, CA: Celestial Arts, 1980.

Jackson, Blair. *Goin' down the Road: A Grateful Dead Traveling Companion.* New York: Harmony, 1992.

Official Website of the Grateful Dead. Accessed April 20, 2012. Available from http://www.dead.net

Palmer, Robert. *Rock & Roll: An Unruly History.* New York: Harmony, 1995.

Ruhlmann, William. *The History of the Grateful Dead.* New York: Gallery, 1990.

University of California Santa Cruz Library. The Grateful Dead Archive. Accessed April 20, 2012. Available from http://library.ucsc.edu/gratefuldeadarchive/gda-home

White, Timothy. "Dead on Arrival! Grateful Dead." In *Rock Lives. Profiles & Interviews.* New York: Henry Holt, 1990.

Womack, David. *Aesthetics of the Grateful Dead.* Palo Alto, CA: Flying Public Press, 1991.

Gray Panthers

The Gray Panthers seek to redefine old age in America. Maggie Kuhn (1905–1995), who founded the Gray Panthers in 1970, emphasized that ageism diminishes all people by stigmatizing the young and old as less than full members of society. The mission statement of the Gray Panthers states: "Work for social and economic justice and peace for all people. "

The Gray Panthers work with other organizations—notably AARP (formerly the American Association of Retired Persons)—on issues of common interest (for example, preserving Social Security), but they are distinctive in placing their primary emphasis on activism, particularly on behalf of those not normally involved in the political process. Philosophically, the Gray Panthers are to the left of AARP, which is more middle of the road. In order to appeal to a wide range of senior interests, AARP is allied with a variety of businesses and services. Since their beginning, the Gray Panthers have advocated social change, inspired by the dynamic example of Kuhn, who urged people to "speak your mind—even if your voice shakes. When you least expect it, someone may actually listen to what you have to say. Well-aimed slingshots can topple giants."

Kuhn had been an advocate for many causes during her life, but the organization that made her famous came about when she was forced to retire from the job she loved as an executive of the United Presbyterian Church. Infuriated by the wasteful nature of bureaucracies that mandated retirement for workers at sixty-five, Kuhn began the process of organizing an advocacy group for older Americans. She recalled the awakening of her consciousness in her autobiography, *No Stone Unturned* (1991): "Something clicked in my mind and I saw that my problem was not mine alone. I came to feel a great kinship with my peers and to believe that something was fundamentally wrong with a system that had no use for us." She believed that the talents, energy, and wisdom of older Americans were being wasted.

TAKING ACTION

Kuhn began to hold meetings with five friends to find ways to address the problem, and the group grew from six to 100 members in a year. The original name of the group was the Consultation of Older Persons, which was changed to the Gray Panthers when a member of the media suggested it to Kuhn. The name change confused and intimidated some people, because it recalled the Black Panthers, a militant activist organization of the civil rights movement. The new organization was helped significantly by consumer advocate Ralph Nader, who incorporated his own seniors group (Retired Professional Action Group) into the Gray Panthers. His organization had investigated the hearing aid industry, and he published an exposé, "Paying through the Ear." Nader also contributed $25,000 to the Gray Panthers, which helped significantly as they began their campaign for nursing home reform. Their efforts (in conjunction with the National Citizen Coalition for Nursing Home Reform) produced a handbook, *Nursing Homes: A Citizens' Action Guide*, which documented nursing home abuses. By 1974 the Gray Panthers were making their presence felt across the country.

Annoyed by television talk-show host Johnny Carson's character Aunt Blabby, Kuhn turned her guest spot on the show in 1974 into a tour de force, charming Carson and, not incidentally, promoting the Gray Panthers. In 1975 the Gray Panthers established a National Media Watch Task Force, which documented ageist stereotyping in broadcasting. That action led the National Association of Broadcasters to amend the Television Code of Ethics to include "age along with race and sex." In 1978 the Gray Panthers won perhaps their most satisfying reward: the Age Discrimination in Employment Act was passed, raising the mandatory retirement age from sixty-five to seventy.

GROWING LARGER AND STRONGER

The 1980s were a successful decade for the organization. The nation's political shift to the right during the Ronald Reagan era spurred many activist groups, and the Panthers' membership reached an all-time high of 80,000. While the Gray Panthers had a much lower profile than AARP, Kuhn possessed a keen sense of what the media would pick up on, and she always provided them with good copy. She once said, "Old age is an excellent time for outrage. My goal is to say or do at least one outrageous thing every week." In that same spirit, membership materials affirm that "the Gray Panthers movement is in the trenches fighting for the values in which we believe—taking the far out positions which lead to real change."

The Gray Panthers always had a strong bond with organized labor, and members walked the picket line in the successful 1997 United Parcel Service strike. In addition, the Gray Panthers asked all their members who were union retirees to identify themselves as such so that the organization could continue to solidify its close relationship with the AFL-CIO and other unions in its quest for social and economic justice. Many members of the Panthers are lifetime activists, participating in union and progressive politics at a level of commitment that makes them extremely skillful as organizers. Networking is crucial to the success of the Gray Panthers: rather than employing the high-power lobbying techniques of AARP to influence members of Congress, the organization uses its modest resources to work directly with other progressive organizations such as Food First (the Institute for Food and Development Policy).

THE PASSING OF KUHN

In 1995 the Tenth Biennial Convention honored Kuhn, who had passed away in April on what would have been her ninetieth birthday: August 3, 1995. The Gray Panthers celebrated her memory in ceremonies across the country. The Panthers' most important achievement after Kuhn's passing was a joint event with the United States Student Association, the first "Age and Youth in Action Summit," in Washington, D.C., in 1996. The next year, the Gray Panthers regrouped and focused attention on producing a successful convention. With the election of a new national chair—fifty-five-year-old Catherine DeLorey, president of the Women's Health Institute—the organization sought to reaffirm its intergenerational character as it moved into the twenty-first century.

Under the Gray Panthers' reorganization plan of 1997, a new deputy director and a director of public policy and media were added to the national staff. New Yorker and longtime activist Judy Lear was named chair of the national board, and the Gray Panthers continue to focus on health care, the environment, peace, civil rights, civil liberties, jobs, and economic security. As an internationally recognized nongovernmental organization (NGO), the Gray Panthers also work with the United Nations on securing peace and social justice around the world.

Mary Hess

SEE ALSO: *AARP (American Association of Retired Persons); Civil Rights Movement; Nader, Ralph.*

BIBLIOGRAPHY

Brazil, Eric. "Gray Panthers Hope to Attract New Blood." *San Francisco Examiner*, September 27, 1997.

Gottlieb, Martin, and Kurt Eichenwald. "A Hospital Chain's Brass Knuckles, and the Backlash." *New York Times*, May 11, 1997.

Gray Panthers. "Age and Youth in Action." Final Report. Washington, DC: Gray Panthers, 1996.

Gray Panthers. "Bridging Generations for a New Social Contract." Report. Washington, DC: Gray Panthers, 1997.

Hessel, Dieter T., ed. *Maggie Kuhn on Aging: A Dialogue.* Philadelphia: Westminster Press, 1977.

Kay, Jane Holtz. "Asphalt Nation: How the Automobile Took Over America and How We Can Take It Back." *New York Times*, July 20, 1997.

Kuhn, Maggie. *No Stone Unturned: The Life and Times of Maggie Kuhn.* New York: Ballantine Books, 1991.

Sanjek, Roger. *Gray Panthers.* Philadelphia: University of Pennsylvania Press, 2009.

Stewart, Charles J.; Craig Allen Smith; and Robert E. Denton Jr. *Persuasion and Social Movements.* Prospect Heights, IL: Waveland Press, 2001.

The Great Depression

Beginning in 1929 and lasting through the 1930s, the Great Depression marked a turning point in American history by establishing the enlarged federal bureaucracy associated with the post–World War II state. While first and foremost an economic event, the Great Depression affected every aspect of American political, social, and cultural life. It was during the Depression that the radio and film industries, in conjunction with developments in documentary photography, reporting, and literature, helped develop a national culture based in uniquely American practices, environments, experiences, and ideals.

While the stock market crash of October 1929 is often viewed as the start of the Great Depression, it was by no means the cause. The crash, and its aftermath of unemployment, bank closures, bankruptcies, and homelessness, was caused by fundamental flaws in the prosperity of the 1920s. The availability and widespread use of credit, the increasingly unequal distribution of wealth, falling farm prices, and the corporate consolidation of American industry all contributed to the overproduction of farm and industrial goods and the overexertion of credit and speculation. In the wake of the crash, American industrial output decreased rapidly, reaching the same level of production in 1932 as in 1913. Employment reached an all-time low, with 13 million people, roughly 25 percent of the population, out of work. For farmers, crop prices had fallen drastically; a bushel of wheat that sold for $3 in 1920 brought only thirty cents in 1932.

DEVELOPMENT OF CULTURAL PROGRAMS

The Depression affected American culture in both the public and private sectors. The federal government, through its New Deal programs, subsidized writers, composers, musicians, performers, painters, sculptors, and other artists. It also developed and encouraged cultural programs that focused attention on the United States and its history, traditions, and native arts and crafts. The Federal Writers Project employed writers, editors, and researchers not only to produce works of fiction, usually with American themes, but also to create several series of books, such as the American Guide Series, consisting of all-purpose guide books for each state of the union.

The Federal Arts Project hired painters and sculptors to create public art for post offices and other public buildings and developed a network of community art centers in cities and towns across the country. The Federal Theater Project sought to bring the dramatic arts to the general public through local programs such as the Living Newspaper, in which local news stories were acted out in community theaters. Additional programs employed musicians, composers, architects, and other artists. Preservation programs, such as the Index of American Design and the Library of Congress's Archive of Folk Song, sought to preserve the inherently American character of folk arts. In all, the cultural programs of the New Deal focused attention on the unique aspects of American culture, not only in past arts and crafts but also in the creation of new works of art.

RADIO AND LEISURE TIME

The broadcasting and motion picture industries responded to the economic realities of the Depression and the government-sponsored trend toward reinforcing traditional American values. In the 1930s radio dominated Americans' leisure time. Nearly one-third of all Americans owned at least one radio, and even those who did not own a radio usually had access to one through family, friends, or neighbors. The potential radio audience for any program was estimated at 60 million people. As a result of these vast audiences and the huge profits to be made, the radio industry became big business, with production companies selling "prepackaged" shows to sponsors and stations and with syndicates and networks developing and growing.

During the 1930s comedians were the most popular radio personalities. Jack Benny, Fanny Brice, George Burns and Gracie Allen, Bob Hope, Milton Berle, and Jimmy Durante all had popular radio shows. Musical shows were also a favorite of audiences, as almost every station presented remote broadcasts from hotel ballrooms featuring dance orchestras and jazz bands such as Paul Whiteman ("The King of Jazz"); Ralph Ginsberg and the Palmer House Ensemble; and Phil Spitalny and his All-Girl Orchestra, featuring Evelyn and her Magic Violin.

Daytime programming was dominated by the soap opera, so named because most were sponsored by soap manufacturers. Writer James Thurber described soap operas as "a kind of sandwich, whose recipe is simple enough. . . . Between thick slices of advertising, spread twelve minutes of dialogue, add predicament, villainy, and female suffering in equal measure, throw in a dash of nobility, sprinkle with tears, season with organ music, cover with a rich announcer sauce, and serve five times a week."

In contrast to daytime serial dramas, evening dramas featured much better production values and more sophisticated material performed by famous actors. The *Texaco Star Theater*, the *Philip Morris Playhouse*, *Grand Central Station*, and other hour-long programs presented serious dramatic fare, but the most popular shows were the half-hour-long crime-suspense-adventure shows, including *Sam Spade*, *Jack Armstrong: The All-American Boy*, *The Thin Man*, *Sergeant Preston of the Yukon*, *The Green Hornet*, *The Shadow*, and *The Lone Ranger*. Even news reporting took on a more entertaining flavor as radio newscasters became celebrities, including such names as Lowell Thomas, Edward R. Murrow, and Floyd Gibbons, who introduced himself as "the fastest talking man in radio." Forty percent of all Americans preferred to get their news and information from radio, more than any other single source.

Radio took on a whole new importance in the wake of the Depression, primarily through the use of the medium by President Franklin D. Roosevelt. In his "fireside chats," Roosevelt addressed the country directly from the White House. This mediated communication, due to the intimacy associated with radio broadcasting, and developed a more personal relationship between the president and the public than ever before, reinforcing the expansion of federal, especially executive, authority. Radio became much more than a source of local information and entertainment; it became a vital tool of the government to promote and support its programs. Roosevelt's first fireside chat (1933), explaining the purpose of the bank holiday and subsequent banking legislation, produced enough confidence in Roosevelt and the government that the following day bank deposits outnumbered withdrawals for the first time since the stock market crash almost four years earlier.

Soup Kitchen Line. *A line of unemployed men looking for a meal at a soup kitchen was a common sight across the United States in the 1930s during the Great Depression.* UNIVERSAL HISTORY ARCHIVE/GETTY IMAGES.

Radio not only informed people but also brought them under the influence of a centralized medium that homogenized the information it was disseminating. As Warren Susman argues in his essay "The Culture of the Thirties," radio "helped mold uniform national responses; it helped create or reinforce uniform national values and beliefs in a way that no previous medium had ever been able to do." Illustrating one such uniform national response was the euphoria witnessed in communities, both black and white, over Joe Louis's heavyweight title fights in 1937 and 1938. Informing the public became such a vital part of the radio industry, and so accepted by the public, that a fake "emergency bulletin" aired as part of Orson Welles's 1938 radio production of H. G. Wells's *War of the Worlds* created pandemonium in towns and cities across the United States.

THE GOLDEN AGE OF TURBULENCE

As a result of the Depression, Hollywood experienced a decline in movie attendance, and it compensated by using the latest technology to its fullest impact to produce movies that would appeal to adult males, the segment of the movie audience that had declined the most. War films such as *All Quiet on the Western Front* (1930) and *The Dawn Patrol* (1930); horror films such as *Dracula* (1931), *Frankenstein* (1931), and *King Kong* (1933); and gangster movies such as *Little Caesar* (1930), *The Public Enemy* (1931), and *Scarface* (1932) all took advantage of sound technology to enhance the film-going experience.

Movies such as Marlene Dietrich's *Blonde Venus* (1932), Jean Harlow's *Red Dust* (1932), and Irene Dunne's *Back Street* (1932) challenged the prevailing notions of respectable women's roles. Even the glamorous Greta Garbo, in her sound film debut, did not play a socialite but rather a prostitute. The long awaited moment when Garbo first spoke on film was in *Anna Christie* (1930), as she addressed a waiter in a waterfront dive: "Gimme a whiskey, ginger ale on the side. And don't be stingy, baby!"

Even a film as superficial as *Gold Diggers of 1933* implied that for women there were limited career paths. In the film's most memorable song, "We're in the Money," chorus girls joke that if they have to give up performing they would have to enter into the world's oldest profession: "We're in the money. We're in the money. We've got a lot of what it takes to get along." Even comedies emphasized this tendency toward anarchy and sex. The most popular film comedians, the Marx Brothers and Mae West, relied heavily on sound to convey their primarily verbal humor, yet both also depended on visuals for the strong physical presence necessary in both slapstick comedy and body-enhancing sexual innuendo.

This "golden age of turbulence," according to film historian Robert Sklar in *Movie-Made America: A Cultural History of American Movies*, lasted from 1930 through 1934 when Hollywood, under pressure from civic organizations such as the Catholic Church's League of Decency, discovered there was as much, if not more, profit to be made by supporting traditional American values as there was in challenging them. With the 1934 introduction of the Breen Office (officially the Production Code Administration but popularly named after Joseph Breen, the film industry's self-imposed censor, who had absolute power), the movie industry stopped challenging traditional values and instead became a staunch supporter of social order.

THE GOLDEN AGE OF ORDER

The Breen Office brought about the "golden age of order," in which the social order was restored in films that reinforced traditional notions about social roles and American ideals. Screwball comedies set among the upper classes, such as *Bringing Up Baby* (1938) and *The Philadelphia Story* (1940), replaced the anarchic vision of the Marx Brothers and the brazen sexuality of West. Gangster movies focused not on the lawless but on the government agent, the G-man. And Hollywood began producing socially conscious films such as *The Grapes of Wrath* (1940) and the films of Frank Capra.

Capra best exemplifies the "age of order" with his morality plays set among the common people of America. He produced films that encouraged Americans to reaffirm their beliefs in democracy, community, and humanity. In his "American trilogy," featuring *Mr. Deeds Goes to Town* (1936), *Mr. Smith Goes to Washington* (1939), and *Meet John Doe* (1941), Capra presents American democracy at its best with each protagonist (Deeds, Smith, and Doe) overcoming challenges to honesty and decency through perseverance. In *Mr. Deeds*, Gary Cooper stars as Longfellow Deeds, who plans to use his inherited millions by establishing farmers on their own small plots of land in an attempt to re-create the Jeffersonian vision of the democratic yeoman farmer. In *Mr. Smith*, Jimmy Stewart stars as Jefferson Smith, a junior senator who envisions a boys' camp in the western wilderness to teach boys the virtues of independence, self-sufficiency, and frontier democracy.

In *John Doe*, Cooper once again stars, this time as Long John Willoughby, a down-and-out baseball player recruited by a big-city newspaper to play the role of John Doe, a "common" man who has threatened to end his life as a protest against modern society. John Doe not only becomes a circulation booster, but his simple ideas about neighborly consideration and the "little guys" watching out for each other are readily picked up by an eager public searching for solutions to the Depression. The John Doe Movement, with the establishment of John Doe clubs, is manipulated by tyrannical newspaper owner D. B. Norton, who aspires to political office. Norton and Willoughby come into conflict when Norton's machinations are revealed, and Willoughby seeks to stop him. Norton exposes the "fake" John Doe, and the movement crumbles. In the end, Willoughby seeks to follow through on "John Doe's" original promise to jump off the city hall tower on Christmas Eve.

Like all Capra movies, the honest and decent hero survives the attacks against him through the faith of a loving woman and the eventual realization of "the people." Capra reaffirms traditional ideas about self-help and the private function of charity in the face of adversity, as opposed to more modern ideas in which the federal government assumes responsibility for the health and welfare of individual citizens. Despite the revolutionary medium of motion pictures, late 1930s movies overwhelmingly reinforced traditional values.

Ultimately, the reaction to the Great Depression, by the federal government and mass-media industries, served to maintain traditional American values in the face of economic, political, and social change.

Charles J. Shindo

SEE ALSO: All Quiet on the Western Front*; Benny, Jack; Berle, Milton; Brice, Fanny;* Bringing Up Baby*; Burns, George, and Gracie Allen; Capra, Frank; Cooper, Gary; Dietrich, Marlene;*

Dracula; Dunne, Irene; Frankenstein; Garbo, Greta; The Grapes of Wrath*; The Great Recession; Harlow, Jean; Hope, Bob;* King Kong*; The Lone Ranger; Louis, Joe; The Marx Brothers; Murrow, Edward R.; New Deal;* The Philadelphia Story*; Radio; Radio Drama; Screwball Comedies; The Shadow; Soap Operas; Stewart, Jimmy; Stock Market Crashes;* War of the Worlds*; Welles, Orson; West, Mae; Whiteman, Paul; World War II.*

BIBLIOGRAPHY

Hilmes, Michele. *Radio Voices: American Broadcasting, 1922–1952.* Minneapolis: University of Minnesota Press, 1997.

McElvaine, Robert S. *The Great Depression: America, 1929–1941.* New York: Times Books, 1984.

Nishi, Dennis. *The Great Depression.* San Diego, CA: Greenhaven Press, 2001.

Shindo, Charles J. *Dust Bowl Migrants in the American Imagination.* Lawrence: University Press of Kansas, 1997.

Sklar, Robert. *Movie-Made America: A Cultural History of American Movies.* New York: Vintage Books, 1975.

Susman, Warren I. *Culture as History: The Transformation of American Society in the Twentieth Century.* New York: Pantheon Books, 1985.

The Great Recession

Beginning in December 2007 the world economy began to decline, and in September 2008 matters became even worse. Many countries experienced a recession, or period of economic crisis, including Germany, Ireland, Italy, Japan, New Zealand, Switzerland, the United Kingdom, and the United States. Although some countries were affected more than others, all experienced higher unemployment, a federal debt crisis, and a rise in food and oil prices.

There are two different meanings for the term *recession.* The economic definition is when a nation's gross domestic product (GDP) is in the negative for two or more consecutive quarters. The other definition is simpler: a period of reduced economic activity that can be felt long after the actual economic recession is over. As of 2012 in the United States, effects of the recession could still be felt, such as high unemployment, a decline in property values, an increase in home foreclosures and personal bankruptcy, and a rise in food and oil cost—although the true economic recession ended in the summer of 2009. Once a recession ends, hardship remains, much like that following the Great Depression of the 1930s. Some economists see an economic recession as an unavoidable part of the modern business cycle, whereas a depression is considered a collapse of the economy or a sustained downward cycle.

CONTRIBUTORY FACTORS

The National Bureau of Economic Research (NBER) is a nonprofit organization that predicts recessions and other economic trends in the United States. In December 2008 the NBER declared that the United States had been in recession for nearly a year. Global economists predicted that this Great Recession was the worst since the Great Depression. There were many factors leading up to the Great Recession, but one of the main reasons lay in risky lending practices concerning home mortgages and personal loans. U.S. mortgages were held by banks in the United States and in other countries around the world. As early as 2000, economists predicted that the United States might experience a recession. In a June 2005 special report, the *Economist* magazine stated:

> Never before have real house prices risen so fast, for so long, in so many countries. Property markets have been frothing from America, Britain and Australia to France, Spain and China. Rising property prices helped to prop up the world economy after the stock-market bubble burst in 2000. What if the housing boom now turns to bust? . . . The global boom in house prices has been driven by two common factors: historically low interest rates have encouraged home buyers to borrow more money; and households have lost faith in equities after stockmarkets plunged, making property look attractive." That same year Alan Greenspan, the U.S. Federal Reserve chairman, commented on real estate as having a lot of local bubbles, both in the United States and globally.

These subprime lending practices provided high interest rates for higher risk consumers. Consequently, too much easy credit with a lack of regulation created an abundance of homeowners unable to make their payments. The losses in these subprime loans led to exposure of other risky loans, and the proverbial "bubble" burst. Both commercial and investment banks in the United States and abroad suffered huge losses. Home prices decreased, leading to there being many homeowners with a mortgage debt higher than their property values. On September 15, 2008, Lehman Brothers Holdings Inc., the fourth-largest investment bank in the United States, declared bankruptcy. Other major lenders teetered on the brink of oblivion as well.

Another major factor leading up to the Great Recession was an increase in both food and oil prices, which were likely caused by a reduction in world incomes and growth. In January 2008 oil prices broke the $100-a-barrel mark, and by July 2008 they peaked at more than $145 a barrel, with prices reaching $4 a gallon nationwide in the United States. In February 2008 Reuters news agency reported that global inflation was at a historic level with ten- to twenty-year highs. American political Economist Robert Reich, who served on President Barack Obama's economic transition advisory board, attributed the U.S. economic troubles to inequality between the upper and middle classes. In a Huffington Post interview, he said, "Stagnant middle-class wages led households to pull equity from their homes and overload on debt to maintain living standards." As the economy began failing at the turn of the millennium with stock market, dot-com industry, and real estate bubbles bursting, the number of suburban, middle-class households below the poverty line increased by more than 50 percent.

In September 2010 the International Monetary Fund (IMF) stated that global financial problems would not end until unemployment decreased, and it urged countries to simultaneously cut spending and generate more jobs. In Ambrose Evans-Pritchard's *Telegraph* article, Olivier Blanchard, the IMF's chief economist stated, "Long term unemployment is alarmingly high: in the United States, half the unemployed have been out of work for over six months, something we have not seen since the Great Depression." In October 2009 U.S. unemployment peaked at 10 percent, still 15 percent less than that of the Great Depression.

SOCIAL CONSEQUENCES

While many families lost their savings and homes, corporate institutions such as Bank of America and General Motors were labeled as essential to the economy. To keep these giant corporations from going bankrupt, the U.S. government instituted a series of bailouts funded by American taxpayers, sparking resentment among middle-class workers. Adding insult to injury, CEOs from many of these companies were offered "golden parachutes" in the form of lucrative exit deals written into their contracts upon termination. In essence the rich seemed to stay rich while the middle class became poorer.

These feelings of disproportionate distribution of wealth led to multiple protests in many countries, including China, France, Greece, Russia, the United Kingdom, and the United States. The Great Recession led to the development of two major political movements in the United States—the Tea Party and Occupy Wall Street. The Tea Party, a Republican populist movement made public in 2009, argues for limited government but struggles to maintain the concept of the worker as an honorable, self-made, middle-class American. A competing ideology around middle-class populism arose in the Occupy Wall Street protest, which began in New York City but spread nationwide. The numerous Occupy movements embraced a central slogan: "We are the 99 percent." Despite being politically diverse, the group tends to espouse socialist policies that address the increasing gap between the working class and the wealthiest 1 percent of the country. Although the two political movements appeared to be very different, they shared an opposition to government bailouts, banking practices, and an international military presence subsidized by taxpayers.

Another social consequence of the Great Recession has been an increased frugality among many Americans. A nationwide belt-tightening forced delayed retirements and unplanned withdrawals from long-term savings. Consumers were reluctant to spend money on luxuries such as vacations, new cars, and high-end electronics. In most cases, money was diverted to pay for housing, food, clothing, education, and other necessities.

As of 2012 there were slight increases to the GDP, but unemployment remained high at about 8 percent. Although some new jobs were created, jobs lost from the industrial and manufacturing sectors were replaced by either highly specialized or low-wage employment opportunities. Additionally, the housing market remained unstable, and energy costs continued to rise, further stagnating the economy.

Don Peck comments in an article in the *Atlantic*:

> The Great Recession may be over, but this era of high joblessness is probably just beginning. Before it ends, it will likely change the life course and character of a generation of young adults. It will leave an indelible imprint on many blue-collar men. It could cripple marriage as an institution in many communities. It may already be plunging many inner cities into a despair not seen for decades. Ultimately, it is likely to warp our politics, our culture, and the character of our society for years to come.

Both the finance and construction industries, which boomed before the housing bubble burst, led to a disproportionately high unemployment of male workers at 75 percent of the eight million jobs lost since 2008. While both education and health care have been hit hard, this higher rate of male unemployment has had a major effect on the traditional concept of marriage. More men are staying at home, taking care of children, and breaking the stereotypical gender barriers.

Another repercussion of the Great Recession is a national decline in the divorce rate. While marital conflict is not on the decline, divorces are not cheap, so even couples who do not get along can easily find themselves sticking together to avoid the added expense of separating. Another side effect of the recession is a drop in the birth rate, as the average cost of raising a child in today's world according to *CNNMoney* in 2010 is an estimated $226,920, up nearly 35 percent from 2000.

One interesting side effect of a recession that can be seen as positive is the creation of new jobs as past jobs become obsolete. As the global market economy shifts from commercial office space and retail shopping centers, many laid-off employees work from home, become entrepreneurs, or seek further education. In today's current marketplace, job switching has become commonplace, and employees are used to periods of joblessness in between their work experiences. Consequently, the slang word *funemployment* has become a common word in today's economy to describe these breaks between jobs subsidized by the nation's unemployment system. As of 2012, in most professions, the concept of working one job from college graduation until retirement is virtually unheard of.

ARTS AND ENTERTAINMENT

As with most global crises, arts and entertainment imitate real life. Television shows ranging from cable miniseries to local news focus on the economy's effects on everyday life. Homer and Marge Simpson sell their house when they cannot afford mortgage payments, Michael Scott is wary of telling his workers that their branch may be downsized in *The Office*, and Ray Drecker becomes a male escort to supplement his declining pay as a high school gym teacher on the HBO series *Hung*.

In an MSNBC article, financial blogger and *Bailout Nation* author Barry Ritholtz discusses a 180-degree shift in popular culture references to the economy. Most recessions since World War II have been short, so their effects on TV and movies were minimal, but with the length of this last one, Great Recession allusions are rampant in all aspects of entertainment. The past trend of coping with economic problems was to escape reality with lavish musicals during the Great Depression or decadent lifestyles depicted in such 1980s television shows as *Dynasty* or *Dallas*. Ritholtz explains, "On the one hand, it's good when it becomes part of popular culture because people are talking about it and thinking about it." On the other hand, he continues, "It's bad when people are obsessing about it to the point of absurdity."

Ron Horton

SEE ALSO: *Bank Failures/Subprime Mortgages;* Dallas*; Divorce;* Dynasty*; General Motors; The Great Depression; Housing Market Bubble; Obama, Barack;* The Office*;* The Simpsons*; Stock Market Crashes; World War II.*

BIBLIOGRAPHY

Evans-Pritchard, Ambrose. "IMF Fears 'Social Explosion' from World Jobs Crisis." *Telegraph*, September 13, 2010. Telegraph Media Group. Accessed June 2012. Available from http://www.telegraph.co.uk/finance/financialcrisis/8000561/IMF-fears-social-explosion-from-world-jobs-crisis.html

Linn, Allison. "Lasting Recession Works Way into Pop Culture." *Still Made in America*, July 23, 2009. MSNBC. Accessed June 2012. Available from http://www.msnbc.msn.com/id/31971034/ns/business-us_business/t/lasting-recession-works-way-pop-culture/#.T9GmG8g-fDd

McCarthy, Ryan. "How American Income Inequality Hit Levels Not Seen since the Depression." Huffington Post, October 22, 2010.

Peck, Don. "How a New Jobless Era Will Transform America." *Atlantic*, March 2010.

Ritholtz, Barry, with Aaron Task. *Bailout Nation*. Hoboken, NJ: John Wiley and Sons, 2009.

The Great Train Robbery

The Great Train Robbery (1903) is an eleven-minute film directed and photographed by Edwin S. Porter. Added to the National Film Registry in 1990, it is a milestone in the history of American film. *The Great Train Robbery* was the first movie created with new, innovative techniques such as shooting on location, panning the camera to follow the actors as they moved, and cutting back and forth between scenes to show events occurring in different places. Based on an actual train robbery by outlaw Butch Cassidy and his gang in 1900, *The Great Train Robbery* was a huge hit.

Robert C. Sickels

SEE ALSO: Butch Cassidy and the Sundance Kid*; Silent Movies; The Western.*

BIBLIOGRAPHY

Kauffmann, Stanley. "The Great Train Robbery." *New Republic* 213, no. 10 (1995): 27–28.

Kirby, Lynne. *Parallel Tracks: The Railroad and Silent Cinema*. Durham, NC: Duke University Press, 1997.

Kobel, Peter, and the Library of Congress. *Silent Movies: The Birth of Film and the Triumph of Movie Culture*. New York: Little, Brown, 2007.

The Great War

SEE: *World War I.*

Greb, Harry *(1894–1926)*

Edward Henry "Harry" Greb epitomized the Roaring Twenties. Middleweight boxing champion by 1923, "The Human Windmill" lived hard, played harder, and fought hardest.

Greb made the sports pages for his myriad, perhaps even historically unparalleled, accomplishments inside of the ring, and he made the front pages for his antics outside of it. Affairs with married women, car crashes, drunken brawls, lawsuits: Greb was the original media bad boy. He once fought fellow Hall of Famer Mickey Walker outside a pub, several hours *after* their bruising title fight (Greb won the title fight; Walker the street brawl). His nonstop attack and indomitable fighting spirit seemed to carry over from the ring to his personal life, and in spite of his negative press (and perhaps because of it), Greb was a beloved sports icon. According to boxing historian Bert Randolph Sugar, Ernest Hemingway once accused another writer who did not know who Greb was of "not knowing one of our greatest Americans."

Max Kellerman

SEE ALSO: *Boxing; Hemingway, Ernest; The Twenties.*

BIBLIOGRAPHY

Fair, James R. *Give Him to the Angels: The Story of Harry Greb*. New York: Smith and Durrell, 1946.

Paxton, Bill. *The Fearless Harry Greb: Biography of a Tragic Hero of Boxing*. Jefferson, NC: McFarland, 2009.

Greed

The bowdlerization of Erich von Stroheim's *Greed* (1924) is almost more famous than the film itself. An adaptation of *McTeague*, Frank Norris's epic novel of avarice, desire, and disintegration, the film stars Gibson Gowland as the dentist McTeague, ZaSu Pitts as the wife he murders for money, and Jean Hersholt as the brute Marcus with whom he fights—to their mutual destruction—in Death Valley, California. In realizing a cherished dream to do literal justice to the book, Stroheim broke new ground in cinematic realism—both in characterization and with the use of actual locations in San Francisco and Death Valley—but emerged with a forty-two-reel, ten-hour film. Producer Irving Thalberg, a nemesis with whom Stroheim had previously tangled, ordered cuts; Stroheim tried to oblige. Ultimately, however, the film was taken away from him, and the cuts became a massacre. The final version of the film was a little short of two and half hours, with much careful detail lost and the dramatic balance seriously upset by the removal of subplots and subsidiary characters.

In 1979 filmmaker Kim Eveleth was conducting research for his documentary on von Stroheim, *The Man You Love to Hate*, and discovered a cache of stills from *Greed* that had been lost for decades. In 1999 a partially restored version of the film was shown on Turner Classic Movies with those stills substituting for the portions that had been destroyed in 1924. Despite the massacre, *Greed* remains a powerful masterpiece of silent cinema from one of the medium's few geniuses.

Robyn Karney

SEE ALSO: *Norris, Frank; Silent Movies; Thalberg, Irving G..*

BIBLIOGRAPHY

Curtiss, Thomas Quinn. *Erich von Stroheim*. New York: Farrar, Straus & Giroux, 1971.

Koszarski, R. *The Man You Love to Hate*. UK: Oxford University Press, 1983.

Rosenbaum, Jonathan. *Essential Cinema: On the Necessity of Film Canons.* Baltimore, MD: Johns Hopkins University Press, 2004.

Roud, Richard. *Cinema: A Critical Dictionary.* London: Secker & Warburg, 1980.

Weinberg, Herman G. *The Complete* Greed *of Erich von Stroheim.* New York: Arno Press, 1972.

Greeley, Andrew *(1928–)*

A self-described "faintly comic Celtic Lancelot" and "perennial dissident priest," Catholic priest, sociologist, and writer Andrew Greeley has stirred frequent controversy within and outside the church, producing enormous amounts of written work in widely different fields. Beginning late in the 1950s and continuing at a relentless pace thereafter, Greeley has published countless articles in newspapers, magazines, and scholarly journals, as well as more than 100 books that range from obscure sociological tracts on religion and ethnicity in the United States to racy best-selling novels filled with sex and corruption to works on relationships, photography, and mysteries. If a central theme ties his work together, it may be his possibly quixotic crusade to "free the riches of the Catholic tradition from the stranglehold of a decrepit and corrupt bureaucracy" and to bring a sense of "God's merciful love" to readers. Although it seemed as if Greeley would never slow down, he was forced to do so after receiving a traumatic brain injury in 2008.

A lifelong resident of Chicago, Greeley has been a professor at both the University of Chicago and the University of Arizona as well as a longtime researcher at Chicago's National Opinion Research Center (NORC). He was embroiled in numerous controversies, offending persons of all political stripes. His advocacy of liberalization of church policies on birth control, divorce, and women in the priesthood angered a conservative Catholic hierarchy, while his opposition to abortion and support of priestly celibacy offended many liberals. Despite his success as a writer of best-selling novels, he claims his primary occupation as parish priest and cites his popular books as his most successful outreach.

RELIGIOUS BELIEFS

As a youth, Greeley attended Catholic schools and admired the works of G. K. Chesterton, Graham Greene, and other Catholic writers. He decided he wanted to be a priest while in second grade, and he was ordained in 1954. While serving as an assistant pastor in Chicago, he began writing articles for religious publications under a pseudonym and later under his own name. His first book, *The Church and the Suburbs* (1959), grew out of two of his articles that examined the effects of increased affluence on religious belief. In 1962 he earned a doctorate in sociology from the University of Chicago. His sociological work, often based on surveys generated at NORC, has included studies of Catholic education, the priesthood, the paranormal, ethnicity and alcoholism, and Irish Americans. Religious works such as *The Mary Myth* (1977) suggest the "womanliness of God," a recurrent theme in Greeley's nonfiction and fiction. Books such as *Unsecular Man* (1972) make a case for the persistence of religious belief in a supposedly secular age.

One of Greeley's main offenses against conventional Catholic doctrine has been to suggest that sex is a sacrament and an expression of God's love rather than a sin when it is not a means of procreation. His outspokenness on this and other similar issues brought him into conflict with leading church authorities, including John Cardinal Cody of Chicago. Greeley's most critically acclaimed work of popular nonfiction, *The Making of the Popes, 1978: The Politics of Intrigue in the Vatican* (1979), examines papal politics in Rome in the style of Theodore White. Analyzing the papacy as White analyzes politics, Greeley deglamorizes, demystifies, and exposes the papal selection process as an unfair practice in which popes are chosen secretly, undemocratically, and often ineptly. Although the book sold only moderately well, it earned plaudits for its close observation, detailed reporting (much of it thanks to a source Greeley termed "Deep Purple"), and analysis of a rite that has remained shrouded in secrecy for centuries.

CHANGING GEARS

In the mid-1970s, convinced that the power of storytelling and emotion rather than dry exposition and philosophy were key to religious belief, Greeley began writing poetry and fiction. His first two novels sold poorly, but his third, *The Cardinal Sins* (1981), made him an overnight celebrity. The story of two boyhood friends, one who goes on to become a simple parish priest and the other who becomes a cardinal, is laced with sex and corruption. It remained on best-seller lists for more than a year, selling more than three million copies. Greeley followed with dozens of other novels, many of them best sellers that often included sex, corruption, and violence. His books are generally set in Chicago, featuring religious or mystical characters. Like *The Cardinal Sins*, many were better received by the public than by critics, who often complain that Greeley's writing is stiff and his characters two-dimensional.

Catholic officials (many of whom, Greeley claims, have never read the books) often criticize the novels for their sex scenes, although Greeley has defended his depiction of sex as tasteful and claims that his own surveys demonstrate that his books brought a majority of Catholic readers closer to the church. He describes his novels as "comedies of grace"—parables of God's grace through love—and "the most effective priestly activity in which I have ever engaged," and he blames the anger of his priestly critics on their envy of the wealth and fame that his books have brought him. Though he has owned expensive houses and cars, he claims he has given away most of his earnings to charity.

Upon reaching his seventieth birthday in 1998, Greeley, who attributed his productivity to celibacy and long hours at the computer terminal, said that he would like to slow down somewhat. The previous decade had shown little evidence of declining energy. During that period, he produced more than a score of both nonfiction and fiction books. Although the latter earned many unfavorable reviews, they continued to receive an enthusiastic reception from loyal fans. According to Greeley, readers who write to him often tell him that his stories have had "an enormous impact on their personal and religious lives, giving them new hope and a new (or renewed) sense of God's forgiving love." Among his later works is a series of eighteen mysteries—somewhat reminiscent of Chesterton's Father Brown series—featuring the adventures of Father Blackwood (Blackie) Ryan, monsignor, who represents the best attributes of Catholic priests: "intelligence, pragmatism, zeal, wisdom and wit" rather than the selfishness and insensitivity of the other priests portrayed in the books. Greeley also contributed popular books on relationships during this period, including *Sexual Intimacy: Love and Play* (1988) and *Faithful Attraction: Discovering Intimacy, Love, and Fidelity in American Marriage* (1991).

Greeley continued to write in a variety of genres in the first years of the twenty-first century. In addition to *Jesus: A Meditation on His Stories and His Relationships with Women* (2007), Greeley explored prayer, Catholicism, God in film, and conservative Christians. His final book on sociology was *Religion in Europe at the End of the Second Millennium: A Sociological Profile* (2003). Blackie Ryan was made a bishop in 1997, and Greeley published seven books in that series in the twenty-first century, ending it with *The Archbishop of Andalusia* in 2008. In addition, he completed twelve books in the Nuala McGrail series, which he had begun in 1994, and produced several stand-alone novels. Greeley dealt with the sex scandal among priests in 2004 in the novel *The Priestly Sins* and in the nonfiction book *Priests: A Calling in Crisis*.

In November 2008, Greeley's coat became caught in a taxi door as he disembarked. Unaware, the driver moved away, throwing Greeley to the ground, where he struck his head and suffered a severe brain injury. Although his last book, *Chicago Catholics and Their Struggle within Their Church*, was published in 2010, his public life ended with the accident, which left him unable to write.

Daniel Lindley

SEE ALSO: *Best Sellers; Celebrity; Romance Novels; Sex Scandals.*

BIBLIOGRAPHY

"Andrew Greeley." *Contemporary Authors Online*. Detroit, MI: Gale, 2009.

Becker, Allienne R. *The Divine and Human Comedy of Andrew M. Greeley*. Westport, CT: Greenwood, 2000.

Carnes, Mark C., ed. *Invisible Giants: Fifty Americans Who Shaped the Nation but Missed the History Books*. New York: Oxford University Press, 2002.

Greeley, Andrew. *Confessions of a Parish Priest: An Autobiography*. New York: Simon & Schuster, 1986.

Shafer, Ingrid H. *Eros and the Womanliness of God: Andrew Greeley's Romances of Renewal*. Chicago: Loyola University Press, 1986.

Shafer, Ingrid H., ed. *The Incarnate Imagination: Essays in Theology, the Arts and Social Sciences in Honor of Andrew Greeley: A Festschrift*. Bowling Green, OH: Bowling Green State University Popular Press, 1988.

Green, Al *(1946–)*

Admirers of eight-time Grammy winner and Rock and Roll Hall of Fame inductee Al Green call him "the quintessential soul man." Green, who was born in Arkansas and grew up in Michigan, toured as a youngster with his father in a family gospel quartet. In the mid-1960s Green formed his own group, the Creations, and he later became lead singer for the Soul Mates. A solo career with Memphis, Tennessee–based Hi Records rocketed him to fame in the 1970s, resulting in his becoming "that decade's most popular purveyor of soul music," according to the Rock and Roll Hall of Fame. Over a period of eight years, Green cowrote thirteen charting singles, including "Tired of Being Alone" and "Let's Stay Together." Fourteen of Green's albums have appeared on the Top 200 charts, and five went gold.

After being ordained in 1976, Green became the proprietor of the Full Gospel Tabernacle in Memphis and began serving as its pastor. His ongoing interest in music led to his recording nine best-selling gospel albums in the 1980s. In the early years of the twenty-first century, Green continued to make music while ministering to his congregation at Full Gospel Tabernacle. Although he gave up performing R&B music when he become a minister, he eventually returned to recording secular music. Early in the twenty-first century, he released *I Can't Stop* (2003) and *Everything's OK* (2005), and he began touring again. In 2011 Green released *The Best of the Gospel Sessions*, featuring music he had recorded between 1981 and 1987.

Courtney Bennett

SEE ALSO: *Funk; Gospel Music; Grammy Awards; Rhythm and Blues; Soul Music.*

BIBLIOGRAPHY

"Al Green: 1995, Performer." Rock and Roll Hall of Fame and Museum. Accessed March 18, 2012. Available from http://rockhall.com/inductees/al-green/bio

Awkward, Michael. *Soul Covers: Rhythm and Blues Remakes and the Struggle for Artistic Identity*. Durham, NC: Duke University Press, 2007.

Mosher, Craig. "Ecstatic Sounds: The Influence of Pentecostalism on Rock and Roll." *Popular Music and Society* 31, no. 1 (2008).

The Green Bay Packers

As the most successful franchise of the National Football League (NFL), with thirteen titles since 1929, the Green Bay Packers overcame early financial hardship and a location in the smallest city with a professional sports team to become one of the most popular teams in all of American sports. In addition to their thirteen league titles, the Packers have placed twenty-one members into the Professional Football Hall of Fame and are the only NFL franchise to win three straight league titles, having done so twice (1929–1931 and 1965–1967). With this long history of success, the Packers have even given a nickname to their hometown, Green Bay, Wisconsin: Titletown, USA. The city has undoubtedly earned its strong connection to the club, as city leaders and citizens have aided the team many times since it was founded.

FORMATION

Founded by Earl L. "Curly" Lambeau and George Calhoun in 1919, the Packers owe their team name to the Indian Packing Company, a meat-packing firm in Green Bay. The company, which employed Lambeau at the time as a meat cutter, provided the initial funds for necessary equipment and allowed the club to use its private athletic fields for practice sessions. The team chose to use "Packers" as its name, and Lambeau was elected as vice president and coach, a position he held for thirty years. In their first season the Packers won ten of eleven games against

Vince Lombardi. Vince Lombardi leads his Green Bay Packers in a pregame prayer. Lombardi sealed his legend by coaching the Packers to three consecutive NFL championships in the 1960s. VERNON BIEVER/GETTY IMAGES.

other club teams in the Wisconsin area, but after this auspicious start even bigger things were on the horizon.

In 1921 Calhoun and Lambeau secured a franchise in the national professional football league that had formed a year earlier, which was the precursor to the modern NFL. Following this grand leap, a long string of financial troubles beset the team, the first of which allowed Lambeau to take full ownership of the club in 1922. The financial difficulties continued throughout the 1920s, and during this decade Lambeau sought citywide assistance for the club and formed the Green Bay Football Corporation with financial help from business leaders throughout Green Bay and the surrounding region.

Once the corporation was established, and with it a more stable financial base, Lambeau was able to secure the services of better players and acquire first-rate equipment, allowing the team to become more competitive in the growing professional football world of the late 1920s. By 1929 the Packers had won the first of three consecutive NFL titles during what is commonly known as the Iron Man era of professional football, when players commonly played both offense and defense for the entire game. Following these early championships, legal problems in the mid-1930s led the club into financial problems once more, but the local business community again came to the rescue with an infusion of capital, and the team was saved.

In 1935 a new weapon was added to the Packers' arsenal of great football players: a young end from the University of Alabama named Don Hutson. He became an immediate star in the fledgling NFL, so great that he was named to the 75th Anniversary Team in 1994, nearly fifty years after his retirement. Hutson led the league in receiving seven times and scoring five times and also set an all-time record in 1945, personally scoring twenty-nine points in one period. In the Hutson era, the Packers won three more NFL titles (1936, 1939, and 1944). During this period the Packers gained national recognition with their success on the gridiron, and fans throughout the country began to follow the team and the legendary Hutson.

LOMBARDI ERA

Following Hutson's retirement in 1945, the Packers' fortunes on the field declined, along with their gate receipts. By 1949 the club was yet again struggling financially, this time nearing complete bankruptcy. The situation led Lambeau to search for greener pastures, and he left the club to coach the Chicago Cardinals. However, the community would not forsake its beloved Packers, and in 1950 a giant public stock sale was organized that raised $125,000 to save the club from dissolution. This sale, the third such effort by the club since 1923 and the first to be open to the public, formed a stable financial base for the franchise that has continued since. While the club was only moderately successful throughout the remainder of the 1950s, the ground had been laid for greater success.

In 1959 the Packers hired Vince Lombardi, an assistant coach from the New York Giants, to become only the fifth head coach of the team in forty years. Over the next nine years, Lombardi became a legend in Green Bay and throughout the country because of the success to which he led his teams and for the unswerving loyalty he demonstrated to players, friends, and colleagues. By Lombardi's third season as coach (1961) he had transformed the Packers from a mediocre club to NFL champions, a feat the team repeated four more times—in 1962, 1965, 1966, and 1967—under his leadership. Within this span the Packers won the first two Super Bowls in 1966 and 1967, setting in motion the development of the Super Bowl as America's premier one-day sporting spectacle. The team's dominance was so commanding that the NFL named the Super Bowl championship trophy after the legendary Packers leader: the Vince Lombardi Trophy. This honor could be attributed in part to Lombardi's phenomenal success as a coach in division and league championship games alone: his teams won nine out of ten such games.

During the Lombardi era, Green Bay was blessed not only with exceptional coaching but with a collection of Hall of Fame–caliber players seldom matched in the history of the NFL. Lombardi himself was inducted into the Hall of Fame in 1971, and ten players who played for him in Green Bay are now also enshrined. These players are Jim Taylor, Forrest Gregg, Bart Starr, Ray Nitschke, Herb Adderley, Willie Davis, Jim Ringo, Paul Hornung, Willie Wood, and Henry Jordan. Starr led the Lombardi-era teams as quarterback and later followed his legendary mentor as Packers head coach from 1975 to 1983. His successor in that position was his Green Bay teammate and fellow Hall of Fame member Gregg, who led the team from 1984 to 1987, having previously taken the Cincinnati Bengals to Super Bowl XVI in 1982.

All of Lombardi's players praised their demanding coach for pushing them to give their very best but also for his undying loyalty to those men who showed their dedication to him. Lombardi's influence has remained evident in the way that many coaches and business executives have continued to follow his axioms, while some even continue to play taped speeches he made regarding leadership, effort, and teamwork.

UPS AND DOWNS

Following the Lombardi era, the Packers slipped into another period of on-field mediocrity, although fans in Green Bay and throughout Wisconsin continued to support the team unfailingly with their attendance at games in Lambeau Field. During this period some critics, skeptical of the Packers' location in a small midwestern city, blamed the team's poor performance on its hometown. However, the residents of Green Bay, as well as Packers fans throughout Wisconsin and across the country, never lost hope that the team would return to greatness. Following the Starr and Gregg coaching periods, Green Bay hired noted offensive innovator Lindy Infante to coach the team, but nobody was able to emulate the success of coaching legends Lambeau and Lombardi. As a result, the Packers remained a second-division team in the National Football Conference (NFC) Central Division throughout the 1970s and 1980s, making the league playoffs only twice between 1968 and 1992.

In 1992 the Packers hired Mike Holmgren, the offensive coordinator of the San Francisco 49ers, as head coach, and a new era of success dawned. By Holmgren's third season new players had been brought in—through the college draft, shrewd trades, and free agency—who helped lead the Packers back into the NFL elite. These players included Brett Favre, a young quarterback acquired from the Atlanta Falcons, and Reggie White, a talented veteran defensive leader who was signed as a free agent from the Philadelphia Eagles. These players led the Packers on the field as Holmgren and his coaching staff devised schemes that confounded opponents into numerous strategic errors, in a manner similar to the Lombardi era.

In 1994 the Packers returned to the playoffs for the first time since 1983, and by 1997 the team had risen to the top of the league, winning Super Bowl XXXI. In 1998 the Packers again reached the Super Bowl but lost to the Denver Broncos in one of the closest and most hard-fought battles the game had seen in many years. During this dramatic run of success, Favre proved the greatest beneficiary of Holmgren's coaching, moving from a reserve player with the Falcons to winning the NFL's Most Valuable Player Award for three consecutive seasons from 1995 to 1997.

MODERN PACKERS

Since the mid-1990s the franchise has gone through upheavals and successes. Holmgren accepted a position as head coach and general manager of the Seattle Seahawks and left the Packers in early 1999. After his departure, the team's sometimes mediocre performance caused great unrest among Packers fans. The arrival in 2006 of Mike McCarthy as head coach has brought stability to the team, particularly in regard to the position of quarterback.

In 2005 Green Bay drafted University of California quarterback Aaron Rodgers in the first round to become an understudy to—and ultimately replace—longtime fan favorite Favre. In 2006 and 2007 Favre toyed with retirement and kept the Packers management in limbo by not announcing his decision until the last moment, making season preparations more and more difficult. In 2008 the situation reached a breaking point, and Favre was traded to the New York Jets. After his departure, Rodgers became the starting quarterback of the storied franchise. At the end of the 2010–2011 season, he led the Packers to victory in Super Bowl XLV.

Through all of the team's successes and hardships, the citizens of Green Bay and fans throughout the United States have always supported the Packers. The team has enjoyed unparalleled fan support, ranging from consistent sellouts at Lambeau Field to the financial aid of the stock sales that have made the team the only publicly held franchise in professional sports. The Packers have become an institution in American sport, and a "pilgrimage" to Lambeau Field is among the most cherished events for many professional football fans throughout the country. Legions of Packers fans have come to be known as "Cheeseheads" for their devotion to the club and for the comical cheese wedge–shaped hats they wear in honor of the state's most famous dairy product. The cheese-adorned paraphernalia, which Packers fans wear in concert with the club's green and yellow colors, are among the most popular sport souvenirs in the country. No other professional franchise enjoys the complete support of its community in quite the same manner as the Green Bay Packers.

G. Allen Finchum

SEE ALSO: *College Football; Lombardi, Vince;* Monday Night Football*; Professional Football; Sports Heroes; Starr, Bart; Super Bowl.*

BIBLIOGRAPHY

Packer Legends in Facts: The Green Bay Packers 75th Year in the NFL Anniversary. Germantown, WI: Tech Data Publications, 1995.

Povletich, William. *Green Bay Packers: Legends in Green and Gold*. Charleston, SC: Arcadia, 2005.

Schaap, Dick. *Green Bay Replay, the Packers Return to Glory.* New York: Avon Books, 1997.

Green Day

Green Day emerged from the Berkeley, California, punk scene in the late 1980s and has since become one of the most popular and influential rock bands in America. Often credited alongside fellow California band the Offspring with bringing punk music into the mainstream in the 1990s, Green Day rose to stardom with its pop-tinged take on the simple template laid out by bands such as the Ramones and the Clash. In the early 2000s, Green Day expanded their sound beyond the bounds of punk, most notably with the 2004 release of *American Idiot*, a rock opera tracing the coming of age of an antihero named Jesus of Suburbia.

Group members include lead singer, songwriter, and guitarist Billie Joe Armstrong, bassist and backing vocalist Mike Dirnt, and drummer Tré Cool, all of whom were born in 1972. Armstrong and Dirnt were elementary school classmates and began singing together when they were fifteen. Cool joined the group in 1991 as a replacement for original drummer John Kiffmeyer. Armstrong is the group's undisputed leader. Commenting on his unusually high level of motivation, Cool has said that the front man wants nothing more than to be "the rock god from hell."

Green Day, which is a slang term for the day after being high on marijuana, started out in 1987 under the more benign name Sweet Children. Three years later, when independent Bay Area label Lookout! Records released the band's first album, *39/Smooth*, Armstrong and company changed their name to avoid confusion with another group. In 1992 they released *Kerplunk*, which sold about 50,000 copies and earned the band a contract with Reprise Records. Though the signing alienated some fans, who regarded it as selling out, it brought the band increased exposure.

Green Day became a household name in 1994, with its major-label debut, *Dookie*. Featuring three number one singles—"Longview," "Basket Case," and "When I Come Around"—the album sold fifteen million copies. Following the success of *Dookie*, Green Day released *Insomniac* (1995), *Nimrod* (1997), and *Warning* (2000). Though those albums sold well, none matched the success of *Dookie*, and the band struggled to regain its footing both artistically and commercially.

The beginning of the twenty-first century was not as productive for Green Day as the 1990s had been. In 2001 the group released a greatest hits album rather than come up with new material. When Green Day did begin working on a new album, tentatively titled *Cigarettes and Valentines*, it was not a smooth process. After they had laid down twenty tracks, the masters were stolen from their studio. Instead of rerecording the songs, the band decided to start a new project, which developed into *American Idiot*.

Modeled after the Who's *Tommy* (1969), *American Idiot* was Armstrong's personal declaration of war against President George W. Bush, whom he reviled for instigating the war in Iraq. The thirteen tracks on the album tell the story of Jesus of Suburbia, a disillusioned youth who finds moral direction on the streets of urban America. Enthusiastically received by both critics and fans, *American Idiot* debuted at number one upon its release in 2004, despite being overtly political and more challenging than the band's earlier work. The album won the Grammy for Best Rock Album and garnered six MTV Music Awards.

Green Day followed up *American Idiot* in 2009 with a second rock opera, *21st Century Breakdown*, which David Fricke of *Rolling Stone* calls a "compound bomb of classic-rock ecstasy, no-mercy punk assault and pop-song wiles." It chronicles the lives of Christian and Gloria, a couple dealing with the unraveling of their relationship amid the insanity of the contemporary political and social scene. Another unmitigated success, *21st Century Breakdown* won the Grammy for Best Rock Album and charted at number one in fourteen different countries. Green Day released *Last Night on Earth: Live in Tokyo* that same year and followed it up with *Awesome as Fuck* (2011), a live concert DVD.

In April 2010 a musical stage adaptation of *American Idiot* opened on Broadway at the St. James Theatre after a successful run in Berkeley. Although it received mixed reviews from critics, the production was a hit with fans and drew especially large crowds when Armstrong stepped in to play St. Jimmy, Jesus of Suburbia's alter ego. Melissa Etheridge also played the role for a portion of the show's extended run before Armstrong returned for the final stretch of the production, which closed in April 2011.

Elizabeth Rholetter Purdy

SEE ALSO: *Broadway; Gulf Wars; The Musical; Punk; The Ramones; Rock and Roll; The Who.*

BIBLIOGRAPHY

Fricke, David. "Green Day Fights On." *Rolling Stone*, May 28, 2009.

Harding, Cortney. "Green Day: The Great Green Way." *Billboard*, April 24, 2010, 20.

Lynskey, Dorian. *33 Revolutions Per Minute: A History of Protest Songs from Billie Holiday to Green Day*. New York: Ecco/HarperCollins, 2011.

Green Lantern

Green Lantern is one of the oldest and most popular comic-book superheroes. The character first appeared in DC comic books in 1940. Wielding a magic power ring capable of performing a variety of feats, Green Lantern spent his early years championing the interests of common citizens against crooked stockbrokers, greedy businessmen, and corrupt politicians before taking on America's enemies in World War II.

Although Green Lantern's initial comic-book series was canceled in 1949, DC Comics revived and revised the character ten years later and has kept him in publication ever since. The "modern" Green Lantern uses his power ring in the service of an intergalactic police force. In 1970 Green Lantern's comic book became a vehicle for "relevant" stories that critiqued America's social ills. This focus received widespread media attention in 2001 and 2002, when one of the comic's characters, a young intern named Terry Berg, revealed that he was gay and subsequently fell victim to a homophobic attack. *The Green Lantern* was the first comic to deal with such abominable hate crimes.

The Green Lantern underwent another popular revival in 2011, beginning with the release of the Warner Brothers film *Green Lantern*, starring Ryan Reynolds. The film garnered mixed reviews but debuted at number one in the box office. A video game and an animated television series followed shortly thereafter, amid rumors that a sequel to the film was in production.

Bradford Wright

SEE ALSO: *Comic Books; DC Comics; Video Games; World War II.*

BIBLIOGRAPHY

Daniels, Les. *DC Comics: Sixty Years of the World's Favorite Comic Book Heroes.* Boston: Little, Brown, 1995.

Dryden, Jane, and Mark D. White, eds. *Green Lantern and Philosophy.* Hoboken, NJ: John Wiley, 2011.

O'Neil, Dennis. *Secret Origins of the Super DC Heroes.* New York: Warner, 1976.

Greenberg, Hank *(1911–1986)*

Noted as the first Jewish baseball star, Hank Greenberg became a hero to a generation of Jewish fans and led the way for greater Jewish opportunities in baseball. Greenberg debuted at first base for the Detroit Tigers in 1933 and faced anti-Semitism from fans and opposing teams. Yet "Hammerin' Hank" withstood this and managed to win two Most Valuable Player awards, earn four batting titles, hit fifty-eight home runs in 1938, and get inducted into the Baseball Hall of Fame in 1956. Greenberg fought more than four years in World War II, and he set a precedent after the war by becoming the first Jewish owner and general manager in baseball. His popularity changed America's perspective on Jews, and he has come to symbolize a hero who overcame prejudice to lead his baseball team, his country, and his faith.

Nathan R. Meyer

SEE ALSO: *Baseball; The Detroit Tigers; World Series; World War II.*

BIBLIOGRAPHY

Greenberg, Hank, and Ira Berkow. *Hank Greenberg: The Story of My Life.* New York: Times Books, 1989.

Sommer, Shelley. *Hammerin' Hank Greenberg: Baseball Pioneer.* Honesdale, PA: Calkins Creek, 2011.

Greene, Graham *(1952–)*

Thanks largely to his Academy Award nomination for Best Supporting Actor for his performance as Kicking Bird in *Dances with Wolves* (1990), Graham Greene is one of the most recognized Native American actors. Greene, a full-blooded Oneida Sioux, was born on the Six Nations Reserve near Brantford, Ontario, Canada. At age sixteen he left the reserve to pursue a variety of careers, including being a welder, drafter, and roadie. He began acting in Toronto in 1974 and landed his first film roles in the early 1980s, in *Running Brave* (1983) and *Revolution* (1985). In 1989 he received the Dora Mavor Moore Award of Toronto for best actor for his performance in the play *Dry Lips Oughta Move to Kapuskasing.*

Following *Dances with Wolves,* he has gone on to appear in numerous films, such as *Clearcut* (1991), *Thunderheart* (1992), *Die Hard with a Vengeance* (1995), *The Green Mile* (1999), and *New Moon* (2009). Greene has also been a presence on television: in addition to appearing in *Lonesome Dove: The Series* (1992) and *Northern Exposure* (1990), he starred in the 1992 HBO film *The Last of His Tribe* and has many other TV credits.

Eugenia Griffith DuPell

SEE ALSO: Northern Exposure; Twilight.

BIBLIOGRAPHY

Johnson, Brian D. "Dances with Oscar: Canadian Actor Graham Greene Tastes Stardom." *Maclean's,* March 25, 1991, 60–61.

Malinowski, Sharon, ed. *Notable Native Americans.* New York: Gale Research, 1995.

Pollock, Sean R., ed. *Newsmakers '97: The People behind Today's Headlines.* Detroit, MI: Gale Research, 1998.

Greenpeace

Formed in 1971 by a group of Canadian and expatriate American Sierra Club members who wanted a more active form of environmentalism, Greenpeace is a global environmental organization with offices in forty countries and international headquarters in Amsterdam. Its major campaigns include climate change, forests, nuclear weapons and nuclear power, agriculture, toxic pollution, and ocean ecology. Its mission combines both environmental and peace issues.

Since its inception Greenpeace has been involved in hundreds of highly publicized direct-action campaigns against major polluters and government nuclear testing. Its flamboyant protests in the cause of ocean ecology in the 1970s heightened public awareness to environmental abuses around the world and drew millions of people to its membership list. Political pressure exercised by Greenpeace led to a global treatise protecting whales and dolphins. The organization shocked public sentiment into action with graphic footage of baby seals being bludgeoned to death. In 2009 Greenpeace, one of the world's largest, wealthiest, and most successful environmental groups, had a membership totaling more than 2.9 million people worldwide.

Greenpeace relies heavily on canvassing, telemarketing, and direct-mail campaigns for mobilization, retention, and fundraising. Not allied with any political party, it accepts no corporate donations, and 90 percent of its revenues come from membership dues and other contributions. To promote its confrontational tactics, Greenpeace operates an international information service that consists of four units: hard news and features, film and video, photo desk, and publications. It also runs mass media crusades, drafts and lobbies for international conventions, participates in educational campaigns, and sells Greenpeace merchandise such as T-shirts and posters. Greenpeace concerts, albums, and compact discs, featuring such groups as U2, R.E.M., and other major acts, market the organization's message to the world's youth.

The elemental principle behind the operation of Greenpeace is the American Quaker tradition of "bearing witness"—drawing attention to objectionable activity by unwavering presence at the site of abuse. The organization has a "navy" of three ships and several inflatable vessels, an "air force" of one hot air balloon, and an "action bus." Its bold protests have included sailing into nuclear testing zones; intercepting whaling vessels;

Greenpeace Protest. *Members of Greenpeace sit chained to the gate of the French Embassy in Mexico City in September 1995 to protest the French government's decision to resume nuclear testing in the South Pacific.* DAVID HERNANDEZ/AFP/GETTY IMAGES.

and hanging banners from bridges, skyscrapers, and smokestacks. In the 1970s and 1980s, these demonstrations drew enormous media attention, and Greenpeace became a model for other organizations by utilizing mass media to influence public opinion. As a result of its campaign against the killing of harp seals, people around the globe changed their buying habits and stopped purchasing products made out of the seal pelts.

In 1985, after protests against nuclear testing in the South Pacific, the French government sabotaged the organization's flagship, the *Rainbow Warrior*, in New Zealand. The sinking killed Fernando Pereira, a Greenpeace photographer, and sparked worldwide condemnation against France. This incident resulted in a doubling of the group's membership and a tripling of its revenues. It became the organization of choice for many high-profile celebrities and the pet issue for many politicians. The French government eventually paid Greenpeace $8 million in compensation for the destruction of the *Rainbow Warrior*.

During the 1990s Greenpeace increasingly moved into the corporate boardrooms, law offices, and scientific laboratories of the mainstream, but direct action—nonviolently confronting polluters and marine mammal killers—is what Greenpeace is best known for in the public mind. As Chris Rose, program director of Greenpeace UK in 1993 pointed out, "The moral imperative of demonstrators and direct action to save whales on the high seas was set against rationalizations and sales images of conventional commerce, and the whales won." The mythology of Moby Dick and Captain Ahab that had dominated human consciousness about whaling for more than a century had been destroyed. The story became one of courageous whales fighting men in giant boats.

In the first decade of the 2000s Greenpeace sought to bring public attention to the dangers of climate change. For example, in July 2009 three activists scaled Mount Rushmore and hung a banner that said "Stop Global Warming" next to the carved face of Abraham Lincoln. The group came under fire for issuing an erroneous statement in 2009 that arctic ice would disappear by 2030. The Greenpeace website later clarified that their findings indicated that the Arctic would have ice-free summers by that date rather than be permanently ice free. The outgoing leader of Greenpeace, Gerd Leipold, apologized for the mistake but defended the group's use of emotionally charged statements to bring urgent issues to the public's attention. Greenpeace continued to warn that the survival of polar bears and other species depended on halting the rate of climate change.

Greenpeace's media exploits and public relations drives have been the centerpiece of its strategies and the prototypes for other social movements striving to assert a presence in the electronic age. With its reputation as an effective, persistent, and uncompromising environmental organization, grown from its prowess as an efficient publicity machine, Greenpeace has been instrumental in alerting people around the world to environmental evils. Together with other organizations, it has succeeded in moving the protection of the environment from a marginal to a central public and moral concern.

Ken Kempcke

SEE ALSO: *Civil Disobedience; Consciousness Raising Groups; Eco-Terrorism; Environmentalism; Global Warming; Protest Groups; R.E.M.; U2.*

BIBLIOGRAPHY

Brown, Michael, and John May. *The Greenpeace Story*. New York: Dorling Kindersley, 1991.

Rose, Chris. "Beyond the Struggle for Proof: Factors Changing the Environmental Movement." *Environmental Values* 2 (1993): 185–198.

Wapner, Paul. "Politics beyond the State: Environmental Activism and World Civic Politics." *World Politics* 47, no. 3 (1995): 311–330.

Weyler, Rex. *Greenpeace: How a Group of Ecologists, Journalists, and Visionaries Changed the World.* Emmaus, PA: Rodale, 2004.

Greenwich Village

Greenwich Village's known history dates back to the sixteenth century, when it was a marshland called Sapokanikan by Native Americans who fished in the trout stream known as Minetta Brook. When the Dutch first settled on Manhattan in 1621, naming the area New Netherlands, all but a small area on the southeastern tip of the island was left untouched by the Europeans. When the colony passed to British hands in 1664 and became New York, a few farms and estates emerged some miles to the north of the city; the settlement evolved into a country hamlet, first designated Grin'wich in 1713 Common Council records.

The village was transformed in the late 1820s, when yellow fever caused thousands of city dwellers to flee from New York to the Greenwich countryside. Many of these displaced city folk enjoyed the country, and throughout the following decade the village grew as businesses and residents moved their permanent homes there.

As the population of Manhattan grew, the city felt the need for northern expansion in an orderly fashion. The city council adopted a grid plan in March 1817 that would have placed gridded streets running from river to river, cutting through the heart of the fledgling village. The village people were outraged. During the year that the grid war waged, an anonymous sixty-two-page pamphlet was submitted to the city laying out an argument against the plan. Soon after, the council backed down and limited the grid to the east of what is now Sixth Avenue and north of what is currently Fourteenth Street.

During the early nineteenth century, as New York University grew on the east side of Washington Square, religious denominations commissioned buildings with elaborate decorative schemes, and the neighborhood soon became the site of art clubs, private picture galleries, learned societies, literary salons, and libraries. Fine hotels, shopping emporia, and theaters also proliferated. The character of the neighborhood changed markedly at the close of the nineteenth century when German, Irish, and Italian immigrants found work in the breweries, warehouses, and coal and lumber yards near the Hudson River and in the southeastern corner of the neighborhood. Older residences were subdivided into cheap lodging hotels and multifamily dwellings or demolished for higher-density tenements.

The village at the turn of the twentieth century was a picturesque and ethnically diverse area. By the start of World War I it was widely known as a bohemian enclave with secluded side streets, low rents, and a tolerance for radicalism and nonconformity. Attention became increasingly focused on artists and writers noted for their boldly innovative work. The bohemian atmosphere helped to make Greenwich Village an attraction for tourists. Entrepreneurs provided amusements ranging from evenings in artists' studios to bacchanalian costume balls. During Prohibition local speakeasies attracted uptown patrons. Decrepit row houses were remodeled into artistic flats for the well-to-do, and in 1926 luxury apartment towers appeared at the northern edge of Washington Square. The stock market crash of 1929 halted the momentum of new construction.

During the 1930s galleries and collectors promoted the cause of contemporary art. Sculptor Gertrude Whitney Vanderbilt opened a museum dedicated to modern American art, which is now the New York Studio School, on West Eighth Street. The New School for Social Research, on West Twelfth Street since the late 1920s, inaugurated the University in Exile to help European scholars in 1933.

The Village had become the center for the Beat movement by the 1950s, with galleries along Eighth Street, coffeehouses on MacDougal Street, and storefront theaters on Bleecker Street. Gatherings and unorthodox artistic, theatrical, and musical events were staged at the Judson Memorial Church. During the 1960s a homosexual community formed around Christopher Street; in 1969 a confrontation by the police culminated in a riot known as the Stonewall Rebellion, regarded as the beginning of the nationwide movement for gay and lesbian rights. Greenwich Village became a rallying place for antiwar protesters in the 1970s and for activity mobilized by the AIDS epidemic in the 1980s.

By the first decade of the 2000s high rents made it difficult for young artists to live in the neighborhood that had once been a famous center of the arts. Greenwich Village, however, retains its reputation as a hip place in the popular imagination. From 1994 to 2004 a hit television sitcom called *Friends*, about a group of quirky people in their twenties, was set there.

Anna Notaro

SEE ALSO: *AIDS; The Beat Generation; The Big Apple;* Friends*;* The Masses*; Stonewall Rebellion.*

BIBLIOGRAPHY

Banes, Sally. *Greenwich Village 1963: Avant-Garde Performance and the Effervescent.* Durham, NC: Duke University Press, 1993.

Beard, Rick, and Leslie Cohen Berlowitz, eds. *Greenwich Village: Culture and Counterculture.* New Brunswick, NJ: Rutgers University Press, 1993.

Gold, Joyce. *From Trout Stream to Bohemia: A Walking Guide to Greenwich Village History.* New York: Old Warren Road Press, 1988.

Gross, Steve, and Susan Daley. *Old Greenwich Village: An Architectural Portrait.* Washington, DC: Preservation Press, 1993.

Harris, Luther S. *Around Washington Square: An Illustrated History of Greenwich Village.* Baltimore, MD: Johns Hopkins University Press, 2003.

Kellerman, Regina M., ed. *The Architecture of the Greenwich Village Waterfront: An Archival Research Study Undertaken by the Greenwich Village Society for Historic Preservation.* New York: New York University Press, 1989.

Kugelmass, Jack. *Masked Culture: The Greenwich Village Halloween Parade.* New York: Columbia University Press, 1994.

McDarrah, Fred W., and Gloria S. McDarrah. *Beat Generation: Glory Days in Greenwich.* New York: Simon & Schuster, 1996.

Rotolo, Suze. *A Freewheelin' Time: A Memoir of Greenwich Village in the Sixties*. New York: Broadway, 2008.

Selzer, Jack. *Kenneth Burke in Greenwich Village: Conversing with the Moderns, 1915–1931*. Wisconsin Project on American Writers. Madison: University of Wisconsin Press, 1996.

Ware, Caroline F. *Greenwich Village 1920–1930: A Comment on American Civilization in the Post-War Years*. Berkeley: University of California Press, 1994.

Greeting Cards

Greeting cards, with their preprinted sentiments and pretty pictures, have in many ways replaced more traditional and personalized forms of communication such as letter writing. Premade cards cater to the needs of busy Americans and their willingness to mark an increasing number of holidays and events in largely commercialized ways. Rather than writing lengthy missives by hand, Americans since the turn of the twentieth century have found it easier to purchase premade cards that they need only sign, address, and mail, or, in the twenty-first century, simply e-mail.

FIRST CARDS

The earliest objects resembling greeting cards were handmade valentines, popular in Europe and America in the eighteenth and nineteenth centuries. By the 1840s English and German chromolithographers had both developed techniques allowing them to publish full-color postcards, commemorating primarily Christmas and Valentine's Day. The cards enjoyed great commercial success in America as well as Europe, beginning what would become a pervasive American habit of sending manufactured rather than personal correspondence. The popularity of these early holiday cards was encouraged by Americans' increasing mobility and their need to communicate with friends and relatives now miles rather than blocks away; they also appealed to the needs of busy people.

After the Civil War the United States experienced what historian Leigh Eric Schmidt has termed the "commercialization of the calendar," characterized by the growing prevalence of business-inspired holidays marked in increasingly homogenous ways. In about 1866 Louis Prang, a Boston printmaker, perfected the "chromo" process and was able to produce finely detailed printed images in full, bright colors. Prang applied his talents to media of all sorts, including advertising trade cards, fine art prints, and calendars. He produced his first Christmas cards in 1874, marking the beginning of American greeting card production that gradually supplanted European imports. Soon Prang added birthday, New Year's, and Easter cards. These early cards, still in postcard form, were often embellished with detailed surface embossing, applied glitter, and silky fringe.

In the first decade of the twentieth century, American producers completely overtook European manufacturers, creating a new standard for greeting cards and establishing their most enduring form: the folded piece of paper with a picture on the front, a written sentiment or verse inside, and a size-matched envelope. Early manufacturers included the A. M. Davis Company; Rust Craft Publishers; the Keating Company; the Gibson Art Company; Hall Brothers; and American Greetings, which in 1913 banded together to form the National Association of Greeting Card Manufacturers (later called the Greeting Card Association). The card producers' success relied on Americans' increasing willingness to acknowledge more and more holidays. Mother's Day, Father's Day, and St. Patrick's Day were soon added to the modern celebratory schedule. The greeting card industry worked with the floral, jewelry, and confectionery industries to cement in the collective American

Selecting a Birthday Card. *A young girl peruses a rack of birthday cards looking for just the right one to send her greeting.* DAVID L. MOORE/ALAMY.

psyche the importance of celebrating holidays—and to make Americans feel comfortable about relying on premade commodities to do so.

THE GENERAL MOTORS OF EMOTION

The most enduring of the early greeting card manufacturers were Hallmark, American Greetings, and Gibson Greetings, all founded between 1850 and 1910. Hallmark, established in 1914 in Kansas City, Missouri, by Joyce C. Hall and his brother Rollie, was the most successful of the three. By 1995 the company possessed 42 percent of the market, followed by American Greetings with 35 percent and Gibson with 8 percent. Hallmark, with revenues estimated at $3.8 billion in 1994, has been called the General Motors of emotion. The company cultivated an image as a producer of down-home, conservative sentiments. J. C. Hall was a close friend of Walt Disney and often incorporated wholesome Disney images into his cards, along with the works of other traditional illustrators such as Norman Rockwell. In addition, Hallmark sponsored television's well-known drama series *Hallmark Hall of Fame* and coined its iconic slogan: "When you care enough to send the very best." To critics, Hallmark has achieved a dubious reputation as a purveyor of bland, mass-produced feelings that reflect the most banal of Middle American thoughts.

Greeting cards both tapped into and reflected changing American sentiments, aesthetic preferences, and preoccupations throughout the twentieth century. During the Depression some Mother's Day cards came embellished with a precious piece of lace, and special Mother's Day cards during World War II were made and sent to women who had lost their sons in the war. Continuing to tap into the contemporary zeitgeist, card companies in the late 1970s responded to a growing American cynicism, producing "alternative" humor lines alongside their more conservative and sentimental staples. By the mid-1980s larger companies began to capitalize on baby boomers' growing desire for self-expression and feelings of individuality by developing more specific lines of greeting cards. By the 1990s Hallmark itself had its own alternative humor line called Shoebox Greetings. Its Mahogany line targeted African American audiences in an effort to open up the world of greeting cards to nonwhite sensibilities. Hallmark's Recovery line offered cards for former addicts, and the Thinking of You line included cards for such late-twentieth-century concerns as downsizing, divorce, PMS, the needs of caregivers, and struggles with weight loss.

Women purchased more than 85 percent of all greeting cards in 1998, helping Hallmark earn some $3.7 billion in revenue, while American Greetings took in $2.2 billion. Card companies responded to the encroachment of computers into their businesses by setting up in-store kiosks for customers to create their own computer-generated cards. Hallmark and a number of other companies developed computer programs that allowed individualized cards to be produced at home.

The greeting card industry continued to evolve in the early twenty-first century as people began sending digital greeting cards through social media such as Facebook or websites such as Hallmark and Blue Mountain. Even though paper greeting cards continue to sell well, their electronic cousins have cut into sales. Greeting card companies have responded by introducing more innovative features, including cards that play preprogrammed songs or allow the sender to record a personal message.

Wendy Woloson

SEE ALSO: *Baby Boomers; Christmas; Consumerism; Disney (Walt Disney Company); Facebook; Father's Day;* Hallmark Hall of Fame; *Mother's Day; Rockwell, Norman; Social Media; Valentine's Day.*

BIBLIOGRAPHY

Chase, Ernest Dudley. *The Romance of Greeting Cards.* Cambridge, MA: University Press, 1956.

"Fewer Holiday Cards Make Their Way via Snail Mail." *USA Today*, December 18, 2011.

Hall, Joyce, and Curtiss Anderson. *When You Care Enough.* Kansas City, MO: Hallmark, 1979.

Hirshey, Gerri. "Happy [ ] Day to You." *New York Times Magazine*, July 2, 1995.

Schmidt, Leigh Eric. *Consumer Rites: The Buying and Selling of American Holidays.* Princeton, NJ: Princeton University Press, 1995.

Shank, Barry. *A Token of My Affection: Greeting Cards and American Business Culture.* New York: Columbia University Press, 2004.

Stern, Ellen Stock. *The Very Best from Hallmark.* New York: Abrams, 1988.

Gregory, Dick *(1932–)*

Dick Gregory brought a unique approach to political activism: he was one of the first African Americans to use his celebrity to promote a variety of political causes. Starting in the 1950s, he intertwined his political beliefs with his work as an athlete, a comedian, an author, an actor, and a nutritionist. As one of the first black comedians to work in top-of-the-line white nightclubs and on television, Gregory was credited with defining black issues for a mainstream white audience. He reached millions with his popular satirical comedy, bringing to light such issues as racism, civil rights, segregation, and nonviolence.

Gregory also used his humor to promote his ideals in his movie appearances and books. In the 1960s he used his visibility as an entertainer to bring political causes—such as the civil rights movement; the antiwar movement; and the fight against violence, hunger, drug and alcohol abuse, and poor health care—to popular attention. He combined his celebrity with what could be termed attention-seeking tactics such as fasts for political causes.

EARLY YEARS

Born Richard Claxton Gregory on October 12, 1932, he was raised in poverty in St. Louis, Missouri. Gregory realized the power of politics at an early age: while in high school he was president of his graduating class and organizer of a march against conditions in segregated schools. With his interest in activism, he soon learned the benefits of combining fame with politics. An athletic scholarship to Southern Illinois University in Carbondale, Illinois, helped him achieve fame on the track team as a half-mile runner, and in 1953 he was the first black student awarded the school's outstanding athlete of the year award. Gregory used his prominence to desegregate Carbondale's only movie theater.

While in the U.S. Army, Gregory performed comedy shows, and by the late 1950s he had begun working in Chicago nightclubs. He parlayed a one-night gig at the prestigious Playboy Club into a six-week run that brought him national recognition, winning him coverage in *Time* magazine and an appearance on the popular *Jack Paar Show*. He subsequently had gigs at numerous nightclubs, at concerts, and on other television shows. His unique ability to use humor and wit to publicize political discourse to a large cross-section of the general population also brought the attention of Medgar Evers and Martin Luther King Jr., who asked him to become more involved with the civil rights movement. He performed at benefits for groups such as the National Association for the Advancement of Colored People and Congress of Racial Equality. He became involved with King's Southern Christian Leadership Conference programs, and in 1963 he helped collect and deliver 14,000 pounds of food to people in Leflore County, Mississippi. A strong advocate of King's nonviolent movement, he was often jailed with King for civil disobedience.

LIFE AS AN ACTIVIST

In the 1960s Gregory wrote a number of books that continued his campaign for the civil rights movement. He titled his 1964 autobiographical work *Nigger* as a shock tactic. His method seemed effective, as the book sold well. Gregory ran for mayor of Chicago in 1966 and for president of the United States in 1968. Those experiences were recounted in his book *Write Me In!* He continued his fight to promote civil rights and his theories on how the government tried to kill the civil rights movement and its leaders in books such as *No More Lies: The Myth and the Reality of American History* and *Code Name "Zorro": The Murder of Martin Luther King*, which he coauthored with Mark Lane. In addition to his books, Gregory made social commentary comedy records to spread his message even further. One of his records was the first talk record to sell more than a million copies.

By the late 1960s and early 1970s Gregory had expanded his activism to address additional issues including the Vietnam War, health care, capital punishment, Native American land and fishing rights, violence, and world hunger. He began using fasts to bring attention to issues. In the tradition of Mohandas Gandhi, Gregory began one of his many fasts in 1967 to protest the Vietnam War. His forty-day fast was sprawled over the media. Since that first fast, Gregory has fasted numerous times for political causes, including one fast that lasted seventy-one days.

In addition to his more traditional political causes, Gregory became one of the first celebrities to strongly advocate vegetarianism, becoming an expert on nutrition and a marathon runner in the 1970s. He jogged across the country to gain recognition for his political analysis of health and nutrition issues and his belief that nutritional solutions can help alleviate world hunger. In 1973 he published *Dick Gregory's Natural Diet for Folks Who Eat: Cookin' with Mother Nature* and in 1984 formed Dick Gregory Health Enterprises, Inc., around his nutritional product, the chemical-free, dairy-free Bahamian Diet. He focused his health work on the African American community, blaming their lower life expectancy on poor nutrition and alcohol and drug addiction. To do his part to alleviate world hunger, he donated 2,600 pounds of his nutritional formula to starving Ethiopians. Gregory's approach to nutrition brought together issues of healthy eating, world hunger, and racism.

RECOGNITION AND AWARDS

Throughout the 1990s Gregory continued fighting for and gaining recognition for a wide spectrum of political causes. In 1992 he started the Campaign for Human Dignity initiative to fight crime in St. Louis, an action that won him a spot on the city's walk of fame. Despite being credited with opening the door for many black comedians, Gregory for the most part stepped away from the entertainment business. Instead, his ability to combine wit, intelligence, humor, and political conviction continued to help support many political causes. In 1995, however, he returned to the Broadway stage with a one-man show, *Dick Gregory Live!*

The next decade brought both ups and downs. In 2000 Gregory was diagnosed with a rare form of lymphoma. Doctors caught it early, however, and his prognosis was good. That same year saw the publication of another memoir—or "updated autobiography," as Gregory calls it—*Callus on My Soul*, as well as an evening of tribute at the John F. Kennedy Center for the Performing Arts, with Bill Cosby serving as the host of the ceremony. Other awards and honorifics continued to arrive: Gregory was a 2001 Candle in the Dark honoree for Morehouse College; a 2001 honoree of the Jackie Robinson Foundation, as well as being awarded the foundation's first-ever Lifetime Achievement Award; a 2005 honoree of the National Association of Black Owned Broadcasters, where he was given the Mickey Leland Public Service Award for his work on world hunger; and a 2005 inductee to the International Civil Rights Walk of Fame, along with other such luminaries as Harry Belafonte and Hank Aaron.

Gregory also maintained his involvement in political activism into the twenty-first century. On September 10, 2010, he announced a fast in protest of the government's official report on the September 11, 2001, terrorist attacks.

Tova Stabin

SEE ALSO: *Aaron, Hank; Belafonte, Harry; Broadway; Cancer; Civil Disobedience; Civil Rights Movement; Cosby, Bill; Dieting; King, Martin Luther, Jr.; 9/11; Paar, Jack; Stand-Up Comedy; Television; Vegetarianism; Vietnam; War on Drugs.*

BIBLIOGRAPHY

Buyukmihci, Hope Sawyer. "A Thinking Man's Journey." *AV Magazine*, June 1, 1994, 17.

Gregory, Dick. *Nigger: An Autobiography*. New York: Dutton, 1964.

Gregory, Dick. *No More Lies: The Myth and the Reality of American History*. New York: Harper & Row, 1971.

Gregory, Dick. *Dick Gregory's Political Primer*. New York: Harper & Row, 1972.

Gregory, Dick, and James R. McGraw. *Up from Nigger*. New York: Stein and Day, 1976.

Gregory, Dick, and Shelia P. Moses. *Callus on My Soul: A Memoir*. New York: Kensington, 2000.

Gretzky, Wayne *(1953–)*

The greatest hockey player of his generation and one of the greatest of all time, Wayne Gretzky's greatest contribution to the sport is the role he played in popularizing it throughout the

United States. The National Hockey League (NHL) has successfully expanded in California and across the Sun Belt (often, it must be said, at the expense of the game's Canadian roots); NHL-licensed apparel is worn by millions of American young people; and an increasing percentage of players joining professional teams are from the United States.

Gretzky was born in Brantford, Ontario, and began skating at two-and-a-half years of age. His father, Walter, taught him to play hockey. Even as a small child, Gretzky's hockey skills were remarkable—at age ten he scored 378 goals in sixty-nine games for a local peewee team, attracting the attention of professional scouts and the national media. The upstart World Hockey Association (WHA) began signing players at a younger age than the established NHL, and in 1978 Gretzky agreed to a contract with the Indianapolis Racers, becoming a pro at seventeen. Like many other WHA teams, the Racers were underfinanced, and owner Nelson Skalbania was forced to sell the skinny center to the Edmonton Oilers in one of the most ill-conceived transactions in the annals of professional sports.

In Edmonton, Gretzky joined a team with a number of promising young players. After one year the Oilers organization joined the NHL, and Gretzky was able to demonstrate his talents to a larger audience. Despite doubters who pointed to his slight build and lack of speed, Gretzky won the Rookie of the Year award in 1979–1980, his first season with the NHL. In his second campaign he broke Phil Esposito's single-season points record, and in his third he smashed his own record with an astonishing ninety-two goals and 212 points. In a sport where fifty goals in a season of eighty games denoted a superstar, Gretzky raised the level of superlatives by reaching the mark of fifty goals in thirty-nine games. In the mid-1980s the Edmonton Oilers were one of the most exciting and successful teams in league history, winning the Stanley Cup in 1984, 1985, 1987, and 1988.

Wayne Gretzky. *Wayne Gretzky hoists the Stanley Cup in 1984 after the Edmonton Oilers defeated the New York Islanders.* **BRUCE BENNETT STUDIOS/GETTY IMAGES.**

By 1988, however, Gretzky's talents could command more in salary than a small-market team like the Oilers claimed they could afford, and he was dispatched to Los Angeles for a package of players, draft choices, and $15 million. The trade, which was a disaster for Edmonton fans, turned out to be a gift to professional hockey in general and the Los Angeles Kings in particular. With Gretzky's marquee presence in a major media center, the profile of the sport was raised enormously in California and throughout the United States. Gretzky's amiable features appeared in national endorsements, and he hosted *Saturday Night Live*, gave interviews to Johnny Carson, and was even cast in a television soap opera. The Forum arena was sold out for the entire season, celebrities flocked to games, and more American children started to play hockey.

The same level of success on the ice was harder to come by. Despite leading the Kings to the Stanley Cup finals in 1993, where they lost to the Montreal Canadiens, Gretzky found team management unable to assemble a supporting cast of players as talented as he had enjoyed in Edmonton. At his request, he was traded to the St. Louis Blues in 1996, but this proved to be an unhappy experience, and after that season he signed with the New York Rangers. Once more his arrival in a large American market sparked media interest, but again his skills—declining with age though still considerable—were insufficient to lift his team to Stanley Cup–winning form. Gretzky retired from the game on April 18, 1999.

At the time of his retirement, Gretzky held sixty-one NHL individual records. He won the scoring championship ten times and was voted Most Valuable Player (MVP) nine times. He was voted to the All-Star team eighteen times and was the game's MVP three times. Along with his four Stanley Cups, he played a leading role in three of his country's Canada Cup victories. He was voted into the Hockey Hall of Fame, and his jersey number (99) was retired by all the teams in the NHL in 2000. Statues of Gretzky stand outside arenas in both Edmonton and Los Angeles.

In 2000 Gretzky became part owner of the Phoenix Coyotes, a team that he coached from 2005 to 2009 without much success, missing the playoffs every year. He left the Coyotes in 2009 when the team's ownership changed hands. As an executive Gretzky was involved with Team Canada at the Olympics, winning gold in Salt Lake City in 2002 and 2010. He continues to prosper in business—his name is attached to restaurants, a winery, and numerous commercial endorsements.

Gerry Bowler

SEE ALSO: *Advertising; Carson, Johnny; Hockey; National Hockey League (NHL); Olympics;* Saturday Night Live; *Sports Heroes; Television.*

BIBLIOGRAPHY

Messier, Mark; Walter Gretzky; Brett Hull; et al. *Wayne Gretzky: The Making of the Great One*. New York: Beckett Publications, 1988.

Grey, Zane *(1872–1939)*

Considered the creator of the modern Western novel, author Zane Grey had a significant and lasting influence on American culture. His work shaped the imagery of the West in the popular imagination. Many evaluations of the genre concentrate on the literary attributes of its writers. These literary considerations tend to outweigh the cultural resonance of the Western's popular appeal and often lead to the underrating of Grey's work in particular. In addition to his ability to establish place and evoke the landscape of the mythical West, Grey endowed his work with a sense of popular history. He also negotiated cultural tensions that revolve around such issues as the coming of modernity, marriage, religion, and the returning veterans of World War I, which appealed to an exceptionally broad range of readers.

Grey's stories were serialized in *Ladies' Home Journal* as well as *Collier's*, *Country Gentleman*, and *McCall's Magazine*, and many of his books were translated into films, some made by his own company. He insisted that his movies be filmed on location, thus introducing a very particular visual depiction of the West that still endures.

Grey was born in Zanesville, Ohio, in 1872. He studied dentistry at the University of Pennsylvania and then practiced in New York, where he published his first novel, *Betty Zane*, with his own money in 1903. His first books, set in Ohio, are based on family history of the pioneer period. While filled with adventure, they do not really convey the sense of the Wild West in a cohesive or effective form.

In 1907, while in New York, Grey met Charles Jesse "Buffalo" Jones, a conservationist who labored to save the American bison from extinction. He joined Jones on a trip to Arizona and across the Painted Desert and the Grand Canyon, where he met and lived with Native Americans, cowboys, and Texas rangers; thereafter his writing contained authentic and convincing descriptions of the West. He wrote his first account of his travels in *Last of the Plainsmen* (1908) but did not become successful as a writer until the publication of *The Heritage of the Desert* (1910), which established his individual style. In the prefatory note in *Last of the Plainsmen*, Grey writes:

> As a boy I read of [frontiersman Daniel] Boone with a throbbing heart, and the silent moccasined, vengeful [scout and Indian fighter Lewis] Wetzel I loved. I pored over the deeds of vengeful men—[General George] Custer and [trapper and scout Kit] Carson, those heroes of the plains. And as a man I came to see the wonder, the tragedy of their lives, and to write about them.

ADVENTURES IN EVOCATIVE SETTINGS

Grey's novels use the frontier west of the ninety-eighth meridian to create a new landscape for the West. This rugged and exacting territory, inhabited by extremes of good and evil, legitimates violence yet offers redemption. It also provided Grey with a fictional space in which to address the anxieties of the period about which he was writing and to offer the prospect of escape from them. *The Heritage of the Desert* opens with intense religious imagery projected onto a desert landscape and leads into a dramatic romantic adventure. The eastern hero is nursed back to health by a Mormon and falls in love with his half-Navajo, half-Spanish adopted daughter. The girl needs to be rescued from an impending marriage to the villain, a circumstance that culminates in a climactic shoot out.

It was with *Riders of the Purple Sage* (1912), however, that Grey made his name. Originally rejected by publishers because of its harsh treatment of Mormon culture, the novel went on to sell two million copies. At the height of Grey's popularity, between 1917 and 1924, his novels made literary journal *Bookman*'s top-ten best-seller list every year. *The U.P. Trail* (1918) and *The Man of the Forest* (1920), his two major best sellers, illustrate the appeal of his work. *The U.P. Trail* is based very specifically on the history of the Union Pacific Railroad between 1864 and 1869 and incorporates the endurance of the pony express rider and the introduction of the telegraph to the West. The background to the narrative accords with popular memory. *The Man of the Forest* is set in 1885 within living memory, and the story follows the integration of a woodsman into the community of the West through his romance with a spirited eastern girl. She finds her full potential in the West and is ready to build a homestead in "Paradise Park."

Novels such as *The Desert of Wheat* (1919), *The Call of the Canyon* (1924), *The Vanishing American* (1925), *Under Tonto Rim* (1926), and *The Shepherd of Guadaloupe* (1930) are set contemporaneously and deal with modern issues and recent changes. They therefore establish the ethos of the West as a living idea rather than a lost ideal.

Grey continued to travel throughout his career and incorporated his experience of landscape and knowledge of oral history directly into his fiction. He published fifty-four novels in his lifetime, and more were released posthumously. For the most part, they have very simple adventure plots but are structured into thrilling and romantic episodes sustained by their evocative settings.

The formula Grey established for the modern Western is one of moral regeneration or redemption, with heroic individuals proving themselves by living up to a basic code of American values. His characters live by a code of the West that differentiates between hero and villain and leads to inevitable confrontation. He presents the Western hero in a manner that would become a central convention. He pays much attention to details of dress, appearance, and stance of his heroic characters. In *Riders of the Purple Sage*, for example, Lassiter is the mysterious gunfighter delineated by his fast draw, costume, honor, and shady past. Here Grey introduces the professional gunman as a hero, but in the majority of his Westerns, the older heroes are ready to be reincorporated into society or commit themselves to very independent heroines. In most cases these women also come to recognize higher moral values through their experience in the West.

WOMEN AND NATIVE AMERICANS

Although women are largely absent in the action of the Western, Grey's novels often feature a female protagonist. Heroines true to romantic formula are introduced at a stage where they have lost their social identity, which is restored in the course of the narrative through their own test of character in the Western landscape and not merely by the hero. In *Riders of the Purple Sage*, Jane Withersteen attempts to stand up to the patriarchal Mormon power structure in which she has been orphaned. Part of the oppression she faces is the terrorism of a gang of outlaws, especially the Masked Rider, who is revealed to be a girl brought up in the immoral culture of men.

Grey is often accused of priggishness in his depiction of his heroes, and this tendency is also found in his heroines. He perfected two extremes of a heroine: the cold, flirtatious, eastern sophisticate who reveals her deep and passionate love for the hero and the practical, unladylike western girl, whose seeming promiscuity proves to be a blind.

These simplistic characters and his constant appeal to religious symbolism and heightened moral codes lead Grey's stories very easily into the realm of melodrama and sentimentality, in which the stories address particular fantasies of freedom away from the corruption and constraints of city life. His characters frequently confront the dilemmas of modern life, as does the flapper heroine of *Code of the West* (1934), who chooses marriage to the hero because she recognizes his worth. More pointedly, a similarly drawn heroine in *The Call of the Canyon* (1924) marries a shell-shocked World War I veteran and chooses the harsher but more essentially American West in which to raise a family. The western landscape, with its promise of abundant riches, offers the protagonists a chance to remake their lives according to higher moral values, in contrast to their old lives and the lives of those around them.

Grey is often accused of being either ambivalent or complacent about the Native Americans in his stories. For *The Vanishing American* (1925), he adopts a melancholy stance regarding the inevitable fate of the Native American culture; while the nobility of the Indian is part of the Western myth, he cannot win against the dishonesty of the white man. Regret at the passing of the bison herds and other species of wildlife and their habitats can also be detected in Grey's writings, and *The Vanishing American* gives evidence of his grounding in other contemporary concerns, such as corruption in the U.S. Bureau of Indian Affairs, which is exposed by the narrative.

After 1925 Grey no longer appeared on the best-seller list, but his influence continued during the 1940s and 1950s through films based on his books, as well as through *Zane Grey's Western Magazine* and television's *Zane Grey Theater* (1956–1961). However, the Western film as a high-budget production went into decline after 1930 until the formula was successfully reworked in director John Ford's film, *Stagecoach* (1939). Although based on a short story by Ernest Haycox, the film—shot in Arizona and famously featuring Monument Valley—is a perfect expression of Grey's articulation of the West. The revitalized formula, of which Ford was the master, explores the psychological depth of its characters at a time when the morality and romance of the 1920s Westerns seemed old-fashioned and melodramatic to Great Depression audiences with more complex concerns.

Grey continued to publish fiction until his death in 1939 and sold his version of the winning of the West to an international audience, sustaining a myth that remains embedded in popular culture.

Nickianne Moody

SEE ALSO: *Best Sellers; Country Gentlemen; Ford, John; The Great Depression;* McCall's Magazine*;* Stagecoach*; Television; The Western; World War I.*

BIBLIOGRAPHY

Blake, K. S. "Zane Grey and Images of the American West." *Geographical Review* 85, no. 2 (1995).

Cawelti, J. G. *Adventure, Mystery and Romance.* Chicago: University of Chicago Press, 1976.

Gruber, F. *Zane Grey.* Cleveland, OH: World, 1970.

Jackson, Carlton. *Zane Grey.* Boston: Twayne, 1989.

Kimball, Arthur G. *Ace of Hearts: The Westerns of Zane Grey.* Forth Worth: Texas Christian University Press, 1993.

May, Stephen. *Zane Grey: Romancing the West.* Athens: Ohio University Press, 1997.

Ronald, Ann. *Zane Grey.* Boise, ID: Boise State University Press, 1975.

Scott, Kenneth William. *Zane Grey, Born to the West: A Reference Guide.* Boston: Hall, 1979.

Varner, Paul. *Historical Dictionary of Westerns in Literature.* Lanham, MD: Scarecrow Press, 2010.

Greyhound Buses

There is barely a town or a city in the United States that is not served by Greyhound bus lines, which began operating in 1914. Since then, the company has become a romantic emblem of America, showcasing its wide open spaces and its freedom to travel cheaply and explore the horizons of the country.

Swedish immigrant Carl Eric Wickman began the enterprise in Hibbing, Minnesota, shuttling miners to and from work in a seven-passenger Hupmobile. He quickly expanded his operation and began buying out competitors; by 1935 the Greyhound Corporation owned 1,726 buses running more than 46,000 route miles.

Although their surrounding neighborhoods may have come to seem dilapidated, bus stations often served as the focal point of many a downtown district. Even in this age of the frequent flyer, Greyhound transported nearly eighteen million passengers in 2010. In 1999 Greyhound merged with a Canadian bus company called Laidlaw, Inc., and in 2007 a British company called FirstGroup PLC purchased the combined transportation company. The Greyhound line, however, retained its name and logo. The well-known slogan "Go Greyhound . . . and leave the driving to us" rests within the public's collective consciousness, and the familiar red, white, and blue bus with its painted profile of an outstretched racing dog has become as much a part of popular culture as any single icon of the road.

Robert Kuhlken

SEE ALSO: *Advertising; Air Travel.*

BIBLIOGRAPHY

Gabrick, Robert. *Go the Greyhound Way: The Romance of the Road.* Hudson, WI: Iconografix, 2009.

Jackson, Carlton. *Hounds of the Road: A History of the Greyhound Bus Company.* Bowling Green, OH: Bowling

Green University Popular Press, 1984.

Schisgall, Oscar. *The Greyhound Story: From Hibbing to Everywhere.* New York: Doubleday, 1985.

Grey's Anatomy

Medical dramas have been a programming staple almost since the beginning of television—but few have achieved a level of popularity that would match *Grey's Anatomy.* In the first five seasons following its 2005 debut, ABC's weekly glimpse into life at Seattle Grace Hospital ranked consistently among the top twelve network programs, based on total audience. Although real-time audiences decreased in seasons six and seven, *Grey's Anatomy* remained the most recorded program on television, and DVD sales continued to be strong. One way or another, millions of viewers followed the continuing story of Meredith Grey's medical career and personal relationships.

The *Grey's Anatomy* phenomenon expanded beyond weekly television to include original online episodes; daily reruns on the Lifetime Network; numerous fan forums; and tie-in products such as calendars, soundtrack CDs, and companion books. Some of this popularity was leveraged in 2007 to the spin-off series *Private Practice,* featuring one of the *Grey's* characters. As Sarah Wendell explains in "Diagnostic Notes, Case Histories, and Profiles of Acute Hybridity in *Grey's Anatomy,*" the series has succeeded in combining mainstream success (which is measured by the number of viewers) with cult status (which is measured by the intensity of fan engagement). This "hybridity" translates into tangible benefits that keep *Grey's Anatomy* consistently among the ten most profitable series on television.

The most obvious factor contributing to its popularity is its skillful mixture of life-and-death crises, romantic complications, and career dilemmas. The series begins with new intern Grey (played by Ellen Pompeo) arriving at Seattle Grace and follows her through a series of personal and professional challenges that include, during the first seven seasons, love affairs, pregnancy, miscarriage, a near-death experience, losing her mother, finding her father, tampering with a clinical trial, suspension and reinstatement, and adopting a child. The other important characters, who include Grey's fellow residents as well as several of the hospital's attending physicians and teachers, all have strong personalities that lead to complicated relationships, and together they all cope with dramatic developments ranging from a mass murder to a merger with another hospital.

As with any long-running series, *Grey's Anatomy* experienced challenges behind the scenes, including a highly publicized incident involving actors Isaiah Washington and T. R. Knight. In 2006 Washington used an anti-gay slur in reference to Knight, and in response, Knight made his sexual identity public. Producers decided in 2007 not to renew Washington's contract, and Knight—who felt his character's screen time was unfairly reduced following the incident—requested to be written out of the show in 2008. Katherine Heigl, who won an Emmy for her role as one of Grey's colleagues, was outspoken about her frustrations with the show and finally chose to leave in 2010. New characters were also added, however, and series creator Shonda Rhimes continued to introduce unexpected complications for the ensemble. Rhimes and the writing staff frequently explore difficult and topical issues in individual episodes and story arcs. Grey, for example, copes with her own infertility and with the aftermath of her mother's early-onset Alzheimer's, while fellow resident Cristina Yang chooses career over motherhood and terminates an unplanned pregnancy against her husband's wishes.

Apart from the personal dramas that drive *Grey's Anatomy,* the series also strives to portray the stress that accompanies medical training and practice, along with the challenges confronting contemporary hospitals. As Andrew Holtz notes in *The Real "Grey's Anatomy,"* "medicine, or more specifically hospital practice and the training of young surgeons, form the cauldron of stress and crisis and challenge in which the characters react and act, fight and love, achieve and stumble." By focusing on surgery instead of general medical practice, *Grey's* creates dramatic immediacy and also opens the window into a world that most patients never see. Similarly, the series portrays one of the most difficult and demanding educational experiences in all of medicine: surgical residency. Although the series exaggerates the pace and intensity of events to heighten dramatic effect—the experiences faced by Grey and her friends really do reflect the high-pressure, high-stakes world that real-life residents must navigate.

Cynthia Giles

SEE ALSO: *Emmy Awards; Television.*

BIBLIOGRAPHY

Burkhead, Cynthia, and Hillary Robson, eds. *Grace under Pressure: "Grey's Anatomy" Uncovered.* Newcastle, UK: Cambridge Scholars Publishing, 2008.

Holtz, Andrew. *The Real "Grey's Anatomy": A Behind-the-Scenes Look at the Real Lives of Surgical Residents.* New York: Berkley Books, 2010.

Wendell, Sarah. "Diagnostic Notes, Case Histories, and Profiles of Acute Hybridity in *Grey's Anatomy.*" In *"Grey's Anatomy" 101: Seattle Grace, Unauthorized,* ed. Leah Wilson, 53–63. Dallas, TX: BenBella Books, 2007.

Grier, Pam *(1949–)*

In the 1970s African American actress Pam Grier emerged as a tough heroine in the genre of blaxploitation films. With Hollywood's history of relegating African Americans to demeaning or minor roles, she quickly stood out as a groundbreaker. While she went on to minor television and movie roles, Grier enjoyed something of a comeback in 1997, when she starred in the movie *Jackie Brown,* directed by Quentin Tarantino.

Grier started her career in "B" movies such as *Beyond the Valley of the Dolls* (1970), and she soon rose to stardom playing grassroots vigilantes in *Coffy* (1972) and *Foxy Brown* (1974). While some critics faulted her movies for their violence, sensationalism, and reliance on her attractive physique, many recognized them as vanguard vehicles for portraying African Americans as smart and self-sufficient, as well as giving women an important place as strong, confident, and active players. The women's rights and civil rights movements of the time likely contributed to the success of Grier's films. She later reflected on the sociopolitical significance of her roles: "I embodied the grassroots avenger," she told David Eimer of the *Independent* in 1998. "You kind of expected me to come in and win."

By the late 1970s Grier was ready to expand her acting horizons. In 1977 she appeared in *Greased Lightning,* a biopic featuring Richard Pryor and Beau Bridges. Unfortunately the movie failed to launch her mainstream career, and she soon found herself playing minor roles in numerous movies and television shows, including the gritty police drama *Fort Apache the Bronx* (1981) and the television series *Crime Story* (1986–1988). In 1988 Grier was forced to put her acting career on hold when she was diagnosed with stage-four cervical cancer. Although initially given only eighteen months to live, she eventually recovered from the disease, and by the early 1990s she had begun to work again, appearing primarily in small stage productions.

Grier reemerged from obscurity in the late 1990s, when Tarantino approached her about *Jackie Brown*. He wrote it specifically for her, intent on revitalizing the kind of tough African American heroine that the actress had made famous during the early 1970s. The movie was successful, introducing Grier to a new generation of moviegoers. She went on to appear in a range of television and movie roles. In 2004 she became a cast member of the new series *The L Word* (2004–2009) on the Showtime cable network. The popular show ran for six seasons.

The year 2010 was a busy one for Grier. She guest starred in three episodes of the long-running television series *Smallville* (2001–2011); appeared in the movies *The Invited* and *Just Wright*; and her memoir, *Foxy: My Life in Three Acts*, was released. In her book she offers blunt reflections on her past love affairs, her fight against cancer, and the discrimination she continued to experience even after she became famous. Talented and enduring, Grier continues to find steady acting work in movies such as *Larry Crowne* (2011) and *Woman Thou Art Loosed: On the 7th Day* (2012).

Geri Speace

SEE ALSO: *"B" Movies; Blaxploitation Films; Cancer; Civil Rights Movement; Hollywood; Pryor, Richard; Sex Symbol; Tarantino, Quentin.*

BIBLIOGRAPHY

Eimer, David. "A Star Is Reborn." *Independent* (London), March 8, 1998.

Grier, Pam, and Andrea Cagan. *Foxy: My Life in Three Acts.* New York: Grand Springboard Press, 2010.

Kennedy, Lisa. "She Was 'Foxy' before Anyone Else." *Denver Post*, May 16, 2010.

Smith, Jessie Carney, ed. *Notable Black American Women, Book II.* Detroit, MI: Gale Research, 1996.

Speace, Geri. *Newsmakers*, vol. 98, no. 3. Detroit, MI: Gale Research, 1998.

Griffin, Kathy *(1960–)*

Comedian Kathy Griffin is known for ridiculing pop culture and its obsession with celebrities. Since coming to prominence on the NBC situation comedy *Suddenly Susan* in the 1990s, Griffin has hosted numerous TV specials and parlayed her self-deprecating wit into a Bravo reality series, *Kathy Griffin: My Life on the D-List*. In 2009 she became a best-selling author with the publication of a memoir, *Official Book Club Selection*. Not shy about courting controversy, Griffin has often been the target of censure for her comments and actions.

Kathleen Mary Griffin was born on November 4, 1960, in Oak Park, Illinois, the fifth and last child of John and Margaret Griffin. Early in life she developed a love for doing stand-up comedy, which she discovered by telling the neighbors stories about her family. Though her parents were Catholics, she despised the strict nuns who taught her at St. Bernadine's Elementary School, and she eventually became an outspoken atheist.

Griffin moved with her parents to Los Angeles, where she studied acting at the prestigious Lee Strasberg Institute and then joined the improvisational comedy group the Groundlings. She landed a few small TV roles in the 1980s. Bit parts followed in several major series (including *The Fresh Prince of Bel-Air*, *Mad about You*, *Ellen*, *Seinfeld*, and *ER*) and motion pictures, including *Pulp Fiction* (1994) and *The Cable Guy* (1996).

Griffin's big break came in 1996 when she won the role of Vicki Groener, Brooke Shields's acid-tongued sidekick on *Suddenly Susan* (1996–2000). In 1998 she hosted the first of many TV specials, *Kathy Griffin: A Hot Cup of Talk* on HBO. After *Suddenly Susan* went off the air, she appeared in several Bravo comedy specials.

In August 2005 the network launched *Kathy Griffin: My Life on the D-List*, a tongue-in-cheek reality show that chronicled her struggles to rise above the bottom in Hollywood. Her parents appeared on the show—a June 2007 episode covered her father's death—as did Matthew Moline, the computer designer she married in 2001. *My Life on the D-List*, which won the Primetime Emmy for Outstanding Reality Program in 2007 and 2008, ran until summer 2010.

Griffin first courted public outrage as host of E! Entertainment Television's coverage of the Golden Globe Awards in 2005, when she joked that ten-year-old actress Dakota Fanning had gone into rehab. In her 2007 Emmy acceptance speech, she ridiculed celebrities who "thank Jesus for this award," and concluded, "So all I can say is suck it, Jesus, this award is my god now!" The Catholic League for Religious and Civil Rights pressured the Academy of Television Arts and Sciences into removing her comments from the telecast of the ceremony. For her part, Griffin maintained that she was attacking hypocritical celebrities, not Christ.

Griffin has been outspoken in her distaste for certain public figures, including Sarah Palin, whom she lampooned with her portrayal of former Tea Party candidate Tammy Jean Albertson on a 2011 episode of *Glee*. She also derided Palin's daughter Willow, claiming that the latter had posted antigay comments on her Facebook page. An outspoken advocate of lesbian, gay, bisexual, and transgender (LGBT) rights, Griffin in March 2010 helped organize a Washington, D.C., rally to protest the military's "Don't Ask, Don't Tell" policy.

Since her 2006 divorce from Moline, whom she publicly accused of stealing money from her, Griffin has been linked romantically with a number of men, including Apple Computer cofounder Steve Wozniak and former National Football League (NFL) practice squad wide receiver Isaiah Mustafa. She and Wozniak, with whom she remains friends, have been involved in several charitable activities, such as the establishment of a school for underprivileged children in Mexico. Griffin did a USO tour of Afghanistan in 2003, and she regularly performs shows for returning veterans at army hospitals.

Official Book Club Selection: A Memoir According to Kathy Griffin debuted at number one on the *New York Times* best-seller list in September 2009. Griffin is a staple on the Bravo network, having hosted thirteen stand-up TV specials as of early 2012, with another two already green-lit by the network. Bravo also launched *Kathy*, a regular one-hour talk show, in May 2012.

Judson Knight

SEE ALSO: *Apple Computer; Best Sellers; Cable TV; Celebrity; Daytime Talk Shows; DeGeneres, Ellen; Emmy Awards;* ER; *Facebook; Gay Liberation Movement;* Glee; *Hollywood; Palin, Sarah; Reality Television;* Seinfeld; *Sitcom; Stand-Up Comedy; Television; War in Afghanistan.*

BIBLIOGRAPHY

Avery, Laura, ed. *Newsmakers, Vol. 4.* Detroit, MI: Gale, 2004.

Griffin, Kathy. *Official Book Club Selection: A Memoir According to Kathy Griffin.* New York: Ballantine, 2009.

KathyGriffin.net. Accessed February 2012. Available from http://www.kathygriffin.net/

Piepenburg, Erik. "Comic with Short Fuse and Some Long Feuds." *New York Times*, March 10, 2011, C3(L).

Griffin, Merv *(1925–2007)*

Merv Griffin earned his place in the public consciousness as the host of *The Merv Griffin Show*, a highly popular television show that ran for more than twenty years. Griffin, who was born in San Mateo, California, began his entertainment career as a singer on the radio. In the late 1940s he began touring with the Freddy Martin and His Orchestra. Griffin then parlayed his quick wit and affable personality into movie-acting opportunities as well as work hosting television game shows and travel programs in the 1950s.

In 1962 Griffin became the host of his own daytime talk show, *The Merv Griffin Show*, on NBC. The program was cancelled after its first season, but it returned to the air and at various times from 1965 through 1986. It was syndicated by Westinghouse Broadcasting Company and Metromedia and broadcast on CBS. Known for his jovial, friendly style, Griffin was disparaged as a "softball" questioner by some and accused of being more concerned with ingratiating himself with his guests than with being a "tough" interviewer. Nevertheless, he did sometimes court controversy, as during the Vietnam War when he presented guests who held antiwar views.

Griffin was also an important influence on daytime television through the highly popular game shows that he produced. They included two of the most successful games shows in the history of television: *Jeopardy!*, which premiered in 1964, and *Wheel of Fortune*, which debuted in 1975. In 1986 Griffin sold his production company, Merv Griffin Enterprises, to the Coca-Cola company for $250 million. As part of the deal, however, he retained the rights to the *Jeopardy!* theme song, which he had composed.

In the late 1980s Griffin acquired and operated a number of high-profile hotels and casinos across the country. He sold most of his casino rights in 1993 to Sun International, and by 2003 he had also sold the Beverly Hilton Hotel, which he had refurbished. In 2005 Griffin was honored with lifetime achievement awards from the Daytime Emmys and the Museum of Television and Radio. At his death in 2007, his net worth was reported to be more than $1 billion.

Steven Kotok

SEE ALSO: *Coca-Cola; Daytime Talk Shows; Emmy Awards; Game Shows;* Jeopardy!*; Martin, Freddy; Syndication; Television; Vietnam;* Wheel of Fortune.

BIBLIOGRAPHY

Druxman, Michael B. *Merv.* New York: Leisure Books, 1980.

Griffin, Merv, and Peter Barsocchini. *Merv: An Autobiography.* New York: Simon & Schuster, 1980.

Severo, Richard, and Edward Wyatt. "Merv Griffin, Television Innovator Dies at 82." *New York Times*, August 13, 2007.

Griffith, D. W. *(1875–1948)*

Considered the father of the motion picture and the first great artist of the cinema, director D. W. Griffith revolutionized filmmaking. His most significant and controversial movie, *The Birth of a Nation* (1915), established the feature-length film and the Hollywood star system. After a private viewing at the White House, President Woodrow Wilson reportedly remarked that the film "was like writing history with lightning." *The Birth of a*

D. W. Griffith. *With his technical innovation and artistic vision, D. W. Griffith made his mark in the early twentieth century as America's first great filmmaker.* APIC/GETTY IMAGES.

Nation was not only the longest and most expensive movie to date but also the most popular movie of its time and perhaps the most politically explosive film in American history.

David Wark Griffith was born on January 22, 1875, in the town of Crestwood in Oldham County, Kentucky. He was an aspiring actor from 1897 to 1907, traveling from Portland, Oregon, to Boston, Massachusetts, working in stock companies under the name Lawrence Griffith. In 1906, while in Boston, he married his first wife, Linda Arvidson Johnson. His days as a stage actor were unremarkable.

In 1908 the famed director Edwin S. Porter introduced Griffith to his associates at the Biograph Company on Fourteenth Street in Manhattan. It was here that the young actor gave up performing to sell stories and, ultimately, to begin making movies himself. Along with his trusted and accomplished cameraman, G. W. "Billy" Bitzer, Griffith worked at a frenzied pace. From August 1908 through August 1911, he completed an astonishing 326 one-reel films.

Through these early years, Griffith experimented with different camera angles, editing, and narrative styles. He used close-ups to produce greater emotional drama and sharp cuts between scenes to quicken a story's pace, believing that action rather than written titles should propel the movie's plot. In 1912 Griffith made a short film, *The New York Hat*, with Lionel Barrymore and a young Mary Pickford based on a story submitted by sixteen-year-old Anita Loos, soon to be the most sought-after scenarist in Hollywood. Griffith stayed with Biograph just one more year, but he made his longest and most elaborate film to date in 1913, *Judith of Bethulia*. At four reels, it was four times longer than the standard movie.

THE BIRTH OF A NATION

Griffith reportedly convinced Bitzer to leave Biograph by telling him that he, Griffith, planned to make the greatest film in history. As an independent, Griffith acted as director, producer, distributor, and press agent for his epic *Birth of a Nation*. Based on Thomas F. Dixon's novel *The Clansman* (1905), Griffith's movie faithfully depicted the Reconstruction Era that immediately followed the American Civil War as a period in which African American men were perceived to threaten the purity of the white race—politically, socially, and sexually.

From 1915 to 1946, a reported 200 million people saw the film. During the first weeks of the movie's release, Americans lined up along sidewalks—and in New York City paid the extraordinary price of $2 a seat—for a chance to see the most talked-about movie of the year. With more than twelve reels of film, it ran a record two hours long. The movie cost more than $100,000 to film but grossed an astonishing $18 million.

The technical innovations that Griffith employed to make his film have continued to impress viewers and film historians alike since 1915. For example, Griffith had Bitzer set up his camera at ground level to capture the power and frantic torrent of horse hoofs at full gallop on a dusty road, a technique that illustrated the capabilities of the movie camera if freed from its stationary position in front of a stage. Using an array of camera angles such as closeups, long shots, and cutbacks Griffith proved that directors could make long movies and still hold an audience's attention. He also utilized parallel editing—cross-cutting footage of different events—to achieve suspense and create the illusion of simultaneous action.

Repugnant to modern audiences yet reflecting widespread white American sentiments at the time, the overt racist and nativist imagery, specifically the sympathetic portrayal of the Ku Klux Klan, throughout *Birth of a Nation* provoked the nascent National Association for the Advancement of Colored People (NAACP) to rally black and white people around the country to picket theaters showing the movie. Surprised by the strong reaction to the film and believing it threatened his freedom of speech and, perhaps more importantly, his artistic integrity, Griffith released the antibigotry epic *Intolerance* in 1916. As seminal and popular as *Birth of a Nation* was, *Intolerance* proved to have a stronger effect on other directors. Among those under Griffith's influence was the famous Russian director Sergei Eisenstein, who believed the American's style of rapid-fire editing had advanced filmmaking by a decade.

Griffith directed another twenty-six features between 1917 and 1931 but never again enjoyed adulation as the world's most brilliant director. He ended his career working from his studio in Mamaroneck, a suburb of New York City, to be closer to the financial center of the movie industry.

Ray Haberski Jr.

SEE ALSO: The Birth of a Nation*; Civil Rights Movement; Gish, Dorothy; Gish, Lillian;* Intolerance*; Ku Klux Klan; Loos, Anita; Pickford, Mary; Silent Movies; United Artists.*

BIBLIOGRAPHY

Barry, Iris. *D. W. Griffith: American Film Master*. New York: Museum of Modern Art, 1965.

Carter, Everett. "Cultural History Written with Lightning: The Significance of *The Birth of a Nation*." In *Hollywood as Historian: American Film in a Cultural Context*, ed. Peter Rollins, 9–19. Lexington: University Press of Kentucky, 1998.

Cripps, Thomas. *The Reaction of the Negro to the Motion Picture "The Birth of a Nation"*. Indianapolis: Bobbs-Merrill, 1963.

Franklin, John Hope. "*Birth of a Nation*—Propaganda as History." In *Hollywood's America: United States History through Its Films*, ed. Steven Mintz and Randy Roberts. New York: Brandywine Press, 1993.

Graham, Cooper C. *D. W. Griffith and the Biograph Company*. Metuchen, NJ: Scarecrow Press, 1985.

Gunning, Thomas. *D. W. Griffith and the Rise of the Narrative Film*. Urbana: University of Illinois Press, 1991.

Litwack, Leon F. "*The Birth of a Nation*." In *Past Imperfect: History According to the Movies*, ed. Mark C. Carnes, 136–141. New York: Henry Holt, 1995.

Schickel, Richard. *D. W. Griffith: An American Life*. New York: Simon & Schuster, 1984.

Stern, Seymour. "*The Birth of a Nation*." Special Griffith issue. *Film Culture* 36 (1965).

Stokes, Melvyn. *D. W. Griffith's "The Birth of a Nation": A History of "the Most Controversial Motion Picture of All Time."* New York: Oxford University Press, 2007.

Williams, Martin. *Griffith: First Artist of the Movies*. New York: Oxford University Press, 1980.

Griffith, Nanci *(1953–)*

Almost alone among commercially successful singer-songwriters within folk and country music, Nanci Griffith represents a refreshing contrast to the sometimes bland offerings of the music industry's hit-making machinery. She defies easy categorization into the standard pigeonholes, once describing her own style of music as "folkabilly." Invoking the muses of the folk genre has turned into a one-woman crusade to resurrect what's good and true among the earthier forms of the American song canon. She cites Carolyn Hester as an influential figure in her early career but also draws inspiration from the Carter Family, Buddy Holly, and the Everly Brothers.

After producing nineteen albums by 2009 and surviving two bouts with cancer, Griffith still seems to be steaming ahead at full throttle. She is no longer scaling the heights but rather traversing the summit ridge of her creative powers, and several of her releases have been met with widespread critical acclaim. By all accounts, Griffith is even more popular in Great Britain than in the United States. Perhaps this stems from her own Anglo ancestry or because of her residential choices: she has maintained a loft in Dublin for more than a decade and divides her time between Ireland and a small farm south of Nashville, Tennessee.

A SONGWRITING TRADITION

Nanci Caroline Griffith was born July 6, 1953, near Austin, Texas—a town full of good music—where she penetrated the competitive ranks of a near-legendary songwriting tradition. She has portrayed her parents as "beatniks" who enthusiastically supported her attempts to become a folksinger. Griffith's first paid gig was at age fourteen, when she played at the local Red Lion. She graduated from Austin's Holy Cross High School, where she strummed guitar for folk mass, then stayed in the neighborhood by enrolling at the University of Texas. Griffin began playing every Sunday night—and continued to play for five years—at the Hole in the Wall, a dingy little bar across the street from campus. The bar became her proving ground—as she once described it, if you can get loud beer-drinkers to hush up a moment and listen to your songs, then you must be doing something right. Griffith tried teaching kindergarten for a while, but by this time her heart was firmly attached to her true calling.

Griffith's first album was recorded in 1978 and was subsequently reissued by folk-oriented Philo/Rounder Records. A good representation from her early forays into record making is the album *Once in a Very Blue Moon* (1984). In 1987 she switched to the predominantly country label MCA, and over the next five years released a series of rich offerings with more production input than the spare earlier records. During this time, Griffith assembled a first-rate touring band—the Blue Moon Orchestra—that has stayed together and backed her efforts for decades.

Since 1992 Griffith has recorded on the Elektra label, which has given her wide latitude to experiment with new ambitions and soundscapes. Unanimously well received by critics was a 1994 album, the very personal and heartfelt *Flyer*. In 1994 Griffith won a Grammy Award for her 1993 album *Other Voices, Other Rooms*, which pays tribute to songwriters she admires. Her 1998 release, *Other Voices, Too (A Trip Back to Bountiful)*, serves as a continuation of this project. She has also recorded with artists as diverse as Bruce Cockburn, John Gorka, The Chieftains, and Hootie and the Blowfish. Her songs have been covered—often as hit records—by many other performers, including Willie Nelson, Suzy Bogguss, and Kathy Mattea.

The mid-1990s began a difficult period in Griffith's life: she successfully battled breast cancer and then overcame thyroid cancer at the end of the decade. Her artistic reputation suffered briefly with the release of two albums that were not critically well received: *Hearts in Mind* (2004) and *Ruby's Torch* (2006), both of which experimented with a more jazzy torch-singer style. Griffith later admitted, "During the past few years, I'd lost something in my heart for writing songs." In 2009 she returned to her folk roots with the release of the acclaimed album *The Loving Kind.*

SONGWRITER, STORYTELLER

Stylistically, Griffith is capable of assuming many postures. Her voice, at once so full and supple, can be delicate and hesitant one moment and growling with anger or unassailable determination the next. That soft Texas twang is never too far away. A true storyteller, she likes to experiment with dialect and playful pronunciation. She has great range of expression and uses her vocal chords like a richly textured instrument. Whether accompanied only by acoustic guitar or backed with a full string orchestra, Griffith is able to reach out to listeners through song.

Thematically, Griffith takes on the broad sweep of land and life, especially the trials of the common person trying to negotiate the lonely distances of modern times. There are accounts of working in orchards and on street corners, of dusty towns, drive-in movies, and dashboard lights. She writes of rivers and lakes and fields of bluebonnets, geographical metaphors for place; there are also railroads and highways and always the alternative of moving on. She accusingly points to racism, violence, and the inexcusable folly of warfare as pernicious tragedies society can ill afford.

An avid reader, Griffith credits writers such as Larry McMurtry, Carson McCullers, and Eudora Welty as major inspirations. Her own stories put to song are situated squarely within the great literary tradition of the South, where the people, the lives they lead, and the land they live on are all worthy of notice. But there is something sad and melancholy about this artist's persona, reflecting bittersweet memories of lost loves and roads not taken. There have been some hard times, perhaps even a few regrets. In her songs, there is more than a hint of autobiography, thereby lending authenticity to the emotional impact. Her characters often live alone, their broken or half-baked dreams seeing them through one day at a time. Yet there is always hope, the yearning for fulfillment and intimacy never quite extinguished. Such an undeniably romantic vision is usually sustained at great cost. Griffith seems to understand that love is a choice people make—though she can never bring herself to venture a decision.

Fortunately, her fans do not face the same dilemma. In one of those paradoxes of popular culture, it seems the more things become homogenized and mass produced, the more people yearn for interaction with a genuine and distinct expression of artistry. Well loved by a devoted group of admirers, Griffith has one of the more active newsgroups on the Internet. Members of NanciNet discuss everything from favorite albums and musical influences to the social and political commentary inherent in Griffith's songs. Numerous websites pay tribute to her artistic achievements. For this reclusive, self-avowed folksinger, such grassroots activism by the people must be gratifying indeed.

Robert Kuhlken

SEE ALSO: *Alternative Country Music; The Beat Generation; The Carter Family; Country Music; The Everly Brothers; Folk Music; Grammy Awards; Holly, Buddy; McMurtry, Larry; Nelson, Willie.*

BIBLIOGRAPHY

Griffith, Nanci, and Joe Jackson. *Nanci Griffith's Other Voices: A Personal History of Folk Music.* New York: Three Rivers Press, 1998.

Kingsbury, Paul. *The Encyclopedia of Country Music: The Ultimate Guide to the Music.* New York: Oxford University Press, 2004.

Vaughan, Andrew. *Who's Who in New Country Music.* New York: St. Martin's Press, 1989.

Grimek, John *(1910–1998)*

During John Grimek's career as a weightlifter, bodybuilder, and magazine editor—which began in the late 1920s and ended in the mid-1980s—he saw weight training change from an activity shunned by athletes and exercise scientists into one universally embraced by these groups. Further, because of his remarkable combination of muscle mass, athleticism, and flexibility, he was one of the main instigators of this change in attitude. In the mid-1920s, when young Grimek first began to lift, following the example of his older brother, George, in Perth Amboy, New Jersey, there were very few men and virtually no women in the United States who trained with heavy weights. It was not that heavy lifting was unknown; it was that lifting was anathema throughout the culture. How such nonsense came to be believed by so many people is important to an understanding of the role Grimek played in demystifying the notion of heavy lifting.

Beginning in the second half of the nineteenth century, several influential writers began to argue that the lifting of heavy weights would make a person slow and inflexible, and a new term came into the English language: *muscle-bound.* These writers, who included Dr. Dio Lewis, William Blaikie, and Dr. Dudley Allen Sargent, warned prospective weight trainers not to work themselves so hard that they ended up getting weighed down and slowed down by their musculature. The arguments of these men, who misunderstood genetics as thoroughly as they misunderstood physiology, were soon bolstered by a group of unscrupulous lifters who had built muscular bodies with weight training and wanted to use those bodies to make money. These lifters realized that it would be difficult to prosper by selling barbells and dumbbells through the mail because such weights were expensive to manufacture and costly to ship. However, they also realized that if they denounced heavy weight training in their mail-order advertisements, they could then either sell equipment that was very light (e.g., rubber expanders) or simply sell a course of instruction explaining how to do various callisthenic exercises that required no apparatus.

Together, the misguided writers and the dishonest entrepreneurs gave birth to the myth of the muscle-bound weightlifter, and almost all coaches, athletes, and trainers came to believe that the worst thing an athlete could do was to lift heavy weights. Thus it was that throughout the first half of the twentieth century, young men such as Grimek were looked on with suspicion and even hostility as they pursued their dreams of size and strength. Perhaps because of the belief that weights would make a person slow and "tie him up," many lifters during that period worked on their flexibility and athleticism so they could disprove the belief. As for Grimek, disproving the critics became especially important, as he gained muscular size very quickly and easily. In a few short years, his robust constitution and genetic predisposition combined to produce a body of previously unsurpassed perfection.

COMPETITIVE BODYBUILDING

During most of the 1930s, there were no bodybuilding contests, and the only place where a young lifter/builder could compete in the "iron game" was on the weightlifting platform. Grimek's first competition was the New Jersey State Championships in Newark, which he won easily, lifting in the heavyweight class (a total of 710 pounds). Later that same year he entered the U.S. National Championships and exceeded the national record in the press, with 242.5 pounds. He moved to York, Pennsylvania, in 1936 to train with the York Barbell Club and to work for the York Barbell Company. By winning the National Championships that year, he qualified for the 1936 Olympic Games in Berlin.

For the next several years, Grimek continued in competition, reaching his best total in 1940 at the National Championships with a press of 285 pounds, a snatch of 250 pounds, and a clean and jerk of 325 pounds. On the same night, he won his first Mr. America title, and by that time he was far more famous in the small subculture of heavy lifting as a bodybuilder than as a weightlifter. In order for him to compete with the true heavyweights in America and around the world, some of whom weighed up to 300 pounds, it would have been necessary for Grimek to gain 40 or 50 pounds, which would have spoiled the symmetry of his already legendary physique. Robert (Bob) Hoffman, the coach of the York Barbell Club team and the owner of the York Barbell Company, analyzed the situation correctly:

> I frequently say that a man can't have everything. John Grimek has more than his share and has done more than his share for weightlifting. . . . He became a weightlifter to prove that there is power in a shapely physique. . . . Grimek would be stronger if he was heavier, but he would not have his present physique. I think his physique does weightlifting and the entire cause of weight training more good than would his winning of the world's championship.

One of the ways Grimek helped the "cause of weight training" was to serve as the prime example of flexible muscle in Hoffman's magazine, *Strength & Health*, for which Grimek worked as a writer/editor. From 1932 on, in every issue of his magazine, Hoffman hammered away at the myth of the muscle-bound lifter, and Grimek was his biggest weapon. Photographs of Grimek's flexibility and stories of his athleticism filled the pages of *Strength & Health* and helped to convince skeptical readers that heavy weights would help them, as Hoffman always said, "in their chosen sport."

Another important way in which Grimek helped the "cause" was by taking part in the many exhibitions arranged by Hoffman. Whenever Hoffman was asked to bring some lifters and put on an exhibition, he would accept if at all possible. He knew that only by exposing the public to the truth that heavy lifting would help a man or a woman at his or her chosen sport could he hope to dispel the myth of the muscle-bound lifter. All of these exhibitions chipped away at the myth, as audiences saw for themselves how quick and flexible the lifters were, but in the spring of 1940 Hoffman took a group of lifters, including Grimek, to Springfield College in Massachusetts. What happened there became a pivotal event in the destruction of the myth.

DEMONSTRATIONS OF AGILITY

Fraysher Ferguson, a student at Springfield College (where most of the country's YMCA directors were trained), invited Hoffman to bring lifters to Springfield for an exhibition because none of his professors believed him when he said that his lifting helped him as an athlete. One of those professors was Dr. Peter Karpovich, the most widely respected physical educator in America at that time and an avowed enemy of heavy lifting. The hall was packed with students and staff that day, and after Hoffman introduced the two top lifters, Grimek and world heavyweight champion John Davis, Davis did some heavy lifting, and Grimek gave a posing exhibition. Although physiques such as Grimek's had become common by the last decades of the twentieth century, none of the people in attendance in 1940 had ever seen a man with such huge, defined muscles.

Following the exhibition, Hoffman invited questions, and the students turned to Dr. Karpovich. True to form, he rose and asked if "Mr. Grimek would mind scratching the back of his neck." After drawing a laugh by saying his neck didn't itch, Grimek obliged, then went on to perform a series of stunts that included standing on a low stool and touching the floor, straight-legged, with his fingertips, and then doing a full side-to-side leg split. Davis then did a back flip while holding a 50-pound dumbbell in each hand. The audience burst into shocked applause at each new shattering stunt, and afterward Karpovich came down and privately apologized, vowing to undertake research studies that would help him understand how he could have been so mistaken. Indeed, though World War II intervened, when Karpovich returned to his lab in the late 1940s, he directed a series of studies that proved to his satisfaction that far from slowing a person down, weight training increased a person's speed. In time, these studies were published in the most important journals in the field, and the muscle-bound theory was gradually laid to rest.

It is doubtful whether a person with significantly less muscle mass could have caused such a change in the thinking of those who saw Grimek perform his feats of flexibility. If anyone appeared visually to symbolize the word *muscle-bound*, it was Grimek during the 1930s and 1940s. That Grimek was both limber and graceful flew in the face of the myth that more muscle equated to less agility. Part of Grimek's power as a performer came from his dramatic ability to pose his body. Many who saw him in his prime have said that his posing was a "ballet of power," in which he moved from pose to pose in a fluid, natural manner.

Most historians of physical culture place Grimek above all bodybuilders before or since in his mastery of physical display. According to Joe Weider, who began his publishing empire in 1940, Grimek was an innovator who developed and mastered the modern style of posing. Films that remain of Grimek on the platform reveal a performance that combined grace, power, drama, masculinity, and beauty. He was never defeated in bodybuilding competition, and he was the man to whom all other lifters/builders would point when they were told, "Lifting will make you muscle-bound." As Grimek himself told a group of skeptical YMCA directors after an exhibition in which he posed and performed his seemingly miraculous stunts, "Can you do what I do? If you can't, then you're the ones who are muscle-bound."

Jan Todd
Terry Todd

SEE ALSO: *Bodybuilding; Schwarzenegger, Arnold.*

BIBLIOGRAPHY

Fair, John. *Muscletown USA: Bob Hoffman and the Manly Culture of York Barbell.* University Park: Pennsylvania State University Press, 1999.

Miller, Carl. *The Miller Fitness Plan.* Santa Fe, NM: Sunstone Press, 2005.

Todd, Jan, and Terry Todd, eds. "John Grimek: The Man." *Iron Game History* 6, special commemorative issue (1999).

Grisham, John *(1955–)*

Primarily known for legal thrillers, best-selling author John Grisham made a mark on Hollywood when his books were turned into films, and in the twenty-first century he diversified his talents to include children's books, literary fiction, and nonfiction. While working as a lawyer and a Mississippi state legislator, Grisham took three years to write his first novel, *A Time to Kill* (1989; film 1996). More than two dozen publishers rejected the book before Wynwood Press agreed to print 5,000 copies in 1989, 1,000 of which Grisham bought and sold himself at library and bookstore events. Grisham's fortunes changed with his second novel, *The Firm* (1991; film 1993), which he wrote based on guidelines he found in a *Writer's Digest* article. Paramount paid $600,000 for film rights before the book had a publisher, leading to a bidding war that landed Grisham a three-book contract with Doubleday.

At this point Grisham closed his law practice and began writing full time. He wrote his third book, *The Pelican Brief* (1993; film 1993), in only 100 days. He took six months to write his next book, *The Client* (1993; film 1994). Shortly after its release, *The Client* was at number one on the *New York Times* hardcover best-seller list, while *The Pelican Brief*, *The Firm*, and *A Time to Kill* were all within the first five slots on the paperback best-seller list. Since then, Grisham has published a book or two a year, most of them legal thrillers and all best sellers. In 2001 he published a literary novel, *A Painted House*, and in 2006 he released *The Innocent Man: Murder and Injustice in a Small Town*, the true story of a man wrongly sentenced to death. He broke into children's books in 2010 with his Theodore Boone series.

Grisham's influence has extended beyond the world of publishing, as many of his books have been made into films, including *The Firm*, *The Pelican Brief*, *The Client*, and *A Time to Kill*. The films have been helmed by such popular and acclaimed directors as Joel Schumacher, Sydney Pollack, and Francis Ford Coppola. Actors involved in the projects include big names such as Susan Sarandon, Holly Hunter (who was nominated for an Academy Award for Best Supporting Actress for her role in *The Firm*), Tommy Lee Jones, Tom Cruise, Gene

Hackman, Denzel Washington, Julia Roberts, Matt Damon, Danny DeVito, and Claire Danes. *The Gingerbread Man*, a film released in 1998, was based on Grisham's first original screenplay. *The Client* was adapted into a television series in 1995, and *The Firm* was adapted into a series that premiered in 2012.

As best sellers, Grisham's novels received a great deal of critical attention, and the reviews were mixed. He was most often criticized for writing formulaic novels and sacrificing character development for plot. Still, even his critics admitted that he wrote a thrilling page-turner. He was often compared to Scott Turow, another best-selling author of legal thrillers including *Presumed Innocent* (1987) and *Burden of Proof* (1990). Grisham and Turow, whose first book appeared in the year Grisham finished *A Time to Kill*, are credited with creating a legal thriller boom in the 1990s, increasing the profile and output of authors such as Richard North Patterson, Steve Martini, and Brad Meltzer.

Grisham's books appeal to a sense of paranoia that prevailed in the 1990s and into the new millennium. His books and the films they inspire center on protagonists who are fighting corruption and confronting other people's self-serving interests. In *The Firm*, Mitchell McDeere only finds out after he and his wife become used to their new high-class lifestyle that the firm he works for is corrupt, and the FBI agents who should be helping him only compound his troubles. In *The Pelican Brief*, law student Darby Shaw stumbles on the truth behind the assassination of two Supreme Court justices and finds herself pursued not only by the man behind the assassinations but also by various government representatives. Other novels deal with class-action lawsuits, the death penalty, and blackmail. Grisham's relatable underdog protagonists strive and struggle to do the morally right thing against business and governmental powers that seem unstoppable.

John Grisham. *A master of the legal thriller, John Grisham's first best seller was* The Firm *(1991), which sold more than seven million copies.* JIM SPELLMAN/WIREIMAGE/GETTY IMAGES.

In an era when corruption was a regular part of the daily news, Grisham's popularity remained strong. His sales were on par with big name authors such as James Patterson, Stephen King, and Danielle Steel. Grisham's influence reached into the entire entertainment industry, and this momentum had him poised to continue to be a strong presence in both the literary and film worlds.

Adrienne Furness

SEE ALSO: *Academy Awards; Best Sellers; Cruise, Tom; Damon, Matt; Hackman, Gene; Hollywood; King, Stephen; Paperbacks; Roberts, Julia; Sarandon, Susan; Television; Washington, Denzel.*

BIBLIOGRAPHY

Ferranti, Jennifer. "Grisham's Law." *Saturday Evening Post*, March/April 1997, 42–45.

"Grisham, John." *Current Biography*, September 1993, 21–24.

"Grisham, John." *Encyclopedia of World Biography*. Detroit, MI: Gale, 1998.

Memmott, Carol. "Grisham's 'Kid Lawyer' Approaches the Bench." *USA Today*, May 24, 2010, D1.

Moore, Dennis. "For Grisham, a Time to Remember." *USA Today*, June 22, 2009, D1.

Olsen, Mark. "Grishamovies." *Film Comment*, March/April 1998, 76–80.

Zaleski, Jeff. "The Grisham Business." *Publishers Weekly*, January 19, 1998, 248–251.

Grits

Made from finely ground dried and hulled corn kernels, or hominy, grits are a central feature of southern foodways. They are commonly eaten for breakfast and complemented by a wide variety of condiments, including redeye gravy, butter, cheese, ham, bacon, salmon, shrimp, and sausage. While generally boiled to a porridgelike consistency, grits can also be served with milk and sugar or even cold-sliced and fried.

Generations of southerners have enjoyed grits since Native Americans first introduced Virginia colonists to unrefined hominy, but this southern staple apparently has less popularity outside the region. Packaged instant or quick grits are a key ingredient in southern cooking and an enduring feature of southern identity. Indeed, grits are an important element of the southern distinctiveness and celebrated in the region through festival, humor, literature, and song. To cite just two examples, the cooking time of the ubiquitous dish is featured as a key point of evidence in the movie *My Cousin Vinny* (1992), and kneeling on uncooked grits is used as a punishment in Sue Monk Kidd's southern novel *The Secret Life of Bees* (2002).

Stephen C. Kenny

SEE ALSO: *Foodies; Organic Food.*

BIBLIOGRAPHY

Egerton, John, and Ann Bleidt Egerton. *Southern Food: At Home, on the Road, in History.* Chapel Hill: University of North Carolina Press, 1993.

McIntosh, Sue McEwen. *Glorious Grits: America's Favorite Comfort Food.* Birmingham, AL: Oxmoor House, 2009.

Wilson, Charles Reagan, and William R. Ferris, eds. *Encyclopedia of Southern Culture.* Chapel Hill: University of North Carolina Press, 1989.

Grizzard, Lewis *(1946–1994)*

Lewis McDonald Grizzard Jr. was a popular and sometimes controversial newspaper columnist who gained fame in the 1980s and 1990s with his popular syndicated newspaper column. Throughout his career, Grizzard's wit entertained readers with commentary that was unabashedly pro-Southern. His love for his alma mater, the University of Georgia; his attitude toward Yankees; and his well-known marital failures all provided material for his columns, numerous books, audiocassettes, and personal and television appearances. But it was in his life-and-death struggle with heart disease that he touched the hearts of his loyal readers.

Born on October 20, 1946, Grizzard grew up in the small town of Moreland, Georgia. He attended the University of Georgia in Athens, but because he accepted a job with the *Atlanta Journal-Constitution* in his senior year, he did not graduate until years later. Despite his delayed graduation, he was awarded the Distinguished Alumni Award from his alma mater's College of Journalism and Mass Communication.

Before settling down as a syndicated newspaper columnist, Grizzard worked as a sports editor at newspapers in Atlanta and Chicago. By the time of his death in 1994, his columns had appeared in more than 200 newspapers across the United States, and he had authored numerous books of his collected humor. Many of Grizzard's books found their way to the *New York Times* best-sellers list, and most remained in print years after his death. True to his persona as a southern "good ol' boy," he never used a word processor or computer, preferring a manual typewriter instead.

While his humor won him fame, Grizzard often endured conflicting attitudes toward his work. Some condemned his brand of humor as sexist, homophobic, jaded, and cynical, while others praised him as a great storyteller and a modern-day Mark Twain. A publisher once compared him to American writer William Faulkner, who was also from the South, but implied that Grizzard was more attuned to the average person. Grizzard met criticism of his work with an honesty that marked his writing and humor as distinctly his own. His popularity quickly spread from syndicated columns to books, audiotapes, and personal appearances. Probably his best-known appearance was on the sitcom *Designing Women*, in which he played Julia and Suzanne Sugarbaker's (Dixie Carter and Delta Burke) half-brother.

Despite his commercial success, Grizzard experienced difficulties in his personal life. He had three failed marriages, which he often wrote about in his columns and books. He married his fourth wife, Dedra, just days before his death. Grizzard had one stepdaughter and no children of his own.

After years of illnesses and surgeries, Grizzard died in 1994 from complications following heart surgery in Atlanta. After his death, the Lewis Grizzard Museum was established in his hometown of Moreland, where visitors could view some of his personal items, such as his baseball glove, his letter jacket, and his childhood rocking chair. In 2011 the museum closed, and its collection was moved to the Old Mill Museum, also in Moreland, where it was incorporated with the Old Mill's growing collection of artifacts from Grizzard's life.

Kimberley H. Kidd

SEE ALSO: *Faulkner, William; The* New York Times*; Twain, Mark.*

BIBLIOGRAPHY

Grizzard, Lewis. *I Took a Lickin' and Kept on Tickin'.* New York: Villard Books, 1993.

Grizzard, Lewis, and Chuck Perry. *Don't Fence Me In: An Anecdotal Biography of Lewis Grizzard.* Atlanta, GA: Longstreet Press, 1995.

Schemmel, William. *Off the Beaten Path Georgia: A Guide to Unique Places*, 9th ed. Guilford, CT: Globe Pequot Press, 2009.

Groening, Matt *(1954–)*

When Matt Groening graduated from Evergreen State University, Washington, in 1977, he expected to become a writer, but cartooning became his claim to fame. By 1991, as the creator of the animated television series *The Simpsons* and the nationally syndicated comic strip *Life in Hell*, Groening not only had received his first two Emmys but also had been listed as one of *Forbes* magazine's top forty earners in the entertainment industry.

After college, the struggles that Groening had as a writer in Los Angeles led him to create *Life in Hell*, a comic strip about Binky, a hostile, frustrated rabbit. (Rabbits were the only recognizable animals that Groening could draw.) Instead of correspondence, Groening sent his relatives and friends his first comics to communicate his feelings. His early efforts to market his comics included trying to sell booklets of comic strips in the punk section of the record store where he worked.

In 1978 a magazine called *Wet*, which showcased unconventional graphics, ran a few installments of the strip. The Los Angeles *Reader*, a weekly alternative paper, hired Groening in 1980 as circulation manager, and it began to run *Life in Hell* regularly. Groening transformed Binky from a grouchy pessimist to a hapless victim. He added several characters—Binky's son, Bongo; his girlfriend, Sheba; and Akbar and Jeff, identical fez-wearing entrepreneurs. By 1983 the strip was being published in twenty papers, and its success led to Groening's first book, *Love Is Hell*, published in 1984. By 1997 he had published twelve *Life in Hell* books, and the comic was regularly appearing in more than 200 newspapers.

In 1985 Groening resigned from the *Reader* along with Deborah Caplan, who worked in the paper's advertising department. Together they created a company, Life in Hell, Inc., to handle the business side of Groening's projects. Groening and Caplan married in 1986 and had two children (Homer and Abraham), but the couple divorced in 1999.

SUCCESS WITH *THE SIMPSONS*

In 1987 James L. Brooks—creator of the television shows *Taxi* (1978–1983) and *The Mary Tyler Moore Show* (1970–1977) and director of *Terms of Endearment* (1983) and *As Good as It Gets* (1997)—approached Groening to create short animated segments of *Life in Hell* for the Fox network's *Tracey Ullman Show* (1987–1990). Groening agreed to do segments for the show, but, unwilling to relinquish the rights to *Life in Hell*, he created an entirely new set of characters—a family called the Simpsons. The family consisted of parents Homer and Marge, son Bart, and daughters Lisa and baby Maggie (Groening named characters after members of his own family: his parents, Homer and Margaret, and his sisters, Lisa and Maggie).

By 1989 the Simpsons had become so popular on *The Tracey Ullman Show* that Fox commissioned thirteen episodes for a new program to air in the 1989 fall season. After a delay, the first episode of *The Simpsons* went on the air in January 1990. Within two months, the show was ranked in the Nielsen's top fifteen most-watched shows on American television. The creator, developer, animator, director, and executive producer of *The Simpsons*, Groening won an Emmy Award for Outstanding Animated Program for the first and second seasons of the program. He won again in 1995, 1997, 1998, 2000, 2001, 2003, 2006, and 2008. In 1997 Groening was awarded the George Foster Peabody Award for excellence in broadcasting for *The Simpsons*.

LATER CREATIONS

To broaden the appeal of *The Simpsons*, Groening started the Bongo Comics Group in 1993. Four of the company's first publications were the monthly comic books *Simpsons Comics*, *BartMan*, *Itchy & Scratchy*, and *Radioactive Man* (Bart Simpson's favorite comic-book hero). In 1995 Groening founded Zongo Comics to publish the work of alternative independent artists. Zongo Comics included the titles *Jimbo*, *Fleener*, and *Hop-ster's Tracks*.

Groening's views on life are deeply integrated into *The Simpsons*. As he explained in a 1993 interview with the *Washington Post*, the Simpsons are a blue-collar family, like such cartoon greats as the Flintstones and the Rubbles. Although the characters encounter exaggerated events, the writers have them react as real people would, conveying "real emotions." Episodes of *The Simpsons* are replete with cultural references, from "Dr. Zaius" (the song referring to the 1968 film *Planet of the Apes* sung to the tune of Falco's 1985 hit "Rock Me Amadeus") to Mayor Quimby's Kennedyesque Boston accent.

In 1999 Groening's *Futurama* premiered on Fox, chronicling the adventures of Fry, a pizza-delivery guy who is accidentally frozen in 1999 and wakes up to find himself in 2999. The lasting popularity of the show results from what Brian Doherty calls Groening's "twisted, absurdly honest, densely reverential" sense of humor. The series has been supplemented by a number of *Futurama* videos and a video game.

The Simpsons have long been one of the most recognizable television families in the world. Bart Simpson even made *Time* magazine's list of the 100 most important people of the twentieth century as one of the top twenty artists and entertainers. Groening's show has not only captured the television market but has also overwhelmed the commercial market, with the Simpsons appearing as toys, in their own video game, on T-shirts, as product endorsers, and on the Internet. The popularity of *The Simpsons* has continued into the twenty-first century, including *The Simpsons Movie* and a companion video game in 2007.

Adam Wathen

SEE ALSO: *Animated Films; Barry, Lynda; Brooks, James L.; Comic Books; Comics; Emmy Awards;* The Flintstones*;* The Mary Tyler Moore Show*;* Planet of the Apes*;* The Simpsons*;* Taxi*; Television;* Time*; Video Games.*

BIBLIOGRAPHY

Doherty, Brian. "Matt Groening." *Mother Jones* 24, no. 2 (1999).

"The Groening of America: Once a Doodler on the Fringe, Bart's Bad Boy Is Now a Millionaire Slob." *Washington Post*, May 13, 1993.

Hile, Kevin S., ed. *Something about the Author*, vol. 81. Detroit, MI: Gale Research, 1995.

Lenburg, Jeff. *Legends of Animation: Matt Groening.* New York: Chelsea House, 2011.

"Matt Groening." *Contemporary Theatre, Film and Television*, vol. 17. Detroit, MI: Gale Research, 1997.

Riley, Sam G., ed. *Biographical Dictionary of American Newspaper Columnists.* Westport, CT: Greenwood Press, 1995.

Grunge

Grunge is the name given to the hard rock music produced by bands such as Nirvana and Soundgarden, in Seattle, Washington, from the mid-1980s through the mid-1990s. Whereas the term provides a convenient blanket description, it also hides fairly substantial stylistic differences between the bands. Few, if any, of those groups ever described themselves as grunge, and the stereotyping of grunge as humorless and angst-ridden is a serious distortion. Nonetheless, the same media scrutiny that bred those misrepresentations turned grunge into a worldwide phenomenon that shaped not only music but also other aspects of popular culture, such as fashion.

INDEPENDENT MOVEMENT

Through the late 1970s and early 1980s, punk and hard-core rock had embraced a do-it-yourself attitude in defiant opposition to the bombast and big money of heavy metal and arena rock. However, as the hard-core and punk movements began to wane in the mid-1980s, many of those independent bands retained their amplifiers and distortion pedals but began slowing the tempos of their songs considerably. As a result, many bands (intentionally or not) began to reproduce the sound of the arena rock bands on which they had originally turned their backs. Although this trend occurred throughout the United States, it became particularly noticeable in two groups of musicians in

Soundgarden. *Soundgarden received a Grammy nomination for their 1989 album* Louder than Love. EBET ROBERTS/REDFERNS/GETTY IMAGE.

Seattle: the Melvins and Green River. Hailing from Aberdeen, Washington, the Melvins played a particularly sludgy form of hard rock, touring with their friend Kurt Cobain at the wheel of their tour bus before he formed Nirvana. Green River also received some attention in independent music circles, before splitting up to re-form as Mudhoney and Mother Love Bone.

Those two groups nicely illustrate the two poles of the grunge movement. Fronted by flamboyant lead singer Andrew Wood, Mother Love Bone's music clearly indicated the band's commercial ambitions, and after just a handful of shows they secured a contract with PolyGram Records—a situation amounting to heresy in the independent music scene. After Wood's death in 1990 from drug-related causes, members of the band secured the talents of San Diego, California–based singer Eddie Vedder and formed Pearl Jam.

In contrast to Mother Love Bone, Mudhoney openly satirized the entire notion of rock stardom. Its sound was considerably rougher, with front man Mark Arm's vocals closer to a hoarse shout than to singing. Taking their name from the title of a soft-core film directed by Russ Meyer, they embraced a faux sexism that simultaneously spoofed and celebrated the excesses of big-name rock bands.

Soundgarden fell somewhere between the blatant commercialism of Pearl Jam and the unpolished garage sound of Mudhoney. Lead singer Chris Cornell possessed a powerful falsetto that went well beyond that of Black Sabbath's Ozzy Osbourne, his most obvious influence. Soundgarden built its reputation as an independent band, satirizing the misogyny of heavy metal in songs such as "Big Dumb Sex," but a lot of listeners seemed to miss the joke. The group's 1989 album, *Louder than Love*, was nominated for a Grammy, and *Superunknown*, released in 1994, debuted at number one on the Billboard charts. By that time the band's sound was closer to Metallica or Guns 'N' Roses (with whom they had once toured) than to Mudhoney or Nirvana. Soundgarden broke up in 1997.

COMMERCIAL SUCCESS

It is likely that many of these bands would have vanished quietly, or perhaps not even formed at all, if it were not for Sub Pop Records. Founders Bruce Pavitt and Jonathan Poneman recognized the strength of the Seattle music scene and, like Berry Gordon, whose Motown label had popularized the pop and rhythm and blues of Detroit, Michigan, in the 1960s, they set out to promote their city's bands. From the label's inception, they showed an ambition previously absent from independent labels. Sub Pop's first release, a compilation of bands that, for the most part, were not from Seattle at all, described the label as "the new thing, the big thing, the God thing: a mighty multinational entertainment conglomerate based in the Pacific Northwest." Most people thought it was a joke, but Pavitt and Poneman were not kidding.

Many independent record labels in America had been releasing excellent music that never achieved any degree of commercial success, but Pavitt and Poneman were shrewd marketers with an unrivaled gift for generating hype. They hired a British press agent to promote their bands and paid a correspondent from the British music newspaper *Melody Maker* to come to Seattle. They believed—correctly—that the best way to promote their bands in the United States was through a reputation that was built abroad. Soon the city was renowned as one of the foremost centers of independent music in the world.

Nonetheless, by early 1991 Sub Pop was nearing bankruptcy. Its salvation came from the wholly unexpected success of Nirvana's second full-length album, *Nevermind*. When David Geffen's DGC label signed Nirvana, the contract stipulated that Sub Pop would receive a 2 percent royalty if the album sold more than 250,000 copies. Most observers expected it would sell a fraction of that number. However, "Smells Like Teen Spirit," the album's first single, became an overnight anthem, combining an infectious riff with a heavy guitar sound and lyrics that expressed a wry world weariness. A few months earlier, Nirvana had been known to only a small number of independent music cognoscenti; now they were receiving airtime on Top 40 rock and alternative stations throughout the world. Within a year *Nevermind* had sold four million albums. Pearl Jam's *Ten* was released the same month as Nirvana's album, and although sales were initially slower, it sold an equal number of copies during its first year.

With the success of Nirvana and Pearl Jam, journalists, film crews, and fashion designers began flocking to Seattle to cash in on the music, which the world outside Seattle was calling grunge. The flannel shirt became the ultimate symbol of grunge couture, although flannels had been popular for years in the national hard-core scene because they were cheap, comfortable, and durable. Soon, upscale stores were selling "designer grunge," a bizarre inversion of a look essentially the opposite of retail fashion. Seattle bands on tour often found crowds dressed in flannels, ripped jeans, and Doc Marten boots: "more Seattle than Seattle," as one musician observed.

IRONIC ROCK STARS

Many bands who had prided themselves on a punk ethos now found themselves signing very lucrative contracts. A popular T-shirt in Seattle depicted the irony. It featured a large picture of a heroin syringe with the caption "I came to Seattle to score, and all I got was a lousy recording contract." The standard defense was an equally ironic pose. Cobain appeared on the cover of *Rolling Stone* with a hand-lettered T-shirt that read "Corporate magazines still suck"—an allusion to the bumper sticker "Corporate music still sucks." Even Mudhoney signed with a major label and, in concert, began changing the lyrics of their song "Touch Me, I'm Sick" to "Fuck Me, I'm Rich." Although those might have been effective comebacks, they did nothing to disguise or alter the fundamental fact that bands that had begun by satirizing rock stars suddenly became rock stars.

One reason for that irony is the music that influenced grunge. While most independent music up until that time ignored commercial hard rock (or at least pretended to), grunge reveled in it. Cobain said, "We just accepted the fact that we liked the music we grew up on: Alice Cooper, the MC5, Kiss. . . . We're paying homage to all the music we loved as kids, and we haven't denied the punk-rock energy that inspired us as teenagers." However, with commercial success, many bands began to spend more time polishing their recordings in the studio. That effectively destroyed the "Seattle sound," much of which came from producer Jack Endino, who used a simple four-track recorder to achieve a deliberately rough sound. Cobain himself admitted that he thought the production of *Nevermind* was a little too slick. Punk energy was often filtered out by producers looking to make a more palatable recording.

By 1994 many of the original grunge bands had cut their hair and begun to release more mainstream albums. Effectively, grunge ended with the suicide of Cobain in the spring of 1994. Nonetheless, it had already forced an essential change in the recording industry; major labels became much more willing to sign new acts, even if they did not fit into a preconceived commercial formula.

POST-GRUNGE

As grunge waned, the more commercial "post-grunge" movement surged, and many former grunge musicians enjoyed continued success. Pearl Jam averaged one new album every two years from 1991 through 2011. Nirvana drummer Dave Grohl's band, Foo Fighters, amassed seven albums and eleven Grammy Awards between 1995 and 2011. In 2002 excerpts from Cobain's notebooks were published as *Journals* and spent eleven weeks atop the *New York Times* best-seller list. Also in 2002 Nirvana's *Greatest Hits* debuted at number three on Billboard's Top 200 list. In 2003 the *New York Times* reported that, while it had never entirely lost its appeal, Nirvana was experiencing greater success than it had since Cobain's death. Though the creation of pure grunge music ended in the early 1990s because it could not coexist with its own mainstream success, that success and the appeal of grunge's original raw rebellion lives on.

Bill Freind

SEE ALSO: *Alternative Rock; Cooper, Alice; Doc Martens; Generation X; Heavy Metal; KISS; Motown; MTV; Nirvana; Osbourne, Ozzy; Pearl Jam; Punk; Rock and Roll; Top 40.*

BIBLIOGRAPHY

Azerrad, Michael. *Come as You Are: The Story of Nirvana*. New York: Doubleday, 1993.

Humphrey, Clark. *Loser: The Real Seattle Music Story*. Portland, OR: Feral House, 1995.

Moore, Thurston, and Michael Lavine. *Grunge*. New York: Abrams Image, 2009.

Nelson, Chris. "Nine Years after Cobain's Death, Big Sales for All Things Grunge." *New York Times*, January 13, 2003.

Yarm, Mark. *Everybody Loves Our Town: An Oral History of Grunge*. New York: Crown Archetype, 2011.

Grusin, Dave *(1934–)*

Combining classical music training, jazz virtuosity, and a popular culture sensibility, Dave Grusin became one of the most prolific composers of the late twentieth century. Born and raised in Littleton, Colorado, Grusin majored in classical piano at the University of Colorado. However, he had an affinity for jazz, and he played with visiting artists such as Art Pepper and singer Anita O'Day. After moving to New York to pursue an academic career, Grusin took a job touring with singer Andy Williams. He became Williams's musical director and moved to Los Angeles to work on *The Andy Williams Show*. Grusin left the show in 1964 to score the Norman Lear and Bud Yorkin film, *Divorce American Style*. He subsequently scored *The Graduate* in 1967.

Grusin soon became one of Hollywood's premier composers. He was nominated for an Academy Award for his scores in eight films, including *Heaven Can Wait*, *On Golden Pond*, *Tootsie*, and *The Fabulous Baker Boys*. He won an Academy Award for *The Milagro Beanfield War*. Grusin's work has also been familiar to television audiences—he wrote the theme songs for *Good Times*, *Maude*, *Baretta*, and *St. Elsewhere*. Despite his cinematic successes, Grusin has remained true to his jazz roots. Highly respected in the jazz community, his recording and performing career has spanned three decades, and he has won ten Grammy Awards.

Grusin has continued to record in the early twenty-first century. He entered the high-tech world of iPad music apps in

2011 with the release of the album application *An Evening with Dave Grusin*, which was simultaneously released as a live album and on Blu-ray disc. Selections include his own music from films such as *Tootsie* and *On Golden Pond* and selections from *West Side Story*.

Victoria Price

SEE ALSO: *Academy Awards;* Good Times*;* The Graduate*; Grammy Awards; iPad; Jazz; Lear, Norman;* Maude*;* St. Elsewhere*;* Tootsie*;* West Side Story*; Williams, Andy.*

BIBLIOGRAPHY

Bruno, Antony. "iPad Albums?" *Billboard*, April 16, 2011.

Carr, Ian; Digby Fairweather; Brian Priestley; et al. *Jazz: The Rough Guide*. London: Rough Guides, 1995.

Guaraldi, Vince *(1928–1976)*

Vince Guaraldi was one of the finest jazz pianists of the 1950s and 1960s. Eventually the leader of his own group, his résumé also included time with jazz greats Cal Tjader and Duke Ellington. In 1963 Guaraldi won a Grammy for his song "Cast Your Fate to the Wind," and although he recorded many successful albums and had a thriving concert career, he will forever be known as the composer for the Charlie Brown television specials. His music for *A Boy Named Charlie Brown* and *A Charlie Brown Christmas* became irrevocably linked to the Peanuts franchise. Several of his songs—including "Linus and Lucy," "Red Baron," and "Great Pumpkin Waltz"—became standard music for all Peanuts specials.

Guaraldi's music introduced children to jazz, and his upbeat, bouncy style seemed a perfect fit to the characters created by Charles Schulz. Although Guaraldi died unexpectedly in 1976, performers from Wynton Marsalis to David Benoit still play his compositions, and his albums continue to sell.

Geoff Peterson

SEE ALSO: *Comics; Ellington, Duke; Grammy Awards; Jazz;* Peanuts.

BIBLIOGRAPHY

Gioia, Ted. *West Coast Jazz: Modern Jazz in California, 1945–1960*. New York: Oxford University Press, 1992.

Hamlin, Jesse. "Guaraldi's 'Peanuts' Legacy Lives On: Late Pianist's Music Still Makes Money." *San Francisco Chronicle*, February 11, 1997, E1.

Sullivan, James. "Peanuts' Composer's Legacy." *San Francisco Chronicle*, October 18, 1998, 44.

The Guardian Angels

Founded by Curtis Sliwa in 1979, the Guardian Angels is a volunteer organization dedicated to protecting law-abiding citizens from violent crime on the New York City subways. The organization spread throughout the United States, and chapters were established in cities in Canada, South America, Australia, and Europe. The members, who wear a uniform that includes a red beret and a white sweatshirt, carry no weapons but undergo training in martial arts, first aid, and citizen's arrest laws. While law enforcement agencies have tended toward skepticism about the Angels' effectiveness in crime prevention, their presence has frequently shamed authorities into improving policing on subway systems. Revelations in 1992 that Sliwa had staged some of the Angels' much-publicized successes caused the decline of many chapters.

Chris Routledge

SEE ALSO: *Martial Arts; Neighborhood Watch.*

BIBLIOGRAPHY

Bumgarner, Jeffrey B. *Icons of Crime Fighting: Relentless Pursuers of Justice*. Westport, CT: Greenwood Press, 2008.

Haskins, James. *The Guardian Angels*. Hillside, NJ: Enslow Publishers, 1983.

Sliwa, Curtis, and Murray Schwartz. *Street Smart: The Guardian Angel Guide to Safe Living*. Reading, MA: Addison Wesley Publishing, 1982.

Gucci

The history of the Gucci fashion house illustrates the precariousness of luxury brand names. Guccio Gucci founded his leather business in Florence in 1906, having been inspired by the beautiful leather luggage of guests at the Ritz Hotel in London, where he had worked in the kitchen. After World War II, when leather was scarce, Gucci printed his company's interlocked-G's logo on canvas luggage and accessories in bright red and green. This phenomenal success in placing high prices on what was inherently less expensive to produce fueled the imagination of the second-generation Guccis. Interlocked Gs were licensed shamelessly, and any number of products enjoyed Gucci cachet, despite degenerating quality.

In the 1970s Gucci leather loafers with a gilt horse snaffle were an expensive favorite of the nouveau riche. By the 1980s the luxury brand had become a bad joke. In the 1990s some selectivity was restored: American fashion designer and Gucci creative director Tom Ford was garnering hype for vulgar but media-generating clothes, and Gucci seemed a business reborn. In 2001 a French holding company called Pinault-Printemps-Redoute (PPR) took over Gucci, and Ford left the fashion house in 2004. Italian designer Frida Giannini became Gucci's creative director in 2006. Under her leadership, sales grew, and Gucci again regained the status of one of the world's most desired luxury brands.

Richard Martin

SEE ALSO: *Retro Fashion.*

BIBLIOGRAPHY

Jebreal, Rula. *Gucci: The Making of.* New York: Rizzoli, 2011.

McKnight, Gerald. *Gucci: A House Divided*. New York: D. I. Fine, 1987.

Guest, Christopher *(1948–)*

Actor, director, writer, and musician Christopher Guest is best known for his work on *This Is Spinal Tap* (1984) and a host other successful mockumentaries, including *Waiting for Guffman* (1997), *Best in Show* (2000), *A Mighty Wind* (2003), and *For Your Consideration* (2006). Guest's movies frequently rely on his trademark style of using documentary techniques to follow a set of self-involved, insecure characters as they seek notoriety in their self-contained worlds. *This Is Spinal Tap*, for example, spoofs a fictional metal band touring in support of an album called *Smell the Glove*; *Best in Show* satirizes contestants as they prepare for the Mayflower Kennel Club Dog Show. Guest's films have attracted a devoted cult following and have earned lavish critical praise.

Guest was born in New York City on February 5, 1948, to an American mother and a British father who passed on to his son the hereditary title Fifth Baron Haden-Guest, of Saling. Guest grew up in New York but also spent time in England, where he became a fan of comedic actor Peter Sellers and comedy troupe Monty Python. After learning several instruments, Guest toured with Arlo Guthrie and other folk musicians in the 1960s. He attended Bard College and New York University, then enrolled in the Tisch School of the Arts. In 1984 he married actress Jamie Lee Curtis; they have two children.

Guest's career in the 1970s included writing and acting for stage and screen. In 1978 he debuted his fake glam rocker character Nigel Tufnel, who later appeared in *This Is Spinal Tap*, on a television sketch comedy show. Although the movie *This Is Spinal Tap* has become a cult classic and has been preserved in the U.S. National Film Registry, it was largely ignored upon its initial release. In 1984 Guest joined *Saturday Night Live* as an actor and a writer. He played several recurring characters, including Frankie from the "Willie and Frankie" skits, which were among the best-received sketches from that season. The skit consisted of Guest's Frankie and Billy Crystal's Willie recalling excruciatingly painful injuries, at the end of which one or the other would say, "I hate when that happens."

Guest returned to the big screen in 1987 to play a six-fingered villain in *The Princess Bride*. His directorial debut was *The Big Picture* (1989), a comedy starring Kevin Bacon, with Martin Short as a strange Hollywood agent. In the late 1990s Guest turned again to the mockumentary format, directing and acting in *Waiting for Guffman*, *Best in Show*, *A Mighty Wind*, and the film-awards spoof *For Your Consideration*. All of these films pulled from a core group of experienced film and improvisational actors, including Eugene Levy (who cowrote scripts and character backstories with Guest), Parker Posey, Fred Willard, Catherine O'Hara, Bob Balaban, Jane Lynch, John Michael Higgins, Jennifer Coolidge, and Ed Begley Jr., as well Spinal Tap bandmates Harry Shearer and Michael McKean. Guest's mockumentaries are known for affording glimpses of the (very real) human propensity for unhealthy relationships, bloated egos, depressive career paths, and quixotic star searches. Along the way, he underscores people's tendencies to mistreat friends, romanticize hidden desperations, and hoard kitschy collectibles.

Stephen P. Davis

SEE ALSO: *Crystal, Billy; Folk Music; Guthrie, Arlo; Hollywood; Mockumentaries;* Monty Python's Flying Circus*;* Saturday Night Live*; Sellers, Peter; Spinal Tap.*

BIBLIOGRAPHY

Muir, John Kenneth. *Best in Show: The Films of Christopher Guest and Company*. New York: Applause Books, 2004.

Guiding Light

The longest-running soap opera in broadcast history, Procter & Gamble's (P&G's) *The Guiding Light*, premiered on radio in 1937. Although recognized as one of the many soaps developed by the legendary Irna Phillips, a 1946 lawsuit ruled that a former writer, Emmons Carlson, share credit for its creation. The veteran soap's logo, a rotating lighthouse beacon, was an apt metaphor for its significance as a guidepost in the cultural lives of generations of fans and for the genre itself. However, the daytime drama was canceled in 2009, as it could not buck the downward ratings spiral plaguing the genre.

The Reverend John Ruthledge (Arthur Peterson) served as the program's central character for years, not only counseling family and flock in the fictional hamlet of Five Points but also comforting the nation's radio audiences through economic depression and war. He also preached against such evils as racism. When the show moved production from Chicago to Los Angeles, Peterson resigned, Ruthledge was killed off, and Five Points was transformed into the town of Selby Flats, California. The original thrust of the program was left far behind, and a new set of characters, the Bauers, became the core family in *The Guiding Light*'s new incarnation. The ratings suffered and, with Hollywood thought to be the culprit, the production migrated once again, this time eastward to New York.

The television version of *The Guiding Light* premiered on CBS in 1952 and ran parallel with continuing radio broadcasts for the next four years. Meta Bauer (Jone Allison; later Ellen Demming), who would maintain a presence for four decades, emerged as a popular young heroine at this juncture. When Phillips exited the show in 1958, she eliminated Meta's stepdaughter by having her crippled and then killed in a traffic accident, eliciting a howl of protest from viewers. The proprietorial involvement of soap opera fans thus made its existence known to the creators.

The 1960s saw *The Guiding Light*'s setting shift once again, this time to the midwestern town of Springfield. Agnes Nixon, future creator of *All My Children*, took over the reins as head writer and proceeded to afflict matriarch Bertha Bauer (Charita Bauer) with cervical cancer, a trendsetting idea that had both P&G and CBS worried about negative fallout. However, the only consequence was to educate female viewers about the need for a yearly Pap smear. Nixon was also instrumental in bringing racial integration to Springfield, with Billy Dee Williams and Cicely Tyson—and later James Earl Jones and Ruby Dee—inhabiting the roles of Dr. Jim and Martha Frazier, a professional, African American couple. This new strand happily failed to validate the misgivings of executives who thought ratings might suffer; rather, it influenced other soaps to strive for racial diversity. In the 1970s the husband-and-wife writing team of Jerome and Bridget Dobson offered a timely marital rape story based on the real-life Rideout case. The installment, involving the nefarious Roger Thorpe (Michael Zaslow) and his wife Holly Lindsey (Maureen Garrett), was imitated by such programs as *Days of Our Lives* and *Another World*. In 1978 the series title was simplified to *Guiding Light*.

The writing turnover continued in the 1980s. *General Hospital* had recently set the standard for appealing to baby boomers, and *Guiding Light* was now duty-bound to follow its lead. When writer Douglas Marland left *General Hospital* due to creative differences, *Guiding Light* snapped him up. After listening to his own teenage niece's romantic fantasies, Marland paired teen Morgan Richards (Kristin Vigard; later Jennifer Cooke) with much older medical student Kelly Nelson (John Wesley Shipp) and added a jealous gold digger, Nola Reardon (Lisa Brown). While she was still a minor, Morgan slept with Kelly, but CBS balked, albeit briefly, at allowing them to marry. The story turned the coupling of innocent teenage girls with experienced older men into a soap opera staple.

The newly introduced Reardons provided a working-class presence, and after Nola manipulated Kelly into believing he had fathered her unborn child while in a drunken stupor, and as she contemplated abortion, a series of vignettes in which she imagined herself the heroine of such classic films as *Dark Victory* and *Casablanca* delighted fans and prompted mimicry on other programs. In 1982 Marland's tenure with the show ended when he challenged the dismissal of a favorite actor. During this period, scholar Michael Intintoli had ventured behind the scenes at *Guiding Light*, generating a published study titled *Taking Soaps Seriously*. Among other things, Intintoli chronicled the creators' concerns about targeting youthful demographics.

Various writers tried their hand in Marland's wake, continuing to highlight tangled teen romances. The Lewis oil dynasty and the upper-crust Spauldings had been added to the cast of characters in the early 1980s, with the Spauldings, especially, slowly displacing the Bauers at *Guiding Light*'s core. But it was brazen Reva Shayne (Kim Zimmer) who emerged as the program's vixen-turned-heroine by marrying her former father-in-law, Lewis patriarch H. B. (Larry Gates), and finally settling on her former brother-in-law Josh Lewis (Robert Newman) for an on-again, off-again, "super couple" turn.

Guiding Light began the 1990s at a cracking pace with the resurrection of villain Roger Thorpe and the death of Reva, and the pace further quickened under executive producer Jill Farren Phelps. A blackout story produced new and intriguing character links. Later, soaps such as *All My Children* and *Sunset Beach* attempted similar shakeups with their own disaster scenarios. Phelps angered fans by killing off matriarch Maureen Bauer (Ellen Parker) in response to focus group data, but the working-class Coopers, led by Vietnam veteran Buzz (Justin Deas), gained a foothold. The super-coupling of Buzz's daughter Harley (Beth Ehlers) and her fellow police officer encouraged replication a few years later on *Another World*. A planned love story between Buzz's other daughter, virginal Lucy (Sonia Satra), and drifter Matt Reardon (Kurt McKinney) did not materialize after Matt's affair with forty-something divorcée Vanessa Chamberlain (Maeve Kinkead). Fans enthralled with the May/September romance wanted more, and writers obligingly shepherded the pair into matrimony and parenthood. Lucy was eventually raped by a cross-dressing psychopath in a story line that had Internet fans fuming about women's victimization and creeping sensationalism.

Guiding Light's top-tier ratings of the 1950s and 1960s had dipped downward with the baby boom influx. Caught lagging behind in its attempts to lure this generation and then even younger viewers, the show failed to recoup its losses during the next two decades. The 1990s saw a parade of personnel, including Phelps and several older actors, axed, while Reva was brought back, first as a spirit and, later, fully embodied—an absurdity that actually gave the show a boost. However, when producer Paul Rauch went further and tried to ape the fantasy-oriented NBC soap *Days of Our Lives* by cloning Reva, Internet fans, who named the clone "Cleva," bristled.

In 2004, as budgets were slashed due to the continued ratings slide, former soap actress Ellen Wheeler was hired as executive producer. She proceeded to let several veterans go and highlighted the younger cast, including half-cousins Jonathan Randall (Tom Pelphrey) and Tammy Winslow (Stephanie Gatschet), who were romantically linked in a controversial story line. Wheeler inserted exterior locations and handheld cameras as part of her "youthification" efforts. Although many faithful viewers kept "turning on the light," the program aired its final episode on September 18, 2009.

Christine Scodari

SEE ALSO: All My Children; Another World; Casablanca; Days of Our Lives; General Hospital; *Nixon, Agnes; Phillips, Irna; Radio Drama; Soap Operas.*

BIBLIOGRAPHY

Allen, Robert Clyde. *Speaking of Soap Operas*. Chapel Hill: University of North Carolina Press, 1985.

Browne, Ray B., and Pat Browne. *The Guide to United States Popular Culture*. Bowling Green, OH: Bowling Green State University Popular Press, 2001.

Intintoli, Michael James. *Taking Soaps Seriously: The World of "Guiding Light."* New York: Praeger, 1984.

Matelski, Marilyn J. *The Soap Opera Evolution: America's Enduring Romance with Daytime Drama*. Jefferson, NC: McFarland, 1988.

Museum of Television and Radio, eds. *Worlds without End: The Art and History of the Soap Opera*. New York: Harry N. Abrams, 1997.

Poll, Julie, and Caelie M. Haines. *"Guiding Light": The Complete Family Album—Anniversary Edition*. Los Angeles: General Publishing Group, 1997.

Scodari, Christine. "'No Politics Here': Age and Gender in Soap Opera 'Cyberfandom.'" *Women's Studies in Communication*, Fall 1998, 168–187.

Waggett, Gerard J. *Soap Opera Encyclopedia*. New York: Harper Paperbacks, 1997.

Gulf Wars

Located in the Middle East along the borders of Kuwait and Iran, Iraq is about twice the size of Idaho. Historically a part of the Ottoman Empire, Iraq became a British protectorate following World War II. By 1958 the country had become a nominal republic, but Iraq was actually ruled by a series of strongmen such as Saddam Hussein. Within Iraq attention was focused on civil war for most of the 1980s. In August 1990 Iraq invaded Kuwait and declared it a province of Iraq. The importance of the Kuwaiti oil fields and the proximity of Saudi Arabia, a strong American ally and an important player in the global oil industry, made it imperative for American interests that Iraq be promptly expelled from Kuwait.

The first Gulf War is still considered a marvel of modern technology as a result of sophisticated weaponry and technological advances in how news was brought to the masses through the use of satellites, cellular phones, and new filming techniques. Throughout the Gulf War viewers were instantly transported to the deserts of Iraq and were able to witness reporters dodging Tomahawk missiles. They saw firsthand what it looked like when U.S. Patriot missiles intercepted Iraqi Scud missiles. Only two decades earlier, journalists had been forced to ship reports and videos from Vietnam by plane.

The military was also extremely different in 1990. During the Vietnam War the majority of recruits had been drafted or had signed up only because enlisting gave them a choice of military branches. The military was often rotated in and out for tours that lasted no longer than a year. By the first Gulf War, the draft had been abolished, and forces consisted of an all-volunteer military. Military officials contended that the U.S. military had become more professional and highly trained.

A new government was installed in Iraq in 2005 under a new constitution. After being convicted of multiple crimes against humanity, including the murder of 148 Shi'ites in 1982, Saddam Hussein was executed by hanging on December 30, 2006. The American presence in Iraq was reduced drastically in 2009, and the United States pulled out in mid-December 2011 as part of President Barack Obama's efforts to bring the wars in the Middle East to a close. In 2012, along with other key terrorists, Khalid Sheikh Mohammed, the alleged mastermind of the 9/11 terrorist attacks on the United States, was imprisoned in Guantánamo, awaiting trial by a military tribunal.

FIRST GULF WAR

Iraq invaded Kuwait on August 2, 1990. President George H. W. Bush announced that the invasion would not be tolerated, and King Fahd of Saudi Arabia formally asked the United States for assistance in protecting Saudi oil fields. On August 7 Operation Desert Shield commenced, and the first American forces arrived in Kuwait the same day. Those forces consisted of two F-15 squadrons, Maritime Pre-positioned Squadrons 2 and 3 (rerouted from Diego Garcia and Guam), two carrier battle groups, the 82nd Airborne Division, and the Airborne Warning and Control System (AWACS) unit. Operation Desert Storm and the air phase of the war began on January 17.

The war was carried out in a massive show of coordinated force. All forces, which numbered 12,000 troops, were under the command of General H. Norman Schwarzkopf Jr. The troops were equipped with 700 tanks, 1,400 armored fighting vehicles, and 600 artillery pieces. U.S. troops were reinforced by 32,000 Arab forces and 400 tanks. Hundreds of planes were scattered across airfields in Saudi Arabia, Turkey, and Qatar. The U.S. Navy had blockaded the area, and aircraft carriers and long-range bombers were put in place.

At the end of October, Bush doubled the forces but did not make an official announcement until November 8. On November 29 the United Nations (UN) Security Council authorized ejecting Iraq from Kuwait by "all means necessary." On December 6 the XVIII Airborne Corps, consisting of an airborne division, an air assault division, two heavy divisions, an armored cavalry regiment, and combat support services, arrived in the Persian Gulf.

In January 1991 the U.S. Congress authorized the use of force in the Persian Gulf with bipartisan support for the president's efforts. Three days later, the UN demanded that Iraq withdraw from Kuwait. The situation heated up over the course of the month. Air attacks focused on Baghdad, and the Allied forces launched an Apache strike on January 17. The following day, Israeli aircraft suffered heavy losses during an attack on an Iraqi missile site. That same day, the United States launched a major air attack from Turkey. There was much concern about the dangers involved in low-altitude airstrikes, and the British abandoned the strategy after suffering heavy losses. Schwarzkopf considered but ultimately abandoned an amphibious landing along the Kuwait/Iraq border.

By the end of January, Allied forces had recaptured Khafji. In February battleships began targeting airfields in Baghdad. On February 13 more than 200 civilians were killed in an airstrike. One week later Bush demanded that Iraq withdraw from Kuwait by noon on February 23. By that date Army Special Forces had infiltrated deep within Iraq, and a major ground attack began the following day. The Iraqi counterattack left twenty-eight Americans dead and another ninety-eight wounded. On February 26 the Iraqis fled Kuwait City. On March 2 the 24th Infantry Division met the Hammurabi Division in battle, and Americans destroyed 600 Iraqi vehicles. A permanent ceasefire led to the release of most American prisoners of war (POWs) on March 5.

With the war at an end, the UN Security Council voted to allow Saddam Hussein to retain power in Iraq. In June participants in the Gulf War were honored in a victory parade in Washington, D.C. Some $50 billion in sophisticated weaponry was sold to Middle Eastern nations after the war, setting the stage for future hostilities. While former President Bush was visiting Kuwait in April 1993, fourteen terrorists were arrested in an assassination attempt. President Bill Clinton responded by ordering a retaliatory strike against Iraq.

ROLE OF THE MEDIA

In the 1950s television became a major part of the political scene. By the 1960s, amid acceleration of the war in Vietnam, television had become the major source of news for most Americans. Well aware of the importance of the still relatively new medium, government officials quickly learned to put a "media spin" on political events. Because the media had shown the harsh realities of war, politicians blamed the media rather than themselves when public opinion turned away from support of an American presence in Vietnam and began demanding that the war be brought to an end.

Lessons learned from Vietnam became extremely important in coverage of the first Gulf War, and the government was determined to control what the media conveyed to the public. Instead of providing free access to journalists, the media were placed in press pools and kept away from the front lines in what many Americans believed to be a clear violation of the First Amendment's guarantee of freedom of the press. Communications expert Bosah Ebo contends that the media became boosters for the official government position on the Gulf War and insists that a new generation raised on video violence in games such as *Mortal Kombat* perceived of news of the war as entertainment rather than as harsh reality. The media cemented that notion by comparing missile attacks to fireworks on the Fourth of July or lit-up Christmas trees. The Kuwaiti government even hired a public relations firm to promote the image of Iraq as barbaric.

SECOND GULF WAR

With Saddam Hussein still in power in Iraq, efforts to resist what officials saw as outside interference continued in the years following the first Gulf War. The peace agreement had stipulated that all weapons of mass destruction be destroyed, but Iraqis refused to cooperate with UN inspectors. By the summer of

1998, officials had ceased even the semblance of cooperation. Citing a long history of abuses by Iraq and calling for the ousting of Saddam Hussein, Congress passed the Iraq Liberation Act, and Clinton signed it on October 31, 1998. In December the president ordered four days of air strikes against Iraq. UN weapons inspectors refused to return to Iraq. By that time it seemed likely that there would be a second war in the Persian Gulf. The likelihood of that occurrence increased drastically with the election of George W. Bush in 2000.

The terrorist attacks of 9/11 and the subsequent passage of the USA Patriot Act gave Bush extended authority to act against Iraq and other nations that harbored terrorists. In his State of the Union Address in January 2002, Bush identified Iraq as an "axis of evil" and warned Congress and the American people that he would take a proactive stance on fighting terror. He ordered Secretary of State Condoleezza Rice to work out a strategy for possible war in Iraq and began holding regular briefings with General Tommy Franks, who held responsibility for U.S. military forces in the Middle East, on ways to bring down Hussein.

Allegedly convinced that Iraq was harboring large stores of nuclear and chemical weapons, on October 10, 2002, Bush sought and won permission from Congress to use force against Iraq. The following month, the UN Security Council agreed that Iraq's refusal to cooperate with weapons inspectors constituted an international peace threat and resolved to head off another war. Within seventeen days of adopting UN Resolution 1441, UN MOVIC teams arrived in Baghdad. Even when faced with invasion, Iraq continued to refuse to cooperate with weapons inspectors. By January 1, 2003, 25,000 American troops were on their way to the Persian Gulf.

The War in Iraq did not sit well with some Americans, who saw an enormous difference in attacking Iraq after the evasion of Kuwait and attacking Iraq as a sovereign nation. Tens of thousands of protestors around the world also took to the streets to protest the invasion. Former allies agreed, and many of them refused to participate in the new attack on Iraq. Both France and Russia warned that they would veto authorization of force.

By March 5 more than 200,000 American troops, five carrier groups, and 1,000 aircraft were in place or on their way to the Middle East. On March 17 Bush issued an ultimatum instructing Saddam Hussein to leave Iraq or face invasion. Operation Iraqi Freedom officially launched on March 19 with the bombing of Baghdad. Throughout the second Gulf War, counterinsurgency efforts created major problems for U.S. forces. The marines mitigated those efforts to some extent by forming alliances with local tribes. By 2003 Saddam Hussein's regime had collapsed.

CULTURAL IMPACTS

By the early twenty-first century, the U.S. news media had evolved into what many saw as a mixture of real news and entertainment. Musicians were particularly adamant about not joining what they saw as the whitewashing of war. During a 2003 concert in London, Natalie Maines, lead singer of the Dixie Chicks, the highest-selling female group in U.S. history, announced that she was ashamed that George W. Bush was from Texas. The conservative country music community responded by boycotting the Dixie Chicks, who subsequently received death threats. The rock, rap, and hip-hop communities, on the other hand, tended to be largely supportive of critiques of the war and the Bush administration. When Bruce Springsteen called for a Bush impeachment, his next album, *Devils & Dust*, went to the top of the Billboard charts. Green Day's *American Idiot*, a scathing indictment of Bush and the war, netted the group the Grammy for Best Rock Album, six MTV Music Awards, and a Broadway rock opera. When Eminem called Bush a "monster," his album *Encore* sold more than five million copies in the United States. When Pearl Jam's *World Wide Suicide* accused Bush of "writing checks that others pay," it reached number one on Billboard's modern rock chart.

Journalists paid a heavy price for their coverage of the War in Iraq. By 2009, 255 journalists had been killed, and the majority of those were local journalists. While many were killed covering battles, most journalists were murdered by insurgents and bounty hunters. A few were killed by friendly fire. The war also took a heavy financial toll on the media. American networks spent from $5 million to $10 million a year on coverage. By 2009 only CNN and the BBC maintained a full presence in Iraq.

A plethora of memoirs and journalistic accounts chronicled the War in Iraq, but there was no fiction that was considered definitive. A number of movies dealt with the war. The best known of those was Kathryn Bigelow's *The Hurt Locker*, an examination of an elite American bomb squad. The film won six Academy Awards, including Best Picture of 2008. *Turtles Can Fly* (2004), which was shot in Iraq after the ousting of Saddam Hussein, depicts Kurdish refugees on the eve of the American invasion of Iraq. *The War Tapes* (2006) uses footage shot by National Guard troops serving in Iraq. *The Ground Truth* (2006) follows all stages of the War in Iraq. The documentary *No End in Sight* (2007) consists of interviews with critics of the decision to go to war in Iraq.

Elizabeth Rholetter Purdy

SEE ALSO: *Academy Awards; Cell Phones; Eminem; Grammy Awards; Green Day; MTV; 9/11; Obama, Barack; Pearl Jam; Satellites; Springsteen, Bruce; Television; Video Games; Vietnam; War in Afghanistan.*

BIBLIOGRAPHY

Atkinson, Rick. *Crusade: The Untold Story of the Persian Gulf War.* New York: Houghton Mifflin, 1993.

CIA. "Iraq." *World Factbook.* Accessed May 2012. Available from https://www.cia.gov/library/publications/the-world-factbook/geos/iz.html

Cordesman, Anthony H. *The War after the War: Strategic Lessons of Iraq and Afghanistan.* Washington, DC: CSIS Press, 2004.

Denton, Robert E. *The Media and the Persian Gulf War.* Westport, CT: Praeger, 1993.

Ebo, Bosah. "War as Popular Culture: The Gulf Conflict and the Technology of Illusionary Entertainment." *Journal of American Culture* 18, no. 3 (1995).

Felman, Marc D. *The Military/Media Clash and the New Principles of War, Media Spin.* Maxwell Air Force Base, AL: School of Advanced Airpower Studies, Air University, 1992.

Gause, F. Gregory, III. *The International Relations of the Persian Gulf.* New York: Cambridge University Press, 2010.

Hoskins, Andrew. *Televising War: From Vietnam to Iraq.* New York: Continuum, 2004.

Katz, J. "Rock, Rap and Movies Bring You the News." *Rolling Stone*, March 5, 1992, 33.

Kreps, Sarah E. *Coalitions of Convenience: United States Military Interventions after the Cold War*. New York: Oxford University Press, 2011.

Lebovic, James H. *The Limits of U.S. Military Capability: Lessons from Vietnam and Iraq*. Baltimore, MD: Johns Hopkins University Press, 2010.

Leslie, Paul. *The Gulf War as Popular Entertainment: An Analysis of the Military-Industrial Media Complex*. Lewiston, NY: E. Mellen Press, 1997.

Nacos, Brigitte L.; Yaeli Bloch-Elkon; and Robert Y. Shapiro. *Selling Fear: Counterterrorism, the Media, and Public Opinion*. Chicago: University of Chicago Press, 2011.

Osgood, Kenneth, and Andrew K. Frank, eds. *Selling War in a Media Age: The Presidency and Public Opinion in the American Century*. Gainesville: University Press of Florida, 2010.

Pillar, Paul R. *Intelligence and U.S. Foreign Policy: Iraq, 9/11, and Misguided Reform*. New York: Columbia University Press, 2011.

Slocum, J. David. *Hollywood and War: The Film Reader*. New York: Routledge, 2006.

Stewart, Richard W. *War in the Persian Gulf: Operation Desert Shield and Desert Storm, August 1990–March 1991*. Washington, DC: Center of Military History, U.S. Army, 2010.

Thrall, A. Trevor. *War in the Media Age*. Cresskill, NJ: Hampton, 2000.

Thussu, Daya Kishan, and Des Freedman, eds. *War and the Media: Reporting Conflict 24/7*. Thousand Oaks, CA: Sage, 2003.

Tyler, Patrick. *A World of Trouble: The White House and the Middle East—From the Cold War to the War on Terror*. New York: Farrar, Straus & Giroux, 2009.

Tyrangiel, Josh, and Andrea Sachs. "In the Line of Fire." *Time*, May 29, 2006, 60–65.

Gunsmoke

In a 1993 *TV Guide* article, *Gunsmoke*, the longest-running Western drama, as well as the longest-running prime-time show with continuing characters in history (1955–1975), was named one of the all-time best television programs. The magazine was succinct: "No contest, this was THE TV Western." The series marked a revolutionary approach to a familiar Western formula, and its popularity, which led to extensive merchandising that included Matt Dillon dolls, *Gunsmoke* trading cards, and comic books, precipitated a rash of TV Westerns—so much so that at one point there were approximately thirty prime-time contributions to the genre.

RADIO BROADCASTS

Originating as the vanguard of the adult Western, the show had its genesis as a CBS radio drama that began in 1952 and endeavored to bring realism—and considerable violence—to standard heroics. Indeed, the show claims in its opening narration to be "the story of the violence that moved west with young America, and the story of a man who moved with it." The premise involved the denizens of Dodge City, Kansas, circa 1873, who are protected by Marshal Matt Dillon (William Conrad), a tough but fair lawman, who often struggles to reconcile the differences between the law and his personal feelings. Dillon is assisted by the crusty but soft-hearted Doc Adams (Howard McNear) and loved by Kitty Russell (Georgia Ellis), the owner of the Long Branch Saloon.

Praised as being better acted and scripted than other radio Westerns, the show enjoyed immense popularity, and its twice-weekly broadcasts were transmitted to U.S. forces abroad during the Korean War. The recipient of several broadcasting awards, *Gunsmoke* had been extensively researched by its writers, who injected such a sense of veracity into the scripts that the head of the chamber of commerce of Dodge City is said to have written the producers inquiring as to what years Dillon served as sheriff.

TELEVISION SHOW

While the radio version continued to run until 1961, the television version of the show debuted as a half-hour drama on September 10, 1955, introduced by John Wayne as "a new kind of Western." And so it proved. The opening episode, titled "Matt Gets It," has its leading character getting shot and, as one critic described it, "left lying in the dusty streets of Dodge, ministered to by a cheap dance hall girl and a seedy looking doctor, while his crippled deputy stood by." This was a gritty and realistic departure from the formula wherein the heroes of other popular shows such as *The Lone Ranger* and *Hopalong Cassidy* were always larger than life and escaped such indignity.

Gunsmoke. *The cast of* Gunsmoke *circa 1962 included, clockwise from left, James Arness, Milburn Stone, Amanda Blake, Ken Curtis, and Burt Reynolds. The television version of* Gunsmoke *ran for twenty seasons from 1955 to 1975.* HULTON ARCHIVE/GETTY IMAGES.

The television incarnation also featured different actors. While the radio actors had been considered, the producers felt that the visual medium made strongly attractive physical attributes a major requirement, particularly for the role of Dillon. Among the several replacements considered, who were either rejected or who themselves turned down the offer because TV was still viewed by some as an unworthy medium, were Raymond Burr, Richard Boone, and Robert Stack. While the rumor that Wayne was approached to play Dillon was without foundation, the big screen's most famous Western star did suggest a young actor who he had worked with named James Arness.

ACTORS

Beyond bit parts, Arness's claim to fame was playing the title character in director Howard Hawks's sci-fi classic, *The Thing from Another World* (1951). His commanding 6-foot, 7-inch frame and strong, silent demeanor, however, secured him the role. Feature film veteran Milburn Stone was cast as Doc Adams, and Amanda Blake inherited the role of Kitty, both of them staying with the show for most of its run.

Prior to his feature film career and TV star turn in *McCloud*, Dennis Weaver played Dillon's first deputy, Chester Goode. He was replaced in 1964 by Ken Curtis, a former singer with the Tommy Dorsey band who played scruffy hillbilly deputy Festus Haggen. Also of note was Burt Reynolds's pre-superstar turn as half-breed blacksmith Quint Asper from 1962 to 1965, during which time many opportunities were found to feature him without his shirt. After Reynolds's departure, Roger Ewing joined the show as the young novice, followed by Buck Taylor (son of actor Dub Taylor), who arrived in 1967 to play the humble gunsmith Newly O'Brien.

Debuting opposite the popular *George Gobel Show*, television's *Gunsmoke* was not an immediate hit, but its popularity rose steadily, taking it to number eight in the ratings in its second season. By its third season (1957–1958), it displaced the ever-popular *I Love Lucy* to become number one and remained there for the next four seasons. The series and its cast were all nominated for Emmys that year, with the show winning for best dramatic series. (Weaver later won an Emmy in 1959, as did Stone in 1968.)

RADIO AND TELEVISION DIFFERENCES

While the majority of the *Gunsmoke* radio episodes conveniently served as fodder for the teleplays, their brutality had to be toned down for the small screen. Whereas Conrad's Dillon was a hardened, abrasive, and often pessimistic loner who could make tragic mistakes, Arness rendered the television Dillon as a man of few words, vulnerable, often restraining his personal feelings in order to do the right thing, and never making a mistake. Likewise, whereas Ellis's Kitty was portrayed as a toughened whore and barfly who was nevertheless Dillon's confidante, Blake became "Miss" Kitty, the owner of the Long Branch Saloon who had both soft and tough characteristics.

Owing to the restraint of the writing, many have speculated over the Dillon–Miss Kitty friendship, but the chemistry between them, and the many plot lines requiring their sacrifices for each other, indicated deep and abiding love. That they never married is easily explained: as long as he remained a lawman, Dillon would not want to risk leaving Kitty a widow. Finally, whereas McNear's Adams could be guilty of greed and cynicism on radio, Stone transformed the television character into an irreproachable ideal of the dedicated, kindly, and wise country doctor.

Like the radio show before it, the substance of *Gunsmoke* lay in its morality, which pitted the good people of Dodge City against the ugly forces of lawlessness. In remaining true to a realistic approach, however, the writers not only avoided sentimentality and pat endings but also made sure that, just as in life, the evildoers were not always brought to justice. Then, too, in response to the antiviolence movement of the 1970s, the show's emphasis shifted from physical confrontation and gunplay to dramatic situations that were more character- and issue-driven. *Gunsmoke* began dealing with race, religion, and other social conflicts and evolved into a sort of dramatic anthology series with the interaction between the regular characters taking a back seat to conflicts faced by characters (often played by guest stars) who were passing through Dodge.

CANCELLATION UPROAR

Despite these changes, the central characters and setting of *Gunsmoke* took on a mythic status in America's collective consciousness. This lofty position was confirmed by events in the late 1960s. Despite its expansion to an hour and the transition to color by 1966, the show so declined in ratings that CBS decided to cancel it at the end of the 1966–1967 season, the producers claiming it to be the victim of program fatigue. Public response, however, was immediate and vehement. Letter-writing campaigns were mounted, and CBS affiliates in the Midwest threatened to boycott all the network's programs unless *Gunsmoke* returned. Senator Robert C. Byrd even went so far as to criticize the network's decision from the floor of Congress. The end result was that CBS president William Paley interceded and in a last-ditch effort switched the show to Monday nights, where it miraculously zoomed in popularity until its run finally ended in 1975. It was the last prime-time Western series on television.

TELEVISION MOVIES

After its initial run, *Gunsmoke* was revived in a succession of TV movies, beginning with *Gunsmoke: Return to Dodge* in 1987, which up to that date was the most expensive made-for-TV movie of all time. Costing $3.5 million, it featured Arness, Blake, and Taylor. The story has Kitty, who had left Dodge a year before the series' cancellation, back in her hometown, New Orleans. Dillon has retired from the law to become a trapper, and O'Brien is the new sheriff.

The TV movie's popularity led to four further sequels in the early 1990s. In *Gunsmoke: The Last Apache* (1990), Dillon learns that he had sired a daughter by Mike (Michael Learned), the woman he had become romantically involved with while suffering from amnesia in an earlier episode of the series, and sets out to look for the girl, who has been taken by a Native American tribe. The movie was dedicated to Blake, who had recently died from AIDS. *Gunsmoke: To the Last Man* (1992) concerns feuding in the Pleasant Valley Wars of the 1880s and the death of Mike. *Gunsmoke: The Long Ride* was broadcast in 1993, while the last, *Gunsmoke: One Man's Justice* (1994), finds Dillon owning his own ranch. It also reveals details of his background and the fact that he had been motivated to become a lawman because his father, a Texas Ranger, had been shot in the back and killed.

SUPPORTING CAST

Gunsmoke retained an extensive supporting cast of townspeople and supplied many character actors with the opportunity to play a variety of roles over the years. Victor French, later of *Little House on the Prairie* and *Highway to Heaven* fame, played several different characters in the course of the run and directed five episodes. Morgan Woodward, Jack Elam, Denver Pyle, Jim Davis, Claude Akins, Strother Martin, and Lane Bradbury appeared in multiple roles, while one of Jeanette Nolan's roles—as itinerant Dirty Sally—resulted in a short-lived spin-off series in 1974. (Interestingly, having been rejected for the television series, Conrad went on to star in *Cannon, Nero Wolfe*, and *Jake and the Fat Man* on TV, while McNear was Floyd the barber in TV's *The Andy Griffith Show*.)

Gunsmoke was in television's top ten most watched programs for multiple seasons and was named in first or second place as best Western series by the *Motion Picture Daily* annual television poll throughout its run. A 1966 episode titled "The Jailer," starring Bette Davis, was ranked in the top half by *TV Guide*'s 100 Greatest (Television) Episodes of All Time. All the leading actors were inducted into the National Cowboy Hall of Fame, while Arness received an International Broadcasting Award as man of the year in 1973 and in 1989 was voted the number six television star of all time by *People* magazine. The series also won several awards for writing and technical achievement in the course of its long run.

Rick Moody

SEE ALSO: The Andy Griffith Show*; Burr, Raymond; Davis, Bette; Dorsey, Tommy; Emmy Awards; Hawks, Howard; Hopalong Cassidy;* I Love Lucy*; The Lone Ranger; Made-for-Television Movies;* People*; Radio; Reynolds, Burt; Television;* TV Guide*; Wayne, John; The Western.*

BIBLIOGRAPHY

Barabas, SuzAnne, and Gabor Barabas. *Gunsmoke*. Jefferson, NC: McFarland, 1990.

Brooks, Tim, and Earle Marsh. *The Complete Dictionary to Prime Time Network and Cable TV Shows, 1946–Present*, 9th ed. New York: Ballantine Books, 2007.

Guthrie, Arlo *(1947–)*

Folksinger Arlo Guthrie has preserved the musical and political heritage he learned from his father, Woody Guthrie. He debuted at the 1967 Newport Folk Festival, where he introduced the talking blues composition "Alice's Restaurant Massacree," an eighteen-minute antiwar song that became a favorite among draft resistors and provided the title for both his first album and a feature film in 1969. His popularity soared with his appearance at Woodstock in 1969, and it peaked with the release of the single "City of New Orleans" (1972).

In the mid-1970s Guthrie reembraced his folk roots, touring and recording with the band Shenandoah until the early 1990s. In 1991 he opened a community center for HIV/AIDS patients at the Stockbridge, Massachusetts, church in which much of *Alice's Restaurant* was filmed. After landing a role in Steven Bochco's short-lived television series *Byrds of Paradise* (1994), Guthrie released *Mystic Journey* (1996) on his own label, Rising Son Records. He produced and toured with An American Scrapbook, a symphonic arrangement of his own and other American folk songs between 1998 and 2004. In 2006 Guthrie and his family rode the train from Chicago to New Orleans, Louisiana, on a tour titled "Arlo Guthrie and Friends: Ridin' on the City of New Orleans." It raised more than $140,000, which was put toward helping New Orleans recover from the devastation of Hurricane Katrina. Since the 1990s he has also toured frequently under his own name, often playing with members of his family.

In his early years, Guthrie's politics were decidedly left wing, but beginning in the 1990s, he began to shift toward libertarianism, and he endorsed Ron Paul for the 2008 Republican Party nomination for president. Guthrie frequently posts political comments on his website. Although these musings generally are aligned with conservative values, he spoke in 2011 on behalf of Wisconsin public-employee unions that were under fire from Republican lawmakers.

Bryan Garman

SEE ALSO: *AIDS; Bochco, Steven; Folk Music; Guthrie, Woody; Hurricane Katrina; Newport Jazz and Folk Festivals; Woodstock.*

BIBLIOGRAPHY

Guthrie, Arlo. *Mooses Come Walking*. San Francisco: Chronicle Books 1995.

Harrington, Richard. "Arlo Guthrie's Storied Career." *Washington Post*, August 12, 2005.

Guthrie, Woody *(1912–1967)*

Folksinger, composer, writer, and homegrown radical, Woody Guthrie became the self-appointed folk spokesman for Dust Bowl migrants and agricultural workers during the Great Depression. His pro-labor, anticapitalist stance attracted many radical and left-leaning liberals during the 1930s and 1940s, but his lasting fame came from his influence on the folk revival of the 1960s, especially on Bob Dylan. Guthrie was best known for ballads, such as "This Land Is Your Land," "This Train Is Bound for Glory," and "The Union Maid," and his music extended beyond the bounds of radical protest to become American folk classics.

PROTEST THROUGH SINGING AND WRITING

Born in Okemah, Oklahoma, in 1912 and named in honor of the presidential nominee Woodrow Wilson, Guthrie spent his childhood in several different households in various parts of Oklahoma and Texas. His mother suffered from a neurological disease called Huntington's chorea (or Huntington's disease, the same disease with which Guthrie himself later struggled for fifteen years before finally succumbing to it in 1967), and he was often left to his own devices. In 1933, at the age of twenty-one, he married his best friend's sister, but a necessary search for work, coupled with a restless nature, took him on the road, traveling along with many other "Okies" and "Arkies"—displaced farmers and others—who headed to California in search of work.

In Los Angeles, Guthrie found work with his cousin Jack "Oklahoma" Guthrie, the singing cowboy, and together they presented *The Oklahoma and Woody Show* on KFVD. Woody's popularity grew as he attracted an audience of transplanted Southwesterners who enjoyed his traditional songs and "cornpone philosophy." He also became politically educated at KFVD, encouraged by the station owner, Frank Burke, who also produced the radical newspaper the *Light*, for which Guthrie occasionally wrote.

Guthrie's national notoriety developed when he wrote and performed songs about the influx of Dust Bowl migrants into California and contributed to the communist newspaper *People's World*. In 1940 he released his first album, *Dust Bowl Ballads*. The album included "I Ain't Got No Home in This World Anymore," a parody of a traditional Baptist hymn; "Vigilante Man," describing the vigilante tactics of farm labor employers; "Pretty Boy Floyd," about the exploits of the Oklahoma outlaw Charles Arthur Floyd; "Goin' Down This Road Feelin' Bad," a song used in the film version of *The Grapes of Wrath* (1940); and "Tom Joad," a song about that film's hero figure that Guthrie wrote after seeing it.

Guthrie's reputation as a spokesman for the down-and-out was reinforced through his association with folklorist Alan Lomax of the Library of Congress and singer Pete Seeger. With Lomax, Guthrie recorded songs and stories for the Library of Congress, and with Seeger he joined the Almanac Singers, a folk-oriented protest group. Lomax, Guthrie, and Seeger collaborated on a collection of folk songs published as *Hard Hitting Songs for Hard Hit People* (1967). Guthrie also appeared on numerous radio programs, including *Pipe Smoking Time* and *Cavalcade of America*. Hired for one month by the Bonneville Power Administration in 1941, he composed twenty-six songs about the hydroelectric construction projects of the Pacific Northwest, including "Roll on Columbia," "The Grand Coulee Dam," and "Pastures of Plenty." In 1943 he published the autobiographical *Bound for Glory* (made into a 1976 film by Hal Ashby, starring David Carradine as Guthrie).

Throughout the late 1940s and early 1950s, Guthrie continued to write protest songs, such as "1913 Massacre," about a strike in Calumet, Michigan, and "Deportee" (also known as "Plane Wreck at Los Gatos"), about a plane crash involving Mexican deportees. He also began writing songs for children, such as "Take Me for a Ride in the Car-Car" and "Put Your Finger in the Air." Guthrie's *People's World* columns were collected in *Woody Sez* (1975), and a second literary work, *Seeds of Man*, appeared in 1976. A volume of previously unpublished writings, *Pastures of Plenty: A Self-Portrait*, was published in 1990.

Throughout his writings, Guthrie expressed his belief in justice and his faith that it could be brought to prevail through action. For him personally, action took the form of singing and writing, best exemplified by the slogan proudly displayed on his guitar: "This Machine Kills Fascists." His sense of the role of a folksinger as a crusader for the less fortunate and as a critic of society's oppressors and manipulators had greater influence on the course of American popular music than his style of singing or any one composition. His philosophy—that "a folk song is what's wrong and how to fix it"—permeates the protest music of the late twentieth century, from anti–Vietnam War songs of the 1960s to songs of victimization in the 1990s.

WIDESPREAD INFLUENCE

From the late 1950s onward, Guthrie's influence on a successive crop of folksingers was evident. It began with "Ramblin'" Jack Elliott (who often claimed to be Guthrie's son); the Weavers, who had a national hit with the Guthrie song "So Long, It's Been Good to Know Ya"; and Dylan, who arrived at his fascination for Guthrie through Elliott. Dylan visited the dying Guthrie in New York in 1961 and composed "Song to Woody," a tribute using the melody of Guthrie's "1913 Massacre." Guthrie's influence on Dylan is most readily seen in the younger man's early albums, such as *Bob Dylan* (1962), *The Freewheelin' Bob Dylan* (1963), and *The Times They Are A-Changin'* (1964), as well as in the style of the monochrome cover photograph of the latter album. Protest music of the 1960s owed much to this remarkable individual, whose compositions were revived by new folk groups, such as Peter, Paul, and Mary, while Phil Ochs and Barry McGuire adopted Guthrie's style in their own original songs. Guthrie's son, Arlo, began performing in the 1960s, presenting his father's work as well as his own songs, such as "Alice's Restaurant" (1967).

Reverence for Guthrie continued into the late 1980s and 1990s, with such performers as Bruce Springsteen and John Mellencamp attributing their own development to his influence in a documentary tribute recording titled *A Vision Shared: A Tribute to Woody Guthrie and Leadbelly* (1988). Springsteen credited Guthrie with the development of his own social consciousness: "For me, Woody Guthrie was that sense of idealism, along with a sense of realism that said, 'maybe you can't save the world, but you can change the world.'" Guthrie's influence on Springsteen is best demonstrated in *Nebraska* (1982) and the Dust Bowl–inspired *The Ghost of Tom Joad* (1995). Mellencamp, believing that later contributions to protest music pale in comparison to Guthrie's, said, "None of us are ever going to make the impact that Woody made." Mellencamp's pro–family farmer songs on *Scarecrow* (1985) illustrate Guthrie's impact, and Mellencamp even sports a Guthriesque antifascist statement on his guitar in the music video "Your Life Is Now" (1998). *A Vision Shared* also features, among others, Emmylou Harris, Arlo Guthrie, Seeger, and the Irish rock band U2, whose lead singer Bono stated that "the thing Woody Guthrie left behind to me was a sense of the poetry of ordinary lives . . . I see Woody Guthrie as a poet."

In 1998 a new collection of Guthrie songs, *Mermaid Avenue*, unveiled lyrics written in the late 1940s and early 1950s, with music composed by the British singer-songwriter Billy Bragg and the American neocountry rock band Wilco. Augmented with performances by Natalie Merchant, the album is the result of a collaboration between the musicians and Guthrie's daughter, Nora, who initiated the project and opened up the Guthrie archives to them. The result introduced Guthrie's music to yet another generation of listeners. A follow-up album, *Mermaid Avenue Vol. II*, was released in 2000, followed by *Vol. III* in 2012.

Charles J. Shindo

SEE ALSO: *Dylan, Bob; Folk Music;* The Grapes of Wrath*; The Great Depression; Guthrie, Arlo; Labor Unions; Leadbelly; Mellencamp, John; Ochs, Phil; Peter, Paul, and Mary; Protest Groups; Seeger, Pete; Springsteen, Bruce; U2; Vietnam; The Weavers.*

BIBLIOGRAPHY

Cray, Ed, and Studs Terkel. *Ramblin' Man: The Life and Times of Woody Guthrie*. New York: Norton, 2004.

Greenway, John. "Woody Guthrie: The Land, the Man, the Understanding." *American West* 3, no. 4 (1966): 25–30, 74–78.

Guthrie, Woody. *Woody Guthrie Folk Songs*, ed. Pete Seeger. New York: Ludlow Music, 1963.

Guthrie, Woody; Marjorie Guthrie; and Harold Leventhal, eds. *The Woody Guthrie Songbook*. New York: Grosset and Dunlap, 1976.

Klein, Joe. *Woody Guthrie: A Life*. New York: Alfred A. Knopf, 1980.

Miller, Terry E. *Folk Music in America: A Reference Guide*. New York: Garland, 1986.

Reuss, Richard A. "Woody Guthrie and His Folk Tradition." *Journal of American Folklore* 83, no. 329 (1970): 273–303.

Yurchenco, Henrietta, and Marjorie Guthrie. *A Mighty Hard Road*. New York: McGraw-Hill, 1970.

Guy, Buddy *(1936–)*

Perhaps the greatest showman to ever play blues guitar, Buddy Guy is a crucial link between blues and rock and roll. Virtually unknown to the general public for most of his early career, Guy has been universally hailed by rock musicians from the United States and Great Britain. Guitarists Stevie Ray Vaughan and Jimi Hendrix cited him as a prime influence, and Eric Clapton stated in *Musician Magazine* in 1986 that Guy "is by far and without a doubt the best guitar player alive."

Buddy Guy. *Buddy Guy performs in France in 1978. His music connected that of Chicago blues pioneers and modern blues-based rock guitarists.* DAVID REDFERN/STAFF/REDFERNS/GETTY IMAGES.

The reason for such praise stems not only from Guy's technical skill but also from his astounding and often unpredictable antics onstage. He holds nothing back during a performance, torturing his guitar into sonic oblivion and singing himself into a frenzy. Although others have been known to play with their teeth and parade through audiences, Guy was one of the first to do so. Before he came to Chicago, blues was played sitting down.

MUSIC CAREER BEGINS

Born on July 30, 1936, in Lettsworth, Louisiana, into a family of sharecroppers, George "Buddy" Guy spent much of his spare time during childhood listening to Muddy Waters, Howlin' Wolf, and Sonny Boy Williamson on the radio. As Guy grew older, he began hanging out at the Temple Roof Garden, a club in Baton Rouge, where he would see B. B. King; Bobby Bland; and his biggest inspiration, Guitar Slim.

Guitar Slim (Eddie Jones) had a number one rhythm-and-blues single with "The Things (That) I Used to Do" in 1954 and was the top draw of the southern Chitlin' Circuit of black clubs. Slim was a wild man on stage, wearing outlandish costumes with matching wigs, swinging from the rafters and dancing through crowds on a 150-foot guitar cable. "When I saw him . . . I'd made up my mind," Guy confirms in Donald E. Wilcox's biography, *Damn Right I've Got the Blues*. "I wanted to play like B. B. but act like Guitar Slim." Around this time an uncle bought Guy his first real guitar.

By the mid-1950s Guy was playing around Louisiana behind local musicians "Big Poppa" John Tilley and Raful Neal. In 1957 he recorded a demo tape at radio station WXOK in Baton Rouge and decided to try to make it big in Chicago. He brought his tape to Chess Records, the top label in town, but got nowhere. After months of struggling he finally got to sit in with Otis Rush. He began to play regular gigs around town, and his frantic stage show soon set him apart from the crowd.

UNIQUE STYLE BRINGS RECOGNITION

"Buddy's act was not premeditated or contrived," Wilcox writes. "His style was merely a natural by-product of being self-taught, having a compulsion to play, and being insecure enough to feel that if he didn't dazzle and hypnotize his audience with the flamboyant techniques he'd seen work for Guitar Slim, he'd be buried by competition from guitarists who were better technicians." Word of the crazy kid from Louisiana spread, and Chess producer and songwriter Willie Dixon soon recognized Guy's talent. Dixon brought him in and immediately put him to work as a session musician with Waters, Howlin' Wolf, Williamson, and Koko Taylor.

Chess tried recording Guy as a solo artist but failed to find the right niche. R&B ballads, jazz instrumentals, soul, and novelty dance tunes were all recorded during the early 1960s, but none was released as a single. Guy wanted to record a set similar to his live shows, boosting his guitar's volume and cutting loose, but Chess would not take the chance. Meanwhile, Guy's reputation spread to Great Britain, where young rockers such as Clapton and the Rolling Stones were seeking out Chess singles and learning about Guy. His tour of England in 1965 brought exposure to a generation of musicians eager to soak it up, repackage it, and turn around and sell it to the U.S. public as the hip new thing. "[Chess founder] Leonard Chess would eventually realize his mistake in not recognizing Buddy's appeal in the clubs, or that much of the appeal of the British rock bands was based on the kind of 'noise' that Buddy was producing live," Wilcox notes. "Still, Chess had not yet released a single album by Buddy Guy. What saved Buddy at Chess was his versatility."

SLOW START

Guy was invited to play with harmonica player Junior Wells on his Delmark album *Hoodoo Man Blues* in 1965. Delmark, a small jazz label, was not interested in producing singles and encouraged the band to play as if it were a live show. The result was the first recording of a Chicago blues band in its natural environment, and the album became the best-selling record in the label's history. On the first pressing Guy was listed only as Friendly Chap because of his contract with Chess.

After leaving Chess in frustration in the late 1960s, Guy recorded for Vanguard Records and continued to play with Wells. In 1972 Clapton convinced Atlantic Records to record Guy and Wells, and *Buddy Guy and Junior Wells Play the Blues* was the result. The album should have been Guy's breakthrough, but Clapton's work as producer was hampered by his heroin addiction. The album was not completed for two years and was virtually ignored.

Guy continued to record on various small labels, often in Europe, through the 1970s and 1980s, and he bought the Checkerboard Lounge on Chicago's South Side. He later opened Buddy Guy's Legends just south of Chicago's Loop, which soon became the city's premier club. Guy was known to join in on the Monday night jam sessions when he was in town.

Guy often jammed with prominent guitarists such as Clapton, Vaughan, and Robert Cray, and his higher profile helped him land a contract with England's Silvertone Records, which released *Damn Right, I've Got the Blues* in 1991. With guests such as Clapton and his fellow British musician Jeff Beck, the album was criticized by purists as leaning too far toward rock. Still, it won a Grammy Award as Best Contemporary Blues Album, and Guy collected five W. C. Handy Awards in 1992. The next year he was the second musician to receive *Billboard*'s Century Award, the magazine's highest honor for artistic achievement. Guy recorded with Silvertone through 1998, influencing a new generation of young guitarists, including Jonny Lang and Kenny Wayne Shepherd.

PRODUCTIVITY CONTINUES

The twenty-first century brought Guy both recognition for a lengthy and impressive career as well as more award-winning new recordings. *Rolling Stone* named him number thirty on its list of the 100 Greatest Guitarists of All-Time. His 2001 release *Sweet Tea* was his first to win the number one blues album award from *Billboard* and has since been called "one of the most profound blues recordings of the last decade" by *Guitar Player* magazine. In 2003 he was awarded the National Medal of the Arts, the highest government award for art and art patrons, and in 2005 he was inducted into the Rock and Roll Hall of Fame. He followed these accolades with his 2008 album *Skin Deep*, his second number one blues album and, at the time, the highest-charting album of his career, coming in at number sixty-eight on the Billboard 200.

Guy's 2010 album *Living Proof* entered the charts at number forty-six, became his third number one blues album, and won the 2011 Grammy—his sixth—for Best Contemporary Blues Album. He continued to spread the love of blues to yet another generation: approached before a show in 2011 by twelve-year-old Quinn Sullivan to autograph a guitar, Guy called Sullivan up onstage to play with him that evening and went on to produce Sullivan's debut album and promote the young star. The two often toured together.

Jon Klinkowitz

SEE ALSO: *Bland, Bobby "Blue"; Blues; Clapton, Eric; Cray, Robert; Grammy Awards; Handy, W. C.; Hendrix, Jimi; Howlin' Wolf; Jazz; King, B. B.; Rhythm and Blues; Rock and Roll; The Rolling Stones; Vaughan, Stevie Ray; Waters, Muddy.*

BIBLIOGRAPHY

DeCurtis, Anthony. "Living Legends." *Rolling Stone*, September 21, 1989, 89–99.

Guy, Buddy, with David Ritz. *When I Left Home: My Story.* Boston: Da Capo Press, 2012.

Murray, Charles Shaar. "Strat Cats." *Guitar World*, July 1991, 80ff.

Obrecht, Jas, ed. *Blues Guitar: The Men Who Made the Music.* San Francisco: GPI Books, 1990.

Whiteis, David. "Buddy Guy: 50 Million Riff Thieves Can't Be Wrong." *Down Beat*, October 1991, 22–23.

Wilcox, Donald E.; Buddy Guy; and Rick Siciliano. *Damn Right I've Got the Blues: Buddy Guy and the Blues Roots of Rock-and-Roll.* San Francisco: Woodford Press, 1993.

Gymnastics

Once an exercise for warriors preparing for battle, gymnastics has evolved into one of the most avidly followed Olympic events and a popular conditioning activity for all ages. Though male gymnasts are admired for their strength and skill, it is largely women's gymnastics that captivates audiences and inspires thousands of children to take up the sport.

ORIGINS OF MODERN GYMNASTICS

Derived from the Greek word *gymnos* (naked), the combination of acrobatics and tumbling that we call gymnastics was devised by the Greeks as an exercise to balance the mind and body and learn skills useful in battle. Other ancient cultures, notably the Chinese, Indians, and Persians, performed similar conditioning exercises. It was in the early eighteenth century that the benefits of gymnastics were popularized in Europe when Friedrich Jahn established *Turnvereins* (gymnastics clubs) all over Germany. American clubs in the style of Jahn's clubs were opened in Cincinnati, Ohio, in 1848 and in St. Louis, Missouri, in 1865.

By 1881 the European Gymnastics Federation was established in Belgium (renamed International Gymnastics Federation, or FIG, in 1921), and gymnastics became an Olympic event in 1896. Women's Olympic gymnastics began in 1928. Olympic events involve performing athletic feats of leaping, swinging, and tumbling on a variety of apparatus, judged on the basis of the Code of Points, established and regularly updated by the FIG. For men there are six types of official apparatus: the floor exercise, the pommel horse, the still rings, the vault, the horizontal bar, and the parallel bars. Women do the floor exercise as well, along with the vault, the uneven parallel bars, and the balance beam.

Gymnastics underwent an enormous leap in popularity in the early 1970s. In the 1972 Olympics, Soviet Union gymnast Olga Korbut dazzled both judges and spectators around the world with her athletic and aggressive style, performing a back flip on the balance beam for the first time ever. In 1976 Romanian Nadia Comaneci became the first person in history to earn perfect scores at an Olympics gymnastic event.

The dramatic performances of these skilled athletes and many others created a shift in perspective for women's gymnastics. No longer simply a demonstration of graceful motion juxtaposed with the male gymnast's display of power and strength, women's gymnastics became a powerful sport in its own right. The new respect for women gymnasts was accompanied by a surge in the popularity of gymnastics in the general population. In 1972 approximately 15,000 amateur athletes learned acrobatics and tumbling at gymnastics clubs in the United States. A decade later there were about 150,000, and the number continues to increase considerably after each Summer Olympics. Whether it is Olympic hopefuls training to compete or children learning to tumble at the local community center, gymnastics has taken its place in American society.

HAZARDS OF COMPETITIVE GYMNASTICS

The new popularity of the sport caused many to be concerned. Competitive gymnastics can be a grueling sport, causing injuries to muscle, bone, and ligament. A 1990 study of Swedish male gymnasts found that they had as many degenerated discs in their spines as the average sixty-five-year-old man. While male gymnasts reach their peak of performance in their late teens and early twenties, female gymnasts peak while they are thirteen to sixteen, a time when bones and other bodily structures have not fully formed. Some trainers and parents worry about a dangerous "female athlete triad": eating disorders, delayed onset of menstruation, and premature osteoporosis. It is not uncommon for young gymnasts to begin their training at age five. By the time they are teenagers, they may be working out for five hours a day. Such demanding schedules, combined with supercompetitive coaching, have pushed young gymnasts to injury and beyond. Small slips while practicing flips and leaps have resulted in several cases of paralysis, the most famous being Sang Lan of China, who fell in a practice session during the 1998 Goodwill Games, breaking her neck.

In response to concerns about the physical and emotional effects of competition on very young girls, the Olympic Committee has changed its rules, making sixteen the minimum age for Olympic teams. Parents and many coaches have also tried to refocus the sport on fun and personal accomplishment and away from the intense competition that drives athletes to risk injury and permanent damage.

Gymnastics continued to grow more popular, especially among young girls, who find needed role models in the strong young women who fly so gracefully through the air at the Olympics. The limits of the sport keep expanding. When Korbut performed her back somersault on the balance beam in 1972, the move was revolutionary. In less than three decades, ten-year-olds did it in gymnastics class, and elite gymnasts in competition were performing three back flips in a row. Perhaps that is the real romance of such athletic displays: the ability of a vulnerable young girl to increase the limits of human physical achievement.

Many female gymnasts have become household names in the United States because of their successes at the Olympic Games. In 1970 Cathy Rigby became the first American to win a medal (silver) on the beam. Fourteen years later, Mary Lou Retton became the first American Olympian to become all-around champion. Shannon Miller became the first American to win that same title back-to-back (1993 and 1994). One of the most exciting moments in Olympic gymnast history occurred in 1996 when Kerri Strug helped her team win the first American gold medal in women's gymnastics. After teammate Dominique Moceanu fell twice during her vaults, responsibility for the win seemed to fall on Strug's shoulders. Even though she injured her ankle when she also fell during her first vault, Strug completed her second vault before collapsing in pain.

Men's gymnastics has also become extremely popular. Some thirty million viewers watched the American team in Beijing in 2008. However, interest in gymnastics began declining among high school males, and many colleges faced budget cuts that led them to eliminate male gymnastic programs. In 2011 there were only seventeen male gymnastic programs in the United States compared to the hundreds of football and basketball programs across the country. Since collegiate teams often serve as training grounds for Olympic athletes, this decline may bode ill for further American men's success in gymnastics at the Olympics.

Tina Gianoulis

SEE ALSO: *Basketball; Olympics; Rigby, Cathy; Sports Heroes.*

BIBLIOGRAPHY

Kauffman, Helen, and Matthew Smith. "Well, Doc, Ya Ain't No Nadia Comaneci . . . (Gymnastics Is the Latest White-Collar Rage)." *Los Angeles Magazine*, May 1980, 115.

Miller, Ernestine G. *Making Her Mark: Firsts and Milestones in Women's Sports*. Chicago: Contemporary Books, 2002.

O'Reilly, Jean, and Susan K. Cahn, eds. *Women and Sports in the United States: A Documentary Reader*. Boston: Northeastern University Press, 2007.

Sander, Libby. "As Men's Gymnastics Programs Dwindle, Backers Try to Save Them." *Chronicle of Higher Education*, May 1, 2011.

Silverstein, Herma. *Mary Lou Retton and the New Gymnasts*. New York: F. Watts, 1985.

Smither, Graham Buxton. *Behind the Scenes of Gymnastics*. New York: Proteus Press, 1980.

H

Hackett, Buddy *(1924–2003)*

Though primarily known in the late twentieth century for his nightclub comedy, Buddy Hackett was a versatile performer whose career spanned more than half the twentieth century. He was always a welcome guest on the talk-show circuit because he told funny stories to which audiences could relate. He performed in films, television, and cable specials and also wrote a book of poetry. Hackett was offered the opportunity to replace Curly in *The Three Stooges*, but he turned it down, preferring to remain a solo act. He frequently made his short stature, rotund build, and Jewishness the subject of his humor. His stand-up was risqué in an old-fashioned way; little of the anger and social commentary of such comedians as Lenny Bruce, Richard Pryor, or Chris Rock was to be found in his acts. Hackett's cherubic face, twinkling eyes, and gentle self-mockery took much of the sting from his profane language.

Buddy Hackett. *Buddy Hackett began his comedy career performing his stand-up routine at Jewish resorts in the Catskill Mountains in the 1940s.* **HULTON ARCHIVE/GETTY IMAGES.**

Hackett was born Leonard Hacker in Brooklyn, New York. After serving in the U.S. Army, he tried his luck as an upholsterer (like his father) and as a waiter. Comedy, however, was his calling. He honed his craft at the resorts of the Catskill Mountains, 100 miles northwest of New York City in the area known as the Borscht Belt. Many American Jews came there to vacation in an atmosphere where Jewish culture was celebrated and Jewish humor brought distraction from the troubles of the city. In the Catskills, Hackett made his reputation in venues such as the Concord Resort Hotel.

CAREER ON TELEVISION

When Hackett made his premiere television appearance, television was enjoying its first golden age. His nightclub style fit perfectly with the DuMont series *School House*. The premise came straight from vaudeville: the main character was a teacher (Kenny Delmar) who played host to a variety of unruly "students," actually comedians doing their shtick. Hackett was among the ever-changing cast, which also included Wally Cox and Arnold Stang. *School House* aired only from January through April 1949.

In the 1950s situation comedy developed into television's dominant form. From September 1956 to March 1957, Hackett starred in NBC's live sitcom *Stanley*, playing Stanley Peck, a newsstand owner who constantly gets in trouble trying to help other people. Future variety-series star Carol Burnett played Stanley's girlfriend, Celia. The show was not a success, however. By 1960 Hackett had begun making appearances as a guest on television talk shows, variety shows, and game shows, including *The Steve Allen Show*, *The Garry Moore Show*, and *What's My Line?* He continued to be a presence on such programs into the 1980s, and he made more than two dozen appearances on both *Hollywood Squares* and *The Tonight Show Starring Johnny Carson*.

MOVIES AND STAND-UP

In the 1960s Hackett made a number of memorable appearances in film, including *The Music Man* (1962) and *The Wonderful World of the Brothers Grimm* (1962). With his manic performance in Stanley Kramer's *It's a Mad, Mad, Mad, Mad*

World (1963), Hackett stood out among the film's overcrowded cast. He may best be remembered during this period for the role of Tennessee Steinmetz in Walt Disney's *The Love Bug* (1968), the tale of a Volkswagen named Herbie with a mind of its own.

The greatest showcase of Hackett's acting ability came in 1978 with NBC's *Bud and Lou*, a made-for-television movie of the comedy duo of Bud Abbott and Lou Costello. Hackett shone as Costello starring opposite Harvey Korman's Abbott. Although the film re-created many of the team's classic bits, it was the portrayal of their often strained relationship and the sadness of Costello's later life that allowed Hackett to show that he could embody a complex dramatic character.

Stand-up comedy remained the backbone of Hackett's career. He frequently played casinos in Las Vegas, Nevada, and Atlantic City, New Jersey. In 1983 a new generation discovered his Catskills roots with the Home Box Office (HBO) special *Buddy Hackett—Live and Uncensored*. New fans learned that the funny little guy from Disney's *The Love Bug* could swear and speak graphically and hilariously about his bodily functions. The program was so successful that in 1986 HBO's live comedy series *On Location* featured the episode "Buddy Hackett II—On Stage at Caesar's Atlantic City."

Hackett lent his distinct raspy voice to several animated productions, most notably Disney's *The Little Mermaid* (1989) and the straight-to-video sequel, *The Little Mermaid 2: Return to the Sea* (2000). His character, a seagull named Scuttle, was patterned after him. Scuttle shares Buddy's hefty build and habit of talking out of the side of his mouth. Much less successful was CBS's *Fish Police*, a failed attempt to cash in on the success of Fox's *The Simpsons*. *Fish Police* ran for only a few weeks in 1992.

A COMEDY LEGEND

In 1997 Hackett appeared in the PBS *Great Performances* special "The College of Comedy with Alan King." Fellow Catskills veteran King moderated a discussion of comedy with Hackett, Tim Conway, Paul Rodriguez, and Judy Gold. Hackett showed off his willingness to joke about politically incorrect subjects like Alzheimer's disease and disability. As always, his high spirits and self-deprecation kept the humor from being insulting. Hackett earned a mark of pop-culture distinction when, in 1995, he was the subject of a gag on *The Simpsons* (in the episode "Lisa's Wedding."). In the gag, a television newscast announces the search for a series of outlaw celebrities, including "The Artist Formerly Known as Buddy Hackett."

Fifty years after his television debut, Hackett's last appearance was playing Uncle Lonnie on *Action* (1999–2000), a show about a filmmaker trying to claw his way back to the top. Hackett died in 2003 at the age of seventy-eight from complications of diabetes.

David L. Hixson

SEE ALSO: *Abbott and Costello; Allen, Steve; Atlantic City; Borscht Belt; Bruce, Lenny; Burnett, Carol; Cable TV; Carson, Johnny; Conway, Tim; Disney (Walt Disney Company); Gleason, Jackie;* Hollywood Squares*; Korman, Harvey; Las Vegas; Paar, Jack; Pryor, Richard; Rock, Chris;* The Simpsons*; Stand-Up Comedy;* The Tonight Show*; Vaudeville;* What's My Line?

BIBLIOGRAPHY

Claxton, William. *Laugh: Portraits of the Greatest Comedians and the Funny Stories They Tell Each Other.* New York: William Morrow, 1999.

Frommer, Myrna Katz, and Harvey Frommer. *It Happened in the Catskills: An Oral History in the Words of Busboys, Bellhops, Guests, Proprietors, Comedians, Agents and Others Who Lived It.* New York: Harcourt & Brace, 1996.

Hackett, Buddy. *The Truth about Golf and Other Lies.* Garden City, NY: Doubleday, 1968.

Hackett, Buddy. *The Naked Mind of Buddy Hackett.* Los Angeles: Nash Publications, 1974.

Kanfer, Stefan. *A Summer World: The Attempt to Build a Jewish Eden in the Catskills from the Days of the Ghetto to the Rise and Decline of the Borscht Belt.* New York: Farrar, Straus & Giroux, 1989.

Richman, Irwin. *Borscht Belt Bungalows: Memories of Catskill Summers.* Philadelphia: Temple University Press, 1998.

Hackman, Gene *(1930–)*

American actor and multiple Academy Award–winner Gene Hackman demonstrates considerable range in his performances. Even when he plays the villain, he retains an amiable integrity that makes his acting compelling.

Born in 1930 in San Bernardino, California, Hackman was raised in Danville, Illinois. He studied journalism at the University of Illinois but then dropped out to pursue acting at the Pasadena Playhouse in California. After a few years performing in summer stock and off-Broadway productions, he had a breakthrough as an actor in 1964—the year that brought him his first Broadway role and a part in the film *Lilith*.

Hackman quickly gained critical recognition and Academy Award nominations for his roles in *Bonnie and Clyde* (1967) and *I Never Sang for My Father* (1970). He went on to win the Academy Award for Best Actor for his portrayal of the gritty, unconventional detective Popeye Doyle in *The French Connection* (1971). Hackman's roles have been quite diverse, ranging from the mousy surveillance expert involved in a murder in *The Conversation* (1974) to the unintentionally slapstick blind hermit in *Young Frankenstein* (1974) to the delightfully overplayed Lex Luthor in *Superman: The Movie* (1978). Playing an inspirational basketball coach in *Hoosiers* (1986) revived his career from a slight slump.

In 1989 Hackman received acclaim and another Academy Award nomination for his role in *Mississippi Burning* (1988), a film about the civil rights era. In the 1990s he found considerable success playing psychologically complex antagonists in movies such as *Unforgiven* (1992), for which he won an Academy Award for Best Supporting Actor. Other notable films include *Crimson Tide* (1995), *Extreme Measures* (1996), and *The Royal Tenenbaums* (2001).

In 2008 the seventy-eight-year-old Hackman announced his retirement from acting—but not from creative pursuits. He and his writing partner Daniel Lenihan have published three historical novels, and in 2011 Hackman released the Western novel *Payback at Morning Peak*, for which he was listed as the sole author. In addition to writing fiction, Hackman spends his time painting.

Christian L. Pyle

SEE ALSO: *Academy Awards;* Bonnie and Clyde*; Broadway; Civil Rights Movement;* The French Connection*; Hollywood;* Hoosiers*; Movie Stars;* Unforgiven*; The Western.*

BIBLIOGRAPHY

Hackman, Gene. *Payback at Morning Peak.* New York: Pocket Books, 2011.

Hunter, Allan. *Gene Hackman.* New York: St. Martin's Press, 1987.

Munn, Michael. *Gene Hackman.* London: Robert Hale, 1997.

Hacky Sack

In 1972 John Stalberger and Mike Marshall met by chance in a park in Oregon City, Oregon, and after "hacking around" for a while by trying to keep a small bag in the air with their feet, they had the idea for a new play product. Although Marshall died in 1975, Stalberger carried on with the project, and in 1979 he secured a patent for the Hacky Sack. At that point the product looked more like a pouch than a ball, and it was used mainly by high school and college students for casual recreation.

Hacky Sacks caught on, however, and in 1983 Stalberger sold the patent to Wham-O, maker of famously fun items such as the Frisbee, the hula hoop, and the Slip 'n Slide. Wham-O wanted to market the Hacky Sack for soccer training, so the bag was given a more ball-like shape. Meanwhile, Hacky Sack enthusiasts had developed their own ways of using the product, and because the original name was now owned by Wham-O, they adopted the term *footbag.* The World Footbag Association (WFA) was formed in 1983 and served as the organizer of the World Footbag Championships from 1984 until 1993.

Despite Wham-O's control of the Hacky Sack name, competitors continued making and marketing a variety of footbags, which continued to be popularly referred to as "hacky sacks." Footbags with crocheted covers (called "granny sacks") have become popular for informal play, whereas more sophisticated covers have evolved for competitive use. Bags are also distinguished by their filling. Granny sacks usually contain plastic pellets, and professional-grade footbags often contain metallic shot. Bags called "sand hacks" are favored by beginners because they are easier to control.

Simple circle games are still the favorite amateur activity, but competitive footbag has continued to develop as an organized sport. The WFA shifted its focus to promotional activities such as team tours, and official events came to be managed by the volunteer International Footbag Players' Association (IFPA). Competitive activities include footbag net, which is similar to volleyball or tennis, and freestyle footbag, in which footbag tricks are combined into acrobatic routines. Freestyle elements include kicks, stalls, spins, and complex maneuvers known as dexterities.

Whether casual or competitive, footbag is an inexpensive, entertaining, healthful, and very portable pastime. It is no surprise, then, that this American invention has become popular around the world.

Cynthia Giles

SEE ALSO: *Frisbee; Hula Hoop.*

BIBLIOGRAPHY

Chetwynd, Josh. *The Secret History of Balls: The Stories behind the Things We Love to Catch, Whack, Throw, Kick, Bounce and Bat.* New York: Perigee Trade, 2011.

Sach, Jacqueline, and Cynthia L. Copeland. *The Hacky Sack Handbook.* Kennebunkport, ME: Applesauce Press, 2008.

Haggard, Merle *(1937–)*

Country singer, songwriter, and guitarist Merle Haggard was among the founders of the popular and distinctive "Bakersfield sound." Although Nashville, Tennessee, was, and is, the undisputed capital of country music, Bakersfield, California, emerged as its rival by the early 1960s. This "second Nashville," was noted for an element of western swing that produced a more up-tempo style than the Nashville sound. Haggard, along with Buck Owens, Tommy Collins, Red Simpson, and Billy Mize, formed the core of this western expression of country music, and Haggard and Owens rode the sound to stardom.

After helping to establish this new honky-tonk music, known for its harder edge and barroom themes, Haggard branched out into other styles of music and by the 1970s had joined the ranks of country's crossover artists. His career represents a combination of change and tradition: despite the diversity of his music, he always tries to maintain his ties to traditional country music, which has earned him the reputation of contemporary country's music-historian.

Haggard showed an interest in music from a very early age, but his early life was not indicative of future success. He was born into poverty in Oakdale, California, in 1937. His parents had migrated westward from Oklahoma to escape the Dust Bowl and seek work as itinerant farmers. His father died when Haggard was very young, and the boy lived a rough and reckless childhood. As a teenager he alternated between odd jobs and reform school. As a young man, he spent time in jail for various petty crimes. An arrest for burglary finally landed him in San Quentin Penitentiary for three years, an experience that gave him the resolve needed to change his life.

After being paroled in 1960 (Governor Ronald Reagan granted him a full pardon in 1972), he went to Bakersfield and worked a series of odd jobs (mostly manual labor), while moonlighting as a guitarist in the raucous nightclubs and bars in the "beer-can hill" area. Over time, his troubled youth became one of his greatest assets, as he churned out hit after hit revolving around themes of barrooms, prisons, and life on the margins of society.

RISE TO FAME

Haggard landed a job as guitarist for a band led by singer Wynn Stewart and eventually signed his first recording contract with Tally Records. His first hit was "Sing a Sad Song" (1963), followed by a Top 10 single "(My Friends Are Gonna Be) Strangers." The success of this tune brought him a deal with Capitol Records, and by the mid-1960s Haggard was becoming a country-music sensation with his songs of drinking, cheating, and breaking the law.

Merle Haggard. Merle Haggard performs in concert in 1985. EBET ROBERTS/REDFERNS/GETTY IMAGES.

During these years, he married Bonnie Owens, a musician also under contract with Tally, and he assembled a band, the Strangers. Soon Merle Haggard and the Strangers were producing a string of hits, including "Swingin' Doors" and "The Bottle Let Me Down," both recorded in 1967. That same year, he had his first number one single with "I'm a Lonesome Fugitive." Several more of his songs reached the top of the charts in the late 1960s, among them "Branded Man" (1967) and "Mama Tried" (1968). These successes earned him his first Top Male Vocalist of the Year award from the Academy of Country Music. His outlaw image set a trend in the industry—several artists emerged during these years who sought popularity by cultivating a reputation of lawlessness.

Yet, just as he had risen to fame as an outlaw, Haggard soon became a patriotic hero to a large and different sector of the country. He attracted national attention and caused controversy with the release of "Okie from Muskogee" in 1969, a song that centered on life in a small Oklahoma town and championed the attitudes of the "silent majority" during the social tumult wrought by the Vietnam War. The song, which declared "we don't burn our draft cards down on Main Street," and "we don't smoke marijuana in Muskogee," became an anthem for those Americans who had tired of social unrest and viewed protest against the country's policies in Southeast Asia, or American society generally, as a lack of patriotism. Haggard later claimed to be somewhat surprised by the attention the song received, asserting that it had been written as a satire. Nevertheless, in 1970 he recorded "The Fightin' Side of Me," also based on the theme of patriotism.

ESTABLISHED ARTIST

By the early 1970s the country music industry was undergoing great change as audiences responded to new styles that combined country with elements of other musical genres. Nashville, alert to the trend, introduced a wave of crossover artists who could sell records on multiple charts, whereas more traditional musicians were given correspondingly less play time. Haggard responded well to these changes, revealing perhaps his greatest talent: his ability to maintain his reputation as a traditional country musician and survive the seemingly constant changes in audience taste. His enormously successful single "If We Make It through December" (1973) established him as one of the industry's top crossover artists by reaching the pop charts.

He complemented this success with tribute albums to earlier country music icons. The first of these tribute albums was *Same Train, a Different Time* (1969), dedicated to the music of the "singing brakeman," Jimmie Rodgers. It was followed by an album recognizing Bob Wills's contributions to country music, *A Tribute to the Best Damn Fiddle Player in the World* (1970). Soon afterward Haggard branched out into areas far removed from the honky-tonk style of his early career. His concept albums were well-received: *Land of Many Churches* (1971), a double album focusing on gospel recordings, and *I Love Dixie Blues* (1973), recorded in New Orleans. These brought him recognition and respect both from fans and his peers in the industry for his versatility.

By the late 1970s, Haggard was a fixture of the country music scene, making numerous television appearances and even a cameo appearance in the Clint Eastwood movie *Bronco Billy* (1980). These years brought increased recording success and national popularity. In 1977 Haggard signed with MCA Records, with which he produced even more number one hits, including "Think I'll Just Stay Here and Drink" and "Rainbow Stew." Haggard recorded celebrated duet albums in the early 1980s with George Jones and his idol Willie Nelson, both of which generated hits: "Yesterday's Wine" with Jones and "Pancho and Lefty" with Nelson. The album *Pancho and Lefty* earned Haggard and Nelson a nomination from the Country Music Association for Best Album of the Year.

Haggard signed with Curb Records in 1990, and he continued to compose, record, and tour at the end of the decade. He was inducted into the Country Music Hall of Fame in 1994. His album *Merle Haggard 1996* represents a musical overview of his entire career, offering a wide variety of styles and duets with country stars young and old.

Haggard released *If I Could Only Fly* in 2000 to critical acclaim and followed it up the next year with *Roots, Volume 1*. In 2005 he released *Chicago Wind*. Two years later he changed gears and released his first bluegrass disc, *The Bluegrass Sessions*. In 2008 Haggard underwent successful lung surgery to remove a tumor. In response to what he saw as a chance for a fresh start for the country with the election of Barack Obama as U.S. president and for himself following the surgery, Haggard wrote "Hopes Are High." He continued to work, releasing *I Am What I Am* in 2010 and *Working in Tennessee* in 2011.

"The Hag," as his fans came to call him over the years, has received almost every major award offered by the country music establishment, and his band, the Strangers, has shared in the fame, garnering numerous accolades from the country music industry, including several awards for Touring Band of the Year. Haggard's unique blending of tradition and change have proved to be a recipe for overwhelming success. He has earned almost forty number one hits over the course of his career, and in 2010 his lifetime achievements were recognized by the John F. Kennedy Center for the Performing Arts.

Jeffrey W. Coker

SEE ALSO: *Bluegrass; Country Music; Eastwood, Clint; Jones, George; Marijuana; Nelson, Willie; Obama, Barack; Owens, Buck; Reagan, Ronald; Rodgers, Jimmie.*

BIBLIOGRAPHY

Byworth, Terry. *The History of Country & Western Music*. New York: Bison Books, 1984.

Fine, Jason. "The Fighter." *Rolling Stone*, October 1, 2009.

Haggard, Merle, and Peggy Russell. *Sing Me Back Home: My Story*. New York: Times Books, 1981.

Haslan, Gerald W. *Workin' Man Blues: Country Music in California*. Berkeley: University of California Press, 1999.

Malone, Bill C. *Country Music U.S.A*, rev. ed. Austin: University of Texas Press, 1985.

Hagler, Marvelous Marvin *(1954–)*

A ring announcer once told Marvin Hagler that if he wanted to be announced as "Marvelous Marvin," he should go change his name. So Hagler—known outside of boxing circles for his bald head, goatee, menacing stare, and muscular physique—did just that, legally changing his name to "Marvelous Marvin Hagler." During the 1980s, when athletes' incomes skyrocketed and attitudes toward athletes in the media changed from idolatry to suspicion and scorn, Hagler came to symbolize the throwback fighter of yesteryear. While his nemesis Sugar Ray Leonard fought his first professional fight in 1977 on national television for a five-figure purse, Hagler began his professional career in obscurity, fighting for very little money. Leonard was the media darling whose career was carefully orchestrated; Hagler was the blue-collar champion who earned everything he ever received.

As a struggling middleweight contender unable to get a title shot, Hagler was once told that he had three things going against him—he was black, he was left-handed, and he was good. In fact, that statement was only partly true. Hagler is in fact African American, but while he could fight southpaw, he could also fight right-handed, and he was not just good, he was great. As a result of his being better than just good, he was able to rise above the obscurity to which most talented black left-handers have been relegated throughout boxing history.

Hagler and Leonard fought for their first world titles on the same card but not against each other. Hagler fought the preliminary bout against middleweight champion Vito Antuofermo for $40,000 and failed to gain the middleweight title when he was awarded a draw in a fight most observers felt he won, while Leonard fought the main event for $1 million and won the welterweight title with a fifteenth-round knockout against Wilfred Benitez.

When Leonard retired in 1982 due to a detached retina, Hagler, who was by then the undisputed middleweight champion of the world, took Leonard's place as the biggest star in boxing. Wins in highly publicized bouts against fellow Hall of Famers Roberto Duran and Thomas Hearns led to endorsement deals, most notably for Right Guard deodorant. Right Guard used Hagler's instantly recognizable face and the association of his face with brutality, and made an ironic, comic television commercial in which Hagler, perched atop a horse and dressed in equestrian attire, declares that anything less than Right Guard would be "uncivilized." Hagler, the everyman champion, had finally reached the superstar plateau that Leonard had occupied in his own heyday.

When Leonard eventually returned to the ring in 1987, he and Hagler met in one of the most anticipated fights in the history of boxing. During negotiations for the bout, Hagler insisted on more money than Leonard. Leonard complied, and Hagler received $12 million to Leonard's $11 million. In exchange, Hagler agreed to a twelve-round rather than a fifteen-round distance. The shorter distance theoretically benefitted Leonard, the naturally smaller fighter who was required to expend more energy than Hagler to remain competitive in the bout. As it turned out, Leonard started the fight quickly and Hagler came on strong later. Marvelous Marvin's late-rounds rally was not enough, and Leonard won the split decision, taking Hagler's middleweight title.

Unlike almost all other former champions, Hagler never made a comeback. Instead he moved to Italy, where the blue-collar throwback fighter became a popular and successful Italian action-movie star, starring in films such as *Indio* and *Indio 2*. In the twenty-first century, Hagler appeared as himself on the American screen in various documentaries, including *Ring of*

Fire: The Emile Griffith Story (2005) and *ESPN 25: Who's #1?* (2006).

Max Kellerman

SEE ALSO: *Advertising; Boxing; Leonard, Sugar Ray; Sports Heroes.*

BIBLIOGRAPHY

Gloeckner, Carolyn. *Marvin Hagler*. Mankato, MN: Crestwood House, 1985.

Kimball, George. *Four Kings: Leonard, Hagler, Hearns, Duran, and the Last Great Era of Boxing*. Ithaca, NY: McBooks Press, 2008.

Schulian, John. *Sometimes They Even Shook Your Hand: Portraits of Champions Who Walked among Us*. Lincoln: University of Nebraska/Bison Press, 2011.

Haight-Ashbury

There are few crossroads with the name recognition of the San Francisco intersection of Haight and Ashbury. A seemingly enchanted place, the Haight-Ashbury district begins at the top of a rise that gradually makes its way west to the beach. The fog drifts up past Golden Gate Park with ritual regularity, settling over the gingerbread Victorians and the Monterey pines. In the space of a little under five years, the Haight traced an arc from a quaint if somewhat dilapidated working-class neighborhood to the Mecca of the psychedelic counterculture and back again. By the early 1970s there was no longer any indication that the street had once hosted a vibrant alternative society. It had collapsed utterly under the weight of its own inner contradictions.

Composed of an eighteen-block stretch of Haight Street ending at Golden Gate Park to the west, Haight-Ashbury, or the Hashbury as it was affectionately dubbed, was the result of happenstance, proximity, and the peculiar tolerance of San Francisco—a city well known for a certain moral lassitude, left over from the gold rush era when it was a lascivious rough-and-tumble city of dubious morality—which was heralded as the Babylon of the west. The city's reputation made it an attractive spot for bohemians; waves of disaffected artists made habitual migrations to the City by the Bay throughout its history—most notably the Beats of the 1950s, who made it a prime destination in the worldwide beatnik circuit, along with Paris, Tangiers, New York, and Los Angeles.

HAVEN FOR BEATNIKS AND HIPPIES

In 1963 beatniks were fleeing North Beach to take advantage of the cheap rents and available storefronts of the Haight. But a sea change took place between the scruffy existential Beats and the earliest denizens of the Haight: LSD. Haight-Ashbury was the site of a remarkable syncretism, an admixture of influences that coalesced over time into the psychedelic eddy that Haight Street became. Like the collection of thrift-store finery and period costumes the original hippies fancied, their philosophy was fashioned from Eastern mysticism, comic books, science fiction, and the Beat writers who acted as a filtering agent through which the younger poets picked and chose their reading. Similarly, acid rock emerged out of a grab bag of styles: be-bop jazz improvisation, folk, and bluegrass modalities dabbed on a heavy impasto of garage-rock primitivism. For the hippies, LSD was their communion, and rock music their liturgy.

At first the scene was remarkably self-supporting, with small venues catering to a local group of cognoscenti. By 1966 new arrivals had flooded the Haight, with an estimated 15,000 hippies in residence. More disturbing, but at this point hardly a blip on the radar, were the runaway teens who flocked to the Haight as if guided by some special teen-alienation magnet.

Haight-Ashbury. *Hippies hang out in San Francisco's Haight-Ashbury district, the center point of the counterculture movement in the Summer of Love in 1967.* MICHAEL OCHS ARCHIVES/GETTY IMAGES.

Shops, boutiques, restaurants, and clubs sprang up to cater to the new arrivals, and an activist collective, the Diggers, provided for the needs of the more indigent among them with a soup kitchen, crash pads, and, later, a free store.

THE SUMMER OF LOVE

The year 1967 started off optimistically enough with the first "Be-In," a massive free concert and showcase of the local musicians. It was by all accounts a magical event. The next logical phase, or so it seemed to the movers and shakers of the community, was to invite the youth of America to the Haight for the summer. They envisioned a kind of hippie training: the youth would come, get turned on, and return from whence they came with the blueprint for a new culture. It didn't quite turn out that way. Young people did arrive for the summer, but they were not the beautiful people the Haight habitués anticipated. "They had bad teeth and acne scars and it was easy to see why they hadn't been voted homecoming king or queen back in Oshkosh or Biloxi or wherever they'd come from," writes Jay Stevens in *Storming Heaven, LSD and the American Dream.* "These kids were rejects; they'd come here because they were losers, and while that had a certain Christian appropriateness, it was not what the Council for the Summer of Love had expected."

By summer's end, the dream of a self-sufficient urban conclave of tripping Luddites had dissolved in a miasma of hard drugs, runaways, and incipient neglect. The fragile social infrastructure the counterculture had built was overcome by the onslaught. Tour buses and sightseers flooded the district, as did reporters. Their dispatches only added to the throng of destitute, addled kids. The indiscriminate use of every variety of drug was legion, as were drug busts, hence informing and informers. "The language was Love," wrote Hunter S. Thompson, "but the style was paranoia." That October the Diggers held a mock burial of the "Hippie, son of Media" in Golden Gate Park. It was a pointed bit of street theater, but it was after the fact. The wave had surged and broken, leaving human jetsam in its wake. By then the Haight-Ashbury pioneers had already fled to higher ground.

By 1971 Haight Street was once again a depressed commercial district with a couple of struggling mom-and-pop enterprises that predated the hippies. Then came the lean years, the urban blight and street violence, but through the district's darkest hour, tour buses continued to visit the neighborhood, offering a glimpse of what had been. By the 1990s boutiques, used clothing stores, and coffee shops lined the street. Bookstores, head shops, and galleries peddled 1960s nostalgia to the new generation of adherents—college students and European tourists who looked on the street as a holy relic. And with the newfound prosperity, old problems reasserted themselves. Homeless celebrants ranged through the park and panhandled on the street corners, their ranks swelled by a second wave of runaway kids: teenage adherents of the Grateful Dead, punk rockers, racist skinheads. Predictably street violence and drug abuse were not short in following.

Haight Street now lives on marketing the allure of that brief, heady period. There is no longer a pretense that Haight-Ashbury is anything but what it appears to be: an urban commercial center that attracts visitors because of its once-colorful history. In addition to the many bookstores, exclusive boutiques, hip restaurants, and music clubs of the district, visitors can find a few shops that still peddle hippie-influenced merchandise. Ironically, this new business cycle has thrived longer than the cultural movement on which its products are based. Without its idealistic communitarian ethos, the Haight-Ashbury is certainly more resilient, but what was at one time disturbing or thrilling is now little more than a titillation, a pleasant way to spend an afternoon.

Michael Baers

SEE ALSO: *The Beat Generation; Bluegrass; Comic Books; Consciousness Raising Groups; The Fifties; Folk Music; Golden Gate Bridge; The Grateful Dead; Hippies; Jazz; LSD; Marijuana; Psychedelia; Punk; Rock and Roll; Science Fiction Publishing; Teenagers; Thompson, Hunter S.*.

BIBLIOGRAPHY

Cohen, Katherine Powell. *San Francisco's Haight-Ashbury.* Images of America: California. Charleston, SC: Arcadia Publishing, 2008.

Didion, Joan. *Slouching towards Bethlehem.* New York: Farrar, Straus & Giroux, 1968.

Hoskyns, Barney. *Beneath the Diamond Sky.* New York: Simon & Schuster, 1997.

Perry, Charles. *The Haight-Ashbury.* New York: Rolling Stone Press, 1984.

Stevens, Jay. *Storming Heaven, LSD and the American Dream.* New York: Grove Press, 1987.

Von Hoffman, Nicholas. *We Are the People Our Parents Warned Us Against.* Chicago: Quadrangle Books, 1968.

Hair

A new milestone in Broadway history was set in 1968 when *Hair*, the first rock musical, opened to mass popularity. Tackling controversial and explosive issues of the era in a theatrically innovative fashion, the brash and exciting musical ran for a little longer than four years at New York's Biltmore Theater. The show eventually spawned a total of fourteen national companies and produced eleven cast albums in different languages worldwide. A concept musical reflecting the antiestablishment energy of the 1960s American "hippie" youth culture, *Hair* was seen by more than four million people in its first two years of production, and the show ultimately grossed over $22 million in revenue. The revolutionary musical generated several hit radio singles and brought to public attention a number of talented performers. The enormous success of *Hair* paved the way for a series of ambitious rock musicals, including *Jesus Christ Superstar* in the 1970s and *Rent* in the mid-1990s.

BRINGING THE COUNTERCULTURE TO STAGE

The project that eventually came to be known as *Hair* evolved in 1965 from the creative minds of the Broadway performers Gerome Ragni and James Rado. Although they had never formally written a musical project before, the two coauthors were fascinated by the as yet untapped theatrical potential of the 1960s youth culture and began to do field research in New York City. Ragni and Rado interviewed and documented the lifestyles of hippies who had rejected dominant social mores and values, choosing instead to fight for abstract principles such as freedom, justice, and liberty. Celebrating the newly arriving "Age of Aquarius," these youth held decided opposition to U.S. military involvement in Vietnam; carried a fondness for marijuana and other experimental drugs; cherished a newfound sense of sexual freedom; and positioned themselves firmly against environmental destruction, racial segregation, and religious dogma.

Ragni and Rado were also enticed by the opportunity to breathe new life into the musical theater scene. Such daring musicals as *West Side Story* (1957), *Fiddler on the Roof* (1964), and *Cabaret* (1966) had already begun to experiment with form, relying less on text and placing more emphasis on music and dance. In 1968 *Hair* would come to alter the formal possibilities for musicals by explicitly drawing on experimental theatrical techniques, including those pioneered by such visionaries as Antonin Artuad and Jerzy Grotowski, and on the energy of the avant-garde downtown New York theater scene. In contrast to *Oklahoma!* (1943), which had revolutionized Broadway theaters in the 1940s, *Hair* was less concerned with character and plot, instead focusing on thematic content and the depiction of lifestyle.

After completing the bulk of their field research, Ragni and Rado decided to collaborate with the Canadian composer Galt MacDermot, who wrote the amiable and infectious rock tunes that would bring *Hair* to public endearment. The nearly incoherent plot centers on Claude, a young man who has been drafted to service in Vietnam; his friend Berger, who has "dropped out" of society; and their friend Sheila, an antiwar student at New York University. Joseph Papp of the New York Shakespeare Festival took an interest in the experimental script and decided to produce it at his Public Theater in downtown New York. Papp's off-Broadway run of *Hair: An American Tribal Love Rock Musical* at the Public Theater was only a modest success, however. Ragni and Rado came into frequent conflict with director Gerald Freedman, who chose to concentrate on the book of the musical and to polish its look rather than attempt to convey onstage the "authenticity" of the youth counterculture.

BREAKING THEATRICAL TABOOS

Upon the completion of the run of *Hair* at the Public Theater, Michael Butler, a young, wealthy political with a pressing concern for the welfare of Native Americans, took an interest in producing the experimental musical. Butler financially backed the show at the Cheetah, a popular dance hall discotheque in Manhattan. The unsuccessful run proved that the show needed to be overhauled before being brought to Broadway. Tom O'Horgan, a director who had honed an impressive amount of experience in his work at the avant-garde New York theater LaMama, was hired to revamp the show; Robin Wagner, Jules Fisher, and Nancy Potts were hired to rework the scenic design, lighting design, and costume design, respectively. O'Horgan virtually wiped the show clean of its narrative and concentrated more intently on the concept. Thirteen songs were added to enhance the show's pro-love, pro-sex, pro-drugs, and racial harmony message.

In its new form, the show fearlessly broke certain taboos of the theater. Headed by the two authors in the leading roles, the young and talented cast demolished the "fourth wall" of the theater by entering through the audience to arrive onstage. The cast often switched roles interchangeably. For the first time on the mainstream stage, audiences witnessed drug use, explicit language, an openly gay character, and drag queens. During the infamous "Be-In" scene, the cast stripped nude under blinking strobe lights to the shock and surprise of the spectators. The show's popularity was enormous, and in April 1970 the members of the original cast performed a free, jam-packed show in New York's Central Park.

For all its experimental bravery, *Hair* was met with derision by distinguished theatrical critics and lost the Tony Award for Best Musical to a more traditional musical, *1776*. Nonetheless, *Hair* brought to attention a series of gifted performers, including Ben Vereen, Diane Keaton, Melba Moore, and Nell Carter, each of whom went on to greater success in areas of film, television, and music. The musical also spawned a series of spin-off albums (such as *DisinHAIRited*) that consisted largely of outtake material that had been excised on the show's path to Broadway. As performed by such groups as the Fifth Dimension and the Cowsills, the infectious songs "Let the Sunshine In," "Good Morning Starshine," and "Aquarius" soon topped the American pop charts.

After generating an impressive number of road shows, *Hair* closed on Broadway in 1972. The show was revived in 1977, but by then the material no longer seemed as topical and original as it had in 1968. In 1979 the musical was reworked as a critically acclaimed film directed by Milos Forman, and in 1988 some of the original cast members rejoined at the United Nations to celebrate the musical's twentieth anniversary reunion concert. A European tour of the musical continued to prove successful into the 1990s, and in 1998 an off-off-Broadway revival of *Hair* marked the show's thirtieth anniversary. In 2009 a new Broadway revival updated the show by exploring some of the ambivalence experienced by the play's characters. The production won the Tony Award for Best Revival of a Musical. The following year, the show opened in London to good reviews.

As evidenced by the success of the rock musical *Rent* in 1995, the impact of *Hair* has been long lasting. A document of a profoundly turbulent and explosive era in American history, *Hair* forever changed not only the look and the sound of the Broadway musical but also its very possibilities.

Jason King

SEE ALSO: *Broadway;* Fiddler on the Roof*; Hairstyles; Hippies;* Jesus Christ Superstar*; Marijuana; The Musical;* Oklahoma!*; Ragni, Gerome, and James Rado;* Rent*; Rock and Roll; Tony Awards; Vietnam;* West Side Story.

BIBLIOGRAPHY

Davis, Lorrie, and Rachel Gallagher. *Letting Down My Hair.* New York: Arthur Fields, 1973.

Grode, Eric. Hair: *The Story of the Show That Defined a Generation.* Philadelphia: Running Press, 2010.

Horn, Barbara Lee. *The Age of* Hair: *Evolution and Impact of Broadway's First Rock Musical.* New York: Greenwood Press, 1991.

Hair Extensions

Hair has always been an important part of human identity, and the styling of hair has been a significant art form in many cultures. Hair extensions, swatches of human or synthetic hair attached to natural hair in order to add length and volume, have been used by both women and men for thousands of years, from ancient Egypt to Victorian England. During the mid-1990s extensions received a boost in popularity as celebrities such as singer Victoria Beckham and model Tyra Banks admitted to enhancing their hairstyles. The use of extensions became widespread, and even men, such as tennis star Andre Agassi and actor Hugh Jackman, began to use them to lengthen their hair.

While celebrity extensions were made of human hair and glued or woven in pricey salons, those who wanted to imitate their flamboyant styles could find affordable clip-on extensions in natural or brightly artificial colors in local drugstores. Extensions covered any imperfections in natural hair and allowed dramatic hairstyle changes to be created quickly and simply. They remained popular throughout the beginning of the twenty-first century, both as a celebrity style statement and as a way to add a bit of glamour to an average life.

Though media coverage of modern hair extensions tended to view them in a lighthearted manner as a fun way to change a person's image, there were political implications to the style as well. Some of the first women in the twentieth century to wear extensions in their hair were African Americans, who used the artificial hair to lengthen and straighten tight curls into styles more common in a predominantly white culture. Though numerous black celebrities, such as singer Beyoncé Knowles and actress Halle Berry, were famous for their hair extensions, many within the African American community expressed concern about the damaging effects of such styles on the self-esteem of black women and girls. Other social critics focused on the ethical issues of the almost billion-dollar human hair industry, revealing that most of the hair used to fill the enormous demand for natural extensions came from impoverished communities in countries such as India and China. Little, if any, of the wealth generated went to the women who gave their hair so that others could be fashionable.

Tina Gianoulis

SEE ALSO: *Agassi, Andre; Banks, Tyra; Hairstyles; Hollywood; Supermodels.*

BIBLIOGRAPHY

Cooper, Carol. "Hair R Us." *Whole Earth*, Summer 2001, 55.

Lamont, Elizabeth. "Faking It: Even if You Weren't Born with Long, Gorgeous Hair, It Can Be Yours in an Instant." *Harper's Bazaar*, October 2002, 130.

Lennon, Christine. "The Tress Goddess." *W*, April 2009, 86.

Zoepf, Katherine. "The Locks Market." *Allure*, March 2009, 114.

Hairstyles

Human beings have styled and adorned their hair since the beginning of recorded history. This styling has different and often contradictory purposes. As an intrinsic yet malleable part of the body, the hair and its styling can serve as an intimate form of self-expression. However, hair is also a public and visible part of personal presentation, and, as such, a hairstyle can become a public, even a political, statement.

As part of the physical body, hair has a role in sexuality, and it is often one of the first things noticed in a prospective sexual partner. Hair is also a major component of fashion, one of the ways in which society dictates how its members should look. Because of its many interpretations, a hairstyle can serve as a medium of conformity or rebellion; it can lure or rebuff prospective mates; and it can be a constant source of frustrating labor for the individual who cannot get it to behave.

Though hairstyles have constantly changed, and those changes have often been seen as radical innovations, most styles have come and gone many times. The straight hairstyle that became popular for women in the late 1990s and early in the first decade of the 2000s and was de rigueur in the late 1960s and early 1970s is basically the same style that was considered appropriate for unmarried girls in medieval Europe. Though hairstyles are constantly changing, there are usually strictly enforced cultural norms, beyond which it is forbidden to deviate. These norms are enforced by rules in schools and on the job as well as by social pressure.

HAIR AS A SOCIAL INDICATOR

Throughout history hair has been shaped and decorated to announce its wearer's place in society. In ancient Egypt nobility was denoted by a bald, shaved head, which was then covered by thick, black wigs made of braided and decorated wool, palm fibers, or human hair. Ancient Romans made marble wigs for their statues in order to update them as hairstyles changed. They changed often according to one Roman writer: "It would be easier to count the acorns on an oak tree . . . than to count the number of new hairstyles that appear every day."

In fifteenth-century Europe a high forehead was prized, and Elizabethan women plucked their hair out to the very tops of their heads. Queen Elizabeth I herself had more than eighty red wigs to make sure that her hairstyle was always in perfect condition. Louis XIV brought wigs into fashion in early eighteenth-century France when he wore them to conceal his balding head. In the late 1700s Madame de Pompadour, mistress of Louis XV, led French fashion with the elaborate hairstyle that

Dolly Parton Wears a Beehive. *Dolly Parton sports a beehive hairdo in the 1960s.* MICHAEL OCHS ARCHIVES/GETTY IMAGES.

was named for her. Women of the day wore flowers, feathers, jewels, and even model ships in hair that was piled high and held in place with beef fat. This pomade often attracted insects, and folklore of bugs and even mice living in the depths of elaborately styled hair persisted right up to the beehives of the 1950s.

THE TWENTIETH CENTURY

Up until World War I, respectable women in the United States wore their hair primly up on their heads, but by the 1920s women were entering a freer era, as documented in F. Scott Fitzgerald's story "Bernice Bobs Her Hair." Men often express a preference for long, flowing hair on women, and a by-product of the twentieth-century waves of feminism has been the popularity of short hairstyles, announcing a new independence from men. The short bobs of the Roaring Twenties were appropriate for the breezy informality of the times as well as being a sort of feminist statement, freeing suffragists and their sisters from the time-consuming triviality of hair care. Many women's hair trends of the twenty-first century have been modeled after the styles of this period, perhaps reflecting a resurgence of feminist ideals.

The 1930s and 1940s marked a return to glamour, with cascading tresses. These were reined in somewhat during World War II by a severe, all-business style that reflected women's role working on the home front. In the 1950s and early 1960s big hair was back, with beehives and stiffly lacquered curls. Many women teased their hair to get the desired volume or wore rats, balls of hair or netting that were placed underneath to increase hair height.

As the hippie counterculture rose at the end of the 1960s, the natural look came into vogue, and women who had once tortured their hair into tight curls began to iron it or roll it on beer cans and toilet paper rolls to achieve the lank straightness prized both on fashion runways and at university sit-ins. Men, too, began to wear their hair long in the late 1960s, and long, straight hair became a symbol of the youthful culture of protest and revolution. The Broadway musical that first appeared in 1968 and claimed to define the generation was called, simply, *Hair*.

With the punk movement of the 1980s, hair fashion exploded beyond any modern precedent. Expressing the nihilistic angst of youth rebelling against complacency, punks made themselves look freakishly dramatic. Both women and men dyed their hair bright blues, purples, and oranges, using gel or dramatic cuts to create sculpted spikes of hair. Some wore their hair in Mohawks, imitating the traditional hairstyle of an American Indian tribe who shaved the sides of the scalp, leaving a sheaf of hair standing in the middle. Though conservative society despaired, the punk rockers did much to liberate the boundaries of fashion, and many of the cropped, angular styles that they pioneered remain popular in the twenty-first century.

MEN

Though women are usually considered the primary slaves to fashion, men are also quite attentive to their hair, and men's hairstyles have often been the focus of media scrutiny. Whether it was the slicked-back ducktails of the 1950s, the revolutionary shaggy bangs of the early 1960s Beatles' haircut, or the defiantly shoulder- and waist-length tresses of the hippies of the late 1960s and 1970s, men have frequently used hairstyle as rebellion and self-expression.

Sometimes male hair experimentation has drawn more dramatic reactions than women's changing styles. Perhaps because women are expected to follow fashion, even to look ridiculous in its name, women are allowed more flexibility in hairstyle. A man who deviates from the narrow range of conservative hairstyles permitted for men faces derision and worse. Long-haired hippies of the 1970s were mocked, threatened, even beaten because of the length of their hair. Schools and businesses have also been slow to permit men freedom to wear their hair in unconventional styles.

Male-pattern baldness, and the desire to conceal it, has long been a motivating factor in the hairstyles of older men. Some men try drugs or hair transplants to fight hair loss, while others attempt the often-ridiculed approach of growing one side long and combing it over the top of the head to cover bald spots (a method called a comb over). Male baby boomers, entrenched in middle age in the 1990s, brought into fashion a neat ponytail, even pairing it with a balding pate, making a discreet statement about its wearer's hipness. In the twenty-first century, however, balding males have largely embraced their dwindling follicle count, choosing to buzz or completely shave away what hair remains on their heads.

AFRICAN AMERICANS

Almost all modern hair fashion in the United States is predicated on the fairly straight or wavy European hair type. Those whose hair is by nature very different from that model, such as African Americans, are hard put to force their hair into the prescribed styles. For African Americans especially, hair has been an intensely political issue. Because all things black have been long stigmatized by white U.S. culture, blacks tried for decades with chemicals, machines, and intensive labor to change their hair, even calling natural, tightly curled black hair bad hair and straighter hair good hair (the 2009 documentary *Good Hair*, hosted by comedian Chris Rock, explores the history of these notions in depth).

In the late 1960s, with the rise of the civil rights movement, a notion of black pride took hold, and many blacks began to grow their hair out in Afros, or naturals, which sometimes stood several inches out from the head. In the 1970s and 1980s, inspired by the politics and culture of the Jamaican Rastafarians, some blacks began to let their hair grow long and gather naturally into dreadlocks, soft ropes of hair that retain their shape as they grow.

Initially, many whites found both Afros and dreadlocks on blacks to be threatening, perhaps both because they often go along with radical antiracist politics and because they represent a new positive black-identified culture that might challenge the dominion of white culture. One reaction of white culture to this challenge has been to repress such expressions of ethnic identity, such as forbidding certain hairstyles in the workplace, but another reaction has been to appropriate them.

Many blacks were outraged in 1979 when actress Bo Derek appeared in the film *10* wearing her hair in cornrows, or many small braids close to the head. Cornrow braids had long been a traditional African American hairstyle, but the media and much of the white public greeted Derek's style as an innovation. Though cornrows enjoyed a brief popularity among whites, few credited the black community as its source. Similarly, in the 1980s, some young counterculture whites, seeking a rebellious political statement, or identifying with black struggles, trained their hair to grow in an approximation of dreadlocks. While some blacks may find this imitation to be a kind of support, many consider it to be insulting and ignorant.

CELEBRITY INFLUENCE

If European styles were historically shaped by kings and courtesans, U.S. styles have been most consistently influenced by film and television stars. Dynamic actress Louise Brooks led the way to the boyish bobs of the 1920s, while blond bombshell Jean Harlow and redhead Rita Hayworth made flowing curls a fashion favorite. Veronica Lake popularized her trademark look by letting her blond hair cascade in front of one eye. In more recent years Farrah Fawcett's shaggy mane became the most imitated style of the 1970s, and in the early 1990s women flocked to hairdressers requesting the style known as the "Rachel" worn by Jennifer Aniston's character on the television series *Friends*.

Men, too, imitate the hairstyles popularized in the media, whether Michael Jackson's 1980s Jeri curls or the slick retro look of playboy advertising executive Don Draper from the hit television show *Mad Men*, which debuted in 2007. Even lack of hair became a fashion as some shaved their heads after seeing the style on Irish singer Sinead O'Connor, actress Sigourney Weaver in *Aliens* (1986), or Demi Moore in *G.I. Jane* (1997). Beleaguered pop singer Britney Spears made headlines in 2007 after spontaneously shaving her head.

HAIR CARE INDUSTRY

Hairstyle is not only a personal choice, a fashion statement, or even political action—it is also a multimillion dollar industry. As people struggle to coax their hair into the latest style, the popular color, or the perfect statement of their own values, they purchase a variety of hair products and fashion magazines and spend hundreds of dollars a year on hairdressers. There is even computer software that allows users to view themselves in various hairstyles before making the crucial decision.

The hair care industry often relies on a culturally induced insecurity about looks, particularly among women, as well as the notion that a different look will bring happiness and fulfillment. The media feeds this insecurity with its ads ("Is it true blonds have more fun?"), talk-show makeovers, and slavish reportage of celebrity fashion. As more images bombard the public, it becomes harder and harder to find the personal element of style. Whether it is African Americans reclaiming a cultural heritage, 1970s lesbians recognizing each other by their close-cropped hair, or punk rockers throwing a purple spiky head in the face of convention, however, there always seems to be room for genuine identity to peek through the rigidity of fashion.

Tina Gianoulis

SEE ALSO: *The Beatles; Broadway; Brooks, Louise; Civil Rights Movement; Clairol Hair Coloring; Fawcett, Farrah; Feminism;* Friends*;* Hair*; Hair Extensions; Hamill, Dorothy; Harlow, Jean; Hayworth, Rita; Hippies; Hollywood; Jackson, Michael; Lake, Veronica;* Mad Men*; Moore, Demi; Punk; Rock, Chris; Sassoon, Vidal; Spears, Britney; Television; Weaver, Sigourney; World War II.*

BIBLIOGRAPHY

Astley, Amy. "The Politics of Hair." *Vogue*, December 1994, 229.

Bryer, Robin. *The History of Hair: Fashion and Fantasy down the Ages*. London: Wilson, 2000.

Cooper, Wendy. *Hair: Sex, Society, Symbolism*. New York: Stein and Day, 1971.

Fiell, Charlotte. *Hairstyles: Ancient to Present*. London: Fiell, 2010.

McCracken, Grant David. *Big Hair: A Journey into the Transformation of Self.* Woodstock, NY: Overlook Press, 1996.

Sherrow, Victoria. *Encyclopedia of Hair: A Cultural History*. Westport, CT: Greenwood Press, 2006.

Halas, George "Papa Bear" *(1895–1983)*

George Stanley Halas was known as "Papa Bear" to almost anyone familiar with the Chicago Bears football team—and rightly so. For sixty-one years Halas was affiliated with the Bears in one capacity or another—he named the Bears, played for the Bears, coached the Bears, and owned the Bears. By the time he retired as a coach in 1968, he had compiled the best coaching record in the history of professional football: 321 wins, 142 losses, and 31 ties. Halas's teams became known as the "Monsters of the Midway," winning eleven championships with their highly physical brand of football. His greatest moment probably came in the 1940 championship game when his underdog Bears crushed the Washington Redskins 73–0. Halas served as the first president of the National Football Conference from 1970 until his death.

Lloyd Chiasson Jr.

SEE ALSO: *The Chicago Bears; National Football League (NFL); Professional Football.*

BIBLIOGRAPHY

Carroll, Bob. *Total Football: The Official Encyclopedia of the National Football League*. New York: HarperCollins, 1997.

Mausser, Wayne. *Chicago Bears, Facts and Trivia*. South Bend, IN: E. B. Houchin, 1995.

McCaskey, Patrick, and Mike Sandrolini. *Bear with Me: A Family History of George Halas and the Chicago Bears*. Chicago: Triumph Books, 2009.

Vass, George. *George Halas and the Chicago Bears*. Chicago: Regnery Press, 1971.

Whittingham, Richard. *The Chicago Bears: An Illustrated History*. Chicago: Rand McNally, 1979.

Whittingham, Richard. *Bears in Their Own Words: Chicago Bear Greats Talk about the Team, the Game, the Coaches, and the Times of Their Lives*. Chicago: Contemporary Books, 1991.

Whittingham, Richard; Ed McCaskey; and Walter Payton. *The Bears: A 75-Year Celebration*. Rochester, MN: Taylor Publishing, 1994.

Haley, Alex *(1921–1992)*

In 1976 author Alex Haley accomplished something no black person had been able to do before: he got Americans to view history from a black perspective. The vehicle he used was *Roots:*

The Saga of an American Family, his 688-page fictional interpretation of the genealogy of his family, beginning with a kidnapped African boy brought to Maryland as a slave in the mid-1700s. It was not the first time Haley had successfully shown readers life from the black perspective. Before *Roots*, he wrote *The Autobiography of Malcolm X*, a story about the transformation of Malcolm Little from a street-savvy hustler to Malcolm X, a Black Muslim who went from hating whites to becoming an advocate of integration just before he was assassinated by fellow Black Muslims.

Haley was a college dropout who began his career while in the U.S. Coast Guard working as a mess boy waiting on white officers. He began by composing love letters for shipmates who did not feel up to the task and then moved on to write articles for magazines. One of his articles, "Hope Springs Eternal," appeared in the *Atlantic* in January 1955. While it focused on one of his great-aunts, the article mentioned his grandmother's having "a paper tracing her family back to a freed slave," a hint of the phenomenal family saga Haley would interpret a decade later in *Roots*.

About halfway through Haley's twenty-year coast guard career, the admiral he served as a steward was so impressed by one of his articles that he successfully petitioned the coast guard to create the rating of journalist for Haley. After retiring from the coast guard in 1959, Haley became a freelance writer, eventually conducting the first *Playboy* interview (with Miles Davis) and several others, including Martin Luther King Jr.; Cassius Clay (later to become Muhammad Ali); Sammy Davis Jr.; Johnny Carson; and George Lincoln Rockwell, a racist and anti-Semitic neo-Nazi.

THE AUTOBIOGRAPHY OF MALCOLM X

Just as a modest article about a great-aunt eventually became *Roots*, Haley's interview with Malcolm X and an earlier article about the Nation of Islam for *Reader's Digest* led to his collaboration with Malcolm X to write *The Autobiography of Malcolm X*. The book was set in type when Malcolm X was assassinated on February 24, 1965, and Haley immediately wrote a lengthy epilogue explaining how he and Malcolm X had collaborated on it. *The Autobiography of Malcolm X* became a best-seller and was adopted in college literature courses around the country.

The *Autobiography* was published at a time of growing racial divisions in the United States and rising interest in African American leaders. Malcolm X was routinely written about in the mainstream press, and his pronouncements were well publicized. His assassination increased interest in his life, although the book, because it tells the story of redemption and transformation, transcends that tragedy. Spike Lee based his 1992 movie *Malcolm X* on Haley's book.

ROOTS

When *Roots* appeared in 1976, it too became an immediate best seller. News accounts tell of Haley appearing at an autograph session expecting to find hundreds of people, only to be swamped by thousands. He had succeeded in giving African Americans more than a sense of identity; he had given them a history. The book appeared during the nation's bicentennial year, and Haley dedicated it "as a birthday offering to my country within which most of *Roots* happened." It is worth repeating the subtitle of the book, *The Saga of an American Family*, for it demonstrates that Haley was trying to make a broad statement about everyone's roots, not just those of African Americans, and he struck a chord. It was as if the entire country was having an identity crisis, and readers of any race could better understand their own lives through the multigenerational saga Haley had written.

Roots consumed Haley both during the research and the writing, as well as after the book was published. He spent about twelve years doing research, even traveling in the hold of a ship to get a feel for how slaves must have felt when they were being transported in chains from Africa to North America. He became even more popular after *Roots* appeared as a six-night, twelve-hour miniseries on television, a show watched by 130 million people. Haley was overwhelmed with speaking engagements and requests he could never satisfy.

Upon his death in 1992, Haley left behind 700 pages of notes outlining a novel based on the life of his grandmother, Queen, who was the illegitimate daughter of a slave owner. David Stevens, a British screenwriter who had been in talks with Haley about a screen adaptation of the unfinished book, compiled a manuscript from Haley's notes and his own recollection of their conversations, and it was published as *Alex Haley's Queen: The Story of an American Family*, in 1993. That same year the novel was adapted as a miniseries on CBS television, starring Halle Berry as Queen.

While in recent years there has been significant critical debate over the factuality of Haley's accounts in *Roots* (a controversy supported by the fact that Haley was twice sued for plagiarizing significant portions of the novel), the fact remains that his works forced Americans to analyze their heritage in such an uncompromising way that discussions of race were forever altered. He gave the world two classics in his lifetime, and those works will remain his legacy.

R. Thomas Berner

SEE ALSO: *Ali, Muhammad; Best Sellers; Carson, Johnny; Davis, Miles; Lee, Spike; Made-for-Television Movies; Malcolm X;* Playboy*;* Roots.

BIBLIOGRAPHY

Berner, R. Thomas. *The Literature of Journalism: Text and Context*. State College, PA: Strata Publishing, 1999.

Haley, Alex. *The Autobiography of Malcolm X*. New York: Grove Press, 1965.

Haley, Alex. *Roots: The Saga of an American Family*. Garden City, NY: Doubleday, 1976.

Haley, Alex. *The Playboy Interviews*, ed. Murray Fisher. New York: Ballantine, 1993.

Haley, Alex, and David Stevens. *Alex Haley's Queen: The Story of an American Family*. New York: William Morrow, 1993.

Kern-Foxworth, Marilyn. "Alex Haley." In *Dictionary of Literary Biography*, vol. 38. *Afro-American Writers after 1955*. Detroit, MI: Gale Research, 1985.

Shirley, David, and Heather Lehr Wagner. *Alex Haley: Author*. Philadelphia: Chelsea House, 2005.

Haley, Bill *(1925–1981)*

Often referred to as the founding father of rock and roll, Bill Haley was the first performer to become famous in the new genre. William John Clifton Haley was born near Detroit, Michigan, but raised in rural Pennsylvania. He left school in 1940, after completing the eighth grade. Coming of age during World War II, Haley was spared military service because of impaired sight in his left eye. He had become interested in country-and-western music as a child, and during the war he began to perform on a semiprofessional basis.

By late 1943 Haley was a regular member of a country band, and for the next several years he sang, yodeled, and played rhythm guitar in bands such as the Down Homers. In 1946 he struck out on his own with a group he called the Range Drifters. After a year of unprofitable touring, the Range Drifters broke up, and Haley found work of a different kind. He spent the next few years as a disc jockey in Pennsylvania. On one station he was able to indulge his growing appreciation of "race music," or rhythm and blues (R&B), when the station owner began a daring policy of mixing genres—playing country, pop, and R&B shows on any given day.

FROM COUNTRY TO POP

Haley capitalized on his growing popularity in Pennsylvania and surrounding states by forming a new band, the Four Aces of Western Swing. As the name indicates, the band attempted to bring two musical genres together. Along with occasional personnel changes over the years, the band also changed its name. By 1950 it was Bill Haley and His Saddlemen and was recording actively on a variety of labels. Increasingly, Haley's repertoire included covers of R&B hits, such as the popular "Rocket 88"

Bill Haley and His Comets. *Bill Haley poses surrounded by the Comets in 1955, the year that "Rock around the Clock" became a hit.* MICHAEL OCHS ARCHIVES/GETTY IMAGES.

that the Saddlemen released in 1951. The following year Haley moved to the Essex label and changed the band's name for the last time. Bill Haley and His Comets was a much better name for a band that by then sought to minimize its country-and-western influences and aim for pop stardom.

The Comets had their first real hit, "Crazy Man, Crazy," in 1953. The next year the band released several records, including "Rock around the Clock," all of which were met with only tepid responses. It was only in the summer of 1955 that "Rock around the Clock" finally became a national hit. Its innovative use as theme music in *The Blackboard Jungle*, a powerful motion picture about juvenile delinquency in a New York high school, brought the song (and Haley) to the attention of millions of theatergoers in a few weeks' time. Decca, Haley's label, quickly rereleased "Rock around the Clock," which raced to the number one position on the *Billboard* singles charts in July 1955.

Some commentators define the beginning of the rock-and-roll era as the moment when "Rock around the Clock" became the number one pop single in America, ostensibly the first rock-and-roll hit on the pop charts. However, it is arguable that Haley's "Crazy Man, Crazy" in 1953, as well as 1954's "Shake, Rattle and Roll" were the first rock-and-roll hits. The first number one pop hit that would later be acknowledged as a rock-and-roll song was probably the Crew Cuts' summer 1954 cover of "Sh-Boom," originally by the doo-wop group the Chords. ("Rock around the Clock" had its dismal first release at about the same time that the Crew Cuts' "Sh-Boom" was rising to number one.)

ROCK PIONEERS

Bill Haley and His Comets enjoyed some indisputable firsts, however. They were the first rock-and-roll band to achieve stardom due to their music's exposure in a movie. In 1956 they became the first band to star in rock-and-roll exploitation films: New York DJ Alan Freed's *Rock around the Clock* and *Don't Knock the Rock*. Haley's success in the pop music business was inseparable from his stature as a media star, a correlation that would come to be routine for later rock giants such as Elvis Presley and the Beatles.

Unfortunately for Haley, rock and roll changed rapidly during the late 1950s, leaving him and the Comets behind. After "Shake, Rattle and Roll" and the rerelease of "Rock around the Clock," Haley had only two more major hits. "Burn That Candle" came out in 1955, and "See You Later, Alligator" was released in 1956. Aside from a few minor songs to follow, the group was essentially washed up in the United States before the end of 1956. The Comets' career as a world-beater was over in less than two years.

Unfortunately, Haley encountered problems outside the United States as well. His world tour of 1958 resulted in teen riots and antirock editorials in more than one nation. Haley continued to record singles and albums at a furious pace and sold a large number of them around the world. In Mexico and elsewhere in Latin America he made and sold many Spanish- and English-language records. On occasion he would tour Europe and South America, places where his popularity had not diminished. He continued to tour in the 1970s, but with longer periods of retirement in between. In 1979 he played for Britain's Queen Elizabeth II in a Royal Command Performance, a high point of his career.

For many fans of rock and roll, Haley remains one of the most important and influential musicians of his generation. For others, he is an obscure curiosity who was unable to change with the times. It is beyond dispute that popular music was heavily influenced by his innovation of mixing country instruments and vocal styles with R&B, a trend that was fully developed by the much younger and more charismatic Presley. On February 9, 1981, Bill Haley died of a heart attack in his home in Harlingen, Texas. He was fifty-five.

David Lonergan

SEE ALSO: The Blackboard Jungle; *The Fifties; Freed, Alan "Moondog"; Pop Music; Presley, Elvis; Rhythm and Blues; Rock and Roll.*

BIBLIOGRAPHY

Candelaria, Lorenzo, and Daniel Kingman. *American Music: A Panorama.* Detroit, MI: Gale Cengage Learning, 2011.

Haley, John W., and John von Hoelle. *Sound and Glory: The Incredible Story of Bill Haley, the Father of Rock 'n' Roll and the Music That Shook the World.* Wilmington, DE: Dyne-American Publishing, 1990.

Nite, Norm N. *Rock On Almanac: The First Four Decades of Rock 'n' Roll: A Chronology*, 2nd ed. New York: HarperCollins, 1992.

Swenson, John. *Bill Haley: The Daddy of Rock and Roll.* New York: Stein and Day, 1983.

Hall and Oates

Comprising singer Daryl Hall and guitarist-vocalist John Oates, the middle-of-the-road, Philadelphia-based pop duo Hall and Oates rose to fame in the mid-1970s with emotive ballads such as "Sarah Smile" and "She's Gone." Initially dubbed "blue-eyed soul" by some critics, stressing that the twosome was a white act singing "black music," Hall and Oates veered toward a more rock-oriented sound at the end of the 1970s, resulting in a slew of platinum singles and albums, such as *Private Eyes* (1981) and *H_2O* (1982). By 1984 their sales had made them the biggest-selling duo in history, replacing the 1960s rock-and-roll act the Everly Brothers. Despite such success, Hall and Oates parted ways after the phenomenally successful 1984 effort *Big Bam Boom.* After the breakup, most of the duo's backing musicians went on to form the house band for television's *Saturday Night Live*, while Hall embarked on a solo career and the thickly mustachioed Oates remained in relative obscurity until a Hall and Oates reunion in the 1990s.

Oates shaved off the mustache in 1990, and the reunion proved fortuitous because it set the stage for the following decades, in which Hall and Oates continued to wield a strong influence on the modern music scene. Chris Norris suggested in *New York* magazine that the two can now be considered a "DNA strand" in the genres of post-rock, post-soul, and post-rap. Hall and Oates have remained busy in the early twenty-first century, releasing *Do It for Love* (2003), *Our Kind of Soul* (2004), and *Home for Christmas* (2006). Between 2001 and 2009 they also released more than eight compilation albums. The box set *Do What You Want, Be What You Are: The Music of Daryl Hall and John Oates* was released in 2009.

Shaun Frentner

SEE ALSO: *The Everly Brothers; Pop Music; Rock and Roll;* Saturday Night Live.

BIBLIOGRAPHY

Gooch, Brad. *Hall and Oates.* New York: Ballantine, 1984.

Norris, Chris. "Daryl Hall." *New York*, January 3, 2011.

Tosches, Nick. *Hall and Oates: Dangerous Dances.* New York: St. Martin's Press, 1984.

Tosches, Nick. *Hall and Oates: Suburban Contemporary: An Authorized Biography.* New York: St. Martin's Press, 1984.

Hallmark Hall of Fame

The *Hallmark Hall of Fame* specials are among the high points of each television season. The dramas, usually movie length, feature fine actors in quality adaptations of recent Broadway shows or older classic plays, as well as screenplays based on popular books. The presentations are shown during holiday seasons, which are peak card-giving periods and times that the sponsor, Hallmark Cards, wants to get its name before the public. While the programs are praised for their quality, by industry standards they are not always big hits in terms of ratings. Nevertheless, Hallmark has been steadfast in its support because the quality of the programs enhances the company's reputation for quality.

The first special was presented on December 24, 1951, as a "thank-you" to the consumers who had sent Hallmark cards over the holidays. The host, Sarah Churchill, briefly thanked the viewers for their support of Hallmark Cards; then Gian Carlo Menotti's Christmas opera *Amahl and the Night Visitors* was shown without further interruption. It was the first opera to be shown on television.

Each succeeding year Hallmark has presented some of the most acclaimed programs of any given season. Many of the first specials were plays by William Shakespeare, such as *Hamlet* (1953 with Maurice Evans and restaged in 1970 with Richard Chamberlain), *MacBeth* (1954), and *Taming of the Shrew* (1956), but the first programs also included nonclassical plays such as *Alice in Wonderland* (1955), *Born Yesterday* (1956), and *Victoria Regina* (1961). The series has been responsible for bringing to television viewers such exceptional plays as *Anastasia* (1967), *Winter of Our Discontent* (1983), *The Secret Garden* (1987), *Stones for Ibarra* (1988), *April Morning* (1988), and *Sarah, Plain and Tall* (1991), which was the highest-rated movie of the season. Two years later the sequel, *Skylark* (1993), was aired. Also presented in 1993 was *To Dance with the White Dog*, which was the top-rated movie for the 1993–1994 season.

Hallmark Hall of Fame has showcased other plays by Shakespeare, including *Richard II* and *The Tempest*, as well as six plays by George Bernard Shaw, including *Pygmalion*, *Saint Joan*, and *Caesar and Cleopatra.* More current works have included Rod Serling's *A Storm in Summer*, James Costigan's *Little Moon of Alban*, John Neufeld's *Lisa Bright and Dark*, and Sherman Yellen's *Beauty and the Beast.*

In addition to critical acclamations, some of the presentations have won praise for their depiction of current social problems. Two such acclaimed specials were *Promise* (1986), which concerns the difficulties faced by a man caring for his mentally ill brother, and *My Name Is Bill W* (1989), which chronicles the life of the founder of Alcoholics Anonymous.

Both specials starred James Garner and James Woods. In the first decade of the 2000s the award-winning *Front of the Class* (2009) depicts a man with Tourette's syndrome who overcomes his difficulties to become a gifted classroom teacher. Other presentations have tackled important historic events. The Emmy-nominated program *The Courageous Heart of Irena Sendler* (2009) tells the story of a Polish woman who saved 2,500 Jewish children during the Holocaust.

Often cited as epitomizing the company slogan, "when you care enough to send the very best," *Hallmark Hall of Fame* received a Peabody in 1965, and Joyce Hall, president of Hallmark Cards, was inducted into the Television Hall of Fame in 1985. The long-running series completed its sixtieth anniversary season in 2011. Many of the movies from the *Hallmark Hall of Fame* library are shown on the Hallmark Movie Channel, a cable network that was launched in 2008. Like its sister station, the Hallmark Channel, the Hallmark Movie Channel focuses on family-friendly programming.

Denise Lowe

SEE ALSO: *Cable TV; Garner, James; Greeting Cards; Made-for-Television Movies; Serling, Rod; Television.*

BIBLIOGRAPHY

UCLA Film and Television Archive. *Hallmark Hall of Fame: The First 50 Years.* Los Angeles: Archive, 2001.

Halloween

The modern holiday of Halloween evolved from a number of ancient traditions. Harvest festivals, solemn religious observance, remembrance of the dead, children's frolics, and anarchistic high jinks have distilled into a uniquely American holiday celebrated on October 31 with candy, costumes, and an increasing number of spine-chilling decorations.

Many historians believe that Halloween has its origins as early as the fifth century BCE in the Celtic festival of Samhain, which marked the end of harvest and acknowledged the thin line between life and death. Theories differ as to the meaning behind the disguises and pranks that became associated with the celebration, but some historians believe they were intended to confuse and distract the spirits of the dead thought to roam the world on Samhain. The Catholic Church, seeking to suppress indigenous religious practices, reinvented Samhain as All Saints' Day, which was established on November 1; the day before it became All Hallows Eve, or Hallowe'en.

Ancient traditions of costumes, gifts of food, and trickery came to the United States with a wave of Irish immigrants during the mid-1800s, but it was not until the 1930s that the phrase "trick or treat" began appearing in newspaper articles and public discourse. By the 1950s the tradition of Halloween as a children's holiday had become firmly established, with groups of costumed youngsters roaming the night, going door to door requesting candy and promising mischief if none was forthcoming. The threat was generally intended in a lighthearted way, but some revelers, especially older children, used the holiday as an opportunity for vandalism, leading some communities to place age limits on trick-or-treaters.

During the 1970s, a number of stories surfaced about dangerous items such as razor blades being hidden in Halloween treats. Although most of these are urban legends, parents began to doubt the wisdom of allowing their children out alone on Halloween. In 1982 the poisoning of seven people in Chicago as a result of criminal tampering with bottles of the pain medication Tylenol caused parents to be even more fearful for the

Halloween. *Costumed revelers take to the streets for a Halloween parade in New York City.* WENDELL TEODORO/WIREIMAGE/GETTY IMAGES.

safety of their children. Many became reluctant to allow random trick-or-treating and instead took their children to shopping centers or held private Halloween parties at home.

Once Halloween became an occasion for in-home parties, adults became more involved in the holiday. By the early 2000s, sales of elaborately ghoulish Halloween decorations had skyrocketed, placing the holiday just behind Christmas in public adornment. Adults began to buy expensive costumes, and the number of public Halloween festivities increased. Some conservative Christian groups have spoken out against Halloween as blatant devil worship, while other people have used the occasion to construct controversial haunted houses that feature bloody depictions of sinful behavior and its consequences.

Halloween has evolved somewhat differently in Latin countries, which have followed more closely the Catholic tradition of All Souls' Day, celebrating the time between October 31 and November 2 as Día de los Muertos, a joyful homage to ancestors' continuing presence among the living. Mexicans and other Latin Americans honor the dead with picnics at family gravesites, humorous images of skeletons, and edible skulls, making death a familiar part of life. As more people from Latin American countries immigrate to the United States, the Latin version of Day of the Dead has also moved across the border, and the vibrantly decorated graveyards, sugar skulls, and festive parties of Día de los Muertos have joined scary masks and candy treats as a part of American Halloween.

Tina Gianoulis

SEE ALSO: *Christmas; Consumerism; Fourth of July Celebrations;* Halloween*; Thanksgiving; Urban Legends.*

BIBLIOGRAPHY

Bannatyne, Lesley Pratt. *Halloween Nation: Behind the Scenes of America's Fright Night.* Gretna, LA: Pelican, 2011.

Feldman, Ellen. "Halloween." *American Heritage* 52, no. 7 (2001): 63.

Markale, Jean. *The Pagan Mysteries of Halloween: Celebrating the Dark Half of the Year.* Rochester, VT: Inner Traditions International, 2001.

Halloween

Nothing less than a horror-film renaissance was spawned by the release of director John Carpenter's *Halloween* in 1978. *Halloween* also gave independent film producers something to scream about. With a budget of around $300,000 and no major studio behind them, executive producers Irwin Yablans and Moustapha Akkad backed the film, which Carpenter cowrote with Debra Hill (who also served as producer). The film went on to earn an estimated $55 million, siring several sequels, comic books, novels, and some worthy and unworthy imitators well into the twenty-first century.

The plot of *Halloween* is deceptively simple. The film begins in the sleepy town of Haddonfield, Illinois, on Halloween night, 1963. Six-year-old Michael Myers has just murdered his sister with a butcher knife. Cut to fifteen years later, when Michael has reached the age of twenty-one within the walls of a mental hospital and is under the care of Dr. Loomis (played with fidgety obsessiveness by Donald Pleasence). Loomis describes Myers as a monster who must never be released. Of course, he escapes on the day before Halloween and returns to Haddonfield to finish what he started. With Loomis giving chase, Myers (described as "the Shape" in the credits, played by Nick Castle) returns home. Myers's modus operandi is consistent: he goes after high school girls, including Laurie Strode (Jamie Lee Curtis in her first and most recognizable screen role), who is revealed in *Halloween II* (1981) to be Myers's younger sister.

A NEW TWIST ON HORROR

With a lean budget and only one star (Pleasence), Carpenter had to depend upon skill and luck to author a film with a tone that is as eerie as it is unprecedented in horror. His musical score is the sparsest imaginable, but the tinkling piano keys above the menacing drone of electronically produced strings and brass set a terrifying mood. In fact, the *Halloween* theme has become one of the most recognizable scores in film history. Thanks to cinematographer Dean Cundey, *Halloween*'s bright but somehow claustrophobic daylight exterior shots make even the quiet neighborhoods of Haddonfield seem ominous. The shadowy interiors of Haddonfield's houses reveal only part of the terror within them, making the threat seem even greater.

By placing the horror within a mundane, middle-class suburb, *Halloween* creates the giddy unease of an urban legend. The chants of trick-or-treat rhymes at the beginning of the film, the sexual precocity of the teenage characters, the babysitting nightmare, the legendary murder fifteen years before—these all elicit campfire ghost story responses without seeming like mere plot devices. Carpenter's greatest innovation, as well as his most copied, is his use of the monster/stalker's point of view. Audiences accustomed to the traditional syntax of horror films—the empty dark space over the heroine's shoulder, the fake-terror-relief-then-real-terror economy in horror movies by William Castle and Roger Corman—were introduced to something new. By offering the point of view of the monster, Carpenter elevates audience tension. Finally, there is the monster himself: created by production designer Tommy Lee Wallace simply by painting a cheap William Shatner mask white, this false face became a blank slate that could hold infinite horrors in the imagination of the audience.

TEENAGE TERROR

Many audience members were the same age as the teenagers being murdered and mutilated in the film, and they responded emphatically to the psychosexual themes. Like the many imitators and their sequels that followed—*Friday the 13th* (1980), *Prom Night* (1980)—*Halloween* features teenagers being maimed and slaughtered before, during, or after intercourse. Sex becomes foreplay for the climax(es) of these films: the murders of promiscuous (and mainly female) teenagers.

Despite the apparent Puritanism and sexism of *Halloween* and its cousins, University of California at Berkeley professor Carol Clover finds an almost feminist formula in them. In the book *Men, Women, and Chain Saws: Gender in the Modern Horror Film* (1992), Clover points out that it is, after all, Laurie Strode who survives *Halloween*:

> The image of the distressed female most likely to linger in memory is the image of the one who did not die: the survivor, or Final Girl. She is the one who encounters the mutilated bodies of her friends and

perceives the full extent of the preceding horror and of her own peril; who is chased, cornered, wounded; whom we see scream, stagger, fall, rise and scream again. . . . She alone looks death in the face; but she alone also finds the strength either to stay the killer long enough to be rescued (ending A) or to kill him herself (ending B). But in either case, from 1974 on, the survivor has been female.

IMITATORS AND SEQUELS

Over the years, a number of sequels and remakes have established *Halloween* as the preeminent horror franchise, perhaps rivaled only by the *Friday the 13th* series. Following the release of *Halloween II* in 1981, producers Carpenter and Hill decided that the Michael Myers murder spree had run its course and enlisted former designer Wallace to concoct a script featuring neither Myers nor his maniacal pursuit of his younger sister. *Halloween III: Season of the Witch* (1982) was poorly received by fans and critics for whom the title *Halloween* had become synonymous with Myers and his increasingly brutal killing techniques. Beginning with *Halloween 4: The Return of Michael Myers* (1988), every film in the series features some variant of Myers inflicting terror upon his surviving family members. In all, eight *Halloween* films were produced from 1978 to 2002, though there is little continuity between installments due to numerous writer, director, and cast changes.

In 2007 musician and filmmaker Rob Zombie wrote, produced, and directed a remake of the original *Halloween*. Zombie took several liberties with the plotline, most notably in humanizing Myers by delving into the details of his dysfunctional home life and his prolonged institutionalization following the murder of a school bully and his sister and her boyfriend. The reimagined *Halloween* was the highest-grossing film in the franchise and was followed by *Halloween II* in 2009, which received similar treatment from Zombie. Just like its twisted protagonist, Myers, *Halloween* appears to be a film franchise that will not die.

Tim Arnold

SEE ALSO: *Corman, Roger;* Friday the 13th*; Halloween; Horror Movies; Slasher Movies; Teenagers; Urban Legends.*

BIBLIOGRAPHY

Clover, Carol J. *Men, Women, and Chain Saws: Gender in the Modern Horror Film.* Princeton, NJ: Princeton University Press, 1992.

Harper, Jim. *Legacy of Blood: A Comprehensive Guide to Slasher Movies.* Manchester, UK: Headpress, 2004.

Nowell, Richard. *Blood Money: A History of the First Teen Slasher Film Cycle.* New York: Continuum, 2011.

Waller, Gregory A., ed. *American Horrors: Essays on the Modern American Horror Film.* Urbana: University of Illinois Press, 1987.

Halston *(1932–1990)*

Halston's (born Roy Halston Frowick) first claim to fame was the simple and much-imitated pillbox hat that Jacqueline Kennedy wore at the 1961 presidential inauguration. The designer's success continued in the 1970s. Within the maelstrom of Paris fashions, youthquake, minis, and maxis, Halston reasserted the unadorned cut and practicality of American sportswear: easy, simple, and eternal. In 1972 his plain Ultrasuede shirtwaist sold 60,000 copies.

Halston's flowing movement and versatile layers allowed women of all sizes and shapes to find him their perfect designer; he ultimately claimed that he would design for every woman in America, including custom-order clients such as Liza Minnelli, Martha Graham, and Elizabeth Taylor. In 1982, when Halston initiated Halston III for JCPenney, the designer was dropped from other stores that did not want him to design for their elite clientele and for everyone. Brilliant and charismatic, Halston could make and market anything, except genuine democracy in American fashion. In 2011 the screenwriter Whitney Sudler-Smith produced a documentary about the designer called *Ultrasuede: In Search of Halston.*

Richard Martin

SEE ALSO: *Graham, Martha; Minnelli, Liza; Onassis, Jacqueline Lee Bouvier Kennedy; Taylor, Elizabeth.*

BIBLIOGRAPHY

Bluttal, Steven, and Patricia Mears. *Halston.* London: Phaidon Press, 2001.

Gaines, Steven S. *Simply Halston: The Untold Story.* New York: Putnam, 1991.

Minnelli, Liza, and Polly Mellen. "Halston, 1932–1990." *Vogue*, July 1990.

Hamburger

In the mid-twentieth century the hamburger emerged as a symbol of American democracy and prosperity. As fast food became dominant on the American landscape, the hamburger provided an inexpensive serving of meat to millions of people. To consume a hamburger was, in a sense, to fulfill the promise of democracy and to enact one's Americanness.

Hamburger. *Brought to the United States by German immigrants in the late 1890s, the hamburger has come to epitomize the classic American meal.* JUSTIN SULLIVAN/GETTY IMAGES.

BIRTH OF THE BURGER

The hamburger, or "burger," minimally defined as a cooked ground beef patty between two pieces of bread, was born in America sometime around 1890. Loosely based on the ground beef steak popular in Hamburg, Germany, the hamburger gained national repute at the 1904 St. Louis, Missouri, World's Fair. In the 1920s the White Castle chain of restaurants helped popularize the hamburger, which was becoming a common food in many regions. In the 1930s and 1940s the Great Depression and World War II severely impacted the ability of most Americans to purchase meat, but after the war America's economy began to boom, and the hamburger rode the crest of a wave of prosperity. Simple to prepare and available in every corner of America, the hamburger made meat cheaply available to a nation familiar with hunger and rationing. It celebrated the end of the war, the democratization of wealth, and America's robust economy.

By 1954, when Ray Kroc bought McDonald's, the hamburger was becoming popular nationwide at diners and roadside stands. With the rapid diffusion of McDonald's franchises in the 1960s, and later with a national advertising campaign for the Big Mac, the hamburger began to take on increased cultural importance. Because of its popularity, its standardization, and its heavy representation on television, it came to be identified as the most American food. It appeared alongside celebrities and the American flag and was heralded in television drama, movies, and rock and roll.

The hamburger's surge in importance coincided with widespread ownership of automobiles. Together, the burger and the car appealed to and reinforced American affinities for speed and convenience. Drive-in and drive-through restaurants proliferated, buoyed by their staple food, the hamburger. The burger could be prepared rapidly, eaten without utensils, and eaten on the run. In the new culture of fast food, it could be eaten alone, breaking many ethnic traditions of social dining.

As the quintessential American food, the hamburger was the main format by which Americans ingested beef and, in the same bite, the mythologies of beef. In addition to prosperity, beef was linked to manliness and patriarchy, to domination over nature, to physical strength, to athletic prowess, and to being a "red-blooded" or an authentic American. The low cost and widespread availability of hamburgers ensured that all citizens could symbolically—and democratically—impart these national ideals.

DIVERSIFICATION OF THE BURGER

Beef's popularity peaked in 1976, when each American ate 127 pounds of it per year, with the hamburger patty as its most popular shape. In the late 1970s new consciousness about dietary fat markedly reduced the hamburger's popularity. By the 1980s red-meat consumption was considerably reduced, and many medical studies were linking red meat consumption to cancer and heart disease. While the cattle industry responded with a multimillion-dollar ad campaign—"Beef: Real Food for Real People"—fast-food restaurants began to diversify their offerings. While the beef hamburger remained the bedrock of fast food, salads, chicken, fish, and burritos made inroads into the market.

By 1995 Americans consumed twenty-nine billion hamburgers a year: an average of 120 per capita. Together, fast-food chains and cattle ranches formed one of the largest industries in America, impacting ecosystems, water resources, and land ownership of large parts of the country in its push for a supply of inexpensive beef—the key to success for the fast-food hamburger. By converting much of the western wilderness into ranchland and by securing water rights and government subsidies, cattle ranchers could profitably sell beef at less than a dollar per pound. Powered by the popularity of hamburgers, an enormous cattle industry transformed millions of acres of wilderness. Barbed-wire fences, cattle manure, grazing, and drought caused by the diversion of water sources radically altered land from Texas to Oregon. From the 1960s onward, parts of Latin American rain forests were also cleared to raise beef for American fast-food burgers.

By the close of the twentieth century, the traditional hamburger was in decline. Environmentalists alleged that the hamburger was a major threat to ecosystems, and health advocates warned Americans to reduce their intake of red meat. The small but growing popularity of vegetarianism also challenged the hamburger, and even though most Americans did not disavow meat altogether, many reduced their intake. While the beef burger was waning in popularity, other versions of the burger were ascendant: the hamburger was being reinterpreted. Burgers were being made with fish, chicken, turkey, soybeans, or grains. In the 1990s the veggie burger, a grain-based burger, rapidly increased in popularity.

DECLINE AND RESURRECTION

The hamburger industry was dealt another blow with the publication of the book *Fast Food Nation* (2001) by investigative reporter Eric Schlosser. The book provided an unflattering yet honest look at the beef and fast-food industries and encouraged readers to stop eating ground beef and eating at fast-food restaurants. *Fast Food Nation* became an international best seller and was on the *New York Times* best-seller list for more than two years. On the heels of *Fast Food Nation* came the documentary film *Super Size Me* (2004), in which filmmaker Morgan Spurlock experimented on himself by limiting his food intake to three fast-food meals from McDonald's per day for thirty days. This diet led to health problems and a weight gain of some 24 pounds. The film was a success and received numerous awards, including an Academy Award nomination for Best Documentary.

As if the publicity from *Fast Food Nation* and *Super Size Me* was not damaging enough to the hamburger, in the first decade of the 2000s *E. coli* outbreaks from tainted ground beef sickened a number of Americans and sparked nationwide fear. Also of concern was the appearance of bovine spongiform encephalopathy (BSE), more commonly known as mad cow disease. Eating infected beef can lead to variant Creutzfeldt-Jakob disease in humans, which can be fatal. Though rare, the fear associated with mad cow disease was enough to impact the beef industry. The first U.S. cow found to have mad cow disease was in 2003 in the state of Washington. As a result of the find, a number of countries banned U.S. beef imports, and sales plunged.

Americans, however, still love their hamburgers and will find a way to eat them. With many of the problems of the commercial beef industry exposed, conscientious burger lovers turned toward the organic beef industry. Demand and sales of organic products have risen during the first two decades of the 2000s: according to the Organic Trade Association, sales of organic beef reached about $10 million in 2003 and $100 million by 2009. In addition, there were plenty of burger consumers who were not scared off by stories of tainted beef or unsanitary cattle production, Fast-food restaurants continued to thrive, including McDonald's, which enjoyed increasing sales; its 2011 sales grew about 4.8 percent over those of 2010.

Dylan Clark

SEE ALSO: *Automobile; Burger King; Diners; Fast Food; The Great Depression; McDonald's; The* New York Times*; Rock and Roll;* Super Size Me*; Television; Vegetarianism; White Castle; World War II; World's Fairs.*

BIBLIOGRAPHY

Levi-Strauss, Claude. *The Raw and the Cooked*, tr. John and Doreen Weightman. New York: Harper & Row, 1969.

McDonald, Ronald L. *The Complete Hamburger: The History of America's Favorite Sandwich*. Secaucus, NJ: Carol, 1997.

Rifkin, Jeremy. *Beyond Beef: The Rise and Fall of the Cattle Culture*. New York: Dutton, 1992.

Robbins, John. *Diet for a New America*. Walpole, NH: Stillpoint, 1987.

Schlosser, Eric. *Fast Food Nation*. New York: Houghton Mifflin, 2001.

Trager, James. *The Food Chronology*. New York: Henry Holt, 1995.

Hamill, Dorothy *(1956–)*

Easily recognizable for the pixie haircut that is her trademark, Dorothy Hamill created one of the first true media frenzies surrounding a figure skater. Hamill reigned as a national, world, and Olympic champion in the 1970s and helped develop the popularity of professional ice-skating shows. During the 1976 Olympics, girls all over the world copied her hairstyle, which led to Hamill becoming a spokesperson for hair care products.

Born in Chicago to Chalmers and Carol Hamill, she became interested in skating at the age of eight. She began taking lessons with former Czech champion Otto Gold in 1965. Almost immediately the Hamill family decided that their talented daughter should train seriously, with the goal of competing at the national level. Hamill passed her first preliminary moves figure skating test to compete in 1965. By 1967 she had switched coaches to train with Swiss coach Gustave Lussi. She later studied with former U.S. champion Sonya Klopfer Dunfield.

Hamill became the U.S. National Ladies Novice Champion in 1969, at the age of twelve, and continued to move up the skating ranks. The teenager soon began training with Carlo Fassi, who had also coached champion Peggy Fleming, and advanced to the Senior Ladies Division. In her first U.S. Figure Skating Championships in 1971, she placed a very respectable fifth place. By 1973 she had matured so much that she barely lost the national championship to Janet Lynn. The same year, Hamill came in fourth in the World Figure Skating Championships.

In 1974 Hamill represented the United States as national champion at the world championships, which were held in Munich, Germany. During the competition an incident occurred that will long be remembered by the skating fans who witnessed it. The audience for the long program, upset by low scores given to local skater, Gerti Schanderl, began booing as Hamill prepared to skate. Although they were not booing her, Hamill became so upset she left the ice in tears. A few moments later she again took the ice, having declined the opportunity to compose herself and skate later in the competition. Showing the determination that had already gotten her so far, Hamill skated almost flawlessly and finished with the silver medal behind Christine Erath of East Germany.

During the 1975 season, Hamill defended her national title and again finished second at the World Figure Skating Championships, this time to Dianne deLeeuw of the Netherlands. Things continued to heat up throughout the season before the 1976 Olympic Games in Austria. Hamill and world champions deLeeuw and Erath remained neck in neck, with no clear favorite for the Olympic gold medal. In the media frenzy before the games, however, it became clear that Hamill was the press and audience favorite. Her parents and coach tried to insulate Hamill from the spotlight as she continued to train for the Olympics. When the games were over, Hamill had been crowned the new Olympic champion. She then captured the world championships, and the interest in Hamill and her professional and private life grew. She became a commercial spokesperson for Short & Sassy hair care products, which capitalized on her famous haircut.

After she turned professional, Hamill continued to command the spotlight while skating with the Ice Capades although not to the extent she had during the Olympics. She starred in ice shows and popular television specials, such as *Romeo and Juliet on Ice*. Hamill was largely responsible for bringing worldwide interest to professional ice shows.

When her first marriage to actor Dean Paul Martin broke up, she married sports medicine specialist Kenneth Forsythe. In 1993, after she had skated with the Ice Capades for several years, Hamill, her husband, and businessman Ben C. Tinsdale purchased the show; their first production was *Cinderella . . . Frozen in Time*. Although the show was a success, Ice Capades did not prosper as hoped, and a conglomerate acquired it in 1994.

Hamill helped increase interest in figure skating, both on the amateur and the professional levels. She became one of the first real superstars of figure skating. Along the way she also became an icon to young girls all over the world.

Jill A. Gregg

SEE ALSO: *Fleming, Peggy; Ice Shows; Olympics; Skating.*

BIBLIOGRAPHY

Dolan, Edward F., and Richard B. Lyttle. *Dorothy Hamill: Olympic Skating Champion*. New York: Doubleday, 1979.

Gustaitis, Joseph Alan. *Figure Skating*. New York: Crabtree Publishing, 2010.

Malone, John Williams. *The Encyclopedia of Figure Skating*. New York: Facts On File, 1998.

Milton, Steve. *Skate: 100 Years of Figure Skating*. North Pomfret, VT: Trafalgar Square, 1996.

Hammerstein, Oscar, II

SEE: *Rodgers and Hammerstein.*

Hammett, Dashiell *(1894–1961)*

For a writer who published only five novels, Dashiell Hammett made a strong and lasting impression on twentieth-century literature. He is considered a founding father of the hard-boiled school of detective fiction—a tough, unsentimental style of American crime writing. He introduced unforgettable characters, such as Sam Spade in *The Maltese Falcon* (1930) and Nick and Nora Charles in *The Thin Man* (1934). His novels remained in print long after his death, along with many of the short stories and novelettes he wrote for the *Black Mask* detective pulp magazine. The film version of *The Maltese Falcon* (1941), starring Humphrey Bogart, can still be seen regularly on television or video. All six of the *Thin Man* films, starring the memorable acting team of William Powell and Myrna Loy, are also easily accessible.

WRITING CAREER

Born in Maryland on May 27, 1894, Samuel Dashiell Hammett dropped out of school while in his early teens, worked as an operative for the Pinkerton Detective Agency in Baltimore, and served as a driver in the Ambulance Corps during World War I. In the early 1920s, married and living in San Francisco, he began submitting stories to magazines and soon became a regular contributor to *Black Mask*. Using a restrained yet tough vernacular first-person style, he wrote a series about a plump, middle-aged operative anonymously known as the "Continental Op," who worked for the Continental Detective Agency in San Francisco. Based in part on his own experiences as a Pinkerton detective, the stories offered action, gunplay, romance, and melodrama. When Joseph T. Shaw took over as *Black Mask* editor in 1926, Shaw quickly decided that Hammett was the best writer he had. Shaw promoted Hammett to star contributor and tried to persuade other writers to follow in his footsteps.

Of the several dozen stories Hammett wrote for the pulp, nearly thirty were about the Continental Op, who also figured in his first two novels: *Red Harvest* (1929) and *The Dain Curse* (1929). After being serialized in *Black Mask*, both novels were published by Alfred A. Knopf. *The Maltese Falcon* began that same year as a serial and was published as a book by Knopf in 1930, followed by *The Glass Key* in 1931. Hammett's final novel, *The Thin Man*, first appeared in *Redbook* in 1933 and later as a book (with a few allegedly risqué lines restored) in 1934. Both critics and readers were enthusiastic about Hammett's books, and his reputation soon spread beyond the pulpwood and mystery novel ghettos. *The Maltese Falcon* was early added to the prestigious Modern Library list, and Hammett's fiction was found in glossy, high-paying magazines such as *Collier's*.

Hammett's literary reputation slipped during the 1930s and early 1940s—despite the success of his creations would have in movies and radio. In the early 1940s Frederic Dannay, the literary half of Ellery Queen, began reprinting Hammett's old pulp stories in *Ellery Queen's Mystery Magazine*. Several paperback reprint collections soon followed, bolstering Hammett's standing and gaining a new audience for his written work.

FILM AND RADIO ADAPTATIONS

Sam Spade soon took his first step into another medium. In 1931 Warner Brothers produced an adaptation of *The Maltese Falcon* starring silent movie star Ricardo Cortez as Spade. Warner Brothers ineptly adapted *The Maltese Falcon* as *Satan Met a Lady* (1936), a comedy featuring Warren William as the sleuth. In 1941 director John Huston persuaded the studio to let him write and direct a new version of *The Maltese Falcon* that would stick closely to the Hammett original. This film became the definitive adaptation of the novel, gave Humphrey Bogart the role that rejuvenated his career, and helped establish film noir as a genre. Hammett, who sold all motion picture rights to his book in 1931, never profited directly from the two later adaptations.

In 1943 Edward G. Robinson became the first voice actor on the radio to play Sam Spade in a broadcast of the *Lux Radio Theatre*. Bogart himself reprised the role in an early 1946 half-hour version for a short-lived show called *Academy Award*. That same year *The Adventures of Sam Spade*, a less gloomy re-creation of Hammett's tough world, became a regular weekly show. The new Spade differed significantly from Hammett's original, but the character was tough, whimsical, and appealing—and the show became a hit. Produced by William Spier, the show was mostly written by Gil Doud and Bob Tallman. Howard Duff, who had not yet begun his movie career, was cast as Spade. Duff had a distinctive radio voice that could sound hard-boiled but still get the most out of his frequent gag lines.

The Adventures of Sam Spade remained on the air until 1950, when sponsors and networks became wary of Hammett's political troubles. *The Adventures of the Thin Man* radio show, which had been broadcast fairly regularly from 1941 to 1950, also fell victim to the graylisting of the era. A third Hammett radio show, *The Fat Man*, was heard from early 1946 to early 1951. Besides allowing the use of his name and the nickname of the villain from *The Maltese Falcon* for the main character, Hammett had nothing to do with the production. It, too, ended along with the other shows.

PERSONAL LIFE, LEGAL TROUBLES, AND DEATH

Hammett moved to Hollywood in 1930 and remained there throughout the decade, working on screenplays and screen stories. He contributed original screen stories for the sequels to the film adaptation of *The Thin Man*. Hammet's other avocations were drinking and Lillian Hellman—neither of which contributed significantly to his well-being—although Hellman was supposedly the inspiration for Nora in *The Thin Man*.

Long suspected of holding extreme left-wing views, Hammett was subpoenaed in 1951. The questioning had to do with four suspected Communists who had jumped bail and vanished. Hammett, a bail bond trustee for an organization called the Civil Rights Congress, was asked to provide the names of contributors to the fund. Although he reportedly didn't know any, he nevertheless refused to name names. Convicted for contempt, Hammett spent nearly six months in a federal prison. He suffered from tuberculoses for much of his life, and he died of lung cancer in New York on January 10, 1961.

Ron Goulart

SEE ALSO: Black Mask*; Blacklisting; Bogart, Humphrey; Communism; Detective Fiction; Hard-Boiled Detective Fiction; Hellman, Lillian; Huston, John;* The Maltese Falcon*; Powell, William; Pulp Magazines; Queen, Ellery; Radio; Radio Drama; Red Scare;* Redbook*; Robinson, Edward G.*

BIBLIOGRAPHY

DeAndrea, William L. *Encyclopedia Mysteriosa.* New York: Prentice Hall, 1994.

Goulart, Ron. *The Dime Detectives.* New York: Mysterious Press, 1988.

Nolan, William F. *Dashiell Hammett: A Casebook.* Santa Barbara, CA: McNally & Loftin, 1969.

Hancock, Herbie *(1940–)*

Herbie Hancock has forged a career that has pushed the envelope of jazz music and, in doing so, has reached a wider audience than any other jazz musician ever has. His 1973 album, *Headhunters,* is the top-selling jazz record in history. This Chicago native is easily among the most eclectic musicians of any genre. He has worked within the field of jazz—playing free, bebop, and fusion styles—and outside—performing world music, hip-hop, funk, and dance music. Along with Miles Davis, Hancock helped create the style known as jazz fusion in the late 1960s and, as a solo artist during the early 1970s, he was one of the first to pioneer the use of synthesizers within jazz. And on his 1983 hit single "Rockit," he introduced the mainstream pop world to turntable scratching, an element of hip-hop music that uses a turntable and an album as a musical instrument by manually manipulating the sounds it makes. Throughout his long career, Hancock has continually evolved and challenged genre boundaries in all forms of music.

Herbie Hancock. *Herbie Hancock performs in San Francisco, California, in 1981.* MICHAEL OCHS ARCHIVES/GETTY IMAGES.

A child prodigy, Hancock studied music in school and, at age eleven, performed with the Chicago Symphony Orchestra at a young people's concert. He later formed a high school jazz group, played with the likes of Donald Byrd and Coleman Hawkins at local Chicago jazz clubs, and then left for New York City in 1961 to join and record with Byrd's combo. Soon after working with Byrd, Hancock was offered a solo contract with the jazz label Blue Note, which released his 1962 debut, *Takin' Off.* The album spawned the hit, and soon-to-be jazz standard, "Watermelon Man," positioning Hancock as an important jazz band composer. During the 1960s he wrote such classics as "Maiden Voyage," "Dolphin Dance," and "I Have a Dream" (a tribute to Martin Luther King Jr.).

After an extended stint in Davis's second legendary quintet (which also included Wayne Shorter, Ron Carter, and Tony Williams), Hancock released a number of solo albums. He then formed his first important group, Mwandishi, which included Joe Henderson, Johnny Coles, Garnett Brown, Albert "Tootie" Heath, and Buster Williams. From 1969 to 1972 Mwandishi explored funk and rock fusion and was one of the first jazz groups to use a synthesizer, specifically the Moog. Displeased with the poor commercial reception of the records this group produced, Hancock disbanded Mwandishi, but not before he released *Sextant* in 1973, a landmark album that heavily incorporated the synthesizer into the band's laid-back funk vamps.

Hancock then formed the Headhunters, an instrumental jazz/pop/rock/funk combo (featuring Hancock, Bennie Maupin, Paul Jackson, Harvey Mason, and Bill Summers) that became hugely popular. That group's 1973 album, *Headhunters,* sold more records than any jazz record had ever sold before, beginning a steady stream of success for Hancock that included seventeen albums charting from 1973 to 1984. Due to his widespread popularity, many charges of "selling out" were leveled against him—charges that he dismissed as "elitist." His popularity culminated with the release of 1983's "Rockit," an electro-funk breakdancing staple that featured the turntable wizardry of Grandmaster D.S.T., marking the first time the art of the hip-hop DJ was heard by a mainstream audience. This song has been cited as a major inspiration for a generation of hip-hop DJs and artists that followed.

During the rest of the 1980s and 1990s, Hancock released a handful of modest-selling albums, which included the world music fusion of *Dis Is Da Drum* and, in 1998, an album by the reformed Headhunters. In the early first decade of the 2000s he produced an album that ventured into a fusion of jazz and electronic music and a later one that focused on pop music. His Joni Mitchell tribute *River: The Joni Letters* (2007) won a pair of Grammy Awards. It was followed by *The Imagine Project* (2010), an album of covers featuring several guest performers, which also won a Grammy.

Kembrew McLeod

SEE ALSO: *Davis, Miles; Funk; Grammy Awards; Hawkins, Coleman; Hip-Hop; Jazz; King, Martin Luther, Jr.; Mitchell, Joni; Pop Music; Rap.*

BIBLIOGRAPHY

Gluck, Bob. *You'll Know When You Get There: Herbie Hancock and the Mwandishi Band.* Chicago: University of Chicago Press, 2012.

Mercer, Michelle. *Footprints: The Life and Work of Wayne Shorter.* New York: J. P. Tarcher/Penguin, 2004.

Porter, Lewis; Michael Ullman; and Edward Hazell. *Jazz: From Its Origins to the Present.* Englewood Cliffs, NJ: Prentice Hall, 1992.

Vincent, Rickey. *Funk: The Music, the People, and the Rhythm of the One.* New York: St. Martin's Griffin, 1996.

H&M

In the second half of the twentieth century, Swedish budget retail chain H&M (Hennes & Mauritz) built a successful international fashion empire by producing cheap clothing for young audiences. Not only does H&M release several seasonal lines per year, as do many more expensive retailers, but the store effectively tracks international trends and reproduces hip styles at extremely low prices.

H&M founder Erling Persson decided to open a Swedish department store in the years following World War II. Inspired by the inexpensive, high-volume stores he observed on a trip to the United States, he opened Hennes ("Hers") department store in Västerås, Sweden, in 1947. The store was expanded to include menswear in 1968, changing its name to Hennes & Mauritz ("Hers and His"). H&M began expanding outside of Sweden in 1968, opening stores in Norway and Denmark. By the late 1970s, H&M was known throughout Europe for its moderately priced, well-made clothing, and the company began a more aggressive international expansion plan, opening stores in the United Kingdom and in other mainland European countries. Indeed, as of 2011, the German and UK markets were even more profitable than the Swedish market.

In March 2000, H&M opened its first U.S. store on New York City's Fifth Avenue. Although there was some question as to whether Americans would warm up to an unknown brand name, H&M went on to be a major success in the United States. As of 2010 there were more than 150 American H&M branches, including nine stores in Manhattan alone. In 2004 H&M began supplementing its regular clothing lines with yearly capsule collections designed by big-name international designers. The first such collection, by French couturier Karl Lagerfeld, was made available at select stores in November 2004, with inventories depleted within an hour. Since then, H&M has presented collections by designers Stella McCartney, Viktor & Rolf, Madonna, Roberto Cavalli, Comme des Garçons, Matthew Williamson, Jimmy Choo, Sonia Rykiel, Lanvin, Versace, and Marni.

Internationally, H&M is the second-largest global clothing retailer, falling just behind the Spanish-based company Inditex (which owns the brand Zara), and outselling the American company Gap Inc. As of 2011 H&M employed more than 90,000 employees worldwide, operating thousands of stores in forty-three countries worldwide. Still based in Stockholm, the company's design team outsources its raw materials and production to European and Asian factories, some of which have been recently cited for labor and health violations. The company announced that it planned to expand its website sales to American customers sometime in 2012, which would also make available H&M's less prominent housewares line, currently sold only online.

Jenny Ludwig

SEE ALSO: *The Gap; Madonna; Versace, Gianni.*

BIBLIOGRAPHY

Curan, Catherine. "Swedish Invasion Begins in NYC: H&M to Open Four Stores, but Lacks Name Recognition." *Crain's New York Business*, February 21, 2000, 1.

"Erling Persson, 85; Founded Clothing Chain." *New York Times*, November 1, 2002.

Handy, W. C. *(1873–1958)*

A major contributor to American music, W. C. Handy is often hailed as the father of the blues. Handy grew up immersed in the folk music of African Americans, a music nurtured by American slaves whose roots were in the various African cultures from which they were torn. A trained musician, he translated this "primitive" music into compositions that revealed the richness and diversity of the black musical tradition. His "Memphis Blues" was the first published blues tune, and he left a legacy of musical compositions to which much of the modern blues can trace its roots.

William Christopher Handy was born on November 16, 1873, in Florence, Alabama. Both his father and grandfather were clergymen and were eager for young Handy to follow in their footsteps, but Handy developed an early love for music. In his autobiography, *Father of the Blues* (1941), he recalls that his father stated that he would rather follow his son's hearse than have him become a musician. Still, Handy persevered, taking vocal lessons from a church singer and secretly buying a cornet and taking lessons from its former owner. By the time he was a teenager, he had amassed a good deal of training in music and, at age fifteen, joined a traveling minstrel show that began a tour of the South. The tour soon fell apart, however, and Handy returned home.

In 1892 Handy graduated from the Huntsville Teachers Agricultural and Mechanical College and began working as a teacher—until he found out that he could make more money working for the Bessemer pipe works factory in Birmingham, Alabama. When wages there were cut, Handy left the factory and returned to music. He organized a group called the Lauzette Quartet, and they went to Chicago to play at the World's Fair—only to find when they arrived that the fair had been postponed until the next year. Dejected, they traveled to St. Louis, Missouri, where they found little work and eventually disbanded. Now on his own, Handy eked out a living playing his cornet and soaking up the ambiance of the city's impoverished black population.

Shortly thereafter, Handy, whose reputation as a talented horn player was spreading, had the good fortune to be hired to play for wealthy southerners in Henderson, Kentucky. "I had my change that day in Henderson," Handy writes in his autobiography. "My change was from a hobo and a member of a road gang to a professional musician." He also found an opportunity to study with a local music teacher, who taught him more about music in a few short months than he had learned so far on his own.

CAMPAIGN SONG

In 1896 Mahara's Minstrels, a minstrel group Handy would later direct, asked Handy to join them, and he traveled extensively with the group until 1900 and from 1902 to 1904. During its travels, the group played to an Alabama audience that included Handy's father. "Sonny," his father told him, "I haven't been in a show since I professed religion. I enjoyed it. I am very proud of you and forgive you for becoming a musician." Handy's band played for both white and black audiences, and during one performance, a white audience asked the group to play some blues. Accustomed to playing popular hits from Broadway and Tin Pan Alley, the band was unable to comply, and a local group of three black musicians took the stage and played what the audience wanted. Handy decided that he had learned an important lesson. He decided to look into the blues.

In 1909 Handy wrote a campaign song titled "Mr. Crump," for Edward H. "Boss" Crump, who was running for mayor of Memphis, Tennessee. Handy's band played the song at rallies, and audiences danced to it. The song includes the following lyrics:

> Mr. Crump won't 'low no easy riders here.
> We doan care what Mr. Crump don't 'low,
> We gon'to bar'l-house anyhow.
> Mr. Crump can go and catch hisself some air.

Crump won the election, and Handy published the song, with some new words, in 1912 as "The Memphis Blues." It was the first written composition to use the flatted thirds and sevenths, the "blue notes." In 1914 popular and successful ballroom dancers Vernon and Irene Castle heard their musical director, composer and conductor James Reese Europe, play the "Memphis Blues" during the intermissions of their shows. The Castles loved the rhythm and developed a slow dance to it called the fox trot.

Following the success of his song, Handy decided to specialize in the blues, a type of music that was little known outside the South at that time. Handy had a great musical memory, coupled with a well-developed musical knowledge. He freely acknowledged the roots of his blues being in black folk songs. As quoted by Stefan Grosman in his book *Mel Bay Complete Country Blues Guitar Book/CD Set*, Handy explained:

> Each one of my blues is based on some old Negro song of the South. . . . Something that sticks in my mind, that I hum to myself when I'm not thinking about it. Some old song that is a part of the memories of my childhood and of my race. I can tell you the exact song I used as a basis for any one of my blues.

At the time, the blues had not yet taken on the classical form by which it was later known. The twelve- or sixteen-bar form in which chords I, IV, and V are used in a set pattern, open to variations, was basically established by Handy as he wrote down the music he heard on his band tours. Handy's blues are more polished than the "primitive" blues that preceded him and were played well into the twentieth century by musicians such as John Lee Hooker.

PUBLISHING COMPANY

Handy had a bad experience with the white publishing house that handled his first song, "Memphis Blues," so in 1913 he founded his own publishing company, Pace and Handy Music Publishers, with partner Harry Pace. Handy assumed the position of secretary-treasurer, Pace served as president, and Handy's brother was vice president. In 1921 Pace left, and Handy renamed the company Handy Brothers Music Company. Despite having his own publishing company, Handy still had a hard time getting his music distributed. In his autobiography he recalls the following encounter with a retailer:

> At the time I approached him his windows were displaying "At The Ball" by J. Lubrie Hill, a colored composer who had gone to New York from Memphis some time earlier. Around it were grouped copies of recent successes by such Negro composers as [Robert Allen] Cole and [J. Rosamond] Johnson, Scott Joplin, and the [Bert] Williams and [George] Walker musical comedies. So when he suggested that his trade wouldn't stand for his selling my work, I pointed out as tactfully as I could that the majority of his musical hits of the moment had come from the Gotham-Attucks Co., a firm of Negro publishers in New York. I'll never forget his smile. "Yes," he said pleasantly. "I know that—but my customers don't."

Handy's "St. Louis Blues" (1914) is the most recorded song in musical history. At the time of his death in 1958, it was still earning him $25,000 per year. King Edward VIII of England once requested that it be played for him on bagpipes, and it even became the Ethiopian fight song in the 1930s. American blues singer Bessie Smith, with jazz trumpeter Louis Armstrong on cornet, immortalized the work. Armstrong later recorded the tune a number of times, even playing it as a tango.

In 1917 Handy moved to New York City where he recorded with his Memphis Orchestra. He began his own recording company in 1922, but it soon failed. Handy's written output faltered as a result of increasing eye problems, but he continued playing cornet and recorded with a number of top jazz musicians, including Henry "Red" Allen and Jelly Roll Morton.

In 1928 Handy organized the first program of all-black music (jazz, blues, ragtime, spirituals, and semiclassical music) to play in New York's Carnegie Hall. That concert is one of the only elements of Handy's life that is re-created accurately in his film biography *St. Louis Blues* (1958), which stars Nat King Cole as Handy. Largely inaccurate, the film served to spark rerecordings of many of his tunes. Shortly before Handy's death, Armstrong and the All Stars recorded an album of Handy tunes, and Handy was recorded reflecting on his career and on Armstrong. The album, *Louis Armstrong Plays W. C. Handy* (1954), is a fine correction to the movie.

During Handy's lifetime, the fact that the blues were so identifiably black in origin and so different from the usual Tin Pan Alley tunes eventually worked in his favor. Many people put the word *blues* in songs, but not everyone could write an authentic-sounding blues tune. Handy could and did. The blues became part of jazz and the basis of rock and roll. Handy's music is inseparable from twentieth-century world music, a fact recognized by the city of Memphis, in which Handy is a legend. There is a park named in his honor, and a statue of Handy stands prominently. Handy is also in the Alabama Music Hall of

Fame in Tuscumbia, and he was featured on a six-cent postage stamp issued in 1969.

Frank A. Salamone

SEE ALSO: *Armstrong, Louis; Blues; Broadway; Carnegie Hall; Cole, Nat King; Hooker, John Lee; Jazz; Joplin, Scott; Morton, Jelly Roll; Smith, Bessie; Walker, George; Williams, Bert.*

BIBLIOGRAPHY

Grosman, Stefan. *Mel Bay Complete Country Blues Guitar Book/CD Set*, 246. Pacific, MO: Mel Bay Publications, 1992.

Handy, W. C. Introduction to *Beale Street: Where the Blues Began*, by George Washington Lee. New York: Ballou, 1934.

Handy, W. C. *Father of the Blues*, ed. Arna Bontemps. New York: Da Capo Press, 1991.

Montgomery, Elizabeth Rider. *William C. Handy: Father of the Blues*. Champaign, IL: Garrard Publishing, 1968.

Sotiropoulos, Karen. *Staging Race: Black Performers in Turn of the Century America*. Cambridge, MA: Harvard University Press, 2006.

Hanks, Tom *(1956–)*

One of only two men to ever win back-to-back Academy Awards for Best Actor, Tom Hanks has proven that he is one of the most talented and versatile actors of the late twentieth and early twenty-first centuries. From his early days as cross-dressing Kip in the television show *Bosom Buddies* (1980–1982), Hanks went on to win Oscars for two vastly diverse roles. First, he won Best Actor for 1993's *Philadelphia*, in which he played Andrew Beckett, a gay lawyer dismissed from his law firm after being diagnosed with AIDS. In 1994 Hanks brought home a second statue for his portrayal of the title character in *Forrest Gump*, an amiable Southerner with questionable intelligence and the good fortune to be present at a number of important historical events. For his role as Beckett, Hanks lost so much weight that he lent grim reality to the deteriorating physical condition of the gay lawyer. In *Forrest Gump* the actor developed a slow drawl that perfectly presented Gump's drawn-out mental processes and childish naïveté.

In 2002, at the age of forty-six, Hanks became the youngest actor in American history to be awarded the American Film Institute's Life Achievement Award. According to Harris polls, he was the number one actor in 2002, 2004, and 2005. Even movies such as *Larry Crown* (2011), which was considered a major box-office failure, did not tarnish Hanks's reputation in Hollywood. The movie did, however, cause some critics to question whether or not Hanks could continue to play romantic leads.

PROFESSIONAL LIFE

Not one to be satisfied with making history, Hanks followed up his two Oscar wins with an Oscar-worthy performance that allowed him to bring a lifelong dream close to reality by playing astronaut Jim Lowell in *Apollo 13* (1995). He was also nominated for his performance in 1998's *Saving Private Ryan*, Steven Spielberg's gripping World War II drama. While continuing to act, he also took on multiple producing and directing roles in both film and television. Such roles allowed him to continue to pursue his lifelong interest in space exploration and World War II.

Hanks met the turn of the twenty-first century by taking on the title role in *Cast Away*. Playing Fed Ex executive Chuck Noland, he spends most of his on-camera time alone on a desert island following a plane crash. His only companion is a Wilson volleyball, which becomes his sounding board. In order to appear emaciated, Hanks lost 55 pounds for the role, which netted him a fourth Oscar nomination. He took on a different kind of challenge in *The Terminal* (2004). In what director Spielberg considers Hanks's best performance, he plays Viktor Navorski, an immigrant from the fictional country of Krakozhia, who is forced to live at Kennedy Airport due to a technical error that will not allow him to enter the United States. Two years later Hanks again changed course with the role of cryptologist Dr. Robert Langdon in Dan Brown's *The Da Vinci Code*. Some critics spent more time criticizing his hair than rating his acting. With shorter hair, Hanks reprised the role in 2009 in *Angels and Demons*.

Hanks takes on the role of Professor G. H. Dorr in the crime caper *The Ladykillers* (2004) and pursues Leonardo DiCaprio, appearing as a multifaceted criminal, in *Catch Me if You Can* (2002). He appears against type in both *Road to Perdition* (2002), in which he portrays hit man Michael Sullivan, and *Charlie Wilson's War* (2010), in which he plays the title role of the sleazy Texas politician. Hanks takes on the tragedy of September 11 in *Extremely Loud and Incredibly Close* (2011), which illustrates the grief of children who lost parents when terrorists attacked the United States in 2001. He limited his role to producing in such films as *My Big Fat Greek Wedding* (2002), *Evan Almighty* (2007), *Mamma Mia!* (2008), *Where the Wild Things Are* (2009), and *My Life in Ruins* (2009).

PERSONAL LIFE

Hanks was born July 9, 1956, in Concord, California. When he was five years old, his parents divorced. Hanks and his older siblings lived with his father, while the youngest child remained with his mother. The divorce was followed by multiple sets of step-parents and frequent moves. As the perennial new kid on the block, Hanks learned that people liked him when he made them laugh, so he became a clown. In 1978 he married Samantha Lewes, with whom he has two children, son Colin and daughter Elizabeth. They divorced in 1985. Colin is also an actor, and he and his father worked together in *The Great Buck Howard* (2009). In 1985, while filming the comedy *Volunteers*, Tom Hanks met Rita Wilson, and they were married in 1988. Hanks and Wilson have two sons, Chester and Truman. While accepting the Academy Award for *Forrest Gump* in 1994, Hanks brought tears to many eyes with his acknowledgement of their mutual love and respect.

The years between *Bosom Buddies* and his two Academy Awards were full of both successes and failures for Hanks. Director Ron Howard gave him his first shot at superstardom by casting him opposite mermaid Daryl Hannah in *Splash* (1984). He followed these movies with comedies, such as *The Man with One Red Shoe* (1985) and *The Money Pit* (1986), that endeared him to fans but were panned by critics. In 1988, however, Hanks won over the critics with the role of Josh Baskin in Penny Marshall's *Big*. This story of a young boy who gets his wish to grow up overnight was the perfect vehicle for Hanks because it allowed him to combine his youthful appeal with a mature performance, garnering a Best Actor Oscar nomination.

Unfortunately, Hanks followed up his success in *Big* with less successful roles in *Punchline* (1988), *Turner and Hooch* (1989), and *The Bonfire of the Vanities* and *Joe versus the Volcano* (both 1990). His return to critical acclaim came in 1992 with the role of Jimmy Dugan in Marshall's *A League of Their Own*. While the female stars were the focus in this tale of a women's baseball team, Hanks more than held his own as the bitter, tobacco-chewing, has-been manager of the team.

VERSATILITY

Hanks's versatility is the key to his success as an actor. The physically and mentally draining role of the gay lawyer in *Philadelphia* was immediately followed by a love story that was to become a classic: *Sleepless in Seattle* (1993). *Sleepless* drew on the earlier classic love story of *An Affair to Remember* (1957) for its plot. Instead of star-crossed lovers, Hanks and Meg Ryan play potential lovers who never get together until the final scene, which takes place at the Empire State Building in New York City.

The phenomenal success of *Forrest Gump* was followed by the Disney favorite *Toy Story* (1995). Hanks lent his voice to Woody, a computer-generated cowboy puppet displaced in his boy's affections by spaceman Buzz Lightyear (the voice of Tim Allen). Even in this children's tale, Hanks presents a character to whom his audience can relate and offers friendship as a moral lesson and proof of character development. He reprised his role as the lovable Woody in the third installment of Pixar's Toy Story franchise in 2010 and signed on to do *Toy Story 4* (2015).

Hanks appears in five different roles in Robert Zemeckis's motion-capture endeavor, *The Polar Express* (2004), which brings the beloved children's classic to the big screen. That same year, he provided the voice of Mailbox Elvis in *Elvis Has Left the Building*. Other efforts directed at young audiences include *The Ant Bully* (2006), the tale of a young boy who magically shrinks after attacking ants with his water gun.

Adding producer, writer, and director to his list of accomplishments, Hanks created his own movie with *That Thing You Do* (1996), a charming, simple story of a one-hit 1960's rock band. *From the Earth to the Moon*, a 1998 mini-series, proved to be even more ambitious; in several installments, the miniseries followed the entire history of the space program. The miniseries genre has also allowed Hanks to take a close look at American history, visiting the presidency of second president John Adams and the World War II era to critical acclaim.

In 2001 Hanks produced the ten-episode series *Band of Brothers* for HBO, which told the story of the Easy Company of the 101st Airborne during World War II. He continued to address World War II in 2010 with *The Pacific*. Hanks served as executive producer for the *25th Anniversary Rock and Roll Hall of Fame Concert* (2009), a four-hour television special that took place in New York's Madison Square Garden. He has also produced a number of documentaries, including *The American Experience: Return with Honor* (2000) and *We Stand Alone Together* (2001). In 2012, Hanks was working on *K Blows Top*, which chronicles thirteen days in the life of Soviet premier Nikita Khrushchev in 1959, and he portrayed the role of Dr. Henry Goose in the 2012 movie *Cloud Atlas*, based on the 2004 novel by British author David Mitchell.

Hanks has frequently been compared to Jimmy Stewart, an actor who was so well loved that the Los Angeles airport was renamed to honor him after his death in 1997. Hanks and Stewart are, indeed, similar in their appeal to both men and women and in their versatility. It is likely that Hanks will go down in history as the most popular and the most critically acclaimed actor of the latter half of the twentieth century and of the first decades of the twenty-first century.

Elizabeth Rholetter Purdy

SEE ALSO: *Academy Awards; Apollo Missions; DiCaprio, Leonardo;* Forrest Gump*; Howard, Ron;* A League of Their Own*; Ryan, Meg; Sitcom; Stewart, Jimmy; Television;* Toy Story.

BIBLIOGRAPHY

Beckman, Della, ed. *The Tom Hanks Handbook*. Brisbane, Australia: Emero, 2010.

McAvoy, Jim. *Tom Hanks*. Philadelphia: Chelsea House, 2000.

Nikart, Ray. *Tom Hanks*. New York: St. Martin's Press, 1987.

Parish, James Robert. *Tom Hanks: Actor*. New York: Facts On File, 2004.

Passero, Kathy. "That Thing He Does: The Perpetual Appeal of Tom Hanks." *Biography*, July 1998, 30–37.

Pfeiffer, Lee, and Michael Lewis. *The Films of Tom Hanks*. Secaucus, NJ: Carol Publishing, 1996.

Quinlan, David. *Tom Hanks: A Career in Orbit*. London: B. T. Botsford, 1997.

Seccia, Kevin. *Punching Tom Hanks*. New York: St. Martin's, 2011.

Trakin, Roy. *Tom Hanks: Journey to Stardom*. New York: St. Martin's Paperbacks, 1995.

Travers, Peter. "Tom Hanks." *Rolling Stone*, November 15, 2007.

Hanna-Barbera

William Hanna and Joseph Barbera, both through their own creativity and that of their studio, were second only to Walt Disney in the number of memorable, durable, and famous characters they introduced to the art of American animation. Known and loved throughout the world, Hanna-Barbera cartoons differed from those of the Walt Disney Company in exclusively mining contemporary American life for their ideas, permeating the popular culture with images that reflected it in cartoon form. The team's output was prodigious, and many of their creations famous, but they will forever be synonymous with the world's most popular cat-and-mouse duo, Tom and Jerry. Tom and Jerry's hilarious adversarial relationship serviced more than 100 cartoon shorts and won Academy Awards for seven of them, of which *Johann Mouse* (1952) is perhaps the most outstanding.

EARLY YEARS OF THE PARTNERSHIP

Born in 1910 in Melrose, New Mexico, Hanna began his professional career at age twenty, working as a story editor, lyricist, and composer for an independent studio. Barbera, born in New York City in 1911, was an accountant and a freelance magazine cartoonist. The two men met at Metro-Goldwyn-Mayer (MGM) in 1937, the year they both joined the studio and, with Fred

Quimby, created Tom and Jerry. The imaginative narrative line of the cartoons, in which Jerry Mouse emerges the victor of the battles, pushed the frontiers of animated entertainment and risked using more sadistic imagery than usual in the genre at the time. Jerry had the distinction of being taught to dance "The Worry Song" by Gene Kelly in a stunning sequence, combining live action and animation, in MGM's *Anchors Aweigh* (1945). For Kelly's *Invitation to the Dance* (1956), Hanna, Barbera, and Quimby directed the third segment of the film, in which cartoon characters and Kelly dance to Nikolay Rimsky-Korsakov's "Scheherazade."

In 1957 MGM closed its cartoon division, whereupon Hanna and Barbera set up their own production company, Hanna-Barbera, and launched themselves into a new medium—television. They created the first cartoons for television at a time when many people thought such a feat could not be done, partly because the expense of the animation process seemed feasible only for feature films. Hanna and Barbera, however, devised a less expensive technique by reducing the size of the storyboards, and if the results lacked the detail and background of animated features, they were nonetheless highly successful.

The Ruff and Reddy Show premiered on National Broadcasting Company (NBC) television in 1957, paving the way for several decades of Hanna-Barbera cartoons and Saturday morning viewing rituals and creating characters who became entrenched in American popular culture, recurring in syndication and cartoons for decades. Among the best known were Yogi ("smarter than the average bear") Bear and his sidekick, Boo Boo Bear, as well as Augie Doggie and Doggie Daddy, Huckleberry Hound, Quick Draw McGraw, and Snagglepuss. Perhaps the most famous and durable Hanna-Barbera creation was *The Flintstones* (1960–1966). When it aired in 1960, it was the first animated half-hour prime-time sitcom on television. Modeled after *The Honeymooners*, *The Flintstones* earned Hanna-Barbera a permanent place in American television history. As the first animated cartoon featuring human characters, the series laid the groundwork for such later shows as *The Simpsons* (1989–) and *King of the Hill* (1997–2010).

Joseph Barbera and William Hanna. *Joseph Barbera, left, and William Hanna are surrounded by the Jetson family, one of their many animated creations, in 1990.* FOTOS INTERNATIONAL/GETTY IMAGES.

Besides the lovable and goofy characters of its early years, Hanna-Barbera productions created action and super-hero cartoons in the 1960s. One of the first of these was *Jonny Quest* (1964–1965). Jonny goes on adventures with his scientist father and companions Hadji and Race Bannon. The show was revamped in the 1990s with a focus on computer animation. Other heroes of the time were Space Ghost, the Herculoids, Birdman, the Mighty Mightor, and animated versions of the comic-book super team the Fantastic Four. However, parents' groups eventually objected to the violence, and Hanna-Barbera returned to making more humorous cartoons.

EXPANDING THEIR REPERTOIRE

The company turned out products at an extraordinary rate and embraced computerized systems. Of its later cartoon characters, Scooby-Doo (named after lyrics of a Frank Sinatra song) was the most popular. A cowardly and often ravenous Great Dane, Scooby-Doo, stars in *Scooby-Doo Where Are You!* (1969) with four teenage costars. They travel around in a psychedelic van called the Mystery Machine, solving mysteries that usually have a supernatural slant. Scooby and the gang enjoyed several incarnations over the next several decades. Also popular in the late 1960s and early 1970s were *Dastardly and Muttley in Their Flying Machines* (1969), *The Perils of Penelope Pitstop* (1969–1971), *Josie and the Pussycats* (1970), and *Help! . . . It's the Hair Bear Bunch* (1971). Hanna-Barbera's biggest success of the 1980s was *The Smurfs*, featuring small blue creatures whose names (Handy and Vanity, for example) match their dominant traits. Led by the red-clad Papa Smurf, the Smurfs constantly fight against the evil Gargomel.

Besides the Smurfs, Hanna-Barbera did animated versions of nationally popular live-action shows. Cartoon versions of *Happy Days*, *Laverne and Shirley*, *Mork & Mindy*, and *The Dukes of Hazzard* appeared on Saturday mornings courtesy of Hanna-Barbera. Some shows, such as *Josie and the Pussycats* and *The Pebbles and Bamm-Bamm Show* (1971), incorporated contemporary rock music. Though not as memorable as the Disney classics, the songs keyed into the tastes of their audiences at the time, especially the preteen audience.

During the 1960s, Hanna-Barbera expanded its activities to make a handful of feature films, beginning with *Hey There, It's Yogi Bear* (1964) and ending with *Jetsons: The Movie* (1990), featuring the characters from the TV series of the same name. If individual Hanna-Barbera characters did not reach quite the icon status of Mickey Mouse, they were more typically American and of this world than Disney's famous creations. The Jetsons, for example, are space-age counterparts to the Flintstones, both archetypal American families. The shows exploit the conflicts that typically occur in American homes, while adding gags appropriate to the period in which they were created. The contemporaneous approach was what probably made these two cartoon families the most famous and memorable of the Hanna-Barbera stable.

Hanna and Barbera won many awards. In addition to their Oscars, there were Emmys, and in 1988, fifty years after they met, they received the Governor's Award from the National Academy of Television Arts and Sciences. That same year the company was absorbed into the Great American Broadcasting company, with Barbera as president. Perhaps the duo's greatest honor is the impact they had on the American public. Their TV cartoon series were significant in the lives of countless American children, who entered adulthood still able to sing part, if not all, of the theme songs and reciting such catch phrases as "Yabba dabba do," "Smarter than the average bear," "Jane, stop this crazy thing!" and "Heavens to Murgatroyd," which had their origins in Hanna-Barbera cartoons. Hanna and Barbera's long-lasting impact on American culture is shown by the fact that movies based on Hanna-Barbera cartoons were still being produced in the twenty-first century. Among these were the live-action features *Scooby-Doo* (2002) and *Scooby-Doo 2: Monsters Unleashed* (2004) and the animated feature *Yogi Bear* (2010).

Hanna died in 2001, and Barbera died in 2006. In the half century during which they were partners, they had one of the most productive collaborations in the history of American television.

P. Andrew Miller

SEE ALSO: *Academy Awards; Animated Films; Disney (Walt Disney Company);* Dukes of Hazzard*; Emmy Awards;* The Fantastic Four*;* The Flintstones*;* Happy Days*;* The Honeymooners*; Kelly, Gene;* Laverne and Shirley*; MGM (Metro-Goldwyn-Mayer);* Mork & Mindy*; Saturday Morning Cartoons;* The Simpsons*; Sinatra, Frank; Television.*

BIBLIOGRAPHY

Beck, Jerry. *The Hanna-Barbera Treasury: Rare Art and Mementos from Your Favorite Cartoon Classics.* San Rafael, CA: Insight Editions, 2007.

Sennett, Ted. *The Art of Hanna-Barbera.* New York: Viking Studio Books, 1989.

Hansberry, Lorraine *(1930–1965)*

A black American playwright who produced only two plays before her death from cancer at age thirty-four, Lorraine Hansberry nonetheless made a tremendous contribution to the American stage and to African American culture. Her first and best-known play, *A Raisin in the Sun* (1959), winner of the New York Drama Critics' Circle Award, is now considered a landmark of American drama. The story of the struggling Younger family, who aspire to a better life, *A Raisin in the Sun* was the first Broadway production by a black woman, and its commercial success opened the stage doors to other black writers.

The Sign in Sidney Brustein's Window, Hansberry's challenging but commercially disappointing second play, followed in 1964. Posthumously produced plays *To Be Young, Gifted and Black* (1969), *Les Blancs* (1970), and *What Use Are Flowers?* (1972), adapted by her ex-husband and literary executor Robert Nemiroff, confirm Hansberry's great ability to combine artistic integrity and skill with commitment to social reform.

Barbara Tepa Lupack

SEE ALSO: *Broadway; Poitier, Sidney.*

BIBLIOGRAPHY

Carter, Steven R. *Hansberry's Drama: Commitment amid Complexity.* Urbana: University of Illinois Press, 1991.

Cheney, Anne. *Lorraine Hansberry.* Boston: Twayne, 1984.

Leeson, Richard M. *Lorraine Hansberry: A Research and Production Sourcebook.* Westport, CT: Greenwood Press, 1997.

Happy Days

For ten years, from 1974 to 1984, a fictional image of suburban Milwaukee, Wisconsin, brought the 1950s back to America through ABC's *Happy Days*. The picture of the world that was painted by this television comedy shaped a whole generation's image of the 1950s. It was a world of drive-ins and leather jackets, of cars and girls, but mostly of hanging out and solving day-to-day problems. It was noticeably *not* the 1950s of Joseph McCarthy and Korea. In the first seasons of the show, a number of episodes focused on specific 1950s topics, such as electioneering for Adlai Stevenson, beatniks, rock-and-roll shows, and gangs. After that, *Happy Days* settled into its stride to present a more general backdrop of the period, against which the Cunninghams and Fonzie developed as characters.

In addition to *Laverne and Shirley* and *Joanie Loves Chachi*, *Happy Days* spawned a Saturday-morning cartoon show, *The Fonz and the Happy Days Gang*. Also, the much-loved 1978–1982 sitcom *Mork & Mindy* was based on an episode of *Happy Days*. Indeed, the series was influential in setting the standard for popular comedies during the later 1970s and through the 1980s.

Happy Days was created by Garry Marshall, a veteran comedy writer who had worked on *The Dick Van Dyke Show* and produced *The Odd Couple*. Marshall produced a pilot for ABC in 1971 titled *New Family in Town*. The network was not interested, and the pilot later surfaced as a segment of *Love, American Style*. Aired on February 25, 1972, it was titled "Love and the Happy Day" and featured Ron Howard, Marion Ross, Harold Gould, and Susan Neher as a 1950s family acquiring their first TV set. In the meantime, however, film director George Lucas had seen the pilot and used it as the inspiration for his tremendously popular movie *American Graffiti* (1973), with Howard as a 1950s "Everyteen." The success of the movie rekindled ABC's interest in Marshall's original pilot.

RICHIE

Over its lifetime, *Happy Days* was really at least three shows. This early incarnation was much like the 1950s comedies it emulated, offering a basic and likable story. The first two seasons focused on the life of Richie Cunningham (Howard) and his family, which consisted of his dad, Howard Cunningham (Tom Bosley), owner of a hardware store; his mom, Marion (Ross); and his little sister, Joanie (Erin Moran). Early on there was also

Happy Days. *Ron Howard, Henry Winkler, and Marion Ross appear in an episode of* Happy Days *from 1975.* FOTOS INTERNATIONAL/HULTON ARCHIVE/GETTY IMAGES.

a basketball-wielding, monosyllabic older brother, Chuck (Gavan O'Herlihy), but he left the collective memory when cast changes were made after the second season. Outside of the family home, Richie's social life was lived primarily at Arnold's Drive-in, where he hung out with his friends Potsie Weber (Anson Williams) and Ralph Malph (Donny Most) and consulted with his leather-jacketed mentor, Fonzie (Henry Winkler). The Fonz soon became an audience favorite.

By the third season, things on *Happy Days* had changed. The show went to the top of the ratings and became the foundation for ABC's rise as the powerhouse of television in the 1970s. No longer just a show about the antics of high school kids, the series began to focus on the relationship of Fonzie and Richie, their mutual admiration and dependency, and the growth and development of Fonzie.

Eventually both the fictional Richie Cunningham and the actor Howard grew up and left the show, leaving it to feature a younger generation of characters and an adult Fonzie in its final years. While attention was transferred to Joanie and her friends in high school, still within the basic format, the dynamic of the show changed as Fonzie's transformation from rebellious youth to mentor and folk hero became complete.

Two things were true at the outset of this show. Before Howard would accept a role as another television youth (after practically growing up on the *Andy Griffith Show*), he made Marshall promise that his character would be allowed to age each year through high school into college. Fonzie had originally been envisioned by Marshall—and portrayed by Winkler—as a brooding, rebellious dropout. In one of those great bits of television folklore, the ABC network had decreed that Fonzie should wear a cloth jacket rather than the "threatening" leather one. Marshall suggested a compromise, permitting Fonzie to wear the leather jacket when he rode or worked on his motorcycle. So in the beginning, Fonzie was not seen without his motorcycle. Eventually, however, Fonzie rode his motorcycle less and less but continued to wear his leather jacket.

FONZIE

Fonzie was originally intended as a minor character. Because he proved to be extremely popular with the audience, the decision was made to emphasize the role. He moved into an apartment above the Cunninghams' garage in 1975. The move enabled Fonzie to maintain his independence but allowed the scriptwriters to involve him in the Cunninghams' domestic life. The Chuck character was no longer necessary, because Fonzie would fill the role as big brother to Richie.

As *Happy Days* moved into its second and third years, Fonzie received ever more attention. He made *Happy Days* unique and distanced the show from the middle-class family. In many ways the middle years of this show seemed simultaneously antiauthority yet accepting of it. Fonzie epitomized all that the middle-class 1950s were supposed to fear. He was cool, he was a dropout, and he got all the women. Fonzie was the working-class character and the leader of the youth pack around Arnold's Drive-in, the youth Mecca in *Happy Days'* Milwaukee. When Fonzie first came to the forefront, he was the prototypical "hood," whose menace served as a counterpoint to the goodness of Richie and his friends.

This new Fonzie was a more human Fonzie, one who could show his feelings and vulnerability without sacrificing the essential toughness of his character. In this permutation, he became a combination of father confessor and guru to Richie's pals. Fonzie was the epitome of cool (almost to the point of caricature), the one who can dispense advice, settle disputes, and serve as role model. This was all a far cry from the standard 1950s sitcom, where only parents could dispense wisdom to children and working-class, noneducated teens were perceived as a threat rather than a role model.

This new dynamic powered the show to its huge success. The rest of the characters, too, were pulled up with Fonzie. Over time, however, it got to be too much. It had too much formula and not enough pizzazz—so much so that several years of episodes would feature a trip (e.g., to a dude ranch, to Hollywood) where Fonzie can save the day by riding a bull or water skiing over a shark. He became one of the family and was thus diluted into a stereotype, a "good" role model, as the character was gradually stripped of most of his threatening qualities.

This was not all bad, and the interaction between Richie and Fonzie provided the opportunity to broaden the show's topics, while Ralph and Potsie were relegated to comic relief. In the fall of 1977, Richie, Potsie, and Ralph began college at the University of Wisconsin in Milwaukee. Joining the cast that season were Scott Baio as Fonzie's enterprising young cousin, Charles "Chachi" Arcola, who became Joanie's boyfriend, and Lynda Goodfriend as Richie's girlfriend, Lori Beth Allen.

FINAL SEASONS

Howard and Most left the series in 1980, written out by having Richie and Ralph leave to join the army. In May 1981 Richie married Lori Beth by proxy, and their baby, Richie Jr., was born in the fall of 1981. Meanwhile Fonzie had become a teacher of auto shop at good old Jefferson High. Joining the cast were Ted McGinley as Marion's nephew Roger, who became Jefferson's new basketball coach and English teacher, and Cathy Silvers (1980–1983) as Joanie's boy-crazy girlfriend, Jenny Piccalo. In the fall of 1982 Fonzie found himself falling in love with a divorcée named Ashley (played by Linda Purl). Ashley's daughter was played by Heather O'Rourke.

In addition, Crystal Bernard joined the show as Howard Cunningham's niece, K. C., who lived with the Cunninghams. One reason for this addition was that Joanie was not at home, having moved to her own (short-lived and unsuccessful) spin-off, *Joanie Loves Chachi*. By the fall of 1983, in what would be the final season of *Happy Days*, Fonzie had become the dean of boys at George S. Patton Vocational High. Joanie and Chachi, whose spin-off had flopped, came back to Milwaukee, and plans were made for their wedding. Also returning were Richie and Ralph, who showed up in a special two-part episode.

Increasingly, over its ten-year run, the life of the show took on a more 1970s feel in clothes, in language, and occasionally in story line. It retained the music and basic settings but seemed to stop caring about the period that was its inspiration. Although Fonzie rose to prominence, it was always Richie who provided the focus and balance for the show. When he left, the show was never the same again, and many would say it never recovered, despite staying on the air for four more seasons.

Although it appeared at the same time as such reality-based comedies as *All in the Family* and *M*A*S*H*, *Happy Days* opted for lighter humor and interaction. Due primarily to Fonzie, who became such a cultural icon that his leather jacket is part of the Smithsonian Institution collections, this show became a part of social consciousness. For the generation of Vietnam and Watergate, it represented a perfect combination: a nostalgic reflection on an earlier time when life seemed less difficult, with a strong character who can solve the problems and who, while allowing us to see his failings, can retain that strength. Last but not least, *Happy Days* reflected the problems of everyday life, placed at a safe remove and tempered by humor.

Frank E. Clark

SEE ALSO: All in the Family*;* American Graffiti*;* The Andy Griffith Show*; The Fifties; Howard, Ron;* Laverne and Shirley*; Lucas, George; Marshall, Garry;* M*A*S*H*;* Mork & Mindy*;* The Odd Couple*; Rock and Roll; Sitcom; Teen Idols; Television; Vietnam; Watergate.*

BIBLIOGRAPHY

Castleman, Harry, and Walter J. Podrazik. *Harry and Wally's Favorite Shows: A Fact-Filled Opinionated Guide to the Best and Worst on TV*. New York: Prentice Hall, 1989.

Marc, David, and Robert J. Thompson. *Prime Time, Prime Movers: From "I Love Lucy" to "L.A. Law"—America's Greatest TV Shows and the People Who Created Them*. Boston: Little, Brown, 1992.

Marcus, Daniel. *"Happy Days" and "Wonder Years": The Fifties and the Sixties in Contemporary Cultural Politics*. New Brunswick, NJ: Rutgers University Press, 2004.

McNeil, Alex. *Total Television: A Comprehensive Guide to Programming from 1948 to the Present*, 3rd ed. New York: Penguin Books, 1991.

Putterman, Barry. *On Television and Comedy: Essays on Style, Theme, Performer and Writer*. Jefferson, NC: McFarland, 1995.

Happy Hour

Happy hour is the two-hour period before dinner when bars offer discounted alcoholic beverages. In the 1920s *happy hour* was navy slang for the scheduled period of on-ship entertainment. After the passage of the Volstead Act (Prohibition) in 1920, civilians held "cocktail hours" at speakeasies and in their own homes to fortify themselves before dinner. Post-Prohibition cocktail lounges continued the custom of predinner cocktails. "Happy hour" became a common term around 1960 after it appeared in a 1959 *Saturday Evening Post* article on military life. Owing its name to the word *happy* as in "slightly drunk," happy hour subsequently became known more as an after-work ritual than as a prelude to the evening. In the 1980s bars offered complimentary appetizers for happy hour in response to the heightened enforcement of drunk-driving laws. The military reflected these changes, too, when in 1984 General John A. Wickham Jr. abolished happy hour at U.S. military base clubs.

Happy hour remains a staple of many bars in the twenty-first century, and some companies have seen it as an ideal way to draw in new customers. In 2010, for example, the brewer Anheuser-Busch, which was lagging considerably behind other global brands, tried to raise its profile by hosting a national happy hour. Using free samples of Budweiser beer, the "Grab Some Buds" campaign targeted the under-thirty market that the company was trying to bolster. In an attempt to boost sagging profits during the economic downturn that started in 2008, restaurants such as the Cheesecake Factory, P.F. Chang's, and Ruby Tuesday also began staging happy hours, which featured reduced prices on both booze and appetizers.

Daryl Umberger

SEE ALSO: *Beer; Cocktail Parties; Leisure Time; The Martini; Prohibition; The* Saturday Evening Post.

BIBLIOGRAPHY

Abel, Ernest L. *Alcohol Wordlore and Folklore.* Buffalo, NY: Prometheus Books, 1987.

Cassidy, Frederick, ed. *Dictionary of American Regional English.* Cambridge, MA: Harvard University Press, 1985.

Kirby, David. "Not-So-Happy-Hour: Industry Hit Hard by Drunk Driving Proposals." *Restaurant Business,* April 1, 1998, 16.

"Latest Ad Strategy to Freshen Budweiser's Image: Free Beer." *USA Today,* September 22, 2010.

Lighter, J. E. *Random House Historical Dictionary of American Slang.* New York: Random House, 1994.

Mariani, John. *The Dictionary of American Food and Drink.* New York: Hearst Books, 1994.

Hard-Boiled Detective Fiction

Hard-boiled detective fiction is often defined in terms of what it is not. It is not set in an English village; the solution is not reached by analyzing clues. To paraphrase Raymond Chandler, one of its most famous writers, it is not about dukes and Venetian vases or hand-wrought dueling pistols or curare or tropical fish. Hard-boiled detective fiction emerged in the 1920s in the United States as an antidote to such things. It exploits familiar urban and industrial settings; its heroes, and now heroines, are ordinary people, working alone.

Hard-boiled detective fiction can be recognized by four main elements: the language, the setting, the detective, and the detection. The first of these is what links hard-boiled detective fiction with other literature of the period. Hard-boiled language describes things rather than ideas: it reports what happened and what was said, not how it felt, and adjectives are kept to a minimum. Perhaps the most famous writer of nondetective fiction in this style is Ernest Hemingway, and many writers of hard-boiled detective fiction have said that they began by imitating him.

This style was also affected by financial concerns. Hard-boiled detective fiction first appeared in the "pulp" magazines and novelettes that were popular during the 1920s; the writers for these magazines were paid by the word, and editors were keen to eliminate unnecessary description that would cost them money. Some pulp writers, such as Horace McCoy and Dashiell Hammett, continued to use this pared-down style in their later novels, while others, such as Chandler, thought that readers would actually enjoy description if it were done well. Chandler's language still reports only what happened and what was said, but settings and people are described in a poetic and often complex way. Since the 1980s some hard-boiled writers, such as James Ellroy, have tried to eliminate the single narrative voice altogether; Ellroy presents his readers with transcripts of newspaper and radio reports about the investigation, heightening the illusion of realism and objectivity.

The setting for hard-boiled detective fiction is almost always urban. Perhaps because of its origins in the period of Prohibition and the Great Depression of the 1920s, the cities it describes tend to be dark, dangerous places run by corrupt politicians and gangster syndicates. Early writers of hard-boiled detective fiction considered themselves to be describing city life in a new, realistic way. The sort of crime that takes place in their stories also could be read about in newspapers. The people in the stories were like people the readers knew or had heard about; they seemed to speak as people really spoke. As Chandler noted, the world they describe is "not a very fragrant world, but it is the world you live in."

The hero of hard-boiled detective stories is most often, though not always, a private detective. It is generally thought that he first appeared in *Black Mask* magazine in 1922 in the form of Carroll John Daly's Race Williams. Sara Paretsky, who began her V. I. Warshawski series in the 1980s, was among the first to create a hard-boiled detective heroine. Before then the protagonist was always a man, and the audience for the stories he appeared in was almost exclusively male. In the 1990s the African American author Walter Mosley further expanded the genre by creating a black amateur detective named Ezekiel "Easy" Rawlins, who must navigate the tough streets of segregated inner-city Los Angeles as he reluctantly pursues his investigations.

The origins of the hard-boiled detective hero are in the frontier heroes of the nineteenth century, and it could be argued that both types of hero bring order to the lives of the people they choose to help. Where they differ is that the frontier hero assists in establishing new settlements and a new civilization, while the hard-boiled detective only patches up an old and corrupt one. Despite the efforts of such writers as Paretsky and Mosley, since the mid-1970s the police procedural has been the dominant detective fiction form. While the language and action of these novels often owes much to the hard-boiled style, the emphasis on the police implies that the lone, hard-boiled private detective is no longer a convincing defense against society's many ills.

The fourth defining characteristic of hard-boiled detective fiction is the method of detection itself. In keeping with origins in Western and romance stories, the hard-boiled detective is usually presented as being on a quest, and the quest itself, rather than its solution, forms the main source of interest for readers. Even in the best examples of the genre, the solution to the mystery is often unsatisfactory or contrived, but rather than wanting to know what has already happened, readers want to find out what will happen next. More particularly, they want to know how the detective will deal with physical and moral difficulties encountered along the way.

From Race Williams to V. I. Warshawski to Easy Rawlins, hard-boiled detective fiction reassures readers that individuals can succeed where government law enforcement has failed. Hard-boiled detectives are ordinary people who take extraordinary risks for the sake of what they see as right. They suggest to their fans that however mundane their lives may seem and however dangerous the world appears, they too have a little of what it takes to be heroic.

Chris Routledge

SEE ALSO: The Big Sleep*;* Black Mask*; Chandler, Raymond; Detective Fiction; Hammett, Dashiell; Hemingway, Ernest;* The Maltese Falcon*; McCoy, Horace; Mosley, Walter; Paretsky, Sara;* The Postman Always Rings Twice*; Prohibition; Pulp Magazines; Spillane, Mickey.*

BIBLIOGRAPHY

Abbott, Megan E. *The Street Was Mine: White Masculinity in Hardboiled Fiction and Film Noir.* New York: Palgrave Macmillan, 2002.

Cawelti, John G. *Adventure, Mystery, and Romance: Formula Stories as Art and Popular Culture.* Chicago: University of Chicago Press, 1976.

Chandler, Raymond. *Pearls Are a Nuisance.* London: Pan Books, 1980.

Geherin, David. *The American Private Eye: The Image in Fiction.* New York: Ungar, 1985.

Horsley, Lee. *The Noir Thriller.* London: Palgrave Macmillan, 2001.

Messent, Peter, ed. *Criminal Proceedings: The Contemporary American Crime Novel.* London: Pluto, 1997.

Moore, Lewis D. *Cracking the Hard-Boiled Detective: A Critical History from the 1920s to the Present.* Jefferson, NC: McFarland, 2006.

O'Brien, Geoffrey. *Hardboiled America: Lurid Paperbacks and the Masters of Noir.* New York: Da Capo Press, 1997.

Harding, Tonya *(1970–)*

Known more for her athleticism than her grace, Tonya Harding was one of the top skaters in women's figure skating in the 1990s. In 1991 she was the first American woman to land a triple axel in competition. She won two U.S. Figure Skating Championships and placed second in the 1991 World Figure Skating Championships. Harding was fighting hard for a spot on the U.S. Olympic team in 1994 when her ex-husband Jeff Gillooly and his friends attacked Nancy Kerrigan, Harding's major competitor during a competition. Kerrigan had to withdraw from the competition, and Harding won one of the coveted Olympic slots. Kerrigan was also given a slot. Almost immediately, however, word broke that Gillooly was responsible for the attack on Kerrigan, and speculation about Harding's involvement was rife. The much-hyped "duel" between Kerrigan and Harding at the 1994 Olympics fizzled when Harding performed poorly. While Kerrigan performed well, Ukrainian skater Oksana Baiul won the gold. Capitalizing on the public fascination with the rivalry, a television film, *Tonya and Nancy,* appeared in 1994.

Even though Harding avoided imprisonment, she was stripped of her U.S. championship title and received a lifetime ban from sanctioned competitions. She was also fined $160,000 and sentenced to 500 hours of community service. Harding twice attempted suicide after years of failures and major depression. She told the story of her life, which she says includes child molestation and abuse, to biographer Lynda Prouse. Harding continues to insist that she took no part in the attack on Kerrigan. According to sportswriter Joan Ryan, Harding's unforgivable sin among her fellow skaters was that "she had no class" and "refused to allow anybody to give her some."

Mary Hess

SEE ALSO: *Ice Shows; Kerrigan, Nancy; Made-for-Television Movies; Media Feeding Frenzies; Olympics; Skating; Tabloids.*

BIBLIOGRAPHY

Baughman, Cynthia, ed. *Women on Ice: Feminist Essays on the Tonya Harding/Nancy Kerrigan Spectacle.* New York: Routledge, 1995.

Brennan, Christie. *Inside Edge: A Revealing Journey into the Secret World of Figure Skating.* New York: Anchor Books, 1997.

Frey, Jennifer. "Harding, Kerrigan: Another Sad Performance." *Washington Post,* February 8, 1998.

Prouse, Lynda D. *The Tonya Tapes.* New York: World Audience Publishing, 2008.

Ryan, Joan. *Little Girls in Pretty Boxes: The Making and Breaking of Elite Gymnasts and Figure Skaters.* New York: Doubleday, 1995.

Hardy, Andy

SEE: *Andy Hardy.*

The Hardy Boys

The Hardy Boys is one of the best-selling children's book series in history. Written for young adults, the books feature teenage brothers Frank and Joe Hardy, who solve exciting mysteries. First published in 1927, the Hardy Boys was extremely popular in the twentieth century, selling more than fifty million copies and spawning new series for older and younger readers, television shows, and an animated series. The books have also been translated into more than a dozen languages. The Hardy Boys continue to be popular in the twenty-first century as new generations of readers discover the brothers' adventures.

The Hardy Boys series was created by the Stratemeyer Syndicate, a book production company that also produced other book series for tweens and teens, such as Nancy Drew, Tom Swift, and the Bobbsey Twins. The company was founded and led by Edward Stratemeyer who, in addition to writing books himself, used ghostwriters who worked from outlines that Stratemeyer provided. The books were then published under pseudonyms.

The Hardy Boys books, all published under the name Franklin W. Dixon, first took shape in 1926 when Stratemeyer noticed the rising popularity of detective fiction among adults. He pitched the Hardy Boys to his publishers at Grosset & Dunlap, expressing the belief that children would be just as interested in detective stories as adults. His proposal outlined a series of adventures that would center on two teenage brothers who solved exciting mysteries. Stratemeyer tapped one of his seasoned ghostwriters, Leslie McFarlane, to launch the series. McFarlane welcomed the opportunity to originate a series rather than merely add to a preexisting one. In his autobiography, *Ghost of the Hardy Boys,* he explains, "It seemed to me that the Hardy boys deserved something better than the slapdash treatment [prior assignments] had been getting. It was still hack work, no doubt, but did the new series have to be all that hack? There was, after all, the chance to contribute a little style." McFarlane was the Hardy Boys' primary ghostwriter for twenty years before retiring. By then the series was well established and well loved and easily survived the transition to other writers.

The books in the Hardy Boys series follow a formula, just like other series produced by the Stratemeyer Syndicate, which makes it easy for different authors to write the books and for audiences to believe that one author wrote all the books of a series. All the books are the same length with the same number of chapters. Each one refers briefly, near the beginning of the book, to the previous book in the series, and near the end each mentions something about the upcoming book. The regular characters have integrity and are of good moral character.

MYSTERIES FOR KIDS

In each book Frank and Joe usually stumble upon a clue that leads them into an investigation, often with the help of their chum Chet Morton and the support of their dad, a well-known private detective. The brothers enjoy unfettered mobility, and on motorcycles, in their boat the *Sleuth*, in planes, on trains, and in automobiles, the Hardy Boys go wherever their cases lead them. In early books they stay mostly in or near their hometown of Bayport, a fictional city on the eastern seaboard, but in later books they travel to foreign countries. The books also offer readers the vicarious thrill of gadgetry; the Hardy Boys have a laboratory where they use microscopes, fingerprinting kits, and other tools to analyze clues. They can fix anything, and they keep abreast of technological innovations, such as short-wave radios (which were new in the 1940s) and voice-printing techniques (which were new in the 1970s).

Hardy Boys Mystery. The Tower Treasure *was one of dozens of Hardy Boys tales in the children's mystery series that debuted in 1927.* STEVE LISS/TIME LIFE PICTURES/GETTY IMAGES.

The Hardy Boys' milieu is "exciting but clean," as dictated by Stratemeyer. Bayport is full of criminals, yet it remains a fundamentally safe community. The crimes committed are wicked but not gruesome; Frank and Joe fight the villains with their fists but never shoot or stab them. The heroes do not smoke, drink alcohol, or have sex. Although Stratemeyer provided the brothers with "girlfriends," the relationships are innocent and superficial; indeed, the action is decidedly gender exclusive, with women and girls barely appearing in the series, except for the more substantial character of the boys' bossy but lovable Aunt Gertrude. The Hardy Boys live in a male-oriented and self-referential world, rich in adventure yet devoid of any real threats to the reader's peace of mind. And, of course, by the end of each adventure-filled story, Frank and Joe solve the mystery.

While the Stratemeyer Syndicate had already established that formula book series could be successful, the Hardy Boys series was unique in that the mystery genre was adapted for a teenage audience. Scholar Carol Billman notes in her book *The Secret of the Stratemeyer Syndicate*, the Hardy Boys provided "the novel lure of the detective mystery [fused] with the earlier adventure tale tradition," a combination that proved appealing, and the series became immensely popular with young readers. Educators, however, were not fans, and they mounted strong opposition. Even before the birth of the Hardy Boys, books produced by the Stratemeyer Syndicate were shunned by librarians and teachers for their sensationalism, flatly formulaic structure, and minimal literary value.

CHANGES AT STRATEMEYER SYNDICATE

In 1930 Stratemeyer died, and his daughters, Harriet Stratemeyer Adams and Edna Stratemeyer, took over management of the company. The sisters noticed that earlier Stratemeyer Syndicate series, such as Tom Swift and the Rover Boys, had seen their sales plummet when the heroes grew older and got married. Determined to keep the Hardy Boys vital, they decreed that Frank and Joe would not suffer the tragedy of maturing. They aged only from their mid-teens to their late teens and thereafter dwelled in a state of arrested development. As the twentieth century progressed and social norms changed, humorists had fun spoofing the Hardy Boys' spotless purity. Books, articles, and plays mocked the boys' utter cluelessness about sex and questioned their sexual identity. This is the theme of the satirical novel, *A Ghost in the Closet: A Hardly Boys Mystery* (1995) by Mabel Maney and the musical stage play, *The Secret of the Old Queen*, by Timothy Cope and Paul Boesing. For teenagers, however, the Hardy Boys' adventures remained compelling and entertaining.

In 1942 Edna got married and retired, leaving Harriet in charge. In 1959 the Stratemeyer Syndicate launched a massive revision project to modernize its series and to erase the most egregious of the racial stereotyping that was rampant in its books published before the 1950s. Ranging from simple edits to completely rewritten stories, the revisions scrubbed away the original narrative flavor, along with outdated cultural references to things such as automats and running boards.

In 1982 Harriet Adams died, and in 1984 book publisher Simon & Schuster acquired the Stratemeyer Syndicate. The new owner revitalized the Hardy Boys series, adding new dimensions to plots, locales, and characterizations and changing the age of the target audience. The original series had been aimed at boys from fourteen to sixteen years old, and even though the Stratemeyer Syndicate had "modernized" the series in the early 1960s, it had not changed the fundamental formula of the series. As a result, in the late twentieth century the revitalized books were a better fit for boys ages eight to eleven years old, and Simon & Schuster packaged and promoted the series to this age group.

Simon & Schuster also expanded the Hardy Boys franchise with multiple spin-off series aimed at older and younger groups of readers. For tween and teen boys, the publisher introduced the Hardy Boys Case Files (1987–1998), with increased levels of danger and violence. The Hardy Boys' cases now included murders, while the boys demonstrated a heightened awareness of the opposite sex (but still no sexual activity). The Nancy Drew and Hardy Boys Supermysteries, launched in 1988, featured collaborations between Frank and Joe and their popular girl-detective counterpart, and another collaboration was attempted in 1992 when the publisher briefly paired the Hardy Boys with Tom Swift. For younger children, ages nine to twelve, Simon & Schuster debuted the Clues Brothers series in 1997, featuring Frank and Joe as children, ages nine and eight. This series endured for seventeen books and concluded in 2000.

The year 2005 was especially significant for the Hardy Boys. Simon & Schuster ended the original series with the 190th title and launched a new Hardy Boys series with completely original stories, under the title Hardy Boys Undercover Brothers. It is narrated in the first person, with Frank and Joe alternating chapters. Also in 2005, the Hardy Boys appeared for the first time in the newly popular graphic novel format, released by Papercutz publishers. The first volume of the graphic novel series, *Ocean of Osyria*, was simultaneously serialized by Papercutz as a standard thirty-two-page comic book, released in three volumes during 2005. In 2010 Papercutz launched a second series, the Hardy Boys: New Case Files (not to be confused with Simon & Schuster's Hardy Boys Case Files series). Also in 2010 the publisher revived a young-readers series with the Hardy Boys: Secret Files.

TELEVISION

The Hardy Boys moved to television for the first time in 1956. They appeared on episodes of *The Mickey Mouse Club* (1955–1959), as two short serials, starring Tommy Kirk and Tim Considine. In 1967 CBS aired a pilot for an hour-long series starring Tim Matheson as Joe and Richard Gates as Frank, but it did not fare well and no more episodes were made. In 1969 the Hardy Boys reemerged as the stars of a Saturday morning cartoon on ABC, characterized as leaders of a pop-music group who solve mysteries between gigs. Reflecting the social inclusivity of the era, the show included a girl and an African American boy in the Hardy Boys' band, along with old friend Chet Morton (renamed "Chubby"). The animated Hardy Boys was a failure, lasting only one season.

In 1977 the Hardy Boys fared better on a television. Universal Studios' *The Hardy Boys/Nancy Drew Mysteries* was a prime-time series that alternated episodes of the Hardy Boys' adventures with those of Nancy Drew in an hour-long format, on Sunday nights. Actors Shaun Cassidy and Parker Stevenson became teen idols by playing Joe and Frank. The series lasted three seasons. While the program was on the air, Universal Studios licensed a great deal of tie-in merchandise, including a lunch box, Halloween costumes, a board game, jigsaw puzzles, a model kit of the boys' van, and numerous posters and T-shirts with the actors' likenesses on them.

In 1995 Nelvana/New Line television produced a half-hour Hardy Boys series, again with a companion Nancy Drew series. Paul Popowich and Colin K. Gray played the brothers. The series received lukewarm reviews, and its popularity was further hindered by its floating status in syndication on a fledgling network. Without a prime-time slot or heavy promotion, the show died after only one season.

In the early twenty-first century the Hardy Boys had two primary groups of fans: children who read the various book series and graphic novels and adults who collected the older printed editions and collectible items from the series' ninety-year lifespan. As contemporary children's books, the Hardy Boys was no longer the massively popular franchise that it once was, but thanks to Simon & Schuster's commitment to constantly renovating and revitalizing the series, Hardy Boys' adventures will likely continue for years to come.

Ilana Nash

SEE ALSO: *Best Sellers; The Bobbsey Twins; Detective Fiction; Graphic Novels;* The Mickey Mouse Club*; Nancy Drew; Stratemeyer, Edward; Teen Idols; Teenagers; Tom Swift Series; Tweens.*

BIBLIOGRAPHY

Billman, Carol. *The Secret of the Stratemeyer Syndicate: Nancy Drew, the Hardy Boys, and the Million Dollar Fiction Factory.* New York: Ungar Publishing, 1986.

Connelly, Mark. *The Hardy Boys Mysteries, 1927–1979: A Cultural and Literary History.* Jefferson, NC: McFarland, 2008.

Greenwald, Marilyn S. *The Secret of the Hardy Boys: Leslie McFarlane and the Stratemeyer Syndicate.* Athens: University of Ohio Press, 2004.

Kismaric, Carole, and Marvin Heiferman. *The Mysterious Case of Nancy Drew & the Hardy Boys.* New York: Simon & Schuster, 1998.

McFarlane, Leslie. *Ghost of the Hardy Boys: An Autobiography.* New York: Two Continents, 1976.

Prager, Arthur. *Rascals at Large or the Clue in the Old Nostalgia.* Garden City, NY: Doubleday, 1971.

Hare Krishna

Of the colorful and exotic features of the U.S. urban landscape during the hippie era in the late 1960s and 1970s, none perhaps was so striking as the small bands of men with shaved heads and saffron robes and women in saris gathering at love-ins or on street corners. Together they danced to the sound of Indian drums as they recited their mantra—"Hare Krishna, hare Krishna, Krishna Krishna, hare hare; hare Rama, hare Rama, Rama Rama, hare hare"—and solicited alms.

The worldwide Krishna movement was founded by one elderly man from India who came to the United States with a vision, determination, and hardly a penny to his name. Born in 1896, Abhay Charan De had already studied economics and

English at the University of Calcutta when he became a disciple and the eventual successor of Bhaktisiddhanta Sarasvati Swami, the tenth in a line of gurus. These gurus began in the late fifteenth century with Lord Chaitanya Mahaprabhu, who had founded a religious system within Hinduism particularly devoted to the god Krishna.

THE DEITY KRISHNA

A divinity with many of the attributes of the trickster archetype, Krishna appears in India's epic poem the *Mahabharata* as charioteer to his friend Arjuna. A great battle has begun in which, Arjuna realizes, he will have friends and relatives on both sides. He asks Krishna whether he ought to fight or not, and Krishna explains why he should do so, in a classic discourse about reality and illusion (the source of Ralph Waldo Emerson's lines "If the red slayer thinks he slays / And the slain thinks he is slain"). This interlude on the eve of the battle is also the setting for the *Bhagavad-Gita*, or "Song of God," a central text in Hindu religious literature.

Chaitanya and his successors revered Krishna as the essential manifestation of God and prescribed a way of life that eschewed earthly sensory pleasures in favor of meditative practice, study of the *Bhagavad-Gita* and other holy books, and the chanting of the Hare Krishna mantra. As such, the followers of Krishna might have been simply one of many Indian sects within Hinduism. The crucial difference came when Abhay Charan De, now called Bhaktivedanta Swami Prabhupada, brought his teaching to the United States, arriving in New York on a freighter in 1965.

ISKCON

Starting with evening lectures on the *Bhagavad-Gita*, Bhaktivedanta Swami soon attracted a small but enthusiastic band of followers who became the International Society for Krishna Consciousness (ISKCON) in 1966; two years later the group acquired a farm in West Virginia, which they dubbed New Vrindavan (after the town in India that was believed to be Krishna's birthplace) and which later grew to 1,000 acres. In 1972, to educate the increasing number of Hare Krishna children, ISKCON started the Gurukula School, and its enrollment grew to 150 over the next three years. By the time of Bhaktivedanta Swami's death in 1977, the Krishna movement boasted 10,000 full-time members worldwide, 5,000 of them in the United States alone, and could claim several million others who came to worship at ISKCON temples.

Those who joined the communities were expected to abstain from drugs, including alcohol, tobacco, coffee, and tea. Sexual relations were permitted only for couples married by an ordained minister in Krishna Consciousness; there was to be no courtship or dating as such, either within the community or with outsiders. Also forbidden were gambling and frivolous games and sports; children, however, were encouraged to play games such as a Krishna version of hopscotch called Hopping to the Spiritual World, I Love Krishna, and the Hanuman Hop. For adults the everyday routine included six temple ceremonies, several hours of classes, work within the temple compound for three hours in the morning, and *sankirtana*—public chanting, preaching, and solicitation of alms—for another three hours each afternoon.

TURMOIL

Many devotees saw in the Krishna communities a welcome refuge from a prior life of adolescent turmoil, insecurity, and drug use. But relatives and friends of converts, alarmed by the strictures of the temple regimen and the apparently hypnotic effect of chanting the Hare Krishna 108 mantras sixteen times a day, sometimes brought accusations of brainwashing and coercion, particularly when children were involved. The grandparents of one boy whose mother had joined the movement spent sixteen months finding him and restoring him to his father, ultimately resorting to counterdemonstrations at Chicago's O'Hare International Airport, a favorite *sankirtana* site.

Such clashes of worldviews raised troublesome civil liberties issues for the courts and generated adverse publicity for the movement. The public backlash made it harder to raise money openly for Krishna Consciousness, so that sales of books and incense on the street came to be divorced from preaching (some males donned toupees to cover their shaved heads), seeming to defeat the purpose of *sankirtana*.

Anticipating his death, Bhaktivedanta Swami had designated eleven gurus to preside over districts within the worldwide organization, as well as a Governing Body Commission (GBC), which was to be ISKCON's central administrative committee. A crisis of conflicting authority soon erupted between the GBC and several of the regional gurus, four of whom resigned during the next decade. There was also bad press from a California police raid, which turned up a large cache of firearms on a ranch owned by the movement, and from the murder of a former member, turned vocal critic, at the New Vrindavan compound.

In 2000 a lawsuit was brought against ISKCON, seeking $400 million in damages on behalf of people who were allegedly abused as children at the movement's boarding schools during the 1970s and 1980s. The initial suit was dismissed, but a second one was filed soon after. Rather than spending the massive sums of money it would take to defend itself in court, ISKCON reorganized under Chapter 11 bankruptcy laws. Leaders said they intended to set up a fund to help anyone who had experienced past abuse.

ISKCON survived, making changes to accommodate members unable or unwilling to join the temple communities (including outreach to expatriate Indians) and broadening its product line to include vegetarian specialty foods and restaurants. A new generation found the Krishna Conscious lifestyle an appealing alternative to what one convert, a former heavy-metal musician, describes as "fashion, cliques, sex, drugs, and loud music." As sociologist E. Burke Rochford explains it, "ISKCON's ability to adapt to what have often been the most adverse circumstances points to the flexibility and ultimate resiliency of the movement. It is these qualities, combined with the deep faith and commitment of the devotees themselves, which will be the Krishna movement's greatest assets as it approaches the twenty-first century." In the early 2010s ISKCON's website claimed that it had more than 500 temples and 250,000 followers worldwide.

Nick Humez

SEE ALSO: *Cults; Hippies; Vegetarianism.*

BIBLIOGRAPHY

Bhaktivedanta Swami Prabhupada, A. C. *Krsna Consciousness: The Topmost Yoga System*. Boston: ISKCON Press, 1970.

Bhaktivedanta Swami Prabhupada, A. C., ed. *The Bhagavad-gita as It Is*. New York: Macmillan, 1972.

Bhaktivedanta Swami Prabhupada, A. C., and John Lennon. *Search for Liberation*. Los Angeles: Bhaktivedanta Book Trust, 1981.

Daner, Francine Jeanne. *The American Children of Krsna: A Study of the Hare Krsna Movement*. New York: Holt, Rinehart and Winston, 1976.

Goswami, Mukunda. *Miracle on Second Avenue: Hare Krishna Arrives in the West: New York, San Francisco, and London 1966–1969*. Badger, CA: Torchlight Publishing, 2011.

Hiltebeitel, Alf. *The Ritual of Battle: Krishna in the Mahabharata*. Ithaca, NY: Cornell University Press, 1976.

Hubner, John, and Lindsey Gruson. *Monkey on a Stick: Murder, Madness and the Hare Krishnas*. San Diego, CA: Harcourt Brace Jovanovich, 1988.

Muster, Nori J. *Betrayal of the Spirit: My Life behind the Headlines of the Hare Krishna Movement*. Urbana: University of Illinois Press, 1997.

Rochford, E. Burke. *Hare Krishna in America*. New Brunswick, NJ: Rutgers University Press, 1985.

Yanoff, Morris. *Where Is Joey?: Lost among the Hare Krishnas*. Chicago: Swallow Press, 1981.

Haring, Keith *(1958–1990)*

Among the most popular and frequently reproduced graphic images to have emerged from the 1980s are the broad cartoonish outlines of a baby on all fours, a boxlike barking dog, and a series of identical funny little men striking a variety of energetic poses. These figures—featureless yet evocative through outline alone—had their genesis in the spontaneous ink drawings Keith Haring began making in 1980. Out of these drawings, the artist told his biographer John Gruen, his "entire future vocabulary was born." Seeking the incompatible goals of immediate acceptance with the masses and critical recognition from the art establishment, Haring lived fast, painted furiously, and died tragically young.

Growing up in Kutztown, Pennsylvania, where as a young child he drew pictures with his father, Haring was obsessed with the art of Walt Disney, Dr. Seuss, and Charles Schulz's earliest Charlie Brown comics. Television cartoons and the cartoonish sitcoms of the 1960s fascinated him, and he started a local Monkees fan club. In junior high school he won an award for a drawing on adding-machine tape. The drawing pitted the hippies against the police—a sign, perhaps, of his budding rebelliousness. After high school Haring briefly attended the Ivy School of Professional Art in Pittsburgh and worked at thc Pittsburgh Arts and Crafts Center. During this period he was influenced profoundly by Robert Henri's book *The Art Spirit* (1923), which echoed Haring's own artistic musings, and by a 1977 retrospective of Pierre Alechinsky, whose work, said Haring, "was the closest thing I had ever seen to what I was doing with these self-generative little shapes."

In 1978 Haring moved to New York City to attend the School for Visual Arts, where his introduction to semiotics, or the study of signs, made a deep impression. He was fascinated by the graffiti in the New York streets and subways and was by 1980 making graffiti himself, eventually collaborating with and promoting other graffiti artists. In the early 1980s he became well known for a series of surreptitious drawings he made in the New York subway stations on the empty black panels placed there to cover up old advertisements; the barking dog, the "Radiant Baby," and the active little men, which became fixtures in much of his later work, were all present here. The opening of his big 1982 show at New York's Shafrazi Gallery, attended by famous painters and graffiti artists alike, was a sensation.

Haring often created the art for his gallery shows on-site a few days before their opening. Onlookers were amazed at his ability to complete huge projects quickly with nary a false brushstroke, whether on paper, tarpaulins, canvas, or building facades. Large-scale projects ranged from a section of the Berlin Wall to the walls of museums, hospitals, and churches, generally with the blessing of property owners and often for socially conscious causes. His collaborators included Andy Warhol and William S. Burroughs, both of whom he considered mentors, and armies of neighborhood children. Haring dabbled in body painting and designed sculpture. Commercial projects included a painting of a car for BMW, ads for Absolut Vodka, and watch faces for Swatch.

In 1986 Haring, wanting as usual to communicate to a wide audience, opened the Pop Shop in New York City to sell inflatable babies, toy radios, buttons, embroidered patches, and T-shirts bearing his and others' designs; a similar venture in Tokyo failed. His work was extremely popular in Europe and Japan, and as early as 1983 the artist noticed imitations of his work "springing up all over the world." Throughout much of the late 1970s and 1980s, he was immersed in recreational drugs and sex; the New York club scene; and friendships with celebrities such as Madonna, Brooke Shields, Warhol, and Timothy Leary. Haring died from AIDS in 1990 at the age of thirty-one.

At the close of the twentieth century, Haring's artistic legacy was still being debated. Calvin Tomkins, writing in the *New Yorker*, described Haring's natural gift as "the ability to cover and animate a surface with strong, simple, cartoon-style images that had an iconic resonance." Kurt Andersen, writing in the same publication, found Haring's work unpretentious and unimportant and saw in Haring all the salient artistic features of the 1980s: "a return to figurative style, the disappearance of distinctions between high and low, and the rise of full-bore marketing and of the overnight sensation." A major retrospective at New York's Whitney Museum of American Art in 1997 revealed Haring to be a more versatile and, often, sexually provocative artist than his mass-produced images would suggest. Certainly he was a master of line drawing, a tireless worker, and an adept self-promoter. While antecedents from Fernand Léger to R. Crumb may be cited, Haring's immediately recognizable work bears his own unique imprint.

Craig Bunch

SEE ALSO: *AIDS; Burroughs, William S.; Crumb, Robert; Disney (Walt Disney Company); Dr. Seuss; Graffiti; Leary, Timothy; Madonna; The Monkees;* Peanuts; *Swatch Watches; Warhol, Andy.*

BIBLIOGRAPHY

Andersen, Kurt. "The Culture Industry." *New Yorker*, July 7, 1997, 23–24.

Gruen, John. *Keith Haring: The Authorized Biography*. New York: Prentice Hall, 1991.

Haring, Keith. *Art in Transit: Subway Drawings by Keith Haring*. New York: Harmony, 1984.

Haring, Keith. *Keith Haring Journals.* New York: Viking, 1996.

Lewisohn, Cedar. *Street Art: The Graffiti Revolution.* London: Tate, 2008.

Sussman, Elisabeth, et al. *Keith Haring.* New York: Whitney Museum of American Art, 1997.

Tomkins, Calvin. "The Time of His Life." *New Yorker*, July 8, 1996, 66–67.

The Harlem Globetrotters

Since 1927 the Harlem Globetrotters have toured continually, showcasing the skills of African American basketball players and developing an entertaining blend of athletics and comedy. In the process they have helped to introduce basketball throughout the world, inspired athletes of all races, and laid the groundwork for the freewheeling "showtime" style of play that has contributed to the growth of basketball's popularity since the early 1970s. The comedic basketball style of the Globetrotters is a product of American racial segregation and discrimination. Their fancy dribbling, flamboyant passing, and spectacular leaping are seminal expressions of an African American athletic style. Their comedic routines (called "reems" by the Globetrotters) draw upon older minstrel show traditions and Sambo stereotypes of African Americans as childish clowns. Both of these dimensions of the Globetrotter—one forward looking and celebrating African American creativity and excellence; the other looking backward and reinforcing racist images—have contributed to their success.

A BASKETBALL SPECTACLE

On their early tours, the Globetrotters and owner/booking agent/coach Abe Saperstein (a Jewish immigrant of Polish parentage), crammed into a small coupe and drove throughout the upper Midwest, taking on town teams for a percentage of the gate. They rarely had money for hotels, and when they did, they often found themselves barred because of their race. The same was true for restaurants. They generally played two games in each city—a day game for a black audience and a night game for a white audience. In some locales, the Globetrotters were treated as an anthropological exhibit by people who had never

Harlem Globetrotters. *The Harlem Globetrotters team in the mid-1970s included stars Curly Neal, kneeling, second from left, and Meadowlark Lemon, kneeling, second from right.* HULTON ARCHIVE/GETTY IMAGES.

met anyone of African ancestry. Unlike other African Americans who had to endure similar indignities, the Globetrotters could also enjoy the subversive pleasure of getting paid to consistently beat white teams on the court.

The exact origins of the Globetrotters' move toward comedic basketball have been shrouded by Saperstein's myth-making; however, it is clear that the primary motivation was to increase the likelihood of a return engagement by not running up the score against inferior competitors and to provide extra entertainment for fans who were bored by lopsided contests. By the late 1930s basketball tricks and comedy were an integral part of most performances by the Globetrotters. The lead comedians—such as Reece "Goose" Tatum and Meadow "Meadowlark" Lemon—enjoyed the laughter, attention, and extra money that their performances brought them. Rather than complaining about assaults to their dignity, they seized opportunities to expand upon the traditional reems.

Despite the fact that their humor could easily be interpreted as reinforcing negative racial stereotypes, few Globetrotters have publicly expressed misgivings. One notable exception is Connie Hawkins, a basketball Hall-of-Famer who spent four years in the 1960s with the Globetrotters. In a 1972 biography, *Foul*, by David Wolf, Hawkins complains that the Globetrotters were "acting like Uncle Toms. Grinnin and smilin and dancin around—that's the way they told us to act, and that's the way a lot of white people like to think we really are." Hawkins's observations help to explain how the Globetrotters' humor contributed to the team's success by undercutting the racial implications of their superiority as basketball players.

The formula has been very successful. In the 1930s and 1940s the Globetrotters' tours expanded to encompass the entire North American continent. In 1950 they undertook their first European visit. The following year they embarked on a world tour. The U.S. State Department found that the Globetrotters' happy-go-lucky style was an effective counter to communist propaganda about American race relations. The armed forces provided logistical support for the Globetrotters on overseas trips during the Cold War.

The demand for the Globetrotters was so great in the 1950s that the team fielded three separate units in the United States, as well as an all-star international squad. Since 1954 the Globetrotters have made numerous television appearances and have starred in their own cartoon series (1970–1973) and a variety show (1974). Although their cultural import has diminished, the Globetrotters continue to tour, make appearances on television and in advertisements, and secure lucrative corporate sponsorships.

INFLUENCE ON BASKETBALL

As straight basketball players, the Globetrotters were once formidable and influential. Prior to the integration of the National Basketball Association (NBA) in 1950 (a move that Saperstein resisted), playing for the Globetrotters was nearly the only way that an African American could make a living playing basketball. The Globetrotters' victory in the 1940 World Tournament of Basketball demonstrated that they were among the best professional teams in the United States. Wins over the National Basketball League champions, the Minneapolis Lakers, in 1948 and 1949 further enhanced the Globetrotters' reputation and struck a blow for racial equality. Even after the integration of the NBA, the Globetrotters had to be taken seriously as a straight basketball team. From 1950 to 1962 they played an annual series against teams of college all-stars, winning 162 games and losing only forty-four. Since the conclusion of this series, the Globetrotters have all but abandoned straight basketball in favor of comedy and entertainment.

Many changes have occurred during the long history of the Globetrotters. While the team has always been predominately African American, several white players have also joined its ranks. In 1985 the team signed its first female player, Lynette Woodard. That same year Joyce Walker was added to the roster. In 1995 Orlando Antigua became the first Hispanic Globetrotters player. In 1993, for the first time in its history, the team was owned by an African American, Mannie Jackson. In 2005 the documentary *The Harlem Globetrotters: The Team That Changed the World* chronicled the team's history using interviews with former players, coaches, and fans, including comedian Bill Cosby and former Secretary of State Henry Kissinger.

Though the team had amassed 22,000 victories by 2006, the Globetrotters' style of play has proved more important than their ability to beat top teams. Against real competitors, they generally dropped the reems but retained the rest of their repertoire. Where most of the white teams in the first half of the twentieth century played a stilted, regimented game, the Globetrotters freelanced and had fun. In recent years, no-look and behind-the-back passes, thrilling dunks, flashy dribbling, and risky plays have enhanced defensive moves developed and displayed during years of barnstorming. Such moves have now entered mainstream basketball as key elements of an African American athletic aesthetic.

Perhaps the Globetrotters' greatest impact has been in demonstrating how basketball skills can be a form of entertainment. NBA stars like Earvin "Magic" Johnson often cite the Globetrotters, particularly master dribbler Marques Haynes, as an inspiration. Much of basketball's growth in popularity since the 1970s has been due to casual fans who savor those moments that most resemble the Globetrotters at their best. Players who induce smiles and laughter not with comedic set pieces but with a surprising pass, a crossover dribble, or an acrobatic shot in the heat of competition are an important part of the Globetrotters' legacy.

Thomas J. Mertz

SEE ALSO: *Basketball; Cold War; Cosby, Bill; Johnson, Earvin "Magic"; Minstrel Shows; National Basketball Association (NBA); Television.*

BIBLIOGRAPHY

Christgau, John. *Tricksters in the Madhouse: Lakers versus Globetrotters, 1948*. Lincoln: University of Nebraska Press, 2004.

Lemon, Meadowlark, and Jerry B. Jenkins. *Meadowlark.* Nashville, TN: Thomas Nelson Publishers, 1987.

Nelson, George. *Elevating the Game: Black Men and Basketball.* New York: HarperCollins, 1992.

Wiggins, David K., and Patrick B. Miller. *The Unlevel Playing Field: A Documentary History of the African American Experience in Sport*. Urbana: University of Illinois Press, 2003.

Wilker, Josh. *The Harlem Globetrotters*. Philadelphia: Chelsea House Publishers, 1997.

Wolf, David. *Foul! The Connie Hawkins Story*. New York: Holt, Rinehart and Winston, 1972.

Harlem Renaissance

Post–World War I Harlem, New York, was the undisputed center of a complex cultural movement out of which emerged a proliferation of black intellectuals, writers, musicians, actors, and visual artists. Variously called the Harlem Renaissance, the Negro Renaissance, and the New Negro Movement, it was an artistic flowering that coincided with sociopolitical expressions of black pride—the rise of the "New Negro" and Garveyism—in much the same way as the Black Arts and Black Power movements emerged simultaneously in the 1960s. Although scholars posit differing views on when it began and ended, most agree that the movement was at its height between the dawning of the Jazz Age in 1919 and the stock market crash in 1929.

Harlem, the area James Weldon Johnson dubbed the black "culture capital," was a fitting center for this outpouring of creativity, in part because it held one of the largest settlements of African Americans in any area outside the South and because of the prevailing zeitgeist of racial affirmation. Intellectuals such as Johnson and Alain Locke saw Harlem as a place of great opportunity where blacks could, according to Locke, shed the "chrysalis of the Negro problem." Locke's 1925 landmark essay "The New Negro" announced the demise of the "Old Negro" and became a kind of cultural manifesto for artists of that generation and the next.

The creation of a "Negro" Harlem was indeed remarkable, a curious mix of affluence and poverty, of black creativity and black exploitation. On the one hand, music, literature, plays, and paintings depicting black life flourished. Black entrepreneurship thrived, and on the political front, the National Association for the Advancement of Colored People (NAACP, 1909) continued its work as the largest civil rights organization in the United States, alongside the National Urban League (1911) and the more controversial politics of Marcus Garvey, who was laying the groundwork for his project of African colonization. On the other hand, even well-intentioned white patrons helped to perpetuate stereotypes of black life that resulted in the paradoxical "Negro vogue" of the 1920s when white spectators went "slumming" in Harlem to see blacks perform in Jim Crow nightclubs. They patronized small bars and cabarets formerly frequented only by blacks and, according to Langston Hughes in his autobiography *The Big Sea*, were given "ringside tables to sit and stare at the Negro customers—like amusing animals in the zoo."

MUSIC

Yet these very contradictions helped to make Harlem the exciting city within a city that it was then and the cultural icon it has since become, in terms of both the place itself and the artists associated with it. It was a place and a time of burgeoning African American music—notably the blues and jazz—and a long list of black performers were recording their own compositions and appearing in black musicals, in concerts, and on radio programs. Classic jazz composers and performers all over the United States were increasingly drawn to New York as the nation's music center. Articles and books devoted exclusively to jazz were being published, and recording companies specializing in jazz were established.

Black female blues and jazz singers, though held in high regard by their fans, were often considered "unrespectable" and their music "low culture" by some members of the black bourgeoisie. The blues revivals of the 1960s and 1980s reflected a major shift in that thinking. Both popular and lesser-known performers of the 1920s were rediscovered through new releases of their recordings that reached broader audiences. Angela Davis, in *Blues Legacies and Black Feminism*, notes that "with the globalization of music distribution . . . the scope of black music and its historically broad cultural implications can no longer be confined to African American communities." Indeed, in 1987 Congress passed a resolution declaring jazz "a rare and valuable national treasure."

LITERARY SCENE

Writers such as Hughes, Claude McKay, Nella Larsen, Jessie Redmon Fauset, Countee Cullen, Zora Neale Hurston, and Jean Toomer appeared on the literary scene, forming a kind of literati that they themselves jokingly referred to as the "Niggerati." Publishers clamored for anything "Negro," as Larsen observed, and white patrons such as Carl Van Vechten and Charlotte Osgood Mason (self-proclaimed the "Godmother" because of her financial support of artists) saw to it that they got what they wanted. Indeed, the overwhelming popularity of Van Vechten's own controversial novel *Nigger Heaven* (1926), depicting a seamy side of black life in Harlem, epitomized what publishers believed "Negro" actually meant. Similarly early productions of work by white playwrights Eugene O'Neill and Frederick Ridgely Torrence were instrumental in creating interest in the plays of black writers and also in bringing talented young black actors, singers, and dancers to the stage.

Eubie Blake and Noble Sissle's 1921 musical comedy *Shuffle Along* was the first black Broadway show of the decade, and Hughes cites it as the show that gave a "scintillating send-off to the Negro vogue." At various points during its first run, it showcased the talents of Paul Robeson; Florence Mills; and the exotic, controversial entertainer Josephine Baker. Aaron Douglas designed posters advertising the work of various writers and entertainers but is best known for his contributions to major periodicals, including the *Crisis* and *Opportunity*, official publications of the NAACP and the National Urban League, respectively. The simultaneity of art and politics is vividly represented in the use of these two magazines, devoted in part to sociopolitical reporting of black experience but also to the artistic endeavors of the young black literati.

IMPACT

A black cultural flowering was taking place in other major cities at the same time. However, despite the ongoing debates about whether or not the Harlem Renaissance is a misnomer, whether or not it was a successful movement or any kind of movement at all, black Harlem of the 1920s has become a symbolic "figure" that resonates across time and space, as well as across gender, racial, and cultural boundaries. According to James De Jongh, in the epilogue of *Vicious Modernisms: Black Harlem and the Literary Imagination*,"many writers of European and Asian as well as African descent have found the idea of Harlem to be relevant to their preoccupations and employed the figure of black Harlem in significant ways." Striking examples are 1970s "blaxploitation" films, in which Harlem is seen as a haven for drug dealing and other illicit operations, teeming with violence. Later black filmmakers, especially males, have modeled their notions of the "Hood"—any black poor and working-class urban community—on a symbolic figuration of Harlem.

Although not necessarily set in Harlem, some of the most popular films—such as *Boyz N the Hood* (1991)—attempt to reinterpret the concept of the black urban environment promulgated by earlier popular movies such as *Shaft* (1971) and *Superfly* (1972) with images of racially self-aware men who are connected to, rather than alienated from, family and community. Harlem, reinterpreted, provides the actual setting for one of Spike Lee's major films, *Jungle Fever* (1991), and the opening of *She's Gotta Have It* (1986) pays homage to Hurston, a writer rediscovered—indeed reclaimed—by black feminists and co-opted by a host of academicians in a wide range of disciplines. Similarly, novels and short stories set in Harlem continue to be published, and *The Music of Black Americans: A History* cites Quincy Jones's *Back on the Block* (1989) as the album that "took his listeners back to the old inner-city neighborhood" to learn the history of black music.

In many ways, this idea of Harlem has shaped later generations' views of individual Renaissance artists, thereby determining who emerges as most representative of the place and the period. At the time, however, the issue of representation was hotly debated. Many of the black intelligentsia believed that the cultural arts were a means to correct the distorted images of blacks and to advance their political agendas. Charles S. Johnson, editor of *Opportunity*, set strict guidelines for literary submissions to the magazine. Garvey was critical of those he believed "prostituted" their intelligence and art by succumbing to the demands of white audiences. W. E. B. Du Bois espoused the idea that "all Art is propaganda and ever must be."

Whereas some tried in various ways to escape the stigma of "blackness," others, such as Hughes, one of the chief poets of the period, turned to the folk as a source of material for their work. Hughes proclaimed that the younger black artists were determined to portray their "dark-skinned selves without fear or shame" regardless of what audiences, black or white, thought. This is the attitude that has had the most profound effect on a hip-hop generation of youths who have both reclaimed and reinvented black cultural traditions in their language, music, and dress.

With the stock market crash came the end of an era and, as Hughes put it, the end of the gay times. By then, some of its most enthusiastic proponents were growing disillusioned with the concept of the "New Negro." Some had simply moved on to take up their careers elsewhere. Garvey was convicted of mail fraud, spent two years in an Atlanta prison, and was deported in 1927. However, though the "Negro vogue" ended, art and activism did not. Renewed interest in the Harlem Renaissance and in individual artists has prompted a plethora of scholarship, biographies, docudramas, plays, and personal sojourns into the past, such as Alice Walker's search for Hurston's resting place.

Black American music has helped to lessen the gap between "high" and "low" culture. A shift in views about paintings depicting black life might best be exemplified in Palmer Hayden, whose work was dismissed during his own day as simplistic and naive but who notable black artists such as Romare Bearden later extolled as the "leading folklorist" among them. This revival of interest focuses on the Harlem Renaissance as a pivotal period in African American culture that intersects with a rich cultural past and a promising future. Through their music, drama, art, and literature, blacks in Harlem's heyday confronted blackness head-on in a profound desire for self-discovery and, in so doing, left Harlem its most enduring cultural legacy.

Jacquelyn Y. McLendon

SEE ALSO: *Baker, Josephine; Black Panthers; Blaxploitation Films; Blues; Broadway; Civil Rights Movement; The Cotton Club; Cullen, Countee; Docudrama; Du Bois, W. E. B.; Fauset, Jessie Redmon; Garvey, Marcus; Hip-Hop; Hughes, Langston; Hurston, Zora Neale; Jazz; Johnson, James Weldon; Lee, Spike; Locke, Alain; McKay, Claude; The Musical; O'Neill, Eugene;* Opportunity*; Radio; Robeson, Paul;* Shaft*; Stock Market Crashes; Van Vechten, Carl; Walker, Alice; World War I.*

BIBLIOGRAPHY

Bearden, Romare, and Harry Henderson. *A History of African-American Artists from 1792 to the Present.* New York: Pantheon Books, 1993.

Davis, Angela. *Blues Legacies and Black Feminism: Gertrude "Ma" Rainey, Bessie Smith, and Billie Holiday.* New York: Pantheon Books, 1998.

De Jongh, James. *Vicious Modernism: Black Harlem and the Literary Imagination.* New York: Cambridge University Press, 1990.

Dyson, Michael Eric. *Reflecting Black: African American Cultural Criticism.* Minneapolis: University of Minnesota Press, 1993.

Huggins, Nathan Irvin. *Harlem Renaissance.* New York: Oxford University Press, 2007.

Hughes, Langston. *The Big Sea.* New York: Hill and Wang, 1940.

Southern, Eileen. *The Music of Black Americans: A History,* 3rd ed. New York: W. W. Norton, 1997.

Harlequin Romances

In a market where 56 percent of all U.S. households do not purchase even one book per year, romance novel readers spend an average of $1,200 a year on their habit, whether for escape or titillation. Although compilers of best-seller lists generally scorn romance novels, the genre accounts for more than 40 percent of all paperback sales in North America and has grown in popularity worldwide. Using strict, formulaic guidelines and innovative marketing, Canadian publisher Harlequin Enterprises at one time controlled 85 percent of the romance market, making a lasting mark on the genre. Supermarket or variety store customers are quick to recognize the company's mildly lurid covers, with titles such as *Savage Promise* or *A Fierce Encounter*, on sale near the checkout stand.

FOUNDATION OF AN EMPIRE

Harlequin Enterprises began as a small reprint house in Winnipeg, Manitoba, in 1949 under the leadership of Richard and Mary Bonnycastle. The Bonnycastles bought reprint rights to a variety of out-of-print books in the United States and Great Britain, republishing the works for Canadian audiences. When Mary noticed the popularity of the romance novels from British publisher Mills and Boon, she suggested that Harlequin focus solely on romances. Her idea was so successful that by 1971 Harlequin had bought Mills and Boon and had begun to amass its own stable of romance writers.

In the 1970s Larry Heisey, a marketing specialist who had previously worked at Procter and Gamble, created Harlequin's most innovative and successful marketing strategy. Reasoning that almost the entire readership of romance novels was women, he figured that the same techniques that sold cleaning products—a clearly recognizable brand name and convenient one-stop availability—could sell novels. He developed the Harlequin Presents series with uniform, trademark covers that differed only by title, author, and the racy art. He marketed the books in places where women already shopped: grocery, drug, and variety stores.

With Heisey's skillful marketing practices, Harlequin's profits began to rise. In 1975 the company was bought by publishing giant Torstar, which also owned the *Toronto Star* newspaper. In 1984 Harlequin, troubled by competition from Silhouette Books, Simon & Schuster's new romance division, slid around antitrust laws in the United States to acquire Silhouette. The move helped Harlequin capture a huge share of the romance market, which many claimed was on the verge of dying.

Social critics predicted the death of the pulp romance novel after the start of the women's liberation movement. They claimed women would no longer be hypnotized by the same gauzy fantasy romances that had helped them escape in repressive times. Yet, spurred by its acquisition of Silhouette and expansion abroad, Harlequin continued to grow. By the 1990s it had become the world's largest publisher of romance fiction, releasing over sixty new titles per month and selling more than 150 million books per year in twenty-three languages and in over 100 countries.

A NOVEL FORMULA

Harlequin has transformed the writing of romance novels into a science. With strict guidelines for length (exactly 192 pages for Harlequin Presents novels) and content (avoiding harsh realities and such topics as drugs, terrorism, politics, sports, and alcoholic heroes), Harlequin does not allow much room for creativity. The novels loosely follow the same general formula: a young, beautiful heroine with a romantic name, such as Selena, Storm, or Ariana, meets a rakishly handsome, often older or darkly brooding man with a romantic name such as Bolt, Jake, or Brodie. The couple encounters difficulties—perhaps she is unsure whether he is a hero or villain—but by the end they are passionately reconciled. By the twenty-first century Harlequin had broadened the formula to include older heroines, divorced women, single mothers, women of color, and other characters who were more representative of real women. However, happy endings continued to be a requirement.

Company research shows that the average Harlequin romance reader is a thirty-nine-year-old woman. In general, 53 percent of romance readers have had some college education and 45 percent work outside the home. With an ever sharp eye on the consumer market, Harlequin continues to branch out, offering several series of novels, each with its own set of guidelines, to appeal to distinct markets. Writing guidelines for the Romance line recommend avoiding explicit sexual description, whereas guidelines for the Temptation line suggest creating realistic love scenes that are fun and erotic. The Superromance and American Romance lines offer longer, more sophisticated novels, whereas the Love Inspired line consists of Christian romances that feature faith and passion with equal prominence.

CRITICISM AND APPEAL

The romance novel has not been immune to ideological battles over sex waged in the late twentieth and early twenty-first centuries. Feminists have disagreed whether pornography and sexually explicit romances are indicative of women's liberation. Some have criticized Harlequin's Christian romances for equating female liberation with unhappiness and lack of fulfillment. In spite of claims of antifeminism or association with the religious right, Harlequin continued to print three new Love Inspired novels each month. In 2011 the publisher introduced the Heartwarming line to reach readers who wanted neither explicit sex nor conservative themes.

The publisher also has attempted to appeal to men. Some of the company's more successful undertakings include the Golden Eagle adventure and Worldwide Mystery lines. In 2005 Harlequin partnered with NASCAR to bring a series of romances to car-racing fans, more than 40 percent of whom are women.

The Harlequin formula seems to have worked in many countries. In 1992 the company's romances sold in Hungary at the astounding rate of 17,800 per day. Readers from non-Western cultures such as Japan and the Philippines welcome Harlequin novels with few alterations apart from translation. Covers with Caucasian couples in rapt embrace sell as rapidly in Asia as in Canada. Despite attempts to diversify Harlequin romances, however, the heroes and heroines are almost universally white.

CONTROVERSY OVER WRITERS' RIGHTS

Perhaps Harlequin writers, most of whom are women, have the fewest illusions about the genre. Signed to restrictive contracts, they are required to choose pen names, often romantic ones such as Desiree or Jasmine, to add to the fanciful image of their books. The practical side to the requirement is that if an author leaves for another publishing house, her pen name remains property of Harlequin Enterprises and may be used to represent the work of other writers. The practice effectively prevents Harlequin authors from retaining the following they gained under their pen name.

Another conflict between the publisher and its authors is the issue of the reversion of rights. Most publishers allow copyright on out-of-print works to return to the author. However, Harlequin has often been unwilling to return rights to its authors, citing its ownership of their pen names.

Although writers and agents have lobbied for increased rights, Harlequin not only has refused but also has retaliated by snubbing recalcitrant writers and threatening to convert its agreements to work-for-hire contracts. Under a traditional contract, Harlequin writers receive an advance fee ($2,000 to $3,000 for beginners and as much as $15,000 for veterans), as well as royalties after the book is published (as much as $40,000). Under a work-for-hire contract, a publisher buys an author's work outright with no further compensation, no matter how high the sales. In spite of threats, such organizations as the Authors Guild and Novelists, Inc., continue to investigate Harlequin's questionable policies, including the legality of its 1984 acquisition of Silhouette.

Notwithstanding the drama around Harlequin's corporate policies, the publisher continues to crank out volumes of lushly improbable escape for readers. In contrast to sports or action movies, which are often geared toward men, romance novels provide an exotic world in which female characters are surrounded by adventure and receive passionate rewards. Like magazine serials, and to a lesser extent television soap operas,

Harlequin romances are meant to be taken lightly, as an escape from readers' mundane lives. Their popularity is an indication of the extent to which people continue to crave alternate realities.

Tina Gianoulis

SEE ALSO: *Best Sellers; Divorce; Feminism; Paperbacks; Pornography; Pulp Magazines; Religious Right; Romance Novels; Sexual Revolution; Soap Operas.*

BIBLIOGRAPHY

Darbyshire, Peter. "The Politics of Love: Harlequin Romance and the Christian Right." *Journal of Popular Culture* 35, no. 4 (2002): 75–87.

Harlequin Enterprises Limited. Accessed March 2, 2012. Available from http://www.harlequin.com

Linden, Dana Wechsler, and Matt Rees. "I'm Hungry, but Not for Food." *Forbes*, July 6, 1992, 70.

Mallet, Gina. "The Greatest Romance on Earth." *Canadian Business*, August 1993, 18.

Pollack, Richard. "Romance Slaves of Harlequin." *Nation*, March 16, 1992, 33.

Harley-Davidson

Few material objects have the mystique of a Harley-Davidson motorcycle. The very name conjures a warehouse of connotations: the loud rumble of the Harley engine; black-leather riding apparel; and, of course, the Hells Angels and other stereotypically unsavory biker gangs. Over the years, the "hog," as the bike is affectionately known by its riders, developed a reputation as the preferred transportation of outlaws. Thus, a gritty subculture grew up around the motorcycle and established it as an iconic badge in America and abroad. Though the Harley-Davidson has remained the ride of choice for hard-core bikers, its image was transformed by the end of the 1990s. Once feared and despised by law-abiding middle- and upper-class Americans, it became a well-polished, sporty recreational vehicle for "weekend warriors." Ironically, the Harley—with its rough-hewn history and lore—is now a status symbol among the wealthy.

A MOTORIZED BICYCLE

The original makers of the Harley-Davidson motorcycle never set out to target the fringe element of the market, nor did they consciously create the wild image that developed around the bike. Soon after the twentieth century dawned, draftsman William Harley and his pattern-maker friend Arthur Davidson simply wanted to design and manufacture a motorized bicycle that would eliminate the need for pedals. They were assisted in their endeavor by Ole Evinrude, a German draftsman who later became known for his superior outboard boat motors. Evinrude, who had worked in a French factory, provided the duo with some De Dion engine drawings as a starting point. Davidson created the patterns for a small air-cooled engine, while Harley designed the bicycle. In need of an experienced mechanic, they called upon Davidson's brother, Walter, a machinist for a Kansas railroad, to come home to Milwaukee, Wisconsin. Another brother, William, later joined the operation.

The Davidsons' father, a cabinet maker named William C. Davidson, assisted the entrepreneurs by fixing up a 10-by-15-

Harley-Davidson Motorcycle. *A service technician tunes up a Harley at a dealership in Chicago, Illinois, in 2001. The Harley-Davidson name, logo, and line of iconic motorcycles has been a part of American culture for more than 100 years.* TIM BOYLE/GETTY IMAGES.

foot shed in the backyard as their first factory, with "Harley-Davidson Motor Company" painted on the door. It was officially opened in Milwaukee in 1903, and the Harley-Davidson Motor Company was incorporated in 1907. The Harley-Davidson company website (http://www.harley-davidson.com) proposes two possible reasons why Harley's name comes first: because he built the actual cycle or as a gentlemanly gesture by the Davidsons. Harley became the company's chief engineer and treasurer, while Arthur Davidson was secretary and general sales manager. Walter Davidson was appointed company president, and William Davidson held the position of works manager.

Nicknamed the "Silent Gray Fellow," the original Harley-Davidson motorcycle was a far cry from the thundering, macho vehicle it later became. Initially, the company installed large mufflers to subdue the noise and tried to sell the bikes as practical family transportation (an optional sidecar could be attached). The product instead caught on with sportsmen.

BECOMING A CULTURAL ICON

Once it had started regular production by 1905, the Harley-Davidson firm moved its factory to Chestnut Street, now called Juneau Avenue, in Milwaukee, where the corporate offices still stand. A Davidson relative, James McLay, lent the firm the money to build the 2,380-square-foot shop. In 1907 Harley-Davidson produced 150 motorcycles; within two years the number had increased to 1,149; and by 1912 the company was cranking out more than 9,500 vehicles annually. The company's sales and reputation grew because of the rugged strength and reliability of the bikes, and the firm started to make its mark in racing competitions. By the mid-1910s, Harley-Davidson was the third-largest motorcycle manufacturer in the country. Harley-Davidson had the top-selling motorcycles in the United States by 1920, with dealerships in sixty-seven countries.

With Arthur Davidson concentrating on sales strategy and Bill Harley focusing on testing and development, the company prospered. When its main competitor, Indian, closed its doors in 1953, Harley-Davidson became the sole remaining American motorcycle company. In 1957 the legendary Sportster model was first released. Harley-Davidson was producing more than 105,000 bikes a year by 1995, and demand was steadily growing. Part of the company's success was due to Davidson's initiative in setting up a network of dealers that were only allowed to sell Harley-Davidson motorcycles, with an accompanying dedication to those dealers that their profits would always come first. In addition, the company boasted a strong product guarantee. Harley-Davidson even survived during difficult economic times, thanks to its foreign sales and the fact that it supplied the U.S. Postal Service and numerous police departments.

In both World War I and II, Harley-Davidsons were used to run dispatch on the front lines. In fact, nearly all of the company's output during World War II went to support the Allied forces. At that time, soldiers began the practice of chopping off parts—including headlights and fenders—to make the machines go faster. Thus, the word *chopper* came to refer to an altered Harley. Eventually it was expected that hog owners would personalize their bikes—not only by making them into choppers but also with custom paint jobs or fenders and other unique touches. As for the nickname *hog*, there are a couple of theories regarding its origin. One notes that a Harley racing enthusiast around 1920 used to do his victory laps with his pet pig accompanying him on the bike.

HELL ON WHEELS

In 1947 the image of the outlaw biker gained full momentum when an article in *Life* magazine detailed the horrors of a rebel motorcycle gang that terrorized a town in California. No longer seen simply as a vehicle for sporting enthusiasts, the Harley was now linked with the Hells Angels, a group of criminal-element bikers who took their name from a 1930 Howard Hughes film about combat pilots. This was bad publicity for Harley-Davidson, and the media continued to beef up the stereotype with films such as Marlon Brando's *The Wild One* (1954), about the biker subculture. Unfortunately, the stories surrounding biker gangs—rape, robbery, beatings, and looting—often contained more truth than fiction. In the 1960s journalist Hunter S. Thompson infiltrated the ranks of the Hells Angels and wrote a book about his experiences called *Hell's Angels: The Strange and Terrible Saga of the Outlaw Motorcycle Gang* (1966). After his exposé was published, Thompson was mercilessly beaten up by a members of the gang.

During the 1960s and 1970s, the preferred vehicle for a mainstream motorcycle enthusiast was usually a lower-priced Japanese model, derogatorily nicknamed a "rice burner" and denounced by Harley riders as watered-down imitations of "true" motorcycles. However, foreign bikes were more accepted in polite society because they were free of the stigma of the Harley, which had come to symbolize low-class, dirty deviants. Magazines such as *Easy Rider*, featuring half-naked cover models, contributed to the bike's sleazy connotations. In the 1980s, however, the image of the Harley rider began to change again. Though the leather-clad antisocial gang members still existed, more and more "yuppie" bikers were taking to the open road. Not only did these yuppies like the fact that the Harley was a well-made American vehicle, but they were also undoubtedly intrigued by its outlaw image.

ROLLING INTO THE FUTURE

Harley-Davidsons soon became a recreational vehicle for successful businessmen, much like a boat or Jet Ski. The bikes could be seen lined up outside hip nightspots in major cities on weekends or streaming down highways as the yuppie riders left town. Harley accessory boutiques mushroomed in upscale shopping districts around the country. The company set up a slick website and appropriated events such as Daytona Bike Week in Florida and the annual motorcycle rally and races in Sturgis, South Dakota, for generating corporate publicity.

In 1993 Turner Original Productions produced a television special titled *Harley-Davidson: The American Motorcycle*, narrated by actor James Caan and featuring celebrities such as David Crosby, Peter Fonda, Wynonna Judd, and a leather-clad Larry Hagman, all touting their love of the bike and its aura. *The Tonight Show* host Jay Leno became another well-known aficionado. As the Harley-Davidson celebrated its 100th anniversary, it had returned to its roots as a bike used by genteel sportsmen.

As the twenty-first century rolls on, so does the Harley-Davidson tradition. Transmissions and engines are still manufactured in Milwaukee, though final assembly and shipping occur in York, Pennsylvania, or Kansas City, Missouri. In 2001 Harley-Davidson introduced the V-Rod, a hybrid that falls somewhere between the sport bike and road cruiser. It has become much more difficult to reproduce the signature uneven rhythm of the original motors in new fuel-injected engines, but the company went so far as to try to patent the sound before finally dropping the issue. By 2003 Harley-Davidson was producing 295,000 units per year. Much of the twenty-first century's marketing efforts have been directed at selling luxury models, such as the Road Glide Custom. Harley-Davidson luxury models are selling particularly well in the oil-rich Middle East, where customers are purchasing the VRSC-F V-Rod Muscle, a bike deemed perfect for dusty desert roads.

Geri Speace

SEE ALSO: *Brando, Marlon; Hells Angels; Leisure Time; Thompson, Hunter S.;* The Wild One; *Yuppies.*

BIBLIOGRAPHY

Bolfert, Thomas C. *The Big Book of Harley Davidson: Official Publication.* Milwaukee, WI: Harley-Davidson, 1991.

Harley-Davidson Motor Company. Access March 7, 2012. Available from http://www.harley-davidson.com

Joans, Barbara. *Bike Lust: Harleys, Women, and American Society.* Madison: University of Wisconsin Press, 2001.

Johnson, David. "Family Affair: Four Men, One Dream." *Cycle World,* September 1993, 60.

Leffingwell, Randy. *Harley-Davidson: Myth & Mystique.* Osceola, WI: Motorbooks Publishers & Wholesalers, 1995.

Norris, Martin. *Rolling Thunder: The Harley-Davidson Legend.* London: Quintet Publishing, 1992.

Teerlink, Richard. *More than a Motorcycle: The Leadership Journey at Harley-Davidson.* Boston: Harvard Business School Press, 2000.

Thompson, Hunter S. *Hell's Angels: The Strange and Terrible Saga of the Outlaw Motorcycle Gangs.* New York: Ballantine Books, 1966.

Wagner, Herbert. *Harley-Davidson 1930–1941: Revolutionary Motorcycles & Those Who Rode Them.* Atglen, PA: Schiffer Publishing, 1996.

Wicks, Frank. "Between the Horse and the Car." *Mechanical Engineering,* 125, no. 7 (2003).

Harlow, Jean *(1911–1937)*

Known for her platinum blond hair, low-cut gowns, and buxom figure, Jean Harlow was Hollywood's original blond bombshell. Her bold sexuality—she refused to wear undergarments, for example—made her both a box-office hit and an icon of modern sexual freedom. But it was not only Harlow's starring roles—in such films as *Platinum Blonde* (1931), *Red Dust* (1932), and *China Seas* (1935)—that made news. The unexplained suicide of her husband, MGM executive Paul Bern, and her own mysterious death from uremia at age twenty-six made Harlow a tragic symbol of the fleeting pleasures of Hollywood stardom.

Samantha Barbas

SEE ALSO: *MGM (Metro-Goldwyn-Mayer); Monroe, Marilyn; Sex Symbol.*

BIBLIOGRAPHY

Bret, David. *Jean Harlow: Tarnished Angel.* London: JR Books, 2009.

Shulman, Irving. *Harlow: An Intimate Biography.* New York: Dell, 1964.

Stenn, David. *Bombshell: The Life and Death of Jean Harlow.* New York: Doubleday, 1993.

Harmonica Bands

Although harmonica bands and orchestras have generally been forgotten, the harmonica was one of the most popular musical instruments from the 1920s through the 1940s. Its cheapness made it ideal for teaching music to children during the Great Depression, and harmonica youth orchestras were influential in instilling discipline. In the years between the two world wars—a period some call the golden age of the mouth organ in America—sales of the tiny, inexpensive instrument increased dramatically. Bands of harmonica players became famous on the vaudeville circuit, on radio, and in Hollywood films. Whole orchestras of harmonica-playing youth were organized in cities all over the United States, and public schools offered harmonica instruction courses. The craze finally hit its peak in 1947 when the Harmonicats' rendition of "Peg o' My Heart" became the number one hit of that year.

EARLY FANS

America's fascination with harmonica bands began during the Boy Council of Philadelphia's 1923 Boys' Week celebration when philanthropist Albert Hoxie organized a harmonica contest. The same year, Hohner Company, a German manufacturer of harmonicas, began sending experts to public schools to teach children how to play the instrument. In 1924 more than 10,000 children participated in the Boys' Week contest, and in the following years harmonica youth bands began forming, including one led by Hoxie himself, called the Philadelphia Harmonica Band.

Hoxie's band, which consisted of about sixty young men, followed a military model, with the musicians wearing marching band uniforms, attaining specific ranks, and ending each show with "Stars and Stripes Forever." The band, which lasted until 1936, traveled around the country and played for presidents and visiting dignitaries. It also performed at events such as the Philadelphia celebration of Charles Lindbergh's transatlantic flight, the heavyweight championship fight between Jack Dempsey and Gene Tunney, and president Franklin D. Roosevelt's inaugural parade.

Hoxie also sent harmonica assistants to schools during the Depression to encourage children to play the affordable instrument. His efforts paid off. By the end of the 1930s, more than 150 harmonica youth orchestras existed in Chicago alone; 1,200 public school children had learned to play the harmonica in Dayton, Ohio; and 115,127 children in Los Angeles were enrolled in the harmonica band program between 1927 and 1937. During the Depression, Boy Scouts could earn merit badges for harmonica playing, and over 2,000 harmonica bands were formed in the United States.

GOLDEN AGE

Hoxie's efforts were not the only reason for the appeal of harmonica bands in schools. Until the 1920s the harmonica had been based on the diatonic scale; therefore, it was limited to the notes in the key to which it was tuned. However, in the mid-1920s, Hohner developed the polyphonia, bass, chord, and chromatic models, which expanded the range of the instrument and improved the overall sound of harmonica bands. Vaudeville acts such as the Harmonica Rascals, which combined music and slapstick comedy, began using the new instruments as early as 1927. Other bands soon followed, making the harmonica even more popular as fans were inspired to try it for themselves.

Critics likened the Harmonica Rascals, formed by harmonica player Borrah Minevitch, to the Three Stooges with mouth organs. Audiences loved the group, whose image was based on the ragamuffin/tramp motif. The band's act centered on Johnny Puleo, who was just over 4 feet tall. Puleo played the largest harmonica available, the polyphonia, for comic effect. The band was so successful that until the end of World War II, Minevitch simultaneously ran three separate groups by the same name, each with its own little person, in different regions of the country. Besides appearing in vaudeville, the Harmonica Rascals had a weekly radio program and filmed several movies between 1935 and 1943.

Other 1930s bands inspired by the Harmonica Rascals include the Harmonica Scamps, a vaudeville band that featured an African American little person, and the Harmonicuties, an all-girl band boasting a female little person. The Harmonica Harlequins, whose members dressed in clown outfits, formed in 1934 as a competitor to the Harmonica Rascals. The Harlequins worked the vaudeville circuit, played on the radio, and made records. Other bands from the 1930s were the Cappy Barra Harmonica Ensemble and the Philharmonicas, both of whom specialized in big band arrangements; the Harlemonicats, a jazz trio; the Stagg McMann Trio; the Harmonica Hi-Hats; and the Harmonica Lads.

POSTWAR GROUPS

World War II ended the golden age of the harmonica. A ban on German goods prohibited the importation of harmonicas from Germany, where the highest-quality instruments were made. Youth orchestras disbanded and schools halted their instructional programs.

Large professional groups pared down to smaller units, usually trios. The most famous materialized when former Harmonica Rascals Jerry Murad and Don Les teamed up with musician Al Fiore to form the Harmonicats in the mid-1940s. Their 1947 version of "Peg o' My Heart"—recorded as a B side—stayed at number one on the Billboard chart for twenty-six weeks. The record subsequently sold more than twenty million copies, becoming the second-most popular 78 of all time, surpassed only by Bing Crosby's "White Christmas." The record's success even convinced the Musicians' Union to accept the harmonica as a legitimate instrument and to allow harmonica players to join.

The Harmonicats went on to record thirty-six albums. Murad kept the trio alive until his death in 1996, although Les retired in 1972 and Fiore, in 1982. Although other harmonica bands performed after World War II, none could match the success of "Peg o' My Heart." The Don Henry trio had a minor hit in the 1950s with their version of "The Saber Dance." Puleo formed the Harmonica Gang, which appeared on television with Milton Berle, Dean Martin, and Perry Como in the 1950s and played live at the Latin Quarter in New York and the Stardust in Las Vegas. Puleo's group recorded seven albums until he retired in 1973. Harmonica player Dave Doucette had some success with the Stereomonics, a quintet, in 1968 and with the Big Harp in 1975.

The success of harmonica bands on the vaudeville stage inspired many future soloists and session players such as Richard Hayman, Pete Pedersen, Mike Chimes, Leo Diamond, Alan Shackner, and Charles Newman. The world-famous soloist Larry Adler elevated the tiny instrument to near-classical status by playing in concert halls. During the postwar era, the instrument became a favorite among blues artists, especially in the burgeoning Chicago blues scene, where players such as Little Walter, whom many consider the greatest blues harmonica player of all time, made a name for themselves. Well-known rock and country musicians, such as Bob Dylan, John Lennon, and Johnny Cash, have reintroduced the harmonica to a wider audience. John Popper, front man for the rock band Blues Traveler, formed in 1987, is considered a harmonica virtuoso.

Richard Levine

SEE ALSO: *Berle, Milton; Blues; Boy Scouts of America; Cash, Johnny; Como, Perry; Crosby, Bing; Dempsey, Jack; Dylan, Bob; The Great Depression; Hollywood; Jazz; Las Vegas; Lennon, John; Lindbergh, Charles; Martin, Dean; The Three Stooges; Vaudeville; World War II.*

BIBLIOGRAPHY

Field, Kim. *Harmonicas, Harps, and Heavy Breathers.* New York: Simon & Schuster, 1993.

Glover, Tony; Scott Dirks; and Ward Gaines. *Blues with a Feeling: The Little Walter Story.* New York: Routledge, 2002.

Hohner USA. "Artist Gallery." Accessed February 28, 2012. Available from http://www.hohnerusa.com/index.php?390

Krampert, Peter. *The Encyclopedia of the Harmonica.* Arlington Heights, IL: Tatanka, 1998.

Oliver, Paul. *The Story of the Blues.* Boston: Northwestern University Press, 1998.

Harper's

Harper's magazine, one of America's most culturally significant periodicals, was founded in 1850 under the name *Harper's New Monthly* magazine. It was published by the New York–based Harper & Brothers, the largest publishing company in nineteenth-century America. Initially conceived of as a miscellany—a collection of reprints from other publications—consisting mostly of fiction, *Harper's* gained a broad middle-class audience by positioning itself as the Victorian reader's gateway to refinement and respectability. By the twentieth century *Harper's* had transformed itself into the magazine of choice for an elite, well-educated readership whose opinions and tastes helped to shape the nation's political debates and social trends.

With an antebellum circulation of 200,000, *Harper's* was easily the best-read and most influential magazine of its time, and its list of nineteenth-century contributors reads like a roll call of some of the era's finest British and American fiction writers. In spite of its long record of prosperity, by the end of World War I, *Harper's* was in financial trouble, its circulation down to 75,000. Over the course of the first few decades of the twentieth century, the genteel, culturally ambitious, middle-class readership upon which *Harper's* had based its success had fragmented. A number of forces, including a widening income gap between rich and poor, increasing cultural diversity through immigration, the rise of the suburbs, and the impact of emerging technologies such as film and radio, split the relatively unified nineteenth-century reading public into lowbrow, middlebrow, and highbrow audiences. Those periodicals that were able to maintain a mass national circulation, such as *Ladies' Home Journal* and the *Saturday Evening Post*, did so by cutting prices and simplifying article content in order to appeal to the largest possible audience, while relying on extensive advertising to compensate for lost subscription revenue.

Rather than follow the lead of the mass-market magazines to try to regain its position as market leader, *Harper's* decided to redefine itself as the journal for the well-educated and the well-read, seeking serious, though not scholarly, discussion of the issues of the day. In 1925 editor Thomas Wells redesigned the magazine, slimming it down and removing most of the elaborate artwork. The new *Harper's* assumed a distinctly progressive but never radically political tone. Most significantly, the amount of fiction, long the magazine's hallmark, was reduced and replaced by nonfiction articles debating major social and political issues to satisfy its readership.

As mid-twentieth-century editor Frederick Lewis Allen noted, the types of issues discussed in the magazine's pages evolved

Harper's *Magazine, 1897.* *When this 1897 issue of* Harper's *was published, it was the most widely read and influential magazine in the United States.* **MPI/GETTY IMAGES.**

with the changing interests of its audience. In the 1920s *Harper's* was full of articles on the social upheaval of the modern era. Numerous articles voiced concerns about the role of the newly enfranchised and emancipated woman and her impact on family life. Other writers—such as James Truslow Adams in "Is Science a Blind Alley?"—expressed fears about the decline of religion in the face of rapid technological change. By the 1930s, motivated by the Great Depression and the specter of war in Europe, *Harper's* turned toward political and economic issues, such as the rise of German and Japanese power abroad and the possibility of social unrest among the unemployed and alienated at home.

WARS AND TRANSFORMATIONS

The entrance of the United States into World War II solidified the magazine's increasingly global focus. *Harper's* wholeheartedly supported the war effort, and writer Henry L. Stimson defended the bombings of Hiroshima and Nagasaki in its pages. Editor Lewis H. Lapham has noted that throughout the 1950s and 1960s *Harper's* was a significant forum for America's Cold War intellectuals, including Arthur Schlesinger Jr., Van Wyck Brooks, Richard Hofstadter, and Henry Steele Commager. Later, as the role of the public intellectual waned, and as public cynicism waxed in the Vietnam and Watergate eras, *Harper's* responded again, by changing to a more journalistic, exposé-oriented style.

In 1965 *Harper's* magazine was acquired by the Minneapolis Star and Tribune Company, which was buying up Harper & Row (the successor to Harper & Brothers) stock. By 1980 the magazine was once again in debt. When the new owners considered terminating *Harper's*, the John D. and Catherine T. MacArthur Foundation and the Atlantic Richfield Company provided funds to set up the Harper's Magazine Foundation, headed by John R. MacArthur, to publish the magazine independently of its parent and make it less reliant on subscription and advertising revenues.

In 1984, under the leadership of Lapham, *Harper's* was again redesigned. In a pair of editorials, Lapham invoked the nineteenth-century origins of the magazine, comparing the situation of Americans of the 1850s facing a new national industrial economy to that of his own readers as the country became integrated into a new global economic order. He vowed to continue to provide a national forum for debate on issues of social and political importance. Interestingly, Lapham also reaffirmed the original mission of *Harper's* as a miscellany, but with a difference. While the editors of 1850 had offered their readers what they felt was the best in entertaining and useful information, Lapham announced new departments that would offer representative statistics or small excerpts from significant publications or public documents in a context often designed to startle the reader and to demystify or even mock the offered text. That change alone, from a tone of Victorian earnestness to one of postmodern irony, speaks volumes about the altered self-image of the writer-intellectual, transforming from ardent educator to alienated commentator over the course of the magazine's 134-year history. Lapham promised to continue to steer a middle course between the banalities of mass-market journalism and the jargon of highly specialized publications, as the magazine had tried to do since its inception.

By the end of the twentieth century, the magazine's major goal had become to provide a national forum for debate on those forces and trends with global origins and impact for its elite readership, but that goal may have become problematic.

There is always some difficulty inherent in identifying national interests as being those of such a comparatively small group of readers. In 1998 *Harper's* had a circulation of 216,630, a respectable number but one that was hardly comparable to the million-plus circulations of mass-market periodicals and only slightly higher than the magazine's highest circulation in the nineteenth century.

Lapham stepped down as editor of *Harper's* in 2005 to start the history periodical *Lapham's Quarterly*. By that time he had become thoroughly disgusted with the George W. Bush administration and with the tendency of the media to gear its message to "the interests of twelve-year-olds." Roger Hodge took over as editor. He, in turn, was replaced by Ellen Rosenbush, in 2010. In 2012, *Harper's* had an annual readership of approximately 220,000 and offered both Internet and digital access for smartphones, portable media players, and tablets. The male/female ratio of the current readership was 65/35, and the median age of readers was 54.8 years. Some 94.6 percent of all readers had college degrees, and 63.9 percent had postgraduate degrees. More than three-fourths of all readers were involved in professional or managerial positions.

Anne Sheehan

SEE ALSO: *Advertising; The Great Depression; The* Saturday Evening Post*; World War I; World War II.*

BIBLIOGRAPHY

Charvat, William. *The Profession of Authorship in America, 1800–1870*, ed. Matthew J. Bruccoli. Columbus: Ohio State University Press, 1968.

Exman, Eugene. *The Brothers Harper*. New York: Harper & Row, 1965.

Exman, Eugene. *The House of Harper: One Hundred and Fifty Years of Publishing*. New York: Harper & Row, 1967.

Harper, J. Henry. *The House of Harper: A Century of Publishing in Franklin Square*. New York: Harper & Brothers Publishers, 1912.

Lapham, Lewis H. "Letter to the Reader." *Harper's*, January 1984, 10, 12.

Lapham, Lewis H. "In the American Grain." *Harper's*, February 1984, 6–8, 10.

Mott, Frank Luther. *A History of American Magazines, Volume II: 1850–1865*. Cambridge, MA: Harvard University Press, 1938.

Nourie, Alan, and Barbara Nourie, eds. *American Mass-Market Magazines*. New York: Greenwood Press, 1990.

Peterson, Theodore. *Magazines in the Twentieth Century*. Urbana: University of Illinois Press, 1964.

Phegley, Jennifer. *Educating the Proper Woman Reader: Victorian Family Literary Magazines and the Cultural Health of the Nation*. Columbus: Ohio State University Press, 2004.

Tebbel, John. *A History of Book Publishing in the United States*, 4 vols. New York: R. R. Bowker, 1975–81.

Harry, Deborah

SEE: *Blondie.*

Harry Potter

The Harry Potter franchise, which consists of seven novels, eight motion pictures, and countless independently released books, accessories, and memorabilia, began in 1997 when first-time British author Joanne Rowling, under the pen name J. K. Rowling, published *Harry Potter and the Philosopher's Stone* in the United Kingdom. In 1998 Scholastic brought Rowling's book to the United States under the title *Harry Potter and the Sorcerer's Stone*. Over the next decade, the Potter franchise grew with remarkable vigor, creating a template for later young-adult fantasy series. As of 2012 the series was the most successful in history, with the books selling more than 450 million copies and the movies grossing more than $7.7 billion.

THE NARRATIVE

The main story line, for both the film and book series, revolves around the constant physical and mental struggle between the protagonist, Harry Potter, and the antagonist, the unspeakably evil Lord Voldemort. Potter is orphaned as an infant when Voldemort kills his parents, and Potter is sent to live with his only remaining relatives, an aunt, uncle, and cousin who treat him unkindly. On his eleventh birthday Harry is shocked when Rubeus Hagrid, a softhearted giant entrusted with Harry's care, shows up and reveals to Potter that he is in fact a wizard. Harry is enrolled at the Hogwarts School of Witchcraft and Wizardry, a boarding school in Scotland that serves as the predominant setting for the rest of the series. There, Potter meets most of the other central characters, including his two closest companions, Hermione Granger and Ron Weasley.

Whereas most fantasy novels take place in some fictional landscape and time, Rowling sets her stories in a contemporary English setting. In Rowling's England, ordinary humans (labeled "muggles") are oblivious to the existence of the wizards, their school, and their struggles. Potter has to navigate both worlds as an adolescent; in one he is an outsider, and in the other a hero—"The Boy Who Lived," the only one who can stop Voldemort. The series' appeal lies squarely in this dichotomy: readers can live vicariously through Harry's adventures as a hero among wizards who is mistreated and misunderstood when among ordinary human beings. For young readers, Harry's tale is a story of hope and perseverance.

BOOK SERIES

When she sold the first Harry Potter novel in 1997, Rowling was offered a £2,500 advance by Bloomsbury (roughly $4,000). Rowling had already completed a large portion of the series by this point, as she had been submitting *The Philosopher's Stone* to publishers for several years to no avail. With much of the series penned, the books were released in rapid succession: *Harry Potter and the Chamber of Secrets* in 1998 (1999 in the United States); *Harry Potter and the Prisoner of Azkaban* in July 1999 (September in the United States); and *Harry Potter and the Goblet of Fire*, released in both markets in July 2000. These early installments focus primarily on fully rendering Potter's world and establishing his relationships with the other characters.

The fifth installment, *Harry Potter and the Order of the Phoenix* (2003), develops Harry's role as a leader, as he organizes his fellow classmates in a campaign to save Hogwarts and its beloved headmaster, Albus Dumbledore. The novel also establishes the trajectory of the remaining novels, revealing that neither Harry nor Voldemort can live unless the other dies. The book sold five million copies in the United States alone on the day of its release.

By the release of the sixth installment, *Harry Potter and the Half-Blood Prince*, in July 2005, the Harry Potter craze had reached its apex. Along with a list of fan sites numbering in the hundreds, the Potter series also became the first books to engender a tradition of overnight camping for midnight premieres—a phenomenon normally associated with major film and music releases. Following just such a release, *Harry Potter and the Half-Blood Prince* had sold about nine million copies globally by the close of its first day.

The seventh installment, *Harry Potter and the Deathly Hallows*, was not released until July 2007. But in the two years leading up to its release, several fan-fiction and speculative analysis titles were released, all hazarding guesses about the content of the final Potter novel and speculating on the series' end: namely, whether Harry would live or die. Upon its release, *The Deathly Hallows* sold eleven million copies in twenty-four hours.

THE FILMS

In 1998 Warner Brothers purchased the film rights for the first four Harry Potter novels. The movies, the first of which premiered after the release of the fourth book, brought even more attention to the series. The first movie, *Harry Potter and the Philosopher's Stone* (again, called *Sorcerer's Stone* in the United States), starred Brit Daniel Radcliffe as Harry Potter and featured an exclusively British cast. Directed by Chris Columbus, it premiered in 2001. *Harry Potter and the Chamber of Secrets* (2002) was also directed by Columbus, but he decided against directing the third film and was replaced by Alfonso Cuarón. *Harry Potter and the Prisoner of Azkaban* was released in 2004. Shooting for *Harry Potter and the Goblet of Fire* (directed by Mike Newell) began before the third film's release and premiered just a year later, in 2005. *Harry Potter and the Order of the Phoenix* was released in 2007, under yet another director, David Yates. Yates was kept on to direct the remaining films, thanks to the success of the fifth installment. The films enjoyed unprecedented popular success, and although, predictably, they could not please all of Rowling's devoted readers, they fostered a deeper fan base than the novels could on their own.

By the last three films, the Harry Potter movie franchise reliably produced blockbusters. *Harry Potter and the Half-Blood Prince* (2009) grossed $394 million in five days, breaking the record for first-week box-office sales. The final book, *Harry Potter and the Deathly Hallows*, was adapted into two separate films: *Part 1* in 2010 and *Part 2* in 2011. *Part 2* broke the opening-weekend record by grossing $483.2 million in three days. All told, the eight Harry Potter films carried a budget of $1.15 billion and grossed $7.7 billion at the box office (more than any other franchise to that point).

In 2010 Universal Studios and Warner Brothers completed construction on a $200 million, 20-acre Harry Potter–themed park in Universal's Orlando resort in Florida. The theme park includes a reconstruction of both Hogwarts Castle and Hogsmeade village—where visitors can dine in re-creations of restaurants and taverns frequently mentioned in Rowling's novels. Universal credited the Potter attractions with a 20 percent increase in overall attendance and a 41 percent increase in overall revenue for its Orlando theme park.

CULTURAL IMPACTS

Together, the releases of books and movies spanned fourteen years. Many devotees were Harry's age when they started reading the books, and they essentially grew up alongside him. The books dominated the best-seller lists and galvanized a resurgence in recreational reading among children and teens. With their success, publishers began looking at children's and young adult books as lucrative business endeavors. Colleges began offering entire classes devoted solely to the series, fostering critical attention usually reserved for more canonical children's texts. Though critics were split on its lasting literary value, the Harry Potter franchise grew from a series of fantasy novels into a cultural touchstone, effectively defining an entire generation of culture in the process.

Brian Black>

SEE ALSO: *Best Sellers; Blockbusters; Hollywood; Teenagers.*

BIBLIOGRAPHY

Anelli, Melissa. *Harry, a History.* New York: Pocket Books, 2008.

"*Harry Potter* Tale Is Fastest-Selling Book in History." *New York Times*, July 23, 2007.

Irwin, William. *The Ultimate Harry Potter and Philosophy.* Hoboken, NJ: Wiley, 2010.

Mulholland, Neil. *The Psychology of Harry Potter.* New York: Smart Pop, 2007.

Thompson, Susan. "Business Big Shot: Harry Potter Author JK Rowling." *Times* (London), April 2, 2008.

Hart, Lorenz

SEE: *Rodgers and Hart.*

Havlicek, John *(1940–)*

Of all the players in the illustrious history of the Boston Celtics, perhaps none is more closely associated with a single moment than John Havlicek. Legions of Celtics fans can imitate team announcer Johnny Most's raspy yell when Havlicek came up with a crucial steal as time ran out in the seventh and deciding game of the 1965 Eastern Division Finals against the perennial rival Philadelphia 76ers: "Havlicek Stole the Ball! Havlicek Stole the Ball!" The steal preserved a one-point win for Boston and paved the way for another National Basketball Association (NBA) championship.

It seems ironic that Havlicek is so renowned for that one play, for his career was marked by a longevity and consistency that few players in NBA history have been able to match. His steal came early in a distinguished career that endured for sixteen seasons. He played on eight NBA championship teams and appeared in thirteen All-Star games. Havlicek's trademark was his amazing endurance—he remained in perpetual motion on both offense and defense throughout entire games.

At 6 feet, 5 inches, Havlicek was able to play both guard and forward, using his size and strength to overpower smaller guards and his quickness to beat larger, slower forwards with drives to the basket and swift passes. In addition to his physical stamina, he was an avid student of the game. Longtime Boston sportswriter Bob Ryan notes in *The Boston Celtics* that Havlicek's "physical abilities were exceeded by his extraordinary basketball mind. If he saw his opponents run a play, he made a note of the hand signal or verbal call that initiated it. Thereafter he always got the jump on it. He couldn't understand why other players didn't retain basketball knowledge equally well."

A three-sport star in high school, Havlicek initially played both baseball and basketball at Ohio State University. He eventually gave up baseball so that he could concentrate on basketball, but his versatility and athletic ability were such that he was drafted by both the National Football League's Cleveland Browns (seventh round) and the Celtics (first round) following his graduation from Ohio State in 1962. Havlicek was the last player cut by the Browns when he tried out as a wide receiver, which allowed him to devote himself solely to basketball.

Havlicek joined the Celtics in the midst of the team's run of eight consecutive championships between 1959 and 1966. In his first four seasons, a time when the Celtics were loaded with veteran players, he assumed the role of the "sixth man," coming off the bench late in the first quarter of games to provide instant scoring. He became an even more central figure on the team during the 1967–1968 and 1968–1969 championship seasons, as some of the veteran players began showing signs of age. In 1967–1968, for example, Havlicek scored forty of Boston's 100 points in a hard-fought seventh-game victory over Philadelphia in the Eastern Division Finals, which put the Celtics into the NBA Finals.

The early 1970s were more difficult for the Celtics, partly because of the retirement of legendary center Bill Russell in 1969, but Havlicek raised his level of play to new heights. In 1970–1971 and 1971–1972, he had the best scoring seasons of his career and led the league in minutes played. In 1972–1973, the Celtics posted their best regular-season record in their history (68–14), but they lost in the Eastern Conference Finals against the New York Knicks, hampered by a shoulder injury that Havlicek had suffered in the third game of the series.

Havlicek, or "Hondo" as he came to be known by Celtics fans in homage to the John Wayne movie of the same name, concluded his career as a leader and elder statesman for a younger generation of Celtics during the championship seasons of 1973–1974 and 1975–1976, both of which offered a number of memorable moments. In the 1973–1974 NBA Finals, the Celtics defeated the Milwaukee Bucks in a seven-game series that included one overtime and one double-overtime game. Havlicek was named Most Valuable Player of that series. In the 1975–1976 NBA Finals, the Celtics faced the Phoenix Suns, who played Boston to a 2–2 tie in the first four games. The fifth game—regarded as one of the greatest games in NBA history—went to three overtimes and was won 128–126 by Boston, thanks in no small part to several key baskets by Havlicek. The Celtics then closed out the series in the sixth game.

Following the 1975–1976 season, the Celtics' nucleus began to disperse for various reasons. Havlicek retired following the 1977–1978 season, one of the worst in Boston history, at the age of thirty-seven. True to form, he scored an impressive twenty-nine points in his final game at the Boston Garden. At the time of his retirement, he was the sixth-leading scorer in NBA history (26,395 points). In addition, he held the Celtics' record for career games (1,270) and was second in team history in career minutes (46,471), third in career points, second in career assists (6,114), and third in career rebounds (8,007). He was elected to the Naismith Memorial Basketball Hall of Fame in 1983 and made the NBA's list of its fifty greatest players of all time in 1996.

Jason George

SEE ALSO: *Basketball; The Boston Celtics; Knight, Bobby; National Basketball Association (NBA); Russell, Bill; Sports Heroes.*

BIBLIOGRAPHY

Fitzgerald, Joe. *That Championship Feeling: The Story of the Boston Celtics.* New York: Scribner, 1975.

Garner, Joe. *And the Crowd Goes Wild: Relive the Most Celebrated Sporting Events Ever Broadcast.* Naperville, IL: Sourcebooks, 1999.

Ryan, Bob. *The Boston Celtics: The History, Legends, and Images of America's Most Celebrated Team.* Reading, MA: Addison-Wesley Publishing, 1989.

Hawaii Five-O

By the time the final episode aired in April 1980, the original *Hawaii Five-O* was the longest continuously running police drama in the history of television. The show premiered in September 1968 and retained loyal viewers for most of its 284 episodes. Producer Leonard Freeman, the main creative force behind the show, brought together the elements that made the show a hit: a well-chosen cast that went virtually unchanged for ten years, dynamic music, and the lush scenery of Hawaii.

The primary appeal of the show was its main character, the tough, no-nonsense Steve McGarrett, who was the head of the Five-O. McGarrett's elite special investigating unit deals with crimes that are too big for conventional police forces, and he answers only to "the governor and God." Freeman's original title for the series was *The Man*, because every criminal in the Aloha State knew that McGarrett was "the man." And when the wrong element came to the Hawaiian shores, McGarrett is quick to let them know, "You're on my rock now." In the pilot, recurring nemesis Wo Fat describes McGarrett as "the proverbial character you would not want to meet in a dark alley."

Jack Lord played the role of McGarrett with intensity. Lord was a driven perfectionist who dedicated himself to the show. Lord's McGarrett was a larger-than-life character who struck fear into the hearts of the islands' criminal element and inspired fierce loyalty from the men and women he commanded. After Freeman's death in 1974, Lord became the guiding force behind the show.

McGarrett's right-hand man was Danny "Danno" Williams, played by James MacArthur. In the pilot Danno was played by Tim O'Kelly, but when he did not get a favorable rating from a test audience in New York, Freeman replaced him with MacArthur before the regular series began filming. MacArthur proved to be a crucial ingredient in the successful chemistry of the show. The best-remembered and most often repeated line from *Hawaii Five-O* was McGarrett's clipped command, "Book 'em, Danno." For eleven seasons, Williams was a loyal and stolid sidekick to McGarrett. MacArthur tired of the role and left the show at the end of the 1978–1979 season; the

***Jack Lord in* Hawaii Five-O.** *Jack Lord, left, was the star of* Hawaii Five-O, *a police drama that ran for twelve seasons on CBS.* HULTON ARCHIVE/GETTY IMAGES.

successful formula was lost, and the series could only limp along for one additional year.

While the network required that the two lead characters be played by *haoles* (Caucasians from the mainland), the other members of the Five-O team were played by local actors. Kam Fong Chun (credited as Kam Fong), who had served on the Honolulu Police Department for more than fifteen years before turning to acting, played Chin Ho Kelly for ten seasons. For the first five years of the series, local musician and stand-up comic Gilbert "Zoulou" Kauhi (credited as Zulu) played KonoKalakaua. After Zulu's departure two new characters were introduced: Ben Kokua, played by Al Harrington, and Duke Lukela, played by Herman Wedemeyer.

In addition to dealing justice to murderers and mobsters, the Hawaii Five-O team was occasionally called on to save the free world from communism. McGarrett fights his own cold war against Chinese spy Wo Fat, played by Khigh Dhiegh. Wo Fat matches wits with McGarrett in the series pilot, "Cocoon," and in several episodes during the series. In the final episode of the series, titled "Woe to Wo Fat," their conflict comes to a resolution when McGarrett personally locks Wo Fat behind bars.

The cast played out their dramas in the midst of the photogenic scenery of the Hawaiian Islands. Producer Freeman insisted that the series be filmed entirely on location in Hawaii. Some members of the Hawaiian tourism industry initially were concerned that the weekly portrayals of murder and corruption would make the islands seem too dangerous. However, the small screen visions of palm trees and blue skies enticed many viewers to take a firsthand look. As *Hawaii Five-O* became a hit, tourism soared.

Following the series finale in 1980, CBS began searching for ways to capitalize on its lasting cultural influence. The show went into syndication for several years until the network ordered a complete remake in 2010. Originally planned as a sequel, the reimagined *Hawaii Five-O* instead kept many of the original elements of the show, including its character names and well-known score—Morton Stevens's driving theme music earned him Emmy Awards for the episodes "Hookman" and "A Thousand Pardons, You're Dead"—but also incorporated the big-budget production values common to contemporary crime dramas like *Law & Order: SVU* and *NCIS*. The remake proved popular with viewers, winning the 2011 People's Choice Award for Favorite New TV Drama.

Randy Duncan

SEE ALSO: *Emmy Awards;* Law & Order: SVU*; Syndication; Television.*

BIBLIOGRAPHY

Rhodes, Karen. *Booking "Hawaii Five-O": An Episode Guide*

and Critical History of the 1968–1980 Television Detective Series. Jefferson, NC: McFarland, 1997.

Hawkins, Coleman *(1904–1969)*

The first jazzman to win fame as a tenor saxophonist, Coleman Hawkins joined Fletcher Henderson's band in 1923 and was already its star when young trumpeter Louis Armstrong was added a year later. Unmatched on the tenor sax—an instrument once ignored by jazz musicians—Hawkins brought his distinctive warm tone to slow ballads like "Body and Soul" and a surging profusion of notes to fast numbers. In the 1930s he worked for five years in Europe, enhancing his international reputation. When bebop appeared on the scene in the 1940s, the innovative Hawkins recorded in this new jazz form with alto saxman Charlie Parker and trumpeter Dizzy Gillespie. Hawkins's primary interest remained conventional swing, working often with his favorite trumpet man, Roy Eldridge, in both Europe and America.

Benjamin Griffith

SEE ALSO: *Armstrong, Louis; Big Bands; Gillespie, Dizzy; Henderson, Fletcher; Jazz; Kansas City Jazz; Parker, Charlie; Swing Dancing.*

BIBLIOGRAPHY

Atkins, Ronald, ed. *All That Jazz*. New York: Smithmark, 1996.

Balliett, Whitney. *American Musicians*. New York: Oxford University Press, 1986.

Giddins, Gary. *Visions of Jazz: The First Century*. New York: Oxford University Press, 1998.

Hentoff, Nat, and Albert J. McCarthy, eds. *Jazz*. New York: Da Capo Press, 1975.

Hawks, Howard *(1896–1977)*

Howard Hawks is considered one of Hollywood's greatest directors. He made forty-six films and has the distinction of being one of the few directors to work in every major genre, including crime (*Scarface*, 1932); war (*The Road to Glory*, 1936 and *Air Force*, 1943); comedy (*Bringing Up Baby*, 1938); biopics (*Sergeant York*, 1941); Westerns (*Red River*, 1948 and *Rio Bravo*, 1959); science fiction (*The Thing from Another World*, 1951); film noir (*The Big Sleep*, 1946); and musicals (*Gentleman Prefer Blondes*, 1953). His films are among the most popular still shown on U.S. television.

Hawks started in film as a prop man for Paramount in 1919. Within six years he had risen to editor, scriptwriter, and assistant director. He directed his first feature film in 1926. His first all-talking film was produced four years later, a First National release titled *The Dawn Patrol*. The most important film during his early years was *Scarface*, starring Paul Muni and Ann Dvorak. Though finished in 1930, the film was not released until 1932 because the producer, Howard Hughes, fought over censorship issues with the Hays Office, the administrative body that oversaw the industry's Production Code. The group found the film too violent and amoral. Upon its release, it was a critical and popular success and was instrumental in establishing the crime genre.

Other films for which Hawks is praised include *Only Angels Have Wings* (1939), *His Girl Friday* (1940), and *To Have and Have Not* (1944). The director is noted for his visual style and recurring character types and themes. One common type of character in his films—especially in his movies about crime and the West—is the strong male who is not a member of society, seeks companionship with other males, and sees women as a threat. Another typical role is the weak and timid man who is easily intimidated and humiliated by women. This character usually appears in comedies and musicals.

In 1974 the Academy of Motion Picture Arts and Sciences presented Hawks with an Honorary Award for a master American filmmaker whose creative efforts hold a distinguished place in world cinema.

Frances Gateward

SEE ALSO: *Academy Awards;* The Big Sleep; Bringing Up Baby; Gentlemen Prefer Blondes; *Hollywood; Hughes, Howard;* The Thing.

BIBLIOGRAPHY

Hillier, Jim, and Peter Wollen, eds. *Howard Hawks, American Artist*. London: BFI Publishing, 1996.

McCarthy, Todd. *Howard Hawks: The Grey Fox of Hollywood*. New York: Grove Press, 1997.

Pippin, Robert B. *Hollywood Westerns and American Myth: The Importance of Howard Hawks and John Ford for Political Philosophy*. New Haven, CT: Yale University Press, 2010.

Wollen, Peter. *Signs and Meaning in the Cinema*. Bloomington: Indiana University Press, 1972.

Wood, Robin. *Howard Hawks*. London: BFI Publishing, 1981.

Hayward, Susan *(1917–1975)*

Stardom and the first of five Oscar nominations came to former photographer's model Susan Hayward with *Smash-Up: The Story of a Woman* (1947). From then on the gifted, husky-voiced, and ravishing redhead—despite playing a range of parts that included sultry temptresses, rich bitches, and intrepid heroines—became uniquely identified with suffering, both harrowing and poignant but always gutsy. A huge box-office draw during the 1950s, she won hearts portraying singer Jane Froman, who was crippled in an air crash; was superb as singer Lillian Roth suffering from alcoholism in *I'll Cry Tomorrow* (1955); won her Academy Award for *I Want to Live!* (1958), in which she went to the gas chamber; and was the natural choice to star in the remakes of *Back Street* (1961) and *Dark Victory* (retitled *Stolen Hours*, 1963).

Born Edythe Marrener in Brooklyn, New York, she suffered much offscreen too—including a stormy marriage, custody battles, and a suicide attempt—before dying of a brain tumor at the age of fifty-seven.

Robyn Karney

SEE ALSO: *Academy Awards.*

BIBLIOGRAPHY

Andersen, Charles P. *A Star Is a Star, Is a Star, Is a Star! The Lives and Loves of Susan Hayward.* Garden City, NY: Doubleday, 1980.

Holston, Kim R. *Susan Hayward: Her Films and Life.* Jefferson, NC: McFarland, 2002.

Linet, Beverly. *Portrait of a Survivor: Susan Hayward.* New York: Atheneum, 1980.

Hayworth, Rita *(1918–1987)*

Considered by some to be the most glamorous Hollywood screen idol of the 1940s, Rita Hayworth was given the name "love goddess" by *Life* magazine. As her career began to blossom, she was transformed from a half-Spanish performer into an American classic and the favorite pinup girl to thousands of American service members during World War II. Perhaps best known for her role as the femme fatale Gilda in director Charles Vidor's 1946 film of the same name, Hayworth embodied a dangerous combination of vulnerable femininity and cynical temptress.

She was born Margarita Carmen Cansino in Brooklyn, New York, to an Irish mother and Spanish father. The Cansinos were a family of professional dancers. "They had me dancing almost as soon as I could walk," Hayworth later recalled. As a voluptuous thirteen-year-old, Hayworth became her father's co-star and began captivating audiences with her sensual stage presence. In 1933 she was spotted by executives from Fox Studios and was given her first break as a dancer in the epic *Dante's Inferno.*

Rita Hayworth. *Hayworth's glamorous image was carefully crafted by Hollywood executives, who made her into a top screen idol in the 1940s.* A. L. WHITEY SCHAFER/JOHN KOBAL FOUNDATION/GETTY IMAGES.

After a string of second-rate movies, Hayworth's contract at Fox was terminated when her mentor, Winfield Sheehan, was fired and she was subsequently dropped. She then met the middle-aged Edward Judson, a shrewd businessman who saw her as a marketable product. They married in 1937. Judson negotiated her contract at Columbia Pictures, where she was to work for the next twenty years for tyrannical president Harry Cohn, who treated her as a "combination daughter, slave and financial investment." Between them, Judson and Cohn created her new image, removing all traces of her Latin ancestry: her surname was changed to the Anglo Hayworth, a new spelling of her mother's maiden name; her low hairline was lifted by electrolysis; and her hair was dyed auburn. Those flowing auburn locks became Hayworth's trademark.

SUCCESSFUL MOVIES

At Columbia, Hayworth's break as a serious actress came with the film *Only Angels Have Wings* (1939) with Cary Grant. Her success in this picture and a subsequent photo shoot for *Life* magazine turned her into a recognized celebrity. She headlined in a couple of musicals with Fred Astaire—*You'll Never Get Rich* (1941) and *You Were Never Lovelier* (1942)—that emphasized her dancing prowess, and her star power expanded even more. Astaire allegedly named her as his favorite dancing partner. Hayworth had her biggest success to date with the movie *Cover Girl* (1944) with Gene Kelly. Divorced from Judson since 1942, Hayworth announced she had married noted director and wunderkind Orson Welles during the shooting of *Cover Girl.* Gossip columnists were puzzled by the match between Welles and Hayworth, but the couple was famously smitten with each other. In 1944 Hayworth gave birth to a baby girl, Rebecca, but within a few years the marriage had ended.

In 1946 Hayworth starred in the film noir *Gilda.* The movie is a tale of a destructive love triangle—or, in the words of the leading man Glenn Ford, about "how hate can be as exciting an emotion as love." Her mesmerizing dance routine to the song "Put the Blame on Mame," in which she performs a partial striptease, removing two long black satin gloves and throwing them to the crowd, is probably the scene most associated with the actress. In a concession to the film censors, the script later reveals Gilda's virtue—she had only pretended to be a tramp to incense her lover. The film was a box-office smash.

CAREER MISCALCULATIONS

In 1947 Cohn assigned Hayworth to work with her estranged husband, Welles, on *The Lady from Shanghai.* Hayworth played the "praying mantis" Elsa, a twisted version of Gilda upon whose fame Welles was hoping to cash in. Welles, in a characteristically maverick move, had Hayworth's hair cropped short and bleached blond for the part. Her new hair was not a success with her fans or with her boss at Columbia. The film, a complicated thriller, flopped. Cohn rushed through Hayworth's next movie, *The Loves of Carmen,* for a quick release to soften the blow.

In 1948 Hayworth went on a trip to Europe, where she met and fell in love with the international playboy Prince Aly Khan. Their subsequent marriage made Hayworth a princess.

The prince had been entranced by the film *Gilda*, as was often the case with the men in her life. Hayworth remarked sadly to a friend, "Every man I've known has fallen in love with Gilda and wakened with me."

FINAL YEARS

Hayworth's comeback movie *Affair in Trinidad* (1952), in which she once again starred with Ford, was the last time she played the central sex symbol. She worked consistently throughout the 1950s, earning praise for her roles in films such as *Salome* (1953), *Pal Joey* (1957), and *They Came to Cordura* (1959). Her personal life, however, continued along a disastrous path, with two more marriages that both ended in divorce. She worked infrequently during the 1960s, and rumors about her supposed alcoholism began to gain strength at the end of the decade. Her last film was *The Wrath of God* at MGM (Metro-Goldwyn-Mayer) in 1972. Hayworth tried to pursue a Broadway career in the 1970s, but she had trouble remembering her lines. She was eventually diagnosed with Alzheimer's disease in 1980, and many of the debilitating symptoms she had struggled with in the previous years were finally attributed to the illness. She died in 1987.

Hayworth was a typical product of Hollywood, transformed from Margarita Cansino and relentlessly promoted by husbands, directors, and studio bosses. Adored by men but also admired by women, she was the symbol of American glamour and beauty of the time. Although she played a catalog of siren roles, including the legendary Carmen and Salome, in reality she was the exact reverse: unassuming, reserved, and eager to please. Ultimately, Hayworth was the hardest role for the reserved Cansino, and playing it took its toll upon her life.

Candida Taylor

SEE ALSO: *Film Noir; Ford, Glenn; Grant, Cary; Hollywood; Kelly, Gene; MGM (Metro-Goldwyn-Mayer); The Pin-Up; Sex Symbol; Welles, Orson; World War II.*

BIBLIOGRAPHY

Friedrich, Otto. *City of Nets: A Portrait of Hollywood in the 1940s.* London: Headline, 1987.

Kobal, John. *Rita Hayworth: The Time, the Place and the Woman.* London: Allen, 1977.

Leaming, Barbara. *If This Was Happiness: A Biography of Rita Hayworth.* London: Weidenfeld and Nicolson, 1989.

McLeanz, Adrienne L. *Being Rita Hayworth: Labor, Identity, and Hollywood Stardom.* New Brunswick, NJ: Rutgers University Press, 2004.

Morella, Joe, and Edward Z. Epstein. *Rita: The Life of Rita Hayworth.* New York: Delacorte Press, 1983.

Ringgold, Gene. *The Films of Rita Hayworth—The Legend and Career of a Love Goddess.* Secaucus: NJ: Citadel Press, 1974.

Hearst, Patty *(1954–)*

The granddaughter of newspaper publisher William Randolph Hearst, Patty Hearst was abducted from her Berkeley college residence in February 1974 at the age of twenty, sparking the biggest manhunt since the Lindbergh kidnapping. Surprisingly, Hearst was next spotted in bank surveillance footage, brandishing automatic weapons during robberies. She released statements renouncing her family and indicating that she had sided with her captors, members of the revolutionary Symbionese Liberation Army (SLA). Los Angeles police had a televised shootout with SLA members; six members of the group were killed. Hearst, who now called herself "Tania," fled.

One of the most bizarre twists of the kidnapping concerned the publication of an adult novel, *Black Abductor*, written under a pseudonym and published by an obscure San Diego publisher that later disappeared. The novel, written two years before the Hearst kidnapping, had many similarities to events surrounding it. Those parallels gave rise to conspiracy theories that suggested Hearst had engineered her own kidnapping or that her father had engineered it to further his own law-and-order political agenda. No evidence of such involvement has ever been documented.

Hearst was apprehended in September 1975. At her trial, famed defense attorney F. Lee Bailey maintained that she had been brainwashed by SLA leaders through psychological torture and was therefore not responsible for her crime spree. She was nonetheless convicted and sentenced to prison in 1977. Two years later her sentence was commuted by President Jimmy Carter. The story created a sensation in the media of the day. Hearst later married her prison guard and retired to life as a middle-class homemaker. By the 1990s, however, she had become resigned to her notoriety, acting in films such as *Bio-Dome* (1996) and *Pecker* (1998). She also guest starred on such television series as *Boston Common* (1996) and *Veronica Mars* (2006).

Andrew Milner

SEE ALSO: *Celebrity; Firearms; Hearst, William Randolph; Lindbergh, Charles; Television; Waters, John.*

BIBLIOGRAPHY

Alexander, Shana. *Anyone's Daughter: The Times and Trials of Patty Hearst.* New York: Viking, 1979.

Boulton, David. *The Making of Tania Hearst.* London: New English Library, 1975.

Botting, James. *Bullets, Bombs, and Fast Talk: Twenty-Five Years of FBI War Stories.* Washington, DC: Potomac Books, 2008.

Hearst, Patricia, and Alvin Moscow. *Every Secret Thing.* New York: Doubleday, 1982.

Reeves, Kenneth J. *The Trial of Patty Hearst.* Trial transcript. San Francisco: Great Fidelity Press, 1976.

Third, Amanda. "Nuclear Terrorists: Patty Hearst and the Terrorist Family." *Hecate* 28, no. 2 (2002): 82–99.

Weed, Steven, and Scott Swanton. *My Search for Patty Hearst.* New York: Crown, 1976.

Hearst, William Randolph *(1863–1951)*

Larger-than-life American publisher William Randolph Hearst acquired his first newspaper, the *San Francisco Examiner*, in 1886. Over the next two decades, he built a media empire that revolutionized journalism. His dictatorial style and sensational approach to the news generated both fortune and controversy. Hearst's seemingly limitless ambition led him to campaign for social reforms; serve in Congress; run for the presidency; famously ignite the Spanish-American War; and become, according to biographer Ben Procter, "arguably the best-known American, not just in the United States but around the world."

In the eyes of many, Hearst personified the American dream. Born to Phoebe Apperson, a Missouri schoolteacher, and George Hearst, a self-made millionaire miner and rancher, William Randolph Hearst parlayed family support, fierce independence, and a sense for drama into enormous wealth and power. In 1880 his father acquired the *Examiner* as payment for a gambling debt. "I am convinced," Hearst wrote to his father from Harvard six years later, "that I could run a newspaper successfully. Now, if you should make over to me the *Examiner*—with enough money to carry out my schemes—I'll tell you what I would do."

HEARST VERSUS PULITZER

At its height, Hearst's empire published twenty-eight newspapers and nine magazines. His motto was simply "Get Results." Within a year he doubled the *Examiner*'s circulation. He modeled it after Joseph Pulitzer's newspapers, emphasizing human interest, crusading for worthy causes, and making up news stories if there were none to be found. Hearst also made it a policy to pay for talent. He invested in stars such as Thomas Nast, Stephen Crane, Mark Twain, and the great "sob sister" investigator Annie Laurie.

In 1895 he bought the *New York Journal* and entered into a circulation war with Pulitzer. Within a year the *Journal*'s circulation tripled. Not even the comics pages escaped the competitive frenzy. Pulitzer ran the popular strip *The Yellow Kid*. Hearst hired the cartoonist away. When Pulitzer hired a new cartoonist, the two newspapers' advertising departments plastered the city with yellow promotional flyers. The campaign gave rise to the term *yellow journalism*, which subsequently became a derisive reference to the sort of sensational excesses in news coverage that characterized the Hearst-Pulitzer circulation war.

A legendary anecdote, perhaps apocryphal, describes the excessive competition between the two men, the increasing power of the press, and Hearst's reckless force of will. From roughly 1895 until the end of the Spanish-American War in 1898, Hearst and Pulitzer attempted to attract readers with trumped-up anti-Spanish atrocity stories from Cuba. Although Spain had consented to U.S. demands with respect to Cuban politics, Hearst sent artist Frederic Remington to the island. Remington cabled Hearst to say "everything is quiet. There is no trouble here. There will be no war. Wish to return." Hearst replied: "Please remain. You furnish the pictures, I'll furnish the war."

SENSATIONAL STORIES

Hearst's newspapers were distinguished largely by their style. They were among the first to use striking photographs and illustrations. They specialized in flashy headlines and sensational reports of topics such as fires, crime, sex, and sports. Hearst encouraged his editors to conduct endless streams of lotteries, giveaways, and serials. He formed a "murder squad" of writers who chased criminals and a "detective corps" of investigative reporters who were paid to keep check on people in positions of power. Hearst also demanded his newspapers serve the masses. They ran stories calling for improved police and fire protection and better roads, sewers, schools, and hospitals. They promoted the eight-hour workday and public assistance after the 1906 San Francisco earthquake.

Overt political stances taken by Hearst publications eventually provoked accusations of opportunism. Critics maintained that Hearst abused his First Amendment rights. They accused him of recklessness and insatiable greed, suggesting that he sparked the Spanish-American War just to sell his newspapers. Readers also grew wary of Hearst's tactics, boycotting his newspapers in the wake of the assassination of President William McKinley in 1901 because they believed that relentlessly inflammatory articles and editorials endorsed by Hearst inspired the assassin.

Although he was often denounced for his nationalist politics, Hearst's publications helped construct an American national identity, especially within burgeoning early-twentieth-century immigrant communities. In his efforts to reach the widest possible audience, Hearst directed his editors to seize upon the human element in the news—to encourage writers to craft stories that emphasized similarities among Americans by underlining universal fears and desires.

ECCENTRIC KINGMAKER

By the time he entered into politics at the turn of the twentieth century, Hearst was well practiced at using his media outlets to fuel his political interests. Although many believed he orchestrated both Theodore and Franklin D. Roosevelt's successful presidential campaigns, he largely failed to realize his own political ambitions. He served two terms as a U.S. representative but lost bids to become governor of New York and mayor of New York City.

Despite his unsuccessful foray into formal politics, Hearst and his movie-star mistress Marion Davies often entertained world leaders and celebrities at his California estate, San Simeon, a museumlike place many referred to simply as Hearst Castle. People accepted invitations to visit San Simeon out of friendship, curiosity, and fear. Hearst reveled in his role as eccentric kingmaker, unabashedly using his media power to promote his friends and ruin his enemies. In the end, however, he seemed to consider more people enemies than friends. He gained a reputation as a xenophobe, a red-baiter, and a fascist. He vehemently opposed anything or anyone who interfered with his profits, forbidding his employees to unionize, fighting against taxation, and demonizing hemp growers with a famous "reefer madness" campaign because they posed a threat to the profits he made supplying timber to the paper-making industry.

Hearst's life inspired the 1941 Orson Welles's film *Citizen Kane*, a stirring portrait of a media tycoon ruined by his own excesses. After a Hollywood preview, Hearst launched a full-scale campaign against the movie and its director, effectively blocking the film's distribution by threatening lawsuits, running venomous reviews, and yanking advertising.

Even into his eighties, Hearst maintained firm control over his newspapers, regularly sending out memos to editors across the country. His print-media companies were among the first to enter radio and television broadcasting. He also produced movie newsreels and is widely credited with creating the comic strip syndication business. Hearst's King Features Syndicate became one of the largest distributors of comics and text features in the world. Threatening, inspiring, and domineering, Hearst was a genius entrepreneur with an appreciation for the value of information who was ahead of his time.

Adrienne Russell

SEE ALSO: *Advice Columns;* Citizen Kane*; Hearst, Patty; Sex Scandals; Tabloids; Twain, Mark; Welles, Orson; The Yellow Kid.*

BIBLIOGRAPHY

Goldsmith, Bonnie. *William Randolph Hearst: Newspaper Magnate.* Edina, MN: ABDO, 2010.

Hearst, William Randolph, Jr., and Jack Casserly. *The Hearsts: Father and Son.* Niwot: CO: Roberts Rinehart, 1991.

Procter, Ben. *William Randolph Hearst: The Early Years 1863–1910.* New York: Oxford University Press, 1998.

Swanberg, W. A. *Citizen Hearst.* New York: Scribner, 1961.

Heavy Metal

Heavy metal, a genre of rock music that first gained widespread popularity during the 1980s, has not only exerted a powerful influence on the development of rock music but also shaped the cultural tastes and style of its many fans. Originating with such bands as Black Sabbath and Led Zeppelin in the late 1960s and early 1970s, heavy metal has evolved to encompass numerous subgenres over the decades, among them thrash metal, death metal, and "grindcore," to name but a few. The heavy metal sound is generally characterized by loud and distorted guitars and vocals, while its image is defined by aggressive male posturing and a preoccupation with sexuality, identity, and the corrosion of traditional social institutions. While it sometimes caused controversy and even outrage among the establishment for its perceived negative influence on youth, heavy metal expanded the range of recognized images and sounds in rock and roll, developing a formula that combined musical virtuosity with social rebellion. Although metal groups have rarely achieved Top 40 success even at the height of the genre's popularity, their albums and concerts outsold all their contemporaries and outlasted them in influence.

GAINING POPULARITY

Historically, the term *heavy metal* refers to radioactive elements or powerful artillery units. Although heavy metal music was not directly named to signify either of these traditions, the bands have always welcomed the associated imagery. Rock critic (and future Angry Samoans front man) Mike Saunders is believed to have been the first writer to use the term *heavy metal* to refer to a specific style of music when he reviewed the Sir Lord Baltimore album *Kingdom Come* (1970) for the May 1971 issue of *Creem.* Rock critics soon began applying the label to other bands, notably British groups Deep Purple, Led Zeppelin, and Black Sabbath. These three are considered to have laid the groundwork for the genre's subsequent development. Deep Purple brought classical influences, Led Zeppelin adapted and applied the African American blues hook, and Black Sabbath lent an air of dark mysticism to its work. Each stressed the importance of distorted guitar sound and long guitar solos.

Heavy metal might never have reached beyond a fanatical cult following if not for a reintroduction of the genre's principles by British and American chart-friendly bands at the beginning of the 1980s. From overseas came Def Leppard, Judas Priest, Iron Maiden, and Ozzy Osbourne (the original vocalist of Black Sabbath). Homegrown American metal of this era included KISS, Van Halen, and Mötley Crüe. This second generation of heavy metal artists was better groomed and less gloomy than its

Metallica in Concert. *Cliff Burton, left, and James Hetfield of the rock band Metallica perform their brand of head-banging heavy metal in 1985.* PETE CRONIN/REDFERNS/GETTY IMAGES.

predecessors, and these bands' heavy metal was about lifestyle as well as music. Their songs were played on MTV as often as on the radio, and for the first time, heavy metal records found a market among women and minorities. However, the music never lost its core following of white, teenage suburban males. Record sales remained more stable than for any other genre of the 1980s, and bands from the expanding array of heavy metal groups often dominated the top five album spots. Pop and rap acts incorporated guitar solos, a revived blues tradition, and power chords. MTV premiered *Headbanger's Ball* in 1986, and the show quickly became its top-rated offering. Throughout the decade, heavy metal dominated summer tour attractions such as the "Monsters of Rock" and "US Festival."

With so much commercial success, heavy metal was bound to splinter. Bands that toned down their anger and the volume on their guitars came to be referred to as "glam metal" or "pretty metal." Groups such as Bon Jovi, Warrant, and Poison sold albums on their hair-sprayed, long locks, and sexually risqué lyrics. Bon Jovi produced the third-best-selling album of the decade in 1986 with *Slippery When Wet*. By contrast, bands such as Metallica, Slayer, and Megadeth were intent on preserving a rawer, purer form of heavy metal and gained mainstream recognition in the late 1980s. Termed "speed metal" or "thrash" because of their blistering drum beats, these bands infused an animal, punk-rock sensibility into heavy metal, playing loud and hard, growling or screaming, and delving into the psychological and pathological.

Crunching along amid the mainstream were the gloomy "dark metal" bands, a subgenre of throwbacks to the early days—led by Judas Priest and Iron Maiden—who employed visual and lyrical images of fantastic worlds, monsters, and heroes. In Scandinavia, bands such as Celtic Frost and Venom became associated with black metal, a genre known for espousing demonic, anti-Christian ideas. At around this time, the British band Napalm Death pioneered a new subgenre, grindcore, with the release of its 1987 album *Scum*. This uniquely coarse style was characterized primarily by rapid tempos and growling, unintelligible lyrics.

CARVING ITS OWN NICHE

In the United States, the rise of heavy metal appeared to coincide with a period of cultural mistrust in the 1970s. The divorce rate was increasing, and a U.S. president had resigned. While disco and light rock dominated the airwaves, heavy metal, like punk rock, built a following by tearing down discredited social institutions. The thrill of a heavy metal concert or a punk show lies at least partially in the bold flaunting of as many rules of decency as possible. Whereas punk called for a rebellious stance against conformity, with a simplicity in its attack on social mores, heavy metal insisted on musicianship and even virtuosity. Guitar heroes of the heavy metal age needed to display stage presence, pure speed, and a thorough knowledge of blues and classical music. Heavy metal publicized its heroes through extravagant concert productions and live videos.

The enormous negative reaction of mainstream America to heavy metal music indicates just how influential it was. Tipper Gore, wife of Senator Al Gore, formed the Parents' Music Resource Center (PMRC) in the early 1980s to examine the effects of modern music lyrics on American youth. The PMRC took Osbourne to court for "Suicide Solution," a song it claimed encouraged and glorified suicide (Osbourne maintained that it warns of the dangers of drink). Its next target was Judas Priest—the PMRC claimed that when they played Judas Priest's 1978 album *Stained Class* backward, it found satanic messages. Though each case was resolved in the musicians' favor, critics continued to connect heavy metal to Satanism, violence, and drug use. Black Sabbath's use of symbols such as the inverted cross as well as Iron Maiden's album *The Number of the Beast* seemed to invite such attacks. The bands almost always pointed to the ultimately positive message of their work—while they openly dabbled in the occult, for example, the good guy always won.

The graphic imagery of one of heavy metal's most lasting offspring, speed metal, horrifies many casual listeners. "Landmine has taken my sight / . . . taken my arms / taken my legs . . . " shouts Metallica in 1989's "One." Again, a closer examination of the song reveals an antiwar theme. Heavy metal artists never denied that they lead a life laced with sex and drugs—Van Halen's 1978 debut single "Running with the Devil," long considered a prototype of the genre, celebrates a life led with no regard for social convention or restriction. "We're not like this because we're in a rock band," said Van Halen's David Lee Roth in one interview, "we're in a rock band because we're like this."

Whether or not one gives any credence to the supposed sociological or psychological messages claimed by its adherents, heavy metal indubitably advanced rock and roll by breaking visual and lyrical taboos. Though eventually commercially successful in their own right, heavy metal bands climbed to that success through the ranks of the counterculture and proved that there was much more to the American popular music scene than reaching the Top 40. Its hard core, purist nature continued to demand "authenticity" from aspiring heavy metal musicians. The guitar heroes of heavy metal upped the ante for rock stars of their era by insisting on classical training and technical prowess, while their feral and sexual lead singers reminded fans and singers that the essence of rock and roll lay in excess.

EVOLVING WITH THE TIMES

Heavy metal musicians continued to innovate. The 1990s witnessed a proliferation of new heavy metal subgenres, both in the United States and abroad. American bands such as Sleep revolutionized a new form of doom metal known as "stoner metal." Scandinavia saw a new generation of black metal bands during this period, notably Mayhem, Darkthrone, and Gorgoroth. Nu metal, known for its mingling of heavy metal, funk, rap, and dance music forms, began to gain popularity in the late 1990s with the emergence of such bands as Limp Bizkit, Linkin Park, and Korn. In the first decade of the twenty-first century, new iterations of earlier metal styles began to emerge; noteworthy among these was djent, which drew inspiration from progressive metal styles of the 1980s. At the same time, doom metal bands such as Sunn O))) continued to expand the limits of what heavy metal could sound like, incorporating such styles as drone and ambient into more traditional metal styles.

Colby Vargas

SEE ALSO: *Black Sabbath; Blues; Bon Jovi; Electric Guitar; Funk; Iron Maiden; Judas Priest; KISS; Led Zeppelin; Mötley Crüe; MTV; Osbourne, Ozzy; Punk; Rap; Rock and Roll; Steppenwolf; Van Halen.*

BIBLIOGRAPHY

Arnett, Jeffrey Jensen. *Metalheads: Heavy Metal Music and Adolescent Alienation*. Boulder, CO: Westview Press, 1996.

Bangs, Lester. "Heavy Metal." *The Rolling Stone Illustrated History of Rock & Roll.* New York: Rolling Stone, 1980.

Bashe, Philip. *Heavy Metal Thunder: The Music, Its History, Its Heroes.* Garden City, NY: Doubleday, 1985.

Cope, Andrew L. *Black Sabbath and the Rise of Heavy Metal Music.* Burlington, VT: Ashgate, 2010.

Jonze, Tim. "A Handy Guide to Heavy Metal." *Guardian*, April 14, 2009.

Walser, Robert. *Running with the Devil: Power, Gender, and Madness in Heavy Metal Music.* Hanover, NH: University Press of New England, 1993.

Weinstein, Deena. *Heavy Metal: The Music and Its Culture.* New York: Da Capo Press, 2000.

Hee Haw

This long-running (1969–1992) television series kept the comedy-variety genre alive into the 1990s with its mix of down-home humor and musical performances from top country-and-western acts. *Hee Haw* was one of the first shows to draw a southern rural audience to network television. Sketches set in fictional "Kornfield Kounty" affectionately parodied the lives of farmers, moonshiners, and small-town dwellers. Hosts Roy Clark and Buck Owens were established country stars who brought musical credibility to the comedic proceedings. The series garnered consistently high ratings, both during its CBS run and as one of the pioneer successes in first-run syndication. *Hee Haw* had the longest run of original syndicated episodes of any television series.

This quintessential show of the South was actually the product of two Canadians and a New York City–born Italian American. In 1967 producer Sam Lovullo (the New Yorker) was working on *The Jonathan Winters Show* (1967–1969) for CBS when writers John Aylesworth and Frank Peppiatt were brought onboard. *The Jonathan Winters Show* was a comedy-variety series with an audience composed mostly of urban northeasterners. Lovullo noticed that ratings, particularly in the South, rose significantly when the musical guests were country-and-western stars such as Roy Clark and Jimmy Dean. At the same time CBS was seeing ratings success with rural situation comedies such as *The Beverly Hillbillies* (1962–1971) and *Green Acres* (1965–1971). A rural variety show seemed a logical move for the network, so Aylesworth and Peppiatt created the concept; personal manager and fellow Canadian Bernie Brillstein came up with the name *Hee Haw*. When CBS canceled *The Jonathan Winters Show* after the 1968–1969 season, they sent Lovullo, Ayleswoth, and Peppiatt to Nashville, Tennessee, to produce the new show in the country music capital of America.

Hosts Clark and Owens were natural choices. Clark was a virtuoso on guitar and banjo. His amiable comedic personality had previously been showcased on *The Jonathan Winters Show* and *The Beverly Hillbillies*. Owens was one of Nashville's premier songwriter-performers. At the time of *Hee Haw*'s creation, he was hosting a regionally syndicated television variety series and looking for a vehicle with which to reach a national audience. He too had appeared on *The Jonathan Winters Show*. Owens's and Clark's wide-ranging abilities helped blend together the series' mix of country music and broad sketches.

The cast included a number of comedians and musicians with a country background and style. Writer-actor Archie Campbell, twins Jim and Jon Hager, Louis "Grandpa" Jones, Lulu Roman, David "Stringbean" Akeman, and former real-life moonshiner Junior Samples were among the original group to populate such sketches as "The General Store" and "The Kornfield." In 1970 the show acquired perhaps its most prized catch: comedienne Minnie Pearl. Her trademark gingham dresses, hat with price tag attached, and gently humorous anecdotes on rural life became staples of the show. In later years George "Goober" Lindsey (of *The Andy Griffith Show*), Misty Rowe, actor Slim Pickens, and even Jonathan Winters would spend time in *Hee Haw*'s ensemble.

HEE HAW'S DEBUT AND THE EARLY YEARS

The show debuted June 15, 1969, and was an instant ratings success. The traditional music and "down-home" humor struck a chord with audiences weary of social unrest and uninterested in seeing television taboos shattered by comedians such as the Smothers Brothers. Though originally a summer replacement series, *Hee Haw* was added to CBS's prime-time lineup in December 1969.

During its run *Hee Haw*'s guest list was a virtual who's who of country music in the 1960s, 1970s, and 1980s. Merle Haggard, George Jones, Tammy Wynette, Ray Charles, Waylon Jennings, Charlie Rich, Ronnie Milsap, Johnny Cash, and Boxcar Willie all graced the *Hee Haw* stage. Singers such as Garth Brooks, Randy Travis, and Vince Gill, who would see great success in the country music boom of the 1990s, made some of their first national television appearances on *Hee Haw*. Even non-country performers visited the Korn field: pop vocalists Sammy Davis Jr. and Phil Harris; baseball legends Mickey Mantle, Johnny Bench, and Roger Maris; and actors Ernest Borgnine, Leslie Nielsen, and John Ritter all made appearances.

SYNDICATION

CBS, tired of its rural image, canceled *Hee Haw* after the 1971–1972 season. Also axed that year were *The Beverly Hillbillies*, *Green Acres*, and *Mayberry RFD* (1968–1971). The producers wasted no time in finding a new home for the show. *Hee Haw* debuted in first-run syndication September 18, 1971. Most markets aired it Saturdays at 7 p.m., a time slot ceded to local stations as a result of the Federal Communications Commission's Prime Time Access Rule, which forbade off-network reruns on affiliates during prime time. These stations needed programming, and *Hee Haw* was a prepackaged, proven hit.

Hee Haw was so popular it spawned a spin-off in the fall of 1978. *Hee Haw Honeys* starred regulars Misty Rowe, Gailard Sartain, Lulu Roman, and Kenny Price along with young actress Kathie Lee Johnson, who would become better known by her married name, Kathie Lee Gifford. Their characters—Misty, Willie Billie, Lulu, Kenny, and Kathie Honey—are a Nashville family who own a country nightclub. Like its parent show, *Hee Haw Honeys* featured musical guests and cornpone humor. It failed to match the older show's success, lasting only twenty-six episodes.

Hee Haw remained relatively unchanged until 1991. Slipping ratings inspired Gaylord Entertainment, the owners of the show, to revamp the format. Much of the cast was replaced. The old "Korn field" set was gone, and a new, bright, modern stage appeared. The look was reminiscent of the 1980s pop music series *Solid Gold*. Longtime viewers felt angry and betrayed. Ratings fell precipitously, and the series was canceled. The last original *Hee Haw* aired May 30, 1992.

Although production ended, the series was far from gone. Reruns of the classic episodes began airing on the Nashville Network. *Hee Haw* quickly became one of the cable network's most popular offerings. A live-stage version at the Grand Ole Opry in Nashville brought the Korn field briefly back to life. *Hee Haw* is still treasured by fans of traditional country music and down-home, simple good times.

David Hixson

SEE ALSO: *Bench, Johnny;* The Beverly Hillbillies*; Brooks, Garth; Cable TV; Cash, Johnny; Charles, Ray; Country Music;* Grand Ole Opry*; Haggard, Merle; Jennings, Waylon; Jones, George; Mantle, Mickey; Maris, Roger; Owens, Buck; Pearl, Minnie; Rich, Charlie; Syndication; Television; Winters, Jonathan; Wynette, Tammy.*

BIBLIOGRAPHY

Beck, Ken. "*Hee Haw* Is Back—Packaged for the 90s." *Courier-Journal,* January 9, 1997.

Bessman, Jim. "*Hee Haw* Returns on TV, Video, and in New Book." *Billboard,* November 23, 1996.

Jones, Loyal. *Country Music Humorists and Comedians.* Urbana: University of Illinois Press, 2008.

Lovullo, Sam, and Marc Eliot. *Life in the Kornfield: My 25 Years at "Hee Haw."* New York: Boulevard Books, 1996.

Moses, Edward. "*Hee Haw* Gives Boot to Hillbilly Look: TV Show Faces 90s, Aging Market; Slow Sales Force Format Updating." *Billboard,* August 31, 1991.

Wohland, Chris. "*Hee Haw* Goes to Town: In Its 24th Season, the Country Variety Show Is Shucking the Cornfield for a New Suburban Image." *Atlanta Journal & Constitution,* June 5, 1992.

Hefner, Hugh *(1926–)*

If America experienced a sexual revolution in the latter half of the twentieth century, then one of the first shots surely was fired by Hugh Marston Hefner in 1953, the year that he introduced *Playboy* magazine to the world. The first issue of the magazine featured a centerfold of a nude Marilyn Monroe (who had posed years earlier, before attaining the stardom she enjoyed in 1953), and it sold well enough to guarantee that other issues would follow in the months, years, and decades to come.

PLAYBOY EVOLVES

The "shocking" new magazine was based in Chicago, the city where Hefner, the older of two sons, had grown up in a typical middle-class household. After army service and college, Hefner married Mildred Williams in 1949 and tried unsuccessfully to earn a living as a freelance cartoonist. He then landed a low-level job with *Esquire* magazine, the most prestigious men's magazine of the day, featuring articles and photo layouts on elegant clothing, sports cars, and other interests that appealed to males. Nude photos in American periodicals in the early 1950s were limited to a few nudist and art photography magazines that skirted the edge of the law and were sold under the counter at newsstands, when they were available at all.

Within a year after *Playboy*'s premiere, Hefner's life had undergone significant changes. He was devoting all of his time to the magazine, except for the attention he gave to the beautiful and sexually available young women who worked for, or posed for, the magazine. The Hefners separated in 1955, with divorce to follow in 1959. As the magazine's circulation continued to grow, Hefner began to adopt the lifestyle epitomized by his publication's title. He *became* a playboy, and he had the business sense to realize that being a public embodiment of what the magazine was all about could attract even more readers. *Playboy* was, from the beginning, more than just a "skin magazine." There were the nude pictorials, of course—generally three per issue, including the centerfold "Playmate of the Month." But like *Esquire* before it, *Playboy* featured articles about luxury cars, fine food, wine, stereo equipment—in short, everything the modern playboy would want to own. And if, as was likely, the reader's income was insufficient to support the described lifestyle—well, he could always dream, and *Playboy* would be there to provide the material for his fantasies.

Hefner's playboy image shifted into high gear in 1959 with his purchase of a seventy-room mansion on Chicago's Gold Coast. After extensive remodeling (including installation of a huge circular revolving bed in the master bedroom), the Playboy Mansion was open for business, and its business was pleasure—pleasure for its sole permanent resident and for his many and frequent guests. Engraved on a brass plate on the mansion's front door was the Latin phrase "Si non oscillas, noli tintinnare," which the host loosely translated to mean "If you don't swing, don't ring."

Hugh Hefner. *From left, Kristina Shannon, Karissa Shannon, and Crystal Harris surround Hugh Hefner at the* Playboy *founder's birthday party in 2009.* DENISE TRUSCELLO/WIREIMAGE/GETTY IMAGES.

Beginning in 1962 the magazine's articles on the good life began to be accompanied by a dose of philosophy, *Playboy* style. The December issue of that year included the first installment of Hefner's "Playboy Philosophy." There would be twenty-five installments in all (amounting to about 150,000 words) before the series ended in 1966. In these columns Hefner defended his magazine's content and values, assailed his critics, and espoused liberal positions on various social issues: he was in favor of increased sex education, legalized abortion, and freedom of expression, and he opposed censorship, prudery, and archaic sex laws. In addition to decrying the sexual puritanism of American life, Hefner was also an early and vocal advocate of civil rights for minorities. The magazine's editorial content reflected this view, as did Hefner's policy for booking entertainers at his mansion, his chain of Playboy Clubs that began in 1960, and his syndicated television shows (*Playboy's Penthouse*, 1959–1960, and *Playboy after Dark*, 1968–1970). Hefner brought in black entertainers (such as Sammy Davis Jr., Dick Gregory, and Nancy Wilson) at a time when having black acts in a predominantly white venue just was not done.

MOVING TO THE BACKGROUND

Hefner's empire went through some tough times in the late 1970s and 1980s. Circulation of the magazine declined, partly due to competition from publications such as *Penthouse* and *Hustler*, both of which were often more sexually graphic than Hefner wanted *Playboy* to be. Further, the close relationship existing between the administration of President Ronald Reagan (who came into office in 1981) and fundamentalist Christian groups like the Reverend Jerry Falwell's Moral Majority made for a political climate that was inhospitable to sexual liberationists like Hefner.

Hefner unloaded the Chicago Playboy Mansion in the early 1980s and moved full time into Playboy Mansion West, an estate he had purchased in Los Angeles. After suffering a mild stroke in 1985, he began turning over day-to-day operation of his empire to his daughter, Christie, whom he had brought into the business ten years earlier. Christie worked as chair and CEO of Playboy Enterprises, Inc., from 1988 to 2009, although her father remained listed as editor-in-chief of the magazine.

Hefner was married a second time in 1989 to former Playmate of the Year Kimberley Conrad. The union produced two children, but the couple separated in January 1998, allowing Hefner to return once again to his playboy lifestyle. He remained in tabloid headlines for his revolving cast of girlfriends, and in 2005 Hefner's simultaneous relationship with three playmates—Holly Madison, Bridget Marquardt, and Kendra Wilkinson—became the subject of the popular reality television show *The Girls Next Door*. The show lasted six seasons but ultimately unraveled late in the first decade of the 2000s along with Hefner's relationship with the three women. In its final season, *The Girls Next Door* introduced his new playmate love interests, Crystal Harris and twins Karissa and Kristina Shannon. Hefner and Harris were engaged to be wed in late 2011, but Harris called off the wedding just days before its scheduled date.

After relinquishing his role as CEO of *Playboy*, Hefner spent much of his time and energy on various charity efforts. The Playboy Foundation and the Hugh M. Hefner Foundation have supported such causes as First Amendment rights, breast cancer awareness, HIV/AIDS research, environmental conservation, and civil liberties since their founding in the 1960s. In 2012 Hefner was named Humanitarian of the Year by the children's charity Angelwish.

Despite declining sales of *Playboy* and his own advanced age (having celebrated his eightieth birthday with a lavish ceremony at the Playboy Mansion in 2006), Hefner remains a celebrated, if controversial, icon of American independence and entrepreneurialism, and his playmates continue to inspire fascination and admiration in both their male and female audiences. His historical role in the global cultural landscape was underscored by the release of the 2009 documentary *Hugh Hefner: Playboy, Activist and Rebel*. The television series *The Playboy Club*, revolving around the original Playboy Club in 1960's Chicago, had a brief run in 2011, and in 2012 came news that Warner Brothers was taking over a project on Hefner that had languished for years at Universal Studios. The studio was bringing in noted producer Jerry Weintraub to complete the Hefner biopic *Playboy*.

Justin Gustainis

SEE ALSO: *Cable TV;* Esquire; *Monroe, Marilyn;* Penthouse; *The Pin-Up;* Playboy; *Pornography; Reality Television; Sex Symbol; Sexual Revolution; Television; Varga Girl.*

BIBLIOGRAPHY

Brady, Frank. *Hefner*. New York: Macmillan, 1974.

Byer, Stephen. *Hefner's Gonna Kill Me When He Reads This.* Chicago: Allen-Bennett Publishers, 1972.

Edgren, Gretchen. *The Playboy Book: Forty Years*. Santa Monica, CA: General Publishing Group, 1998.

St. James, Izabella. *Bunny Tales: Behind Closed Doors at the Playboy Mansion*. Philadelphia: Running Press, 2006.

Watts, Steven. *Mr. Playboy: Hugh Hefner and the American Dream*. Hoboken, NJ: John Wiley & Sons, 2008.

Hellman, Lillian *(1905–1984)*

One of the most daring and inventive playwrights of her generation, Lillian Hellman's own life was the stuff of drama. As Carl Rollyson writes in *Lillian Hellman: Her Legend and Her Legacy*, "The key to Lillian Hellman's character, to what made her a legend in her own time, was her sense of herself as a grande dame." Indeed Hellman is not only remembered for her work—award-winning plays such as *The Children's Hour* (1934), *The Little Foxes* (1939), and *Watch on the Rhine* (1941)—but for her audacious persona.

A tough-talking, cigarette-smoking Jewish woman from New Orleans, Louisiana, Hellman loved attention. She got it through her plays, through her difficult relationship with the brilliant writer Dashiell Hammett, and through her left-wing politics. When called before the House Un-American Activities Committee, Hellman refused to be a friendly witness, uttering her most famous line: "I cannot and will not cut my conscience to fit this year's fashions."

In her advancing years, Hellman wrote three extraordinary memoirs, making her very public life even more so. When a story from one of them was made into a major motion picture, *Julia* (1977), starring Jane Fonda and Vanessa Redgrave, Hellman became a heroine to a new generation of women. Hellman liked money; she also liked fame. She got both and became, in the process, a one-of-a kind American icon.

Victoria Price

SEE ALSO: *Broadway; Communism; Fonda, Jane; Hammett, Dashiell; The Hollywood Ten;* Julia*; McCarthyism.*

BIBLIOGRAPHY

Griffin, Alice, and Geraldine Thorsten. *Understanding Lillian Hellman.* Columbia: University of South Carolina Press, 1999.

Hellman, Lillian. *An Unfinished Woman.* Boston: Little, Brown, 1969.

Hellman, Lillian. *Pentimento: A Book of Portraits.* Boston: Little, Brown, 1973.

Hellman, Lillian. *Scoundrel Time.* Boston: Little, Brown, 1976.

Rollyson, Carl. *Lillian Hellman: Her Legend and Her Legacy.* New York: St. Martin's Press, 1988.

Wright, William C. *Lillian Hellman: The Image, the Woman.* New York: Simon & Schuster, 1986.

Hello, Dolly!

Hello, Dolly! occupies an enduring place in popular American culture. A musical adaptation of playwright Thornton Wilder's *The Matchmaker*, it has become one of the most popular Broadway musicals since its opening in 1964. The original production furnished Carol Channing with a trademark role as Dolly Gallagher Levi, a turn-of-the-twentieth-century New York widow, matchmaker, and "fixer" for all occasions. Dolly's second-act entrance at the Harmonia Gardens Restaurant, where she sings the title song as she descends a red-carpeted staircase into the company of her admirers for a show-stopping production number, has become one of the classic scenes of the musical theater.

With music and lyrics by Jerry Herman, book by Michael Stewart, and choreography and direction by Gower Champion, *Hello, Dolly!* played 2,844 performances in its initial New York run. The show won multiple Tony Awards, including for best musical, book, score, actress (Channing), and director-choreographer. Channing's costars in the original cast included David Burns, Eileen Brennan, and Charles Nelson Reilly. The 1969 film version, which Herman considers definitive, stars Barbra Streisand and Walter Matthau, was directed by Gene Kelly, and marks the last of the big Hollywood musicals. The show is still often performed on Broadway and worldwide.

William A. Everett

SEE ALSO: *Broadway; Kelly, Gene; The Musical; Streisand, Barbra; Tony Awards; Wilder, Thornton.*

BIBLIOGRAPHY

Green, Stanley, and Elaine Schmidt. *Hollywood Musicals Year by Year.* Milwaukee, WI: Hal Leonard Corporation, 2000.

Hirshberg, Jack. Hello, Dolly! *Journal.* Twentieth Century Fox Film Corporation, 1969.

Suskin, Steven. *Opening Night on Broadway: A Critical Quotebook of the Golden Era of the Musical Theatre,* Oklahoma! *(1943) to* Fiddler on the Roof *(1964).* New York: Schirmer Books, 1990.

Hells Angels

During the height of their notoriety, the motorcycle gang Hells Angels made headlines from coast to coast, with stories appearing in the *New York Times*, *Newsweek*, *Time*, *True*, the *Nation*, and a host of other publications. With their death's-head emblem, outré habits, and the mystique of modern-day Quantrill's raiders, the Angels were tantalizing to the press. In fact, their seedy allure was heightened by the press to such a degree that it spawned a national and then international fascination with outlaw motorcyclists. From magazines and books, the Angels' story spread inexorably to movie theaters, and biker movies became so popular that they inspired a rash of films based on the Angels' true-life exploits. Predictably, the fictional amplification of their misdeeds bears only a faint resemblance to the real-life models, increasing their fascination so much that the Angels have established charters throughout Europe and beyond.

POST–WORLD WAR II BEGINNINGS

The movement started in California after World War II, "when most ex-GIs wanted to get back to an orderly pattern: college, marriage, a job, children—all the peaceful extras that come with a sense of security," writes Hunter S. Thompson, whose book *Hell's Angels: A Strange and Terrible Saga* is perhaps the definitive work on the Angels. Not everybody felt that way, however: "There were thousands of veterans in 1945 who flatly rejected the idea of going back to their prewar pattern. They wanted more action, and one of the ways to look for it was on a big motorcycle." In California, where the weather is clement year-round and a premium is placed on mobility of all kinds, these young men congregated in groups, adopting such names as the Booze Fighters or the Market Street Commandos. They regularly made runs to resort towns throughout the state—trips that were always tinged by menace. These were the culprits who tore up the agricultural town of Hollister, California, in 1947 in the first motorcycle riot, coverage of which inspired producer Stanley Kramer and actor Marlon Brando to make *The Wild One* in 1954.

In Fontana, California, a steel town east of Los Angeles, the original Hells Angels emerged out of the wreckage of an earlier club, the Booze Fighters. They were blue-collar types, scornful of normalcy. Among motorcycle outlaws, the Angels were soon known as the toughest and most obdurate—kings of violence and depravity. For many years the San Bernardino Angels were the de facto leaders, bestowing new charters at their whim. However, the Berdoo Angels, as they were called, who had a reputation for inspired depravity, persisted in their folly a little too long. They became the victims of massive police harassment, and soon the chapter had been decimated by an exodus to Oakland, California. By the early 1960s a large concentration of Angels had gathered in the Bay Area.

MEDIA ATTENTION BRINGS NOTORIETY

For all their colorful ways, it took until the mid-1960s for the Angels to come to the attention of the state law enforcement apparatus. The occasion was a Labor Day run to Monterey, California, that had resulted in allegations of rape, and although the defendants were eventually acquitted, the state attorney general's office was alarmed enough to launch a six-month investigation. Much of the report was unfounded or so prejudiced as to be beyond credulity, and the Angels might have faded back into obscurity were it not for a sole *New York Times* correspondent in Los Angeles who filed a lurid dispatch. Appearing in the *Times* gave the bikers credibility. *Newsweek* and *Time* weighed in with their own alarms. Other publications followed, and soon the bikers had grown accustomed to the media's presence and were earnestly trying to capitalize on their newfound fame.

The heightened publicity had benefits and drawbacks. The Angels truly enjoyed seeing themselves in print, and their presence acquired a certain amount of hip cachet in bohemian circles throughout the Bay; however, police harassment had increased exponentially, and many of the outlaws were summarily dismissed by their employers as a result of the ensuing hysteria. Some Angels grew restive over the fact that they had failed to profit from the storm of controversy that had swept over them. They also had become self-conscious. Oakland President Sonny Barger, having grown accustomed to giving well-attended press conferences, took himself seriously enough to attack a peace march in Oakland, the first time the Angels had shown even the faintest interest in politics. The attack and its subsequent notoriety heralded a drop in media interest, but Hollywood was just catching on.

From the philosophical 1969 *Easy Rider* (not so much a biker film as a paean to the myth of the outlaw biker), arguably the best of the lot, to the outlandish *Werewolves on Wheels* (1971), the myth of the nefarious yet noble biker was worked through all its possible permutations to varying degrees of success or profit. First of the group was *The Wild Angels* (1966), starring Peter Fonda and Nancy Sinatra. Director Roger Corman, always quickest to the draw, had cobbled together a story from elements of the Lynch Report. In its story of paying tribute to a fallen comrade (based on the death of a Sacramento Angel that January), *The Wild Angels* came closest to portraying the Angels in their natural state. The film has an equivocal tone, part denunciation, part hero worship, and it set the standard for the rash of biker films that would follow.

The Born Losers (1967), released the following year, concentrates on the Angels' reputation for gang rape and is a slightly less sympathetic account. The group's participation in the havoc at Altamont—a Rolling Stones concert at which a member of a Hells Angels chapter hired to act as security guards stabbed a man—was captured on film as part of the movie *Gimme Shelter* (1970). After that incident, the Angels' screen persona degenerated further.

INTERNATIONAL GROWTH

Since the coverage of the Hollister motorcycle riot in 1947, the relationship between the media and the bikers has always been symbiotic. The Angels' appeal was archetypal—the vanishing outlaw beset on all sides by an increasingly regimented society. It is arguable that had the national news media, and then Hollywood, not exploited the Angels' very existence, the group would have remained a local phenomenon. As it was, Hells Angels clubs sprang up in the United Kingdom, Germany, Scandinavian countries, and even the Soviet Union, where Angels rode World War II–era army surplus machines when they rode anything. In 1994 the Angels made news when a rival gang blew up the Swedish Hells Angels clubhouse near Oslo with hand-launched rockets stolen from a Swedish military base. The Hells Angels phenomenon was truly international in scope.

As for the California Hells Angels, they persisted at the fringes of society, often making headlines for their role in various drug-smuggling conspiracies, but the threat and the allure were gone. They seemed more like picturesque anachronisms than voracious, threatening marauders. By the 2010s there were magazines devoted to outlaw motorcyclists, and an annual run to Sturgis, North Dakota, is usually a well-organized, fairly tame event, drawing participants from around the world. In 2011, however, two bikers—one from the Hells Angels and one from a rival gang—were stabbed during an altercation in downtown Sturgis. Because of the Angels' recurring association with such incidents, whenever a big Harley piloted by an Angel in a cutoff jean jacket and the ubiquitous death's-head patch pulls past on the freeway, the frisson is palpable. One can only imagine the fear and trepidation such a sight would have inspired in the summer of 1965.

Michael Baers

SEE ALSO: *Altamont; Brando, Marlon;* Easy Rider*; Harley-Davidson; Hughes, Howard; Leather Jacket;* The Nation*; The* New York Times*;* Newsweek*; The Rolling Stones; Thompson, Hunter S.;* Time*;* The Wild One.

BIBLIOGRAPHY

Barger, Sonny; Keith Zimmerman; and Kent Zimmerman. *Hell's Angel: The Life and Times of Sonny Barger and the Hell's Angels Motorcycle Club.* New York: William Morrow, 2000.

Dobyns, Jay, and Nils Johnson-Shelton. *No Angel: My Harrowing Undercover Journey to the Inner Circle of the Hells Angels.* New York: Crown, 2009.

Lavigne, Yves. *Hell's Angels: Taking Care of Business.* Toronto: Deneau & Wayne, 1987.

Lavigne, Yves. *Hell Angels: "Three Can Keep a Secret if Two Are Dead".* Secaucus: NJ: Carol Publishing Group, 1990.

Lavigne, Yves. *Hell's Angels: Into the Abyss.* Toronto: HarperCollins, 1996.

McClure, Michael, and Frank Reynolds. *Freewheelin Frank, Secretary of the Angels as Told to Michael McClure.* New York: Grove Press, 1967.

Morgan, Raymond C. *The "Angels" Do Not Forget.* San Diego, CA: Law and Justice Publishers, 1979.

Thompson, Hunter S. *Hell's Angels: A Strange and Terrible Saga.* New York: Ballantine, 1967.

Hemingway, Ernest *(1899–1961)*

At the height of his popularity, Ernest Hemingway was hailed as the greatest writer of American literature; a hero of several wars; a world-class sportsman in the fields of bullfighting, boxing, hunting, and fishing; and a connoisseur of food, wine, writing, and painting. He was viewed as a colossus who strode across all fields of action, excelling in manly pursuits. At his worst, Hemingway was derided as a writer who specialized in evasion and repression; an illiterate, inarticulate ox who avoided literary circles to disguise his own limitations; a bully, misogynist, and homophobe; a self-aggrandizing egotist and poseur; a belligerent and jealous writer; and an overpaid, glorified journalist who succumbed to dementia in later years and who finally took his own life when he realized that he could no longer write.

EARLY INFLUENCES AND STYLE

Born Ernest Miller Hemingway in Oak Park, Illinois, on July 21, 1899, Hemingway developed his characteristically terse style by writing for the *Kansas City (Missouri) Star* in 1917. During World War I he volunteered as a Red Cross ambulance driver in Italy, where he was badly wounded while attempting to save a soldier's life. Hemingway's war experiences and his severe injuries seem to have carved a deep scar in the young man's psyche, and he suffered from insomnia and a fear of sleeping in the dark. His early writing reveals a preoccupation with violence and wounds and a terror of death. The honesty with which Hemingway wrote about naked emotions in the 1920s was immediately greeted as a major innovation in modern writing. His rapid development and swift rise to acclaim were derived from his willingness to learn from older writers. While living in Paris among expatriates, he sought, and followed, the advice of Gertrude Stein, James Joyce, Ezra Pound, Ford Madox Ford, and F. Scott Fitzgerald.

Though most famous for his stark narrative style and realistic dialogue, Hemingway was certainly not the first to write plainly and simply; he did not singlehandedly overthrow the decadent conventions of the Victorian novel. Many predecessors, including Mark Twain, Stein, and Sherwood Anderson, had cleared the path that Hemingway boldly strode. He drove verbal terseness and austerity to its limit, setting an unsurpassable standard, while avoiding Stein's and Anderson's eccentricities. Hemingway's early prose was taut and brittle, achieving its effects through extremely subtle suggestion while refusing to be "literary." He jettisoned the worn accoutrements of alliteration, assonance, simile, and metaphor to look directly at life and report only what he saw, unencumbered by literary conventions.

Ernest Hemingway. *Ernest Hemingway is considered among the most famous but most polarizing authors in American literary history.* PHOTOQUEST/GETTY IMAGES.

This does not mean, however, that Hemingway's fiction was stripped of emotion, as it may seem to a careless reader. He generally refrained from describing emotion, avoiding phrases such as "he felt" or "she thought" and discarding adverbs and adjectives. Instead he suggested the characters' emotions by reporting what they saw, noticed, or did. For instance, in the short story "Big Two-Hearted River," Hemingway conveys the anxiety of a veteran, Nick Adams, returning home from the war and trying to repress his painful memories. The author did this not by telling us that Nick is trying to repress his thoughts but rather by meticulously reporting Nick's concentration on mundane but consoling activities such as fishing and making lunch. Such indirect and subtle effects were quite powerful when done well, but could result in long, pointless passages when done badly, as in some of his later works.

Also notable in his early writing is a willingness to portray what his characters really felt rather than what they were supposed to feel. He did not care to write edifying stories: if his character felt empty and hollow after an event that was supposed to make a respectable man feel sad, the story gained power through its honest realism. The most successful products of Hemingway's method were his short stories. His first novel, *The Sun Also Rises* (1926), also managed to sustain the dramatic tension and power of his shorter works. Hemingway made extensive revisions at Fitzgerald's suggestion, and the book revealed remarkable parallels with Fitzgerald's *The Great Gatsby* (1925). Ironically, Hemingway soon displaced Fitzgerald as the major new author of the postwar generation.

Fitzgerald had been feted as *the* author of the Jazz Age, and he appealed to collegiate readers stateside. Hemingway became known as the author of the Lost Generation (though the phrase, made famous by Stein, referred cynically to the same generation as Fitzgerald's Jazz Age). He made a stronger impression on war veterans, and *The Sun Also Rises* became the most significant work of the growing genre of postwar novels about world-weary veterans. The book was amazingly influential: young women began talking like the flippant heroine, Brett Ashley, and young men started acting like Jake Barnes or Hemingway's other male characters, muttering tough-sounding understatements and donning the repressive sackcloth of machismo. His portrayal of the wounded, taciturn hero resounded among men who might not ordinarily read serious literature and validated an archetype in popular culture perpetuated by such Hollywood icons as John Wayne, Charles Bronson, and Clint Eastwood.

Hemingway's next novel, *A Farewell to Arms* (1929), returned to the themes of the wounded soldier and the pastoral charms of escape. It was a best seller, as were all of his subsequent books, and it secured his reputation as a major author. Unfortunately, *A Farewell to Arms* marked the end of Hemingway's rapid development and uncompromised artistic integrity. In 1932 he published *Death in the Afternoon*, a handbook on the art of bullfighting. Treating bullfighting as a tragic ritual, the book provides many insights into Hemingway's views on death, performance, courage, and art—all important themes in his fiction. Although the book has interesting digressions on literature, it also has entire chapters devoted to specific bullfighting techniques or appraisals of long-dead bullfighters, which makes for tedious reading.

VULNERABILITIES AND DIGRESSIONS

But the real subject of the book is not bullfighting; it is Hemingway. In *Fame Became of Him*, John Raeburn identifies nine personae that Hemingway projected in *Death in the Afternoon* and in later autobiographical works: world traveler, arbiter of taste, bon vivant, heroic artist, exposer of sham, initiated insider, battle-scarred stoic, sportsman, and manly man. Three of these—arbiter of taste, world traveler, and bon vivant—form a cluster of roles typical of the literary gentleman. Writers can often be counted on to offer tips on wine, dining, arts, and travel. In these roles Hemingway was similar to the effete, foppish dilettantes whom he usually detested, such as Ford Madox Ford or Henry James. To a lesser extent, the roles of heroic artist, exposer of sham, and initiated insider are also common among writers. The heroic artist who suffers for his muse was a familiar pose of the Romantics (particularly Byron), and the exposer of sham has a long pedigree in satirical writing. The battle-scarred stoic had become a common, though resonant, figure in postwar writing. The initiated insider was partly related to the veteran figure, but initiation into a select fraternity of like-minded fellows became quintessentially Hemingway. He pretended to follow a code of conduct that was all the more dignified for being unspoken, above defense, and inscrutable to outsiders.

The uniqueness and popularity of Hemingway's public personality lay in joining these highbrow roles with those of sportsman and manly man. Readers knew of his interest in fishing, hunting, and bullfighting from his early fiction, where these sports were embraced as pastoral pleasures of escape for the physically or mentally wounded and solitary pastimes for the taciturn. But when described as Hemingway's own hobbies in his nonfiction, they lost the therapeutic element—presumably because Hemingway was loath to admit any psychological wounds—and became games of competition, obligatory tasks of masculinity, demonstrations of cojones. Indeed, Hemingway seemed to devote his life from the 1930s onward to proving his cojones, perhaps embarrassed by theories that Jake Barnes, the protagonist of *The Sun Also Rises* whose penis is shot off in the war, was an autobiographical character. In later works Hemingway seemed to dissociate himself from such vulnerable characters and also alienated himself from other writers, whom he considered an unmanly lot, by quarreling with, defaming, and even threatening almost every major writer of his generation. He derided homosexuals in *Death in the Afternoon*, dismissing the artistry of Stein, Oscar Wilde, André Gide, Walt Whitman, and Francisco Goya on the theory that they were inherently flawed and therefore disqualified as artists.

Hemingway's masculine posturing proved enormously popular. Soon after *Death in the Afternoon* came out, he began a series of essays for the newly founded men's magazine *Esquire*, which was marketed toward a sophisticated, though not intellectual, audience. He wrote essays for *Esquire* on topics such as fishing, hunting, and wine. He even wrote beer ads disguised as essays. Whereas *Death in the Afternoon* had a professed artistic impetus in Hemingway's desire to view death in order to write truly about the experience, the *Esquire* articles lacked any artistic purpose and were pointedly nonliterary. Hemingway was beginning to fashion a new character, whose name was also Ernest Hemingway.

He continued this farce in another book of nonfiction, *Green Hills of Africa* (1935). A personal account of a safari adventure, it reads more like a novel than *Death in the Afternoon*, sporting vivid descriptions of action and dialogue. But Hemingway's writing falters progressively as the book becomes more about himself: it simply promotes the legend of his virility without revealing anything intimate about him. The *Esquire* experience and his swelling fame distorted his self-awareness and blurred his ability to distinguish fact from fiction. His self-aggrandizing grew more frequent as the burgeoning medium of photojournalism got bigger and flashier. Hemingway's striking demeanor and handsome, husky appearance made him a favorite of glossy magazines, such as *Life* and *Look*, that wedded big, colorful photos to the trenchant aphorisms Hemingway was happy to provide.

Another product of Hemingway's African adventure was the short story "The Snows of Kilimanjaro," which told of a writer who, dying of gangrene while hunting in Africa, realizes too late that he has squandered his talent. The protagonist laments "poor Scott Fitzgerald" as a writer ruined by his fascination with the rich. Through this jab at Fitzgerald, Hemingway sought to deflect any suspicion that the ruined writer of the story might represent himself. Whether or not he needed this decoy to write with his old frankness, he wrought a rich and complex story. However, most critics recognized that the declining writer was Hemingway himself, and soon his decline would become obvious to everyone.

COMPARISONS AND COMMERCIALISM

When Hemingway finally returned to novel writing in 1937 with *To Have and Have Not*, he was a very different writer from the artistic innovator of the 1920s. Whereas his earlier fiction masterfully portrayed vulnerable characters through extremely subtle prose that seemed to mirror the repressed nature of the characters themselves, in *To Have and Have Not* repression triumphs over revelation. Masking his own vulnerabilities, Hemingway also masks those of his characters, stripping them of human interest. His latest protagonist, Harry Morgan, a tough-talking smuggler in trouble with the Mafia and the government, betrays no weakness and awakens no pathos. After losing his arm in an accident, he stoically responds, "[If] you lose an arm, you lose an arm."

The novel was barely distinguishable from pulp fiction. Hemingway's halfhearted attempts at political significance made the work more embarrassing than redeeming. During the Depression, critics from the New Left favored novels of social relevance, such as those of John Steinbeck or Sinclair Lewis. Many writers of the 1920s, such as Fitzgerald and Thornton Wilder, had fallen out of critical favor because of their indifference to politics. Hemingway, who seemed to appeal to the common man because of his simple prose and simple pleasures, was urged by some critics to write more socially relevant stories. He capitulated with *To Have and Have Not* and found favor with the more naive members of the Left, but most critics recognized the novel as politically simplistic. Although it was a best seller, and Hemingway was more popular than ever, his critical reputation sank.

Whereas William Faulkner had spent the 1930s producing one masterpiece after another in the most astonishing series of achievements in American literature since Henry James, Hemingway had churned out a preponderance of facile nonfiction, mostly in slick popular magazines. Always jealously competitive, Hemingway responded to the challenge of Faulkner's achievement and set out to regain the championship he had held in the 1920s. The result was *For Whom the Bell Tolls* (1940), his longest and most ambitious work. The novel seems to have been intended as his masterpiece, embracing a wider range of themes than any of his previous novels. However, Hemingway's carefully crafted style was ill suited for such a broad canvas, and the novel's sheer bulk diluted the potency of his prose. The novel was almost as politically simplistic as *To Have and Have Not*. Although Hemingway strove to weave grand themes of nature, technology, and the unity of humankind, his truer, deeper preoccupations were still with the solitary man proving his mettle and facing death alone. The hero, Robert Jordan, was cut from the same cloth as earlier Hemingway heroes—solitary, glum, absinthe-drinking men. Jordan was a professor of Spanish, but the intellectual side of the character was sketchy, unconvincing, and incongruent with his more familiar Hemingwayesque traits. The intended effect of the novel was unachieved, and Hemingway failed to unify his themes and symbols. Nevertheless, the novel was extraordinarily popular, selling 360,000 copies and generating a movie.

Hemingway continued to make money by writing for *Collier's* magazine as a war correspondent in Europe during World War II. The 1940s were highly profitable for the author and brought him fame as a war hero (although the extent of his military participation is disputed). He did not return to writing novels until 1950. At the pinnacle of fame, and arrogance, Hemingway consented to an interview with *New Yorker* writer Lillian Ross in which he boasted about his forthcoming work and his enduring position as the "champ" in American fiction. This memorable character sketch, titled "How Do You Like It, Now, Gentlemen?" was very different from the usual adulatory articles honoring Hemingway as a champion sportsman and manly man. Although affectionate, the sketch revealed his eccentricities and egotism. He called himself Papa, posing as the wise, grizzled old man of American letters. He claimed that he had once lived with a bear in Montana, where they drank and slept together.

But what proved to be most embarrassing to Hemingway was his boast that his forthcoming novel would be his best ever. When *Across the River and into the Trees* appeared four months later, it was almost unanimously regarded as the worst novel of his career. It was an abysmal work, so poorly written that it seemed a parody of his own style, riddled with pet words such as *good, true*, and *well.* Though not without redeeming qualities, it is best enjoyed as a parody of the famous Hemingway style from the master's own pen.

The contrast between Hemingway's published boastfulness and the critics' sudden disfavor became even more painful when Faulkner won the Nobel Prize in Literature in 1950. Five years earlier Faulkner had been a well-kept secret, and Hemingway (in his role as initiated insider and arbiter of taste) had been able to confide to Jean-Paul Sartre and others that Faulkner was a better writer than himself. Once Faulkner won the Nobel Prize and myriad belated accolades tumbled his way, Hemingway could no longer regard himself as the champ of American letters. Consequently, he turned on Faulkner, declaring that no one ever wrote a decent novel after winning the Nobel Prize.

Meanwhile, Hemingway labored over a long autobiographical novel, *Islands in the Stream*, which came out in 1970, nine years after his death. The novel was disjointed, tedious, and uninspired. Hemingway, aging, alcoholic, and unhealthy, seemed to be losing his talent. However, he adapted the last part of the novel and published it as an independent work in 1952 in *Life* as *The Old Man and the Sea*. A painfully poignant tale of an aged fisherman who catches the biggest marlin of his life and loses it to sharks, the story was told in a beautifully simple, chaste style that surpassed anything Hemingway had written since the 1920s. Struggling with artistic and physical decline, he had made one final effort to write truly and succeeded by reaching inside himself to wrench out the painful theme of failure. "Man was not made for defeat. A man can be destroyed, but not defeated." The *Life* issue that first carried the story sold five million copies, and the story was instantly hailed as a masterpiece. In 1954 Hemingway won the Nobel Prize in Literature, largely based on *The Old Man and the Sea*.

Throughout the 1950s Hemingway worked on a novel, *The Garden of Eden*, but remained unhappy with it and withheld publication. He also discovered a cache of memoirs he had begun in the 1920s and proceeded to revise and expand them into a book called *A Moveable Feast*. The rediscovered writings reminded Hemingway of his youth, when he was establishing his reputation as a bold new artist of uncompromised integrity, and made it painfully clear that the aging writer had squandered his talent for the gratifications of fame. Although he had accused Fitzgerald and Faulkner of ruining their talent on stories for the *Saturday Evening Post* and movies for Hollywood, Hemingway had compromised his own talent even more grotesquely by creating an absurd fabrication of himself. His public persona had infected most of the characters he had created since the 1920s. Realizing that he could no longer write nor maintain his own egotistical standards, Hemingway shot himself on July 2, 1961.

The adulation continued for years after his death, and posthumous novels, stories, and nonfiction continued to appear well into the 1990s. But biographies also appeared, and emerging evidence gradually revealed Hemingway to be a despicable man motivated by egotism, jealousy, and a sexual insecurity that led him to ridicule others and prove his own manhood ad absurdum. Such macho posturing already seemed out of place in the 1960s and was deemed utterly ridiculous by the 1990s, though academic interest in Hemingway continued to thrive under deconstructive and feminist approaches to literature.

By the turn of the millennium it seemed unlikely that Hemingway would ever regain the swollen stature of his middle period. However, his influence over American literature is immense and ubiquitous. As one of the major prose stylists of the English language, he has bred more imitators than any other American writer. But few authors have been able to attain the suggestive power and subtlety of Hemingway's finest work. Faulkner captures it in his stark, brittle potboiler *Sanctuary*, and Fitzgerald employs a certain Hemingwayesque subtlety amid the softly echoing motifs of *Tender Is the Night*. More often, however, such efforts are merely verbal imitations by inferior authors who simply borrowed the outward trappings of conscientious monosyllables and tough dialogue for their otherwise conventional narratives and perfunctory symbolism. Hemingway's best fiction set a standard that few could attain, not even the later Hemingway.

Ernest Hemingway's popularity has not waned in the twenty-first century, and he has been called the world's greatest writer since William Shakespeare. Both his work and his personality continue to be critiqued, and his influence on writers such as J. D. Salinger is a constant topic of debate. *To Have and Have Not* was remade into a film in 2002, and *After the Storm* became a television movie in 2006. One of the most interesting aspects of the modern interest in Hemingway has been psychiatric examination of the personality traits that caused him to take his own life. It leads to the conclusion that he may have been bipolar and that he suffered from a dependency on alcohol, had likely experienced a traumatic brain injury, was borderline narcissistic, and had become psychotic by the time of his death.

Douglas Cooke

SEE ALSO: *Anderson, Sherwood; Best Sellers; Celebrity;* Esquire; *Faulkner, William; Fitzgerald, F. Scott; Key West; Pulp Magazines; Suicide; Twain, Mark; The Twenties; World War I.*

BIBLIOGRAPHY

Baker, Carlos. *Ernest Hemingway: A Life Story.* New York: Scribner, 1969.

Berman, Ronald. *Translating Modernism: Fitzgerald and Hemingway.* Tuscaloosa: University of Alabama Press, 2009.

Burgess, Anthony. *Ernest Hemingway and His World.* New York: Scribner, 1978.

Cirino, Mark, and Mark P. Ott. *Ernest Hemingway and the Geography of Memory.* Kent, OH: Kent State University Press, 2010.

Hemingway, Ernest. *To Have and Have Not.* New York: Scribner, 1937.

Hemingway, Ernest. *The Old Man and the Sea.* New York: Scribner, 1952.

Lamb, Robert Paul. *Art Matters: Hemingway, Craft, and the Creation of the Modern Short Story.* Baton Rouge: Louisiana State University Press, 2010.

Larson, Kelli A. *Ernest Hemingway: A Reference Guide, 1974–1989.* Boston: G. K. Hall, 1990.

Martin, Christopher. "Ernest Hemingway: A Psychological Autopsy of a Suicide." *Psychiatry: Interpersonal and Biological Processes* 69, no. 4 (2006): 351–361.

Raeburn, John. *Fame Became of Him: Hemingway as Public Writer.* Bloomington: Indiana University Press, 1984.

Wagner-Martin, Linda. *Ernest Hemingway: A Reference Guide.* Boston: G. K. Hall, 1977.

Weeks, Robert P., ed. *Hemingway: A Collection of Critical Essays.* Englewood Cliffs, NJ: Prentice Hall, 1962.

Hemlines

Hemlines have been equated with both fashion and culture, defining particular decades, generations, economies, media, and gendered ideologies, thereby working as imagistic markers within systems of popular culture. Couture culture's system of design traditionally has fed the contents of fashion magazines with fantasy imagery fabricating a "look," color, or hemline for readers. Such is the case with Christian Dior's New Look of 1947, the essential feature of which was the full skirt fish-tailing from cinched waist to mid-calf. This silhouette was adapted for department-store and catalogue sales and home-sewing patterns, thus becoming part of popular fashion.

Hollywood's studio system of the 1930s and 1940s established a primary place for designers, whose costumes glamorized the female star, made her a screen icon, and typified the genre character she played, especially in melodrama and film noir. Two films released in 1957, *Designing Woman* and *Funny Face*, parodied the arbitrariness of the fashion system and its fixation on the viewable woman.

THE MID-TWENTIETH CENTURY

Television sitcoms of the 1950s and 1960s conventionalized the look of the well turned-out wife and mom, dressing her in the essential style and hemline seen in the costuming of Gracie Allen (*The George Burns and Gracie Allen Show*), Lucille Ball (*I Love Lucy*), Harriet Nelson (*The Adventures of Ozzie and Harriet*), and Barbara Billingsley (*Leave It to Beaver*). Weekly, these original sitcom women performed their domestic roles wearing variations of the New Look's vertical line, most commonly the shirtmaker dress of trim bodice and sleeves, tailored collar, buttoned front, and mid-calf skirt flaring out from a defined waist. A crinoline often underpinned the full skirt. But, whether flaring or straight, their dresses typically were accessorized by that symbol of the proper woman, a neat strand of cultured pearls. The middlebrow American homemaker represented in these sitcoms was a picture of postwar comfort, consumerism, and suburbia. She was also a trickster who juggled her husband's money to maintain her image by shopping for fashionable clothes.

British designer Mary Quant's radical miniskirt of the 1960s, emerging out of a "swinging" London of Carnaby Street and boutique-store culture, countered the Americanized femininity of Lucy and her sitcom generation.

Boutique culture's eclecticism prevailed into the 1970s, displacing the long-or-short hemline dilemma with fashionable options, notably the "maxi," which fell to the ankle or below. Mid-calf lengths, known as the "midi," were reincarnated in looser styles and fabrics. By the 1980s the long-or-short hemline dilemma had become passé though still part of fashion rhetoric in style magazines and department store flyers promoting "seasons," "the new" or "the latest" in ready-to-wear labels and commercial brands.

Asymmetrical hemlines in variation (a short front with dipping back, or a side-to-side diagonal) signaled the compromise of designers in the 1980s and early 1990s. Similarly, the flash effect of vertical off-side slits, which could be used for every skirt length from maxi to mini, made one leg visible and emphasized the thigh. Manufactured in office wear as well as evening garb, this style allowed for greater mobility but also a loss of skirt-control when the wearer sat down. The ladylike posture of crossed legs became an instinctive defense against exposure. The vertical side-slit was less about utility than about projecting a feminine essence—reminiscent of the New Look, if more sexualized.

THE LATE 20TH CENTURY

In the late 1990s the hemline debate was given timely twists and fell victim to self-conscious parody in the popular television series *Ally McBeal*. Ally's short skirts (the micro-mini in tailored form) are a feminine tool to test, sometimes to arrest, the sexist patriarchal structures of the legal system and courtroom. Anne Hollander argues in *Sex and Suits*, "The first [1960s] function of small, short modern skirts was to put women's clothed bodies into a complete physical correspondence with men's . . . visual assumption of public equality for men and women." Ally McBeal's ultra short skirts brought forward this struggle for the contemporary young woman within American culture who presumably strives to be taken seriously as a professional and also to be desirable to men. Ally's short hemlines and sputtering naive persona externalize the cultural tentativeness that followed a long line of fashionable sitcom figures, from Lucy and Gracie as maneuvering wives in the 1950s to Mary Tyler Moore's single woman negotiating with male newsroom colleagues and boyfriends in the 1970s.

Ally McBeal's character is popular culture's good girl reincarnated, whose short skirts do not render her sexually secure or successful. At the same time, Ally's quirkiness exudes what the cool if neurotic bad girl of 1950s "B" movies had to suppress. The "bad but beautiful" movie genre persona of actress Ida Lupino in *Women's Prison* (1955) is embodied by her simple, sophisticated costuming. In her pencil-slim, mid-calf dark skirt and crisp white blouses, Lupino's mean prison warden metes out a professional woman's control. Unable to handle power, in this tale of morality she is not only asexual but also must die. It is the decent women prisoners, garbed in striped shirtmaker dresses, midi-length, who are domesticated and make sacrifices in order to survive. In the moment of her destruction, the warden's clean blouse and midi skirt give way to a straitjacket, her cold femininity and existence erased.

American film, television, and magazines can be charted historically through fashion and hemlines for shifts and slippage in the popular imagery and ideologies of femininity. One slippage is the persistence of retro hemlines and looks. In 1998 *Vogue Patterns*, a magazine for home sewers, launched a Vintage Vogue Collection of their patterns from the late 1930s to mid-1940s, a service said by the editor to be based on contemporary readers' "wishes" and "needs." Pleated, straight, and A-line skirts all fall below the knee or to mid-calf in these designs, a conservative reordering in the face of Ally McBeal's minis and the trendy knit maxi skirt of the 1990s.

THE EARLY TWENTY-FIRST CENTURY

In the early twenty-first century the fashion industry recycled familiar hemline lengths. Minis were rehashed as microminis, and pencil skirts grazing the knee or calf were tapered to emphasize the body's curves. Stylists play a prominent role in such repackaging of fashion, with the make-over a staple of popular television shows (such as *What Not to Wear*). Moms and working women, who have given up on the fashion game, are re-styled in age- and work-appropriate fashion, with hemlines settling around the knees, more or less. Encouraging women to trade pants for skirts includes the expectation that they will wear towering heels that hobble mobility. This return to conventional notions of femininity is a far cry from couturier Yves St. Laurent's liberating revival of the pantsuit in the mid-1960s for office and evening wear, although the pantsuit became a safe uniform, as does all fashion sooner or later.

Today's mass industrialization of fashion poaches styles from designer runways, televised red-carpet events (such as the Oscars and the Grammy Awards), and street gear, typically coded for sexual appeal over function. This credo is most apparent in the footwear accessorizing the micromini. Both the low-heeled, knee-high boot and the stiletto invite the spectator to gaze up the space of thigh to the imagined area beyond the buttocks-grazing hemline. That gap of thigh between boot-top and micro-mini sexualizes women, teens, and girls as figures of public display, in a period that categorizes these age groups as demographics amid a mass culture of standardized spectacle. Whether hemlines swing high or low, fashion is fickle and political, and highly invested in trolling the female body for points of consuming interest—from necklines to hemlines.

Joan Nicks

SEE ALSO: *Academy Awards;* The Adventures of Ozzie and Harriet; Ally McBeal; *Ball, Lucille; Grammy Awards;* I Love Lucy; Leave It to Beaver; *Minnelli, Liza; Retro Fashion;* Vogue.

BIBLIOGRAPHY

Breward, Christopher. *The Culture of Fashion.* New York: Manchester University Press, 1995.

Gaines, Jane, and Charlotte Herzog, eds. *Fabrications: Costume and the Female Body.* New York: Routledge, 1990.

Hollander, Anne. *Sex and Suits.* New York: Alfred A. Knopf, 1994.

Henderson, Fletcher *(1897–1952)*

A bandleader, composer, and arranger, Fletcher Henderson was one of the definers and shapers of jazz music in the swing era of the 1940s and 1950s. After graduating from Atlanta University with majors in chemistry and math, Henderson moved to New York for postgraduate study in 1920. There he accepted a job as a pianist with W. C. Handy, and his career goals changed. In 1923 he assembled a band widely recognized as the first large jazz orchestra, one that included such celebrated sidemen as Louis Armstrong, Coleman Hawkins, and Benny Carter. His most lasting work came in the swing era as an arranger for the Dorsey brothers and Benny Goodman. His style of big band jazz featured the reeds pitted against the brass section as well as highly rhythmic passages of ensemble chords by the entire band. Typical Henderson arrangements can be heard on recordings of "King Porter Stomp" and "Sometimes I'm Happy" by the Goodman band.

Benjamin Griffith

SEE ALSO: *Armstrong, Louis; Big Bands; Dorsey, Jimmy; Dorsey, Tommy; Goodman, Benny; Handy, W. C.; Hawkins, Coleman; Jazz; Race Music; Savoy Ballroom.*

BIBLIOGRAPHY

Atkins, Ronald, ed. *All That Jazz: The Illustrated Story of Jazz Music.* New York: Smithmark, 1996.

Collier, James Lincoln. *Benny Goodman and the Swing Era.* New York: Oxford University Press, 1989.

Simon, George T. *The Big Bands.* New York: Macmillan, 1974.

Smith, Jessie Carney. *Encyclopedia of African American Popular Culture, Vol. 1.* Santa Barbara, CA: Greenwood, 2011.

Hendrix, Jimi *(1942–1970)*

Jimi Hendrix was the quintessential 1960s rock star. A black superstar in a predominantly white industry and an American who first found success in Great Britain, Hendrix embodied many of the contradictions of the late 1960s music scene. As a

Jimi Hendrix at Woodstock. *Jimi Hendrix performs at Woodstock in 1969.* MICHAEL OCHS ARCHIVES/GETTY IMAGES.

guitar player, he single-handedly redefined the genre's most important instrument and is widely considered the best to have ever played it. As a performer, he combined showmanship and musicianship in equal parts and played the best-remembered sets of the two best-remembered music festivals of the period. His death at age twenty-seven from an overdose of prescription drugs completed the picture of what became a cultural archetype of the late twentieth century: that of the enormously talented, misunderstood rock star, whose meteoric rise to fame is matched by a tragic fall and early death.

Hendrix was born Johnny Allen Hendrix in Seattle, Washington, on November 27, 1942, to seventeen-year-old Lucille Hendrix. His father, Al, was in the army. His early childhood was one of nonstop confusion, as he lodged with a variety of family members in houses and hotels as far away as Texas, California, and Vancouver. In 1946 Al changed his son's name to James Marshall. Lucille died in 1958 when Hendrix was fifteen, the same year he got his first guitar. He played in the high school band until he dropped out of school in 1960. Arrested for riding in a stolen car, Hendrix received a suspended sentence by promising to enlist in the military. He became a parachutist in the 101st Airborne in 1961. He soon tired of the military life and was discharged after breaking his ankle in 1962. At this point he became a professional musician, setting up his own group in Nashville, Tennessee, with army buddy Billy Cox and backing up a variety of rhythm-and-blues (R&B) artists who came through town. In the spring of 1963, Hendrix left Nashville as part of "Gorgeous" George Odell's band.

For the next three years, Hendrix played backup for many of the biggest names in R&B, such as the Isley Brothers, Little Richard, Ike and Tina Turner, King Curtis, Sam and Dave, even though he made no significant recordings. Anxious to make his own music, he settled in New York City in 1965 and by early 1966 was focusing his efforts on his own band, Jimmy James and the Blue Flames. The band performed in the Greenwich Village folk-rock club Café Wha? for a pittance in front of a scant audience, but his astonishing command of blues, soul, and rock guitar styles greatly impressed fellow musicians, such as Mike Bloomfield, John Hammond Jr., and a small group of cognoscenti. In September 1966 Animals bassist Brian "Chas" Chandler, who was looking to make his mark as a manager and producer, signed Hendrix and took him to England.

FORMS THE JIMI HENDRIX EXPERIENCE

London, England, was in the midst of a blues craze, led by musicians John Mayall and Eric Clapton and the group the Rolling Stones. It was immediately apparent that Hendrix's talent greatly exceeded that of the top local guitarists: Clapton, Jeff Beck, and Pete Townshend, all of whom made a point of seeing Hendrix wherever he was playing. After sitting in at London's hippest clubs, Hendrix formed the Jimi Hendrix Experience with two young white Englishmen, bassist Noel Redding and drummer Mitch Mitchell. The group's first single was "Hey Joe." Hendrix soon demonstrated his skill as a composer, writing the group's next single, "Purple Haze"—probably his best-known composition. His generous use of guitar effects—unusual intervals like flatted fifths and sharp ninths, and bizarre lyrical themes—perfectly suited him to lead the psychedelic movement that was starting to sweep through rock and roll.

The Jimi Hendrix Experience released its first album, *Are You Experienced?* in the spring of 1967. It was a tour de force, replete with complex guitar sounds that had never been heard before. By then, following the Beatles' lead, every British band was scrambling to pile up as many weird sounds and special effects as they could, but none had Hendrix's touch for making consistent musical sense with them. Like musician Stevie Wonder a few years later, Hendrix humanized electronic effects, using the rapidly advancing technology of the late 1960s to communicate timeless emotions. And when it suited the material, he could create perfectly beautiful music without any effects at all (as in "The Wind Cries Mary," the group's third single). The album also contains his first protest song, "I Don't Live Today," which he often dedicated in concert to the American Indian. And he was not above exploiting the stereotype of the macho black male, as in "Fire."

The U.S. release of *Are You Experienced?* was supplemented with the group's first three singles; two blues numbers were excised, helping to create the myth of Hendrix as a purely intuitive talent. A highly anticipated performance at the Monterey Pop Festival in June 1967 marked the Jimi Hendrix Experience's American debut, complete with guitar-burning theatrics, and cemented Hendrix's reputation as an international star, although his wild appearance and demeanor tended to be promoted at the expense of his musicianship. A second album, *Axis: Bold as Love*, followed close behind the first; it contained his most-covered composition, "Little Wing," the individualist anthem "If 6 Was 9," and an experimental tape collage, "EXP."

By the end of 1967 Hendrix's relationship with Chandler had deteriorated, and he took over the production reins himself for the group's next album, *Electric Ladyland*, at the same time keeping to a heavy touring schedule. Released as a double long-playing record (LP) in October 1968, the album's sprawl offended some critics, and the UK cover, featuring photos of twenty-one nude women, caused some controversy, but the album went to the top of the charts thanks to hard rock classics, including "Voodoo Chile (Slight Return)" and "All Along the Watchtower." *Electric Ladyland* was the only number-one album Hendrix ever had in the United States. Despite its commercial success, the Jimi Hendrix Experience was having problems. Hendrix was arrested in Sweden in January 1968 after smashing up his hotel room, a lawsuit by unscrupulous producer Ed Chalpin was holding up the band's royalties, and Redding was more interested in a side project. The group broke up in June 1969 after abortive attempts at a fourth album.

OVERWHELMED BY PROBLEMS

Even without a steady band, Hendrix's mystique was enough to earn him headliner status at the Woodstock Music and Art Fair. Unfortunately, being the final act at a chaotic three-day show meant that he and his barely rehearsed rag-tag group finally went on stage at 8 a.m. on Monday when most of the crowd had already left. If not for the sound and film crews on hand, Hendrix's performance might have gone virtually unnoticed. As it was, his ear-splitting rendition of "The Star-Spangled Banner" became the symbol of the peace-and-love counterculture celebration. Offstage, however, Hendrix was overwhelmed by problems. He was arrested for taking drugs into Canada; his Band of Gypsys group with Buddy Miles and Billy Cox fell apart shortly after forming; and nearly every dollar he made touring was needed to build his own state-of-the-art recording studio, Electric Lady Studios. Several more attempts at recording went sour, even though a new band stabilized around Cox and Mitchell. In mid-1970, after the studio was completed, Hendrix made a serious push to finish a new album, tentatively titled *First Rays of the New Rising Sun*. Recording was complicated by a judgment awarding Chalpin rights to one album's worth of Hendrix material. The award was based on a 1965 contract Hendrix had signed with Chalpin that Chandler had inadvertently failed to buy out, and several songs intended for *First Rays* wound up on a hastily assembled live recording, *Band of Gypsys*, released in April 1970. Although seriously flawed, the album includes "Machine Gun," an antiwar number with a lengthy, breathtaking guitar solo. *Band of Gypsys* was the last album Hendrix would live to see released.

In August 1970 Hendrix reluctantly left New York for a European tour. He played in front of his largest audience yet at the Isle of Wight Festival, but the tour fell apart a few days later when Cox experienced paranoid delusions after taking LSD. On September 18, after spending several days visiting friends, Hendrix took several prescription sleeping pills belonging to girlfriend Monica Dannemann, fell asleep, and never woke up. He choked to death in the ambulance en route to the hospital. Hendrix was the first well-known rock star to die of a drug overdose. What seemed a tragic isolated accident at the time soon became just another cliché surrounding the fast-paced rock-and-roll lifestyle: Singer and songwriter Janis Joplin died of a heroin overdose two weeks later, and Jim Morrison, a lyricist and lead singer for the rock band the Doors, followed in less than a year, giving anti-hippie pundits plenty of ammunition to attack rock music as hedonistic and self-destructive.

Hendrix's three complete albums and countless live appearances had changed popular music more than any superficial moralizing could undo. Beyond his direct imitators—Stevie Ray Vaughan, Ernie Isley, Robin Trower, Funkadelic's Eddie Hazel and Mike Hampton—Hendrix's influence extended directly and indirectly to all pre-punk guitar players; Led Zeppelin and a horde of hard rock and heavy metal bands made their careers exploring areas Hendrix had opened up. In rock and roll, almost any black man with a guitar was compared with Hendrix, including musicians as dissimilar as Vernon Reid and Prince. Criticism is necessarily reductive: A white rock band will often be compared to the Beatles, the Rolling Stones, or the Velvet Underground; a white male solo artist to Bob Dylan, Jim Morrison, or Bruce Springsteen; a female singer to Janis Joplin or Joni Mitchell. But for black men in rock, Jimi Hendrix is the only archetype available.

David B. Wilson

SEE ALSO: *Clapton, Eric; Electric Guitar; Heavy Metal; Joplin, Janis; Led Zeppelin; LSD; Psychedelia; Rhythm and Blues; Rock and Roll; Woodstock.*

BIBLIOGRAPHY

Cross, Charles R. *Room Full of Mirrors: A Biography of Jimi Hendrix*. New York: Hyperion, 2005.

Henderson, David. *'Scuse Me While I Kiss the Sky: Jimi Hendrix, Voodoo Child*, rev. ed. New York: Atria Books, 2008.

Shapiro, Harry, and Caesar Glebbeek. *Jimi Hendrix: Electric Gypsy*. New York: St. Martin's, 1991.

Unterberger, Richie. *The Rough Guide to Jimi Hendrix*. London: Rough Guides, 2009.

Henry Aldrich

The quintessential teenager of the 1940s, Henry Aldrich was born as a character on the Broadway stage in 1938. He reached his widest audience through radio, a string of "B" movies, and a television series. Henry, who was likable, clean-cut, and monumentally prone to mishap, influenced a whole generation of teen characters on the radio, in movies, and even in comic books.

While college youths had become popular culture stereotypes in the 1920s, high school kids did not receive much notice until a decade later. Swing music and the jitterbug craze helped thrust them into the forefront of society. Writer Clifford Goldsmith introduced Henry in his play *What a Life!* According to radio historian John Dunning, Goldsmith "was virtually penniless and making his living on the high school lecture circuit when he wrote the play." In 1938 the then immensely popular crooner Rudy Vallee invited Goldsmith to write some skits about the Aldrich family for his weekly radio variety show. Next came a similar invitation from Kate Smith's variety show, and by the autumn of 1939 *The Aldrich Family* was a regular weekly radio program, sponsored by Jell-O on NBC.

The Aldrich family lives in a typical small town and consists of Henry, his parents, and his older sister, Mary. His high school pal Homer is underfoot virtually all the time. The opening of the show became one of the best known, and most quoted, in radio. Henry's long-suffering mom calls him—"Henry, Henry Aldrich!"—and he replies, in his harried adolescent croak, "Coming, Mother!" Ezra Stone, who had created the role on the stage, was the first radio Henry, with Jackie Kelk as Homer. House Jameson, who also played the radio detective known as the Crime Doctor, was the head of the household.

The show, though it touched on real family situations, was played for rather broad comedy. Preoccupied with girls, cars, and school, Henry sees no reason why he cannot have all the rights and perks of the adult he feels he will become any day. His anxious and elaborate schemes and his frequent dreams of glory lead him into all sorts of unforeseen complications. His parents, of course, rarely understand him and often act as though he might have contracted some rare disease that causes him to run amok on occasion or behave as if he might even be an alien invader masquerading as their son.

Paramount Pictures turned Goldsmith's play into a movie in 1939, casting Jackie Cooper as Henry. The script was by Charles Brackett and writer-director Billy Wilder, whose several brilliant creations included the same year's *Ninotchka* starring Greta Garbo. Cooper appeared in the second film in the series in 1941, with Eddie Bracken as his sidekick, and then turned the role over to Jimmy Lydon. Less handsome and gawkier than Cooper, Lydon made nine Henry Aldrich films. John Litel, who had also been girl detective Nancy Drew's screen father, was Sam Aldrich, and Olive Blakeney played Henry's mom. She later became Lydon's offscreen mother-in-law.

Henry and his kin were early arrivals on television, with *The Aldrich Family* premiering on NBC on October 2, 1949. An actor named Robert Casey was the first of five juveniles who took turns enacting the role of Henry. Kelk moved from radio to TV to play Homer, and Jameson returned to repeat Sam Aldrich. Three actresses portrayed Mrs. Aldrich: Lois Wilson (1949–1950, 1951), Nancy Carroll (1950–1951), and Barbara Robbins (1951–1953). Jean Muir, a movie actress in the 1930s and 1940s, had been scheduled to take over the part in 1950, but because of her liberal sympathies she found herself listed in *Red Channels*, the right-wing publication dedicated to rooting out alleged communist sympathizers from the entertainment business. She was subsequently blacklisted by the sponsor and the network and never got the chance to say, "Henry, Henry Aldrich!" *The Aldrich Family* remained on radio and television until 1953, when Henry stepped aside to make way for a new breed of teenage stereotypes.

Ron Goulart

SEE ALSO: *"B" Movies; Blacklisting; Broadway; Garbo, Greta; Jell-O; McCarthyism; Radio; Sitcom; Smith, Kate; Teenagers; Television; Vallee, Rudy; Wilder, Billy.*

BIBLIOGRAPHY

Dunning, John. *Tune In Yesterday*. Englewood Cliffs, NJ: Prentice-Hall, 1976.

Eames, John Douglas. *The Paramount Story*. New York: Crown Publishers, 1985.

Halliwell, Leslie. *Halliwell's Film and Video Guide*. New York: Scribner's, 1987.

Henson, Jim *(1936–1990)*

Puppeteer and filmmaker-director Jim Henson was the genius behind the world-famous puppet creations known as the Muppets. By the end of the twentieth century, Henson's name was synonymous with modern puppetry, children's television programming, and family-based entertainment. With his talented team of artists, he revolutionized the ancient art of puppetry by fusing it with twentieth-century technology—first through his television shows *Sesame Street* (1969–) and *The Muppet Show* (1976–1981), then through films and computer animation. Yet Henson was not famous solely for his technical innovations. His work expressed a strong moral vision—humorous, uplifting, full of tolerance and love—that viewed all individuals as worthy of respect. It was this vision, expressed through his lifelike puppets, that transcended lines of age and culture. Henson's work has been seen in some 120 countries and has brought him praise as the twentieth century's greatest entertainer-educator. The Jim Henson Company sold the rights to the Muppets to Disney in 2004.

While *Sesame Street* has never been off the air since its debut in 1969, a new generation growing up in the early twenty-first century had not been officially introduced to the Muppets. Actor Jason Segel changed all that in 2011. A lifelong fan of Henson and the Muppets, Segel almost single-handedly resurrected them by convincing Disney that it was time to bring them back to the big screen. Segel starred in *The Muppets*, which introduced Walter, a new Muppet, roughly based on Segel himself. The plot of the movie centers on the Muppets trying to save their old theater from a greedy oil tycoon. Resurrecting the Muppets brings just a little of the Henson magic back to those who still regret that he left the world too soon.

Brian Granger

SEE ALSO: *Animated Films; Disney (Walt Disney Company); The Muppets; Public Television (PBS);* Sesame Street*; Television.*

BIBLIOGRAPHY

Abate, Michelle Ann. "Taking Silliness Seriously: Jim Henson's *The Muppet Show*, the Anglo-American Tradition of Nonsense and Cultural Critique." *Journal of Popular Culture* 42, no. 4 (2009).

Finch, Christopher. *Of Muppets and Men: The Making of "The Muppet Show."* New York: Muppet Press/Alfred A. Knopf, 1981.

Finch, Christopher. *Jim Henson: The Works*. New York: Random House, 1993.

Graham, Anissa M., ed. *Kermit Culture: Critical Perspectives on Jim Henson's Muppets*. Jefferson, NC: McFarland, 2009.

Krull, Kathleen. *Jim Henson: The Guy Who Played with Puppets*. New York: Random House, 2011.

Hep Cats

An important term in the history of African American slang, *hep cat* was used to describe a jazz aficionado in the marijuana-using urban subculture of the 1940s and 1950s. A hep cat's essential qualities included a free-spirited rejection of societal convention, intense creativity, and an unflagging rejection of all things "square." First entering the language in the late 1930s, the term was an amalgam of "hep," an older term meaning "smart" or "aware," and "cat," slang for "man." Its roots stretch back to the Wolof language of Africa, where "hepi" meant "to see," and "hipi" meant "to open one's eyes," while "hipicat" translated as "wise" or "informed." As *hep cat* was appropriated by white beatniks in the 1950s, African Americans turned to fresher terminology like *hip* and *hipster*. Continuing to evolve with stylistic changes in American musical and drug-related subcultures, its roots survive in terms such as *hippie* and *hip-hop*.

Steve Burnett

SEE ALSO: *Hip-Hop; Hippies; Jazz; Slang.*

BIBLIOGRAPHY

Alvarez, Luis. *The Power of the Zoot: Youth Culture and Resistance during World War II*. Berkeley: University of California Press, 2008.

Jonnes, Jill. *Hep-Cats, Narcs, and Pipe Dreams: A History of America's Romance with Illegal Drugs*. New York: Scribner, 1996.

Major, Clarence, ed. *Juba to Jive: A Dictionary of African-American Slang*. New York: Penguin Books, 1994.

Thorne, Tony. *The Dictionary of Contemporary Slang*. New York: Pantheon Books, 1990.

Hepburn, Audrey *(1929–1993)*

From her first starring role as a princess in *Roman Holiday* (1953), Belgian-born Audrey Hepburn, the daughter of an Anglo-Irish banker and a Dutch aristocrat, was lauded for bringing a stately "European" elegance to Hollywood. Billy Wilder, her director in 1954's *Sabrina*, declared: "After so many drive-in waitresses in movies, here is class." Hepburn's androgynous looks and waifish physique—photographer Cecil Beaton called her "the gamine, the urchin, the lost Barnardo boy"—challenged and redefined the dominant popular image of femininity in the 1950s, the curvaceous, all-American bombshell typified by Marilyn Monroe. Hepburn often played royalty (*Roman Holiday*; *War and Peace*, 1956) or a poor, modest girl who achieves a fairy-tale rise to high society (*Sabrina*; *Funny Face*, 1957; *My Fair Lady*, 1964). Though cast somewhat against type as a scandalous socialite in *Breakfast at Tiffany's* (1961), Hepburn's Holly Golightly, as Robyn Karney observes in *A Star Danced: The Life of Audrey Hepburn*, "passed into the iconography of the 1960s."

Hepburn gave up Hollywood in the late 1960s and moved to Switzerland, devoting the rest of her life to humanitarian causes, particularly to her work as goodwill ambassador for UNICEF. When she was not traveling, she lived quietly at her home La Paisible (place of peace) with her companion Robert Wolders, the widower of actress Merle Oberon. In her last role in Steven Spielberg's *Always* (1989), Hepburn fittingly played an angel.

Martyn Bone

SEE ALSO: *Androgyny;* Breakfast at Tiffany's*; Hollywood; Monroe, Marilyn; Movie Stars;* My Fair Lady*; Sex Symbol; Spielberg, Steven.*

BIBLIOGRAPHY

Karney, Robyn. *A Star Danced: The Life of Audrey Hepburn*. London: Bloomsbury, 1993.

Mosley, Rachel. *Growing Up with Audrey Hepburn: Text, Audience, Resonance*. New York: Manchester University Press, 2002.

Hepburn, Katharine *(1907–2003)*

Always a role model for female independence, self-determination, and integrity, actress Katharine Hepburn is thought by many to be one of the most monumental and enduring of all of Hollywood's stars. At the time of her death, Hepburn held the record for Oscar wins for acting (four). Her twelve Academy Award nominations for acting held the record until 2003, when Meryl Streep surpassed her.

Hepburn spent her early years in Hartford, Connecticut, where her parents were liberal intellectuals who did not raise their children according to traditional sex roles but encouraged them to excel at all their endeavors and expand their boundaries. Her father was a successful surgeon, and her mother an active suffragette, giving Hepburn an expanded view of women's roles from an early age.

Hepburn was drawn to acting early and participated in local productions before attending Bryn Mawr College and appearing in college theatricals. She graduated in 1928 and made her Broadway debut in *The Warrior's Husband* (1932), for which she garnered critical praise. She was then approached by Hollywood, but thinking that Hollywood was not "legitimate," she demanded an extremely high salary, which, to her amazement, RKO accepted. Hepburn made her screen debut in 1932 in *Bill of Divorcement*, starring John Barrymore; the film was both a critical and box-office success. Upon her arrival in Hollywood, she refused to conform to the standard starlet mold. She preferred wearing slacks to revealing dresses, avoided publicity, and closely guarded her private life. She shunned the party crowd of Hollywood and demanded to be dealt with respectfully.

Hepburn's first Academy Award was for her third film, *Morning Glory* (1933), in which she played an aspiring actress-understudy who, after many manipulations, becomes an overnight success when the veteran actress has a breakdown that necessitates the understudy taking her place. The same year Hepburn appeared as Jo in *Little Women*, a role that she found personally rewarding. One of her next projects was the screwball comedy *Bringing Up Baby* (1938), which ranks as one of the best examples of the genre. Hepburn portrayed the madcap heiress Susan Vance, who falls in love with an absentminded paleontologist (Cary Grant) and enlists his aid in caring for a tame leopard named Baby to keep Grant's character from marrying his staid assistant. Later that same year Hepburn appeared in *Holiday*, again with Grant.

For some reason, film exhibitors branded Hepburn "box-office poison" despite her many successes, and she left Hollywood for Broadway, where she appeared in *The Philadelphia Story* (1939), forgoing a salary in favor of a percentage of the profits and screen rights. It was a huge hit and enabled Hepburn to return to Hollywood with the upper hand. She sold the screen rights to Metro-Goldwyn-Mayer (MGM) but maintained creative control, which allowed her to choose the director and her costars (Grant and Jimmy Stewart). The film broke attendance records and won Hepburn the New York Film Critics' Circle Award as well as her third Oscar nomination.

Hepburn's next film, *Woman of the Year* (1942), paired her for the first time with Spencer Tracy and began a twenty-five-year relationship that ended only with Tracy's death. On-screen they were a remarkable team and made eight more films together: *Keeper of the Flame* (1942); *Without Love* (1945); *The Sea of Grass* (1947); *State of the Union* (1948); *Adam's Rib* (1949); *Pat and Mike* (1952); *Desk Set* (1957); and their final film, *Guess Who's Coming to Dinner?* (1967). Offscreen they remained devoted to each other and were seldom seen apart. Hepburn did appear in several films without Tracy during this period. In *The African Queen* (1951) she portrayed an uptight spinster who falls in love with Humphrey Bogart's reprobate supply boat "captain." She also appeared in *Summertime* (1955), *The Rainmaker* (1956), *Suddenly, Last Summer* (1959), and *Long Day's Journey into Night* (1962).

Katharine Hepburn. *Hepburn won four Academy Awards in her long and distinguished Hollywood career.* HULTON ARCHIVE/GETTY IMAGES.

Hepburn retired from the screen for several years as Tracy became more ill, but both returned in 1967 to appear in their last picture together, *Guess Who's Coming to Dinner?* for which she won her second Oscar. She won her third Academy Award for *The Lion in Winter* (1968), in which she portrayed Eleanor of Aquitaine, and her fourth for *On Golden Pond* (1981), for which she also won a British Academy of Film and Television Arts Award.

While Hepburn's work on television was not as extensive, her performances were of consistent quality. She received Emmy nominations for her performances in *The Glass Menagerie* (1973) and *The Corn Is Green* (1979) and won an Emmy for her portrayal of an elderly woman in *Love among the Ruins* (1975). She also starred in several television movies, including *Mrs. Delafield Wants to Marry* (1986), *Laura Lansing Slept Here* (1988), *The Man Upstairs* (1992), and *This Can't Be Love* (1994).

In 1999 the American Film Institute ranked Hepburn number one on its list of greatest female American screen legends of all time. She died at her home in Connecticut in 2003 at the age of ninety-six. Afterward President George W. Bush paid tribute to her by saying, "Katharine Hepburn delighted audiences with her unique talent for more than six decades. She was known for her intelligence and wit and will be remembered as one of the nation's artistic treasures."

Denise Lowe

SEE ALSO: *Academy Awards;* The African Queen*; Barrymore, John; Bogart, Humphrey;* Bringing Up Baby*; Broadway; Celebrity Couples; Emmy Awards;* The Glass Menagerie*; Grant, Cary; Hollywood; Made-for-Television Movies; Movie Stars;* The Philadelphia Story*; Stewart, Jimmy; Television; Tracy, Spencer.*

BIBLIOGRAPHY

Felder, Deborah G. *The 100 Most Influential Women of All Time*. New York: Citadel Press, 1996.

Hepburn, Katharine. *Me*. New York: Alfred A. Knopf, 1991.

Mann, William J. *Kate: The Woman Who Was Hepburn*. New York: Henry Holt, 2006.

Martin, Jean, ed. *Who's Who of Women in the Twentieth Century*. New York: Crescent Books, 1995.

McHenry, Robert, ed. *Famous American Women*. New York: Dover Publications, 1980.

Herbert, Frank *(1920–1986)*

Many literary critics have ranked science fiction writer Frank Herbert among such well-respected authors of imaginary worlds as J. R. R. Tolkien, C. S. Lewis, and Isaac Asimov. Though Herbert wrote more than twenty novels and several short stories, his fame was linked to his series of books called the Dune

Chronicles. His premier book in the series, *Dune* (1965), won the first-ever Nebula Award and shared a Hugo Award, both for Best Novel. Although initially rejected by twenty publishers, the book became one of the best-selling science fiction books in history, with some twelve million copies sold. By the beginning of the twenty-first century, the book had not yet gone out of print.

Intended as the beginning of a trilogy, *Dune* instead spawned five sequels, with a sixth left unfinished at the time of Herbert's death in 1986. *Dune* was made into a major motion picture in 1984. The series, set on the planet of Arrakis, or Dune, follows the history of the Atreides family over thousands of years. The Dune saga is considered one of the greatest science fiction stories ever written.

Frank Patrick Herbert was born in Tacoma, Washington, on October 8, 1920. He attended the University of Washington for a year in the mid-1940s as he worked as a reporter and an editor for such newspapers as the *Glendale (California) Star*, the *Oregon Statesman*, the *Seattle Star*, and the *San Francisco Examiner*. By the late 1960s and early 1970s, he had taken a job as an educational writer for the *Seattle Post-Intelligencer*. Shortly thereafter, however, he was able devote his whole attention to his novel writing, although he did continue to lecture and act as a social and ecological consultant.

ECOLOGICAL BEGINNINGS

A strong believer in self-reliance and ecological harmony, Herbert generated his own energy on his small farm with solar heating, methane gas from chicken dung, and wind power (from an improved windmill design for which he was awarded a U.S. patent). He wove many of his ecological ideas into his novels. Throughout his work he provides his readers with complex adventure plots and probing questions about the cosmos, human nature, and society.

Dune is a work of extraordinary complexity, telling the story of the desert planet Arrakis and its inhabitants. Set in the future, the novel introduces a universe that is controlled by two opposing political powers, the Imperium and the Great Houses. The interstellar civilization is a precarious balance between the political, military, and economic forces of the largest powers as well as the disruptive smaller independent organizations, including the Spacing Guild (which has a monopoly on interplanetary travel), the Bene Gesserit order, the massive CHOAM trading company, and the Bene Tleilax. The story is a remarkable metaphor of late twentieth-century U.S. society with the blending and balancing of political and economic forces with religious, cultural, and business interests—and, of course, the ever-present but largely ignored ecological phenomena. With *Dune* Herbert successfully created a complete and detailed imaginary world that captured the audience's attention.

POPULARITY OF *DUNE*

The success of *Dune* was a turning point in science fiction publishing. The book's popularity broadened the audience of the genre and "paved the way for large advances, bigger printings, best-seller status, and heavy subsidiary sales for many other writers," according to Willis E. McNelly in *The Dune Encyclopedia*. The ecological thinking examined in *Dune* made it a college campus cult classic, in fashion with Tolkien's *Lord of the Rings* or the original *Star Trek* television series. The attention directed toward *Dune* in the 1970s and 1980s was in many ways the predecessor of the type of fandom that sprang up around *The X-Files* in the 1990s.

Many young people strived to become more ecologically minded, patterning themselves after Herbert's character Liet-Kynes, the planetary ecologist, who was aware of and concerned with the consequences of human actions on the environment. The novel also attracted those interested in the effects of drugs on behavior. The book discussed a substance called spice (mélange), which increased awareness and cerebral functions and allowed Mentats (human computers) to pursue their vocation in a world that banned thinking machines. Users of controlled substances claimed many of the same effects as those discussed in *Dune*. Although illegal, hallucinogens called "smart drugs" were used in areas of California to aid complex problem solving, and another street drug, named Ecstasy, reportedly improved sexual awareness and pleasure.

Although there was intense interest in turning *Dune* into a movie, with a script written by David Lynch and an estimated $40 million to $50 million budget, the resultant film flopped in 1984. But the disappointing film did not damage the cultlike interest in Herbert's original material. In 2000 New Amsterdam Entertainment, in cooperation with the Sci-Fi Channel (now SyFy Channel), aired a miniseries adaptation of *Dune* called *Frank Herbert's Dune*. Its success led to a sequel miniseries titled *Frank Herbert's Children of Dune* (2003). The miniseries were two of the highest-rated programs ever broadcast on the cable channel.

DUNE AS INSPIRATION

Herbert's Dune Chronicles went on to inspire other artists, including several popular musicians. Iron Maiden, a heavy metal band, performed what they called a Dune song, "To Tame a Land," on their 1983 *Piece of Mind* album. The Blind Guardian released a Dune-inspired song, "Traveler in Time," from *Tales from the Twilight World* in 1991. A German techno band called itself Dune. The band's electronic instrumentals were popular in U.S. techno dance clubs in the mid-1990s, where the oft repeated refrain of "the spice must flow" could be heard.

Some of the jargon found in *Dune* even infiltrated popular speech. Many analogies were made between the *Dune* story line, with its obsession over the spice mélange, and the Middle Eastern oil reserves and their influence on the global economy. "The spice must flow," a quote from a third-grade guild navigator, was referred to quite often in its modern version "the oil must flow." In addition, statements such as "long live the fighters," "the gom jabbar," and "fear is the mind killer" became as ingrained in popular jargon as "may the force be with you" from the *Star Wars* movies and "Grokking" and "Sharing Water" from Robert Heinlein's science fiction novel *Stranger in a Strange Land*.

The Dune story also permeated U.S. popular culture when it was adapted into several games. In 1979 Avalon Hill created Dune the Board Game, which was based on the novel. Five years later Parker Brothers developed a board game titled Dune, which was based on the movie. Computer versions of the Dune saga soon appeared on the market. In 1992 the first computer-related game combined both strategy and adventure. A sequel, titled *Dune II: The Building of a Dynasty*, followed shortly thereafter. An improvement over the first, *Dune II* became an even bigger hit. It was awarded the 1993 Strategy Game of the Year Award.

The continuing success of *Dune II* led to the introduction of *Dune 2000*, released in 1998. *Dune 2000* was a real-time strategy game that could be played singly on CD-ROM, over the Internet, or over local area networks. The game focused on military strategy and political intrigue. Five Ring Publishing produced Dune: The Eye of the Storm, a customizable card game, which was popular in the 1990s. Though the games followed much of the Dune saga, none incorporated any serious consideration of ecology, which was one of Herbert's central ideas in the series.

DUNE AFTER HERBERT'S DEATH

With the collaboration of Herbert's son Brian and Kevin J. Anderson, the Dune universe continued to grow. Together the two wrote more than a dozen books based upon the original works. The two prequel series, Prelude to Dune (1999–2001) and Legends of Dune (2002–2004), were both trilogies and spent time on the *New York Times* best-seller list. The duo also published *Hunters of Dune* (2006) and *Sandworms of Dune* (2007), a continuation of Herbert's saga that was based upon an outline and notes he left behind. In addition, the two planned a series of four books called Heroes of Dune, which included *Paul of Dune* (2008) and *The Winds of Dune* (2009), as well as other books meant to fill in gaps left by the original novels. These new books, while entertaining and, more importantly, commercially successful, lacked the brilliance, complexity, and sheer intellectual audacity of the originals.

Herbert had considered *Dune* a "training manual for consciousness." Others agreed with his sentiment, and the Dune Chronicles have been used in architecture, literature, and philosophy courses at universities across the country. Herbert attributed the popularity of *Dune* in college classrooms to the genre of science fiction, which he noted "lends itself to that because we're dealing with ideas a great deal of the time." Indeed, Herbert's greatest contribution was perhaps his imaginative ideas.

Craig T. Cobane

SEE ALSO: *Best Sellers; Cable TV; Environmentalism; Iron Maiden; Lewis, C. S.; Lynch, David; Science Fiction Publishing;* Star Trek*; Television; Tolkien, J. R. R.;* The X-Files.

BIBLIOGRAPHY

DiTommaso, Lorenzo. "History and Historical Effects in Frank Herbert's *Dune*." *Science-Fiction Studies* 19, no. 3 (1992): 311–325.

Ellis, R. J. "Frank Herbert's *Dune* and the Discourse of Apocalyptic Ecologism in the United States." In *Science Fiction Roots and Branches: Contemporary Critical Approaches*, ed. Rhys Garnett and R. J. Ellis. New York: St. Martin's, 1990.

Levack, Daniel J. H., and Mark Willard. *Dune Master: A Frank Herbert Bibliography*. Westport, CT: Meckler, 1988.

Liddell, Elisabeth, and Michael Liddell. "*Dune*: A Tale of Two Texts." In *Cinema and Fiction: New Modes of Adapting 1950–90*, ed. John Orr and Colin Nicholson. Edinburgh: Edinburgh University Press, 1992.

McNelly, Willis E., ed. *The Dune Encyclopedia*. New York: Putnam, 1984.

Miller, David M. *Frank Herbert*. San Bernardino, CA: Borgo Press, 1984.

Minowitz, Peter. "Prince versus Prophet: Machiavellianism in Frank Herbert's *Dune* Epic." In *Political Science Fiction*, ed. Donald M. Hassler and Clyde Wilcox. Columbia: University of South Carolina Press, 1997.

O'Reilly, Timothy. *Frank Herbert*. New York: Ungar, 1981.

Touponce, William. *Frank Herbert*. Boston: Twayne, 1988.

Westfahl, Gary. *The Greenwood Encyclopedia of Science Fiction and Fantasy: Themes, Works, and Wonders*. Westport, CT: Greenwood Press, 2005.

Hercules: The Legendary Journeys

Initially conceived in 1993 as a made-for-TV movie, *Hercules: The Legendary Journeys* became a syndicated television series for the 1995–1996 television season. Starring Kevin Sorbo as the half-god Hercules, the series combined action, special effects, and camp to create one of the most popular syndicated shows of the 1990s, rivaling the *Star Trek* franchise and *Baywatch* for ratings. In fact, the show spawned a number of spin-offs and imitators.

The show's executive producers, Sam Raimi (the writer and director of cult movie favorite *The Evil Dead*, 1981) and Rob Tapert, combined unlikely elements to make the show a success. The show deviated from previous incarnations of the Greek hero played by such musclemen as Steve Reeves and Lou Ferrigno. Sorbo, though lean and muscular, was not just a muscle-bound hero. Despite beating up villains and groups of bad guys in highly choreographed and often farcical fights, he was chiefly portrayed as a hero with heart. The show's title narration told the story: it was a time when the gods were cruel and played with mortals. Hercules, son to Zeus and the mortal Alcmene, stood up for the common man against his family, the gods.

Simply portraying Hercules as champion of the people did not totally account for the show's popularity. Many reviewers gave credit to the fact that the show used pop culture references and a healthy dose of camp to entertain a broad spectrum of the television audience. For instance, the show did not care about historical or mythological accuracy. It went instead for hipness and, at times, silliness. In one episode titled "Porkules," Hercules is transformed into a superstrong pig. Ares, the god of war, is always dressed in leather, as is the goddess Discord. Their choice of attire is the source of many double entendres about their possibly kinky preferences. Apollo, the sun god, is portrayed riding a type of golden snowboard and talking like a contemporary teenager.

The show offered plenty of action. Almost every episode featured Hercules and Iolaus, or one of the other heroes, battling a group of armed men. These scenes feature Hercules and his cohorts butting heads, throwing men through the air, doing flips, and throwing old-fashioned punches. Although violent, most shows had no deaths, but occasionally a battle scene was just that—a battle with fatalities. At times Hercules faced off against special effects monsters such as Echidna. The show also displayed wit and imagination. The producers did a postmodern episode that featured the cast looking for actor Kevin Sorbo. Another episode was a retelling of the movie *Some Like It Hot* (1959). The producers and writers of the show were not afraid to take chances.

Besides Hercules, the show had a cast of regular characters. Hercules' constant sidekick throughout the first five seasons was

Iolaus, played by Michael Hurst. Ares, played by Kevin Smith; Autolycus, the King of Thieves, played by Bruce Campbell; and Salmoneus, played by Robert Trebor, were also regulars. On some occasions the show focused only on supporting characters. The show also featured Xena, Warrior Princess, a character that inspired a spin-off of her own, ultimately becoming more popular than *Hercules*. The two shows shared supporting casts, with stars occasionally crossing over from one show to the other. The characters were also the costars of an animated movie. *Hercules* also produced a second spin-off, *Young Hercules* (1998–1999)—broadcast on Saturday mornings on the Fox network—that chronicled the adventures of the juvenile Hercules and Iolaus.

After *Hercules* scored big in the ratings, other companies brought out mythic figures to try to cash in on the show's success. However, shows such as *The Adventures of Sinbad* (1996–1998) and *Tarzan: The Epic Adventures* (1996) did not have the popular appeal of *Hercules*. Besides television, Hercules and Xena found a home on the Internet, generating numerous fan pages. Computer games and multiplayer online games also featured these characters.

In 1997 Sorbo, who had always been known for his clean living and healthy lifestyle, unaccountably suffered an aneurysm that was followed by a series of strokes. The actor began suffering from persistent weakness, dizziness, migraines, vision loss, and panic attacks. He slowly recovered, though he suffered permanent nerve damage. In 1998 he married actress Sam Jenkins, who had played the roles of Serena and the Golden Hind on *Hercules: The Legendary Journeys*. Sorbo has since returned to acting, appearing in several television shows, including *Andromeda* (2000–2005), *The O.C.* (2003–2007), *Hawaii Five-0* (2010–), and *The Super-Hero Squad Show* (2009–).

P. Andrew Miller

SEE ALSO: Baywatch*; Camp; Computer Games;* Hawaii Five-O*; The Internet; Made-for-Television Movies; Postmodernism; Reeves, Steve; Saturday Morning Cartoons; Snowboarding;* Some Like It Hot*;* Star Trek*; Syndication; Tarzan; Teenagers; Television;* Xena, Warrior Princess.

BIBLIOGRAPHY

Freeman, Michael. "Mything in Action." *Mediaweek*, April 29, 1996.

Gliatto, Tom, and Kirsten Warner. "Sorbo the Greek: As TV's New Hercules, Minnesota's Kevin Sorbo Gives the Mythic Muscleman a Sensitive Spin." *People Weekly*, July 3, 1995.

Sorbo, Kevin. *True Strength: My Journey from Hercules to Mere Mortal and How Nearly Dying Saved My Life*. Cambridge, MA: Da Capo/Perseus, 2011.

Herman, Woody *(1913–1987)*

Along with Benny Goodman and Artie Shaw, Woody Herman was one of a triumvirate of clarinet-playing band leaders in the big band era. Playing a high-pitched instrument that could cut through the sound of the ensemble in those days of poor amplification, Herman for more than fifty years headed one of the most popular and innovative of the bands in the swing era. His greatest contributions to jazz history came from his ability to organize and sustain a talented big band that was wholly dedicated to the cutting edge of jazz during the severe economic trials of the Great Depression. His band, Herman's Herd, spawned a number of great jazz soloists as well as writers and arrangers of major importance.

Born Woodrow Charles Thomas Herrmann to German parents in Milwaukee, Wisconsin, in 1913, Herman seemed destined for the spotlight from the age of nine. He toured the state of Wisconsin for eight weeks as one of a troupe of musicians who played a live prologue to the screening of silent films. Soon Herman began studying the alto sax and clarinet. His teacher was Art Beuch, whom he later described as "an old German fellow who would take nothing but hard work." Beuch's advice to the budding jazzman was "practice until you turn blue and your lip is numb and your teeth hurt and you may accomplish something."

When Herman began playing in local dance bands in high school, he became dedicated to the life of a jazzman. He left home at seventeen with a band led by Tom Gerun, playing in a reed section that included Tony Martin, who later gained fame as a singer and film star. After unsuccessfully trying to form his own band, Herman joined the Isham Jones orchestra in 1934 and was featured on tenor sax, clarinet, and vocals on the band's Decca records. When the band folded two years later, the twenty-three-year-old persuaded key sidemen to join a band he was organizing on his own. In that year—the depth of the Great Depression—Herman ran his band on a cooperative, share-the-profit basis. Featuring the blues as well as some pop songs in their repertoire, the band slowly gained fame, soon to be enhanced in 1939 by their biggest hit, the upbeat blues piece "Woodchopper's Ball," which ultimately reached the five million mark in sales.

Woody Herman. *Woody Herman, one of the most popular bandleaders of the 1930s and 1940s, continued to perform into the 1980s.* DAVID REDFERN/REDFERNS/GETTY IMAGES.

Although still overshadowed by the Count Basie, Duke Ellington, and Benny Goodman bands, Woody Herman's Herd had begun to attract national attention. Dave Dexter, writing in *DownBeat* magazine in January 1940, suggested that a part of the band's problem in finding major bookings was the delay caused by the band members (as shareholders) voting on each booking proposition.

In 1941 the band filmed a musical short for Warner Brothers in Brooklyn, New York, and later that year they went to Los Angeles to be featured in a Universal picture called *What's Cookin'?* The Andrews Sisters and Donald O'Connor also appeared in this "typical wartime musical," as Herman called it.

When the band began a new recording contract with Columbia in 1945, it demonstrated the strong influence of the new bebop style of jazz played by Charlie Parker and Dizzy Gillespie. Joining the band at this time were three devout boppers: Neal Hefti, Shorty Rogers, and Pete Candoli, and Herman's First Herd was soon widely known as one of the most advanced and innovative bands of its era. Davey Tough, the perfect drummer for the new Herd, received belated acclaim when he raised the band to new heights in 1944 and 1945 on a series of nationwide radio programs. His unique style can be heard on such Columbia hits as "Apple Honey," "Laura," and "I Wonder."

In 1946 the great Russian composer Igor Stravinsky composed *Ebony Concerto* expressly for the Herman band, adding to the band's prestige after a sold-out performance in Carnegie Hall. That year the band won the *DownBeat, Metronome, Billboard*, and *Esquire* polls. Gunther Schuller, in his book *The Swing Era*, attributes this great success to the highly original arrangements by Ralph Burns and Hefti and to the band's playing "night after night, with an infectious exuberance, an almost physically palpable excitement and a never-say-die energy."

In 1986, still active at age seventy-three after fifty years as bandleader, Herman led his band on a jazz cruise aboard the SS *Norway* and, after spending time in the hospital with heart problems, led the Herd in November at the Kennedy Center awards ceremony in Washington, D.C. He died in October of the following year.

Benjamin Griffith

SEE ALSO: *The Andrews Sisters; Basie, Count; Big Bands; Blues; Carnegie Hall; Ellington, Duke; Gillespie, Dizzy; Goodman, Benny; The Great Depression; Hollywood; Jazz; The Musical; Parker, Charlie; Radio; Shaw, Artie; Silent Movies; Swing Dancing.*

BIBLIOGRAPHY

Lees, Gene. *Leader of the Band: The Life of Woody Herman.* New York: Oxford Press, 1995.

Schuller, Gunther. *The Swing Era.* New York: Oxford Press, 1989.

Simon, George T. *The Big Bands.* New York: Macmillan, 1974.

Studwell, William E., and Mark Baldin. *The Big Band Reader: Songs Favored by Swing Era Orchestras and Other Popular Ensembles.* New York: Haworth Press, 2000.

Troup, Stewart, and Woody Herman. *The Woodchopper's Ball.* New York: E. P. Dutton, 1990.

Voce, Steve. *Woody Herman.* London: Apollo Press, 1986.

Herpes

Herpes simplex viruses I (oral) and II (genital) are persistent, embarrassing, and often devastating sexually transmitted diseases. Symptoms can include small, painful blisters or lesions around the lips, nose, mouth (cold sores), or genitals; fever; headaches; swollen lymph glands; and feelings of isolation and depression. Herpes spreads through direct contact with infected areas and is only detectable with a blood test, as the virus can remain dormant indefinitely. After an initial outbreak, herpes symptoms can disappear for months, only to recur during periods of stress or when the immune system becomes weakened.

Between 50 and 80 percent of the American adult population is infected with a form of herpes, yet only one-third of these carriers ever experience symptoms. Using condoms during sex can cut the risk of developing herpes by half. There is no known cure for herpes, but it is not life threatening, and advances in treatment have made living with herpes more manageable and less stigmatizing. Researchers have continued to search for a vaccine, particularly after it was discovered that having genital herpes raises the risk for contracting HIV/AIDS threefold.

Tony Brewer

SEE ALSO: *AIDS; Safe Sex.*

BIBLIOGRAPHY

Ebel, Charles. *Managing Herpes: How to Live and Love with a Chronic STD.* Research Triangle Park, NC: American Social Health Association, 1998.

Johnston, Christine; D. M. Koelle; and A. Wald. "HSV-2: In Pursuit of a Vaccine." *Journal of Clinical Investigation* 121, no. 12 (2011).

Kudesia, Goura, and T. G. Wreghitt. *Clinical and Diagnostic Virology.* New York: Cambridge University Press, 2009.

Hersey, John *(1914–1993)*

Born in China to missionaries, John Hersey began his journalism career as a correspondent for *Time* and went on to cover World War II for that magazine and *Life*. He had already won a Pulitzer Prize for his World War II novel *A Bell for Adano* (1944) when in 1946 the *New Yorker* magazine published in a single issue his most famous and enduring work, titled simply *Hiroshima*. The nonfiction story describes the experiences of six survivors of the United States' 1945 atomic bombing of the Japanese city. The bomb killed an estimated 140,000 people and injured thousands more. Forty years after *Hiroshima* appeared, Hersey updated the story with an epilogue telling how the lives of the six survivors focused on in the original story had progressed. Overall, he published twenty-five books during his career.

R. Thomas Berner

SEE ALSO: *The* New Yorker*; World War II.*

BIBLIOGRAPHY

Hersey, John. *Hiroshima.* New York: Random House, 1989.

Sanders, David. *John Hersey Revisited.* Boston: Twayne Publishers, 1991.

Hess, Joan *(1949–)*

Joan Hess has infused her mystery writing with her knowledge of her home state of Arkansas and its regional culture. She has two main mystery series, both set in Arkansas—the first features Claire Malloy, a bookstore proprietor who is the widow of an English professor, and the second is set in the town of Maggody and centers on Arly Hanks, who returns to Maggody after an unsuccessful marriage. Both series are marked by a kind of off-center humor that enlivens the action and rounds out the characters. Among the books in the Claire Malloy series are *Strangled Prose* (1986), *The Murder at the Murder at the Mimosa Inn* (1986), *Dear Miss Demeanor* (1987), *A Diet to Die For* (1989), and *A Holly Jolly Murder* (1997). Among the Arly Hanks books are *Malice in Maggody* (1987), *Mischief in Maggody* (1988), *Maggody in Manhattan* (1992), *O Little Town of Maggody* (1993), and *The Maggody Militia* (1996).

Between 2000 and 2012 Hess wrote six new Claire Malloy books, including *Deader Homes and Gardens* (2012). She has also been busy with Arly Hanks, releasing five new books between 2000 and 2010, including *The Merry Wives of Maggody* (2009). Under the name Joan Hadley, Hess published two books featuring the character Theo Bloomer, but she has not published a book in that series since 1988. Hess has won the American Mystery Award and has been nominated for numerous other awards. She has also served as president of the American Crime Writers League.

Frank A. Salamone

SEE ALSO: *Best Sellers; Detective Fiction.*

BIBLIOGRAPHY

"Joan Hess." *Contemporary Authors Online*. Detroit, MI: Gale, 2010.

Van Dover, J. K., and John F. Jebb. *Isn't Justice Always Unfair? The Detective in Southern Literature*. Bowling Green, OH: Bowling Green University Popular Press, 1996.

Heston, Charlton *(1923–2008)*

"'Hard' is what I do best," Charlton Heston once told a photographer. "I don't do 'nice.'" Strange words, perhaps, coming from an actor who specialized in playing symbols of rectitude such as Moses, Judah Ben-Hur, and even Jehovah himself. Yet this steely-eyed, jut-jawed performer excelled at infusing his heroic portrayals with an almost fearsome iconic power. He brought a comparable flintiness to his civic life as a firearms activist and an itinerant right-wing gadfly.

Heston was born John Charles Carter on October 4, 1923, in Evanston, Illinois. A speech and drama graduate of Northwestern University, he was a stolid if unspectacular presence in Westerns and war pictures of the 1950s. He became well known playing Moses in Cecil B. DeMille's 1956 epic *The Ten Commandments*. That biblical classic started him on a long string of historical parts, including the title roles in *Ben-Hur* (1959), for which he earned an Academy Award for best actor, and *El Cid* (1961). He also played a muscular Michelangelo in *The Agony and the Ecstasy* (1965).

In 1968 Heston made *Planet of the Apes*, a film *Entertainment Weekly* called "the *Citizen Kane* of guilty pleasures." As George Taylor, an astronaut stranded on a world ruled by simians, Heston chews the scenery with the voracity of a starving dog attacking a T-bone steak. Glowering, grimacing, and barking at his ape captors through clenched teeth, Heston is the apotheosis of Nixonian macho. "Damn you! God damn you all to hell!" he rails into the empty sky at the film's climax.

Planet of the Apes proved a career turning point for Heston—the precise moment he made the transformation from respected leading man to endearing camp figure. He solidified that newfound status with two early 1970s science fiction films, *The Omega Man* in 1971 and *Soylent Green* two years later. Both pictures traded on his macho persona, affording him copious amounts of screen time with his shirt off and an automatic weapon in his hand. The reactionary subtext was unmistakable. In the first film he fights off an army of hippie zombies; in the second he vainly tries to save the planet from government-sponsored euthanasia. In both movies he ends up prostrate, sacrificing his own life for humanity, in a crucifixion pose.

There were other prominent roles for Heston in the 1970s. He did a string of disaster movies, most notably *Earthquake* (1974), but turned down the lead in *Jaws* when he had tired of the genre. After growing too old to carry a picture by himself, he settled comfortably into character actor status. He was used, effectively, by Kenneth Branagh as the Player King in the British auteur's 1997 production of *Hamlet*.

Charlton Heston. *Charlton Heston, the heroic star of some of Hollywood's most enduring epic movies of the 1950s and 1960s, was also known for his political activism.* SILVER SCREEN COLLECTION/ HULTON ARCHIVE/GETTY IMAGES.

For the most part, however, Heston concentrated on political endeavors during his later years. He spoke out often and endlessly on right-wing causes, from family values to white pride. "I'm pissed off when Indians say they're Native Americans," he complained to *Time* in 1998. "*I'm* a Native American, for chrisakes!"

Especially dear to Heston's heart was the right to gun ownership. In 1997 Moses, as his critics invariably derided him, was elected first vice president of the National Rifle Association (NRA). The next year the actor ascended to the presidency itself, ousting a candidate who was deemed too conservative by the NRA rank and file. While liberals may have shuddered at the thought of Heston being considered a moderate alternative, the actor continued to provide them with red meat for their fund-raising letters. In speeches he publicly called for the return of a society where one could "love without being kinky . . . be white without feeling guilty" and other back-to-the-future nostrums.

Heston received the Kennedy Center Lifetime Achievement Award in 1997, but his professional output began a sharp decline in the late 1990s, as he underwent hip replacement surgery and prostate cancer treatments. He was diagnosed with Alzheimer's disease in 2002 and subsequently stepped down from his position in the NRA before being awarded the highest civilian honor in the United States, the Presidential Medal of Freedom, by George W. Bush in 2003. Heston died of complications from pneumonia at his home in Beverly Hills, California, on April 5, 2008. His legacy is commemorated by the Charlton Heston Award—presented annually by the American Film Institute—of which he was the first recipient in 2003.

Robert E. Schnakenberg

SEE ALSO: *Academy Awards;* Ben-Hur*;* Citizen Kane*; DeMille, Cecil B.; Disaster Movies;* Entertainment Weekly*; Firearms;* Jaws*;* Planet of the Apes*;* The Ten Commandments*;* Time*.*

BIBLIOGRAPHY

Heston, Charlton. *In the Arena.* New York: Simon & Schuster, 1995.

Mulrine, Anna. "Moses Fights for Gun Rights." *U.S. News & World Report,* May 19, 1997.

Raymond, Emilie. *From My Cold, Dead Hands: Charlton Heston and American Politics.* Lexington: University Press of Kentucky, 2006.

Schilling, Mary-Kaye. "Charlton Heston: Treasured Chest." *Entertainment Weekly,* September 5, 1997.

Higginson, Major Henry Lee *(1834–1919)*

A Boston Brahmin who had been a major in the Civil War, Henry Lee Higginson was the sole founder of the Boston Symphony Orchestra in 1881. He set the example for other businesspeople to establish a tradition of noblesse oblige in the performing arts that in Europe had initially been the province of landed aristocracy.

Higginson approached the task with a unique blend of "boosterism," sound business principles, and overtones of evangelical Christianity and patriotism. He would not tolerate any deviance from the high musical and operational standards he set by the professionals he engaged. Higginson believed firmly that men who had survived the Civil War (he himself had been wounded) had a moral obligation to make America a better country, which meant creating better cultural institutions. It also meant a willingness for an aristocracy—in America it would be composed of businessmen—to step forward and take responsibility for those developments.

Milton Goldin

SEE ALSO: *The Boston Symphony Orchestra.*

BIBLIOGRAPHY

Goldin, Milton. *The Music Merchants.* New York: Macmillan, 1969.

Grimm, Robert T. *Notable American Philanthropists: Biographies of Giving and Volunteering.* Westport, CT: Greenwood Press, 2002.

Johnson, H. Earle. *Symphony Hall, Boston.* Boston: Little, Brown, 1950.

High Definition TV

High definition television (HDTV) refers either to a set of digital television (DTV) standards offering substantially higher picture and sound quality than traditional television systems (standard-definition TV, or SDTV) or to a TV set that supports those standards. Although some HDTV sets are available in standard (nearly square) screen sizes, the overwhelming majority of sets are widescreen, which eliminates most or all of the black bordering, known as the letterbox effect, when watching movies delivered in their original wide format.

The term *high definition* is not in itself new. It was used for a series of television systems produced in the 1930s and 1940s; these included the British 240i and 405i black-and-white systems introduced in 1936 and the American 525i National Television System Committee (NTSC) system from 1941. However, the term can be misleading, as these systems were not high definition by today's standards. The name was intended as a comparison to previous systems. These early versions of HDTV broadcasting used analog technology, but modern HDTV is transmitted digitally and uses video compression.

Modern HD technology arose from an increased desire among the average consumer to replicate the theater-going experience at home. From the 1970s—when color television sets first became commonplace in the average household—to the early twenty-first century, filming technology had significantly advanced, as had the media on which the resulting footage was distributed. Most significantly, both recording and playback devices had transitioned from analog systems to digital systems. While the analog systems were cassette based, the new digital systems relied on optical disc formats—first the highly unpopular laser disc (LD) in the 1980s, then the widely accepted standard digital video (or versatile) disc (DVD) in the 1990s, and most recently the ultra-high-quality Blu-ray Disc (BD) in the first decade of the 2000s. Each format offered picture and sound quality increasingly true to real-life experience.

The transmission of broadcast television also underwent a change from analog to digital beginning in the early 1990s. The Advanced Television Systems Committee (ATSC), which replaced the NTSC, set into action an initiative to transition to digital-only cable systems, switching off almost all analog systems and replacing them with digital systems on June 12, 2009. The handful of regions unable to comply at that time were given an extension until September 1, 2015.

Newer televisions were equipped for the conversion, but older TVs required an adaptor to process the new transmission standards. Since the 1950s television had been broadcast in, and therefore TVs could only render at, either 480i (United States) or 576i (Europe). Digital-only broadcast necessitated a higher line limit, with 625i becoming the new standard. Old TVs just were not able to compete, giving rise to HDTV sets.

The first digital HDTVs became available to consumers in 1995. Rather than the old cathode-ray tube (CRT) construction, these televisions used one of two new constructions: liquid crystal display (LCD) or plasma. Both contained fewer, smaller parts, allowing for unprecedentedly thin TVs. Unlike previous format wars, both LCD and plasma survived, joined later by the organic light-emitting diode (OLED). Plasma TVs were brighter and produced truer colors but used a glass that caused an unpleasant glare. LCD and LED television sets suffered fewer glare issues and were cheaper to produce. None of them, however, was cheap to purchase. Prices on early LCD HDTV sets began in the $2,000–$5,000 range, with many plasma sets costing more than $10,000.

With movie ticket prices rising and HDTV quickly gaining popularity, people began staying home for their entertainment experience. Cable and satellite television providers recognized this and worked toward broadcasting in HD. Though full-time HD broadcast stations would not be available until a few years later, the HDTV system had its public launch in the United States over a digital signal on October 29, 1998, during the live coverage of astronaut John Glenn's return mission to space aboard the space shuttle *Discovery*. By the end of the first decade of the 2000s, most major networks were broadcasting in both SD and HD.

Michele Lellouche

SEE ALSO: *Cable TV; New 3-D; Television.*

BIBLIOGRAPHY

Albiniak, Paige. "HDTV: Launched and Counting." *Broadcasting and Cable* (BNET), November 2, 1998.

Blaszczyk, Regina Lee. *American Consumer Society, 1865–2005: From Hearth to HDTV.* Wheeling, IL: Harlan Davidson, 2009.

Cianci, Philip J. *High Definition Television: The Creation, Development, and Implementation of HDTV Technology.* Jefferson, NC: McFarland, 2012.

"Digital TV: A Cringely Crash Course." Public Broadcasting Service. Accessed June 2012. Available from http://www.pbs.org/opb/crashcourse

Drummond, Mike. "Engadget Primed: HDTV Technologies Detailed, Past and Future." Accessed June 2012. Available from http://www.engadget.com/2011/11/11/engadget-primed-hdtv-technologies-detailed-past-and-future/

Dupagne, Michel, and Peter Benjamin Seel. *High-Definition Television: A Global Perspective.* Ames: Iowa State University Press, 1998.

Ives, John. "Image Formats for HDTV." *EBU Technical Review*, July 2004.

High Noon

Director Fred Zinnemann's film *High Noon* was made during the anti-communist McCarthy era. Consequently it has been invested with political significance beyond the striking simplicity of its plot. The allegorical claims that are made for it originated with its screenwriter, Carl Foreman—a victim of Senator Joseph McCarthy's paranoid hunt for communist sympathizers in Hollywood—who professed to see his script as an allegory of his own situation. Zinnemann denied this interpretation, considering it the story of a man driven to act in accordance with his own conscience, while conceding that the town in which the action takes place is "a symbol of democracy gone soft." The nature of the film's message continues to challenge the film scholars, historians, and critics who examine and analyze it. In the annals of popular culture, however, it remains a classic Western, one of the best of all time. To legions of ordinary moviegoers *High Noon* conjures the lasting image of Gary Cooper's weary and reluctant hero, the young Grace Kelly's ice-maiden beauty, Dimitri Tiomkin's haunting theme song, "Do Not Forsake Me, O My Darling," and Floyd Crosby's atmospheric black-and-white photography.

Foreman based his screenplay on "The Tin Star," a two-page magazine story. Played out in "real time"—the 90 minutes in which the incidents take place correspond to the 85-minute running-time of the film—denoted by Zinnemann's artful use of a clock as a marker that contributes to the tension, the story begins 10:40 a.m. on a Sunday morning in the fictional frontier town of Hadleyville. Marshal Will Kane (Gary Cooper) is at his

***Gary Cooper and Grace Kelly in* High Noon.** *Gary Cooper, left, and Grace Kelly star in a scene from* High Noon *in 1952.* JOHN KOBAL FOUNDATION/GETTY IMAGES.

own wedding reception, prior to retiring and leaving town to start life afresh with his young Quaker bride, Amy (Grace Kelly). During the festivities, however, Kane is warned that Frank Miller (Ian MacDonald), a murderer whom Kane had helped to convict, has been released from the penitentiary. Miller is heading for Hadleyville to exact revenge by killing Kane and will arrive on the 12:00 noon train. Three of Miller's old cohorts are already waiting at the otherwise deserted train depot to escort him into town for the fatal shoot-out.

COUNTDOWN

Amy implores her new husband to leave town immediately. Determined to face down Miller and rid the town of the killer's malevolent influence, however, he ignores her pleadings, and those of others, including Helen Ramirez (Katy Jurado), his former lover. Ramirez urges Kane to take his new bride and escape to safety. For about an hour, from around 10:45 a.m. up to just before noon, Kane attempts to drum up support from the townspeople, but nobody is willing to stand by him. A number of people begin to throw their belongings into wagons, preparing to leave town temporarily before the trouble starts at noon; even Kane's deputy, resentful at having been passed over for the job in favor of a stranger, deserts him. Amy, too, prepares to leave—on the same train that is bringing Miller to town—and, while waiting at the hotel, learns from the clerk that many inhabitants of Hadleyville would like to see Miller kill her husband because they want a return to the kind of town where saloons and gambling are allowed to flourish.

The noon train arrives on time. Frightened and alone, but wedded irrevocably to his own moral code, Kane makes out his will and prepares to face the gunmen, who ride into town. He ambushes one, and kills a second in a shoot-out. Hearing the gunfire Amy rushes to her husband's aid, shooting another of Miller's henchmen in the back. She is seized by Miller himself as a hostage, however. During the struggle that ensues in Amy trying to free herself, Kane is able to shoot Miller dead. He throws his badge in the dust and rides out of the deserted town with his wife.

When *High Noon* was released it was not an immediate hit. In the strained climate of the times, that gesture of Kane's—throwing away his badge—was interpreted by some as an insult to federal authority and led to accusations of subversion. As Zinnemann interpreted it, Kane's action was simply intended as "a gesture of contempt for a craven community." The film captured the public imagination only gradually, but its excellence was recognized in the winning of four Academy Awards (Music Score, Title Song, Editing, and Best Actor) and three nominations (Picture, Screenplay, and Director). Over the years it came to gross several million dollars.

CHANGING THE GENRE

While widely viewed as a classic Western, several commentators consider *High Noon* a realist Western, providing a depiction of a place and its people that was undoubtedly representative of a hundred towns across the frontier during the 1870s. It can also be read as a commentary on the genre itself, one that observes the classical unities of time and action. Some have even credited the film with inaugurating a new subgenre, the adult Western, in its mature treatment of its otherwise familiar good-versus-evil theme. What cannot be denied, however, is that *High Noon* changed the Western genre by both streamlining and rethinking it as both an extension and a commentary upon the classic tradition.

As opposed to the ultimate redemption of townspeople in such later films as *The Magnificent Seven*, the citizens of Hadleyville are craven to the end. This is, of course, in direct opposition to the mythology of the West, in which the venality of the common man is redeemed by a folk hero whose bravery in the face of overwhelming odds inspires the townspeople to rise above themselves for the common good. On the other hand, the contradictory currents running through the town (development versus frontier lawlessness) and the ambivalence of the citizens who, each for their own reasons, refuse to side with Kane can be taken to represent the currents of the American political climate in the 1950s. This interpretation is underpinned by the deliberate vagueness of the town's location and the film's exact historical time period. Thus on an allegorical level Hadleyville could be any town at any point in history, where the common man falls prey to cowardice and fear, and the high moral courage of the few is severely tested. The chronological symmetry of the film and the relentless progress of the ever-present clock not only helps create and maintain tension, but counterpoints Kane's agonizingly slow progress in trying to recruit help and decide his course of action.

GARY COOPER'S CHARACTERIZATION

In its characterizations, the film offers an antimythological touch that sets it apart from most examples of the Western genre. Will Kane does not conform to the usual heroic figure that audiences of the 1950s had come to expect. Both the character and the man who portrays him are somewhat past their prime. Cooper, who was not in the best of health, appeared haggard and drawn. He conveyed an air of world-weariness—precisely the quality that director Zinnemann had in mind. The female characters also depart from the female stereotype found in most Westerns. Though both Helen and Amy are emotionally involved with Will and are diametrically opposed (Helen is a fiery Hispanic businesswoman, Amy a Nordically cool and devout Quaker pacifist), both are highly principled and intelligent and cannot be pigeonholed. They are allowed to move the action forward by their principled stands and are able to bond across ethnic lines while respecting their differences. Both survive the action and give strong evidence of strength and independence. This was not only rare in traditional Westerns but also flew in the face of 1950s American social convention when women had not yet assumed positions of power.

In the opinion of many, *High Noon* has continued to stand head and shoulders above most frontier Westerns in its depiction of ethical conflicts and ideas that cannot be confined to one particular genre, place, or time, but that always seem to manifest themselves in their most elemental form in the Western. The film has been credited as a significant influence on later Westerns, inspiring such thoughtful and revisionist films as *Pat Garrett and Billy the Kid* (1973), *Butch Cassidy and the Sundance Kid* (1969), *The Wild Bunch* (1969), *High Plains Drifter* (1973), *The Shootist* (1976), and *Unforgiven* (1992), all of which dealt with the ending of the Western way of life and the death of the six-gun mentality.

Steve Hanson

SEE ALSO: Butch Cassidy and the Sundance Kid*; Cooper, Gary; Kelly, Grace;* The Magnificent Seven*; McCarthyism;* Unforgiven*; The Western;* The Wild Bunch.

BIBLIOGRAPHY

Bodeen, DeWitt. "High Noon." In *Magill's Survey of Cinema—English Language Films, First Series*, ed. Frank N. Magill. Englewood Cliffs, NJ: Salem Press, 1980.

Combs, Richard. "When the Big Hand Is on the Twelve . . . or 7 Ambiguities of Time." *Monthly Film Bulletin*, June 1986, 188.

Foster, Gwendolyn. "The Women in *High Noon*: A Metanarrative of Difference." *Film Criticism*, Spring 1994, 72–81.

Prince, Stephen. "Historical Perspective and the Realist Aesthetic in *High Noon*." *Film Criticism*, Spring 1994, 59–71.

Reynolds, D. J. "Taking Care of Things: Evolution in the Treatment of a Western Theme, 1947–1957." *Literature/Film Quarterly*, July 1990, 202–208.

Zinnemann, Fred. *A Life in the Movies*. New York: Scribner, 1992.

High School Musical

High School Musical, the Disney Channel's film phenomenon, is widely credited with initiating a pervasive interest in musical theater and film among preteens and teenagers. Originally airing on the Disney Channel in January 2006, the film focuses on the troubled relationship of Troy Bolton (played by Zac Efron) and Gabrielle Montez (played by Vanessa Hudgens), two high school students whose rival social circles attempt to spoil their romance by sabotaging their performance in the school musical. The story features several choreographed musical performances of original songs based around the basic theme of breaking free from the status quo. The creative team responsible for the musical aspects of show included director and choreograph Kenny Ortega, writer Peter Barsocchini, and composer David Lawrence. The film and accompanying soundtrack proved so popular (the soundtrack alone sold well over three million copies and was named *Billboard*'s Soundtrack Album of the Year) that two sequels, several live theater tours, a series of video games and books, and a range of spin-offs on international television followed.

High School Musical focuses on the romance of Troy, the basketball player, and Gabrielle, the science geek. The two meet at a New Year's Eve party, where they team up in a karaoke duet. When Gabrielle later appears as the new girl at Troy's high school, the story evolves into the couple's search for identity as well as love, and they both audition for the school's musical play. Competition annoys the resident theater stars, Sharpay and her brother Ryan (played by Ashley Tisdale and Lucas Grabeel), who try to stop the couple from supplanting them. Troy and Gabrielle eventually change the attitudes of their feuding friends, who then help them land the leads in the school musical.

High School Musical 2 (2007), which became the most-watched show in basic cable history with more than seventeen million viewers, continues the story, as Troy, Gabrielle, and their friends land summer jobs at Sharpay's country club and Troy is forced to resist Sharpay's advances as the group prepares for a new theater production. *High School Musical 3: Senior Year* (released theatrically in 2008) finishes the saga as Troy and Gabrielle plan for their future, the prom, and graduation. When Gabrielle leaves early for college, Troy faces the decision of doing what his father expects (playing basketball for the University of Albuquerque) or staying true to himself and following a dream that includes musical theater. Seeking Gabrielle's advice, he visits her at college and discovers he can have both—basketball and musical theater—at a college near her.

In many ways *High School Musical* echoes back to the "let's put on a show" musicals of the mid-twentieth century, such as *Babes in Arms* (1939) and *Strike Up the Band* (1940), where characters not only perform a play but frequently break into song to illustrate a plot point. The film led a new generation to discover musical theater by introducing characters to which twenty-first-century teens could relate. Although Ryan Murphy, creator of *Glee* (2009–), claims not to have been influenced by the *High School Musical* films, his musical television series owes some of its acceptance and success to viewers being willing to watch a series based around a musical theme. NBC followed with their musical theater series, *Smash*, in 2012.

With the *High School Musical* franchise, Disney found a merchandising gold mine. By developing a style of programming that showcases and promotes its own merchandise, Disney reached a preteen and teenage audience who buy posters and clothing as well as DVDs and CDs that, in turn, create demand for further sequels. Not only did Disney expand the franchise with additional movies, but it also found marketing venues through on-ice, Broadway, and independent high school productions based on the film. The movies have become popular in overseas markets as well, where productions are altered to suit the culture of the host country. Disney theme parks also feature attractions based on the movies, which continually expand the franchise's audience.

The original *High School Musical* film earned a number of awards, including two prime-time Emmy Awards, three Teen Choice Awards, and a Television Critics Association Award. Although the sequels generally received less critical acclaim, they continued to enjoy widespread popularity among teenagers. Some critics have complained that the films present an idealized version of the high school experience, but most reviewers applauded their overall message of pursuing one's dreams even in the face of peer pressure to do otherwise.

Linda Martindale

SEE ALSO: *Amusement Parks; Broadway; Cable TV; Compact Discs; Disney (Walt Disney Company); Emmy Awards;* Glee; *Ice Shows; The Musical; Teenagers; Television; Video Games.*

BIBLIOGRAPHY

Giroux, Henry A., and Grace Pollock. *The Mouse That Roared: Disney and the End of Innocence*. New York: Rowman & Littlefield, 2010.

Meltzer, Melissa. "We're Soaring, We're Flying!: For Every Generation, There Is a Musical." Slate, March 31, 2006. Accessed May 2012. Available from http://www.slate.com

Potter, Anna. "It's a Small World after All: New Media Constellations and Disney's Rising Star." *International Journal of Cultural Studies* 15, no. 2 (2012): 117–130.

Highway System

In the mid-1950s, at a time when automobile manufacturers in Detroit, Michigan, sold 7.92 million cars in one year and 70 percent of American families owned automobiles, the American road system was noted for its inadequacies. There were no four-lane highways except for eastern toll roads, and only cities had expressways. President Dwight D. Eisenhower, who once made the trip from coast to coast using the nation's roads, is credited with originating the interstate highway system. Building the system was more expensive and more elaborate than funding most New Deal programs. The new highways shifted economic power to the Sun Belt, bypassing the main streets and roadside towns that once had served as way stations and homogenizing American roadside culture. By making longer commutes possible, highways changed how many Americans worked.

EARLY ROADS

Americans have long had a fascination with transcontinental travel and with linking both coasts by road. Physician H. Nelson Jackson made the first continental crossing by automobile in 1903, driving from San Francisco to New York in sixty-five days. As early as 1911, Congress introduced legislation calling for seven national highways, one of which was transcontinental.

American travelers of the early twentieth century were often more familiar with Europe than with their own country. New York socialite Emily Post's account of her 1915 cross-country automobile trip illustrates how little faith Americans had in the transcontinental road system. Asked the best road to take across the country, Post's well-traveled friend replied, "the Union Pacific [Railroad]. . . . Once you get beyond the Mississippi the roads are trails of mud and sand. . . . Tell me, where do you think you are going to stop? These are not towns; they are only names on a map, or at best two shacks and a saloon!"

Post's friend's concern was well placed. Most of the improved roads early in the century were near cities, and often "improved" meant merely that the road was graded. There was no asphalt or concrete, and brick and gravel roads were scarce. Bumpy and dusty in dry weather, roads often became impassable for motorists when it rained.

CONNECTING THE COASTS

The formation of the Lincoln Highway Association in 1913 led to the construction of the first coast-to-coast highway at a cost of $10 million. Completed in 1915, the highway ran from San Francisco to New York. Sensing the commercial importance of a continuous route, towns and cities competed for the highway to run through their towns. Called America's Main Street, the Lincoln Highway overlapped much of the Oregon Trail, slashing a sixty- to ninety-day transcontinental automobile trip to twenty to thirty days. Despite the improvements, the two-lane routes, with their low speed limits and stop-and-go traffic, continued to hamper the trucking industry.

Americans in the late 1920s were eager to use the new roads to visit popular tourist attractions such as the Henry Ford Museum and Greenfield Village. The completion of long-span bridges such as the San Francisco–Oakland Bay Bridge; the Golden Gate Bridge; and the Mark Twain Memorial Bridge in Hannibal, Missouri, further eased road travel during the 1930s. Yet the Lincoln Highway (U.S. Route 30) and the William Penn Highway (U.S. Route 22) remained a nightmare to drive, especially through rough terrain such as the Allegheny Mountains of western Pennsylvania. During winter the narrow roads' sharp curves and steep grades made travel so treacherous that trucking companies rerouted their shipping hundreds of miles in order to avoid problems.

Toll roads were the first major development in the highway system. The Pennsylvania Turnpike, which opened in 1940, became "the first long-distance, high-speed, limited-access, four-lane divided road—the direct conceptual predecessor of the interstate system," writes Dan Cupper in "The Road to the Future." At the time, only 11,070 out of three million miles of roadway were wider than two lanes. The turnpike marked a revolution in road design, and on opening day, motorists waited up to four hours to try out the new highway.

EISENHOWER'S VISION

After decades of false starts by Congress on the issue of highway development, Eisenhower in 1954 became the first to make progress toward a national highway system. Like many other Americans who fought in Europe during World War II, he had been impressed by Adolf Hitler's autobahns, Germany's modern, broad four-lane highways. Eisenhower sought to create a national transport system to facilitate military movement and evacuation during the Cold War. The Formosa Strait crisis of 1955, in which U.S.–Chinese tensions rose over the perceived threat of mainland communists to Taiwan, underscored the need for such a system. Although there was little danger of large-scale military conflict with China, the incident raised concerns about America's ability to evacuate large cities such as Washington, D.C.

Eisenhower had a personal connection to building the highway system. In 1919, as a lieutenant colonel, he had joined an army truck convoy on a cross-country trip to test army vehicles. Traveling from Washington, D.C., mostly along the Lincoln Highway, the convoy of almost 300 men took sixty-two days to reach San Francisco. Biographer Stephen Ambrose writes that Eisenhower considered it "a lark. He camped out for the entire summer, hunting and fishing, playing practical jokes and poker, and thoroughly enjoying himself." However, he also learned just how "miserable the American road network was—the convoy hardly averaged five miles per hour."

Eisenhower faced many of the same obstacles that had hindered road builders for two decades. The federal and state governments continued to dispute whose responsibility it was to pay for the system. The high price of urban land acquisition drove costs higher, and construction stalled as funding methods were debated. Yet Eisenhower, writes Ambrose, "envisioned a road network that would link all U.S. cities with populations of 50,000 or more with defense installations." The main part of the system would be composed of farm-to-city routes, with highways that traveled around cities rather than through them.

In order to gain congressional votes for the 1956 Interstate Highway Bill, the president's administration negotiated a large share of expenditures for big cities that largely opposed the bill. Eisenhower considered funding the system by levying a tax on city-bound automobiles, but he soon abandoned the idea. His vision of prohibiting billboards along the new highways also failed to materialize.

SOCIAL AND ECONOMIC IMPACT

Regardless of its imperfections, the new highway system had enormous impact. Economic power shifted away from the small towns that routes once passed through, and new sectors of the economy grew around beltways. City freeways changed patterns of urban life as planners sacrificed entire neighborhoods to make way for new roads. Highways also facilitated the spread of the suburbs, which caused a middle-class exodus from the cities. The era of highway building ended around 1969 due to backlash against destruction of neighborhoods. Congress began diverting money toward mass transit, slowing funding for maintenance of the highway system.

The man who shared Eisenhower's vision, Francis Turner, was caught in the backlash as he became head of the Federal Highway Administration. The former secretary to the committee charged with implementing the highway system praised the construction of farm-to-city routes and derided mass, or rapid, transit, calling it "rabbit transit." Nevertheless, many Americans decried the changes in roadside culture, citing the highway system as a homogenizing factor. Drake Hokanson in *The Lincoln Highway* writes that highways made it possible to "cross the entire state of Wyoming and never smell sagebrush," giving Americans instead a "great franchised monoculture that extends from sea to sea."

American writers have long paid homage to the road. "O public road," serenaded poet Walt Whitman in 1855, "You express me better than I can express myself." In *The Grapes of Wrath* (1939), novelist John Steinbeck portrayed the road as symbolic of the Okies' search for prosperity during the Great Depression. Beat writer Jack Kerouac, especially in *On the Road* (1957), portrayed the new highways as a place to find adventure. Subsequently, Kerouac's vision was made palatable for mainstream consumption and popularized in such productions as the existential television drama *Route 66* (1960–1964). Named after the highway that ran through the American Southwest, *Route 66* featured two young drifters who drove a Corvette through small towns and cities, encountering outcasts and dreamers.

A TECHNOLOGICAL ACHIEVEMENT

Not all Americans lamented the construction of the new highway system. Long-haul truckers and travelers could drive from one coast to the other in less than a week. With even-numbered roads traveling east–west and odd-numbered ones heading north–south, even those unfamiliar with a particular area generally found the new system easy to navigate. Many regarded the new roadways as technological marvels and the "roads to the future." Designers mitigated delays by creating cloverleaf intersections, in which two highways interchange through a system of ramps that resembles a four-leaf clover. Early postcards of highway systems with the legend "America's Super Highway" portrayed the sort of regard for highways that seemed inconceivable in later years.

Because highways have become an integral part of the American landscape, changes to the system are seldom felt, though they may be easily measured. By the turn of the twenty-first century, the average motorist traveled about 3,000 miles a year on the interstate system. The number of accidents per year remained more or less constant before and after the construction of the interstates; however, the number of vehicles tripled between the 1950s and 1990s. By 2012 the Interstate Highway System covered 46,876 miles at a total cost of $425 billion. Although the system constitutes just 1.1 percent of all American roads, it supports 24 percent of all highway travel in the United States.

Even more expansive than Eisenhower and his contemporaries had dreamed, the highway system marked a new era of settlement in America. Although the pioneers had been replaced by drivers with cars named after explorers, such as DeSoto and Cadillac, the spirit of adventure remained. Highway culture mitigated fears of the unknown through roadside tourist attractions, familiar brand-name advertising, and restaurant and hotel chains. Although many Americans look back upon the 1950s as a dull and sterile decade, the era nevertheless marked the taming of a new frontier.

Daryl Umberger

SEE ALSO: *Automobile; The Beat Generation; Billboards; Cadillac; Cold War; The Corvette; The Fifties; Ford, Henry; Gas Stations; Golden Gate Bridge; The Great Depression; New Deal;* On the Road*; Route 66; Steinbeck, John; Twain, Mark; World War II.*

BIBLIOGRAPHY

Ambrose, Stephen E. *Eisenhower: Soldier, General of the Army, President-Elect, 1890–1952, Vol. 1.* New York: Simon & Schuster, 1983.

Ambrose, Stephen E. *Eisenhower: The President, Vol. 2.* New York: Simon & Schuster, 1984.

Block, Lawrence. "How Have We Changed?" *American Heritage*, December 1994, 62.

Cupper, Dan. "The Road to the Future." *American Heritage*, May/June 1990, 102–111.

Hokanson, Drake. *The Lincoln Highway: Main Street across America.* Iowa City: Iowa University Press, 1988.

Kammen, Michael G. *Mystic Chords of Memory: The Transformation of Tradition in American Culture.* New York: Alfred A. Knopf, 1991.

Karnes, Thomas L. *Asphalt and Politics: A History of the American Highway System.* Jefferson, NC: McFarland, 2009.

Lockridge, Deborah, and Jack Roberts. "How We Got Our Highway System." *Overdrive*, July 1996, 54–57.

Patton, Phil. *Open Road: A Celebration of the American Highway.* New York: Simon & Schuster, 1986.

Patton, Phil. "Agents of Change." *American Heritage*, December 1994, 88–109.

Perrier, Dianne. *Onramps and Overpasses: A Cultural History of Interstate Travel.* Gainesville: University of Florida, 2009.

Radal, Dave. "Trail Lore Connects E. Iowans: Lincoln Highway's Reputation Outlasts the Original Pavement." *Cedar Rapids Gazette*, September 27, 1998, 1.

Rose, Mark H. *Interstate: Express Highway Politics, 1941–1956.* Lawrence: Regents Press of Kansas, 1979.

Sky, Theodore. *The National Road and the Difficult Path to Sustainable National Investment.* Newark, NJ: University of Delaware Press, 2011.

Hijuelos, Oscar *(1951–)*

A New Yorker with Cuban heritage, Oscar Hijuelos has written, among other works, best-selling epic family sagas of the twentieth-century Cuban American experience. His debut, *Our House in the Last World* (1983), charts the cultural identity crisis of two brothers and their Cuban-born parents in New York during the years after World War II. The Pulitzer Prize–winning *The Mambo Kings Play Songs of Love* (1989) flamboyantly depicts 1950s New York as a musical, multicultural melting pot. The

Irish-Cuban protagonist of *The Fourteen Sisters of Emilio Montez O'Brien* (1993) is torn between fulfilling the mainstream American Dream of movie stardom and the doting, redeeming love of his all-female family.

All of Hijuelos's novels, including even the more understated and contemplative *Mr. Ives' Christmas* (1995), exhibit a troubled fascination with the cultural hegemony of Hollywood. It is therefore appropriately ironic that the 1992 Warner Brothers production, *The Mambo Kings*, brought Hijuelos's work to a wider, moviegoing public. The book also became a stage musical in 2005. In 2002 Hijuelos and his wife, Lori Marie Carlson, visited Cuba, where they were struck by the country's extreme wealth and extreme poverty. That experience inspired them to coedit *Burnt Sugar Caña Quemada: Contemporary Cuban Poetry in English and Spanish* (2006). Hijuelos produced *Dark Dude*, a novel for young adults, in 2008. Other works include *A Simple Habana Melody: From When the World Was Good* (2002), *Beautiful Maria of My Soul* (2010), and *Thoughts without Cigarettes* (2011).

Martyn Bone

SEE ALSO: *Best Sellers; Hollywood; Latin Jazz; World War II.*

BIBLIOGRAPHY

Borinsky, Alicia. *One-Way Tickets: Writers and the Culture of Exile.* San Antonio, TX: Trinity University Press, 2011.

Kevane, Bridget A. *Latino Literature in America: Literature as Windows to World Cultures.* Westport, CT: Greenwood, 2003.

Hiking

As views of nature in the United States began to change during the twentieth century, so too did the recreational practice of hiking. During the last century hiking was linked to a love of the outdoors and was a means by which to express a connection to the land. But as the meaning of the American landscape for U.S. citizens changed with time, so too did the popular meaning of hiking.

The idea of hiking for amusement would not gain widespread attention until the presidency of Theodore Roosevelt (1901–1909). With the ear of the nation, Roosevelt became the greatest proponent of outdoor appreciation. While earlier politicians had urged the American public to exploit natural resources, farm, and conquer wilderness, Roosevelt often called for the preservation of nature. Deeply influenced by the British Imperial fashion of becoming a "man" by entering and besting nature, Roosevelt traveled to many wild places. In the Dakotas, Michigan, and other parts of the United States, Roosevelt "roughed it" by camping and hunting. He helped to popularize a masculinity based not on comfort and cultivation but upon strength and the ability to tolerate hardship. By entering into nature's realm, it was possible to prove a "rugged individualism."

Roosevelt's regard for nature and individualism coincided with and helped forge America's emerging sense of itself as a new kind of nation. American democratic ideals clashed with the popular concepts of privilege and elitism of the European aristocracy. Fearing European "flabbiness" and "slothful ease," Roosevelt and others promoted contact with nature so as to cultivate in American citizens a "vigorous manliness" and a "life of strenuous endeavor."

At the same time, the United States began to grow into an industrial giant, reaping seemingly limitless resources from a great expanse. To hike was to enter nature and to appreciate the land. The United States was coming to see itself as a nation favored by God, and its land was part of God's gift to the nation. Roosevelt, along with naturalists such as John Muir and Aldo Leopold, was also concerned with preserving the stunning beauty of the United States.

Europe had annihilated much of its wilderness, and American citizens and corporations had already plundered millions of acres. The still-popular writings of Henry David Thoreau and Muir, the paintings of Thomas Moran, and later the photography of Ansel Adams revealed new ways of seeing the natural world. A powerful "wilderness cult" became the vanguard of a movement to protect millions of acres of wilderness. This movement somewhat slowed resource extraction and greatly accelerated forest recreation. From all these ideas, hiking eventually came into being.

Ironically, it was the popularity of the automobile that gave hiking its greatest boost. As the twentieth century aged, the proliferation of cars brought millions of American citizens to the

Hiking in Shenandoah National Forest. *A hiker makes his way from Mary's Rock and Thornton Gap in Shenandoah National Park in 2011.* **BENJAMIN C. TANKERSLEY FOR THE WASHINGTON POST/GETTY IMAGES.**

forests and parks. In the 1950s widespread car ownership, new parks, and new ideas about recreation in nature resulted in an explosion in visits to wilderness preserves. At this time hiking was typically a short jaunt from the car, followed by a picnic. Though adventurous, hiking was closely affiliated with the prevailing notion that leisure was to be relaxing and peaceful.

People often see wilderness as the antithesis of civilization. As such, hiking in the wilderness offers salvation from a variety of social ills. For example, urbanites throughout the past century sometimes went hiking to have contact with a natural world that they seldom saw. Overdeveloped suburbs and concrete jungles of urban blight left some people alienated from the natural world. Hiking could renew the spirit. In the 1970s the fitness movement and the environmental movement changed the practice of hiking. Better and lighter equipment—the external frame backpack, the down sweater, and the lighter hiking boots—helped to increase enjoyment of overnight adventures.

In the 1970s and 1980s hiking grew exponentially. As the nation sought to move beyond the pain of the Vietnam War and as environmentalism grew in popularity, communing with nature was a way of living simply and finding harmony with the earth. By being in the woods, many hikers were enacting their environmental beliefs and getting back to nature. Groups such as the Sierra Club not only lobbied the government to preserve the wilderness but also recruited hikers as part of their preservation strategy. Hikers were easily converted to conservation, and they helped to change the way the wilderness was used.

From the 1970s onward, hiking was extended to all parts of the continent, as places once looked upon as wastelands were seen and experienced as sites of stark, arid beauty. In a sense, these areas were symbolically reclaimed for nature through the act of hiking. Land once considered useless for anything but resource extraction could be transformed by hiking—hiking literally made use of the land.

Dylan Clark

SEE ALSO: *Adams, Ansel; Automobile; Camping.*

BIBLIOGRAPHY

Benson, W. Todd. *Theodore Roosevelt's Conservation Legacy.* Haverford, PA: Infinity Publishing, 2003.

Devall, Bill, and George Sessions. *Deep Ecology.* Salt Lake City, UT: Peregrine Smith Books, 1985.

Gruen, Lori, and Dale Jamieson, eds. *Reflecting on Nature: Readings in Environmental Philosophy.* New York: Oxford University Press, 1994.

Nash, Roderick. *Wilderness and the American Mind.* New Haven, CT: Yale University Press, 1982.

Thoreau, Henry David. *The Portable Thoreau,* ed. Carl Bode. New York: Viking, 1964.

Hill, Anita

SEE: *Anita Hill–Clarence Thomas Senate Hearings.*

Hill Street Blues

First airing on January 15, 1981, and ending its broadcast television run on May 12, 1987, *Hill Street Blues* broke new ground to become one of the most critically acclaimed television dramas ever. The show won twenty-six Emmy Awards for NBC. Police dramas had been a staple, if not a cliché, since the beginning of prime-time television broadcasting, with shows such as *CHiPS* and *Dragnet* setting the standard from the 1950s onward. These series featured straitlaced, tight-lipped cops upholding the law in a black-and-white world where every crime was solved within thirty minutes. The focus changed radically when NBC president Fred Silverman, his network mired in third place, gave Steven Bochco free rein to create and produce a show that would reinvent television police drama. As Robert J. Thompson, director of the Center for the Study of Popular Television at Syracuse University, summarized it, "What Bochco did in 1981 was change the television cop show by making it more realistic."

LANDMARK STYLE, COMPLEX CHARACTERS

Bochco had chosen television over work in film, and both he and the medium benefited. After graduating from the Carnegie Institute of Technology (now Carnegie Mellon University), Bochco had a film script produced at Universal Studios in 1971. By the time *Silent Running* (a knockoff of *2001: A Space Odyssey*), starring Bruce Dern, was released, Bochco had decided to leave film for television. He told British ITV's distinguished *South Bank Show* presenter Melvyn Bragg, "In a week and a half I wrote a script. . . . It was a shocking experience for me. It was so devalued by the actors involved, and . . . it made me determine somehow to get more control over the things I wrote." Seeking that control in television, Bochco wrote several scripts for the *NBC Sunday Mystery Movie*, *Columbo* (also produced at Universal Studios), between 1971 and 1973 and, with these writing credits to back him up, he created or produced several television pilots and series for NBC, including *The Invisible Man* (1975), *Delvecchio* (1976), and *Paris* (1979). With his television apprenticeship behind him and NBC's Nielsen ratings in the doldrums in the late 1970s and early 1980s, Bochco got his opportunity. The result was *Hill Street Blues.*

Much of the show's style derived from police documentary films, particularly Susan and Alan Raymond's *Police Tapes* (1977) and Frederick Wiseman's *Law and Order* (1969). The cinema verité style adopted for *Hill Street Blues* had previously been seen on television only in the news, and it lent a startling immediacy and realism to prime-time drama. *Hill Street* employed shaky, handheld cameras and grainy film stock that appeared to be the result of preexposing, or "flashing," the stock. The result was a low-contrast, shadowy, and claustrophobic world, well suited to the characters and story lines. Interior shots were particularly tight, busy with supporting cast members and extras going about police business in the background, while close shots of the main characters filled the foreground. This heightened realism had a profound influence on the genre and altered the style of successive series, which were quick to apply the new gritty, hard-edged approach of *Hill Street.*

In addition to its landmark style, *Hill Street*'s plot lines and subject matter were also new to prime-time network dramas. Law and order were negotiated in interrogation rooms and courtrooms, and the lines between criminal and cop were often blurred. The serial nature of *Hill Street* was also critical to this more naturalistic treatment of the criminal justice system. While such prime-time soap operas as *Dallas* had serial plots, the impulse of most police dramas was to present a self-contained story in a closed thirty-minute format or, as Bochco had learned with *Columbo*, a two-hour movie slot. But the plots and the characters that filled *Hill Street* were too complex for quick resolution.

The characters, too, were innovative, exhibiting human dimensions of weakness as well as strength that came to dictate character-driven cop series such as the contemporaneous *Cagney and Lacey* and, notably, of course, Bochco's later *NYPD Blue*. Bochco, rather curiously, described his characters in a 1997 *New York Times* interview as "broad-brushed, almost comedic. . . . " Foremost among the ensemble cast was Precinct Captain Frank Furillo, played by Daniel J. Travanti. Furillo is an unwaveringly ethical leader, a recovering alcoholic (as was Travanti) eventually married to sane and professional public defender Joyce Davenport, played by Veronica Hamel. Other characters are more idiosyncratic. Frank's shrill ex-wife (played by Bochco's wife, Barbara Bosson) is arrested for marijuana possession in one episode. Sergeant Phil Esterhaus (Michael Conrad) dies of a heart attack *in medias coitus*. And Detective Mick Belker (Bruce Weitz) is not above biting suspects to subdue them. Other cast members included Charles Haid, Michael Warren, Taurean Blacque, Kiel Martin, Ed Marinaro, Joe Spano, Rene Enriquez, James B. Sikking, and Dennis Franz as Detective Norman Buntz. Franz's relationship with Bochco crossed over into *NYPD Blue*.

IMITATORS

Hill Street Blues, along with the sitcom *Cheers*, made NBC's Thursday lineup unbeatable and helped the network climb back into the Nielsen ratings race by the mid-1980s. Mike Post's theme music became a hit on radio, just as his theme for *The Rockford Files* had done in the 1970s. By the end of the decade *Hill Street* had spawned innumerable imitators, including *St. Elsewhere* (often called "*Hill Street* in a hospital"). Bochco continued experimenting with the form, creating a show about minor league ballplayers called *Bay City Blues*, but he was not infallible. The 1990 musical drama *Cop Rock*, in which characters launched into song in the middle of an arrest or a court proceeding, was a bizarre and unfortunate mistake. *NYPD Blue*, Bochco's series for ABC, first aired in October 1994 and continued to push the envelope where content was concerned, airing mild nudity, which caused some affiliates to cancel or preempt the show. The furor died down after the first season, and *NYPD Blue* became a huge and ongoing critical and ratings success. Bochco then broke new ground yet again with *Murder One* (1995), a one-season serial that followed one murder trial to its conclusion and carried unmistakable resonances of the O. J. Simpson case.

In a 1995 interview in the *New York Times*, Bochco, referring to *Murder One*, clarified his vision for television drama. "What we're trying to do," he said, "is create a long term impact. One which requires its viewership to defer gratification for a while, to control that impulse in anticipation of a more complex and fully satisfying closure down the road. It's the same commitment you make when you open up to the first page of a novel." And Travanti reminisced in a 1997 interview in the *Washington Post*, "It's nice to know that in a minor key, we are legendary." Unlike most such legends, however, *Hill Street Blues* indubitably had an impact on American cultural expectations of the genre, and the successful series that have followed in its wake stand on its shoulders.

Tim Arnold

SEE ALSO: *Bochco, Steven;* Cagney and Lacey*;* Cheers*;* Columbo*;* Dragnet*; Emmy Awards;* NYPD Blue*; Simpson, O. J.; Simpson Trial;* St. Elsewhere.

BIBLIOGRAPHY

Douglas, Pamela. *Writing the TV Drama Series: How to Succeed as a Professional Writer in TV*, 2nd ed. Studio City, CA: Michael Wiese Productions, 2007.

Thompson, Robert J. *Television's Second Golden Age: From "Hill Street Blues" to "ER"*. Syracuse, NY: Syracuse University Press, 1996.

Hillerman, Tony *(1925–2008)*

Starting with his first published book, *The Blessing Way* (1970), Tony Hillerman's highly regarded series of police procedural detective novels based on Navajo customs and culture brought a unique perspective to the detective fiction genre. His two Native American detectives, Joe Leaphorn and Jim Chee, pursue their investigations in and around the Navajo reservation that covers parts of Arizona, New Mexico, and Utah. Hillerman's major innovation to detective fiction was to transplant an essentially European American method of detection into the Native American cultural context. This approach revealed the European American method's shortcomings and addressed Native American concerns by showing that a detective must have intimate knowledge of the specific culture in which a crime takes place. Without that knowledge of cultural difference, the so-called analytical method of detection cannot be used successfully to solve a mystery. For a white writer even to consider entering such a difficult cultural arena as this is remarkable in itself, but Hillerman managed it with great sensitivity and subtlety. This was confirmed in 1987, when he was made a Special Friend of the Dineh by the Navajo Tribal Council.

Hillerman was born and brought up in a small farming settlement near Konawa, Oklahoma. His father and uncle ran a farm and a general store during the 1930s. Hillerman attributed his skill as a storyteller to the social gatherings on the front porch of the store, describing his mother in particular as a great storyteller. He escaped Dust Bowl–struck Potawatomie County first by attending Oklahoma State University and later, having dropped out of his chemical engineering degree to help on the farm, by enlisting in the army and going to fight in Europe.

Hillerman was involved in the D-day landings and, according to his October 2008 obituary in the *Guardian* newspaper, received silver and bronze stars for valor. He was awarded the Purple Heart after being injured by a mine. Extracts from his wartime letters home were published as a story by a journalist with the *Daily Oklahoman*, and it is this that pushed Hillerman toward writing as a career. After the war he returned to the University of Oklahoma, where he gained a bachelor of arts degree in journalism. Suitably qualified, he found work as a journalist for newspapers and news bureaus in Oklahoma, Texas, and New Mexico. His decision to begin writing fiction coincided with his return to academic study. After completing a master of arts degree in 1965, he became a faculty member at the University of New Mexico in Albuquerque, where he eventually became chair of the Department of Journalism.

Hillerman published eighteen Leaphorn and Chee mystery novels, the last being *The Shape Shifter* (2006). In 1995 he departed from detective fiction to write a novel, *Finding Moon*, based in Asia at the time of the fall of Saigon. He wrote detective short stories and nonfiction essays and books on subjects such as the southwestern states, Navajo culture, and the process of writing. He also wrote two children's books, edited various collections of essays about the West, and (with Rosemary Herbert) was the editor of *The Oxford Book of American Detective Stories* (1996) and *A New Omnibus of Crime* (2009). In 2001 he published a memoir, *Seldom Disappointed*.

For a man who grew up in relative poverty and cultural isolation, Hillerman achieved remarkable success, both in his career on the faculty of the University of New Mexico and, especially, as a writer of detective fiction. Critical responses to his fiction are almost universally good, although he has been described as preachy. Hillerman served as president of the Mystery Writers of America (MWA). Among his awards were a Malice Domestic Lifetime Achievement Award (2002); an Owen Wister Award for Lifetime Achievement, from the Western Writers of America (2008); and in 1991, the MWA Grandmaster Award and the French Grand Prix de Littérature Policière. He won the prestigious MWA Edgar Allan Poe Award for *Dance Hall of the Dead* in 1973.

Chris Routledge

SEE ALSO: *Detective Fiction; Wister, Owen.*

BIBLIOGRAPHY

Carlson, Michael. "Tony Hillerman." Obituary in the *Guardian*, October 31, 2008. Accessed January 25, 2012. Available from http://www.guardian.co.uk/books/2008/oct/31/tony-hillerman-obituary

Erisman, Fred. "Tony Hillerman." *Western Writers Series*. No. 87. Boise, ID: Boise State University, 1989.

Herbert, Rosemary. "Tony Hillerman." *The Fatal Art of Entertainment: Interviews with Mystery Writers*, 85–111. New York: G. K. Hall, 1994.

Murray, David. "Reading the Signs: Detection and Anthropology in the Work of Tony Hillerman." In *Criminal Proceedings: The Contemporary American Crime Novel*, ed. Peter Messent, 127–149. London: Pluto Press, 1997.

Reilly, John M. *Tony Hillerman: A Critical Companion*. Westport, CT: Greenwood Press, 1996.

The Hills

MTV's wildly popular reality show *The Hills*, along with its predecessor *Laguna Beach: The Real Orange County* and its sequel *The City*, represented a new format for television programming. Combining the slick production values and organized drama of a scripted show with the intimate immediacy of the reality genre, *The Hills* became a must-see program for millions of viewers during the six seasons it ran, from 2006 through 2010.

The Hills was a spin-off of *Laguna Beach*, which ran on MTV from 2004 to 2006. *Laguna Beach* itself had been MTV's response to the popular Fox scripted drama *The O.C.*, purporting to show the reality of life among the young, beautiful, and privileged in a wealthy beach community in Southern California's Orange County. *The Hills* takes up where *Laguna Beach* ends, with *Laguna Beach* star Lauren Conrad moving to Los Angeles to take a job with *Teen Vogue*.

In addition to Conrad, who narrates the show, the original core cast of *The Hills* included Lauren's roommate Heidi Montag, her coworker Whitney Port, and her neighbor Audrina Patridge. Love interests of the four include Jason Wahler, Spencer Pratt, Justin Brescia, and Brody Jenner. Conrad, Montag, and Port left the show after several seasons and were replaced by Kristin Cavallari, Stephanie Pratt, and Lo Bosworth.

Like many MTV reality shows, *The Hills* features a cast of glamorous young people living and working together, dating, breaking up, forming friendships, and betraying friends, much like the plot on any soap opera. However, instead of actors playing roles, the dramatic tension on *The Hills* is intensified by the supposition that the events unfolding on the screen and the emotional responses of the cast are real. Unlike other reality shows, there is no "confessional" where actors talk directly to the camera, and the presence of a film crew is not overt. Many scenes seem either rehearsed or so fortuitous as to be unbelievable as reality programming, such as a phone call that comes at exactly the right moment to be caught on camera.

However, fans seemed more than willing to suspend their disbelief; throughout its run, *The Hills* averaged three million viewers per episode, and many more streamed the show on their computers the day after it was aired on TV. The show was especially popular with teenagers and young women, who avidly compared notes in Internet chat rooms and fan websites, cheering for their favorite couples, booing their villains, and debating continually whether the show was real or not and whether they should care.

The last episode of *The Hills* aired on July 13, 2010, and the show's long run ended with a wink to the reality-or-not controversy. In the last scene, Jenner says goodbye to Cavallari, who is leaving for Europe. Cavallari's limo drives off, and the camera lingers on Jenner, who stands with the Hollywood hills in the background. After a moment the hills move away, revealing themselves as a backdrop, and the camera pans out showing that the scene has taken place on a studio lot, in what appears to be a visual admission that *The Hills* was all fiction.

The stars of *The Hills* moved on to other projects. Conrad launched two lines of clothing, the high-end Paper Crown and the more affordable LC Lauren Conrad. In 2009 she published *L.A. Candy*, a young adult novel about a young woman's experiences on a reality television show. Port launched her own fashion line, Whitney Eve, and moved to New York City, where she appeared on another MTV reality show, *The City*, which focused on more beautiful people working at glamorous jobs.

Both Conrad and Cavallari have admitted in interviews that large parts of *The Hills* were scripted, though others, such as Kelly Cutrone, a New York publicist who appeared on the show for a time, insist that it was not. Though the controversy continues, it is clear that programs such as *The Hills* are part of the changing face of television. Networks, ever eager to cut costs, see reality programming as a way to avoid the demands of high-priced union actors and writers. And if reality itself gets inconvenient or boring, enhanced—or heightened—reality shows such as *The Hills* seem to provide the best of both worlds, even if they do breed a more cynical audience in the process.

Tina Gianoulis

SEE ALSO: *MTV; Reality Television; Television.*

BIBLIOGRAPHY

Amsden, David. "Run for *The Hills*: MTV's Heightened Reality Spinoff, *The City*, Is Coming to New York." *New York*, January 5, 2009, 30.

"*The Hills* Have Lies." Accessed May 2012. Available from http://realscreen.com/2007/12/01/page24c-20071201/

Weiss, Joanna. "A Reality Check on *The Hills*." *Boston Globe*, April 5, 2008. Accessed May 2012. Available from http://www.boston.com/ae/tv/articles/2008/04/05/a_reality_check_on_the_hills/?page=full

Hilton, Paris *(1981–)*

Few people in the news epitomize the twenty-first-century cult of celebrity more perfectly than socialite Paris Hilton, one of the heirs to the vast Hilton Hotel fortune. First exposed to public view when a video of her sexual activity with a boyfriend was leaked on the Internet, Hilton instantly became the sort of celebrity whom American society loves to hate: superficial, self-centered, and absurd. Paparazzi obsessively follow her, and the public is fascinated by her privileged lifestyle. A child of wealth and excess, Hilton came of age early in the first decade of the 2000s, an era of irony and technology, and she managed to turn her often-ridiculed image of clueless bimbo into a multimillion-dollar industry of Paris Hilton products. Her blithe, fun-loving image and her revealing fashions have been especially influential with preteen and teenage girls.

The name Hilton has long been the hallmark of luxury hotel accommodations. Paris Hilton's great-grandfather was Conrad Hilton (1887–1979), an entrepreneur from New Mexico who bought his first hotel in 1919 and built a worldwide financial empire before his death. Conrad stunned the public and his relatives by leaving the majority of his fortune to charity, but his son, Barron, successfully contested the will, preserving much of the family wealth. Barron and his wife, Marilyn, had eight children, one of whom was Richard. In 1979 Richard married Kathy Avanzino, and they had four children, the oldest of whom is Paris.

Paris Whitney Hilton was born in New York, New York, in 1981. Given her family's wealth, she immediately faced a life of privilege, social activity, and media exposure. Along with attending fashionable parties, she began modeling at charity events as a child and got a contract with a modeling agency while she was still in her teens. Because the family moved frequently among luxurious homes around the country, Hilton's education was often interrupted. Although she attended several prestigious schools, she did not graduate from high school and later completed the General Educational Development (GED) test.

Hilton unsuccessfully tried acting, obtaining small roles in movies such as the horror film *Nine Lives* (2002). It was, however, her social life that attracted the attention of the press. Along with her younger sister, Nicky, Hilton became a regular at lavish parties and red-carpet receptions, and the press was captivated by her style-setting glamour.

Adulation of Hilton's looks, style, and trendy lifestyle always went hand in hand with criticism of the shallow values and conspicuous consumption of that lifestyle, and the same media that created her celebrity mocked her as unworthy of it. In 2003 Hilton's growing popularity received a blow when a videotape showing her and former boyfriend Rick Salomon engaged in sex appeared on the Internet. Hilton first denied being in the video, then sued Salomon for publishing and profiting from it.

VARIOUS BUSINESS VENTURES

Also in 2003 Hilton capitalized on her privileged image by starring in *The Simple Life*, a Fox network reality television show featuring Hilton and party-circuit friend Nicole Richie as they interacted with simpler folk in a variety of situations. In the first season they join a family on an Arkansas farm, where they learn to milk cows while wearing impossibly inappropriate fashions. The young stars constantly demonstrate their complete lack of practical knowledge (they cannot remember to carry cash and think that Wal-Mart is a store that sells walls), and audiences found their fish-out-of-water naïveté comic and endearing. *The Simple Life* drew thirteen million viewers for its first episodes and lasted five seasons, ending in 2007.

The popularity Hilton gained on *The Simple Life* led to even more media demand. She not only filmed controversially sexy commercials for Guess? jeans and Carl's Jr. hamburgers, but she also launched her own lines of clothing, fragrance, shoes, nail polish, and dog fashions. In 2004 she opened Club Paris nightspots in Las Vegas, Nevada, and Orlando, Florida, and in 2006 she recorded a single, "Stars Are Blind," and an album, *Paris*, which together sold almost 200,000 copies.

In 2007 scandal once again placed Hilton in the middle of public controversy. Driving illegally with a suspended license, she was stopped by police for reckless driving and sentenced to forty-five days in jail. The sentence horrified Hilton, who protested in tears and polarized the public into those who thought the punishment too harsh and those who demanded the justice system not favor the rich. The furor increased when a Los Angeles County sheriff, accustomed to accommodating celebrities, converted the sentence to house arrest, but a judge restored the jail time, and Hilton spent slightly more than three weeks locked up.

With her arrest and other such incidents, Hilton's image as pampered bad girl became firmly established. Along with similarly stereotyped friends, such as singer Britney Spears and actress Lindsay Lohan, she was frequently portrayed in the media as an out-of-control degenerate. The 2007 *Guinness Book of World Records* lists Hilton as the World's Most Overrated Person, and a November 2006 *New York Post* captioned a photo of Hilton, Spears, and Lohan, "Bimbo Summit."

In 2007 in a move that might be considered poetic justice, Barron Hilton announced his intention to leave 97 percent of his almost $2.5 billion fortune to a charitable foundation, drastically reducing bequests to heirs. Journalists speculated that his actions were, in part, a condemnation of his granddaughter's reckless lifestyle.

In 2008 Paris Hilton returned to television with *Paris Hilton's My New BFF*, a reality competition in which contestants vie to be Hilton's latest BFF (best friend forever). The show received some scathing reviews, but it was popular enough to spawn a second season and spin-offs in the United Kingdom and Dubai. In 2011 another reality show, *The World According to Paris*, began with the repercussions of Hilton's 2010 Las Vegas arrest for possession of cocaine. The show never found a consistent audience and was canceled after one season.

Tina Gianoulis

SEE ALSO: *Celebrity; The Internet; Lohan, Lindsay; Reality Television; Sex Scandals; Spears, Britney; Teenagers; Television; Wal-Mart.*

BIBLIOGRAPHY

Hilton, Paris; Merle Ginsberg; and Jeff Vespa. *Confessions of an Heiress: A Tongue-in-Chic Peek behind the Pose.* New York: Fireside, 2004.

Learmonth, Michael. "Newsies Ride Paris Wheel." *Daily Variety*, June 11, 2007, 1.

Newkey-Burden, Chas. *Paris Hilton: Life on the Edge.* London: John Blake, 2007.

Oppenheimer, Jerry. *House of Hilton: From Conrad to Paris; A Drama of Wealth, Power and Privilege.* New York: Crown, 2006.

Setoodeh, Ramin. "Ms. Hilton Gets Serious. Please Stop Laughing." *Newsweek*, October 22, 2007, 58.

Himes, Chester *(1909–1984)*

American writer Chester Himes is the author of the acclaimed Harlem Cycle crime novels. His featured characters, African American detectives Coffin Ed Johnson and Grave Digger Jones, deal with transgressors ruthlessly and violently, brandishing huge guns to settle disputes. The absurdity of the level of violence the two detectives both mete out and suffer is presented as representative of the wider absurdity of the lives of African Americans in the United States—and perhaps the absurdities of Himes's own life. Whatever Johnson and Jones do, they cannot end the cycle of crime and violence that grips black city life, just as, in Himes's view, whatever African Americans do, they cannot escape the cycle of racism that controls their lives.

Himes was born into a respectable, middle-class family in Jefferson City, Missouri, in 1909. His dark-skinned father was a college professor at the Lincoln Institute in Missouri and later at Alcorn College in Mississippi. His light-skinned mother was a descendant of wealthy southern whites and was immensely proud of it, often criticizing her husband for his dark skin. After Himes's father lost his job at Alcorn, the family moved to St. Louis, Missouri, and later to Cleveland, Ohio. After graduating from high school, Himes began studying at Ohio State University in 1926.

At predominately white Ohio State, Himes faced discrimination, and he soon rejected what he called the "light-bright-and-damn-near-white" social clique at the university in favor of friends he made among gamblers, pimps, and prostitutes off campus. His grades began to fall, and after an ill-advised prank, he was expelled in 1927. He then began a short but formative career as a criminal, selling bootleg whiskey during Prohibition and taking part in robberies. Eventually Himes participated in an armed robbery for which he was sentenced to twenty years in the Ohio State Penitentiary. With encouragement from his devoted mother, Himes began to write in prison, and his stories were published magazines such as *Abbott's Monthly*, owned by and marketed to African Americans. He also managed to sell an occasional story to *Esquire* magazine, from which he concealed his racial origins.

In 1936 Himes was paroled, after serving seven and a half years. He began trying to earn a living from his writing, continuing to submit work to magazines. When he and his first wife, Jean, moved to California during World War II, he worked in the shipyards and began his first novel, *If He Hollers Let Him Go*, which was published in 1945. It dealt with the social and psychological burdens of being black in a white society. In the following several years, Himes wrote autobiographical protest novels but struggled to find publishers. His parents died; his marriage to Jean failed; and his various affairs with white women, most notably with Vandi Haygood, ended in disaster. In 1953 Himes sailed to France, living briefly in Paris, London, and Mallorca, before returning to Paris.

In 1957 Himes met Marcel Duhamel, who recruited him to write detective stories for the publishing house Gallimard, which published American hard-boiled novels under the famous imprint, La Série Noire. The first of these, *For Love of Imabelle* (1957), later published in the United States as *A Rage in Harlem*, won the prestigious Grand Prix de Littérature Policière, the highest honor for crime fiction in France. The novel made Himes famous overnight. He wrote a total of ten detective novels, nine involving detectives Johnson and Jones, one of which, *Plan B*, was published posthumously in 1993.

The Harlem Cycle novels allowed Himes to address the themes of racism and violence that had made his earlier novels unpopular. Racism is present among both blacks and whites, and as such his novels represent the growing awareness among African Americans in the 1950s of race and class, although his attitude toward women is far from progressive. His detectives are only too aware of the absurdity of their real task. They must protect whites and white society from black criminals and the latent chaos of Harlem so that they do not become too afraid to go there. If that should happen, black criminals and con artists would be deprived of their income.

Even though the Harlem Cycle crime novels won awards and sold well from the start, it is only since the 1980s that they received the critical attention they deserve. Himes's elaborate hierarchies of good and evil characters, signaled by their skin color, and his experiments with nonlinear time and simultaneous plot events in his novels have informed the work of later novelists, such as Ishmael Reed. Himes's crime novels are an angry continuation of his early challenges to America and a significant contribution to the development of American detective fiction.

His works also include two autobiographies, *A Quality of Hurt* (1972) and *My Life of Absurdity* (1976). In 1998 Himes was posthumously inducted into Chicago State University's International Literary Hall of Fame for Writers of African Descent.

Chris Routledge

SEE ALSO: *Detective Fiction;* Esquire*; Hard-Boiled Detective Fiction; Mosley, Walter; Reed, Ishmael; World War II.*

BIBLIOGRAPHY

Muller, Gilbert H. *Chester Himes.* Boston: Twayne, 1989.

Sallis, James. *Chester Himes: A Life.* New York: Walker, 2001.

Skinner, Robert E. *Two Guns from Harlem: The Detective Fiction of Chester Himes.* Bowling Green, OH: Bowling Green State University Popular Press, 1989.

Soitos, Stephen F. *The Blues Detective: A Study of African American Detective Fiction.* Amherst: University of Massachusetts Press, 1996.

The *Hindenburg*

The May 1937 explosion of the German airship *Hindenburg* is one of the most memorable disasters of the twentieth century, outshining other more serious and costly catastrophes. Of the ninety-seven passengers and crew on board, thirty-six lost their lives in the conflagration. Images of its fiery denouement have made their way through the pop culture pantheon, onto T-shirts and album covers (most famously, the eponymous debut of Led Zeppelin), while the mystery of the *Hindenburg*'s final flight has inspired a feature film (1975) and numerous documentaries. Various theories on the cause of the explosion blame a hydrogen leak, electrostatic discharges in the air igniting the ship's highly flammable fabric covering, or an anti-Nazi act of sabotage.

A NASA scientist claimed to have resolved the dispute in favor of the flammable covering thesis in 1997, but doubters remained. "For reasons which are not clear to me even now, however," writes Michael Mooney in his history of the flight, "the *Hindenburg* disaster seemed to sear the memory of everyone even remotely connected to it." Maybe it was a conjunction of the times, the fragile peace preceding World War II, and the spectacular manner of the airship's end. Or perhaps it was because the *Hindenburg* was destroyed in direct view of the assembled press, with cameras clicking and newsreel film rolling and radio announcers squawking excitedly into their microphones, their coverage competing with the screams of the dying. "Here it comes, ladies and gentlemen, and what a sight it is, a thrilling one, a marvelous sight," exclaimed radio announcer Herb Morrison for the benefit of his listeners in Chicago as the *Hindenburg* prepared to dock over a Lakehurst, New Jersey, airfield. Only moments later his tenor changed abruptly from enthusiasm to abject terror. "It burst into flame!" cried the horror-stricken reporter. "It burst into flame and it's falling . . . this is one of the worst. . . . It's a terrific crash, ladies and gentlemen . . . the smoke and its flames now and the frame is crashing to the ground, not quite to the mooring mast, oh, the humanity!" Morrison broke down, finding himself unable to continue.

Spectators on the ground claimed they saw a small explosion toward the stern followed by an enormous secondary burst.

***The* Hindenburg.** *The* Hindenburg *disaster in 1937 ended the era of the airship as a mode of passenger transportation.* SAM SHERE/GETTY IMAGES.

The lighter-than-air *Hindenburg* plummeted toward earth, passengers leaping from the observation platform as it descended. Others managed to flee from the wreckage once it came to rest on the airfield—some parting the white-hot aluminum superstructure with their bare hands. The unlucky were trapped in the burning superstructure or were mortally wounded while escaping.

Zeppelin travel had attracted people who disliked sea travel and those for whom time was of the essence; a great many were attracted by the sheer novelty of airships. Until the *Hindenburg* disaster, zeppelins had provided safe, fast transport between the Americas and Germany for close to twenty years. (Only Germany had managed to master the art of the zeppelin, with French and English efforts ending in failure.) Having served a year of regular flights between Germany and New York, the *Hindenburg*, 804 feet long with a cruising speed of 78 miles per hour, was the largest and most advanced of the airships, providing comfortable, luxurious passage in a fraction of the time it would take the fastest steamer to traverse the Atlantic.

INVESTIGATION AND AFTERMATH

According to the dramatic sabotage legend, a letter had arrived at the German Embassy in Washington, D.C., the day before the flight warning of a saboteur among the paying passengers. As a result, security was unusually thorough, and Captain Ernst Lehmann, the newly appointed director of the Zeppelin Company (his predecessor having resigned in disgrace), and two SS officials scrutinized the passengers. By journey's end, Captain Lehmann was convinced the letter was a figment of SS paranoia. Nothing of import had transpired.

He did not know that Erich Spehl, a young rigger on the ship whose job it was to tend to the bags of highly flammable hydrogen within the aluminum superstructure, had surreptitiously planted a bomb within Gas Cell IV long before the ship had left its hangar. It was left to Spehl to rip open the gas bag shortly before landing and set the timer on his rudimentary bomb. It was not Spehl's intention to kill anyone: The innocent farm lad was motivated to perform his "act of genius" by his older, more sophisticated girlfriend, under whose tutelage Spehl had grown violently opposed to the Nazi regime. As the *Hindenburg* circled to position itself for landing, Spehl slit the gas bag and set the bomb's timer so that it would explode long after the passengers and crew should have disembarked. Unfortunately, the timer malfunctioned, or in his haste, Spehl set it wrong. The *Hindenburg* was just preparing to dock when the bomb exploded, burning the silk bag and allowing air to rush in and mix with the highly flammable hydrogen.

Regardless of whether the explosion was caused by such a saboteur, a more dramatic black eye for the Nazi regime could scarcely have been planned. The disaster was featured in newsreels within the week, and it made a phenomenal spectacle, the bright white flames leaping into the dark sky as the silhouetted bulk of the zeppelin descended gracefully toward the earth. The German government, hoping to avoid an international incident, ascribed the disaster to "an act of God." A binational commission was convened, but the Germans had been expressly warned not to find any evidence of sabotage. The FBI, in turn, played along, but the commission met nightly, and convictions were aired off the record. The decision to sweep the entire mess under the rug abruptly brought any further experiments with passenger airships to an end.

Michael Baers

SEE ALSO: *Air Travel; Disaster Movies; FBI (Federal Bureau of Investigation); Led Zeppelin; Radio.*

BIBLIOGRAPHY

As Reported by the New York Times: Great Moments of the Century: Catastrophes. New York: Arno Press, 1976.

Greystone Communications. *The* Hindenburg. New York: A & E Home Video, 1996. Videocassette (VHS).

Hoehling, A. A. *Who Destroyed the* Hindenburg? Boston: Little, Brown, 1962.

Mooney, Michael M. *The* Hindenburg. New York: Dodd, Mead, 1972.

Sherman, Jill. *The* Hindenburg *Disaster*. Edina, MN: ABDO, 2010.

Stacey, Thomas. *The* Hindenburg. San Diego, CA: Lucent Books, 1990.

Hip-Hop

Hip-hop describes both a musical genre and a cultural revolution. It originated in the 1970s in the predominately African American and Hispanic American neighborhoods of New York City's Bronx, which was home to pioneer hip-hop artists such as Afrika Bambaataa, Grandmaster Flash and the Furious Five, Kool Herc, and the Sugarhill Gang. Born on the coattails of the civil rights movement, hip-hop began as a cultural statement, a chance for the disenfranchised to finally have a voice. The term *hip-hop* derives from the slang for *hip*, as in "new" or "cool," and *hoppin'*, as in "happening" or reminiscent of the hopping dance accompanying bass-driven percussive music. First used by disco disc jockeys in a derogatory manner, the name stuck and began surfacing in music, lyrics, art, and culture.

There is debate about who came up with the term. It is attributed to either Grandmaster Flash's Keith "Cowboy" Wiggins making a syncopated, marching sound with the words "hip, hop, hip, hop" or Sugarhill Gang's 1979 song "Rappers Delight," which begins with the repetitive phrase "hip hip hop, a you don't stop." Either way, Bambaataa was the first to define the four distinct elements of hip-hop culture: DJ'ing, MC'ing, B-boying, and graffiti painting.

DISSECTING HIP-HOP

Disc jockeys, or DJs, create the music or beats by playing small bits of songs accentuating the bass and percussion parts in a process called "looping," or "sampling." DJs use two separate turntables, vinyl records, and a mixer, allowing them to switch back and forth between the two records or play both at once. DJs sometimes also keep one track playing while scratching the other record back and forth, which creates an entirely different rhythm on top of the one playing. DJ Kool Herc, a Jamaican immigrant, created the break-beat style in which the upbeat, percussive sections of disco, funk, and reggae songs are isolated and looped to create a solid, repetitive, danceable beat. He would then rap with the music, directing his break-boys, or B-boys, to dance.

Dance crews are groups that would meet to create and practice new break-dancing moves to perform in competition against other crews for bragging rights. Break dancing consists of waiting for the breaks in the beats to dance in time with the hopping music, oftentimes spinning on the ground with one's legs, back, or head. The moves used include popping, locking, strobing, waving, headspins, and windmills. Popping, a form of flexing and relaxing the muscles in a jerking fashion, was popularized by Sam Solomon of the Electric Boogaloos Crew. Locking, or holding a dance move in a locked position momentarily before making another move, was originated by Don Campbell and his dance crew the Lockers. The Rock Steady Crew with Jamie White and Santiago Torres helped popularize moves such as the windmill, spinning on the back and shoulders, and the headspin. These moves were derived from both gymnastics and the Brazilian martial art form Capoeira. The TV show *Soul Train*, as well as movies such as *Wild Style* (1983), *Beat Street* (1984), *Breakin'* (1984), and *Krush Groove* (1985), included these dance crews and helped to transform break dancing from a localized phenomenon into a worldwide craze.

An emcee, or MC, recites rhythmic, often rhyming lyrics in sixteen-bar measures, called either "rapping" or "spitting bars," over the music. It is reminiscent of the call-and-response technique of African poets or Jamaican toasting. Melle Mel is credited with being the first to use the word *MC*, in reference to his performance. Later MCs would mimic the rhythms using their lips, mouth, tongue, and voice projected against cupped palms, an art called beat boxing. Early beat boxers included Doug E. Fresh and Biz Markie.

HIP-HOP CULTURE

DJs such as Kool Herc created block parties by taking over abandoned buildings, vacant lots, or open spaces, where they tapped into power lines and set up speakers, turntables, and microphones. Many MCs, B-boys, and DJs, such as Bambaataa, were former gang members, searching for a way to release their frustrations over being underprivileged, disenfranchised, and stuck in a cycle of poverty. Bambaataa started the Greater Zulu Nation as a gang outreach program centered on hip-hop, which provided a positive group environment and a creative way for members to vent their emotions and frustrations through music, art, and dance.

Hip-hop began in poor neighborhoods where vacant buildings were rampant, providing canvases for graffiti artists to paint their signatures, or "tags," as a means of marking territory, communicating with other taggers, or simply showing that they had been there. Early hip-hop culture and New York graffiti artists are described in depth in the 1984 documentary *Style Wars*. Different graffiti styles are named for their styles, such as block, wavy, bubble, and wildstyle (made popular by tagger Tracy 168, whose numbers stand for the artist's street of origin). Other early graffiti pioneers included Taki 183, Zephyr, and Fab 5 Freddy. Freddy was a member of the Brooklyn graffiti group the Fabulous 5, and he bridged the gap between hip-hop culture and the art/punk scene occurring simultaneously in New York. He helped to legitimize graffiti in the art community, hosting shows with the likes of Jean-Michel Basquiat, Andy Warhol, and Keith Haring. Freddy's ties to both hip-hop and punk are evident in punk-pop artist Blondie's song "Rapture" (1981), which was the first rap video to appear on MTV. The song references his name, and the video shows him painting graffiti.

A WIDER AUDIENCE

Freddy went on to host *Yo MTV Raps*, which premiered in 1988. The show forever changed the face of hip-hop music by spreading it to a much wider audience, but many cultural aspects were lost in translation. Viewers were drawn to the smooth beats, slick rhymes, acrobatic dances, and urban art, but as outsiders, they could not identify with the cultural message.

Hip-hop's evolution from inner-city New York to the world stage in the late 1980s and early 1990s divided the musical genre into two categories: old school and new school. The old school hip-hop of Bambaataa, Grandmaster Flash, and the Sugarhill Gang focused on the issues of poverty, oppression, crime, inequality, and other injustices in their neighborhoods. New school hip-hop artists such as Gang Starr, KRS-One, and Run-DMC kept the signature sound, but their focus became more far reaching. Though they continued to rap about their native New York, they addressed other issues with which a wider hip-hop audience could relate. These new school artists inspired other groups of musicians, such as A Tribe Called Quest, De La Soul, and the Jungle Brothers, who pioneered a new sound with roots in both jazz and the hippie bands of the 1960s.

A MEDIA DARLING

As the genre progressed, the hip-hop movement spread south to other urban centers, notably Atlanta, Georgia, with bands such as Arrested Development, Goodie Mob, and OutKast. Goodie Mob's Cee Lo Green left to form Gnarls Barkley with producer Brian "Danger Mouse" Burton, creating an entirely new alternative sound. Green also went on to work as a host on the TV singing competition show *The Voice*. Danger Mouse has also broadened the genre by remixing the work of both hip-hop artists and indie rock bands. One of his most famous works is a mixing of Jay-Z's *The Black Album* (2003) with the Beatles' *The Beatles* (1968), widely referred to as "the White Album," to create a new product called *The Grey Album* (2004). These mixes, or "mash ups," are another example of how the hip-hop genre continues to branch out from its localized beginnings to reach new audiences.

Rap is not the only element of hip-hop to branch out. B-boying turned into a hip-hop dance craze with television shows such as *The Grind* (1992–1997) and *Randy Jackson Presents: America's Best Dance Crew* (2008–) and the documentary *Planet B-Boy* (2007). These sparked a wave of parodies, such the *South Park* episode "Randy Got Served," in which the boys form a dance crew to battle one another in a dance-off. The sketch-comedy show *In Living Color* (1990–1994) included hip-hop dancers known as the Fly Girls, with whom pop superstar Jennifer Lopez got her start as a dancer and singer. Hip-hop dance has gone from the streets of the Bronx to nightclubs worldwide; it has been seen on national television, performed in high school gym classes, and used in workout videos such as *Dance Off the Inches: Hip Hop Party* and *Hip Hop Abs*.

GRAFFITI ART

Graffiti art is another element of hip-hop that has branched out globally with a new generation of taggers taking their art to greater heights. Like their predecessor *Style Wars*, films such as *Beautiful Losers* (2008) and *Exit through the Gift Shop* (2010) detail the rise of graffiti in the United States and beyond, focusing on renowned artists such as Shepard Fairey, Invader, and Banksy. The artwork of Banksy, who has never divulged his true identity, is highly coveted.

Graffiti began as a product of the streets, but the hip-hop movement helped to elevate it from an urban expression to an accepted form of art. It has been used by advertising agencies to sell products. Clothing and video game designer Mark Ecko noted this phenomenon in a 2006 interview with National Public Radio's Robert Siegel:

> If you're in Sao Paulo, Brazil, or if you're in Newark, New Jersey, or Carney, Nebraska, or Detroit . . . you're going to see street art, and the motif of street art, even if it's being marketed to you by soft drink companies or media companies and motion graphics, or whatever at the front of their music videos. It has really become the visual language of youth culture.

INTO THE MAINSTREAM

Hip-hop even has its own game show, MTV's *Hip Hop Squares* (2012–) with Nick Cannon and Biz Markie. MTV's website describes the show as follows: "*Hip Hop Squares* stays true to the tic-tac-toe format of the original game show, while infusing it with some of the biggest and most charismatic personalities in Hip Hop culture today, which transcends genre and crosses into the mainstream."

Along with game shows and the like, video games reflect every aspect of hip-hop culture: *Get on Da Mic* presents famous songs in a karaoke fashion, *Scratch: The Ultimate DJ* allows players to drop beats and scratch with a realistic turntable controller, *Mark Ecko's Getting Up: Contents under Pressure* creates a virtual city canvas on which to paint, and *Dance Central* enables users to leave their controllers behind to perform full-bodied hip-hop dance moves.

UNDERGROUND OUTPOSTS

Although hip-hop has developed an international sheen, there are still underground pockets taking the genre in new directions. What began as a product of the African American and Hispanic American culture has now crossed over to all races of people. There are numerous white hip-hop artists, such as Sage Francis, Aesop Rock, Cage, and Slug. England also has its share of hip-hop acts, some natives of the country and others transplants, including M.I.A., Dylan "Dizzee Rascal" Mills, and Lady Sovereign. New York, of course, still has a thriving hip-hop scene with artists such as Kool Keith, Mos Def, Prince Paul, and Talib Kweli. Mos Def has gone on to become a renowned Hollywood actor, starring in *16 Blocks* (2006), *The Hitchhiker's Guide to the Galaxy* (2005), and the Showtime series *Dexter* (2006–).

The Bay Area in California, notably Oakland, is another major hip-hop enclave with artists such as Del the Funky Homosapien, Dan the Automator, Freestyle Fellowship, Jurassic 5, and the Pharcyde. Meanwhile, the Los Angeles area has spawned artists such as Aceyalone, the Beat Junkies, Madlib, and Saul Williams. Acts from the various hip-hop cultures often collaborate, creating unique forms of music.

Although MCs have been referred to as rappers, rap music is an entirely different genre from hip-hop, with its own subcategories divided by philosophy, politics, and region. *National Geographic* writer Tom Pryor has described the differences between hip-hop and rap thusly:

> If hip-hop culture has metastasized from its urban American roots into the global juggernaut it is today, then that's largely thanks to the insistent, irresistible appeal of rap: the most high profile of the three elements that comprise the movement. While "B-boying" and graffiti art have also found worldwide constituencies, rap's easily replicated "two turntables and a microphone" formula has had an enormous impact on our rapidly urbanizing world. From the *favellas* of Sao Paulo to the slums of Dar Es Salaam to the suburbs of Marseille to the high rises of Tokyo, rap is truly a global music.

Over the years, the lines between hip-hop and rap have blurred, forming an enormous, somewhat homogenized entity. Hip-hop is now a big business with more attention paid to public image, product endorsements, and record deals than actual social change. At its core, however, it remains a vital way to express frustrations over inequality and injustice.

Ron Horton

SEE ALSO: *Blondie; Civil Rights Movement; Disc Jockeys; Game Shows; Graffiti; Lopez, Jennifer; MTV; Rap; Run-DMC; Sampling;* Soul Train*; Television; Video Games; Warhol, Andy.*

BIBLIOGRAPHY

Alridge, Derrick; James B. Stewart; and V. P. Franklin, eds. *Message in the Music: Hip Hop, History, and Pedagogy.* Washington, DC: ASALH Press, 2010.

Chang, Jeff. *Can't Stop Won't Stop: A History of the Hip Hop Generation.* New York: St. Martin's Press, 2005.

Kitwana, Bakari. *Why White Kids Love Hip-Hop: Wankstas, Wiggers, Wannabes, and the New Reality of Race in America.* New York: Basic Books, 2005.

Pryor, Tom. "Hip Hop Music." National Geographic World Music. Accessed June 2012. Available from http://worldmusic.nationalgeographic.com/view/page.basic/genre/content.genre/hip_hop_730

Style Wars: The Original Hip Hop Documentary. Accessed June 2012. Available from http://www.stylewars.com

Toop, David. *Rap Attack: African Rap to Global Hip Hop,* 3rd ed. London: Serpent's Tail, 2000.

"Video Game Makes Everybody a Graffiti Artist." National Public Radio, February 14, 2006. Accessed June 2012. Available from http://www.npr.org/templates/story/story.php?storyId=5206181

Hippies

The post–World War II baby boom generation was something of an anomaly both to parents and to the children they would eventually raise. Growing up amid the contradictory conditions of prosperity and paranoia that prevailed during the 1950s, this young generation became tired of abundance and yearned for a more "authentic" life. Their quest initiated outlandish fashions and tastes; broke taboos; and, together with an eager television and music business, monopolized the culture industry, saturating public discourse with hedonistic and sentimental idioms. With the objective of a new classless society based on sincerity and trust, some of these young people adopted the term *hip* from beatnik slang and donned the flowery, flamboyant posture of "hippies."

Hippies at Woodstock. A hippie couple attends Woodstock in 1969, four years after the term hippie *was first used in print to describe the new generation of beatniks who had moved from North Beach into the Haight-Ashbury district of San Francisco, California.* RALPH ACKERMAN/GETTY IMAGES.

RISE OF THE HIPPIE MOVEMENT

By the mid-1960s, hippies had begun to appear in high schools, at colleges, and in enclaves around the country. Their unique combination of hedonism and morality depended on the spin they placed on the "generation gap" that separated them from their elders: in high moral gear, hippies projected every conceivable social and ethical defect of society onto their parents—the generation who, having survived depression and war, clung to middle-class prosperity and values. From the perspective of the young, this "materialism" was evidence of the bleak life of "straight" society and of the moral bankruptcy that spawned war, environmental damage, racism, and sexual persecution.

Starting around 1964 and increasing steadily into the early 1970s, hippies began gathering in lower-income, inner-city neighborhoods (the same areas their parents had worked hard to escape), such as the East Village in New York and particularly Haight-Ashbury in San Francisco, and later formed communes and settlements in the countryside. Largely white, middle class, and educated, hippies whipped up their own philosophy of natural living, easy sexual and social relations, sincerity, and hedonism through a blend of Eastern mysticism, left-wing social critique, and beatnik appropriations of African American slang. To the hippies, "squares" were "uptight," out of touch with their feelings and with each other, and it was this isolation from human feeling that had made them such aggressive, authoritarian, and often brutal people. The hippie lifestyle was not only more fun but it was also morally superior.

Drugs played a special part in this hedonistic moral rebirth. By "blowing one's mind," drugs allowed a user to see through the fake values of middle-class materialism and into the profound layers of one's innermost being. The hippie political outlook was just as fanciful. Hippies imagined the older generation working together in a massive authoritarian conspiracy called "the Establishment" or "the Man." They believed that the main objective of the recognized social order was to restrain and control the innocent love of life, nature, and happiness that defined hippie life. The Vietnam War provided a ready target for hippie opposition and rebellion: the words *peace* and *love* became symbolically loaded terms, lumping together a call for military withdrawal from Vietnam, an attitude of mutual acceptance and trust among people, and a sense of personal awareness and happiness. The famous photograph of a hippie protester inserting flowers into the rifle barrels of a line of National Guard troops demonstrates the unique style of hippie morality, which connected personal feeling with political intent.

THE HEYDAY OF HIPPIEDOM

It is possible to bracket a viable and active hippie counterculture between 1965 and 1973. Over this period, a few important dates stand out: in 1966 the Beatles, having already made long hair an important emblem of youth culture, released *Sergeant Pepper's Lonely Hearts Club Band*, rock's first concept album. The jacket featured the band in lavish, mock Napoleonic military garb, a look that coined much early hippie camp and whimsy. One song in particular, "A Day in the Life," crystallized the hallucinatory drug-induced sense of the absurd that was to become known as "psychedelic." The song weaves together two quite different sounds; one, sung by Paul McCartney, takes an everyday, commonsensical tone, "woke up, got out of bed, dragged a comb across my head," while the other, sung by John Lennon, interrupts McCartney's narrative to coo dreamily, "Ahhhhhhh . . . I'd love to turn . . . you . . . on." The song seemed to split reality into two, the mundane and the fantastic, the square and the hip. Along with another track on the record, "Lucy in the Sky with Diamonds," *Sergeant Pepper* was thought to advocate psychedelic drug use as the necessary bridge from the drab world of old straights to the lush and expressive world of the young and the free.

In 1967 the Monterey Pop Festival provided the first in a series of major outdoor rock concerts, and in 1969 the Woodstock Music and Arts Festival provided the movement's thrilling climax. Hundreds of thousands of hippies clogged the region around the concert trying to get in, and after airlifts of food, water, and flowers from state troopers, the event subsided without incident, a testimony to the solidarity and mutual goodwill of a counterculture guided by feelings of love and peace. However, over time the climate of the counterculture changed: hippie urban frolicking turned into serious homelessness and poverty, and the drug culture grew into an organized and dangerous underworld. Petty criminals, drifters, and profiteers overran many of the hippie hangouts and communes. The Manson murders and a violent outbreak of violence and murder at a concert at Altamont, California, in 1969 brought to the fore a growing tension within hippie culture between middle-class and idealistic hippies and a growing criminal drug culture with no idealistic pretensions to speak of.

More than the criminal underclass, the hippie movement faced a far greater challenge from the same force that had brought it into existence: the mainstream media, which commercialized hippie culture and dulled its radical edge. By 1970 psychedelic styles were a common feature of advertising, bell-bottom pants were marketed to children, and even conservatives were seen to sport sideburns and long hair. When Lyndon B. Johnson was photographed in retirement on his farm with hair down to his shoulders, it was clear that the counterculture had become mainstream culture.

Indeed, hippies now exist primarily in fiction. Movies such as *Almost Famous* (2000), about a young writer who tours with a rock band in 1973, and novels such as *Drop City* (2003) by T. C. Boyle, about a California commune in 1970, continue to draw on the hippie movement of the past to dish up colorful characters and events for mass entertainment.

Sam Binkley

SEE ALSO: *Altamont; Baby Boomers; The Beat Generation; The Beatles; Bellbottoms; Communes; Haight-Ashbury; Hairstyles; Hoffman, Abbie; Lennon, John; LSD; Manson, Charles; Marijuana; McCartney, Paul; Psychedelia; Vietnam; Woodstock; Yippies.*

BIBLIOGRAPHY

Bisbort, Alan, and Parke Puterbaugh. *Groovy, Man: Tripping through the Psychedelic Years.* Los Angeles: General Publishing Group, 1998.

Gitlin, Todd. *The Sixties: Years of Hope, Days of Rage.* New York: Bantam Books, 1993.

Miles, Barry. *Hippie.* New York: Sterling, 2004.

Miller, Timothy. *The Hippies and American Values.* Knoxville: University of Tennessee Press, 1991.

Willis, Ellen. *Beginning to See the Light: Pieces of a Decade.* New York: Random House, 1981.

Wolfe, Tom. *The Electric Kool-Aid Acid Test.* New York: Farrar, Straus & Giroux, 1968.

Hipsters

First used in the 1940s and 1950s to refer to the disaffected nonconformists of the Beat generation, the term *hipster* was revived during the first decade of the twenty-first century. Hipsters, in their postmodern incarnation, are anything from a trendy youth subculture to a lucrative advertising demographic to privileged poseurs laying claim to a bohemian, counterculture identity. The term *hipster* arises from the slang words *hep* and *hip*, meaning informed or in the know, commonly used by African American jazz musicians during the 1920s and 1930s.

One of the earliest published uses of the word *hipster* to describe members of U.S. jazz culture was in an article by Louisiana-born writer Anatole Broyard titled "A Portrait of the Hipster," which appeared in the *Partisan Review* in 1948. Broyard describes the hipster largely in terms of the underground world of jazz, marijuana, jive talk, and unselfconscious understanding of the authentically hip. However, the ruination of the hipster, according to Broyard, was acceptance by the mainstream.

The image of the hipster as a rebel was reinforced during the 1950s by writers such as Jack Kerouac, who wrote in his autobiographical novel *On the Road* of "the sordid hipsters of America, a new Beat generation that I was slowly joining." Beat poet Allen Ginsberg's "Howl" includes the line, "angelheaded hipsters burning for the ancient heavenly connection to the starry dynamo in the machinery of night." Midcentury hipsters were subversives, artists, and radicals who lived on society's fringes. But beatniks in black turtlenecks reading poetry in coffeehouses gave way in the 1960s to hippies, who grew their hair long, dressed in flamboyant colors, and used hallucinogenic drugs such as LSD and marijuana to expand their awareness. Hippies challenged mainstream culture, developing antiwar and free speech movements and espousing open relationships and free love.

At the end of the twentieth century, the press began to label certain liberal, urban young adults as hipsters. These children and grandchildren of rebellious generations have rejected society in their own way, by embracing a bohemian lifestyle, avant-garde art forms, and eccentric styles of dress. Rather than espousing the existential angst of the beatniks or the utopian earnestness of the hippies, twenty-first-century hipsters express their disaffection largely through self-deprecating ennui and irony. Born into an atmosphere of instant, worldwide communication; intrusive media; and constantly superseded technology, hipsters often reject the slick and packaged in favor of the unpolished and experimental.

Although hipsters sometimes hold a satirical affection for aspects of mainstream popular culture, they are most closely associated with independent (indie) music. Small do-it-yourself bands that generally do not record on major labels often have small followings of devoted hipster fans. Some indie bands, such as Death Cab for Cutie, have achieved mainstream success, but in general hipsters prefer lesser-known, local groups. Similarly, hipsters often appreciate the edginess and obscurity of indie films, such as the quirky 1999 comedy *Being John Malkovich*, directed by Spike Jonze. Director Todd Berger's 2009 indie dark comedy *The Scenesters* focuses on hipsters who frequent the trendy music club scene.

Congregating in fashionable neighborhoods, such as the Williamsburg area of Brooklyn, New York; Wicker Park in Chicago; and Capitol Hill in Seattle, Washington, hipsters have espoused tolerance and openness, sometimes engaging in bisexual relationships and wearing gender-bending styles. Satiric eccentricity permeates hipster identity, from dress to language.

With a carefully chosen carelessness that mocks everything from preppy to punk, hipsters often don retro-style tight jeans, cartoon T-shirts, chunky sweaters, and trucker baseball caps. Hipsters have even created new slang terms, replacing *cool* with *deck* to refer to all things good or desirable (the opposite of *deck* is *fin*, which in another era might have been translated as *lame* or *square*). More recently, Dublin, Ireland; Oslo, Norway; and Atlanta, Georgia, rank as the world's top hipster cities.

As hipster style reached its peak, however, it sparked two predictable reactions—targeting by advertisers and backlash. Corporations saw in hipsters a profitable demographic and thus developed products, from high-priced retro-chic fashions at stores such as Urban Outfitters to cool candy such as Dentyne Ice chewing gum and Hershey's Ice Breakers mints. The most successful such marketing was done by Pabst Brewing Company, which began sponsoring indie events where hipsters congregated, making Pabst Blue Ribbon (called "PBR" for short) the unofficial hipster beer.

Critics have criticized hipsters as pretentious, hypocritical, and self-obsessed. Satiric books have appeared such as *Field Guide to the Urban Hipster* and *The Hipster Handbook* in 2003 and *Stuff Hipsters Hate* and *Look at This F*cking Hipster* in 2010. Websites with titles such as *The Self-Hating Hipster* have revealed that hipsters, too, have mixed feelings about their image. It remains to be seen if Broyard was right in his assertion that no counterculture movement can survive acceptance by the mainstream.

Tina Gianoulis

SEE ALSO: *The Beat Generation; Beer;* Being John Malkovich*; Ginsberg, Allen; Hippies; Indie Music; Jazz; LSD; Marijuana;* On the Road*; Retro Fashion.*

BIBLIOGRAPHY

Fletcher, Dan. "Brief History: Hipsters." *Time*, July 29, 2009.

Greif, Mark; Kathleen Ross; and Dayna Tortorici, eds. *What Was the Hipster? A Sociological Investigation.* New York: n+1 Foundation, 2010.

Lanham, Robert; Bret Nicely; and Jeff Bechtel. *The Hipster Handbook.* New York: Anchor, 2003.

Malone, Bernie. "So Much for Brooklyn—Dublin Tops Charts for World's Top Hipster Cities." *Irish Central*, May 17, 2012.

Mande, Joe. *Look at This F+cking Hipster.* New York: St. Martin's Griffin Press, 2010.

Rayner, Alex. "Why Do People Hate Hipsters?" *Guardian*, October 14, 2010.

Hiroshima

SEE: *Hersey, John.*

Hirschfeld, Albert *(1903–2003)*

Beginning in 1927, Al Hirschfeld's instantly recognizable pen-and-ink drawings for the *New York Times* chronicled the worlds of theater, film, television (when it came along), and indeed virtually every area of performance-based artistry in the last three-quarters of the twentieth century. His mastery of the sinuous line, which he used to reveal the essence of a performer or role, was unparalleled. Hirschfeld's work has been compared to that of Honoré Daumier and Henri de Toulouse-Lautrec. He studied art in Europe and traveled to Japan, where he learned the Japanese art style that influenced his work. Calling himself not a caricaturist but a "characterist," Hirschfeld relied on wit and humor, never malice, to bring life to his subjects and a smile to the faces of those who read the *New York Times.* When his daughter, Nina, was born in 1945, Hirschfeld began hiding her name in the folds of clothing or elsewhere, prompting many admirers to an even closer reading of his eloquent drawings.

Hirschfeld left an enduring mark on twentieth-century pop culture. In 1991 he produced the designs for a set of U.S. postage stamps honoring great American humorists. Several years later he drew a set of *TV Guide* covers featuring the stars of *Seinfeld* in its final 1997–1998 season. In 1996 filmmaker Susan W. Dryfoos made a documentary of his life, *The Line King.* That same year he received the Milton Caniff Lifetime Achievement Award and was designated as one of New York City's landmarks. Hirschfeld died in his Manhattan home on January 20, 2003, at the age of ninety-nine after working on a sketch of the Marx Brothers.

Craig Bunch

SEE ALSO: *Celebrity; Celebrity Caricature; The Marx Brothers; The* New York Times*;* Seinfeld*; Television;* TV Guide.

BIBLIOGRAPHY

Bell, Clare. *Hirschfeld's New York.* New York: H. N. Abrams and the Museum of the City of New York, 2001.

Hirschfeld, Al. *Hirschfeld: Art and Recollections from Eight Decades.* New York: Scribner, 1991.

Leopold, David. *Hirschfeld's Hollywood: The Film Art of Al Hirschfeld.* New York: H. N. Abrams and the Academy of Motion Picture Arts and Sciences, 2001.

Shepard, Richard F., and Mel Gussow. "Al Hirschfeld, 99 Dies; He Drew Broadway." *New York Times*, January 21, 2003.

Hispanic Magazine

Described as a "Latino version of *People*" at the time of its 1988 debut, *Hispanic* was one of the first general interest magazines for Hispanic Americans to be printed in English and nationally distributed. Launched in Washington, D.C., by Cuban-born Fred Estrada, with former New Mexico governor Jerry Apodaca as his publisher, *Hispanic* initially revolved around celebrity photo spreads and articles that were roundly dismissed as "fluff." The debut issue featured Raquel Welch on its cover, as Estrada's son Alfredo would later lament. After a dismal first year of receipts, *Hispanic* underwent extensive reformatting. Becoming far more career- and professional-oriented, the magazine's new focus was on the achievements of Hispanic business leaders and politicians such as Secretary of Housing and Urban Development Henry Cisneros, with regular articles on corporate America and its relationship to Hispanics.

The shift was successful. By its third year, *Hispanic* was turning a profit. Reformatting was so successful, in fact, that

Hispanic was often confused with its competitor, the California-based *Hispanic Business* (founded in 1979).

While many print periodicals faced increasing difficulty in an era of expanding media technology, *Hispanic* remained solvent throughout the 1990s, largely due to the rapidly increasing demographic of Hispanic Americans, whose numbers were growing at five times the rate of the general population. It was a trend that advertisers had taken more than two decades to grasp. Whereas in 1977 the total national ad expenditures in all Hispanic print media were only about $650,000, by 1997 that figure had skyrocketed to $492 million. As Alfredo Estrada noted, referring to the "lean" early years, "the idea that Hispanics spoke English was heresy [in those days] . . . even now, some advertising agencies remain wedded to the idea that the only effective way to reach Hispanics is in Spanish." Indeed, in 1992 *Hispanic* challenged *Forbes* magazine for its claim that the Hispanic market was practically nonexistent. Why then, asked a Hispanic writer, had 70 of the Fortune 500 companies invested in it?

Early pioneering Latino magazines may not have survived long enough to witness the exponential growth in advertising revenue, but the fact that they existed at all certainly paved the way for publications such as *Hispanic*. In turn, the hard work of the Estrada family broke down barriers for later competitors, some of whom were based in large entertainment and publishing conglomerates, such as *People en Español*, launched by Time Warner in 1996, and *Latina*, which was first published by African American–owned Essence Communications in 1996.

In the 1990s *Hispanic* saw several changes in operation strategies and long-term goals, which seemed to both expand and focus its efforts at once. The publication instituted, for example, the "Latina Excellence Awards," in an effort to "honor Hispanic American women who have made significant contributions in their chosen field of endeavor," as well as the "Schools of Excellence Awards," to pay tribute to secondary-school principals with unique academic and enrichment programs for Hispanic students.

Other changes included relocating its family-owned publishing headquarters, in 1994, from Washington, D.C., to Austin, Texas. The consortium (which now owned Florida-based *Vista* as well), also joined the new wave of publishers offering titles for Latinas; its quarterly supplement, *Moderna*, became a stand-alone publication in 1996.

In 1999 *Hispanic*'s circulation was a solid 250,000, and the future looked promising. Estrada remained chairman and founder, while Alfredo, a former lawyer and graduate of Harvard University, served as editor and publisher. When the elder Estrada heard one advertiser note that the flood of new publications for Latinos had finally "brought credibility to Hispanic print," he asked, incredulous, "What am I, chopped chorizo?"

Despite that statement of bravado by the publication's founder, the magazine was not able to survive the onslaught of competitors. In 2004 a Mexican company called Editorial Televisa took over *Hispanic*, and in June 2010 the magazine folded.

Kristal Brent Zook

SEE ALSO: People.

BIBLIOGRAPHY

Estrada, Alfredo J. "The Decade of *Hispanic*." *Hispanic*, December 1997, 70.

Kanellos, Nicolás, ed. *The Hispanic-American Almanac: A Reference Work on Hispanics in the United States*, 2nd ed. Detroit: Gale Publishing, 1997.

Manley, Lorne. "Mixing Business with Pleasure." *Folio*, November 15, 1993, 56.

Hiss, Alger *(1904–1996)*

Alger Hiss's life up to 1948 seemed, on the surface, to be an American success story. He attended Johns Hopkins University and Harvard Law School and was a stellar student at both institutions. He pursued a law career and later joined the State Department in Washington, D.C. Then accusations that he was a Soviet spy blocked his road to success. He worked relentlessly to clear his name but to no avail. He died haunted by the specter of accusations brought against him during a period in America of political infighting and mass hysteria.

EARLY CAREER

Hiss met Felix Frankfurter, a professor and future Supreme Court justice, while attending Harvard. After graduating, Hiss served as a law clerk to Justice Oliver Wendell Holmes, pursuing what he thought would be a successful career in law. He then began a private law practice in Boston and New York. The election of President Franklin D. Roosevelt brought Hiss to Washington in 1933 to work on the New Deal as part of the Agricultural Adjustment Administration. A year later he served as a lawyer for the Nye Committee, a U.S. Senate panel that was investigating the arms industry. In 1936 he joined the State Department.

Whittaker Chambers, a self-proclaimed former communist who would later testify against Hiss in front of the House Committee on Un-American Activities (HUAC), visited Adolf Berle, the assistant secretary of state, in 1939. Chambers claimed he knew of "fellow travelers" in the federal government. Although Chambers made similar claims in follow-up interviews with the Federal Bureau of Investigation (FBI), fingering Hiss as a communist, the government did not immediately act on the allegations.

In the years that followed, Hiss participated in the 1944 Dumbarton Oaks Conference, which laid the framework for the United Nations and an international economic order. He also accompanied President Roosevelt to the historic 1945 conference of major Allied leaders in Yalta. In 1947 Hiss became president of the Carnegie Endowment for International Peace after being recruited by John Foster Dulles, a New York lawyer who later became President Dwight D. Eisenhower's hard-line anticommunist secretary of state.

TESTIMONY AND INDICTMENT

In 1948 Chambers testified before HUAC, alleging that he had known Hiss in the 1930s and that both of them had been communists. He claimed Hiss was part of an underground that had existed in the federal government during Roosevelt's administration and that tried to direct federal policy according to communist designs. However, Chambers denied witnessing any espionage at the time.

In response to the allegations, Hiss demanded, and received, an opportunity to appear before HUAC. He denied the charges of communism, as well as having known Chambers. Although Hiss gave an impressive performance, one member of HUAC, a freshman Republican congressman named Richard M. Nixon, wanted to look deeper into the matter. The committee agreed to let Nixon continue with the investigation in order to determine if Chambers and Hiss had known each other.

Chambers was summoned to testify in executive session, where he gave details (some accurate, some not) about Hiss and his wife. In a secret session, HUAC members examined Hiss, who backtracked on his denial of having met Chambers, claiming he had met a man called George Crosley who might have been Chambers. However, he denied knowing Crosley as a communist. In a face-to-face confrontation, Hiss confirmed that Chambers was the Crosley he had known in the 1930s, also challenging Chambers to repeat his allegations outside the congressional hearing so Hiss could file a defamation lawsuit.

After Chambers publicly repeated his charge that Hiss was a communist, Hiss, as promised, sued him for defamation. During the pretrial discovery phase of the lawsuit, Chambers made new accusations. Reversing his earlier testimony, he said that Hiss had spied for the Soviet Union, using Chambers as a courier. To back up his dramatic accusation, Chambers produced various documents, including what he said were copies of government (mostly State Department) documents allegedly typed by Hiss and turned over to Chambers for the Soviets' use. He also produced microfilm of State Department documents that, he alleged, Hiss had desired to send to the Soviets. When asked why he had not turned the evidence over to HUAC before, Chambers claimed he had hidden it in a hollowed-out pumpkin on his farm until he felt able to present it.

Although federal prosecutors believed the espionage allegations, the statute of limitations had expired. However, a New York grand jury indicted Hiss for allegedly committing perjury about espionage and his relationship with Chambers. In Hiss's two trials, the prosecution backed up Chambers's story by trying to show that Hiss's typewriter had been used to write some of the documents in Chambers's possession. Hiss countered by attacking Chambers's credibility and by using an impressive list of character witnesses, including Justices Frankfurter (Hiss's former teacher) and Stanley Reed and Adlai E. Stevenson, governor of Illinois. The first trial in 1949 ended with a hung jury (the vote was eight to four for conviction). At a second trial, Hiss was convicted, and he subsequently served forty four months in prison.

For the remainder of his life, Hiss denied having spied for the Soviets. He wrote two books defending his innocence and had many supporters who thought that his prosecution was a conservative effort to smear the New Deal and the Democrats. According to the pro-Hiss view, the case was a product of the anticommunist hysteria of the times. When Nixon resigned from the presidency in 1974, Hiss's supporters argued that if Nixon was capable of the "dirty tricks" of the Watergate period, he certainly could have fabricated the case against Hiss. After the collapse of the Soviet Union, a former Soviet general in charge of certain secret archives announced that there was no evidence that Hiss had been a spy, although he later added that such evidence might have been overlooked or destroyed.

Hiss's opponents cite Soviet documents that seem to confirm Chambers's account of a 1930s spy ring in Washington. Hiss's enemies also point to recently declassified U.S. government translations of secret Soviet communications, one of which contains a description of an agent that could fit only four people, one of whom was Hiss. Historians and others continue to debate the veracity of Chambers's claims as part of the continuing reassessment of events during the Cold War.

Eric Longley

SEE ALSO: *Communism; FBI (Federal Bureau of Investigation); New Deal.*

BIBLIOGRAPHY

Alonso, Karen. *The Alger Hiss Communist Spy Trial: A Headline Court Case.* Berkeley Heights, NJ: Enslow Publishers, 2001.

Chambers, Whittaker. *Witness.* Washington, DC: Regnery Publishing, 1987.

Gay, James Thomas. "The Alger Hiss Spy Case." *American History* 33, no. 2 (1998): 26.

Hiss, Alger. *In the Court of Public Opinion.* New York: A. A. Knopf, 1957.

Hiss, Alger. *Recollections of a Life.* New York: Seaver Books, 1988.

Klehr, Harvey; John Earl Haynes; and Fridrikh Igorevich Firsov. *The Secret World of American Communism*, tr. Timothy D. Sergay. New Haven, CT: Yale University Press, 1995.

Tanenhaus, Sam. *Whittaker Chambers: A Biography.* New York: Random House, 1997.

Weinstein, Allen. *Perjury: The Hiss-Chambers Case.* New York: Alfred A. Knopf, 1978.

Hitchcock, Alfred *(1899–1980)*

Universally acknowledged as the master of suspense, British-born film director Alfred Hitchcock reached the zenith of his accomplishments within the American film industry with a series of now classic psychological thrillers that remain a constant presence in the cultural landscape of the moviegoer. Regarded as one of the major artists of Hollywood's Golden Age, Hitchcock created and perfected his own genre of thriller, one that was by turns romantic, comedic, and macabre. In fact, his unique gift for creating suspense has given the adjective *Hitchcockian* to the English language. A supreme cinematic stylist, it was said that Hitchcock filmed murder scenes as if they were love scenes and love scenes as if they were murder scenes.

Thanks to his hosting of the television series *Alfred Hitchcock Presents* during the 1950s, Hitchcock became probably the only film director whose face was recognizable to the general public. Although, master showman that he was, he made a fleeting trademark appearance in virtually every one of his films, giving audiences the added frisson of trying to spot him on the screen. His mastery of film technique, refined in the silent era, combined with his ability to, as he put it, "play the audience like an organ," made his films extremely popular—so popular, in fact, that the respect of his critics and peers was not immediately forthcoming. In the twenty-first century, however, his place in the cinematic pantheon is secure, and his work continues to exert an overwhelming influence on upcoming generations of filmmakers. For better or worse, Hitchcock's most lasting impact may prove to have been the floodgate of still-escalating violence that he unleashed on-screen in his 1960 masterpiece, *Psycho*.

EARLY CAREER

Alfred Joseph Hitchcock was born in suburban London on August 13, 1899. Raised in a Catholic household by an emotionally repressed father, he was a painfully shy child. Years later he would often repeat the story of how his father had instructed the local police to place the boy in a cell for a short time in order to demonstrate what happens to bad little boys who misbehave. A recurring theme of his films is a fear of the police. Young Hitchcock developed an interest in art, but his first job was as a technical clerk in a telegraph company.

In 1919 he joined the Islington branch of the Famous Players-Lasky film company as a designer of title cards. He was hired as an assistant director for the production company run by Michael Balcon and Victor Saville in 1923, where he met Alma Reville, a film editor whom he married three years later. Reville would remain his collaborator and confidante for the remainder of his life. After starting to write scripts, Hitchcock was sent to work on a German-British coproduction at the UFA studios, famous home of the German expressionist cinema, which would eventually reveal its influence in his own work.

By 1925 Hitchcock had worked on half a dozen British silent films in various capacities as assistant director, art director, editor, and coscriptwriter. That year he directed his first solo feature, *The Pleasure Garden*, but it was his third, *The Lodger* (1927), that began to earn him his early reputation. Starring Ivor Novello, the British composer of Ruritanian musical romances and matinee idol of the musical stage, the tale concerns a mysterious stranger wrongly thought to be the murderer Jack the Ripper. Many years later Hitchcock said of the film, "It was the first time I exercised my style . . . you might almost say it was my first picture."

Alfred Hitchcock. *Often regarded as the greatest British filmmaker, Alfred Hitchcock directed more than fifty feature films in a career spanning six decades.* RON GALELLA, LTD./WIREIMAGE/ GETTY IMAGES.

He returned to the thriller form six pictures and three years later with *Blackmail*, the first British talkie or, more accurately, part-talkie (it had begun shooting as a silent). Alternating thrillers with dramas and comedies for a time, Hitchcock truly hit his stride in 1934 with *The Man Who Knew Too Much*, a fast-paced story of kidnapping and espionage, filled with memorable set pieces such as the assassination attempt during a concert at the Royal Albert Hall. He remade it in 1956 starring James Stewart, Doris Day, VistaVision, and the song "Que Sera Sera," but, despite its massive box-office success, critics continue to agree that the early version was the more refined and effective.

BRITISH PERIOD

The Man Who Knew Too Much launched what is now referred to as Hitchcock's British period, in which he turned out one successful thriller after another, notably *The 39 Steps* (1935) and one of the most famous of British films, *The Lady Vanishes* (1938). The former, one of several screen versions of John Buchan's novel, starred Robert Donat and Madeleine Carroll and set the tone for many Hitchcock classics to follow: a combination of comedy, action, and romance along with the theme of an innocent man hounded by the police as well as the arch-villain.

Though it would take a generation for the more intellectual film critics to catch up with the public that made these movies hits, Hitchcock's films were remarkable for the craft with which they so skillfully hooked audiences and kept them in suspense for the length of the movie. The director paid immaculate attention to working out every detail and often claimed that, with the script and storyboard complete, the actual filming itself was anticlimactic. He called upon the fullest vocabulary of cinema, from casting and camerawork to editing and sound, to tell his stories and was a great believer in the power of montage, which he employed masterfully.

HOLLYWOOD

Inevitably, Hollywood beckoned, and Hitchcock signed a contract with producer David O. Selznick. Their first collaboration, *Rebecca* (1940), from the novel by Daphne Du Maurier, starred Joan Fontaine and Laurence Olivier and was largely British in flavor. It won Hitchcock the first of his five Academy Award nominations for Best Director, earned seven additional nominations (including one for Judith Anderson's immortal Mrs. Danvers), and carried off the best picture and cinematography Oscars. *Rebecca* was an unqualified triumph, but Hitchcock chafed under the oppressively hands-on methods of his producer and yearned for artistic independence.

Meanwhile (sometimes on loan to other studios), he directed American films that continued his cycle of spy-chase thrillers but, in keeping with the World War II years, cunningly carried anti-Nazi propaganda messages. Such movies include *Foreign Correspondent* (1940, with Joel McCrea in the title role as an American war correspondent tangling with Nazi thugs), *Saboteur* (1942, with Robert Cummings interacting with Fifth Columnists), and *Lifeboat* (1944, with Tallulah Bankhead and others surviving a German torpedo and seeking safety). *Notori-*

ous (1946), the second of three films with Ingrid Bergman and four with Cary Grant, depicts the infiltration of a group of Nazi conspirators in South America in one of the director's most stylish thriller-romances.

Sometimes cited by Hitchcock as his personal favorite, *Shadow of a Doubt* (1943), which starred Joseph Cotten as a killer escaping detection by visiting his adoring relatives, brilliantly dramatizes the terrors that can lurk in the shadows of a seemingly normal small town. It was this penchant for perceiving the disturbance underneath the surface that helped Hitchcock's movies resonate so powerfully. Perhaps the most famous demonstration of this disjunction would come in *North by Northwest* (1959), where Grant, seemingly safe on a sunny day, surrounded by miles of empty farm fields, suddenly finds himself attacked by a machine-gunning airplane. Before the rich collection of war years thrillers, there was a beguiling and polished foray into domestic comedy drama with *Mr. and Mrs. Smith* (1940, with Carole Lombard and Robert Montgomery) and the romantic and sophisticated suspense tale *Suspicion* (1941, Grant and Fontaine), which pointed the way toward Hitchcock's fertile 1950s period.

POSTWAR FILMS

The postwar decade kicked off with the adaptation of Patricia Highsmith's novel *Strangers on a Train* (1951), in which Farley Granger and Robert Walker swap murders. The film climaxes with one of Hitchcock's most famous and memorable visual set pieces, a chase in a fairground. It was filmed in black and white, as was *I Confess* (1953, with Montgomery Clift as a priest who receives an unwelcome confession). To date, the master of suspense had only ventured into color twice—*Rope* (1948) and, one of his rare failures, *Under Capricorn* (1949). Now, he capitulated to color for the remainder of his career, with the well-judged exceptions of the Henry Fonda vehicle, *The Wrong Man* (1956), and his most famous film, *Psycho*. Along with color, his taste for blond leading ladies took on an almost obsessional aura. This led, during the 1950s, to films with Grace Kelly, Day, Eva Marie Saint, Kim Novak, Janet Leigh, Julie Andrews, and the previously unknown Tippi Hedren (whose career swiftly took off after roles in *The Birds* [1963] and *Marnie* [1964] and petered out just as quickly).

His professional reputation secure, Hitchcock gained his artistic independence and entered a high period in which he turned out success after success, some better than others, but all of them entertaining. However, along with *North by Northwest*, which ended the 1950s, the two masterpieces of the decade emerged from his three-picture collaboration with Stewart and marked a new dimension of interior psychological darkness that, in each case, infused every frame of an absorbing plotline. The films were, of course, *Rear Window* (1954) and *Vertigo* (1958), both of which deal with obsession under the deceptive guise of a straightforward thriller. The first, with Stewart laid up with a broken leg and witnessing a murder across the way as a result of spying on his neighbors, hints at voyeurism; the second, in which he turns the lookalike of an illicit dead love into an exact copy of her predecessor (both played by Novak), deals in guilt and sick delusion. *Vertigo*, for sheer artistic expertise, combined with Stewart's grim, haunted performance and the disturbing undertones of the piece, is quite possibly the most substantial of the postwar Hitchcock oeuvre, but the public impact of his first movie for the new decade would go on to top all his recent accomplishments.

HORROR FILMS

The director's first excursion into unabashed horror, *Psycho* (1960) sent shock waves that continue to reverberate through the genre. The murder of Leigh in the shower has been imitated, suggested, and ripped off in countless films since and has become part of the cinema's iconography. In certain cases, such as *Dressed to Kill* (1980), director Brian De Palma made no secret of the fact that he was drawing on the association in open homage to Hitchcock. *Psycho*, which drew on the Ed Gein multiple murder case for its inspiration, caused much controversy on its release and has since been analyzed endlessly by film historians and academics. When a shot-by-shot color remake by director Gus Van Sant, made ostensibly as the highest form of compliment to the original, emerged late in 1998, a rash of fresh argument was unleashed, as many bemoaned the pointlessness of the exercise or, indeed, the travesty that many considered it to be. The original is generally considered Hitchcock's last great film, attracting additional reverence for the contribution of his frequent collaborators Bernard Herrmann (who composed the pulsating score) and Saul Bass, the great designer of opening titles. Several of the Hitchcock masterpieces owe a debt to these two creative artists, and the Bass titles for *Vertigo* remain a work of art in their own right.

The follow-up to *Psycho*, *The Birds* (1963), was less highly regarded but is a durable and complex experiment in terror and a monument to technical expertise. In the late 1990s it, too, became the subject for renewed examination and analysis, notably by the controversial feminist academic Camille Paglia, who admired it greatly. There were only five more films after *The Birds*—a varied quintet that signaled a decline in the director's prodigious powers—and he bowed out, somewhat disappointingly, with *Family Plot* in 1976. By then, however, thanks to TV's *Alfred Hitchcock Presents*, he had cemented his image in the public consciousness as the endearingly roly-poly master of dryly witty gallows humor.

In his later years Hitchcock had the pleasure of being lionized by the newer generations of filmmakers and the wistful experience of attaining honors that long earlier should have been his. Although, inexplicably, he never won an Oscar for directing, the Academy of Motion Picture Arts and Sciences did ultimately honor him with the Irving Thalberg Award in recognition of his work, and he was also the recipient of the American Film Institute Lifetime Achievement Award.

Knighted in 1980 by Queen Elizabeth II, Sir Alfred Hitchcock died a few months later at his home in Bel Air, California. Decades after his last great film, Hitchcock remains a symbol of a certain kind of entertainment and excitement in a darkened movie theater. He is still one of the most admired and emulated of moviemakers, but his many imitators have never remotely replicated his consummate artistry or penetrated the personal and private obsessions that drew him to stories of innocence accused, double identities, morbid romance, and the other themes and undercurrents now recognized as Hitchcockian. If the mid-twentieth century has rightly been called the Age of Anxiety, then Hitchcock was the quintessential artist of his time.

Preston Neal Jones

SEE ALSO: *Bergman, Ingrid; Clift, Montgomery; Cotten, Joseph; Day, Doris; Fonda, Henry; Grant, Cary; Hollywood; Kelly, Grace; Lombard, Carole; McCrea, Joel;* North by Northwest*; Novak, Kim; Olivier, Laurence;* Psycho*;* Rear Window*;*

Selznick, David O.; Silent Movies; Stewart, Jimmy; Vertigo; *World War II.*

BIBLIOGRAPHY

Bogdanovich, Peter. *Who the Devil Made It: Conversations with Legendary Film Directors.* New York: Ballantine, 1998.

Chandler, Charlotte. *It's Only a Movie: Alfred Hitchcock: A Personal Biography.* New York: Simon & Schuster, 2005.

Freeman, David. *The Last Days of Alfred Hitchcock.* Woodstock, NY: Overlook Press, 1984.

Gottlieb, Sidney, ed. *Hitchcock on Hitchcock: Selected Writings and Interviews.* Berkeley: University of California Press, 1997.

Leff, Leonard J. *Hitchcock and Selznick: The Rich and Strange Collaboration of Alfred Hitchcock and David O. Selznick in Hollywood.* New York: Weidenfeld & Nicholson, 1987.

Smith, Steven C. *A Heart at Fire's Center: The Life and Music of Bernard Herrmann.* Berkeley: University of California Press, 1991.

Spoto, Donald. *The Dark Side of Genius: The Life of Alfred Hitchcock.* Boston: Little, Brown, 1983.

Taylor, John Russell. *Hitch: The Life and Times of Alfred Hitchcock.* New York: Pantheon, 1978.

Truffaut, François. *Hitchcock.* New York: Simon & Schuster, 1984.

Hite, Shere *(1942–)*

Shere Hite burst upon the American scene in 1976 with the publication of her first book, *The Hite Report: A Nationwide Study on Female Sexuality.* Since then, she has authored a number of other best-selling books on sex and relationships, delighting her publishers, intriguing or infuriating her public, and frustrating many social scientists, who consider her research to be seriously flawed.

Hite was born Shirley Diana Gregory in St. Joseph, Missouri, in 1942. Her parents divorced when she was three years old. Her mother remarried a truck driver named Raymond Hite, and he adopted young Shirley. When her mother's second marriage ended in divorce, Hite went to live with her grandparents. She later earned a bachelor's degree and a master's degree in history from the University of Florida. She then moved to New York City, where she dropped out of a doctoral program at Columbia University, worked as a model, and eventually joined the National Organization for Women (NOW). Feminism led Hite to the realization that female sexuality had rarely been studied scientifically, and the determination to change that fact set Hite on the path that ultimately led to the writing and publication of *The Hite Report.*

Before writing *The Hite Report,* Hite gathered data by having members of the general public complete a survey. She mailed her survey to women who were members of women's rights groups, political groups, and professional organizations. She also solicited female survey takers by participating in television talk-show interviews and offering an address to which women viewers could write in and request a survey. Of the 100,000 surveys that Hite sent out, she received 4,500 completed surveys back. So, after targeting specific female populations, Hite received only a response of 4.5 percent.

Hite's method of data gathering received much criticism from those versed in the techniques of survey administration. Her approach involved what is referred to in social science as a "self-selecting sample"—that is, the only people included in the "sample" (the pool of respondents) are those who chose to participate by completing and returning the survey. Such respondents are likely to be both few in number and extreme in their views on the subject of the survey, since only those with the strongest opinions will usually take the time to fill out and mail a survey.

Despite the criticism, Hite used similar methods to gather data for all of her subsequent books, and it may explain the results that she reports. She found that 70 percent of her responding women who had been married more than five years reported having an affair, and 76 percent of them claimed not to have feelings of guilt about their infidelity. More than 95 percent of women surveyed for Hite's third book claimed to have suffered "emotional and psychological harassment" from their men, and 98 percent replied that they desired "basic changes" in their relationships with husbands or lovers.

These, and similar results, which Hite freely generalizes to all American women, are usually at odds with other surveys that used traditional methods. For example, Hite's statistic about a 70 percent infidelity rate is in sharp contrast to a survey funded by *Playboy* that found 34 percent of married women reporting infidelity and a study sponsored by *Redbook* magazine that reported the figure to be 29 percent.

As Hite continued to produce books using similar survey methods, she garnered enormous antipathy from the press and other critics who also continued to condemn her methods and her conclusions. Her books include *The Hite Report on Male Sexuality* (1981) and *The Hite Report: Women and Love; A Cultural Revolution in Progress* (1987). In the 1980s, Hite moved to Paris, and her books began to take on more of a "self-help" aspect, such as her 1989 work *Good Guys, Bad Guys: The Hite Guide to Smart Choices,* cowritten with Kate Colleran.

In the 1990s her first novel, *The Divine Comedy of Ariadne and Jupiter* (1994), was published, and she set up a website, through which she offered her services as a business consultant and a personal consultant. In 1994 *The Hite Report on the Family: Growing Up under Patriarchy* was published, and her autobiography, *The Hite Report on Shere Hite: Voice of a Daughter in Exile* appeared in 2000. In her autobiography Hite explains that she moved to Europe and eventually became a German citizen because of the vitriolic attacks she endured from U.S. critics. In 2006, thirty years after the *Hite Report* appeared, *The Shere Hite Reader: New and Selected Writings on Sex, Globalization, and Private Life* was published.

Justin Gustainis

SEE ALSO: *Best Sellers; Feminism;* Ms.*; National Organization for Women (NOW);* Playboy*;* Redbook*; Sexual Revolution.*

BIBLIOGRAPHY

Bindel, Julie. "Shere Hite: 'We Need to Make a Film about Me.'" *Guardian,* May 13, 2011. Accessed May 2, 2012. Available from http://www.guardian.co.uk/books/2011/may/13/shere-hite-film-feminist-sex

Hite, Shere. *The Hite Report: A Nationwide Study on Female Sexuality.* New York: Macmillan, 1976.

Hite, Shere. *The Hite Report on Male Sexuality*. New York: Knopf, 1981.

Hite, Shere. *The Hite Report: Women and Love; A Cultural Revolution in Progress*. New York: Knopf, 1987.

Hite, Shere. *The Divine Comedy of Ariadne and Jupiter*. London: Peter Owen, 1994.

Hite, Shere. *The Hite Report on the Family: Growing Up under Patriarchy*. London: Bloomsbury, 1994.

Hite, Shere. *The Hite Report on Shere Hite: Voice of a Daughter in Exile*. London: Arcadia, 2000.

Hite, Shere. *The Shere Hite Reader: New and Selected Writings on Sex, Globalization, and Private Life*. New York: Seven Stories Press, 2006.

Hite, Shere. "Why I Became a German." *New Statesman*, November 17, 2003. Accessed May 2, 2012. Available from http://www.newstatesman.com/node/146720

Hite, Shere, and Kate Colleran. *Good Guys, Bad Guys: The Hite Guide to Smart Choices*. New York: Carroll & Graf, 1991.

Smith, Joan. "Shere Hite: On Female Sexuality in the 21st Century." *Independent* (London, April 30, 2006). Accessed May 2, 2012. Available from http://www.independent.co.uk/news/people/profiles/shere-hite-on-female-sexuality-in-the-21st-century

Wallis, Claudia. "Back Off, Buddy: A New Hite Report Stirs Up a Furor over Sex and Love in the '80s." *Time*, October 12, 1987, 68.

Hobo

SEE: *Tramps.*

Hockey

North American hockey is a fast and violent game played on ice that originated in Canada in the mid-nineteenth century. Players, wearing skates and heavy pads, use sticks to propel a flat rubber disk known as a puck. It is thought that hockey derives its name from the French word for a shepherd's crook, in reference to the shape of the sticks, which have a curved playing end. The origins of ice hockey are much debated and have been sought in several other sports, such as hurley, shinty, bandy, field hockey (played with a small, hard ball), and the Native American MicMac game, but there seems to be general agreement that the earliest match that can be identified with any certainty as hockey was played in 1855 on a frozen harbor by soldiers of the Royal Canadian Regiment in Kingston, Ontario. It remained an outdoor game for the next twenty years, played by nine-man teams, and—influenced by the rules of rugby—allowing no forward passing.

Students at Montreal's McGill University played the first indoor game in 1875 and developed the first hockey league in 1877. In 1883 the McGill team won the first game to be termed a "world championship," and ten years later teams were competing in a national championship for the Stanley Cup, which was donated by Canada's governor general, Lord Stanley. By then, the game had spread across the border to Yale and Johns Hopkins Universities in the United States and to Europe.

TURNING PRO

In the spirit of most sport during the Victorian era—a time when competing for financial gain was considered ungentlemanly and socially unacceptable—hockey flourished as an amateur game. This changed in the first decade of the twentieth century with the advent of professional hockey. The world's first professional team, the Portage Lakers of Houghton, Michigan, was American, albeit composed of imported Canadian players. It was organized in 1903 by J. L. Gibson, a dentist who, in 1904, established the first professional circuit, the International Pro Hockey League. Other leagues soon sprang up in Canada: the Ontario Professional League, the Pacific Coast Hockey Association (PCHA), and the National Hockey Association (NHA). By this time most teams were using only seven players a side, but the NHA, for reasons of economy, dropped yet another man from the ice, and six a side eventually became the standard team composition.

The most innovative of the leagues was the PCHA, formed by the wealthy Patrick family. They led the way in building arenas for indoor hockey played on artificial ice. They also pioneered rules that allowed the goalie to move about, permitted forward passing, and awarded an "assist" credit to those players setting up a goal-scorer. The league expanded to the American Northwest, and in 1917 the Seattle Metropolitans became the first U.S. team to win the Stanley Cup.

DAWN OF THE NHL

In 1917 the NHA gave way to the National Hockey League (NHL), which would become the dominant professional league in the world. Beginning in Canada, the NHL had teams in Toronto, Montreal, Hamilton, and Ottawa, and after 1926, when it shrewdly bought out the Pacific Coast League and acquired all its players for $250,000, it had no rival. It began to admit American franchises, starting with the Boston Bruins in 1924, followed by short-lived teams such as the Pittsburgh Pirates, Philadelphia Quakers, St. Louis Eagles, and New York (later Brooklyn) Americans. American teams that endured included three that entered in 1926: the New York Rangers, the Detroit Cougars (later the Falcons, later the Red Wings), and the Chicago Blackhawks. Canadian franchises that flourished for a time, only to disappear, included the Ottawa Senators (which won four Stanley Cups during the 1920s), Hamilton Tigers, Montreal Wanderers, Montreal Maroons, and Quebec Bulldogs.

At the end of World War II, only six teams remained in the NHL, but many consider the period between 1942 and 1967 to have been the golden age of hockey. It was certainly the era of elegant skaters and scorers such as Maurice "Rocket" Richard and Jean Beliveau of the Montreal Canadiens, Frank Mahovlich of the Toronto Maple Leafs, and Andy Bathgate of the Rangers and of powerful forwards such as Johnny "The Beast" Bucyk of the Bruins and Gordie Howe and "Terrible" Ted Lindsay of the Red Wings. There has never been a trio of goaltenders to match Chicago's Glen Hall, Montreal's Jacques Plante (inventor of the goalie mask), and Detroit's Terry Sawchuk. Rock-hard defensemen like Doug Harvey and Elmer "Moose" Vasko contended with players who had perfected the slap shot (which could propel the puck upward of 100 miles per hour): shooters such as Bobby "The Golden Jet" Hull and Bernie "Boom Boom" Geoffrion.

NHL EXPANSION

The expansion of the NHL to six more American cities in 1967 and the 1971 addition of twelve more teams in the rival World

Hockey Association (WHA) diluted the quality of the sport. Players of exceptional talent, however, such as the magical Bobby Orr, could still shine. Orr revolutionized his position when he became the first defenseman to win the NHL scoring trophy. The bidding wars for players that ensued during the 1970s drove up salaries and costs, thus causing many franchises to go under during the decade, and the frenzy stopped only in 1979 when the WHA folded and its four remaining teams were accepted into the NHL. One of the players who came from the WHA during this period was Wayne Gretzky of the Edmonton Oilers. He went on to set innumerable scoring records in the 1980s and 1990s before retiring amid fanfare in 1999.

Up until the 1980s the overwhelming majority of professional players were Canadian, but developments in world hockey soon began to change that. An amateur team from the United States had caused an upset in the 1960 Winter Olympics when it returned with the gold medal, but that victory did not have nearly the impact of the 1980 "Miracle on Ice" when an underdog American squad, amid Cold War tensions, defeated the seemingly unstoppable Soviets to reach the Olympic finals. After the "miraculous" victory, the Americans went on to beat Finland for the gold. A number of players on this team later played in the NHL, and their example encouraged many more young Americans to take up the game and do well at it. These new recruits to the big league were joined by a flood of highly skilled players from newly democratized countries in eastern Europe seeking employment in North America.

There was plenty of work for the newcomers. The NHL was committed to a relentless policy of expansion, targeted particularly in the American West and the Sun Belt, with the expectation that, by 2001, there would be thirty teams in the league, twenty-four of them in the United States. The aim was to penetrate large media markets that would provide the kind of giant television contracts that U.S. networks were handing to the professional baseball, basketball, and football leagues. The NHL had not yet hit television pay dirt by 1999 (largely because Americans still preferred watching televised bowling and stock car races to seeing hockey on the small screen), while spiraling costs had caused the demise of small-market clubs in Canada and stretched the resources of many franchises in America.

THE GAME'S FUTURE

As the new millennium approached, the fate of hockey looked uncertain. College hockey in the United States, and women's hockey throughout the world, seemed set for more success; in Russia, however, once-mighty teams were in a state of poverty-stricken postcommunist collapse. Canada seemed destined to breed great players while being unable to afford to watch them play in person—franchises such as the Winnipeg Jets and Quebec Nordiques had been moved to the United States, becoming the Phoenix Coyotes and the Colorado Avalanche, respectively. In the United States, the question was whether the NHL could afford to continue with so little financial assistance from television revenue.

In the twenty-first century some clarity emerged. A lockout by NHL owners resulted in the loss of the entire 2004–2005 season and a labor agreement that ensured more financial stability. More television money was secured, though the league remained funded largely by gate receipts. The resolute stand against franchises moving out of the American Sun Belt dissolved when the Atlanta Thrashers were sold to a Winnipeg group that renamed the team the Jets. In eastern Europe the KHL, a largely Russian league that included teams from Kazakhstan, Belarus, Slovakia, and Latvia, was formed, providing some competition for the services of international players. National squads compete for world championships in the spring. Because these games conflict with the NHL schedule, they do not always involve players of the highest caliber. However, recent Olympics have produced epic clashes, particularly between Canadian and American teams, in both men's and women's competitions. The International Ice Hockey Federation claims fifty-one member nations, drawn from every continent. Faster than football, more violent than pro wrestling, at once graceful and crude, hockey has moved from its Canadian origins to be a global phenomenon.

Gerry Bowler

SEE ALSO: *Gretzky, Wayne; Howe, Gordie; Hull, Bobby; National Hockey League (NHL); 1980 U.S. Olympic Hockey Team; Olympics; Orr, Bobby; Sports Heroes; Television.*

BIBLIOGRAPHY

Coffey, Wayne R. *1980 U.S. Hockey Team*. Woodbridge, CT: Blackbirch Press, 1993.

Dryden, Ken, and Roy MacGregor. *Home Game*. Toronto, ON: McClelland and Stewart, 1991.

Farrington, S. Kip, Jr. *Skates, Sticks, and Men: The Story of Amateur Hockey in the United States*. New York: McKay, 1971.

Hockey's Heritage. Dubuque, IA: Kendall/Hunt, 1982.

Hubbard, Kevin, and Stan Fischler. *Hockey America*. Indianapolis, IN: Masters Press, 1997.

McFarlane, Brian. *One Hundred Years of Hockey*. Toronto, ON: Deneau, 1989.

McKinley, Michael; Derik Murray; Ken Koo; et al. *Hockey Hall of Fame Legends: The Official Book*. Chicago: Triumph Books, 1995.

Potvin, Denis, and Stan Fischler. *Power on Ice*. New York: Harper & Row, 1977.

Powers, John, and Arthur C. Kaminsky. *One Goal: A Chronicle of the 1980 U.S. Olympic Hockey Team*. New York: Harper & Row, 1984.

Rockwell, Bart. *World's Strangest Hockey Stories*. Mahwah, NJ: Watermill Press, 1993.

Wendel, Tim. *Going for the Gold: How the U.S. Won at Lake Placid*. Westport, CT: L. Hill, 1980.

Whitehead, Eric. *The Patricks, Hockey's Royal Family*. Garden City, NY: Doubleday, 1980.

Hoffman, Abbie *(1936–1989)*

Abbie Hoffman, one of the most colorful figures to emerge from the social turmoil of the 1960s, put his personal stamp on the activism of the decade with his insistence that radical politics find expression in personal attitudes as well as in political positions. Linking the spirited hedonism of the hippies with the politics of the civil rights movement, the New Left, and the antiwar movement, Hoffman's attitude was pure hippie. *Revolution for the Hell of It* (1968) is the title of his first and most influential book. His doctrine of absurdity and wit, combined with an unmatched media savvy, marked him for the elite ranks

Abbie Hoffman. *Abbie Hoffman speaks at a Black Panther rally in New Haven, Connecticut, in 1971.* DAVID FENTON/GETTY IMAGES.

of the counterculture. A hippie, an activist, a visionary, and a knave, Hoffman left an enduring legacy of influence and controversy.

Hoffman was born in Worcester, Massachusetts, in 1936, and his life was an extraordinary patchwork of triumphs, calamities, and accidents. After fighting the Ku Klux Klan in Mississippi, he moved to New York, where he joined the hippie counterculture and undertook a series of flamboyant public stunts designed to infuse the growing hippie mob with political purpose. After organizing protests at the Democratic National Convention in 1968, he went underground in 1973, reappeared in 1980 to resume his activist work, and committed suicide in 1989.

In 1967 Hoffman left the Deep South for Manhattan's Lower East Side, where he joined the "diggers," a group of hippie community pranksters and activists, and opened a store to sell craft products produced in Mississippi homesteads. Together with social activist Jerry Rubin, Hoffman formed the Yippies (Youth International Party was offered as the formal name only when pressed by reporters) and began a campaign of high-profile stunts meant to focus media attention on the movement. He understood what the media wanted, and he set out to give it to them, aiming to swell the ranks of the movement with new conscripts through publicity.

His actions, promoted with press releases and high-level media contacts to ensure maximum hype, emphasized the whimsy and humorous characteristic of hippies. In one incident, his group dumped a bunch of dollar bills onto the floor of the New York Stock Exchange from the visitors' gallery, causing mayhem as investors squabbled over the cash. In another, it sent soot bombs to Con Edison to protest pollution standards. The group also mailed more than 3,000 marijuana cigarettes to people randomly selected from the phone book, one of whom turned out to be a prominent journalist. A celebration of the spring equinox at Grand Central drew more than 6,000 hippies to a midnight gathering at the cavernous station, where police in riot gear waited nervously outside as hippies ran wild, tearing the hands off clocks, dancing, and squealing "Yippeee!!" Hoffman's Exorcism of the Pentagon was another landmark event, drawing 50,000 hippies to Virginia in an effort to levitate the entire Pentagon complex through magical means. The hippies joined hands, forming a human chain around the building as television crews filmed the colorful event.

A SPLINTERING MOVEMENT

However, the tone of Yippie activism changed at the 1968 Democratic National Convention in Chicago. Yippies gathered there to offer a "festival of life" to counter what they called the "convention of death," but their innocence and prankishness turned into an ugly riot as the demonstration was consumed by police violence. Outside the convention, where Hubert Humphrey was clinching the Democratic nomination for president, hippies, antiwar activists, and others massed, chanted, and sang. When Chicago mayor Richard J. Daley ordered police to disperse the throng, widespread panic and bloodshed resulted, lending credibility to the conservative call for law and order then being touted by Republican presidential candidate Richard Nixon.

Hoffman and seven others were arrested and later stood trial as "the Chicago Eight" for conspiring to incite the riot. After Black Panther Bobby Seale was remanded for separate trial by Judge Julius Hoffman, the group became known as the Chicago Seven (which included Rubin and other Yippies and antiwar activists), achieving nationwide notoriety. Despite receiving 175 contempt citations during the trial, the seven were ultimately found innocent, and other charges of crossing state lines to incite a riot were dropped on appeal in 1973.

By the early 1970s, however, Hoffman had other problems. Faced with accusations of egoism and showmanship from the organized left and charged with chauvinism and authoritarianism from feminists, hippies, and other cultural factions, he found himself standing at the center of a splintering movement. His response was to resign in an open letter addressed to the movement in 1971, and in 1974, fearing a lifetime jail term on a cocaine possession charge, he went into hiding. Even underground, however, he retained his media savvy, granting a well-publicized interview to *Playboy* magazine, in which he pledged to maintain his resistance and organize an underground movement aimed at toppling the U.S. government.

After undergoing plastic surgery and taking up a prominent role incognito as a community environmental activist in Canada, Hoffman came out of hiding in 1980 to face charges. He served only a short term before he was once again free to resume his activism. His public stunts secured his lasting reputation as a spirited activist, cemented by the wide circulation of his books. *Revolution for the Hell of It, Steal This Book* (1971), and *Woodstock Nation* (1969) were, and continue to be, staple reading for activists and latter-day hippies. His later titles include *Steal This Urine Test* (1987), a commentary on the drug-testing craze of the 1980s, and *Square Dancing in the Ice Age* (1982).

Sam Binkley

SEE ALSO: *Black Panthers; The Chicago Seven; Environmentalism; Flag Clothing; Ku Klux Klan;* Playboy*; Suicide; Woodstock; Yippies.*

BIBLIOGRAPHY

Becker, Theodore L., and Anthony L. Dodson. *Live This Book: Abbie Hoffman's Philosophy for a Free and Green America.* Chicago: Nobel Press, 1991.

Hoffman, Abbie. *Revolution for the Hell of It.* New York: Dial Press, 1968.

Hoffman, Abbie. *The Autobiography of Abbie Hoffman.* New York: Four Walls Eight Windows, 2000.

Hoffman, Abbie; Izak Haber; and Bert Cohen. *Steal This Book.* New York: Pirate Editions, 1971.

Hoffman, Abbie, and Daniel Simon. *The Best of Abbie Hoffman.* New York: Four Walls Eight Windows, 1989.

Hoffman, Jack, and Daniel Simon. *Run Run Run: The Lives of Abbie Hoffman.* New York: Putnam, 1994.

Jezer, Marty. *Abbie Hoffman: American Rebel.* New Brunswick, NJ: Rutgers University Press, 1992.

Raskin, Jonah. *For the Hell of It: The Life and Times of Abbie Hoffman.* Berkeley: University of California Press, 1996.

Sloman, Larry. *Steal This Dream: Abbie Hoffman and the Countercultural Revolution in America.* New York: Doubleday, 1998.

Hoffman, Dustin *(1937–)*

Beginning in the late 1960s, Dustin Hoffman established himself as one of his generation's finest film actors and helped usher method acting into the American cinema mainstream. From his first screen success as Benjamin Braddock in *The Graduate* (1967), Hoffman appeared in a series of diverse films that showcased his great range and indicated the rise of the character actor as superstar. He and actors such as Gene Hackman, Jack Nicholson, and Robert De Niro symbolized a new breed of movie star who was known more for fully inhabiting their characters than for their perfect profiles. Hoffman was, at times, criticized for being difficult to work with, but none could criticize his ability to employ the teachings of the method tradition that stressed the performer's ability to temporarily "become" his character.

Born on August 8, 1937, in Los Angeles, Dustin Hoffman, named after silent-screen cowboy star Dustin Farnum, was the son of a Columbia Pictures set decorator and an aspiring actress. He developed an early interest in performing, and he began acting at age twelve when he played Tiny Tim in a school production of *A Christmas Carol.* He was an accomplished pianist and enrolled in the Los Angeles Conservatory of Music (which later became the California Institute for the Arts) to study classical and jazz piano.

By 1957 he was devoting less time to music and more time to acting. He studied at the famed Pasadena Playhouse and later moved to New York. He attended the Actor's Studio, where he developed his craft alongside his roommates, future film stars Robert Duvall and Hackman. Under the direction of noted acting teacher Lee Strasberg, Hoffman learned the method's performance goal of becoming rather than acting. To support himself he took on a series of jobs, including janitor, waiter, and weaver of Hawaiian leis. He even worked as a hospital attendant in a psychiatric ward, where he observed patient behavior in an effort to improve his dramatic technique. Hoffman established himself as a respected New York theater actor in the early 1960s by appearing in acclaimed works such as *The Journey of the Fifth Horse* (1966) and the British comedy *Eh?* (1966). Hoffman's ultimate goal, however, was to become a film star.

THE GRADUATE

After years of honing his craft, Hoffman became an overnight sensation in 1967 with the release of director Mike Nichols's *The Graduate.* The film, based on a 1963 novel of the same name written by Charles Webb, features an innocent college graduate (Hoffman) who is seduced by an older woman (Anne Bancroft). In the novel the character of college graduate Benjamin Braddock is a handsome, well-bred, surfer type, but Nichols gave the role to the short, dark Hoffman. At age thirty Hoffman was also a decade older than the character. His performance as the confused and depressed college graduate who has an affair with a friend of his parents, the infamous Mrs. Robinson, captured the mood of American youth of the late 1960s who had grown disenchanted with their parents' generation.

In his book, *Dustin Hoffman: Hollywood's Anti-Hero,* author Jeff Lenburg quotes a university student who wrote a letter to the *New York Times* shortly after the film's release that demonstrates the impact it had upon the youth culture. The student writes, "I identified with Ben. . . . I thought of him as a spiritual brother. He was confused about his future and about his place in the world, as I am. It's a film one digs, rather than understands intellectually." The baby boomer generation's uncertainty of the future was best captured in the film's final scene, where Ben and Elaine (Mrs. Robinson's daughter) flee her wedding and her mother only to realize the uncertainty of their final destination. Hoffman was nominated for an Academy Award for his portrayal of the embodiment of 1960s youth angst, and the film garnered six additional nominations, winning the award for best direction.

MORE SUCCESSFUL ROLES

Following his early success in *The Graduate*, Hoffman appeared in a number of landmark films. In 1969 he starred as the tubercular small-time street hustler Ratso Rizzo in *Midnight Cowboy*. The controversial film about male prostitution was an enormous hit. It received seven Academy Award nominations, including one for Hoffman as Best Actor, and it won Best Picture, Best Director, and Best Writing. *Midnight Cowboy* was the first X-rated film to win the Academy Award for Best Picture (it was downgraded to an R rating the following decade).

In *Little Big Man* (1970) Hoffman plays 121-year-old Jack Crabb, who looks back on his life in the early West, and in *Lenny* (1974) he portrays the doomed comedian Lenny Bruce, a role for which Hoffman received his third Academy Award nomination. In 1976 he and Robert Redford starred as *Washington Post* reporters Carl Bernstein and Bob Woodward in the Watergate drama *All the President's Men*. In 1980 Hoffman won the Academy Award for Best Actor for his performance as a divorced father engaged in a child-custody battle in *Kramer vs. Kramer* (1979).

In *Tootsie* (1982) Hoffman mocks his reputation as a difficult actor by playing a man who disguises himself in drag to get a job on a soap opera. The movie was wildly popular with audiences, and Hoffman received his fifth Academy Award nomination for his performance. In 1984 he returned to the stage for a widely praised performance as Willy Loman in *Death of a Salesman*. For *Rain Man* (1988) Hoffman masterfully depicted an autistic savant. The film, which also stars Tom Cruise, earned eight Academy Award nominations. It won four awards, including Best Picture, Best Director (Barry Levinson), and Best Actor for Hoffman.

Hoffman remained a popular performer in the 1990s, appearing in several large, studio films, including *Dick Tracy* (1990), *Billy Bathgate* (1991), *Outbreak* (1995), *Sleepers* (1996), and *Mad City* (1997). In 1991 he memorably portrayed the revenge-seeking Captain Hook opposite an adult Peter Pan (Robin Williams) in director Steven Spielberg's *Hook*. Hoffman scored another hit and another Academy Award nomination for *Wag the Dog* (1997), playing a Hollywood producer attempting to cover up a presidential sex scandal.

In the first decade of the 2000s Hoffman often chose roles in family-oriented and animated films, such as *Racing Stripes* (2005), *Mr. Magorium's Wonder Emporium* (2007), and *Horton Hears a Who!* (2008). He also joined actors Ben Stiller, De Niro, and Barbra Streisand in the popular comedy *Meet the Fockers* in 2004, which was followed by the sequel *Little Fockers* in 2010. He received critical praise for his comedic performance as Shifu in the computer-animated *Kung Fu Panda* (2008) and its sequel, *Kung Fu Panda 2* (2011). Hoffman's filmography also contains one of Hollywood's most notorious disasters—the comedic misfire *Ishtar* (1987). In 2011–2012 he appeared in his first television series, *Luck*, opposite Nick Nolte. The HBO drama featured Hoffman as an ex-con and a professional gambler in the world of horse racing.

Hoffman remains a star after more than forty years in film because he invests all his portrayals with sensitivity and realism. In 1999 he earned one of cinema's highest honors when he received the American Film Institute's Life Achievement Award. Through his method-acting skills and nonflashy, realistic appearance, Hoffman opened mainstream American film to a style of performance that had seldom been achieved before on-screen.

Charles Coletta

SEE ALSO: *Academy Awards; Baby Boomers; Bruce, Lenny; Cruise, Tom; De Niro, Robert;* Death of a Salesman*; Duvall, Robert;* The Graduate*; Hackman, Gene;* Midnight Cowboy*; Nicholson, Jack; Redford, Robert; Spielberg, Steven; Stiller, Ben; Streisand, Barbra;* Tootsie*; The* Washington Post*; Watergate; Williams, Andy.*

BIBLIOGRAPHY

Brode, Douglas. *The Films of Dustin Hoffman*. Secaucus, NJ: Citadel Press, 1983.

Lenburg, Jeff. *Dustin Hoffman: Hollywood's Anti-Hero*. New York: St. Martin's Press, 1983.

Hogan, Ben *(1912–1997)*

With his perfect swing, golfer Ben Hogan achieved a kind of mythic stature in the collective mind of the American public. During his career Hogan won sixty-three tournaments, including nine major championships. He was the Professional Golfers' Association (PGA) Tour's leading money-winner five times, won the Vardon Trophy for lowest scoring average three times, and in 1974 was one of the first inductees into the World Golf Hall of Fame. As incredible as that record is, the folklore concerning Hogan's arduous rise to the top of his profession and his famed comeback after a near-fatal auto accident nearly transcends it.

Perhaps the most famous photograph of Hogan (included in *The Hogan Mystique*, 1994) captures much of the essence of the mystique: a shot of Hogan's flawless swing taken at its height and from the golfer's back, it extends outward to feature an attentive gallery on two sides of a tree-lined fairway. Thus, Hogan's face is not shown; his personal identity is subordinated to a frozen image of the mechanical perfection of his golfing prowess. Throughout his career Hogan was notoriously aloof from competitors, the press, and even his public. In addition, the peak years of his achievement preceded the wide coverage of golf by television; therefore, he was not captured repeatedly in widely distributed images as were Arnold Palmer, Jack Nicklaus, Gary Player, and Lee Treviño. Hogan became, though, something of an icon to these later figures, and what they admired was Hogan's game and the story of the literally painful way in which it had been developed.

The son of a blacksmith, Hogan was born in small-town Dublin, Texas, in 1912 and moved with his family to Fort Worth in 1921. His father, who had suffered from depression and alcoholism, committed suicide around this time, and Hogan's family was immediately plunged into poverty. In order to help out financially, young Ben became a caddie at Glen Garden Country Club. There he discovered the sport that would change his life. At Glen Garden he met a fellow caddie, Byron Nelson, with whom he quickly became a fierce competitor.

Hogan turned professional in 1929 but would achieve success only after years of relative obscurity. Throughout this early period, his status on the PGA Tour was always subordinate to that of Nelson. Hogan was not in effect a natural golfer and only realized his famous swing by regularly practicing until his hands literally bled. Perfection resulting from a puritan work ethic, long a central ingredient in American mythology, would become an essential element of the Hogan mystique. This grim self-creation was also a key factor in his legendary aloofness; always struggling to improve, he never felt that he had time for, nor did he see any point in, small talk with his playing partners or courting tournament galleries.

FIRST TOURNAMENT WIN

Hogan did not win his first tournament on the tour until 1940, when he won a total of four. He followed that with five victories in 1941, but his new success was interrupted when he was drafted into the U.S. Army in 1943. It was in the immediate postwar period that Hogan began to dominate the PGA Tour and his legend started to take form. He won his first major title, the PGA tournament, in 1946. In 1948 he repeated his success in the PGA and, in a rare exhibition of golfing perfection, won his first of four U.S. Open championships. Just as he seemed finally to have reached the peak of his success and his career, he was nearly killed in an automobile accident in February 1949. His doctors were not certain, first, that he would live, or next, that he would walk again, and finally, that he would play competitive golf again. After doing all three, Hogan returned to the tour in January 1950. In that year he won his second U.S. Open: the often-recounted Hogan comeback was under way, and the final ingredient, that of the courageous underdog who survived extreme adversity, was added to the Hogan mystique.

The story would prove so compelling that Hollywood would have to film it, even if inadequately. *Follow the Sun*, supposedly the story of Hogan's life and climaxing with his comeback, was released in 1951. Its script was clichéd, and Glenn Ford, as Hogan, was miscast. In the words of Hogan biographer Curt Sampson: "Ford, an unathletic man whose hobby was gardening, held the club as if it were a trowel and swung it like a rake."

In 1953 Hogan reached the pinnacle of his golfing career when he won the U.S. Open, his second Masters Tournament, and his first British Open, thus sweeping three of professional golf's four major events (he did not enter the PGA tournament that year). The British Open win in Carnoustie, Scotland, especially contributed to the Hogan myth. Already known as Bantam Ben, he was nicknamed the Wee Ice Mon by Scottish fans who were simultaneously paying tribute to his determined concentration and his triumph over physical adversity. (Hogan was, in fact, of average height.) In July of that year, he was treated to a ticker tape parade down Broadway in New York City.

Hogan wrote a popular five-part series on the basic elements of the correct golf swing for *Sports Illustrated* beginning March 11, 1957. After retiring from competitive golf in 1971, he fittingly devoted his time to manufacturing and selling golf clubs until his death on July 25, 1997.

James R. Giles

SEE ALSO: *Ford, Glenn; Golf; Hollywood; The Masters Golf Tournament; Nicklaus, Jack; Palmer, Arnold; Sports Heroes;* Sports Illustrated*; Treviño, Lee; Vardon, Harry; World War II.*

BIBLIOGRAPHY

Campbell, Malcolm, and J. M. Fox. *The Random House International Encyclopedia of Golf.* New York: Random House, 1991.

Davis, Martin, ed. *The Hogan Mystique: Classic Photographs of the Great Ben Hogan by Jules Alexander.* New York: Broadway Books, 1994.

Diaz, Jaime. "One of a Kind." *Sports Illustrated*, August 4, 1997, G6–G10.

Dodson, James. *Ben Hogan: An American Life.* New York: Doubleday, 2004.

Matuz, Roger. *Inside Sports: Golf—Your Ultimate Tour Guide.* Detroit, MI: Visible Ink, 1997.

Nelson, Byron. "The Mystique Lives On." *Sports Illustrated*, August 4, 1997, 26–29.

Sampson, Curt. *Hogan.* New York: Broadway Books, 1996.

Hogan, Hulk *(1953–)*

Though Hulk Hogan had limited talent as an in-ring performer, his sculpted physique and incredible charisma made him one of the greatest drawing cards in the modern era of professional wrestling, which began when he joined the World Wrestling Federation (WWF, which became World Wrestling Entertainment, or WWE, in 2002) in 1983. Hogan became a crossover celebrity, with appearances on magazine covers, roles in movies and on TV, and guest spots on talk shows.

To those who did not follow wrestling, Hogan *was* the sport. From 1983 to 2006, with a few bumps in the road, Hogan was one of the biggest stars in the business in terms of generating ticket sales, headlining pay-per-view events, moving merchandise, and driving television ratings. However, after leaving the WWE in 2006, he endured a series of professional and personal setbacks that took a toll on his health and left him nearly bankrupt.

THE RISE

Born Terry Bollea, Hogan began weightlifting as a teenager while living in Tampa, Florida. After studying business administration and music at the University of South Florida, he was discovered by two professional wrestlers while playing bass in a rock band. Hogan started wrestling in the southern United States under names such as Terry "the Hulk" Boulder and Sterling Golden. He first hit the big time with the WWF in the early 1980s. With "heel" manager Classy Freddie Blassie at his side, Hogan played a muscular, egotistical blond villain. As was then common, he left one wrestling territory and moved to the next: the American Wrestling Association (AWA), based in Minneapolis, Minnesota.

Though Hogan had wrestled in both the WWF and AWA, his trips to Japan were what created the phenomenon known as "Hulkamania." Japanese wrestling fans immediately took to Hogan, and he became a superstar. He extended his success with a small but very noticeable part in *Rocky III*; his character, Thunderlips, is paired with Rocky in a boxer-versus-wrestler charity match. By 1983 Hogan was the biggest name in professional wrestling, but there was more to come.

Hulk Hogan. *Hulk Hogan has parlayed his popularity as a professional wrestler into a career as an actor, product pitchman, and reality television star.* © WALLY MCNAMEE/CORBIS.

SUPERSTARDOM

In late 1983 WWF owner Vince McMahon lured Hogan from the AWA and made him the star of his nationally expanding organization. In 1984 Hogan defeated the evil Iron Sheik in less than ten minutes at New York's Madison Square Garden to become the WWF champion. He began starring in wrestling shows across the country as the WWF became nationally syndicated and featured on cable programs. His feud with Rowdy Roddy Piper led first to the "brawl to settle it all," broadcast live on MTV, and then WrestleMania in March 1985, the first wrestling event to be broadcast nationally on closed-circuit TV. Hogan teamed with TV actor Mr. T in the main event to defeat Piper and his partner, Paul "Mr. Wonderful" Orndorff.

The success of WrestleMania soon earned Hogan and McMahon a show on NBC called *Saturday Night's Main Event*, which aired until 1992. Hogan's image was everywhere: on T-shirts, on the cover of a record album, in wrestling videos, and on TV shows. He was used to merchandise everything from dolls to jigsaw puzzles to ice cream bars. After his hugely successful match against Andre the Giant at WrestleMania III in March 1987, NBC broadcast their rematch in prime time in February 1988. More than thirty million people watched, as wrestling returned to prime time.

Hogan continued to roll, winning championships and headlining pay-per-view events, including an epic encounter with former tag-team partner Randy "Macho Man" Savage at WrestleMania V in 1989. He also found time to star in the movie *No Holds Barred* (1989), which failed to impress critics or draw much of an audience.

In the early 1990s, however, Hogan encountered difficulty when a doctor affiliated with the WWF was arrested for selling illegal steroids. The case expanded to include McMahon, with Hogan as a witness for the government. He went on *The Arsenio Hall Show* and denied being a steroid user or abuser, confessing only to a limited use of steroids for medical purposes. Friends and former wrestlers, including "Superstar" Billy Graham, called Hogan a liar; they were proved right when, at the steroids trial, Hogan confessed to additional use. After Hogan won the main event at WrestleMania VIII in 1992, he disappeared from wrestling as the steroid scandal intensified. A brief comeback proved to be a flop—his physique had shrunk and so too had his popularity. Hogan severed his relationship with the WWF, and it seemed his career was over.

REBORN

After some movie and television work, including the short-lived TV show *Thunder in Paradise* (1994), Hogan returned to the U.S. wrestling scene in the summer of 1994 just as the verdict of "not guilty" came down in the WWF steroids case. He went to work for Ted Turner's World Championship Wrestling (WCW) and had an immediate impact on ratings and pay-per-view revenue.

After failing to toughen up his image, Hogan finally "turned" on the fans in 1996 and adopted the persona of Hollywood Hogan, forming a group of wrestlers called the New World Order (NWO). The NWO soon became the hottest gimmick in wrestling, and Hogan was the focus of the promotion. Behind the scenes, he was acting as the de facto "head booker," deciding which wrestlers received TV time, wins, and championship belts. Hogan also demonstrated his star power by drawing celebrities such as National Basketball Association players Dennis Rodman and Karl Malone into the ring. One of the most memorable of these celebrity fights was between Hogan and *Tonight Show* host Jay Leno in a pay-per-view event in August 1998. Hogan used Leno's show in the fall of 1998 to announce that he was running for president. It was, like most developments in wrestling, a short-term stunt designed to boost ratings. Soon after, Hogan briefly went on hiatus from the WCW.

Hogan returned to the ring in January 1999 to regain the WCW title in an infamous match against Kevin Nash. He "knocked down" Nash with just one finger and then pinned him. The incident became known as the "Fingerpoke of Doom," and Nash's dive caused hundreds of thousands of viewers to switch allegiance to the rival WWF. Hogan's star power declined in the aftermath of this debacle. He left the WCW in 2000, and the company shut down the following year.

Hogan returned to the WWF to challenge Dwayne "The Rock" Johnson at WrestleMania X8 in Toronto in 2002. Hogan was billed as the heel, but during the match, fans cheered for the aging star. Though it was not a great physical match, the intensity from the crowd surpassed anything else from the event. Hogan lost to "The Rock," but his renewed fan support allowed him to regain the championship for a short time. Hogan and McMahon created a story line in which they were feuding leading up to a match at WrestleMania XIX, but behind the scenes, the heat between them was real.

From 2003 to 2006 Hogan would come and go from the WWE, showing up long enough to headline a pay-per-view event or be inducted into the WWE Hall of Fame in 2005. He needed wrestling and McMahon even less when he landed a reality TV show in 2005 titled *Hogan Knows Best*, which was broadcast on VH1.

THE FALL

Hogan Knows Best focused on Hogan's family, particularly his attempts to help his daughter, Brooke, succeed as a Britney Spears–type pop star and his son, Nick, pursue a career as a race-car driver. The show, which was about as "real" as wrestling, aired only until 2007.

Early in Hogan's career, everything he touched turned to gold. After leaving the WWE, however, his luck went south. He cohosted *American Gladiators* with Muhammad Ali's daughter Laila, but low ratings resulted in only a two-season run (2008–2009). In 2008 Country Music Television broadcast *Hulk Hogan's Celebrity Championship Wrestling*, which featured contestants such as former child stars Danny Bonaduce and Todd Bridges. This effort lasted only seven episodes. A 2011 show on TruTV, *Micro Championship Wrestling*, which featured little people as wrestlers, also lasted less than a season. Additionally, his 2011 video game, *Hulk Hogan's Main Event*, was named the worst offering of the year by several critics. Hogan returned to wrestling in January 2010, joining the fledgling Total Nonstop Action Wrestling (TNA) as both a wrestler and head booker. The signing of Hogan was supposed to bolster the company, but his impact turned out to be minimal.

Away from his work, Hogan's fortunes were equally dismal. In August 2007 Nick was involved in a serious auto accident, which left his passenger severely injured. Nick later pleaded no contest to criminal charges and was sentenced to time in prison. Hogan's wife of more than twenty years, Linda, filed for divorce just weeks after the accident. The divorce and the lawsuits related to Nick's car crash left Hogan nearly bankrupt, damaging a legacy he had spent decades building.

Patrick Jones

SEE ALSO: *Leno, Jay; MTV; Piper, "Rowdy" Roddy; Reality Television; Savage, Randy "Macho Man"; Spears, Britney; Television; Turner, Ted; World Wrestling Federation.*

BIBLIOGRAPHY

Hedegaard, Erik. "Hulk at Twilight." *Rolling Stone*, April 30, 2009, 50.

Hogan, Hulk, and Mark Dagostino. *My Life outside the Ring*. New York: St. Martin's, 2009.

Hogan, Hulk, and Michael Jan Friedman. *Hollywood Hulk Hogan*. New York: Pocket Books: World Wrestling Entertainment, 2002.

Hogan, Linda. *Wrestling the Hulk: My Life against the Ropes*. New York: William Morrow, 2011.

Reynolds, R. D., and Bryan Alvarez. *The Death of WCW*. Toronto: ECW Press, 2004.

Hogan's Heroes

The television show *Hogan's Heroes* was seen by most people in one of two ways: either as a cutting-edge situation comedy or as a testament to how desensitized to human suffering U.S. television viewers had become by the 1960s. The basic plot of the popular series centers on U.S. Colonel Robert Hogan, played by Bob Crane, and a band of other prisoners of war (POWs), who have established a secret complex within and below the grounds of Stalag 13, a Nazi concentration camp. From there they engage in sabotage and rescue operations against the Third Reich. Every bed is a passageway, every coffee pot a radio. For six seasons on CBS, Hogan and his group used a stash of supplies to confound Adolf Hitler's hapless forces in and around Düsseldorf, Germany.

Hogan's Heroes is loosely based on the play *Stalag 17* (1951), triggering a lawsuit by its producers, but the series also contains elements of the 1963 hit movie *The Great Escape*. Hogan's team is composed of demolition expert Andrew Carter (Larry Hovis), radio operator Ivan Kinchlow (Ivan Dixon), all-around procurer Peter Newkirk (Richard Dawson), and chef Louis LeBeau (Robert Clary). Their primary nemesis is Wilhelm Klink (Werner Klemperer), a pompous colonel who seeks promotion to general by constantly reminding his superiors that "no one has ever escaped from Stalag 13!" He is aided by Sergeant Major Hans Schultz (John Banner), who regularly stumbles across Hogan's escapades but, unable to fathom the consequences of his perceptions, manages to ignore them by chanting the mantra "I see nothing!" Among Klink's regular superiors are General Albert Burkhalter (Leon Askin) and Gestapo Major Wolfgang Hochstetter (Howard Cain). The show never actually features Hitler as a character, but he is impersonated twice—once on radio and once in person—to great comic effect.

While *Hogan's Heroes* was a popular show, it was also a lightning rod for controversy. In 1965, when the program first aired, organized reaction to the involvement of the United States in Vietnam was intensifying. It did not help matters much that corporate America was making huge amounts of money and the "silent majority" was settling back once a week to revel in the light-hearted high jinks, as a fun-loving bunch of POWs confounded their dumb but lovable Nazi tormentors.

This was not new territory. *McHale's Navy*, which debuted in 1962, features Ernest Borgnine as the commander of a U.S. patrol torpedo boat crewed by a load of drunks and petty thieves and catered to by an escaped Japanese POW named Fuji, who they hide from their dumbfounded commanding officer Admiral Binghamton (Joe Flynn). But the members of *McHale's Navy* rarely fight the enemy face-to-face. By comparison, a whole concentration camp of prisoners, who could have left at any time and chose not to, policed by representatives of a system of imbecility that appeared to stretch all the way to the top of the chain of command, was more than many people, particularly those less than a generation removed from the war, could stand.

The show's defenders countered that it was meant to be nothing more than slapstick entertainment. Indeed, the action of the show was extremely unrealistic—in one episode they smuggle a whole German army tank into camp, while in another Hogan convinces Klink and Burkhalter that the war is over. Supporters also pointed out that Clary had spent most of his early life in a concentration camp and thought ridicule a more than appropriate treatment of the Nazis. But those defenses mattered little to the show's critics, and *Hogan's Heroes* was regularly attacked throughout its run.

Barry Morris

SEE ALSO: McHale's Navy; *Sitcom; Television; World War II.*

BIBLIOGRAPHY

Cash, LaVerne. *New Beginnings: A Hogan's Heroes Story.* North Charleston, SC: BookSurge, 2004.

Royce, Brenda Scott. *Hogan's Heroes: Behind the Scenes at Stalag 13.* Los Angeles: Renaissance, 1998.

Shive, Nathan. *The Official "Hogan's Heroes" Companion.* New York: Macmillan, 1995.

Holbrook, Hal *(1925–)*

On April 6, 1959, a thirty-four-year-old actor took the stage in the role of a seventy-two-year-old Mark Twain. From his hair to his shoes, from his voice to his movements, Hal Holbrook became, from that night on, a living version of the icon of American literature. What was so extraordinary about this innovative dramatic event was that no actor had ever done a one-person show in which he actually embodied a historical figure. Holbrook's feat was a masterpiece of creativity; his acting was electrifying, and he received standing ovations every night. Holbrook thus initiated the one-actor play based on a historical, political, or literary personage. Although he has also earned acclaim as an accomplished film and television actor, it is for his landmark performance as Twain that he has remained most famous. In the process, Holbrook has played a crucial role in advancing the public's knowledge of Twain's writings.

Holbrook was born in Cleveland, Ohio, in 1925, but he was raised by his grandfather in Hartford, Connecticut. He attended Culver Military Academy and later Denison University, where he majored in acting. After his graduation, he and his first wife, actress Ruby Holbrook, toured the southwestern United States, playing William Shakespeare works in small-town high schools. These road shows ceased after two children arrived, and Holbrook returned to New York to act in the CBS television daytime series *The Brighter Day* from 1954 to 1959.

It was during these years that the young actor first developed his Twain persona, basing his performance on Twain's own lectures. With the encouragement of his former drama teacher at Denison, Ed Wright, Holbrook expanded his routine into a full-length show, which debuted off-Broadway as *Mark Twain, Tonight!* in 1959. The performance was a critical and popular success, and it earned Holbrook a Vernon Rice Award. In 1966 he starred in a revival of the play at Broadway's Longacre Theatre, a performance that garnered him a Tony Award. Holbrook brought the play back to Broadway two more times, once in 1977 and again in 2005. In November 2010, on the occasion of the 175th anniversary of Twain's birth, an eighty-five-year-old Holbrook again took the stage as the venerated author at the Clemens Center in Elmira, New York.

Along with his stage work in *Twain* and other plays, including *King Lear* and *Death of a Salesman*, Holbrook has been a well-respected television and film actor since the 1950s. He is the recipient of five Emmy Awards, including for his portrayal of Abraham Lincoln in *Sandburg's Lincoln* (1973); for his Kennedy-like senator in *The Senator* (1976); for his performance as Commander Bucher on the ill-fated *Pueblo* (1973); and for his part as the informational host of *Portrait of America: Alaska* (1989). He also accepted the challenge to be cast in the very first television drama dealing with homosexuals in the critically acclaimed *That Certain Summer* (1972). Holbrook portrayed Lincoln again in the *North and South* TV miniseries in 1985 and 1986; Reese Watson in *Designing Women* (with his third wife, Dixie Carter) from 1986 to 1989; and "Wild Bill" McKenzie in several *Perry Mason Mystery* episodes in the 1990s.

Holbrook also acted in numerous motion pictures, including a memorable turn as "Deep Throat" in the award-winning *All the President's Men.* In the 1990s he appeared in such films as *The Firm* (1993) and *The Bachelor* (1999), while also continuing to play a range of dramatic roles on television. Holbrook later received an Oscar nomination for Best Supporting Actor for his part in the acclaimed film *Into the Wild* (2007). In 2011 his autobiography, *Harold: The Boy Who Became Mark Twain* was released. Reviewing the work for the *Washington Post*, Louis Bayard recalled the daring of Holbrook's decision to play Twain, while describing the actor's career as a "uniquely American pilgrimage."

Toby Irene Cohen

SEE ALSO: *Academy Awards; Broadway; Emmy Awards; Television; Twain, Mark.*

BIBLIOGRAPHY

Bayard, Louis. "Review of *Harold: The Boy Who Become Mark Twain.*" *Washington Post*, October 14, 2011.

Holbrook, Hal. *Harold: The Boy Who Became Mark Twain.* New York: Farrar, Straus & Giroux, 2011.

Holden, William *(1918–1981)*

After actor William Holden was discovered in the late 1930s, he became one of the most dependable and likable leading men of 1950s Hollywood. He personified the mild-mannered charm of the Dwight D. Eisenhower era while, at his best, infusing integrity and feeling into a period that seemed bland and conformist. During his forty-three years as an actor, he had more than seventy roles, which he played with varying blends of wryness, cynicism, and good humor that were particularly successful in the mid-1950s.

Before joining the U.S. Air Force during World War II, Holden appeared in several feature films, including *Golden Boy* (1939) and *Our Town* (1940), exhibiting a homely and good-natured appeal. After returning from the war, he earned roles in a number of forgettable Westerns. He received an important break as a late replacement for Montgomery Clift in Billy Wilder's *Sunset Boulevard* (1950), showing a seedier side to his good looks by playing a failed Hollywood scriptwriter turned gigolo. Though the film was not a popular success, his role in *Born Yesterday* (1950) and his Oscar-winning performance in the prison camp comedy *Stalag 17* (1953) substantially raised his profile.

The lovable rogue of *Stalag 17* epitomizes Holden's best roles—characters who are relatively mild mannered yet opportunistic, brave if necessary but averse to confrontation. A series of parts as cads, lovers, and reluctant heroes followed in

***William Holden in* The Bridge on the River Kwai.** *William Holden starred in the classic World War II drama* The Bridge on the River Kwai *in 1957.* SILVER SCREEN COLLECTION/GETTY IMAGES.

The Moon Is Blue (1953), *Sabrina* (1954), *The Country Girl* (1954), *The Bridges at Toko-Ri* (1954), *Love Is a Many Splendored Thing* (1955), *Picnic* (1955), and *Bridge on the River Kwai* (1957)—most of which were highly successful. One of the top ten box-office stars from 1954 to 1956, Holden negotiated a deal that gave him 10 percent of the gross of *Bridge on the River Kwai*.

As his looks began to fade and 1960s audiences sought younger, more overt rebels, Holden was no longer a box-office certainty. Increasingly grizzled and marked by the alcoholism that would kill him in his sixties, he was still capable of outstanding performances—most notably as a sadistic, psychopathic cowboy in *The Wild Bunch* (1969) and as the fading anchorman wearily clinging to job and wife in *Network* (1976).

Like John Wayne or Robert Mitchum, Holden was most successful when he did not need to "act" but merely characterized a form of masculinity that appealed to 1950s audiences. Though his persona was not as attached to the uncompromising code of the Old West as Wayne's or as superhumanly laid back as Mitchum's, his masculinity had a broad appeal. His characters' good nature was tempered by skepticism and suspicion, which gave an edge to his heroism, and he often made moral choices with self-preservation in mind. He reflected the experiences of a generation of men who had been at war and knew the dangers of moral absolutes and strict codes of behavior (essentially the subject of *Bridge on the River Kwai*), and he flourished in the space between the bad-guy heroes of 1930s and 1940s gangster movies and the youth-oriented antiheroes of the 1960s, subtly embodying the hopes and fears of American men in the 1950s.

Kyle Smith

SEE ALSO: The Bridge on the River Kwai; *Clift, Montgomery; Mitchum, Robert; Movie Stars;* Network; Sunset Boulevard; *Wayne, John;* The Wild Bunch; *Wilder, Billy.*

BIBLIOGRAPHY

Capua, Michelangelo. *William Holden: A Biography*. Jefferson, NC: McFarland, 2010.

Parish, James Robert, and Don E. Stanke. *The All-Americans*. New Rochelle, NY: Arlington House, 1977.

Thomas, Bob. *Golden Boy: The Untold Story of William Holden*. London: Weidenfeld & Nicolson, 1983.

Holiday, Billie *(1915–1959)*

Billie Holiday, perhaps one of the foremost American song stylists and often called the greatest American jazz singer, was born Eleanora Harris on April 7, 1915, in Philadelphia. After her birth to Sadie Harris, the facts about Holiday are often in dispute, due in large part to Holiday's own tendency to spin tales about her life that have small kernels of truth but cannot be accepted wholesale as fact. The truth about her life is as interesting, if not more so, than her invention—recent biographers benefitted from extensive oral interviews done for a projected biography by Linda Kuehl (who died before completing it).

Listening to these recordings is a parallel version of Holiday's tumultuous and heartfelt life, one that expresses her beauty and soulfulness. However, as writer Hettie Jones warns, "Sometimes you are afraid to listen to this lady." Her short life was consumed by trouble: the wrong men, alcohol, heroin, racism, and just plain hard times, yet her personality was so winning that it shone through her vocals and she was well loved by her friends. What is certain is that the singer gave as good as she got; alternately tough-minded and intensely vulnerable, she helped create the mystique of Lady Day and nurtured it throughout her career.

Her autobiography, *Lady Sings the Blues* (1956; written by the *New York Post*'s William Dufty), is the prime source for the Holiday mythology. She bragged that she had never even read it, yet enough of her salty humor and dramatic timing made it into the book to capture an audience that was more than ready to accept it. What was painful to Holiday was often transformed in the narrative; the circumstances of her birth being a good example. Her mother told her that her father was Clarence Holiday, a talented guitarist best known for his work with Fletcher Henderson's band, and Holiday states in the book that "Mom and pop were just a couple of kids when I was born." They were never married nor lived together; Clarence acknowledged Eleanora, though their relationship was strained and awkward as he was married to another woman and disliked having his daughter around as evidence of his past.

Billie Holiday. *Considered one of America's greatest jazz singers, Billie Holiday, made her recording debut in 1933 when she was eighteen years old.* MICHAEL OCHS ARCHIVES/GETTY IMAGES.

HARSH CHILDHOOD

Growing up in Fell's Point, a tough waterfront neighborhood in Baltimore, Maryland, Eleanora experienced a brief, brutal childhood—her mother, forced to take work in New York as a maid, left her daughter in the care of abusive relatives. Only her great-grandmother (who she recalls with special fondness in *Lady*) was a source of solace to the little girl. Picked up for truancy, she was sent to the House of Good Shepherd for Colored Girls, a Catholic residential facility, where she was baptized and found some stability after a succession of "stepfathers" and being shunted around. Her recollections of Good Shepherd were mixed; she was glad to escape the harsh institution. Sadie was not able to handle her daughter, having enough problems of her own, and the breaking point came when the eleven-year-old girl was raped by a neighbor. She was returned to Good Shepherd but stayed only a short while before returning home.

The seminal event of young Eleanora's life was the discovery of jazz—she absorbed her first musical education listening to her lifelong idol, Louis Armstrong, on a Victrola in a neighborhood brothel. "I heard a record by, as we call him, Pops, and it was called 'West End Blues' and . . . he sang 'Ooh be doo,' and I would wonder why he didn't sing any words and he had the most beautiful thing." She always credited Armstrong as her major influence as a singer, although she was certainly influenced by Bessie Smith and others. Billie loved Armstrong and performed with him on a number of occasions.

Now fifteen, Eleanora became a prostitute in madam Alice Dean's house and soon was declared out of control by her guardian. Her exodus from Baltimore marked a turning point in her life when she made her way to New York to join her mother, who was employed as a maid. She was picked up in a Harlem vice raid along with Sadie, charged with prostitution, and spent a short time in a workhouse. After her discharge she found that she could make a good living as a singer in clubs, and she perfected her craft in juke joints. At this time she adopted her father's surname and chose the name Billie after silent film actress Billie Dove.

Holiday loved the club life, and she also took to marijuana, which was commonplace in the music world—aficionados were called "vipers," and "sticks" were cheap and easy to find. She had a prodigious tolerance for all substances, including alcohol, marijuana, and heroin. It would be a mistake to focus on Holiday as a singer ruined by addictions, yet there is no doubt her appetites shortened her life and harmed her voice. She was part of a culture that accepted drugs easily—one critic called them "an occupational hazard."

LADY DAY

The discovery of Holiday has been claimed by more than one person, and she herself told a story about auditioning as a dancer at the Harlem jazz club Pod and Jerry's and being hired as a singer, which in actuality was more fancy than fact. What is true is that in early 1933, white jazz writer and producer John Hammond was astonished when he heard Holiday sing, but it was not until November of that year that he was finally able to schedule a recording session and later signed her to Columbia Records.

In 1937 Holiday met saxophonist Lester Young, her soul mate musically and personally: their friendship was one of Holiday's deepest and most enduring relationships. It was Young who named her Lady Day (the "Day" from Holiday) and christened Sadie as Duchess when he lived with them after he first came to New York. Holiday called him Prez (short for "President," since she considered him the greatest), and their careers would intertwine over the years with memorable recordings to prove it. Holiday liked and supported other female singers: she and Ella Fitzgerald admired each other; she also befriended the young Lena Horne.

Holiday may have sung the blues, but she was primarily a jazz singer and one of the best interpreters of pop music. She disliked the title of her autobiography for that reason (the publisher chose it). In the words of the musicians who almost universally admired her: "She had ears"—meaning she understood the music thoroughly, earning the respect of Count Basie, Artie Shaw, and many others.

Her signature song, "Strange Fruit," is indescribably wrenching—an indictment of lynching so potent it silenced audiences whenever she performed it. With "Strange Fruit" her artistry confronted the fashionable jazz world of Café Society with the brutal reality of racism that black musicians knew firsthand. Lillian Smith told Holiday that the song inspired her to write her novel of the same name. Touring the South with Shaw's band, Holiday felt the force of Jim Crow. In her autobiography she states, "It got to the point where I hardly ever ate, slept, or went to the bathroom without having a major NAACP-type production."

RELATIONSHIP STRUGGLES

Many songs Holiday performed, including "The Man I Love," "Tain't Nobody's Business if I Do," and "My Man," often have been held up as an example of how Lady Day felt about the men in her life. Holiday was often exploited and abused by many people she trusted, but her choices reflected her deep ambivalence about love, as well as a measure of masochism. Musicians who worked with her loved her and deplored her boyfriends. One, Bobby Tucker, a faithful accompanist, called them pimps because they "lived off her," particularly the brutal John Levy and husband Louis McKay, who managed the singer by facilitating her drug habit and draining her financial resources. Hospitalized several times and jailed at Alderson Federal Reformatory in 1947, Holiday was penalized for her high-profile troubles. She lost her New York City cabaret license, which paradoxically opened up venues such as Carnegie Hall (where she performed several legendary concerts in 1948) but severely restricted her ability to make a living.

The 1972 film *Lady Sings the Blues*, a showcase for singer Diana Ross crafted for her by Berry Gordy as a new venue for Motown, distorted Holiday's life and created a love story from McKay's viewpoint (he served as a technical adviser on the picture). Despite Ross's strong performance, the film failed to create a convincing portrait and was critically panned. It did generate new interest in Holiday and her recordings, however, which translated into diverse appreciations of the singer, such as Alice Adams's novel *Listening to Billie* and an Australian film, *Billy's Holiday* (a fantasy wherein a male fan discovers he can sing like his favorite singer).

ICONIC IMAGE

Images of Holiday are ubiquitous on such items as T-shirts and posters: the "Lady with the Gardenia" (the flower she often wore in her hair), dressed to kill in elegant gowns, is an icon that has not only endured but has also become ever more popular, much as Marilyn Monroe or Elvis Presley has. In her discography, the Verve recordings (beginning in 1946) are often touted as her greatest, with her voice at its mature best and her spirit radiant in songs she made standards: "All of Me"; "Autumn in New York"; "Don't Explain"; and the song she coauthored, "God Bless the Child," best reflect Holiday's essential personality—an artist, first and foremost. A last recording, the controversial "Lady in Satin," shows the singer diminished but still innovating, working with a lush orchestral accompaniment.

Holiday's death on July 17, 1959, followed a long, sad decline precipitated by the death of Sadie and accelerated by her addiction. Hospitalized in New York in May 1959, Holiday was arrested for possession of narcotics in her hospital bed, a last indignity. In a 1956 interview, she told Mike Wallace why she thought jazz greats die young: "We try to live a hundred days in one day, and we try to please so many people. Like myself, I want to bend this note, bend that note, sing this way, sing that way, and get all the feeling, eat all the good foods, and travel all over in one day, and you can't do it."

Legendary stylist Frank Sinatra once stated that "Billie Holiday was, and still remains, the greatest single musical influence on me." Her friend, writer Leonard Feather, says of Holiday that "her voice was the voice of living intensity, of soul in the true sense of that greatly abused word. As a human being, she was sweet, sour, kind, mean, generous, profane, lovable, and impossible, and nobody who knew her expects to see anyone quite like her ever again."

Mary Hess

SEE ALSO: *Basie, Count; Big Bands; Fitzgerald, Ella; Gordy, Berry; Henderson, Fletcher; Horne, Lena; Jazz; Monroe, Marilyn; Motown; Presley, Elvis; Rhythm and Blues; Ross, Diana, and the Supremes; Shaw, Artie; Sinatra, Frank.*

BIBLIOGRAPHY

Baraka, Amiri. *Black Music*. New York: Morrow, 1968.

Chilton, John. *Billie's Blues: The True Story of the Immortal Billie Holiday*. London: Quartet Books, 1975.

Clarke, Donald. *Billie Holiday: Wishing on the Moon*. New York: Da Capo Press, 2002.

Davis, Angela Y. *Blues Legacies & Black Feminism: Gertrude "Ma" Rainey, Bessie Smith & Billie Holiday*. New York: Pantheon, 1998.

De Veaux, Alexis. *Don't Explain: A Song of Billie Holiday*. New York: Harper, 1980.

Gourse, Leslie. *Louis' Children: American Jazz Singers*. New York: Quill, 1984.

Gourse, Leslie. *The Billie Holiday Companion: Seven Decades of Commentary*. New York: Schirmer Books, 1997.

Holiday, Billie, and William Dufty. *Lady Sings the Blues*. New York: Doubleday, 1956.

James, Burnett. *Billie Holiday*. New York: Hippocrene, 1984.

Jones, Hettie. *Big Star Fallin' Mama: Five Women in Black Music*. New York: Viking Press, 1974.

Nicholson, Stuart. *Billie Holiday*. Boston: Northeastern University Press, 1995.

O'Meally, Robert G. *Lady Day: The Many Faces of Billie Holiday*. New York: Arcade, 1991.

Vail, Ken. *Lady Day's Diary: The Life of Billie Holiday 1937–1959*. Chessington, UK: Castle Communications, 1996.

White, John. *Billie Holiday*. New York: Universe Books, 1987.

Holiday Inns

Kemmons Wilson transformed roadside accommodations by building or franchising look-alike motels known as Holiday Inns. In 1952 entrepreneur Wilson, a high school dropout and home builder, opened the first Holiday Inn in Memphis, Tennessee, after returning from a road trip to Washington, D.C., with his wife and five children. During the trip Wilson had been disappointed with the typical motel or roadside cabin of the day, which tended to be overpriced, cramped units charging $2 extra for each child. Wilson's first motel, opened at the start of the postwar auto travel boom, was the prototype for the thousands of Holiday Inns that later formed a global giant much imitated by newer hotel-motel chains. At its height, Holiday Inn was opening a new facility every three days.

Wilson retired in 1979, and eighteen years later Holiday Inns Inc. was acquired for more than $2.2 billion by the British firm Bass PLC, which, by the end of the twentieth century, was operating or franchising more than 2,700 Holiday Inns and other hotels in ninety countries. Holiday Inns caught the public's fancy by offering uniformly family-friendly, unsurprising, and moderately priced accommodations, with each motel easily recognizable because of its large green-and-white sign.

By the twenty-first century, Holiday Inn was the largest division of the InterContinental Hotel Group, with 1,319 Holiday Inns and 2,018 Holiday Inn Expresses in operation worldwide. Quality had become inconsistent, however, and the chain was in danger of becoming marginalized. The response was to convince investors to ante up $1 billion for the most comprehensive brand refreshment in history. The refreshment included a new logo, new bedding and showers, and new advertising and marketing. The brand update was completed by the end of 2010, with plans to open 362 new Holiday Inns and 631 new Holiday Inn Expresses.

Michael Posner

SEE ALSO: *Highway System; Leisure Time.*

BIBLIOGRAPHY

Van Dyk, Deirdre. "Dreaming of a Rebound." *Time*, October 1, 2009.

Walton, William B., and Mel Lorentzen. *Innkeeper*. Wheaton, IL: Tyndale House Publishers, 1987.

Wilson, Kemmons, and Robert Kerr. *Half Luck and Half Brains: The Kemmons Wilson, Holiday Inn Story*. Nashville, TN: Hambleton-Hill, 1996.

Holliday, Judy *(1921–1965)*

In a relatively brief stage and screen career, Judy Holliday elevated the stock character of the dumb blond to a complex combination of naïveté, common sense, intelligence, and vulnerability. Born Judith Tuvim in New York City on June 21, 1921, Holliday started out in 1938 as a telephone operator at Orson Welles's Mercury Theatre. This led to friendships with Betty Comden, Adolph Green, and others, and they all formed a cabaret act called "The Revuers." After starting in nightclubs in New York's Greenwich Village, the act moved to the city's posh establishments and eventually to a sixteen-week run on the radio for NBC and an extended stay at Radio City Music Hall.

"The Revuers" headed for Hollywood in 1944 but failed to gain much notice. Although Holliday managed to land supporting roles in three films for Twentieth Century Fox, her contract was not renewed. She headed back to New York, where she was cast in the 1945 play *Kiss Them for Me* as Alice, a dumb blond. Holliday was praised by critics for rendering her character's sensitivity and vulnerability, and audiences loved her too. However, the play lasted only fourteen weeks.

In 1946 Holliday replaced Jean Arthur in *Born Yesterday* when Arthur left the play in Philadelphia. She learned the part of Billie Dawn in three days, and the play was a sensation when it opened on Broadway at the Lyceum Theater on February 4, 1946. Her performance helped her win the part of Doris Attinger in the MGM (Metro-Goldwyn-Mayer) film *Adam's Rib* (1949) with Spencer Tracy and Katharine Hepburn. According to Hollywood legend, this role was really Holliday's screen test for Harry Cohn, the tyrannical boss at Columbia Pictures. Following her success in *Adam's Rib*, she starred as Billie Dawn in the film version of *Born Yesterday* (1950). Holliday won the Academy Award for Best Actress, beating out Bette Davis, Gloria Swanson, Celeste Holm, and Anne Bancroft.

In 1952 Holliday's career was slowed when she was accused of communist leanings by the McCarran Committee. However, she did perform in a series of movies, including *The Marrying Kind* (1952), *It Should Happen to You* (1954), *Phffft* (1954), and *Solid Gold Cadillac* (1956). Holliday returned to Broadway in 1956, cast as the lonely telephone operator in *Bells Are Ringing*, a musical by Comden, Green, and Jule Styne that ran for three years. She then reprised her role opposite Dean Martin in the 1960 film version by MGM. It would be her last movie. In 1963 she was diagnosed with breast cancer, and following a two-year struggle, she died on June 7, 1965, two weeks before her forty-fourth birthday.

James R. Belpedio

SEE ALSO: *Academy Awards; Communism; Hepburn, Katharine; Martin, Dean; Tracy, Spencer; Welles, Orson.*

BIBLIOGRAPHY

Bordman, Gerald Martin, and Thomas S. Hischak. *The Oxford Companion to American Theatre*, 3rd ed. New York: Oxford University Press, 2004.

Thomson, David. *A Biographical Dictionary of Film*, 3rd ed. New York: Alfred A. Knopf, 1998.

Holly, Buddy *(1936–1959)*

As a songwriter, performer, and musician, Buddy Holly remains one of the most influential rock-and-roll entertainers of all time. Artists such as the Beatles, the Rolling Stones, Bob Dylan, the Byrds, Eric Clapton, Pete Townshend, Elton John, and Bruce Springsteen all acknowledged Holly's impact on their music. His career was tragically brief, lasting from September 1957 (when "That'll Be the Day" became a chart-topper) to February 3, 1959 (when he died in a plane crash in Iowa). However, as Holly biographer Philip Norman has pointed out, in that short period, "he created a blueprint for enlightened rock stardom that every modern newcomer with any pretense at self-respect still aspires to follow."

Holly's musical legend is replete with many firsts: He was the first rock performer to insist on artistic control over his material. He was the first to write his own songs, arrange them, and supervise his own studio sessions. He was the first to master the technical aspects of recording, achieving effects with echo, double-tracking, and overdubbing. He was the first to eschew the "pretty boy" looks of most performers in the 1950s, adopting a more bookwormish countenance that featured black horn-rim glasses. And he was the first rock performer capable of attracting faithful male fans and not just a female audience. Holly was only twenty-two years old when he died, but he left behind a legacy that has steadily grown in stature, making him one of the genuine legends of popular music.

BORN TO PERFORM

Born on September 7, 1936, in Lubbock, Texas, Holly was influenced by country and western music and rhythm and blues. At age five, he made his first onstage appearance, joining his brothers Larry and Travis for a talent contest in which they won $5. Holly took guitar, violin, and piano lessons, though he taught himself boogie-woogie rhythms on the piano. By age twelve, he was entertaining friends with Hank Williams's songs, and he formed the bluegrass duo Buddy and Bob with his friend Bob Montgomery in 1949. That year, after learning to play the banjo and mandolin, Holly laid down the first song of his career, "My Two Timin' Woman," on a home tape recorder. Holly and Montgomery were a sensation in Lubbock by 1952, and they recorded two songs in Holly's home that year and another in

1953. Additionally in 1953, they performed on KDAV radio, added Larry Welborn on bass, and were given their own program, *The Buddy and Bob Show*. KDAV disc jockey "Hipockets" Duncan became their manager, securing shows for them in west Texas. Fiddler Sonny Curtis and steel guitarist Don Guess were added in 1954, and the newly expanded band recorded songs in Lubbock and Wichita Falls. That same year, with drummer Jerry Allison now also in the mix, the band got a taste of the big time by opening concerts in Texas for Bill Haley & His Comets and Elvis Presley. Holly was intrigued by Presley's rock-and-roll style but continued to play country music.

Holly's group landed its first recording contract in December 1955, with Decca Records. The band, now minus Montgomery, recorded four songs in a Nashville studio on January 26, 1956. From that session, Decca released "Blue Days, Black Nights," backed with "Love Me," under the name Buddy Holly and the Three Tunes. However, by September 1956, Holly had left Decca because of the label's insistence that he continue playing country music and because of differences his band members had with Decca's session men. In late 1956, Holly, Allison, and Welborn traveled to Clovis, New Mexico, where they recorded two songs at a local studio. After returning to Lubbock, Holly formed the Crickets with Allison and Wiki Sullivan, who played rhythm guitar. On February 25, 1957, they returned to Clovis and recorded the classic "That'll Be the Day," trading their country stylings for a definitive rock-and-roll sound. Numerous record companies rejected the song until Brunswick Records finally released it in May 1957. With Clovis studio owner Norman Petty now managing the Crickets and Joe B. Mauldin having joined them as the bassist, "That'll Be the Day" received heavy promotion and reached number one by September 1957.

FAME AND FORTUNE

On the heels of the release of "That'll Be the Day," Buddy Holly and the Crickets spent three months touring the United States, playing such venues as the Apollo Theater in New York and the Howard Theater in Washington, D.C. Holly's band recorded an impressive body of work in 1957, including such classics as "Words of Love," "Maybe Baby," "Not Fade Away," "Everyday," "Oh Boy," and "Peggy Sue." Holly was experimental in the studio, using a variety of new production techniques, such as overdubbed vocals and double-tracked guitar parts. In 1957, "Peggy Sue" reached number three on the charts in the United States and "Oh Boy" hit number ten. The group closed out this watershed year by playing on the *Ed Sullivan Show*, an appearance it repeated in January 1958.

The Crickets also kicked off 1958 by recording "Rave On" in New York and touring Australia for six days in January and then recording "Well . . . All Right" in February. In early March, Holly's group toured England, where their songs were topping the charts, before returning to America to join a tour assembled by disc jockey Alan Freed that included Jerry Lee Lewis and Chuck Berry. As if 1958 had not been busy enough, Holly also married Maria Elena Santiago, recorded "Heartbeat," "Wishing," and "Love's Made a Fool of You," and held recording sessions that included Waylon Jennings, Phil Everly, and King Curtis.

By the time Holly's group toured the Northeast and Canada in October 1958, tension was growing between Holly and the band's manager, Petty. In addition, there was friction among Holly and the band members because of Holly's expressed desire to become a solo artist. Holly broke ties with Petty during the tour, and the other members of the Crickets opted to remain with the manager rather than Holly. On October 21, 1958, Holly worked with producer Dick Jacobs and studio musicians to record "True Love Ways," "It Doesn't Matter Anymore," "Raining in My Heart," and "Moondreams."

"THE DAY THE MUSIC DIED"

Holly assembled a new band, also called the Crickets, for the "Winter Dance Party" tour of the Midwest, which began on January 23, 1959, in Milwaukee, Wisconsin. The tour also included Ritchie Valens, the Big Bopper, and Dion and the Belmonts. On February 2, the tour played at the Surf Ballroom in Clear Lake, Iowa. Amid bitter weather conditions following that fateful show, Holly, Valens, and the Big Bopper chartered a small plane to take them to the next date in Moorhead, Minnesota. The idea was to avoid taking the tour bus, which had previously broken down and had a defective heater. Shortly after takeoff, about five miles north of Clear Lake, the plane crashed in a cornfield, killing Holly, Valens, the Big Bopper, and the pilot. Don McLean later memorialized the date as "the day the music died" in his classic song "American Pie."

Holly's popularity skyrocketed after his death—as late as the 1980s, his unreleased material was still being issued. Paul McCartney purchased the Holly song catalogue in the 1970s and began sponsoring annual Buddy Holly Week celebrations. Holly fan clubs, magazines, books, and websites abound, movies and musicals based on his life have been produced, and a statue of him was erected in Lubbock. There are also two memorials in Clear Lake, Iowa—one is a large, gray stone located at the Surf Ballroom, and the other, placed at the crash site, is a guitar and three records fashioned out of stainless steel.

Dennis Russell

SEE ALSO: *Berry, Chuck; Big Bopper; Electric Guitar; "La Bamba"; Lewis, Jerry Lee; Rock and Roll; Teen Idols; Valens, Ritchie.*

BIBLIOGRAPHY

Amburn, Ellis. *Buddy Holly: A Biography*. New York: St. Martin's Press, 1995.

Goldrosen, John, and John Beecher. *Remembering Buddy: The Definitive Biography*. New York: Penguin, 1987.

Lehmer, Larry. *The Day the Music Died: The Last Tour of Buddy Holly, the Big Bopper, and Ritchie Valens*. New York: Schirmer Trade Books, 2004.

Norman, Philip. *Rave On: The Biography of Buddy Holly*. New York: Simon & Schuster, 1996.

Tobler, John. *The Buddy Holly Story*. New York: Beaufort Books, 1979.

Hollywood

In America, Hollywood is often portrayed as a promised land—a sun-kissed playground with the weather of a modern-day Eden. Known for its central role in the U.S. film industry, the small district of the city of Los Angeles is more than a place: it is an idea that has captivated the American imagination. Hollywood represents a land where anything can be bought and nothing is out of reach. Even after its downtown area became a sleazy mixture of tourist attractions and dilapidated office buildings in the late twentieth century, Hollywood continues to be America's capital of glamour. Inextricably linked to its golden age, the district is known for a bygone era when enormous film studios lined side streets, talent agencies occupied office buildings, and swank restaurants and nightclubs occupied busy thoroughfares.

EARLY HISTORY AND DEVELOPMENT

In 1887 Kansas real estate tycoon Horace Henderson Wilcox began mapping out the streets of a town built especially for stolid midwesterners who were sick of ice and snow. The Wilcoxes, themselves pious midwesterners, banned saloons and offered land gratis to any church willing to locate there. The embryonic community was nestled 12 miles from the Pacific Ocean at the foot of a ridge of gentle hills, which sheltered farms from the brutal desert winds. It was an idyllic setting, and Wilcox's homesick wife named it Hollywood after the country place of a family friend.

Brad Pitt and Angelina Jolie at the Academy Awards. *Angelina Jolie waves as she and Brad Pitt walk the red carpet at 2012 Academy Awards in Hollywood, California, which has served as the epicenter of the film industry since the early twentieth century.* JEFF KRAVITZ/FILMMAGIC/GETTY IMAGES.

In 1903 future *Los Angeles Times* publisher Harry Chandler and general and railroad tycoon Moses Hazeltine Sherman formed a syndicate that incorporated the city's vacant fields as an independent municipality—a prime example of the land speculation that remains typical of Los Angeles. The duo built a trolley line from downtown and a thirty-three-room Spanish-style hotel on the unpaved Hollywood Boulevard. However, the population at the time was a mere 500. In order to attract what they considered solid citizens (midwestern farmers), Chandler and Sherman continued in the pious tradition of the Wilcoxes by outlawing saloons. In 1910 the Hollywood Board of Trustees also banned movie theaters, though none existed there at the time.

ARRIVAL OF THE FILM INDUSTRY

The film industry came to Los Angeles in 1907, the result of a fluke. Winter storms prompted producer William Selig of the Chicago-based Selig Studios to go west in search of an alternate location to film. Selig made *The Count of Monte Cristo* (1908), the first motion picture shot in California, in Laguna Beach and was so taken by the area that he returned the following year, setting up shop in a converted Chinese laundry east of downtown.

Soon film companies were flocking to Los Angeles for financial and legal reasons. The weather accommodated outdoor shoots year round, and the Los Angeles basin afforded a wealth of natural scenery. "It was all rather pristine and primeval," Otto Friedrich writes in *City of Nets*. "Cops and robbers chased each other through the streets and directors improvised their stories as they went along." A further incentive lay in Los Angeles's remote location: Independent film producers were at war with inventor Thomas Alva Edison's syndicate, which sought to milk the industry ad infinitum by enforcing patents on film and projection equipment. In remote Los Angeles, collecting royalties would be difficult for Edison.

At first, the majority of studios settled in Edendale, a hilly and somewhat congested area just west of downtown Hollywood. In 1911 the Nestor Film Company became the first film studio to establish itself in Hollywood proper. By that time, the city of Los Angeles had subsumed Hollywood, rendering the prohibition against movie theaters null and void. Thus, film production in the 1920s was wholly centered in Hollywood, with a scattering of studios established to the north in Burbank or southwest in Culver City. Movie stars staked their claim to the geographic high ground, moving from downtown (the adjacent Silver Lake was the neighborhood of choice for the earliest silent stars) to the Hollywood Hills and to the lush western canyons of Beverly Hills.

THE SILENT ERA

As the film industry continued to grow in the 1910s and 1920s, Hollywood's legend began to spread. By some accounts (most notably Kenneth Anger's lurid, sensationalistic *Hollywood Babylon* [1975]), the silent era was a never-ending party of dope, booze, and aggressive promiscuity. Even in this innocent time, drugs were an acceptable subject for pictures. In 1916, for instance, actor Douglas Fairbanks Sr. starred in *The Mystery of the Leaping Fish* as Coke Ennyday, a besotted detective who liberally used "joy powder." However, the cavalier attitude met with tragic results in 1920, when popular starlet Olive Thomas committed suicide in Paris after she had failed to procure heroin. In 1921 comedian Fatty Arbuckle was arrested for the death of aspiring starlet Virginia Rappe as a result of "rough sex," and the following year director William Desmond Taylor was murdered in his home.

Studio publicists worked overtime at damage control, even as newspapers owned by media mogul William Randolph Hearst played up such salacious stories in pursuit of an ever-wider readership. In the wake of public outrage, Hollywood production heads reluctantly appointed William H. Hays, a Republican functionary, as arbiter of public morality. Though studio heads were slow to adopt such new regulations, the notorious Hays Office and its West Coast enforcer Joseph Breen would pass judgment on all Hollywood products in the 1930s and 1940s. Hays declared that movies needed purifying, both in content and cast. To aid in the latter, he released a blacklist (considered by many as the predecessor to the anticommunist blacklists of the McCarthy era) that ended the careers of many screen idols, such as actor Wallace Reid, one of Paramount's biggest stars (he died in a sanitarium the following year), and actresses Juanita Hansen and Alma Rubens, both popular leading ladies who died shortly after appearing on Hays's list.

At the time, the 1920s were considered a golden age in Hollywood, though they proved merely a holding pattern until the next big thing—sound—came along. In short order, talkies separated new talent from the old. Actors who had succeeded on their looks but had no training in elocution, had undesirable speaking voices, or had thick regional accents disappeared. Actress Clara Bow, born and raised in Brooklyn, New York, found her career prospects hampered when she blew out the microphones during her first sound scene. One of Hollywood's most successful leading men, actor John Gilbert, was said to be similarly affected after sound technicians neutered his tenor voice; by the mid-1930s, he had succumbed to alcoholism.

THE GOLDEN AGE

With the advent of sound, the movies—and Hollywood itself—began to mature. No longer a curiosity, movies began to reflect American consciousness, values, and lore. Warner Brothers specialized in gangster films, Universal made its living off of horror films, MGM created lighthearted fare, and Columbia made wisecracking screwball comedies. It seemed that films that failed to tap into deep-seated American archetypes were destined to sink from view in a matter of weeks.

As instruments of Americans' unconscious desires, film stars became demigods and demigoddesses reflecting American virtues and vices. For a time, the places where film industry figures staged their debauches became as well known as the stars who patronized them. Establishments such as Chasen's, Musso & Frank's, the Brown Derby, and the Montmartre evoked an era when film deals were made over three-martini lunches and stars relaxed after a day of shooting at exclusive watering holes. At lunch time, crowds would gather around Hollywood eateries in the hopes of catching a glimpse of actor Cary Grant or actress Marlene Dietrich.

Even as the country struggled through the Great Depression, Hollywood wallowed in abundance. Far from taking umbrage with celebrity antics, the public took Hollywood high living as a reassuring sign that better times lay ahead. "Around the globe Hollywood became Tinseltown, a land of dreams and luxury," writes Ronald L. Davis in *The Glamour Factory*. "For the American public, raised on an ethic that emphasized success, material wealth, and social mobility, Hollywood embodied a national ideal."

Although Los Angeles was not alone in having luxurious movie palaces, the theaters that lined Hollywood Boulevard became world famous, especially for the red-carpet events they so frequently hosted. Grauman's Chinese Theatre became a national landmark for its premieres and the famous footprints and handprints embedded in concrete around the box office. Although neighboring theaters El Capitan and the Egyptian fared poorly in the second half of the twentieth century, Mann's has remained a Hollywood institution. Along with Musso & Frank's, the theater marks one of the last vestiges of Hollywood's glamour years.

DECLINE OF THE STUDIO SYSTEM

By 1939 movies were the nation's eleventh-largest industry, grossing $700 million in a single year and attracting more than fifty million Americans to the theaters every week. But the studios that had built an empire in Hollywood soon ran into trouble. After two decades of staving off U.S. Department of Justice antitrust lawsuits, Hollywood moguls divested themselves of their theater holdings and ended their unreasonable, but lucrative, booking practices, such as forcing theater owners to buy films in blocs. In addition, the star system that moguls had pinned their fortunes on backfired with disastrous results. Stars demanded enormous salaries and began packaging their own deals, in effect usurping the role of the studios, which now were at the mercy of actors, agents, and managers.

Television also contributed to the demise of the studio system. Large studios ignored the threat posed by the small screen, watching their profits evaporate during the 1950s and early 1960s as movies grew further out of touch with the postwar audience. However, film noir, one of cinema's most enduring and symbolically rich genres, fell perfectly in step with the mood of paranoia and desperation sweeping the country. The genre's richness was unintentional, constructed by "B" movies and programmers, not the epic, sweeping dramas that studios had proudly produced.

NEW HOLLYWOOD

Ironically "B" movie actors and directors, more attuned to the changing times, saved major film studios by ushering in New Hollywood. The era became for many the last golden age of American moviemaking. By the early 1960s Hollywood profits had withered, and oil and insurance companies (such as Gulf & Western) snapped up film production companies as an opportunity to diversify their investments. Desperately seeking salvation from the financial doldrums, executives began to take gamble on new ideas.

Director Mike Nichols's *The Graduate* (1967) redefined the parameters of what could be shown on screen. The casting of actor Dustin Hoffman in the lead opened up opportunities for actors such as Robert De Niro and Al Pacino, both of whom differed from the traditional image of the fair-haired, muscular film star, to be treated as legitimate leading men. *Bonnie and Clyde* (1967), *Easy Rider* (1969), and *Midnight Cowboy* (1969) soon followed—all films that would have been unthinkable ten years earlier. Executives, who were scornful of the new generation's politics and artistic influences, were forced to change with the times.

The 1970s proved a time of great artistic ferment in Hollywood. Directors, who at times had been relegated to the role of glorified technicians by the major studios, were now heroes. With their newfound power, they explored territory that only a decade earlier would have been strictly forbidden. As director Robert Altman put it, "Suddenly there was a moment when it seemed as if the pictures you wanted to make, they wanted to make." Directors Martin Scorsese, Francis Ford Coppola, William Friedkin, Hal Ashby, and Peter Bogdanovich burst into prominence, making edgy, uncompromising films. However, as film budgets grew more outrageous and as directors, fueled by a combination of drugs and hubris, grew more stunning in their arrogance, studio executives, nursing a decade of bruised egos, once again took control of Hollywood.

BLOCKBUSTERS AND REVITALIZATION

By the 1970s, after a decade of war and civil unrest, the nation wanted entertainment—and not just the sort television could provide. Americans wanted spectacle. The death knell of New Hollywood was the success of two films: *Jaws* (1975) and *Star Wars* (1977). A few years later, producer Don Simpson had turned spectacle into a science, producing a string of mindless but entertaining hits. His first, *Flashdance* (1983), had a simple plot: a blue-collar dancer yearns to be ballerina. Film critics decried his other equally simple-minded films—*Top Gun* (1986), *Beverly Hills Cop* (1984), and *Days of Thunder* (1990). Nevertheless, Simpson's work, the so-called high-concept film, was king. Event films, or blockbusters, became a Hollywood staple throughout the 1980s and 1990s. Not much more than glorified genre films, these all-American spectacles of excess featured sex, violence, and mind-boggling special effects.

The trend evolved in the first decade of the 2000s and the 2010s as filmmakers found ways of making new money out of old projects. Studios issued remakes of popular films from the previous century, such as *3:10 to Yuma* (2007), *The Manchurian Candidate* (2004), *The Karate Kid* (2010), and *Halloween* (2007). Filmmakers also issued digitally remade versions of classic films, such as 3-D versions of *Titanic* (1997) and *Star Wars* (1977).

As Hollywood Boulevard moldered through the 1990s, only a few relics of the glory years remained among the cheap tourist gift shops, homeless people, and Scientology buildings. The new millennium saw a revitalization of Hollywood's infrastructure, including the opening of the new Kodak Theatre (now called the Dolby Theatre) in 2001 on the site of the old Hollywood Hotel. The theater became internationally known as the new home of the Academy Awards. In 2006 Los Angeles made Hollywood into an official district, further legitimizing the historic location. The district remains a magnet for tourists, many of whom wish to see the iconic Hollywood sign (an accidental remnant of a failed housing project).

Although only one studio, Paramount (a subsidiary of Viacom), remains within Hollywood's borders, the district's landscape remains a powerful symbol. In 1949 producer David O. Selznick mused, "Hollywood's like Egypt. Full of crumbling pyramids. It'll never come back. It'll just keep on crumbling until finally the wind blows the last studio prop across the sand." He was both right and wrong. Although multinational corporations have bought all of the major film studios that created Hollywood and have relocated them elsewhere, the idea of a place where dreams come true, where anyone can become a star, is ineffable.

Michael Baers

SEE ALSO: *Academy Awards; Altman, Robert; Arbuckle, Fatty; "B" Movies; Blacklisting;* Bonnie and Clyde*; Bow, Clara; Celebrity; De Niro, Robert; Dietrich, Marlene;* Easy Rider*; Edison, Thomas Alva; Fairbanks, Douglas, Sr.; Film Noir;* The Graduate*; Grant, Cary; The Great Depression;* Halloween*; Hoffman, Dustin; The Hollywood Ten;* Jaws*;* Midnight Cowboy*; Movie Palaces; Movie Stars; Pacino, Al; Scorsese, Martin; Selznick, David O.; Silent Movies;* Star Wars*; Studio System; Television;* Variety.

BIBLIOGRAPHY

Anger, Kenneth. *Hollywood Babylon.* New York: Dell Publishing, 1975.

Biskind, Peter. *Easy Riders, Raging Bulls: How the Sex-Drugs-and-Rock-n-Roll Generation Saved Hollywood.* New York: Simon & Schuster, 1998.

Davis, Ronald L. *The Glamour Factory.* Dallas, TX: Southern Methodist University Press, 1993.

Fleming, Charles. *High Concept: Don Simpson and the Hollywood Culture of Excess.* New York: Doubleday, 1998.

Friedrich, Otto. *City of Nets.* New York: Harper & Row, 1986.

Gabler, Neal. *An Empire of Their Own: How the Jews Invented Hollywood.* New York: Crown Publishers, 1988.

McDougal, Dennis. *The Last Mogul: Lew Wasserman, MCA, and the Hidden History of Hollywood.* New York: Da Capo Press, 2001.

Schatz, Thomas. *The Genius of the System: Hollywood Filmmaking in the Studio Era.* New York: Pantheon Books, 1988.

Scott, Allen John. *On Hollywood: The Place, the Industry.* Princeton, NJ: Princeton University Press, 2005.

Sommer, Robin Langley. *Hollywood: The Glamour Years (1919–1941).* New York: Gallery Books, 1987.

Thomson, David. *The Whole Equation: A History of Hollywood.* New York: Random House, 2004.

Wallace, David. *Lost Hollywood.* New York: St. Martin's Press, 2001.

Hollywood Squares

One of television's most popular game shows during its fifteen-year run, from 1966 to 1981, *Hollywood Squares* combined high camp, humor, and a modicum of intellect to become an audience favorite. As described in *Entertainment Weekly*'s "The Best Game Shows of All Time," "Nine celebs sat inside a three-story ticktacktoe board and parried questions with wacky ad-libs (which turned out to be scripted)." Hosted by the good-natured Peter Marshall, the squares were occupied by "A"- and "B"-list stars from film, television, and music. The center square, however, was the hub of the show. First occupied by Ernest Borgnine, the center square came to be the domain of the acerbically witty and very camp Paul Lynde and was later taken over by the inimitable Joan Rivers.

A hip new *Hollywood Squares* debuted in 1998 with Tom Bergeron as host and Whoopi Goldberg in the coveted center square, proving that pop culture always has a place for amiable schlock. Goldberg left the show in 2002. A rotating roster filled the center spot until 2004, the final season, when the center square was taken over by comedian Martin Mull.

Victoria Price

SEE ALSO: *Camp;* Entertainment Weekly*; Game Shows; Goldberg, Whoopi; Marie, Rose; Rivers, Joan; Television.*

BIBLIOGRAPHY

"The Best Game Shows of All Time." In *The 100 Greatest TV Shows of All Time*, 70–71. New York: Entertainment Weekly Books, 1998.

Holms, John Pynchon, and Ernest Wood. *The TV Game Show Almanac.* Radnor, PA: Chilton Book, 1995.

Shaw, Jessica. "Question: What Campy Celebrity-Studded Game Show Is Making Whoopi with a $25 Million Face-Lift? Answer: You Need to Ask?" *Entertainment Weekly*, September 18, 1998.

Spring, Greg. "'Squares' Rolling Like a 'Wheel.'" *Electronic Media* 18, no. 13 (1999).

Watson, Bret. "When It Was Hip to Be Square." *Entertainment Weekly*, October 18, 1996.

The Hollywood Ten

In the fall of 1947, a group of ten prominent artists working in film, who were to enter American history as the Hollywood Ten, were subpoenaed by the House Un-American Activities Committee (HUAC) as part of investigations into "the extent of Communist infiltration in the Hollywood motion picture industry." Taking the First Amendment, the Hollywood Ten denied HUAC's constitutional legitimacy as well as its right to inquire into an individual's personal and political beliefs and refused to answer any of the committee's questions. In their prepared statements, they went so far as to compare the activities of the committee to those of Nazi Germany and stated that HUAC heralded the onset of a new fascism within American life.

The Ten's refusal to cooperate in admitting to their political affiliations resulted in their being tried at the federal court in Washington, D.C., in April 1948. Found guilty of contempt, writer-producer Herbert Biberman; director Edward Dmytryk; producer-writer Adrian Scott; and screenwriters Alvah Bessie, Lester Cole, Ring Lardner Jr., John Howard Lawson, Albert Maltz, Samuel Ornitz, and Dalton Trumbo were each sentenced to one year in jail and a $1,000 fine. They were blacklisted by the film industry and for many years were able to work only by living abroad or under cover of a pseudonym. (Robert Rich, for example, who won an Oscar for his script for *The Brave One* in 1956, was actually Trumbo.)

The Hollywood Ten became a benchmark for resistance against the investigative powers of the congressional committees during the Cold War, but their treatment left a shameful blot on the community that ostracized them. It was an omen for a much wider process that expanded to all sectors of American society and eventually all but destroyed the liberal left in America. The cultural consequences of their indictment and the subsequent blacklisting of many of their distinguished peers were serious—Hollywood was deprived of many of its finest and most intelligent creative talents, and the climate of fear that came to prevail led to blandness, even sterility, of artistic expression and new ideas for fully a decade.

NAMING NAMES

Matters grew worse when Dmytryk recanted his position and agreed to cooperate with the HUAC. He was released early from jail, admitted past membership of the Communist Party, and took himself to England. Ironically, Dmytryk is admired for the socially conscious, humane stance of some of his best work, including the antifascist drama *Hitler's Children* (1943) and *Crossfire* (1947), a serious attempt to address anti-Semitism. He returned from exile in 1951, stood as a witness in the HUAC's second round of hearings into Hollywood, and named names. He was not alone. Altogether over this dark period in Hollywood's history, some 300 "witnesses" confessed to their own past communist affiliations, and many also incriminated their fellows. Among the more celebrated who failed to take the First Amendment were writers Clifford Odets, Isabel Lennart, and Budd Schulberg; actors Sterling Hayden and Larry Parks; and, famously, the great director Elia Kazan, whose appearance to receive a special Oscar at the 1999 Academy Awards ceremony opened old wounds and provoked furious controversy.

The fate of the Hollywood Ten exemplified that of anyone who refused to cooperate with the HUAC. The refusal of any individual to name names before the committee was interpreted as evidence of communist or fellow-traveling sympathies, and the fate of the Ten instigated an ignominious cycle of cowardice and betrayal in the Hollywood community. The FBI put many creative artists under surveillance, and at least two victims of the hearings committed suicide. The roll call of those either "named" by their peers or blacklisted on suspicion is long, shocking, and substantial.

Among the many who suffered the harsh artistic, economic, and social consequences of blacklisting were writers Ben Barzman, Waldo Salt, Dashiell Hammett, and Lillian Hellman; director Joseph Losey; writer-directors Carl Foreman, Jules Dassin, and Abraham Polonsky; actors Anne Revere and Gale Sondergaard; satirist Dorothy Parker; and Paula Miller (second wife of method acting teacher Lee Strasberg). Foreman, Dassin, and Losey in particular continued to forge careers in Europe; the more fortunate actors found work on the stage, while others were forced into retirement. Actor John Garfield died in 1952, aged thirty-nine, from a heart attack said to have been caused by the strain of the investigations.

BACK TO WORK

Blacklisting began to fade in the late 1950s, along with the rest of the McCarthyite hysteria that had for so many years held Americans under threat. Many of the previously blacklisted writers and directors were able to return openly to Hollywood, where their achievements were a salutary lesson in the loss that films had suffered by their absence. Thanks to the insistence of Kirk Douglas and Otto Preminger, Trumbo was the first screenwriter to reemerge under his own name on the credits of, respectively, *Spartacus* and *Exodus* (both 1960).

Robert Rossen added *The Hustler* (1961) to his distinguished body of work pre-1951. Polonsky, whose career had been completely ruined by the hearings and his subsequent exile, came back to make only his second of three films, the highly regarded Western *Tell Them Willie Boy Is Here* (1969), and Lardner wrote the Academy Award–winning screenplay for *M*A*S*H* (1970). Foreman, who had just completed the screenplay for *High Noon* (1952) when he was blacklisted, never returned from Britain but was posthumously acknowledged in 1985 for his previously uncredited Oscar-winning work on *The Bridge on the River Kwai* (1957). Salt received the Oscar for *Midnight Cowboy* (1969), shared it for *Coming Home* (1978), and was nominated for *Serpico* (1973).

The unwavering courage of the Hollywood Ten and others continues to stand as a historic reproach to the movie moguls who caved in to McCarthyite demands to "clean up" their industry.

Nathan Abrams

SEE ALSO: *Academy Awards; Blacklisting; Cold War; Communism; FBI (Federal Bureau of Investigation); Garfield, John; Hammett, Dashiell; Hellman, Lillian;* High Noon*; Hollywood; Lardner, Ring;* M*A*S*H*; McCarthyism; Parker, Dorothy; Preminger, Otto;* Spartacus.

BIBLIOGRAPHY

Bentley, Eric, ed. *Thirty Years of Treason: Excerpts from Hearings before the House Committee on Un-American Activities, 1938–1968.* New York: Viking, 1971.

Ceplair, Larry, and Steven Englund. *The Inquisition in Hollywood: Politics in the Film Community 1930–1960.* New York: Anchor/Doubleday, 1980.

Dmytryk, Edward. *Odd Man Out: A Memoir of the Hollywood Ten.* Carbondale: Southern Illinois University Press, 1996.

Kahn, Gordon. *Hollywood on Trial: The Story of the Ten Who Were Indicted.* New York: Boni & Gaer, 1948.

Navasky, Victor S. *Naming Names.* New York: Viking, 1980.

Holocaust

Over the span of four nights, between April 16 and 19, 1978, approximately 120 million Americans watched at least some of an NBC miniseries that graphically portrayed the genocide of six million Jews during the Nazi era. Commercial prime-time television may have seemed an unlikely venue for this kind of subject matter, but *Holocaust* aired at a moment in American network history when more serious topics began to get a toehold in that broadcasting time slot. The phenomenal and unprecedented success the year before of the miniseries *Roots* paved the way for *Holocaust*. In fact, NBC gave the production its go-ahead during the week that *Roots* aired. That series' record-breaking Nielsen numbers apparently gave the network confidence that if American viewers were willing to sit through night after night of brutal, realistic depictions of slavery in America, then they might also brave the images of genocide.

Producer Herbert Bodkin, director Marvin Chomsky (who had directed an episode of *Roots*), and writer Gerald Green wanted to avoid reproducing *Roots* in a Jewish context, however. While the earlier series was shot entirely on the Hollywood back lot, *Holocaust* was filmed in Europe. The Mauthausen concentration camp in Germany stood in for Auschwitz, thus giving camp scenes a chilling sense of verisimilitude. Some responses to the project during its production were challenging. In Germany and Austria, many local technicians declined to work on the shoot. Swastikas occasionally appeared on sets. Officials in Hungary, Czechoslovakia, and Yugoslavia refused permission to film in their countries, arguing that the script contained "Zionist" elements.

Holocaust also differed from *Roots* in that it avoided filling its cast with highly recognizable stars. The producers didn't want viewers to be distracted by the star power of performers but rather to accept the actors as the characters they played. *Holocaust*'s cast included then-little-known players such as Meryl Streep, James Woods, and Michael Moriarty.

Like *Roots*, *Holocaust* used the family melodrama genre to tell its sweeping tale of human misery and survival. The series focused on two German families: the Weisses, who are thoroughly assimilated German Jews, and the Dorfs. Most of the Weisses are sent to concentration camps. The artist son (Woods) finds himself in Tereisen, the Nazis' "model" camp for high-profile Jews, especially those with artistic talent. The narrative focuses on the utter squalor and horror of the place and the attempt by artists to document their experience there. The Weisses' daughter (Blanche Baker) is raped and then put into a hospital for the mentally ill, where the Nazi policies toward "mental defectives" ensure that she is quickly killed. Mr. and Mrs. Weiss, along with their Catholic daughter-in-law (Streep), end up in Auschwitz. A particularly graphic scene portrays the supposed "showers" the women were to have; the audience views a portrayal of them being gassed. Only the youngest son (Timothy Bottoms) survives. He escapes a concentration camp and joins Jewish partisans fighting the Germans. The Dorf family includes Erik (Moriarty), an unemployed lawyer, and his ambitious wife, who persuades him to take a job with the Nazi security forces. Dorf rises quickly through Nazi ranks, becoming an aide to top architect of the Final Solution, Heinrich Heydrich (David Warner).

The miniseries received many of the same criticisms heaped on *Roots*: it took one of history's greatest human horrors and turned it into a soap opera. It made the unimaginable too easily accessible. It gave audiences only abject Jewish passivity on the one hand and heroic, active Jewish resistance on the other hand. Other critics praised the production for not flinching from brutality: there was no turning away from scenes of mass murder, torture, and death camp ovens. The realism proved too much for some midwestern NBC affiliates, which found the portrayal of naked women driven to the gas chambers too graphic and asked the network to delete the offending scenes in their markets. Commentators complimented the series for not portraying the Nazis as boot-clicking, saluting caricatures. Instead, the actors played their characters as ordinary people who too easily followed the instructions of a fascist regime. Notably, the actors did not attempt German accents.

By March 1979, thirty-one countries had bought rights to the film. While *Holocaust* was a success in North America, it became a phenomenon of historic proportions when broadcast in West Germany in January 1979. Nearly half of the population watched at least some of the series, the vast majority responding to it positively. Germans had been exposed to relatively little information about the Nazi period or the Holocaust since the end of the war. The broadcast of *Holocaust* partially broke that silence, opening up debate among family, friends, and coworkers and generating new discussions by broadcast and print media and among academicians. The miniseries was preceded by the showing of documentaries and followed by television debates and phone-in programs. Almost overnight, Germans, especially secondary school students, were demanding discussion of Germany's Nazi past. Those born after World War II argued that there were links between that past and modern-day terrorism.

In the political arena, the showing of *Holocaust* may have also been instrumental in influencing the Bundestag to vote to discontinue a policy of statute of limitations for Nazi war crimes. Polls taken in West Germany revealed that the number of people who wanted the prosecutions to continue increased by 24 percent after watching *Holocaust*. In Austria, the number of people who accepted that the Nazis had indeed perpetrated mass murder rose from 72 percent to more than 80 percent.

In North America *Holocaust* demonstrated that network television could tackle weighty issues of human tragedy. In Germany the miniseries might have caused an entire nation to reflect seriously on its historical demons.

Aniko Bodroghkozy

SEE ALSO: *Docudrama; Hollywood; Made-for-Television Movies; Movie Stars;* Roots; *Streep, Meryl; Television; World War II.*

BIBLIOGRAPHY

Doneson, E. Judith. *The Holocaust in American Film.* New York: Syracuse University Press, 2002.

Markovits, Andrei S., and Rebecca S. Hayden. "Holocaust before and after the Event: Reactions in West Germany and Austria." *New German Critique* 19, no. 53 (1980).

Rabinbach, Anson, and Jack Zipos, eds. *Germans and Jews since the Holocaust: The Changing Situation in West Germany.* New York: Cambridge University Press, 2005.

Shandler, Jeffrey. *While America Watches: Televising the Holocaust.* New York: Oxford University Press, 1999.

Holyfield, Evander *(1962–)*

The only fighter in history to hold the world heavyweight boxing championship five times, Evander Holyfield might unfortunately be remembered not only for his achievements—which include thirty-eight wins with twenty-five knockouts, seven losses, and two draws—but also as the boxer whose ears Mike Tyson bit partially off in June 1997. In the 1990s Holyfield and Tyson portrayed the diametrically opposing images of professional boxers. Holyfield rejected the snarling pit-bull image projected by Tyson and so many other boxers and instead presented the calm, reasoned demeanor of a serious professional.

Holyfield, raised in Atlanta, Georgia, was the youngest of nine children brought up by a single mother. A scrawny child who sat on the bench during most of his sophomore football season because he was so small (5 feet, 4 inches tall, at 115 pounds), Holyfield grew to 6 feet, 2 inches and trained hard to reach about 212 pounds. Nevertheless, he was still considered small in the world of heavyweight boxing, where opponents weighing 230 pounds regularly entered the ring. Undaunted by his many doubters, who thought his lighter weight meant he was not as powerful as his opponents, Holyfield steadily rose through the heavyweight ranks to become the undisputed heavyweight champion in 1990. Losing his title in 1992, he reclaimed it from Riddick Bowe in 1993. Having lost his title a second time, in 1994 to Michael Moorer, Holyfield discovered that he had a heart problem and was forced to retire.

A devout Christian, Holyfield had always given much of the credit for his success in the ring to God and to his spiritual upbringing. Relying on his faith and continuing his rigorous training schedule, he made it back to the ring. He was poised to win the heavyweight title in 1997 from Tyson, who had recently reentered the ring after his stint in prison for a rape conviction. When Tyson bit off a portion of Holyfield's left ear, after having done the same to Holyfield's right ear, the fight was stopped. Holyfield won a rematch later that year. In 1999 Holyfield fought Lennox Lewis to a draw in one meeting but lost the title to him later that same year. In 2000 Lewis was stripped of the title through a court decision. Also in 2000, Holyfield recovered the title in a match against John Ruiz. In 2001, however, Ruiz won the title in a controversial draw.

Ignoring the advice of family and friends to retire, Holyfield won the title for a fifth time, in 2010, beating out Francois Botha. Holyfield now lives on a large estate outside Atlanta and continues to be involved in his church and with the Evander Holyfield Foundation. He also owns a cable company, a record company, and a clothing company and sponsors the Georgia Amateur Boxing team.

D. Byron Painter

SEE ALSO: *Ali, Muhammad; Boxing; Tyson, Mike.*

BIBLIOGRAPHY

Chappell, Kevin. "A 109-Room Showplace at Home with Evander Holyfield and His New Bride." *Ebony*, April 2004.

"Evander Holyfield Credits God, Wife, and Family for Championship." *Jet*, December 9, 1996, 46–51.

Hauser, Thomas. *A Beautiful Sickness: Reflections on the Sweet Science.* Fayetteville: University of Arkansas Press, 2001.

Holyfield, Evander, and Lee Gruenfeld. *Becoming Holyfield: A Fighter's Journey.* New York: Atria Books, 2008.

Holyfield, Evander, and Bernard Holyfield. *Holyfield: The Humble Warrior.* Nashville, TN: T. Nelson Publishers, 1996.

Ryan, Jeff. "Holy Revival." *Sport*, December 1997, 34–39.

Home Improvement

SEE: *DIY/Home Improvement.*

Home Improvement

The ABC network sitcom *Home Improvement* first aired on September 17, 1991, and ran for eight seasons, through May 1999. During only its second season, the show was renewed for three additional seasons, an unusual decision in the television industry. Based on the stand-up comedy routine of its star, Tim Allen (born Timothy Allen Dick in 1953), *Home Improvement* initially reflected Allen's love of power tools, cars, and Sears department stores, as well as mirroring his own family situation. Allen portrayed Tim Taylor, the host of cable TV's *Tool Time*. His wife, Jill, was portrayed by Patricia Richardson. More than just comedy, though, *Home Improvement* epitomized the concerns of the largest generation in history, the baby boomers.

The Taylors are a representation of the average American family of the 1990s, and their struggles, although treated with lighthearted humor, reflect the struggles of the show's demographic. In the main, three fundamental concerns of the boomer generation were examined on a weekly basis: relationships, family, and the search for spirituality.

TRADITIONAL ROLES

One trend that *Home Improvement* influenced was a return to more defined gender roles. While women in the 1960s and

1970s discarded their bras and retained their own last names within marriage and men grew their hair long and explored the sensitive side of their natures, couples in the 1990s rediscovered the fundamental differences between the sexes. *Home Improvement* gave propulsion to such best-selling pop psychology books as John Gray's *Men Are from Mars, Women Are from Venus* (1992), with its, at times, stereotypical gender roles.

On *Tool Time,* buxom tool girl Heidi (Debbe Dunning) seems more like window dressing than a flesh-and-blood character. In the Taylor household, Tim grunts, works on cars, is obsessed with "more power," and does not read unless a book has the word *illustrated* in the title. He is into sports and often does not listen to his wife. Jill, on the other hand, does not understand cars and calls tools "thing-a-ma-jigs." An example of Mars-Venus stereotyping is seen in the episode "Shooting Three to Make Tutu," where Jill wants Tim to take one of their sons to the ballet, but he has plans to take him to a basketball game instead. In this episode, and others like it, real men do not like ballet (or opera), and women do not like sports.

The series, however, wasn't content merely to stereotype male-female relationships and, in stretching itself, made the characters search for an identity beyond roles. Jill loses a job, finds another, struggles to keep family and job together ("Abandoned Family"), and decides to go back to college. Tim deals with the death of a mentor ("Arriverderci, Binford") and the arrival of a new boss; he faces work rivalries and an inferiority complex with Bob Vila ("What about Bob"). In other episodes, *Home Improvement* breaks the stereotype of the dumb male that it had helped to perpetuate. The formula that had always put Tim in the wrong is overthrown as Jill realizes her own shortcomings (e.g., "Heavy Meddle" and "Slip Sleddin' Away").

The three boys (Zachery Ty Bryan, Taran Noah Smith, Jonathan Taylor Thomas) grow older and deal with issues of their own: identity, dating, sex, drugs, and pulling away from mom and dad. Al Borland (Richard Karn), originally cast as a foil to Tim, becomes even more sensitive—the man every woman wants, the representative of the 1990s Iron John manhood movement (e.g., the episode "Reel Men," for male bonding). Heidi is given more to do as she juggles work with a new baby.

As Tim was fond of saying on *Tool Time,* "It's not just about home improvement, it's about male improvement," and *Home Improvement* could be said to be about marriage improvement. Episodes did not shy away from tough topics that boomers were having to confront in their own marriages, such as sexual temptation on both sides ("Eye on Tim" and "Jill's Passion"), legal separation of friends and family members ("He Ain't Heavy, He's Just Irresponsible"), marriage counseling, lack of intimacy, and taking each other for granted ("Taking Jill for Granite").

SHOW GROWTH

Home Improvement reflected the concerns of an aging baby boomer population. It resisted a sitcom staple that infuses life into dying ratings: an impending pregnancy. Instead, it went in the opposite direction and began pulling in extended family. Boomers became increasingly aware of aging parents, and so the series introduced Tim's mother and brothers, Jill's parents and sisters. In "Taps," the audience vicariously experiences the death of a parent as Jill loses her father. In "No Place Like Home," Tim deals with his mother selling the home in which he grew up. In the final season, Jill faces an emergency hysterectomy ("Love's Labor Lost"), forcing her into menopause, a condition with which female audience members could readily identify.

During the 1990s the baby boomers were frantically searching for who they were and where they fit into the cosmos. The idealistic 1960s had faded, along with their bell-bottom jeans, leaving many to wonder where their ideals had gone. Their search for spiritual values is found in Wilson (Earl Hindman), the Taylors' over-the-fence neighbor. He regularly hands out spiritual platitudes with as much profundity as a fortune cookie, but Wilson develops along with the show and audiences see more of his family, hear the story of his dead wife ("My Dinner with Wilson"), and watch romance bloom in his life. Wilson's wisdom, like spirituality in the latter 1990s, draws on many wells, including Buddha, Jesus Christ, Mark Twain, William Shakespeare, Mohandas Gandhi, and Galileo Galilei. A running gag, and a technical challenge to the crew, was Wilson's partially obscured face, reflective of the boomers' belief that spirituality has many faces and none is clearly illumined.

Home Improvement won many awards, including Emmys, People's Choice, and TV Guide Reader's Poll, as did its two central stars, Allen and Richardson. Allen won the People's Choice Award for Favorite Male Performer in a Television Series for the eight years of *Home Improvement*'s run. He won the Golden Globe Award for Funniest Actor in a Television Series in 1997 and was nominated again in 1998. Richardson was nominated four times for an Emmy as Outstanding Lead Actress in a Comedy Series and twice for the Golden Globe Award. The show held a mirror up to the baby boomer generation, and the baby boomer generation made sure that the Taylors knew they were America's family.

Cheryl A. Smith

SEE ALSO: *Baby Boomers; Emmy Awards; Sitcom; Stand-Up Comedy; Television.*

BIBLIOGRAPHY

Allen, Tim. *Don't Stand Too Close to a Naked Man.* New York: Hyperion, 1994.

Allen, Tim. *I'm Not Really Here.* New York: Hyperion, 1996.

Arkush, Michael. *Tim Allen Laid Bare: Unauthorized.* New York: Avon Books, 1995.

Dougherty, Terri. *Tim Allen.* San Diego, CA: Lucent Books, 2003.

Lichter, Robert S.; Linda Lichter; and Stanley Rothman. *Prime Time: How TV Portrays American Culture.* Washington, DC: Regnery Publications, 1994.

Home Shopping Network/QVC

Home Shopping Network (HSN) and Quality, Value, Convenience (QVC) were responsible for a historic change in American consumer habits and have become as much essential features of television as have religious channels. These two cable television channels feature live broadcasts of themed sales presentations, seven days a week, twenty-four hours per day. At any time, viewers can call a toll-free telephone number, speak with presenters live on the air, and order products. During their early history, home shopping networks generally appealed to lower-income viewers. Products chiefly consisted of cheap items that were often discontinued and usually overstocked. Hosts appeared on camera only every fifteen minutes. The rest of the time was devoted to scrolling product offerings. Over time, such celebrities as Susan Lucci and Joan Rivers began to be heavily associated with television shopping channels, and they served to draw in customers.

Home Shopping Network got its start in 1977 when a Clearwater, Florida, radio station agreed to accept an advertiser's merchandise in lieu of payment of an overdue bill. Saddled with 112 electric can openers, the station manager offered them for sale on the air. When they sold out instantly and callers clamored for other products, he established a regularly scheduled radio show called *Suncoast Bargaineers*. In 1981 the show moved to a local-access cable channel in the Tampa Bay area and was given a new name: Home Shopping Channel. In 1985 it was renamed Home Shopping Club (HSC) and transmitted twenty-four hours per day through cable and broadcast television to a national audience, becoming a publicly quoted company (the Home Shopping Network [HSN]) on the American Stock Exchange in 1986.

In 1990 HSN stock became available on the New York Stock Exchange, and in 1995 Barry Diller, former chairman of the board and CEO of Paramount Pictures and Fox, was welcomed as chairman of the board of HSN. James Held, senior vice president of Bloomingdale's department store, was named president and CEO. In 1997 HSN's parent company (HSN, Inc.) acquired a controlling interest in Ticketmaster, the world's largest special events ticketing company. In 1998, after purchasing the majority of Universal Studios Inc.'s television assets, HSN, Inc., changed its name to USA Networks, Inc., and purchased the remainder of Ticketmaster. That year also saw the premiere of Home Shopping Channel in Spanish, the result of a partnership with Univision. With 4,000 employees and more than five million active customers, HSN had by 1998 become an electronic retailing giant rivaled only by QVC, another media conglomerate.

HSN faced its first major competition in the electronic retailing forum in 1986. QVC was founded in West Chester, Pennsylvania, by Joseph Segel, founder of the Franklin Mint. With revenues of more than $112 million, QVC, which became known to faithful viewers as "the Q," broke the American record for first full-fiscal-year sales by a new public company and, like HSN, QVC broadcasted live seven days a week, twenty-four hours per day. The focus was on the soft-sell approach, and the products sold were often household names such as Kodak and Panasonic. By 1993 the company boasted access to more than 80 percent of all U.S. cable-subscribing households. Reaching 64 million cable households and three million satellite dishes in the United States alone, QVC made more than $2 billion in sales in 1997 as the result of eighty-four million phone calls and fifty-six million orders. The company, through a 1997 joint venture with BSkyB in the United Kingdom and Ireland, reached an additional 6.6 million households, broadcasting live seventeen hours per day.

QVC became best known for its jewelry sales, which accounted for 35 percent of its programming time, and made it one of the world's largest purveyors of 14-carat gold and sterling silver jewelry. At times derogatorily referred to as QVCZ, the channel brought cubic zirconium to the forefront of the shopping public's consciousness with its sales of Diamonique, a low-cost alternative to diamonds.

HOME SHOPPING TRENDS

Home shopping evolved from the world of impulse buying to become a relevant, meaningful form of shopping by the late 1990s. The customer base of HSN and QVC covers a range of socioeconomic groups. These customers share the common characteristics of having access to cable and possessing above-average amounts of disposable income. The products offered on the channels vary from hour to hour because of the varying demographics of viewers at a given time. Because the channels offer unconditional, money-back guarantees on their products, consumers are able to shop with confidence. Many Americans now prefer to shop from home for the sake of convenience, but for bedridden or other homebound individuals in the pre-online shopping era, QVC and HSN offerred a viable link to the outside world. Instead of relying solely on caregivers for their shopping needs, homebound people had access to a significant means to independence.

The regular hosts of home shopping programs came to provide viewers with a sense of companionship because, unlike ordinary news or talk show hosts, the electronic retailers take calls directly from the viewing audience and, indeed, consider it their job to chat with the callers and not always push a hard sell. Many viewers avidly follow the hairstyles of the hosts and devour personal details, speculating about their offscreen lives with the fervor of soap-opera fans.

Early critics of home shopping held that it was tantamount to the downfall of Western civilization because it gave already television-dependent people yet another excuse to avoid the outside world. They found fault with the hyper-enthusiasm of the product-selling hosts, claiming that viewers were not even permitted to formulate their own emotional responses to the products because the hosts, like deadpan singers in a Greek chorus, force-feed reactions to the audience. The elimination of any room for (mis)interpretation, however, is precisely what has appealed to so many consumers. Because every feature of a given product is described in detail, and the sometimes skeptical questions of callers answered candidly, live on the air, viewers feel secure in their understanding of the benefits and drawbacks of the product. Home shopping television may have helped Internet shopping in its infancy. By the time retailers began to offer their wares on the Internet in the mid-1990s, channels like QVC and HSN had already acclimated Americans to the concept of remote shopping. Consumers were, thus, less leery of giving their credit card numbers to a disembodied voice (in the case of home shopping channels) or to a faceless computer screen.

Both QVC and HSN are doing amazingly well in the twenty-first century. QVC reaches eighty-four million American homes and has an employee base of 12,000. The channel takes in more than a million calls a year. The average price of a product is $50, but some items sell for thousands of dollars. QVC has extended its base and now offers a regular programming schedule. HSN reinvented itself in 2009, revamping both image and programming and tripling sales in the process. The new focus is on tie-ins with entertainment and popular culture. When HSN offered fragrances by singer Mary J. Blige, the network sold more than 60,000 units within six hours. A partnership with Sony and the Julia Roberts movie *Eat Pray Love* led to more than 100 of 400 brand-connected items selling out completely.

HSN now reaches more than ninety-five million homes, with access provided by cable, the iPhone, the iPod, android phones, and social networks, such as Facebook and Twitter. This continued success indicates that home shopping networks will continue to attract audiences of predominantly female viewers as the century progresses.

Tilney Marsh

SEE ALSO: *Cable TV; Consumerism; Department Stores; Facebook; iPod / iTunes; Kodak; Online Shopping; Rivers, Joan; Roberts, Julia; Rogers, Kenny; Twitter.*

BIBLIOGRAPHY

Gudelunas, D. "QVC: Television Retail and Ritual." *American and Comparative Culture* 25, no. 12 (2002).

Hampp, Andrew. "How a Marriage of Pop Culture, Shopping Gave HSN a New Start." *Advertising Age* 81, no. 30 (2010).

Lavine, Kim. *Mommy Millionaire: How I Turned My Kitchen Table Idea into a Million Dollars and How You Can Too!* New York: St. Martin's, 2007.

Levine, Kathy, and Jane Scovell. *It's Better to Laugh . . . Life, Good Luck, Bad Hair Days, and QVC.* New York: Pocket Books, 1995.

McCauley, Stephen. "Selling Anything, Enthusiastically, at 3 a.m." *New York Times*, July 26, 1998, 27.

Zemke, Ron, and Chip R. Bell. *Service Magic: The Art of Amazing Your Customers.* Chicago: Dearborn Trade Publishers, 2003.

The Honeymooners

The Honeymooners is one of the best-remembered and most imitated comedies in the history of television. Although the series ran for only one year in prime time (during the 1955–1956 season on CBS), it succeeded remarkably in syndication and on video and DVD. Generations of viewers identified with Jackie Gleason's portrayal of Ralph Kramden, the aggravated bus driver from Brooklyn, New York, whose dreams of advancement were continually upended.

The Honeymooners was among the last of the urban, working-class comedies on 1950s television. As the nation experienced postwar prosperity, so did the families on television. The Nelsons on *The Adventures of Ozzie and Harriet* (1952–1966), the Andersons on *Father Knows Best* (1954–1960), and the Cleavers on *Leave It to Beaver* (1957–1963) all lived in the tree-lined, secure suburbs. By 1955 even the prototypical proletariat family on television's *The Goldbergs* (1949–1956) had moved out of the city.

THE STORY LINE

The Kramdens, however, were the exception. Ralph and his exasperated wife, Alice (Audrey Meadows), were stuck in the urban chaos—a cold-water apartment above a noisy, New York street, without any creature comforts of Dwight Eisenhower–era conformity. Their main possessions were a plain dining table and a depression icebox. They shared their lower-class frustrations with the upstairs neighbors, the Nortons. Slow-witted Ed (Art Carney) worked in the sewers, while his wife Trixie (Joyce

The Honeymooners. *From left to right, Audrey Meadows, Jackie Gleason, Art Carney, and Joyce Randolph perform a scene from* The Honeymooners *in 1956.* PARAMOUNT/GETTY IMAGES.

Randolph) commiserated with Alice about their common hardships. Unlike the suburban couples on television, the Kramdens and the Nortons were childless, just trying to keep themselves above water.

Much of the comedy revolved around the couples' schemes to get rich quick. In the classic episode "Better Living through Television," Ed and Ralph appear in a television commercial to sell Happy Housewife Helpers. The yearning to get out of near poverty reflected Gleason's own boyhood: he had grown up in the same Brooklyn environment as Ralph. Gleason wanted his show to be based in reality, so he instructed his writers to "make it the way people really live. If it isn't credible, nobody's going to laugh."

Gleason introduced Ralph and Alice (first played by Pert Kelton) on his DuMont variety series, *Cavalcade of Stars*. Gleason's original writers, Joe Bigelow and Harry Crane, wanted to call the sketch "The Beast," but Gleason understood that underneath Ralph's blustery exterior was a tremendous need for affection. In the opening monologue of this October 5, 1951, telecast, he saluted another Ralph, Ralph Branca of the Brooklyn Dodgers, who served the infamous home-run pitch to Bobby Thomson during the 1951 playoff game against the New York Giants. Like his namesake Branca, Kramden would suffer the blows of fate; but no matter what, his love for Alice endured. From the beginning Ralph proclaimed to her, "Baby, you're the greatest!" The six-minute live sketch, also featuring Carney as a policeman, proved so popular that Gleason and company created new struggles for the couple. Soon afterward, the physically agile Carney joined the regular cast with actress Elaine Stritch as the first Trixie.

SERIES' EXPANSION

In 1952 William Paley of CBS stole Gleason and his staff from the downtrodden DuMont network. Gleason was given a much larger budget to produce a weekly live extravaganza on Saturday nights. A younger actress, Meadows, was hired to replace Kelton, who was blacklisted amid political accusations. Gleason had created many memorable characters—Joe the Bartender, the Poor Soul, and Reginald Van Gleason III—but the audiences wanted more of the Kramdens. Within a few months *The Honeymooners* sketches grew from ten minutes to more than thirty.

In 1955 the Buick Motor Company offered Gleason more than $6 million to produce *The Honeymooners* as a weekly situation comedy for two years. The corpulent comedian formed his own production company and used a new film technology, the Electronicam process, to record the series live on film. The program was shot two times a week before an audience of 1,100 people. During the first season Gleason was disturbed by the amount of rehearsal time and felt that these recorded episodes lacked the spontaneity and originality of the live sketches. He discontinued the series after thirty-nine programs and decided to return to the live, variety format. He sold the films and syndication rights to CBS for $1.5 million.

The Honeymooners remained a prominent part of Gleason's succeeding variety series, with the writers trying to do something unusual with the trusted material. During the 1956–1957 season of *The Jackie Gleason Show*, the Kramdens and the Nortons took a live musical trip to Europe. At the end of the season Carney left the series, and Gleason did not revive the sketch until his 1960s extravaganza, *Jackie Gleason: The American Scene Magazine*. When Carney was available, Gleason revived the sketch on videotape, often with new cast members. Sue Ane Langdon and Sheila MacRae played Alice, while Patricia Wilson and Jean Kean were recruited for Trixie. Despite the changes, the familiar catchphrases remained: "One of these days . . . Pow! Right in the kisser!" and "Bang! Zoom"—Ralph's stock phrases to Alice—as well as Ed's greeting to Ralph, "Hey, Ralphie boy."

SYNDICATION

After his variety series ended in 1970, Gleason produced four more *Honeymooners* specials with Carney and the returning Meadows. But Ralph remained fixed in the popular imagination because the thirty-nine episodes of *The Honeymooners* were a perennial success in syndication. For more than twenty years a local station in Manhattan played them every night. There was great celebration among fans when the Museum of Broadcasting and Gleason unearthed the live sketches during the mid-1980s. Those lost episodes found another life on cable television and the home video and DVD market.

The Honeymooners remained a touchstone in the twenty-first century. The characters have been referenced by other television series such as *King of Queens*, *The Simpsons*, and *Futurama*. In 2005 *The Honeymooners* was adapted into a feature film with an African American cast. This version starred Cedric the Entertainer as Ralph and Mike Epps as Norton.

Whether as a recorded situation comedy or a live sketch, *The Honeymooners* stood as a comic reflection of urban, postwar America. The United States was a land of opportunity for dreamers such as Ralph, even though success remained elusive. The search for the American dream turned Arthur Miller's salesman, Willy Loman, into a tragic hero; the same quest made Gleason's bus driver a comic archetype. His bravado and anxieties can be felt in all subsequent, working-class underdogs on television—Fred Flintstone, Archie Bunker, Roseanne, and Homer Simpson.

Ron Simon

SEE ALSO: The Adventures of Ozzie and Harriet*; Blacklisting; Cable TV;* Father Knows Best*;* The Flintstones*; Gleason, Jackie;* Leave It to Beaver*; Live Television; Meadows, Audrey; Miller, Arthur; Paley, William S.;* Roseanne*;* The Simpsons*; Sitcom; Television.*

BIBLIOGRAPHY

Bacon, James. *How Sweet It Is: The Jackie Gleason Story*. New York: St. Martin's Press, 1985.

Crescenti, Peter, and Bob Columbe. *The Official Honeymooners Treasury*. New York: Perigee Books, 1985.

Henry, William. *The Great One: The Life and Legend of Jackie Gleason*. New York: Doubleday, 1992.

McCrohan, Donna. *The Honeymooners' Companion*. New York: Workman, 1978.

McCrohan, Donna, and Peter Crescenti. *The Honeymooners Lost Episodes*. New York: Workman, 1986.

Meadows, Audrey, and Joseph A. Daley. *Love, Alice: My Life as a Honeymooner*. New York: Crown, 1994.

Waldron, Vince. *Classic Sitcoms*. New York: Macmillan, 1987.

Hoodies

The hoodie is a long-sleeved sweatshirt with a hood that can be pulled tightly around the face with a drawstring. The first hoodies were made by Champion in the 1930s for laborers working in the harsh winter cold of upstate New York. From these humble, utilitarian beginnings, the garment was adopted by track runners and football players in the 1960s and 1970s as workout gear. *New York Times* writer Denis Wilson credits film character Rocky Balboa with launching the hoodie's cultural rise in popularity: "Simultaneously a workingman's hero, a street thug, and a striving athlete . . . Rocky came to embody the underdog, and his bare-bones workout gear reflected his origins . . . a well-worn gray hooded sweatshirt. . . . As Rocky pulled himself out of anonymity, he brought with him what would become a mainstay of American fashion: the hoodie."

Over the following decades, hoodies remained increasingly popular in sports culture, and by the 1990s every organization from high schools and universities to professional sports teams had a hoodie boasting its logo. This trend was also employed in more extreme sports, such as surfing, skating, and snowboarding. These sports continued to use the garment for function as well as fashion. The hoodie provided warmth on the slopes and dryness after exiting the water, and it provided obscurity for skateboarders trespassing on private property, all the while advertising a team or company logo.

Another group that adopted the hoodie as a staple garment is the urban culture surrounding drugs, graffiti artists, and so-called stick-up kids seeking the shield of a hooded garment while committing crimes. One individual who took this desire for isolation and anonymity to a far more sinister level was Ted Kaczynski, the Unabomber, whose only recorded sighting spawned the famous police sketch of a mustached man in dark glasses with a hooded sweatshirt shrouding his face.

By the turn of the twenty-first century, hoodies found their place in high fashion. Ralph Lauren, Sean "P. Diddy" Combs, Gucci, Versace, and many other designers produced them for the runways and the streets. In the 2010 Huffington Post article "Hoodies Hailed as Defining Fashion Trend," designer Rick Owens sums up the phenomenon: "I like the simplicity and universal application: Christ wore a hood, the Unabomber wore a hood, Grace Jones wore a hood, and Dante wore a hood."

The hoodie went from fashion trend to political statement overnight on February 26, 2012, when a hoodie-wearing African American teenager named Trayvon Martin was shot and killed by George Zimmerman, a twenty-eight-year-old off-duty neighborhood watch volunteer in a Sanford, Florida, gated community. Using Florida's "Stand Your Ground" law, shooter Zimmerman claimed self defense and was not initially charged. The case remained local for ten days until the family's attorney hired a publicist and appealed to Change.org in a call for justice for their son. Within weeks they had millions of supporters, many of them high-profile politicians, athletes, and celebrities. President Barack Obama promoted his 2012 campaign with hoodies, stating: "If I had a son, he would look like Trayvon." Illinois Representative Bobby Rush was escorted off the House floor for wearing a hoodie; the Miami Heat posted a picture online of the team wearing hoodies; Combs, Jamie Foxx, and other "A"-list celebrities used their Twitter accounts to post pictures of themselves in hoodies; and the Roots' drummer Questlove helped support the "Million Hoodie March" in New York's Union Square, calling for an arrest in the case. Geraldo Rivera drew much criticism by stating that wearing the hoodie was equally as responsible for Martin's death as Zimmerman was.

On April 11, 2012, Zimmerman turned himself in to police after being charged with second-degree murder. Supporters of Martin still use the hoodie as a symbol of unity against racial profiling and as a call for justice in the American legal system.

Ron Horton

SEE ALSO: *Combs, Sean "P. Diddy"; Gucci; Lauren, Ralph; Rivera, Geraldo;* Rocky; *Sweatshirt; Versace, Gianni.*

BIBLIOGRAPHY

Blow, Charles. "The Curious Case of Trayvon Martin." *New York Times*, March 18, 2012.

Glynn, Casey. "Trayvon Martin Shooting Sparks 'Hoodie' Movement." CBS News. Accessed June 2012. Available from http://www.cbsnews.com/2300-504083_162-10011784.html

Wilson, Denis. "A Look under the Hoodie." *New York Times*, December 23, 2006.

Wilson, Denis. "The History of the Hoodie." *Rolling Stone*, April 3, 2012.

Hooker, John Lee *(1917–2001)*

The undisputed king of boogie, John Lee Hooker not only achieved commercial success—a rare feat among blues singers—but he also maintained it for more than five decades, recording more than 100 albums. His one-chord, droning grooves lent themselves, as Robert Palmer writes in *Deep Blues*, to "building up a cumulative, trancelike effect." Although he attempted to redefine himself later in life, much to the detriment of the legendary style and talent that had made him famous, Hooker was always an original whose contributions to music in the twentieth century belonged in a category all their own.

Born near Clarksdale, Mississippi, on August 22, 1917, Hooker was primarily influenced by his stepfather, Will Moore, a Louisiana-born guitarist who played in a style very different from that of other Delta players. Occasional visits by such legendary bluesmen as Blind Lemon Jefferson, Charley Patton, and Blind Blake (who all knew Moore) certainly influenced young John Lee's style as well, especially his singing. Leaving home at fourteen, Hooker settled in Memphis, where he worked as an usher in a Beale Street movie theater while moonlighting as an entertainer at neighborhood house parties. After a seven-year stint working for a cesspool draining company in Cincinnati, Ohio, he relocated to Detroit, Michigan, in 1943. With the city's factories operating at peak wartime production, jobs were not hard to find. Hooker continued to limit his musical forays to occasional sit-ins and weekend gigs at various Hastings Street clubs.

One night an African American record store owner heard Hooker playing in a friend's living room and took him to see Bernie Bessman, a local record distributor. Bessman helped to record Hooker's first single, the seminal "Boogie Chillen," a primitive effort featuring only guitar and vocals. Issued by Modern Records in 1948, "the thing caught afire," as Hooker later remembered. "When it come out, every jukebox you went to, every place you went to, every drugstore you went, everywhere you went, department stores, they were playin' it in there. And I was workin' in Detroit in a factory there for a while. Then I quit my job I said, 'No, I ain't workin' no more'" With the success of follow-up efforts "Hobo Blues," "Hoogie

Boogie," and "Crawling King Snake Blues" over the next year, Hooker never regretted his decision.

Although contractually bound to Modern Records during this period, Hooker recorded for many other labels using a variety of pseudonyms, including Texas Slim, Delta John, Johnny Lee, Johnny Williams, and even Little Pork Chops. He finally reached an exclusive agreement with Vee-Jay Records in 1955, recording thereafter only under his own name. The format of his music, however, changed dramatically with the addition of a backup band, often including the superb duo of guitarist Eddie Taylor and harmonica player Jimmy Reed. While most of Hooker's Vee-Jay material lacked the spark of his initial recordings, he did reenter the charts in 1958 with "I Love You Honey," in 1960 with "No Shoes," and finally in 1962 with "Boom Boom."

After cranking out "Big Legs, Tight Skirt," his last hit for Vee-Jay, in 1964, Hooker underwent another round of label hopping, recording for Verve, Chess, and BluesWay, among others. His 1960s recordings presented him in a variety of contexts—folk bluesman, old-time boogie master, or quasi-rock-and-roll artist—always in an attempt to appeal to the changing blues-rock audience. Hooker became a major figure in both the British blues invasion (with two major groups, the Yardbirds and the Animals, both tackling "Boom Boom") and the American folk-blues revival, with acoustic recordings and frequent coffeehouse appearances. In 1970 he teamed up with the rock group Canned Heat for the hit album *Hooker 'n' Heat.* Some of his subsequent recordings, however, appeared to be blatant attempts to recapture the album's popularity and place Hooker squarely within the rock-and-roll genre. In 1980 Hooker was inducted into the Blues Hall of Fame, and he was honored for his contributions to rock music by being inducted into the Rock and Roll Hall of Fame in 1991.

Bandmate and slide guitarist extraordinaire Roy Rogers organized a 1989 recording session that eventually became *The Healer*, a major comeback album for Hooker. Once again, he returned to the spotlight, partly because of superstar guests who appeared on the album, including Bonnie Raitt, Keith Richards, Carlos Santana, Robert Cray, and Los Lobos. The disc won a Grammy Award as best traditional blues recording and set the stage for another all-star session, *Mr. Lucky* (1991), which featured guitarists Albert Collins and Johnny Winter, among others. Enjoying his newfound wealth and fame, Hooker went into semiretirement after the album's release. He continued, however, to record and tour when inspired, even appearing in television commercials for Pepsi.

In 2000 Hooker was awarded a fifth Grammy, in recognition of his lifetime achievements. The following year, just before beginning a European tour, he became ill and died on June 21 at the age of eighty-three. Hooker had finished recording the music for a new album, *Face to Face*, which was released in 2003. Three years later *John Hooker—Bits and Pieces About*, a DVD/CD set, and *Hooker*, a four-CD boxed set of his greatest works, were released.

Marc R. Sykes

SEE ALSO: *Blues; Collins, Albert; Cray, Robert; Los Lobos; Raitt, Bonnie; Rock and Roll; Santana; The Yardbirds.*

BIBLIOGRAPHY

Gioia, Ted. *Delta Blues: The Life and Times of the Mississippi Masters Who Revolutionized American Music.* New York: W. W. Norton, 2008.

Oakley, Giles. *The Devil's Music: A History of the Blues.* London: BBC, 1983.

Palmer, Robert. *Deep Blues.* New York: Viking, 1981.

Hoosiers

Basketball in many parts of the country is like religion, and *Hoosiers*, a 1986 film written by Angelo Pizzo and directed by David Anspaugh, is a clear homage to that sentiment. Set against an idyllic rural Indiana backdrop, *Hoosiers* traces the pursuit of the state basketball championship by tiny Hickory High School. The film looks at first glance like the classic David versus Goliath sports movie, with a predictably familiar ending, but, in this case, predictability neither lessens the impact of the drama nor detracts from the audience's response to the emotions revealed on the screen.

Some very prominent actors were drawn to this small-budget production. Gene Hackman portrays Norman Dale, a former college coach who was fired for striking a player in a moment of rage. The troubled Dale, now head coach of the Hickory Huskers, has come to Indiana as his last chance to work in the game he loves. The always excellent Hackman gives a convincing portrayal of a man who, throughout the action of the film, attempts to contain his competitive nature and learn to trust others. Barbara Hershey plays Myra Fleener, a teacher who tries to draw the team's star, Jimmy Chitwood, away from basketball and into the classroom. A relationship develops between Coach Dale and Fleener, despite their differences on the future of Chitwood. Dennis Hopper tackles the role of Shooter, the town drunk who constantly recounts the glory days of his high school basketball career. The relationship between Dale and Shooter that develops illustrates Dale's attempts to give somebody a second chance—something that he himself had been denied years before. Hopper's performance earned him an Oscar nomination.

Hoosiers was based on the true story of little Milan High School, which shocked the Indiana basketball world by winning the state championship in 1954 on a last-second shot. True to form, the Hickory Huskers also make the improbable run through the series, defeating larger schools and better teams. Star player Jimmy Chitwood, played by Maris Valainis, makes the winning shot as time runs out to immortalize himself and his team in the town of Hickory and all of Indiana.

Though no surprises appear in this familiar underdog story, *Hoosiers* is still able to maintain the tension and excitement needed to entertain audiences. The film provides an accurate depiction of life in rural Indiana in the 1950s, with several high school students forced by necessity to work on the farm instead of playing basketball. The all-white Huskers battle a city team made up of largely black players and a black coach in the championship game, another accurate portrayal of social life in the Midwest in the 1950s. *Hoosiers* also clearly demonstrates the importance of high school athletics to small, rural communities. Almost the entire town would caravan to every away game and to each step of the state tournament. The community meeting held to determine the fate of Coach Dale midway through his season, and the Saturday morning discussions at the barber shop illustrate just how important the team is and how much civic pride athletics can create.

Jay Parrent

SEE ALSO: *Basketball; Hackman, Gene; Hopper, Dennis.*

BIBLIOGRAPHY

Didinger, Ray, and Glen Macnow. *The Ultimate Book of Sports Movies: Featuring the 100 Greatest Sports Films of All Time.* Philadelphia: Running Press, 2009.

Harris, Ann. "*Hoosiers.*" In *Magill's Cinema Annual.* Englewood Cliffs, NJ: Salem Press, 1987.

Kauffmann, Stanley. Review of *Hoosiers. New Republic*, April 6, 1987, 26–27.

Hoover, J. Edgar *(1895–1972)*

When J. Edgar Hoover died in 1972, the *New York Times* wrote of him, "For nearly a half century, J. Edgar Hoover and the Federal Bureau of Investigation were indistinguishable. That was at once his strength and its weakness." Hoover was a strong personality, fiercely patriotic, highly organized, and controlling. As head of the Federal Bureau of Investigation (FBI) from the presidency of Calvin Coolidge until the presidency of Richard Nixon, he transformed the face of the U.S. Justice Department and became the definition of law enforcement in America, for better or worse.

EARLY LIFE AND CAREER

Hoover was born into a solidly middle-class neighborhood in Washington, D.C. His father was in the coast guard and later worked as a low-level employee of the federal government. Brought up to the exacting standards of his strict mother, Hoover determined that he would surpass his unambitious father. He remained devoted to his mother, living with her in the house in which he was born until her death in 1938.

Hoover received both a bachelor's and a master's of law degree at George Washington University and went to work for the government. He worked at the Library of Congress until the advent of World War I. In 1917, seeking to avoid the draft, which would force him to leave his aging parents, he obtained a clerical job at the Department of Justice, from which he moved up quickly. An extremely moralistic man, Hoover was virulently anticommunist and antiradical, and he gained prestige in the Justice Department by overseeing its wartime campaign against American radicals. In 1924 he took over as director of the Bureau of Investigation of the Justice Department (renamed Federal Bureau of Investigation in 1935).

When Hoover took over as director, the Bureau of Investigation was a slack organization, largely made up of political appointees and "hacks" who were not law enforcement professionals. He immediately began to revamp the organization, firing much of the staff and retraining those who remained. He eliminated the seniority system of promotions and instituted a merit system, with regular performance reviews. Over the course of his almost fifty-year directorship, he succeeded in turning the FBI into one of the world's most efficient crime-fighting organizations, with a state-of-the-art criminal lab, an ingenious fingerprint filing system designed by Hoover himself, and a prestigious training school for law enforcement agents.

ACHIEVEMENTS AND LEGACY

Hoover is perhaps most famous for his success against the gangsters of the Prohibition era, arresting renowned crime figures such as Al Capone and John Dillinger, and for his post–World War II activity against the Communist Party and the Ku Klux Klan. He was infamous for abusing the power of his agency and exceeding its jurisdiction. If he turned the FBI into a crack crime-fighting force, he also turned it into an internal secret surveillance tool.

Hoover's FBI employed tactics of infiltration, provocation, illegal wiretapping, and even burglary to amass volumes of damaging information about public figures and private citizens. Even presidents and their families were not exempt from FBI scrutiny. This information was kept by the director in secret files that were allegedly used to control the activities of government officials, influence the outcome of elections, and quash public dissent. In the 1960s, with the support of President Lyndon Johnson, Hoover created counterintelligence programs (COINTELPROs) to infiltrate and disrupt the activities of many leftist organizations, including the Black Panthers and Students for a Democratic Society.

Hoover and his G-men were hailed as heroes during the gangster-fighting days of Prohibition. Although they garnered much popular support during the anticommunist 1950s, with the rise of the New Left in the 1960s, more people began to question the authority of the FBI. On March 8, 1971, a small group calling itself the Citizens' Commission to Investigate the FBI broke into the agency's offices in the town of Media, Pennsylvania. They found and publicized files proving the illegal activities involved in the FBI's COINTELPROs, changing the public image of Hoover's FBI from dashing G-men to secret police.

PERSONAL LIFE

Throughout his life Hoover was dogged by rumors of homosexuality. He was a dandified dresser who was never romantically associated with women but who did form intimate attachments with men, notably Clyde Tolson, his second in command at the FBI, with whom he had a long, close friendship that some compared to marriage. Hoover violently denied any allegations that he had sexual relations with men, and his strict moral code would have certainly forbidden either the relations themselves or the acknowledgment of them. In the 1993 biography *Official and Confidential: The Secret Life of J. Edgar Hoover*, Anthony Summers argues that Hoover was unquestionably homosexual, but historians generally agree that there is no firm evidence for this claim; Richard Hack's 2004 biography *Puppetmaster: The Secret Life of J. Edgar Hoover* actively refutes it. In the 2011 film *J. Edgar*, directed by Clint Eastwood, Hoover's relationship with Tolson has a strong element of eroticism, but the film does not suggest that the two men ever consummated their affections.

Hoover died suddenly in 1972 of undiagnosed heart disease. He had been a religious man, an unbending moralist, obsessed with details and with eradicating any threats to the American way of life as he defined it. Though Hoover had used his agency to enforce Johnson's civil rights legislation and to root out the Ku Klux Klan, he was personally a racial bigot, and the FBI had a poor record of hiring minorities. While Hoover transformed the FBI into an effective and efficient government agency, the criticism he received later in his life and after his death for extending the powers of the FBI made many wary of giving one man so much power. Because of Hoover's long tenure, FBI directors are now limited to a single ten-year term.

Tina Gianoulis

SEE ALSO: *Black Panthers; Capone, Al; Civil Rights Movement; Communism; Dillinger, John; Eastwood, Clint; FBI (Federal Bureau of Investigation); Gay Men; Ku Klux Klan; Mafia/Organized Crime; New Left; Prohibition; Red Scare; Students for a Democratic Society (SDS); World War I; World War II.*

BIBLIOGRAPHY

DeLoach, Cartha. *Hoover's FBI: The Inside Story by Hoover's Trusted Lieutenant.* Washington, DC: Regnery Publications, 1995.

Hack, Richard. *Puppetmaster: The Secret Life of J. Edgar Hoover.* New York: New Millennium, 2004.

Keller, William W. *The Liberals and J. Edgar Hoover: Rise and Fall of a Domestic Intelligence State.* Princeton, NJ: Princeton University Press, 1989.

O'Reilly, Kenneth. *Hoover and the Un-Americans: The FBI, HUAC, and the Red Menace.* Philadelphia: Temple University Press, 1983.

O'Reilly, Kenneth, and David Gallen. *Black Americans: The FBI Files.* New York: Carroll and Graf, 1994.

Potter, Claire Bond. *War on Crime: Bandits, G-men and the Politics of Mass Culture.* New Brunswick, NJ: Rutgers University Press, 1998.

Powers, Richard. *G-men: Hoover's FBI in American Pop Culture.* Carbondale: Southern Illinois University Press, 1983.

Summers, Anthony. *Personal and Confidential: The Secret Life of J. Edgar Hoover.* New York: Putnam, 1993.

Theoharis, Athan G., and John Stuart. *The Boss: J. Edgar Hoover and the Great American Inquisition.* Philadelphia: Temple University Press, 1988.

Hoover Dam

The Colorado River bobs and jukes through the crisp sandstone of the western high plains. Early explorers saw it as a defining characteristic of Arizona and much of the semiarid western United States. Over time the river has become a monument to American riverine technology, as aqueducts and hydroelectric dams use the Colorado to make the American West a hydraulic society. The first of the incursions into the river is also the most famous: Hoover Dam.

Opened in 1935, Hoover Dam stands as a larger-than-life symbol of fluctuating meaning for generations of Americans. Even without such symbolic significance, the dam remains among the nation's most impressive engineering achievements.

A major part of the dam's significance derives from the structure itself. The dam, which has long-since repaid the $165 million cost for construction, is a National Historic Landmark and has been rated by the American Society of Civil Engineers as one of America's Seven Modern Civil Engineering Wonders. The massive structure, the highest concrete arch gravity dam in the United States, rises to 726 feet and contains approximately 4 million cubic yards of concrete. If placed in a monument 100 feet square, the concrete would reach 2.5 miles high—higher than the Empire State Building. The dam impounds Lake Mead, one of the world's largest manmade lakes.

As proposed in 1910, the mammoth Boulder Dam (as it was first called) served as the linchpin of a western land-use policy known as reclamation. After policy makers and developers finally conceded that a serious lack of rainfall stood in the way of their dreams of the "garden of the West," they sought a way to turn their adversity into opportunity. Reclamation grew out of the impulse to reclaim these dry, barren regions by applying human ingenuity to the few existing waterways, including the Colorado. In 1912 five western states agreed on the Colorado Compact, which parceled up the great river's flow among the signees—including at least two states that never made contact with the river. Most of the flow, including the electricity made at Hoover Dam, would be managed by the Six Companies contractors to power development more than 300 miles away in Southern California. Since the late 1990s the majority of Hoover Dam's power has been passed over wires to Los Angeles.

The symbolic significance of this immense structure became obvious immediately, which led developers to name it after President Herbert Hoover (an engineer who had been a great supporter of the project). Upon its completion in 1935 (all structures were finished by early the next year), Hoover Dam became a symbol of America's technological prowess, firmly placing the United States with the great civilizations in world history. One observer described it as the "Great Pyramid of the

Hoover Dam. *The Hoover Dam, which opened in 1935, took more than five years and nearly $50 million to build. The landmark dam, a major tourist attraction, has been rated by the American Society of Civil Engineers as one of America's Seven Modern Civil Engineering Wonders.* ETHAN MILLER/GETTY IMAGES.

American Desert, the Ninth Symphony of our day" and "a visual symphony written in steel and concrete . . . magnificently original, strong, simple, and majestic as the greatest works of art of all time and all peoples, and as eloquently expressive of our own as anything ever achieved." Particularly during the Great Depression, Hoover Dam's restoration of national confidence led to its appearance throughout popular culture, including advertisements and numerous collectible mementos.

Hoover Dam remains a symbol in contemporary America; however, the changing attitude of river-management technology has altered its image. In the twenty-first century some observers see Hoover Dam as the symbol of all the development that has prohibited the Colorado from reaching the ocean for decades. This view has prompted many American communities to advocate for the removal of dams instead of the building of them. Particularly in the northwestern United States, efforts to save salmon and the native communities that rely on them have gathered steam. Although activists are not exactly sure how one of the large dams would be removed, many environmentalists call for it to happen—particularly Glen Canyon Dam, a similar dam on the Colorado.

The reality of dams has become clear: as the great dams begin to clog with silt, Hoover and other dams may have only a limited life. Marc Reisner, in his book *Cadillac Desert* , notes that "we set out to tame the rivers and ended up killing them." He suggests that Hoover and others might eventually be viewed as "uniquely productive, creative vandalism." In other societies, however, dam building remains a link to development. Particularly in China, massive construction efforts clearly build on the monuments of the American past.

In terms of structural design, Hoover Dam will always serve as a symbol of the modern era—an icon of pop culture, even serving as a backdrop in a James Bond film. For many Americans, achievements such as this sleek yet powerful dam led the way to a century of innovation and development.

Brian Black

SEE ALSO: *Empire State Building; Environmentalism; The Great Depression; James Bond Films.*

BIBLIOGRAPHY

Hiltzik, Michael. *Colossus: Hoover Dam and the Making of the American Century.* New York: Free Press, 2010.

Hundley, Norris. *Water and the West.* Berkeley: University of California Press, 2009.

Jackson, Donald C. *Building the Ultimate Dam.* Lawrence: University Press of Kansas, 1995.

Miller, Char. *Water in the 21st Century West.* Corvallis: Oregon State University Press, 2009.

Reisner, Marc. *Cadillac Desert: The American West and Its Disappearing Water.* New York: Viking, 1993.

Stevens, Joseph E. *Hoover Dam.* Norman: University of Oklahoma Press, 1988.

Hopalong Cassidy

A multimedia cowboy hero, Hopalong Cassidy first appeared in a series of magazine stories that were published in 1905 and 1906. Clarence E. Mulford, who lived in Brooklyn, New York, at the time and had never been to the West, created Cassidy as a tough, tobacco-chewing redhead. He bossed the hands at the Bar-20 Ranch and got his nickname from a permanent limp caused by a gunshot wound in his leg. The more familiar image of this popular American fictional hero, however, is the one personified in movies and on television by silver-haired actor William Boyd. Boyd's Hopalong Cassidy was a dapper, soft-spoken cowboy who almost always wore black and was taken into the hearts of millions of kids. The later television incarnation of Hopalong spawned one of the first merchandising sensations inspired by that medium.

Mulford, who worked for many years in a civil service job, sold his earliest Hopalong Cassidy stories to a travel monthly called *Outing Magazine*. The first collection of those stories in book form was titled *Bar 20* and came out in 1907. All told, Mulford wrote more than two dozen novels and story collections about his limping, hard-bitten cowhand between then and 1941. Much of the material appeared initially in such pulp fiction magazines as *Argosy* and *Short Stories*. A dedicated researcher and collector of Western lore, Mulford did eventually travel extensively in the western states but, despite the popularity of his books, he is remembered today chiefly as the man who coined the name that others used to create an almost entirely different hero.

Producer Harry Sherman transformed Hoppy into a screen hero. An entrepreneur since silent movie days and one of the financial backers of *The Birth of a Nation* (1915), Sherman bought the screen rights to the Mulford books and then put together a movie production outfit to make the films, which were distributed by Paramount Pictures. The actor Sherman chose to play Cassidy was also a veteran of the silents. A protégé of Cecil B. DeMille, Boyd became a star in the 1920s in such films as *The Volga Boatman* (1926) and *The Yankee Clipper* (1927), but by the mid-1930s his fortunes had declined, and he was appearing in lower-budget action films. The first movie in Sherman's cowboy series was *Hop-a-long Cassidy*, released in 1935. In this film the prematurely gray Boyd actually does limp, but in later adventures he lost the limp, as well as the hyphens.

A formula was established from the beginning. Hoppy always had two sidekicks—one young and handsome (played originally by James Ellison), the other, crusty and humorous (first portrayed by Gabby Hayes). Known as a hell-raiser in real life, Boyd reformed as the series progressed, and Hopalong, who soon acquired the black outfit that was to become his trademark, also underwent changes. As a movie hero, he never drank, smoked, or swore, and his relations with women were almost always nothing more than avuncular. A hit from the first, the Hoppy series eventually stretched to sixty-six titles. As one film historian noted, the pictures, "long on human interest, short on violence, were especially popular with family audiences."

Hopalong first moved into comic books at the end of 1942, as a backup feature in Fawcett's *Master Comics*. The following year Fawcett started a *Hopalong Cassidy* comic book, which they kept going until 1954.

In the late 1940s Boyd took over the production of the Hoppy films and also bought the rights to all of the earlier Sherman productions. This proved to be an especially wise move. In 1949 NBC started showing the movies nationally, every Friday night from 8 to 9 p.m., and, as the number of American households with television sets grew, so did Hoppy's popularity. "The show became a hit very quickly," writes Richard

O'Brien in *The Story of American Toys*, "and almost as quickly a wide variety of manufacturers leaped aboard Hopalong's bandwagon. There were Hopalong Cassidy costumes, tin windups, toy soldiers, binoculars, dart boards, knives, badges, shooting galleries, and of course a wide variety of guns and holsters." A comic strip began in 1950, drawn by Dan Spiegle and distributed by King Features.

In 1952 Boyd, who had last played Hoppy in 1948, produced and starred in a *Hopalong Cassidy* television series. It ran on NBC until the end of 1954, with movie veteran Edgar Buchanan as the hero's crusty sidekick. A radio show had been put together in 1948, but it wasn't until the character became a craze through TV that it showed up on national radio—first on the Mutual Broadcasting System and then on CBS. Andy Clyde, the resident old coot sidekick from the later movies, repeated his role as California Carlson on the radio networks. The show was last heard late in 1952. During the heyday of Hoppy, Boyd became a national celebrity and his personal appearances drew enormous crowds of dedicated kids. He gradually faded away, although the comic book, taken over by DC Comics, continued publication until 1959. By the time he retired, Boyd—who controlled all the merchandising on the character—was a multimillionaire. He died in 1972.

Ron Goulart

SEE ALSO: Argosy; The Birth of a Nation; *Comic Books; Comics; DC Comics; DeMille, Cecil B.; Hollywood; Movie Stars; Pulp Magazines; Radio; Silent Movies; Television; Toys; The Western.*

BIBLIOGRAPHY

Keltner, Howard. *Golden Age Comic Books Index: 1935–1955.* Gainesville: Author, 1998.

Nevins, Francis M. *The Films of Hopalong Cassidy.* Waynesville, NC: World of Yesterday, 1988.

O'Brien, Richard. *The Story of American Toys.* New York: Artabras, 1990.

Sampson, Robert. *Yesterday's Faces,* vol. 1. Bowling Green, OH: Bowling Green University Popular Press, 1983.

Young, William H., and Nancy K. Young. *World War II and the Postwar Years in America: A Historical and Cultural Encyclopedia.* Santa Barbara, CA: ABC-CLIO, 2010.

Hope, Bob *(1903–2003)*

Entertainer Bob Hope was unquestionably an American show-business icon, as demonstrated by his multidecade, multigenerational success. Hope's entertainment persona was evident in nearly every decade of the twentieth century. He performed in some seventy movies and had an unprecedented contract of at least fifty-five years with NBC. He entertained American troops in both war and peacetime and was hailed as "America's most prized ambassador of goodwill throughout the world" when presented with the Congressional Gold Medal by President John F. Kennedy.

The fifth of seven sons, he was born Leslie Townes Hope in Eltham, England, on May 29, 1903, and died 100 years later, on July 27, 2003. His father, William Henry Hope, was a stonemason who decided on an impulse to migrate with his family to Cleveland, Ohio. His Welsh mother, Avis Townes Hope, who had been a concert singer, instilled in him a love for music and entertaining. Hope would later claim that he first warmed to an audience laughing at him when his voice cracked while singing at a backyard family reunion. In 1920, by virtue of his father's naturalization, "Bob"—the name by which the world would later know him—and his brothers also became U.S. citizens.

ON THE STAGE

After high school Hope took dancing lessons from African American entertainer King Rastus Brown and from vaudeville hoofer Johnny Root. A natural, Hope soon began teaching classes. He also worked briefly as a newspaper reporter and tried amateur boxing under the name of Packy East. At eighteen Hope persuaded his girlfriend, Mildred Rosequist, to become his dance partner. Appearing at nearby vaudeville houses, they worked their way to the generous wages of $8 a night. But the partnership would not last long: when Rosequist's mother finally saw their act, she thought it was too risqué for her daughter.

Hope then teamed up with a friend, Lloyd Durbin. After developing their act in local bookings, they were hired by the

Bob Hope. *Bob Hope moved from a career in vaudeville into radio, movies, and television to become a comedy icon who entertained generations of Americans.* MICHAEL OCHS ARCHIVES/ GETTY IMAGES.

Bandbox Theater in Cleveland as a "cheap act" for the Fatty Arbuckle Show. Arbuckle, who headlined the touring revue, loved Hope and Durbin's comedy-and-dance act and helped the boys get better bookings. Following the accidental death of Durbin, Hope took on another partner, George Byrne, with whom he developed a blackface act.

After several career reversals, Hope and Byrne were almost ready to give it all up when they were hired to emcee Marshall Walker's Whiz Bang revue in New Castle, Pennsylvania. Hope went onstage alone and entertained the audience with his adlibbed wisecracks. He was using for the first time a technique that would prove good enough to last through seven decades: not only parrying and jousting with anything an audience member or fellow comic could throw at him but also being brave enough to wait onstage in front of the toughest audience until everyone understood his jokes.

In 1929 Hope went to New York and was given a movie screen test but was told that his "ski nose" had killed his chances. With material from legendary gagster Al Boasberg, Hope continued his career onstage, appearing in *The Antics of 1931*. His performance impressed the audiences and led to an even better theatrical gig, *The Ballyhoo of 1932*, in which Hope was encouraged to ad-lib to his heart's content. But his first major recognition, by critics and the public, came in 1933 for his wisecracking role as Huckleberry Haines in the highly successful Broadway musical *Roberta*. Not only did Hope's professional life change during this time but so did his personal life. One of his coperformers in the musical, George Murphy, introduced him to a young singer, Dolores Reade. After a brief courtship, Dolores and Bob got married in February 1934. They went on to adopt four children and later had four grandchildren.

RADIO

Along with his vaudeville show at New York's Capitol Theater came his first radio appearance, on the *Capitol Family Hour* (hosted by Major Edward J. Bowes), which originated from the theater every morning. After guest spots and semiregular work on a couple of shows, Hope was signed on by Pepsodent toothpaste for his own show on NBC. He went on to become a huge radio star and was a Tuesday-night regular for about the next eighteen years.

On his half-hour program, Hope opened with a monologue that fired off barbs about current news events and usually set the tone for the rest of the show. Every time a news story broke, everybody would look forward to hearing what Hope was going to say about it on his next show. With his "and I wanna tell you" catchphrase, he inaugurated a comedy style in which no joke, whether resulting in irrepressible laughs or just a smile, was any more important than the next one coming up.

MOVIES

In 1937 Hope traveled to Hollywood to film *The Big Broadcast of 1938*, in which he sang the Oscar-winning song "Thanks for the Memory" as a duet with Shirley Ross. The song became his signature theme. Between 1934 and 1936 he had appeared in eight comedy shorts, all filmed in New York, but his first screen hit would not come until 1939, with *The Cat and the Canary*. In the next year, he struck it big with *Road to Singapore* (1940), the first of seven successful "Road" pictures he was to make over the years with Bing Crosby and Dorothy Lamour. These popular films featured in-jokes about the private lives of Hope and Crosby.

Relying heavily on rapid quips and topical wisecracks, Hope built his own style of screen comedy, which would reach a peak in the Western parody *The Paleface* (1948). His films of the 1950s were a mixed bag and were less and less profitable. Writers-directors Norman Panama and Melvin Frank suggested that Hope should start playing straight dramatic roles. The advice resulted in Hope playing Eddie Foy Sr. in *The Seven Little Foys* (1955), a role that gave him the chance to combine drama and humor. Hope's last dramatic role was as New York City mayor Jimmy Walker in *Beau James* (1957). In the same year, Hope started working as his own producer and brought forward successes including *Alias Jesse James* (1959) and *The Facts of Life* (1960), with Lucille Ball as his costar.

In the 1960s, however, the public began to find Hope's films increasingly less entertaining. With *Boy, Did I Get a Wrong Number* (1966) and *The Private Navy of Sgt. O'Farrell* (1968), he dissatisfied even his most loyal fans. Besides, Hope's conservative political ideas were at odds with the general frame of mind concerning the Vietnam War. At that point, Hope was criticized severely for not being able to separate his stage persona from his political beliefs. When traveling to entertain the troops, he found for the first time a welcome that was less than enthusiastic, and his overall career was never quite the same from then on.

TELEVISION AND THE TROOPS

Television came calling as early as the 1930s, but Hope was not at all convinced that the "new" entertainment medium would succeed. He participated in an experimental show for CBS, in the first commercial television broadcast on the West Coast in 1947, and as a surprise guest on Ed Sullivan's *Toast of the Town* in 1949. But his formal debut on NBC television would only happen on Easter Sunday in 1950. Douglas Fairbanks Jr., Beatrice Lillie, and Dinah Shore were Bob's guest stars in the special *Star Spangled Revue*, sponsored by Frigidaire. His annual trips overseas to entertain the U.S. troops, which had started full bore during World War II and lasted through Korea and Vietnam and to the Persian Gulf conflict of 1990–1991, soon became a regular Christmas television event.

For sixty consecutive years Hope aired his specials with NBC-TV stars. But his jokes were gradually becoming outdated and predictable, his style getting more and more insipid. In 1996 NBC announced the end of its contract with Hope. That year's *Bob Hope: Laughing with the Presidents* was his final Christmas special.

Hope's work with NBC guaranteed him a place in the *Guinness Book of Records* as the entertainer with the longest-term television contract. He is also in *Guinness* as the most honored entertainer in the world, for he received more than 2,000 awards and citations for humanitarian and professional efforts, including fifty-four honorary doctorates. Although he never received an Oscar for his acting, Hope frequently emceed the ceremonies, and he won special Academy Awards five times (1940, 1944, 1952, 1959, and 1965) for humanitarian action and contribution to the industry. In July 1976, by order of Her Majesty Queen Elizabeth II, Hope was made an Honorary Commander of the Order of the British Empire (CBE) for his services to British troops around the world during World War II, and his lifetime professional achievements were acknowledged by Kennedy Center Honors in 1985.

Hope was an avid golfer, and his name became associated with the Bob Hope Desert Classic, an annual event that produced millions of dollars for charity. The extensive list of his golfing buddies includes presidents Dwight D. Eisenhower, Richard Nixon, Gerald Ford, Ronald Reagan, George H. W. Bush, and Bill Clinton.

Hope, who over the years assumed the stature of a national institution, authored several humorous books about his career and travels. He was honored and befriended by U.S. presidents since Franklin D. Roosevelt. President Lyndon B. Johnson honored Hope with the Medal of Freedom, and President and Mrs. Jimmy Carter hosted a White House reception in celebration of his seventy-fifth birthday. Harry Truman played the piano for him, and Clinton bestowed on him a Medal of the Arts. In his nineties Hope remained active and honored: the Library of Congress named the Bob Hope Gallery of American Entertainment after him, and his 100th birthday celebration took place back where it all began, in Hollywood, as the corner of Hollywood and Vine was renamed Bob Hope Square.

His long years dedicated to the entertainment industry brought him more than honorary accolades. These years were also extremely profitable for the entertainer. With his fortune estimated at hundreds of millions, mostly in real estate, securities, oil and gas wells, Thoroughbred horses, and a broadcasting company, Hope passed away as one of the richest performers, in every sense, ever.

Bianca Freire-Medeiros

SEE ALSO: *Academy Awards; Ball, Lucille; Celebrity; Crosby, Bing; Fairbanks, Douglas, Jr.; Golf; Gulf Wars; Hollywood; Lamour, Dorothy; Radio; Reagan, Ronald; Shore, Dinah; Sullivan, Ed; Television; Vaudeville; Vietnam; World War II.*

BIBLIOGRAPHY

Mielke, Randall G. *Road to Box Office: The Seven Film Comedies of Bing Crosby, Bob Hope, and Dorothy Lamour, 1940–1962.* Jefferson, NC: McFarland, 1997.

Morella, Joe; Edward Z. Epstein; and Eleanor Clark. *The Amazing Careers of Bob Hope: From Gags to Riches.* New York: W. H. Allen, 1974.

Quirk, Lawrence J. *Bob Hope: The Road Well-Traveled.* New York: Applause Theatre Book Publications, 1998.

Hopkins, Sam "Lightnin'" *(1912–1982)*

Blues guitarist Sam "Lightnin'" Hopkins enjoyed a six-decade career that took him from the streets of Houston to festival stages around the world. As a youngster, Hopkins worked with guitarist Blind Lemon Jefferson as a "guide boy" before striking out on his own in 1946. For the next several years, he had a string of national rhythm-and-blues hits for the Aladdin, Modern, and Mercury labels, including "Katie Mae," "Shotgun Blues," and "Lightnin's Boogie." As musical styles changed, however, Hopkins found himself out of vogue, and eventually he landed back in Houston.

"Rediscovered" in the early 1960s and repackaged as a folk-blues artist, Hopkins found a role in the forefront of the blues revival, starring at university coffeehouses, on television programs, and on European tours. He continued to record for a variety of labels, including Vee-Jay, Arhoolie, and Verve. In 1967 filmmaker Les Blank captured Hopkins's eccentric lifestyle in the documentary *The Blues Accordin' to Lightnin' Hopkins.* Hopkins died in Houston in 1982.

Marc R. Sykes

SEE ALSO: *Blues; Rhythm and Blues.*

BIBLIOGRAPHY

Govenar, Alan B. *Lightnin' Hopkins: His Life and Blues.* Chicago: Chicago Review Press, 2010.

Oakley, Giles. *The Devil's Music: A History of the Blues.* New York: Da Capo Press, 1997.

Palmer, Robert. *Deep Blues.* New York: Viking, 1981.

Hopper, Dennis *(1936–2010)*

An accomplished actor, director, writer, photographer, and art collector, Dennis Hopper was among the most original and iconoclastic figures in American pop culture. From his early days as a young Hollywood rebel to his emergence as a counterculture icon, Hopper exerted a profound cultural influence on Hollywood, opening the way for the new, independent, youth-oriented cinema that took hold in the 1970s. Although his career was derailed by years of drug and alcohol abuse, as well as a string of failed marriages, Hopper reemerged during the 1980s and 1990s as one of Hollywood's most intriguing character actors, lending his inimitable charisma to a number of acclaimed film and television productions.

As a star-struck boy born and raised on a farm in Kansas, Hopper dreamed of becoming a Hollywood actor. When his family moved to San Diego, California, teenage Hopper fell in with a drug-using party crowd. But he also found an outlet for his acting ambitions by working at the Old Globe Theatre and the La Jolla Playhouse, where he was cast in his first professional role. At eighteen Hopper was signed to a seven-year contract with Warner Brothers. He soon appeared in a small role in *Rebel without a Cause* (1955) and became a close friend of James Dean and Natalie Wood.

Hopper's breakthrough film was *Giant* (1956), starring Dean, Rock Hudson, and Elizabeth Taylor, and for most of the next ten years he was known as a rebellious but gifted and successful young actor. It was not until he tried his hand at directing that he became a Hollywood icon. In 1969 Hopper and his good friends Peter Fonda and Jack Nicholson made *Easy Rider*, a film that reflected the attitudes of nearly a decade of the counterculture from which it sprang. *Easy Rider* captured the imagination of a generation, shone the spotlight on future megastar Nicholson, and caused convulsive changes in the thinking of the established movie industry.

Hopper used his heightened success and influence to direct *The Last Movie* (1971) on location in Peru, but the result was a muddled drama that was a commercial and critical disaster. Hopper then dropped out of the limelight for almost fifteen years, doing drugs in New Mexico, working on personal projects, and making foreign films. Among his most memorable acting roles from these years was his portrayal of a crazed war photographer in Francis Ford Coppola's *Apocalypse Now* (1979).

Hopper returned to Hollywood respectability with an astonishingly brilliant portrait of psychologically disturbed brutality in David Lynch's indie favorite, *Blue Velvet* (1986). That same year he made *Hoosiers*, another independent film, which earned him an Oscar nomination, while also appearing in the disturbing drama *River's Edge*. By the early 1990s Hopper had reinvented himself as one of the industry's busiest performers, bringing his unique combination of dramatic intensity and wild energy to a range of film and television roles. In 1993 he played Clifford Worley in *True Romance*; a year later, he starred as an explosives expert turned criminal in the action thriller *Speed* (1994). Over the remainder of the decade, Hopper appeared in more than twenty roles, including a memorable turn as William S. Burroughs in the PBS documentary series *American Masters* in 1999. Late in his career, Hopper played recurring roles on the popular TV series *24* and *Crash*. He died of prostate cancer on May 29, 2010.

Victoria Price

SEE ALSO: Apocalypse Now*;* Blue Velvet*; Burroughs, William S.; Cancer;* Crash*; Dean, James;* Easy Rider*;* Giant*; Hollywood;* Hoosiers*; Hudson, Rock; Lynch, David; Nicholson, Jack; Public Television (PBS);* Rebel without a Cause*; Taylor, Elizabeth; Television;* 24*; Wood, Natalie.*

BIBLIOGRAPHY

Biskind, Peter. "'I Was Scared to Death of Dennis.'" *Times* (London), June 5, 2010, 40–41.

Hoberman, J. *Dennis Hopper: From Method to Madness.* Minneapolis, MN: Walker Art Center, 1988.

Monaco, James, and the Editors of Baseline. *Encyclopedia of Film.* New York: Perigee, 1991.

Rodriguez, Elena. *Dennis Hopper: A Madness to His Method.* New York: St. Martin's Press, 1988.

Sellers, Robert. *Hollywood Hellraisers: The Wild Lives and Fast Times of Marlon Brando, Dennis Hopper, Warren Beatty, and Jack Nicholson.* New York: Skyhorse, 2010.

Thomson, David. *A Biographical Dictionary of Film.* New York: Alfred A. Knopf, 1994.

Wloszczyna, Susan. "Dennis Hopper Lived Like a Revved-up Rebel." *USA Today*, May 31, 2010, 2D.

Hopper, Edward *(1882–1967)*

Born in 1882 in Nyack, New York, Edward Hopper developed a style of realist painting that art critic Rolf Günter Renner suggests revealed the limits that humanity and nature impose on each other. This tension is put into sharp relief in one of Hopper's best-known paintings, *Gas, 1940*, which shows a lone attendant checking the pumps at a Mobil gas station bordered by woods. Hopper is perhaps most widely recognized for his *Nighthawks* (1942), a painting of two men and a woman in a diner late at night, which entered the popular realm as a poster, "Boulevard of Broken Dreams," with the men transformed into James Dean and Humphrey Bogart, the counterman to Elvis Presley, and the woman to Marilyn Monroe. Hopper's figures in *Nighthawks* and other paintings display an edginess and detachment from the moment, possibly in search of something grander. The poster commodified this alienation through the figures of tragic, troubled movie stars.

Hopper studied illustration at a commercial art school for two years before switching to the New York School of Art in 1901. There, he worked most closely with Robert Henri, a member of the Ashcan school. Hopper's studies of people seem to build on the urban gaze of Ashcan school painter John Sloan, whose etchings hover between reportage and voyeurism.

Hopper traveled to Europe three times between 1906 and 1910. Thereafter, he settled in New York City and summered at South Truro, Massachusetts, near Cape Cod, with his wife, Josephine (Jo) Verstille Nivison, whom he married in 1924.

Until the mid-1920s Hopper worked as a commercial artist. In 1925 he painted *House by the Railroad.* The painting captures Hopper's themes of loneliness, detachment, and alienation. Ann Temkin, curator of New York's Museum of Modern Art, where the painting resides, notes in a 2008 audio text on the museum's website that "the loneliness of the house is what really comes through in the painting." According to Gail Levin, Hopper's biographer, the eerie mood of this painting led to its being used as a model for the house in Alfred Hitchcock's 1960 film *Psycho.*

The German filmmaker Wolfgang Hastert has suggested that Hopper's paintings are like storyboards for films. In a short film on the painter he draws comparisons to Hopper's work and films such as *Paris, Texas*, by Wim Wenders, and *Blue Velvet* by David Lynch. The brooding nature of Hopper's work lends itself to such comparisons, and his use of light and shadow

Edward Hopper. *Edward Hopper is perhaps best know for his 1942 painting of a lonely diner scene titled* Nighthawks. **FRED W. MCDARRAH/GETTY IMAGES.**

could be compared to the technical dimensions of film noir. One reason Hopper's work draws such analogies is that much of it deals self-consciously with the process of looking. In many of Hopper's paintings, the field of sight is clearly from the outside looking in or the inside looking out. For instance, in *Office in a Small City* (1953), Hopper lets us look from the outside at a man at work, and simultaneously, at the vision before that man from his office window.

Hopper's wife was a constant presence in his life and paintings. The photographer Arnold Newman has suggested that his 1960 photograph of Hopper at South Truro, in which Jo dances in the distant background while Hopper grimaces at the camera, is indicative of their relationship, with Jo always in the background. But Jo was a constant figure in Hopper's paintings, and Renner suggests that paintings such as *Girlie Show* (1941), *New York Movie* (1939), *Summertime* (1943), and *Western Motel* (1957)—all of which feature a woman similar in appearance to Jo—reveal a sexual tension, perhaps unfulfilled desire, in Hopper's work. Renner further suggests that *New York Office* (1962), in which a woman is framed in light through a large office window, shows Hopper finally realizing sexual fantasies by dominating the female figure through the act of painting.

The initial attraction of Hopper's paintings for many might well be a surface appeal to an idealized American past. The paintings, however, retain their allure because they stretch the imagination beyond their initial appeal into often forgotten realms of American life.

Ian Gordon

SEE ALSO: *Ashcan School;* Blue Velvet*; Bogart, Humphrey; Dean, James; Film Noir; Hitchcock, Alfred; Lynch, David; Monroe, Marilyn; Presley, Elvis;* Psycho.

BIBLIOGRAPHY

Berman, Avis, and Edward Hopper . *Edward Hopper's New York.* San Francisco: Pomegranate, 2005.

Edward Hopper: The Silent Witness. Directed by Wolfgang Hastert. West Long Branch, NJ: Kultur International Films, 1994.

Goodrich, Lloyd. *Edward Hopper.* New York: Abrams, 1971.

Levin, Gail. *Edward Hopper: An Intimate Biography.* New York: Knopf, 1995.

Renner, Rolf Günter. *Edward Hopper, 1882–1967: Transformation of the Real.* Cologne, Germany: Taschen, 1993.

Temkin, Ann. Excerpt from audio commentary on Museum of Modern Art collection, 2008. Accessed December 19, 2011. Available from http://www.moma.org/collection/object.php?object_id=78330

Hopscotch

Children in Europe and in North, Central, and South America, as well as in Russia, China, and India, play the same hopping game, with only minor variations, variously called hopscotch, potsy, paradise, heaven and hell, airplane, and hop-round. The game is played on a pattern chalked on a sidewalk or traced in dirt. The pattern consists of several single and occasional side-by-side squares or circles, which are often sequentially numbered. Play begins when a player tosses an object (usually a rock) into the pattern and then hops into the pattern, careful to skip the square containing the rock and to land without touching the lines in all the empty squares. Scholars believe that the game may be up to a thousand years old, suggesting that the pattern derives from the figure of the labyrinth, a motif found as far back as the Iron Age, through which youth were required to walk during an initiation ceremony.

Dorothy Jane Mills

SEE ALSO: *Leapfrog; Leisure Time; Toys.*

BIBLIOGRAPHY

Bancroft, Jessie H. *Games.* New York: Macmillan, 1937.

Lankford, Mary D. *Hopscotch around the World.* New York: Morrow, 1992.

Sutton-Smith, Brian. *The Folkgames of Children.* Austin: University of Texas, 1972.

Horne, Lena *(1917–2010)*

The career of singer and entertainer Lena Horne evolved with, and mirrored, the times. From the Jim Crow years in the South, to the 1950s McCarthy blacklists, to the Mississippi marches for civil rights, Horne was there as a performer and a sympathizer, despite the fact that her career often suffered according to the extent of her involvement. From her beginnings at the age of sixteen as a chorus girl at Harlem, New York's whites-only Cotton Club in the 1930s, Horne developed a reputation as a moderately talented singer with a tendency to coast on beauty and charm.

But Horne was troubled because her celebrity image did not appear to match her personal beliefs. It seemed that every decision she faced about roles to take or songs to sing resonated with symbolic reference to race. Too refined (and "too white") to be taken seriously as a blues singer, she honed her image as a cabaret artist, only to be criticized for a perceived lack of warmth in her vocal delivery that was itself partly based on the "down and dirty" stereotype she could not fulfill. Her marriage to a white man, music arranger Lennie Hayton, also contributed to her reputation, as her African American fans were offended by her perceived betrayal of faith. Horne's autobiography, *Lena*, written in 1965, captures all these experiences in memorable detail, reading like a textbook on the combined effects of race and class in American cultural life during the twentieth century.

As a movie actress under contract to Metro-Goldwyn-Mayer (MGM) in the 1940s and 1950s, Horne found that her skin color held her back from playing African American roles, for which she wasn't "black" enough, and white roles, for which she was too "colored." When she tried using dark makeup on her fair skin, she felt it looked like the blackface used in a minstrel show. Max Factor was called in to create a special foundation color for Horne called "light Egyptian," later used for white actresses playing mulattos. One option Horne did not especially like was to play Latin parts, though she did so in the otherwise forgettable film *Panama Hattie* (1942).

In fulfillment of her contract with MGM, she was frequently asked to perform "guest numbers" as a chanteuse, elegantly gowned and leaning against a pillar. These sequences would then be edited out of the films for showings to white audiences in the South. Horne found greater satisfaction in all-black films such as the fanciful religious fable *Cabin in the Sky* (1943) and *Stormy Weather* (1943), for which she was lent to Twentieth Century Fox, based on the life of dancer Bill "Bojangles" Robinson. The title song to *Stormy Weather* became Horne's theme song in the years to come.

Over the next thirty years, Horne stayed busy performing in posh clubs in New York, Hollywood, and Las Vegas; making television appearances on the popular shows of the day, including those of Ed Sullivan and Perry Como; and taking part in numerous political benefits. One goal she seemed unable to fulfill was finding the right part in a Broadway show. Although she enjoyed singing the songs of Harold Arlen and Yip Harburg in the musical *Jamaica*, which opened in 1957, she hated her part—that of a silly island woman in love with American consumer goods. It took another two decades and several personal tragedies (Horne lost her father, her son, and her husband to fatal illnesses within a few short months in 1970–1971) for Horne to find the right role.

In 1981, at age sixty-three, when other performers might have been ready to retire, she opened in *Lena Horne: The Lady and Her Music*, which was to become the longest-running one-woman show in Broadway history. She held the audience's rapt attention from the opening phrase of her first song—Cole Porter's aptly titled "From This Moment On." The public was reintroduced to a woman it never really knew, who evinced a bold sense of humor and the ability to laugh at herself. After her Broadway success, Horne's recording career also blossomed, with releases such as *We'll Be Together Again* (1994) and *Being Myself* (1998), which she produced at the age of eighty-one. Horne's renditions of old standards such as "My Buddy" and "Willow Weep for Me" mix poignancy with wit, echoing the experiences of a full and courageous life.

Horne's many awards include a Grammy Lifetime Achievement Award in 1989 and Best Vocal Performance Grammy Awards for pop in 1981 and for jazz in 1995. As the first African American to sign a long-term contract with a major Hollywood studio, Horne is honored on the International Civil Rights Walk of Fame at the Martin Luther King Jr. National Historic Site for battling racism in the entertainment industry. A musical about her, *Stormy Weather*, premiered in 2007. Horne died in 2010 at the age of ninety-two. The following year the Academy Awards ceremony featured a tribute to her by actress Halle Berry.

Sue Russell

SEE ALSO: *Academy Awards; Broadway; Civil Rights Movement; Como, Perry; The Cotton Club; Grammy Awards; Hollywood; Jazz; King, Martin Luther, Jr.; McCarthyism; MGM (Metro-Goldwyn-Mayer); Porter, Cole; Sullivan, Ed.*

BIBLIOGRAPHY

Buckley, Gail Lumet. *The Hornes: An American Family*. New York: Applause Theatre & Cinema Books, 2002.

Gavin, James. *Stormy Weather: The Life of Lena Horne*. New York: Atria Books, 2010.

Haskins, James, and Kathleen Benson. *Lena: A Personal and Professional Biography of Lena Horne*. New York: Stein and Day, 1984.

Horne, Lena, and Richard Schickel. *Lena*. London: André Deutsch, 1966.

Horror Movies

No popular genre has been more reflective of America's cultural mood swings than the horror movie. At the same time, no popular genre has been more conducive to the expression of idiosyncratic nightmare visions. If these claims seem contradictory, even vaguely paradoxical, that is hardly surprising. For the horror genre consists of a group of texts as diverse as they are numerous, as controversial as they are popular, as conservative (or progressive) in their overt messages as they are progressive (or conservative) in their subtler implications. Although the horror genre may be lacking in firm boundaries or essential features, its rich and storied history, which goes back to the beginning of the twentieth century, exhibits a remarkable degree of coherence.

There are at least three reasons why this is so. First, what initially appear to be utterly dissimilar entries often turn out to conform in crucial ways, whether formally, stylistically, or thematically. Second, as is typically the case with pop cultural phenomena, market forces have dictated that the most commercially successful entries spawn a host of unimaginative imitators. This, in turn, has led to a fairly reliable boom-and-bust periodization of the genre. Third and most important, what all horror movies have in common is the intention to transform—through metaphor, symbol, and code—real-life fears into terrifying narratives; uncanny images; and, above all, representations of monstrosity. Not all horror movies succeed in realizing this intention, but the fact that they try places them squarely within the genre.

EARLY HISTORY

The horror film genre has its roots in the English gothic novels of the eighteenth and nineteenth centuries. After the Selig Polyscope Company produced a brief adaptation of *Dr. Jekyll and Mr. Hyde* in 1908, the stage was set for Robert Wiene's masterpiece of German Expressionist cinema, *The Cabinet of Dr. Caligari* (1919). *Nosferatu*, F. W. Murnau's silent magnum opus starring an emaciated Max Schreck as the decidedly unglamorous and unromantic undead Count, followed in 1922.

Universal Pictures, heavily influenced by the dark, shadowy style, imported a number of Germany's most gifted film technicians in an effort to stave off bankruptcy. It worked, and in just a few years, Universal had become the king of the sound horror movie. Classic versions of *The Phantom of the Opera* (1925), *Dracula* (1931), and *Frankenstein* (1931) made household names out of actors Lon Chaney, Bela Lugosi, and Boris Karloff, respectively. These pictures were exceedingly popular, partially because audiences were desperate for entertaining diversions as the Great Depression loomed. Although sober admonitions are issued against such human foibles as avarice; impetuosity; and, especially, scientific hubris, the source of the threat in these films is nearly always supernatural. To reassure viewers that everything will turn out all right, the monster is always soundly defeated in the end.

POSTWAR INCARNATIONS

Universal's reign ended toward the beginning of World War II, and the studio eventually stooped to the level of self-parody

Halloween. *The masked killer Michael Myers wields a knife in a still from the 1978 horror film* Halloween, *directed by John Carpenter.* FOTOS INTERNATIONAL/COURTESY OF GETTY IMAGES.

with such entries as *Frankenstein Meets the Wolf Man* (1943) and *Bud Abbott and Lou Costello Meet Frankenstein* (1948). However, during this period, RKO producer Val Lewton wisely encouraged his directors to avoid straightforward depictions of violence and attempt instead to encourage viewers to conjure their own images of horror by means of suggestion and innuendo. Jacques Tourneur's *Cat People* (1942) is without a doubt the most highly acclaimed Lewton production, but the influence of his cinematic approach and techniques extended all the way into the 1960s, as evidenced by Robert Wise's masterful *The Haunting* (1963).

America's Cold War anxieties, coupled with advancements in special effects, gave rise to a cycle of highly successful science fiction horror movies in the middle of the twentieth century. Some of these films, notably *The Thing from Another World* (1951) and *Invasion of the Body Snatchers* (1956), focus on man's brave (i.e., patriotic) battle against a hostile alien threat. Others, such as *Them!* (1954) and *Godzilla* (1956), reflect American fears of atomic explosion and radioactive fallout. However, it was a return to traditional horror film iconography that proved most responsible for the genre's huge popularity boom in the late 1950s.

A small British studio, Hammer Films, took advantage of the industry's greater permissiveness with respect to the depiction of violence and sexual activities. Starting with *The Curse of Frankenstein* in 1957, Hammer released a string of colorful and lurid versions of the Universal classics. These included a successful cycle of Dracula films, beginning with *Horror of Dracula* (1958), which features Christopher Lee as Dracula and Peter Cushing as Van Helsing. American International Pictures (AIP) quickly followed suit, churning out a series of low-budget, teen-oriented horror films, such as *I Was a Teenage Werewolf* (1957). AIP also acted as distributor for Mario Bava's atmospheric Italian masterpiece *Black Sunday* (1960) and Roger Corman's cycle of Edgar Allan Poe adaptations, most of which star Vincent Price as a mentally unstable aristocrat. In these color gothics, lavish set designs and extravagant costumes serve to reflect the decadence of Poe's characters. Price also stars in William Castle's best-known gimmick horror film, *The Tingler* (1959), which made use of "Percepto" technology—really just theater seats equipped with electric buzzers—to shock audience members during key scenes.

In 1960 two films—Alfred Hitchcock's *Psycho* and Michael Powell's *Peeping Tom*—effectively initiated a whole new era in horror cinema by making their monsters not just human but psychologically realistic. The killers in these movies—both seemingly normal young men—are driven by instinctual drives and irresistible compulsions to commit murder against sexually transgressive women. Making disturbing connections between male-upon-female voyeurism and the objectification of women, between gender confusion and murder as a substitute for sex, these two films suggest in the most vehement terms that monstrosity is as likely to be located within (at least if you are a male) as without.

CRAZY KILLERS

The majority of horror movies to come out in the 1960s and 1970s perpetuated these ideas, though independent producer-director Herschell Gordon Lewis took such concepts to grisly extremes. His low-budget, independently produced "splatter films"—given such transparent names as *Blood Feast* (1963) and *Color Me Blood Red* (1965)—make up for their lack of narrative suspense with an abundance of gory close-ups. Although Lewis's films appealed only to a small number of hard-core horror fans, they achieved a kind of cult status and, whether directly or indirectly, have exerted a powerful influence on the genre.

The year 1968 marked the undeniable birth of the modern horror movie. *Rosemary's Baby*, Roman Polanski's paranoid urban gothic, stars Mia Farrow as an ingenuous young newlywed who moves into a Manhattan apartment building only to discover that her kind old neighbors are really devil-worshipping witches. Conspiring with Rosemary's husband and obstetrician (among others), they have affected a diabolical plan to make Rosemary the mother of Satan's child. Based on the best-selling novel by Ira Levin, *Rosemary's Baby* effectively taps into fears and anxieties surrounding pregnancy and childbirth. Because the film is shot almost entirely from Rosemary's point of view, it succeeds in conveying her growing sense of alienation and despair as she struggles to find someone she can trust in a huge, unfriendly city.

Also appearing in 1968 was George Romero's *Night of the Living Dead,* among the most distressing horror movies of all time and the film that launched the "zombie" subgenre. Made for only $114,000 and unrated at the time of its release, this no-frills black-and-white film centers on a small group of isolated individuals who try, with little success, to stave off the murderous advances of an ever-growing army of flesh-eating zombies. Although notable for its excessive gore and apocalyptic overtones, *Night of the Living Dead* works primarily because it conveys so well the claustrophobia and hysteria of the trapped party and vividly portrays the horror of seeing members of one's own family turned into monsters. Not without sociopolitical implications, Romero's film also serves to register the dissatisfaction of America's "silent majority" and illustrates the breakdown of patriarchal order under highly stressful conditions.

Rosemary's Baby and *Night of the Living Dead* were followed by a slew of movies that locate the source of horror within the nuclear family. If *Psycho* and *Peeping Tom* make the monstrous human, these films bring the monstrous home, turning it into something not so much human as familiar. More than ever before, generic horror conventions were now being put to use, especially by auteur directors, in the service of the social statement. This period delivered such films as *Deathdream* (1974), Bob Clark's tale of a young soldier killed in combat in Vietnam who is temporarily brought back to life—unfortunately, as a vampiric zombie—by his mother's passionate prayers. Larry Cohen's *It's Alive* (1974) presents the Frankenstein legend in distinctly modern terms, giving the role of ambivalent creator to the father of a grotesquely deformed baby-on-a-rampage.

A NEW LEVEL OF TERROR

The apex of this horror-in-the-family movement was the 1974 release of Tobe Hooper's slasher-splatter masterpiece *The Texas Chain Saw Massacre* (1974), in which a male family of insane slaughterhouse workers lays waste to a group of vapid teenagers. The tagline on the movie poster reads, "Who will survive, and what will be left of them?" To further suggest the horror awaiting the viewer, radio ads featured a group of people repeating, "Keep remembering—it's only a movie." Like *Psycho* and many other films, *The Texas Chain Saw Massacre* is loosely based on the true story of Ed Gein, who murdered two people in 1957 and robbed several graves, using the body parts to decorate his home. The cultural effect of *The Texas Chain Saw Massacre* was such that the film became part of the New York Museum of Modern Art's permanent collection.

The Texas Chain Saw Massacre inspired several equally grisly and low-budget "family horror" films, such as Wes Craven's *The Hills Have Eyes* (1977), in which cannibalistic mutants descend upon a family vacationing in the desert. In Italy, meanwhile, legendary horror film directors Bava, Dario Argento, and Lucio Fulci made successful contributions to the splatter subgenre with such entries as *Bay of Blood* (1971), *Deep Red* (1975), and *Zombie* (1979), respectively.

By far the most acclaimed and talked-about horror movie of the 1970s and 1980s was William Friedkin's *The Exorcist* (1973). Winner of two Academy Awards and nominated for eight others, this film was the subject of intense media scrutiny from the time of its initial release. Loosely based on a reported real-life exorcism, the film chronicles the efforts of a disenchanted priest to save the life of a young girl who has been possessed by demonic forces. The display of Christian iconography in the presence of foul sexual language, nauseating special effects, and graphic exhibitions of self-mutilation outraged many religious groups. However, stripped of its demonic-possession theme, *The Exorcist* provides a moving commentary on, among other issues, the uselessness of modern medicine when confronted with unknown illnesses; the crises of guilt and responsibility faced by single mothers; and the difficulty parents have comprehending and responding to their often aggressive, hormonal children.

Although inspired by *The Exorcist* and highly successful in its own right, Richard Donner's "satanic child" film *The Omen* (1976) lacks its predecessor's underlying concern with domestic issues. Instead, it terrifies viewers with threats of the apocalypse and, what ultimately amounts to the same end, the infiltration of evil agents into the political sphere.

Many of the "revenge of nature" films that came out in the late 1970s after the massive success of Steven Spielberg's PG-rated *Jaws* (1975) are family horror stories at heart. Following a tradition that stretches at least to Hitchcock's *The Birds* (1963) and arguably all the way to James Whale's *Frankenstein* (1931), these pictures—*Squirm* (1976), *Piranha* (1978), and *Alligator* (1980), to name a few—externalize the manifest source of the horror, all the while insinuating that what should be most feared is something lurking within the individual, the family, or the community at large.

THE *HALLOWEEN* INFLUENCE

John Carpenter's blockbuster *Halloween* (1978) officially launched the slasher—or, more precisely, the stalker—subgenre. The *Psycho*/*Peeping Tom* elements, though still operative, are overshadowed by a life-or-death game of terror waged between the psycho killer (now masked, now superhuman) and the film's only surviving female. Partly to create space for sequels, partly to exploit the insecurity and paranoia of modern viewers, open-ended narratives soon became the order of the day. *Halloween* spawned the campier, bloodier, and just-as-popular *Friday the 13th* (1980) and a series of progressively less original and less successful variants.

Because of their emphasis on male-against-female violence and the heinous nature of the crimes they depict, the slasher and splatter subgenres have repeatedly been accused of exploitation, misogyny, and even sadism. Craven's *The Last House on the Left* (1972), Meir Zarchi's *I Spit on Your Grave* (1978), and Abel Ferrara's *The Driller Killer* (1979) were all banned in England under the controversial "video nasties" bill that cleared Parliament in 1984. Brian De Palma's *Dressed to Kill* (1980) raised the ire of feminists by featuring a male transvestite who murders (punishes?) women for their promiscuity and/or sex appeal. John McNaughton's *Henry: Portrait of a Serial Killer* (1990), denied an R rating by the Motion Picture Association of America despite favorable reviews by such prominent critics as Roger Ebert, was released unrated after sitting on a distributor's shelf for four years.

That there are misogynist messages in many of these films is undeniable; recently, however, attention has been drawn to the fact that in a number of slasher-splatter movies, female ingenuity and the employment of self-defense are actually championed. Nowhere is this more apparent than in the rape-revenge cycle of horror movies that appeared in the late 1970s and early 1980s.

Simultaneous with the American slasher cycle, Canadian writer-director David Cronenberg attained a degree of mainstream success with disturbing and highly original works such as *The Brood* (1979), *Scanners* (1981), *Videodrome* (1983), *The Fly* (1986), and *Dead Ringers* (1988). These films have been praised *and* criticized for elevating "body horror"—or, more specifically, sexually based "venereal horror"—to an art form.

Director Sam Raimi gave new life to the "haunted house" subgenre with his low-budget "splatstick" cult favorites *The Evil Dead* (1982) and *Evil Dead II* (1987), which manage to find humor in the gore. However, not all the films in the haunted house subgenre are low-budget, independently produced affairs. In his much-heralded adaptation of Stephen King's *The Shining* (1980), for example, Stanley Kubrick uses haunted-house conventions primarily as a means of exploring the real-life horrors of alcoholism, child abuse, and domestic violence.

SLASHERS, PARODIES, AND DEAD ENDS

Although the proportion of horror movies within the overall film population continued to increase well into the 1980s, staleness had set in by the end of the decade. *Halloween* was up to its fourth sequel in 1989 and *Friday the 13th* its seventh, and the overuse of narrative and technical conventions caused a decline in viewer interest. However, with Jonathan Demme's Academy Award–winning *The Silence of the Lambs* (1991) selling the mystique of the serial killer to mainstream audiences, the horror-thriller-suspense hybrid received a massive boost in popularity. The mid-1990s saw the release of glossy, big-budget, star-powered films such as *Copycat* (1995), *Se7en* (1995), and *Kiss the Girls* (1997), which focus on the gruesome handiwork of charismatic, creative serial killers and reflect the public fascination with those who allegedly commit mass murder on principle rather than because of some underlying psychosexual disorder.

Other, more conventional horror movies of this period seek to supernaturalize the serial killer. Inspired by Craven's modern classic *A Nightmare on Elm Street* (1984), in which a once-human child murderer takes revenge on those who lynched him by invading the dreams of their offspring, films such as *Child's Play* (1988), *The Exorcist III* (1990), *The Frighteners* (1996), and *Fallen* (1998) either give supernatural powers to a serial killer or give serial-killer characteristics to a supernatural being. Another Craven movie, *Scream*, was a sleeper hit in 1996 and became the first in a slew of neo-stalkers. These self-reflexive works, which include *Scream 2* (1997), *Halloween H20* (1998), and *Urban Legend* (1998), contrive to satirize stalker-film conventions while still providing genuine scares. They succeed in this task only insofar as they are able to avoid too heavy a reliance on the very conventions they are mocking. Even though almost all the neo-stalker films in the late 1990s did quite well at the box office, many critics viewed the ever-increasing emphasis on parody, intertextuality, and pastiche as signs that the genre had exhausted itself and that a dark age in horror cinema was imminent.

In 1999, the minimalist, low-budget *The Blair Witch Project* began as a film festival entry and became a worldwide phenomenon. The film centers on university students who set out to film a documentary project chronicling the legend of the Blair Witch, a woman who supposedly killed a series of children and still haunts the forest surrounding Burkettsville, Maryland. Consisting of a series of interviews with historical experts and denizens of the town, the film follows the students as they explore the forest sites of Blair Witch encounters. Soon the characters become lost in the forest and find evidence that they are being stalked by some unseen entity. Then they disappear. Adding to the horror is the conceit that the story is factual, that the filmmakers actually did disappear and their footage, the content of the movie, was found a year after their disappearance. *The Blair Witch Project* became one of the most successful independent films in history, grossing $248 million. As a result, it initiated the "found footage" subgenre, which includes such films as *Cloverfield* (2007), the *Paranormal Activity* series (2007–2012), and *Chronicle* (2012).

REMAKES AND REANIMATED CORPSES

Film studios in the first decade of the 2000s adhered to predictable franchise films, releasing, among others, the *Final Destination* movies, a remastered and extended version of *The Exorcist*, and the resurrection of industry giants Freddy Krueger from *A Nightmare on Elm Street* and Jason Voorhees from *Friday the 13th* in 2003's *Freddy vs. Jason*. Additionally, remakes of earlier horror hits seemed commonplace. Driven by advances in special effects, updated versions of *The Texas Chain Saw Massacre* and *Dawn of the Dead* were released in 2003 and 2004, respectively.

The decade also saw creative reinterpretations of many of the genre's foundational films, including *Friday the 13th* (2009), *A Nightmare on Elm Street* (2010), *The Amityville Horror* (2005), and *The Wolfman (2010)*. Most notably, the horror industry gravitated toward two subgenres: splatter and zombie films.

Splatter films celebrate gore and fuel fear through the extent and randomness of the violence, and films such as *Saw* (2004), *Hostel* (2005), *Wolf Creek* (2005), and *The Human Centipede* (2009), as well as their sequels, tap into society's subconscious and use graphic violence to tease out its darker curiosities. Although such films were routinely attacked by critics, they succeeded at the box office.

Many horror films aspire to make a social comment, and this is particularly the case with zombie movies, which typically signal the fall of civilization, either through disease or supernatural causes. The 2004 remake of Romero's *Dawn of the Dead* follows the exploits of survivors who find haven in a shopping mall. The undead creatures are upgraded: unlike their movie ancestors, they no longer are slow and weak but instead have superhuman speed fueled by their bloodlust. Films such as *28 Days Later* (2002) follow this trend, portraying zombies more as diseased psychotics than lumbering creatures.

The decade was also notable for a series of American remakes of Japanese horror films. Led by box-office hits *The Ring* (2002) and *The Grudge* (2004), these movies center on the wronged dead seeking revenge on their killers and slaughtering the innocents who stand in their way.

In 2008 the first book in Stephenie Meyer's best-selling *Twilight* trilogy was successfully adapted to film. It concerns innocent teen Bella Swan (Kristen Stewart), who falls in love with a century-old teenage vampire, Edward Cullen (Robert Pattinson). Their involvement is threatened by his lust for blood, as well as the danger posed by other vampires, and is further complicated by Bella's love for her childhood friend Jacob (Taylor Lautner), who happens to be a werewolf. The sequels to the film—*New Moon* (2009), *Eclipse* (2010), *Breaking Dawn–Part I* (2011), and *Breaking Dawn–Part II* (2012)—were also box-office hits.

Judging from the horror movie revivals, it seems safe to declare that no matter how grim the future of the genre may seem at times, it will not be killed any time soon. After all, there are always young people who are desperate to consume accessible texts in which their ambivalent attitudes toward society, family, and self are given imaginative and relatively safe communal expression.

Steven Schneider

SEE ALSO: Alien*; American International Pictures; "B" Movies; Corman, Roger; Crawford, Joan; Cult Films; Dr. Jekyll and Mr. Hyde; Dracula;* The Exorcist*; Frankenstein;* Friday the 13th*;* Halloween*; Hitchcock, Alfred;* I Was a Teenage Werewolf*;* Jaws*; Karloff, Boris;* King Kong*; Kubrick, Stanley; Lorre, Peter; Lugosi, Bela; The Mummy;* Night of the Living Dead*;* The Phantom of the Opera*; Price, Vincent;* Psycho*;* Rosemary's Baby*;* Scream*;* The Silence of the Lambs*; Slasher Movies;* Them!*;* The Thing*;* Twilight*; The Wolfman.*

BIBLIOGRAPHY

Grant, Barry K., ed. *Planks of Reason: Essays on the Horror Film.* Metuchen, NJ: Scarecrow Press, 1984.

Hantke, Steffen. *American Horror Film: The Genre at the Turn of the Millennium.* Jackson: University Press of Mississippi, 2010.

Jancovich, Mark. *Horror.* London: B. T. Batsford, 1992.

Jess-Cooke, Carolyn. *Film Sequels: Theory and Practice from Hollywood to Bollywood.* Edinburgh: Edinburgh University Press, 2009.

Kellner, Douglas, and Michael Ryan. *Camera Politica: The Politics and Ideology of Contemporary Hollywood Film.* Bloomington: Indiana University Press, 1988.

Lyden, John. *Film as Religion: Myths, Morals, and Rituals.* New York: New York University Press, 2003.

Magistrale, Tony. *Abject Terrors: Surveying the Modern and Postmodern Horror Film.* New York: Peter Lang Publishing, 2005.

Prawer, S. S. *Caligari's Children: The Film as Tale of Terror.* New York: Oxford University Press, 1980.

Skal, David J. *The Monster Show: A Cultural History of Horror.* New York: W. W. Norton, 1993.

Tudor, Andrew. *Monsters and Mad Scientists: A Cultural History of the Horror Movie.* Oxford, UK: Basil Blackwell, 1989.

Waller, Gregory, ed. *American Horrors: Essays on the Modern American Horror Film.* Urbana: University of Illinois Press, 1987.

Williams, Tony. *Hearths of Darkness: The Family in the American Horror Film.* Madison, NJ: Fairleigh Dickinson University Press, 1996.

Wood, Robin. *Hollywood from Vietnam to Reagan.* New York: Columbia University Press, 1986.

Hot Dogs

Long a staple of sports arenas and backyard cookouts, the unpretentious hot dog is one of the favorite sandwiches among people in the United States. More than twenty billion of them are consumed in the country each year. Traditionally, the sausage is made of beef, pork, veal, chicken, or turkey, with or without skin, and commonly placed in a bun. Regular hot dogs are about 6 inches long, although they are also available in 2-inch cocktail and foot-long varieties.

The sausage was allegedly married to the ubiquitous bun when Harry Stevens (1855–1934), who sold ice cream at the New York Polo Grounds, instructed his crew to sell frankfurters on rolls. The sandwich did not become famous, however, until it came to New York's Coney Island amusement park. There Charles Feltman (1841–1910), who is also sometimes credited with melding the sausage and roll, served the sandwich first out of a moving wagon and later at his restaurant. Polish immigrant Nathan Handwerker (1892–1974), once an employee at Feltman's, sparked interest in the hot dog when he sold his dogs for a nickel (half the price of Feltman's) at his hot dog stand just steps away from the subway stop on Coney Island.

Interest in hot dogs was so great that German immigrant Oscar Mayer (1859–1955) began marketing them in supermarkets in the 1930s. Not only was his company the first to sell hot dogs through supermarkets, but it was also the first to specifically target children as consumers of the food. Beginning in 1936 the Oscar Mayer Weinermobile—an automobile that resembles a hot dog on a bun—has driven across the country promoting its hot dogs to children. The vehicle has been redesigned six times since that original version.

In its simplest iteration a hot dog consists of a frankfurter in an oblong-shaped bun, and it can be topped with mustard, ketchup, onions, pickles, cheese, sauerkraut, chili, slaw, beans, and a variety of ingredients specific to particular locations or restaurants. Legend has it that the hot sausage sandwiches were given their descriptive moniker by sports cartoonist T. A. "Tad" Dorgan (1877–1929), who at the turn of the twentieth century caricatured the wieners as dachshund dogs. The term *hot dog* first appeared in print in *The Oxford English Dictionary* in 1900.

As people in the United States have gotten more health conscious in the twenty-first century, some members of the medical establishment have targeted hot dogs as unhealthful. In 2011 the Harvard School of Public Health announced that eating 2 ounces of hot dogs a day has been linked to the development of type 2 diabetes. Regardless of the risk, the U.S. public's love affair with the hot dog does not seem to be waning. According to the National Hot Dog and Sausage Council, at Los Angeles's Dodger Stadium alone, two million hot dogs were sold in 2011.

Robert E. Schnakenberg

SEE ALSO: *Baseball; Coney Island; Fast Food; Hamburger.*

BIBLIOGRAPHY

American Eats: History on a Bun. DVD. New York: A&E Television Network, 2002.

Herbst, Sharon Taylor. *The New Food Lover's Companion.* New York: Barron's Educational Series, 1995.

Horowitz, Roger. *Putting Meat on the American Table: Taste, Technology, Transformation.* Baltimore, MD: Johns Hopkins University Press, 2006.

Hot Pants

Hot pants were a short-lived fashion of the early 1970s that evoked the unconventional attitudes of the youth that had burgeoned in the 1960s. An adaptation of the 1960s mini skirt, hot pants offered the wearer a measure of modesty that the mini could not provide. For those who wanted their panties to be concealed, the stylish solution lay in short, tight, sometimes cuffed hot pants. Designed to be worn either as an item of clothing in their own right or as the revealed undergarment of maxi-length outfits, hot pants looked smartest when worn with tights (fishnets or opaques) and platform boots. The open fronts and side slits of maxi outfits permitted legs and hot pants to be visible, effecting a mod look and attitude that signified the trendiness of the wearer in that period.

Joan Nicks

SEE ALSO: *Disco; Retro Fashion.*

BIBLIOGRAPHY

Gunn, Tim, and Ada Calhoun. *Tim Gunn's Fashion Bible: The Fascinating History of Everything in Your Closet.* New York: Gallery Books, 2012.

Peril, Lynn. "Hot Pants." In *Girl Culture: An Encyclopedia,* ed. Claudia A. Mitchell and Jacqueline Reid-Walsh. Westport, CT: Greenwood Press, 2008, 362–363.

Steele, Valerie. *Fifty Years of Fashion: New Look to Now.* New Haven, CT: Yale University Press, 1997.

Hot Rods

Americans love speed. It suffuses their culture, coloring every aspect of it from food to mail service. It should come as no surprise, then, that the automobile holds a hallowed space in the American myth. Nowhere is this more evident than in the realm of the hot rod. The popularity of the hot rod ties in with the American preoccupation with youth, speed, and individualism, and the people who pioneered the hot rod have become recognized as master artists outside of this very specific milieu. More than eighty years after its invention, the hot rod is still omnipresent on the road and off.

SOMETHING FROM NOTHING

Hot rod culture emerged in the early 1940s—the war years—particularly in Los Angeles. As Tom Wolfe writes of the period in *The Kandy-Kolored Tangerine-Flake Streamline Baby* (1965), "Family life was dislocated, as the phrase goes, but the money was pouring in, and the kids began to work up their own style of life—as they've been doing ever since." In these early years, aesthetics and necessity joined to create a new form of car. Owing to war rationing, cars and car parts were scarce, and underage enthusiasts resorted to junkyard salvaging, creating hybridized vehicles with primitively hopped-up engines.

The aggressively declassé activities of these youngsters, who engaged in illegal drag-racing competitions and ostentatiously public congregations at drive-in restaurants, created an atmosphere of public alarm, not unlike that which accompanied the Hells Angels two decades later. Part of the public opprobrium had to do with appearances. Hot-rodders cultivated a distinctly sinister look, chopping (lowering the top of the car) and channeling (lowering the body itself down between the wheels) their rides.

Hot-rodders reduced the 1932 Ford Roadster, one of the most popular objects of customizing of all time, to little more than a streamlined square that was brightly painted and wedded to 30-inch tires and an enormous chrome engine. Nor did frequent contretemps between police and illicit road racers improve the hot-rodders' reputation. A whole hot rod culture had emerged around the rituals of customizing, cruising, and drag racing. In the Los Angeles area, drag racing took place on a deserted stretch of road in Culver City nicknamed "Thunder Alley," and large-scale police raids were not uncommon.

A CULTURAL MOVEMENT

The public might have viewed hot-rodders with distaste, but a middling movie writer named Robert Petersen was fascinated by the religious fervor with which teenagers were pouring money into their cars. In the late 1940s, Petersen started *Hot Rod* magazine, which eventually ballooned into Petersen Publishing, a publishing empire devoted to automotive speed and beauty. By the early 1960s, models, T-shirts, toy cars, stickers, music groups, and movies were part of the marketplace. In short, any product tangentially associated with hot-rodding was produced and rapidly consumed. However, even after hot-rodding had been "rationalized," as Wolfe puts it, subjected to capitalism's "efficient exploitation," its antisocial qualities remained central to its allure.

This brazen nose-thumbing quality was best expressed by Ed "Big Daddy" Roth. He was a customizer who specialized in baroque, grotesque creations that were exemplified in automobiles with names such as the Beatnik Bandit and Mysterion and in T-shirts called Weirdo or Monster (harkening back to the pieced-together Frankenstein quality of early hot rods) that featured bizarre hot-rodding creatures alongside slogans such as "Mother Is Wrong" or "Born to Lose." Writes Wolfe:

> Roth pointed out that the kids have a revealing vocabulary. They use the words "rotten," "bad," and "tough" in a very fey, ironic way. Often a particularly baroque and sleek custom car will be called a "big, bad Merc" (for Mercury) or something like that. In this case "bad" means "good," but it also retains some of the original meaning of "bad." The kids know that to adults, like their own parents, this car is going to look sinister and somehow like an assault on their style of life.

MAINSTREAM RECOGNITION

The first act in the narrative of the avant-garde artist involves producing work that is virtually ignored. Then comes recognition, then absorption into the mainstream. So it was that the superstars of customizing—Roth, Daryl Starbird, George Barris—started their careers as pariahs and ended with Detroit, Michigan, car makers wooing them as highly valued consultants.

In fact, Detroit had been assiduously following their careers for some time. Barris recounted for Wolfe that those big-time stylists knew all about cars he had customized as far back as 1945. Stylistic innovations such as tail fins, bubbletops, frenched headlights, and concealed headlights all derived from the customizers. The early era of muscle cars—Rivieras, Sting Rays, Barracudas, and Chargers—drew freely upon hot rod aesthetics.

By the twenty-first century, hot rods were recognized as an art form, with Roth and his peers exhibiting their work in museums and galleries. Even clothing designer Ralph Lauren had joined the game, showing his car collection in a 2011 Paris exhibition titled "L'Art de L'Automobile." Celebrity hot rod enthusiast Jay Leno has also brought attention to the hobby. His collection of cars has been publicized on television and his interactive website, *Jay Leno's Garage*. Reality television shows such as *American Hot Rod* (2004–2008) chronicle the making of specialty cars and have brought the hobby back into mainstream consciousness. Furthermore, ever since Petersen put on the first hot rod car show in 1948, such happenings have become commonplace. The National Street Rod Association annually hosts the Street Rod Nationals in Kentucky; in 2006, the event drew more than 10,000 cars and more than 30,000 spectators. Hot rod clubs continue to flourish, fueled by each new generation of teenage boys.

Indeed, the tradition continues unbroken since its dawn during the World War II era. Hot-rodding is now more about craft than rebellion, but its outlaw implications still hold true. A custom car is, by its very nature, a menace—and therein lies its continuing allure.

Michael Baers

SEE ALSO: *Automobile; The Beach Boys; Drag Racing; Leno, Jay; Muscle Cars; Reality Television; Wolfe, Tom.*

BIBLIOGRAPHY

Blair, John, and Stephen J. McParland. *The Illustrated Discography of Hot Rod Music.* Ann Arbor, MI: Popular Culture, 1990.

Felsen, Henry Gregor. *Street Rod.* New York: Random House, 1953.

Genat, Robert, and Robin Genat. *Hot Rod Nights: Boulevard Cruisin' in the USA.* Osceola, WI: Motorbooks International, 1998.

Gifford, Barry. *H-o-t R-o-d.* San Francisco: Chronicle Books, 1997.

Medley, Tom, and LeRoi Smith. *Tex Smith's Hot Rod History: Tracing America's Most Popular Automotive Hobby.* Osceola, WI: Motorbooks International, 1994.

Ross, Ken. *Art of the Hot Rod.* Minneapolis, MN: Motor Books, 2008.

Roth, Ed, and Howie "Pyro" Kusten. *Confessions of a Rat Fink: The Life and Times of Ed "Big Daddy" Roth.* New York: Pharos Books, 1992.

Roth, Ed, and Tony Thacker. *Hot Rods.* Osceola, WI: Motorbooks International, 1995.

Szatmary, D. P. *Rockin' in Time: a Social History of Rock-and-Roll.* New York: Prentice Hall, 2006.

Wolfe, Tom. *The Kandy-Kolored Tangerine Flake Streamline Baby.* New York: Farrar, Straus & Giroux, 1963.

Wolfe, Tom. *The Pump House Gang.* New York: Farrar, Straus & Giroux, 1968.

Houdini, Harry *(1874–1926)*

Before there was a Doug Henning, a David Copperfield, or a Siegfried & Roy, Harry Houdini was the celebrity magician without peer. A global figure thanks to his relentless touring, he was the first entertainer to take full advantage of the emergent mass media, engaging in death-defying public stunts that cannily made use of newspapers, radio, and film. Had Houdini simply been another skilled magician, he might have been forgotten along with the generation of vaudevillians from which he sprang, but the magnitude of his exploits, his tormented personality, and his untimely demise created an allure that has not dimmed over the passing decades. Houdini was a figure out of Greek tragedy: the indestructible warrior with an Achilles' heel.

HUMBLE BEGINNINGS

Born Ehrich Weiss in Budapest, Hungary, Houdini was the son of a rabbinical scholar of somewhat dubious credentials who moved his family to America in 1878 after securing a position as rabbi at a small synagogue in Appleton, Wisconsin. Ultimately, Mayer Weiss was not to the liking of his small-town flock. Perhaps it was his advanced age, European conceits, or habit of conducting services in German, but for whatever reason, the congregation cut him loose, and the Weiss family, now numbering seven, moved to Milwaukee, Wisconsin, barely scraping by on Mayer's earnings. Young Ehrich felt the family's poverty acutely and was hurt by his father's humiliation; in his later years, he would take pains to ennoble the hapless rabbi. When the family had finally settled in New York City, Ehrich found work as a tie-cutter at the age of fourteen. His ailing father was soon laboring alongside Ehrich in the tie factory. It

Harry Houdini. *In addition to being a skilled magician, Harry Houdini was a master at using the media to publicize his ambitious stunts, gaining as a result international celebrity in the early twentieth century.* **HULTON ARCHIVE/GETTY IMAGES.**

was with a measure of relief that Ehrich and his family witnessed the passing of the ill and unhappy head of the household in 1892.

Houdini possessed a meager education, but he retained as part of his father's legacy a deep respect for learning, and it was a book that changed his life. While reading the autobiography of eighteenth-century French magician Jean Eugène Robert-Houdin, a teenage Ehrich discovered not only a fascination with all things illusory but also a template on which to build his own life story. Robert-Houdin appears to have replaced the unsuccessful Rabbi Weiss as Ehrich's father figure, and the young man excised vast chunks of the autobiography to fill in the holes of his own shabby persona, even borrowing the dead magician's moniker.

A LEGEND IS BORN

With his father dead, Ehrich was no longer constrained in his job choices by filial piety, and he embarked on his career as a professional magician as one half of the Houdini Brothers. Harry (possibly a version of his nickname, Eiri), with his young wife, Bess Rahner, acting as his assistant, plied the length and breadth of the country in the 1890s, playing dime museums, burlesque shows, traveling carnivals, and medicine shows. One trick in particular, a bait and switch, was a favorite with audiences, and the astute Houdini was soon specializing in a variety of escape tricks, which had the added advantage of familiarity in their resemblance to the stunts in many spiritualist mediums. The escape tricks were especially well suited to Houdini—a small, compact man who had an enthusiasm for sports—for they demanded strenuous exertion, muscular control, and prodigious endurance. For several years, he labored in obscurity and was in the midst of rethinking his career options when he was offered a position on a vaudeville circuit by theater impresario Martin Beck.

At the turn of the twentieth century, vaudeville was the height of mass entertainment, and palatial theaters were being built to house the various acts. For an entertainer such as Houdini, accustomed to making $25 a week, vaudeville was a quantum leap in remuneration and prestige. Under the management of Beck, Houdini was soon gaining nationwide notoriety and commanding a substantial salary. To promote his act, he had started to make a practice of escaping from jails and police stations, miraculously freeing himself from manacles and cells alike. Houdini was always eager to keep one step ahead of the competition: as a refinement, he began to perform his escapes in the nude or dressed only in a loincloth, flabbergasting the police and sparking the public's curiosity with each successive news story.

GOING GLOBAL

When he sailed for England in the summer of 1900, Houdini had established himself as the "Handcuff King," adept at unshackling himself under a variety of conditions. He created a sensation in Great Britain and then in Europe as a whole. In fact, Europe embraced his act with such enthusiasm that he stayed a full five years. Houdini continued his practice of escaping from jail cells and offering prizes to people who could produce locks he could not pick. This almost led to public humiliation in Birmingham, England, when a local judo expert and teacher of physiognomy devised a system of shackles that left the magician nearly immobilized. During the torturous trick, Houdini struggled with his bonds, finally freeing himself, though not without casting a pall of suspicion over the escape with the filing marks he produced in his efforts.

Returning to the United States in 1905, Houdini was alarmed by the legion of shameless imitators that had sprung up in his absence. He forsook handcuffs, leaving them to the copycats, and concentrated on new escapes. Houdini had always known the importance of remaining in the public eye, and he began to perform high-visibility stunts in which he escaped from straitjackets, bags, and crates—whatever could be thrown off a bridge. He toured for the next ten years, constantly refining his act, innovating, and pushing his body to the limits of endurance. This period saw the introduction of the milk-can escape; the Chinese water torture (perhaps the best remembered of his escapes and the most frequently imitated today); the vanishing elephant; and, for outdoor performances, an aerial straitjacket act. In terms of cinematic potential, the aerial straitjacket escape was a vast improvement on his previous publicity stunts: with his ankles secured by heavy rope, he was hauled to the top of a skyscraper and, suspended above the crowd, was left to wriggle free.

HOLLYWOOD CALLS

With the advent of film, Houdini realized that vaudeville's days were numbered. By 1918 he was hard at work on his first film. Houdini moved to Los Angeles, and until his death in 1926, he generally shunned live performances for film acting. Perhaps his best-known movie is *The Grim Game* (1919). Not content simply to star in movies, he started his own production company, which lost money at an alarming rate.

While Houdini the movie star carried on with his work in a desultory fashion, Houdini the whistle-blower was waging a fierce battle against the forces of hokum. Besides being a possessor of tremendous energy, he had a streak of the pedant in him. He had met the author Arthur Conan Doyle, the creator of the Sherlock Holmes character and a believer in spiritualism. Houdini, who had earned his living artfully faking his way out of impossible situations, was skeptical of such beliefs. He had made a parlor game out of unmasking mediums, and now he directed his scorn at one Mina Crandon—better known as Margery—a society woman who, with the aid of her deceased brother, Walter, had impressed *Scientific American* as a legitimate medium. Houdini would have none of it. In a series of séances where he deduced one trick after another, he reduced Margery to fuming impotence and irrevocably splintered the *Scientific American* panel.

THE FINAL ACT

In December 1925 Houdini launched a two-and-a-half-hour extravaganza, *Magic*, on Broadway. It was his first big tour in a number of years. The first act consisted of nothing but magic tricks—he even went so far as to pull a rabbit out of a hat to prove he was a magician—followed by an exposé of spiritualism and then an escape act. For the status-conscious Houdini, *Magic* was a step up. This was a proper theater—not a vaudeville house—and when the show opened, it placed Houdini in direct competition with the lions of Broadway.

The show ran through the spring, with time out for Houdini to take his antispiritualist campaign to Washington, D.C., where he testified before Congress. During this break he had a chance to unmask another fraud, a fakir named Rahman Bey, who allowed himself to be submerged in a coffin for an hour, claiming he had achieved the feat by putting himself in a trance. Again, Houdini would have none of it. After training himself to ration oxygen, Houdini remained underwater in a glass-fronted coffin for an hour and a half, and he did so without being in a "trance." It was his last unmasking.

When the *Magic* tour resumed in the fall of 1926, Houdini seemed rundown. If the testimony of his friends can be believed, he had also become convinced of his imminent death and tearfully bade goodbye to several of his acquaintances. In Albany, New York, he broke his ankle while being hoisted into the Chinese water torture apparatus and continued the tour on crutches. When he arrived in Detroit, Michigan, he had a temperature of 102 degrees. Persevering through the night's performance despite his condition, he collapsed backstage immediately afterward. Soon he was hospitalized with a ruptured appendix. After surgery, peritonitis set in, and the master escapologist died six days later, on October 31.

A MYSTERIOUS ENDING

Lore contends that the ruptured appendix resulted from a punch to the stomach. Houdini took great pride in his physical condition and often asked men to punch him to prove the strength of his abdomen muscles. In Detroit, a man asked him if his muscles were as strong as advertised, and Houdini said they were. The man punched his stomach, but Houdini was not expecting the blow and, therefore, was not prepared. It is unclear if this incident really took place, but it does add to the eeriness surrounding his death.

Houdini was a transitional figure in the cultural pantheon, marking the end of the Victorian era and the beginning of the modern one. He was a textbook case of repressed neurosis in which Sigmund Freud would have delighted. For a man whose very livelihood depended on nerves of steel, Houdini was notoriously emotional. Vain and egotistical, he left a trail of broken friendships and hurt feelings in his wake. Houdini was an immigrant of humble origins who was obsessed by status, once buying a dress commissioned by the recently deceased Queen Victoria so that his mother might wear it while entertaining her old-world relatives. Despite his flaws, Houdini was smart enough to embrace the expanding technological universe. A lover of gadgetry, he filled his house with a surfeit of modern appliances. Professionally, he did not allow the thrust of progress to leave him stranded, as it had so many of his confederates in vaudeville.

Indeed, Houdini was a complex man. In the archetypal pattern of a tragic hero, he was struck down by his blind ambition, but it was this same ambition—in the form of his extraordinary feats—that gave life to a legend that continues on.

Michael Baers

SEE ALSO: *Broadway; Burlesque; Doyle, Arthur Conan; Vaudeville;* Weird Tales.

BIBLIOGRAPHY

Kellock, Harold. *Houdini: His Life Story from the Recollections and Documents of Beatrice Houdini.* New York: Blue Ribbon Books, 1928.

Meyer, Bernard. *Houdini: A Mind in Chains.* New York: E. P. Dutton, 1976.

Milbourne, Christopher. *Houdini, the Untold Story.* New York: Thomas Y. Crowell, 1969.

Mullin, Rita T. *Harry Houdini: Death-Defying Showman.* New York: Sterling, 2007.

Silverman, Kenneth. *Houdini!!! The Career of Ehrich Weiss.* New York: HarperCollins, 1996.

Housing Market Bubble

A housing market bubble (or real estate or property bubble) is a type of economic bubble that occurs periodically in local and global markets. It is typically characterized by swift increases in assessments of housing property until prices for homes reach unsustainable levels, after which they decline. In comparison to stock market bubbles, housing market bubbles take longer to deflate: the decline in prices is slower because the real estate market is less liquid—in other words, houses cannot be sold, or exchanged for cash, as quickly as stocks can. A drop in commercial real estate properties generally moves in tandem with the decline of residential property values. In addition to decreasing the value of homes, any collapse of the housing bubble adversely affects lending institutions, home builders, general contractors, home supply retail outlets, and other related entities.

Schools of economic thought differ on whether housing market bubbles have broad macroeconomic significance and can be predicted and avoided. Some argue that a house price index such as the Case-Shiller index can identify such bubbles in advance. Others argue that housing bubbles cannot be identified and, as they are a normal part of the economic cycle, should not be prevented. The economists who hold this latter view believe the government and the central bank should be responsible for cleaning up after the bubble bursts.

RECENT HOUSING MARKET BUBBLES

In the United States, the real estate boom ended in the second quarter of 2006. As mortgage rates began to rise significantly for the first time in years, first-time buyers were priced out of the market. Other home buyers and speculative investors in real estate lost confidence in the market because the data indicated that property values would not continue rising as they had in previous years. Resort property buyers and trade-up buyers likewise became hesitant to enter the market. Many areas with multiple foreclosures, including Southern California, suburban Las Vegas, and several counties throughout Florida and Arizona, saw property values dip by more than 20 percent. In many cases, such decreases left homeowners owing more on their mortgages than the houses were worth. By the end of 2010, more than eleven million American residential properties (or slight over 23 percent of all U.S. homes) were in negative equity.

Housing market bubbles during this period spread to other countries, such as Argentina, Australia, the Baltic States, Bulgaria, China, Croatia, France, Greece, India, Ireland, Israel, Italy, Lebanon, the Netherlands, New Zealand, Norway, Poland, Romania, Russia, Singapore, South Africa, South Korea, Spain, Sweden, Ukraine, and the United Kingdom. As was the case in the United States, these housing market bubbles in other countries were followed by severe price decreases or housing price crashes that resulted in many owners holding mortgages that exceeded the value of their homes. In the United Kingdom property values had declined by 35 percent below their mid-2007 peak values.

CAUSES

Housing prices, like those of all goods and services, are driven by supply and demand. Prices for homes tend to go up with either an increase in demand or a decrease in supply. The demand might increase because of any of the following factors: an upturn in general economic growth and prosperity that enables consumers to have more disposable income; an increase in the population of a specific demographic segment that creates more first-time buyers; or low interest rates. Easy access to credit because of liberal underwriting standards also brings more buyers to the market, while a short-term relationship between the mortgage broker and the borrower encourages the latter to take excessive risks. A lack of financial literacy as well as speculative and risky behavior by home buyers and property investors can also cause a bubble. In sum, all critical stakeholders—buyers, borrowers, lenders, builders, and investors—are involved in the excessive risk taking and speculative behavior that causes this phenomenon.

Many economists agree that the housing market bubble of the first decade of the 2000s was caused in part by a combination of predatory lending practices and increased buyer speculation. Predatory lending occurs when a financial institution encourages a borrower to take a mortgage carrying high fees and high interest rates, thus reducing the equity the borrower acquires in the property when making monthly payments on the loan. Many of the borrowers who agree to such mortgages do not fully understand the terms of the agreement to which they have committed themselves.

As U.S. banks were more likely to lend to buyers who might default on their loans, at the same time Americans were more willing than they had been in the past to take on multiple mortgages. With property values soaring, it made sense to many buyers to take on a mortgage, no matter what the terms, if one could sell the property at a sizable profit within a few years. More than a third of the U.S. home mortgages initiated in 2006 went to people who already owned at least one home, and buyers owning three or more homes were the fastest-growing segment of homeowners between 2000 and 2006. Most of these speculators were allowed to use small down payments and subprime credit to acquire properties during this period. The housing market bubble of 2006 was especially acute in Arizona, California, Florida, and Nevada, where home prices doubled between 2000 and 2006 and investors constituted about half of all mortgage-backed home purchases.

WHY THE BUBBLES BURST

Typically, housing market bubbles burst when excessive risk taking becomes pervasive throughout the market. During such times, the demand decreases even as supplies continue to increase, resulting in a drop in prices. Caught up in the buying frenzy, builders add large numbers of new homes to the market but eventually run out of buyers. Values of other properties plateau and then begin to drop. Owners who have taken on risky mortgages become keen to cut their losses, so they, too, put their houses on the market. As a result, there are considerably more sellers than buyers, and prices continue to drop.

The losses are not just limited to homeowners—mortgage lenders, mortgage investors, and property investors begin to realize losses as well. To cover their losses, lending institutions raise interest rates, pricing many buyers out of the market. People committed to mortgages with variable interest rates watch their monthly payments escalate and often default on their loans, making banks less likely to lend to new buyers at advantageous rates. The once-hyperactive housing market then grinds to a halt, as numerous houses become available but remain on the market because buyers have no reason to hope their value will increase in the near future.

In 2006 the multiple-home owners began defaulting on the risky loans as housing prices plunged. Buyers with at least three properties accounted for more than a fourth of all seriously delinquent mortgage balances in the United States. Although housing bubbles may be identifiable in progress, they can be definitively measured only in hindsight, after a market correction.

The U.S. Treasury Department and the Housing and Urban Development (HUD) administer programs to assist homeowners who are at risk of foreclosure or are struggling with their monthly mortgage payments. Some programs modify or refinance homeowners' loans to lower payments. Other programs offer temporary reduction or suspension of mortgage payments for twelve months for the unemployed. Homeowners who are interested in transitioning to more affordable housing may be eligible for a short sale or deed-in-lieu foreclosure. Finally, there are redemption programs that allow consumers to reclaim their home after it has been already sold at a foreclosure by paying the outstanding mortgage balance and all costs incurred during the foreclosure process.

Abhijit Roy

SEE ALSO: *Bank Failures/Subprime Mortgages; Consumerism; The Great Recession; Suburbia.*

BIBLIOGRAPHY

"Building Wealth: Homes in Japan Last for Only 30 Years. The Government Wants to Change That." *Economist*, January 5, 2008, 73–74.

Calabresi, Massimo, and Stephen Gandel. "How to Save the Housing Market: Destroy Houses." *Time*, September 5, 2011, 46–52.

Carter, Adrienne. "Selling Your Home in Slow Market." *Money*, November 2004, 61–62.

Handley, Meg. "Has the Housing Market Found Its Footing?" *US News Digital Weekly*, September 9, 2011, 7.

Kirby, Jason. "Housing Prices Start to Fall: What's Next?" *Maclean's*, August 4, 2008, 45.

Kiviat, Barbara. "The Bust Hits Home." *Time*, September 24, 2007, 52–54.

Leonard, William Torbert. *Masquerade in Black*. Metuchen, NJ: Scarecrow Press, 1986.

Shiller, R. *Irrational Exuberance*. New York: Crown Business, 2006.

Houston, Whitney *(1963–2012)*

Singer Whitney Houston, a beauty with a clear and soaring soprano voice, became a megastar in the 1980s. She was born in Newark, New Jersey, the daughter of gospel singer Cissy Houston and a cousin to singing star Dionne Warwick, and began singing herself at age eleven with the New Hope Baptist Choir. In her teens she sang backup for Chaka Khan and Lou Rawls, but at eighteen she became a successful model and appeared in television comedies while pursuing her singing career. This took off when she was signed exclusively by Clive Davis of Arista Records. Under his careful management, she launched her first album, *Whitney Houston*, in 1985. It sold fourteen million copies, setting a debut album record. She became a household name and, by the late 1990s was the recipient of six Grammy Awards and twenty-one American Music Awards.

In 1992 Houston married singer Bobby Brown and embarked on a film career, starring opposite Kevin Costner in *The Bodyguard*. She acted on-screen again in *Waiting to Exhale* (1995), directed by actor Forest Whitaker and featuring an all-female African American cast, and in *The Preacher's Wife* (1996) with Denzel Washington. All three movies yielded massive hit songs, most notably "I Will Always Love You." Houston's commanding, multi-octave range allowed her to sing a wide range of material—gospel; R&B; pop; rock; and, most popularly, love ballads. By the late 1990s, despite commercial competition from performers such as Mariah Carey and Céline Dion, Houston was still popular, both at home and in Britain.

In the first decade of the 2000s, however, Houston's personal problems began to overshadow her undeniable talents. Although she renewed her contract with Arista for a massive sum of $100 million and found success with the reissue of her 1991 Super Bowl performance of "The Star-Spangled Banner" after the attacks of September 11, 2011, Houston's repeated failures to appear at scheduled events, rapid weight loss, numerous run-ins with the law, and generally erratic behavior led many to suspect that she was battling drug addiction (something she later admitted in a 2009 interview with Oprah Winfrey). She entered a drug rehabilitation facility in 2004 for prescription drug abuse, and in 2005 Houston and Brown starred in the short-lived reality show *Being Bobby Brown*. The couple's odd on-camera behavior led to further speculation and rumors, and Houston subsequently divorced Brown and reentered rehab again, largely disappearing from the public spotlight until 2009, when she released the album *I Look to You*. The album was well received and sparked a 2010 world tour that was touted as a "comeback" for Houston, though many critics and fans complained that her voice had noticeably deteriorated.

Houston was found dead in a Beverly Hills hotel room on February 11, 2012, the cause an apparent accidental drowning caused by cocaine and alcohol use. The news, coming the day before the Grammy Awards show, was met with a mixture of deep sadness and grim acknowledgment, prompting a number of tributes from musicians of all styles. Though many felt that Houston's tragic death could (and perhaps should) have been avoided, most chose to focus on her legacy as one of the most influential female vocalists of all time.

Brian Granger

SEE ALSO: *Brown, Bobby; Celebrity; Celebrity Couples; Gospel Music; Grammy Awards; Hollywood; Movie Stars; Pop Music; Reality Television; Rhythm and Blues; Rock and Roll; Super Bowl; Television; Washington, Denzel; Winfrey, Oprah.*

BIBLIOGRAPHY

Bego, Mark. *Whitney Houston!: The Spectacular Rise and Tragic Fall of the Woman Whose Voice Inspired a Generation*. New York: Skyhorse Publishing, 2012.

Parish, James Robert. *Whitney Houston: The Unauthorized Biography*. London: Aurum, 2003.

Whitburn, Joel. *The Billboard Book of Top 40 Hits*. New York: Billboard Books, 1996.

How the West Was Won

Featuring narration by Spencer Tracy; individual segments directed by Henry Hathaway, John Ford, and George Marshall; and an engaging story and thrilling action sequences, MGM's *How the West Was Won* (1962) is widely considered one of Hollywood's greatest epics. The gigantic all-star cast included movie giants such as Henry Fonda, Karl Malden, Gregory Peck, George Peppard, Debbie Reynolds, Jimmy Stewart, Eli Wallach, John Wayne, Richard Widmark, and Walter Brennan. The film won Academy Awards for Best Film Editing and Best Sound and was nominated for five others, including Best Picture.

The film episodically tells the story of three generations of the Prescott family, who migrate westward over a fifty-year period during the nineteenth century. This was the first theatrical release featuring Cinerama, a filming technique that employs three cameras sharing a single shutter in order to replicate the scope of the human eye. The process is far less impressive on TV. In theaters, however, the film, much of which was shot on location in various spots throughout the American West, is spectacular. Despite Cinerama's initial popularity, few films after *How the West Was Won* successfully utilized the process, which ultimately resulted in its demise. *How the West Was Won* nevertheless remains a classic example of big-budget Hollywood filmmaking at its best.

In 2000 *How the West Was Won* was made available on DVD for a new generation. Eight years later, Warner Home Video released a three-disc set, an ultimate edition, and a two-disc Blu-ray version. The remastered film, which includes a documentary on the history of Cinerama, employed the Smile-Box process in an effort to reproduce the Cinerama effects of the original version, but it was not altogether successful.

Robert C. Sickels

SEE ALSO: *Academy Awards; Blockbusters; Fonda, Henry; Ford, John; Peck, Gregory; Stewart, Jimmy; Tracy, Spencer; Wayne, John; The Western.*

BIBLIOGRAPHY

Cameron, Ian, and Douglas Pye, eds. *The Book of Westerns*. New York: Continuum, 1996.

Darby, William. *John Ford's Westerns: A Thematic Analysis, with Filmography*. Jefferson, NC: McFarland, 1996.

Hall, Sheldon. "*How the West Was Won*: History, Spectacle, and the American Mountains." In *The Book of Westerns*, ed. Ian Cameron and Douglas Pye. New York: Continuum, 1996.

Lucas, Tim. "The Wide, Wide West." *Sight and Sound* 18, no. 12 (2008).

Howard, Ron *(1954–)*

Ron Howard began his career in show business at the tender age of eighteen months and spent much of the rest of his childhood starring in television sitcoms. Unlike the typical child actor, he found financial success and artistic respect as an adult—but from the other side of the film camera, as a director and producer of hit Hollywood movies. Throughout his career, whether he was playing an adorable kid or making a film about politics, he is known for making work that is wholesome, accessible, and almost always popular with audiences.

ACTING CAREER

Born Ronald William Howard on March 1, 1954, in Duncan, Oklahoma, Howard became a child actor thanks to his showbiz parents, Jean Speegle and Rance Howard. Credited initially as Ronny Howard, he appeared in TV shows, specials, and films. At age six he began playing homespun Opie Taylor on *The Andy Griffith Show* (1960–1968). Audiences watched Howard grow up on screen as Opie, the freckle-faced, redheaded son of a kindly, widowed sheriff in an ostensibly wholesome yet quietly segregated North Carolina town.

After taking several lesser TV roles, Howard portrayed Richie Cunningham, a clean-cut teenager growing up in an idealized middle-class midwestern family, on the nostalgic sitcom *Happy Days* (1974–1984). Richie was famous for exclaiming "Fonzie!" at the highjinks of his family's upstairs tenant, Arthur Fonzarelli (played by Henry Winkler). Like Opie, Richie was a wholesome boy, who spent his time eating his mom's home-cooked meals, visiting soda fountains with his friends, and taking various sweethearts to sock hops. Howard's face and name soon became permanently identified with the image of all-American youth.

Howard also appeared in films. Some of his most prominent roles were in director George Lucas's coming-of-age film *American Graffiti* (1973) and in actor John Wayne's last film, *The Shootist* (1976). Rather than accept the child actor's usual fate of having new work measured against old reruns, Howard risked a jump behind the camera. He began directing TV projects and made his film directorial debut with *Grand Theft Auto* (1977).

Since 1982, when he hosted *Saturday Night Live* (1975–) and let comedian Eddie Murphy chide him for having played Opie, Howard has seldom faced the camera. Guest appearances as himself and reunions of *The Andy Griffith Show* in 1986 and 2003 and of *Happy Days* in 1992 and 2005 have proved the exception. Howard has also voiced characters for the animated TV series *The Simpsons* (1989–) and served as the narrator for the sitcom *Arrested Development* (2003–2006), which he also executive produced.

DIRECTORIAL WORK

His breakthrough as a director came with his film comedy *Night Shift* (1982), in which former costar Winkler and actors Michael Keaton and Shelley Long lead a morgue-based prostitution ring. The director also received considerable praise for *Splash!* (1984), starring Tom Hanks as a man smitten by a mermaid, played by Daryl Hannah. Critics enjoyed the cast and gags but faulted the film's excessive length.

In *Cocoon* (1985) Howard combined humor and pathos in a story of love, aging, and dignity. The lighter, more predictable social comedy *Gung Ho* (1986) was less successful. His quirky fantasy-adventure *Willow* (1988) tended to please filmgoers but confuse or anger critics, who faulted its seemingly random mishmash of myth and fairy tale. Howard again saw mixed reviews for the comedy *Parenthood* (1989), starring comedian Steve Martin. The firefighting adventure *Backdraft* (1991) became yet another top-grossing, special-effects-driven film that critics derided.

Howard has been criticized for overly facile historical messages. For example, *Far and Away* (1992), an epic love story starring Tom Cruise and Nicole Kidman, set during the settling of the American frontier, was seen by some critics as an alarmingly old-fashioned and naive take on westward expansion. Several of Howard's movies have included ritualistic flag-waving and American-as-apple-pie scenes that, with heady soundtracks and heart-wrenching cinematography, soar to an almost propagandistic level. Such a critique applies to the otherwise widely acclaimed *Apollo 13* (1995), a tense, documentary-style drama about a nearly disastrous NASA moon shot. Nevertheless, *Apollo 13* had nine Academy Awards nominations and earned Howard a Directors Guild of America Award.

As a director, Howard has experimented with different genres. In 1996 he created the dark thriller *Ransom*, and in 1999 he toyed with metamedia in *EdTV*. In 2001 he won a slew of awards nominations for *A Beautiful Mind*, which told the story of a Nobel laureate's struggle with schizophrenia. The picture received four Academy Awards, including Best Director and Best Picture. The film's star, Russell Crowe, also appeared in Howard's Depression-era boxing movie *Cinderella Man* (2005). The sharp historical drama *Frost/Nixon* (2008) and lighter fare such as *The Dilemma* (2011) have added breadth to Howard's oeuvre.

Even Howard's subpar work has usually generated box-office success, such as *Dr. Seuss's How the Grinch Stole Christmas* (2000), which became a top-grossing film despite uninspired direction and horribly slapstick performances. Many have claimed that Howard proved the adage that books are better than their movies with *The Da Vinci Code* (2006) and *Angels & Demons* (2009). Some critics panned these adaptations of author Dan Brown's best-selling novels for their anti-Catholic slant, while others gave them mixed reviews for their look, feel, and pacing.

PRODUCTION CREDITS AND AWARDS

Howard and longtime friend and producer Brian Grazer formed Imagine Entertainment in 1986 to produce dozens of films, including *Liar Liar* (1997), *8 Mile* (2002), *J. Edgar* (2011), and *Cowboys & Aliens* (2011), and TV series such as *Felicity* (1998–2002), *24* (2001–2010), and *Arrested Development* (2003–2006).

Although Howard studied film for two years at the University of Southern California and did not graduate, his honors and distinctions have more than made up for his lack of a diploma. He received the American Cinematheque Award in 1990; the U.S. government's National Medal of Arts in 2003; the American Cinema Editors USA Award and the Golden Eddie Filmmaker of the Year Award, both in 2006; and the American Society of Cinematographers and Board of the Governors Award in 2007. He has received several other lifetime achievement distinctions and festival honors.

Stephen P. Davis

SEE ALSO: *Academy Awards;* American Graffiti*;* The Andy Griffith Show*;* Arrested Development*; Child Stars; Cruise, Tom;* The Da Vinci Code*; Hanks, Tom;* Happy Days*; Hollywood;* Laverne and Shirley*; Lucas, George; Martin, Steve; Murphy, Eddie;* Saturday Night Live*;* The Simpsons*; Sitcom; Soda Fountains; Television;* 24*; Wayne, John.*

BIBLIOGRAPHY

Gray, Beverly. *Ron Howard: From Mayberry to the Moon . . . and Beyond.* Nashville, TN: Rutledge Hill Press, 2003.

Weinraub, Bernard. "The Dark Underbelly of Ron Howard." *New York Times*, November 12, 1996.

The Howdy Doody Show

Howdy Doody was the name of a twenty-seven-inch, big-eared, freckle-faced wooden puppet. Howdy appeared in a starring capacity on an immensely popular children's television show of the same name that ran on NBC from 1947 to 1960. It was broadcast live from 30 Rockefeller Plaza in New York City.

The Howdy Doody Show was the creation of Robert E. Smith (1917–1998), a former radio personality who appeared along with his wooden counterpart at first on a weekly basis and later five days a week from Monday through Friday, starting at 5:30 in the evening. Howdy, clad in a red bandanna, dungarees, and a checkered shirt, would exchange banter with Smith, whose on-screen persona was that of Buffalo Bob Smith. Howdy also interacted with the colorful denizens of Doodyville, among whom were Phineas T. Bluster, the crusty mayor of Doodyville; Flub-a-Dub, a zoological pastiche comprising eight different animals allegedly caught by Buffalo Bob himself in a South American jungle; Princess Summerfall Winterspring, a puppet at first but later a real person played by Judy Tyler; Clarabell the Clown (first played by Bob Keeshan, also known as Captain Kangaroo), a virtual mute who engaged in Harpo Marx–like antics and frequently brandished a seltzer bottle with which he would squirt Buffalo Bob; and miscellaneous others. Hallmarks of the show were the Peanut Gallery, a kiddy audience between the ages of three and eight; the call and response between Bob and the Peanut Gallery, which had the former shouting, "Say, kids, what time is it?" to which the galvanized gallery would respond, "It's Howdy Doody time"; and the Howdy Doody theme song, the music of which was borrowed from "Tar-ra-ra-boom-de-ay."

The Howdy Doody Show holds a number of records. It was, for example, the first daily show on NBC to feature live music and the first to be broadcast in color. When it placed Buffalo Bob in New York and Howdy in Chicago for a special broadcast to celebrate NBC's having become a transcontinental network, it became the first show to employ the split-screen technique. And as Smith himself put it, "We were the first show on every day in quite a few markets. . . . There was no daytime television, just a test pattern until 5:30. We were the first show to reach 1,000 shows, then 2,000."

The importance of *The Howdy Doody Show* is not confined to record-breaking firsts, however. Howdy, Buffalo Bob, and the rest of the cast made an indelible impression on their baby boomer fans. In 1970 Smith received a call from a graduate student at the University of Pennsylvania who asked him to come to the campus to do a show. At first he thought it was a hoax, but the student was serious. Smith agreed, and a *Howdy Doody* revival was born. As reported in Smith's Associated Press obituary, columnist Bob Greene wrote in 1987 that the show "may have been the most important cultural landmark for my generation."

Howdy Doody resides at Smith's former home in Flat Rock, North Carolina. A replica, known as Double Doody, now resides at the Smithsonian Institution.

William F. O'Connor

SEE ALSO: *Baby Boomers;* Captain Kangaroo*; The Fifties; The Marx Brothers; Smithsonian Institution; Television; Toys.*

BIBLIOGRAPHY

Associated Press. "'Buffalo Bob' Smith Dead at 80." CBS News. Accessed November 2, 2011. Available from http://www.cbsnews.com/2100-207_162-15058.html

Davis, Stephen. *Say Kids, What Time Is It?: Notes from the Peanut Gallery.* Boston: Little, Brown, 1987.

"*Howdy Doody* Host Delighted a Generation." *Ottawa Citizen,* July 31, 1998, B-5.

Smith, Buffalo Bob, and Donna McCrohan. *Howdy and Me: Buffalo Bob's Own Story.* New York: Plume, 1990.

Von Schilling, James Arthur. *The Magic Window: American Television, 1939–1953.* New York: Haworth Press, 2003.

Williams, Scott. "Happy Birthday, Howdy Doody." *Pittsburgh Post-Gazette.* December 27, 1997, C-7.

Howe, Gordie *(1928–)*

Most professional hockey players retire in their thirties—but not Gordie Howe. This legendary figure played into his fifties, setting numerous records along the way. As a result of his accomplishments, he became known as "Mr. Hockey." His name and prowess generated fan interest in a sport that received much less attention than football, basketball, and baseball until recent years. In 1946, at the age of eighteen, Howe began his professional career as a right-wing forward with the Detroit Red Wings of the National Hockey League (NHL). He retired in 1980 at the age of fifty-two—it was his third and final retirement.

Howe was born on March 31, 1928, in Floral, Saskatchewan, Canada, the fourth of nine children. He played amateur hockey and one year in the minors before reaching the

Gordie Howe. *Gordie Howe's long and successful professional career earned him the nickname "Mr. Hockey." He's the only player to have competed in the National Hockey League in five different decades.* DENIS BRODEUR/NHLI/GETTY IMAGES.

NHL. Howe's first three years with Detroit were not stellar, but in the early 1950s, he came into his own and became the first player to win three consecutive scoring titles. His other records included being the league's top scorer six times and earning the league's most valuable player award six times. When he ended his career with the Red Wings following the 1970–1971 season (his first retirement), he had set numerous NHL records, including for games played (1,767), goals (801), and assists (1,049). Although Wayne Gretzky later broke many of Howe's records, his marks for most seasons (twenty-six) and oldest person to play in an NHL game (fifty-two) have stood the test of time. Additionally, he played on four Stanley Cup championship teams. In 2008 Howe was honored with the NHL Lifetime Achievement Award.

Ambidextrous and possessing incredible strength, Howe had a playing style that has been described as a combination of effortless and deceptively fast skating and outstanding stick-handling. When he started as a professional, his father said he worried that his son might kill someone in an on-ice skirmish because of his strength and his ability to use both hands. As a young man, Howe had impressed his father with his strength while working summers on construction crews; he could easily carry 90-pound cement sacks with either hand.

Howe's staying power was equally impressive. After a two-year retirement following the 1970–1971 season, he returned to professional hockey with the Houston Aeros of the World Hockey Association (WHA) at age forty-five. The physician who gave him his team physical described Howe's pulse rate as comparable to that of a man half his age. His dedication as a player is revealed in a story about the 1950 Stanley Cup semifinal series, when his head was slammed into a sideboard. The blow knocked him unconscious, and he had to be transported to the hospital for immediate brain surgery. As he was wheeled into the operating room, he apologized to the team manager for being unable to help the team more that night.

Despite seeming introverted, Howe was an extrovert on the ice, practicing what he called "religious hockey"—a philosophy in which he considered it better to give than to receive. His NHL record of 1,685 penalty minutes attests to this. According to *Fischler's Ice Hockey Encyclopedia*, former Red Wings teammate Carl Brewer once called Howe the "dirtiest player who ever lived. A great player, but also the dirtiest. He'd gouge your eye out if you gave him a chance, carve you up. He's both big and tough and used his size to intimidate guys."

Following his first retirement, Howe was elected to the Hockey Hall of Fame in 1972. Two years later he made his comeback with the Aeros so that he could play with his sons, Mark and Marty, who had also been signed by the team. The three Howes led the Aeros to WHA titles in both 1974 and 1975. In 1974, at age forty-six, Howe was named the league's most valuable player. He again left professional hockey in 1979, but he came back once more at age fifty-one in 1979, this time to play for the Hartford Whalers of the NHL. He spent one season with the Whalers before calling it quits for good in 1980.

In celebration of the fiftieth anniversary of his professional hockey debut and to become the only pro hockey player ever to play in six consecutive decades, Howe briefly came out of retirement in October 1997. The sixty-nine-year-old played an opening shift with the Detroit Vipers of the International Hockey League. Perhaps NHL great Dave Keon described Howe best in a quote in *Fischler's Ice Hockey Encyclopedia*. Referring to the state of the NHL during Howe's heyday, he observed that there were "four strong teams in this league and two weak teams ones—and the strong ones are Toronto, Chicago, Montreal, and Gordie Howe."

Mary Lou Nemanic

SEE ALSO: *Gretzky, Wayne; Hockey; Hull, Bobby; National Hockey League (NHL); Orr, Bobby; Sports Heroes.*

BIBLIOGRAPHY

Duff, Bob, and Bill Roose. *Nine: A Salute to Mr. Hockey, Gordie Howe.* Detroit, MI: Olympia Entertainment, 2007.

Fischler, Stan, and Shirley Fischler. *Fischler's Ice Hockey Encyclopedia.* New York: Crowell, 1979.

Hollander, Zander, ed. *The Complete Encyclopedia of Hockey.* Detroit, MI: Gale Research, 1993.

Libby, Bill. *Great Stanley Cup Playoffs.* New York: Random House, 1972.

Swift, E. M. "On and On and On and . . . " *Sports Illustrated,* January 17, 1994, 40–43.

Howlin' Wolf *(1910–1976)*

Standing more than 6 feet tall and weighing almost 300 pounds, Howlin' Wolf was "one of the most menacingly forceful singers of his time," according to author Giles Oakley in his book *The Devil's Music: A History of the Blues.* Born Chester Arthur Burnett, Howlin' Wolf was a farmer until his eighteenth birthday. His life was dramatically altered by a chance meeting with Delta blues legend Charley Patton. The marriage of his half-sister, Mary, to harmonica player Sonny Boy Williamson further shaped Howlin' Wolf's musical style.

Howlin' Wolf's 1950s songs for Chess Records stand as some of the finest blues ever produced. "I Ain't Superstitious," "Little Red Rooster," and "Spoonful," for example, were all big hits. Howlin' Wolf died on January 10, 1976, in Illinois. In 1991 he was inducted into the Rock and Roll Hall of Fame.

Marc R. Sykes

SEE ALSO: *Blues; Clapton, Eric; The Rolling Stones.*

BIBLIOGRAPHY

Oakley, Giles. *The Devil's Music: A History of the Blues.* New York: British Broadcasting Corporation, 1983.

Palmer, Robert. *Deep Blues.* New York: Viking, 1981.

Segrest, James, and Mark Hoffman. *Moanin' at Midnight: The Life and Times of Howlin' Wolf.* New York: Pantheon Books, 2005.

Hubbard, L. Ron *(1911–1986)*

Best known as the founder of the Church of Scientology, LaFayette Ron Hubbard was noted chiefly in literary circles as a talented and prolific author of pulp fiction from the time of his first sale in 1934 until the early 1950s. Survival for writers during the penny-a-word days meant that being prolific was a job requirement, which Hubbard more than met. His stories appeared in magazines devoted to high adventure, mystery, or science fiction. Perhaps his two most famous stories in the latter genre were "Fear" (1940) and "Typewriter in the Sky" (1940). Because of his skills at weaving the fantastic into plausible narratives, Hubbard, like sci-fi writers Robert Heinlein and Isaac Asimov, filled the pages of *Astounding Science Fiction*, the leading periodical in its field.

DIANETICS AND SCIENTOLOGY

John Wood Campbell, editor of *Astounding Science Fiction*, was so taken with Hubbard's ideas for developing human potential that he printed the writer's 16,000-word article "Dianetics" in the May 1950 issue. Hubbard's thesis traced all human misery and misunderstanding to the distorted and confused signals received by the fetus in the womb. He contended that individuals could "clear" themselves of misapprehensions and inhibitions by submitting to an auditing process, a kind of question-and-answer session conducted by a practitioner of Dianetics. According to Scientology literature, the term *Dianetics* is a combination of the Greek words *dia* (through) and *nous* (soul).

The text was widely ridiculed by medical professionals—especially psychiatrists, who claimed with some justification that Hubbard's new science had appropriated certain psychological tenets for its own purposes. Nonetheless, "Dianetics" created a sufficient stir, and Hubbard soon expanded it into a full-length book, *Dianetics: The Modern Science of Mental Health* (1950). The book sold well (it is still in print) and aroused interest in becoming "clear."

Soon Hubbard found himself in the Dianetics business, training auditors and charging fees for their services. By 1954, in a move some considered a way to gain mainstream respectability and circumvent prosecution for quackery, Hubbard had evolved Dianetics into a religion, dubbed Scientology. Those who claim to heal under the auspices of religion are not customarily held to the same rigorous standards as medical professionals. Thus, healing has been a longtime tradition in many religions. For example, in the early 1950s, faith healers, such as televangelist Oral Roberts, were as prevalent on television as professional wrestlers.

For years a possibly apocryphal story has circulated in science fiction circles that at a gathering of his fellow writers, the young Hubbard had declared that one way to become rich would be to found a new religion. (Some state that Hubbard participated in such a discussion, but another man made the infamous pronouncement.) Whether or not it was his intention, Hubbard indeed prospered. By the early twenty-first century, there were thousands of Scientology churches around the world.

CONTROVERSIAL LEGACY

Almost as long as it has been in existence, Scientology has been an object of controversy, accused of cultic brainwashing and tax evasion, among other charges. In response to public attacks and government investigations, the Church of Scientology has defended itself rigorously in court and in the media, weathering each storm largely unscathed. Despite the many books and periodical articles (including a 1991 cover story in *Time* magazine) attempting to debunk Scientology's precepts and to expose its unscrupulous practices, Scientology continues to thrive. Perhaps the most media-savvy church in existence, the Church of Scientology uses everything from television to cyberspace to promote its methodology, to attack what it views as the evils of psychiatry, and to engage in positive public relations.

Hubbard eventually went into seclusion, remaining the subject of rumors and speculation until his death was announced in 1986. His legacy is carried on largely by celebrities, whom church publicists continually point to as examples of prominent men and women in the arts who feel that Scientology has been of immeasurable benefit in their personal and professional lives. Among these artists are film actors John Travolta and Tom Cruise, jazz musician Chick Corea, and composer Mark Isham.

Despite the number of celebrity converts, Scientology is far from a mainstream belief system. The church insists that new members isolate themselves from their former lives. It also generally adopts Hubbard's stance that all critiques of Scientology stem from a worldwide conspiracy rooted in the U.S. government and the psychiatric profession. Moreover, the church collects large portions of members' assets, which critics frequently argue makes it is more like an investment scheme or a pyramid swindle than a religion. In fact, in 2009 a French court found the Church of Scientology guilty of organized fraud. Although the United States has accepted Scientology as a religion since 1993 (thus affording it tax-exempt status), a number of countries have refused to grant it any special allowances.

Among the most controversial of Scientology's claims is that most illnesses of the body and mind are psychosomatic and should be cured through church teachings rather than by medications or other mainstream medical treatment. There have been a number of high-profile incidents in which church members reportedly refused necessary psychiatric care, most notably the 1990 suicide of Noah Lottick and the 1995 death of Lisa McPherson in a Scientology medical facility. In 2012 member Debbie Cook publicly spoke about her forced incarceration and mistreatment at a Scientology base in California. However, because of the church's refusal to let outsiders in, and its hostility toward inquiries, these accusations are notoriously difficult to verify.

Marc R. Sykes

SEE ALSO: *Asimov, Isaac;* Astounding Science Fiction*; Cruise, Tom; Cults; Depression; est; New Age Spirituality; Science Fiction Publishing; Televangelism;* Time*; Travolta, John.*

BIBLIOGRAPHY

Atack, Jon. *A Piece of Blue Sky: Scientology, Dianetics and L. Ron Hubbard Exposed.* New York: Carol Publications, 1990.

Behar, Richard. "The Thriving Cult of Greed and Power." *Time*, May 6, 1991, 50.

Corydon, Bent, and Brian Ambry. *L. Ron Hubbard: Messiah or Madman?* Fort Lee, NJ: Barricade Books, 1996.

Hubbard, L. Ron. *Fear.* New York: Gnome Press, 1951.

Hubbard, L. Ron. *Typewriter in the Sky.* New York: Gnome Press, 1951.

Hubbard, L. Ron. *Dianetics: The Modern Science of Mental Health.* Los Angeles: Bridge Publications, 1992.

Hubbard, L. Ron. *What Is Scientology? The Comprehensive Reference on the World's Fastest Growing Religion.* Los Angeles: Bridge Publications, 1992.

Hubbard, L. Ron. *Scientology, a New Slant on Life.* Los Angeles: Bridge Publications, 1997.

Hubbard, L. Ron. *The Problems of Work: Scientology Applied to the Workaday World.* Los Angeles: Bridge Publications, 2007.

Hudson, Rock *(1925–1985)*

Actor Rock Hudson's unmistakable masculinity made him a screen idol of the 1950s and 1960s. Hudson was a traditionally handsome figure and a romantic hero. He was brought into film as the heir to leading men Clark Gable and Gary Cooper. His broad shouldered, six-foot-five-inch frame, and dark brooding eyes gave him an enormous screen presence. He won Golden Globes for World Film Favorite five times, made the "top 10 stars of the year" a record eight times, and was the recipient of numerous other awards. He also earned the respect of critics, in particular for his fine performances in *Magnificent Obsession* (1954) and *Giant* (1956), garnering an Oscar nomination for the latter.

Born Roy Scherer Jr., on November 17, 1925, in Winnetka, Illinois, Hudson was a member of a blue-collar family. His father was an automobile mechanic and his mother a telephone operator. Hudson's years at New Trier High School were ordinary: he sang in the school's glee club, and residents of the city remember him as a shy boy who delivered newspapers, ran errands, and worked as a golf caddy.

Rock Hudson. *Rock Hudson appeared in nearly seventy motion pictures and starred in several television productions during a career that spanned over four decades.* PHOTOSHOT/GETTY IMAGES.

Hudson was drafted into the navy during World War II. After a military discharge in 1946, he briefly returned to Winnetka and worked at several odd jobs. Then, inspired by the movie *The Hurricane*, he moved to Los Angeles to pursue an acting career. He applied to the University of Southern California's dramatics program but was rejected due to poor grades. Pursuing his dream of becoming a film star, Hudson sent out numerous résumés and photographs to movie studios. He received only one response, from talent scout Henry Willson, a representative of movie mogul David O. Selznick.

Willson renamed the ruggedly handsome young man "Rock Hudson"—"Rock" for the Rock of Gibraltar, and "Hudson" for the famous New York river. Hudson was introduced to the Hollywood studios but got off to a slow start. In fact, his screen test for Twentieth Century Fox studios was so bad that it was shown to beginning classes as a classic example of poor acting.

Hudson finally landed his first acting job in 1948. It was a one-line bit part in Raoul Walsh's *Fighter Squadron* (1948). According to Hollywood legend, Hudson needed thirty-eight takes to get that one line correct. But he learned to act on the job, and within six years he had appeared in twenty-eight pictures. The roles, however, were primarily characters lacking depth.

A STAR IS BORN

During the 1950s Hudson was cast in longer parts in a series of adventure and "B" pictures. After his appearance in the movie *Magnificent Obsession*, his career took off. In 1954 *Modern Screen* magazine cited Hudson as the most popular actor of the year, and in 1955 *Look* magazine named him as the top male movie star. That same year he was wed to Phyllis Gates, but the marriage lasted only three years, and Hudson did not remarry.

Under director George Stevens, Hudson was able to give real depth to the characterization of Texas rancher Bick Benedict in the movie *Giant* and earned an Academy Award nomination. After Richard Brooks's notable *Something of Value* and a moving performance in *A Farewell to Arms* (1957), the actor moved into comedy roles, usually paired with singer/actress Doris Day. While these films varied in quality, they allowed Hudson the opportunity to explore his comedic talents. Utilizing innuendo, the films bridged the gap between humor and permissiveness. From 1959 to 1965 he portrayed humorous characters in *Pillow Talk* (1959), *Come September* (1961), *Lover Come Back* (1961), *Send Me No Flowers* (1964), *Man's Favorite Sport* (1964), and *Strange Bedfellows* (1964). Hudson subsequently appeared in a number of unsuccessful and mediocre films.

In his fifties, Hudson made the jump to television. Initially he was not interested in a small-screen career, but the series *McMillan and Wife* (1971), in which he starred as the police commissioner of San Francisco, proved to be a hit and ran for several years. He made few notable films afterward, and he appeared in two television miniseries, *The Martian Chronicles* (1980) and *The Star Maker* (1981). He was also cast in the poorly conceived, short-lived TV series *The Devlin Connection* (1982). His last recurring television role was in *Dynasty* (beginning in 1981).

Hudson made his final screen appearance in the 1984 television film *The Las Vegas Strip Wars*. The following year, while in Paris seeking medical treatment for an undisclosed illness, Hudson collapsed. The news broke that he had been diagnosed with AIDS. Friends stated he had discovered that he had the disease in mid-1984 but chose to continue acting on *Dynasty* while secretly undergoing treatment. For years Hudson, his managers, and the studios had avoided the issue of his homosexuality. His illness, however, brought it into the open. Acquaintances often described Hudson as gay, but he refused to publicly comment on or acknowledge the reports. Hudson became the first major public figure to declare he had AIDS.

His last appearance at a benefit hosted by his former leading lady Doris Day revealed the horrifying truth of AIDS in vivid and unflinching detail. Before his death Hudson stated, "I am not happy that I am sick. I am not happy that I have AIDS. But if that is helping others, I can at least know that my own misfortune has had some positive worth." Hudson passed away at his home in Beverly Hills, California, on October 2, 1985.

Michael A. Lutes

SEE ALSO: *AIDS; "B" Movies; Cooper, Gary; Day, Doris;* Dynasty; *Gable, Clark; Gay Men;* Giant; *Selznick, David O.; Sex Symbol; Taylor, Elizabeth.*

BIBLIOGRAPHY

Barrios, Richard. *Screened Out: Playing Gay in Hollywood from Edison to Stonewall.* New York: Routledge, 2003.

Bego, Mark. *Rock Hudson: Public and Private; An Unauthorized Biography.* New York: New American Library, 1986.

Clark, Tom, and Dick Kleiner. *Rock Hudson: Friend of Mine.* New York: Pharos Books, 1989.

Gates, Phyllis, and Bob Thomas. *My Husband Rock Hudson: The Real Story of Rock Hudson's Marriage to Phyllis Gates.* New York: Doubleday, 1987.

Oppenheimer, Jerry, and Jack Vitek. *Idol Rock Hudson: The True Story of an American Film Hero.* New York: Villard Books, 1986.

Royce, Brenda Scott. *Rock Hudson: A Bio-bibliography.* Westport, CT: Greenwood Press, 1995.

The Huffington Post

Founded in 2005 by Arianna Huffington, Jonah Peretti, and Kenneth Lerer, the Huffington Post is an online newspaper and news aggregation website. Its slogan is "The Internet Newspaper: News, Blogs, Video, Community." The site began as a liberal-minded forum, though it rejects the label of "leftist" and claims to be "beyond left and right" politically. Nonetheless, its popularity soared immediately among those readers looking for an answer to the Drudge Report, an aggregation website with a conservative tone.

Cofounder and namesake Arianna Huffington had been a political media fixture decades before the launch of the Huffington Post. Throughout her career, the Greek-born Huffington worked as a radio and television host and commentator, published books and articles on a variety of subjects, and even ran for political office. She rose to political notoriety through her marriage to Michael Huffington, a Republican California politician. She became a recognized conservative commentator in the 1990s, appearing on numerous media outlets to champion Republican causes, but by the end of the decade her views had shifted to the Left. Soon after her own unsuccessful political run in the 2003 run-off election for California governor, Huffington established an Internet presence that would become the Huffington Post.

The Huffington Post started by offering local news for major U.S. cities, then branched out to the United Kingdom and Canada. The Huffington Post has won several awards, including the Webby Award for Best Politics Blog in 2006 and 2008. In 2011 the site was purchased by AOL for $315 million, and Huffington became president and editor-in-chief of the AOL Huffington Post Media Group. *Time* included her as one of the world's 100 most influential people in 2006 and 2011.

One of the most often cited sources of online news, the Huffington Post offers content such that the site appears at the top of Internet searches. From the start, the Huffington Post's audience grew so rapidly that it earned the reputation of causing a decline of print newspapers. Readers are drawn to the convenience of obtaining news online with up-to-the-minute coverage and video links. The paper's popularity also derives from its substantial coverage of entertainment, lifestyles, and other popular subjects, with sections on women's news, the green movement, black voices, Latino voices, dining, comedy, high school events, weddings, and sports.

Another reason for the Huffington Post's popularity is its interactive element, which aims to create a community of readers sharing the news. For example, users can join the site and comment on news stories through blogs. Bloggers include celebrities who, according to the site, "contribute in real-time on a wide-range of topics." Among celebrities listed are Larry Page, Bill Maher, Robert Redford, Madonna, Alec Baldwin, Scarlett Johansson, Russell Simmons, Bill Gates, and Charlie Rose. Huffington credits the success of its blogs to a timely editing process that ensures offensive content is quickly removed.

Another technique that creates a community of readers is a section called "Social News." Through this tool the site encourages users to connect to Facebook, Twitter, and Tumblr in order to share the Huffington Post's articles with friends. The site also produces a sense of participation by giving virtual "badges" to reward users who frequently contribute their opinions or flag inappropriate comments. The Huffington Post also offers RSS ("rich site summary," or in the popularized interpretation of the acronym, "really simple syndication"), enabling readers to easily find information on specific news topics. A topic can be entered into the Huffington Post

In an age of advertisement inundation, the low level of intrusion from ads is another appealing characteristic of the news source. Though income is generated through advertising, readers have the option of opening or ignoring the site's "sponsored links." The costs of running the Huffington Post are fewer than those for print newspapers because much of the material is obtained free through aggregation of other sites and from material supplied by unpaid bloggers, along with the fact that there are no printing or physical distribution costs. The site, therefore, makes a profit with less advertising pitch, though the purchase of the site by AOL may bring about an increased focus on revenue and more dominant ads. For now, the Huffington Post's staff creates attractive layouts to present its articles by combining a little original writing with video clips, blogs, and excerpts from other sites, and the reader gets a broad sampling of sources for the news without annoying pop-up ads.

Sharon Brown

SEE ALSO: *Baldwin, Alec; Blogging; Facebook; The Internet; Redford, Robert; Social Media;* Time; *Twitter.*

BIBLIOGRAPHY

"America Online Has Bought the Huffington Post for $315 Million and Put Its Co-founder, Arianna Huffington, in Charge of All AOL News Content." *National Review*, March 7, 2011, 8.

Huffington, Arianna. *The Huffington Post Complete Guide to Blogging*. New York: Simon & Schuster, 2008.

Keller, Bill. "All the Aggregation That's Fit to Aggregate."*New York Times Magazine*, March 13, 2011, 11(L).

Lieberman, David, and Donna Leinwand. "AOL Empire Takes on New Shape, MONEYAOL Inc. and the Huffington Post Merger." *USA Today*, February 8, 2011, 01B.

"Mail Online Overtakes Huffington Post as World's Second Most Popular Newspaper." *News of the Media*. Accessed November 29, 2011. Available from http://newsofthemedia.com/2011/04/mail-online-overtakes-huffington-post-worlds-popular-newspaper-site/

Hughes, Howard *(1905–1976)*

When he passed away on April 5, 1976, billionaire financier Howard Hughes was considered the world's most mysterious man. Rumors abounded about the strange way he looked, his eccentricities, and the odd way he lived. But before he became a man on the run, moving from continent to continent with his cadre of Mormon aides, Hughes was the embodiment of the Jazz Age wealthy playboy, the 1930s-era aviation hero, the 1940s and 1950s millionaire-as-superstar, and the 1960s Las Vegas casino mogul. Along the way he also riled censors and packed movie houses with several milestone films that pushed the boundaries of sex and violence.

Born in Houston, Texas, on Christmas Eve 1905, Howard Robard Hughes Jr. was the son of an oilman who had developed a drill bit that revolutionized oil drilling the world over. The Hughes rock bit, or rollerbit, was the foundation of the family fortune that Hughes Jr. inherited at age eighteen. That fortune financed Hughes's earliest Hollywood ventures, which began in 1926 and climaxed with the monumental World War I aviation epic *Hell's Angels* in 1930. Because its production spanned the silent and talkie eras, the early sound movie required reshoots and a new leading lady. Hughes chose the unknown starlet Jean Harlow. He also took over as director. By the time of its lavish premiere, "Hughes's Folly," as it was called, was the costliest movie of its time. With its dazzling aviation sequences and Harlow's presence, it also proved a crowd-pleaser, establishing Hughes as a major filmmaking force. But after producing several significant films of the early 1930s, including *The Front Page* and the violent *Scarface*, he turned his attention to the skies.

His love of aviation had begun at age fourteen with a $5 flight in a Curtiss flying boat. An astute flight student, he made headlines in 1932 when he was discovered working under an alias as a baggage handler for American Airlines. With Hughes Aircraft Company, he developed and built the planes in which he made various speed records. Those efforts led to the development of the first retractable landing gear, flushed rivets, streamlined airplane designs, and advances in high-altitude flying. His July 1938 flight around the world, in three days, nineteen hours, enshrined him as a ticker-tape hero and the country's most famous aviator since Charles Lindbergh. Hughes's romances with Ginger Rogers, Katharine Hepburn, and others gave the matinee-idol-handsome Hughes a reputation as a ladies' man.

His interest in women, and the female figure, was evident when he returned to filmmaking with the audacious Western *The Outlaw*. Producer-director Hughes was so determined to glorify his leading lady's bust line that he once stopped production in order to design a better brassiere for newcomer Jane Russell. He spent two years editing the movie and battling censors and finally opened *The Outlaw* in 1943. Inexplicably, he pulled it from distribution after eight record-breaking weeks. Rereleased in later years, the film, which remains noteworthy for its early depiction of cleavage, denoted Hughes's obsessive nature and eccentricities.

The 1940s saw Hughes wielding his power and wealth to romance a "Who's Who" of Hollywood luminaries, including Bette Davis, Ava Gardner, Rita Hayworth, and Lana Turner. Expanding his empire, he became principal shareholder of TWA Airlines in 1939. In 1947 he defiantly faced a Senate subcommittee hearing involving the HK-1, Hercules. Popularly known as the Spruce Goose, the government-funded eight-story plane had not been completed in time to ferry soldiers over the ocean during World War II. When government sources doubted it would fly at all, Hughes personally proved them wrong. Though the flight of November 2, 1947, lasted less than one minute, it was a benchmark in aviation history.

Yet Hughes was already on a dark, downward spiral, as symbolized by his July 1946 crash while test piloting an XF-11 photo reconnaissance plane. Obsessive-compulsive disorder (OCD) had not yet been diagnosed, but Hughes has since been identified as a classic OCD sufferer. This biologically based condition led to his dependence on drugs, which were first given to him following the 1946 crash.

Hughes ventured back into filmmaking in 1948, purchasing a controlling interest in RKO Pictures. The studio legacy included such revered titles as *King Kong*, *Citizen Kane*, and the Fred Astaire–Ginger Rogers musicals. Under Hughes, filmmakers were dismayed to learn that they had to cast his assorted girlfriends, including Terry Moore. But during his tenure, he personally salvaged a career that became legendary: following a notorious September 1948 marijuana arrest, Robert Mitchum thought his career was over, but Hughes stood by the actor and went on to cast him in a string of enjoyable crime thrillers. Hughes, who never did set foot on the studio lot, eventually became sole owner of RKO, which he sold in 1955. Shortly afterward, he became so reclusive that when he and actress Jean Peters secretly married in 1957, both used assumed names.

In the 1960s, as his companies pioneered space and satellite ventures, Hughes lived behind the blackened windows of the Desert Inn penthouse suite, amassing a then-unsurpassed Las Vegas desert kingdom of casinos and hotels. He left the city in the dead of night in November 1970 and thereafter was a man on the run. Pursued by various government agencies, attorneys, process servers, and the media, he was so isolated that the publishing world fell for an elaborate hoax perpetrated by writer Clifford Irving, who claimed he was working with Hughes on his autobiography.

Following Hughes's death and the ensuing battle for his money, revelations surfaced detailing his germ phobia, food fetishes, and drug usage. That the once dashing, adventurous Hughes had died weighing just 93 pounds, with broken hypodermic needles embedded in his arms, was proof that money does not buy happiness. Meanwhile, the hoaxes continued, most notably that of the "Mormon will." The fraudulent document left money to gas station attendant Melvin Dummar, whose saga was the impetus for the 1980 film *Melvin and Howard*. In 2004 Martin Scorsese directed Leonardo DiCaprio as Hughes in the title role of the film *The Aviator*, which focused on Hughes's extraordinary abilities as an engineer and a pilot. The movie was nominated for eleven Academy Awards and won five. The film's story ended in 1947, long before Hughes's decline into madness, allowing him to shine as the greatly talented magnetic man that he was, once upon a time.

Pat H. Broeske

SEE ALSO: *Astaire, Fred, and Ginger Rogers; Celebrity; Celebrity Couples;* Citizen Kane*; Davis, Bette; DiCaprio, Leonardo; Gardner, Ava; Harlow, Jean; Hayworth, Rita; Hepburn, Katharine; Hollywood;* King Kong*; Las Vegas; Lindbergh, Charles; Mitchum, Robert; Russell, Jane; Scorsese, Martin; Silent Movies; Turner, Lana; United Artists; World War I; World War II.*

BIBLIOGRAPHY

Bartlett, Donald L., and James B. Steele. *Empire: The Life, Legend and Madness of Howard Hughes*. New York: W. W. Norton, 1979.

Brown, Peter Harry, and Pat H. Broeske. *Howard Hughes: The Untold Story*. New York: Dutton, 2004.

Dietrich, Noah, and Bob Thomas. *Howard: The Amazing Mr. Hughes*. Greenwich, CT: Fawcett, 1972.

Phelan, James. *Howard Hughes: The Hidden Years*. New York: Random House, 1976.

Hughes, John

SEE: *Brat Pack; The Breakfast Club.*

Hughes, Langston *(1902–1967)*

With his essay "The Negro Artist and the Racial Mountain" (1926), writer Langston Hughes helped to define the spirit that motivated the Harlem Renaissance, a black cultural movement of the 1920s. In the essay, he argues against blacks seeking integration at the expense of racial pride and proclaims that instead "we younger Negro artists who create now intend to express our individual dark-skinned selves without fear or shame." It was a bold statement for those racially unsettling times, which were marked by lynchings and riots. Perhaps his determination to affirm, indeed revel in, black culture had something to do with his father's hatred of black people, a sentiment that affected Hughes profoundly. He writes in his autobiography *The Big Sea* (1940) that "my father hated Negroes. I think he hated himself, too, for being a Negro."

Unlike his father, Hughes was seduced early in life by the joie de vivre of a people who simply could have been bitter because their lives were filled with injustice. In nearly everything he wrote—and he wrote more than fifty books in every conceivable genre—he sought to capture the complexities of, and pay homage to, such people, especially those who were poor or of modest means. He believed that they "had as much in their lives to put into books as did those more fortunate." Thus, the black folk idiom, the rhythm and tones of its language and music, was the only choice for Hughes, and he became the poet laureate of the people for one simple reason: he spoke their language.

AFFECTION FOR HIS PEOPLE

Hughes himself had very humble beginnings, and it may well have been his memory of his roots that fed his desire to be in touch with the masses. He was born James Langston Hughes on February 1, 1902, in Joplin, Missouri, to James Nathaniel and Carrie Mercer Langston Hughes, who separated soon after his birth. He lived on and off with his mother but stayed primarily with his grandmother for the first twelve years of his life. After his grandmother's death, he lived with friends of hers whom he referred to as Auntie and Uncle Reed, then went to live again with his mother, who had remarried and given birth to another son.

In the loneliness of his childhood, Hughes turned to books. Though there was never much money, his mother took him to see plays and introduced him to literature. His grandmother, meanwhile, had been a great storyteller. Her staunch pride sometimes prevented them from having enough to eat, but the stories she told about heroic blacks seemed to instill a similar pride in Hughes that would later manifest itself in his deep affection for his people and in the tales he told.

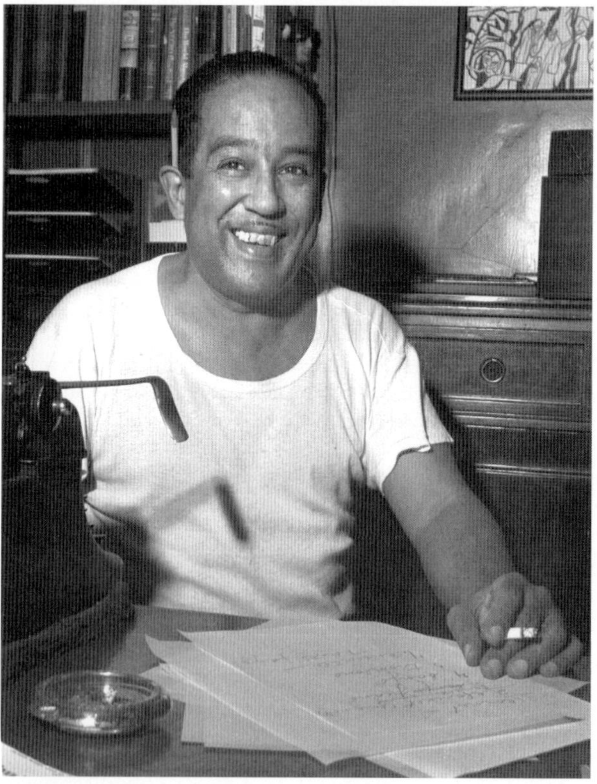

Langston Hughes. *Langston Hughes is one of the most revered and widely studied writers to come out of the Harlem Renaissance.* FRED STEIN ARCHIVE/ARCHIVE PHOTOS/GETTY IMAGES.

His early poems were imitations of the works of Paul Laurence Dunbar and Carl Sandburg, but he eventually began to find his own voice, drawing on his observations of the people and culture that so fascinated him. For example, the inspiration for "When Sue Wears Red," which extols the majestic beauty of African American women, was a "little brownskin girl" from the South whom he had met at a high school dance.

SPREADING HIS MESSAGE

At age seventeen Hughes wrote one of his best-loved and most enduring poems, "The Negro Speaks of Rivers," published in *Crisis* in 1921, the first of his works to appear in a national publication. It was later set to music by composer Howard Swanson, and Marian Anderson performed it at Carnegie Hall. His collection of blues and jazz poems, *The Weary Blues* (1926), was an unprecedented use of those particular cultural forms, winning him first prize in *Opportunity* magazine's literary contest and establishing him as an influential writer whose art was deeply rooted in racial pride. Hughes's biographer, Arnold Rampersad, comments that poems such as "The Negro Speaks of Rivers," "Mother to Son," and "Harlem" are "virtual anthems of black America."

Hughes's participation in the Harlem Renaissance, major though it was, constitutes only a small part of his literary career. His influence extended beyond the African American community. For example, his appointment by President Lyndon Johnson as the American representative to the First World Festival of Negro Arts, held in Dakar, Senegal, in April of 1966, attests to his having achieved a widespread international reputation. According to Rampersad, Senegal's poet-president Léopold Sédar Senghor considered Hughes important to the concept of négritude, saying that "we considered Langston to be the greatest black American poet because it was Langston Hughes who best answered to our definition." Senghor believed Hughes to be a "model . . . for the world." Rampersad also notes that the *New York Times* reported that while Hughes was attending the festival, "young writers from all over Africa followed him about the city and haunted his hotel the way American youngsters dog favorite baseball players."

A COMPLEX LEGACY

Certain aspects of Hughes's life remain enigmatic. In recent years, some scholars have proposed the theory that he was a deeply closeted homosexual and have analyzed supposed clues to his sexuality in his poetry. Many gay literary critics have been eager to claim the poet as one of their own. In contrast, Rampersad believes that he was a person who was not much interested in sex rather than one who was trying to hide his orientation. Filmmakers have also explored the question of whether Hughes was gay in movies such as *Looking for Langston* (1989) and *Brother to Brother* (2004). Because Hughes himself was highly secretive about his sexuality, this debate may never be completely resolved.

The impact of Hughes's work did not diminish with his death in 1967. Many scholars have come to see him as black America's most original poet; long before the black arts movement of the 1960s, his poetry reflected the idea that black music is essential to the artistic creation of an authentic "black" voice. Further, the kind of fusion of black music and literary forms that has come to be associated with his poetry is reflected in much of the black popular music of the 1970s, 1980s, and 1990s. His poem "Afro-American Fragments" inspired the title of a music CD made in 1995 by Ensemble Sans Frontiére, which pays tribute to Hughes and musicians Dizzy Gillespie, Charles Mingus, and Miles Davis. Perhaps the blues revival of the 1980s and Congress's 1987 resolution declaring jazz a "rare and valuable national treasure" helped to secure Hughes's acceptance by mainstream literary audiences. He is the only African American to be included in the *Voices & Visions* PBS series, which explores the lives and works of thirteen famous American poets.

The last line of *The Big Sea* reads, "Literature is a big sea full of many fish. I let down my nets and pulled. I'm still pulling." One has only to look at his legacy of poetry, drama, musicals, libretti, fiction, and nonfiction to know that even now, the poet of the people is "still pulling."

Jacquelyn Y. McLendon

SEE ALSO: *Anderson, Marian; Blues;* The Crisis; *Harlem Renaissance; Jazz; The Twenties.*

BIBLIOGRAPHY

Hughes, Langston. *The Big Sea.* New York: Hill and Wang, 1940.

Rampersad, Arnold. *The Life of Langston Hughes*, vols. 1 and 2. New York: Oxford University Press, 1986, 1988.

Rampersad, Arnold, and David Roessel, eds. *The Collected Poems of Langston Hughes.* New York: Vintage Classics, 1995.

Hula Hoop

Although a simple concept in terms of toy design, the hula hoop is one of the most popular mid-twentieth-century fads. Marketed by the toy manufacturer Wham-O, the hula hoop was introduced to the public in California in 1958 and quickly became popular throughout America. Children and fun-loving adults could be seen reeling and wiggling, trying to spin the 4-foot plastic hoops around their waists. The craze crossed both oceans; within a year hula hoops were a mania in Europe, the Middle East, and Japan. Approximately 100 million hoops were sold in the first year of the toy's production.

When two young chemists working for Phillips Petroleum discovered a durable, heat-resistant, and inexpensive plastic (Marlex), the material turned out to be perfect for the production of the kind of hoops that were used in exercise gyms. American children loved the challenge of gyrating like a hula dancer to keep the colored, lightweight plastic ring aloft. The hula hoop craze introduced the public to the plastics industry that would produce everything from baby toys to automobile parts as the twentieth century progressed.

Hula hoops have never disappeared from toy stores, but today they fill another niche in American culture as well: they are often used in exercise programs. First Lady Michelle Obama championed the toy in her HealthierUS School Challenge program in 2009. In addition, the toy can be found in several categories of Guinness World Records, including longest time of nonstop hula hooping, biggest hoop used, most hula-hoopers at one gathering, and most hoops used at once. In 1999 the toy was among the first inducted in the National Toy Hall of Fame. There's even an international World Hoop Day, started in 2007.

Sharon Brown

SEE ALSO: *Hacky Sack; Leisure Time; Toys.*

BIBLIOGRAPHY

Asakawa, Gil, and Leland Rucker. *The Toy Book.* New York: Knopf, 1992.

Hamill, Sean. "Hooping Already Has Its Own Jane Fonda." *New York Times*, March 11, 2010, E10.

"Hula Hooping: Facts, Fitness, Dance & Workout Information, History of Hoops, More!" Accessed November 2011. Available from http://www.hulahooping.com/

James, Kari, and Jamie Bennett. *Hoop-La!: The Ultimate Book of Hoop Tricks.* New York: Grosset & Dunlap, 2002.

Hull, Bobby *(1939–)*

To become a legend, a hockey player needs something special in addition to great playing abilities. His speed and the incredible force of his slap shots have given Bobby Hull, the Chicago Blackhawks' famous number nine, a unique profile. One of the finest hockey players ever to take to the ice, the "Golden Jet" became a three-time National Hockey League (NHL) point-scoring champion and a two-time Most Valuable Player (MVP) while playing left wing for the Blackhawks. He is still considered the best left-winger in the history of hockey.

Bobby Hull. *Nicknamed the "Golden Jet," Bobby Hull was known for much of his twenty-three-year career for his fearsome slap shot.* MELCHIOR DIGIACOMO/GETTY IMAGES.

Born Robert Marvin Hull Jr. on January 3, 1939, in Pointe Anne, Ontario, Hull progressed quickly through the minor-league hockey ranks. At the age of ten, he was already considered a potential NHL player. After playing junior hockey in Hespeler and Woodstock, Ontario, he joined the St. Catharines TeePees, where he was coached by Rudy Pilous, his future Blackhawks coach.

Hull was nicknamed the Golden Jet because of his blond hair, speed, power, and charisma. He joined the Chicago Blackhawks for the 1957–1958 season and played as their left wing from 1957 to 1972. His brother, Dennis, also played for the Hawks from 1964 to 1977. Although Hull's first two seasons were not particularly brilliant, with only thirty-one goals (thirteen in the first year and eighteen in the second), he used the time to increase his speed and perfect his unique slap shot. He was considered the NHL's fastest skater, clocked at 28.3 miles per hour with the puck and 29.7 without it. His booming slap shot—clocked once at 118.3 miles per hour, around 35 miles per hour above the league average—was thought to be the league's hardest. That "high-velocity piece of lead," as goalie Jacques Plante called it, could easily thrust a goalie backward into the net.

Gradually, Hull became a top player for his team. With thirty-nine goals in his third season and thirty-one in his fourth, he led Chicago to their first Stanley Cup in twenty-three years in 1961. The following year he matched the NHL's fifty-goal scoring record before raising it for the first time ever to fifty-four in the 1965–1966 season. During the 1968–1969 season, he raised the bar to fifty-eight while playing part of the time with his mouth wired shut because of a broken jaw. In sixteen NHL seasons, Hull scored 610 goals and added 560 assists (for a total of 1,170 points) in regular season play, plus 62 goals and 67 assists (129 points) during the Stanley Cup playoffs. He led the NHL in goals scored in seven different seasons.

Hull displayed the combined skills of some of the game's best players: he perfected Boom-Boom Geoffrion's slap shot; he had the speed of Howie Morenz, the goal-scoring abilities of Maurice "Rocket" Richard, and the strength and control of Gordie Howe. Not surprisingly, Hull was voted hockey's Player of the Decade in a 1970 Associated Press poll of writers and sportscasters. He won the Ross Trophy three times, the Lady Byng Memorial Trophy once, the Hart Memorial Trophy twice, and the Lester Patrick Trophy in 1969 for the outstanding contribution he had made to hockey in the United States. He was a regular choice in All-Star selections, named ten times to the First NHL All-Star Team and twice to the Second Team.

In 1972 a contract dispute with the Hawks management led to a major surprise when Hull jumped to the Winnipeg Jets of the upstart World Hockey Association (WHA). The Jets were offering high salaries to attract stars, and Hull's new contract made him hockey's first millionaire. It was a major setback for the Blackhawks: his departure may have cost the organization close to $1 billion over ten years because of drops in attendance. The NHL tried legal action to block the move and then arranged to punish Hull by leaving him off of Team Canada in

1972. His decision made history, however: by switching from a hallowed NHL team to an unknown league, he immediately raised the interest of spectators in WHA hockey. He remained a top player with Winnipeg, scoring 77 goals during 78 games in the 1974–1975 season and adding 303 goals and 638 points to his career numbers.

In 1980 and 1981 Hull tried to return to NHL hockey with the New York Rangers but did not make the team. The celebrated figure's time was past. In 1983 he was inducted into the Hockey Hall of Fame. In his retirement Hull farmed and ran cattle-breeding operations across Canada. His son, Brett Hull, achieved renown of his own while playing for the Dallas Stars.

Henri Paratte

SEE ALSO: *Hockey; Howe, Gordie; National Hockey League (NHL); Orr, Bobby; Sports Heroes.*

BIBLIOGRAPHY

Diamond, Dan, and Eric Zweig. *Hockey's Glory Days: The 1950s and '60s.* Kansas City, MO: Andrews McMeel Publishing, 2003.

Hull, Bobby, and Roy G. Nelson. *Bobby Hull's Hockey Made Easy.* New York: Beaufort Books, 1983.

Hunt, Jim. *Bobby Hull.* Chicago: Follett, 1966.

Hunt, Jim. *Bobby Hull: The First Million Dollar Hockey Player.* Markham, Ontario, Canada: Simon & Schuster, 1974.

May, Julian. *Bobby Hull, Hockey's Golden Jet.* Mankato, MN: Crestwood, 1974.

Hulu

Founded in 2007, the website Hulu is one of the premier video-streaming sites for popular television shows and movies. Featuring content from more than 350 media companies, as well as an increasing array of original programming, Hulu offers a two-tiered experience: its free version allows users to stream several episodes from the current season of popular shows on their computers, and its subscription service, Hulu Plus, offers high-definition streams of full seasons (current and previous) that can be played on Hulu-enabled devices such as tablets, smartphones, and gaming consoles. With more than thirty million visitors per month, the site has been touted as a free or inexpensive alternative to a traditional cable or satellite television subscription. In mid-2012, however, rumors surfaced that the company was considering a new model that would restrict usage to cable or satellite TV subscribers only.

Hulu began as a joint venture between media giants NBC Universal and News Corporation (Fox) and Internet companies AOL, MSN, MySpace, and Yahoo! Former Amazon.com executive Jason Kilar, who helped expand Amazon's business model to include video and DVD sales, was named chief executive officer in June 2007, and the service was made available to all Internet users in the United States in March 2008. At that time, Hulu's content (episodes from 250 television series and 100 full-length feature films) was supported by a group of ten advertisers; by the end of the year, the site boasted 100 different advertisers, featured episodes from more than 1,000 different shows, and was named Website of the Year by the Associated Press. In mid-2009 Disney-owned ABC purchased a 27 percent stake in the company and contributed a number of shows and movies from its affiliated stations to Hulu's growing content library. Hulu launched its premium subscription service, Hulu Plus, in November 2010, and within a year, the service had more than a million subscribers, a number that has since grown exponentially.

In 2011 Hulu announced a string of new content partnerships, including Viacom (owner of Comedy Central, MTV, BET, TV Land, and other popular channels), Criterion (curator of the Criterion Collection, a series of meticulously restored classic films), Miramax, Univision, and the CW. Additionally during that year, Hulu launched a similar streaming service in Japan; introduced a feature that allowed users to comment on and share short video clips on Facebook; and began producing a documentary series, *A Day in the Life*, with documentarian Morgan Spurlock (*Super Size Me*). This was followed by the political drama *Battleground* in early 2012. With more than $400 million in yearly revenues and viewers streaming movies and shows more than 800 million times every month, Hulu is the second-largest Internet video service, behind only YouTube.

Jacob Schmitt

SEE ALSO: *Advertising; Amazon.com; The Internet; Smartphones;* Super Size Me*; Television; YouTube.*

BIBLIOGRAPHY

Dana, Rebecca, and Emily Steel. "Can Hulu Find Its Mojo with Viewers?" Wall Street Journal, March 11, 2008. Accessed March 2008. Available from http://online.wsj.com/article/SB120519822483125987.html

Garrahan, Matthew. "Hulu Goes for Original Series to Win Adherents." *Financial Times*, May 21, 2012.

"Hulu's Evolution." *New York Times*, April 17, 2012.

Rose, Frank. "Free, Legal and Online: Why Hulu Is the New Way to Watch TV." *Wired*, September 22, 2008. Accessed August 9, 2012. Available from http://www.wired.com/entertainment/theweb/magazine/16-10/mf_hulu?currentPage=all

Stelter, Brian. "Serving Up Television without the TV Set." *New York Times*, March 10, 2008, C1.

Hunt, Helen *(1963–)*

Helen Hunt began a prolific acting career as a child, appearing in several television series and made-for-TV movies, beginning with her debut in *Pioneer Woman* (1973). Fame finally found her with *Mad about You* (1992–1999), an NBC sitcom about the evolving relationship of the Buchmans, a young married couple. As Jamie Buchman, a role that earned her several Emmys, Hunt explored the difficult marital and career challenges of the 1990s. Her success with both the public and the critics in *Mad about You* and in the movie *The Waterdance* (1992) earned Hunt leading roles in the special-effects blockbuster *Twister* (1996) and the moving comedy-drama *As Good as It Gets* (1997), for which she won an Academy Award.

Hunt has pursued a number of different projects since winning the Oscar. The following year she played Viola, a comic figure who masquerades as a eunuch to win the favor of a duke, in William Shakespeare's *Twelfth Night* at Lincoln Center in New York City. In 2000 she appeared in four feature-length films, including *Cast Away* with Tom Hanks and *Pay It Forward* with Kevin Spacey. She then took a break from film to return to the stage, acting alongside John Turturro in Yasmina Reza's *Life x 3*, which opened to mixed reviews at Broadway's Circle in the Square Theatre in April 2003.

Returning once again to television, Hunt played Janine Roby in *Empire Falls* (2005), an HBO miniseries based on Richard Russo's Pulitzer Prize–winning novel. In 2006 she was part of a critically acclaimed ensemble cast in Emilio Estevez's *Bobby*, a film that reimagines the hours leading up to the assassination of Robert Kennedy in 1968.

Hunt turned her attention to directing in the latter half of the decade. *Then She Found Me* (2007), her big-screen directorial debut starring Matthew Broderick and Colin Firth, received mixed reviews. She also directed an episode of Showtime's series *Californication* in 2012.

Christian L. Pyle

SEE ALSO: *Academy Awards; Broadway; Emmy Awards; Hanks, Tom; Lincoln Center for the Performing Arts; Made-for-Television Movies; Sitcom; Television.*

BIBLIOGRAPHY

Associated Press. "Helen Hunt Gets Comfy in the Director's Chair." MSNBC, March 12, 2008. Accessed April 19, 2012. Available from http://today.msnbc.msn.com/id/23599619/ns/today-entertainment/t/helen-hunt-gets-comfy-directors-chair

Hunter, Evan

SEE: *McBain, Ed.*

Hunter, Tab *(1931–)*

Tab Hunter was a teen idol and movie actor who was popular in the 1950s. He was tall, blond, tan, and athletically built, and the press called him "Golden Boy." Hunter was typical of the Hollywood actors of the time who enjoyed careers in the wake of the so-called studio star system: he was handsome and engaging, with boyish charm, but he had a limited acting range.

A native of New York, Hunter was born Arthur Andrew Kelm. He later changed his last name to Gelien, his mother's maiden name. When he was fifteen, he lied about his age so he could join the coast guard but was discharged when his real age was revealed. At eighteen, while working for a Southern California riding academy, a friend suggested that he try show business. He got an agent, Henry Willson, who Hollywoodized his name, changing it to Tab Hunter.

In 1952 Hunter caught moviegoers' attention as a shipwrecked sailor opposite glamorous Linda Darnell in *Island of Desire*. In 1955 he portrayed a marine caught up in a love triangle in *Battle Cry*, which was a box-office hit. He quickly became a darling of the fan magazines, which photographed him on dates with beautiful young actresses, such as Natalie Wood and Debbie Reynolds. Along with being thrust into the spotlight, Hunter was shoved into the recording studio: "If you can carry a tune at all, we'd like you to record it," a Dot Records executive told him. At that time the airwaves were pivotal to the teen idol phenomenon. Hunter's resulting musical foray, "Young Love," was the top single in the United States for six weeks in 1957. Then under contract with Warner Brothers, he went on to record for their label.

In 1958 Hunter tried his hand at television, appearing in the episode "Portrait of a Murderer" for the series *Playhouse 90* (1956–1961). That same year he held his own opposite Tony Award–winning actress Gwen Verdon in the movie version of the hit musical, *Damn Yankees*. In the candid 1959 movie, *That Kind of Woman*, he was convincing as an idealistic soldier in love with another man's mistress, played by Sophia Loren.

Hunter's movies, however, became less prestigious as his fans matured. Moreover, even though he had successfully weathered innuendo wrought by negative press in 1955 when the scandal magazine *Confidential* detailed his arrest at a "pajama party," where "boys were dancing with boys and girls with girls," it was his arrest and subsequent 1960 trial for beating his dog that alienated fans and the media. The jury acquitted Hunter, but offers of work dwindled afterward. Turning to television, he played a bachelor-artist in the short-lived *The Tab Hunter Show* (1960–1961). By the mid-1960s, his stardom had waned.

To survive the 1970s Hunter made movies in Europe, toured the American heartland performing in dinner theater, and appeared on television game shows. In 1977 he briefly joined the cast of the quirky television series, *Forever Fernwood* (1977–1978). Lampooning himself, he played a character who falls into a vat of Rust-Oleum, undergoes plastic surgery, and

Tab Hunter. *Tab Hunter reached the peak of his stardom as a teen idol in the 1950s.* SILVER SCREEN COLLECTION/GETTY IMAGES.

awakes to discover that he looks like Tab Hunter. In the 1981 movie *Polyester* Hunter portrays the love interest of a disillusioned housewife, played by the 300-pound female impersonator, Divine. Directed by offbeat filmmaker John Waters, the movie became a cult favorite. As a result, Hunter reunited with Divine in *Lust in the Dust*, a 1985 Western spoof that he coproduced. He subsequently appeared in small roles in obscure films.

In 2005 Hunter's autobiography, *Tab Hunter Confidential: The Making of a Movie Star*, was published, drawing positive reviews from critics. In his book Hunter confirms his homosexuality and chronicles the double life he led throughout his career, dating female actresses at the behest of the studios and keeping his romantic life private in order to maintain an image that was considered proper in Hollywood.

Pat H. Broeske

SEE ALSO: *Gay Men; Hollywood;* Playhouse 90*; Studio System; Teen Idols; Waters, John; Wood, Natalie.*

BIBLIOGRAPHY

Broeske, Pat H. "With Hot Films, Tab Hunter's No Longer out in the Cold." *Orange County Register*, March 10, 1985.

Bronson, Fred. *The Billboard Book of Number One Hits*. New York: Billboard Publications, 1988.

Estrin, Eric. "Has Nonsuccess Spoiled Tab Hunter?" *Los Angeles Magazine*, October 1981, 134–144.

Hamilton, William. "Did Success Spoil Tab Hunter?" *New York Times*, September 18, 2005. Accessed on May 2, 2012. Available from http://www.nytimes.com/2005/09/18/fashion/sundaystyles/18tab.html?pagewanted=all

Huntley, Chet *(1911–1974)*

As part of the most successful television broadcasting team in television history, Chet Huntley (with coanchor David Brinkley) was responsible for NBC's winning the news ratings war against CBS and ABC in the 1960s. From 1956 to 1970, when Huntley retired, the *Huntley/Brinkley Report* was a household staple for millions of Americans. By 1960 the program was America's top-rated news show and remained there until 1969. The two men formed an unlikely but successful team. Huntley's resonate voice and straightforward style was a perfect match to Brinkley's more cryptic, somewhat cynical, approach. Their balanced reporting style was perhaps best epitomized by their well-known sign-off line: "Goodnight, Chet." "Goodnight, David, and goodnight for NBC News."

Lloyd Chiasson Jr.

SEE ALSO: *Brinkley, David; Cronkite, Walter; Live Television; Television; Television Anchors.*

BIBLIOGRAPHY

Barnouw, Erik. *Tube of Plenty: The Evolution of American Television*. New York: Oxford University Press, 1982.

Bliss, Edward, Jr. *Now the News: The Story of Broadcast Journalism*. New York: Columbia University Press, 1991.

Emery, Michael, and Edwin Emery. *The Press and America: An Interpretive History of the Mass Media*, 7th ed. Englewood Cliffs, NJ: Prentice Hall, 1992.

Johnston, Lyle. *"Good Night, Chet": A Biography of Chet Huntley*. Jefferson, NC: McFarland, 2003.

Weaver, Pat. *The Best Seat in the House: The Golden Years in Radio and Television*. New York: Knopf, 1994.

Hurricane Katrina

In late August 2005 Hurricane Katrina caused major damage in Alabama, Florida, Mississippi, and Louisiana. There is no official death toll for Katrina, but it is known that more than 1,800 people lost their lives and in excess of 700 individuals were still listed as missing in 2011. With close to a million refugees, Hurricane Katrina was the greatest displacement of American citizens since the Dust Bowl era.

Of all the cities impacted by this category five hurricane, New Orleans, Louisiana, saw the most extensive devastation. Although New Orleans mayor Ray Nagin had imposed a mandatory evacuation of the city several days before Katrina hit, the city lacked resources to assist those who were too old, infirm, or poor to leave on their own. An estimated 20 percent of the population of New Orleans remained in the city when the hurricane made landfall on Monday, August 29, 2005. Makeshift shelters were set up in the city's Superdome and Convention Center, but these became overcrowded, unsanitary, and unsafe as conditions worsened.

Shortly after the hurricane hit the city, waves on the Mississippi River were reported up to 40 feet high and levees faltered, flooding water into New Orleans. Over the next two days, floodwaters continued to rise, covering 80 percent of the city. U.S. Department of Health and Human Services secretary Michael O. Leavitt declared a public health emergency in the four states affected by the storm. The U.S. National Guard was deployed to help with rescue and evacuation, but some of these troops, fresh from Iraq and Afghanistan, were criticized for treating evacuees as if they were hostile combatants rather than victims. Exacerbating the situation was the mass looting in the streets and gang violence erupting in and around the Superdome and Convention Center, which forced police and troops to focus on damage control instead of search and rescue. On the September 4, 2005, police shot and killed four people on Danziger Bridge. Initially, the police officers claimed that they were defending themselves from armed civilians; however, an investigation revealed that the officers fired without cause and that the department attempted to cover up the murders by providing false statements and fabricating evidence. In 2011 the five New Orleans police officers were found guilty of a variety of charges, including deprivation of rights under color of law, conspiracy, counts of obstruction of justice, and civil rights conspiracy.

The Federal Emergency Management Agency (FEMA), headed by Mike Brown, was criticized by victims and media alike for its inadequate and unequal response to the crisis. Proof surfaced that FEMA knew years ahead of time that the New Orleans levees could not withstand anything above a category three hurricane. It was evident days before Katrina hit the Gulf Coast that the hurricane would surpass that level. Jefferson Parish president Aaron Broussard commented, "We have been abandoned by our own country. . . . The aftermath of Hurricane Katrina will go down as one of the worst abandonments of Americans on American soil ever in U.S. history."

Brown eventually stepped down from his position, leaving Congress and the president to investigate how this situation spiraled so far out of control. President George W. Bush received much scrutiny for vacationing at his Texas ranch through August 30, when he was aware of the impending hurricane. In a televised news conference, Bush gave the following explanation: "Katrina exposed serious problems in our response capability at all levels of government, and to the extent the federal government didn't fully do its job right, I take responsibility." This failure on the government's part, to respond in an equal and timely manner to the Hurricane Katrina disaster, left many Americans questioning their leaders' ability to handle a national crisis.

Hurricane Katrina sparked a wave of artistic responses. Musical tributes were organized to help victims and displaced musicians return to their homeland. Documentary movies such as *Trouble the Water* and Spike Lee's *When the Levees Broke: A Requiem in Four Acts* depicted scenes during and after the hurricane, with firsthand accounts of survivor stories as well as the tragic deaths that surrounded them. Lee followed *Requiem* with *If God Is Willing and Da Creek Don't Rise*, which focuses on the rebuilding efforts following Katrina. The film juxtaposes the almost storybook 2009 Super Bowl victory of the New Orleans Saints against the lingering conflicts between many of the citizens. The piece also exposes an array of issues stemming from the demolition of public housing projects; the closing of public hospitals and schools; the failure of local, state, and federal agencies to provide adequate post-storm assistance; increased crime rates; allegations of police corruption; and the poor oversight by the Army Corps of Engineers that allowed for the levees to be breached.

On April 11, 2010, HBO launched a miniseries centered on the New Orleans music scene called *Treme*, named for the historic Seventh Ward neighborhood still struggling to rebuild from the hurricane. Treme, the first city where free people of color could own property prior to the American Civil War, was a vibrant part of the New Orleans musical community. The miniseries shadows one of the main criticisms against FEMA: its focus on rebuilding more affluent neighborhoods while leaving residents of less fortunate neighborhoods, such as Treme and the lower Ninth Ward, to fend for themselves.

A number of nonfiction books were written immediately after the Hurricane Katrina disaster. Pulitzer Prize–winning *Times Picayune* writer Jed Horne wrote *Breach of Faith*. Published in 2006, this narrative describes life in the city during and after Katrina. Much like the aftermath of 9/11, it took several years after the tragedy for fiction works to appear. In 2011 Jesmyn Ward won the National Book Award for her novel *Salvage the Bones*, the story of one poor black family's struggle to survive the trials and tribulations of Hurricane Katrina.

Many of the artistic expressions highlighted how race and class were big factors that underlie most of the tragedies associated with Hurricane Katrina. The outcry from African American leaders, citizens, and intellectuals produced various investigations, legal disputes, and public outrage over the conduct of the initial evacuations and subsequent reconstruction efforts. In 2009 the U.S. Court of Appeals for the Fifth Circuit ruled that the Army Corps of Engineers was liable for the damages suffered in the Lower Ninth Ward and St. Bernard Parish.

Reconstruction and repopulation of New Orleans has been gradual, and the population has yet to recover. It has been estimated that the city's population has regained approximately 70 percent of its pre-storm population, sitting at 363,000 of the 455,155 residents in 2005; however, much of the population growth occurred in areas that were not decimated by the flooding. Once ranked the twenty-sixth largest city, New Orleans ranked forty-sixth in 2010. The storm effectively reshaped the city, leading to a wealthier and less diverse population. The 2010 census figures show that there were approximately 24,000 fewer white residents and 118,000 fewer black residents than the last census, while the Hispanic population increased by nearly 65 percent. Part of the disparity can be attributed to people relocating to the city for construction jobs, but many of the original residents may never return.

Although Mississippi was also devastated by the hurricane, leading to the entire state being declared a disaster area, Katrina's historical and cultural impact is intricately linked with New Orleans. Far beyond its human costs, it revealed the staggering inadequacies of government agencies to respond to natural disasters as well as the racial and class stratification that exists in many American cities.

Ron Horton

SEE ALSO: *Gulf Wars; New Orleans Rhythm and Blues; 9/11; War in Afghanistan.*

BIBLIOGRAPHY

CNN Reports: Katrina—State of Emergency. Kansas City, MO: Andrews McMeel Publishing, 2005.

Dyson, Michael Eric. *Come Hell or High Water: Hurricane Katrina and the Color of Disaster.* New York; Basic Civitas Books, 2006.

Hartman, Chester, and Gregory D. Aquires. *There Is No Such Thing as a Natural Disaster: Race, Class, and Hurricane Katrina.* New York: Routledge, 2006.

Horne, Jed. *Breach of Faith: Hurricane Katrina and the Near Death of a Great American City.* New York: Random House, 2006.

Treme. Home Box Office (HBO). Accessed April 2012. Available from http://www.hbo.com/treme/index.html

Trouble the Water. Zeitgeist Films. Accessed April 2012. Available from http://www.troublethewaterfilm.com

Troutee, David Dante. *After the Storm: Black Intellectuals Explore the Meaning of Hurricane Katrina.* New York: New Press, 2006.

Ward, Jesmyn. *Salvage the Bones.* New York: Bloomsbury, 2011.

Hurston, Zora Neale *(1903–1960)*

A prolific novelist, folklorist, and anthropologist, Zora Neale Hurston was one of the inspiring personalities of the Harlem Renaissance. Her diverse interests intertwine in her most influential novel, *Their Eyes Were Watching God* (1937), in which the narration of a black woman's quest for self-identity is interspersed with folktales that Hurston collected during a research trip supervised by noted anthropologist Franz Boas. In 1943 her autobiography, *Dust Tracks on a Road* (1942), won the Anisfield-Wolf Book Award for the best book on race relations.

Although this award made her a well-known public figure, Hurston always refused the role of spokesperson for the African American community. She held controversial views on race, which led her to write an article against school desegregation in 1955. In the years following her death in 1960, notably in the 1980s and 1990s, Hurston's work achieved a prominent position in the American literary canon.

Luca Prono

SEE ALSO: *Harlem Renaissance; The Twenties.*

BIBLIOGRAPHY

Bloom, Harold, ed. *Zora Neale Hurston*. New York: Chelsea House Publishers, 1986.

Gates, Henry Louis, Jr. *The Signifying Monkey: A Theory of African-American Literary Criticism*. New York: Oxford University Press, 1988.

Hemenway, Robert E. *Zora Neale Hurston: A Literary Biography*. Urbana: University of Illinois Press, 1977.

Plant, Deborah G. *Zora Neale Hurston: A Biography of the Spirit*. Westport, CT: Praeger Publishers, 2007.

Walker, Alice. *In Search of Our Mothers' Gardens*. San Diego, CA: Harcourt Brace Jovanovich, 1983.

Hustler

As the twentieth century drew to a close, the American pornography industry was raking in $10 billion a year. About $1 billion of that cash flow was generated by magazine sales. One of the most provocative and controversial of the so-called men's magazines was Larry Flynt's *Hustler*. The raunchy periodical, founded on its publisher's oft-stated desire to cater to the "erotic imaginations of real people," helped redefine the "mainstream" of porn and wielded an influence far beyond the cloistered realm of XXX literature.

MORE EXPLICIT THAN PLAYBOY

At its essence the *Hustler* story is inseparable from that of its founder, Larry Flynt. A child bootlegger from the mountains of Kentucky, Flynt escaped the torpor of Appalachia at age fifteen by joining the U.S. Army. Upon leaving the service and surviving a failed first marriage, he established a profitable chain of go-go bars. In 1972 he moved into publishing, starting up an eponymous newsletter for his Hustler club. The new periodical, later expanded into a glossy magazine, became notorious for its explicit depiction of female genitalia. Whereas other men's magazines of the time, such as *Playboy* and *Penthouse*, bathed their nude models in a gauzy glow that obstructed the view of their "naughty bits," Flynt's *Hustler* examined every nook and cranny of the distaff form with an almost gynecological zeal. The approach shocked many in the beginning—no doubt a part of Flynt's plan all along—but had soon resulted in expanded parameters for what could and could not be shown in a newsstand periodical.

A host of imitators cropped up in the wake of *Hustler*'s initial success. Often they bore titles that aped the magazine's pornoscenti cachet, titles such as *Swank*, *Gent*, and *High Society*. But few of these publications could match Flynt's élan or his flair for generating publicity. In 1975 he created a furor by running telephoto pictures of a naked Jackie Onassis sunbathing in Greece. Amid howls from the world's opinion elites, Flynt gleefully cashed his checks. The scandalous photo spread helped attract 1.3 million readers to *Hustler*—and allowed a former strip club owner from Appalachia to rake in more than $30 million a year.

Not surprisingly, Flynt's ability to reach a mass audience made him a ripe target for all manner of detractors. Foremost among these were American feminists, to whom Flynt gave plenty of ammunition. *Hustler*'s visual features repeatedly portrayed sex as ugly and dirty, with women depicted in rape fantasies, smeared with excrement, or likened to pieces of meat. One infamous cover showed a woman being fed into a meat grinder. The backlash to such content was swift and visceral. In an op-ed piece for the *New York Times*, Gloria Steinem compared *Hustler* to a Ku Klux Klan publication and derided Flynt for printing images of women being "beaten, tortured and raped" and "subject to degradations from bestiality to sexual slavery."

African Americans and other minority groups also heaped scorn on *Hustler* for its monthly parade of cartoons and features that were blatantly racist, bigoted, or putridly scatological. Even fellow pornographers had little tolerance for this type of material. To all of these critics a defiant Flynt had the same answer: "We're an equal opportunity offender," he declared repeatedly, adopting the rhetoric of civil rights law to defend his cause. "Every month we try to figure out who we haven't offended yet."

Hustler has not lacked for high-profile defenders. One of Flynt's most ardent apologists has been the outspoken author and academic Camille Paglia, who lauded the maverick publisher as "a hero" who "forces people to confront their own buried snobbery about the South and working-class culture." Paglia went on to laud *Hustler* for "being totally frank, playing no more games, laying it out for everyone to see."

A CONTROVERSIAL CAREER

Nevertheless, such "explicitness" has cost *Hustler* dearly among mainstream advertisers, almost all of whom have shunned the magazine despite having no qualms about gracing the pages of *Playboy* and *Penthouse*. Even more damaging, Flynt has found himself hauled into court on numerous occasions to defend the magazine against indecency charges. The legal cost of defending *Hustler* over the years has been estimated at $50 million. It was during one such trial, in 1978, that *Hustler*'s publisher nearly paid the ultimate price for his commitment to pornography. Joseph Paul Franklin shot Flynt twice from close range with a high-powered rifle outside a courthouse where he was being prosecuted for obscenity. Flynt survived the attack but lost the use of his legs permanently.

The after-effects of the assassination attempt nearly sank *Hustler*, as a devastated Flynt briefly found religion under the tutelage of President Jimmy Carter's evangelical sister, Ruth Carter Stapleton. The bizarre life change found its way onto the pages of the magazine, which suffered a drop in circulation. Flynt's subsequent addiction to painkillers, with the attendant high spending, resulted in a severe money crunch.

In the 1980s Flynt reconsidered his spiritual awakening and opted to return *Hustler* to its raunchy roots. He placed advertisements in the Hollywood trade press offering $1 million to any top television or film actress who would pose nude in the pages of the magazine. Spurred by the advent of videocassette recorders, he started producing porno videotapes under the *Hustler* imprimatur. The first entry depicted an eighteen-year-old medically certified virgin being deflowered in front of the cameras. "She was holding out for the right man," Flynt crowed, "but the right price won out."

Hustler's ability to keep publishing such sordid material was nearly compromised during the Reagan era, when Moral Majority leader Jerry Falwell sued Flynt for libel over a scatological ad parody depicting the preacher in an outhouse having sex with his mother. A lower court ruled in Falwell's favor, but in 1988 the U.S. Supreme Court reversed the decision and upheld Flynt's right to satirize a public figure. Some First Amendment advocates began hailing Flynt as a poster child for free speech, though many other civil libertarians felt uncomfortable with the association.

Flynt's defenders were plainly cheered by the appearance in 1996 of a reverential biopic, *The People vs. Larry Flynt*, directed by Academy Award–winner Milos Forman and starring *Cheers* hayseed Woody Harrelson as the eponymous pornographer. The film sugarcoated many of the more tawdry facts of Flynt's life while avoiding the issues of *Hustler*'s racism and misogyny entirely. Though dismissed as a tendentious mess by some critics and savaged by feminists as a whitewash, the feature nonetheless proved a major hit and gave the bumptious publisher a brief ripple of renewed popularity.

WADING INTO POLITICS

Flynt used his newfound status as a media darling to his own advantage in 1998, injecting himself into the debate over the impeachment of President Bill Clinton. In the October issue of the *Washington Post*, he offered $1 million to anyone willing to admit to having an affair with a member of Congress. His target, he claimed, was the "hypocrisy" of conservatives who were pursuing Clinton for lying about sex, while leading less than pure lives themselves. By December Flynt had bagged his first victim when Representative Robert Livingston, the Republicans' choice to be Speaker of the House, resigned after investigators hired by *Hustler* determined that he had been unfaithful to his wife. In 2003 Flynt ran unsuccessfully for governor of California, and in 2007 he exposed conservative Senator David Vitter of Louisiana as the client of a prostitute. In the months leading up to the 2012 presidential election, Flynt continued to try to influence politics by offering a reward to anyone who could provide proof that conservative candidates had been guilty of extramarital affairs.

In the meantime, Flynt's pornography empire was changing as Americans shifted from print to technology-based media. Like newspapers, many magazines saw their ad revenues and circulation numbers fall. Pornography was hit especially hard, as so much free porn was available on the Internet. In 2011 Flynt predicted that *Hustler* as a magazine would probably survive only another two or three years; at that point the publication generated only 5 percent of the parent company's income. Given Flynt's past, the magazine's ending isn't likely to slow him down.

Robert E. Schnakenberg

SEE ALSO: *Academy Awards; Advertising; Celebrity;* Cheers; *Divorce; Feminism; Firearms; Hollywood; The Internet; Moral Majority; Onassis, Jacqueline Lee Bouvier Kennedy;* Penthouse; Playboy; *Pornography; Reagan, Ronald; Sex Scandals; Sex Symbol; Strip Joints/Striptease; Television; Videos; The* Washington Post.

BIBLIOGRAPHY

Flynt, Larry. *An Unseemly Man: My Life as a Pornographer, Pundit, and Social Outcast.* New York: Dove Books, 1997.

Flynt, Larry, and David Eisenbach. *One Nation under Sex: How the Private Lives of Presidents, First Ladies, and Their Lovers Changed the Course of American History.* New York: Palgrave Macmillan, 2011.

Smolla, Rodney A. *Jerry Falwell v. Larry Flynt: The First Amendment on Trial.* New York: St. Martin's, 1988.

Huston, John *(1906–1987)*

The multifaceted John Huston entered modern cinema history in 1941 when he wrote the screenplay for *The Maltese Falcon*, also making his directorial debut. The film established his reputation, began a significant working relationship with Hum-

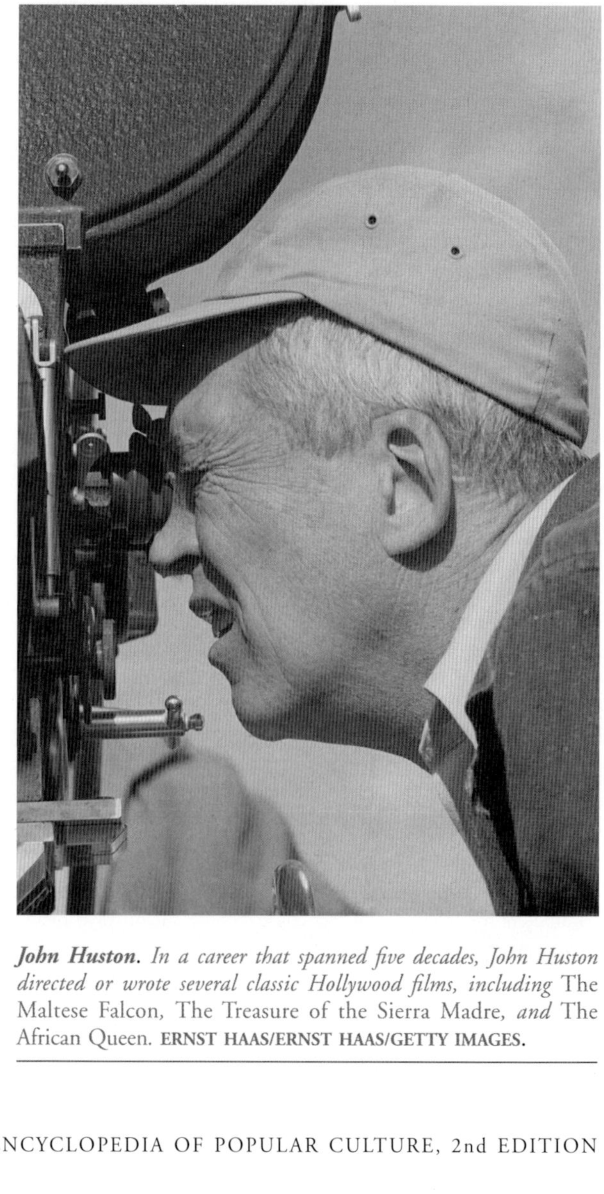

John Huston. *In a career that spanned five decades, John Huston directed or wrote several classic Hollywood films, including* The Maltese Falcon, The Treasure of the Sierra Madre, *and* The African Queen. **ERNST HAAS/ERNST HAAS/GETTY IMAGES.**

phrey Bogart, and pointed to his preference for mining literary sources for his material—in this case, Dashiell Hammett.

In the course of a long and decidedly erratic career, Huston dealt memorably with human greed in *The Treasure of the Sierra Madre* (1948), winning Oscars for his screenplay and direction, and *Key Largo* (1948). Plaudits greeted *The Asphalt Jungle* (1950), often considered his best film, and he entranced audiences by pairing Katharine Hepburn's missionary and Bogart's booze-drenched river trader as companions in adversity in *The African Queen* (1952)—an idea beguilingly echoed by Deborah Kerr's nun marooned on a wartime Pacific island with Robert Mitchum's marine in *Heaven Knows, Mr. Allison* (1957). (*The African Queen* was voted one of the 100 best American films of the century by the American Film Institute in 1998.) Huston acted frequently from the 1960s on, and while many look fondly on his genial Noah in *The Bible*, which he directed in 1966, it is his tycoon in Roman Polanski's *Chinatown* (1974), oozing cruelty and corruption, that is burnt in the collective memory.

A VARIED FILMOGRAPHY

As a director, Huston's films reflect his wide interests and, like the man, often present a rough exterior beneath which hovers tenderness, or even romantic idealism. Most of his heroes are either fiercely independent, social misfits, or both: the artist Toulouse-Lautrec, played by José Ferrer in *Moulin Rouge* (1952); Gregory Peck's Captain Ahab in *Moby Dick* (1956), the eponymous *Freud* (a tortured and miscast Montgomery Clift, 1962); and Stacy Keach's disintegrating prizefighter in *Fat City* (1972, one of Huston's quality films in a period of failures). His best work reflects a sense of irony and a sharp attention to character, focused in a decisive narrative style, as in *The Man Who Would be King* (1975), adapted from Rudyard Kipling and one of his last real successes. Some of the films are offbeat and tend to misfire, though the imagery of elephants and the accompanying doom-laden message of *Roots of Heaven* (1958) are interesting. While comedy barely features in his oeuvre, he ventured successfully into parody with the spoof adventure-thriller *Beat the Devil* (1953, with Bogart again).

Although married five times, Huston created a heavily masculine on-screen world; with a handful of exceptions, women are largely peripheral in his films. As David Thomson accurately observes in *A Biographical Dictionary of Film*, "There is no real female challenge to the smoke-room atmosphere of the films. But there is a list of female onlookers as wan and powerless as Jacqueline Bisset in *Under the Volcano*, Elizabeth Taylor in *Reflections in a Golden Eye*, and Dominique Sanda in *The Mackintosh Man*." One might add a dozen others, but the casting of his daughter Anjelica in *Prizzi's Honor* (1985), one of his last and most entertaining films, helped her win an Oscar.

Huston's failures, ranging from the pretentiously arty, such as *Under the Volcano* (1984), through the tedious, slapdash, and irredeemably dreadful, such as *The List of Adrian Messenger* (1963), are numerous and seriously tarnish his reputation. In truth, it is almost impossible to define the particular gift, characteristic, or achievement that led to his enduring position as a Hollywood—indeed, an American—legend, and perhaps it is to the man himself that history must look for the answer. It was not only his huge frame and powerfully craggy face that made him larger than life, but also his hell-raising extroversion and colorful exploits, coupled with courage and an adventurous nature (as well as a mean streak).

EARLY LIFE

Huston was born in Nevada, Missouri, on August 5, 1906, the son of the distinguished actor Walter Huston; he later fathered sons, Tony and Danny, who became a screenwriter and film director, respectively. Huston had a peripatetic childhood, traveling the vaudeville circuit with his father and the horse-racing circuit with his mother (they divorced when he was three). He left school at fourteen to become a boxer, and at nineteen he embarked on a short-lived career as a stage actor in New York, also marrying the first of his wives.

For the next twelve years or so, Huston led an unsettled life that embraced a period as an officer with the Mexican cavalry, small parts in a few films, and reporting for the New York *Graphic*. A fruitless stint as a contract scriptwriter in Hollywood followed before he took off for a nomadic and often poverty-stricken existence in London and Paris, where he studied painting. Back in Hollywood by 1937, he settled in as a writer at Warner Brothers, applying himself seriously to his work, which included collaborations on films such as *Jezebel* (1938), *Dr. Ehrlich's Magic Bullet* (1940), *High Sierra* (1941), and *Sergeant York* (1941).

Professionally, the sheer length, breadth, and range of Huston's filmography astonishes: in a career that began in 1929 with an acting role in *The Shakedown* and ended with his directing of *The Dead* in 1987, he accrued dozens of credits in his various capacities as screenwriter, director, and/or actor. He joined the army in 1942 and made three of the most acclaimed documentaries ever to emerge from World War II. The most searing of these, *Let There Be Light* (1946), dealing with the treatment and rehabilitation of shellshocked soldiers, was banned by the War Department because of its sensitive subject and was first shown publicly in the early 1980s.

In 1947, along with William Wyler and others, Huston formed the Committee for the First Amendment to counteract the House Un-American Committee's Hollywood witch hunt. The following year, with the expiration of his Warner Brothers contract, he formed Horizon Pictures with independent producer Sam Spiegel, and in 1952, no longer able to tolerate the McCarthyite atmosphere, he bought a vast country estate in Ireland. He resided there for twenty years with his family, living the hunting-shooting-fishing life of a squire between films. In 1972 he moved to Mexico, married and divorced for the last time, and made nine more films, including his only musical, *Annie* (1982).

In 1987, increasingly ill with emphysema and keeping himself alive with an oxygen tank and sheer will, Huston directed *The Dead*. Adapted from James Joyce by Huston's son Tony and starring his daughter Anjelica, this delicate and elegiac piece marked the exit of one of American cinema's great warriors.

Robyn Karney

SEE ALSO: The African Queen*;* Annie*; Bogart, Humphrey;* Chinatown*;* The Maltese Falcon*; McCarthyism; Mitchum, Robert; Peck, Gregory; Taylor, Elizabeth;* The Treasure of the Sierra Madre.

BIBLIOGRAPHY

Finler, Joel W. *The Movie Directors Story*. New York: Crescent Books, 1986.

Flynn, Tracy; Tony Flynn; and Roddy Flynn. *John Huston:*

Essays on a Restless Director. Jefferson, NC: McFarland, 2010.

Grobel, Lawrence. *The Hustons*. New York: Scribner, 1989.

Huston, John. *An Open Book*. New York: Alfred A. Knopf, 1980.

Huston, John, and Robert Emmet Long. *John Huston: Interviews*. Jackson: University Press of Mississippi, 2001.

Thomson, David. *A Biographical Dictionary of Film*. New York: Alfred A. Knopf, 1994.

Hutton, Ina Ray *(1916–1984)*

A pioneer in bringing women musicians onto the jazz scene, svelte Ina Ray Hutton, "The Blonde Bombshell of Rhythm," led an all-girl swing band, the Melodears, from 1934 through 1939 and again in a television series in 1956. Although her idea was ahead of its time, when the Melodears opened a set with their theme song, "Gotta Have Your Love," few would dispute critic George Simon's claim that "without a doubt, the sexiest of all big bandleaders was Ina Ray Hutton."

The Chicago-born Ina Ray, elder sister of June Hutton (who sang with Tommy Dorsey's Pied Pipers), entered show business at a young age, singing and tap dancing with Gus Edwards's vaudeville revues at the Palace Theater in New York City. Four years later she was in the chorus line of the Ziegfeld Follies and George White's Scandals. Her background in dance prepared her for her special style of leading a band, which was more choreography than conducting.

Changing mind-sets in that era was difficult, and Simon, reviewing an appearance by Hutton's Melodears, wrote: "Only God can make a tree, and only men can play good jazz." Fans of the Melodears praised the band's soloists: Betty Sattley on tenor sax; Alyse Wells, who played several instruments; and Betty Roudebush on piano. Another musician in the band, Ruth Lowe, later wrote two great Frank Sinatra hits: "I'll Never Smile Again" and "Put Your Dreams Away."

After the Melodears folded in 1939, Hutton fronted a band of male musicians in the 1940s, one critic describing her technique as "waving her long baton in a languorous, seductive sort of way." If Hutton's beauty had attracted the crowds, the critic added, good dance music by the band held them there. By 1943, as the band continued to find a wider audience, it took on an international flavor with the addition of the Kim Loo sisters. Stuart Foster was a popular soloist in the band. One of the leading musicians in the group, tenor saxophonist and arranger George Paxton, went on to form his own orchestra in 1944, but his greatest success came in heading a recording company and a successful music publishing businesses.

In the early 1950s Hutton returned to her original concept, leading a jazz orchestra of female musicians. Aired nationally on NBC beginning in July 1956, her half-hour variety show had no male regulars or guests. The musicians included Mickey Anderson, clarinet; Deedie Ball, piano; Harriet Blackburn and Lois Cronin, trombone; Janie Davis, Peggy Fairbanks, and Helen Hammond, trumpet; Evie Howeth and Margaret Rinker, drums; and Helen Smith, Judy Van Ever, Zoe Ann Willey, and Helen Wooley, reed section. The show ended in September 1956.

Benjamin Griffith

SEE ALSO: *Big Bands; Dorsey, Tommy; Jazz; Sinatra, Frank; Vaudeville;* The Ziegfeld Follies.

BIBLIOGRAPHY

Esposito, Tony, ed. *Golden Era of the Big Bands*. Miami, FL: Warner Brothers, 1995.

McGee , Kristin A. *Some Liked It Hot: Jazz Women in Film and Television, 1928–1959*. Middletown, CT: Wesleyan University Press, 2009.

Simon, George T. *The Big Bands*. New York: Macmillan, 1974.

Hybrid Cars

Who Killed the Electric Car? asked the title of a 2007 pseudo-documentary. A more appropriate question today might be "Who will be given credit for the rebirth of the electric car?" As the cost of fossil fuels becomes increasingly prohibitive, consumers see their improbable, century-long ride in the petroleum-powered internal combustion engine coming to an end. Issues relating to energy management are today clearly imbued with a green or environmental consciousness, making renewable options for transportation a very likely option for the future.

Electric or hybrid cars (grouped together here as EVs) were introduced in the United States in 1905 when H. Piper applied for a patent on a vehicular power train that used electricity to augment a gasoline engine. Piper's technology actually followed the work of French inventors: for a ten-year period beginning in 1897, the Compagnie Parisienne des Voitures Electriques (Paris Electric Car Company) built a number of electric and hybrid vehicles. One well-known model was the 1903 Krieger. Although these vehicles used electric power, some also ran on alcohol.

By the late 1800s a few large suppliers had steered urban transit toward electric vehicles. The Columbia Automobile and Electric Vehicle companies worked with smaller companies in most northeastern cities to create regional interests that established cab fleets and central charging stations in 1899. In Philadelphia the era of electric transportation began with Electrobat, a prototype cleared for a test drive on Broad Street in August 1894. But the path of American transportation took a very different turn during World War I. Great new supplies of petroleum transformed gasoline into an abundant and inexpensive source of energy. This spurred inventors to focus on perfecting gasoline-powered engines.

During a century of overwhelming supplies of cheap petroleum, EVs held little interest in America. Even the oil shortage of the 1970s and its skyrocketing fuel costs did not radically alter energy use. Americans increased their use of electricity at an even greater rate than their oil consumption, and utilities struggled to meet the demand, leading them to dismiss energy conservation measures proposed by President Jimmy Carter and later by President Bill Clinton. However, a small surge in hybrid development occurred in 1993 when the Clinton administration announced the formation of the Partnership for a New Generation of Vehicles. This group consisted of the "Big Three" automobile manufacturers (General Motors, Ford, and Chrysler) and about 350 smaller technical firms. Their goal was to create operating prototypes by 2004.

The film *Who Killed the Electric Car?* tells the story of General Motors' brief but popular effort to develop the EV-1 in

California during the early 1990s. The movie leaves little doubt that industry and government colluded to discontinue this experiment and to invest in another decade of supersize SUVs. By the turn of the twenty-first century, though, particularly thanks to foreign manufacturers, Americans looked at EVs as a bona fide transportation option.

Similar to the first designs in the 1890s, today's hybrid autos combine gas power with the use of an electric battery that allows the vehicle to consume much less petroleum. The hybrid rebirth began when Toyota began to sell the Prius in Japan in 1997; the Prius has the distinction of being the world's first mass-produced hybrid car. Since its introduction, the five-passenger Prius has been the world's most popular hybrid. It uses a separate generator to keep the electric battery pack charged; thus, owners never need to plug in their cars for recharging.

Other hybrids include the Honda Insight, developed in Japan in the 1990s and first sold in the United States as a 2000 model, and the Honda Civic Hybrid, which was introduced in the United States as a 2003 model and employs an electric motor that assists the gasoline engine during acceleration or times of heavy load but does not move the car on its own. Ford and Chevrolet have chosen to leap directly to plug-in electric models.

Obvious changes have indicated a new dawn for electric-powered automobiles. The major stimulus has, of course, been high petroleum prices. These costs coupled with new awareness of the detrimental effect of the internal combustion engine on the environment have made many consumers interested in purchasing one of the hybrid or "flex-fuel" models in production. In addition, federal and state tax incentives have been used to help offset the higher costs of hybrid vehicles. The result has been that hybrids are more popular today than at any other time in history.

Brian Black

SEE ALSO: *Automobile; Electric Trains; Environmentalism; Ford Motor Company; Gas Stations; General Motors; Sport Utility Vehicles (SUVs); World War I.*

BIBLIOGRAPHY

Black, Brian. *Crude Reality*. New York: Rowman & Littlefield, 2012.

Brinkley, Douglas. *Wheels for the World: Henry Ford, His Company and a Century of Progress*. New York: Viking 2003.

Gorman, Hugh. *Redefining Efficiency: Pollution Concerns*. Akron, OH: University of Akron Press, 2001.

Jackson, Kenneth T. *Crabgrass Frontier*. New York: Oxford University Press, 1985.

Kay, Jane Holtz. *Asphalt Nation*. Berkeley: University of California Press, 1997.

McShane, Clay. *Down the Asphalt Path*. New York: Columbia University Press, 1994.

Motavalli, Jim. *Forward Drive: The Race to Build "Clean" Cars for the Future*. San Francisco: Sierra Club Books, 2001.

Yergin, Daniel. *The Quest*. New York: Crown, 2011.